Current Law

Legislation Citator

STATUTE CITATOR 2009

STATUTORY INSTRUMENT CITATOR 2009

Current Law

Legislation Citator

STATUTE CITATOR 2009

STATUTORY INSTRUMENT CITATOR 2009

Sweet & Maxwell Editorial and Production Team

Lucy Naisbitt
Rajnikant Bhaidas

SWEET & MAXWELL

 THOMSON REUTERS

Published and typeset in 2010 by Thomson Reuters (Legal) Limited
(Registered in England & Wales, Company No 1679046. Registered Office and address for service:
100 Avenue Road, London, NW3 3PF) trading as Sweet & Maxwell.

For further information on our products and services, visit:
www.sweetandmaxwell.co.uk

Printed and bound in Great Britain by TJ International, Padstow, Cornwall.

A CIP catalogue record for this book is available from The British Library

ISBN 978-0-414-04190-5

No forests were destroyed to make this product;
farmed timber was used and then replanted.

PREFACE

The Sweet & Maxwell Current Law Service

The Current Law Service began in 1947 and provides a comprehensive guide to developments in case law, primary legislation and secondary legislation in the United Kingdom and mainland Europe. The Current Law service presently consists of the Monthly Digest and the Yearbook, Current Law Statutes Annotated and the Bound Volumes, European Current Law, Current Law Week, the Case Citator and the Legislation Citator.

Also available is Current Legal Information, which contains an archive of Yearbooks dating back to 1986 and the present year's cumulated Monthly Digests, as well as a range of other Sweet & Maxwell current awareness products such as the Case Citator, the Legal Journals Index and the Financial Journals Index.

The Legislation Citator

The Legislation Citator comprises the Statute Citator and the Statutory Instrument Citator and has been published annually in this format since 2005. The Citators list all amendments, modifications, repeals, etc. to primary and secondary legislation made in the years indicated.

Quarterly updates to these Citators are available in Current Law Statutes Annotated. This Volume of Legislation Citator contains the Statute Citator 2009 and the Statutory Instrument Citator 2009.

The Statute Citator

The material within the Statute Citator is arranged in chronological order and the following information is provided:

(i) Statutes passed during the specified period;

(ii) Statutes affected during the specified period by Statute or Statutory Instrument;

(iii) Statutes judicially considered during the specified period;

(iv) Statutes repealed and amended during the specified period; and

(v) Statutes under which Statutory Instruments have been made during this period.

The Statutory Instrument Citator

The material within the Statutory Instrument Citator is arranged in chronological order and the following information is provided:

(i) Statutory Instruments amended, repealed, modified, etc. by Statute passed or Statutory Instrument issued during the specified period;

(ii) Statutory Instruments judicially considered during the specified period;

(iii) Statutory Instruments consolidated during the specified period; and

(iv) Statutory Instruments made under the powers of any Statutory Instrument issued during this period.

How To Use The Legislation Citator

The following example entries of the Statute and Statutory Instrument Citators indicate how to determine developments which have occurred to the piece of legislation in which you are interested. Entries to the Citators are arranged chronologically.

Statute Citator

7. Business Rates Supplement Act 2009 — Chapter number, name of Act and year

Commencement Orders: SI 2009/2892 Art.2 — Commencement orders bringing provisions into force

Royal Assent July 02, 2009 — Date of Royal Assent

s.12, enabling SI 2009/2542 — Statutory Instruments made under the powers of s.1 of the Act

s.2, see *R. v Brown* [2009] Crim.L.R. 43 — Case judicially considering s.2

s.3, amended: 2010 c.3 s.2 — s.3 amended by Act (s.2 of Ch.3 of 2010) and two SIs

s.3, enabling: SI 2009/82; SI 2010/70

s.4, repealed: 2010 c.3 Sch.4 — s.4 repealed by Sch.4 of Ch.3 of 2010

s.4A added: SI 2009/42 — s.4A added by SI Number 42 of 2009

SI Citator

3264 Agriculture (Cross compliance) Regulations 2009 — Number, name and year of SI

Reg.2, amended: SI 2010/65 Art.2 — reg.2 amended by art.2 of SI number 65 of 2010

Reg.3, revoked: 2010 c.23 Sch.15 — reg.3 revoked by Sch.15 of Ch.23 of 2010

Reg.4, see *R v. Smith* [2010] C.O.D. 54 — Case judicially considering reg.4

CONTENTS

TABLE OF ABBREVIATIONS

Publishers name follows reports and journals.

(HMCE = HM Customs and Excise; HMSO = Her Majesty's Stationery Office; S&M = Sweet & Maxwell; TSO = The Stationery Office.) All other names are in full.

A. & B. = Accounting & Business *(Association of Chartered Certified Accountants)*

A. & S.L. = Air & Space Law *(Turpin Distribution Serv Ltd)*

A.C. = Law Reports Appeal Cases *(Incorporated Council of Law Reporting)*

A.C.D. = Administrative Court Digest *(Sweet & Maxwell Ltd)*

A.E.L.N. = Alliance Environmental Law News *(Turpin Distribution Serv Ltd)*

A.I. & L. = Artificial Intelligence and Law *(Kluwer Law International)*

A.I.B. Review = Allied Irish Banks Review *(Allied Irish Banks Plc)*

A.J.I.C.L. = African Journal of International and Comparative Law *(Edinburgh University Press Ltd)*

A.J.I.L. = Journal African De Droit International *(ISAL Publications)*

A.L.E.R. = American Law and Economic Review *(Oxford University Press)*

A.L.P.S.P. = Association of Learned & Professional Society Publishers *(Learned Publishing)*

A.L.Q. = Arab Law Quarterly *(Brill Academic Publishers)*

A.P.J.H.R.L. = Asia-Pacific Journal on Human Rights and the Law *(Martinus Nijhoff Publishers)*

A.P.L.R. = Asia Pacific Law Review *(Butterworth Tolley Publishing)*

AALL Spectrum = American Association of Law Libraries Spectrum *(American Association of Law Libraries)*

AIDA P.I.B. = AIDA Pollution Insurance Bulletin *(Dr Carl Martin Roos)*

AVMA M. & L.J. = Action for Victims of Medical Accidents Medical & Legal Journal *(Action for Victims of Medical Accidents Services Ltd)*

Accountancy = Accountancy *(Institute of Chartered Accountants in England and Wales)*

Accountancy Irl. = Accountancy Ireland *(Institute of Chartered Accountants in Ireland)*

Accountant = Accountant *(Lafferty Publications Ltd)*

Acquisitions M. = Acquisitions Monthly *(Thomson Financial Services)*

Actuary = Actuary *(Institute of Actuaries)*

Ad. & Fos. = Adoption & Fostering *(British Agencies for Adoption & Fostering)*

Ad. & Mar. L. & P. = Advertising & Marketing Law & Practice *(Frank Cass & Co Ltd)*

Adviser = Adviser *(National Association of Citizens Advice Bureaux)*

All E.R. = All England Law Reports *(Butterworth Tolley Publishing)*

All E.R. (EC) = All England Law Reports European Cases *(Butterworth Tolley Publishing)*

All. E.R. (Comm) = All England Law Reports (Commercial Cases) *(Butterworth Tolley Publishing)*

Amex. B.R. = Amex Bank Review *(American Express Bank Ltd)*

Arb. L.M. = Arbitration Law Monthly *(Informa Publishing Group Ltd)*

Arbitration = Arbitration *(Chartered Institute of Arbitrators)*

Arbitration Int. = Arbitration International *(Turpin Distribution Serv Ltd)*

Arch. Rev. = Archbold Review *(Sweet & Maxwell Ltd)*

Aslib P. = Aslib Proceedings *(Aslib Information Management)*

Ass. = Assurances *(Assurances Publications Ltd)*

Australian L.L. = Australian Law Librarian *(Australian Law Librarians' Group)*

B.C.C. = British Company Cases *(Sweet & Maxwell Ltd)*

B.C.L.C. = Butterworths Company Law Cases *(Butterworth Tolley Publishing)*

B.F.I.T. = Bulletin For International Taxation *(IBFD Publications BV)*

B.H.R.C. = Butterworths Human Rights Cases *(Butterworth Tolley Publishing)*

B.I.L.A.J. = British Insurance Law Association Journal *(British Insurance Law Association)*

B.J.I.B. & F.L. = Butterworths Journal of International Banking & Financial Law *(Butterworth Tolley Publishing)*

B.L.G.R. = Butterworths Local Government Reports *(Butterworth Tolley Publishing)*

B.L.R. = Building Law Reports *(Informa Publishing Group Ltd)*

B.M.L.R. = Butterworths Medico-Legal Reports *(Butterworth Tolley Publishing)*

B.P.I.R. = Bankruptcy and Personal Insolvency Reports *(Jordan & Sons Ltd)*

B.S. = Balance Sheet *(Risk Publications)*

B.S.L.R. = BIO-Science Law Review *(Lawtext Publishing Limited)*

B.T.C. = British Tax Cases *(Croner CCH Group Ltd)*

B.T.R. = British Tax Review *(Sweet & Maxwell Ltd)*

B.V.C. = British Value Added Tax Reporter *(Croner CCH Group Ltd)*

Bank. Law = Bankers' Law *(Guthrum House Ltd)*

Banker = Banker *(Financial Times Finance)*

Bar Review = Bar Review *(Sweet & Maxwell/Round Hall)*

Ben. File = Benefits File *(Wyatt Company (UK) Ltd)*

Bookseller = Bookseller *(Bookseller)*

Bracton L.J. = Bracton Law Journal *(Exeter University)*

Brit. J. Criminol. = British Journal of Criminology *(Oxford University Press)*

Build. L.M. = Building Law Monthly *(Informa Publishing Group Ltd)*

Building = Building *(Tower Publishing Services Ltd)*

Bus. L.B. = Business Law Bulletin *(Sweet & Maxwell Ltd/W. Green)*

Bus. L.R. = Business Law Review *(Turpin Distribution Serv Ltd)*

Busy P. = Busy Practitioner *(Bloomsbury Publishing Plc)*

Buyer = Buyer *(Informa Publishing Group Ltd)*

TABLE OF ABBREVIATIONS

C. & F.L.U. = Child & Family Law Update *(SLS Legal Publications (NI))*

C. Mag. = Chambers Magazine *(Chambers & Partners Publishing)*

C. Risk = Clinical Risk *(Royal Society of Medicine Press)*

C.C. Law = Current Criminal Law *(Sally Ramage)*

C.C.L. Rep. = Community Care Law Reports *(Legal Action Group)*

C.C.L. Rev. = Carbon & Climate Law Review *(Lexxion Verlagsgesellschaft mbH)*

C.C.N. = Civil Costs Newsletter *(Butterworth Tolley Publishing)*

C.E.C. = European Community Cases *(Sweet & Maxwell Ltd)*

C.F.L.Q. = Child and Family Law Quarterly *(Jordan & Sons Ltd)*

C.G. = Corporate Governance *(John Wiley & Sons Ltd)*

C.H.R.L.D. = Commonwealth Human Rights Law Digest *(Interights)*

C.I.L. = Contemporary Issues in Law *(Lawtext Publishing Limited)*

C.I.L.L. = Construction Industry Law Letter *(Informa Publishing Group Ltd)*

C.I.P.A.J. = Chartered Institute of Patent Agents Journal *(The Chartered Institute of Patent Agents)*

C.J.I.L. = Chinese Journal of International Law *(Oxford University Press)*

C.J.Q. = Civil Justice Quarterly *(Sweet & Maxwell Ltd)*

C.J.R.B. = Commercial Judicial Review Bulletin *(Chancery Law Publishing Ltd)*

C.L. & J. = Criminal Law & Justice Weekly *(Butterworth Tolley Publishing)*

C.L. & P.R. = Charity Law and Practice Review *(Key Haven Publications Plc)*

C.L. Int. = Competition Law International *(International Bar Association)*

C.L. Pract. = Commercial Law Practitioner *(Sweet & Maxwell/Round Hall)*

C.L.B. = Commonwealth Law Bulletin *(Informa Publishing Group Ltd)*

C.L.C. = Commercial Law Cases *(Sweet & Maxwell Ltd)*

C.L.E. = Commercial Law of Europe *(Sweet & Maxwell Ltd)*

C.L.J. = Cambridge Law Journal *(Cambridge University Press)*

C.L.M.D. = Current Law Monthly Digest *(Sweet & Maxwell Ltd/W. Green)*

C.L.O.S. = Criminal Law Online Service *(First Law)*

C.L.S. = Current Law Statutes *(Sweet & Maxwell Ltd/W. Green)*

C.L.S. Rev. = Computer Law & Security Review *(Elsevier)*

C.L.W.R. = Common Law World Review *(Portland Press Ltd)*

C.L.Y. = Current Law Year Book *(Sweet & Maxwell Ltd)*

C.M. = Compliance Monitor *(Informa Publishing Group Ltd)*

C.M.L. Rev. = Common Market Law Review *(Turpin Distribution Serv Ltd)*

C.M.L.J. = Capital Markets Law Journal *(Oxford University Press)*

C.M.L.R. = Common Market Law Reports *(Sweet & Maxwell Ltd)*

C.M.L.R. (AR) = Common Markets Law Reports *(Sweet & Maxwell Ltd)*

C.N. = Construction Newsletter *(Bloomsbury Publishing Plc)*

C.O.B. = Compliance Officer Bulletin *(Sweet & Maxwell Ltd)*

C.P. Rep. = Civil Procedure Reports *(Sweet & Maxwell Ltd)*

C.P.L.J. = Conveyancing and Property Law Journal *(Sweet & Maxwell/Round Hall)*

C.P.L.R. = Civil Practice Law Reports *(XPL Publishing)*

C.P.N. = Civil Procedure News *(Sweet & Maxwell Ltd)*

C.R. & I. = Corporate Rescue and Insolvency *(Butterworth Tolley Publishing)*

C.R.N.I. = Competition and Regulation in Network Industries *(Intersentia)*

C.S.R. = Company Secretary's Review *(Butterworth Tolley Publishing)*

C.T.L.R. = Computer and Telecommunications Law Review *(Sweet & Maxwell Ltd/ESC Publishing)*

C.T.R. = Corporate Tax Review *(Key Haven Publications Plc)*

C.W. = Copyright World *(Informa Publishing Group Ltd)*

CPD Papers = Criminal Law Week - CPD Extended Papers *(S&M)*

Cambrian L.R. = Cambrian Law Review *(University College of Wales)*

Can. Ins. = Canadian Insurance *(Stone & Cox Ltd)*

Ch. = Law Reports Chancery Division *(Incorporated Council of Law Reporting)*

Charity. F = Charity Finance *(Plaza Publishing Limited)*

Civ. P.B. = Civil Practice Bulletin *(Sweet & Maxwell Ltd/W. Green)*

Clarity = Clarity *(Cripps Harries Hall)*

Co. L.J. = Commercial Litigation Journal *(Legalease Ltd)*

Co. L.N. = Company Law Newsletter *(Sweet & Maxwell Ltd)*

Com. Jud. J. = Commonwealth Judicial Journal *(Commonwealth Magistrates & Judges Association)*

Com. Lawyer = The Commonwealth Lawyer *(Commonwealth Lawyers' Association)*

Comm. Leases = Commercial Leases *(Informa Publishing Group Ltd)*

Comms. L. = Communications Law *(Bloomsbury Publishing Plc)*

Comp. L. Rev. = Competition Law Review *(Competition Law Scholars Forum)*

Comp. L.I. = Competition Law Insight *(Informa Publishing Group Ltd)*

Comp. L.J. = Competition Law Journal *(Jordan Publishing Ltd)*

Comp. Law. = Company Lawyer *(Sweet & Maxwell Ltd)*

Comps. & Law = Computers & Law *(Society for Computers and Law)*

Con. L.R. = Construction Law Reports *(Butterworth Tolley Publishing)*

Cons. I.L. = Construction Law International *(International Bar Association)*

Cons. L. Today = Consumer Law Today *(Informa Publishing Group Ltd)*

Cons. Law = Construction Law *(Eclipse/Butterworth Tolley Publishing)*

Const. L.J. = Construction Law Journal *(Sweet & Maxwell Ltd)*

Conv. = Conveyancer and Property Lawyer *(Sweet & Maxwell Ltd)*

Converg. = Convergence *(International Bar Association)*

Corp. Brief. = Corporate Briefing *(Informa Publishing Group Ltd)*

Costs L.R. = Costs Law Reports *(XPL Publishing)*

TABLE OF ABBREVIATIONS

Counsel = Counsel *(Butterworth Tolley Publishing)*

Cov. L.J. = Coventry Law Journal *(Coventry University)*

Cr. App. R. = Criminal Appeal Reports *(Sweet & Maxwell Ltd)*

Cr. App. R. (S.) = Criminal Appeal Reports (Sentencing) *(Sweet & Maxwell Ltd)*

Crim. L.B. = Criminal Law Bulletin *(Sweet & Maxwell Ltd/W. Green)*

Crim. L.F. = Criminal Law Forum *(Springer)*

Crim. L.N. = Criminal Law News *(Sally Ramage)*

Crim. L.R. = Criminal Law Review *(Sweet & Maxwell Ltd)*

Crim. Law. = Criminal Lawyer *(Bloomsbury Publishing Plc)*

D.E. & E.S.L.R. = Digital Evidence and Electronic Signature Law Review *(Pario Communications Ltd)*

D.F.I. = Derivatives & Financial Instruments *(IBFD Publications BV)*

D.L. = Daily List *(TSO)*

D.P.I. = Data Protection Ireland *(Privacy & Data Protection)*

D.P.L. & P. = Data Protection Law & Policy *(Cecile Park Publishing Ltd)*

D.R.I. = Dispute Resolution International *(International Bar Association)*

D.U.L.J. = Dublin University Law Journal *(Sweet & Maxwell/Round Hall)*

Data Base Reps. = Data Base Reports *(Insurance Information Institute)*

De Voil I.T.I. = De Voil Indirect Tax Intelligence *(Butterworth Tolley Publishing)*

Delphi Mag. = Delphi Magazine *(ITEC)*

Denning L.J. = Denning Law Journal *(University of Buckingham)*

E-doc = E-doc Magazine *(AIIM International)*

E. & L. = Education and the Law *(Taylor & Francis Ltd)*

E. & P. = International Journal of Evidence & Proof *(Vathek Publishing)*

E. & S.L.J. = Entertainment and Sports Law Journal *(Warwick)*

E. St. A.L. = European State Aid Law Quarterly *(Lexxion Verlagsgesellschaft mbH)*

E.B. & F.L.J. = European Banking & Financial Law Journal *(Intersentia NV)*

E.B.L. Rev. = European Business Law Review *(Turpin Distribution Serv Ltd)*

E.B.O.R. = European Business Organization Law Review *(Cambridge University Press)*

E.C. Law = European Company Law *(Kluwer Law International)*

E.C.A. = Elderly Client Adviser *(Ark Publishing)*

E.C.C. = European Commercial Cases *(Sweet & Maxwell Ltd)*

E.C.D.R. = European Copyright and Design Reports *(Sweet & Maxwell Ltd)*

E.C.F.R. = European Company and Financial Law Review *(Rhenus Medien Logistik GmbH & Co)*

E.C.L. & P. = E-Commerce Law & Policy *(Cecile Park Publishing Ltd)*

E.C.L. Rep. = E-Commerce Law Reports *(Cecile Park Publishing Ltd)*

E.C.L. Review = European Constitutional Law Review *(Cambridge University Press)*

E.C.L.R. = European Competition Law Review *(Sweet & Maxwell Ltd/ESC Publishing)*

E.E.E.L.R. = European Energy and Environmental Law Review *(Turpin Distribution Serv Ltd)*

E.F.A. Rev. = European Foreign Affairs Review *(Turpin Distribution Serv Ltd)*

E.F.F.L.R. = European Food and Feed Law Review *(Lexxion Verlagsgesellschaft mbH)*

E.F.P.L. & P. = E-Finance & Payments Law & Policy *(Cecile Park Publishing Ltd)*

E.G. = Estates Gazette *(Estates Gazette Ltd)*

E.G.L.R. = Estates Gazette Law Reports *(Estates Gazette Ltd)*

E.H.L.R. = Environmental Health Law Reports *(Sweet & Maxwell Ltd)*

E.H.R.L.R. = European Human Rights Law Review *(Sweet & Maxwell Ltd)*

E.H.R.R. = European Human Rights Reports *(Sweet & Maxwell Ltd)*

E.I.P.R. = European Intellectual Property Review *(Sweet & Maxwell Ltd/ESC Publishing)*

E.J.C. = European Journal of Criminology *(Sage Publications Ltd)*

E.J.C.L. = Electronic Journal of Comparative Law *(Electronic Journal of Comparative Law)*

E.J.H.L. = European Journal of Health Law *(Martinus Nijhoff Publishers)*

E.J.I.L. = European Journal of International Law *(Oxford University Press)*

E.J.L. & E. = European Journal of Law & Economics *(Springer)*

E.J.L.E. = European Journal of Legal Education *(Routledge Taylor & Francis Group)*

E.J.M.L. = European Journal of Migration and Law *(Martinus Nijhoff Publishers)*

E.J.S.S. = European Journal of Social Security *(Intersentia NV)*

E.L. Rev. = European Law Review *(Sweet & Maxwell Ltd)*

E.L.J. = European Law Journal *(John Wiley & Sons Ltd)*

E.L.L.J. = European Labour Law Journal *(Intersentia NV)*

E.L.M. = Environmental Law & Management *(Lawtext Publishing Limited)*

E.L.R. = Education Law Reports *(Jordan & Sons Ltd)*

E.L.R.I. = Employment Law Review - Ireland *(First Law)*

E.M.L.R. = Entertainment and Media Law Reports *(Sweet & Maxwell Ltd/ESC Publishing)*

E.N.P.R. = European National Patent Reports *(Sweet & Maxwell Ltd)*

E.O.R. = Equal Opportunities Review *(Michael Rubenstein Publishing)*

E.P.G. = Environmental Policy and Governance *(John Wiley & Sons Ltd)*

E.P.L. = European Public Law *(Turpin Distribution Serv Ltd)*

E.P.L.I. = Education, Public Law and the Individual *(Education Law Association Ltd)*

E.P.O.R. = European Patent Office Reports *(Sweet & Maxwell Ltd)*

E.P.P.P.L.R. = European Public Private Partnership Law Review *(Lexxion Verlagsgesellschaft mbH)*

E.R.C.L. = European Review of Contract Law *(Walter de Gruyter GmbH & Co. KG)*

E.R.P.L. = European Review of Private Law *(Turpin Distribution Serv Ltd)*

E.T.M.R. = European Trade Marks Reports *(Sweet & Maxwell Ltd)*

EC C.P.N. = European Commission Competition Policy Newsletter *(Commission of The European Communities)*

EC E.M. = EC Energy Monthly *(Financial Times Finance)*

EC T.J. = EC Tax Journal *(Key Haven Publications Plc)*

TABLE OF ABBREVIATIONS

EC T.R. = EC Tax Review *(Turpin Distribution Serv Ltd)*

EDI L.R. = Electronic Data Interchange Law Review *(Turpin Distribution Serv Ltd)*

ENDS = ENDS Report *(Environmental Data Services Ltd)*

EU Focus = EU Focus *(Sweet & Maxwell Ltd)*

Ecc. L.J. = Ecclesiastical Law Journal *(Cambridge University Press)*

Ed. C.R. = Education Case Reports *(Sweet & Maxwell Ltd)*

Ed. L.M. = Education Law Monitor *(Informa Publishing Group Ltd)*

Ed. Law = Education Law Journal *(Jordan & Sons Ltd)*

Edin. L.R. = Edinburgh Law Review *(Edinburgh University Press Ltd)*

Emp. L.B. = Employment Law Bulletin *(Sweet & Maxwell Ltd/W. Green)*

Emp. L.J. = Employment Law Journal *(Legalease Ltd)*

Employ. L. = Employer's Law *(Reed Business Information Ltd)*

Enc. C.S.P. = Encyclopedia of Current Sentencing Practice *(Sweet & Maxwell Ltd)*

Enc. E.U.L. = Encyclopedia of European Union Law *(Sweet & Maxwell Ltd)*

Enc. F.S.L. = Encyclopedia of Financial Services Law *(Sweet & Maxwell Ltd)*

Enc. I.T.L. = Encyclopedia of Information Technology Law *(Sweet & Maxwell Ltd)*

Enc. P.L. & P. = Encyclopedia of Planning Law & Practice *(Sweet & Maxwell Ltd)*

Ent. L.R. = Entertainment Law Review *(Sweet & Maxwell Ltd/ESC Publishing)*

Env. I.B. = Environment In Business *(Butterworth Tolley Publishing)*

Env. L. Rev. = Environmental Law Review *(Vathek Publishing)*

Env. L.M. = Environmental Law Monthly *(Informa Publishing Group Ltd)*

Env. L.R. = Environmental Law Reports *(Sweet & Maxwell Ltd)*

Env. Law = Environmental Law *(UKELA)*

Env. Liability = Environmental Liability *(Lawtext Publishing Limited)*

Eu. L.F. = European Legal Forum *(IPR Verlag GmbH)*

Eu. L.R. = European Law Reports *(Hart Publishing Ltd)*

Eur. J. Crime Cr. L. Cr. J. = European Journal of Crime, Criminal Law and Criminal Justice *(Martinus Nijhoff Publishers)*

Euro. C.J. = European Competition Journal *(Hart Publishing Ltd)*

Euro. C.L. = European Current Law *(Sweet & Maxwell Ltd)*

Euro. Law. = European Lawyer *(Polyview Media Limited)*

Euro. News. = European Newsletter *(Sweet & Maxwell Ltd)*

Euro. T.S. = European Tax Service *(BNA International Inc)*

Euro. Tax. = European Taxation *(IBFD Publications BV)*

Euromoney = Euromoney *(Euromoney Institutional Investor Plc)*

F. & C.L. = Finance & Credit Law *(Informa Publishing Group Ltd)*

F. & D. = Finance & Development *(Finance & Development)*

F. & D.L.M. = Food & Drink Law Monthly *(Agra Europe)*

F.C.R. = Family Court Reporter *(Butterworth Tolley Publishing)*

F.I. = Fraud Intelligence *(Informa Publishing Group Ltd)*

F.I.T.A.R. = Financial Instruments Tax & Accounting Review *(Informa Publishing Group Ltd)*

F.L.N. = Family Law Newsletter *(Butterworth Tolley Publishing)*

F.L.R. = Family Law Reports *(Jordan & Sons Ltd)*

F.O.I. = Freedom of Information *(Privacy & Data Protection)*

F.R.I. = Financial Regulation International *(Informa Publishing Group Ltd)*

F.S.R. = Fleet Street Reports *(Sweet & Maxwell Ltd)*

Fairplay = Fairplay *(Fairplay Publications Ltd)*

Fam. = Law Reports Family Division *(Incorporated Council of Law Reporting)*

Fam. L.B. = Family Law Bulletin *(Sweet & Maxwell Ltd/W. Green)*

Fam. L.J. = Family Law Journal *(Legalease Ltd)*

Fam. L.R. = Family Law Reports (Greens) *(Sweet & Maxwell Ltd/W. Green)*

Fam. Law = Family Law *(Jordan & Sons Ltd)*

Farm Law = Farm Law *(Agra Europe)*

Farm T.B. = Farm Tax Brief *(Informa Publishing Group Ltd)*

Fem. L.S. = Feminist Legal Studies *(Turpin Distribution Serv Ltd)*

Focus = Focus *(Zurich International (UK) Ltd)*

G.A.R. = Global Arbitration Review *(Law Business Research Ltd)*

G.C. = Global Crime *(Routledge Taylor & Francis Group)*

G.C.L.R. = Global Competition Litigation Review *(Sweet & Maxwell Ltd/ESC Publishing)*

G.C.R. = Global Competition Review *(Law Business Research Ltd)*

G.L.S.I. = Gazette of the Law Society Ireland *(The Law Society)*

G.P.R.I.T. = Geneva Papers on Risk & Insurance: Theory *(Geneva Association)*

G.T. & C.J. = Global Trade and Customs Journal *(Kluwer Law International)*

G.W.D. = Greens Weekly Digest *(Sweet & Maxwell Ltd/W. Green)*

Go. J.I.L. = Gottingen Journal of International Law *(Universitatsverlag Gottingen)*

Gov. = Governance *(Plaza Publishing)*

Guide = Guide *(Sweet & Maxwell Ltd)*

H. & S.B. = Health and Safety Bulletin *(Butterworth Tolley Publishing)*

H. & S.M. = Health & Safety Monitor *(Schofield Publishing)*

H. & S.W. = Health & Safety at Work *(Butterworth Tolley Publishing)*

H.C.L.M. = High Court Litigation Manual *(Sweet & Maxwell Ltd)*

H.C.W.I.B. = House of Commons Weekly Information Bulletin *(TSO)*

H.J.R.L. = Hague Journal on the Rule of Law *(TMC Asser Press)*

H.L.M. = Housing Law Monitor *(Informa Publishing Group Ltd)*

H.L.R. = Housing Law Reports *(Sweet & Maxwell Ltd)*

H.R. & I.L.D. = Human Rights & International Legal Discourse *(Intersentia)*

H.R.A. = Human Rights Alerter *(Sweet & Maxwell Ltd)*

H.R.C.D. = Human Rights Case Digest *(Sweet & Maxwell Ltd)*

H.R.L. Rev. = Human Rights Law Review *(Oxford University Press)*

H.R.L.R. = Human Rights Law Reports *(Sweet & Maxwell Ltd)*

H.S. at W. = Health & Safety at Work *(Bloomsbury Publishing Plc)*

H.S.I. = Halsbury's Statutory Instruments *(Legal Library Services Ltd)*

Halsbury S. = Halsbury's Statutes *(Legal Library Services Ltd)*

Hert. L.J. = Hertfordshire Law Journal *(University of Hertfordshire)*

Hous. L.R. = Greens Housing Law Reports *(Sweet & Maxwell Ltd/W. Green)*

Howard Journal = Howard Journal of Criminal Justice *(John Wiley & Sons Ltd)*

I. & C.T.L. = Information & Communications Technology Law *(Taylor & Francis Ltd)*

I. & P.E. = Investment & Pensions Europe *(IPE International Publishers Ltd)*

I. & R.I. = Insolvency and Restructuring International *(International Bar Association)*

I. & R.L.B. = Insurance & Reinsurance Law Briefing *(Sweet & Maxwell Ltd)*

I.B.L.J. = International Business Law Journal *(Sweet & Maxwell Ltd)*

I.B.L.Q. = Irish Business Law Quarterly *(Clarus Press)*

I.B.N. = International Bar News *(International Bar Association)*

I.C. = Investors Chronicle *(Investors Chronicle Publications Ltd)*

I.C.C.L.R. = International Company and Commercial Law Review *(Sweet & Maxwell Ltd/ESC Publishing)*

I.C.L. Rev. = International Construction Law Review *(Informa Publishing Group Ltd)*

I.C.L.B. = International Corporate Law Bulletin *(Turpin Distribution Serv Ltd)*

I.C.L.J. = Irish Criminal Law Journal *(Sweet & Maxwell/Round Hall)*

I.C.L.M.D. = Irish Current Law Monthly Digest *(Sweet & Maxwell/Round Hall)*

I.C.L.Q. = International & Comparative Law Quarterly *(Cambridge University Press)*

I.C.L.S.A. = Irish Current Law Statutes Annotated *(Sweet & Maxwell/Round Hall)*

I.C.R. = Industrial Cases Reports *(Incorporated Council of Law Reporting)*

I.E.L.J. = Irish Employment Law Journal *(Sweet & Maxwell/Round Hall)*

I.E.L.R. = International Energy Law Review *(Sweet & Maxwell Ltd)*

I.F.L. = International Family Law *(Jordan & Sons Ltd)*

I.F.L. Rev. = International Financial Law Review *(Euromoney Institutional Investor Plc)*

I.F.O.S.S.L.R. = International Free and Open Source Software Law Review *(Editorial Committee Board)*

I.H.L. = In-House Lawyer *(Legalease Ltd)*

I.H.P. = In-House Perspective *(International Bar Association)*

I.I.R. = International Insolvency Review *(John Wiley & Sons Ltd)*

I.J.C.L. = International Journal of Constitutional Law *(Oxford University Press)*

I.J.C.L.E. = International Journal of Clinical Legal Education *(Northumbria Law Press)*

I.J.C.L.P. = International Journal of Communications Law and Policy *(Institute for Information, Telecommunications and Media Law)*

I.J.D.G. = International Journal of Disclosure and Governance *(Palgrave Macmillan)*

I.J.D.L. = International Journal of Discrimination and the Law *(A B Academic Publishers)*

I.J.F.L. = Irish Journal of Family Law *(Sweet & Maxwell/Round Hall)*

I.J.H.R. = International Journal of Human Rights *(Taylor & Francis Ltd)*

I.J.L. & I.T. = International Journal of Law & Information Technology *(Oxford University Press)*

I.J.L.B.E. = International Journal of Law in the Built Environment *(Emerald Group Publishing Limited)*

I.J.L.C.J. = International Journal of Law Crime and Justice *(Elsevier)*

I.J.L.P. = International Journal of the Legal Profession *(Taylor & Francis Ltd)*

I.J.M.C.L. = International Journal of Marine & Coastal Law *(Martinus Nijhoff Publishers)*

I.J.R.L. = International Journal of Refugee Law *(Oxford University Press)*

I.J.S.L. = International Journal for the Semiotics of Law *(Turpin Distribution Serv Ltd)*

I.J.T.J. = International Journal of Transitional Justice *(Oxford University Press)*

I.L. & S. = Islamic Law and Society *(Brill Academic Publishers)*

I.L. Pr. = International Litigation Procedure *(Sweet & Maxwell Ltd)*

I.L.D. = Immigration Law Digest *(Immigration Advisory Service)*

I.L.J. = Industrial Law Journal *(Oxford University Press)*

I.L.T. = Irish Law Times *(Sweet & Maxwell/Round Hall)*

I.N.L.R. = Immigration and Nationality Law Reports *(Jordan & Sons Ltd)*

I.O.L.R. = International Organizations Law Review *(Martinus Nijhoff Publishers)*

I.P. & T. = Intellectual Property and Technology *(Butterworth Tolley Publishing)*

I.P. News. = Intellectual Property Newsletter *(Informa Publishing Group Ltd)*

I.P.D. = Intellectual Property Decisions *(Informa Publishing Group Ltd)*

I.P.E.L.J. = Irish Planning and Environmental Law Journal *(Sweet & Maxwell/Round Hall)*

I.P.Q. = Intellectual Property Quarterly *(Sweet & Maxwell Ltd)*

I.R.L.C.T. = International Review of Law Computers & Technology *(Taylor & Francis Ltd)*

I.R.L.R. = Industrial Relations Law Reports *(Eclipse/Butterworth Tolley Publishing)*

I.R.V. = International Review of Victimology *(A B Academic Publishers)*

I.S.L.J. = International Sports Law Journal *(TMC Asser Press)*

I.S.L.R. = International Sports Law Review *(Sweet & Maxwell Ltd)*

I.S.L.Rev. = Irish Student Law Review *(The Honourable Society of Kings' Inn)*

I.T. Rep. = International Tax Report *(Informa Publishing Group Ltd)*

I.T. Rev. = International Tax Review *(Euromoney Institutional Investor Plc)*

I.T.E.L.R. = International Trust and Estate Law Reports *(Bloomsbury Publishing Plc)*

I.T.L. Rep. = International Tax Law Reports *(Butterworth Tolley Publishing)*

I.T.P.J. = International Transfer Pricing Journal *(IBFD Publications BV)*

I.V.M. = International VAT Monitor *(IBFD Publications BV)*

I.W.R. = Information World Review *(Learned Information Ltd)*

IDS D.W. = IDS Diversity at Work *(Sweet & Maxwell/IDS)*

IDS Emp. L. Brief = IDS Employment Law Brief *(Sweet & Maxwell/IDS)*

IDS P.B. = IDS Pensions Bulletin *(Sweet & Maxwell/IDS)*

IDS P.L.R. = IDS Pensions Law Reports *(Sweet & Maxwell/IDS)*

IIC = International Review of Intellectual Property and Competition Law *(IPR Verlag GmbH)*

INSOL W. = INSOL World *(INSOL International)*

IT L.T. = IT Law Today *(Informa Publishing Group Ltd)*

Imm. A.R. = Immigration Appeal Reports *(TSO)*

Ind. L.R. = Independent Law Review *(Clarus Press)*

Ind. T.R. = Industrial Tribunal Reports *(HMSO)*

Info. T.L.R. = Information Technology Law Reports *(Lawtext Publishing Limited)*

Info. Today = Information Today *(Learned Information Europe Ltd)*

Ins. L.M. = Insurance Law Monthly *(Informa Publishing Group Ltd)*

Insolv. Int. = Insolvency Intelligence *(Sweet & Maxwell Ltd)*

Int. A.L.R. = International Arbitration Law Review *(Sweet & Maxwell Ltd)*

Int. C.L. Rev. = International Community Law Review *(Martinus Nijhoff Publishers)*

Int. C.L.R. = International Criminal Law Review *(Martinus Nijhoff Publishers)*

Int. C.R. = International Corporate Rescue *(Chase Cambria Co (Publishing) Ltd)*

Int. I.R. = International Insurance Report *(Risk & Insurance Research Group Ltd)*

Int. J. Comp. L.L.I.R. = International Journal of Comparative Labour Law and Industrial Relations *(Turpin Distribution Serv Ltd)*

Int. J.F.L. = International Journal of Franchising Law *(Claerhout Publishing Ltd)*

Int. J.L.C. = International Journal of Law in Context *(Cambridge University Press)*

Int. J.L.P.F. = International Journal of Law, Policy and the Family *(Oxford University Press)*

Int. M.L. = International Maritime Law *(Lawtext Publishing Limited)*

Int. Rel. = International Relations *(Sage Publications Ltd)*

Int. T.L.R. = International Trade Law & Regulation *(Sweet & Maxwell Ltd/ESC Publishing)*

Intertax = Intertax *(Turpin Distribution Serv Ltd)*

Ir. T.R. = Irish Tax Review *(Institute of Taxation in Ireland)*

Irish Jurist = Irish Jurist *(Sweet & Maxwell/Round Hall)*

J. Com. Mar. St. = Journal of Common Market Studies *(John Wiley & Sons Ltd)*

J. Crim. L. = Journal of Criminal Law *(Portland Customer Services)*

J. Env. L. = Journal of Environmental Law *(Oxford University Press)*

J. Int. P. = Journal of International Trust and Corporate Planning *(Jordan & Sons Ltd)*

J. Law & Soc. = Journal of Law and Society *(John Wiley & Sons Ltd)*

J. Leg. Hist. = Journal of Legal History *(Frank Cass & Co Ltd)*

J. Priv. Int. L. = Journal of Private International Law *(Hart Publishing Ltd)*

J. Soc. Wel. & Fam. L. = Journal of Social Welfare and Family Law *(Taylor & Francis Ltd)*

J.A.L. = Journal of African Law *(Cambridge University Press)*

J.B.L. = Journal of Business Law *(Sweet & Maxwell Ltd)*

J.B.R. = Journal of Banking Regulation *(Palgrave Macmillan)*

J.C. & S.L. = Journal of Conflict & Security Law *(Oxford University Press)*

J.C.L. & E. = Journal of Competition Law & Economics *(Oxford University Press)*

J.C.L.L.E. = Journal of Commonwealth Law and Legal Education *(Taylor & Francis Ltd)*

J.C.L.P. = Journal of Competition Law & Policy *(OECD Publications Service (Databeuro Ltd))*

J.C.L.S. = Journal of Corporate Law Studies *(Hart Publishing Ltd)*

J.C.T.1 = J.C.T.1 *(Sweet & Maxwell/JCT)*

J.C.T.2 = J.C.T.2 *(Sweet & Maxwell/JCT)*

J.C.T.3 = J.C.T.3 *(Sweet & Maxwell/JCT)*

J.C.T.4 = J.C.T.4 *(Sweet & Maxwell/JCT)*

J.C.T.5 = J.C.T.5 *(Sweet & Maxwell/JCT)*

J.D. = Journal of Documentation *(Emerald Group Publishing Limited)*

J.E.C.L. & Pract. = Journal of European Competition Law & Practice *(Oxford University Press)*

J.E.E.P.L. = Journal for European Environmental & Planning Law *(Brill Academic Publishers)*

J.E.L.S. = Journal of Empirical Legal Studies *(John Wiley & Sons Ltd)*

J.E.R.L. = Journal of Energy & Natural Resources Law *(International Bar Association)*

J.F.C. = Journal of Financial Crime *(Emerald Group Publishing Limited)*

J.F.R. & C. = Journal of Financial Regulation and Compliance *(Emerald Group Publishing Limited)*

J.G.L.R. = Jersey and Guernsey Law Review *(The Jersey and Guernsey Law Review Ltd)*

J.H.L. = Journal of Housing Law *(Sweet & Maxwell Ltd)*

J.I.A.N.L. = Journal of Immigration Asylum and Nationality Law *(Bloomsbury Publishing Plc)*

J.I.B. Law = Journal of International Biotechnology Law *(Walter de Gruyter GmbH & Co. KG)*

J.I.B.L.R. = Journal of International Banking Law and Regulation *(Sweet & Maxwell Ltd/ESC Publishing)*

J.I.C.J. = Journal of International Criminal Justice *(Oxford University Press)*

J.I.E.L. = Journal of International Economic Law *(Oxford University Press)*

J.I.L. & C. = Journal of Islamic Law and Culture *(Taylor & Francis Ltd)*

J.I.L.T. = Journal of Information, Law & Technology *(CTI Law Technology Centre)*

J.I.M.L. = Journal of International Maritime Law *(Lawtext Publishing Limited)*

J.I.P.L.P. = Journal of Intellectual Property Law & Practice *(Oxford University Press)*

J.I.T.L. & P. = Journal of International Trade Law & Policy *(Emerald Group Publishing Limited)*

J.J. = Justice Journal *(Justice)*

J.L.E. & O. = Journal of Law, Economics & Organization *(Oxford University Press)*

J.L.M &. E. = Journal of Law, Medicine & Ethics *(John Wiley & Sons Ltd)*

J.L.S. = Journal of Legislative Studies *(Taylor & Francis Ltd)*

J.L.S.S. = Journal of the Law Society of Scotland *(The Law Society of Scotland)*

TABLE OF ABBREVIATIONS

J.M.H.L. = Journal of Mental Health Law *(Northumbria Law Press)*

J.M.L. = Journal of Media Law *(Hart Publishing Ltd)*

J.M.L.C. = Journal of Money Laundering Control *(Emerald Group Publishing Limited)*

J.O. & R. = Journal of Obligations and Remedies *(Northumbria Law Press)*

J.P.I. Law = Journal of Personal Injury Law *(Sweet & Maxwell Ltd)*

J.P.L. = Journal of Planning & Environment Law *(Sweet & Maxwell Ltd)*

J.P.N. = Justice of the Peace & Local Government Law *(Butterworth Tolley Publishing)*

J.R. = Judicial Review *(Hart Publishing Ltd)*

J.R.S. = Journal of Refugee Studies *(Oxford University Press)*

J.S.I.J. = Judicial Studies Instiutute Journal *(Judicial Studies Institute)*

J.S.S.L. = Journal of Social Security Law *(Sweet & Maxwell Ltd)*

J.W.E.L. & B. = Journal of World Energy Law & Business *(Oxford University Press)*

J.W.I.P. = Journal of World Intellectual Property *(John Wiley & Sons Ltd)*

J.W.T. = Journal of World Trade *(Turpin Distribution Serv Ltd)*

Jour. G.M. = Journal of General Management *(Braybrooke Press Ltd)*

Jur. Rev. = Juridical Review *(Sweet & Maxwell Ltd/W. Green)*

Juris. = Jurisprudence *(Hart Publishing Ltd)*

K.I.R. = Knights Industrial Reports *(Charles Knight Publishing)*

K.L.J. = King's Law Journal *(Hart Publishing Ltd)*

KIM Legal = Knowledge and Information Management *(Ark Group)*

Kemp & Kemp = Kemp & Kemp The Quantum of Damages *(Sweet & Maxwell Ltd)*

Kemp News = Kemp News *(Sweet & Maxwell Ltd)*

L & T.R. = Landlord and Tenant Reports *(Sweet & Maxwell Ltd)*

L. & F.M.R. = Law & Financial Markets Review *(Hart Publishing Ltd)*

L. & H. = Law & Humanities *(Hart Publishing Ltd)*

L. & T. Review = Landlord & Tenant Review *(Sweet & Maxwell Ltd)*

L. Ex. = Legal Executive *(ILEX Publishing & Advertising Services Ltd)*

L.C.B. = Legal Compliance Bulletin *(Law Society Publishing)*

L.F. = Litigation Funding *(Law Society Publishing)*

L.G.D. = Law, Social Justice & Global Development *(Electronic Law Journals)*

L.G.L.R. = Local Government Law Reports *(Sweet & Maxwell Ltd)*

L.I.M. = Legal Information Management *(Cambridge University Press)*

L.I.T. = Law, Innovation and Technology *(Hart Publishing Ltd)*

L.J.I.L. = Leiden Journal of International Law *(Cambridge University Press)*

L.L.I.D. = Lloyd's List Insurance Day *(Informa Publishing Group Ltd)*

L.L.R. = London Law Review *(London Law Review)*

L.M.C.L.Q. = Lloyd's Maritime and Commercial Law Quarterly *(Informa Publishing Group Ltd)*

L.M.L.N. = Lloyd's Maritime Law Newsletter *(Informa Publishing Group Ltd)*

L.P. & R. = Law, Probability & Risk *(Oxford University Press)*

L.P.I.C.T. = Law & Practice of International Courts and Tribunals *(Martinus Nijhoff Publishers)*

L.Q.R. = Law Quarterly Review *(Sweet & Maxwell Ltd)*

L.R. = Licensing Review *(Benedict Books)*

L.S. = Legal Studies *(John Wiley & Sons Ltd)*

L.S. & P. = Law, Science and Policy *(A B Academic Publishers)*

L.S.G. = Law Society's Gazette *(The Law Society's Hall)*

L.T.I. = Legal Technology Insider *(Legal Technology Insider)*

Law & Just. = Law & Justice *(Edmund Plowden Trust)*

Law & Phil. = Law & Philosophy *(Springer)*

Law & Pol. = Law & Policy *(John Wiley & Sons Ltd)*

Law Teach. = Law Teacher *(Sweet & Maxwell Ltd)*

Lawyer = Lawyer *(Centaur Communications Group)*

Lawyer = Lawyer *(Centaur Communications Group)*

Leg. = Legisprudence *(Hart Publishing Ltd)*

Legal Action = Legal Action *(Legal Action Group)*

Legal Bus. = Legal Business *(Legalease Ltd)*

Legal Ethics = Legal Ethics *(Hart Publishing Ltd)*

Legal I.E.I. = Legal Issues of Economic Integration *(Turpin Distribution Serv Ltd)*

Legal M. = Legal Marketing *(Ark Publishing)*

Legal Week = Legal Week *(Legal Week Global Media)*

Link AWS = Link Association of Women Solicitors *(Association of Women Solicitors)*

Liverpool L.R. = Liverpool Law Review *(Kluwer Law International)*

Lloyd's List = Lloyd's List *(Informa Publishing Group Ltd)*

Lloyd's Rep. = Lloyd's Law Reports *(Informa Publishing Group Ltd)*

Lloyd's Rep. Bank. = Lloyd's Law Reports Banking *(Informa Publishing Group Ltd)*

Lloyd's Rep. I.R. = Lloyd's Law Reports Insurance & Reinsurance *(Informa Publishing Group Ltd)*

Lloyd's Rep. Med. = Lloyd's Law Reports Medical *(Informa Publishing Group Ltd)*

Lloyd's Rep. P.N. = Lloyd's Law Reports Professional Negligence *(Informa Publishing Group Ltd)*

M. EC News. = Mercer European Community Newsletter *(William M Mercer Ltd)*

M.D.U. Jour. = Medical Defence Union Journal *(The Medical Defence Union)*

M.F.G. = Mortgage Finance Gazette *(Metropolis International Group Ltd)*

M.F.S. = Managing for Success *(Law Management Section/The Law Society)*

M.I. = Managing Information *(Aslib Information Management)*

M.I.P. = Managing Intellectual Property *(Euromoney Institutional Investor Plc)*

M.J.L.S. = Mountbatten Journal of Legal Studies *(Southampton Institute)*

M.L.J.I. = Medico-Legal Journal of Ireland *(Sweet & Maxwell/Round Hall)*

M.L.N. = Media Lawyer Newsletter *(The Press Association)*

M.L.R. = Modern Law Review *(John Wiley & Sons Ltd)*

M.R.I. = Maritime Risk International *(Informa Publishing Group Ltd)*

Maastricht J. = Maastricht Journal of European and Comparative Law *(Intersentia NV)*

Magistrate = Magistrate *(Magistrates Association)*

Med. L. Int. = Medical Law International *(A B Academic Publishers)*

Med. L. Rev. = Medical Law Review *(Oxford University Press)*

Med. Leg. J. = Medico-Legal Journal *(XPL Publishing)*

Med. Sci. Law = Medicine, Science & the Law *(The Royal Society of Medicine Press)*

Money L.B. = Money Laundering Bulletin *(Informa Publishing Group Ltd)*

N.I.E.R. = National Institute of Economic Review *(The National Institute of Economic Review)*

N.I.L.Q. = Northern Ireland Legal Quarterly *(School of Law)*

N.I.L.R. = Northern Ireland Law Reports *(Butterworth Tolley Publishing)*

N.I.L.R. = Netherlands International Law Review *(Cambridge University Press)*

N.J.I.L. = Nordic Journal of International Law *(Martinus Nijoff Publishers)*

N.L.J. = New Law Journal *(Butterworths Tolley Publishing)*

N.P.C. = New Property Cases *(New Property Cases Ltd)*

N.Q.H.R. = Netherlands Quarterly of Human Rights *(Intersentia NV)*

N.S.A.I.L. = Non-State Actors and International Law *(Martinus Nijhoff Publishers)*

Nott. L.J. = Nottingham Law Journal *(Nottingham Law School)*

O. & I.T. Rev. = Offshore & International Taxation Review *(Key Haven Publications Plc)*

O.D. and I.L. = Ocean Development and International Law *(Taylor & Francis Ltd)*

O.G.J.F.I. = Open Government: A Journal on Freedom of Information *(Liverpool John Moores University)*

O.J.L.S. = Oxford Journal of Legal Studies *(Oxford University Press)*

O.P.L.R. = Occupational Pensions Law Reports *(Eclipse/Butterworth Tolley Publishing)*

O.R. & R. = Operational Risk & Regulation *(Incisive Media Plc)*

O.U.C.L.J. = Oxford University Commonwealth Law Journal *(Hart Publishing Ltd)*

Observer = OECD Observer *(Databeuro Ltd)*

Occ. Pen. = Occupational Pensions *(Eclipse/Butterworth Tolley Publishing)*

Offshore Red = Offshore Red *(ClearView Financial Media Ltd)*

P. & C.R. = Property, Planning and Compensation Reports *(Sweet & Maxwell Ltd)*

P. & D.P. = Privacy & Data Protection *(Privacy & Data Protection)*

P. & S. = Punishment & Society *(Sage Publications Ltd)*

P.A.D. = Planning Appeal Decisions *(Sweet & Maxwell Ltd)*

P.C. & L. = Psychology, Crime & Law *(Taylor & Francis Ltd)*

P.C.B. = Private Client Business *(Sweet & Maxwell Ltd)*

P.C.P. = Private Client Practitioner *(PAM Insight Ltd)*

P.C.R. = Proceeds of Crime Review *(Wildy & Sons Ltd)*

P.G.A.M. = Public General Acts & Measures *(TSO)*

P.H.B. = Parliament House Book *(Sweet & Maxwell Ltd/W. Green)*

P.I. = Personal Injury (Wiley) *(John Wiley & Sons Ltd)*

P.I. Comp. = Personal Injury Compensation *(Informa Publishing Group Ltd)*

P.I.L.J. = Personal Injury Law Journal *(Legalease Ltd)*

P.I.P. = Property in Practice *(Property Section/The Law Society)*

P.I.Q.R. = Personal Injuries and Quantum Reports *(Sweet & Maxwell Ltd)*

P.L. = Public Law *(Sweet & Maxwell Ltd)*

P.L. & B.I.N. = Privacy Laws & Business International Newsletter *(Privacy Laws & Business)*

P.L. & B.U.K.N. = Privacy Laws & Business United Kingdom Newsletter *(Privacy Laws & Business)*

P.L.B. = Property Law Bulletin (S&M) *(Sweet & Maxwell Ltd)*

P.L.C. = Practical Law Companies *(Practical Law Company Ltd)*

P.L.C.R. = Planning Law Case Reports *(Sweet & Maxwell Ltd)*

P.L.J. = Property Law Journal *(Legalease Ltd)*

P.L.R. = Estates Gazette Planning Law Reports *(Estates Gazette)*

P.N. = Professional Negligence *(Bloomsbury Publishing Plc)*

P.N.L.R. = Professional Negligence and Liability Reports *(Sweet & Maxwell Ltd)*

P.P.L.R. = Public Procurement Law Review *(Sweet & Maxwell Ltd)*

P.S.T. = Pension Scheme Trustee *(Informa Publishing Group Ltd)*

P.T. = Pensions Today *(Informa Publishing Group Ltd)*

P.T.P.R. = Personal Tax Planning Review *(Key Haven Publications Plc)*

P.W. = Patent World *(Informa Publishing Group Ltd)*

PS = Probate Section *(Probate Section/The Law Society)*

Palmer's C.L. = Palmer's Company Law *(Sweet & Maxwell Ltd)*

Parl. Aff. = Parliamentary Affairs *(Oxford University Press)*

Pay Mag. = Pay Magazine *(Wolters Kluwer (UK) Ltd)*

Pen. = Pensions *(Palgrave Macmillan)*

Pen. L.R. = Pensions Law Reports *(Incomes Data Services Ltd)*

Pen. Law. = Pension Lawyer *(Association of Penion Lawyers)*

Pen. World = Pensions World *(Butterworth Tolley Publishing)*

Pharm. L.I. = Pharmaceutical Law Insight *(Informa Publishing Group Ltd)*

Pol. J. = Police Journal *(Portland Press Ltd)*

Post Mag. = Post Magazine *(Incisive Media Plc)*

Prison Serv. J. = Prison Service Journal *(Governor, H.M. Prison Leyhill)*

Probat. J. = Probation Journal *(Sage Publications Ltd)*

Prof. L. = Professional Lawyer *(Chancery Law Publishing Ltd)*

Prop. L.B. = Property Law Bulletin (W Green) *(Sweet & Maxwell Ltd/W. Green)*

Q.A. = Quarterly Account *(Institute of Money Advisers)*

Q.B. = Law Reports Queen's Bench *(Incorporated Council of Law Reporting)*

Q.R. = Quantum Reports *(Sweet & Maxwell Ltd)*

Q.R.T.L. = Quarterly Review of Tort Law *(Clarus Press)*

R. & B.C.P. = Renton & Brown's Criminal Procedure *(Sweet & Maxwell Ltd/W. Green)*

R. & B.C.P.L. = Renton & Brown's Criminal Procedure Legislation *(Sweet & Maxwell Ltd/W. Green)*

R. & B.S.O. = Renton & Brown's Statutory Offences *(Sweet & Maxwell Ltd/W. Green)*

R.A. = Rating Appeals *(Rating Publishers Ltd)*

R.A.D.I.C. = African Journal of International and Comparative Law *(African Society of International and Comparative Law)*

R.L.R. = Restitution Law Review *(Marenex Productions)*

R.P.C. = Reports of Patent, Design and Trade Mark Cases *(Sweet & Maxwell Ltd)*

R.T.R. = Road Traffic Reports *(Sweet & Maxwell Ltd)*

R.V.R. = Rating and Valuation Reporter *(Rating Publishers Ltd)*

R.W.L.R. = Rights of Way Law Review *(Rights of Way Law Review)*

Ratio Juris = Ratio Juris *(John Wiley & Sons Ltd)*

Reactions = Reactions *(Euromoney Institutional Investor Plc)*

Recovery = Recovery *(Association of Business Recovery Professionals)*

Reins. = Reinsurance *(Incisive Media Plc)*

Rep. B. = Reparation Bulletin *(Sweet & Maxwell Ltd/W. Green)*

Rep. L.R. = Reparation Law Reports *(Sweet & Maxwell Ltd/W. Green)*

Res Publica = Res Publica *(Kluwer Law International)*

Rev. C.E.E. Law = Review of Central and East European Law *(Martinus Nijhoff Publishers)*

S. & L.S. = Social & Legal Studies *(Sage Publications Ltd)*

S. & T.I. = Shipping & Transport International *(Guthrum House Ltd)*

S. & T.L.I. = Shipping & Transport Lawyer International *(Guthrum House Ltd)*

S. News = Sentencing News *(Sweet & Maxwell Ltd)*

S.B.T. & F. = Small Business Tax & Finance *(Cyan Publishing Services)*

S.C. = Session Cases *(Sweet & Maxwell Ltd/W. Green)*

S.C.C.R. = Scottish Criminal Case Reports *(The Law Society of Scotland)*

S.C.L. = Scottish Criminal Law *(Sweet & Maxwell Ltd/W. Green)*

S.C.L.R. = Scottish Civil Law Reports *(The Law Society of Scotland)*

S.C.P. = Supreme Court Practice, The *(Sweet & Maxwell Ltd)*

S.E.G.J. = Law Society Solicitors' European Group Journal *(Butterworth Tolley Publishing)*

S.F.L.L. = Scottish Family Law Legislation *(Sweet & Maxwell Ltd/W. Green)*

S.H.R.J. = Scottish Human Rights Journal *(Sweet & Maxwell Ltd/W. Green)*

S.I. = Statutory Instruments *(TSO)*

S.J. = Solicitors Journal *(Waterlow Professional Publishing)*

S.J.L.B. = Solicitors Journal LawBrief *(Waterlow Professional Publishing)*

S.L. Rev. = Student Law Review *(Routledge-Cavendish)*

S.L.A. & P. = Sports Law Administration & Practice *(Ivy House Sports Law Publications Ltd)*

S.L.C.R. = Scottish Land Court Reports *(The Law Society of Scotland)*

S.L.G. = Scottish Law Gazette *(Scottish Law Agents Society)*

S.L.L.P. = Scottish Licensing Law and Practice *(Licensing Services Ltd)*

S.L.T. = Scots Law Times *(Sweet & Maxwell Ltd/W. Green)*

S.P.C.L.R. = Scottish Private Client Law Review *(Sweet & Maxwell Ltd/W. Green)*

S.T.C. = Simon's Tax Cases *(Butterworth Tolley Publishing)*

S.T.L. = Shipping and Trade Law *(Informa Publishing Group Ltd)*

S.W.T.I. = Simon's Weekly Tax Intelligence *(Butterworth Tolley Publishing)*

SCOLAG = SCOLAG *(Scottish Legal Action Group)*

SCRIPT-ed = SCRIPT-ed *(University of Edinburgh)*

Soc. L. = Socialist Lawyer *(Haldane Society of Socialist Lawyers)*

Sol. = Solutions *(Dispute Resolution Section/The Law Society)*

Stat. L.R. = Statute Law Review *(Oxford University Press)*

Sudebnik = Sudebnik *(Wildy & Sons Ltd)*

T. & E.P. = Trust & Estates Practitioner *(Tru-Est Limited)*

T. & T. = Trusts & Trustees *(Oxford University Press)*

T.B. = Technical Bulletin *(Association of Business Recovery Professionals)*

T.B.S.P.I. = Technical Bulletin of the Society of Practitioners of Insolvency *(Association of Business Recovery Professionals)*

T.C. = Tax Cases *(TSO)*

T.C.L.R. = Technology and Construction Law Reports *(Sweet & Maxwell Ltd)*

T.E.L. & T.J. = Trusts and Estates Law & Tax Journal *(Legalease Ltd)*

T.E.L.L. = Tolley's Employment Law-Line *(Butterworth Tolley Publishing)*

T.I.A. = Troubled Insurer Alert *(Evandale Publishing Co Ltd)*

T.L.J. = Travel Law Journal *(The Travel Law Centre)*

T.M.I.F. = Tax Management International Forum *(BNA International Inc)*

T.P.A. & A. = Tolley's Practical Audit & Accounting *(Butterworth Tolley Publishing)*

T.P.I. e-commerce = Tax Planning International e-commerce *(BNA International Inc)*

T.P.I.I.T. = Tax Planning International Indirect Taxes *(BNA International Inc)*

T.P.I.J. = Transfer Pricing International Journal *(BNA International Inc)*

T.P.I.R. = Tax Planning International Review *(BNA International Inc)*

T.P.T.N. = Tolley's Practical Tax Newsletter *(Butterworth Tolley Publishing)*

T.W. = Trademark World *(Informa Publishing Group Ltd)*

Tax A. = Tax Adviser *(Croner CCH Group Ltd)*

Tax J. = Tax Journal *(Butterworth Tolley Publishing)*

Tax. = Taxation *(Butterworth Tolley Publishing)*

Taxline = Taxline *(ICAEW)*

The Sentence = The Sentence *(Sentencing Guidelines Secretariat)*

Theo. Crim. = Theoretical Criminology *(Sage Publications Ltd)*

TABLE OF ABBREVIATIONS

Tort & Ins. L.J. = Tort and Insurance Law Journal *(Tort and Insurance Practice Section)*

Tort. L.R. = Tort Law Review *(Sweet & Maxwell Ltd/ESC Publishing)*

Tr. & Est. = Trusts & Estates *(Informa Publishing Group Ltd)*

Trans. L.T. = Transnational Legal Theory *(Hart Publishing Ltd)*

Tribunals = Tribunals *(Judicial Studies Board)*

Tru. L.I. = Trust Law International *(Bloomsbury Publishing Plc)*

U.K.C.L.R. = UK Competition Law Reports *(Jordan & Sons Ltd)*

U.K.H.R.R. = United Kingdom Human Rights Reports *(Jordan & Sons Ltd)*

U.L.R. = Utilities Law Review *(Lawtext Publishing Limited)*

UCL Juris. Rev. = UCL Jurisprudence Review *(University College London)*

UK Prac. Dir. = UK Practice Directions *(TSO)*

UK Pre. Pro. = UK Preaction Protocols *(TSO)*

V. & D.R. = Value Added Tax and Duties Tribunals Reports *(TSO)*

V.A.T.T.R. = Value Added Tax Tribunal Reports *(TSO)*

VAT Dig. = VAT Digest *(Bloomsbury Publishing Plc)*

W. Comp. = World Competition *(Turpin Distribution Serv Ltd)*

W.C.R.R. = World Communications Regulation Report *(BNA International Inc)*

W.D.P.R. = World Data Protection Report *(BNA International Inc)*

W.E.C. & I.P.R. = World E-Commerce & IP Report *(BNA International Inc)*

W.I.P.O.J. = WIPO Journal *(Sweet and Maxwell)*

W.I.P.R. = World Intellectual Property Report *(BNA International Inc)*

W.L. = Water Law *(Lawtext Publishing Limited)*

W.L.L.R. = World Licensing Law Report *(BNA International Inc)*

W.L.R. = Weekly Law Reports *(Incorporated Council of Law Reporting)*

W.L.T.B. = Woodfall Landlord & Tenant Bulletin *(Sweet & Maxwell Ltd)*

W.M. = Wastes Management *(IWM Business Services Ltd)*

W.O.G.L.R. = World Online Gambling Law Report *(Cecile Park Publishing Ltd)*

W.S.L.R. = World Sports Law Report *(Cecile Park Publishing Ltd)*

W.T.J. = World Tax Journal *(IBFD Publications BV)*

W.T.L.R. = Wills & Trusts Law Reports *(Legalease Ltd)*

Wel. & Fam. L. & P. = Welfare and Family: Law & Practice *(XPL Publishing)*

Welf. R. Bull. = Welfare Rights Bulletin *(Child Poverty Action Group Ltd)*

Woodfall = Woodfall: Landlord & Tenant *(Sweet & Maxwell Ltd)*

World I.L.R. = World Internet Law Report *(BNA International Inc)*

World T.R. = World Trade Review *(Cambridge University Press)*

Writ = Writ *(Law Society of Northern Ireland)*

Y.J. = Youth Justice *(Sage Publications Ltd)*

ALPHABETICAL TABLE OF STATUTES

This table lists all the Statutes cited in the Statute Citator

Abolition of Feudal Tenure etc (Scotland) Act 2000 (asp 5)
Access to Health Records Act 1990 (c.23)
Access to Justice Act 1999 (c.22)
Acquisition of Land (Authorisation Procedure) (Scotland) Act 1947 (c.42)
Acquisition of Land Act 1981 (c.67)
Administration of Estates (Small Payments) Act 1965 (c.32)
Administration of Estates Act 1925 (c.23)
Administration of Justice (Miscellaneous Provisions) Act 1933 (c.36)
Administration of Justice (Scotland) Act 1972 (c.59)
Administration of Justice Act 1960 (c.65)
Administration of Justice Act 1969 (c.58)
Administration of Justice Act 1982 (c.53)
Administration of Justice Act 1985 (c.61)
Adoption (Intercountry Aspects) Act 1999 (c.18)
Adoption (Scotland) Act 1978 (c.28)
Adoption Act 1976 (c.36)
Adoption and Children (Scotland) Act 2007 (asp 4)
Adoption and Children Act 2002 (c.38)
Adults with Incapacity (Scotland) Act 2000 (asp 4)
Age-Related Payments Act 2004 (c.10)
Agricultural Holdings (Scotland) Act 1991 (c.55)
Agricultural Holdings Act 1986 (c.5)
Agricultural Marketing Act 1958 (c.47)
Agricultural Produce (Grading and Marking) Act 1928 (c.19)
Agricultural Produce (Grading and Marking) Amendment Act 1931 (c.40)
Agricultural Wages Act 1948 (c.47)
Agriculture (Miscellaneous Provisions) Act 1972 (c.62)
Agriculture (Safety, Health and Welfare Provisions) Act 1956 (c.49)
Agriculture Act 1967 (c.22)
Agriculture Act 1970 (c.40)
Agriculture and Horticulture Act 1964 (c.28)
Air Force Act 1955 (c.19)
Aircraft and Shipbuilding Industries Act 1977 (c.3)
Airports Act 1986 (c.31)
Alcoholic Liquor Duties Act 1979 (c.4)
An Act for inclosing lands in the parish of Saint Mary in the town and county of Nottingham in the town of Nottingham. 1845 (c.7)
Ancient Monuments and Archaeological Areas Act 1979 (c.46)
Animal Boarding Establishments Act 1963 (c.43)
Animal Health Act 1981 (c.22)
Animal Health and Welfare (Scotland) Act 2006 (asp 11)
Animal Welfare Act 2006 (c.45)
Animals (Scientific Procedures) Act 1986 (c.14)
Animals (Scotland) Act 1987 (c.9)
Animals Act 1971 (c.22)
Antarctic Act 1994 (c.15)
Anti-social Behaviour Act 2003 (c.38)
Antisocial Behaviour etc (Scotland) Act 2004 (asp 8)
Anti-terrorism, Crime and Security Act 2001 (c.24)
Apprenticeships, Skills, Children and Learning Act 2009 (c.22)
Appropriation (No.2) Act 2007 (c.10)
Appropriation (No.2) Act 2009 (c.9)
Appropriation Act 2007 (c.1)
Appropriation Act 2008 (c.3)
Appropriation Act 2009 (c.2)
Arbitration Act 1950 (c.27)
Arbitration Act 1996 (c.23)

Architects (Registration) Act 1931 (c.33)
Architects Act 1997 (c.22)
Armed Forces (Pensions and Compensation) Act 2004 (c.32)
Armed Forces Act 1966 (c.45)
Armed Forces Act 1976 (c.52)
Armed Forces Act 1981 (c.55)
Armed Forces Act 1991 (c.62)
Armed Forces Act 1996 (c.46)
Armed Forces Act 2001 (c.19)
Armed Forces Act 2006 (c.52)
Army Act 1955 (c.18)
Asylum and Immigration (Treatment of Claimants, etc.) Act 2004 (c.19)
Asylum and Immigration Act 1996 (c.49)
Asylum and Immigration Appeals Act 1993 (c.23)
Atomic Energy Authority Act 1986 (c.3)
Atomic Weapons Establishment Act 1991 (c.46)
Attachment of Earnings Act 1971 (c.32)
Attempted Rape, etc., Act (Northern Ireland) 1960 (c.3)
Audit Commission Act 1998 (c.18)
Autism Act 2009 (c.15)
Aviation and Maritime Security Act 1990 (c.31)
Aviation Security Act 1982 (c.36)
Bail Act 1976 (c.63)
Bank Charter Act 1844 (c.32)
Bank Notes (Scotland) Act 1845 (c.38)
Bank of England Act 1946 (c.27)
Bank of England Act 1998 (c.11)
Banker's (Ireland) Act 1845 (c.37)
Bankers (Northern Ireland) Act 1928 (c.15)
Bankers Books Evidence Act 1879 (c.11)
Banking (Special Provisions) Act 2008 (c.2)
Banking Act 2009 (c.1)
Banking and Financial Dealings Act 1971 (c.80)
Bankruptcy (Scotland) Act 1985 (c.66)
Bankruptcy Act 1914 (c.59)
Bankruptcy and Diligence etc (Scotland) Act 2007 (asp 3)
Behring Sea Award Act 1894 (c.2)
Betting and Gaming Duties Act 1981 (c.63)
Bills of Exchange Act 1882 (c.61)
Biological Weapons Act 1974 (c.6)
Births and Deaths Registration Act 1926 (c.48)
Births and Deaths Registration Act 1953 (c.20)
Borders, Citizenship and Immigration Act 2009 (c.11)
Breastfeeding etc (Scotland) Act 2005 (asp 1)
Breeding of Dogs Act 1973 (c.60)
British Aerospace Act 1980 (c.26)
British Nationality (Hong Kong) Act 1997 (c.20)
British Nationality Act 1948 (c.56)
British Nationality Act 1981 (c.61)
British Overseas Territories Act 2002 (c.8)
British Settlements Act 1887 (c.54)
British Settlements Act 1945 (c.7)
British Steel Act 1988 (c.35)
British Telecommunications Act 1981 (c.38)
Broadcasting Act 1990 (c.42)
Broadcasting Act 1996 (c.55)
Brunei (Appeals) Act 1989 (c.36)
Budget (Scotland) Act 2007 (asp 9)
Budget (Scotland) Act 2008 (asp 2)
Budget (Scotland) Act 2009 (asp 2)
Building (Scotland) Act 2003 (asp 8)
Building Act 1984 (c.55)
Building Societies (Funding) and Mutual Societies (Transfers) Act 2007 (c.26)

ALPHABETICAL TABLE OF STATUTES

ALPHABETICAL TABLE OF STATUTORY INSTRUMENTS

This table lists all the Statutory Instruments cited in the Statutory Instruments Citator

A63 Trunk Road (Barlby Junction to Bridge Farm) (Detrunking) Order 2004 (3435)

A63 Trunk Road (Osgodby Bypass) Order 2004 (3436)

A77 Trunk Road (Haggstone Climbing Lane and Glen App Carriageway Improvement) (Temporary Prohibition of Traffic, Temporary Prohibition of Overtaking and Temporary Speed Restriction) Order 2007 (SSI 441)

A830 Trunk Road (Arisaig to Kinsadel) (40/30mph Speed Limit) Order 2003 (SSI 240)

Abernant Mine (Diesel Vehicles) Special Regulations 1963 (1335)

Aberpergwm Mine (Diesel Vehicles) Special Regulations 1970 (613)

Abertawe Bro Morgannwg University National Health Service Trust (Establishment) Order 2008 (716)

Absent Voting (Transitional Provisions) (Scotland) Regulations 2008 (48)

Access for Community Air Carriers to Intra-Community Air Routes (Amendment and Other Provisions) Regulations 1993 (3040)

Access for Community Air Carriers to Intra-Community Air Routes (Second Amendment and other Provisions) Regulations 1994 (1731)

Access for Community Air Carriers to Intra-Community Air Routes Regulations 1992 (2993)

Access to Information (Post-Commencement Adoptions) (Wales) Regulations 2005 (2689)

Access to Justice (Northern Ireland) Order 2003 (435)

Access to Justice Act 1999 (Destination of Appeals) (Family Proceedings) Order 2009 (871)

Accession (Immigration and Worker Authorisation) Regulations 2006 (3317)

Accession (Immigration and Worker Registration) Regulations 2004 (1219)

Accounts and Audit Regulations 2003 (533)

Act of Adjournal (Criminal Procedure Rules) 1996 (513)

Act of Sederunt (Child Care and Maintenance Rules) 1997 (291)

Act of Sederunt (Child Support Rules) 1993 (920)

Act of Sederunt (Commissary Business) 1975 (539)

Act of Sederunt (Debt Arrangement and Attachment (Scotland) Act 2002) 2002 (SSI 560)

Act of Sederunt (Fees of Messengers-at-Arms) (No.2) 2002 (SSI 566)

Act of Sederunt (Fees of Sheriff Officers) (No.2) 2002 (SSI 567)

Act of Sederunt (Fees of Solicitors in the Sheriff Court) (Amendment and Further Provisions) 1993 (3080)

Act of Sederunt (Fees of Witnesses and Shorthand Writers in the Sheriff Court) 1992 (1878)

Act of Sederunt (Lands Valuation Appeal Court) 2007 (SSI 539)

Act of Sederunt (Proceedings for Determination of Devolution Issues Rules) 1999 (1347)

Act of Sederunt (Proceedings in the Sheriff Court under the Debtors (Scotland) Act 1987) 1988 (2013)

Act of Sederunt (Registration Appeal Court) 2007 (SSI 113)

Act of Sederunt (Rules of the Court of Session 1994) 1994 (1443)

Act of Sederunt (Sections 25 to 29 of the Law Reform (Miscellaneous Provisions) (Scotland) Act 1990) (Association of Commercial Attorneys) 2009 (SSI 163)

Act of Sederunt (Sheriff Court Ordinary Cause Rules) 1993 (1956)

Act of Sederunt (Sheriff Court Rules) (Miscellaneous Amendments) 2009 (SSI 294)

Act of Sederunt (Small Claim Rules) 2002 (SSI 133)

Act of Sederunt (Summary Applications, Statutory Applications and Appeals etc Rules) 1999 (929)

Act of Sederunt (Summary Cause Rules) 2002 (SSI 132)

Action Programme for Nitrate Vulnerable Zones (Scotland) Amendment Regulations 2008 (SSI 394)

Action Programme for Nitrate Vulnerable Zones (Scotland) Regulations 2008 (SSI 298)

Addition of Vitamins, Minerals and Other Substances (England) Regulations 2007 (1631)

Addition of Vitamins, Minerals and Other Substances (Scotland) Regulations 2007 (SSI 325)

Addition of Vitamins, Minerals and Other Substances (Wales) Regulations 2007 (1984)

Additional Pension and Social Security Pensions (Home Responsibilities) (Amendment) Regulations 2001 (1323)

Adjudications by Case Tribunals and Interim Case Tribunals (Wales) Regulations 2001 (2288)

Administration Charges (Summary of Rights and Obligations) (England) Regulations 2007 (1258)

Administrative Justice and Tribunals Council (Listed Tribunals) (Scotland) Order 2007 (SSI 436)

Administrative Justice and Tribunals Council (Listed Tribunals) Order 2007 (2951)

Adopted Children Register and Parental Order Register (Form of Entry) (Scotland) Regulations 1995 (3158)

Adoption (Designation of Overseas Adoptions) (Variation) (Scotland) Order 1995 (1614)

Adoption (Designation of Overseas Adoptions) Order 1973 (19)

Adoption (Disclosure of Information and Medical Information about Natural Parents) (Scotland) Regulations 2009 (SSI 268)

Adoption (Northern Ireland) Order 1987 (2203)

Adoption Agencies (Scotland) Regulations 1996 (3266)

Adoption Agencies (Scotland) Regulations 2009 (SSI 154)

Adoption Agencies (Wales) Regulations 2005 (1313)

Adoption Agencies Regulations 2005 (389)

Adoption Allowance (Scotland) Regulations 1996 (3257)

Adoption of Children from Overseas (Scotland) Regulations 2001 (SSI 236)

Adoption Support Agencies (England) and Adoption Agencies (Miscellaneous Amendments) Regulations 2005 (2720)

Adoption Support Agencies (Wales) Regulations 2005 (1514)

Adoptions with a Foreign Element (Scotland) Regulations 2009 (SSI 182)

Annesley Mine (Endless Rope Haulage) Special Regulations 1973 (1041)

Antarctic Regulations 1995 (490)

Anthrax Order 1991 (2814)

Anti-Pollution Works Regulations 1999 (1006)

Appeals (Excluded Decisions) (Amendment) Order 2008 (2780)

Appeals (Excluded Decisions) Order 2008 (2707)

Arkwright Mine (Endless Rope Haulage) Special Regulations 1976 (484)

Arley Mine (Diesel Vehicles) Special Regulations 1966 (979)

Armed Forces (Discharge and Transfer to the Reserve Forces) Regulations 2009 (832)

Armed Forces (Entry, Search and Seizure) Order 2003 (2273)

Armed Forces (Entry, Search and Seizure) Order 2006 (3243)

Armed Forces (Forfeiture of Service) Regulations 2009 (833)

Armed Forces (Pensions) (Prescribed Modification) Order 2009 (262)

Armed Forces (Protection of Children of Service Families) Regulations 1996 (1174)

Armed Forces (Review of Court Martial Sentence) (Supplementary Provision) Regulations 2009 (1169)

Armed Forces (Terms of Service) (Amendment) Regulations 2009 (831)

Armed Forces Act 2006 (Transitional Provisions etc) Order 2009 (1059)

Armed Forces and Reserve Forces (Compensation Scheme) Order 2005 (439)

Armed Forces Early Departure Payments Scheme Order 2005 (437)

Armed Forces Pension Scheme Order 2005 (438)

Armed Forces Proceedings (Costs) Regulations 2005 (3478)

Army Terms of Service Regulations 2007 (3382)

Arrangements to Look After Children (Scotland) Regulations 1996 (3262)

Artist's Resale Right Regulations 2006 (346)

Ash Grove No.1 Mine (Diesel Vehicles) Special Regulations 1973 (1206)

Ashington Mine (Endless Rope Haulage) Special Regulations 1971 (1578)

Askern Mine (Endless Rope Haulage) Special Regulations 1974 (2218)

Assembly Learning Grant (Further Education) Regulations 2008 (538)

Assembly Learning Grants (European Institutions) (Wales) (Amendment) (No.2) Regulations 2008 (3114)

Assembly Learning Grants (European Institutions) (Wales) (Amendment) Regulations 2008 (1324)

Assembly Learning Grants (European Institutions) (Wales) (Amendment) Regulations 2009 (2157)

Assembly Learning Grants (European Institutions) (Wales) Regulations 2008 (18)

Assembly Learning Grants and Loans (Higher Education) (Wales) (Amendment) Regulations 2006 (1863)

Assembly Learning Grants and Loans (Higher Education) (Wales) (Amendment) Regulations 2007 (2312)

Assembly Learning Grants and Loans (Higher Education) (Wales) (Amendment) Regulations 2008 (2140)

Assembly Learning Grants and Loans (Higher Education) (Wales) (No.2) Regulations 2008 (3170)

Assembly Learning Grants and Loans (Higher Education) (Wales) Regulations 2008 (1273)

Association of Law Costs Draftsmen Order 2006 (3333)

Assured and Protected Tenancies (Lettings to Students) Regulations 1998 (1967)

Astley Green Mine (Steam Boilers) Special Regulations 1965 (1915)

Asylum and Immigration Tribunal (Procedure) Rules 2005 (230)

Asylum Support (Amendment) Regulations 2008 (760)

Asylum Support (Amendment) Regulations 2009 (485)

Asylum Support Regulations 2000 (704)

Atomic Weapons Establishment (AWE) Aldermaston Byelaws 2007 (1066)

Aujeszky's Disease Order 1983 (344)

Authorised Investment Funds (Tax) (Amendment No.2) Regulations 2008 (1463)

Authorised Investment Funds (Tax) (Amendment) Regulations 2009 (2036)

Authorised Investment Funds (Tax) Regulations 2006 (964)

Avian Influenza (Preventive Measures) (England) Regulations 2006 (2701)

Avian Influenza (Vaccination) (England) Regulations 2006 (2703)

Avian Influenza and Influenza of Avian Origin in Mammals (England) (No.2) Order 2006 (2702)

Aylesbury Vale (Parish Electoral Arrangements and Electoral Changes) Order 2007 (480)

Babbacombe Cliff Lift Railway (Amendment) Regulations 1955 (725)

Babbacombe Cliff Light Railway Order 1923 (1624)

Babbington Mine (Endless Rope Haulage) Special Regulations 1973 (1074)

Baddesley Mine (Endless Rope Haulage) Special Regulations 1976 (27)

Bagworth Mine (Endless Rope Haulage) Special Regulations 1973 (1499)

Bagworth Mine (Pass-Byes) (Revocation) Special Regulations 1969 (727)

Bahama Islands (Procedure in Appeals to Privy Council) Order 1964 (2042)

Bahamas (Procedure in Appeals to Privy Council) (Amendment) Order 1973 (1081)

Bail (Amendment) Act 1993 (Prescription of Prosecuting Authorities) Order 1994 (1438)

Bank Administration (Scotland) Rules 2009 (350)

Bank Administration (Sharing Information) Regulations 2009 (314)

Bank Administration Rules (Northern Ireland) 2009 (63)

Bank Insolvency (No.2) Rules (Northern Ireland) 2009 (122)

Bank Insolvency (Scotland) Rules 2009 (351)

Banking Act 1987 (Exempt Transactions) Regulations 1988 (646)

Banking Act 2009 (Bank Administration) (Modification for Application to Banks in Temporary Public Ownership) Regulations 2009 (312)

Banking Act 2009 (Bank Administration) (Modification for Application to Multiple Transfers) Regulations 2009 (313)

Banking Act 2009 (Parts 2 and 3 Consequential Amendments) Order 2009 (317)

Banking Act 2009 (Restriction of Partial Property Transfers) Order 2009 (322)

Banking Act 2009 (Third Party Compensation Arrangements for Partial Property Transfers) Regulations 2009 (319)

Bankruptcy and Diligence etc (Scotland) Act 2007 (Commencement No.3, Savings and Transitionals) Order 2008 (SSI 115)

Bankruptcy Fees (Scotland) Regulations 1993 (486)

Barbados (Procedure in Appeals to Privy Council) Order 1966 (1456)

Barking, Havering and Redbridge Hospitals National Health Service Trust (Establishment) Order 2000 (1413)

Bates Mine (Diesel Vehicles) Special Regulations 1961 (1273)

Bates Mine (Endless Rope Haulage) Special Regulations 1973 (1689)

Bedfordshire (Coroners) Order 1997 (494)

Bedfordshire (Structural Changes) Order 2008 (907)

Bedfordshire Fire Services (Combination Scheme) Order 1996 (2918)

Beer Regulations 1993 (1228)

Beet Seed (England) Regulations 2002 (3171)

Beet Seed (Wales) Regulations 2005 (3037)

Belarus (Restrictive Measures) (Overseas Territories) Order 2006 (1909)

Benefices Rules 1899 (141)

Bentinck Mine (Diesel Engined Stone Dusting Machine) Regulations 1976 (2046)

Bentinck Mine (Endless Rope Haulage) Special Regulations 1972 (1952)

Bentley Mine (Endless Rope Haulage) Regulations 1977 (203)

Berwick upon Tweed (Closure of Spittal Quay) Harbour Revision Order 2009 (3382)

Berwick Upon Tweed Harbour Revision (Constitution) Order 2009 (1231)

Bestwood Mine (Diesel Vehicles) Special Regulations 1961 (241)

Betting, Gaming, Lotteries and Amusements (Northern Ireland) Order 1985 (1204)

Bevercotes Mine (Diesel Vehicles) Special Regulations 1965 (1194)

Billingham Mine (Explosives) Special Regulations 1960 (724)

Bilsthorpe Mine (Endless Rope Haulage) Special Regulations 1974 (1176)

Bilston Glen Mine (Endless Rope Haulage) Special Regulations 1976 (1609)

Biocidal Products Regulations 2001 (880)

Biofuel (Labelling) Regulations 2004 (3349)

Birch Coppice Mine (Endless Rope Haulage) Special Regulations 1976 (28)

Blackdene Mine (Storage Battery Locomotives) Special Regulations 1969 (1876)

Blackdene Mine (Storage Battery Locomotives) Special Regulations 1976 (1827)

Blackhall Mine (Diesel Vehicles) Special Regulations 1965 (41)

Blaengwrach New Mine (Diesel Vehicles) Special Regulations 1963 (1470)

Blaenserchan Mine (Diesel Vehicles) Regulations 1977 (917)

Blidworth Mine (Man-riding) (Revocation) Special Regulations 1970 (1122)

Blood Safety and Quality Regulations 2005 (50)

Bluetongue Regulations 2008 (962)

Bogside Mine (Endless Rope Haulage) Special Regulations 1976 (482)

Bold Mine (Diesel Vehicles) Special Regulations 1963 (28)

Boldon Mine (Diesel Vehicles) Special Regulations 1962 (1729)

Bolsolver Mine (Endless Rope Haulage) Special Regulations 1976 (485)

Bolton Primary Care Trust (Establishment) Order 2001 (3662)

Book of Scottish Connections Regulations 2008 (SSI 386)

Boulby Mine (Diesel Vehicles) Regulations 1979 (1532)

Bradford & Bingley plc Compensation Scheme Order 2008 (3249)

Bradford & Bingley plc Transfer of Securities and Property etc Order 2008 (2546)

Brandon Pit House Mine (Diesel Vehicles) Special Regulations 1965 (539)

Brenkley Mine (Endless Rope Haulage) Special Regulations 1969 (559)

Brightling Mine (Diesel Vehicles) Special Regulations 1962 (1094)

British Antarctic Territory Court of Appeal (Appeal to Privy Council) Order 1965 (592)

British Citizenship (Designated Service) (Amendment) Order 2008 (135)

British Citizenship (Designated Service) Order 2006 (1390)

British Coal Staff Superannuation Scheme (Modification) Regulations 1994 (2576)

British Indian Ocean Territory (Appeals to Privy Council) Order 1983 (1888)

British Nationality (General) Regulations 2003 (548)

British Protectorates, Protected States and Protected Persons Order 1982 (1070)

British Railways Board (Totnes and Ashburton) Light Railway (Transfer) Order 1969 (508)

British Railways Board (Totnes and Ashburton) Light Railway Order 1967 (1756)

Broadcasting and Communications (Jersey) Order 2004 (308)

Brucellosis (England) Order 2000 (2055)

Brucellosis (Scotland) Regulations 2000 (SSI 364)

Brucellosis and Tuberculosis (Scotland) Compensation Amendment Order 1998 (2181)

Brucellosis and Tuberculosis Compensation (Scotland) Amendment Order 1981 (1448)

Brucellosis and Tuberculosis Compensation (Scotland) Amendment Order 1996 (1358)

Brucellosis and Tuberculosis Compensation (Scotland) Order 1978 (1485)

Brunei (Appeals) Order 1989 (2396)

Building (Amendment No.2) Regulations 2009 (2397)

Building (Approved Inspectors etc.) Regulations 2000 (2532)

Building (Procedure) (Scotland) Regulations 2004 (SSI 428)

Building (Scotland) Regulations 2004 (SSI 406)

Building and Approved Inspectors (Amendment) Regulations 2009 (1219)

Building Regulations 2000 (2531)

Building Societies (Accounts and Related Provisions) Regulations 1998 (504)

Building Societies (Business Names) Regulations 1998 (3186)

Building Societies (Insolvency and Special Administration) Order 2009 (805)

Building Societies (Transfer of Business) Regulations 1998 (212)

Bullcliffe Wood Mine (Suspended Chair Haulage Apparatus) Special Regulations 1970 (36)

Burma (Financial Sanctions) Regulations 2005 (1526)

Burma (Freezing of Funds) (Amendment) Regulations 2003 (1810)

Burma (Freezing of Funds) Regulations 2000 (1472)

Burma (Restrictive Measures) (Overseas Territories) (Amendment) Order 2004 (3333)

Burma (Restrictive Measures) (Overseas Territories) Order 2004 (1979)

ALPHABETICAL TABLE OF STATUTORY INSTRUMENTS

Commercial Agents (Council Directive) Regulations 1993 (3053)

Commission for Healthcare Audit and Inspection (Defence Medical Services) Regulations 2008 (1181)

Commission for Healthcare Audit and Inspection (Explanation, Statements of Action and Co-operation) Regulations 2004 (557)

Commission for Healthcare Audit and Inspection (Membership) Regulations 2003 (3279)

Commission for Social Care Inspection (Children's Rights Director) Regulations 2004 (615)

Commission for Social Care Inspection (Explanation and Co-operation) Regulations 2004 (555)

Commission for Social Care Inspection (Fees and Frequency of Inspections) Regulations 2007 (556)

Commission for Social Care Inspection (Membership) Regulations 2003 (3190)

Common Agricultural Policy (Wine) (England and Northern Ireland) (Amendment) Regulations 2003 (114)

Common Agricultural Policy (Wine) (England and Northern Ireland) (Amendment) Regulations 2004 (1046)

Common Agricultural Policy (Wine) (England and Northern Ireland) (Amendment) Regulations 2005 (2992)

Common Agricultural Policy (Wine) (England and Northern Ireland) (Amendment) Regulations 2006 (1499)

Common Agricultural Policy (Wine) (England and Northern Ireland) (Amendment) Regulations 2007 (1943)

Common Agricultural Policy (Wine) (England and Northern Ireland) Regulations 2001 (686)

Common Agricultural Policy Schemes (Cross-Compliance) (Scotland) Regulations 2004 (SSI 518)

Common Agricultural Policy Single Farm Payment and Support Schemes (Scotland) Regulations 2005 (SSI 143)

Common Agricultural Policy Single Payment and Support Schemes (Amendment No.2) Regulations 2006 (301)

Common Agricultural Policy Single Payment and Support Schemes (Amendment) (No.3) Regulations 2006 (989)

Common Agricultural Policy Single Payment and Support Schemes (Amendment) Regulations 2005 (1087)

Common Agricultural Policy Single Payment and Support Schemes (Amendment) Regulations 2006 (239)

Common Agricultural Policy Single Payment and Support Schemes (Amendment) Regulations 2007 (3182)

Common Agricultural Policy Single Payment and Support Schemes (Amendment) Regulations 2008 (1139)

Common Agricultural Policy Single Payment and Support Schemes (Cross-compliance) (England) (Amendment) Regulations 2006 (3254)

Common Agricultural Policy Single Payment and Support Schemes (Cross-compliance) (England) (Amendment) Regulations 2007 (2500)

Common Agricultural Policy Single Payment and Support Schemes (Cross-compliance) (England) (Amendment) Regulations 2008 (80)

Common Agricultural Policy Single Payment and Support Schemes (Cross-compliance) (England) Regulations 2005 (3459)

Common Agricultural Policy Single Payment and Support Schemes (Integrated Administration and Control System) Regulations 2005 (218)

Common Agricultural Policy Single Payment and Support Schemes (Wales) Regulations 2005 (360)

Common Agricultural Policy Single Payment and Support Schemes Regulations 2005 (219)

Common Agricultural Policy Single Payment Scheme (Set-aside) (England) (Amendment) Regulations 2005 (3460)

Common Agricultural Policy Single Payment Scheme (Set-aside) (England) (Amendment) Regulations 2007 (633)

Common Agricultural Policy Single Payment Scheme (Set-aside) (England) Regulations 2004 (3385)

Commonhold (Land Registration) Rules 2004 (1830)

Commonhold Regulations 2004 (1829)

Commons Registration (England) Regulations 2008 (1961)

Commons Registration (General) Regulations 1966 (1471)

Commonwealth Countries and Republic of Ireland (Immunities and Privileges) Order 1985 (1983)

Communications (Bailiwick of Guernsey) Order 2003 (3195)

Communications (Bailiwick of Guernsey) Order 2004 (307)

Communications (Isle of Man) Order 2003 (3198)

Communications (Jersey) Order 2003 (3197)

Communications (Television Licensing) Regulations 2004 (692)

Community Bus (Amendment) Regulations 1996 (3087)

Community Bus (Amendment) Regulations 1997 (2917)

Community Bus (Amendment) Regulations 2008 (1465)

Community Bus Regulations 1986 (1245)

Community Care (Personal Care and Nursing Care) (Scotland) Regulations 2002 (SSI 303)

Community Care, Services for Carers and Children's Services (Direct Payments) (England) Regulations 2003 (762)

Community Care, Services for Carers and Children's Services (Direct Payments) (Wales) Regulations 2004 (1748)

Community Charges (Administration and Enforcement) Regulations 1989 (438)

Community Interest Company Regulations 2005 (1788)

Community Investment Tax Relief (Accreditation of Community Development Finance Institutions) Regulations 2003 (96)

Community Legal Service (Asylum and Immigration Appeals) Regulations 2005 (966)

Community Legal Service (Cost Protection) Regulations 2000 (824)

Community Legal Service (Costs) Regulations 2000 (441)

Community Legal Service (Financial) Regulations 2000 (516)

Community Legal Service (Funding) (Counsel in Family Proceedings) Order 2001 (1077)

Community Legal Service (Funding) Order 2000 (627)

Community Legal Service (Funding) Order 2007 (2441)

Community Right to Buy (Definition of Excluded Land) (Scotland) Order 2006 (SSI 486)

Community Right to Buy (Forms) (Scotland) Regulations 2004 (SSI 233)

Justice of the Peace Courts (Sheriffdom of North Strathclyde) etc Amendment Order 2009 (SSI 409)

Justice of the Peace Courts (Sheriffdom of North Strathclyde) etc Order 2009 (SSI 331)

Justice of the Peace Courts (Sheriffdom of South Strathclyde, Dumfries and Galloway) Order 2009 (SSI 115)

Justice of the Peace Courts (Sheriffdom of Tayside, Central and Fife) Order 2008 (SSI 363)

Kaupthing Singer & Friedlander Limited Transfer of Certain Rights and Liabilities Order 2008 (2674)

Kellingley Mine (Diesel Vehicles) Special Regulations 1964 (567)

Kellingley Mine (Endless Rope Haulage) Special Regulations 1974 (2219)

Kellingley Mine (Steam Boilers) Regulations 1985 (1162)

Killoch Mine (Endless Rope Haulage) Special Regulations 1976 (1608)

Kiribati Appeals to Judicial Committee Order 1979 (720)

Kiveton Park Mine (Diesel Vehicles) Special Regulations 1974 (2224)

Lambton "D" Mine (Diesel Vehicles) Special Regulations 1963 (132)

Land Charges Rules 1974 (1286)

Land Management Contracts (Menu Scheme) (Scotland) Regulations 2005 (SSI 225)

Land Managers Skills Development Grants (Scotland) Regulations 2008 (SSI 162)

Land Registration (Official Searches) Rules 1988 (629)

Land Registration (Proper Office) Order 2008 (3201)

Land Registration (Proper Office) Order 2009 (1393)

Land Registration (Scotland) Rules 2006 (SSI 485)

Land Registration Fee Order 1986 (1399)

Land Registration Fee Order 1988 (665)

Land Registration Fee Order 1990 (172)

Land Registration Fee Order 2006 (1332)

Land Registration Rules 1925 (1093)

Land Registration Rules 1990 (314)

Land Registration Rules 2003 (1417)

Landfill (Scotland) Regulations 2003 (SSI 235)

Landfill Tax Regulations 1996 (1527)

Landlord and Tenant (Determination of Rateable Value Procedure) Rules 1954 (1255)

Lands Tribunal (Fees) (Amendment) Rules 2002 (770)

Lands Tribunal (Fees) Rules 1996 (1021)

Lands Tribunal (Statutory Undertakers Compensation Jurisdiction) Order 1952 (161)

Lands Tribunal for Scotland Rules 1971 (218)

Lands Tribunal for Scotland Rules 2003 (SSI 452)

Lands Tribunal Rules 1975 (299)

Lands Tribunal Rules 1996 (1022)

Landsbanki Freezing (Amendment) Order 2008 (2766)

Landsbanki Freezing Order 2008 (2668)

Langley Park Mine (Diesel Vehicles) Special Regulations 1965 (272)

Large and Medium-sized Companies and Groups (Accounts and Reports) Regulations 2008 (410)

Lasting Powers of Attorney, Enduring Powers of Attorney and Public Guardian Regulations 2007 (1253)

Law Reform (Miscellaneous Provisions) (Northern Ireland) Order 2005 (1452)

Lea Hall Mine (Diesel Vehicles) Special Regulations 1962 (735)

Leader Grants (Scotland) Regulations 2008 (SSI 66)

Leasehold Valuation Tribunals (Procedure) (England) Regulations 2003 (2099)

Lebanon and Syria (United Nations Measures) (Overseas Territories) Order 2006 (311)

Ledston Luck Mine (Diesel Vehicles) Special Regulations 1963 (1117)

Ledston Luck Mine (Rope Hauled Sledge) Special Regulations 1972 (1389)

Legal Advice and Assistance (Duty Solicitor) (Remuneration) Regulations 1989 (341)

Legal Advice and Assistance (Scope) Regulations 1989 (550)

Legal Advice and Assistance at Police Stations (Remuneration) Regulations 1989 (342)

Legal Advice and Assistance Regulations 1989 (340)

Legal Aid (Scotland) (Children) Regulations 1997 (690)

Legal Aid in Contempt of Court Proceedings (Scotland) (Fees) Regulations 1992 (1228)

Legal Aid in Contempt of Court Proceedings (Scotland) Regulations 1992 (1227)

Legal Aid in Criminal and Care Proceedings (Costs) Regulations 1989 (343)

Legal Aid in Criminal and Care Proceedings (General) Regulations 1989 (344)

Legal Aid, Advice and Assistance (Northern Ireland) Order 1981 (228)

Legal Officers (Annual Fees) Order 2008 (1969)

Legal Officers Fees Order 1974 (1837)

Legal Services Ombudsman (Extension of Remit) Regulations 2004 (2757)

Legal Services Ombudsman (Jurisdiction) (Amendment) Order 1998 (935)

Legal Services Ombudsman (Jurisdiction) (Amendment) Order 1999 (2905)

Legal Services Ombudsman (Jurisdiction) (Amendment) Order 2005 (489)

Legal Services Ombudsman (Jurisdiction) (Amendment) Order 2006 (3362)

Legal Services Ombudsman (Jurisdiction) Order 1990 (2485)

Legislative and Regulatory Reform (Regulatory Functions) Order 2007 (3544)

Legislative Reform (Health and Safety Executive) Order 2008 (960)

Less Favoured Area Support Scheme (Scotland) Regulations 2001 (SSI 50)

Less Favoured Area Support Scheme (Scotland) Regulations 2002 (SSI 139)

Less Favoured Area Support Scheme (Scotland) Regulations 2003 (SSI 129)

Less Favoured Area Support Scheme (Scotland) Regulations 2004 (SSI 70)

Less Favoured Area Support Scheme (Scotland) Regulations 2005 (SSI 569)

Less Favoured Area Support Scheme (Scotland) Regulations 2007 (SSI 439)

Licensed Conveyancers (Compensation for Inadequate Professional Services) Order 2000 (643)

Licensed Dealers (Conduct of Business) Rules 1983 (585)

Licensing (Northern Ireland) Order 1996 (3158)

Licensing Act 2003 (Fees) Regulations 2005 (79)

Licensing Act 2003 (Licensing authority's register) (other information) Regulations 2005 (43)

Licensing Act 2003 (Premises licences and club premises certificates) Regulations 2005 (42)

Licensing and Management of Houses in Multiple Occupation (Additional Provisions) (England) Regulations 2007 (1903)

I

Markham Mine (Diesel Vehicles) Regulations 1976 (1734)
Marley Hill Mine (Diesel Vehicles) Special Regulations 1964 (379)
Marriage (Prescription of Forms) (Scotland) Regulations 1997 (2349)
Materials and Articles in Contact with Food (England) Regulations 2007 (2790)
Materials and Articles in Contact with Food (Scotland) Regulations 2007 (SSI 471)
Materials and Articles in Contact with Food (Wales) Regulations 2007 (3252)
Matrimonial Causes (Costs) Rules 1979 (399)
Matrimonial Causes Rules 1977 (344)
Measham Mine (Endless Rope Haulage) Special Regulations 1974 (2220)
Measuring Container Bottles (EEC Requirements) Regulations 1977 (932)
Measuring Equipment (Capacity Measures and Testing Equipment) Regulations 1995 (735)
Measuring Equipment (Intoxicating Liquor) Regulations 1983 (1656)
Measuring Equipment (Liquid Fuel and Lubricants) Regulations 1995 (1014)
Measuring Equipment (Liquid Fuel delivered from Road Tankers) Regulations 1983 (1390)
Measuring Equipment (Measures of Length) Regulations 1986 (1682)
Measuring Instruments (Automatic Catchweighers) Regulations 2006 (1257)
Measuring Instruments (Automatic Discontinuous Totalisers) Regulations 2006 (1255)
Measuring Instruments (Automatic Gravimetric Filling Instruments) Regulations 2006 (1258)
Measuring Instruments (Automatic Rail-weighbridges) Regulations 2006 (1256)
Measuring Instruments (Beltweighers) Regulations 2006 (1259)
Measuring Instruments (Capacity Serving Measures) Regulations 2006 (1264)
Measuring Instruments (Cold-water Meters) Regulations 2006 (1268)
Measuring Instruments (EEC Requirements) (Fees) Regulations 2004 (1300)
Measuring Instruments (EEC Requirements) (Gas Volume Meters) Regulations 1988 (296)
Measuring Instruments (EEC Requirements) Regulations 1988 (186)
Measuring Instruments (Liquid Fuel and Lubricants) Regulations 2006 (1266)
Measuring Instruments (Liquid Fuel delivered from Road Tankers) Regulations 2006 (1269)
Measuring Instruments (Material Measures of Length) Regulations 2006 (1267)
Meat (Official Controls Charges) (England) Regulations 2008 (447)
Meat (Official Controls Charges) (Scotland) Regulations 2008 (SSI 98)
Meat (Official Controls Charges) (Wales) Regulations 2008 (601)
Meat Products (England) Regulations 2003 (2075)
Meat Products (Scotland) Regulations 2004 (SSI 6)
Meat Products (Wales) Regulations 2004 (1396)
Medical Devices (Consultation Requirements) (Fees) Regulations 1995 (449)
Medical Devices Regulations 2002 (618)
Medical Profession (Miscellaneous Amendments) Order 2008 (3131)
Medicines (Advertising) Regulations 1994 (1932)
Medicines (Exemption from Licences) (Special and Transitional Cases) Order 1971 (1450)
Medicines (Homoeopathic Medicinal Products for Human Use) Regulations 1994 (105)
Medicines (Pharmacies) (Applications for Registration and Fees) Amendment Regulations 2007 (3282)
Medicines (Pharmacies) (Applications for Registration and Fees) Amendment Regulations 2008 (2946)
Medicines (Pharmacies) (Applications for Registration and Fees) Regulations 1973 (1822)
Medicines (Pharmacy and General Sale Exemption) Order 1980 (1924)
Medicines (Products for Human Use) (Fees) Regulations 2009 (389)
Medicines (Products for Human Use-Fees) Regulations 2008 (552)
Medicines (Sale or Supply) (Miscellaneous Provisions) Regulations 1980 (1923)
Medicines (Surgical Materials) Order 1971 (1267)
Medicines (Traditional Herbal Medicinal Products for Human Use) Regulations 2005 (2750)
Medicines for Human Use (Clinical Trials) Regulations 2004 (1031)
Medicines for Human Use (Fees and Miscellaneous Amendments) Regulations 2003 (2321)
Medicines for Human Use (Manufacturing, Wholesale Dealing and Miscellaneous Amendments) Regulations 2005 (2789)
Medicines for Human Use (Marketing Authorisations Etc.) Regulations 1994 (3144)
Mental Capacity (Deprivation of Liberty Assessments, Standard Authorisations and Disputes about Residence) (Wales) Regulations 2009 (783)
Mental Capacity (Deprivation of Liberty Standard Authorisations, Assessments and Ordinary Residence) Regulations 2008 (1858)
Mental Capacity Act 2005 (Independent Mental Capacity Advocates) (General) Regulations 2006 (1832)
Mental Capacity Act 2005 (Independent Mental Capacity Advocates) (Wales) Regulations 2007 (852)
Mental Health (Advance Statements) (Prescribed Class of Persons) (Scotland) (No.2) Regulations 2004 (SSI 429)
Mental Health (Approval of Persons to be Approved Mental Health Professionals) (Wales) Regulations 2008 (2436)
Mental Health (Approved Mental Health Professionals) (Approval) (England) Regulations 2008 (1206)
Mental Health (Care and Treatment) (Scotland) Act 2003 (Consequential Provisions) Order 2005 (2078)
Mental Health (Hospital, Guardianship and Treatment) (England) Regulations 2008 (1184)
Mental Health (Northern Ireland) Order 1986 (595)
Mental Health (Patient Representation) (Prescribed Persons) (Scotland) (No.2) Regulations 2004 (SSI 430)
Mental Health Act 1983 (Independent Mental Health Advocates) (England) Regulations 2008 (3166)
Mental Health Act 2007 (Consequential Amendments) Order 2008 (2828)
Mental Health Review Tribunal for Wales Rules 2008 (2705)
Mental Health Review Tribunal Rules 1983 (942)
Mental Health Tribunal for Scotland (Appointment of General Members) Regulations 2004 (SSI 375)
Mental Health Tribunal for Scotland (Appointment of Medical Members) Regulations 2004 (SSI 374)

ALPHABETICAL TABLE OF STATUTORY INSTRUMENTS

Smoke Control Areas (Exempt Fireplaces) (Scotland) Order 2001 (SSI 16)

Smoke Control Areas (Exempted Fireplaces) (England) (No.2) Order 2008 (2343)

Smoke Control Areas (Exempted Fireplaces) (England) (No.2) Order 2009 (2190)

Smoke Control Areas (Exempted Fireplaces) (England) Order 2009 (449)

Smoke Control Areas (Exempted Fireplaces) (No.2) Order 1990 (2457)

Smoke Control Areas (Exempted Fireplaces) (Scotland) Order 1982 (448)

Smoke Control Areas (Exempted Fireplaces) (Scotland) Order 1983 (1573)

Smoke Control Areas (Exempted Fireplaces) (Scotland) Order 1984 (1805)

Smoke Control Areas (Exempted Fireplaces) (Scotland) Order 1985 (315)

Smoke Control Areas (Exempted Fireplaces) (Scotland) Order 1987 (383)

Smoke Control Areas (Exempted Fireplaces) (Scotland) Order 1989 (888)

Smoke Control Areas (Exempted Fireplaces) (Scotland) Order 1999 (SSI 58)

Smoke Control Areas (Exempted Fireplaces) (Wales) Order 2008 (3101)

Smoke Control Areas (Exempted Fireplaces) Order 1991 (2892)

Smoke Control Areas (Exempted Fireplaces) Order 1992 (2811)

Smoke Control Areas (Exempted Fireplaces) Order 1993 (2277)

Smoke Control Areas (Exempted Fireplaces) Order 1996 (1108)

Smoke Control Areas (Exempted Fireplaces) Order 1997 (3009)

Smoke-free (Exemptions and Vehicles) Regulations 2007 (765)

Snibston Mine (Diesel Vehicles) Special Regulations 1976 (480)

Snibston Mine (Endless Rope Haulage) Special Regulations 1976 (82)

Social Fund (Applications and Miscellaneous Provisions) Regulations 2008 (2265)

Social Fund Cold Weather Payments (General) Regulations 1988 (1724)

Social Fund Winter Fuel Payment (Temporary Increase) Regulations 2008 (1778)

Social Fund Winter Fuel Payment Regulations 2000 (729)

Social Security (Australia) Order 2000 (3255)

Social Security (Benefit) (Members of the Forces) Regulations 1975 (493)

Social Security (Categorisation of Earners) Regulations 1978 (1689)

Social Security (Claims and Payments) Regulations 1987 (1968)

Social Security (Contributions) Regulations 1979 (591)

Social Security (Contributions) Regulations 2001 (1004)

Social Security (Crediting and Treatment of Contributions, and National Insurance Numbers) Regulations 2001 (769)

Social Security (Credits) Regulations 1975 (556)

Social Security (Disability Living Allowance) Regulations 1991 (2890)

Social Security (General Benefit) Regulations 1982 (1408)

Social Security (Graduated Retirement Benefit) (No.2) Regulations 1978 (393)

Social Security (Graduated Retirement Benefit) Regulations 2005 (454)

Social Security (Housing Costs Special Arrangements) (Amendment and Modification) Regulations 2008 (3195)

Social Security (Immigration and Asylum) Consequential Amendments Regulations 2000 (636)

Social Security (Incapacity Benefit Work-focused Interviews) Regulations 2008 (2928)

Social Security (Incapacity Benefit) (Transitional) Regulations 1995 (310)

Social Security (Incapacity Benefit) Regulations 1994 (2946)

Social Security (Incapacity for Work) (General) Regulations 1995 (311)

Social Security (Industrial Injuries) (Prescribed Diseases) Regulations 1985 (967)

Social Security (Invalid Care Allowance) Regulations 1976 (409)

Social Security (Jobcentre Plus Interviews) Regulations 2001 (3210)

Social Security (Jobcentre Plus Interviews) Regulations 2002 (1703)

Social Security (Maternity Allowance) Regulations 1987 (416)

Social Security (Miscellaneous Amendments) (No.6) Regulations 2008 (2767)

Social Security (Northern Ireland) Order 1998 (1506)

Social Security (Overlapping Benefits) Regulations 1979 (597)

Social Security (Payments on account, Overpayments and Recovery) Regulations 1988 (664)

Social Security (Recovery of Benefits) (Lump Sum Payments) Regulations 2008 (1596)

Social Security (Recovery of Benefits) (Northern Ireland) Order 1997 (1183)

Social Security (Reduced Rates of Class 1 Contributions, Rebates and Minimum Contributions) Order 2006 (1009)

Social Security (Widow's Benefit and Retirement Pensions) Regulations 1979 (642)

Social Security (Widow's Benefit, Retirement Pensions and Other Benefits) (Transitional) Regulations 1979 (643)

Social Security (Work-focused Interviews) Regulations 2000 (897)

Social Security and Child Support (Decisions and Appeals) Regulations 1999 (991)

Social Security Benefit (Computation of Earnings) Regulations 1996 (2745)

Social Security Benefit (Dependency) Regulations 1977 (343)

Social Security Benefit (Persons Abroad) Regulations 1975 (563)

Social Security Benefits Up-rating Order 2008 (632)

Social Security Benefits Up-rating Order 2009 (497)

Social Security Benefits Up-rating Regulations 2008 (667)

Social Security Contributions (Decisions and Appeals) (Amendment) Regulations 2001 (4023)

Social Security Contributions (Decisions and Appeals) Regulations 1999 (1027)

Social Security Contributions (Intermediaries) Regulations 2000 (727)

Social Security Contributions (Transfer of Functions, etc.) (Northern Ireland) Order 1999 (671)

Solicitors (Non-Contentious Business) Remuneration Order 1994 (2616)

Solicitors Recognised Bodies Order 1991 (2684)

Solicitors Remuneration Order 1972 (1139)

Solsgirth Nos 1 & 2 Mine (Endless Rope Haulage) Special Regulations 1976 (1607)

Somalia (United Nations Sanctions) (Overseas Territories) Order 2002 (2631)

South Crofty Mine (Locomotives) Special Regulations 1965 (759)

South Georgia and South Sandwich Islands (Appeals to Privy Council) Order 1985 (450)

South Wales Fire Services (Combination Scheme) Order 1995 (3230)

Southampton Airport (Designation) (Detention and Sale of Aircraft) Order 1972 (189)

Sovereign Base Areas of Akrotiri and Dhekelia (Appeals to Privy Council) Order in Council 1961 (59)

Special Annual Allowance Charge (Application to Members of Currently-Relieved Non-UK Pension Schemes) Order 2009 (2031)

Special Commissioners (Amendment of the Taxes Management Act 1970) Regulations 1999 (3294)

Special Commissioners (Jurisdiction and Procedure) (Amendment) Regulations 1999 (3292)

Special Commissioners (Jurisdiction and Procedure) (Amendment) Regulations 2000 (288)

Special Commissioners (Jurisdiction and Procedure) (Amendment) Regulations 2003 (968)

Special Commissioners (Jurisdiction and Procedure) (Amendment) Regulations 2005 (341)

Special Commissioners (Jurisdiction and Procedure) Regulations 1994 (1811)

Special Educational Needs Tribunal Regulations 2001 (600)

Special Waste Regulations 1996 (972)

Specified Animal Pathogens (Scotland) Order 2009 (SSI 45)

Specified Animal Pathogens (Wales) Order 2008 (1270)

Specified Animal Pathogens Amendment (Scotland) Order 2007 (SSI 30)

Specified Animal Pathogens Order 1998 (463)

Specified Animal Pathogens Order 2008 (944)

Specified Body (Consumer Claims) Order 2005 (2365)

Specified Diseases (Notification) Order 1996 (2628)

Specified Sugar Products (England) Regulations 2003 (1563)

Specified Sugar Products (Scotland) Regulations 2003 (SSI 527)

Specified Sugar Products (Wales) Regulations 2003 (3047)

Spirit Drinks Regulations 2008 (3206)

Spring Traps Approval Order 1995 (2427)

St Helena Constitution Order 1988 (1842)

St Helena Constitution Order 1989 (155)

St Helena Court of Appeal (Appeal to Privy Council) Order 1964 (1846)

St Mary's Music School (Aided Places) (Scotland) Regulations 2001 (SSI 223)

Staffing of Maintained Schools (Wales) Regulations 2006 (873)

Stafford Mine (Diesel Vehicles) Special Regulations 1965 (1699)

Stakeholder Pension Schemes Regulations 2000 (1403)

Stamp Duty (Collection and Recovery of Penalties) Regulations 1999 (2537)

Stamp Duty and Stamp Duty Reserve Tax (Investment Exchanges and Clearing Houses) (European Central Counterparty Limited and the Turquoise Multilateral Trading Facility) Regulations 2008 (1814)

Stamp Duty and Stamp Duty Reserve Tax (Investment Exchanges and Clearing Houses) Regulations (No.10) 2009 (1831)

Stamp Duty and Stamp Duty Reserve Tax (Investment Exchanges and Clearing Houses) Regulations (No.2) 2009 (194)

Stamp Duty and Stamp Duty Reserve Tax (Investment Exchanges and Clearing Houses) Regulations (No.3) 2009 (397)

Stamp Duty Land Tax (Administration) Regulations 2003 (2837)

Stamp Duty Land Tax (Appeals) Regulations 2004 (1363)

Stamp Duty Land Tax (Exemption of Certain Acquisitions of Residential Property) Regulations 2008 (2339)

Stamp Duty Land Tax (Variation of Part 4 of the Finance Act 2003) Regulations 2008 (2338)

Stamp Duty Reserve Tax Regulations 1986 (1711)

Standards Committee (England) Regulations 2008 (1085)

Standing Civilian Courts (Evidence) Rules 2006 (2891)

Standing Civilian Courts Order 1997 (172)

State Pension Credit Regulations 2002 (1792)

Statistics of Trade (Customs and Excise) Regulations 1992 (2790)

Statutory Auditors and Third Country Auditors Regulations 2007 (3494)

Statutory Maternity Pay (General) Regulations 1986 (1960)

Statutory Paternity Pay and Statutory Adoption Pay (Weekly Rates) Regulations 2002 (2818)

Statutory Rules (Northern Ireland) Order 1973 (1513)

Statutory Rules (Northern Ireland) Order 1979 (1573)

Strategic Investment and Regeneration of Sites (Northern Ireland) Order 2003 (410)

Street Works (Charges for Unreasonably Prolonged Occupation of the Highway) (England) Regulations 2001 (1281)

Street Works (Charges for Unreasonably Prolonged Occupation of the Highway) (England) Regulations 2009 (303)

Street Works (Charges for Unreasonably Prolonged Occupation of the Highway) (Wales) Regulations 2009 (1268)

Street Works (Fixed Penalty) (England) Regulations 2007 (1952)

Street Works (Fixed Penalty) (Wales) Regulations 2008 (102)

Street Works (Inspection Fees) (England) Regulations 2002 (2092)

Street Works (Inspection Fees) (Wales) Regulations 2006 (1532)

Street Works (Maintenance) Regulations 1992 (1691)

Street Works (Qualifications of Supervisors and Operatives) Regulations 1992 (1687)

Street Works (Registers, Notices, Directions and Designations) (England) Regulations 2007 (1951)

Street Works (Registers, Notices, Directions and Designations) (Wales) (No.2) Regulations 2008 (540)

Street Works (Registers, Notices, Directions and Designations) (Wales) Regulations 2008 (101)

Street Works (Registers, Notices, Directions and Designations) Regulations 1992 (2985)

Street Works (Reinstatement) Regulations 1992 (1689)

Street Works (Sharing of Costs of Works) (England) Regulations 2000 (3314)

Street Works (Sharing of Costs of Works) (Wales) Regulations 2005 (1721)

Street Works Register (Registration Fees) Regulations 1999 (1048)

Students Allowances (Scotland) Regulations 2007 (SSI 153)

STATUTE CITATOR 2009

The Statute Citator covers the period 2009 and is up to date to **March 1, 2010**. It covers both public and local Statutes and comprises in a single table:

    (i) Statutes passed during this period;
    (ii) Statutes affected during this period by Statute or Statutory Instrument;
    (iii) Statutes judicially considered during this period;
    (iv) Statutes repealed and amended during this period; and
    (v) Statutes under which Statutory Instruments have been made during this period.

The material is arranged in numerical order under the relevant year.

Definitions of legislative effects:

"added"	: new provisions are inserted by subsequent legislation
"amended"	: text of legislation is modified by subsequent legislation
"applied"	: brought to bear, or exercised by subsequent legislation
"consolidated"	: used where previous Acts in the same subject area are brought together in subsequent legislation, with or without amendments
"disapplied"	: an exception made to the application of an earlier enactment
"enabling"	: giving power for the relevant SI to be made
"referred to"	: direction from other legislation without specific effect or application
"repealed"	: rescinded by subsequent legislation
"restored"	: reinstated by subsequent legislation (where previously repealed/revoked)
"substituted"	: text of provision is completely replaced by subsequent legislation
"varied"	: provisions modified in relation to their application to specified areas or circumstances, however the text itself remains unchanged

ACTS OF THE SCOTTISH PARLIAMENT

2000

asp 1. Public Finance and Accountability (Scotland) Act 2000
referred to: 2009 asp 2 s.9
s.4, applied: 2009 asp 2 s.3, s.6

asp 4. Adults with Incapacity (Scotland) Act 2000
applied: 2009 c.24 s.43, SI 2009/457 Reg.9
Part 2, applied: SSI 2009/352 Sch.1 para.14
s.1, applied: SSI 2009/352 Sch.1 para.10
s.28, applied: SSI 2009/352 Sch.1 para.14
s.28A, applied: SSI 2009/352 Sch.1 para.14
s.28B, applied: SSI 2009/352 Sch.1 para.14

asp 5. Abolition of Feudal Tenure etc (Scotland) Act 2000
Sch.12 Part 1 para.24, repealed: 2009 asp 6 Sch.3 para.11

asp 7. Ethical Standards in Public Life etc (Scotland) Act 2000
s.28, enabling: SSI 2009/286
s.32, enabling: SSI 2009/287
Sch.3, amended: 2009 asp 12 Sch.2 para.3, SSI 2009/286 Art.2

asp 8. Education and Training (Scotland) Act 2000
s.1, enabling: SSI 2009/176
s.2, enabling: SSI 2009/176

asp 10. National Parks (Scotland) Act 2000
s.12, applied: SSI 2009/53 Reg.2

2000–cont.

asp 10. National Parks (Scotland) Act 2000–*cont.*
Sch.2 para.15, amended: SI 2009/1941 Sch.1 para.186

asp 11. Regulation of Investigatory Powers (Scotland) Act 2000
s.2, amended: SI 2009/1941 Sch.1 para.187
s.8, enabling: SSI 2009/340

2001

asp 7. Convention Rights (Compliance) (Scotland) Act 2001
s.10, repealed (in part): 2009 asp 9 Sch.6

asp 8. Regulation of Care (Scotland) Act 2001
Part 1, applied: SI 2009/1547 Sch.1 para.16, Sch.1 para.19, SSI 2009/154 Sch.1 para.14
s.7, applied: SI 2009/1547 Sch.1 para.22
s.12, applied: SI 2009/1547 Sch.1 para.22
s.18, applied: SI 2009/1547 Sch.1 para.22
s.21, applied: SI 2009/1547 Sch.3 para.2
s.22, applied: SI 2009/1547 Sch.3 para.2
s.25, amended: SSI 2009/131 Art.4, Art.5
s.25, applied: SSI 2009/118 Reg.15
s.25, enabling: SSI 2009/131
s.27, applied: SSI 2009/118 Reg.15
s.28, applied: SSI 2009/130
s.28, enabling: SSI 2009/32, SSI 2009/130

2001– cont.

asp 8. Regulation of Care (Scotland) Act 2001–*cont.*
s.29, applied: SI 2009/1547 Sch.3 para.2, SSI 2009/90, SSI 2009/91, SSI 2009/118
s.29, enabling: SSI 2009/32, SSI 2009/90, SSI 2009/91, SSI 2009/118, SSI 2009/349
s.44, applied: SSI 2009/350
s.44, enabling: SSI 2009/350
s.78, applied: SSI 2009/130, SSI 2009/131
Sch.3 para.25, repealed: 2009 asp 9 Sch.6

asp 10. Housing (Scotland) Act 2001
s.58, amended: SI 2009/1941 Sch.1 para.191
s.82, amended: SI 2009/1941 Sch.1 para.191
s.83, amended: SI 2009/1941 Sch.1 para.191
Sch.1 para.8, amended: SSI 2009/248 Sch.1 para.9
Sch.7 Part 2 para.4, amended: SI 2009/1941 Sch.1 para.191
Sch.7 Part 2 para.6, amended: SI 2009/1941 Sch.1 para.191
Sch.7 Part 2 para.8, amended: SI 2009/1941 Sch.1 para.191
Sch.7 Part 2 para.9, amended: SI 2009/1941 Sch.1 para.191
Sch.7 Part 2 para.10, amended: SI 2009/1941 Sch.1 para.191
Sch.7 Part 2 para.12, amended: SI 2009/1941 Sch.1 para.191
Sch.8 para.2, amended: SI 2009/1941 Sch.1 para.191
Sch.8 para.3, amended: SI 2009/1941 Sch.1 para.191
Sch.8 para.7, amended: SI 2009/1941 Sch.1 para.191

asp 13. International Criminal Court (Scotland) Act 2001
varied: SI 2009/317 Sch.1

2002

asp 1. Scottish Local Government (Elections) Act 2002
s.1, repealed: 2009 asp 10 Sch.1 para.3

asp 3. Water Industry (Scotland) Act 2002
s.25, amended: SI 2009/1941 Sch.1 para.200
s.42, applied: 2009 asp 2 Sch.5
s.43, amended: SI 2009/1941 Sch.1 para.200
s.56, amended: 2009 asp 12 s.74
Sch.7 para.3, repealed: 2009 asp 6 Sch.3 para.13

asp 5. Community Care and Health (Scotland) Act 2002
s.1, enabling: SSI 2009/137, SSI 2009/138
s.2, enabling: SSI 2009/138
s.23, applied: SSI 2009/137, SSI 2009/138
s.23, enabling: SSI 2009/138
Sch.1 para.2, substituted: SSI 2009/137 Art.2

asp 11. Scottish Public Services Ombudsman Act 2002
s.3, enabling: SSI 2009/236
s.21, amended: 2009 c.21 Sch.5 para.15
s.24, applied: SSI 2009/236
Sch.2 Part 2 para.27, amended: SI 2009/1941 Sch.1 para.201
Sch.2 Part 2 para.38A, added: 2009 asp 12 Sch.2 para.4
Sch.2 Part 2 para.66, repealed: SSI 2009/236 Art.2

asp 13. Freedom of Information (Scotland) Act 2002
applied: SSI 2009/440 Reg.12
s.47, referred to: SSI 2009/440 Reg.12
s.47, varied: SSI 2009/440 Sch.1 para.1, Sch.1 para.2
s.48, referred to: SSI 2009/440 Reg.12
s.48, varied: SSI 2009/440 Sch.1 para.1, Sch.1 para.3
s.49, referred to: SSI 2009/440 Reg.12

2002– cont.

asp 13. Freedom of Information (Scotland) Act 2002– *cont.*
s.49, varied: SSI 2009/440 Sch.1 para.1, Sch.1 para.4
s.50, referred to: SSI 2009/440 Reg.12
s.50, varied: SSI 2009/440 Sch.1 para.1, Sch.1 para.5
s.51, referred to: SSI 2009/440 Reg.12
s.51, varied: SSI 2009/440 Sch.1 para.1, Sch.1 para.6
s.53, referred to: SSI 2009/440 Reg.12
s.53, varied: SSI 2009/440 Sch.1 para.1, Sch.1 para.7
s.54, referred to: SSI 2009/440 Reg.12
s.54, varied: SSI 2009/440 Sch.1 para.1
s.55, referred to: SSI 2009/440 Reg.12
s.55, varied: SSI 2009/440 Sch.1 para.1, Sch.1 para.8
s.56, referred to: SSI 2009/440 Reg.12
s.56, varied: SSI 2009/440 Sch.1 para.1
s.63, applied: SSI 2009/440 Reg.12
Sch.1 Part 7 para.81A, added: 2009 asp 12 Sch.2 para.5
Sch.3 para.1, varied: SSI 2009/440 Sch.1 para.9
Sch.3 para.7, varied: SSI 2009/440 Sch.1 para.9

asp 17. Debt Arrangement and Attachment (Scotland) Act 2002
varied: SI 2009/317 Sch.1
Part 1, applied: 2009 asp 12 Sch.1 para.5, 2009 c.23 Sch.1 para.9
s.2, enabling: SSI 2009/234, SSI 2009/258
s.4, enabling: SSI 2009/234, SSI 2009/258
s.5, enabling: SSI 2009/234, SSI 2009/258
s.6, enabling: SSI 2009/234, SSI 2009/258
s.7, enabling: SSI 2009/234, SSI 2009/258
s.62, enabling: SSI 2009/234, SSI 2009/258

2003

asp 1. Local Government in Scotland Act 2003
Commencement Orders: SSI 2009/275 Art.2
s.62, enabling: SSI 2009/275

asp 2. Land Reform (Scotland) Act 2003
s.33, applied: SSI 2009/207 Art.2
s.33, enabling: SSI 2009/207
s.34, amended: SI 2009/1941 Sch.1 para.218
s.37, applied: SSI 2009/156 Reg.2, Reg.3, SSI 2009/207 Art.2
s.37, referred to: SSI 2009/156 Reg.4
s.37, enabling: SSI 2009/156
s.44, applied: SSI 2009/156 Reg.2
s.48, applied: SSI 2009/156 Reg.5
s.48, enabling: SSI 2009/156
s.49, applied: SSI 2009/156 Reg.6
s.49, enabling: SSI 2009/156
s.69A, applied: SSI 2009/160 Reg.2
s.71, amended: SI 2009/1941 Sch.1 para.218
s.73, applied: SSI 2009/160 Reg.2
s.73, enabling: SSI 2009/160
s.82, applied: SSI 2009/160 Reg.3
s.82, enabling: SSI 2009/160
s.98, applied: SSI 2009/207
s.98, enabling: SSI 2009/207

asp 3. Water Environment and Water Services (Scotland) Act 2003
applied: 2009 asp 6 Sch.1 para.4
Part 1, applied: 2009 asp 6 Sch.1 para.10
Part 1 c.2, applied: 2009 asp 6 s.48
s.2, amended: 2009 asp 6 Sch.3 para.14
s.2, varied: SSI 2009/420 Reg.3
s.3, applied: SSI 2009/266 Reg.7
s.4, applied: 2009 asp 6 s.8
s.6, applied: 2009 asp 6 s.23

2003– cont.

asp 3. Water Environment and Water Services (Scotland) Act 2003–*cont.*
s.7, referred to: 2009 asp 6 s.23
s.9, applied: 2009 asp 6 s.28
s.20, enabling: SSI 2009/420
s.21, applied: SSI 2009/420
s.25, enabling: SSI 2009/420
s.26, applied: 2009 asp 6 s.52
s.28, varied: SSI 2009/420 Reg.3
s.36, applied: SSI 2009/420
s.36, enabling: SSI 2009/420
Sch.2, enabling: SSI 2009/420

asp 4. Public Appointments and Public Bodies etc (Scotland) Act 2003
s.3, enabling: SSI 2009/390
s.18, applied: SSI 2009/390
Sch.2, amended: 2009 asp 5 Sch.1 para.2, 2009 asp 12 Sch.2 para.6, SSI 2009/390 Art.2

asp 5. Protection of Children (Scotland) Act 2003
applied: SI 2009/1547 Sch.1 para.20
referred to: SSI 2009/4 Art.4
s.1, applied: SI 2009/1633 Reg.3, SI 2009/2558 Reg.3
s.11, applied: SSI 2009/154 Sch.1 para.14
s.17, applied: SSI 2009/39 Art.2, SSI 2009/316 Art.2
s.17, referred to: SSI 2009/4 Art.4
s.17, varied: SSI 2009/337 Art.4
s.17, enabling: SSI 2009/39, SSI 2009/316
Sch.1 para.1, amended: 2009 asp 9 Sch.5 para.4
Sch.1 para.2, amended: 2009 asp 9 Sch.5 para.4

asp 7. Criminal Justice (Scotland) Act 2003
s.14, applied: SSI 2009/31 Art.2, SSI 2009/71 Sch.1, SSI 2009/134 Art.2
s.14, enabling: SSI 2009/31, SSI 2009/71, SSI 2009/134
s.16, enabling: SSI 2009/142
s.19, repealed (in part): 2009 asp 9 Sch.6
s.21, amended: SI 2009/1182 Sch.5 para.11
s.22, referred to: SI 2009/37 Sch.1 para.2
s.88, applied: SSI 2009/134

asp 8. Building (Scotland) Act 2003
Commencement Orders: SSI 2009/150 Art.2, Art.3
disapplied: SI 2009/822 Art.3
s.1, enabling: SSI 2009/119
s.8, enabling: SSI 2009/119
s.24, enabling: SSI 2009/117
s.28, referred to: SI 2009/2037 Art.5
s.33, enabling: SSI 2009/117
s.54, enabling: SSI 2009/117, SSI 2009/150
s.59, enabling: SSI 2009/150
Sch.1 para.4, enabling: SSI 2009/119
Sch.6 para.12, repealed: SSI 2009/248 Sch.2

asp 9. Title Conditions (Scotland) Act 2003
Commencement Orders: SSI 2009/190 Art.2
s.2, applied: SI 2009/729 Art.5
s.3, applied: SI 2009/729 Art.5
s.5, applied: SI 2009/729 Art.5
s.10, applied: SI 2009/729 Art.5
s.11, applied: SI 2009/729 Art.5
s.13, applied: SI 2009/729 Art.5
s.14, applied: SI 2009/729 Art.5
s.16, applied: SI 2009/729 Art.5
s.18, applied: SI 2009/729 Art.5
s.46A, added: 2009 asp 12 s.68
s.59, applied: SI 2009/729 Art.5
s.60, applied: SI 2009/729 Art.5
s.61, applied: SI 2009/729 Art.5

2003– cont.

asp 9. Title Conditions (Scotland) Act 2003– *cont.*
s.67, applied: SI 2009/729 Art.5
s.68, disapplied: SI 2009/729 Art.5
s.69, disapplied: SI 2009/729 Art.5
s.70, applied: SI 2009/729 Art.5
s.71, applied: SI 2009/729 Art.4
s.72, referred to: SI 2009/729 Art.5
s.98, disapplied: SI 2009/729 Art.5
s.100, disapplied: SI 2009/729 Art.5
s.104, disapplied: SI 2009/729 Art.5
s.105, applied: SI 2009/729 Art.5
s.129, enabling: SSI 2009/190

asp 13. Mental Health (Care and Treatment) (Scotland) Act 2003
s.41, referred to: SI 2009/1887 Sch.2
s.53, referred to: SI 2009/1887 Sch.2
s.64, applied: SI 2009/1887 Sch.2
s.65, applied: SI 2009/1887 Sch.2
s.66, referred to: SI 2009/1887 Sch.2
s.127, referred to: SI 2009/1887 Sch.2
s.179, referred to: SI 2009/1887 Sch.2
s.193, applied: SI 2009/1887 Reg.7, Reg.8
s.221, referred to: SI 2009/1887 Sch.2
s.224, referred to: SI 2009/1887 Sch.2
s.311, applied: SSI 2009/31 Sch.1 para.15, SSI 2009/71 Sch.1 para.15
s.311, referred to: SI 2009/37 Sch.1 para.1, Sch.1 para.2, Sch.1 para.3
s.311, repealed: 2009 asp 9 Sch.6
s.312, repealed: 2009 asp 9 Sch.6
s.313, applied: SSI 2009/31 Sch.1 para.15, SSI 2009/71 Sch.1 para.15
s.313, referred to: SI 2009/37 Sch.1 para.1, Sch.1 para.2, Sch.1 para.3
s.313, repealed: 2009 asp 9 Sch.6
s.319, repealed: 2009 asp 9 Sch.6
s.326, amended: 2009 asp 9 Sch.5 para.6
s.328, applied: SSI 2009/284 Sch.1
s.329, applied: SI 2009/457 Reg.9
Sch.2 Part 1 para.1, enabling: SSI 2009/359

asp 15. Salmon and Freshwater Fisheries (Consolidation) (Scotland) Act 2003
s.8, amended: SSI 2009/85 Sch.2 para.10
s.69, amended: SSI 2009/85 Sch.2 para.10

2004

asp 3. Vulnerable Witnesses (Scotland) Act 2004
s.12, applied: SSI 2009/284 Sch.1

asp 4. Education (Additional Support for Learning) (Scotland) Act 2004
applied: SSI 2009/154 Reg.24, Sch.1 para.14, SSI 2009/182 Reg.5, Reg.24
s.1, amended: 2009 asp 7 s.1, s.6, s.8
s.5, amended: 2009 asp 7 s.9
s.6, amended: 2009 asp 7 s.8
s.7, amended: 2009 asp 7 s.1
s.8A, added: 2009 asp 7 s.7
s.10, amended: 2009 asp 7 s.1
s.11, amended: 2009 asp 7 s.1
s.12, amended: 2009 asp 7 s.1
s.13, amended: 2009 asp 7 s.17
s.14A, added: 2009 asp 7 s.10
s.15, amended: 2009 asp 7 s.2, s.11
s.16, amended: 2009 asp 7 s.3, s.12
s.18, amended: 2009 asp 7 s.1, s.18, s.19
s.19, amended: 2009 asp 7 s.1, s.18, s.19
s.26, amended: 2009 asp 7 s.13, s.14, s.15, s.16
s.26A, added: 2009 asp 7 s.22

2004–cont.

asp 4. Education (Additional Support for Learning) (Scotland) Act 2004–*cont.*
s.27A, added: 2009 asp 7 s.23
s.29, amended: 2009 asp 7 s.5
Sch.1 para.11, amended: 2009 asp 7 s.20
Sch.1 para.11A, added: 2009 asp 7 s.21
Sch.2 para.2, amended: 2009 asp 7 s.1
Sch.2 para.4, amended: 2009 asp 7 s.1
Sch.2 para.6, amended: 2009 asp 7 s.1
Sch.2 para.7, amended: 2009 asp 7 s.1

asp 6. Nature Conservation (Scotland) Act 2004
s.1, applied: 2009 asp 12 s.59
s.3, referred to: 2009 asp 6 s.23

asp 8. Antisocial Behaviour etc (Scotland) Act 2004
s.83, amended: SSI 2009/33 Art.2
s.83, enabling: SSI 2009/33
s.128, amended: SSI 2009/248 Sch.1 para.10
s.141, applied: SSI 2009/33
s.141, enabling: SSI 2009/33

asp 9. Local Governance (Scotland) Act 2004
s.3, enabling: SSI 2009/36
s.3A, added: 2009 asp 10 s.2
s.15, enabling: SSI 2009/205
s.16, amended: 2009 asp 10 s.2
s.16, applied: SSI 2009/205
s.16, enabling: SSI 2009/36, SSI 2009/205

asp 11. Tenements (Scotland) Act 2004
Sch.1, amended: 2009 asp 12 s.69

2005

asp 1. Breastfeeding etc (Scotland) Act 2005
s.1, amended: SSI 2009/248 Sch.1 para.11

asp 3. Water Services etc (Scotland) Act 2005
s.13, amended: SI 2009/1941 Sch.1 para.248
s.14, applied: 2009 asp 2 Sch.5

asp 5. Fire (Scotland) Act 2005
s.6, referred to: SSI 2009/241 Art.4
s.43, applied: SSI 2009/235 Art.2
s.43, enabling: SSI 2009/235

asp 7. Gaelic Language (Scotland) Act 2005
Sch.1 para.11, amended: SI 2009/1941 Sch.1 para.249

asp 9. Protection of Children and Prevention of Sexual Offences (Scotland) Act 2005
s.1, amended: 2009 asp 9 Sch.5 para.7
s.1, applied: 2009 asp 9 Sch.1 para.4
s.1, referred to: SI 2009/37 Sch.1 para.2, Sch.1 para.4
s.2, applied: SI 2009/37 Reg.4, Reg.6
s.9, applied: 2009 asp 9 s.56, Sch.1 para.4, Sch.4 para.13
s.9, referred to: SI 2009/37 Sch.1 para.2, Sch.1 para.4
s.10, applied: 2009 asp 9 s.56, Sch.1 para.4, Sch.4 para.14
s.10, referred to: SI 2009/37 Sch.1 para.2, Sch.1 para.4
s.11, applied: 2009 asp 9 s.56, Sch.1 para.4, Sch.4 para.15
s.11, referred to: SI 2009/37 Sch.1 para.2, Sch.1 para.4
s.12, applied: 2009 asp 9 s.56, Sch.1 para.4, Sch.4 para.16
s.12, referred to: SI 2009/37 Sch.1 para.2, Sch.1 para.4
Sch.1 para.1, repealed: 2009 asp 9 Sch.6

2005–cont.

asp 10. Charities and Trustee Investment (Scotland) Act 2005
s.34, applied: SI 2009/26 Sch.1, SI 2009/263 Art.5, SI 2009/442 Art.5, SI 2009/468 Sch.1, SI 2009/1345 Art.5, SI 2009/1355 Sch.1, SI 2009/1808 Art.5, SI 2009/1813 Sch.1, SI 2009/2722 Reg.3
s.56, amended: SI 2009/1941 Sch.1 para.250
s.58, amended: SI 2009/1941 Sch.1 para.250
s.81, applied: SSI 2009/121 Reg.2, Reg.7
s.83, applied: SSI 2009/121
s.83, enabling: SSI 2009/121
s.102, enabling: SSI 2009/28, SSI 2009/386
s.103, applied: SSI 2009/28, SSI 2009/386
s.106, amended: SI 2009/1941 Sch.1 para.250
Sch.4 Part 1 para.6, repealed: SI 2009/1941 Sch.2

asp 12. Transport (Scotland) Act 2005
Sch.1 para.12, amended: SI 2009/1941 Sch.1 para.251

asp 14. Management of Offenders etc (Scotland) Act 2005
Commencement Orders: SSI 2009/240 Art.2; SSI 2009/269 Art.2
s.24, enabling: SSI 2009/240, SSI 2009/269

asp 16. Licensing (Scotland) Act 2005
s.2, applied: SSI 2009/248 Art.3
s.27, enabling: SSI 2009/270
s.45, applied: SSI 2009/248 Art.3
s.50, amended: SSI 2009/256 Art.4
s.56, applied: SSI 2009/248 Art.3
s.56, varied: SSI 2009/277 Art.7
s.71, varied: SSI 2009/277 Art.7
s.72, applied: SSI 2009/277 Art.4
s.72, varied: SSI 2009/277 Art.7
s.73, varied: SSI 2009/277 Art.7
s.74, varied: SSI 2009/277 Art.7
s.75, varied: SSI 2009/277 Art.7
s.76, varied: SSI 2009/277 Art.7
s.77, varied: SSI 2009/277 Art.7
s.78, varied: SSI 2009/277 Art.7
s.79, varied: SSI 2009/277 Art.7
s.80, varied: SSI 2009/277 Art.7
s.81, varied: SSI 2009/277 Art.7
s.82, referred to: SSI 2009/277 Art.7
s.82, varied: SSI 2009/277 Art.7
s.83, referred to: SSI 2009/277 Art.7
s.83, varied: SSI 2009/277 Art.7
s.84, referred to: SSI 2009/277 Art.7
s.84, varied: SSI 2009/277 Art.7
s.85, varied: SSI 2009/277 Art.7
s.86, varied: SSI 2009/277 Art.7
s.87, varied: SSI 2009/277 Art.7
s.88, referred to: SSI 2009/277 Art.7
s.88, varied: SSI 2009/277 Art.7
s.89, varied: SSI 2009/277 Art.7
s.90, varied: SSI 2009/277 Art.7
s.91, varied: SSI 2009/277 Art.7
s.92, varied: SSI 2009/277 Art.7
s.93, varied: SSI 2009/277 Art.7
s.145, enabling: SSI 2009/248, SSI 2009/277
s.146, applied: SSI 2009/248, SSI 2009/270
s.146, enabling: SSI 2009/248, SSI 2009/270, SSI 2009/277
Sch.3 para.13, amended: SSI 2009/270 Reg.2

2006

asp 1. Housing (Scotland) Act 2006
Commencement Orders: SSI 2009/122 Art.3, Art.7

2006– cont.

asp 1. Housing (Scotland) Act 2006– *cont.*
s.179, repealed: 2009 asp 12 Sch.2 para.7
s.191, enabling: SSI 2009/122
s.195, enabling: SSI 2009/122
Sch.6 Part 1 para.2, disapplied: SSI 2009/122 Art.7
Sch.6 Part 1 para.3, disapplied: SSI 2009/122 Art.7
Sch.6 Part 1 para.6, disapplied: SSI 2009/122 Art.7
Sch.6 Part 1 para.12, disapplied: SSI 2009/122 Art.7

asp 10. Police, Public Order and Criminal Justice (Scotland) Act 2006
referred to: 2009 c.26 s.115
s.2, applied: SI 2009/2570 Art.9
s.34, applied: SI 2009/2570 Art.10
s.53, amended: 2009 c.26 s.104, Sch.8 Part 11
s.53, applied: 2009 c.26 s.104
s.61, applied: 2009 c.26 s.104
s.66, amended: 2009 c.26 s.104
s.68, applied: 2009 c.26 s.106
s.102, enabling: SSI 2009/340
Sch.1 para.15, amended: SI 2009/1941 Sch.1 para.261
Sch.4 para.3, amended: SI 2009/1941 Sch.1 para.261

asp 11. Animal Health and Welfare (Scotland) Act 2006
s.19, applied: SSI 2009/141 Reg.21
s.20, applied: SSI 2009/47, SSI 2009/141 Reg.21
s.20, enabling: SSI 2009/47
s.21, applied: SSI 2009/141 Reg.21
s.22, applied: SSI 2009/141 Reg.21
s.23, applied: SSI 2009/141 Reg.21
s.24, applied: SSI 2009/141 Reg.21
s.25, applied: SSI 2009/141 Reg.21
s.26, applied: SSI 2009/141
s.26, enabling: SSI 2009/141
s.27, applied: SSI 2009/141
s.27, enabling: SSI 2009/141
s.29, applied: SSI 2009/141 Reg.21
s.40, applied: SSI 2009/141 Reg.4, Reg.21
s.51, applied: SSI 2009/47, SSI 2009/141
s.51, enabling: SSI 2009/141

asp 12. Interests of Members of the Scottish Parliament Act 2006
s.19, amended: SI 2009/1941 Sch.1 para.262

asp 14. Local Electoral Administration and Registration Services (Scotland) Act 2006
Commencement Orders: SSI 2009/2 Art.2, Art.3
s.21, enabling: SSI 2009/35
s.22, enabling: SSI 2009/35
s.23, enabling: SSI 2009/35
s.24, enabling: SSI 2009/35
s.33, enabling: SSI 2009/35
s.55, enabling: SSI 2009/314
s.58, enabling: SSI 2009/64
s.60, applied: SSI 2009/64, SSI 2009/314
s.61, enabling: SSI 2009/2, SSI 2009/35
s.62, enabling: SSI 2009/94
s.63, enabling: SSI 2009/2

asp 17. Planning etc (Scotland) Act 2006
Commencement Orders: SSI 2009/70 Sch.1, Art.2; SSI 2009/100 Art.2, Sch.1; SSI 2009/179 Art.2; SSI 2009/219 Sch.1, Art.2
s.20, amended: SSI 2009/256 Art.5
s.21, amended: SSI 2009/256 Art.5
s.54, referred to: SSI 2009/101 Art.3
s.58, applied: SSI 2009/256

2006– cont.

asp 17. Planning etc (Scotland) Act 2006– *cont.*
s.58, enabling: SSI 2009/18, SSI 2009/101, SSI 2009/222, SSI 2009/256, SSI 2009/344
s.59, enabling: SSI 2009/70, SSI 2009/100, SSI 2009/179, SSI 2009/219

2007

asp 3. Bankruptcy and Diligence etc (Scotland) Act 2007
Commencement Orders: SSI 2009/67 Art.3, Art.4, Art.5, Art.6, Sch.1, Sch.2; SSI 2009/369 Art.3, Sch.1
varied: SI 2009/317 Sch.1
Part 8, applied: SSI 2009/382 r.2
s.38, amended: 2009 c.1 s.253
s.39, amended: 2009 c.1 s.253
s.42, amended: 2009 c.1 s.253
s.43, amended: 2009 c.1 s.253
s.44, amended: 2009 c.1 s.253
s.47, amended: 2009 c.1 s.253, SI 2009/1941 Sch.1 para.267
s.60, referred to: SSI 2009/67 Art.4
s.80, referred to: SSI 2009/67 Art.5, SSI 2009/129 Art.4
s.148, applied: SSI 2009/68 Reg.3
s.148, enabling: SSI 2009/68, SSI 2009/396
s.152, amended: SSI 2009/129 Art.2
s.152, referred to: SSI 2009/129 Art.3, Art.4
s.176, applied: SSI 2009/382 Sch.1
s.179, applied: SSI 2009/382 Sch.1
s.179, enabling: SSI 2009/382
s.181, applied: SSI 2009/382 Sch.1
s.182, applied: SSI 2009/382 Sch.1
s.182, enabling: SSI 2009/382
s.183, applied: SSI 2009/382 Sch.1
s.183, enabling: SSI 2009/382
s.185, applied: SSI 2009/382 Sch.1
s.186, applied: SSI 2009/382 Sch.1
s.188, applied: SSI 2009/382 Sch.1
s.188, enabling: SSI 2009/382
s.189, applied: SSI 2009/382 Sch.1
s.189, enabling: SSI 2009/382
s.190, applied: SSI 2009/382 Sch.1
s.191, applied: SSI 2009/382 Sch.1
s.194, applied: SSI 2009/382 Sch.1
s.224, applied: SSI 2009/129
s.224, enabling: SSI 2009/66, SSI 2009/67, SSI 2009/68, SSI 2009/129, SSI 2009/369, SSI 2009/396
s.225, enabling: SSI 2009/66, SSI 2009/129
s.227, enabling: SSI 2009/67, SSI 2009/369

asp 4. Adoption and Children (Scotland) Act 2007
Commencement Orders: SSI 2009/147 Art.2, Sch.1; SSI 2009/267 Art.2
applied: SSI 2009/154 Reg.6, SSI 2009/268 Reg.6, SSI 2009/284 r.2, Sch.1
Part 1 c.2, applied: SSI 2009/182 Reg.9
s.3, enabling: SSI 2009/152
s.8, enabling: SSI 2009/154, SSI 2009/182
s.9, applied: SSI 2009/152 Reg.4, Reg.6, Reg.8, Reg.9, SSI 2009/268 Reg.3, Reg.4
s.9, disapplied: SSI 2009/152 Reg.4
s.9, referred to: SSI 2009/152 Reg.5
s.9, enabling: SSI 2009/152
s.13, enabling: SSI 2009/152
s.14, applied: SSI 2009/154 Reg.6, SSI 2009/182 Reg.9, Reg.42, Reg.46, SSI 2009/284 Sch.1

asp 4. Adoption and Children (Scotland) Act 2007– *cont.*

s.15, disapplied: SSI 2009/182 Reg.9

s.17, applied: SSI 2009/182 Reg.50, SSI 2009/284 Sch.1

s.18, applied: SSI 2009/182 Reg.5, Reg.26, SSI 2009/ 267 Art.9

s.18, varied: SSI 2009/182 Reg.54

s.19, applied: SSI 2009/182 Reg.33, Reg.50, SSI 2009/284 Sch.1

s.20, applied: SSI 2009/154 Reg.19, SSI 2009/284 Sch.1

s.20, varied: SSI 2009/182 Reg.55

s.20, enabling: SSI 2009/154

s.21, applied: SSI 2009/284 Sch.1

s.21, disapplied: SSI 2009/182 Reg.6, Reg.9

s.21, varied: SSI 2009/182 Reg.56

s.22, applied: SSI 2009/284 Sch.1

s.22, disapplied: SSI 2009/182 Reg.9

s.22, varied: SSI 2009/182 Reg.56

s.23, applied: SSI 2009/284 Sch.1

s.23, varied: SSI 2009/182 Reg.56

s.24, applied: SSI 2009/284 Sch.1

s.24, disapplied: SSI 2009/182 Reg.9

s.25, disapplied: SSI 2009/182 Reg.9

s.25, varied: SSI 2009/182 Reg.6, Reg.57

s.26, disapplied: SSI 2009/182 Reg.9

s.26, varied: SSI 2009/182 Reg.57

s.28, varied: SSI 2009/182 Reg.9, Reg.58

s.29, applied: SSI 2009/182 Reg.5, SSI 2009/267 Art.20, SSI 2009/284 Sch.1

s.29, referred to: SSI 2009/182 Reg.45

s.29, varied: SSI 2009/182 Reg.9, Reg.59

s.30, applied: SSI 2009/182 Reg.5, SSI 2009/267 Art.20, SSI 2009/284 Sch.1

s.30, referred to: SSI 2009/182 Reg.45

s.30, varied: SSI 2009/182 Reg.9, Reg.60

s.31, applied: SSI 2009/284 Sch.1

s.31, varied: SSI 2009/182 Reg.61, SSI 2009/267 Art.20

s.32, applied: SSI 2009/284 Sch.1

s.34, disapplied: SSI 2009/182 Reg.9

s.35, applied: SSI 2009/267 Art.16

s.36, applied: SSI 2009/284 Sch.1

s.37, enabling: SSI 2009/154

s.38, enabling: SSI 2009/268

s.45, applied: SSI 2009/152 Reg.8, Reg.9

s.49, applied: SSI 2009/152 Reg.5, Reg.7, Reg.8, Reg.9

s.49, enabling: SSI 2009/152

s.53, varied: SSI 2009/182 Reg.9

s.54, varied: SSI 2009/182 Reg.9

s.55, applied: SSI 2009/154 Reg.24

s.55, varied: SSI 2009/182 Reg.9

s.58, applied: SSI 2009/182 Reg.3, Reg.4, Reg.5, Reg.6

s.58, enabling: SSI 2009/182

s.59, applied: SSI 2009/182 Reg.7, Reg.9, Reg.49, Reg.50, SSI 2009/284 Sch.1

s.59, enabling: SSI 2009/182

s.61, enabling: SSI 2009/182

s.67, applied: SSI 2009/267 Art.12

s.68, applied: SSI 2009/182 Reg.31, Reg.37

s.69, enabling: SSI 2009/170

s.71, referred to: SSI 2009/168 Art.3

s.71, enabling: SSI 2009/152, SSI 2009/168

s.74, enabling: SSI 2009/268

s.75, applied: SSI 2009/284 Sch.1

asp 4. Adoption and Children (Scotland) Act 2007– *cont.*

s.76, applied: SSI 2009/284 Sch.1

s.80, applied: SSI 2009/154 Reg.6, Reg.14, Reg.15, Reg.17, Sch.1 para.15, SSI 2009/284 Sch.1

s.81, applied: SSI 2009/154 Sch.1 para.14

s.81, referred to: SSI 2009/267 Art.13, Art.17

s.82, applied: SSI 2009/154 Sch.1 para.14

s.82, referred to: SSI 2009/154 Reg.21, Reg.23, SSI 2009/182 Reg.46, SSI 2009/267 Art.13, Art.17

s.83, applied: SSI 2009/284 Sch.1

s.84, applied: SSI 2009/284 Sch.1

s.89, applied: SSI 2009/284 Sch.1

s.92, applied: SSI 2009/267 Art.15, Art.21, SSI 2009/284 Sch.1

s.92, varied: SSI 2009/267 Art.15, Art.21

s.93, applied: SSI 2009/267 Art.15, SSI 2009/284 Sch.1

s.93, varied: SSI 2009/267 Art.15

s.94, applied: SSI 2009/267 Art.15, Art.21, SSI 2009/284 Sch.1

s.94, varied: SSI 2009/267 Art.15, Art.21

s.95, applied: SSI 2009/169 Reg.3, SSI 2009/284 Sch.1

s.95, enabling: SSI 2009/169

s.96, applied: SSI 2009/284 Sch.1

s.97, applied: SSI 2009/284 Sch.1

s.98, applied: SSI 2009/267 Art.15, Art.21, SSI 2009/284 Sch.1

s.104, enabling: SSI 2009/283, SSI 2009/284

s.105, applied: SSI 2009/284 Sch.1

s.106, applied: SSI 2009/154 Reg.13, Reg.22

s.106, enabling: SSI 2009/154

s.108, applied: SSI 2009/268 Reg.6, SSI 2009/284 Sch.1

s.108, enabling: SSI 2009/283, SSI 2009/284

s.110, enabling: SSI 2009/210

s.114, enabling: SSI 2009/283, SSI 2009/284

s.116, enabling: SSI 2009/429

s.117, applied: SSI 2009/268

s.117, enabling: SSI 2009/152, SSI 2009/154, SSI 2009/210, SSI 2009/267, SSI 2009/268

s.119, applied: SSI 2009/284 Sch.1

s.121, enabling: SSI 2009/147, SSI 2009/267

Sch.1 para.1, varied: SSI 2009/182 Reg.9

Sch.1 para.1, enabling: SSI 2009/314

Sch.1 para.2, varied: SSI 2009/182 Reg.9

Sch.1 para.3, varied: SSI 2009/182 Reg.9

Sch.1 para.4, applied: SSI 2009/284 Sch.1

Sch.1 para.4, varied: SSI 2009/182 Reg.9

Sch.1 para.6, enabling: SSI 2009/314

Sch.1 para.7, applied: SSI 2009/284 Sch.1

asp 5. Legal Profession and Legal Aid (Scotland) Act 2007

applied: SSI 2009/163 Sch.1

s.6, applied: SSI 2009/17 Art.2

s.47, applied: SSI 2009/163 Sch.1

s.78, enabling: SSI 2009/17

asp 6. Criminal Proceedings etc (Reform) (Scotland) Act 2007

Commencement Orders: SSI 2009/116 Sch.1, Art.3; SSI 2009/432 Sch.1, Art.3, Sch.2

s.56, enabling: SSI 2009/342

s.59, applied: SSI 2009/115, SSI 2009/180, SSI 2009/331, SSI 2009/332

s.59, enabling: SSI 2009/115, SSI 2009/180, SSI 2009/331, SSI 2009/332

s.64, applied: SSI 2009/20, SSI 2009/115, SSI 2009/ 180, SSI 2009/331, SSI 2009/332

2007– cont.

asp 6. Criminal Proceedings etc (Reform) (Scotland) Act 2007– *cont.*
s.64, referred to: SSI 2009/409
s.64, enabling: SSI 2009/20, SSI 2009/115, SSI 2009/180, SSI 2009/331, SSI 2009/332, SSI 2009/409
s.65, applied: SSI 2009/115 Art.4, SSI 2009/331 Art.4, SSI 2009/332 Art.4
s.65, enabling: SSI 2009/20, SSI 2009/115, SSI 2009/180, SSI 2009/331, SSI 2009/332, SSI 2009/409
s.66, applied: SSI 2009/115 Art.6, SSI 2009/331 Art.6, SSI 2009/332 Art.6
s.81, applied: SSI 2009/342
s.81, enabling: SSI 2009/20, SSI 2009/115, SSI 2009/180, SSI 2009/331, SSI 2009/332, SSI 2009/409
s.82, applied: SSI 2009/342
s.82, enabling: SSI 2009/115, SSI 2009/180, SSI 2009/331, SSI 2009/332, SSI 2009/342
s.84, enabling: SSI 2009/116, SSI 2009/238, SSI 2009/432

asp 9. Budget (Scotland) Act 2007
s.3, amended: SSI 2009/120 Art.2
s.7, applied: SSI 2009/120
s.7, enabling: SSI 2009/120
Sch.1, amended: SSI 2009/120 Art.3
Sch.2 Part 2, amended: SSI 2009/120 Art.4

asp 14. Protection of Vulnerable Groups (Scotland) Act 2007
applied: SI 2009/26 Sch.1, SI 2009/263 Art.5, SI 2009/442 Art.5, SI 2009/468 Sch.1, SI 2009/1345 Art.5, SI 2009/1355 Sch.1, SI 2009/1808 Art.5, SI 2009/1813 Sch.1, SI 2009/2722 Reg.3
s.1, applied: SI 2009/1633 Reg.3, SI 2009/2558 Reg.3
s.30, referred to: SI 2009/1182 Art.1
s.30A, added: SI 2009/1182 Sch.5 para.12
s.30A, referred to: SI 2009/1182 Art.9
s.39, amended: 2009 c.26 s.81
s.40, amended: 2009 c.26 s.81
s.87, enabling: SSI 2009/4, SSI 2009/337, SSI 2009/375
s.97, amended: 2009 c.26 s.81
s.100, enabling: SSI 2009/4, SSI 2009/337, SSI 2009/375
Sch.4 para.30, applied: SSI 2009/337 Art.2
Sch.4 para.30, referred to: SSI 2009/375 Art.2
Sch.5, amended: 2009 c.26 s.81

asp 17. Custodial Sentences and Weapons (Scotland) Act 2007
Commencement Orders: SSI 2009/197 Art.2, Sch.1, Art.3
Part 2, referred to: 2009 c.25 Sch.22 para.36
s.65, enabling: SSI 2009/197
s.67, enabling: SSI 2009/197

2008

asp 2. Budget (Scotland) Act 2008
s.3, amended: SSI 2009/120 Art.5
s.6, repealed: 2009 asp 2 s.8
s.7, applied: SSI 2009/120
s.7, enabling: SSI 2009/120
Sch.1, amended: SSI 2009/120 Art.6
Sch.2 Part 1, amended: SSI 2009/120 Art.7
Sch.2 Part 2, amended: SSI 2009/120 Art.7
Sch.2 Part 3, amended: SSI 2009/120 Art.7
Sch.2 Part 4, amended: SSI 2009/120 Art.7

2008– cont.

asp 2. Budget (Scotland) Act 2008– *cont.*
Sch.2 Part 6, amended: SSI 2009/120 Art.7
Sch.2 Part 7, amended: SSI 2009/120 Art.7
Sch.3, amended: SSI 2009/120 Art.8
Sch.4 Part 3, amended: SSI 2009/120 Art.9
Sch.5, amended: SSI 2009/120 Art.10

asp 4. Glasgow Commonwealth Games Act 2008
Commencement Orders: SSI 2009/377 Art.2, Sch.1
s.49, enabling: SSI 2009/377

asp 5. Public Health etc (Scotland) Act 2008
Commencement Orders: SSI 2009/9 Art.2, Sch.1, Sch.2; SSI 2009/319 Art.2, Sch.1; SSI 2009/404 Sch.1, Sch.3, Art.2
s.3, enabling: SSI 2009/301
s.5, enabling: SSI 2009/301
s.71, enabling: SSI 2009/320
s.95, applied: SSI 2009/388 Reg.2
s.95, enabling: SSI 2009/388
s.96, applied: SSI 2009/388 Reg.2
s.96, enabling: SSI 2009/388
s.100, enabling: SSI 2009/388
s.101, enabling: SSI 2009/388
s.122, applied: SSI 2009/301, SSI 2009/388
s.122, enabling: SSI 2009/9, SSI 2009/319, SSI 2009/404
s.128, enabling: SSI 2009/9, SSI 2009/319, SSI 2009/404
Sch.3 Part 1, referred to: SSI 2009/319 Sch.2 para.2

asp 6. Judiciary and Courts (Scotland) Act 2008
Commencement Orders: SSI 2009/83 Art.2; SSI 2009/192 Art.2, Sch.1; SSI 2009/318 Art.2, Sch.1
referred to: SSI 2009/83 Art.1
Part 2 c.3, applied: SSI 2009/311 Art.2
s.9, applied: SSI 2009/311 Art.2
s.60, applied: SI 2009/2231 Art.2
s.60, referred to: SI 2009/2231 Art.3
s.71, applied: SSI 2009/334
s.71, enabling: SSI 2009/303
s.74, enabling: SSI 2009/334
s.75, enabling: SSI 2009/311
s.76, enabling: SSI 2009/83, SSI 2009/192, SSI 2009/318
Sch.3 para.2, referred to: SSI 2009/303 Reg.2, Reg.3
Sch.3 para.3, applied: SSI 2009/303
Sch.3 para.3, enabling: SSI 2009/303

asp 7. Scottish Register of Tartans Act 2008
Commencement Orders: SSI 2009/5 Art.2
s.4, applied: SSI 2009/6 Sch.1
s.6, applied: SSI 2009/6 Sch.1
s.8, applied: SSI 2009/6 Sch.1
s.9, applied: SSI 2009/6 Sch.1
s.10, applied: SSI 2009/6 Sch.1
s.13, applied: SSI 2009/6 Sch.1
s.14, applied: SSI 2009/6, SSI 2009/6 Sch.1
s.14, enabling: SSI 2009/6
s.18, enabling: SSI 2009/5

2009

asp 1. Scottish Parliamentary Pensions Act 2009
Royal Assent, February 25, 2009

asp 2. Budget (Scotland) Act 2009
Royal Assent, March 10, 2009
s.3, amended: SSI 2009/434 Art.2
s.7, applied: SSI 2009/434
s.7, enabling: SSI 2009/434
Sch.1, amended: SSI 2009/434 Art.3

2009– cont.

asp 2. Budget (Scotland) Act 2009– *cont.*
Sch.2 Part 1, amended: SSI 2009/434 Art.4
Sch.2 Part 4, amended: SSI 2009/434 Art.4
Sch.2 Part 7, amended: SSI 2009/434 Art.4
Sch.2 Part 11, amended: SSI 2009/434 Art.4
Sch.3, amended: SSI 2009/434 Art.5

asp 3. Disabled Persons Parking Places (Scotland) Act 2009
Royal Assent, April 1, 2009

asp 4. Damages (Asbestos-related Conditions) (Scotland) Act 2009
Commencement Orders: SSI 2009/172 Art.2
Royal Assent, April 17, 2009
s.4, enabling: SSI 2009/172

asp 5. Health Boards (Membership and Elections) (Scotland) Act 2009
Commencement Orders: SSI 2009/242 Art.2
Royal Assent, April 22, 2009
s.4, enabling: SSI 2009/242
s.11, enabling: SSI 2009/433

asp 6. Flood Risk Management (Scotland) Act 2009
Commencement Orders: SSI 2009/393 Art.2, Art.3, Art.4, Art.5, Sch.1

2009– cont.

asp 6. Flood Risk Management (Scotland) Act 2009– *cont.*
Royal Assent, June 16, 2009
s.94, enabling: SSI 2009/393
s.97, enabling: SSI 2009/393

asp 7. Education (Additional Support for Learning) (Scotland) Act 2009
Royal Assent, June 25, 2009

asp 8. Offences (Aggravation by Prejudice) (Scotland) Act 2009
Royal Assent, July 8, 2009

asp 9. Sexual Offences (Scotland) Act 2009
Royal Assent, July 14, 2009

asp 10. Scottish Local Government (Elections) Act 2009
Royal Assent, July 21, 2009

asp 11. Convention Rights Proceedings (Amendment) (Scotland) Act 2009
Royal Assent, July 23, 2009

asp 12. Climate Change (Scotland) Act 2009
Commencement Orders: SSI 2009/341 Art.2
Royal Assent, August 4, 2009
s.100, enabling: SSI 2009/341

ACTS OF THE PARLIAMENT OF ENGLAND, WALES & THE UNITED KINGDOM

1567

15. Incest Act 1567
see *HM Advocate v L* 2009 S.L.T. 127 (HCJ), Lord Osborne

7 & 8 Will. 3 (1695)

12. Statute of Frauds (Ireland) 1695
s.6, disapplied: SI 2009/555 Art.5

11 Geo. 3 (1771)

31. White Herring Fisheries Act 1771
repealed: 2009 c.23 s.234, Sch.22 Part 5

32 Geo. 3 (1792)

60. Libel Act 1792
repealed: 2009 c.25 Sch.23 Part 2

59 Geo. 3 (1819)

8. Criminal Libel Act 1819
s.1, amended: 2009 c.25 Sch.21 para.65, Sch.23 Part 2

5 Geo. 4 (1824)

83. Vagrancy Act 1824
s.4, see *Akhurst v DPP* [2009] EWHC 806 (Admin), (2009) 173 J.P. 499 (DC), Goldring, L.J.

6 Geo. 4 (1825)

22. Jurors (Scotland) Act 1825
s.3, applied: SSI 2009/293 Art.3

2 & 3 Will. 4 (1832)

71. Prescription Act 1832
s.3, see *Salvage Wharf Ltd v G&S Brough Ltd* [2009] EWCA Civ 21, [2009] 3 W.L.R. 990 (CA (Civ Div)), Tuckey, L.J.

3 & 4 Will. 4 (1833)

41. Judicial Committee Act 1833
s.4, applied: SI 2009/1379 Sch.2, SI 2009/1751 Sch.1
s.24, enabling: SI 2009/224

85. Saint Helena Act 1833
applied: SI 2009/1751 Sch.1
s.112, enabling: SI 2009/888, SI 2009/1751, SI 2009/3008

6 & 7 Will. 4 (1836)

71. Tithe Act 1836
applied: SI 2009/2106 Sch.1 Part 1

7 Will. 4 & 1 Vict. (1837)

37. Chartered Companies act 1837
referred to: SI 2009/500 Sch.1 Part 1

1 & 2 Vict. (1837-38)

110. Judgments Act 1838
s.17, see *Gater Assets Ltd v Nak Naftogaz Ukrainiy* [2008] EWHC 1108 (Comm), [2009] Bus. L.R. 396 (QBD (Comm)), Beatson, J.
s.17, referred to: SI 2009/2477 r.88

2 & 3 Vict. (1839)

45. Highway (Railway Crossing) Act 1839
disapplied: SI 2009/1100 Art.3, SI 2009/1300 Art.3

3 & 4 Vict. (1840)

97. Railway Regulation Act 1840
disapplied: SI 2009/1300 Art.3

4 & 5 Vict. (1841)

38. Schools Sites Act 1841
see *Burgess-Lumsden v Aberdeenshire Council*
2009 S.L.T. (Sh Ct) 117 (Sh Ct (Grampian)
(Aberdeen)), Sheriff D J Cusine
s.2, see *Burgess-Lumsden v Aberdeenshire Council*
2009 S.L.T. (Sh Ct) 117 (Sh Ct (Grampian)
(Aberdeen)), Sheriff D J Cusine

5 & 6 Vict. (1842)

55. Railway Regulation Act 1842
disapplied: SI 2009/1300 Art.3

6 & 7 Vict. (1843)

96. Libel Act 1843
s.4, repealed: 2009 c.25 Sch.23 Part 2
s.5, repealed: 2009 c.25 Sch.23 Part 2
s.6, repealed: 2009 c.25 Sch.23 Part 2
s.7, amended: 2009 c.25 Sch.21 para.66

7 & 8 Vict. (1844)

32. Bank Charter Act 1844
s.6, repealed: 2009 c.1 s.245
s.12, repealed: 2009 c.1 s.214

69. Judicial Committee Act 1844
s.1, enabling: SI 2009/224, SI 2009/3204, SI 2009/
3205, SI 2009/3206, SI 2009/3207

8 & 9 Vict. (1845)

**7. An Act for inclosing lands in the parish of Saint
Mary in the town and county of Nottingham in
the town of Nottingham. 1845**
s.53, applied: SI 2009/1300 Art.35, Art.46

16. Companies Clauses Consolidation Act 1845
disapplied: SI 2009/2579 Art.5, SI 2009/2604
Art.5

18. Lands Clauses Consolidation Act 1845
s.58, applied: SI 2009/1114 Sch.1

20. Railways Clauses Consolidation Act 1845
s.6, amended: SI 2009/1307 Sch.1 para.2
s.16, referred to: SI 2009/2728 Sch.1
s.68, applied: SI 2009/3281 Art.3
s.71, applied: SI 2009/3281 Art.3
s.72, applied: SI 2009/3281 Art.3
s.73, applied: SI 2009/3281 Art.3
s.77, applied: SI 2009/3281 Art.3
s.78, amended: SI 2009/1307 Sch.1 para.3
s.78, applied: SI 2009/3281 Art.3
s.78A, applied: SI 2009/3281 Art.3
s.79, applied: SI 2009/3281 Art.3
s.79A, applied: SI 2009/3281 Art.3
s.79B, applied: SI 2009/3281 Art.3
s.80, applied: SI 2009/3281 Art.3
s.81, applied: SI 2009/3281 Art.3
s.82, applied: SI 2009/3281 Art.3

8 & 9 Vict. (1845)–cont.

20. Railways Clauses Consolidation Act 1845–*cont.*
s.83, applied: SI 2009/3281 Art.3
s.84, applied: SI 2009/3281 Art.3
s.85, applied: SI 2009/3281 Art.3
s.85A, applied: SI 2009/3281 Art.3
s.85B, applied: SI 2009/3281 Art.3
s.85C, applied: SI 2009/3281 Art.3
s.85D, applied: SI 2009/3281 Art.3
s.85E, applied: SI 2009/3281 Art.3
s.145, applied: SI 2009/3281 Art.3
Sch.1, applied: SI 2009/3281 Art.3
Sch.2, applied: SI 2009/3281 Art.3
Sch.3, applied: SI 2009/3281 Art.3

37. Banker's (Ireland) Act 1845
s.8, repealed: 2009 c.1 s.212
s.9, repealed: 2009 c.1 s.214
s.23, repealed: 2009 c.1 s.214
s.26, amended: 2009 c.1 s.214
s.28, repealed: 2009 c.1 s.214
Sch.A, repealed: 2009 c.1 s.214
Sch.B, repealed: 2009 c.1 s.214

38. Bank Notes (Scotland) Act 1845
s.1, repealed: 2009 c.1 s.212
s.2, repealed: 2009 c.1 s.214
s.3, repealed: 2009 c.1 s.214
s.4, repealed: 2009 c.1 s.214
s.5, repealed: 2009 c.1 s.214
s.6, repealed: 2009 c.1 s.214
s.7, repealed: 2009 c.1 s.214
s.8, repealed: 2009 c.1 s.214
s.9, repealed: 2009 c.1 s.214
s.10, repealed: 2009 c.1 s.214
s.11, repealed: 2009 c.1 s.214
s.12, repealed: 2009 c.1 s.214
s.13, repealed: 2009 c.1 s.214
s.14, repealed: 2009 c.1 s.214
s.15, repealed: 2009 c.1 s.214
s.17, repealed: 2009 c.1 s.214
s.18, amended: 2009 c.1 s.214
s.19, repealed: 2009 c.1 s.214
s.20, repealed: 2009 c.1 s.214
s.23, repealed: 2009 c.1 s.214
Sch.A, repealed: 2009 c.1 s.214
Sch.B, repealed: 2009 c.1 s.214

9 & 10 Vict. (1846)

clxiii. Midland Railways, Nottingham and Mansfield, Act 1846
applied: SI 2009/1300 Sch.16 para.9

10 & 11 Vict. (1847)

16. Commissioners Clauses Act 1847
s.15, applied: SI 2009/1231 Art.2
s.48, applied: SI 2009/1231 Art.2
s.53, applied: SI 2009/1231 Art.2
s.56, applied: SI 2009/1231 Art.2
s.58, applied: SI 2009/1231 Art.2
s.59, applied: SI 2009/1231 Art.2
s.60, applied: SI 2009/1231 Art.2
s.62, applied: SI 2009/1231 Art.2
s.63, applied: SI 2009/1231 Art.2
s.64, applied: SI 2009/1231 Art.2
s.65, applied: SI 2009/1231 Art.2
s.67, applied: SI 2009/1231 Art.2
s.69, applied: SI 2009/1231 Art.2
s.70, applied: SI 2009/1231 Art.2

10 & 11 Vict. (1847) – cont.

16. Commissioners Clauses Act 1847 – *cont.*
s.71, applied: SI 2009/1231 Art.2
s.72, applied: SI 2009/1231 Art.2
s.73, applied: SI 2009/1231 Art.2
s.74, applied: SI 2009/1231 Art.2
s.75, applied: SI 2009/1231 Art.2
s.76, applied: SI 2009/1231 Art.2
s.77, applied: SI 2009/1231 Art.2
s.78, applied: SI 2009/1231 Art.2
s.79, applied: SI 2009/1231 Art.2
s.80, applied: SI 2009/1231 Art.2
s.81, applied: SI 2009/1231 Art.2
s.82, applied: SI 2009/1231 Art.2
s.83, applied: SI 2009/1231 Art.2
s.85, applied: SI 2009/1231 Art.2
s.86, applied: SI 2009/1231 Art.2
s.87, applied: SI 2009/1231 Art.2
s.88, applied: SI 2009/1231 Art.2
s.96, applied: SI 2009/1231 Art.2
s.97, applied: SI 2009/1231 Art.2
s.99, applied: SI 2009/1231 Art.2
s.100, applied: SI 2009/1231 Art.2
s.101, applied: SI 2009/1231 Art.2
s.102, applied: SI 2009/1231 Art.2
s.104, applied: SI 2009/1231 Art.2
s.109, applied: SI 2009/1231 Art.2
s.110, applied: SI 2009/1231 Art.2
s.111, applied: SI 2009/1231 Art.2

27. Harbours, Docks, and Piers Clauses Act 1847
referred to: SI 2009/2325 Art.3
applied: SI 2009/2325 Art.3, SSI 2009/27 Art.3
s.1, applied: SI 2009/2325 Art.3, SSI 2009/27 Art.3
s.3, varied: SI 2009/2325 Art.3, SSI 2009/27 Art.3
s.26, applied: SI 2009/2325 Art.3
s.27, applied: SI 2009/2325 Art.3, SSI 2009/27 Art.3
s.29, applied: SI 2009/2325 Art.3, SSI 2009/27 Art.3
s.30, applied: SI 2009/2325 Art.3
s.32, applied: SI 2009/2325 Art.3, SSI 2009/27 Art.3
s.33, applied: SI 2009/2325 Art.3
s.34, applied: SI 2009/2325 Art.3, SSI 2009/27 Art.3
s.35, applied: SI 2009/2325 Art.3, SSI 2009/27 Art.3
s.36, applied: SI 2009/2325 Art.3
s.37, applied: SI 2009/2325 Art.3, SSI 2009/27 Art.3
s.38, applied: SI 2009/2325 Art.3, SSI 2009/27 Art.3
s.39, applied: SI 2009/2325 Art.3, SSI 2009/27 Art.3
s.40, applied: SI 2009/2325 Art.3, SSI 2009/27 Art.3
s.41, applied: SI 2009/2325 Art.3, SSI 2009/27 Art.3
s.43, applied: SI 2009/2325 Art.3, Art.19, SSI 2009/27 Art.3
s.44, applied: SI 2009/2325 Art.3, Art.19, SSI 2009/27 Art.3
s.45, applied: SI 2009/2325 Art.3, Art.19, SSI 2009/27 Art.3
s.46, applied: SI 2009/2325 Art.3, Art.19, SSI 2009/27 Art.3
s.47, applied: SI 2009/2325 Art.3
s.51, applied: SI 2009/2325 Art.3, SSI 2009/27 Art.3
s.52, applied: SI 2009/2325 Art.3, Art.27

10 & 11 Vict. (1847) – cont.

27. Harbours, Docks, and Piers Clauses Act 1847 – *cont.*
s.53, applied: SI 2009/2325 Art.3, SSI 2009/27 Art.3
s.53, referred to: SI 2009/2325 Art.3
s.53, varied: SSI 2009/27 Art.3
s.54, applied: SI 2009/2325 Art.3, SSI 2009/27 Art.3
s.55, applied: SI 2009/2325 Art.3, SSI 2009/27 Art.3
s.56, applied: SI 2009/2325 Art.3, SSI 2009/27 Art.3
s.56, varied: SSI 2009/27 Art.3
s.57, applied: SI 2009/2325 Art.3, Art.35, SSI 2009/27 Art.3
s.58, applied: SI 2009/2325 Art.3, Art.33, SSI 2009/27 Art.3, Art.17
s.59, applied: SI 2009/2325 Art.3, SSI 2009/27 Art.3
s.60, applied: SI 2009/2325 Art.3
s.61, applied: SI 2009/2325 Art.3, SSI 2009/27 Art.3
s.62, applied: SI 2009/2325 Art.3, SSI 2009/27 Art.3
s.63, applied: SI 2009/2325 Art.3, SSI 2009/27 Art.3
s.63, varied: SI 2009/2325 Art.3, SSI 2009/27 Art.3
s.64, applied: SI 2009/2325 Art.3, SSI 2009/27 Art.3
s.65, applied: SI 2009/2325 Art.3, SSI 2009/27 Art.3
s.66, applied: SI 2009/2325 Art.3, SSI 2009/27 Art.3
s.68, applied: SI 2009/2325 Art.3, SSI 2009/27 Art.3
s.69, applied: SI 2009/2325 Art.3, SSI 2009/27 Art.3
s.69, varied: SI 2009/2325 Art.3, SSI 2009/27 Art.3
s.70, applied: SI 2009/2325 Art.3, SSI 2009/27 Art.3
s.70, varied: SSI 2009/27 Art.3
s.71, applied: SI 2009/2325 Art.3, SSI 2009/27 Art.3
s.71, varied: SSI 2009/27 Art.3
s.72, applied: SI 2009/2325 Art.3, SSI 2009/27 Art.3
s.73, applied: SI 2009/2325 Art.3, SSI 2009/27 Art.3
s.73, varied: SSI 2009/27 Art.3
s.74, applied: SI 2009/2325 Art.3, SSI 2009/27 Art.3
s.75, applied: SI 2009/2325 Art.3
s.76, applied: SI 2009/2325 Art.3
s.78, applied: SI 2009/2325 Art.3
s.79, applied: SI 2009/2325 Art.3
s.80, applied: SI 2009/2325 Art.3
s.81, applied: SI 2009/2325 Art.3
s.82, applied: SI 2009/2325 Art.3
s.83, applied: SI 2009/2325 Art.3, Art.24
s.83, referred to: SI 2009/2325 Art.22, Art.24
s.83, varied: SI 2009/2325 Art.24
s.84, applied: SI 2009/2325 Art.3
s.85, applied: SI 2009/2325 Art.3
s.86, applied: SI 2009/2325 Art.3
s.87, applied: SI 2009/2325 Art.3
s.88, applied: SI 2009/2325 Art.3
s.89, applied: SI 2009/2325 Art.3
s.90, applied: SI 2009/2325 Art.3
s.91, applied: SI 2009/2325 Art.3

10 & 11 Vict. (1847) – cont.

27. Harbours, Docks, and Piers Clauses Act 1847– cont.
s.92, applied: SI 2009/2325 Art.3, SSI 2009/27 Art.3
s.93, applied: SI 2009/2325 Art.3
s.94, applied: SI 2009/2325 Art.3
s.95, applied: SI 2009/2325 Art.3
s.96, applied: SI 2009/2325 Art.3
s.97, applied: SI 2009/2325 Art.3
s.98, applied: SI 2009/2325 Art.3
s.99, applied: SI 2009/2325 Art.3
s.100, applied: SI 2009/2325 Art.3
s.101, applied: SI 2009/2325 Art.3
s.102, applied: SI 2009/2325 Art.3
s.103, applied: SI 2009/2325 Art.3
s.104, applied: SI 2009/2325 Art.3
s.109, applied: SI 2009/2325 Art.3

89. Town Police Clauses Act 1847
s.37, see *R. (on the application of Newcastle City Council) v Berwick-upon-Tweed BC* [2008] EWHC 2369 (Admin), [2009] R.T.R. 34 (QBD (Admin)), Christopher Symons Q.C.

11 & 12 Vict. (1848)

lxxxviii. Midland Railway, Ripley Branches, Act 1848
applied: SI 2009/1300 Sch.16 para.9

20 & 21 Vict. (1857)

44. Crown Suits (Scotland) Act 1857
referred to: SI 2009/2231 Art.3
81. Burial Act 1857
s.25, disapplied: SI 2009/1300 Art.28

24 & 25 Vict. (1861)

100. Offences against the Person Act 1861
see *Downs v Secretary of State for Environment, Food and Rural Affairs* [2008] EWHC 2666 (Admin), [2009] Env. L.R. 19 (QBD (Admin)), Collins, J.
s.16, applied: SI 2009/1168 Sch.1 para.1
s.18, see *Attorney General's Reference (No.14 of 2008), Re* [2008] EWCA Crim 1532, [2009] 1 Cr. App. R. (S.) 62 (CA (Crim Div)), Lord Phillips of Worth Matravers, L.C.J.; see *R. v Clark-Webber (Georgina)* [2009] EWCA Crim 514, [2009] 2 Cr. App. R. (S.) 95 (CA (Crim Div)), Aikens L.J.; see *R. v Cross (Adam Stuart)* [2008] EWCA Crim 1194, [2009] 1 Cr. App. R. (S.) 34 (CA (Crim Div)), Dyson, L.J.; see *R. v Gore (Raymond)* [2009] EWCA Crim 1424, [2009] 1 W.L.R. 2454 (CA (Crim Div)), Lord Judge, L.C.J.; see *R. v Owen (Simon Matthew Winston)* [2008] EWCA Crim 1724, [2009] 1 Cr. App. R. (S.) 64 (CA (Crim Div)), Hooper, L.J.
s.20, see *Attorney General's Reference (No.48 of 2008), Re* [2008] EWCA Crim 2514, [2009] 2 Cr. App. R. (S.) 1 (CA (Crim Div)), Lord Judge, L.C.J.; see *R. v Gore (Raymond)* [2009] EWCA Crim 1424, [2009] 1 W.L.R. 2454 (CA (Crim Div)), Lord Judge, L.C.J.; see *R. v Kent (Darran Douglas)* [2008] EWCA Crim 3057, [2009] 2 Cr. App. R. (S.) 39 (CA (Crim Div)), Hooper, L.J.; see *R. v Owen (Simon Matthew Winston)* [2008] EWCA Crim 1724, [2009] 1

24 & 25 Vict. (1861) – cont.

100. Offences against the Person Act 1861 – cont.
s.20 – cont.
Cr. App. R. (S.) 64 (CA (Crim Div)), Hooper, L.J.
s.21, referred to: SI 2009/37 Sch.1 para.2, Sch.1 para.4
s.24, see *R. v Jamieson (Nicholas Steven)* [2008] EWCA Crim 2761, [2009] 2 Cr. App. R. (S.) 26 (CA (Crim Div)), Hallett, LJ
s.32, varied: SI 2009/1100 Art.3, SI 2009/1300 Art.3
s.33, varied: SI 2009/1100 Art.3, SI 2009/1300 Art.3
s.34, varied: SI 2009/1100 Art.3, SI 2009/1300 Art.3
s.35, see *R. v Lambert (Robert John)* [2008] EWCA Crim 2109, [2009] 1 Cr. App. R. (S.) 92 (CA (Crim Div)), Hallett, L.J. DBE
s.47, referred to: SSI 2009/182 Sch.1 para.16
s.52, applied: 2009 asp 9 Sch.1 para.32
s.52, referred to: SI 2009/37 Sch.1 para.2, Sch.1 para.4
s.53, applied: 2009 asp 9 Sch.1 para.32
s.53, referred to: SI 2009/37 Sch.1 para.2, Sch.1 para.4
s.54, applied: 2009 asp 9 Sch.1 para.32
s.54, referred to: SI 2009/37 Sch.1 para.2, Sch.1 para.4
s.55, referred to: SI 2009/37 Sch.1 para.2, Sch.1 para.4
s.61, applied: 2009 asp 9 Sch.1 para.32
s.61, referred to: SI 2009/37 Sch.1 para.2, Sch.1 para.4
s.62, applied: 2009 asp 9 Sch.1 para.32
s.62, referred to: SI 2009/37 Sch.1 para.2, Sch.1 para.4

25 & 26 Vict. (1862)

37. Crown Private Estates Act 1862
s.1, applied: 2009 asp 6 s.91, 2009 c.23 s.145, s.185, s.308
53. Land Registry Act 1862
referred to: SI 2009/500 Sch.1 Part 1

26 & 27 Vict. (1863)

49. Duchy of Cornwall, Management Act 1863
s.39, applied: SI 2009/2325 Art.40

27 & 28 Vict. (1864)

114. Improvement of Land Act 1864
s.73, amended: SI 2009/1307 Sch.1 para.4

28 & 29 Vict. (1865)

18. Criminal Procedure Act 1865
s.3, see *R. v Greene (Jeremy Herbert)* [2009] EWCA Crim 2282, Times, October 28, 2009 (CA (Crim Div)), Scott Baker, L.J.
63. Colonial Laws Validity Act 1865
see *R. (on the application of Bancoult) v Secretary of State for Foreign and Commonwealth Affairs* [2008] UKHL 61, [2009] 1 A.C. 453 (HL), Lord Hoffmann
73. Naval and Marine Pay and Pensions Act 1865
s.3, disapplied: SI 2009/1059 Art.198

30 & 31 Vict. (1867)

133. Consecration of Churchyards Act 1867
applied: SI 2009/2107 Sch.2 para.1

31 & 32 Vict. (1868)

37. Documentary Evidence Act 1868
applied: SI 2009/229 Art.3, SI 2009/2748 Art.3
varied: 2009 c.22 Sch.9 para.13
s.2, see *West Midlands Probation Board v French*
[2008] EWHC 2631 (Admin), [2009] 1 W.L.R.
1715 (DC), Scott Baker, L.J.
Sch.1, referred to: SI 2009/229 Art.3
Sch.1, varied: 2009 c.22 Sch.9 para.13

40. Partition Act 1868
see *Official Receiver for Northern Ireland v Rooney*
[2009] 2 F.L.R. 1437 (Ch D (NI)), Weir, J.

64. Land Registers (Scotland) Act 1868
s.25, enabling: SSI 2009/171

101. Titles to Land Consolidation (Scotland) Act 1868
s.155, applied: SSI 2009/68 Reg.3
s.155, enabling: SSI 2009/68, SSI 2009/396
s.159, applied: SSI 2009/68 Reg.3, Reg.3A
s.159, enabling: SSI 2009/68, SSI 2009/396
s.159A, applied: SSI 2009/68 Reg.3
s.159A, enabling: SSI 2009/68, SSI 2009/396

119. Regulation of Railways Act 1868
disapplied: SI 2009/1100 Art.3, SI 2009/1300 Art.3

34 & 35 Vict. (1871)

48. Promissory Oaths Act 1871
s.2, amended: SSI 2009/334 Art.2

78. Regulation of Railways Act 1871
disapplied: SI 2009/1300 Art.3

96. Pedlars Act 1871
applied: SI 2009/2999 Reg.45
s.3, amended: SI 2009/2999 Reg.45

36 & 37 Vict. (1873)

48. Regulation of Railways Act 1873
disapplied: SI 2009/1100 Art.3

66. Supreme Court of Judicature Act 1873
see *Masri v Consolidated Contractors
International Co SAL* [2008] EWCA Civ 303,
[2009] Q.B. 450 (CA (Civ Div)), Ward, L.J.

38 & 39 Vict. (1875)

17. Explosives Act 1875
referred to: SI 2009/669 Sch.1 Part 2

18. Seal Fishery Act 1875
repealed: 2009 c.23 s.234, Sch.22 Part 5

55. Public Health Act 1875
s.153, applied: SI 2009/721 Sch.3 para.1

39 & 40 Vict. (1876)

36. Customs Consolidation Act 1876
s.42, applied: SI 2009/37 Sch.1 para.4, SI 2009/1168
Sch.1 para.1, SI 2009/1547 Sch.3 para.7, SSI
2009/182 Sch.1 para.4, Sch.1 para.19
s.42, referred to: SI 2009/37 Sch.1 para.2

70. Sheriff Courts (Scotland) Act 1876
s.54, enabling: SSI 2009/292

40 & 41 Vict. (1877)

53. Prisons (Scotland) Act 1877
s.30, applied: SSI 2009/380 r.3

41 & 42 Vict. (1878)

73. Territorial Waters Jurisdiction Act 1878
s.3, disapplied: 2009 c.23 s.319

42 & 43 Vict. (1879)

11. Bankers Books Evidence Act 1879
s.7, applied: SI 2009/2041 r.71

42. Valuation of Lands (Scotland) Amendment Act 1879
s.7, applied: SSI 2009/295 Art.2
s.7, enabling: SSI 2009/295

44 & 45 Vict. (1881)

60. Newspaper Libel and Registration Act 1881
s.1, amended: SI 2009/1941 Sch.1 para.1
s.4, amended: 2009 c.25 Sch.21 para.67, Sch.23 Part 2
s.9, amended: SI 2009/1941 Sch.1 para.1
s.9, applied: SI 2009/2392 Sch.1 para.6
s.11, amended: SI 2009/1941 Sch.1 para.1
s.13, substituted: SI 2009/1941 Sch.1 para.1
s.14, applied: SI 2009/2392 Reg.5
s.14, repealed: SI 2009/1941 Sch.1 para.1
s.15, substituted: SI 2009/1941 Sch.1 para.1
s.18, amended: SI 2009/1941 Sch.1 para.1

45 & 46 Vict. (1882)

61. Bills of Exchange Act 1882
applied: 2009 c.1 s.254
s.53, amended: 2009 c.1 s.254
s.75A, repealed: 2009 c.1 s.254
s.92, applied: 2009 c.10 s.101, s.102, SI 2009/470
Reg.39, Reg.58

47 & 48 Vict. (1884)

55. Pensions and Yeomanry Pay Act 1884
s.4, varied: SI 2009/1059 Sch.1 para.3

48 & 49 Vict. (1885)

69. Criminal Law Amendment Act 1885
s.2, applied: 2009 asp 9 Sch.1 para.31, Sch.1 para.34
s.2, referred to: SI 2009/37 Sch.1 para.2, Sch.1 para.4
s.3, applied: 2009 asp 9 Sch.1 para.31, Sch.1 para.34
s.3, referred to: SI 2009/37 Sch.1 para.2, Sch.1 para.4
s.4, applied: 2009 asp 9 Sch.1 para.31
s.4, referred to: SI 2009/37 Sch.1 para.1, Sch.1 para.2, Sch.1 para.4
s.5, applied: 2009 asp 9 Sch.1 para.31, Sch.1 para.34
s.5, referred to: SI 2009/37 Sch.1 para.2, Sch.1 para.4
s.7, applied: 2009 asp 9 Sch.1 para.31, Sch.1 para.34
s.7, referred to: SI 2009/37 Sch.1 para.2, Sch.1 para.4
s.8, applied: 2009 asp 9 Sch.1 para.31, Sch.1 para.34
s.8, referred to: SI 2009/37 Sch.1 para.2, Sch.1 para.4
s.11, referred to: SI 2009/37 Sch.1 para.2, Sch.1 para.4

48 & 49 Vict. (1885) – cont.

69. Criminal Law Amendment Act 1885–*cont.*
s.77, applied: 2009 asp 9 Sch.1 para.31, Sch.1 para.34
s.77, referred to: SI 2009/37 Sch.1 para.2, Sch.1 para.4

49 & 50 Vict. (1886)

29. Crofters Holdings (Scotland) Act 1886
applied: SSI 2009/122 Art.7
38. Riot (Damages) Act 1886
see *Bedfordshire Police Authority v Constable* [2008] EWHC 1375 (Comm), [2009] Lloyd's Rep. I.R. 39 (QBD (Comm)), Walker, J.; see *Bedfordshire Police Authority v Constable* [2009] EWCA Civ 64, [2009] 2 All E.R. (Comm) 200 (CA (Civ Div)), Longmore, L.J.; see *Yarl's Wood Immigration Ltd v Bedfordshire Police Authority* [2008] EWHC 2207 (Comm), [2009] 1 All E.R. 886 (QBD (Comm)), Beatson, J.

50 & 51 Vict. (1887)

40. Savings Banks Act 1887
s.10, amended: SSI 2009/65 Sch.1
s.10B, amended: SSI 2009/65 Sch.1
54. British Settlements Act 1887
enabling: SI 2009/888, SI 2009/1737, SI 2009/1751, SI 2009/3008
55. Sheriffs Act 1887
Sch.2A, amended: SI 2009/837 Art.11

51 & 52 Vict. (1888)

21. Law of Distress Amendment Act 1888
s.8, enabling: SI 2009/873
48. Companies Clauses Consolidation Act 1888
disapplied: SI 2009/2579 Art.5, SI 2009/2604 Art.5
64. Law of Libel Amendment Act 1888
s.3, repealed: 2009 c.25 Sch.23 Part 2
s.4, repealed: 2009 c.25 Sch.23 Part 2
s.8, amended: 2009 c.25 Sch.21 para.68

52 & 53 Vict. (1889)

57. Regulation of Railways Act 1889
disapplied: SI 2009/1300 Art.3

53 & 54 Vict. (1890)

37. Foreign Jurisdiction Act 1890
applied: SI 2009/700 Sch.1 Part II
39. Partnership Act 1890
see *Hodson v Hodson* [2009] EWHC 430 (Ch), [2009] P.N.L.R. 23 (Ch D), Arnold, J.; see *Kovats v TFO Management LLP* [2009] I.C.R. 1140 (EAT), Birtles, J.; see *Tann v Herrington* [2009] EWHC 445 (Ch), [2009] Bus. L.R. 1051 (Ch D), Bernard Livesey Q.C.
referred to: SI 2009/3015 Art.5
s.1, see *Hodson v Hodson* [2009] EWHC 430 (Ch), [2009] P.N.L.R. 23 (Ch D), Arnold, J.
s.1, amended: SI 2009/1941 Sch.1 para.2
s.21, see *Longmuir v Moffat* [2009] CSIH 19, 2009 S.C. 329 (IH (Ex Div)), Lord Osborne

53 & 54 Vict. (1890) – cont.

39. Partnership Act 1890–*cont.*
s.32, see *HLB Kidsons (A Firm) v Lloyd's Underwriters* [2008] EWHC 2415 (Comm), [2009] 1 All E.R. (Comm) 760 (QBD (Comm)), Judge Mackie Q.C.
s.37, see *HLB Kidsons (A Firm) v Lloyd's Underwriters* [2008] EWHC 2415 (Comm), [2009] 1 All E.R. (Comm) 760 (QBD (Comm)), Judge Mackie Q.C.
s.38, see *HLB Kidsons (A Firm) v Lloyd's Underwriters* [2008] EWHC 2415 (Comm), [2009] 1 All E.R. (Comm) 760 (QBD (Comm)), Judge Mackie Q.C.
s.44, see *HLB Kidsons (A Firm) v Lloyd's Underwriters* [2008] EWHC 2415 (Comm), [2009] 1 All E.R. (Comm) 760 (QBD (Comm)), Judge Mackie Q.C.

54 & 55 Vict. (1891)

8. Tithe Act 1891
referred to: SI 2009/500 Sch.1 Part 1
37. Fisheries Act 1891
s.13, repealed: 2009 c.23 s.234, Sch.22 Part 5
39. Stamp Act 1891
applied: SI 2009/2971 Reg.32
s.13, amended: SI 2009/56 Sch.1 para.2
s.13A, amended: SI 2009/56 Sch.1 para.3
s.13A, repealed (in part): SI 2009/56 Sch.1 para.3
s.122, amended: SI 2009/56 Sch.1 para.4
Sch.1, see *Hameed v Qayyum* [2008] EWHC 2274 (Ch), [2009] B.P.I.R. 35 (Ch D), Judge Purle Q.C.

55 & 56 Vict. (1892)

6. Colonial Probates Act 1892
see *Hamblett (Deceased), Re* [2009] W.T.L.R. 559 (HC (NZ)), Asher, J.
23. Foreign Marriage Act 1892
applied: SI 2009/700 Art.3, Sch.1 Part VI
43. Military Lands Act 1892
s.14, enabling: SI 2009/3284
s.16, applied: SI 2009/3284
s.17, applied: SI 2009/3284, SI 2009/3284 Reg.7
s.18, applied: SI 2009/3284

1893

i. Manchester, Sheffield and Lincolnshire Railway (Extension to London &c.) Act 1893
applied: SI 2009/1300 Art.88
5. Regimental Debts Act 1893
varied: SI 2009/1059 Sch.1 para.1
s.2, amended: SI 2009/2054 Sch.1 para.1
s.23, varied: SI 2009/1059 Sch.1 para.1
s.29A, varied: SI 2009/1059 Sch.1 para.1
17. North Sea Fisheries Act 1893
repealed: 2009 c.23 s.234, Sch.22 Part 5

57 & 58 Vict. (1894)

2. Behring Sea Award Act 1894
repealed: 2009 c.23 s.234, Sch.22 Part 5
44. Heritable Securities (Scotland) Act 1894
s.5, see *Royal Bank of Scotland Plc v Wilson* [2009] CSIH 36, 2009 S.L.T. 729 (IH (Ex Div)), Lord Nimmo Smith

58 & 59 Vict. (1895)

14. Courts of Law Fees (Scotland) Act 1895
s.2, enabling: SSI 2009/87, SSI 2009/88, SSI 2009/89

21. Seal Fisheries (North Pacific) Act 1895
repealed: 2009 c.23 s.234, Sch.22 Part 5

60 & 61 Vict. (1897)

38. Public Health (Scotland) Act 1897
applied: SSI 2009/319 Sch.2 para.2
disapplied: SSI 2009/319 Sch.2 para.2
Part II, referred to: SSI 2009/319 Art.3
Part V, referred to: SSI 2009/319 Art.3
s.3, referred to: SSI 2009/319 Art.3
s.72, referred to: SSI 2009/319 Art.3
s.166, referred to: SSI 2009/319 Art.3

61 & 62 Vict. (1898)

36. Criminal Evidence Act 1898
s.6, varied: SI 2009/1059 Sch.1 para.2

39. Vagrancy Act 1898
s.1, referred to: SI 2009/37 Sch.1 para.2, Sch.1 para.4

60. Inebriates Act 1898
repealed (in part): SSI 2009/248 Sch.2

62 & 63 Vict. (1899)

19. Electric Lighting (Clauses) Act 1899
s.10, applied: SI 2009/640 Reg.4

2 Edw. 7 (1902)

8. Cremation Act 1902
see *R. (on the application of Ghai) v Newcastle City Council* [2009] EWHC 978 (Admin), Times, May 18, 2009 (QBD (Admin)), Cranston, J.
s.2, see *R. (on the application of Ghai) v Newcastle City Council* [2009] EWHC 978 (Admin), Times, May 18, 2009 (QBD (Admin)), Cranston, J.
s.7, referred to: 2009 c.25 s.20
s.8, see *R. (on the application of Ghai) v Newcastle City Council* [2009] EWHC 978 (Admin), Times, May 18, 2009 (QBD (Admin)), Cranston, J.
s.10, amended: 2009 c.25 Sch.21 para.1

6 Edw. 7 (1906)

40. Marriage with Foreigners Act 1906
applied: SI 2009/700 Art.3

41. Marine Insurance Act 1906
s.63, see *Dornoch Ltd v Westminster International BV* [2009] EWHC 889 (Admlty), [2009] 2 All E.R. (Comm) 399 (QBD (Admlty)), Tomlinson, J.
s.79, see *Dornoch Ltd v Westminster International BV* [2009] EWHC 1782 (Admlty), [2009] 2 Lloyd's Rep. 420 (QBD (Admlty)), Tomlinson, J.; see *Dornoch Ltd v Westminster International BV* [2009] EWHC 889 (Admlty), [2009] 2 All E.R. (Comm) 399 (QBD (Admlty)), Tomlinson, J.

7 Edw. 7 (1907)

24. Limited Partnerships Act 1907
applied: SI 2009/1940 Art.3, SI 2009/2160 r.3
referred to: SI 2009/1940 Art.3

7 Edw. 7 (1907) – cont.

24. Limited Partnerships Act 1907 – *cont.*
s.5, amended: SI 2009/1940 Art.8
s.8, substituted: SI 2009/1940 Art.4
s.8A, added: SI 2009/1940 Art.5
s.8B, added: SI 2009/1940 Art.6
s.8C, added: SI 2009/1940 Art.7
s.9, amended: SI 2009/1941 Sch.1 para.3
s.9, applied: SI 2009/2160 r.3
s.10, amended: SI 2009/1941 Sch.1 para.3
s.14, amended: SI 2009/1941 Sch.1 para.3
s.15, substituted: SI 2009/1941 Sch.1 para.3
s.16, amended: SI 2009/1941 Sch.1 para.3
s.16, applied: SI 2009/2392 Sch.2 para.4, Sch.2 para.5, Sch.2 para.6
s.17, applied: SI 2009/1940 Art.9
s.17, enabling: SI 2009/2160

51. Sheriff Courts (Scotland) Act 1907
Appendix 1, amended: SSI 2009/107 Sch.2, SSI 2009/285 Sch.1, SSI 2009/294 Sch.1
Appendix 3, added: SSI 2009/285 Sch.2
s.3, see *Napoli v Stone* 2009 S.L.T. (Sh Ct) 125 (Sh Ct (Grampian) (Portree)), Sheriff Principal Sir S S T Young, Bt, QC
s.27, see *B v B* 2009 Fam. L.R. 129 (Sh Ct (South Strathclyde) (Ayr)), Sheriff Principal B A Lockhart
s.40, enabling: SSI 2009/81, SSI 2009/103, SSI 2009/162, SSI 2009/321, SSI 2009/379
s.50, see *Manning v Manning* [2009] CSIH 67, 2009 S.L.T. 743 (IH (Ex Div)), Lord Clarke
Sch.1, applied: SSI 2009/284 Sch.1
Sch.1, referred to: SSI 2009/294 r.6
Sch.1 Part 1 para.2, amended: SSI 2009/164 r.2
Sch.1 Part 3 para.1, amended: SSI 2009/285 r.2
Sch.1 Part 3 para.2A, added: SSI 2009/294 r.2
Sch.1 Part 3 para.2A, substituted: SSI 2009/294 r.2
Sch.1 Part 5 para.1, varied: SSI 2009/284 Sch.1
Sch.1 Part 5 para.2, varied: SSI 2009/284 Sch.1
Sch.1 Part 5 para.3, varied: SSI 2009/284 Sch.1
Sch.1 Part 5 para.4, varied: SSI 2009/284 Sch.1
Sch.1 Part 5 para.5, varied: SSI 2009/284 Sch.1
Sch.1 Part 5 para.6, varied: SSI 2009/284 Sch.1
Sch.1 Part 5 para.7, varied: SSI 2009/284 Sch.1
Sch.1 Part 5 para.8, varied: SSI 2009/284 Sch.1
Sch.1 Part 5 para.9, varied: SSI 2009/284 Sch.1
Sch.1 Part 5 para.10, varied: SSI 2009/284 Sch.1
Sch.1 Part 5 para.89, varied: SSI 2009/284 Sch.1
Sch.1 Part 5 para.90, varied: SSI 2009/284 Sch.1
Sch.1 Part 5 para.90A, varied: SSI 2009/284 Sch.1
Sch.1 Part 5 para.91, varied: SSI 2009/284 Sch.1
Sch.1 Part 5 para.92, varied: SSI 2009/284 Sch.1
Sch.1 Part 5 para.93, varied: SSI 2009/284 Sch.1
Sch.1 Part 5 para.94, varied: SSI 2009/284 Sch.1
Sch.1 Part 5 para.95, varied: SSI 2009/284 Sch.1
Sch.1 Part 5 para.96, varied: SSI 2009/284 Sch.1
Sch.1 Part 5 para.97, varied: SSI 2009/284 Sch.1
Sch.1 Part 5 para.98, varied: SSI 2009/284 Sch.1
Sch.1 Part 6 paraA.3, amended: SSI 2009/107 r.3
Sch.1 Part 6 paraA.6, repealed: SSI 2009/107 r.3
Sch.1 Part 6 paraA.8, added: SSI 2009/107 r.3
Sch.1 Part 7 para.3, amended: SSI 2009/294 r.2
Sch.1 Part 13 para.1, amended: SSI 2009/285 r.2
Sch.1 Part 13 para.2, amended: SSI 2009/285 r.2
Sch.1 Part 15, applied: SSI 2009/284 Sch.1
Sch.1 Part 15 para.7, added: SSI 2009/294 r.14
Sch.1 Part 19 para.2, amended: SSI 2009/294 r.10
Sch.1 Part 19 para.2, repealed (in part): SSI 2009/294 r.10

7 Edw. 7 (1907)– cont.

51. Sheriff Courts (Scotland) Act 1907– cont.
Sch.1 Part 20 para.3, amended: SSI 2009/ 294 r.10
Sch.1 Part 21 para.1, amended: SSI 2009/ 285 r.2
Sch.1 Part 27 para.8, amended: SSI 2009/ 294 r.16
Sch.1 Part 31 para.1, varied: SSI 2009/ 284 Sch.1
Sch.1 Part 31 para.2, varied: SSI 2009/ 284 Sch.1
Sch.1 Part 31 para.2A, varied: SSI 2009/ 284 Sch.1
Sch.1 Part 31 para.3, varied: SSI 2009/ 284 Sch.1
Sch.1 Part 31 para.4, varied: SSI 2009/ 284 Sch.1
Sch.1 Part 31 para.5, varied: SSI 2009/ 284 Sch.1
Sch.1 Part 31 para.6, varied: SSI 2009/ 284 Sch.1
Sch.1 Part 31 para.7, varied: SSI 2009/ 284 Sch.1
Sch.1 Part 31 para.8, varied: SSI 2009/ 284 Sch.1
Sch.1 Part 31 para.9, varied: SSI 2009/ 284 Sch.1
Sch.1 Part 31 para.10, varied: SSI 2009/ 284 Sch.1
Sch.1 Part 31 para.11, varied: SSI 2009/ 284 Sch.1
Sch.1 Part 33 para.3, amended: SSI 2009/ 284 r.3
Sch.1 Part 33A para.3, amended: SSI 2009/ 284 r.3
Sch.1 Part 33A para.57A, added: SSI 2009/ 284 r.3
Sch.1 Part 33A para.65A, added: SSI 2009/ 284 r.3
Sch.1 Part 36, added: SSI 2009/ 285 r.2
Sch.1 Part 36 paraA.1, added: SSI 2009/ 285 r.2
Sch.1 Part 36 paraB.1, added: SSI 2009/ 285 r.2
Sch.1 Part 36 paraC.1, added: SSI 2009/ 285 r.2
Sch.1 Part 36 paraD.1, added: SSI 2009/ 285 r.2
Sch.1 Part 36 paraE.1, added: SSI 2009/ 285 r.2
Sch.1 Part 36 paraF.1, added: SSI 2009/ 285 r.2
Sch.1 Part 36 paraH.1, added: SSI 2009/ 285 r.2
Sch.1 Part 36 paraJ.1, added: SSI 2009/ 285 r.2
Sch.1 Part 36 paraK.1, added: SSI 2009/ 285 r.2
Sch.1 Part 36 paraL.1, added: SSI 2009/ 285 r.2
Sch.1 Part 36 para.17A, amended: SSI 2009/ 285 r.2
Sch.1 Part 36 para.19, added: SSI 2009/ 285 r.2
Sch.1 Part 45, applied: SSI 2009/ 284 Sch.1

8 Edw. 7 (1908)

45. Punishment of Incest Act 1908
s.1, applied: 2009 asp 9 Sch.1 para.30
s.1, referred to: SI 2009/ 37 Sch.1 para.2, Sch.1 para.4
s.2, referred to: SI 2009/ 37 Sch.1 para.2, Sch.1 para.4

1 & 2 Geo. 5 (1911)

6. Perjury Act 1911
s.4, amended: 2009 c.24 Sch.6 para.19
s.5, applied: 2009 c.23 s.263
28. Official Secrets Act 1911
s.9, applied: SI 2009/ 2056 Sch.1 para.4

2 & 3 Geo. 5 (1912-13)

10. Seal Fisheries (North Pacific) Act 1912
repealed: 2009 c.23 s.234, Sch.22 Part 5

3 & 4 Geo. 5 (1913)

16. Foreign Jurisdiction Act 1913
applied: SI 2009/ 700 Sch.1 Part II
37. National Insurance Act 1913
repealed (in part): SSI 2009/ 319 Sch.3 Part 1

4 & 5 Geo. 5 (1914)

59. Bankruptcy Act 1914
applied: SI 2009/ 645 Art.7

4 & 5 Geo. 5 (1914)– cont.

59. Bankruptcy Act 1914– cont.
s.133, enabling: SI 2009/ 645

5 & 6 Geo. 5 (1914-15)

89. Finance (No.2) Act 1915
s.47, applied: 2009 c.4 s.1280

6 & 7 Geo. 5 (1916)

12. Local Government (Emergency Provisions) Act 1916
s.5, repealed (in part): SSI 2009/ 319 Sch.3 Part 1

10 & 11 Geo. 5 (1920)

33. Maintenance Orders (Facilities for Enforcement) Act 1920
applied: SI 2009/ 1109 Reg.8
41. Census Act 1920
s.1, applied: SI 2009/ 3210
s.1, enabling: SI 2009/ 3210
s.2, applied: SI 2009/ 277 Reg.5, SI 2009/ 3201 Reg.5
s.3, applied: SI 2009/ 3210 Art.4
Sch.1 para.6, referred to: SI 2009/ 3210
65. Employment of Women, Young Persons, and Children Act 1920
applied: SI 2009/ 605 Reg.3

11 & 12 Geo. 5 (1921)

58. Trusts (Scotland) Act 1921
s.19, applied: 2009 asp 1 Sch.1 para.8

12 & 13 Geo. 5 (1922)

56. Criminal Law Amendment Act 1922
see *H v Griffiths* [2009] HCJAC 15, 2009 S.L.T. 199 (HCJ), Lord Eassie

15 & 16 Geo. 5 (1925)

19. Trustee Act 1925
s.23, referred to: SI 2009/ 500 Sch.1 Part 1
s.27, see *MCP Pension Trustees Ltd v AON Pension Trustees Ltd* [2009] EWHC 1351 (Ch), [2009] Pens. L.R. 247 (Ch D), Jeremy Cousins Q.C.
s.61, see *Adams v Bridge* [2009] Pens. L.R. 153 (Pensions Ombudsman), Judge not applicable; see *Kemp v Sims* [2008] EWHC 2579 (Ch), [2009] Pens. L.R. 83 (Ch D), Norris, J.
20. Law of Property Act 1925
applied: SI 2009/ 153 Reg.27, SI 2009/ 995 Reg.27
s.1, see *Alexander-David v Hammersmith and Fulham LBC* [2009] EWCA Civ 259, [2009] 3 All E.R. 1098 (CA (Civ Div)), Waller, L.J.
s.4, amended: 2009 c.18 s.1, Sch.1
s.27, see *Bateman v Hyde* [2009] EWHC 81 (Ch), [2009] B.P.I.R. 737 (Ch D (Manchester)), Judge Pelling Q.C.
s.49, see *Aribisala v St James Homes (Grosvenor Dock) Ltd* [2008] EWHC 456 (Ch), [2009] 1 W.L.R. 1089 (Ch D), Floyd, J; see *Midill (97PL) Ltd v Park Lane Estates Ltd* [2008] EWCA Civ 1227, [2009] 1 W.L.R. 2460 (CA (Civ Div)), Keene, L.J.
s.53, see *Hameed v Qayyum* [2008] EWHC 2274 (Ch), [2009] B.P.I.R. 35 (Ch D), Judge Purle Q.C.; see *Hanchett-Stamford v Attorney*

15 & 16 Geo. 5 (1925) – cont.

20. Law of Property Act 1925 – *cont.*
   s.53– *cont.*
     General [2008] EWHC 330 (Ch), [2009] Ch. 173 (Ch D (Bristol)), Lewison, J.; see *McLaughlin v Duffill* [2008] EWCA Civ 1627, [2009] 3 W.L.R. 1139 (CA (Civ Div)), Sir Andrew Morritt (Chancellor)
   s.53, disapplied: SI 2009/555 Art.3
   s.62, see *Hall v Moore* [2009] EWCA Civ 201, [2009] 24 E.G. 86 (CA (Civ Div)), Rix, L.J.; see *Thornhill v Sita Metal Recycling Ltd* [2009] EWHC 2037 (QB), [2009] Env. L.R. 35 (QBD), Judge Seymour Q.C.
   s.74, amended: SI 2009/1941 Sch.1 para.4
   s.78, see *Hutchinson's Application, Re* [2009] UKUT 182 (LC) (UT (Lands)), George Bartlett Q.C. (President, LTr)
   s.84, see *Hutchinson's Application, Re* [2009] UKUT 182 (LC) (UT (Lands)), George Bartlett Q.C. (President, LTr); see *Practice Direction (UT (Lands): Lands Tribunal: Interim Practice Directions and Guidance)* [2009] R.V.R. 208 (UT (Lands)), Carnwath, L.J. (SP)
   s.84, amended: SI 2009/1307 Sch.1 para.5
   s.84, applied: SI 2009/1114 Sch.1
   s.84, referred to: SI 2009/1114 Sch.1
   s.101, see *Horsham Properties Group Ltd v Clark* [2008] EWHC 2327 (Ch), [2009] 1 W.L.R. 1255 (Ch D), Briggs, J.
   s.121, repealed (in part): 2009 c.18 s.4, Sch.1
   s.162, repealed: 2009 c.18 s.4, Sch.1
   s.164, repealed: 2009 c.18 s.13, Sch.1
   s.165, repealed: 2009 c.18 s.13, Sch.1
   s.166, repealed: 2009 c.18 s.13, Sch.1
   s.205, see *Clarence House Ltd v National Westminster Bank Plc* [2009] EWHC 77 (Ch), [2009] 1 W.L.R. 1651 (Ch D), Judge Hodge Q.C.

21. Land Registration Act 1925
   referred to: SI 2009/500 Sch.1 Part 1

23. Administration of Estates Act 1925
   s.46, varied: SI 2009/135 Art.2

33. Church of Scotland (Property and Endowments) Act 1925
   s.32, amended: SSI 2009/319 Sch.3 Part 1

71. Public Health Act 1925
   s.14, applied: SI 2009/721 Sch.3 para.2

86. Criminal Justice Act 1925
   s.33, applied: SI 2009/209 Reg.118, SI 2009/216 Reg.10, SI 2009/261 Reg.52, SI 2009/1299 Reg.44, SI 2009/1361 Reg.19, SI 2009/1372 Reg.44, SI 2009/1551 Reg.19, SI 2009/1611 Reg.24, SI 2009/2470 Reg.24, SI 2009/2902 Reg.24, SI 2009/3219 Art.40, SI 2009/3263 Reg.12, SI 2009/3364 Art.43
   s.33, referred to: SI 2009/842 Reg.28

16 & 17 Geo. 5 (1926)

28. Mining Industry Act 1926
   s.20, amended: SI 2009/1941 Sch.1 para.5

48. Births and Deaths Registration Act 1926
   s.4, amended: 2009 c.25 Sch.21 para.3
   s.5, amended: 2009 c.25 Sch.21 para.4

18 & 19 Geo. 5 (1928)

13. Currency and Bank Notes Act 1928
   s.9, repealed: 2009 c.1 s.214

18 & 19 Geo. 5 (1928) – cont.

15. Bankers (Northern Ireland) Act 1928
   s.1, repealed: 2009 c.1 s.214
   s.3, repealed: 2009 c.1 s.214
   Sch.1, repealed: 2009 c.1 s.214

19. Agricultural Produce (Grading and Marking) Act 1928
   disapplied: SI 2009/1361 Reg.22, SI 2009/1551 Reg.22, SSI 2009/225 Reg.24

32. Petroleum (Consolidation) Act 1928
   s.4, applied: SI 2009/515 Sch.8 Part 4
   s.4, disapplied: SI 2009/515 Reg.10
   s.5, applied: SI 2009/716 Reg.7
   s.19, applied: SI 2009/515 Sch.8 Part 4, SI 2009/716 Reg.7

20 & 21 Geo. 5 (1930)

25. Third Parties (Rights against Insurers) Act 1930
   see *Law Society v Shah* [2007] EWHC 2841 (Ch), [2009] Ch. 223 (Ch D), Floyd, J

21 & 22 Geo. 5 (1931)

28. Finance Act 1931
   s.28, applied: SI 2009/2269 Reg.17
   Sch.2, applied: SI 2009/2269 Reg.17

33. Architects (Registration) Act 1931
   referred to: SI 2009/500 Sch.1 Part 1

40. Agricultural Produce (Grading and Marking) Amendment Act 1931
   disapplied: SI 2009/1361 Reg.22, SI 2009/1551 Reg.22, SSI 2009/225 Reg.24

49. Finance (No.2) Act 1931
   s.22, applied: 2009 c.4 s.1280

23 & 24 Geo. 5 (1932-33)

12. Children and Young Persons Act 1933
   s.1, applied: SI 2009/1168 Sch.1 para.1
   s.1, referred to: SI 2009/37 Sch.1 para.2, Sch.1 para.4
   s.12D, amended: 2009 c.21 s.22, Sch.6
   Sch.1, amended: 2009 c.25 Sch.21 para.53
   Sch.1, applied: SSI 2009/154 Sch.1 para.14

36. Administration of Justice (Miscellaneous Provisions) Act 1933
   s.2, amended: 2009 c.25 s.116, Sch.23 Part 3
   s.2, applied: SI 2009/3328 Reg.4
   Sch.2 para.1, amended: 2009 c.25 s.116, Sch.23 Part 3

24 & 25 Geo. 5 (1933-34)

36. Petroleum (Production) Act 1934
   see *Bocardo SA v Star Energy UK Onshore Ltd* [2008] EWHC 1756 (Ch), [2009] 1 All E.R. 517 (Ch D), Peter Smith, J.; see *Bocardo SA v Star Energy UK Onshore Ltd* [2009] EWCA Civ 579, [2009] 3 W.L.R. 1010 (CA (Civ Div)), Jacob, L.J.
   s.2, applied: 2009 c.23 s.77
   s.3, see *Bocardo SA v Star Energy UK Onshore Ltd* [2009] EWCA Civ 579, [2009] 3 W.L.R. 1010 (CA (Civ Div)), Jacob, L.J.
   s.10, see *Bocardo SA v Star Energy UK Onshore Ltd* [2009] EWCA Civ 579, [2009] 3 W.L.R. 1010 (CA (Civ Div)), Jacob, L.J.

24 & 25 Geo. 5 (1933-34) – cont.

41. Law Reform (Miscellaneous Provisions) Act 1934
see *Rabone v Pennine Care NHS Trust* [2009] EWHC 1827 (QB), [2009] LS Law Medical 503 (QBD (Manchester)), Simon, J.

26 Geo. 5 & Edw. 8 (1935-36)

27. Petroleum (Transfer of Licences) Act 1936
s.1, applied: SI 2009/515 Sch.8 Part 4
s.1, disapplied: SI 2009/515 Reg.10
49. Public Health Act 1936
s.6, applied: SI 2009/3051 Reg.2, SI 2009/3230 Reg.2, SI 2009/3238 Reg.2, SI 2009/3255 Reg.2, SI 2009/3376 Reg.2, SI 2009/3378 Reg.2, SI 2009/3379 Reg.2

1 Edw. 8 & 1 Geo. 6 (1936-37)

lvii. National Trust Act 1937
see *National Trust for Places of Historic Interest or Natural Beauty v Fleming* [2009] EWHC 1789 (Ch), [2009] N.P.C. 97 (Ch D), Henderson, J.
33. Diseases of Fish Act 1937
repealed (in part): SI 2009/463 Sch.2 para.1, SSI 2009/85 Sch.2 para.1
37. Children and Young Persons (Scotland) Act 1937
s.12, applied: SSI 2009/31 Sch.1 para.7, SSI 2009/71 Sch.1 para.7
s.12, referred to: SI 2009/37 Sch.1 para.2, Sch.1 para.4
s.110, amended: SSI 2009/248 Sch.2

1 & 2 Geo. 6 (1937-38)

12. Population (Statistics) Act 1938
Sch.1 para.1, amended: 2009 c.24 Sch.6 para.20
36. Infanticide Act 1938
s.1, amended: 2009 c.25 s.57
s.1, referred to: SI 2009/37 Sch.1 para.2, Sch.1 para.4

2 & 3 Geo. 6 (1938-39)

5. Infanticide Act (Northern Ireland) 1939
s..1, amended: 2009 c.25 s.58
75. Compensation (Defence) Act 1939
s.18, applied: SSI 2009/319 Art.3
82. Personal Injuries (Emergency Provisions) Act 1939
applied: SI 2009/226 Sch.1, SI 2009/227 Sch.1
s.1, enabling: SI 2009/438
s.2, enabling: SI 2009/438

3 & 4 Geo. 6 (1939-40)

42. Law Reform (Miscellaneous Provisions) (Scotland) Act 1940
s.3, see *Farstad Supply AS v Enviroco Ltd* [2009] CSIH 35, 2009 S.C. 489 (IH (Ex Div)), Lord Osborne

6 & 7 Geo. 6 (1942-43)

39. Pensions Appeal Tribunals Act 1943
s.5, see *R. (on the application of Bunce) v Pensions Appeal Tribunal* [2009] EWCA Civ 451, Times, April 15, 2009 (CA (Civ Div)), Laws, L.J.

6 & 7 Geo. 6 (1942-43) – cont.

39. Pensions Appeal Tribunals Act 1943– *cont.*
s.6A, enabling: SI 2009/459
s.6C, enabling: SI 2009/459
s.6D, enabling: SI 2009/459
s.11A, enabling: SI 2009/459
Sch.1 para.2, amended: 2009 c.3 Sch.4 para.1
Sch.1 para.2B, amended: 2009 c.3 Sch.4 para.1
Sch.1 para.5, enabling: SSI 2009/353

8 & 9 Geo. 6 (1944-45)

7. British Settlements Act 1945
enabling: SI 2009/888, SI 2009/1737, SI 2009/1751
15. Public Health (Scotland) Act 1945
s.1, amended: SSI 2009/319 Sch.2 para.1
s.1, applied: SSI 2009/319 Sch.2 para.2
28. Law Reform (Contributory Negligence) Act 1945
see *Deans v Glasgow Housing Association Ltd* 2009 Hous. L.R. 82 (Sh Ct (Glasgow)), Sheriff A R Mackenzie
s.1, see *St George v Home Office* [2008] EWCA Civ 1068, [2009] 1 W.L.R. 1670 (CA (Civ Div)), Ward, L.J.
43. Requisitioned Land and War Works Act 1945
s.47, amended: SI 2009/1307 Sch.1 para.7
s.48, amended: SI 2009/1307 Sch.1 para.8
s.59, amended: SI 2009/1307 Sch.1 para.9

9 & 10 Geo. 6 (1945-46)

27. Bank of England Act 1946
s.4, disapplied: 2009 c.1 s.247
36. Statutory Instruments Act 1946
applied: SI 2009/2108 Reg.23
varied: 2009 c.25 s.176
s.1, applied: SI 2009/1182 Art.10
s.6, applied: SI 2009/3210
45. United Nations Act 1946
see *A v HM Treasury* [2008] EWCA Civ 1187, [2009] 3 W.L.R. 25 (CA (Civ Div)), Sir Anthony Clarke, M.R.
s.1, see *Hay v HM Treasury* [2009] EWHC 1677 (Admin), [2009] Lloyd's Rep. F.C. 547 (QBD (Admin)), Owen, J.
s.1, enabling: SI 2009/699, SI 2009/886, SI 2009/888, SI 2009/1746, SI 2009/1747, SI 2009/1749, SI 2009/3213
73. Hill Farming Act 1946
s.23, amended: 2009 asp 12 Sch.2 para.1
s.23A, added: 2009 asp 12 s.58

10 & 11 Geo. 6 (1946-47)

xxxv. London Midland and Scottish Railway Act 1947
applied: SI 2009/1300 Sch.16 para.9
19. Polish Resettlement Act 1947
s.1, enabling: SI 2009/436
24. Naval Forces (Enforcement of Maintenance Liabilities) Act 1947
s.1, applied: SI 2009/1059 Art.198
33. Foreign Marriage Act 1947
applied: SI 2009/700 Sch.1 Part VI
41. Fire Services Act 1947
s.26, enabling: SI 2009/1226, SSI 2009/184
42. Acquisition of Land (Authorisation Procedure) (Scotland) Act 1947
applied: 2009 asp 6 s.66

10 & 11 Geo. 6 (1946-47) – cont.

44. Crown Proceedings Act 1947
see *Al Rawi v Security Service* [2009] EWHC 2959
(QB),Times, November 24, 2009 (QBD),Silber,J.
s.17, applied: SI 2009/2657 r.24
s.35, see *Advocate General for Scotland v
Montgomery* [2009] S.T.C. 2387 (OH), Lady Paton
s.38, varied: SI 2009/847 Reg.16, SI 2009/1495
Reg.23, SI 2009/1747 Art.25

11 & 12 Geo. 6 (1947-48)

29. National Assistance Act 1948
see *X v Hounslow LBC* [2009] EWCA Civ 286,
[2009] 2 F.L.R. 262 (CA (Civ Div)), Sir
Anthony Clarke, M.R.
s.21, see *R. (on the application of Wilson) v Coventry
City Council* [2008] EWHC 2300 (Admin),
(2009) 12 C.C.L. Rep. 7 (QBD (Admin)), Judge
Pelling Q.C.; see *R. (on the application of Z) v
Hillingdon LBC* [2009] EWHC 1398 (Admin),
(2009) 12 C.C.L. Rep. 429 (QBD (Admin)),
Timothy Brennan Q.C.
s.22, applied: SI 2009/632 Reg.2, SSI 2009/73
Reg.2
s.22, enabling: SI 2009/597, SI 2009/632, SSI 2009/
72, SSI 2009/73, SSI 2009/381
s.24, amended: 2009 c.21 Sch.1 para.1
s.29, see *R. (on the application of Z) v Hillingdon
LBC* [2009] EWHC 1398 (Admin), (2009) 12
C.C.L. Rep. 429 (QBD (Admin)), Timothy
Brennan Q.C.

38. Companies Act 1948
s.28, applied: SI 2009/1941 Sch.3 para.1

43. Children Act 1948
s.1, see *Pierce v Doncaster MBC* [2008] EWCA Civ
1416, [2009] 1 F.L.R. 1189 (CA (Civ Div)), Sedley,
L.J.

47. Agricultural Wages Act 1948
applied: SI 2009/603 Sch.1 para.1
Sch.2, amended: SI 2009/837 Art.24

**53. Nurseries and Child-Minders Regulation Act
1948**
s.1, applied: SI 2009/1547 Sch.1 para.19
s.5, applied: SI 2009/1547 Sch.1 para.19

56. British Nationality Act 1948
s.3, applied: SI 2009/3015 Art.247

12, 13 & 14 Geo. 6 (1948-49)

42. Lands Tribunal Act 1949
s.1, amended: SI 2009/1307 Sch.1 para.11
s.1, repealed (in part): SI 2009/1307 Sch.1 para.11
s.1, substituted: SI 2009/1307 Sch.1 para.11
s.2, amended: SI 2009/1307 Sch.1 para.12
s.2, applied: SI 2009/1307 Art.3
s.2, repealed (in part): SI 2009/1307 Sch.1 para.12
s.3, amended: SI 2009/1307 Sch.1 para.13
s.3, repealed (in part): SI 2009/1307 Sch.1 para.13
s.3, enabling: SSI 2009/259, SSI 2009/260
s.4, amended: SI 2009/1307 Sch.1 para.14
s.6, amended: SI 2009/1307 Sch.1 para.15
s.7, amended: SI 2009/1307 Sch.1 para.16
s.9, amended: SI 2009/1307 Sch.1 para.17

54. Wireless Telegraphy Act 1949
see *Floe Telecom Ltd (In Administration) v Office of
Communications* [2009] EWCA Civ 47, [2009]
Bus. L.R. 1116 (CA (Civ Div)), Mummery, L.J.

55. Prevention of Damage by Pests Act 1949
s.4, applied: SI 2009/665 Art.2

12, 13 & 14 Geo. 6 (1948-49) – cont.

55. Prevention of Damage by Pests Act 1949 *–cont.*
s.28, amended: SSI 2009/319 Sch.3 Part 1

74. Coast Protection Act 1949
s.2, amended: 2009 c.23 s.193, Sch.14 para.2, Sch.22
Part 4
s.24, amended: SI 2009/1307 Sch.1 para.18
s.34, applied: 2009 c.23 Sch.9 para.9
s.34, repealed (in part): 2009 c.23 Sch.8 para.1,
Sch.22 Part 2
s.34, varied: 2009 c.23 Sch.9 para.2
s.35, repealed (in part): 2009 c.23 Sch.8 para.1,
Sch.22 Part 2
s.36, repealed (in part): 2009 c.23 Sch.8 para.1,
Sch.22 Part 2
s.36A, referred to: 2009 c.23 Sch.9 para.3
s.36A, repealed (in part): 2009 c.23 Sch.8 para.1,
Sch.22 Part 2
s.45, amended: 2009 c.23 Sch.14 para.3, Sch.22 Part 4
s.47, repealed (in part): 2009 c.23 Sch.22 Part 2
s.49, amended: 2009 c.23 Sch.8 para.1, Sch.14
para.4, Sch.22 Part 4
s.49, repealed (in part): 2009 c.23 Sch.22 Part 2
Sch.1 Part I para.1, amended: 2009 c.23 Sch.14
para.5, Sch.22 Part 4

76. Marriage Act 1949
applied: SI 2009/2107 Sch.2 para.1
s.27, amended: SI 2009/2821 Art.2
s.27, enabling: SI 2009/2806
s.27A, amended: SI 2009/2821 Art.3
s.27B, amended: SI 2009/2821 Art.4
s.30, substituted: SI 2009/2821 Art.5
s.31, amended: SI 2009/2821 Art.6
s.31, enabling: SI 2009/2806
s.33, amended: SI 2009/2821 Art.7
s.41, amended: SI 2009/2821 Art.8
s.57, amended: SI 2009/2821 Art.9
s.58, amended: SI 2009/2821 Art.10
s.73, amended: SI 2009/2821 Art.11
s.74, substituted: SI 2009/2821 Art.12
s.74, enabling: SI 2009/2806
s.75, amended: SI 2009/2821 Art.13
s.78, amended: SI 2009/2821 Art.14
s.78, enabling: SI 2009/2806

88. Registered Designs Act 1949
see *Central Vista (M) Sdn Bhd v Pemi Trade sro*
[2009] E.C.D.R. 21 (Designs Registry), Edward
Smith
applied: SI 2009/1969 Art.8
s.11ZA, see *Central Vista (M) Sdn Bhd v Pemi
Trade sro* [2009] E.C.D.R. 21 (Designs
Registry), Edward Smith
s.13, enabling: SI 2009/2747
s.36, enabling: SI 2009/546
s.37, enabling: SI 2009/2747

**97. National Parks and Access to the Countryside
Act 1949**
Part IV, referred to: 2009 c.23 s.307
s.16, applied: SI 2009/3264 Sch.2 para.1, SI 2009/
3365 Sch.2 para.1
s.51, applied: 2009 c.23 s.298, s.305, Sch.20 para.9
s.52, applied: 2009 c.23 s.305
s.55, applied: 2009 c.23 s.298, s.305, Sch.20 para.9
s.55A, added: 2009 c.23 s.302
s.55A, applied: 2009 c.23 s.298
s.55B, added: 2009 c.23 s.302
s.55C, added: 2009 c.23 s.302
s.55D, added: 2009 c.23 s.302
s.55E, added: 2009 c.23 s.302

12, 13 & 14 Geo. 6 (1948-49) – cont.

97. National Parks and Access to the Countryside Act 1949– cont.
s.55F, added: 2009 c.23 s.302
s.55G, added: 2009 c.23 s.302
s.55H, added: 2009 c.23 s.302
s.55I, added: 2009 c.23 s.302
s.55I, applied: 2009 c.23 Sch.20 para.10
s.55J, added: 2009 c.23 s.302
s.107, amended: SI 2009/1307 Sch.1 para.19
s.111, applied: 2009 c.23 s.307
Sch.1A para.1, added: 2009 c.23 Sch.19
Sch.1A para.2, added: 2009 c.23 Sch.19
Sch.1A para.3, added: 2009 c.23 Sch.19
Sch.1A para.4, added: 2009 c.23 Sch.19
Sch.1A para.5, added: 2009 c.23 Sch.19
Sch.1A para.6, added: 2009 c.23 Sch.19
Sch.1A para.7, added: 2009 c.23 Sch.19
Sch.1A para.8, added: 2009 c.23 Sch.19
Sch.1A para.9, added: 2009 c.23 Sch.19
Sch.1A para.10, added: 2009 c.23 Sch.19
Sch.1A para.11, added: 2009 c.23 Sch.19
Sch.1A para.12, added: 2009 c.23 Sch.19
Sch.1A para.13, added: 2009 c.23 Sch.19
Sch.1A para.14, added: 2009 c.23 Sch.19
Sch.1A para.15, added: 2009 c.23 Sch.19
Sch.1A para.16, added: 2009 c.23 Sch.19
Sch.1A para.17, added: 2009 c.23 Sch.19
Sch.1A para.18, added: 2009 c.23 Sch.19

14 Geo. 6 (1950)

15. Finance Act 1950
s.39, amended: 2009 c.4 Sch.1 para.294
27. Arbitration Act 1950
s.26, see *National Ability SA v Tinna Oils & Chemicals Ltd* [2009] EWCA Civ 1330, Times, December 24, 2009 (CA (Civ Div)), Thomas, L.J.
29. Employment and Training (Northern Ireland) Act 1950
s.1, applied: 2009 c.22 s.109
37. Maintenance Orders Act 1950
s.4, amended: 2009 c.24 Sch.7 Part 1
s.4, repealed (in part): 2009 c.24 Sch.7 Part 1
s.9, amended: 2009 c.24 Sch.7 Part 1
s.9, repealed (in part): 2009 c.24 Sch.7 Part 1

14 & 15 Geo. 6 (1950-51)

35. Pet Animals Act 1951
s.1, applied: SSI 2009/141 Reg.3
s.5, applied: SSI 2009/141 Reg.4
65. Reserve and Auxiliary Forces (Protection of Civil Interests) Act 1951
s.14, amended: SSI 2009/248 Sch.1 para.1
s.18, amended: SSI 2009/248 Sch.1 para.1
s.27, amended: SI 2009/1941 Sch.1 para.6
s.38, amended: SI 2009/1941 Sch.1 para.6, SSI 2009/248 Sch.1 para.1

15 & 16 Geo. 6 & 1 Eliz. 2 (1951-52)

10. Income Tax Act 1952
s.228, applied: 2009 c.10 Sch.54 para.9
52. Prison Act 1952
applied: SI 2009/1922 Art.14
s.6, applied: 2009 c.20 s.3
s.39, varied: SI 2009/1096 r.71
s.40, varied: SI 2009/1096 r.71

15 & 16 Geo. 6 & 1 Eliz. 2 (1951-52) – cont.

52. Prison Act 1952– cont.
s.40A, varied: SI 2009/1096 r.71
s.40B, varied: SI 2009/1096 r.71
s.40C, varied: SI 2009/1096 r.71
s.40D, varied: SI 2009/1096 r.71
s.40E, varied: SI 2009/1096 r.71
s.40F, varied: SI 2009/1096 r.71
s.41, varied: SI 2009/1096 r.71
s.42, varied: SI 2009/1096 r.71
s.43, varied: SI 2009/1059 Sch.1 para.4
s.47, applied: SI 2009/703 Art.2
s.47, enabling: SI 2009/3082
Sch.A1 para.4, applied: SI 2009/570 Art.2
Sch.A1 para.4, enabling: SI 2009/570
66. Defamation Act 1952
s.17, repealed (in part): 2009 c.25 Sch.23 Part 2
67. Visiting Forces Act 1952
referred to: SI 2009/822 Art.3
s.7, amended: 2009 c.25 Sch.21 para.5, Sch.21 para.54
s.8, applied: SI 2009/705
s.8, enabling: SI 2009/705
s.13, applied: SI 2009/1059 Art.181
Sch.1 para.1, amended: 2009 c.25 Sch.21 para.54

1 & 2 Eliz. 2 (1952-53)

20. Births and Deaths Registration Act 1953
applied: 2009 c.25 s.5, s.10, s.40
referred to: 2009 c.24 s.56
Part II, applied: 2009 c.25 s.20
s.1, amended: 2009 c.24 Sch.6 para.2
s.1, enabling: SI 2009/2165
s.2, amended: 2009 c.24 Sch.6 para.3, 2009 c.25 Sch.21 para.7
s.2A, added: 2009 c.24 Sch.6 para.4
s.2B, added: 2009 c.24 Sch.6 para.4
s.2C, added: 2009 c.24 Sch.6 para.4
s.2D, added: 2009 c.24 Sch.6 para.4
s.2E, added: 2009 c.24 Sch.6 para.4
s.4, amended: 2009 c.24 Sch.6 para.5
s.5, amended: 2009 c.24 Sch.6 para.6
s.6, repealed: 2009 c.24 Sch.6 para.7, Sch.7 Part 5
s.7, repealed (in part): 2009 c.24 Sch.6 para.8, Sch.7 Part 5
s.8, amended: 2009 c.24 Sch.6 para.9
s.9, amended: 2009 c.24 Sch.6 para.10
s.9, enabling: SI 2009/2165
s.10, see *A v H* [2009] EWHC 636 (Fam), [2009] 4 All E.R. 641 (Fam Div), Sir Christopher Sumner
s.10, amended: 2009 c.24 Sch.6 para.11
s.10, repealed (in part): 2009 c.24 Sch.6 para.11, Sch.7 Part 5
s.10, enabling: SI 2009/2165
s.10A, amended: 2009 c.24 Sch.6 para.12
s.10A, repealed (in part): 2009 c.24 Sch.6 para.12, Sch.7 Part 5
s.10A, enabling: SI 2009/2165
s.10B, added: 2009 c.24 Sch.6 para.13
s.10C, added: 2009 c.24 Sch.6 para.13
s.14, enabling: SI 2009/2165
s.15, enabling: SI 2009/2165
s.16, amended: 2009 c.25 Sch.21 para.8
s.17, amended: 2009 c.25 Sch.21 para.9
s.18, amended: 2009 c.25 Sch.21 para.10
s.19, amended: 2009 c.25 Sch.21 para.11

1 & 2 Eliz. 2 (1952-53)–cont.

20. Births and Deaths Registration Act 1953–*cont.*
s.19, substituted: 2009 c.25 Sch.21 para.11
s.20, amended: 2009 c.25 Sch.21 para.12, Sch.23 Part 1
s.21, repealed: 2009 c.25 Sch.21 para.13, Sch.23 Part 1
s.22, substituted: 2009 c.25 Sch.21 para.14
s.23, amended: 2009 c.25 Sch.21 para.15
s.23A, amended: 2009 c.25 Sch.21 para.16
s.23A, repealed (in part): 2009 c.25 Sch.21 para.16, Sch.23 Part 1
s.24, amended: 2009 c.25 Sch.21 para.17
s.26, amended: SI 2009/2821 Art.15
s.29, amended: 2009 c.25 Sch.21 para.18
s.29, repealed (in part): 2009 c.25 Sch.21 para.18, Sch.23 Part 1
s.33A, added: 2009 c.25 Sch.21 para.19
s.34, amended: 2009 c.24 Sch.6 para.14
s.34, repealed (in part): 2009 c.25 Sch.21 para.20, Sch.23 Part 1
s.36, amended: 2009 c.24 Sch.6 para.15
s.39, amended: 2009 c.24 Sch.6 para.16
s.39, enabling: SI 2009/2165
s.39A, added: 2009 c.24 Sch.6 para.17
s.41, amended: 2009 c.24 Sch.6 para.18, 2009 c.25 Sch.21 para.21

26. Local Government (Miscellaneous Provisions) Act 1953
s.5, applied: SI 2009/721 Sch.3 para.3

36. Post Office Act 1953
s.87, referred to: SSI 2009/79 Art.6

37. Registration Service Act 1953
s.20, applied: SI 2009/2165

47. Emergency Laws (Miscellaneous Provisions) Act 1953
s.10, varied: SI 2009/1059 Sch.1 para.5

2 & 3 Eliz. 2 (1953-54)

40. Protection of Animals (Amendment) Act 1954
s.1, applied: SSI 2009/141 Reg.4

56. Landlord and Tenant Act 1954
see *Somerfield Stores Ltd v Spring (Sutton Coldfield) Ltd* [2009] EWHC 2384 (Ch), [2009] 48 E.G. 104 (Ch D (Birmingham)), Judge Purle Q.C.
Part II, see *Brooker v Unique Pub Properties Ltd* [2009] EWHC 2599 (Ch), [2009] 49 E.G. 72 (Ch D), Judge Iain Hughes QC
s.24, see *Newham LBC v Thomas-Van Staden* [2008] EWCA Civ 1414, [2009] L. & T.R. 5 (CA (Civ Div)), Moore-Bick, L.J.; see *Windsor Life Assurance Co Ltd v Lloyds TSB Bank Plc* [2009] 47 E.G. 134 (CC (Central London)), Judge Peter Cowell
s.25, see *Newham LBC v Thomas-Van Staden* [2008] EWCA Civ 1414, [2009] L. & T.R. 5 (CA (Civ Div)), Moore-Bick, L.J.
s.28, see *Newham LBC v Thomas-Van Staden* [2008] EWCA Civ 1414, [2009] L. & T.R. 5 (CA (Civ Div)), Moore-Bick, L.J.
s.29, see *Windsor Life Assurance Co Ltd v Lloyds TSB Bank Plc* [2009] 47 E.G. 134 (CC (Central London)), Judge Peter Cowell
s.30, see *Patel v Keles* [2009] EWCA Civ 1187, Times, December 08, 2009 (CA (Civ Div)), Waller, L.J. (V-P); see *Somerfield Stores Ltd v Spring (Sutton Coldfield) Ltd* [2009] EWHC 2384 (Ch), [2009] 48 E.G. 104 (Ch D (Birmingham)), Judge Purle Q.C.
s.37, amended: SI 2009/1307 Sch.1 para.20

2 & 3 Eliz. 2 (1953-54)–cont.

56. Landlord and Tenant Act 1954–*cont.*
s.46, amended: SI 2009/1941 Sch.1 para.7
s.64, see *Windsor Life Assurance Co Ltd v Lloyds TSB Bank Plc* [2009] 47 E.G. 134 (CC (Central London)), Judge Peter Cowell
s.69, amended: 2009 c.20 Sch.6 para.1

68. Pests Act 1954
s.8, enabling: SI 2009/2166

70. Mines and Quarries Act 1954
s.143, enabling: SI 2009/693

3 & 4 Eliz. 2 (1954-55)

18. Army Act 1955
applied: 2009 c.25 s.157, Sch.22 para.18, Sch.22 para.19, Sch.22 para.20, SI 2009/993 Reg.10, SI 2009/1059 Art.2, Art.3, Art.27, Art.48, Art.55, Art.63, Art.66, Art.69, Art.70, Art.72, Art.157, Art.195, Art.197, SI 2009/1091 Reg.9, Reg.10, SI 2009/1109 Reg.13, SI 2009/1112 Reg.12, SI 2009/1209 Sch.2 para.2, Sch.2 para.10, SI 2009/1211 Sch.2 para.6, Sch.2 para.11, SI 2009/1212 Reg.4, Reg.5, Reg.6, SI 2009/1216 Sch.2 para.5, SI 2009/2041 Sch.2 para.2, Sch.2 para.11, Sch.2 para.28, Sch.2 para.33, SI 2009/2055 Reg.17, SI 2009/2056 Sch.4 para.11, SI 2009/2057 Sch.1 para.2, Sch.1 para.5, Sch.1 para.9
referred to: SI 2009/989 Sch.1
Part I, applied: SI 2009/831 Sch.1 para.7, Sch.1 para.8, SI 2009/1089 Sch.1 para.7, Sch.1 para.8, SI 2009/1209 Sch.2 para.10, SI 2009/1211 Sch.2 para.11, SI 2009/2041 Sch.2 para.11
Part II, applied: 2009 c.25 Sch.22 para.15, Sch.22 para.21, SI 2009/1109 Reg.12, Reg.13
Part III, applied: SI 2009/1059 Art.158
s.2, disapplied: SI 2009/2057 Sch.1 para.3, Sch.1 para.10
s.9, applied: SI 2009/832 Sch.1 para.20, SI 2009/1059 Art.193, SI 2009/1091 Reg.9, Sch.1 para.21
s.9, varied: SI 2009/832 Reg.9, Reg.13, SI 2009/1091 Reg.13
s.10, varied: SI 2009/832 Reg.9
s.11, applied: SI 2009/832 Sch.1 para.17, SI 2009/1091 Sch.1 para.18
s.12, applied: SI 2009/832 Sch.1 para.17, SI 2009/1091 Sch.1 para.18
s.17, applied: SI 2009/833 Sch.1 para.4, Sch.1 para.5, SI 2009/1059 Art.192, SI 2009/1090 Sch.1 para.4, Sch.1 para.5
s.18, applied: SI 2009/2057 Sch.1 para.8, Sch.1 para.9
s.19, applied: SI 2009/1059 Art.200
s.24, applied: 2009 c.25 s.159, SI 2009/1059 Art.42, Art.77, SI 2009/2056 Sch.4 para.24
s.25, applied: 2009 c.25 s.159, SI 2009/1059 Art.42, Art.77, SI 2009/1109 Reg.12, SI 2009/2056 Sch.4 para.24
s.26, applied: 2009 c.25 s.159, SI 2009/1059 Art.42, Art.77, SI 2009/2056 Sch.4 para.24
s.27, applied: SI 2009/1059 Art.77
s.28, applied: SI 2009/1059 Art.77
s.29, applied: SI 2009/1059 Art.15, Art.77
s.29A, applied: SI 2009/1059 Art.15, Art.77
s.30, applied: 2009 c.25 s.159, SI 2009/1059 Art.15, Art.42, Art.77, SI 2009/2056 Sch.4 para.24
s.31, applied: 2009 c.25 s.159, SI 2009/1059 Art.17, Art.42, Art.77, SI 2009/2056 Sch.4 para.24
s.32, applied: 2009 c.25 s.159, SI 2009/1059 Art.17, Art.42, Art.77, SI 2009/2056 Sch.4 para.24
s.33, applied: SI 2009/1059 Art.15, Art.77

3 & 4 Eliz. 2 (1954-55)–cont.

18. Army Act 1955–*cont.*

s.34, applied: SI 2009/1059 Art.15, Art.77

s.34A, applied: SI 2009/1059 Art.15, Art.77, Art.177

s.34B, applied: SI 2009/1059 Art.15, Art.77

s.35, applied: SI 2009/1059 Art.15, Art.77

s.36, applied: SI 2009/1059 Art.15, Art.77

s.37, applied: SI 2009/833 Sch.1 para.2, SI 2009/1059 Art.15, Art.42, Art.77, Art.181, Art.192, Art.199, Art.201, SI 2009/1090 Sch.1 para.2, SI 2009/1109 Reg.12, SI 2009/2056 Sch.4 para.24

s.37, disapplied: SI 2009/1059 Art.15

s.38, applied: SI 2009/1059 Art.15, Art.77, Art.199, Art.201, SI 2009/1109 Reg.12

s.39, applied: SI 2009/1059 Art.15, Art.77

s.40, applied: SI 2009/1059 Art.77

s.41, applied: SI 2009/1059 Art.77

s.42, applied: SI 2009/1059 Art.15, Art.77

s.43, applied: SI 2009/1059 Art.15, Art.77

s.43A, applied: SI 2009/1059 Art.15, Art.77

s.44, applied: SI 2009/1059 Art.15, Art.77, SI 2009/1109 Reg.13

s.44A, applied: SI 2009/1059 Art.15, Art.42, Art.77, SI 2009/1109 Reg.13

s.44B, applied: SI 2009/1059 Art.15, Art.77

s.45, applied: SI 2009/1059 Art.15, Art.77

s.46, applied: SI 2009/1059 Art.15, Art.77

s.47, applied: SI 2009/1059 Art.77

s.48, applied: SI 2009/1059 Art.77

s.48A, applied: SI 2009/1059 Art.42, Art.77, SI 2009/2056 Sch.4 para.24

s.49, applied: SI 2009/1059 Art.42, Art.77, SI 2009/2056 Sch.4 para.24

s.50, applied: SI 2009/1059 Art.15, Art.77

s.51, applied: SI 2009/1059 Art.15, Art.77

s.52, applied: SI 2009/1059 Art.15, Art.77

s.53, applied: SI 2009/1059 Art.15, Art.77

s.54, applied: SI 2009/1059 Art.15, Art.77

s.54, disapplied: SI 2009/1059 Art.15

s.55, applied: SI 2009/1059 Art.15, Art.77

s.56, applied: SI 2009/1059 Art.15, Art.77

s.57, applied: SI 2009/1059 Art.13, Art.77, Art.178

s.58, applied: SI 2009/1059 Art.77

s.59, applied: SI 2009/1059 Art.77

s.60, applied: SI 2009/1059 Art.15, Art.77

s.61, applied: SI 2009/1059 Art.13, Art.15, Art.23, Art.77

s.62, applied: SI 2009/1059 Art.15, Art.77

s.63, applied: SI 2009/1059 Art.77

s.63A, applied: SI 2009/1059 Art.77

s.64, applied: SI 2009/1059 Art.77

s.65, applied: SI 2009/1059 Art.15, Art.77

s.66, applied: SI 2009/1059 Art.15, Art.77

s.68, applied: SI 2009/1059 Art.15, Art.42, SI 2009/2056 Sch.4 para.24

s.68A, applied: SI 2009/2056 Sch.4 para.24

s.69, applied: SI 2009/1059 Art.15, Art.77

s.70, applied: SI 2009/37 Sch.1 para.1, Sch.1 para.2, SI 2009/991 Art.4, SI 2009/992 Art.4, SI 2009/1059 Art.12, Art.89, Art.110, SI 2009/2055 Reg.17

s.70, referred to: SI 2009/37 Sch.1 para.3, Sch.1 para.4, SI 2009/1059 Art.129

s.70, varied: 2009 c.25 Sch.22 para.8

s.71, applied: SI 2009/2041 Sch.2 para.19

s.71A, applied: SI 2009/1059 Art.85, SI 2009/2041 Sch.2 para.19

s.71AA, applied: SI 2009/2041 Sch.2 para.19

s.71B, applied: SI 2009/1059 Art.158

s.74, applied: SI 2009/1059 Art.31, Art.35, Art.36, Art.37, Art.38, Art.39, SI 2009/2056 Sch.4 para.8

3 & 4 Eliz. 2 (1954-55)–cont.

18. Army Act 1955–*cont.*

s.74, referred to: SI 2009/1059 Art.33

s.74A, applied: SI 2009/1059 Art.31

s.75, applied: SI 2009/1059 Art.35, Art.37, Art.38, Art.39, SI 2009/2042 Reg.10

s.75A, applied: SI 2009/1059 Art.36, Art.38

s.75B, applied: SI 2009/1059 Art.36

s.75C, applied: SI 2009/1059 Art.37

s.75C, referred to: SI 2009/1059 Art.37

s.75C, varied: SI 2009/1059 Art.37

s.75F, applied: SI 2009/1059 Art.40

s.75F, varied: SI 2009/1059 Art.40

s.75G, applied: SI 2009/1059 Art.40

s.75J, applied: SI 2009/1059 Art.15, Art.21

s.75J, varied: SI 2009/1059 Art.40

s.75K, applied: SI 2009/1059 Art.31, Art.41

s.75K, varied: SI 2009/1059 Art.41

s.76, applied: SI 2009/990 Art.4, SI 2009/1059 Art.27, Art.40, Art.41, Art.46, Art.47, Art.65, SI 2009/2041 Sch.2 para.27, Sch.2 para.28

s.76A, applied: SI 2009/1059 Art.27, Art.47

s.76AA, applied: SI 2009/1059 Art.54, Art.65, SI 2009/2041 Sch.2 para.31

s.76B, applied: SI 2009/1059 Art.27, Art.46, Art.47, Art.55, Art.65, SI 2009/1216 Sch.2 para.2, SI 2009/2041 Sch.2 para.25

s.81, applied: SI 2009/833 Sch.1 para.3, Sch.1 para.4, SI 2009/1059 Art.25, Art.192, SI 2009/1090 Sch.1 para.3, Sch.1 para.4

s.83B, applied: SI 2009/989 Sch.1, SI 2009/1059 Art.44, Art.47, Art.49, Art.119, SI 2009/2041 Sch.2 para.27

s.83BB, applied: SI 2009/1059 Art.46, Art.47, Art.49, Art.51

s.83ZA, applied: SI 2009/1109 Reg.13

s.83ZE, applied: SI 2009/1059 Art.63

s.83ZH, applied: SI 2009/1059 Art.69

s.91A, applied: SI 2009/1059 Art.7, Art.40, Art.41, Art.76, SI 2009/2041 Sch.2 para.8

s.94, see *Times Newspapers Ltd v R* [2008] EWCA Crim 2559, [2009] 1 W.L.R. 1015 (CMAC), Latham, L.J.

s.98, applied: SI 2009/1059 Art.27

s.99A, referred to: SI 2009/1209 Sch.2 para.9, SI 2009/2041 Sch.2 para.10

s.101, applied: SI 2009/1059 Art.178

s.101, varied: 2009 c.25 Sch.22 para.20

s.113AA, applied: SI 2009/1059 Art.176

s.113C, applied: SI 2009/1059 Art.129

s.115, applied: SI 2009/1059 Art.71, Art.73

s.115A, applied: SI 2009/1059 Art.82

s.115B, applied: SI 2009/1059 Art.82

s.116A, applied: SI 2009/1059 Art.80, Art.81, Art.83, SI 2009/1922 Sch.2 para.15, SI 2009/2054 Sch.2 para.17

s.116A, varied: SI 2009/1922 Sch.2 para.15

s.116B, applied: SI 2009/1059 Art.80, Art.81, Art.83

s.118A, applied: SI 2009/1059 Art.138, Art.140, Art.142

s.118ZA, applied: SI 2009/1059 Art.138, Art.139

s.118ZA, referred to: SI 2009/1059 Art.146

s.119, applied: SI 2009/1059 Art.35, Art.151, Art.153, Art.183

s.120, applied: SI 2009/1059 Art.93, Art.109, Art.117

s.122, applied: SI 2009/1059 Art.149, Art.150, Art.151

s.132, applied: SI 2009/1059 Art.17, Art.45, Art.48, Art.53

s.132, referred to: SI 2009/1059 Art.17

3 & 4 Eliz. 2 (1954-55)–cont.

18. Army Act 1955–*cont.*
s.133, applied: SI 2009/1059 Art.26
s.133A, applied: SI 2009/2054 Sch.2 para.4
s.133A, varied: SI 2009/1212 Reg.5
s.134, applied: SI 2009/1059 Art.25
s.135, applied: SI 2009/1059 Art.65, Art.75
s.137, applied: SI 2009/1059 Art.65, Art.75
s.138, applied: SI 2009/1059 Art.160
s.145, applied: SI 2009/1059 Art.198
s.146, applied: SI 2009/1059 Art.198
s.147, applied: SI 2009/1059 Art.198
s.150, applied: SI 2009/1059 Art.198
s.150A, applied: SI 2009/1059 Art.198
s.150AA, applied: SI 2009/1059 Art.198
s.151, applied: SI 2009/1059 Art.198
s.151A, applied: SI 2009/1059 Art.198
s.153, applied: SI 2009/1093 Reg.6
s.161, applied: SI 2009/1059 Art.200
s.171, applied: SI 2009/1059 Art.200
s.180, applied: SI 2009/2054 Sch.2 para.9
s.180, referred to: SI 2009/2054 Sch.2 para.11, Sch.2 para.12, Sch.2 para.13
s.186, applied: SI 2009/1059 Art.181
s.187, applied: SI 2009/1059 Art.39, Art.182, SI 2009/1108 Sch.1 para.1
s.188, applied: SI 2009/1059 Art.39, Art.181
s.188, referred to: SI 2009/1059 Art.181
s.190A, applied: SI 2009/1059 Art.39
s.190B, applied: SI 2009/1059 Art.183
s.191, applied: SI 2009/1059 Art.200
s.192, applied: SI 2009/1059 Art.200
s.192, varied: SI 2009/2054 Sch.2 para.14
s.193, applied: SI 2009/1059 Art.200
s.194, applied: SI 2009/1059 Art.200
s.195, applied: SI 2009/1059 Art.200
s.196, applied: SI 2009/1059 Art.200
s.197, applied: SI 2009/1059 Art.200
s.198, applied: SI 2009/1059 Art.200
s.204, applied: SI 2009/1059 Art.202
s.209, applied: SI 2009/1059 Art.2, SI 2009/2055 Reg.17
s.209, referred to: SI 2009/1059 Art.19
s.220, referred to: SI 2009/1059 Art.199
s.225, applied: SI 2009/1109 Reg.13
Sch.1 para.5, applied: SI 2009/2057 Sch.1 para.3, Sch.1 para.5, Sch.1 para.7
Sch.5A para.3, applied: SI 2009/1059 Art.108
Sch.5A para.4, applied: 2009 c.25 Sch.22 para.15, Sch.22 para.21, SI 2009/1059 Art.11, Art.108, Art.117, Art.134, Art.167, Art.168, Art.169, Art.170, Art.171, Art.172, Art.173, Art.186
Sch.5A para.4, varied: SI 2009/1059 Art.167
Sch.5A para.5, applied: SI 2009/1059 Art.165
Sch.5A para.5, disapplied: 2009 c.25 s.158
Sch.5A para.5, varied: SI 2009/1059 Art.173
Sch.5A para.10, applied: SI 2009/2041 Sch.2 para.19
Sch.5A para.11, applied: SI 2009/1059 Art.155, Art.156, Art.157
Sch.5A para.13, applied: SI 2009/1059 Art.108, Art.134, Art.197
Sch.5A para.14, applied: SI 2009/1059 Art.91, Art.108, Art.134, Art.197, SI 2009/2041 Sch.2 para.24
Sch.7 Part I para.4A, applied: SI 2009/832 Sch.1 para.20, SI 2009/1059 Art.193, SI 2009/1091 Reg.10, Sch.1 para.21
Sch.7 Part I para.4A, varied: SI 2009/832 Reg.10, Reg.13, SI 2009/1091 Reg.13

3 & 4 Eliz. 2 (1954-55)–cont.

18. Army Act 1955–*cont.*
Sch.7 Part I para.4B, varied: SI 2009/832 Reg.10
Sch.7 Part I para.5, applied: SI 2009/832 Sch.1 para.17, SI 2009/1091 Sch.1 para.18

19. Air Force Act 1955
applied: 2009 c.25 s.157, Sch.22 para.18, Sch.22 para.19, Sch.22 para.20, Sch.22 para.21, SI 2009/993 Reg.10, SI 2009/1059 Art.2, Art.3, Art.27, Art.48, Art.55, Art.63, Art.67, Art.69, Art.70, Art.72, Art.142, Art.157, Art.195, Art.197, SI 2009/1091 Reg.11, SI 2009/1109 Reg.13, SI 2009/1112 Reg.12, SI 2009/1209 Sch.2 para.2, Sch.2 para.10, SI 2009/1211 Sch.2 para.6, Sch.2 para.11, SI 2009/1212 Reg.4, Reg.5, Reg.6, SI 2009/1216 Sch.2 para.5, SI 2009/2041 Sch.2 para.2, Sch.2 para.11, Sch.2 para.28, Sch.2 para.33, SI 2009/2055 Reg.17, SI 2009/2056 Sch.4 para.11, SI 2009/2057 Sch.1 para.2, Sch.1 para.9
referred to: 2009 c.25 Sch.22 para.20, SI 2009/989 Sch.1
Part I, applied: SI 2009/831 Sch.1 para.10, SI 2009/1089 Sch.1 para.10, SI 2009/1209 Sch.2 para.10, SI 2009/1211 Sch.2 para.11, SI 2009/2041 Sch.2 para.11
Part II, applied: 2009 c.25 Sch.22 para.21, SI 2009/1109 Reg.12, Reg.13
Part III, applied: SI 2009/1059 Art.158
s.2, disapplied: SI 2009/2057 Sch.1 para.3, Sch.1 para.10
s.9, applied: SI 2009/832 Sch.1 para.20, SI 2009/1059 Art.193, SI 2009/1091 Reg.11, Sch.1 para.21
s.9, varied: SI 2009/832 Reg.11, Reg.13, SI 2009/1091 Reg.13
s.10, varied: SI 2009/832 Reg.11
s.11, applied: SI 2009/832 Sch.1 para.17, SI 2009/1091 Sch.1 para.18
s.12, applied: SI 2009/832 Sch.1 para.17, SI 2009/1091 Sch.1 para.18
s.17, applied: SI 2009/833 Sch.1 para.4, Sch.1 para.5, SI 2009/1059 Art.192, SI 2009/1090 Sch.1 para.4, Sch.1 para.5
s.18, applied: SI 2009/2057 Sch.1 para.8, Sch.1 para.9
s.19, applied: SI 2009/1059 Art.200
s.24, applied: 2009 c.25 s.159, SI 2009/1059 Art.42, Art.77, SI 2009/2056 Sch.4 para.24
s.25, applied: 2009 c.25 s.159, SI 2009/1059 Art.42, Art.77, SI 2009/1109 Reg.12, SI 2009/2056 Sch.4 para.24
s.26, applied: 2009 c.25 s.159, SI 2009/1059 Art.42, Art.77, SI 2009/2056 Sch.4 para.24
s.27, applied: SI 2009/1059 Art.77
s.28, applied: SI 2009/1059 Art.77
s.29, applied: SI 2009/1059 Art.15, Art.77
s.29A, applied: SI 2009/1059 Art.15, Art.77
s.30, applied: 2009 c.25 s.159, SI 2009/1059 Art.15, Art.42, Art.77, SI 2009/2056 Sch.4 para.24
s.31, applied: 2009 c.25 s.159, SI 2009/1059 Art.17, Art.42, Art.77, SI 2009/2056 Sch.4 para.24
s.32, applied: 2009 c.25 s.159, SI 2009/1059 Art.17, Art.42, Art.77, SI 2009/2056 Sch.4 para.24
s.33, applied: SI 2009/1059 Art.15, Art.77
s.34, applied: SI 2009/1059 Art.15, Art.77
s.34A, applied: SI 2009/1059 Art.15, Art.77, Art.177
s.34B, applied: SI 2009/1059 Art.15, Art.77
s.35, applied: SI 2009/1059 Art.15, Art.77
s.36, applied: SI 2009/1059 Art.15, Art.77

3 & 4 Eliz. 2 (1954-55)–cont.

19. Air Force Act 1955–*cont.*

s.37, applied: SI 2009/833 Sch.1 para.2, SI 2009/
1059 Art.15, Art.42, Art.77, Art.181, Art.192,
Art.199, Art.201, SI 2009/1090 Sch.1 para.2, SI
2009/1109 Reg.12, SI 2009/2056 Sch.4 para.24

s.37, disapplied: SI 2009/1059 Art.15

s.38, applied: SI 2009/1059 Art.15, Art.77, Art.199,
Art.201, SI 2009/1109 Reg.12

s.39, applied: SI 2009/1059 Art.15, Art.77

s.40, applied: SI 2009/1059 Art.77

s.41, applied: SI 2009/1059 Art.77

s.42, applied: SI 2009/1059 Art.15, Art.77

s.43, applied: SI 2009/1059 Art.15, Art.77

s.43A, applied: SI 2009/1059 Art.15, Art.77

s.44, applied: SI 2009/1059 Art.15, Art.77, SI 2009/
1109 Reg.13

s.44A, applied: SI 2009/1059 Art.15, Art.42, Art.77,
SI 2009/1109 Reg.13

s.44B, applied: SI 2009/1059 Art.15, Art.77

s.45, applied: SI 2009/1059 Art.15, Art.77

s.46, applied: SI 2009/1059 Art.15, Art.77

s.47, applied: SI 2009/1059 Art.77

s.48, applied: SI 2009/1059 Art.77

s.48A, applied: SI 2009/1059 Art.42, Art.77, SI
2009/2056 Sch.4 para.24

s.49, applied: SI 2009/1059 Art.42, Art.77, SI 2009/
2056 Sch.4 para.24

s.50, applied: SI 2009/1059 Art.15, Art.77

s.51, applied: SI 2009/1059 Art.15, Art.77

s.52, applied: SI 2009/1059 Art.15, Art.77

s.53, applied: SI 2009/1059 Art.15, Art.77

s.54, applied: SI 2009/1059 Art.15, Art.77

s.54, disapplied: SI 2009/1059 Art.15

s.55, applied: SI 2009/1059 Art.15, Art.77

s.56, applied: SI 2009/1059 Art.15, Art.77

s.57, applied: SI 2009/1059 Art.13, Art.77, Art.178

s.58, applied: SI 2009/1059 Art.77

s.59, applied: SI 2009/1059 Art.77

s.60, applied: SI 2009/1059 Art.15, Art.77

s.61, applied: SI 2009/1059 Art.13, Art.15, Art.23,
Art.77

s.62, applied: SI 2009/1059 Art.15, Art.77

s.63, applied: SI 2009/1059 Art.77

s.63A, applied: SI 2009/1059 Art.77

s.64, applied: SI 2009/1059 Art.77

s.65, applied: SI 2009/1059 Art.15, Art.77

s.66, applied: SI 2009/1059 Art.15, Art.77

s.68, applied: SI 2009/1059 Art.15, Art.42, SI 2009/
2056 Sch.4 para.24

s.68A, applied: SI 2009/2056 Sch.4 para.24

s.69, applied: SI 2009/1059 Art.15, Art.77

s.70, applied: SI 2009/37 Sch.1 para.1, Sch.1 para.2,
SI 2009/991 Art.4, SI 2009/992 Art.4, SI 2009/
1059 Art.12, Art.89, Art.110, SI 2009/2055 Reg.17

s.70, referred to: SI 2009/37 Sch.1 para.3, Sch.1
para.4, SI 2009/1059 Art.129

s.70, varied: 2009 c.25 Sch.22 para.8

s.71, applied: SI 2009/1059 Art.31, SI 2009/2041
Sch.2 para.19

s.71A, applied: SI 2009/1059 Art.85, SI 2009/2041
Sch.2 para.19

s.71AA, applied: SI 2009/2041 Sch.2 para.19

s.71B, applied: SI 2009/1059 Art.158

s.74, applied: SI 2009/1059 Art.31, Art.35, Art.36,
Art.37, Art.38, Art.39, SI 2009/2056 Sch.4 para.8

s.74, referred to: SI 2009/1059 Art.33

s.74A, applied: SI 2009/1059 Art.31

s.75, applied: SI 2009/1059 Art.35, Art.37, Art.38, SI
2009/2042 Reg.10

3 & 4 Eliz. 2 (1954-55)–cont.

19. Air Force Act 1955–*cont.*

s.75A, applied: SI 2009/1059 Art.36, Art.38, Art.39

s.75B, applied: SI 2009/1059 Art.36

s.75C, applied: SI 2009/1059 Art.37

s.75C, referred to: SI 2009/1059 Art.37

s.75C, varied: SI 2009/1059 Art.37

s.75F, applied: SI 2009/1059 Art.40

s.75F, varied: SI 2009/1059 Art.40

s.75G, applied: SI 2009/1059 Art.40

s.75J, applied: SI 2009/1059 Art.15, Art.21

s.75J, varied: SI 2009/1059 Art.40

s.75K, applied: SI 2009/1059 Art.31, Art.41

s.75K, varied: SI 2009/1059 Art.41

s.76, applied: SI 2009/990 Art.4, SI 2009/1059
Art.27, Art.40, Art.41, Art.46, Art.47, Art.65,
SI 2009/2041 Sch.2 para.27, Sch.2 para.28

s.76A, applied: SI 2009/1059 Art.27, Art.47

s.76AA, applied: SI 2009/1059 Art.54, Art.65

s.76B, applied: SI 2009/1059 Art.27, Art.46, Art.47,
Art.55, Art.65, SI 2009/1216 Sch.2 para.2, SI
2009/2041 Sch.2 para.25

s.81, applied: SI 2009/833 Sch.1 para.3, Sch.1 para.4,
SI 2009/1059 Art.25, Art.192, SI 2009/1090
Sch.1 para.3, Sch.1 para.4

s.83B, applied: SI 2009/989 Sch.1, SI 2009/1059
Art.44, Art.47, Art.49, Art.119, SI 2009/2041
Sch.2 para.27

s.83BB, applied: SI 2009/1059 Art.46, Art.47,
Art.49, Art.51

s.83ZA, applied: SI 2009/1109 Reg.13

s.83ZE, applied: SI 2009/1059 Art.63

s.83ZH, applied: SI 2009/1059 Art.69

s.91A, applied: SI 2009/1059 Art.7, Art.40, Art.41,
Art.76, SI 2009/2041 Sch.2 para.8

s.98, applied: SI 2009/1059 Art.27

s.101, applied: SI 2009/1059 Art.178

s.113AA, applied: SI 2009/1059 Art.176

s.113C, applied: SI 2009/1059 Art.129

s.115, applied: SI 2009/1059 Art.71, Art.73

s.115A, applied: SI 2009/1059 Art.82

s.115B, applied: SI 2009/1059 Art.82

s.116A, applied: SI 2009/1059 Art.80, Art.81,
Art.83, SI 2009/1922 Sch.2 para.15

s.116A, varied: SI 2009/1922 Sch.2 para.15

s.116B, applied: SI 2009/1059 Art.80, Art.81, Art.83

s.118A, applied: SI 2009/1059 Art.138, Art.140,
Art.142

s.118ZA, applied: SI 2009/1059 Art.138, Art.139

s.118ZA, referred to: SI 2009/1059 Art.146

s.119, applied: SI 2009/1059 Art.35, Art.151, Art.153,
Art.183

s.120, applied: SI 2009/1059 Art.93, Art.109, Art.117

s.132, applied: SI 2009/1059 Art.17, Art.45, Art.48,
Art.53

s.132, referred to: SI 2009/1059 Art.17

s.133, applied: SI 2009/1059 Art.26

s.133A, applied: SI 2009/2054 Sch.2 para.4

s.133A, varied: SI 2009/1212 Reg.5

s.134, applied: SI 2009/1059 Art.25

s.135, applied: SI 2009/1059 Art.65, Art.75

s.137, applied: SI 2009/1059 Art.65, Art.75

s.138, applied: SI 2009/1059 Art.160

s.145, applied: SI 2009/1059 Art.198

s.146, applied: SI 2009/1059 Art.198

s.147, applied: SI 2009/1059 Art.198

s.150, applied: SI 2009/1059 Art.198

s.150A, applied: SI 2009/1059 Art.198

s.151, applied: SI 2009/1059 Art.198

3 & 4 Eliz. 2 (1954-55)–cont.

19. Air Force Act 1955–*cont.*
s.151A, applied: SI 2009/ 1059 Art.198
s.153, applied: SI 2009/1093 Reg.6
s.161, applied: SI 2009/ 1059 Art.200
s.171, applied: SI 2009/ 1059 Art.200
s.180, applied: SI 2009/2054 Sch.2 para.9
s.180, referred to: SI 2009/ 2054 Sch.2 para.11, Sch.2 para.12, Sch.2 para.13
s.186, applied: SI 2009/ 1059 Art.181
s.187, applied: SI 2009/1059 Art.39, Art.182, SI 2009/ 1108 Sch.1 para.1
s.188, applied: SI 2009/1059 Art.39, Art.181
s.190A, applied: SI 2009/1059 Art.39
s.190B, applied: SI 2009/1059 Art.183
s.191, applied: SI 2009/1059 Art.200
s.192, applied: SI 2009/1059 Art.200
s.193, applied: SI 2009/1059 Art.200
s.194, applied: SI 2009/1059 Art.200
s.195, applied: SI 2009/1059 Art.200
s.196, applied: SI 2009/1059 Art.200
s.197, applied: SI 2009/1059 Art.200
s.198, applied: SI 2009/1059 Art.200
s.204, applied: SI 2009/1059 Art.202
s.209, applied: SI 2009/1059 Art.2, SI 2009/2055 Reg.17
s.209, referred to: SI 2009/1059 Art.19
s.218, referred to: SI 2009/1059 Art.199
s.223, applied: SI 2009/1109 Reg.13
Sch.1 para.5, applied: SI 2009/2057 Sch.1 para.3, Sch.1 para.5, Sch.1 para.7
Sch.5A para.3, applied: SI 2009/1059 Art.108
Sch.5A para.4, applied: SI 2009/1059 Art.11, Art.108, Art.117, Art.134, Art.167, Art.168, Art.169, Art.170, Art.171, Art.172, Art.173, Art.186
Sch.5A para.4, varied: SI 2009/1059 Art.167
Sch.5A para.5, applied: SI 2009/1059 Art.165
Sch.5A para.5, disapplied: 2009 c.25 s.158
Sch.5A para.5, varied: SI 2009/1059 Art.173
Sch.5A para.10, applied: SI 2009/2041 Sch.2 para.19
Sch.5A para.11, applied: SI 2009/1059 Art.155, Art.156
Sch.5A para.13, applied: SI 2009/1059 Art.108, Art.134, Art.197
Sch.5A para.14, applied: SI 2009/1059 Art.91, Art.108, Art.134, Art.197, SI 2009/2041 Sch.2 para.24

4 & 5 Eliz. 2 (1955-56)

49. Agriculture (Safety, Health and Welfare Provisions) Act 1956
s.25, amended: SSI 2009/319 Sch.3 Part 1
59. Underground Works (London) Act 1956
s.3, amended: SI 2009/1307 Sch.1 para.22
s.4, amended: SI 2009/1307 Sch.1 para.23
60. Valuation and Rating (Scotland) Act 1956
s.6, see *Lothian Assessor v Belhaven Brewery Co Ltd* 2009 S.C. 120 (LVAC), The Lord Justice Clerk (Gill)
s.6, applied: SSI 2009/42 Reg.3
s.6A, applied: SSI 2009/112, SSI 2009/196
s.6A, enabling: SSI 2009/112, SSI 2009/196
s.7B, applied: SSI 2009/42 Reg.3
69. Sexual Offences Act 1956
see *Director of the Assets Recovery Agency v Virtosu* [2008] EWHC 149 (QB), [2009] 1 W.L.R. 2808 (QBD), Tugendhat, J.

4 & 5 Eliz. 2 (1955-56)–cont.

69. Sexual Offences Act 1956–*cont.*
s.1, applied: 2009 asp 9 Sch.1 para.28, SI 2009/1059 Art.40, Art.42, SI 2009/1547 Sch.2 para.1
s.1, referred to: SI 2009/37 Sch.1 para.1, Sch.1 para.2, Sch.1 para.4
s.2, applied: SI 2009/1059 Art.42, SI 2009/1547 Sch.2 para.1
s.2, referred to: SI 2009/37 Sch.1 para.2, Sch.1 para.4
s.3, applied: SI 2009/1059 Art.42, SI 2009/1547 Sch.2 para.1
s.3, referred to: SI 2009/37 Sch.1 para.2, Sch.1 para.4
s.4, applied: SI 2009/1059 Art.42, SI 2009/1547 Sch.2 para.1
s.4, referred to: SI 2009/37 Sch.1 para.2, Sch.1 para.4
s.5, applied: 2009 asp 9 Sch.1 para.29, SI 2009/1059 Art.42, SI 2009/1547 Sch.2 para.1
s.5, referred to: SI 2009/37 Sch.1 para.1, Sch.1 para.2, Sch.1 para.4
s.6, applied: 2009 asp 9 Sch.1 para.29, SI 2009/1059 Art.42, SI 2009/1547 Sch.2 para.1
s.6, referred to: SI 2009/37 Sch.1 para.2, Sch.1 para.4
s.7, applied: SI 2009/1059 Art.42, SI 2009/1547 Sch.2 para.2
s.7, referred to: SI 2009/37 Sch.1 para.2, Sch.1 para.4
s.8, referred to: SI 2009/37 Sch.1 para.2, Sch.1 para.4
s.9, applied: SI 2009/1059 Art.42, SI 2009/1547 Sch.2 para.2
s.9, referred to: SI 2009/37 Sch.1 para.2, Sch.1 para.4
s.10, applied: 2009 asp 9 Sch.1 para.28, SI 2009/1059 Art.42, SI 2009/1547 Sch.2 para.2
s.10, referred to: SI 2009/37 Sch.1 para.2, Sch.1 para.4
s.11, applied: 2009 asp 9 Sch.1 para.28, SI 2009/1059 Art.42, SI 2009/1547 Sch.2 para.2
s.11, referred to: SI 2009/37 Sch.1 para.2, Sch.1 para.4
s.12, applied: 2009 asp 9 Sch.1 para.28, SI 2009/1547 Sch.2 para.2
s.12, referred to: SI 2009/37 Sch.1 para.2, Sch.1 para.4
s.13, applied: SI 2009/1547 Sch.2 para.2
s.13, referred to: SI 2009/37 Sch.1 para.2, Sch.1 para.4
s.14, applied: 2009 asp 9 Sch.1 para.28, SI 2009/1547 Sch.2 para.1
s.14, referred to: SI 2009/37 Sch.1 para.2, Sch.1 para.4
s.15, applied: 2009 asp 9 Sch.1 para.28, SI 2009/1547 Sch.2 para.1
s.15, referred to: SI 2009/37 Sch.1 para.2, Sch.1 para.4
s.16, applied: 2009 asp 9 Sch.1 para.28, SI 2009/1059 Art.42, SI 2009/1547 Sch.2 para.1
s.16, referred to: SI 2009/37 Sch.1 para.2, Sch.1 para.4
s.17, applied: SI 2009/1059 Art.42, SI 2009/1547 Sch.2 para.1
s.17, referred to: SI 2009/37 Sch.1 para.2, Sch.1 para.4
s.19, applied: SI 2009/1059 Art.42, SI 2009/1547 Sch.2 para.1
s.19, referred to: SI 2009/37 Sch.1 para.2, Sch.1 para.4

4 & 5 Eliz. 2 (1955-56) – cont.

69. Sexual Offences Act 1956–*cont.*

s.20, applied: SI 2009/1059 Art.42, SI 2009/1547 Sch.2 para.1

s.20, referred to: SI 2009/37 Sch.1 para.2, Sch.1 para.4

s.21, applied: SI 2009/1059 Art.42, SI 2009/1547 Sch.2 para.2

s.21, referred to: SI 2009/37 Sch.1 para.2, Sch.1 para.4

s.22, applied: SI 2009/1059 Art.42, SI 2009/1547 Sch.2 para.2

s.22, referred to: SI 2009/37 Sch.1 para.2, Sch.1 para.4

s.23, applied: SI 2009/1059 Art.42, SI 2009/1547 Sch.2 para.2

s.23, referred to: SI 2009/37 Sch.1 para.2, Sch.1 para.4

s.24, applied: SI 2009/1059 Art.42, SI 2009/1547 Sch.2 para.1

s.24, referred to: SI 2009/37 Sch.1 para.2, Sch.1 para.4

s.25, applied: SI 2009/1547 Sch.2 para.1

s.25, referred to: SI 2009/37 Sch.1 para.2, Sch.1 para.4

s.26, applied: SI 2009/1059 Art.42, SI 2009/1547 Sch.2 para.1

s.26, referred to: SI 2009/37 Sch.1 para.2, Sch.1 para.4

s.27, applied: SI 2009/1059 Art.42, SI 2009/1547 Sch.2 para.2

s.27, referred to: SI 2009/37 Sch.1 para.2, Sch.1 para.4

s.28, applied: 2009 asp 9 Sch.1 para.29, SI 2009/1059 Art.42, SI 2009/1547 Sch.2 para.1

s.28, referred to: SI 2009/37 Sch.1 para.2, Sch.1 para.4

s.29, applied: SI 2009/1059 Art.42, SI 2009/1547 Sch.2 para.2

s.29, referred to: SI 2009/37 Sch.1 para.2, Sch.1 para.4

s.30, applied: SI 2009/1547 Sch.2 para.2

s.30, referred to: SI 2009/37 Sch.1 para.2, Sch.1 para.4

s.31, applied: SI 2009/1547 Sch.2 para.2

s.31, referred to: SI 2009/37 Sch.1 para.2, Sch.1 para.4

s.32, applied: SI 2009/1059 Art.42

5 & 6 Eliz. 2 (1957)

11. Homicide Act 1957

s.2, see *R. v Stewart (James)* [2009] EWCA Crim 593, [2009] 1 W.L.R. 2507 (CA (Crim Div)), Lord Judge, L.C.J.; see *R. v Wood (Clive)* [2008] EWCA Crim 1305, [2009] 1 W.L.R. 496 (CA (Crim Div)), Sir Igor Judge (President, QB)

s.2, amended: 2009 c.25 s.52

s.3, repealed: 2009 c.25 s.56, Sch.23 Part 2

31. Occupiers Liability Act 1957

see *George v Coastal Marine 2004 Ltd (t/a Mashfords)* [2009] EWHC 816 (Admlty), [2009] 2 Lloyd's Rep. 356 (QBD (Admlty)), Gloster, J.; see *Smith v Northamptonshire CC* [2009] UKHL 27, [2009] 4 All E.R. 557 (HL), Lord Hope of Craighead; see *Young (now Phillips) v Merthyr Tydfil CBC* [2009] P.I.Q.R. P23 (CC (Cardiff)), Judge Curran Q.C.

s.2, see *George v Coastal Marine 2004 Ltd (t/a Mashfords)* [2009] EWHC 816 (Admlty), [2009] 2 Lloyd's Rep. 356 (QBD (Admlty)), Gloster, J.

5 & 6 Eliz. 2 (1957) – cont.

42. Parish Councils Act 1957

s.5, applied: SI 2009/721 Sch.3 para.4

52. Geneva Conventions Act 1957

s.1, amended: 2009 c.6 s.1

s.6, amended: 2009 c.6 s.1

s.6A, amended: 2009 c.6 s.1

s.7, amended: 2009 c.6 s.1

s.8, applied: 2009 c.6 s.3

Sch.7, added: 2009 c.6 Sch.1

53. Naval Discipline Act 1957

applied: 2009 c.25 s.157, Sch.22 para.18, Sch.22 para.19, Sch.22 para.20, SI 2009/993 Reg.10, SI 2009/1059 Art.2, Art.3, Art.8, Art.14, Art.17, Art.18, Art.19, Art.23, Art.27, Art.48, Art.55, Art.63, Art.68, Art.69, Art.70, Art.72, Art.96, Art.97, Art.99, Art.136, Art.142, Art.144, Art.157, Art.197, SI 2009/1109 Reg.13, SI 2009/1211 Sch.2 para.6, SI 2009/1212 Reg.4, Reg.5, Reg.6, SI 2009/1216 Sch.2 para.5, Sch.2 para.8, SI 2009/2041 Sch.2 para.1, Sch.2 para.2, Sch.2 para.18, Sch.2 para.21, Sch.2 para.28, Sch.2 para.33, SI 2009/2055 Reg.17, SI 2009/2056 Sch.4 para.11

referred to: 2009 c.25 Sch.22 para.20, SI 2009/989 Sch.1, SI 2009/1059 Art.32, SI 2009/2041 Sch.2 para.3

Part I, applied: 2009 c.25 Sch.22 para.15, Sch.22 para.21, SI 2009/1109 Reg.12, Reg.13

Part IV, applied: SI 2009/1059 Art.158

s.2, applied: 2009 c.25 s.159, SI 2009/1059 Art.42, Art.77, SI 2009/2056 Sch.4 para.24

s.3, applied: 2009 c.25 s.159, SI 2009/1059 Art.42, Art.77, SI 2009/1109 Reg.12, SI 2009/2056 Sch.4 para.24

s.4, applied: 2009 c.25 s.159, SI 2009/1059 Art.42, Art.77, SI 2009/2056 Sch.4 para.24

s.5, applied: 2009 c.25 s.159, SI 2009/1059 Art.15, Art.42, Art.77, SI 2009/2056 Sch.4 para.24

s.6, applied: SI 2009/1059 Art.15, Art.77

s.7, applied: SI 2009/1059 Art.15, Art.77

s.8, applied: SI 2009/1059 Art.77

s.9, applied: 2009 c.25 s.159, SI 2009/1059 Art.42, Art.77, SI 2009/2056 Sch.4 para.24

s.10, applied: 2009 c.25 s.159, SI 2009/1059 Art.42, Art.77, SI 2009/2056 Sch.4 para.24

s.11, applied: SI 2009/1059 Art.15, Art.77

s.12, applied: SI 2009/1059 Art.15, Art.77

s.12A, applied: SI 2009/1059 Art.15, Art.77, Art.177

s.12B, applied: SI 2009/1059 Art.15, Art.77

s.13, applied: SI 2009/1059 Art.15, Art.77

s.14, applied: SI 2009/1059 Art.15, Art.77

s.14A, applied: SI 2009/1059 Art.15, Art.77

s.15, applied: SI 2009/1059 Art.77, SI 2009/1109 Reg.12

s.16, applied: SI 2009/833 Sch.1 para.2, SI 2009/1059 Art.42, Art.77, Art.181, Art.192, Art.198, Art.199, Art.201, SI 2009/1090 Sch.1 para.2, SI 2009/2056 Sch.4 para.24

s.17, applied: SI 2009/1059 Art.15, Art.77, Art.198, Art.199, Art.201, SI 2009/1109 Reg.12

s.18, applied: SI 2009/1059 Art.15, Art.77

s.19, applied: SI 2009/1059 Art.42, Art.77, SI 2009/2056 Sch.4 para.24

s.20, applied: SI 2009/1059 Art.42, Art.77, SI 2009/2056 Sch.4 para.24

s.21, applied: SI 2009/1059 Art.15, Art.77

s.22, applied: SI 2009/1059 Art.15, Art.77

s.23, applied: SI 2009/1059 Art.77

s.24, applied: SI 2009/1059 Art.77

s.25, applied: SI 2009/1059 Art.15, Art.77

5 & 6 Eliz. 2 (1957)–cont.

53. Naval Discipline Act 1957–*cont.*

s.26, applied: SI 2009/1059 Art.77

s.27, applied: SI 2009/1059 Art.15, Art.77

s.28, applied: SI 2009/1059 Art.15, Art.77

s.29, applied: SI 2009/1059 Art.15, Art.77, SI 2009/1109 Reg.13

s.29A, applied: SI 2009/1059 Art.15, Art.42, Art.77, SI 2009/1109 Reg.13

s.29B, applied: SI 2009/1059 Art.15, Art.77

s.30, applied: SI 2009/1059 Art.15, Art.77

s.31, applied: SI 2009/1059 Art.15, Art.77

s.32, applied: SI 2009/1059 Art.77

s.33, applied: SI 2009/1059 Art.77

s.33A, applied: SI 2009/1059 Art.15, Art.77

s.33B, applied: SI 2009/1059 Art.15, Art.77

s.33C, applied: SI 2009/1059 Art.15, Art.77

s.34, applied: SI 2009/1059 Art.15, Art.77

s.34A, applied: SI 2009/1059 Art.13, Art.15, Art.23, Art.77

s.35, applied: SI 2009/1059 Art.15, Art.77

s.35A, applied: SI 2009/1059 Art.77

s.35B, applied: SI 2009/1059 Art.77

s.36, applied: SI 2009/1059 Art.77

s.36A, applied: SI 2009/1059 Art.15, Art.77

s.37, applied: SI 2009/1059 Art.15, Art.77

s.38, applied: SI 2009/1059 Art.13, Art.77, Art.178

s.39, applied: SI 2009/1059 Art.15, Art.77

s.40, applied: SI 2009/1059 Art.15, Art.42, Art.77, SI 2009/2056 Sch.4 para.24

s.41, applied: SI 2009/2056 Sch.4 para.24

s.42, applied: SI 2009/37 Sch.1 para.1, Sch.1 para.2, SI 2009/991 Art.4, SI 2009/992 Art.4, SI 2009/1059 Art.89, Art.110, SI 2009/2055 Reg.17

s.42, referred to: SI 2009/37 Sch.1 para.3, Sch.1 para.4, SI 2009/1059 Art.129

s.43, applied: SI 2009/832 Sch.1 para.19, SI 2009/1059 Art.55, Art.56, Art.137, SI 2009/1091 Sch.1 para.20, SI 2009/1109 Reg.13, SI 2009/2041 Sch.2 para.19

s.43A, applied: SI 2009/1059 Art.85, SI 2009/2041 Sch.2 para.19

s.43AA, applied: SI 2009/2041 Sch.2 para.19

s.43B, applied: SI 2009/1059 Art.158

s.45, applied: SI 2009/1059 Art.31, Art.35, Art.36, Art.37, Art.38, Art.39, SI 2009/2056 Sch.4 para.8

s.45, referred to: SI 2009/1059 Art.33

s.45A, applied: SI 2009/1059 Art.31

s.47A, applied: SI 2009/1059 Art.35, Art.37, Art.38, Art.39, SI 2009/2042 Reg.10

s.47B, applied: SI 2009/1059 Art.36, Art.38

s.47C, applied: SI 2009/1059 Art.36

s.47D, applied: SI 2009/1059 Art.37

s.47D, referred to: SI 2009/1059 Art.37

s.47D, varied: SI 2009/1059 Art.37

s.47G, applied: SI 2009/1059 Art.40

s.47G, varied: SI 2009/1059 Art.40

s.47H, applied: SI 2009/1059 Art.40

s.47K, applied: 2009 c.25 Sch.22 para.15, Sch.22 para.21, SI 2009/1059 Art.15, Art.21

s.47K, varied: SI 2009/1059 Art.40

s.47L, applied: SI 2009/1059 Art.31, Art.41

s.47L, varied: SI 2009/1059 Art.41

s.48, applied: SI 2009/1059 Art.12

s.48, varied: 2009 c.25 Sch.22 para.8

s.52, applied: SI 2009/1059 Art.17, Art.45, Art.48

s.52, referred to: SI 2009/1059 Art.17

s.52B, applied: SI 2009/990 Art.4, SI 2009/1059 Art.27, Art.40, Art.41, Art.46, Art.47, Art.65, SI 2009/2041 Sch.2 para.27

5 & 6 Eliz. 2 (1957)–cont.

53. Naval Discipline Act 1957–*cont.*

s.52C, applied: SI 2009/1059 Art.27, Art.46, Art.47

s.52D, applied: SI 2009/1059 Art.27, Art.46, Art.47, Art.54, Art.55, Art.65, SI 2009/1216 Sch.2 para.2, SI 2009/2041 Sch.2 para.25

s.52EE, applied: SI 2009/1059 Art.65

s.52FF, applied: SI 2009/1109 Reg.13

s.52FK, applied: SI 2009/1059 Art.63

s.52FN, applied: SI 2009/1059 Art.69

s.52I, applied: SI 2009/989 Sch.1, SI 2009/1059 Art.25, Art.44, Art.46, Art.47, Art.49, Art.119, SI 2009/2041 Sch.2 para.27

s.52II, applied: SI 2009/1059 Art.46, Art.47, Art.49, Art.51

s.58A, applied: SI 2009/1059 Art.40, Art.41, Art.76, SI 2009/2041 Sch.2 para.8

s.63A, applied: SI 2009/1059 Art.80, Art.81, Art.82, Art.83, SI 2009/1922 Sch.2 para.15

s.63A, varied: SI 2009/1922 Sch.2 para.15

s.63B, applied: SI 2009/1059 Art.80, Art.81, Art.82, Art.83

s.65, applied: SI 2009/1059 Art.178

s.68, applied: SI 2009/1059 Art.27

s.71, applied: SI 2009/1059 Art.176

s.71AC, applied: SI 2009/1059 Art.129

s.71B, applied: SI 2009/1059 Art.71, Art.73

s.74, applied: SI 2009/833 Sch.1 para.3, Sch.1 para.4, SI 2009/1059 Art.25, Art.192, SI 2009/1090 Sch.1 para.3, Sch.1 para.4

s.75, applied: SI 2009/1059 Art.198

s.76, applied: SI 2009/1059 Art.160

s.77, applied: SI 2009/1059 Art.160

s.81, applied: SI 2009/1059 Art.55, Art.136, Art.137

s.85A, applied: SI 2009/1059 Art.137, Art.138, Art.139

s.85A, referred to: SI 2009/1059 Art.146

s.86, applied: SI 2009/1059 Art.138, Art.140, Art.142

s.88, disapplied: SI 2009/1059 Art.35

s.88, varied: SI 2009/1059 Art.151, Art.153, Art.183

s.90, applied: SI 2009/1059 Art.55, Art.93, Art.96, Art.99, Art.136, Art.137, Art.142, SI 2009/2041 Sch.2 para.21

s.91, applied: SI 2009/1059 Art.93, Art.109, Art.117, Art.136, Art.137, SI 2009/2041 Sch.2 para.21

s.91B, applied: SI 2009/1059 Art.55, Art.62, Art.70, Art.72, Art.93, Art.98, Art.99, Art.137, Art.143, SI 2009/2041 Sch.2 para.21

s.94, applied: SI 2009/1059 Art.136

s.100, referred to: SI 2009/1059 Art.199

s.101, applied: SI 2009/1093 Reg.6

s.103, applied: SI 2009/1059 Art.39

s.104, applied: SI 2009/1059 Art.183

s.105, applied: SI 2009/1059 Art.181

s.108, applied: SI 2009/1059 Art.39, Art.181

s.109, applied: SI 2009/1059 Art.39, Art.182, SI 2009/1108 Sch.1 para.1

s.118, applied: SI 2009/1059 Art.2, SI 2009/2055 Reg.17

s.128B, applied: SI 2009/1059 Art.198

s.128C, applied: SI 2009/1059 Art.198

s.128E, applied: SI 2009/1059 Art.198

s.128F, applied: SI 2009/2054 Sch.2 para.4

s.128F, varied: SI 2009/1212 Reg.5

s.129, applied: SI 2009/1059 Art.25, Art.26

s.129D, applied: SI 2009/833 Sch.1 para.4, Sch.1 para.5, SI 2009/1059 Art.192, SI 2009/1090 Sch.1 para.4, Sch.1 para.5

s.130, applied: SI 2009/2054 Sch.2 para.9

5 & 6 Eliz. 2 (1957)–cont.

53. Naval Discipline Act 1957–*cont.*
s.130, referred to: SI 2009/2054 Sch.2 para.11, Sch.2 para.12, Sch.2 para.13
Sch.4A, applied: 2009 c.25 Sch.22 para.15, Sch.22 para.21, SI 2009/1059 Art.11, Art.91, Art.108, Art.157, SI 2009/2041 Sch.2 para.24
Sch.4 para.4A, referred to: SI 2009/1059 Art.19
Sch.4A para.4, applied: SI 2009/1059 Art.108, Art.117, Art.134, Art.167, Art.168, Art.169, Art.170, Art.171, Art.172, Art.173, Art.186
Sch.4A para.4, varied: SI 2009/1059 Art.167
Sch.4A para.5, applied: SI 2009/1059 Art.165
Sch.4A para.5, disapplied: 2009 c.25 s.158
Sch.4A para.5, varied: SI 2009/1059 Art.173
Sch.4A para.10, applied: SI 2009/2041 Sch.2 para.19
Sch.4A para.11, applied: SI 2009/1059 Art.155, Art.156
Sch.4A para.13, applied: SI 2009/1059 Art.134, Art.197
Sch.4A para.14, applied: SI 2009/1059 Art.134, Art.197

58. Registration of Births, Deaths and Marriages (Special Provisions) Act 1957
s.1, varied: SI 2009/1059 Sch.1 para.6
s.1, enabling: SI 2009/1736
s.2, varied: SI 2009/1059 Sch.1 para.6
s.2, enabling: SI 2009/1736
s.4, enabling: SI 2009/1736
s.5, varied: SI 2009/1059 Sch.1 para.6
s.6, enabling: SI 2009/1736

6 & 7 Eliz. 2 (1957-58)

24. Land Drainage (Scotland) Act 1958
s.1, amended: 2009 asp 6 Sch.3 para.1
s.2, amended: 2009 asp 6 Sch.3 para.1
s.18, amended: 2009 asp 6 Sch.3 para.1

30. Land Powers Defence Act 1958
s.10, amended: SI 2009/1307 Sch.1 para.25
s.18, amended: SI 2009/1307 Sch.1 para.26
s.22, repealed: SI 2009/1307 Sch.1 para.27
s.25, amended: SI 2009/1307 Sch.1 para.28
s.25, repealed (in part): SI 2009/1307 Sch.1 para.28
Sch.4 para.3, amended: SI 2009/1307 Sch.1 para.29

39. Maintenance Orders Act 1958
s.4, see *Practice Direction (Fam Div: Family Proceedings: Allocation of Appeals)* [2009] 1 W.L.R. 1107 (Fam Div), Sir Mark Potter (President, Fam)
s.4, amended: SI 2009/871 Art.2

47. Agricultural Marketing Act 1958
disapplied: SI 2009/1361 Reg.22, SI 2009/1551 Reg.22, SSI 2009/225 Reg.24

51. Public Records Act 1958
applied: 2009 c.1 s.55, SI 2009/807 Sch.1 para.11
Sch.1 Part 2, amended: 2009 c.13 Sch.1 para.28, Sch.2 para.11, 2009 c.20 Sch.1 para.19, 2009 c.22 Sch.12 para.1, 2009 c.23 Sch.2 para.1, SI 2009/1744 Art.2
Sch.1 para.3A, enabling: SI 2009/1744
Sch.1 para.4, amended: SI 2009/1307 Sch.1 para.30

53. Variation of Trusts Act 1958
s.1, see *Wyndham v Egremont* [2009] EWHC 2076 (Ch), [2009] W.T.L.R. 1473 (Ch D), Blackburne, J.

65. Children Act 1958
s.4, applied: SI 2009/1547 Sch.1 para.17
s.14, applied: SI 2009/1547 Sch.2 para.1

6 & 7 Eliz. 2 (1957-58)–cont.

69. Opencast Coal Act 1958
s.40, amended: SI 2009/1307 Sch.1 para.32
s.51, applied: SI 2009/229 Art.4
s.52, applied: SI 2009/229 Art.4
s.52, repealed (in part): SI 2009/1307 Sch.1 para.33
Sch.3 para.1, amended: SI 2009/1307 Sch.1 para.34

7 & 8 Eliz. 2 (1958-59)

2. Mental Health Act 1959
see *M, Re* [2009] EWHC 2525 (Fam), (2009) 12 C.C.L. Rep. 635 (CP), Munby, J.
s.128, referred to: SI 2009/37 Sch.1 para.4

15. Coroners Act (Northern Ireland) 1959
see *Forde's Application for Judicial Review, Re* [2009] N.I. 29 (QBD (NI)), Gillen, J.
s.2, amended: 2009 c.3 Sch.4 para.2
s.13, amended: 2009 c.25 s.49
s.17A, substituted: 2009 c.25 Sch.11 para.1
s.17C, substituted: 2009 c.25 Sch.11 para.1
s.18, varied: SI 2009/1059 Sch.1 para.7
s.19, repealed: 2009 c.25 Sch.11 para.2, Sch.23 Part 1
s.20, repealed: 2009 c.25 Sch.11 para.2, Sch.23 Part 1

54. Weeds Act 1959
applied: SI 2009/3365 Sch.1 para.1
s.1A, applied: SI 2009/3365 Sch.1 para.1
s.2, applied: SI 2009/3264 Sch.1 para.1, SI 2009/3365 Sch.1 para.1

56. Rights of Light Act 1959
s.2, see *Salvage Wharf Ltd v G&S Brough Ltd* [2009] EWCA Civ 21, [2009] 3 W.L.R. 990 (CA (Civ Div)), Tuckey, L.J.
s.2, amended: SI 2009/1307 Sch.1 para.35
s.2, referred to: SI 2009/1114 Sch.1

57. Street Offences Act 1959
s.1, amended: 2009 c.26 s.16, s.17
s.1, applied: 2009 c.26 s.16
s.1A, added: 2009 c.26 s.17
s.2, repealed: 2009 c.26 s.16, Sch.8 Part 2
Sch.1 Part 1 para.1, added: 2009 c.26 Sch.1
Sch.1 Part 2 para.2, added: 2009 c.26 Sch.1
Sch.1 Part 2 para.3, added: 2009 c.26 Sch.1
Sch.1 Part 2 para.4, added: 2009 c.26 Sch.1
Sch.1 Part 3 para.5, added: 2009 c.26 Sch.1
Sch.1 Part 3 para.6, added: 2009 c.26 Sch.1
Sch.1 Part 3 para.7, added: 2009 c.26 Sch.1
Sch.1 Part 3 para.8, added: 2009 c.26 Sch.1
Sch.1 Part 4 para.9, added: 2009 c.26 Sch.1
Sch.1 Part 4 para.10, added: 2009 c.26 Sch.1
Sch.1 Part 4 para.11, added: 2009 c.26 Sch.1
Sch.1 Part 4 para.12, added: 2009 c.26 Sch.1

72. Mental Health Act 1959
s.128, applied: SI 2009/1059 Art.42, SI 2009/1547 Sch.2 para.2
s.128, referred to: SI 2009/37 Sch.1 para.1, Sch.1 para.2

8 & 9 Eliz. 2 (1959-60)

3. Attempted Rape, etc., Act (Northern Ireland) 1960
s.2, applied: 2009 asp 9 Sch.1 para.27

30. Occupiers Liability (Scotland) Act 1960
s.2, see *Anderson v Scottish Ministers* [2009] CSOH 92, 2009 Rep. L.R. 122 (OH), Lord Bannatyne; see *Porter v Scottish Borders Council* 2009 Rep. L.R. 46 (OH), Temporary Judge Morag Wise, Q.C.

8 & 9 Eliz. 2 (1959-60) – cont.

33. Indecency with Children Act 1960
s.1, applied: 2009 asp 9 Sch.1 para.26, SI 2009/1059 Art.42, SI 2009/1547 Sch.2 para.1
s.1, referred to: SI 2009/37 Sch.1 para.2, Sch.1 para.4

46. Corporate Bodies Contracts Act 1960
s.2, substituted: SI 2009/1941 Sch.1 para.8

58. Charities Act 1960
referred to: SI 2009/500 Sch.1 Part 1

62. Caravan Sites and Control of Development Act 1960
see *Brightlingsea Haven Ltd v Morris* [2008] EWHC 1928 (QB), [2009] 2 P. & C.R. 11 (QBD), Jack, J.
Part I, applied: SSI 2009/213 Reg.1
s.9, see *Brightlingsea Haven Ltd v Morris* [2008] EWHC 1928 (QB), [2009] 2 P. & C.R. 11 (QBD), Jack, J.
s.24, see *South Cambridgeshire DC v Gammell* [2008] EWCA Civ 1159, [2009] B.L.G.R. 141 (CA (Civ Div)), Keene, L.J.

65. Administration of Justice Act 1960
s.2, applied: SI 2009/1603 r.11
s.12, see *N (A Child) (Family Proceedings: Disclosure), Re* [2009] EWHC 1663 (Fam), [2009] 2 F.L.R. 1152 (Fam Div), Munby, J.

67. Public Bodies (Admission to Meetings) Act 1960
applied: SI 2009/467 Reg.9
s.1, applied: 2009 c.20 s.49, SI 2009/779 Sch.3 para.8

9 & 10 Eliz. 2 (1960-61)

27. Carriage by Air Act 1961
s.2, enabling: SI 2009/3018

33. Land Compensation Act 1961
see *Spirerose Ltd v Transport for London* [2008] EWCA Civ 1230, [2009] 1 P. & C.R. 20 (CA (Civ Div)), Carnwath, L.J.
applied: SI 2009/1300 Art.39
varied: SI 2009/2364 Art.27, SI 2009/2728 Art.14
Part I, applied: SI 2009/1300 Art.11, Art.12, Art.20, Art.22, Art.25, Art.35, Art.36, Art.37, Art.41, Art.51, Art.76, Sch.16 para.5, SI 2009/2364 Art.8, Art.9, Art.16, Art.23, Art.24, Art.25, Art.29, Art.35, SI 2009/2728 Art.9, Art.10, Art.11, Art.12, Art.16
s.1, amended: SI 2009/1307 Sch.1 para.37
s.2, repealed: SI 2009/1307 Sch.1 para.38
s.2, varied: SI 2009/995 Sch.6 para.7
s.3, repealed: SI 2009/1307 Sch.1 para.38
s.4, see *Moyce v National Grid Electricity Transmission Plc* [2009] R.V.R. 141 (Lands Tr), George Bartlett Q.C. (President)
s.4, amended: SI 2009/1307 Sch.1 para.39
s.4, repealed (in part): SI 2009/1307 Sch.1 para.39
s.4, varied: SI 2009/995 Sch.6 para.7
s.5, see *Greenweb Ltd v Wandsworth LBC* [2008] EWCA Civ 910, [2009] 1 W.L.R. 612 (CA (Civ Div)), Buxton, L.J.; see *Pattle v Secretary of State for Transport* [2009] UKUT 141 (LC), [2009] R.V.R. 328 (UT (Lands)), Judge Huskinson; see *Sadiq v Stoke-on-Trent City Council* [2009] R.V.R. 178 (Lands Tr), George Bartlett Q.C.; see *Spirerose Ltd v Transport for London* [2008] EWCA Civ 1230, [2009] 1 P. & C.R. 20 (CA (Civ Div)), Carnwath, L.J.
s.5, amended: SI 2009/1307 Sch.1 para.40
s.5, referred to: SI 2009/995 Sch.6 para.6

9 & 10 Eliz. 2 (1960-61) – cont.

33. Land Compensation Act 1961 – *cont.*
s.5, varied: SI 2009/153 Sch.6 para.6
s.5A, amended: SI 2009/1307 Sch.1 para.41
s.10A, see *Sadiq v Stoke-on-Trent City Council* [2009] R.V.R. 178 (Lands Tr), George Bartlett Q.C.
s.14, see *Greenweb Ltd v Wandsworth LBC* [2008] EWCA Civ 910, [2009] 1 W.L.R. 612 (CA (Civ Div)), Buxton, L.J.; see *Spirerose Ltd v Transport for London* [2009] UKHL 44, [2009] 1 W.L.R. 1797 (HL), Lord Scott of Foscote
s.15, see *Greenweb Ltd v Wandsworth LBC* [2008] EWCA Civ 910, [2009] 1 W.L.R. 612 (CA (Civ Div)), Buxton, L.J.
s.16, see *Urban Edge Group Ltd v London Underground Ltd* [2009] UKUT 103 (LC), [2009] R.V.R. 361 (UT (Lands)), George Bartlett Q.C.
s.17, see *Greenweb Ltd v Wandsworth LBC* [2008] EWCA Civ 910, [2009] 1 W.L.R. 612 (CA (Civ Div)), Buxton, L.J.; see *Spirerose Ltd v Transport for London* [2009] UKHL 44, [2009] 1 W.L.R. 1797 (HL), Lord Scott of Foscote
s.17, amended: SI 2009/1307 Sch.1 para.42
s.31, amended: SI 2009/1307 Sch.1 para.43
s.35, amended: SI 2009/1307 Sch.1 para.44

34. Factories Act 1961
s.29, see *Baker v Quantum Clothing Group* [2009] EWCA Civ 499, [2009] P.I.Q.R. P19 (CA (Civ Div)), Sedley, L.J.
s.39, amended: SI 2009/605 Reg.4
s.39, applied: SI 2009/605 Reg.3
s.122, repealed (in part): SI 2009/605 Reg.4
s.125, amended: SI 2009/605 Reg.4
s.126, amended: SI 2009/605 Reg.4
s.127, amended: SI 2009/605 Reg.4
s.137, repealed: SI 2009/605 Reg.2
s.140, repealed: SI 2009/605 Reg.3
s.141, amended: SI 2009/605 Reg.3
s.141, referred to: SI 2009/605 Reg.3
s.141, varied: SI 2009/605 Reg.3
s.176, amended: SI 2009/605 Reg.4
s.178, amended: SSI 2009/65 Sch.1
s.182, repealed (in part): SSI 2009/319 Sch.3 Part 1

39. Criminal Justice Act 1961
s.22, amended: SI 2009/1096 r.71
s.22, varied: SI 2009/1059 Sch.1 para.8, SI 2009/1096 r.71

41. Flood Prevention (Scotland) Act 1961
applied: 2009 asp 6 s.63
repealed: 2009 asp 6 s.70
s.2, applied: 2009 asp 6 s.19
s.4, applied: 2009 asp 6 s.67, s.69, s.79

55. Crown Estate Act 1961
applied: 2009 c.23 Sch.6 para.9

60. Suicide Act 1961
s.2, see *R. (on the application of Purdy) v DPP* [2008] EWHC 2565 (Admin), [2009] H.R.L.R. 7 (DC), Scott Baker, L.J.; see *R. (on the application of Purdy) v DPP* [2009] EWCA Civ 92, [2009] 1 Cr. App. R. 32 (CA (Civ Div)), Lord Judge, L.C.J.; see *R. (on the application of Purdy) v DPP* [2009] UKHL 45, [2009] 3 W.L.R. 403 (HL), Lord Phillips of Worth Matravers
s.2, amended: 2009 c.25 s.59
s.2, applied: 2009 c.25 s.61, Sch.12 para.1
s.2A, added: 2009 c.25 s.59
s.2B, added: 2009 c.25 s.59
Sch.1 Part I, amended: 2009 c.25 Sch.23 Part 2

9 & 10 Eliz. 2 (1960-61)–cont.

62. Trustee Investments Act 1961
s.11, amended: 2009 c.20 Sch.6 para.2
s.11, applied: SI 2009/3093 Reg.13

64. Public Health Act 1961
s.45, amended: SI 2009/1307 Sch.1 para.45
s.45, applied: SI 2009/721 Sch.3 para.5
s.81, applied: SI 2009/721 Sch.3 para.5

10 & 11 Eliz. 2 (1961-62)

9. Local Government (Financial Provisions etc.) (Scotland) Act 1962
s.4, applied: SSI 2009/42 Reg.3, Reg.5
s.4, see *English Speaking Union Scottish Branches Educational Fund v Edinburgh City Council* [2009] CSOH 139, 2009 S.L.T. 1051 (OH), Lord Bonomy

12. Education Act 1962
applied: SI 2009/1555 Reg.4, SI 2009/2737 Reg.3

14. Electoral Law Act (Northern Ireland) 1962
s.11, amended: SI 2009/225 Art.2
s.11, applied: SI 2009/225 Art.3
s.11, disapplied: SI 2009/225 Art.2
s.28, referred to: SI 2009/225 Art.3
s.65, amended: SI 2009/3014 Art.2
s.65, applied: SI 2009/3014 Art.2

19. West Indies Act 1962
s.5, enabling: SI 2009/701, SI 2009/1379, SI 2009/1755
s.7, enabling: SI 2009/701, SI 2009/1379, SI 2009/1755

27. Recorded Delivery Service Act 1962
see *Kodak Processing Companies Ltd v Shoredale Ltd* [2009] CSIH 71, 2009 S.L.T. 1151 (IH (Ex Div)), Lord Osborne

37. Building Societies Act 1962
referred to: SI 2009/500 Sch.1 Part 1

38. Town and Country Planning Act 1962
see *Urban Edge Group Ltd v London Underground Ltd* [2009] UKUT 103 (LC), [2009] R.V.R. 361 (UT (Lands)), George Bartlett Q.C.

46. Transport Act 1962
s.92, amended: SI 2009/1941 Sch.1 para.9

56. Local Government (Records) Act 1962
s.2, amended: 2009 c.20 Sch.6 para.3
s.8, amended: 2009 c.20 Sch.6 para.3

58. Pipe-lines Act 1962
s.48, amended: SI 2009/1307 Sch.1 para.48
s.67, repealed (in part): SI 2009/1307 Sch.1 para.49
Sch.2 Part I para.4, amended: SI 2009/1307 Sch.1 para.50
Sch.3 para.3, amended: SI 2009/1307 Sch.1 para.51

1963

18. Stock Transfer Act 1963
s.1, amended: SI 2009/1941 Sch.1 para.10

41. Offices, Shops and Railway Premises Act 1963
referred to: SI 2009/669 Sch.1 Part 1
s.49, repealed: SI 2009/605 Reg.2

43. Animal Boarding Establishments Act 1963
s.3, applied: SSI 2009/141 Reg.4

51. Land Compensation (Scotland) Act 1963
s.12, varied: SSI 2009/266 Sch.4 para.46
s.25, see *Hallam Land Management Ltd v Scottish Ministers* [2009] CSIH 22, 2009 S.C. 347 (IH (Ex Div)), Lord Osborne

1964

5. International Headquarters and Defence Organisations Act 1964
applied: SI 2009/822 Art.3
s.1, applied: SI 2009/704
s.1, enabling: SI 2009/704
Sch.1 para.7, enabling: SI 2009/705

14. Plant Varieties and Seeds Act 1964
s.16, enabling: SI 2009/1274, SI 2009/1356, SI 2009/2342, SI 2009/2980, SSI 2009/223, SSI 2009/226, SSI 2009/306, SSI 2009/330
s.36, enabling: SI 2009/1274, SI 2009/1356, SI 2009/2342, SI 2009/2980, SSI 2009/223, SSI 2009/226, SSI 2009/330

26. Licensing Act 1964
referred to: SI 2009/500 Sch.1 Part 1

28. Agriculture and Horticulture Act 1964
disapplied: SI 2009/1361 Reg.22, SI 2009/1551 Reg.22, SSI 2009/225 Reg.24

29. Continental Shelf Act 1964
s.1, applied: SI 2009/785 Art.17, SSI 2009/140 Art.17
s.8, amended: 2009 c.23 Sch.4 para.1

36. Business Tenancies Act (Northern Ireland) 1964
s.25, amended: SI 2009/1941 Sch.1 para.13

40. Harbours Act 1964
applied: 2009 c.23 s.78, SI 2009/2579 Art.4, SI 2009/2604 Art.4
enabling: SI 2009/1231
s.14, amended: SI 2009/1941 Sch.1 para.12
s.14, applied: 2009 c.23 s.75, SI 2009/2207, SI 2009/3382
s.14, referred to: SI 2009/2207
s.14, enabling: SI 2009/1231, SI 2009/2207, SI 2009/2259, SI 2009/2325, SI 2009/2579, SI 2009/2604, SI 2009/3382
s.16, amended: 2009 c.23 Sch.21 para.2
s.16, applied: 2009 c.23 s.75
s.16, referred to: SSI 2009/27
s.16, enabling: SSI 2009/27
s.26, applied: SI 2009/2207 Art.19
s.30, applied: SSI 2009/27 Art.29
s.30, disapplied: SI 2009/2207 Art.19, SI 2009/2325 Art.31, SSI 2009/27 Art.29
s.42A, added: 2009 c.23 Sch.21 para.3
s.42B, added: 2009 c.23 Sch.21 para.3
s.42C, added: 2009 c.23 Sch.21 para.4
s.42D, added: 2009 c.23 Sch.21 para.4
s.44, amended: SI 2009/269 Reg.2
s.54, amended: 2009 c.23 Sch.21 para.3
s.57, amended: SI 2009/1941 Sch.1 para.12
s.57, applied: SSI 2009/27 Art.4
Sch.2 para.9B, referred to: SI 2009/1231 Sch.2 para.13, SI 2009/2207 Sch.2 para.13, SI 2009/2325 Art.32
Sch.3 Part I para.1, amended: SI 2009/269 Reg.4
Sch.3 Part I para.10, amended: SI 2009/269 Reg.5
Sch.3 Part I para.10, applied: SSI 2009/27
Sch.3 Part I para.10A, added: SI 2009/269 Reg.6
Sch.3 Part I para.15, amended: SI 2009/269 Reg.7
Sch.3 Part I para.16, amended: SI 2009/269 Reg.8
Sch.3 Part I para.17, amended: SI 2009/269 Reg.9
Sch.3 Part I para.18, amended: 2009 c.23 Sch.21 para.5
Sch.3 Part I para.18, repealed (in part): 2009 c.23 Sch.21 para.5, Sch.22 Part 8
Sch.3 Part I para.19, amended: SI 2009/269 Reg.10
Sch.3 Part I para.20, amended: SI 2009/269 Reg.11
Sch.3 Part II para.28, substituted: 2009 c.23 Sch.21 para.6

1964– cont.

40. Harbours Act 1964– *cont.*
Sch.3 Part II para.29, amended: 2009 c.23 Sch.21 para.6

41. Succession (Scotland) Act 1964
see *Price v Baxter* 2009 Fam. L.R.138 (Sh Ct (South Strathclyde) (Hamilton)), Sheriff T McCartney; see *Savage v Purches* 2009 S.L.T. (Sh Ct) 36 (Sh Ct (Tayside) (Falkirk)), Sheriff P Arthurson; see *Windram, Applicant* 2009 Fam. L.R. 157 (Sh Ct (Lothian) (Jedburgh)), Sheriff J M Scott, QC
s.8, see *Savage v Purches* 2009 S.L.T. (Sh Ct) 36 (Sh Ct (Tayside) (Falkirk)), Sheriff P Arthurson
s.9, see *Savage v Purches* 2009 S.L.T. (Sh Ct) 36 (Sh Ct (Tayside) (Falkirk)), Sheriff P Arthurson

55. Perpetuities and Accumulations Act 1964
s.1, varied: 2009 c.18 s.12
s.2, varied: 2009 c.18 s.12
s.3, varied: 2009 c.18 s.12
s.4, varied: 2009 c.18 s.12
s.5, varied: 2009 c.18 s.12
s.6, varied: 2009 c.18 s.12
s.7, varied: 2009 c.18 s.12
s.8, varied: 2009 c.18 s.12
s.9, varied: 2009 c.18 s.12
s.10, varied: 2009 c.18 s.12
s.11, varied: 2009 c.18 s.12
s.12, varied: 2009 c.18 s.12
s.13, repealed: 2009 c.18 s.13, Sch.1
s.15, amended: 2009 c.18 s.16

56. Housing Act 1964
s.9, applied: SI 2009/484 Art.4

81. Diplomatic Privileges Act 1964
applied: SI 2009/222 Art.2
Sch.1, applied: SI 2009/1748 Art.7, Art.9, Art.14, Art.15, Art.16

84. Criminal Procedure (Insanity) Act 1964
s.4A, see *R. v B* [2008] EWCA Crim 1997, [2009] 1 W.L.R. 1545 (CA (Crim Div)), Toulson, L.J.
s.6, amended: 2009 c.25 s.52
Sch.1A Part 1, referred to: SI 2009/1887 Sch.2

1965

12. Industrial and Provident Societies Act 1965
see *Dairy Farmers of Britain Ltd, Re* [2009] EWHC 1389 (Ch), [2009] 4 All E.R. 241 (Ch D (Companies Ct)), Henderson, J.
applied: 2009 c.4 s.431, s.682, s.821, SI 2009/1085 Reg.13
referred to: 2009 c.1 s.131, s.159
s.1, amended: SI 2009/1941 Sch.1 para.14
s.7E, amended: SI 2009/1941 Sch.1 para.14
s.7F, amended: SI 2009/1941 Sch.1 para.14
s.7F, repealed (in part): SI 2009/1941 Sch.1 para.14
s.39, amended: SI 2009/1941 Sch.1 para.14
s.52, amended: SI 2009/1941 Sch.1 para.14
s.53, amended: SI 2009/1941 Sch.1 para.14
s.55, substituted: SI 2009/1941 Sch.1 para.14

19. Teaching Council (Scotland) Act 1965
s.4A, repealed: SSI 2009/386 Art.2
s.5, repealed (in part): SSI 2009/386 Art.2
s.6A, repealed: SSI 2009/386 Art.2
Sch.1 Part II para.8, repealed (in part): SSI 2009/386 Art.2
Sch.1 Part II para.16A, repealed: SSI 2009/386 Art.2
Sch.1 Part II para.17, amended: SSI 2009/386 Art.2

1965– cont.

20. Criminal Evidence Act 1965
see *R. v Horncastle (Michael Christopher)* [2009] UKSC 14 (SC), Lord Phillips (President)

22. Law Commissions Act 1965
s.3A, added: 2009 c.14 s.1
s.3B, added: 2009 c.14 s.2

32. Administration of Estates (Small Payments) Act 1965
s.6, referred to: 2009 asp 1 Sch.1 para.107

36. Gas Act 1965
s.10, amended: SI 2009/1307 Sch.1 para.54
s.23, amended: SI 2009/1307 Sch.1 para.55
s.28, amended: SI 2009/1307 Sch.1 para.56
s.28, repealed (in part): SI 2009/1307 Sch.1 para.56
Sch.2 Part II para.8, amended: SI 2009/1307 Sch.1 para.57
Sch.2 Part II para.12, amended: SI 2009/1307 Sch.1 para.57

37. Carriage of Goods by Road Act 1965
see *Hatzl v XL Insurance Co Ltd* [2009] EWCA Civ 223, [2009] 3 All E.R. 617 (CA (Civ Div)), Rix, L.J.

49. Registration of Births, Deaths and Marriages (Scotland) Act 1965
s.13, enabling: SSI 2009/315
s.18, enabling: SSI 2009/315
s.21, enabling: SSI 2009/315
s.22, enabling: SSI 2009/315
s.32, enabling: SSI 2009/315
s.37, enabling: SSI 2009/64
s.39B, enabling: SSI 2009/315
s.39D, enabling: SSI 2009/64
s.39E, enabling: SSI 2009/64
s.43, enabling: SSI 2009/315
s.54, applied: SSI 2009/64, SSI 2009/315
s.54, enabling: SSI 2009/315

51. National Insurance Act 1965
s.36, amended: SI 2009/497 Art.12, SI 2009/2206 Reg.3
s.37, amended: SI 2009/2206 Reg.4
s.37, varied: SI 2009/497 Art.12

56. Compulsory Purchase Act 1965
applied: SI 2009/1300 Art.30, Art.32, Art.40, SI 2009/2364 Art.28, SI 2009/2728 Art.15
referred to: SI 2009/2364 Art.20, SI 2009/2728 Art.6
varied: SI 2009/1300 Sch.7 para.3, SI 2009/2728 Sch.2 para.3
Part I, applied: SI 2009/1300 Art.30, Art.45, Sch.7 para.3, SI 2009/2364 Art.14, Art.30, SI 2009/2728 Art.17, Sch.2 para.3
Part I, referred to: SI 2009/1300 Art.36, Art.37, Art.40
s.1, varied: SI 2009/1300 Art.30, SI 2009/2364 Art.18, Sch.5 para.3, SI 2009/2728 Art.4
s.2, varied: SI 2009/1300 Art.30, SI 2009/2364 Art.18, Sch.5 para.3, SI 2009/2728 Art.4
s.3, varied: SI 2009/1300 Art.30, SI 2009/2364 Art.18, Sch.5 para.3, SI 2009/2728 Art.4
s.4, varied: SI 2009/1300 Art.30, SI 2009/2364 Art.18, Sch.5 para.3, SI 2009/2728 Art.4
s.5, see *Oakglade Investments Ltd v Greater Manchester Passenger Transport Executive* [2009] R.V.R. 39 (Lands Tr), George Bartlett Q.C. (President); see *Union Railways (North) Ltd v Kent CC* [2009] EWCA Civ 363, [2009] 30 E.G. 68 (CA (Civ Div)), Ward, L.J.
s.5, amended: SI 2009/1307 Sch.1 para.60

1965– cont.

56. Compulsory Purchase Act 1965–*cont.*
s.5, varied: SI 2009/1300 Art.30, SI 2009/2364 Art.18, Sch.5 para.3, SI 2009/2728 Art.4

s.6, amended: SI 2009/1307 Sch.1 para.61

s.6, varied: SI 2009/1300 Art.30, SI 2009/2364 Art.18, Sch.5 para.3, SI 2009/2728 Art.4

s.7, see *Spirerose Ltd v Transport for London* [2008] EWCA Civ 1230, [2009] 1 P. & C.R. 20 (CA (Civ Div)), Carnwath, L.J.

s.7, applied: SI 2009/1300 Sch.7 para.2, SI 2009/2364 Sch.5 para.2

s.7, substituted: SI 2009/2364 Sch.5 para.4

s.7, varied: SI 2009/1300 Art.30, Sch.7 para.4, SI 2009/2364 Art.18, Sch.5 para.3, SI 2009/2728 Art.4, Sch.2 para.4

s.8, amended: SI 2009/1307 Sch.1 para.62

s.8, applied: SI 2009/1300 Art.32, Sch.7 para.2, SI 2009/2364 Art.20, Sch.5 para.2, SI 2009/2728 Art.6

s.8, disapplied: SI 2009/1300 Art.40, SI 2009/2364 Art.28, SI 2009/2728 Art.15

s.8, substituted: SI 2009/2364 Sch.5 para.5

s.8, varied: SI 2009/1300 Art.30, Sch.7 para.5, SI 2009/2364 Art.18, Sch.5 para.3, SI 2009/2728 Art.4, Sch.2 para.5

s.9, varied: SI 2009/1300 Art.30, Sch.7 para.6, SI 2009/2364 Art.18, Sch.5 para.3, Sch.5 para.6, SI 2009/2728 Art.4, Sch.2 para.6

s.10, see *Union Railways (North) Ltd v Kent CC* [2009] EWCA Civ 363, [2009] 30 E.G. 68 (CA (Civ Div)), Ward, L.J.

s.10, amended: SI 2009/1307 Sch.1 para.63

s.10, applied: SI 2009/1300 Art.22, Art.36, Art.37, SI 2009/2364 Art.14, Art.24, Art.25, SI 2009/2728 Art.10, Art.12

s.10, varied: SI 2009/1300 Art.30, SI 2009/2364 Art.18, Sch.5 para.3, SI 2009/2728 Art.4

s.11, amended: SI 2009/1307 Sch.1 para.64

s.11, applied: SI 2009/1300 Art.36, Art.41, Sch.12 para.42, Sch.13 para.3, Sch.14 para.4, SI 2009/2364 Art.29, Sch.9 para.4, Sch.10 para.42, SI 2009/2728 Art.10, Art.16

s.11, varied: SI 2009/1300 Art.30, Sch.7 para.7, SI 2009/2364 Art.18, Sch.5 para.3, Sch.5 para.7, SI 2009/2728 Art.4, Sch.2 para.7

s.12, varied: SI 2009/1300 Art.30, Sch.7 para.7, SI 2009/2364 Art.18, Sch.5 para.3, Sch.5 para.7, SI 2009/2728 Art.4, Sch.2 para.7

s.13, applied: SI 2009/1300 Art.36, Art.37, SI 2009/2364 Art.24, Art.25, SI 2009/2728 Art.10, Art.11, Art.12

s.13, varied: SI 2009/1300 Art.30, Sch.7 para.7, SI 2009/2364 Art.18, Sch.5 para.3, Sch.5 para.7, SI 2009/2728 Art.4, Sch.2 para.7

s.14, varied: SI 2009/1300 Art.30, SI 2009/2364 Art.18, Sch.5 para.3, SI 2009/2728 Art.4

s.15, amended: SI 2009/1307 Sch.1 para.65

s.15, varied: SI 2009/1300 Art.30, SI 2009/2364 Art.18, Sch.5 para.3, SI 2009/2728 Art.4

s.16, amended: SI 2009/1307 Sch.1 para.66

s.16, varied: SI 2009/1300 Art.30, SI 2009/2364 Art.18, Sch.5 para.3, SI 2009/2728 Art.4

s.17, amended: SI 2009/1307 Sch.1 para.67

s.17, varied: SI 2009/1300 Art.30, SI 2009/2364 Art.18, Sch.5 para.3, SI 2009/2728 Art.4

s.18, amended: SI 2009/1307 Sch.1 para.68

s.18, varied: SI 2009/1300 Art.30, SI 2009/2364 Art.18, Sch.5 para.3, SI 2009/2728 Art.4

s.19, amended: SI 2009/1307 Sch.1 para.69

1965– cont.

56. Compulsory Purchase Act 1965–*cont.*
s.19, varied: SI 2009/1300 Art.30, SI 2009/2364 Art.18, Sch.5 para.3, SI 2009/2728 Art.4

s.20, amended: SI 2009/1307 Sch.1 para.70

s.20, varied: SI 2009/1300 Art.30, Sch.7 para.8, SI 2009/2364 Art.18, Sch.5 para.3, Sch.5 para.8, SI 2009/2728 Art.4, Sch.2 para.8

s.21, varied: SI 2009/1300 Art.30, SI 2009/2364 Art.18, Sch.5 para.3, SI 2009/2728 Art.4

s.22, see *Union Railways (North) Ltd v Kent CC* [2009] EWCA Civ 363, [2009] 30 E.G. 68 (CA (Civ Div)), Ward, L.J.

s.22, varied: SI 2009/1300 Art.30, Sch.7 para.9, SI 2009/2364 Art.18, Sch.5 para.3, Sch.5 para.9, SI 2009/2728 Art.4, Sch.2 para.9

s.23, varied: SI 2009/1300 Art.30, SI 2009/2364 Art.18, Sch.5 para.3, SI 2009/2728 Art.4

s.24, varied: SI 2009/1300 Art.30, SI 2009/2364 Art.18, Sch.5 para.3, SI 2009/2728 Art.4

s.25, varied: SI 2009/1300 Art.30, SI 2009/2364 Art.18, Sch.5 para.3, SI 2009/2728 Art.4

s.26, varied: SI 2009/1300 Art.30, SI 2009/2364 Art.18, Sch.5 para.3, SI 2009/2728 Art.4

s.27, varied: SI 2009/1300 Art.30, SI 2009/2364 Art.18, Sch.5 para.3, SI 2009/2728 Art.4

s.28, varied: SI 2009/1300 Art.30, SI 2009/2364 Art.18, Sch.5 para.3, SI 2009/2728 Art.4

s.29, varied: SI 2009/1300 Art.30, SI 2009/2364 Art.18, Sch.5 para.3, SI 2009/2728 Art.4

s.30, varied: SI 2009/1300 Art.30, SI 2009/2364 Art.18, Sch.5 para.3, SI 2009/2728 Art.4

s.31, varied: SI 2009/1300 Art.30, SI 2009/2364 Art.18, Sch.5 para.3, SI 2009/2728 Art.4

s.32, varied: SI 2009/1300 Art.30, SI 2009/2364 Art.18, Sch.5 para.3, SI 2009/2728 Art.4

Sch.1 para.4, amended: SI 2009/1307 Sch.1 para.71

Sch.1 para.10, varied: SI 2009/1300 Sch.7 para.6, SI 2009/2364 Sch.5 para.6, SI 2009/2728 Sch.2 para.6

Sch.2, applied: SI 2009/1114 Sch.1

Sch.2 para.1, amended: SI 2009/1307 Sch.1 para.72

Sch.2 para.2, varied: SI 2009/1300 Sch.7 para.6, SI 2009/2364 Sch.5 para.6, SI 2009/2728 Sch.2 para.6

Sch.2 para.4, amended: SI 2009/1307 Sch.1 para.72

Sch.3 para.3, varied: SI 2009/1300 Art.30

Sch.4 para.2, varied: SI 2009/1300 Sch.7 para.6, SI 2009/2364 Sch.5 para.6, SI 2009/2728 Sch.2 para.6

Sch.4 para.5, amended: SI 2009/1307 Sch.1 para.73

Sch.4 para.6, amended: SI 2009/1307 Sch.1 para.73

Sch.4 para.7, varied: SI 2009/1300 Sch.7 para.6, SI 2009/2364 Sch.5 para.6, SI 2009/2728 Sch.2 para.6

Sch.7 Part 1, amended: SI 2009/1307 Sch.1 para.74

57. Nuclear Installations Act 1965
s.1, applied: SI 2009/515 Sch.13

s.3, amended: 2009 c.23 Sch.14 para.6, Sch.22 Part 4

s.3, applied: SI 2009/515 Sch.13

64. Commons Registration Act 1965
see *Hall v Moore* [2009] EWCA Civ 201, [2009] 24 E.G. 86 (CA (Civ Div)), Rix, L.J.

s.13, see *Betterment Properties (Weymouth) Ltd v Dorset CC* [2008] EWCA Civ 22, [2009] 1 W.L.R. 334 (CA (Civ Div)), Laws, L.J.

s.14, see *Betterment Properties (Weymouth) Ltd v Dorset CC* [2008] EWCA Civ 22, [2009] 1 W.L.R. 334 (CA (Civ Div)), Laws, L.J.

1965– cont.

64. Commons Registration Act 1965– *cont.*
s.22, see *Betterment Properties (Weymouth) Ltd v Dorset CC* [2008] EWCA Civ 22, [2009] 1 W.L.R. 334 (CA (Civ Div)), Laws, L.J.

69. Criminal Procedure (Attendance of Witnesses) Act 1965
s.2, see *R. v Popat (Harish)* [2008] EWCA Crim 1921, (2009) 172 J.P. 24 (CA (Crim Div)), Hughes, L.J.
s.3, see *R. v Popat (Harish)* [2008] EWCA Crim 1921, (2009) 172 J.P. 24 (CA (Crim Div)), Hughes, L.J.

1966

4. Mines (Working Facilities and Support) Act 1966
s.8, see *Bocardo SA v Star Energy UK Onshore Ltd* [2008] EWHC 1756 (Ch), [2009] 1 All E.R. 517 (Ch D), Peter Smith, J.; see *Bocardo SA v Star Energy UK Onshore Ltd* [2009] EWCA Civ 579, [2009] 3 W.L.R. 1010 (CA (Civ Div)), Jacob, L.J.

20. Supplementary Benefit Act (enacted as the Ministry of Social Security Act) 1966
s.5, amended: 2009 c.25 s.53

35. Family Provision Act 1966
s.1, applied: SI 2009/135
s.1, enabling: SI 2009/135

36. Veterinary Surgeons Act 1966
applied: SI 2009/2474 Sch.1
s.5A, referred to: SI 2009/2999 Reg.31
s.5C, applied: SI 2009/2474 Sch.1
s.5CA, applied: SI 2009/2474 Sch.1
s.5CB, applied: SI 2009/2474 Sch.1
s.5CC, applied: SI 2009/2474 Sch.1
s.5D, applied: SI 2009/2474 Sch.1
s.5D, enabling: SI 2009/2474
s.17, applied: SI 2009/224 Sch.1
s.17, enabling: SI 2009/224
s.19, disapplied: SI 2009/1217 Art.2
s.19, enabling: SI 2009/1217, SI 2009/2769
s.25, applied: SI 2009/2474
s.25, enabling: SI 2009/2474
Sch.1B para.5, referred to: SI 2009/2999 Reg.31
Sch.1B para.6, referred to: SI 2009/2999 Reg.31

38. Sea Fisheries Regulation Act 1966
referred to: 2009 c.23 s.188
repealed: 2009 c.23 s.187, Sch.22 Part 4
s.1, applied: 2009 c.23 s.16, s.188

42. Local Government Act 1966
s.11, amended: 2009 c.20 Sch.6 para.4

45. Armed Forces Act 1966
applied: SI 2009/1059 Art.195, SI 2009/1091 Reg.12, SI 2009/2057 Sch.1 para.13
s.4, applied: SI 2009/832 Sch.1 para.20, SI 2009/1059 Art.193, SI 2009/1091 Reg.12, Sch.1 para.21
s.4, varied: SI 2009/832 Reg.12, Reg.13, SI 2009/1091 Reg.13
s.5, varied: SI 2009/832 Reg.12
s.6, applied: SI 2009/832 Sch.1 para.17, SI 2009/1091 Sch.1 para.18
s.7, applied: SI 2009/832 Sch.1 para.17, SI 2009/1091 Sch.1 para.18
s.9, disapplied: SI 2009/2057 Sch.1 para.3, Sch.1 para.14
s.10, applied: SI 2009/2057 Sch.1 para.12, Sch.1 para.13

51. Local Government (Scotland) Act 1966
s.24, applied: SSI 2009/42 Reg.3

1966– cont.

51. Local Government (Scotland) Act 1966– *cont.*
s.24A, applied: SSI 2009/42 Reg.3
s.25A, applied: SSI 2009/42 Reg.5
s.38, repealed: SSI 2009/248 Sch.2

1967

7. Misrepresentation Act 1967
see *Trident Turboprop (Dublin) Ltd v First Flight Couriers Ltd* [2008] EWHC 1686 (Comm), [2009] 1 All E.R. (Comm) 16 (QBD (Comm)), Aikens, J.
s.3, see *Trident Turboprop (Dublin) Ltd v First Flight Couriers Ltd* [2008] EWHC 1686 (Comm), [2009] 1 All E.R. (Comm) 16 (QBD (Comm)), Aikens, J.

8. Plant Health Act 1967
s.2, enabling: SI 2009/587, SI 2009/594, SI 2009/1376, SI 2009/3020, SSI 2009/153
s.3, enabling: SI 2009/587, SI 2009/594, SI 2009/1376, SI 2009/3020, SSI 2009/153
s.4, enabling: SSI 2009/153

10. Forestry Act 1967
applied: SI 2009/3365 Sch.1 para.1
s.5, amended: SI 2009/1307 Sch.1 para.76
s.9, see *Palm Developments Ltd v Secretary of State for Communities and Local Government* [2009] EWHC 220 (Admin), [2009] 2 P. & C.R. 16 (QBD (Admin)), Cranston, J.
s.9, applied: SI 2009/3264 Sch.1 para.1, SI 2009/3365 Sch.1 para.1
s.24, applied: SI 2009/3264 Sch.1 para.1, SI 2009/3365 Sch.1 para.1
s.31, amended: SI 2009/1307 Sch.1 para.77
s.39, applied: SI 2009/2829 Sch.1

13. Parliamentary Commissioner Act 1967
see *R. (on the application of Bradley) v Secretary of State for Work and Pensions* [2008] EWCA Civ 36, [2009] Q.B. 114 (CA (Civ Div)), Wall, L.J.
applied: 2009 c.22 s.217
s.4, enabling: SI 2009/1754
s.5, see *R. (on the application of Bradley) v Secretary of State for Work and Pensions* [2008] EWCA Civ 36, [2009] Q.B. 114 (CA (Civ Div)), Wall, L.J.
s.11, disapplied: 2009 c.22 s.217
Sch.2, amended: 2009 c.20 Sch.1 para.20, 2009 c.22 Sch.3 para.20, Sch.12 para.2, 2009 c.23 Sch.2 para.2, 2009 c.25 Sch.21 para.79, Sch.23 Part 4, 2009 c.26 s.81, SI 2009/1754 Art.2, SI 2009/2748 Sch.1 para.1, SI 2009/3019 Art.10
Sch.3 para.6, varied: SI 2009/1059 Sch.1 para.9
Sch.4, amended: SI 2009/1836 Sch.1 para.1

22. Agriculture Act 1967
s.49, amended: SI 2009/1307 Sch.1 para.78
s.49, repealed (in part): SI 2009/1307 Sch.1 para.78

48. Industrial and Provident Societies Act 1967
s.3, amended: SI 2009/1941 Sch.1 para.16

54. Finance Act 1967
s.5, repealed (in part): SSI 2009/248 Sch.2

58. Criminal Law Act 1967
s.4, see *R. v Sherif (Abdul)* [2008] EWCA Crim 2653, [2009] 2 Cr. App. R. (S.) 33 (CA (Crim Div)), Latham, L.J.
s.4, applied: 2009 c.25 s.159

60. Sexual Offences Act 1967
s.4, applied: SI 2009/1059 Art.42, SI 2009/1547 Sch.2 para.2

1967– cont.

60. Sexual Offences Act 1967– *cont.*
s.4, referred to: SI 2009/37 Sch.1 para.2, Sch.1 para.4
s.5, applied: SI 2009/1059 Art.42, SI 2009/1547 Sch.2 para.2
s.5, referred to: SI 2009/37 Sch.1 para.2, Sch.1 para.4

77. Police (Scotland) Act 1967
s.1, applied: SI 2009/1922 Art.14, SI 2009/3069 Reg.3
s.26, enabling: SSI 2009/372
s.32, enabling: SSI 2009/41, SSI 2009/55, SSI 2009/80
s.33, applied: SI 2009/3070 Reg.5
s.33, referred to: 2009 c.11 s.29
s.34, referred to: 2009 c.11 s.29
s.39, applied: SI 2009/3269 Art.2
s.39, enabling: SI 2009/3269
s.41, applied: SI 2009/3269 Art.2, SSI 2009/31 Sch.1 para.8, SSI 2009/71 Sch.1 para.8
s.41, enabling: SI 2009/3269
s.48, enabling: SSI 2009/55
Sch.3, applied: SI 2009/3070 Reg.5
Sch.3 para.2, applied: SI 2009/3070 Reg.5

80. Criminal Justice Act 1967
s.9, applied: SI 2009/1209 r.60, r.73, SI 2009/1211 r.61, r.74, SI 2009/2041 r.75, r.88
s.9, varied: SI 2009/1209 r.60, SI 2009/1211 r.61, SI 2009/2041 r.75
s.10, applied: SI 2009/989 Sch.1
s.10, varied: SI 2009/1209 r.61, SI 2009/1211 r.62, SI 2009/2041 r.76
s.11, varied: SI 2009/1059 Sch.1 para.11
s.13, varied: SI 2009/1059 Sch.1 para.11
s.72, varied: SI 2009/1059 Sch.1 para.10
s.89, applied: SI 2009/1209 r.60, SI 2009/1211 r.61, SI 2009/2041 r.75

83. Sea Fisheries (Shellfish) Act 1967
applied: 2009 c.23 s.173
s.1, amended: 2009 c.23 s.202, s.203
s.1, applied: 2009 c.23 s.166, s.172, s.173, s.188, s.192, s.214, SSI 2009/443
s.1, repealed (in part): 2009 c.23 Sch.22 Part 5
s.1, enabling: SSI 2009/443
s.3, amended: 2009 c.23 s.204, s.205, s.206, s.207
s.3, applied: SSI 2009/443, SSI 2009/443 Art.5
s.4, amended: 2009 c.23 s.208, Sch.22 Part 5
s.4, applied: SSI 2009/443
s.4ZA, added: 2009 c.23 s.209
s.7, amended: 2009 c.23 s.205, s.210, s.211
s.7, applied: 2009 c.23 s.166, s.173, s.192
s.16, applied: 2009 c.23 s.156
s.17, amended: 2009 c.23 s.212, s.213
s.17, referred to: 2009 c.23 s.156
s.20, amended: 2009 c.23 s.213
s.22, amended: 2009 c.23 s.206
Sch.1, applied: SSI 2009/443
Sch.1 para.1, applied: SSI 2009/443
Sch.1 para.2, applied: SSI 2009/443
Sch.1 para.4, amended: 2009 c.23 s.214
Sch.1 para.4, repealed (in part): 2009 c.23 Sch.22 Part 5
Sch.1 para.5, repealed (in part): 2009 c.23 s.214, Sch.22 Part 5
Sch.1 para.6, amended: 2009 c.23 s.214
Sch.1 para.6, substituted: 2009 c.23 s.202

84. Sea Fish (Conservation) Act 1967
s.1, amended: 2009 c.23 s.194, Sch.15 para.1

1967– cont.

84. Sea Fish (Conservation) Act 1967– *cont.*
s.1, applied: 2009 c.23 s.166
s.2, applied: 2009 c.23 s.166
s.3, amended: 2009 c.23 s.195, Sch.14 para.7, Sch.15 para.2, Sch.22 Part 4
s.3, applied: 2009 c.23 s.166
s.3, enabling: SSI 2009/165
s.4, amended: 2009 c.23 s.4, s.196, s.197
s.4, applied: 2009 c.23 s.4, s.7, s.284
s.4, varied: 2009 c.23 s.4
s.4A, added: 2009 c.23 s.6
s.4A, applied: 2009 c.23 s.6, s.7, s.284
s.4A, varied: 2009 c.23 s.6
s.4AA, varied: 2009 c.23 s.5
s.4B, applied: 2009 c.23 s.4, s.6, s.7
s.5, amended: 2009 c.23 s.198, Sch.15 para.3
s.5, applied: 2009 c.23 s.166, SSI 2009/38 Art.4
s.5, enabling: SI 2009/2721, SSI 2009/38
s.5A, enabling: SI 2009/2721
s.6, applied: 2009 c.23 s.166
s.9, amended: 2009 c.23 s.8
s.9, applied: 2009 c.23 s.8
s.11, amended: 2009 c.23 s.199, Sch.15 para.4, Sch.22 Part 5
s.11, repealed (in part): 2009 c.23 Sch.22 Part 5
s.12, substituted: 2009 c.23 s.200
s.13, repealed: 2009 c.23 Sch.22 Part 4
s.15, amended: 2009 c.23 s.199
s.15, repealed (in part): 2009 c.23 Sch.22 Part 5
s.15, enabling: SI 2009/1675, SI 2009/2721, SSI 2009/38, SSI 2009/165
s.16, amended: 2009 c.23 s.199
s.16, repealed (in part): 2009 c.23 Sch.22 Part 4
s.17, repealed: 2009 c.23 Sch.22 Part 4
s.20, enabling: SI 2009/2721
s.22, amended: 2009 c.23 s.196, Sch.22 Part 4
s.24, applied: 2009 c.23 s.323

88. Leasehold Reform Act 1967
Part I, applied: SI 2009/2096 Art.3
s.1AA, referred to: SI 2009/2096 Art.3
s.2, see *Grosvenor Estates Ltd v Prospect Estates Ltd* [2008] EWCA Civ 1281, [2009] 1 W.L.R. 1313 (CA (Civ Div)), Mummery, L.J.
s.8, see *Ackerman v Lay* [2008] EWCA Civ 1428, [2009] 1 W.L.R. 1556 (CA (Civ Div)), Tuckey, L.J.
s.9, see *Mansal Securities Ltd, Re* [2009] 20 E.G. 104 (Lands Tr), Norman Rose FRICS; see *Pitts v Earl Cadogan* [2008] UKHL 71, [2009] 2 W.L.R. 12 (HL), Lord Hoffmann
s.20, amended: SI 2009/1307 Sch.1 para.83
s.21, amended: SI 2009/1307 Sch.1 para.84
s.28, amended: 2009 c.20 Sch.6 para.5
s.31, amended: SI 2009/1307 Sch.1 para.85
Sch.2 para.8, amended: SI 2009/1307 Sch.1 para.86
Sch.4A para.3A, applied: SI 2009/2097 Reg.4, Reg.5, Reg.6, Reg.7
Sch.4A para.3A, enabling: SI 2009/2097
Sch.4A para.4A, applied: SI 2009/2097 Reg.8, Reg.9, Reg.10, SI 2009/2098, SI 2009/2098 Art.2, Art.3, Art.4, Art.5, Art.6, Art.7, Art.8, Art.9
Sch.4A para.4A, enabling: SI 2009/2097, SI 2009/2098
Sch.4A para.5, enabling: SI 2009/2097

1968

13. National Loans Act 1968
s.12, amended: SI 2009/1941 Sch.1 para.18

14. Public Expenditure and Receipts Act 1968
s.5, enabling: SSI 2009/65
Sch.3 para.1, enabling: SSI 2009/65

18. Consular Relations Act 1968
s.12, enabling: SI 2009/1741

19. Criminal Appeal Act 1968
see *R. v Adams (Terrance)* [2008] EWCA Crim 914,
  [2009] 1 W.L.R. 301 (CA (Crim Div)), Latham,
  L.J.
s.9, applied: 2009 c.25 s.124
s.10, applied: 2009 c.25 s.124
s.11, see *R. v Bukhari (Daniyal)* [2008] EWCA
  Crim 2915, [2009] 2 Cr. App. R. (S.) 18 (CA
  (Crim Div)), Moore-Bick, L.J.
s.11, amended: 2009 c.25 s.140
s.11A, added: 2009 c.25 s.140
s.16, see *R. v Norman (Leslie)* [2008] EWCA Crim
  1810, [2009] 1 Cr. App. R. 13 (CA (Crim Div)),
  Thomas, L.J.
s.23, see *R. v Erskine (Kenneth)* [2009] EWCA
  Crim 1425, [2009] 2 Cr. App. R. 29 (CA (Crim
  Div)), Lord Judge, L.C.J.
s.29, see *R. v Fortean (Jerry)* [2009] EWCA Crim
  437, Times, March 4, 2009 (CA (Crim Div)),
  Hughes, L.J. (V-P)
s.31, amended: 2009 c.25 Sch.21 para.69
s.31A, amended: 2009 c.25 s.110

20. Court Martial Appeals Act 1968
applied: SI 2009/1059 Art.165, SI 2009/2657 r.66,
  r.68
referred to: 2009 c.25 Sch.22 para.22
varied: SI 2009/1059 Art.173
Part III, applied: SI 2009/2044 Art.10
s.5, applied: SI 2009/992 Art.3
s.8, applied: SI 2009/1059 Art.108
s.8, varied: SI 2009/1059 Art.108
s.9, disapplied: SI 2009/1059 Art.110
s.12, varied: SI 2009/1059 Art.111
s.13, disapplied: SI 2009/1059 Art.112
s.13, varied: SI 2009/2041 r.162
s.14, disapplied: SI 2009/1059 Art.113
s.14, varied: SI 2009/2041 r.162
s.14A, disapplied: SI 2009/1059 Art.114
s.14A, varied: SI 2009/2041 r.162
s.15, applied: SI 2009/1059 Art.115
s.15, varied: SI 2009/2041 r.162
s.16, applied: SI 2009/1059 Art.80, Art.81
s.16, varied: SI 2009/2041 r.162
s.16, enabling: SI 2009/1213
s.16A, applied: SI 2009/1059 Art.116
s.16A, disapplied: SI 2009/1059 Art.117
s.16A, varied: SI 2009/2041 r.162
s.17, applied: SI 2009/1059 Art.120
s.17, varied: SI 2009/1059 Art.118
s.18, applied: SI 2009/1059 Art.25, Art.26
s.19, applied: SI 2009/1059 Art.119, Art.121, SI
  2009/2041 r.61
s.19, varied: SI 2009/1059 Art.119
s.19, enabling: SI 2009/2041
s.20, applied: SI 2009/1059 Art.121
s.20, referred to: SI 2009/1059 Art.119
s.21, varied: SI 2009/1059 Art.120
s.22, disapplied: SI 2009/1059 Art.120
s.22, varied: SI 2009/1059 Art.120
s.23, applied: SI 2009/1059 Art.80, Art.81
s.23A, applied: SI 2009/1059 Art.80
s.24, applied: SI 2009/1059 Art.121
s.24, varied: SI 2009/1059 Art.121

20. Court Martial Appeals Act 1968– *cont.*
s.25, applied: SI 2009/1059 Art.121
s.25A, applied: SI 2009/1059 Art.122
s.25A, varied: SI 2009/1059 Art.122
s.25B, applied: SI 2009/1059 Art.80, Art.81,
  Art.122
s.25B, varied: SI 2009/1059 Art.122
s.31, varied: SI 2009/1059 Art.123
s.32, applied: SI 2009/1109 Reg.11
s.34, applied: SI 2009/1059 Art.124
s.34, varied: SI 2009/1059 Art.124
s.36, amended: 2009 c.25 Sch.21 para.70
s.37, varied: SI 2009/1059 Art.125
s.39, amended: SI 2009/2044 Art.9
s.39, referred to: SI 2009/2044 Art.32
s.41, varied: SI 2009/1059 Art.126
s.42, amended: SI 2009/2044 Art.9
s.42, referred to: SI 2009/2044 Art.32
s.46, applied: SI 2009/1059 Art.160
s.47, applied: SI 2009/1059 Art.126
s.47, varied: SI 2009/1059 Art.126
s.49, applied: SI 2009/992 Art.8
s.49, enabling: SI 2009/2657
s.50, varied: SI 2009/1059 Art.127
s.54, varied: SI 2009/1059 Art.128

27. Firearms Act 1968
see *Attorney General's Reference (No.43 of 2009),*
  Re [2009] EWCA Crim 1925, Times, October 9,
  2009 (CA (Crim Div)), Lord Judge, L.C.J.
applied: SI 2009/515 Sch.8 Part 9
referred to: SI 2009/669 Sch.1 Part 1
s.4, see *R. v Jalloh (Mohammed Kandeh)* [2009]
  EWCA Crim 456, [2009] 2 Cr. App. R. (S.) 92
  (CA (Crim Div)), Hooper, L.J.
s.5, see *R. v Kirby (Paul St John)* [2009] EWCA
  Crim 14, [2009] 2 Cr. App. R. (S.) 49 (CA
  (Crim Div)), Moses, L.J.
s.16, see *Attorney General's Reference (No.43 of*
  2009), Re [2009] EWCA Crim 1925, Times,
  October 9, 2009 (CA (Crim Div)), Lord Judge,
  L.C.J.
s.16A, see *R. v Oddy (Gary)* [2009] EWCA Crim
  245, [2009] 2 Cr. App. R. (S.) 78 (CA (Crim
  Div)), Rix, L.J.
s.21, see *R. v Gambrah (Frank)* [2008] EWCA Crim
  2786, [2009] 2 Cr. App. R. (S.) 16 (CA (Crim
  Div)), Moore-Bick, L.J.
s.51A, see *Attorney General's Reference (No.45 of*
  2008), Re [2008] EWCA Crim 2019, [2009] 1 Cr.
  App. R. (S.) 89 (CA (Crim Div)), Gage, L.J.; see
  R. v Havill (Ricky Douglas) [2008] EWCA Crim
  2952, [2009] 2 Cr. App. R. (S.) 35 (CA (Crim
  Div)), Lord Judge, L.C.J.; see *R. v Smith*
  (Dave Devon) [2009] EWCA Crim 472, [2009]
  2 Cr. App. R. (S.) 87 (CA (Crim Div)), Rix, L.J.
s.51A, applied: 2009 c.25 s.125, SI 2009/1059 Art.13
s.54, amended: 2009 c.26 s.110

29. Trade Descriptions Act 1968
referred to: SI 2009/669 Sch.1 Part 2
s.24, see *Ferguson v British Gas Trading Ltd* [2009]
  EWCA Civ 46, [2009] 3 All E.R. 304 (CA (Civ
  Div)), Sedley, L.J.

41. Countryside Act 1968
s.15, applied: SI 2009/3264 Sch.2 para.1, SI 2009/
  3365 Sch.2 para.1

46. Health Services and Public Health Act 1968
s.63, amended: 2009 c.21 Sch.1 para.2
s.63, referred to: SI 2009/1511 Sch.1
s.64, referred to: SI 2009/1511 Sch.1

1968– *cont.*

48. International Organisations Act 1968
s.1, enabling: SI 2009/887, SI 2009/1748, SSI 2009/44
s.6, disapplied: SI 2009/222 Art.3
s.6, enabling: SI 2009/222
s.10, applied: SI 2009/887, SI 2009/1748, SSI 2009/44
Sch.1 Part IV, disapplied: SI 2009/222 Art.3, SI 2009/1748 Art.14, Art.15, Art.16, SSI 2009/44 Sch.1 para.6, Sch.1 para.7, Sch.3 para.6, Sch.3 para.7, Sch.4 para.7, Sch.4 para.8, Sch.6 para.6, Sch.6 para.7, Sch.7 para.6, Sch.8 para.6, Sch.8 para.7, Sch.8 para.11, Sch.9 para.6, Sch.9 para.7, Sch.12 para.8

49. Social Work (Scotland) Act 1968
Part II, applied: SSI 2009/183 Sch.1 para.12
s.5, enabling: SSI 2009/210, SSI 2009/290
s.6A, applied: SSI 2009/268 Reg.6
s.13ZA, see *M, Applicant* 2009 S.L.T. (Sh Ct) 185 (Sh Ct (North Strathclyde) (Kilmarnock)), Sheriff I S McDonald
s.16, applied: SI 2009/1547 Sch.1 para.14
s.17, applied: SI 2009/1547 Sch.3 para.2
s.44, applied: SI 2009/1547 Sch.1 para.13
s.60, applied: SI 2009/1547 Sch.3 para.2
s.61, applied: SI 2009/1547 Sch.3 para.2
s.62, applied: SI 2009/1547 Sch.1 para.21, Sch.3 para.2
s.71, applied: SI 2009/1547 Sch.3 para.2
s.87, applied: SSI 2009/72, SSI 2009/73 Reg.2, SSI 2009/381

50. Hearing Aid Council Act 1968
s.3, see *R. (on the application of Hidden Hearing Ltd) v Hearing Aid Council* [2009] EWHC 63 (Admin), (2009) 106 B.M.L.R. 110 (QBD (Admin)), Simon, J.
s.14, see *R. (on the application of Hidden Hearing Ltd) v Hearing Aid Council* [2009] EWHC 63 (Admin), (2009) 106 B.M.L.R. 110 (QBD (Admin)), Simon, J.

52. Caravan Sites Act 1968
see *Brightlingsea Haven Ltd v Morris* [2008] EWHC 1928 (QB), [2009] 2 P. & C.R. 11 (QBD), Jack, J.; see *Doherty v Birmingham City Council* [2008] UKHL 57, [2009] 1 A.C. 367 (HL), Lord Hope of Craighead
s.4, see *Doran v Liverpool City Council* [2009] EWCA Civ 146, [2009] 1 W.L.R. 2365 (CA (Civ Div)), Jacob, L.J.
s.13, see *Brightlingsea Haven Ltd v Morris* [2008] EWHC 1928 (QB), [2009] 2 P. & C.R. 11 (QBD), Jack, J.

54. Theatres Act 1968
s.4, amended: 2009 c.25 Sch.23 Part 2
s.7, amended: 2009 c.25 Sch.23 Part 2
s.8, amended: 2009 c.25 Sch.23 Part 2

55. Friendly and Industrial and Provident Societies Act 1968
s.4, applied: 2009 c.20 s.40
s.4, disapplied: 2009 c.20 s.40
s.4A, applied: 2009 c.20 s.40
s.9, referred to: 2009 c.20 s.44
s.9, varied: 2009 c.20 s.44
s.13, referred to: 2009 c.20 s.44
s.18, varied: 2009 c.20 s.44

60. Theft Act 1968
s.1, applied: SI 2009/2773 Sch.1, SI 2009/2781 Sch.1
s.9, see *R. v Downer* [2009] EWCA Crim 1361, [2009] 2 Cr. App. R. 28 (CA (Crim Div)), Scott Baker, L.J.

1968– *cont.*

60. Theft Act 1968– *cont.*
s.9, applied: SI 2009/1547 Sch.2 para.2
s.9, referred to: SI 2009/37 Sch.1 para.2, Sch.1 para.4
s.11, applied: SI 2009/2773 Sch.1, SI 2009/2781 Sch.1
s.13, applied: SI 2009/2773 Sch.1, SI 2009/2781 Sch.1
s.17, see *R. v Stapleton (Rosie)* [2008] EWCA Crim 1308, [2009] 1 Cr. App. R. (S.) 38 (CA (Crim Div)), Latham, L.J.
s.17, applied: SI 2009/2773 Sch.1, SI 2009/2781 Sch.1
s.21, applied: 2009 c.4 s.1304
s.22, applied: SI 2009/2773 Sch.1, SI 2009/2781 Sch.1
s.25, applied: SI 2009/2773 Sch.1, SI 2009/2781 Sch.1
s.26, applied: SI 2009/2056 Sch.1 para.4
Sch.1 para.2, amended: 2009 c.23 s.228
Sch.1 para.2, repealed (in part): 2009 c.23 Sch.22 Part 5

65. Gaming Act 1968
s.8, see *R. v Kelly (Derek)* [2008] EWCA Crim 137, [2009] 1 W.L.R. 701 (CA (Crim Div)), Thomas, L.J.
s.14, see *Revenue and Customs Commissioners v Rank Group* [2009] EWHC 1244 (Ch), [2009] S.T.C. 2304 (Ch D), Norris, J.
s.21, see *Revenue and Customs Commissioners v Rank Group* [2009] EWHC 1244 (Ch), [2009] S.T.C. 2304 (Ch D), Norris, J.
s.52, see *R. v Kelly (Derek)* [2008] EWCA Crim 137, [2009] 1 W.L.R. 701 (CA (Crim Div)), Thomas, L.J.

67. Medicines Act 1968
applied: SSI 2009/183 Sch.1 para.11
referred to: 2009 c.21 s.40
Part II, applied: SI 2009/389 Sch.3 para.6
s.2A, applied: SI 2009/389 Sch.5 para.2, Sch.5 para.4
s.4, applied: SI 2009/389 Sch.5 para.2, Sch.5 para.4
s.7, applied: SSI 2009/45 Art.5
s.7, disapplied: SI 2009/3062 Art.2
s.8, disapplied: SI 2009/3062 Art.2
s.15, enabling: SI 2009/3062
s.21, referred to: SI 2009/389 Reg.37
s.22, referred to: SI 2009/389 Reg.37
s.27, referred to: SI 2009/389 Reg.37
s.30, applied: SI 2009/389 Reg.18
s.44, applied: SI 2009/389 Sch.5 para.4
s.50, applied: SI 2009/389 Reg.14
s.51, applied: SI 2009/389 Reg.5, Sch.1 para.31, Sch.2 para.7
s.57, enabling: SI 2009/1165, SI 2009/3062
s.58, applied: SI 2009/1165, SI 2009/3062
s.58, enabling: SI 2009/1165, SI 2009/3062
s.61, enabling: SI 2009/3063
s.75, applied: SI 2009/716 Reg.14
s.75, enabling: SI 2009/2502, SI 2009/3071
s.76, enabling: SI 2009/3071
s.104, applied: SI 2009/716 Reg.3
s.105, applied: SI 2009/716 Reg.3
s.109, referred to: SI 2009/669 Sch.1 Part 1
s.129, applied: SI 2009/389, SI 2009/1165, SI 2009/2502, SI 2009/3062, SI 2009/3063, SI 2009/3071, SI 2009/3222
s.129, enabling: SI 2009/1165, SI 2009/2502, SI 2009/3062, SI 2009/3063, SI 2009/3071

1968–cont.

67. Medicines Act 1968–*cont.*
s.130, applied: SI 2009/716 Reg.3
Sch.1A para.6, substituted: 2009 c.21 Sch.3 para.1
Sch.2 para.5, referred to: SI 2009/389 Reg.37
Sch.2 para.6, referred to: SI 2009/389 Reg.37
Sch.2 para.7, referred to: SI 2009/389 Reg.37

70. Law Reform (Miscellaneous Provisions) (Scotland) Act 1968
s.10, amended: SI 2009/2054 Sch.1 para.6
s.10, applied: SI 2009/2054 Sch.2 para.2
s.12, amended: SI 2009/2054 Sch.1 para.6

73. Transport Act 1968
s.23A, amended: SI 2009/1941 Sch.1 para.20
s.56, amended: 2009 c.20 Sch.6 para.6
s.96, applied: SI 2009/483 Art.2
s.96, referred to: SI 2009/491 Sch.1 Part 1, SI 2009/492 Sch.2
s.97, applied: SI 2009/483 Art.2
s.97, referred to: SI 2009/491 Sch.1 Part 1, SI 2009/492 Sch.2
s.97AA, referred to: SI 2009/491 Sch.1 Part 1
s.98, applied: SI 2009/483 Art.2
s.98, referred to: SI 2009/491 Sch.1 Part 1, SI 2009/492 Sch.1 Part 1
s.99, applied: SI 2009/483 Art.3
s.99, referred to: SI 2009/491 Sch.1 Part 1, SI 2009/492 Sch.1 Part 1
s.99A, applied: SI 2009/493 Reg.3, Reg.4
s.99B, referred to: SI 2009/493 Reg.4
s.99C, applied: SI 2009/483 Art.2
s.99C, referred to: SI 2009/491 Sch.1 Part 1, SI 2009/492 Sch.1 Part 1
s.99ZC, applied: SI 2009/483 Art.3
s.99ZD, applied: SI 2009/483 Art.3
s.99ZD, referred to: SI 2009/491 Sch.1 Part 1, SI 2009/492 Sch.1 Part 1
s.99ZE, referred to: SI 2009/491 Sch.1 Part 1
s.99ZF, applied: SI 2009/483 Art.3
s.105, applied: SI 2009/1300 Sch.13 para.14
s.115, amended: SI 2009/1307 Sch.1 para.90

77. Sea Fisheries Act 1968
s.7, amended: 2009 c.23 s.239, Sch.22 Part 6
s.7, repealed (in part): 2009 c.23 s.239, Sch.22 Part 6
s.15, amended: 2009 c.23 s.202
s.15, applied: SSI 2009/443
s.15, repealed (in part): 2009 c.23 Sch.22 Part 5

1969

2. Local Government Grants (Social Need) Act 1969
s.1, amended: 2009 c.20 Sch.6 para.7

10. Mines and Quarries (Tips) Act 1969
s.34, applied: SSI 2009/319 Art.3

24. Tattooing of Minors Act 1969
applied: SI 2009/1085 Reg.13

48. Post Office Act 1969
s.86, repealed (in part): SI 2009/1941 Sch.2

51. Development of Tourism Act 1969
referred to: SI 2009/669 Sch.1 Part 2

54. Children and Young Persons Act 1969
s.12AA, applied: SI 2009/1547 Sch.1 para.8
s.32, amended: 2009 c.26 Sch.7 para.18, Sch.8 Part 2
s.32, applied: SI 2009/1547 Sch.3 para.7

1969–cont.

57. Employers Liability (Compulsory Insurance) Act 1969
see *Durham v BAI (Run Off) Ltd* [2008] EWHC 2692 (QB), [2009] 2 All E.R. 26 (QBD), Burton, J.
s.3, amended: 2009 c.20 Sch.6 para.8

58. Administration of Justice Act 1969
s.12, applied: SI 2009/1603 r.11, r.43
s.13, applied: SI 2009/1603 r.11, r.43

1970

9. Taxes Management Act 1970
see *Monro v Revenue and Customs Commissioners* [2008] EWCA Civ 306, [2009] Ch. 69 (CA (Civ Div)), Mummery, L.J.; see *Morgan v Revenue and Customs Commissioners* [2009] UKFTT 78 (TC), [2009] S.F.T.D. 160 (FTT (Tax)), Nuala Brice (Chairman)
applied: 2009 c.10 Sch.22 para.16, Sch.52 para.11
referred to: SI 2009/470 Reg.31
varied: SI 2009/317 Sch.1
Part IV, substituted: 2009 c.10 Sch.52 para.4
Part V, applied: 2009 c.8 s.24, 2009 c.10 Sch.46 para.10, SI 2009/2998 Reg.5
Part V, amended: SI 2009/56 Sch.1 para.26
Part VI, applied: 2009 c.8 s.12, s.13, SI 2009/470 Reg.37, SI 2009/2997 Reg.20
s.1, applied: SI 2009/470 Reg.10
s.2, applied: SI 2009/196 Art.9
s.4, applied: SI 2009/56 Art.5, SI 2009/196 Art.9
s.4, repealed: SI 2009/56 Sch.1 para.6
s.4A, applied: SI 2009/56 Art.5
s.4A, repealed: SI 2009/56 Sch.1 para.6
s.5, repealed: SI 2009/56 Sch.1 para.6
s.6, repealed (in part): SI 2009/56 Sch.1 para.6
s.7, applied: 2009 c.10 Sch.53 para.3, SI 2009/470 Reg.35
s.8, amended: 2009 c.10 Sch.19 para.9
s.8, applied: 2009 c.10 Sch.53 para.3, Sch.55 para.1, SI 2009/403 Art.10, SI 2009/470 Reg.28, Reg.29, Reg.30, Reg.31, Reg.35, Reg.40
s.8A, see *Revenue and Customs Commissioners' Application (Section 20 Notice: Financial Institution No.5), Re (TC 9)* [2009] UKFTT 68 (TC), [2009] S.T.C. (S.C.D.) 488 (Sp Comm), John F Avery Jones
s.8A, amended: 2009 c.10 Sch.19 para.9
s.8A, applied: 2009 c.10 Sch.55 para.1, SI 2009/403 Art.10
s.9, see *Eyretel Unapproved Pension Scheme Trustees v Revenue and Customs Commissioners* [2009] S.T.C. (S.C.D.) 17 (Sp Comm), J F Avery Jones (Chairman)
s.9, amended: 2009 c.10 Sch.19 para.9
s.9, applied: SI 2009/470 Reg.31
s.9A, see *Clarke v Revenue and Customs Commissioners* [2009] S.T.C. (S.C.D.) 278 (Sp Comm), Charles Hellier; see *Lee v Revenue and Customs Commissioners* [2009] S.T.C. (S.C.D.) 1 (Sp Comm), David Williams
s.9A, applied: SI 2009/470 Reg.31
s.12, amended: 2009 c.4 Sch.1 para.296
s.12, repealed: SI 2009/2035 Sch.1 para.2
s.12AA, amended: 2009 c.10 Sch.19 para.9
s.12AA, applied: 2009 c.10 Sch.55 para.1, SI 2009/403 Art.10
s.12AA, repealed (in part): SI 2009/2035 Sch.1 para.3

1970–cont.

9. Taxes Management Act 1970–cont.

s.12AB, amended: 2009 c.10 Sch.19 para.9

s.12AE, repealed: 2009 c.4 Sch.3 Part 1

s.12B, amended: SI 2009/56 Sch.1 para.7, SI 2009/2035 Sch.1 para.4

s.12B, varied: SI 2009/470 Reg.32

s.13, applied: SI 2009/470 Reg.33

s.15, applied: SI 2009/470 Reg.33

s.16, applied: SI 2009/470 Reg.33

s.16A, applied: SI 2009/470 Reg.33

s.17, amended: 2009 c.4 Sch.1 para.298

s.18, amended: 2009 c.4 Sch.1 para.299

s.19, amended: 2009 c.4 Sch.1 para.300

s.19, repealed (in part): 2009 c.4 Sch.3 Part 1

s.19A, see *Clarke v Revenue and Customs Commissioners* [2009] S.T.C. (S.C.D.) 278 (Sp Comm), Charles Hellier; see *Sokoya v Revenue and Customs Commissioners* [2009] UKFTT 163 (TC), [2009] S.F.T.D. 480 (FTT (Tax)), Roger Berner

s.19A, amended: SI 2009/56 Sch.1 para.8

s.19A, applied: SI 2009/404 Art.3

s.20, see *Chemists (A Firm) v Revenue and Customs Commissioners* [2009] UKFTT 66 (TC), [2009] S.T.C. (S.C.D.) 472 (Sp Comm), Nicholas Aleksander; see *Clarke v Revenue and Customs Commissioners* [2009] S.T.C. (S.C.D.) 278 (Sp Comm), Charles Hellier; see *Eclipse Film Partners No.35 LLP v Revenue and Customs Commissioners* [2009] S.T.C. (S.C.D.) 293 (Sp Comm), Edward Sadler; see *Pattullo, Petitioner* [2009] CSOH 137 (OH), Lord Bannatyne; see *Paulden Activities Ltd, Petitioners* [2009] CSOH 55, [2009] S.T.C. 1884 (OH), Lord Kinclaven; see *Revenue and Customs Commissioners' Application (Section 20 Notice: Financial Institution No.5), Re (TC 9)* [2009] UKFTT 68 (TC), [2009] S.T.C. (S.C.D.) 488 (Sp Comm), John F Avery Jones; see *Revenue and Customs Commissioners' Application (Section 20 Notice: Financial Institution No.8), Re (TC 11)* [2009] UKFTT 70 (TC), [2009] S.T.I. 1805 (Sp Comm), John F Avery Jones; see *Revenue and Customs Commissioners' Application (Section 20 Notice: Financial Institutions Nos.6 and 7), Re (TC 10)* [2009] UKFTT 69 (TC), [2009] S.T.C. (S.C.D.) 493 (Sp Comm), John F Avery Jones; see *Revenue and Customs Commissioners v Wilson* [2009] S.T.C. (S.C.D.) 130 (Sp Comm), Theodore Wallace

s.20, amended: SI 2009/56 Sch.1 para.9

s.20, applied: SI 2009/275 Art.3, SI 2009/404 Art.4, Art.9, Art.10

s.20A, applied: SI 2009/470 Reg.33

s.20B, amended: SI 2009/56 Sch.1 para.10

s.20B, applied: SI 2009/275 Art.3, SI 2009/404 Art.10

s.20BA, applied: SI 2009/470 Reg.33

s.20BB, amended: SI 2009/56 Sch.1 para.11

s.20BB, applied: SI 2009/275 Art.3, SI 2009/404 Art.10, SI 2009/470 Reg.33

s.20BB, referred to: SI 2009/404 Art.4

s.20C, see *R. (on the application of Mercury Tax Group Ltd) v Revenue and Customs Commissioners* [2008] EWHC 2721 (Admin), [2009] S.T.C. 743 (QBD (Admin)), Underhill, J.

s.20D, applied: SI 2009/404 Art.10

s.22, repealed: SI 2009/2035 Sch.1 para.5

s.25, amended: 2009 c.10 Sch.22 para.11

1970–cont.

9. Taxes Management Act 1970–cont.

s.28, amended: 2009 c.10 Sch.22 para.11

s.28, repealed: SI 2009/2035 Sch.1 para.6

s.28A, amended: SI 2009/56 Sch.1 para.17

s.28A, varied: SI 2009/470 Reg.34

s.28AA, varied: SI 2009/470 Reg.34

s.28AB, varied: SI 2009/470 Reg.34

s.28B, see *Eclipse Film Partners No.35 LLP v Revenue and Customs Commissioners* [2009] S.T.C. (S.C.D.) 293 (Sp Comm), Edward Sadler

s.28B, amended: SI 2009/56 Sch.1 para.18

s.28B, varied: SI 2009/470 Reg.34

s.28C, applied: SI 2009/470 Reg.34

s.28C, varied: SI 2009/470 Reg.34

s.28D, varied: SI 2009/470 Reg.34

s.28E, varied: SI 2009/470 Reg.34

s.28F, varied: SI 2009/470 Reg.34

s.28ZA, amended: SI 2009/56 Sch.1 para.12

s.28ZA, repealed (in part): SI 2009/56 Sch.1 para.12

s.28ZB, amended: SI 2009/56 Sch.1 para.13

s.28ZB, repealed (in part): SI 2009/56 Sch.1 para.13

s.28ZC, repealed: SI 2009/56 Sch.1 para.14

s.28ZD, amended: SI 2009/56 Sch.1 para.15

s.28ZE, amended: SI 2009/56 Sch.1 para.16

s.29, see *Coll v Revenue and Customs Commissioners* [2009] UKFTT 61 (TC), [2009] S.F.T.D. 101 (FTT (Tax)), Michael Tildesley OBE; see *Lee v Revenue and Customs Commissioners* [2009] S.T.C. (S.C.D.) 1 (Sp Comm), David Williams; see *Pattullo, Petitioner* [2009] CSOH 137 (OH), Lord Bannatyne

s.29, varied: SI 2009/470 Reg.34

s.30, applied: 2009 c.10 Sch.53 para.5

s.30, varied: SI 2009/470 Reg.34

s.30A, varied: SI 2009/470 Reg.34

s.30B, varied: SI 2009/470 Reg.34

s.31, amended: SI 2009/56 Sch.1 para.19

s.31, repealed (in part): 2009 c.4 Sch.3 Part 1

s.31, varied: SI 2009/470 Reg.34

s.31A, repealed (in part): SI 2009/56 Sch.1 para.20

s.31A, varied: SI 2009/470 Reg.34

s.31B, repealed: SI 2009/56 Sch.1 para.21

s.31B, varied: SI 2009/470 Reg.34

s.31C, repealed: SI 2009/56 Sch.1 para.21

s.31C, varied: SI 2009/470 Reg.34

s.31D, repealed: SI 2009/56 Sch.1 para.21

s.31D, varied: SI 2009/470 Reg.34

s.32, amended: SI 2009/56 Sch.1 para.22

s.32, varied: SI 2009/470 Reg.34

s.32A, varied: SI 2009/470 Reg.34

s.33, see *Monro v Revenue and Customs Commissioners* [2008] EWCA Civ 306, [2009] Ch. 69 (CA (Civ Div)), Mummery, L.J.

s.33, amended: SI 2009/56 Sch.1 para.23

s.33, substituted: 2009 c.10 Sch.52 para.1

s.33, varied: SI 2009/470 Reg.34

s.33A, amended: SI 2009/56 Sch.1 para.24

s.33A, substituted: 2009 c.10 Sch.52 para.1

s.33A, varied: SI 2009/470 Reg.34

s.34, applied: SI 2009/2997 Reg.20

s.34, varied: SI 2009/470 Reg.34

s.35, applied: SI 2009/2997 Reg.20

s.35, varied: SI 2009/470 Reg.34

s.36, see *Adams v Revenue and Customs Commissioners* [2009] UKFTT 80 (TC), [2009] S.F.T.D. 184 (FTT (Tax)), Theodore Wallace; see *Bird v Revenue and Customs*

1970– cont.

9. Taxes Management Act 1970–*cont.*
s.36–*cont.*
    Commissioners [2009] S.T.C. (S.C.D.) 81 (Sp Comm), Sir Stephen Oliver Q.C.; see *Coll v Revenue and Customs Commissioners* [2009] UKFTT 61 (TC), [2009] S.F.T.D. 101 (FTT (Tax)), Michael Tildesley OBE; see *Rouf (t/a New Balaka Restaurant) v General Commissioners of Income Tax* [2009] CSIH 6, [2009] S.T.C. 1307 (IH (Ex Div)), Lord Osborne
s.36, amended: 2009 c.10 Sch.1 para.6, Sch.51 para.41
s.36, applied: SI 2009/2997 Reg.20
s.36, disapplied: SI 2009/403 Art.7
s.36, varied: SI 2009/470 Reg.34
s.37, varied: SI 2009/470 Reg.34
s.37A, amended: 2009 c.10 Sch.1 para.6
s.37A, varied: SI 2009/470 Reg.34
s.38, varied: SI 2009/470 Reg.34
s.39, varied: SI 2009/470 Reg.34
s.40, varied: SI 2009/470 Reg.34
s.41, varied: SI 2009/470 Reg.34
s.41A, varied: SI 2009/470 Reg.34
s.41B, varied: SI 2009/470 Reg.34
s.41C, varied: SI 2009/470 Reg.34
s.42, amended: 2009 c.4 Sch.1 para.302, Sch.3 Part 1
s.42, repealed (in part): 2009 c.4 Sch.3 Part 1
s.42, varied: SI 2009/470 Reg.34
s.43, varied: SI 2009/470 Reg.34
s.43A, amended: 2009 c.10 Sch.1 para.6, Sch.52 para.5
s.43A, varied: SI 2009/470 Reg.34
s.43B, varied: SI 2009/470 Reg.34
s.43C, varied: SI 2009/470 Reg.34
s.44, see *Wright v Revenue and Customs Commissioners* [2009] UKFTT 227 (TC), [2009] S.F.T.D. 748 (FTT (Tax)), Theodore Wallace
s.44, repealed: SI 2009/56 Sch.1 para.25
s.44, varied: SI 2009/470 Reg.34
s.45, repealed: SI 2009/56 Sch.1 para.25
s.45, varied: SI 2009/470 Reg.34
s.46, repealed: SI 2009/56 Sch.1 para.25
s.46, varied: SI 2009/470 Reg.34
s.46A, repealed: SI 2009/56 Sch.1 para.25
s.46A, varied: SI 2009/470 Reg.34
s.46B, amended: 2009 c.4 Sch.1 para.303
s.46B, repealed: SI 2009/56 Sch.1 para.25
s.46B, varied: SI 2009/470 Reg.34
s.46C, repealed: SI 2009/56 Sch.1 para.25
s.46C, varied: SI 2009/470 Reg.34
s.46D, amended: SI 2009/1307 Sch.1 para.96
s.46D, varied: SI 2009/470 Reg.34
s.47, applied: SI 2009/1114 Art.6
s.47, varied: SI 2009/470 Reg.34
s.47A, applied: SI 2009/1114 Art.6
s.47A, varied: SI 2009/470 Reg.34
s.47B, amended: SI 2009/1307 Sch.1 para.97
s.47B, varied: SI 2009/470 Reg.34
s.47C, added: SI 2009/56 Sch.1 para.27
s.47C, varied: SI 2009/470 Reg.34
s.48, applied: SI 2009/2998 Reg.5
s.48, referred to: SI 2009/2998 Reg.5
s.48, substituted: SI 2009/56 Sch.1 para.28
s.48, varied: SI 2009/470 Reg.34
s.49, see *R. (on the application of Cook) v General Commissioners of Income Tax* [2009] EWHC 590 (Admin), [2009] S.T.C. 1212 (QBD (Admin)), Dyson, L.J.

1970– cont.

9. Taxes Management Act 1970–*cont.*
s.49, applied: SI 2009/2997 Reg.20
s.49, substituted: SI 2009/56 Sch.1 para.29
s.49, varied: SI 2009/470 Reg.34
s.49A, added: SI 2009/56 Sch.1 para.30
s.49A, varied: SI 2009/470 Reg.34
s.49B, added: SI 2009/56 Sch.1 para.30
s.49B, varied: SI 2009/470 Reg.34
s.49C, added: SI 2009/56 Sch.1 para.30
s.49C, varied: SI 2009/470 Reg.34
s.49D, added: SI 2009/56 Sch.1 para.30
s.49D, varied: SI 2009/470 Reg.34
s.49E, added: SI 2009/56 Sch.1 para.30
s.49E, varied: SI 2009/470 Reg.34
s.49F, added: SI 2009/56 Sch.1 para.30
s.49F, varied: SI 2009/470 Reg.34
s.49G, added: SI 2009/56 Sch.1 para.30
s.49G, varied: SI 2009/470 Reg.34
s.49H, added: SI 2009/56 Sch.1 para.30
s.49H, varied: SI 2009/470 Reg.34
s.49I, added: SI 2009/56 Sch.1 para.30
s.49I, varied: SI 2009/470 Reg.34
s.50, amended: SI 2009/56 Sch.1 para.31
s.50, disapplied: SI 2009/2998 Reg.5
s.50, varied: SI 2009/470 Reg.34
s.51, varied: SI 2009/470 Reg.34
s.52, varied: SI 2009/470 Reg.34
s.53, repealed: SI 2009/56 Sch.1 para.32
s.53, varied: SI 2009/470 Reg.34
s.54, amended: SI 2009/56 Sch.1 para.33
s.54, applied: SI 2009/2997 Reg.20
s.54, varied: SI 2009/470 Reg.34
s.55, amended: SI 2009/56 Sch.1 para.34
s.55, applied: 2009 c.10 Sch.53 para.4, Sch.53 para.15, Sch.56 para.1, SI 2009/470 Reg.36
s.55, repealed (in part): SI 2009/56 Sch.1 para.34
s.55, varied: SI 2009/470 Reg.34
s.56, substituted: SI 2009/56 Sch.1 para.35
s.56, varied: SI 2009/56 Sch.3 para.11, SI 2009/470 Reg.34
s.56A, repealed: SI 2009/56 Sch.1 para.36
s.56A, varied: SI 2009/470 Reg.34
s.56B, repealed: SI 2009/56 Sch.1 para.36
s.56B, varied: SI 2009/470 Reg.34
s.56C, repealed: SI 2009/56 Sch.1 para.36
s.56C, varied: SI 2009/470 Reg.34
s.56D, repealed: SI 2009/56 Sch.1 para.36
s.56D, varied: SI 2009/470 Reg.34
s.57, amended: SI 2009/56 Sch.1 para.37
s.57, repealed (in part): SI 2009/56 Sch.1 para.37
s.57, varied: SI 2009/470 Reg.34
s.57A, varied: SI 2009/470 Reg.34
s.57B, varied: SI 2009/470 Reg.34
s.58, repealed: SI 2009/56 Sch.1 para.38
s.58, varied: SI 2009/56 Sch.3 para.11, SI 2009/470 Reg.34
s.59, varied: SI 2009/470 Reg.34
s.59A, amended: 2009 c.10 Sch.19 para.9
s.59A, applied: 2009 c.10 s.111, Sch.53 para.1, Sch.53 para.2, Sch.53 para.15, Sch.54 para.13
s.59B, amended: 2009 c.10 Sch.19 para.9
s.59B, applied: 2009 c.10 s.111, Sch.53 para.15, Sch.54 para.13, Sch.56 para.1, SI 2009/470 Reg.35, Reg.36
s.59B, disapplied: SI 2009/470 Reg.35
s.59B, referred to: 2009 c.10 Sch.56 para.1
s.59B, varied: SI 2009/470 Reg.35, Reg.40

1970–cont.

9. Taxes Management Act 1970–*cont.*

s.59C, amended: SI 2009/56 Sch.1 para.39, SI 2009/571 Sch.1 para.11

s.59C, applied: 2009 c.10 s.108, SI 2009/470 Reg.36

s.59C, varied: 2009 c.10 s.68

s.59D, applied: 2009 c.10 s.111

s.59DA, amended: SI 2009/56 Sch.1 para.40

s.59E, applied: 2009 c.10 Sch.56 para.1

s.60, varied: 2009 c.8 s.22

s.61, varied: 2009 c.8 s.22

s.62, varied: 2009 c.8 s.22

s.63, applied: SI 2009/3024 Art.4, SSI 2009/403 Art.3

s.63, varied: 2009 c.8 s.22

s.63A, varied: 2009 c.8 s.22

s.64, varied: 2009 c.8 s.22

s.65, varied: 2009 c.8 s.22

s.66, applied: SI 2009/470 Reg.57

s.66, varied: 2009 c.8 s.22

s.67, applied: SI 2009/470 Reg.57

s.67, varied: 2009 c.8 s.22

s.68, varied: 2009 c.8 s.22

s.69, varied: 2009 c.8 s.22, SI 2009/470 Reg.69

s.70, see *Advocate General for Scotland v Montgomery* [2009] S.T.C. 2387 (OH), Lady Paton

s.70, varied: 2009 c.8 s.22

s.70A, varied: 2009 c.8 s.22

s.71, amended: 2009 c.4 Sch.3 Part 1

s.72, applied: SI 2009/470 Reg.38

s.74, applied: SI 2009/470 Reg.38

s.75, applied: SI 2009/470 Reg.38

s.76, applied: SI 2009/470 Reg.38

s.86, applied: SI 2009/470 Reg.39, Reg.58, Reg.63

s.87A, amended: 2009 c.4 Sch.1 para.305

s.90, amended: 2009 c.4 Sch.1 para.306

s.90, applied: SI 2009/470 Reg.39

s.90, repealed (in part): 2009 c.4 Sch.3 Part 1

s.91, applied: SI 2009/470 Reg.39

s.93, amended: SI 2009/56 Sch.1 para.41, SI 2009/2035 Sch.1 para.7

s.93, applied: SI 2009/470 Reg.40

s.93, referred to: SI 2009/470 Reg.40

s.93A, amended: SI 2009/56 Sch.1 para.42

s.95, see *Coll v Revenue and Customs Commissioners* [2009] UKFTT 61 (TC), [2009] S.F.T.D. 101 (FTT (Tax)), Michael Tildesley OBE; see *Revenue and Customs Commissioners v Khawaja* [2008] EWHC 1687 (Ch), [2009] 1 W.L.R. 398 (Ch D), Mann, J.; see *Stockler v Revenue and Customs Commissioners* [2009] EWHC 2306 (Ch), [2009] S.T.C. 2602 (Ch D), Sir John Lindsay; see *Stockler v Revenue and Customs Commissioners* [2009] S.T.C. (S.C.D.) 333 (Sp Comm), John Clark

s.95, referred to: SI 2009/470 Reg.40

s.95, varied: SI 2009/470 Reg.40

s.95A, see *Stockler v Revenue and Customs Commissioners* [2009] S.T.C. (S.C.D.) 333 (Sp Comm), John Clark

s.97, varied: SI 2009/470 Reg.40

s.97AA, see *Sokoya v Revenue and Customs Commissioners* [2009] UKFTT 163 (TC), [2009] S.F.T.D. 480 (FTT (Tax)), Roger Berner

s.97AA, amended: SI 2009/56 Sch.1 para.43

s.97AA, referred to: SI 2009/404 Art.3

1970–cont.

9. Taxes Management Act 1970–*cont.*

s.98, see *Revenue and Customs Commissioners v Wilson* [2009] S.T.C. (S.C.D.) 130 (Sp Comm), Theodore Wallace

s.98, amended: 2009 c.4 Sch.1 para.307, Sch.3 Part 1, 2009 c.10 Sch.15 para.95, Sch.17 para.2, Sch.17 para.10, Sch.25 para.9, SI 2009/2035 Sch.1 para.8

s.98, repealed (in part): 2009 c.10 Sch.17 para.2

s.98, varied: SI 2009/470 Reg.13

s.98A, applied: SI 2009/470 Reg.59

s.98B, amended: SI 2009/56 Sch.1 para.44

s.99, varied: SI 2009/470 Reg.13

s.100, applied: SI 2009/470 Reg.13, SI 2009/2034 Reg.22

s.100, repealed (in part): 2009 c.10 Sch.57 para.13

s.100, varied: SI 2009/470 Reg.13

s.100A, applied: SI 2009/470 Reg.13, SI 2009/2034 Reg.22

s.100A, varied: SI 2009/470 Reg.13

s.100B, amended: SI 2009/56 Sch.1 para.45, SI 2009/571 Sch.1 para.12

s.100B, applied: SI 2009/470 Reg.13, SI 2009/2034 Reg.22

s.100B, varied: SI 2009/470 Reg.13

s.100C, amended: SI 2009/56 Sch.1 para.46

s.100C, applied: SI 2009/470 Reg.13

s.100C, repealed (in part): SI 2009/56 Sch.1 para.46

s.100C, varied: SI 2009/470 Reg.13

s.100D, varied: SI 2009/470 Reg.13

s.101, amended: SI 2009/56 Sch.1 para.47

s.102, applied: SI 2009/2034 Reg.22

s.102, varied: SI 2009/470 Reg.13

s.103, amended: SI 2009/56 Sch.1 para.48

s.103, applied: SI 2009/2034 Reg.22

s.103, varied: SI 2009/470 Reg.13

s.103A, varied: SI 2009/470 Reg.13

s.103ZA, added: 2009 c.10 Sch.57 para.13

s.104, varied: SI 2009/470 Reg.13

s.105, varied: SI 2009/470 Reg.13

s.107A, amended: SI 2009/571 Sch.1 para.13

s.108, amended: SI 2009/1890 Art.3

s.108, applied: 2009 c.10 Sch.15 para.17, Sch.15 para.21, Sch.15 para.29, Sch.15 para.33, Sch.46 para.13, Sch.49 para.7

s.109, see *Advocate General for Scotland v Montgomery* [2009] S.T.C. 2387 (OH), Lady Paton

s.109A, added: 2009 c.4 Sch.1 para.308

s.110, repealed: SI 2009/3054 Sch.1 para.1

s.111, repealed: SI 2009/3054 Sch.1 para.1

s.112, amended: SI 2009/56 Sch.1 para.49

s.112, applied: SI 2009/470 Reg.13

s.112, repealed (in part): SI 2009/56 Sch.1 para.49

s.112, varied: SI 2009/470 Reg.13

s.113, varied: SI 2009/470 Reg.13

s.114, applied: 2009 c.10 Sch.46 para.13, Sch.49 para.7

s.114, varied: SI 2009/470 Reg.13

s.115, amended: SI 2009/56 Sch.1 para.50

s.115, applied: 2009 c.10 Sch.46 para.13, Sch.49 para.7

s.115, repealed (in part): SI 2009/56 Sch.1 para.50

s.115, varied: SI 2009/470 Reg.13

s.115A, varied: SI 2009/470 Reg.13

s.118, see *Sokoya v Revenue and Customs Commissioners* [2009] UKFTT 163 (TC), [2009] S.F.T.D. 480 (FTT (Tax)), Roger Berner

s.118, amended: 2009 c.4 Sch.1 para.309, SI 2009/56 Sch.1 para.51

1970– cont.

9. Taxes Management Act 1970–*cont.*
s.118, applied: SI 2009/2034 Reg.22
s.118, varied: SI 2009/470 Reg.13
Sch.1 Part I, repealed: SI 2009/56 Sch.1 para.52
Sch.1 Part II, repealed: SI 2009/56 Sch.1 para.52
Sch.1 Part III, repealed: SI 2009/56 Sch.1 para.52
Sch.1 AB para.1, added: 2009 c.10 Sch.52 para.2
Sch.1 AB para.2, added: 2009 c.10 Sch.52 para.2
Sch.1 AB para.3, added: 2009 c.10 Sch.52 para.2
Sch.1 AB para.3, referred to: 2009 c.10 Sch.52 para.10
Sch.1 AB para.3, varied: 2009 c.10 Sch.52 para.10
Sch.1 AB para.4, added: 2009 c.10 Sch.52 para.2
Sch.1 AB para.5, added: 2009 c.10 Sch.52 para.2
Sch.1 AB para.6, added: 2009 c.10 Sch.52 para.2
Sch.1 AB para.7, added: 2009 c.10 Sch.52 para.2
Sch.1 AB para.8, added: 2009 c.10 Sch.52 para.2
Sch.1 AB para.9, added: 2009 c.10 Sch.52 para.2
Sch.1 A para.1, amended: 2009 c.10 Sch.52 para.6, Sch.52 para.17
Sch.1 A para.2, amended: SI 2009/2035 Sch.1 para.9
Sch.1 A para.2, repealed (in part): SI 2009/2035 Sch.1 para.9
Sch.1 A para.2A, amended: SI 2009/56 Sch.1 para.54
Sch.1 A para.4, amended: 2009 c.10 Sch.52 para.7
Sch.1 A para.6, applied: SI 2009/404 Art.5
Sch.1 A para.6, referred to: SI 2009/404 Art.5
Sch.1 A para.6A, amended: SI 2009/56 Sch.1 para.55
Sch.1 A para.6A, referred to: SI 2009/404 Art.5
Sch.1 A para.7, amended: SI 2009/56 Sch.1 para.56
Sch.1 A para.9, amended: SI 2009/56 Sch.1 para.57
Sch.1 A para.10, repealed: SI 2009/56 Sch.1 para.58
Sch.1 A para.11, repealed: SI 2009/56 Sch.1 para.58
Sch.1 B para.2, applied: 2009 c.10 Sch.6 para.2, Sch.54 para.7
Sch.3, repealed: SI 2009/56 Sch.1 para.59
Sch.3A, applied: SI 2009/470 Reg.13
Sch.3 para.1, repealed: SI 2009/56 Sch.1 para.59
Sch.3 para.2, repealed: SI 2009/56 Sch.1 para.59
Sch.3 para.3, repealed: SI 2009/56 Sch.1 para.59
Sch.3 para.4, repealed: SI 2009/56 Sch.1 para.59
Sch.3 para.5, repealed: SI 2009/56 Sch.1 para.59
Sch.3 para.6, repealed: SI 2009/56 Sch.1 para.59
Sch.3 para.7, repealed: SI 2009/56 Sch.1 para.59
Sch.3 para.8, repealed: SI 2009/56 Sch.1 para.59
Sch.3 para.9, repealed: SI 2009/56 Sch.1 para.59
Sch.3 para.10, amended: 2009 c.4 Sch.1 para.310, Sch.3 Part 1
Sch.3 para.10, repealed: SI 2009/56 Sch.1 para.59
Sch.3A Part I para.1, varied: SI 2009/470 Reg.13
Sch.3A Part I para.2, varied: SI 2009/470 Reg.13
Sch.3A Part II para.3, varied: SI 2009/470 Reg.13
Sch.3A Part III para.4, amended: SI 2009/56 Sch.1 para.61
Sch.3A Part III para.4, varied: SI 2009/470 Reg.13
Sch.3A Part III para.5, varied: SI 2009/470 Reg.13
Sch.3A Part III para.6, varied: SI 2009/470 Reg.13
Sch.3A Part III para.7, varied: SI 2009/470 Reg.13
Sch.3A Part IV para.8, varied: SI 2009/470 Reg.13
Sch.3A Part IV para.9, varied: SI 2009/470 Reg.13
Sch.3A Part V para.10, varied: SI 2009/470 Reg.13
Sch.3A Part V para.11, amended: SI 2009/56 Sch.1 para.62
Sch.3A Part V para.11, varied: SI 2009/470 Reg.13
Sch.3ZA para.10, repealed: 2009 c.10 Sch.52 para.8

1970– cont.

30. Conservation of Seals Act 1970
s.10, amended: 2009 c.23 Sch.11 para.1
s.10, applied: 2009 c.23 s.9

34. Marriage (Registrar General's Licence) Act 1970
s.2, enabling: SI 2009/2806
s.18, enabling: SI 2009/2806

35. Conveyancing and Feudal Reform (Scotland) Act 1970
s.9, applied: SI 2009/1917 Reg.9, SSI 2009/266 Sch.4 para.46
s.24, see *Royal Bank of Scotland Plc v Wilson* [2009] CSIH 36, 2009 S.L.T. 729 (IH (Ex Div)), Lord Nimmo Smith
s.50, repealed (in part): SI 2009/1307 Sch.4
Sch.3 para.9, see *Royal Bank of Scotland Plc v Wilson* [2009] CSIH 36, 2009 S.L.T. 729 (IH (Ex Div)), Lord Nimmo Smith
Sch.7, see *Royal Bank of Scotland Plc v Wilson* [2009] CSIH 36, 2009 S.L.T. 729 (IH (Ex Div)), Lord Nimmo Smith

39. Local Authorities (Goods and Services) Act 1970
s.1, amended: 2009 c.20 Sch.6 para.9
s.1, applied: 2009 c.22 Sch.12 para.3

40. Agriculture Act 1970
s.66, applied: SI 2009/716 Reg.3
s.66, enabling: SI 2009/28, SI 2009/106, SI 2009/2825, SI 2009/2881, SSI 2009/21, SSI 2009/373
s.68, enabling: SI 2009/28, SI 2009/106, SSI 2009/21
s.69, enabling: SI 2009/28, SI 2009/106, SSI 2009/21
s.74A, enabling: SI 2009/28, SI 2009/106, SI 2009/2825, SI 2009/2881, SSI 2009/21, SSI 2009/373
s.84, applied: SI 2009/28, SI 2009/106, SI 2009/2881, SSI 2009/21, SSI 2009/373
s.84, enabling: SI 2009/28, SI 2009/106, SI 2009/2825, SI 2009/2881, SSI 2009/21, SSI 2009/373
s.92, repealed: 2009 asp 6 Sch.3 para.2
s.94, repealed: 2009 asp 6 Sch.3 para.2

41. Equal Pay Act 1970
see *Carl v University of Sheffield* [2009] 3 C.M.L.R. 21 (EAT), Judge Peter Clark; see *Chief Constable of West Midlands v Blackburn* [2008] EWCA Civ 1208, [2009] I.R.L.R. 135 (CA (Civ Div)), Scott Baker, L.J.; see *Coventry City Council v Nicholls* [2009] I.R.L.R. 345 (EAT), Elias, J (President); see *Hartlepool BC v Dolphin* [2009] I.R.L.R. 168 (EAT), Judge McMullen Q.C.; see *Sodexo Ltd v Gutridge* [2009] EWCA Civ 729, [2009] I.C.R. 1486 (CA (Civ Div)), Pill, L.J.; see *Suffolk Mental Health Partnership NHS Trust v Hurst* [2009] EWCA Civ 309, [2009] I.C.R. 1011 (CA (Civ Div)), Pill, L.J.
s.1, see *Carl v University of Sheffield* [2009] 3 C.M.L.R. 21 (EAT), Judge Peter Clark; see *Dumfries and Galloway Council v North* [2009] I.C.R. 1363 (EAT), Lady Smith; see *Hartlepool BC v Dolphin* [2009] I.R.L.R. 168 (EAT), Judge McMullen Q.C.; see *Hartlepool BC v Llewellyn* [2009] I.C.R. 1426 (EAT), Underhill, J. (President); see *Hovell v Ashford and St Peter's Hospital NHS Trust* [2009] EWCA Civ 670, [2009] I.C.R. 1545 (CA (Civ Div)), Mummery, L.J.; see *Hovell v Ashford and St Peter's Hospital NHS Trust* [2009] I.C.R. 254 (EAT), Judge Peter Clark; see *North Cumbria Acute Hospitals NHS Trust v Potter* [2009] I.R.L.R.

1970– cont.

41. Equal Pay Act 1970–*cont.*
s.1–*cont.*
176 (EAT), Nelson, J.; see *Redcar and Cleveland BC v Bainbridge* [2008] EWCA Civ 885, [2009] I.C.R. 133 (CA (Civ Div)), Mummery, L.J.
s.2, see *Slack v Cumbria CC* [2009] EWCA Civ 293, [2009] 3 C.M.L.R. 8 (CA (Civ Div)), Mummery, L.J.; see *Sodexo Ltd v Gutridge* [2009] EWCA Civ 729, [2009] I.C.R. 1486 (CA (Civ Div)), Pill, L.J.
s.2ZA, see *Slack v Cumbria CC* [2009] EWCA Civ 293, [2009] 3 C.M.L.R. 8 (CA (Civ Div)), Mummery, L.J.; see *Sodexo Ltd v Gutridge* [2009] EWCA Civ 729, [2009] I.C.R. 1486 (CA (Civ Div)), Pill, L.J.; see *Sodexo Ltd v Gutridge* [2009] I.C.R. 70 (EAT), Elias, J.
s.7A, applied: SI 2009/1059 Art.196
s.7AB, applied: SI 2009/1059 Art.196
s.7AC, applied: SI 2009/1059 Art.196

42. Local Authority Social Services Act 1970
applied: 2009 c.15 s.2, s.3
s.1, referred to: 2009 c.15 s.3
s.1A, referred to: 2009 c.15 s.2, s.3
s.7, applied: 2009 c.15 s.3
Sch.1, amended: 2009 c.22 s.195

44. Chronically Sick and Disabled Persons Act 1970
s.2, see *R. (on the application of Z) v Hillingdon LBC* [2009] EWHC 1398 (Admin), (2009) 12 C.C.L. Rep. 429 (QBD (Admin)), Timothy Brennan Q.C.
s.17, referred to: SI 2009/1511 Sch.1
s.21, applied: SSI 2009/79 Art.7, Art.8

45. Matrimonial Proceedings and Property Act 1970
s.37, see *Hameed v Qayyum* [2008] EWHC 2274 (Ch), [2009] B.P.I.R. 35 (Ch D), Judge Purle Q.C.

1971

19. Carriage of Goods by Sea Act 1971
Sch.1, see *Bulk & Metal Transport (UK) LLP v Voc Bulk Ultra Handymax Pool LLC (Voc Gallant)* [2009] EWHC 288 (Comm), [2009] 2 All E.R. (Comm) 377 (QBD (Comm)), Judge Mackie Q.C.

22. Animals Act 1971
s.2, see *Freeman v Higher Park Farm* [2008] EWCA Civ 1185, [2009] P.I.Q.R. P6 (CA (Civ Div)), Tuckey, L.J.
s.5, see *Freeman v Higher Park Farm* [2008] EWCA Civ 1185, [2009] P.I.Q.R. P6 (CA (Civ Div)), Tuckey, L.J.

23. Courts Act 1971
Sch.2 Part IA, amended: 2009 c.25 Sch.21 para.22, SI 2009/56 Sch.1 para.63, SI 2009/1307 Sch.1 para.98

24. Coinage Act 1971
s.6, amended: SI 2009/2748 Sch.1 para.2
s.8, amended: SI 2009/2748 Sch.1 para.2
s.12, repealed (in part): 2009 c.1 s.214
Sch.2, amended: 2009 c.1 s.214

29. National Savings Bank Act 1971
referred to: 2009 c.10 s.125
s.4, enabling: SI 2009/2460
s.17, applied: 2009 c.10 s.125
s.20, applied: 2009 c.10 s.125

30. Unsolicited Goods and Services Act 1971
referred to: SI 2009/669 Sch.1 Part 1

1971– cont.

32. Attachment of Earnings Act 1971
applied: SI 2009/470 Reg.51

36. Civil Evidence Act (Northern Ireland) 1971
s.7, varied: SI 2009/1059 Sch.1 para.12
s.9, varied: SI 2009/1059 Sch.1 para.12

38. Misuse of Drugs Act 1971
see *Allison v HM Advocate* 2009 S.C.L. 167 (HCJ), Lord Osborne; see *Glasgow Housing Association Ltd v Hetherington* 2009 S.L.T. (Sh Ct) 64 (Sh Ct (Glasgow)), Sheriff I Miller
applied: SI 2009/716 Reg.3, SSI 2009/183 Sch.1 para.4
s.2, applied: SI 2009/1168 Sch.1 para.1, SI 2009/3209
s.2, enabling: SI 2009/3209
s.3, applied: SI 2009/1168 Sch.1 para.1
s.4, see *Xiao Pu Du v HM Advocate* 2009 S.C.C.R. 779 (HCJ), Lord Eassie
s.4, applied: SI 2009/716 Reg.3, SI 2009/1168 Sch.1 para.1
s.4, referred to: SI 2009/37 Sch.1 para.2, Sch.1 para.4
s.5, applied: SI 2009/1168 Sch.1 para.1
s.5, repealed (in part): 2009 c.26 Sch.7 para.122, Sch.8 Part 13
s.6, applied: SI 2009/1168 Sch.1 para.1
s.7, applied: SI 2009/716 Reg.3, SSI 2009/3135
s.7, enabling: SI 2009/3135, SI 2009/3136
s.10, enabling: SI 2009/3136
s.22, enabling: SI 2009/3136
s.23, see *MacAuley (Alexander) v HM Advocate* 2009 S.C.C.R. 566 (HCJ), Lord Justice General Hamilton
s.23, amended: 2009 c.26 Sch.8 Part 12
s.23, repealed (in part): 2009 c.26 Sch.8 Part 12
s.27, applied: 2009 c.25 s.164
s.31, amended: 2009 c.26 Sch.8 Part 13
s.31, applied: SI 2009/3136
s.31, repealed (in part): 2009 c.26 Sch.8 Part 13
s.31, enabling: SI 2009/3136
s.38, repealed (in part): 2009 c.26 Sch.8 Part 13
Sch.2 Part II para.1, amended: SI 2009/3209 Art.2
Sch.2 Part II para.2A, amended: SI 2009/3209 Art.2
Sch.2 Part III para.1, amended: SI 2009/3209 Art.2
Sch.3 Part IV para.21, amended: 2009 c.3 Sch.4 para.8

40. Fire Precautions Act 1971
see *R. v Nevins (John)* [2009] EWCA Crim 1033, [2009] 2 Cr. App. R. (S.) 112 (CA (Crim Div)), Goldring, L.J.

48. Criminal Damage Act 1971
s.1, applied: SI 2009/2773 Sch.1, SI 2009/2781 Sch.1
s.2, applied: SI 2009/2773 Sch.1, SI 2009/2781 Sch.1
s.3, applied: SI 2009/2773 Sch.1, SI 2009/2781 Sch.1

56. Pensions (Increase) Act 1971
applied: SI 2009/692 Art.4
s.1, applied: SI 2009/692 Art.3
Sch.2 Part II para.61, amended: 2009 c.25 Sch.21 para.23

58. Sheriff Courts (Scotland) Act 1971
s.3, enabling: SSI 2009/293
s.11B, amended: SSI 2009/334 Art.3
s.19, amended: SSI 2009/334 Art.3
s.32, enabling: SI 2009/29, SSI 2009/29, SSI 2009/107, SSI 2009/109, SSI 2009/164, SSI 2009/284, SSI 2009/285, SSI 2009/294, SSI 2009/320, SSI 2009/323, SSI 2009/365, SSI 2009/382, SSI 2009/402, SSI 2009/403, SSI 2009/449

1971– cont.

58. Sheriff Courts (Scotland) Act 1971–*cont.*
s.33, applied: SSI 2009/ 323

s.34, applied: SSI 2009/ 29, SSI 2009/ 107, SSI 2009/ 109, SSI 2009/ 164, SSI 2009/ 284, SSI 2009/ 285, SSI 2009/ 294, SSI 2009/ 320, SSI 2009/ 365, SSI 2009/ 382, SSI 2009/ 402, SSI 2009/ 403, SSI 2009/ 449

s.38, see *Mono Seal Plus Ltd v Young* 2009 S.L.T. (Sh Ct) 31 (Sh Ct (Grampian) (Tain)), Sheriff Principal Sir S S T Young, Bt, QC; see *Napoli v Stone* 2009 S.L.T. (Sh Ct) 125 (Sh Ct (Grampian) (Portree)), Sheriff Principal Sir S S T Young, Bt, QC

s.43, enabling: SSI 2009/ 293

60. Prevention of Oil Pollution Act 1971
s.3, see *Amoco (UK) Exploration Co v Frame* 2009 J.C. 65 (HCJ), Lord Osborne

s.6, see *Amoco (UK) Exploration Co v Frame* 2009 J.C. 65 (HCJ), Lord Osborne

s.19, amended: 2009 c.23 Sch.14 para.8, SI 2009/ 1941 Sch.1 para.22

s.19, repealed (in part): 2009 c.23 Sch.22 Part 4

69. Medicines Act 1971
s.1, enabling: SI 2009/ 389, SI 2009/ 3222

77. Immigration Act 1971
see *Odelola v Secretary of State for the Home Department* [2008] EWCA Civ 308, [2009] 1 W.L.R. 126 (CA (Civ Div)), Buxton, L.J.

applied: SI 2009/ 3032 Art.2, SI 2009/ 3323 Art.2

s.3, see *OP (Colombia) v Secretary of State for the Home Department* [2009] Imm. A.R. 233 (AIT), CMG Ockelton (Deputy President); see *R. (on the application of Oczelik) v Secretary of State for the Home Department* [2009] EWCA Civ 260, [2009] Imm. A.R. 554 (CA (Civ Div)), Sedley, L.J.

s.3, amended: 2009 c.11 s.50

s.3, applied: 2009 c.11 s.50

s.3C, see *JH (Zimbabwe) v Secretary of State for the Home Department* [2009] EWCA Civ 78, [2009] Imm. A.R. 499 (CA (Civ Div)), Laws, L.J.; see *R. (on the application of Oczelik) v Secretary of State for the Home Department* [2009] EWCA Civ 260, [2009] Imm. A.R. 554 (CA (Civ Div)), Sedley, L.J.

s.5, see *JN (Cameroon) v Secretary of State for the Home Department* [2009] EWCA Civ 307, [2009] Imm. A.R. 615 (CA (Civ Div)), Rix, L.J.

s.8B, enabling: SI 2009/ 3044

Sch.2, see *MS (Palestinian Territories) v Secretary of State for the Home Department* [2009] EWCA Civ 17, [2009] Imm. A.R. 464 (CA (Civ Div)), Rix, L.J.

Sch.2 para.21, see *R. (on the application of A) v Secretary of State for Health* [2009] EWCA Civ 225, (2009) 12 C.C.L. Rep. 213 (CA (Civ Div)), Ward, L.J.

Sch.3 para.2, see *R. (on the application of SK (Zimbabwe)) v Secretary of State for the Home Department* [2008] EWCA Civ 1204, [2009] 1 W.L.R. 1527 (CA (Civ Div)), Laws, L.J.

80. Banking and Financial Dealings Act 1971
applied: 2009 c.2 s.20, SI 2009/ 366 Reg.7, SI 2009/ 443 Reg.2, SI 2009/ 445 Reg.2, SI 2009/ 988 Art.11, SI 2009/ 2818 Sch.1 para.4, SI 2009/ 3056 Sch.3 para.6, SI 2009/ 3243 Reg.2, SI 2009/ 3245 Reg.2, SI 2009/ 3246 Reg.2, SI 2009/ 3293 Reg.2

1972

11. Superannuation Act 1972
applied: 2009 c.13 Sch.1 para.16, 2009 c.20 Sch.1 para.7, 2009 c.22 Sch.3 para.6, Sch.11 para.8

s.1, applied: 2009 c.13 Sch.1 para.16, Sch.1 para.21, 2009 c.20 Sch.1 para.7, Sch.1 para.8, 2009 c.22 Sch.3 para.6, Sch.11 para.8, 2009 c.23 Sch.1 para.19

s.1, varied: 2009 c.13 Sch.1 para.21, 2009 c.20 Sch.1 para.8

s.7, applied: SI 2009/ 276 Reg.1, SI 2009/ 837 Art.12, Art.13, SI 2009/ 1025, SI 2009/ 3150, SSI 2009/ 93, SSI 2009/ 186, SSI 2009/ 187

s.7, enabling: SI 2009/ 447, SI 2009/ 1025, SI 2009/ 3093, SI 2009/ 3150, SSI 2009/ 93, SSI 2009/ 186, SSI 2009/ 187

s.10, applied: SI 2009/ 309 Reg.8, SI 2009/ 381, SI 2009/ 1298, SI 2009/ 2446, SSI 2009/ 19

s.10, enabling: SI 2009/ 381, SI 2009/ 1298, SI 2009/ 2446, SSI 2009/ 19, SSI 2009/ 208

s.12, enabling: SI 2009/ 381, SI 2009/ 1025, SI 2009/ 1226, SI 2009/ 2446, SI 2009/ 3150, SSI 2009/ 19, SSI 2009/ 184, SSI 2009/ 186, SSI 2009/ 187, SSI 2009/ 208

s.16, applied: SI 2009/ 1226

s.16, enabling: SSI 2009/ 184

s.24, applied: SI 2009/ 309 Reg.8

s.24, enabling: SI 2009/ 3150, SSI 2009/ 93, SSI 2009/ 187

Sch.1, amended: 2009 c.13 Sch.1 para.16, 2009 c.20 Sch.1 para.7, 2009 c.22 Sch.3 para.22, Sch.12 para.4, 2009 c.23 Sch.1 para.19, 2009 c.25 Sch.23 Part 5, 2009 c.26 s.81

Sch.3, enabling: SI 2009/ 381, SI 2009/ 2446, SI 2009/ 3093, SSI 2009/ 19, SSI 2009/ 186, SSI 2009/ 208

18. Maintenance Orders (Reciprocal Enforcement) Act 1972
Part I, applied: SI 2009/ 1109 Reg.8

s.19, applied: SSI 2009/ 29

s.31, referred to: SSI 2009/ 29

27. Road Traffic (Foreign Vehicles) Act 1972
s.1, applied: SI 2009/ 493 Reg.3, Reg.4

s.2, referred to: SI 2009/ 493 Reg.4

s.3, applied: SI 2009/ 483 Art.2

s.3, referred to: SI 2009/ 491 Sch.1 Part 1, SI 2009/ 492 Sch.1 Part 1

58. National Health Service (Scotland) Act 1972
s.28, amended: SSI 2009/ 319 Sch.3 Part 1

s.32, repealed: SSI 2009/ 319 Sch.3 Part 1

s.34, repealed (in part): SSI 2009/ 319 Sch.3 Part 1

Sch.4 para.1, repealed: SSI 2009/ 319 Sch.3 Part 1

Sch.4 para.2, repealed: SSI 2009/ 319 Sch.3 Part 1

Sch.4 para.3, repealed: SSI 2009/ 319 Sch.3 Part 1

Sch.4 para.4, repealed: SSI 2009/ 319 Sch.3 Part 1

Sch.4 para.5, repealed: SSI 2009/ 319 Sch.3 Part 1

Sch.4 para.6, repealed: SSI 2009/ 319 Sch.3 Part 1

Sch.4 para.7, repealed: SSI 2009/ 319 Sch.3 Part 1

59. Administration of Justice (Scotland) Act 1972
s.1, see *Manning v Manning* [2009] CSIH 67, 2009 S.L.T. 743 (IH (Ex Div)), Lord Clarke; see *Sovereign Dimensional Survey Ltd v Cooper* [2009] CSIH 12, 2009 S.C. 382 (IH (Ex Div)), Lord Reed

61. Land Charges Act 1972
s.3, amended: SI 2009/ 1941 Sch.1 para.23

62. Agriculture (Miscellaneous Provisions) Act 1972
s.20, applied: SSI 2009/ 153

63. Industry Act 1972
s.10, amended: SI 2009/ 1941 Sch.1 para.24

1972– cont.

65. National Debt Act 1972

s.3, enabling: SI 2009/ 1263

s.10, applied: SI 2009/ 1263, SI 2009/ 1263 Reg.2

s.10, enabling: SI 2009/ 1263

s.11, enabling: SI 2009/ 1263

66. Poisons Act 1972

s.9, referred to: SI 2009/ 669 Sch.1 Part 1

68. European Communities Act 1972

see *R. (on the application of Age UK) v Secretary of State for Business, Innovation and Skills* [2009] EWHC 2336 (Admin), [2009] I.R.L.R. 1017 (QBD (Admin)), Blake, J

applied: 2009 c.2 Sch.2 Part 2, 2009 c.9 Sch.2 Part 25, SI 2009/ 551

s.1, applied: SI 2009/ 1757

s.1, referred to: SI 2009/ 220 Art.3, SI 2009/ 1181 Art.2, SI 2009/ 1757 Art.2, SI 2009/ 1759 Art.4, SI 2009/ 3211 Art.3

s.1, enabling: SI 2009/ 220, SI 2009/ 1181, SI 2009/ 1757, SI 2009/ 1759, SI 2009/ 3211

s.2, see *National Grid Electricity Transmission Plc v ABB Ltd* [2009] EWHC 1326 (Ch), [2009] U.K.C.L.R. 838 (Ch D), Sir Andrew Morritt (Chancellor); see *R. (on the application of Cukurova Finance International Ltd) v HM Treasury* [2008] EWHC 2567 (Admin), [2009] Eu. L.R. 317 (QBD (Admin)), Moses, L.J.; see *S&I Electronics Plc v Revenue and Customs Commissioners* [2009] UKFTT 108 (TC), [2009] S.F.T.D. 241 (FTT (Tax)), Charles Hellier (Chairman)

s.2, applied: 2009 c.23 s.60, s.294, SI 2009/ 108, SI 2009/ 1122, SI 2009/ 1297, SI 2009/ 1299, SI 2009/ 1349, SI 2009/ 1495, SI 2009/ 1802, SI 2009/ 3100, SI 2009/ 3130, SI 2009/ 3235, SI 2009/ 3277, SI 2009/ 3378, SSI 2009/ 436

s.2, referred to: SI 2009/ 205, SI 2009/ 481, SI 2009/ 496, SI 2009/ 594, SI 2009/ 1034, SI 2009/ 1122, SI 2009/ 1223, SI 2009/ 1348, SI 2009/ 1386, SI 2009/ 1495, SI 2009/ 1742, SI 2009/ 1847, SI 2009/ 1850, SI 2009/ 2043, SI 2009/ 2427, SI 2009/ 3020, SI 2009/ 3051, SI 2009/ 3232, SI 2009/ 3238, SI 2009/ 3251, SI 2009/ 3252, SI 2009/ 3254, SSI 2009/ 7, SSI 2009/ 30, SSI 2009/ 215, SSI 2009/ 427, SSI 2009/ 438

s.2, enabling: SI 2009/ 6, SI 2009/ 7, SI 2009/ 11, SI 2009/ 41, SI 2009/ 47, SI 2009/ 64, SI 2009/ 108, SI 2009/ 138, SI 2009/ 153, SI 2009/ 192, SI 2009/ 209, SI 2009/ 216, SI 2009/ 221, SI 2009/ 261, SI 2009/ 269, SI 2009/ 318, SI 2009/ 360, SI 2009/ 372, SI 2009/ 383, SI 2009/ 386, SI 2009/ 389, SI 2009/ 390, SI 2009/ 392, SI 2009/ 463, SI 2009/ 507, SI 2009/ 515, SI 2009/ 534, SI 2009/ 551, SI 2009/ 581, SI 2009/ 592, SI 2009/ 663, SI 2009/ 693, SI 2009/ 707, SI 2009/ 716, SI 2009/ 717, SI 2009/ 726, SI 2009/ 793, SI 2009/ 818, SI 2009/ 842, SI 2009/ 847, SI 2009/ 859, SI 2009/ 875, SI 2009/ 890, SI 2009/ 892, SI 2009/ 995, SI 2009/ 1034, SI 2009/ 1056, SI 2009/ 1088, SI 2009/ 1117, SI 2009/ 1119, SI 2009/ 1122, SI 2009/ 1164, SI 2009/ 1176, SI 2009/ 1210, SI 2009/ 1273, SI 2009/ 1297, SI 2009/ 1299, SI 2009/ 1309, SI 2009/ 1349, SI 2009/ 1361, SI 2009/ 1372, SI 2009/ 1373, SI 2009/ 1381, SI 2009/ 1485, SI 2009/ 1495, SI 2009/ 1504, SI 2009/ 1551, SI 2009/ 1557, SI 2009/ 1567, SI 2009/ 1574, SI 2009/ 1580, SI 2009/ 1581, SI 2009/ 1591, SI 2009/ 1610, SI 2009/ 1611, SI 2009/ 1632, SI 2009/ 1735, SI 2009/ 1771, SI 2009/ 1773, SI 2009/ 1802, SI 2009/ 1846, SI 2009/ 1896, SI 2009/ 1899, SI 2009/ 1900, SI 2009/ 1906, SI

1972– cont.

68. European Communities Act 1972–*cont.*

s.2, enabling:–*cont.*

2009/ 1910, SI 2009/ 1912, SI 2009/ 1914, SI 2009/ 1925, SI 2009/ 1927, SI 2009/ 1941, SI 2009/ 1972, SI 2009/ 2021, SI 2009/ 2048, SI 2009/ 2151, SI 2009/ 2163, SI 2009/ 2194, SI 2009/ 2258, SI 2009/ 2263, SI 2009/ 2297, SI 2009/ 2301, SI 2009/ 2331, SI 2009/ 2399, SI 2009/ 2400, SI 2009/ 2401, SI 2009/ 2402, SI 2009/ 2426, SI 2009/ 2437, SI 2009/ 2438, SI 2009/ 2461, SI 2009/ 2462, SI 2009/ 2470, SI 2009/ 2475, SI 2009/ 2559, SI 2009/ 2560, SI 2009/ 2561, SI 2009/ 2712, SI 2009/ 2743, SI 2009/ 2766, SI 2009/ 2792, SI 2009/ 2796, SI 2009/ 2797, SI 2009/ 2798, SI 2009/ 2820, SI 2009/ 2824, SI 2009/ 2861, SI 2009/ 2890, SI 2009/ 2956, SI 2009/ 2957, SI 2009/ 2970, SI 2009/ 2974, SI 2009/ 2979, SI 2009/ 2992, SI 2009/ 2999, SI 2009/ 3015, SI 2009/ 3042, SI 2009/ 3046, SI 2009/ 3063, SI 2009/ 3064, SI 2009/ 3081, SI 2009/ 3100, SI 2009/ 3101, SI 2009/ 3102, SI 2009/ 3104, SI 2009/ 3128, SI 2009/ 3129, SI 2009/ 3130, SI 2009/ 3131, SI 2009/ 3145, SI 2009/ 3155, SI 2009/ 3157, SI 2009/ 3159, SI 2009/ 3160, SI 2009/ 3182, SI 2009/ 3200, SI 2009/ 3214, SI 2009/ 3216, SI 2009/ 3222, SI 2009/ 3230, SI 2009/ 3255, SI 2009/ 3263, SI 2009/ 3264, SI 2009/ 3266, SI 2009/ 3270, SI 2009/ 3275, SI 2009/ 3277, SI 2009/ 3307, SI 2009/ 3342, SI 2009/ 3344, SI 2009/ 3365, SI 2009/ 3376, SI 2009/ 3379, SI 2009/ 3391, SSI 2009/ 1, SSI 2009/ 7, SSI 2009/ 8, SSI 2009/ 85, SSI 2009/ 99, SSI 2009/ 155, SSI 2009/ 173, SSI 2009/ 221, SSI 2009/ 225, SSI 2009/ 227, SSI 2009/ 228, SSI 2009/ 229, SSI 2009/ 231, SSI 2009/ 232, SSI 2009/ 233, SSI 2009/ 262, SSI 2009/ 263, SSI 2009/ 266, SSI 2009/ 305, SSI 2009/ 333, SSI 2009/ 335, SSI 2009/ 339, SSI 2009/ 343, SSI 2009/ 376, SSI 2009/ 391, SSI 2009/ 410, SSI 2009/ 411, SSI 2009/ 412, SSI 2009/ 415, SSI 2009/ 417, SSI 2009/ 428, SSI 2009/ 437, SSI 2009/ 439, SSI 2009/ 440, SSI 2009/ 446, SSI 2009/ 447

s.6, applied: 2009 c.11 s.7

Sch.2 para.1, applied: 2009 c.25 s.143

Sch.2 para.1 A, applied: SI 2009/ 205, SI 2009/ 481, SI 2009/ 496, SI 2009/ 995, SI 2009/ 1223, SI 2009/ 1386, SI 2009/ 2427, SI 2009/ 2992, SI 2009/ 3051, SI 2009/ 3100, SI 2009/ 3251, SSI 2009/ 438

Sch.2 para.1 A, referred to: SI 2009/ 153, SI 2009/ 1348

Sch.2 para.1 A, enabling: SI 2009/ 47, SI 2009/ 108, SI 2009/ 261, SI 2009/ 360, SI 2009/ 463, SI 2009/ 594, SI 2009/ 793, SI 2009/ 842, SI 2009/ 847, SI 2009/ 890, SI 2009/ 1122, SI 2009/ 1273, SI 2009/ 1361, SI 2009/ 1495, SI 2009/ 1551, SI 2009/ 1557, SI 2009/ 1574, SI 2009/ 1610, SI 2009/ 1742, SI 2009/ 1771, SI 2009/ 1773, SI 2009/ 1847, SI 2009/ 1850, SI 2009/ 2043, SI 2009/ 2151, SI 2009/ 2163, SI 2009/ 2301, SI 2009/ 2470, SI 2009/ 3015, SI 2009/ 3020, SI 2009/ 3130, SI 2009/ 3131, SI 2009/ 3157, SI 2009/ 3232, SI 2009/ 3238, SI 2009/ 3255, SI 2009/ 3270, SI 2009/ 3271, SI 2009/ 3376, SI 2009/ 3378, SI 2009/ 3391, SSI 2009/ 7, SSI 2009/ 30, SSI 2009/ 85, SSI 2009/ 215, SSI 2009/ 225, SSI 2009/ 227, SSI 2009/ 228, SSI 2009/ 229, SSI 2009/ 231, SSI 2009/ 262, SSI 2009/ 266, SSI 2009/ 335, SSI 2009/ 339, SSI 2009/ 417, SSI 2009/ 427, SSI 2009/ 428, SSI 2009/ 436, SSI 2009/ 440, SSI 2009/ 446

68. European Communities Act 1972– *cont.*
Sch.2 para.2, applied: SI 2009/1176, SI 2009/1581, SI 2009/1802, SI 2009/1941, SSI 2009/266
Sch.2 para.2, varied: 2009 c.25 s.143

70. Local Government Act 1972
applied: SI 2009/3157 Reg.4
Part V, applied: SI 2009/1254 Art.6, SI 2009/2467 Art.6
Part VA, referred to: 2009 c.20 s.71
s.1, applied: SI 2009/2565 Art.2
s.6, amended: 2009 c.20 Sch.4 para.2
s.11A, amended: 2009 c.20 Sch.4 para.3
s.12A, amended: 2009 c.20 Sch.4 para.3
s.12B, amended: 2009 c.20 Sch.4 para.3
s.54, applied: SI 2009/367, SI 2009/889, SI 2009/2717, SI 2009/2718, SI 2009/3047, SI 2009/3052
s.58, applied: SI 2009/367, SI 2009/889, SI 2009/2717, SI 2009/2718, SI 2009/3047, SI 2009/3052
s.58, enabling: SI 2009/367, SI 2009/889, SI 2009/2717, SI 2009/2718, SI 2009/3047, SI 2009/3052
s.70, amended: 2009 c.20 Sch.6 para.11
s.73, amended: 2009 c.20 Sch.4 para.3
s.74, applied: SI 2009/276 Reg.12
s.80, amended: 2009 c.20 Sch.6 para.12
s.85, amended: 2009 c.20 Sch.6 para.13
s.86, amended: 2009 c.20 Sch.6 para.14
s.92, amended: 2009 c.20 Sch.6 para.15
s.92, applied: SI 2009/1254 Art.6, SI 2009/2467 Art.6
s.98, amended: 2009 c.20 Sch.6 para.16
s.99, amended: 2009 c.20 Sch.6 para.17
s.100A, applied: 2009 c.23 s.151
s.100A, varied: 2009 c.20 s.49, SI 2009/1254 Sch.1 para.7, SI 2009/2467 Sch.1 para.7
s.100B, applied: 2009 c.20 s.49, 2009 c.23 s.151
s.100B, varied: 2009 c.20 s.49
s.100C, applied: 2009 c.23 s.151
s.100C, varied: 2009 c.20 s.49
s.100D, applied: 2009 c.23 s.151
s.100D, varied: 2009 c.20 s.49
s.100E, varied: 2009 c.20 s.49
s.100EA, varied: 2009 c.20 s.49
s.100EA, enabling: SI 2009/352
s.100F, varied: 2009 c.20 s.49
s.100G, varied: 2009 c.20 s.49
s.100H, varied: 2009 c.20 s.49
s.100I, varied: 2009 c.20 s.49, SI 2009/1254 Sch.1 para.7, SI 2009/2467 Sch.1 para.7
s.100J, amended: 2009 c.20 Sch.6 para.18
s.100J, varied: 2009 c.20 s.49
s.100K, varied: 2009 c.20 s.49
s.101, amended: 2009 c.20 Sch.6 para.19
s.101, applied: 2009 c.23 s.20
s.101, repealed (in part): 2009 c.23 Sch.22 Part 4, SI 2009/1375 Art.2
s.101, varied: 2009 c.2 s.10
s.103, disapplied: 2009 c.23 s.180
s.104, applied: 2009 c.23 s.151
s.106, applied: 2009 c.23 s.151, SI 2009/467 Reg.10
s.111, see *Ramblers Association v Coventry City Council* [2008] EWHC 796 (Admin), [2009] 1 All E.R. 130 (QBD (Admin)), Michael Supperstone Q.C.
s.111, applied: SI 2009/467 Reg.14
s.112, applied: SI 2009/467 Reg.10
s.114, applied: SI 2009/467 Reg.10
s.115, applied: SI 2009/467 Reg.10
s.116, applied: SI 2009/467 Reg.10

70. Local Government Act 1972– *cont.*
s.117, applied: SI 2009/467 Reg.10
s.120, applied: SI 2009/1300 Art.86
s.140, applied: SI 2009/467 Reg.14
s.142, amended: 2009 c.20 Sch.6 para.20
s.146A, amended: 2009 c.20 Sch.6 para.21
s.151, applied: SI 2009/369 Reg.9, SI 2009/467 Reg.14
s.173, applied: SI 2009/467 Reg.14
s.173A, applied: SI 2009/467 Reg.14
s.174, applied: SI 2009/467 Reg.14
s.175, amended: 2009 c.20 Sch.6 para.22
s.175, applied: SI 2009/467 Reg.14
s.176, amended: 2009 c.20 Sch.6 para.23
s.176, applied: SI 2009/467 Reg.14
s.177, applied: SI 2009/467 Reg.14
s.177A, applied: SI 2009/467 Reg.14
s.178, applied: SI 2009/467 Reg.14
s.222, see *Birmingham City Council v Shafi* [2008] EWCA Civ 1186, [2009] 1 W.L.R. 1961 (CA (Civ Div)), Sir Anthony Clarke, M.R.
s.223, amended: 2009 c.20 Sch.6 para.24
s.224, amended: 2009 c.20 Sch.6 para.25
s.225, amended: 2009 c.20 Sch.6 para.26
s.228, amended: 2009 c.20 Sch.6 para.27
s.228, applied: SI 2009/467 Reg.9
s.229, amended: 2009 c.20 Sch.6 para.28
s.230, amended: 2009 c.20 Sch.6 para.29
s.231, amended: 2009 c.20 Sch.6 para.30
s.232, amended: 2009 c.20 Sch.6 para.31
s.233, amended: 2009 c.20 Sch.6 para.32
s.233, applied: SI 2009/2268 Reg.22
s.233, referred to: SI 2009/2268 Reg.22
s.234, amended: 2009 c.20 Sch.6 para.33
s.236, amended: 2009 c.20 Sch.6 para.34
s.236, applied: SI 2009/2325 Art.24
s.236, varied: SI 2009/2325 Art.24
s.236B, amended: 2009 c.20 Sch.6 para.35
s.238, amended: 2009 c.20 Sch.6 para.36
s.238, applied: SI 2009/2325 Art.24
s.239, amended: 2009 c.20 Sch.6 para.37
s.248, amended: 2009 c.20 s.27, s.28
s.249, amended: 2009 c.20 s.29
s.250, applied: 2009 c.2 s.29, 2009 c.23 s.70, SI 2009/2301 Sch.3 para.4
s.250, varied: 2009 c.23 s.161, SI 2009/3130 Sch.1 para.3
s.270, amended: 2009 c.20 Sch.6 para.38
Sch.2 Part I para.7, amended: 2009 c.20 Sch.4 para.4
Sch.3 para.10, amended: 2009 c.20 Sch.4 para.5
Sch.11 para.1, repealed: 2009 c.20 Sch.4 para.6, Sch.7 Part 3
Sch.11 para.3, repealed: 2009 c.20 Sch.4 para.6, Sch.7 Part 3
Sch.11 para.4, amended: 2009 c.20 Sch.4 para.6, Sch.7 Part 3
Sch.12 Part IA para.6A, amended: 2009 c.20 Sch.6 para.39
Sch.12 Part II para.10, applied: SI 2009/467 Reg.9
Sch.12 Part II para.13, applied: SI 2009/467 Reg.9
Sch.12 Part VI para.39, applied: 2009 c.23 s.151, SI 2009/467 Reg.9
Sch.12 Part VI para.39, disapplied: SI 2009/467 Reg.8
Sch.12 Part VI para.40, applied: 2009 c.23 s.151, SI 2009/467 Reg.9

1972– cont.

70. Local Government Act 1972–cont.

Sch.12 Part VI para.41, applied: 2009 c.23 s.151, SI 2009/467 Reg.9

Sch.12 Part VI para.42, applied: 2009 c.23 s.151, SI 2009/467 Reg.9

Sch.12 Part VI para.43, applied: 2009 c.23 s.151, SI 2009/467 Reg.9

Sch.12 Part VI para.44, applied: SI 2009/467 Reg.9

Sch.12A Part I para.1, varied: SI 2009/1254 Sch.1 para.7, SI 2009/2467 Sch.1 para.7

Sch.12A Part I para.2, varied: SI 2009/1254 Sch.1 para.7, SI 2009/2467 Sch.1 para.7

Sch.12A Part I para.2A, varied: SI 2009/1254 Sch.1 para.7, SI 2009/2467 Sch.1 para.7

Sch.12A Part I para.3, varied: SI 2009/1254 Sch.1 para.7, SI 2009/2467 Sch.1 para.7

Sch.12A Part I para.4, varied: SI 2009/1254 Sch.1 para.7, SI 2009/2467 Sch.1 para.7

Sch.12A Part I para.5, varied: SI 2009/1254 Sch.1 para.7, SI 2009/2467 Sch.1 para.7

Sch.12A Part I para.6, varied: SI 2009/1254 Sch.1 para.7, SI 2009/2467 Sch.1 para.7

Sch.12A Part I para.6A, varied: SI 2009/1254 Sch.1 para.7, SI 2009/2467 Sch.1 para.7

Sch.12A Part I para.6B, varied: SI 2009/1254 Sch.1 para.7, SI 2009/2467 Sch.1 para.7

Sch.12A Part I para.7, varied: SI 2009/1254 Sch.1 para.7, SI 2009/2467 Sch.1 para.7

Sch.12A Part I para.7A, varied: SI 2009/1254 Sch.1 para.7, SI 2009/2467 Sch.1 para.7

Sch.12A Part I para.7B, varied: SI 2009/1254 Sch.1 para.7, SI 2009/2467 Sch.1 para.7

Sch.12A Part I para.7C, varied: SI 2009/1254 Sch.1 para.7, SI 2009/2467 Sch.1 para.7

Sch.12A Part I para.8, varied: SI 2009/1254 Sch.1 para.7, SI 2009/2467 Sch.1 para.7

Sch.12A Part I para.9, varied: SI 2009/1254 Sch.1 para.7, SI 2009/2467 Sch.1 para.7

Sch.12A Part I para.10, varied: SI 2009/1254 Sch.1 para.7, SI 2009/2467 Sch.1 para.7

Sch.12A Part I para.11, varied: SI 2009/1254 Sch.1 para.7, SI 2009/2467 Sch.1 para.7

Sch.28A para.1, added: 2009 c.20 s.28

Sch.28A para.2, added: 2009 c.20 s.28

Sch.28A para.3, added: 2009 c.20 s.28

Sch.28A para.4, added: 2009 c.20 s.28

Sch.28A para.5, added: 2009 c.20 s.28

Sch.28A para.6, added: 2009 c.20 s.28

Sch.28A para.7, added: 2009 c.20 s.28

Sch.28A para.8, added: 2009 c.20 s.28

Sch.28A para.9, added: 2009 c.20 s.28

Sch.28A para.10, added: 2009 c.20 s.28

Sch.28A para.11, added: 2009 c.20 s.28

71. Criminal Justice Act 1972

s.60, amended: SI 2009/1307 Sch.1 para.100

1973

13. Supply of Goods (Implied Terms) Act 1973

referred to: SI 2009/669 Sch.1 Part 2

18. Matrimonial Causes Act 1973

see *Ansari v Ansari* [2008] EWCA Civ 1456, [2009] 3 W.L.R. 1092 (CA (Civ Div)), Longmore, L.J.; see *Hudson v Leigh* [2009] EWHC 1306 (Fam), [2009] 2 F.L.R. 1129 (Fam Div), Bodey, J.; see *Stodgell v Stodgell* [2008] EWHC 1925 (Admin), [2009] 2 F.L.R. 218 (QBD (Admin)), Holman, J.

applied: SI 2009/845 Art.3, Art.4

1973– cont.

18. Matrimonial Causes Act 1973–cont.

s.12, see *Hudson v Leigh* [2009] EWHC 1306 (Fam), [2009] 2 F.L.R. 1129 (Fam Div), Bodey, J.; see *Westminster City Council v C* [2008] EWCA Civ 198, [2009] Fam. 11 (CA (Civ Div)), Thorpe, L.J.

s.13, see *Hudson v Leigh* [2009] EWHC 1306 (Fam), [2009] 2 F.L.R. 1129 (Fam Div), Bodey, J.

s.23, see *M v M (Maintenance Pending Suit: Enforcement on Dismissal of Suit)* [2008] EWHC 2153 (Fam), [2009] 1 F.L.R. 790 (Fam Div), Bodey, J.

s.23, applied: SI 2009/1555 Sch.4 para.1, SI 2009/2737 Sch.5 para.1, Sch.6 para.1, SI 2009/3359 Sch.2 para.1

s.24, see *Ben Hashem v Ali Shayif* [2008] EWHC 2380 (Fam), [2009] 1 F.L.R. 115 (Fam Div), Munby, J.; see *Ben Hashem v Ali Shayif* [2009] EWHC 864 (Fam), [2009] 2 F.L.R. 896 (Fam Div), Munby, J.

s.25, see *Barron v Woodhead* [2008] EWHC 810 (Ch), [2009] 1 F.L.R. 747 (Ch D (Newcastle)), Judge Behrens; see *Behzadi v Behzadi* [2008] EWCA Civ 1070, [2009] 2 F.L.R. 649 (CA (Civ Div)), Rix, L.J.; see *Ben Hashem v Ali Shayif* [2008] EWHC 2380 (Fam), [2009] 1 F.L.R. 115 (Fam Div), Munby, J.; see *C v C* [2007] EWHC 2033 (Fam), [2009] 1 F.L.R. 8 (Fam Div), Moylan, J.; see *C v C* [2009] EWHC 1491 (Fam), [2009] W.T.L.R. 1419 (Fam Div), Munby, J.; see *R. v K* [2009] EWCA Crim 1640, [2009] S.T.C. 2553 (CA (Crim Div)), Moore-Bick, L.J.; see *Radmacher v Granatino* [2008] EWHC 1532 (Fam), [2009] 1 F.L.R.1478 (Fam Div), Baron, J.; see *Radmacher v Granatino* [2009] EWCA Civ 649, [2009] 2 F.L.R. 1181 (CA (Civ Div)), Thorpe, L.J.; see *W v H* [2008] EWHC 2038 (Fam), [2009] 1 F.L.R. 254 (Fam Div), Eleanor King, J; see *Williams v Thompson Leatherdale (A Firm)* [2008] EWHC 2574 (QB), [2009] 2 F.L.R. 730 (QBD), Field, J.

s.25B, applied: SI 2009/1555 Sch.4 para.1, SI 2009/2737 Sch.5 para.1, Sch.6 para.1, SI 2009/3359 Sch.2 para.1

s.25E, applied: SI 2009/1555 Sch.4 para.1, SI 2009/2737 Sch.5 para.1, Sch.6 para.1, SI 2009/3359 Sch.2 para.1

s.28, see *Whitehouse-Piper v Stokes* [2008] EWCA Civ 1049, [2009] 1 F.L.R. 983 (CA (Civ Div)), Thorpe, L.J.

s.31, see *Horne v Horne* [2009] EWCA Civ 487, [2009] 2 F.L.R. 1031 (CA (Civ Div)), Thorpe, L.J.; see *M v M (Maintenance Pending Suit: Enforcement on Dismissal of Suit)* [2008] EWHC 2153 (Fam), [2009] 1 F.L.R. 790 (Fam Div), Bodey, J.; see *McFarlane v McFarlane* [2009] EWHC 891 (Fam), [2009] 2 F.L.R. 1322 (Fam Div), Charles, J.; see *W v W* [2009] 1 F.L.R. 92 (CC (Romford)), Judge Platt

s.34, see *Radmacher v Granatino* [2008] EWHC 1532 (Fam), [2009] 1 F.L.R. 1478 (Fam Div), Baron, J.

s.37, see *Ansari v Ansari* [2008] EWCA Civ 1456, [2009] 3 W.L.R. 1092 (CA (Civ Div)), Longmore, L.J.

26. Land Compensation Act 1973

Part I, see *Scholes v Kirklees Council* [2009] R.V.R. 196 (Lands Tr), Judge Huskinson

s.3, amended: SI 2009/1307 Sch.1 para.102

s.16, amended: SI 2009/1307 Sch.1 para.103

s.26, applied: SI 2009/1300 Art.86

1973 – cont.

26. Land Compensation Act 1973–*cont.*
s.30, amended: SI 2009/1307 Sch.1 para.104
s.33A, amended: SI 2009/1307 Sch.1 para.105
s.33I, amended: SI 2009/1307 Sch.1 para.106
s.38, amended: SI 2009/1307 Sch.1 para.107
s.44, varied: SI 2009/1300 Sch.7 para.2, SI 2009/2364 Sch.5 para.2, SI 2009/2728 Sch.2 para.2
s.52, see *Clemdell Ltd v Dorset CC* [2009] R.V.R. 318 (Lands Tr), Judge Reid Q.C.
s.52ZC, amended: SI 2009/1307 Sch.1 para.108
s.54, amended: SI 2009/1307 Sch.1 para.109
s.56, amended: SI 2009/1307 Sch.1 para.110
s.58, amended: SI 2009/1307 Sch.1 para.111
s.58, varied: SI 2009/1300 Sch.7 para.2, SI 2009/2364 Sch.5 para.2, SI 2009/2728 Sch.2 para.2
s.61, amended: SI 2009/1307 Sch.1 para.112

33. Protection of Wrecks Act 1973
applied: SI 2009/2394 Art.2
s.1, applied: SI 2009/2394
s.1, enabling: SI 2009/2394
s.3, enabling: SI 2009/2394

35. Employment Agencies Act 1973
see *Accenture Services Ltd v Revenue and Customs Commissioners* [2009] EWHC 857 (Admin), [2009] S.T.C. 1503 (QBD (Admin)), Sales, J
s.9, amended: SI 2009/2999 Reg.46
s.9, applied: SI 2009/603 Sch.1 para.4
s.13, amended: 2009 c.20 Sch.6 para.40
s.13, applied: SI 2009/3297 Reg.11

37. Water Act 1973
Sch.8 para.43, repealed (in part): SI 2009/463 Sch.2 para.2, SSI 2009/85 Sch.2 para.2

41. Fair Trading Act 1973
referred to: SI 2009/669 Sch.1 Part 2
s.137, amended: SI 2009/1941 Sch.1 para.26

43. Hallmarking Act 1973
referred to: SI 2009/669 Sch.1 Part 2
s.1, amended: SI 2009/2040 Sch.1 para.2
s.4, amended: SI 2009/2040 Sch.1 para.3
s.5, amended: SI 2009/2040 Sch.1 para.4
s.17, applied: SI 2009/2040
s.17, enabling: SI 2009/2040
s.21, applied: SI 2009/2040
s.22, amended: SI 2009/2040 Sch.1 para.5
s.22, varied: SI 2009/2040 Art.2
Sch.1 Part I para.1, amended: SI 2009/2040 Sch.1 para.6
Sch.1 Part II para.6, amended: SI 2009/2040 Sch.1 para.6
Sch.1 Part II para.9A, added: SI 2009/2040 Sch.1 para.6
Sch.1 Part II para.12, amended: SI 2009/2040 Sch.1 para.6
Sch.1 Part II para.12A, amended: SI 2009/2040 Sch.1 para.6
Sch.1 Part II para.12D, added: SI 2009/2040 Sch.1 para.6
Sch.2 Part I para.2, amended: SI 2009/2040 Sch.1 para.7
Sch.2 Part I para.3, amended: SI 2009/2040 Sch.1 para.7
Sch.2 Part II para.13, amended: SI 2009/2040 Sch.1 para.7
Sch.2 Part II para.14, amended: SI 2009/2040 Sch.1 para.7
Sch.2 Part II para.15, amended: SI 2009/2040 Sch.1 para.7
Sch.2 Part III para.19, amended: SI 2009/2040 Sch.1 para.7

1973 – cont.

45. Domicile and Matrimonial Proceedings Act 1973
s.5, see *A v L* [2009] EWHC 1448 (Fam), [2009] 2 F.L.R. 1496 (Fam Div), Sir Mark Potter (President, Fam)
s.8, see *Williamson v Williamson* 2009 Fam. L.R. 153 (Sh Pr), Sheriff Principal R A Dunlop, QC; see *Williamson v Williamson* 2009 Fam. L.R. 44 (Sh Ct (Tayside) (Kirkcaldy)), Sheriff AG McCulloch
Sch.1 para.9, see *A v L* [2009] EWHC 1448 (Fam), [2009] 2 F.L.R. 1496 (Fam Div), Sir Mark Potter (President, Fam)
Sch.3 para.9, see *A v L* [2009] EWHC 1448 (Fam), [2009] 2 F.L.R. 1496 (Fam Div), Sir Mark Potter (President, Fam)

50. Employment and Training Act 1973
s.2, applied: 2009 c.20 s.123, 2009 c.22 s.69, s.108, SI 2009/212 Reg.2, SI 2009/1555 Reg.121, Reg.138, SI 2009/1562, SI 2009/1562 Art.2, SI 2009/2737 Reg.73, Reg.88, SI 2009/3355 Reg.6, Reg.7
s.8, applied: SI 2009/3355 Reg.6, Reg.7
s.10, applied: SI 2009/3355 Reg.6, Reg.7

51. Finance Act 1973
applied: SI 2009/718, SI 2009/856, SI 2009/866
enabling: SI 2009/718, SI 2009/719, SI 2009/856, SI 2009/861, SI 2009/866
s.32, repealed: SI 2009/2035 Sch.1 para.10
s.41, repealed: SI 2009/56 Sch.1 para.65
s.56, applied: SI 2009/861, SI 2009/2258
s.56, enabling: SI 2009/372, SI 2009/383, SI 2009/389, SI 2009/398, SI 2009/496, SI 2009/718, SI 2009/719, SI 2009/842, SI 2009/855, SI 2009/856, SI 2009/861, SI 2009/866, SI 2009/879, SI 2009/2043, SI 2009/2053, SI 2009/2258, SI 2009/2297, SI 2009/2427, SI 2009/2492, SI 2009/3140, SI 2009/3222, SSI 2009/8, SSI 2009/230, SSI 2009/305, SSI 2009/416
Sch.15 para.2, amended: 2009 c.4 Sch.1 para.312
Sch.15 para.4, amended: SI 2009/2860 Art.2

52. Prescription and Limitation (Scotland) Act 1973
see *Hamilton v Dumfries and Galloway Council* [2009] CSIH 13, 2009 S.C. 277 (IH (Ex Div)), Lord Reed
varied: SI 2009/317 Sch.1
s.1, see *Burgess-Lumsden v Aberdeenshire Council* 2009 S.L.T. (Sh Ct) 117 (Sh Ct (Grampian) (Aberdeen)), Sheriff D J Cusine
s.17, applied: 2009 asp 4 s.3
s.18, applied: 2009 asp 4 s.3
s.19A, see *A v N* [2009] CSIH 29, 2009 S.C. 449 (IH (1 Div)), The Lord President (Hamilton)
s.19B, amended: 2009 c.26 s.62
s.19C, amended: 2009 c.26 s.62
s.19D, added: 2009 c.25 s.171
s.19D, applied: 2009 c.25 s.163
s.23A, amended: SSI 2009/410 Reg.3
Sch.3, see *Burgess-Lumsden v Aberdeenshire Council* 2009 S.L.T. (Sh Ct) 117 (Sh Ct (Grampian) (Aberdeen)), Sheriff D J Cusine

56. Land Compensation (Scotland) Act 1973
s.27, applied: SSI 2009/122 Art.7

60. Breeding of Dogs Act 1973
s.1, applied: SSI 2009/141 Reg.3
s.3, applied: SSI 2009/141 Reg.4

63. Government Trading Funds Act 1973
applied: SI 2009/81
s.1, applied: SI 2009/81, SI 2009/2622

1973– cont.

63. Government Trading Funds Act 1973– *cont.*
s.l, enabling: SI 2009/81, SI 2009/469, SI 2009/647, SI 2009/1362, SI 2009/2622, SSI 2009/450
s.2, enabling: SI 2009/1362, SI 2009/2622
s.2A, enabling: SI 2009/1362
s.2AA, enabling: SI 2009/1362
s.2C, enabling: SI 2009/469
s.6, applied: SI 2009/81, SI 2009/2622
s.6, enabling: SI 2009/81, SI 2009/647, SI 2009/ 1362, SI 2009/2622, SSI 2009/450

65. Local Government (Scotland) Act 1973
s.17, enabling: SSI 2009/368, SSI 2009/442
s.74, see *Multi-Link Leisure Developments Ltd v North Lanarkshire Council* [2009] CSOH 114, 2009 S.L.T. 1170 (OH), Lord Glennie
s.210, applied: 2009 asp 6 Sch.2 para.7, 2009 c.23 s.70, SI 2009/2301 Sch.3 para.6
s.210, varied: SI 2009/3130 Sch.1 para.3
Sch.7A Part II para.2, amended: SI 2009/1941 Sch.1 para.27

1974

6. Biological Weapons Act 1974
s.4, applied: SI 2009/2056 Sch.1 para.4

7. Local Government Act 1974
applied: SI 2009/309 Reg.8, Reg.14, Reg.18
s.23, amended: 2009 c.21 Sch.5 para.5
s.23A, amended: 2009 c.21 Sch.5 para.6
s.25, amended: 2009 c.20 Sch.6 para.41
s.26C, amended: 2009 c.20 Sch.6 para.41
s.26D, amended: 2009 c.21 Sch.5 para.7
s.29, amended: 2009 c.21 Sch.5 para.8
s.30, amended: 2009 c.21 Sch.5 para.9
s.31A, amended: 2009 c.23 Sch.14 para.9
s.31A, repealed (in part): 2009 c.23 Sch.22 Part 4
s.32, amended: 2009 c.21 Sch.5 para.10
s.33ZA, amended: 2009 c.21 Sch.5 para.11
s.34A, added: 2009 c.21 Sch.5 para.2
s.34B, added: 2009 c.21 Sch.5 para.2
s.34C, added: 2009 c.21 Sch.5 para.2
s.34D, added: 2009 c.21 Sch.5 para.2
s.34E, added: 2009 c.21 Sch.5 para.2
s.34F, added: 2009 c.21 Sch.5 para.2
s.34G, added: 2009 c.21 Sch.5 para.2
s.34H, added: 2009 c.21 Sch.5 para.2
s.34I, added: 2009 c.21 Sch.5 para.2
s.34J, added: 2009 c.21 Sch.5 para.2
s.34K, added: 2009 c.21 Sch.5 para.2
s.34L, added: 2009 c.21 Sch.5 para.2
s.34M, added: 2009 c.21 Sch.5 para.2
s.34N, added: 2009 c.21 Sch.5 para.2
s.34O, added: 2009 c.21 Sch.5 para.2
s.34P, added: 2009 c.21 Sch.5 para.2
s.34Q, added: 2009 c.21 Sch.5 para.2
s.34R, added: 2009 c.21 Sch.5 para.2
s.34S, added: 2009 c.21 Sch.5 para.2
s.34T, added: 2009 c.21 Sch.5 para.2
Sch.4 para.1, amended: 2009 c.21 Sch.5 para.12, 2009 c.22 s.223
Sch.5 para.5, amended: 2009 c.22 s.261
Sch.5A para.1, added: 2009 c.21 Sch.5 para.3
Sch.5A para.2, added: 2009 c.21 Sch.5 para.3
Sch.5A para.3, added: 2009 c.21 Sch.5 para.3
Sch.5A para.4, added: 2009 c.21 Sch.5 para.3

23. Juries Act 1974
referred to: SI 2009/500 Sch.2 Part 1
s.l, applied: 2009 c.25 s.8

1974– cont.

23. Juries Act 1974– *cont.*
s.ll, see *R. v B* [2008] EWCA Crim 1997, [2009] 1 W.L.R. 1545 (CA (Crim Div)), Toulson, L.J.
s.19, amended: 2009 c.25 Sch.21 para.24
s.22, repealed (in part): 2009 c.25 Sch.23 Part 1
Sch.1 Part I, applied: SI 2009/2041 r.33
Sch.1 Part II, applied: 2009 c.25 Sch.6 para.1, SI 2009/2041 r.33
Sch.1 Part II para.8, varied: SI 2009/1059 Sch.1 para.13

24. Prices Act 1974
referred to: SI 2009/669 Sch.1 Part 2
s.4, applied: SI 2009/3231
s.4, enabling: SI 2009/3231

37. Health and Safety at Work etc Act 1974
applied: SI 2009/515 Reg.14, Reg.15, Reg.16, Reg.17, SI 2009/711 Sch.1 para.47, SI 2009/716 Reg.14, SI 2009/1927 Reg.9
referred to: SI 2009/669 Sch.1 Part 1
see *LH Access Technology Ltd v HM Advocate* [2009] HCJAC 11, 2009 S.C.L. 622 (HCJ), Lady Paton; see *R. v Dodd (Costs)* [2009] 2 Costs L.R. 368 (Sup Ct Costs Office), Costs Judge Gordon-Saker; see *R. v LCH Contracts Ltd* [2009] EWCA Crim 902, [2009] 2 Cr. App. R. (S.) 101 (CA (Crim Div)), Maurice Kay, L.J.
s.l, applied: SI 2009/716 Reg.16
s.2, applied: SI 2009/716 Reg.16
s.2, see *Ahmed v Amnesty International* [2009] I.C.R. 1450 (EAT), Underhill, J. (President); see *R. v Chargot Ltd (t/a Contract Services)* [2008] UKHL 73, [2009] 1 W.L.R. 1 (HL), Lord Hoffmann; see *R. v TDG (UK) Ltd* [2008] EWCA Crim 1963, [2009] 1 Cr. App. R. (S.) 81 (CA (Crim Div)), Gage, L.J.
s.3, applied: SI 2009/716 Reg.16
s.3, see *HM Advocate v Munro & Sons (Highland) Ltd* [2009] HCJAC 10, 2009 S.L.T. 233 (HCJ), Lord Nimmo Smith; see *R. v Chargot Ltd (t/a Contract Services)* [2008] UKHL 73, [2009] 1 W.L.R. 1 (HL), Lord Hoffmann
s.4, applied: SI 2009/716 Reg.16
s.5, applied: SI 2009/716 Reg.16
s.6, applied: SI 2009/716 Reg.16
s.7, applied: SI 2009/716 Reg.16
s.7, see *R. v TDG (UK) Ltd* [2008] EWCA Crim 1963, [2009] 1 Cr. App. R. (S.) 81 (CA (Crim Div)), Gage, L.J.
s.8, applied: SI 2009/716 Reg.16
s.9, applied: SI 2009/716 Reg.16
s.10, applied: SI 2009/716 Reg.16
s.ll, applied: SI 2009/1595(b), SI 2009/1927(b), SI 2009/515 Reg.8, Sch.13, SI 2009/515(b), SI 2009/ 605, SI 2009/606, SI 2009/693, SI 2009/716, SI 2009/716 Reg.16
s.ll, referred to: SI 2009/515 Sch.7
s.12, applied: SI 2009/716 Reg.16
s.13, applied: SI 2009/716 Reg.16
s.14, applied: SI 2009/716 Reg.16
s.15, applied: SI 2009/716 Reg.16
s.15, enabling: SI 2009/605, SI 2009/606, SI 2009/ 693, SI 2009/716, SI 2009/1348, SI 2009/1927
s.16, applied: SI 2009/716 Reg.14, Reg.16
s.17, applied: SI 2009/716 Reg.14, Reg.16
s.18, applied: SI 2009/716 Reg.14, Reg.16
s.18, enabling: SI 2009/693, SI 2009/1927
s.19, applied: 2009 c.25 s.7, SI 2009/716 Reg.14, Reg.16
s.20, applied: SI 2009/716 Reg.14, Reg.16

1974– cont.

37. Health and Safety at Work etc Act 1974– *cont.*

s.21, applied: SI 2009/665 Art.2, SI 2009/716 Reg.14, Reg.16

s.22, applied: SI 2009/665 Art.2, SI 2009/716 Reg.14, Reg.16

s.23, applied: SI 2009/716 Reg.14, Reg.16

s.24, applied: SI 2009/515 Reg.17, SI 2009/716 Reg.14, Reg.16

s.25, applied: SI 2009/716 Reg.14, Reg.16

s.25A, applied: SI 2009/716 Reg.14, Reg.16

s.26, applied: SI 2009/716 Reg.14, Reg.16

s.27, applied: SI 2009/716 Reg.14, Reg.16

s.27A, applied: SI 2009/716 Reg.14, Reg.16

s.28, amended: 2009 c.20 Sch.6 para.42

s.28, applied: SI 2009/716 Reg.14, Reg.16

s.29, applied: SI 2009/716 Reg.16

s.30, applied: SI 2009/716 Reg.16

s.31, applied: SI 2009/716 Reg.16

s.32, applied: SI 2009/716 Reg.16

s.33, applied: SI 2009/716 Reg.14, Reg.16, SI 2009/1927 Reg.9

s.33, see *HM Advocate v Munro & Sons (Highland) Ltd* [2009] HCJAC 10, 2009 S.L.T. 233 (HCJ), Lord Nimmo Smith

s.34, amended: 2009 c.25 Sch.21 para.25

s.34, applied: SI 2009/716 Reg.14, Reg.16, SI 2009/1927 Reg.9

s.35, applied: SI 2009/716 Reg.14, Reg.16, SI 2009/1927 Reg.9

s.36, applied: SI 2009/716 Reg.14, Reg.16, SI 2009/1927 Reg.9

s.37, applied: SI 2009/716 Reg.14, Reg.16, SI 2009/1927 Reg.9

s.37, see *R. v Chargot Ltd (t/a Contract Services)* [2008] UKHL 73, [2009] 1 W.L.R. 1 (HL), Lord Hoffmann

s.38, applied: SI 2009/716 Reg.14, Reg.16, SI 2009/1927 Reg.9

s.39, applied: SI 2009/716 Reg.14, Reg.16, SI 2009/1927 Reg.9

s.40, applied: SI 2009/716 Reg.14, Reg.16, SI 2009/1927 Reg.9

s.40, see *R. v Chargot Ltd (t/a Contract Services)* [2008] UKHL 73, [2009] 1 W.L.R. 1 (HL), Lord Hoffmann

s.41, applied: SI 2009/716 Reg.14, Reg.16, SI 2009/1927 Reg.9

s.42, applied: SI 2009/716 Reg.14, Reg.16, SI 2009/1927 Reg.9

s.43, applied: SI 2009/716 Reg.16

s.43, enabling: SI 2009/515, SI 2009/1348, SI 2009/1595, SI 2009/1927

s.43A, applied: SI 2009/716 Reg.16

s.44, applied: SI 2009/716 Reg.16

s.45, applied: SI 2009/716 Reg.16

s.46, applied: SI 2009/716 Reg.16

s.47, applied: SI 2009/716 Reg.14, Reg.16

s.48, applied: SI 2009/716 Reg.16

s.49, applied: SI 2009/716 Reg.16

s.50, applied: SI 2009/605, SI 2009/606, SI 2009/693, SI 2009/716, SI 2009/716 Reg.16, SI 2009/1348, SI 2009/1927

s.51, applied: SI 2009/716 Reg.16

s.51A, applied: SI 2009/716 Reg.16

s.52, applied: SI 2009/716 Reg.16

s.53, applied: SI 2009/716 Reg.16

s.54, applied: SI 2009/716 Reg.16

s.80, applied: SI 2009/716 Reg.16

s.81, applied: SI 2009/716 Reg.16

1974– cont.

37. Health and Safety at Work etc Act 1974– *cont.*

s.82, applied: SI 2009/716 Reg.16

s.82, enabling: SI 2009/515, SI 2009/693, SI 2009/716, SI 2009/1348, SI 2009/1595, SI 2009/1927

s.84, enabling: SI 2009/1750

Sch.3 para.1, enabling: SI 2009/693, SI 2009/716, SI 2009/1348, SI 2009/1927

Sch.3 para.2, enabling: SI 2009/716, SI 2009/1348

Sch.3 para.3, enabling: SI 2009/716, SI 2009/1348

Sch.3 para.4, enabling: SI 2009/693, SI 2009/1348

Sch.3 para.5, enabling: SI 2009/693

Sch.3 para.6, enabling: SI 2009/693, SI 2009/1348, SI 2009/1927

Sch.3 para.7, enabling: SI 2009/693, SI 2009/1348

Sch.3 para.8, enabling: SI 2009/1348

Sch.3 para.9, enabling: SI 2009/693, SI 2009/1348

Sch.3 para.11, enabling: SI 2009/693, SI 2009/1348

Sch.3 para.12, enabling: SI 2009/1348

Sch.3 para.13, enabling: SI 2009/693, SI 2009/1348

Sch.3 para.14, enabling: SI 2009/693, SI 2009/1348

Sch.3 para.15, enabling: SI 2009/606, SI 2009/716, SI 2009/1348, SI 2009/1927

Sch.3 para.16, enabling: SI 2009/693, SI 2009/716, SI 2009/1348, SI 2009/1927

Sch.3 para.20, enabling: SI 2009/1348, SI 2009/1927

39. Consumer Credit Act 1974

see *Heath v Southern Pacific Mortgage Ltd* [2009] EWHC 103 (Ch), [2009] Bus. L.R. 984 (Ch D (Birmingham)), Judge Purle Q.C.; see *Maple Leaf Macro Volatility Master Fund v Rouvroy* [2009] EWHC 257 (Comm), [2009] 2 All E.R. (Comm) 287 (QBD (Comm)), Andrew Smith, J.

referred to: SI 2009/669 Sch.1 Part 1

s.2, amended: SI 2009/1835 Sch.1 para.2

s.15, see *TRM Copy Centres (UK) Ltd v Lanwall Services Ltd* [2009] UKHL 35, [2009] 1 W.L.R. 1375 (HL), Lord Hope of Craighead

s.16, amended: SI 2009/1941 Sch.1 para.28

s.16, applied: SI 2009/470 Reg.21

s.18, see *Heath v Southern Pacific Mortgage Ltd* [2009] EWHC 103 (Ch), [2009] Bus. L.R. 984 (Ch D (Birmingham)), Judge Purle Q.C.

s.21, disapplied: SI 2009/209 Reg.26

s.39, disapplied: SI 2009/209 Reg.26

s.40A, repealed: SI 2009/1835 Sch.1 para.3

s.41, amended: SI 2009/1835 Sch.1 para.4

s.41, repealed (in part): SI 2009/1835 Sch.1 para.4

s.41A, repealed: SI 2009/1835 Sch.1 para.6

s.41ZA, added: SI 2009/1835 Sch.1 para.5

s.41ZB, added: SI 2009/1835 Sch.1 para.5

s.51, applied: SI 2009/209 Reg.52

s.66, applied: SI 2009/209 Reg.52

s.76, applied: SI 2009/209 Reg.52

s.83, applied: SI 2009/209 Reg.52

s.84, applied: SI 2009/209 Reg.52

s.87, applied: SI 2009/209 Reg.52

s.139, see *Nolan v Wright* [2009] EWHC 305 (Ch), [2009] 3 All E.R. 823 (Ch D), Judge Hodge Q.C.

s.182, amended: SI 2009/1835 Sch.1 para.7

s.182, repealed (in part): SI 2009/1835 Sch.1 para.7

s.188, see *Heath v Southern Pacific Mortgage Ltd* [2009] EWCA Civ 1135, Times, November 20, 2009 (CA (Civ Div)), Waller, L.J. (V-P)

s.189, amended: SI 2009/1835 Sch.1 para.8

Sch.A1 Part 1 para.1, repealed: SI 2009/1835 Sch.1 para.9

Sch.A1 Part 2 para.2, applied: SI 2009/1835 Art.3

1974–cont.

39. Consumer Credit Act 1974–*cont.*

Sch.A1 Part 2 para.2, repealed: SI 2009/1835 Sch.1 para.9

Sch.A1 Part 2 para.3, applied: SI 2009/1835 Art.3

Sch.A1 Part 2 para.3, repealed: SI 2009/1835 Sch.1 para.9

Sch.A1 Part 2 para.4, repealed: SI 2009/1835 Sch.1 para.9

Sch.A1 Part 2 para.5, repealed: SI 2009/1835 Sch.1 para.9

Sch.A1 Part 2 para.6, repealed: SI 2009/1835 Sch.1 para.9

Sch.A1 Part 3 para.7, repealed: SI 2009/1835 Sch.1 para.9

Sch.A1 Part 4 para.8, repealed: SI 2009/1835 Sch.1 para.9

Sch.A1 Part 4 para.9, repealed: SI 2009/1835 Sch.1 para.9

Sch.A1 Part 4 para.10, repealed: SI 2009/1835 Sch.1 para.9

Sch.A1 Part 4 para.11, repealed: SI 2009/1835 Sch.1 para.9

Sch.A1 Part 4 para.12, repealed: SI 2009/1835 Sch.1 para.9

Sch.A1 Part 4 para.13, repealed: SI 2009/1835 Sch.1 para.9

Sch.A1 Part 4 para.14, repealed: SI 2009/1835 Sch.1 para.9

Sch.A1 Part 4 para.15, repealed: SI 2009/1835 Sch.1 para.9

Sch.A1 Part 4 para.16, repealed: SI 2009/1835 Sch.1 para.9

Sch.2, see *Heath v Southern Pacific Mortgage Ltd* [2009] EWCA Civ 1135, Times, November 20, 2009 (CA (Civ Div)), Waller, L.J. (V-P)

40. Control of Pollution Act 1974

applied: SI 2009/2325 Art.17

s.60, applied: SI 2009/665 Art.2, SI 2009/1300 Art.78, SI 2009/2364 Art.38

s.61, applied: SI 2009/665 Art.2, SI 2009/1300 Art.78, SI 2009/2364 Art.38

s.61, disapplied: SI 2009/1300 Art.78

s.65, applied: SI 2009/1300 Art.78, SI 2009/2364 Art.38

s.65, disapplied: SI 2009/1300 Art.78

46. Friendly Societies Act 1974

s.82, amended: SI 2009/1941 Sch.1 para.29

s.84, amended: SI 2009/1941 Sch.1 para.29

s.111, amended: SI 2009/1941 Sch.1 para.29

47. Solicitors Act 1974

s.11, applied: SI 2009/1365 Art.3

s.11, varied: SI 2009/1589 Art.3, Sch.1

s.13, varied: SI 2009/1589 Art.3, Sch.1

s.13A, varied: SI 2009/1589 Art.3, Sch.1

s.13B, varied: SI 2009/1589 Art.3, Sch.1

s.13ZA, applied: SI 2009/1365 Art.3

s.13ZB, applied: SI 2009/1365 Art.3

s.16, varied: SI 2009/1589 Art.3, Sch.1

s.22, applied: SI 2009/3250 Art.5

s.23, amended: SI 2009/1941 Sch.1 para.30

s.23, applied: SI 2009/3250 Art.5

s.24, applied: SI 2009/3250 Art.5

s.26, applied: SI 2009/3250 Art.5

s.28, applied: SI 2009/1365 Art.3

s.28, referred to: SI 2009/1589 Art.4

s.28, varied: SI 2009/1589 Art.4

s.32, varied: SI 2009/1589 Art.3, Sch.1

s.33A, varied: SI 2009/1589 Art.3

s.34, varied: SI 2009/1589 Art.3, Art.5

1974–cont.

47. Solicitors Act 1974–*cont.*

s.36, see *Law Society v Shah* [2007] EWHC 2841 (Ch), [2009] Ch. 223 (Ch D), Floyd, J

s.36, applied: SI 2009/503 Art.4

s.36, referred to: SI 2009/503 Art.5

s.36, varied: SI 2009/503 Art.4

s.36A, applied: SI 2009/503 Art.4

s.41, varied: SI 2009/1589 Art.5

s.42, varied: SI 2009/1589 Art.5

s.43, applied: SI 2009/503 Art.4

s.44B, varied: SI 2009/503 Art.4, SI 2009/1589 Art.3, Sch.1

s.44BA, varied: SI 2009/1589 Art.5

s.44BC, varied: SI 2009/1589 Art.5

s.44C, applied: SI 2009/503 Art.4

s.44C, varied: SI 2009/1589 Art.3, Sch.1

s.44D, see *Napier v Pressdram Ltd* [2009] EWCA Civ 443, [2009] C.P. Rep. 36 (CA (Civ Div)), Hughes, L.J.

s.44D, applied: SI 2009/503 Art.4

s.44D, varied: SI 2009/1589 Art.3, Sch.1

s.44E, see *Napier v Pressdram Ltd* [2009] EWCA Civ 443, [2009] C.P. Rep. 36 (CA (Civ Div)), Hughes, L.J.

s.44E, varied: SI 2009/1589 Art.3, Sch.1

s.47, varied: SI 2009/503 Art.4, SI 2009/1589 Art.3, Sch.1

s.56, applied: SI 2009/1931

s.56, varied: SI 2009/503 Art.4

s.56, enabling: SI 2009/1931

s.66, varied: SI 2009/503 Art.4

s.68, varied: SI 2009/1589 Art.3

s.70, see *Mastercigars Direct Ltd v Withers LLP* [2007] EWHC 2733 (Ch), [2009] 1 W.L.R. 881 (Ch D), Morgan, J.

s.73, see *Mastercigars Direct Ltd v Withers LLP* [2007] EWHC 2733 (Ch), [2009] 1 W.L.R. 881 (Ch D), Morgan, J.

s.81A, applied: SI 2009/3250 Art.9

s.83, varied: SI 2009/1589 Art.3

s.84, varied: SI 2009/1589 Art.3, Sch.1

Sch.1A, applied: SI 2009/1931 Art.5

Sch.1 Part I para.1, varied: SI 2009/1589 Art.3, Sch.1

Sch.1 Part II para.6B, applied: SI 2009/503 Art.4

Sch.2, referred to: SI 2009/503 Art.5

53. Rehabilitation of Offenders Act 1974

applied: 2009 c.23 Sch.1 para.9, SI 2009/1209 r.96, SI 2009/1211 r.86, SI 2009/2041 r.114, SI 2009/3297 Reg.5

varied: SI 2009/1059 Sch.1 para.14

s.1, applied: SSI 2009/210 Sch.3 para.10

s.4, enabling: SI 2009/1818, SSI 2009/271, SSI 2009/334

s.5, amended: 2009 c.26 s.18

s.6, amended: 2009 c.26 s.18

s.7, amended: 2009 c.25 s.158

s.7, enabling: SI 2009/1818

s.10, applied: SSI 2009/271, SSI 2009/334

s.10, enabling: SI 2009/1818

Sch.2 para.4, enabling: SI 2009/1818

Sch.2 para.6, enabling: SI 2009/1818

1975

7. Finance Act 1975

applied: SI 2009/1114 Art.6

s.48, amended: 2009 c.10 s.105

s.57, repealed: SI 2009/56 Sch.1 para.67

1975–cont.

14. Social Security Act 1975
referred to: SI 2009/500 Sch.1 Part 1
s.126A, varied: SI 2009/497 Art.4

20. District Courts (Scotland) Act 1975
repealed: SSI 2009/332 Art.7
s.1A, repealed (in part): SSI 2009/115 Sch.3, SSI 2009/331 Sch.3
s.5, repealed (in part): SSI 2009/115 Sch.3, SSI 2009/331 Sch.3
s.7, repealed (in part): SSI 2009/115 Sch.3, SSI 2009/331 Sch.3
s.8, repealed (in part): SSI 2009/115 Sch.3, SSI 2009/331 Sch.3
s.17, repealed (in part): SSI 2009/115 Sch.3, SSI 2009/331 Sch.3
s.18, repealed (in part): SSI 2009/115 Sch.3, SSI 2009/331 Sch.3
s.20, repealed (in part): SSI 2009/115 Sch.3, SSI 2009/331 Sch.3
s.23, repealed (in part): SSI 2009/115 Sch.3, SSI 2009/331 Sch.3

22. Oil Taxation Act 1975
s.2, amended: 2009 c.10 Sch.43 para.3
s.2, repealed (in part): 2009 c.10 Sch.43 para.3
s.3, amended: 2009 c.4 Sch.1 para.314, Sch.3 Part 1, 2009 c.10 Sch.41 para.1
s.6, amended: 2009 c.10 Sch.45 para.3
s.8, amended: SI 2009/730 Art.15
s.9, repealed (in part): 2009 c.10 Sch.45 para.1
s.12, amended: 2009 c.10 Sch.42 para.2, Sch.42 para.6
Sch.1 para.1, amended: 2009 c.10 Sch.42 para.7
Sch.1 para.2, amended: 2009 c.10 Sch.42 para.7
Sch.1 para.3, amended: 2009 c.10 Sch.42 para.7
Sch.1 para.4, amended: 2009 c.10 Sch.42 para.7
Sch.1 para.5, amended: 2009 c.10 Sch.42 para.7
Sch.1 para.6, added: 2009 c.10 Sch.42 para.7
Sch.1 para.7, added: 2009 c.10 Sch.42 para.7
Sch.2 para.1, amended: 2009 c.10 Sch.51 para.18, SI 2009/56 Sch.1 para.70
Sch.2 para.1, applied: 2009 c.10 Sch.52 para.11
Sch.2 para.2, applied: 2009 c.10 Sch.55 para.1
Sch.2 para.3, amended: SI 2009/56 Sch.1 para.71
Sch.2 para.6, amended: SI 2009/56 Sch.1 para.72
Sch.2 para.8, amended: SI 2009/56 Sch.1 para.73
Sch.2 para.10, amended: 2009 c.10 Sch.51 para.19
Sch.2 para.11, applied: 2009 c.10 Sch.56 para.1
Sch.2 para.12, amended: 2009 c.10 Sch.51 para.20
Sch.2 para.12A, amended: 2009 c.10 Sch.51 para.21
Sch.2 para.12B, added: 2009 c.10 Sch.51 para.22
Sch.2 para.13, applied: 2009 c.10 Sch.56 para.1
Sch.2 para.14, amended: SI 2009/56 Sch.1 para.74, SI 2009/777 Art.2
Sch.2 para.14A, added: SI 2009/56 Sch.1 para.75
Sch.2 para.14B, added: SI 2009/56 Sch.1 para.75
Sch.2 para.14C, added: SI 2009/56 Sch.1 para.75
Sch.2 para.14D, added: SI 2009/56 Sch.1 para.75
Sch.2 para.14E, added: SI 2009/56 Sch.1 para.75
Sch.2 para.14F, added: SI 2009/56 Sch.1 para.75
Sch.2 para.14G, added: SI 2009/56 Sch.1 para.75
Sch.2 para.14H, added: SI 2009/56 Sch.1 para.75
Sch.2 para.14I, added: SI 2009/56 Sch.1 para.75
Sch.3 para.9, repealed: 2009 c.10 Sch.45 para.1
Sch.3 para.10, repealed: 2009 c.10 Sch.45 para.1
Sch.4 para.3, repealed: 2009 c.10 Sch.45 para.1
Sch.5 para.2, amended: 2009 c.10 Sch.51 para.23
Sch.5 para.2C, amended: 2009 c.10 Sch.42 para.3
Sch.5 para.5, amended: SI 2009/56 Sch.1 para.77

1975–cont.

22. Oil Taxation Act 1975–*cont.*
Sch.5 para.6, amended: SI 2009/56 Sch.1 para.78
Sch.5 para.7, amended: SI 2009/56 Sch.1 para.79
Sch.5 para.8, amended: SI 2009/56 Sch.1 para.80
Sch.5 para.9, amended: 2009 c.10 Sch.51 para.24, SI 2009/56 Sch.1 para.81
Sch.5 para.9, repealed (in part): 2009 c.10 Sch.51 para.24
Sch.5 para.10, added: SI 2009/56 Sch.1 para.82
Sch.6 para.1, amended: 2009 c.10 Sch.51 para.25
Sch.6 para.2, amended: 2009 c.10 Sch.51 para.25, SI 2009/56 Sch.1 para.83
Sch.7 para.1, amended: 2009 c.10 Sch.51 para.26, SI 2009/56 Sch.1 para.84
Sch.8 para.3, amended: SI 2009/56 Sch.1 para.85

23. Reservoirs Act 1975
applied: 2009 asp 6 s.85
s.1, amended: 2009 asp 6 s.84
s.1, applied: SI 2009/3042 Reg.36
s.2, amended: 2009 asp 6 s.84
s.2, applied: 2009 asp 6 s.85
s.12C, added: 2009 asp 6 s.89
s.12ZA, added: 2009 asp 6 s.88
s.15, amended: 2009 asp 6 s.86
s.18, amended: SI 2009/1307 Sch.1 para.113
s.22B, added: 2009 asp 6 s.86
s.27B, added: 2009 asp 6 s.90
Sch.1, amended: 2009 asp 6 s.84

24. House of Commons Disqualification Act 1975
Sch.1 Part I, amended: SI 2009/56 Sch.1 para.86
Sch.1 Part II, amended: 2009 c.13 Sch.1 para.8, 2009 c.20 Sch.1 para.22, 2009 c.23 Sch.2 para.3, SI 2009/1307 Sch.1 para.114, SI 2009/1834 Sch.1 para.1
Sch.1 Part III, amended: 2009 c.13 Sch.2 para.9, 2009 c.22 Sch.3 para.21, Sch.12 para.5, Sch.15 para.7, 2009 c.25 Sch.21 para.26, Sch.23 Part 5, SI 2009/56 Sch.1 para.86, SI 2009/1941 Sch.1 para.31

25. Northern Ireland Assembly Disqualification Act 1975
Sch.1 Part II, amended: 2009 c.13 Sch.1 para.8, SI 2009/56 Sch.1 para.87, SI 2009/1307 Sch.1 para.115, SI 2009/1834 Sch.1 para.2
Sch.1 Part III, amended: 2009 c.13 Sch.2 para.9, 2009 c.22 Sch.12 para.6, 2009 c.25 Sch.21 para.27, Sch.23 Part 5, SI 2009/1941 Sch.1 para.32

26. Ministers of the Crown Act 1975
s.1, enabling: SI 2009/229, SI 2009/2748
s.2, enabling: SI 2009/229, SI 2009/2748

30. Local Government (Scotland) Act 1975
s.7B, applied: SSI 2009/3 Art.2
s.7B, enabling: SSI 2009/3
s.9A, enabling: SSI 2009/76
s.37, enabling: SSI 2009/3

47. Litigants in Person (Costs and Expenses) Act 1975
s.1, amended: SI 2009/1307 Sch.1 para.116

51. Salmon and Freshwater Fisheries Act 1975
s.1, amended: 2009 c.23 s.215, Sch.22 Part 5
s.1, repealed (in part): 2009 c.23 Sch.22 Part 5
s.2, amended: 2009 c.23 s.216
s.3, repealed: 2009 c.23 Sch.16 para.2, Sch.22 Part 5
s.4, amended: 2009 c.23 Sch.22 Part 5
s.4, repealed (in part): 2009 c.23 Sch.22 Part 5
s.5, amended: 2009 c.23 Sch.16 para.3
s.6, repealed: 2009 c.23 Sch.16 para.4, Sch.22 Part 5
s.7, repealed: 2009 c.23 Sch.16 para.4, Sch.22 Part 5

1975– cont.

51. Salmon and Freshwater Fisheries Act 1975– cont.

s.8, repealed: 2009 c.23 Sch.16 para.4, Sch.22 Part 5

s.16, repealed: 2009 c.23 Sch.16 para.5, Sch.22 Part 5

s.17, repealed: 2009 c.23 Sch.16 para.6, Sch.22 Part 5

s.18, amended: 2009 c.23 Sch.16 para.7

s.19, repealed: 2009 c.23 Sch.22 Part 5

s.20, repealed: 2009 c.23 Sch.16 para.8, Sch.22 Part 5

s.21, repealed: 2009 c.23 Sch.22 Part 5

s.22, repealed: 2009 c.23 Sch.22 Part 5

s.23, repealed: 2009 c.23 Sch.22 Part 5

s.24, repealed: 2009 c.23 Sch.22 Part 5

s.25, amended: 2009 c.23 s.217, s.219, Sch.16 para.9, Sch.22 Part 5

s.25, disapplied: SI 2009/3344 Reg.10, Reg.11

s.25, repealed (in part): 2009 c.23 Sch.22 Part 5

s.26, amended: 2009 c.23 s.218, s.219, Sch.16 para.10

s.27, amended: 2009 c.23 s.219, Sch.16 para.11

s.27A, added: 2009 c.23 s.219

s.27A, amended: 2009 c.23 s.219

s.27B, added: 2009 c.23 s.219

s.27B, amended: 2009 c.23 s.219

s.31, amended: 2009 c.23 s.220, Sch.22 Part 5

s.32, repealed (in part): 2009 c.23 Sch.22 Part 5

s.33, amended: 2009 c.23 s.220, Sch.16 para.12

s.34, amended: 2009 c.23 Sch.16 para.13, Sch.22 Part 5

s.35, amended: 2009 c.23 s.220

s.35, repealed (in part): 2009 c.23 Sch.22 Part 5

s.40A, added: 2009 c.23 s.221

s.40B, added: 2009 c.23 s.222

s.41, amended: 2009 c.23 s.221, s.223, Sch.16 para.14, SI 2009/463 Sch.2 para.3, SSI 2009/85 Sch.2 para.3

Sch.1 para.1, repealed: 2009 c.23 Sch.22 Part 5

Sch.1 para.2, repealed: 2009 c.23 Sch.22 Part 5

Sch.1 para.3, repealed: 2009 c.23 Sch.22 Part 5

Sch.1 para.4, repealed: 2009 c.23 Sch.22 Part 5

Sch.1 para.5, repealed: 2009 c.23 Sch.22 Part 5

Sch.1 para.6, repealed: 2009 c.23 Sch.22 Part 5

Sch.2 para.1, amended: 2009 c.23 Sch.16 para.16

Sch.2 para.2, amended: 2009 c.23 Sch.16 para.16

Sch.2 para.3, amended: 2009 c.23 Sch.16 para.16

Sch.2 para.4, amended: 2009 c.23 Sch.16 para.16

Sch.2 para.5, amended: 2009 c.23 Sch.16 para.16

Sch.2 para.7, amended: 2009 c.23 Sch.16 para.16

Sch.2 para.9, amended: 2009 c.23 Sch.16 para.16

Sch.2 para.10, amended: 2009 c.23 Sch.16 para.16

Sch.2 para.11, amended: 2009 c.23 s.217, Sch.22 Part 5

Sch.2 para.12, repealed: 2009 c.23 s.217, Sch.22 Part 5

Sch.2 para.13, amended: 2009 c.23 Sch.16 para.16

Sch.2 para.14A, added: 2009 c.23 s.217

Sch.2 para.15, amended: 2009 c.23 Sch.16 para.16

Sch.2 para.17, amended: 2009 c.23 Sch.16 para.16

Sch.4 Part I para.1, amended: 2009 c.23 s.219, s.220, Sch.16 para.17, Sch.22 Part 5

Sch.4 Part II para.7, amended: 2009 c.23 Sch.16 para.17

Sch.4 Part II para.9, amended: 2009 c.23 Sch.16 para.17

Sch.4 Part II para.10, amended: 2009 c.23 Sch.16 para.17

Sch.4 Part II para.11, amended: 2009 c.23 Sch.16 para.17

1975– cont.

52. Safety of Sports Grounds Act 1975

see *Chief Constable of Greater Manchester v Wigan Athletic AFC Ltd* [2008] EWCA Civ 1449, [2009] 1 W.L.R. 1580 (CA (Civ Div)), Sir Andrew Morritt (Chancellor)

applied: SI 2009/373 Art.2, SI 2009/1394 Art.2, SI 2009/1501 Art.2

s.1, enabling: SI 2009/373, SI 2009/1394, SI 2009/1501

s.10, applied: SI 2009/665 Art.2

s.18, applied: SI 2009/373, SI 2009/1394, SI 2009/1501

55. Statutory Corporations (Financial Provisions) Act 1975

s.5, repealed (in part): SI 2009/484 Sch.2

Sch.2, repealed (in part): SI 2009/484 Sch.2

60. Social Security Pensions Act 1975

s.59, applied: SI 2009/692 Art.6

s.59, enabling: SI 2009/692

s.59A, applied: SI 2009/692 Art.5

s.63, enabling: SI 2009/2206

63. Inheritance (Provision for Family and Dependants) Act 1975

see *Barron v Woodhead* [2008] EWHC 810 (Ch), [2009] 1 F.L.R. 747 (Ch D (Newcastle)), Judge Behrens; see *Baynes v Hedger* [2009] EWCA Civ 374, [2009] 2 F.L.R. 767 (CA (Civ Div)), Sir Andrew Morritt (Chancellor); see *Webster v Webster* [2008] EWHC 31 (Ch), [2009] 1 F.L.R. 1240 (Ch D (Leeds)), Judge Behrens

s.1, see *Baynes v Hedger* [2009] EWCA Civ 374, [2009] 2 F.L.R. 767 (CA (Civ Div)), Sir Andrew Morritt (Chancellor); see *Challinor v Challinor* [2009] EWHC 180 (Ch), [2009] W.T.L.R. 931 (Ch D), Judge David Cooke; see *Lindop v Agus* [2009] EWHC 1795 (Ch), [2009] W.T.L.R. 1175 (Ch D (Leeds)), Judge Behrens

s.3, see *Barron v Woodhead* [2008] EWHC 810 (Ch), [2009] 1 F.L.R. 747 (Ch D (Newcastle)), Judge Behrens; see *Challinor v Challinor* [2009] EWHC 180 (Ch), [2009] W.T.L.R. 931 (Ch D), Judge David Cooke

s.19, applied: 2009 c.10 Sch.53 para.8, Sch.54 para.10

65. Sex Discrimination Act 1975

see *Wilson v Health and Safety Executive* [2009] EWCA Civ 1074, Times, October 26, 2009 (CA (Civ Div)), Sedley, L.J.

referred to: SI 2009/500 Sch.1 Part 1

s.1, see *Carl v University of Sheffield* [2009] 3 C.M.L.R. 21 (EAT), Judge Peter Clark; see *Hartlepool BC v Llewellyn* [2009] I.C.R. 1426 (EAT), Underhill, J. (President)

s.76, see *Tradition Securities and Futures SA v X* [2009] I.C.R. 88 (EAT), Bean, J.

s.85, applied: SI 2009/1059 Art.196

68. Industry Act 1975

s.37, amended: SI 2009/1941 Sch.1 para.33

70. Welsh Development Agency Act 1975

s.27, amended: SI 2009/1941 Sch.1 para.34

Sch.4 Part IV para.15, amended: SI 2009/1307 Sch.1 para.117

76. Local Land Charges Act 1975

s.14, enabling: SI 2009/2494

1976

14. Fatal Accidents and Sudden Deaths Inquiry (Scotland) Act 1976
 see *Global Santa Fe Drilling (North Sea) Ltd v Lord Advocate* [2009] CSIH 43, 2009 S.C. 575 (IH (1 Div)), Lord President Hamilton; see *Niven v Lord Advocate* [2009] CSOH 110, 2009 S.L.T. 876 (OH), Lord Malcolm
 applied: 2009 c.25 s.12, s.13
 s.1, see *Niven v Lord Advocate* [2009] CSOH 110, 2009 S.L.T. 876 (OH), Lord Malcolm
 s.1A, added: 2009 c.25 s.50
 s.2, amended: 2009 c.25 s.50
 s.3, amended: 2009 c.25 s.50
 s.6, amended: 2009 c.25 s.50
31. Legitimacy Act 1976
 s.1, see *A v H* [2009] EWHC 636 (Fam), [2009] 4 All E.R. 641 (Fam Div), Sir Christopher Sumner
35. Police Pensions Act 1976
 s.1, applied: SSI 2009/185
 s.1, enabling: SI 2009/2060, SSI 2009/185
 s.3, enabling: SSI 2009/185
 s.7, amended: 2009 c.26 s.81
 s.7, enabling: SSI 2009/185
 s.11, see *R. (on the application of Ashton) v Police Medical Appeal Board* [2008] EWHC 1833 (Admin), [2009] I.C.R. 51 (QBD (Admin)), Charles, J.
 s.11, amended: 2009 c.26 s.81
 s.11A, added: 2009 c.26 s.10
36. Adoption Act 1976
 s.34, applied: SSI 2009/154 Sch.1 para.14
52. Armed Forces Act 1976
 applied: 2009 c.25 Sch.22 para.19, Sch.22 para.20, SI 2009/1059 Art.157
 s.7, applied: SI 2009/1059 Art.53
 Sch.3 para.6, applied: SI 2009/1059 Art.52
 Sch.3 para.18, applied: SI 2009/1059 Art.129, Art.134
 Sch.3 para.20, applied: SI 2009/1059 Art.176
57. Local Government (Miscellaneous Provisions) Act 1976
 s.15, amended: SI 2009/1307 Sch.1 para.119
 s.24, amended: SI 2009/1307 Sch.1 para.120
 s.44, amended: 2009 c.20 Sch.6 para.43
 s.45, varied: SI 2009/2863 Reg.4
 s.46, see *R. (on the application of Newcastle City Council) v Berwick-upon-Tweed BC* [2008] EWHC 2369 (Admin), [2009] R.T.R. 34 (QBD (Admin)), Christopher Symons Q.C.
 s.46, varied: SI 2009/2863 Reg.4
 s.48, applied: SI 2009/2863 Reg.4
 s.48, varied: SI 2009/2863 Reg.4
 s.49, varied: SI 2009/2863 Reg.4
 s.50, varied: SI 2009/2863 Reg.4
 s.51, varied: SI 2009/2863 Reg.4
 s.52, varied: SI 2009/2863 Reg.4
 s.53, varied: SI 2009/2863 Reg.4
 s.54, varied: SI 2009/2863 Reg.4
 s.57, see *R. (on the application of Newcastle City Council) v Berwick-upon-Tweed BC* [2008] EWHC 2369 (Admin), [2009] R.T.R. 34 (QBD (Admin)), Christopher Symons Q.C.
 s.57, varied: SI 2009/2863 Reg.4
 s.58, varied: SI 2009/2863 Reg.4
 s.60, varied: SI 2009/2863 Reg.4
 s.61, varied: SI 2009/2863 Reg.4
 s.68, varied: SI 2009/2863 Reg.4
 s.70, varied: SI 2009/2863 Reg.4
 s.72, varied: SI 2009/2863 Reg.4

1976– cont.

57. Local Government (Miscellaneous Provisions) Act 1976– *cont.*
 s.73, varied: SI 2009/2863 Reg.4
 s.74, varied: SI 2009/2863 Reg.4
 s.75, varied: SI 2009/2863 Reg.4
 s.76, varied: SI 2009/2863 Reg.4
 s.77, varied: SI 2009/2863 Reg.4
 s.78, varied: SI 2009/2863 Reg.4
 s.79, varied: SI 2009/2863 Reg.4
 s.80, varied: SI 2009/2863 Reg.4
 Sch.1 Part II para.7, amended: SI 2009/1307 Sch.1 para.121
58. International Carriage of Perishable Foodstuffs Act 1976
 applied: SI 2009/711 Sch.1 para.1, Sch.1 para.2
 s.3, applied: SI 2009/711 Art.3
 s.4, applied: SI 2009/711 Art.3
63. Bail Act 1976
 s.4, amended: 2009 c.25 Sch.21 para.74, 2009 c.26 Sch.7 para.19, Sch.8 Part 2
 s.7, see *R. (on the application of Thomas) v Greenwich Magistrates' Court* [2009] EWHC 1180 (Admin), (2009) 173 J.P. 345 (QBD (Admin)), Hickinbottom, J.
 s.7, amended: 2009 c.25 Sch.21 para.74
 Sch.1 Part I para.4, varied: SI 2009/1059 Sch.1 para.15
 Sch.1 Part I para.6ZA, added: 2009 c.25 s.114
 Sch.1 Part I para.9, amended: 2009 c.25 s.114
 Sch.1 Part II para.4, varied: SI 2009/1059 Sch.1 para.15
67. Sexual Offences (Scotland) Act 1976
 s.2A, applied: 2009 asp 9 Sch.1 para.24
 s.2A, referred to: SI 2009/37 Sch.1 para.2, Sch.1 para.4
 s.2B, applied: 2009 asp 9 Sch.1 para.24
 s.2B, referred to: SI 2009/37 Sch.1 para.2, Sch.1 para.4
 s.2C, applied: 2009 asp 9 Sch.1 para.24
 s.2C, referred to: SI 2009/37 Sch.1 para.2, Sch.1 para.4
 s.3, applied: 2009 asp 9 Sch.1 para.24
 s.3, referred to: SI 2009/37 Sch.1 para.1
 s.4, applied: 2009 asp 9 Sch.1 para.24
 s.4, referred to: SI 2009/37 Sch.1 para.2, Sch.1 para.4
 s.5, applied: 2009 asp 9 Sch.1 para.24
 s.10, applied: 2009 asp 9 Sch.1 para.24
74. Race Relations Act 1976
 see *Coutinho v Rank Nemo (DMS) Ltd* [2009] EWCA Civ 454, [2009] I.C.R. 1296 (CA (Civ Div)), Mummery, L.J.; see *R. (on the application of E) v JFS Governing Body* [2009] EWCA Civ 626, [2009] 4 All E.R. 375 (CA (Civ Div)), Sedley, L.J.
 referred to: SI 2009/500 Sch.1 Part 1
 s.1, see *Carl v University of Sheffield* [2009] 3 C.M.L.R. 21 (EAT), Judge Peter Clark; see *R. (on the application of E) v JFS Governing Body* [2009] EWCA Civ 626, [2009] 4 All E.R. 375 (CA (Civ Div)), Sedley, L.J.; see *R. (on the application of E) v JFS Governing Body* [2009] UKSC 15 (SC), Lord Phillips (President)
 s.3, see *R. (on the application of E) v JFS Governing Body* [2009] UKSC 15 (SC), Lord Phillips (President)
 s.3, applied: SI 2009/3050 Art.3
 s.3A, see *Richmond Pharmacology Ltd v Dhaliwal* [2009] I.C.R. 724 (EAT), Underhill, J.

1976–cont.

74. Race Relations Act 1976–*cont.*
s.9, disapplied: SI 2009/1743 Art.4
s.20, applied: SI 2009/1914 Reg.12
s.41, see *Ahmed v Amnesty International* [2009] I.C.R. 1450 (EAT), Underhill, J. (President)
s.54A, see *Abbey National Plc v Chagger* [2009] I.C.R. 624 (EAT), Underhill, J.
s.57, varied: SI 2009/1059 Sch.1 para.16
s.71, see *R. (on the application of C) v Secretary of State for Justice* [2008] EWCA Civ 882, [2009] Q.B. 657 (CA (Civ Div)), Buxton, L.J.; see *South Cambridgeshire DC v Gammell* [2008] EWCA Civ 1159, [2009] B.L.G.R. 141 (CA (Civ Div)), Keene, L.J.
s.75, applied: SI 2009/1059 Art.196
s.78, varied: SI 2009/1059 Sch.1 para.16
Sch.1A Part I para.26, substituted: SSI 2009/248 Sch.1 para.2
Sch.1A Part II, amended: 2009 c.20 Sch.6 para.44, 2009 c.22 Sch.6 para.1, Sch.12 para.7, 2009 c.23 Sch.2 para.4, 2009 c.25 Sch.23 Part 4, 2009 c.26 s.2, SI 2009/3019 Art.11

76. Energy Act 1976
referred to: SI 2009/669 Sch.1 Part 2, Sch.1 Part 6
s.6, see *R. (on the application of Mabanaft Ltd) v Secretary of State for Trade and Industry* [2009] EWCA Civ 224, [2009] Eu. L.R. 799 (CA (Civ Div)), Arden, L.J.

77. Weights and Measures etc Act 1976
referred to: SI 2009/669 Sch.1 Part 2

78. Industrial Common Ownership Act 1976
s.2, amended: SI 2009/1941 Sch.1 para.35

80. Rent (Agriculture) Act 1976
s.5, amended: 2009 c.20 Sch.6 para.45

86. Fishery Limits Act 1976
s.1, amended: 2009 c.23 Sch.4 para.2
s.1, referred to: 2009 c.23 Sch.4 para.2
s.1, repealed (in part): 2009 c.23 Sch.4 para.2, Sch.22 Part 1
Sch.1 para.1, repealed: 2009 c.23 Sch.22 Part 4

1977

3. Aircraft and Shipbuilding Industries Act 1977
s.9, amended: SI 2009/1941 Sch.1 para.36
s.56, amended: SI 2009/1941 Sch.1 para.36

5. Social Security (Miscellaneous Provisions) Act 1977
s.12, enabling: SI 2009/706
s.24, enabling: SI 2009/706

7. Nuclear Industry (Finance) Act 1977
s.3, amended: SI 2009/1941 Sch.1 para.37

15. Marriage (Scotland) Act 1977
s.2, amended: SI 2009/1892 Sch.1 para.1
s.3, enabling: SSI 2009/64, SSI 2009/315
s.6, enabling: SSI 2009/315
s.19, enabling: SSI 2009/64
s.25, applied: SSI 2009/64, SSI 2009/315

30. Rentcharges Act 1977
s.6, amended: SI 2009/1307 Sch.1 para.123
s.7, amended: SI 2009/1307 Sch.1 para.124
s.13, amended: SI 2009/1307 Sch.1 para.125

37. Patents Act 1977
see *Ratiopharm GmbH v Napp Pharmaceutical Holdings Ltd* [2009] EWCA Civ 252, [2009] R.P.C. 18 (CA (Civ Div)), Jacob, L.J.
s.1, see *Blacklight Power Inc v Comptroller-General of Patents* [2008] EWHC 2763 (Pat), [2009] Bus. L.R. 748 (Ch D (Patents Ct)), Floyd, J; see

1977–cont.

37. Patents Act 1977–*cont.*
s.1–*cont.*
Symbian Ltd v Comptroller General of Patents, Designs and Trademarks [2008] EWCA Civ 1066, [2009] Bus. L.R. 607 (CA (Civ Div)), Jacob, L.J.
s.2, see *Edwards Lifesciences AG v Cook Biotech Inc* [2009] EWHC 1304 (Pat), [2009] F.S.R. 27 (Ch D (Patents Ct)), Kitchin, J.
s.4A, see *Laboratorios Almirall SA v Boehringer Ingelheim International GmbH* [2009] EWHC 102 (Pat), [2009] F.S.R. 12 (Ch D (Patents Ct)), Judge Fysh Q.C.
s.14, see *Blacklight Power Inc v Comptroller-General of Patents* [2008] EWHC 2763 (Pat), [2009] Bus. L.R. 748 (Ch D (Patents Ct)), Floyd, J; see *Generics (UK) Ltd v H Lundbeck A/S* [2009] UKHL 12, [2009] Bus. L.R. 828 (HL), Lord Phillips of Worth Matravers; see *Laboratorios Almirall SA v Boehringer Ingelheim International GmbH* [2009] EWHC 102 (Pat), [2009] F.S.R. 12 (Ch D (Patents Ct)), Judge Fysh Q.C.
s.30, see *Siemens Schweiz AG v Thorn Security Ltd* [2008] EWCA Civ 1161, [2009] R.P.C. 3 (CA (Civ Div)), Mummery, L.J.
s.33, see *Siemens Schweiz AG v Thorn Security Ltd* [2008] EWCA Civ 1161, [2009] R.P.C. 3 (CA (Civ Div)), Mummery, L.J.
s.40, see *Kelly v GE Healthcare Ltd* [2009] EWHC 181 (Pat), [2009] R.P.C. 12 (Ch D (Patents Ct)), Floyd, J
s.41, see *Kelly v GE Healthcare Ltd* [2009] EWHC 181 (Pat), [2009] R.P.C. 12 (Ch D (Patents Ct)), Floyd, J
s.55, applied: 2009 c.4 s.923
s.56, applied: 2009 c.4 s.923
s.57, applied: 2009 c.4 s.923
s.57A, applied: 2009 c.4 s.923
s.58, applied: 2009 c.4 s.923
s.59, applied: 2009 c.4 s.923
s.60, see *Corevalve Inc v Edwards Lifesciences AG* [2009] EWHC 6 (Pat), [2009] F.S.R. 8 (Ch D (Patents Ct)), Peter Prescott Q.C.
s.68, see *Siemens Schweiz AG v Thorn Security Ltd* [2008] EWCA Civ 1161, [2009] R.P.C. 3 (CA (Civ Div)), Mummery, L.J.
s.72, see *Corevalve Inc v Edwards Lifesciences AG* [2009] EWHC 6 (Pat), [2009] F.S.R. 8 (Ch D (Patents Ct)), Peter Prescott Q.C.; see *Generics (UK) Ltd v H Lundbeck A/S* [2009] UKHL 12, [2009] Bus. L.R. 828 (HL), Lord Phillips of Worth Matravers; see *Laboratorios Almirall SA v Boehringer Ingelheim International GmbH* [2009] EWHC 102 (Pat), [2009] F.S.R. 12 (Ch D (Patents Ct)), Judge Fysh Q.C.; see *TNS Group Holdings Ltd v Nielsen Media Research Inc* [2009] EWHC 1160 (Pat), [2009] F.S.R. 23 (Ch D (Patents Ct)), Arnold, J.
s.90, enabling: SI 2009/2746
s.123, enabling: SI 2009/546, SI 2009/2089
s.124, enabling: SI 2009/2746
Sch.A2 para.3, see *Practice Notice (PO: Inventions involving human embryonic cells)* [2009] Bus. L.R. 627 (PO), Sean Dennehey

42. Rent Act 1977
see *Truro Diocesan Board of Finance Ltd v Foley* [2008] EWCA Civ 1162, [2009] 1 W.L.R. 2218 (CA (Civ Div)), May, L.J.
s.14, amended: 2009 c.20 Sch.6 para.46

1977–cont.

42. Rent Act 1977–cont.
s.98, see *Whitehouse v Lee* [2009] EWCA Civ 375, [2009] L. & T.R. 29 (CA (Civ Div)), Waller, L.J.

43. Protection from Eviction Act 1977
s.3A, amended: 2009 c.20 Sch.6 para.47

45. Criminal Law Act 1977
s.1, see *R. (on the application of Minshall) v Marylebone Magistrates' Court* [2008] EWHC 2800 (Admin), [2009] 2 All E.R. 806 (QBD (Admin)), Pitchford, J.; see *R. v Kenning (David Matthew)* [2008] EWCA Crim 1534, [2009] Q.B. 221 (CA (Crim Div)), Lord Phillips of Worth Matravers, L.C.J.
s.1, applied: SI 2009/1059 Art.42
s.1A, amended: 2009 c.25 s.72
s.3, see *R. v Kelleher (James Gerard)* [2008] EWCA Crim 3055, [2009] 2 Cr. App. R. (S.) 25 (CA (Crim Div)), Lord Judge, L.C.J.; see *R. v Patel (Sophia)* [2009] EWCA Crim 67, [2009] 2 Cr. App. R. (S.) 67 (CA (Crim Div)), Hughes, L.J.
s.51, see *R. v McMenemy (Claire)* [2009] EWCA Crim 42, [2009] 2 Cr. App. R. (S.) 57 (CA (Crim Div)), Keene, L.J.
s.54, applied: 2009 asp 9 Sch.1 para.23, SI 2009/1547 Sch.2 para.1
s.54, referred to: SI 2009/37 Sch.1 para.2, Sch.1 para.4

50. Unfair Contract Terms Act 1977
see *Barclays Bank Plc v Kufner* [2008] EWHC 2319 (Comm), [2009] 1 All E.R. (Comm) 1 (QBD (Comm)), Field, J.; see *Regus (UK) Ltd v Epcot Solutions Ltd* [2008] EWCA Civ 361, [2009] 1 All E.R. (Comm) 586 (CA (Civ Div)), Sir Mark Potter (President, Fam); see *Trident Turboprop (Dublin) Ltd v First Flight Couriers Ltd* [2008] EWHC 1686 (Comm), [2009] 1 All E.R. (Comm) 16 (QBD (Comm)), Aikens, J.
referred to: SI 2009/669 Sch.1 Part 2
s.11, see *Trident Turboprop (Dublin) Ltd v First Flight Couriers Ltd* [2009] EWCA Civ 290, [2009] 3 W.L.R. 861 (CA (Civ Div)), Waller, L.J. (V-P)
s.16, see *Langstane Housing Association Ltd v Riverside Construction (Aberdeen) Ltd* [2009] CSOH 52, 2009 S.C.L.R. 639 (OH), Lord Glennie
s.17, see *Langstane Housing Association Ltd v Riverside Construction (Aberdeen) Ltd* [2009] CSOH 52, 2009 S.C.L.R. 639 (OH), Lord Glennie
s.26, see *Trident Turboprop (Dublin) Ltd v First Flight Couriers Ltd* [2008] EWHC 1686 (Comm), [2009] 1 All E.R. (Comm) 16 (QBD (Comm)), Aikens, J.

1978

19. Oaths Act 1978
s.1, applied: SI 2009/1110 r.16, SI 2009/1209 r.20, SI 2009/1216 r.14, SI 2009/2041 r.21
s.1, varied: SI 2009/1098 r.21, SI 2009/1110 r.16, SI 2009/1209 r.20, SI 2009/1211 r.28, SI 2009/1216 r.14, SI 2009/2657 r.15
s.3, applied: SI 2009/1110 r.16, SI 2009/1209 r.20, SI 2009/1216 r.14, SI 2009/2041 r.21
s.3, varied: SI 2009/1098 r.21, SI 2009/1211 r.28, SI 2009/2657 r.15
s.4, applied: SI 2009/1110 r.16, SI 2009/1209 r.20, SI 2009/1216 r.14, SI 2009/2041 r.21

1978–cont.

19. Oaths Act 1978–cont.
s.4, varied: SI 2009/1098 r.21, SI 2009/1211 r.28, SI 2009/2657 r.15
s.5, applied: SI 2009/1110 r.16, SI 2009/1209 r.20, r.59, SI 2009/1211 r.60, SI 2009/1216 r.14, SI 2009/2041 r.21, r.74
s.5, varied: SI 2009/1098 r.21, SI 2009/1211 r.28, SI 2009/2657 r.15
s.6, applied: SI 2009/1110 r.16, SI 2009/1209 r.20, SI 2009/1216 r.14, SI 2009/2041 r.21
s.6, varied: SI 2009/1098 r.21, SI 2009/1110 r.16, SI 2009/1209 r.20, SI 2009/1211 r.28, SI 2009/1216 r.14, SI 2009/2657 r.15

22. Domestic Proceedings and Magistrates Courts Act 1978
s.19, amended: SI 2009/871 Art.3
s.29, see *Practice Direction (Fam Div: Family Proceedings: Allocation of Appeals)* [2009] 1 W.L.R. 1107 (Fam Div), Sir Mark Potter (President, Fam)
s.29, amended: SI 2009/871 Art.3

23. Judicature (Northern Ireland) Act 1978
s.2, amended: 2009 c.3 Sch.4 para.10
s.3, amended: 2009 c.3 Sch.4 para.11
s.7, amended: 2009 c.3 Sch.4 para.12
s.8, amended: 2009 c.3 Sch.4 para.13
s.12, amended: 2009 c.3 Sch.2
s.12, applied: 2009 c.3 Sch.5 para.10
s.12, substituted: 2009 c.3 Sch.2
s.12B, applied: 2009 c.3 Sch.5 para.11
s.12B, disapplied: 2009 c.3 Sch.5 para.11
s.12B, substituted: 2009 c.3 Sch.2
s.14, amended: 2009 c.3 Sch.4 para.14
s.25A, amended: 2009 c.11 s.53
s.70, amended: 2009 c.3 Sch.4 para.15
s.74, amended: 2009 c.3 Sch.4 para.16
s.103, amended: 2009 c.3 Sch.4 para.17
s.119, amended: 2009 c.3 Sch.4 para.18
s.122, amended: 2009 c.3 Sch.2
s.122, substituted: 2009 c.3 Sch.2

28. Adoption (Scotland) Act 1978
s.6, see *Highland Council v B* 2009 Fam. L.R. 101 (Sh Ct (Grampian) (Inverness)), Sheriff Principal Sir S S T Young, Bt, QC
s.14, applied: SSI 2009/267 Art.3, Art.4, SSI 2009/283 r.3, SSI 2009/284 r.4
s.15, applied: SSI 2009/267 Art.3, Art.4, SSI 2009/283 r.3, SSI 2009/284 r.4
s.16, see *Highland Council v B* 2009 Fam. L.R. 101 (Sh Ct (Grampian) (Inverness)), Sheriff Principal Sir S S T Young, Bt, QC
s.17, applied: SSI 2009/267 Art.6, SSI 2009/283 r.3, SSI 2009/284 r.4
s.18, see *Highland Council v B* 2009 Fam. L.R. 101 (Sh Ct (Grampian) (Inverness)), Sheriff Principal Sir S S T Young, Bt, QC
s.18, applied: SSI 2009/267 Art.18, SSI 2009/283 r.3, SSI 2009/284 r.4
s.20, applied: SSI 2009/267 Art.19, SSI 2009/283 r.3, SSI 2009/284 r.4
s.24, see *Highland Council v B* 2009 Fam. L.R. 101 (Sh Ct (Grampian) (Inverness)), Sheriff Principal Sir S S T Young, Bt, QC
s.25, applied: SSI 2009/267 Art.3
s.28, applied: SSI 2009/267 Art.4, SSI 2009/284 r.4
s.29, applied: SSI 2009/267 Art.4, SSI 2009/283 r.3, SSI 2009/284 r.4
s.47, applied: SSI 2009/267 Art.10, SSI 2009/283 r.3

1978–cont.

28. Adoption (Scotland) Act 1978–*cont.*
s.49, applied: SSI 2009/267 Art.11, SSI 2009/283 r.3, SSI 2009/284 r.4
s.60, applied: SSI 2009/267 Art.12, SSI 2009/314
s.65, applied: SSI 2009/267 Art.12
Sch.1 para.1, enabling: SSI 2009/314

29. National Health Service (Scotland) Act 1978
applied: SSI 2009/183 Sch.1 para.4
referred to: 2009 asp 5 s.5
Part I, applied: SSI 2009/352 Sch.1 para.10
Part II, applied: SSI 2009/352 Sch.1 para.10
s.2, amended: 2009 asp 5 s.2
s.2, applied: SI 2009/2737 Reg.24, SSI 2009/154 Reg.24, SSI 2009/182 Reg.5, Reg.24, SSI 2009/183 Reg.6, Sch.1 para.13
s.2, enabling: SSI 2009/183, SSI 2009/209, SSI 2009/302, SSI 2009/352
s.17N, applied: SSI 2009/183 Sch.1 para.4
s.17P, enabling: SSI 2009/308
s.25, enabling: SSI 2009/96, SSI 2009/308
s.26, enabling: SSI 2009/308
s.27, applied: SSI 2009/183 Reg.12, Sch.1 para.4
s.27, enabling: SSI 2009/37, SSI 2009/177, SSI 2009/183, SSI 2009/209, SSI 2009/308
s.28, enabling: SSI 2009/183
s.28A, enabling: SSI 2009/183
s.29, see *Kelly v Shetland Health Board* [2009] CSIH 3, 2009 S.C. 248 (IH (Ex Div)), Lord Wheatley; see *Martin v Greater Glasgow Primary Care NHS Trust* [2009] CSIH 10, 2009 S.C. 417 (IH (1 Div)), Lord President Hamilton
s.29, applied: SSI 2009/183 Sch.1 para.11
s.29A, applied: SSI 2009/183 Sch.1 para.11
s.29B, applied: SSI 2009/183 Reg.7, Sch.1 para.7, Sch.1 para.11
s.29C, applied: SSI 2009/183 Sch.1 para.11
s.30, applied: SSI 2009/183 Reg.7, Sch.1 para.7, Sch.1 para.11
s.32B, applied: SSI 2009/183 Reg.7
s.32D, enabling: SSI 2009/183
s.32E, enabling: SSI 2009/183
s.69, applied: SSI 2009/183 Sch.1 para.9, Sch.1 para.10
s.69, enabling: SSI 2009/37, SSI 2009/177
s.70, enabling: SSI 2009/86, SSI 2009/288
s.73, enabling: SSI 2009/86, SSI 2009/288
s.74, enabling: SSI 2009/86, SSI 2009/288
s.75A, enabling: SSI 2009/37, SSI 2009/124, SSI 2009/177
s.77, amended: 2009 asp 5 s.3
s.84B, amended: SI 2009/1941 Sch.1 para.39
s.98, enabling: SSI 2009/177
s.105, amended: 2009 asp 5 s.2
s.105, applied: SSI 2009/352
s.105, enabling: SSI 2009/37, SSI 2009/86, SSI 2009/96, SSI 2009/124, SSI 2009/166, SSI 2009/177, SSI 2009/183, SSI 2009/209, SSI 2009/288, SSI 2009/302, SSI 2009/308, SSI 2009/352
s.106, enabling: SSI 2009/183, SSI 2009/209, SSI 2009/308
s.108, enabling: SSI 2009/37, SSI 2009/86, SSI 2009/96, SSI 2009/124, SSI 2009/166, SSI 2009/177, SSI 2009/183, SSI 2009/209, SSI 2009/288, SSI 2009/308
Sch.1 Part I para.2, amended: 2009 asp 5 s.6
Sch.1 Part I para.2, repealed (in part): 2009 asp 5 s.6
Sch.1 Part I para.2, substituted: 2009 asp 5 s.1
Sch.1 Part I para.2, enabling: SSI 2009/302

1978–cont.

29. National Health Service (Scotland) Act 1978–*cont.*
Sch.1 Part I para.2A, amended: 2009 asp 5 s.1
Sch.1 Part I para.3, amended: 2009 asp 5 s.1
Sch.1 Part I para.3, repealed (in part): 2009 asp 5 s.1
Sch.1 Part I para.3A, added: 2009 asp 5 s.1
Sch.1 Part I para.4, amended: 2009 asp 5 Sch.1 para.1
Sch.1 Part I para.6, enabling: SSI 2009/166
Sch.1 Part II para.10A, added: 2009 asp 5 s.1
Sch.1 Part II para.10A, referred to: SSI 2009/302 Reg.4
Sch.1 Part II para.10A, enabling: SSI 2009/302
Sch.1 Part II para.11, amended: 2009 asp 5 s.1
Sch.1 Part II para.11, enabling: SSI 2009/183, SSI 2009/209, SSI 2009/302
Sch.1 Part II para.12, amended: 2009 asp 5 s.1
Sch.1A para.1, added: 2009 asp 5 s.2
Sch.1A para.2, added: 2009 asp 5 s.2
Sch.1A para.3, added: 2009 asp 5 s.2
Sch.1A para.4, added: 2009 asp 5 s.2
Sch.1A para.5, added: 2009 asp 5 s.2
Sch.1A para.5, applied: SSI 2009/352 Sch.1 para.15
Sch.1A para.6, added: 2009 asp 5 s.2
Sch.1A para.6, applied: SSI 2009/352 Sch.1 para.50
Sch.1A para.7, added: 2009 asp 5 s.2
Sch.1A para.8, added: 2009 asp 5 s.2
Sch.1A para.9, added: 2009 asp 5 s.2
Sch.1A para.10, added: 2009 asp 5 s.2
Sch.1A para.11, added: 2009 asp 5 s.2
Sch.1A para.11, applied: SSI 2009/352 Reg.5, Sch.1 para.57
Sch.1A para.12, added: 2009 asp 5 s.2
Sch.1A para.12, enabling: SSI 2009/352
Sch.5 para.8, enabling: SSI 2009/166
Sch.11 para.2, enabling: SSI 2009/86, SSI 2009/288
Sch.11 para.2A, enabling: SSI 2009/86, SSI 2009/288

30. Interpretation Act 1978
see *Odelola v Secretary of State for the Home Department* [2008] EWCA Civ 308, [2009] 1 W.L.R. 126 (CA (Civ Div)), Buxton, L.J.
s.5, see *R. (on the application of Ashton) v Police Medical Appeal Board* [2008] EWHC 1833 (Admin), [2009] I.C.R. 51 (QBD (Admin)), Charles, J.; see *R. v L* [2008] EWCA Crim 1970, [2009] 1 All E.R. 786 (CA (Crim Div)), Hughes, L.J.
s.7, see *Gidden v Chief Constable of Humberside* [2009] EWHC 2924 (Admin), (2009) 173 J.P. 609 (DC), Elias, L.J.
s.7, applied: SI 2009/463 Reg.44, SI 2009/717 Reg.39, SI 2009/890 Reg.4, SI 2009/1100 Art.80, SI 2009/1299 Reg.32, SI 2009/1300 Art.80, SI 2009/1372 Reg.32, SI 2009/1964 Reg.24, SI 2009/2085 Reg.16, SI 2009/2163 Reg.38, SI 2009/2364 Art.40, SI 2009/2728 Art.21, SI 2009/2890 Reg.41, SI 2009/3130 Reg.10, SI 2009/3344 Reg.24, SSI 2009/85 Reg.47
s.11, applied: SI 2009/350 r.4, SI 2009/357 r.4
s.14, applied: 2009 c.20 s.59, 2009 c.23 s.159
s.16, see *Odelola v Secretary of State for the Home Department* [2008] EWCA Civ 308, [2009] 1 W.L.R. 126 (CA (Civ Div)), Buxton, L.J.; see *Odelola v Secretary of State for the Home Department* [2009] UKHL 25, [2009] 1 W.L.R. 1230 (HL), Lord Hope of Craighead
s.16, applied: SI 2009/1059 Art.4, SI 2009/1379 Sch.2

1978–cont.

30. Interpretation Act 1978–*cont.*
s.16, referred to: SI 2009/1751 Sch.1
s.17, see *DPP v Inegbu* [2008] EWHC 3242 (Admin), [2009] 1 W.L.R. 2327 (DC), Latham, L.J.
s.17, applied: SI 2009/359 Sch.1 para.1
s.17, disapplied: 2009 c.4 Sch.2 para.6
s.20A, applied: SI 2009/717 Sch.2 para.7
Sch.1, see *R. v L* [2008] EWCA Crim 1970, [2009] 1 All E.R. 786 (CA (Crim Div)), Hughes, L.J.

31. Theft Act 1978
s.3, applied: SI 2009/2773 Sch.1, SI 2009/2781 Sch.1

33. State Immunity Act 1978
s.2, see *NML Capital Ltd v Argentina* [2009] EWHC 110 (Comm), [2009] Q.B. 579 (QBD (Comm)), Blair, J.
s.3, see *NML Capital Ltd v Argentina* [2009] EWHC 110 (Comm), [2009] Q.B. 579 (QBD (Comm)), Blair, J.; see *Orascom Telecom Holding SAE v Chad* [2008] EWHC 1841 (Comm), [2009] 1 All E.R. (Comm) 315 (QBD (Comm)), Burton, J.
s.11, see *NML Capital Ltd v Argentina* [2009] EWHC 110 (Comm), [2009] Q.B. 579 (QBD (Comm)), Blair, J.
s.11, varied: 2009 c.7 s.21
s.12, see *Norsk Hydro ASA v State Property Fund of Ukraine* [2002] EWHC 2120 (Admin), [2009] Bus. L.R. 558 (QBD (Admin)), Gross, J.; see *Wilhelm Finance Inc v Ente Administrador Del Astillero Rio Santiago* [2009] EWHC 1074 (Comm), [2009] 1 C.L.C. 867 (QBD (Comm)), Teare, J.
s.13, see *ETI Euro Telecom International NV v Bolivia* [2008] EWCA Civ 880, [2009] 1 W.L.R. 665 (CA (Civ Div)), Tuckey, L.J.; see *Orascom Telecom Holding SAE v Chad* [2008] EWHC 1841 (Comm), [2009] 1 All E.R. (Comm) 315 (QBD (Comm)), Burton, J.
s.14, see *Wilhelm Finance Inc v Ente Administrador Del Astillero Rio Santiago* [2009] EWHC 1074 (Comm), [2009] 1 C.L.C. 867 (QBD (Comm)), Teare, J.
s.17, see *Orascom Telecom Holding SAE v Chad* [2008] EWHC 1841 (Comm), [2009] 1 All E.R. (Comm) 315 (QBD (Comm)), Burton, J.

35. Import of Live Fish (Scotland) Act 1978
s.1, amended: SSI 2009/85 Sch.2 para.4

37. Protection of Children Act 1978
s.1, applied: 2009 asp 9 Sch.1 para.11
s.1, referred to: SI 2009/37 Sch.1 para.2, Sch.1 para.4
s.1A, amended: 2009 c.25 s.69
s.4, applied: 2009 c.25 s.67
Sch.1, applied: 2009 c.25 s.67

40. Rating (Disabled Persons) Act 1978
applied: SSI 2009/42 Reg.3

47. Civil Liability (Contribution) Act 1978
see *Crooks v Newdigate Properties Ltd (formerly UPUK Ltd)* [2009] EWCA Civ 283, [2009] C.P. Rep. 34 (CA (Civ Div)), Arden, L.J.; see *Greene Wood & McClean LLP v Templeton Insurance Ltd* [2008] EWHC 1593 (Comm), [2009] Lloyd's Rep. I.R. 61 (QBD (Comm)), Teare, J.; see *Greene Wood & McClean LLP v Templeton Insurance Ltd* [2009] EWCA Civ 65, [2009] 1 W.L.R. 2013 (CA (Civ Div)), Sir Anthony Clarke, M.R.; see *Pritchard Joyce & Hinds (A Firm) v Batcup* [2009] EWCA Civ 369, [2009] P.N.L.R. 28 (CA (Civ Div)), Sedley, L.J.

1978–cont.

47. Civil Liability (Contribution) Act 1978–*cont.*
s.1, see *Cook v Green* [2009] B.C.C. 204 (Ch D (Manchester)), Judge Pelling Q.C.

1979

2. Customs and Excise Management Act 1979
applied: 2009 c.26 s.102
varied: SI 2009/261 Reg.18
s.1, amended: SI 2009/56 Sch.1 para.89
s.1, applied: SI 2009/886 Art.11, SI 2009/1749 Art.13
s.50, applied: SI 2009/1168 Sch.1 para.1
s.68, applied: SI 2009/1168 Sch.1 para.1
s.94, amended: SI 2009/56 Sch.1 para.90
s.118A, enabling: SI 2009/2051
s.138, applied: SI 2009/1749 Art.13
s.145, applied: SI 2009/1749 Art.13
s.146, applied: SI 2009/1749 Art.13
s.146A, see *Revenue and Customs Prosecutions Office v NE Plastics Ltd* [2008] EWHC 3560 (Admin), [2009] 2 Cr. App. R. 21 (DC), Maurice Kay, L.J.
s.146A, applied: SI 2009/1749 Art.13
s.147, applied: SI 2009/1749 Art.13
s.148, applied: SI 2009/1749 Art.13
s.150, applied: SI 2009/1749 Art.13
s.151, applied: SI 2009/1749 Art.13
s.152, applied: SI 2009/1749 Art.13
s.154, applied: SI 2009/1749 Art.13
s.155, applied: SI 2009/1749 Art.13
s.157A, added: 2009 c.26 s.98
s.164A, added: 2009 c.26 s.99
s.170, see *Attorney General's Reference (No.2 of 2008), Re* [2008] EWCA Crim 2953, [2009] Lloyd's Rep. F.C. 189 (CA (Crim Div)), Hooper, L.J.; see *R. (on the application of Minshall) v Marylebone Magistrates' Court* [2008] EWHC 2800 (Admin), [2009] 2 All E.R. 806 (QBD (Admin)), Pitchford, J.; see *R. v M* [2009] EWCA Crim 214, [2009] 2 Cr. App. R. (S.) 66 (CA (Crim Div)), Toulson, L.J.
s.170, applied: SI 2009/261 Reg.17, SI 2009/1168 Sch.1 para.1, SI 2009/1547 Sch.3 para.7, SSI 2009/182 Sch.1 para.4, Sch.1 para.19
s.170, referred to: SI 2009/37 Sch.1 para.2, Sch.1 para.4
s.170A, amended: SI 2009/56 Sch.1 para.91
Sch.4 para.12, amended: 2009 c.23 Sch.22 Part 5, SI 2009/463 Sch.2 para.4, SSI 2009/85 Sch.2 para.5

3. Customs and Excise Duties (General Reliefs) Act 1979
s.13, enabling: SI 2009/3172

4. Alcoholic Liquor Duties Act 1979
s.4, amended: SSI 2009/248 Sch.2
s.5, amended: 2009 c.10 s.11
s.5A, added: SI 2009/730 Art.16
s.36, amended: 2009 c.10 s.11
s.62, amended: 2009 c.10 s.11
Sch.1, amended: 2009 c.10 s.11

5. Hydrocarbon Oil Duties Act 1979
applied: SI 2009/1748 Art.12, Art.15
s.6, amended: 2009 c.10 s.15, s.16
s.6AA, amended: 2009 c.10 s.15, s.16
s.6AD, amended: 2009 c.10 s.15, s.16
s.8, amended: 2009 c.10 s.15, s.16
s.11, amended: 2009 c.10 s.15, s.16, s.121
s.14, amended: 2009 c.10 s.15, s.16
s.14A, amended: 2009 c.10 s.15, s.16

1979–cont.

5. Hydrocarbon Oil Duties Act 1979– *cont.*
s.14D, amended: 2009 c.10 s.121

7. Tobacco Products Duty Act 1979
s.7C, amended: SI 2009/56 Sch.1 para.93
Sch.1, substituted: 2009 c.10 s.12

10. Public Lending Right Act 1979
s.3, enabling: SI 2009/3259

17. Vaccine Damage Payments Act 1979
applied: SI 2009/2516 Art.2
s.1, enabling: SI 2009/2516
s.2, varied: SI 2009/2516 Art.3
s.2, enabling: SI 2009/2516

29. International Monetary Fund Act 1979
s.2, applied: SI 2009/1830, SI 2009/1830 Art.2
s.2, enabling: SI 2009/1830

33. Land Registration (Scotland) Act 1979
s.9, see *PMP Plus Ltd v Keeper of the Registers of Scotland* 2009 S.L.T. (Lands Tr) 2 (Lands Tr (Scot)), Lord McGhie
s.20, see *Wright v Shoreline Management Ltd* 2009 S.L.T. (Sh Ct) 83 (Sh Ct (Tayside) (Arbroath)), Sheriff Principal R A Dunlop, QC
s.21, see *Wright v Shoreline Management Ltd* 2009 S.L.T. (Sh Ct) 83 (Sh Ct (Tayside) (Arbroath)), Sheriff Principal R A Dunlop, QC
s.25, see *PMP Plus Ltd v Keeper of the Registers of Scotland* 2009 S.L.T. (Lands Tr) 2 (Lands Tr (Scot)), Lord McGhie
s.28, see *Upton Park Homes Ltd v Macdonalds, Solicitors* [2009] CSOH 159 (OH), Lord Uist

34. Credit Unions Act 1979
referred to: 2009 c.1 s.131, s.159
s.6, amended: SI 2009/1941 Sch.1 para.40
s.31, applied: 2009 c.1 s.89, s.131, s.159
s.31, referred to: 2009 c.1 s.134, s.167

38. Estate Agents Act 1979
referred to: SI 2009/669 Sch.1 Part 2
s.7, amended: SI 2009/1836 Sch.1 para.3
s.7, applied: SI 2009/1836 Art.2
s.7, repealed (in part): SI 2009/1836 Sch.1 para.3

41. Pneumoconiosis etc (Workers Compensation) Act 1979
see *Crossett v Upper Clyde Shipbuilders Ltd (In Liquidation)* 2009 S.C.L.R. 77 (OH), Lady Dorrian; see *Renfrew v Lithgows Ltd* 2009 Rep. L.R. 19 (OH), Lord Woolman
s.1, enabling: SI 2009/747
s.7, applied: SI 2009/747
s.7, enabling: SI 2009/747

46. Ancient Monuments and Archaeological Areas Act 1979
applied: SI 2009/1300 Art.25, SI 2009/3365 Sch.1 para.1
s.2, applied: SI 2009/3264 Sch.1 para.1, SI 2009/3365 Sch.1 para.1
s.8, amended: SI 2009/1307 Sch.1 para.127
s.17, amended: SI 2009/1307 Sch.1 para.128
s.47, amended: SI 2009/1307 Sch.1 para.129

50. European Assembly (Pay and Pensions) Act 1979
s.1, amended: SI 2009/1485 Reg.2
s.2, repealed: SI 2009/1485 Reg.2
s.3, amended: SI 2009/1485 Reg.2
s.3A, amended: 2009 c.13 s.5, SI 2009/1485 Reg.2
s.4, amended: SI 2009/1485 Reg.2
s.7, repealed (in part): SI 2009/1485 Reg.2
s.8, amended: SI 2009/1485 Reg.2

1979–cont.

53. Charging Orders Act 1979
s.1, see *N (A Child) (Financial Provision: Dependency), Re* [2009] EWHC 11 (Fam), [2009] 1 W.L.R. 1621 (Fam Div), Munby, J.
s.3, see *Nationwide Building Society v Wright* [2009] EWCA Civ 811, [2009] 2 B.C.L.C. 695 (CA (Civ Div)), Maurice Kay, L.J.

54. Sale of Goods Act 1979
referred to: SI 2009/669 Sch.1 Part 2
s.14, see *Douglas v Glenvarigill Co Ltd* [2009] CSOH 17, 2009 S.C.L.R. 379 (OH), Lord Glennie; see *KG Bominflot Bunkergesellschaft fur Mineralole mbh & Co KG v Petroplus Marketing AG (The Mercini Lady)* [2009] EWHC 1088 (Comm), [2009] 2 All E.R. (Comm) 827 (QBD (Comm)), Field, J.
s.50, see *Westbrook Resources Ltd v Globe Metallurgical Inc* [2008] EWHC 241 (Comm), [2009] 1 All E.R. (Comm) 193 (QBD (Comm)), Tomlinson, J.

55. Justices of the Peace Act 1979
referred to: SI 2009/500 Sch.1 Part 1

1980

1. Petroleum Revenue Tax Act 1980
s.1, applied: 2009 c.10 Sch.55 para.1

6. Foster Children Act 1980
s.10, applied: SI 2009/1547 Sch.1 para.17
s.16, applied: SI 2009/1547 Sch.2 para.1

13. Slaughter of Animals (Scotland) Act 1980
s.6, amended: SSI 2009/319 Sch.2 para.3
s.14, repealed (in part): SSI 2009/319 Sch.2 para.3
s.22, amended: SSI 2009/319 Sch.2 para.3

21. Competition Act 1980
s.11, amended: SI 2009/1941 Sch.1 para.42
s.12, amended: SI 2009/1941 Sch.1 para.42

23. Consular Fees Act 1980
s.1, enabling: SI 2009/700, SI 2009/1745

24. Limitation Amendment Act 1980
s.11, see *Rogers v East Kent Hospitals NHS Trust* [2009] EWHC 54 (QB), [2009] LS Law Medical 153 (QBD), Griffith Williams, J.
s.14, see *Rogers v East Kent Hospitals NHS Trust* [2009] EWHC 54 (QB), [2009] LS Law Medical 153 (QBD), Griffith Williams, J.

26. British Aerospace Act 1980
s.14, amended: SI 2009/1941 Sch.1 para.43

27. Import of Live Fish (England and Wales) Act 1980
s.1, amended: SI 2009/463 Sch.2 para.5

33. Industry Act 1980
s.3, amended: SI 2009/1941 Sch.1 para.44

34. Transport Act 1980
s.64, varied: SI 2009/2863 Reg.4

43. Magistrates Courts Act 1980
applied: SI 2009/261 Reg.49, SI 2009/2163 Reg.21, SI 2009/2297 Reg.39, Reg.41, SI 2009/2890 Reg.21, Reg.23, SI 2009/3101 Reg.19, SI 2009/3255 Reg.12, Reg.33, SI 2009/3376 Reg.12, Reg.33, SI 2009/3391 Art.7
referred to: SI 2009/500 Sch.1 Part 1
Part III, applied: SI 2009/1850 Art.10, SI 2009/3391 Art.11
s.8A, see *Brett v DPP* [2009] EWHC 440 (Admin), [2009] 1 W.L.R. 2530 (DC), Leveson, L.J.
s.19, amended: 2009 c.25 Sch.17 para.4, Sch.21 para.80, Sch.23 Part 5
s.19, varied: SI 2009/1059 Sch.1 para.18

1980 – cont.

43. Magistrates Courts Act 1980–*cont.*
  s.24, see *W v Warrington Magistrates' Court* [2009] EWHC 1538 (Admin), (2009) 173 J.P. 561 (DC), Pill, L.J.
  s.46, applied: SI 2009/209 Reg.118
  s.51, see *R. (on the application of Taylor) v Commissioner of Police of the Metropolis* [2009] EWHC 264 (Admin), (2009) 173 J.P. 121 (QBD (Admin)), Lloyd Jones, J.
  s.55, see *R. (on the application of Taylor) v Commissioner of Police of the Metropolis* [2009] EWHC 264 (Admin), (2009) 173 J.P. 121 (QBD (Admin)), Lloyd Jones, J.
  s.64, see *R. (on the application of Perinpanathan) v City of Westminster Magistrates' Court* [2009] EWHC 762 (Admin), (2009) 173 J.P. 379 (DC), Goldring, L.J.; see *R. (on the application of Taylor) v Commissioner of Police of the Metropolis* [2009] EWHC 264 (Admin), (2009) 173 J.P. 121 (QBD (Admin)), Lloyd Jones, J.
  s.65, see *Practice Direction (Fam Div: Family Proceedings: Written Reasons)* [2009] 1 W.L.R. 1109 (Sup Ct), Lord Judge, L.C.J.
  s.77, applied: SI 2009/1850 Art.10, SI 2009/3391 Art.11
  s.78, applied: SI 2009/1850 Art.10, SI 2009/3391 Art.11
  s.89, amended: 2009 c.24 Sch.2 para.1
  s.90, amended: 2009 c.24 Sch.2 para.1
  s.90, applied: SSI 2009/317 Art.13
  s.101, see *DPP v Wright* [2009] EWHC 105 (Admin), [2009] 3 All E.R. 726 (DC), Sir Anthony May (President, QB)
  s.111, amended: SI 2009/871 Art.4
  s.111, applied: SI 2009/1896 Sch.1 para.6, SI 2009/1899 Sch.1 para.6, SI 2009/2194 Reg.9
  s.111A, see *Practice Direction (Fam Div: Family Proceedings: Allocation of Appeals)* [2009] 1 W.L.R. 1107 (Fam Div), Sir Mark Potter (President, Fam); see *Practice Direction (Fam Div: Family Proceedings: Appeals)* [2009] 1 W.L.R. 1103 (Fam Div), Sir Mark Potter (President, Fam)
  s.111A, added: SI 2009/871 Art.4
  s.112, amended: SI 2009/871 Art.4
  s.112, substituted: SI 2009/871 Art.4
  s.117, amended: 2009 c.25 Sch.21 para.75
  s.125D, varied: SI 2009/1059 Sch.1 para.18
  s.127, see *Birmingham City Council v Dixon* [2009] EWHC 761 (Admin), (2009) 173 J.P. 233 (DC), Richards, L.J.
  s.127, disapplied: SI 2009/886 Art.12, SI 2009/1749 Art.14
  s.142, see *Zykin v Crown Prosecution Service* [2009] EWHC 1469 (Admin), (2009) 173 J.P. 361 (DC), Bean, J.
  s.144, see *Jain v Trent SHA* [2009] UKHL 4, [2009] 1 A.C. 853 (HL), Lord Scott of Foscote
  s.144, applied: SI 2009/637, SI 2009/858, SI 2009/3362
  s.144, enabling: SI 2009/637, SI 2009/858, SI 2009/2025, SI 2009/2197, SI 2009/2937, SI 2009/3362
  s.145, see *Jain v Trent SHA* [2009] UKHL 4, [2009] 1 A.C. 853 (HL), Lord Scott of Foscote
  s.145, enabling: SI 2009/858, SI 2009/3362
  Sch.3, applied: SI 2009/209 Reg.118, SI 2009/261 Reg.52, SI 2009/1299 Reg.44, SI 2009/1361 Reg.19, SI 2009/1372 Reg.44, SI 2009/1551 Reg.19, SI 2009/1611 Reg.24, SI 2009/2470 Reg.24, SI 2009/2902 Reg.24, SI 2009/3219

1980 – cont.

43. Magistrates Courts Act 1980–*cont.*
  Sch.3, applied:–*cont.*
    Art.40, SI 2009/3263 Reg.12, SI 2009/3364 Art.43
  Sch.3, referred to: SI 2009/842 Reg.28
  Sch.6A, amended: 2009 c.25 Sch.21 para.28, Sch.23 Part 1
  Sch.7 para.30, repealed: 2009 c.26 Sch.8 Part 2

44. Education (Scotland) Act 1980
  applied: 2009 c.4 s.71, SI 2009/470 Reg.6, Reg.19
  s.23, see *East Renfrewshire DC v Glasgow City Council* 2009 S.C. 197 (OH), Lord Penrose
  s.23, amended: 2009 asp 7 s.4
  s.31, applied: SSI 2009/182 Reg.24
  s.31, referred to: SSI 2009/182 Reg.5
  s.49, enabling: SSI 2009/188, SSI 2009/309
  s.53, applied: SSI 2009/178 Reg.3, Reg.4
  s.53, enabling: SSI 2009/178
  s.73, applied: SI 2009/1555 Reg.120, Reg.137, SI 2009/2737 Reg.72, Reg.85
  s.73, enabling: SI 2009/470, SSI 2009/102, SSI 2009/181, SSI 2009/188, SSI 2009/189, SSI 2009/309
  s.73B, applied: SI 2009/1555 Reg.120, Reg.137, SI 2009/2737 Reg.72, Reg.85
  s.73B, enabling: SI 2009/470, SSI 2009/102, SSI 2009/189
  s.74, applied: SI 2009/1555 Reg.120, Reg.137, SI 2009/2737 Reg.72, Reg.85
  s.74, enabling: SSI 2009/102, SSI 2009/181, SSI 2009/188, SSI 2009/189, SSI 2009/309
  s.84, amended: SSI 2009/65 Sch.1
  s.98A, applied: SSI 2009/4 Art.4
  s.100, applied: SI 2009/1633 Reg.3, SI 2009/2558 Reg.3

46. Solicitors (Scotland) Act 1980
  see *Scottish Solicitors' Discipline Tribunal v Auditor of the Court of Session* [2009] CSOH 101, 2009 S.L.T. 1104 (OH), Lady Dorrian
  s.54, see *Y v Law Society of Scotland* [2009] CSIH 32, 2009 S.C. 430 (IH (Ex Div)), Lord Carloway
  s.64, see *Y v Law Society of Scotland* [2009] CSIH 32, 2009 S.C. 430 (IH (Ex Div)), Lord Carloway

47. Criminal Appeal (Northern Ireland) Act 1980
  s.10., amended: 2009 c.25 s.141
  s.10A, added: 2009 c.25 s.141
  s.45, amended: 2009 c.25 Sch.21 para.71

48. Finance Act 1980
  s.120, applied: SI 2009/1263 Reg.2
  Sch.17 Part I para.5, amended: SI 2009/56 Sch.1 para.95
  Sch.17 Part III para.11, repealed: 2009 c.10 Sch.43 para.3
  Sch.17 Part III para.15, amended: 2009 c.10 Sch.45 para.3

51. Housing Act 1980
  s.89, see *Admiral Taverns (Cygnet) Ltd v Daniel* [2008] EWCA Civ 1501, [2009] 1 W.L.R. 2192 (CA (Civ Div)), Tuckey, L.J.; see *Admiral Taverns (Cygnet) Ltd v Daniel* [2008] EWHC 1688 (QB), [2009] 1 P. & C.R. 6 (QBD), Teare, J.

58. Limitation Act 1980
  see *Byrne v Motor Insurers' Bureau* [2008] EWCA Civ 574, [2009] Q.B. 66 (CA (Civ Div)), Waller, L.J.; see *FJ Chalke Ltd v Revenue and Customs Commissioners* [2009] EWHC 952 (Ch), [2009] S.T.C. 2027 (Ch D), Henderson, J.; see *Shore v Sedgwick Financial Services Ltd* [2008] EWCA Civ 863, [2009] Bus. L.R. 42 (CA (Civ Div)), Buxton, L.J.; see *Whiston v London SHA*

1980 – cont.

58. Limitation Act 1980–*cont.*

see–*cont.*

[2009] EWHC 956 (QB), [2009] LS Law Medical 355 (QBD), Eady, J.; see *Yorkshire Bank Finance Ltd v Mulhall* [2008] EWCA Civ 1156, [2009] 2 All E.R. (Comm) 164 (CA (Civ Div)), Sir Anthony May (President, QB)

applied: SI 2009/1941 Art.11

s.2, see *Spencer v Secretary of State for Work and Pensions* [2008] EWCA Civ 750, [2009] Q.B. 358 (CA (Civ Div)), Waller, L.J.

s.7, see *National Ability SA v Tinna Oils & Chemicals Ltd* [2009] EWCA Civ 1330, Times, December 24, 2009 (CA (Civ Div)), Thomas, L.J.

s.8, see *Nolan v Wright* [2009] EWHC 305 (Ch), [2009] 3 All E.R. 823 (Ch D), Judge Hodge Q.C.

s.9, see *Oakglade Investments Ltd v Greater Manchester Passenger Transport Executive* [2009] R.V.R. 39 (Lands Tr), George Bartlett Q.C. (President)

s.10, see *Crooks v Newdigate Properties Ltd (formerly UPUK Ltd)* [2009] EWCA Civ 283, [2009] C.P. Rep. 34 (CA (Civ Div)), Arden, L.J.

s.11, see *Giles v Rhind* [2008] EWCA Civ 118, [2009] Ch. 191 (CA (Civ Div)), Buxton, L.J.; see *Raggett v Society of Jesus Trust 1929 for Roman Catholic Purposes* [2009] EWHC 909 (QB), (2009) 108 B.M.L.R. 147 (QBD), Swift, J DBE

s.14, see *D v Harrow LBC* [2008] EWHC 3048 (QB), [2009] 1 F.L.R. 719 (QBD), Eady, J.; see *Pierce v Doncaster MBC* [2008] EWCA Civ 1416, [2009] 1 F.L.R. 1189 (CA (Civ Div)), Sedley, L.J.; see *Raggett v Society of Jesus Trust 1929 for Roman Catholic Purposes* [2009] EWHC 909 (QB), (2009) 108 B.M.L.R. 147 (QBD), Swift, J DBE; see *Rogers v East Kent Hospitals NHS Trust* [2009] EWHC 54 (QB), [2009] LS Law Medical 153 (QBD), Griffith Williams, J.

s.14A, see *Shore v Sedgwick Financial Services Ltd* [2008] EWCA Civ 863, [2009] Bus. L.R. 42 (CA (Civ Div)), Buxton, L.J.; see *Williams v Lishman Sidwell Campbell & Price Ltd* [2009] EWHC 1322 (QB), [2009] P.N.L.R. 34 (QBD), Judge Reddihough

s.15, see *Ofulue v Bossert* [2009] UKHL 16, [2009] 1 A.C. 990 (HL), Lord Hope of Craighead

s.20, see *Yorkshire Bank Finance Ltd v Mulhall* [2008] EWCA Civ 1156, [2009] 2 All E.R. (Comm) 164 (CA (Civ Div)), Sir Anthony May (President, QB)

s.24, see *National Ability SA v Tinna Oils & Chemicals Ltd* [2009] EWCA Civ 1330, Times, December 24, 2009 (CA (Civ Div)), Thomas, L.J.; see *Yorkshire Bank Finance Ltd v Mulhall* [2008] EWCA Civ 1156, [2009] 2 All E.R. (Comm) 164 (CA (Civ Div)), Sir Anthony May (President, QB)

s.27A, amended: 2009 c.26 s.62

s.27B, amended: 2009 c.26 s.62

s.27C, added: 2009 c.25 s.171

s.27C, applied: 2009 c.25 s.163

s.28, see *Byrne v Motor Insurers' Bureau* [2008] EWCA Civ 574, [2009] Q.B. 66 (CA (Civ Div)), Waller, L.J.

s.29, see *FJ Chalke Ltd v Revenue and Customs Commissioners* [2009] EWHC 952 (Ch), [2009] S.T.C. 2027 (Ch D), Henderson, J.; see *Ofulue v Bossert* [2008] EWCA Civ 7, [2009] Ch. 1 (CA (Civ Div)), May, L.J.; see *Ofulue v Bossert*

1980 – cont.

58. Limitation Act 1980–*cont.*

s.29–*cont.*

[2009] UKHL 16, [2009] 1 A.C. 990 (HL), Lord Hope of Craighead

s.32, see *Bocardo SA v Star Energy UK Onshore Ltd* [2008] EWHC 1756 (Ch), [2009] 1 All E.R. 517 (Ch D), Peter Smith, J.; see *FJ Chalke Ltd v Revenue and Customs Commissioners* [2009] EWHC 952 (Ch), [2009] S.T.C. 2027 (Ch D), Henderson, J.; see *Giles v Rhind* [2008] EWCA Civ 118, [2009] Ch. 191 (CA (Civ Div)), Buxton, L.J.; see *Harris v Society of Lloyd's* [2008] EWHC 1433 (Comm), [2009] Lloyd's Rep. I.R. 119 (QBD (Comm)), David Steel, J.; see *Williams v Lishman Sidwell Campbell & Price Ltd* [2009] EWHC 1322 (QB), [2009] P.N.L.R. 34 (QBD), Judge Reddihough

s.33, see *B v Ministry of Defence* [2009] EWHC 1225 (QB), Times, June 10, 2009 (QBD), Foskett, J.; see *Cain v Francis* [2008] EWCA Civ 1451, [2009] Q.B. 754 (CA (Civ Div)), Sir Andrew Morritt (Chancellor); see *D v Harrow LBC* [2008] EWHC 3048 (QB), [2009] 1 F.L.R. 719 (QBD), Eady, J.; see *Pierce v Doncaster MBC* [2008] EWCA Civ 1416, [2009] 1 F.L.R. 1189 (CA (Civ Div)), Sedley, L.J.; see *Raggett v Society of Jesus Trust 1929 for Roman Catholic Purposes* [2009] EWHC 909 (QB), (2009) 108 B.M.L.R. 147 (QBD), Swift, J DBE; see *Rogers v East Kent Hospitals NHS Trust* [2009] EWHC 54 (QB), [2009] LS Law Medical 153 (QBD), Griffith Williams, J.; see *Whiston v London SHA* [2009] EWHC 956 (QB), [2009] LS Law Medical 355 (QBD), Eady, J.

s.35, see *Giles v Rhind* [2008] EWCA Civ 118, [2009] Ch. 191 (CA (Civ Div)), Buxton, L.J.; see *Law Society v Shah* [2008] EWHC 2515 (Ch), [2009] 1 W.L.R. 2254 (Ch D), Norris, J.; see *Parker v SJ Berwin & Co* [2008] EWHC 3017 (QB), [2009] P.N.L.R. 17 (QBD), Hamblen, J

s.38, see *National Ability SA v Tinna Oils & Chemicals Ltd* [2009] EWCA Civ 1330, Times, December 24, 2009 (CA (Civ Div)), Thomas, L.J.

60. Civil Aviation Act 1980

s.4, amended: SI 2009/1941 Sch.1 para.45

62. Criminal Justice (Scotland) Act 1980

s.80, referred to: SI 2009/37 Sch.1 para.2, Sch.1 para.4

65. Local Government, Planning and Land Act 1980

s.2, amended: 2009 c.20 Sch.1 para.2, 2009 c.20 Sch.6 para.49

s.98, amended: 2009 c.20 Sch.6 para.50, SI 2009/1941 Sch.1 para.46

s.99, amended: 2009 c.20 Sch.6 para.51

s.100, amended: 2009 c.20 Sch.6 para.52, SI 2009/1941 Sch.1 para.46

s.141, amended: SI 2009/1941 Sch.1 para.46

s.159, amended: SSI 2009/319 Sch.2 para.4, SSI 2009/404 Sch.2

s.159, applied: SSI 2009/319 Art.3

s.167, amended: SI 2009/1307 Sch.1 para.131

s.170, amended: SI 2009/1941 Sch.1 para.46

s.185, applied: SI 2009/2325 Art.23

Sch.16 para.5BZA, added: 2009 c.20 Sch.6 para.53

Sch.16 para.5BZB, added: 2009 c.20 Sch.6 para.53

Sch.28 Part IV para.23, amended: SI 2009/1307 Sch.1 para.132

Sch.33 para.3, repealed: SI 2009/1307 Sch.4

1980–cont.

66. Highways Act 1980

see *Young (now Phillips) v Merthyr Tydfil CBC* [2009] P.I.Q.R. P23 (CC (Cardiff)), Judge Curran Q.C.

applied: SI 2009/3365 Sch.1 para.1

referred to: SI 2009/721 Art.2

s.1, applied: 2009 c.20 s.123, SI 2009/3042 Reg.36

s.10, enabling: SI 2009/50, SI 2009/51, SI 2009/52, SI 2009/53, SI 2009/282, SI 2009/283, SI 2009/284, SI 2009/727, SI 2009/1370, SI 2009/1505, SI 2009/2716, SI 2009/3192, SI 2009/3375

s.12, enabling: SI 2009/282, SI 2009/283, SI 2009/284, SI 2009/1370, SI 2009/1505, SI 2009/2716, SI 2009/3375

s.16, enabling: SI 2009/776

s.17, enabling: SI 2009/776

s.18, enabling: SI 2009/977

s.19, enabling: SI 2009/776

s.41, see *Jones v Rhondda Cynon Taff CBC* [2008] EWCA Civ 1497, [2009] R.T.R. 13 (CA (Civ Div)), Laws, L.J.; see *Young (now Phillips) v Merthyr Tydfil CBC* [2009] P.I.Q.R. P23 (CC (Cardiff)), Judge Curran Q.C.

s.41, applied: SI 2009/721 Sch.1 para.1

s.41, enabling: SI 2009/50, SI 2009/51, SI 2009/283, SI 2009/727

s.58, see *Jones v Rhondda Cynon Taff CBC* [2008] EWCA Civ 1497, [2009] R.T.R. 13 (CA (Civ Div)), Laws, L.J.

s.62, applied: SI 2009/721 Sch.1 para.1

s.63, applied: SI 2009/721 Sch.1 para.1, Sch.1 para.2

s.64, applied: SI 2009/721 Sch.1 para.1, SI 2009/1300 Art.4, SI 2009/2364 Art.3

s.65, applied: SI 2009/721 Sch.1 para.1

s.66, applied: SI 2009/721 Sch.1 para.1

s.68, applied: SI 2009/721 Sch.1 para.1

s.69, applied: SI 2009/721 Sch.1 para.1

s.70, applied: SI 2009/721 Sch.1 para.1

s.71, applied: SI 2009/721 Sch.1 para.1

s.75, applied: SI 2009/721 Sch.1 para.1

s.76, applied: SI 2009/721 Sch.1 para.1

s.77, applied: SI 2009/721 Sch.1 para.1

s.78, applied: SI 2009/721 Sch.1 para.1

s.80, applied: SI 2009/721 Sch.1 para.1

s.81, applied: SI 2009/721 Sch.1 para.1

s.84, applied: SI 2009/721 Sch.1 para.1

s.90, applied: SI 2009/721 Sch.1 para.1

s.90G, applied: SI 2009/721 Sch.1 para.1

s.90GA, applied: SI 2009/721 Sch.1 para.1

s.92, applied: SI 2009/721 Sch.1 para.1

s.96, applied: SI 2009/721 Sch.1 para.1

s.97, applied: SI 2009/721 Sch.1 para.1

s.99, applied: SI 2009/721 Sch.1 para.1

s.100, applied: SI 2009/721 Sch.1 para.1

s.101, applied: SI 2009/721 Sch.1 para.1

s.102, applied: SI 2009/721 Sch.1 para.1

s.103, applied: SI 2009/721 Sch.1 para.1

s.104, applied: SI 2009/721 Sch.1 para.1

s.105, applied: SI 2009/721 Sch.1 para.1

s.106, applied: SI 2009/2826 Sch.1, SI 2009/2891 Sch.1

s.106, enabling: SI 2009/1505, SI 2009/2826, SI 2009/2891, SI 2009/3405

s.112, applied: SI 2009/721 Sch.1 para.2

s.114, applied: SI 2009/721 Sch.1 para.1

s.115H, applied: SI 2009/721 Sch.1 para.1

1980–cont.

66. Highways Act 1980–*cont.*

s.129A, see *Ramblers Association v Coventry City Council* [2008] EWHC 796 (Admin), [2009] 1 All E.R. 130 (QBD (Admin)), Michael Supperstone Q.C.

s.131A, applied: SI 2009/3264 Sch.1 para.1, SI 2009/3365 Sch.1 para.1

s.133, applied: SI 2009/721 Sch.1 para.1

s.134, applied: SI 2009/3264 Sch.1 para.1, SI 2009/3365 Sch.1 para.1

s.137, applied: SI 2009/3264 Sch.1 para.1, SI 2009/3365 Sch.1 para.1

s.139, applied: SI 2009/721 Sch.1 para.1

s.140, applied: SI 2009/721 Sch.1 para.1

s.141, applied: SI 2009/721 Sch.1 para.1

s.143, applied: SI 2009/721 Sch.1 para.4

s.144, applied: SI 2009/721 Sch.1 para.5

s.146, applied: SI 2009/3264 Sch.1 para.1, SI 2009/3365 Sch.1 para.1

s.150, applied: SI 2009/721 Sch.1 para.1

s.154, applied: SI 2009/721 Sch.1 para.4

s.167, applied: SI 2009/721 Sch.1 para.1, Sch.1 para.6

s.169, applied: SI 2009/721 Sch.1 para.1

s.171, applied: SI 2009/721 Sch.1 para.1

s.178, applied: SI 2009/721 Sch.1 para.1

s.184, applied: SI 2009/1300 Art.4, SI 2009/2364 Art.3

s.185, applied: SI 2009/721 Sch.1 para.4

s.254, enabling: SI 2009/1505

s.261, amended: SI 2009/1307 Sch.1 para.134

s.262, amended: SI 2009/1307 Sch.1 para.135

s.271, amended: SI 2009/1307 Sch.1 para.136

s.288, applied: SI 2009/721 Sch.1 para.3

s.294, applied: SI 2009/721 Sch.1 para.9

s.301A, applied: SI 2009/721 Sch.1 para.7

s.307, amended: SI 2009/1307 Sch.1 para.137

s.326, enabling: SI 2009/776, SI 2009/977

s.338, applied: SI 2009/721 Sch.1 para.9

s.339, applied: SI 2009/721 Sch.1 para.9

Sch.2 para.1, applied: SI 2009/2826 Art.1, SI 2009/2891 Art.1

Sch.19 Part II para.7, amended: SI 2009/1307 Sch.1 para.138

1981

14. Public Passenger Vehicles Act 1981

applied: SI 2009/711 Sch.1 para.4, Sch.1 para.5, Sch.1 para.7, Sch.1 para.14, Sch.1 para.18, Sch.1 para.21, SI 2009/1885 Art.2, Sch.4 para.1

referred to: SI 2009/669 Sch.1 Part 2

s.4A, applied: SI 2009/3243 Reg.6

s.4C, amended: 2009 c.20 Sch.6 para.54

s.5, enabling: SI 2009/443

s.6, amended: SI 2009/818 Reg.2

s.6, referred to: SI 2009/491 Sch.1 Part 1

s.6, enabling: SI 2009/141

s.10, applied: SI 2009/711 Art.4

s.10, enabling: SI 2009/877

s.12, applied: SI 2009/483 Art.2, SI 2009/1964 Reg.3, Reg.10, Reg.23

s.12, referred to: SI 2009/491 Sch.1 Part 1, SI 2009/492 Sch.1 Part 1

s.14, enabling: SI 2009/787 Reg.3

s.17A, applied: SI 2009/445 Reg.13, SI 2009/3293 Reg.13

s.18, referred to: SI 2009/491 Sch.1 Part 1

s.18, enabling: SI 2009/786

1981–cont.

14. Public Passenger Vehicles Act 1981–*cont.*
s.24, varied: SI 2009/1300 Art.57
s.25, applied: SI 2009/1300 Art.66
s.25, varied: SI 2009/1300 Art.57
s.50, amended: SI 2009/1885 Sch.1 para.2
s.52, applied: SI 2009/711 Art.4
s.52, enabling: SI 2009/365, SI 2009/366, SI 2009/787, SI 2009/877, SI 2009/878, SSI 2009/151
s.54, amended: SI 2009/1885 Sch.1 para.3
s.54, applied: SI 2009/443 Reg.5
s.60, applied: SI 2009/711 Art.4
s.60, varied: SI 2009/1300 Art.57
s.60, enabling: SI 2009/141, SI 2009/365, SI 2009/366, SI 2009/786, SI 2009/787, SI 2009/877, SI 2009/878, SI 2009/2863, SI 2009/3245, SSI 2009/151
s.61, applied: SI 2009/141, SI 2009/365, SI 2009/443, SI 2009/786, SI 2009/787, SI 2009/877, SI 2009/878, SI 2009/1964, SI 2009/2863, SI 2009/3245, SSI 2009/151
s.65, referred to: SI 2009/491 Sch.1 Part 1
Sch.2A, enabling: SI 2009/1964
Sch.2A para.12, amended: SI 2009/1885 Sch.1 para.4
Sch.2A para.12, repealed (in part): SI 2009/1885 Sch.1 para.4
Sch.3 para.1, varied: SI 2009/1059 Sch.1 para.19

20. Judicial Pensions Act 1981
s.10, amended: SI 2009/1307 Sch.1 para.140
s.10, repealed (in part): SI 2009/1307 Sch.1 para.140
s.16, amended: SI 2009/1307 Sch.1 para.141

22. Animal Health Act 1981
applied: SI 2009/3219 Art.39, SI 2009/3255 Reg.18, Reg.39, SI 2009/3364 Art.42, SI 2009/3376 Reg.18, Reg.39, SSI 2009/45 Art.2, SSI 2009/446 Reg.18, Reg.39
referred to: SSI 2009/45 Art.6
s.1, enabling: SI 2009/260, SI 2009/441, SI 2009/2614, SI 2009/2713, SI 2009/2940, SI 2009/3083, SI 2009/3219, SI 2009/3234, SI 2009/3271, SI 2009/3364, SSI 2009/45, SSI 2009/173, SSI 2009/174, SSI 2009/229, SSI 2009/232, SSI 2009/394, SSI 2009/414, SSI 2009/417, SSI 2009/445
s.7, enabling: SI 2009/3083, SI 2009/3234, SSI 2009/45, SSI 2009/173, SSI 2009/232, SSI 2009/394
s.8, enabling: SI 2009/260, SI 2009/441, SI 2009/2940, SI 2009/3219, SI 2009/3271, SI 2009/3364, SSI 2009/173, SSI 2009/174, SSI 2009/229, SSI 2009/232, SSI 2009/414, SSI 2009/417, SSI 2009/445
s.11, enabling: SSI 2009/174
s.15, enabling: SI 2009/2713, SSI 2009/173, SSI 2009/232
s.17, enabling: SSI 2009/173
s.21, applied: SI 2009/2614, SI 2009/2614 Art.2
s.21, enabling: SI 2009/2614
s.22, applied: SI 2009/2614 Art.3
s.22, referred to: SI 2009/2614 Art.5
s.23, enabling: SSI 2009/173
s.25, enabling: SSI 2009/173, SSI 2009/232
s.28, enabling: SSI 2009/173
s.28C, applied: SSI 2009/141 Reg.21
s.28F, applied: SSI 2009/141 Reg.4, Reg.21
s.32, see *R. (on the application of Partridge Farms Ltd) v Secretary of State for the Environment, Food and Rural Affairs* [2009] EWCA Civ 284, [2009] Eu. L.R. 816 (CA (Civ Div)), Ward, L.J.

1981–cont.

22. Animal Health Act 1981–*cont.*
s.32, applied: SSI 2009/173 Art.4, SSI 2009/232 Art.3, Art.16, Art.18
s.32, enabling: SSI 2009/173, SSI 2009/232
s.34, enabling: SSI 2009/232
s.35, enabling: SSI 2009/45, SSI 2009/173, SSI 2009/394
s.72, enabling: SI 2009/2614, SSI 2009/173
s.83, enabling: SI 2009/2713, SI 2009/3219, SI 2009/3364, SSI 2009/173, SSI 2009/232, SSI 2009/414
s.84, enabling: SI 2009/839
s.86, enabling: SI 2009/2614
s.87, enabling: SI 2009/3083, SI 2009/3234, SSI 2009/45, SSI 2009/174, SSI 2009/229, SSI 2009/232
s.88, varied: SSI 2009/232 Art.3
s.88, enabling: SI 2009/3083, SI 2009/3234, SSI 2009/45, SSI 2009/173, SSI 2009/174, SSI 2009/232, SSI 2009/394

28. Licensing (Alcohol Education and Research) Act 1981
Sch.1 para.3, amended: 2009 c.21 Sch.3 para.2
Sch.1 para.3A, added: 2009 c.21 Sch.3 para.2
Sch.1 para.3B, added: 2009 c.21 Sch.3 para.2
Sch.1 para.4, amended: 2009 c.21 Sch.3 para.2
Sch.1 para.4A, added: 2009 c.21 Sch.3 para.2

29. Fisheries Act 1981
s.19, repealed (in part): 2009 c.23 Sch.22 Part 5
s.22, repealed (in part): 2009 c.23 Sch.22 Part 5
s.28, repealed: 2009 c.23 Sch.22 Part 5
s.30, amended: 2009 c.23 s.293
s.30, applied: 2009 c.23 s.294, SSI 2009/317 Art.20
s.30, referred to: SSI 2009/317 Art.1
s.30, enabling: SI 2009/1847, SI 2009/1850, SI 2009/3391, SSI 2009/304, SSI 2009/317, SSI 2009/338, SSI 2009/413
Sch.4 Part I para.2, repealed: 2009 c.23 Sch.22 Part 5
Sch.4 Part I para.4, repealed: 2009 c.23 Sch.22 Part 5
Sch.4 Part I para.6, amended: 2009 c.23 Sch.16 para.18, Sch.22 Part 5
Sch.4 Part I para.10, repealed: 2009 c.23 Sch.22 Part 4
Sch.4 Part I para.12, amended: 2009 c.23 Sch.15 para.5
Sch.4 Part I para.13, amended: 2009 c.23 Sch.15 para.5
Sch.4 Part I para.16, amended: 2009 c.23 Sch.15 para.5
Sch.4 Part I para.17B, added: 2009 c.23 Sch.14 para.10
Sch.4 Part II para.28, repealed: 2009 c.23 Sch.22 Part 5
Sch.4 Part II para.33, amended: 2009 c.23 Sch.15 para.5

38. British Telecommunications Act 1981
s.85, amended: SI 2009/1941 Sch.1 para.47

47. Criminal Attempts Act 1981
see *R. v R* [2008] EWCA Crim 619, [2009] 1 W.L.R. 713 (CA (Crim Div)), Moses, L.J.
s.1, see *R. v Kenning (David Matthew)* [2008] EWCA Crim 1534, [2009] Q.B. 221 (CA (Crim Div)), Lord Phillips of Worth Matravers, L.C.J.
s.1, amended: 2009 c.25 Sch.21 para.58
s.1, applied: SI 2009/1059 Art.42

1981 – cont.

49. Contempt of Court Act 1981
s.2, see *Scottish Daily Record and Sunday Mail Ltd v Thomson* [2009] HCJAC 24, 2009 J.C. 175 (HCJ), Lord Nimmo Smith
s.8, see *Attorney General v Seckerson* [2009] EWHC 1023 (Admin), [2009] E.M.L.R. 20 (QBD (Admin)), Pill, L.J.
s.11, see *Times Newspapers Ltd v R* [2008] EWCA Crim 2559, [2009] 1 W.L.R. 1015 (CMAC), Latham, L.J.
s.14, see *Slade v Slade* [2009] EWCA Civ 748, Times, August 20, 2009 (CA (Civ Div)), Ward, L.J.
Sch.1 para.1A, varied: SI 2009/1059 Sch.1 para.20

54. Senior Courts Act 1981
see *R. (on the application of B) v X Crown Court* [2009] EWHC 1149 (Admin), [2009] P.N.L.R. 30 (QBD (Admin)), Hickinbottom, J.
referred to: SI 2009/500 Sch.2 Part 1
s.29, varied: SI 2009/1059 Sch.1 para.21
s.31A, amended: 2009 c.11 s.53
s.49, see *Kaupthing Singer and Friedlander Ltd (In Administration), Re* [2009] EWHC 740 (Ch), [2009] 2 Lloyd's Rep. 154 (Ch D), Sir Andrew Morritt (Chancellor)
s.51, see *Roach v Home Office* [2009] EWHC 312 (QB), [2009] 3 All E.R. 510 (QBD), Davis, J.
s.81, amended: 2009 c.25 Sch.21 para.76
s.82, amended: 2009 c.25 Sch.23 Part 3
s.84, enabling: SI 2009/3361
s.86, enabling: SI 2009/3361
s.127, enabling: SI 2009/1893

54. Supreme Court Act 1981
s.8, see *T v B* [2008] EWHC 3000 (Fam), [2009] 1 F.L.R. 1231 (Fam Div), Sir Mark Potter (President, Fam)
s.9, see *Bailey v Dargue* [2008] EWHC 2903 (Ch), [2009] B.P.I.R. 1 (Ch D (Manchester)), Judge Hodge Q.C.
s.21, see *Metvale Ltd v Monsanto International Sarl (The MSC Napoli)* [2008] EWHC 3002 (Admlty), [2009] 1 All E.R. (Comm) 1158 (QBD (Admlty)), Teare, J.
s.29, see *R. (on the application of B) v X Crown Court* [2009] EWHC 1149 (Admin), [2009] P.N.L.R. 30 (QBD (Admin)), Hickinbottom, J.; see *R. (on the application of Securiplan Plc) v Security Industry Authority* [2008] EWHC 1762 (Admin), [2009] 2 All E.R. 211 (DC), Maurice Kay, L.J.
s.29, varied: SI 2009/1059 Sch.1 para.21
s.31, see *Merger Action Group v Secretary of State for Business, Enterprise and Regulatory Reform* 2009 S.L.T. 10 (CAT), Barling, J. (President)
s.33, see *EDO Corp v Ultra Electronics Ltd* [2009] EWHC 682 (Ch), [2009] Bus. L.R. 1306 (Ch D), Bernard Livesey Q.C.
s.34, see *Parkinson v Hawthorne* [2008] EWHC 3499 (Ch), [2009] 1 W.L.R. 1665 (Ch D), Patten, J.
s.35A, see *Knight v Axa Assurances* [2009] EWHC 1900 (QB), [2009] Lloyd's Rep. I.R. 667 (QBD), Sharp, J.; see *Maher v Groupama Grand Est* [2009] EWHC 38 (QB), [2009] 1 W.L.R. 1752 (QBD), Blair, J.
s.37, see *Birmingham City Council v Shafi* [2008] EWCA Civ 1186, [2009] 1 W.L.R. 1961 (CA (Civ Div)), Sir Anthony Clarke, M.R.; see *Masri v Consolidated Contractors International Co SAL* [2008] EWCA Civ 303,

1981 – cont.

54. Supreme Court Act 1981–*cont.*
s.37–*cont.*
[2009] Q.B. 450 (CA (Civ Div)), Ward, L.J.; see *Sheffield United Football Club Ltd v West Ham United Football Club Plc* [2008] EWHC 2855 (Comm), [2009] 1 Lloyd's Rep. 167 (QBD (Comm)), Teare, J.
s.45, see *R. v M* [2008] EWCA Crim 1901, [2009] 1 W.L.R. 1179 (CA (Crim Div)), Toulson, L.J.
s.51, see *Dean & Dean (A Firm) v Angel Airlines SA* [2009] EWHC 447 (Ch), [2009] B.P.I.R. 409 (Ch D), Patten, J.; see *Equitas Ltd v Horace Holman & Co Ltd* [2008] EWHC 2287 (Comm), [2009] 1 B.C.L.C. 662 (QBD (Comm)), Andrew Smith, J.; see *Harrison v Harrison* [2009] EWHC 428 (QB), [2009] 1 F.L.R. 1434 (QBD), Mackay, J.
Sch.1 para.3, see *Judge v Judge* [2008] EWCA Civ 1458, [2009] 1 F.L.R. 1287 (CA (Civ Div)), Longmore, L.J.

55. Armed Forces Act 1981
s.4, applied: SI 2009/833 Sch.1 para.4, SI 2009/1090 Sch.1 para.4
Sch.3 Part I para.2, varied: SI 2009/1059 Sch.1 para.22

56. Transport Act 1981
s.10, amended: SI 2009/1941 Sch.1 para.48
s.13, amended: SI 2009/1941 Sch.1 para.48
s.14, amended: SI 2009/1941 Sch.1 para.48

61. British Nationality Act 1981
applied: 2009 c.11 s.58, SI 2009/421 Reg.28, SI 2009/700 Sch.1 Part VIII, SI 2009/2958 Art.6
Part IV, applied: SI 2009/847 Reg.1, SI 2009/1495 Reg.1, SI 2009/1747 Art.1, SI 2009/2794 Reg.3
s.1, amended: 2009 c.11 s.42
s.1, applied: 2009 c.11 s.48
s.1, referred to: SSI 2009/182 Reg.20, Reg.21
s.2, applied: SI 2009/2958 Art.6
s.3, amended: 2009 c.11 s.43
s.3, repealed (in part): 2009 c.11 Sch.1 Part 2
s.4, applied: 2009 c.11 s.48
s.4B, amended: 2009 c.11 s.44, Sch.1 Part 2
s.4C, amended: 2009 c.11 s.45, Sch.1 Part 2
s.4C, applied: 2009 c.11 s.58
s.4D, added: 2009 c.11 s.46
s.6, see *MH v Secretary of State for the Home Department* [2009] EWCA Civ 287, [2009] 1 W.L.R. 2049 (CA (Civ Div)), Sir Anthony Clarke, M.R.
s.6, amended: 2009 c.11 s.40
s.6, applied: 2009 c.11 s.48
s.31, applied: SI 2009/2795 Sch.1 para.12, Sch.1 para.13, Sch.1 para.20, Sch.2 para.16
s.41, amended: 2009 c.11 s.41
s.41, enabling: SI 2009/3363
s.41A, added: 2009 c.11 s.47
s.42, applied: SI 2009/421 Reg.26
s.50, amended: 2009 c.11 s.49, SI 2009/2958 Art.3
s.50, enabling: SI 2009/2744
s.50A, added: 2009 c.11 s.48
s.50A, disapplied: 2009 c.11 s.48
Sch.1, applied: 2009 c.11 s.58
Sch.1 para.1, see *MH v Secretary of State for the Home Department* [2009] EWCA Civ 287, [2009] 1 W.L.R. 2049 (CA (Civ Div)), Sir Anthony Clarke, M.R.
Sch.1 para.1, amended: 2009 c.11 s.39, Sch.1 Part 2
Sch.1 para.1, applied: 2009 c.11 s.58
Sch.1 para.1, repealed (in part): 2009 c.11 s.39, Sch.1 Part 2

1981– cont.

61. British Nationality Act 1981– *cont.*

Sch.1 para.2, amended: 2009 c.11 s.39

Sch.1 para.2, repealed (in part): 2009 c.11 s.39, Sch.1 Part 2

Sch.1 para.2, substituted: 2009 c.11 s.39

Sch.1 para.2A, added: 2009 c.11 s.39

Sch.1 para.3, applied: 2009 c.11 s.58

Sch.1 para.3, substituted: 2009 c.11 s.40

Sch.1 para.4, substituted: 2009 c.11 s.40

Sch.1 para.4A, added: 2009 c.11 s.40

Sch.1 para.4B, added: 2009 c.11 s.41

Sch.1 para.9, amended: 2009 c.11 s.49

Sch.1 para.11, added: 2009 c.11 s.49

Sch.6, amended: SI 2009/2744 Art.2

63. Betting and Gaming Duties Act 1981

s.17, amended: 2009 c.10 s.20, s.115

s.19, repealed (in part): 2009 c.10 s.113

s.21, amended: 2009 c.10 s.22

s.22, amended: 2009 c.10 s.22

s.23, amended: 2009 c.10 s.21, s.22

s.23, repealed (in part): 2009 c.10 s.22

s.25, amended: 2009 c.10 s.116

s.26E, repealed (in part): 2009 c.10 s.113

s.26H, amended: 2009 c.10 s.115

s.26M, amended: SI 2009/56 Sch.1 para.97

s.33, amended: 2009 c.10 s.116

Sch.1 para.15, amended: SI 2009/571 Sch.1 para.16

Sch.3 Part I para.5, amended: 2009 c.10 s.20

Sch.4 Part II para.7A, amended: SI 2009/56 Sch.1 para.98

Sch.4A para.6, amended: SI 2009/56 Sch.1 para.99

64. New Towns Act 1981

applied: SI 2009/803 Art.6

s.78, applied: SI 2009/229 Art.4

Sch.6 Part II para.6, amended: SI 2009/1307 Sch.1 para.143

Sch.7 para.1, amended: SI 2009/1307 Sch.1 para.144

Sch.7 para.3, amended: SI 2009/1307 Sch.1 para.144

66. Compulsory Purchase (Vesting Declarations) Act 1981

applied: SI 2009/1300 Art.31, SI 2009/2364 Sch.9 para.4

referred to: SI 2009/1300 Art.45

varied: SI 2009/2364 Art.19, SI 2009/2728 Art.5

s.3, varied: SI 2009/1300 Art.31, SI 2009/2728 Art.5

s.4, applied: SI 2009/1300 Art.36, Art.45, SI 2009/2728 Art.10, Art.17

s.5, varied: SI 2009/2728 Art.5

s.7, varied: SI 2009/1300 Art.31, SI 2009/2728 Art.5

s.8, varied: SI 2009/1300 Art.31

s.10, amended: SI 2009/1307 Sch.1 para.146

s.10, varied: SI 2009/1300 Art.31

s.11, amended: SI 2009/1307 Sch.1 para.147

Sch.1 Part I para.2, varied: SI 2009/1300 Art.31

Sch.1 Part I para.4, amended: SI 2009/1307 Sch.1 para.148

Sch.1 Part I para.8, amended: SI 2009/1307 Sch.1 para.148

Sch.1 Part I para.9, amended: SI 2009/1307 Sch.1 para.148

Sch.1 Part II para.11, varied: SI 2009/1300 Art.31

Sch.1 Part II para.12, varied: SI 2009/1300 Art.31

Sch.2 para.3, varied: SI 2009/1300 Art.31

1981– cont.

67. Acquisition of Land Act 1981

applied: SI 2009/153 Sch.6 para.5, SI 2009/995 Sch.6 para.5, SI 2009/1300 Art.30, SI 2009/2364 Art.18, SI 2009/2728 Art.4

varied: SI 2009/1300 Art.30

s.4, amended: SI 2009/1307 Sch.1 para.150

s.4, applied: SI 2009/2364 Art.30

s.5A, applied: 2009 c.7 Sch.2 para.8

s.5B, referred to: 2009 c.7 Sch.2 para.8

s.17, amended: 2009 c.20 Sch.6 para.55

Sch.2 Part III para.3, amended: SI 2009/1307 Sch.1 para.151

69. Wildlife and Countryside Act 1981

see *Powell v Secretary of State for the Environment, Food and Rural Affairs* [2009] EWHC 643 (Admin), [2009] J.P.L. 1513 (QBD (Admin)), Michael Supperstone Q.C.

applied: SI 2009/3365 Sch.1 para.1

Part II, applied: 2009 c.23 s.158, SI 2009/153 Sch.1 para.5, SI 2009/995 Sch.1 para.5

Part II, amended: 2009 c.23 Sch.11 para.2

s.7, applied: SSI 2009/419 Reg.3, Reg.5

s.7, enabling: SI 2009/1733, SSI 2009/419

s.16, amended: 2009 c.23 s.10

s.16, applied: 2009 c.23 s.10

s.22, applied: SSI 2009/418

s.22, enabling: SI 2009/780, SSI 2009/418

s.26, applied: SI 2009/780(b), SI 2009/780, SSI 2009/418

s.27, amended: 2009 c.23 s.193, Sch.14 para.11, Sch.22 Part 4

s.28, see *R. (on the application of Boggis) v Natural England* [2008] EWHC 2954 (Admin), [2009] 3 All E.R. 879 (QBD (Admin)), Blair, J.

s.28, amended: 2009 c.23 Sch.13 para.2

s.28, applied: SI 2009/153 Sch.1 para.4, SI 2009/995 Sch.1 para.4

s.28A, amended: 2009 c.23 Sch.13 para.3

s.28B, amended: 2009 c.23 Sch.13 para.5

s.28C, amended: 2009 c.23 Sch.13 para.6

s.28CA, added: 2009 c.23 Sch.13 para.7

s.28CB, added: 2009 c.23 Sch.13 para.8

s.28D, amended: 2009 c.23 Sch.13 para.9

s.28E, applied: SI 2009/197 Reg.2, Sch.1 para.1, Sch.1 para.7, Sch.1 para.11, SI 2009/3264 Sch.1 para.1, SI 2009/3365 Sch.1 para.1

s.28F, applied: SI 2009/197 Sch.1 para.1

s.28F, enabling: SI 2009/197

s.28K, applied: SI 2009/197 Reg.2, Sch.1 para.1

s.28L, referred to: SI 2009/197 Sch.1 para.2, Sch.1 para.7, Sch.1 para.9, Sch.1 para.10, Sch.1 para.11, Sch.1 para.12, Sch.1 para.13, Sch.1 para.14, Sch.1 para.15, Sch.1 para.16, Sch.1 para.17, Sch.1 para.18, Sch.1 para.19, Sch.1 para.20, Sch.1 para.21, Sch.1 para.22

s.28L, enabling: SI 2009/197

s.28P, applied: SI 2009/3264 Sch.1 para.1, SI 2009/3365 Sch.1 para.1

s.31, applied: SI 2009/3264 Sch.1 para.1, SI 2009/3365 Sch.1 para.1

s.35, amended: 2009 c.23 Sch.13 para.10

s.35A, added: 2009 c.23 Sch.13 para.11

s.36, applied: 2009 c.23 Sch.12 para.2

s.36, repealed (in part): 2009 c.23 Sch.11 para.2, Sch.22 Part 3

s.37, applied: 2009 c.23 Sch.12 para.3

s.37, repealed (in part): 2009 c.23 Sch.11 para.2, Sch.22 Part 3

s.37A, applied: 2009 c.23 s.158

1981– cont.

69. Wildlife and Countryside Act 1981– *cont.*
s.52, amended: 2009 c.23 Sch.13 para.4
s.67, amended: 2009 c.23 Sch.22 Part 3
Sch.4, amended: SI 2009/780 Art.2, SSI 2009/418 Art.2
Sch.4, applied: SI 2009/780 Art.2
Sch.4, referred to: SSI 2009/419 Reg.2
Sch.12 para.1, repealed (in part): 2009 c.23 Sch.11 para.2, Sch.22 Part 3
Sch.12 para.2, repealed (in part): 2009 c.23 Sch.11 para.2, Sch.22 Part 3
Sch.12 para.3, repealed (in part): 2009 c.23 Sch.11 para.2, Sch.22 Part 3
Sch.12 para.4, repealed (in part): 2009 c.23 Sch.11 para.2, Sch.22 Part 3
Sch.12 para.5, repealed (in part): 2009 c.23 Sch.11 para.2, Sch.22 Part 3
Sch.12 para.6, repealed (in part): 2009 c.23 Sch.11 para.2, Sch.22 Part 3
Sch.12 para.7, repealed (in part): 2009 c.23 Sch.11 para.2, Sch.22 Part 3
Sch.12 para.8, repealed (in part): 2009 c.23 Sch.11 para.2, Sch.22 Part 3
Sch.12 para.9, repealed (in part): 2009 c.23 Sch.11 para.2, Sch.22 Part 3
Sch.14 para.1, see *R. (on the application of Winchester College) v Hampshire CC* [2008] EWCA Civ 431, [2009] 1 W.L.R. 138 (CA (Civ Div)), Ward, L.J.

1982

10. Industrial Training Act 1982
s.11, applied: SI 2009/548, SI 2009/549
s.11, referred to: SI 2009/548, SI 2009/549
s.11, enabling: SI 2009/548, SI 2009/549
s.12, applied: SI 2009/548 Art.16, SI 2009/549 Art.16
s.12, enabling: SI 2009/548, SI 2009/549

16. Civil Aviation Act 1982
s.6, applied: SI 2009/41 Sch.2 para.10
s.17, amended: SI 2009/41 Reg.33
s.23, amended: SI 2009/1941 Sch.1 para.51
s.36, amended: SSI 2009/319 Sch.3 Part 1
s.44, amended: SI 2009/1307 Sch.1 para.153
s.47, applied: SI 2009/3015 Art.219
s.50, amended: SI 2009/1307 Sch.1 para.154
s.51, amended: SI 2009/1307 Sch.1 para.155
s.60, enabling: SI 2009/1735, SI 2009/1742, SI 2009/3015
s.61, enabling: SI 2009/1735, SI 2009/1742, SI 2009/3015
s.64, amended: SI 2009/41 Reg.33
s.65, applied: SI 2009/3015 Art.230
s.69A, amended: SI 2009/41 Reg.34
s.69A, applied: SI 2009/3015 Art.230
s.77, applied: SI 2009/3015 Art.215
s.77, enabling: SI 2009/3015
s.84, amended: SI 2009/41 Reg.33
s.86, applied: SI 2009/2301 Sch.1 para.2, SI 2009/3015 Art.8
s.88, applied: SI 2009/2350 Art.3
s.88, enabling: SI 2009/2350
s.101, enabling: SI 2009/3015
s.102, enabling: SI 2009/1742
s.105, amended: SI 2009/41 Reg.35, SI 2009/1307 Sch.1 para.156, SI 2009/1941 Sch.1 para.51
s.105, repealed (in part): SI 2009/1307 Sch.1 para.156

1982– cont.

16. Civil Aviation Act 1982– *cont.*
Sch.2 para.4, amended: 2009 asp 6 Sch.3 para.3
Sch.8 para.5, amended: SI 2009/1307 Sch.1 para.157
Sch.9 Part II para.9, amended: SI 2009/1307 Sch.1 para.158
Sch.13, enabling: SI 2009/1742, SI 2009/3015

27. Civil Jurisdiction and Judgments Act 1982
Part I, applied: SI 2009/1109 Reg.8
s.1, amended: SI 2009/3131 Reg.3
s.1, applied: SI 2009/3131 Reg.46
s.1, repealed (in part): SI 2009/3131 Reg.3
s.3A, repealed: SI 2009/3131 Reg.4
s.3B, repealed: SI 2009/3131 Reg.4
s.4, amended: SI 2009/3131 Reg.5
s.4A, added: SI 2009/3131 Reg.5
s.4A, applied: SI 2009/3131 Reg.47
s.4A, varied: SI 2009/3131 Reg.47
s.5, amended: SI 2009/3131 Reg.6
s.5A, added: SI 2009/3131 Reg.6
s.5A, applied: SI 2009/3131 Reg.47
s.5A, varied: SI 2009/3131 Reg.47
s.6, amended: SI 2009/871 Art.5, SI 2009/3131 Reg.7
s.6A, added: SI 2009/3131 Reg.7
s.6A, applied: SI 2009/3131 Reg.47
s.7, amended: SI 2009/3131 Reg.8
s.7, applied: SI 2009/3131 Reg.47
s.8, amended: SI 2009/3131 Reg.9
s.8, applied: SI 2009/3131 Reg.47
s.9, amended: SI 2009/3131 Reg.10
s.9, repealed (in part): SI 2009/3131 Reg.10
s.10, amended: SI 2009/3131 Reg.11
s.11, amended: SI 2009/3131 Reg.12
s.11A, added: SI 2009/3131 Reg.12
s.11A, varied: SI 2009/3131 Reg.47
s.13, amended: SI 2009/3131 Reg.13
s.13, referred to: SI 2009/1109 Reg.9
s.14, amended: SI 2009/3131 Reg.14
s.14, repealed (in part): SI 2009/3131 Reg.14
s.15, amended: SI 2009/3131 Reg.15
s.18, amended: 2009 c.26 Sch.7 para.114, Sch.8 Part 5
s.18, disapplied: SI 2009/3131 Reg.47
s.24, amended: SI 2009/3131 Reg.16
s.25, see *ETI Euro Telecom International NV v Bolivia* [2008] EWCA Civ 880, [2009] 1 W.L.R. 665 (CA (Civ Div)), Tuckey, L.J.; see *N v R* [2008] EWHC 1347 (Fam), [2009] 2 F.L.R. 342 (Fam Div), Black, J.
s.25, amended: SI 2009/3131 Reg.17
s.31, see *NML Capital Ltd v Argentina* [2009] EWHC 110 (Comm), [2009] Q.B. 579 (QBD (Comm)), Blair, J.
s.34, see *Karafarin Bank v Mansoury-Dara* [2009] EWHC 1217 (Comm), [2009] 2 Lloyd's Rep. 289 (QBD (Comm)), Teare, J.
s.41, repealed (in part): SI 2009/3131 Reg.18
s.41A, added: SI 2009/3131 Reg.18
s.42, amended: SI 2009/3131 Reg.19
s.43, amended: SI 2009/3131 Reg.20
s.43A, added: SI 2009/3131 Reg.20
s.44, amended: SI 2009/3131 Reg.21
s.44A, added: SI 2009/3131 Reg.22
s.46, amended: SI 2009/3131 Reg.23
s.48, applied: SI 2009/3131 Reg.47
s.48, enabling: SSI 2009/449, SSI 2009/450
s.50, amended: SI 2009/3131 Reg.24
Sch.3C, repealed: SI 2009/3131 Reg.25

1982– cont.

27. Civil Jurisdiction and Judgments Act 1982– *cont.*

Sch.4, see *Royal Bank of Scotland Plc v Davidson* [2009] CSOH 134 (OH), Lord Drummond Young

Sch.4 para.3, see *JS Swan (Printing) Ltd v Kall Kwik UK Ltd* [2009] CSOH 99, 2009 S.C.L.R. 688 (OH), Lord Hodge

Sch.8 para.2, see *Mackie (t/a 197 Aerial Photography) v Askew* 2009 S.L.T. (Sh Ct) 146 (Sh Ct (South Strathclyde) (Ayr)), Sheriff Principal B A Lockhart

29. Supply of Goods and Services Act 1982

referred to: SI 2009/ 669 Sch.1 Part 2

s.4, see *JG Pears (Newark) Ltd v Omega Proteins Ltd* [2009] EWHC 1070 (Comm), [2009] 2 Lloyd's Rep. 339 (QBD (Comm)), Judge Mackie Q.C.

s.11, see *Trident Turboprop (Dublin) Ltd v First Flight Couriers Ltd* [2008] EWHC 1686 (Comm), [2009] 1 All E.R. (Comm) 16 (QBD (Comm)), Aikens, J.

s.15, see *Mastercigars Direct Ltd v Withers LLP* [2007] EWHC 2733 (Ch), [2009] 1 W.L.R. 881 (Ch D), Morgan, J.

30. Local Government (Miscellaneous Provisions) Act 1982

s.2, applied: 2009 c.26 Sch.3 para.1, Sch.3 para.2, Sch.3 para.3, Sch.3 para.4

s.33, amended: 2009 c.20 Sch.6 para.56

s.41, see *Hall v Sandwell MBC* [2009] EWCA Civ 1064, [2009] R.V.R. 316 (CA (Civ Div)), Aikens, L.J.

s.41, amended: 2009 c.20 Sch.6 para.56

Sch.3, applied: 2009 c.26 Sch.3 para.1, Sch.3 para.2, Sch.3 para.3

Sch.3 para.2, amended: 2009 c.26 s.27

Sch.3 para.2A, added: 2009 c.26 s.27

Sch.3 para.9, amended: 2009 c.26 s.27

Sch.3 para.10, amended: SI 2009/ 2999 Reg.47

Sch.3 para.10, applied: SI 2009/ 2999 Reg.47

Sch.3 para.12, amended: 2009 c.26 s.27, SI 2009/ 2999 Reg.47

Sch.3 para.13, amended: 2009 c.26 s.27

Sch.3 para.19, amended: 2009 c.26 s.27

Sch.3 para.25A, added: 2009 c.26 s.27

Sch.3 para.27, amended: 2009 c.26 s.27

Sch.3 para.27A, added: 2009 c.26 s.27

Sch.3 para.28, applied: 2009 c.26 Sch.3 para.3

Sch.3 para.29, applied: 2009 c.26 Sch.3 para.3

Sch.4, applied: SI 2009/ 2999 Reg.45

Sch.4 para.9, applied: SI 2009/ 1300 Art.76

31. Firearms Act 1982

referred to: SI 2009/ 669 Sch.1 Part 1

36. Aviation Security Act 1982

Part IIA, added: 2009 c.26 s.79

s.24AA, added: 2009 c.26 s.79

s.24AB, added: 2009 c.26 s.79

s.24AC, added: 2009 c.26 s.79

s.24AD, added: 2009 c.26 s.79

s.24AE, added: 2009 c.26 s.79

s.24AF, added: 2009 c.26 s.79

s.24AH, added: 2009 c.26 s.79

s.24AI, added: 2009 c.26 s.79

s.24AJ, added: 2009 c.26 s.79

s.24AK, added: 2009 c.26 s.79

s.24AL, added: 2009 c.26 s.79

s.24AM, added: 2009 c.26 s.79

s.24AN, added: 2009 c.26 s.79

1982– cont.

36. Aviation Security Act 1982– *cont.*

s.24AO, added: 2009 c.26 s.79

s.24AP, added: 2009 c.26 s.79

s.24AQ, added: 2009 c.26 s.79

s.24AR, added: 2009 c.26 s.79

s.24AS, added: 2009 c.26 s.79

s.24AT, added: 2009 c.26 s.79

s.25, repealed: 2009 c.26 Sch.8 Part 7

s.25A, applied: 2009 c.26 Sch.6 para.14

s.25A, repealed: 2009 c.26 Sch.8 Part 7

s.25AA, added: 2009 c.26 Sch.6 para.4

s.25B, applied: 2009 c.26 Sch.6 para.14

s.25B, substituted: 2009 c.26 Sch.6 para.5

s.26, amended: 2009 c.26 Sch.6 para.6, Sch.8 Part 7

s.26, applied: 2009 c.26 Sch.6 para.14

s.27, amended: 2009 c.26 Sch.6 para.7

s.28, amended: 2009 c.26 Sch.6 para.8

s.29, amended: 2009 c.26 Sch.6 para.9

s.29A, applied: 2009 c.26 Sch.6 para.14

s.29A, substituted: 2009 c.26 Sch.6 para.10

s.29B, applied: 2009 c.26 Sch.6 para.14

s.29B, substituted: 2009 c.26 Sch.6 para.10

s.29C, applied: 2009 c.26 Sch.6 para.14

s.29C, substituted: 2009 c.26 Sch.6 para.10

s.29D, applied: 2009 c.26 Sch.6 para.14

s.29D, substituted: 2009 c.26 Sch.6 para.10

s.30, applied: 2009 c.26 Sch.6 para.15

s.30, repealed: 2009 c.26 Sch.6 para.11, Sch.8 Part 7

s.31, amended: 2009 c.26 Sch.6 para.12, Sch.8 Part 7

s.31, applied: 2009 c.26 Sch.6 para.14

s.39, amended: 2009 c.26 Sch.6 para.13

Sch.1 para.7, amended: SI 2009/ 1307 Sch.1 para.159

Sch.1 para.9, amended: SI 2009/ 1307 Sch.1 para.159

Sch.1 para.10, amended: SI 2009/ 1307 Sch.1 para.159

39. Finance Act 1982

Sch.18 para.8, amended: SI 2009/ 56 Sch.1 para.101

Sch.18 para.10, amended: SI 2009/ 571 Sch.1 para.18

Sch.18 para.10, repealed (in part): SI 2009/ 571 Sch.1 para.18

Sch.19 Part I para.7, amended: SI 2009/ 56 Sch.1 para.102

41. Stock Transfer Act 1982

Sch.1 para.7, amended: 2009 c.20 Sch.6 para.57

42. Derelict Land Act 1982

s.1, applied: SI 2009/ 3098, SI 2009/ 3098 Art.2

s.1, enabling: SI 2009/ 3098

43. Local Government and Planning (Scotland) Act 1982

s.27, amended: SSI 2009/ 248 Sch.1 para.3

45. Civic Government (Scotland) Act 1982

Part I, applied: SSI 2009/ 145 Art.4

s.1, varied: SI 2009/ 2863 Reg.5, SSI 2009/ 145 Art.3

s.2, varied: SI 2009/ 2863 Reg.5, SSI 2009/ 145 Art.3

s.3, varied: SI 2009/ 2863 Reg.5, SSI 2009/ 145 Art.3

s.4, varied: SI 2009/ 2863 Reg.5, SSI 2009/ 145 Art.3

s.5, varied: SI 2009/ 2863 Reg.5, SSI 2009/ 145 Art.3

s.6, varied: SI 2009/ 2863 Reg.5, SSI 2009/ 145 Art.3, Sch.1 para.2

s.7, applied: SSI 2009/ 145 Art.4, SSI 2009/ 197 Art.3

s.7, varied: SI 2009/ 2863 Reg.5, SSI 2009/ 145 Art.3

s.8, varied: SI 2009/ 2863 Reg.5, SSI 2009/ 145 Art.3

s.10, see *Sneddon v Renfrewshire Council* [2009] CSIH 40, 2009 S.C. 539 (IH (Ex Div)), Lord Osborne

s.10, varied: SI 2009/ 2863 Reg.5

1982– cont.

45. Civic Government (Scotland) Act 1982–*cont.*
s.11, varied: SI 2009/2863 Reg.5
s.12, varied: SI 2009/2863 Reg.5
s.13, varied: SI 2009/2863 Reg.5
s.14, varied: SI 2009/2863 Reg.5
s.19, referred to: SSI 2009/146 Art.5
s.20, varied: SI 2009/2863 Reg.5
s.21, varied: SI 2009/2863 Reg.5
s.23, varied: SI 2009/2863 Reg.5
s.27A, amended: SSI 2009/218 Art.2
s.27A, applied: SSI 2009/197 Art.3, SSI 2009/218 Art.3
s.27A, referred to: SSI 2009/217 Art.3
s.27A, enabling: SSI 2009/218
s.27C, enabling: SSI 2009/217
s.44, applied: SSI 2009/145
s.44, enabling: SSI 2009/145
s.52, applied: 2009 asp 9 s.56, Sch.1 para.10, Sch.4 para.11, SI 2009/1547 Sch.3 para.2, SSI 2009/182 Sch.1 para.2, Sch.1 para.5
s.52, referred to: SI 2009/37 Sch.1 para.2, Sch.1 para.4
s.52A, applied: 2009 asp 9 s.56, Sch.1 para.10, Sch.4 para.12, SI 2009/1547 Sch.3 para.2, SSI 2009/182 Sch.1 para.2, Sch.1 para.5
s.52A, referred to: SI 2009/37 Sch.1 para.2, Sch.1 para.4
s.57, see *Wilson v Barbour* [2009] HCJAC 30, 2009 S.L.T. 437 (HCJ), Lady Paton
s.126, referred to: SI 2009/37 Sch.1 para.2
s.127, referred to: SI 2009/37 Sch.1 para.2
s.128, referred to: SI 2009/37 Sch.1 para.2
s.129, referred to: SI 2009/37 Sch.1 para.2
Sch.1 para.5, varied: SSI 2009/145 Sch.1 para.3
Sch.1 para.18, see *Sneddon v Renfrewshire Council* [2009] CSIH 40, 2009 S.C. 539 (IH (Ex Div)), Lord Osborne
Sch.1 para.18, referred to: SSI 2009/145 Art.4, SSI 2009/197 Art.3
Sch.1 para.20, varied: SSI 2009/145 Sch.1 para.4
48. Criminal Justice Act 1982
s.32, varied: SI 2009/1059 Sch.1 para.23
49. Transport Act 1982
s.13, amended: SI 2009/1941 Sch.1 para.52
s.70, amended: 2009 c.24 Sch.7 Part 1
52. Industrial Development Act 1982
Part II, applied: 2009 c.4 s.149, s.853
s.7, applied: 2009 c.4 s.102, s.1252
s.8, amended: 2009 c.5 s.1, SI 2009/712 Art.2, SI 2009/1227 Art.2, SI 2009/1228 Art.2
s.8, applied: 2009 c.4 s.102, s.1252, SI 2009/712, SI 2009/1227, SI 2009/1228
s.8, referred to: SI 2009/1227 Art.2, SI 2009/1228 Art.2
s.8, enabling: SI 2009/712, SI 2009/1227, SI 2009/1228
53. Administration of Justice Act 1982
s.8, see *Burgess v Napier University* [2009] CSOH 6, 2009 Rep. L.R. 55 (OH), Lady Dorrian; see *Kerr v Stiell Facilities Ltd* [2009] CSOH 67, 2009 S.L.T. 851 (OH), Lord Hodge; see *Renfrew v Lithgows Ltd* 2009 Rep. L.R. 19 (OH), Lord Woolman
s.9, see *Burgess v Napier University* [2009] CSOH 6, 2009 Rep. L.R. 55 (OH), Lady Dorrian; see *Renfrew v Lithgows Ltd* 2009 Rep. L.R. 19 (OH), Lord Woolman
s.20, see *Sprackling v Sprackling* [2008] EWHC 2696 (Ch), [2009] W.T.L.R. 897 (Ch D), Norris, J.

1982– cont.

53. Administration of Justice Act 1982–*cont.*
s.21, see *Frear v Frear* [2008] EWCA Civ 1320, [2009] 1 F.L.R. 391 (CA (Civ Div)), Sir Andrew Morritt

1983

2. Representation of the People Act 1983
see *Pilling v Reynolds* [2008] EWHC 316 (QB), [2009] 1 All E.R. 163 (DC), Tugendhat, J.
Part III, applied: SSI 2009/352 Sch.1 para.10, Sch.1 para.55
s.3, varied: SI 2009/1059 Sch.1 para.24
s.3A, varied: SI 2009/1059 Sch.1 para.24
s.9, applied: 2009 c.12 s.30
s.9B, enabling: SI 2009/725
s.10, amended: 2009 c.12 s.33
s.10, applied: 2009 c.12 s.30, SI 2009/2395 Art.3
s.10, referred to: 2009 c.12 s.34
s.10A, amended: 2009 c.12 s.33, Sch.6 para.1, Sch.7
s.10A, applied: 2009 c.12 s.30, s.34
s.10A, referred to: 2009 c.12 s.34
s.10ZB, amended: 2009 c.12 s.33, Sch.7
s.13, amended: 2009 c.12 s.23, Sch.6 para.2
s.13A, amended: 2009 c.12 s.33, Sch.6 para.3, Sch.7
s.13A, applied: 2009 c.12 s.30
s.13A, referred to: 2009 c.12 s.34
s.13B, enabling: SI 2009/186
s.13BA, enabling: SI 2009/813
s.13BB, added: 2009 c.12 s.23
s.13BB, amended: 2009 c.12 s.33
s.13D, amended: 2009 c.12 s.33
s.41, applied: SSI 2009/352 Sch.1 para.2
s.43, amended: 2009 asp 10 Sch.1 para.1
s.43, repealed (in part): 2009 asp 10 Sch.1 para.1
s.53, enabling: SI 2009/725, SSI 2009/128
s.57, applied: SSI 2009/12 Art.2
s.57, enabling: SSI 2009/12
s.63, amended: 2009 c.12 s.25, Sch.7
s.65A, amended: 2009 c.12 Sch.6 para.4
s.70, amended: 2009 c.12 Sch.6 para.5
s.76A, amended: 2009 c.12 Sch.6 para.6, Sch.7
s.76ZA, added: 2009 c.12 s.21
s.86, see *Finch v Richardson* [2008] EWHC 3067 (QB), [2009] 1 W.L.R. 1338 (QBD), Tugendhat, J.
s.90ZA, amended: 2009 c.12 Sch.6 para.7
s.120, varied: SSI 2009/352 Reg.6
s.121, varied: SSI 2009/352 Reg.6
s.122, varied: SSI 2009/352 Reg.6
s.123, varied: SSI 2009/352 Reg.6
s.124, varied: SSI 2009/352 Reg.6
s.125, varied: SSI 2009/352 Reg.6
s.126, varied: SSI 2009/352 Reg.6
s.127, varied: SSI 2009/352 Reg.6
s.128, see *Aehmed v Legal Services Commission* [2009] EWCA Civ 572, [2009] 3 Costs L.R. 425 (CA (Civ Div)), Sedley, L.J.
s.128, varied: SSI 2009/352 Reg.6
s.129, varied: SSI 2009/352 Reg.6
s.130, varied: SSI 2009/352 Reg.6
s.131, varied: SSI 2009/352 Reg.6
s.132, varied: SSI 2009/352 Reg.6
s.133, varied: SSI 2009/352 Reg.6
s.134, varied: SSI 2009/352 Reg.6
s.135, varied: SSI 2009/352 Reg.6
s.135A, varied: SSI 2009/352 Reg.6
s.136, varied: SSI 2009/352 Reg.6
s.137, varied: SSI 2009/352 Reg.6

1983–cont.

2. Representation of the People Act 1983–*cont.*
s.138, varied: SSI 2009/352 Reg.6
s.139, varied: SSI 2009/352 Reg.6
s.140, varied: SSI 2009/352 Reg.6
s.141, varied: SSI 2009/352 Reg.6
s.142, varied: SSI 2009/352 Reg.6
s.143, varied: SSI 2009/352 Reg.6
s.144, varied: SSI 2009/352 Reg.6
s.145, varied: SSI 2009/352 Reg.6
s.145A, varied: SSI 2009/352 Reg.6
s.146, varied: SSI 2009/352 Reg.6
s.147, varied: SSI 2009/352 Reg.6
s.148, varied: SSI 2009/352 Reg.6
s.149, varied: SSI 2009/352 Reg.6
s.150, varied: SSI 2009/352 Reg.6
s.151, varied: SSI 2009/352 Reg.6
s.152, varied: SSI 2009/352 Reg.6
s.153, varied: SSI 2009/352 Reg.6
s.154, varied: SSI 2009/352 Reg.6
s.155, varied: SSI 2009/352 Reg.6
s.156, varied: SSI 2009/352 Reg.6
s.157, varied: SSI 2009/352 Reg.6
s.158, varied: SSI 2009/352 Reg.6
s.159, varied: SSI 2009/352 Reg.6
s.160, varied: SSI 2009/352 Reg.6
s.161, varied: SSI 2009/352 Reg.6
s.162, varied: SSI 2009/352 Reg.6
s.163, varied: SSI 2009/352 Reg.6
s.164, varied: SSI 2009/352 Reg.6
s.165, varied: SSI 2009/352 Reg.6
s.166, varied: SSI 2009/352 Reg.6
s.167, see *Finch v Richardson* [2008] EWHC 3067 (QB), [2009] 1 W.L.R. 1338 (QBD), Tugendhat, J.
s.167, varied: SSI 2009/352 Reg.6
s.168, varied: SSI 2009/352 Reg.6
s.169, varied: SSI 2009/352 Reg.6
s.170, varied: SSI 2009/352 Reg.6
s.171, varied: SSI 2009/352 Reg.6
s.172, varied: SSI 2009/352 Reg.6
s.173, varied: SSI 2009/352 Reg.6
s.173A, varied: SSI 2009/352 Reg.6
s.174, varied: SSI 2009/352 Reg.6
s.175, varied: SSI 2009/352 Reg.6
s.176, varied: SSI 2009/352 Reg.6
s.177, varied: SSI 2009/352 Reg.6
s.178, varied: SSI 2009/352 Reg.6
s.179, varied: SSI 2009/352 Reg.6
s.180, varied: SSI 2009/352 Reg.6
s.180A, varied: SSI 2009/352 Reg.6
s.181, varied: SSI 2009/352 Reg.6
s.182, varied: SSI 2009/352 Reg.6
s.183, varied: SSI 2009/352 Reg.6
s.184, varied: SSI 2009/352 Reg.6
s.185, amended: SSI 2009/248 Sch.2
s.185, varied: SSI 2009/352 Reg.6
s.186, varied: SSI 2009/352 Reg.6
s.201, amended: 2009 c.12 s.33
s.201, applied: SI 2009/186, SI 2009/725, SI 2009/813, SSI 2009/128
s.202, referred to: SI 2009/725
s.204, repealed (in part): SSI 2009/248 Sch.2
Sch.1 Part 1, amended: 2009 c.12 Sch.6 para.8, Sch.7
Sch.1 Part 1 para.3, amended: 2009 c.12 Sch.6 para.8
Sch.1 Part II para.6, amended: 2009 c.12 s.24, Sch.6 para.8
Sch.1 Part II para.6, repealed (in part): 2009 c.12 Sch.7

1983–cont.

2. Representation of the People Act 1983–*cont.*
Sch.1 Part II para.9, amended: 2009 c.12 Sch.6 para.8
Sch.1 Part II para.11, amended: 2009 c.12 s.24
Sch.1 Part II para.12, amended: 2009 c.12 s.24
Sch.1 Part II para.14, amended: 2009 c.12 s.24, Sch.6 para.8
Sch.1 Part II para.14A, amended: 2009 c.12 Sch.6 para.8
Sch.1 Part V para.53A, added: 2009 c.12 s.24
Sch.1 Part V para.58, substituted: 2009 c.12 s.25
Sch.2 para.1, amended: 2009 c.12 s.33
Sch.2 para.1, repealed (in part): 2009 c.12 s.33, Sch.7
Sch.2 para.5, enabling: SI 2009/725
Sch.2 para.5A, enabling: SSI 2009/128
Sch.2 para.10B, enabling: SI 2009/725
Sch.2 para.11, enabling: SI 2009/725
Sch.2 para.12, enabling: SSI 2009/128
Sch.2 para.13, amended: 2009 c.12 s.33
Sch.4A Part 3 para.14, amended: 2009 c.12 s.22

18. Nuclear Material (Offences) Act 1983
s.1, varied: SI 2009/3203 Art.3, Sch.1 para.4
s.1A, varied: SI 2009/3203 Art.3, Sch.1 para.5
s.1B, varied: SI 2009/3203 Art.3, Sch.1 para.6
s.1C, varied: SI 2009/3203 Art.3, Sch.1 para.7
s.1D, varied: SI 2009/3203 Art.3, Sch.1 para.8
s.2, varied: SI 2009/3203 Art.3, Sch.1 para.9
s.2A, varied: SI 2009/3203 Art.3, Sch.1 para.10
s.3, varied: SI 2009/3203 Art.3, Sch.1 para.11
s.3A, varied: SI 2009/3203 Art.3
s.4, varied: SI 2009/3203 Art.3, Sch.1 para.12
s.6, varied: SI 2009/3203 Art.3
s.7, enabling: SI 2009/3203
s.8, varied: SI 2009/3203 Art.3, Sch.1 para.13
Sch.1, varied: SI 2009/3203 Art.3

20. Mental Health Act 1983
see *Attorney General's Reference (No.20 of 2008), Re* [2008] EWCA Crim 1383, [2009] 1 Cr. App. R. (S.) 58 (CA (Crim Div)), Lord Philips, L.C.J.; see *McFaddens (A Firm) v Platford* [2009] EWHC 126 (TCC), [2009] P.N.L.R. 26 (QBD (TCC)), Judge Toulmin Q.C.; see *R. (on the application of Rayner) v Secretary of State for the Home Department* [2008] EWCA Civ 176, [2009] 1 W.L.R. 310 (CA (Civ Div)), Ward, L.J.; see *R. v Collier (Martin Graham)* [2009] EWCA Crim 160, [2009] 2 Cr. App. R. (S.) 61 (CA (Crim Div)), Moses, L.J.; see *W Primary Care Trust v B* [2009] EWHC 1737 (Fam), (2009) 12 C.C.L. Rep. 488 (Fam Div), Roderic Wood, J.
applied: 2009 c.25 s.125, 2009 c.26 s.45, SI 2009/1059 Art.80, SI 2009/1209 r.75, SI 2009/1213 Reg.7, SI 2009/2041 r.90, SI 2009/3112 Reg.17
Part IV, applied: SI 2009/462 Sch.4 para.2, Sch.4 para.5
Part IVA, applied: SI 2009/462 Sch.4 para.2
Part III, see *X v NHS Trust* [2008] EWCA Civ 1354, [2009] 2 All E.R. 792 (CA (Civ Div)), Laws, L.J.
s.2, see *GJ v Foundation Trust* [2009] EWHC 2972 (Fam), (2009) 12 C.C.L. Rep. 600 (CP), Charles, J.
s.3, see *GJ v Foundation Trust* [2009] EWHC 2972 (Fam), (2009) 12 C.C.L. Rep. 600 (CP), Charles, J.; see *R. v Norman (Leslie)* [2008] EWCA Crim 1810, [2009] 1 Cr. App. R. 13 (CA (Crim Div)), Thomas, L.J.; see *Savage v South Essex Partnership NHS Foundation Trust* [2008] UKHL 74, [2009] 1 A.C. 681 (HL), Lord Scott of Foscote
s.8, applied: SI 2009/1887 Sch.2

1983– cont.

1983– cont.

20. Mental Health Act 1983–*cont.*
s.8, referred to: SI 2009/1887 Sch.2
s.12, applied: SI 2009/783 Reg.4
s.12, referred to: SI 2009/1511 Sch.1
s.17, referred to: SI 2009/1887 Sch.2
s.17B, referred to: SI 2009/1887 Sch.2
s.35, applied: 2009 c.26 s.45
s.37, see *Gray v Thames Trains Ltd* [2008] EWCA
    Civ 713, [2009] 2 W.L.R. 351 (CA (Civ Div)),
    Sir Anthony Clarke, M.R.; see *R. (on the*
    application of P) v Secretary of State for Justice
    [2009] EWCA Civ 701, [2009] U.K.H.R.R. 1496
    (CA (Civ Div)), Ward, L.J.; see *R. (on the*
    application of Rayner) v Secretary of State for
    the Home Department [2008] EWCA Civ 176,
    [2009] 1 W.L.R. 310 (CA (Civ Div)), Ward, L.J.;
    see *R. v Norman (Leslie)* [2008] EWCA Crim
    1810, [2009] 1 Cr. App. R. 13 (CA (Crim Div)),
    Thomas, L.J.; see *X v NHS Trust* [2008] EWCA
    Civ 1354, [2009] 2 All E.R. 792 (CA (Civ Div)),
    Laws, L.J.
s.40, see *X v NHS Trust* [2008] EWCA Civ 1354,
    [2009] 2 All E.R. 792 (CA (Civ Div)), Laws, L.J.
s.40, referred to: SI 2009/1887 Sch.2
s.41, see *R. (on the application of Rayner) v*
    Secretary of State for the Home Department
    [2008] EWCA Civ 176, [2009] 1 W.L.R. 310 (CA
    (Civ Div)), Ward, L.J.; see *R. v Norman (Leslie)*
    [2008] EWCA Crim 1810, [2009] 1 Cr. App. R. 13
    (CA (Crim Div)), Thomas, L.J.
s.42, see *R. (on the application of Rayner) v*
    Secretary of State for the Home Department
    [2008] EWCA Civ 176, [2009] 1 W.L.R. 310 (CA
    (Civ Div)), Ward, L.J.
s.42, applied: SI 2009/1887 Reg.7, Reg.8
s.47, see *R. (on the application of F) v Secretary of*
    State for the Home Department [2008] EWCA
    Civ 1457, (2009) 12 C.C.L. Rep. 245 (CA (Civ
    Div)), Waller, L.J. (V-P); see *R. (on the*
    application of N) v Mental Health Review
    Tribunal [2008] EWHC 3383 (Admin), (2009)
    106 B.M.L.R. 64 (QBD (Admin)), Justice
    Plender
s.47, varied: SI 2009/1059 Sch.1 para.25
s.48, see *R. (on the application of P) v Secretary of*
    State for Justice [2009] EWCA Civ 701, [2009]
    U.K.H.R.R. 1496 (CA (Civ Div)), Ward, L.J.
s.49, see *R. (on the application of N) v Mental Health*
    Review Tribunal [2008] EWHC 3383 (Admin),
    (2009) 106 B.M.L.R. 64 (QBD (Admin)),
    Justice Plender
s.57, applied: SI 2009/462 Sch.4 para.2
s.61, applied: SI 2009/462 Sch.4 para.3
s.64H, applied: SI 2009/462 Sch.4 para.4
s.69, see *R. (on the application of N) v Mental Health*
    Review Tribunal [2008] EWHC 3383 (Admin),
    (2009) 106 B.M.L.R. 64 (QBD (Admin)),
    Justice Plender
s.70, see *R. (on the application of N) v Mental Health*
    Review Tribunal [2008] EWHC 3383 (Admin),
    (2009) 106 B.M.L.R. 64 (QBD (Admin)),
    Justice Plender
s.73, see *R. (on the application of Rayner) v*
    Secretary of State for the Home Department
    [2008] EWCA Civ 176, [2009] 1 W.L.R. 310 (CA
    (Civ Div)), Ward, L.J.
s.73, applied: SI 2009/1887 Reg.7, Reg.8
s.75, see *R. (on the application of Rayner) v*
    Secretary of State for the Home Department
    [2008] EWCA Civ 176, [2009] 1 W.L.R. 310 (CA
    (Civ Div)), Ward, L.J.

20. Mental Health Act 1983–*cont.*
s.75, applied: SI 2009/1887 Reg.7, Reg.8
s.77, amended: SI 2009/1307 Sch.1 para.161
s.78, enabling: SI 2009/3348
s.117, amended: 2009 c.21 Sch.1 para.3
s.117, applied: SI 2009/1887 Reg.9, Reg.10
s.118, applied: SI 2009/462 Sch.4 para.2, Sch.4
    para.5
s.119, applied: SI 2009/462 Sch.4 para.5
s.120, applied: SI 2009/462 Sch.4 para.6, Sch.4
    para.7, Sch.4 para.8, Sch.4 para.9, Sch.4 para.10,
    SI 2009/1360 Art.3
s.121, applied: SI 2009/462 Sch.4 para.11, Sch.4
    para.13, Sch.4 para.14
s.126, referred to: SI 2009/37 Sch.1 para.2, Sch.1
    para.4
s.127, referred to: SI 2009/37 Sch.1 para.2, Sch.1
    para.4
s.128, referred to: SI 2009/37 Sch.1 para.2, Sch.1
    para.4
s.129, referred to: SI 2009/37 Sch.1 para.2, Sch.1
    para.4
s.130A, enabling: SI 2009/2376
s.130C, enabling: SI 2009/2376
s.134A, applied: SI 2009/462 Sch.4 para.11
s.134A, varied: SI 2009/462 Sch.4 para.12, Sch.4
    para.14
Sch.2 para.5, added: SI 2009/1307 Sch.1 para.162
30. Diseases of Fish Act 1983
repealed (in part): SI 2009/463 Sch.2 para.6, SSI
    2009/85 Sch.2 para.6
34. Mobile Homes Act 1983
see *Doherty v Birmingham City Council* [2008]
    UKHL 57, [2009] 1 A.C. 367 (HL), Lord Hope
    of Craighead
s.5, see *Doherty v Birmingham City Council* [2008]
    UKHL 57, [2009] 1 A.C. 367 (HL), Lord Hope of
    Craighead
35. Litter Act 1983
s.5, applied: SI 2009/721 Sch.3 para.6
Sch.1, applied: SI 2009/721 Sch.3 para.6
40. Education (Fees and Awards) Act 1983
s.1, applied: SI 2009/3201 Reg.4
s.1, enabling: SSI 2009/188, SSI 2009/309
s.2, enabling: SSI 2009/188, SSI 2009/309
41. Health and Social Services and Social Security
    Adjudications Act 1983
s.17, see *R. (on the application of B) v Cornwall CC*
    [2009] EWHC 491 (Admin), (2009) 12 C.C.L.
    Rep. 381 (QBD (Admin)), Hickinbottom, J.;
    see *R. (on the application of Domb) v*
    Hammersmith and Fulham LBC [2008]
    EWHC 3277 (Admin), [2009] B.L.G.R. 340
    (QBD (Admin)), Sir Michael Harrison
44. National Audit Act 1983
s.6, applied: 2009 c.11 s.29, 2009 c.20 Sch.1 para.13
s.8, applied: 2009 c.20 Sch.1 para.13
Sch.3, applied: 2009 c.13 Sch.1 para.1
Sch.3 para.1, amended: SI 2009/1941 Sch.1 para.54
47. National Heritage Act 1983
s.36, amended: SI 2009/1307 Sch.1 para.163
54. Medical Act 1983
see *R. (on the application of British Medical*
    Association) v General Medical Council [2008]
    EWHC 2602 (Admin), Times, January 19, 2009
    (QBD (Admin)), Burnett, J.
applied: SI 2009/2722 Reg.3, SI 2009/2739 Sch.1
Part V, applied: SI 2009/2739 Sch.1
s.18, applied: SI 2009/2739 Sch.1

1983– cont.

54. Medical Act 1983– *cont.*

s.18A, applied: SI 2009/2739 Sch.1

s.27A, applied: SI 2009/2739 Sch.1

s.27B, applied: SI 2009/2739 Sch.1

s.29A, enabling: SI 2009/2739

s.29E, enabling: SI 2009/2739

s.29J, applied: SI 2009/2739

s.29J, enabling: SI 2009/2739

s.30, applied: SI 2009/2739 Sch.1

s.31, applied: SI 2009/2739 Sch.1

s.31, referred to: SI 2009/2764

s.31, enabling: SI 2009/2764

s.31A, applied: SI 2009/2739 Sch.1

s.31A, referred to: SI 2009/2763

s.31A, enabling: SI 2009/2763

s.32, applied: SI 2009/2739 Sch.1

s.35C, see *R. (on the application of Zygmunt) v General Medical Council* [2008] EWHC 2643 (Admin), [2009] LS Law Medical 219 (QBD (Admin)), Mitting, J.

s.35C, amended: 2009 c.26 s.81

s.35C, applied: SI 2009/2739 Sch.1

s.35CC, enabling: SI 2009/1913

s.35D, applied: SI 2009/2739 Sch.1

s.39, applied: SI 2009/2739 Sch.1

s.41, applied: SI 2009/2739 Sch.1

s.41, enabling: SI 2009/2739

s.41C, applied: SI 2009/2739 Sch.1

s.44, applied: SI 2009/2739 Sch.1

s.44B, applied: SI 2009/2739 Sch.1

s.44C, applied: SI 2009/2739 Sch.1

s.47, see *Cheatle v General Medical Council* [2009] EWHC 645 (Admin), [2009] LS Law Medical 299 (QBD (Admin)), Cranston, J.

Sch.1 Part III para.19A, enabling: SI 2009/2751

Sch.1 Part III para.19B, enabling: SI 2009/2751

Sch.1 Part III para.19C, enabling: SI 2009/2751

Sch.1 Part III para.19D, enabling: SI 2009/2751

Sch.1 Part III para.19E, enabling: SI 2009/2751

Sch.1 Part III para.23B, enabling: SI 2009/2751

Sch.1 Part III para.24, applied: SI 2009/2751

Sch.3B para.3, applied: SI 2009/2752

Sch.3B para.3, referred to: SI 2009/2752

Sch.3B para.3, enabling: SI 2009/2752

Sch.4 para.1, applied: SI 2009/2765 Sch.1

Sch.4 para.1, enabling: SI 2009/1913, SI 2009/2765

56. Oil Taxation Act 1983

s.6, amended: 2009 c.10 Sch.41 para.2

s.9, amended: 2009 c.10 Sch.45 para.2

s.9, repealed (in part): 2009 c.10 Sch.45 para.2

s.13, repealed: 2009 c.10 Sch.45 para.2

s.14, repealed: 2009 c.10 Sch.45 para.2

Sch.1 Part II para.8, amended: 2009 c.10 Sch.41 para.3

Sch.3 para.3, repealed: 2009 c.10 Sch.45 para.2

Sch.5 para.1, repealed: 2009 c.10 Sch.45 para.2

Sch.5 para.2, repealed: 2009 c.10 Sch.45 para.2

Sch.5 para.3, repealed: 2009 c.10 Sch.45 para.2

Sch.5 para.4, repealed: 2009 c.10 Sch.45 para.2

Sch.5 para.5, repealed: 2009 c.10 Sch.45 para.2

Sch.5 para.6, repealed: 2009 c.10 Sch.45 para.2

Sch.5 para.7, repealed: 2009 c.10 Sch.45 para.2

1984

3. Occupiers Liability Act 1984

s.1, amended: 2009 c.23 s.306

1984– cont.

12. Telecommunications Act 1984

referred to: SSI 2009/79 Art.6, SSI 2009/95 Art.5, SSI 2009/146 Art.5, SSI 2009/149 Art.3

Sch.2 para.1, applied: SI 2009/640 Reg.3

Sch.2 para.4, amended: SI 2009/1307 Sch.1 para.164

Sch.2 para.4, repealed (in part): SI 2009/1307 Sch.1 para.164

Sch.2 para.11, amended: 2009 c.23 s.80, Sch.22 Part 2

Sch.2 para.11, applied: 2009 c.23 Sch.9 para.11, Sch.9 para.12

Sch.2 para.11, repealed (in part): 2009 c.23 s.80, Sch.22 Part 2

Sch.2 para.11, varied: 2009 c.23 Sch.9 para.11

Sch.2 para.23, applied: 2009 c.23 s.87

16. Foreign Limitation Periods Act 1984

s.2, see *Harley v Smith* [2009] EWHC 56 (QB), [2009] 1 Lloyd's Rep. 359 (QBD), Foskett, J.

s.8, amended: SI 2009/3064 Reg.3

22. Public Health (Control of Disease) Act 1984

s.2, applied: SI 2009/3051 Reg.2, SI 2009/3230 Reg.2, SI 2009/3238 Reg.2, SI 2009/3255 Reg.2, SI 2009/3376 Reg.2, SI 2009/3378 Reg.2, SI 2009/3379 Reg.2

s.7, applied: SI 2009/3051 Reg.2, SI 2009/3230 Reg.2, SI 2009/3238 Reg.2, SI 2009/3255 Reg.2, SI 2009/3376 Reg.2, SI 2009/3378 Reg.2, SI 2009/3379 Reg.2

s.45C, applied: SI 2009/38

s.45C, enabling: SI 2009/38

s.45F, enabling: SI 2009/38

s.45P, enabling: SI 2009/38

s.45Q, applied: SI 2009/38

23. Registered Homes Act 1984

s.30, see *Jain v Trent SHA* [2009] UKHL 4, [2009] 1 A.C. 853 (HL), Lord Scott of Foscote

24. Dentists Act 1984

applied: SI 2009/2722 Reg.3

s.1, amended: SI 2009/1182 Sch.1 para.1

s.1, repealed (in part): SI 2009/1182 Sch.1 para.1

s.1, enabling: SI 2009/1808

s.2, amended: SI 2009/1182 Sch.1 para.2

s.2, repealed (in part): SI 2009/1182 Sch.1 para.2

s.2, enabling: SI 2009/1813

s.2A, amended: SI 2009/1182 Sch.1 para.3

s.2A, repealed (in part): SI 2009/1182 Sch.1 para.3

s.2B, substituted: SI 2009/1182 Sch.1 para.4

s.2C, amended: SI 2009/1182 Sch.1 para.5

s.2E, added: SI 2009/1182 Sch.1 para.6

s.3, applied: SI 2009/1358 Art.2

s.3, varied: SI 2009/1182 Art.7

s.27, amended: 2009 c.26 s.81, SI 2009/1182 Sch.1 para.7

s.36N, amended: 2009 c.26 s.81, SI 2009/1182 Sch.1 para.8

s.41, amended: SI 2009/1182 Sch.1 para.9

s.50C, amended: SI 2009/1182 Sch.1 para.10

s.50C, applied: SI 2009/1813

s.50C, enabling: SI 2009/1813

s.51, amended: SI 2009/1182 Sch.1 para.11

s.53, amended: SI 2009/1182 Sch.1 para.12

Sch.1 Part I para.1A, applied: SI 2009/1808 Art.6

Sch.1 Part I para.1A, substituted: SI 2009/1182 Sch.1 para.13

Sch.1 Part I para.1B, substituted: SI 2009/1182 Sch.1 para.13

Sch.1 Part I para.1B, enabling: SI 2009/1808

1984–cont.

24. Dentists Act 1984–*cont.*

Sch.1 Part I para.2, repealed: SI 2009/ 1182 Sch.1 para.13

Sch.1 Part I para.3, repealed: SI 2009/ 1182 Sch.1 para.13

Sch.1 Part I para.4, repealed: SI 2009/ 1182 Sch.1 para.13

Sch.1 Part I para.6, amended: SI 2009/ 1182 Sch.1 para.13

Sch.1 Part I para.8, amended: SI 2009/ 1182 Sch.1 para.13

Sch.1 Part I para.8, repealed (in part): SI 2009/ 1182 Sch.1 para.13

Sch.1 Part I para.8, enabling: SI 2009/ 1813

Sch.1 Part I para.8A, added: SI 2009/ 1182 Sch.1 para.13

26. Inshore Fishing (Scotland) Act 1984

s.1, enabling: SSI 2009/444

27. Road Traffic Regulation Act 1984

applied: 2009 asp 3 s.3, SI 2009/1300 Art.49, Art.50, SI 2009/2364 Art.34

referred to: SI 2009/271 Art.5, SI 2009/1300 Art.49, Art.50

s.1, applied: SSI 2009/ 146

s.1, enabling: SI 2009/ 3300, SI 2009/ 3350, SI 2009/ 3394, SSI 2009/ 13, SSI 2009/ 15, SSI 2009/ 79, SSI 2009/ 95, SSI 2009/ 146, SSI 2009/ 148, SSI 2009/ 149, SSI 2009/ 204, SSI 2009/ 241, SSI 2009/ 313, SSI 2009/ 367

s.2, enabling: SI 2009/ 3300, SI 2009/ 3350, SI 2009/ 3394, SSI 2009/ 13, SSI 2009/ 15, SSI 2009/ 22, SSI 2009/ 23, SSI 2009/ 24, SSI 2009/ 25, SSI 2009/ 56, SSI 2009/ 57, SSI 2009/ 58, SSI 2009/ 59, SSI 2009/ 62, SSI 2009/ 77, SSI 2009/ 78, SSI 2009/ 79, SSI 2009/ 95, SSI 2009/ 123, SSI 2009/ 125, SSI 2009/ 126, SSI 2009/ 127, SSI 2009/ 136, SSI 2009/ 146, SSI 2009/ 148, SSI 2009/ 149, SSI 2009/ 157, SSI 2009/ 158, SSI 2009/ 159, SSI 2009/ 161, SSI 2009/ 195, SSI 2009/ 198, SSI 2009/ 199, SSI 2009/ 200, SSI 2009/ 201, SSI 2009/ 204, SSI 2009/ 237, SSI 2009/ 241, SSI 2009/ 252, SSI 2009/ 253, SSI 2009/ 254, SSI 2009/ 255, SSI 2009/ 272, SSI 2009/ 274, SSI 2009/ 278, SSI 2009/ 279, SSI 2009/ 280, SSI 2009/ 281, SSI 2009/ 282, SSI 2009/ 289, SSI 2009/ 296, SSI 2009/ 297, SSI 2009/ 298, SSI 2009/ 299, SSI 2009/ 313, SSI 2009/ 324, SSI 2009/ 325, SSI 2009/ 326, SSI 2009/ 327, SSI 2009/ 346, SSI 2009/ 347, SSI 2009/ 354, SSI 2009/ 355, SSI 2009/ 356, SSI 2009/ 360, SSI 2009/ 361, SSI 2009/ 362, SSI 2009/ 363, SSI 2009/ 364, SSI 2009/ 367, SSI 2009/ 370, SSI 2009/ 384, SSI 2009/ 398, SSI 2009/ 421, SSI 2009/ 422, SSI 2009/ 423, SSI 2009/ 424, SSI 2009/ 430, SSI 2009/ 431, SSI 2009/ 451, SSI 2009/ 452, SSI 2009/ 453, SSI 2009/ 454, SSI 2009/ 455

s.3, enabling: SI 2009/ 3350, SI 2009/ 3394

s.4, enabling: SI 2009/ 3350, SI 2009/ 3394, SSI 2009/ 22, SSI 2009/ 23, SSI 2009/ 24, SSI 2009/ 25, SSI 2009/ 56, SSI 2009/ 57, SSI 2009/ 58, SSI 2009/ 59, SSI 2009/ 62, SSI 2009/ 77, SSI 2009/ 78, SSI 2009/ 123, SSI 2009/ 125, SSI 2009/ 126, SSI 2009/ 127, SSI 2009/ 157, SSI 2009/ 158, SSI 2009/ 159, SSI 2009/ 161, SSI 2009/ 195, SSI 2009/ 198, SSI 2009/ 199, SSI 2009/ 200, SSI 2009/ 201, SSI 2009/ 237, SSI 2009/ 252, SSI 2009/ 253, SSI 2009/ 254, SSI 2009/ 255, SSI 2009/ 272, SSI 2009/ 274, SSI 2009/ 278, SSI 2009/ 279, SSI 2009/ 280, SSI 2009/ 281, SSI 2009/ 282, SSI 2009/ 289, SSI 2009/ 296, SSI

1984–cont.

27. Road Traffic Regulation Act 1984–*cont.*

s.4, enabling:–*cont.*

2009/ 297, SSI 2009/ 298, SSI 2009/ 299, SSI 2009/ 324, SSI 2009/ 325, SSI 2009/ 326, SSI 2009/ 327, SSI 2009/ 346, SSI 2009/ 347, SSI 2009/ 354, SSI 2009/ 355, SSI 2009/ 356, SSI 2009/ 360, SSI 2009/ 361, SSI 2009/ 362, SSI 2009/ 363, SSI 2009/ 364, SSI 2009/ 370, SSI 2009/ 384, SSI 2009/ 398, SSI 2009/ 421, SSI 2009/ 422, SSI 2009/ 423, SSI 2009/ 424, SSI 2009/ 430, SSI 2009/ 431, SSI 2009/ 451, SSI 2009/ 452, SSI 2009/ 453, SSI 2009/ 454, SSI 2009/ 455

s.5, referred to: SI 2009/ 491 Sch.1 Part 1, SI 2009/ 492 Sch.1 Part 1

s.8, referred to: SI 2009/ 491 Sch.1 Part 1, SI 2009/ 492 Sch.1 Part 1

s.11, referred to: SI 2009/ 491 Sch.1 Part 1, SI 2009/ 492 Sch.1 Part 1

s.14, applied: SI 2009/ 1267 Reg.10, SSI 2009/ 16, SSI 2009/ 22, SSI 2009/ 23, SSI 2009/ 24, SSI 2009/ 25, SSI 2009/ 56, SSI 2009/ 57, SSI 2009/ 58, SSI 2009/ 59, SSI 2009/ 62, SSI 2009/ 77, SSI 2009/ 78, SSI 2009/ 92, SSI 2009/ 123, SSI 2009/ 125, SSI 2009/ 126, SSI 2009/ 127, SSI 2009/ 157, SSI 2009/ 158, SSI 2009/ 159, SSI 2009/ 161, SSI 2009/ 175, SSI 2009/ 195, SSI 2009/ 198, SSI 2009/ 199, SSI 2009/ 200, SSI 2009/ 201, SSI 2009/ 237, SSI 2009/ 252, SSI 2009/ 253, SSI 2009/ 254, SSI 2009/ 255, SSI 2009/ 265, SSI 2009/ 272, SSI 2009/ 274, SSI 2009/ 278, SSI 2009/ 279, SSI 2009/ 289

s.14, enabling: SI 2009/ 2681, SI 2009/ 2684, SI 2009/ 2735, SI 2009/ 2736, SI 2009/ 2740, SI 2009/ 2741, SI 2009/ 2742, SI 2009/ 2753, SI 2009/ 2754, SI 2009/ 2755, SI 2009/ 2756, SI 2009/ 2758, SI 2009/ 2770, SI 2009/ 2771, SI 2009/ 2776, SI 2009/ 2778, SI 2009/ 2782, SI 2009/ 2787, SI 2009/ 2788, SI 2009/ 2789, SI 2009/ 2790, SI 2009/ 2791, SI 2009/ 2799, SI 2009/ 2802, SI 2009/ 2803, SI 2009/ 2804, SI 2009/ 2807, SI 2009/ 2808, SI 2009/ 2812, SI 2009/ 2815, SI 2009/ 2828, SI 2009/ 2830, SI 2009/ 2831, SI 2009/ 2832, SI 2009/ 2833, SI 2009/ 2834, SI 2009/ 2835, SI 2009/ 2836, SI 2009/ 2837, SI 2009/ 2838, SI 2009/ 2839, SI 2009/ 2840, SI 2009/ 2841, SI 2009/ 2842, SI 2009/ 2843, SI 2009/ 2844, SI 2009/ 2845, SI 2009/ 2846, SI 2009/ 2847, SI 2009/ 2848, SI 2009/ 2850, SI 2009/ 2851, SI 2009/ 2852, SI 2009/ 2853, SI 2009/ 2854, SI 2009/ 2855, SI 2009/ 2856, SI 2009/ 2857, SI 2009/ 2865, SI 2009/ 2866, SI 2009/ 2867, SI 2009/ 2868, SI 2009/ 2869, SI 2009/ 2870, SI 2009/ 2872, SI 2009/ 2882, SI 2009/ 2883, SI 2009/ 2884, SI 2009/ 2885, SI 2009/ 2893, SI 2009/ 2895, SI 2009/ 2897, SI 2009/ 2899, SI 2009/ 2900, SI 2009/ 2901, SI 2009/ 2903, SI 2009/ 2904, SI 2009/ 2905, SI 2009/ 2906, SI 2009/ 2907, SI 2009/ 2910, SI 2009/ 2911, SI 2009/ 2912, SI 2009/ 2913, SI 2009/ 2914, SI 2009/ 2916, SI 2009/ 2917, SI 2009/ 2918, SI 2009/ 2919, SI 2009/ 2920, SI 2009/ 2921, SI 2009/ 2923, SI 2009/ 2924, SI 2009/ 2925, SI 2009/ 2926, SI 2009/ 2928, SI 2009/ 2929, SI 2009/ 2931, SI 2009/ 2932, SI 2009/ 2933, SI 2009/ 2934, SI 2009/ 2935, SI 2009/ 2936, SI 2009/ 2941, SI 2009/ 2942, SI 2009/ 2943, SI 2009/ 2944, SI 2009/ 2945, SI 2009/ 2946, SI 2009/ 2948, SI 2009/ 2949, SI 2009/ 2951, SI 2009/ 2952, SI 2009/ 2953, SI 2009/ 2959, SI 2009/ 2960, SI 2009/ 2961, SI 2009/ 2962, SI 2009/ 2963, SI

1984–cont.

27. Road Traffic Regulation Act 1984–*cont.*
s.14, enabling:–*cont.*

2009/2965, SI 2009/2966, SI 2009/2967, SI
2009/2968, SI 2009/2986, SI 2009/2987, SI
2009/2988, SI 2009/2989, SI 2009/2990, SI
2009/2991, SI 2009/2994, SI 2009/3002, SI
2009/3004, SI 2009/3025, SI 2009/3026, SI
2009/3027, SI 2009/3028, SI 2009/3031, SI
2009/3034, SI 2009/3035, SI 2009/3036, SI
2009/3037, SI 2009/3038, SI 2009/3039, SI
2009/3057, SI 2009/3058, SI 2009/3059, SI
2009/3060, SI 2009/3065, SI 2009/3067, SI
2009/3076, SI 2009/3077, SI 2009/3078, SI
2009/3079, SI 2009/3080, SI 2009/3089, SI
2009/3090, SI 2009/3091, SI 2009/3092, SI
2009/3099, SI 2009/3106, SI 2009/3107, SI
2009/3108, SI 2009/3109, SI 2009/3110, SI
2009/3114, SI 2009/3115, SI 2009/3116, SI 2009/
3118, SI 2009/3119, SI 2009/3120, SI 2009/3121, SI 2009/
3122, SI 2009/3123, SI 2009/3124, SI 2009/
3125, SI 2009/3126, SI 2009/3137, SI 2009/3138,
SI 2009/3181, SI 2009/3183, SI 2009/3185, SI
2009/3194, SI 2009/3195, SI 2009/3196, SI
2009/3197, SI 2009/3198, SI 2009/3199, SI
2009/3260, SI 2009/3261, SI 2009/3262, SI
2009/3278, SI 2009/3279, SI 2009/3280, SI
2009/3282, SI 2009/3285, SI 2009/3287, SI
2009/3288, SI 2009/3289, SI 2009/3290, SI
2009/3291, SI 2009/3292, SI 2009/3295, SI
2009/3296, SI 2009/3299, SI 2009/3301, SI
2009/3302, SI 2009/3303, SI 2009/3304, SI
2009/3305, SI 2009/3306, SI 2009/3308, SI
2009/3309, SI 2009/3310, SI 2009/3311, SI
2009/3324, SI 2009/3325, SI 2009/3326, SI
2009/3327, SI 2009/3330, SI 2009/3349, SI
2009/3353, SI 2009/3356, SI 2009/3357, SI
2009/3360, SI 2009/3368, SI 2009/3369, SI
2009/3370, SI 2009/3371, SI 2009/3372, SI
2009/3373, SI 2009/3374, SI 2009/3383, SI
2009/3384, SI 2009/3385, SI 2009/3386, SI
2009/3387, SI 2009/3388, SI 2009/3392, SI
2009/3393, SI 2009/3395, SI 2009/3396, SI
2009/3397, SI 2009/3398, SI 2009/3399, SI
2009/3400, SI 2009/3401, SI 2009/3402, SI
2009/3404, SI 2009/3407, SI 2009/3408, SI
2009/3411, SI 2009/3412, SI 2009/3413, SI
2009/3414, SI 2009/3415, SI 2009/3416, SI
2009/3417, SI 2009/3418, SI 2009/3419, SI
2009/3421, SI 2009/3422, SI 2009/3423, SI
2009/3424, SI 2009/3425, SI 2009/3426, SI
2009/3427, SI 2009/3428, SI 2009/3429, SI
2009/3430, SI 2009/3431, SI 2009/3432, SI
2009/3433, SI 2009/3434, SI 2009/3435, SI
2009/3436, SI 2009/3437, SI 2009/3438, SI
2009/3439, SI 2009/3440, SI 2009/3441, SI
2009/3442, SI 2009/3443, SI 2009/3444, SI
2009/3445, SI 2009/3446, SI 2009/3447, SI
2009/3448, SI 2009/3449, SI 2009/3450, SI
2009/3451, SI 2009/3452, SI 2009/3453, SI
2009/3454, SI 2009/3455, SI 2009/3456, SI
2009/3457, SI 2009/3458, SI 2009/3459, SI
2009/3460, SI 2009/3461, SI 2009/3462, SI
2009/3463, SI 2009/3464, SI 2009/3465, SI
2009/3466, SI 2009/3467, SSI 2009/16, SI
2009/22, SSI 2009/23, SSI 2009/24, SSI 2009/
25, SSI 2009/56, SSI 2009/57, SSI 2009/58, SSI
2009/59, SSI 2009/62, SSI 2009/77, SSI 2009/
78, SSI 2009/92, SSI 2009/123, SSI 2009/125,
SSI 2009/126, SSI 2009/127, SSI 2009/136, SSI
2009/157, SSI 2009/158, SSI 2009/159, SSI 2009/
161, SSI 2009/175, SSI 2009/195, SSI 2009/198,
SSI 2009/199, SSI 2009/200, SSI 2009/201, SSI
2009/237, SSI 2009/252, SSI 2009/253, SSI
2009/254, SSI 2009/255, SSI 2009/265, SSI
2009/272, SSI 2009/274, SSI 2009/278, SSI
2009/279, SSI 2009/280, SSI 2009/281, SSI
2009/282, SSI 2009/289, SSI 2009/296, SSI
2009/297, SSI 2009/298, SSI 2009/299, SSI
2009/324, SSI 2009/325, SSI 2009/326, SSI
2009/327, SSI 2009/346, SSI 2009/347, SSI
2009/354, SSI 2009/355, SSI 2009/356, SSI
2009/360, SSI 2009/361, SSI 2009/362, SSI
2009/363, SSI 2009/364, SSI 2009/384, SSI
2009/398, SSI 2009/421, SSI 2009/422, SSI
2009/423, SSI 2009/424, SSI 2009/430, SSI
2009/431, SSI 2009/451, SSI 2009/452, SSI
2009/453, SSI 2009/454

1984–cont.

27. Road Traffic Regulation Act 1984–*cont.*
s.15, applied: SSI 2009/136

s.15, enabling: SI 2009/3386

s.16, referred to: SI 2009/491 Sch.1 Part 1, SI 2009/
492 Sch.1 Part 1

s.16A, enabling: SI 2009/2898, SI 2009/2922, SI
2009/3066, SSI 2009/370, SSI 2009/425, SSI
2009/455

s.17, referred to: SI 2009/491 Sch.1 Part 1, SI 2009/
492 Sch.1 Part 1

s.17, enabling: SI 2009/1421, SI 2009/1568, SI 2009/
1569, SI 2009/1570, SI 2009/1571, SI 2009/1631,
SI 2009/1814, SI 2009/2247, SI 2009/3061

s.18, referred to: SI 2009/491 Sch.1 Part 1, SI 2009/
492 Sch.1 Part 1

s.20, referred to: SI 2009/491 Sch.1 Part 1, SI 2009/
492 Sch.1 Part 1

s.25, referred to: SI 2009/491 Sch.1 Part 1, SI 2009/
492 Sch.1 Part 1

s.32, applied: SI 2009/1300 Art.50, SI 2009/2364
Art.34

s.33, applied: 2009 asp 3 s.6, s.7, s.8

s.45, applied: 2009 asp 3 s.4, s.5

s.64, applied: SI 2009/271 Art.5, SI 2009/1300
Art.18, Art.49, SSI 2009/113 Art.2

s.65, applied: SI 2009/271 Art.5, SI 2009/1300
Art.49

s.72, applied: SI 2009/721 Sch.3 para.7

s.82, enabling: SSI 2009/385, SSI 2009/405

s.83, enabling: SSI 2009/385, SSI 2009/405

s.84, enabling: SI 2009/2772, SI 2009/3117, SSI
2009/14, SSI 2009/46, SSI 2009/84, SSI 2009/
111, SSI 2009/239, SSI 2009/329, SSI 2009/348,
SSI 2009/351, SSI 2009/385, SSI 2009/405

s.88, applied: SSI 2009/264

s.88, referred to: SI 2009/491 Sch.1 Part 1, SI 2009/
492 Sch.1 Part 1

s.88, enabling: SSI 2009/264

s.89, referred to: SI 2009/491 Sch.1 Part 1, SI 2009/
492 Sch.1 Part 1

s.121A, applied: 2009 c.20 s.123

s.121A, referred to: SI 2009/3245 Reg.7

s.122, applied: 2009 asp 3 s.4, s.5, s.6, s.7, s.8, SI 2009/
1300 Art.49

s.124, enabling: SI 2009/1116, SSI 2009/14, SSI
2009/46, SSI 2009/79, SSI 2009/95, SSI 2009/
111, SSI 2009/146, SSI 2009/204, SSI 2009/239,
SSI 2009/329, SSI 2009/348, SSI 2009/351, SSI
2009/385, SSI 2009/405

s.134, applied: SI 2009/1116, SI 2009/1421, SI 2009/
1568, SI 2009/1569, SI 2009/1570, SI 2009/1571,
SI 2009/1631, SI 2009/1814, SI 2009/2247, SI
2009/3061

1984–cont.

27. Road Traffic Regulation Act 1984–*cont.*
s.140, applied: SSI 2009/22 Art.4, SSI 2009/23 Art.4, SSI 2009/24 Art.4, SSI 2009/25 Art.4, SSI 2009/56 Art.4, SSI 2009/57 Art.4, SSI 2009/58 Art.4, SSI 2009/59 Art.4, SSI 2009/123 Art.4, SSI 2009/125 Art.4, SSI 2009/126 Art.4, SSI 2009/127 Art.4, SSI 2009/157 Art.4, SSI 2009/158 Art.4, SSI 2009/159 Art.4, SSI 2009/161 Art.4, SSI 2009/195 Art.3, SSI 2009/198 Art.4, SSI 2009/199 Art.4, SSI 2009/200 Art.4, SSI 2009/201 Art.4, SSI 2009/252 Art.4, SSI 2009/253 Art.4, SSI 2009/254 Art.4, SSI 2009/255 Art.4, SSI 2009/279 Art.4
Sch.4 Part IV para.22, amended: SI 2009/1307 Sch.1 para.165
Sch.9 Part III para.21, enabling: SI 2009/1116
Sch.9 Part III para.22, enabling: SI 2009/1116
Sch.9 Part III para.23, enabling: SI 2009/1116
Sch.9 Part III para.25, enabling: SI 2009/1116
Sch.9 Part IV para.27, enabling: SI 2009/2740, SI 2009/2772, SI 2009/2831, SI 2009/2946, SI 2009/3309, SI 2009/3327, SI 2009/3350, SI 2009/3386, SI 2009/3393, SI 2009/3429, SI 2009/3436

28. County Courts Act 1984
s.2, enabling: SI 2009/3320
s.10, referred to: SI 2009/500 Sch.2 Part 1
s.60, amended: 2009 c.20 Sch.6 para.58
s.60, referred to: SI 2009/500 Sch.2 Part 1

36. Mental Health (Scotland) Act 1984
s.68, see *Scottish Ministers v Mental Health Tribunal for Scotland* [2009] CSIH 33, 2009 S.C. 510 (IH (Ex Div)), Lord Clarke
s.105, referred to: SI 2009/37 Sch.1 para.2, Sch.1 para.4
s.108, referred to: SI 2009/37 Sch.1 para.2, Sch.1 para.4
s.109, referred to: SI 2009/37 Sch.1 para.2, Sch.1 para.4

37. Child Abduction Act 1984
s.1, referred to: SI 2009/37 Sch.1 para.2, Sch.1 para.4
s.2, see *R. v Norman (Leslie)* [2008] EWCA Crim 1810, [2009] 1 Cr. App. R. 13 (CA (Crim Div)), Thomas, L.J.
s.2, referred to: SI 2009/37 Sch.1 para.2, Sch.1 para.4
s.3, see *R. v Norman (Leslie)* [2008] EWCA Crim 1810, [2009] 1 Cr. App. R. 13 (CA (Crim Div)), Thomas, L.J.
s.6, applied: SI 2009/1547 Sch.3 para.2
s.6, referred to: SI 2009/37 Sch.1 para.2, Sch.1 para.4
Sch.1 para.2, amended: 2009 c.26 Sch.7 para.20, Sch.8 Part 2

38. Cycle Tracks Act 1984
s.4, applied: SI 2009/721 Sch.3 para.8
s.5, amended: SI 2009/1307 Sch.1 para.166
s.5, applied: SI 2009/721 Sch.3 para.8

39. Video Recordings Act 1984
referred to: SI 2009/669 Sch.1 Part 1
s.22, applied: 2009 c.25 s.63

42. Matrimonial and Family Proceedings Act 1984
Part III, see *Agbaje v Agbaje* [2009] EWCA Civ 1, [2009] 3 W.L.R. 835 (CA (Civ Div)), Ward, L.J.
s.13, see *Agbaje v Agbaje* [2009] EWCA Civ 1, [2009] 3 W.L.R. 835 (CA (Civ Div)), Ward, L.J.
s.16, see *Agbaje v Agbaje* [2009] EWCA Civ 1, [2009] 3 W.L.R. 835 (CA (Civ Div)), Ward, L.J.

1984–cont.

42. Matrimonial and Family Proceedings Act 1984–*cont.*
s.32, see *Judge v Judge* [2008] EWCA Civ 1458, [2009] 1 F.L.R. 1287 (CA (Civ Div)), Longmore, L.J.
s.33, enabling: SI 2009/3320
s.40, enabling: SI 2009/636, SI 2009/857, SI 2009/2027

43. Finance Act 1984
s.115, amended: SI 2009/56 Sch.1 para.104
s.116, amended: SI 2009/56 Sch.1 para.105
s.127, repealed: SI 2009/56 Sch.1 para.106
Sch.22 para.1, repealed: SI 2009/56 Sch.1 para.107
Sch.22 para.2, repealed: SI 2009/56 Sch.1 para.107
Sch.22 para.3, repealed: SI 2009/56 Sch.1 para.107
Sch.22 para.4, repealed: SI 2009/56 Sch.1 para.107
Sch.22 para.5, repealed: SI 2009/56 Sch.1 para.107
Sch.22 para.6, repealed: SI 2009/56 Sch.1 para.107
Sch.22 para.7, repealed: SI 2009/56 Sch.1 para.107
Sch.22 para.8, repealed: SI 2009/56 Sch.1 para.107

47. Repatriation of Prisoners Act 1984
see *R. (on the application of Shields) v Secretary of State for Justice* [2008] EWHC 3102 (Admin), [2009] 3 W.L.R. 765 (QBD (Admin)), Sir Anthony May (President, QB)
s.1, varied: SI 2009/1059 Sch.1 para.26

51. Inheritance Tax Act 1984
Part V c.II, applied: 2009 c.10 Sch.53 para.7
Part VIII, amended: SI 2009/56 Sch.1 para.114
Part V, see *Nelson Dance Family Settlement Trustees v Revenue and Customs Commissioners* [2009] EWHC 71 (Ch), [2009] S.T.C. 802 (Ch D), Sales, J
s.4, see *Richardson v Revenue and Customs Commissioners* [2009] S.T.C. (S.C.D.) 202 (Sp Comm), Richard Barlow
s.5, amended: SI 2009/730 Art.13
s.6, amended: SI 2009/730 Art.14
s.7, see *Ogden v Trustees of the RHS Griffiths 2003 Settlement* [2008] EWHC 118 (Ch), [2009] Ch. 162 (Ch D (Birmingham)), Lewison, J.
s.13, amended: SI 2009/1890 Art.4
s.35A, amended: SI 2009/56 Sch.1 para.109
s.35A, applied: SI 2009/275 Art.3
s.41, see *Hamblett (Deceased), Re* [2009] W.T.L.R. 559 (HC (NZ)), Asher, J.
s.54A, amended: SI 2009/56 Sch.1 para.110
s.64, substituted: SI 2009/730 Art.13
s.79A, amended: SI 2009/56 Sch.1 para.111
s.79A, applied: SI 2009/275 Art.3
s.91, amended: 2009 c.4 Sch.1 para.316
s.94, amended: 2009 c.4 Sch.1 para.317
s.103, amended: SI 2009/1890 Art.4
s.104, see *Brander v Revenue and Customs Commissioners* [2009] UKFTT 101 (TC), [2009] S.F.T.D. 374 (FTT (Tax)), J Gordon Reid Q.C.; see *Nelson Dance Family Settlement Trustees v Revenue and Customs Commissioners* [2009] EWHC 71 (Ch), [2009] S.T.C. 802 (Ch D), Sales, J
s.105, see *Brander v Revenue and Customs Commissioners* [2009] UKFTT 101 (TC), [2009] S.F.T.D. 374 (FTT (Tax)), J Gordon Reid Q.C.; see *Nelson Dance Family Settlement Trustees v Revenue and Customs Commissioners* [2009] EWHC 71 (Ch), [2009] S.T.C. 802 (Ch D), Sales, J

1984– cont.

51. Inheritance Tax Act 1984– *cont.*

s.107, see *Brander v Revenue and Customs Commissioners* [2009] UKFTT 101 (TC), [2009] S.F.T.D. 374 (FTT (Tax)), J Gordon Reid Q.C.

s.110, see *Nelson Dance Family Settlement Trustees v Revenue and Customs Commissioners* [2009] EWHC 71 (Ch), [2009] S.T.C. 802 (Ch D), Sales, J

s.112, see *Nelson Dance Family Settlement Trustees v Revenue and Customs Commissioners* [2009] EWHC 71 (Ch), [2009] S.T.C. 802 (Ch D), Sales, J

s.115, amended: 2009 c.10 s.122

s.116, amended: 2009 c.10 s.122

s.125, amended: 2009 c.10 s.122

s.125, applied: 2009 c.10 s.122

s.131, amended: 2009 c.10 Sch.51 para.6

s.142, see *Lau v Revenue and Customs Commissioners* [2009] S.T.C. (S.C.D.) 352 (Sp Comm), Michael Tildesley

s.146, amended: 2009 c.10 Sch.51 para.7

s.146, applied: 2009 c.10 Sch.53 para.8, Sch.54 para.10, Sch.54 para.11

s.147, applied: 2009 c.10 Sch.53 para.9, Sch.54 para.12

s.150, amended: 2009 c.10 Sch.51 para.8

s.150, applied: 2009 c.10 Sch.54 para.11

s.154, varied: SI 2009/1059 Sch.1 para.27

s.160, see *Bower v Revenue and Customs Commissioners* [2008] EWHC 3105 (Ch), [2009] S.T.C. 510 (Ch D), Lewison, J.

s.174, amended: SI 2009/3001 Reg.125

s.179, amended: 2009 c.10 Sch.51 para.9

s.199, see *Nelson Dance Family Settlement Trustees v Revenue and Customs Commissioners* [2009] EWHC 71 (Ch), [2009] S.T.C. 802 (Ch D), Sales, J

s.211, see *Hamblett (Deceased), Re* [2009] W.T.L.R. 559 (HC (NZ)), Asher, J.

s.216, see *Cairns v Revenue and Customs Commissioners* [2009] UKFTT 67 (TC), [2009] S.T.C. (S.C.D.) 479 (Sp Comm), J Gordon Reid Q.C.; see *Nelson Dance Family Settlement Trustees v Revenue and Customs Commissioners* [2009] EWHC 71 (Ch), [2009] S.T.C. 802 (Ch D), Sales, J

s.216, applied: 2009 c.10 Sch.55 para.1, Sch.56 para.1

s.217, applied: 2009 c.10 Sch.55 para.1

s.219, amended: SI 2009/56 Sch.1 para.112

s.219, applied: SI 2009/275 Art.3, SI 2009/3054 Art.4

s.219, repealed: SI 2009/3054 Sch.1 para.2

s.219A, applied: SI 2009/3054 Art.4

s.219A, repealed: SI 2009/3054 Sch.1 para.2

s.219B, amended: SI 2009/56 Sch.1 para.113

s.219B, applied: SI 2009/3054 Art.4

s.219B, repealed: SI 2009/3054 Sch.1 para.2

s.220, repealed: SI 2009/3054 Sch.1 para.2

s.221, see *Smith v Revenue and Customs Commissioners* [2009] S.T.C. (S.C.D.) 386 (Sp Comm), Judith Powell

s.222, amended: SI 2009/56 Sch.1 para.115, SI 2009/1307 Sch.1 para.167

s.223, substituted: SI 2009/56 Sch.1 para.116

s.223A, added: SI 2009/56 Sch.1 para.117

s.223B, added: SI 2009/56 Sch.1 para.117

s.223C, added: SI 2009/56 Sch.1 para.117

s.223D, added: SI 2009/56 Sch.1 para.117

s.223E, added: SI 2009/56 Sch.1 para.117

1984– cont.

51. Inheritance Tax Act 1984– *cont.*

s.223F, added: SI 2009/56 Sch.1 para.117

s.223G, added: SI 2009/56 Sch.1 para.117

s.223H, added: SI 2009/56 Sch.1 para.117

s.223I, added: SI 2009/56 Sch.1 para.117

s.224, substituted: SI 2009/56 Sch.1 para.118

s.225, repealed: SI 2009/56 Sch.1 para.119

s.225A, repealed: SI 2009/56 Sch.1 para.119

s.226, applied: 2009 c.10 Sch.56 para.1

s.227, see *Nelson Dance Family Settlement Trustees v Revenue and Customs Commissioners* [2009] EWHC 71 (Ch), [2009] S.T.C. 802 (Ch D), Sales, J

s.227, applied: 2009 c.10 Sch.53 para.7, Sch.56 para.1

s.229, applied: 2009 c.10 Sch.53 para.7, Sch.56 para.1

s.230, applied: 2009 c.10 Sch.53 para.14

s.233, see *Richardson v Revenue and Customs Commissioners* [2009] S.T.C. (S.C.D.) 202 (Sp Comm), Richard Barlow

s.233, referred to: 2009 c.4 s.949

s.234, amended: SI 2009/1890 Art.4

s.235, amended: 2009 c.10 s.105

s.235, applied: 2009 c.10 s.122

s.237, see *Nelson Dance Family Settlement Trustees v Revenue and Customs Commissioners* [2009] EWHC 71 (Ch), [2009] S.T.C. 802 (Ch D), Sales, J

s.240, amended: 2009 c.10 Sch.51 para.11

s.240A, added: 2009 c.10 Sch.51 para.12

s.241, amended: 2009 c.10 Sch.51 para.13

s.241, applied: 2009 c.10 s.122

s.245, amended: SI 2009/56 Sch.1 para.120

s.245A, amended: SI 2009/56 Sch.1 para.121, SI 2009/3054 Sch.1 para.2

s.245A, applied: SI 2009/3054 Art.4

s.245A, repealed (in part): SI 2009/3054 Sch.1 para.2

s.247, see *Cairns v Revenue and Customs Commissioners* [2009] UKFTT 67 (TC), [2009] S.T.C. (S.C.D.) 479 (Sp Comm), J Gordon Reid Q.C.

s.249, amended: SI 2009/56 Sch.1 para.122

s.251, repealed: SI 2009/56 Sch.1 para.123

s.252, amended: SI 2009/56 Sch.1 para.124

s.272, amended: SI 2009/56 Sch.1 para.125, SI 2009/730 Art.13

Sch.3, amended: 2009 c.23 Sch.2 para.5

Sch.6 para.2, see *Davies v Revenue and Customs Commissioners* [2009] UKFTT 138 (TC), [2009] W.T.L.R. 1151 (FTT (Tax)), Judith Powell

54. Roads (Scotland) Act 1984

s.2, enabling: SSI 2009/54, SSI 2009/389, SSI 2009/401

s.5, enabling: SSI 2009/250, SSI 2009/357, SSI 2009/399, SSI 2009/406

s.7, see *Robbie the Pict v Service* [2009] HCJAC 49, 2009 S.C.L. 944 (HCJ), Lord Carloway

s.7, enabling: SSI 2009/10

s.8, see *Robbie the Pict v Service* [2009] HCJAC 49, 2009 S.C.L. 944 (HCJ), Lord Carloway

s.8, enabling: SSI 2009/10

s.9, applied: SSI 2009/11

s.9, enabling: SSI 2009/11

s.10, enabling: SSI 2009/10

s.12, applied: SSI 2009/249

s.12, enabling: SSI 2009/249, SSI 2009/251, SSI 2009/358, SSI 2009/366, SSI 2009/397, SSI 2009/400, SSI 2009/407, SSI 2009/408

54. Roads (Scotland) Act 1984–*cont.*

s.16, see *Hamilton v Dumfries and Galloway Council* [2009] CSIH 13, 2009 S.C. 277 (IH (Ex Div)), Lord Reed

s.20A, applied: SSI 2009/10, SSI 2009/11, SSI 2009/249, SSI 2009/250

s.21, see *Boyack Homes Ltd v Fife Council* [2009] CSIH 7, 2009 S.L.T. 406 (IH (1 Div)), Lord Wheatley

s.32, amended: 2009 asp 6 Sch.3 para.4

s.35, see *Boyack Homes Ltd v Fife Council* [2009] CSIH 7, 2009 S.L.T. 406 (IH (1 Div)), Lord Wheatley

s.55A, applied: SSI 2009/10, SSI 2009/11, SSI 2009/249, SSI 2009/250

s.62, enabling: SSI 2009/113

s.70, enabling: SSI 2009/11, SSI 2009/249, SSI 2009/251, SSI 2009/358, SSI 2009/366, SSI 2009/400, SSI 2009/407, SSI 2009/408

s.71, applied: SSI 2009/11, SSI 2009/249

s.143, see *Robbie the Pict v Service* [2009] HCJAC 49, 2009 S.C.L. 944 (HCJ), Lord Carloway

s.151, see *Hamilton v Dumfries and Galloway Council* [2009] CSIH 13, 2009 S.C. 277 (IH (Ex Div)), Lord Reed

s.152, enabling: SSI 2009/54, SSI 2009/389, SSI 2009/401

Sch.1 Part I, applied: SSI 2009/11, SSI 2009/249, SSI 2009/250

Sch.1 Part II, applied: SSI 2009/10

Sch.3, referred to: SSI 2009/10 Art.3

55. Building Act 1984

applied: SI 2009/3019 Art.2

s.1, enabling: SI 2009/466, SI 2009/1219, SI 2009/2397, SI 2009/2465

s.3, enabling: SI 2009/1219, SI 2009/2397, SI 2009/2465

s.14, amended: SI 2009/3019 Art.8

s.14, applied: SI 2009/1219, SI 2009/2397

s.16, applied: SI 2009/1219 Reg.7

s.34, enabling: SI 2009/1219, SI 2009/2397, SI 2009/2465

s.35, enabling: SI 2009/1219, SI 2009/2465

s.35A, enabling: SI 2009/2397, SI 2009/2465

s.42, applied: SI 2009/3019 Art.3

s.44, applied: SI 2009/3019 Art.3

s.47, applied: SI 2009/1219 Reg.5

s.47, enabling: SI 2009/1219, SI 2009/2465

s.50, applied: SI 2009/1219 Reg.8

s.51A, applied: SI 2009/1219 Reg.5

s.54, applied: SI 2009/1219 Reg.5

s.77, referred to: SI 2009/2037 Art.5

s.79, referred to: SI 2009/2037 Art.5

s.126, amended: SI 2009/1941 Sch.1 para.55

s.134, applied: SI 2009/3019 Art.3

Sch.1 para.1, enabling: SI 2009/1219, SI 2009/2397, SI 2009/2465

Sch.1 para.2, enabling: SI 2009/1219, SI 2009/2397, SI 2009/2465

Sch.1 para.4, enabling: SI 2009/466, SI 2009/1219, SI 2009/2397, SI 2009/2465

Sch.1 para.4A, enabling: SI 2009/1219, SI 2009/2397, SI 2009/2465

Sch.1 para.7, enabling: SI 2009/1219, SI 2009/2397, SI 2009/2465

Sch.1 para.8, enabling: SI 2009/1219, SI 2009/2397, SI 2009/2465

Sch.1 para.10, enabling: SI 2009/1219, SI 2009/2397, SI 2009/2465

55. Building Act 1984–*cont.*

Sch.4 para.2, applied: SI 2009/1219 Reg.8

56. Foster Children (Scotland) Act 1984

s.1, applied: SSI 2009/154 Sch.1 para.14

s.7, applied: SSI 2009/154 Sch.1 para.14

s.10, applied: SI 2009/1547 Sch.1 para.17, SSI 2009/154 Sch.1 para.14

s.12, applied: SSI 2009/154 Sch.1 para.14

s.15, applied: SI 2009/1547 Sch.3 para.2

58. Rent (Scotland) Act 1984

s.9, see *William Grant & Son Distillers Ltd v McClymont* [2009] CSIH 8, 2009 S.L.T. 305 (IH (Ex Div)), Lord Eassie

s.10, amended: SSI 2009/248 Sch.1 para.4

s.106, applied: SSI 2009/122 Art.7

59. Ordnance Factories and Military Services Act 1984

s.14, amended: SI 2009/1941 Sch.1 para.56

60. Police and Criminal Evidence Act 1984

see *R. v Horncastle (Michael Christopher)* [2009] UKSC 14 (SC), Lord Phillips (President); see *R. v Ibrahim (Muktar)* [2008] EWCA Crim 880, [2009] 1 W.L.R. 578 (CA (Crim Div)), Sir Igor Judge (President, QB); see *Revenue and Customs v Financial Investment Advisers* [2009] Lloyd's Rep. F.C. 221 (Central Crim Ct), Judge Peter Thornton Q.C.

applied: 2009 c.11 s.22, s.23, 2009 c.23 s.252

s.8, see *Bates v Chief Constable of Avon and Somerset* [2009] EWHC 942 (Admin), (2009) 173 J.P. 313 (DC), Richards, L.J.; see *Power-Hynes v Norwich Magistrates' Court* [2009] EWHC 1512 (Admin), (2009) 173 J.P. 573 (DC), Stanley Burnton, L.J.; see *R. (on the application of Redknapp) v Commissioner of the City of London Police* [2008] EWHC 1177 (Admin), [2009] 1 W.L.R. 2091 (DC), Latham, L.J.

s.9, see *Power-Hynes v Norwich Magistrates' Court* [2009] EWHC 1512 (Admin), (2009) 173 J.P. 573 (DC), Stanley Burnton, L.J.; see *R. (on the application of Faisaltex Ltd) v Preston Crown Court* [2008] EWHC 2832 (Admin), [2009] 1 W.L.R. 1687 (DC), Keene, L.J.; see *R. (on the application of Redknapp) v Commissioner of the City of London Police* [2008] EWHC 1177 (Admin), [2009] 1 W.L.R. 2091 (DC), Latham, L.J.

s.9, referred to: SI 2009/2056 Sch.1 para.3

s.11, referred to: SI 2009/2056 Sch.1 para.14

s.15, see *Bates v Chief Constable of Avon and Somerset* [2009] EWHC 942 (Admin), (2009) 173 J.P. 313 (DC), Richards, L.J.; see *Power-Hynes v Norwich Magistrates' Court* [2009] EWHC 1512 (Admin), (2009) 173 J.P. 573 (DC), Stanley Burnton, L.J.

s.15, applied: 2009 c.1 s.194, 2009 c.25 s.43

s.16, see *Bates v Chief Constable of Avon and Somerset* [2009] EWHC 942 (Admin), (2009) 173 J.P. 313 (DC), Richards, L.J.; see *R. (on the application of Redknapp) v Commissioner of the City of London Police* [2008] EWHC 1177 (Admin), [2009] 1 W.L.R. 2091 (DC), Latham, L.J.

s.16, applied: 2009 c.1 s.194, 2009 c.25 s.43

s.17, see *Baker v Crown Prosecution Service* [2009] EWHC 299 (Admin), (2009) 173 J.P. 215 (DC), Sir Anthony May (President, QB)

s.19, see *Bates v Chief Constable of Avon and Somerset* [2009] EWHC 942 (Admin), (2009) 173 J.P. 313 (DC), Richards, L.J.

1984– cont.

60. Police and Criminal Evidence Act 1984– *cont.*
s.21, applied: 2009 c.25 s.43
s.22, see *Scopelight Ltd v Chief Constable of Northumbria* [2009] EWHC 958 (QB), [2009] 2 Cr. App. R. 22 (QBD), Sharp, J.
s.24, applied: SI 2009/886 Art.12, SI 2009/1749 Art.14
s.30CA, amended: 2009 c.26 Sch.8 Part 13
s.36, amended: 2009 c.26 Sch.7 para.123, Sch.8 Part 13
s.36, repealed (in part): 2009 c.26 Sch.8 Part 13
s.37, varied: 2009 c.11 s.31
s.37A, varied: 2009 c.11 s.31
s.37B, varied: 2009 c.11 s.31
s.38, amended: 2009 c.25 Sch.21 para.77
s.39, amended: 2009 c.26 Sch.8 Part 13
s.39, repealed (in part): 2009 c.26 Sch.8 Part 13
s.46A, amended: 2009 c.25 s.107, s.108, Sch.23 Part 3
s.46A, referred to: SI 2009/3253 Art.4
s.46ZA, amended: 2009 c.25 s.107
s.46ZA, referred to: SI 2009/3253 Art.4
s.46ZA, repealed (in part): 2009 c.25 s.107, Sch.23 Part 3
s.54, applied: SI 2009/1922 Sch.2 para.6, SI 2009/2056 Art.17, Sch.4 para.11
s.54A, applied: SI 2009/1922 Sch.2 para.7
s.54B, added: 2009 c.25 s.108
s.54C, added: 2009 c.25 s.108
s.55, applied: SI 2009/1922 Sch.2 para.8
s.55, repealed (in part): 2009 c.26 Sch.8 Part 13
s.55A, applied: SI 2009/1922 Sch.2 para.9
s.56, applied: SI 2009/1922 Sch.2 para.10
s.58, see *Gearing v DPP* [2008] EWHC 1695 (Admin), [2009] R.T.R. 7 (DC), Latham, L.J.
s.58, applied: SI 2009/1922 Sch.2 para.11
s.61, applied: SI 2009/1922 Sch.2 para.12
s.61, repealed (in part): 2009 c.26 Sch.8 Part 13
s.61A, applied: SI 2009/1922 Sch.2 para.13
s.62, applied: SI 2009/1922 Sch.2 para.14
s.63, applied: SI 2009/1922 Sch.2 para.15
s.63, repealed (in part): 2009 c.26 Sch.8 Part 13
s.64, see *S v United Kingdom (30562/04)* (2009) 48 E.H.R.R. 50 (ECHR (Grand Chamber)), Judge Costa (President)
s.64, applied: SI 2009/1922 Sch.2 para.17
s.64A, applied: SI 2009/1922 Sch.2 para.18
s.73, amended: 2009 c.25 Sch.17 para.13
s.74, see *R. v Downer* [2009] EWCA Crim 1361, [2009] 2 Cr. App. R. 28 (CA (Crim Div)), Scott Baker, L.J.; see *R. v O'Dowd (Kevin)* [2009] EWCA Crim 905, [2009] 2 Cr. App. R. 16 (CA (Crim Div)), Scott Baker, L.J.
s.74, amended: 2009 c.25 Sch.17 para.14
s.75, amended: 2009 c.25 Sch.17 para.15
s.76, see *Public Prosecution Service v Duddy* [2009] N.I. 19 (CA (NI)), Lord Kerr L.C.J.; see *R. v Sherif (Abdul)* [2008] EWCA Crim 2653, [2009] 2 Cr. App. R. (S.) 33 (CA (Crim Div)), Latham, L.J.
s.78, see *DPP v Agyemang* [2009] EWHC 1542 (Admin), (2009) 173 J.P. 487 (QBD (Admin)), Richards, L.J.; see *Gearing v DPP* [2008] EWHC 1695 (Admin), [2009] R.T.R. 7 (DC), Latham, L.J.; see *R. v D* [2008] EWCA Crim 1156, [2009] 2 Cr. App. R. 17 (CA (Crim Div)), Rix, L.J.; see *R. v Downer* [2009] EWCA Crim 1361, [2009] 2 Cr. App. R. 28 (CA (Crim Div)), Scott Baker, L.J.; see *R. v Ibrahim (Muktar)* [2008] EWCA Crim 880, [2009] 1 W.L.R. 578

1984– cont.

60. Police and Criminal Evidence Act 1984– *cont.*
s.78– *cont.*
(CA (Crim Div)), Sir Igor Judge (President, QB); see *R. v Kamuhuza (Martin)* [2008] EWCA Crim 3060, (2009) 173 J.P. 55 (CA (Crim Div)), Thomas, L.J.; see *R. v Sherif (Abdul)* [2008] EWCA Crim 2653, [2009] 2 Cr. App. R. (S.) 33 (CA (Crim Div)), Latham, L.J.; see *R. v Woodhouse (Rupert Giles)* [2009] EWCA Crim 498, (2009) 173 J.P. 337 (CA (Crim Div)), Rix, L.J.
s.80, see *R. v L* [2008] EWCA Crim 973, [2009] 1 W.L.R. 626 (CA (Crim Div)), Lord Phillips, L.C.J.
s.82, varied: SI 2009/1059 Sch.1 para.28
s.101, see *R. v Woodhouse (Rupert Giles)* [2009] EWCA Crim 498, (2009) 173 J.P. 337 (CA (Crim Div)), Rix, L.J.
s.113, applied: SI 2009/1922 Sch.2 para.7, Sch.2 para.16, Sch.2 para.17, Sch.2 para.18, SI 2009/2056 Art.17, Art.34, Sch.4 para.11
s.113, varied: SI 2009/1059 Sch.1 para.28
s.113, enabling: SI 2009/1922
s.114, applied: 2009 c.11 s.23
s.114A, amended: SI 2009/2748 Sch.1 para.3
Sch.1, see *R. (on the application of Faisaltex Ltd) v Preston Crown Court* [2008] EWHC 2832 (Admin), [2009] 1 W.L.R. 1687 (DC), Keene, L.J.; see *Revenue and Customs v Financial Investment Advisers* [2009] Lloyd's Rep. F.C. 221 (Central Crim Ct), Judge Peter Thornton Q.C.
Sch.1 para.4, see *R. (on the application of Faisaltex Ltd) v Preston Crown Court* [2008] EWHC 2832 (Admin), [2009] 1 W.L.R. 1687 (DC), Keene, L.J.
Sch.1 para.11, see *R. (on the application of Faisaltex Ltd) v Preston Crown Court* [2008] EWHC 2832 (Admin), [2009] 1 W.L.R. 1687 (DC), Keene, L.J.
Sch.1 para.12, see *R. (on the application of Faisaltex Ltd) v Preston Crown Court* [2008] EWHC 2832 (Admin), [2009] 1 W.L.R. 1687 (DC), Keene, L.J.; see *R. (on the application of Redknapp) v Commissioner of the City of London Police* [2008] EWHC 1177 (Admin), [2009] 1 W.L.R. 2091 (DC), Latham, L.J.
Sch.1 para.14, see *R. (on the application of Faisaltex Ltd) v Preston Crown Court* [2008] EWHC 2832 (Admin), [2009] 1 W.L.R. 1687 (DC), Keene, L.J.

1985

6. Companies Act 1985
see *Dairy Farmers of Britain Ltd, Re* [2009] EWHC 1389 (Ch), [2009] 4 All E.R. 241 (Ch D (Companies Ct)), Henderson, J.
applied: SI 2009/645 Art.7, SI 2009/1801 Sch.8 para.3, Sch.8 para.9, Sch.8 para.15, Sch.8 para.16, Sch.8 para.17, SI 2009/1804 Sch.1 para.15, Sch.1 para.16, Sch.1 para.18, Sch.1 para.22, Sch.1 para.35, SI 2009/2436 Sch.2 para.10, Sch.2 para.13, Sch.2 para.21, Sch.2 para.22, Sch.2 para.37, SI 2009/2579 Art.4, Art.5, Art.6, Art.7, Art.8, SI 2009/2604 Art.4, Art.5, Art.6, Art.7, Art.8, SSI 2009/27
disapplied: SI 2009/814 Art.3, SI 2009/3226 Sch.1 para.28
referred to: SI 2009/1801 Sch.8 para.31, SI 2009/1804 Sch.1 para.34, SI 2009/2101 Sch.4 para.2, SI 2009/2436 Sch.2 para.1, Sch.2 para.40, SI 2009/2492 Sch.1 para.2
varied: SI 2009/317 Sch.1

6. Companies Act 1985–*cont.*

Part XA, applied: SI 2009/2436 Sch.2 para.20

Part XI, referred to: SI 2009/669 Sch.1 Part 5

Part XII, applied: SI 2009/214 Reg.11, SI 2009/1917 Sch.1 para.2, Sch.1 para.3, Sch.1 para.4, SI 2009/2101 Sch.4 para.1, SI 2009/2492 Sch.1 para.1

Part XII, referred to: 2009 c.1 s.252

Part XIV, applied: SI 2009/214 Sch.1, SI 2009/1801 Sch.1, SI 2009/1804 Sch.2 para.4, SI 2009/2436 Sch.1 para.16

Part XV, applied: SI 2009/2436 Sch.1 para.16

Part XVII, applied: SI 2009/2469 r.7

Part XXII c.II, applied: SI 2009/2579 Art.3, SI 2009/2604 Art.3

Part XXIII, applied: SI 2009/2101 Sch.4 para.1

Part XXIII c.I, applied: SI 2009/1801 Sch.8 para.2

s.10, applied: SI 2009/214 Reg.9

s.14, applied: SI 2009/1941 Art.11

s.18, applied: SI 2009/2436 Sch.2 para.2, Sch.2 para.3, Sch.2 para.4

s.35, applied: SI 2009/2436 Sch.2 para.6

s.36A, applied: SI 2009/2436 Sch.2 para.7

s.38, applied: SI 2009/1804 Sch.1 para.2

s.92, see *Choudhary v Bhatter* [2009] EWCA Civ 1176, Times, November 20, 2009 (CA (Civ Div)), Ward, L.J.

s.139, applied: SI 2009/2425 Reg.9

s.151, see *AMG Global Nominees (Private) Ltd v SMM Holdings Ltd* [2008] EWCA Civ 1278, [2009] B.C.C. 767 (CA (Civ Div)), Sir Andrew Morritt C.; see *Corporate Development Partners LLC v E-Relationship Marketing Ltd* [2007] EWHC 436 (Ch), [2009] B.C.C. 295 (Ch D), Rimer, J.

s.152, see *AMG Global Nominees (Private) Ltd v SMM Holdings Ltd* [2008] EWCA Civ 1278, [2009] B.C.C. 767 (CA (Civ Div)), Sir Andrew Morritt C.

s.153, see *Corporate Development Partners LLC v E-Relationship Marketing Ltd* [2007] EWHC 436 (Ch), [2009] B.C.C. 295 (Ch D), Rimer, J.

s.155, see *Cook v Green* [2009] B.C.C. 204 (Ch D (Manchester)), Judge Pelling Q.C.

s.156, see *Cook v Green* [2009] B.C.C. 204 (Ch D (Manchester)), Judge Pelling Q.C.

s.221, see *Secretary of State for Business Enterprise and Regulatory Reform v Art IT Plc* [2008] EWHC 258 (Ch), [2009] 1 B.C.L.C. 262 (Ch D (Companies Ct)), Judge Toulmin Q.C.; see *Secretary of State for Trade and Industry v Hall* [2006] EWHC 1995 (Ch), [2009] B.C.C. 190 (Ch D (Companies Ct)), Evans-Lombe, J.

s.262, amended: SI 2009/1342 Art.23

s.263, see *Progress Property Co Ltd v Moore* [2009] EWCA Civ 629, [2009] Bus. L.R. 1535 (CA (Civ Div)), Mummery, L.J.

s.288, applied: SI 2009/214 Reg.9, SI 2009/814 Art.7

s.306, referred to: SI 2009/1941 Art.9

s.307, referred to: SI 2009/1941 Art.9

s.363, applied: SI 2009/214 Reg.9, SI 2009/1804 Sch.1 para.15, SI 2009/2101 Sch.4 para.1

s.364, applied: SI 2009/1804 Sch.1 para.15

s.386, applied: SI 2009/2436 Sch.2 para.24

s.390, applied: SI 2009/2436 Sch.2 para.30, Sch.2 para.32

s.394, applied: SI 2009/2436 Sch.2 para.33

s.394A, applied: SI 2009/2436 Sch.2 para.33

s.400, applied: SI 2009/1804 Sch.1 para.17

6. Companies Act 1985–*cont.*

s.403, applied: SI 2009/1804 Sch.1 para.21, SI 2009/1917 Sch.1 para.7

s.405, applied: SI 2009/1804 Sch.1 para.20, SI 2009/1917 Sch.1 para.6

s.416, applied: SI 2009/1804 Sch.1 para.17

s.419, applied: SI 2009/1804 Sch.1 para.21, SI 2009/1917 Sch.1 para.7

s.434, amended: SI 2009/1941 Sch.1 para.57

s.437, amended: SI 2009/1941 Sch.1 para.57

s.441, amended: SI 2009/1941 Sch.1 para.57

s.447, see *Secretary of State for Business Enterprise and Regulatory Reform v Art IT Plc* [2008] EWHC 258 (Ch), [2009] 1 B.C.L.C. 262 (Ch D (Companies Ct)), Judge Toulmin Q.C.; see *Secretary of State for Business Enterprise and Regulatory Reform v Sullman* [2008] EWHC 3179 (Ch), [2009] 1 B.C.L.C. 397 (Ch D), Norris, J.

s.447, applied: SI 2009/214 Sch.1, SI 2009/1801 Sch.1

s.447A, amended: SI 2009/1941 Sch.1 para.57

s.448A, amended: SI 2009/1941 Sch.1 para.57

s.453, amended: SI 2009/1941 Sch.1 para.57

s.458, applied: SI 2009/2436 Sch.2 para.38

s.458, disapplied: SI 2009/2436 Sch.2 para.38

s.459, see *Allied Business & Financial Consultants Ltd, Re* [2009] EWCA Civ 751, [2009] B.C.C. 822 (CA (Civ Div)), Waller, L.J.; see *McCarthy Surfacing Ltd, Re* [2008] EWHC 2279 (Ch), [2009] B.C.C. 464 (Ch D), Michael Furness Q.C.; see *McLean v Zonal Retail Data Systems Ltd* [2009] CSOH 12, 2009 S.C.L.R. 763 (OH), Lord Hodge; see *Miller v Bayliss* [2009] EWHC 2063 (Ch), [2009] B.P.I.R. 1438 (Ch D), Alison Foster QC; see *Robertson, Petitioner (No 2)* [2009] CSIH 59, 2009 S.C.L.R. 773 (IH (1 Div)), The Lord President (Hamilton)

s.651, applied: SI 2009/1804 Sch.1 para.23

s.652, applied: SI 2009/1804 Sch.1 para.25

s.652A, applied: SI 2009/1804 Sch.1 para.25

s.653, applied: SI 2009/1804 Sch.1 para.23, Sch.1 para.25

s.654, applied: SI 2009/1804 Sch.1 para.22A, Sch.1 para.26

s.656, applied: SI 2009/1804 Sch.1 para.22A

s.663, enabling: SI 2009/645

s.690A, applied: SI 2009/1801 Sch.8 para.15, Sch.8 para.16

s.691, applied: SI 2009/214 Reg.9, SI 2009/1801 Sch.8 para.9, Sch.8 para.12, Sch.8 para.15, Sch.8 para.16

s.691, disapplied: SI 2009/1801 Sch.8 para.14

s.692, applied: SI 2009/214 Reg.9, SI 2009/1801 Sch.8 para.15, Sch.8 para.16

s.697, applied: SI 2009/1801 Sch.8 para.14

s.699A, applied: SI 2009/1801 Sch.8 para.4

s.699AA, applied: SI 2009/1801 Sch.8 para.23

s.700, applied: SI 2009/1801 Sch.8 para.23, Sch.8 para.24

s.701, applied: SI 2009/1801 Sch.8 para.23, Sch.8 para.24

s.702, applied: SI 2009/1801 Sch.8 para.23, Sch.8 para.24

s.703, applied: SI 2009/1801 Sch.8 para.23

s.703P, applied: SI 2009/1801 Sch.8 para.27, Sch.8 para.28

s.703Q, applied: SI 2009/1801 Sch.8 para.29

s.707B, applied: SI 2009/2436 Sch.2 para.40

1985–cont.

6. Companies Act 1985–*cont.*
s.707B, referred to: SI 2009/1801 Sch.8 para.31, SI 2009/1804 Sch.1 para.34
s.708, applied: SI 2009/1804 Sch.1 para.36
s.708, referred to: SI 2009/1804 Sch.1 para.36
s.710A, referred to: SI 2009/1804 Sch.1 para.33
s.714, applied: SI 2009/1801 Sch.8 para.10
s.723B, applied: SI 2009/1801 Reg.25, Sch.8 para.21, Sch.8 para.22, SI 2009/1804 Sch.1 para.12, Sch.1 para.13, SI 2009/2400 Sch.2 para.12, Sch.2 para.13, Sch.2 para.14, Sch.2 para.15
s.723B, varied: SI 2009/1804 Sch.1 para.11
s.723D, applied: SI 2009/2400 Sch.2 para.12
s.723E, applied: SI 2009/1801 Sch.8 para.21, SI 2009/2400 Sch.2 para.12, Sch.2 para.13
s.726, see *Jirehouse Capital v Beller* [2008] EWCA Civ 908, [2009] 1 W.L.R. 751 (CA (Civ Div)), Mummery, L.J.
s.726, varied: SI 2009/1941 Art.13
s.727, see *Paycheck Services 3 Ltd, Re* [2008] EWHC 2200 (Ch), [2009] Bus. L.R. 1 (Ch D (Companies Ct)), Mark Cawson Q.C.
s.735, applied: SI 2009/490 Art.3
s.736, see *Enviroco Ltd v Farstad Supply A/S* [2009] EWHC 906 (Ch), [2009] 2 Lloyd's Rep. 666 (Ch D), Gabriel Moss Q.C.
s.736A, see *Enviroco Ltd v Farstad Supply A/S* [2009] EWHC 906 (Ch), [2009] 2 Lloyd's Rep. 666 (Ch D), Gabriel Moss Q.C.
Sch.7 Part I para.3, applied: SI 2009/2436 Sch.2 para.20
Sch.15D para.9, amended: SI 2009/1941 Sch.1 para.58
Sch.15D para.34, amended: SI 2009/1941 Sch.1 para.58
Sch.15D para.35, amended: SI 2009/1941 Sch.1 para.58
Sch.15D para.38, amended: SI 2009/1941 Sch.1 para.58
Sch.15D para.42, amended: SI 2009/1941 Sch.1 para.58
Sch.21A para.1, applied: SI 2009/1801 Sch.8 para.3, Sch.8 para.6, Sch.8 para.7, Sch.8 para.14
Sch.21A para.2, applied: SI 2009/214 Reg.9
Sch.21A para.5, applied: SI 2009/1801 Sch.8 para.6
Sch.21A para.6, applied: SI 2009/1801 Sch.8 para.7
Sch.21A para.7, applied: SI 2009/1801 Sch.8 para.15, Sch.8 para.16
Sch.21A para.8, applied: SI 2009/1801 Sch.8 para.17
Sch.21C Part I para.2, applied: SI 2009/1801 Sch.8 para.25
Sch.21C Part I para.3, applied: SI 2009/1801 Sch.8 para.25
Sch.21C Part II, applied: SI 2009/1801 Sch.8 para.26
Sch.21D Part I, applied: SI 2009/1801 Sch.8 para.23
Sch.21D Part I para.2, applied: SI 2009/1801 Sch.8 para.8
Sch.21D Part II, applied: SI 2009/1801 Sch.8 para.24
Sch.21D Part II para.10, applied: SI 2009/1801 Sch.8 para.8
Sch.24, applied: SI 2009/1804 Sch.1 para.35
7. Business Names Act 1985
referred to: SI 2009/669 Sch.1 Part 5
9. Companies Consolidation (Consequential Provisions) Act 1985
applied: SI 2009/1941 Art.12

1985–cont.

12. Mineral Workings Act 1985
s.7, amended: SI 2009/1307 Sch.1 para.169
s.8, amended: SI 2009/1307 Sch.1 para.170
13. Cinemas Act 1985
s.1, referred to: SI 2009/669 Sch.1 Part 3
s.2, referred to: SI 2009/669 Sch.1 Part 3
s.3, referred to: SI 2009/669 Sch.1 Part 3
s.5, referred to: SI 2009/669 Sch.1 Part 3
s.6, referred to: SI 2009/669 Sch.1 Part 3
s.7, referred to: SI 2009/669 Sch.1 Part 3
s.8, referred to: SI 2009/669 Sch.1 Part 3
s.9, referred to: SI 2009/669 Sch.1 Part 3
s.10, referred to: SI 2009/669 Sch.1 Part 3
s.11, referred to: SI 2009/669 Sch.1 Part 3
s.12, referred to: SI 2009/669 Sch.1 Part 3
s.13, referred to: SI 2009/669 Sch.1 Part 3
s.14, referred to: SI 2009/669 Sch.1 Part 3
s.15, referred to: SI 2009/669 Sch.1 Part 3
s.16, referred to: SI 2009/669 Sch.1 Part 3
17. Reserve Forces (Safeguard of Employment) Act 1985
Sch.2 para.2, amended: 2009 c.3 Sch.4 para.19
21. Films Act 1985
see *Revenue and Customs Commissioners v Micro Fusion 2004-1 LLP* [2009] EWHC 1082 (Ch), [2009] S.T.C. 1741 (Ch D), Davis, J.
Sch.1, applied: 2009 c.4 s.1197, s.1206
Sch.1 para.1, amended: 2009 c.4 Sch.1 para.319
Sch.1 para.4, enabling: SI 2009/3009
23. Prosecution of Offences Act 1985
see *R. v Lambert (Goldan)* [2009] EWCA Crim 700, [2009] 2 Cr. App. R. 32 (CA (Crim Div)), Thomas, L.J.
s.6, see *R. v Rollins (Neil)* [2009] EWCA Crim 1941, Times, October 20, 2009 (CA (Crim Div)), Richards, L.J.
s.10, see *R. (on the application of Purdy) v DPP* [2008] EWHC 2565 (Admin), [2009] H.R.L.R. 7 (DC), Scott Baker, L.J.; see *R. (on the application of Purdy) v DPP* [2009] EWCA Civ 92, [2009] 1 Cr. App. R. 32 (CA (Civ Div)), Lord Judge, L.C.J.
s.15, applied: 2009 c.11 s.31
s.16, see *Dowler v Merseyrail* [2009] EWHC 558 (Admin), (2009) 173 J.P. 332 (DC), Goldring, L.J.; see *Emohare v Thames Magistrates Court* [2009] EWHC 689 (Admin), (2009) 173 J.P. 303 (QBD (Admin)), Goldring, L.J.; see *R. (on the application of Crowch) v DPP* [2008] EWHC 948 (Admin), [2009] P.N.L.R. 1 (QBD (Admin)), Davis, J.; see *R. (on the application of Pluckrose) v Snaresbrook Crown Court* [2009] EWHC 1506 (Admin), (2009) 173 J.P. 492 (DC), Pill, L.J.
s.18, see *Balshaw v Crown Prosecution Service* [2009] EWCA Crim 470, [2009] 1 W.L.R. 2301 (CA (Crim Div)), Moses, L.J.
s.19, see *R. (on the application of Crowch) v DPP* [2008] EWHC 948 (Admin), [2009] P.N.L.R. 1 (QBD (Admin)), Davis, J.
s.19, enabling: SI 2009/2720
s.19A, see *R. (on the application of B) v X Crown Court* [2009] EWHC 1149 (Admin), [2009] P.N.L.R. 30 (QBD (Admin)), Hickinbottom, J.
s.19A, enabling: SI 2009/2720
s.19B, enabling: SI 2009/2720
s.20, enabling: SI 2009/2720
s.21, see *R. v Dodd (Costs)* [2009] 2 Costs L.R. 368 (Sup Ct Costs Office), Costs Judge Gordon-Saker

1985– cont.

23. Prosecution of Offences Act 1985– *cont.*
s.22A, repealed: 2009 c.26 Sch.8 Part 13
s.22B, amended: 2009 c.26 Sch.8 Part 13
s.25, see *R. v Lambert (Goldan)* [2009] EWCA
Crim 700, [2009] 2 Cr. App. R. 32 (CA (Crim
Div)),Thomas, L.J.

29. Enduring Powers of Attorney Act 1985
see *J (Enduring Power of Attorney), Re* [2009]
EWHC 436 (Ch), [2009] 2 All E.R. 1051 (CP),
Lewison, J.

37. Family Law (Scotland) Act 1985
see *M v M* [2009] CSIH 62, 2009 S.L.T. 750 (IH (Ex
Div)), Lady Paton; see *Smith v Smith* [2009]
CSOH 2, 2009 Fam. L.R. 39 (OH), Lord
Malcolm
s.8, see *Smith v Smith* [2009] CSOH 2, 2009 Fam.
L.R. 39 (OH), Lord Malcolm
s.9, see *Smith v Smith* [2009] CSOH 2, 2009 Fam.
L.R. 39 (OH), Lord Malcolm; see *Turner v
Turner* 2009 Fam. L.R. 124 (Sh Ct (Tayside)
(Kirkcaldy)), Sheriff A G McCulloch; see
Willson v Willson 2009 Fam. L.R. 18 (OH),
Lord Drummond Young
s.12, see *B v B* 2009 S.L.T. (Sh Ct) 43 (Sh Ct
(Lothian) (Edinburgh)), Sheriff Principal E F
Bowen, QC
s.13, see *B v B* 2009 S.L.T. (Sh Ct) 43 (Sh Ct
(Lothian) (Edinburgh)), Sheriff Principal E F
Bowen, QC
s.16, see *B v B* 2009 S.L.T. (Sh Ct) 43 (Sh Ct
(Lothian) (Edinburgh)), Sheriff Principal E F
Bowen, QC; see *Turner v Turner* 2009 Fam.
L.R. 124 (Sh Ct (Tayside) (Kirkcaldy)), Sheriff
A G McCulloch
s.18, see *B v B* 2009 S.L.T. (Sh Ct) 43 (Sh Ct
(Lothian) (Edinburgh)), Sheriff Principal E F
Bowen, QC; see *Brown v Robertson* 2009 Fam.
L.R. 13 (Sh Ct (South Strathclyde) (Dumfries)),
Sheriff Principal B A Lockhart; see *M v M*
[2009] CSIH 62, 2009 S.L.T. 750 (IH (Ex Div)),
Lady Paton; see *M v M* [2009] CSOH 65, 2009
S.L.T. 608 (OH), Lady Clark of Calton
s.28, see *Jamieson v Rodhouse* 2009 Fam. L.R. 34
(Sh Ct (Tayside) (Kirkcaldy)), Sheriff K R W
Hogg

44. Sexual Offences Act 1985
repealed: 2009 c.26 Sch.8 Part 2

48. Food and Environment Protection Act 1985
applied: 2009 asp 2 Sch.2 Part 6, 2009 c.23 s.323
Part II, applied: 2009 c.23 s.323, Sch.9 para.9, SI
2009/153 Sch.3 para.1, SI 2009/995 Sch.3 para.1
Part IV, applied: 2009 c.23 s.323
s.5, amended: 2009 c.23 Sch.8 para.2
s.5, applied: 2009 c.23 Sch.9 para.12
s.5, repealed (in part): 2009 c.23 Sch.8 para.2,
Sch.22 Part 2
s.5, varied: 2009 c.23 Sch.9 para.4, Sch.9 para.12
s.6, amended: 2009 c.23 Sch.8 para.2
s.6, applied: 2009 c.23 Sch.9 para.12
s.6, repealed (in part): 2009 c.23 Sch.8 para.2,
Sch.22 Part 2
s.6, varied: 2009 c.23 Sch.9 para.4, Sch.9 para.12
s.7, varied: 2009 c.23 Sch.9 para.4
s.7A, amended: 2009 c.23 Sch.8 para.2
s.7A, repealed (in part): 2009 c.23 Sch.8 para.2,
Sch.22 Part 2
s.7A, varied: 2009 c.23 Sch.9 para.4
s.8, amended: 2009 c.23 Sch.8 para.2, Sch.22 Part 2
s.8, applied: 2009 c.23 Sch.9 para.4
s.8, varied: 2009 c.23 Sch.9 para.4

1985– cont.

48. Food and Environment Protection Act 1985–
cont.
s.8A, added: 2009 c.23 Sch.8 para.5
s.8A, varied: 2009 c.23 Sch.9 para.4
s.9, amended: 2009 c.23 Sch.8 para.2, Sch.8 para.6
s.9, repealed (in part): 2009 c.23 Sch.8 para.2,
Sch.22 Part 2
s.9, varied: 2009 c.23 Sch.9 para.4
s.10, referred to: 2009 c.23 Sch.9 para.6
s.10, varied: 2009 c.23 Sch.9 para.4
s.11, amended: 2009 c.23 Sch.8 para.2
s.11, varied: 2009 c.23 Sch.9 para.4
s.12, varied: 2009 c.23 Sch.9 para.4
s.13, varied: 2009 c.23 Sch.9 para.4
s.14, applied: 2009 c.23 Sch.9 para.7
s.14, varied: 2009 c.23 Sch.9 para.4
s.15, varied: 2009 c.23 Sch.9 para.4
s.21, repealed (in part): 2009 c.23 Sch.8 para.2,
Sch.22 Part 2
s.24, amended: 2009 c.23 Sch.8 para.2, Sch.22 Part
2
s.24, repealed (in part): 2009 c.23 Sch.8 para.2,
Sch.22 Part 2
s.25, repealed (in part): 2009 c.23 Sch.22 Part 2
s.26, repealed: 2009 c.23 Sch.22 Part 2
s.26, varied: 2009 c.23 Sch.9 para.8
Sch.3 para.1, applied: 2009 c.23 Sch.9 para.5
Sch.3 para.2, applied: 2009 c.23 Sch.9 para.5
Sch.3 para.3, applied: 2009 c.23 Sch.9 para.5
Sch.3 para.4, applied: 2009 c.23 Sch.9 para.5
Sch.3 para.5, applied: 2009 c.23 Sch.9 para.5
Sch.3 para.6, applied: 2009 c.23 Sch.9 para.5
Sch.3 para.7, applied: 2009 c.23 Sch.9 para.5
Sch.3 para.8, applied: 2009 c.23 Sch.9 para.5
Sch.3 para.9, applied: 2009 c.23 Sch.9 para.5
Sch.3 para.10, applied: 2009 c.23 Sch.9 para.5
Sch.3 para.11, applied: 2009 c.23 Sch.9 para.5
Sch.3 para.12, applied: 2009 c.23 Sch.9 para.5
Sch.3 para.13, applied: 2009 c.23 Sch.9 para.5
Sch.3 para.14, applied: 2009 c.23 Sch.9 para.5
Sch.3 para.15, applied: 2009 c.23 Sch.9 para.5
Sch.3 para.16, applied: 2009 c.23 Sch.9 para.5
Sch.3 para.17, applied: 2009 c.23 Sch.9 para.5

50. Representation of the People Act 1985
s.3, enabling: SI 2009/725

51. Local Government Act 1985
s.10, applied: 2009 c.20 s.2, s.35, s.123, SI 2009/1360
Art.2
s.72, amended: 2009 c.20 Sch.6 para.60
s.73, substituted: 2009 c.20 Sch.6 para.61
Sch.8 para.15, applied: SI 2009/3051 Reg.2, SI
2009/3230 Reg.2, SI 2009/3238 Reg.2, SI
2009/3255 Reg.2, SI 2009/3378 Reg.2, SI
2009/3379 Reg.2
Sch.8 para.19, repealed: 2009 c.23 Sch.22 Part 4

56. Interception of Communications Act 1985
see *Liberty v United Kingdom (58243/00)* (2009) 48
E.H.R.R. 1 (ECHR), Judge Garlicki (President)
s.3, see *Liberty v United Kingdom (58243/00)*
(2009) 48 E.H.R.R. 1 (ECHR), Judge Garlicki
(President)

60. Child Abduction and Custody Act 1985
see *A v B (Abduction: Rights of Custody:
Declaration of Wrongful Removal)* [2008]
EWHC 2524 (Fam), [2009] 1 F.L.R. 1253 (Fam
Div), Bodey, J.; see *RC (Child Abduction)
(Brussels II Revised: Article 11(7)), Re* [2009] 1
F.L.R. 574 (Fam Div), Singer, J.; see *Z,*

1985–cont.

60. Child Abduction and Custody Act 1985–*cont.*
see–*cont.*
Petitioner [2009] CSOH 136, 2009 Fam. L.R. 162 (OH), Lady Smith
s.2, enabling: SI 2009/702
s.13, enabling: SI 2009/702

61. Administration of Justice Act 1985
s.9, referred to: SI 2009/500 Art.1
s.9, enabling: SI 2009/500
s.9A, referred to: SI 2009/500 Art.1
Sch.2 para.6, referred to: SI 2009/503 Art.5
Sch.2 para.9, varied: SI 2009/1589 Art.6
Sch.2 para.10, varied: SI 2009/1589 Art.6
Sch.2 para.14, varied: SI 2009/503 Art.4
Sch.2 para.14A, applied: SI 2009/503 Art.4
Sch.2 para.14B, applied: SI 2009/503 Art.4
Sch.2 para.18A, varied: SI 2009/503 Art.4
Sch.2 para.36, amended: SI 2009/2035 Sch.1 para.60

62. Oil and Pipelines Act 1985
s.6, amended: SI 2009/1941 Sch.1 para.59

66. Bankruptcy (Scotland) Act 1985
applied: 2009 c.25 s.165, SI 2009/457 Reg.9
s.3, see *Accountant in Bankruptcy (Brown's Trustee) v Brown* [2009] CSIH 2, 2009 S.C. 236 (IH (Ex Div)), Lord Nimmo Smith
s.6, amended: SI 2009/1941 Sch.1 para.60
s.7, amended: 2009 c.26 Sch.7 para.47
s.9, see *Gerrard, Petitioner* [2009] CSOH 76, 2009 S.C. 593 (OH), Lord Glennie
s.16, see *Barlow v City Plumbing Supplies Holdings Ltd* [2009] CSOH 5, 2009 S.C.L.R. 350 (OH), Lord Hardie
s.17, see *Barlow v City Plumbing Supplies Holdings Ltd* [2009] CSOH 5, 2009 S.C.L.R. 350 (OH), Lord Hardie
s.31A, amended: 2009 c.26 Sch.7 para.48, Sch.8 Part 4
s.31AA, added: 2009 c.26 Sch.7 para.49
s.31B, amended: 2009 c.26 Sch.7 para.50
s.31BA, added: 2009 c.26 Sch.7 para.51
s.31C, amended: 2009 c.26 Sch.7 para.52
s.34, see *Accountant in Bankruptcy (Brown's Trustee) v Brown* [2009] CSIH 2, 2009 S.C. 236 (IH (Ex Div)), Lord Nimmo Smith
s.49, applied: SI 2009/806 r.41
s.65, see *Accountant in Bankruptcy (Brown's Trustee) v Brown* [2009] CSIH 2, 2009 S.C. 236 (IH (Ex Div)), Lord Nimmo Smith
s.69A, enabling: SSI 2009/97
s.72, enabling: SSI 2009/97
s.73, enabling: SSI 2009/97

67. Transport Act 1985
applied: SI 2009/711 Sch.1 para.7, Sch.1 para.14, Sch.1 para.16, SI 2009/1300 Art.57, SI 2009/1885 Art.2, Sch.4 para.1
disapplied: SI 2009/1300 Art.57
Part I, referred to: SSI 2009/146 Art.5
s.2, referred to: SSI 2009/95 Art.5, SSI 2009/149 Art.3
s.6, applied: SI 2009/107 Sch.1 para.2, Sch.2 para.4, SI 2009/443 Reg.3, Reg.6, SI 2009/445 Reg.5, Reg.7, Reg.24, SI 2009/579 Sch.1 para.2, SI 2009/711 Sch.1 para.14, SI 2009/3245 Reg.3, Reg.4, Reg.5, Reg.6, SI 2009/3246 Reg.9, SI 2009/3293 Reg.5, Reg.7, Reg.24
s.6, disapplied: SI 2009/1300 Art.58
s.6, referred to: SI 2009/443 Reg.6

1985–cont.

67. Transport Act 1985–*cont.*
s.6, varied: SI 2009/443 Reg.6, SI 2009/3245 Reg.4, Reg.7, Reg.8
s.6, enabling: SI 2009/443, SI 2009/3245
s.6A, amended: SI 2009/1885 Sch.1 para.6
s.6A, applied: SI 2009/443 Reg.3
s.6A, repealed (in part): SI 2009/1885 Sch.1 para.6
s.6A, enabling: SI 2009/443
s.6B, applied: SI 2009/3245 Reg.10
s.6B, disapplied: SI 2009/3245 Reg.11
s.6B, enabling: SI 2009/3245
s.7, applied: SI 2009/711 Sch.1 para.15
s.8, applied: SI 2009/711 Sch.1 para.15
s.9, amended: SI 2009/1885 Sch.1 para.7
s.9, applied: SI 2009/107 Sch.1 para.1, SI 2009/711 Sch.1 para.15
s.9, repealed (in part): SI 2009/1885 Sch.1 para.7
s.12, applied: SI 2009/2863 Reg.3, Reg.4, Reg.5
s.12, enabling: SI 2009/2863
s.13, enabling: SI 2009/2863
s.16, see *R. (on the application of Newcastle City Council) v Berwick-upon-Tweed BC* [2008] EWHC 2369 (Admin), [2009] R.T.R. 34 (QBD (Admin)), Christopher Symons Q.C.
s.18, applied: SI 2009/365 Reg.4
s.18, referred to: SI 2009/366 Reg.4
s.19, applied: SI 2009/365 Reg.8, Reg.13, SI 2009/711 Art.4, Sch.1 para.18, Sch.1 para.19
s.20, applied: SI 2009/365 Reg.8, Reg.12
s.21, enabling: SI 2009/365
s.22, applied: SI 2009/711 Art.4, Sch.1 para.18, Sch.1 para.19, SI 2009/3244 Sch.1 para.1, Sch.1 para.6
s.23, applied: SI 2009/366 Reg.9, Reg.10, Reg.13
s.23, enabling: SI 2009/366
s.23A, enabling: SI 2009/365, SI 2009/366
s.26, applied: SI 2009/107 Sch.1 para.2
s.27A, amended: 2009 c.20 Sch.6 para.63
s.27A, applied: SI 2009/107 Sch.1 para.2
s.64, amended: 2009 c.20 Sch.6 para.64
s.75, applied: SI 2009/107 Sch.2 para.5, SI 2009/579 Sch.1 para.3
s.79, applied: SI 2009/107 Sch.2 para.5, SI 2009/579 Sch.1 para.3
s.89, applied: SI 2009/3244 Reg.3, SI 2009/3246 Reg.9
s.89, disapplied: SI 2009/3244 Reg.3
s.89, referred to: SI 2009/3244 Reg.3
s.91, applied: SI 2009/3246 Reg.9
s.91, disapplied: SI 2009/3244 Reg.4
s.91, referred to: SI 2009/3244 Reg.4
s.93, amended: 2009 c.20 Sch.6 para.65
s.94, enabling: SI 2009/575
s.106, amended: 2009 c.20 Sch.6 para.66
s.108, applied: SI 2009/107 Sch.2 para.1
s.117, amended: SI 2009/1885 Sch.1 para.8
s.125, applied: SI 2009/2816 Art.4
s.126, applied: SI 2009/711 Art.4
s.126, enabling: SI 2009/878
s.130, applied: SI 2009/3244 Reg.6, Reg.7, Sch.1 para.3
s.130, disapplied: SI 2009/3244 Reg.5
s.131, referred to: SI 2009/3244 Reg.6, Reg.7
s.134, applied: SI 2009/711 Art.4
s.134, enabling: SI 2009/365, SI 2009/366, SI 2009/878
s.137, amended: 2009 c.20 Sch.6 para.67, SI 2009/1941 Sch.1 para.61
Sch.4 para.1, amended: SI 2009/1885 Sch.1 para.9

1985– cont.

67. Transport Act 1985–*cont.*

Sch.4 para.2, applied: SI 2009/ 1885 Art.3

Sch.4 para.8, amended: SI 2009/ 1885 Sch.1 para.9

Sch.4 para.9, repealed: SI 2009/ 1885 Sch.1 para.9

Sch.4 para.17, added: SI 2009/ 1885 Sch.1 para.9

Sch.4 para.18, added: SI 2009/ 1885 Sch.1 para.9

68. Housing Act 1985

see *Bracknell Forest BC v Green* [2009] EWCA Civ 238, [2009] C.P. Rep. 31 (CA (Civ Div)), Mummery, L.J.; see *R. (on the application of Bath) v North Somerset Council* [2008] EWHC 630 (Admin), [2009] H.L.R. 1 (QBD (Admin)), Sir Robin Auld

Part IV, see *Jones v Merton LBC* [2008] EWCA Civ 660, [2009] 1 W.L.R. 1269 (CA (Civ Div)), Arden, L.J.

Part V, see *Hanoman v Southwark LBC* [2008] EWCA Civ 624, [2009] 1 W.L.R. 374 (CA (Civ Div)), Sir Anthony Clarke, M.R.; see *Hanoman v Southwark LBC* [2009] UKHL 29, [2009] 1 W.L.R. 1367 (HL), Lord Phillips of Worth Matravers

s.4, amended: 2009 c.20 Sch.6 para.68

s.6A, amended: SI 2009/ 1941 Sch.1 para.62

s.21, see *Alexander-David v Hammersmith and Fulham LBC* [2009] EWCA Civ 259, [2009] 3 All E.R. 1098 (CA (Civ Div)), Waller, L.J.

s.27AB, amended: SI 2009/ 1941 Sch.1 para.62

s.36, referred to: SI 2009/ 2096 Art.3

s.51, amended: SI 2009/ 1941 Sch.1 para.62

s.82, see *Bracknell Forest BC v Green* [2009] EWCA Civ 238, [2009] C.P. Rep. 31 (CA (Civ Div)), Mummery, L.J.

s.85, see *Jones v Merton LBC* [2008] EWCA Civ 660, [2009] 1 W.L.R. 1269 (CA (Civ Div)), Arden, L.J.; see *Knowsley Housing Trust v White* [2008] UKHL 70, [2009] 1 A.C. 636 (HL), Lord Hoffmann

s.89, see *Newport City Council v Charles* [2008] EWCA Civ 1541, [2009] 1 W.L.R. 1884 (CA (Civ Div)), Laws, L.J.

s.103, see *Peabody Trust Governors v Reeve* [2008] EWHC 1432 (Ch), [2009] L. & T.R. 6 (Ch D), Gabriel Moss Q.C.

s.121, see *Knowsley Housing Trust v White* [2008] UKHL 70, [2009] 1 A.C. 636 (HL), Lord Hoffmann; see *Manchester City Council v Benjamin* [2008] EWCA Civ 189, [2009] 1 W.L.R. 2202 (CA (Civ Div)), Dyson, L.J.

s.122, see *Hanoman v Southwark LBC* [2009] UKHL 29, [2009] 1 W.L.R. 1367 (HL), Lord Phillips of Worth Matravers; see *Knowsley Housing Trust v White* [2008] UKHL 70, [2009] 1 A.C. 636 (HL), Lord Hoffmann

s.124, see *Hanoman v Southwark LBC* [2009] UKHL 29, [2009] 1 W.L.R. 1367 (HL), Lord Phillips of Worth Matravers

s.140, see *Ryan v Islington LBC* [2009] EWCA Civ 578, Times, July 29, 2009 (CA (Civ Div)), Waller, L.J.

s.151B, referred to: SI 2009/ 2096 Art.3

s.153A, see *Hanoman v Southwark LBC* [2008] EWCA Civ 624, [2009] 1 W.L.R. 374 (CA (Civ Div)), Sir Anthony Clarke, M.R.; see *Hanoman v Southwark LBC* [2009] UKHL 29, [2009] 1 W.L.R. 1367 (HL), Lord Phillips of Worth Matravers

s.153B, see *Hanoman v Southwark LBC* [2008] EWCA Civ 624, [2009] 1 W.L.R. 374 (CA (Civ Div)), Sir Anthony Clarke, M.R.; see *Hanoman v Southwark LBC* [2009] UKHL 29, [2009] 1

1985– cont.

68. Housing Act 1985–*cont.*

s.153B–*cont.*

W.L.R. 1367 (HL), Lord Phillips of Worth Matravers

s.155, see *Hanoman v Southwark LBC* [2008] EWCA Civ 624, [2009] 1 W.L.R. 374 (CA (Civ Div)), Sir Anthony Clarke, M.R.

s.156, referred to: SI 2009/ 2096 Art.3

s.171B, amended: SI 2009/ 1941 Sch.1 para.62

s.181, see *Hanoman v Southwark LBC* [2008] EWCA Civ 624, [2009] 1 W.L.R. 374 (CA (Civ Div)), Sir Anthony Clarke, M.R.

s.207, see *Aardvark SRE Ltd v Sedgefield BC* [2008] EWCA Civ 1109, [2009] R.V.R. 93 (CA (Civ Div)), Richards, L.J.

s.269, amended: SI 2009/ 1307 Sch.1 para.172

s.296, amended: SI 2009/ 1307 Sch.1 para.173

s.450B, enabling: SI 2009/ 602

s.450C, enabling: SI 2009/ 602

s.450D, enabling: SI 2009/ 601

s.550, amended: SI 2009/ 1307 Sch.1 para.174

s.584B, amended: SI 2009/ 1307 Sch.1 para.175

s.609, see *Cantrell v Wycombe DC* [2008] EWCA Civ 866, [2009] H.L.R. 14 (CA (Civ Div)), Moore-Bick, L.J.

s.622, amended: SI 2009/ 1941 Sch.1 para.62

Sch.2, see *Bracknell Forest BC v Green* [2009] EWCA Civ 238, [2009] C.P. Rep. 31 (CA (Civ Div)), Mummery, L.J.; see *Manchester City Council v Benjamin* [2008] EWCA Civ 189, [2009] 1 W.L.R. 2202 (CA (Civ Div)), Dyson, L.J.; see *Newport City Council v Charles* [2008] EWCA Civ 1541, [2009] 1 W.L.R. 1884 (CA (Civ Div)), Laws, L.J.

Sch.4 para.4, see *Manchester City Council v Benjamin* [2008] EWCA Civ 189, [2009] 1 W.L.R. 2202 (CA (Civ Div)), Dyson, L.J.

Sch.5 para.11, amended: SI 2009/ 1307 Sch.1 para.176

69. Housing Associations Act 1985

s.74, repealed (in part): SI 2009/ 484 Sch.2

s.75, amended: SI 2009/ 484 Sch.1 para.3

s.76A, repealed (in part): SI 2009/ 484 Sch.2

s.78, repealed (in part): SI 2009/ 484 Sch.2

s.84, amended: SI 2009/ 484 Sch.1 para.6

s.84, repealed (in part): SI 2009/ 484 Sch.2

s.85, amended: SI 2009/ 484 Sch.1 para.7, Sch.2

s.88, amended: SI 2009/ 484 Sch.1 para.8

s.88, repealed (in part): SI 2009/ 484 Sch.1 para.8, Sch.2

s.89, amended: SI 2009/ 484 Sch.1 para.9

s.90, amended: SI 2009/ 484 Sch.1 para.10, Sch.2

s.91, repealed (in part): SI 2009/ 484 Sch.2

s.92, repealed (in part): SI 2009/ 484 Sch.2

s.93, repealed (in part): SI 2009/ 484 Sch.2

s.94, repealed (in part): SI 2009/ 484 Sch.2

s.95, repealed (in part): SI 2009/ 484 Sch.2

s.96, repealed (in part): SI 2009/ 484 Sch.2

s.97, repealed (in part): SI 2009/ 484 Sch.2

s.98, repealed (in part): SI 2009/ 484 Sch.2

s.99, repealed (in part): SI 2009/ 484 Sch.2

s.100, repealed (in part): SI 2009/ 484 Sch.2

s.101, amended: SI 2009/ 1941 Sch.1 para.63

s.102, amended: SI 2009/ 1941 Sch.1 para.63

s.106, amended: 2009 c.20 Sch.6 para.69

Sch.6 para.1, repealed (in part): SI 2009/ 484 Sch.2

Sch.6 para.2, repealed (in part): SI 2009/ 484 Sch.2

Sch.6 para.3, repealed (in part): SI 2009/ 484 Sch.2

Sch.6 para.4, repealed (in part): SI 2009/ 484 Sch.2

1985– cont.

69. Housing Associations Act 1985– cont.
Sch.6 para.5, repealed (in part): SI 2009/484 Sch.2
Sch.6 para.6, repealed (in part): SI 2009/484 Sch.2
Sch.6 para.6A, repealed (in part): SI 2009/484 Sch.2
Sch.6 para.7, repealed (in part): SI 2009/484 Sch.2
Sch.6 para.8, repealed (in part): SI 2009/484 Sch.2
Sch.6 para.9, repealed (in part): SI 2009/484 Sch.2

70. Landlord and Tenant Act 1985
s.18, see *Morshead Mansions Ltd v Di Marco* [2008] EWCA Civ 1371, [2009] 1 B.C.L.C. 559 (CA (Civ Div)), Mummery, L.J.
s.20C, amended: SI 2009/1307 Sch.1 para.177
s.27A, see *Buckley v Bowerbeck Properties Ltd* [2009] 1 E.G.L.R. 43 (LVT), Peter Korn (Chairman)
s.28, amended: SI 2009/1941 Sch.1 para.64
s.38, see *Buckley v Bowerbeck Properties Ltd* [2009] 1 E.G.L.R. 43 (LVT), Peter Korn (Chairman)
s.38, amended: 2009 c.20 Sch.6 para.70

72. Weights and Measures Act 1985
applied: SSI 2009/183 Sch.1 para.4
referred to: SI 2009/669 Sch.1 Part 4
s.3, amended: SI 2009/2748 Sch.1 para.4
s.8, amended: SI 2009/3046 Reg.3
s.15, enabling: SI 2009/2463, SI 2009/3045
s.86, enabling: SI 2009/2463
s.94, amended: SI 2009/2748 Sch.1 para.4
s.94, enabling: SI 2009/3045
Sch.2 Part V, amended: SI 2009/2748 Sch.1 para.4
Sch.4 Part I para.2, substituted: SI 2009/663 Reg.2
Sch.5 Part I para.3, amended: SI 2009/663 Reg.2
Sch.5 Part I para.3, repealed (in part): SI 2009/663 Reg.2
Sch.6 Part II para.5, amended: SI 2009/663 Reg.2
Sch.7 para.3, amended: SI 2009/663 Reg.2
Sch.7 para.5, amended: SI 2009/663 Reg.2

73. Law Reform (Miscellaneous Provisions) (Scotland) Act 1985
s.4, see *Kodak Processing Companies Ltd v Shoredale Ltd* [2009] CSIH 71, 2009 S.L.T. 1151 (IH (Ex Div)), Lord Osborne
s.11, repealed: 2009 c.1 s.254

1986

3. Atomic Energy Authority Act 1986
s.9, amended: SI 2009/1941 Sch.1 para.67

5. Agricultural Holdings Act 1986
see *Mason v Boscawen* [2008] EWHC 3100 (Ch), [2009] 1 W.L.R. 2139 (Ch D (Bristol)), Lewison, J.
Sch.2 para.4, see *Mason v Boscawen* [2008] EWHC 3100 (Ch), [2009] 1 W.L.R. 2139 (Ch D (Bristol)), Lewison, J.
Sch.2 para.4, amended: 2009 c.10 s.79
Sch.3, see *Mason v Boscawen* [2008] EWHC 3100 (Ch), [2009] 1 W.L.R. 2139 (Ch D (Bristol)), Lewison, J.
Sch.6 Part I para.3, applied: SI 2009/2762 Art.2, SI 2009/3232 Art.2
Sch.6 Part I para.4, enabling: SI 2009/2762, SI 2009/3232

10. Local Government Act 1986
s.6, amended: 2009 c.20 Sch.6 para.71
s.9, amended: 2009 c.20 Sch.6 para.71

1986– cont.

14. Animals (Scientific Procedures) Act 1986
see *Secretary of State for the Home Department v British Union for the Abolition of Vivisection* [2008] EWCA Civ 870, [2009] 1 W.L.R. 636 (CA (Civ Div)), Lord Phillips of Worth Matravers, L.C.J.
applied: 2009 c.2 Sch.2 Part 2, 2009 c.9 Sch.2 Part 9, SI 2009/2297 Reg.3, Reg.25, Sch.7 para.49
s.24, see *Secretary of State for the Home Department v British Union for the Abolition of Vivisection* [2008] EWCA Civ 870, [2009] 1 W.L.R. 636 (CA (Civ Div)), Lord Phillips of Worth Matravers, L.C.J.

20. Horticultural Produce Act 1986
disapplied: SI 2009/1361 Reg.22, SI 2009/1551 Reg.22, SSI 2009/225 Reg.24

31. Airports Act 1986
s.13, amended: SI 2009/1941 Sch.1 para.68
s.26, amended: SI 2009/1941 Sch.1 para.68
s.35, enabling: SI 2009/3015
s.41, amended: SI 2009/1941 Sch.1 para.68
s.63, applied: SI 2009/2576 Art.2
s.63, enabling: SI 2009/2576
s.77, amended: 2009 c.4 Sch.1 para.321
s.82, amended: SI 2009/1941 Sch.1 para.68

33. Disabled Persons (Services, Consultation and Representation) Act 1986
s.2, amended: 2009 c.21 Sch.1 para.4

35. Protection of Military Remains Act 1986
s.1, applied: SI 2009/3380
s.1, enabling: SI 2009/3380
s.3, amended: SI 2009/1941 Sch.1 para.69

38. Outer Space Act 1986
applied: SI 2009/3015 Art.168

41. Finance Act 1986
s.66, amended: SI 2009/1890 Art.7
s.78, amended: 2009 c.4 Sch.1 para.323
s.79, amended: 2009 c.4 Sch.1 para.324
s.80D, added: 2009 c.10 Sch.37 para.2
s.80D, repealed: 2009 c.10 Sch.37 para.2
s.87, applied: 2009 c.10 Sch.56 para.1
s.88, amended: 2009 c.10 Sch.37 para.3
s.89AB, added: 2009 c.10 Sch.37 para.5
s.89AB, repealed: 2009 c.10 Sch.37 para.5
s.90, amended: SI 2009/1890 Art.7
s.92, amended: SI 2009/1890 Art.7
s.93, applied: 2009 c.10 Sch.56 para.1
s.96, applied: 2009 c.10 Sch.56 para.1
s.98, applied: 2009 c.10 Sch.55 para.1, Sch.56 para.1
s.99, amended: 2009 c.4 Sch.1 para.325, SI 2009/1890 Art.7

44. Gas Act 1986
Part I, applied: SI 2009/1905 Art.27
s.7, applied: SI 2009/2195 Art.2
s.7A, applied: SI 2009/1905 Art.5
s.7B, applied: SI 2009/3190 Reg.8
s.7B, enabling: SI 2009/3190
s.8, referred to: SI 2009/3190 Reg.6
s.19A, amended: SI 2009/1349 Reg.4
s.19C, amended: SI 2009/1349 Reg.4
s.27B, added: SI 2009/1349 Reg.2
s.27C, added: SI 2009/1349 Reg.2
s.27D, added: SI 2009/1349 Reg.2
s.33BC, applied: SI 2009/1904, SI 2009/1905
s.33BC, enabling: SI 2009/1904, SI 2009/1905
s.33F, amended: SI 2009/1941 Sch.1 para.70
s.47, enabling: SI 2009/3190
s.48, amended: SI 2009/1941 Sch.1 para.70

1986– cont.

44. Gas Act 1986–*cont.*
s.51, amended: SI 2009/ 1941 Sch.1 para.70
s.55, amended: SI 2009/ 1941 Sch.1 para.70
s.60, amended: 2009 c.4 Sch.1 para.327
s.61, amended: SI 2009/ 1941 Sch.1 para.70
Sch.3 Part II para.8, amended: SI 2009/ 1307 Sch.1 para.179
Sch.3 Part III para.22, amended: SI 2009/ 1307 Sch.1 para.179

45. Insolvency Act 1986
see *D/S Norden A/S v Samsun Logix Corp* [2009] EWHC 2304 (Ch), [2009] B.P.I.R. 1367 (Ch D (Companies Ct)), Guy Newey Q.C.; see *MacPlant Services Ltd v Contract Lifting Services (Scotland) Ltd* 2009 S.C. 125 (OH), Lord Hodge; see *Official Receiver v Southey* [2009] B.P.I.R. 89 (Ch D (Bankruptcy Ct)), Registrar Baister; see *Perpetual Trustee Co Ltd v BNY Corporate Trustee Services Ltd* [2009] EWHC 1912 (Ch), [2009] 2 B.C.L.C. 400 (Ch D), Sir Andrew Morritt (Chancellor)
applied: 2009 c.1 s.93, s.136, s.233, s.234, 2009 c.4 s.10, s.12, SI 2009/ 356 r.204, r.209, r.262, SI 2009/ 457 Reg.3, Reg.8, SI 2009/ 1801 Reg.69, Reg.70, SI 2009/ 2477 r.40, r.45, r.60, r.70, r.71, r.76, r.92, r.102, r.120, r.126, r.127
referred to: 2009 c.1 s.166, SI 2009/ 351 r.4, SI 2009/ 356 r.6, SI 2009/ 806 r.18, r.40, SI 2009/ 1941 Art.8, SI 2009/ 2477 r.119
varied: SI 2009/ 357 r.60
Part I, applied: SI 2009/ 356 r.7, r.10, r.20, SI 2009/ 357 r.41, SI 2009/ 457 Reg.5, SI 2009/ 806 r.40, SI 2009/ 1801 Reg.71
Part II, applied: SI 2009/ 356 r.7, SI 2009/ 1801 Reg.71
Part IV, applied: 2009 c.1 s.103
Part V, applied: 2009 c.1 s.103
Part VIIA, applied: SI 2009/ 457 Reg.7, Reg.11
Part VIII, applied: SI 2009/ 645 Art.7
Part II, see *William Hare Ltd v Shepherd Construction Ltd* [2009] EWHC 1603 (TCC), [2009] B.L.R. 447 (QBD (TCC)), Coulson, J.
s.1, amended: SI 2009/ 1941 Sch.1 para.71
s.1, applied: 2009 c.1 s.113, s.154
s.1, referred to: 2009 c.1 s.113
s.1, varied: 2009 c.1 s.154
s.1A, varied: 2009 c.1 s.154
s.2, applied: SI 2009/ 356 r.7
s.2, varied: 2009 c.1 s.154
s.3, see *Official Receiver v Baars* [2009] B.P.I.R. 524 (Ch D), Registrar Derrett
s.3, varied: 2009 c.1 s.113, s.154
s.4, varied: 2009 c.1 s.154, SI 2009/ 3056 Sch.1 para.2
s.4A, varied: 2009 c.1 s.154
s.4B, varied: 2009 c.1 s.154
s.5, varied: 2009 c.1 s.113, s.154
s.6, see *Beloit Walmsley Ltd, Re* [2008] EWHC 1888 (Ch), [2009] 1 B.C.L.C. 584 (Ch D (Manchester)), Judge Pelling Q.C.
s.6, varied: 2009 c.1 s.154
s.6A, varied: 2009 c.1 s.154
s.7, applied: SI 2009/ 351 r.101
s.7, varied: 2009 c.1 s.154
s.7A, amended: SI 2009/ 1941 Sch.1 para.71
s.7A, varied: 2009 c.1 s.154
s.7B, varied: 2009 c.1 s.154
s.14, amended: SI 2009/ 1941 Sch.1 para.73
s.14, applied: SI 2009/ 2477 r.43
s.15, amended: SI 2009/ 1941 Sch.1 para.73

1986– cont.

45. Insolvency Act 1986–*cont.*
s.15, applied: SI 2009/ 2477 r.37
s.17, applied: SI 2009/ 2477 r.43
s.18, see *Newscreen Media Group Plc (In Liquidation), Re* [2009] EWHC 944 (Ch), [2009] 2 B.C.L.C. 353 (Ch D (Companies Ct)), Bernard Livesey Q.C.
s.18, amended: SI 2009/ 1941 Sch.1 para.73
s.18, applied: SI 2009/ 2477 r.35
s.20, see *Newscreen Media Group Plc (In Liquidation), Re* [2009] EWHC 944 (Ch), [2009] 2 B.C.L.C. 353 (Ch D (Companies Ct)), Bernard Livesey Q.C.
s.21, see *Secretary of State for Trade and Industry v Hall* [2006] EWHC 1995 (Ch), [2009] B.C.C. 190 (Ch D (Companies Ct)), Evans-Lombe, J.
s.21, amended: SI 2009/ 1941 Sch.1 para.73
s.21, applied: SI 2009/ 2477 r.17
s.22, applied: SI 2009/ 2477 r.27, r.31, r.80
s.22, referred to: SI 2009/ 2477 r.28
s.23, applied: SI 2009/ 2477 r.33, r.36
s.23, referred to: SI 2009/ 2477 r.35
s.24, amended: SI 2009/ 1941 Sch.1 para.73
s.25, applied: SI 2009/ 2477 r.34
s.27, amended: SI 2009/ 1941 Sch.1 para.73
s.28, substituted: SI 2009/ 1941 Sch.1 para.74
s.29, see *Dairy Farmers of Britain Ltd, Re* [2009] EWHC 1389 (Ch), [2009] 4 All E.R. 241 (Ch D (Companies Ct)), Henderson, J.
s.29, amended: SI 2009/ 1941 Sch.1 para.74
s.37, see *Dairy Farmers of Britain Ltd, Re* [2009] EWHC 1389 (Ch), [2009] 4 All E.R. 241 (Ch D (Companies Ct)), Henderson, J.
s.39, applied: SI 2009/ 1801 Reg.63
s.43, amended: SI 2009/ 1941 Sch.1 para.74
s.51, amended: SI 2009/ 1941 Sch.1 para.74
s.51, applied: SI 2009/ 1917 Reg.20
s.53, applied: SI 2009/ 1917 Reg.20
s.54, applied: SI 2009/ 1917 Reg.20
s.55, varied: SI 2009/ 3056 Sch.1 para.2
s.61, amended: SI 2009/ 1941 Sch.1 para.74
s.70, amended: SI 2009/ 1941 Sch.1 para.74
s.72A, see *Dairy Farmers of Britain Ltd, Re* [2009] EWHC 1389 (Ch), [2009] 4 All E.R. 241 (Ch D (Companies Ct)), Henderson, J.
s.73, substituted: SI 2009/ 1941 Sch.1 para.75
s.74, amended: SI 2009/ 1941 Sch.1 para.75
s.75, referred to: SI 2009/ 1941 Art.9
s.75, repealed: SI 2009/ 1941 Sch.1 para.75
s.76, amended: SI 2009/ 1941 Sch.1 para.75
s.76, repealed (in part): SI 2009/ 1941 Sch.1 para.75
s.77, amended: SI 2009/ 1941 Sch.1 para.75
s.78, amended: SI 2009/ 1941 Sch.1 para.75
s.79, see *Charit-Email Technology Partnership LLP v Vermillion International Investments Ltd* [2009] EWHC 388 (Ch), [2009] B.P.I.R. 762 (Ch D), Sir Andrew Morritt (Chancellor)
s.79, amended: SI 2009/ 1941 Sch.1 para.75
s.80, amended: SI 2009/ 1941 Sch.1 para.75
s.80, referred to: SI 2009/ 1941 Art.11
s.83, amended: SI 2009/ 1941 Sch.1 para.75
s.84, applied: 2009 c.1 s.118
s.85, see *Gardiner v Secretary of State for Business Enterprise and Regulatory Reform* [2009] B.C.C. 742 (Ch D (Birmingham)), District Judge Dowling
s.95, amended: SI 2009/ 864 Art.3

1986– cont.

45. Insolvency Act 1986– *cont.*

s.98, see *Gardiner v Secretary of State for Business Enterprise and Regulatory Reform* [2009] B.C.C. 742 (Ch D (Birmingham)), District Judge Dowling

s.98, amended: SI 2009/ 864 Art.3

s.98, applied: SI 2009/ 356 r.72

s.110, amended: SI 2009/ 1941 Sch.1 para.75

s.122, amended: SI 2009/ 1941 Sch.1 para.75

s.123, see *MacPlant Services Ltd v Contract Lifting Services (Scotland) Ltd* 2009 S.C. 125 (OH), Lord Hodge

s.123, applied: 2009 c.1 s.93, s.166

s.124, see *MacPlant Services Ltd v Contract Lifting Services (Scotland) Ltd* 2009 S.C. 125 (OH), Lord Hodge

s.124, amended: SI 2009/ 1941 Sch.1 para.75

s.124A, see *Secretary of State for Business, Enterprise and Regulatory Reform v Amway (UK) Ltd* [2009] EWCA Civ 32, [2009] B.C.C. 781 (CA (Civ Div)), Rix, L.J.; see *Secretary of State for Trade and Industry v Hall* [2006] EWHC 1995 (Ch), [2009] B.C.C. 190 (Ch D (Companies Ct)), Evans-Lombe, J.

s.124A, applied: 2009 c.1 s.96

s.126, amended: SI 2009/ 1941 Sch.1 para.75

s.126, varied: SI 2009/ 3056 Sch.1 para.2

s.127, see *Power v Brown* [2009] EWHC 9 (Ch), [2009] B.P.I.R. 340 (Ch D), Gabriel Moss Q.C.; see *R. (on the application of BERR) v Lowe* [2009] EWCA Crim 194, [2009] 2 Cr. App. R. (S.) 81 (CA (Crim Div)), Thomas, L.J.

s.127, varied: 2009 c.1 s.103

s.128, varied: 2009 c.1 s.103, SI 2009/ 3056 Sch.1 para.2

s.130, amended: SI 2009/ 1941 Sch.1 para.75

s.130, applied: SI 2009/ 351 r.8, SI 2009/ 356 r.16

s.130, varied: 2009 c.1 s.103, SI 2009/ 3056 Sch.1 para.2

s.135, applied: 2009 c.4 s.322, s.357, SI 2009/ 317 Art.6, SI 2009/ 356 r.20, SI 2009/ 357 r.40

s.135, varied: 2009 c.1 s.103, s.145

s.141, see *Gresham International Ltd (In Liquidation) v Moonie* [2009] EWHC 1093 (Ch), [2009] 2 B.C.L.C. 256 (Ch D), Peter Smith, J.

s.141, applied: 2009 c.1 s.101

s.141, varied: 2009 c.1 s.103

s.142, applied: 2009 c.1 s.101

s.142, varied: 2009 c.1 s.103

s.143, see *Ruttle Plant Hire Ltd v Secretary of State for the Environment, Food and Rural Affairs* [2008] EWHC 238 (TCC), [2009] 1 All E.R. 448 (QBD (TCC)), Ramsey, J.

s.143, applied: SI 2009/ 356 r.203

s.143, varied: 2009 c.1 s.103, SI 2009/ 3056 Sch.1 para.2

s.144, varied: 2009 c.1 s.103, SI 2009/ 3056 Sch.1 para.2

s.145, varied: 2009 c.1 s.103

s.146, varied: 2009 c.1 s.103

s.147, varied: 2009 c.1 s.103

s.148, amended: SI 2009/ 1941 Sch.1 para.75

s.148, varied: 2009 c.1 s.103

s.149, amended: SI 2009/ 1941 Sch.1 para.75

s.149, varied: 2009 c.1 s.103

s.150, varied: 2009 c.1 s.103

s.152, varied: 2009 c.1 s.103

s.153, varied: 2009 c.1 s.103

1986– cont.

45. Insolvency Act 1986– *cont.*

s.154, varied: 2009 c.1 s.103, SI 2009/ 805 Sch.1 para.13

s.155, varied: 2009 c.1 s.103

s.156, varied: 2009 c.1 s.103

s.157, varied: 2009 c.1 s.103

s.158, varied: 2009 c.1 s.103

s.159, amended: SI 2009/ 1941 Sch.1 para.75

s.159, varied: 2009 c.1 s.103

s.160, amended: SI 2009/ 1941 Sch.1 para.75

s.160, varied: 2009 c.1 s.103

s.161, varied: 2009 c.1 s.103

s.162, amended: SI 2009/ 1941 Sch.1 para.75

s.162, varied: 2009 c.1 s.103

s.165, varied: SI 2009/ 3056 Sch.1 para.2

s.166, amended: SI 2009/ 864 Art.3

s.167, see *Ruttle Plant Hire Ltd v Secretary of State for the Environment, Food and Rural Affairs* [2008] EWHC 238 (TCC), [2009] 1 All E.R. 448 (QBD (TCC)), Ramsey, J.

s.167, varied: 2009 c.1 s.103, SI 2009/ 3056 Sch.1 para.2

s.168, applied: 2009 c.1 s.100, s.101, s.102, SI 2009/ 356 r.109

s.168, varied: 2009 c.1 s.103, s.145

s.169, applied: 2009 c.1 s.101

s.169, varied: 2009 c.1 s.103

s.170, varied: 2009 c.1 s.103

s.172, see *Managa Properties Ltd v Brittain* [2009] EWHC 157 (Ch), [2009] 1 B.C.L.C. 689 (Ch D (Companies Ct)), Charles Hollander Q.C.

s.172, varied: 2009 c.1 s.103

s.174, varied: 2009 c.1 s.103

s.175, varied: 2009 c.1 s.103

s.176, varied: 2009 c.1 s.103

s.176A, see *Courts Plc (In Liquidation), Re* [2008] EWHC 2339 (Ch), [2009] 1 W.L.R. 1499 (Ch D (Companies Ct)), Blackburne, J.; see *International Sections Ltd (In Liquidation), Re* [2009] EWHC 137 (Ch), [2009] B.C.C. 574 (Ch D (Birmingham)), Judge Purle Q.C.

s.176A, applied: SI 2009/ 350 r.21, r.27, SI 2009/ 351 r.21, r.41, r.44, SI 2009/ 356 r.34, r.96, SI 2009/ 357 r.29, r.35, SI 2009/ 806 r.20, r.26

s.176A, varied: 2009 c.1 s.103, s.145

s.176ZA, varied: 2009 c.1 s.103

s.177, varied: 2009 c.1 s.103

s.178, see *Shaw v Doleman* [2009] EWCA Civ 279, [2009] Bus. L.R. 1175 (CA (Civ Div)), Mummery, L.J.

s.178, referred to: SI 2009/ 357 r.61

s.178, varied: 2009 c.1 s.103, s.145

s.179, varied: 2009 c.1 s.103, s.145

s.180, varied: 2009 c.1 s.103, s.145

s.181, varied: 2009 c.1 s.103, s.145

s.182, varied: 2009 c.1 s.103, s.145

s.183, disapplied: 2009 c.1 s.134

s.183, varied: 2009 c.1 s.103

s.184, applied: SI 2009/ 356 r.279

s.184, disapplied: 2009 c.1 s.134

s.184, varied: 2009 c.1 s.103

s.185, varied: 2009 c.1 s.103

s.186, varied: 2009 c.1 s.103

s.187, amended: SI 2009/ 1941 Sch.1 para.75

s.187, varied: 2009 c.1 s.103, SI 2009/ 805 Sch.1 para.13

s.188, applied: SI 2009/ 1801 Reg.63

s.188, varied: 2009 c.1 s.103, s.145

s.189, applied: SI 2009/ 356 r.262

1986– cont.

45. Insolvency Act 1986– *cont.*
s.189, varied: 2009 c.1 s.103
s.190, varied: 2009 c.1 s.103
s.191, varied: 2009 c.1 s.103
s.192, varied: 2009 c.1 s.103
s.193, amended: SI 2009/1941 Sch.1 para.75
s.193, varied: 2009 c.1 s.103
s.194, varied: 2009 c.1 s.103
s.195, amended: SI 2009/1941 Sch.1 para.75
s.195, applied: 2009 c.1 s.109, SI 2009/356 r.42
s.195, varied: 2009 c.1 s.103
s.196, amended: SI 2009/1941 Sch.1 para.75
s.196, varied: 2009 c.1 s.103
s.197, varied: 2009 c.1 s.103
s.198, varied: 2009 c.1 s.103
s.199, varied: 2009 c.1 s.103
s.200, varied: 2009 c.1 s.103
s.205, referred to: 2009 c.1 s.116
s.206, see *R. (on the application of BERR) v Lowe*
   [2009] EWCA Crim 194, [2009] 2 Cr. App. R. (S.)
   81 (CA (Crim Div)), Thomas, L.J.
s.206, varied: 2009 c.1 s.103
s.207, varied: 2009 c.1 s.103
s.208, varied: 2009 c.1 s.103
s.209, varied: 2009 c.1 s.103
s.210, varied: 2009 c.1 s.103
s.211, varied: 2009 c.1 s.103
s.212, see *Paycheck Services 3 Ltd, Re* [2009]
   EWCA Civ 625, [2009] S.T.C. 1639 (CA (Civ
   Div)), Ward, L.J.
s.212, disapplied: 2009 c.1 s.111
s.212, varied: 2009 c.1 s.103
s.213, see *Overnight Ltd (In Liquidation), Re* [2009]
   EWHC 601 (Ch), [2009] Bus. L.R. 1141 (Ch D),
   Sir Andrew Morritt (Chancellor)
s.213, applied: SI 2009/350 r.38, SI 2009/357 r.57, SI
   2009/806 r.37
s.213, referred to: SI 2009/314 Reg.8
s.213, varied: 2009 c.1 s.103, s.145
s.214, applied: 2009 c.1 s.120, SI 2009/350 r.38, SI
   2009/357 r.57, SI 2009/806 r.37, SI 2009/814
   Art.7, SI 2009/3226 Sch.5 para.2
s.214, referred to: SI 2009/314 Reg.8
s.214, varied: 2009 c.1 s.103, s.145
s.214A, applied: SI 2009/806 r.37
s.214A, varied: 2009 c.1 s.103
s.215, applied: SI 2009/350 r.38, SI 2009/357 r.57, SI
   2009/806 r.37
s.215, varied: 2009 c.1 s.103
s.215S, varied: 2009 c.1 s.103
s.216, see *Glasgow City Council v Craig* 2009 S.L.T.
   212 (OH), Lord Glennie
s.216, applied: SI 2009/351 r.91, r.96, SI 2009/356
   r.182, r.187
s.216, varied: 2009 c.1 s.103, SI 2009/805 Sch.1
   para.13
s.217, see *Glasgow City Council v Craig* 2009 S.L.T.
   212 (OH), Lord Glennie
s.217, varied: 2009 c.1 s.103, SI 2009/805 Sch.1
   para.13
s.218, amended: SI 2009/1941 Sch.1 para.75
s.218, varied: 2009 c.1 s.103, SI 2009/805 Sch.1
   para.13
s.219, amended: SI 2009/1941 Sch.1 para.75
s.219, varied: 2009 c.1 s.103, SI 2009/805 Sch.1
   para.13
s.220, substituted: SI 2009/1941 Sch.1 para.76

1986– cont.

45. Insolvency Act 1986– *cont.*
s.221, see *OJSC Ank Yugraneft, Re* [2008] EWHC
   2614 (Ch), [2009] 1 B.C.L.C. 298 (Ch D
   (Companies Ct)), Christopher Clarke, J.
s.221, amended: SI 2009/1941 Sch.1 para.76
s.225, amended: SI 2009/1941 Sch.1 para.76
s.226, repealed (in part): SI 2009/1941 Sch.1 para.76
s.229, amended: SI 2009/1941 Sch.1 para.76
s.229, repealed (in part): SI 2009/1941 Sch.1 para.76
s.231, varied: 2009 c.1 s.103
s.232, varied: 2009 c.1 s.103
s.233, varied: 2009 c.1 s.103, s.145
s.234, varied: 2009 c.1 s.103, s.145
s.235, see *Bernard L Madoff Investment Securities
   LLC, Re* [2009] EWHC 442 (Ch), [2009] 2
   B.C.L.C. 78 (Ch D), Lewison, J.
s.235, applied: SI 2009/356 r.203, SI 2009/2477 r.27,
   r.80
s.235, varied: 2009 c.1 s.103, s.145
s.236, applied: SI 2009/356 r.204, r.241, SI 2009/357
   r.61, SI 2009/2477 r.109, r.112, r.113, r.115, r.116, r.117
s.236, varied: 2009 c.1 s.103, s.145
s.237, applied: SI 2009/2477 r.117
s.237, varied: 2009 c.1 s.103, s.145
s.238, varied: 2009 c.1 s.103, s.145
s.239, see *Klempka v Miller* [2008] EWHC 3654
   (Ch), [2009] B.P.I.R. 549 (Ch D (Leeds)),
   Anthony Elleray Q.C.; see *Wilson v Masters
   International Ltd* [2009] EWHC 1753 (Ch),
   [2009] 2 B.C.L.C. 485 (Ch D (Companies Ct)),
   Mark Cawson Q.C.
s.239, varied: 2009 c.1 s.103, s.145
s.240, varied: 2009 c.1 s.103, s.145
s.241, see *Wilson v Masters International Ltd* [2009]
   EWHC 1753 (Ch), [2009] 2 B.C.L.C. 485 (Ch D
   (Companies Ct)), Mark Cawson Q.C.
s.241, varied: 2009 c.1 s.103, s.145
s.242, varied: 2009 c.1 s.103, s.145
s.243, see *Anderson v Dickens* 2009 S.C.L.R. 609
   (OH), Temporary Judge Sir D Edward, QC
s.243, varied: 2009 c.1 s.103, s.145
s.244, varied: 2009 c.1 s.103, s.145
s.245, varied: 2009 c.1 s.103, s.145
s.246, varied: 2009 c.1 s.103, s.145
s.247, applied: 2009 c.4 s.431, s.682, s.821
s.249, applied: SI 2009/814 Art.7, SI 2009/2477 r.55,
   SI 2009/3226 Sch.5 para.2
s.251, amended: SI 2009/1941 Sch.1 para.77
s.251U, applied: SI 2009/457 Reg.3, Reg.4
s.251U, enabling: SI 2009/457, SI 2009/1553
s.262, see *Tradition (UK) Ltd v Ahmed* [2008]
   EWHC 2946 (Ch), [2009] B.P.I.R. 626 (Ch D),
   Andrew Simmonds Q.C.
s.267, see *Dean & Dean (A Firm) v Angel Airlines
   SA* [2009] EWHC 447 (Ch), [2009] B.P.I.R. 409
   (Ch D), Patten, J.; see *Truex v Toll* [2009] EWHC
   396 (Ch), [2009] 1 W.L.R. 2121 (Ch D
   (Bankruptcy Ct)), Proudman, J; see *Watts v
   Newham LBC* [2009] EWHC 377 (Ch), [2009]
   B.P.I.R. 718 (Ch D), Stephen Smith Q.C.; see
   Wicks v Russell [2008] EWHC 2713 (Ch),
   [2009] B.P.I.R. 194 (Ch D (Birmingham)),
   Judge Purle Q.C.
s.268, see *Watts v Newham LBC* [2009] EWHC 377
   (Ch), [2009] B.P.I.R. 718 (Ch D), Stephen Smith
   Q.C.
s.281, see *R. (on the application of Mohammed) v
   Southwark LBC* [2009] EWHC 311 (Admin),
   [2009] B.P.I.R. 882 (QBD (Admin)), Geraldine
   Andrews QC

1986–cont.

45. Insolvency Act 1986–*cont.*

s.282, see *Ella v Ella* [2008] EWHC 3258 (Ch), [2009] B.P.I.R. 441 (Ch D), Sir Edward Evans-Lombe; see *Official Receiver v McKay* [2009] EWCA Civ 467, [2009] B.P.I.R. 1061 (CA (Civ Div)), Mummery, L.J.; see *Official Receiver v Mitterfellner* [2009] B.P.I.R. 1075 (Ch D), Chief Registrar Baister; see *Paulin v Paulin* [2009] EWCA Civ 221, [2009] 3 All E.R. 88 (CA (Civ Div)), Longmore, L.J.; see *Revenue and Customs Commissioners v Cassells* [2008] EWHC 3180 (Ch), [2009] S.T.C. 1047 (Ch D), Sir Andrew Morritt (Chancellor); see *Wicks v Russell* [2008] EWHC 2713 (Ch), [2009] B.P.I.R. 194 (Ch D (Birmingham)), Judge Purle Q.C.

s.283A, see *Lewis v Metropolitan Property Realisations Ltd* [2008] EWHC 2760 (Ch), [2009] 1 F.L.R. 631 (Ch D), Proudman, J; see *Lewis v Metropolitan Property Realisations Ltd* [2009] EWCA Civ 448, [2009] 4 All E.R. 141 (CA (Civ Div)), Laws, L.J.

s.284, see *Bateman v Hyde* [2009] EWHC 81 (Ch), [2009] B.P.I.R. 737 (Ch D (Manchester)), Judge Pelling Q.C.; see *Nationwide Building Society v Wright* [2009] EWCA Civ 811, [2009] 2 B.C.L.C. 695 (CA (Civ Div)), Maurice Kay, L.J.; see *Power v Brown* [2009] EWHC 9 (Ch), [2009] B.P.I.R. 340 (Ch D), Gabriel Moss Q.C.

s.285, see *R. (on the application of Mohammed) v Southwark LBC* [2009] EWHC 311 (Admin), [2009] B.P.I.R. 882 (QBD (Admin)), Geraldine Andrews QC

s.290, see *Rottmann, Re* [2008] EWHC 1794 (Ch), [2009] Bus. L.R. 284 (Ch D), Judge Kaye Q.C.

s.292, see *Donaldson v O'Sullivan* [2008] EWCA Civ 879, [2009] 1 W.L.R. 924 (CA (Civ Div)), Ward, L.J.

s.297, see *Donaldson v O'Sullivan* [2008] EWCA Civ 879, [2009] 1 W.L.R. 924 (CA (Civ Div)), Ward, L.J.

s.298, see *Donaldson v O'Sullivan* [2008] EWCA Civ 879, [2009] 1 W.L.R. 924 (CA (Civ Div)), Ward, L.J.

s.303, see *Bank of Baroda v Patel* [2008] EWHC 3390 (Ch), [2009] 2 F.L.R. 753 (Ch D), Sales, J; see *Donaldson v O'Sullivan* [2008] EWCA Civ 879, [2009] 1 W.L.R. 924 (CA (Civ Div)), Ward, L.J.; see *Miller v Bayliss* [2009] EWHC 2063 (Ch), [2009] B.P.I.R. 1438 (Ch D), Alison Foster QC; see *Supperstone v Hurst* [2009] EWHC 1271 (Ch), [2009] 1 W.L.R. 2306 (Ch D), Bernard Livesey Q.C.

s.305, see *Lewis v Metropolitan Property Realisations Ltd* [2008] EWHC 2760 (Ch), [2009] 1 F.L.R. 631 (Ch D), Proudman, J

s.306, see *Raymond Saul & Co v Holden* [2008] EWHC 2731 (Ch), [2009] Ch. 313 (Ch D), Richard Snowden QC

s.306, amended: 2009 c.26 Sch.7 para.54

s.306A, amended: 2009 c.26 Sch.7 para.54, Sch.8 Part 4

s.306AA, added: 2009 c.26 Sch.7 para.55

s.306B, amended: 2009 c.26 Sch.7 para.56

s.306BA, added: 2009 c.26 Sch.7 para.57

s.306C, amended: 2009 c.26 Sch.7 para.58

s.307, applied: SI 2009/470 Reg.80

s.310, applied: SI 2009/470 Reg.80

1986–cont.

45. Insolvency Act 1986–*cont.*

s.314, see *Gresham International Ltd (In Liquidation) v Moonie* [2009] EWHC 1093 (Ch), [2009] 2 B.C.L.C. 256 (Ch D), Peter Smith, J.

s.323, see *Bateman v Williams* [2009] B.P.I.R. 748 (CC (Wrexham)), Judge Jarman Q.C.; see *Richards (A Bankrupt), Re* [2009] EWHC 1760 (Ch), [2009] B.P.I.R. 973 (Ch D (Manchester)), David Richards, J.

s.330, see *Lewis v Metropolitan Property Realisations Ltd* [2008] EWHC 2760 (Ch), [2009] 1 F.L.R. 631 (Ch D), Proudman, J

s.335A, see *Turner v Avis* [2009] 1 F.L.R. 74 (Ch D (Liverpool)), Judge Pelling Q.C.

s.336, see *Haghighat (A Bankrupt), Re* [2009] EWHC 90 (Ch), [2009] 1 F.L.R. 1271 (Ch D), George Bompas Q.C.

s.337, see *Haghighat (A Bankrupt), Re* [2009] EWHC 90 (Ch), [2009] 1 F.L.R. 1271 (Ch D), George Bompas Q.C.

s.339, see *Miller v Bayliss* [2009] EWHC 2063 (Ch), [2009] B.P.I.R. 1438 (Ch D), Alison Foster QC; see *Papanicola v Fagan* [2008] EWHC 3348 (Ch), [2009] B.P.I.R. 320 (Ch D), Judge Raynor QC; see *Tomlinson v Harrington* [2009] B.P.I.R. 331 (Ch D (Bankruptcy Ct)), Registrar Simmonds

s.341, see *Marsh, Re* [2009] B.P.I.R. 834 (CC (Portsmouth)), District Judge Cawood

s.346, see *Nationwide Building Society v Wright* [2009] EWCA Civ 811, [2009] 2 B.C.L.C. 695 (CA (Civ Div)), Maurice Kay, L.J.; see *Tagore Investments SA v Official Receiver* [2008] EWHC 3495 (Ch), [2009] B.P.I.R. 392 (Ch D), Mann, J.

s.363, see *Donaldson v O'Sullivan* [2008] EWCA Civ 879, [2009] 1 W.L.R. 924 (CA (Civ Div)), Ward, L.J.; see *Expandable Ltd v Rubin* [2007] EWHC 2463 (Ch), [2009] B.C.C. 443 (Ch D), Patten, J.

s.366, see *Rottmann, Re* [2008] EWHC 1794 (Ch), [2009] Bus. L.R. 284 (Ch D), Judge Kaye Q.C.

s.367, see *Rottmann, Re* [2008] EWHC 1794 (Ch), [2009] Bus. L.R. 284 (Ch D), Judge Kaye Q.C.

s.375, see *Bailey v Dargue* [2008] EWHC 2903 (Ch), [2009] B.P.I.R. 1 (Ch D (Manchester)), Judge Hodge Q.C.; see *Haghighat (A Bankrupt), Re* [2009] EWHC 934 (Ch), [2009] B.P.I.R. 785 (Ch D), George Bompas Q.C.; see *Revenue and Customs Commissioners v Cassells* [2008] EWHC 3180 (Ch), [2009] S.T.C. 1047 (Ch D), Sir Andrew Morritt (Chancellor)

s.382, see *Wicks v Russell* [2008] EWHC 2713 (Ch), [2009] B.P.I.R. 194 (Ch D (Birmingham)), Judge Purle Q.C.

s.386, varied: 2009 c.1 s.103, s.145

s.387, varied: 2009 c.1 s.103, s.145

s.388, amended: SI 2009/1941 Sch.1 para.78

s.388, applied: SI 2009/214 Sch.1

s.389, varied: 2009 c.1 s.103, s.145

s.389A, amended: SI 2009/1941 Sch.1 para.78, SI 2009/3081 Reg.2

s.389A, enabling: SI 2009/3081

s.390, amended: SI 2009/1941 Sch.1 para.78, SI 2009/3081 Reg.2

s.390, applied: SI 2009/351 r.8, r.31, r.50, r.99, SI 2009/356 r.43, r.106

s.390, varied: 2009 c.1 s.103, s.145

s.390, enabling: SI 2009/3081

s.391, applied: SI 2009/487 Art.4, SI 2009/2477 r.24

85

1986–cont.

45. Insolvency Act 1986–*cont.*
s.391, varied: 2009 c.1 s.145
s.392, enabling: SI 2009/3081
s.393, amended: SI 2009/3081 Reg.2
s.393, applied: SI 2009/3081 Reg.5
s.393, enabling: SI 2009/3081
s.399, applied: SI 2009/214 Sch.1
s.411, amended: 2009 c.1 s.125, s.160, SI 2009/805 Art.13
s.411, applied: 2009 c.1 s.95, s.100, s.107, s.142, s.259, SI 2009/314 Reg.8, SI 2009/356, SI 2009/2469
s.411, enabling: SI 2009/350, SI 2009/351, SI 2009/356, SI 2009/357, SI 2009/482, SI 2009/642, SI 2009/662, SI 2009/806, SI 2009/2375, SI 2009/2469, SI 2009/2472, SI 2009/2477
s.412, see *Trustee in Bankruptcy of St John Poulton v Ministry of Justice* [2009] EWHC 2123 (Ch), [2009] B.P.I.R. 1512 (Ch D), Judge Hazel Marshall Q.C.
s.412, enabling: SI 2009/482, SI 2009/642, SI 2009/2472
s.413, applied: SI 2009/356, SI 2009/642, SI 2009/2469, SI 2009/2472
s.413, disapplied: 2009 c.1 s.125, s.160, SI 2009/805 Art.16
s.414, amended: 2009 c.1 s.126, s.161, SI 2009/805 Art.14
s.414, enabling: SI 2009/487, SI 2009/645
s.415, enabling: SI 2009/645
s.415A, enabling: SI 2009/487, SI 2009/3081
s.418, enabling: SI 2009/465
s.419, enabling: SI 2009/3081
s.420, applied: 2009 c.1 s.132, s.163, s.259
s.421A, see *Wicks v Russell* [2008] EWHC 2713 (Ch), [2009] B.P.I.R. 194 (Ch D (Birmingham)), Judge Purle Q.C.
s.423, see *4 Eng Ltd v Harper* [2009] EWHC 2633 (Ch), Times, November 6, 2009 (Ch D), Sales, J; see *Dornoch Ltd v Westminster International BV* [2009] EWHC 1782 (Admlty), [2009] 2 Lloyd's Rep. 420 (QBD (Admlty)), Tomlinson, J.; see *Giles v Rhind* [2008] EWCA Civ 118, [2009] Ch. 191 (CA (Civ Div)), Buxton, L.J.; see *Papanicola v Fagan* [2008] EWHC 3348 (Ch), [2009] B.P.I.R. 320 (Ch D), Judge Raynor QC; see *Treasury Solicitor v Doveton* [2008] EWHC 2812 (Ch), [2009] B.P.I.R. 352 (Ch D), Mark Herbert Q.C.
s.423, varied: 2009 c.1 s.103, s.145, SI 2009/805 Sch.1 para.13
s.424, varied: 2009 c.1 s.103, s.145, SI 2009/805 Sch.1 para.13
s.425, varied: 2009 c.1 s.103, s.145, SI 2009/805 Sch.1 para.13
s.426, see *Gerrard, Petitioner* [2009] CSOH 76, 2009 S.C. 593 (OH), Lord Glennie; see *SwissAir Schweizerische Luftverkehr-Aktiengesellschaft, Re* [2009] EWHC 2099 (Ch), [2009] B.P.I.R. 1505 (Ch D (Companies Ct)), David Richards, J.
s.426, amended: 2009 c.1 s.129, s.165
s.426, applied: 2009 c.1 s.129, s.165
s.429, applied: SI 2009/26 Sch.1, SI 2009/263 Art.5, SI 2009/442 Art.5, SI 2009/468 Sch.1, SI 2009/1345 Art.5, SI 2009/1355 Sch.1, SI 2009/1808 Art.5, SI 2009/1813 Sch.1, SI 2009/2722 Reg.3
s.430, varied: 2009 c.1 s.103, s.145
s.431, applied: SI 2009/2477 r.128
s.431, varied: 2009 c.1 s.103, s.145
s.432, varied: 2009 c.1 s.103, s.145
s.433, amended: 2009 c.1 s.128, s.162

1986–cont.

45. Insolvency Act 1986–*cont.*
s.433, varied: 2009 c.1 s.103, s.145
s.434D, added: SI 2009/1941 Sch.1 para.81
s.434E, added: SI 2009/1941 Sch.1 para.81
s.435, amended: SI 2009/1941 Sch.1 para.82
s.436, see *Raymond Saul & Co v Holden* [2008] EWHC 2731 (Ch), [2009] Ch. 313 (Ch D), Richard Snowden QC
s.436, amended: SI 2009/1941 Sch.1 para.82
s.436, substituted: SI 2009/1941 Sch.1 para.82
s.436, varied: SI 2009/3056 Sch.1 para.2
s.437, amended: SI 2009/1941 Sch.1 para.83
s.441, disapplied: SI 2009/1941 Sch.1 para.84
Sch.A1 Part I para.3, amended: SI 2009/1941 Sch.1 para.71
Sch.A1 Part III para.12, varied: SI 2009/3056 Sch.1 para.2
Sch.A1 Part III para.13, varied: SI 2009/3056 Sch.1 para.2
Sch.A1 Part III para.14, varied: SI 2009/3056 Sch.1 para.2
Sch.A1 Part III para.15, varied: SI 2009/3056 Sch.1 para.2
Sch.A1 Part III para.16, applied: SI 2009/1801 Reg.63
Sch.A1 Part III para.16, varied: SI 2009/3056 Sch.1 para.2
Sch.A1 Part III para.17, varied: SI 2009/3056 Sch.1 para.2
Sch.A1 Part III para.18, varied: SI 2009/3056 Sch.1 para.2
Sch.A1 Part III para.19, varied: SI 2009/3056 Sch.1 para.2
Sch.A1 Part III para.20, amended: SI 2009/1941 Sch.1 para.71
Sch.A1 Part III para.20, varied: SI 2009/3056 Sch.1 para.2
Sch.A1 Part III para.21, varied: SI 2009/3056 Sch.1 para.2
Sch.A1 Part III para.22, varied: SI 2009/3056 Sch.1 para.2
Sch.A1 Part III para.23, varied: SI 2009/3056 Sch.1 para.2
Sch.A1 Part V para.34, amended: SI 2009/1941 Sch.1 para.71
Sch.B1, see *Kayley Vending Ltd, Re* [2009] EWHC 904 (Ch), [2009] B.C.C. 578 (Ch D (Birmingham)), Judge Cooke; see *Somerfield Stores Ltd v Spring (Sutton Coldfield) Ltd* [2009] EWHC 2384 (Ch), [2009] 48 E.G. 104 (Ch D (Birmingham)), Judge Purle Q.C.; see *William Hare Ltd v Shepherd Construction Ltd* [2009] EWHC 1603 (TCC), [2009] B.L.R. 447 (QBD (TCC)), Coulson, J.
Sch.B1, applied: 2009 c.4 s.10, s.323, SI 2009/1801 Reg.71
Sch.B1, referred to: SI 2009/806 r.40
Sch.B1 Part 1 para.1, varied: SI 2009/357 r.60
Sch.B1 Part 1 para.2, varied: SI 2009/357 r.60
Sch.B1 Part 1 para.3, varied: SI 2009/357 r.60
Sch.B1 Part 1 para.4, varied: SI 2009/357 r.60
Sch.B1 Part 1 para.5, varied: SI 2009/357 r.60
Sch.B1 Part 1 para.6, varied: SI 2009/357 r.60
Sch.B1 Part 1 para.7, varied: SI 2009/357 r.60
Sch.B1 Part 1 para.8, varied: SI 2009/357 r.60
Sch.B1 Part 1 para.9, varied: SI 2009/357 r.60
Sch.B1 Part 2 para.10, applied: SI 2009/1941 Art.8, SI 2009/2472 r.2
Sch.B1 Part 2 para.10, varied: SI 2009/357 r.60

1986–cont.

45. Insolvency Act 1986–*cont.*

Sch.B1 Part 2 para.11, varied: SI 2009/357 r.60

Sch.B1 Part 2 para.12, varied: SI 2009/357 r.60

Sch.B1 Part 2 para.13, varied: SI 2009/357 r.60

Sch.B1 para.3, see *Somerfield Stores Ltd v Spring (Sutton Coldfield) Ltd* [2009] EWHC 2384 (Ch), [2009] 48 E.G.104 (Ch D (Birmingham)), Judge Purle Q.C.

Sch.B1 Part 3 para.14, applied: SI 2009/350 r.13, SI 2009/357 r.12, r.15, SI 2009/853 Reg.1, SI 2009/1941 Art.8, SI 2009/2472 r.2

Sch.B1 Part 3 para.14, varied: SI 2009/357 r.60

Sch.B1 Part 3 para.15, varied: SI 2009/357 r.60

Sch.B1 Part 3 para.16, varied: SI 2009/357 r.60

Sch.B1 Part 3 para.17, varied: SI 2009/357 r.60

Sch.B1 Part 3 para.18, varied: SI 2009/357 r.60

Sch.B1 Part 3 para.19, varied: SI 2009/357 r.60

Sch.B1 Part 3 para.20, varied: SI 2009/357 r.60

Sch.B1 Part 3 para.21, varied: SI 2009/357 r.60

Sch.B1 Part 4 para.22, applied: SI 2009/853 Reg.1, SI 2009/1941 Art.8, SI 2009/2472 r.2

Sch.B1 Part 4 para.22, varied: SI 2009/357 r.60

Sch.B1 Part 4 para.23, varied: SI 2009/357 r.60

Sch.B1 Part 4 para.24, varied: SI 2009/357 r.60

Sch.B1 Part 4 para.25, varied: SI 2009/357 r.60

Sch.B1 Part 4 para.26, varied: SI 2009/357 r.60

Sch.B1 Part 4 para.27, varied: SI 2009/357 r.60

Sch.B1 Part 4 para.28, varied: SI 2009/357 r.60

Sch.B1 Part 4 para.29, varied: SI 2009/357 r.60

Sch.B1 Part 4 para.30, varied: SI 2009/357 r.60

Sch.B1 Part 4 para.31, varied: SI 2009/357 r.60

Sch.B1 Part 4 para.32, varied: SI 2009/357 r.60

Sch.B1 Part 4 para.33, varied: SI 2009/357 r.60

Sch.B1 Part 4 para.34, varied: SI 2009/357 r.60

Sch.B1 Part 5 para.35, varied: SI 2009/357 r.60

Sch.B1 Part 5 para.36, varied: SI 2009/357 r.60

Sch.B1 Part 5 para.37, applied: 2009 c.4 s.323

Sch.B1 Part 5 para.37, varied: SI 2009/357 r.60

Sch.B1 Part 5 para.38, applied: 2009 c.1 s.114, 2009 c.4 s.323

Sch.B1 Part 5 para.38, varied: SI 2009/357 r.60

Sch.B1 Part 5 para.39, varied: SI 2009/357 r.60

Sch.B1 Part 6 para.40, applied: 2009 c.1 s.119

Sch.B1 Part 6 para.40, varied: 2009 c.1 s.145, SI 2009/357 r.60

Sch.B1 Part 6 para.41, varied: 2009 c.1 s.145, SI 2009/357 r.60

Sch.B1 Part 6 para.42, applied: 2009 c.1 s.119

Sch.B1 Part 6 para.42, varied: 2009 c.1 s.145, SI 2009/357 r.60

Sch.B1 Part 6 para.43, varied: 2009 c.1 s.145, SI 2009/357 r.60, SI 2009/3056 Sch.1 para.2

Sch.B1 Part 6 para.44, varied: 2009 c.1 s.145, SI 2009/357 r.60

Sch.B1 Part 6 para.45, applied: SI 2009/1801 Reg.63

Sch.B1 Part 6 para.45, varied: SI 2009/357 r.60

Sch.B1 Part 7 para.46, varied: 2009 c.1 s.145, SI 2009/357 r.60

Sch.B1 Part 7 para.47, varied: 2009 c.1 s.145, SI 2009/357 r.60

Sch.B1 Part 7 para.48, varied: 2009 c.1 s.145, SI 2009/357 r.60

Sch.B1 Part 7 para.49, applied: 2009 c.1 s.147, SI 2009/350 r.21, r.22, r.23, r.25, r.26, SI 2009/357 r.29, r.30, r.31, r.33, r.34, SI 2009/806 r.20, r.21, r.22, r.24, r.25

Sch.B1 Part 7 para.49, referred to: SI 2009/350 r.23

1986–cont.

45. Insolvency Act 1986–*cont.*

Sch.B1 Part 7 para.49, varied: 2009 c.1 s.145, SI 2009/357 r.60

Sch.B1 Part 7 para.50, applied: SI 2009/806 r.41

Sch.B1 Part 7 para.50, referred to: SI 2009/357 r.61

Sch.B1 Part 7 para.50, varied: 2009 c.1 s.145, SI 2009/357 r.60

Sch.B1 Part 7 para.51, applied: SI 2009/806 r.41

Sch.B1 Part 7 para.51, referred to: SI 2009/357 r.61

Sch.B1 Part 7 para.51, varied: 2009 c.1 s.145, SI 2009/357 r.60

Sch.B1 Part 7 para.52, applied: SI 2009/350 r.24, SI 2009/357 r.32, SI 2009/806 r.23, r.41

Sch.B1 Part 7 para.52, referred to: SI 2009/357 r.61

Sch.B1 Part 7 para.52, varied: 2009 c.1 s.145, SI 2009/357 r.60

Sch.B1 Part 7 para.53, applied: SI 2009/806 r.41

Sch.B1 Part 7 para.53, referred to: SI 2009/357 r.61

Sch.B1 Part 7 para.53, varied: 2009 c.1 s.145, SI 2009/357 r.60

Sch.B1 Part 7 para.54, applied: SI 2009/806 r.41

Sch.B1 Part 7 para.54, referred to: SI 2009/357 r.61

Sch.B1 Part 7 para.54, varied: 2009 c.1 s.145, SI 2009/357 r.60

Sch.B1 Part 7 para.55, applied: SI 2009/806 r.41

Sch.B1 Part 7 para.55, referred to: SI 2009/357 r.61

Sch.B1 Part 7 para.55, varied: 2009 c.1 s.145, SI 2009/357 r.60

Sch.B1 Part 7 para.56, applied: SI 2009/806 r.41

Sch.B1 Part 7 para.56, referred to: SI 2009/357 r.61

Sch.B1 Part 7 para.56, varied: 2009 c.1 s.145, SI 2009/357 r.60

Sch.B1 Part 7 para.57, applied: SI 2009/806 r.41

Sch.B1 Part 7 para.57, referred to: SI 2009/357 r.61

Sch.B1 Part 7 para.57, varied: 2009 c.1 s.145, SI 2009/357 r.60

Sch.B1 Part 7 para.58, applied: SI 2009/806 r.41

Sch.B1 Part 7 para.58, referred to: SI 2009/357 r.61

Sch.B1 Part 7 para.58, varied: 2009 c.1 s.145, SI 2009/357 r.60

Sch.B1 Part 8 para.59, varied: 2009 c.1 s.145, SI 2009/357 r.60, SI 2009/805 Sch.1 para.29, SI 2009/3056 Sch.1 para.2

Sch.B1 Part 8 para.60, varied: 2009 c.1 s.145, SI 2009/357 r.60, SI 2009/805 Sch.1 para.29

Sch.B1 Part 8 para.61, varied: 2009 c.1 s.145, SI 2009/357 r.60, SI 2009/805 Sch.1 para.29

Sch.B1 Part 8 para.62, varied: 2009 c.1 s.145, SI 2009/357 r.60, SI 2009/805 Sch.1 para.29

Sch.B1 Part 8 para.63, applied: 2009 c.1 s.138, s.139, s.147

Sch.B1 Part 8 para.63, varied: 2009 c.1 s.145, SI 2009/357 r.60, SI 2009/805 Sch.1 para.29

Sch.B1 Part 8 para.64, varied: 2009 c.1 s.145, SI 2009/357 r.60, SI 2009/805 Sch.1 para.29

Sch.B1 Part 8 para.65, applied: SI 2009/806 r.41

Sch.B1 Part 8 para.65, referred to: SI 2009/357 r.61

Sch.B1 Part 8 para.65, varied: 2009 c.1 s.145, SI 2009/357 r.60

Sch.B1 Part 8 para.66, varied: 2009 c.1 s.145, SI 2009/357 r.60

Sch.B1 Part 8 para.67, varied: 2009 c.1 s.145, SI 2009/357 r.60, SI 2009/3056 Sch.1 para.2

Sch.B1 Part 8 para.68, varied: 2009 c.1 s.145, SI 2009/357 r.60, SI 2009/3056 Sch.1 para.2

Sch.B1 Part 8 para.69, varied: 2009 c.1 s.145, SI 2009/357 r.60

Sch.B1 Part 8 para.70, varied: 2009 c.1 s.145, SI 2009/357 r.60

1986– cont.

45. Insolvency Act 1986–*cont.*

Sch.B1 Part 8 para.71, varied: 2009 c.1 s.145, SI 2009/357 r.60

Sch.B1 Part 8 para.72, varied: 2009 c.1 s.145, SI 2009/357 r.60

Sch.B1 Part 8 para.73, varied: 2009 c.1 s.145, SI 2009/357 r.60

Sch.B1 Part 8 para.74, varied: 2009 c.1 s.145, SI 2009/357 r.60

Sch.B1 Part 8 para.75, varied: 2009 c.1 s.145, SI 2009/357 r.60

Sch.B1 Part 9 para.76, varied: SI 2009/357 r.60

Sch.B1 Part 9 para.77, varied: SI 2009/357 r.60

Sch.B1 Part 9 para.78, varied: SI 2009/357 r.60

Sch.B1 Part 9 para.79, varied: SI 2009/357 r.60

Sch.B1 Part 9 para.80, applied: 2009 c.1 s.153, SI 2009/350 r.25, r.36, SI 2009/357 r.33, r.48, SI 2009/806 r.24, r.35

Sch.B1 Part 9 para.80, referred to: SI 2009/806 r.41

Sch.B1 Part 9 para.80, varied: 2009 c.1 s.145, SI 2009/357 r.60

Sch.B1 Part 9 para.81, varied: SI 2009/357 r.60

Sch.B1 Part 9 para.82, varied: SI 2009/357 r.60

Sch.B1 Part 9 para.83, applied: SI 2009/1941 Art.8, SI 2009/2472 r.2

Sch.B1 Part 9 para.83, varied: SI 2009/357 r.60

Sch.B1 Part 9 para.84, applied: 2009 c.1 s.154, SI 2009/350 r.37, SI 2009/357 r.49, SI 2009/805 Sch.1 para.30

Sch.B1 Part 9 para.84, referred to: SI 2009/350 r.37

Sch.B1 Part 9 para.84, varied: 2009 c.1 s.145, SI 2009/357 r.60

Sch.B1 Part 9 para.85, varied: 2009 c.1 s.145, SI 2009/357 r.60

Sch.B1 Part 9 para.86, varied: 2009 c.1 s.145, SI 2009/357 r.60

Sch.B1 Part 10 para.87, varied: 2009 c.1 s.145, SI 2009/357 r.60

Sch.B1 Part 10 para.88, applied: SI 2009/806 r.41

Sch.B1 Part 10 para.88, referred to: SI 2009/357 r.61

Sch.B1 Part 10 para.88, varied: 2009 c.1 s.145, SI 2009/357 r.60

Sch.B1 Part 10 para.89, varied: 2009 c.1 s.145, SI 2009/357 r.60

Sch.B1 Part 10 para.90, varied: 2009 c.1 s.145, SI 2009/357 r.60

Sch.B1 Part 10 para.91, applied: SI 2009/350 r.31, SI 2009/806 r.30, r.41

Sch.B1 Part 10 para.91, referred to: SI 2009/357 r.39, r.61

Sch.B1 Part 10 para.91, varied: 2009 c.1 s.145, SI 2009/357 r.60

Sch.B1 Part 10 para.91A, varied: SI 2009/357 r.60

Sch.B1 Part 10 para.91B, varied: SI 2009/357 r.60

Sch.B1 Part 10 para.92, varied: SI 2009/357 r.60

Sch.B1 Part 10 para.93, varied: SI 2009/357 r.60

Sch.B1 Part 10 para.94, varied: SI 2009/357 r.60

Sch.B1 Part 10 para.95, varied: SI 2009/357 r.60

Sch.B1 Part 10 para.96, varied: 2009 c.1 s.145, SI 2009/357 r.60

Sch.B1 Part 10 para.97, varied: SI 2009/357 r.60

Sch.B1 Part 10 para.98, varied: 2009 c.1 s.145, SI 2009/357 r.60

Sch.B1 Part 10 para.99, varied: 2009 c.1 s.145, SI 2009/357 r.60

Sch.B1 Part 11 para.100, varied: 2009 c.1 s.145, SI 2009/357 r.60

Sch.B1 Part 11 para.101, varied: 2009 c.1 s.145, SI 2009/357 r.60

1986– cont.

45. Insolvency Act 1986–*cont.*

Sch.B1 Part 11 para.102, varied: 2009 c.1 s.145, SI 2009/357 r.60

Sch.B1 Part 11 para.103, varied: 2009 c.1 s.145, SI 2009/357 r.60

Sch.B1 Part 11 para.104, varied: 2009 c.1 s.145, SI 2009/357 r.60

Sch.B1 Part 11 para.105, varied: SI 2009/357 r.60

Sch.B1 Part 11 para.106, varied: 2009 c.1 s.145, SI 2009/357 r.60

Sch.B1 Part 11 para.107, applied: SI 2009/350 r.23, SI 2009/357 r.31, SI 2009/806 r.22

Sch.B1 Part 11 para.107, varied: 2009 c.1 s.145, SI 2009/357 r.60

Sch.B1 Part 11 para.108, varied: 2009 c.1 s.145, SI 2009/357 r.60

Sch.B1 Part 11 para.109, varied: 2009 c.1 s.145, SI 2009/357 r.60

Sch.B1 Part 11 para.110, varied: 2009 c.1 s.145, SI 2009/357 r.60

Sch.B1 Part 11 para.111, amended: SI 2009/1941 Sch.1 para.72

Sch.B1 Part 11 para.111, varied: 2009 c.1 s.145, SI 2009/357 r.60

Sch.B1 Part 11 para.111A, varied: 2009 c.1 s.145, SI 2009/357 r.60

Sch.B1 Part 11 para.112, varied: 2009 c.1 s.145, SI 2009/357 r.60

Sch.B1 Part 11 para.113, varied: 2009 c.1 s.145, SI 2009/357 r.60

Sch.B1 Part 11 para.114, varied: 2009 c.1 s.145, SI 2009/357 r.60

Sch.B1 Part 11 para.115, varied: 2009 c.1 s.145, SI 2009/357 r.60

Sch.B1 Part 11 para.116, varied: 2009 c.1 s.145, SI 2009/357 r.60

Sch.B1 Part 11 para.117, varied: SI 2009/357 r.60

Sch.B1 Part 11 para.119, varied: SI 2009/357 r.60

Sch.B1 para.13, see *Kayley Vending Ltd, Re* [2009] EWHC 904 (Ch), [2009] B.C.C. 578 (Ch D (Birmingham)), Judge Cooke

Sch.B1 para.43, see *Kaupthing Singer & Friedlander Ltd (In Administration), Re* [2009] EWHC 2308 (Ch), (2009) 153(38) S.J.L.B. 30 (Ch D (Companies Ct)), Norris, J.; see *Somerfield Stores Ltd v Spring (Sutton Coldfield) Ltd* [2009] EWHC 2384 (Ch), [2009] 48 E.G. 104 (Ch D (Birmingham)), Judge Purle Q.C.; see *Sunberry Properties Ltd v Innovate Logistics Ltd (In Administration)* [2008] EWCA Civ 1321, [2009] B.C.C. 164 (CA (Civ Div)), Mummery, L.J.

Sch.B1 para.68, see *Lehman Brothers International (Europe) (In Administration), Re* [2008] EWHC 2869 (Ch), [2009] B.C.C. 632 (Ch D (Companies Ct)), Blackburne, J.

Sch.B1 para.74, see *Lehman Brothers International (Europe) (In Administration), Re* [2008] EWHC 2869 (Ch), [2009] B.C.C. 632 (Ch D (Companies Ct)), Blackburne, J.

Sch.B1 para.88, see *Clydesdale Financial Services v Smailes* [2009] EWHC 1745 (Ch), [2009] B.C.C. 810 (Ch D), David Richards, J.

Sch.1 para.1, varied: 2009 c.1 s.145

Sch.1 para.2, varied: 2009 c.1 s.145

Sch.1 para.3, varied: 2009 c.1 s.145

Sch.1 para.4, varied: 2009 c.1 s.145

Sch.1 para.5, varied: 2009 c.1 s.145

Sch.1 para.6, varied: 2009 c.1 s.145

Sch.1 para.7, varied: 2009 c.1 s.145

1986–cont.

45. Insolvency Act 1986–*cont.*

Sch.1 para.8, varied: 2009 c.1 s.145
Sch.1 para.9, varied: 2009 c.1 s.145
Sch.1 para.10, varied: 2009 c.1 s.145
Sch.1 para.11, varied: 2009 c.1 s.145
Sch.1 para.12, varied: 2009 c.1 s.145
Sch.1 para.13, varied: 2009 c.1 s.145
Sch.1 para.14, varied: 2009 c.1 s.145
Sch.1 para.15, varied: 2009 c.1 s.145
Sch.1 para.16, varied: 2009 c.1 s.145
Sch.1 para.17, varied: 2009 c.1 s.145
Sch.1 para.18, varied: 2009 c.1 s.145
Sch.1 para.19, varied: 2009 c.1 s.145
Sch.1 para.20, varied: 2009 c.1 s.145
Sch.1 para.21, varied: 2009 c.1 s.145
Sch.1 para.22, varied: 2009 c.1 s.145
Sch.1 para.23, varied: 2009 c.1 s.145
Sch.3, see *Gresham International Ltd (In Liquidation) v Moonie* [2009] EWHC 1093 (Ch), [2009] 2 B.C.L.C. 256 (Ch D), Peter Smith, J.
Sch.4, see *Official Receiver v Baars* [2009] B.P.I.R. 524 (Ch D), Registrar Derrett
Sch.4, applied: SI 2009/350 r.42, SI 2009/806 r.41
Sch.4A, applied: SI 2009/263 Art.5, SI 2009/442 Art.5, SI 2009/468 Sch.1, SI 2009/1345 Art.5, SI 2009/1355 Sch.1, SI 2009/1808 Art.5, SI 2009/1813 Sch.1, SI 2009/2722 Reg.3
Sch.4ZB, applied: SI 2009/450 Art.2
Sch.4 Part I para.1, varied: 2009 c.1 s.103
Sch.4 Part I para.2, varied: 2009 c.1 s.103
Sch.4 Part I para.3, varied: 2009 c.1 s.103
Sch.4 Part I para.3A, varied: 2009 c.1 s.103
Sch.4 Part II para.4, varied: 2009 c.1 s.103
Sch.4 Part II para.5, varied: 2009 c.1 s.103
Sch.4 para.3A, see *Gresham International Ltd (In Liquidation) v Moonie* [2009] EWHC 1093 (Ch), [2009] 2 B.C.L.C. 256 (Ch D), Peter Smith, J.
Sch.4 Part III para.6, varied: 2009 c.1 s.103
Sch.4 Part III para.6A, varied: 2009 c.1 s.103
Sch.4 Part III para.7, varied: 2009 c.1 s.103
Sch.4 Part III para.8, varied: 2009 c.1 s.103
Sch.4 Part III para.9, varied: 2009 c.1 s.103
Sch.4 Part III para.10, varied: 2009 c.1 s.103
Sch.4 Part III para.11, varied: 2009 c.1 s.103
Sch.4 Part III para.12, varied: 2009 c.1 s.103
Sch.4 Part III para.13, varied: 2009 c.1 s.103, s.145
Sch.5 para.3, see *Lewis v Metropolitan Property Realisations Ltd* [2008] EWHC 2760 (Ch), [2009] 1 F.L.R. 631 (Ch D), Proudman, J
Sch.5 para.8, see *Lewis v Metropolitan Property Realisations Ltd* [2008] EWHC 2760 (Ch), [2009] 1 F.L.R. 631 (Ch D), Proudman, J
Sch.6 para.1, varied: 2009 c.1 s.103, s.145
Sch.6 para.2, varied: 2009 c.1 s.103, s.145
Sch.6 para.3, varied: 2009 c.1 s.103, s.145
Sch.6 para.3A, varied: 2009 c.1 s.103, s.145
Sch.6 para.3B, varied: 2009 c.1 s.103, s.145
Sch.6 para.3C, varied: 2009 c.1 s.103, s.145
Sch.6 para.3D, varied: 2009 c.1 s.103, s.145
Sch.6 para.4, varied: 2009 c.1 s.103, s.145
Sch.6 para.5, varied: 2009 c.1 s.103, s.146
Sch.6 para.5A, varied: 2009 c.1 s.103, s.145
Sch.6 para.5B, varied: 2009 c.1 s.103, s.145
Sch.6 para.5C, varied: 2009 c.1 s.103, s.145
Sch.6 para.6, varied: 2009 c.1 s.103, s.145
Sch.6 para.7, varied: 2009 c.1 s.103, s.145
Sch.6 para.8, varied: 2009 c.1 s.103, s.145

1986–cont.

45. Insolvency Act 1986–*cont.*

Sch.6 para.9, varied: 2009 c.1 s.103, s.145
Sch.6 para.10, varied: 2009 c.1 s.103, s.145
Sch.6 para.11, varied: 2009 c.1 s.103, s.145
Sch.6 para.12, varied: 2009 c.1 s.103, s.145
Sch.6 para.13, varied: 2009 c.1 s.103, s.145
Sch.6 para.14, varied: 2009 c.1 s.103, s.145
Sch.6 para.15, varied: 2009 c.1 s.103, s.145
Sch.6 para.15A, varied: 2009 c.1 s.103, s.145
Sch.6 para.16, varied: 2009 c.1 s.103, s.145
Sch.8 para.27, amended: 2009 c.1 s.125
Sch.8 para.27, applied: SI 2009/356 r.260, SI 2009/2477 r.119
Sch.8 para.27, enabling: SI 2009/482
Sch.9, see *Trustee in Bankruptcy of St John Poulton v Ministry of Justice* [2009] EWHC 2123 (Ch), [2009] B.P.I.R. 1512 (Ch D), Judge Hazel Marshall Q.C.
Sch.9 para.30, enabling: SI 2009/482
Sch.10, amended: SI 2009/1941 Sch.1 para.80
Sch.10, varied: 2009 c.1 s.103, s.145
Sch.11 Part I para.2, amended: SI 2009/1941 Sch.1 para.83
Sch.11 Part I para.3, amended: SI 2009/1941 Sch.1 para.83
Sch.11 Part I para.4, amended: SI 2009/1941 Sch.1 para.83
Sch.11 Part I para.5, amended: SI 2009/1941 Sch.1 para.83
Sch.11 Part I para.6, amended: SI 2009/1941 Sch.1 para.83
Sch.11 Part I para.7, amended: SI 2009/1941 Sch.1 para.83
Sch.11 Part V para.22, amended: SI 2009/1941 Sch.1 para.83

46. Company Directors Disqualification Act 1986

see *Secretary of State for Business Enterprise and Regulatory Reform v Aaron* [2008] EWCA Civ 1146, [2009] Bus. L.R. 809 (CA (Civ Div)), Buxton, L.J.
applied: SI 2009/26 Sch.1, SI 2009/263 Art.5, SI 2009/314 Reg.8, SI 2009/442 Art.5, SI 2009/457 Reg.9, SI 2009/468 Sch.1, SI 2009/1345 Art.5, SI 2009/1355 Sch.1, SI 2009/1808 Art.5, SI 2009/1813 Sch.1, SI 2009/2722 Reg.3, SSI 2009/352 Sch.1 para.10
referred to: 2009 c.1 s.121
s.3, amended: SI 2009/1941 Sch.1 para.85
s.5, amended: SI 2009/1941 Sch.1 para.85
s.6, see *Official Receiver v Key* [2009] B.C.C. 11 (CC (Nottingham)), District Judge Mithani; see *Secretary of State for Business Enterprise and Regulatory Reform v Aaron* [2008] EWCA Civ 1146, [2009] Bus. L.R. 809 (CA (Civ Div)), Buxton, L.J.; see *Secretary of State for Business, Enterprise and Regulatory Reform v Poulter* [2009] B.C.C. 608 (Ch D), Registrar Derrett; see *Secretary of State for Trade and Industry v Hall* [2006] EWHC 1995 (Ch), [2009] B.C.C. 190 (Ch D (Companies Ct)), Evans-Lombe, J.
s.7, see *Gardiner v Secretary of State for Business Enterprise and Regulatory Reform* [2009] B.C.C. 742 (Ch D (Birmingham)), District Judge Dowling; see *Secretary of State for Business Enterprise and Regulatory Reform v Aaron* [2008] EWCA Civ 1146, [2009] Bus. L.R. 809 (CA (Civ Div)), Buxton, L.J.
s.7, applied: 2009 c.1 s.121, s.155

1986– cont.

46. Company Directors Disqualification Act 1986– *cont.*

s.8, see *Secretary of State for Business Enterprise and Regulatory Reform v Aaron* [2008] EWCA Civ 1146, [2009] Bus. L.R. 809 (CA (Civ Div)), Buxton, L.J.; see *Secretary of State for Business Enterprise and Regulatory Reform v Sullman* [2008] EWHC 3179 (Ch), [2009] 1 B.C.L.C. 397 (Ch D), Norris, J.

s.8, amended: SI 2009/1941 Sch.1 para.85
s.9, repealed (in part): SI 2009/1941 Sch.1 para.85
s.10, amended: SI 2009/1941 Sch.1 para.85
s.11, amended: SI 2009/1941 Sch.1 para.85
s.12, amended: SI 2009/1941 Sch.1 para.85
s.12A, amended: SI 2009/1941 Sch.1 para.85
s.15, amended: SI 2009/1941 Sch.1 para.85
s.18, amended: SI 2009/1941 Sch.1 para.85
s.18, referred to: SI 2009/2471 Reg.9
s.18, enabling: SI 2009/2471
s.20, amended: SI 2009/1941 Sch.1 para.85
s.21, amended: SI 2009/1941 Sch.1 para.85
s.21A, added: 2009 c.1 s.121
s.21B, added: 2009 c.1 s.155
s.21C, added: SI 2009/805 Art.12
s.22, amended: SI 2009/1941 Sch.1 para.85
s.22A, amended: SI 2009/1941 Sch.1 para.85
s.22B, amended: SI 2009/1941 Sch.1 para.85
s.22C, amended: SI 2009/1941 Sch.1 para.85
s.22D, added: SI 2009/1941 Sch.1 para.85
Sch.1 Part I para.1, amended: SI 2009/1941 Sch.1 para.85
Sch.1 Part I para.3, amended: SI 2009/1941 Sch.1 para.85
Sch.1 Part I para.4, substituted: SI 2009/1941 Sch.1 para.85
Sch.1 Part I para.4A, substituted: SI 2009/1941 Sch.1 para.85
Sch.1 Part I para.5A, repealed: SI 2009/1941 Sch.1 para.85
Sch.1 Part II para.8, amended: SI 2009/1941 Sch.1 para.85
Sch.1 Part II para.9, amended: SI 2009/1941 Sch.1 para.85
Sch.1 Part II para.10, amended: SI 2009/1941 Sch.1 para.85
Sch.2 Part 1 para.7, amended: SI 2009/1941 Sch.1 para.85
Sch.3 para.1, amended: SI 2009/1941 Sch.1 para.85

47. Legal Aid (Scotland) Act 1986

s.8, amended: SSI 2009/143 Reg.4
s.11, amended: SSI 2009/143 Reg.4
s.11, applied: SSI 2009/143 Reg.6, Reg.7
s.11, enabling: SSI 2009/143
s.12, enabling: SSI 2009/49
s.15, amended: SSI 2009/143 Reg.4
s.17, amended: SSI 2009/143 Reg.4
s.17, applied: SSI 2009/143 Reg.5
s.17, enabling: SSI 2009/49, SSI 2009/143
s.18, see *West of Scotland Housing Association Ltd v Daly* 2009 Hous. L.R. 101 (Sh Ct (Glasgow)), Sheriff Principal J A Taylor
s.19, see *Young v Bohannon* [2009] CSOH 90, 2009 S.L.T. 928 (OH), Lord Brodie
s.33, enabling: SSI 2009/203, SSI 2009/312
s.34, applied: SSI 2009/17 Art.2
s.36, enabling: SSI 2009/143, SSI 2009/203, SSI 2009/312
s.37, applied: SSI 2009/143

1986– cont.

50. Social Security Act 1986

s.63, varied: SI 2009/497 Art.4
Sch.10 Part I para.35, repealed: 2009 c.24 Sch.7 Part 1
Sch.10 Part I para.36, repealed: 2009 c.24 Sch.7 Part 1

52. Dockyard Services Act 1986

s.1, amended: SI 2009/1941 Sch.1 para.86

53. Building Societies Act 1986

applied: 2009 c.1 s.87, SI 2009/509 Art.3, SI 2009/805 Sch.1 para.5, SI 2009/2997 Reg.10
referred to: 2009 c.1 s.130, s.158, s.251
s.5, disapplied: SI 2009/805 Sch.1 para.29
s.6, disapplied: SI 2009/805 Sch.1 para.29
s.7, disapplied: SI 2009/805 Sch.1 para.29
s.9B, referred to: 2009 c.1 s.251
s.54, repealed (in part): SI 2009/1941 Sch.1 para.87
s.57, amended: SI 2009/1941 Sch.1 para.87
s.65, amended: SI 2009/1941 Sch.1 para.87
s.70, amended: SI 2009/1941 Sch.1 para.87
s.75, enabling: SI 2009/1391
s.81, applied: SI 2009/509 Art.7
s.85, applied: SI 2009/805 Sch.1 para.32
s.86, amended: SI 2009/805 Art.7
s.88, amended: SI 2009/805 Art.4
s.88, varied: SI 2009/805 Sch.1 para.20
s.89A, added: SI 2009/805 Art.5
s.90, applied: SI 2009/806 r.40
s.90B, applied: 2009 c.1 s.86, s.259
s.90C, added: SI 2009/805 Art.2
s.90C, applied: SI 2009/805 Sch.1 para.1, Sch.1 para.6, Sch.1 para.24, SI 2009/806 r.40, SI 2009/814 Art.11
s.90C, referred to: SI 2009/805 Sch.1 para.2, Sch.1 para.32
s.90D, added: SI 2009/805 Art.6
s.90D, applied: SI 2009/806 r.13
s.90E, added: SI 2009/805 Art.6
s.91, amended: SI 2009/805 Art.8
s.92, amended: SI 2009/805 Art.9
s.93, disapplied: 2009 c.1 s.84
s.94, disapplied: 2009 c.1 s.84
s.95, disapplied: 2009 c.1 s.84
s.96, disapplied: 2009 c.1 s.84
s.97, amended: SI 2009/1941 Sch.1 para.87
s.97, applied: 2009 c.4 s.824, SI 2009/509 Art.7
s.97, disapplied: 2009 c.1 s.84
s.97, varied: SI 2009/509 Art.4, Art.6, Art.8, Art.11, Art.12
s.98, disapplied: 2009 c.1 s.84
s.98, varied: SI 2009/509 Art.9
s.99, disapplied: 2009 c.1 s.84
s.99A, disapplied: 2009 c.1 s.84
s.100, disapplied: 2009 c.1 s.84
s.100, varied: SI 2009/509 Art.10
s.100A, disapplied: 2009 c.1 s.84
s.100A, varied: SI 2009/509 Art.11
s.101, disapplied: 2009 c.1 s.84
s.101, varied: SI 2009/509 Art.12
s.101A, disapplied: 2009 c.1 s.84
s.101A, varied: SI 2009/509 Art.12
s.102, amended: SI 2009/1941 Sch.1 para.87
s.102, disapplied: 2009 c.1 s.84
s.102A, disapplied: 2009 c.1 s.84
s.102B, disapplied: 2009 c.1 s.84
s.102B, varied: SI 2009/509 Art.13
s.102C, disapplied: 2009 c.1 s.84
s.102C, repealed (in part): SI 2009/1941 Sch.2

1986–cont.

53. Building Societies Act 1986–cont.
s.102C, varied: SI 2009/509 Art.13
s.102D, disapplied: 2009 c.1 s.84
s.103, amended: SI 2009/805 Art.10
s.104A, amended: SI 2009/1941 Sch.1 para.87
s.107, amended: SI 2009/1941 Sch.1 para.87
s.110, amended: SI 2009/1941 Sch.1 para.87
s.119, amended: SI 2009/805 Art.11, SI 2009/1941 Sch.1 para.87
s.119, applied: 2009 c.1 s.87, s.130, s.158, SI 2009/774 Art.5, SI 2009/814 Art.11
Sch.2 Part III para.30, varied: SI 2009/509 Art.5
Sch.15A, applied: SI 2009/806 r.40
Sch.15 Part I para.2, amended: SI 2009/1941 Sch.1 para.87
Sch.15 Part IV para.57, amended: SI 2009/1941 Sch.1 para.87
Sch.15A Part I para.1, amended: SI 2009/1941 Sch.1 para.87
Sch.15A Part II para.16, amended: SI 2009/1941 Sch.1 para.87
Sch.15A Part III para.38, amended: SI 2009/1941 Sch.1 para.87
Sch.17 Part I para.3, referred to: SI 2009/509 Art.18

55. Family Law Act 1986
see *B v B* 2009 S.L.T. (Sh Ct) 24 (Sh Ct (Tayside) (Dunfermline)), Sheriff I D Dunbar; see *Westminster City Council v C* [2008] EWCA Civ 198, [2009] Fam. 11 (CA (Civ Div)), Thorpe, L.J.
s.15, see *B v B* 2009 S.L.T. (Sh Ct) 24 (Sh Ct (Tayside) (Dunfermline)), Sheriff I D Dunbar
s.58, see *Hudson v Leigh* [2009] EWHC 1306 (Fam), [2009] 2 F.L.R. 1129 (Fam Div), Bodey, J.
s.60, see *Practice Direction (Fam Div: Family Proceedings: Allocation of Appeals)* [2009] 1 W.L.R. 1107 (Fam Div), Sir Mark Potter (President, Fam)
s.60, amended: SI 2009/871 Art.6

56. Parliamentary Constituencies Act 1986
s.3, applied: SI 2009/698
s.4, enabling: SI 2009/698

60. Financial Services Act 1986
referred to: SI 2009/500 Sch.1 Part 1
s.54, see *Financial Services Compensation Scheme Ltd v Abbey National Treasury Services Plc* [2008] EWHC 1897 (Ch), [2009] Bus. L.R. 465 (Ch D), David Richards, J.

62. Salmon Act 1986
s.24, amended: SSI 2009/85 Sch.2 para.7
s.32, amended: 2009 c.23 s.229, Sch.22 Part 5
s.32, repealed (in part): 2009 c.23 Sch.22 Part 5
s.33, repealed (in part): 2009 c.23 Sch.22 Part 5
s.37, repealed: 2009 c.23 Sch.22 Part 4
s.38, repealed: SI 2009/463 Sch.2 para.7
Sch.4 para.6, repealed (in part): SI 2009/463 Sch.2 para.7, SSI 2009/85 Sch.2 para.7

64. Public Order Act 1986
s.5, see *DPP v Dykes* [2008] EWHC 2775 (Admin), (2009) 173 J.P. 88 (QBD (Admin)), Calvert-Smith, J.
s.5, applied: SI 2009/2773 Sch.2, SI 2009/2781 Sch.2

1987

4. Ministry of Defence Police Act 1987
applied: SI 2009/1609 Reg.2
s.1, enabling: SI 2009/1609

1987–cont.

4. Ministry of Defence Police Act 1987–cont.
s.2, applied: SI 2009/3050 Art.3
s.3A, enabling: SI 2009/3069
s.4, enabling: SI 2009/3069
s.4A, enabling: SI 2009/3070

9. Animals (Scotland) Act 1987
s.1, see *Welsh v Brady* [2009] CSIH 60, 2009 S.L.T. 747 (IH (Ex Div)), Lord Nimmo Smith

12. Petroleum Act 1987
s.21, applied: SI 2009/1374 Art.2, SI 2009/2099 Art.2, SI 2009/2927 Art.2
s.22, enabling: SI 2009/1374, SI 2009/2099, SI 2009/2927
s.24, applied: SI 2009/2099(b), SI 2009/1374(b), SI 2009/2927

16. Finance Act 1987
s.62, amended: SI 2009/56 Sch.1 para.127
s.63, amended: SI 2009/56 Sch.1 para.128
s.63, substituted: 2009 c.10 Sch.39 para.2
s.66, amended: SI 2009/56 Sch.1 para.129
Sch.12 para.1, substituted: 2009 c.10 Sch.39 para.3
Sch.12 para.2, substituted: 2009 c.10 Sch.39 para.3
Sch.12 para.3, amended: 2009 c.10 Sch.39 para.3, SI 2009/56 Sch.1 para.130
Sch.12 para.4, repealed: 2009 c.10 Sch.39 para.3
Sch.14 Part I para.2, amended: SI 2009/56 Sch.1 para.131

18. Debtors (Scotland) Act 1987
applied: SI 2009/470 Reg.51
referred to: SI 2009/3024 Art.5
Part IIIA, applied: SSI 2009/67 Art.6
s.1, applied: SI 2009/3024 Art.5
s.5, applied: SI 2009/3024 Art.5
s.15, see *McCormack v Hamilton Academical Football Club Ltd* [2009] CSIH 16, 2009 S.C. 313 (IH (Ex Div)), Lord Wheatley
s.15K, see *McCormack v Hamilton Academical Football Club Ltd* [2009] CSIH 16, 2009 S.C. 313 (IH (Ex Div)), Lord Wheatley
s.49, enabling: SSI 2009/98, SSI 2009/133, SSI 2009/395
s.53, amended: SSI 2009/98 Reg.2, SSI 2009/395 Reg.2
s.53, enabling: SSI 2009/98, SSI 2009/133, SSI 2009/395
s.63, amended: SSI 2009/98 Reg.2, SSI 2009/395 Reg.2
s.63, enabling: SSI 2009/98, SSI 2009/133, SSI 2009/395
s.73B, applied: SSI 2009/68 Reg.4
s.73B, enabling: SSI 2009/68
s.73C, enabling: SSI 2009/104, SSI 2009/107
s.73D, varied: SSI 2009/110 Reg.2
s.73G, applied: SSI 2009/68 Reg.4
s.73G, varied: SSI 2009/110 Reg.2
s.73G, enabling: SSI 2009/68
s.73H, applied: SSI 2009/66 Art.3
s.73J, varied: SSI 2009/110 Reg.2
s.73M, applied: SSI 2009/66 Art.4
s.73M, enabling: SSI 2009/107
s.73Q, applied: SSI 2009/66 Art.5
s.73Q, enabling: SSI 2009/107
s.73S, applied: SSI 2009/68 Reg.4
s.73S, enabling: SSI 2009/68
s.106, referred to: SI 2009/3024 Art.5
Sch.2, amended: SSI 2009/98 Sch.1, SSI 2009/395 Sch.1

26. Housing (Scotland) Act 1987
Part IV, applied: SSI 2009/122 Art.5, Art.6, Art.7

1987– cont.

26. Housing (Scotland) Act 1987–*cont.*
Part XIII, applied: SSI 2009/ 122 Art.7
Part I, see *EA (Nigeria) v Secretary of State for the Home Department* [2009] Imm. A.R. 242 (AIT), CMG Ockelton (Deputy President)
s.52, see *McCreight v West Lothian Council* [2009] CSIH 4, 2009 S.C. 258 (IH (2 Div)), The Lord Justice Clerk (Gill)
s.68, see *Fotheringham v Hillcrest Housing Association Ltd* 2009 Hous. L.R. 99 (Lands Tr (Scot)), J N Wright, QC
s.71, see *McCreight v West Lothian Council* [2009] CSIH 4, 2009 S.C. 258 (IH (2 Div)), The Lord Justice Clerk (Gill)
s.88, applied: SSI 2009/ 122 Art.7
s.89, disapplied: SSI 2009/ 122 Art.4
s.90, disapplied: SSI 2009/ 122 Art.4
s.91, disapplied: SSI 2009/ 122 Art.4
s.92, disapplied: SSI 2009/ 122 Art.4
s.93, disapplied: SSI 2009/ 122 Art.4
s.94, disapplied: SSI 2009/ 122 Art.4
s.95, disapplied: SSI 2009/ 122 Art.4
s.96, disapplied: SSI 2009/ 122 Art.4
s.97, disapplied: SSI 2009/ 122 Art.4
s.98, disapplied: SSI 2009/ 122 Art.4
s.99, disapplied: SSI 2009/ 122 Art.4
s.100, disapplied: SSI 2009/ 122 Art.4
s.101, disapplied: SSI 2009/ 122 Art.4
s.102, disapplied: SSI 2009/ 122 Art.4
s.103, disapplied: SSI 2009/ 122 Art.4
s.104, disapplied: SSI 2009/ 122 Art.4
s.105, disapplied: SSI 2009/ 122 Art.4
s.106, disapplied: SSI 2009/ 122 Art.4
s.113, see *Todd v Clapperton* [2009] CSOH 112, 2009 S.L.T. 837 (OH), Lord Bannatyne
s.135, see *Glasgow Housing Association Ltd v Du* 2009 Hous. L.R. 91 (Sh Ct (Glasgow)), Temporary Sheriff Principal C G McKay
s.191, enabling: SSI 2009/ 139
s.192, enabling: SSI 2009/ 139
s.204, enabling: SSI 2009/ 43
s.236, disapplied: SSI 2009/ 122 Art.5
s.236A, disapplied: SSI 2009/ 122 Art.5
s.237, disapplied: SSI 2009/ 122 Art.5
s.237A, disapplied: SSI 2009/ 122 Art.5
s.238, disapplied: SSI 2009/ 122 Art.5
s.239, disapplied: SSI 2009/ 122 Art.5
s.239A, disapplied: SSI 2009/ 122 Art.5
s.240, disapplied: SSI 2009/ 122 Art.5
s.240A, disapplied: SSI 2009/ 122 Art.5
s.240B, disapplied: SSI 2009/ 122 Art.5
s.241, disapplied: SSI 2009/ 122 Art.5
s.242, disapplied: SSI 2009/ 122 Art.5
s.243, disapplied: SSI 2009/ 122 Art.5
s.244, disapplied: SSI 2009/ 122 Art.6
s.245, disapplied: SSI 2009/ 122 Art.5
s.246, disapplied: SSI 2009/ 122 Art.5
s.247, disapplied: SSI 2009/ 122 Art.5
s.248, disapplied: SSI 2009/ 122 Art.5
s.249, disapplied: SSI 2009/ 122 Art.5
s.250, disapplied: SSI 2009/ 122 Art.5
s.250A, disapplied: SSI 2009/ 122 Art.5
s.251, disapplied: SSI 2009/ 122 Art.5
s.252, disapplied: SSI 2009/ 122 Art.5
s.253, disapplied: SSI 2009/ 122 Art.5
s.254, disapplied: SSI 2009/ 122 Art.5
s.255, disapplied: SSI 2009/ 122 Art.5
s.256, disapplied: SSI 2009/ 122 Art.5

1987– cont.

26. Housing (Scotland) Act 1987–*cont.*
s.256A, disapplied: SSI 2009/ 122 Art.5
s.311, applied: SSI 2009/ 122 Art.7
s.313, applied: SSI 2009/ 319 Art.3
Sch.2 para.7, see *Robb v Tayside Joint Police Board* 2009 S.L.T. (Lands Tr) 23 (Lands Tr (Scot)), J N Wright QC
Sch.8, disapplied: SSI 2009/ 122 Art.4
Sch.8 Part I, applied: SSI 2009/ 122 Art.7
Sch.10 para.1, see *Todd v Clapperton* [2009] CSOH 112, 2009 S.L.T. 837 (OH), Lord Bannatyne
Sch.15 Part II para.3, applied: SSI 2009/ 139 Sch.1 para.2
Sch.19, disapplied: SSI 2009/ 122 Art.4, Art.5, Art.6

31. Landlord and Tenant Act 1987
applied: SI 2009/ 2767 Sch.1
Part IV, applied: SI 2009/ 2767 Sch.1
s.12D, amended: SI 2009/ 1307 Sch.1 para.181
s.14, amended: SI 2009/ 1307 Sch.1 para.182
s.20, amended: SI 2009/ 1941 Sch.1 para.88
s.33, amended: SI 2009/ 1307 Sch.1 para.183
s.34, amended: SI 2009/ 1307 Sch.1 para.184
s.58, amended: 2009 c.20 Sch.6 para.72

34. Motor Cycle Noise Act 1987
referred to: SI 2009/ 669 Sch.1 Part 2

38. Criminal Justice Act 1987
s.3, amended: SI 2009/ 1941 Sch.1 para.89

41. Criminal Justice (Scotland) Act 1987
s.54, amended: SI 2009/ 1941 Sch.1 para.90

43. Consumer Protection Act 1987
applied: SI 2009/ 2824 Reg.6
referred to: SI 2009/ 669 Sch.1 Part 2
Part II, referred to: SI 2009/ 669 Sch.2 Part 1
Part III, referred to: SI 2009/ 669 Sch.2 Part 1
s.11, applied: SI 2009/ 716 Reg.14, SI 2009/ 1347, SI 2009/ 2824 Reg.6, SI 2009/ 3367
s.11, enabling: SI 2009/ 796, SI 2009/ 1346, SI 2009/ 1347, SI 2009/ 2562, SI 2009/ 2824, SI 2009/ 3367
s.12, applied: SI 2009/ 716 Reg.14
s.12, disapplied: SI 2009/ 2824 Reg.6

45. Parliamentary and other Pensions Act 1987
referred to: 2009 c.13 s.5
s.2, enabling: SI 2009/ 1920, SI 2009/ 3154

49. Territorial Sea Act 1987
s.3, repealed (in part): 2009 c.23 Sch.22 Part 3
Sch.1 para.3, repealed: 2009 c.23 Sch.22 Part 5
Sch.1 para.6, repealed: 2009 c.23 Sch.22 Part 3

51. Finance (No.2) Act 1987
s.102, applied: SI 2009/ 711, SI 2009/ 711 Art.3, Art.4, Art.5, Art.6, Art.7, Art.8, Art.9
s.102, enabling: SI 2009/ 711

53. Channel Tunnel Act 1987
s.11, amended: SI 2009/ 1941 Sch.1 para.91
s.11, enabling: SI 2009/ 2081
s.46, amended: SI 2009/ 1307 Sch.1 para.186
Sch.5 Part III para.3, amended: SI 2009/ 1307 Sch.1 para.187
Sch.5 Part III para.6, amended: SI 2009/ 1307 Sch.1 para.187
Sch.5 Part III para.8, amended: SI 2009/ 1307 Sch.1 para.187

1988

1. Income and Corporation Taxes Act 1988
see *PA Holdings Ltd v Revenue and Customs Commissioners* [2009] UKFTT 95 (TC), [2009] S.F.T.D. 209 (FTT (Tax)), David

1988–cont.

1. Income and Corporation Taxes Act 1988–*cont.*

see–*cont.*

Williams (Chairman); see *Paycheck Services 3 Ltd, Re* [2008] EWHC 2200 (Ch), [2009] Bus. L.R. 1 (Ch D (Companies Ct)), Mark Cawson Q.C.

Part II, applied: SI 2009/2034 Reg.15

Part VI c.I, referred to: 2009 c.4 s.533

Part VI c.II, referred to: 2009 c.4 s.533

Part VI c.III, referred to: 2009 c.4 s.533

Part VII c.I, applied: SI 2009/1555 Sch.4 para.5, SI 2009/2158 Reg.10, SI 2009/3359 Sch.2 para.4

Part VII c.I, referred to: SI 2009/2737 Sch.5 para.5, Sch.6 para.4

Part X c.II, amended: 2009 c.4 Sch.1 para.108

Part X c.II, applied: 2009 c.4 s.39, s.264, s.269

Part X c.IV, applied: 2009 c.4 s.521D, s.39, s.371, s.530, s.1082, s.1211

Part XI, applied: 2009 c.4 s.784

Part XII c.I, applied: 2009 c.4 s.931W

Part XII c.V, applied: 2009 c.4 s.461

Part XIII c.II, applied: 2009 c.4 s.567

Part XVII c.IV, applied: 2009 c.4 s.486D, s.521E, s.486E, s.870, 2009 c.10 Sch.16 para.7, Sch.16 para.14, Sch.16 para.15

Part XVII c.V, applied: 2009 c.10 Sch.22 para.6, SI 2009/3001 Sch.1 para.5

Part XVIII, applied: 2009 c.4 s.931H, s.931J, s.931R, s.793, 2009 c.10 Sch.16 para.7

Part XVIII, referred to: 2009 c.4 s.533

s.6, amended: 2009 c.4 Sch.3 Part 1

s.6, repealed (in part): 2009 c.4 Sch.3 Part 1

s.7, applied: 2009 c.4 s.971

s.8, repealed: 2009 c.4 Sch.3 Part 1

s.9, see *Sun Life Assurance Co of Canada (UK) Ltd v Revenue and Customs Commissioners* [2009] EWHC 60 (Ch), [2009] S.T.C. 768 (Ch D), Patten, J.

s.9, amended: 2009 c.4 Sch.3 Part 1

s.9, repealed (in part): 2009 c.4 Sch.3 Part 1

s.11, repealed (in part): 2009 c.4 Sch.3 Part 1

s.11AA, repealed: 2009 c.4 Sch.3 Part 1

s.12, repealed (in part): 2009 c.4 Sch.3 Part 1

s.13, amended: 2009 c.10 Sch.14 para.3

s.13, referred to: 2009 c.10 s.8

s.15, repealed: 2009 c.4 Sch.3 Part 1

s.16, see *Morgan v Revenue and Customs Commissioners* [2009] UKFTT 78 (TC), [2009] S.F.T.D. 160 (FTT (Tax)), Nuala Brice (Chairman)

s.18, see *Morgan v Revenue and Customs Commissioners* [2009] UKFTT 78 (TC), [2009] S.F.T.D. 160 (FTT (Tax)), Nuala Brice (Chairman); see *Test Claimants in the FII Group Litigation v Revenue and Customs Commissioners* [2008] EWHC 2893 (Ch), [2009] S.T.C. 254 (Ch D), Henderson, J.

s.18, repealed: 2009 c.4 Sch.3 Part 1

s.19, see *Genovese v Revenue and Customs Commissioners* [2009] S.T.C. (S.C.D.) 373 (Sp Comm), John Clark; see *PA Holdings Ltd v Revenue and Customs Commissioners* [2009] UKFTT 95 (TC), [2009] S.F.T.D. 209 (FTT (Tax)), David Williams (Chairman)

s.20, see *PA Holdings Ltd v Revenue and Customs Commissioners* [2009] UKFTT 95 (TC), [2009] S.F.T.D. 209 (FTT (Tax)), David Williams (Chairman)

s.21A, repealed: 2009 c.4 Sch.3 Part 1

s.21B, repealed: 2009 c.4 Sch.3 Part 1

1988–cont.

1. Income and Corporation Taxes Act 1988–*cont.*

s.21C, repealed: 2009 c.4 Sch.3 Part 1

s.23, varied: 2009 c.10 Sch.6 para.1

s.24, amended: 2009 c.4 Sch.1 para.13, Sch.3 Part 1

s.24, referred to: 2009 c.10 Sch.6 para.1

s.24, repealed (in part): 2009 c.4 Sch.3 Part 1

s.25, varied: 2009 c.10 Sch.6 para.1

s.30, repealed: 2009 c.4 Sch.3 Part 1

s.31ZA, repealed: 2009 c.4 Sch.3 Part 1

s.31ZB, repealed: 2009 c.4 Sch.3 Part 1

s.31ZC, repealed: 2009 c.4 Sch.3 Part 1

s.34, repealed: 2009 c.4 Sch.3 Part 1

s.35, repealed: 2009 c.4 Sch.3 Part 1

s.36, repealed: 2009 c.4 Sch.3 Part 1

s.37, repealed: 2009 c.4 Sch.3 Part 1

s.37A, repealed: 2009 c.4 Sch.3 Part 1

s.38, repealed: 2009 c.4 Sch.3 Part 1

s.39, repealed: 2009 c.4 Sch.3 Part 1

s.40, repealed: 2009 c.4 Sch.3 Part 1

s.42, amended: 2009 c.4 Sch.1 para.18, SI 2009/56 Sch.1 para.133

s.42, repealed (in part): 2009 c.4 Sch.3 Part 1

s.46, repealed: 2009 c.4 Sch.3 Part 1

s.53, repealed: 2009 c.4 Sch.3 Part 1

s.55, repealed: 2009 c.4 Sch.3 Part 1

s.56, amended: 2009 c.4 Sch.1 para.22

s.70, repealed: 2009 c.4 Sch.3 Part 1

s.70A, repealed: 2009 c.4 Sch.3 Part 1

s.72, see *RIG Holdings LP v Aeroflex Test Solutions Ltd (formerly IFR Systems Ltd)* [2009] EWHC 1440 (QB), [2009] S.T.C. 2521 (QBD), Jack, J.

s.72, repealed: 2009 c.4 Sch.3 Part 1

s.74, see *Morgan v Revenue and Customs Commissioners* [2009] UKFTT 78 (TC), [2009] S.F.T.D. 160 (FTT (Tax)), Nuala Brice (Chairman)

s.74, repealed: 2009 c.4 Sch.3 Part 1

s.75, see *Dawsongroup Ltd v Revenue and Customs Commissioners* [2009] UKFTT 137 (TC), [2009] S.F.T.D. 435 (FTT (Tax)), Colin Bishopp

s.75, repealed: 2009 c.4 Sch.3 Part 1

s.75A, repealed: 2009 c.4 Sch.3 Part 1

s.75B, repealed: 2009 c.4 Sch.3 Part 1

s.76, amended: 2009 c.4 Sch.1 para.30, Sch.3 Part 1, 2009 c.10 Sch.7 para.24

s.76, applied: 2009 c.4 s.383, s.985, s.999, s.1013, s.1021, s.1080, s.1153, s.1158, s.1162, s.1168, s.1297, s.1298, s.1304

s.76, referred to: 2009 c.4 s.390, s.391, s.1161

s.76A, repealed: 2009 c.4 Sch.3 Part 1

s.76B, repealed: 2009 c.4 Sch.3 Part 1

s.76ZA, added: 2009 c.4 Sch.1 para.31

s.76ZB, added: 2009 c.4 Sch.1 para.32

s.76ZC, added: 2009 c.4 Sch.1 para.33

s.76ZD, added: 2009 c.4 Sch.1 para.34

s.76ZE, added: 2009 c.4 Sch.1 para.35

s.76ZE, repealed (in part): SI 2009/2035 Sch.1 para.12

s.76ZF, added: 2009 c.4 Sch.1 para.36

s.76ZG, added: 2009 c.4 Sch.1 para.37

s.76ZH, added: 2009 c.4 Sch.1 para.38

s.76ZI, added: 2009 c.4 Sch.1 para.39

s.76ZJ, added: 2009 c.4 Sch.1 para.40

s.76ZK, added: 2009 c.4 Sch.1 para.41

s.76ZL, added: 2009 c.4 Sch.1 para.42

s.76ZL, applied: 2009 c.4 s.1288

s.76ZM, added: 2009 c.4 Sch.1 para.43

s.76ZN, added: 2009 c.4 Sch.1 para.44

1988– cont.

1988– cont.

1. Income and Corporation Taxes Act 1988– *cont.*
s.76ZN, amended: 2009 c.10 Sch.11 para.60
s.76ZN, repealed (in part): 2009 c.10 Sch.11 para.60
s.76ZO, added: 2009 c.4 Sch.1 para.45
s.76ZO, repealed: 2009 c.10 Sch.11 para.61
s.79, repealed: 2009 c.4 Sch.3 Part 1
s.79A, repealed: 2009 c.4 Sch.3 Part 1
s.79B, repealed: 2009 c.4 Sch.3 Part 1
s.82A, repealed: 2009 c.4 Sch.3 Part 1
s.82B, repealed: 2009 c.4 Sch.3 Part 1
s.83, repealed: 2009 c.4 Sch.3 Part 1
s.83A, repealed: 2009 c.4 Sch.3 Part 1
s.84, repealed: 2009 c.4 Sch.3 Part 1
s.84A, amended: 2009 c.4 Sch.3 Part 1
s.84A, repealed (in part): 2009 c.4 Sch.3 Part 1
s.85, repealed: 2009 c.4 Sch.3 Part 1
s.85A, repealed: 2009 c.4 Sch.3 Part 1
s.85B, repealed: 2009 c.4 Sch.3 Part 1
s.86, repealed: 2009 c.4 Sch.3 Part 1
s.86A, repealed: 2009 c.4 Sch.3 Part 1
s.87, repealed: 2009 c.4 Sch.3 Part 1
s.87A, repealed: 2009 c.4 Sch.3 Part 1
s.88, repealed: 2009 c.4 Sch.3 Part 1
s.88D, repealed: 2009 c.4 Sch.3 Part 1
s.89, repealed: 2009 c.4 Sch.3 Part 1
s.90, repealed: 2009 c.4 Sch.3 Part 1
s.91, repealed: 2009 c.4 Sch.3 Part 1
s.91A, repealed: 2009 c.4 Sch.3 Part 1
s.91B, repealed: 2009 c.4 Sch.3 Part 1
s.91BA, repealed: 2009 c.4 Sch.3 Part 1
s.91C, repealed: 2009 c.4 Sch.3 Part 1
s.92, repealed: 2009 c.4 Sch.3 Part 1
s.93, repealed: 2009 c.4 Sch.3 Part 1
s.94, repealed: 2009 c.4 Sch.3 Part 1
s.95, repealed: 2009 c.4 Sch.3 Part 1
s.95ZA, amended: 2009 c.4 Sch.1 para.75, 2009 c.10 Sch.14 para.5
s.97, repealed: 2009 c.4 Sch.3 Part 1
s.98, repealed: 2009 c.4 Sch.3 Part 1
s.99, repealed: 2009 c.4 Sch.3 Part 1
s.100, see *Revenue and Customs Commissioners v Micro Fusion 2004-1 LLP* [2009] EWHC 1082 (Ch), [2009] S.T.C. 1741 (Ch D), Davis, J.
s.100, repealed: 2009 c.4 Sch.3 Part 1
s.101, repealed: 2009 c.4 Sch.3 Part 1
s.102, amended: SI 2009/56 Sch.1 para.134
s.102, repealed: 2009 c.4 Sch.3 Part 1
s.103, repealed: 2009 c.4 Sch.3 Part 1
s.104, repealed: 2009 c.4 Sch.3 Part 1
s.105, repealed: 2009 c.4 Sch.3 Part 1
s.106, repealed: 2009 c.4 Sch.3 Part 1
s.110, repealed: 2009 c.4 Sch.3 Part 1
s.111, see *Morgan v Revenue and Customs Commissioners* [2009] UKFTT 78 (TC), [2009] S.F.T.D. 160 (FTT (Tax)), Nuala Brice (Chairman)
s.111, repealed (in part): 2009 c.4 Sch.3 Part 1
s.114, repealed: 2009 c.4 Sch.3 Part 1
s.115, repealed: 2009 c.4 Sch.3 Part 1
s.116, amended: 2009 c.4 Sch.1 para.86
s.116, referred to: 2009 c.4 s.1256
s.116, repealed (in part): 2009 c.4 Sch.3 Part 1
s.118ZA, repealed: 2009 c.4 Sch.3 Part 1
s.119, see *Bute v Revenue and Customs Commissioners* [2009] CSIH 42, [2009] S.T.C. 2138 (IH (Ex Div)), Lord Osborne
s.119, repealed: 2009 c.4 Sch.3 Part 1
s.120, repealed: 2009 c.4 Sch.3 Part 1

1. Income and Corporation Taxes Act 1988– *cont.*
s.121, repealed: 2009 c.4 Sch.3 Part 1
s.122, see *Bute v Revenue and Customs Commissioners* [2009] CSIH 42, [2009] S.T.C. 2138 (IH (Ex Div)), Lord Osborne
s.122, repealed: 2009 c.4 Sch.3 Part 1
s.125, repealed: 2009 c.4 Sch.3 Part 1
s.128, repealed (in part): 2009 c.4 Sch.3 Part 1
s.130, see *Dawsongroup Ltd v Revenue and Customs Commissioners* [2009] UKFTT 137 (TC), [2009] S.F.T.D. 435 (FTT (Tax)), Colin Bishopp
s.130, amended: 2009 c.4 Sch.1 para.94, Sch.3 Part 1
s.144A, see *Chilcott v Revenue and Customs Commissioners* [2009] S.T.C. (S.C.D.) 148 (Sp Comm), John Clark
s.152, amended: SI 2009/56 Sch.1 para.135
s.152, applied: SI 2009/275 Art.3
s.152, repealed (in part): SI 2009/56 Sch.1 para.135
s.154, see *Smith v Revenue and Customs Commissioners* [2009] UKFTT 210 (TC), [2009] S.F.T.D. 731 (FTT (Tax)), Nuala Brice
s.162, see *Smith v Revenue and Customs Commissioners* [2009] UKFTT 210 (TC), [2009] S.F.T.D. 731 (FTT (Tax)), Nuala Brice
s.168, see *Smith v Revenue and Customs Commissioners* [2009] UKFTT 210 (TC), [2009] S.F.T.D. 731 (FTT (Tax)), Nuala Brice
s.187, amended: 2009 c.4 Sch.1 para.95
s.198, see *Revenue and Customs Commissioners v Banerjee* [2009] EWHC 1229 (Ch), [2009] 3 All E.R. 930 (Ch D), Henderson, J.; see *Revenue and Customs Commissioners v Banerjee* [2009] EWHC 62 (Ch), [2009] 3 All E.R. 915 (Ch D), Henderson, J.
s.208, see *Test Claimants in the FII Group Litigation v Revenue and Customs Commissioners* [2008] EWHC 2893 (Ch), [2009] S.T.C. 254 (Ch D), Henderson, J.
s.208, repealed: 2009 c.4 Sch.3 Part 1
s.209, amended: 2009 c.4 Sch.1 para.97
s.209, referred to: 2009 c.4 s.448, s.465, s.931B, s.931D
s.212, amended: 2009 c.4 Sch.1 para.98
s.213, amended: SI 2009/2797 Reg.2
s.213, applied: 2009 c.4 s.345, s.346
s.213, referred to: 2009 c.4 s.631, s.632, SI 2009/2797 Reg.1
s.213A, applied: 2009 c.4 s.345, s.346
s.213A, referred to: 2009 c.4 s.631, s.632
s.214, amended: 2009 c.4 Sch.1 para.99
s.214, applied: 2009 c.4 s.346
s.215, amended: SI 2009/56 Sch.1 para.136
s.215, applied: SI 2009/275 Art.3
s.217, repealed (in part): SI 2009/2035 Sch.1 para.13
s.226, repealed (in part): SI 2009/2035 Sch.1 para.14
s.230A, added: 2009 c.4 Sch.1 para.100
s.230A, applied: 2009 c.4 s.132
s.231, amended: 2009 c.10 Sch.14 para.6
s.231AA, amended: 2009 c.4 Sch.1 para.101
s.231AB, amended: 2009 c.4 Sch.1 para.102
s.234, amended: SI 2009/2035 Sch.1 para.15
s.234A, amended: SI 2009/1890 Art.3
s.234A, applied: SI 2009/2034 Reg.21, Reg.23
s.234A, disapplied: 2009 c.8 s.9
s.250, repealed (in part): SI 2009/2035 Sch.1 para.16
s.252, referred to: 2009 c.10 Sch.53 para.6
s.256, repealed: 2009 c.10 Sch.1 para.2

1988–cont.

1. Income and Corporation Taxes Act 1988–*cont.*
s.256A, repealed: 2009 c.10 Sch.1 para.2
s.256B, repealed: 2009 c.10 Sch.1 para.2
s.257, amended: 2009 c.10 s.3
s.257, referred to: 2009 c.10 s.3
s.257, repealed: 2009 c.10 Sch.1 para.2
s.257A, see *Adams v Revenue and Customs Commissioners* [2009] UKFTT 80 (TC), [2009] S.F.T.D. 184 (FTT (Tax)), Theodore Wallace
s.257A, repealed: 2009 c.10 Sch.1 para.2
s.257AA, repealed: 2009 c.10 Sch.1 para.2
s.257AB, repealed: 2009 c.10 Sch.1 para.2
s.257B, repealed: 2009 c.10 Sch.1 para.2
s.257BA, repealed: 2009 c.10 Sch.1 para.2
s.257BB, repealed: 2009 c.10 Sch.1 para.2
s.257C, disapplied: 2009 c.10 s.3
s.257C, repealed: 2009 c.10 Sch.1 para.2
s.258, see *Adams v Revenue and Customs Commissioners* [2009] UKFTT 80 (TC), [2009] S.F.T.D. 184 (FTT (Tax)), Theodore Wallace
s.265, repealed: 2009 c.10 Sch.1 para.2
s.266, amended: 2009 c.10 Sch.1 para.3
s.266, repealed (in part): 2009 c.10 Sch.1 para.3
s.270, see *Paycheck Services 3 Ltd, Re* [2008] EWHC 2200 (Ch), [2009] Bus. L.R. 1 (Ch D (Companies Ct)), Mark Cawson Q.C.
s.272, repealed (in part): SI 2009/2035 Sch.1 para.17
s.273, applied: SI 2009/1555 Sch.4 para.4, Sch.4 para.5, SI 2009/2158 Reg.9, Reg.10, SI 2009/2737 Sch.5 para.4, Sch.5 para.5, Sch.6 para.3, Sch.6 para.4, SI 2009/3359 Sch.2 para.3, Sch.2 para.4
s.273, repealed: 2009 c.10 Sch.1 para.2
s.274, amended: 2009 c.10 Sch.1 para.4
s.274, repealed (in part): 2009 c.10 Sch.1 para.4
s.278, repealed: 2009 c.10 Sch.1 para.2
s.307, applied: 2009 c.4 s.540
s.336, see *Grace v Revenue and Customs Commissioners* [2008] EWHC 2708 (Ch), [2009] S.T.C. 213 (Ch D), Lewison, J.; see *Grace v Revenue and Customs Commissioners* [2009] EWCA Civ 1082, [2009] S.T.C. 2707 (CA (Civ Div)), Waller, L.J.
s.337, repealed: 2009 c.4 Sch.3 Part 1
s.337A, amended: 2009 c.4 Sch.1 para.104
s.337A, repealed (in part): 2009 c.4 Sch.3 Part 1
s.338, applied: 2009 c.4 s.463
s.342, amended: 2009 c.4 Sch.1 para.105
s.342A, amended: 2009 c.4 Sch.1 para.106
s.343, amended: 2009 c.4 Sch.1 para.107, SI 2009/56 Sch.1 para.137
s.343, repealed (in part): SI 2009/56 Sch.1 para.137
s.375, applied: 2009 c.10 Sch.54 para.8
s.375, referred to: 2009 c.10 Sch.54 para.8
s.376A, amended: SI 2009/56 Sch.1 para.138
s.378, amended: SI 2009/56 Sch.1 para.139
s.392A, amended: 2009 c.4 Sch.1 para.108
s.392A, applied: 2009 c.4 s.461, s.1153, s.1158
s.392A, referred to: 2009 c.4 s.1223
s.392B, amended: 2009 c.4 Sch.1 para.109
s.393, see *Sun Life Assurance Co of Canada (UK) Ltd v Revenue and Customs Commissioners* [2009] EWHC 60 (Ch), [2009] S.T.C. 768 (Ch D), Patten, J.
s.393, amended: 2009 c.4 Sch.1 para.110

1988–cont.

1. Income and Corporation Taxes Act 1988–*cont.*
s.393, applied: 2009 c.4 s.1048, s.1056, s.1062, s.1096, s.1105, s.1111, s.1153, s.1158, s.1209, s.1210, s.1211, SI 2009/2971 Reg.4
s.393A, amended: 2009 c.4 Sch.1 para.111, 2009 c.10 s.62
s.393A, applied: 2009 c.4 s.461, s.463, s.1048, s.1056, s.1096, s.1105, s.1153, s.1210, 2009 c.10 Sch.6 para.3, SI 2009/2971 Reg.4
s.393A, disapplied: SI 2009/2971 Reg.4
s.393A, varied: 2009 c.10 Sch.6 para.3
s.393B, applied: 2009 c.4 s.1048, s.1056
s.396, amended: 2009 c.4 Sch.1 para.112, SI 2009/3001 Reg.126
s.397, amended: 2009 c.4 Sch.1 para.113, SI 2009/2860 Art.3
s.398, amended: 2009 c.4 Sch.1 para.114
s.399, amended: 2009 c.4 Sch.3 Part 1
s.399, repealed (in part): 2009 c.4 Sch.3 Part 1
s.400, amended: 2009 c.4 Sch.1 para.116
s.400, applied: 2009 c.4 s.326
s.400, referred to: 2009 c.4 s.464
s.401, repealed: 2009 c.4 Sch.3 Part 1
s.402, applied: 2009 c.4 s.443
s.403, amended: 2009 c.4 Sch.1 para.118
s.403, applied: 2009 c.4 s.443, s.457, s.1048, s.1056, s.1105, s.1153, s.1210
s.403, referred to: 2009 c.4 s.753
s.403C, applied: 2009 c.4 s.364
s.403D, see *Philips Electronics UK Ltd v Revenue and Customs Commissioners* [2009] UKFTT 226 (TC) (FTT (Tax)), John F Avery Jones
s.403ZC, amended: 2009 c.4 Sch.1 para.119
s.403ZD, amended: 2009 c.4 Sch.1 para.120
s.403ZE, amended: 2009 c.4 Sch.1 para.121
s.404, amended: 2009 c.4 Sch.1 para.122
s.404, applied: 2009 c.4 s.775, s.793, s.818
s.406, see *Philips Electronics UK Ltd v Revenue and Customs Commissioners* [2009] UKFTT 226 (TC) (FTT (Tax)), John F Avery Jones
s.407, amended: 2009 c.4 Sch.1 para.123
s.411, see *Philips Electronics UK Ltd v Revenue and Customs Commissioners* [2009] UKFTT 226 (TC) (FTT (Tax)), John F Avery Jones
s.411ZA, added: 2009 c.4 Sch.1 para.124
s.413, applied: 2009 c.4 s.371
s.413, referred to: 2009 c.4 s.521D, s.371, s.530, 2009 c.10 Sch.15 para.86
s.414, amended: 2009 c.4 Sch.3 Part 1
s.414, varied: 2009 c.4 s.376
s.416, see *Kellogg Brown & Root Holdings (UK) Ltd v Revenue and Customs Commissioners* [2009] EWHC 584 (Ch), [2009] S.T.C. 1359 (Ch D), Sir Andrew Morritt (Chancellor)
s.416, applied: 2009 c.4 s.784
s.416, referred to: SI 2009/2034 Reg.15
s.416, varied: SI 2009/2813 Sch.1
s.417, applied: 2009 c.4 s.519, 2009 c.10 Sch.15 para.82
s.417, referred to: SI 2009/2813 Sch.1
s.419, applied: 2009 c.10 Sch.55 para.24
s.431, amended: 2009 c.4 Sch.1 para.126, Sch.3 Part 1
s.431G, amended: 2009 c.4 Sch.1 para.127
s.431H, amended: 2009 c.4 Sch.1 para.128
s.432A, amended: 2009 c.4 Sch.1 para.130
s.432A, varied: 2009 c.4 s.393
s.432AA, amended: 2009 c.4 Sch.1 para.131
s.432AA, applied: 2009 c.4 s.203, s.1153

1. Income and Corporation Taxes Act 1988–*cont.*
s.432AB, amended: 2009 c.4 Sch.1 para.132
s.432AB, applied: 2009 c.4 s.1153
s.432AB, referred to: 2009 c.4 s.1158
s.432E, amended: 2009 c.10 Sch.23 para.5
s.432YA, amended: 2009 c.4 Sch.1 para.129
s.432ZA, applied: 2009 c.4 s.394
s.434, amended: 2009 c.4 Sch.1 para.133
s.434A, amended: 2009 c.4 Sch.1 para.134, Sch.3 Part 1
s.434AZA, added: 2009 c.10 Sch.23 para.3
s.434AZA, referred to: 2009 c.10 Sch.23 para.3
s.434AZB, added: 2009 c.10 Sch.23 para.3
s.434AZC, added: 2009 c.10 Sch.23 para.3
s.436A, amended: 2009 c.4 Sch.1 para.135
s.440, amended: 2009 c.4 Sch.1 para.136
s.440, referred to: 2009 c.4 s.336, s.337, s.636
s.440A, amended: 2009 c.4 Sch.1 para.137
s.440B, amended: 2009 c.4 Sch.1 para.138
s.440C, amended: 2009 c.4 Sch.1 para.139
s.442, amended: 2009 c.4 Sch.1 para.140
s.442A, amended: 2009 c.4 Sch.1 para.141
s.444A, amended: SI 2009/56 Sch.1 para.140
s.444AB, referred to: 2009 c.10 s.47
s.444ABD, amended: 2009 c.4 Sch.1 para.144
s.444AEA, amended: 2009 c.4 Sch.1 para.145, Sch.3 Part 1
s.444AEB, amended: 2009 c.4 Sch.1 para.146
s.444AEC, amended: 2009 c.4 Sch.1 para.147
s.444AECA, amended: 2009 c.4 Sch.1 para.148, Sch.3 Part 1
s.444AECB, amended: 2009 c.4 Sch.1 para.149
s.444AECC, amended: 2009 c.4 Sch.1 para.150
s.444AED, amended: 2009 c.4 Sch.1 para.151, SI 2009/56 Sch.1 para.143
s.444AF, amended: 2009 c.4 Sch.1 para.152, Sch.3 Part 1
s.444AH, amended: 2009 c.4 Sch.1 para.153
s.444AK, amended: 2009 c.4 Sch.1 para.154
s.444AZA, amended: 2009 c.4 Sch.1 para.142, Sch.3 Part 1, SI 2009/56 Sch.1 para.141
s.444AZB, amended: 2009 c.4 Sch.1 para.143, Sch.3 Part 1, SI 2009/56 Sch.1 para.142
s.444BA, amended: 2009 c.4 Sch.1 para.155
s.444BA, applied: SI 2009/2039 Reg.3, Reg.5
s.444BA, referred to: SI 2009/2039 Reg.3
s.444BA, varied: SI 2009/2039 Reg.4
s.444BB, amended: 2009 c.4 Sch.1 para.156
s.444BC, amended: SI 2009/1890 Art.5
s.461, amended: SI 2009/56 Sch.1 para.144
s.461A, applied: 2009 c.4 s.775, s.793, s.818
s.461C, amended: SI 2009/56 Sch.1 para.145
s.465, amended: SI 2009/56 Sch.1 para.146
s.468, applied: 2009 c.4 s.493
s.468A, applied: 2009 c.4 s.493
s.469, amended: SI 2009/23 Art.2
s.469, repealed (in part): 2009 c.4 Sch.3 Part 1, SI 2009/23 Art.2
s.472A, repealed: 2009 c.4 Sch.3 Part 1
s.473, repealed: 2009 c.4 Sch.3 Part 1
s.475, amended: 2009 c.4 Sch.1 para.160, Sch.3 Part 1
s.475, repealed (in part): 2009 c.4 Sch.3 Part 1
s.477A, referred to: 2009 c.4 s.465
s.477A, repealed (in part): 2009 c.4 Sch.3 Part 1
s.477B, repealed: 2009 c.4 Sch.3 Part 1
s.486, amended: 2009 c.4 Sch.3 Part 1
s.486, applied: SI 2009/2971 Reg.30

1. Income and Corporation Taxes Act 1988–*cont.*
s.486, referred to: 2009 c.4 s.465
s.486, repealed (in part): 2009 c.4 Sch.3 Part 1
s.487, repealed: 2009 c.4 Sch.3 Part 1
s.488, applied: 2009 c.4 s.260
s.491, repealed: 2009 c.4 Sch.3 Part 1
s.492, amended: 2009 c.4 Sch.1 para.166
s.494, amended: 2009 c.4 Sch.1 para.167
s.494, applied: 2009 c.4 s.297
s.494, referred to: 2009 c.4 s.464
s.494A, amended: 2009 c.4 Sch.1 para.169
s.494AA, amended: 2009 c.4 Sch.1 para.168
s.500, amended: 2009 c.4 Sch.1 para.170
s.501A, amended: 2009 c.4 Sch.1 para.171, 2009 c.10 s.90
s.502, amended: 2009 c.10 Sch.45 para.4
s.502, referred to: 2009 c.10 Sch.15 para.59, Sch.15 para.74
s.502B, applied: 2009 c.10 Sch.33 para.6
s.502B, disapplied: 2009 c.10 Sch.33 para.5
s.502C, disapplied: 2009 c.10 Sch.33 para.7
s.502D, applied: 2009 c.10 Sch.33 para.8
s.502GD, added: 2009 c.10 Sch.33 para.1
s.503, amended: 2009 c.4 Sch.1 para.172
s.503, applied: 2009 c.4 s.264
s.504, repealed: 2009 c.4 Sch.3 Part 1
s.505, amended: 2009 c.4 Sch.1 para.174, Sch.3 Part 1, 2009 c.10 Sch.14 para.4, SI 2009/3001 Reg.126
s.505, repealed (in part): 2009 c.4 Sch.3 Part 1, 2009 c.10 Sch.14 para.4
s.506, applied: SI 2009/548 Art.10, SI 2009/549 Art.10
s.506A, amended: SI 2009/1029 Reg.2
s.506C, amended: 2009 c.4 Sch.1 para.175, SI 2009/56 Sch.1 para.147
s.506C, enabling: SI 2009/1029
s.508, applied: 2009 c.4 s.88
s.509, repealed: 2009 c.4 Sch.3 Part 1
s.510A, amended: 2009 c.4 Sch.1 para.177
s.518, amended: 2009 c.4 Sch.1 para.178
s.524, repealed: 2009 c.4 Sch.3 Part 1
s.525, repealed: 2009 c.4 Sch.3 Part 1
s.526, repealed: 2009 c.4 Sch.3 Part 1
s.528, repealed: 2009 c.4 Sch.3 Part 1
s.531, repealed: 2009 c.4 Sch.3 Part 1
s.532, repealed: 2009 c.4 Sch.3 Part 1
s.533, repealed: 2009 c.4 Sch.3 Part 1
s.539, see *Mayes v Revenue and Customs Commissioners* [2009] S.T.C. (S.C.D.) 181 (Sp Comm), David Williams
s.541, see *Drummond v Revenue and Customs Commissioners* [2009] EWCA Civ 608, [2009] S.T.C. 2206 (CA (Civ Div)), Arden, L.J.; see *Smith v Revenue and Customs Commissioners* [2009] S.T.C. (S.C.D.) 132 (Sp Comm), Theodore Wallace
s.549, see *Mayes v Revenue and Customs Commissioners* [2009] S.T.C. (S.C.D.) 181 (Sp Comm), David Williams
s.552A, amended: SI 2009/56 Sch.1 para.148
s.554, see *Mayes v Revenue and Customs Commissioners* [2009] S.T.C. (S.C.D.) 181 (Sp Comm), David Williams
s.556, repealed: 2009 c.4 Sch.1 para.186
s.558, repealed (in part): 2009 c.4 Sch.3 Part 1
s.566, applied: SI 2009/470 Reg.59
s.568, amended: 2009 c.4 Sch.1 para.188, Sch.3 Part 1
s.570, amended: 2009 c.4 Sch.1 para.189

1988–cont.

1. Income and Corporation Taxes Act 1988–*cont.*

s.571, amended: 2009 c.4 Sch.1 para.190, Sch.3 Part 1

s.576D, amended: SI 2009/2859 Art.2

s.577, repealed: 2009 c.4 Sch.3 Part 1

s.577A, repealed: 2009 c.4 Sch.3 Part 1

s.578, repealed: 2009 c.4 Sch.3 Part 1

s.578A, amended: 2009 c.10 Sch.11 para.62

s.578A, repealed (in part): 2009 c.4 Sch.3 Part 1, 2009 c.10 Sch.11 para.62

s.578B, amended: 2009 c.10 Sch.11 para.63

s.578B, repealed (in part): 2009 c.4 Sch.3 Part 1, 2009 c.10 Sch.11 para.63

s.579, repealed: 2009 c.4 Sch.3 Part 1

s.580, repealed: 2009 c.4 Sch.3 Part 1

s.582, repealed: 2009 c.4 Sch.3 Part 1

s.584, repealed (in part): 2009 c.4 Sch.3 Part 1, SI 2009/56 Sch.1 para.149

s.586, repealed: 2009 c.4 Sch.3 Part 1

s.587, repealed: 2009 c.4 Sch.3 Part 1

s.587B, amended: 2009 c.4 Sch.1 para.199, SI 2009/3001 Reg.126

s.587B, referred to: 2009 c.4 s.1223, s.1262

s.588, repealed: 2009 c.4 Sch.3 Part 1

s.589A, repealed: 2009 c.4 Sch.3 Part 1

s.589B, repealed (in part): 2009 c.4 Sch.3 Part 1

s.591C, see *Thorpe v Revenue and Customs Commissioners* [2009] EWHC 611 (Ch), [2009] S.T.C. 2107 (Ch D), Sir Edward Evans-Lombe

s.596A, see *Thorpe v Revenue and Customs Commissioners* [2009] EWHC 611 (Ch), [2009] S.T.C. 2107 (Ch D), Sir Edward Evans-Lombe

s.600, see *Thorpe v Revenue and Customs Commissioners* [2009] EWHC 611 (Ch), [2009] S.T.C. 2107 (Ch D), Sir Edward Evans-Lombe

s.615, applied: 2009 c.4 s.1290

s.617, repealed: 2009 c.4 Sch.3 Part 1

s.660A, see *Buck v Revenue and Customs Commissioners* [2009] S.T.C. (S.C.D.) 6 (Sp Comm), Stephen Oliver Q.C.; see *Eyretel Unapproved Pension Scheme Trustees v Revenue and Customs Commissioners* [2009] S.T.C. (S.C.D.) 17 (Sp Comm), JF Avery Jones (Chairman)

s.660B, see *Bird v Revenue and Customs Commissioners* [2009] S.T.C. (S.C.D.) 81 (Sp Comm), Sir Stephen Oliver Q.C.

s.660G, see *Bird v Revenue and Customs Commissioners* [2009] S.T.C. (S.C.D.) 81 (Sp Comm), Sir Stephen Oliver Q.C.; see *Buck v Revenue and Customs Commissioners* [2009] S.T.C. (S.C.D.) 6 (Sp Comm), Stephen Oliver Q.C.

s.686, see *Eyretel Unapproved Pension Scheme Trustees v Revenue and Customs Commissioners* [2009] S.T.C. (S.C.D.) 17 (Sp Comm), JF Avery Jones (Chairman); see *Peter Clay Discretionary Trust Trustees v Revenue and Customs Commissioners* [2008] EWCA Civ 1441, [2009] Ch. 296 (CA (Civ Div)), Arden, L.J.

s.687A, referred to: 2009 c.4 s.976

s.695, repealed: 2009 c.4 Sch.3 Part 1

s.696, repealed: 2009 c.4 Sch.3 Part 1

s.697, repealed: 2009 c.4 Sch.3 Part 1

s.698, repealed: 2009 c.4 Sch.3 Part 1

s.699A, repealed: 2009 c.4 Sch.3 Part 1

s.700, amended: 2009 c.4 Sch.1 para.209, Sch.3 Part 1

s.700, repealed (in part): 2009 c.4 Sch.3 Part 1, SI 2009/2035 Sch.1 para.18

1. Income and Corporation Taxes Act 1988–*cont.*

s.701, repealed: 2009 c.4 Sch.3 Part 1

s.702, repealed: 2009 c.4 Sch.3 Part 1

s.703, see *Ebsworth v Revenue and Customs Commissioners* [2009] UKFTT 199 (TC), [2009] S.F.T.D. 602 (FTT (Tax)), Adrian Shipwright; see *Grogan v Revenue and Customs Commissioners* [2009] UKFTT 238 (TC) (FTT (Tax)), Theodore Wallace

s.703, amended: 2009 c.4 Sch.3 Part 1, SI 2009/56 Sch.1 para.150

s.704, see *Ebsworth v Revenue and Customs Commissioners* [2009] UKFTT 199 (TC), [2009] S.F.T.D. 602 (FTT (Tax)), Adrian Shipwright

s.705, amended: SI 2009/56 Sch.1 para.151

s.705, repealed (in part): SI 2009/56 Sch.1 para.151

s.705A, repealed: SI 2009/56 Sch.1 para.152

s.705B, repealed: SI 2009/56 Sch.1 para.152

s.706, applied: SI 2009/56 Art.5, SI 2009/196 Art.9

s.706, repealed: SI 2009/56 Sch.1 para.152

s.708, repealed: SI 2009/2035 Sch.1 para.19

s.709, see *Ebsworth v Revenue and Customs Commissioners* [2009] UKFTT 199 (TC), [2009] S.F.T.D. 602 (FTT (Tax)), Adrian Shipwright

s.709, amended: 2009 c.4 Sch.1 para.213, SI 2009/56 Sch.1 para.153

s.728, repealed: SI 2009/2035 Sch.1 para.20

s.730, see *Revenue and Customs Commissioners v Mercury Tax Group Ltd* [2009] S.T.C. (S.C.D.) 307 (Sp Comm), John F Avery Jones

s.730, amended: 2009 c.4 Sch.1 para.214

s.730, repealed: 2009 c.10 Sch.25 para.9

s.730A, see *DCC Holdings (UK) Ltd v Revenue and Customs Commissioners* [2008] EWHC 2429 (Ch), [2009] S.T.C. 77 (Ch D), Norris, J.

s.736B, amended: 2009 c.4 Sch.1 para.215, 2009 c.10 Sch.29 para.2

s.736B, applied: 2009 c.4 s.541

s.736B, referred to: 2009 c.4 s.539

s.736B, repealed (in part): 2009 c.10 Sch.24 para.9

s.736C, amended: 2009 c.4 Sch.1 para.216

s.736C, repealed: 2009 c.10 Sch.24 para.8

s.736D, repealed: 2009 c.10 Sch.24 para.8

s.739, see *Burns v Revenue and Customs Commissioners* [2009] S.T.C. (S.C.D.) 165 (Sp Comm), Howard M Nowlan

s.741, see *Burns v Revenue and Customs Commissioners* [2009] S.T.C. (S.C.D.) 165 (Sp Comm), Howard M Nowlan

s.747, see *Vodafone 2 v Revenue and Customs Commissioners* [2008] EWHC 1569 (Ch), [2009] Ch. 123 (Ch D), Evans-Lombe, J.

s.747, amended: 2009 c.4 Sch.1 para.217, 2009 c.10 Sch.16 para.22

s.747, applied: 2009 c.4 s.521E, s.870

s.748, see *Vodafone 2 v Revenue and Customs Commissioners* [2008] EWHC 1569 (Ch), [2009] Ch. 123 (Ch D), Evans-Lombe, J.

s.748, applied: 2009 c.4 s.521E

s.748, repealed (in part): 2009 c.10 Sch.16 para.1

s.749, amended: 2009 c.10 Sch.16 para.22

s.749A, amended: 2009 c.10 Sch.16 para.22

s.750, amended: 2009 c.10 Sch.16 para.22

s.751, amended: 2009 c.4 Sch.1 para.218

s.751AA, added: 2009 c.10 Sch.16 para.23

s.751B, amended: 2009 c.10 Sch.16 para.24, SI 2009/56 Sch.1 para.154

1988–cont.

1. Income and Corporation Taxes Act 1988–*cont.*
s.752, applied: 2009 c.4 s.521E
s.754, amended: SI 2009/56 Sch.1 para.155
s.754, repealed (in part): SI 2009/56 Sch.1 para.155, SI 2009/2035 Sch.1 para.21
s.754A, repealed: 2009 c.10 Sch.16 para.2
s.755A, amended: 2009 c.4 Sch.1 para.219
s.755B, amended: SI 2009/1890 Art.5
s.755D, applied: 2009 c.4 s.486E, s.931E
s.755D, varied: 2009 c.4 s.931E
s.756, see *Vodafone 2 v Revenue and Customs Commissioners* [2008] EWHC 1569 (Ch), [2009] Ch. 123 (Ch D), Evans-Lombe, J.
s.756A, repealed: SI 2009/3001 Sch.2
s.756B, repealed: SI 2009/3001 Sch.2
s.756C, repealed: SI 2009/3001 Sch.2
s.757, repealed: SI 2009/3001 Sch.2
s.758, repealed: SI 2009/3001 Sch.2
s.759, applied: SI 2009/3001 Reg.30, Reg.43
s.759, repealed: SI 2009/3001 Sch.2
s.760, repealed: SI 2009/3001 Sch.2
s.761, amended: 2009 c.4 Sch.1 para.220
s.761, repealed: SI 2009/3001 Sch.2
s.762, repealed: SI 2009/3001 Sch.2
s.762A, repealed: SI 2009/3001 Sch.2
s.762ZA, repealed: SI 2009/3001 Sch.2
s.762ZB, repealed: SI 2009/3001 Sch.2
s.763, repealed: SI 2009/3001 Sch.2
s.764, repealed: SI 2009/3001 Sch.2
s.765, repealed: 2009 c.10 Sch.17 para.1
s.765A, repealed: 2009 c.10 Sch.17 para.1
s.766, repealed: 2009 c.10 Sch.17 para.1
s.767, repealed: 2009 c.10 Sch.17 para.1
s.767C, applied: SI 2009/404 Art.6
s.768B, amended: 2009 c.4 Sch.1 para.221, Sch.3 Part 1
s.768C, amended: 2009 c.4 Sch.1 para.222, Sch.3 Part 1
s.768D, amended: 2009 c.4 Sch.1 para.223
s.768E, amended: 2009 c.4 Sch.1 para.224
s.770, see *DSG Retail Ltd v Revenue and Customs Commissioners* [2009] UKFTT 31 (TC), [2009] S.T.C. (S.C.D.) 397 (Sp Comm), John F Avery Jones
s.774, amended: 2009 c.4 Sch.1 para.225
s.774, repealed (in part): SI 2009/2035 Sch.1 para.22
s.774A, applied: 2009 c.10 Sch.25 para.4
s.774B, amended: 2009 c.4 Sch.1 para.226
s.774C, applied: 2009 c.10 Sch.25 para.4
s.774D, amended: 2009 c.4 Sch.1 para.227
s.774E, amended: 2009 c.4 Sch.1 para.228, 2009 c.10 Sch.25 para.9
s.774G, amended: 2009 c.4 Sch.1 para.229
s.775A, amended: 2009 c.4 Sch.1 para.230
s.775A, repealed: 2009 c.10 Sch.25 para.9
s.776, amended: 2009 c.4 Sch.1 para.231
s.777, amended: SI 2009/2859 Art.2
s.779, amended: 2009 c.4 Sch.1 para.232, Sch.3 Part 1
s.779, repealed (in part): 2009 c.4 Sch.3 Part 1
s.780, amended: 2009 c.4 Sch.1 para.233
s.781, amended: 2009 c.4 Sch.1 para.234, Sch.3 Part 1
s.782, amended: 2009 c.4 Sch.3 Part 1
s.783, amended: SI 2009/56 Sch.1 para.156
s.783, repealed (in part): SI 2009/56 Sch.1 para.156
s.785, amended: 2009 c.4 Sch.1 para.236

1988–cont.

1. Income and Corporation Taxes Act 1988–*cont.*
s.785A, repealed: 2009 c.10 Sch.25 para.9
s.785C, amended: 2009 c.4 Sch.1 para.239, 2009 c.10 Sch.32 para.9
s.785C, repealed (in part): 2009 c.10 Sch.32 para.9
s.785C, varied: 2009 c.10 Sch.32 para.11
s.785D, amended: 2009 c.4 Sch.1 para.240
s.785ZA, amended: 2009 c.4 Sch.1 para.237
s.785ZB, amended: 2009 c.4 Sch.1 para.238, 2009 c.10 Sch.25 para.9, SI 2009/2860 Art.3
s.786, amended: 2009 c.4 Sch.1 para.241, 2009 c.10 Sch.25 para.9
s.787, amended: 2009 c.4 Sch.1 para.242, Sch.3 Part 1
s.787, repealed (in part): 2009 c.4 Sch.3 Part 1
s.788, amended: 2009 c.4 Sch.3 Part 1
s.788, applied: 2009 c.4 s.1266, SI 2009/226, SI 2009/227, SI 2009/228, SI 2009/3011, SI 2009/3012, SI 2009/3013
s.788, varied: 2009 c.10 s.56
s.788, enabling: SI 2009/226, SI 2009/227, SI 2009/228, SI 2009/3011, SI 2009/3012, SI 2009/3013
s.789, varied: 2009 c.10 s.56
s.790, see *Bayfine UK Products v Revenue and Customs Commissioners* [2009] S.T.C. (S.C.D.) 43 (Sp Comm), John F Avery Jones
s.790, amended: 2009 c.4 Sch.3 Part 1
s.790, varied: 2009 c.10 s.56
s.791, varied: 2009 c.10 s.56
s.792, varied: 2009 c.10 s.56
s.793, varied: 2009 c.10 s.56
s.793A, varied: 2009 c.10 s.56
s.794, varied: 2009 c.10 s.56
s.795, amended: 2009 c.4 Sch.1 para.245
s.795, referred to: 2009 c.4 s.464
s.795, repealed (in part): 2009 c.10 Sch.14 para.7
s.795, varied: 2009 c.10 s.56
s.795A, see *Hill Samuel Investments Ltd v Revenue and Customs Commissioners* [2009] S.T.C. (S.C.D.) 315 (Sp Comm), John F Avery Jones (Chairman)
s.795A, varied: 2009 c.10 s.56
s.796, varied: 2009 c.10 s.56
s.797, amended: 2009 c.4 Sch.1 para.246
s.797, varied: 2009 c.10 s.56
s.797A, amended: 2009 c.4 Sch.1 para.247, Sch.3 Part 1
s.797A, varied: 2009 c.10 s.56
s.797B, amended: 2009 c.4 Sch.1 para.248
s.797B, varied: 2009 c.10 s.56
s.798, varied: 2009 c.10 s.56
s.798A, amended: 2009 c.4 Sch.1 para.249, 2009 c.10 s.60
s.798A, varied: 2009 c.10 s.56
s.798B, amended: 2009 c.10 s.60
s.798B, varied: 2009 c.10 s.56
s.798C, varied: 2009 c.10 s.56
s.799, amended: 2009 c.10 s.57, Sch.14 para.8
s.799, varied: 2009 c.10 s.56, Sch.16 para.8
s.800, varied: 2009 c.10 s.56
s.801, amended: 2009 c.10 s.57
s.801, applied: 2009 c.10 Sch.16 para.8
s.801, repealed (in part): 2009 c.10 Sch.16 para.2
s.801, varied: 2009 c.10 s.56
s.801A, varied: 2009 c.10 s.56
s.801B, varied: 2009 c.10 s.56
s.801C, applied: 2009 c.4 s.931R, 2009 c.10 Sch.16 para.8
s.801C, referred to: 2009 c.4 s.931R

1988–cont.

1. **Income and Corporation Taxes Act 1988**–*cont.*
s.801C, repealed: 2009 c.10 Sch.16 para.2
s.801C, varied: 2009 c.10 s.56
s.802, varied: 2009 c.10 s.56
s.803, varied: 2009 c.10 s.56
s.803A, applied: 2009 c.10 Sch.16 para.8
s.803A, repealed (in part): 2009 c.10 Sch.16 para.2
s.803A, varied: 2009 c.10 s.56
s.804, varied: 2009 c.10 s.56
s.804A, amended: 2009 c.4 Sch.1 para.250
s.804A, varied: 2009 c.10 s.56
s.804B, varied: 2009 c.10 s.56
s.804C, amended: 2009 c.4 Sch.1 para.251
s.804C, varied: 2009 c.10 s.56
s.804D, varied: 2009 c.10 s.56
s.804E, varied: 2009 c.10 s.56
s.804F, varied: 2009 c.10 s.56
s.804G, added: 2009 c.10 s.59
s.804G, varied: 2009 c.10 s.56
s.804ZA, varied: 2009 c.10 s.56
s.804ZB, varied: 2009 c.10 s.56
s.804ZC, varied: 2009 c.10 s.56
s.805, varied: 2009 c.10 s.56
s.806, amended: 2009 c.10 s.59
s.806, varied: 2009 c.10 s.56
s.806A, amended: 2009 c.4 Sch.1 para.252
s.806A, repealed: 2009 c.10 Sch.14 para.9
s.806A, varied: 2009 c.10 s.56
s.806B, amended: 2009 c.4 Sch.1 para.253, Sch.3 Part 1
s.806B, repealed: 2009 c.10 Sch.14 para.9
s.806B, varied: 2009 c.10 s.56
s.806C, repealed: 2009 c.10 Sch.14 para.9
s.806C, varied: 2009 c.10 s.56
s.806D, repealed: 2009 c.10 Sch.14 para.9
s.806D, varied: 2009 c.10 s.56
s.806E, repealed: 2009 c.10 Sch.14 para.9
s.806E, varied: 2009 c.10 s.56
s.806F, repealed: 2009 c.10 Sch.14 para.9
s.806F, varied: 2009 c.10 s.56
s.806G, repealed: 2009 c.10 Sch.14 para.9
s.806G, varied: 2009 c.10 s.56
s.806H, repealed: 2009 c.10 Sch.14 para.9
s.806H, varied: 2009 c.10 s.56
s.806J, repealed: 2009 c.10 Sch.14 para.9
s.806J, varied: 2009 c.10 s.56
s.806K, amended: 2009 c.4 Sch.1 para.254
s.806K, repealed: 2009 c.10 Sch.14 para.9
s.806K, varied: 2009 c.10 s.56
s.806L, amended: 2009 c.4 Sch.1 para.255, Sch.3 Part 1
s.806L, varied: 2009 c.10 s.56
s.806M, varied: 2009 c.10 s.56
s.807, varied: 2009 c.10 s.56
s.807A, amended: 2009 c.4 Sch.1 para.256
s.807A, repealed (in part): 2009 c.10 Sch.24 para.9
s.807A, varied: 2009 c.10 s.56
s.807B, added: 2009 c.4 Sch.1 para.257
s.807B, applied: 2009 c.4 s.827
s.807B, referred to: 2009 c.4 s.782
s.807B, varied: 2009 c.10 s.56
s.807C, added: 2009 c.4 Sch.1 para.258
s.807C, varied: 2009 c.10 s.56
s.807D, added: 2009 c.4 Sch.1 para.259
s.807D, varied: 2009 c.10 s.56
s.807E, added: 2009 c.4 Sch.1 para.260
s.807E, varied: 2009 c.10 s.56
s.807F, added: 2009 c.4 Sch.1 para.261

1988–cont.

1. **Income and Corporation Taxes Act 1988**–*cont.*
s.807F, varied: 2009 c.10 s.56
s.807G, substituted: 2009 c.4 Sch.1 para.262
s.807G, varied: 2009 c.10 s.56
s.808, varied: 2009 c.10 s.56
s.808A, varied: 2009 c.10 s.56
s.808B, varied: 2009 c.10 s.56
s.809, varied: 2009 c.10 s.56
s.810, varied: 2009 c.10 s.56
s.811, amended: 2009 c.4 Sch.1 para.263, 2009 c.10 s.59
s.811, applied: 2009 c.4 s.486
s.811, referred to: 2009 c.4 s.464
s.811, varied: 2009 c.10 s.56
s.812, varied: 2009 c.10 s.56
s.813, varied: 2009 c.10 s.56
s.814, varied: 2009 c.10 s.56
s.815, repealed: SI 2009/2035 Sch.1 para.23
s.815, varied: 2009 c.10 s.56
s.815A, varied: 2009 c.10 s.56
s.815AA, varied: 2009 c.10 s.56
s.815AZA, amended: 2009 c.4 Sch.1 para.264
s.815AZA, varied: 2009 c.10 s.56
s.815B, varied: 2009 c.10 s.56
s.815C, varied: 2009 c.10 s.56
s.816, varied: 2009 c.10 s.56
s.817, repealed: 2009 c.4 Sch.3 Part 1
s.821, amended: 2009 c.4 Sch.3 Part 1
s.824, amended: 2009 c.10 Sch.19 para.10
s.826, amended: 2009 c.4 Sch.1 para.267, Sch.3 Part 1
s.826, applied: 2009 c.4 s.1057, s.1060, s.1106, s.1109, s.1155, s.1203
s.826, repealed (in part): 2009 c.4 Sch.3 Part 1, 2009 c.10 Sch.14 para.10
s.827, amended: SI 2009/571 Sch.1 para.20
s.827, repealed: 2009 c.4 Sch.3 Part 1
s.828, amended: 2009 c.4 Sch.1 para.269, Sch.3 Part 1
s.828, disapplied: 2009 c.10 Sch.22 para.14
s.830, amended: SI 2009/2860 Art.3
s.830, repealed (in part): 2009 c.4 Sch.3 Part 1
s.831, amended: 2009 c.4 Sch.1 para.271
s.832, amended: 2009 c.4 Sch.3 Part 1, SI 2009/56 Sch.1 para.157
s.832, repealed (in part): 2009 c.4 Sch.3 Part 1
s.834, amended: 2009 c.4 Sch.1 para.273
s.834A, added: 2009 c.4 Sch.1 para.274
s.834A, amended: SI 2009/3001 Reg.126, Sch.2
s.834A, applied: 2009 c.4 s.1307
s.834A, varied: 2009 c.4 s.1307
s.834B, added: 2009 c.4 Sch.1 para.275
s.834C, added: 2009 c.4 Sch.1 para.276
s.835, applied: 2009 c.10 Sch.6 para.1
s.837C, see *Spowage v Revenue and Customs Commissioners* [2009] UKFTT 142 (TC), [2009] S.F.T.D. 393 (FTT (Tax)), J Gordon Reid Q.C.
s.838, applied: 2009 c.4 s.768, s.773, 2009 c.10 Sch.46 para.18
s.838, varied: 2009 c.10 Sch.46 para.18
s.839, amended: SI 2009/2192 Reg.2
s.839, applied: 2009 c.4 s.168, s.419, s.1316, 2009 c.10 Sch.3 para.8, SI 2009/1926 Reg.11, SI 2009/2192 Reg.2, SI 2009/2971 Reg.2, SI 2009/3001 Reg.76, Reg.82
s.840, applied: 2009 c.4 s.1316
s.840ZA, amended: 2009 c.10 Sch.19 para.10

1988–cont.

1. Income and Corporation Taxes Act 1988–*cont.*
s.842, amended: 2009 c.4 Sch.1 para.277, 2009 c.10 Sch.22 para.11, SI 2009/3001 Reg.126
s.842, applied: SI 2009/2034 Reg.6, Reg.12
Sch.A1 Part I para.1, repealed: 2009 c.4 Sch.3 Part 1
Sch.A1 Part II para.2, repealed: 2009 c.4 Sch.3 Part 1
Sch.A1 Part II para.3, repealed: 2009 c.4 Sch.3 Part 1
Sch.A1 Part II para.4, repealed: 2009 c.4 Sch.3 Part 1
Sch.A1 Part II para.5, repealed: 2009 c.4 Sch.3 Part 1
Sch.A1 Part II para.6, repealed: 2009 c.4 Sch.3 Part 1
Sch.A1 Part III para.7, repealed: 2009 c.4 Sch.3 Part 1
Sch.A1 Part III para.8, repealed: 2009 c.4 Sch.3 Part 1
Sch.A1 Part III para.9, repealed: 2009 c.4 Sch.3 Part 1
Sch.A1 Part III para.10, repealed: 2009 c.4 Sch.3 Part 1
Sch.4AA para.1, repealed: 2009 c.4 Sch.3 Part 1
Sch.4AA para.2, repealed: 2009 c.4 Sch.3 Part 1
Sch.4AA para.3, repealed: 2009 c.4 Sch.3 Part 1
Sch.4AA para.4, repealed: 2009 c.4 Sch.3 Part 1
Sch.4AA para.5, repealed: 2009 c.4 Sch.3 Part 1
Sch.4AA para.6, repealed: 2009 c.4 Sch.3 Part 1
Sch.4AA para.7, repealed: 2009 c.4 Sch.3 Part 1
Sch.4AA para.8, repealed: 2009 c.4 Sch.3 Part 1
Sch.4AA para.9, repealed: 2009 c.4 Sch.3 Part 1
Sch.4AA para.10, repealed: 2009 c.4 Sch.3 Part 1
Sch.4AA para.11, repealed: 2009 c.4 Sch.3 Part 1
Sch.4AA para.12, repealed: 2009 c.4 Sch.3 Part 1
Sch.4AA para.13, repealed: 2009 c.4 Sch.3 Part 1
Sch.5 para.1, repealed: 2009 c.4 Sch.3 Part 1
Sch.5 para.2, repealed: 2009 c.4 Sch.3 Part 1
Sch.5 para.3, repealed: 2009 c.4 Sch.3 Part 1
Sch.5 para.4, repealed: 2009 c.4 Sch.3 Part 1
Sch.5 para.5, repealed: 2009 c.4 Sch.3 Part 1
Sch.5 para.6, repealed: 2009 c.4 Sch.3 Part 1
Sch.5 para.7, repealed: 2009 c.4 Sch.3 Part 1
Sch.5 para.8, repealed: 2009 c.4 Sch.3 Part 1
Sch.5 para.9, repealed: 2009 c.4 Sch.3 Part 1
Sch.5 para.10, repealed: 2009 c.4 Sch.3 Part 1
Sch.5 para.11, repealed: 2009 c.4 Sch.3 Part 1
Sch.5 para.12, repealed: 2009 c.4 Sch.3 Part 1
Sch.9 Part I para.5, varied: SI 2009/56 Sch.1 para.158
Sch.14 Part II para.6, amended: 2009 c.10 Sch.1 para.5
Sch.15 Part I para.14, repealed (in part): SI 2009/2035 Sch.1 para.24
Sch.15 Part II para.21, amended: SI 2009/56 Sch.1 para.159
Sch.16 para.2, see *ECL Solutions Ltd v Revenue and Customs Commissioners* [2009] S.T.C. (S.C.D.) 90 (Sp Comm), Theodore Wallace
Sch.16 para.4, see *ECL Solutions Ltd v Revenue and Customs Commissioners* [2009] S.T.C. (S.C.D.) 90 (Sp Comm), Theodore Wallace
Sch.17 Part II para.7, amended: SI 2009/56 Sch.1 para.160
Sch.17A para.6, see *Marks & Spencer Plc v Revenue and Customs Commissioners* [2009] UKFTT 64 (TC), [2009] S.F.T.D.1 (FTT (Tax)), John F Avery Jones

1988–cont.

1. Income and Corporation Taxes Act 1988–*cont.*
Sch.18, applied: 2009 c.4 s.519, s.772, 2009 c.10 Sch.15 para.86
Sch.18 para.1, amended: 2009 c.10 Sch.9 para.2
Sch.18 para.1, disapplied: 2009 c.4 s.519
Sch.18 para.1, varied: 2009 c.4 s.772
Sch.18 para.1A, added: 2009 c.10 Sch.9 para.3
Sch.18 para.1A, varied: 2009 c.4 s.772
Sch.18 para.2, varied: 2009 c.4 s.772
Sch.18 para.3, varied: 2009 c.4 s.772
Sch.18 para.4, varied: 2009 c.4 s.772
Sch.18 para.5, varied: 2009 c.4 s.772
Sch.18 para.5A, varied: 2009 c.4 s.772
Sch.18 para.5B, amended: 2009 c.10 Sch.9 para.4
Sch.18 para.5B, varied: 2009 c.4 s.772
Sch.18 para.5C, varied: 2009 c.4 s.772
Sch.18 para.5D, varied: 2009 c.4 s.772
Sch.18 para.5E, varied: 2009 c.4 s.772
Sch.18 para.5F, varied: 2009 c.4 s.772
Sch.18 para.6, varied: 2009 c.4 s.772
Sch.18 para.7, varied: 2009 c.4 s.772
Sch.18A Part 2 para.13, amended: 2009 c.4 Sch.1 para.281
Sch.19ABA Part 2, amended: 2009 c.4 Sch.1 para.282
Sch.19ABA Part 2 para.9, amended: 2009 c.4 Sch.1 para.282
Sch.19ABA Part 3, amended: 2009 c.4 Sch.1 para.282
Sch.19ABA Part 3 para.23, amended: 2009 c.4 Sch.1 para.282
Sch.19B Part II para.6, amended: 2009 c.4 Sch.1 para.283
Sch.19C Part 2 para.6, amended: 2009 c.4 Sch.1 para.284
Sch.23A para.2, amended: 2009 c.10 Sch.14 para.11
Sch.23A para.2, repealed (in part): 2009 c.10 Sch.14 para.11
Sch.23A para.4, amended: 2009 c.4 Sch.1 para.285, 2009 c.10 Sch.14 para.12, Sch.29 para.1
Sch.23A para.4, applied: 2009 c.4 s.1221
Sch.23A para.4A, added: 2009 c.10 Sch.29 para.1
Sch.23A para.7, amended: 2009 c.4 Sch.1 para.285
Sch.23A para.7A, amended: 2009 c.4 Sch.1 para.285
Sch.23A para.7A, applied: 2009 c.4 s.540, s.1248
Sch.23A para.8, enabling: SI 2009/2811
Sch.24, see *Vodafone 2 v Revenue and Customs Commissioners* [2008] EWHC 1569 (Ch), [2009] Ch. 123 (Ch D), Evans-Lombe, J.
Sch.24 para.1, amended: 2009 c.4 Sch.1 para.286, 2009 c.10 Sch.16 para.2
Sch.24 para.1, applied: 2009 c.4 s.870
Sch.24 para.1, repealed (in part): 2009 c.10 Sch.16 para.2
Sch.24 para.2, repealed (in part): 2009 c.10 Sch.16 para.2
Sch.24 para.4, applied: 2009 c.4 s.870
Sch.24 para.4, repealed (in part): 2009 c.10 Sch.16 para.2
Sch.24 para.9, amended: 2009 c.10 Sch.16 para.2
Sch.24 para.10, repealed (in part): 2009 c.10 Sch.16 para.2
Sch.24 para.12, amended: 2009 c.4 Sch.1 para.286
Sch.25 Part I, applied: 2009 c.4 s.521B, 2009 c.10 Sch.16 para.8
Sch.25 Part I para.1, repealed: 2009 c.10 Sch.16 para.1

1988– cont.

1. Income and Corporation Taxes Act 1988– *cont.*

Sch.25 Part I para.2, amended: 2009 c.4 Sch.1 para.287

Sch.25 Part I para.2, disapplied: 2009 c.10 Sch.9 para.8

Sch.25 Part I para.2, repealed: 2009 c.10 Sch.16 para.1

Sch.25 Part I para.2A, repealed: 2009 c.10 Sch.16 para.1

Sch.25 Part I para.2B, repealed: 2009 c.10 Sch.16 para.1

Sch.25 Part I para.3, repealed: 2009 c.10 Sch.16 para.1

Sch.25 Part I para.4, amended: 2009 c.4 Sch.1 para.287

Sch.25 Part I para.4, repealed: 2009 c.10 Sch.16 para.1

Sch.25 Part I para.4A, repealed: 2009 c.10 Sch.16 para.1

Sch.25 Part II, applied: 2009 c.10 Sch.16 para.17

Sch.25 Part II para.6, amended: 2009 c.10 Sch.16 para.10

Sch.25 Part II para.6, repealed (in part): 2009 c.10 Sch.16 para.10

Sch.25 Part II para.6, varied: 2009 c.10 Sch.16 para.17

Sch.25 Part II para.8, amended: 2009 c.10 Sch.16 para.10

Sch.25 Part II para.11B, amended: SI 2009/1890 Art.3

Sch.25 Part II para.12, amended: 2009 c.4 Sch.1 para.287, 2009 c.10 Sch.16 para.10

Sch.25 Part II para.12A, repealed: 2009 c.10 Sch.16 para.10

Sch.25 para.6, see *Vodafone 2 v Revenue and Customs Commissioners* [2008] EWHC 1569 (Ch), [2009] Ch. 123 (Ch D), Evans-Lombe, J.

Sch.26, see *Vodafone 2 v Revenue and Customs Commissioners* [2008] EWHC 1569 (Ch), [2009] Ch. 123 (Ch D), Evans-Lombe, J.

Sch.26 para.1, amended: 2009 c.4 Sch.1 para.288

Sch.27 Part I, substituted: 2009 c.4 Sch.1 para.289

Sch.27 Part I para.1, amended: 2009 c.4 Sch.1 para.289, Sch.3 Part 1

Sch.27 Part I para.1, repealed: SI 2009/3001 Sch.2

Sch.27 Part I para.2, repealed: SI 2009/3001 Sch.2

Sch.27 Part I para.3, amended: 2009 c.4 Sch.1 para.289

Sch.27 Part I para.3, repealed: SI 2009/3001 Sch.2

Sch.27 Part I para.4, amended: 2009 c.4 Sch.1 para.289

Sch.27 Part I para.4, repealed: SI 2009/3001 Sch.2

Sch.27 Part I para.5, amended: 2009 c.4 Sch.1 para.289, 2009 c.10 Sch.14 para.13

Sch.27 Part I para.5, repealed: SI 2009/3001 Sch.2

Sch.27 Part II para.6, repealed: SI 2009/3001 Sch.2

Sch.27 Part II para.7, repealed: SI 2009/3001 Sch.2

Sch.27 Part II para.8, repealed: SI 2009/3001 Sch.2

Sch.27 Part II para.9, repealed: SI 2009/3001 Sch.2

Sch.27 Part II para.10, repealed: SI 2009/3001 Sch.2

Sch.27 Part II para.11, repealed: SI 2009/3001 Sch.2

Sch.27 Part II para.12, repealed: SI 2009/3001 Sch.2

Sch.27 Part II para.13, repealed: SI 2009/3001 Sch.2

Sch.27 Part II para.14, repealed: SI 2009/3001 Sch.2

Sch.27 Part III, applied: 2009 c.10 Sch.22 para.15

1988– cont.

1. Income and Corporation Taxes Act 1988– *cont.*

Sch.27 Part III para.15, repealed: SI 2009/3001 Sch.2

Sch.27 Part III para.16, amended: SI 2009/56 Sch.1 para.161

Sch.27 Part III para.16, repealed: SI 2009/3001 Sch.2

Sch.27 Part IV para.17, repealed: SI 2009/3001 Sch.2

Sch.27 Part IV para.18, repealed: SI 2009/3001 Sch.2

Sch.27 Part IV para.19, amended: SI 2009/56 Sch.1 para.161

Sch.27 Part IV para.19, repealed: SI 2009/3001 Sch.2

Sch.27 Part IV para.20, amended: SI 2009/56 Sch.1 para.161

Sch.27 Part IV para.20, repealed: SI 2009/3001 Sch.2

Sch.27 Part IV para.21, repealed: SI 2009/3001 Sch.2

Sch.28AA, see *DSG Retail Ltd v Revenue and Customs Commissioners* [2009] UKFTT 31 (TC), [2009] S.T.C. (S.C.D.) 397 (Sp Comm), John F Avery Jones

Sch.28AA, applied: 2009 c.4 s.931P, s.161, s.445, s.446, s.447, s.693, s.694, s.721, s.728, s.729, s.731, s.736, s.739, s.740, s.742, s.743, s.846

Sch.28AA, disapplied: 2009 c.4 s.340, s.447, s.625, s.775, SI 2009/2971 Reg.19, Reg.22, SI 2009/3227 Reg.4, Reg.6

Sch.28AA, see *DSG Retail Ltd v Revenue and Customs Commissioners* [2009] UKFTT 31 (TC), [2009] S.T.C. (S.C.D.) 397 (Sp Comm), John F Avery Jones

Sch.28AA, amended: 2009 c.4 Sch.1 para.291

Sch.28 Part I para.1, repealed: SI 2009/3001 Sch.2

Sch.28 Part I para.2, repealed: SI 2009/3001 Sch.2

Sch.28 Part I para.3, repealed: SI 2009/3001 Sch.2

Sch.28 Part I para.4, repealed: SI 2009/3001 Sch.2

Sch.28 Part I para.5, repealed: SI 2009/3001 Sch.2

Sch.28 Part II para.6, repealed: SI 2009/3001 Sch.2

Sch.28 Part II para.7, repealed: SI 2009/3001 Sch.2

Sch.28 Part II para.8, repealed: SI 2009/3001 Sch.2

Sch.28 Part III para.9, repealed: SI 2009/3001 Sch.2

Sch.28AA para.1, amended: 2009 c.4 Sch.1 para.291

Sch.28AA para.1, applied: 2009 c.4 s.455, s.508, s.698

Sch.28AA para.1, referred to: 2009 c.4 s.162, s.508

Sch.28AA para.2, amended: 2009 c.4 Sch.1 para.291

Sch.28AA para.3, applied: 2009 c.10 Sch.17 para.12

Sch.28AA para.5, amended: 2009 c.10 Sch.14 para.14, Sch.15 para.96

Sch.28AA para.6A, amended: 2009 c.4 Sch.1 para.291

Sch.28AA para.6D, applied: 2009 c.4 s.452

Sch.28AA para.6E, amended: 2009 c.4 Sch.1 para.291, Sch.3 Part 1

Sch.28AA para.8, repealed (in part): 2009 c.4 Sch.3 Part 1

Sch.28AA para.10, disapplied: 2009 c.4 s.161

Sch.28AA para.12, amended: SI 2009/56 Sch.1 para.162

Sch.28AA para.12, repealed (in part): SI 2009/56 Sch.1 para.162

Sch.28AA para.13, disapplied: 2009 c.4 s.161

1988– cont.

1. Income and Corporation Taxes Act 1988–*cont.*
Sch.28AA para.14, amended: 2009 c.4 Sch.1 para.291
Sch.28A Part I para.5, amended: SI 2009/1890 Art.8
Sch.28A Part II para.6, amended: 2009 c.4 Sch.1 para.290
Sch.28A Part II para.6, repealed (in part): 2009 c.4 Sch.3 Part 1
Sch.28A Part II para.6A, amended: 2009 c.4 Sch.1 para.290
Sch.28A Part III para.7, amended: 2009 c.4 Sch.1 para.290
Sch.28A Part IV para.9, amended: 2009 c.4 Sch.1 para.290
Sch.28A Part IV para.10, amended: 2009 c.4 Sch.1 para.290
Sch.28A Part IV para.11, amended: 2009 c.4 Sch.1 para.290, Sch.3 Part 1
Sch.28A Part IV para.11, repealed (in part): 2009 c.4 Sch.3 Part 1
Sch.28A Part IV para.12, amended: 2009 c.4 Sch.1 para.290
Sch.28A Part V para.13, amended: 2009 c.4 Sch.1 para.290
Sch.28A Part V para.13, repealed (in part): 2009 c.4 Sch.3 Part 1
Sch.28A Part VI para.16, amended: 2009 c.4 Sch.1 para.290
Sch.28A Part VI para.16, repealed (in part): 2009 c.4 Sch.3 Part 1
Sch.29 para.32, amended: SI 2009/2035 Sch.1 para.60
Sch.30 para.2, repealed: 2009 c.4 Sch.3 Part 1
Sch.30 para.3, repealed: 2009 c.4 Sch.3 Part 1
Sch.30 para.4, repealed: 2009 c.4 Sch.3 Part 1
Sch.30 para.5, repealed: 2009 c.4 Sch.3 Part 1
Sch.30 para.7, amended: 2009 c.4 Sch.1 para.292

7. Social Security Act 1988
s.13, referred to: SI 2009/295
s.13, enabling: SI 2009/295

9. Local Government Act 1988
s.17, amended: SI 2009/1941 Sch.1 para.93
Sch.2 Part 1, amended: 2009 c.20 Sch.6 para.73

12. Merchant Shipping Act 1988
s.36, repealed (in part): 2009 c.23 Sch.22 Part 2

13. Coroners Act 1988
applied: 2009 c.25 Sch.22 para.2, Sch.22 para.4
repealed: 2009 c.25 Sch.23 Part 1
s.1, amended: 2009 c.20 Sch.7 Part 4
s.1, applied: 2009 c.25 Sch.22 para.5, SI 2009/837 Art.28
s.1, referred to: 2009 c.25 Sch.22 para.1, Sch.22 para.3
s.2, referred to: 2009 c.25 Sch.22 para.1, Sch.22 para.3
s.3, referred to: 2009 c.25 Sch.22 para.1, Sch.22 para.3
s.4, referred to: 2009 c.25 Sch.22 para.1, Sch.22 para.3
s.4A, referred to: 2009 c.25 Sch.22 para.1, Sch.22 para.3
s.5, referred to: 2009 c.25 Sch.22 para.1, Sch.22 para.3
s.6, referred to: 2009 c.25 Sch.22 para.1, Sch.22 para.3
s.7, referred to: 2009 c.25 Sch.22 para.1, Sch.22 para.3
s.8, varied: SI 2009/1059 Sch.1 para.29

1988– cont.

13. Coroners Act 1988– *cont.*
s.16, see *Moss v HM Coroner for the North and South Districts of Durham and Darlington* [2008] EWHC 2940 (Admin), (2009) 173 J.P. 65 (QBD (Admin)), Underhill, J.
s.16, amended: 2009 c.25 Sch.22 para.9
s.17, amended: 2009 c.25 Sch.22 para.9

15. Public Utility Transfers and Water Charges Act 1988
s.1, amended: SI 2009/1941 Sch.1 para.94

19. Employment Act 1988
referred to: SI 2009/500 Sch.1 Part 1
s.26, enabling: SI 2009/1562

22. Scotch Whisky Act 1988
repealed: SI 2009/2890 Reg.2

26. Landlord and Tenant Act 1988
s.1, see *Landlord Protect Ltd v St Anselm Development Co Ltd* [2009] EWCA Civ 99, [2009] 2 P. & C.R. 9 (CA (Civ Div)), Waller, L.J.

33. Criminal Justice Act 1988
see *Crown Prosecution Service v Moulden* [2008] EWCA Crim 2648, [2009] 1 W.L.R. 1173 (CA (Crim Div)), Pill, L.J.; see *Escobar v DPP* [2008] EWHC 422 (Admin), [2009] 1 W.L.R. 64 (DC), Maurice Kay, L.J.; see *R. v Stapleton (Rosie)* [2008] EWCA Crim 1308, [2009] 1 Cr. App. R. (S.) 38 (CA (Crim Div)), Latham, L.J.; see *Stodgell v Stodgell* [2008] EWHC 1925 (Admin), [2009] 2 F.L.R. 218 (QBD (Admin)), Holman, J.
Part IV, see *Escobar v DPP* [2008] EWHC 422 (Admin), [2009] 1 W.L.R. 64 (DC), Maurice Kay, L.J.
Part VI, see *Ilyas v Aylesbury Vale DC* [2008] EWCA Crim 1303, [2009] 1 Cr. App. R. (S.) 59 (CA (Crim Div)), Scott Baker, L.J.; see *R. v Sangha (Bhovinder Singh)* [2008] EWCA Crim 2562, [2009] S.T.C. 570 (CA (Crim Div)), Richards, L.J.
s.32, applied: SI 2009/2657 r.14
s.32, varied: SI 2009/2569 Art.3
s.36, applied: 2009 c.25 s.124
s.40, see *R. v Roberts (Patrice)* [2008] EWCA Crim 1304, [2009] 1 Cr. App. R. 20 (CA (Crim Div)), Latham, L.J. (VP, CA Crim)
s.71, see *Bullen v United Kingdom (3383/06)* [2009] Lloyd's Rep. F.C. 210 (ECHR), Judge Garlicki (President); see *R. v Allpress (Sylvia)* [2008] EWCA Crim 8, [2009] 2 Cr. App. R. (S.) 58 (CA (Crim Div)), Latham, L.J. (VP, CA Crim); see *R. v Bukhari (Daniyal)* [2008] EWCA Crim 2915, [2009] 2 Cr. App. R. (S.) 18 (CA (Crim Div)), Moore-Bick, L.J.; see *R. v Sangha (Bhovinder Singh)* [2008] EWCA Crim 2562, [2009] S.T.C. 570 (CA (Crim Div)), Richards, L.J.
s.72, see *R. v Shahid (Abdul)* [2009] EWCA Crim 831, [2009] 2 Cr. App. R. (S.) 105 (CA (Crim Div)), Hallett, L.J.
s.72A, see *R. (on the application of Minshall) v Marylebone Magistrates' Court* [2008] EWHC 2800 (Admin), [2009] 2 All E.R. 806 (QBD (Admin)), Pitchford, J.
s.72AA, see *Crown Prosecution Service v Moulden* [2008] EWCA Crim 2648, [2009] 1 W.L.R. 1173 (CA (Crim Div)), Pill, L.J.; see *Ilyas v Aylesbury Vale DC* [2008] EWCA Crim 1303, [2009] 1 Cr. App. R. (S.) 59 (CA (Crim Div)), Scott Baker, L.J.; see *R. v Shahid (Abdul)* [2009] EWCA Crim 831, [2009] 2 Cr. App. R. (S.) 105 (CA (Crim Div)), Hallett, L.J.

1988–cont.

33. Criminal Justice Act 1988–cont.
s.74, see *Ilyas v Aylesbury Vale DC* [2008] EWCA Crim 1303, [2009] 1 Cr. App. R. (S.) 59 (CA (Crim Div)), Scott Baker, L.J.; see *R. v Shahid (Abdul)* [2009] EWCA Crim 831, [2009] 2 Cr. App. R. (S.) 105 (CA (Crim Div)), Hallett, L.J.; see *Sinclair v Glatt* [2009] EWCA Civ 176, [2009] 1 W.L.R. 1845 (CA (Civ Div)), Longmore, L.J.

s.75, see *Escobar v DPP* [2008] EWHC 422 (Admin), [2009] 1 W.L.R. 64 (DC), Maurice Kay, L.J.

s.77, see *Sinclair v Glatt* [2009] EWCA Civ 176, [2009] 1 W.L.R. 1845 (CA (Civ Div)), Longmore, L.J.

s.80, see *Revenue and Customs Prosecutions Office v May* [2009] EWHC 1826 (QB), [2009] S.T.C. 2466 (QBD), Judge Mackie Q.C.

s.82, see *Revenue and Customs Prosecutions Office v May* [2009] EWHC 1826 (QB), [2009] S.T.C. 2466 (QBD), Judge Mackie Q.C.

s.83, see *Escobar v DPP* [2008] EWHC 422 (Admin), [2009] 1 W.L.R. 64 (DC), Maurice Kay, L.J.; see *R. v Ford (Laurence Peter)* [2008] EWCA Crim 966, [2009] 1 Cr. App. R. (S.) 13 (CA (Crim Div)), Hallett, L.J.; see *R. v Younis (Shaed)* [2008] EWCA Crim 2950, [2009] 2 Cr. App. R. (S.) 34 (CA (Crim Div)), Thomas, L.J.

s.84, see *R. v Allpress (Sylvia)* [2009] EWCA Crim 8, [2009] 2 Cr. App. R. (S.) 58 (CA (Crim Div)), Latham, L.J. (VP, CA Crim); see *R. v Shahid (Abdul)* [2009] EWCA Crim 831, [2009] 2 Cr. App. R. (S.) 105 (CA (Crim Div)), Hallett, L.J.

s.102, see *R. v Shahid (Abdul)* [2009] EWCA Crim 831, [2009] 2 Cr. App. R. (S.) 105 (CA (Crim Div)), Hallett, L.J.; see *Sinclair v Glatt* [2009] EWCA Civ 176, [2009] 1 W.L.R. 1845 (CA (Civ Div)), Longmore, L.J.

s.133, see *R. (on the application of Harris) v Secretary of State for the Home Department* [2008] EWCA Civ 808, [2009] 2 All E.R. 1 (CA (Civ Div)), Sir Mark Potter (President, Fam)

s.141, amended: 2009 c.26 Sch.7 para.119, Sch.8 Part 10

s.141, referred to: 2009 c.26 s.102

s.141, repealed (in part): 2009 c.26 Sch.7 para.119, Sch.8 Part 10

s.141ZB, added: 2009 c.26 s.102

s.141ZB, referred to: 2009 c.26 s.102

s.141ZC, added: 2009 c.26 s.102

s.141ZD, added: 2009 c.26 s.102

s.146, enabling: SI 2009/2569

s.160, see *R. v Clinch (Simon)* [2008] EWCA Crim 1630, [2009] 1 Cr. App. R. (S.) 49 (CA (Crim Div)), Scott Baker, L.J.

s.160, applied: 2009 asp 9 Sch.1 para.8

s.160, referred to: SI 2009/37 Sch.1 para.2, Sch.1 para.4

s.160A, amended: 2009 c.25 s.69

Sch.13 para.8, referred to: SI 2009/2569 Art.3

Sch.13 para.8, enabling: SI 2009/994, SI 2009/2569

34. Legal Aid Act 1988
referred to: SI 2009/500 Sch.1 Part 1

35. British Steel Act 1988
s.11, amended: 2009 c.4 Sch.1 para.329

s.15, amended: SI 2009/1941 Sch.1 para.95

1988–cont.

36. Court of Session Act 1988
s.5, enabling: SSI 2009/63, SSI 2009/82, SSI 2009/104, SSI 2009/105, SSI 2009/114, SSI 2009/135, SSI 2009/283, SSI 2009/323, SSI 2009/382, SSI 2009/383, SSI 2009/387, SSI 2009/450

s.45, applied: SI 2009/859 Reg.10, SI 2009/1914 Reg.23, SI 2009/2570 Art.7, SSI 2009/446 Reg.6

s.47, see *M v M* [2009] CSOH 65, 2009 S.L.T. 608 (OH), Lady Clark of Calton

39. Finance Act 1988
referred to: SI 2009/56 Sch.1 para.163

s.33, repealed: 2009 c.10 Sch.1 para.6

s.65, repealed: 2009 c.4 Sch.3 Part 1

s.66, repealed: 2009 c.4 Sch.3 Part 1

s.66A, repealed: 2009 c.4 Sch.3 Part 1

s.72, repealed: 2009 c.4 Sch.3 Part 1

s.73, repealed (in part): 2009 c.4 Sch.3 Part 1

s.105, repealed (in part): 2009 c.10 Sch.17 para.3

s.130, amended: SI 2009/56 Sch.1 para.164

s.130, referred to: SI 2009/56 Sch.1 para.164

s.133, repealed: SI 2009/56 Sch.1 para.165

s.134, repealed: SI 2009/56 Sch.1 para.165

s.135, repealed: SI 2009/56 Sch.1 para.165

Sch.3 Part I para.8, repealed: 2009 c.10 Sch.1 para.6

Sch.3 Part I para.10, repealed: 2009 c.10 Sch.1 para.6

Sch.6 para.1, repealed: 2009 c.4 Sch.3 Part 1

Sch.6 para.2, repealed: 2009 c.4 Sch.3 Part 1

Sch.6 para.3, repealed: 2009 c.4 Sch.3 Part 1

Sch.6 para.4, repealed: 2009 c.4 Sch.3 Part 1

Sch.6 para.5, repealed: 2009 c.4 Sch.3 Part 1

Sch.6 para.6, repealed: 2009 c.4 Sch.3 Part 1

Sch.6 para.49, repealed: 2009 c.4 Sch.3 Part 1

Sch.7 para.1, repealed: 2009 c.4 Sch.3 Part 1

Sch.7 para.2, repealed: 2009 c.4 Sch.3 Part 1

Sch.7 para.3, repealed: 2009 c.4 Sch.3 Part 1

Sch.7 para.4, repealed: 2009 c.4 Sch.3 Part 1

Sch.7 para.5, repealed: 2009 c.4 Sch.3 Part 1

Sch.12 para.3, amended: 2009 c.4 Sch.1 para.337

Sch.12 para.3, repealed (in part): 2009 c.4 Sch.3 Part 1

Sch.13 Part I para.12, repealed: SI 2009/3001 Sch.2

40. Education Reform Act 1988
referred to: SI 2009/669 Sch.1 Part 2

s.129, amended: SI 2009/1941 Sch.1 para.96

s.129B, amended: SI 2009/1941 Sch.1 para.96

s.156, amended: SI 2009/1941 Sch.1 para.96

s.192, amended: SI 2009/1941 Sch.1 para.96

s.216, enabling: SI 2009/667, SI 2009/710, SSI 2009/60, SSI 2009/61

s.232, enabling: SI 2009/710

Sch.6 para.1, applied: 2009 c.22 s.100

41. Local Government Finance Act 1988
applied: SI 2009/2269 Reg.38, SI 2009/3343 Reg.9

Part I, applied: SI 2009/2270 Reg.2

Part III, applied: SI 2009/2268 Reg.15, SI 2009/2269 Reg.42, Reg.44, SI 2009/2270 Reg.3, Reg.11, SI 2009/2543 Sch.1 para.2, Sch.1 para.3, Sch.2 para.7

Part III, referred to: SI 2009/2270 Reg.11

s.41, referred to: 2009 c.7 s.30

s.42, applied: SI 2009/2268 Reg.4, SI 2009/3343 Reg.13

s.42, enabling: SI 2009/2268

s.43, applied: 2009 c.7 s.1, s.11, s.13, s.25, SI 2009/354 Art.2, SI 2009/3343 Reg.4, Reg.9, Reg.10, Sch.2 para.2, Sch.2 para.3, Sch.2 para.4, Sch.2 para.5, Sch.2 para.8

s.43, disapplied: SI 2009/3343 Sch.2 para.4

1988– cont.

41. Local Government Finance Act 1988–*cont.*
s.43, enabling: SI 2009/ 354, SI 2009/ 3175, SI 2009/ 3176
s.44, applied: SI 2009/ 3343 Reg.4, Reg.10, Reg.13, Sch.2 para.2, Sch.2 para.3, Sch.2 para.4, Sch.2 para.5
s.44A, applied: 2009 c.7 s.12, SI 2009/ 3343 Reg.13
s.45, applied: 2009 c.7 s.1, s.11, s.12, s.14, s.18, s.25, SI 2009/ 3343 Reg.4, Reg.9, Reg.10, Sch.2 para.2, Sch.2 para.3, Sch.2 para.4, Sch.2 para.5
s.45, referred to: 2009 c.7 Sch.1 para.14
s.45, enabling: SI 2009/ 255, SI 2009/ 353
s.45A, applied: 2009 c.7 s.11, SI 2009/ 3343 Reg.4, Reg.9, Sch.2 para.2, Sch.2 para.3, Sch.2 para.4, Sch.2 para.5
s.47, applied: 2009 c.7 s.13, SI 2009/ 3343 Sch.2 para.2, Sch.2 para.3, Sch.2 para.5, Sch.2 para.8
s.47, disapplied: SI 2009/ 3343 Sch.2 para.4
s.47, enabling: SI 2009/ 3176
s.49, applied: 2009 c.7 s.13, SI 2009/ 3343 Sch.2 para.2, Sch.2 para.3, Sch.2 para.5, Sch.2 para.8
s.49, disapplied: SI 2009/ 3343 Sch.2 para.4
s.50, applied: 2009 c.7 s.17
s.53, applied: SI 2009/ 2268 Reg.18, SI 2009/ 3343 Reg.1, Reg.3
s.53, enabling: SI 2009/ 2268
s.54, applied: SI 2009/ 3343 Reg.9, Sch.2 para.2, Sch.2 para.3, Sch.2 para.4, Sch.2 para.5
s.54, referred to: SI 2009/ 3343 Reg.10
s.55, applied: 2009 c.7 s.12
s.55, enabling: SI 2009/ 2268, SI 2009/ 2269
s.57A, applied: 2009 c.7 s.13, SI 2009/ 3343 Reg.2
s.57A, enabling: SI 2009/ 3343
s.58, applied: SI 2009/ 2268 Reg.25
s.60, enabling: SI 2009/ 3147
s.62, enabling: SI 2009/ 2154
s.62A, applied: 2009 c.7 s.21
s.63, applied: 2009 c.7 s.17
s.64, referred to: 2009 c.7 s.30
s.74, amended: 2009 c.20 Sch.6 para.75, Sch.7 Part 4
s.78, applied: 2009 c.2 Sch.2 Part 2
s.78, applied: 2009 c.9 Sch.2 Part 10
s.88B, amended: 2009 c.20 Sch.6 para.76
s.89, amended: 2009 c.20 Sch.7 Part 4
s.89, applied: 2009 c.7 Sch.3 para.2, SI 2009/ 5 Reg.3
s.90, amended: 2009 c.7 Sch.3 para.4
s.90, applied: SI 2009/ 2543 Sch.1 para.2, Sch.1 para.3, Sch.2 para.7
s.90, referred to: 2009 c.7 s.22, s.29, Sch.3 para.4
s.91, amended: 2009 c.20 Sch.7 Part 4
s.91, applied: SI 2009/ 5 Reg.4
s.99, applied: 2009 c.7 Sch.3 para.2
s.111, amended: 2009 c.20 Sch.6 para.77
s.112, amended: 2009 c.20 Sch.6 para.78
s.140, enabling: SI 2009/ 3147, SI 2009/ 3343
s.143, applied: SI 2009/ 3343
s.143, enabling: SI 2009/ 204, SI 2009/ 353, SI 2009/ 354, SI 2009/ 355, SI 2009/ 461, SI 2009/ 1597, SI 2009/ 2154, SI 2009/ 2268, SI 2009/ 2269, SI 2009/ 3095, SI 2009/ 3147, SI 2009/ 3175, SI 2009/ 3177, SI 2009/ 3343
s.144, referred to: 2009 c.7 s.30
s.145, referred to: 2009 c.7 s.30
s.146, enabling: SI 2009/ 255, SI 2009/ 355, SI 2009/ 1597, SI 2009/ 2154
Sch.4A, applied: SI 2009/ 2268 Reg.14, SI 2009/ 2270 Reg.4
Sch.4A, referred to: SI 2009/ 2270 Reg.2

1988– cont.

41. Local Government Finance Act 1988–*cont.*
Sch.4A para.1, applied: SI 2009/ 2268 Reg.14, SI 2009/ 2269 Reg.42, Reg.43, Reg.44
Sch.4A para.3, applied: SI 2009/ 2268 Reg.14
Sch.4A para.4, applied: SI 2009/ 2268 Reg.14
Sch.5, see *Ebury (Valuation Officer) v Church Council of the Central Methodist Church* [2009] UKUT 138 (LC), [2009] R.A. 239 (UT (Lands)), George Bartlett Q.C.
Sch.5 para.11, see *Ebury (Valuation Officer) v Church Council of the Central Methodist Church* [2009] UKUT 138 (LC), [2009] R.A. 239 (UT (Lands)), George Bartlett Q.C.
Sch.6 para.2, see *Chilton-Merryweather (Listing Officer) v Hunt* [2008] EWCA Civ 1025, [2009] Env. L.R. 16 (CA (Civ Div)), Waller, L.J.; see *Kendrick (Valuation Officer), Re* [2009] R.A. 145 (Lands Tr), George Bartlett Q.C. (President, LTr)
Sch.6 para.2, referred to: SI 2009/ 3343 Sch.1 para.3
Sch.6 para.2A, applied: SI 2009/ 3177 Art.2
Sch.6 para.2A, enabling: SI 2009/ 3177
Sch.8 Part II para.4, enabling: SI 2009/ 3095, SI 2009/ 3147
Sch.8 Part II para.5, applied: SI 2009/ 2543 Sch.2 para.3
Sch.8 Part II para.6, enabling: SI 2009/ 1597, SI 2009/ 2154, SI 2009/ 3095, SI 2009/ 3147
Sch.9 para.1, applied: 2009 c.7 s.21
Sch.9 para.1, enabling: SI 2009/ 204, SI 2009/ 355, SI 2009/ 461, SI 2009/ 1597, SI 2009/ 2154
Sch.9 para.2, applied: 2009 c.7 s.21
Sch.9 para.2, enabling: SI 2009/ 355, SI 2009/ 1597, SI 2009/ 2154
Sch.9 para.3, applied: 2009 c.7 s.21
Sch.9 para.3, enabling: SI 2009/ 1597, SI 2009/ 2154
Sch.9 para.4, applied: 2009 c.7 s.21
Sch.9 para.4, enabling: SI 2009/ 1597, SI 2009/ 2154
Sch.9 para.4A, applied: 2009 c.7 s.21
Sch.9 para.5, applied: SI 2009/ 2269 Reg.17
Sch.9 para.5A, referred to: 2009 c.7 Sch.2 para.8
Sch.9 para.5B, referred to: 2009 c.7 Sch.2 para.8
Sch.9 para.5C, referred to: 2009 c.7 Sch.2 para.8
Sch.9 para.5D, referred to: 2009 c.7 Sch.2 para.8
Sch.9 para.5E, referred to: 2009 c.7 Sch.2 para.8
Sch.9 para.5F, applied: 2009 c.7 Sch.2 para.8
Sch.9 para.6, see *Southwark LBC v Cherry Advertising* [2009] R.V.R. 38 (MC), District Judge Zani
Sch.9 para.6, applied: SI 2009/ 2268 Reg.24
Sch.9 para.6, enabling: SI 2009/ 2268
Sch.11, applied: SI 2009/ 2268 Reg.25, SI 2009/ 2271 Reg.3
Sch.11 Part 1, applied: SI 2009/ 2269 Reg.6
Sch.11 Part 1 paraA.3, enabling: SI 2009/ 2269
Sch.11 Part 1 paraA.4, referred to: SI 2009/ 2267 Reg.2
Sch.11 Part 1 paraA.19, enabling: SI 2009/ 2269
Sch.11 Part 3 para.9, applied: SI 2009/ 2269 Reg.4
Sch.11 para.8, enabling: SI 2009/ 2269
Sch.11 para.9, varied: SI 2009/ 2269 Reg.42
Sch.11 para.10A, varied: SI 2009/ 2269 Reg.43
Sch.11 para.11, amended: SI 2009/ 1307 Sch.1 para.188
Sch.11 para.11, enabling: SI 2009/ 2269
Sch.11 para.12, enabling: SI 2009/ 2269
Sch.11 para.14, amended: SI 2009/ 1307 Sch.1 para.188
Sch.11 para.15, enabling: SI 2009/ 2269

1988–cont.

41. Local Government Finance Act 1988–cont.
Sch.11 para.16, enabling: SI 2009/2269

43. Housing (Scotland) Act 1988
see *Fotheringham v Hillcrest Housing Association Ltd* 2009 Hous. L.R. 99 (Lands Tr (Scot)), J N Wright, QC
s.2, amended: SI 2009/1941 Sch.1 para.97
s.2, applied: SI 2009/537 Art.2
s.43, see *Fotheringham v Hillcrest Housing Association Ltd* 2009 Hous. L.R. 99 (Lands Tr (Scot)), J N Wright, QC

48. Copyright, Designs and Patents Act 1988
see *Magical Marking Ltd v Holly* [2008] EWHC 2428 (Ch), [2009] E.C.C. 10 (Ch D), Norris, J.
Part I, applied: SI 2009/1969 Art.12
s.12, see *Phonographic Performance Ltd, Re* [2008] EWHC 2715 (Ch), [2009] R.P.C. 7 (Ch D), Kitchin, J.
s.16, see *Magical Marking Ltd v Holly* [2008] EWHC 2428 (Ch), [2009] E.C.C. 10 (Ch D), Norris, J.
s.17, see *Magical Marking Ltd v Holly* [2008] EWHC 2428 (Ch), [2009] E.C.C. 10 (Ch D), Norris, J.
s.35, applied: SI 2009/20
s.48, referred to: SI 2009/1511 Sch.1
s.69, amended: SI 2009/2979 Reg.12
s.72, see *Phonographic Performance Ltd, Re* [2008] EWHC 2715 (Ch), [2009] R.P.C. 7 (Ch D), Kitchin, J.
s.107, see *Scopelight Ltd v Chief Constable of Northumbria* [2009] EWCA Civ 1156, Times, November 11, 2009 (CA (Civ Div)), Ward, L.J.
s.107A, referred to: SI 2009/669 Sch.1 Part 1
s.114, applied: SI 2009/1969 Art.17
s.116, see *Phonographic Performance Ltd, Re* [2008] EWHC 2715 (Ch), [2009] R.P.C. 7 (Ch D), Kitchin, J.
s.116, amended: SI 2009/1941 Sch.1 para.98
s.118, see *Phonographic Performance Ltd, Re* [2008] EWHC 2715 (Ch), [2009] R.P.C. 7 (Ch D), Kitchin, J.
s.119, see *Phonographic Performance Ltd, Re* [2008] EWHC 2715 (Ch), [2009] R.P.C. 7 (Ch D), Kitchin, J.
s.128A, see *Phonographic Performance Ltd, Re* [2008] EWHC 2715 (Ch), [2009] R.P.C. 7 (Ch D), Kitchin, J.
s.128B, see *Phonographic Performance Ltd, Re* [2008] EWHC 2715 (Ch), [2009] R.P.C. 7 (Ch D), Kitchin, J.
s.143, enabling: SI 2009/20
s.157, enabling: SI 2009/2749
s.159, enabling: SI 2009/2745
s.198A, referred to: SI 2009/669 Sch.1 Part 1
s.204, applied: SI 2009/1969 Art.17
s.208, enabling: SI 2009/2745
s.226, see *Virgin Atlantic Airways Ltd v Premium Aircraft Interiors UK Ltd* [2009] EWHC 26 (Pat), [2009] E.C.D.R. 11 (Ch D (Patents Ct)), Lewison, J.
s.231, applied: SI 2009/1969 Art.17
s.250, enabling: SI 2009/546
s.281, amended: SI 2009/3348 Art.3
s.296ZF, see *R. v Higgs (Neil Stanley)* [2008] EWCA Crim 1324, [2009] 1 W.L.R. 73 (CA (Crim Div)), Jacob, L.J.
Sch.2 para.6, applied: SI 2009/20
Sch.2 para.17, amended: SI 2009/2979 Reg.12

1988–cont.

48. Copyright, Designs and Patents Act 1988–cont.
Sch.2A para.1, amended: SI 2009/1941 Sch.1 para.98
Sch.2A para.16, enabling: SI 2009/20
Sch.7 para.35, repealed: SI 2009/1941 Sch.2

49. Health and Medicines Act 1988
s.7, amended: SI 2009/1941 Sch.1 para.99
s.17, enabling: SSI 2009/308

50. Housing Act 1988
see *Hughes v Borodex Ltd* [2009] EWHC 565 (Admin), [2009] 26 E.G. 114 (QBD (Admin)), Collins, J.; see *Knowsley Housing Trust v White* [2008] UKHL 70, [2009] 1 A.C. 636 (HL), Lord Hoffmann
s.9, see *Knowsley Housing Trust v White* [2008] UKHL 70, [2009] 1 A.C. 636 (HL), Lord Hoffmann
s.13, see *Hughes v Borodex Ltd* [2009] EWHC 565 (Admin), [2009] 26 E.G. 114 (QBD (Admin)), Collins, J.
s.19A, see *Truro Diocesan Board of Finance Ltd v Foley* [2008] EWCA Civ 1162, [2009] 1 W.L.R. 2218 (CA (Civ Div)), May, L.J.
s.21, see *Truro Diocesan Board of Finance Ltd v Foley* [2008] EWCA Civ 1162, [2009] 1 W.L.R. 2218 (CA (Civ Div)), May, L.J.
s.34, see *Truro Diocesan Board of Finance Ltd v Foley* [2008] EWCA Civ 1162, [2009] 1 W.L.R. 2218 (CA (Civ Div)), May, L.J.
s.45, see *Truro Diocesan Board of Finance Ltd v Foley* [2008] EWCA Civ 1162, [2009] 1 W.L.R. 2218 (CA (Civ Div)), May, L.J.
s.74, amended: 2009 c.20 Sch.6 para.79
s.107, referred to: SI 2009/500 Sch.1 Part 1
Sch.1 Part I para.8, enabling: SI 2009/1825
Sch.1 Part I para.12, amended: 2009 c.20 Sch.6 para.79
Sch.1 para.2, see *Hughes v Borodex Ltd* [2009] EWHC 565 (Admin), [2009] 26 E.G. 114 (QBD (Admin)), Collins, J.
Sch.2, see *Knowsley Housing Trust v Prescott* [2009] EWHC 924 (QB), [2009] L. & T.R. 24 (QBD (Liverpool)), Blair, J.; see *R. (on the application of Weaver) v London & Quadrant Housing Trust* [2008] EWHC 1377 (Admin), [2009] 1 All E.R. 17 (DC), Richards, L.J.
Sch.2A para.3, see *Redstone Mortgages Plc v Welch* [2009] 36 E.G. 98 (CC (Birmingham)), Judge Worster
Sch.6 Part III para.31, repealed (in part): SI 2009/484 Sch.2
Sch.6 Part III para.35, repealed (in part): SI 2009/484 Sch.2
Sch.9 Part I para.2, amended: SI 2009/1941 Sch.1 para.100
Sch.10 Part III para.22, amended: SI 2009/1307 Sch.1 para.189

52. Road Traffic Act 1988
see *Agheampong v Allied Manufacturing (London) Ltd* [2009] Lloyd's Rep. I.R. 379 (CC (London)), Judge Dean Q.C.
applied: SI 2009/711 Sch.1 para.21, Sch.1 para.25, Sch.1 para.32, Sch.1 para.34, SI 2009/1885 Art.2, Sch.4 para.1
Part III, applied: SI 2009/365 Reg.4, Reg.5, SI 2009/366 Reg.4, SI 2009/2793 Reg.2
Part V, referred to: 2009 c.17 s.4
s.1, see *Lynn (Graham Stuart) v HM Advocate* 2009 S.C.L. 324 (HCJ), Lord Clarke

1988– cont.

52. Road Traffic Act 1988– *cont.*
s.1, applied: SSI 2009/ 31 Sch.1 para.22, SSI 2009/ 71 Sch.1 para.22
s.1, referred to: SI 2009/ 669 Sch.1 Part 3
s.2, referred to: SI 2009/ 669 Sch.1 Part 3
s.2A, referred to: SI 2009/ 669 Sch.1 Part 3
s.2B, see *R. v Larke (Ann)* [2009] EWCA Crim 870, [2009] R.T.R. 33 (CA (Crim Div)), Scott Baker, L.J.
s.2B, applied: SSI 2009/ 31 Sch.1 para.23, SSI 2009/ 71 Sch.1 para.23
s.2B, referred to: SI 2009/ 669 Sch.1 Part 3
s.3, referred to: SI 2009/ 491 Sch.1 Part 1, SI 2009/ 669 Sch.1 Part 3
s.3A, applied: SSI 2009/ 31 Sch.1 para.24, SSI 2009/ 71 Sch.1 para.24
s.3A, referred to: SI 2009/ 669 Sch.1 Part 3
s.3ZA, referred to: SI 2009/ 669 Sch.1 Part 3
s.3ZB, applied: SSI 2009/ 31 Sch.1 para.25, SSI 2009/ 71 Sch.1 para.25
s.3ZB, referred to: SI 2009/ 669 Sch.1 Part 3
s.4, referred to: SI 2009/ 491 Sch.1 Part 1, SI 2009/ 669 Sch.1 Part 3
s.5, applied: SI 2009/ 1922 Art.12
s.5, referred to: SI 2009/ 491 Sch.1 Part 1, SI 2009/ 669 Sch.1 Part 3
s.6, applied: SI 2009/ 1922 Art.12
s.6, referred to: SI 2009/ 669 Sch.1 Part 3
s.6A, applied: SI 2009/ 1922 Art.12
s.6A, referred to: SI 2009/ 669 Sch.1 Part 3
s.6B, applied: SI 2009/ 1922 Art.12
s.6B, referred to: SI 2009/ 669 Sch.1 Part 3
s.6C, applied: SI 2009/ 1922 Art.12
s.6C, referred to: SI 2009/ 669 Sch.1 Part 3
s.6D, see *DPP v Wilson* [2009] EWHC 1988 (Admin), [2009] R.T.R. 29 (DC), Thomas, L.J.
s.6D, applied: SI 2009/ 1922 Art.12
s.6D, referred to: SI 2009/ 669 Sch.1 Part 3
s.6E, applied: SI 2009/ 1922 Art.12
s.6E, referred to: SI 2009/ 669 Sch.1 Part 3
s.7, see *Morris v DPP* [2008] EWHC 2788 (Admin), (2009) 173 J.P. 41 (QBD (Admin)), Slade, J.; see *R. v Bryan (Julian)* [2008] EWCA Crim 1568, [2009] R.T.R. 4 (CA (Crim Div)), Scott Baker, L.J.
s.7, applied: SI 2009/ 1922 Art.12
s.7, referred to: SI 2009/ 669 Sch.1 Part 3
s.7A, applied: SI 2009/ 1922 Art.12
s.7A, referred to: SI 2009/ 669 Sch.1 Part 3
s.8, applied: SI 2009/ 1922 Art.12
s.8, referred to: SI 2009/ 669 Sch.1 Part 3
s.9, applied: SI 2009/ 1922 Art.12
s.9, referred to: SI 2009/ 669 Sch.1 Part 3
s.10, applied: SI 2009/ 1922 Art.12
s.10, referred to: SI 2009/ 669 Sch.1 Part 3
s.11, referred to: SI 2009/ 669 Sch.1 Part 3
s.12, referred to: SI 2009/ 491 Sch.1 Part 1, SI 2009/ 669 Sch.1 Part 3
s.13, referred to: SI 2009/ 491 Sch.1 Part 1, SI 2009/ 669 Sch.1 Part 3
s.13A, referred to: SI 2009/ 669 Sch.1 Part 3
s.14, referred to: SI 2009/ 491 Sch.1 Part 1, SI 2009/ 492 Sch.1 Part 1, SI 2009/ 669 Sch.1 Part 3
s.15, referred to: SI 2009/ 491 Sch.1 Part 1, SI 2009/ 492 Sch.1 Part 1, SI 2009/ 669 Sch.1 Part 3
s.15A, referred to: SI 2009/ 669 Sch.1 Part 3
s.15B, referred to: SI 2009/ 669 Sch.1 Part 3
s.16, referred to: SI 2009/ 491 Sch.1 Part 1, SI 2009/ 492 Sch.1 Part 1, SI 2009/ 669 Sch.1 Part 3

1988– cont.

52. Road Traffic Act 1988– *cont.*
s.17, referred to: SI 2009/ 669 Sch.1 Part 3
s.18, referred to: SI 2009/ 491 Sch.1 Part 1, SI 2009/ 492 Sch.1 Part 1, SI 2009/ 669 Sch.1 Part 3
s.19, referred to: SI 2009/ 491 Sch.1 Part 1, SI 2009/ 492 Sch.1 Part 1, SI 2009/ 669 Sch.1 Part 3
s.19A, referred to: SI 2009/ 669 Sch.1 Part 3
s.20, referred to: SI 2009/ 669 Sch.1 Part 3
s.21, referred to: SI 2009/ 669 Sch.1 Part 3
s.22, referred to: SI 2009/ 491 Sch.1 Part 1, SI 2009/ 492 Sch.1 Part 1, SI 2009/ 669 Sch.1 Part 3
s.22A, referred to: SI 2009/ 669 Sch.1 Part 3
s.23, referred to: SI 2009/ 669 Sch.1 Part 3
s.24, referred to: SI 2009/ 669 Sch.1 Part 3
s.25, referred to: SI 2009/ 669 Sch.1 Part 3
s.26, referred to: SI 2009/ 669 Sch.1 Part 3
s.27, referred to: SI 2009/ 669 Sch.1 Part 3
s.28, referred to: SI 2009/ 669 Sch.1 Part 3
s.29, referred to: SI 2009/ 669 Sch.1 Part 3
s.30, referred to: SI 2009/ 669 Sch.1 Part 3
s.31, referred to: SI 2009/ 669 Sch.1 Part 3
s.32, referred to: SI 2009/ 669 Sch.1 Part 3
s.33, referred to: SI 2009/ 491 Sch.1 Part 1, SI 2009/ 669 Sch.1 Part 3
s.34, referred to: SI 2009/ 491 Sch.1 Part 1, SI 2009/ 492 Sch.1 Part 1, SI 2009/ 669 Sch.1 Part 3
s.34A, referred to: SI 2009/ 669 Sch.1 Part 3
s.35, referred to: SI 2009/ 491 Sch.1 Part 1, SI 2009/ 492 Sch.1 Part 1, SI 2009/ 669 Sch.1 Part 3
s.36, see *R. (on the application of Pluckrose) v Snaresbrook Crown Court* [2009] EWHC 1506 (Admin), (2009) 173 J.P. 492 (DC), Pill, L.J.; see *Robbie the Pict v Crown Prosecution Service* [2009] EWHC 1176 (Admin), Times, May 14, 2009 (QBD (Admin)), Davis, J.
s.36, referred to: SI 2009/ 491 Sch.1 Part 1, SI 2009/ 492 Sch.1 Part 1, SI 2009/ 669 Sch.1 Part 3
s.37, referred to: SI 2009/ 669 Sch.1 Part 3
s.38, referred to: SI 2009/ 669 Sch.1 Part 3
s.39, referred to: SI 2009/ 669 Sch.1 Part 3
s.40, referred to: SI 2009/ 669 Sch.1 Part 3
s.40A, referred to: SI 2009/ 491 Sch.1 Part 1, SI 2009/ 492 Sch.1 Part 1, SI 2009/ 669 Sch.1 Part 3
s.41, referred to: SI 2009/ 669 Sch.1 Part 3
s.41, enabling: SI 2009/ 141, SI 2009/ 142, SI 2009/ 1806, SI 2009/ 2196, SI 2009/ 3220, SI 2009/ 3221
s.41A, referred to: SI 2009/ 491 Sch.1 Part 1, SI 2009/ 492 Sch.2, SI 2009/ 669 Sch.1 Part 3
s.41B, referred to: SI 2009/ 491 Sch.1 Part 1, SI 2009/ 492 Sch.2, SI 2009/ 669 Sch.1 Part 3
s.41C, referred to: SI 2009/ 669 Sch.1 Part 3
s.41D, referred to: SI 2009/ 491 Sch.1 Part 1, SI 2009/ 492 Sch.1 Part 1, SI 2009/ 669 Sch.1 Part 3
s.42, referred to: SI 2009/ 491 Sch.1 Part 1, SI 2009/ 492 Sch.2, SI 2009/ 669 Sch.1 Part 3
s.43, referred to: SI 2009/ 669 Sch.1 Part 3
s.44, referred to: SI 2009/ 669 Sch.1 Part 3
s.45, applied: SI 2009/ 711 Art.5, Sch.1 para.25
s.45, referred to: SI 2009/ 669 Sch.1 Part 3
s.45, enabling: SI 2009/ 643, SI 2009/ 802
s.46, applied: SI 2009/ 711 Art.5
s.46, referred to: SI 2009/ 669 Sch.1 Part 3
s.46, enabling: SI 2009/ 643, SI 2009/ 802
s.46A, referred to: SI 2009/ 669 Sch.1 Part 3
s.46B, referred to: SI 2009/ 669 Sch.1 Part 3
s.47, referred to: SI 2009/ 491 Sch.1 Part 1, SI 2009/ 492 Sch.1 Part 1, SI 2009/ 669 Sch.1 Part 3
s.48, referred to: SI 2009/ 669 Sch.1 Part 3

1988– cont.

52. Road Traffic Act 1988–*cont.*
s.49, applied: SI 2009/711 Art.5, Sch.1 para.28, Sch.1 para.33
s.49, referred to: SI 2009/669 Sch.1 Part 3
s.49, enabling: SI 2009/799, SI 2009/3220
s.49A, referred to: SI 2009/669 Sch.1 Part 3
s.50, referred to: SI 2009/669 Sch.1 Part 3
s.51, applied: SI 2009/711 Art.5
s.51, referred to: SI 2009/669 Sch.1 Part 3
s.51, enabling: SI 2009/799, SI 2009/3220
s.52, referred to: SI 2009/669 Sch.1 Part 3
s.53, referred to: SI 2009/491 Sch.1 Part 1, SI 2009/669 Sch.1 Part 3
s.54, referred to: SI 2009/669 Sch.1 Part 3
s.54, enabling: SI 2009/2084
s.55, referred to: SI 2009/669 Sch.1 Part 3
s.56, referred to: SI 2009/669 Sch.1 Part 3
s.57, referred to: SI 2009/669 Sch.1 Part 3
s.58, applied: SI 2009/717 Sch.3 para.2
s.58, referred to: SI 2009/669 Sch.1 Part 3
s.59, applied: SI 2009/711 Sch.1 para.29
s.59, referred to: SI 2009/669 Sch.1 Part 3
s.60, referred to: SI 2009/669 Sch.1 Part 3
s.61, applied: SI 2009/711 Art.5, Sch.1 para.32
s.61, referred to: SI 2009/669 Sch.1 Part 3
s.61, enabling: SI 2009/815, SI 2009/863, SI 2009/865, SI 2009/2084
s.62, referred to: SI 2009/669 Sch.1 Part 3
s.63, referred to: SI 2009/491 Sch.1 Part 1, SI 2009/669 Sch.1 Part 3
s.63, enabling: SI 2009/815
s.63A, applied: SI 2009/711 Art.5, Sch.1 para.28, Sch.1 para.29, Sch.1 para.33
s.63A, referred to: SI 2009/669 Sch.1 Part 3
s.63A, enabling: SI 2009/799
s.64, referred to: SI 2009/491 Sch.1 Part 1, SI 2009/669 Sch.1 Part 3
s.64A, amended: SI 2009/818 Reg.3
s.64A, referred to: SI 2009/669 Sch.1 Part 3
s.64A, repealed (in part): SI 2009/818 Reg.3
s.65, referred to: SI 2009/669 Sch.1 Part 3
s.65A, amended: SI 2009/818 Reg.3
s.65A, referred to: SI 2009/669 Sch.1 Part 3
s.65A, repealed (in part): SI 2009/818 Reg.3
s.66, referred to: SI 2009/669 Sch.1 Part 3
s.66A, referred to: SI 2009/669 Sch.1 Part 3
s.67, referred to: SI 2009/491 Sch.1 Part 1, SI 2009/669 Sch.1 Part 3
s.67A, referred to: SI 2009/669 Sch.1 Part 3
s.67B, referred to: SI 2009/669 Sch.1 Part 3
s.68, referred to: SI 2009/491 Sch.1 Part 1, SI 2009/669 Sch.1 Part 3
s.68, referred to: SI 2009/669 Sch.1 Part 3
s.69, referred to: SI 2009/669 Sch.1 Part 3
s.69, applied: SI 2009/493 Reg.3, Reg.4
s.69, referred to: SI 2009/669 Sch.1 Part 3
s.69A, referred to: SI 2009/669 Sch.1 Part 3
s.70, referred to: SI 2009/669 Sch.1 Part 3
s.70, applied: SI 2009/493 Reg.3, Reg.4
s.70, referred to: SI 2009/669 Sch.1 Part 3
s.71, referred to: SI 2009/669 Sch.1 Part 3
s.71, applied: SI 2009/483 Art.2
s.71, referred to: SI 2009/491 Sch.1 Part 1, SI 2009/492 Sch.1 Part 1, SI 2009/669 Sch.1 Part 3
s.72, applied: SI 2009/711 Art.5
s.72, referred to: SI 2009/669 Sch.1 Part 3
s.72, referred to: SI 2009/493 Reg.4, SI 2009/669 Sch.1 Part 3

1988– cont.

52. Road Traffic Act 1988–*cont.*
s.72A, referred to: SI 2009/669 Sch.1 Part 3
s.73, referred to: SI 2009/669 Sch.1 Part 3
s.74, referred to: SI 2009/669 Sch.1 Part 3
s.75, referred to: SI 2009/669 Sch.1 Part 3
s.76, referred to: SI 2009/491 Sch.1 Part 1, SI 2009/669 Sch.1 Part 3
s.77, referred to: SI 2009/669 Sch.1 Part 3
s.78, referred to: SI 2009/491 Sch.1 Part 1, SI 2009/669 Sch.1 Part 3
s.79, referred to: SI 2009/669 Sch.1 Part 3
s.80, referred to: SI 2009/669 Sch.1 Part 3
s.81, referred to: SI 2009/669 Sch.1 Part 3
s.82, referred to: SI 2009/669 Sch.1 Part 3
s.83, referred to: SI 2009/669 Sch.1 Part 3
s.84, referred to: SI 2009/669 Sch.1 Part 3
s.85, amended: SI 2009/818 Reg.3
s.85, referred to: SI 2009/669 Sch.1 Part 3
s.85, repealed (in part): SI 2009/818 Reg.3
s.86, amended: SI 2009/818 Reg.3
s.86, referred to: SI 2009/669 Sch.1 Part 3
s.87, referred to: SI 2009/491 Sch.1 Part 1, SI 2009/492 Sch.1 Part 1, SI 2009/669 Sch.1 Part 3
s.88, applied: SI 2009/365 Reg.2
s.88, referred to: SI 2009/669 Sch.1 Part 3
s.89, referred to: SI 2009/669 Sch.1 Part 3
s.89, enabling: SI 2009/788, SI 2009/2362
s.89A, referred to: SI 2009/669 Sch.1 Part 3
s.90, referred to: SI 2009/669 Sch.1 Part 3
s.91, referred to: SI 2009/669 Sch.1 Part 3
s.91, enabling: SI 2009/788
s.92, referred to: SI 2009/669 Sch.1 Part 3
s.93, referred to: SI 2009/669 Sch.1 Part 3
s.94, referred to: SI 2009/669 Sch.1 Part 3
s.94A, referred to: SI 2009/491 Sch.1 Part 1, SI 2009/669 Sch.1 Part 3
s.95, referred to: SI 2009/669 Sch.1 Part 3
s.96, referred to: SI 2009/491 Sch.1 Part 1, SI 2009/669 Sch.1 Part 3
s.97, applied: SI 2009/788
s.97, referred to: SI 2009/669 Sch.1 Part 3
s.97, enabling: SI 2009/788
s.98, referred to: SI 2009/669 Sch.1 Part 3
s.98A, referred to: SI 2009/669 Sch.1 Part 3
s.99, referred to: SI 2009/669 Sch.1 Part 3
s.99, enabling: SI 2009/788
s.99A, referred to: SI 2009/669 Sch.1 Part 3
s.99B, referred to: SI 2009/669 Sch.1 Part 3
s.99C, referred to: SI 2009/669 Sch.1 Part 3
s.99D, referred to: SI 2009/669 Sch.1 Part 3
s.99E, referred to: SI 2009/669 Sch.1 Part 3
s.99ZA, referred to: SI 2009/669 Sch.1 Part 3
s.99ZB, referred to: SI 2009/669 Sch.1 Part 3
s.99ZC, referred to: SI 2009/669 Sch.1 Part 3
s.100, referred to: SI 2009/669 Sch.1 Part 3
s.101, referred to: SI 2009/669 Sch.1 Part 3
s.102, referred to: SI 2009/669 Sch.1 Part 3
s.102A, referred to: SI 2009/669 Sch.1 Part 3
s.103, referred to: SI 2009/491 Sch.1 Part 1, SI 2009/669 Sch.1 Part 3
s.104, referred to: SI 2009/669 Sch.1 Part 3
s.105, referred to: SI 2009/669 Sch.1 Part 3
s.105, repealed (in part): 2009 c.26 Sch.8 Part 13
s.105, enabling: SI 2009/788
s.106, referred to: SI 2009/669 Sch.1 Part 3
s.107, referred to: SI 2009/669 Sch.1 Part 3
s.108, referred to: SI 2009/669 Sch.1 Part 3
s.109, referred to: SI 2009/669 Sch.1 Part 3

1988– cont.

52. Road Traffic Act 1988– *cont.*
s.109A, referred to: SI 2009/669 Sch.1 Part 3
s.109B, referred to: SI 2009/669 Sch.1 Part 3
s.109C, referred to: SI 2009/669 Sch.1 Part 3
s.114, referred to: SI 2009/491 Sch.1 Part 1
s.115, see *R. (on the application of Hume) v Carmarthen Magistrates Court* [2008] EWHC 3272 (Admin), [2009] R.T.R. 15 (QBD (Admin)), Cranston, J.
s.117, see *R. (on the application of Hume) v Carmarthen Magistrates Court* [2008] EWHC 3272 (Admin), [2009] R.T.R. 15 (QBD (Admin)), Cranston, J.
s.119, see *R. (on the application of Hume) v Carmarthen Magistrates Court* [2008] EWHC 3272 (Admin), [2009] R.T.R. 15 (QBD (Admin)), Cranston, J.
s.123, amended: 2009 c.17 s.1, Sch.1 para.2, Sch.2
s.123, referred to: SI 2009/669 Sch.1 Part 3
s.123A, amended: 2009 c.17 s.1
s.123A, referred to: SI 2009/669 Sch.1 Part 3
s.124, amended: 2009 c.17 s.3
s.124, referred to: SI 2009/669 Sch.1 Part 3
s.125, referred to: SI 2009/669 Sch.1 Part 3
s.125A, referred to: SI 2009/669 Sch.1 Part 3
s.125B, referred to: SI 2009/669 Sch.1 Part 3
s.125ZA, referred to: SI 2009/669 Sch.1 Part 3
s.126, referred to: SI 2009/669 Sch.1 Part 3
s.127, amended: 2009 c.17 Sch.1 para.3
s.127, referred to: SI 2009/669 Sch.1 Part 3
s.127, repealed (in part): 2009 c.17 Sch.2
s.128, amended: 2009 c.17 Sch.1 para.1
s.128, referred to: SI 2009/669 Sch.1 Part 3
s.128, repealed (in part): 2009 c.17 Sch.2
s.128A, referred to: SI 2009/669 Sch.1 Part 3
s.128ZA, added: 2009 c.17 s.1
s.128ZA, referred to: SI 2009/669 Sch.1 Part 3
s.128ZB, added: 2009 c.17 s.2
s.128ZB, referred to: SI 2009/669 Sch.1 Part 3
s.129, amended: 2009 c.17 Sch.1 para.6
s.129, applied: SI 2009/844 Reg.3
s.129, referred to: SI 2009/669 Sch.1 Part 3
s.129, repealed (in part): 2009 c.17 Sch.2
s.129, enabling: SI 2009/844
s.130, amended: 2009 c.17 Sch.1 para.5
s.130, referred to: SI 2009/669 Sch.1 Part 3
s.130, repealed (in part): 2009 c.17 Sch.2
s.131, amended: SI 2009/1885 Sch.1 para.11
s.131, referred to: SI 2009/669 Sch.1 Part 3
s.131, repealed (in part): SI 2009/1885 Sch.1 para.11
s.131A, added: 2009 c.17 Sch.1 para.7
s.131A, referred to: SI 2009/669 Sch.1 Part 3
s.131A, repealed: 2009 c.17 Sch.2
s.132, referred to: SI 2009/669 Sch.1 Part 3
s.132, enabling: SI 2009/844
s.133, referred to: SI 2009/669 Sch.1 Part 3
s.133A, referred to: SI 2009/669 Sch.1 Part 3
s.133B, referred to: SI 2009/669 Sch.1 Part 3
s.133C, referred to: SI 2009/669 Sch.1 Part 3
s.133D, referred to: SI 2009/669 Sch.1 Part 3
s.133ZA, amended: SI 2009/1885 Sch.1 para.12
s.133ZA, referred to: SI 2009/669 Sch.1 Part 3
s.134, referred to: SI 2009/669 Sch.1 Part 3
s.135, referred to: SI 2009/669 Sch.1 Part 3
s.136, referred to: SI 2009/669 Sch.1 Part 3
s.137, referred to: SI 2009/669 Sch.1 Part 3
s.138, referred to: SI 2009/669 Sch.1 Part 3
s.139, referred to: SI 2009/669 Sch.1 Part 3

1988– cont.

52. Road Traffic Act 1988– *cont.*
s.140, referred to: SI 2009/669 Sch.1 Part 3
s.141, referred to: SI 2009/669 Sch.1 Part 3
s.141, enabling: SI 2009/844
s.141A, referred to: SI 2009/669 Sch.1 Part 3
s.142, amended: 2009 c.17 s.1
s.142, referred to: SI 2009/669 Sch.1 Part 3
s.143, see *Agheampong v Allied Manufacturing (London) Ltd* [2009] Lloyd's Rep. I.R. 379 (CC (London)), Judge Dean Q.C.; see *Sedgefield BC v Crowe* [2008] EWHC 1814 (Admin), [2009] R.T.R. 10 (DC), Maurice Kay, L.J.
s.143, referred to: SI 2009/491 Sch.1 Part 1, SI 2009/492 Sch.1 Part 1, SI 2009/669 Sch.1 Part 3
s.144, amended: 2009 c.20 Sch.6 para.80
s.144, referred to: SI 2009/669 Sch.1 Part 3
s.144A, referred to: SI 2009/669 Sch.1 Part 3
s.144B, referred to: SI 2009/669 Sch.1 Part 3
s.144C, referred to: SI 2009/669 Sch.1 Part 3
s.144D, referred to: SI 2009/669 Sch.1 Part 3
s.145, referred to: SI 2009/669 Sch.1 Part 3
s.146, referred to: SI 2009/669 Sch.1 Part 3
s.147, referred to: SI 2009/669 Sch.1 Part 3
s.148, referred to: SI 2009/669 Sch.1 Part 3
s.149, referred to: SI 2009/669 Sch.1 Part 3
s.150, referred to: SI 2009/669 Sch.1 Part 3
s.151, see *Cameron v Gellatly* [2009] CSOH 82, 2009 S.C. 639 (OH), Lord Malcolm
s.151, referred to: SI 2009/669 Sch.1 Part 3
s.152, referred to: SI 2009/669 Sch.1 Part 3
s.153, referred to: SI 2009/669 Sch.1 Part 3
s.154, referred to: SI 2009/669 Sch.1 Part 3
s.155, referred to: SI 2009/669 Sch.1 Part 3
s.156, referred to: SI 2009/669 Sch.1 Part 3
s.159A, referred to: SI 2009/669 Sch.1 Part 3
s.160, referred to: SI 2009/669 Sch.1 Part 3
s.161, referred to: SI 2009/669 Sch.1 Part 3
s.162, referred to: SI 2009/669 Sch.1 Part 3
s.162A, amended: SI 2009/1885 Sch.1 para.13
s.162A, referred to: SI 2009/669 Sch.1 Part 3
s.163, referred to: SI 2009/491 Sch.1 Part 1, SI 2009/492 Sch.1 Part 1, SI 2009/669 Sch.1 Part 3
s.164, amended: 2009 c.24 Sch.7 Part 4
s.164, referred to: SI 2009/491 Sch.1 Part 1, SI 2009/669 Sch.1 Part 3
s.165, referred to: SI 2009/491 Sch.1 Part 1, SI 2009/669 Sch.1 Part 3
s.165A, referred to: SI 2009/669 Sch.1 Part 3
s.165B, referred to: SI 2009/669 Sch.1 Part 3
s.166, referred to: SI 2009/669 Sch.1 Part 3
s.167, referred to: SI 2009/669 Sch.1 Part 3
s.168, referred to: SI 2009/491 Sch.1 Part 1, SI 2009/669 Sch.1 Part 3
s.169, referred to: SI 2009/669 Sch.1 Part 3
s.170, referred to: SI 2009/491 Sch.1 Part 1, SI 2009/669 Sch.1 Part 3
s.171, referred to: SI 2009/669 Sch.1 Part 3
s.172, see *R. (on the application of Taylor) v Southampton Magistrates Court* [2008] EWHC 3006 (Admin), (2009) 172 J.P. 17 (QBD (Admin)), Toulson, L.J.
s.172, referred to: SI 2009/669 Sch.1 Part 3
s.173, applied: SI 2009/2773 Sch.1, SI 2009/2781 Sch.1
s.173, referred to: SI 2009/669 Sch.1 Part 3
s.174, referred to: SI 2009/669 Sch.1 Part 3
s.175, referred to: SI 2009/669 Sch.1 Part 3
s.176, referred to: SI 2009/669 Sch.1 Part 3
s.177, referred to: SI 2009/669 Sch.1 Part 3

1988– cont.

52. Road Traffic Act 1988–*cont.*
s.178, referred to: SI 2009/669 Sch.1 Part 3
s.179, referred to: SI 2009/669 Sch.1 Part 3
s.180, referred to: SI 2009/669 Sch.1 Part 3
s.181, referred to: SI 2009/491 Sch.1 Part 1, SI 2009/669 Sch.1 Part 3
s.182, referred to: SI 2009/669 Sch.1 Part 3
s.183, referred to: SI 2009/669 Sch.1 Part 3
s.184, applied: SI 2009/1922 Art.12
s.184, referred to: SI 2009/669 Sch.1 Part 3
s.184, varied: SI 2009/1059 Sch.1 para.30
s.185, referred to: SI 2009/669 Sch.1 Part 3
s.186, referred to: SI 2009/669 Sch.1 Part 3
s.187, referred to: SI 2009/669 Sch.1 Part 3
s.188, referred to: SI 2009/669 Sch.1 Part 3
s.189, referred to: SI 2009/669 Sch.1 Part 3
s.190, referred to: SI 2009/669 Sch.1 Part 3
s.191, referred to: SI 2009/669 Sch.1 Part 3
s.192, referred to: SI 2009/669 Sch.1 Part 3
s.192A, referred to: SI 2009/669 Sch.1 Part 3
s.193, referred to: SI 2009/669 Sch.1 Part 3
s.193A, referred to: SI 2009/669 Sch.1 Part 3
s.194, referred to: SI 2009/669 Sch.1 Part 3
s.195, applied: SI 2009/141, SI 2009/142, SI 2009/643, SI 2009/788, SI 2009/799, SI 2009/802, SI 2009/815, SI 2009/863, SI 2009/865, SI 2009/1806, SI 2009/2084, SI 2009/2196, SI 2009/2362, SI 2009/3220, SI 2009/3221
s.195, referred to: SI 2009/669 Sch.1 Part 3
s.196, referred to: SI 2009/669 Sch.1 Part 3
s.197, referred to: SI 2009/669 Sch.1 Part 3
Sch.1, referred to: SI 2009/669 Sch.1 Part 3
Sch.2, referred to: SI 2009/669 Sch.1 Part 3
Sch.2A, referred to: SI 2009/669 Sch.1 Part 3
Sch.3, referred to: SI 2009/669 Sch.1 Part 3
Sch.4, referred to: SI 2009/669 Sch.1 Part 3

53. Road Traffic Offenders Act 1988
see *Gidden v Chief Constable of Humberside* [2009] EWHC 2924 (Admin), (2009) 173 J.P. 609 (DC), Elias, L.J.
applied: SI 2009/1885 Art.2, Sch.4 para.1
referred to: SI 2009/500 Sch.1 Part 1
Part III, applied: SI 2009/483 Art.2, Art.3
s.1, see *Gidden v Chief Constable of Humberside* [2009] EWHC 2924 (Admin), (2009) 173 J.P. 609 (DC), Elias, L.J.
s.1, applied: SI 2009/493 Reg.19
s.6, see *Burwell v DPP* [2009] EWHC 1069 (Admin), (2009) 173 J.P. 351 (QBD (Admin)), Keene, L.J.
s.6, applied: SI 2009/493 Reg.19
s.11, applied: SI 2009/493 Reg.19
s.12, applied: SI 2009/493 Reg.19
s.15, see *DPP v Wilson* [2009] EWHC 1988 (Admin), [2009] R.T.R. 29 (DC), Thomas, L.J.
s.16, see *Brett v DPP* [2009] EWHC 440 (Admin), [2009] 1 W.L.R. 2530 (DC), Leveson, L.J.
s.18, amended: 2009 c.17 s.1, Sch.1 para.4
s.18, repealed (in part): 2009 c.17 Sch.2
s.20, see *Robbie the Pict v Crown Prosecution Service* [2009] EWHC 1176 (Admin), Times, May 14, 2009 (QBD (Admin)), Davis, J.; see *Robbie the Pict v Service* [2009] HCJAC 49, 2009 S.C.L. 944 (HCJ), Lord Carloway
s.27, amended: 2009 c.24 Sch.7 Part 4
s.30C, amended: SI 2009/1885 Sch.1 para.15
s.34, amended: 2009 c.25 Sch.21 para.90
s.34A, amended: 2009 c.25 Sch.21 para.90, Sch.22 para.31

1988– cont.

53. Road Traffic Offenders Act 1988– *cont.*
s.34A, referred to: 2009 c.25 Sch.22 para.30
s.34B, amended: 2009 c.25 Sch.21 para.90, Sch.22 para.32
s.34B, referred to: 2009 c.25 Sch.22 para.30
s.34BA, amended: SI 2009/1885 Sch.1 para.16
s.34BA, referred to: 2009 c.25 Sch.22 para.30
s.34C, referred to: 2009 c.25 Sch.22 para.30
s.34D, amended: 2009 c.25 Sch.21 para.90
s.34F, amended: SI 2009/1885 Sch.1 para.17
s.35, amended: 2009 c.25 Sch.21 para.90
s.35A, added: 2009 c.25 Sch.16 para.2
s.35A, varied: 2009 c.25 Sch.22 para.34
s.35B, added: 2009 c.25 Sch.16 para.2
s.35C, added: 2009 c.25 Sch.16 para.2
s.35C, varied: 2009 c.25 Sch.22 para.35
s.35D, added: 2009 c.25 Sch.16 para.2
s.37, amended: 2009 c.25 Sch.21 para.90
s.42, amended: 2009 c.25 Sch.21 para.90
s.44, see *Warring-Davies v Crown Prosecution Service* [2009] EWHC 1172 (Admin), [2009] R.T.R. 35 (DC), Maurice Kay, L.J.
s.47, amended: 2009 c.25 Sch.21 para.90, Sch.22 para.33
s.51, enabling: SI 2009/483
s.52, applied: SI 2009/495 Sch.1
s.53, enabling: SI 2009/488, SI 2009/1487
s.54, applied: SI 2009/495 Reg.3
s.55, applied: SI 2009/495 Reg.6
s.56, applied: SI 2009/495 Reg.9, Sch.1
s.62, referred to: SI 2009/491 Sch.1 Part 1
s.70, applied: SI 2009/495 Reg.6, Sch.1
s.71, applied: SI 2009/495 Reg.7
s.84, enabling: SI 2009/494, SI 2009/495
s.88, applied: SI 2009/483, SI 2009/488, SI 2009/494, SI 2009/495, SI 2009/1487
s.88, enabling: SI 2009/488, SI 2009/494, SI 2009/495
s.90A, applied: SI 2009/491 Art.3, Art.4, Art.5
s.90A, referred to: SI 2009/491 Art.6
s.90A, enabling: SI 2009/491
s.90B, enabling: SI 2009/491, SI 2009/492
s.90C, applied: SI 2009/491 Art.7, SI 2009/498 Art.2
s.90C, enabling: SI 2009/491, SI 2009/498
s.90D, applied: SI 2009/483 Art.2, SI 2009/493 Reg.3, Reg.4
s.90D, referred to: SI 2009/491 Sch.1 Part 1, SI 2009/492 Sch.1 Part 1, SI 2009/493 Reg.4
s.90E, applied: SI 2009/491, SI 2009/492, SI 2009/498
s.90E, enabling: SI 2009/491, SI 2009/492
Sch.3, amended: SI 2009/483 Sch.1 para.1, Sch.1 para.2, Sch.1 para.3, Sch.1 para.4, Sch.1 para.5, Sch.1 para.6, Sch.1 para.7

54. Road Traffic (Consequential Provisions) Act 1988
Sch.3 para.22, repealed: SI 2009/818 Reg.4
Sch.3 para.29, repealed: 2009 c.26 Sch.8 Part 2

1989

5. Security Service Act 1989
see *A v B (Investigatory Powers Tribunal: Jurisdiction)* [2009] EWCA Civ 24, [2009] 3 W.L.R. 717 (CA (Civ Div)), Laws, L.J.

15. Water Act 1989
s.83, amended: SI 2009/1941 Sch.1 para.101
s.141, amended: SSI 2009/85 Sch.2 para.8

1989– cont.

15. Water Act 1989–*cont.*
s.189, amended: SI 2009/1941 Sch.1 para.101
Sch.17 para.1, repealed (in part): 2009 c.23 Sch.22 Part 4
Sch.17 para.3, repealed (in part): SI 2009/463 Sch.2 para.8, SSI 2009/85 Sch.2 para.8
Sch.17 para.5, repealed: 2009 c.23 Sch.22 Part 4
Sch.17 para.7, repealed (in part): 2009 c.23 Sch.22 Part 5
Sch.17 para.8, repealed (in part): SI 2009/463 Sch.2 para.8, SSI 2009/85 Sch.2 para.8
Sch.25 para.66, repealed (in part): 2009 c.23 Sch.22 Part 3
Sch.27 Part I, amended: SI 2009/463 Sch.2 para.8, SSI 2009/85 Sch.2 para.8

26. Finance Act 1989
s.33, repealed (in part): 2009 c.10 Sch.1 para.6
s.43, repealed: 2009 c.4 Sch.3 Part 1
s.44, repealed: 2009 c.4 Sch.3 Part 1
s.57, repealed (in part): SI 2009/2035 Sch.1 para.60
s.67, applied: 2009 c.4 s.1290
s.82, amended: 2009 c.4 Sch.1 para.341, 2009 c.10 Sch.23 para.2
s.82D, amended: 2009 c.4 Sch.1 para.342
s.82E, amended: 2009 c.4 Sch.1 para.343
s.83, amended: 2009 c.4 Sch.1 para.344, 2009 c.10 Sch.23 para.1
s.83, referred to: 2009 c.4 s.464
s.83A, see *Legal & General Assurance Society Ltd v Revenue and Customs Commissioners* [2009] UKFTT 225 (TC), [2009] S.F.T.D. 701 (FTT (Tax)), John F Avery Jones
s.83YC, amended: 2009 c.4 Sch.1 para.345
s.83YD, amended: 2009 c.4 Sch.1 para.346
s.83YF, amended: 2009 c.4 Sch.1 para.347
s.83ZA, referred to: 2009 c.4 s.699, s.906
s.85, amended: 2009 c.4 Sch.1 para.348
s.85A, amended: 2009 c.4 Sch.1 para.349, Sch.3 Part 1, 2009 c.10 Sch.14 para.16
s.86, applied: 2009 c.4 s.1297
s.88, see *Sun Life Assurance Co of Canada (UK) Ltd v Revenue and Customs Commissioners* [2009] EWHC 60 (Ch), [2009] S.T.C. 768 (Ch D), Patten, J.
s.88, amended: 2009 c.4 Sch.3 Part 1
s.88, applied: 2009 c.4 s.563
s.89, see *Sun Life Assurance Co of Canada (UK) Ltd v Revenue and Customs Commissioners* [2009] EWHC 60 (Ch), [2009] S.T.C. 768 (Ch D), Patten, J.
s.89, amended: 2009 c.4 Sch.1 para.351, Sch.3 Part 1, 2009 c.10 Sch.14 para.17
s.114, repealed: 2009 c.4 Sch.3 Part 1
s.123, repealed (in part): SI 2009/2035 Sch.1 para.60
s.178, amended: 2009 c.10 s.105
s.178, applied: SI 2009/470 Reg.39, Reg.58, Reg.63
s.178, repealed (in part): 2009 c.10 s.105
s.178, enabling: SI 2009/199, SI 2009/2032
s.182, amended: SI 2009/56 Sch.1 para.167
s.182, repealed (in part): SI 2009/56 Sch.1 para.167
Sch.5, applied: 2009 c.4 s.1000
Sch.12 Part I para.2, repealed: SI 2009/2035 Sch.1 para.25
Sch.12 Part II para.5, repealed: SI 2009/2035 Sch.1 para.60

29. Electricity Act 1989
applied: 2009 c.23 s.79
Part I, applied: SI 2009/1905 Art.27

1989– cont.

29. Electricity Act 1989–*cont.*
s.1, applied: SI 2009/785 Art.33
s.2, applied: SI 2009/785 Art.33
s.3, applied: SI 2009/785 Art.33
s.3A, applied: SI 2009/785 Art.33
s.3B, applied: SI 2009/785 Art.33
s.3C, applied: SI 2009/785 Art.33
s.3D, applied: SI 2009/785 Art.33
s.4, applied: SI 2009/785 Art.33
s.4, disapplied: SI 2009/1600 Art.3, SI 2009/2344 Art.3
s.5, applied: SI 2009/785 Art.33, SI 2009/1600, SI 2009/2344
s.5, enabling: SI 2009/1600, SI 2009/2344
s.6, applied: SI 2009/785 Art.16, Art.33, Art.49, SI 2009/1600 Art.4, SI 2009/1905 Art.5, SI 2009/2344 Art.4, Art.5, SSI 2009/140 Art.16, Art.49
s.6A, applied: SI 2009/785 Art.33, SI 2009/3191 Reg.8
s.6A, varied: SI 2009/1340 Reg.28
s.6A, enabling: SI 2009/3191
s.6B, applied: SI 2009/785 Art.33
s.6B, varied: SI 2009/1340 Reg.28
s.6C, applied: SI 2009/785 Art.33
s.6C, enabling: SI 2009/1340
s.6D, applied: SI 2009/785 Art.33
s.6D, enabling: SI 2009/1340
s.6E, applied: SI 2009/785 Art.33
s.7, applied: SI 2009/785 Art.33
s.7A, applied: SI 2009/785 Art.33
s.7B, applied: SI 2009/785 Art.33
s.8, applied: SI 2009/785 Art.33
s.8A, applied: SI 2009/785 Art.33
s.9, applied: SI 2009/785 Art.33
s.10, applied: SI 2009/785 Art.33
s.11, applied: SI 2009/785 Art.33
s.11A, applied: SI 2009/785 Art.33
s.12, applied: SI 2009/785 Art.33
s.12A, applied: SI 2009/785 Art.33
s.12B, applied: SI 2009/785 Art.33
s.13, applied: SI 2009/785 Art.33
s.14, applied: SI 2009/785 Art.33
s.14A, applied: SI 2009/785 Art.33
s.15, applied: SI 2009/785 Art.33
s.15A, applied: SI 2009/785 Art.33
s.16, applied: SI 2009/785 Art.33
s.16A, applied: SI 2009/785 Art.33
s.17, see *William Old International Ltd v Arya* [2009] EWHC 599 (Ch), [2009] 2 P. & C.R. 20 (Ch D), Judge Pelling Q.C.
s.17, applied: SI 2009/785 Art.33
s.18, applied: SI 2009/785 Art.33
s.18A, applied: SI 2009/785 Art.33
s.19, applied: SI 2009/785 Art.33
s.20, applied: SI 2009/785 Art.33
s.21, applied: SI 2009/785 Art.33
s.22, applied: SI 2009/785 Art.33
s.23, applied: SI 2009/785 Art.33
s.24, applied: SI 2009/785 Art.33
s.25, applied: SI 2009/785 Art.33, Art.49, SSI 2009/140 Art.49
s.25, varied: SSI 2009/140 Art.49
s.26, applied: SI 2009/785 Art.33, Art.49
s.26, varied: SSI 2009/140 Art.49
s.27, applied: SI 2009/785 Art.33, Art.49
s.27, varied: SSI 2009/140 Art.49
s.27A, applied: SI 2009/785 Art.33, Art.44, Art.49, SSI 2009/140 Art.44

1989– cont.

29. Electricity Act 1989– *cont.*

s.27A, varied: SSI 2009/140 Art.49

s.27B, applied: SI 2009/785 Art.33, Art.49

s.27B, varied: SSI 2009/140 Art.49

s.27C, applied: SI 2009/785 Art.33, Art.49

s.27C, varied: SSI 2009/140 Art.49

s.27D, applied: SI 2009/785 Art.33, Art.49

s.27D, varied: SSI 2009/140 Art.49

s.27E, applied: SI 2009/785 Art.33, Art.49

s.27E, varied: SSI 2009/140 Art.49

s.27F, applied: SI 2009/785 Art.33, Art.49

s.27F, varied: SSI 2009/140 Art.49

s.28, applied: SI 2009/785 Art.33, Art.49, SSI 2009/
140 Art.49

s.28, varied: SSI 2009/140 Art.49

s.29, applied: SI 2009/785 Art.33

s.29, enabling: SI 2009/639

s.30, applied: SI 2009/785 Art.33

s.31, applied: SI 2009/785 Art.33

s.32, applied: SI 2009/785 Art.3, Art.6, Art.9,
Art.15, Art.36, SSI 2009/140 Art.3, Art.15,
Art.36

s.32, referred to: SSI 2009/140 Art.33

s.32, enabling: SI 2009/785, SSI 2009/140, SSI
2009/276

s.32A, applied: SI 2009/785 Art.3, Art.6, Art.9,
Art.15, Art.36, SSI 2009/140 Art.3, Art.15,
Art.36

s.32A, referred to: SSI 2009/140 Art.33

s.32A, enabling: SI 2009/785, SSI 2009/140

s.32B, applied: SI 2009/785 Art.3, Art.6, Art.9,
Art.15, Art.16, Art.36, SSI 2009/140 Art.3,
Art.15, Art.16, Art.23, Art.24, Art.35, Art.36,
Art.37, Art.38, Art.39, Art.40, Art.41, Art.53,
Sch.4 para.3

s.32B, referred to: SI 2009/785 Art.14, Art.15,
Art.16, Art.23, Art.24, Art.35, Art.36, Art.37,
Art.38, Art.39, Art.40, Art.41, Art.53, Sch.4
para.3, SSI 2009/140 Art.14, Art.33

s.32B, enabling: SI 2009/785, SSI 2009/140

s.32BA, applied: SI 2009/785 Art.3, Art.6, Art.9,
Art.15, Art.36, SSI 2009/140 Art.3, Art.15,
Art.36

s.32BA, referred to: SSI 2009/140 Art.33

s.32BA, enabling: SI 2009/785, SSI 2009/140

s.32C, applied: SI 2009/785 Art.3, Art.6, Art.9,
Art.15, Art.36, SSI 2009/140 Art.3, Art.15,
Art.36

s.32C, referred to: SSI 2009/140 Art.33

s.32C, enabling: SI 2009/785, SSI 2009/140

s.32D, applied: SI 2009/785 Art.3, Art.6, Art.9,
Art.15, Art.36, SSI 2009/140, SSI 2009/140
Art.3, Art.15, Art.36, SSI 2009/276

s.32D, referred to: SI 2009/785, SSI 2009/785 Art.33,
SSI 2009/140 Art.33

s.32D, enabling: SI 2009/785, SSI 2009/140, SSI
2009/276

s.32E, applied: SI 2009/785 Art.3, Art.6, Art.9,
Art.15, Art.36, SSI 2009/140 Art.3, Art.15,
Art.36

s.32E, referred to: SSI 2009/140 Art.33

s.32E, enabling: SI 2009/785, SSI 2009/140

s.32F, amended: SI 2009/556 Art.2

s.32F, applied: SI 2009/785 Art.3, Art.6, Art.9,
Art.15, Art.36, SSI 2009/140 Art.3, Art.15,
Art.36

s.32F, referred to: SSI 2009/140 Art.33

s.32F, enabling: SI 2009/785, SSI 2009/140

1989– cont.

29. Electricity Act 1989– *cont.*

s.32G, applied: SI 2009/785 Art.3, Art.6, Art.9,
Art.15, Art.36, SSI 2009/140 Art.3, Art.15,
Art.36

s.32G, referred to: SSI 2009/140 Art.33

s.32G, enabling: SI 2009/785, SSI 2009/140

s.32H, applied: SI 2009/785 Art.3, Art.6, Art.9,
Art.15, Art.36, SSI 2009/140 Art.3, Art.15,
Art.36

s.32H, referred to: SSI 2009/140 Art.33

s.32H, enabling: SI 2009/785, SSI 2009/140

s.32I, amended: SI 2009/556 Art.2

s.32I, applied: SI 2009/785 Art.3, Art.6, Art.9,
Art.15, Art.36, SSI 2009/140 Art.3, Art.15,
Art.36

s.32I, referred to: SSI 2009/140 Art.33

s.32I, enabling: SI 2009/785, SSI 2009/140

s.32J, applied: SI 2009/785 Art.3, Art.6, Art.9,
Art.15, Art.36, SSI 2009/140 Art.3, Art.15,
Art.36

s.32J, referred to: SSI 2009/140 Art.33

s.32J, enabling: SI 2009/785, SSI 2009/140

s.32K, amended: SI 2009/556 Art.2

s.32K, applied: SI 2009/785 Art.3, Art.6, Art.9,
Art.15, Art.36, SSI 2009/140 Art.3, Art.15,
Art.36

s.32K, referred to: SSI 2009/140 Art.33

s.32K, enabling: SI 2009/785, SSI 2009/140

s.32L, applied: SI 2009/785, SI 2009/785 Art.3,
Art.6, Art.9, Art.15, Art.36, SSI 2009/140, SSI
2009/140 Art.3, Art.15, Art.36, SSI 2009/276

s.32L, referred to: SSI 2009/140 Art.33

s.32L, enabling: SI 2009/785, SSI 2009/140

s.32M, applied: SI 2009/785 Art.3, Art.6, Art.9,
Art.36, SSI 2009/140 Art.3, Art.36

s.32M, referred to: SSI 2009/140 Art.33

s.32M, enabling: SI 2009/785, SSI 2009/140

s.33, applied: SI 2009/785 Art.33

s.34, applied: SI 2009/785 Art.33

s.35, applied: SI 2009/785 Art.33

s.36, amended: 2009 c.23 s.12

s.36, applied: 2009 c.23 s.12, SI 2009/785 Art.33,
Art.58, SSI 2009/140 Art.58

s.36A, amended: 2009 c.23 s.12

s.36A, applied: 2009 c.23 s.12, SI 2009/785 Art.33

s.36B, amended: 2009 c.23 s.12

s.36B, applied: 2009 c.23 s.12, SI 2009/785 Art.33

s.37, applied: SI 2009/640 Reg.4, SI 2009/785
Art.33

s.37, disapplied: SI 2009/640 Reg.3

s.37, enabling: SI 2009/640

s.38, applied: SI 2009/785 Art.33

s.39, applied: SI 2009/785 Art.33

s.39A, applied: SI 2009/785 Art.33

s.39B, applied: SI 2009/785 Art.33

s.40, applied: SI 2009/785 Art.33

s.40A, applied: SI 2009/785 Art.33

s.40B, applied: SI 2009/785 Art.33

s.41, applied: SI 2009/785 Art.33

s.41A, applied: SI 2009/785 Art.33, SI 2009/1904,
SI 2009/1905

s.41A, enabling: SI 2009/1904, SI 2009/1905

s.42, applied: SI 2009/785 Art.33

s.42A, applied: SI 2009/785 Art.33

s.42AA, applied: SI 2009/785 Art.33

s.42AB, applied: SI 2009/785 Art.33

s.42B, applied: SI 2009/785 Art.33

s.42C, amended: SI 2009/1941 Sch.1 para.102

s.42C, applied: SI 2009/785 Art.33

1989– cont.

29. Electricity Act 1989–*cont.*
s.43, applied: SI 2009/ 785 Art.33
s.43A, applied: SI 2009/ 785 Art.33
s.43B, applied: SI 2009/ 785 Art.33
s.44, applied: SI 2009/ 785 Art.33
s.44A, applied: SI 2009/ 785 Art.33
s.44B, added: SI 2009/ 1349 Reg.3
s.44B, applied: SI 2009/ 785 Art.33
s.44C, added: SI 2009/ 1349 Reg.3
s.44C, applied: SI 2009/ 785 Art.33
s.44D, added: SI 2009/ 1349 Reg.3
s.44D, applied: SI 2009/ 785 Art.33
s.45, applied: SI 2009/ 785 Art.33
s.46, applied: SI 2009/ 785 Art.33
s.46A, applied: SI 2009/ 785 Art.33
s.47, applied: SI 2009/ 785 Art.33
s.48, applied: SI 2009/ 785 Art.33
s.49, applied: SI 2009/ 785 Art.33
s.49A, applied: SI 2009/ 785 Art.33
s.50, applied: SI 2009/ 785 Art.33
s.51, applied: SI 2009/ 785 Art.33
s.52, applied: SI 2009/ 785 Art.33
s.53, applied: SI 2009/ 785 Art.33
s.54, applied: SI 2009/ 785 Art.33
s.55, applied: SI 2009/ 785 Art.33
s.56, applied: SI 2009/ 785 Art.33
s.56A, applied: SI 2009/ 785 Art.33
s.56B, applied: SI 2009/ 785 Art.33
s.56C, applied: SI 2009/ 785 Art.33
s.56CA, applied: SI 2009/ 785 Art.33
s.56CB, applied: SI 2009/ 785 Art.33
s.56D, applied: SI 2009/ 785 Art.33
s.56E, applied: SI 2009/ 785 Art.33
s.56F, applied: SI 2009/ 785 Art.33
s.56FA, applied: SI 2009/ 785 Art.33
s.56FB, applied: SI 2009/ 785 Art.33
s.56FC, applied: SI 2009/ 785 Art.33
s.56G, applied: SI 2009/ 785 Art.33
s.57, applied: SI 2009/ 785 Art.33
s.58, applied: SI 2009/ 785 Art.33
s.59, applied: SI 2009/ 785 Art.33
s.60, applied: SI 2009/ 785 Art.33
s.60, enabling: SI 2009/ 640, SI 2009/ 1340, SI 2009/ 3191
s.61, applied: SI 2009/ 785 Art.33
s.62, applied: SI 2009/ 785 Art.33
s.63, applied: SI 2009/ 785 Art.33
s.64, applied: SI 2009/ 785 Art.33
s.65, applied: SI 2009/ 785 Art.33
s.66, applied: SI 2009/ 785 Art.33
s.67, applied: SI 2009/ 785 Art.33
s.68, applied: SI 2009/ 785 Art.33
s.69, applied: SI 2009/ 785 Art.33
s.70, applied: SI 2009/ 785 Art.33
s.71, amended: SI 2009/ 1941 Sch.1 para.102
s.71, applied: SI 2009/ 785 Art.33
s.72, applied: SI 2009/ 785 Art.33
s.73, applied: SI 2009/ 785 Art.33
s.74, applied: SI 2009/ 785 Art.33
s.75, amended: SI 2009/ 1941 Sch.1 para.102
s.75, applied: SI 2009/ 785 Art.33
s.76, applied: SI 2009/ 785 Art.33
s.77, amended: SI 2009/ 1941 Sch.1 para.102
s.77, applied: SI 2009/ 785 Art.33
s.78, applied: SI 2009/ 785 Art.33
s.79, applied: SI 2009/ 785 Art.33
s.80, applied: SI 2009/ 785 Art.33
s.81, applied: SI 2009/ 785 Art.33

1989– cont.

29. Electricity Act 1989–*cont.*
s.82, applied: SI 2009/ 785 Art.33
s.83, applied: SI 2009/ 785 Art.33
s.84, applied: SI 2009/ 785 Art.33
s.85, applied: SI 2009/ 785 Art.33
s.86, applied: SI 2009/ 785 Art.33
s.87, applied: SI 2009/ 785 Art.33
s.88, applied: SI 2009/ 785 Art.33
s.89, applied: SI 2009/ 785 Art.33
s.90, applied: SI 2009/ 785 Art.33
s.91, applied: SI 2009/ 785 Art.33
s.92, applied: SI 2009/ 785 Art.33
s.93, applied: SI 2009/ 785 Art.33
s.94, applied: SI 2009/ 785 Art.33
s.95, applied: SI 2009/ 785 Art.33
s.96, applied: SI 2009/ 785 Art.33
s.97, applied: SI 2009/ 785 Art.33
s.98, applied: SI 2009/ 785 Art.33
s.99, applied: SI 2009/ 785 Art.33
s.100, applied: SI 2009/ 785 Art.33
s.101, applied: SI 2009/ 785 Art.33
s.102, applied: SI 2009/ 785 Art.33
s.103, applied: SI 2009/ 785 Art.33
s.104, applied: SI 2009/ 785 Art.33
s.105, applied: SI 2009/ 785 Art.33
s.106, applied: SI 2009/ 785 Art.33
s.107, applied: SI 2009/ 785 Art.33
s.108, applied: SI 2009/ 785 Art.33
s.108A, applied: SI 2009/ 785 Art.33
s.109, applied: SI 2009/ 785 Art.33
s.110, applied: SI 2009/ 785 Art.33
s.111, applied: SI 2009/ 785 Art.33
s.112, applied: SI 2009/ 785 Art.33
s.113, applied: SI 2009/ 785 Art.33
Sch.3 Part II para.9, amended: SI 2009/ 1307 Sch.1 para.191
Sch.4 para.6, see *Patersons of Greenoakhill Ltd v SP Transmission Ltd* [2009] CSOH 155 (OH), Lord Glennie
Sch.4 para.7, see *Patersons of Greenoakhill Ltd v SP Transmission Ltd* [2009] CSOH 155 (OH), Lord Glennie; see *Welford v EDF Energy Networks (LPN) Plc* [2009] R.V.R. 10 (Lands Tr), George Bartlett Q.C. (President, LTr)
Sch.4 para.7, amended: SI 2009/ 1307 Sch.1 para.192
Sch.4 para.8, see *Patersons of Greenoakhill Ltd v SP Transmission Ltd* [2009] CSOH 155 (OH), Lord Glennie
Sch.4 para.11, amended: SI 2009/ 1307 Sch.1 para.192
Sch.4 para.12, amended: SI 2009/ 1307 Sch.1 para.192
Sch.7 para.2, applied: SSI 2009/ 140 Art.36
Sch.8 para.1, disapplied: 2009 c.23 s.12
Sch.8 para.1, varied: 2009 c.23 s.12
Sch.8 para.2, varied: 2009 c.23 s.12
Sch.8 para.3, varied: 2009 c.23 s.12
Sch.8 para.4, varied: 2009 c.23 s.12
Sch.8 para.5, varied: 2009 c.23 s.12
Sch.8 para.5A, varied: 2009 c.23 s.12
Sch.8 para.6, varied: 2009 c.23 s.12
Sch.8 para.7, varied: 2009 c.23 s.12
Sch.8 para.7A, varied: 2009 c.23 s.12
Sch.8 para.8, varied: 2009 c.23 s.12
Sch.9 para.1, varied: 2009 c.23 s.12
Sch.16 para.1, repealed (in part): 2009 asp 6 Sch.3 para.5

1989– *cont.*

29. Electricity Act 1989– *cont.*
Sch.16 para.3, applied: SI 2009/229 Art.4

33. Extradition Act 1989
see *R. (on the application of Bary) v Secretary of State for the Home Department* [2009] EWHC 2068 (Admin), Times, October 14, 2009 (DC), Scott Baker, L.J.
Sch.1 para.1, see *R. (on the application of Bary) v Secretary of State for the Home Department* [2009] EWHC 2068 (Admin), Times, October 14, 2009 (DC), Scott Baker, L.J.

34. Law of Property (Miscellaneous Provisions) Act 1989
s.2, see *Brightlingsea Haven Ltd v Morris* [2008] EWHC 1928 (QB), [2009] 2 P. & C.R. 11 (QBD), Jack, J.; see *Hanoman v Southwark LBC* [2008] EWCA Civ 624, [2009] 1 W.L.R. 374 (CA (Civ Div)), Sir Anthony Clarke, M.R.; see *Herbert v Doyle* [2008] EWHC 1950 (Ch), [2009] W.T.L.R. 589 (Ch D), Mark Herbert Q.C.; see *Looe Fuels Ltd v Looe Harbour Commissioners* [2008] EWCA Civ 414, [2009] L. & T.R. 3 (CA (Civ Div)), Rix, L.J.; see *McLaughlin v Duffill* [2008] EWCA Civ 1627, [2009] 3 W.L.R. 1139 (CA (Civ Div)), Sir Andrew Morritt (Chancellor); see *Mirza v Mirza* [2009] EWHC 3 (Ch), [2009] 2 F.L.R. 115 (Ch D (Birmingham)), Stephen Smith Q.C.
s.2, amended: SI 2009/1342 Art.24

36. Brunei (Appeals) Act 1989
s.1, applied: SI 2009/224 Sch.1
s.1, enabling: SI 2009/224

37. Football Spectators Act 1989
referred to: 2009 c.26 s.115
s.11, applied: SI 2009/1395
s.11, enabling: SI 2009/1395
s.14, amended: 2009 c.26 s.103
s.14E, amended: 2009 c.26 s.104, Sch.8 Part 11
s.14E, applied: 2009 c.26 s.104
s.14J, applied: 2009 c.26 s.105
s.19, amended: 2009 c.26 s.103, Sch.8 Part 11
s.19, applied: 2009 c.26 s.104, s.105
s.20, applied: 2009 c.26 s.105
s.21A, amended: 2009 c.26 s.103
Sch.1 para.1, amended: 2009 c.26 s.107

40. Companies Act 1989
varied: SI 2009/317 Sch.1
s.82, applied: SI 2009/214 Sch.1
s.84, applied: SI 2009/214 Sch.1, SI 2009/1801 Sch.1
s.89, applied: SI 2009/1801 Sch.1
s.112, amended: SI 2009/1941 Sch.1 para.103
s.154, amended: SI 2009/853 Reg.2
s.155, amended: SI 2009/853 Reg.2
s.155, enabling: SI 2009/853
s.158, amended: SI 2009/853 Reg.2
s.158, enabling: SI 2009/853
s.159, amended: SI 2009/853 Reg.2
s.161, amended: SI 2009/853 Reg.2
s.161, varied: SI 2009/853 Reg.2
s.163, amended: SI 2009/853 Reg.2
s.164, amended: SI 2009/853 Reg.2
s.165, amended: SI 2009/853 Reg.2
s.167, amended: SI 2009/853 Reg.2
s.170, amended: SI 2009/853 Reg.2
s.175, amended: SI 2009/853 Reg.2
s.177, amended: SI 2009/853 Reg.2
s.180, amended: SI 2009/853 Reg.2
s.185, enabling: SI 2009/853
s.186, enabling: SI 2009/853

1989– *cont.*

40. Companies Act 1989– *cont.*
s.187, enabling: SI 2009/853
s.188, amended: SI 2009/853 Reg.2
s.191, amended: SI 2009/853 Reg.2
s.213, amended: SI 2009/1941 Sch.1 para.103

41. Children Act 1989
see *B (A Child) (Residence: Second Appeal), Re* [2009] EWCA Civ 545, [2009] 2 F.L.R. 632 (CA (Civ Div)), Wall, L.J.; see *Holmes-Moorhouse v Richmond upon Thames LBC* [2009] UKHL 7, [2009] 1 W.L.R. 413 (HL), Lord Hoffmann; see *Marsh, Re* [2009] B.P.I.R. 834 (CC (Portsmouth)), District Judge Cawood; see *Practice Direction (Fam Div: Family Proceedings: Appeals)* [2009] 1 W.L.R. 1103 (Fam Div), Sir Mark Potter (President, Fam); see *R (A Child) (Fact-Finding Hearing), Re* [2009] EWCA Civ 1619, [2009] 2 F.L.R. 83 (CA (Civ Div)), Thorpe, L.J.; see *R. (on the application of Liverpool City Council) v Hillingdon LBC* [2009] EWCA Civ 43, [2009] 1 F.L.R. 1536 (CA (Civ Div)), Rix, L.J.; see *RC (Child Abduction) (Brussels II Revised: Article 11(7)), Re* [2009] 1 F.L.R. 574 (Fam Div), Singer, J.; see *RD (Child Abduction) (Brussels II Revised: Articles 11(7) and 19), Re* [2009] 1 F.L.R. 586 (Fam Div), Singer, J.; see *Stodgell v Stodgell* [2008] EWHC 1925 (Admin), [2009] 2 F.L.R. 218 (QBD (Admin)), Holman, J.; see *T (A Child) v Wakefield MDC* [2008] EWCA Civ 199, [2009] Fam. 1 (CA (Civ Div)), Thorpe, L.J.
applied: SI 2009/2057 Reg.5, SSI 2009/154 Sch.1 para.14
Part II, see *X (Children) (Parental Order: Foreign Surrogacy), Re* [2008] EWHC 3030 (Fam), [2009] Fam. 71 (Fam Div), Hedley, J.
Part III, see *R. (on the application of M) v Lambeth LBC* [2008] EWCA Civ 1445, [2009] 1 F.L.R. 1325 (CA (Civ Div)), Ward, L.J.
Part IV, applied: SI 2009/1547 Sch.1 para.7
Part X, applied: SI 2009/1547 Sch.1 para.19
Part XA, applied: SI 2009/1547 Sch.1 para.19
Part II, see *X (Children) (Parental Order: Foreign Surrogacy), Re* [2008] EWHC 3030 (Fam), [2009] Fam. 71 (Fam Div), Hedley, J.
Part III, see *R. (on the application of M) v Lambeth LBC* [2008] EWCA Civ 1445, [2009] 1 F.L.R. 1325 (CA (Civ Div)), Ward, L.J.
s.1, see *B (Children) (Sexual Abuse: Standard of Proof), Re* [2008] UKHL 35, [2009] 1 A.C. 11 (HL), Lord Hoffmann; see *D (Children) (Non-Accidental Injury), Re* [2009] EWCA Civ 472, [2009] 2 F.L.R. 668 (CA (Civ Div)), Thorpe, L.J.
s.4, amended: 2009 c.24 Sch.6 para.21
s.4, enabling: SI 2009/2026
s.4ZA, amended: 2009 c.24 Sch.6 para.22
s.8, see *G (A Child) (Residence: Restriction on Further Applications), Re* [2008] EWCA Civ 1468, [2009] 1 F.L.R. 894 (CA (Civ Div)), Ward, L.J.
s.15, see *H v C* [2009] EWHC 1527 (Fam), [2009] 2 F.L.R. 1540 (Fam Div), Judge Kevin Barnett
s.15, applied: SI 2009/1555 Reg.42, SI 2009/2737 Reg.31, Reg.96, SI 2009/3359 Reg.26
s.17, see *R. (on the application of Clue) v Birmingham City Council* [2008] EWHC 3036 (Admin), [2009] 1 All E.R. 1039 (QBD (Admin)), Charles, J.; see *R. (on the application of G) v Southwark LBC* [2009] UKHL 26, [2009] 1 W.L.R. 1299 (HL), Lord

41. Children Act 1989– *cont.*

s.17– *cont.*

Hope of Craighead; see *R. (on the application of M) v Barnet LBC* [2008] EWHC 2354 (Admin), [2009] 2 F.L.R. 725 (QBD (Admin)), Judge Michael Kay QC; see *R. (on the application of M) v Lambeth LBC* [2008] EWCA Civ 1445, [2009] 1 F.L.R. 1325 (CA (Civ Div)), Ward, L.J.; see *R. (on the application of M) v Lambeth LBC* [2009] UKSC 8, [2009] 1 W.L.R. 2557 (SC), Lord Hope (Deputy President)

s.17, amended: 2009 c.24 Sch.7 Part 1

s.17, applied: 2009 c.24 s.39

s.17A, amended: 2009 c.24 Sch.7 Part 1

s.17A, applied: SI 2009/ 1887 Reg.4, Reg.7, Reg.9, Reg.11, Reg.14, Reg.17

s.17A, enabling: SI 2009/ 1887

s.20, see *R. (on the application of A) v Coventry City Council* [2009] EWHC 34 (Admin), [2009] 1 F.L.R. 1202 (QBD (Admin)), Antony Edwards-Stuart Q.C.; see *R. (on the application of Collins) v Knowsley MBC* [2008] EWHC 2551 (Admin), [2009] 1 F.L.R. 493 (QBD (Admin)), Michael Supperstone Q.C.; see *R. (on the application of G) v Southwark LBC* [2009] UKHL 26, [2009] 1 W.L.R. 1299 (HL), Lord Hope of Craighead; see *R. (on the application of Liverpool City Council) v Hillingdon LBC* [2008] EWHC 1702 (Admin), [2009] 1 F.C.R. 252 (QBD (Admin)), James Goudie Q.C.; see *R. (on the application of Liverpool City Council) v Hillingdon LBC* [2009] EWCA Civ 43, [2009] 1 F.L.R. 1536 (CA (Civ Div)), Rix, L.J.; see *R. (on the application of M) v Barnet LBC* [2008] EWHC 2354 (Admin), [2009] 2 F.L.R. 725 (QBD (Admin)), Judge Michael Kay QC; see *R. (on the application of M) v Lambeth LBC* [2008] EWCA Civ 1445, [2009] 1 F.L.R. 1325 (CA (Civ Div)), Ward, L.J.; see *R. (on the application of M) v Lambeth LBC* [2009] UKSC 8, [2009] 1 W.L.R. 2557 (SC), Lord Hope (Deputy President); see *S v Rochdale MBC* [2008] EWHC 3283 (Fam), [2009] 1 F.L.R. 1090 (Fam Div), Munby, J.

s.21, amended: 2009 c.26 Sch.7 para.21, Sch.8 Part 2

s.22, see *R. (on the application of Collins) v Knowsley MBC* [2008] EWHC 2551 (Admin), [2009] 1 F.L.R. 493 (QBD (Admin)), Michael Supperstone Q.C.

s.22, applied: 2009 c.22 s.218, SI 2009/ 1511 Reg.3, SI 2009/ 1555 Sch.4 para.2, SI 2009/ 1563 Reg.2, SI 2009/ 1797 Art.3, SI 2009/ 2158 Reg.13, SI 2009/ 2737 Sch.5 para.2

s.23, see *R. (on the application of A) v Coventry City Council* [2009] EWHC 34 (Admin), [2009] 1 F.L.R. 1202 (QBD (Admin)), Antony Edwards-Stuart Q.C.; see *R. (on the application of Collins) v Knowsley MBC* [2008] EWHC 2551 (Admin), [2009] 1 F.L.R. 493 (QBD (Admin)), Michael Supperstone Q.C.; see *R. (on the application of M) v Lambeth LBC* [2008] EWCA Civ 1445, [2009] 1 F.L.R. 1325 (CA (Civ Div)), Ward, L.J.

s.23, applied: SI 2009/ 1555 Reg.42, SI 2009/ 2737 Reg.31, Reg.96, SI 2009/ 3359 Reg.26

s.23, enabling: SI 2009/ 394, SI 2009/ 395

s.23A, see *R. (on the application of G) v Southwark LBC* [2009] UKHL 26, [2009] 1 W.L.R. 1299 (HL), Lord Hope of Craighead

s.23A, applied: SI 2009/ 1511 Reg.3

s.23C, applied: 2009 c.22 s.92, s.252, SI 2009/ 2274 Reg.1, Reg.2, Reg.3, SI 2009/ 2737 Reg.31, Reg.96, SI 2009/ 3359 Reg.26

41. Children Act 1989– *cont.*

s.23C, enabling: SI 2009/ 2274

s.23CA, applied: 2009 c.22 s.92, s.252

s.23D, applied: 2009 c.22 s.252

s.24, applied: SI 2009/ 1511 Reg.3, SI 2009/ 1555 Reg.42, SI 2009/ 2737 Reg.31, Reg.96, SI 2009/ 3359 Reg.26

s.27, see *R. (on the application of G) v Southwark LBC* [2009] UKHL 26, [2009] 1 W.L.R. 1299 (HL), Lord Hope of Craighead

s.29, amended: 2009 c.24 Sch.7 Part 1

s.31, see *B (A Child) (Fact-Finding Hearing: Evidence), Re* [2008] EWCA Civ 1547, [2009] 2 F.L.R. 14 (CA (Civ Div)), Thorpe, L.J.; see *B (Children) (Sexual Abuse: Standard of Proof), Re* [2008] UKHL 35, [2009] 1 A.C. 11 (HL), Lord Hoffmann; see *D (Children) (Non-Accidental Injury), Re* [2009] EWCA Civ 472, [2009] 2 F.L.R. 668 (CA (Civ Div)), Thorpe, L.J.; see *G (Children) (Fact-Finding Hearing), Re* [2009] EWCA Civ 10, [2009] 1 F.L.R. 1145 (CA (Civ Div)), Thorpe, L.J.; see *J (A Child) (Care Proceedings: Injuries), Re* [2009] EWHC 1383 (Fam), [2009] 2 F.L.R. 99 (Fam Div), Hogg, J.; see *L (A Child) (Fact-Finding Hearing), Re* [2009] EWCA Civ 1008, [2009] 3 F.C.R. 527 (CA (Civ Div)), Waller, L.J.; see *M (Children) (Fact-Finding Hearing: Burden of Proof), Re* [2008] EWCA Civ 1261, [2009] 1 F.L.R. 1177 (CA (Civ Div)), Sir Mark Potter (President, Fam); see *S-B (Children) (Care Proceedings: Standard of Proof), Re* [2009] UKSC 17 (SC), Lord Hope (Deputy President); see *T (A Child) (Care Order), Re* [2009] EWCA Civ 121, [2009] 3 All E.R. 1078 (CA (Civ Div)), Sir Mark Potter (President); see *T (A Child) v Wakefield MDC* [2008] EWCA Civ 199, [2009] Fam. 1 (CA (Civ Div)), Thorpe, L.J.

s.31, applied: SI 2009/ 1547 Sch.1 para.1, SSI 2009/ 154 Sch.1 para.14

s.33, see *P-B (Children) (Contact Order: Committal: Penal Notice), Re* [2009] EWCA Civ 143, [2009] 2 F.L.R. 66 (CA (Civ Div)), Thorpe, L.J.

s.34, see *P-B (Children) (Contact Order: Committal: Penal Notice), Re* [2009] EWCA Civ 143, [2009] 2 F.L.R. 66 (CA (Civ Div)), Thorpe, L.J.

s.34, applied: SI 2009/ 1107 Reg.5

s.37, see *H (Abduction), Re* [2009] EWHC 1735 (Fam), [2009] 2 F.L.R. 1513 (Fam Div), Roderic Wood, J.

s.38, see *A (A Child) (Residential Assessment), Re* [2009] EWHC 865 (Fam), [2009] 2 F.L.R. 443 (Fam Div), Munby, J.; see *H (Abduction), Re* [2009] EWHC 1735 (Fam), [2009] 2 F.L.R. 1513 (Fam Div), Roderic Wood, J.; see *S (A Child) (Residential Assessment), Re* [2008] EWCA Civ 1078, [2009] 2 F.L.R. 397 (CA (Civ Div)), Mummery, L.J.

s.44, see *L LBC v G* [2007] EWHC 2640 (Fam), [2009] 1 F.L.R. 414 (Fam Div), McFarlane, J.

s.44, applied: SSI 2009/ 154 Sch.1 para.14

s.47, amended: 2009 c.26 Sch.8 Part 13

s.47, repealed (in part): 2009 c.26 Sch.8 Part 13

s.49, applied: SI 2009/ 1547 Sch.3 para.1

s.50, applied: SI 2009/ 1547 Sch.3 para.1

s.63, applied: SI 2009/ 1547 Sch.2 para.1

s.66, applied: SSI 2009/ 154 Sch.1 para.14

s.67, applied: SSI 2009/ 154 Sch.1 para.14

s.68, applied: SSI 2009/ 154 Sch.1 para.14

1989– cont.

41. Children Act 1989– *cont.*

s.68, enabling: SI 2009/2541

s.69, applied: SI 2009/1547 Sch.1 para.17, SSI 2009/154 Sch.1 para.14

s.70, applied: SI 2009/1547 Sch.2 para.1

s.79C, enabling: SI 2009/2541, SI 2009/3265

s.79M, enabling: SI 2009/2541

s.87D, enabling: SI 2009/2724

s.91, see *C (A Child) (Litigant in Person: s.91 (14) Order)*, Re [2009] EWCA Civ 674, [2009] 2 F.L.R. 1461 (CA (Civ Div)), Thorpe, L.J.; see *C (Children) (Contact Order: Variation: Implementation)*, Re [2008] EWCA Civ 1389, [2009] 1 F.L.R. 869 (CA (Civ Div)), Thorpe, L.J.; see *G (A Child) (Residence: Restriction on Further Applications)*, Re [2008] EWCA Civ 1468, [2009] 1 F.L.R. 894 (CA (Civ Div)), Ward, L.J.

s.92, enabling: SI 2009/3319

s.94, see *Practice Direction (Fam Div: Family Proceedings: Allocation of Appeals)* [2009] 1 W.L.R. 1107 (Fam Div), Sir Mark Potter (President, Fam)

s.94, amended: SI 2009/871 Art.7

s.97, see *R. (on the application of Dacre) v Westminster Magistrates' Court* [2008] EWHC 1667 (Admin), [2009] 1 W.L.R. 2241 (DC), Latham, L.J.; see *X (A Child) (Residence and Contact: Rights of Media Attendance)*, Re [2009] EWHC 1728 (Fam), [2009] E.M.L.R. 26 (Fam Div), Sir Mark Potter (President, Fam)

s.97, enabling: SI 2009/858

s.98, see *P (Care Proceedings: Disclosure)*, Re [2008] EWHC 2197 (Fam), [2009] 2 F.L.R. 1039 (Fam Div), Judge Hunt

s.104, amended: SI 2009/1892 Sch.1 para.2

s.104, applied: SI 2009/2274

s.104, enabling: SI 2009/394, SI 2009/395, SI 2009/1887, SI 2009/2026, SI 2009/2274, SI 2009/2541, SI 2009/2724, SI 2009/3265

Sch.1, see *H v C* [2009] EWHC 1527 (Fam), [2009] 2 F.L.R. 1540 (Fam Div), Judge Kevin Barnett; see *N (A Child) (Financial Provision: Dependency)*, Re [2009] EWHC 11 (Fam), [2009] 1 W.L.R. 1621 (Fam Div), Munby, J.; see *Tv B* [2008] EWHC 3000 (Fam), [2009] 1 F.L.R. 1231 (Fam Div), Sir Mark Potter (President, Fam)

Sch.1, applied: SI 2009/1555 Reg.42, SI 2009/2737 Reg.31, Reg.96, SI 2009/3359 Reg.26

Sch.1 para.15, see *R. (on the application of H) v Essex CC* [2009] EWHC 353 (Admin), [2009] 2 F.L.R. 91 (QBD (Admin)), Sir George Newman

Sch.2 Part II para.12A, applied: SI 2009/395 Reg.4

Sch.2 Part II para.12A, enabling: SI 2009/394, SI 2009/395

Sch.2 Part III para.21, amended: 2009 c.24 Sch.7 Part 1

Sch.2 para.19, see *A LBC v Department for Children, Schools and Families* [2009] EWCA Civ 41, [2009] 3 W.L.R. 1169 (CA (Civ Div)), Thorpe, L.J.

Sch.2 para.19B, see *R. (on the application of G) v Southwark LBC* [2009] UKHL 26, [2009] 1 W.L.R. 1299 (HL), Lord Hope of Craighead; see *S (A Child) (Eligible Child)*, Re [2008] EWCA Civ 1140, [2009] 1 F.L.R. 378 (CA (Civ Div)), Ward, L.J.

Sch.3 para.6, see *T (A Child) v Wakefield MDC* [2008] EWCA Civ 199, [2009] Fam. 1 (CA (Civ Div)), Thorpe, L.J.

1989– cont.

41. Children Act 1989– *cont.*

Sch.5 Part I para.1, applied: SI 2009/1547 Sch.1 para.16, Sch.2 para.1

Sch.6 Part I para.1, applied: SI 2009/1547 Sch.1 para.16

Sch.6 Part I para.2, applied: SI 2009/1547 Sch.2 para.1

Sch.6 Part I para.4, applied: SI 2009/1547 Sch.1 para.16

Sch.9A para.4, enabling: SI 2009/2541

Sch.11 Part I, enabling: SI 2009/3319

Sch.14 Part 5 para.15, applied: SI 2009/1547 Sch.1 para.7

42. Local Government and Housing Act 1989

Part I, applied: SI 2009/1255 Reg.14

s.2, amended: 2009 c.20 Sch.7 Part 1

s.2, applied: 2009 c.20 s.16

s.2, repealed (in part): 2009 c.20 Sch.7 Part 1

s.3, amended: 2009 c.20 Sch.7 Part 1, SSI 2009/205 Art.2

s.3, applied: SSI 2009/352 Sch.1 para.11

s.3, repealed (in part): 2009 c.20 Sch.7 Part 1

s.3A, amended: 2009 c.20 Sch.7 Part 1

s.3A, repealed (in part): 2009 c.20 Sch.7 Part 1

s.4, amended: 2009 c.20 Sch.6 para.81

s.5, amended: 2009 c.23 Sch.14 para.13, Sch.22 Part 4

s.5, repealed (in part): 2009 c.23 Sch.22 Part 4

s.9, applied: SI 2009/40 Art.3

s.9, enabling: SI 2009/40

s.13, amended: 2009 c.20 Sch.6 para.81, 2009 c.23 Sch.14 para.14

s.13, applied: 2009 c.23 s.151

s.13, repealed (in part): 2009 c.23 Sch.22 Part 4

s.15, disapplied: 2009 c.20 s.89, s.114

s.16, disapplied: 2009 c.20 s.114

s.17, disapplied: 2009 c.20 s.114

s.20, amended: 2009 c.20 Sch.6 para.81

s.21, amended: 2009 c.20 Sch.6 para.81

s.21, referred to: 2009 c.20 s.20

s.67, amended: SI 2009/1941 Sch.1 para.104

s.68, amended: SI 2009/1941 Sch.1 para.104

s.150, applied: SI 2009/369

s.150, enabling: SI 2009/369

s.152, amended: 2009 c.20 Sch.6 para.81

s.152, applied: SI 2009/369

s.152, enabling: SI 2009/369

s.157, amended: 2009 c.20 Sch.6 para.81

s.186, see *Hughes v Borodex Ltd* [2009] EWHC 565 (Admin), [2009] 26 E.G. 114 (QBD (Admin)), Collins, J.

Sch.1, disapplied: 2009 c.20 s.114

Sch.1 para.2, amended: 2009 c.20 Sch.6 para.81, 2009 c.23 Sch.14 para.15

Sch.1 para.2, repealed (in part): 2009 c.23 Sch.22 Part 4

Sch.1 para.4, amended: 2009 c.20 Sch.6 para.81

Sch.10, see *Hughes v Borodex Ltd* [2009] EWHC 565 (Admin), [2009] 26 E.G. 114 (QBD (Admin)), Collins, J.

Sch.10 para.10, see *Hughes v Borodex Ltd* [2009] EWHC 565 (Admin), [2009] 26 E.G. 114 (QBD (Admin)), Collins, J.

Sch.10 para.11, see *Hughes v Borodex Ltd* [2009] EWHC 565 (Admin), [2009] 26 E.G. 114 (QBD (Admin)), Collins, J.

Sch.11 para.11, see *Hughes v Borodex Ltd* [2009] EWHC 565 (Admin), [2009] 26 E.G. 114 (QBD (Admin)), Collins, J.

1989– cont.

44. Opticians Act 1989
applied: SI 2009/2722 Reg.3
s.1, enabling: SI 2009/442
s.13D, amended: 2009 c.26 s.81
s.13I, applied: SI 2009/442 Art.5, Art.7
s.13L, applied: SI 2009/442 Art.7
Sch.1 para.1A, referred to: SI 2009/442 Art.6
Sch.1 para.1B, enabling: SI 2009/442

45. Prisons (Scotland) Act 1989
s.14, enabling: SSI 2009/380
s.22, applied: SI 2009/1887 Sch.1
s.22, referred to: SI 2009/1887 Sch.2
s.26, applied: SI 2009/1887 Sch.1
s.26, referred to: SI 2009/1887 Sch.2
s.39, enabling: SSI 2009/380

1990

6. Education (Student Loans) Act 1990
applied: SI 2009/470 Reg.16, Reg.19, SI 2009/1555
  Reg.5, SI 2009/2737 Reg.4
s.4, varied: 2009 c.22 s.258
Sch.2 para.1, varied: 2009 c.22 s.258
Sch.2 para.2, varied: 2009 c.22 s.258
Sch.2 para.3, varied: 2009 c.22 s.258
Sch.2 para.3A, varied: 2009 c.22 s.258
Sch.2 para.4, varied: 2009 c.22 s.258
Sch.2 para.5, varied: 2009 c.22 s.258
Sch.2 para.6, varied: 2009 c.22 s.258

8. Town and Country Planning Act 1990
applied: SI 2009/452 Reg.6, Reg.13, SI 2009/785
  Art.58, SI 2009/1300 Sch.11 para.1, SI 2009/
  2325 Art.17, SI 2009/3342 Reg.2, SI 2009/3365
  Sch.1 para.1
referred to: 2009 c.7 s.3, SI 2009/3342 Reg.2
Part III, applied: SI 2009/1300 Art.24
Part XI, applied: SI 2009/1300 Sch.14 para.4
Part XII, applied: SI 2009/3342 Reg.54
s.33, disapplied: SI 2009/1799 Reg.28
s.59, enabling: SI 2009/453, SI 2009/1024, SI 2009/
  1304, SI 2009/2193, SI 2009/2261
s.60, enabling: SI 2009/2193
s.61, enabling: SI 2009/453, SI 2009/1024, SI 2009/
  2193
s.62, enabling: SI 2009/1024, SI 2009/2261
s.65, enabling: SI 2009/453
s.69, applied: SI 2009/3342 Reg.47
s.69, varied: SI 2009/3342 Reg.47
s.69, enabling: SI 2009/1024
s.70, see *R. (on the application of Sainsbury's*
  Supermarkets Ltd) v Wolverhampton City
  Council [2009] EWCA Civ 835, [2009] 44 E.G.
  210 (CA (Civ Div)), Ward, L.J.
s.71, enabling: SI 2009/2261
s.74, enabling: SI 2009/453, SI 2009/2261
s.77, disapplied: SI 2009/3342 Reg.6
s.78, applied: SI 2009/452 Reg.3
s.78, enabling: SI 2009/453
s.79, enabling: SI 2009/453
s.83, amended: 2009 c.20 Sch.5 para.2
s.90, applied: SI 2009/1300 Art.24, SI 2009/2364
  Art.15
s.96A, enabling: SI 2009/2261
s.97, applied: SI 2009/3342 Reg.51
s.106, see *R. (on the application of Buglife: The*
  Invertebrate Conservation Trust) v Thurrock
  Thames Gateway Development Corp [2009]
  EWCA Civ 29, [2009] 2 P. & C.R. 8 (CA (Civ
  Div)), Pill, L.J.; see *R. (on the application of*

1990– cont.

8. Town and Country Planning Act 1990– *cont.*
s.106– *cont.*
  Sainsbury's Supermarkets Ltd) v Wolverhamp-
  ton City Council [2009] EWCA Civ 835, [2009]
  44 E.G. 210 (CA (Civ Div)), Ward, L.J.; see *R. (on*
  the application of Sainsbury's Supermarkets
  Ltd) v Wolverhampton City Council [2009]
  EWHC 134 (Admin), [2009] J.P.L. 1354 (QBD
  (Admin)), Elias, J.; see *Rastrum Ltd v Secretary*
  of State for Communities and Local Government
  [2009] EWHC 184 (Admin), [2009] J.P.L. 1159
  (QBD (Admin)), Sir George Newman; see *Ridge-*
  land Properties Ltd v Bristol City Council
  [2009] UKUT 102 (LC), [2009] R.V.R. 252 (UT
  (Lands)), PR Francis FRICS; see *Southampton*
  City Council v Hallyard Ltd [2008] EWHC 916
  (Ch), [2009] 1 P. & C.R. 5 (Ch D), Morgan, J.; see
  Watson v Croft Promo-Sport Ltd [2009] EWCA
  Civ 15, [2009] 3 All E.R. 249 (CA (Civ Div)), Sir
  Andrew Morritt (Chancellor)
s.109, amended: SI 2009/1307 Sch.1 para.194
s.118, amended: SI 2009/1307 Sch.1 para.195
s.146, amended: SI 2009/1307 Sch.1 para.196
s.149, see *Aardvark SRE Ltd v Sedgefield BC* [2008]
  EWCA Civ 1109, [2009] R.V.R. 93 (CA (Civ
  Div)), Richards, L.J.
s.150, applied: SI 2009/1300 Art.86
s.152, amended: SI 2009/1307 Sch.1 para.197
s.153, amended: SI 2009/1307 Sch.1 para.198
s.153, repealed (in part): SI 2009/1307 Sch.1
  para.198
s.154, amended: SI 2009/1307 Sch.1 para.199
s.155, amended: SI 2009/1307 Sch.1 para.200
s.156, amended: SI 2009/1307 Sch.1 para.201
s.159, amended: SI 2009/1307 Sch.1 para.202
s.160, amended: SI 2009/1307 Sch.1 para.203
s.161, applied: SI 2009/1300 Art.86
s.163, amended: SI 2009/1307 Sch.1 para.204
s.166, amended: SI 2009/1307 Sch.1 para.205
s.171B, see *Basingstoke and Deane BC v Secretary*
  of State for Communities and Local Government
  [2009] EWHC 1012 (Admin), [2009] J.P.L. 1585
  (QBD (Admin)), Collins, J.
s.174, see *R. (on the application of Perrett) v*
  Secretary of State for Communities and Local
  Government [2009] EWHC 234 (Admin),
  [2009] J.P.L. 1151 (QBD (Admin)), Mitting, J.
s.178, see *R. (on the application of McCarthy) v*
  Basildon DC [2009] EWCA Civ 13, [2009]
  B.L.G.R. 1013 (CA (Civ Div)), Pill, L.J.
s.186, see *Shopsearch UK Ltd v Greenwich LBC*
  [2009] R.V.R. 198 (Lands Tr), NJ Rose, FRICS
s.186, amended: SI 2009/1307 Sch.1 para.206
s.187B, see *South Cambridgeshire DC v Gammell*
  [2008] EWCA Civ 1159, [2009] B.L.G.R. 141
  (CA (Civ Div)), Keene, L.J.
s.192, see *Rastrum Ltd v Secretary of State for*
  Communities and Local Government [2009]
  EWHC 184 (Admin), [2009] J.P.L. 1159 (QBD
  (Admin)), Sir George Newman
s.198, see *Palm Developments Ltd v Secretary of*
  State for Communities and Local Government
  [2009] EWHC 220 (Admin), [2009] 2 P. & C.R.
  16 (QBD (Admin)), Cranston, J.
s.205, amended: SI 2009/1307 Sch.1 para.207
s.210, applied: SI 2009/3264 Sch.1 para.1, SI 2009/
  3365 Sch.1 para.1
s.211, applied: SI 2009/3264 Sch.1 para.1, SI 2009/
  3365 Sch.1 para.1

1990–cont.

8. Town and Country Planning Act 1990–*cont.*

s.215, see *Picton v South Northamptonshire Council* [2009] R.V.R. 193 (Lands Tr), George Bartlett Q.C. (President, LTr); see *Toni & Guy (South) Ltd v Hammersmith and Fulham LBC* [2009] EWHC 203 (Admin), Times, March 27, 2009 (QBD (Admin)), Wyn Williams, J.

s.215, referred to: SI 2009/2037 Art.5

s.223, amended: SI 2009/1307 Sch.1 para.208

s.226, see *R. (on the application of Sainsbury's Supermarkets Ltd) v Wolverhampton City Council* [2009] EWCA Civ 835, [2009] 44 E.G. 210 (CA (Civ Div)), Ward, L.J.; see *R. (on the application of Sainsbury's Supermarkets Ltd) v Wolverhampton City Council* [2009] EWHC 134 (Admin), [2009] J.P.L. 1354 (QBD (Admin)), Elias, J.

s.250, amended: SI 2009/1307 Sch.1 para.209

s.252, amended: 2009 c.20 Sch.6 para.82

s.259, applied: SI 2009/849 Art.2

s.264, applied: SI 2009/1300 Art.24, SI 2009/2364 Art.15

s.265, applied: SI 2009/229 Art.4

s.271, applied: SI 2009/1300 Art.41, Sch.11 para.1, Sch.13 para.3, SI 2009/2364 Art.29, Sch.8 para.1, Sch.9 para.4, SI 2009/2728 Art.16, Sch.6 para.1, Sch.6 para.3

s.271, disapplied: SI 2009/2364 Sch.8 para.1, SI 2009/2728 Sch.6 para.5

s.271, varied: SI 2009/2728 Sch.6 para.2

s.272, applied: SI 2009/1300 Art.41, Sch.11 para.1, Sch.13 para.3, SI 2009/2364 Art.29, Sch.8 para.1, Sch.9 para.4, SI 2009/2728 Art.16, Sch.6 para.1, Sch.6 para.3

s.272, disapplied: SI 2009/2364 Sch.8 para.1, SI 2009/2728 Sch.6 para.5

s.272, varied: SI 2009/2728 Sch.6 para.2

s.273, applied: SI 2009/1300 Sch.11 para.1, SI 2009/2364 Sch.8 para.1, SI 2009/2728 Sch.6 para.1, Sch.6 para.3

s.273, disapplied: SI 2009/2364 Sch.8 para.1, SI 2009/2728 Sch.6 para.5

s.273, varied: SI 2009/2728 Sch.6 para.2

s.274, applied: SI 2009/1300 Sch.11 para.1, SI 2009/2364 Sch.8 para.1, SI 2009/2728 Sch.6 para.1

s.274, disapplied: SI 2009/2364 Sch.8 para.1, SI 2009/2728 Sch.6 para.5

s.274, varied: SI 2009/2728 Sch.6 para.2

s.275, applied: SI 2009/1300 Sch.11 para.1, SI 2009/2364 Sch.8 para.1

s.275, disapplied: SI 2009/2364 Sch.8 para.1, SI 2009/2728 Sch.6 para.5

s.275, referred to: SI 2009/2728 Sch.6 para.1

s.275, varied: SI 2009/2728 Sch.6 para.2

s.276, applied: SI 2009/1300 Sch.11 para.1, SI 2009/2364 Sch.8 para.1

s.276, disapplied: SI 2009/2364 Sch.8 para.1, SI 2009/2728 Sch.6 para.5

s.276, referred to: SI 2009/2728 Sch.6 para.1

s.276, varied: SI 2009/2728 Sch.6 para.2

s.277, applied: SI 2009/1300 Sch.11 para.1, SI 2009/2364 Sch.8 para.1

s.277, disapplied: SI 2009/2364 Sch.8 para.1, SI 2009/2728 Sch.6 para.5

s.277, referred to: SI 2009/2728 Sch.6 para.1

s.277, varied: SI 2009/2728 Sch.6 para.2

s.278, applied: SI 2009/1300 Sch.11 para.1, SI 2009/2364 Sch.8 para.1

s.278, disapplied: SI 2009/2364 Sch.8 para.1, SI 2009/2728 Sch.6 para.5

1990–cont.

8. Town and Country Planning Act 1990–*cont.*

s.278, referred to: SI 2009/2728 Sch.6 para.1

s.278, varied: SI 2009/2728 Sch.6 para.2

s.279, applied: SI 2009/1300 Sch.11 para.1, SI 2009/2364 Sch.8 para.1, SI 2009/2728 Sch.6 para.1

s.279, disapplied: SI 2009/2364 Sch.8 para.1, SI 2009/2728 Sch.6 para.5

s.279, varied: SI 2009/2728 Sch.6 para.2

s.280, amended: SI 2009/1307 Sch.1 para.210

s.280, applied: SI 2009/1300 Sch.11 para.1, SI 2009/2364 Sch.8 para.1, SI 2009/2728 Sch.6 para.1

s.280, disapplied: SI 2009/2364 Sch.8 para.1, SI 2009/2728 Sch.6 para.5

s.280, varied: SI 2009/2728 Sch.6 para.2

s.281, applied: SI 2009/2364 Sch.8 para.1

s.281, disapplied: SI 2009/2364 Sch.8 para.1

s.282, amended: SI 2009/1307 Sch.1 para.211

s.282, applied: SI 2009/1300 Sch.11 para.1, SI 2009/2364 Sch.8 para.1, SI 2009/2728 Sch.6 para.1

s.282, disapplied: SI 2009/2364 Sch.8 para.1, SI 2009/2728 Sch.6 para.5

s.282, varied: SI 2009/2728 Sch.6 para.2

s.284, varied: SI 2009/3342 Reg.54

s.288, see *Bovale Ltd v Secretary of State for Communities and Local Government* [2009] EWCA Civ 171, [2009] 1 W.L.R. 2274 (CA (Civ Div)), Waller, L.J. (V-P)

s.288, applied: SI 2009/3342 Reg.54

s.288, varied: SI 2009/3342 Reg.54

s.289, see *R. (on the application of Perrett) v Secretary of State for Communities and Local Government* [2009] EWHC 234 (Admin), [2009] J.P.L. 1151 (QBD (Admin)), Mitting, J.

s.303, applied: SI 2009/851

s.303, enabling: SI 2009/851

s.319A, applied: SI 2009/452 Reg.3, Reg.4, Reg.11, Reg.18, SI 2009/454 Reg.2

s.319A, enabling: SI 2009/454

s.323, enabling: SI 2009/452

s.329, applied: SI 2009/3342 Reg.53

s.333, enabling: SI 2009/380, SI 2009/452, SI 2009/453, SI 2009/454, SI 2009/2193, SI 2009/2261

Sch.1 para.7, amended: 2009 c.20 Sch.5 para.3

Sch.3 para.1, see *Greenweb Ltd v Wandsworth LBC* [2008] EWCA Civ 910, [2009] 1 W.L.R. 612 (CA (Civ Div)), Buxton, L.J.

Sch.4A para.1, enabling: SI 2009/1304

Sch.6 para.1, enabling: SI 2009/380

Sch.7 para.12, amended: 2009 c.20 Sch.5 para.4

Sch.8 Part I para.2, applied: SI 2009/2364 Art.29

Sch.9, applied: SI 2009/3342 Reg.48

Sch.9 para.1, applied: SI 2009/3342 Reg.51

Sch.9 para.2, applied: SI 2009/3342 Reg.51

Sch.9 para.3, applied: SI 2009/3342 Reg.51, Reg.54

Sch.9 para.3, varied: SI 2009/3342 Reg.51

Sch.9 para.4, varied: SI 2009/3342 Reg.51

Sch.13 para.21, applied: SI 2009/1300 Art.86

Sch.14 Part I para.1, amended: 2009 c.20 Sch.6 para.82

9. Planning (Listed Buildings and Conservation Areas) Act 1990

s.1, applied: SI 2009/2108 Reg.12

s.2, enabling: SI 2009/2711

s.10, applied: SI 2009/1026, SI 2009/2262

s.31, amended: SI 2009/1307 Sch.1 para.212

s.48, referred to: SI 2009/2037 Art.5

s.91, enabling: SI 2009/2262

s.93, enabling: SI 2009/1026, SI 2009/2262, SI 2009/2711

1990– cont.

10. Planning (Hazardous Substances) Act 1990
s.4, enabling: SI 2009/1901
s.5, enabling: SI 2009/1901
s.23, applied: SI 2009/1901 Reg.4
s.25, varied: SI 2009/849 Art.2
s.37, varied: SI 2009/849 Art.2
s.38, varied: SI 2009/849 Art.2
s.39, amended: SI 2009/1941 Sch.1 para.116
s.40, enabling: SI 2009/1901
Sch.1 para.6, varied: SI 2009/849 Art.2

11. Planning (Consequential Provisions) Act 1990
Sch.4 para.1, enabling: SI 2009/849

16. Food Safety Act 1990
applied: SI 2009/2163
referred to: SSI 2009/437 Reg.2
enabling: SI 2009/793, SI 2009/2163
s.1, applied: SI 2009/716 Reg.3
s.1, enabling: SI 2009/3378
s.2, applied: SI 2009/1584 Reg.11, SI 2009/3230
   Reg.5, SI 2009/3379 Reg.5, SSI 2009/261
   Reg.11, SSI 2009/437 Reg.5
s.2, varied: SI 2009/1795 Reg.11, SI 2009/3230
   Reg.5, SI 2009/3238 Reg.16, SI 2009/3378
   Reg.16, SI 2009/3379 Reg.5, SSI 2009/436
   Reg.16, SSI 2009/437 Reg.5
s.3, applied: SI 2009/205 Reg.24, SI 2009/481
   Reg.24, SI 2009/1584 Reg.11, SSI 2009/30
   Reg.21, SSI 2009/261 Reg.11
s.3, varied: SI 2009/793 Reg.21, SI 2009/1223
   Reg.5, SI 2009/1386 Reg.5, SI 2009/1795
   Reg.11, SI 2009/2163 Reg.39, SI 2009/3051
   Reg.4, SI 2009/3235 Reg.5, SI 2009/3238
   Reg.16, SI 2009/3254 Reg.4, SI 2009/3378
   Reg.16, SSI 2009/215 Reg.5, SSI 2009/427
   Reg.4, SSI 2009/435 Reg.5, SSI 2009/436 Reg.16
s.6, enabling: SI 2009/793, SI 2009/2163, SI 2009/
   2779
s.9, applied: SI 2009/1223 Reg.5, SI 2009/1584
   Reg.11, SI 2009/3235 Reg.6, SI 2009/3238
   Reg.17, SI 2009/3378 Reg.17, SI 2009/3379
   Reg.5, SSI 2009/261 Reg.11, SSI 2009/435
   Reg.6, SSI 2009/436 Reg.17, SSI 2009/437 Reg.5
s.9, referred to: SI 2009/3230 Reg.5
s.9, varied: SI 2009/1223 Reg.5, SI 2009/1386 Reg.5,
   SI 2009/1795 Reg.11, SI 2009/3230 Reg.5, SI
   2009/3379 Reg.5, SSI 2009/215 Reg.5, SSI
   2009/437 Reg.5
s.10, applied: SI 2009/665 Art.2
s.11, applied: SI 2009/3255 Reg.12, SI 2009/3376
   Reg.12, SSI 2009/446 Reg.12
s.12, applied: SI 2009/665 Art.2, SI 2009/3255
   Reg.12, SI 2009/3376 Reg.12, SSI 2009/446
   Reg.12
s.13, applied: SI 2009/3255 Reg.12, SI 2009/3376
   Reg.12, SSI 2009/446 Reg.12
s.14, applied: SI 2009/1386 Reg.5, SI 2009/1584
   Reg.11, SSI 2009/215 Reg.5, SSI 2009/261
   Reg.11, SSI 2009/435 Reg.5
s.15, applied: SI 2009/1386 Reg.5, SI 2009/1584
   Reg.11, SSI 2009/215 Reg.5, SSI 2009/261
   Reg.11, SSI 2009/435 Reg.5
s.16, enabling: SI 2009/205, SI 2009/481, SI 2009/
   793, SI 2009/891, SI 2009/1092, SI 2009/1223, SI
   2009/1386, SI 2009/1584, SI 2009/1598, SI 2009/
   1795, SI 2009/1897, SI 2009/1925, SI 2009/2163,
   SI 2009/2201, SI 2009/2538, SI 2009/2705, SI
   2009/2801, SI 2009/2880, SI 2009/2938, SI
   2009/2939, SI 2009/3051, SI 2009/3105, SI
   2009/3235, SI 2009/3238, SI 2009/3251, SI
   2009/3252, SI 2009/3254, SI 2009/3377, SI

1990– cont.

16. Food Safety Act 1990–*cont.*
s.16, enabling:–*cont.*
   2009/3378, SSI 2009/30, SSI 2009/167, SSI
   2009/215, SSI 2009/225, SSI 2009/261, SSI
   2009/273, SSI 2009/328, SSI 2009/374, SSI
   2009/426, SSI 2009/427, SSI 2009/435, SSI
   2009/436, SSI 2009/438
s.17, enabling: SI 2009/205, SI 2009/481, SI 2009/
   793, SI 2009/891, SI 2009/1092, SI 2009/1223, SI
   2009/1386, SI 2009/1584, SI 2009/1598, SI 2009/
   1795, SI 2009/1897, SI 2009/1925, SI 2009/2163,
   SI 2009/2201, SI 2009/2538, SI 2009/2705, SI
   2009/2801, SI 2009/2880, SI 2009/2938, SI
   2009/2939, SI 2009/3051, SI 2009/3105, SI
   2009/3235, SI 2009/3238, SI 2009/3251, SI
   2009/3252, SI 2009/3254, SI 2009/3377, SI
   2009/3378, SSI 2009/30, SSI 2009/167, SSI
   2009/215, SSI 2009/225, SSI 2009/261, SSI
   2009/273, SSI 2009/328, SSI 2009/374, SSI
   2009/426, SSI 2009/427, SSI 2009/435, SSI
   2009/436, SSI 2009/438
s.18, enabling: SI 2009/1584, SI 2009/1795, SSI
   2009/261
s.19, enabling: SI 2009/1584, SI 2009/1795, SSI
   2009/261
s.20, applied: SI 2009/1584 Reg.11, SSI 2009/30
   Reg.21, SSI 2009/261 Reg.11
s.20, referred to: SI 2009/793 Reg.21
s.20, varied: SI 2009/793 Reg.21, SI 2009/1223
   Reg.5, SI 2009/1386 Reg.5, SI 2009/1795
   Reg.11, SI 2009/2163 Reg.39, SI 2009/3051
   Reg.4, SI 2009/3230 Reg.5, SI 2009/3235
   Reg.5, SI 2009/3238 Reg.16, SI 2009/3254
   Reg.4, SI 2009/3378 Reg.16, SI 2009/3379
   Reg.5, SSI 2009/215 Reg.5, SSI 2009/427
   Reg.4, SSI 2009/435 Reg.5, SSI 2009/436
   Reg.16, SSI 2009/437 Reg.5
s.21, applied: SI 2009/1584 Reg.11, SSI 2009/261
   Reg.11
s.21, referred to: SI 2009/793 Reg.21
s.21, varied: SI 2009/793 Reg.21, SI 2009/1223
   Reg.5, SI 2009/1386 Reg.5, SI 2009/1795
   Reg.11, SI 2009/2163 Reg.39, SI 2009/3051
   Reg.4, SI 2009/3230 Reg.5, SI 2009/3235
   Reg.5, SI 2009/3238 Reg.16, SI 2009/3254
   Reg.4, SI 2009/3378 Reg.16, SI 2009/3379
   Reg.5, SSI 2009/215 Reg.5, SSI 2009/427
   Reg.4, SSI 2009/435 Reg.5, SSI 2009/436
   Reg.16, SSI 2009/437 Reg.5
s.22, varied: SI 2009/3238 Reg.16, SI 2009/3378
   Reg.16, SSI 2009/436 Reg.16
s.26, enabling: SI 2009/205, SI 2009/481, SI 2009/
   793, SI 2009/1223, SI 2009/1386, SI 2009/1584,
   SI 2009/1598, SI 2009/1795, SI 2009/1897, SI
   2009/1925, SI 2009/2163, SI 2009/2705, SI
   2009/2801, SI 2009/2880, SI 2009/2938, SI
   2009/3051, SI 2009/3105, SI 2009/3235, SI
   2009/3238, SI 2009/3251, SI 2009/3252, SI
   2009/3254, SI 2009/3377, SI 2009/3378, SSI
   2009/30, SSI 2009/215, SSI 2009/261, SSI
   2009/273, SSI 2009/374, SSI 2009/426, SSI
   2009/427, SSI 2009/435, SSI 2009/436, SSI
   2009/438
s.29, applied: SI 2009/205 Reg.22, SI 2009/481
   Reg.22, SI 2009/3230 Reg.4, SI 2009/3379
   Reg.4, SSI 2009/30 Reg.19, SSI 2009/437
   Reg.4, SSI 2009/446 Reg.38
s.29, referred to: SI 2009/793 Reg.21
s.29, varied: SI 2009/793 Reg.21, SI 2009/2163
   Reg.39, SI 2009/3230 Reg.5, SI 2009/3379
   Reg.5, SSI 2009/437 Reg.5

1990– cont.

16. Food Safety Act 1990–*cont.*

s.30, applied: SI 2009/205 Reg.22, Reg.24, SI 2009/481 Reg.22, Reg.24, SI 2009/1584 Reg.11, SSI 2009/30 Reg.19, Reg.21, SSI 2009/261 Reg.11

s.30, referred to: SI 2009/793 Reg.21

s.30, varied: SI 2009/793 Reg.21, SI 2009/1223 Reg.5, SI 2009/1386 Reg.5, SI 2009/1795 Reg.11, SI 2009/2163 Reg.39, SI 2009/3051 Reg.4, SI 2009/3230 Reg.5, SI 2009/3235 Reg.5, SI 2009/3238 Reg.16, SI 2009/3254 Reg.4, SI 2009/3378 Reg.16, SI 2009/3379 Reg.5, SSI 2009/215 Reg.5, SSI 2009/427 Reg.4, SSI 2009/435 Reg.5, SSI 2009/436 Reg.16, SSI 2009/437 Reg.5

s.31, enabling: SI 2009/205, SI 2009/481, SI 2009/1598, SI 2009/1897, SSI 2009/30, SSI 2009/273

s.32, applied: SI 2009/3378 Reg.16, SSI 2009/435 Reg.5

s.32, referred to: SI 2009/793 Reg.21

s.32, varied: SI 2009/793 Reg.21, SI 2009/3230 Reg.5, SI 2009/3235 Reg.5, SI 2009/3238 Reg.16, SI 2009/3379 Reg.5, SSI 2009/436 Reg.16, SSI 2009/437 Reg.5

s.33, applied: SI 2009/1386 Reg.5, SI 2009/1584 Reg.11, SI 2009/3378 Reg.16, SI 2009/3379 Reg.5, SSI 2009/215 Reg.5, SSI 2009/261 Reg.11, SSI 2009/427 Reg.4, SSI 2009/435 Reg.5

s.33, referred to: SI 2009/1386 Reg.5

s.33, varied: SI 2009/1223 Reg.5, SI 2009/1386 Reg.5, SI 2009/1795 Reg.11, SI 2009/3051 Reg.4, SI 2009/3230 Reg.5, SI 2009/3235 Reg.5, SI 2009/3238 Reg.16, SI 2009/3254 Reg.4, SI 2009/3378 Reg.16, SI 2009/3379 Reg.5, SSI 2009/215 Reg.5, SSI 2009/427 Reg.4, SSI 2009/435 Reg.5, SSI 2009/436 Reg.16, SSI 2009/437 Reg.5

s.34, applied: SI 2009/1584 Reg.11, SI 2009/1795 Reg.11, SI 2009/3238 Reg.16, SI 2009/3378 Reg.16, SSI 2009/435 Reg.5

s.34, varied: SI 2009/3235 Reg.5, SSI 2009/436 Reg.16

s.35, applied: SI 2009/1584 Reg.11, SI 2009/1795 Reg.11, SI 2009/3238 Reg.16, SI 2009/3378 Reg.16, SSI 2009/261 Reg.11, SSI 2009/435 Reg.5

s.35, varied: SI 2009/1223 Reg.5, SI 2009/1386 Reg.5, SI 2009/1795 Reg.11, SI 2009/3051 Reg.4, SI 2009/3230 Reg.5, SI 2009/3235 Reg.5, SI 2009/3238 Reg.16, SI 2009/3254 Reg.4, SI 2009/3378 Reg.16, SI 2009/3379 Reg.5, SSI 2009/215 Reg.5, SSI 2009/427 Reg.4, SSI 2009/435 Reg.5, SSI 2009/436 Reg.16, SSI 2009/437 Reg.5

s.36, applied: SI 2009/1584 Reg.11, SSI 2009/30 Reg.21, SSI 2009/261 Reg.11

s.36, varied: SI 2009/793 Reg.21, SI 2009/1223 Reg.5, SI 2009/1386 Reg.5, SI 2009/1795 Reg.11, SI 2009/3051 Reg.4, SI 2009/3230 Reg.5, SI 2009/3235 Reg.5, SI 2009/3238 Reg.16, SI 2009/3254 Reg.4, SI 2009/3378 Reg.16, SI 2009/3379 Reg.5, SSI 2009/215 Reg.5, SSI 2009/427 Reg.4, SSI 2009/435 Reg.5, SSI 2009/436 Reg.16, SSI 2009/437 Reg.5

s.36A, applied: SI 2009/1584 Reg.11, SSI 2009/30 Reg.21, SSI 2009/261 Reg.11

s.36A, varied: SI 2009/793 Reg.21, SI 2009/1223 Reg.5, SI 2009/1386 Reg.5, SI 2009/1795 Reg.11, SI 2009/3051 Reg.4, SI 2009/3230 Reg.5, SI 2009/3235 Reg.5, SI 2009/3238 Reg.16, SI 2009/3254 Reg.4, SI 2009/3378 Reg.16, SI 2009/3379 Reg.5, SSI 2009/215

1990– cont.

16. Food Safety Act 1990–*cont.*

s.36A, varied:–*cont.*
Reg.5, SSI 2009/427 Reg.4, SSI 2009/435 Reg.5, SSI 2009/436 Reg.16, SSI 2009/437 Reg.5

s.37, varied: SI 2009/2163 Reg.23

s.43, applied: SI 2009/1584 Sch.2 para.3, SI 2009/1795 Sch.2 para.3, SSI 2009/261 Sch.2 para.26

s.44, applied: SI 2009/205 Reg.24, SI 2009/481 Reg.24, SI 2009/1584 Reg.11, SSI 2009/30 Reg.21, SSI 2009/261 Reg.11

s.44, referred to: SI 2009/793 Reg.21

s.44, varied: SI 2009/793 Reg.21, SI 2009/1223 Reg.5, SI 2009/1386 Reg.5, SI 2009/1795 Reg.11, SI 2009/2163 Reg.39, SI 2009/3051 Reg.4, SI 2009/3230 Reg.5, SI 2009/3235 Reg.5, SI 2009/3238 Reg.16, SI 2009/3254 Reg.4, SI 2009/3378 Reg.16, SI 2009/3379 Reg.5, SSI 2009/215 Reg.5, SSI 2009/427 Reg.4, SSI 2009/435 Reg.5, SSI 2009/436 Reg.16, SSI 2009/437 Reg.5

s.45, enabling: SI 2009/2779

s.46, varied: SI 2009/793 Reg.21, SI 2009/2163 Reg.39

s.48, applied: SI 2009/205, SI 2009/481, SI 2009/793, SI 2009/891, SI 2009/1092, SI 2009/1223, SI 2009/1386, SI 2009/1584, SI 2009/1598, SI 2009/1795, SI 2009/1897, SI 2009/2201, SI 2009/2538, SI 2009/2705, SI 2009/2779, SI 2009/2801, SI 2009/2880, SI 2009/2938, SI 2009/3051, SI 2009/3105, SI 2009/3235, SI 2009/3238, SI 2009/3252, SI 2009/3254, SI 2009/3378, SSI 2009/30, SSI 2009/215, SSI 2009/273, SSI 2009/328, SSI 2009/374, SSI 2009/427, SSI 2009/435, SSI 2009/436, SSI 2009/438

s.48, enabling: SI 2009/205, SI 2009/481, SI 2009/793, SI 2009/1223, SI 2009/1386, SI 2009/1584, SI 2009/1598, SI 2009/1795, SI 2009/1897, SI 2009/1925, SI 2009/2163, SI 2009/2538, SI 2009/2705, SI 2009/2779, SI 2009/2801, SI 2009/2880, SI 2009/2938, SI 2009/3051, SI 2009/3105, SI 2009/3235, SI 2009/3238, SI 2009/3251, SI 2009/3252, SI 2009/3254, SI 2009/3377, SI 2009/3378, SSI 2009/30, SSI 2009/215, SSI 2009/261, SSI 2009/273, SSI 2009/328, SSI 2009/374, SSI 2009/426, SSI 2009/427, SSI 2009/435, SSI 2009/436, SSI 2009/438

s.48A, applied: SI 2009/2163, SI 2009/3251, SSI 2009/167, SSI 2009/261, SSI 2009/426

s.50, varied: SI 2009/793 Reg.21

s.58, applied: SI 2009/1584 Reg.11, SSI 2009/261 Reg.11

s.58, varied: SI 2009/1795 Reg.11

Sch.1 para.1, enabling: SI 2009/1584, SI 2009/1598, SI 2009/1795, SI 2009/1897, SSI 2009/261

Sch.1 para.4, enabling: SI 2009/1584, SI 2009/1598, SI 2009/1795, SI 2009/1897, SSI 2009/261

18. Computer Misuse Act 1990

see *Culkin v Wirral Independent Appeal Panel* [2009] EWHC 868 (Admin), [2009] E.L.R. 287 (QBD (Admin)), Nicol, J.

s.1, see *Burwell v DPP* [2009] EWHC 1069 (Admin), (2009) 173 J.P. 351 (QBD (Admin)), Keene, L.J.

s.11, see *Burwell v DPP* [2009] EWHC 1069 (Admin), (2009) 173 J.P. 351 (QBD (Admin)), Keene, L.J.

19. National Health Service and Community Care Act 1990

Part I, applied: SI 2009/3050 Art.2

s.18, referred to: SI 2009/1511 Sch.1

1990– cont.

19. National Health Service and Community Care Act 1990– *cont.*

s.46, applied: SI 2009/ 1887 Reg.6

s.47, see *R. (on the application of F) v Wirral BC* [2009] EWHC 1626 (Admin), [2009] B.L.G.R. 905 (QBD (Admin)), McCombe, J.

23. Access to Health Records Act 1990

s.3, amended: 2009 c.25 Sch.21 para.29

27. Social Security Act 1990

s.15, enabling: SI 2009/ 1816, SSI 2009/ 48, SSI 2009/ 392

29. Finance Act 1990

s.25, see *Simpson (East Berkshire Sports Foundation Trustee) v Revenue and Customs Commissioners* [2009] S.T.C. (S.C.D.) 226 (Sp Comm), Howard M Nowlan

s.67, repealed (in part): 2009 c.10 Sch.16 para.5

s.68, repealed (in part): 2009 c.10 Sch.17 para.3

s.76, repealed: 2009 c.4 Sch.3 Part 1

s.78, repealed: 2009 c.4 Sch.3 Part 1

s.90, repealed (in part): SI 2009/ 2035 Sch.1 para.60

s.122, repealed: 2009 c.10 Sch.51 para.43

s.124, repealed: SI 2009/ 3054 Sch.1 para.16

s.125, repealed (in part): SI 2009/ 2035 Sch.1 para.26

s.126, repealed (in part): 2009 c.4 Sch.3 Part 1

s.128, applied: SI 2009/ 718

Sch.14 Part I para.2, repealed: 2009 c.4 Sch.3 Part 1

Sch.14 Part I para.10, repealed: SI 2009/ 3001 Sch.2

Sch.14 Part I para.11, repealed: SI 2009/ 3001 Sch.2

Sch.14 Part II para.15, repealed: SI 2009/ 2035 Sch.1 para.60

31. Aviation and Maritime Security Act 1990

Sch.2 para.7, amended: SI 2009/ 1307 Sch.1 para.213

Sch.2 para.8, amended: SI 2009/ 1307 Sch.1 para.213

Sch.2 para.9, amended: SI 2009/ 1307 Sch.1 para.213

35. Enterprise and New Towns (Scotland) Act 1990

s.4, amended: SI 2009/ 1941 Sch.1 para.117

s.8, amended: SI 2009/ 1941 Sch.1 para.117

s.25, applied: 2009 asp 2 Sch.5

s.26, applied: 2009 asp 2 Sch.5

s.36, amended: SI 2009/ 1941 Sch.1 para.117

36. Contracts (Applicable Law) Act 1990

s.4A, added: SI 2009/ 3064 Reg.2

s.4B, added: SSI 2009/ 410 Reg.2

s.8, amended: SSI 2009/ 410 Reg.2

37. Human Fertilisation and Embryology Act 1990

see *L v Human Fertilisation and Embryology Authority* [2008] EWHC 2149 (Fam), [2009] Eu. L.R. 107 (Fam Div), Charles, J.

applied: SI 2009/ 1397 Reg.3, SI 2009/ 1892 Sch.4 para.1, Sch.4 para.2, Sch.4 para.3, Sch.4 para.4

referred to: SI 2009/ 2478 Art.1

s.1, applied: SI 2009/ 1892 Sch.4 para.2

s.3, see *Yearworth v North Bristol NHS Trust* [2009] EWCA Civ 37, [2009] 3 W.L.R. 118 (CA (Civ Div)), Lord Judge, L.C.J.

s.3ZA, applied: SI 2009/ 2478 Art.2

s.4, see *Yearworth v North Bristol NHS Trust* [2009] EWCA Civ 37, [2009] 3 W.L.R. 118 (CA (Civ Div)), Lord Judge, L.C.J.

s.4A, applied: SI 2009/ 1892 Sch.4 para.2

s.8B, applied: SI 2009/ 1891 Reg.4

s.8C, applied: SI 2009/ 1891 Reg.4

s.9, applied: SI 2009/ 1892 Sch.4 para.7

s.10, applied: SI 2009/ 1892 Sch.4 para.9

1990– cont.

37. Human Fertilisation and Embryology Act 1990– *cont.*

s.12, see *Yearworth v North Bristol NHS Trust* [2009] EWCA Civ 37, [2009] 3 W.L.R. 118 (CA (Civ Div)), Lord Judge, L.C.J.

s.13, applied: SI 2009/ 1892 Sch.4 para.1

s.14, applied: SI 2009/ 1582 Reg.3, Reg.4, SI 2009/ 2478 Art.2

s.14, enabling: SI 2009/ 1582, SI 2009/ 2581

s.18, applied: SI 2009/ 1892 Sch.4 para.8, Sch.4 para.9

s.18A, applied: SI 2009/ 1892 Sch.4 para.8, Sch.4 para.9

s.19, applied: SI 2009/ 1397 Reg.4, Reg.8, SI 2009/ 1892 Sch.4 para.8, Sch.4 para.9

s.19, referred to: SI 2009/ 1892 Sch.4 para.9

s.19, enabling: SI 2009/ 1397, SI 2009/ 2088

s.19A, applied: SI 2009/ 1892 Sch.4 para.9

s.19A, referred to: SI 2009/ 1397 Reg.17

s.19B, applied: SI 2009/ 1892 Sch.4 para.9

s.19C, applied: SI 2009/ 1892 Sch.4 para.9, Sch.4 para.12

s.20, applied: SI 2009/ 1891 Reg.20, SI 2009/ 1892 Sch.4 para.9, Sch.4 para.11

s.20A, applied: SI 2009/ 1892 Sch.4 para.11

s.20A, enabling: SI 2009/ 1891

s.20B, applied: SI 2009/ 1892 Sch.4 para.11

s.20B, enabling: SI 2009/ 1891

s.21, applied: SI 2009/ 1892 Sch.4 para.11

s.22, applied: SI 2009/ 1892 Sch.4 para.12

s.24, see *L v Human Fertilisation and Embryology Authority* [2008] EWHC 2149 (Fam), [2009] Eu. L.R. 107 (Fam Div), Charles, J.

s.28, see *X (Children) (Parental Order: Foreign Surrogacy), Re* [2008] EWHC 3030 (Fam), [2009] Fam. 71 (Fam Div), Hedley, J.

s.30, see *X (Children) (Parental Order: Foreign Surrogacy), Re* [2008] EWHC 3030 (Fam), [2009] Fam. 71 (Fam Div), Hedley, J.

s.30, amended: SI 2009/ 1892 Sch.1 para.3

s.30, applied: SI 2009/ 2232 Art.4, SI 2009/ 2233 Art.2

s.31, applied: SI 2009/ 1892 Sch.4 para.5

s.31, referred to: SI 2009/ 1892 Sch.4 para.13

s.31ZA, applied: SI 2009/ 1892 Sch.4 para.13

s.31ZB, applied: SI 2009/ 1892 Sch.4 para.5

s.33A, disapplied: SI 2009/ 2232 Art.4

s.39, applied: SI 2009/ 1892 Sch.4 para.6

s.40, applied: SI 2009/ 1892 Sch.4 para.6

s.41, applied: SI 2009/ 1397 Reg.10, SI 2009/ 1891 Reg.22

s.43, enabling: SI 2009/ 1918

s.45, applied: SI 2009/ 1918

s.45, enabling: SI 2009/ 1397, SI 2009/ 1582, SI 2009/ 1891, SI 2009/ 1918, SI 2009/ 2088, SI 2009/ 2581

Sch.1 para.5, amended: 2009 c.21 Sch.3 para.3

Sch.1 para.5A, added: 2009 c.21 Sch.3 para.3

Sch.1 para.5B, added: 2009 c.21 Sch.3 para.3

Sch.2 para.1, applied: SI 2009/ 1892 Sch.4 para.1, SI 2009/ 2478 Art.2

Sch.2 para.1A, applied: SI 2009/ 1892 Sch.4 para.4

Sch.2 para.1ZA, applied: SI 2009/ 1892 Sch.4 para.1

Sch.2 para.1ZB, applied: SI 2009/ 1892 Sch.4 para.1

Sch.2 para.2, applied: SI 2009/ 1892 Sch.4 para.3, SI 2009/ 2478 Art.2

Sch.2 para.3, applied: SI 2009/ 1892 Sch.4 para.2

1990– cont.

37. Human Fertilisation and Embryology Act 1990– *cont.*

Sch.3, see *Yearworth v North Bristol NHS Trust* [2009] EWCA Civ 37, [2009] 3 W.L.R. 118 (CA (Civ Div)), Lord Judge, L.C.J.

Sch.3, applied: SI 2009/1892 Sch.4 para.1, Sch.4 para.2, Sch.4 para.3

Sch.3 para.5, applied: SI 2009/1892 Sch.4 para.4

Sch.3B para.2, applied: SI 2009/1892 Sch.4 para.7

Sch.3B para.3, applied: SI 2009/1892 Sch.4 para.7

Sch.3B para.4, applied: SI 2009/1892 Sch.4 para.7

Sch.3B para.5, applied: SI 2009/1892 Sch.4 para.6

Sch.3B para.6, applied: SI 2009/1892 Sch.4 para.6

Sch.3B para.7, applied: SI 2009/1892 Sch.4 para.6

Sch.3B para.8, applied: SI 2009/1892 Sch.4 para.6

Sch.3B para.9, applied: SI 2009/1892 Sch.4 para.6

Sch.3B para.10, applied: SI 2009/1892 Sch.4 para.6

Sch.3B para.11, applied: SI 2009/1892 Sch.4 para.6

Sch.3ZA Part 1, referred to: SI 2009/479 Sch.1 para.1

Sch.3ZA Part 1 para.1, referred to: SI 2009/479 Sch.1 para.1

Sch.3ZA Part 1 para.3, referred to: SI 2009/479 Sch.1 para.1

Sch.3ZA Part 2, applied: SI 2009/479 Sch.1 para.1

40. Law Reform (Miscellaneous Provisions) (Scotland) Act 1990

referred to: SSI 2009/163 Sch.1

s.7, applied: SI 2009/26 Sch.1, SI 2009/263 Art.5, SI 2009/442 Art.5, SI 2009/468 Sch.1, SI 2009/1345 Art.5, SI 2009/1355 Sch.1, SI 2009/1808 Art.5, SI 2009/1813 Sch.1, SI 2009/2722 Reg.3

s.24, see *Woodside (Alexander) v HM Advocate* [2009] HCJAC 19, 2009 S.L.T. 371 (HCJ), The Lord Justice Clerk (Gill)

s.25, applied: SSI 2009/163, SSI 2009/163 Sch.1

s.26, applied: SSI 2009/163, SSI 2009/163 Sch.1

s.27, enabling: SSI 2009/163

s.33, applied: SSI 2009/17 Art.2

41. Courts and Legal Services Act 1990

see *Napier v Pressdram Ltd* [2009] EWCA Civ 443, [2009] C.P. Rep. 36 (CA (Civ Div)), Hughes, L.J.

applied: SI 2009/2401 Reg.39

s.1, applied: SI 2009/577

s.1, enabling: SI 2009/577

s.21, varied: SI 2009/3250 Art.7

s.22, varied: SI 2009/3250 Art.7

s.23, varied: SI 2009/3250 Art.7

s.24, varied: SI 2009/3250 Art.7

s.53, applied: SI 2009/3233 Art.5

s.55, applied: SI 2009/1588 Art.2, SI 2009/3250 Art.6

s.55, enabling: SI 2009/1588

s.58AA, added: 2009 c.25 s.154

s.71, applied: SI 2009/1098 r.18, SI 2009/1209 r.26, SI 2009/1211 r.41, SI 2009/2041 r.39, SI 2009/2044 Art.12, SI 2009/2657 r.18

s.89, varied: SI 2009/503 Art.4

s.89, enabling: SI 2009/1589

s.105, amended: SI 2009/1941 Sch.1 para.118

s.113, applied: SI 2009/3250 Art.9

s.119, referred to: SI 2009/1976 r.11

s.120, amended: 2009 c.25 s.154

s.120, applied: SI 2009/1588, SI 2009/1589

s.120, enabling: SI 2009/577

Sch.3 para.7, varied: SI 2009/3250 Art.7

Sch.4 Part I para.1, applied: SI 2009/3250 Art.6

Sch.4 Part II para.9, applied: SI 2009/3250 Art.6

Sch.4 Part III para.17, applied: SI 2009/3250 Art.6

1990– cont.

41. Courts and Legal Services Act 1990– *cont.*

Sch.4 Part IV para.25, applied: SI 2009/3250 Art.6

Sch.8 Part II para.16, amended: SI 2009/501 Art.2

Sch.8 Part II para.16, applied: SI 2009/501

Sch.8 Part II para.16, enabling: SI 2009/501

Sch.9 para.4, applied: SI 2009/3233

Sch.9 para.4, enabling: SI 2009/1588

Sch.9 para.6, applied: SI 2009/3250 Art.6

Sch.10 para.7, repealed: SI 2009/1307 Sch.4

Sch.11, amended: 2009 c.25 Sch.21 para.30, SI 2009/56 Sch.1 para.168, SI 2009/1307 Sch.1 para.214, SI 2009/1834 Sch.1 para.3

Sch.14 Part II para.6, referred to: SI 2009/503 Art.5

Sch.14 Part II para.14, amended: SI 2009/1589 Art.7

42. Broadcasting Act 1990

s.58, amended: SI 2009/1968 Art.4

s.71, amended: SI 2009/1968 Art.4

s.135, amended: SI 2009/1941 Sch.1 para.119

s.141, amended: SI 2009/1941 Sch.1 para.119

s.166, amended: 2009 c.25 Sch.23 Part 2

Sch.2 Part I para.1, amended: SI 2009/1941 Sch.1 para.119

43. Environmental Protection Act 1990

applied: SI 2009/2325 Art.17

Part IIA, see *R. (on the application of Thames Water Utilities Ltd) v Bromley Magistrates' Court* [2008] EWHC 1763 (Admin), [2009] 1 W.L.R. 1247 (DC), Carnwath, L.J.

Part III, see *R. (on the application of Thames Water Utilities Ltd) v Bromley Magistrates' Court* [2008] EWHC 1763 (Admin), [2009] 1 W.L.R. 1247 (DC), Carnwath, L.J.

s.29, amended: SI 2009/1799 Sch.2 para.1

s.30, amended: SI 2009/1941 Sch.1 para.120

s.33, see *Environment Agency v Thorn International UK Ltd* [2008] EWHC 2595 (Admin), [2009] Env. L.R. 10 (DC), Moses, L.J.; see *MacLachlan v Harris* [2009] HCJAC 68, 2009 S.L.T. 1074 (HCJ), Lady Paton; see *R. (on the application of Thames Water Utilities Ltd) v Bromley Magistrates' Court* [2008] EWHC 1763 (Admin), [2009] 1 W.L.R. 1247 (DC), Carnwath, L.J.; see *R. v Kelleher (James Gerard)* [2008] EWCA Crim 3055, [2009] 2 Cr. App. R. (S.) 25 (CA (Crim Div)), Lord Judge, L.C.J.; see *R. v Trafalgar Leisure Ltd* [2009] EWCA Crim 217, [2009] Env. L.R. 29 (CA (Crim Div)), Pill, L.J.; see *WRG Waste Services Ltd v Donaldson* 2009 J.C. 253 (HCJ), Lord Wheatley

s.33, amended: SI 2009/1799 Sch.2 para.1, SSI 2009/247 Reg.3

s.33A, amended: SI 2009/1799 Sch.2 para.1

s.33B, amended: SI 2009/1799 Sch.2 para.1

s.34, see *Environment Agency v Inglenorth Ltd* [2009] EWHC 670 (Admin), [2009] Env. L.R. 33 (DC), Sir Anthony May (President, QB); see *R. v Trafalgar Leisure Ltd* [2009] EWCA Crim 217, [2009] Env. L.R. 29 (CA (Crim Div)), Pill, L.J.; see *Wandsworth LBC v Rashid* [2009] EWHC 1844 (Admin), (2009) 173 J.P. 547 (DC), Pill, L.J.

s.34, amended: SI 2009/1799 Sch.2 para.1

s.34, applied: 2009 asp 12 s.80, s.81

s.34, disapplied: 2009 asp 12 s.79

s.59, amended: SI 2009/1799 Sch.2 para.1

s.75, see *Environment Agency v Inglenorth Ltd* [2009] EWHC 670 (Admin), [2009] Env. L.R. 33 (DC), Sir Anthony May (President, QB); see *Environment Agency v Thorn International UK*

1990–cont.

43. Environmental Protection Act 1990–*cont.*
s.75–*cont.*
  Ltd [2008] EWHC 2595 (Admin), [2009] Env.
  L.R. 10 (DC), Moses, L.J.
s.78A, enabling: SSI 2009/202
s.78E, referred to: SI 2009/2037 Art.5
s.78YC, enabling: SSI 2009/202
s.79, applied: SI 2009/1300 Art.78, SI 2009/2364
  Art.38
s.79, referred to: SI 2009/2037 Art.5, SI 2009/2264
  Reg.5
s.80, see *Dobson v Thames Water Utilities Ltd* [2009]
  EWCA Civ 28, [2009] 3 All E.R. 319 (CA (Civ
  Div)), Waller, L.J. (V-P); see   *R. (on the
  application of Chiltern DC) v Wren Davis Ltd*
  [2008] EWHC 2164 (Admin), [2009] Env. L.R.
  D5 (QBD (Admin)), Sir George Newman
s.80, applied: SI 2009/665 Art.2
s.80, referred to: SI 2009/2037 Art.5
s.81, referred to: SI 2009/2037 Art.5
s.82, see *Dobson v Thames Water Utilities Ltd* [2009]
  EWCA Civ 28, [2009] 3 All E.R. 319 (CA (Civ
  Div)), Waller, L.J. (V-P)
s.82, applied: SI 2009/1300 Art.78, SI 2009/2364
  Art.38
s.82, referred to: SI 2009/2037 Art.5
s.84, amended: SSI 2009/319 Sch.3 Part 1
s.84, repealed (in part): SSI 2009/319 Sch.3 Part 1
s.86, enabling: SI 2009/2677
s.89, applied: SI 2009/2677 Art.2
s.111, applied: SI 2009/153 Sch.3 para.1
s.128, amended: 2009 c.23 s.313
s.132, amended: 2009 c.23 s.313
s.134, amended: 2009 c.23 s.313
s.143, see *MacLachlan v Harris* [2009] HCJAC 68,
  2009 S.L.T. 1074 (HCJ), Lady Paton
s.146, repealed (in part): 2009 c.23 Sch.22 Part 2
s.153, amended: SI 2009/1506 Art.2, SSI 2009/75
  Art.2
s.153, enabling: SI 2009/1506, SSI 2009/75
s.157, see *MacLachlan v Harris* [2009] HCJAC 68,
  2009 S.L.T. 1074 (HCJ), Lady Paton
44. Caldey Island Act 1990
s.3, repealed: 2009 c.25 Sch.23 Part 1
s.4, repealed (in part): 2009 c.25 Sch.23 Part 1

1991

22. New Roads and Street Works Act 1991
applied: SI 2009/1300 Art.4
referred to: SI 2009/721 Art.2, SI 2009/2364 Art.3
Part III, applied: SI 2009/1300 Art.4, Art.70, Sch.11
  para.1, Sch.11 para.2, Sch.12, SI 2009/2364 Art.3,
  Sch.8 para.1, Sch.8 para.2, Sch.10 para.5, SI 2009/
  2728 Sch.6 para.5
Part III, referred to: SI 2009/2728 Sch.7 para.3
s.48, varied: SI 2009/1300 Art.4
s.49, varied: SI 2009/1300 Art.4
s.50, applied: SI 2009/1267 Reg.6, Reg.33
s.50, varied: SI 2009/1300 Art.4
s.51, varied: SI 2009/1300 Art.4
s.52, varied: SI 2009/1300 Art.4
s.53, applied: SI 2009/721 Sch.2 para.1
s.53, disapplied: SI 2009/1267 Reg.36
s.53, varied: SI 2009/1300 Art.4
s.53A, varied: SI 2009/1300 Art.4
s.54, applied: SI 2009/303 Reg.4, Reg.9, SI 2009/
  721 Art.4, Sch.2 para.1, SI 2009/1268 Reg.3,
  Reg.8, SI 2009/1300 Art.4

1991–cont.

22. New Roads and Street Works Act 1991–*cont.*
s.54, disapplied: SI 2009/1267 Reg.36
s.54, referred to: SI 2009/2364 Art.3
s.54, varied: SI 2009/1300 Art.4, SI 2009/2364
  Art.3
s.55, applied: SI 2009/303 Reg.4, Reg.9, Reg.10, SI
  2009/721 Art.4, Sch.2 para.1, SI 2009/1268
  Reg.3, Reg.8, Reg.9, SI 2009/1300 Art.4
s.55, disapplied: SI 2009/1267 Reg.36
s.55, referred to: SI 2009/2364 Art.3
s.55, varied: SI 2009/1300 Art.4, SI 2009/2364
  Art.3
s.56, applied: SI 2009/721 Sch.2 para.1
s.56, disapplied: SI 2009/1267 Reg.36, SI 2009/
  1300 Art.4, SI 2009/2364 Art.3
s.56, varied: SI 2009/1300 Art.4
s.56A, applied: SI 2009/721 Sch.2 para.1
s.56A, disapplied: SI 2009/1300 Art.4, SI 2009/
  2364 Art.3
s.56A, varied: SI 2009/1300 Art.4
s.57, applied: SI 2009/303 Reg.4, Reg.9, SI 2009/
  721 Art.4, Sch.2 para.1, SI 2009/1268 Reg.3,
  Reg.8, SI 2009/1300 Art.4
s.57, disapplied: SI 2009/1267 Reg.36
s.57, referred to: SI 2009/2364 Art.3
s.57, varied: SI 2009/1300 Art.4
s.58, applied: SI 2009/721 Sch.2 para.1, SI 2009/
  1267 Reg.14, Reg.33
s.58, disapplied: SI 2009/1300 Art.4, SI 2009/2364
  Art.3
s.58, varied: SI 2009/1267 Reg.37, SI 2009/1300
  Art.4
s.58A, applied: SI 2009/721 Sch.2 para.1
s.58A, disapplied: SI 2009/1300 Art.4, SI 2009/
  2364 Art.3
s.58A, varied: SI 2009/1300 Art.4
s.59, applied: SI 2009/721 Sch.2 para.1, SI 2009/
  1300 Art.4, Art.70
s.59, referred to: SI 2009/2364 Art.3
s.59, varied: SI 2009/1300 Art.4
s.60, applied: SI 2009/721 Sch.2 para.1, SI 2009/
  1300 Art.4, Art.70
s.60, referred to: SI 2009/2364 Art.3
s.60, varied: SI 2009/1300 Art.4
s.61, applied: SI 2009/721 Sch.2 para.1, SI 2009/
  1267 Reg.33
s.61, varied: SI 2009/1300 Art.4
s.62, varied: SI 2009/1300 Art.4
s.63, applied: SI 2009/1267 Reg.33
s.63, varied: SI 2009/1300 Art.4
s.64, applied: SI 2009/1267 Reg.33
s.64, varied: SI 2009/1300 Art.4
s.65, applied: SI 2009/721 Sch.2 para.1, Sch.2 para.2
s.65, varied: SI 2009/1300 Art.4
s.66, applied: SI 2009/721 Sch.2 para.1
s.66, disapplied: SI 2009/1267 Reg.36
s.66, varied: SI 2009/1300 Art.4
s.67, applied: SI 2009/2257 Reg.8, Reg.9
s.67, varied: SI 2009/1300 Art.4
s.67, enabling: SI 2009/2257
s.68, applied: SI 2009/721 Sch.2 para.1, SI 2009/
  1300 Art.4
s.68, referred to: SI 2009/2364 Art.3
s.68, varied: SI 2009/1300 Art.4
s.69, applied: SI 2009/1300 Art.4
s.69, referred to: SI 2009/2364 Art.3
s.69, varied: SI 2009/1300 Art.4
s.70, applied: SI 2009/721 Sch.2 para.1, SI 2009/
  1267 Reg.33

1991– cont.

22. New Roads and Street Works Act 1991–*cont.*
s.70, varied: SI 2009/1300 Art.4
s.71, varied: SI 2009/1300 Art.4
s.72, applied: SI 2009/721 Sch.2 para.1, SI 2009/1300 Art.4
s.72, varied: SI 2009/1300 Art.4
s.73, varied: SI 2009/1300 Art.4
s.73A, disapplied: SI 2009/1300 Art.4, SI 2009/2364 Art.3
s.73A, varied: SI 2009/1267 Reg.37, SI 2009/1300 Art.4
s.73B, disapplied: SI 2009/1300 Art.4, SI 2009/2364 Art.3
s.73B, varied: SI 2009/1300 Art.4
s.73C, disapplied: SI 2009/1300 Art.4, SI 2009/2364 Art.3
s.73C, varied: SI 2009/1300 Art.4
s.73D, varied: SI 2009/1300 Art.4
s.73E, varied: SI 2009/1300 Art.4
s.73F, varied: SI 2009/1300 Art.4
s.74, applied: SI 2009/303 Reg.7, Reg.11, SI 2009/1267 Reg.16, SI 2009/1268 Reg.6, Reg.10
s.74, varied: SI 2009/1267 Reg.37, SI 2009/1300 Art.4
s.74, enabling: SI 2009/303, SI 2009/1178, SI 2009/1268
s.74A, varied: SI 2009/1300 Art.4
s.74B, varied: SI 2009/1300 Art.4
s.75, applied: SI 2009/721 Sch.2 para.1, SI 2009/1300 Art.4
s.75, referred to: SI 2009/2364 Art.3
s.75, varied: SI 2009/1300 Art.4
s.75, enabling: SI 2009/104, SI 2009/258
s.76, applied: SI 2009/1300 Art.4
s.76, referred to: SI 2009/2364 Art.3
s.76, varied: SI 2009/1300 Art.4
s.77, applied: SI 2009/1300 Art.4
s.77, referred to: SI 2009/2364 Art.3
s.77, varied: SI 2009/1300 Art.4
s.78, varied: SI 2009/1300 Art.4
s.78A, disapplied: SI 2009/1300 Art.4, SI 2009/2364 Art.3
s.78A, varied: SI 2009/1300 Art.4
s.79, varied: SI 2009/1300 Art.4
s.80, applied: SI 2009/1267 Reg.33
s.80, varied: SI 2009/1300 Art.4
s.81, applied: SI 2009/721 Sch.2 para.1, Sch.2 para.3
s.81, varied: SI 2009/1300 Art.4
s.82, applied: SI 2009/721 Sch.2 para.1, Sch.2 para.3
s.82, varied: SI 2009/1300 Art.4
s.83, applied: SI 2009/721 Sch.2 para.4
s.83, varied: SI 2009/1300 Art.4
s.84, applied: SI 2009/721 Sch.2 para.4
s.84, varied: SI 2009/1300 Art.4
s.85, applied: SI 2009/721 Sch.2 para.4, SI 2009/1300 Art.35, Sch.11 para.2, Sch.12 para.5, SI 2009/2364 Art.23, Sch.8 para.2, SI 2009/2728 Art.9
s.85, varied: SI 2009/1300 Art.4
s.86, referred to: SI 2009/1300 Art.4, SI 2009/2364 Art.3
s.86, varied: SI 2009/1300 Art.4
s.87, applied: SI 2009/721 Sch.2 para.1, SI 2009/1300 Art.4, SI 2009/2364 Art.3
s.87, varied: SI 2009/1300 Art.4
s.88, applied: SI 2009/721 Sch.2 para.4
s.88, varied: SI 2009/1267 Reg.37, SI 2009/1300 Art.4

1991– cont.

22. New Roads and Street Works Act 1991–*cont.*
s.89, varied: SI 2009/1267 Reg.37, SI 2009/1300 Art.4
s.90, applied: SI 2009/721 Sch.2 para.5
s.90, varied: SI 2009/1300 Art.4
s.91, varied: SI 2009/1300 Art.4
s.92, varied: SI 2009/1300 Art.4
s.93, applied: SI 2009/1300 Art.4
s.93, varied: SI 2009/1267 Reg.37, SI 2009/1300 Art.4
s.94, applied: SI 2009/721 Sch.2 para.1
s.94, varied: SI 2009/1300 Art.4
s.95, varied: SI 2009/1300 Art.4
s.95A, varied: SI 2009/1300 Art.4
s.96, varied: SI 2009/1300 Art.4
s.97, varied: SI 2009/1300 Art.4
s.97, enabling: SI 2009/303, SI 2009/1178, SI 2009/1268
s.98, applied: SI 2009/303 Reg.15, SI 2009/1267 Reg.39, SI 2009/1268 Reg.14
s.98, varied: SI 2009/1300 Art.4
s.99, varied: SI 2009/1300 Art.4
s.100, varied: SI 2009/1300 Art.4
s.101, varied: SI 2009/1300 Art.4
s.102, varied: SI 2009/1300 Art.4
s.103, varied: SI 2009/1300 Art.4
s.104, varied: SI 2009/1300 Art.4
s.104, enabling: SI 2009/104, SI 2009/258, SI 2009/303, SI 2009/1178, SI 2009/1268, SI 2009/2257
s.105, varied: SI 2009/1267 Reg.37, SI 2009/1300 Art.4
s.106, varied: SI 2009/1300 Art.4
s.112A, applied: SSI 2009/26 Reg.3
s.112A, referred to: SSI 2009/26 Reg.3
s.112A, enabling: SSI 2009/26
s.134, enabling: SSI 2009/74
s.163, enabling: SSI 2009/26
s.163A, applied: SSI 2009/26, SSI 2009/74
Sch.2 para.1, applied: SI 2009/721 Art.4
Sch.2 para.10, applied: SI 2009/721 Art.4
Sch.3A, applied: SI 2009/1267 Reg.33
Sch.3A, disapplied: SI 2009/1300 Art.4, SI 2009/2364 Art.3
Sch.3A para.1, applied: SI 2009/721 Sch.2 para.1
Sch.3A para.1, varied: SI 2009/1267 Reg.37
Sch.3A para.2, applied: SI 2009/303 Reg.10, SI 2009/721 Sch.2 para.1, SI 2009/1268 Reg.9
Sch.3A para.2, varied: SI 2009/1267 Reg.37
Sch.3A para.3, applied: SI 2009/721 Sch.2 para.1
Sch.3A para.3, varied: SI 2009/1267 Reg.37
Sch.3A para.4, applied: SI 2009/721 Sch.2 para.1
Sch.3A para.4, varied: SI 2009/1267 Reg.37
Sch.3A para.5, applied: SI 2009/721 Sch.2 para.1
Sch.3A para.5, varied: SI 2009/1267 Reg.37
Sch.3A para.6, varied: SI 2009/1267 Reg.37
Sch.4, applied: SI 2009/1267 Reg.33
Sch.4 para.2, applied: SI 2009/1267 Reg.33
Sch.4 para.3, applied: SI 2009/1267 Reg.33
Sch.4 para.5, applied: SI 2009/1267 Reg.33

23. Children and Young Persons (Protection from Tobacco) Act 1991
s.3A, added: 2009 c.21 s.22
s.5, amended: 2009 c.21 Sch.4 para.1

28. Natural Heritage (Scotland) Act 1991
s.2, amended: SI 2009/1941 Sch.1 para.121

29. Property Misdescriptions Act 1991
referred to: SI 2009/669 Sch.1 Part 2

31. Finance Act 1991
s.33, repealed (in part): SI 2009/2035 Sch.1 para.60
s.43, repealed: 2009 c.4 Sch.3 Part 1
s.65, amended: 2009 c.4 Sch.1 para.356
s.68, repealed: 2009 c.4 Sch.3 Part 1
s.116, applied: SI 2009/35 Reg.3, SI 2009/194 Reg.3, SI 2009/397 Reg.3, SI 2009/1344 Reg.3, SI 2009/1462 Reg.3, SI 2009/1601 Reg.3, SI 2009/1827 Reg.3, SI 2009/1828 Reg.3, SI 2009/1831 Reg.3, SI 2009/1832 Reg.3, SI 2009/2954 Reg.3, SI 2009/2975 Reg.3, SI 2009/2976 Reg.3, SI 2009/2977 Reg.3, SI 2009/3088 Reg.3
s.116, enabling: SI 2009/35, SI 2009/194, SI 2009/397, SI 2009/1115, SI 2009/1344, SI 2009/1462, SI 2009/1601, SI 2009/1827, SI 2009/1828, SI 2009/1831, SI 2009/1832, SI 2009/2954, SI 2009/2975, SI 2009/2976, SI 2009/2977, SI 2009/3088
s.117, applied: SI 2009/35 Reg.3, SI 2009/194 Reg.3, SI 2009/397 Reg.3, SI 2009/1344 Reg.3, SI 2009/1462 Reg.3, SI 2009/1601 Reg.3, SI 2009/1827 Reg.3, SI 2009/1828 Reg.3, SI 2009/1831 Reg.3, SI 2009/1832 Reg.3, SI 2009/2954 Reg.3, SI 2009/2975 Reg.3, SI 2009/2976 Reg.3, SI 2009/2977 Reg.3, SI 2009/3088 Reg.3
s.117, enabling: SI 2009/35, SI 2009/194, SI 2009/397, SI 2009/1115, SI 2009/1344, SI 2009/1462, SI 2009/1601, SI 2009/1827, SI 2009/1828, SI 2009/1831, SI 2009/1832, SI 2009/2954, SI 2009/2975, SI 2009/2976, SI 2009/2977, SI 2009/3088
s.121, repealed (in part): 2009 c.4 Sch.3 Part 1
Sch.10 para.3, repealed: 2009 c.4 Sch.3 Part 1
Sch.15 para.3, repealed: 2009 c.4 Sch.3 Part 1

34. Planning and Compensation Act 1991
referred to: SI 2009/3342 Reg.20, Reg.30, Reg.37
Sch.2 para.2, applied: SI 2009/3342 Reg.42
Sch.2 para.2, disapplied: SI 2009/3342 Reg.42
Sch.2 para.4, disapplied: SI 2009/3342 Reg.43
Sch.2 para.5, varied: SI 2009/3342 Reg.45
Sch.2 para.7, applied: SI 2009/3342 Reg.2
Sch.2 para.9, applied: SI 2009/3342 Reg.54
Sch.18 Part II, amended: SI 2009/1307 Sch.1 para.215

40. Road Traffic Act 1991
see *R. v Bannister (Craig)* [2009] EWCA Crim 1571, Times, August 24, 2009 (CA (Crim Div)), Thomas, L.J.

45. Coal Mining Subsidence Act 1991
s.6, amended: SI 2009/1307 Sch.1 para.217
s.40, amended: SI 2009/1307 Sch.1 para.218
s.52, amended: SI 2009/1307 Sch.1 para.219

46. Atomic Weapons Establishment Act 1991
s.1, amended: SI 2009/1941 Sch.1 para.122

48. Child Support Act 1991
see *Secretary of State for Work and Pensions v Wincott* [2009] EWCA Civ 113, [2009] 1 F.L.R. 1222 (CA (Civ Div)), Sedley, L.J.; see *Treharne v Secretary of State for Work and Pensions* [2008] EWHC 3222 (QB), [2009] 1 F.L.R. 853 (QBD), Cranston, J.
applied: SI 2009/1109 Reg.10, SI 2009/3151 Reg.12, Reg.13
s.4, see *W v Secretary of State for Work and Pensions* [2009] CSIH 21, 2009 S.C. 340 (IH (1 Div)), Lord President Hamilton
s.4, applied: SI 2009/2909 Reg.5
s.7, applied: SI 2009/2909 Reg.5
s.14, enabling: SI 2009/396, SI 2009/3151
s.14A, amended: 2009 c.24 s.55
s.17, applied: SI 2009/2909 Reg.5

48. Child Support Act 1991– *cont.*
s.17, enabling: SI 2009/396, SI 2009/2909
s.23, amended: 2009 c.3 Sch.4 para.22
s.26, amended: 2009 c.24 Sch.6 para.23
s.28J, enabling: SI 2009/396, SI 2009/3151
s.29, see *Bird v Secretary of State for Work and Pensions* [2008] EWHC 3159 (Admin), [2009] 2 F.L.R. 660 (QBD (Admin)), Slade, J.
s.29, amended: 2009 c.24 s.54
s.29, applied: SI 2009/3151 Reg.3
s.32A, enabling: SI 2009/1815
s.32C, enabling: SI 2009/1815
s.32D, enabling: SI 2009/1815
s.32E, enabling: SI 2009/1815
s.32F, enabling: SI 2009/1815
s.32H, enabling: SI 2009/1815
s.32I, enabling: SI 2009/1815
s.32J, enabling: SI 2009/1815
s.32K, enabling: SI 2009/1815
s.33, see *Bird v Secretary of State for Work and Pensions* [2008] EWHC 3159 (Admin), [2009] 2 F.L.R. 660 (QBD (Admin)), Slade, J.
s.39A, see *Secretary of State for Work and Pensions v McCulloch* 2009 S.L.T. (Sh Ct) 115 (Sh Ct (Glasgow)), Sheriff Principal J A Taylor
s.39B, amended: 2009 c.24 s.51, Sch.5 para.2
s.39C, amended: 2009 c.24 s.51, Sch.5 para.3
s.39CA, added: 2009 c.24 s.51
s.39CB, added: 2009 c.24 s.51
s.39D, amended: 2009 c.24 Sch.5 para.4
s.39DA, added: 2009 c.24 s.51
s.39E, amended: 2009 c.24 Sch.5 para.5, Sch.7 Part 4
s.39E, repealed (in part): 2009 c.24 Sch.5 para.5, Sch.7 Part 4
s.39F, substituted: 2009 c.24 Sch.5 para.6
s.39G, repealed: 2009 c.24 Sch.5 para.7, Sch.7 Part 4
s.40B, repealed: 2009 c.24 Sch.5 para.8, Sch.7 Part 4
s.41, applied: SI 2009/3151 Reg.5
s.41C, applied: SI 2009/3151 Reg.5, Reg.6
s.41C, enabling: SI 2009/3151
s.43A, enabling: SI 2009/3151
s.44, amended: SI 2009/1941 Sch.1 para.123
s.50, enabling: SI 2009/396
s.51, enabling: SI 2009/396, SI 2009/1815, SI 2009/2909, SI 2009/3151
s.52, amended: 2009 c.24 Sch.5 para.9
s.52, applied: SI 2009/736, SI 2009/1815
s.52, enabling: SI 2009/736, SI 2009/1815, SI 2009/2909, SI 2009/3151
s.54, amended: 2009 c.24 Sch.7 Part 1
s.54, enabling: SI 2009/396, SI 2009/736, SI 2009/1815, SI 2009/2909, SI 2009/3151
s.55, applied: SI 2009/2909 Reg.3
s.55, enabling: SI 2009/396, SI 2009/2909
Sch.1 Part I para.5, amended: 2009 c.24 Sch.7 Part 1
Sch.1 Part I para.5, enabling: SI 2009/736
Sch.1 Part I para.5, enabling: SI 2009/396
Sch.1 Part I para.6, enabling: SI 2009/736
Sch.1 Part I para.9, enabling: SI 2009/736
Sch.4 para.4, amended: 2009 c.3 Sch.4 para.23, SI 2009/1307 Sch.1 para.226
Sch.4B Part I para.4, enabling: SI 2009/736
Sch.4B Part I para.5, enabling: SI 2009/736

52. Ports Act 1991
s.1, amended: SI 2009/1941 Sch.1 para.124
s.3, amended: SI 2009/1941 Sch.1 para.124
s.9, amended: SI 2009/1941 Sch.1 para.124

1991–cont.

52. Ports Act 1991–*cont.*
s.12, amended: SI 2009/1941 Sch.1 para.124
s.21, amended: SI 2009/1941 Sch.1 para.124
s.22, amended: SI 2009/1941 Sch.1 para.124
s.40, amended: SI 2009/1941 Sch.1 para.124

53. Criminal Justice Act 1991
see *Gibson v Secretary of State for Justice* [2008] EWCA Civ 177, [2009] Q.B. 204 (CA (Civ Div)), Sir Anthony Clarke, M.R.; see *R. (on the application of Noone) v Governor of Drake Hall Prison* [2008] EWCA Civ 1097, [2009] 1 W.L.R. 1321 (CA (Civ Div)), Sir Anthony Clarke, M.R.
Part II, applied: SI 2009/1059 Art.100, SI 2009/1887 Sch.1
s.24, amended: 2009 c.24 Sch.2 para.2, Sch.7 Part 1
s.33, see *Gibson v Secretary of State for Justice* [2008] EWCA Civ 177, [2009] Q.B. 204 (CA (Civ Div)), Sir Anthony Clarke, M.R.
s.33, applied: 2009 c.25 Sch.22 para.43
s.35, see *R. (on the application of Black) v Secretary of State for the Home Department* [2009] UKHL 1, [2009] 1 A.C. 949 (HL), Lord Phillips of Worth Matravers
s.35, amended: 2009 c.25 s.145
s.35, applied: 2009 c.25 Sch.22 para.43
s.35, varied: 2009 c.25 s.145, Sch.22 para.43
s.37, see *Gibson v Secretary of State for Justice* [2008] EWCA Civ 177, [2009] Q.B. 204 (CA (Civ Div)), Sir Anthony Clarke, M.R.
s.37, amended: 2009 c.25 s.145
s.37, applied: 2009 c.25 Sch.22 para.43
s.37, referred to: SI 2009/1887 Sch.2
s.37, repealed (in part): 2009 c.25 s.145, Sch.23 Part 5
s.37, varied: 2009 c.25 s.145, Sch.22 para.43
s.39, see *Dunn v Parole Board* [2008] EWCA Civ 374, [2009] 1 W.L.R. 728 (CA (Civ Div)), Smith, L.J.; see *Gibson v Secretary of State for Justice* [2008] EWCA Civ 177, [2009] Q.B. 204 (CA (Civ Div)), Sir Anthony Clarke, M.R.
s.40A, see *West Midlands Probation Board v French* [2008] EWHC 2631 (Admin), [2009] 1 W.L.R. 1715 (DC), Scott Baker, L.J.
s.49, varied: 2009 c.25 Sch.22 para.34
s.50, repealed: 2009 c.25 Sch.23 Part 5
s.65, amended: SI 2009/2054 Sch.1 para.11
s.86B, referred to: SI 2009/576 Art.3
s.86B, enabling: SI 2009/576

55. Agricultural Holdings (Scotland) Act 1991
s.22, see *North Berwick Trust v Miller* [2009] CSIH 15, 2009 S.C. 305 (IH (2 Div)), The Lord Justice Clerk (Gill)
s.24, see *North Berwick Trust v Miller* [2009] CSIH 15, 2009 S.C. 305 (IH (2 Div)), The Lord Justice Clerk (Gill)
s.76, amended: SI 2009/1941 Sch.1 para.125

56. Water Industry Act 1991
see *R. (on the application of Thames Water Utilities Ltd) v Bromley Magistrates' Court* [2008] EWHC 1763 (Admin), [2009] 1 W.L.R. 1247 (DC), Carnwath, L.J.
applied: 2009 c.23 s.17, SI 2009/2477 r.7, r.8, r.92, r.120, r.126
referred to: SI 2009/2477 r.119
Part II c.I, applied: SI 2009/3042 Reg.36
Part II c.IA, applied: SI 2009/3042 Reg.36
s.23, applied: SI 2009/2477
s.24, applied: SI 2009/2477, SI 2009/2477 r.8
s.25, applied: SI 2009/2477

1991–cont.

56. Water Industry Act 1991–*cont.*
s.26, applied: SI 2009/2477, SI 2009/2477 r.8
s.32, applied: SI 2009/2396 Art.1
s.67, enabling: SI 2009/3101
s.77, applied: SI 2009/3101 Reg.7
s.77, enabling: SI 2009/3101
s.80, applied: SI 2009/3101 Reg.16, Reg.17, Sch.4 para.2
s.80, referred to: SI 2009/3101 Reg.18, Sch.5 para.2
s.87, applied: SI 2009/359 Sch.1 para.1
s.87, referred to: SI 2009/359 Sch.1 para.1
s.88, applied: SI 2009/359 Sch.1 para.1
s.88, referred to: SI 2009/359 Sch.1 para.1
s.89, applied: SI 2009/359 Sch.1 para.1
s.89, referred to: SI 2009/359 Sch.1 para.1
s.90, applied: SI 2009/359 Sch.1 para.1
s.90, referred to: SI 2009/359 Sch.1 para.1
s.91, applied: SI 2009/359 Sch.1 para.1
s.94, see *Dobson v Thames Water Utilities Ltd* [2009] EWCA Civ 28, [2009] 3 All E.R. 319 (CA (Civ Div)), Waller, L.J. (V-P)
s.101A, see *R. (on the application of Dwr Cymru Cyfyngedig (Welsh Water)) v Environment Agency* [2009] EWHC 435 (Admin), [2009] 2 All E.R. 919 (QBD (Admin)), Wyn Williams, J.
s.106, see *Barratt Homes Ltd v Dwr Cymru Cyfyngedig (Welsh Water)* [2008] EWCA Civ 1552, [2009] Env. L.R. 25 (CA (Civ Div)), Pill, L.J.; see *Barratt Homes Ltd v Dwr Cymru Cyfyngedig (Welsh Water)* [2009] UKSC 13, Times, December 14, 2009 (SC), Lord Phillips (President)
s.106, applied: SI 2009/1300 Art.21, SI 2009/2364 Art.13
s.107, see *Barratt Homes Ltd v Dwr Cymru Cyfyngedig (Welsh Water)* [2009] UKSC 13, Times, December 14, 2009 (SC), Lord Phillips (President)
s.155, amended: SI 2009/1941 Sch.1 para.126
s.168, applied: SI 2009/721 Sch.1 para.1
s.213, enabling: SI 2009/3101
s.219, amended: SI 2009/1941 Sch.1 para.126
s.219, applied: SI 2009/3042 Reg.36
Sch.3, applied: SI 2009/2477
Sch.3 Part I para.4, amended: SI 2009/1941 Sch.1 para.126
Sch.6 Part II para.11, amended: SI 2009/1307 Sch.1 para.221
Sch.7, applied: SI 2009/359 Sch.1 para.1
Sch.9 para.4, amended: SI 2009/1307 Sch.1 para.222
Sch.9 para.4, substituted: SI 2009/1307 Sch.1 para.222
Sch.11 para.8, amended: SI 2009/1307 Sch.1 para.223
Sch.12 para.3, amended: SI 2009/1307 Sch.1 para.224
Sch.14 para.2, amended: SI 2009/1307 Sch.1 para.225

57. Water Resources Act 1991
applied: SI 2009/153 Sch.3 para.1, SI 2009/995 Sch.3 para.1, SI 2009/1300 Art.21, SI 2009/3365 Sch.1 para.1
referred to: SI 2009/2364 Art.13
Part II c.II, applied: SI 2009/1300 Art.71
Part II c.II, referred to: SI 2009/271 Art.4
s.24, applied: SI 2009/3264 Sch.1 para.1, SI 2009/3344 Reg.12, SI 2009/3365 Sch.1 para.1
s.24, disapplied: SI 2009/3344 Reg.21

57. Water Resources Act 1991–*cont.*
s.25, applied: SI 2009/3344 Reg.12
s.25, disapplied: SI 2009/3344 Reg.21
s.30, applied: SI 2009/1300 Art.71
s.61, amended: SI 2009/1307 Sch.1 para.228
s.62, amended: SI 2009/1307 Sch.1 para.229
s.63, amended: SI 2009/1307 Sch.1 para.230
s.82, enabling: SI 2009/1264, SI 2009/1266
s.85, see *R. v L* [2008] EWCA Crim 1970, [2009] 1
All E.R. 786 (CA (Crim Div)), Hughes, L.J.
s.85, amended: SI 2009/1799 Sch.2 para.2
s.85, applied: SI 2009/1300 Art.21, SI 2009/2364
Art.13
s.88, applied: SI 2009/2902 Reg.14
s.88, varied: SI 2009/2902 Reg.14
s.91, applied: SI 2009/2902 Reg.13
s.93, amended: SI 2009/3104 Reg.3
s.93, repealed (in part): SI 2009/3104 Reg.3
s.94, repealed: SI 2009/3104 Reg.4
s.95, repealed: SI 2009/3104 Reg.4
s.96, repealed (in part): SI 2009/3104 Reg.4
s.97, applied: SI 2009/46
s.97, enabling: SI 2009/46
s.102, applied: SI 2009/1266
s.102, enabling: SI 2009/1264, SI 2009/1266
s.109, amended: 2009 c.23 s.82
s.109, applied: 2009 c.23 Sch.9 para.10
s.109, disapplied: SI 2009/1300 Art.5
s.115, amended: 2009 c.23 Sch.16 para.21
s.116, substituted: 2009 c.23 Sch.16 para.22
s.161, substituted: SI 2009/3104 Reg.5
s.161A, substituted: SI 2009/3104 Reg.5
s.161ZA, substituted: SI 2009/3104 Reg.5
s.161ZB, substituted: SI 2009/3104 Reg.5
s.161ZC, substituted: SI 2009/3104 Reg.5
s.168, enabling: SI 2009/271
s.190, applied: SI 2009/2902 Reg.21
s.191A, applied: SI 2009/2902 Reg.21
s.191B, applied: SI 2009/2902 Reg.21
s.210, amended: 2009 c.23 s.225
s.211, amended: 2009 c.23 s.226
s.212, amended: 2009 c.23 s.227, Sch.16 para.23,
Sch.22 Part 5
s.212, repealed (in part): 2009 c.23 Sch.22 Part 5
s.217, see *R. v L* [2008] EWCA Crim 1970, [2009] 1
All E.R. 786 (CA (Crim Div)), Hughes, L.J.
s.219, enabling: SI 2009/1264, SI 2009/1266
Sch.9 para.3, amended: SI 2009/1307 Sch.1
para.231
Sch.9 para.4, amended: SI 2009/1307 Sch.1
para.231
Sch.10 para.3, referred to: SI 2009/2902 Reg.15
Sch.10 para.6, referred to: SI 2009/2902 Reg.15
Sch.10 para.11, applied: SI 2009/2902 Reg.15
Sch.10 para.11, varied: SI 2009/2902 Reg.15
Sch.12 Part I para.1, repealed: SI 2009/3104 Reg.4
Sch.12 Part I para.2, repealed: SI 2009/3104 Reg.4
Sch.12 Part II para.3, repealed: SI 2009/3104 Reg.4
Sch.12 Part II para.4, repealed: SI 2009/3104 Reg.4
Sch.12 Part II para.5, repealed: SI 2009/3104 Reg.4
Sch.12 Part II para.6, repealed: SI 2009/3104 Reg.4
Sch.12 Part II para.7, repealed: SI 2009/3104 Reg.4
Sch.18 para.4, amended: SI 2009/1307 Sch.1
para.232
Sch.18 para.4, substituted: SI 2009/1307 Sch.1
para.232
Sch.19 para.1, applied: SI 2009/271
Sch.19 para.3, enabling: SI 2009/271

57. Water Resources Act 1991–*cont.*
Sch.19 para.8, amended: SI 2009/1307 Sch.1
para.233
Sch.20 para.6, amended: SI 2009/1307 Sch.1
para.234
Sch.21 para.3, amended: SI 2009/1307 Sch.1
para.235
Sch.21 para.5, amended: SI 2009/1307 Sch.1
para.235
Sch.23 para.2, amended: SI 2009/1307 Sch.1
para.236
Sch.25 para.5, amended: 2009 c.23 s.84, Sch.11
para.3
Sch.25 para.6, amended: 2009 c.23 s.224, Sch.16
para.24, Sch.22 Part 5
Sch.25 para.6, repealed (in part): 2009 c.23 Sch.22
Part 5
Sch.25 para.7, repealed: 2009 c.23 Sch.22 Part 5
Sch.27 para.1, added: 2009 c.23 s.225
Sch.27 para.2, added: 2009 c.23 s.225
Sch.27 para.3, added: 2009 c.23 s.225
Sch.27 para.4, added: 2009 c.23 s.225
Sch.27 para.5, added: 2009 c.23 s.225
Sch.27 para.6, added: 2009 c.23 s.225
Sch.27 para.7, added: 2009 c.23 s.225
Sch.27 para.8, added: 2009 c.23 s.225
Sch.27 para.9, added: 2009 c.23 s.225
Sch.27 para.10, added: 2009 c.23 s.225
58. Statutory Water Companies Act 1991
s.9, amended: SI 2009/1941 Sch.1 para.127
s.10, amended: SI 2009/1941 Sch.1 para.127
s.11, amended: SI 2009/1941 Sch.1 para.127
s.12, amended: SI 2009/1941 Sch.1 para.127
s.13, amended: SI 2009/1941 Sch.1 para.127
s.13, repealed (in part): SI 2009/1941 Sch.1 para.127
s.15, amended: SI 2009/1941 Sch.1 para.127
59. Land Drainage Act 1991
s.1, applied: SI 2009/3042 Reg.36
s.3, applied: SI 2009/1170, SI 2009/1723
s.3, enabling: SI 2009/1170, SI 2009/1723, SI 2009/
3468
s.14, amended: SI 2009/1307 Sch.1 para.238
s.22, amended: SI 2009/1307 Sch.1 para.239
s.23, disapplied: SI 2009/1300 Art.5
s.29, amended: SI 2009/1307 Sch.1 para.240
s.46, amended: SI 2009/1307 Sch.1 para.241
s.64, amended: SI 2009/1307 Sch.1 para.242
Sch.1, applied: SI 2009/1723 Sch.1
Sch.2 para.3, applied: SI 2009/1723 Sch.1
Sch.3 para.1, applied: SI 2009/1170 Sch.1, SI 2009/
1723 Sch.1
Sch.3 para.2, applied: SI 2009/1170, SI 2009/1723
Sch.3 para.4, applied: SI 2009/1170 Sch.1, SI 2009/
1723 Sch.1
Sch.3 para.5, applied: SI 2009/1170 Art.1, Sch.1, SI
2009/1723 Sch.1
**60. Water Consolidation (Consequential Provisions)
Act 1991**
Sch.1 para.16, repealed: 2009 c.23 Sch.22 Part 4
Sch.1 para.41, repealed: SI 2009/1941 Sch.2
62. Armed Forces Act 1991
Part III, applied: SI 2009/1107 Reg.10
s.10, applied: SI 2009/1059 Art.130
s.17, applied: SI 2009/1107 Reg.3, Reg.4, Reg.6,
Reg.12, Reg.13
s.17, referred to: SI 2009/1107 Reg.4, Reg.13
s.17, enabling: SI 2009/1107
s.18, applied: 2009 c.25 Sch.22 para.15, Sch.22
para.21, SI 2009/1107 Reg.14

1991– cont.

62. Armed Forces Act 1991– *cont.*
s.18, enabling: SI 2009/1107
s.19, applied: SI 2009/1107 Reg.3, Reg.15
s.19, referred to: SI 2009/1107 Reg.6, Reg.15
s.19, enabling: SI 2009/1107
s.20, applied: 2009 c.25 Sch.22 para.15, Sch.22 para.21, SI 2009/1107 Reg.7, Reg.8, Reg.15, Reg.16, Reg.17
s.20, referred to: SI 2009/1059 Art.203
s.20, enabling: SI 2009/1107
s.21, applied: SI 2009/1107 Reg.9
s.22, applied: SI 2009/1107 Reg.7, Reg.8, Reg.9, Reg.10
s.22, enabling: SI 2009/1107
s.22A, applied: SI 2009/1107 Reg.12
65. Dangerous Dogs Act 1991
s.3, see *R. v Richards (Jamal)* [2008] EWCA Crim 1427, [2009] 1 Cr. App. R. (S.) 48 (CA (Crim Div)), Aikens, J.
67. Export and Investment Guarantees Act 1991
s.1, amended: 2009 c.5 s.2
s.1, applied: 2009 c.5 s.2
s.2, applied: 2009 c.4 s.91, s.1245

1992

3. Severn Bridges Act 1992
s.8, referred to: SI 2009/3358 Art.2
s.9, applied: SI 2009/3358 Art.1
s.9, enabling: SI 2009/3358
4. Social Security Contributions and Benefits Act 1992
applied: SI 2009/470 Reg.29, SI 2009/497 Art.6, SI 2009/610 Art.2, SI 2009/2131 Sch.2 para.5, SI 2009/3328 Reg.8
referred to: 2009 c.24 s.58
Part I, applied: 2009 c.4 s.1203, s.1302, SI 2009/1562 Art.2, SI 2009/2131 Sch.2 para.5, SI 2009/3328 Reg.8
Part I, referred to: SI 2009/593
Part VII, applied: SI 2009/1555 Reg.121, Reg.138, SI 2009/2737 Reg.73, Reg.88, SSI 2009/48 Reg.6
Part IX, applied: SI 2009/1555 Reg.42, SI 2009/2737 Reg.31, Reg.96, SI 2009/3359 Reg.26
Part XI, applied: SI 2009/391 Reg.3, SI 2009/2108 Reg.27
Part XII, applied: SI 2009/212 Reg.2
Part XIIZA, applied: SI 2009/212 Reg.2
Part XIIZB, applied: SI 2009/212 Reg.2
s.1, see *Oleochem (Scotland) Ltd v Revenue and Customs Commissioners* [2009] S.T.C. (S.C.D.) 205 (Sp Comm), J Gordon Reid Q.C.
s.1, applied: 2009 c.4 s.1292
s.3, enabling: SI 2009/600, SI 2009/2678
s.5, enabling: SI 2009/111, SI 2009/591
s.11, amended: SI 2009/593 Art.2
s.13, amended: SI 2009/593 Art.3
s.13A, applied: SI 2009/659
s.15, amended: SI 2009/593 Art.4
s.18, amended: SI 2009/593 Art.4
s.20, amended: 2009 c.24 Sch.7 Part 2
s.22, enabling: SI 2009/2206
s.23A, applied: SI 2009/1377 Art.2, SI 2009/2206 Reg.15
s.30A, see *Sheffield Forgemasters International Ltd v Fox* [2009] I.C.R. 333 (EAT), Silber, J.
s.30A, applied: SI 2009/212 Reg.2
s.30B, applied: SI 2009/497 Art.6
s.30DD, enabling: SI 2009/792

1992– cont.

4. Social Security Contributions and Benefits Act 1992– *cont.*
s.30E, enabling: SI 2009/2343
s.35, applied: 2009 c.24 s.15, SI 2009/212 Reg.2
s.35A, applied: SI 2009/497 Art.1
s.36, applied: SI 2009/212 Reg.2
s.37, applied: SI 2009/212 Reg.2
s.37, referred to: SI 2009/775 Art.3
s.38, applied: SI 2009/212 Reg.2
s.39A, applied: SI 2009/212 Reg.2
s.39A, referred to: SI 2009/775 Art.3
s.39B, applied: SI 2009/212 Reg.2
s.40, applied: SI 2009/212 Reg.2
s.41, applied: SI 2009/212 Reg.2
s.44, amended: SI 2009/497 Art.4
s.44, applied: SI 2009/212 Reg.2
s.44C, enabling: SI 2009/2206
s.47, applied: SI 2009/497 Art.6
s.48, enabling: SI 2009/2206
s.48A, applied: SI 2009/212 Reg.2
s.48B, applied: SI 2009/212 Reg.2
s.48BB, applied: SI 2009/212 Reg.2
s.48C, applied: SI 2009/497 Art.6
s.51, applied: SI 2009/212 Reg.2
s.54, enabling: SI 2009/2206
s.55A, applied: SI 2009/212 Reg.2
s.55A, varied: SI 2009/497 Art.4
s.60, enabling: SI 2009/2206
s.60A, enabling: SI 2009/2206
s.62, enabling: SI 2009/2206
s.63, amended: 2009 c.24 Sch.7 Part 2
s.64, applied: SI 2009/212 Reg.2, SSI 2009/48 Reg.6
s.68, applied: SI 2009/212 Reg.2
s.70, applied: 2009 c.8 s.3, SI 2009/212 Reg.2
s.71, applied: SI 2009/212 Reg.2, SSI 2009/48 Reg.6
s.73, see *M's Guardian v Advocate General for Scotland* [2009] CSOH 91, 2009 S.C. 643 (OH), Lord Woolman
s.73, amended: 2009 c.24 s.14
s.77, applied: SI 2009/1555 Reg.42, SI 2009/2737 Reg.31, Reg.96, SI 2009/3359 Reg.26
s.77, enabling: SI 2009/3268
s.79, applied: SI 2009/497 Art.3
s.80, amended: SI 2009/497 Art.8
s.80, varied: 2009 c.24 s.37
s.81, varied: 2009 c.24 s.37
s.82, repealed: 2009 c.24 s.15, Sch.7 Part 2
s.88, disapplied: 2009 c.24 s.58
s.88, repealed: 2009 c.24 Sch.7 Part 2
s.89, disapplied: 2009 c.24 s.58
s.89, repealed: 2009 c.24 Sch.7 Part 2
s.90, repealed: 2009 c.24 s.15, Sch.7 Part 2
s.90, enabling: SI 2009/607
s.91, disapplied: 2009 c.24 s.58
s.91, repealed: 2009 c.24 Sch.7 Part 2
s.92, disapplied: 2009 c.24 s.58
s.92, repealed: 2009 c.24 Sch.7 Part 2
s.94, applied: SI 2009/212 Reg.2
s.103, applied: SSI 2009/48 Reg.6
s.104, applied: SI 2009/212 Reg.2, SSI 2009/48 Reg.6
s.105, applied: SSI 2009/48 Reg.6
s.107, applied: SI 2009/497 Art.6
s.108, enabling: SI 2009/1396
s.113, enabling: SI 2009/607, SI 2009/810
s.114, amended: 2009 c.24 Sch.7 Part 2

1992– cont.

**4. Social Security Contributions and Benefits Act
1992**– *cont.*

s.117, see *Oleochem (Scotland) Ltd v Revenue and
Customs Commissioners* [2009] S.T.C. (S.C.D.)
205 (Sp Comm), J Gordon Reid Q.C.

s.117, enabling: SI 2009/696

s.122, enabling: SI 2009/ 111, SI 2009/607, SI 2009/
659, SI 2009/ 810, SI 2009/1396, SI 2009/2206

s.123, referred to: 2009 c.24 s.36

s.123, repealed (in part): 2009 c.24 Sch.7 Part 1

s.123, enabling: SI 2009/362, SI 2009/480, SI 2009/
583, SI 2009/614, SI 2009/1488, SI 2009/1575, SI
2009/1848, SI 2009/2608, SI 2009/2655, SI
2009/3152, SI 2009/3228, SI 2009/3257

s.124, amended: 2009 c.24 s.3, s.5

s.124, applied: 2009 c.24 s.9, SI 2009/212 Reg.2, SI
2009/1555 Reg.60, SI 2009/2737 Reg.40

s.124, disapplied: 2009 c.24 s.9

s.124, repealed: 2009 c.24 Sch.7 Part 1

s.124, enabling: SI 2009/583, SI 2009/2655, SI
2009/3152, SI 2009/3228

s.126, amended: SI 2009/497 Art.18

s.126, repealed: 2009 c.24 Sch.7 Part 1

s.127, repealed: 2009 c.24 Sch.7 Part 1

s.130, applied: SI 2009/212 Reg.2, SI 2009/1555
Reg.60, SI 2009/2737 Reg.40

s.130, enabling: SI 2009/583

s.130A, enabling: SI 2009/614, SI 2009/1488

s.131, applied: SI 2009/212 Reg.2

s.131, enabling: SI 2009/362, SI 2009/583

s.132, enabling: SI 2009/583

s.135, enabling: SI 2009/362, SI 2009/583, SI 2009/
1488, SI 2009/3228, SI 2009/3257

s.136, enabling: SI 2009/480, SI 2009/583, SI 2009/
1488, SI 2009/1575, SI 2009/1676, SI 2009/1848,
SI 2009/2608, SI 2009/2655, SI 2009/3228

s.136A, enabling: SI 2009/583, SI 2009/2655

s.137, enabling: SI 2009/362, SI 2009/480, SI 2009/
583, SI 2009/614, SI 2009/1488, SI 2009/1575, SI
2009/1676, SI 2009/1848, SI 2009/2608, SI
2009/2655, SI 2009/3152, SI 2009/3228, SI
2009/3257

s.138, amended: 2009 c.24 s.17, s.19

s.138, enabling: SI 2009/1488, SI 2009/1489, SI
2009/2649

s.139, amended: 2009 c.24 s.19

s.140, amended: 2009 c.24 s.19

s.140ZA, added: 2009 c.24 s.16

s.140ZB, added: 2009 c.24 s.16

s.140ZC, added: 2009 c.24 s.16

s.141, applied: SI 2009/391 Reg.3

s.142, enabling: SI 2009/3268

s.150, amended: 2009 c.24 s.37

s.157, amended: SI 2009/497 Art.9

s.171B, see *Sheffield Forgemasters International
Ltd v Fox* [2009] I.C.R. 333 (EAT), Silber, J.

s.171C, see *Sheffield Forgemasters International
Ltd v Fox* [2009] I.C.R. 333 (EAT), Silber, J.

s.171D, enabling: SI 2009/2343

s.171G, enabling: SI 2009/2343

s.175, applied: 2009 c.24 s.7, s.9, s.36

s.175, referred to: SI 2009/295

s.175, enabling: SI 2009/ 111, SI 2009/295, SI 2009/
362, SI 2009/480, SI 2009/583, SI 2009/591, SI
2009/600, SI 2009/607, SI 2009/614, SI 2009/
659, SI 2009/696, SI 2009/792, SI 2009/810, SI
2009/1396, SI 2009/1488, SI 2009/1489, SI
2009/1575, SI 2009/1676, SI 2009/1848, SI
2009/2206, SI 2009/2343, SI 2009/2608, SI

1992– cont.

**4. Social Security Contributions and Benefits Act
1992**– *cont.*

s.175, enabling:– *cont.*
2009/2649, SI 2009/2655, SI 2009/2678, SI
2009/3152, SI 2009/3228, SI 2009/3229, SI
2009/3257, SI 2009/3268

s.176, applied: SI 2009/591, SI 2009/792

Sch.1 para.3A, applied: 2009 c.4 s.1018

Sch.1 para.3B, amended: SI 2009/56 Sch.1 para.169

Sch.1 para.3B, applied: 2009 c.4 s.1018

Sch.1 para.6, applied: SI 2009/470 Reg.59

Sch.1 para.6, referred to: SI 2009/600

Sch.1 para.6, enabling: SI 2009/ 111, SI 2009/600, SI
2009/2028

Sch.1 para.8, enabling: SI 2009/600, SI 2009/659

Sch.2 para.3, referred to: 2009 c.10 Sch.6 para.2

Sch.3 Part I para.5A, enabling: SI 2009/2206

Sch.4 Part I, referred to: SI 2009/497 Art.3

Sch.4 Part I, substituted: SI 2009/497 Sch.1

Sch.4 Part II, substituted: SI 2009/497 Sch.1

Sch.4 Part III, referred to: SI 2009/497 Art.3

Sch.4 Part III, amended: SI 2009/797 Art.2

Sch.4 Part III, referred to: SI 2009/497 Art.3

Sch.4 Part III, substituted: SI 2009/497 Sch.1

Sch.4 Part III para.1, substituted: SI 2009/497 Sch.1

Sch.4 Part III para.2, substituted: SI 2009/497
Sch.1

Sch.4 Part III para.3, substituted: SI 2009/497
Sch.1

Sch.4 Part III para.4, substituted: SI 2009/497
Sch.1

Sch.4 Part III para.5, amended: SI 2009/797 Art.2

Sch.4 Part III para.5, substituted: SI 2009/497
Sch.1

Sch.4 Part III para.6, substituted: SI 2009/497
Sch.1

Sch.4 Part III para.7, substituted: SI 2009/497 Sch.1

Sch.4 Part III para.8, substituted: SI 2009/497
Sch.1

Sch.4 Part IV, referred to: SI 2009/497 Art.3

Sch.4 Part IV, substituted: SI 2009/497 Sch.1

Sch.4 Part IV para.1, substituted: SI 2009/497 Sch.1

Sch.4 Part IV para.3, repealed: 2009 c.24 Sch.7 Part
2

Sch.4 Part IV para.3, substituted: SI 2009/497 Sch.1

Sch.4 Part IV para.4, substituted: SI 2009/497
Sch.1

Sch.4 Part IV para.8, substituted: SI 2009/497 Sch.1

Sch.4 Part IV para.9, repealed: 2009 c.24 Sch.7 Part
2

Sch.4 Part IV para.9, substituted: SI 2009/497 Sch.1

Sch.4 Part V, referred to: SI 2009/497 Art.3

Sch.4 Part V, substituted: SI 2009/497 Sch.1

Sch.4 Part V para.1, substituted: SI 2009/497 Sch.1

Sch.4 Part V para.2, substituted: SI 2009/497 Sch.1

Sch.4 Part V para.3, substituted: SI 2009/497 Sch.1

Sch.4 Part V para.4, substituted: SI 2009/497 Sch.1

Sch.4 Part V para.5, substituted: SI 2009/497 Sch.1

Sch.4 Part V para.6, substituted: SI 2009/497 Sch.1

Sch.4 Part V para.7, substituted: SI 2009/497 Sch.1

Sch.4 Part V para.8, substituted: SI 2009/497 Sch.1

Sch.4 Part V para.9, substituted: SI 2009/497 Sch.1

Sch.4 Part V para.10, substituted: SI 2009/497 Sch.1

Sch.4 Part V para.11, substituted: SI 2009/497 Sch.1

Sch.4 Part V para.12, substituted: SI 2009/497 Sch.1

Sch.4B Part IV para.11, enabling: SI 2009/2206

Sch.5 paraA.1, varied: SI 2009/497 Art.4

Sch.5 para.1, varied: SI 2009/497 Art.4

1992–cont.

4. Social Security Contributions and Benefits Act 1992–*cont.*
Sch.5 para.2, varied: SI 2009/497 Art.4
Sch.5 para.2, enabling: SI 2009/2206
Sch.5 para.2A, varied: SI 2009/497 Art.4
Sch.5 para.3, varied: SI 2009/497 Art.4
Sch.5 para.3A, varied: SI 2009/497 Art.4
Sch.5 para.3B, varied: SI 2009/497 Art.4
Sch.5 para.3C, varied: SI 2009/497 Art.4
Sch.5 para.4, varied: SI 2009/497 Art.4
Sch.5 para.5, varied: SI 2009/497 Art.4
Sch.5 para.5A, varied: SI 2009/497 Art.4
Sch.5 para.6, varied: SI 2009/497 Art.4
Sch.5 para.6A, varied: SI 2009/497 Art.4
Sch.5 para.7, varied: SI 2009/497 Art.4
Sch.5 para.7A, varied: SI 2009/497 Art.4
Sch.5 para.7B, varied: SI 2009/497 Art.4
Sch.5 para.7C, varied: SI 2009/497 Art.4
Sch.5 para.8, varied: SI 2009/497 Art.4
Sch.5 para.9, varied: SI 2009/497 Art.4
Sch.5A para.2, varied: SI 2009/497 Art.4
Sch.7 Part I para.2, enabling: SI 2009/2343
Sch.7 Part I para.4, amended: SI 2009/661 Art.2
Sch.7 Part I para.4, enabling: SI 2009/661
Sch.7 Part II para.9, applied: SI 2009/497 Art.6
Sch.7 Part V para.13, applied: SI 2009/497 Art.6
Sch.7 Part V para.13, varied: SI 2009/497 Art.4
Sch.8 Part I para.2, amended: SI 2009/497 Art.7
Sch.8 Part I para.2, enabling: SI 2009/664
Sch.8 Part I para.4, applied: SI 2009/212 Reg.2, SSI 2009/48 Reg.6
Sch.8 Part I para.6, amended: SI 2009/497 Art.7
Sch.8 Part II para.7, applied: SI 2009/212 Reg.2, SSI 2009/48 Reg.6

5. Social Security Administration Act 1992
Part I, amended: 2009 c.24 s.2
Part III, added: 2009 c.24 s.16
Part VII, added: 2009 c.24 s.18
Part VII, added: 2009 c.24 s.20
s.1, enabling: SI 2009/471, SI 2009/1490, SI 2009/3268
s.2A, amended: 2009 c.24 s.3, s.34, s.35, Sch.1 para.24
s.2A, repealed (in part): 2009 c.24 Sch.7 Part 1, Sch.7 Part 3
s.2A, enabling: SI 2009/1541
s.2AA, amended: 2009 c.24 s.34, s.35
s.2AA, repealed (in part): 2009 c.24 Sch.7 Part 1, Sch.7 Part 3
s.2B, repealed: 2009 c.24 Sch.7 Part 3
s.2D, added: 2009 c.24 s.2
s.2D, repealed (in part): 2009 c.24 Sch.7 Part 1
s.2E, added: 2009 c.24 s.2
s.2E, repealed (in part): 2009 c.24 Sch.7 Part 1
s.2F, added: 2009 c.24 s.2
s.2G, added: 2009 c.24 s.2
s.2H, added: 2009 c.24 s.2
s.5, amended: 2009 c.24 s.22
s.5, repealed (in part): 2009 c.24 s.22, Sch.7 Part 1, Sch.7 Part 3
s.5, enabling: SI 2009/604, SI 2009/607, SI 2009/609, SI 2009/1488, SI 2009/1490, SI 2009/2655, SI 2009/3229, SI 2009/3268
s.6, enabling: SI 2009/1488
s.7, amended: 2009 c.24 s.22
s.7A, enabling: SI 2009/1490
s.12, enabling: SI 2009/2655, SI 2009/3033
s.12A, enabling: SI 2009/713

1992–cont.

5. Social Security Administration Act 1992–*cont.*
s.15A, amended: 2009 c.24 Sch.7 Part 1
s.15A, repealed (in part): 2009 c.24 Sch.7 Part 1
s.15A, enabling: SI 2009/583
s.16, amended: 2009 c.24 s.22
s.71, see *R. (on the application of Child Poverty Action Group) v Secretary of State for Work and Pensions* [2009] EWCA Civ 1058, Times, October 21, 2009 (CA (Civ Div)), Sedley, L.J.; see *R. (on the application of Child Poverty Action Group) v Secretary of State for Work and Pensions* [2009] EWHC 341 (Admin), [2009] 3 All E.R. 633 (QBD (Admin)), Michael Supperstone Q.C.
s.71, amended: 2009 c.24 s.22
s.71, applied: SI 2009/609 Reg.2, Reg.3
s.71, repealed (in part): 2009 c.24 Sch.7 Part 1
s.73, applied: 2009 c.8 s.3
s.74, amended: 2009 c.24 Sch.2 para.3, Sch.7 Part 1
s.74, applied: SI 2009/609 Reg.2, Reg.3
s.74A, amended: 2009 c.24 Sch.7 Part 1
s.75, enabling: SI 2009/2608
s.78, see *AM (Ethiopia) v Entry Clearance Officer* [2009] UKSC 16 (SC), Lord Hope (Deputy President)
s.78, amended: 2009 c.24 Sch.7 Part 1
s.78, applied: SI 2009/609 Reg.2, Reg.3
s.105, amended: 2009 c.24 Sch.7 Part 1
s.106, repealed: 2009 c.24 Sch.7 Part 1
s.108, repealed: 2009 c.24 Sch.7 Part 1
s.109, amended: 2009 c.24 Sch.7 Part 1
s.110ZA, amended: SI 2009/2035 Sch.1 para.27, SI 2009/3054 Sch.1 para.3
s.110ZA, referred to: SI 2009/404 Art.9
s.111A, see *R. v Tilley* [2009] EWCA Crim 1426, [2009] 2 Cr. App. R. 31 (CA (Crim Div)), Scott Baker, L.J.
s.113, enabling: SI 2009/600
s.115B, amended: SI 2009/1941 Sch.1 para.129
s.121B, applied: SI 2009/3024 Art.4, SSI 2009/403 Art.3
s.121D, amended: SI 2009/56 Sch.1 para.171
s.121F, amended: 2009 c.8 s.18
s.124, amended: SSI 2009/65 Sch.1
s.124, repealed (in part): 2009 c.24 Sch.7 Part 1
s.124B, amended: SSI 2009/65 Sch.1
s.126, amended: 2009 c.24 Sch.7 Part 1
s.132A, enabling: SI 2009/208, SI 2009/612
s.134, see *Hanoman v Southwark LBC* [2008] EWCA Civ 624, [2009] 1 W.L.R. 374 (CA (Civ Div)), Sir Anthony Clarke, M.R.; see *Hanoman v Southwark LBC* [2009] UKHL 29, [2009] 1 W.L.R. 1367 (HL), Lord Phillips of Worth Matravers
s.134, enabling: SI 2009/3389
s.139, enabling: SI 2009/3389
s.139A, amended: 2009 c.2 Sch.1 para.4
s.139C, amended: 2009 c.2 Sch.1 para.5
s.139D, amended: 2009 c.2 Sch.1 para.6
s.140B, enabling: SI 2009/30, SI 2009/2564, SI 2009/2580
s.140C, enabling: SI 2009/30, SI 2009/2564
s.140F, enabling: SI 2009/30, SI 2009/2564, SI 2009/2580
s.141, applied: SI 2009/593, SI 2009/696
s.141, enabling: SI 2009/593
s.142, enabling: SI 2009/593
s.148, applied: SI 2009/608, SI 2009/795
s.148, enabling: SI 2009/608

5. **Social Security Administration Act 1992**–*cont.*
s.148A, enabling: SI 2009/610
s.150, applied: SI 2009/497, SI 2009/607, SI 2009/
692, SI 2009/797, SI 2009/798
s.150, referred to: SI 2009/692, SI 2009/797, SI
2009/798
s.150, varied: 2009 c.24 s.23, SI 2009/497 Art.4
s.150, enabling: SI 2009/497, SI 2009/797
s.150A, applied: SI 2009/497, SI 2009/607
s.150A, enabling: SI 2009/497
s.151, applied: SI 2009/692
s.151, enabling: SI 2009/497
s.155, disapplied: SI 2009/607 Reg.2, SI 2009/810
Reg.2
s.155, enabling: SI 2009/607, SI 2009/810
s.159, repealed: 2009 c.24 Sch.7 Part 1
s.159B, referred to: SSI 2009/48 Reg.6
s.160, repealed: 2009 c.24 Sch.7 Part 1
s.163, repealed (in part): 2009 c.24 Sch.7 Part 1
s.170, amended: 2009 c.24 Sch.4 para.9, Sch.7 Part 3
s.172, applied: SI 2009/604, SI 2009/609, SI 2009/
614, SI 2009/1396
s.173, applied: SI 2009/471, SI 2009/1490, SI 2009/
1494, SI 2009/2608, SI 2009/3229, SI 2009/3389
s.176, applied: SI 2009/30, SI 2009/471, SI 2009/
614, SI 2009/1488, SI 2009/1848, SI 2009/2564,
SI 2009/2580, SI 2009/3389
s.179, repealed (in part): 2009 c.24 Sch.7 Part 1
s.189, amended: 2009 c.24 s.2
s.189, applied: SI 2009/30, SI 2009/2564, SI 2009/
2580
s.189, enabling: SI 2009/30, SI 2009/208, SI 2009/
471, SI 2009/497, SI 2009/583, SI 2009/604, SI
2009/607, SI 2009/608, SI 2009/609, SI 2009/
612, SI 2009/797, SI 2009/810, SI 2009/1488, SI
2009/1490, SI 2009/1494, SI 2009/1541, SI 2009/
2564, SI 2009/2580, SI 2009/2608, SI 2009/
2655, SI 2009/3033, SI 2009/3229, SI 2009/
3268, SI 2009/3389
s.190, amended: 2009 c.24 s.21
s.190, applied: SI 2009/497, SI 2009/593, SI 2009/
692, SI 2009/797
s.191, repealed (in part): 2009 c.24 Sch.7 Part 1
s.191, enabling: SI 2009/471, SI 2009/583, SI 2009/
604, SI 2009/607, SI 2009/609, SI 2009/810, SI
2009/1488, SI 2009/1490, SI 2009/1541, SI 2009/
2608, SI 2009/2655, SI 2009/3033, SI 2009/3229,
SI 2009/3389
Sch.3A para.2, amended: SI 2009/56 Sch.1
para.172
Sch.3A para.2, repealed (in part): SI 2009/56 Sch.1
para.172
Sch.9 para.1, enabling: SI 2009/664
6. **Social Security (Consequential Provisions) Act
1992**
Sch.2 para.3, repealed (in part): 2009 c.24 Sch.7
Part 1
Sch.2 para.108, repealed: 2009 c.24 Sch.7 Part 1
Sch.3 Part II para.15, enabling: SI 2009/2206
7. **Social Security Contributions and Benefits
(Northern Ireland) Act 1992**
applied: SI 2009/2131 Sch.2 para.5
referred to: 2009 c.10 Sch.6 para.2
Part I, applied: 2009 c.4 s.1203, s.1302, SI 2009/2131
Sch.2 para.5
s.1, applied: 2009 c.4 s.1292
s.3, enabling: SI 2009/600, SI 2009/2679
s.5, enabling: SI 2009/111, SI 2009/591
s.11, amended: SI 2009/593 Art.2

7. **Social Security Contributions and Benefits
(Northern Ireland) Act 1992**–*cont.*
s.13, amended: SI 2009/593 Art.3
s.15, amended: SI 2009/593 Art.4
s.18, amended: SI 2009/593 Art.4
s.77, enabling: SI 2009/3268
s.113, enabling: SI 2009/810
s.117, enabling: SI 2009/696
s.121, enabling: SI 2009/111, SI 2009/810, SI 2009/
2679
s.138, enabling: SI 2009/3268
s.171, enabling: SI 2009/111, SI 2009/591, SI 2009/
600, SI 2009/696, SI 2009/810, SI 2009/2679, SI
2009/3268
s.172, applied: SI 2009/591
Sch.1 para.3A, applied: 2009 c.4 s.1018
Sch.1 para.3B, amended: SI 2009/56 Sch.1 para.174
Sch.1 para.3B, applied: 2009 c.4 s.1018
Sch.1 para.6, referred to: SI 2009/600
Sch.1 para.6, enabling: SI 2009/111, SI 2009/600, SI
2009/2028
Sch.1 para.8, enabling: SI 2009/600
Sch.4 Part III, amended: SI 2009/798 Art.2
8. **Social Security Administration (Northern
Ireland) Act 1992**
s.1, enabling: SI 2009/3268
s.5, enabling: SI 2009/3268
s.50, amended: 2009 c.3 Sch.4 para.24
s.104ZA, amended: SI 2009/2035 Sch.1 para.28, SI
2009/3054 Sch.1 para.4
s.104ZA, referred to: SI 2009/404 Art.9
s.107, enabling: SI 2009/600
s.109B, amended: SI 2009/1941 Sch.1 para.130
s.115C, amended: SI 2009/56 Sch.1 para.176
s.115E, amended: 2009 c.8 s.18
s.129, applied: SI 2009/593, SI 2009/696
s.129, enabling: SI 2009/593
s.132, enabling: SI 2009/798
s.135, disapplied: SI 2009/810 Reg.2
s.135, enabling: SI 2009/810
s.165, enabling: SI 2009/593, SI 2009/798, SI 2009/
810, SI 2009/3268
s.166, applied: SI 2009/593, SI 2009/798
s.167, enabling: SI 2009/810
12. **Taxation of Chargeable Gains Act 1992**
see *Blackburn v Revenue and Customs
Commissioners* [2008] EWCA Civ 1454, [2009]
S.T.C. 188 (CA (Civ Div)), Sedley, L.J.; see *Grays
Timber Products Ltd v Revenue and Customs
Commissioners* [2009] CSIH 11, [2009] S.T.C.
889 (IH (Ex Div)), Lord Osborne
applied: 2009 c.4 s.264, s.491, s.888, s.895, s.898,
s.899, s.900, 2009 c.10 Sch.22 para.18, Sch.61
para.10, Sch.61 para.11, Sch.61 para.12, SI 2009/
391 Reg.3, SI 2009/3001 Reg.10, Reg.33, Reg.39,
Reg.44, Reg.100, Sch.1 para.4, SI 2009/3227
Reg.3
disapplied: 2009 c.4 s.514
referred to: 2009 c.4 s.892, SI 2009/3001 Reg.39
varied: SI 2009/317 Sch.1, SI 2009/3001 Reg.47
Part VI, applied: 2009 c.10 Sch.13 para.4
s.1, amended: 2009 c.4 Sch.1 para.359
s.2, varied: SI 2009/3001 Reg.22
s.3, applied: SI 2009/824 Art.2
s.3, enabling: SI 2009/824
s.10, varied: SI 2009/3001 Reg.22
s.10A, varied: SI 2009/3001 Reg.23
s.10B, amended: 2009 c.4 Sch.1 para.360
s.10B, applied: 2009 c.4 s.19, s.900

1992–cont.

12. **Taxation of Chargeable Gains Act 1992**–*cont.*
s.10B, varied: SI 2009/3001 Reg.22
s.12, varied: SI 2009/3001 Reg.20
s.13, referred to: SI 2009/3001 Reg.18
s.13, repealed (in part): SI 2009/56 Sch.1 para.178
s.13, varied: SI 2009/3001 Reg.24
s.14A, amended: 2009 c.10 Sch.27 para.12
s.16, disapplied: SI 2009/3001 Reg.42
s.17, disapplied: 2009 c.4 s.653
s.18, see *Kellogg Brown & Root Holdings (UK) Ltd v Revenue and Customs Commissioners* [2009] EWHC 584 (Ch), [2009] S.T.C. 1359 (Ch D), Sir Andrew Morritt (Chancellor)
s.24, amended: SI 2009/730 Art.4
s.25A, amended: 2009 c.10 Sch.32 para.3
s.26, applied: 2009 c.4 s.418, s.522
s.28, see *Kellogg Brown & Root Holdings (UK) Ltd v Revenue and Customs Commissioners* [2009] EWHC 584 (Ch), [2009] S.T.C. 1359 (Ch D), Sir Andrew Morritt (Chancellor); see *Underwood v Revenue and Customs Commissioners* [2008] EWCA Civ 1423, [2009] S.T.C. 239 (CA (Civ Div)), Lord Neuberger of Abbotsbury
s.30, see *HBOS Treasury Services Ltd v Revenue and Customs Commissioners* [2009] UKFTT 261 (TC) (FTT (Tax)), Howard M Nowlan
s.30, referred to: 2009 c.10 Sch.23 para.8
s.32, amended: 2009 c.10 Sch.23 para.8
s.33A, amended: 2009 c.4 Sch.1 para.361
s.35, amended: 2009 c.10 Sch.40 para.2
s.37, see *Drummond v Revenue and Customs Commissioners* [2009] EWCA Civ 608, [2009] S.T.C. 2206 (CA (Civ Div)), Arden, L.J.; see *Smith v Revenue and Customs Commissioners* [2009] S.T.C. (S.C.D.) 132 (Sp Comm), Theodore Wallace
s.37, applied: 2009 c.4 s.670
s.37, disapplied: 2009 c.4 s.672
s.37, referred to: SI 2009/3001 Reg.45
s.38, see *Drummond v Revenue and Customs Commissioners* [2009] EWCA Civ 608, [2009] S.T.C. 2206 (CA (Civ Div)), Arden, L.J.; see *Smith v Revenue and Customs Commissioners* [2009] S.T.C. (S.C.D.) 132 (Sp Comm), Theodore Wallace
s.38, applied: 2009 c.4 s.667, s.668, s.670, s.672, s.898, SI 2009/3001 Reg.99
s.38, referred to: 2009 c.4 s.1157
s.39, see *Drummond v Revenue and Customs Commissioners* [2009] EWCA Civ 608, [2009] S.T.C. 2206 (CA (Civ Div)), Arden, L.J.
s.39, applied: 2009 c.4 s.670
s.39, disapplied: 2009 c.4 s.672
s.39, referred to: 2009 c.4 s.1157
s.40, amended: 2009 c.4 Sch.1 para.362
s.41, amended: 2009 c.4 Sch.1 para.363, Sch.3 Part 1
s.42, applied: 2009 c.4 s.667, s.668, s.670, SI 2009/3001 Reg.45
s.48, amended: 2009 c.4 Sch.1 para.364
s.55, amended: 2009 c.10 Sch.40 para.3
s.56, applied: SI 2009/3001 Reg.40
s.58, amended: 2009 c.10 Sch.22 para.9
s.59, amended: 2009 c.4 Sch.1 para.365, 2009 c.10 Sch.22 para.9
s.59A, amended: 2009 c.10 Sch.22 para.9
s.60, amended: 2009 c.10 Sch.22 para.9
s.61, amended: 2009 c.10 Sch.22 para.9
s.62, amended: 2009 c.10 Sch.22 para.9
s.62, applied: SI 2009/3001 Reg.34

1992–cont.

12. **Taxation of Chargeable Gains Act 1992**–*cont.*
s.62, disapplied: SI 2009/3001 Reg.34
s.63, amended: 2009 c.10 Sch.22 para.9
s.63A, amended: 2009 c.10 Sch.22 para.9
s.64, amended: 2009 c.10 Sch.22 para.9
s.65, amended: 2009 c.10 Sch.22 para.9
s.66, amended: 2009 c.10 Sch.22 para.9
s.67, amended: 2009 c.10 Sch.22 para.9
s.68, amended: 2009 c.10 Sch.22 para.9
s.68A, amended: 2009 c.10 Sch.22 para.9
s.68B, amended: 2009 c.10 Sch.22 para.9
s.68C, amended: 2009 c.10 Sch.22 para.9
s.69, amended: 2009 c.10 Sch.22 para.9
s.69A, amended: 2009 c.10 Sch.22 para.9
s.70, amended: 2009 c.10 Sch.22 para.9
s.71, amended: 2009 c.10 Sch.22 para.9
s.72, amended: 2009 c.10 Sch.22 para.9
s.73, amended: 2009 c.10 Sch.22 para.9
s.74, amended: 2009 c.10 Sch.22 para.9
s.75, amended: 2009 c.10 Sch.22 para.9
s.76, amended: 2009 c.10 Sch.22 para.9
s.76A, amended: 2009 c.10 Sch.22 para.9
s.76B, amended: 2009 c.10 Sch.22 para.9
s.77, see *Eyretel Unapproved Pension Scheme Trustees v Revenue and Customs Commissioners* [2009] S.T.C. (S.C.D.) 17 (Sp Comm), JF Avery Jones (Chairman); see *Smallwood v Revenue and Customs Commissioners* [2009] EWHC 777 (Ch), [2009] S.T.C. 1222 (Ch D), Mann, J.
s.77, amended: 2009 c.10 Sch.22 para.9
s.78, amended: 2009 c.10 Sch.22 para.9
s.79, amended: 2009 c.10 Sch.22 para.9
s.79A, amended: 2009 c.10 Sch.22 para.9
s.79B, amended: 2009 c.10 Sch.22 para.9
s.80, amended: 2009 c.10 Sch.22 para.9
s.81, amended: 2009 c.10 Sch.22 para.9
s.82, amended: 2009 c.10 Sch.22 para.9
s.83, amended: 2009 c.10 Sch.22 para.9
s.83A, amended: 2009 c.10 Sch.22 para.9
s.84, amended: 2009 c.10 Sch.22 para.9
s.85, amended: 2009 c.10 Sch.22 para.9
s.85A, amended: 2009 c.10 Sch.22 para.9
s.86, see *Burton v Revenue and Customs Commissioners* [2009] UKFTT 203 (TC), [2009] S.F.T.D. 682 (FTT (Tax)), Theodore Wallace; see *Smallwood v Revenue and Customs Commissioners* [2009] EWHC 777 (Ch), [2009] S.T.C. 1222 (Ch D), Mann, J.
s.86, amended: 2009 c.10 Sch.22 para.9
s.86A, amended: 2009 c.10 Sch.22 para.9
s.87, see *Burton v Revenue and Customs Commissioners* [2009] UKFTT 203 (TC), [2009] S.F.T.D. 682 (FTT (Tax)), Theodore Wallace
s.87, amended: 2009 c.10 Sch.22 para.9
s.87, applied: SI 2009/3001 Reg.20
s.87, varied: SI 2009/3001 Reg.20
s.87A, amended: 2009 c.10 Sch.22 para.9
s.87A, applied: SI 2009/3001 Reg.20
s.87A, varied: SI 2009/3001 Reg.20
s.87B, amended: 2009 c.10 Sch.22 para.9
s.87B, varied: SI 2009/3001 Reg.20
s.87C, amended: 2009 c.10 Sch.22 para.9
s.87C, varied: SI 2009/3001 Reg.20
s.88, amended: 2009 c.10 Sch.22 para.9
s.88, varied: SI 2009/3001 Reg.20
s.89, amended: 2009 c.10 Sch.22 para.9

1992– cont.

12. Taxation of Chargeable Gains Act 1992–*cont.*

s.89, varied: SI 2009/3001 Reg.20

s.90, amended: 2009 c.10 Sch.22 para.9

s.90, varied: SI 2009/3001 Reg.20

s.90A, amended: 2009 c.10 Sch.22 para.9

s.90A, varied: SI 2009/3001 Reg.20

s.91, amended: 2009 c.10 Sch.22 para.9

s.92, amended: 2009 c.10 Sch.22 para.9

s.93, amended: 2009 c.10 Sch.22 para.9

s.94, amended: 2009 c.10 Sch.22 para.9

s.95, amended: 2009 c.10 Sch.22 para.9

s.96, amended: 2009 c.10 Sch.22 para.9

s.96, varied: SI 2009/3001 Reg.20

s.97, see *Burton v Revenue and Customs Commissioners* [2009] UKFTT 203 (TC), [2009] S.F.T.D. 682 (FTT (Tax)), Theodore Wallace

s.97, amended: 2009 c.10 Sch.22 para.9

s.97, varied: SI 2009/3001 Reg.20

s.98, amended: 2009 c.10 Sch.22 para.9

s.98, varied: SI 2009/3001 Reg.20

s.98A, amended: 2009 c.10 Sch.22 para.9

s.99, amended: 2009 c.10 Sch.22 para.9

s.99A, amended: 2009 c.10 Sch.22 para.9

s.99AA, amended: 2009 c.10 Sch.22 para.9

s.99B, amended: 2009 c.10 Sch.22 para.9

s.100, amended: 2009 c.10 Sch.22 para.9

s.101, amended: 2009 c.10 Sch.22 para.9

s.101A, amended: 2009 c.10 Sch.22 para.9

s.101B, amended: 2009 c.10 Sch.22 para.9

s.101C, amended: 2009 c.10 Sch.22 para.9

s.102, amended: 2009 c.10 Sch.22 para.9

s.103, amended: 2009 c.10 Sch.22 para.9

s.103A, added: 2009 c.10 Sch.22 para.8

s.103A, amended: 2009 c.10 Sch.22 para.9

s.103A, referred to: 2009 c.10 Sch.22 para.13

s.104, varied: SI 2009/3001 Reg.43

s.108, amended: SI 2009/3001 Reg.127, Sch.2

s.116, see *Klincke v Revenue and Customs Commissioners* [2009] UKFTT 156 (TC), [2009] S.F.T.D. 466 (FTT (Tax)), Sir Stephen Oliver (Chamber President)

s.116, amended: 2009 c.4 Sch.1 para.366

s.116, referred to: 2009 c.4 s.339, s.424, s.435

s.116A, added: 2009 c.4 Sch.1 para.367

s.116B, added: 2009 c.4 Sch.1 para.367

s.116B, amended: 2009 c.10 Sch.24 para.5

s.116B, applied: 2009 c.10 Sch.24 para.14

s.116B, referred to: 2009 c.4 s.521A, s.522

s.117, see *Klincke v Revenue and Customs Commissioners* [2009] UKFTT 156 (TC), [2009] S.F.T.D. 466 (FTT (Tax)), Sir Stephen Oliver (Chamber President)

s.117, amended: 2009 c.4 Sch.1 para.368

s.117, applied: 2009 c.4 s.131

s.125, amended: SI 2009/730 Art.5

s.126, applied: 2009 c.4 s.129

s.127, see *Adams v Revenue and Customs Commissioners* [2009] UKFTT 80 (TC), [2009] S.F.T.D. 184 (FTT (Tax)), Theodore Wallace

s.127, applied: 2009 c.4 s.129, s.339, s.424, s.435, s.670

s.127, referred to: SI 2009/3001 Reg.37

s.128, applied: 2009 c.4 s.129, s.339, s.424, s.435, SI 2009/3001 Reg.47

s.129, applied: 2009 c.4 s.129, s.339, s.424, s.435

s.130, applied: 2009 c.4 s.129, s.339, s.424, s.435

1992– cont.

12. Taxation of Chargeable Gains Act 1992–*cont.*

s.131, see *Adams v Revenue and Customs Commissioners* [2009] UKFTT 80 (TC), [2009] S.F.T.D. 184 (FTT (Tax)), Theodore Wallace

s.131, applied: 2009 c.4 s.129

s.132, see *Klincke v Revenue and Customs Commissioners* [2009] UKFTT 156 (TC), [2009] S.F.T.D. 466 (FTT (Tax)), Sir Stephen Oliver (Chamber President)

s.132, applied: 2009 c.4 s.129

s.133, applied: 2009 c.4 s.129

s.133A, applied: 2009 c.4 s.129

s.134, applied: 2009 c.4 s.129

s.135, see *Adams v Revenue and Customs Commissioners* [2009] UKFTT 80 (TC), [2009] S.F.T.D. 184 (FTT (Tax)), Theodore Wallace

s.135, applied: 2009 c.4 s.129, s.339, 2009 c.10 Sch.8 para.12, SI 2009/3001 Reg.35

s.135, disapplied: SI 2009/3001 Reg.35

s.135, referred to: 2009 c.4 s.129, s.339, SI 2009/3001 Reg.39, Reg.47

s.136, applied: 2009 c.4 s.129, SI 2009/3001 Reg.36

s.136, disapplied: SI 2009/3001 Reg.36

s.136, referred to: 2009 c.4 s.129, 2009 c.10 Sch.8 para.12, SI 2009/3001 Reg.39, Reg.47

s.137, see *Adams v Revenue and Customs Commissioners* [2009] UKFTT 80 (TC), [2009] S.F.T.D. 184 (FTT (Tax)), Theodore Wallace; see *Coll v Revenue and Customs Commissioners* [2009] UKFTT 61 (TC), [2009] S.F.T.D. 101 (FTT (Tax)), Michael Tildesley OBE

s.137, varied: 2009 c.4 s.129

s.138, see *Adams v Revenue and Customs Commissioners* [2009] UKFTT 80 (TC), [2009] S.F.T.D. 184 (FTT (Tax)), Theodore Wallace

s.138, amended: SI 2009/56 Sch.1 para.179

s.138, applied: SI 2009/275 Art.3

s.138A, see *Adams v Revenue and Customs Commissioners* [2009] UKFTT 80 (TC), [2009] S.F.T.D. 184 (FTT (Tax)), Theodore Wallace

s.139, referred to: 2009 c.4 s.892

s.140A, referred to: 2009 c.4 s.892

s.140E, referred to: 2009 c.4 s.892

s.143, amended: 2009 c.4 Sch.1 para.369

s.143, applied: 2009 c.4 s.981

s.151, enabling: SI 2009/1550, SI 2009/1994

s.151E, added: 2009 c.4 Sch.1 para.370

s.151E, repealed: 2009 c.4 Sch.2 para.71, Sch.3 Part 2

s.151F, added: 2009 c.4 Sch.1 para.370

s.151F, amended: SI 2009/2860 Art.4

s.151F, repealed: 2009 c.4 Sch.2 para.71, Sch.3 Part 2

s.151G, added: 2009 c.4 Sch.1 para.370

s.156, amended: 2009 c.4 Sch.1 para.371, Sch.3 Part 1

s.156ZA, added: 2009 c.4 Sch.1 para.372

s.156ZB, added: 2009 c.4 Sch.1 para.372

s.158, amended: 2009 c.4 Sch.3 Part 1, SI 2009/730 Art.6

s.161, amended: 2009 c.4 Sch.1 para.374

s.162, applied: SI 2009/3001 Reg.41, Reg.46

s.164A, see *Pegasus Management Holdings SCA v Ernst & Young (A Firm)* [2008] EWHC 2720 (Ch), [2009] P.N.L.R. 11 (Ch D), Lewison, J.

1992– cont.

12. Taxation of Chargeable Gains Act 1992– *cont.*
s.164N, see *Pegasus Management Holdings SCA v Ernst & Young (A Firm)* [2008] EWHC 2720 (Ch), [2009] P.N.L.R. 11 (Ch D), Lewison, J.
s.165, applied: 2009 c.4 s.849, SI 2009/3001 Reg.41
s.169E, amended: SI 2009/2035 Sch.1 para.30
s.169G, repealed (in part): SI 2009/2035 Sch.1 para.31
s.170, see *Limitgood Ltd v Revenue and Customs Commissioners* [2009] EWCA Civ 177, [2009] S.T.C. 980 (CA (Civ Div)), Mummery, L.J.
s.170, amended: 2009 c.4 Sch.3 Part 1, SI 2009/1890 Art.3
s.170, applied: 2009 c.4 s.335, s.618, s.624, s.773, SI 2009/2971 Reg.1, Reg.2
s.171, amended: 2009 c.4 Sch.1 para.376
s.171, applied: 2009 c.4 s.773, s.830
s.171, repealed (in part): 2009 c.10 Sch.24 para.9
s.171A, applied: 2009 c.4 s.773
s.171A, substituted: 2009 c.10 Sch.12 para.1
s.171B, applied: 2009 c.4 s.773
s.171C, applied: 2009 c.4 s.773
s.172, applied: 2009 c.4 s.773
s.173, applied: 2009 c.4 s.773
s.174, applied: 2009 c.4 s.773
s.175, amended: 2009 c.10 Sch.40 para.4
s.175, applied: 2009 c.4 s.773
s.176, amended: SI 2009/1890 Art.9
s.176, applied: 2009 c.4 s.773
s.177, applied: 2009 c.4 s.773
s.177A, applied: 2009 c.4 s.773
s.177B, applied: 2009 c.4 s.773
s.178, applied: 2009 c.4 s.773
s.179, see *Johnston Publishing (North) Ltd v Revenue and Customs Commissioners* [2008] EWCA Civ 858, [2009] 1 W.L.R. 1349 (CA (Civ Div)), Tuckey, L.J.
s.179, applied: 2009 c.4 s.773, s.899, SI 2009/2971 Reg.7, Reg.18
s.179, disapplied: SI 2009/2971 Reg.6, Reg.7, Reg.17, Reg.18
s.179A, amended: 2009 c.10 Sch.12 para.2
s.179A, applied: 2009 c.4 s.773
s.179B, applied: 2009 c.4 s.773
s.180, applied: 2009 c.4 s.773
s.181, applied: 2009 c.4 s.773
s.195A, added: 2009 c.10 Sch.40 para.5
s.195B, added: 2009 c.10 Sch.40 para.5
s.195C, added: 2009 c.10 Sch.40 para.5
s.195D, added: 2009 c.10 Sch.40 para.5
s.195E, added: 2009 c.10 Sch.40 para.5
s.196, amended: 2009 c.10 Sch.40 para.6
s.198, amended: 2009 c.10 Sch.40 para.10, Sch.40 para.11
s.198A, added: 2009 c.10 Sch.40 para.12
s.198B, added: 2009 c.10 Sch.40 para.12
s.198C, added: 2009 c.10 Sch.40 para.12
s.198D, added: 2009 c.10 Sch.40 para.12
s.198E, added: 2009 c.10 Sch.40 para.12
s.198F, added: 2009 c.10 Sch.40 para.12
s.198G, added: 2009 c.10 Sch.40 para.12
s.201, applied: 2009 c.4 s.135, s.258, s.273
s.201, repealed (in part): 2009 c.4 Sch.3 Part 1
s.203, amended: 2009 c.4 Sch.1 para.378
s.210A, amended: 2009 c.4 Sch.1 para.379
s.211ZA, amended: SI 2009/56 Sch.1 para.180
s.212, amended: SI 2009/3001 Reg.127
s.212, repealed (in part): SI 2009/3001 Sch.2

1992– cont.

12. Taxation of Chargeable Gains Act 1992– *cont.*
s.213, amended: SI 2009/56 Sch.1 para.181
s.215, applied: SI 2009/2971 Reg.14
s.216, applied: SI 2009/2971 Reg.14
s.223, amended: SI 2009/730 Art.7, Art.8
s.225B, added: SI 2009/730 Art.9
s.225C, added: SI 2009/730 Art.10
s.235, repealed: SI 2009/2035 Sch.1 para.32
s.239, amended: SI 2009/1890 Art.4
s.239, substituted: SI 2009/730 Art.11
s.239ZA, added: SI 2009/730 Art.11
s.241, amended: 2009 c.4 Sch.1 para.380, Sch.3 Part 1
s.241, applied: 2009 c.4 s.264
s.251, amended: 2009 c.4 Sch.3 Part 1
s.251, repealed (in part): 2009 c.4 Sch.3 Part 1
s.253, amended: 2009 c.4 Sch.1 para.382
s.256, amended: SI 2009/23 Art.3
s.258, amended: SI 2009/730 Art.12
s.260, applied: SI 2009/3001 Reg.41
s.261B, amended: SI 2009/56 Sch.1 para.182
s.261C, amended: SI 2009/56 Sch.1 para.183
s.263B, amended: 2009 c.10 Sch.13 para.2
s.263CA, added: 2009 c.10 Sch.13 para.3
s.263CA, applied: 2009 c.10 Sch.13 para.4
s.263CA, varied: 2009 c.10 Sch.13 para.4
s.272, see *Gray's Timber Products Ltd v Revenue and Customs Commissioners* [2009] CSIH 11, [2009] S.T.C. 889 (IH (Ex Div)), Lord Osborne
s.272, referred to: 2009 c.4 s.491
s.272, varied: SI 2009/3001 Reg.10
s.275B, amended: 2009 c.4 Sch.1 para.383
s.286, see *Kellogg Brown & Root Holdings (UK) Ltd v Revenue and Customs Commissioners* [2009] EWHC 584 (Ch), [2009] S.T.C. 1359 (Ch D), Sir Andrew Morritt (Chancellor)
s.286A, added: 2009 c.4 Sch.1 para.384
s.287, disapplied: 2009 c.10 Sch.22 para.14
s.288, amended: 2009 c.4 Sch.1 para.385, 2009 c.10 Sch.22 para.10, SI 2009/56 Sch.1 para.184
s.288, applied: 2009 c.10 Sch.13 para.4
s.288, referred to: SI 2009/3227 Reg.3
Sch.A1 para.5, see *Chappell v Revenue and Customs Commissioners* [2009] S.T.C. (S.C.D.) 11 (Sp Comm), John F Avery Jones
Sch.1 para.1, repealed (in part): SI 2009/2035 Sch.1 para.33
Sch.1 para.2, repealed (in part): SI 2009/2035 Sch.1 para.33
Sch.3 para.1, amended: 2009 c.10 Sch.40 para.7
Sch.4C para.1, varied: SI 2009/3001 Reg.20
Sch.4C para.1A, varied: SI 2009/3001 Reg.20
Sch.4C para.2, varied: SI 2009/3001 Reg.20
Sch.4C para.3, varied: SI 2009/3001 Reg.20
Sch.4C para.4, varied: SI 2009/3001 Reg.20
Sch.4C para.5, varied: SI 2009/3001 Reg.20
Sch.4C para.6, varied: SI 2009/3001 Reg.20
Sch.4C para.7, varied: SI 2009/3001 Reg.20
Sch.4C para.7A, varied: SI 2009/3001 Reg.20
Sch.4C para.7B, varied: SI 2009/3001 Reg.20
Sch.4C para.8, varied: SI 2009/3001 Reg.20
Sch.4C para.8A, varied: SI 2009/3001 Reg.20
Sch.4C para.8AA, varied: SI 2009/3001 Reg.20
Sch.4C para.8B, varied: SI 2009/3001 Reg.20
Sch.4C para.8C, varied: SI 2009/3001 Reg.20
Sch.4C para.9, varied: SI 2009/3001 Reg.20
Sch.4C para.10, varied: SI 2009/3001 Reg.20
Sch.4C para.11, varied: SI 2009/3001 Reg.20

12. Taxation of Chargeable Gains Act 1992–*cont.*
Sch.4C para.12, varied: SI 2009/3001 Reg.20
Sch.4C para.12A, varied: SI 2009/3001 Reg.20
Sch.4C para.13, varied: SI 2009/3001 Reg.20
Sch.4C para.13A, varied: SI 2009/3001 Reg.20
Sch.4C para.14, varied: SI 2009/3001 Reg.20
Sch.4ZA para.14, repealed: SI 2009/2035 Sch.1 para.34
Sch.4ZA para.15, repealed: SI 2009/2035 Sch.1 para.34
Sch.4ZA para.16, repealed: SI 2009/2035 Sch.1 para.34
Sch.5 para.2, see *Burton v Revenue and Customs Commissioners* [2009] UKFTT 203 (TC), [2009] S.F.T.D. 682 (FTT (Tax)), Theodore Wallace
Sch.5 para.10, repealed: SI 2009/2035 Sch.1 para.35
Sch.5B para.1, amended: 2009 c.10 Sch.8 para.2
Sch.5B para.1A, amended: 2009 c.10 Sch.8 para.3
Sch.5B para.1A, repealed (in part): 2009 c.10 Sch.8 para.3
Sch.5B para.9, amended: 2009 c.10 Sch.8 para.4
Sch.5B para.13, see *Blackburn v Revenue and Customs Commissioners* [2008] EWCA Civ 1454, [2009] S.T.C. 188 (CA (Civ Div)), Sedley, L.J.
Sch.5B para.16, repealed (in part): 2009 c.10 Sch.8 para.5
Sch.7AC Part I para.2, applied: 2009 c.4 s.642
Sch.7AC Part II para.8, applied: 2009 c.4 s.591
Sch.7AC Part V para.34, repealed (in part): 2009 c.4 Sch.3 Part 1
Sch.7AD para.7, amended: SI 2009/3001 Reg.127
Sch.7A para.1, see *Limitgood Ltd v Revenue and Customs Commissioners* [2009] EWCA Civ 177, [2009] S.T.C. 980 (CA (Civ Div)), Mummery, L.J.
Sch.7D Part 1 para.2, amended: 2009 c.4 Sch.1 para.387
Sch.8, amended: 2009 c.4 Sch.1 para.388
Sch.8 para.5, amended: 2009 c.4 Sch.1 para.388
Sch.8 para.5, repealed (in part): 2009 c.4 Sch.3 Part 1
Sch.8 para.6, amended: 2009 c.4 Sch.1 para.388
Sch.8 para.7, amended: 2009 c.4 Sch.1 para.388
Sch.8 para.7A, amended: 2009 c.4 Sch.3 Part 1
Sch.10 para.2, repealed (in part): SI 2009/2035 Sch.1 para.60
Sch.10 para.14, repealed (in part): 2009 c.4 Sch.3 Part 1, SI 2009/3001 Sch.2

13. Further and Higher Education Act 1992
applied: 2009 c.4 s.71
s.17, amended: 2009 c.22 Sch.8 para.2
s.19, amended: 2009 c.22 s.256, Sch.6 para.3
s.19A, added: 2009 c.22 s.256
s.26, applied: SI 2009/499 Art.3
s.26, varied: SI 2009/1514 Art.3, SI 2009/1515 Art.3, SI 2009/1543 Art.3, SI 2009/1841 Art.3, SI 2009/3153 Art.3, SI 2009/3237 Art.3, SI 2009/3239 Art.3
s.27, enabling: SI 2009/499, SI 2009/1514, SI 2009/1515, SI 2009/1543, SI 2009/1841, SI 2009/2633, SI 2009/3153, SI 2009/3237, SI 2009/3239
s.29, amended: 2009 c.22 Sch.6 para.4
s.31, amended: 2009 c.22 Sch.6 para.5, SI 2009/1941 Sch.1 para.131
s.33A, added: 2009 c.22 Sch.8 para.3
s.33B, added: 2009 c.22 Sch.8 para.3
s.33C, added: 2009 c.22 Sch.8 para.3

13. Further and Higher Education Act 1992–*cont.*
s.33D, added: 2009 c.22 Sch.8 para.3
s.33E, added: 2009 c.22 Sch.8 para.3
s.33F, added: 2009 c.22 Sch.8 para.3
s.33G, added: 2009 c.22 Sch.8 para.3
s.33H, added: 2009 c.22 Sch.8 para.3
s.33I, added: 2009 c.22 Sch.8 para.3
s.33J, added: 2009 c.22 Sch.8 para.3
s.33K, added: 2009 c.22 Sch.8 para.3
s.33L, added: 2009 c.22 Sch.8 para.3
s.33M, added: 2009 c.22 Sch.8 para.3
s.33N, added: 2009 c.22 Sch.8 para.3
s.34, amended: 2009 c.22 Sch.8 para.4
s.51A, added: 2009 c.22 s.44
s.52, amended: 2009 c.22 s.44
s.52A, amended: 2009 c.22 Sch.8 para.5
s.54, amended: 2009 c.22 Sch.6 para.6
s.56A, amended: 2009 c.22 Sch.6 para.7, Sch.8 para.6
s.56AA, added: 2009 c.22 Sch.6 para.8
s.56B, amended: 2009 c.22 Sch.6 para.9, Sch.16 Part 2
s.56C, amended: 2009 c.22 Sch.6 para.10, Sch.8 para.7, Sch.16 Part 2
s.56D, added: 2009 c.22 Sch.6 para.11
s.56E, added: 2009 c.22 Sch.8 para.8
s.56F, added: 2009 c.22 Sch.8 para.8
s.56G, added: 2009 c.22 Sch.8 para.8
s.56H, added: 2009 c.22 Sch.8 para.8
s.56H, applied: 2009 c.22 s.73
s.56I, added: 2009 c.22 Sch.8 para.8
s.56I, applied: 2009 c.22 s.73
s.56J, added: 2009 c.22 Sch.8 para.8
s.65, applied: SI 2009/1555 Reg.6, Reg.14, Reg.135, Reg.152, SI 2009/2737 Reg.5, Reg.13, Reg.86, Reg.110
s.76, amended: 2009 c.22 s.259, Sch.16 Part 11
s.85AA, added: 2009 c.22 s.244
s.85AB, added: 2009 c.22 s.244
s.85AC, added: 2009 c.22 s.244
s.85AD, added: 2009 c.22 s.244
s.85B, amended: 2009 c.22 s.245
s.85D, added: 2009 c.22 s.247
s.88, amended: 2009 c.22 Sch.8 para.9
s.88A, amended: 2009 c.22 Sch.8 para.10
s.89, amended: 2009 c.22 s.244, Sch.8 para.11
s.90, amended: 2009 c.22 Sch.8 para.12
s.91, amended: 2009 c.22 Sch.8 para.13
s.91, applied: SI 2009/3297 Reg.11
s.91, referred to: SI 2009/3050 Art.2, Art.3
s.92, amended: 2009 c.22 Sch.8 para.14
Sch.4 para.1, amended: 2009 c.22 Sch.8 para.15
Sch.4 para.1, substituted: 2009 c.22 Sch.8 para.15
Sch.4 para.1A, amended: 2009 c.22 Sch.6 para.12, Sch.8 para.15
Sch.4 para.1B, added: 2009 c.22 Sch.8 para.15
Sch.4 para.1B, amended: 2009 c.22 Sch.8 para.15
Sch.4 para.2, amended: 2009 c.22 Sch.8 para.15
Sch.4 para.3, amended: 2009 c.22 Sch.8 para.15
Sch.4 para.4, amended: 2009 c.22 Sch.8 para.15
Sch.4 para.5, amended: 2009 c.22 Sch.8 para.15
Sch.4 para.6, amended: 2009 c.22 Sch.8 para.15
Sch.4 para.7, amended: 2009 c.22 Sch.8 para.15
Sch.4 para.8, amended: 2009 c.22 Sch.8 para.15
Sch.4 para.9, amended: 2009 c.22 Sch.8 para.15
Sch.4 para.10, amended: 2009 c.22 Sch.8 para.15
Sch.4 para.11, amended: 2009 c.22 Sch.8 para.15
Sch.4 para.12, amended: 2009 c.22 Sch.8 para.15

1992– cont.

14. Local Government Finance Act 1992
see *R. (on the application of Mohammed) v Southwark LBC* [2009] EWHC 311 (Admin), [2009] B.P.I.R. 882 (QBD (Admin)), Geraldine Andrews QC
applied: SI 2009/ 2269 Reg.38
Part I, applied: SI 2009/ 2269 Reg.43, SI 2009/ 2270 Reg.4, Reg.11, SI 2009/ 3193 Sch.1 para.26
s.3, applied: SI 2009/ 2270 Reg.11
s.6, see *Pogonowska v Camden LBC* [2008] EWHC 3212 (Admin), [2009] R.V.R. 138 (QBD (Admin)), Timothy Corner Q.C.; see *R. (on the application of Kinsley) v Barnet Magistrates Court* [2009] EWHC 464 (Admin), [2009] R.V.R. 133 (QBD (Admin)), Judge Raynor Q.C.
s.8, see *R. (on the application of Salmon) v Feltham Magistrates' Court* [2008] EWHC 3507 (Admin), [2009] R.V.R. 160 (QBD (Admin)), Stadlen, J.; see *Watts v Preston City Council* [2009] EWHC 2179 (Admin), [2009] R.A. 334 (QBD (Admin)), Langstaff, J.
s.11, applied: SI 2009/ 3193 Sch.1 para.26
s.11, referred to: SI 2009/ 3193 Sch.1 para.16
s.11A, applied: SI 2009/ 3193 Sch.1 para.16, Sch.1 para.26
s.13A, applied: SI 2009/ 3193 Sch.1 para.16, Sch.1 para.26
s.16, see *R. (on the application of Kinsley) v Barnet Magistrates Court* [2009] EWHC 464 (Admin), [2009] R.V.R. 133 (QBD (Admin)), Judge Raynor Q.C.; see *R. (on the application of Salmon) v Feltham Magistrates' Court* [2008] EWHC 3507 (Admin), [2009] R.V.R. 160 (QBD (Admin)), Stadlen, J.
s.16, applied: SI 2009/ 2269 Reg.21, Reg.43, SI 2009/ 3193 Sch.1 para.26
s.16, referred to: SI 2009/ 2269 Reg.21
s.17, applied: SI 2009/ 2270 Reg.11
s.22, applied: SI 2009/ 2270 Reg.4, Reg.12
s.24, see *Chilton-Merryweather (Listing Officer) v Hunt* [2008] EWCA Civ 1025, [2009] Env. L.R. 16 (CA (Civ Div)), Waller, L.J.
s.24, enabling: SI 2009/ 2270
s.27, applied: SI 2009/ 2269 Reg.17
s.30, applied: SI 2009/ 3193 Sch.1 para.7, Sch.1 para.13
s.32, amended: SI 2009/ 206 Reg.3, SI 2009/ 267 Reg.2
s.32, applied: SI 2009/ 5 Reg.3, Reg.6
s.32, varied: SI 2009/ 206 Reg.3, SI 2009/ 267 Reg.2
s.32, enabling: SI 2009/ 206, SI 2009/ 267
s.33, amended: SI 2009/ 206 Reg.4, SI 2009/ 267 Reg.3
s.33, enabling: SI 2009/ 206, SI 2009/ 267
s.34, applied: SI 2009/ 5 Reg.6
s.35, referred to: SI 2009/ 5 Reg.6
s.36, applied: SI 2009/ 3193 Sch.1 para.9
s.37, applied: SI 2009/ 3193 Reg.9
s.37, varied: SI 2009/ 5 Reg.6
s.40, applied: SI 2009/ 119 Sch.1 para.3, Sch.2 para.3, SI 2009/ 3193 Sch.1 para.8
s.41, applied: SI 2009/ 5 Reg.6, SI 2009/ 3193 Sch.1 para.10
s.41, disapplied: SI 2009/ 467 Reg.12
s.43, applied: SI 2009/ 119 Sch.1 para.3, Sch.2 para.3, SI 2009/ 3193 Reg.9
s.43, varied: SI 2009/ 206 Reg.5, SI 2009/ 267 Reg.4
s.43, enabling: SI 2009/ 206, SI 2009/ 267
s.44, varied: SI 2009/ 206 Reg.6, SI 2009/ 267 Reg.5
s.44, enabling: SI 2009/ 206, SI 2009/ 267

1992– cont.

14. Local Government Finance Act 1992– *cont.*
s.50, disapplied: SI 2009/ 467 Reg.12
s.52B, applied: SI 2009/ 1849
s.52D, applied: SI 2009/ 1849
s.52E, applied: SI 2009/ 1849
s.52F, applied: SI 2009/ 1849
s.52F, enabling: SI 2009/ 1849
s.52X, varied: SI 2009/ 5 Reg.6
s.52Y, varied: SI 2009/ 5 Reg.6
s.80A, added: 2009 asp 12 s.65
s.80A, applied: 2009 asp 12 s.66
s.113, enabling: SI 2009/ 206, SI 2009/ 267, SI 2009/ 2270, SI 2009/ 3193
s.116, enabling: SI 2009/ 3193
Sch.2, see *R. (on the application of Salmon) v Feltham Magistrates' Court* [2008] EWHC 3507 (Admin), [2009] R.V.R. 160 (QBD (Admin)), Stadlen, J.
Sch.2 para.1, enabling: SI 2009/ 3193
Sch.2 para.2, enabling: SI 2009/ 3193
Sch.2 para.4, enabling: SI 2009/ 3193
Sch.2 para.14, enabling: SI 2009/ 3193
Sch.2 para.22, added: 2009 asp 12 s.65
Sch.3 para.1, referred to: SI 2009/ 3193 Sch.1 para.17
Sch.3 para.3, applied: SI 2009/ 2269 Reg.21
Sch.3 para.6, enabling: SI 2009/ 3193
Sch.4 para.6, amended: 2009 c.24 Sch.7 Part 1
Sch.4 para.12, amended: 2009 c.24 Sch.2 para.4
Sch.8 para.6, amended: 2009 c.24 Sch.7 Part 1
Sch.12 Part I para.1, enabling: SSI 2009/50, SSI 2009/ 132
Sch.12 Part I para.2, applied: SSI 2009/50, SSI 2009/ 132
Sch.12 Part II para.9, applied: SSI 2009/50 Art.3
Sch.12 Part II para.9, enabling: SSI 2009/ 50
18. Licensing (Amendment) (Scotland) Act 1992
repealed: SSI 2009/ 248 Sch.2
19. Local Government Act 1992
Part II, applied: 2009 c.20 s.63, s.64, Sch.3 para.1
s.12, repealed: 2009 c.20 s.66, Sch.7 Part 3
s.13, repealed: 2009 c.20 Sch.7 Part 3
s.14, repealed: 2009 c.20 Sch.7 Part 3
s.14A, repealed: 2009 c.20 Sch.7 Part 3
s.14B, repealed: 2009 c.20 Sch.7 Part 3
s.15, amended: 2009 c.20 Sch.3 para.2
s.15, applied: SI 2009/ 529, SI 2009/ 530, SI 2009/ 531
s.15, repealed (in part): 2009 c.20 Sch.7 Part 3
s.15A, repealed: 2009 c.20 Sch.7 Part 3
s.16, repealed: 2009 c.20 Sch.7 Part 3
s.17, referred to: 2009 c.20 s.146
s.17, repealed: 2009 c.20 Sch.7 Part 3
s.17, substituted: 2009 c.20 Sch.3 para.2
s.17, enabling: SI 2009/ 529, SI 2009/ 530, SI 2009/ 531
s.19, added: 2009 c.20 Sch.3 para.2
s.19, referred to: 2009 c.20 s.146
s.19, repealed: 2009 c.20 Sch.7 Part 3
s.25, repealed: 2009 c.20 Sch.7 Part 3
s.26, added: 2009 c.20 Sch.3 para.2
s.26, referred to: 2009 c.20 s.146
s.26, repealed: 2009 c.20 Sch.7 Part 3
s.27, repealed (in part): 2009 c.20 Sch.7 Part 3
s.28, amended: 2009 c.20 Sch.7 Part 3
s.28, repealed (in part): 2009 c.20 Sch.7 Part 3
Sch.2 para.1, repealed: 2009 c.20 s.66, Sch.7 Part 3
Sch.2 para.2, repealed: 2009 c.20 s.66, Sch.7 Part 3
Sch.2 para.3, repealed: 2009 c.20 s.66, Sch.7 Part 3
Sch.2 para.4, repealed: 2009 c.20 s.66, Sch.7 Part 3

19. Local Government Act 1992–*cont.*
Sch.2 para.5, repealed: 2009 c.20 s.66, Sch.7 Part 3
Sch.2 para.6, repealed: 2009 c.20 s.66, Sch.7 Part 3
Sch.2 para.7, repealed: 2009 c.20 s.66, Sch.7 Part 3
Sch.2 para.8, repealed: 2009 c.20 s.66, Sch.7 Part 3
Sch.2 para.9, repealed: 2009 c.20 s.66, Sch.7 Part 3
Sch.2 para.10, repealed: 2009 c.20 s.66, Sch.7 Part 3
Sch.2 para.11, repealed: 2009 c.20 s.66, Sch.7 Part 3
Sch.2 para.12, repealed: 2009 c.20 s.66, Sch.7 Part 3

34. Sexual Offences (Amendment) Act 1992
s.2, varied: SI 2009/1059 Sch.1 para.32
s.4, varied: SI 2009/1059 Sch.1 para.32
s.6, varied: SI 2009/1059 Sch.1 para.32

35. Timeshare Act 1992
referred to: SI 2009/669 Sch.1 Part 1

36. Sea Fisheries (Wildlife Conservation) Act 1992
s.1, amended: 2009 c.23 s.11, Sch.22 Part 4

37. Further and Higher Education (Scotland) Act 1992
s.12, amended: SI 2009/1941 Sch.1 para.132
s.18, amended: SSI 2009/28 Art.2
s.36, applied: 2009 c.4 s.71
s.45, enabling: SSI 2009/194
s.56, applied: 2009 c.4 s.71
s.60, enabling: SSI 2009/194

40. Friendly Societies Act 1992
applied: 2009 c.4 s.764
s.66, amended: SI 2009/1941 Sch.1 para.133
s.75, amended: SI 2009/1941 Sch.1 para.133
s.86, amended: SI 2009/1941 Sch.1 para.133
s.91, amended: SI 2009/1941 Sch.1 para.133
s.106, amended: SI 2009/1941 Sch.1 para.133
s.116, referred to: SI 2009/1085 Reg.13
Sch.10 Part I para.2, amended: SI 2009/1941 Sch.1 para.133
Sch.10 Part IV para.68, amended: SI 2009/1941 Sch.1 para.133

41. Charities Act 1992
s.58, amended: SI 2009/508 Art.3
s.58, enabling: SI 2009/508, SI 2009/1060
s.60, amended: SI 2009/508 Art.4
s.60B, amended: SI 2009/508 Art.5
s.60B, enabling: SI 2009/508
s.61, amended: SI 2009/508 Art.6
s.61, enabling: SI 2009/508
s.64, enabling: SI 2009/1060
s.77, applied: SI 2009/1060
s.77, enabling: SI 2009/508, SI 2009/1060

42. Transport and Works Act 1992
s.1, applied: SI 2009/1300
s.1, enabling: SI 2009/872, SI 2009/1100, SI 2009/1300, SI 2009/2364, SI 2009/2728, SI 2009/3281
s.3, applied: SI 2009/1300
s.3, enabling: SI 2009/1300
s.5, applied: SI 2009/1300
s.5, enabling: SI 2009/872, SI 2009/1100, SI 2009/1300, SI 2009/2364, SI 2009/2728, SI 2009/3281
s.6, applied: SI 2009/1300 Art.18
s.11, applied: SI 2009/1300, SI 2009/2364, SI 2009/2728
s.23, amended: SI 2009/229 Sch.2 para.1
s.53, amended: SI 2009/1307 Sch.1 para.243
Sch.1 para.1, enabling: SI 2009/1100, SI 2009/1300, SI 2009/2364, SI 2009/3281
Sch.1 para.2, enabling: SI 2009/1100, SI 2009/1300, SI 2009/2364
Sch.1 para.3, enabling: SI 2009/1300, SI 2009/2364, SI 2009/2728

42. Transport and Works Act 1992–*cont.*
Sch.1 para.4, enabling: SI 2009/1300, SI 2009/2364, SI 2009/2728
Sch.1 para.5, enabling: SI 2009/2728
Sch.1 para.7, enabling: SI 2009/1100, SI 2009/1300, SI 2009/2364, SI 2009/2728
Sch.1 para.8, enabling: SI 2009/1100, SI 2009/1300, SI 2009/2364, SI 2009/3281
Sch.1 para.9, enabling: SI 2009/1100, SI 2009/1300
Sch.1 para.10, enabling: SI 2009/1300, SI 2009/2364
Sch.1 para.11, enabling: SI 2009/1100, SI 2009/1300, SI 2009/2364, SI 2009/2728
Sch.1 para.12, enabling: SI 2009/872, SI 2009/1100, SI 2009/1300
Sch.1 para.13, enabling: SI 2009/1100, SI 2009/1300
Sch.1 para.15, enabling: SI 2009/872, SI 2009/1100, SI 2009/1300, SI 2009/3281
Sch.1 para.16, enabling: SI 2009/1100, SI 2009/1300, SI 2009/2364, SI 2009/2728
Sch.1 para.17, enabling: SI 2009/872, SI 2009/1100, SI 2009/1300, SI 2009/3281

48. Finance (No.2) Act 1992
varied: SI 2009/317 Sch.1
s.2, applied: SI 2009/1022 Art.2
s.2, enabling: SI 2009/1023
s.4, amended: 2009 c.10 s.112, 2009 c.26 s.98, s.99, Sch.8 Part 9
s.42, see *Revenue and Customs Commissioners v Micro Fusion 2004-1 LLP* [2009] EWHC 1082 (Ch), [2009] S.T.C. 1741 (Ch D), Davis, J.
s.75, amended: SI 2009/56 Sch.1 para.186
s.75, repealed: SI 2009/56 Sch.1 para.186
s.76, repealed: SI 2009/56 Sch.1 para.186
Sch.5 para.2, repealed: 2009 c.10 Sch.1 para.6
Sch.5 para.8, repealed (in part): 2009 c.10 Sch.1 para.6
Sch.5 para.9, repealed (in part): 2009 c.10 Sch.1 para.6
Sch.12, amended: 2009 c.4 Sch.1 para.390
Sch.12 para.2, amended: SI 2009/1890 Art.3
Sch.12 para.2, varied: SI 2009/317 Art.4
Sch.12 para.3, amended: 2009 c.4 Sch.1 para.390, Sch.3 Part 1
Sch.12 para.3, referred to: 2009 c.4 s.464
Sch.16 para.1, repealed: SI 2009/56 Sch.1 para.186
Sch.16 para.2, repealed: SI 2009/56 Sch.1 para.186
Sch.16 para.3, repealed: SI 2009/56 Sch.1 para.186
Sch.16 para.4, repealed: SI 2009/56 Sch.1 para.186
Sch.16 para.5, repealed: SI 2009/56 Sch.1 para.186
Sch.16 para.6, repealed: SI 2009/56 Sch.1 para.186
Sch.16 para.7, repealed: SI 2009/56 Sch.1 para.186
Sch.16 para.8, repealed: SI 2009/56 Sch.1 para.186
Sch.17 para.8, amended: SI 2009/56 Sch.1 para.187
Sch.17 para.8, repealed (in part): SI 2009/56 Sch.1 para.187

52. Trade Union and Labour Relations (Consolidation) Act 1992
disapplied: SI 2009/1743 Art.4
Part IV c.III, applied: SI 2009/2108 Reg.31, Reg.32
s.1, applied: SI 2009/3050 Art.3
s.10, amended: SI 2009/1941 Sch.1 para.134
s.47, see *UNISON v Bakhsh* [2009] I.R.L.R. 418 (EAT), Underhill, J.
s.108B, see *UNISON v Bakhsh* [2009] I.R.L.R. 418 (EAT), Underhill, J.
s.117, amended: SI 2009/1941 Sch.1 para.134
s.131, amended: SI 2009/1941 Sch.1 para.134
s.176, amended: SI 2009/3274 Sch.1

1992– cont.

52. Trade Union and Labour Relations (Consolidation) Act 1992– *cont.*

s.188, see *United States v Nolan* [2009] I.R.L.R. 923 (EAT), Slade, J.

s.189, see *United States v Nolan* [2009] I.R.L.R. 923 (EAT), Slade, J.

s.199, applied: SI 2009/ 771, SI 2009/ 3223

s.199, enabling: SI 2009/ 771

s.200, applied: SI 2009/ 771, SI 2009/ 771 Art.2, SI 2009/ 3223, SI 2009/ 3223 Art.2

s.200, enabling: SI 2009/ 771, SI 2009/ 3223

s.212A, amended: 2009 c.22 Sch.1 para.13

s.237, see *Sehmi v Gate Gourmet London Ltd* [2009] I.R.L.R. 807 (EAT), Underhill, J. (President)

s.237, amended: 2009 c.22 Sch.1 para.14

s.237, disapplied: SI 2009/ 307 Sch.1 para.10

s.238, amended: 2009 c.22 Sch.1 para.15

s.280, applied: SI 2009/ 2133 Reg.42

s.287, applied: SI 2009/ 1743 Art.4

53. Tribunals and Inquiries Act 1992

applied: 2009 c.20 s.76

s.6, amended: 2009 c.3 Sch.4 para.25

s.8, applied: SI 2009/ 546, SSI 2009/ 353

s.9, enabling: SI 2009/ 455, SSI 2009/ 212

s.11, see *Calltel Telecom Ltd v Revenue and Customs Commissioners* [2008] EWHC 2107 (Ch), [2009] Bus. L.R. 513 (Ch D), Briggs, J.; see *Wild (t/a Audrey's Pianos) v Revenue and Customs Commissioners* [2008] EWHC 3401 (Ch), [2009] S.T.C. 566 (Ch D), Lewison, J.

s.11, amended: SI 2009/ 1307 Sch.1 para.245

Sch.1 Part I, amended: SI 2009/ 56 Sch.1 para.188, SI 2009/ 1307 Sch.1 para.246, SI 2009/ 1834 Sch.1 para.4, SI 2009/ 1835 Sch.1 para.10

Sch.1 Part II, amended: SI 2009/ 56 Sch.1 para.188

60. Sea Fish (Conservation) Act 1992

s.5, repealed (in part): 2009 c.23 Sch.22 Part 5

1993

8. Judicial Pensions and Retirement Act 1993

Sch.1 Part II, amended: 2009 c.25 Sch.21 para.31, SI 2009/ 56 Sch.1 para.190, SI 2009/ 1307 Sch.1 para.248, SI 2009/ 1834 Sch.1 para.5

Sch.5, amended: SI 2009/ 56 Sch.1 para.191, SI 2009/ 1307 Sch.1 para.249

Sch.7 para.5, amended: SI 2009/ 1307 Sch.1 para.250

9. Prisoners and Criminal Proceedings (Scotland) Act 1993

s.1, applied: SI 2009/ 1887 Sch.1

s.1AA, applied: SI 2009/ 1887 Sch.1

s.12, referred to: SI 2009/ 1887 Sch.2

s.16, see *HM Advocate v D* [2009] HCJAC 51, 2009 J.C. 215 (HCJ), Lord Nimmo Smith

s.27, varied: 2009 c.25 Sch.22 para.35

10. Charities Act 1993

s.2A, amended: SI 2009/ 1834 Sch.1 para.7, Sch.1 para.8

s.2A, repealed (in part): SI 2009/ 1834 Sch.1 para.8

s.2B, amended: SI 2009/ 1834 Sch.1 para.7, Sch.1 para.9

s.2B, repealed (in part): SI 2009/ 1834 Sch.1 para.9

s.2C, amended: SI 2009/ 1834 Sch.1 para.7, Sch.1 para.10

s.2C, repealed (in part): SI 2009/ 1834 Sch.1 para.10

s.2D, amended: SI 2009/ 1834 Sch.1 para.7, Sch.1 para.11

s.2D, applied: SI 2009/ 1976 r.31

1993– cont.

10. Charities Act 1993– *cont.*

s.6, repealed (in part): SI 2009/ 1941 Sch.1 para.139

s.7, amended: SI 2009/ 1941 Sch.1 para.139

s.31, amended: SI 2009/ 3348 Art.4

s.40, amended: SI 2009/ 508 Art.8

s.40, enabling: SI 2009/ 508

s.42, amended: SI 2009/ 508 Art.9

s.42, enabling: SI 2009/ 508

s.43, amended: SI 2009/ 508 Art.10

s.43, enabling: SI 2009/ 508

s.45, amended: SI 2009/ 508 Art.11

s.45, enabling: SI 2009/ 508

s.63, amended: SI 2009/ 1941 Sch.1 para.139

s.64, amended: SI 2009/ 1941 Sch.1 para.139

s.65, applied: SI 2009/ 1941 Art.6

s.65, repealed: SI 2009/ 1941 Sch.1 para.139

s.69A, applied: 2009 c.22 Sch.3 para.19, Sch.4 para.9, SI 2009/ 649 Reg.5

s.69D, amended: SI 2009/ 1941 Sch.1 para.139

s.72, amended: SI 2009/ 1941 Sch.1 para.139

s.86, applied: SI 2009/ 508

s.86, enabling: SI 2009/ 508

s.97, amended: SI 2009/ 1834 Sch.1 para.12, SI 2009/ 1941 Sch.1 para.139

s.97, enabling: SI 2009/ 508

Sch.1 D, applied: SI 2009/ 1976 r.26

Sch.1 B para.1, applied: SI 2009/ 1834 Art.3

Sch.1 B para.1, repealed: SI 2009/ 1834 Sch.1 para.13

Sch.1 B para.2, repealed: SI 2009/ 1834 Sch.1 para.13

Sch.1 B para.3, repealed: SI 2009/ 1834 Sch.1 para.13

Sch.1 B para.4, repealed: SI 2009/ 1834 Sch.1 para.13

Sch.1 B para.5, repealed: SI 2009/ 1834 Sch.1 para.13

Sch.1 B para.6, repealed: SI 2009/ 1834 Sch.1 para.13

Sch.1 B para.7, repealed: SI 2009/ 1834 Sch.1 para.13

Sch.1 B para.8, repealed: SI 2009/ 1834 Sch.1 para.13

Sch.1 B para.9, repealed: SI 2009/ 1834 Sch.1 para.13

Sch.1 B para.10, repealed: SI 2009/ 1834 Sch.1 para.13

Sch.1 C para.1, amended: SI 2009/ 1834 Sch.1 para.14

Sch.1 C para.2, amended: SI 2009/ 1834 Sch.1 para.14

Sch.1 C para.3, amended: SI 2009/ 1834 Sch.1 para.14

Sch.1 C para.4, amended: SI 2009/ 1834 Sch.1 para.14

Sch.1 C para.5, amended: SI 2009/ 1834 Sch.1 para.14, SI 2009/ 1941 Sch.1 para.139, SI 2009/ 3348 Art.4

Sch.1 C para.6, amended: SI 2009/ 1834 Sch.1 para.14

Sch.1 C para.7, amended: SI 2009/ 1834 Sch.1 para.14

Sch.1 D para.1, amended: SI 2009/ 1834 Sch.1 para.15

Sch.1 D para.2, amended: SI 2009/ 1834 Sch.1 para.15

Sch.1 D para.3, amended: SI 2009/ 1834 Sch.1 para.15

Sch.1 D para.4, amended: SI 2009/ 1834 Sch.1 para.15

Sch.1 D para.5, amended: SI 2009/ 1834 Sch.1 para.15

Sch.1 D para.6, amended: SI 2009/ 1834 Sch.1 para.15

Sch.1 D para.6, repealed (in part): SI 2009/ 1834 Sch.1 para.15

10. Charities Act 1993– *cont.*
Sch.1D para.7, amended: SI 2009/1834 Sch.1 para.15
Sch.2, amended: 2009 c.22 Sch.12 para.8, Sch.16 Part 4
Sch.5B para.4, amended: SI 2009/1941 Sch.1 para.139

11. Clean Air Act 1993
s.20, applied: SI 2009/2302 Art.2
s.20, disapplied: SI 2009/449 Art.2
s.20, referred to: SI 2009/2190 Art.2, SI 2009/3224 Art.2, SSI 2009/214 Art.2
s.20, enabling: SI 2009/2191, SI 2009/3225
s.21, enabling: SI 2009/449, SI 2009/2190, SI 2009/2302, SI 2009/3224, SSI 2009/214
s.41A, amended: SI 2009/1799 Sch.2 para.3
s.63, enabling: SI 2009/3225

12. Radioactive Substances Act 1993
s.10, applied: SI 2009/2902 Reg.13
s.13, applied: SI 2009/2902 Reg.13
s.30, amended: SSI 2009/319 Sch.2 para.5
s.47, amended: 2009 c.23 Sch.14 para.17, Sch.22 Part 4
Sch.3 Part I para.3, repealed: 2009 c.23 Sch.22 Part 4
Sch.3 Part I para.10A, added: 2009 c.23 Sch.14 para.18

21. Osteopaths Act 1993
applied: SI 2009/2722 Reg.3
s.1, enabling: SI 2009/263
s.3, enabling: SI 2009/1993
s.6, enabling: SI 2009/1993
s.20, amended: 2009 c.26 s.81
s.24, applied: SI 2009/263 Art.7, SI 2009/468 Sch.1
s.35, applied: SI 2009/468, SI 2009/1993
s.35, enabling: SI 2009/468, SI 2009/1993
s.36, applied: SI 2009/1993
Sch.1 Part I para.1A, applied: SI 2009/263 Art.6
Sch.1 Part I para.1B, enabling: SI 2009/263
Sch.1 Part II para.16, enabling: SI 2009/468
Sch.1 Part II para.17, applied: SI 2009/468 Sch.1
Sch.1 Part II para.17, enabling: SI 2009/468
Sch.1 Part II para.25, enabling: SI 2009/468
Sch.1 Part II para.30, enabling: SI 2009/468
Sch.1 Part II para.30A, added: SI 2009/1182 Sch.5 para.1
Sch.1 Part II para.34, enabling: SI 2009/468
Sch.1 Part II para.34A, added: SI 2009/1182 Sch.5 para.1
Sch.1 Part II para.38, enabling: SI 2009/468
Sch.1 Part II para.38A, added: SI 2009/1182 Sch.5 para.1

23. Asylum and Immigration Appeals Act 1993
s.1, see *R. (on the application of PE (Cameroon)) v Secretary of State for the Home Department* [2009] UKSC 7, [2009] 3 W.L.R. 1253 (SC), Lord Hope (Deputy President)

25. Local Government (Overseas Assistance) Act 1993
s.1, amended: 2009 c.20 Sch.6 para.83

28. Leasehold Reform, Housing and Urban Development Act 1993
see *Elizabeth Court (Bournemouth) Ltd v Revenue and Customs Commissioners* [2008] EWHC 2828 (Ch), [2009] S.T.C. 682 (Ch D), Sir Andrew Morritt (Chancellor); see *Howard de Walden Estates Ltd v Aggio* [2008] UKHL 44, [2009] 1 A.C. 39 (HL), Lord Hoffmann

28. Leasehold Reform, Housing and Urban Development Act 1993– *cont.*
s.4A, see *Elizabeth Court (Bournemouth) Ltd v Revenue and Customs Commissioners* [2008] EWHC 2828 (Ch), [2009] S.T.C. 682 (Ch D), Sir Andrew Morritt (Chancellor)
s.4A, amended: SI 2009/1941 Sch.1 para.140
s.4A, applied: SI 2009/1085 Reg.4
s.4B, see *Elizabeth Court (Bournemouth) Ltd v Revenue and Customs Commissioners* [2008] EWHC 2828 (Ch), [2009] S.T.C. 682 (Ch D), Sir Andrew Morritt (Chancellor)
s.4C, see *Elizabeth Court (Bournemouth) Ltd v Revenue and Customs Commissioners* [2008] EWHC 2828 (Ch), [2009] S.T.C. 682 (Ch D), Sir Andrew Morritt (Chancellor)
s.4C, amended: SI 2009/1941 Sch.1 para.140
s.5, see *Howard de Walden Estates Ltd v Aggio* [2008] UKHL 44, [2009] 1 A.C. 39 (HL), Lord Hoffmann
s.5, amended: SI 2009/1941 Sch.1 para.140
s.12A, amended: SI 2009/1941 Sch.1 para.140
s.24, see *Goldeagle Properties Ltd v Thornbury Court Ltd* [2008] EWCA Civ 864, [2009] H.L.R. 13 (CA (Civ Div)), Tuckey, L.J.
s.29, amended: SI 2009/1941 Sch.1 para.140
s.39, see *Howard de Walden Estates Ltd v Aggio* [2008] UKHL 44, [2009] 1 A.C. 39 (HL), Lord Hoffmann
s.42, see *Ackerman v Lay* [2008] EWCA Civ 1428, [2009] 1 W.L.R. 1556 (CA (Civ Div)), Tuckey, L.J.
s.56, see *Nailrile Ltd v Earl Cadogan* [2009] R.V.R. 95 (Lands Tr), George Bartlett Q.C. (President)
s.57, see *Howard de Walden Estates Ltd v Aggio* [2008] UKHL 44, [2009] 1 A.C. 39 (HL), Lord Hoffmann
s.61A, see *Ackerman v Lay* [2008] EWCA Civ 1428, [2009] 1 W.L.R. 1556 (CA (Civ Div)), Tuckey, L.J.
s.87, disapplied: SI 2009/512 Art.4
s.87, enabling: SI 2009/512
s.91, see *Howard de Walden Estates Ltd v Aggio* [2008] UKHL 44, [2009] 1 A.C. 39 (HL), Lord Hoffmann
s.100, enabling: SI 2009/512
s.101, see *Howard de Walden Estates Ltd v Aggio* [2008] UKHL 44, [2009] 1 A.C. 39 (HL), Lord Hoffmann
Sch.6, see *Pitts v Earl Cadogan* [2008] UKHL 71, [2009] 2 W.L.R. 12 (HL), Lord Hoffmann
Sch.6 para.3, see *Pitts v Earl Cadogan* [2008] UKHL 71, [2009] 2 W.L.R. 12 (HL), Lord Hoffmann
Sch.6 para.4, see *Pitts v Earl Cadogan* [2008] UKHL 71, [2009] 2 W.L.R. 12 (HL), Lord Hoffmann
Sch.12 para.5, see *Ackerman v Lay* [2008] EWCA Civ 1428, [2009] 1 W.L.R. 1556 (CA (Civ Div)), Tuckey, L.J.
Sch.13, see *Nailrile Ltd v Earl Cadogan* [2009] R.V.R. 95 (Lands Tr), George Bartlett Q.C. (President); see *Pitts v Earl Cadogan* [2008] UKHL 71, [2009] 2 W.L.R. 12 (HL), Lord Hoffmann
Sch.13 para.3, see *Pitts v Earl Cadogan* [2008] UKHL 71, [2009] 2 W.L.R. 12 (HL), Lord Hoffmann
Sch.13 para.4, see *Pitts v Earl Cadogan* [2008] UKHL 71, [2009] 2 W.L.R. 12 (HL), Lord Hoffmann

1993– cont.

34. Finance Act 1993
s.69, repealed: 2009 c.4 Sch.3 Part 1
s.92, amended: 2009 c.10 Sch.18 para.2
s.92B, amended: 2009 c.10 Sch.18 para.3
s.92B, applied: 2009 c.10 Sch.18 para.8, Sch.18 para.9
s.92C, amended: 2009 c.10 Sch.18 para.4
s.92C, applied: 2009 c.10 Sch.18 para.8, Sch.18 para.9
s.92D, applied: 2009 c.10 Sch.18 para.9
s.92D, substituted: 2009 c.10 Sch.18 para.5
s.92DA, disapplied: 2009 c.10 Sch.18 para.8
s.92DB, referred to: 2009 c.10 Sch.18 para.12
s.92DC, applied: 2009 c.10 Sch.18 para.10
s.92DC, disapplied: 2009 c.10 Sch.18 para.10
s.92DD, applied: 2009 c.10 Sch.18 para.11
s.92DD, referred to: 2009 c.10 Sch.18 para.12
s.92DD, varied: 2009 c.10 Sch.18 para.11
s.92DE, applied: 2009 c.10 Sch.18 para.12
s.92E, amended: 2009 c.10 Sch.18 para.6
s.107, repealed (in part): 2009 c.10 Sch.1 para.6
s.108, repealed: 2009 c.4 Sch.3 Part 1
s.109, repealed (in part): 2009 c.4 Sch.3 Part 1
s.110, repealed: 2009 c.4 Sch.3 Part 1
s.123, repealed: 2009 c.4 Sch.3 Part 1
s.171, amended: 2009 c.10 Sch.19 para.11
s.182, enabling: SI 2009/2889
s.185, amended: 2009 c.10 Sch.45 para.3
s.187, amended: SI 2009/56 Sch.1 para.193
s.187, applied: SI 2009/275 Art.3, SI 2009/3054 Art.5
s.187, repealed (in part): SI 2009/3054 Sch.1 para.5
Sch.6 para.11, repealed: 2009 c.4 Sch.3 Part 1
Sch.20B para.1, substituted: 2009 c.10 Sch.45 para.3
Sch.20B para.2, substituted: 2009 c.10 Sch.45 para.3
Sch.20B para.3, substituted: 2009 c.10 Sch.45 para.3
Sch.20B para.4, substituted: 2009 c.10 Sch.45 para.3
Sch.20B para.5, substituted: 2009 c.10 Sch.45 para.3
Sch.20B para.6, substituted: 2009 c.10 Sch.45 para.3
Sch.20B para.7, substituted: 2009 c.10 Sch.45 para.3
Sch.20B para.8, substituted: 2009 c.10 Sch.45 para.3
Sch.20B para.9, substituted: 2009 c.10 Sch.45 para.3
Sch.20B para.10, substituted: 2009 c.10 Sch.45 para.3
Sch.20B para.11, amended: SI 2009/56 Sch.1 para.194
Sch.20B para.11, repealed (in part): SI 2009/56 Sch.1 para.194
Sch.20B para.11, substituted: 2009 c.10 Sch.45 para.3
Sch.20B para.12, amended: SI 2009/56 Sch.1 para.194
Sch.20B para.12, substituted: 2009 c.10 Sch.45 para.3
Sch.21 Part I para.1, repealed: SI 2009/3054 Sch.1 para.5
Sch.21 Part I para.2, repealed: SI 2009/3054 Sch.1 para.5
Sch.21 Part I para.3, amended: SI 2009/56 Sch.1 para.195
Sch.21 Part I para.3, applied: SI 2009/275 Art.3

1993– cont.

34. Finance Act 1993– cont.
Sch.21 Part I para.3, repealed: SI 2009/3054 Sch.1 para.5
Sch.21 Part I para.4, repealed: SI 2009/3054 Sch.1 para.5
Sch.21 Part I para.5, repealed: SI 2009/3054 Sch.1 para.5
Sch.21 Part I para.6, amended: SI 2009/56 Sch.1 para.195
Sch.21 Part I para.6, applied: SI 2009/275 Art.3
Sch.21 Part I para.6, repealed: SI 2009/3054 Sch.1 para.5
Sch.21 Part I para.7, repealed: SI 2009/3054 Sch.1 para.5
Sch.21 Part I para.8, repealed: SI 2009/3054 Sch.1 para.5
Sch.21 Part I para.9, repealed: SI 2009/3054 Sch.1 para.5
Sch.21 Part I para.10, repealed: SI 2009/3054 Sch.1 para.5
Sch.21 Part I para.11, repealed: SI 2009/3054 Sch.1 para.5
Sch.21 Part I para.12, repealed: SI 2009/3054 Sch.1 para.5
Sch.21 Part II para.13, repealed: SI 2009/3054 Sch.1 para.5
Sch.21 Part II para.14, repealed: SI 2009/3054 Sch.1 para.5

36. Criminal Justice Act 1993
Part V, see *R. (on the application of Uberoi) v Westminster Magistrates' Court* [2008] EWHC 3191 (Admin), [2009] 1 W.L.R. 1905 (DC), May, L.J.
s.52, see *R. (on the application of Uberoi) v Westminster Magistrates' Court* [2008] EWHC 3191 (Admin), [2009] 1 W.L.R. 1905 (DC), May, L.J.
s.61, see *R. (on the application of Uberoi) v Westminster Magistrates' Court* [2008] EWHC 3191 (Admin), [2009] 1 W.L.R. 1905 (DC), May, L.J.
s.61A, added: SI 2009/1941 Sch.1 para.141

38. Welsh Language Act 1993
see *Practice Direction (UT: First-tier and Upper Tribunals: Welsh Language)* [2009] 1 W.L.R. 331 (UT), Carnwath, L.J. (SP)
s.18, applied: SI 2009/2058
s.25, enabling: SI 2009/2058
s.26, applied: SI 2009/2165, SI 2009/2806
s.26, enabling: SI 2009/781
s.27, enabling: SI 2009/781

39. National Lottery etc Act 1993
s.27, amended: SI 2009/1941 Sch.1 para.142

42. Cardiff Bay Barrage Act 1993
Sch.2 para.13, amended: SI 2009/1307 Sch.1 para.252
Sch.5 para.6, amended: SI 2009/1307 Sch.1 para.253
Sch.7 para.16, amended: SI 2009/1307 Sch.1 para.254
Sch.7 para.27, amended: SI 2009/1307 Sch.1 para.254

43. Railways Act 1993
Part I, applied: SI 2009/1300 Sch.14 para.19, SI 2009/3281 Art.12
s.6, referred to: SI 2009/2726 Art.3
s.7, enabling: SI 2009/2726, SI 2009/3336
s.16A, disapplied: SI 2009/2726 Art.16
s.16A, referred to: SI 2009/2726 Art.4
s.16A, enabling: SI 2009/2726

43. Railways Act 1993–*cont.*
s.16B, enabling: SI 2009/2726, SI 2009/3336
s.17, referred to: SI 2009/2726 Art.5
s.18, referred to: SI 2009/2726 Art.5
s.20, enabling: SI 2009/2726, SI 2009/3336
s.22A, referred to: SI 2009/2726 Art.5
s.23, applied: SI 2009/2726 Art.6, SI 2009/3335 Art.3
s.23, enabling: SI 2009/2726
s.24, enabling: SI 2009/2726, SI 2009/3335
s.25, amended: 2009 c.20 Sch.6 para.85, SI 2009/1941 Sch.1 para.143
s.37, disapplied: SI 2009/2726 Art.12
s.39, disapplied: SI 2009/2726 Art.13
s.41, disapplied: SI 2009/2726 Art.14
s.59, amended: SI 2009/1941 Sch.1 para.143
s.65, amended: SI 2009/1941 Sch.1 para.143
s.114, amended: SI 2009/1941 Sch.1 para.143
s.143, enabling: SI 2009/3336
s.145, amended: SI 2009/1122 Sch.1 para.1
s.149, amended: 2009 c.20 Sch.6 para.86
s.151, amended: SI 2009/1941 Sch.1 para.143
s.151, enabling: SI 2009/2726, SI 2009/3336
Sch.5, applied: SI 2009/2726 Art.15
Sch.6 Part I para.1, amended: SI 2009/1941 Sch.1 para.143
Sch.6 Part I para.4, amended: SI 2009/1941 Sch.1 para.143
Sch.6 Part I para.7, amended: SI 2009/1941 Sch.1 para.143
Sch.6 Part I para.8, amended: SI 2009/1941 Sch.1 para.143
Sch.6 Part I para.9, amended: SI 2009/1941 Sch.1 para.143
Sch.6 Part I para.10, amended: SI 2009/1941 Sch.1 para.143

45. Scottish Land Court Act 1993
Sch.1 para.15, disapplied: SSI 2009/376 Reg.10

46. Health Service Commissioners Act 1993
applied: SI 2009/309 Reg.8, Reg.14, Reg.18, Reg.20, Reg.21, Sch.1 para.8
s.2, enabling: SI 2009/883
s.2B, amended: 2009 c.21 s.12
s.3, see *R. (on the application of Attwood) v Health Service Commissioner* [2008] EWHC 2315 (Admin), [2009] 1 All E.R. 415 (QBD (Admin)), Burnett, J.
s.3, amended: 2009 c.21 s.12
s.3, applied: SI 2009/462 Sch.4 para.17
s.7, amended: 2009 c.21 s.12
s.14, amended: 2009 c.21 s.12
s.18, amended: 2009 c.21 Sch.5 para.13
s.19, amended: 2009 c.21 s.12
Sch.2 para.3, repealed: 2009 c.21 Sch.6

48. Pension Schemes Act 1993
applied: SI 2009/497 Art.6
varied: SI 2009/317 Sch.1
Part III, applied: SI 2009/608 Art.2, SI 2009/2108 Reg.9
Part III c.I, applied: SI 2009/2108 Reg.5
Part IV c.IV, applied: 2009 asp 1 Sch.1 para.91
s.1, applied: 2009 c.18 s.20, SI 2009/1907 Reg.2
s.1, enabling: SI 2009/1907
s.8, applied: 2009 asp 1 Sch.1 para.77
s.11, enabling: SI 2009/615
s.12C, enabling: SI 2009/615, SI 2009/2930
s.14, applied: 2009 asp 1 Sch.1 para.105

48. Pension Schemes Act 1993–*cont.*
s.15, applied: 2009 asp 1 Sch.1 para.105, SI 2009/497 Art.5
s.15, varied: SI 2009/497 Art.5
s.15A, applied: 2009 asp 1 Sch.1 para.105
s.16, applied: 2009 asp 1 Sch.1 para.105
s.17, applied: SI 2009/497 Art.5
s.19, see *Easterly Ltd v Headway Plc* [2009] EWCA Civ 793, [2009] Pens. L.R. 279 (CA (Civ Div)), Lord Neuberger of Abbotsbury
s.20, enabling: SI 2009/615
s.21, enabling: SI 2009/2930
s.24B, enabling: SI 2009/846
s.24C, enabling: SI 2009/846
s.28, enabling: SI 2009/2930
s.32A, enabling: SI 2009/2930
s.45, enabling: SI 2009/615
s.46, see *Head v Social Security Commissioner* [2009] EWHC 950 (Admin), [2009] Pens. L.R. 207 (QBD (Admin)), Nicol, J.; see *Wilkinson v Secretary of State for Work and Pensions* [2009] EWCA Civ 1111, [2009] Pens. L.R. 369 (CA (Civ Div)), Longmore, L.J.
s.47, see *Easterly Ltd v Headway Plc* [2009] EWCA Civ 793, [2009] Pens. L.R. 279 (CA (Civ Div)), Lord Neuberger of Abbotsbury
s.55, referred to: 2009 asp 1 Sch.1 para.72
s.71, enabling: SI 2009/2930
s.81, see *Easterly Ltd v Headway Plc* [2009] EWCA Civ 793, [2009] Pens. L.R. 279 (CA (Civ Div)), Lord Neuberger of Abbotsbury
s.93A, applied: 2009 asp 1 Sch.1 para.75
s.93A, referred to: 2009 asp 1 Sch.1 para.75
s.95, applied: 2009 asp 1 Sch.1 para.75
s.96, applied: 2009 asp 1 Sch.1 para.77
s.101C, enabling: SI 2009/615, SI 2009/2930
s.101D, enabling: SI 2009/615
s.101E, enabling: SI 2009/615
s.101F, enabling: SI 2009/615
s.109, applied: SI 2009/477, SI 2009/477 Art.2
s.109, enabling: SI 2009/477
s.113, enabling: SI 2009/1906
s.127, amended: SI 2009/1941 Sch.1 para.144
s.146, see *R. (on the application of Parish) v Pensions Ombudsman* [2009] EWHC 32 (Admin), [2009] Pens. L.R. 91 (QBD (Admin)), Keith, J.
s.149, repealed (in part): SI 2009/1941 Sch.1 para.144
s.163, repealed (in part): 2009 c.18 s.4, Sch.1
s.168, enabling: SI 2009/615
s.181, applied: 2009 c.18 s.20
s.181, enabling: SI 2009/615, SI 2009/846, SI 2009/2930
s.182, enabling: SI 2009/615, SI 2009/846, SI 2009/1907, SI 2009/2930
s.183, enabling: SI 2009/615, SI 2009/846, SI 2009/2930
s.185, applied: SI 2009/846, SI 2009/1906, SI 2009/1907, SI 2009/2930
s.186, applied: SI 2009/846
Sch.3 para.2, applied: SI 2009/3267 Art.2
Sch.3 para.2, enabling: SI 2009/3267
Sch.4 para.1, varied: 2009 c.1 s.103, s.145
Sch.4 para.2, varied: 2009 c.1 s.103, s.145
Sch.4 para.3, varied: 2009 c.1 s.103, s.145
Sch.4 para.4, varied: 2009 c.1 s.103, s.145

49. Pension Schemes (Northern Ireland) Act 1993
varied: SI 2009/317 Sch.1

1993– cont.

49. Pension Schemes (Northern Ireland) Act 1993– *cont.*
s.123, amended: SI 2009/1941 Sch.1 para.145
s.145, repealed (in part): SI 2009/1941 Sch.1 para.145
Sch.3 para.4, amended: SI 2009/1941 Sch.1 para.145
Sch.7 para.20, repealed: SI 2009/1941 Sch.2

50. Statute Law (Repeals) Act 1993
Sch.2 Part I para.8, repealed: 2009 c.23 Sch.22 Part 5

1994

9. Finance Act 1994
Part I c.IV, referred to: 2009 c.10 Sch.5 para.8
Part IV c.V, applied: 2009 c.4 s.905
s.7, substituted: SI 2009/56 Sch.1 para.197
s.8, applied: 2009 c.4 s.1303
s.9, applied: 2009 c.4 s.1303, 2009 c.10 s.108
s.10, applied: 2009 c.4 s.1303
s.10A, applied: 2009 c.4 s.1303
s.11, applied: 2009 c.4 s.1303
s.13A, added: SI 2009/56 Sch.1 para.198
s.14, amended: SI 2009/56 Sch.1 para.199
s.14, repealed (in part): SI 2009/56 Sch.1 para.199
s.14A, added: SI 2009/56 Sch.1 para.200
s.15, amended: SI 2009/56 Sch.1 para.201
s.15A, added: SI 2009/56 Sch.1 para.202
s.15B, added: SI 2009/56 Sch.1 para.202
s.15C, added: SI 2009/56 Sch.1 para.202
s.15D, added: SI 2009/56 Sch.1 para.202
s.15E, added: SI 2009/56 Sch.1 para.202
s.15F, added: SI 2009/56 Sch.1 para.202
s.16, amended: SI 2009/56 Sch.1 para.203
s.17, amended: SI 2009/56 Sch.1 para.204
s.30, amended: 2009 c.10 s.17, Sch.5 para.2, SI 2009/193 Art.2
s.30, repealed (in part): 2009 c.10 Sch.5 para.2
s.30, enabling: SI 2009/193
s.38, enabling: SI 2009/2045
s.39, applied: 2009 c.10 Sch.5 para.8
s.39, substituted: 2009 c.10 Sch.5 para.3
s.42, amended: 2009 c.10 Sch.5 para.4
s.42, enabling: SI 2009/2045
s.51A, enabling: SI 2009/219
s.59, amended: SI 2009/56 Sch.1 para.205
s.59, repealed (in part): SI 2009/56 Sch.1 para.205
s.59A, added: SI 2009/56 Sch.1 para.206
s.59B, added: SI 2009/56 Sch.1 para.206
s.59C, added: SI 2009/56 Sch.1 para.206
s.59D, added: SI 2009/56 Sch.1 para.206
s.59E, added: SI 2009/56 Sch.1 para.206
s.59F, added: SI 2009/56 Sch.1 para.206
s.59G, added: SI 2009/56 Sch.1 para.206
s.60, amended: SI 2009/56 Sch.1 para.207
s.60, applied: SI 2009/56 Sch.3 para.9
s.60, repealed (in part): SI 2009/56 Sch.1 para.207
s.63, amended: SI 2009/1890 Art.4
s.72, see *Homeserve Membership Ltd (formerly Homeserve GB Ltd) v Revenue and Customs Commissioners* [2009] EWHC 1311 (Ch), [2009] S.T.C. 2366 (Ch D), Blackburne, J.
s.73, amended: SI 2009/56 Sch.1 para.208
s.77, repealed (in part): 2009 c.10 Sch.1 para.6
s.113, repealed (in part): 2009 c.4 Sch.3 Part 1, SI 2009/23 Art.4
s.134, repealed: 2009 c.10 Sch.16 para.5

1994– cont.

9. Finance Act 1994– *cont.*
s.141, repealed: 2009 c.4 Sch.3 Part 1
s.144, repealed: 2009 c.4 Sch.3 Part 1
s.145, repealed: 2009 c.4 Sch.3 Part 1
s.151, see *Prudential Plc v Revenue and Customs Commissioners* [2009] EWCA Civ 622, [2009] S.T.C. 2459 (CA (Civ Div)), Mummery, L.J.
s.165, see *Bayfine UK Products v Revenue and Customs Commissioners* [2009] S.T.C. (S.C.D.) 43 (Sp Comm), John F Avery Jones
s.166, see *Bayfine UK Products v Revenue and Customs Commissioners* [2009] S.T.C. (S.C.D.) 43 (Sp Comm), John F Avery Jones
s.167, see *Bayfine UK Products v Revenue and Customs Commissioners* [2009] S.T.C. (S.C.D.) 43 (Sp Comm), John F Avery Jones
s.215, repealed: 2009 c.4 Sch.3 Part 1
s.219, amended: 2009 c.4 Sch.1 para.392, 2009 c.10 Sch.14 para.18
s.219, referred to: 2009 c.4 s.1285
s.219, repealed (in part): 2009 c.10 Sch.14 para.18
s.220, amended: 2009 c.4 Sch.1 para.393
s.225, amended: 2009 c.4 Sch.1 para.394
s.226, amended: 2009 c.4 Sch.1 para.395
s.229, amended: 2009 c.4 Sch.1 para.396
s.229, enabling: SI 2009/2889
s.249, repealed: 2009 c.4 Sch.3 Part 1
s.250, repealed: 2009 c.4 Sch.3 Part 1
Sch.5A Part 1, added: 2009 c.10 Sch.5 para.5
Sch.5A Part 2, added: 2009 c.10 Sch.5 para.5
Sch.5A Part 3, added: 2009 c.10 Sch.5 para.5
Sch.6 para.1, enabling: SI 2009/2051
Sch.6 para.6, amended: SI 2009/56 Sch.1 para.209
Sch.6 para.8, amended: SI 2009/56 Sch.1 para.209
Sch.6 para.8, applied: SI 2009/56 Sch.3 para.9
Sch.6 para.10, applied: SI 2009/56 Sch.3 para.9
Sch.6A Part II para.2, amended: SI 2009/219 Art.2
Sch.7 Part I para.1, amended: 2009 c.10 Sch.50 para.1
Sch.7 Part I para.2, repealed: SI 2009/3054 Sch.1 para.6
Sch.7 Part I para.3, repealed: SI 2009/3054 Sch.1 para.6
Sch.7 Part II para.4, repealed: SI 2009/3054 Sch.1 para.6
Sch.7 Part III para.8, amended: 2009 c.10 Sch.51 para.2
Sch.7 Part IV para.12, applied: 2009 c.4 s.1303
Sch.7 Part IV para.13, applied: 2009 c.4 s.1303
Sch.7 Part IV para.14, amended: SI 2009/571 Sch.1 para.21
Sch.7 Part IV para.14, applied: 2009 c.4 s.1303
Sch.7 Part IV para.15, amended: SI 2009/571 Sch.1 para.21
Sch.7 Part IV para.15, applied: 2009 c.4 s.1303, 2009 c.10 s.108
Sch.7 Part IV para.16, applied: 2009 c.4 s.1303
Sch.7 Part IV para.17, amended: SI 2009/571 Sch.1 para.21
Sch.7 Part IV para.17, applied: 2009 c.4 s.1303, SI 2009/3054 Art.6
Sch.7 Part IV para.17, repealed (in part): SI 2009/3054 Sch.1 para.6
Sch.7 Part IV para.18, applied: 2009 c.4 s.1303
Sch.7 Part IV para.18A, applied: 2009 c.4 s.1303
Sch.7 Part IV para.19, applied: 2009 c.4 s.1303
Sch.7 Part V para.21, applied: 2009 c.4 s.1303
Sch.7 Part V para.22, amended: 2009 c.10 Sch.51 para.3

1994– cont.

9. Finance Act 1994– *cont.*
Sch.7 Part VI para.26, amended: 2009 c.10 Sch.51 para.4
Sch.14 para.5, repealed: 2009 c.4 Sch.3 Part 1
Sch.16 Part IV para.10, repealed: SI 2009/2035 Sch.1 para.60
Sch.22 Part I para.4, amended: SI 2009/56 Sch.1 para.211
Sch.22 Part I para.7, amended: SI 2009/56 Sch.1 para.212
Sch.22 Part I para.8, amended: SI 2009/56 Sch.1 para.213
Sch.24 para.20, amended: 2009 c.4 Sch.3 Part 1

15. Antarctic Act 1994
s.9, enabling: SI 2009/2354
s.25, enabling: SI 2009/2354
s.32, enabling: SI 2009/2354

17. Chiropractors Act 1994
applied: SI 2009/2722 Reg.3
s.3, applied: SI 2009/27 Sch.1
s.3, enabling: SI 2009/27, SI 2009/2305
s.6, applied: SI 2009/27 Sch.1
s.6, enabling: SI 2009/27, SI 2009/2305
s.20, amended: 2009 c.26 s.81
s.35, applied: SI 2009/26, SI 2009/27, SI 2009/27 Sch.1, SI 2009/2305, SI 2009/2738, SI 2009/2738 Sch.1
s.35, enabling: SI 2009/26, SI 2009/27, SI 2009/2305, SI 2009/2738
s.36, applied: SI 2009/2305, SI 2009/2738
s.43, enabling: SI 2009/2305
Sch.1 Part II para.16, applied: SI 2009/2738 Sch.1
Sch.1 Part II para.16, enabling: SI 2009/26, SI 2009/2738
Sch.1 Part II para.17, applied: SI 2009/26 Sch.1, SI 2009/2738 Sch.1
Sch.1 Part II para.17, enabling: SI 2009/26, SI 2009/2738
Sch.1 Part II para.25, enabling: SI 2009/26
Sch.1 Part II para.30, applied: SI 2009/2738 Sch.1
Sch.1 Part II para.30, enabling: SI 2009/26, SI 2009/2738
Sch.1 Part II para.30A, added: SI 2009/1182 Sch.5 para.2
Sch.1 Part II para.30A, applied: SI 2009/2738 Sch.1
Sch.1 Part II para.30A, enabling: SI 2009/2738
Sch.1 Part II para.34, enabling: SI 2009/26
Sch.1 Part II para.34A, added: SI 2009/1182 Sch.5 para.2
Sch.1 Part II para.36, referred to: SI 2009/26 Sch.1
Sch.1 Part II para.38, enabling: SI 2009/26
Sch.1 Part II para.38A, added: SI 2009/1182 Sch.5 para.2
Sch.1 Part II para.40, referred to: SI 2009/26 Sch.1

18. Social Security (Incapacity for Work) Act 1994
s.4, enabling: SI 2009/1488
s.12, enabling: SI 2009/1488
Sch.1 Part I para.25, repealed: 2009 c.24 Sch.7 Part 2
Sch.1 Part I para.26, repealed: 2009 c.24 Sch.7 Part 2
Sch.1 Part I para.27, repealed: 2009 c.24 Sch.7 Part 2

19. Local Government (Wales) Act 1994
Sch.15 para.26, repealed (in part): SI 2009/1375 Art.2
Sch.16 para.26, repealed: 2009 c.23 Sch.22 Part 4
Sch.16 para.65, repealed (in part): 2009 c.23 Sch.22 Part 3

1994– cont.

19. Local Government (Wales) Act 1994– *cont.*
Sch.17 Part II para.23, repealed: 2009 c.25 Sch.23 Part 1

21. Coal Industry Act 1994
s.26, see *Bute v Revenue and Customs Commissioners* [2009] CSIH 42, [2009] S.T.C. 2138 (IH (Ex Div)), Lord Osborne
s.36, amended: SI 2009/1941 Sch.1 para.147
s.36, repealed (in part): SI 2009/1941 Sch.1 para.147
s.47, amended: SI 2009/1307 Sch.1 para.256
s.59, amended: SI 2009/1307 Sch.1 para.257
s.65, amended: SI 2009/1941 Sch.1 para.147
Sch.1B para.4, amended: SI 2009/1307 Sch.1 para.258
Sch.1B para.4, substituted: SI 2009/1307 Sch.1 para.258
Sch.3 para.2, amended: SI 2009/1941 Sch.1 para.147
Sch.7 Part I para.6, amended: SI 2009/1307 Sch.1 para.259

22. Vehicle Excise and Registration Act 1994
applied: SI 2009/717 Reg.5, Sch.3 para.4, Sch.5 para.6, Sch.5 para.8, Sch.5 para.9, SI 2009/1300 Art.48
s.3, amended: 2009 c.10 Sch.4 para.2
s.7B, amended: SI 2009/56 Sch.1 para.215
s.19, amended: 2009 c.10 Sch.4 para.3
s.19, repealed (in part): 2009 c.10 Sch.4 para.3
s.21, applied: SI 2009/717 Reg.6, Sch.3 para.1, Sch.3 para.5
s.22, amended: 2009 c.10 s.120
s.22, enabling: SI 2009/880
s.22A, applied: SI 2009/711 Art.6, Sch.1 para.39
s.22A, enabling: SI 2009/880
s.23, enabling: SI 2009/811
s.34, applied: SI 2009/483 Art.2
s.42, referred to: SI 2009/491 Sch.1 Part 1, SI 2009/492 Sch.1 Part 1
s.43, referred to: SI 2009/491 Sch.1 Part 1, SI 2009/492 Sch.1 Part 1
s.44, applied: SI 2009/2773 Sch.1, SI 2009/2781 Sch.1
s.44, referred to: SI 2009/491 Sch.1 Part 1
s.51, enabling: SI 2009/881
s.57, enabling: SI 2009/811, SI 2009/880, SI 2009/881, SI 2009/3103
s.61A, applied: SI 2009/711 Art.6, Sch.1 para.40
s.61A, enabling: SI 2009/881
s.61B, applied: SI 2009/711 Art.6, Sch.1 para.42
s.61B, enabling: SI 2009/880, SI 2009/3103
s.62, amended: 2009 c.10 Sch.4 para.4
Sch.1 Part I para.1, amended: 2009 c.10 s.13, s.14
Sch.1 Part IA para.1A, amended: 2009 c.10 Sch.4 para.5
Sch.1 Part IA para.1B, amended: 2009 c.10 s.13, s.14
Sch.1 Part IA para.1C, amended: 2009 c.10 Sch.4 para.5
Sch.1 Part IB para.1H, amended: 2009 c.10 Sch.4 para.5
Sch.1 Part IB para.1J, amended: 2009 c.10 s.13, s.14
Sch.1 Part IB para.1K, amended: 2009 c.10 Sch.4 para.5
Sch.1 Part IB para.1M, amended: 2009 c.10 Sch.4 para.5
Sch.2 para.25, substituted: 2009 c.10 Sch.4 para.6
Sch.3 para.24, repealed (in part): SI 2009/818 Reg.4

23. Value Added Tax Act 1994
applied: 2009 c.10 Sch.3 para.1, Sch.3 para.20, Sch.3 para.24, Sch.53 para.10

1994– cont.

23. Value Added Tax Act 1994– *cont.*
s.2, amended: 2009 c.10 Sch.3 para.25
s.2, applied: 2009 c.10 s.9, Sch.3 para.1
s.5, see *Bath Festivals Trust Ltd v Revenue and Customs Commissioners* [2009] B.V.C. 2194 (V&DTr (London)), JC Gort (Chairman); see *Community Housing Association Ltd v Revenue and Customs Commissioners* [2009] EWHC 455 (Ch), [2009] S.T.C. 1324 (Ch D), Sales, J
s.6, amended: 2009 c.10 Sch.36 para.2
s.6, enabling: SI 2009/1967
s.7, see *Arachchige v Revenue and Customs Commissioners* [2009] B.V.C. 2003 (V&DTr (London)), Charles Hellier (Chairman)
s.7, amended: 2009 c.10 Sch.36 para.3
s.7, repealed (in part): 2009 c.10 Sch.36 para.3
s.7, enabling: SI 2009/215
s.7A, added: 2009 c.10 Sch.36 para.4
s.8, see *R. (on the application of Medical Protection Society) v Revenue and Customs Commissioners* [2009] EWHC 2780 (Admin), [2009] B.V.C. 943 (QBD (Admin)), Sales, J
s.8, amended: 2009 c.10 Sch.36 para.5
s.8, repealed (in part): 2009 c.10 Sch.36 para.5
s.8, enabling: SI 2009/3241
s.9, substituted: 2009 c.10 Sch.36 para.6
s.21, amended: SI 2009/730 Art.17
s.24, enabling: SI 2009/586
s.25, see *Revenue and Customs Commissioners v Raj Restaurant* [2009] S.T.C. 729 (IH (Ex Div)), Lord Nimmo Smith
s.25, enabling: SI 2009/217, SI 2009/586, SI 2009/2978
s.26, see *S&I Electronics Plc v Revenue and Customs Commissioners* [2009] UKFTT 108 (TC), [2009] S.F.T.D. 241 (FTT (Tax)), Charles Hellier (Chairman)
s.26, enabling: SI 2009/586, SI 2009/820
s.26B, enabling: SI 2009/586, SI 2009/3241
s.29A, see *University of Cambridge v Revenue and Customs Commissioners* [2009] EWHC 434 (Ch), [2009] S.T.C. 1288 (Ch D), Sir Andrew Morritt (Chancellor)
s.29A, enabling: SI 2009/1359
s.30, enabling: SI 2009/2093, SI 2009/2972
s.31, see *Allen Carr's Easyway (International) Ltd v Revenue and Customs Commissioners* [2009] UKFTT 181 (TC), [2009] S.F.T.D. 523 (FTT (Tax)), JC Gort
s.33, applied: SI 2009/1177 Art.2, Art.3
s.33, enabling: SI 2009/1177
s.33A, applied: SI 2009/403 Art.3
s.35, enabling: SI 2009/1967
s.36, enabling: SI 2009/586
s.39, amended: 2009 c.10 s.77
s.39, enabling: SI 2009/3241
s.39A, added: 2009 c.10 s.77
s.41, applied: 2009 asp 2 s.1, s.2
s.43, amended: 2009 c.10 Sch.36 para.7
s.43A, amended: SI 2009/1890 Art.4
s.43A, applied: 2009 c.10 Sch.3 para.16
s.43AA, applied: 2009 c.10 Sch.3 para.16
s.43B, applied: 2009 c.10 Sch.3 para.16
s.43C, applied: 2009 c.10 Sch.3 para.16
s.43D, applied: 2009 c.10 Sch.3 para.16
s.47, see *Oriel Support Ltd v Revenue and Customs Commissioners* Times, March 25, 2009 (V&DTr (London)), John Clark (Chairman)

1994– cont.

23. Value Added Tax Act 1994– *cont.*
s.51, enabling: SI 2009/1966
s.53, enabling: SI 2009/3166
s.57, amended: SI 2009/1030 Art.2
s.57, enabling: SI 2009/1030
s.58B, enabling: SI 2009/2978
s.59, applied: 2009 c.4 s.1303, 2009 c.10 s.108
s.59A, applied: 2009 c.10 s.108
s.60, applied: 2009 c.4 s.1303, SI 2009/571 Art.7
s.61, applied: 2009 c.4 s.1303, SI 2009/571 Art.7
s.62, applied: 2009 c.4 s.1303
s.63, applied: 2009 c.4 s.1303
s.64, applied: 2009 c.4 s.1303
s.65, applied: 2009 c.4 s.1303
s.66, amended: SI 2009/571 Sch.1 para.23
s.66, applied: 2009 c.4 s.1303
s.67, applied: 2009 c.4 s.1303, SI 2009/403 Art.9
s.67A, applied: 2009 c.4 s.1303
s.68, applied: 2009 c.4 s.1303
s.69, amended: SI 2009/571 Sch.1 para.24
s.69, applied: 2009 c.4 s.1303
s.69A, amended: SI 2009/571 Sch.1 para.25
s.69A, applied: 2009 c.4 s.1303
s.69B, amended: SI 2009/571 Sch.1 para.26
s.69B, applied: 2009 c.4 s.1303
s.70, applied: 2009 c.4 s.1303
s.73, see *Bestline Data Ltd v Revenue and Customs Commissioners* [2009] UKFTT 42 (TC), [2009] S.F.T.D. 78 (FTT (Tax)), David Demack
s.74, applied: 2009 c.4 s.1303
s.76, see *Revenue and Customs Commissioners v Raj Restaurant* [2009] S.T.C. 729 (IH (Ex Div)), Lord Nimmo Smith
s.77, see *R. (on the application of Medical Protection Society) v Revenue and Customs Commissioners* [2009] EWHC 2780 (Admin), [2009] B.V.C. 943 (QBD (Admin)), Sales, J
s.77, applied: SI 2009/403 Art.4
s.77, disapplied: SI 2009/403 Art.9
s.78, see *FJ Chalke Ltd v Revenue and Customs Commissioners* [2009] EWHC 952 (Ch), [2009] S.T.C. 2027 (Ch D), Henderson, J.; see *Grattan Plc v Revenue and Customs Commissioners* [2009] UKFTT 184 (TC), [2009] S.F.T.D. 590 (FTT (Tax)), Sir Stephen Oliver Q.C.; see *John Wilkins (Motor Engineers) Ltd v Revenue and Customs Commissioners* [2009] UKUT 175 (TCC), [2009] S.T.C. 2485 (UT (Tax)), Warren, J.
s.78, applied: SI 2009/403 Art.5
s.79, applied: 2009 c.4 s.1286
s.80, see *FJ Chalke Ltd v Revenue and Customs Commissioners* [2009] EWHC 952 (Ch), [2009] S.T.C. 2027 (Ch D), Henderson, J.; see *Grattan Plc v Revenue and Customs Commissioners* [2009] UKFTT 184 (TC), [2009] S.F.T.D. 590 (FTT (Tax)), Sir Stephen Oliver Q.C.
s.80, applied: SI 2009/403 Art.6
s.82, amended: SI 2009/56 Sch.1 para.217
s.82, substituted: SI 2009/56 Sch.1 para.218
s.83, see *Loughborough University v Revenue and Customs Commissioners* [2009] UKFTT 91 (TC), [2009] S.F.T.D. 200 (FTT (Tax)), Richard Barlow; see *Oxfam v Revenue and Customs Commissioners* [2009] EWHC 3078 (Ch), Times, December 31, 2009 (Ch D), Sales, J
s.83, amended: 2009 c.10 s.77, SI 2009/56 Sch.1 para.217, Sch.1 para.219
s.83, applied: SI 2009/56 Sch.3 para.4
s.83A, added: SI 2009/56 Sch.1 para.220

1994– cont.

23. Value Added Tax Act 1994– *cont.*

s.83A, amended: SI 2009/56 Sch.1 para.217

s.83B, added: SI 2009/56 Sch.1 para.220

s.83B, amended: SI 2009/56 Sch.1 para.217

s.83C, added: SI 2009/56 Sch.1 para.220

s.83C, amended: SI 2009/56 Sch.1 para.217

s.83D, added: SI 2009/56 Sch.1 para.220

s.83D, amended: SI 2009/56 Sch.1 para.217

s.83E, added: SI 2009/56 Sch.1 para.220

s.83E, amended: SI 2009/56 Sch.1 para.217

s.83F, added: SI 2009/56 Sch.1 para.220

s.83F, amended: SI 2009/56 Sch.1 para.217

s.83G, see *John Wilkins (Motor Engineers) Ltd v Revenue and Customs Commissioners* [2009] UKUT 175 (TCC), [2009] S.T.C. 2485 (UT (Tax)), Warren, J.

s.83G, added: SI 2009/56 Sch.1 para.220

s.83G, amended: SI 2009/56 Sch.1 para.217

s.84, see *Calltel Telecom Ltd v Revenue and Customs Commissioners* [2008] EWHC 2107 (Ch), [2009] Bus. L.R. 513 (Ch D), Briggs, J.

s.84, amended: SI 2009/56 Sch.1 para.217, Sch.1 para.221

s.84, applied: SI 2009/56 Sch.3 para.9

s.84, repealed (in part): SI 2009/56 Sch.1 para.221

s.85, amended: SI 2009/56 Sch.1 para.217, Sch.1 para.222

s.85A, added: SI 2009/56 Sch.1 para.223

s.85A, amended: SI 2009/56 Sch.1 para.217

s.85B, added: SI 2009/56 Sch.1 para.223

s.85B, amended: SI 2009/56 Sch.1 para.217

s.85B, disapplied: SI 2009/56 Sch.3 para.10

s.86, amended: SI 2009/56 Sch.1 para.217

s.86, repealed: SI 2009/56 Sch.1 para.224

s.87, amended: SI 2009/56 Sch.1 para.217

s.87, repealed: SI 2009/56 Sch.1 para.224

s.89, see *Mason v Boscawen* [2008] EWHC 3100 (Ch), [2009] 1 W.L.R. 2139 (Ch D (Bristol)), Lewison, J.

s.96, amended: 2009 c.10 Sch.36 para.8, SI 2009/56 Sch.1 para.225

s.96, enabling: SI 2009/1359, SI 2009/2093, SI 2009/2972

s.97, amended: 2009 c.10 Sch.3 para.25, Sch.36 para.9, SI 2009/56 Sch.1 para.226

s.97, repealed (in part): SI 2009/56 Sch.1 para.226

s.97A, amended: 2009 c.10 Sch.36 para.10

Sch.1 para.1, amended: SI 2009/1031 Art.3

Sch.1 para.4, amended: SI 2009/1031 Art.3

Sch.1 para.15, enabling: SI 2009/1031

Sch.3 para.1, amended: SI 2009/1031 Art.4

Sch.3 para.2, amended: SI 2009/1031 Art.4

Sch.3 para.9, enabling: SI 2009/1031

Sch.3B Part 4 para.20, amended: SI 2009/56 Sch.1 para.227

Sch.4A Part 1 para.1, added: 2009 c.10 Sch.36 para.11

Sch.4A Part 1 para.2, added: 2009 c.10 Sch.36 para.11

Sch.4A Part 1 para.3, added: 2009 c.10 Sch.36 para.11

Sch.4A Part 1 para.4, added: 2009 c.10 Sch.36 para.11

Sch.4A Part 1 para.4, repealed: 2009 c.10 Sch.36 para.15

Sch.4A Part 1 para.5, added: 2009 c.10 Sch.36 para.11

Sch.4A Part 1 para.6, added: 2009 c.10 Sch.36 para.11

1994– cont.

23. Value Added Tax Act 1994– *cont.*

Sch.4A Part 1 para.7, added: 2009 c.10 Sch.36 para.11

Sch.4A Part 1 para.8, added: 2009 c.10 Sch.36 para.11

Sch.4A Part 2 para.9, added: 2009 c.10 Sch.36 para.11

Sch.4A Part 2 para.9A, added: 2009 c.10 Sch.36 para.11, Sch.36 para.15

Sch.4A Part 3 para.10, added: 2009 c.10 Sch.36 para.11

Sch.4A Part 3 para.11, added: 2009 c.10 Sch.36 para.11

Sch.4A Part 3 para.12, added: 2009 c.10 Sch.36 para.11

Sch.4A Part 3 para.13, added: 2009 c.10 Sch.36 para.11

Sch.4A Part 3 para.13A, added: 2009 c.10 Sch.36 para.11, Sch.36 para.17

Sch.4A Part 3 para.14, added: 2009 c.10 Sch.36 para.11

Sch.4A Part 3 para.14A, added: 2009 c.10 Sch.36 para.11, Sch.36 para.15

Sch.4A Part 3 para.15, added: 2009 c.10 Sch.36 para.11

Sch.4A Part 3 para.16, added: 2009 c.10 Sch.36 para.11

Sch.5 para.1, repealed: 2009 c.10 Sch.36 para.12

Sch.5 para.2, repealed: 2009 c.10 Sch.36 para.12

Sch.5 para.3, repealed: 2009 c.10 Sch.36 para.12

Sch.5 para.4, repealed: 2009 c.10 Sch.36 para.12

Sch.5 para.5, repealed: 2009 c.10 Sch.36 para.12

Sch.5 para.5A, repealed: 2009 c.10 Sch.36 para.12

Sch.5 para.6, repealed: 2009 c.10 Sch.36 para.12

Sch.5 para.7, repealed: 2009 c.10 Sch.36 para.12

Sch.5 para.7A, repealed: 2009 c.10 Sch.36 para.12

Sch.5 para.7B, repealed: 2009 c.10 Sch.36 para.12

Sch.5 para.7C, repealed: 2009 c.10 Sch.36 para.12

Sch.5 para.8, repealed: 2009 c.10 Sch.36 para.12

Sch.5 para.9, repealed: 2009 c.10 Sch.36 para.12

Sch.5 para.10, repealed: 2009 c.10 Sch.36 para.12

Sch.7A, see *University of Cambridge v Revenue and Customs Commissioners* [2009] EWHC 434 (Ch), [2009] S.T.C. 1288 (Ch D), Sir Andrew Morritt (Chancellor)

Sch.7A Part II, amended: SI 2009/1359 Art.3, Art.4, Art.5

Sch.8 Part I, amended: SI 2009/2093 Art.3

Sch.8 Part II, added: SI 2009/2093 Art.4

Sch.8 Part II, amended: SI 2009/2972 Art.3, Art.4, Art.5, Art.6, Art.7

Sch.8 Group 1, see *Procter & Gamble UK v Revenue and Customs Commissioners* [2009] EWCA Civ 407, [2009] S.T.C. 1990 (CA (Civ Div)), Mummery, L.J.

Sch.9, see *Friendly Loans Ltd v Revenue and Customs Commissioners* [2009] UKFTT 247 (TC) (FTT (Tax)), Michael Tildesley (Chairman)

Sch.9 Part II, repealed: 2009 c.10 s.113

Sch.9 Group 1, see *Acrylux Ltd v Revenue and Customs Commissioners* [2009] UKFTT 223 (TC), [2009] S.F.T.D. 763 (FTT (Tax)), Malcolm Gammie Q.C.

Sch.9 Group 2, see *Bank of Ireland v Revenue and Customs Commissioners* [2009] B.V.C. 2171 (V&DTr (London)), JC Gort (Chairman); see *InsuranceWide.com Services Ltd v Revenue and Customs Commissioners* [2009] EWHC 999 (Ch), [2009] S.T.C. 2219 (Ch D), Sir

1994– cont.

23. Value Added Tax Act 1994– *cont.*

Sch.9 Group 2–*cont.*

Edward Evans-Lombe; see *Royal Bank of Scotland Group Plc v Revenue and Customs Commissioners* [2009] B.V.C. 2212 (V&DTr (London)), John F Avery Jones (Chairman)

Sch.9 Group 4, see *Revenue and Customs Commissioners v Rank Group* [2009] EWHC 1244 (Ch), [2009] S.T.C. 2304 (Ch D), Norris, J.

Sch.9 Group 5, see *HBOS Plc v Revenue and Customs Commissioners* [2009] S.T.C. 486 (IH (Ex Div)), Lord Nimmo Smith

Sch.9 Group 7, see *Allen Carr's Easyway (International) Ltd v Revenue and Customs Commissioners* [2009] UKFTT 181 (TC), [2009] S.F.T.D. 523 (FTT (Tax)), JC Gort; see *Ultralase Medical Aesthetics Ltd v Revenue and Customs Commissioners* [2009] UKFTT 187 (TC), [2009] S.F.T.D. 541 (FTT (Tax)), David S Porter

Sch.10, applied: 2009 c.10 s.79

Sch.10A, see *Arachchige v Revenue and Customs Commissioners* [2009] B.V.C. 2003 (V&DTr (London)), Charles Hellier (Chairman)

Sch.10 Part 1 para.3, amended: SI 2009/1966 Art.3

Sch.10 Part 1 para.21, amended: SI 2009/1966 Art.4

Sch.10 Part 1 para.25, amended: SI 2009/1966 Art.5

Sch.10 Part 1 para.26, substituted: SI 2009/1966 Art.6

Sch.10 Part 1 para.27, amended: SI 2009/1966 Art.7

Sch.10 Part 1 para.34, amended: SI 2009/1966 Art.8

Sch.10 para.2, see *Mason v Boscawen* [2008] EWHC 3100 (Ch), [2009] 1 W.L.R. 2139 (Ch D (Bristol)), Lewison, J.; see *Shurgard Storage Centres UK Ltd v Revenue and Customs Commissioners* [2009] B.V.C. 2139 (V&DTr (London)), Rodney P Huggins (Chairman)

Sch.10 para.3A, see *Shurgard Storage Centres UK Ltd v Revenue and Customs Commissioners* [2009] B.V.C. 2139 (V&DTr (London)), Rodney P Huggins (Chairman)

Sch.11 para.2, amended: 2009 c.10 s.78

Sch.11 para.2, enabling: SI 2009/586, SI 2009/2978, SI 2009/3241

Sch.11 para.2A, applied: 2009 c.10 Sch.3 para.22

Sch.11 para.2A, enabling: SI 2009/3241

Sch.11A para.10, amended: SI 2009/571 Sch.1 para.27

Sch.12, applied: SI 2009/196 Art.9

Sch.12 para.1, repealed: SI 2009/56 Sch.1 para.228

Sch.12 para.2, applied: SI 2009/56 Art.5

Sch.12 para.2, repealed: SI 2009/56 Sch.1 para.228

Sch.12 para.3, repealed: SI 2009/56 Sch.1 para.228

Sch.12 para.4, repealed: SI 2009/56 Sch.1 para.228

Sch.12 para.5, repealed: SI 2009/56 Sch.1 para.228

Sch.12 para.6, repealed: SI 2009/56 Sch.1 para.228

Sch.12 para.7, applied: SI 2009/56 Art.5

Sch.12 para.7, repealed: SI 2009/56 Sch.1 para.228

Sch.12 para.8, repealed: SI 2009/56 Sch.1 para.228

Sch.12 para.9, repealed: SI 2009/56 Sch.1 para.228

Sch.12 para.10, repealed: SI 2009/56 Sch.1 para.228

Sch.14 para.12, repealed: SI 2009/56 Sch.1 para.229

26. Trade Marks Act 1994

applied: SI 2009/1969 Art.8

referred to: SI 2009/669 Sch.1 Part 1

s.3, see *Hotel Cipriani SRL v Cipriani (Grosvenor Street) Ltd* [2008] EWHC 3032 (Ch), [2009] R.P.C. 9 (Ch D), Arnold, J.; see *Hull Daily*

1994– cont.

26. Trade Marks Act 1994– *cont.*

s.3– *cont.*

Mail's Application No.2409366 [2009] R.P.C. 8 (App Person), Richard Arnold Q.C.; see *Starfire Publishing Ltd v Ordo Templi Orientis* [2009] R.P.C. 14 (App Person), Anna Carboni

s.5, see *esure Insurance Ltd v Direct Line Insurance Plc* [2008] EWCA Civ 842, [2009] Bus. L.R. 438 (CA (Civ Div)), Arden, L.J.; see *Intel Corp Inc v CPM United Kingdom Ltd (C-252/07)* [2009] Bus. L.R. 1079 (ECJ (1st Chamber)), Judge Jann (President)

s.10, see *Daimler AG v Sany Group Co Ltd* [2009] EWHC 1003 (Ch), [2009] E.T.M.R. 58 (Ch D), Geoffrey Hobbs Q.C.; see *R. v Boulter (Gary)* [2008] EWCA Crim 2375, [2009] E.T.M.R. 6 (CA (Crim Div)), Toulson, L.J.

s.41, enabling: SI 2009/2089

s.54, enabling: SI 2009/2464

s.56, see *Hotel Cipriani SRL v Cipriani (Grosvenor Street) Ltd* [2008] EWHC 3032 (Ch), [2009] R.P.C. 9 (Ch D), Arnold, J.

s.64, see *AVON GRIPSTER Trade Mark* [2009] R.P.C. 17 (TMR), Allan James

s.76, see *Munroe v Intel Corp* [2009] R.P.C. 16 (App Person), Geoffrey Hobbs Q.C.

s.77, see *Munroe v Intel Corp* [2009] R.P.C. 16 (App Person), Geoffrey Hobbs Q.C.

s.78, enabling: SI 2009/546, SI 2009/2089

s.79, enabling: SI 2009/2089

s.88, amended: SI 2009/3348 Art.5

Sch.4 para.1, amended: SI 2009/1941 Sch.2

33. Criminal Justice and Public Order Act 1994

see *R. v Ibrahim (Muktar)* [2008] EWCA Crim 880, [2009] 1 W.L.R. 578 (CA (Crim Div)), Sir Igor Judge (President, QB)

s.9, see *R. (on the application of Pounder) v HM Coroner for North and South Districts of Durham and Darlington* [2009] EWHC 76 (Admin), [2009] 3 All E.R. 150 (QBD (Admin)), Blake, J

s.25, amended: 2009 c.25 Sch.17 para.3, Sch.23 Part 5

s.25, referred to: SI 2009/991 Art.4, SI 2009/992 Art.4

s.34, see *R. v Ibrahim (Muktar)* [2008] EWCA Crim 880, [2009] 1 W.L.R. 578 (CA (Crim Div)), Sir Igor Judge (President, QB)

s.34, applied: SI 2009/990 Sch.1

s.34, referred to: SI 2009/990 Sch.2

s.34, varied: SI 2009/990 Sch.1

s.35, see *R. v Anwoir (Ilham)* [2008] EWCA Crim 1354, [2009] 1 W.L.R. 980 (CA (Crim Div)), Latham, L.J.; see *R. v Tabbakh (Hassan)* [2009] EWCA Crim 464, (2009) 173 J.P. 201 (CA (Crim Div)), Hughes, LJ. (V-P)

s.35, applied: SI 2009/990 Sch.1

s.35, referred to: SI 2009/990 Sch.2

s.35, varied: SI 2009/990 Sch.1

s.36, applied: SI 2009/990 Sch.1

s.36, referred to: SI 2009/990 Sch.2

s.36, varied: SI 2009/990 Sch.1

s.37, applied: SI 2009/990 Sch.1

s.37, referred to: SI 2009/990 Sch.2

s.37, varied: SI 2009/990 Sch.1

s.38, applied: SI 2009/990 Sch.1

s.38, referred to: SI 2009/990 Sch.2

s.38, varied: SI 2009/990 Art.5, Sch.1

s.39, varied: SI 2009/1059 Sch.1 para.33

s.39, enabling: SI 2009/990

1994– cont.

33. Criminal Justice and Public Order Act 1994–
cont.
s.51, applied: 2009 c.25 s.159
Sch.8 Part I, amended: 2009 c.23 Sch.22 Part 5

37. Drug Trafficking Act 1994
see *Gibson v Revenue and Customs Prosecution Office* [2008] EWCA Civ 645, [2009] Q.B. 348 (CA (Civ Div)), May, L.J.; see *R. v Griffin (Dion Howard)* [2009] EWCA Crim 569, [2009] 2 Cr. App. R. (S.) 89 (CA (Crim Div)), Aikens, L.J.
s.2, see *Attorney General's Reference (No.2 of 2008), Re* [2008] EWCA Crim 2953, [2009] Lloyd's Rep. F.C. 189 (CA (Crim Div)), Hooper, L.J.; see *R. v Allpress (Sylvia)* [2009] EWCA Crim 8, [2009] 2 Cr. App. R. (S.) 58 (CA (Crim Div)), Latham, L.J. (VP, CA Crim)
s.4, see *R. v Briggs-Price (Robert William)* [2009] UKHL 19, [2009] 1 A.C. 1026 (HL), Lord Phillips of Worth Matravers
s.5, see *R. v Griffin (Dion Howard)* [2009] EWCA Crim 569, [2009] 2 Cr. App. R. (S.) 89 (CA (Crim Div)), Aikens, L.J.
s.16, see *R. v Griffin (Dion Howard)* [2009] EWCA Crim 569, [2009] 2 Cr. App. R. (S.) 89 (CA (Crim Div)), Aikens, L.J.
s.17, see *R. v Griffin (Dion Howard)* [2009] EWCA Crim 569, [2009] 2 Cr. App. R. (S.) 89 (CA (Crim Div)), Aikens, L.J.; see *R. v Younis (Shaed)* [2008] EWCA Crim 2950, [2009] 2 Cr. App. R. (S.) 34 (CA (Crim Div)), Thomas, L.J.

39. Local Government etc (Scotland) Act 1994
s.5, amended: 2009 asp 10 s.1
s.5, repealed (in part): 2009 asp 10 Sch.1 para.2
s.27, applied: SSI 2009/112
s.27, enabling: SSI 2009/112
s.153, amended: 2009 asp 12 s.67
s.153, enabling: SSI 2009/42
Sch.13 para.56, repealed: 2009 asp 6 Sch.3 para.6

40. Deregulation and Contracting Out Act 1994
Part II, applied: SI 2009/1941 Art.7
s.22, repealed: SSI 2009/248 Sch.2
s.69, applied: 2009 c.13 Sch.1 para.21, 2009 c.23 s.21, s.171
s.69, varied: 2009 c.20 Sch.1 para.8
s.69, enabling: SI 2009/721
s.70, see *De-Winter Heald v Brent LBC* [2009] EWCA Civ 930, [2009] H.R.L.R. 34 (CA (Civ Div)), Sedley, L.J.
s.70, applied: SI 2009/721
s.70, enabling: SI 2009/721
s.74, amended: SI 2009/1941 Sch.1 para.148
s.77, applied: SI 2009/721
s.77, enabling: SI 2009/721
s.79, amended: SI 2009/1941 Sch.1 para.148
s.79A, amended: 2009 c.20 Sch.6 para.87
Sch.15, applied: 2009 c.23 s.21
Sch.15 para.1, varied: 2009 c.23 s.171
Sch.15 para.2, varied: 2009 c.23 s.171
Sch.15 para.3, varied: 2009 c.23 s.171
Sch.15 para.4, varied: 2009 c.23 s.171
Sch.15 para.5, varied: 2009 c.23 s.171
Sch.15 para.6, varied: 2009 c.23 s.171
Sch.15 para.7, varied: 2009 c.23 s.171
Sch.15 para.8, varied: 2009 c.23 s.171
Sch.15 para.9, varied: 2009 c.23 s.171
Sch.15 para.10, varied: 2009 c.23 s.171
Sch.16 para.1, amended: SI 2009/1941 Sch.1 para.148

1995

x. London Local Authorities Act 1995
s.11, see *R. (on the application of Clear Channel UK Ltd) v Hammersmith and Fulham LBC* [2009] EWHC 465 (Admin), [2009] 22 E.G. 120 (QBD (Admin)), Irwin, J.

4. Finance Act 1995
s.5, amended: SI 2009/56 Sch.1 para.231
s.15, repealed: 2009 c.10 Sch.5 para.6
s.76, repealed (in part): 2009 c.4 Sch.3 Part 1
s.117, repealed: 2009 c.4 Sch.3 Part 1
s.120, repealed: 2009 c.4 Sch.3 Part 1
s.121, repealed: 2009 c.4 Sch.3 Part 1
s.125, repealed: 2009 c.4 Sch.3 Part 1
s.126, repealed (in part): 2009 c.4 Sch.3 Part 1
s.127, amended: 2009 c.4 Sch.1 para.401
s.127, repealed (in part): 2009 c.4 Sch.3 Part 1
s.134, repealed: SI 2009/3001 Sch.2
s.140, repealed: 2009 c.4 Sch.3 Part 1
Sch.5 para.7, repealed: SI 2009/3054 Sch.1 para.16
Sch.6 para.2, repealed: 2009 c.4 Sch.3 Part 1
Sch.18 para.2, repealed: 2009 c.4 Sch.3 Part 1

7. Requirements of Writing (Scotland) Act 1995
see *Park, Petitioners* [2009] CSOH 122, 2009 S.L.T. 871 (OH), Temporary Judge MG Thomson Q.C.
s.1, see *Aisling Developments Ltd v Persimmon Homes Ltd* 2009 S.L.T. 494 (OH), Lord Glennie
s.1, disapplied: SI 2009/555 Art.4
s.3, see *Gibson v Royal Bank of Scotland Plc* [2009] CSOH 14, 2009 S.L.T. 444 (OH), Lord Emslie
s.12, amended: SI 2009/1941 Sch.1 para.151

10. Home Energy Conservation Act 1995
s.2, applied: SI 2009/486 Reg.3, Reg.4

18. Jobseekers Act 1995
applied: SI 2009/1562 Art.2, SSI 2009/48 Reg.6
Part I, applied: SI 2009/212 Reg.2, SI 2009/1555 Reg.121, Reg.138, SI 2009/2737 Reg.73, Reg.88
Part I, added: 2009 c.24 Sch.1 para.3
Part I, added: 2009 c.24 Sch.1 para.4
Part I, added: 2009 c.24 s.25
s.1, amended: 2009 c.24 s.4, Sch.1 para.8
s.1A, added: 2009 c.24 s.4
s.1A, applied: 2009 c.24 s.9
s.1A, repealed (in part): 2009 c.24 Sch.7 Part 1
s.1B, added: 2009 c.24 s.4
s.2, amended: 2009 c.24 s.12, Sch.1 para.9, Sch.2 para.6
s.2, repealed (in part): 2009 c.24 Sch.7 Part 1
s.3, amended: 2009 c.24 Sch.1 para.10, Sch.7 Part 1
s.3, repealed (in part): 2009 c.24 Sch.7 Part 1
s.3, enabling: SI 2009/2655
s.3A, amended: 2009 c.24 Sch.1 para.11, Sch.2 para.7
s.3A, repealed (in part): 2009 c.24 Sch.7 Part 1
s.3A, enabling: SI 2009/2655
s.4, amended: 2009 c.24 Sch.1 para.12
s.4, enabling: SI 2009/362, SI 2009/583, SI 2009/1488, SI 2009/1575, SI 2009/2655, SI 2009/3228, SI 2009/3257
s.5, enabling: SI 2009/1488
s.8, amended: 2009 c.24 s.32, s.33, Sch.1 para.2
s.8, repealed (in part): 2009 c.24 Sch.7 Part 3
s.9, amended: 2009 c.24 s.31, s.32, Sch.1 para.13
s.9, repealed (in part): 2009 c.24 Sch.7 Part 3
s.10, amended: 2009 c.24 s.32, Sch.1 para.14
s.12, enabling: SI 2009/480, SI 2009/583, SI 2009/1488, SI 2009/1575, SI 2009/2655, SI 2009/3228
s.13, enabling: SI 2009/3228
s.14, amended: 2009 c.24 Sch.1 para.15

1995–cont.

18. Jobseekers Act 1995–*cont.*

s.15, amended: 2009 c.24 Sch.1 para.16

s.15A, amended: 2009 c.24 Sch.1 para.17

s.15A, repealed (in part): 2009 c.24 Sch.1 para.17, Sch.7 Part 3

s.15B, added: 2009 c.24 Sch.1 para.18

s.16, amended: 2009 c.24 s.32, Sch.7 Part 1, Sch.7 Part 3

s.18C, added: 2009 c.24 Sch.1 para.5

s.18D, added: 2009 c.24 Sch.1 para.5

s.19, amended: 2009 c.24 s.32

s.19, repealed (in part): 2009 c.24 Sch.7 Part 3

s.19, substituted: 2009 c.24 Sch.1 para.6

s.19, enabling: SI 2009/480, SI 2009/2710

s.20, substituted: 2009 c.24 Sch.1 para.6

s.20, enabling: SI 2009/480

s.20A, amended: 2009 c.24 s.32

s.20A, substituted: 2009 c.24 Sch.1 para.7

s.20A, enabling: SI 2009/480, SI 2009/2710

s.20B, substituted: 2009 c.24 Sch.1 para.7

s.20B, enabling: SI 2009/480

s.20C, amended: 2009 c.24 Sch.1 para.19

s.20E, added: 2009 c.24 s.32

s.20E, varied: 2009 c.24 s.32

s.22, amended: 2009 c.24 Sch.1 para.20

s.26, amended: 2009 c.24 Sch.7 Part 1

s.28, amended: 2009 c.24 Sch.7 Part 1

s.29, amended: 2009 c.24 s.28

s.29, applied: 2009 c.24 Sch.3 para.5

s.31, repealed: 2009 c.24 Sch.7 Part 1

s.35, amended: 2009 c.24 Sch.1 para.21

s.35, enabling: SI 2009/362, SI 2009/480, SI 2009/583, SI 2009/1488, SI 2009/1575, SI 2009/2655, SI 2009/2710, SI 2009/3228, SI 2009/3257

s.36, amended: 2009 c.24 s.1, Sch.1 para.22, Sch.3 para.3, Sch.7 Part 3

s.36, enabling: SI 2009/362, SI 2009/480, SI 2009/583, SI 2009/1488, SI 2009/1575, SI 2009/2655, SI 2009/2710, SI 2009/3228, SI 2009/3257

s.37, amended: 2009 c.24 s.25, s.29, Sch.3 para.3

Sch.A1 para.1, added: 2009 c.24 Sch.3 para.2

Sch.A1 para.1, applied: 2009 c.24 Sch.3 para.5

Sch.A1 para.2, added: 2009 c.24 Sch.3 para.2

Sch.A1 para.2, applied: 2009 c.24 Sch.3 para.5

Sch.A1 para.3, added: 2009 c.24 Sch.3 para.2

Sch.A1 para.3, applied: 2009 c.24 Sch.3 para.5

Sch.A1 para.4, added: 2009 c.24 Sch.3 para.2

Sch.A1 para.5, added: 2009 c.24 Sch.3 para.2

Sch.A1 para.5, applied: 2009 c.24 Sch.3 para.5

Sch.A1 para.6, added: 2009 c.24 Sch.3 para.2

Sch.A1 para.6, applied: 2009 c.24 Sch.3 para.5

Sch.A1 para.7, added: 2009 c.24 Sch.3 para.2

Sch.A1 para.7, amended: 2009 c.24 Sch.1 para.19

Sch.A1 para.8, added: 2009 c.24 Sch.3 para.2

Sch.A1 para.9, added: 2009 c.24 Sch.3 para.2

Sch.A1 para.9, repealed (in part): 2009 c.24 Sch.7 Part 3

Sch.A1 para.10, added: 2009 c.24 Sch.3 para.2

Sch.1, added: 2009 c.24 Sch.1 para.23

Sch.1 para.1, enabling: SI 2009/583, SI 2009/3228

Sch.1 para.2, amended: 2009 c.24 Sch.1 para.23

Sch.1 para.3, enabling: SI 2009/480

Sch.1 para.8, substituted: 2009 c.24 Sch.1 para.23

Sch.1 para.8, enabling: SI 2009/583

Sch.1 para.8A, amended: 2009 c.24 Sch.1 para.23

Sch.1 para.8A, enabling: SI 2009/583, SI 2009/1488, SI 2009/3228

Sch.1 para.8B, added: 2009 c.24 s.29

1995–cont.

18. Jobseekers Act 1995–*cont.*

Sch.1 para.9, enabling: SI 2009/583

Sch.1 para.14, amended: 2009 c.24 Sch.1 para.23

Sch.1 para.14A, added: 2009 c.24 s.30

Sch.1 para.19, added: 2009 c.24 s.34

Sch.1 para.19, amended: 2009 c.24 Sch.3 para.3

Sch.2 para.24, referred to: 2009 c.24 s.58

Sch.2 para.24, repealed: 2009 c.24 Sch.7 Part 2

Sch.2 para.25, repealed: 2009 c.24 Sch.7 Part 2

Sch.2 para.26, repealed: 2009 c.24 Sch.7 Part 2

Sch.2 para.27, repealed: 2009 c.24 Sch.7 Part 2

Sch.2 para.30, repealed: 2009 c.24 Sch.7 Part 1

Sch.2 para.31, repealed: 2009 c.24 Sch.7 Part 1

Sch.2 para.32, repealed: 2009 c.24 Sch.7 Part 1

21. Merchant Shipping Act 1995

applied: SI 2009/700 Sch.1 Part II, Sch.1 Part XIII, SI 2009/2325 Art.35

Part IX, applied: SSI 2009/27 Art.7

Part X, applied: SI 2009/2793 Reg.2

s.1, applied: SI 2009/153 Reg.31

s.85, applied: SI 2009/2796 Reg.13

s.85, enabling: SI 2009/1210, SI 2009/2021

s.86, enabling: SI 2009/1210, SI 2009/2021

s.94, see *Club Cruise Entertainment & Travelling Services Europe BV v Department for Transport (The Van Gogh)* [2008] EWHC 2794 (Comm), [2009] 1 All E.R. (Comm) 955 (QBD (Comm)), Flaux, J.

s.95, see *Club Cruise Entertainment & Travelling Services Europe BV v Department for Transport (The Van Gogh)* [2008] EWHC 2794 (Comm), [2009] 1 All E.R. (Comm) 955 (QBD (Comm)), Flaux, J.

s.97, see *Club Cruise Entertainment & Travelling Services Europe BV v Department for Transport (The Van Gogh)* [2008] EWHC 2794 (Comm), [2009] 1 All E.R. (Comm) 955 (QBD (Comm)), Flaux, J.

s.108, amended: 2009 c.25 Sch.21 para.33

s.130A, enabling: SI 2009/1176

s.130B, enabling: SI 2009/1176

s.130C, enabling: SI 2009/1176

s.130D, applied: SI 2009/1176

s.130D, enabling: SI 2009/1176

s.131, amended: SI 2009/1210 Reg.3

s.131, applied: SI 2009/2796 Reg.15

s.143, amended: SI 2009/1941 Sch.1 para.152

s.143, varied: SI 2009/2796 Reg.15

s.145, varied: SI 2009/2796 Reg.12

s.146, varied: SI 2009/2796 Reg.16

s.163A, amended: SI 2009/1941 Sch.1 para.152

s.173, amended: SI 2009/1941 Sch.1 para.152

s.187, see *Krysia Maritime Inc v Intership Ltd (The Krysia)* [2008] EWHC 1880 (Admlty), [2009] 1 All E.R. (Comm) 292 (QBD (Admlty)), Aikens, J.

s.190, see *Gold Shipping Navigation Co SA v Lulu Maritime Ltd* [2009] EWHC 1365 (Admlty), [2009] 2 Lloyd's Rep. 484 (QBD (Admlty)), Teare, J.

s.205, enabling: SI 2009/1371

s.258, applied: SI 2009/2796 Reg.10

s.258, varied: SI 2009/2796 Reg.10

s.259, applied: SI 2009/2796 Reg.7

s.259, varied: SI 2009/2796 Reg.10

s.260, varied: SI 2009/2796 Reg.10

s.261, varied: SI 2009/2796 Reg.10

s.262, varied: SI 2009/2796 Reg.10

s.263, varied: SI 2009/2796 Reg.10

1995–cont.

21. Merchant Shipping Act 1995–*cont.*
s.264, varied: SI 2009/2796 Reg.10
s.265, varied: SI 2009/2796 Reg.10
s.266, varied: SI 2009/2796 Reg.10
s.271, amended: 2009 c.25 Sch.21 para.34
s.271, applied: SI 2009/700 Sch.1 Part XIII
s.273, amended: 2009 c.25 Sch.21 para.35
s.284, referred to: SI 2009/2796 Reg.12
s.284, varied: SI 2009/2796 Reg.12
s.302, varied: SI 2009/2796 Reg.20
s.306, referred to: SI 2009/1176
s.313, applied: SI 2009/3042 Reg.36
Sch.3A para.11, substituted: SI 2009/1941 Sch.1 para.152
Sch.7, applied: SI 2009/995 Reg.7
Sch.7, referred to: SSI 2009/266 Reg.6
Sch.7 Part I, applied: SI 2009/153 Reg.7
Sch.13 para.11, repealed: 2009 c.23 Sch.22 Part 5
Sch.13 para.12, repealed: 2009 c.23 Sch.22 Part 5
Sch.13 para.38, repealed (in part): 2009 c.23 Sch.22 Part 5

23. Goods Vehicles (Licensing of Operators) Act 1995
applied: SI 2009/711 Sch.1 para.44, SI 2009/1885 Art.2, Sch.4 para.1
s.2, applied: SI 2009/483 Art.2
s.2, referred to: SI 2009/491 Sch.1 Part 1, SI 2009/492 Sch.1 Part 1
s.3, referred to: SI 2009/491 Sch.1 Part 1
s.13, applied: SI 2009/804 Reg.3
s.17, applied: SI 2009/804 Reg.3
s.22, amended: SI 2009/1941 Sch.1 para.153
s.24, amended: SI 2009/1885 Sch.1 para.19
s.24, applied: SI 2009/804 Reg.3
s.25, applied: SI 2009/804 Reg.3
s.28, amended: SI 2009/1941 Sch.1 para.153
s.29, amended: SI 2009/1885 Sch.1 para.20
s.29, repealed (in part): SI 2009/1885 Sch.1 para.20
s.35, amended: SI 2009/1885 Sch.1 para.21
s.37, amended: SI 2009/1885 Sch.1 para.22
s.38, referred to: SI 2009/491 Sch.1 Part 1
s.45, applied: SI 2009/711 Art.7
s.45, enabling: SI 2009/804
s.57, applied: SI 2009/711 Art.7, SI 2009/804, SI 2009/1965
s.57, enabling: SI 2009/804
s.58, amended: SI 2009/1941 Sch.1 para.153
Sch.1A, enabling: SI 2009/1965
Sch.1A para.11, amended: SI 2009/1885 Sch.1 para.23
Sch.1A para.11, repealed (in part): SI 2009/1885 Sch.1 para.23
Sch.3 para.5, varied: SI 2009/1059 Sch.1 para.34

24. Crown Agents Act 1995
s.6, amended: SI 2009/1941 Sch.1 para.154
s.14, amended: SI 2009/1941 Sch.1 para.154

25. Environment Act 1995
referred to: SI 2009/3342 Reg.20, Reg.30, Reg.37
s.2, amended: SI 2009/463 Sch.2 para.9, SSI 2009/85 Sch.2 para.9
s.6, amended: 2009 c.23 s.230
s.6, repealed (in part): SI 2009/463 Sch.2 para.9, SSI 2009/85 Sch.2 para.9
s.13, amended: 2009 c.23 Sch.16 para.26
s.25, repealed (in part): 2009 asp 6 Sch.3 para.7
s.27, applied: 2009 asp 6 s.78
s.41, amended: 2009 asp 12 Sch.2 para.2, SI 2009/890 Sch.8 para.1

1995–cont.

25. Environment Act 1995–*cont.*
s.41, applied: SI 2009/890 Reg.13, Reg.14, Reg.55, Reg.65
s.41, repealed (in part): SI 2009/3381 Reg.13
s.48, applied: 2009 asp 2 Sch.5
s.56, amended: SI 2009/3381 Reg.13, SSI 2009/247 Reg.5
s.63, enabling: SI 2009/557
s.84, applied: SI 2009/486 Reg.4
s.102, repealed: 2009 c.23 Sch.22 Part 4
s.108, applied: SI 2009/153 Reg.31, SI 2009/216 Reg.7, SI 2009/261 Reg.45, SI 2009/995 Reg.31
Sch.7 para.1, enabling: SI 2009/557
Sch.7 para.2, enabling: SI 2009/557
Sch.8 para.7, amended: 2009 c.20 Sch.4 para.7
Sch.13, applied: SI 2009/3342 Reg.47
Sch.13 para.9, applied: SI 2009/3342 Reg.42
Sch.13 para.9, disapplied: SI 2009/3342 Reg.42
Sch.13 para.11, applied: SI 2009/3342 Reg.2
Sch.13 para.11, varied: SI 2009/3342 Reg.45
Sch.13 para.13, applied: SI 2009/3342 Reg.2
Sch.13 para.16, applied: SI 2009/3342 Reg.54
Sch.14, applied: SI 2009/3342 Reg.47
Sch.14 para.6, applied: SI 2009/3342 Reg.42
Sch.14 para.6, disapplied: SI 2009/3342 Reg.42
Sch.14 para.8, applied: SI 2009/3342 Reg.2
Sch.14 para.9, applied: SI 2009/3342 Reg.2, Reg.54
Sch.14 para.9, varied: SI 2009/3342 Reg.45
Sch.15 para.2, amended: SI 2009/463 Sch.2 para.9, SSI 2009/85 Sch.2 para.9
Sch.15 para.2, repealed (in part): 2009 c.23 Sch.22 Part 4
Sch.15 para.4, repealed (in part): SI 2009/463 Sch.2 para.9, SSI 2009/85 Sch.2 para.9
Sch.15 para.5, repealed: 2009 c.23 Sch.22 Part 4
Sch.15 para.8, repealed: 2009 c.23 Sch.22 Part 5
Sch.15 para.9, repealed: 2009 c.23 Sch.22 Part 5
Sch.15 para.15, repealed: 2009 c.23 Sch.22 Part 5
Sch.15 para.22, repealed: 2009 c.23 Sch.22 Part 5
Sch.15 para.23, repealed (in part): SI 2009/463 Sch.2 para.9, SSI 2009/85 Sch.2 para.9
Sch.15 para.24, repealed: 2009 c.23 Sch.22 Part 4

26. Pensions Act 1995
see *R. (on the application of Bradley) v Secretary of State for Work and Pensions* [2008] EWCA Civ 36, [2009] Q.B. 114 (CA (Civ Div)), Wall, L.J.
applied: 2009 asp 1 Sch.1 para.7
varied: SI 2009/317 Sch.1
Part I, see *R. (on the application of Bradley) v Secretary of State for Work and Pensions* [2008] EWCA Civ 36, [2009] Q.B. 114 (CA (Civ Div)), Wall, L.J.
s.4, amended: SI 2009/1941 Sch.1 para.155
s.10, applied: SI 2009/1888 Reg.2
s.10, enabling: SI 2009/615
s.11, amended: SI 2009/1682 Sch.1 para.1
s.22, amended: SI 2009/1941 Sch.1 para.155
s.29, amended: SI 2009/1941 Sch.1 para.155
s.33, see *Adams v Bridge* [2009] Pens. L.R. 153 (Pensions Ombudsman), Judge not applicable
s.36, see *Adams v Bridge* [2009] Pens. L.R. 153 (Pensions Ombudsman), Judge not applicable
s.40, enabling: SI 2009/615
s.47, applied: SI 2009/3247 Reg.6
s.50, referred to: 2009 asp 1 Sch.1 para.104
s.67, see *Walker Morris Trustees Ltd v Masterson* [2009] EWHC 1955 (Ch), [2009] Pens. L.R. 307 (Ch D), Peter Smith, J.
s.68, enabling: SI 2009/615, SI 2009/1906

1995– cont.

26. Pensions Act 1995–*cont.*
s.73, enabling: SI 2009/ 1906
s.74, enabling: SI 2009/ 615, SI 2009/ 2930
s.75, see *Easterly Ltd v Headway Plc* [2008] EWHC 2573 (Ch), [2009] Pens. L.R. 1 (Ch D), Sir Andrew Morritt (Chancellor); see *Scottish Solicitors' Staff Pension Fund Trustees v Crichton* [2009] CSOH 85, 2009 S.L.T. 1175 (OH), Lord Glennie
s.75, enabling: SI 2009/ 1906
s.91, disapplied: 2009 asp 1 Sch.1 para.106
s.91, enabling: SI 2009/ 2930
s.120, applied: SI 2009/ 1906, SI 2009/ 2930
s.124, enabling: SI 2009/ 615, SI 2009/ 1906, SI 2009/ 2930
s.174, enabling: SI 2009/ 615, SI 2009/ 1906, SI 2009/ 2930

32. Olympic Symbol etc (Protection) Act 1995
referred to: SI 2009/ 669 Sch.1 Part 1

35. Criminal Appeal Act 1995
s.12A, applied: SI 2009/ 2657 r.25, r.45, r.51
s.12A, referred to: SI 2009/ 1059 Art.184
s.12B, varied: SI 2009/ 1059 Art.184

36. Children (Scotland) Act 1995
applied: SSI 2009/ 210 Reg.45, SSI 2009/ 268 Reg.6, SSI 2009/ 284 Sch.1
Part II, applied: SSI 2009/ 210 Reg.5, Reg.13, Reg.29, Reg.34, Reg.40
Part II c.2, applied: SSI 2009/ 210 Reg.8, Reg.11, Reg.27, Reg.36
Part II c.3, applied: SSI 2009/ 210 Reg.8, Reg.11, Reg.27, Reg.36
Part II c.4, applied: SSI 2009/ 210 Reg.8, Reg.11, Reg.27, Reg.36
s.1, applied: SI 2009/ 2057 Reg.5
s.1, referred to: SSI 2009/ 154 Sch.1 para.11, Sch.1 para.12, SSI 2009/ 267 Art.13, Art.17
s.2, referred to: SSI 2009/ 154 Sch.1 para.11, Sch.1 para.12, SSI 2009/ 267 Art.13, Art.17, SSI 2009/ 284 Sch.1
s.3, amended: 2009 c.24 Sch.6 para.25
s.4, applied: SSI 2009/ 154 Reg.16, Reg.17
s.4, enabling: SSI 2009/ 191
s.11, applied: SSI 2009/ 182 Reg.28, SSI 2009/ 210 Sch.4 para.6
s.13, see *S v Argyll and Clyde Acute Hospitals NHS Trust* [2009] CSOH 43, 2009 S.L.T. 1016 (OH), Lord Brodie
s.17, applied: SSI 2009/ 210 Reg.5, Reg.11, Reg.13, Reg.20, Reg.27, Reg.29, Reg.33, Reg.34, Reg.36, Reg.38, Reg.40, Reg.41, Sch.4 para.6
s.17, referred to: SSI 2009/ 210 Reg.3, Reg.8, Reg.10, Reg.21, Reg.34, Reg.35, Reg.36, Reg.37, Reg.42, Reg.44, Reg.48, Sch.2 para.7
s.17, enabling: SSI 2009/ 210, SSI 2009/ 290
s.22, applied: 2009 c.24 s.39
s.25, applied: SSI 2009/ 210 Reg.8, Reg.47
s.26, applied: 2009 asp 9 s.43
s.31, enabling: SSI 2009/ 210, SSI 2009/ 290
s.42, enabling: SSI 2009/ 211, SSI 2009/ 307
s.51, see *K v Authority Reporter* [2009] CSIH 76, 2009 S.L.T. 1019 (IH (Ex Div)), Lord Kingarth
s.52, see *M v Scottish Children's Reporter for Renfrewshire* [2009] CSIH 49, 2009 Fam. L.R. 106 (IH (Ex Div)), Lord Osborne
s.52, applied: SSI 2009/ 284 Sch.1
s.54, referred to: SSI 2009/ 284 Sch.1
s.56, applied: SSI 2009/ 210 Reg.7
s.57, applied: SI 2009/ 1547 Sch.1 para.10

1995– cont.

36. Children (Scotland) Act 1995–*cont.*
s.70, see *Highland Council v B* 2009 Fam. L.R. 101 (Sh Ct (Grampian) (Inverness)), Sheriff Principal Sir S S T Young, Bt, QC
s.70, applied: SI 2009/ 1547 Sch.1 para.13, SSI 2009/ 210 Reg.33, SSI 2009/ 284 Sch.1
s.70, referred to: SSI 2009/ 210 Sch.4 para.6
s.73, applied: SSI 2009/ 154 Reg.13, Reg.22, Reg.23, SSI 2009/ 210 Reg.45, SSI 2009/ 284 Sch.1
s.75, applied: SSI 2009/ 284 Sch.1
s.76, applied: SI 2009/ 1547 Sch.1 para.11, SSI 2009/ 284 Sch.1
s.81, applied: SI 2009/ 1547 Sch.3 para.2
s.83, applied: SI 2009/ 1547 Sch.3 para.2
s.85, see *D v Children's Reporter* 2009 Fam. L.R. 88 (Sh Ct (South Strathclyde) (Stranraer)), Sheriff K Robb
s.86, applied: SI 2009/ 1547 Sch.1 para.14, SSI 2009/ 154 Sch.1 para.14, SSI 2009/ 267 Art.13, Art.14
s.86A, applied: SSI 2009/ 267 Art.14
s.87, applied: SSI 2009/ 267 Art.14
s.88, applied: SI 2009/ 1107 Reg.5, SSI 2009/ 267 Art.14
s.89, applied: SI 2009/ 1547 Sch.3 para.2, SSI 2009/ 267 Art.14
s.93, see *D v Children's Reporter* 2009 Fam. L.R. 88 (Sh Ct (South Strathclyde) (Stranraer)), Sheriff K Robb
s.93, applied: SSI 2009/ 284 Sch.1
s.101, applied: SSI 2009/ 284 Sch.1
s.103, enabling: SSI 2009/ 191, SSI 2009/ 210, SSI 2009/ 211, SSI 2009/ 290

38. Civil Evidence Act 1995
Sch.1 para.18, repealed: SI 2009/ 3054 Sch.1 para.16

39. Criminal Law (Consolidation) (Scotland) Act 1995
s.1, applied: 2009 asp 9 Sch.1 para.7, SSI 2009/ 31 Sch.1 para.16, SSI 2009/ 71 Sch.1 para.16
s.1, referred to: SI 2009/ 37 Sch.1 para.2, Sch.1 para.4
s.2, applied: 2009 asp 9 Sch.1 para.7, SSI 2009/ 31 Sch.1 para.16, SSI 2009/ 71 Sch.1 para.16
s.2, referred to: SI 2009/ 37 Sch.1 para.2, Sch.1 para.4
s.3, applied: 2009 asp 9 s.53, Sch.1 para.7, Sch.1 para.20, SSI 2009/ 31 Sch.1 para.16, SSI 2009/ 71 Sch.1 para.16
s.3, referred to: SI 2009/ 37 Sch.1 para.2, Sch.1 para.4
s.3, repealed: 2009 asp 9 Sch.6
s.4, see *H v Griffiths* [2009] HCJAC 15, 2009 S.L.T. 199 (HCJ), Lord Eassie
s.4, amended: 2009 asp 9 Sch.5 para.1
s.5, see *H v Griffiths* [2009] HCJAC 15, 2009 S.L.T. 199 (HCJ), Lord Eassie; see *Watson v King* [2009] HCJAC 14, 2009 S.L.T. 228 (HCJ), Lord Eassie
s.5, applied: 2009 asp 9 s.53, Sch.1 para.20, SSI 2009/ 31 Sch.1 para.16, SSI 2009/ 71 Sch.1 para.16, SSI 2009/ 182 Sch.1 para.3
s.5, referred to: SI 2009/ 37 Sch.1 para.1, Sch.1 para.2, Sch.1 para.4
s.5, repealed: 2009 asp 9 Sch.6
s.6, see *H v Griffiths* [2009] HCJAC 15, 2009 S.L.T. 199 (HCJ), Lord Eassie
s.6, applied: 2009 asp 9 s.53, Sch.1 para.20, SSI 2009/ 31 Sch.1 para.16, SSI 2009/ 71 Sch.1 para.16, SSI 2009/ 182 Sch.1 para.3
s.6, referred to: SI 2009/ 37 Sch.1 para.2, Sch.1 para.4

1995– cont.

39. Criminal Law (Consolidation) (Scotland) Act 1995– cont.
s.6, repealed: 2009 asp 9 Sch.6
s.7, applied: SSI 2009/31 Sch.1 para.16, SSI 2009/71 Sch.1 para.16
s.7, referred to: SI 2009/37 Sch.1 para.2, Sch.1 para.4
s.7, repealed (in part): 2009 asp 9 Sch.6
s.8, applied: 2009 asp 9 Sch.1 para.7, SSI 2009/31 Sch.1 para.16, SSI 2009/71 Sch.1 para.16
s.8, referred to: SI 2009/37 Sch.1 para.2, Sch.1 para.4
s.9, amended: 2009 asp 9 Sch.5 para.1
s.9, applied: 2009 asp 9 Sch.1 para.7
s.9, referred to: SI 2009/37 Sch.1 para.2, Sch.1 para.4
s.10, amended: 2009 asp 9 Sch.5 para.1
s.10, applied: 2009 asp 9 Sch.1 para.7, SSI 2009/31 Sch.1 para.16, SSI 2009/71 Sch.1 para.16
s.10, referred to: SI 2009/37 Sch.1 para.2, Sch.1 para.4
s.11, referred to: SI 2009/37 Sch.1 para.2, Sch.1 para.4
s.12A, added: 2009 asp 9 Sch.5 para.1
s.13, amended: 2009 asp 9 Sch.5 para.1
s.13, applied: 2009 asp 9 Sch.1 para.20, SSI 2009/31 Sch.1 para.16, SSI 2009/71 Sch.1 para.16, SSI 2009/182 Sch.1 para.2, Sch.1 para.3
s.13, referred to: SI 2009/37 Sch.1 para.2, Sch.1 para.4
s.13, repealed (in part): 2009 asp 9 Sch.6
s.14, repealed: 2009 asp 9 Sch.6
s.16A, referred to: 2009 asp 9 s.53
s.16A, repealed: 2009 asp 9 Sch.6
s.16B, applied: SI 2009/1547 Sch.3 para.7
s.16B, referred to: 2009 asp 9 s.53, s.56
s.16B, repealed: 2009 asp 9 Sch.6
s.19, amended: SSI 2009/248 Sch.1 para.5, Sch.2
s.23, amended: SSI 2009/248 Sch.1 para.5
s.26C, added: 2009 c.11 s.24
s.30, amended: SI 2009/1941 Sch.1 para.156
s.44, applied: 2009 c.23 s.263
s.49, see *Donnelly (Stephen) v HM Advocate* 2009 S.C.C.R. 512 (HCJ), Lord Carloway
s.50A, applied: SSI 2009/31 Sch.1 para.20, SSI 2009/71 Sch.1 para.20

40. Criminal Procedure (Consequential Provisions) (Scotland) Act 1995
Sch.4 para.89, repealed (in part): 2009 c.10 Sch.50 para.2

42. Private International Law (Miscellaneous Provisions) Act 1995
s.11, see *Knight v Axa Assurances* [2009] EWHC 1900 (QB), [2009] Lloyd's Rep. I.R. 667 (QBD), Sharp, J.; see *Maher v Groupama Grand Est* [2009] EWHC 38 (QB), [2009] 1 W.L.R. 1752 (QBD), Blair, J.; see *Middle Eastern Oil v National Bank of Abu Dhabi* [2008] EWHC 2895 (Comm), [2009] 1 Lloyd's Rep. 251 (QBD (Comm)), Teare, J.
s.12, see *Middle Eastern Oil v National Bank of Abu Dhabi* [2008] EWHC 2895 (Comm), [2009] 1 Lloyd's Rep. 251 (QBD (Comm)), Teare, J.
s.14, see *Maher v Groupama Grand Est* [2009] EWHC 38 (QB), [2009] 1 W.L.R. 1752 (QBD), Blair, J.

43. Proceeds of Crime (Scotland) Act 1995
varied: SI 2009/317 Sch.1
Part II, applied: 2009 c.25 s.164

1995– cont.

45. Gas Act 1995
Sch.4 para.2, applied: SI 2009/229 Art.4
Sch.4 para.2, repealed (in part): 2009 asp 6 Sch.3 para.8

46. Criminal Procedure (Scotland) Act 1995
referred to: SSI 2009/342 Art.2
s.3, amended: 2009 asp 9 Sch.5 para.2
s.7, amended: 2009 asp 9 Sch.5 para.2
s.14, see *Gillies v Ralph* 2009 J.C. 25 (HCJ), Lord Wheatley; see *Stone (Carole Barbara) v HM Advocate* 2009 S.C.C.R. 71 (HCJ), Lord Osborne
s.19A, amended: 2009 asp 9 Sch.5 para.2
s.23C, see *M v Watson* [2009] HCJ 3, 2009 S.L.T. 1030 (HCJ), Lord Brodie
s.23D, see *M v Watson* [2009] HCJ 3, 2009 S.L.T. 1030 (HCJ), Lord Brodie
s.24A, amended: 2009 asp 9 Sch.5 para.2
s.32, see *M v Watson* [2009] HCJ 3, 2009 S.L.T. 1030 (HCJ), Lord Brodie
s.55, applied: SSI 2009/448 Art.2
s.57, see *Scottish Ministers v Mental Health Tribunal for Scotland* [2009] CSIH 33, 2009 S.C. 510 (IH (Ex Div)), Lord Clarke
s.57A, referred to: SI 2009/1887 Sch.2
s.70, applied: SI 2009/209 Reg.118, SI 2009/216 Reg.10, SI 2009/261 Reg.52, SI 2009/3263 Reg.12
s.70, referred to: SI 2009/842 Reg.28
s.92, see *Carswell (Derek Henry) v HM Advocate* 2009 J.C. 59 (HCJ), Lord Justice General Hamilton; see *Hunt v Aitken* 2009 S.C.L. 25 (HCJ), Lord Reed
s.99, see *Carswell (Derek Henry) v HM Advocate* 2009 J.C. 59 (HCJ), Lord Justice General Hamilton
s.103, see *McIntyre (Colin McLean) v HM Advocate* [2009] HCJAC 63, 2009 S.C.L. 982 (HCJ), Lord Osborne
s.106, see *Fraser (Nat Gordon) v HM Advocate* [2009] HCJAC 27, 2009 S.L.T. 441 (HCJ), The Lord Justice Clerk (Gill)
s.110, see *McIntyre (Colin McLean) v HM Advocate* [2009] HCJAC 63, 2009 S.C.L. 982 (HCJ), Lord Osborne
s.116, referred to: SSI 2009/448 Art.2
s.118, see *Ahmed (Shaban) v HM Advocate* 2009 S.C.L. 183 (HCJ), Lord Osborne; see *HM Advocate v D* [2009] HCJAC 51, 2009 J.C. 215 (HCJ), Lord Nimmo Smith
s.124, see *McIntyre (Colin McLean) v HM Advocate* [2009] HCJAC 63, 2009 S.C.L. 982 (HCJ), Lord Osborne
s.134, applied: SSI 2009/115 Art.6, SSI 2009/331 Art.6, SSI 2009/332 Art.6
s.136, applied: SI 2009/41 Reg.30, SI 2009/847 Reg.14, SI 2009/886 Art.12, SI 2009/1495 Reg.21, SI 2009/1747 Art.22, SI 2009/3263 Reg.10
s.136, disapplied: SI 2009/886 Art.12, SI 2009/1749 Art.14
s.137, applied: SSI 2009/115 Art.6, SSI 2009/331 Art.6, SSI 2009/332 Art.6
s.137ZA, applied: SSI 2009/115 Art.6, SSI 2009/331 Art.6, SSI 2009/332 Art.6
s.141, applied: SSI 2009/225 Reg.21
s.143, see *MacLachlan v Harris* [2009] HCJAC 68, 2009 S.L.T. 1074 (HCJ), Lady Paton
s.143, applied: SI 2009/3263 Reg.12
s.144, see *Robbie the Pict v Service* [2009] HCJAC 49, 2009 S.C.L. 944 (HCJ), Lord Carloway

1995– cont.

46. Criminal Procedure (Scotland) Act 1995– *cont.*

s.178, see *Hunt v Aitken* 2009 S.C.L. 25 (HCJ), Lord Reed

s.179, see *Hunt v Aitken* 2009 S.C.L. 25 (HCJ), Lord Reed

s.179, amended: SSI 2009/108 Art.2

s.184, referred to: SSI 2009/448 Art.2

s.188, see *Lawrie & Symington Ltd v Donaldson* [2009] HCJAC 50, 2009 J.C. 296 (HCJ), Lord Carloway; see *S v McGowan* [2009] HCJAC 62, 2009 S.L.T. 922 (HCJ), Lord Hardie

s.189, see *HM Advocate v D* [2009] HCJAC 51, 2009 J.C. 215 (HCJ), Lord Nimmo Smith

s.192, see *Akram (John Ahmar Hussain) v HM Advocate* [2009] HCJAC 67, 2009 S.L.T. 805 (HCJ), Lord Osborne

s.194B, see *Akram (John Ahmar Hussain) v HM Advocate* [2009] HCJAC 67, 2009 S.L.T. 805 (HCJ), Lord Osborne

s.194B, applied: SSI 2009/448 Art.2

s.194E, see *Akram (John Ahmar Hussain) v HM Advocate* [2009] HCJAC 67, 2009 S.L.T. 805 (HCJ), Lord Osborne

s.194K, enabling: SSI 2009/448

s.199, referred to: 2009 asp 9 s.48

s.210A, amended: 2009 asp 9 Sch.5 para.2

s.210A, repealed (in part): 2009 asp 9 Sch.6

s.211, amended: SSI 2009/342 Art.7

s.221, disapplied: SSI 2009/317 Art.13

s.222, applied: SI 2009/1850 Art.10, SSI 2009/317 Art.13

s.222, varied: SI 2009/3391 Art.11

s.223A, added: SSI 2009/342 Art.3

s.223A, enabling: SSI 2009/345

s.223B, added: SSI 2009/342 Art.3

s.223C, added: SSI 2009/342 Art.3

s.223D, added: SSI 2009/342 Art.3

s.223E, added: SSI 2009/342 Art.3

s.223F, added: SSI 2009/342 Art.3

s.223G, added: SSI 2009/342 Art.3

s.223H, added: SSI 2009/342 Art.3

s.223I, added: SSI 2009/342 Art.3

s.223J, added: SSI 2009/342 Art.3

s.223K, added: SSI 2009/342 Art.3

s.223L, added: SSI 2009/342 Art.3

s.223M, added: SSI 2009/342 Art.3

s.223N, added: SSI 2009/342 Art.3

s.223O, added: SSI 2009/342 Art.3

s.223P, added: SSI 2009/342 Art.3

s.223Q, added: SSI 2009/342 Art.3

s.223R, added: SSI 2009/342 Art.3

s.223S, added: SSI 2009/342 Art.3

s.223T, added: SSI 2009/342 Art.3

s.225, applied: 2009 asp 6 s.69

s.226B, amended: SSI 2009/342 Art.5

s.226F, enabling: SSI 2009/110

s.226HA, added: SSI 2009/342 Art.4

s.226I, amended: SSI 2009/342 Art.6

s.228, applied: SI 2009/1887 Sch.1

s.228, referred to: SI 2009/1887 Sch.2

s.229, applied: SI 2009/1887 Sch.1

s.229, referred to: SI 2009/1887 Sch.2

s.229A, applied: SI 2009/1887 Sch.1

s.229A, referred to: SI 2009/1887 Sch.2

s.230, amended: SI 2009/1182 Sch.5 para.3

s.230, applied: SI 2009/1887 Sch.1

s.230, referred to: SI 2009/1887 Sch.2

s.234B, applied: SI 2009/1887 Sch.1

1995– cont.

46. Criminal Procedure (Scotland) Act 1995– *cont.*

s.247, disapplied: 2009 c.25 s.158

s.248C, repealed (in part): 2009 c.25 Sch.21 para.91, Sch.23 Part 4

s.248D, added: 2009 c.25 Sch.16 para.3

s.248D, varied: 2009 c.25 Sch.22 para.35

s.248E, added: 2009 c.25 Sch.16 para.3

s.259, see *Allison v HM Advocate* 2009 S.C.L. 167 (HCJ), Lord Osborne; see *Cowie (Colin Alexander) v HM Advocate* [2009] HCJAC 76 (HCJ), The Lord Justice Clerk (Gill); see *HM Advocate v Khder (Nazim Saber)* 2009 S.C.C.R. 187 (Sh Ct (Glasgow)), Sheriff JKM Mitchell; see *McIntyre (Ian Wayne) v HM Advocate* [2009] HCJAC 32, 2009 S.L.T. 716 (HCJ), Lord Wheatley; see *McPhee (William McAllister) v HM Advocate* [2009] HCJAC 54, 2009 J.C. 308 (HCJ), Lord Eassie

s.260, see *Hughes (Sean Stephen) v HM Advocate* [2009] HCJAC 35, 2009 J.C. 201 (HCJ), Lord Eassie; see *McIntyre (Ian Wayne) v HM Advocate* [2009] HCJAC 32, 2009 S.L.T. 716 (HCJ), Lord Wheatley

s.263, see *Ahmed (Shaban) v HM Advocate* 2009 S.C.L. 183 (HCJ), Lord Osborne

s.275, see *D v HM Advocate* [2009] HCJAC 95 (HCJ), Lady Paton

s.288C, amended: 2009 asp 9 Sch.5 para.2

s.293, see *Lowrie (James) v HM Advocate* [2009] HCJAC 71, 2009 S.C.L. 1317 (HCJ), Lord Eassie

s.293, applied: 2009 asp 9 Sch.1 para.14, Sch.1 para.34, Sch.4 para.18

s.305, enabling: SSI 2009/108, SSI 2009/144, SSI 2009/243, SSI 2009/244, SSI 2009/322, SSI 2009/345

s.307, amended: SI 2009/1182 Sch.5 para.3

s.307, varied: SI 2009/1059 Sch.1 para.35

Sch.1, referred to: SI 2009/1547 Sch.3 para.2, SSI 2009/154 Sch.1 para.14, SSI 2009/182 Sch.1 para.2

Sch.1 para.1A, added: 2009 asp 9 Sch.5 para.2

Sch.1 para.1B, added: 2009 asp 9 Sch.5 para.2

Sch.1 para.1C, added: 2009 asp 9 Sch.5 para.2

Sch.1 para.1D, added: 2009 asp 9 Sch.5 para.2

Sch.1 para.2B, referred to: SSI 2009/182 Sch.1 para.2

Sch.1 para.4A, added: 2009 asp 9 Sch.5 para.2

Sch.1 para.4B, added: 2009 asp 9 Sch.5 para.2

Sch.4, referred to: SI 2009/1887 Sch.2

Sch.5, amended: SSI 2009/248 Sch.2

Sch.6 para.4, amended: SI 2009/1182 Sch.5 para.3

Sch.9, amended: SSI 2009/248 Sch.1 para.6, Sch.2

Sch.11 para.1, added: SSI 2009/342 Art.8

Sch.11 para.2, added: SSI 2009/342 Art.8

Sch.11 para.3, added: SSI 2009/342 Art.8

Sch.11 para.4, added: SSI 2009/342 Art.8

Sch.11 para.5, added: SSI 2009/342 Art.8

Sch.11 para.6, added: SSI 2009/342 Art.8

Sch.11 para.7, added: SSI 2009/342 Art.8

Sch.12 Part I para.1, added: SSI 2009/342 Art.8

Sch.12 Part I para.2, added: SSI 2009/342 Art.8

Sch.12 Part I para.3, added: SSI 2009/342 Art.8

Sch.12 Part I para.4, added: SSI 2009/342 Art.8

Sch.12 Part I para.5, added: SSI 2009/342 Art.8

Sch.12 Part I para.6, added: SSI 2009/342 Art.8

Sch.12 Part I para.7, added: SSI 2009/342 Art.8

Sch.12 Part II para.8, added: SSI 2009/342 Art.8

Sch.12 Part II para.9, added: SSI 2009/342 Art.8

Sch.12 Part II para.10, added: SSI 2009/342 Art.8

46. Criminal Procedure (Scotland) Act 1995–*cont.*
Sch.12 Part II para.11, added: SSI 2009/342 Art.8
Sch.12 Part II para.12, added: SSI 2009/342 Art.8
Sch.12 Part II para.13, added: SSI 2009/342 Art.8
Sch.12 Part II para.14, added: SSI 2009/342 Art.8
Sch.12 Part II para.15, added: SSI 2009/342 Art.8
Sch.12 Part II para.16, added: SSI 2009/342 Art.8
Sch.12 Part II para.17, added: SSI 2009/342 Art.8
Sch.12 Part II para.18, added: SSI 2009/342 Art.8
Sch.12 Part II para.19, added: SSI 2009/342 Art.8
Sch.12 Part II para.20, added: SSI 2009/342 Art.8
Sch.12 Part II para.21, added: SSI 2009/342 Art.8
Sch.12 Part II para.22, added: SSI 2009/342 Art.8
Sch.12 Part II para.23, added: SSI 2009/342 Art.8
Sch.12 Part II para.24, added: SSI 2009/342 Art.8
Sch.12 Part II para.25, added: SSI 2009/342 Art.8
Sch.12 Part II para.26, added: SSI 2009/342 Art.8
Sch.12 Part II para.27, added: SSI 2009/342 Art.8
Sch.12 Part II para.28, added: SSI 2009/342 Art.8
Sch.12 Part II para.29, added: SSI 2009/342 Art.8
Sch.12 Part II para.30, added: SSI 2009/342 Art.8
Sch.12 Part II para.31, added: SSI 2009/342 Art.8
Sch.12 Part II para.32, added: SSI 2009/342 Art.8
Sch.12 Part II para.33, added: SSI 2009/342 Art.8
Sch.12 Part II para.34, added: SSI 2009/342 Art.8
Sch.12 Part II para.35, added: SSI 2009/342 Art.8
Sch.12 Part II para.36, added: SSI 2009/342 Art.8
Sch.12 Part II para.37, added: SSI 2009/342 Art.8
Sch.12 Part II para.38, added: SSI 2009/342 Art.8
Sch.12 Part II para.39, added: SSI 2009/342 Art.8
Sch.12 Part II para.40, added: SSI 2009/342 Art.8
Sch.12 Part II para.41, added: SSI 2009/342 Art.8
Sch.12 Part II para.42, added: SSI 2009/342 Art.8
Sch.12 Part II para.43, added: SSI 2009/342 Art.8
Sch.12 Part II para.44, added: SSI 2009/342 Art.8
Sch.12 Part II para.45, added: SSI 2009/342 Art.8
Sch.12 Part II para.46, added: SSI 2009/342 Art.8
Sch.12 Part III para.47, added: SSI 2009/342 Art.8

50. Disability Discrimination Act 1995
see *Booth v Oldham MBC* [2009] EWCA Civ 880,
[2009] Pens. L.R. 325 (CA (Civ Div)), Laws, L.J.;
see *Kingston upon Hull City Council v
Matuszowicz* [2009] EWCA Civ 22, [2009] 3
All E.R. 685 (CA (Civ Div)), Sedley, L.J.; see
SCA Packaging Ltd v Boyle [2009] I.R.L.R. 54
(CA (NI)), Kerr, L.C.J.; see *Sneddon v
Renfrewshire Council* [2009] CSIH 40, 2009
S.C. 539 (IH (Ex Div)), Lord Osborne; see
Stockton on Tees BC v Aylott [2009] I.C.R. 872
(EAT), Slade, J.
referred to: SI 2009/669 Sch.1 Part 7
Part III, see *R. (on the application of N) v
Independent Appeal Panel of Barking and
Dagenham LBC* [2009] EWCA Civ 108, [2009]
B.L.G.R. 711 (CA (Civ Div)), Rix, L.J.
s.1, see *Chief Constable of Dumfries and Galloway v
Adams* [2009] I.C.R. 1034 (EAT (SC)), Lady
Smith; see *Child Support Agency (Dudley) v
Truman* [2009] I.C.R. 576 (EAT), Judge Peter
Clark; see *SCA Packaging Ltd v Boyle* [2009]
I.R.L.R. 54 (CA (NI)), Kerr, L.C.J.
s.1, applied: 2009 c.22 s.218, SI 2009/2816 Art.4, SI
2009/3200 Sch.1 para.5
s.3A, see *Child Support Agency (Dudley) v Truman*
[2009] I.C.R. 576 (EAT), Judge Peter Clark; see
Stockton on Tees BC v Aylott [2009] I.C.R. 872
(EAT), Slade, J.

50. Disability Discrimination Act 1995–*cont.*
s.4A, see *Eastern and Coastal Kent Primary Care
Trust v Grey* [2009] I.R.L.R. 429 (EAT), Silber, J.;
see *Stafford and Rural Homes Ltd v Hughes*
(2009) 107 B.M.L.R. 155 (EAT), Judge Reid Q.C.
s.17A, see *Stockton on Tees BC v Aylott* [2009] I.C.R.
872 (EAT), Slade, J.
s.18B, see *Stafford and Rural Homes Ltd v Hughes*
(2009) 107 B.M.L.R. 155 (EAT), Judge Reid Q.C.
s.24, see *Child Support Agency (Dudley) v Truman*
[2009] I.C.R. 576 (EAT), Judge Peter Clark; see
Stockton on Tees BC v Aylott [2009] I.C.R. 872
(EAT), Slade, J.
s.28B, see *R. (on the application of N) v
Independent Appeal Panel of Barking and
Dagenham LBC* [2009] EWCA Civ 108, [2009]
B.L.G.R. 711 (CA (Civ Div)), Rix, L.J.; see *S v K
School* 2009 S.L.T. (Sh Ct) 86 (Sh Ct (Glasgow)),
Temporary Sheriff Principal C G McKay
s.28C, see *D v Bedfordshire CC* [2008] EWHC 2664
(Admin), [2009] E.L.R. 1 (QBD (Admin)), Sir
George Newman; see *Governors of X
Endowed Primary School v Special
Educational Needs and Disability Tribunal*
[2009] EWHC 1842 (Admin), [2009] I.R.L.R.
1007 (QBD (Admin)), Lloyd-Jones J.; see *S v K
School* 2009 S.L.T. (Sh Ct) 86 (Sh Ct (Glasgow)),
Temporary Sheriff Principal C G McKay
s.28G, see *D v Bedfordshire CC* [2008] EWHC
2664 (Admin), [2009] E.L.R. 1 (QBD
(Admin)), Sir George Newman; see *D v
Bedfordshire CC* [2009] EWCA Civ 678, [2009]
E.L.R. 361 (CA (Civ Div)), Rix, L.J.
s.28M, amended: 2009 c.22 s.221
s.36, varied: SI 2009/2863 Reg.4, Reg.5
s.36A, varied: SI 2009/2863 Reg.4, Reg.5
s.37A, varied: SI 2009/2863 Reg.4
s.38, varied: SI 2009/2863 Reg.4, Reg.5
s.40, applied: SI 2009/143
s.40, referred to: SI 2009/491 Sch.1 Part 1
s.40, enabling: SI 2009/143
s.41, applied: SI 2009/711 Sch.1 para.48
s.41, referred to: SI 2009/491 Sch.1 Part 1
s.41, enabling: SI 2009/143
s.42, applied: SI 2009/711 Sch.1 para.49
s.44, applied: SI 2009/711 Sch.1 para.50
s.45, applied: SI 2009/711 Art.8, SI 2009/876
s.45, enabling: SI 2009/876
s.49A, see *R. (on the application of AM) v
Birmingham City Council* [2009] EWHC 688
(Admin), (2009) 12 C.C.L. Rep. 407 (QBD
(Admin)), Cranston, J.; see *R. (on the
application of B) v DPP* [2009] EWHC 106
(Admin), [2009] 1 W.L.R. 2072 (DC), Toulson,
L.J.
s.67, enabling: SI 2009/876
s.68, varied: SI 2009/1059 Sch.1 para.36
Sch.1, see *Governors of X Endowed Primary School
v Special Educational Needs and Disability
Tribunal* [2009] EWHC 1842 (Admin), [2009]
I.R.L.R. 1007 (QBD (Admin)), Lloyd-Jones J.
Sch.1 para.2, see *Chief Constable of Dumfries and
Galloway v Adams* [2009] I.C.R. 1034 (EAT
(SC)), Lady Smith; see *SCA Packaging Ltd v
Boyle* [2009] UKHL 37, [2009] 4 All E.R. 1181
(HL (NI)), Lord Hope of Craighead
Sch.1 para.6, see *SCA Packaging Ltd v Boyle* [2009]
I.R.L.R. 54 (CA (NI)), Kerr, L.C.J.; see *SCA
Packaging Ltd v Boyle* [2009] UKHL 37, [2009]

1995– cont.

50. Disability Discrimination Act 1995–*cont.*
Sch.1 para.6–*cont.*
4 All E.R. 1181 (HL (NI)), Lord Hope of Craighead
Sch.3 para.3, see *Kingston upon Hull City Council v Matuszowicz* [2009] EWCA Civ 22, [2009] 3 All E.R. 685 (CA (Civ Div)), Sedley, L.J.
Sch.8 para.53, amended: SI 2009/1941 Sch.2

53. Criminal Injuries Compensation Act 1995
s.5, see *Practice Direction (Sup Ct: Upper Tribunal: Judicial Review Jurisdiction)* [2009] 1 W.L.R. 327 (Sup Ct), Lord Judge, L.C.J.
s.11, amended: 2009 asp 9 Sch.5 para.3

1996

6. Chemical Weapons Act 1996
s.24, applied: SSI 2009/44 Sch.7 para.8

8. Finance Act 1996
see *DCC Holdings (UK) Ltd v Revenue and Customs Commissioners* [2008] EWHC 2429 (Ch), [2009] S.T.C. 77 (Ch D), Norris, J.
varied: SI 2009/317 Sch.1
Part III, referred to: 2009 c.10 Sch.60 para.1
Part III, see *Waste Recycling Group Ltd v Revenue and Customs Commissioners* [2008] EWCA Civ 849, [2009] S.T.C. 200 (CA (Civ Div)), Sir Andrew Morritt C.
s.40, see *Waste Recycling Group Ltd v Revenue and Customs Commissioners* [2008] EWCA Civ 849, [2009] S.T.C. 200 (CA (Civ Div)), Sir Andrew Morritt C.
s.42, amended: 2009 c.10 s.18
s.43C, repealed: 2009 c.10 Sch.60 para.10
s.46, amended: SI 2009/56 Sch.1 para.233
s.49, amended: 2009 c.10 Sch.60 para.12
s.49, enabling: SI 2009/1930
s.51, enabling: SI 2009/1930
s.54, amended: SI 2009/56 Sch.1 para.234
s.54, repealed (in part): SI 2009/56 Sch.1 para.234
s.54A, added: SI 2009/56 Sch.1 para.235
s.54B, added: SI 2009/56 Sch.1 para.235
s.54C, added: SI 2009/56 Sch.1 para.235
s.54D, added: SI 2009/56 Sch.1 para.235
s.54E, added: SI 2009/56 Sch.1 para.235
s.54F, added: SI 2009/56 Sch.1 para.235
s.54G, added: SI 2009/56 Sch.1 para.235
s.55, amended: SI 2009/56 Sch.1 para.236
s.55, repealed (in part): SI 2009/56 Sch.1 para.236
s.56, amended: SI 2009/56 Sch.1 para.237
s.56, applied: SI 2009/56 Sch.3 para.9
s.56, repealed (in part): SI 2009/56 Sch.1 para.237
s.59, amended: SI 2009/1890 Art.4
s.62, repealed: 2009 c.10 Sch.60 para.4
s.62, enabling: SI 2009/1930
s.64, see *Waste Recycling Group Ltd v Revenue and Customs Commissioners* [2008] EWCA Civ 849, [2009] S.T.C. 200 (CA (Civ Div)), Sir Andrew Morritt C.
s.65, see *Waste Recycling Group Ltd v Revenue and Customs Commissioners* [2008] EWCA Civ 849, [2009] S.T.C. 200 (CA (Civ Div)), Sir Andrew Morritt C.
s.65A, added: 2009 c.10 Sch.60 para.2
s.65A, applied: SI 2009/1929 Art.3
s.65A, enabling: SI 2009/1929
s.70, amended: SI 2009/56 Sch.1 para.238
s.71, amended: 2009 c.10 Sch.60 para.3
s.80, repealed: 2009 c.4 Sch.3 Part 1

1996– cont.

8. Finance Act 1996–*cont.*
s.81, repealed: 2009 c.4 Sch.3 Part 1
s.82, see *DCC Holdings (UK) Ltd v Revenue and Customs Commissioners* [2008] EWHC 2429 (Ch), [2009] S.T.C. 77 (Ch D), Norris, J.
s.82, repealed: 2009 c.4 Sch.3 Part 1
s.83, repealed: 2009 c.4 Sch.3 Part 1
s.84, see *DCC Holdings (UK) Ltd v Revenue and Customs Commissioners* [2008] EWHC 2429 (Ch), [2009] S.T.C. 77 (Ch D), Norris, J.
s.84, repealed: 2009 c.4 Sch.3 Part 1
s.84A, repealed: 2009 c.4 Sch.3 Part 1
s.85, see *DCC Holdings (UK) Ltd v Revenue and Customs Commissioners* [2008] EWHC 2429 (Ch), [2009] S.T.C. 77 (Ch D), Norris, J.
s.85, repealed: 2009 c.4 Sch.3 Part 1
s.85A, repealed: 2009 c.4 Sch.3 Part 1
s.85B, repealed: 2009 c.4 Sch.3 Part 1
s.85C, repealed: 2009 c.4 Sch.3 Part 1
s.86, repealed: 2009 c.4 Sch.3 Part 1
s.87, repealed: 2009 c.4 Sch.3 Part 1
s.87A, repealed: 2009 c.4 Sch.3 Part 1
s.88, repealed: 2009 c.4 Sch.3 Part 1
s.88A, repealed: 2009 c.4 Sch.3 Part 1
s.89, repealed: 2009 c.4 Sch.3 Part 1
s.90, repealed: 2009 c.4 Sch.3 Part 1
s.90A, repealed: 2009 c.4 Sch.3 Part 1
s.91, repealed: 2009 c.4 Sch.3 Part 1
s.91A, repealed: 2009 c.4 Sch.3 Part 1
s.91B, repealed: 2009 c.4 Sch.3 Part 1
s.91C, repealed: 2009 c.4 Sch.3 Part 1
s.91D, repealed: 2009 c.4 Sch.3 Part 1
s.91E, repealed: 2009 c.4 Sch.3 Part 1
s.91F, repealed: 2009 c.4 Sch.3 Part 1
s.91G, repealed: 2009 c.4 Sch.3 Part 1
s.91H, repealed: 2009 c.4 Sch.3 Part 1
s.91I, repealed: 2009 c.4 Sch.3 Part 1
s.92, repealed: 2009 c.4 Sch.3 Part 1
s.92A, repealed: 2009 c.4 Sch.3 Part 1
s.93, repealed: 2009 c.4 Sch.3 Part 1
s.93A, repealed: 2009 c.4 Sch.3 Part 1
s.93B, repealed: 2009 c.4 Sch.3 Part 1
s.93C, repealed: 2009 c.4 Sch.3 Part 1
s.94, repealed: 2009 c.4 Sch.3 Part 1
s.94A, repealed: 2009 c.4 Sch.3 Part 1
s.94B, repealed: 2009 c.4 Sch.3 Part 1
s.95, repealed: 2009 c.4 Sch.3 Part 1
s.96, repealed: 2009 c.4 Sch.3 Part 1
s.97, see *DCC Holdings (UK) Ltd v Revenue and Customs Commissioners* [2008] EWHC 2429 (Ch), [2009] S.T.C. 77 (Ch D), Norris, J.
s.97, amended: 2009 c.10 Sch.30 para.5
s.97, repealed: 2009 c.4 Sch.3 Part 1
s.98, repealed: 2009 c.4 Sch.3 Part 1
s.99, repealed: 2009 c.4 Sch.3 Part 1
s.100, applied: 2009 c.10 Sch.13 para.4
s.100, repealed: 2009 c.4 Sch.3 Part 1
s.101, repealed: 2009 c.4 Sch.3 Part 1
s.102, repealed: 2009 c.4 Sch.3 Part 1
s.103, repealed: 2009 c.4 Sch.3 Part 1
s.147, repealed (in part): 2009 c.4 Sch.3 Part 1
s.154, repealed (in part): 2009 c.4 Sch.3 Part 1
s.186, amended: SI 2009/1890 Art.10
s.197, amended: SI 2009/56 Sch.1 para.239
s.197, repealed (in part): 2009 c.10 s.105
s.197, enabling: SI 2009/2032
s.203, amended: 2009 c.4 Sch.1 para.439
Sch.5 Part I, substituted: 2009 c.10 Sch.60 para.6

8. Finance Act 1996–*cont.*

Sch.5 Part I, substituted: 2009 c.10 Sch.60 para.8
Sch.5 Part I para.1, repealed: SI 2009/3054 Sch.1 para.7
Sch.5 Part I para.1A, added: 2009 c.10 Sch.60 para.7
Sch.5 Part I para.1A, enabling: SI 2009/1930
Sch.5 Part I para.1B, added: 2009 c.10 Sch.60 para.11
Sch.5 Part I para.1B, applied: SI 2009/1929 Art.3
Sch.5 Part I para.2, amended: 2009 c.10 Sch.50 para.21
Sch.5 Part I para.2, enabling: SI 2009/1930
Sch.5 Part I para.2A, added: 2009 c.10 Sch.60 para.9
Sch.5 Part I para.2A, enabling: SI 2009/1930
Sch.5 Part I para.3, repealed: SI 2009/3054 Sch.1 para.7
Sch.5 Part II para.4, repealed: SI 2009/3054 Sch.1 para.7
Sch.5 Part III para.14, amended: 2009 c.10 Sch.51 para.38
Sch.5 Part V, applied: 2009 c.4 s.1303
Sch.5 Part V para.19, amended: SI 2009/56 Sch.1 para.240
Sch.5 Part V para.22, amended: SI 2009/571 Sch.1 para.29
Sch.5 Part V para.22, applied: SI 2009/3054 Art.6
Sch.5 Part V para.22, repealed (in part): SI 2009/3054 Sch.1 para.7
Sch.5 Part V para.23, amended: SI 2009/571 Sch.1 para.29
Sch.5 Part VI para.26, applied: 2009 c.4 s.1303
Sch.5 Part VI para.27, applied: 2009 c.4 s.1303, 2009 c.10 s.108
Sch.5 Part VI para.29, amended: 2009 c.10 Sch.51 para.39
Sch.5 Part VII para.33, amended: 2009 c.10 Sch.51 para.40
Sch.5 Part VII para.33, repealed (in part): 2009 c.10 Sch.51 para.40
Sch.5 Part VIII, amended: SI 2009/56 Sch.1 para.240
Sch.5 Part VIII para.59, amended: SI 2009/56 Sch.1 para.240
Sch.6 para.22, repealed: 2009 c.4 Sch.3 Part 1
Sch.7 para.4, repealed (in part): 2009 c.4 Sch.3 Part 1
Sch.7 para.23, repealed: 2009 c.10 Sch.25 para.9
Sch.8 para.1, repealed: 2009 c.4 Sch.3 Part 1
Sch.8 para.2, repealed: 2009 c.4 Sch.3 Part 1
Sch.8 para.3, repealed: 2009 c.4 Sch.3 Part 1
Sch.8 para.4, repealed: 2009 c.4 Sch.3 Part 1
Sch.8 para.5, repealed: 2009 c.4 Sch.3 Part 1
Sch.9 para.1, repealed: 2009 c.4 Sch.3 Part 1
Sch.9 para.1A, repealed: 2009 c.4 Sch.3 Part 1
Sch.9 para.2, repealed: 2009 c.4 Sch.3 Part 1
Sch.9 para.3, repealed: 2009 c.4 Sch.3 Part 1
Sch.9 para.4, repealed: 2009 c.4 Sch.3 Part 1
Sch.9 para.4A, repealed: 2009 c.4 Sch.3 Part 1
Sch.9 para.5, repealed: 2009 c.4 Sch.3 Part 1
Sch.9 para.5A, repealed: 2009 c.4 Sch.3 Part 1
Sch.9 para.5ZA, repealed: 2009 c.4 Sch.3 Part 1
Sch.9 para.6, repealed: 2009 c.4 Sch.3 Part 1
Sch.9 para.6A, repealed: 2009 c.4 Sch.3 Part 1
Sch.9 para.6B, repealed: 2009 c.4 Sch.3 Part 1
Sch.9 para.6C, repealed: 2009 c.4 Sch.3 Part 1
Sch.9 para.6D, repealed: 2009 c.4 Sch.3 Part 1
Sch.9 para.7, repealed: 2009 c.4 Sch.3 Part 1
Sch.9 para.8, repealed: 2009 c.4 Sch.3 Part 1

8. Finance Act 1996–*cont.*

Sch.9 para.9, repealed: 2009 c.4 Sch.3 Part 1
Sch.9 para.10, repealed: 2009 c.4 Sch.3 Part 1
Sch.9 para.10A, repealed: 2009 c.4 Sch.3 Part 1
Sch.9 para.11, repealed: 2009 c.4 Sch.3 Part 1
Sch.9 para.11A, repealed: 2009 c.4 Sch.3 Part 1
Sch.9 para.11B, repealed: 2009 c.4 Sch.3 Part 1
Sch.9 para.12, repealed: 2009 c.4 Sch.3 Part 1
Sch.9 para.12A, repealed: 2009 c.4 Sch.3 Part 1
Sch.9 para.12B, repealed: 2009 c.4 Sch.3 Part 1
Sch.9 para.12C, repealed: 2009 c.4 Sch.3 Part 1
Sch.9 para.12D, repealed: 2009 c.4 Sch.3 Part 1
Sch.9 para.12E, repealed: 2009 c.4 Sch.3 Part 1
Sch.9 para.12F, repealed: 2009 c.4 Sch.3 Part 1
Sch.9 para.12G, repealed: 2009 c.4 Sch.3 Part 1
Sch.9 para.12H, repealed: 2009 c.4 Sch.3 Part 1
Sch.9 para.12I, repealed: 2009 c.4 Sch.3 Part 1
Sch.9 para.12J, repealed: 2009 c.4 Sch.3 Part 1
Sch.9 para.13, repealed: 2009 c.4 Sch.3 Part 1
Sch.9 para.14, repealed: 2009 c.4 Sch.3 Part 1
Sch.9 para.14A, repealed: 2009 c.4 Sch.3 Part 1
Sch.9 para.15, see *DCC Holdings (UK) Ltd v Revenue and Customs Commissioners* [2008] EWHC 2429 (Ch), [2009] S.T.C. 77 (Ch D), Norris, J.
Sch.9 para.15, repealed: 2009 c.4 Sch.3 Part 1
Sch.9 para.16, repealed: 2009 c.4 Sch.3 Part 1
Sch.9 para.17, repealed: 2009 c.4 Sch.3 Part 1
Sch.9 para.18, repealed: 2009 c.4 Sch.3 Part 1
Sch.9 para.19, repealed: 2009 c.4 Sch.3 Part 1
Sch.9 para.19A, repealed: 2009 c.4 Sch.3 Part 1
Sch.9 para.19B, repealed: 2009 c.4 Sch.3 Part 1
Sch.9 para.20, repealed: 2009 c.4 Sch.3 Part 1
Sch.10 para.1, repealed: 2009 c.4 Sch.3 Part 1
Sch.10 para.1A, repealed: 2009 c.4 Sch.3 Part 1
Sch.10 para.1B, repealed: 2009 c.4 Sch.3 Part 1
Sch.10 para.2, repealed: 2009 c.4 Sch.3 Part 1
Sch.10 para.2A, repealed: 2009 c.4 Sch.3 Part 1
Sch.10 para.2B, repealed: 2009 c.4 Sch.3 Part 1
Sch.10 para.3, repealed: 2009 c.4 Sch.3 Part 1
Sch.10 para.4, repealed: 2009 c.4 Sch.3 Part 1
Sch.10 para.5, repealed: 2009 c.4 Sch.3 Part 1
Sch.10 para.6, repealed: 2009 c.4 Sch.3 Part 1
Sch.10 para.7, repealed: 2009 c.4 Sch.3 Part 1
Sch.10 para.8, repealed: 2009 c.4 Sch.3 Part 1
Sch.10 para.9, repealed: 2009 c.4 Sch.3 Part 1
Sch.11 Part I para.1, repealed: 2009 c.4 Sch.3 Part 1
Sch.11 Part I para.2, repealed: 2009 c.4 Sch.3 Part 1
Sch.11 Part I para.3, repealed: 2009 c.4 Sch.3 Part 1
Sch.11 Part I para.3A, repealed: 2009 c.4 Sch.3 Part 1
Sch.11 Part I para.4, repealed: 2009 c.4 Sch.3 Part 1
Sch.11 Part I para.5, repealed: 2009 c.4 Sch.3 Part 1
Sch.11 Part I para.6, repealed: 2009 c.4 Sch.3 Part 1
Sch.11 Part II para.7, repealed: 2009 c.4 Sch.3 Part 1
Sch.11 Part II para.8, repealed: 2009 c.4 Sch.3 Part 1
Sch.13, see *Astall v Revenue and Customs Commissioners* [2009] EWCA Civ 1010, [2009] B.T.C. 631 (CA (Civ Div)), Arden, L.J.
Sch.13 para.2, see *Astall v Revenue and Customs Commissioners* [2009] EWCA Civ 1010, [2009] B.T.C. 631 (CA (Civ Div)), Arden, L.J.
Sch.13 para.3, see *Astall v Revenue and Customs Commissioners* [2009] EWCA Civ 1010, [2009] B.T.C. 631 (CA (Civ Div)), Arden, L.J.
Sch.14 para.5, repealed: 2009 c.4 Sch.3 Part 1
Sch.14 para.7, repealed: 2009 c.4 Sch.3 Part 1
Sch.14 para.20, repealed: 2009 c.4 Sch.3 Part 1

1996– cont.

8. Finance Act 1996–*cont.*

Sch.14 para.31, repealed: 2009 c.4 Sch.3 Part 1

Sch.15 Part I para.2, repealed: 2009 c.4 Sch.3 Part 1

Sch.15 Part I para.3, repealed: 2009 c.4 Sch.3 Part 1

Sch.15 Part I para.3A, repealed: 2009 c.4 Sch.3 Part 1

Sch.15 Part I para.4, repealed: 2009 c.4 Sch.3 Part 1

Sch.15 Part I para.5, amended: 2009 c.4 Sch.1 para.444

Sch.15 Part I para.6, amended: 2009 c.4 Sch.1 para.444

Sch.15 Part I para.9, amended: 2009 c.4 Sch.1 para.444

Sch.15 Part I para.10, repealed: 2009 c.4 Sch.3 Part 1

Sch.15 Part I para.11, amended: 2009 c.4 Sch.1 para.444

Sch.15 Part I para.11A, amended: 2009 c.4 Sch.1 para.444

Sch.15 Part I para.12, amended: 2009 c.4 Sch.1 para.444

Sch.15 Part I para.13, repealed: 2009 c.4 Sch.3 Part 1

Sch.15 Part I para.14, repealed: 2009 c.4 Sch.3 Part 1

Sch.15 Part I para.15, repealed: 2009 c.4 Sch.3 Part 1

Sch.15 Part I para.16, amended: 2009 c.4 Sch.1 para.444

Sch.15 Part I para.17, amended: 2009 c.4 Sch.1 para.444

Sch.15 Part I para.18, repealed: 2009 c.4 Sch.3 Part 1

Sch.15 Part I para.19, amended: 2009 c.4 Sch.1 para.444

Sch.15 Part I para.19, repealed (in part): 2009 c.4 Sch.3 Part 1

Sch.15 Part I para.20, amended: 2009 c.4 Sch.1 para.444

Sch.15 Part I para.20, repealed (in part): 2009 c.4 Sch.3 Part 1

Sch.15 Part I para.21, amended: 2009 c.4 Sch.1 para.444

Sch.15 Part I para.21, repealed (in part): 2009 c.4 Sch.3 Part 1

Sch.20 para.2, repealed: 2009 c.4 Sch.3 Part 1

Sch.20 para.14, repealed (in part): 2009 c.10 Sch.1 para.6

Sch.20 para.33, repealed: 2009 c.4 Sch.3 Part 1

Sch.21 para.2, repealed: 2009 c.4 Sch.3 Part 1

Sch.21 para.3, repealed: 2009 c.4 Sch.3 Part 1

Sch.21 para.4, repealed: 2009 c.10 Sch.1 para.6

Sch.21 para.5, repealed: 2009 c.10 Sch.1 para.6

Sch.21 para.6, repealed: 2009 c.10 Sch.1 para.6

Sch.21 para.15, repealed: 2009 c.4 Sch.3 Part 1

Sch.21 para.20, repealed: 2009 c.4 Sch.3 Part 1

Sch.24 Part II para.11, repealed: 2009 c.4 Sch.3 Part 1

Sch.28 para.6, amended: SI 2009/3001 Sch.2

Sch.36 para.3, repealed (in part): 2009 c.10 Sch.16 para.5

Sch.36 para.4, repealed (in part): 2009 c.10 Sch.16 para.5

13. Non-Domestic Rating (Information) Act 1996

s.1, amended: 2009 c.7 s.12

14. Reserve Forces Act 1996

applied: SI 2009/1059 Art.13, Art.18, Art.19, Art.20, Art.22, Art.201, SI 2009/1212 Reg.3

Part I, applied: 2009 c.9 Sch.2 Part 22

Part III, applied: 2009 c.9 Sch.2 Part 22

Part IV, applied: 2009 c.9 Sch.2 Part 22, SI 2009/832 Reg.8, SI 2009/1091 Reg.8

Part V, applied: 2009 c.9 Sch.2 Part 22, SI 2009/832 Reg.8, SI 2009/1091 Reg.8

1996– cont.

14. Reserve Forces Act 1996–*cont.*

Part VI, applied: SI 2009/832 Reg.8, SI 2009/1091 Reg.8

Part VII, applied: SI 2009/832 Reg.8, SI 2009/1091 Reg.8

s.4, applied: SI 2009/1111 Reg.10

s.13, referred to: SI 2009/1059 Art.195

s.52, applied: SI 2009/832 Reg.8, SI 2009/1089 Sch.1 para.7, Sch.1 para.9, Sch.1 para.11, SI 2009/1091 Reg.8

s.54, applied: SI 2009/832 Reg.8, SI 2009/1091 Reg.8

s.56, applied: SI 2009/832 Reg.8, SI 2009/1091 Reg.8

s.95, applied: 2009 c.25 Sch.22 para.15, Sch.22 para.21, SI 2009/1059 Art.201, SI 2009/1111 Reg.10

s.96, applied: 2009 c.25 Sch.22 para.15, Sch.22 para.21, SI 2009/1059 Art.15, Art.201

s.97, applied: 2009 c.25 Sch.22 para.15, Sch.22 para.21, SI 2009/1059 Art.15, SI 2009/1109 Reg.3

s.98, referred to: SI 2009/1059 Art.201

s.99, applied: SI 2009/1059 Art.201

s.105, referred to: SI 2009/1059 Art.201

s.107, disapplied: SI 2009/1059 Art.201

s.107, referred to: SI 2009/1059 Art.201

s.108, enabling: SI 2009/1111

Sch.1 para.5, applied: 2009 c.25 Sch.22 para.15, Sch.22 para.21

Sch.2 para.4, applied: SI 2009/1059 Art.39, Art.182

Sch.2 para.5, applied: SI 2009/1059 Art.39, Art.182

Sch.2 para.6, applied: SI 2009/1059 Art.39

Sch.3 para.1, applied: SI 2009/1059 Art.200

Sch.3 para.2, applied: SI 2009/1059 Art.200

Sch.3 para.3, applied: SI 2009/1059 Art.200

Sch.3 para.4, applied: SI 2009/1059 Art.200

Sch.3 para.5, applied: SI 2009/1059 Art.200

Sch.3 para.6, applied: SI 2009/1059 Art.200

Sch.3 para.7, applied: SI 2009/1059 Art.200

Sch.3 para.8, applied: SI 2009/1059 Art.200

Sch.7 para.1, applied: SI 2009/1091 Reg.9

Sch.7 para.1, disapplied: SI 2009/832 Reg.9

Sch.7 para.2, applied: SI 2009/832 Reg.9, SI 2009/1091 Reg.9

Sch.7 para.3, disapplied: SI 2009/832 Reg.10, SI 2009/1091 Reg.10

Sch.7 para.4, applied: SI 2009/832 Reg.10, SI 2009/1091 Reg.10

Sch.7 para.5, disapplied: SI 2009/832 Reg.11, SI 2009/1091 Reg.11

Sch.7 para.6, applied: SI 2009/832 Reg.11, SI 2009/1091 Reg.11

Sch.7 para.7, disapplied: SI 2009/832 Reg.12, SI 2009/1091 Reg.12

Sch.7 para.8, applied: SI 2009/832 Reg.12, SI 2009/1091 Reg.12

16. Police Act 1996

s.2, applied: SI 2009/1922 Art.14, SI 2009/3069 Reg.3

s.6, amended: 2009 c.26 s.1

s.6ZB, applied: SI 2009/119 Sch.2 para.3

s.9A, amended: 2009 c.26 Sch.7 para.2

s.9F, amended: 2009 c.26 s.4

s.9FA, amended: 2009 c.26 s.4

s.9G, amended: 2009 c.26 s.4

s.10, amended: 2009 c.26 Sch.7 para.3

s.15, amended: 2009 c.26 Sch.7 para.4

s.18, amended: 2009 c.26 Sch.7 para.5

s.23, substituted: 2009 c.26 s.5

1996–*cont.*

16. Police Act 1996–*cont.*
s.23A, substituted: 2009 c.26 s.5
s.23B, substituted: 2009 c.26 s.5
s.23C, substituted: 2009 c.26 s.5
s.23D, substituted: 2009 c.26 s.5
s.23E, substituted: 2009 c.26 s.5
s.23F, substituted: 2009 c.26 s.5
s.23G, substituted: 2009 c.26 s.5
s.23H, substituted: 2009 c.26 s.5
s.23I, substituted: 2009 c.26 s.5
s.25, see *Chief Constable of Greater Manchester v Wigan Athletic AFCLtd* [2008] EWCA Civ 1449, [2009] 1 W.L.R. 1580 (CA (Civ Div)), Sir Andrew Morritt (Chancellor)
s.27, amended: 2009 c.26 Sch.7 para.6
s.30, amended: 2009 c.26 Sch.7 para.7
s.40B, amended: 2009 c.26 Sch.7 para.133
s.50, amended: 2009 c.26 s.3
s.53, amended: 2009 c.26 s.11
s.53A, amended: 2009 c.26 s.12
s.53B, added: 2009 c.26 s.2
s.53C, added: 2009 c.26 s.2
s.53D, added: 2009 c.26 s.2
s.54, amended: 2009 c.26 s.1
s.54, referred to: 2009 c.11 s.29
s.54, repealed (in part): 2009 c.26 s.2, Sch.8 Part 1
s.55, referred to: 2009 c.11 s.29
s.56, referred to: 2009 c.11 s.29
s.57, amended: 2009 c.26 s.13
s.62, applied: SSI 2009/372
s.63, amended: 2009 c.26 s.10
s.88, applied: SI 2009/3269 Art.2
s.88, enabling: SI 2009/3269
s.89, applied: SI 2009/3269 Art.2
s.89, enabling: SI 2009/3269
s.97, applied: SI 2009/2133 Reg.42
s.97, substituted: 2009 c.26 s.81
s.97A, added: 2009 c.26 s.10
s.101, see *R. (on the application of Ashton) v Police Medical Appeal Board* [2008] EWHC 1833 (Admin), [2009] I.C.R. 51 (QBD (Admin)), Charles, J.
Sch.1, amended: SI 2009/119 Art.3, Art.6
17. Employment Tribunals Act 1996
s.4, amended: SI 2009/789 Art.2
s.4, enabling: SI 2009/789
s.11, see *Tradition Securities & Futures SA v Times Newspapers Ltd* [2009] I.R.L.R. 354 (EAT), Underhill, J.
s.16, amended: 2009 c.24 Sch.7 Part 1
s.17, amended: 2009 c.24 Sch.7 Part 1
s.18, amended: 2009 c.22 Sch.1 para.16, SI 2009/2401 Reg.33
s.18, applied: SI 2009/2401 Reg.39
s.19A, enabling: SSI 2009/109
s.20, amended: SI 2009/2401 Reg.35
s.21, amended: SI 2009/2401 Reg.36
s.21, applied: SI 2009/2401 Reg.35
s.41, applied: SI 2009/789
18. Employment Rights Act 1996
see *Gisda Cyf v Barratt* [2009] EWCA Civ 648, [2009] I.C.R. 1408 (CA (Civ Div)), Mummery, L.J.; see *Kovats v TFO Management LLP* [2009] I.C.R. 1140 (EAT), Birtles, J.
varied: SI 2009/317 Sch.1
see *Gisda Cyf v Barratt* [2009] EWCA Civ 648, [2009] I.C.R. 1408 (CA (Civ Div)), Mummery, L.J.; see *Kovats v TFO Management LLP* [2009] I.C.R. 1140 (EAT), Birtles, J.

1996–*cont.*

18. Employment Rights Act 1996–*cont.*
varied: SI 2009/2108 Reg.33
Part I, varied: SI 2009/2108 Reg.33
Part VIII, applied: SI 2009/2108 Reg.23
Part X, applied: SI 2009/2108 Reg.33, SI 2009/2401 Reg.29
Part X c.I, varied: SI 2009/2108 Reg.33
Part XIV c.II, applied: SI 2009/2401 Reg.27
s.1, varied: SI 2009/2108 Reg.33
s.2, varied: SI 2009/2108 Reg.33
s.3, varied: SI 2009/2108 Reg.33
s.4, varied: SI 2009/2108 Reg.33
s.5, varied: SI 2009/2108 Reg.33
s.6, varied: SI 2009/2108 Reg.33
s.7, varied: SI 2009/2108 Reg.33
s.7A, varied: SI 2009/2108 Reg.33
s.7B, varied: SI 2009/2108 Reg.33
s.8, varied: SI 2009/2108 Reg.33
s.9, varied: SI 2009/2108 Reg.33
s.10, varied: SI 2009/2108 Reg.33
s.11, varied: SI 2009/2108 Reg.33
s.12, varied: SI 2009/2108 Reg.33
s.13, see *Inland Revenue Commissioners v Ainsworth* [2009] UKHL 31, [2009] 4 All E.R. 1205 (HL), Lord Hope of Craighead; see *Patel v Marquette Partners (UK) Ltd* [2009] I.C.R. 569 (EAT), Judge McMullen Q.C.
s.13, varied: SI 2009/2108 Reg.33
s.14, see *Patel v Marquette Partners (UK) Ltd* [2009] I.C.R. 569 (EAT), Judge McMullen Q.C.
s.14, varied: SI 2009/2108 Reg.33
s.15, varied: SI 2009/2108 Reg.33
s.16, varied: SI 2009/2108 Reg.33
s.17, varied: SI 2009/2108 Reg.33
s.18, varied: SI 2009/2108 Reg.33
s.19, varied: SI 2009/2108 Reg.33
s.20, varied: SI 2009/2108 Reg.33
s.21, varied: SI 2009/2108 Reg.33
s.22, varied: SI 2009/2108 Reg.33
s.23, see *Inland Revenue Commissioners v Ainsworth* [2009] UKHL 31, [2009] 4 All E.R. 1205 (HL), Lord Hope of Craighead; see *Small v Boots Co Plc* [2009] I.R.L.R. 328 (EAT), Slade, J.
s.23, varied: SI 2009/2108 Reg.33
s.24, varied: SI 2009/2108 Reg.33
s.25, varied: SI 2009/2108 Reg.33
s.26, varied: SI 2009/2108 Reg.33
s.27, see *Inland Revenue Commissioners v Ainsworth* [2009] UKHL 31, [2009] 4 All E.R. 1205 (HL), Lord Hope of Craighead
s.27, varied: SI 2009/2108 Reg.33
s.31, amended: SI 2009/3274 Sch.1
s.36, varied: SI 2009/2108 Reg.33
s.37, varied: SI 2009/2108 Reg.33
s.38, varied: SI 2009/2108 Reg.33
s.39, varied: SI 2009/2108 Reg.33
s.40, varied: SI 2009/2108 Reg.33
s.41, varied: SI 2009/2108 Reg.33
s.42, varied: SI 2009/2108 Reg.33
s.43, varied: SI 2009/2108 Reg.33
s.43A, applied: SI 2009/2401 Reg.24, Reg.29, Reg.31
s.43B, see *Hibbins v Hesters Way Neighbourhood Project* [2009] 1 All E.R. 949 (EAT), Silber, J.
s.43C, see *Hibbins v Hesters Way Neighbourhood Project* [2009] 1 All E.R. 949 (EAT), Silber, J.
s.43F, enabling: SI 2009/2457
s.43K, varied: SI 2009/2108 Reg.33

1996–cont.

18. Employment Rights Act 1996–*cont.*
s.43KA, varied: SI 2009/2108 Reg.33
s.43M, amended: 2009 c.25 Sch.21 para.36
s.43M, varied: SI 2009/2108 Reg.33
s.44, varied: SI 2009/2108 Reg.33
s.45, varied: SI 2009/2108 Reg.33
s.45A, varied: SI 2009/2108 Reg.33
s.46, varied: SI 2009/2108 Reg.33
s.47, varied: SI 2009/2108 Reg.33
s.47A, varied: SI 2009/2108 Reg.33
s.47AA, varied: SI 2009/2108 Reg.33
s.47B, varied: SI 2009/2108 Reg.33
s.47C, varied: SI 2009/2108 Reg.33
s.47D, varied: SI 2009/2108 Reg.33
s.47E, varied: SI 2009/2108 Reg.33
s.47F, added: 2009 c.22 s.40
s.47F, varied: SI 2009/2108 Reg.33
s.48, amended: 2009 c.22 Sch.1 para.2
s.48, applied: SI 2009/2401 Reg.32
s.48, varied: SI 2009/2108 Reg.33
s.49, applied: SI 2009/2401 Reg.32
s.49, varied: SI 2009/2108 Reg.33
s.49A, varied: SI 2009/2108 Reg.33
s.50, varied: SI 2009/2108 Reg.33
s.51, varied: SI 2009/2108 Reg.33
s.52, varied: SI 2009/2108 Reg.33
s.53, varied: SI 2009/2108 Reg.33
s.54, varied: SI 2009/2108 Reg.33
s.55, varied: SI 2009/2108 Reg.33
s.56, varied: SI 2009/2108 Reg.33
s.57, varied: SI 2009/2108 Reg.33
s.57A, see *Royal Bank of Scotland Plc v Harrison*
[2009] I.C.R. 116 (EAT), Judge Burke Q.C.
s.57A, varied: SI 2009/2108 Reg.33
s.57B, varied: SI 2009/2108 Reg.33
s.58, varied: SI 2009/2108 Reg.33
s.59, varied: SI 2009/2108 Reg.33
s.60, varied: SI 2009/2108 Reg.33
s.61, varied: SI 2009/2108 Reg.33
s.62, varied: SI 2009/2108 Reg.33
s.63, varied: SI 2009/2108 Reg.33
s.63A, varied: SI 2009/2108 Reg.33
s.63B, varied: SI 2009/2108 Reg.33
s.63C, varied: SI 2009/2108 Reg.33
s.63D, added: 2009 c.22 s.40
s.63E, added: 2009 c.22 s.40
s.63F, added: 2009 c.22 s.40
s.63G, added: 2009 c.22 s.40
s.63H, added: 2009 c.22 s.40
s.63I, added: 2009 c.22 s.40
s.63J, added: 2009 c.22 s.40
s.63K, added: 2009 c.22 s.40
s.64, varied: SI 2009/2108 Reg.33
s.65, varied: SI 2009/2108 Reg.33
s.66, varied: SI 2009/2108 Reg.33
s.67, varied: SI 2009/2108 Reg.33
s.68, varied: SI 2009/2108 Reg.33
s.68A, varied: SI 2009/2108 Reg.33
s.69, varied: SI 2009/2108 Reg.33
s.70, varied: SI 2009/2108 Reg.33
s.71, varied: SI 2009/2108 Reg.33
s.72, varied: SI 2009/2108 Reg.33
s.73, varied: SI 2009/2108 Reg.33
s.74, varied: SI 2009/2108 Reg.33
s.75, varied: SI 2009/2108 Reg.33
s.75A, varied: SI 2009/2108 Reg.33
s.75B, varied: SI 2009/2108 Reg.33
s.75C, varied: SI 2009/2108 Reg.33

1996–cont.

18. Employment Rights Act 1996–*cont.*
s.75D, varied: SI 2009/2108 Reg.33
s.76, varied: SI 2009/2108 Reg.33
s.77, varied: SI 2009/2108 Reg.33
s.78, varied: SI 2009/2108 Reg.33
s.79, varied: SI 2009/2108 Reg.33
s.80, varied: SI 2009/2108 Reg.33
s.80A, varied: SI 2009/2108 Reg.33
s.80AA, varied: SI 2009/2108 Reg.33
s.80B, varied: SI 2009/2108 Reg.33
s.80BB, varied: SI 2009/2108 Reg.33
s.80C, varied: SI 2009/2108 Reg.33
s.80D, varied: SI 2009/2108 Reg.33
s.80E, varied: SI 2009/2108 Reg.33
s.80F, enabling: SI 2009/595
s.81, varied: SI 2009/2108 Reg.33
s.82, varied: SI 2009/2108 Reg.33
s.83, varied: SI 2009/2108 Reg.33
s.84, varied: SI 2009/2108 Reg.33
s.85, varied: SI 2009/2108 Reg.33
s.86, varied: SI 2009/2108 Reg.33
s.87, varied: SI 2009/2108 Reg.33
s.88, varied: SI 2009/2108 Reg.33
s.89, varied: SI 2009/2108 Reg.33
s.90, varied: SI 2009/2108 Reg.33
s.91, varied: SI 2009/2108 Reg.33
s.92, varied: SI 2009/2108 Reg.33
s.93, varied: SI 2009/2108 Reg.33
s.94, varied: SI 2009/2108 Reg.33
s.95, see *Bournemouth University Higher
Education Corp v Buckland* [2009] I.C.R. 1042
(EAT), Judge Peter Clark
s.95, varied: SI 2009/2108 Reg.33
s.96, varied: SI 2009/2108 Reg.33
s.97, see *Gisda Cyf v Barratt* [2009] EWCA Civ 648,
[2009] I.C.R. 1408 (CA (Civ Div)), Mummery,
L.J.
s.97, varied: SI 2009/2108 Reg.33
s.98, see *Bournemouth University Higher
Education Corp v Buckland* [2009] I.C.R. 1042
(EAT), Judge Peter Clark; see *Sehmi v Gate
Gourmet London Ltd* [2009] I.R.L.R. 807
(EAT), Underhill, J. (President); see *West
London Mental Health NHS Trust v Sarkar*
[2009] I.R.L.R. 512 (EAT), Judge McMullen
Q.C.
s.98, applied: SI 2009/2108 Reg.33
s.98, varied: SI 2009/2108 Reg.33
s.98A, varied: SI 2009/2108 Reg.33
s.98B, varied: SI 2009/2108 Reg.33
s.98B, amended: 2009 c.25 Sch.21 para.36
s.98B, varied: SI 2009/2108 Reg.33
s.98ZA, varied: SI 2009/2108 Reg.33
s.98ZB, varied: SI 2009/2108 Reg.33
s.98ZC, varied: SI 2009/2108 Reg.33
s.98ZD, varied: SI 2009/2108 Reg.33
s.98ZE, varied: SI 2009/2108 Reg.33
s.98ZF, varied: SI 2009/2108 Reg.33
s.98ZG, varied: SI 2009/2108 Reg.33
s.98ZH, varied: SI 2009/2108 Reg.33
s.99, varied: SI 2009/2108 Reg.33
s.100, varied: SI 2009/2108 Reg.33
s.101, varied: SI 2009/2108 Reg.33
s.101A, varied: SI 2009/2108 Reg.33
s.101B, varied: SI 2009/2108 Reg.33
s.102, varied: SI 2009/2108 Reg.33
s.103, varied: SI 2009/2108 Reg.33
s.103A, varied: SI 2009/2108 Reg.33

1996–cont.

18. Employment Rights Act 1996–*cont.*
s.104, varied: SI 2009/ 2108 Reg.33
s.104A, varied: SI 2009/ 2108 Reg.33
s.104B, varied: SI 2009/ 2108 Reg.33
s.104C, varied: SI 2009/ 2108 Reg.33
s.104D, varied: SI 2009/ 2108 Reg.33
s.104E, added: 2009 c.22 s.40
s.104E, varied: SI 2009/ 2108 Reg.33
s.105, varied: SI 2009/ 2108 Reg.33
s.105, amended: 2009 c.22 Sch.1 para.3, SI 2009/ 2401 Reg.30
s.105, varied: SI 2009/ 2108 Reg.33
s.106, varied: SI 2009/ 2108 Reg.33
s.107, varied: SI 2009/ 2108 Reg.33
s.108, amended: 2009 c.22 Sch.1 para.4, SI 2009/ 2401 Reg.30
s.108, disapplied: SI 2009/ 2108 Reg.33
s.108, varied: SI 2009/ 2108 Reg.33
s.109, varied: SI 2009/ 2108 Reg.33
s.110, varied: SI 2009/ 2108 Reg.33
s.111, see *Cambridge and Peterborough Foundation NHS Trust v Crouchman* [2009] I.C.R. 1306 (EAT), Underhill, J.; see *Radecki v Kirklees MBC* [2009] EWCA Civ 298, [2009] I.C.R. 1244 (CA (Civ Div)), Rix, L.J.; see *Remploy Ltd v Shaw* [2009] I.C.R. 1159 (EAT), Judge McMullen Q.C.
s.111, varied: SI 2009/ 2108 Reg.33
s.112, varied: SI 2009/ 2108 Reg.33
s.113, varied: SI 2009/ 2108 Reg.33
s.114, varied: SI 2009/ 2108 Reg.33
s.115, varied: SI 2009/ 2108 Reg.33
s.116, varied: SI 2009/ 2108 Reg.33
s.117, varied: SI 2009/ 2108 Reg.33
s.118, varied: SI 2009/ 2108 Reg.33
s.119, varied: SI 2009/ 2108 Reg.33
s.120, varied: SI 2009/ 2108 Reg.33
s.121, varied: SI 2009/ 2108 Reg.33
s.122, varied: SI 2009/ 2108 Reg.33
s.123, see *Stuart Peters Ltd v Bell* [2009] I.C.R. 453 (EAT), Judge Burke Q.C.; see *West London Mental Health NHS Trust v Sarkar* [2009] I.R.L.R. 512 (EAT), Judge McMullen Q.C.
s.123, varied: SI 2009/ 2108 Reg.33
s.124, amended: SI 2009/ 3274 Sch.1
s.124, varied: SI 2009/ 2108 Reg.33
s.124A, varied: SI 2009/ 2108 Reg.33
s.125, varied: SI 2009/ 2108 Reg.33
s.126, varied: SI 2009/ 2108 Reg.33
s.127, varied: SI 2009/ 2108 Reg.33
s.127A, varied: SI 2009/ 2108 Reg.33
s.127B, varied: SI 2009/ 2108 Reg.33
s.128, varied: SI 2009/ 2108 Reg.33
s.129, varied: SI 2009/ 2108 Reg.33
s.130, varied: SI 2009/ 2108 Reg.33
s.131, varied: SI 2009/ 2108 Reg.33
s.132, varied: SI 2009/ 2108 Reg.33
s.133, varied: SI 2009/ 2108 Reg.33
s.134, varied: SI 2009/ 2108 Reg.33
s.134A, varied: SI 2009/ 2108 Reg.33
s.136, varied: SI 2009/ 2108 Reg.33
s.137, varied: SI 2009/ 2108 Reg.33
s.138, varied: SI 2009/ 2108 Reg.33
s.139, varied: SI 2009/ 2108 Reg.33
s.140, varied: SI 2009/ 2108 Reg.33
s.141, varied: SI 2009/ 2108 Reg.33
s.142, varied: SI 2009/ 2108 Reg.33
s.143, varied: SI 2009/ 2108 Reg.33

1996–cont.

18. Employment Rights Act 1996–*cont.*
s.144, varied: SI 2009/ 2108 Reg.33
s.145, varied: SI 2009/ 2108 Reg.33
s.146, varied: SI 2009/ 2108 Reg.33
s.147, varied: SI 2009/ 2108 Reg.33
s.148, varied: SI 2009/ 2108 Reg.33
s.149, varied: SI 2009/ 2108 Reg.33
s.150, varied: SI 2009/ 2108 Reg.33
s.151, varied: SI 2009/ 2108 Reg.33
s.152, varied: SI 2009/ 2108 Reg.33
s.154, varied: SI 2009/ 2108 Reg.33
s.167, applied: 2009 c.4 s.81, s.1243
s.171, varied: SI 2009/ 2108 Reg.33
s.172, varied: SI 2009/ 2108 Reg.33
s.173, varied: SI 2009/ 2108 Reg.33
s.174, varied: SI 2009/ 2108 Reg.33
s.175, varied: SI 2009/ 2108 Reg.33
s.176, varied: SI 2009/ 2108 Reg.33
s.177, varied: SI 2009/ 2108 Reg.33
s.178, varied: SI 2009/ 2108 Reg.33
s.179, varied: SI 2009/ 2108 Reg.33
s.181, varied: SI 2009/ 2108 Reg.33
s.186, amended: SI 2009/ 1903 Art.2
s.186, referred to: SI 2009/ 1903 Art.3
s.191, varied: SI 2009/ 2108 Reg.33
s.192, applied: SI 2009/ 1059 Art.196
s.192, varied: SI 2009/ 2108 Reg.33
s.193, varied: SI 2009/ 2108 Reg.33
s.194, amended: 2009 c.22 Sch.1 para.5
s.194, varied: SI 2009/ 2108 Reg.33
s.195, amended: 2009 c.22 Sch.1 para.6
s.195, varied: SI 2009/ 2108 Reg.33
s.196, see *Diggins v Condor Marine Crewing Services Ltd* [2009] I.C.R. 609 (EAT), Judge Burke Q.C.
s.196, varied: SI 2009/ 2108 Reg.33
s.197, varied: SI 2009/ 2108 Reg.33
s.198, varied: SI 2009/ 2108 Reg.33
s.199, see *Diggins v Condor Marine Crewing Services Ltd* [2009] I.C.R. 609 (EAT), Judge Burke Q.C.
s.199, amended: 2009 c.22 Sch.1 para.7
s.199, varied: SI 2009/ 2108 Reg.33
s.200, applied: SI 2009/ 2133 Reg.42
s.200, varied: SI 2009/ 2108 Reg.33
s.201, varied: SI 2009/ 2108 Reg.33
s.202, varied: SI 2009/ 2108 Reg.33
s.203, varied: SI 2009/ 2108 Reg.33
s.204, varied: SI 2009/ 2108 Reg.33
s.205, varied: SI 2009/ 2108 Reg.33
s.206, varied: SI 2009/ 2108 Reg.33
s.207, varied: SI 2009/ 2108 Reg.33
s.209, varied: SI 2009/ 2108 Reg.33
s.218, see *Da Silva v Composite Mouldings & Design Ltd* [2009] I.C.R. 416 (EAT), Judge McMullen Q.C.
s.220, varied: SI 2009/ 2108 Reg.33
s.221, see *British Airways Plc v Williams* [2009] EWCA Civ 281, [2009] I.C.R. 906 (CA (Civ Div)), Ward, L.J.
s.221, varied: SI 2009/ 2108 Reg.33
s.222, varied: SI 2009/ 2108 Reg.33
s.223, varied: SI 2009/ 2108 Reg.33
s.224, see *British Airways Plc v Williams* [2009] EWCA Civ 281, [2009] I.C.R. 906 (CA (Civ Div)), Ward, L.J.
s.224, varied: SI 2009/ 2108 Reg.33
s.225, amended: 2009 c.22 Sch.1 para.8

1996–cont.

18. Employment Rights Act 1996–*cont.*

s.225, varied: SI 2009/2108 Reg.33

s.226, varied: SI 2009/2108 Reg.33

s.227, amended: 2009 c.22 Sch.1 para.9, SI 2009/1903 Art.2

s.227, referred to: SI 2009/1903 Art.3

s.228, varied: SI 2009/2108 Reg.33

s.229, varied: SI 2009/2108 Reg.33

s.232, amended: SSI 2009/248 Sch.1 para.7

s.235, amended: 2009 c.22 Sch.1 para.10

s.236, amended: 2009 c.22 Sch.1 para.11

s.245, varied: SI 2009/2108 Reg.33

Sch.1 para.1, varied: SI 2009/2108 Reg.33

Sch.1 para.2, varied: SI 2009/2108 Reg.33

Sch.1 para.4, varied: SI 2009/2108 Reg.33

Sch.1 para.5, varied: SI 2009/2108 Reg.33

Sch.1 para.6, varied: SI 2009/2108 Reg.33

Sch.1 para.7, varied: SI 2009/2108 Reg.33

Sch.1 para.8, varied: SI 2009/2108 Reg.33

Sch.1 para.9, varied: SI 2009/2108 Reg.33

Sch.1 para.10, varied: SI 2009/2108 Reg.33

Sch.1 para.11, varied: SI 2009/2108 Reg.33

Sch.1 para.12, varied: SI 2009/2108 Reg.33

Sch.1 para.13, varied: SI 2009/2108 Reg.33

Sch.1 para.14, varied: SI 2009/2108 Reg.33

Sch.1 para.15, varied: SI 2009/2108 Reg.33

Sch.1 para.16, varied: SI 2009/2108 Reg.33

Sch.1 para.17, varied: SI 2009/2108 Reg.33

Sch.1 para.18, varied: SI 2009/2108 Reg.33

Sch.1 para.19, varied: SI 2009/2108 Reg.33

Sch.1 para.20, varied: SI 2009/2108 Reg.33

Sch.1 para.21, varied: SI 2009/2108 Reg.33

Sch.1 para.22, varied: SI 2009/2108 Reg.33

Sch.1 para.23, varied: SI 2009/2108 Reg.33

Sch.1 para.24, varied: SI 2009/2108 Reg.33

Sch.1 para.25, varied: SI 2009/2108 Reg.33

Sch.1 para.26, varied: SI 2009/2108 Reg.33

Sch.1 para.27, varied: SI 2009/2108 Reg.33

Sch.1 para.28, varied: SI 2009/2108 Reg.33

Sch.1 para.29, varied: SI 2009/2108 Reg.33

Sch.1 para.30, varied: SI 2009/2108 Reg.33

Sch.1 para.31, varied: SI 2009/2108 Reg.33

Sch.1 para.32, varied: SI 2009/2108 Reg.33

Sch.1 para.33, varied: SI 2009/2108 Reg.33

Sch.1 para.34, varied: SI 2009/2108 Reg.33

Sch.1 para.35, varied: SI 2009/2108 Reg.33

Sch.1 para.36, varied: SI 2009/2108 Reg.33

Sch.1 para.37, varied: SI 2009/2108 Reg.33

Sch.1 para.38, varied: SI 2009/2108 Reg.33

Sch.1 para.39, varied: SI 2009/2108 Reg.33

Sch.1 para.40, varied: SI 2009/2108 Reg.33

Sch.1 para.41, varied: SI 2009/2108 Reg.33

Sch.1 para.42, varied: SI 2009/2108 Reg.33

Sch.1 para.43, varied: SI 2009/2108 Reg.33

Sch.1 para.44, varied: SI 2009/2108 Reg.33

Sch.1 para.45, varied: SI 2009/2108 Reg.33

Sch.1 para.46, varied: SI 2009/2108 Reg.33

Sch.1 para.47, varied: SI 2009/2108 Reg.33

Sch.1 para.48, varied: SI 2009/2108 Reg.33

Sch.1 para.49, varied: SI 2009/2108 Reg.33

Sch.1 para.50, varied: SI 2009/2108 Reg.33

Sch.1 para.51, varied: SI 2009/2108 Reg.33

Sch.1 para.52, varied: SI 2009/2108 Reg.33

Sch.1 para.53, varied: SI 2009/2108 Reg.33

Sch.1 para.54, varied: SI 2009/2108 Reg.33

Sch.1 para.55, varied: SI 2009/2108 Reg.33

Sch.1 para.56, varied: SI 2009/2108 Reg.33

Sch.1 para.58, varied: SI 2009/2108 Reg.33

1996–cont.

18. Employment Rights Act 1996–*cont.*

Sch.1 para.59, varied: SI 2009/2108 Reg.33

Sch.1 para.60, varied: SI 2009/2108 Reg.33

Sch.1 para.61, varied: SI 2009/2108 Reg.33

Sch.1 para.62, varied: SI 2009/2108 Reg.33

Sch.1 para.63, varied: SI 2009/2108 Reg.33

Sch.1 para.64, varied: SI 2009/2108 Reg.33

Sch.1 para.65, varied: SI 2009/2108 Reg.33

Sch.1 para.66, varied: SI 2009/2108 Reg.33

Sch.1 para.67, repealed (in part): 2009 c.24 Sch.7 Part 3

Sch.1 para.67, varied: SI 2009/2108 Reg.33

Sch.1 para.68, varied: SI 2009/2108 Reg.33

Sch.1 para.69, varied: SI 2009/2108 Reg.33

Sch.2 Part I para.7, varied: SI 2009/2108 Reg.33

Sch.2 Part I para.8, varied: SI 2009/2108 Reg.33

Sch.2 Part I para.9, varied: SI 2009/2108 Reg.33

Sch.2 Part I para.10, varied: SI 2009/2108 Reg.33

Sch.2 Part I para.11, varied: SI 2009/2108 Reg.33

Sch.2 Part I para.12, varied: SI 2009/2108 Reg.33

Sch.2 Part I para.13, varied: SI 2009/2108 Reg.33

Sch.2 Part I para.14, varied: SI 2009/2108 Reg.33

Sch.2 Part II para.16, varied: SI 2009/2108 Reg.33

Sch.3 Part I, varied: SI 2009/2108 Reg.33

Sch.3 Part II, varied: SI 2009/2108 Reg.33

19. Law Reform (Year and a Day Rule) Act 1996

s.2, amended: 2009 c.25 Sch.21 para.60

23. Arbitration Act 1996

see *British Telecommunications Plc v SAE Group Inc* [2009] EWHC 252 (TCC), [2009] B.L.R. 231 (QBD (TCC)), Ramsey, J.; see *ETI Euro Telecom International NV v Bolivia* [2008] EWCA Civ 880, [2009] 1 W.L.R. 665 (CA (Civ Div)), Tuckey, L.J.; see *IPCO (Nigeria) Ltd v Nigerian National Petroleum Corp* [2008] EWCA Civ 1157, [2009] Bus. L.R. 545 (CA (Civ Div)), Tuckey, L.J.; see *Sheffield United Football Club Ltd v West Ham United Football Club Plc* [2008] EWHC 2855 (Comm), [2009] 1 Lloyd's Rep. 167 (QBD (Comm)), Teare, J.

Part I, disapplied: SI 2009/273 r.3, SI 2009/1976 r.3

Part III, see *IPCO (Nigeria) Ltd v Nigerian National Petroleum Corp* [2008] EWCA Civ 1157, [2009] Bus. L.R. 545 (CA (Civ Div)), Tuckey, L.J.

s.1, see *Emmott v Michael Wilson & Partners Ltd* [2009] EWHC 1 (Comm), [2009] Bus. L.R. 723 (QBD (Comm)), Teare, J.

s.3, see *Shashoua v Sharma* [2009] EWHC 957 (Comm), [2009] 2 All E.R. (Comm) 477 (QBD (Comm)), Cooke, J.

s.9, see *Accentuate Ltd v Asigra Inc* [2009] EWHC 2655 (QB), [2009] 2 Lloyd's Rep. 599 (QBD), Tugendhat, J.; see *Bovis Homes Ltd v Kendrick Construction Ltd* [2009] EWHC 1359 (TCC), [2009] T.C.L.R. 8 (QBD (TCC)), Coulson, J.; see *City of London v Sancheti* [2008] EWCA Civ 1283, [2009] Bus. L.R. 996 (CA (Civ Div)), Laws, L.J.; see *Mylcrist Builders Ltd v Buck* [2008] EWHC 2172 (TCC), [2009] 2 All E.R. (Comm) 259 (QBD (TCC)), Ramsey, J.; see *Sheffield United Football Club Ltd v West Ham United Football Club Plc* [2008] EWHC 2855 (Comm), [2009] 1 Lloyd's Rep. 167 (QBD (Comm)), Teare, J.

s.14, see *Bulk & Metal Transport (UK) LLP v Voc Bulk Ultra Handymax Pool LLC (Voc Gallant)* [2009] EWHC 288 (Comm), [2009] 2 All E.R. (Comm) 377 (QBD (Comm)), Judge Mackie Q.C.; see *Taylor Woodrow Construction Ltd v*

1996– cont.

23. Arbitration Act 1996–*cont.*
s.14–*cont.*
RMD Kwikform Ltd [2008] EWHC 825 (TCC), [2009] Bus. L.R. 292 (QBD (TCC)), Ramsey, J.
s.16, see *Mylcrist Builders Ltd v Buck* [2008] EWHC 2172 (TCC), [2009] 2 All E.R. (Comm) 259 (QBD (TCC)), Ramsey, J.
s.17, see *Mylcrist Builders Ltd v Buck* [2008] EWHC 2172 (TCC), [2009] 2 All E.R. (Comm) 259 (QBD (TCC)), Ramsey, J.
s.18, see *Mylcrist Builders Ltd v Buck* [2008] EWHC 2172 (TCC), [2009] 2 All E.R. (Comm) 259 (QBD (TCC)), Ramsey, J.
s.32, see *British Telecommunications Plc v SAE Group Inc* [2009] EWHC 252 (TCC), [2009] B.L.R. 231 (QBD (TCC)), Ramsey, J.
s.33, see *O'Donoghue v Enterprise Inns Plc* [2008] EWHC 2273 (Ch), [2009] 1 P. & C.R. 14 (Ch D (Leeds)), Judge Behrens
s.34, see *O'Donoghue v Enterprise Inns Plc* [2008] EWHC 2273 (Ch), [2009] 1 P. & C.R. 14 (Ch D (Leeds)), Judge Behrens
s.38, see *Emmott v Michael Wilson & Partners Ltd* [2009] EWHC 1 (Comm), [2009] Bus. L.R. 723 (QBD (Comm)), Teare, J.
s.40, disapplied: SI 2009/ 1976 r.4
s.42, see *Emmott v Michael Wilson & Partners Ltd* [2009] EWHC 1 (Comm), [2009] Bus. L.R. 723 (QBD (Comm)), Teare, J.
s.44, see *EDO Corp v Ultra Electronics Ltd* [2009] EWHC 682 (Ch), [2009] Bus. L.R. 1306 (Ch D), Bernard Livesey Q.C.; see *ETI Euro Telecom International NV v Bolivia* [2008] EWCA Civ 880, [2009] 1 W.L.R. 665 (CA (Civ Div)), Tuckey, L.J.; see *Sheffield United Football Club Ltd v West Ham United Football Club Plc* [2008] EWHC 2855 (Comm), [2009] 1 Lloyd's Rep. 167 (QBD (Comm)), Teare, J.
s.49, see *Gater Assets Ltd v Nak Naftogaz Ukrainiy* [2008] EWHC 1108 (Comm), [2009] Bus. L.R. 396 (QBD (Comm)), Beatson, J.; see *Welford v EDF Energy Networks (LPN) Plc* [2009] R.V.R. 10 (Lands Tr), George Bartlett Q.C. (President, LTr)
s.60, see *Shashoua v Sharma* [2009] EWHC 957 (Comm), [2009] 2 All E.R. (Comm) 477 (QBD (Comm)), Cooke, J.
s.66, see *National Ability SA v Tinna Oils & Chemicals Ltd* [2009] EWCA Civ 1330, Times, December 24, 2009 (CA (Civ Div)), Thomas, L.J.
s.67, see *Emmott v Michael Wilson & Partners Ltd* [2009] EWHC 1 (Comm), [2009] Bus. L.R. 723 (QBD (Comm)), Teare, J.; see *Michael Wilson & Partners Ltd v Emmott* [2008] EWHC 2684 (Comm), [2009] 1 Lloyd's Rep. 162 (QBD (Comm)), Teare, J.; see *Sheltam Rail Co (Proprietary) Ltd v Mirambo Holdings Ltd* [2008] EWHC 829 (Comm), [2009] Bus. L.R. 302 (QBD (Comm)), Aikens, J.; see *Syska v Vivendi Universal SA* [2008] EWHC 2155 (Comm), [2009] Bus. L.R. 367 (QBD (Comm)), Christopher Clarke, J.
s.68, see *F Ltd v M Ltd* [2009] EWHC 275 (TCC), [2009] 2 All E.R. (Comm) 519 (QBD (TCC)), Coulson, J.; see *O'Donoghue v Enterprise Inns Plc* [2008] EWHC 2273 (Ch), [2009] 1 P. & C.R. 14 (Ch D (Leeds)), Judge Behrens; see *R v V* [2008] EWHC 1531 (Comm), [2009] 1 Lloyd's Rep. 97 (QBD (Comm)), Steel, J.; see *Sheltam Rail Co (Proprietary) Ltd v Mirambo Holdings*

1996– cont.

23. Arbitration Act 1996–*cont.*
s.68–*cont.*
Ltd [2008] EWHC 829 (Comm), [2009] Bus. L.R. 302 (QBD (Comm)), Aikens, J.; see *Trustees of the Edmond Stern Settlement v Levy (t/a Simon Levy Associates)* [2009] EWHC 14 (TCC), [2009] 1 Lloyd's Rep. 345 (QBD (TCC)), Akenhead, J.; see *UR Power GmbH v Kuok Oils & Grains PTE Ltd* [2009] EWHC 1940 (Comm), [2009] 2 Lloyd's Rep. 495 (QBD (Comm)), Gross, J.; see *Van der Giessen-de Noord Shipbuilding Division BV v Imtech Marine & Offshore BV* [2008] EWHC 2904 (Comm), [2009] 1 Lloyd's Rep. 273 (QBD (Comm)), Christopher Clarke, J.
s.69, see *ASM Shipping Ltd of India v TTMI Ltd of England (The Amer Energy)* [2009] 1 Lloyd's Rep. 293 (QBD (Comm)), Flaux, J.; see *Emmott v Michael Wilson & Partners Ltd* [2009] EWHC 1 (Comm), [2009] Bus. L.R. 723 (QBD (Comm)), Teare, J.; see *National Trust for Places of Historic Interest or Natural Beauty v Fleming* [2009] EWHC 1789 (Ch), [2009] N.P.C. 97 (Ch D), Henderson, J.; see *Trustees of the Edmond Stern Settlement v Levy (t/a Simon Levy Associates)* [2009] EWHC 14 (TCC), [2009] 1 Lloyd's Rep. 345 (QBD (TCC)), Akenhead, J.
s.70, see *UR Power GmbH v Kuok Oils & Grains PTE Ltd* [2009] EWHC 1940 (Comm), [2009] 2 Lloyd's Rep. 495 (QBD (Comm)), Gross, J.; see *Van der Giessen-de Noord Shipbuilding Division BV v Imtech Marine & Offshore BV* [2008] EWHC 2904 (Comm), [2009] 1 Lloyd's Rep. 273 (QBD (Comm)), Christopher Clarke, J.
s.72, see *British Telecommunications Plc v SAE Group Inc* [2009] EWHC 252 (TCC), [2009] B.L.R. 231 (QBD (TCC)), Ramsey, J.
s.73, see *O'Donoghue v Enterprise Inns Plc* [2008] EWHC 2273 (Ch), [2009] 1 P. & C.R. 14 (Ch D (Leeds)), Judge Behrens
s.80, see *ASM Shipping Ltd of India v TTMI Ltd of England (The Amer Energy)* [2009] 1 Lloyd's Rep. 293 (QBD (Comm)), Flaux, J.
s.81, see *R v V* [2008] EWHC 1531 (Comm), [2009] 1 Lloyd's Rep. 97 (QBD (Comm)), Steel, J.
s.101, see *Gater Assets Ltd v Nak Naftogaz Ukrainiy* [2008] EWHC 1108 (Comm), [2009] Bus. L.R. 396 (QBD (Comm)), Beatson, J.; see *Norsk Hydro ASA v State Property Fund of Ukraine* [2002] EWHC 2120 (Admin), [2009] Bus. L.R. 558 (QBD (Admin)), Gross, J.
s.103, see *Dallah Real Estate & Tourism Holding Co v Pakistan* [2008] EWHC 1901 (Comm), [2009] 1 All E.R. (Comm) 505 (QBD (Comm)), Aikens, J.; see *IPCO (Nigeria) Ltd v Nigerian National Petroleum Corp* [2008] EWCA Civ 1157, [2009] Bus. L.R. 545 (CA (Civ Div)), Tuckey, L.J.
Sch.3 para.6, repealed: SI 2009/ 1307 Sch.4

24. Treasure Act 1996
applied: 2009 c.25 s.29
disapplied: 2009 c.25 s.29
s.4, referred to: 2009 c.25 s.29
s.7, substituted: 2009 c.25 Sch.21 para.38
s.8, amended: 2009 c.25 Sch.21 para.39
s.8, applied: 2009 c.25 s.26
s.8A, added: 2009 c.25 s.30
s.8A, applied: 2009 c.25 s.30
s.8B, added: 2009 c.25 Sch.21 para.40
s.8C, added: 2009 c.25 Sch.21 para.40

1996–cont.

24. Treasure Act 1996–cont.
s.9, substituted: 2009 c.25 Sch.21 para.41
s.10, amended: 2009 c.25 s.30
s.11, applied: 2009 c.25 s.29, s.31
s.13, repealed: 2009 c.25 Sch.21 para.42, Sch.23 Part 1

25. Criminal Procedure and Investigations Act 1996
s.61, repealed (in part): 2009 c.25 Sch.23 Part 2
s.78, applied: SI 2009/988 Art.4, Art.5, Art.13, Art.14
s.78, varied: SI 2009/1059 Sch.1 para.37
s.78, enabling: SI 2009/988, SI 2009/989

27. Family Law Act 1996
applied: SI 2009/845 Sch.3 Part 4, Sch.4
s.33, see *Haghighat (A Bankrupt), Re* [2009] EWHC 90 (Ch), [2009] 1 F.L.R. 1271 (Ch D), George Bompas Q.C.
s.56, applied: SI 2009/845 Sch.3 Part 3
s.61, amended: SI 2009/871 Art.8
s.63C, applied: SI 2009/2023 Art.3
s.63C, enabling: SI 2009/2023
s.65, enabling: SI 2009/2023

31. Defamation Act 1996
Commencement Orders: SI 2009/2858 Art.3
see *Tesco Stores Ltd v Guardian News & Media Ltd* [2009] E.M.L.R. 5 (QBD), Eady, J.
s.1, see *Metropolitan International Schools Ltd (t/a SkillsTrain and t/a Train2Game) v Designtechnica Corp (t/a Digital Trends)* [2009] EWHC 1765 (QB), [2009] E.M.L.R. 27 (QBD), Eady, J.
s.2, see *Tesco Stores Ltd v Guardian News & Media Ltd* [2009] E.M.L.R. 5 (QBD), Eady, J.; see *Warren v Random House Group Ltd* [2008] EWCA Civ 834, [2009] Q.B. 600 (CA (Civ Div)), Sir Anthony Clarke, M.R.
s.19, enabling: SI 2009/2858
s.20, repealed (in part): 2009 c.25 Sch.23 Part 2
Sch.1 Part II para.13, amended: SI 2009/1941 Sch.1 para.159

40. Party Wall etc Act 1996
see *Reeves v Blake* [2009] EWCA Civ 611, [2009] 38 E.G. 113 (CA (Civ Div)), Mummery, L.J.
s.1, see *Reeves v Blake* [2009] EWCA Civ 611, [2009] 38 E.G. 113 (CA (Civ Div)), Mummery, L.J.
s.6, see *Reeves v Blake* [2009] EWCA Civ 611, [2009] 38 E.G. 113 (CA (Civ Div)), Mummery, L.J.
s.10, see *Reeves v Blake* [2009] EWCA Civ 611, [2009] 38 E.G. 113 (CA (Civ Div)), Mummery, L.J.

41. Hong Kong (War Wives and Widows) Act 1996
s.1, amended: 2009 c.11 s.47, Sch.1 Part 2

43. Education (Scotland) Act 1996
s.6, amended: SI 2009/1941 Sch.1 para.160

46. Armed Forces Act 1996
s.6, varied: SI 2009/1059 Sch.1 para.38

47. Trusts of Land and Appointment of Trustees Act 1996
s.12, see *French v Barcham* [2008] EWHC 1505 (Ch), [2009] 1 W.L.R. 1124 (Ch D), Blackburne, J.
s.13, see *French v Barcham* [2008] EWHC 1505 (Ch), [2009] 1 W.L.R. 1124 (Ch D), Blackburne, J.
s.14, see *Close Invoice Finance Ltd v Pile* [2008] EWHC 1580 (Ch), [2009] 1 F.L.R. 873 (Ch D), Judge Purle Q.C.; see *Turner v Avis* [2009] 1 F.L.R. 74 (Ch D (Liverpool)), Judge Pelling Q.C.

1996–cont.

47. Trusts of Land and Appointment of Trustees Act 1996–cont.
s.15, see *C Putnam & Sons v Taylor* [2009] EWHC 317 (Ch), [2009] B.P.I.R. 769 (Ch D (Birmingham)), Judge Purle Q.C.; see *Close Invoice Finance Ltd v Pile* [2008] EWHC 1580 (Ch), [2009] 1 F.L.R. 873 (Ch D), Judge Purle Q.C.; see *French v Barcham* [2008] EWHC 1505 (Ch), [2009] 1 W.L.R. 1124 (Ch D), Blackburne, J.
Sch.1 para.1, see *Alexander-David v Hammersmith and Fulham LBC* [2009] EWCA Civ 259, [2009] 3 All E.R. 1098 (CA (Civ Div)), Waller, L.J.

49. Asylum and Immigration Act 1996
s.2, see *EN (Serbia) v Secretary of State for the Home Department* [2009] EWCA Civ 630, [2009] I.N.L.R. 459 (CA (Civ Div)), Laws, L.J.

52. Housing Act 1996
see *R. (on the application of Weaver) v London & Quadrant Housing Trust* [2008] EWHC 1377 (Admin), [2009] 1 All E.R. 17 (DC), Richards, L.J.; see *X v Hounslow LBC* [2009] EWCA Civ 286, [2009] 2 F.L.R. 262 (CA (Civ Div)), Sir Anthony Clarke, M.R.
Part I, applied: 2009 c.2 s.44, SI 2009/3050 Art.2
Part VII, see *Holmes-Moorhouse v Richmond upon Thames LBC* [2009] UKHL 7, [2009] 1 W.L.R. 413 (HL), Lord Hoffmann; see *Lambeth LBC v Johnston* [2008] EWCA Civ 690, [2009] H.L.R. 10 (CA (Civ Div)), Smith, L.J.; see *R. (on the application of Aweys) v Birmingham City Council* [2009] UKHL 36, [2009] 1 W.L.R. 1506 (HL), Lord Hope of Craighead; see *R. (on the application of G) v Southwark LBC* [2009] UKHL 26, [2009] 1 W.L.R. 1299 (HL), Lord Hope of Craighead; see *Teixeira v Lambeth LBC* [2008] EWCA Civ 1088, [2009] Eu. L.R. 253 (CA (Civ Div)), Mummery, L.J.; see *Ugiagbe v Southwark LBC* [2009] EWCA Civ 31, [2009] H.L.R. 35 (CA (Civ Div)), Sedley, L.J.
s.2, amended: SI 2009/1941 Sch.1 para.161
s.3, amended: SI 2009/1941 Sch.1 para.161
s.4, amended: SI 2009/1941 Sch.1 para.161
s.6, amended: SI 2009/1941 Sch.1 para.161
s.40, amended: SI 2009/1941 Sch.1 para.161
s.41, amended: SI 2009/1941 Sch.1 para.161
s.45, amended: SI 2009/1941 Sch.1 para.161
s.56, amended: SI 2009/1941 Sch.1 para.161
s.58, amended: SI 2009/1941 Sch.1 para.161
s.59, amended: SI 2009/1941 Sch.1 para.161
s.60, amended: SI 2009/1941 Sch.1 para.161
s.61, amended: SI 2009/1941 Sch.1 para.161
s.63, amended: SI 2009/1941 Sch.1 para.161
s.64, amended: SI 2009/1941 Sch.1 para.161
s.109, see *Pitts v Earl Cadogan* [2008] UKHL 71, [2009] 2 W.L.R. 12 (HL), Lord Hoffmann
s.122, enabling: SI 2009/2459
s.143E, see *R. (on the application of Gilboy) v Liverpool City Council* [2008] EWCA Civ 751, [2009] Q.B. 699 (CA (Civ Div)), Waller, L.J. (V-P)
s.143F, see *R. (on the application of Gilboy) v Liverpool City Council* [2008] EWCA Civ 751, [2009] Q.B. 699 (CA (Civ Div)), Waller, L.J. (V-P)
s.153, see *Kirklees Council v Davis* [2008] EWCA Civ 632, [2009] H.L.R. 3 (CA (Civ Div)), Richards, L.J.
s.153D, see *Wear Valley DC v Robson* [2008] EWCA Civ 1470, [2009] H.L.R. 27 (CA (Civ Div)), Laws, L.J.

1996– cont.

52. Housing Act 1996– *cont.*

s.160A, enabling: SI 2009/ 358, SI 2009/ 393

s.167, see *R. (on the application of Ahmad) v Newham LBC* [2009] UKHL 14, [2009] 3 All E.R. 755 (HL), Lord Hope of Craighead; see *R. (on the application of Faarah) v Southwark LBC* [2008] EWCA Civ 807, [2009] H.L.R. 12 (CA (Civ Div)), Sedley, L.J.

s.172, enabling: SI 2009/ 358, SI 2009/ 393

s.175, see *R. (on the application of Aweys) v Birmingham City Council* [2009] UKHL 36, [2009] 1 W.L.R. 1506 (HL), Lord Hope of Craighead

s.184, see *Lambeth LBC v Johnston* [2008] EWCA Civ 690, [2009] H.L.R. 10 (CA (Civ Div)), Smith, L.J.

s.185, see *Barry v Southwark LBC* [2008] EWCA Civ 1440, [2009] 2 C.M.L.R. 11 (CA (Civ Div)), Arden, L.J.

s.185, enabling: SI 2009/ 358, SI 2009/ 393

s.189, see *Holmes-Moorhouse v Richmond upon Thames LBC* [2009] UKHL 7, [2009] 1 W.L.R. 413 (HL), Lord Hoffmann; see *Lambeth LBC v Johnston* [2008] EWCA Civ 690, [2009] H.L.R. 10 (CA (Civ Div)), Smith, L.J.; see *Simms v Islington LBC* [2008] EWCA Civ 1083, [2009] H.L.R. 20 (CA (Civ Div)), Ward, L.J.

s.191, see *R. (on the application of Aweys) v Birmingham City Council* [2009] UKHL 36, [2009] 1 W.L.R. 1506 (HL), Lord Hope of Craighead; see *Ugiagbe v Southwark LBC* [2009] EWCA Civ 31, [2009] H.L.R. 35 (CA (Civ Div)), Sedley, L.J.

s.193, see *Alexander-David v Hammersmith and Fulham LBC* [2009] EWCA Civ 259, [2009] 3 All E.R. 1098 (CA (Civ Div)), Waller, L.J.; see *Ali v Birmingham City Council* [2009] EWCA Civ 1279, Times, October 30, 2009 (CA (Civ Div)), May, L.J.; see *Boreh v Ealing LBC* [2008] EWCA Civ 1176, [2009] 2 All E.R. 383 (CA (Civ Div)), Wall, L.J.; see *R. (on the application of Aweys) v Birmingham City Council* [2009] UKHL 36, [2009] 1 W.L.R. 1506 (HL), Lord Hope of Craighead

s.202, see *De-Winter Heald v Brent LBC* [2009] EWCA Civ 930, [2009] H.R.L.R. 34 (CA (Civ Div)), Sedley, L.J.

s.204, see *Ali v Birmingham City Council* [2008] EWCA Civ 1228, [2009] 2 All E.R. 501 (CA (Civ Div)), Thomas, L.J.; see *De-Winter Heald v Brent LBC* [2009] EWCA Civ 930, [2009] H.R.L.R. 34 (CA (Civ Div)), Sedley, L.J.

s.215, enabling: SI 2009/ 358, SI 2009/ 393

Sch.1 Part I para.1, amended: SI 2009/ 1941 Sch.1 para.161

Sch.1 Part I para.2, amended: SI 2009/ 1941 Sch.1 para.161

Sch.1 Part I para.3, amended: SI 2009/ 1941 Sch.1 para.161

Sch.1 Part II, amended: SI 2009/ 1941 Sch.1 para.161

Sch.1 Part II para.4, amended: SI 2009/ 1941 Sch.1 para.161

Sch.1 Part II para.7, amended: SI 2009/ 1941 Sch.1 para.161

Sch.1 Part II para.10, amended: SI 2009/ 1941 Sch.1 para.161

Sch.1 Part II para.11, amended: SI 2009/ 1941 Sch.1 para.161

Sch.1 Part II para.12, amended: SI 2009/ 1941 Sch.1 para.161

1996– cont.

52. Housing Act 1996– *cont.*

Sch.1 Part II para.13, amended: SI 2009/ 1941 Sch.1 para.161

Sch.1 Part II para.14, amended: SI 2009/ 1941 Sch.1 para.161

Sch.1 Part II para.15, amended: SI 2009/ 1941 Sch.1 para.161

Sch.3 para.6, repealed: SI 2009/484 Sch.2

Sch.5, amended: SI 2009/1307 Sch.1 para.261

53. Housing Grants, Construction and Regeneration Act 1996

see *North Midland Construction Plc v AE&E Lentjes UK Ltd (formerly Lurgi (UK) Ltd)* [2009] EWHC 1371 (TCC), [2009] B.L.R. 574 (QBD (TCC)), Ramsey, J.

s.3, amended: 2009 c.20 Sch.6 para.88

s.30, enabling: SI 2009/1087, SI 2009/1807

s.105, see *North Midland Construction Plc v AE&E Lentjes UK Ltd (formerly Lurgi (UK) Ltd)* [2009] EWHC 1371 (TCC), [2009] B.L.R. 574 (QBD (TCC)), Ramsey, J.

s.106, repealed (in part): 2009 c.20 s.138, Sch.7 Part 5

s.106A, added: 2009 c.20 s.138

s.107, see *Allen Wilson Joinery Ltd v Privetgrange Construction Ltd* [2008] EWHC 2802 (TCC), [2009] T.C.L.R. 1 (QBD (TCC)), Akenhead, J.

s.107, repealed: 2009 c.20 s.139, Sch.7 Part 5

s.108, see *HS Works Ltd v Enterprise Managed Services Ltd* [2009] EWHC 729 (TCC), [2009] B.L.R. 378 (QBD (TCC)), Akenhead, J.

s.108, amended: 2009 c.20 s.139, s.140

s.108A, added: 2009 c.20 s.141

s.109, amended: 2009 c.20 s.143

s.110, amended: 2009 c.20 s.142, s.143, Sch.7 Part 5

s.110, repealed (in part): 2009 c.20 s.143, Sch.7 Part 5

s.110A, added: 2009 c.20 s.143

s.110B, added: 2009 c.20 s.143

s.111, see *Aedas Architects Ltd v Skanska Construction UK Ltd* (2009) 25 Const. L.J. 670 (OH), Lord McEwan

s.111, substituted: 2009 c.20 s.144

s.112, amended: 2009 c.20 s.144, s.145

s.113, see *William Hare Ltd v Shepherd Construction Ltd* [2009] EWHC 1603 (TCC), [2009] B.L.R. 447 (QBD (TCC)), Coulson, J.

s.146, amended: 2009 c.20 s.138

s.146, enabling: SI 2009/1087, SI 2009/1807

55. Broadcasting Act 1996

s.29, repealed (in part): SI 2009/1968 Art.3

s.132, amended: SI 2009/1941 Sch.1 para.162

Sch.5 para.8, amended: SI 2009/1941 Sch.1 para.162

Sch.6 para.1, amended: SI 2009/1941 Sch.1 para.162

Sch.7 para.1, amended: SI 2009/1941 Sch.1 para.162

Sch.7 para.11, amended: 2009 c.4 Sch.1 para.446

Sch.7 para.21, amended: 2009 c.4 Sch.1 para.446

56. Education Act 1996

applied: 2009 c.4 s.71, 2009 c.22 s.264

varied: 2009 c.22 s.264

Part IV, applied: SI 2009/1563 Reg.2

Part X c.II, substituted: 2009 c.22 s.242

s.4, applied: SI 2009/3050 Art.2

s.5, enabling: SI 2009/1556

s.9, see *Hampshire CC v R* [2009] EWHC 626 (Admin), [2009] E.L.R. 371 (QBD (Admin)), Stadlen, J.

s.12, applied: 2009 c.22 s.215, s.216

s.13, amended: 2009 c.22 Sch.2 para.2, Sch.6 para.13

s.13A, substituted: 2009 c.22 Sch.2 para.3

1996– cont.

56. Education Act 1996–*cont.*

s.15A, amended: 2009 c.22 Sch.2 para.4

s.15B, amended: 2009 c.22 Sch.2 para.5

s.15ZA, added: 2009 c.22 s.41

s.15ZA, applied: 2009 c.22 s.66, s.67, s.72, s.83, s.84, s.95

s.15ZB, added: 2009 c.22 s.41

s.15ZB, applied: 2009 c.22 s.72

s.15ZC, added: 2009 c.22 s.42

s.15ZC, applied: 2009 c.22 s.72

s.16, amended: 2009 c.22 s.126

s.16, varied: 2009 c.22 s.58

s.17A, added: 2009 c.22 s.45

s.17A, applied: 2009 c.22 s.86

s.17B, added: 2009 c.22 s.45

s.17B, applied: 2009 c.22 s.86

s.17C, added: 2009 c.22 s.45

s.17C, applied: 2009 c.22 s.86

s.17D, added: 2009 c.22 s.45

s.17D, applied: 2009 c.22 s.86

s.18, varied: 2009 c.22 s.58

s.18A, added: 2009 c.22 s.48

s.18A, applied: 2009 c.22 s.66, s.67, s.72

s.19, applied: 2009 c.22 s.249, SI 2009/3355 Reg.3

s.29, enabling: SI 2009/1556

s.312, amended: 2009 c.22 Sch.2 para.6

s.312, applied: 2009 c.22 s.218, SI 2009/1555 Reg.45, SI 2009/2737 Reg.28, Reg.93

s.312A, added: 2009 c.22 s.52

s.313, applied: SI 2009/3355 Sch.1 para.4

s.317, enabling: SI 2009/1387

s.321, applied: SI 2009/1563 Reg.2

s.324, see *Hampshire CC v R* [2009] EWHC 626 (Admin), [2009] E.L.R. 371 (QBD (Admin)), Stadlen, J.; see *R. (on the application of M) v East Sussex CC* [2009] EWHC 1651 (Admin), Times, May 12, 2009 (QBD), Timothy Brennan Q.C.

s.324, applied: SI 2009/1511 Reg.3

s.326, see *R. (on the application of M) v East Sussex CC* [2009] EWHC 1651 (Admin), Times, May 12, 2009 (QBD), Timothy Brennan Q.C.

s.328, amended: 2009 c.22 s.52

s.342, enabling: SI 2009/1924, SI 2009/2544

s.391, amended: 2009 c.22 Sch.12 para.10

s.408, amended: 2009 c.22 Sch.12 para.11

s.408, applied: SI 2009/646

s.408, repealed (in part): 2009 c.22 s.223, Sch.16 Part 7

s.408, enabling: SI 2009/646

s.409, repealed: 2009 c.22 s.223, Sch.16 Part 7

s.457, repealed (in part): 2009 c.24 Sch.7 Part 1

s.463, applied: SI 2009/3050 Art.2

s.482, see *R. (on the application of Chandler) v Secretary of State for Children, Schools and Families* [2009] EWHC 219 (Admin), [2009] Eu. L.R. 615 (QBD (Admin)), Forbes, J.

s.482, applied: 2009 c.22 s.77

s.496, amended: 2009 c.22 s.221, Sch.2 para.7

s.497, amended: 2009 c.22 s.221, Sch.2 para.8

s.497A, amended: 2009 c.22 Sch.2 para.9

s.508B, see *D v Bedfordshire CC* [2008] EWHC 2664 (Admin), [2009] E.L.R. 1 (QBD (Admin)), Sir George Newman; see *D v Bedfordshire CC* [2009] EWCA Civ 678, [2009] E.L.R. 361 (CA (Civ Div)), Rix, L.J.

s.508F, added: 2009 c.22 s.57

s.508G, added: 2009 c.22 s.57

s.508H, added: 2009 c.22 s.57

1996– cont.

56. Education Act 1996–*cont.*

s.508I, added: 2009 c.22 s.57

s.509, repealed: 2009 c.22 s.57, Sch.16 Part 1

s.509A, amended: 2009 c.22 Sch.2 para.10

s.509AA, amended: 2009 c.22 s.55, s.56, Sch.2 para.10

s.509AB, amended: 2009 c.22 s.53, s.54, s.55

s.509AB, substituted: 2009 c.22 Sch.2 para.10

s.509AD, amended: 2009 c.22 s.57

s.509AE, added: 2009 c.22 s.56

s.512, amended: 2009 c.3 s.8

s.512, applied: 2009 c.3 s.6, SI 2009/3355 Sch.1 para.3

s.512, referred to: SI 2009/2680 Reg.21

s.512A, applied: SI 2009/2680 Reg.21

s.512ZA, referred to: SI 2009/3144 Art.2

s.512ZB, applied: 2009 c.3 s.6, SI 2009/830 Art.2, SI 2009/1673 Art.2, SI 2009/2300 Art.2, SI 2009/3355 Sch.1 para.3

s.512ZB, referred to: SI 2009/2680 Reg.21

s.512ZB, repealed (in part): 2009 c.24 Sch.7 Part 1

s.512ZB, enabling: SI 2009/830, SI 2009/1673, SI 2009/2300

s.512ZC, added: 2009 c.3 s.7

s.514A, added: 2009 c.22 s.46

s.533, referred to: SI 2009/3144 Art.3

s.537, enabling: SI 2009/646

s.537A, applied: SI 2009/1563 Reg.3, SI 2009/3355 Reg.5, Reg.6, Reg.7, Reg.8, Reg.9

s.537A, enabling: SI 2009/213, SI 2009/646, SI 2009/1563, SI 2009/3355

s.537B, applied: SI 2009/3355 Reg.5, Reg.6, Reg.7, Reg.8

s.537B, enabling: SI 2009/3355

s.550AA, amended: 2009 c.22 s.243

s.554, applied: SI 2009/817

s.554, enabling: SI 2009/817

s.555, applied: SI 2009/817

s.556, enabling: SI 2009/817

s.557, amended: SI 2009/1941 Sch.1 para.163

s.560A, added: 2009 c.22 s.47

s.562, amended: 2009 c.22 s.49

s.562, disapplied: 2009 c.22 s.264

s.562A, added: 2009 c.22 s.50

s.562B, added: 2009 c.22 s.50

s.562C, added: 2009 c.22 s.50

s.562D, added: 2009 c.22 s.50

s.562E, added: 2009 c.22 s.50

s.562F, added: 2009 c.22 s.50

s.562G, added: 2009 c.22 s.50

s.562H, added: 2009 c.22 s.50

s.562I, added: 2009 c.22 s.50

s.562J, added: 2009 c.22 s.50

s.568, enabling: SI 2009/830, SI 2009/1673, SI 2009/2300

s.569, amended: 2009 c.22 s.242

s.569, enabling: SI 2009/646, SI 2009/1301, SI 2009/1338, SI 2009/1387, SI 2009/1563, SI 2009/1924, SI 2009/2544, SI 2009/3355

s.569A, added: 2009 c.22 Sch.2 para.11

s.578, referred to: 2009 c.3 s.12

s.579, amended: 2009 c.22 Sch.2 para.12

s.579, enabling: SI 2009/1301, SI 2009/1338

s.580, amended: 2009 c.22 Sch.2 para.13

Sch.1 para.3A, added: 2009 c.22 s.249

Sch.1 para.6, repealed (in part): 2009 c.22 s.223, Sch.16 Part 7

Sch.1 para.15, enabling: SI 2009/1924

1996–cont.

56. Education Act 1996–*cont.*
  Sch.27 para.3, see *Hampshire CC v R* [2009] EWHC 626 (Admin), [2009] E.L.R. 371 (QBD (Admin)), Stadlen, J.
  Sch.36, applied: SI 2009/817 Art.4

61. Channel Tunnel Rail Link Act 1996
  s.50, amended: SI 2009/229 Sch.2 para.2
  s.50, applied: SI 2009/229 Art.4
  Sch.4 Part III para.6, substituted: SI 2009/1307 Sch.1 para.262
  Sch.4 Part III para.7, substituted: SI 2009/1307 Sch.1 para.262
  Sch.4 Part III para.8, substituted: SI 2009/1307 Sch.1 para.262
  Sch.4 Part III para.9, amended: SI 2009/1307 Sch.1 para.262
  Sch.4 Part III para.9, substituted: SI 2009/1307 Sch.1 para.262
  Sch.4 Part III para.10, substituted: SI 2009/1307 Sch.1 para.262
  Sch.4 Part III para.11, amended: SI 2009/1307 Sch.1 para.262
  Sch.4 Part III para.11, substituted: SI 2009/1307 Sch.1 para.262
  Sch.4 Part III para.12, amended: SI 2009/1307 Sch.1 para.262
  Sch.4 Part III para.12, substituted: SI 2009/1307 Sch.1 para.262
  Sch.4 Part III para.13, substituted: SI 2009/1307 Sch.1 para.262
  Sch.4 Part III para.14, substituted: SI 2009/1307 Sch.1 para.262
  Sch.4 Part III para.15, substituted: SI 2009/1307 Sch.1 para.262
  Sch.4 Part III para.16, substituted: SI 2009/1307 Sch.1 para.262
  Sch.14 para.13, amended: SI 2009/229 Sch.2 para.2
  Sch.14 para.13, applied: SI 2009/229 Art.4
  Sch.15 Part II para.2, amended: SI 2009/229 Sch.2 para.2
  Sch.15 Part II para.2, applied: SI 2009/229 Art.4

1997

7. Northern Ireland Arms Decommissioning Act 1997
  s.2, applied: SI 2009/281, SI 2009/281 Art.2
  s.2, enabling: SI 2009/281

8. Town and Country Planning (Scotland) Act 1997
  applied: 2009 asp 3 s.7, SSI 2009/140 Art.58
  Part V c.II, applied: SSI 2009/101 Art.3
  s.3F, added: 2009 asp 12 s.72
  s.3F, referred to: 2009 asp 12 s.73
  s.8, enabling: SSI 2009/378
  s.16, enabling: SSI 2009/378
  s.19, applied: SSI 2009/53 Reg.2
  s.19, enabling: SSI 2009/53, SSI 2009/343
  s.20, applied: SSI 2009/222 Art.10
  s.20B, enabling: SSI 2009/220
  s.22, applied: SSI 2009/222 Art.10
  s.26, applied: SSI 2009/51 Sch.1
  s.26A, applied: SSI 2009/51
  s.26A, enabling: SSI 2009/51
  s.30, applied: 2009 asp 12 s.70, s.71
  s.30, enabling: SSI 2009/34, SSI 2009/220
  s.31, applied: 2009 asp 12 s.70, s.71
  s.31, enabling: SSI 2009/34
  s.32, enabling: SSI 2009/220

1997–cont.

8. Town and Country Planning (Scotland) Act 1997–*cont.*
  s.34, enabling: SSI 2009/220
  s.35, referred to: SSI 2009/101 Art.2
  s.35B, referred to: SSI 2009/101 Art.2
  s.36, amended: SSI 2009/256 Art.2
  s.36A, referred to: SSI 2009/222 Art.5
  s.38A, enabling: SSI 2009/220
  s.40, enabling: SSI 2009/221, SSI 2009/343
  s.43A, enabling: SSI 2009/220
  s.47, see *Vattenfall Wind Power Ltd v Scottish Ministers* [2009] CSIH 27, 2009 S.C. 444 (IH (2 Div)), The Lord Justice Clerk (Gill)
  s.47, applied: SSI 2009/222 Art.3, Art.7, Art.9
  s.47, referred to: SSI 2009/222 Art.7
  s.47A, disapplied: SSI 2009/222 Art.9
  s.56, applied: SSI 2009/222 Art.10
  s.57, amended: 2009 asp 6 s.65
  s.59, applied: SSI 2009/222 Art.11
  s.60, amended: SSI 2009/256 Art.2
  s.75, see *North Berwick Trust v Miller* [2009] CSIH 15, 2009 S.C. 305 (IH (2 Div)), The Lord Justice Clerk (Gill)
  s.130, applied: SSI 2009/220 Reg.3, SSI 2009/222 Art.9
  s.130, referred to: SSI 2009/222 Art.12
  s.131, enabling: SSI 2009/220
  s.136A, applied: SSI 2009/52 Reg.2
  s.136A, enabling: SSI 2009/52
  s.144B, applied: SSI 2009/213 Reg.2
  s.144B, enabling: SSI 2009/213
  s.145A, applied: SSI 2009/52 Reg.2
  s.145A, enabling: SSI 2009/52
  s.147, enabling: SSI 2009/220
  s.154, applied: SSI 2009/222 Art.9
  s.169, applied: SSI 2009/222 Art.9
  s.179, referred to: SI 2009/2037 Art.5
  s.180, amended: SSI 2009/256 Art.2
  s.180, applied: SSI 2009/220 Reg.3, SSI 2009/222 Art.9
  s.242A, applied: SSI 2009/222 Art.13
  s.252, applied: SSI 2009/257
  s.252, enabling: SSI 2009/257
  s.266, amended: SSI 2009/256 Art.2
  s.267, enabling: SSI 2009/220
  s.275, applied: SSI 2009/52, SSI 2009/53
  s.275, repealed (in part): SSI 2009/404 Sch.4 Part 1
  s.275, enabling: SSI 2009/220, SSI 2009/221, SSI 2009/343
  s.277, amended: SSI 2009/256 Art.2
  Sch.4 para.6, amended: SSI 2009/256 Art.2
  Sch.9 para.7, applied: SSI 2009/222 Art.4
  Sch.10 para.6, applied: SSI 2009/222 Art.4
  Sch.14 para.1, referred to: SSI 2009/101 Art.3
  Sch.14 para.2, referred to: SSI 2009/101 Art.3

9. Planning (Listed Buildings and Conservation Areas) (Scotland) Act 1997
  s.15, amended: SSI 2009/256 Art.3
  s.43, referred to: SI 2009/2037 Art.5

10. Planning (Hazardous Substances) (Scotland) Act 1997
  s.2, enabling: SSI 2009/378
  s.3, enabling: SSI 2009/378
  s.6, applied: SSI 2009/222 Art.15
  s.21, applied: SSI 2009/378 Reg.5
  s.23, applied: SSI 2009/222 Art.15
  s.29, applied: SSI 2009/222 Art.15
  s.38, amended: SI 2009/1941 Sch.1 para.167

1997– cont.

10. Planning (Hazardous Substances) (Scotland) Act 1997– *cont.*
s.39, enabling: SSI 2009/378

11. Planning (Consequential Provisions) (Scotland) Act 1997
Sch.2 para.8, repealed: 2009 asp 6 Sch.3 para.9

12. Civil Procedure Act 1997
s.l, applied: SI 2009/2092, SI 2009/3390
s.2, applied: SI 2009/2092
s.2, enabling: SI 2009/2092, SI 2009/3390
s.5, see *Bovale Ltd v Secretary of State for Communities and Local Government* [2009] EWCA Civ 171, [2009] 1 W.L.R. 2274 (CA (Civ Div)), Waller, L.J. (V-P)
s.9, see *Bovale Ltd v Secretary of State for Communities and Local Government* [2009] EWCA Civ 171, [2009] 1 W.L.R. 2274 (CA (Civ Div)), Waller, L.J. (V-P)

13. United Nations Personnel Act 1997
s.4, amended: 2009 c.6 s.2
s.9, applied: 2009 c.6 s.3

16. Finance Act 1997
s.10, amended: 2009 c.10 s.114
s.ll, amended: 2009 c.10 s.19, SI 2009/56 Sch.1 para.242
s.ll, repealed (in part): 2009 c.10 s.113
s.12, enabling: SI 2009/2046
s.14, amended: 2009 c.10 s.114
s.14, enabling: SI 2009/2046
s.15, amended: 2009 c.10 s.114
s.52, applied: SI 2009/3024 Art.4, SSI 2009/403 Art.3
s.56, repealed (in part): 2009 c.10 Sch.1 para.6
s.65, repealed: 2009 c.4 Sch.3 Part 1
s.66, repealed: 2009 c.4 Sch.3 Part 1
Sch.1 Part I para.6, applied: 2009 c.10 s.114
Sch.1 Part I para.8, amended: SI 2009/56 Sch.1 para.243, SI 2009/1890 Art.4
Sch.1 Part II para.9, amended: SI 2009/56 Sch.1 para.243
Sch.5 Part II para.6, repealed (in part): 2009 c.10 Sch.51 para.43
Sch.5 Part V para.19, amended: SI 2009/56 Sch.1 para.244
Sch.7 para.8, repealed (in part): 2009 c.4 Sch.3 Part 1
Sch.12 Part I para.ll, amended: 2009 c.4 Sch.1 para.448
Sch.13 para.2, repealed: 2009 c.4 Sch.3 Part 1
Sch.13 para.3, repealed: 2009 c.4 Sch.3 Part 1

20. British Nationality (Hong Kong) Act 1997
applied: SI 2009/421 Reg.28
s.l, amended: 2009 c.11 s.47

22. Architects Act 1997
s.4A, referred to: SI 2009/2999 Reg.31
Sch.1A para.3, referred to: SI 2009/2999 Reg.31
Sch.1A para.6, referred to: SI 2009/2999 Reg.31

23. Lieutenancies Act 1997
Sch.1 para.3, amended: SI 2009/837 Art.10

27. Social Security (Recovery of Benefits) Act 1997
see *Allen v Ravenhill Farm Services Ltd* [2009] CSOH 42, 2009 S.L.T. 1084 (OH), Lady Stacey
s.29, enabling: SI 2009/1494
Sch.1 Part I para.2, varied: SI 2009/1059 Sch.1 para.39
Sch.1 Part I para.4, enabling: SI 2009/1494

28. Merchant Shipping and Maritime Security Act 1997
s.24, amended: SI 2009/1941 Sch.1 para.168

1997– cont.

29. Local Government and Rating Act 1997
Part II, applied: SI 2009/276 Reg.l
s.8, applied: SSI 2009/69
s.8, enabling: SSI 2009/69
s.9, applied: SI 2009/532, SI 2009/533, SI 2009/535, SI 2009/538, SI 2009/539, SI 2009/540, SI 2009/542, SI 2009/543
s.14, enabling: SI 2009/532, SI 2009/533, SI 2009/535, SI 2009/536, SI 2009/538, SI 2009/539, SI 2009/540, SI 2009/541, SI 2009/542, SI 2009/543
Sch.2 para.3, applied: SSI 2009/42 Reg.3, SSI 2009/69 Art.3
Sch.2 para.3, enabling: SSI 2009/69
Sch.2 para.4, applied: SSI 2009/42 Reg.5

33. Confiscation of Alcohol (Young Persons) Act 1997
s.l, amended: 2009 c.26 s.29, Sch.8 Part 3
s.l, repealed (in part): 2009 c.26 Sch.8 Part 3

36. Flood Prevention and Land Drainage (Scotland) Act 1997
repealed: 2009 asp 6 Sch.3 para.10

40. Protection from Harassment Act 1997
see *Ferguson v British Gas Trading Ltd* [2009] EWCA Civ 46, [2009] 3 All E.R. 304 (CA (Civ Div)), Sedley, L.J.; see *R. v McDermott (Lee)* [2008] EWCA Crim 2345, [2009] 1 Cr. App. R. (S.) 110 (CA (Crim Div)), Hallett, L.J.; see *Supperstone v Hurst* [2009] EWHC 1271 (Ch), [2009] 1 W.L.R. 2306 (Ch D), Bernard Livesey Q.C.
s.l, see *DPP v Hardy* [2008] EWHC 2874 (Admin), (2009) 173 J.P. 10 (DC), Pill, L.J.
s.2, see *Ferguson v British Gas Trading Ltd* [2009] EWCA Civ 46, [2009] 3 All E.R. 304 (CA (Civ Div)), Sedley, L.J.
s.3, see *Ferguson v British Gas Trading Ltd* [2009] EWCA Civ 46, [2009] 3 All E.R. 304 (CA (Civ Div)), Sedley, L.J.
s.4, see *R. v McDermott (Lee)* [2008] EWCA Crim 2345, [2009] 1 Cr. App. R. (S.) 110 (CA (Crim Div)), Hallett, L.J.
s.4, applied: SI 2009/2055 Reg.3, Reg.5

43. Crime (Sentences) Act 1997
Part II c.II, applied: SI 2009/1887 Sch.l
s.28, see *Wells v Parole Board* [2009] UKHL 22, [2009] 2 W.L.R. 1149 (HL), Lord Hope of Craighead
s.30, see *R. (on the application of Wellington) v Secretary of State for the Home Department* [2008] UKHL 72, [2009] 1 A.C. 335 (HL), Lord Hoffmann; see *R. v Bieber (David Francis)* [2008] EWCA Crim 1601, [2009] 1 W.L.R. 223 (CA (Crim Div)), Lord Phillips of Worth Matravers, L.C.J.
s.34, varied: SI 2009/1059 Sch.1 para.40

44. Education Act 1997
s.19, enabling: SI 2009/1596
s.21, applied: 2009 c.22 s.175
s.21, repealed: 2009 c.22 Sch.12 para.13, Sch.16 Part 4
s.22, repealed: 2009 c.22 Sch.12 para.13, Sch.16 Part 4
s.23, repealed: 2009 c.22 Sch.12 para.13, Sch.16 Part 4
s.24, repealed: 2009 c.22 Sch.12 para.13, Sch.16 Part 4
s.25, repealed: 2009 c.22 Sch.12 para.13, Sch.16 Part 4

1997–cont.

44. Education Act 1997–*cont.*

s.26, repealed: 2009 c.22 Sch.12 para.13, Sch.16 Part 4

s.26A, repealed: 2009 c.22 Sch.12 para.13, Sch.16 Part 4

s.29, amended: 2009 c.22 Sch.12 para.14

s.30, amended: 2009 c.22 Sch.12 para.15

s.30, applied: SI 2009/1220 Art.1

s.30, referred to: SI 2009/1220 Art.2

s.30, repealed (in part): 2009 c.22 Sch.12 para.15, Sch.16 Part 4

s.30, enabling: SI 2009/1220

s.32, amended: 2009 c.22 Sch.12 para.16

s.32, repealed (in part): 2009 c.22 Sch.12 para.16, Sch.16 Part 4

s.32A, amended: 2009 c.22 Sch.12 para.18

s.32A, repealed (in part): 2009 c.22 Sch.12 para.18, Sch.16 Part 4

s.32B, added: 2009 c.22 Sch.12 para.19

s.32C, added: 2009 c.22 Sch.12 para.19

s.32ZA, added: 2009 c.22 Sch.12 para.17

s.35, amended: 2009 c.22 Sch.12 para.20

s.36, repealed: 2009 c.22 Sch.12 para.21, Sch.16 Part 4

s.43, amended: 2009 c.22 s.250

s.45B, added: 2009 c.1 s.45

s.54, amended: 2009 c.22 Sch.12 para.22, Sch.16 Part 4

s.54, enabling: SI 2009/1596

s.58, amended: 2009 c.22 Sch.12 para.23, Sch.16 Part 4

Sch.4 para.1, repealed: 2009 c.22 Sch.12 para.24, Sch.16 Part 4

Sch.4 para.2, repealed: 2009 c.22 Sch.12 para.24, Sch.16 Part 4

Sch.4 para.3, repealed: 2009 c.22 Sch.12 para.24, Sch.16 Part 4

Sch.4 para.4, repealed: 2009 c.22 Sch.12 para.24, Sch.16 Part 4

Sch.4 para.5, repealed: 2009 c.22 Sch.12 para.24, Sch.16 Part 4

Sch.4 para.6, repealed: 2009 c.22 Sch.12 para.24, Sch.16 Part 4

Sch.4 para.7, repealed: 2009 c.22 Sch.12 para.24, Sch.16 Part 4

Sch.4 para.8, repealed: 2009 c.22 Sch.12 para.24, Sch.16 Part 4

Sch.4 para.9, repealed: 2009 c.22 Sch.12 para.24, Sch.16 Part 4

Sch.4 para.10, repealed: 2009 c.22 Sch.12 para.24, Sch.16 Part 4

Sch.4 para.11, repealed: 2009 c.22 Sch.12 para.24, Sch.16 Part 4

Sch.4 para.12, repealed: 2009 c.22 Sch.12 para.24, Sch.16 Part 4

Sch.4 para.13, repealed: 2009 c.22 Sch.12 para.24, Sch.16 Part 4

Sch.4 para.14, repealed: 2009 c.22 Sch.12 para.24, Sch.16 Part 4

Sch.4 para.15, repealed: 2009 c.22 Sch.12 para.24, Sch.16 Part 4

Sch.4 para.16, repealed: 2009 c.22 Sch.12 para.24, Sch.16 Part 4

Sch.4 para.17, repealed: 2009 c.22 Sch.12 para.24, Sch.16 Part 4

Sch.4 para.18, repealed: 2009 c.22 Sch.12 para.24, Sch.16 Part 4

Sch.4 para.19, repealed: 2009 c.22 Sch.12 para.24, Sch.16 Part 4

1997–cont.

44. Education Act 1997–*cont.*

Sch.4 para.20, repealed: 2009 c.22 Sch.12 para.24, Sch.16 Part 4

Sch.7 para.1, repealed: 2009 c.22 Sch.16 Part 4

Sch.7 para.2, repealed: 2009 c.22 Sch.12 para.25, Sch.16 Part 4

Sch.7 para.3, repealed (in part): 2009 c.22 Sch.16 Part 4

Sch.7 para.4, repealed (in part): 2009 c.22 Sch.16 Part 4

Sch.7 para.29, repealed (in part): 2009 c.22 Sch.16 Part 4

48. Crime and Punishment (Scotland) Act 1997

Sch.1 para.18, repealed (in part): 2009 asp 9 Sch.6

50. Police Act 1997

Part V, applied: SI 2009/12 Art.9, SI 2009/2610 Art.21, SI 2009/2680 Reg.3, SI 2009/2793 Reg.2, SI 2009/3297 Reg.12, Reg.13, Reg.16, SSI 2009/4 Art.4

Part V, referred to: SSI 2009/4 Art.4, Art.5

Part III, see *C's Application for Judicial Review, Re* [2009] UKHL 15, [2009] 1 A.C. 908 (HL (NI)), Lord Phillips of Worth Matravers

s.91, amended: SI 2009/1941 Sch.1 para.169

s.93, amended: 2009 c.26 s.6

s.97, see *C's Application for Judicial Review, Re* [2009] UKHL 15, [2009] 1 A.C. 908 (HL (NI)), Lord Phillips of Worth Matravers

s.108, varied: SI 2009/1059 Sch.1 para.41

s.112, amended: 2009 c.26 s.93, Sch.8 Part 8

s.112, enabling: SI 2009/3334, SSI 2009/40, SSI 2009/216

s.113A, amended: 2009 c.26 Sch.8 Part 8, SI 2009/203 Art.3

s.113A, applied: SI 2009/203 Art.21, SI 2009/266 Reg.11, SI 2009/783 Reg.3, SI 2009/3112 Sch.1 para.2, SI 2009/3297 Reg.3, Reg.5, Reg.9, Reg.12, Reg.16

s.113A, referred to: SI 2009/3112 Sch.1 para.2

s.113A, varied: SI 2009/3215 Sch.1 para.2

s.113A, enabling: SI 2009/2428, SI 2009/3297, SI 2009/3334, SSI 2009/40, SSI 2009/216

s.113B, amended: 2009 c.26 Sch.8 Part 8, SI 2009/203 Art.4

s.113B, applied: SI 2009/203 Art.21, SI 2009/266 Reg.11, SI 2009/460 Reg.2, SI 2009/783 Reg.3, SI 2009/1798 Reg.2, SI 2009/1887 Reg.8, Reg.12, SI 2009/2680 Reg.18, Reg.30, Sch.2 para.6, SI 2009/3112 Sch.1 para.2, SI 2009/3297 Reg.3, Reg.5, Reg.6, Reg.9, Reg.12, Reg.16

s.113B, referred to: SI 2009/3112 Sch.1 para.2

s.113B, varied: SI 2009/3215 Sch.1 para.3

s.113B, enabling: SI 2009/460, SI 2009/1798, SI 2009/1882, SI 2009/2495, SI 2009/3297, SI 2009/3334, SSI 2009/40, SSI 2009/216

s.113BA, amended: 2009 c.26 s.81

s.113BA, applied: SI 2009/1882 Reg.5, SI 2009/3297 Reg.7

s.113BA, varied: SI 2009/2610 Art.5, Art.11

s.113BA, enabling: SI 2009/1882, SI 2009/2495, SI 2009/3297

s.113BB, amended: 2009 c.26 s.81

s.113BB, applied: SI 2009/1882 Reg.6, SI 2009/3297 Reg.8

s.113BB, varied: SI 2009/2610 Art.6, Art.12

s.113BB, enabling: SI 2009/1882, SI 2009/2495, SI 2009/3297

s.113C, varied: SSI 2009/337 Art.3, SSI 2009/375 Art.3

s.113CA, amended: 2009 c.26 s.81

1997–cont.

50. Police Act 1997–*cont.*
s.113CB, amended: 2009 c.26 s.81
s.113CD, added: 2009 c.26 s.94
s.113D, varied: SSI 2009/337 Art.3, SSI 2009/375 Art.3
s.113E, applied: SI 2009/3297 Reg.4
s.113E, varied: SI 2009/2610 Art.14, SI 2009/3215 Sch.1 para.4
s.113E, enabling: SI 2009/3297
s.114, amended: 2009 c.26 Sch.8 Part 8
s.114, applied: SI 2009/3297 Reg.3, Reg.5, Reg.9
s.114, varied: SI 2009/3215 Sch.1 para.5
s.114, enabling: SI 2009/3297, SSI 2009/216
s.115, see *R. (on the application of L) v Commissioner of Police of the Metropolis* [2009] UKSC 3, [2009] 3 W.L.R. 1056 (SC), Lord Hope (Deputy President)
s.116, amended: 2009 c.26 Sch.8 Part 8
s.116, applied: SI 2009/3297 Reg.3, Reg.5, Reg.9
s.116, varied: SI 2009/2610 Art.15, SI 2009/3215 Sch.1 para.6
s.116, enabling: SI 2009/3297, SSI 2009/216
s.118, amended: 2009 c.26 s.95
s.118, varied: SI 2009/3215 Sch.1 para.7
s.118, enabling: SI 2009/460, SI 2009/1798, SI 2009/3334
s.119, amended: 2009 c.26 Sch.7 para.118
s.119, varied: SI 2009/2610 Art.7, SI 2009/3215 Sch.1 para.8, Sch.3 para.1
s.120, amended: SI 2009/203 Art.5
s.120, applied: SI 2009/2680 Reg.3
s.120, varied: SI 2009/3215 Sch.1 para.9
s.120A, amended: 2009 c.26 s.96, SI 2009/203 Art.7
s.120A, applied: SI 2009/3297 Reg.13
s.120A, varied: SI 2009/2610 Art.8
s.120AA, amended: SI 2009/203 Art.8
s.120AB, amended: SI 2009/203 Art.9
s.120ZA, amended: SI 2009/203 Art.6
s.120ZA, varied: SI 2009/3215 Sch.1 para.10
s.120ZA, enabling: SI 2009/3297
s.122, amended: SI 2009/203 Art.10
s.122A, varied: SI 2009/3215 Sch.1 para.11
s.124, amended: SI 2009/203 Art.11
s.124, applied: SI 2009/3297 Reg.11
s.124, varied: SI 2009/3215 Sch.1 para.12
s.124, enabling: SI 2009/3297
s.124A, varied: SI 2009/3215 Sch.1 para.13
s.125, varied: SI 2009/3215 Sch.1 para.14
s.125, enabling: SI 2009/1882, SI 2009/2428, SI 2009/2495, SI 2009/3297, SI 2009/3334
s.125B, added: 2009 c.26 s.97
s.126, varied: SI 2009/3215 Sch.1 para.15
58. Finance (No.2) Act 1997
s.21, repealed: 2009 c.4 Sch.3 Part 1
s.22, repealed (in part): 2009 c.10 Sch.14 para.30
s.24, repealed (in part): 2009 c.4 Sch.3 Part 1
s.33, repealed (in part): 2009 c.4 Sch.3 Part 1
s.35, amended: SI 2009/56 Sch.1 para.246
s.40, repealed: 2009 c.4 Sch.3 Part 1
s.48, see *Revenue and Customs Commissioners v Micro Fusion 2004-1 LLP* [2009] EWHC 1082 (Ch), [2009] S.T.C. 1741 (Ch D), Davis, J.
Sch.6 para.12, repealed: 2009 c.4 Sch.3 Part 1
Sch.6 para.13, repealed: 2009 c.4 Sch.3 Part 1
59. Education (Schools) Act 1997
s.2, applied: SI 2009/1561
s.3, applied: SI 2009/1561
s.3, enabling: SI 2009/1560, SI 2009/1561

1997–cont.

66. Plant Varieties Act 1997
Sch.3 para.4, amended: 2009 c.3 Sch.4 para.27
Sch.3 para.5, amended: 2009 c.3 Sch.4 para.27
Sch.3 para.16, amended: 2009 c.3 Sch.4 para.27

1998

11. Bank of England Act 1998
s.1, amended: 2009 c.1 s.239
s.2, amended: 2009 c.1 s.238
s.2A, added: 2009 c.1 s.238
s.2B, added: 2009 c.1 s.238
s.2C, added: 2009 c.1 s.238
s.3, amended: 2009 c.1 s.241, s.242
s.3, repealed (in part): 2009 c.1 s.242
Sch.1 para.1, amended: 2009 c.1 s.243
Sch.1 para.6, amended: 2009 c.1 s.243
Sch.1 para.12, amended: 2009 c.1 s.240
Sch.1 para.13, amended: 2009 c.1 s.241, s.242
Sch.1 para.13, repealed (in part): 2009 c.1 s.242
Sch.3 para.2A, added: 2009 c.1 s.243
Sch.3 para.6, amended: 2009 c.1 s.243
Sch.5 Part IV para.63, repealed: SI 2009/1941 Sch.2
Sch.7 para.3, amended: SI 2009/1941 Sch.1 para.172
14. Social Security Act 1998
applied: 2009 c.8 s.24, SI 2009/607 Reg.2
s.8, applied: SI 2009/810 Reg.2, SI 2009/1377 Art.4
s.8, referred to: SI 2009/1377 Art.3
s.8, repealed (in part): 2009 c.24 Sch.7 Part 1
s.9, applied: SI 2009/1377 Art.3
s.9, enabling: SI 2009/659, SI 2009/713, SI 2009/751, SI 2009/1490, SI 2009/3268
s.10, applied: SI 2009/1377 Art.3
s.10, enabling: SI 2009/1490, SI 2009/3268
s.10A, amended: SI 2009/56 Sch.1 para.248
s.11, applied: SI 2009/1377 Art.3
s.12, applied: SI 2009/1377 Art.3
s.12, enabling: SI 2009/713, SI 2009/751, SI 2009/3268
s.13, applied: SI 2009/1377 Art.3
s.14, applied: SI 2009/1377 Art.3
s.15, applied: SI 2009/1377 Art.3
s.15A, applied: SI 2009/1377 Art.3
s.16, applied: SI 2009/1377 Art.3
s.17, applied: SI 2009/1377 Art.3
s.18, applied: SI 2009/1377 Art.3
s.21, applied: SI 2009/1377 Art.3
s.21, referred to: SI 2009/1377 Art.4
s.22, applied: SI 2009/1377 Art.3
s.22, referred to: SI 2009/1377 Art.4
s.23, applied: SI 2009/1377 Art.3
s.23, referred to: SI 2009/1377 Art.4
s.24A, amended: SI 2009/56 Sch.1 para.249
s.25, applied: SI 2009/1377 Art.3
s.26, applied: SI 2009/1377 Art.3
s.27, applied: SI 2009/1377 Art.3
s.28, applied: SI 2009/1377 Art.3
s.34, amended: 2009 c.24 Sch.7 Part 1
s.38, amended: 2009 c.24 s.20
s.39, amended: SI 2009/56 Sch.1 para.250
s.39ZA, applied: SI 2009/1377 Art.3
s.79, enabling: SI 2009/659, SI 2009/713, SI 2009/751, SI 2009/1490, SI 2009/3268
s.84, enabling: SI 2009/659, SI 2009/1490, SI 2009/3268
Sch.2 para.5A, repealed: 2009 c.24 Sch.7 Part 3
Sch.2 para.6, repealed (in part): 2009 c.24 Sch.7 Part 1

1998– cont.

14. Social Security Act 1998–*cont.*
Sch.2 para.7, amended: 2009 c.24 Sch.7 Part 1
Sch.3 Part I para.3, amended: 2009 c.24 s.1, s.25, s.33, Sch.1 para.25, Sch.3 para.4, Sch.4 para.10
Sch.3 Part I para.3, repealed (in part): 2009 c.24 Sch.7 Part 3
Sch.7 para.95, repealed: 2009 c.24 Sch.7 Part 1
Sch.7 para.97, repealed: 2009 c.24 Sch.7 Part 1
Sch.7 para.141, repealed: 2009 c.24 Sch.7 Part 3
Sch.7 para.142, repealed: 2009 c.24 Sch.7 Part 3
Sch.7 para.145, repealed: 2009 c.24 Sch.7 Part 3

17. Petroleum Act 1998
Part III, applied: 2009 c.23 s.77
Part IV, applied: 2009 c.23 s.77
s.3, applied: 2009 c.23 s.77, SI 2009/2814 Reg.2, Sch.1 para.2
s.4, enabling: SI 2009/2814, SI 2009/3283
s.14, applied: 2009 c.23 Sch.8 para.7
s.17C, amended: SI 2009/1349 Reg.4
s.24, amended: 2009 c.23 Sch.8 para.7
s.24, applied: 2009 c.23 Sch.8 para.7
s.26, applied: SI 2009/2809 Art.2
s.45, amended: 2009 c.23 Sch.8 para.8

18. Audit Commission Act 1998
see *Veolia ES Nottinghamshire Ltd v Nottinghamshire CC* [2009] EWHC 2382 (Admin), Times, October 15, 2009 (QBD (Admin)), Cranston, J.
applied: SI 2009/467 Reg.13
s.3, amended: SI 2009/1941 Sch.1 para.173
s.3, repealed (in part): SI 2009/1941 Sch.1 para.173
s.4, applied: 2009 c.20 s.46
s.27, applied: SI 2009/3322
s.27, enabling: SI 2009/473, SI 2009/3322
s.29, amended: SI 2009/1941 Sch.1 para.173
s.31, amended: SI 2009/1941 Sch.1 para.173
s.31, repealed: 2009 c.20 s.52, Sch.7 Part 2
s.47A, repealed (in part): 2009 c.2 Sch.1 para.8, Sch.4
s.47B, enabling: SI 2009/1360
s.53, amended: SI 2009/1941 Sch.1 para.173
Sch.2 para.1, amended: 2009 c.20 Sch.6 para.89
Sch.2 para.1, referred to: SI 2009/467 Reg.13
Sch.2A Part 2 para.5, applied: SI 2009/1360 Art.2, Art.3
Sch.2A Part 2 para.5, enabling: SI 2009/1360

20. Late Payment of Commercial Debts (Interest) Act 1998
s.4, see *Ruttle Plant Hire Ltd v Secretary of State for the Environment, Food and Rural Affairs* [2008] EWHC 730 (TCC), [2009] 1 All E.R. (Comm) 73 (QBD (TCC)), Coulson, J.

29. Data Protection Act 1998
see *Bernard L Madoff Investment Securities LLC, Re* [2009] EWHC 442 (Ch), [2009] 2 B.C.L.C. 78 (Ch D), Lewison, J.; see *Chief Constable of Humberside v Information Commissioner* [2009] EWCA Civ 1079, Times, October 22, 2009 (CA (Civ Div)), Waller, L.J.; see *Clift v Slough BC* [2009] EWHC 1550 (QB), [2009] 4 All E.R. 756 (QBD), Tugendhat, J.; see *Galloway v Information Commissioner* (2009) 108 B.M.L.R. 50 (Information Tr), Claire Taylor
applied: 2009 c.11 s.19, 2009 c.22 s.215, 2009 c.23 Sch.10 para.9, SI 2009/209 Reg.119, SI 2009/214 Sch.2 para.6, SI 2009/307 Sch.1 para.19, SI 2009/1801 Sch.2 para.6, SI 2009/1919 Reg.11, SI 2009/1976 r.19, SI 2009/2793 Reg.5
disapplied: 2009 c.23 Sch.7 para.13

1998– cont.

29. Data Protection Act 1998–*cont.*
referred to: SI 2009/3157 Reg.9
Part V, applied: 2009 c.22 s.215
s.10, applied: SI 2009/3157 Reg.9, SSI 2009/440 Reg.10
s.16, amended: 2009 c.25 Sch.20 para.1, Sch.23 Part 8
s.17, enabling: SI 2009/1677
s.18, amended: 2009 c.25 Sch.20 para.2
s.18, enabling: SI 2009/1677
s.19, amended: 2009 c.25 Sch.20 para.3
s.19, enabling: SI 2009/1677
s.20, amended: 2009 c.25 Sch.20 para.4, Sch.23 Part 8
s.25, applied: SI 2009/1677
s.26, referred to: SI 2009/1677
s.26, enabling: SI 2009/1677
s.28, applied: SI 2009/1976 r.19, r.22
s.29, see *Chief Constable of Humberside v Information Commissioner* [2009] EWCA Civ 1079, Times, October 22, 2009 (CA (Civ Div)), Waller, L.J.
s.35, see *Parkinson v Hawthorne* [2008] EWHC 3499 (Ch), [2009] 1 W.L.R. 1665 (Ch D), Patten, J.
s.41A, added: 2009 c.25 s.173
s.41B, added: 2009 c.25 s.173
s.41C, added: 2009 c.25 s.173
s.43, amended: 2009 c.25 Sch.20 para.8, Sch.20 para.10
s.44, amended: 2009 c.25 Sch.20 para.9, Sch.20 para.11
s.47, applied: SI 2009/214 Sch.2 para.6, SI 2009/1801 Sch.2 para.6
s.48, amended: 2009 c.25 Sch.20 para.5
s.51, amended: 2009 c.25 s.174
s.52A, added: 2009 c.25 s.174
s.52B, added: 2009 c.25 s.174
s.52C, added: 2009 c.25 s.174
s.52D, added: 2009 c.25 s.174
s.52E, added: 2009 c.25 s.174
s.55A, amended: 2009 c.25 Sch.20 para.13
s.56, amended: 2009 c.26 s.81
s.67, amended: 2009 c.25 Sch.20 para.6
s.67, applied: SI 2009/1677, SI 2009/1811
s.67, enabling: SI 2009/1811
s.69, amended: SI 2009/1182 Sch.5 para.4
s.70, amended: 2009 c.25 Sch.20 para.7
s.75, amended: 2009 c.26 s.81
Sch.1, see *Bernard L Madoff Investment Securities LLC, Re* [2009] EWHC 442 (Ch), [2009] 2 B.C.L.C. 78 (Ch D), Lewison, J.; see *Chief Constable of Humberside v Information Commissioner* [2009] EWCA Civ 1079, Times, October 22, 2009 (CA (Civ Div)), Waller, L.J.
Sch.3 para.10, applied: SI 2009/1811 Art.2
Sch.3 para.10, enabling: SI 2009/1811
Sch.4 para.4, see *Bernard L Madoff Investment Securities LLC, Re* [2009] EWHC 442 (Ch), [2009] 2 B.C.L.C. 78 (Ch D), Lewison, J.
Sch.4 para.5, see *Bernard L Madoff Investment Securities LLC, Re* [2009] EWHC 442 (Ch), [2009] 2 B.C.L.C. 78 (Ch D), Lewison, J.
Sch.7 para.11, amended: 2009 c.25 Sch.20 para.12
Sch.9 para.1, amended: 2009 c.25 Sch.20 para.14
Sch.9 para.1, varied: 2009 c.25 Sch.22 para.46
Sch.9 para.2, amended: 2009 c.25 Sch.20 para.14
Sch.9 para.5, amended: 2009 c.25 Sch.20 para.14

1998– cont.

29. Data Protection Act 1998–*cont.*
Sch.9 para.12, amended: 2009 c.25 Sch.20 para.14, Sch.23 Part 8
Sch.9 para.12, disapplied: 2009 c.22 s.215
Sch.9 para.16, added: 2009 c.25 Sch.20 para.14

30. Teaching and Higher Education Act 1998
applied: SI 2009/470 Reg.4, Reg.6, SI 2009/1555 Reg.96, SI 2009/2737 Reg.66
s.1, enabling: SI 2009/1352, SI 2009/1924
s.3, applied: SI 2009/12 Art.9, SI 2009/2610 Art.21, SI 2009/3200 Reg.5
s.3, enabling: SI 2009/1353
s.4, enabling: SI 2009/1353
s.6, enabling: SI 2009/1350, SI 2009/1354, SI 2009/2161
s.7, applied: SI 2009/1351
s.7, enabling: SI 2009/1351
s.14, enabling: SI 2009/1353, SI 2009/1354, SI 2009/2161
s.15, enabling: SI 2009/1350
s.15A, enabling: SI 2009/1350
s.19, applied: SI 2009/1538 Reg.3
s.22, amended: 2009 c.22 s.257
s.22, applied: SI 2009/470 Reg.5, Reg.15, Reg.21, SI 2009/1555 Reg.5, Reg.6, Reg.25, Reg.26, Reg.29, Reg.115, Reg.116, Reg.118, Reg.120, Reg.132, Reg.133, Reg.135, Reg.137, Reg.140, Reg.149, Reg.150, Reg.152, Reg.159, SI 2009/2274 Reg.3, SI 2009/2737 Reg.2, Reg.4, Reg.5, Reg.68, Reg.70, Reg.72, Reg.84, Reg.85, Reg.86, Reg.88, Reg.101, Reg.108, Reg.109, Reg.110, Reg.117, SI 2009/3359 Reg.9
s.22, enabling: SI 2009/470, SI 2009/862, SI 2009/1555, SI 2009/1576, SI 2009/2156, SI 2009/2157, SI 2009/2158, SI 2009/2737, SI 2009/3359
s.42, applied: SI 2009/1350, SI 2009/1352, SI 2009/1353, SI 2009/1354, SI 2009/2161
s.42, enabling: SI 2009/470, SI 2009/862, SI 2009/1350, SI 2009/1351, SI 2009/1353, SI 2009/1354, SI 2009/1555, SI 2009/1576, SI 2009/1924, SI 2009/2156, SI 2009/2157, SI 2009/2158, SI 2009/2161, SI 2009/2737, SI 2009/3359
s.43, enabling: SI 2009/2156, SI 2009/2157, SI 2009/2158, SI 2009/2737, SI 2009/3359
s.46, amended: 2009 c.22 s.257
s.46, enabling: SI 2009/1354
Sch.1 para.3, enabling: SI 2009/1352
Sch.2, enabling: SI 2009/1350
Sch.2 para.1, amended: 2009 c.26 s.81
Sch.2 para.1, enabling: SI 2009/1354, SI 2009/2161
Sch.2 para.8, applied: SI 2009/1350 Reg.4, Reg.5

31. School Standards and Framework Act 1998
Commencement Orders: 2009 c.22 Sch.16 Part 1
applied: 2009 c.22 s.264
s.1, enabling: SI 2009/828
s.14, amended: 2009 c.22 Sch.14 para.2
s.15, amended: 2009 c.22 Sch.14 para.3
s.18, amended: 2009 c.22 Sch.14 para.4
s.18A, amended: 2009 c.22 Sch.14 para.5
s.19ZA, added: 2009 c.22 Sch.14 para.6
s.21, enabling: SI 2009/2544
s.23A, enabling: SI 2009/1924
s.45A, amended: 2009 c.22 s.202
s.47A, amended: 2009 c.22 s.194
s.47ZA, added: 2009 c.22 s.202
s.52, amended: 2009 c.22 s.253
s.52, applied: SI 2009/1586 Reg.4, Reg.5, Reg.6
s.52, enabling: SI 2009/444, SI 2009/1586
s.53, repealed: 2009 c.22 Sch.16 Part 9

1998– cont.

31. School Standards and Framework Act 1998–*cont.*
s.69, applied: SI 2009/821 Reg.4
s.69, enabling: SI 2009/510, SI 2009/1218, SI 2009/2198, SI 2009/3273, SI 2009/3276
s.71, enabling: SI 2009/48
s.72, enabling: SI 2009/1924, SI 2009/2544, SI 2009/2680, SI 2009/2708
s.84, amended: 2009 c.22 s.43
s.85, enabling: SI 2009/210, SI 2009/211, SI 2009/1844, SI 2009/1845
s.87, applied: SI 2009/821 Reg.9
s.88K, enabling: SI 2009/1099
s.89, applied: SI 2009/821 Reg.2, Reg.7
s.89, enabling: SI 2009/821
s.94, enabling: SI 2009/25, SI 2009/823, SI 2009/1500
s.95, applied: SI 2009/821 Reg.9
s.95, enabling: SI 2009/25, SI 2009/823, SI 2009/1500
s.96, amended: 2009 c.22 s.43
s.97D, enabling: SI 2009/821
s.100, applied: SI 2009/821 Reg.5
s.101, applied: SI 2009/821 Reg.6
s.114A, amended: 2009 c.3 s.8
s.114A, applied: 2009 c.3 s.9
s.124B, applied: SI 2009/1218
s.124B, applied: SI 2009/510, SI 2009/2198, SI 2009/3276
s.128, repealed: 2009 c.22 Sch.16 Part 1
s.138, enabling: SI 2009/444, SI 2009/821, SI 2009/823, SI 2009/828, SI 2009/1099, SI 2009/1218, SI 2009/1500, SI 2009/1556, SI 2009/1586, SI 2009/1924, SI 2009/2544, SI 2009/2680, SI 2009/2708, SI 2009/3273
s.144, enabling: SI 2009/1556
Sch.2 para.10, enabling: SI 2009/1556
Sch.30 para.64, repealed: 2009 c.22 Sch.16 Part 1
Sch.30 para.214, repealed: 2009 c.22 Sch.16 Part 4

32. Police (Northern Ireland) Act 1998
Part VII, referred to: SI 2009/3070 Reg.4
s.29, applied: SI 2009/3269 Art.2
s.29, enabling: SI 2009/3269
s.41, referred to: 2009 c.11 s.29
s.42, referred to: 2009 c.11 s.29
s.50, applied: SI 2009/3069 Reg.3
s.54, applied: SI 2009/3069 Reg.11, Reg.20, Reg.31, Reg.39, Reg.52
s.56, applied: SI 2009/3069 Reg.10, Reg.11, Reg.19, Reg.20, Reg.30, Reg.31, Reg.32, Reg.39, Reg.40, Reg.51, Reg.52, Reg.53
s.57, applied: SI 2009/3069 Reg.10, Reg.11, Reg.19, Reg.20, Reg.30, Reg.31, Reg.32, Reg.39, Reg.40, Reg.52, Reg.53
s.58, applied: SI 2009/3069 Reg.19
s.58A, applied: SI 2009/3069 Reg.19
s.59, applied: SI 2009/3069 Reg.19, Reg.30, Reg.32, Reg.40, Reg.53
s.60, applied: SI 2009/3069 Reg.3
s.66, applied: SI 2009/3269 Art.2
s.66, enabling: SI 2009/3269

36. Finance Act 1998
Commencement Orders: SI 2009/1022 Art.2, Art.3
s.27, repealed (in part): 2009 c.10 Sch.1 para.6
s.33, repealed (in part): 2009 c.4 Sch.3 Part 1
s.36, applied: 2009 c.10 s.111
s.40, repealed: 2009 c.4 Sch.3 Part 1
s.41, repealed (in part): 2009 c.4 Sch.3 Part 1

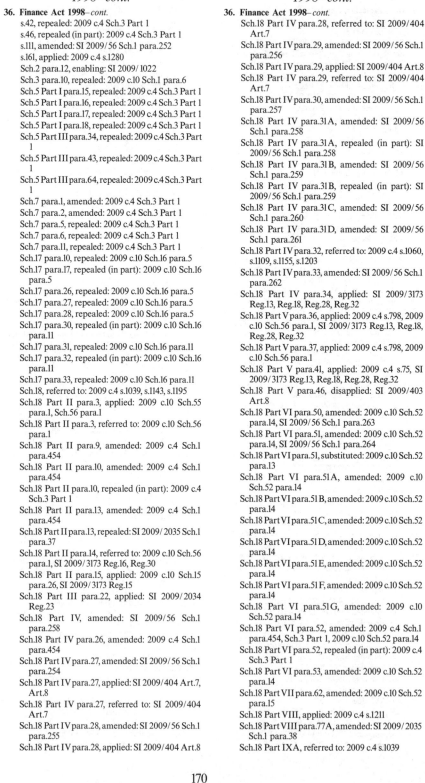

36. Finance Act 1998– *cont.*
s.42, repealed: 2009 c.4 Sch.3 Part 1
s.46, repealed (in part): 2009 c.4 Sch.3 Part 1
s.111, amended: SI 2009/56 Sch.1 para.252
s.161, applied: 2009 c.4 s.1280
Sch.2 para.12, enabling: SI 2009/1022
Sch.3 para.10, repealed: 2009 c.10 Sch.1 para.6
Sch.5 Part I para.15, repealed: 2009 c.4 Sch.3 Part 1
Sch.5 Part I para.16, repealed: 2009 c.4 Sch.3 Part 1
Sch.5 Part I para.17, repealed: 2009 c.4 Sch.3 Part 1
Sch.5 Part I para.18, repealed: 2009 c.4 Sch.3 Part 1
Sch.5 Part III para.34, repealed: 2009 c.4 Sch.3 Part 1
Sch.5 Part III para.43, repealed: 2009 c.4 Sch.3 Part 1
Sch.5 Part III para.64, repealed: 2009 c.4 Sch.3 Part 1
Sch.7 para.1, amended: 2009 c.4 Sch.3 Part 1
Sch.7 para.2, amended: 2009 c.4 Sch.3 Part 1
Sch.7 para.5, repealed: 2009 c.4 Sch.3 Part 1
Sch.7 para.6, repealed: 2009 c.4 Sch.3 Part 1
Sch.7 para.11, repealed: 2009 c.4 Sch.3 Part 1
Sch.17 para.10, repealed: 2009 c.10 Sch.16 para.5
Sch.17 para.17, repealed (in part): 2009 c.10 Sch.16 para.5
Sch.17 para.26, repealed: 2009 c.10 Sch.16 para.5
Sch.17 para.27, repealed: 2009 c.10 Sch.16 para.5
Sch.17 para.28, repealed: 2009 c.10 Sch.16 para.5
Sch.17 para.30, repealed (in part): 2009 c.10 Sch.16 para.11
Sch.17 para.31, repealed: 2009 c.10 Sch.16 para.11
Sch.17 para.32, repealed (in part): 2009 c.10 Sch.16 para.11
Sch.17 para.33, repealed: 2009 c.10 Sch.16 para.11
Sch.18, referred to: 2009 c.4 s.1039, s.1143, s.1195
Sch.18 Part II para.3, applied: 2009 c.10 Sch.55 para.1, Sch.56 para.1
Sch.18 Part II para.3, referred to: 2009 c.10 Sch.56 para.1
Sch.18 Part II para.9, amended: 2009 c.4 Sch.1 para.454
Sch.18 Part II para.10, amended: 2009 c.4 Sch.1 para.454
Sch.18 Part II para.10, repealed (in part): 2009 c.4 Sch.3 Part 1
Sch.18 Part II para.13, amended: 2009 c.4 Sch.1 para.454
Sch.18 Part II para.13, repealed: SI 2009/2035 Sch.1 para.37
Sch.18 Part II para.14, referred to: 2009 c.10 Sch.56 para.1, SI 2009/3173 Reg.16, Reg.30
Sch.18 Part II para.15, applied: 2009 c.10 Sch.15 para.26, SI 2009/3173 Reg.15
Sch.18 Part III para.22, applied: SI 2009/2034 Reg.23
Sch.18 Part IV, amended: SI 2009/56 Sch.1 para.258
Sch.18 Part IV para.26, amended: 2009 c.4 Sch.1 para.454
Sch.18 Part IV para.27, amended: SI 2009/56 Sch.1 para.254
Sch.18 Part IV para.27, applied: SI 2009/404 Art.7, Art.8
Sch.18 Part IV para.27, referred to: SI 2009/404 Art.7
Sch.18 Part IV para.28, amended: SI 2009/56 Sch.1 para.255
Sch.18 Part IV para.28, applied: SI 2009/404 Art.8

36. Finance Act 1998– *cont.*
Sch.18 Part IV para.28, referred to: SI 2009/404 Art.7
Sch.18 Part IV para.29, amended: SI 2009/56 Sch.1 para.256
Sch.18 Part IV para.29, applied: SI 2009/404 Art.8
Sch.18 Part IV para.29, referred to: SI 2009/404 Art.7
Sch.18 Part IV para.30, amended: SI 2009/56 Sch.1 para.257
Sch.18 Part IV para.31A, amended: SI 2009/56 Sch.1 para.258
Sch.18 Part IV para.31A, repealed (in part): SI 2009/56 Sch.1 para.258
Sch.18 Part IV para.31B, amended: SI 2009/56 Sch.1 para.259
Sch.18 Part IV para.31B, repealed (in part): SI 2009/56 Sch.1 para.259
Sch.18 Part IV para.31C, amended: SI 2009/56 Sch.1 para.260
Sch.18 Part IV para.31D, amended: SI 2009/56 Sch.1 para.261
Sch.18 Part IV para.32, referred to: 2009 c.4 s.1060, s.1109, s.1155, s.1203
Sch.18 Part IV para.33, amended: SI 2009/56 Sch.1 para.262
Sch.18 Part IV para.34, applied: SI 2009/3173 Reg.13, Reg.18, Reg.28, Reg.32
Sch.18 Part V para.36, applied: 2009 c.4 s.798, 2009 c.10 Sch.56 para.1, SI 2009/3173 Reg.13, Reg.18, Reg.28, Reg.32
Sch.18 Part V para.37, applied: 2009 c.4 s.798, 2009 c.10 Sch.56 para.1
Sch.18 Part V para.41, applied: 2009 c.4 s.75, SI 2009/3173 Reg.13, Reg.18, Reg.28, Reg.32
Sch.18 Part V para.46, disapplied: SI 2009/403 Art.8
Sch.18 Part VI para.50, amended: 2009 c.10 Sch.52 para.14, SI 2009/56 Sch.1 para.263
Sch.18 Part VI para.51, amended: 2009 c.10 Sch.52 para.14, SI 2009/56 Sch.1 para.264
Sch.18 Part VI para.51, substituted: 2009 c.10 Sch.52 para.13
Sch.18 Part VI para.51A, amended: 2009 c.10 Sch.52 para.14
Sch.18 Part VI para.51B, amended: 2009 c.10 Sch.52 para.14
Sch.18 Part VI para.51C, amended: 2009 c.10 Sch.52 para.14
Sch.18 Part VI para.51D, amended: 2009 c.10 Sch.52 para.14
Sch.18 Part VI para.51E, amended: 2009 c.10 Sch.52 para.14
Sch.18 Part VI para.51F, amended: 2009 c.10 Sch.52 para.14
Sch.18 Part VI para.51G, amended: 2009 c.10 Sch.52 para.14
Sch.18 Part VI para.52, amended: 2009 c.4 Sch.1 para.454, Sch.3 Part 1, 2009 c.10 Sch.52 para.14
Sch.18 Part VI para.52, repealed (in part): 2009 c.4 Sch.3 Part 1
Sch.18 Part VI para.53, amended: 2009 c.10 Sch.52 para.14
Sch.18 Part VII para.62, amended: 2009 c.10 Sch.52 para.15
Sch.18 Part VIII, applied: 2009 c.4 s.1211
Sch.18 Part VIII para.77A, amended: SI 2009/2035 Sch.1 para.38
Sch.18 Part IXA, referred to: 2009 c.4 s.1039

1998– cont.

36. Finance Act 1998–*cont.*

Sch.18 Part IXA para.83A, amended: 2009 c.4 Sch.1 para.454

Sch.18 Part IXA para.83F, amended: 2009 c.4 Sch.1 para.454

Sch.18 Part IXB, referred to: 2009 c.4 s.1143

Sch.18 Part IXBA para.83LA, repealed: 2009 c.4 Sch.3 Part 1

Sch.18 Part IXBA para.83LB, repealed: 2009 c.4 Sch.3 Part 1

Sch.18 Part IXBA para.83LC, repealed: 2009 c.4 Sch.3 Part 1

Sch.18 Part IXBA para.83LD, repealed: 2009 c.4 Sch.3 Part 1

Sch.18 Part IXBA para.83LE, repealed: 2009 c.4 Sch.3 Part 1

Sch.18 Part IXB para.83G, amended: 2009 c.4 Sch.1 para.454, 2009 c.10 Sch.7 para.25

Sch.18 Part IXB para.83H, amended: 2009 c.10 Sch.7 para.25

Sch.18 Part IXB para.83I, amended: 2009 c.10 Sch.7 para.25

Sch.18 Part IXB para.83J, amended: 2009 c.10 Sch.7 para.25

Sch.18 Part IXB para.83K, amended: 2009 c.10 Sch.7 para.25

Sch.18 Part IXB para.83L, amended: 2009 c.10 Sch.7 para.25

Sch.18 Part X para.84, repealed: 2009 c.4 Sch.3 Part 1

Sch.18 Part X para.85, amended: SI 2009/1890 Art.5

Sch.18 Part XI para.88, amended: 2009 c.10 Sch.52 para.16

Sch.18 Part XI para.89, varied: SI 2009/56 Sch.1 para.265

Sch.18 Part XI para.92, repealed (in part): SI 2009/56 Sch.1 para.266

Sch.18 Part XI para.93, repealed: SI 2009/56 Sch.1 para.267

Sch.18 Part XI para.94, repealed: SI 2009/56 Sch.1 para.267

Sch.18 para.33, see *ECL Solutions Ltd v Revenue and Customs Commissioners* [2009] S.T.C. (S.C.D.) 90 (Sp Comm), Theodore Wallace

Sch.18 para.67, see *Marks & Spencer Plc v Revenue and Customs Commissioners* [2009] UKFTT 64 (TC), [2009] S.F.T.D.1 (FTT (Tax)), John F Avery Jones

Sch.18 Part IXC para.83M, repealed: 2009 c.4 Sch.3 Part 1

Sch.18 Part IXC para.83N, repealed: 2009 c.4 Sch.3 Part 1

Sch.18 Part IXC para.83O, repealed: 2009 c.4 Sch.3 Part 1

Sch.18 Part IXC para.83P, repealed: 2009 c.4 Sch.3 Part 1

Sch.18 Part IXC para.83Q, repealed: 2009 c.4 Sch.3 Part 1

Sch.18 Part IXC para.83R, repealed: 2009 c.4 Sch.3 Part 1

Sch.18 Part IXD, referred to: 2009 c.4 s.1195

37. Crime and Disorder Act 1998

see *Birmingham City Council v Dixon* [2009] EWHC 761 (Admin), (2009) 173 J.P. 233 (DC), Richards, L.J.

Part I c.I, applied: SI 2009/1033 Art.2

s.1, see *R. (on the application of Langley) v Preston Crown Court* [2008] EWHC 2623 (Admin), [2009] 1 W.L.R. 1612 (DC), Scott Baker, J.

1998– cont.

37. Crime and Disorder Act 1998–*cont.*

s.1B, see *R. (on the application of Langley) v Preston Crown Court* [2008] EWHC 2623 (Admin), [2009] 1 W.L.R. 1612 (DC), Scott Baker, J.

s.1C, see *R. (on the application of Langley) v Preston Crown Court* [2008] EWHC 2623 (Admin), [2009] 1 W.L.R. 1612 (DC), Scott Baker, J.

s.1I, repealed (in part): 2009 c.25 Sch.23 Part 3

s.4, see *R. (on the application of Langley) v Preston Crown Court* [2008] EWHC 2623 (Admin), [2009] 1 W.L.R. 1612 (DC), Scott Baker, J.

s.5, amended: 2009 c.26 s.108

s.5, applied: SI 2009/3050 Art.2, Art.3

s.5, enabling: SI 2009/1033, SI 2009/3050

s.6, amended: 2009 c.26 s.108

s.6, applied: SI 2009/3050 Art.2, Art.3

s.6, varied: SI 2009/1033 Art.2

s.7, varied: SI 2009/1033 Art.2

s.10, amended: SI 2009/871 Art.9

s.11, amended: 2009 c.25 Sch.21 para.72

s.11, repealed (in part): 2009 c.26 Sch.8 Part 13

s.13, amended: SI 2009/871 Art.9

s.14, repealed: 2009 c.26 Sch.8 Part 13

s.15, repealed: 2009 c.26 Sch.8 Part 13

s.16, amended: 2009 c.26 Sch.7 para.134

s.17, amended: 2009 c.20 Sch.6 para.90, 2009 c.26 s.108

s.18, amended: 2009 c.26 Sch.8 Part 13

s.28, see *DPP v Dykes* [2008] EWHC 2775 (Admin), (2009) 173 J.P. 88 (QBD (Admin)), Calvert-Smith, J.

s.29, applied: SI 2009/1168 Sch.1 para.1

s.30, applied: SI 2009/1168 Sch.1 para.1

s.31, see *DPP v Dykes* [2008] EWHC 2775 (Admin), (2009) 173 J.P. 88 (QBD (Admin)), Calvert-Smith, J.

s.31, applied: SI 2009/1168 Sch.1 para.1

s.32, see *R. v McDermott (Lee)* [2008] EWCA Crim 2345, [2009] 1 Cr. App. R. (S.) 110 (CA (Crim Div)), Hallett, L.J.

s.32, applied: SI 2009/1168 Sch.1 para.1

s.34, see *R. v T* [2009] UKHL 20, [2009] 1 A.C. 1310 (HL), Lord Phillips of Worth Matravers

s.39A, added: 2009 c.22 s.51

s.44, repealed: 2009 c.26 Sch.8 Part 13

s.51, see *R. v Agbobu (Costs)* [2009] 2 Costs L.R. 374 (Sup Ct Costs Office), Costs Judge Gordon-Saker

s.52, amended: 2009 c.25 Sch.21 para.78

s.52, applied: 2009 c.25 s.115

s.57A, amended: 2009 c.25 s.109

s.57B, amended: 2009 c.25 s.106, s.109

s.57B, referred to: SI 2009/3253 Art.4

s.57C, amended: 2009 c.25 s.106, s.109, Sch.23 Part 3

s.57C, applied: SI 2009/3253 Art.4

s.57C, referred to: SI 2009/3253 Art.4

s.57C, repealed (in part): 2009 c.25 s.106, Sch.23 Part 3

s.57D, amended: 2009 c.25 s.106, s.109

s.57D, repealed (in part): 2009 c.25 s.106, Sch.23 Part 3

s.57E, amended: 2009 c.25 s.109

s.57E, referred to: SI 2009/3253 Art.4

s.57E, repealed (in part): 2009 c.25 s.106, Sch.23 Part 3

s.57F, added: 2009 c.25 s.109

s.57F, amended: 2009 c.25 s.109

1998–cont.

37. Crime and Disorder Act 1998–*cont.*
s.66C, applied: SI 2009/2781 Art.2
s.66C, enabling: SI 2009/2781
s.96, applied: SSI 2009/31 Sch.1 para.21, SSI 2009/71 Sch.1 para.21
s.114, enabling: SI 2009/3050
Sch.3 para.2, see *R. v Agbobu (Costs)* [2009] 2 Costs L.R. 374 (Sup Ct Costs Office), Costs Judge Gordon-Saker
Sch.3 para.9, amended: 2009 c.25 Sch.17 para.5, Sch.21 para.81, Sch.23 Part 5
Sch.3 para.9, varied: SI 2009/1059 Sch.1 para.43

38. Government of Wales Act 1998
applied: 2009 c.3 s.9, SI 2009/3104 Reg.7
Sch.13 para.3, amended: SI 2009/1307 Sch.1 para.263
Sch.16 para.32, repealed (in part): SI 2009/484 Sch.2
Sch.16 para.34, repealed (in part): SI 2009/484 Sch.2
Sch.16 para.38, repealed (in part): SI 2009/484 Sch.2
Sch.16 para.39, repealed (in part): SI 2009/484 Sch.2
Sch.16 para.41, repealed (in part): SI 2009/484 Sch.2
Sch.16 para.42, repealed (in part): SI 2009/484 Sch.2
Sch.16 para.43, repealed (in part): SI 2009/484 Sch.2
Sch.16 para.44, repealed (in part): SI 2009/484 Sch.2
Sch.16 para.45, repealed (in part): SI 2009/484 Sch.2
Sch.16 para.46, repealed (in part): SI 2009/484 Sch.2
Sch.16 para.47, repealed (in part): SI 2009/484 Sch.2
Sch.16 para.48, repealed (in part): SI 2009/484 Sch.2
Sch.16 para.49, repealed (in part): SI 2009/484 Sch.2
Sch.16 para.50, repealed (in part): SI 2009/484 Sch.2
Sch.16 para.51, repealed (in part): SI 2009/484 Sch.2

39. National Minimum Wage Act 1998
s.1, enabling: SI 2009/1902
s.2, enabling: SI 2009/1902
s.3, enabling: SI 2009/1902
s.14, applied: SI 2009/603 Sch.1 para.1
s.15, applied: SI 2009/603 Sch.1 para.3
s.19, see *Revenue and Customs Commissioners v Annabel's (Berkeley Square) Ltd* [2009] EWCA Civ 361, [2009] 4 All E.R. 55 (CA (Civ Div)), Mummery, L.J.
s.19, applied: SI 2009/603 Sch.1 para.1, Sch.1 para.2
s.51, enabling: SI 2009/1902

40. Criminal Justice (Terrorism and Conspiracy) Act 1998
Sch.1 Part II para.8, repealed (in part): 2009 asp 9 Sch.6

41. Competition Act 1998
see *Albion Water Ltd v Water Services Regulation Authority* [2009] CAT 12, [2009] Comp. A.R. 223 (CAT), Lord Carlile of Berriew Q.C.
s.2, see *Bookmakers' Afternoon Greyhound Services Ltd v Amalgamated Racing Ltd* [2008] EWHC 1978 (Ch), [2009] U.K.C.L.R. 547 (Ch D), Morgan, J.; see *Bookmakers' Afternoon*

1998–cont.

41. Competition Act 1998–*cont.*
s.2–*cont.*
Greyhound Services Ltd v Amalgamated Racing Ltd [2008] EWHC 2688 (Ch), [2009] U.K.C.L.R. 1 (Ch D), Morgan, J.; see *Bookmakers' Afternoon Greyhound Services Ltd v Amalgamated Racing Ltd* [2009] EWCA Civ 750, [2009] U.K.C.L.R. 863 (CA (Civ Div)), Mummery, L.J.; see *R. (on the application of Cityhook Ltd) v Office of Fair Trading* [2009] EWHC 204 (Admin), [2009] U.K.C.L.R. 657 (QBD (Admin)), Foskett, J.; see *R. (on the application of Cityhook Ltd) v Office of Fair Trading* [2009] EWHC 57 (Admin), [2009] U.K.C.L.R. 255 (QBD (Admin)), Foskett, J.
s.18, see *Albion Water Ltd v Water Services Regulation Authority* [2009] Comp. A.R. 28 (CAT), Lord Carlile of Berriew Q.C.; see *Floe Telecom Ltd (In Administration) v Office of Communications* [2009] EWCA Civ 47, [2009] Bus. L.R. 1116 (CA (Civ Div)), Mummery, L.J.; see *National Grid Plc v Gas and Electricity Markets Authority (Costs)* [2009] CAT 24, [2009] Comp. A.R. 375 (CAT), Vivien Rose (Chairman); see *National Grid Plc v Gas and Electricity Markets Authority* [2009] CAT 14, [2009] Comp. A.R. 282 (CAT), Vivien Rose (Chairman)
s.25, see *R. (on the application of Cityhook Ltd) v Office of Fair Trading* [2009] EWHC 204 (Admin), [2009] U.K.C.L.R. 657 (QBD (Admin)), Foskett, J.; see *R. (on the application of Cityhook Ltd) v Office of Fair Trading* [2009] EWHC 57 (Admin), [2009] U.K.C.L.R. 255 (QBD (Admin)), Foskett, J.
s.33, see *Albion Water Ltd v Water Services Regulation Authority* [2009] CAT 12, [2009] Comp. A.R. 223 (CAT), Lord Carlile of Berriew Q.C.
s.47A, see *BCL Old Co Ltd v BASF SE* [2009] C.P. Rep. 9 (CAT), Barling, J; see *BCL Old Co Ltd v BASF SE* [2009] EWCA Civ 434, [2009] Bus. L.R. 1516 (CA (Civ Div)), Waller, L.J.; see *Devenish Nutrition Ltd v Sanofi-Aventis SA* [2008] EWCA Civ 1086, [2009] Ch. 390 (CA (Civ Div)), Tuckey, L.J.; see *Emerson Electric Co v Morgan Crucible Co Plc* [2009] Comp. A.R. 7 (CAT), Barling, J. (President)
s.54, see *R. (on the application of Cityhook Ltd) v Office of Fair Trading* [2009] EWHC 57 (Admin), [2009] U.K.C.L.R. 255 (QBD (Admin)), Foskett, J.
Sch.8 para.3, see *Albion Water Ltd v Water Services Regulation Authority* [2009] CAT 12, [2009] Comp. A.R. 223 (CAT), Lord Carlile of Berriew Q.C.

42. Human Rights Act 1998
see *A (A Child) (Residential Assessment), Re* [2009] EWHC 865 (Fam), [2009] 2 F.L.R. 443 (Fam Div), Munby, J.; see *Al Rawi v Security Service* [2009] EWHC 2959 (QB), Times, November 24, 2009 (QBD), Silber, J.; see *Clift v Slough BC* [2009] EWHC 1550 (QB), [2009] 4 All E.R. 756 (QBD), Tugendhat, J.; see *Dobson v Thames Water Utilities Ltd* [2009] EWCA Civ 28, [2009] 3 All E.R. 319 (CA (Civ Div)), Waller, L.J. (V-P); see *Dunn v Parole Board* [2008] EWCA Civ 374, [2009] 1 W.L.R. 728 (CA (Civ Div)), Smith, L.J.; see *Gillies v Ralph* 2009 J.C. 25 (HCJ), Lord Wheatley; see *HM Advocate v L* 2009 S.L.T. 127 (HCJ), Lord Osborne; see *Jain v Trent SHA* [2009] UKHL 4, [2009] 1 A.C. 853

1998– cont.

42. Human Rights Act 1998–*cont.*

see–*cont.*

(HL), Lord Scott of Foscote; see *Niven v Lord Advocate* [2009] CSOH 110, 2009 S.L.T. 876 (OH), Lord Malcolm; see *P (A Child) (Adoption: Unmarried Couples), Re* [2008] UKHL 38, [2009] 1 A.C. 173 (HL (NI)), Lord Hoffmann; see *R. (on the application of Barclay) v Secretary of State for Justice* [2008] EWCA Civ 1319, [2009] 2 W.L.R. 1205 (CA (Civ Div)), Pill, L.J.; see *R. (on the application of Barclay) v Secretary of State for Justice* [2009] UKSC 9, [2009] 3 W.L.R. 1270 (SC), Lord Hope (Deputy President); see *R. (on the application of Smith) v Oxfordshire Assistant Deputy Coroner* [2009] EWCA Civ 441, [2009] 3 W.L.R. 1099 (CA (Civ Div)), Sir Anthony Clarke, M.R.; see *Revenue and Customs Commissioners' Application (Approval to Serve 308 Notices on Financial Institutions), Re (TC 174)* [2009] UKFTT 224 (TC), [2009] S.F.T.D. 780 (FTT (Tax)), John Avery Jones; see *S v S* [2008] EWHC 2288 (Fam), [2009] 1 F.L.R. 241 (Fam Div), Munby, J.; see *Wandsworth LBC v Dixon* [2009] EWHC 27 (Admin), [2009] L. & T.R. 28 (QBD (Admin)), Judge Bidder QC; see *Z (Children) (Unsupervised Contact: Allegations of Domestic Violence), Re* [2009] EWCA Civ 430, [2009] 2 F.L.R. 877 (CA (Civ Div)), Wall, L.J.; see *ZT (Kosovo) v Secretary of State for the Home Department* [2009] UKHL 6, [2009] 1 W.L.R. 348 (HL), Lord Phillips of Worth Matravers

applied: 2009 c.1 s.4, 2009 c.25 s.5, SI 2009/2657 r.24

s.1, applied: SI 2009/1800 Sch.2 para.3

s.2, see *R. v Horncastle (Michael Christopher)* [2009] UKSC 14 (SC), Lord Phillips (President)

s.3, see *AS (Somalia) v Entry Clearance Officer (Addis Ababa)* [2009] UKHL 32, [2009] 1 W.L.R. 1385 (HL), Lord Phillips of Worth Matravers; see *Doherty v Birmingham City Council* [2008] UKHL 57, [2009] 1 A.C. 367 (HL), Lord Hope of Craighead; see *Forde's Application for Judicial Review, Re* [2009] N.I. 29 (QBD (NI)), Gillen, J.; see *Hungary v Fenyvesi* [2009] EWHC 231 (Admin), [2009] 4 All E.R. 324 (QBD (Admin)), Sir Anthony May (President, QB); see *McIntyre (Colin McLean) v HM Advocate* [2009] HCJAC 63, 2009 S.C.L. 982 (HCJ), Lord Osborne; see *S&I Electronics Plc v Revenue and Customs Commissioners* [2009] UKFTT 108 (TC), [2009] S.F.T.D. 241 (FTT (Tax)), Charles Hellier (Chairman); see *Truro Diocesan Board of Finance Ltd v Foley* [2008] EWCA Civ 1162, [2009] 1 W.L.R. 2218 (CA (Civ Div)), May, L.J.

s.4, see *M's Guardian v Advocate General for Scotland* [2009] CSOH 91, 2009 S.C. 643 (OH), Lord Woolman; see *Practice Direction (Sup Ct: Upper Tribunal: Judicial Review Jurisdiction)* [2009] 1 W.L.R. 327 (Sup Ct), Lord Judge, L.C.J.

s.4, applied: SI 2009/1603 r.40, SI 2009/2657 r.24, r.46, r.65

s.5, applied: SI 2009/1603 r.26

s.6, see *C's Application for Judicial Review, Re* [2009] UKHL 15, [2009] 1 A.C. 908 (HL (NI)), Lord Phillips of Worth Matravers; see *Doherty v Birmingham City Council* [2008] UKHL 57, [2009] 1 A.C. 367 (HL), Lord Hope of Craighead; see *Martin v Greater Glasgow Primary Care NHS Trust* [2009] CSIH 10, 2009 S.C. 417 (IH (1 Div)), Lord President Hamilton;

1998– cont.

42. Human Rights Act 1998–*cont.*

s.6–*cont.*

see *R. (on the application of Purdy) v DPP* [2009] EWCA Civ 92, [2009] 1 Cr. App. R. 32 (CA (Civ Div)), Lord Judge, L.C.J.; see *R. (on the application of Weaver) v London & Quadrant Housing Trust* [2008] EWHC 1377 (Admin), [2009] 1 All E.R. 17 (DC), Richards, L.J.; see *Wandsworth LBC v Dixon* [2009] EWHC 27 (Admin), [2009] L. & T.R. 28 (QBD (Admin)), Judge Bidder QC

s.6, applied: 2009 c.23 s.291, 2009 c.25 s.48

s.6, disapplied: 2009 c.1 s.244

s.6, referred to: 2009 c.1 s.191

s.7, see *A v B (Investigatory Powers Tribunal: Jurisdiction)* [2009] EWCA Civ 24, [2009] 3 W.L.R. 717 (CA (Civ Div)), Laws, L.J.; see *A v B (Investigatory Powers Tribunal: Jurisdiction)* [2009] UKSC 12 (SC), Lord Phillips (President); see *Beoku-Betts v Secretary of State for the Home Department* [2008] UKHL 39, [2009] 1 A.C. 115 (HL), Lord Bingham of Cornhill; see *Dunn v Parole Board* [2008] EWCA Civ 374, [2009] 1 W.L.R. 728 (CA (Civ Div)), Smith, L.J.; see *M's Guardian v Advocate General for Scotland* [2009] CSOH 91, 2009 S.C. 643 (OH), Lord Woolman; see *R. (on the application of G) v Nottinghamshire Healthcare NHS Trust* [2009] EWCA Civ 795, [2009] H.R.L.R. 31 (CA (Civ Div)), Lord Clarke of Stone-cum-Ebony MR; see *Savage v South Essex Partnership NHS Foundation Trust* [2008] UKHL 74, [2009] 1 A.C. 681 (HL), Lord Scott of Foscote

s.8, see *Dobson v Thames Water Utilities Ltd* [2009] EWCA Civ 28, [2009] 3 All E.R. 319 (CA (Civ Div)), Waller, L.J. (V-P)

s.8, applied: 2009 c.1 s.56

s.12, see *Author of a Blog v Times Newspapers Ltd* [2009] EWHC 1358 (QB), [2009] E.M.L.R. 22 (QBD), Eady, J.; see *Napier v Pressdram Ltd* [2009] EWCA Civ 443, [2009] C.P. Rep. 36 (CA (Civ Div)), Hughes, L.J.; see *Stedman, Re* [2009] EWHC 935 (Fam), [2009] 2 F.L.R. 852 (Fam Div), Eleanor King, J; see *X (A Child) (Residence and Contact: Rights of Media Attendance), Re* [2009] EWHC 1728 (Fam), [2009] E.M.L.R. 26 (Fam Div), Sir Mark Potter (President, Fam)

45. Regional Development Agencies Act 1998

s.1, applied: 2009 c.20 s.123

s.7, substituted: 2009 c.20 s.83

s.7A, applied: 2009 c.20 s.77

s.7B, amended: 2009 c.20 Sch.5 para.6

s.8, repealed: 2009 c.20 Sch.5 para.7, Sch.7 Part 4

s.11, repealed (in part): 2009 c.20 Sch.7 Part 4

s.18, repealed (in part): 2009 c.20 Sch.5 para.8, Sch.7 Part 4

s.19, amended: SI 2009/1941 Sch.1 para.174

Sch.1, amended: SI 2009/837 Art.25

Sch.2 para.7, repealed (in part): 2009 c.20 Sch.7 Part 4

Sch.5 Part II para.4, amended: SI 2009/1307 Sch.1 para.264

Sch.6 para.9, amended: SI 2009/2748 Sch.1 para.5

Sch.6 para.11, amended: SI 2009/2748 Sch.1 para.5

46. Scotland Act 1998

see *Niven v Lord Advocate* [2009] CSOH 110, 2009 S.L.T. 876 (OH), Lord Malcolm

varied: SI 2009/2231 Art.3

1998– cont.

46. Scotland Act 1998–*cont.*

Part I, applied: 2009 asp 1 Sch.2 para.1, Sch.2 para.3, Sch.3 para.13

s.12, applied: SI 2009/548, SI 2009/549

s.12, enabling: SI 2009/1978

s.30, enabling: SI 2009/1380

s.33, applied: SI 2009/1603 r.41

s.51, applied: 2009 c.23 s.14

s.57, see *HM Advocate v McLean (Duncan)* [2009] HCJAC 97 (HCJ), The Lord Justice General (Hamilton)

s.57, applied: 2009 c.23 s.60

s.58, applied: 2009 c.23 s.60

s.64, applied: SI 2009/537 Art.2

s.64, enabling: SI 2009/537

s.65, applied: 2009 asp 2 s.4, s.6

s.81, applied: 2009 asp 1 Sch.1 para.50, Sch.2 para.3

s.82, applied: 2009 asp 1 Sch.1 para.38, Sch.1 para.95, Sch.2 para.3

s.88, applied: SI 2009/548, SI 2009/549

s.100, amended: 2009 asp 11 s.1

s.104, enabling: SI 2009/729, SI 2009/822, SI 2009/1682, SI 2009/1969, SI 2009/2231, SI 2009/2233

s.111, amended: 2009 c.23 s.231

s.112, enabling: SI 2009/729, SI 2009/822, SI 2009/1682, SI 2009/1969, SI 2009/2231, SI 2009/2233

s.113, enabling: SI 2009/729, SI 2009/822, SI 2009/1682, SI 2009/1969, SI 2009/1978, SI 2009/2231, SI 2009/2233

s.114, enabling: SI 2009/2231

s.115, applied: SI 2009/1380, SI 2009/1682, SI 2009/1978

s.115, enabling: SI 2009/537

s.126, applied: 2009 c.23 s.76, s.322, SI 2009/3391 Art.2

Sch.4 Part I para.4A, added: SI 2009/1380 Art.2

Sch.5 Part I para.9, applied: 2009 c.23 s.113

Sch.5 Part II paraA.1, applied: SSI 2009/44 Sch.11 para.7, Sch.13 para.6

Sch.5 Part II paraA.1, disapplied: SSI 2009/44 Sch.9 para.7

Sch.5 Part II paraA.1, referred to: SSI 2009/44 Sch.4 para.7, Sch.5 para.3, Sch.5 para.4, Sch.6 para.6, Sch.6 para.7, Sch.7 para.6, Sch.7 para.7, Sch.8 para.6, Sch.8 para.7, Sch.8 para.8, Sch.8 para.9, Sch.11, Sch.11 para.6, Sch.11 para.8, Sch.12 para.7, Sch.13

Sch.5 Part II paraD.2, applied: 2009 c.23 s.113

Sch.5 Part II paraC.5, applied: SSI 2009/44 Sch.1 para.5, Sch.3 para.5, Sch.7 para.5, Sch.8 para.5, Sch.9 para.5, Sch.11 para.5, Sch.12 para.5, Sch.13 para.4

Sch.5 Part II paraC.5, disapplied: SSI 2009/44 Sch.6 para.5

Sch.6 para.1, see *Allison (Steven Edward) v HM Advocate* [2009] HCJAC 23, 2009 S.L.T. 550 (HCJ), Lord Osborne

Sch.6 para.5, see *Allison (Steven Edward) v HM Advocate* [2009] HCJAC 23, 2009 S.L.T. 550 (HCJ), Lord Osborne

Sch.6 Part V para.33, applied: SI 2009/1603 r.41

Sch.6 Part V para.34, applied: SI 2009/1603 r.41

Sch.6 Part V para.37, enabling: SSI 2009/322, SSI 2009/323

Sch.6 para.13, see *Allison (Steven Edward) v HM Advocate* [2009] HCJAC 23, 2009 S.L.T. 550 (HCJ), Lord Osborne

Sch.7, applied: SI 2009/1978

Sch.7, enabling: SI 2009/537

1998– cont.

46. Scotland Act 1998–*cont.*

Sch.7 para.1, applied: SI 2009/1380, SI 2009/1682

Sch.7 para.2, applied: SI 2009/1380, SI 2009/1682

Sch.7 para.3, applied: SI 2009/1682

Sch.8 para.9, repealed (in part): SI 2009/1307 Sch.4

47. Northern Ireland Act 1998

applied: 2009 c.2 Sch.2 Part 2

referred to: 2009 c.2 Sch.2 Part 2, 2009 c.9 Sch.2 Part 40

s.4, referred to: 2009 c.3 Sch.1 para.8

s.11, applied: SI 2009/1603 r.41

s.16A, applied: 2009 c.3 Sch.1 para.7

s.16A, disapplied: 2009 c.3 Sch.1 para.7

s.17, applied: 2009 c.3 Sch.1 para.6, Sch.1 para.8

s.17, disapplied: 2009 c.3 Sch.1 para.8

s.17, enabling: SI 2009/723

s.18, applied: 2009 c.3 Sch.1 para.8

s.18, disapplied: 2009 c.3 Sch.1 para.6

s.19, applied: SI 2009/2818 Sch.1 para.1

s.21, applied: 2009 c.3 Sch.1 para.8

s.21A, amended: 2009 c.3 Sch.1 para.3

s.21A, applied: 2009 c.3 Sch.1 para.5

s.21A, referred to: 2009 c.3 Sch.1 para.5, Sch.1 para.8

s.21B, amended: 2009 c.3 Sch.1 para.9

s.21C, amended: 2009 c.3 Sch.1 para.10

s.26, applied: 2009 c.23 s.60

s.27, applied: 2009 c.23 s.60

s.28, applied: 2009 c.23 s.27

s.29C, added: 2009 c.3 Sch.6 para.1

s.32, varied: 2009 c.3 Sch.1 para.7

s.34, enabling: SI 2009/256

s.35, enabling: SI 2009/256

s.84, applied: SI 2009/225, SI 2009/3014, SI 2009/3016

s.84, enabling: SI 2009/225, SI 2009/3014, SI 2009/3016

s.85, enabling: SI 2009/884, SI 2009/3017

s.86, amended: 2009 c.3 s.4

s.86, applied: 2009 c.3

s.87, amended: SI 2009/885 Art.2

s.87, referred to: SI 2009/885

s.87, enabling: SI 2009/885

s.96, applied: SI 2009/256

s.98, applied: 2009 c.23 s.322, SI 2009/3391 Art.2

Sch.2 para.4, applied: 2009 c.23 s.113

Sch.2 para.9B, added: 2009 c.8 s.27

Sch.2 para.22, applied: 2009 c.3 Sch.1 para.2

Sch.4A, applied: 2009 c.3 Sch.1 para.8

Sch.4A Part 1 para.1, amended: 2009 c.3 Sch.1 para.4

Sch.4A Part 1 para.1A, amended: 2009 c.3 Sch.1 para.4

Sch.4A Part 1 para.2, amended: 2009 c.3 Sch.1 para.4

Sch.4A Part 1 para.3, amended: 2009 c.3 Sch.1 para.4

Sch.4A Part 1A, applied: 2009 c.3 Sch.1 para.7

Sch.4A Part 1A para.3A, added: 2009 c.3 Sch.1 para.4

Sch.4A Part 1A para.3B, added: 2009 c.3 Sch.1 para.4

Sch.4A Part 1A para.3C, added: 2009 c.3 Sch.1 para.4

Sch.4A Part 1A para.3D, added: 2009 c.3 Sch.1 para.4

Sch.4A Part 3A para.11E, applied: 2009 c.3 Sch.1 para.8

1998–cont.

47. Northern Ireland Act 1998–*cont.*

Sch.4A Part 4 para.12, amended: 2009 c.3 Sch.1 para.4

Sch.4A Part 4 para.13, added: 2009 c.3 Sch.1 para.4

Sch.10 Part V para.33, applied: SI 2009/1603 r.41

Sch.10 Part V para.34, applied: SI 2009/1603 r.41

Sch.10 Part V para.38, enabling: SSI 2009/322, SSI 2009/323

Sch.11 para.2A, added: 2009 c.3 Sch.5 para.4

1999

2. Social Security Contributions (Transfer of Functions, etc.) Act 1999

s.8, see *Patel v Marquette Partners (UK) Ltd* [2009] I.C.R. 569 (EAT), Judge McMullen Q.C.

s.10, amended: SI 2009/56 Sch.1 para.269

s.11, amended: SI 2009/56 Sch.1 para.270

s.12, amended: SI 2009/56 Sch.1 para.271

s.12, repealed (in part): SI 2009/56 Sch.1 para.271

s.13, amended: SI 2009/56 Sch.1 para.272, SI 2009/777 Art.3

s.13, repealed (in part): SI 2009/56 Sch.1 para.272

s.14, amended: SI 2009/56 Sch.1 para.273

s.19, substituted: SI 2009/56 Sch.1 para.274

s.23, enabling: SI 2009/1377

Sch.7 para.2, repealed: SI 2009/56 Sch.1 para.275

Sch.7 para.3, repealed: SI 2009/56 Sch.1 para.275

6. Rating (Valuation) Act 1999

s.1, see *Leda Properties Ltd v Howells (Valuation Officer)* [2009] R.A. 165 (Lands Tr), George Bartlett Q.C. (President, LTr)

7. Northern Ireland (Location of Victims Remains) Act 1999

s.4, amended: 2009 c.25 Sch.21 para.43

8. Health Act 1999

s.60, applied: SI 2009/1182

s.60, referred to: SI 2009/1922 Art.2

s.60, enabling: SI 2009/1182

s.62, enabling: SI 2009/1182

Sch.3, enabling: SI 2009/1182

Sch.3 para.9, applied: SI 2009/1182

10. Tax Credits Act 1999

s.10, applied: SI 2009/2364 Art.35

s.22, applied: SI 2009/2364 Art.35

14. Protection of Children Act 1999

see *D v Buckinghamshire CC* [2008] EWCA Civ 1372, [2009] 1 F.L.R. 881 (CA (Civ Div)), Thorpe, L.J.

s.1, applied: SI 2009/12 Art.2, Art.6, Art.6A, Art.9, SI 2009/1547 Reg.6, SI 2009/1633 Reg.3, SI 2009/2558 Reg.3, SI 2009/2610 Art.21, SI 2009/2611 Art.5, Art.7, SSI 2009/4 Art.4

s.2, applied: SI 2009/12 Art.2, Art.3

s.2A, applied: SI 2009/12 Art.2, Art.3

s.2B, disapplied: SI 2009/12 Art.3

s.2D, applied: SI 2009/12 Art.2, Art.3

s.4, applied: SI 2009/12 Art.6, Art.6A, SI 2009/2611 Art.5

s.4A, applied: SI 2009/2611 Art.5

s.7, applied: SI 2009/2611 Art.5, Art.7

16. Finance Act 1999

s.25, repealed (in part): 2009 c.10 Sch.1 para.6

s.31, repealed: 2009 c.10 Sch.1 para.6

s.32, repealed: 2009 c.10 Sch.1 para.6

s.54, repealed: 2009 c.4 Sch.3 Part 1

s.55, repealed (in part): 2009 c.4 Sch.3 Part 1

s.58, repealed: 2009 c.4 Sch.3 Part 1

s.61, repealed: 2009 c.4 Sch.3 Part 1

1999–cont.

16. Finance Act 1999–*cont.*

s.63, repealed: 2009 c.4 Sch.3 Part 1

s.81, amended: 2009 c.4 Sch.1 para.458

s.81, repealed (in part): 2009 c.4 Sch.3 Part 1

s.88, repealed: 2009 c.10 Sch.16 para.5

s.106, repealed: SI 2009/3054 Sch.1 para.16

s.119, amended: SI 2009/1890 Art.11

s.132, enabling: SI 2009/2050, SI 2009/2978

s.133, enabling: SI 2009/600, SI 2009/2978

Sch.6 para.1, repealed: 2009 c.4 Sch.3 Part 1

Sch.6 para.2, repealed: 2009 c.4 Sch.3 Part 1

Sch.6 para.3, repealed: 2009 c.4 Sch.3 Part 1

Sch.6 para.4, repealed: 2009 c.4 Sch.3 Part 1

Sch.6 para.5, repealed: 2009 c.4 Sch.3 Part 1

Sch.6 para.6, repealed: 2009 c.4 Sch.3 Part 1

Sch.6 para.7, repealed: 2009 c.4 Sch.3 Part 1

Sch.6 para.8, repealed: 2009 c.4 Sch.3 Part 1

Sch.11 para.2, repealed: 2009 c.4 Sch.3 Part 1

Sch.11 para.9, repealed: SI 2009/56 Sch.1 para.277

Sch.13 Part I para.1, amended: SI 2009/1890 Art.11

Sch.17 Part II para.9, amended: SI 2009/56 Sch.1 para.280

Sch.17 Part II para.9, substituted: SI 2009/56 Sch.1 para.279

Sch.17 Part II para.10, substituted: SI 2009/56 Sch.1 para.279

Sch.17 Part II para.11, amended: SI 2009/56 Sch.1 para.281

Sch.17 Part II para.11, repealed (in part): SI 2009/56 Sch.1 para.281

Sch.17 Part II para.11, substituted: SI 2009/56 Sch.1 para.279

Sch.17 Part II para.11A, added: SI 2009/56 Sch.1 para.282

Sch.17 Part II para.11A, substituted: SI 2009/56 Sch.1 para.279

Sch.17 Part II para.12, amended: SI 2009/56 Sch.1 para.283

Sch.17 Part II para.12, repealed (in part): SI 2009/56 Sch.1 para.283

Sch.17 Part II para.12, substituted: SI 2009/56 Sch.1 para.279

Sch.17 Part II para.13, substituted: SI 2009/56 Sch.1 para.279

Sch.17 Part II para.14, substituted: SI 2009/56 Sch.1 para.279

Sch.17 Part II para.15, substituted: SI 2009/56 Sch.1 para.279

Sch.19 Part IV para.19, applied: 2009 c.10 Sch.56 para.1

18. Adoption (Intercountry Aspects) Act 1999

s.1, enabling: SI 2009/2563, SSI 2009/182

s.16, applied: SI 2009/2563

19. Company and Business Names (Chamber of Commerce, Etc.) Act 1999

s.1, amended: SI 2009/1941 Sch.1 para.176

s.2, amended: SI 2009/1941 Sch.1 para.176

s.3, amended: SI 2009/1941 Sch.1 para.176

20. Commonwealth Development Corporation Act 1999

s.16, amended: SI 2009/1941 Sch.1 para.177

s.26, amended: SI 2009/1941 Sch.1 para.177

Sch.2 Part II para.3, amended: SI 2009/1941 Sch.1 para.177

Sch.2 Part II para.5, amended: SI 2009/1941 Sch.1 para.177

Sch.2 Part II para.6, amended: SI 2009/1941 Sch.1 para.177

20. Commonwealth Development Corporation Act 1999–*cont.*

Sch.2 Part II para.7, amended: SI 2009/ 1941 Sch.1 para.177

Sch.2 Part II para.8, repealed: SI 2009/ 1941 Sch.1 para.177

Sch.2 Part II para.9, amended: SI 2009/ 1941 Sch.1 para.177

Sch.2 Part II para.14, amended: SI 2009/ 1941 Sch.1 para.177

Sch.2 Part II para.14, repealed (in part): SI 2009/ 1941 Sch.1 para.177

Sch.2 Part II para.15, amended: SI 2009/ 1941 Sch.1 para.177

Sch.3 para.6, amended: 2009 c.4 Sch.1 para.461

22. Access to Justice Act 1999

see *R. (on the application of Taylor) v Westminster Magistrates Court* [2009] EWHC 1498 (Admin), (2009) 173 J.P. 405 (DC), Pill, L.J.; see *Secretary of State for Business Enterprise and Regulatory Reform v Sullman* [2008] EWHC 3179 (Ch), [2009] 1 B.C.L.C. 397 (Ch D), Norris, J.

s.1, applied: SI 2009/ 2131 Sch.2 para.1

s.2, repealed (in part): 2009 c.25 Sch.23 Part 6

s.6, amended: 2009 c.25 s.149

s.6, enabling: SI 2009/ 1854

s.7, enabling: SI 2009/ 502, SI 2009/ 1894, SI 2009/ 3312

s.8A, added: 2009 c.25 s.149

s.9, amended: 2009 c.25 s.149

s.9, applied: SI 2009/ 2131 Sch.2 para.1

s.10, enabling: SI 2009/ 502, SI 2009/ 1894, SI 2009/ 3312

s.11, see *Ben Hashem v Ali Shayif* [2009] EWHC 864 (Fam), [2009] 2 F.L.R. 896 (Fam Div), Munby, J.; see *Liverpool Freeport Electronics Ltd v Habib Bank Ltd* [2009] EWHC 861 (QB), [2009] 3 Costs L.R. 434 (QBD), Jack, J.

s.11 A, added: 2009 c.25 s.149

s.12, see *R. (on the application of Taylor) v Westminster Magistrates Court* [2009] EWHC 1498 (Admin), (2009) 173 J.P. 405 (DC), Pill, L.J.

s.12, enabling: SI 2009/ 2167, SI 2009/ 2777

s.14, enabling: SI 2009/ 1843, SI 2009/ 2086

s.15, enabling: SI 2009/ 1853, SI 2009/ 2876

s.17, amended: 2009 c.25 s.152, Sch.23 Part 6

s.17, applied: SI 2009/ 3328 Reg.30

s.17, enabling: SI 2009/ 3352

s.17A, amended: 2009 c.25 s.151, s.152, Sch.23 Part 6

s.17A, applied: SI 2009/ 3328 Reg.3

s.17A, enabling: SI 2009/ 3328

s.25, amended: 2009 c.25 s.149, s.153

s.25, applied: SI 2009/ 391, SI 2009/ 1843, SI 2009/ 1854, SI 2009/ 2086, SI 2009/ 3328, SI 2009/ 3329

s.25, referred to: SI 2009/ 1843, SI 2009/ 1854, SI 2009/ 2086

s.25, enabling: SI 2009/ 2875, SI 2009/ 2876, SI 2009/ 2878, SI 2009/ 3328, SI 2009/ 3329, SI 2009/ 3331

s.26, enabling: SI 2009/ 212, SI 2009/ 391, SI 2009/ 1853, SI 2009/ 1894, SI 2009/ 1995, SI 2009/ 2167, SI 2009/ 2777, SI 2009/ 2875, SI 2009/ 2876, SI 2009/ 2878, SI 2009/ 3312, SI 2009/ 3328, SI 2009/ 3329, SI 2009/ 3331, SI 2009/ 3352

s.29, see *Secretary of State for Business Enterprise and Regulatory Reform v Sullman* [2008] EWHC 3179 (Ch), [2009] 1 B.C.L.C. 397 (Ch D), Norris, J.

s.51, varied: SI 2009/ 3250 Art.8

s.52, varied: SI 2009/ 3250 Art.8

22. Access to Justice Act 1999–*cont.*

s.55, see *B (A Child) (Residence: Second Appeal), Re* [2009] EWCA Civ 545, [2009] 2 F.L.R. 632 (CA (Civ Div)), Wall, L.J.

s.56, applied: SI 2009/ 871

s.56, enabling: SI 2009/ 871

s.68, enabling: SSI 2009/ 291

s.71, repealed: 2009 c.25 Sch.23 Part 1

s.104, repealed (in part): 2009 c.25 Sch.23 Part 1

Sch.2 para.1, repealed (in part): 2009 c.25 Sch.23 Part 6

Sch.2 para.1 A, added: 2009 c.25 s.150

Sch.2 para.2, amended: 2009 c.25 s.51, Sch.23 Part 1, 2009 c.26 Sch.7 para.65, Sch.7 para.98

Sch.2 para.3, amended: 2009 c.26 Sch.7 para.65

Sch.2 para.4, added: 2009 c.25 s.51

Sch.3 para.1 A, enabling: SI 2009/ 1995

Sch.3 para.2, enabling: SI 2009/ 2876

Sch.3 para.2A, enabling: SI 2009/ 1995, SI 2009/ 3331

Sch.3 para.3B, enabling: SI 2009/ 2878

Sch.3 para.4, enabling: SI 2009/ 3229, SI 2009/ 3329

Sch.3 para.5, enabling: SI 2009/ 2875

Sch.3 para.6, amended: 2009 c.25 s.151

Sch.3 para.6, applied: SI 2009/ 212 Reg.2, Reg.3, SI 2009/ 391 Reg.2, Reg.3

Sch.3 para.6, enabling: SI 2009/ 391

Sch.3 para.7, amended: 2009 c.25 s.151

Sch.3 para.8, amended: 2009 c.25 s.151

Sch.3 para.8, repealed (in part): 2009 c.25 Sch.23 Part 6

Sch.3 para.8, enabling: SI 2009/ 212

Sch.3A para.1, added: 2009 c.25 Sch.18

Sch.3A para.2, added: 2009 c.25 Sch.18

Sch.3A para.3, added: 2009 c.25 Sch.18

Sch.3A para.4, added: 2009 c.25 Sch.18

Sch.3A para.5, added: 2009 c.25 Sch.18

Sch.3A para.6, added: 2009 c.25 Sch.18

Sch.3A para.7, added: 2009 c.25 Sch.18

Sch.3A para.8, added: 2009 c.25 Sch.18

Sch.4 para.48, repealed: 2009 c.24 Sch.7 Part 1

Sch.8 para.7, varied: SI 2009/ 3250 Art.8

Sch.11 para.38, repealed: 2009 c.20 Sch.7 Part 3

23. Youth Justice and Criminal Evidence Act 1999

Commencement Orders: SI 2009/ 1941 Art.2, Sch.2

Part II c.I, applied: SI 2009/ 2083 Art.11

Part II c.IA, applied: SI 2009/ 2083 Art.11

Part II c.II, applied: SI 2009/ 2083 Art.11

Part II c.III, applied: SI 2009/ 2083 Art.11

Part II c.IV, applied: SI 2009/ 2083 Art.13

Part II c.V, applied: SI 2009/ 2083 Art.11

s.16, amended: 2009 c.25 s.98

s.16, varied: SI 2009/ 2083 Art.4

s.17, amended: 2009 c.25 s.99

s.17, varied: SI 2009/ 2083 Art.4

s.18, varied: SI 2009/ 2083 Art.4

s.19, applied: SI 2009/ 2083 Art.2

s.19, varied: SI 2009/ 2083 Art.4

s.20, applied: 2009 c.25 Sch.22 para.23

s.20, varied: SI 2009/ 2083 Art.4

s.21, amended: 2009 c.25 s.98, s.100, Sch.23 Part 3

s.21, repealed (in part): 2009 c.25 s.100, Sch.23 Part 3

s.21, varied: SI 2009/ 2083 Art.4

s.22, amended: 2009 c.25 s.98, s.100

s.22, repealed (in part): 2009 c.25 s.100, Sch.23 Part 3

s.22, varied: SI 2009/ 2083 Art.4

23. Youth Justice and Criminal Evidence Act 1999– cont.

s.22A, added: 2009 c.25 s.101
s.22A, varied: SI 2009/2083 Art.4
s.23, applied: SI 2009/1209 r.77, SI 2009/2041 r.92
s.23, varied: SI 2009/2083 Art.4
s.24, amended: 2009 c.25 s.102
s.24, varied: SI 2009/2083 Art.4
s.25, applied: SI 2009/1209 r.77, r.79, SI 2009/2041 r.92, r.94
s.25, varied: SI 2009/2083 Art.4
s.26, applied: SI 2009/1209 r.77, SI 2009/2041 r.92
s.26, varied: SI 2009/2083 Art.4
s.27, amended: 2009 c.25 s.102, s.103, Sch.21 para.73, Sch.23 Part 3
s.27, applied: SI 2009/1209 r.77, r.80, r.82, r.83, SI 2009/2041 r.92, r.95, r.97, r.98
s.27, repealed (in part): 2009 c.25 s.103, Sch.23 Part 3
s.27, varied: SI 2009/2083 Art.4
s.29, applied: SI 2009/1209 r.77, r.81, SI 2009/2041 r.92, r.96
s.29, varied: SI 2009/2083 Art.4
s.30, applied: SI 2009/1209 r.77, SI 2009/2041 r.92
s.30, varied: SI 2009/2083 Art.4
s.31, applied: SI 2009/1209 r.59, SI 2009/2041 r.74
s.31, varied: SI 2009/2083 Art.4
s.33, varied: SI 2009/2083 Art.4
s.33A, amended: 2009 c.25 s.104
s.33A, applied: SI 2009/2657 r.14
s.33A, varied: SI 2009/2569 Art.4
s.33B, amended: 2009 c.25 s.104
s.33B, varied: SI 2009/2569 Art.4
s.33BA, added: 2009 c.25 s.104
s.33BA, amended: 2009 c.25 s.104
s.33BA, varied: SI 2009/2569 Art.4
s.33BB, added: 2009 c.25 s.104
s.33BB, amended: 2009 c.25 s.104
s.33BB, varied: SI 2009/2569 Art.4
s.33C, amended: 2009 c.25 s.104
s.33C, varied: SI 2009/2569 Art.4
s.34, applied: SI 2009/2100 r.5, r.6, r.7
s.34, varied: SI 2009/2083 Art.6
s.35, amended: 2009 c.25 s.105
s.35, applied: SI 2009/2100 r.5, r.6, r.7
s.35, varied: SI 2009/2083 Art.6
s.36, applied: SI 2009/2100 r.4, r.5, r.6, r.7
s.36, varied: SI 2009/2083 Art.6
s.37, varied: SI 2009/2083 Art.6
s.37, enabling: SI 2009/2100
s.38, applied: SI 2009/2100 r.6, r.7
s.38, varied: SI 2009/2083 Art.6
s.38, enabling: SI 2009/2100
s.39, varied: SI 2009/2083 Art.6
s.41, applied: SI 2009/2100 r.8
s.41, varied: SI 2009/2083 Art.8
s.42, varied: SI 2009/2083 Art.8
s.43, varied: SI 2009/2083 Art.8
s.43, enabling: SI 2009/2100
s.44, varied: SI 2009/1059 Sch.1 para.44
s.45, varied: SI 2009/2083 Art.13
s.46, applied: SI 2009/2100 r.10, r.11, r.12
s.46, varied: SI 2009/2083 Art.13
s.47, varied: SI 2009/2083 Art.13
s.52, varied: SI 2009/2083 Art.13
s.53, varied: SI 2009/2083 Art.10
s.54, varied: SI 2009/2083 Art.10
s.55, varied: SI 2009/2083 Art.10

23. Youth Justice and Criminal Evidence Act 1999– cont.

s.56, applied: SI 2009/1209 r.59, SI 2009/2041 r.74
s.56, varied: SI 2009/2083 Art.10
s.57, varied: SI 2009/2083 Art.10
s.61, enabling: SI 2009/2083, SI 2009/2569
s.62, varied: SI 2009/2083 Art.12
s.63, applied: SI 2009/2083 Art.13
s.63, varied: SI 2009/2083 Art.12, Art.13, SI 2009/2569 Art.5
s.64, amended: 2009 c.25 s.99
s.65, applied: SI 2009/2083 Art.13
s.65, varied: SI 2009/2083 Art.12, Art.13, SI 2009/2569 Art.5
s.65, enabling: SI 2009/2100
Sch.1A para.1, added: 2009 c.25 Sch.14
Sch.1A para.2, added: 2009 c.25 Sch.14
Sch.1A para.3, added: 2009 c.25 Sch.14
Sch.1A para.4, added: 2009 c.25 Sch.14
Sch.1A para.5, added: 2009 c.25 Sch.14
Sch.1A para.6, added: 2009 c.25 Sch.14
Sch.1A para.7, added: 2009 c.25 Sch.14
Sch.1A para.8, added: 2009 c.25 Sch.14
Sch.1A para.9, added: 2009 c.25 Sch.14
Sch.1A para.10, added: 2009 c.25 Sch.14
Sch.1A para.11, added: 2009 c.25 Sch.14
Sch.1A para.12, added: 2009 c.25 Sch.14
Sch.1A para.13, added: 2009 c.25 Sch.14
Sch.1A para.14, added: 2009 c.25 Sch.14
Sch.1A para.15, added: 2009 c.25 Sch.14
Sch.1A para.16, added: 2009 c.25 Sch.14
Sch.1A para.17, added: 2009 c.25 Sch.14
Sch.1A para.18, added: 2009 c.25 Sch.14
Sch.1A para.19, added: 2009 c.25 Sch.14
Sch.1A para.20, added: 2009 c.25 Sch.14
Sch.1A para.21, added: 2009 c.25 Sch.14
Sch.1A para.22, added: 2009 c.25 Sch.14
Sch.1A para.23, added: 2009 c.25 Sch.14
Sch.1A para.24, added: 2009 c.25 Sch.14
Sch.1A para.25, added: 2009 c.25 Sch.14
Sch.1A para.26, added: 2009 c.25 Sch.14
Sch.1A para.27, added: 2009 c.25 Sch.14
Sch.1A para.28, added: 2009 c.25 Sch.14
Sch.1A para.29, added: 2009 c.25 Sch.14
Sch.1A para.30, added: 2009 c.25 Sch.14
Sch.1A para.31, added: 2009 c.25 Sch.14
Sch.1A para.31, referred to: 2009 c.25 Sch.22 para.24
Sch.1A para.32, added: 2009 c.25 Sch.14
Sch.3 para.4, repealed: SI 2009/1941 Sch.2
Sch.3 para.5, repealed: SI 2009/1941 Sch.2
Sch.3 para.13, repealed: SI 2009/1941 Sch.2
Sch.3 para.14, repealed: SI 2009/1941 Sch.2
Sch.3 para.15, repealed: SI 2009/1941 Sch.2
Sch.4 para.18, repealed: SI 2009/1941 Sch.2
Sch.7 para.6, varied: SI 2009/1059 Sch.1 para.44

24. Pollution Prevention and Control Act 1999

s.2, applied: SI 2009/1799, SI 2009/2301, SI 2009/2902, SI 2009/3130, SI 2009/3381
s.2, enabling: SI 2009/1799, SI 2009/2902, SI 2009/3130, SI 2009/3381, SSI 2009/247, SSI 2009/336
Sch.1, enabling: SI 2009/1799, SI 2009/2902, SI 2009/3381
Sch.1 Part I para.20, applied: SI 2009/1517 Art.2
Sch.1 Part I para.20, enabling: SI 2009/1517

26. Employment Relations Act 1999

see *Diggins v Condor Marine Crewing Services Ltd* [2009] I.C.R. 609 (EAT), Judge Burke Q.C.

26. Employment Relations Act 1999–*cont.*
s.13, see *N v Lewisham LBC* [2009] I.C.R. 1538 (EAT), Burton, J.
s.34, applied: SI 2009/1903 Art.3
s.34, enabling: SI 2009/3274

27. Local Government Act 1999
s.1, amended: 2009 c.20 Sch.6 para.91
s.1, referred to: SI 2009/3272 Art.3
s.1, repealed (in part): 2009 c.2 Sch.1 para.10, Sch.4
s.2, repealed (in part): 2009 c.2 Sch.1 para.11, Sch.4
s.2A, repealed (in part): 2009 c.2 Sch.4
s.3A, repealed (in part): 2009 c.2 Sch.1 para.12, Sch.4
s.4, repealed (in part): 2009 c.2 Sch.4
s.6, repealed (in part): 2009 c.2 Sch.4
s.7, repealed (in part): 2009 c.2 Sch.4
s.8A, repealed (in part): 2009 c.2 Sch.4
s.8B, repealed (in part): 2009 c.2 Sch.4
s.9, repealed (in part): 2009 c.2 Sch.4
s.10, repealed (in part): 2009 c.2 Sch.1 para.13, Sch.4
s.10A, referred to: SI 2009/3272 Art.3
s.10A, repealed (in part): 2009 c.2 Sch.1 para.14, Sch.4
s.13A, repealed (in part): 2009 c.2 Sch.1 para.15, Sch.4
s.15, applied: SI 2009/3272 Art.3
s.15, repealed (in part): 2009 c.2 Sch.1 para.16, Sch.4
s.16, repealed (in part): 2009 c.2 Sch.1 para.17, Sch.4
s.17A, repealed (in part): 2009 c.2 Sch.4
s.17B, repealed (in part): 2009 c.2 Sch.4
s.19, amended: 2009 c.2 Sch.1 para.18
s.23, amended: 2009 c.2 Sch.1 para.19, Sch.4
s.25, referred to: SI 2009/3272 Art.3
s.25, repealed (in part): 2009 c.2 Sch.1 para.20, Sch.4
s.28, amended: 2009 c.2 Sch.1 para.21, Sch.4
s.29, amended: 2009 c.2 Sch.1 para.22, Sch.4
s.29, applied: SI 2009/3272 Art.3
s.29, referred to: SI 2009/3272 Art.3
s.29, repealed (in part): 2009 c.2 Sch.1 para.22, Sch.4
s.33, amended: 2009 c.2 s.36

28. Food Standards Act 1999
s.12, applied: SI 2009/3255 Reg.7, SI 2009/3376 Reg.7, SSI 2009/446 Reg.7
s.19, applied: SI 2009/3255 Reg.7, SI 2009/3376 Reg.7
s.19, varied: SSI 2009/446 Reg.7
s.22, applied: SI 2009/3255 Reg.7, SI 2009/3376 Reg.7, SSI 2009/446 Reg.7

29. Greater London Authority Act 1999
s.2, amended: 2009 c.20 Sch.4 para.9
s.2, applied: 2009 c.20 s.60
s.85, varied: SI 2009/206 Reg.7
s.86, enabling: SI 2009/206
s.88, varied: SI 2009/206 Reg.8
s.88, enabling: SI 2009/206
s.89, varied: SI 2009/206 Reg.9
s.89, enabling: SI 2009/206
s.99, varied: SI 2009/206 Reg.10
s.102, varied: SI 2009/206 Reg.11
s.134, enabling: SI 2009/473, SI 2009/3322
s.157, amended: SI 2009/1941 Sch.1 para.178
s.165, enabling: SI 2009/2168
s.189, amended: SI 2009/1885 Sch.1 para.24
s.189, applied: SI 2009/1885 Art.2, Sch.4 para.1
s.189, repealed (in part): SI 2009/1885 Sch.1 para.24

29. Greater London Authority Act 1999–*cont.*
s.211, amended: 2009 c.20 Sch.6 para.92, SI 2009/1941 Sch.1 para.178
s.220, amended: SI 2009/1941 Sch.1 para.178
s.224, amended: SI 2009/1941 Sch.1 para.178
s.235, amended: SI 2009/1122 Sch.1 para.2
s.306, repealed (in part): 2009 c.20 Sch.7 Part 4
s.342, amended: 2009 c.20 Sch.5 para.10
s.420, enabling: SI 2009/206
s.424, amended: SI 2009/1941 Sch.1 para.178
s.424, referred to: 2009 c.7 s.30
Sch.1 Part I para.1, substituted: 2009 c.20 Sch.4 para.10
Sch.1 Part I para.2, substituted: 2009 c.20 Sch.4 para.10
Sch.1 Part I para.3, substituted: 2009 c.20 Sch.4 para.10
Sch.1 Part I para.4, substituted: 2009 c.20 Sch.4 para.10
Sch.1 Part I para.5, substituted: 2009 c.20 Sch.4 para.10
Sch.1 Part I para.7, amended: 2009 c.20 Sch.4 para.10
Sch.1 Part II para.8, repealed: 2009 c.20 Sch.4 para.10, Sch.7 Part 3
Sch.1 Part II para.9, repealed: 2009 c.20 Sch.4 para.10, Sch.7 Part 3
Sch.10 para.2, amended: 2009 c.20 Sch.5 para.11
Sch.10 para.7, amended: SI 2009/1941 Sch.1 para.178
Sch.12 para.7, enabling: SI 2009/2168
Sch.14 Part I para.1, amended: SI 2009/1941 Sch.1 para.178
Sch.14 Part I para.4, amended: SI 2009/1941 Sch.1 para.178
Sch.14 Part I para.7, amended: SI 2009/1941 Sch.1 para.178
Sch.14 Part I para.8, amended: SI 2009/1941 Sch.1 para.178
Sch.14 Part I para.9, substituted: SI 2009/1941 Sch.1 para.178
Sch.14 Part I para.10, amended: SI 2009/1941 Sch.1 para.178
Sch.32 para.5, amended: SI 2009/1941 Sch.1 para.178

30. Welfare Reform and Pensions Act 1999
see *Slattery v Cabinet Office (Civil Service Pensions)* [2009] EWHC 226 (Ch), [2009] I.C.R. 806 (Ch D), Proudman, J
applied: 2009 asp 1 Sch.3 para.21
referred to: 2009 c.24 s.58
s.1, enabling: SI 2009/615
s.2, enabling: SI 2009/615
s.8, enabling: SI 2009/615
s.11, amended: SI 2009/56 Sch.1 para.284
s.23, applied: SI 2009/3093 Reg.4
s.24, applied: SI 2009/3093 Reg.4
s.27, see *Slattery v Cabinet Office (Civil Service Pensions)* [2009] EWHC 226 (Ch), [2009] I.C.R. 806 (Ch D), Proudman, J
s.28, referred to: 2009 asp 1 Sch.1 para.92
s.29, see *Slattery v Cabinet Office (Civil Service Pensions)* [2009] EWHC 226 (Ch), [2009] I.C.R. 806 (Ch D), Proudman, J
s.29, referred to: 2009 asp 1 Sch.1 para.92, Sch.1 para.93
s.31, see *Slattery v Cabinet Office (Civil Service Pensions)* [2009] EWHC 226 (Ch), [2009] I.C.R. 806 (Ch D), Proudman, J

1999– cont.

30. Welfare Reform and Pensions Act 1999– *cont.*
s.31, applied: 2009 asp 1 Sch.1 para.109
s.31, referred to: 2009 asp 1 Sch.1 para.92
s.41, applied: SI 2009/3093 Reg.4
s.41, enabling: SI 2009/615
s.45, enabling: SI 2009/615
s.60, repealed: 2009 c.24 Sch.7 Part 3
s.72, amended: 2009 c.24 s.2, s.34
s.72, repealed (in part): 2009 c.24 Sch.7 Part 3
s.83, amended: 2009 c.24 Sch.7 Part 3
s.83, applied: SI 2009/2930
s.83, enabling: SI 2009/615, SI 2009/2930
Sch.5 para.2, applied: 2009 asp 1 Sch.3 para.21
Sch.5 para.7, enabling: SI 2009/2930
Sch.7 para.2, repealed (in part): 2009 c.24 Sch.7 Part 3
Sch.7 para.3, repealed: 2009 c.24 Sch.7 Part 3
Sch.7 para.4, repealed (in part): 2009 c.24 Sch.7 Part 3
Sch.7 para.7, repealed (in part): 2009 c.24 Sch.7 Part 3
Sch.7 para.12, repealed: 2009 c.24 Sch.7 Part 3
Sch.7 para.13, repealed: 2009 c.24 Sch.7 Part 3
Sch.7 para.14, repealed: 2009 c.24 Sch.7 Part 1
Sch.8 Part III para.26, repealed: 2009 c.24 Sch.7 Part 2
Sch.8 Part III para.27, repealed: 2009 c.24 Sch.7 Part 1
Sch.8 Part IV para.28, repealed: 2009 c.24 Sch.7 Part 1
Sch.8 Part V para.29, repealed (in part): 2009 c.24 Sch.7 Part 3
Sch.12 Part II para.87, repealed: 2009 c.24 Sch.7 Part 3

31. Contracts (Rights of Third Parties) Act 1999
see *Dolphin Maritime & Aviation Services Ltd v Sveriges Angfartygs Assurans Forening* [2009] EWHC 716 (Comm), [2009] 2 Lloyd's Rep. 123 (QBD (Comm)), Christopher Clarke, J.
s.1, see *Dolphin Maritime & Aviation Services Ltd v Sveriges Angfartygs Assurans Forening* [2009] EWHC 716 (Comm), [2009] 2 Lloyd's Rep. 123 (QBD (Comm)), Christopher Clarke, J.
s.6, amended: SI 2009/1941 Sch.1 para.179
s.9, repealed (in part): SI 2009/1941 Sch.1 para.179

33. Immigration and Asylum Act 1999
see *Yarl's Wood Immigration Ltd v Bedfordshire Police Authority* [2008] EWHC 2207 (Comm), [2009] 1 All E.R. 886 (QBD (Comm)), Beatson, J.
Part VIII, applied: SI 2009/2133 Reg.3
s.10, see *HH (Iraq) v Secretary of State for the Home Department* [2009] I.N.L.R. 148 (AIT), CMG Ockelton (Deputy President); see *R. (on the application of RK (Nepal)) v Secretary of State for the Home Department* [2009] EWCA Civ 359, Times, May 11, 2009 (CA (Civ Div)), Waller, L.J.
s.41, enabling: SI 2009/198, SI 2009/1032, SI 2009/1229, SI 2009/1233
s.65, see *Beoku-Betts v Secretary of State for the Home Department* [2008] UKHL 39, [2009] 1 A.C. 115 (HL), Lord Bingham of Cornhill
s.77, see *Beoku-Betts v Secretary of State for the Home Department* [2008] UKHL 39, [2009] 1 A.C. 115 (HL), Lord Bingham of Cornhill
s.84, see *R. v K* [2008] EWCA Crim 1900, [2009] 1 W.L.R. 694 (CA (Crim Div)), Toulson, L.J.
s.84, applied: SI 2009/506 Art.3
s.84, enabling: SI 2009/506

1999– cont.

33. Immigration and Asylum Act 1999– *cont.*
s.86, enabling: SI 2009/458
s.91, see *R. v K* [2008] EWCA Crim 1900, [2009] 1 W.L.R. 694 (CA (Crim Div)), Toulson, L.J.
s.97, amended: 2009 c.24 Sch.2 para.8
s.103, applied: SI 2009/275 Art.2
s.115, repealed (in part): 2009 c.24 Sch.7 Part 1
s.115, enabling: SI 2009/3228
s.141, amended: 2009 c.11 s.51
s.147, amended: 2009 c.11 s.25
s.152, applied: 2009 c.20 s.3
s.166, enabling: SI 2009/198, SI 2009/506, SI 2009/641, SI 2009/1032, SI 2009/1229, SI 2009/1233, SI 2009/1388, SI 2009/3228
s.167, enabling: SI 2009/3228
Sch.2 para.6, applied: SI 2009/2133 Reg.5
Sch.5 Part I para.9, applied: SI 2009/1976 r.19A
Sch.8 para.1, enabling: SI 2009/641, SI 2009/1388
Sch.8 para.3, enabling: SI 2009/641, SI 2009/1388

2000

1. Northern Ireland Act 2000
applied: 2009 c.2 Sch.2 Part 2
referred to: 2009 c.2 Sch.2 Part 2, 2009 c.9 Sch.2 Part 40

2. Representation of the People Act 2000
Sch.4, applied: SSI 2009/2 Art.3, SSI 2009/35 Reg.13, Reg.15
Sch.4, referred to: SSI 2009/35 Reg.15

6. Powers of Criminal Courts (Sentencing) Act 2000
see *R. v Knight (Kate Marie)* [2008] EWCA Crim 1444, [2009] 1 Cr. App. R. (S.) 57 (CA (Crim Div)), Lord Philips, L.C.J.; see *R. v Sofekun (Ade Tute)* [2008] EWCA Crim 2035, [2009] 1 Cr. App. R. (S.) 78 (CA (Crim Div)), Sir Igor Judge (President, QB)
s.14, disapplied: 2009 c.25 s.158
s.17, amended: 2009 c.25 Sch.17 para.12
s.19, amended: 2009 c.26 Sch.7 para.22
s.41, applied: SI 2009/1887 Sch.1
s.41, referred to: SI 2009/1887 Sch.2
s.51, applied: SI 2009/1887 Sch.1
s.51, referred to: SI 2009/1887 Sch.2
s.52, applied: SI 2009/1887 Sch.1
s.82A, applied: 2009 c.25 s.126
s.91, see *Attorney General's Reference (No.48 of 2008), Re* [2008] EWCA Crim 2514, [2009] 2 Cr. App. R. (S.) 1 (CA (Crim Div)), Lord Judge, L.C.J.; see *Attorney General's Reference (No.49 of 2008), Re* [2008] EWCA Crim 2304, [2009] 1 Cr. App. R. (S.) 109 (CA (Crim Div)), Lord Judge, L.C.J.; see *R. v W* [2009] EWCA Crim 390, [2009] 2 Cr. App. R. (S.) 94 (CA (Crim Div)), Moses, L.J.
s.93, applied: SI 2009/1059 Sch.2 para.6
s.94, applied: SI 2009/1059 Sch.2 para.7
s.96, applied: SI 2009/1059 Sch.2 para.9
s.97, applied: SI 2009/1059 Sch.2 para.9
s.99, varied: SI 2009/1059 Sch.1 para.45
s.101, varied: SI 2009/1059 Art.87
s.103, see *H v Doncaster Youth Court* [2009] EWHC 3463 (Admin), (2009) 173 J.P. 162 (DC), Latham, L.J.
s.104, see *H v Doncaster Youth Court* [2009] EWHC 3463 (Admin), (2009) 173 J.P. 162 (DC), Latham, L.J.

6. Powers of Criminal Courts (Sentencing) Act 2000–*cont.*
s.105, see *H v Doncaster Youth Court* [2009] EWHC 3463 (Admin), (2009) 173 J.P. 162 (DC), Latham, L.J.
s.105, applied: SI 2009/ 2041 r.134
s.106, varied: SI 2009/ 1059 Sch.2 para.10
s.106A, varied: SI 2009/ 1059 Sch.1 para.45
s.109, applied: SI 2009/ 1059 Art.89, Art.110
s.109, disapplied: SI 2009/ 1059 Art.110
s.110, amended: 2009 c.25 Sch.17 para.10
s.110, applied: 2009 c.25 s.125
s.111, amended: 2009 c.25 Sch.17 para.10
s.111, applied: 2009 c.25 s.125
s.113, amended: 2009 c.25 Sch.17 para.10, Sch.23 Part 5
s.114, amended: 2009 c.25 Sch.17 para.10
s.114, varied: SI 2009/ 1059 Sch.1 para.45
s.116, see *H v Doncaster Youth Court* [2009] EWHC 3463 (Admin), (2009) 173 J.P. 162 (DC), Latham, L.J.
s.134, varied: SI 2009/ 1059 Sch.1 para.45
s.139, see *Escobar v DPP* [2008] EWHC 422 (Admin), [2009] 1 W.L.R. 64 (DC), Maurice Kay, L.J.
s.143, applied: 2009 c.25 s.164
s.146, see *R. v Sofekun (Ade Tute)* [2008] EWCA Crim 2035, [2009] 1 Cr. App. R. (S.) 78 (CA (Crim Div)), Sir Igor Judge (President, QB)
s.147, see *R. v Bowling (Stephen David)* [2008] EWCA Crim 1148, [2009] 1 Cr. App. R. (S.) 23 (CA (Crim Div)), Sir Igor Judge; see *R. v Sofekun (Ade Tute)* [2008] EWCA Crim 2035, [2009] 1 Cr. App. R. (S.) 78 (CA (Crim Div)), Sir Igor Judge (President, QB)
s.147A, added: 2009 c.25 Sch.16 para.5
s.147A, varied: 2009 c.25 Sch.22 para.34
s.147B, added: 2009 c.25 Sch.16 para.5
s.154, see *R. v Hills (Christopher Carl)* [2008] EWCA Crim 1871, [2009] 1 Cr. App. R. (S.) 75 (CA (Crim Div)), Latham, L.J.
s.155, see *R. v Bukhari (Daniyal)* [2008] EWCA Crim 2915, [2009] 2 Cr. App. R. (S.) 18 (CA (Crim Div)), Moore-Bick, L.J.
s.160, amended: 2009 c.25 Sch.16 para.5, Sch.21 para.94
Sch.6 para.5, applied: SI 2009/ 1547 Sch.1 para.8
Sch.6 para.6, amended: SI 2009/ 1182 Sch.5 para.5
7. Electronic Communications Act 2000
referred to: SI 2009/ 360 Reg.2, SSI 2009/ 121 Reg.1, SSI 2009/ 141 Reg.2, SSI 2009/ 414 Art.2
s.8, enabling: SI 2009/ 203, SI 2009/ 555, SI 2009/ 2706, SI 2009/ 2821, SI 2009/ 3023
s.9, applied: SI 2009/ 555
s.9, enabling: SI 2009/ 555, SI 2009/ 3023
s.10, enabling: SI 2009/ 2706
s.15, referred to: SSI 2009/ 232 Art.2, SSI 2009/ 266 Reg.2, SSI 2009/ 443 Art.9
8. Financial Services and Markets Act 2000
see *Financial Services Authority v Fox Hayes (A Firm)* [2009] EWCA Civ 76, [2009] 1 B.C.L.C. 603 (CA (Civ Div)), Longmore, L.J.; see *Financial Services Authority v Shepherd* [2009] Lloyd's Rep. F.C. 631 (Ch D), Jules Sher Q.C.; see *Financial Services Compensation Scheme Ltd v Abbey National Treasury Services Plc* [2008] EWHC 1897 (Ch), [2009] Bus. L.R. 465 (Ch D), David Richards, J.; see *R. (on the application of Uberoi) v Westminster Magistrates' Court* [2008] EWHC 3191

8. Financial Services and Markets Act 2000–*cont.*
see–*cont.*
(Admin), [2009] 1 W.L.R. 1905 (DC), May, L.J.; see *Whiteley Insurance Consultants (A Firm), Re* [2008] EWHC 1782 (Ch), [2009] Bus. L.R. 418 (Ch D (Companies Ct)), David Richards, J.
applied: 2009 c.1 s.249, SI 2009/ 209 Reg.13, Sch.5 para.8, Sch.5 para.9, SI 2009/ 322 Art.5, SI 2009/ 1342 Sch.1 para.5, SI 2009/ 1389, SI 2009/ 3056 Reg.17, SI 2009/ 3093 Sch.1
referred to: 2009 c.4 s.210
Part IV, applied: 2009 c.1 s.57, s.186, s.187, s.223, s.232, SI 2009/ 1342 Art.32, Sch.1 para.2, SI 2009/ 2425 Reg.4, SI 2009/ 2997 Reg.14, SI 2009/ 3056 Reg.31
Part IV, referred to: 2009 c.1 s.223
Part VI, applied: SI 2009/ 214 Sch.1, SI 2009/ 1801 Sch.1
Part IX, applied: 2009 c.1 s.202, SI 2009/ 209 Sch.5 para.2
Part XIV, applied: SI 2009/ 209 Reg.86
Part XV, applied: 2009 c.1 s.6, s.123, s.169, s.234, s.246, SI 2009/ 351 r.30, SI 2009/ 356 r.73, SI 2009/ 807 Reg.11, SI 2009/ 1171 Reg.8
Part XVI, applied: SI 2009/ 209 Reg.91
Part XV, see *Financial Services Compensation Scheme Ltd v Abbey National Treasury Services Plc* [2008] EWHC 1897 (Ch), [2009] Bus. L.R. 465 (Ch D), David Richards, J.
s.1, amended: 2009 c.1 s.249
s.2, varied: SI 2009/ 209 Reg.92
s.15, applied: SI 2009/ 356 r.73
s.17, varied: SI 2009/ 209 Reg.92
s.19, see *Financial Services Authority v Bayshore Nominees Ltd* [2009] EWHC 285 (Ch), [2009] Lloyd's Rep. F.C. 398 (Ch D), Floyd, J; see *Financial Services Authority v Shepherd* [2009] Lloyd's Rep. F.C. 631 (Ch D), Jules Sher Q.C.; see *Secretary of State for Business Enterprise and Regulatory Reform v Art IT Plc* [2008] EWHC 258 (Ch), [2009] 1 B.C.L.C. 262 (Ch D (Companies Ct)), Judge Toulmin Q.C.; see *Whiteley Insurance Consultants (A Firm), Re* [2008] EWHC 1782 (Ch), [2009] Bus. L.R. 418 (Ch D (Companies Ct)), David Richards, J.
s.20, see *Whiteley Insurance Consultants (A Firm), Re* [2008] EWHC 1782 (Ch), [2009] Bus. L.R. 418 (Ch D (Companies Ct)), David Richards, J.
s.20, applied: SI 2009/ 1342 Sch.1 para.2
s.21, see *Financial Services Authority v Bayshore Nominees Ltd* [2009] EWHC 285 (Ch), [2009] Lloyd's Rep. F.C. 398 (Ch D), Floyd, J; see *Financial Services Authority v Shepherd* [2009] Lloyd's Rep. F.C. 631 (Ch D), Jules Sher Q.C.; see *R. v Powell (Curtis)* [2008] EWCA Crim 1214, [2009] 1 Cr. App. R. (S.) 30 (CA (Crim Div)), Hughes, L.J.; see *Secretary of State for Business Enterprise and Regulatory Reform v Art IT Plc* [2008] EWHC 258 (Ch), [2009] 1 B.C.L.C. 262 (Ch D (Companies Ct)), Judge Toulmin Q.C.
s.21, applied: SI 2009/ 1342 Sch.1 para.6
s.22, applied: SI 2009/ 2477 r.11, SI 2009/ 3093 Reg.2
s.22, enabling: SI 2009/ 1342, SI 2009/ 1389
s.26, see *Whiteley Insurance Consultants (A Firm), Re* [2008] EWHC 1782 (Ch), [2009] Bus. L.R. 418 (Ch D (Companies Ct)), David Richards, J.
s.28, see *Whiteley Insurance Consultants (A Firm), Re* [2008] EWHC 1782 (Ch), [2009] Bus. L.R. 418 (Ch D (Companies Ct)), David Richards, J.
s.31, applied: SI 2009/ 1342 Sch.1 para.4

2000–cont.

8. Financial Services and Markets Act 2000–*cont.*

s.38, applied: SI 2009/1342 Sch.1 para.3, SI 2009/3093 Sch.1

s.38, enabling: SI 2009/118, SI 2009/264

s.40, applied: SI 2009/1342 Sch.1 para.3

s.41, applied: 2009 c.1 s.7, SI 2009/1800 Sch.2 para.9

s.42, applied: SI 2009/1342 Sch.1 para.3, SI 2009/2997 Reg.14, SI 2009/3226 Art.9

s.43, applied: SI 2009/1342 Sch.1 para.3, SI 2009/2997 Reg.14

s.44, applied: SI 2009/1342 Sch.1 para.3

s.45, amended: 2009 c.1 s.248

s.45, applied: SI 2009/1342 Art.32, Sch.1 para.3

s.49, amended: SI 2009/1342 Art.25

s.51, applied: SI 2009/1342 Art.32

s.52, applied: SI 2009/1342 Sch.1 para.3

s.53, applied: SI 2009/1342 Sch.1 para.3

s.54, applied: SI 2009/1342 Sch.1 para.3

s.55, applied: SI 2009/1342 Sch.1 para.3

s.59, applied: SI 2009/1342 Sch.1 para.3, SI 2009/3226 Art.10

s.60, applied: SI 2009/1342 Sch.1 para.3

s.61, applied: SI 2009/1342 Sch.1 para.3, SI 2009/3226 Art.10

s.62, applied: SI 2009/1342 Sch.1 para.3

s.63, applied: SI 2009/1342 Sch.1 para.3

s.65, disapplied: SI 2009/1342 Art.33

s.66, applied: SI 2009/209 Sch.5 para.1

s.66, varied: SI 2009/209 Sch.5 para.1

s.67, applied: SI 2009/209 Sch.5 para.1

s.68, applied: SI 2009/209 Sch.5 para.1

s.69, applied: SI 2009/209 Sch.5 para.1

s.70, applied: SI 2009/209 Sch.5 para.1

s.74, applied: 2009 c.1 s.19

s.96A, applied: SI 2009/814 Art.7, SI 2009/3226 Sch.5 para.3

s.96B, amended: SI 2009/1941 Sch.1 para.181, SI 2009/2461 Reg.2

s.96B, applied: SI 2009/814 Art.7, SI 2009/3226 Sch.5 para.3

s.107, see *Names at Lloyds, Re* [2008] EWHC 2960 (Ch), [2009] Bus. L.R. 509 (Ch D), Floyd, J

s.108, enabling: SI 2009/1390

s.109, see *Names at Lloyds, Re* [2008] EWHC 2960 (Ch), [2009] Bus. L.R. 509 (Ch D), Floyd, J

s.118, amended: SI 2009/3128 Reg.2

s.118A, amended: SI 2009/3128 Reg.2

s.132, varied: SI 2009/1810 Art.14

s.133, varied: 2009 c.1 s.202, SI 2009/209 Sch.5 para.2, SI 2009/1810 Art.14, Art.16, Art.17

s.133A, varied: SI 2009/1810 Art.14

s.133B, varied: SI 2009/1810 Art.14

s.134, varied: SI 2009/1810 Art.14, Art.18

s.135, varied: SI 2009/1810 Art.14, Art.18

s.136, varied: SI 2009/1810 Art.14, Art.18

s.137, applied: SI 2009/1342 Art.32

s.137, varied: SI 2009/1810 Art.14

s.138, varied: SI 2009/814 Art.9, SI 2009/3226 Art.20

s.146, applied: SI 2009/214 Sch.2 para.7, SI 2009/1801 Sch.2 para.7

s.148, applied: SI 2009/3226 Art.20

s.148, varied: SI 2009/814 Art.9

s.155, disapplied: SI 2009/1342 Art.33

s.155, varied: SI 2009/209 Sch.7 para.3, SI 2009/814 Art.10, SI 2009/3226 Art.21

2000–cont.

8. Financial Services and Markets Act 2000–*cont.*

s.156, see *Financial Services Compensation Scheme Ltd v Abbey National Treasury Services Plc* [2008] EWHC 1897 (Ch), [2009] Bus. L.R. 465 (Ch D), David Richards, J.

s.157, disapplied: SI 2009/1342 Art.33

s.157, varied: SI 2009/814 Art.10, SI 2009/3226 Art.21

s.159, varied: SI 2009/209 Reg.92

s.165, applied: 2009 c.1 s.250

s.165, varied: SI 2009/209 Sch.5 para.3

s.166, applied: SI 2009/214 Sch.1, SI 2009/1801 Sch.1

s.166, varied: SI 2009/209 Sch.5 para.3

s.167, applied: SI 2009/214 Sch.1, SI 2009/1801 Sch.1

s.167, varied: SI 2009/209 Sch.5 para.3

s.168, applied: SI 2009/214 Sch.1, SI 2009/1801 Sch.1

s.168, varied: SI 2009/209 Sch.5 para.3

s.169, varied: SI 2009/209 Sch.5 para.3

s.170, see *Secretary of State for Business Enterprise and Regulatory Reform v Aaron* [2008] EWCA Civ 1146, [2009] Bus. L.R. 809 (CA (Civ Div)), Buxton, L.J.

s.170, varied: SI 2009/209 Sch.5 para.3

s.171, varied: SI 2009/209 Sch.5 para.3

s.172, varied: SI 2009/209 Sch.5 para.3

s.173, varied: SI 2009/209 Sch.5 para.3

s.174, varied: SI 2009/209 Sch.5 para.3

s.175, varied: SI 2009/209 Sch.5 para.3

s.176, varied: SI 2009/209 Sch.5 para.3

s.177, varied: SI 2009/209 Sch.5 para.3

s.178, applied: SI 2009/774 Art.4, Art.5, Art.6

s.178, substituted: SI 2009/534 Sch.1

s.179, substituted: SI 2009/534 Sch.1

s.180, substituted: SI 2009/534 Sch.1

s.181, substituted: SI 2009/534 Sch.1

s.182, substituted: SI 2009/534 Sch.1

s.183, substituted: SI 2009/534 Sch.1

s.184, applied: SI 2009/774 Art.3

s.184, substituted: SI 2009/534 Sch.1

s.185, substituted: SI 2009/534 Sch.1

s.186, substituted: SI 2009/534 Sch.1

s.187, substituted: SI 2009/534 Sch.1

s.188, substituted: SI 2009/534 Sch.1

s.189, substituted: SI 2009/534 Sch.1

s.190, substituted: SI 2009/534 Sch.1

s.191, substituted: SI 2009/534 Sch.1

s.191A, substituted: SI 2009/534 Sch.1

s.191B, substituted: SI 2009/534 Sch.1

s.191C, substituted: SI 2009/534 Sch.1

s.191D, applied: SI 2009/774 Art.4, Art.5, Art.6

s.191D, substituted: SI 2009/534 Sch.1

s.191E, substituted: SI 2009/534 Sch.1

s.191F, substituted: SI 2009/534 Sch.1

s.192, amended: SI 2009/534 Reg.4

s.192, enabling: SI 2009/774

s.203, amended: SI 2009/209 Reg.26

s.203, applied: SI 2009/209 Reg.26

s.203, varied: SI 2009/209 Reg.26

s.210, applied: SI 2009/209 Reg.86

s.211, applied: SI 2009/209 Reg.86

s.212, varied: SI 2009/1804 Sch.2 para.3

s.213, see *Beloit Walmsley Ltd, Re* [2008] EWHC 1888 (Ch), [2009] 1 B.C.L.C. 584 (Ch D (Manchester)), Judge Pelling Q.C.; see *Financial Services Compensation Scheme Ltd v Abbey National Treasury Services Plc* [2008]

2000–cont.

8. **Financial Services and Markets Act 2000**–*cont.*
s.213–*cont.*
EWHC 1897 (Ch), [2009] Bus. L.R. 465 (Ch D),
David Richards, J.
s.213, amended: 2009 c.1 s.170
s.213, applied: 2009 c.1 s.123, SI 2009/317 Art.7, SI
2009/807 Reg.11
s.213, disapplied: SI 2009/1342 Sch.1 para.7
s.213, varied: SI 2009/1804 Sch.2 para.3
s.214, amended: 2009 c.1 s.174
s.214, varied: SI 2009/1804 Sch.2 para.3
s.214A, added: 2009 c.1 s.170
s.214A, varied: SI 2009/1804 Sch.2 para.3
s.214B, added: 2009 c.1 s.171
s.214B, applied: 2009 c.1 s.61, s.83, SI 2009/807
Reg.3, Reg.4
s.214B, varied: 2009 c.1 s.83, SI 2009/1804 Sch.2
para.3
s.214B, enabling: SI 2009/807
s.215, amended: 2009 c.1 s.175
s.215, substituted: 2009 c.1 s.175
s.215, varied: SI 2009/317 Art.5, SI 2009/1804 Sch.2
para.3
s.216, varied: SI 2009/1804 Sch.2 para.3
s.217, varied: SI 2009/1804 Sch.2 para.3
s.218, amended: 2009 c.1 s.170
s.218, varied: SI 2009/1804 Sch.2 para.3
s.218A, added: 2009 c.1 s.176
s.218A, varied: SI 2009/1804 Sch.2 para.3
s.219, amended: 2009 c.1 s.176
s.219, repealed (in part): 2009 c.1 s.176
s.219, varied: SI 2009/1804 Sch.2 para.3
s.220, amended: 2009 c.1 s.123, SI 2009/805 Art.15
s.220, varied: SI 2009/1804 Sch.2 para.3
s.221, varied: SI 2009/1804 Sch.2 para.3
s.221A, added: 2009 c.1 s.179
s.221A, applied: 2009 c.1 s.123
s.221A, varied: SI 2009/1804 Sch.2 para.3
s.222, amended: 2009 c.1 s.179
s.222, varied: SI 2009/1804 Sch.2 para.3
s.223, amended: 2009 c.1 s.171
s.223, varied: SI 2009/1804 Sch.2 para.3
s.223A, added: 2009 c.1 s.172
s.223A, varied: SI 2009/1804 Sch.2 para.3
s.223B, added: 2009 c.1 s.173
s.223B, varied: SI 2009/1804 Sch.2 para.3
s.223C, added: 2009 c.1 s.177
s.223C, varied: SI 2009/1804 Sch.2 para.3
s.224, varied: SI 2009/1804 Sch.2 para.3
s.224A, added: 2009 c.1 s.180
s.224A, varied: SI 2009/1804 Sch.2 para.3
s.225, varied: SI 2009/209 Reg.125
s.226, amended: SI 2009/209 Sch.6 para.1
s.226, varied: SI 2009/209 Reg.125
s.226A, varied: SI 2009/209 Reg.125
s.227, varied: SI 2009/209 Reg.125
s.228, varied: SI 2009/209 Reg.125
s.229, varied: SI 2009/209 Reg.125
s.230, varied: SI 2009/209 Reg.125
s.231, varied: SI 2009/209 Reg.125
s.232, varied: SI 2009/209 Reg.125
s.233, varied: SI 2009/209 Reg.125
s.234, amended: SI 2009/209 Sch.6 para.1
s.234, varied: SI 2009/209 Reg.125
s.234A, varied: SI 2009/209 Reg.125
s.236, amended: SI 2009/1941 Sch.1 para.181
s.237, referred to: SI 2009/2034 Reg.13
s.259, applied: SI 2009/807

2000–cont.

8. **Financial Services and Markets Act 2000**–*cont.*
s.262, enabling: SI 2009/553
s.264, applied: SI 2009/3001 Reg.74
s.270, applied: SI 2009/3001 Reg.74
s.272, applied: SI 2009/3001 Reg.74
s.284, applied: SI 2009/214 Sch.1, SI 2009/1801
Sch.1
s.285, applied: 2009 c.1 s.186, s.187
s.286, applied: SI 2009/853(c)
s.286, enabling: SI 2009/853
s.301A, substituted: SI 2009/534 Sch.2
s.301B, substituted: SI 2009/534 Sch.2
s.301C, substituted: SI 2009/534 Sch.2
s.301D, substituted: SI 2009/534 Sch.2
s.301E, substituted: SI 2009/534 Sch.2
s.301F, substituted: SI 2009/534 Sch.2
s.301G, substituted: SI 2009/534 Sch.2
s.301H, substituted: SI 2009/534 Sch.2
s.301I, substituted: SI 2009/534 Sch.2
s.301J, substituted: SI 2009/534 Sch.2
s.301K, substituted: SI 2009/534 Sch.2
s.301L, substituted: SI 2009/534 Sch.2
s.301M, substituted: SI 2009/534 Sch.2
s.341, varied: SI 2009/209 Sch.5 para.4
s.342, varied: SI 2009/209 Sch.5 para.4
s.343, varied: SI 2009/209 Sch.5 para.4
s.344, varied: SI 2009/209 Sch.5 para.4
s.345, varied: SI 2009/209 Sch.5 para.4
s.346, varied: SI 2009/209 Sch.5 para.4
s.348, see *Financial Services Authority v
Information Commissioner* [2009] EWHC
1548 (Admin), [2009] Bus. L.R. 1287 (QBD
(Admin)), Munby, J.
s.348, applied: SI 2009/209 Reg.119
s.348, varied: SI 2009/209 Sch.5 para.5
s.349, applied: SI 2009/209 Reg.119
s.349, varied: SI 2009/209 Sch.5 para.5
s.349, enabling: SI 2009/2877
s.351, varied: SI 2009/209 Sch.5 para.5
s.352, varied: SI 2009/209 Sch.5 para.5
s.355, varied: SI 2009/317 Art.5, SI 2009/1804 Sch.2
para.3
s.356, varied: SI 2009/1804 Sch.2 para.3
s.357, varied: SI 2009/1804 Sch.2 para.3
s.358, varied: SI 2009/1804 Sch.2 para.3
s.359, varied: SI 2009/209 Sch.5 para.6, SI 2009/
1804 Sch.2 para.3
s.360, varied: SI 2009/1804 Sch.2 para.3
s.361, varied: SI 2009/317 Art.5, SI 2009/1804 Sch.2
para.3
s.362, varied: SI 2009/317 Art.5, SI 2009/1804 Sch.2
para.3
s.362A, varied: SI 2009/1804 Sch.2 para.3
s.363, varied: SI 2009/1804 Sch.2 para.3
s.364, varied: SI 2009/1804 Sch.2 para.3
s.365, varied: SI 2009/1804 Sch.2 para.3
s.366, varied: SI 2009/1804 Sch.2 para.3
s.367, varied: SI 2009/209 Sch.5 para.6, SI 2009/
1804 Sch.2 para.3
s.368, varied: SI 2009/209 Sch.5 para.6, SI 2009/
1804 Sch.2 para.3
s.369, varied: SI 2009/1804 Sch.2 para.3
s.369A, varied: SI 2009/1804 Sch.2 para.3
s.370, varied: SI 2009/317 Art.5, SI 2009/1804 Sch.2
para.3
s.371, varied: SI 2009/1804 Sch.2 para.3
s.372, varied: SI 2009/1804 Sch.2 para.3
s.373, varied: SI 2009/1804 Sch.2 para.3

2000–cont.

8. Financial Services and Markets Act 2000–*cont.*
s.374, varied: SI 2009/1804 Sch.2 para.3
s.375, varied: SI 2009/317 Art.5, SI 2009/1804 Sch.2 para.3
s.376, varied: SI 2009/1804 Sch.2 para.3
s.377, varied: SI 2009/1804 Sch.2 para.3
s.378, varied: SI 2009/1804 Sch.2 para.3
s.379, varied: SI 2009/1804 Sch.2 para.3
s.380, see *Financial Services Authority v Shepherd* [2009] Lloyd's Rep. F.C. 631 (Ch D), Jules Sher Q.C.
s.382, see *Financial Services Authority v Shepherd* [2009] Lloyd's Rep. F.C. 631 (Ch D), Jules Sher Q.C.
s.382, applied: SI 2009/356 r.262
s.387, varied: SI 2009/209 Sch.5 para.7
s.388, varied: SI 2009/209 Sch.5 para.7
s.389, varied: SI 2009/209 Sch.5 para.7
s.390, varied: SI 2009/209 Sch.5 para.7
s.391, applied: SI 2009/209 Reg.11
s.391, varied: SI 2009/209 Sch.5 para.7
s.392, varied: SI 2009/209 Sch.5 para.7
s.393, applied: SI 2009/209 Reg.86
s.393, varied: SI 2009/209 Sch.5 para.7
s.394, varied: SI 2009/209 Sch.5 para.7
s.395, amended: SI 2009/534 Reg.6
s.395, varied: SI 2009/209 Sch.5 para.7
s.396, varied: SI 2009/209 Sch.5 para.7
s.401, see *R. (on the application of Uberoi) v Westminster Magistrates' Court* [2008] EWHC 3191 (Admin), [2009] 1 W.L.R. 1905 (DC), May, L.J.
s.402, see *R. (on the application of Uberoi) v Westminster Magistrates' Court* [2008] EWHC 3191 (Admin), [2009] 1 W.L.R. 1905 (DC), May, L.J.
s.411, repealed (in part): 2009 c.4 Sch.3 Part 1
s.413, applied: SI 2009/209 Sch.5 para.8
s.417, amended: 2009 c.1 s.174, SI 2009/1941 Sch.1 para.181
s.417, applied: SI 2009/814 Art.7, SI 2009/3226 Art.18
s.417, enabling: SI 2009/1390, SI 2009/2877, SI 2009/3075
s.422, substituted: SI 2009/534 Sch.3
s.424, enabling: SI 2009/3075
s.426, enabling: SI 2009/1342
s.427, enabling: SI 2009/1342
s.428, enabling: SI 2009/118, SI 2009/553, SI 2009/774, SI 2009/807, SI 2009/853, SI 2009/1342, SI 2009/1390, SI 2009/3075
s.429, amended: 2009 c.1 s.178
s.429, applied: SI 2009/553
Sch.1 Part I para.1, amended: SI 2009/1941 Sch.1 para.181
Sch.1 Part II para.14, amended: SI 2009/1941 Sch.1 para.181
Sch.1 Part III para.17, applied: SI 2009/209 Reg.92
Sch.1 Part IV para.19, applied: SI 2009/209 Reg.94
Sch.2, applied: SI 2009/3093 Reg.2
Sch.2, referred to: SI 2009/2477 r.11
Sch.2 Part III para.25, enabling: SI 2009/1342, SI 2009/1389
Sch.3, applied: SI 2009/2425 Reg.4
Sch.3 Part I para.5, referred to: SI 2009/2997 Reg.14
Sch.3 Part II, applied: SI 2009/209 Reg.110
Sch.3 Part II para.12, applied: SI 2009/2997 Reg.14
Sch.3 Part II para.15, applied: SI 2009/2997 Reg.14

2000–cont.

8. Financial Services and Markets Act 2000–*cont.*
Sch.6, referred to: SI 2009/1342 Art.32
Sch.11 B Part 1 para.1, added: SI 2009/2461 Sch.1
Sch.11 B Part 1 para.2, added: SI 2009/2461 Sch.1
Sch.11 B Part 1 para.3, added: SI 2009/2461 Sch.1
Sch.11 B Part 1 para.4, added: SI 2009/2461 Sch.1
Sch.11 B Part 1 para.5, added: SI 2009/2461 Sch.1
Sch.11 B Part 1 para.6, added: SI 2009/2461 Sch.1
Sch.11 B Part 2 para.7, added: SI 2009/2461 Sch.1
Sch.11 B Part 2 para.8, added: SI 2009/2461 Sch.1
Sch.11 B Part 2 para.9, added: SI 2009/2461 Sch.1
Sch.11 B Part 2 para.10, added: SI 2009/2461 Sch.1
Sch.11 B Part 2 para.11, added: SI 2009/2461 Sch.1
Sch.11 B Part 2 para.12, added: SI 2009/2461 Sch.1
Sch.13 Part I para.1, varied: SI 2009/1810 Art.14, Art.16
Sch.13 Part II para.2, varied: SI 2009/1810 Art.14, Art.16
Sch.13 Part II para.3, varied: SI 2009/1810 Art.14, Art.16
Sch.13 Part II para.4, varied: SI 2009/1810 Art.14, Art.16
Sch.13 Part II para.5, varied: SI 2009/1810 Art.14, Art.16
Sch.13 Part II para.6, varied: SI 2009/1810 Art.14, Art.16
Sch.13 Part III para.7, varied: SI 2009/1810 Art.14, Art.16
Sch.13 Part IV para.8, varied: SI 2009/1810 Art.14, Art.16
Sch.13 Part IV para.9, varied: SI 2009/1810 Art.14, Art.16
Sch.13 Part IV para.10, varied: SI 2009/1810 Art.14, Art.16
Sch.13 Part IV para.11, varied: SI 2009/1810 Art.14, Art.16
Sch.13 Part IV para.12, varied: SI 2009/1810 Art.14, Art.16
Sch.13 Part IV para.13, varied: SI 2009/1810 Art.14, Art.16
Sch.16 para.2, varied: SI 2009/209 Reg.26
Sch.17 Part I para.1, varied: SI 2009/209 Reg.125
Sch.17 Part II para.2, varied: SI 2009/209 Reg.125
Sch.17 Part II para.3, varied: SI 2009/209 Reg.125
Sch.17 Part II para.4, varied: SI 2009/209 Reg.125
Sch.17 Part II para.5, varied: SI 2009/209 Reg.125
Sch.17 Part II para.6, varied: SI 2009/209 Reg.125
Sch.17 Part II para.7, varied: SI 2009/209 Reg.125
Sch.17 Part II para.8, varied: SI 2009/209 Reg.125
Sch.17 Part II para.9, varied: SI 2009/209 Reg.125
Sch.17 Part II para.10, varied: SI 2009/209 Reg.125
Sch.17 Part II para.11, varied: SI 2009/209 Reg.125
Sch.17 Part IIIA para.16A, varied: SI 2009/209 Reg.125
Sch.17 Part IIIA para.16B, varied: SI 2009/209 Reg.125
Sch.17 Part IIIA para.16C, varied: SI 2009/209 Reg.125
Sch.17 Part IIIA para.16D, varied: SI 2009/209 Reg.125
Sch.17 Part IIIA para.16E, varied: SI 2009/209 Reg.125
Sch.17 Part IIIA para.16F, varied: SI 2009/209 Reg.125
Sch.17 Part IIIA para.16G, varied: SI 2009/209 Reg.125
Sch.17 Part III para.12, varied: SI 2009/209 Reg.125
Sch.17 Part III para.13, amended: SI 2009/209 Sch.6 para.1

2000– cont.

8. Financial Services and Markets Act 2000– *cont.*
Sch.17 Part III para.13, varied: SI 2009/209 Reg.125
Sch.17 Part III para.14, varied: SI 2009/209 Reg.125, Sch.7 para.3
Sch.17 Part III para.15, varied: SI 2009/209 Reg.125
Sch.17 Part III para.16, varied: SI 2009/209 Reg.125
Sch.17 Part IV para.17, varied: SI 2009/209 Reg.125
Sch.17 Part IV para.18, varied: SI 2009/209 Reg.125
Sch.17 Part IV para.19, varied: SI 2009/209 Reg.125
Sch.17 Part IV para.20, varied: SI 2009/209 Reg.125
Sch.17 Part IV para.21, varied: SI 2009/209 Reg.125
Sch.17 Part IV para.22, varied: SI 2009/209 Reg.125
Sch.17 para.14, see *Financial Ombudsman Service Ltd v Heather Moor & Edgecomb Ltd* [2008] EWCA Civ 643, [2009] 1 All E.R. 328 (CA (Civ Div)), Laws, L.J.
Sch.20 para.4, repealed (in part): SI 2009/2035 Sch.1 para.60

11. Terrorism Act 2000
see *Federal Security Services Ltd v Northern Ireland Court Service* [2009] NIQB 15, [2009] Eu. L.R. 739 (QBD (NI)), McCloskey, J.; see *MH (Syria) v Secretary of State for the Home Department* [2009] EWCA Civ 226, [2009] 3 All E.R. 564 (CA (Civ Div)), Ward, L.J.; see *People's Mojahedin Organization of Iran v Council of the European Union (T-284/08)* [2009] 1 C.M.L.R. 44 (CFI (7th Chamber)), Judge Forwood (President)
applied: SI 2009/1593(a)
varied: SI 2009/317 Sch.1
s.3, applied: SI 2009/578
s.3, enabling: SI 2009/578
s.15, applied: SI 2009/209 Reg.13
s.16, applied: SI 2009/209 Reg.13
s.17, applied: SI 2009/209 Reg.13
s.18, applied: SI 2009/209 Reg.13
s.23, applied: 2009 c.25 s.164
s.23A, applied: 2009 c.25 s.164
s.38B, see *R. v Sherif (Abdul)* [2008] EWCA Crim 2653, [2009] 2 Cr. App. R. (S.) 33 (CA (Crim Div)), Latham, L.J.
s.57, see *R. v G* [2009] UKHL 13, [2009] 2 W.L.R. 724 (HL), Lord Phillips of Worth Matravers
s.58, see *R. v G* [2009] UKHL 13, [2009] 2 W.L.R. 724 (HL), Lord Phillips of Worth Matravers
s.63, applied: SI 2009/209 Reg.13
s.111, applied: 2009 c.25 s.164
Sch.2, referred to: SI 2009/578, SI 2009/578 Art.2
Sch.7, applied: SI 2009/1593 Art.3
Sch.8, applied: SI 2009/1593 Art.3
Sch.8 para.7, see *C's Application for Judicial Review, Re* [2009] UKHL 15, [2009] 1 A.C. 908 (HL (NI)), Lord Phillips of Worth Matravers; see *R. v Ibrahim (Muktar)* [2008] EWCA Crim 880, [2009] 1 W.L.R. 578 (CA (Crim Div)), Sir Igor Judge (President, QB)
Sch.8 para.9, see *R. v Ibrahim (Muktar)* [2008] EWCA Crim 880, [2009] 1 W.L.R. 578 (CA (Crim Div)), Sir Igor Judge (President, QB)
Sch.14 para.6, applied: SI 2009/1593(a)
Sch.14 para.7, applied: SI 2009/1593(b), SI 2009/1593(c)
Sch.14 para.7, enabling: SI 2009/1593

12. Limited Liability Partnerships Act 2000
applied: SI 2009/1804 Sch.2 para.1, Sch.2 para.2, SI 2009/1941 Art.13
s.2, amended: SI 2009/1804 Sch.3 para.1
s.2, applied: SI 2009/1804 Sch.1 para.5

2000– cont.

12. Limited Liability Partnerships Act 2000– *cont.*
s.2, repealed (in part): SI 2009/1804 Sch.3 para.1
s.3, amended: SI 2009/1804 Sch.3 para.2
s.3, applied: SI 2009/2101 Sch.1 para.9
s.4, see *Kovats v TFO Management LLP* [2009] I.C.R. 1140 (EAT), Birtles, J.
s.4A, added: SI 2009/1804 Sch.3 para.3
s.8, repealed (in part): SI 2009/1804 Sch.3 para.4
s.9, amended: SI 2009/1804 Sch.3 para.5
s.9, applied: SI 2009/1804 Sch.1 para.5, Sch.1 para.6
s.9, repealed (in part): SI 2009/1804 Sch.3 para.5
s.14, amended: SI 2009/1804 Sch.3 para.6
s.14, enabling: SSI 2009/310
s.15, applied: SI 2009/2455
s.15, enabling: SI 2009/1804, SI 2009/1833, SI 2009/2404, SI 2009/2476, SI 2009/2995
s.17, amended: SI 2009/1804 Sch.3 para.7
s.17, applied: SI 2009/1804, SI 2009/2455
s.17, enabling: SI 2009/1804, SI 2009/1833, SI 2009/2404, SI 2009/2476, SI 2009/2995, SSI 2009/310
s.18, amended: SI 2009/1804 Sch.3 para.8
s.19, amended: SI 2009/1804 Sch.3 para.9
Sch.1 Part I para.3, repealed: SI 2009/1804 Sch.3 para.10
Sch.1 Part I para.4, amended: SI 2009/1804 Sch.3 para.10
Sch.1 Part I para.5, amended: SI 2009/1804 Sch.3 para.10
Sch.1 Part I para.5, applied: SI 2009/2101 Sch.1 para.9
Sch.1 Part I para.5, repealed (in part): SI 2009/1804 Sch.3 para.10
Sch.1 Part I para.8, repealed: SI 2009/1804 Sch.3 para.10
Sch.1 Part II para.9, repealed: SI 2009/1804 Sch.3 para.10
Sch.1 Part II para.10, repealed: SI 2009/1804 Sch.3 para.10

14. Care Standards Act 2000
see *A (A Child) (Residential Assessment), Re* [2009] EWHC 865 (Fam), [2009] 2 F.L.R. 443 (Fam Div), Munby, J.; see *W Primary Care Trust v B* [2009] EWHC 1737 (Fam), (2009) 12 C.C.L. Rep. 488 (Fam Div), Roderic Wood, J.
applied: SI 2009/462 Sch.3 para.11
Part VII, see *R. (on the application of Wright) v Secretary of State for Health* [2009] UKHL 3, [2009] 1 A.C. 739 (HL), Lord Phillips of Worth Matravers
s.5, amended: SI 2009/462 Sch.2 para.4
s.11, amended: SI 2009/462 Sch.2 para.4
s.11, applied: SI 2009/1547 Sch.3 para.1
s.12, amended: SI 2009/462 Sch.2 para.4
s.12, enabling: SI 2009/1895, SI 2009/2541
s.13, applied: SI 2009/1547 Sch.1 para.15
s.14, applied: SI 2009/1547 Sch.1 para.15
s.15, amended: SI 2009/462 Sch.2 para.4
s.16, amended: SI 2009/462 Sch.2 para.4
s.16, enabling: SI 2009/1895, SI 2009/2541, SI 2009/2724
s.20, see *Jain v Trent SHA* [2009] UKHL 4, [2009] 1 A.C. 853 (HL), Lord Scott of Foscote
s.20, applied: SI 2009/1547 Sch.1 para.15
s.22, amended: SI 2009/462 Sch.2 para.4
s.22, enabling: SI 2009/394, SI 2009/1895, SI 2009/2541, SI 2009/3258
s.24, applied: SI 2009/1547 Sch.3 para.1
s.25, applied: SI 2009/1547 Sch.3 para.1
s.26, applied: SI 2009/1547 Sch.3 para.1

2000–cont.

14. Care Standards Act 2000–*cont.*
s.27, applied: SI 2009/1547 Sch.3 para.1
s.29, amended: SI 2009/462 Sch.2 para.4
s.31, amended: SI 2009/462 Sch.2 para.4
s.31, applied: SI 2009/1360 Art.3
s.42, amended: SI 2009/462 Sch.2 para.4
s.43, referred to: SI 2009/2724 Reg.5
s.48, enabling: SI 2009/1895, SI 2009/2541
s.55, amended: SI 2009/462 Sch.2 para.4
s.55, repealed (in part): SI 2009/462 Sch.2 para.4
s.67, applied: SI 2009/1555 Reg.150, SI 2009/2737 Reg.109
s.81, applied: SI 2009/12 Art.2, Art.7, Art.7A, SI 2009/2610 Art.21, SI 2009/2611 Art.6, SSI 2009/4 Art.5
s.81, disapplied: SI 2009/12 Art.7A
s.82, see *Joyce v Secretary of State for Health* [2008] EWHC 1891 (Admin), [2009] 1 All E.R. 1025 (QBD (Admin)), Goldring, J.; see *R. (on the application of Wright) v Secretary of State for Health* [2009] UKHL 3, [2009] 1 A.C. 739 (HL), Lord Phillips of Worth Matravers
s.82, applied: SI 2009/12 Art.2, Art.3
s.83, applied: SI 2009/12 Art.2, Art.3
s.84, applied: SI 2009/12 Art.2, Art.3
s.85, disapplied: SI 2009/12 Art.3
s.86, see *Joyce v Secretary of State for Health* [2008] EWHC 1891 (Admin), [2009] 1 All E.R. 1025 (QBD (Admin)), Goldring, J.
s.86, applied: SI 2009/12 Art.7, Art.7A, SI 2009/2611 Art.6
s.87, applied: SI 2009/12 Art.7
s.89, applied: SI 2009/2611 Art.6
s.113A, amended: SI 2009/462 Sch.2 para.4
s.113A, applied: SI 2009/462 Art.6
s.118, enabling: SI 2009/394, SI 2009/1895, SI 2009/2541, SI 2009/2724
s.118A, enabling: SI 2009/3258

16. Carers and Disabled Children Act 2000
applied: 2009 c.24 s.39

17. Finance Act 2000
varied: SI 2009/317 Sch.1
s.18, repealed (in part): 2009 c.10 Sch.5 para.6
s.39, repealed (in part): 2009 c.10 Sch.1 para.6
s.46, amended: 2009 c.4 Sch.1 para.463
s.46, repealed (in part): 2009 c.4 Sch.3 Part 1
s.50, repealed: 2009 c.4 Sch.3 Part 1
s.69, repealed (in part): 2009 c.4 Sch.3 Part 1
s.88, repealed: 2009 c.4 Sch.3 Part 1
s.89, repealed: 2009 c.4 Sch.3 Part 1
s.101, repealed: 2009 c.10 Sch.12 para.4
s.130, amended: SI 2009/1890 Art.3
s.143, repealed (in part): 2009 c.4 Sch.3 Part 1
Sch.2 para.3, repealed (in part): 2009 c.10 s.22
Sch.6, applied: 2009 c.4 s.1303
Sch.6 Part I para.3, enabling: SI 2009/3338
Sch.6 Part IV para.40, amended: 2009 c.10 Sch.59 para.3
Sch.6 Part IV para.41, amended: 2009 c.10 Sch.59 para.4, SI 2009/571 Sch.1 para.30
Sch.6 Part IV para.42, amended: 2009 c.10 Sch.59 para.5
Sch.6 Part IV para.44, amended: 2009 c.10 s.117, Sch.59 para.6
Sch.6 Part IV para.45A, amended: 2009 c.10 Sch.59 para.7
Sch.6 Part IV para.45B, added: 2009 c.10 Sch.59 para.1
Sch.6 Part IV para.50, enabling: SI 2009/2458

2000–cont.

17. Finance Act 2000–*cont.*
Sch.6 Part V para.55, amended: SI 2009/571 Sch.1 para.30
Sch.6 Part VI para.64, amended: 2009 c.10 Sch.51 para.33
Sch.6 Part VI para.66, amended: 2009 c.10 Sch.51 para.34
Sch.6 Part VI para.70, applied: 2009 c.4 s.1303
Sch.6 Part VII para.80, amended: 2009 c.10 Sch.51 para.35
Sch.6 Part VII para.80, repealed (in part): 2009 c.10 Sch.51 para.35
Sch.6 Part VII para.81, applied: 2009 c.4 s.1303
Sch.6 Part VII para.82, applied: 2009 c.4 s.1303, 2009 c.10 s.108
Sch.6 Part VII para.83, applied: 2009 c.4 s.1303
Sch.6 Part VII para.84, applied: 2009 c.4 s.1303
Sch.6 Part VII para.85, applied: 2009 c.4 s.1303
Sch.6 Part VII para.91, amended: 2009 c.10 Sch.59 para.8
Sch.6 Part VIII para.99, amended: SI 2009/56 Sch.1 para.287
Sch.6 Part IX para.108, amended: 2009 c.10 Sch.51 para.36
Sch.6 Part IX para.108, repealed (in part): 2009 c.10 Sch.51 para.36
Sch.6 Part IX para.109, applied: 2009 c.4 s.1303
Sch.6 Part XI para.121, amended: SI 2009/56 Sch.1 para.288
Sch.6 Part XI para.121, repealed (in part): SI 2009/56 Sch.1 para.288
Sch.6 Part XI para.121A, added: SI 2009/56 Sch.1 para.289
Sch.6 Part XI para.121B, added: SI 2009/56 Sch.1 para.289
Sch.6 Part XI para.121C, added: SI 2009/56 Sch.1 para.289
Sch.6 Part XI para.121D, added: SI 2009/56 Sch.1 para.289
Sch.6 Part XI para.121E, added: SI 2009/56 Sch.1 para.289
Sch.6 Part XI para.121F, added: SI 2009/56 Sch.1 para.289
Sch.6 Part XI para.121G, added: SI 2009/56 Sch.1 para.289
Sch.6 Part XI para.122, amended: SI 2009/56 Sch.1 para.290
Sch.6 Part XI para.122, repealed (in part): SI 2009/56 Sch.1 para.290
Sch.6 Part XI para.123, amended: SI 2009/56 Sch.1 para.291
Sch.6 Part XI para.123, applied: SI 2009/56 Sch.3 para.9
Sch.6 Part XII para.124, amended: SI 2009/571 Sch.1 para.30
Sch.6 Part XII para.124, applied: SI 2009/3054 Art.6
Sch.6 Part XII para.124, repealed: SI 2009/3054 Sch.1 para.8
Sch.6 Part XII para.125, amended: 2009 c.10 Sch.50 para.19, SI 2009/571 Sch.1 para.30
Sch.6 Part XII para.126, repealed: 2009 c.10 Sch.50 para.20
Sch.6 Part XII para.127, amended: SI 2009/571 Sch.1 para.30
Sch.6 Part XII para.127, applied: SI 2009/3054 Art.6
Sch.6 Part XII para.127, repealed: SI 2009/3054 Sch.1 para.8

2000–cont.

17. Finance Act 2000–*cont.*

Sch.6 Part XII para.128, repealed: SI 2009/3054 Sch.1 para.8

Sch.6 Part XII para.129, repealed: SI 2009/3054 Sch.1 para.8

Sch.6 Part XIII para.146, amended: SI 2009/571 Sch.1 para.30

Sch.6 Part XIII para.146, applied: SI 2009/3338

Sch.6 Part XIII para.146, enabling: SI 2009/2458

Sch.6 Part XIV para.147, amended: 2009 c.10 s.117, Sch.59 para.9, SI 2009/56 Sch.1 para.292

Sch.12, see *Revenue and Customs Commissioners v Larkstar Data Ltd* [2008] EWHC 3284 (Ch), [2009] S.T.C. 1161 (Ch D), Sir Donald Rattee

Sch.12 para.1, see *Revenue and Customs Commissioners v Larkstar Data Ltd* [2008] EWHC 3284 (Ch), [2009] S.T.C. 1161 (Ch D), Sir Donald Rattee

Sch.12 Part III para.17, repealed: 2009 c.4 Sch.3 Part 1

Sch.12 Part III para.18, repealed: 2009 c.4 Sch.3 Part 1

Sch.15 Part IV para.36, amended: 2009 c.10 Sch.8 para.8

Sch.15 Part IV para.36, repealed (in part): 2009 c.10 Sch.8 para.8

Sch.15 Part VI para.60, amended: 2009 c.4 Sch.3 Part 1

Sch.15 Part X para.91, amended: SI 2009/56 Sch.1 para.293

Sch.15 Part X para.91, applied: SI 2009/275 Art.3

Sch.15 Part X para.92, amended: SI 2009/56 Sch.1 para.293

Sch.20 Part I para.1, repealed: 2009 c.4 Sch.3 Part 1

Sch.20 Part I para.2, repealed: 2009 c.4 Sch.3 Part 1

Sch.20 Part I para.3, repealed: 2009 c.4 Sch.3 Part 1

Sch.20 Part I para.4, repealed: 2009 c.4 Sch.3 Part 1

Sch.20 Part I para.5, repealed: 2009 c.4 Sch.3 Part 1

Sch.20 Part I para.6, repealed: 2009 c.4 Sch.3 Part 1

Sch.20 Part I para.6A, repealed: 2009 c.4 Sch.3 Part 1

Sch.20 Part I para.7, repealed: 2009 c.4 Sch.3 Part 1

Sch.20 Part I para.8, repealed: 2009 c.4 Sch.3 Part 1

Sch.20 Part I para.8A, repealed: 2009 c.4 Sch.3 Part 1

Sch.20 Part I para.8B, repealed: 2009 c.4 Sch.3 Part 1

Sch.20 Part I para.8C, repealed: 2009 c.4 Sch.3 Part 1

Sch.20 Part I para.8D, repealed: 2009 c.4 Sch.3 Part 1

Sch.20 Part I para.8E, repealed: 2009 c.4 Sch.3 Part 1

Sch.20 Part I para.9, repealed: 2009 c.4 Sch.3 Part 1

Sch.20 Part I para.10, repealed: 2009 c.4 Sch.3 Part 1

Sch.20 Part I para.11, repealed: 2009 c.4 Sch.3 Part 1

Sch.20 Part I para.12, repealed: 2009 c.4 Sch.3 Part 1

Sch.20 Part II para.13, repealed: 2009 c.4 Sch.3 Part 1

Sch.20 Part II para.14, repealed: 2009 c.4 Sch.3 Part 1

Sch.20 Part II para.15, repealed: 2009 c.4 Sch.3 Part 1

Sch.20 Part II para.16, repealed: 2009 c.4 Sch.3 Part 1

Sch.20 Part II para.17, repealed: 2009 c.4 Sch.3 Part 1

2000–cont.

17. Finance Act 2000–*cont.*

Sch.20 Part II para.18, repealed: 2009 c.4 Sch.3 Part 1

Sch.20 Part II para.18A, repealed: 2009 c.4 Sch.3 Part 1

Sch.20 Part II para.19, repealed: 2009 c.4 Sch.3 Part 1

Sch.20 Part II para.20, repealed: 2009 c.4 Sch.3 Part 1

Sch.20 Part III para.21, repealed: 2009 c.4 Sch.3 Part 1

Sch.20 Part III para.22, repealed: 2009 c.4 Sch.3 Part 1

Sch.20 Part III para.23, repealed: 2009 c.4 Sch.3 Part 1

Sch.20 Part III para.24, repealed: 2009 c.4 Sch.3 Part 1

Sch.20 Part III para.25, repealed: 2009 c.4 Sch.3 Part 1

Sch.20 Part III para.26, repealed: 2009 c.4 Sch.3 Part 1

Sch.22, applied: 2009 c.10 Sch.15 para.75

Sch.22 Part IV para.29, enabling: SI 2009/2304

Sch.22 Part IV para.31, enabling: SI 2009/2304

Sch.22 Part IV para.36, enabling: SI 2009/2304

Sch.22 Part V para.43, amended: SI 2009/56 Sch.1 para.294

Sch.22 Part VI para.50, amended: 2009 c.4 Sch.1 para.470

Sch.22 Part VI para.51, amended: 2009 c.4 Sch.1 para.470

Sch.22 Part VII para.61, amended: 2009 c.4 Sch.1 para.470

Sch.22 Part VII para.61, applied: 2009 c.10 Sch.15 para.75

Sch.22 Part VII para.62, amended: 2009 c.4 Sch.1 para.470

Sch.22 Part VII para.62, applied: 2009 c.10 Sch.15 para.75

Sch.22 Part VII para.63, amended: 2009 c.4 Sch.1 para.470

Sch.22 Part XII para.126, amended: SI 2009/56 Sch.1 para.294

Sch.23, applied: 2009 c.4 s.897

Sch.29 Part II para.44, repealed: 2009 c.4 Sch.3 Part 1

Sch.30 para.8, repealed (in part): 2009 c.10 Sch.14 para.30

Sch.30 para.13, repealed: 2009 c.10 Sch.16 para.5

Sch.30 para.21, repealed: 2009 c.10 Sch.14 para.30

Sch.30 para.22, repealed: 2009 c.10 Sch.14 para.30

Sch.31 para.7, repealed (in part): 2009 c.10 Sch.16 para.11

Sch.38, applied: 2009 c.4 s.1287

Sch.38 para.4, amended: SI 2009/56 Sch.1 para.295

19. Child Support, Pensions and Social Security Act 2000

referred to: SI 2009/396 Reg.7

s.16, repealed (in part): 2009 c.24 Sch.7 Part 4

s.62, repealed: 2009 c.24 s.26, Sch.7 Part 3

s.63, repealed: 2009 c.24 s.26, Sch.7 Part 3

s.64, repealed: 2009 c.24 s.26, Sch.7 Part 3

s.65, repealed: 2009 c.24 s.26, Sch.7 Part 3

s.66, repealed: 2009 c.24 s.26, Sch.7 Part 3

20. Government Resources and Accounts Act 2000

s.2, applied: 2009 c.2 s.5, Sch.2 Part 2, Sch.2 Part 3, 2009 c.9 s.3, Sch.2 Part 1, Sch.2 Part 2, Sch.2 Part 3, Sch.2 Part 4, Sch.2 Part 5, Sch.2 Part 6, Sch.2 Part 7, Sch.2 Part 8, Sch.2 Part 9, Sch.2 Part 10,

2000–cont.

20. Government Resources and Accounts Act 2000– *cont.*

s.2, applied:–*cont.*

Sch.2 Part 11, Sch.2 Part 12, Sch.2 Part 13, Sch.2 Part 14, Sch.2 Part 15, Sch.2 Part 16, Sch.2 Part 17, Sch.2 Part 18, Sch.2 Part 19, Sch.2 Part 20, Sch.2 Part 21, Sch.2 Part 22, Sch.2 Part 23, Sch.2 Part 24, Sch.2 Part 25, Sch.2 Part 26, Sch.2 Part 27, Sch.2 Part 28, Sch.2 Part 29, Sch.2 Part 30, Sch.2 Part 31, Sch.2 Part 32, Sch.2 Part 33, Sch.2 Part 34, Sch.2 Part 35, Sch.2 Part 36, Sch.2 Part 37, Sch.2 Part 38, Sch.2 Part 39, Sch.2 Part 40, Sch.2 Part 41, Sch.2 Part 42, Sch.2 Part 43, Sch.2 Part 44, Sch.2 Part 45, Sch.2 Part 46, Sch.2 Part 47, Sch.2 Part 48, Sch.2 Part 49, Sch.2 Part 50, Sch.2 Part 51, Sch.2 Part 52, Sch.2 Part 53, Sch.2 Part 54, Sch.2 Part 55, Sch.2 Part 56, Sch.2 Part 57

s.10, applied: SI 2009/1973, SI 2009/1973 Art.2

s.10, enabling: SI 2009/1973

s.25, applied: SI 2009/476

s.25, enabling: SI 2009/476

21. Learning and Skills Act 2000

referred to: 2009 c.1 s.46

s.1, repealed: 2009 c.22 Sch.6 para.15, Sch.16 Part 2

s.2, repealed: 2009 c.22 Sch.6 para.16, Sch.16 Part 2

s.3, repealed: 2009 c.22 Sch.6 para.17, Sch.16 Part 2

s.3A, repealed: 2009 c.22 Sch.16 Part 2

s.3B, repealed: 2009 c.22 Sch.16 Part 2

s.3C, repealed: 2009 c.22 Sch.16 Part 2

s.3D, repealed: 2009 c.22 Sch.16 Part 2

s.4, repealed: 2009 c.22 Sch.6 para.18, Sch.16 Part 2

s.4A, applied: SI 2009/1602 Reg.8, Reg.9

s.4A, repealed: 2009 c.22 Sch.6 para.19, Sch.16 Part 2

s.4A, enabling: SI 2009/1602

s.4B, applied: SI 2009/1602 Reg.8, Reg.9

s.4B, repealed: 2009 c.22 Sch.6 para.19, Sch.16 Part 2

s.4B, enabling: SI 2009/1602

s.4C, repealed: 2009 c.22 Sch.6 para.19, Sch.16 Part 2

s.4C, enabling: SI 2009/1602

s.5, repealed: 2009 c.22 Sch.6 para.20, Sch.16 Part 2

s.6, repealed: 2009 c.22 Sch.6 para.21, Sch.16 Part 2

s.7, repealed: 2009 c.22 Sch.6 para.22, Sch.16 Part 2

s.8, repealed: 2009 c.22 Sch.6 para.23, Sch.16 Part 2

s.9, repealed: 2009 c.22 Sch.6 para.24, Sch.16 Part 2

s.10, repealed: 2009 c.22 Sch.6 para.25, Sch.16 Part 2

s.11, repealed: 2009 c.22 Sch.6 para.26, Sch.16 Part 2

s.11A, repealed: 2009 c.22 Sch.6 para.27, Sch.16 Part 2

s.12, repealed: 2009 c.22 Sch.6 para.28, Sch.16 Part 2

s.13, repealed: 2009 c.22 Sch.6 para.29, Sch.16 Part 2

s.14, repealed: 2009 c.22 Sch.6 para.30, Sch.16 Part 2

s.14A, repealed: 2009 c.22 Sch.6 para.31, Sch.16 Part 2

s.15, repealed: 2009 c.22 Sch.6 para.32, Sch.16 Part 2

s.16, repealed: 2009 c.22 Sch.6 para.33, Sch.16 Part 2

s.17, repealed: 2009 c.22 Sch.6 para.34, Sch.16 Part 2

s.18, repealed: 2009 c.22 Sch.6 para.35, Sch.16 Part 2

s.18A, repealed: 2009 c.22 Sch.6 para.36, Sch.16 Part 2

s.18B, repealed: 2009 c.22 Sch.6 para.36, Sch.16 Part 2

s.18C, repealed: 2009 c.22 Sch.6 para.36, Sch.16 Part 2

s.19, repealed: 2009 c.22 Sch.16 Part 2

s.20, repealed: 2009 c.22 Sch.16 Part 2

2000–cont.

21. Learning and Skills Act 2000–*cont.*

s.21, repealed: 2009 c.22 Sch.16 Part 2

s.22, repealed: 2009 c.22 Sch.16 Part 2

s.23, repealed: 2009 c.22 Sch.16 Part 2

s.24, repealed: 2009 c.22 Sch.16 Part 2

s.24A, repealed: 2009 c.22 Sch.6 para.37, Sch.16 Part 2

s.24B, repealed: 2009 c.22 Sch.6 para.37, Sch.16 Part 2

s.24C, repealed: 2009 c.22 Sch.6 para.37, Sch.16 Part 2

s.25, repealed: 2009 c.22 Sch.6 para.38, Sch.16 Part 2

s.26, repealed: 2009 c.22 Sch.6 para.39, Sch.16 Part 2

s.27, repealed: 2009 c.22 Sch.6 para.40, Sch.16 Part 2

s.28, repealed: 2009 c.22 Sch.6 para.41, Sch.16 Part 2

s.29, repealed: 2009 c.22 Sch.6 para.42, Sch.16 Part 2

s.31, amended: 2009 c.1 s.21, Sch.1 para.4

s.32, amended: 2009 c.1 Sch.1 para.2, Sch.1 para.5

s.33, amended: 2009 c.1 Sch.1 para.2

s.33A, added: 2009 c.1 s.22

s.33B, added: 2009 c.1 s.23

s.33C, added: 2009 c.1 s.24

s.33D, added: 2009 c.1 s.25

s.33E, added: 2009 c.1 s.26

s.33F, added: 2009 c.1 s.27

s.33G, added: 2009 c.1 s.28

s.33H, added: 2009 c.1 s.29

s.33I, added: 2009 c.1 s.30

s.33J, added: 2009 c.1 s.31

s.33K, added: 2009 c.1 s.32

s.33L, added: 2009 c.1 s.33

s.33M, added: 2009 c.1 s.34

s.33N, added: 2009 c.1 s.35

s.33O, added: 2009 c.1 s.36

s.33P, added: 2009 c.1 s.37

s.33Q, added: 2009 c.1 s.38

s.34, amended: 2009 c.1 Sch.1 para.2, Sch.1 para.6

s.35, amended: 2009 c.1 Sch.1 para.2, Sch.1 para.7

s.36, amended: 2009 c.1 Sch.1 para.2

s.37, amended: 2009 c.1 Sch.1 para.2, Sch.1 para.8

s.38, amended: 2009 c.1 Sch.1 para.2

s.39, amended: 2009 c.1 Sch.1 para.2

s.40, amended: 2009 c.1 Sch.1 para.2, Sch.1 para.9

s.41, amended: 2009 c.1 Sch.1 para.2, Sch.1 para.10

s.96, amended: 2009 c.22 Sch.12 para.27

s.96, applied: SI 2009/1563 Reg.3

s.97, repealed: 2009 c.22 Sch.6 para.43, Sch.16 Part 2

s.98, amended: 2009 c.22 Sch.6 para.44, Sch.12 para.28

s.98, applied: 2009 c.22 s.141, SI 2009/1563 Reg.3

s.98, repealed (in part): 2009 c.22 Sch.6 para.44, Sch.16 Part 2

s.99, amended: 2009 c.22 Sch.6 para.45, Sch.12 para.29

s.99, repealed (in part): 2009 c.22 Sch.6 para.45, Sch.16 Part 2

s.100, amended: 2009 c.22 Sch.6 para.46

s.101, amended: 2009 c.22 Sch.6 para.47

s.101, repealed (in part): 2009 c.22 Sch.6 para.47, Sch.16 Part 2

s.102, amended: 2009 c.22 Sch.6 para.48

s.102, repealed (in part): 2009 c.22 Sch.6 para.48, Sch.16 Part 2

s.103, repealed (in part): 2009 c.22 Sch.16 Part 4

21. Learning and Skills Act 2000– *cont.*
s.113A, repealed (in part): 2009 c.22 Sch.6 para.49, Sch.16 Part 2
s.126, amended: 2009 c.1 s.42
s.127, amended: 2009 c.1 s.42
s.139A, applied: 2009 c.22 s.62, s.101
s.140, applied: 2009 c.22 s.62, s.101
s.141, amended: SI 2009/1941 Sch.1 para.182
s.152, amended: 2009 c.1 s.39
s.152, enabling: SI 2009/1602
Sch.1 para.1, repealed: 2009 c.22 Sch.6 para.50, Sch.16 Part 2
Sch.1 para.2, repealed: 2009 c.22 Sch.6 para.50, Sch.16 Part 2
Sch.1 para.3, repealed: 2009 c.22 Sch.6 para.50, Sch.16 Part 2
Sch.1 para.4, repealed: 2009 c.22 Sch.6 para.50, Sch.16 Part 2
Sch.1 para.5, repealed: 2009 c.22 Sch.6 para.50, Sch.16 Part 2
Sch.1 para.6, repealed: 2009 c.22 Sch.6 para.50, Sch.16 Part 2
Sch.1 para.7, repealed: 2009 c.22 Sch.6 para.50, Sch.16 Part 2
Sch.1 para.8, repealed: 2009 c.22 Sch.6 para.50, Sch.16 Part 2
Sch.1 para.9, repealed: 2009 c.22 Sch.6 para.50, Sch.16 Part 2
Sch.1 para.10, repealed: 2009 c.22 Sch.6 para.50, Sch.16 Part 2
Sch.1 para.11, repealed: 2009 c.22 Sch.6 para.50, Sch.16 Part 2
Sch.1 para.12, repealed: 2009 c.22 Sch.6 para.50, Sch.16 Part 2
Sch.1 para.13, repealed: 2009 c.22 Sch.6 para.50, Sch.16 Part 2
Sch.1 para.14, repealed: 2009 c.22 Sch.6 para.50, Sch.16 Part 2
Sch.1 para.15, repealed: 2009 c.22 Sch.6 para.50, Sch.16 Part 2
Sch.1A Part I para.1, applied: SI 2009/1602 Reg.3, Reg.4, Reg.5
Sch.1A Part I para.1, repealed: 2009 c.22 Sch.6 para.51, Sch.16 Part 2
Sch.1A Part I para.2, applied: SI 2009/1602 Reg.6
Sch.1A Part I para.2, repealed: 2009 c.22 Sch.6 para.51, Sch.16 Part 2
Sch.1A Part II para.3, applied: SI 2009/1602 Reg.10
Sch.1A Part II para.3, repealed: 2009 c.22 Sch.6 para.51, Sch.16 Part 2
Sch.1A Part II para.3, enabling: SI 2009/1602
Sch.1A Part II para.4, applied: SI 2009/1602 Reg.10
Sch.1A Part II para.4, disapplied: SI 2009/1602 Reg.3
Sch.1A Part II para.4, repealed: 2009 c.22 Sch.6 para.51, Sch.16 Part 2
Sch.1A Part I para.5, disapplied: SI 2009/1602 Reg.4
Sch.1A Part II para.5, repealed: 2009 c.22 Sch.6 para.51, Sch.16 Part 2
Sch.1A Part II para.6, disapplied: SI 2009/1602 Reg.5
Sch.1A Part II para.6, repealed: 2009 c.22 Sch.6 para.51, Sch.16 Part 2
Sch.1A Part II para.7, disapplied: SI 2009/1602 Reg.6
Sch.1A Part II para.7, repealed: 2009 c.22 Sch.6 para.51, Sch.16 Part 2
Sch.1A Part II para.8, repealed: 2009 c.22 Sch.6 para.51, Sch.16 Part 2

21. Learning and Skills Act 2000– *cont.*
Sch.1A Part II para.9, repealed: 2009 c.22 Sch.6 para.51, Sch.16 Part 2
Sch.3 para.1, repealed: 2009 c.22 Sch.6 para.52, Sch.16 Part 2
Sch.3 para.2, repealed: 2009 c.22 Sch.6 para.52, Sch.16 Part 2
Sch.3 para.3, repealed: 2009 c.22 Sch.6 para.52, Sch.16 Part 2
Sch.3 para.4, repealed: 2009 c.22 Sch.6 para.52, Sch.16 Part 2
Sch.3 para.5, repealed: 2009 c.22 Sch.6 para.52, Sch.16 Part 2
Sch.3 para.6, repealed: 2009 c.22 Sch.6 para.52, Sch.16 Part 2
Sch.3 para.7, repealed: 2009 c.22 Sch.6 para.52, Sch.16 Part 2
Sch.3 para.8, repealed: 2009 c.22 Sch.6 para.52, Sch.16 Part 2
Sch.3 para.9, repealed: 2009 c.22 Sch.6 para.52, Sch.16 Part 2
Sch.3 para.10, repealed: 2009 c.22 Sch.6 para.52, Sch.16 Part 2
Sch.7A para.1, amended: 2009 c.22 Sch.6 para.53, Sch.16 Part 2
Sch.7A para.3, repealed (in part): 2009 c.22 Sch.6 para.53, Sch.16 Part 2
Sch.7A para.5, repealed (in part): 2009 c.22 Sch.6 para.53, Sch.16 Part 2
Sch.7A para.6, repealed (in part): 2009 c.22 Sch.6 para.53, Sch.16 Part 2
Sch.7A para.7, repealed (in part): 2009 c.22 Sch.6 para.53, Sch.16 Part 2
Sch.9 para.69, repealed: 2009 c.22 Sch.16 Part 4

22. Local Government Act 2000
applied: SI 2009/276 Reg.6, SI 2009/486 Reg.6, SI 2009/1976 r.22
Part III, applied: SI 2009/1255 Reg.3, Reg.14
Part III, disapplied: SI 2009/1255 Reg.14
Part III c.I, applied: 2009 c.23 s.151
s.2, amended: 2009 c.2 Sch.2 para.2
s.4, amended: 2009 c.2 Sch.2 para.3
s.4, repealed (in part): 2009 c.2 Sch.2 para.3, Sch.4
s.6, enabling: SI 2009/714
s.11, applied: 2009 c.23 s.20
s.13, see *R. (on the application of Domb) v Hammersmith and Fulham LBC* [2008] EWHC 3277 (Admin), [2009] B.L.G.R. 340 (QBD (Admin)), Sir Michael Harrison
s.13, applied: 2009 c.23 s.20
s.13, enabling: SI 2009/2983
s.14, applied: 2009 c.23 s.20
s.15, applied: 2009 c.23 s.20
s.16, applied: 2009 c.23 s.20
s.17, applied: 2009 c.23 s.20
s.18, applied: 2009 c.23 s.20
s.20, applied: 2009 c.23 s.20
s.21, amended: 2009 c.20 s.32
s.21, applied: 2009 c.20 s.16, s.17
s.21B, applied: SI 2009/1919 Reg.8, Reg.14, Reg.15
s.21C, applied: SI 2009/1919 Reg.8, Reg.9
s.21D, applied: SI 2009/1919 Reg.8
s.21E, applied: SI 2009/1919 Reg.4
s.21E, referred to: SI 2009/1919 Reg.3
s.21E, enabling: SI 2009/1919
s.21ZA, added: 2009 c.20 s.31
s.22, enabling: SI 2009/1919
s.22A, applied: SI 2009/1919 Reg.9
s.22A, enabling: SI 2009/1919

2000– cont.

22. Local Government Act 2000– *cont.*
s.32, enabling: SI 2009/ 2993
s.39, applied: SI 2009/ 3112 Reg.10
s.49, amended: 2009 c.20 Sch.6 para.93
s.49, applied: SI 2009/ 467 Reg.14
s.53, applied: SI 2009/ 1255 Reg.14
s.53, varied: SI 2009/ 1255 Reg.14
s.53, enabling: SI 2009/ 1255
s.56A, enabling: SI 2009/ 1255
s.57A, applied: SI 2009/ 276 Reg.6, Reg.7, SI 2009/ 1255 Reg.9, Reg.10, Reg.11, Reg.15
s.57A, varied: SI 2009/ 1255 Reg.9, Reg.10
s.57B, applied: SI 2009/ 276 Reg.7, SI 2009/ 1255 Reg.11
s.57B, disapplied: SI 2009/ 1255 Reg.11
s.57C, varied: SI 2009/ 1255 Reg.9, Reg.10
s.57D, applied: SI 2009/ 1255 Reg.3, Reg.4, Reg.5, Reg.6, Reg.7, Reg.8, Reg.9, Reg.10, Reg.11, Reg.12
s.57D, enabling: SI 2009/ 1255
s.58, applied: SI 2009/ 486 Reg.6
s.58, varied: SI 2009/ 1255 Reg.9
s.58, applied: SI 2009/ 1255 Reg.9
s.63, applied: SI 2009/ 1976 r.22
s.65, applied: SI 2009/ 1976 r.22
s.67, applied: SI 2009/ 1255 Reg.12
s.73, enabling: SI 2009/ 2578
s.75, applied: SI 2009/ 276 Reg.5
s.77, enabling: SI 2009/ 2578
s.78A, applied: SI 2009/ 2267 Reg.4, Reg.5
s.79, applied: SI 2009/ 2267 Reg.4, Reg.5
s.81, applied: SI 2009/ 1255 Reg.18
s.81, enabling: SI 2009/ 1255
s.86, enabling: SI 2009/ 2734
s.89, repealed (in part): 2009 c.20 Sch.7 Part 3
s.93, referred to: SI 2009/ 2687 Art.2
s.105, enabling: SI 2009/ 714, SI 2009/ 1255, SI 2009/ 1919, SI 2009/ 2578, SI 2009/ 2983, SI 2009/ 2993
s.106, enabling: SI 2009/ 2983, SI 2009/ 2993

23. Regulation of Investigatory Powers Act 2000
Part I, applied: 2009 c.11 s.19, 2009 c.23 Sch.10 para.9
Part I, disapplied: 2009 c.23 Sch.7 para.13
Part II, applied: SI 2009/ 3404 Art.3
Part II, see *C's Application for Judicial Review, Re* [2009] UKHL 15, [2009] 1 A.C. 908 (HL (NI)), Lord Phillips of Worth Matravers
s.3, amended: 2009 c.26 s.100
s.5, applied: SI 2009/ 989 Sch.1
s.15, referred to: SI 2009/ 989 Sch.1
s.17, see *A v HM Treasury* [2008] EWCA Civ 1187, [2009] 3 W.L.R. 25 (CA (Civ Div)), Sir Anthony Clarke, M.R.
s.17, amended: 2009 c.26 s.100
s.17, applied: SI 2009/ 988 Art.4, Art.13, Art.14
s.22, amended: 2009 c.26 s.7, Sch.7 para.13
s.23, amended: 2009 c.26 s.7, Sch.7 para.14
s.28, see *C's Application for Judicial Review, Re* [2009] UKHL 15, [2009] 1 A.C. 908 (HL (NI)), Lord Phillips of Worth Matravers
s.29, amended: 2009 c.26 s.8
s.29, applied: SI 2009/ 3404 Art.3, Art.4, Art.5, Art.6
s.29, enabling: SI 2009/ 3404
s.33, amended: 2009 c.26 s.9
s.43, referred to: SI 2009/ 3404 Art.5
s.43, varied: SI 2009/ 3404 Art.8
s.43, enabling: SI 2009/ 3404
s.46, enabling: SI 2009/ 3403

2000– cont.

23. Regulation of Investigatory Powers Act 2000– cont.
s.49, see *R. v S* [2008] EWCA Crim 2177, [2009] 1 W.L.R. 1489 (CA (Crim Div)), Sir Igor Judge (President, QB)
s.49, amended: 2009 c.26 Sch.7 para.15
s.49, applied: SI 2009/ 2056 Art.30
s.49, referred to: 2009 c.26 s.26
s.53, see *R. v S* [2008] EWCA Crim 2177, [2009] 1 W.L.R. 1489 (CA (Crim Div)), Sir Igor Judge (President, QB)
s.53, amended: 2009 c.26 s.26
s.58, amended: 2009 c.26 Sch.7 para.16
s.65, see *A v B (Investigatory Powers Tribunal: Jurisdiction)* [2009] EWCA Civ 24, [2009] 3 W.L.R. 717 (CA (Civ Div)), Laws, L.J.; see *A v B (Investigatory Powers Tribunal: Jurisdiction)* [2009] UKSC 12 (SC), Lord Phillips (President)
s.68, amended: 2009 c.26 Sch.7 para.17
Sch.1 Part I para.9ZA, repealed: SI 2009/ 2748 Sch.1 para.6
Sch.1 Part I para.9ZB, added: SI 2009/ 2748 Sch.1 para.6
Sch.1 Part I para.10ZB, added: SI 2009/ 229 Sch.2 para.3
Sch.3, applied: 2009 c.26 s.27

26. Postal Services Act 2000
applied: 2009 c.4 s.12, SI 2009/ 1885 Art.2, Sch.4 para.1
s.4, applied: SSI 2009/ 352 Sch.1 para.21
s.40, amended: SI 2009/ 1941 Sch.1 para.183
s.63, amended: SI 2009/ 1941 Sch.1 para.183
s.80, amended: SI 2009/ 1941 Sch.1 para.183
s.94, amended: SI 2009/ 1885 Sch.1 para.25
s.105, amended: 2009 c.26 s.99
s.125, amended: SI 2009/ 1941 Sch.1 para.183
s.125, referred to: SSI 2009/ 95 Art.5, SSI 2009/ 146 Art.5, SSI 2009/ 149 Art.3
Sch.5 Part II para.8, amended: SI 2009/ 1307 Sch.1 para.266
Sch.5 Part II para.8, substituted: SI 2009/ 1307 Sch.1 para.266
Sch.6 para.5, amended: SI 2009/ 1307 Sch.1 para.267

27. Utilities Act 2000
s.103, applied: SI 2009/ 1904, SI 2009/ 1905
s.103, enabling: SI 2009/ 1904, SI 2009/ 1905

31. Warm Homes and Energy Conservation Act 2000
s.2, see *Friends of the Earth v Secretary of State for Business Enterprise and Regulatory Reform* [2008] EWHC 2518 (Admin), [2009] A.C.D. 25 (QBD (Admin)), McCombe, J.

32. Police (Northern Ireland) Act 2000
s.66, see *Officer O's Application for Judicial Review, Re* [2009] N.I. 55 (QBD (NI)), Gillen, J.

33. Fur Farming (Prohibition) Act 2000
s.5, amended: SI 2009/ 1307 Sch.1 para.268

35. Children (Leaving Care) Act 2000
s.6, amended: 2009 c.24 Sch.7 Part 1

36. Freedom of Information Act 2000
see *BBC v Sugar* [2009] UKHL 9, [2009] 1 W.L.R. 430 (HL), Lord Phillips of Worth Matravers; see *Financial Services Authority v Information Commissioner* [2009] EWHC 1548 (Admin), [2009] Bus. L.R. 1287 (QBD (Admin)), Munby, J.; see *Galloway v Information Commissioner* (2009) 108 B.M.L.R. 50 (Information Tr), Claire Taylor; see *R. (on the application of Hasan) v Secretary of State for Trade and*

2000–cont.

36. Freedom of Information Act 2000–*cont.*
see–*cont.*

Industry [2008] EWCA Civ 1312, [2009] 3 All
E.R. 539 (CA (Civ Div)), Sir Anthony May (President, QB); see *Secretary of State for the Home
Department v British Union for the Abolition of
Vivisection* [2008] EWCA Civ 870, [2009] 1
W.L.R. 636 (CA (Civ Div)), Lord Phillips of
Worth Matravers, L.C.J.

applied: 2009 c.23 s.24, SI 2009/309 Reg.8, SI
2009/1976 r.19, SI 2009/3243 Reg.14, SI 2009/
3342 Reg.16, Reg.36

Part IV, applied: 2009 c.22 s.215

s.1, see *BBC v Sugar* [2009] UKHL 9, [2009] 1
W.L.R. 430 (HL), Lord Phillips of Worth
Matravers; see *Corporate Officer of the House
of Commons v Information Commissioner*
[2008] EWHC 1084 (Admin), [2009] 3 All E.R.
403 (DC), Sir Igor Judge (President, QB)

s.3, applied: SI 2009/814 Art.8, SI 2009/3226 Art.19

s.7, see *BBC v Sugar* [2009] UKHL 9, [2009] 1
W.L.R. 430 (HL), Lord Phillips of Worth
Matravers

s.10, applied: SI 2009/1369 Reg.2

s.10, enabling: SI 2009/1369

s.17, see *Galloway v Information Commissioner*
(2009) 108 B.M.L.R. 50 (Information Tr),
Claire Taylor

s.19, see *Corporate Officer of the House of
Commons v Information Commissioner* [2008]
EWHC 1084 (Admin), [2009] 3 All E.R. 403
(DC), Sir Igor Judge (President, QB)

s.19, applied: 2009 c.13 Sch.1 para.27

s.25, see *Glasgow City Council v Scottish
Information Commissioner* [2009] CSIH 73
(IH (Ex Div)), Lord Reed

s.30, varied: SI 2009/1059 Sch.1 para.46

s.31, see *Galloway v Information Commissioner*
(2009) 108 B.M.L.R. 50 (Information Tr),
Claire Taylor

s.32, amended: 2009 c.25 Sch.21 para.44

s.36, see *Galloway v Information Commissioner*
(2009) 108 B.M.L.R. 50 (Information Tr),
Claire Taylor

s.40, see *Galloway v Information Commissioner*
(2009) 108 B.M.L.R. 50 (Information Tr),
Claire Taylor

s.41, see *Galloway v Information Commissioner*
(2009) 108 B.M.L.R. 50 (Information Tr),
Claire Taylor; see *Secretary of State for the
Home Department v British Union for the
Abolition of Vivisection* [2008] EWCA Civ 870,
[2009] 1 W.L.R. 636 (CA (Civ Div)), Lord
Phillips of Worth Matravers, L.C.J.

s.41, referred to: SI 2009/3243 Reg.14

s.43, see *Financial Services Authority v Information
Commissioner* [2009] EWHC 1548 (Admin),
[2009] Bus. L.R. 1287 (QBD (Admin)), Munby, J.

s.43, referred to: SI 2009/3243 Reg.14

s.44, see *Secretary of State for the Home
Department v British Union for the Abolition of
Vivisection* [2008] EWCA Civ 870, [2009] 1
W.L.R. 636 (CA (Civ Div)), Lord Phillips of
Worth Matravers, L.C.J.

s.44, applied: 2009 c.11 s.19

s.48, applied: 2009 c.22 s.215

s.50, see *BBC v Sugar* [2009] UKHL 9, [2009] 1
W.L.R. 430 (HL), Lord Phillips of Worth
Matravers; see *Corporate Officer of the House
of Commons v Information Commissioner*

2000–cont.

36. Freedom of Information Act 2000–*cont.*
s.50–*cont.*

[2008] EWHC 1084 (Admin), [2009] 3 All E.R.
403 (DC), Sir Igor Judge (President, QB)

s.50, varied: SI 2009/3157 Reg.11

s.51, varied: SI 2009/3157 Reg.11

s.52, varied: SI 2009/3157 Reg.11

s.54, varied: SI 2009/3157 Reg.11

s.55, varied: SI 2009/3157 Reg.11

s.56, varied: SI 2009/3157 Reg.11

s.57, see *Corporate Officer of the House of
Commons v Information Commissioner* [2008]
EWHC 1084 (Admin), [2009] 3 All E.R. 403
(DC), Sir Igor Judge (President, QB)

s.57, varied: SI 2009/3157 Reg.11

s.58, varied: SI 2009/3157 Reg.11

s.59, varied: SI 2009/3157 Reg.11

s.60, applied: SI 2009/1976 r.19, r.22

s.61, varied: SI 2009/3157 Reg.11

s.68, see *BBC v Sugar* [2009] UKHL 9, [2009] 1
W.L.R. 430 (HL), Lord Phillips of Worth
Matravers

s.76, amended: 2009 c.21 Sch.5 para.14

s.76, applied: SI 2009/3157 Reg.11

s.77, applied: 2009 c.22 s.215

s.82, applied: SI 2009/1369

Sch.1 Part II para.19A, added: 2009 c.20 Sch.6
para.94

Sch.1 Part II para.19B, added: 2009 c.20 Sch.6
para.94

Sch.1 Part II para.35A, repealed: 2009 c.23 Sch.22
Part 4

Sch.1 Part II para.35B, added: 2009 c.23 Sch.14
para.19

Sch.1 Part VI, amended: 2009 c.13 Sch.1 para.27,
Sch.2 para.10, 2009 c.20 Sch.1 para.21, Sch.7
Part 3, 2009 c.22 Sch.12 para.30, 2009 c.23
Sch.2 para.6, 2009 c.25 Sch.21 para.82, Sch.23
Part 4, 2009 c.26 s.2, SI 2009/56 Sch.1 para.296

Sch.1 Part VII, amended: SI 2009/56 Sch.1
para.296

Sch.3 para.1, varied: SI 2009/3157 Reg.11

Sch.3 para.8, varied: SI 2009/3157 Reg.11

Sch.3 para.12, applied: SI 2009/3157 Reg.11

Sch.3 para.13, applied: SI 2009/3157 Reg.11

Sch.4 para.3, varied: SI 2009/3157 Reg.11

Sch.4 para.4, varied: SI 2009/3157 Reg.11

37. Countryside and Rights of Way Act 2000
Part I, referred to: 2009 c.23 s.307

Part I c.II, applied: 2009 c.23 s.305

Part I c.III, applied: 2009 c.23 Sch.20 para.1

s.1, amended: 2009 c.23 s.303, Sch.22 Part 7

s.1, applied: 2009 c.23 s.296

s.2, amended: 2009 c.23 s.303

s.2, applied: 2009 c.23 Sch.20 para.2, Sch.20 para.10

s.3, amended: 2009 c.23 s.303

s.3A, added: 2009 c.23 s.303

s.3A, applied: 2009 c.23 s.296, Sch.20 para.6, Sch.20
para.10

s.6, applied: 2009 c.23 Sch.20 para.4

s.7, applied: 2009 c.23 Sch.20 para.4

s.8, applied: 2009 c.23 Sch.20 para.4

s.15, referred to: 2009 c.23 s.296, Sch.20 para.9

s.16, amended: 2009 c.23 s.303, Sch.22 Part 7

s.19, amended: 2009 c.23 Sch.20 para.7

s.19, applied: 2009 c.23 Sch.20 para.8, Sch.20 para.9

s.20, amended: 2009 c.23 s.303, Sch.22 Part 7

s.24, applied: 2009 c.23 s.305

s.25, applied: 2009 c.23 s.305

2000–cont.

37. Countryside and Rights of Way Act 2000–*cont.*
s.27, applied: 2009 c.23 s.305
s.35, applied: 2009 c.23 s.308, Sch.20 para.5, Sch.20 para.9
s.36, applied: 2009 c.23 Sch.20 para.9
s.37, applied: 2009 c.23 Sch.20 para.9
s.40, applied: 2009 c.23 Sch.20 para.9
s.41, varied: 2009 c.23 Sch.20 para.9
s.44, amended: 2009 c.23 s.303
s.45, amended: 2009 c.23 s.303
s.60, applied: SI 2009/486 Reg.4
s.86, applied: SI 2009/1578, SI 2009/1579
s.86, enabling: SI 2009/1578, SI 2009/1579
s.87, enabling: SI 2009/1578, SI 2009/1579
s.88, applied: SI 2009/1578, SI 2009/1579
s.98, see *Betterment Properties (Weymouth) Ltd v Dorset CC* [2008] EWCA Civ 22, [2009] 1 W.L.R. 334 (CA (Civ Div)), Laws, L.J.
s.100, applied: 2009 c.23 s.307
Sch.2, referred to: 2009 c.23 Sch.20 para.2
Sch.3, applied: 2009 c.23 Sch.20 para.4
Sch.11 para.9, applied: SI 2009/197 Reg.2, Sch.1 para.1
Sch.11 para.11, referred to: SI 2009/197
Sch.11 para.11, enabling: SI 2009/197

38. Transport Act 2000
see *Dowler v Merseyrail* [2009] EWHC 558 (Admin), (2009) 173 J.P. 332 (DC), Goldring, L.J.
referred to: SI 2009/3243 Reg.2
Part I, applied: SI 2009/3015 Art.173
Part III, applied: SI 2009/107 Sch.2 para.6
s.5, amended: SI 2009/1941 Sch.1 para.184
s.49, amended: SI 2009/1941 Sch.1 para.184
s.56, amended: SI 2009/1941 Sch.1 para.184
s.58, amended: SI 2009/1941 Sch.1 para.184
s.65, amended: SI 2009/1941 Sch.1 para.184
s.73, applied: SI 2009/2301 Reg.33
s.77, enabling: SI 2009/189
s.108, amended: 2009 c.20 Sch.6 para.96
s.108, applied: 2009 c.20 s.106, s.107, SI 2009/107 Sch.2 para.3
s.108, referred to: SI 2009/3245 Reg.6
s.109, amended: 2009 c.20 Sch.6 para.97
s.109, applied: SI 2009/107 Art.5
s.109C, enabling: SI 2009/109
s.110, applied: SI 2009/107 Sch.2 para.2, SI 2009/579 Sch.1 para.1
s.113, amended: 2009 c.20 Sch.6 para.98
s.113, applied: SI 2009/107 Sch.2 para.3
s.114, applied: SI 2009/443 Reg.6, SI 2009/445 Reg.4, Reg.5, Reg.7, Reg.8, Reg.14, SI 2009/3293 Reg.5, Reg.7, Reg.8, Reg.14
s.114, disapplied: SI 2009/3293 Reg.4
s.115, applied: SI 2009/445 Reg.3, Reg.5, Reg.6, Reg.7, Reg.8, Reg.25, SI 2009/3293 Reg.3, Reg.5, Reg.6, Reg.7, Reg.8, Reg.25
s.116, applied: SI 2009/445 Reg.5, Reg.6, SI 2009/3293 Reg.5, Reg.6
s.118, applied: SI 2009/107 Sch.2 para.4
s.118, referred to: SI 2009/579 Sch.1 para.2
s.119, enabling: SI 2009/3293
s.122, applied: SI 2009/445 Reg.5, Reg.7, Reg.8, SI 2009/3293 Reg.5, Reg.7, Reg.8
s.122, enabling: SI 2009/445, SI 2009/3248, SI 2009/3293
s.124, amended: 2009 c.20 Sch.6 para.99
s.124, applied: SI 2009/107 Sch.2 para.2
s.124, referred to: SI 2009/579 Sch.1 para.1

2000–cont.

38. Transport Act 2000–*cont.*
s.125, applied: SI 2009/3242 Art.3, SI 2009/3243 Reg.4, Reg.5, Reg.6, Reg.11, Reg.12, Reg.14, SI 2009/3246 Reg.5, Reg.8
s.125, referred to: SI 2009/3242 Art.3
s.126A, applied: SI 2009/3242 Art.3, SI 2009/3243 Reg.4, Reg.5, Reg.6, Reg.7
s.126A, enabling: SI 2009/3243
s.126B, applied: SI 2009/3243 Reg.4, Reg.8
s.126B, enabling: SI 2009/3243
s.126C, applied: SI 2009/3243 Reg.9, Reg.10, Reg.11, Reg.12, Reg.13, Reg.14, Reg.15, SI 2009/3246 Reg.8
s.126C, referred to: SI 2009/3243 Reg.14
s.126D, applied: SI 2009/3243 Reg.9, Reg.13
s.126D, referred to: SI 2009/3243 Reg.14
s.126E, enabling: SI 2009/3243
s.127, applied: SI 2009/3245 Reg.5, Reg.6, SI 2009/3246 Reg.5, Reg.6
s.127, referred to: SI 2009/3245 Reg.1
s.129, applied: SI 2009/107 Sch.2 para.4
s.129, referred to: SI 2009/579 Sch.1 para.2
s.130, enabling: SI 2009/3244
s.131, enabling: SI 2009/3244
s.133, enabling: SI 2009/3243
s.134, enabling: SI 2009/3244
s.134B, applied: SI 2009/3246 Reg.3, SI 2009/3247 Reg.4
s.134B, referred to: SI 2009/3247, SI 2009/3247 Reg.3
s.134B, enabling: SI 2009/3246, SI 2009/3247
s.138, applied: SI 2009/107 Sch.2 para.4
s.138, referred to: SI 2009/579 Sch.1 para.2
s.140, applied: SI 2009/107 Sch.2 para.4
s.140, referred to: SI 2009/579 Sch.1 para.2
s.146, enabling: SI 2009/575
s.153, applied: SI 2009/3293 Reg.24
s.153, referred to: SI 2009/445 Reg.24
s.155, amended: SI 2009/1885 Sch.1 para.26
s.155, applied: SI 2009/107 Sch.2 para.4, SI 2009/579 Sch.1 para.2, SI 2009/1885 Art.2, Sch.4 para.1
s.157, amended: 2009 c.20 Sch.6 para.100
s.160, enabling: SI 2009/445, SI 2009/575, SI 2009/3243, SI 2009/3244, SI 2009/3246, SI 2009/3247, SI 2009/3293
s.162, amended: 2009 c.20 Sch.6 para.101
s.163, amended: 2009 c.20 Sch.6 para.102
s.164, amended: 2009 c.20 Sch.6 para.103
s.165, amended: 2009 c.20 Sch.6 para.104
s.165A, amended: 2009 c.20 Sch.6 para.105
s.166, amended: 2009 c.20 Sch.6 para.106
s.166A, amended: 2009 c.20 Sch.6 para.107
s.167, amended: 2009 c.20 Sch.6 para.108
s.168, amended: 2009 c.20 Sch.6 para.109
s.169, applied: SI 2009/107 Sch.2 para.6
s.170, amended: 2009 c.20 Sch.6 para.110
s.170, applied: SI 2009/107 Sch.2 para.6
s.177A, amended: 2009 c.20 Sch.6 para.111
s.178, enabling: SI 2009/2085
s.184, disapplied: SI 2009/2085 Reg.3
s.184, enabling: SI 2009/2085
s.189, enabling: SI 2009/2085
s.193, amended: 2009 c.20 Sch.6 para.112
s.194, amended: 2009 c.20 Sch.6 para.113
s.195, enabling: SI 2009/2085
s.197, enabling: SI 2009/2085
s.198, amended: 2009 c.20 Sch.6 para.114

2000–cont.

38. Transport Act 2000–*cont.*

s.219, see *DPP v Inegbu* [2008] EWHC 3242 (Admin), [2009] 1 W.L.R. 2327 (DC), Latham, L.J.

s.258, repealed (in part): SI 2009/1885 Sch.3

s.267, repealed (in part): SI 2009/1885 Sch.3

Sch.1 Part I para.6, amended: SI 2009/1941 Sch.1 para.184

Sch.1 Part I para.12, amended: SI 2009/1941 Sch.1 para.184

Sch.3 para.1, amended: SI 2009/1941 Sch.1 para.184

Sch.3 para.6, amended: SI 2009/1941 Sch.1 para.184

Sch.5 para.1, repealed (in part): 2009 asp 6 Sch.3 para.12

Sch.7 para.12, amended: 2009 c.4 Sch.1 para.472

Sch.7 para.17, amended: 2009 c.4 Sch.1 para.472

Sch.12 para.2, amended: 2009 c.20 Sch.6 para.115

Sch.12 para.3, amended: 2009 c.20 Sch.6 para.115

Sch.12 para.7, amended: 2009 c.20 Sch.6 para.115

Sch.12 para.8, amended: 2009 c.20 Sch.6 para.115

Sch.12 para.11 A, amended: 2009 c.20 Sch.6 para.115

Sch.12 para.11 B, amended: 2009 c.20 Sch.6 para.115

Sch.12 para.11 C, amended: 2009 c.20 Sch.6 para.115

Sch.20 para.7, see *DPP v Inegbu* [2008] EWHC 3242 (Admin), [2009] 1 W.L.R. 2327 (DC), Latham, L.J.

Sch.26 Part II para.7, amended: 2009 c.4 Sch.1 para.473

Sch.26 Part III para.13, amended: 2009 c.4 Sch.1 para.473

Sch.26 Part III para.17, amended: 2009 c.4 Sch.1 para.473

Sch.26 Part V para.29, amended: 2009 c.4 Sch.1 para.473

Sch.26 Part VI para.35, amended: 2009 c.4 Sch.1 para.473

39. Insolvency Act 2000

Sch.4 Part II para.16, repealed (in part): SI 2009/1941 Sch.2

Sch.4 Part II para.17, repealed: SI 2009/1941 Sch.2

Sch.4 Part II para.18, repealed (in part): SI 2009/1941 Sch.2

Sch.4 Part II para.19, repealed: SI 2009/1941 Sch.2

Sch.4 Part II para.20, repealed: SI 2009/1941 Sch.2

Sch.4 Part II para.21, repealed: SI 2009/1941 Sch.2

41. Political Parties, Elections and Referendums Act 2000

Commencement Orders: 2009 c.20 Sch.7 Part 3, 2009 c.20 s.146

applied: 2009 c.9 Sch.2 Part 57

referred to: 2009 c.12 s.9, s.19, s.43

Part II, applied: 2009 c.20 Sch.1 para.1

Part IV c.III, applied: 2009 c.20 Sch.1 para.1

Part IV c.V, applied: 2009 c.20 Sch.1 para.1

Part IVA, applied: 2009 c.20 Sch.1 para.1

Part VI, applied: 2009 c.20 Sch.1 para.1

Part VII, applied: 2009 c.20 Sch.1 para.1

s.1, amended: 2009 c.12 s.6, Sch.6 para.9

s.2, referred to: 2009 c.20 Sch.1 para.2

s.3, amended: 2009 c.12 s.4, s.5, s.7, Sch.6 para.10

s.3A, added: 2009 c.12 s.5

s.7, applied: SI 2009/186, SI 2009/225, SI 2009/256, SI 2009/725, SI 2009/813, SI 2009/848, SI 2009/1978, SI 2009/3014, SI 2009/3016

s.13, amended: 2009 c.12 Sch.7

s.13, repealed (in part): 2009 c.12 s.8, Sch.7

s.14, amended: 2009 c.12 s.5

s.14, applied: 2009 c.20 s.61

2000–cont.

41. Political Parties, Elections and Referendums Act 2000–*cont.*

s.14, repealed (in part): 2009 c.20 s.61, Sch.7 Part 3

s.15, amended: 2009 c.12 Sch.6 para.11

s.15, repealed: 2009 c.20 s.61, Sch.7 Part 3

s.16, repealed: 2009 c.20 s.61, Sch.7 Part 3

s.17, repealed: 2009 c.20 s.61, Sch.7 Part 3

s.18, applied: 2009 c.12 s.7

s.18, repealed: 2009 c.20 s.66, Sch.7 Part 3

s.19, repealed: 2009 c.20 s.61, Sch.7 Part 3

s.20, repealed: 2009 c.20 s.61, Sch.7 Part 3

s.28, see *Aehmed v Legal Services Commission* [2009] EWCA Civ 572, [2009] 3 Costs L.R. 425 (CA (Civ Div)), Sedley, L.J.

s.47, amended: 2009 c.12 s.13

s.47, repealed (in part): 2009 c.12 s.13, Sch.7

s.52, amended: 2009 c.12 s.20

s.54, see *Electoral Commission v City of Westminster Magistrates' Court* [2009] EWCA Civ 1078, Times, October 28, 2009 (CA (Civ Div)), Waller, L.J.

s.54, amended: 2009 c.12 s.9, s.10, s.20, Sch.6 para.12, Sch.7, SI 2009/185 Sch.1 para.1, SI 2009/1941 Sch.1 para.185

s.54A, added: 2009 c.12 s.9

s.54B, added: 2009 c.12 s.10

s.55, amended: 2009 c.12 Sch.6 para.13

s.56, see *Electoral Commission v City of Westminster Magistrates' Court* [2009] EWCA Civ 1078, Times, October 28, 2009 (CA (Civ Div)), Waller, L.J.

s.56, amended: 2009 c.12 s.9, s.10, s.12, Sch.6 para.14

s.57A, repealed: SI 2009/185 Sch.1 para.2

s.58, see *Electoral Commission v City of Westminster Magistrates' Court* [2009] EWCA Civ 1078, Times, October 28, 2009 (CA (Civ Div)), Waller, L.J.

s.58, amended: 2009 c.12 Sch.6 para.15

s.62, amended: 2009 c.12 s.20, Sch.6 para.16

s.63, amended: 2009 c.12 s.20

s.65, amended: 2009 c.12 s.13, Sch.6 para.17

s.65, repealed (in part): 2009 c.12 Sch.7

s.67, amended: 2009 c.12 Sch.6 para.18

s.71F, amended: 2009 c.12 s.20

s.71GA, added: SI 2009/185 Sch.1 para.3

s.71H, amended: 2009 c.12 Sch.6 para.19, SI 2009/185 Sch.1 para.4

s.71H, varied: SI 2009/185 Sch.1 para.4

s.71HA, added: SI 2009/185 Sch.1 para.5

s.71HZA, added: 2009 c.12 s.11

s.71I, varied: SI 2009/185 Sch.1 para.6

s.71J, varied: SI 2009/185 Sch.1 para.7

s.71L, amended: 2009 c.12 s.11

s.71L, varied: SI 2009/185 Sch.1 para.8

s.71M, amended: 2009 c.12 s.20

s.71O, amended: SI 2009/185 Sch.1 para.9

s.71Q, amended: 2009 c.12 s.20

s.71R, amended: SI 2009/185 Sch.1 para.10

s.71S, amended: 2009 c.12 s.13, SI 2009/185 Sch.1 para.11

s.71S, repealed (in part): 2009 c.12 s.13, Sch.7

s.71U, amended: 2009 c.12 Sch.6 para.20, SI 2009/185 Sch.1 para.12

s.71W, amended: SI 2009/185 Sch.1 para.13

s.71X, amended: SI 2009/185 Sch.1 para.14

s.88, amended: 2009 c.12 s.18

s.88, applied: 2009 c.12 s.18

s.98, applied: 2009 c.20 Sch.1 para.1

s.122, applied: 2009 c.20 Sch.1 para.1

2000– cont.

41. Political Parties, Elections and Referendums Act 2000– *cont.*

s.139, amended: 2009 c.12 Sch.6 para.21

s.140, amended: 2009 c.12 Sch.6 para.21

s.140A, added: 2009 c.12 s.19

s.140A, amended: 2009 c.12 Sch.6 para.21

s.145, amended: 2009 c.12 s.1, Sch.6 para.22, Sch.7

s.146, substituted: 2009 c.12 s.2

s.147, substituted: 2009 c.12 s.3

s.148, amended: 2009 c.12 Sch.6 para.23

s.149, amended: 2009 c.12 Sch.6 para.24, Sch.7

s.155, amended: 2009 c.12 s.20

s.156, amended: 2009 c.12 s.3, Sch.6 para.25, 2009 c.20 Sch.7 Part 3

s.156, repealed (in part): 2009 c.20 Sch.7 Part 3

s.160, amended: 2009 c.12 Sch.6 para.26, SI 2009/185 Sch.1 para.15

s.163, amended: SI 2009/185 Art.2

Sch.1, referred to: 2009 c.12 s.43

Sch.1 para.3, amended: 2009 c.12 Sch.6 para.27

Sch.1 para.6, repealed: 2009 c.20 Sch.7 Part 3

Sch.1 para.7, amended: 2009 c.12 Sch.6 para.27, 2009 c.20 Sch.7 Part 3

Sch.1 para.8, amended: 2009 c.20 Sch.7 Part 3

Sch.1 para.9, repealed (in part): 2009 c.20 Sch.7 Part 3

Sch.1 para.10, amended: 2009 c.20 Sch.7 Part 3

Sch.1 para.11, amended: 2009 c.12 Sch.6 para.27

Sch.1 para.11, repealed (in part): 2009 c.12 Sch.7

Sch.1 para.11A, added: 2009 c.12 s.7

Sch.1 para.11B, added: 2009 c.12 s.7

Sch.1 para.12, amended: 2009 c.20 Sch.7 Part 3

Sch.1 para.24, amended: 2009 c.20 Sch.7 Part 3

Sch.2 para.1, applied: 2009 c.20 Sch.1 para.11, Sch.1 para.12

Sch.3 Part I para.1, repealed: 2009 c.20 s.61, Sch.7 Part 3

Sch.3 Part I para.2, repealed: 2009 c.20 s.61, Sch.7 Part 3

Sch.3 Part I para.3, repealed: 2009 c.20 s.61, Sch.7 Part 3

Sch.3 Part I para.4, repealed: 2009 c.20 s.61, Sch.7 Part 3

Sch.3 Part I para.5, repealed: 2009 c.20 s.61, Sch.7 Part 3

Sch.3 Part I para.6, repealed: 2009 c.20 s.61, Sch.7 Part 3

Sch.3 Part I para.7, repealed: 2009 c.20 s.61, Sch.7 Part 3

Sch.6 para.1A, added: 2009 c.12 s.9

Sch.6 para.1A, amended: 2009 c.12 s.10

Sch.6 para.1A, substituted: 2009 c.12 s.10

Sch.6 para.2, amended: SI 2009/185 Sch.1 para.16

Sch.6 para.6, amended: 2009 c.12 s.9

Sch.6A para.1A, added: 2009 c.12 s.11

Sch.6A para.2, amended: SI 2009/185 Sch.1 para.17

Sch.6A para.3, amended: SI 2009/185 Sch.1 para.17

Sch.7, applied: 2009 c.20 Sch.1 para.1

Sch.7, referred to: 2009 c.12 s.9, s.10

Sch.7 Part I para.1, amended: 2009 c.12 s.14

Sch.7 Part I para.1A, added: 2009 c.12 s.14

Sch.7 Part I para.1B, added: 2009 c.12 s.14

Sch.7 Part I para.4, amended: 2009 c.12 s.20

Sch.7 Part II para.6, amended: 2009 c.12 s.20, Sch.3 para.1, Sch.4 para.1, Sch.6 para.28, Sch.7

Sch.7 Part II para.6A, added: 2009 c.12 Sch.3 para.1

Sch.7 Part II para.6B, added: 2009 c.12 Sch.4 para.1

Sch.7 Part II para.8, amended: 2009 c.12 Sch.4 para.2, Sch.6 para.28

2000– cont.

41. Political Parties, Elections and Referendums Act 2000– *cont.*

Sch.7 Part III para.10, amended: 2009 c.12 s.20, Sch.3 para.2, Sch.4 para.3

Sch.7 Part III para.11, amended: 2009 c.12 Sch.3 para.3

Sch.7 Part III para.12, amended: 2009 c.12 s.13, s.14

Sch.7 Part III para.12, repealed (in part): 2009 c.12 s.13, Sch.7

Sch.7 Part V para.15A, referred to: SI 2009/1509

Sch.7 Part VII para.17, added: 2009 c.12 s.15

Sch.7 Part VII para.18, added: 2009 c.12 s.15

Sch.7 Part VII para.19, added: 2009 c.12 s.15

Sch.7A para.1, amended: 2009 c.12 s.16, Sch.7

Sch.7A para.2, amended: 2009 c.12 s.20

Sch.7A para.4, amended: SI 2009/185 Sch.1 para.18

Sch.7A para.4A, added: 2009 c.12 s.11

Sch.7A para.8, amended: 2009 c.12 s.11

Sch.7A para.9, amended: 2009 c.12 s.11, s.20, SI 2009/185 Sch.1 para.18

Sch.7A para.12, amended: 2009 c.12 s.13, s.16

Sch.7A para.12, repealed (in part): 2009 c.12 Sch.7

Sch.7A para.17, amended: SI 2009/185 Sch.1 para.18

Sch.7A para.18, added: 2009 c.12 s.17

Sch.11, referred to: 2009 c.12 s.9, s.10

Sch.11 Part I para.4, amended: 2009 c.12 s.20, Sch.6 para.29

Sch.11 Part II para.6, amended: 2009 c.12 s.20, Sch.3 para.4, Sch.4 para.4, Sch.7

Sch.11 Part II para.6A, added: 2009 c.12 Sch.3 para.4

Sch.11 Part II para.6B, added: 2009 c.12 Sch.4 para.4

Sch.11 Part II para.7, amended: 2009 c.12 Sch.4 para.5, Sch.6 para.29

Sch.11 Part III para.9, amended: 2009 c.12 Sch.3 para.5

Sch.11 Part III para.9A, added: 2009 c.12 Sch.3 para.5, Sch.4 para.6

Sch.11 Part III para.9A, amended: 2009 c.12 Sch.4 para.6

Sch.11 Part III para.10, amended: 2009 c.12 s.20

Sch.11 Part III para.11, amended: 2009 c.12 Sch.3 para.6

Sch.15, referred to: 2009 c.12 s.9, s.10

Sch.15 Part I para.4, amended: 2009 c.12 s.20, Sch.6 para.30

Sch.15 Part I para.4, repealed (in part): 2009 c.12 Sch.6 para.30, Sch.7

Sch.15 Part II para.6, amended: 2009 c.12 s.20, Sch.3 para.7, Sch.4 para.7, Sch.7

Sch.15 Part II para.6A, added: 2009 c.12 Sch.3 para.7

Sch.15 Part II para.6B, added: 2009 c.12 Sch.4 para.7

Sch.15 Part II para.7, amended: 2009 c.12 Sch.4 para.8, Sch.6 para.30

Sch.15 Part III para.9, amended: 2009 c.12 Sch.3 para.8

Sch.15 Part III para.9A, added: 2009 c.12 Sch.3 para.8

Sch.15 Part III para.9A, amended: 2009 c.12 Sch.4 para.9

Sch.15 Part III para.10, amended: 2009 c.12 s.20

Sch.15 Part III para.11, amended: 2009 c.12 Sch.3 para.9

Sch.19A para.1, added: 2009 c.12 Sch.5

Sch.19A para.1, varied: 2009 c.12 s.19

2000–cont.

41. Political Parties, Elections and Referendums Act 2000–*cont.*
Sch.19A para.2, added: 2009 c.12 Sch.5
Sch.19A para.2, varied: 2009 c.12 s.19
Sch.19A para.3, added: 2009 c.12 Sch.5
Sch.19A para.4, added: 2009 c.12 Sch.5
Sch.19A para.5, added: 2009 c.12 Sch.5
Sch.19A para.6, added: 2009 c.12 Sch.5
Sch.19A para.7, added: 2009 c.12 Sch.5
Sch.19A para.8, added: 2009 c.12 Sch.5
Sch.19A para.9, added: 2009 c.12 Sch.5
Sch.19B para.1, added: 2009 c.12 Sch.1
Sch.19B para.2, added: 2009 c.12 Sch.1
Sch.19B para.3, added: 2009 c.12 Sch.1
Sch.19B para.4, added: 2009 c.12 Sch.1
Sch.19B para.5, added: 2009 c.12 Sch.1
Sch.19B para.6, added: 2009 c.12 Sch.1
Sch.19B para.7, added: 2009 c.12 Sch.1
Sch.19B para.8, added: 2009 c.12 Sch.1
Sch.19B para.9, added: 2009 c.12 Sch.1
Sch.19B para.10, added: 2009 c.12 Sch.1
Sch.19B para.11, added: 2009 c.12 Sch.1
Sch.19B para.12, added: 2009 c.12 Sch.1
Sch.19B para.13, added: 2009 c.12 Sch.1
Sch.19B para.14, added: 2009 c.12 Sch.1
Sch.19B para.15, added: 2009 c.12 Sch.1
Sch.19C Part I para.1, added: 2009 c.12 Sch.2
Sch.19C Part I para.2, added: 2009 c.12 Sch.2
Sch.19C Part I para.3, added: 2009 c.12 Sch.2
Sch.19C Part I para.4, added: 2009 c.12 Sch.2
Sch.19C Part II para.5, added: 2009 c.12 Sch.2
Sch.19C Part II para.6, added: 2009 c.12 Sch.2
Sch.19C Part II para.7, added: 2009 c.12 Sch.2
Sch.19C Part II para.8, added: 2009 c.12 Sch.2
Sch.19C Part II para.9, added: 2009 c.12 Sch.2
Sch.19C Part III para.10, added: 2009 c.12 Sch.2
Sch.19C Part III para.11, added: 2009 c.12 Sch.2
Sch.19C Part III para.12, added: 2009 c.12 Sch.2
Sch.19C Part III para.13, added: 2009 c.12 Sch.2
Sch.19C Part III para.14, added: 2009 c.12 Sch.2
Sch.19C Part IV para.15, added: 2009 c.12 Sch.2
Sch.19C Part V para.16, added: 2009 c.12 Sch.2
Sch.19C Part V para.17, added: 2009 c.12 Sch.2
Sch.19C Part V para.18, added: 2009 c.12 Sch.2
Sch.19C Part V para.19, added: 2009 c.12 Sch.2
Sch.19C Part V para.20, added: 2009 c.12 Sch.2
Sch.19C Part V para.21, added: 2009 c.12 Sch.2
Sch.19C Part VI para.22, added: 2009 c.12 Sch.2
Sch.19C Part VI para.23, added: 2009 c.12 Sch.2
Sch.19C Part VI para.24, added: 2009 c.12 Sch.2
Sch.19C Part VI para.25, added: 2009 c.12 Sch.2
Sch.19C Part VI para.26, added: 2009 c.12 Sch.2
Sch.19C Part VI para.27, added: 2009 c.12 Sch.2
Sch.19C Part VI para.28, added: 2009 c.12 Sch.2
Sch.19C Part VII para.29, added: 2009 c.12 Sch.2
Sch.20, amended: 2009 c.12 s.2, s.3, s.9, s.10, s.11, s.14, s.15, s.19, Sch.3 para.10, Sch.4 para.10, Sch.6 para.31, Sch.7
Sch.20, referred to: 2009 c.12 s.9, s.10
Sch.21 para.9, repealed: 2009 c.20 Sch.7 Part 3
Sch.21 para.10, repealed: 2009 c.20 Sch.7 Part 3
Sch.22, amended: 2009 c.20 s.61, Sch.7 Part 3
43. Criminal Justice and Court Services Act 2000
Part II, applied: SI 2009/37 Reg.2
s.5A, referred to: SI 2009/1059 Art.187
s.5A, varied: SI 2009/1059 Sch.1 para.47
s.26, applied: SI 2009/1547 Reg.4

2000–cont.

43. Criminal Justice and Court Services Act 2000– *cont.*
s.28, see *R. v Barley (Stuart John)* [2008] EWCA Crim 2466, [2009] 2 Cr. App. R. (S.) 2 (CA (Crim Div)), Toulson, L.J.
s.28, applied: SI 2009/1547 Reg.10, SI 2009/1633 Reg.3, SI 2009/2558 Reg.3
s.29, applied: SI 2009/1547 Reg.10, SI 2009/1633 Reg.3, SI 2009/2558 Reg.3
s.29A, applied: SI 2009/1547 Reg.10, SI 2009/1633 Reg.3, SI 2009/2558 Reg.3
s.35, repealed: SI 2009/2611 Art.3
s.36, applied: SI 2009/2611 Art.3
s.42, applied: SI 2009/3297 Reg.11
s.61, referred to: SI 2009/1059 Sch.2 para.6, Sch.2 para.7
s.71, repealed (in part): 2009 c.26 Sch.8 Part 13
Sch.4 para.2, referred to: SI 2009/1547 Reg.4
Sch.7 Part II para.205, repealed: 2009 c.24 Sch.7 Part 3
Sch.7 Part II para.206, repealed: 2009 c.24 Sch.7 Part 3
Sch.7 Part II para.207, repealed: 2009 c.24 Sch.7 Part 3
44. Sexual Offences (Amendment) Act 2000
repealed (in part): 2009 asp 9 Sch.6
s.3, applied: 2009 asp 9 s.53, Sch.1 para.19, Sch.1 para.34, SI 2009/1547 Sch.2 para.1, Sch.3 para.2, SSI 2009/31 Sch.1 para.17, SSI 2009/71 Sch.1 para.17
s.3, referred to: SI 2009/37 Sch.1 para.2, Sch.1 para.4

2001

2. Capital Allowances Act 2001
applied: 2009 c.4 s.212, s.230, s.251, s.264, s.885, s.889, 2009 c.10 Sch.25 para.3, Sch.61 para.13, Sch.61 para.14, SI 2009/2971 Reg.4
referred to: 2009 c.4 s.49, s.815, 2009 c.10 Sch.61 para.13
Part 2, applied: 2009 c.4 s.463, s.804, 2009 c.10 Sch.11 para.31
Part 2, referred to: 2009 c.10 s.24
Part 2 c.4, applied: 2009 c.10 s.24
Part 2 c.8, referred to: 2009 c.4 s.56, s.1251
Part 11 c.2, applied: 2009 c.4 s.927
s.2, amended: 2009 c.4 Sch.1 para.475
s.4, applied: 2009 c.4 s.931
s.12, referred to: 2009 c.10 s.24
s.15, amended: 2009 c.4 Sch.1 para.476
s.15, applied: 2009 c.4 s.1233
s.16, amended: 2009 c.4 Sch.3 Part 1
s.17, amended: 2009 c.4 Sch.1 para.478, Sch.3 Part 1
s.18, amended: 2009 c.4 Sch.1 para.479
s.28, amended: 2009 c.4 Sch.1 para.480
s.33, repealed (in part): 2009 c.10 Sch.11 para.13
s.33A, applied: 2009 c.4 s.60, s.263
s.38, amended: 2009 c.4 Sch.1 para.481
s.38B, amended: 2009 c.10 Sch.11 para.2
s.39, varied: 2009 c.10 s.24
s.45A, enabling: SI 2009/1863
s.45C, enabling: SI 2009/1863
s.45D, amended: 2009 c.10 Sch.11 para.14
s.45D, repealed (in part): 2009 c.10 Sch.11 para.14
s.45H, enabling: SI 2009/1864
s.46, amended: 2009 c.10 Sch.11 para.3
s.46, referred to: 2009 c.10 s.24

2001–*cont.*

2. Capital Allowances Act 2001–*cont.*

s.51A, amended: 2009 c.10 Sch.32 para.12, Sch.32 para.18

s.52, amended: 2009 c.10 Sch.32 para.13, Sch.32 para.19

s.52, varied: 2009 c.10 s.24

s.54, amended: 2009 c.10 Sch.11 para.15

s.55, amended: 2009 c.10 Sch.11 para.16

s.57, amended: 2009 c.10 Sch.32 para.14, Sch.32 para.20

s.61, amended: 2009 c.10 Sch.32 para.1

s.61, applied: 2009 c.10 Sch.61 para.14

s.61, repealed (in part): 2009 c.10 Sch.32 para.1

s.63, amended: 2009 c.4 Sch.1 para.482

s.63, applied: 2009 c.4 s.108

s.65, amended: 2009 c.10 Sch.11 para.17

s.66, amended: 2009 c.10 Sch.11 para.18, Sch.32 para.6

s.70DA, added: 2009 c.10 Sch.32 para.15

s.70DA, referred to: 2009 c.10 Sch.32 para.17

s.70E, amended: 2009 c.10 Sch.32 para.7

s.70G, amended: 2009 c.10 s.126

s.70H, amended: 2009 c.10 s.126, Sch.32 para.16, Sch.52 para.9

s.70O, amended: 2009 c.10 s.126

s.70R, referred to: 2009 c.10 s.24

s.72, applied: 2009 c.4 s.815

s.74, applied: 2009 c.4 s.56, s.1251, 2009 c.10 Sch.11 para.31

s.74, repealed: 2009 c.10 Sch.11 para.4

s.75, repealed: 2009 c.10 Sch.11 para.4

s.76, repealed: 2009 c.10 Sch.11 para.4

s.77, repealed: 2009 c.10 Sch.11 para.4

s.78, repealed: 2009 c.10 Sch.11 para.4

s.79, repealed: 2009 c.10 Sch.11 para.4

s.81, repealed: 2009 c.10 Sch.11 para.5

s.82, repealed: 2009 c.10 Sch.11 para.5

s.82, varied: 2009 c.10 Sch.11 para.32

s.84, amended: 2009 c.10 Sch.11 para.6, Sch.11 para.19

s.86, amended: 2009 c.10 Sch.11 para.20

s.96, amended: 2009 c.10 Sch.11 para.21

s.104A, amended: 2009 c.10 Sch.11 para.7

s.104A, referred to: 2009 c.10 s.24

s.104AA, added: 2009 c.10 Sch.11 para.8

s.104F, added: 2009 c.10 Sch.11 para.9

s.105, amended: 2009 c.4 Sch.1 para.483, 2009 c.10 s.126

s.106, amended: 2009 c.4 Sch.1 para.484

s.108, amended: 2009 c.4 Sch.1 para.485

s.112, amended: 2009 c.4 Sch.1 para.486

s.115, amended: 2009 c.4 Sch.1 para.487

s.122, amended: 2009 c.4 Sch.1 para.488

s.125, amended: 2009 c.4 Sch.1 para.489

s.163, amended: 2009 c.10 Sch.41 para.5

s.165, amended: 2009 c.10 Sch.41 para.6

s.186, amended: 2009 c.10 s.126

s.204, amended: SI 2009/56 Sch.1 para.298

s.208A, added: 2009 c.10 Sch.11 para.10

s.216, amended: 2009 c.10 Sch.32 para.23

s.216, applied: 2009 c.10 Sch.32 para.25

s.216, referred to: 2009 c.10 Sch.32 para.25

s.221, amended: 2009 c.10 Sch.32 para.24

s.221, applied: 2009 c.10 Sch.32 para.26

s.221, referred to: 2009 c.10 Sch.32 para.26

s.227, applied: 2009 c.10 Sch.32 para.25

s.227, referred to: 2009 c.10 Sch.32 para.25

s.228A, applied: 2009 c.10 Sch.32 para.26

2001–*cont.*

2. Capital Allowances Act 2001–*cont.*

s.228A, referred to: 2009 c.10 Sch.32 para.26

s.229A, added: 2009 c.10 Sch.32 para.21

s.229A, referred to: 2009 c.10 Sch.32 para.22

s.248, applied: 2009 c.4 s.264, s.269

s.249, applied: 2009 c.4 s.264, s.269

s.252, amended: 2009 c.4 Sch.1 para.490

s.253, amended: 2009 c.4 Sch.1 para.491

s.253, applied: 2009 c.4 s.1233

s.256, amended: 2009 c.4 Sch.1 para.492

s.257, amended: 2009 c.4 Sch.1 para.493, 2009 c.10 s.126

s.260, amended: 2009 c.4 Sch.1 para.494

s.263, amended: 2009 c.4 Sch.1 para.495

s.265, amended: 2009 c.4 Sch.1 para.496

s.268A, added: 2009 c.10 Sch.11 para.11

s.268B, added: 2009 c.10 Sch.11 para.11

s.268C, added: 2009 c.10 Sch.11 para.11

s.268D, added: 2009 c.10 Sch.11 para.22

s.282, amended: 2009 c.4 Sch.1 para.497

s.291, amended: 2009 c.4 Sch.1 para.498

s.326, amended: 2009 c.4 Sch.1 para.499

s.331, amended: 2009 c.4 Sch.1 para.500

s.353, amended: 2009 c.4 Sch.1 para.501, Sch.3 Part 1

s.354, amended: 2009 c.4 Sch.1 para.502

s.360B, amended: 2009 c.10 s.126

s.360C, amended: 2009 c.10 s.126

s.390, amended: 2009 c.4 Sch.1 para.503

s.392, amended: 2009 c.4 Sch.1 para.504, Sch.3 Part 1

s.392, repealed (in part): 2009 c.4 Sch.3 Part 1

s.393B, amended: 2009 c.4 Sch.3 Part 1

s.393J, amended: 2009 c.4 Sch.1 para.506

s.393T, amended: 2009 c.4 Sch.1 para.507, Sch.3 Part 1

s.393T, repealed (in part): 2009 c.4 Sch.3 Part 1

s.406, amended: 2009 c.4 Sch.1 para.508

s.454, amended: 2009 c.4 Sch.1 para.509

s.455, amended: 2009 c.4 Sch.1 para.510

s.462, amended: 2009 c.4 Sch.1 para.511

s.462, applied: 2009 c.4 s.177, s.909

s.480, applied: 2009 c.4 s.925

s.481, amended: 2009 c.4 Sch.1 para.512

s.483, amended: 2009 c.4 Sch.1 para.513

s.488, amended: 2009 c.4 Sch.1 para.514

s.529, amended: 2009 c.4 Sch.1 para.515, Sch.3 Part 1

s.529, repealed (in part): 2009 c.4 Sch.3 Part 1

s.532, applied: 2009 c.4 s.97

s.534, applied: 2009 c.4 s.149

s.536, amended: 2009 c.4 Sch.1 para.516

s.545, amended: 2009 c.4 Sch.1 para.517

s.558, amended: 2009 c.4 Sch.1 para.518

s.559, amended: 2009 c.4 Sch.1 para.519

s.563, amended: SI 2009/56 Sch.1 para.299

s.563, applied: 2009 c.4 s.177, s.930

s.563, repealed (in part): SI 2009/56 Sch.1 para.299

s.577, amended: 2009 c.4 Sch.1 para.520, Sch.3 Part 1

Sch.A1 Part 1 para.5, amended: 2009 c.4 Sch.1 para.521

Sch.A1 Part 1 para.7, amended: 2009 c.4 Sch.1 para.521

Sch.A1 Part 1 para.8, amended: 2009 c.4 Sch.1 para.521

Sch.A1 Part 1 para.11, amended: 2009 c.4 Sch.1 para.521

Sch.A1 Part 1 para.12, amended: 2009 c.4 Sch.1 para.521

Sch.A1 Part 1 para.14, amended: 2009 c.4 Sch.1 para.521

2001–cont.

2. Capital Allowances Act 2001–*cont.*

Sch.A1 Part 1 para.15, amended: 2009 c.4 Sch.1 para.521

Sch.A1 Part 1 para.16, amended: 2009 c.4 Sch.1 para.521

Sch.A1 Part 2 para.20, amended: 2009 c.4 Sch.1 para.521

Sch.A1 Part 2 para.21, amended: 2009 c.4 Sch.1 para.521

Sch.1 Part 1, amended: 2009 c.4 Sch.1 para.522, 2009 c.10 s.126

Sch.1 Part 2, amended: 2009 c.4 Sch.1 para.522, Sch.3 Part 1, 2009 c.10 Sch.11 para.23

Sch.2 para.5, repealed: 2009 c.4 Sch.3 Part 1, SI 2009/56 Sch.1 para.300

Sch.2 para.14, repealed: 2009 c.4 Sch.3 Part 1

Sch.2 para.16, repealed: 2009 c.4 Sch.3 Part 1

Sch.2 para.17, repealed: 2009 c.4 Sch.3 Part 1

Sch.2 para.18, repealed: 2009 c.4 Sch.3 Part 1

Sch.2 para.19, repealed: 2009 c.4 Sch.3 Part 1

Sch.2 para.20, repealed: 2009 c.4 Sch.3 Part 1

Sch.2 para.40, repealed: 2009 c.4 Sch.3 Part 1

Sch.2 para.45, repealed: 2009 c.4 Sch.3 Part 1

Sch.2 para.46, repealed: 2009 c.4 Sch.3 Part 1

Sch.2 para.48, repealed: 2009 c.4 Sch.3 Part 1

Sch.2 para.49, repealed: 2009 c.4 Sch.3 Part 1

Sch.2 para.50, repealed: 2009 c.4 Sch.3 Part 1

Sch.2 para.51, repealed: 2009 c.4 Sch.3 Part 1

Sch.2 para.52, repealed: 2009 c.4 Sch.3 Part 1

Sch.2 para.96, repealed: 2009 c.4 Sch.3 Part 1

Sch.2 para.104, repealed: 2009 c.4 Sch.3 Part 1

Sch.3 Part 4 para.19, repealed: 2009 c.10 Sch.11 para.24

Sch.3 Part 8 para.91, amended: SI 2009/56 Sch.1 para.301

Sch.3 Part 10 para.105, amended: 2009 c.10 s.126

3. Vehicles (Crime) Act 2001

Commencement Orders: 2009 c.26 Sch.8 Part 13

s.36, repealed: 2009 c.26 Sch.8 Part 13

s.45, repealed (in part): 2009 c.26 Sch.8 Part 13

9. Finance Act 2001

Part 2, applied: 2009 c.4 s.1303

s.16, see *MMC Midlands Ltd v Revenue and Customs Commissioners* [2009] EWHC 683 (Ch), [2009] S.T.C. 1969 (Ch D), Lewison, J.

s.17, see *MMC Midlands Ltd v Revenue and Customs Commissioners* [2009] EWHC 683 (Ch), [2009] S.T.C. 1969 (Ch D), Lewison, J.

s.25, amended: SI 2009/571 Sch.1 para.32

s.32, amended: 2009 c.10 Sch.51 para.28

s.40, amended: SI 2009/56 Sch.1 para.303

s.40, repealed (in part): SI 2009/56 Sch.1 para.303

s.40A, added: SI 2009/56 Sch.1 para.304

s.40B, added: SI 2009/56 Sch.1 para.304

s.40C, added: SI 2009/56 Sch.1 para.304

s.40D, added: SI 2009/56 Sch.1 para.304

s.40E, added: SI 2009/56 Sch.1 para.304

s.40F, added: SI 2009/56 Sch.1 para.304

s.40G, added: SI 2009/56 Sch.1 para.304

s.41, amended: SI 2009/56 Sch.1 para.305

s.41, repealed (in part): SI 2009/56 Sch.1 para.305

s.42, amended: SI 2009/56 Sch.1 para.306

s.42, applied: SI 2009/56 Sch.3 para.9

s.45, amended: SI 2009/571 Sch.1 para.33

s.48, amended: SI 2009/56 Sch.1 para.307

s.70, repealed (in part): 2009 c.4 Sch.3 Part 1

s.73, repealed: 2009 c.4 Sch.3 Part 1

s.75, repealed (in part): 2009 c.4 Sch.3 Part 1

2001–cont.

9. Finance Act 2001–*cont.*

s.77, repealed: 2009 c.10 Sch.12 para.4

s.82, repealed: 2009 c.10 Sch.16 para.5

Sch.3 Part 3 para.14, amended: SI 2009/56 Sch.1 para.308

Sch.3 Part 3 para.14, applied: SI 2009/56 Sch.3 para.9

Sch.4 para.1, amended: SI 2009/571 Sch.1 para.34

Sch.5 para.4, amended: 2009 c.10 Sch.51 para.29

Sch.5 para.4, repealed (in part): 2009 c.10 Sch.51 para.29

Sch.5 para.5, applied: 2009 c.4 s.1303, 2009 c.10 s.108

Sch.5 para.6, applied: 2009 c.4 s.1303

Sch.5 para.7, applied: 2009 c.4 s.1303

Sch.5 para.8, applied: 2009 c.4 s.1303

Sch.5 para.9, applied: 2009 c.4 s.1303

Sch.6 Part 2 para.8, amended: SI 2009/56 Sch.1 para.309

Sch.7 para.1, amended: SI 2009/571 Sch.1 para.35

Sch.7 para.1, applied: SI 2009/3054 Art.6

Sch.7 para.1, repealed: SI 2009/3054 Sch.1 para.9

Sch.7 para.2, amended: 2009 c.10 Sch.50 para.16, SI 2009/571 Sch.1 para.35

Sch.7 para.3, repealed: 2009 c.10 Sch.50 para.17

Sch.7 para.4, amended: SI 2009/571 Sch.1 para.35

Sch.7 para.4, applied: SI 2009/3054 Art.6

Sch.7 para.4, repealed: SI 2009/3054 Sch.1 para.9

Sch.7 para.5, repealed: SI 2009/3054 Sch.1 para.9

Sch.7 para.6, repealed: SI 2009/3054 Sch.1 para.9

Sch.8 para.2, amended: 2009 c.10 Sch.51 para.30

Sch.8 para.6, applied: 2009 c.4 s.1303

Sch.9 para.8, amended: SI 2009/1890 Art.4

Sch.10 para.4, amended: 2009 c.10 Sch.51 para.31

Sch.10 para.4, repealed (in part): 2009 c.10 Sch.51 para.31

Sch.10 para.5, applied: 2009 c.4 s.1303

Sch.15 Part 2 para.26, repealed: 2009 c.10 Sch.8 para.10

Sch.15 Part 2 para.27, repealed: 2009 c.10 Sch.8 para.10

Sch.15 Part 2 para.28, repealed: 2009 c.10 Sch.8 para.10

Sch.22 Part 1 para.1, repealed: 2009 c.4 Sch.3 Part 1

Sch.22 Part 1 para.2, repealed: 2009 c.4 Sch.3 Part 1

Sch.22 Part 1 para.3, repealed: 2009 c.4 Sch.3 Part 1

Sch.22 Part 1 para.4, repealed: 2009 c.4 Sch.3 Part 1

Sch.22 Part 1 para.5, repealed: 2009 c.4 Sch.3 Part 1

Sch.22 Part 1 para.6, repealed: 2009 c.4 Sch.3 Part 1

Sch.22 Part 1 para.7, repealed: 2009 c.4 Sch.3 Part 1

Sch.22 Part 1 para.8, repealed: 2009 c.4 Sch.3 Part 1

Sch.22 Part 1 para.9, repealed: 2009 c.4 Sch.3 Part 1

Sch.22 Part 1 para.10, repealed: 2009 c.4 Sch.3 Part 1

Sch.22 Part 1 para.11, repealed: 2009 c.4 Sch.3 Part 1

Sch.22 Part 2 para.12, repealed: 2009 c.4 Sch.3 Part 1

Sch.22 Part 3 para.13, repealed: 2009 c.4 Sch.3 Part 1

Sch.22 Part 3 para.14, repealed: 2009 c.4 Sch.3 Part 1

Sch.22 Part 3 para.15, repealed: 2009 c.4 Sch.3 Part 1

Sch.22 Part 3 para.16, repealed: 2009 c.4 Sch.3 Part 1

Sch.22 Part 3 para.17, repealed: 2009 c.4 Sch.3 Part 1

Sch.22 Part 3 para.18, repealed: 2009 c.4 Sch.3 Part 1

Sch.22 Part 3 para.19, repealed: 2009 c.4 Sch.3 Part 1

Sch.22 Part 4 para.20, repealed: 2009 c.4 Sch.3 Part 1

Sch.22 Part 4 para.21, repealed: 2009 c.4 Sch.3 Part 1

Sch.22 Part 4 para.22, repealed: 2009 c.4 Sch.3 Part 1

Sch.22 Part 4 para.23, repealed: 2009 c.4 Sch.3 Part 1

Sch.22 Part 4 para.24, repealed: 2009 c.4 Sch.3 Part 1

Sch.22 Part 4 para.25, repealed: 2009 c.4 Sch.3 Part 1

Sch.22 Part 4 para.26, repealed: 2009 c.4 Sch.3 Part 1

2001– cont.

9. Finance Act 2001– *cont.*

Sch.22 Part 4 para.27, repealed: 2009 c.4 Sch.3 Part 1

Sch.22 Part 4 para.28, repealed: 2009 c.4 Sch.3 Part 1

Sch.22 Part 5 para.29, repealed: 2009 c.4 Sch.3 Part 1

Sch.22 Part 5 para.30, repealed: 2009 c.4 Sch.3 Part 1

Sch.22 Part 5 para.31, repealed: 2009 c.4 Sch.3 Part 1

Sch.22 Part 5 para.32, repealed: 2009 c.4 Sch.3 Part 1

Sch.22 Part 5 para.53, repealed: 2009 c.4 Sch.3 Part 1

Sch.22 Part 5 para.54, repealed: 2009 c.4 Sch.3 Part 1

Sch.23 para.1, repealed: 2009 c.4 Sch.3 Part 1

Sch.24 Part 2 para.2, repealed: SI 2009/56 Sch.1 para.310

Sch.27 para.1, repealed (in part): 2009 c.10 Sch.14 para.30

Sch.27 para.4, repealed: 2009 c.10 Sch.14 para.30

Sch.27 para.5, repealed: 2009 c.10 Sch.14 para.30

Sch.29 Part 5 para.27, repealed: SI 2009/56 Sch.1 para.311

Sch.29 Part 5 para.28, repealed: SI 2009/56 Sch.1 para.311

11. Social Security Fraud Act 2001

s.6A, added: 2009 c.24 s.24

s.6B, amended: 2009 c.24 Sch.2 para.10

s.6B, repealed (in part): 2009 c.24 Sch.7 Part 1

s.6B, added: 2009 c.24 s.24

s.6C, added: 2009 c.24 s.24

s.7, amended: 2009 c.24 Sch.2 para.11, Sch.4 para.2, Sch.7 Part 3

s.7, repealed (in part): 2009 c.24 Sch.4 para.2, Sch.7 Part 1, Sch.7 Part 3

s.8, amended: 2009 c.24 s.1, Sch.4 para.3

s.8, repealed (in part): 2009 c.24 Sch.7 Part 3

s.9, amended: 2009 c.24 Sch.4 para.4

s.9, repealed (in part): 2009 c.24 Sch.7 Part 1

s.10, amended: 2009 c.24 Sch.4 para.5

s.11, amended: 2009 c.24 Sch.4 para.6

s.11, repealed (in part): 2009 c.24 Sch.7 Part 1

s.12, repealed (in part): 2009 c.24 Sch.7 Part 3

s.13, amended: 2009 c.24 Sch.4 para.7, Sch.7 Part 3

s.21, amended: 2009 c.24 Sch.4 para.8

12. Private Security Industry Act 2001

Commencement Orders: SI 2009/644 Art.3; SI 2009/1058 Art.3, Art.4

see *Security Industry Authority v Stewart* [2007] EWHC 2338 (Admin), [2009] 1 W.L.R. 466 (DC), Laws, L.J.

applied: SI 2009/2964

s.1, see *R. (on the application of Securiplan Plc) v Security Industry Authority* [2008] EWHC 1762 (Admin), [2009] 2 All E.R. 211 (DC), Maurice Kay, L.J.

s.1, applied: SI 2009/2570 Art.9

s.3, applied: SI 2009/3048 Art.2, Art.3

s.3, enabling: SI 2009/3048

s.4, amended: SI 2009/1941 Sch.1 para.188, SI 2009/3017 Art.2

s.4, enabling: SI 2009/2964

s.5, see *R. (on the application of Securiplan Plc) v Security Industry Authority* [2008] EWHC 1762 (Admin), [2009] 2 All E.R. 211 (DC), Maurice Kay, L.J.

s.8, see *Security Industry Authority v Stewart* [2007] EWHC 2338 (Admin), [2009] 1 W.L.R. 466 (DC), Laws, L.J.

s.8, enabling: SI 2009/600, SI 2009/634, SI 2009/635, SI 2009/2398

s.9, enabling: SI 2009/600, SI 2009/634

2001– cont.

12. Private Security Industry Act 2001– *cont.*

s.11, see *Security Industry Authority v Stewart* [2007] EWHC 2338 (Admin), [2009] 1 W.L.R. 466 (DC), Laws, L.J.

s.15, enabling: SI 2009/633

s.19, see *R. (on the application of Securiplan Plc) v Security Industry Authority* [2008] EWHC 1762 (Admin), [2009] 2 All E.R. 211 (DC), Maurice Kay, L.J.

s.21, see *R. (on the application of Securiplan Plc) v Security Industry Authority* [2008] EWHC 1762 (Admin), [2009] 2 All E.R. 211 (DC), Maurice Kay, L.J.

s.24, applied: SI 2009/633, SI 2009/634, SI 2009/635, SI 2009/1058, SI 2009/2398, SI 2009/2964, SI 2009/3043, SI 2009/3048

s.24, enabling: SI 2009/600, SI 2009/634, SI 2009/2398

s.25, amended: SI 2009/1941 Sch.1 para.188

s.26, enabling: SI 2009/644, SI 2009/1058

Sch.2 Part 1 para.1, applied: SI 2009/3043

Sch.2 Part 1 para.1, enabling: SI 2009/3043

Sch.2 Part 1 para.2, amended: SI 2009/3043 Art.2

Sch.2 Part 1 para.2, referred to: SI 2009/3048 Art.2

Sch.2 Part 1 para.3, amended: SI 2009/3043 Art.3

Sch.2 Part 1 para.3, referred to: SI 2009/3048 Art.3

Sch.2 Part 1 para.3A, amended: SI 2009/3043 Art.4

Sch.2 Part 1 para.3A, referred to: SI 2009/3048 Art.3

Sch.2 Part 1 para.6, referred to: SI 2009/3048 Art.3

Sch.2 Part 2 para.7, applied: SI 2009/3043

Sch.2 Part 2 para.7, enabling: SI 2009/3043

Sch.2 Part 2 para.8, amended: SI 2009/3017 Art.3, SI 2009/3043 Art.5, Art.6, Art.7, SSI 2009/248 Sch.1 para.8

Sch.2 Part 2 para.8, repealed (in part): SSI 2009/248 Sch.2

15. Health and Social Care Act 2001

s.57, applied: SI 2009/212 Reg.2, SI 2009/1887 Reg.2, Reg.3, Reg.5, Reg.6, Reg.7, Reg.8, Reg.9, Reg.10, Reg.11, Reg.12, Reg.14, Reg.16, Reg.17, Reg.18

s.57, disapplied: SI 2009/1887 Reg.10

s.57, enabling: SI 2009/1887

s.64, enabling: SI 2009/1887

16. Criminal Justice and Police Act 2001

see *R. v Gore (Raymond)* [2009] EWCA Crim 1424, [2009] 1 W.L.R. 2454 (CA (Crim Div)), Lord Judge, L.C.J.

s.1, amended: SI 2009/110 Art.2

s.1, enabling: SI 2009/110

s.3, enabling: SI 2009/83

s.48, repealed: 2009 c.26 Sch.8 Part 13

s.49, repealed: 2009 c.26 Sch.8 Part 13

s.50, see *Bates v Chief Constable of Avon and Somerset* [2009] EWHC 942 (Admin), (2009) 173 J.P. 313 (DC), Richards, L.J.

s.52, see *Bates v Chief Constable of Avon and Somerset* [2009] EWHC 942 (Admin), (2009) 173 J.P. 313 (DC), Richards, L.J.

s.56, repealed (in part): SI 2009/1941 Sch.1 para.189

s.57, repealed (in part): SI 2009/1941 Sch.1 para.189

s.64, amended: 2009 c.26 Sch.7 para.115, Sch.8 Part 5

s.64, repealed (in part): SI 2009/1941 Sch.1 para.189

s.65, repealed (in part): SI 2009/1941 Sch.1 para.189

s.66, amended: 2009 c.23 s.253

s.66, repealed (in part): SI 2009/1941 Sch.1 para.189

2001– cont.

16. Criminal Justice and Police Act 2001– *cont.*
s.78, repealed (in part): 2009 c.26 Sch.8 Part 13
s.80, repealed (in part): 2009 c.26 Sch.8 Part 13
s.134, repealed (in part): 2009 c.26 Sch.8 Part 8
s.138, repealed (in part): SI 2009/1941 Sch.2
Sch.1 Part 1 para.42, repealed: SI 2009/1941 Sch.1 para.189
Sch.1 Part 1 para.73L, added: 2009 c.23 s.253
17. International Criminal Court Act 2001
varied: SI 2009/317 Sch.1, SI 2009/1738 Art.2
Part 2, applied: SI 2009/699 Art.2
s.23, applied: SI 2009/699
s.32, varied: SI 2009/1059 Sch.1 para.48
s.35, amended: 2009 c.25 Sch.21 para.45
s.53, amended: 2009 c.25 s.70
s.54, varied: SI 2009/1059 Sch.1 para.48
s.60, amended: 2009 c.25 s.70
s.65A, added: 2009 c.25 s.70
s.65B, added: 2009 c.25 s.70
s.67A, added: 2009 c.25 s.70
s.68, varied: SI 2009/1059 Sch.1 para.48
s.79, referred to: 2009 c.25 s.181
s.79, enabling: SI 2009/1738
19. Armed Forces Act 2001
Part 2, applied: SI 2009/1059 Art.33, Art.65, Art.75, SI 2009/1108 Sch.1 para.3, SI 2009/1209 Sch.2 para.11, SI 2009/2041 Sch.2 para.12, SI 2009/2056 Sch.4 para.10, Sch.4 para.11, Sch.4 para.12, Sch.4 para.15, Sch.4 para.19, Sch.4 para.20, Sch.4 para.23
Part 2, referred to: SI 2009/989 Sch.1
s.2, applied: SI 2009/2056 Sch.4 para.2, Sch.4 para.3, Sch.4 para.15
s.2, disapplied: SI 2009/2056 Sch.4 para.12
s.4, applied: SI 2009/2056 Sch.4 para.4, Sch.4 para.15
s.4, disapplied: SI 2009/2056 Sch.4 para.12
s.4, varied: SI 2009/1059 Art.32
s.5, applied: SI 2009/1059 Art.33, SI 2009/2056 Sch.4 para.5, Sch.4 para.7, Sch.4 para.21, Sch.4 para.23
s.5, varied: SI 2009/1059 Art.33
s.7, applied: SI 2009/1059 Art.33, SI 2009/2056 Sch.4 para.12, Sch.4 para.15, Sch.4 para.25
s.7, disapplied: SI 2009/2056 Sch.4 para.12, Sch.4 para.20, Sch.4 para.23
s.7, referred to: SI 2009/2056 Sch.4 para.20, Sch.4 para.21, Sch.4 para.23
s.7, varied: SI 2009/1059 Art.33
s.8, applied: SI 2009/1059 Art.33, SI 2009/2056 Sch.4 para.25
s.8, varied: SI 2009/1059 Art.33
s.9, applied: SI 2009/1059 Art.33
s.9, varied: SI 2009/1059 Art.33
s.10, applied: SI 2009/1059 Art.31, SI 2009/2056 Sch.4 para.11, Sch.4 para.21
s.10, varied: SI 2009/1059 Art.31
s.26, enabling: SI 2009/993
s.27, referred to: SI 2009/993 Reg.6
s.27, enabling: SI 2009/993
s.28, varied: SI 2009/1059 Sch.1 para.49
s.28, enabling: SI 2009/993
s.30, enabling: SI 2009/991, SI 2009/992
s.32, applied: SI 2009/1059 Art.177, SI 2009/1922 Sch.2 para.14
24. Anti-terrorism, Crime and Security Act 2001
see *A v United Kingdom (3455/05)* (2009) 49 E.H.R.R. 29 (ECHR (Grand Chamber)), Judge Costa (President)

2001– cont.

24. Anti-terrorism, Crime and Security Act 2001– *cont.*
Part 4, see *A v United Kingdom (3455/05)* (2009) 49 E.H.R.R. 29 (ECHR (Grand Chamber)), Judge Costa (President)
s.4, enabling: SI 2009/1392
s.14, enabling: SI 2009/1392
s.17, applied: SI 2009/1361 Reg.7, SI 2009/1551 Reg.7, SSI 2009/225 Reg.4
s.21, see *A v United Kingdom (3455/05)* (2009) 49 E.H.R.R. 29 (ECHR (Grand Chamber)), Judge Costa (President)
s.23, see *A v United Kingdom (3455/05)* (2009) 49 E.H.R.R. 29 (ECHR (Grand Chamber)), Judge Costa (President)
Sch.1 Part 5 para.16, varied: SI 2009/1059 Sch.1 para.50
Sch.3, enabling: SI 2009/1392
Sch.4 Part 2 para.59, repealed: SI 2009/1941 Sch.2

2002

1. International Development Act 2002
applied: 2009 c.2 Sch.2 Part 2, 2009 c.9 Sch.2 Part 25
s.11, applied: SI 2009/1368 Art.3, SI 2009/2947 Art.3
s.11, enabling: SI 2009/1368, SI 2009/2947
7. Homelessness Act 2002
see *R. (on the application of Ahmad) v Newham LBC* [2009] UKHL 14, [2009] 3 All E.R. 755 (HL), Lord Hope of Craighead
8. British Overseas Territories Act 2002
applied: SI 2009/1379 Sch.2
9. Land Registration Act 2002
see *Parkinson v Hawthorne* [2008] EWHC 3499 (Ch), [2009] 1 W.L.R. 1665 (Ch D), Patten, J.
applied: 2009 c.10 Sch.61 para.19, SI 2009/1931, SI 2009/1931 Art.3
s.1, applied: 2009 c.10 Sch.61 para.5
s.1, enabling: SI 2009/1996
s.25, enabling: SI 2009/1996
s.27, applied: SI 2009/845 Art.4
s.27, enabling: SI 2009/1996
s.29, see *Redstone Mortgages Plc v Welch* [2009] 36 E.G. 98 (CC (Birmingham)), Judge Worster
s.41, applied: SI 2009/845 Sch.3 Part 1, Sch.3 Part 4, Sch.4
s.64, applied: SI 2009/845 Sch.3 Part 1
s.66, see *Parkinson v Hawthorne* [2008] EWHC 3499 (Ch), [2009] 1 W.L.R. 1665 (Ch D), Patten, J.
s.86, see *Bateman v Hyde* [2009] EWHC 81 (Ch), [2009] B.P.I.R. 737 (Ch D (Manchester)), Judge Pelling Q.C.
s.100, enabling: SI 2009/1393, SI 2009/2727
s.102, enabling: SI 2009/845
s.106, amended: SI 2009/1941 Sch.1 para.193
s.117, applied: SI 2009/845 Sch.3 Part 1
s.121, substituted: SI 2009/1941 Sch.1 para.193
s.126, enabling: SI 2009/1996
s.127, applied: SI 2009/845, SI 2009/1996, SI 2009/2024
s.127, enabling: SI 2009/1996
s.128, enabling: SI 2009/845, SI 2009/1996
Sch.3 para.2, see *Redstone Mortgages Plc v Welch* [2009] 36 E.G. 98 (CC (Birmingham)), Judge Worster
Sch.10 Part 2 para.6, enabling: SI 2009/1996

2002– cont.

9. Land Registration Act 2002–*cont.*
Sch.10 Part 2 para.8, enabling: SI 2009/ 1996

13. Electoral Fraud (Northern Ireland) Act 2002
s.6, repealed (in part): 2009 c.12 Sch.7

15. Commonhold and Leasehold Reform Act 2002
see *Elizabeth Court (Bournemouth) Ltd v Revenue and Customs Commissioners* [2008] EWHC 2828 (Ch), [2009] S.T.C. 682 (Ch D), Sir Andrew Morritt (Chancellor)
applied: SI 2009/ 2767 Sch.1
s.1, amended: SI 2009/ 1941 Sch.1 para.194
s.5, amended: SI 2009/ 1941 Sch.1 para.194
s.8, amended: SI 2009/ 1941 Sch.1 para.194
s.9, applied: SI 2009/ 845 Sch.3 Part 1
s.13, amended: SI 2009/ 1941 Sch.1 para.194
s.13, enabling: SI 2009/ 2363
s.31, amended: SI 2009/ 1941 Sch.1 para.194
s.31, enabling: SI 2009/ 2363
s.32, enabling: SI 2009/ 2363
s.34, amended: SI 2009/ 1941 Sch.1 para.194
s.36, amended: SI 2009/ 1941 Sch.1 para.194
s.37, amended: SI 2009/ 1941 Sch.1 para.194
s.40, amended: SI 2009/ 1941 Sch.1 para.194
s.51, amended: SI 2009/ 1941 Sch.1 para.194
s.57, amended: SI 2009/ 1941 Sch.1 para.194
s.58, amended: SI 2009/ 1941 Sch.1 para.194
s.58, applied: SI 2009/ 845 Sch.3 Part 1
s.64, enabling: SI 2009/ 2363
s.65, enabling: SI 2009/ 2024
s.69, amended: SI 2009/ 1941 Sch.1 para.194
s.73, amended: SI 2009/ 1941 Sch.1 para.194
s.73, applied: SI 2009/ 1085 Reg.4
s.74, amended: SI 2009/ 1941 Sch.1 para.194
s.74, enabling: SI 2009/ 2767
s.75, referred to: SI 2009/ 2767 Sch.1
s.78, amended: SI 2009/ 1941 Sch.1 para.194
s.86, applied: SI 2009/ 2767 Sch.1
s.87, amended: SI 2009/ 1941 Sch.1 para.194
s.87, applied: SI 2009/ 2767 Sch.1
s.90, applied: SI 2009/ 2767 Sch.1
s.96, applied: SI 2009/ 2767 Sch.1
s.97, applied: SI 2009/ 2767 Sch.1
s.98, applied: SI 2009/ 2767 Sch.1
s.99, applied: SI 2009/ 2767 Sch.1
s.100, applied: SI 2009/ 2767 Sch.1
s.101, applied: SI 2009/ 2767 Sch.1
s.105, amended: SI 2009/ 1941 Sch.1 para.194
s.175, amended: SI 2009/ 1307 Sch.1 para.269
s.175, repealed (in part): SI 2009/ 1307 Sch.1 para.269
s.178, enabling: SI 2009/ 2767
Sch.1 para.2, amended: SI 2009/ 1941 Sch.1 para.194
Sch.1 para.3, amended: SI 2009/ 1941 Sch.1 para.194
Sch.1 para.4, amended: SI 2009/ 1941 Sch.1 para.194
Sch.1 para.7, amended: SI 2009/ 1941 Sch.1 para.194
Sch.3 Part 1 para.1, amended: SI 2009/ 1941 Sch.1 para.195
Sch.3 Part 1 para.1, substituted: SI 2009/ 1941 Sch.1 para.195
Sch.3 Part 1 para.2, amended: SI 2009/ 1941 Sch.1 para.195
Sch.3 Part 1 para.2, enabling: SI 2009/ 2363
Sch.3 Part 1 para.3, amended: SI 2009/ 1941 Sch.1 para.195

2002– cont.

15. Commonhold and Leasehold Reform Act 2002– *cont.*
Sch.3 Part 1 para.4, amended: SI 2009/ 1941 Sch.1 para.195
Sch.3 Part 1 para.4, repealed: SI 2009/ 1941 Sch.1 para.195
Sch.3 Part 2 para.5, amended: SI 2009/ 1941 Sch.1 para.195
Sch.3 Part 2 para.6, amended: SI 2009/ 1941 Sch.1 para.195
Sch.3 Part 2 para.11, amended: SI 2009/ 1941 Sch.1 para.195
Sch.3 Part 2 para.14, amended: SI 2009/ 1941 Sch.1 para.195
Sch.3 Part 2 para.15, substituted: SI 2009/ 1941 Sch.1 para.195
Sch.3 Part 3, amended: SI 2009/ 1941 Sch.1 para.195
Sch.3 Part 3 para.16, amended: SI 2009/ 1941 Sch.1 para.195
Sch.3 Part 3 para.16, enabling: SI 2009/ 2363
Sch.3 Part 3 para.17, amended: SI 2009/ 1941 Sch.1 para.195
Sch.6 para.1, applied: SI 2009/ 2767 Sch.1

16. State Pension Credit Act 2002
see *Patmalniece v Secretary of State for Work and Pensions* [2009] EWCA Civ 621, [2009] 4 All E.R. 738 (CA (Civ Div)), Lord Clarke
s.1, applied: SI 2009/ 212 Reg.2
s.1, referred to: SSI 2009/ 48 Reg.6
s.1, enabling: SI 2009/ 362
s.2, enabling: SI 2009/ 3257
s.5, enabling: SI 2009/ 2655
s.15, enabling: SI 2009/ 583, SI 2009/ 1488, SI 2009/ 1676, SI 2009/ 2655
s.17, enabling: SI 2009/ 362, SI 2009/ 1488, SI 2009/ 1676, SI 2009/ 2655, SI 2009/ 3229, SI 2009/ 3257
s.18A, added: 2009 c.24 s.27
s.19, amended: 2009 c.24 s.27
s.19, enabling: SI 2009/ 583, SI 2009/ 1488, SI 2009/ 2655, SI 2009/ 3257
Sch.1 Part 3 para.13, enabling: SI 2009/ 3229
Sch.2 Part 1 para.2, repealed: 2009 c.24 Sch.7 Part 1
Sch.2 Part 3 para.45, repealed (in part): 2009 c.24 Sch.7 Part 3

17. National Health Service Reform and Health Care Professions Act 2002
s.25, referred to: SI 2009/ 2722 Reg.3

19. National Insurance Contributions Act 2002
Sch.1 para.45, amended: 2009 c.24 s.12

21. Tax Credits Act 2002
applied: 2009 c.8 s.3, SI 2009/ 830 Art.2, SI 2009/ 1673 Art.2, SSI 2009/ 48 Reg.6, SSI 2009/ 178 Reg.3, Reg.4
referred to: 2009 c.24 s.58
Part 1, applied: SI 2009/ 391 Reg.3, SI 2009/ 1555 Reg.42, Reg.45, SI 2009/ 2737 Reg.28, Reg.31, Reg.93, Reg.96, SI 2009/ 3359 Reg.26
s.4, enabling: SI 2009/ 697, SI 2009/ 2887
s.7, applied: SI 2009/ 2300 Art.2, SI 2009/ 2997 Reg.3, SSI 2009/ 178 Reg.3, Reg.4
s.7, enabling: SI 2009/ 697, SI 2009/ 800, SI 2009/ 2887
s.8, enabling: SI 2009/ 697
s.9, enabling: SI 2009/ 800
s.10, enabling: SI 2009/ 1829
s.11, enabling: SI 2009/ 800, SI 2009/ 2887
s.12, applied: SI 2009/ 1544, SI 2009/ 2888
s.12, enabling: SI 2009/ 697, SI 2009/ 2887
s.13, enabling: SI 2009/ 800

2002– cont.

21. Tax Credits Act 2002– *cont.*
s.17, applied: SI 2009/ 2997 Reg.3
s.18, applied: SI 2009/ 2997 Reg.3
s.19, amended: SI 2009/ 56 Sch.1 para.313
s.19, applied: SI 2009/ 2997 Reg.3
s.20, applied: SI 2009/ 2997 Reg.3
s.21, applied: SI 2009/ 2997 Reg.3
s.25, referred to: SI 2009/ 404 Art.9
s.29, amended: 2009 c.10 Sch.58 para.8
s.39, amended: SI 2009/ 56 Sch.1 para.314
s.39, repealed (in part): SI 2009/ 56 Sch.1 para.314
s.41, applied: SI 2009/ 800
s.41, referred to: SI 2009/ 800
s.48, amended: SI 2009/ 56 Sch.1 para.315
s.49, enabling: SI 2009/ 3268
s.50, enabling: SI 2009/ 3268
s.63, amended: SI 2009/ 56 Sch.1 para.316
s.63, repealed (in part): SI 2009/ 56 Sch.1 para.316
s.65, enabling: SI 2009/ 697, SI 2009/ 800, SI 2009/ 1829, SI 2009/ 2887
s.66, applied: SI 2009/ 800
s.67, enabling: SI 2009/ 697, SI 2009/ 800, SI 2009/ 2887
Sch.2, amended: SI 2009/ 56 Sch.1 para.319
Sch.2 para.2, amended: SI 2009/ 56 Sch.1 para.318
Sch.2 para.3, amended: SI 2009/ 56 Sch.1 para.319
Sch.2 para.4, amended: SI 2009/ 56 Sch.1 para.320
Sch.3 para.16, repealed (in part): 2009 c.24 Sch.7 Part 1
Sch.3 para.18, repealed (in part): 2009 c.24 Sch.7 Part 1
Sch.3 para.20, repealed (in part): 2009 c.24 Sch.7 Part 1
Sch.3 para.34, repealed: 2009 c.24 Sch.7 Part 2
Sch.3 para.59, repealed: 2009 c.4 Sch.3 Part 1

22. Employment Act 2002
see *N v Lewisham LBC* [2009] I.C.R. 1538 (EAT), Burton, J.
s.29, applied: SI 2009/ 771 Art.3
s.30, see *Redcar and Cleveland BC v Bainbridge* [2008] EWCA Civ 885, [2009] I.C.R. 133 (CA (Civ Div)), Mummery, L.J.
s.30, applied: SI 2009/ 771 Art.3
s.31, applied: SI 2009/ 771 Art.3
s.32, see *Suffolk Mental Health Partnership NHS Trust v Hurst* [2009] EWCA Civ 309, [2009] I.C.R. 1011 (CA (Civ Div)), Pill, L.J.
s.32, applied: SI 2009/ 771 Art.3
s.33, applied: SI 2009/ 771 Art.3
Sch.1 para.3, amended: SI 2009/ 56 Sch.1 para.322
Sch.1 para.4, amended: SI 2009/ 56 Sch.1 para.323
Sch.1 para.7, amended: SI 2009/ 56 Sch.1 para.324
Sch.1 para.9, amended: SI 2009/ 56 Sch.1 para.325
Sch.2, see *N v Lewisham LBC* [2009] I.C.R. 1538 (EAT), Burton, J.
Sch.2, applied: SI 2009/ 771 Art.3
Sch.2 para.6, see *Suffolk Mental Health Partnership NHS Trust v Hurst* [2009] EWCA Civ 309, [2009] I.C.R. 1011 (CA (Civ Div)), Pill, L.J.; see *Suffolk Mental Health Partnership NHS Trust v Hurst* [2009] I.C.R. 281 (EAT), Elias, J (President)
Sch.3, applied: SI 2009/ 771 Art.3
Sch.4, applied: SI 2009/ 771 Art.3
Sch.7 para.9, repealed: 2009 c.24 Sch.7 Part 3
Sch.7 para.51, repealed: 2009 c.24 Sch.7 Part 3
Sch.7 para.55, repealed: 2009 c.24 Sch.7 Part 3

2002– cont.

23. Finance Act 2002
referred to: 2009 c.4 s.855, s.882, s.890, s.891, s.892, s.893, s.894, s.895, s.896, s.897, s.898, s.899, s.905, s.907
varied: SI 2009/ 317 Sch.1
s.11, repealed: 2009 c.10 s.114
s.38, repealed: 2009 c.4 Sch.3 Part 1
s.53, repealed: 2009 c.4 Sch.3 Part 1
s.54, repealed: 2009 c.4 Sch.3 Part 1
s.55, repealed: 2009 c.4 Sch.3 Part 1
s.56, repealed: 2009 c.4 Sch.3 Part 1
s.60, repealed: 2009 c.4 Sch.3 Part 1
s.64, repealed: 2009 c.4 Sch.3 Part 1
s.65, amended: 2009 c.4 Sch.1 para.531
s.65, repealed (in part): 2009 c.4 Sch.3 Part 1
s.67, repealed (in part): 2009 c.4 Sch.3 Part 1
s.68, repealed: 2009 c.4 Sch.3 Part 1
s.71, repealed: 2009 c.4 Sch.3 Part 1
s.81, amended: 2009 c.4 Sch.1 para.533
s.83, repealed (in part): 2009 c.4 Sch.3 Part 1
s.84, repealed (in part): 2009 c.4 Sch.3 Part 1
s.101, see *Revenue and Customs Commissioners v Micro Fusion 2004-1 LLP* [2009] EWHC 1082 (Ch), [2009] S.T.C. 1741 (Ch D), Davis, J.
s.103, amended: 2009 c.4 Sch.3 Part 1
s.103, repealed (in part): 2009 c.4 Sch.3 Part 1
s.105, repealed (in part): 2009 c.4 Sch.3 Part 1
s.106, repealed: 2009 c.4 Sch.3 Part 1
s.121, repealed: 2009 c.10 Sch.5 para.6
s.135, applied: 2009 c.8 s.11
s.135, enabling: SI 2009/ 2978, SI 2009/ 3218
s.136, applied: SI 2009/ 2029
Sch.9 Part 2 para.4, repealed (in part): 2009 c.4 Sch.3 Part 1, SI 2009/ 3001 Sch.2
Sch.9 Part 3 para.8, repealed (in part): 2009 c.4 Sch.3 Part 1
Sch.12 Part 1 para.1, repealed: 2009 c.4 Sch.3 Part 1
Sch.12 Part 1 para.2, repealed: 2009 c.4 Sch.3 Part 1
Sch.12 Part 1 para.3, repealed: 2009 c.4 Sch.3 Part 1
Sch.12 Part 1 para.4, repealed: 2009 c.4 Sch.3 Part 1
Sch.12 Part 1 para.5, repealed: 2009 c.4 Sch.3 Part 1
Sch.12 Part 1 para.6, repealed: 2009 c.4 Sch.3 Part 1
Sch.12 Part 2 para.7, repealed: 2009 c.4 Sch.3 Part 1
Sch.12 Part 2 para.8, repealed: 2009 c.4 Sch.3 Part 1
Sch.12 Part 2 para.9, repealed: 2009 c.4 Sch.3 Part 1
Sch.12 Part 2A para.10A, repealed: 2009 c.4 Sch.3 Part 1
Sch.12 Part 2A para.10B, repealed: 2009 c.4 Sch.3 Part 1
Sch.12 Part 2A para.10C, repealed: 2009 c.4 Sch.3 Part 1
Sch.12 Part 2 para.10, repealed: 2009 c.4 Sch.3 Part 1
Sch.12 Part 3 para.11, repealed: 2009 c.4 Sch.3 Part 1
Sch.12 Part 4 para.12, repealed: 2009 c.4 Sch.3 Part 1
Sch.12 Part 4 para.13, repealed: 2009 c.4 Sch.3 Part 1
Sch.12 Part 5 para.14, repealed: 2009 c.4 Sch.3 Part 1
Sch.12 Part 5 para.15, repealed: 2009 c.4 Sch.3 Part 1
Sch.12 Part 5 para.16, repealed: 2009 c.4 Sch.3 Part 1
Sch.12 Part 6 para.17, repealed: 2009 c.4 Sch.3 Part 1
Sch.12 Part 6 para.18, repealed: 2009 c.4 Sch.3 Part 1
Sch.12 Part 6 para.19, repealed: 2009 c.4 Sch.3 Part 1
Sch.12 Part 6 para.20, repealed: 2009 c.4 Sch.3 Part 1
Sch.12 Part 6 para.21, repealed: 2009 c.4 Sch.3 Part 1
Sch.13 Part 1 para.1, repealed: 2009 c.4 Sch.3 Part 1
Sch.13 Part 1 para.2, repealed: 2009 c.4 Sch.3 Part 1
Sch.13 Part 1 para.3, repealed: 2009 c.4 Sch.3 Part 1
Sch.13 Part 1 para.4, repealed: 2009 c.4 Sch.3 Part 1
Sch.13 Part 1 para.5, repealed: 2009 c.4 Sch.3 Part 1

2002– cont.

23. Finance Act 2002–*cont.*

Sch.13 Part 1 para.6, repealed: 2009 c.4 Sch.3 Part 1
Sch.13 Part 1 para.7, repealed: 2009 c.4 Sch.3 Part 1
Sch.13 Part 1 para.8, repealed: 2009 c.4 Sch.3 Part 1
Sch.13 Part 1 para.9, repealed: 2009 c.4 Sch.3 Part 1
Sch.13 Part 1 para.10, repealed: 2009 c.4 Sch.3 Part 1
Sch.13 Part 1 para.11, repealed: 2009 c.4 Sch.3 Part 1
Sch.13 Part 1 para.12, repealed: 2009 c.4 Sch.3 Part 1
Sch.13 Part 2 para.13, repealed: 2009 c.4 Sch.3 Part 1
Sch.13 Part 2 para.14, repealed: 2009 c.4 Sch.3 Part 1
Sch.13 Part 2 para.15, repealed: 2009 c.4 Sch.3 Part 1
Sch.13 Part 2 para.15A, repealed: 2009 c.4 Sch.3 Part 1
Sch.13 Part 2 para.16, repealed: 2009 c.4 Sch.3 Part 1
Sch.13 Part 2 para.16A, repealed: 2009 c.4 Sch.3 Part 1
Sch.13 Part 2 para.17, repealed: 2009 c.4 Sch.3 Part 1
Sch.13 Part 2 para.18, repealed: 2009 c.4 Sch.3 Part 1
Sch.13 Part 2 para.18A, repealed: 2009 c.4 Sch.3 Part 1
Sch.13 Part 2 para.19, repealed: 2009 c.4 Sch.3 Part 1
Sch.13 Part 2 para.20, repealed: 2009 c.4 Sch.3 Part 1
Sch.13 Part 3 para.21, repealed: 2009 c.4 Sch.3 Part 1
Sch.13 Part 4 para.22, repealed: 2009 c.4 Sch.3 Part 1
Sch.13 Part 4 para.23, repealed: 2009 c.4 Sch.3 Part 1
Sch.13 Part 5 para.24, repealed: 2009 c.4 Sch.3 Part 1
Sch.13 Part 5 para.25, repealed: 2009 c.4 Sch.3 Part 1
Sch.13 Part 5 para.26, repealed: 2009 c.4 Sch.3 Part 1
Sch.13 Part 5 para.27, repealed: 2009 c.4 Sch.3 Part 1
Sch.13 Part 5 para.28, repealed: 2009 c.4 Sch.3 Part 1
Sch.14 para.1, repealed: 2009 c.4 Sch.3 Part 1
Sch.14 para.2, repealed: 2009 c.4 Sch.3 Part 1
Sch.14 para.3, repealed: 2009 c.4 Sch.3 Part 1
Sch.14 para.4, repealed: 2009 c.4 Sch.3 Part 1
Sch.14 para.5, repealed: 2009 c.4 Sch.3 Part 1
Sch.15 para.1, repealed: 2009 c.4 Sch.3 Part 1
Sch.15 para.2, repealed: 2009 c.4 Sch.3 Part 1
Sch.15 para.3, repealed: 2009 c.4 Sch.3 Part 1
Sch.15 para.4, repealed: 2009 c.4 Sch.3 Part 1
Sch.15 para.5, repealed: 2009 c.4 Sch.3 Part 1
Sch.16 Part 6 para.27, amended: 2009 c.4 Sch.3 Part 1
Sch.18 Part 2 para.4, amended: 2009 c.4 Sch.1 para.539
Sch.18 Part 2 para.5, amended: 2009 c.4 Sch.1 para.539
Sch.18 Part 3 para.9, repealed (in part): 2009 c.4 Sch.3 Part 1
Sch.18 Part 5 para.12, repealed: SI 2009/2035 Sch.1 para.39
Sch.18 Part 5 para.13, amended: SI 2009/56 Sch.1 para.327
Sch.18 Part 5 para.13, repealed (in part): SI 2009/56 Sch.1 para.327
Sch.19 para.6, repealed: 2009 c.10 Sch.11 para.25
Sch.22 Part 1 para.1, repealed: 2009 c.4 Sch.3 Part 1
Sch.22 Part 2 para.2, repealed: 2009 c.4 Sch.3 Part 1
Sch.22 Part 2 para.3, repealed: 2009 c.4 Sch.3 Part 1
Sch.22 Part 2 para.4, repealed: 2009 c.4 Sch.3 Part 1
Sch.22 Part 2 para.5, repealed: 2009 c.4 Sch.3 Part 1
Sch.22 Part 3 para.6, repealed: 2009 c.4 Sch.3 Part 1
Sch.22 Part 3 para.7, repealed: 2009 c.4 Sch.3 Part 1
Sch.22 Part 3 para.8, repealed: 2009 c.4 Sch.3 Part 1
Sch.22 Part 3 para.9, repealed: 2009 c.4 Sch.3 Part 1
Sch.22 Part 3 para.10, repealed: 2009 c.4 Sch.3 Part 1
Sch.22 Part 3 para.11, repealed: 2009 c.4 Sch.3 Part 1
Sch.22 Part 3 para.12, repealed: 2009 c.4 Sch.3 Part 1
Sch.22 Part 4 para.13, repealed: 2009 c.4 Sch.3 Part 1
Sch.22 Part 4 para.14, repealed: 2009 c.4 Sch.3 Part 1
Sch.22 Part 4 para.15, repealed: 2009 c.4 Sch.3 Part 1
Sch.22 Part 5 para.16, repealed: 2009 c.4 Sch.3 Part 1
Sch.22 Part 5 para.17, repealed: 2009 c.4 Sch.3 Part 1

2002– cont.

23. Finance Act 2002–*cont.*

Sch.22 Part 5 para.18, repealed: 2009 c.4 Sch.3 Part 1
Sch.23 Part 1 para.2, repealed: 2009 c.4 Sch.3 Part 1
Sch.23 Part 1 para.3, repealed: 2009 c.4 Sch.3 Part 1
Sch.23 Part 1 para.6, repealed: 2009 c.4 Sch.3 Part 1
Sch.23 Part 1 para.7, repealed: 2009 c.4 Sch.3 Part 1
Sch.23 Part 1 para.9, repealed: 2009 c.4 Sch.3 Part 1
Sch.23 Part 1 para.10, repealed: 2009 c.4 Sch.3 Part 1
Sch.23 Part 1 para.11, repealed: 2009 c.4 Sch.3 Part 1
Sch.23 Part 1 para.12, repealed: 2009 c.4 Sch.3 Part 1
Sch.23 Part 1 para.13, repealed: 2009 c.4 Sch.3 Part 1
Sch.23 Part 1 para.14, repealed: 2009 c.4 Sch.3 Part 1
Sch.23 Part 1 para.15, repealed: 2009 c.4 Sch.3 Part 1
Sch.23 Part 3 para.25, repealed: 2009 c.4 Sch.3 Part 1
Sch.23 Part 3 para.26, amended: 2009 c.4 Sch.1 para.541
Sch.25 Part 1 para.2, repealed: 2009 c.4 Sch.3 Part 1
Sch.25 Part 1 para.3, repealed: 2009 c.4 Sch.3 Part 1
Sch.25 Part 1 para.4, repealed: 2009 c.4 Sch.3 Part 1
Sch.25 Part 1 para.5, repealed: 2009 c.4 Sch.3 Part 1
Sch.25 Part 1 para.6, repealed: 2009 c.4 Sch.3 Part 1
Sch.25 Part 1 para.7, repealed: 2009 c.4 Sch.3 Part 1
Sch.25 Part 1 para.8, repealed: 2009 c.4 Sch.3 Part 1
Sch.25 Part 1 para.9, repealed: 2009 c.4 Sch.3 Part 1
Sch.25 Part 1 para.10, repealed: 2009 c.4 Sch.3 Part 1
Sch.25 Part 1 para.11, repealed: 2009 c.4 Sch.3 Part 1
Sch.25 Part 1 para.12, repealed: 2009 c.4 Sch.3 Part 1
Sch.25 Part 1 para.13, repealed: 2009 c.4 Sch.3 Part 1
Sch.25 Part 1 para.14, repealed: 2009 c.4 Sch.3 Part 1
Sch.25 Part 1 para.15, repealed: 2009 c.4 Sch.3 Part 1
Sch.25 Part 1 para.16, repealed: 2009 c.4 Sch.3 Part 1
Sch.25 Part 1 para.17, repealed: 2009 c.4 Sch.3 Part 1
Sch.25 Part 1 para.18, repealed: 2009 c.4 Sch.3 Part 1
Sch.25 Part 1 para.19, repealed: 2009 c.4 Sch.3 Part 1
Sch.25 Part 1 para.20, repealed: 2009 c.4 Sch.3 Part 1
Sch.25 Part 1 para.21, repealed: 2009 c.4 Sch.3 Part 1
Sch.25 Part 1 para.22, repealed: 2009 c.4 Sch.3 Part 1
Sch.25 Part 1 para.23, repealed: 2009 c.4 Sch.3 Part 1
Sch.25 Part 1 para.24, repealed: 2009 c.4 Sch.3 Part 1
Sch.25 Part 1 para.25, repealed: 2009 c.4 Sch.3 Part 1
Sch.25 Part 1 para.27, repealed: 2009 c.4 Sch.3 Part 1
Sch.25 Part 1 para.28, repealed: 2009 c.4 Sch.3 Part 1
Sch.25 Part 1 para.29, repealed: 2009 c.4 Sch.3 Part 1
Sch.25 Part 1 para.30, repealed: 2009 c.4 Sch.3 Part 1
Sch.25 Part 1 para.31, repealed: 2009 c.4 Sch.3 Part 1
Sch.25 Part 1 para.32, repealed: 2009 c.4 Sch.3 Part 1
Sch.25 Part 1 para.33, repealed: 2009 c.4 Sch.3 Part 1
Sch.25 Part 1 para.34, repealed: 2009 c.4 Sch.3 Part 1
Sch.25 Part 1 para.35, repealed: 2009 c.4 Sch.3 Part 1
Sch.25 Part 1 para.36, repealed: 2009 c.4 Sch.3 Part 1
Sch.25 Part 1 para.40, repealed: 2009 c.4 Sch.3 Part 1
Sch.25 Part 2 para.47, repealed: 2009 c.4 Sch.3 Part 1
Sch.25 Part 2 para.48, repealed: 2009 c.4 Sch.3 Part 1
Sch.25 Part 2 para.50, repealed: 2009 c.4 Sch.3 Part 1
Sch.25 Part 2 para.53, repealed: 2009 c.4 Sch.3 Part 1
Sch.25 Part 3 para.61, repealed: 2009 c.4 Sch.3 Part 1
Sch.25 Part 3 para.61A, repealed: 2009 c.4 Sch.3 Part 1
Sch.25 Part 3 para.62, repealed: 2009 c.4 Sch.3 Part 1
Sch.25 Part 3 para.63, repealed: 2009 c.4 Sch.3 Part 1
Sch.25 Part 3 para.64, repealed: 2009 c.4 Sch.3 Part 1
Sch.26 Part 1 para.1, repealed: 2009 c.4 Sch.3 Part 1
Sch.26 Part 2 para.2, repealed: 2009 c.4 Sch.3 Part 1
Sch.26 Part 2 para.2A, repealed: 2009 c.4 Sch.3 Part 1
Sch.26 Part 2 para.2B, repealed: 2009 c.4 Sch.3 Part 1
Sch.26 Part 2 para.3, repealed: 2009 c.4 Sch.3 Part 1

23. Finance Act 2002–*cont.*

Sch.26 Part 2 para.4, repealed: 2009 c.4 Sch.3 Part 1
Sch.26 Part 2 para.4A, repealed: 2009 c.4 Sch.3 Part 1
Sch.26 Part 2 para.4B, repealed: 2009 c.4 Sch.3 Part 1
Sch.26 Part 2 para.4C, repealed: 2009 c.4 Sch.3 Part 1
Sch.26 Part 2 para.4D, repealed: 2009 c.4 Sch.3 Part 1
Sch.26 Part 2 para.5, repealed: 2009 c.4 Sch.3 Part 1
Sch.26 Part 2 para.5A, repealed: 2009 c.4 Sch.3 Part 1
Sch.26 Part 2 para.6, repealed: 2009 c.4 Sch.3 Part 1
Sch.26 Part 2 para.7, repealed: 2009 c.4 Sch.3 Part 1
Sch.26 Part 2 para.8, repealed: 2009 c.4 Sch.3 Part 1
Sch.26 Part 2 para.9, repealed: 2009 c.4 Sch.3 Part 1
Sch.26 Part 2 para.10, repealed: 2009 c.4 Sch.3 Part 1
Sch.26 Part 2 para.11, repealed: 2009 c.4 Sch.3 Part 1
Sch.26 Part 2 para.12, repealed: 2009 c.4 Sch.3 Part 1
Sch.26 Part 2 para.13, repealed: 2009 c.4 Sch.3 Part 1
Sch.26 Part 3 para.14, repealed: 2009 c.4 Sch.3 Part 1
Sch.26 Part 3 para.15, repealed: 2009 c.4 Sch.3 Part 1
Sch.26 Part 3 para.16, repealed: 2009 c.4 Sch.3 Part 1
Sch.26 Part 4 para.17, repealed: 2009 c.4 Sch.3 Part 1
Sch.26 Part 4 para.17A, repealed: 2009 c.4 Sch.3 Part 1
Sch.26 Part 4 para.17B, repealed: 2009 c.4 Sch.3 Part 1
Sch.26 Part 4 para.17C, repealed: 2009 c.4 Sch.3 Part 1
Sch.26 Part 4 para.18, repealed: 2009 c.4 Sch.3 Part 1
Sch.26 Part 4 para.19, repealed: 2009 c.4 Sch.3 Part 1
Sch.26 Part 4 para.20, repealed: 2009 c.4 Sch.3 Part 1
Sch.26 Part 4 para.21, repealed: 2009 c.4 Sch.3 Part 1
Sch.26 Part 5 para.22, repealed: 2009 c.4 Sch.3 Part 1
Sch.26 Part 6 para.22A, repealed: 2009 c.4 Sch.3 Part 1
Sch.26 Part 6 para.23, repealed: 2009 c.4 Sch.3 Part 1
Sch.26 Part 6 para.24, repealed: 2009 c.4 Sch.3 Part 1
Sch.26 Part 6 para.25, repealed: 2009 c.4 Sch.3 Part 1
Sch.26 Part 6 para.25A, repealed: 2009 c.4 Sch.3 Part 1
Sch.26 Part 6 para.26, repealed: 2009 c.4 Sch.3 Part 1
Sch.26 Part 6 para.27, repealed: 2009 c.4 Sch.3 Part 1
Sch.26 Part 6 para.27A, repealed: 2009 c.4 Sch.3 Part 1
Sch.26 Part 6 para.28, repealed: 2009 c.4 Sch.3 Part 1
Sch.26 Part 6 para.29, repealed: 2009 c.4 Sch.3 Part 1
Sch.26 Part 6 para.30, repealed: 2009 c.4 Sch.3 Part 1
Sch.26 Part 6 para.30A, repealed: 2009 c.4 Sch.3 Part 1
Sch.26 Part 6 para.30B, repealed: 2009 c.4 Sch.3 Part 1
Sch.26 Part 6 para.30C, repealed: 2009 c.4 Sch.3 Part 1
Sch.26 Part 6 para.30D, repealed: 2009 c.4 Sch.3 Part 1
Sch.26 Part 6 para.30E, repealed: 2009 c.4 Sch.3 Part 1
Sch.26 Part 6 para.30F, repealed: 2009 c.4 Sch.3 Part 1
Sch.26 Part 6 para.30G, repealed: 2009 c.4 Sch.3 Part 1
Sch.26 Part 6 para.30H, repealed: 2009 c.4 Sch.3 Part 1
Sch.26 Part 6 para.30I, repealed: 2009 c.4 Sch.3 Part 1
Sch.26 Part 6 para.31, repealed: 2009 c.4 Sch.3 Part 1
Sch.26 Part 6 para.31A, repealed: 2009 c.4 Sch.3 Part 1

23. Finance Act 2002–*cont.*

Sch.26 Part 7 para.32, repealed: 2009 c.4 Sch.3 Part 1
Sch.26 Part 7 para.33, repealed: 2009 c.4 Sch.3 Part 1
Sch.26 Part 7 para.34, repealed: 2009 c.4 Sch.3 Part 1
Sch.26 Part 7 para.35, repealed: 2009 c.4 Sch.3 Part 1
Sch.26 Part 7 para.36, repealed: 2009 c.4 Sch.3 Part 1
Sch.26 Part 7 para.37, repealed: 2009 c.4 Sch.3 Part 1
Sch.26 Part 7 para.38, repealed: 2009 c.4 Sch.3 Part 1
Sch.26 Part 7 para.38A, repealed: 2009 c.4 Sch.3 Part 1
Sch.26 Part 7 para.39, repealed: 2009 c.4 Sch.3 Part 1
Sch.26 Part 7 para.40, repealed: 2009 c.4 Sch.3 Part 1
Sch.26 Part 8 para.41, repealed: 2009 c.4 Sch.3 Part 1
Sch.26 Part 8 para.41A, repealed: 2009 c.4 Sch.3 Part 1
Sch.26 Part 8 para.42, repealed: 2009 c.4 Sch.3 Part 1
Sch.26 Part 8 para.43, repealed: 2009 c.4 Sch.3 Part 1
Sch.26 Part 9 para.43A, repealed: 2009 c.4 Sch.3 Part 1
Sch.26 Part 9 para.43B, repealed: 2009 c.4 Sch.3 Part 1
Sch.26 Part 9 para.44, repealed: 2009 c.4 Sch.3 Part 1
Sch.26 Part 9 para.45, repealed: 2009 c.4 Sch.3 Part 1
Sch.26 Part 9 para.45A, repealed: 2009 c.4 Sch.3 Part 1
Sch.26 Part 9 para.45B, repealed: 2009 c.4 Sch.3 Part 1
Sch.26 Part 9 para.45C, repealed: 2009 c.4 Sch.3 Part 1
Sch.26 Part 9 para.45D, repealed: 2009 c.4 Sch.3 Part 1
Sch.26 Part 9 para.45E, repealed: 2009 c.4 Sch.3 Part 1
Sch.26 Part 9 para.45F, repealed: 2009 c.4 Sch.3 Part 1
Sch.26 Part 9 para.45FA, repealed: 2009 c.4 Sch.3 Part 1
Sch.26 Part 9 para.45G, repealed: 2009 c.4 Sch.3 Part 1
Sch.26 Part 9 para.45H, repealed: 2009 c.4 Sch.3 Part 1
Sch.26 Part 9 para.45HA, repealed: 2009 c.4 Sch.3 Part 1
Sch.26 Part 9 para.45HZA, repealed: 2009 c.4 Sch.3 Part 1
Sch.26 Part 9 para.45I, repealed: 2009 c.4 Sch.3 Part 1
Sch.26 Part 9 para.45J, repealed: 2009 c.4 Sch.3 Part 1
Sch.26 Part 9 para.45JA, repealed: 2009 c.4 Sch.3 Part 1
Sch.26 Part 9 para.45K, repealed: 2009 c.4 Sch.3 Part 1
Sch.26 Part 9 para.45KA, repealed: 2009 c.4 Sch.3 Part 1
Sch.26 Part 9 para.45L, repealed: 2009 c.4 Sch.3 Part 1
Sch.26 Part 9 para.45LA, repealed: 2009 c.4 Sch.3 Part 1
Sch.26 Part 9 para.45M, repealed: 2009 c.4 Sch.3 Part 1
Sch.26 Part 9 para.46, repealed: 2009 c.4 Sch.3 Part 1
Sch.26 Part 9 para.47, repealed: 2009 c.4 Sch.3 Part 1
Sch.26 Part 9 para.48, repealed: 2009 c.4 Sch.3 Part 1
Sch.26 Part 9 para.48A, repealed: 2009 c.4 Sch.3 Part 1
Sch.26 Part 9 para.49, repealed: 2009 c.4 Sch.3 Part 1
Sch.26 Part 9 para.50, repealed: 2009 c.4 Sch.3 Part 1
Sch.26 Part 9 para.50A, repealed: 2009 c.4 Sch.3 Part 1

2002– cont.

23. Finance Act 2002– *cont.*

Sch.26 Part 9 para.51, repealed: 2009 c.4 Sch.3 Part 1

Sch.26 Part 10 para.52, repealed: 2009 c.4 Sch.3 Part 1

Sch.26 Part 10 para.53, repealed: 2009 c.4 Sch.3 Part 1

Sch.26 Part 10 para.54, repealed: 2009 c.4 Sch.3 Part 1

Sch.26 para.15, see *HBOS Treasury Services Ltd v Revenue and Customs Commissioners* [2009] UKFTT 261 (TC) (FTT (Tax)), Howard M Nowlan

Sch.26 para.28, see *HBOS Treasury Services Ltd v Revenue and Customs Commissioners* [2009] UKFTT 261 (TC) (FTT (Tax)), Howard M Nowlan

Sch.27 para.3, repealed: 2009 c.4 Sch.3 Part 1

Sch.27 para.19, repealed: 2009 c.4 Sch.3 Part 1

Sch.27 para.20, repealed: 2009 c.4 Sch.3 Part 1

Sch.28 para.1, repealed: 2009 c.4 Sch.3 Part 1

Sch.28 para.2, amended: 2009 c.4 Sch.1 para.544

Sch.28 para.3, repealed: 2009 c.4 Sch.3 Part 1

Sch.28 para.4, amended: 2009 c.4 Sch.1 para.544

Sch.28 para.5, amended: 2009 c.4 Sch.1 para.544

Sch.28 para.6, amended: 2009 c.4 Sch.1 para.544

Sch.29 Part 1 para.1, repealed: 2009 c.4 Sch.3 Part 1

Sch.29 Part 1 para.2, repealed: 2009 c.4 Sch.3 Part 1

Sch.29 Part 1 para.3, repealed: 2009 c.4 Sch.3 Part 1

Sch.29 Part 1 para.4, repealed: 2009 c.4 Sch.3 Part 1

Sch.29 Part 1 para.5, repealed: 2009 c.4 Sch.3 Part 1

Sch.29 Part 1 para.6, repealed: 2009 c.4 Sch.3 Part 1

Sch.29 Part 2 para.7, repealed: 2009 c.4 Sch.3 Part 1

Sch.29 Part 2 para.8, repealed: 2009 c.4 Sch.3 Part 1

Sch.29 Part 2 para.9, repealed: 2009 c.4 Sch.3 Part 1

Sch.29 Part 2 para.10, repealed: 2009 c.4 Sch.3 Part 1

Sch.29 Part 2 para.11, repealed: 2009 c.4 Sch.3 Part 1

Sch.29 Part 2 para.12, repealed: 2009 c.4 Sch.3 Part 1

Sch.29 Part 3 para.13, repealed: 2009 c.4 Sch.3 Part 1

Sch.29 Part 3 para.14, repealed: 2009 c.4 Sch.3 Part 1

Sch.29 Part 3 para.14A, repealed: 2009 c.4 Sch.3 Part 1

Sch.29 Part 3 para.15, repealed: 2009 c.4 Sch.3 Part 1

Sch.29 Part 3 para.16, repealed: 2009 c.4 Sch.3 Part 1

Sch.29 Part 3 para.17, repealed: 2009 c.4 Sch.3 Part 1

Sch.29 Part 4 para.18, repealed: 2009 c.4 Sch.3 Part 1

Sch.29 Part 4 para.19, repealed: 2009 c.4 Sch.3 Part 1

Sch.29 Part 4 para.20, repealed: 2009 c.4 Sch.3 Part 1

Sch.29 Part 4 para.21, repealed: 2009 c.4 Sch.3 Part 1

Sch.29 Part 4 para.22, repealed: 2009 c.4 Sch.3 Part 1

Sch.29 Part 4 para.23, repealed: 2009 c.4 Sch.3 Part 1

Sch.29 Part 4 para.24, repealed: 2009 c.4 Sch.3 Part 1

Sch.29 Part 4 para.25, repealed: 2009 c.4 Sch.3 Part 1

Sch.29 Part 4 para.26, repealed: 2009 c.4 Sch.3 Part 1

Sch.29 Part 5 para.27, repealed: 2009 c.4 Sch.3 Part 1

Sch.29 Part 5 para.28, repealed: 2009 c.4 Sch.3 Part 1

Sch.29 Part 5 para.29, repealed: 2009 c.4 Sch.3 Part 1

Sch.29 Part 6 para.30, repealed: 2009 c.4 Sch.3 Part 1

Sch.29 Part 6 para.31, repealed: 2009 c.4 Sch.3 Part 1

Sch.29 Part 6 para.32, repealed: 2009 c.4 Sch.3 Part 1

Sch.29 Part 6 para.33, repealed: 2009 c.4 Sch.3 Part 1

Sch.29 Part 6 para.34, repealed: 2009 c.4 Sch.3 Part 1

Sch.29 Part 6 para.35, repealed: 2009 c.4 Sch.3 Part 1

Sch.29 Part 6 para.36, repealed: 2009 c.4 Sch.3 Part 1

Sch.29 Part 7 para.37, repealed: 2009 c.4 Sch.3 Part 1

Sch.29 Part 7 para.38, repealed: 2009 c.4 Sch.3 Part 1

Sch.29 Part 7 para.39, repealed: 2009 c.4 Sch.3 Part 1

Sch.29 Part 7 para.40, repealed: 2009 c.4 Sch.3 Part 1

Sch.29 Part 7 para.41, repealed: 2009 c.4 Sch.3 Part 1

2002– cont.

23. Finance Act 2002– *cont.*

Sch.29 Part 7 para.42, repealed: 2009 c.4 Sch.3 Part 1

Sch.29 Part 7 para.42A, repealed: 2009 c.4 Sch.3 Part 1

Sch.29 Part 7 para.43, repealed: 2009 c.4 Sch.3 Part 1

Sch.29 Part 7 para.44, repealed: 2009 c.4 Sch.3 Part 1

Sch.29 Part 7 para.45, repealed: 2009 c.4 Sch.3 Part 1

Sch.29 Part 8 para.46, repealed: 2009 c.4 Sch.3 Part 1

Sch.29 Part 8 para.47, repealed: 2009 c.4 Sch.3 Part 1

Sch.29 Part 8 para.48, repealed: 2009 c.4 Sch.3 Part 1

Sch.29 Part 8 para.49, repealed: 2009 c.4 Sch.3 Part 1

Sch.29 Part 8 para.50, repealed: 2009 c.4 Sch.3 Part 1

Sch.29 Part 8 para.51, repealed: 2009 c.4 Sch.3 Part 1

Sch.29 Part 8 para.51A, repealed: 2009 c.4 Sch.3 Part 1

Sch.29 Part 8 para.52, repealed: 2009 c.4 Sch.3 Part 1

Sch.29 Part 8 para.53, repealed: 2009 c.4 Sch.3 Part 1

Sch.29 Part 8 para.54, repealed: 2009 c.4 Sch.3 Part 1

Sch.29 Part 9 para.55, repealed: 2009 c.4 Sch.3 Part 1

Sch.29 Part 9 para.56, repealed: 2009 c.4 Sch.3 Part 1

Sch.29 Part 9 para.57, repealed: 2009 c.4 Sch.3 Part 1

Sch.29 Part 9 para.58, repealed: 2009 c.4 Sch.3 Part 1

Sch.29 Part 9 para.59, repealed: 2009 c.4 Sch.3 Part 1

Sch.29 Part 9 para.60, repealed: 2009 c.4 Sch.3 Part 1

Sch.29 Part 9 para.61, repealed: 2009 c.4 Sch.3 Part 1

Sch.29 Part 9 para.62, repealed: 2009 c.4 Sch.3 Part 1

Sch.29 Part 9 para.63, repealed: 2009 c.4 Sch.3 Part 1

Sch.29 Part 9 para.64, repealed: 2009 c.4 Sch.3 Part 1

Sch.29 Part 9 para.65, repealed: 2009 c.4 Sch.3 Part 1

Sch.29 Part 9 para.66, repealed: 2009 c.4 Sch.3 Part 1

Sch.29 Part 9 para.67, repealed: 2009 c.4 Sch.3 Part 1

Sch.29 Part 9 para.68, repealed: 2009 c.4 Sch.3 Part 1

Sch.29 Part 9 para.69, repealed: 2009 c.4 Sch.3 Part 1

Sch.29 Part 9 para.70, repealed: 2009 c.4 Sch.3 Part 1

Sch.29 Part 9 para.71, repealed: 2009 c.4 Sch.3 Part 1

Sch.29 Part 10 para.72, repealed: 2009 c.4 Sch.3 Part 1

Sch.29 Part 10 para.73, repealed: 2009 c.4 Sch.3 Part 1

Sch.29 Part 10 para.73A, repealed: 2009 c.4 Sch.3 Part 1

Sch.29 Part 10 para.74, repealed: 2009 c.4 Sch.3 Part 1

Sch.29 Part 10 para.75, repealed: 2009 c.4 Sch.3 Part 1

Sch.29 Part 10 para.76, repealed: 2009 c.4 Sch.3 Part 1

Sch.29 Part 10 para.77, repealed: 2009 c.4 Sch.3 Part 1

Sch.29 Part 10 para.78, repealed: 2009 c.4 Sch.3 Part 1

Sch.29 Part 10 para.79, repealed: 2009 c.4 Sch.3 Part 1

Sch.29 Part 10 para.80, repealed: 2009 c.4 Sch.3 Part 1

Sch.29 Part 10 para.80A, repealed: 2009 c.4 Sch.3 Part 1

Sch.29 Part 10 para.80B, repealed: 2009 c.4 Sch.3 Part 1

Sch.29 Part 10 para.81, repealed: 2009 c.4 Sch.3 Part 1

Sch.29 Part 10 para.82, repealed: 2009 c.4 Sch.3 Part 1

Sch.29 Part 10 para.83, repealed: 2009 c.4 Sch.3 Part 1

Sch.29 Part 11 para.84, repealed: 2009 c.4 Sch.3 Part 1

Sch.29 Part 11 para.85, repealed: 2009 c.4 Sch.3 Part 1

23. Finance Act 2002–*cont.*

Sch.29 Part 11 para.85A, repealed: 2009 c.4 Sch.3
Part 1

Sch.29 Part 11 para.85B, repealed: 2009 c.4 Sch.3
Part 1

Sch.29 Part 11 para.85C, repealed: 2009 c.4 Sch.3
Part 1

Sch.29 Part 11 para.85D, repealed: 2009 c.4 Sch.3
Part 1

Sch.29 Part 11 para.86, repealed: 2009 c.4 Sch.3
Part 1

Sch.29 Part 11 para.87, repealed: 2009 c.4 Sch.3
Part 1

Sch.29 Part 11 para.87A, repealed: 2009 c.4 Sch.3
Part 1

Sch.29 Part 11 para.88, amended: SI 2009/56 Sch.1
para.328

Sch.29 Part 11 para.88, applied: SI 2009/275 Art.3

Sch.29 Part 11 para.88, repealed: 2009 c.4 Sch.3
Part 1

Sch.29 Part 11 para.89, repealed: 2009 c.4 Sch.3
Part 1

Sch.29 Part 11 para.90, repealed: 2009 c.4 Sch.3
Part 1

Sch.29 Part 11 para.91, repealed: 2009 c.4 Sch.3
Part 1

Sch.29 Part 12 para.92, repealed: 2009 c.4 Sch.3
Part 1

Sch.29 Part 12 para.93, repealed: 2009 c.4 Sch.3
Part 1

Sch.29 Part 12 para.94, repealed: 2009 c.4 Sch.3
Part 1

Sch.29 Part 12 para.95, repealed: 2009 c.4 Sch.3
Part 1

Sch.29 Part 12 para.95A, repealed: 2009 c.4 Sch.3
Part 1

Sch.29 Part 12 para.96, repealed: 2009 c.4 Sch.3
Part 1

Sch.29 Part 12 para.97, repealed: 2009 c.4 Sch.3
Part 1

Sch.29 Part 12 para.98, repealed: 2009 c.4 Sch.3
Part 1

Sch.29 Part 12 para.99, repealed: 2009 c.4 Sch.3
Part 1

Sch.29 Part 12 para.100, repealed: 2009 c.4 Sch.3
Part 1

Sch.29 Part 12 para.101, repealed: 2009 c.4 Sch.3
Part 1

Sch.29 Part 13A para.116A, repealed: 2009 c.4
Sch.3 Part 1

Sch.29 Part 13A para.116B, repealed: 2009 c.4 Sch.3
Part 1

Sch.29 Part 13A para.116C, repealed: 2009 c.4 Sch.3
Part 1

Sch.29 Part 13A para.116D, repealed: 2009 c.4
Sch.3 Part 1

Sch.29 Part 13A para.116E, repealed: 2009 c.4 Sch.3
Part 1

Sch.29 Part 13A para.116F, repealed: 2009 c.4 Sch.3
Part 1

Sch.29 Part 13A para.116G, repealed: 2009 c.4
Sch.3 Part 1

Sch.29 Part 13A para.116H, repealed: 2009 c.4
Sch.3 Part 1

Sch.29 Part 13 para.102, repealed: 2009 c.4 Sch.3
Part 1

Sch.29 Part 13 para.103, repealed: 2009 c.4 Sch.3
Part 1

Sch.29 Part 13 para.104, repealed: 2009 c.4 Sch.3
Part 1

23. Finance Act 2002–*cont.*

Sch.29 Part 13 para.105, repealed: 2009 c.4 Sch.3
Part 1

Sch.29 Part 13 para.106, repealed: 2009 c.4 Sch.3
Part 1

Sch.29 Part 13 para.107, repealed: 2009 c.4 Sch.3
Part 1

Sch.29 Part 13 para.108, repealed: 2009 c.4 Sch.3
Part 1

Sch.29 Part 13 para.109, repealed: 2009 c.4 Sch.3
Part 1

Sch.29 Part 13 para.110, repealed: 2009 c.4 Sch.3
Part 1

Sch.29 Part 13 para.111, repealed: 2009 c.4 Sch.3
Part 1

Sch.29 Part 13 para.112, repealed: 2009 c.4 Sch.3
Part 1

Sch.29 Part 13 para.113, repealed: 2009 c.4 Sch.3
Part 1

Sch.29 Part 13 para.114, repealed: 2009 c.4 Sch.3
Part 1

Sch.29 Part 13 para.115, repealed: 2009 c.4 Sch.3
Part 1

Sch.29 Part 13 para.116, repealed (in part): 2009 c.4
Sch.3 Part 1, 2009 c.10 Sch.16 para.3

Sch.29 Part 13 para.116A, repealed: 2009 c.4 Sch.3
Part 1

Sch.29 Part 14 para.117, repealed: 2009 c.4 Sch.3
Part 1

Sch.29 Part 14 para.118, repealed: 2009 c.4 Sch.3
Part 1

Sch.29 Part 14 para.119, repealed: 2009 c.4 Sch.3
Part 1

Sch.29 Part 14 para.120, repealed: 2009 c.4 Sch.3
Part 1

Sch.29 Part 14 para.121, repealed: 2009 c.4 Sch.3
Part 1

Sch.29 Part 14 para.122, repealed: 2009 c.4 Sch.3
Part 1

Sch.29 Part 14 para.123, repealed: 2009 c.4 Sch.3
Part 1

Sch.29 Part 14 para.124, repealed: 2009 c.4 Sch.3
Part 1

Sch.29 Part 14 para.125, repealed: 2009 c.4 Sch.3
Part 1

Sch.29 Part 14 para.126, repealed: 2009 c.4 Sch.3
Part 1

Sch.29 Part 14 para.127, repealed: 2009 c.4 Sch.3
Part 1

Sch.29 Part 14 para.127A, repealed: 2009 c.4 Sch.3
Part 1

Sch.29 Part 14 para.127B, repealed: 2009 c.4 Sch.3
Part 1

Sch.29 Part 14 para.128, repealed: 2009 c.4 Sch.3
Part 1

Sch.29 Part 14 para.129, repealed: 2009 c.4 Sch.3
Part 1

Sch.29 Part 14 para.130, repealed: 2009 c.4 Sch.3
Part 1

Sch.29 Part 14 para.131, repealed: 2009 c.4 Sch.3
Part 1

Sch.29 Part 14 para.132, repealed: 2009 c.4 Sch.3
Part 1

Sch.29 Part 15 para.133, repealed: 2009 c.4 Sch.3
Part 1

Sch.29 Part 15 para.134, repealed: 2009 c.4 Sch.3
Part 1

Sch.29 Part 15 para.135, repealed: 2009 c.4 Sch.3
Part 1

2002–cont.

23. Finance Act 2002–*cont.*
Sch.29 Part 15 para.136, repealed: 2009 c.4 Sch.3 Part 1
Sch.29 Part 15 para.137, repealed: 2009 c.4 Sch.3 Part 1
Sch.29 Part 15 para.138, repealed: 2009 c.4 Sch.3 Part 1
Sch.29 Part 15 para.139, repealed: 2009 c.4 Sch.3 Part 1
Sch.29 Part 15 para.140, repealed: 2009 c.4 Sch.3 Part 1
Sch.29 Part 15 para.141, repealed: 2009 c.4 Sch.3 Part 1
Sch.29 Part 15 para.142, repealed: 2009 c.4 Sch.3 Part 1
Sch.29 Part 15 para.143, repealed: 2009 c.4 Sch.3 Part 1

24. European Parliamentary Elections Act 2002
s.2, enabling: SI 2009/ 186
s.5, amended: 2009 c.12 s.26
s.5, enabling: SI 2009/ 186
s.6, amended: 2009 c.12 s.27
s.6, applied: SI 2009/ 1120 Sch.1 para.1
s.6, enabling: SI 2009/ 186, SI 2009/ 813, SI 2009/ 848
s.7, applied: SI 2009/ 781
s.7, enabling: SI 2009/ 186, SI 2009/ 813, SI 2009/ 848
s.10, applied: SI 2009/ 190
s.10, enabling: SI 2009/ 190
s.13, applied: SI 2009/ 186, SI 2009/ 190, SI 2009/ 813, SI 2009/848
Sch.1 para.4, amended: SI 2009/837 Art.26

26. Justice (Northern Ireland) Act 2002
disapplied: 2009 c.3 Sch.5 para.11
s.2, amended: 2009 c.3 Sch.3 para.1
s.2, repealed (in part): 2009 c.3 Sch.3 para.1
s.4, repealed: 2009 c.3 Sch.3 para.2
s.5, applied: 2009 c.3 Sch.5 para.12
s.5, substituted: 2009 c.3 Sch.3 para.3
s.5A, amended: 2009 c.3 Sch.3 para.4
s.6, repealed: 2009 c.3 Sch.3 para.5
s.7, amended: 2009 c.3 Sch.3 para.6
s.7, repealed (in part): 2009 c.3 Sch.3 para.6
s.8, substituted: 2009 c.3 Sch.3 para.7
s.9, amended: 2009 c.3 Sch.4 para.33
s.9, referred to: SI 2009/ 890 Reg.88
s.9B, amended: 2009 c.3 Sch.3 para.8
s.9B, repealed (in part): SI 2009/56 Sch.1 para.330
s.9G, applied: 2009 c.3 Sch.5 para.14
s.9G, repealed: 2009 c.3 Sch.3 para.9
s.9H, amended: 2009 c.3 Sch.3 para.10
s.9H, applied: 2009 c.3 Sch.5 para.14
s.9I, amended: 2009 c.3 Sch.3 para.11
s.9I, varied: 2009 c.3 Sch.5 para.15
s.27, applied: SI 2009/ 1747 Art.22
s.30A, added: 2009 c.3 s.3
s.88, amended: 2009 c.3 Sch.3 para.12
s.90, amended: 2009 c.3 Sch.4 para.34
Sch.1, amended: 2009 c.3 Sch.4 para.35, SI 2009/ 56 Sch.1 para.331
Sch.3 para.1, substituted: 2009 c.3 Sch.3 para.13
Sch.3 Part I para.1, substituted: 2009 c.3 Sch.3 para.13
Sch.3 Part I para.2, substituted: 2009 c.3 Sch.3 para.13
Sch.3 para.2, substituted: 2009 c.3 Sch.3 para.13
Sch.3 Part II para.3, substituted: 2009 c.3 Sch.3 para.13

2002–cont.

26. Justice (Northern Ireland) Act 2002–*cont.*
Sch.3 Part II para.4, substituted: 2009 c.3 Sch.3 para.13
Sch.3 para.3, substituted: 2009 c.3 Sch.3 para.13
Sch.3 Part III para.5, substituted: 2009 c.3 Sch.3 para.13
Sch.3 para.4, substituted: 2009 c.3 Sch.3 para.13
Sch.3 Part IV para.6, substituted: 2009 c.3 Sch.3 para.13
Sch.3 para.5, substituted: 2009 c.3 Sch.3 para.13
Sch.3 para.6, substituted: 2009 c.3 Sch.3 para.13
Sch.3 para.7, substituted: 2009 c.3 Sch.3 para.13
Sch.3 para.8, substituted: 2009 c.3 Sch.3 para.13
Sch.3 para.9, substituted: 2009 c.3 Sch.3 para.13
Sch.3 para.10, substituted: 2009 c.3 Sch.3 para.13
Sch.3 para.11, substituted: 2009 c.3 Sch.3 para.13
Sch.3 para.12, substituted: 2009 c.3 Sch.3 para.13
Sch.3 para.13, substituted: 2009 c.3 Sch.3 para.13
Sch.3 para.14, substituted: 2009 c.3 Sch.3 para.13
Sch.3 para.15, substituted: 2009 c.3 Sch.3 para.13
Sch.3 para.16, substituted: 2009 c.3 Sch.3 para.13
Sch.3 para.17, substituted: 2009 c.3 Sch.3 para.13
Sch.3 para.18, substituted: 2009 c.3 Sch.3 para.13
Sch.3 para.19, substituted: 2009 c.3 Sch.3 para.13
Sch.3 para.20, substituted: 2009 c.3 Sch.3 para.13
Sch.3 para.21, substituted: 2009 c.3 Sch.3 para.13
Sch.3 para.22, substituted: 2009 c.3 Sch.3 para.13
Sch.3 para.23, substituted: 2009 c.3 Sch.3 para.13
Sch.3 para.24, substituted: 2009 c.3 Sch.3 para.13
Sch.3 para.25, substituted: 2009 c.3 Sch.3 para.13
Sch.3 para.26, substituted: 2009 c.3 Sch.3 para.13
Sch.3 para.27, substituted: 2009 c.3 Sch.3 para.13
Sch.3 para.28, substituted: 2009 c.3 Sch.3 para.13
Sch.3 para.29, substituted: 2009 c.3 Sch.3 para.13
Sch.3 para.30, substituted: 2009 c.3 Sch.3 para.13
Sch.3 para.31, substituted: 2009 c.3 Sch.3 para.13
Sch.3 para.32, substituted: 2009 c.3 Sch.3 para.13
Sch.3 para.33, substituted: 2009 c.3 Sch.3 para.13
Sch.3 para.34, substituted: 2009 c.3 Sch.3 para.13
Sch.3 para.35, substituted: 2009 c.3 Sch.3 para.13
Sch.3 para.36, substituted: 2009 c.3 Sch.3 para.13
Sch.3 para.37, substituted: 2009 c.3 Sch.3 para.13
Sch.3 para.38, substituted: 2009 c.3 Sch.3 para.13
Sch.3 para.39, substituted: 2009 c.3 Sch.3 para.13
Sch.3 para.40, substituted: 2009 c.3 Sch.3 para.13
Sch.3 para.41, substituted: 2009 c.3 Sch.3 para.13
Sch.3 para.42, substituted: 2009 c.3 Sch.3 para.13
Sch.3A para.12, amended: 2009 c.3 Sch.3 para.14
Sch.4 para.14, repealed: 2009 c.3 Sch.4 para.36
Sch.4 para.17, repealed (in part): 2009 c.3 Sch.4 para.36
Sch.6, amended: 2009 c.3 Sch.4 para.35, SI 2009/ 56 Sch.1 para.332
Sch.12 para.13, repealed: 2009 c.3 Sch.4 para.37
Sch.13, amended: 2009 c.3 Sch.4 para.38

28. Export Control Act 2002
see *R. (on the application of Hasan) v Secretary of State for Trade and Industry* [2008] EWCA Civ 1312, [2009] 3 All E.R. 539 (CA (Civ Div)), Sir Anthony May (President, QB)
s.1, enabling: SI 2009/585, SI 2009/1174, SI 2009/ 1305, SI 2009/ 1852, SI 2009/ 2151, SI 2009/ 2164, SI 2009/2969
s.2, enabling: SI 2009/ 1174, SI 2009/ 1305
s.3, enabling: SI 2009/ 1174
s.4, enabling: SI 2009/ 1174, SI 2009/ 1305, SI 2009/ 2151, SI 2009/ 2969

2002– cont.

28. Export Control Act 2002–*cont.*
s.5, enabling: SI 2009/585, SI 2009/1174, SI 2009/1305, SI 2009/2164, SI 2009/2969
s.7, enabling: SI 2009/585, SI 2009/1174, SI 2009/1305, SI 2009/1852, SI 2009/2151, SI 2009/2164, SI 2009/2969
s.16, enabling: SI 2009/888, SI 2009/3212

29. Proceeds of Crime Act 2002
see *Ahmad (Mohammad) v HM Advocate* [2009] HCJAC 60, 2009 S.L.T. 794 (HCJ), Lord Kingarth; see *Crown Prosecution Service v Campbell* [2009] EWCA Crim 997, Times, June 16, 2009 (CA (Crim Div)), Hooper, L.J.; see *Crown Prosecution Service v Moulden* [2008] EWCA Crim 2648, [2009] 1 W.L.R. 1173 (CA (Crim Div)), Pill, L.J.; see *Director of the Assets Recovery Agency v Virtosu* [2008] EWHC 149 (QB), [2009] 1 W.L.R. 2808 (QBD), Tugendhat, J.; see *Pollock v Harrower* [2009] HCJAC 34, 2009 J.C. 222 (HCJ), Lord Carloway; see *R. v Bukhari (Daniyal)* [2008] EWCA Crim 2915, [2009] 2 Cr. App. R. (S.) 18 (CA (Crim Div)), Moore-Bick, L.J.; see *R. v Islam (Samsul)* [2009] UKHL 30, [2009] 1 A.C. 1076 (HL), Lord Hope of Craighead; see *R. v Leslie (Thomas)* [2009] N.I. 93 (CA (NI)), Girvan, L.J.; see *R. v M* [2009] EWCA Crim 214, [2009] 2 Cr. App. R. (S.) 66 (CA (Crim Div)), Toulson, L.J.; see *R. v Newman (Paul Terence)* [2008] EWCA Crim 816, [2009] 1 Cr. App. R. (S.) 12 (CA (Crim Div)), Thomas, L.J.; see *R. v Roach (Susan Tricia)* [2008] EWCA Crim 2649, [2009] Lloyd's Rep. F.C. 66 (CA (Crim Div)), Toulson, L.J.; see *R. v Shabir (Mohammed)* [2008] EWCA Crim 1809, [2009] 1 Cr. App. R. (S.) 84 (CA (Crim Div)), Hughes, L.J.; see *R. v Stapleton (Rosie)* [2008] EWCA Crim 1308, [2009] 1 Cr. App. R. (S.) 38 (CA (Crim Div)), Latham, L.J.; see *Shah v HSBC Private Bank (UK) Ltd* [2009] EWHC 79 (QB), [2009] 1 Lloyd's Rep. 328 (QBD), Hamblen, J; see *Stone (Carole Barbara) v HM Advocate* 2009 S.C.C.R. 71 (HCJ), Lord Osborne; see *T v B* [2008] EWHC 3000 (Fam), [2009] 1 F.L.R. 1231 (Fam Div), Sir Mark Potter (President, Fam)
applied: 2009 asp 2 Sch.1, Sch.2 Part 5
referred to: 2009 c.25 s.170, SI 2009/975 Art.2
varied: SI 2009/317 Sch.1
Part 2, applied: SI 2009/356 r.262
Part 2, amended: 2009 c.26 s.58
Part 3, applied: SI 2009/356 r.262
Part 3, added: 2009 c.26 s.56
Part 4, applied: SI 2009/356 r.262
Part 4, added: 2009 c.26 s.57
Part 4, amended: 2009 c.26 s.60
Part 7, applied: SI 2009/209 Reg.13
Part 8, applied: 2009 c.25 s.161
Part 8 c.3, applied: SSI 2009/245
Part 5, see *R. v W* [2008] EWCA Crim 2, [2009] 1 W.L.R. 965 (CA (Crim Div)), Laws, L.J.; see *Scottish Ministers v Doig* [2009] CSIH 34, 2009 S.C. 474 (IH (Ex Div)), Lord Kingarth
Part 7, see *R. v W* [2008] EWCA Crim 2, [2009] 1 W.L.R. 965 (CA (Crim Div)), Laws, L.J.
s.6, see *CPS v Nelson* [2009] EWCA Crim 1573, [2009] Lloyd's Rep. F.C. 663 (CA (Crim Div)), Lord Judge, L.C.J.; see *Crown Prosecution Service (Swansea) v Gilleeney* [2009] EWCA Crim 193, [2009] 2 Cr. App. R. (S.) 80 (CA

2002– cont.

29. Proceeds of Crime Act 2002–*cont.*
s.6–*cont.*
(Crim Div)), Pill, L.J.; see *Crown Prosecution Service v Moulden* [2008] EWCA Crim 2648, [2009] 1 W.L.R. 1173 (CA (Crim Div)), Pill, L.J.; see *R. (on the application of BERR) v Lowe* [2009] EWCA Crim 194, [2009] 2 Cr. App. R. (S.) 81 (CA (Crim Div)), Thomas, L.J.
s.7, see *CPS v Nelson* [2009] EWCA Crim 1573, [2009] Lloyd's Rep. F.C. 663 (CA (Crim Div)), Lord Judge, L.C.J.; see *R. (on the application of BERR) v Lowe* [2009] EWCA Crim 194, [2009] 2 Cr. App. R. (S.) 81 (CA (Crim Div)), Thomas, L.J.; see *R. v Islam (Samsul)* [2009] UKHL 30, [2009] 1 A.C. 1076 (HL), Lord Hope of Craighead
s.7, amended: 2009 c.26 Sch.7 para.100
s.9, see *R. v Islam (Samsul)* [2009] UKHL 30, [2009] 1 A.C. 1076 (HL), Lord Hope of Craighead
s.10, see *R. v Roach (Susan Tricia)* [2008] EWCA Crim 2649, [2009] Lloyd's Rep. F.C. 66 (CA (Crim Div)), Toulson, L.J.
s.14, see *Crown Prosecution Service (Swansea) v Gilleeney* [2009] EWCA Crim 193, [2009] 2 Cr. App. R. (S.) 80 (CA (Crim Div)), Pill, L.J.
s.16, see *Crown Prosecution Service (Swansea) v Gilleeney* [2009] EWCA Crim 193, [2009] 2 Cr. App. R. (S.) 80 (CA (Crim Div)), Pill, L.J.
s.23, see *R. v Younis (Shaed)* [2008] EWCA Crim 2950, [2009] 2 Cr. App. R. (S.) 34 (CA (Crim Div)), Thomas, L.J.
s.31, see *Crown Prosecution Service (Swansea) v Gilleeney* [2009] EWCA Crim 193, [2009] 2 Cr. App. R. (S.) 80 (CA (Crim Div)), Pill, L.J.; see *Crown Prosecution Service v Moulden* [2008] EWCA Crim 2648, [2009] 1 W.L.R. 1173 (CA (Crim Div)), Pill, L.J.
s.41, see *Crown Prosecution Service v Campbell* [2009] EWCA Crim 997, Times, June 16, 2009 (CA (Crim Div)), Hooper, L.J.; see *Irwin Mitchell (A Firm) v Revenue and Customs Prosecutions Office* [2008] EWCA Crim 1741, [2009] 1 W.L.R. 1079 (CA (Crim Div)), Toulson, L.J.; see *R. v B* [2008] EWCA Crim 1374, [2009] 1 Cr. App. R. 14 (CA (Crim Div)), Moses, L.J.; see *R. v M* [2008] EWCA Crim 1901, [2009] 1 W.L.R. 1179 (CA (Crim Div)), Toulson, L.J.
s.41A, added: 2009 c.26 s.52
s.42, applied: SI 2009/975 Sch.1
s.44A, added: 2009 c.26 s.52
s.45, applied: SI 2009/975 Sch.1
s.45, repealed: 2009 c.26 s.55, Sch.8 Part 4
s.47A, added: 2009 c.26 s.55
s.47B, added: 2009 c.26 s.55
s.47C, added: 2009 c.26 s.55
s.47D, added: 2009 c.26 s.55
s.47E, added: 2009 c.26 s.55
s.47F, added: 2009 c.26 s.55
s.47G, added: 2009 c.26 s.55
s.47H, added: 2009 c.26 s.55
s.47I, added: 2009 c.26 s.55
s.47J, added: 2009 c.26 s.55
s.47K, added: 2009 c.26 s.55
s.47L, added: 2009 c.26 s.55
s.47M, added: 2009 c.26 s.55
s.47N, added: 2009 c.26 s.55
s.47O, added: 2009 c.26 s.55
s.47P, added: 2009 c.26 s.55

2002– cont.

29. Proceeds of Crime Act 2002–*cont.*
s.47Q, added: 2009 c.26 s.55
s.47R, added: 2009 c.26 s.55
s.47S, added: 2009 c.26 s.55
s.55, amended: 2009 c.26 s.51, s.58
s.67A, added: 2009 c.26 s.58
s.67B, added: 2009 c.26 s.58
s.67C, added: 2009 c.26 s.58
s.67D, added: 2009 c.26 s.58
s.68, applied: SI 2009/975 Sch.1
s.69, see *Crown Prosecution Service v Campbell* [2009] EWCA Crim 997, Times, June 16, 2009 (CA (Crim Div)), Hooper, L.J.; see *Serious Fraud Office v Lexi Holdings Plc (In Administration)* [2008] EWCA Crim 1443, [2009] Q.B. 376 (CA (Crim Div)), Keene, L.J.
s.69, amended: 2009 c.26 s.55, Sch.7 para.67
s.72, amended: 2009 c.26 s.61
s.74, see *King v Serious Fraud Office* [2009] UKHL 17, [2009] 1 W.L.R. 718 (HL), Lord Phillips of Worth Matravers
s.75, see *R. v Islam (Samsul)* [2008] EWCA Crim 1740, [2009] 1 Cr. App. R. (S.) 83 (CA (Crim Div)), Toulson, L.J.
s.76, see *R. v Shabir (Mohammed)* [2008] EWCA Crim 1809, [2009] 1 Cr. App. R. (S.) 84 (CA (Crim Div)), Hughes, L.J.; see *R. v Waller (Steven)* [2008] EWCA Crim 2037, [2009] 1 Cr. App. R. (S.) 76 (CA (Crim Div)), Gage, L.J.
s.79, see *R. v Islam (Samsul)* [2008] EWCA Crim 1740, [2009] 1 Cr. App. R. (S.) 83 (CA (Crim Div)), Toulson, L.J.; see *R. v Islam (Samsul)* [2009] UKHL 30, [2009] 1 A.C. 1076 (HL), Lord Hope of Craighead; see *R. v Roach (Susan Tricia)* [2008] EWCA Crim 2649, [2009] Lloyd's Rep. F.C. 66 (CA (Crim Div)), Toulson, L.J.
s.80, see *R. v Allpress (Sylvia)* [2009] EWCA Crim 8, [2009] 2 Cr. App. R. (S.) 58 (CA (Crim Div)), Latham, L.J. (VP, CA Crim); see *R. v Islam (Samsul)* [2009] UKHL 30, [2009] 1 A.C. 1076 (HL), Lord Hope of Craighead
s.82, amended: 2009 c.26 Sch.7 para.101
s.82, substituted: 2009 c.26 Sch.7 para.101
s.85, amended: 2009 c.26 Sch.7 para.68
s.87, amended: 2009 c.26 Sch.7 para.69, Sch.8 Part 4
s.87A, added: 2009 c.26 Sch.7 para.70
s.92, applied: SSI 2009/244 r.1
s.93, amended: 2009 c.26 Sch.7 para.102
s.101, see *Pollock v Harrower* [2009] HCJAC 34, 2009 J.C. 222 (HCJ), Lord Carloway
s.101, applied: SSI 2009/244 r.1
s.110, applied: SSI 2009/244 r.1
s.120A, added: 2009 c.26 s.53
s.122A, added: 2009 c.26 s.53
s.126, repealed: 2009 c.26 s.56, Sch.8 Part 4
s.131, amended: 2009 c.26 s.59
s.132, amended: 2009 c.26 s.56, Sch.7 para.71
s.139, amended: 2009 c.26 s.61
s.142, see *Pollock v Harrower* [2009] HCJAC 34, 2009 J.C. 222 (HCJ), Lord Carloway
s.148, amended: 2009 c.26 Sch.7 para.103
s.148, substituted: 2009 c.26 Sch.7 para.103
s.153, amended: 2009 c.26 Sch.7 para.72, Sch.8 Part 4
s.153A, added: 2009 c.26 Sch.7 para.73
s.157, amended: 2009 c.26 Sch.7 para.104
s.190A, added: 2009 c.26 s.54
s.191, applied: SI 2009/975 Sch.1
s.193A, added: 2009 c.26 s.54

2002– cont.

29. Proceeds of Crime Act 2002–*cont.*
s.194, applied: SI 2009/975 Sch.1
s.194, repealed: 2009 c.26 s.57, Sch.8 Part 4
s.203, amended: 2009 c.26 s.51, s.60
s.215A, added: 2009 c.26 s.60
s.215B, added: 2009 c.26 s.60
s.215C, added: 2009 c.26 s.60
s.215D, added: 2009 c.26 s.60
s.216, applied: SI 2009/975 Sch.1
s.217, amended: 2009 c.26 s.57, Sch.7 para.74
s.220, amended: 2009 c.26 s.61
s.230, amended: 2009 c.26 Sch.7 para.105
s.230, substituted: 2009 c.26 Sch.7 para.105
s.233, amended: 2009 c.26 Sch.7 para.75
s.235, amended: 2009 c.26 Sch.7 para.76, Sch.8 Part 4
s.235A, added: 2009 c.26 Sch.7 para.77
s.240, see *Director of the Assets Recovery Agency v Virtosu* [2008] EWHC 149 (QB), [2009] 1 W.L.R. 2808 (QBD), Tugendhat, J.; see *Serious Organised Crime Agency v Olden* [2009] EWHC 610 (QB), [2009] Lloyd's Rep. F.C. 375 (QBD), Holroyde, J
s.241, see *Director of the Assets Recovery Agency v Virtosu* [2008] EWHC 149 (QB), [2009] 1 W.L.R. 2808 (QBD), Tugendhat, J.
s.242, see *R. (on the application of the Chief Constable of Greater Manchester) v City of Salford Magistrates' Court* [2008] EWHC 1651 (Admin), [2009] 1 W.L.R. 1023 (DC), Richards, L.J.
s.245A, applied: 2009 c.25 s.164
s.246, applied: 2009 c.25 s.164
s.252, see *Serious Organised Crime Agency v Szepietowski* [2009] EWHC 344 (Ch), [2009] 4 All E.R. 393 (Ch D), Henderson, J.
s.255A, applied: 2009 c.25 s.164
s.256, applied: 2009 c.25 s.164
s.266, see *Serious Organised Crime Agency v Olden* [2009] EWHC 610 (QB), [2009] Lloyd's Rep. F.C. 375 (QBD), Holroyde, J; see *Serious Organised Crime Agency v Szepietowski* [2009] EWHC 344 (Ch), [2009] 4 All E.R. 393 (Ch D), Henderson, J.
s.266, applied: 2009 c.25 s.164
s.278, amended: 2009 c.26 Sch.7 para.106
s.289, amended: 2009 c.26 s.63, Sch.7 para.120
s.289, applied: SSI 2009/246
s.290, applied: SI 2009/975 Sch.1
s.293, applied: SSI 2009/246
s.293, enabling: SSI 2009/246
s.294, see *R. (on the application of the Chief Constable of Greater Manchester) v City of Salford Magistrates' Court* [2008] EWHC 1651 (Admin), [2009] 1 W.L.R. 1023 (DC), Richards, L.J.
s.295, see *R. (on the application of the Chief Constable of Greater Manchester) v City of Salford Magistrates' Court* [2008] EWHC 1651 (Admin), [2009] 1 W.L.R. 1023 (DC), Richards, L.J.
s.295, amended: 2009 c.26 s.64
s.295, applied: 2009 c.25 s.164
s.297, see *R. (on the application of the Chief Constable of Greater Manchester) v City of Salford Magistrates' Court* [2008] EWHC 1651 (Admin), [2009] 1 W.L.R. 1023 (DC), Richards, L.J.
s.297A, added: 2009 c.26 s.65
s.297A, applied: 2009 c.25 s.164
s.297B, added: 2009 c.26 s.65
s.297C, added: 2009 c.26 s.65

2002– cont.

29. Proceeds of Crime Act 2002– *cont.*
s.297D, added: 2009 c.26 s.65
s.297E, added: 2009 c.26 s.65
s.297F, added: 2009 c.26 s.65
s.297G, added: 2009 c.26 s.65
s.298, see *R. (on the application of the Chief Constable of Greater Manchester) v City of Salford Magistrates' Court* [2008] EWHC 1651 (Admin), [2009] 1 W.L.R. 1023 (DC), Richards, L.J.
s.298, amended: 2009 c.26 s.65
s.298, applied: 2009 c.25 s.164
s.299, amended: 2009 c.26 s.65
s.300, amended: 2009 c.26 Sch.7 para.107
s.301, amended: 2009 c.26 Sch.7 para.108
s.302, amended: 2009 c.26 Sch.7 para.109
s.303A, applied: SI 2009/ 975 Sch.1
s.304, see *Director of the Assets Recovery Agency v Virtosu* [2008] EWHC 149 (QB), [2009] 1 W.L.R. 2808 (QBD), Tugendhat, J.
s.305, see *Director of the Assets Recovery Agency v Virtosu* [2008] EWHC 149 (QB), [2009] 1 W.L.R. 2808 (QBD), Tugendhat, J.; see *Serious Organised Crime Agency v Olden* [2009] EWHC 610 (QB), [2009] Lloyd's Rep. F.C. 375 (QBD), Holroyde, J
s.306, see *R. v Roach (Susan Tricia)* [2008] EWCA Crim 2649, [2009] Lloyd's Rep. F.C. 66 (CA (Crim Div)), Toulson, L.J.
s.307, see *Serious Organised Crime Agency v Olden* [2009] EWHC 610 (QB), [2009] Lloyd's Rep. F.C. 375 (QBD), Holroyde, J
s.308, amended: 2009 c.26 Sch.7 para.78
s.308, varied: SI 2009/ 1059 Sch.1 para.51
s.320, repealed: SI 2009/56 Sch.1 para.333
s.327, see *R. v Cave (Dennis James)* [2008] EWCA Crim 1119, [2009] 1 Cr. App. R. (S.) 28 (CA (Crim Div)), Hughes, L.J.; see *R. v W* [2008] EWCA Crim 2, [2009] 1 W.L.R. 965 (CA (Crim Div)), Laws, L.J.
s.328, see *R. v Anwoir (Ilham)* [2008] EWCA Crim 1354, [2009] 1 W.L.R. 980 (CA (Crim Div)), Latham, L.J.; see *R. v Khanani (Abbas Hussain)* [2009] EWCA Crim 276, [2009] Lloyd's Rep. F.C. 310 (CA (Crim Div)), Toulson, L.J.; see *R. v Smale (Christopher)* [2008] EWCA Crim 1235, [2009] 1 Cr. App. R. (S.) 25 (CA (Crim Div)), Toulson, L.J.; see *R. v W* [2008] EWCA Crim 2, [2009] 1 W.L.R. 965 (CA (Crim Div)), Laws, L.J.
s.340, see *HM Advocate v Duffy (Gerald James)* [2009] HCJAC 5, 2009 S.L.T. 47 (HCJ Appeal), Lord Hamilton L.J.G.; see *R. v W* [2008] EWCA Crim 2, [2009] 1 W.L.R. 965 (CA (Crim Div)), Laws, L.J.
s.341, amended: 2009 c.25 Sch.19 para.2, 2009 c.26 Sch.7 para.110
s.341, applied: 2009 c.25 s.168
s.342, amended: 2009 c.25 Sch.19 para.3
s.343, amended: 2009 c.25 Sch.19 para.4, 2009 c.26 s.66, Sch.8 Part 5
s.344, amended: 2009 c.25 Sch.19 para.5, 2009 c.26 s.66, Sch.8 Part 5
s.345, see *R. (on the application of Redknapp) v Commissioner of the City of London Police* [2008] EWHC 1177 (Admin), [2009] 1 W.L.R. 2091 (DC), Latham, L.J.
s.345, amended: 2009 c.25 Sch.19 para.6
s.346, amended: 2009 c.25 Sch.19 para.7

2002– cont.

29. Proceeds of Crime Act 2002– *cont.*
s.350, amended: 2009 c.25 Sch.19 para.8, 2009 c.26 s.66, Sch.8 Part 5
s.351, amended: 2009 c.25 Sch.19 para.9, 2009 c.26 s.66, Sch.8 Part 5
s.352, amended: 2009 c.25 Sch.19 para.10
s.352, applied: SI 2009/ 975 Sch.1
s.353, amended: 2009 c.25 Sch.19 para.11
s.353, applied: SI 2009/ 975 Sch.1
s.355, amended: 2009 c.26 s.66
s.356, amended: 2009 c.25 Sch.19 para.12, 2009 c.26 s.66, Sch.8 Part 5
s.356, repealed (in part): 2009 c.26 s.66, Sch.8 Part 5
s.357, amended: 2009 c.25 Sch.19 para.13
s.358, amended: 2009 c.25 Sch.19 para.14
s.362, amended: 2009 c.25 Sch.19 para.15
s.363, amended: 2009 c.25 Sch.19 para.16
s.364, amended: SI 2009/ 1941 Sch.1 para.196
s.370, amended: 2009 c.25 Sch.19 para.17
s.378, amended: 2009 c.25 Sch.19 para.18
s.378, applied: SI 2009/ 975 Sch.1
s.380, see *S v McGowan* [2009] HCJAC 62, 2009 S.L.T. 922 (HCJ), Lord Hardie
s.388, see *S v McGowan* [2009] HCJAC 62, 2009 S.L.T. 922 (HCJ), Lord Hardie
s.398, amended: SI 2009/ 1941 Sch.1 para.196
s.410, applied: SSI 2009/ 245
s.410, enabling: SSI 2009/ 245
s.417, amended: 2009 c.26 Sch.7 para.79
s.418, amended: 2009 c.26 Sch.7 para.80
s.419, amended: 2009 c.26 Sch.7 para.81, Sch.8 Part 4
s.420, amended: 2009 c.26 Sch.7 para.82
s.421, amended: 2009 c.26 Sch.7 para.83
s.422, amended: 2009 c.26 Sch.7 para.84, Sch.8 Part 4
s.423, amended: 2009 c.26 Sch.7 para.85
s.424, amended: 2009 c.26 Sch.7 para.86
s.425, amended: 2009 c.26 Sch.7 para.87
s.426, amended: 2009 c.26 Sch.7 para.88
s.427, amended: 2009 c.26 Sch.7 para.89, Sch.8 Part 4
s.428, amended: 2009 c.26 Sch.7 para.90
s.429, amended: 2009 c.26 Sch.7 para.91, Sch.8 Part 4
s.430, amended: 2009 c.26 Sch.7 para.92
s.432, amended: 2009 c.26 Sch.7 para.93
s.436, see *Serious Organised Crime Agency v Olden* [2009] EWHC 610 (QB), [2009] Lloyd's Rep. F.C. 375 (QBD), Holroyde, J
s.447, see *King v Serious Fraud Office* [2009] UKHL 17, [2009] 1 W.L.R. 718 (HL), Lord Phillips of Worth Matravers
s.453, enabling: SI 2009/ 975, SI 2009/ 2707
s.453A, amended: 2009 c.26 Sch.7 para.94
s.459, amended: 2009 c.26 Sch.7 para.95
s.459, applied: SSI 2009/ 245, SSI 2009/ 246
s.459, enabling: SI 2009/ 975, SI 2009/ 2707
Sch.10 Part 2 para.3, amended: 2009 c.26 Sch.7 para.111
Sch.10 Part 2 para.9, amended: 2009 c.4 Sch.1 para.547
Sch.10 Part 2 para.11, amended: 2009 c.4 Sch.1 para.547

30. Police Reform Act 2002
see *R. (on the application of Reynolds) v Chief Constable of Sussex* [2008] EWCA Civ 1160, [2009] 3 All E.R. 237 (CA (Civ Div)), Ward, L.J.
s.9, varied: SI 2009/ 2133 Reg.4
s.10, see *R. (on the application of Reynolds) v Chief Constable of Sussex* [2008] EWCA Civ 1160, [2009] 3 All E.R. 237 (CA (Civ Div)), Ward, L.J.
s.19, varied: SI 2009/ 2133 Reg.4

2002– *cont.*

30. Police Reform Act 2002–*cont.*

s.21, see *R. (on the application of Saunders) v Independent Police Complaints Commission* [2008] EWHC 2372 (Admin), [2009] 1 All E.R. 379 (QBD (Admin)), Underhill, J.

s.22, varied: SI 2009/2133 Reg.4

s.23, varied: SI 2009/2133 Reg.4

s.24, varied: SI 2009/2133 Reg.4

s.26, applied: SI 2009/3069 Reg.3

s.27, varied: SI 2009/2133 Reg.4

s.29, applied: SI 2009/3069 Reg.3

s.38, repealed (in part): 2009 c.26 Sch.8 Part 13

s.51, amended: 2009 c.25 s.117

s.84, repealed: 2009 c.26 Sch.8 Part 1

Sch.2 para.1, amended: SI 2009/1941 Sch.1 para.197

Sch.2 para.2, amended: SI 2009/1941 Sch.1 para.197

Sch.3, referred to: SI 2009/3070 Reg.4

Sch.3 Part 3, applied: 2009 c.25 s.47

Sch.3 Part 3 para.16, applied: SI 2009/3069 Reg.11, Reg.20, Reg.30, Reg.31, Reg.32, Reg.39, Reg.40, Reg.51, Reg.52, Reg.53

Sch.3 Part 3 para.17, applied: SI 2009/3069 Reg.10, Reg.11, Reg.20, Reg.30, Reg.31, Reg.32, Reg.39, Reg.40, Reg.51, Reg.52, Reg.53

Sch.3 Part 3 para.18, applied: SI 2009/3069 Reg.10, Reg.11, Reg.20, Reg.30, Reg.31, Reg.32, Reg.39, Reg.40, Reg.51, Reg.52, Reg.53

Sch.3 Part 3 para.19, applied: SI 2009/3069 Reg.10, Reg.11, Reg.20, Reg.30, Reg.31, Reg.32, Reg.39, Reg.40, Reg.51, Reg.52, Reg.53

Sch.3 Part 3 para.19A, applied: SI 2009/3070 Reg.19, Reg.22

Sch.3 Part 3 para.19B, applied: SI 2009/3069 Reg.31, Reg.52

Sch.3 Part 3 para.20H, applied: SI 2009/3069 Reg.42, Reg.51, Reg.53

Sch.3 Part 3 para.22, applied: SI 2009/3069 Reg.19

Sch.3 Part 3 para.23, applied: SI 2009/3069 Reg.19

Sch.3 Part 3 para.24, applied: SI 2009/3069 Reg.19

Sch.3 Part 3 para.27, applied: SI 2009/3069 Reg.19, Reg.30, Reg.32, Reg.40

Sch.3 para.14D, see *R. (on the application of Reynolds) v Chief Constable of Sussex* [2008] EWCA Civ 1160, [2009] 3 All E.R. 237 (CA (Civ Div)), Ward, L.J.

Sch.4 Part 1 para.2, amended: 2009 c.20 Sch.6 para.116

Sch.4 Part 1 para.4B, repealed: 2009 c.26 Sch.8 Part 13

Sch.4 Part 3 para.27A, added: 2009 c.25 s.108

Sch.4 Part 4A para.35A, repealed: 2009 c.26 Sch.8 Part 13

Sch.4 Part 5 para.36, amended: 2009 c.26 Sch.7 para.125

Sch.5 para.5, amended: 2009 c.26 Sch.7 para.27

32. Education Act 2002

applied: SI 2009/2680 Reg.7

referred to: 2009 c.1 s.46

s.1, referred to: SI 2009/558, SI 2009/3144

s.2, enabling: SI 2009/558, SI 2009/3144

s.3, enabling: SI 2009/558

s.4, applied: SI 2009/558, SI 2009/3144

s.11, amended: SI 2009/1941 Sch.1 para.198

s.12, enabling: SI 2009/1924

s.13, amended: SI 2009/1941 Sch.1 para.198

s.19, enabling: SI 2009/1556, SI 2009/1924, SI 2009/2544, SI 2009/2680, SI 2009/2708

2002– *cont.*

32. Education Act 2002– *cont.*

s.21, amended: 2009 c.22 s.194

s.21, enabling: SI 2009/2159, SI 2009/2708

s.24, enabling: SI 2009/1556

s.26, enabling: SI 2009/2680

s.27, applied: SI 2009/2680 Reg.3

s.29, amended: 2009 c.22 s.260

s.30, amended: 2009 c.3 s.2

s.32, applied: SI 2009/572 Reg.3

s.32, enabling: SI 2009/572

s.34, enabling: SI 2009/1924, SI 2009/2544, SI 2009/2680, SI 2009/2708

s.35, applied: 2009 c.22 s.237

s.35, enabling: SI 2009/1924, SI 2009/2544, SI 2009/2680, SI 2009/2708, SI 2009/3161

s.36, applied: 2009 c.22 s.237

s.36, enabling: SI 2009/1924, SI 2009/2544, SI 2009/2680, SI 2009/2708, SI 2009/3161

s.52, see *R. (on the application of A) v Independent Appeal Panel for Sutton LBC* [2009] EWHC 1223 (Admin), [2009] E.L.R. 321 (QBD (Admin)), Hickinbottom, J.

s.62A, amended: 2009 c.22 s.204

s.76, amended: 2009 c.22 Sch.12 para.32, Sch.16 Part 4

s.76, substituted: 2009 c.22 Sch.12 para.32

s.78, applied: 2009 c.22 s.177

s.85, amended: 2009 c.22 Sch.12 para.33

s.85A, amended: 2009 c.22 Sch.12 para.34

s.87, amended: 2009 c.22 s.159, Sch.12 para.35, Sch.16 Part 4

s.87, repealed (in part): 2009 c.22 Sch.12 para.35, Sch.16 Part 4

s.87, enabling: SI 2009/1585

s.90, amended: 2009 c.22 Sch.12 para.36

s.96, amended: 2009 c.22 Sch.12 para.37, Sch.16 Part 4

s.97, amended: 2009 c.1 s.1

s.100, amended: 2009 c.1 s.2, Sch.1 para.12, Sch.1 para.14

s.101, amended: 2009 c.1 s.3, Sch.1 para.12

s.102, amended: 2009 c.1 Sch.1 para.12

s.103, amended: 2009 c.1 Sch.1 para.12

s.105, amended: 2009 c.1 Sch.1 para.12

s.107, amended: 2009 c.1 s.19

s.108, amended: 2009 c.1 Sch.1 para.12, Sch.1 para.15

s.111, amended: 2009 c.1 Sch.1 para.12, Sch.1 para.16, Sch.1 para.17

s.114, amended: 2009 c.1 Sch.1 para.12, Sch.1 para.18

s.116A, added: 2009 c.1 s.4

s.116A, applied: SI 2009/3256 Reg.3

s.116A, enabling: SI 2009/3256

s.116B, added: 2009 c.1 s.5

s.116C, added: 2009 c.1 s.6

s.116D, added: 2009 c.1 s.7

s.116D, applied: SI 2009/3256 Reg.9

s.116D, enabling: SI 2009/3256

s.116E, added: 2009 c.1 s.8

s.116F, added: 2009 c.1 s.9

s.116F, enabling: SI 2009/3256

s.116G, added: 2009 c.1 s.10

s.116H, added: 2009 c.1 s.11

s.116H, applied: SI 2009/3256 Reg.10

s.116H, enabling: SI 2009/3256

s.116I, added: 2009 c.1 s.12

s.116J, added: 2009 c.1 s.13

s.116K, added: 2009 c.1 s.14

s.116L, added: 2009 c.1 s.15

s.116M, added: 2009 c.1 s.16

2002– cont.

32. Education Act 2002–*cont.*
s.116N, added: 2009 c.1 s.17
s.116O, added: 2009 c.1 s.18
s.117, amended: 2009 c.1 Sch.1 para.19
s.118, amended: 2009 c.1 Sch.1 para.12, Sch.1 para.16, Sch.1 para.20
s.120, applied: SI 2009/2132
s.121, referred to: SI 2009/2132
s.122, applied: SI 2009/1974 Art.3, SI 2009/2680 Reg.5
s.122, enabling: SI 2009/2132
s.123, enabling: SI 2009/1974, SI 2009/2132
s.124, enabling: SI 2009/2132
s.125, applied: SI 2009/2132
s.126, applied: SI 2009/2132
s.131, applied: SI 2009/2159, SI 2009/2864
s.131, enabling: SI 2009/2159, SI 2009/2864
s.132, applied: SI 2009/1538 Reg.3
s.132, enabling: SI 2009/3156
s.135, applied: SI 2009/1538 Reg.3
s.136, enabling: SI 2009/1924, SI 2009/2544, SI 2009/2730
s.137, enabling: SI 2009/472, SI 2009/2049
s.142, see *D v Buckinghamshire CC* [2008] EWCA Civ 1372, [2009] 1 F.L.R. 881 (CA (Civ Div)), Thorpe, L.J.; see *R. (on the application of G) v X School Governors* [2009] EWHC 504 (Admin), [2009] I.R.L.R. 434 (QBD (Admin)), Stephen Morris QC; see *Secretary of State for Children, Schools and Families v Philliskirk* [2008] EWHC 2838 (Admin), [2009] E.L.R. 68 (QBD (Admin)), Collins, J.
s.142, applied: SI 2009/12 Art.6, Art.6A, Art.2, Art.4, Art.9, SI 2009/37 Reg.3, Reg.4, SI 2009/1633 Reg.3, SI 2009/2558 Reg.3, SI 2009/2610 Art.18, Art.21, SI 2009/2611 Art.4, Art.7, SI 2009/2680 Sch.2 para.2, SI 2009/3200 Sch.1 para.15
s.142, disapplied: SI 2009/12 Art.4
s.142, referred to: SI 2009/2611 Art.7
s.144, applied: SI 2009/12 Art.6, Art.6A, SI 2009/2611 Art.7
s.145, enabling: SI 2009/472, SI 2009/2049, SI 2009/3156
s.157, applied: SI 2009/1607 Reg.6
s.157, enabling: SI 2009/1924, SI 2009/2544
s.158, referred to: SI 2009/1513 Art.2A, SI 2009/1606 Art.5, Art.6, SI 2009/1607 Reg.2, Reg.4
s.161, applied: 2009 c.4 s.71
s.162A, applied: SI 2009/1513 Art.2A, SI 2009/1607 Reg.1, Reg.4, Reg.5
s.162B, referred to: SI 2009/1606 Art.6
s.162B, enabling: SI 2009/1607
s.167A, applied: SI 2009/1633 Reg.3, SI 2009/2558 Reg.3
s.167C, amended: 2009 c.26 s.81
s.168, enabling: SI 2009/1924, SI 2009/2544
s.169, applied: SI 2009/2558 Reg.2, Reg.3
s.169, enabling: SI 2009/2558
s.181, enabling: SI 2009/825
s.207, amended: 2009 c.22 Sch.2 para.14
s.208A, added: 2009 c.22 Sch.6 para.55
s.210, amended: 2009 c.1 s.20, 2009 c.22 Sch.6 para.56
s.210, enabling: SI 2009/472, SI 2009/572, SI 2009/1585, SI 2009/1607, SI 2009/1924, SI 2009/2049, SI 2009/2159, SI 2009/2544, SI 2009/2558, SI 2009/2680, SI 2009/2708, SI 2009/2730, SI

2002– cont.

32. Education Act 2002–*cont.*
s.210, enabling:–*cont.*
2009/2864, SI 2009/3144, SI 2009/3156, SI 2009/3161, SI 2009/3256
s.214, enabling: SI 2009/2544, SI 2009/2730
s.216, amended: 2009 c.22 Sch.16 Part 4
Sch.2 Part 1, applied: SI 2009/2680 Reg.43
Sch.2 Part 1 para.1, varied: SI 2009/2680 Reg.40
Sch.2 Part 1 para.2, varied: SI 2009/2680 Reg.40
Sch.2 Part 1 para.3, varied: SI 2009/2680 Reg.40
Sch.2 Part 1 para.4, varied: SI 2009/2680 Reg.40
Sch.2 Part 2, applied: SI 2009/2680 Reg.44
Sch.2 Part 2 para.5, varied: SI 2009/2680 Reg.40
Sch.2 Part 2 para.6, varied: SI 2009/2680 Reg.40
Sch.2 Part 2 para.7, varied: SI 2009/2680 Reg.40
Sch.2 Part 2 para.8, varied: SI 2009/2680 Reg.40
Sch.2 Part 2 para.9, varied: SI 2009/2680 Reg.40
Sch.2 Part 2 para.10, varied: SI 2009/2680 Reg.40
Sch.2 Part 2 para.11, added: 2009 c.22 s.237
Sch.2 Part 2 para.11, varied: SI 2009/2680 Reg.40
Sch.2 Part 2 para.21, varied: SI 2009/2680 Reg.40
Sch.17, repealed: 2009 c.22 Sch.16 Part 4
Sch.17 para.5, repealed (in part): 2009 c.22 Sch.16 Part 4
Sch.21 para.69, repealed: 2009 c.22 Sch.16 Part 4

36. Tobacco Advertising and Promotion Act 2002
s.6, amended: 2009 c.21 s.20, Sch.4 para.3
s.7A, added: 2009 c.21 s.21
s.7B, added: 2009 c.21 s.21
s.7C, added: 2009 c.21 s.21
s.7D, added: 2009 c.21 s.21
s.8, amended: 2009 c.21 Sch.4 para.4
s.8, applied: 2009 c.21 s.40
s.9, amended: 2009 c.21 Sch.4 para.5
s.9, applied: 2009 c.21 s.40
s.11, amended: 2009 c.21 Sch.4 para.6
s.11, applied: 2009 c.21 s.40
s.13, amended: 2009 c.21 Sch.4 para.7
s.13, repealed (in part): 2009 c.21 Sch.4 para.7, Sch.6
s.14, amended: 2009 c.21 Sch.4 para.8, Sch.6
s.14, repealed (in part): 2009 c.21 Sch.4 para.8, Sch.6
s.16, amended: 2009 c.21 Sch.4 para.9
s.16, repealed (in part): 2009 c.21 Sch.6
s.17, amended: 2009 c.21 Sch.4 para.10
s.19, amended: 2009 c.21 Sch.4 para.11
s.21, amended: 2009 c.21 Sch.4 para.12
Sch.1 para.1, amended: 2009 c.21 Sch.4 para.13

38. Adoption and Children Act 2002
see *A LBC v Department for Children, Schools and Families* [2009] EWCA Civ 41, [2009] 3 W.L.R. 1169 (CA (Civ Div)), Thorpe, L.J.; see *R. (on the application of G) v Southwark LBC* [2008] EWCA Civ 877, [2009] 1 W.L.R. 34 (CA (Civ Div)), Pill, L.J.
s.1, see *R. (on the application of T) v Newham LBC* [2008] EWHC 2640 (Admin), [2009] 1 F.L.R. 311 (QBD (Admin)), Bennett, J.
s.2, applied: SI 2009/1555 Reg.42, SI 2009/2737 Reg.31, Reg.96, SI 2009/3359 Reg.26
s.3, applied: SI 2009/1555 Reg.42, SI 2009/2737 Reg.31, Reg.96, SI 2009/3359 Reg.26
s.4, applied: SI 2009/1555 Reg.42, SI 2009/2737 Reg.31, Reg.96, SI 2009/3359 Reg.26
s.9, enabling: SI 2009/395, SI 2009/1895, SI 2009/1898, SI 2009/2541
s.10, enabling: SI 2009/1895, SI 2009/1898, SI 2009/2541
s.12, applied: SI 2009/395 Reg.3

2002–cont.

38. Adoption and Children Act 2002–*cont.*

s.12, enabling: SI 2009/395

s.18, see *C (A Child) (Adoption: Parental Consent), Re* [2008] EWHC 2555 (Fam), [2009] Fam. 83 (Fam Div), Eleanor King, J; see *S (A Child) (Placement Order: Revocation), Re* [2008] EWCA Civ 1333, [2009] 1 F.L.R. 503 (CA (Civ Div)), Thorpe, L.J.

s.19, see *C (A Child) (Adoption: Parental Consent), Re* [2008] EWHC 2555 (Fam), [2009] Fam. 83 (Fam Div), Eleanor King, J

s.19, applied: SSI 2009/284 Sch.1

s.20, see *C (A Child) (Adoption: Parental Consent), Re* [2008] EWHC 2555 (Fam), [2009] Fam. 83 (Fam Div), Eleanor King, J

s.20, applied: SSI 2009/284 Sch.1

s.21, applied: SSI 2009/284 Sch.1

s.24, see *S (A Child) (Placement Order: Revocation), Re* [2008] EWCA Civ 1333, [2009] 1 F.L.R. 503 (CA (Civ Div)), Thorpe, L.J.

s.42, see *A LBC v Department for Children, Schools and Families* [2009] EWCA Civ 41, [2009] 3 W.L.R. 1169 (CA (Civ Div)), Thorpe, L.J.

s.47, see *C (A Child) (Adoption: Parental Consent), Re* [2008] EWHC 2555 (Fam), [2009] Fam. 83 (Fam Div), Eleanor King, J

s.52, see *C (A Child) (Adoption: Parental Consent), Re* [2008] EWHC 2555 (Fam), [2009] Fam. 83 (Fam Div), Eleanor King, J

s.52, applied: SSI 2009/284 Sch.1

s.60, applied: SSI 2009/268 Reg.3, Reg.4

s.61, applied: SSI 2009/268 Reg.3, Reg.4

s.62, applied: SSI 2009/268 Reg.3, Reg.4

s.84, see *A LBC v Department for Children, Schools and Families* [2009] EWCA Civ 41, [2009] 3 W.L.R. 1169 (CA (Civ Div)), Thorpe, L.J.

s.85, see *A LBC v Department for Children, Schools and Families* [2009] EWCA Civ 41, [2009] 3 W.L.R. 1169 (CA (Civ Div)), Thorpe, L.J.

s.140, enabling: SI 2009/1895, SI 2009/1898, SI 2009/2541

s.142, enabling: SI 2009/395

40. Enterprise Act 2002

see *Official Receiver v Baars* [2009] B.P.I.R. 524 (Ch D), Registrar Derrett; see *William Hare Ltd v Shepherd Construction Ltd* [2009] EWHC 1603 (TCC), [2009] B.L.R. 447 (QBD (TCC)), Coulson, J.

applied: SI 2009/209 Reg.106

Part 8, referred to: SI 2009/669 Sch.1 Part 2

Part 9, applied: SI 2009/209 Reg.107, Reg.119

s.11, enabling: SI 2009/2079

s.14, applied: SI 2009/209 Reg.106

s.15, applied: SI 2009/209 Reg.106

s.22, applied: SI 2009/2396 Art.1

s.42, see *Merger Action Group v Secretary of State for Business, Enterprise and Regulatory Reform* 2009 S.L.T. 10 (CAT), Barling, J. (President)

s.45, see *Merger Action Group v Secretary of State for Business, Enterprise and Regulatory Reform* 2009 S.L.T. 10 (CAT), Barling, J. (President)

s.45, applied: SI 2009/2396 Art.1

s.47, see *Virgin Media Inc v Competition Commission* [2009] Comp. A.R. 98 (CAT), Barling, J. (President)

s.58, see *Virgin Media Inc v Competition Commission* [2009] Comp. A.R. 98 (CAT), Barling, J. (President)

s.79, amended: SI 2009/1941 Sch.1 para.199

40. Enterprise Act 2002–*cont.*

s.120, see *British Sky Broadcasting Group Plc v Competition Commission (Costs)* [2009] CAT 20, [2009] Comp. A.R. 247 (CAT), Barling, J. (President); see *Merger Action Group v Secretary of State for Business, Enterprise and Regulatory Reform* [2009] Comp. A.R. 167 (CAT), Barling, J; see *Merger Action Group v Secretary of State for Business, Enterprise and Regulatory Reform* 2009 S.L.T. 10 (CAT), Barling, J. (President); see *Tesco Plc v Competition Commission (Costs)* [2009] CAT 26, [2009] Comp. A.R. 429 (CAT), Barling, J. (President); see *Virgin Media Inc v Competition Commission* [2009] Comp. A.R. 98 (CAT), Barling, J. (President)

s.121, enabling: SI 2009/2396

s.129, amended: SI 2009/1941 Sch.1 para.199

s.134, see *Barclays Bank Plc v Competition Commission* [2009] CAT 27, [2009] Comp. A.R. 381 (CAT), Briggs, J.; see *Tesco Plc v Competition Commission* [2009] CAT 6, [2009] Comp. A.R. 168 (CAT), Barling, J. (President); see *Tesco Plc v Competition Commission* [2009] CAT 9, [2009] Comp. A.R. 359 (CAT), Barling, J. (President)

s.136, see *Tesco Plc v Competition Commission* [2009] CAT 9, [2009] Comp. A.R. 359 (CAT), Barling, J. (President)

s.137, see *Tesco Plc v Competition Commission* [2009] CAT 13, [2009] Comp. A.R. 373 (CAT), Barling, J. (President); see *Tesco Plc v Competition Commission* [2009] CAT 9, [2009] Comp. A.R. 359 (CAT), Barling, J. (President)

s.138, see *Tesco Plc v Competition Commission* [2009] CAT 9, [2009] Comp. A.R. 359 (CAT), Barling, J. (President)

s.179, see *Tesco Plc v Competition Commission (Costs)* [2009] CAT 26, [2009] Comp. A.R. 429 (CAT), Barling, J. (President); see *Tesco Plc v Competition Commission* [2009] CAT 13, [2009] Comp. A.R. 373 (CAT), Barling, J. (President); see *Tesco Plc v Competition Commission* [2009] CAT 9, [2009] Comp. A.R. 359 (CAT), Barling, J. (President)

s.188, see *R. v Whittle (Peter)* [2008] EWCA Crim 2560, [2009] U.K.C.L.R. 247 (CA (Crim Div)), Hallett, L.J.

s.223, amended: SI 2009/1941 Sch.1 para.199

s.244, referred to: SI 2009/209 Reg.119

s.249, applied: SI 2009/853 Reg.2

s.255, see *Dairy Farmers of Britain Ltd, Re* [2009] EWHC 1389 (Ch), [2009] 4 All E.R. 241 (Ch D (Companies Ct)), Henderson, J.

s.261, see *Lewis v Metropolitan Property Realisations Ltd* [2008] EWHC 2760 (Ch), [2009] 1 F.L.R. 631 (Ch D), Proudman, J

Sch.8 para.13, amended: SI 2009/1941 Sch.1 para.199

Sch.13 Part 1 para.9D, added: SI 2009/2999 Reg.48

Sch.15, amended: SI 2009/1941 Sch.1 para.199

Sch.17 para.45, referred to: SI 2009/853 Reg.2

41. Nationality, Immigration and Asylum Act 2002

see *MS (Palestinian Territories) v Secretary of State for the Home Department* [2009] EWCA Civ 17, [2009] Imm. A.R. 464 (CA (Civ Div)), Rix, L.J.

Part 5, applied: 2009 c.11 s.58

s.11, applied: 2009 c.11 s.48

s.11, referred to: 2009 c.11 s.48

s.11, repealed: 2009 c.11 Sch.1 Part 2

2002– cont.

41. Nationality, Immigration and Asylum Act 2002– cont.

s.72, see *EN (Serbia) v Secretary of State for the Home Department* [2009] EWCA Civ 630, [2009] I.N.L.R. 459 (CA (Civ Div)), Laws, L.J.; see *R. (on the application of TB (Jamaica)) v Secretary of State for the Home Department* [2008] EWCA Civ 977, [2009] I.N.L.R. 221 (CA (Civ Div)), Thorpe, L.J.

s.82, see *JH (Zimbabwe) v Secretary of State for the Home Department* [2009] EWCA Civ 78, [2009] Imm. A.R. 499 (CA (Civ Div)), Laws, L.J.; see *R. (on the application of AM (Somalia)) v Secretary of State for the Home Department* [2009] EWCA Civ 114, [2009] Imm. A.R. 534 (CA (Civ Div)), Sedley, L.J.; see *R. (on the application of PE (Cameroon)) v Secretary of State for the Home Department* [2009] EWCA Civ 119, [2009] Q.B. 686 (CA (Civ Div)), Sedley, L.J.; see *R. (on the application of PE (Cameroon)) v Secretary of State for the Home Department* [2009] UKSC 7, [2009] 3 W.L.R. 1253 (SC), Lord Hope (Deputy President); see *R. (on the application of RK (Nepal)) v Secretary of State for the Home Department* [2009] EWCA Civ 359, Times, May 11, 2009 (CA (Civ Div)), Waller, L.J.

s.84, see *Beoku-Betts v Secretary of State for the Home Department* [2008] UKHL 39, [2009] 1 A.C. 115 (HL), Lord Bingham of Cornhill; see *R. (on the application of PE (Cameroon)) v Secretary of State for the Home Department* [2009] UKSC 7, [2009] 3 W.L.R. 1253 (SC), Lord Hope (Deputy President)

s.85, see *AS (Somalia) v Entry Clearance Officer (Addis Ababa)* [2009] UKHL 32, [2009] 1 W.L.R. 1385 (HL), Lord Phillips of Worth Matravers

s.86, see *MA (Somalia) v Secretary of State for Home Department* [2009] EWCA Civ 4, [2009] Imm. A.R. 413 (CA (Civ Div)), Laws, L.J.

s.92, see *R. (on the application of PE (Cameroon)) v Secretary of State for the Home Department* [2009] EWCA Civ 119, [2009] Q.B. 686 (CA (Civ Div)), Sedley, L.J.; see *R. (on the application of PE (Cameroon)) v Secretary of State for the Home Department* [2009] UKSC 7, [2009] 3 W.L.R. 1253 (SC), Lord Hope (Deputy President)

s.94, see *G v Secretary of State for the Home Department* 2009 S.C. 373 (OH), Lord Hodge; see *R. (on the application of PE (Cameroon)) v Secretary of State for the Home Department* [2009] EWCA Civ 119, [2009] Q.B. 686 (CA (Civ Div)), Sedley, L.J.; see *R. (on the application of PE (Cameroon)) v Secretary of State for the Home Department* [2009] UKSC 7, [2009] 3 W.L.R. 1253 (SC), Lord Hope (Deputy President); see *ZT (Kosovo) v Secretary of State for the Home Department* [2009] UKHL 6, [2009] 1 W.L.R. 348 (HL), Lord Phillips of Worth Matravers

s.95, see *R. (on the application of PE (Cameroon)) v Secretary of State for the Home Department* [2009] UKSC 7, [2009] 3 W.L.R. 1253 (SC), Lord Hope (Deputy President)

s.96, see *R. (on the application of AM (Somalia)) v Secretary of State for the Home Department* [2009] EWCA Civ 114, [2009] Imm. A.R. 534 (CA (Civ Div)), Sedley, L.J.; see *R. (on the application of PE (Cameroon)) v Secretary of State for the Home Department* [2009] UKSC

2002– cont.

41. Nationality, Immigration and Asylum Act 2002– cont.

s.96– cont.
7, [2009] 3 W.L.R. 1253 (SC), Lord Hope (Deputy President)

s.97, see *R. (on the application of AM (Somalia)) v Secretary of State for the Home Department* [2009] EWCA Civ 114, [2009] Imm. A.R. 534 (CA (Civ Div)), Sedley, L.J.

s.103A, see *JH (Zimbabwe) v Secretary of State for the Home Department* [2009] EWCA Civ 78, [2009] Imm. A.R. 499 (CA (Civ Div)), Laws, L.J.

s.103B, see *JH (Zimbabwe) v Secretary of State for the Home Department* [2009] EWCA Civ 78, [2009] Imm. A.R. 499 (CA (Civ Div)), Laws, L.J.

s.104, applied: SI 2009/1555 Reg.5, Reg.116, Reg.133, Reg.150, SI 2009/2737 Reg.4, Reg.68, Reg.85, Reg.109

s.104, referred to: SI 2009/3359 Reg.8

s.105, see *JN (Cameroon) v Secretary of State for the Home Department* [2009] EWCA Civ 307, [2009] Imm. A.R. 615 (CA (Civ Div)), Rix, L.J.

s.113, see *R. (on the application of PE (Cameroon)) v Secretary of State for the Home Department* [2009] EWCA Civ 119, [2009] Q.B. 686 (CA (Civ Div)), Sedley, L.J.; see *R. (on the application of PE (Cameroon)) v Secretary of State for the Home Department* [2009] UKSC 7, [2009] 3 W.L.R. 1253 (SC), Lord Hope (Deputy President)

s.131, amended: 2009 c.11 s.47

s.145, referred to: SI 2009/37 Sch.1 para.2, Sch.1 para.4

Sch.3 para.1, see *R. (on the application of Clue) v Birmingham City Council* [2008] EWHC 3036 (Admin), [2009] 1 All E.R. 1039 (QBD (Admin)), Charles, J.

Sch.3 para.3, see *R. (on the application of Clue) v Birmingham City Council* [2008] EWHC 3036 (Admin), [2009] 1 All E.R. 1039 (QBD (Admin)), Charles, J.

Sch.3 para.7, amended: 2009 c.11 s.48

2003

1. Income Tax (Earnings and Pensions) Act 2003

applied: 2009 c.4 s.867, s.1009, s.1293, SI 2009/470 Reg.29, Reg.57, SI 2009/600 Reg.7

Part 2, applied: 2009 c.4 s.969, s.1009, SI 2009/391 Reg.3

Part 2 c.4, applied: 2009 c.4 s.1293

Part 3 c.1, applied: 2009 c.4 s.1009, s.1011

Part 3 c.10, applied: SI 2009/470 Reg.29

Part 3 c.5, applied: SI 2009/470 Reg.29

Part 3 c.6, applied: SI 2009/470 Reg.29

Part 3 c.7, applied: SI 2009/470 Reg.29

Part 5 c.2, applied: 2009 c.10 Sch.35 para.2

Part 7 c.2, applied: 2009 c.4 s.1025, s.1027

Part 9, applied: SI 2009/391 Reg.3, SI 2009/1171 Reg.3, Reg.4, Reg.5

Part 10, applied: SI 2009/391 Reg.3

Part 10 c.3, applied: SI 2009/470 Reg.29

Part 11, referred to: 2009 c.10 Sch.58 para.10

s.8, applied: 2009 c.4 s.1011, SI 2009/2031 Art.5, Art.6

s.10, applied: SI 2009/2031 Art.5, Art.6

s.15, applied: 2009 c.4 s.992, s.996

s.18, applied: 2009 c.4 s.1250, s.1289, s.1293

s.18, referred to: 2009 c.4 s.867

s.19, applied: 2009 c.4 s.1250, s.1289

2003– cont.

1. **Income Tax (Earnings and Pensions) Act 2003–**
cont.

s.19, referred to: 2009 c.4 s.867
s.20, applied: 2009 c.4 s.992, s.996
s.43, varied: SI 2009/56 Sch.1 para.335
s.54, applied: 2009 c.4 s.140
s.61, amended: 2009 c.4 Sch.1 para.549
s.86, amended: SI 2009/1890 Art.4
s.105, amended: 2009 c.10 s.71
s.105A, added: 2009 c.10 s.71
s.105B, added: 2009 c.10 s.71
s.111, amended: SI 2009/56 Sch.1 para.336
s.111, repealed (in part): SI 2009/56 Sch.1 para.336
s.116, amended: 2009 c.10 s.54
s.121, amended: 2009 c.10 s.54, Sch.28 para.2
s.122, substituted: 2009 c.10 s.54
s.124A, added: 2009 c.10 s.54
s.139, amended: 2009 c.10 Sch.28 para.6
s.140, amended: 2009 c.10 Sch.28 para.7
s.142, amended: 2009 c.10 Sch.28 para.8
s.142, repealed (in part): 2009 c.10 Sch.28 para.8
s.145, amended: 2009 c.10 Sch.28 para.3
s.147, amended: 2009 c.10 Sch.28 para.4
s.170, repealed (in part): 2009 c.10 Sch.28 para.5
s.178, amended: 2009 c.4 Sch.1 para.550
s.180, amended: 2009 c.4 Sch.1 para.551
s.181, enabling: SI 2009/199
s.210, enabling: SI 2009/695
s.225, applied: 2009 c.4 s.69, s.1234
s.226, applied: 2009 c.4 s.69, s.1234
s.266, amended: 2009 c.10 s.55
s.267, amended: 2009 c.10 s.55
s.291, amended: 2009 c.10 s.56
s.311, referred to: 2009 c.4 s.75
s.318, amended: SI 2009/1544 Reg.2
s.318C, amended: SI 2009/1544 Reg.3, SI 2009/2888 Reg.2
s.318C, repealed (in part): SI 2009/1544 Reg.3
s.318D, enabling: SI 2009/1544, SI 2009/2888
s.320B, added: 2009 c.10 s.55
s.343, amended: SI 2009/1182 Sch.5 para.6
s.345, amended: SI 2009/56 Sch.1 para.337
s.346, amended: 2009 c.10 s.67
s.357, amended: 2009 c.4 Sch.1 para.552
s.360A, applied: 2009 c.4 s.1302
s.393B, enabling: SI 2009/2886
s.395A, added: SI 2009/730 Art.2
s.401, see *A v Revenue and Customs Commissioners* [2009] S.T.C. (S.C.D.) 269 (Sp Comm), Michael Tildesley; see *Crompton v Revenue and Customs Commissioners* [2009] UKFTT 71 (TC), [2009] S.T.C. (S.C.D.) 504 (FTT (Tax)), Richard Barlow
s.420, amended: 2009 c.4 Sch.1 para.553, 2009 c.10 s.126
s.421B, referred to: 2009 c.4 s.1025
s.426, applied: 2009 c.4 s.1009, s.1025, s.1026, s.1027
s.426, disapplied: 2009 c.4 s.1025
s.427, applied: 2009 c.4 s.1027
s.428, applied: 2009 c.4 s.1027
s.428, disapplied: 2009 c.4 s.1027
s.428A, applied: 2009 c.4 s.1026
s.438, applied: 2009 c.4 s.1032, s.1033, s.1034
s.438, disapplied: 2009 c.4 s.1032
s.442A, applied: 2009 c.4 s.1033
s.446E, disapplied: 2009 c.4 s.1026, s.1027
s.446G, disapplied: 2009 c.4 s.1033, s.1034
s.446H, disapplied: 2009 c.4 s.1033, s.1034
s.446K, referred to: 2009 c.4 s.1026, s.1027

2003– cont.

1. **Income Tax (Earnings and Pensions) Act 2003–**
cont.

s.446UA, disapplied: 2009 c.4 s.1009
s.476, applied: 2009 c.4 s.1017, s.1019
s.481, applied: 2009 c.4 s.1019
s.482, applied: 2009 c.4 s.1019
s.488, referred to: 2009 c.4 s.984
s.515, amended: 2009 c.4 Sch.1 para.554, Sch.3 Part 1
s.515, repealed (in part): 2009 c.4 Sch.3 Part 1
s.516, referred to: 2009 c.4 s.999
s.521, referred to: 2009 c.4 s.999
s.556A, added: 2009 c.10 s.67
s.641, referred to: SI 2009/226 Sch.1, SI 2009/227 Sch.1
s.682, amended: 2009 c.10 Sch.58 para.9
s.684, amended: 2009 c.10 Sch.58 para.2, Sch.58 para.3, Sch.58 para.4, Sch.58 para.5, Sch.58 para.6, Sch.58 para.7, SI 2009/56 Sch.1 para.338
s.684, applied: SI 2009/470 Reg.42, Reg.57, Reg.59
s.684, enabling: SI 2009/588, SI 2009/2029
s.685, amended: 2009 c.10 Sch.58 para.9
s.688A, applied: 2009 c.10 Sch.56 para.3
s.691, applied: SI 2009/470 Reg.48
s.702, amended: 2009 c.4 Sch.1 para.555, 2009 c.10 s.126
s.711, applied: SI 2009/403 Art.10
s.715, amended: SI 2009/56 Sch.1 para.339
s.715, repealed (in part): SI 2009/3054 Sch.1 para.10
Sch.1 Part 1, amended: 2009 c.4 Sch.1 para.556, 2009 c.10 s.126
Sch.1 Part 2, amended: 2009 c.4 Sch.3 Part 1, 2009 c.10 Sch.19 para.12, SI 2009/56 Sch.1 para.340
Sch.2, applied: 2009 c.4 s.999
Sch.2, referred to: 2009 c.4 s.984
Sch.2 Part 8 para.68, applied: 2009 c.10 Sch.19 para.14
Sch.2 Part 9 para.78, amended: 2009 c.10 s.126
Sch.2 Part 10 para.82, amended: SI 2009/56 Sch.1 para.341
Sch.2 Part 10 para.85, amended: 2009 c.4 Sch.1 para.557, SI 2009/56 Sch.1 para.342
Sch.2 Part 11 para.89, applied: 2009 c.4 s.993
Sch.2 Part 11 para.100, amended: SI 2009/56 Sch.1 para.343
Sch.3, applied: 2009 c.4 s.999
Sch.3 Part 8 para.41, amended: SI 2009/56 Sch.1 para.345
Sch.3 Part 8 para.44, amended: SI 2009/56 Sch.1 para.346
Sch.3 Part 9 para.49, amended: SI 2009/56 Sch.1 para.347
Sch.4 Part 7 para.29, amended: SI 2009/56 Sch.1 para.349
Sch.4 Part 7 para.32, amended: SI 2009/56 Sch.1 para.350
Sch.4 Part 8 para.37, amended: SI 2009/56 Sch.1 para.351
Sch.5 Part 7 para.48, amended: SI 2009/56 Sch.1 para.353
Sch.5 Part 7 para.48, repealed (in part): SI 2009/56 Sch.1 para.353
Sch.5 Part 7 para.50, repealed (in part): SI 2009/56 Sch.1 para.354
Sch.5 Part 8 para.56, amended: SI 2009/56 Sch.1 para.355
Sch.5 Part 8 para.56, repealed (in part): SI 2009/56 Sch.1 para.355
Sch.5 Part 8 para.57, repealed (in part): SI 2009/56 Sch.1 para.356

2003– cont.

1. Income Tax (Earnings and Pensions) Act 2003–
cont.
Sch.5 Part 8 para.59, amended: SI 2009/56 Sch.1
para.357
Sch.6 Part 1 para.4, repealed: 2009 c.4 Sch.3 Part 1
Sch.6 Part 1 para.5, repealed: 2009 c.4 Sch.3 Part 1
Sch.6 Part 1 para.12, repealed: 2009 c.4 Sch.3 Part 1
Sch.6 Part 1 para.13, repealed: 2009 c.4 Sch.3 Part 1
Sch.6 Part 1 para.35, repealed: 2009 c.10 Sch.1
para.6
Sch.6 Part 1 para.62, repealed: 2009 c.4 Sch.3 Part 1
Sch.6 Part 1 para.63, repealed: 2009 c.4 Sch.3 Part 1
Sch.6 Part 1 para.64, repealed: 2009 c.4 Sch.3 Part 1
Sch.6 Part 1 para.67, repealed: 2009 c.4 Sch.3 Part 1
Sch.6 Part 1 para.69, repealed: 2009 c.4 Sch.3 Part 1
Sch.6 Part 1 para.70, repealed: 2009 c.4 Sch.3 Part 1
Sch.6 Part 1 para.87, repealed: 2009 c.4 Sch.3 Part 1
Sch.6 Part 1 para.109, repealed: 2009 c.4 Sch.3 Part 1
Sch.6 Part 2 para.129, repealed: SI 2009/56 Sch.1
para.358
Sch.6 Part 2 para.142, repealed: SI 2009/56 Sch.1
para.358
Sch.6 Part 2 para.179, repealed: 2009 c.24 Sch.7
Part 1
Sch.6 Part 2 para.244, repealed: 2009 c.4 Sch.3 Part 1
Sch.6 Part 2 para.258, repealed: 2009 c.4 Sch.3 Part 1
Sch.7 Part 4 para.37, amended: SI 2009/2035 Sch.1
para.40
Sch.7 Part 7 para.54, amended: 2009 c.10 s.126
4. Health (Wales) Act 2003
s.3, referred to: SI 2009/2623 Art.3
s.3, enabling: SI 2009/2623
s.8, enabling: SI 2009/2623
6. Police (Northern Ireland) Act 2003
s.30, repealed (in part): 2009 c.26 Sch.7 para.126,
Sch.8 Part 13
Sch.2A para.6, amended: 2009 c.26 Sch.7 para.28
7. European Parliament (Representation) Act 2003
s.12, applied: SI 2009/185
s.12, enabling: SI 2009/185
s.13, enabling: SI 2009/185
s.17, applied: SI 2009/186
s.17, enabling: SI 2009/186, SI 2009/848
s.18, applied: SI 2009/186
s.18, enabling: SI 2009/186, SI 2009/848
s.23, enabling: SI 2009/185, SI 2009/186
s.25, enabling: SI 2009/186
9. Electricity (Miscellaneous Provisions) Act 2003
s.1, amended: SI 2009/1941 Sch.1 para.216
10. Regional Assemblies (Preparations) Act 2003
repealed: 2009 c.20 Sch.7 Part 4
Sch.1 para.2, repealed: 2009 c.25 Sch.23 Part 1
**11. Industrial Development (Financial Assistance)
Act 2003**
repealed: 2009 c.5 s.1
14. Finance Act 2003
varied: SI 2009/317 Sch.1
Part 3, amended: SI 2009/56 Sch.1 para.362
Part 4, applied: 2009 c.4 s.1303, SI 2009/2269
Reg.17, SI 2009/2971 Reg.31
Part 4, referred to: 2009 c.10 Sch.61 para.1, Sch.61
para.8
s.24, amended: SI 2009/56 Sch.1 para.360
s.24, enabling: SI 2009/3164
s.25, applied: 2009 c.4 s.1303
s.26, applied: 2009 c.4 s.1303
s.26, enabling: SI 2009/3164
s.30, amended: SI 2009/56 Sch.1 para.361

2003– cont.

14. Finance Act 2003– *cont.*
s.33, amended: SI 2009/56 Sch.1 para.363
s.33A, added: SI 2009/56 Sch.1 para.364
s.33B, added: SI 2009/56 Sch.1 para.364
s.33C, added: SI 2009/56 Sch.1 para.364
s.33D, added: SI 2009/56 Sch.1 para.364
s.33E, added: SI 2009/56 Sch.1 para.364
s.33F, added: SI 2009/56 Sch.1 para.364
s.34, amended: SI 2009/56 Sch.1 para.365
s.35, amended: SI 2009/56 Sch.1 para.365
s.36, amended: SI 2009/56 Sch.1 para.365
s.37, amended: SI 2009/56 Sch.1 para.365
s.37, substituted: SI 2009/56 Sch.1 para.366
s.40, repealed: 2009 c.4 Sch.3 Part 1
s.41, enabling: SI 2009/3164
s.55, amended: 2009 c.10 s.80
s.55, varied: 2009 c.10 s.10
s.66, amended: SI 2009/1890 Art.3
s.71, amended: 2009 c.10 s.81
s.73C, added: 2009 c.10 Sch.61 para.25
s.74, see *Elizabeth Court (Bournemouth) Ltd v
Revenue and Customs Commissioners* [2008]
EWHC 2828 (Ch), [2009] S.T.C. 682 (Ch D),
Sir Andrew Morritt (Chancellor)
s.74, amended: 2009 c.10 s.80
s.74, substituted: 2009 c.10 s.80
s.76, applied: 2009 c.10 Sch.55 para.1
s.78A, enabling: SI 2009/2095
s.81, applied: 2009 c.10 Sch.55 para.1
s.81, referred to: 2009 c.10 Sch.56 para.1
s.82, amended: SI 2009/56 Sch.1 para.367
s.86, amended: 2009 c.10 Sch.61 para.26
s.86, applied: 2009 c.10 Sch.56 para.1
s.86, referred to: 2009 c.10 Sch.56 para.1
s.90, amended: SI 2009/56 Sch.1 para.368
s.93, amended: SI 2009/3054 Sch.1 para.11
s.93, applied: SI 2009/3054 Art.7
s.94, applied: SI 2009/3054 Art.7
s.94, repealed: SI 2009/3054 Sch.1 para.11
s.103, amended: SI 2009/56 Sch.1 para.369
s.114, enabling: SI 2009/2095
s.115, repealed: SI 2009/56 Sch.1 para.370
s.121, amended: SI 2009/56 Sch.1 para.371
s.122, amended: SI 2009/56 Sch.1 para.372
s.141, repealed: 2009 c.4 Sch.3 Part 1
s.143, repealed: 2009 c.4 Sch.3 Part 1
s.148, amended: 2009 c.4 Sch.1 para.561
s.148, repealed (in part): 2009 c.4 Sch.3 Part 1
s.149, repealed (in part): 2009 c.4 Sch.3 Part 1
s.150, amended: 2009 c.4 Sch.1 para.562, Sch.3 Part 1
s.152, amended: 2009 c.4 Sch.1 para.563
s.153, amended: 2009 c.4 Sch.3 Part 1
s.153, repealed (in part): 2009 c.4 Sch.3 Part 1
s.168, repealed: 2009 c.4 Sch.3 Part 1
s.177, amended: 2009 c.4 Sch.1 para.564
s.178, repealed: 2009 c.4 Sch.3 Part 1
s.179, repealed: 2009 c.4 Sch.3 Part 1
s.180, repealed (in part): 2009 c.4 Sch.3 Part 1
s.184, repealed: 2009 c.4 Sch.3 Part 1
s.195, amended: 2009 c.4 Sch.1 para.565
s.204, enabling: SI 2009/2978, SI 2009/3218
s.205, applied: SI 2009/2029
s.205, enabling: SI 2009/2030
Sch.5 para.2, varied: 2009 c.10 s.10
Sch.7 Part 1, applied: SI 2009/2971 Reg.33
Sch.7 Part 1 para.1, applied: SI 2009/2971 Reg.33
Sch.7 Part 1 para.3, disapplied: SI 2009/2971
Reg.33

2003– cont.

14. Finance Act 2003– *cont.*

Sch.9 para.5, amended: 2009 c.l0 s.81

Sch.9 para.7, amended: 2009 c.l0 s.81

Sch.9 para.13, added: 2009 c.l0 s.82

Sch.9 para.13, referred to: 2009 c.l0 s.82

Sch.9 para.14, added: 2009 c.l0 s.82

Sch.9 para.14, referred to: 2009 c.l0 s.82

Sch.10 Part 1 para.1, varied: 2009 c.l0 Sch.61 para.7

Sch.10 Part 1 para.1A, varied: 2009 c.l0 Sch.61 para.7

Sch.10 Part 1 para.1B, varied: 2009 c.l0 Sch.61 para.7

Sch.10 Part 1 para.2, varied: 2009 c.l0 Sch.61 para.7

Sch.10 Part 1 para.3, varied: 2009 c.l0 Sch.61 para.7

Sch.10 Part 1 para.4, varied: 2009 c.l0 Sch.61 para.7

Sch.10 Part 1 para.5, amended: SI 2009/56 Sch.1 para.374

Sch.10 Part 1 para.5, varied: 2009 c.l0 Sch.61 para.7

Sch.10 Part 1 para.6, varied: 2009 c.l0 Sch.61 para.7

Sch.10 Part 1 para.7, varied: 2009 c.l0 Sch.61 para.7

Sch.10 Part 1 para.8, varied: 2009 c.l0 Sch.61 para.7

Sch.10 Part 2 para.9, amended: 2009 c.l0 Sch.50 para.5

Sch.10 Part 2 para.9, varied: 2009 c.l0 Sch.61 para.7

Sch.10 Part 2 para.10, amended: 2009 c.l0 Sch.50 para.7, SI 2009/56 Sch.1 para.375

Sch.10 Part 2 para.10, substituted: 2009 c.l0 Sch.50 para.6

Sch.10 Part 2 para.10, varied: 2009 c.l0 Sch.61 para.7

Sch.10 Part 2 para.11, varied: 2009 c.l0 Sch.61 para.7

Sch.10 Part 3 para.12, varied: 2009 c.l0 Sch.61 para.7

Sch.10 Part 3 para.13, varied: 2009 c.l0 Sch.61 para.7

Sch.10 Part 3 para.14, amended: SI 2009/56 Sch.1 para.376

Sch.10 Part 3 para.14, applied: SI 2009/3054 Art.7

Sch.10 Part 3 para.14, repealed: SI 2009/3054 Sch.1 para.11

Sch.10 Part 3 para.14, varied: 2009 c.l0 Sch.61 para.7

Sch.10 Part 3 para.15, amended: SI 2009/56 Sch.1 para.377

Sch.10 Part 3 para.15, applied: SI 2009/3054 Art.7

Sch.10 Part 3 para.15, repealed: SI 2009/3054 Sch.1 para.11

Sch.10 Part 3 para.15, varied: 2009 c.l0 Sch.61 para.7

Sch.10 Part 3 para.16, applied: SI 2009/3054 Art.7

Sch.10 Part 3 para.16, repealed: SI 2009/3054 Sch.1 para.11

Sch.10 Part 3 para.16, varied: 2009 c.l0 Sch.61 para.7

Sch.10 Part 3 para.17, varied: 2009 c.l0 Sch.61 para.7

Sch.10 Part 3 para.18, varied: 2009 c.l0 Sch.61 para.7

Sch.10 Part 3 para.19, amended: SI 2009/56 Sch.1 para.378

Sch.10 Part 3 para.19, repealed (in part): SI 2009/56 Sch.1 para.378

Sch.10 Part 3 para.19, varied: 2009 c.l0 Sch.61 para.7

Sch.10 Part 3 para.20, amended: SI 2009/56 Sch.1 para.379

Sch.10 Part 3 para.20, repealed (in part): SI 2009/56 Sch.1 para.379

Sch.10 Part 3 para.20, varied: 2009 c.l0 Sch.61 para.7

Sch.10 Part 3 para.21, amended: SI 2009/56 Sch.1 para.380

Sch.10 Part 3 para.21, varied: 2009 c.l0 Sch.61 para.7

Sch.10 Part 3 para.22, amended: SI 2009/56 Sch.1 para.381

2003– cont.

14. Finance Act 2003– *cont.*

Sch.10 Part 3 para.22, varied: 2009 c.l0 Sch.61 para.7

Sch.10 Part 3 para.23, varied: 2009 c.l0 Sch.61 para.7

Sch.10 Part 3 para.24, amended: SI 2009/56 Sch.1 para.382

Sch.10 Part 3 para.24, varied: 2009 c.l0 Sch.61 para.7

Sch.10 Part 4 para.25, amended: 2009 c.l0 Sch.51 para.15

Sch.10 Part 4 para.25, applied: 2009 c.l0 Sch.56 para.1

Sch.10 Part 4 para.25, varied: 2009 c.l0 Sch.61 para.7

Sch.10 Part 4 para.26, varied: 2009 c.l0 Sch.61 para.7

Sch.10 Part 4 para.27, amended: 2009 c.l0 Sch.51 para.15

Sch.10 Part 4 para.27, varied: 2009 c.l0 Sch.61 para.7

Sch.10 Part 5 para.28, varied: 2009 c.l0 Sch.61 para.7

Sch.10 Part 5 para.29, varied: 2009 c.l0 Sch.61 para.7

Sch.10 Part 5 para.30, varied: 2009 c.l0 Sch.61 para.7

Sch.10 Part 5 para.31, amended: 2009 c.l0 Sch.51 para.15

Sch.10 Part 5 para.31, varied: 2009 c.l0 Sch.61 para.7

Sch.10 Part 5 para.31A, added: 2009 c.l0 Sch.51 para.15

Sch.10 Part 5 para.31A, varied: 2009 c.l0 Sch.61 para.7

Sch.10 Part 5 para.32, varied: 2009 c.l0 Sch.61 para.7

Sch.10 Part 6 para.33, amended: SI 2009/56 Sch.1 para.383

Sch.10 Part 6 para.33, varied: 2009 c.l0 Sch.61 para.7

Sch.10 Part 6 para.34, amended: 2009 c.l0 Sch.51 para.15, SI 2009/56 Sch.1 para.384

Sch.10 Part 6 para.34, varied: 2009 c.l0 Sch.61 para.7

Sch.10 Part 7 para.35, amended: SI 2009/56 Sch.1 para.385, Sch.1 para.386

Sch.10 Part 7 para.35, repealed (in part): SI 2009/56 Sch.1 para.386

Sch.10 Part 7 para.35, varied: 2009 c.l0 Sch.61 para.7

Sch.10 Part 7 para.36, amended: SI 2009/56 Sch.1 para.385

Sch.10 Part 7 para.36, repealed (in part): SI 2009/56 Sch.1 para.387

Sch.10 Part 7 para.36, varied: 2009 c.l0 Sch.61 para.7

Sch.10 Part 7 para.36A, added: SI 2009/56 Sch.1 para.388

Sch.10 Part 7 para.36A, amended: SI 2009/56 Sch.1 para.385

Sch.10 Part 7 para.36A, varied: 2009 c.l0 Sch.61 para.7

Sch.10 Part 7 para.36B, added: SI 2009/56 Sch.1 para.388

Sch.10 Part 7 para.36B, amended: SI 2009/56 Sch.1 para.385

Sch.10 Part 7 para.36B, varied: 2009 c.l0 Sch.61 para.7

Sch.10 Part 7 para.36C, added: SI 2009/56 Sch.1 para.388

2003–cont.

14. Finance Act 2003–*cont.*

Sch.10 Part 7 para.36C, amended: SI 2009/56 Sch.1 para.385

Sch.10 Part 7 para.36C, varied: 2009 c.10 Sch.61 para.7

Sch.10 Part 7 para.36D, added: SI 2009/56 Sch.1 para.388

Sch.10 Part 7 para.36D, amended: SI 2009/56 Sch.1 para.385

Sch.10 Part 7 para.36D, varied: 2009 c.10 Sch.61 para.7

Sch.10 Part 7 para.36E, added: SI 2009/56 Sch.1 para.388

Sch.10 Part 7 para.36E, amended: SI 2009/56 Sch.1 para.385

Sch.10 Part 7 para.36E, varied: 2009 c.10 Sch.61 para.7

Sch.10 Part 7 para.36F, added: SI 2009/56 Sch.1 para.388

Sch.10 Part 7 para.36F, amended: SI 2009/56 Sch.1 para.385

Sch.10 Part 7 para.36F, varied: 2009 c.10 Sch.61 para.7

Sch.10 Part 7 para.36G, added: SI 2009/56 Sch.1 para.388

Sch.10 Part 7 para.36G, amended: SI 2009/56 Sch.1 para.385

Sch.10 Part 7 para.36G, varied: 2009 c.10 Sch.61 para.7

Sch.10 Part 7 para.36H, added: SI 2009/56 Sch.1 para.388

Sch.10 Part 7 para.36H, amended: SI 2009/56 Sch.1 para.385

Sch.10 Part 7 para.36H, varied: 2009 c.10 Sch.61 para.7

Sch.10 Part 7 para.36I, added: SI 2009/56 Sch.1 para.388

Sch.10 Part 7 para.36I, amended: SI 2009/56 Sch.1 para.385

Sch.10 Part 7 para.36I, varied: 2009 c.10 Sch.61 para.7

Sch.10 Part 7 para.37, amended: SI 2009/56 Sch.1 para.385, Sch.1 para.389

Sch.10 Part 7 para.37, varied: 2009 c.10 Sch.61 para.7

Sch.10 Part 7 para.38, amended: SI 2009/56 Sch.1 para.385, Sch.1 para.390

Sch.10 Part 7 para.38, varied: 2009 c.10 Sch.61 para.7

Sch.10 Part 7 para.39, amended: SI 2009/56 Sch.1 para.385, Sch.1 para.391

Sch.10 Part 7 para.39, repealed (in part): SI 2009/56 Sch.1 para.391

Sch.10 Part 7 para.39, varied: 2009 c.10 Sch.61 para.7

Sch.10 Part 7 para.40, amended: SI 2009/56 Sch.1 para.385, Sch.1 para.392

Sch.10 Part 7 para.40, varied: 2009 c.10 Sch.61 para.7

Sch.10 Part 7 para.41, added: SI 2009/56 Sch.1 para.393

Sch.10 Part 7 para.41, amended: SI 2009/56 Sch.1 para.385

Sch.10 Part 7 para.41, varied: 2009 c.10 Sch.61 para.7

Sch.10 Part 7 para.42, added: SI 2009/56 Sch.1 para.393

Sch.10 Part 7 para.42, amended: SI 2009/56 Sch.1 para.385

Sch.10 Part 7 para.42, varied: 2009 c.10 Sch.61 para.7

2003–cont.

14. Finance Act 2003–*cont.*

Sch.10 Part 7 para.43, added: SI 2009/56 Sch.1 para.393

Sch.10 Part 7 para.43, amended: SI 2009/56 Sch.1 para.385

Sch.10 Part 7 para.43, varied: 2009 c.10 Sch.61 para.7

Sch.10 Part 7 para.44, added: SI 2009/56 Sch.1 para.393

Sch.10 Part 7 para.44, amended: SI 2009/56 Sch.1 para.385

Sch.10 Part 7 para.44, varied: 2009 c.10 Sch.61 para.7

Sch.10 Part 7 para.45, added: SI 2009/56 Sch.1 para.393

Sch.10 Part 7 para.45, amended: SI 2009/56 Sch.1 para.385, SI 2009/1307 Sch.1 para.270

Sch.10 Part 7 para.45, varied: 2009 c.10 Sch.61 para.7

Sch.10 Part 7 para.46, added: SI 2009/56 Sch.1 para.393

Sch.10 Part 7 para.46, amended: SI 2009/56 Sch.1 para.385

Sch.10 Part 7 para.46, varied: 2009 c.10 Sch.61 para.7

Sch.11 Part 2 para.4, amended: 2009 c.10 Sch.50 para.9

Sch.11 Part 2 para.5, amended: 2009 c.10 Sch.50 para.11, SI 2009/56 Sch.1 para.394

Sch.11 Part 2 para.5, substituted: 2009 c.10 Sch.50 para.10

Sch.11A para.3, amended: 2009 c.10 Sch.50 para.13, SI 2009/56 Sch.1 para.396

Sch.11A para.3, repealed (in part): 2009 c.10 Sch.50 para.13

Sch.11A para.3A, added: 2009 c.10 Sch.50 para.14

Sch.11A para.8, applied: SI 2009/3054 Art.7

Sch.11A para.8, repealed: SI 2009/3054 Sch.1 para.11

Sch.11A para.9, amended: SI 2009/56 Sch.1 para.397

Sch.11A para.9, applied: SI 2009/3054 Art.7

Sch.11A para.9, repealed: SI 2009/3054 Sch.1 para.11

Sch.11A para.10, applied: SI 2009/3054 Art.7

Sch.11A para.10, repealed: SI 2009/3054 Sch.1 para.11

Sch.11A para.12, amended: SI 2009/56 Sch.1 para.398

Sch.11A para.14, amended: SI 2009/56 Sch.1 para.399

Sch.11A para.14, repealed (in part): SI 2009/56 Sch.1 para.399

Sch.11A para.15, repealed: SI 2009/56 Sch.1 para.400

Sch.12 Part 1 para.3, applied: SI 2009/3024 Art.4, SSI 2009/403 Art.3

Sch.13 Part 1, applied: SI 2009/3054 Art.7

Sch.13 Part 1 para.1, repealed: SI 2009/3054 Sch.1 para.11

Sch.13 Part 1 para.2, amended: SI 2009/56 Sch.1 para.402

Sch.13 Part 1 para.2, applied: SI 2009/275 Art.3

Sch.13 Part 1 para.2, repealed (in part): SI 2009/56 Sch.1 para.402, SI 2009/3054 Sch.1 para.11

Sch.13 Part 1 para.3, repealed: SI 2009/3054 Sch.1 para.11

Sch.13 Part 1 para.4, amended: SI 2009/56 Sch.1 para.403

Sch.13 Part 1 para.4, applied: SI 2009/275 Art.3

2003– cont.

14. Finance Act 2003–*cont.*

Sch.13 Part 1 para.4, repealed: SI 2009/3054 Sch.1 para.11

Sch.13 Part 1 para.5, repealed: SI 2009/3054 Sch.1 para.11

Sch.13 Part 2, applied: SI 2009/3054 Art.7

Sch.13 Part 2 para.6, repealed: SI 2009/3054 Sch.1 para.11

Sch.13 Part 2 para.7, amended: SI 2009/56 Sch.1 para.404

Sch.13 Part 2 para.7, applied: SI 2009/275 Art.3

Sch.13 Part 2 para.7, repealed (in part): SI 2009/56 Sch.1 para.404, SI 2009/3054 Sch.1 para.11

Sch.13 Part 2 para.8, repealed: SI 2009/3054 Sch.1 para.11

Sch.13 Part 2 para.9, amended: SI 2009/56 Sch.1 para.405

Sch.13 Part 2 para.9, applied: SI 2009/275 Art.3

Sch.13 Part 2 para.9, repealed: SI 2009/3054 Sch.1 para.11

Sch.13 Part 2 para.10, amended: SI 2009/56 Sch.1 para.406

Sch.13 Part 2 para.10, applied: SI 2009/275 Art.3

Sch.13 Part 2 para.10, repealed: SI 2009/3054 Sch.1 para.11

Sch.13 Part 2 para.11, amended: SI 2009/56 Sch.1 para.407

Sch.13 Part 2 para.11, applied: SI 2009/275 Art.3

Sch.13 Part 2 para.11, repealed: SI 2009/3054 Sch.1 para.11

Sch.13 Part 2 para.12, repealed: SI 2009/3054 Sch.1 para.11

Sch.13 Part 2 para.13, repealed: SI 2009/3054 Sch.1 para.11

Sch.13 Part 4 para.19, amended: SI 2009/3054 Sch.1 para.11

Sch.13 Part 4 para.20, amended: SI 2009/3054 Sch.1 para.11

Sch.13 Part 4 para.21, repealed (in part): SI 2009/3054 Sch.1 para.11

Sch.13 Part 4 para.22, amended: SI 2009/3054 Sch.1 para.11

Sch.13 Part 4 para.23, amended: SI 2009/3054 Sch.1 para.11

Sch.13 Part 4 para.24, amended: SI 2009/56 Sch.1 para.408

Sch.13 Part 4 para.24, applied: SI 2009/275 Art.3

Sch.13 Part 4 para.24, repealed: SI 2009/3054 Sch.1 para.11

Sch.13 Part 4 para.25, amended: SI 2009/3054 Sch.1 para.11

Sch.13 Part 4 para.26, repealed: SI 2009/3054 Sch.1 para.11

Sch.13 Part 4 para.27, repealed: SI 2009/3054 Sch.1 para.11

Sch.13 Part 5 para.28, repealed: SI 2009/3054 Sch.1 para.11

Sch.13 Part 5 para.29, repealed: SI 2009/3054 Sch.1 para.11

Sch.13 Part 5 para.30, repealed: SI 2009/3054 Sch.1 para.11

Sch.13 Part 5 para.31, repealed: SI 2009/3054 Sch.1 para.11

Sch.13 Part 8 para.53, amended: SI 2009/56 Sch.1 para.409, SI 2009/3054 Sch.1 para.11

Sch.13 Part 8 para.53, repealed (in part): SI 2009/3054 Sch.1 para.11

Sch.14 para.5, amended: SI 2009/56 Sch.1 para.411

Sch.14 para.6, amended: SI 2009/56 Sch.1 para.412

2003– cont.

14. Finance Act 2003–*cont.*

Sch.14 para.6, repealed (in part): SI 2009/56 Sch.1 para.412

Sch.14 para.8, amended: 2009 c.10 Sch.51 para.16

Sch.17 para.1, repealed: SI 2009/56 Sch.1 para.413

Sch.17 para.2, repealed: SI 2009/56 Sch.1 para.413

Sch.17 para.3, repealed: SI 2009/56 Sch.1 para.413

Sch.17 para.4, repealed: SI 2009/56 Sch.1 para.413

Sch.17 para.5, repealed: SI 2009/56 Sch.1 para.413

Sch.17 para.6, repealed: SI 2009/56 Sch.1 para.413

Sch.17 para.7, repealed: SI 2009/56 Sch.1 para.413

Sch.17 para.8, repealed: SI 2009/56 Sch.1 para.413

Sch.17 para.9, repealed: SI 2009/56 Sch.1 para.413

Sch.17 para.10, repealed: SI 2009/56 Sch.1 para.413

Sch.17 para.11, repealed: SI 2009/56 Sch.1 para.413

Sch.17A para.3, applied: 2009 c.10 Sch.55 para.1

Sch.17A para.4, applied: 2009 c.10 Sch.55 para.1

Sch.17A para.8, applied: 2009 c.10 Sch.55 para.1

Sch.22 para.59, repealed: 2009 c.4 Sch.3 Part 1

Sch.22 para.60, repealed: 2009 c.4 Sch.3 Part 1

Sch.22 para.61, repealed: 2009 c.4 Sch.3 Part 1

Sch.22 para.62, repealed: 2009 c.4 Sch.3 Part 1

Sch.22 para.63, repealed: 2009 c.4 Sch.3 Part 1

Sch.22 para.64, repealed: 2009 c.4 Sch.3 Part 1

Sch.22 para.65, repealed: 2009 c.4 Sch.3 Part 1

Sch.22 para.66, repealed: 2009 c.4 Sch.3 Part 1

Sch.22 para.67, repealed: 2009 c.4 Sch.3 Part 1

Sch.22 para.68, repealed: 2009 c.4 Sch.3 Part 1

Sch.22 para.69, repealed: 2009 c.4 Sch.3 Part 1

Sch.22 para.70, repealed: 2009 c.4 Sch.3 Part 1

Sch.22 para.71, repealed: 2009 c.4 Sch.3 Part 1

Sch.22 para.72, repealed: 2009 c.4 Sch.3 Part 1

Sch.22 para.73, repealed: 2009 c.4 Sch.3 Part 1

Sch.23 Part 1 para.1, repealed: 2009 c.4 Sch.3 Part 1

Sch.23 Part 1 para.2, repealed: 2009 c.4 Sch.3 Part 1

Sch.23 Part 1 para.3, repealed: 2009 c.4 Sch.3 Part 1

Sch.23 Part 1 para.4, repealed: 2009 c.4 Sch.3 Part 1

Sch.23 Part 2 para.5, repealed: 2009 c.4 Sch.3 Part 1

Sch.23 Part 2 para.6, repealed: 2009 c.4 Sch.3 Part 1

Sch.23 Part 2 para.7, repealed: 2009 c.4 Sch.3 Part 1

Sch.23 Part 2 para.8, repealed: 2009 c.4 Sch.3 Part 1

Sch.23 Part 2 para.9, repealed: 2009 c.4 Sch.3 Part 1

Sch.23 Part 2 para.10, repealed: 2009 c.4 Sch.3 Part 1

Sch.23 Part 3 para.11, repealed: 2009 c.4 Sch.3 Part 1

Sch.23 Part 3 para.12, repealed: 2009 c.4 Sch.3 Part 1

Sch.23 Part 3 para.13, repealed: 2009 c.4 Sch.3 Part 1

Sch.23 Part 3 para.14, repealed: 2009 c.4 Sch.3 Part 1

Sch.23 Part 3 para.15, repealed: 2009 c.4 Sch.3 Part 1

Sch.23 Part 3 para.16, repealed: 2009 c.4 Sch.3 Part 1

Sch.23 Part 3 para.17, repealed: 2009 c.4 Sch.3 Part 1

Sch.23 Part 4A para.22A, repealed: 2009 c.4 Sch.3 Part 1

Sch.23 Part 4A para.22B, repealed: 2009 c.4 Sch.3 Part 1

Sch.23 Part 4A para.22C, repealed: 2009 c.4 Sch.3 Part 1

Sch.23 Part 4A para.22D, repealed: 2009 c.4 Sch.3 Part 1

Sch.23 Part 4 para.18, repealed: 2009 c.4 Sch.3 Part 1

Sch.23 Part 4 para.19, repealed: 2009 c.4 Sch.3 Part 1

Sch.23 Part 4 para.20, repealed: 2009 c.4 Sch.3 Part 1

Sch.23 Part 4 para.21, repealed: 2009 c.4 Sch.3 Part 1

Sch.23 Part 4 para.22, repealed: 2009 c.4 Sch.3 Part 1

Sch.23 Part 5 para.23, repealed: 2009 c.4 Sch.3 Part 1

Sch.23 Part 5 para.24, repealed: 2009 c.4 Sch.3 Part 1

Sch.23 Part 5 para.25, repealed: 2009 c.4 Sch.3 Part 1

Sch.23 Part 5 para.26, repealed: 2009 c.4 Sch.3 Part 1

Sch.23 Part 5 para.27, repealed: 2009 c.4 Sch.3 Part 1

2003– cont.

14. Finance Act 2003– *cont.*
Sch.23 Part 5 para.28, repealed: 2009 c.4 Sch.3 Part 1
Sch.23 Part 5 para.29, repealed: 2009 c.4 Sch.3 Part 1
Sch.23 Part 5 para.30, repealed: 2009 c.4 Sch.3 Part 1
Sch.23 Part 5 para.31, repealed: 2009 c.4 Sch.3 Part 1
Sch.23 Part 6 para.32, repealed: 2009 c.4 Sch.3 Part 1
Sch.23 Part 6 para.33, repealed: 2009 c.4 Sch.3 Part 1
Sch.24 para.1, repealed: 2009 c.4 Sch.3 Part 1
Sch.24 para.2, repealed: 2009 c.4 Sch.3 Part 1
Sch.24 para.3, repealed: 2009 c.4 Sch.3 Part 1
Sch.24 para.4, repealed: 2009 c.4 Sch.3 Part 1
Sch.24 para.5, repealed: 2009 c.4 Sch.3 Part 1
Sch.24 para.6, repealed: 2009 c.4 Sch.3 Part 1
Sch.24 para.7, repealed: 2009 c.4 Sch.3 Part 1
Sch.24 para.8, repealed: 2009 c.4 Sch.3 Part 1
Sch.24 para.9, repealed: 2009 c.4 Sch.3 Part 1
Sch.24 para.10, repealed: 2009 c.4 Sch.3 Part 1
Sch.24 para.11, repealed: 2009 c.4 Sch.3 Part 1
Sch.25, repealed: 2009 c.4 Sch.3 Part 1
Sch.26 para.5A, amended: 2009 c.4 Sch.1 para.568
Sch.26 para.5A, referred to: 2009 c.4 s.20
Sch.28 Part 2 para.4, repealed (in part): SI 2009/
2035 Sch.1 para.60
Sch.28 Part 2 para.5, repealed (in part): SI 2009/
2035 Sch.1 para.60
Sch.31 Part 1 para.1, repealed: 2009 c.4 Sch.3 Part 1
Sch.31 Part 1 para.2, repealed: 2009 c.4 Sch.3 Part 1
Sch.31 Part 1 para.3, repealed: 2009 c.4 Sch.3 Part 1
Sch.31 Part 1 para.4, repealed: 2009 c.4 Sch.3 Part 1
Sch.31 Part 1 para.5, repealed: 2009 c.4 Sch.3 Part 1
Sch.31 Part 1 para.6, repealed: 2009 c.4 Sch.3 Part 1
Sch.31 Part 1 para.7, repealed: 2009 c.4 Sch.3 Part 1
Sch.31 Part 2 para.8, repealed: 2009 c.4 Sch.3 Part 1
Sch.31 Part 2 para.9, repealed: 2009 c.4 Sch.3 Part 1
Sch.31 Part 2 para.10, repealed: 2009 c.4 Sch.3 Part 1
Sch.31 Part 3 para.11, repealed: 2009 c.4 Sch.3 Part 1
Sch.31 Part 3 para.12, repealed: 2009 c.4 Sch.3 Part 1
Sch.31 Part 3 para.13, repealed: 2009 c.4 Sch.3 Part 1
Sch.31 Part 3 para.14, repealed: 2009 c.4 Sch.3 Part 1
Sch.31 Part 4 para.15, repealed: 2009 c.4 Sch.3 Part 1
Sch.31 Part 5 para.16, repealed: 2009 c.4 Sch.3 Part 1
Sch.31 Part 5 para.17, repealed: 2009 c.4 Sch.3 Part 1
Sch.31 Part 5 para.18, repealed: 2009 c.4 Sch.3 Part 1
Sch.31 Part 5 para.19, repealed: 2009 c.4 Sch.3 Part 1
Sch.31 Part 6 para.20, repealed: 2009 c.4 Sch.3 Part 1
Sch.31 Part 6 para.21, repealed: 2009 c.4 Sch.3 Part 1
Sch.31 Part 6 para.22, repealed: 2009 c.4 Sch.3 Part 1
Sch.31 Part 6 para.23, repealed: 2009 c.4 Sch.3 Part 1
Sch.31 Part 6 para.24, repealed: 2009 c.4 Sch.3 Part 1
Sch.33 para.17, repealed: 2009 c.10 Sch.12 para.4
Sch.35 para.4, repealed: 2009 c.4 Sch.3 Part 1
Sch.37 Part 1 para.1, repealed: 2009 c.4 Sch.3 Part 1
Sch.37 Part 1 para.2, repealed: 2009 c.4 Sch.3 Part 1
Sch.37 Part 1 para.3, repealed: 2009 c.4 Sch.3 Part 1
Sch.37 Part 1 para.4, repealed: 2009 c.4 Sch.3 Part 1
Sch.37 Part 1 para.5, repealed: 2009 c.4 Sch.3 Part 1
Sch.37 Part 2 para.6, repealed: 2009 c.4 Sch.3 Part 1
Sch.41 para.1, repealed: 2009 c.4 Sch.3 Part 1
Sch.41 para.4, repealed: 2009 c.4 Sch.3 Part 1
Sch.41 para.5, repealed (in part): 2009 c.4 Sch.3
Part 1
Sch.42 para.2, repealed (in part): 2009 c.10 Sch.16
para.11

17. Licensing Act 2003
see *R. (on the application of Harpers Leisure
International Ltd) v Chief Constable of Surrey*
[2009] EWHC 2160 (Admin), Times, August
14, 2009 (QBD (Admin)), Charles, J.

2003– cont.

17. Licensing Act 2003– *cont.*
applied: SI 2009/ 665 Art.2
s.4, see *Blackpool BC v Howitt* [2008] EWHC 3300
(Admin), [2009] 4 All E.R. 154 (QBD (Admin)),
Judge Denyer; see *R. (on the application of
Bassetlaw DC) v Worksop Magistrates' Court*
[2008] EWHC 3530 (Admin), (2009) 173 J.P.
599 (QBD (Admin)), Slade, J.
s.8, enabling: SI 2009/ 1809
s.9, see *R. (on the application of Harpers Leisure
International Ltd) v Chief Constable of Surrey*
[2009] EWHC 2160 (Admin), Times, August
14, 2009 (QBD (Admin)), Charles, J.
s.13, amended: 2009 c.26 s.33
s.17, amended: SI 2009/ 2999 Reg.49
s.17, applied: SI 2009/ 1772 Art.1
s.17, repealed (in part): SI 2009/ 2999 Reg.49
s.17, enabling: SI 2009/ 1809, SI 2009/ 3159
s.19, amended: 2009 c.26 Sch.4 para.1
s.19A, added: 2009 c.26 Sch.4 para.2
s.24, amended: 2009 c.26 Sch.7 para.30
s.25A, added: SI 2009/ 1724 Art.3
s.25A, amended: 2009 c.26 Sch.7 para.31
s.34, amended: SI 2009/ 2999 Reg.49
s.34, enabling: SI 2009/ 1809, SI 2009/ 3159
s.35, amended: 2009 c.26 Sch.7 para.32
s.37, amended: SI 2009/ 2999 Reg.49
s.41A, added: SI 2009/ 1772 Art.2
s.41A, applied: SI 2009/ 1772 Art.1
s.41A, enabling: SI 2009/ 1809, SI 2009/ 3159
s.41B, added: SI 2009/ 1772 Art.2
s.41C, added: SI 2009/ 1772 Art.2
s.41D, added: SI 2009/ 1724 Art.4
s.41D, amended: 2009 c.26 Sch.7 para.33
s.42, amended: SI 2009/ 2999 Reg.49
s.47, amended: SI 2009/ 2999 Reg.49
s.51, see *R. (on the application of Harpers Leisure
International Ltd) v Chief Constable of Surrey*
[2009] EWHC 2160 (Admin), Times, August
14, 2009 (QBD (Admin)), Charles, J.
s.52, amended: 2009 c.26 Sch.7 para.34
s.52A, added: SI 2009/ 1724 Art.5
s.52A, amended: 2009 c.26 Sch.7 para.35
s.53C, amended: 2009 c.26 Sch.7 para.36
s.54, enabling: SI 2009/ 1809, SI 2009/ 3159
s.55, enabling: SI 2009/ 1809
s.57, amended: 2009 c.26 Sch.7 para.37
s.69, amended: 2009 c.26 s.33
s.71, amended: SI 2009/ 2999 Reg.49
s.71, applied: SI 2009/ 1772 Art.1
s.71, repealed (in part): SI 2009/ 2999 Reg.49
s.71, enabling: SI 2009/ 1809, SI 2009/ 3159
s.72, amended: 2009 c.26 Sch.7 para.38
s.73A, added: 2009 c.26 Sch.4 para.3
s.73B, added: 2009 c.26 Sch.4 para.4
s.78, amended: 2009 c.26 Sch.7 para.39
s.84, amended: SI 2009/ 2999 Reg.49
s.84, enabling: SI 2009/ 3159
s.85, amended: 2009 c.26 Sch.7 para.40
s.86A, added: SI 2009/ 1772 Art.3
s.86A, applied: SI 2009/ 1772 Art.1
s.86A, enabling: SI 2009/ 1809, SI 2009/ 3159
s.86B, added: SI 2009/ 1772 Art.3
s.86C, added: SI 2009/ 1772 Art.3
s.88, amended: 2009 c.26 Sch.7 para.41
s.91, enabling: SI 2009/ 1809, SI 2009/ 3159
s.92, enabling: SI 2009/ 1809
s.94, amended: 2009 c.26 Sch.7 para.42

2003–cont.

17. Licensing Act 2003–*cont.*
s.100, amended: SI 2009/2999 Reg.49
s.104, amended: SI 2009/2999 Reg.49
s.147A, amended: 2009 c.26 s.28
s.155, repealed (in part): 2009 c.26 Sch.8 Part 3
s.167, amended: 2009 c.26 Sch.7 para.43
s.182, see *R. (on the application of Bassetlaw DC) v Worksop Magistrates' Court* [2008] EWHC 3530 (Admin), (2009) 173 J.P. 599 (QBD (Admin)), Slade, J.
s.193, amended: SI 2009/1724 Art.6, SI 2009/2999 Reg.49
s.194, amended: SI 2009/1724 Art.6, SI 2009/2999 Reg.49
s.197, amended: 2009 c.26 Sch.7 para.44
Sch.1 Part 2 para.11A, added: 2009 c.26 Sch.7 para.23

20. Railways and Transport Safety Act 2003
applied: 2009 c.9 Sch.2 Part 7
referred to: 2009 c.2 Sch.2 Part 2
s.24, amended: 2009 c.26 Sch.7 para.9
s.27, amended: 2009 c.26 Sch.7 para.10
Sch.4 Part 1 para.7, amended: SI 2009/1941 Sch.1 para.217

21. Communications Act 2003
Commencement Orders: SI 2009/2130 Art.2
s.5, applied: SI 2009/17 Reg.8
s.109, applied: SI 2009/584
s.109, enabling: SI 2009/584
s.198, amended: SI 2009/2979 Reg.3
s.204, amended: SI 2009/1968 Art.2
s.204, enabling: SI 2009/1968
s.211, amended: SI 2009/2979 Reg.8
s.232, amended: SI 2009/2979 Reg.6
s.233, repealed (in part): SI 2009/2979 Reg.6
s.329, amended: SI 2009/2979 Reg.8
s.335A, added: SI 2009/2979 Reg.7
s.341, amended: SI 2009/2979 Reg.5
s.361, amended: SI 2009/2979 Reg.9
s.361, repealed (in part): SI 2009/2979 Reg.9
s.362, amended: SI 2009/2979 Reg.10
s.365, enabling: SI 2009/505
s.368A, added: SI 2009/2979 Reg.2
s.368B, added: SI 2009/2979 Reg.2
s.368BA, added: SI 2009/2979 Reg.2
s.368BB, added: SI 2009/2979 Reg.2
s.368C, added: SI 2009/2979 Reg.2
s.368D, added: SI 2009/2979 Reg.2
s.368E, added: SI 2009/2979 Reg.2
s.368F, added: SI 2009/2979 Reg.2
s.368G, added: SI 2009/2979 Reg.2
s.368H, added: SI 2009/2979 Reg.2
s.368I, added: SI 2009/2979 Reg.2
s.368J, added: SI 2009/2979 Reg.2
s.368K, added: SI 2009/2979 Reg.2
s.368L, added: SI 2009/2979 Reg.2
s.368M, added: SI 2009/2979 Reg.2
s.368N, added: SI 2009/2979 Reg.2
s.368NA, added: SI 2009/2979 Reg.2
s.368O, added: SI 2009/2979 Reg.2
s.368P, added: SI 2009/2979 Reg.2
s.368Q, added: SI 2009/2979 Reg.2
s.368R, added: SI 2009/2979 Reg.2
s.402, enabling: SI 2009/505, SI 2009/584, SI 2009/1968
s.405, amended: SI 2009/2979 Reg.11
s.411, enabling: SI 2009/2130

2003–cont.

21. Communications Act 2003–*cont.*
Sch.8, see *T-Mobile (UK) Ltd v Office of Communications* [2008] EWCA Civ 1373, [2009] 1 W.L.R. 1565 (CA (Civ Div)), Tuckey, L.J.
Sch.12 Part 1 para.2, amended: SI 2009/2979 Reg.3
Sch.12 Part 2 para.15, amended: SI 2009/2979 Reg.4
Sch.12 Part 2 para.19, amended: SI 2009/2979 Reg.4
Sch.12 Part 2 para.23A, added: SI 2009/2979 Reg.4

22. Fireworks Act 2003
referred to: SI 2009/669 Sch.1 Part 2

26. Local Government Act 2003
s.9, enabling: SI 2009/2272
s.11, enabling: SI 2009/2272
s.21, enabling: SI 2009/321, SI 2009/560
s.23, amended: 2009 c.20 Sch.6 para.117
s.24, enabling: SI 2009/560
s.31, applied: 2009 c.2 Sch.2 Part 2, 2009 c.9 Sch.2 Part 10, SI 2009/2162 Art.2
s.33, amended: 2009 c.20 Sch.6 para.117
s.36, amended: 2009 c.2 Sch.1 para.24
s.36, applied: 2009 c.2 Sch.2 Part 2, 2009 c.9 Sch.2 Part 10
s.36A, amended: 2009 c.2 Sch.1 para.25
s.36B, amended: 2009 c.2 Sch.1 para.26
s.41, referred to: 2009 c.7 s.30
s.42, applied: 2009 c.7 Sch.2 para.10
s.43, varied: 2009 c.7 Sch.2 para.9
s.44, varied: 2009 c.7 Sch.2 para.9
s.46, varied: 2009 c.7 Sch.2 para.9
s.47, applied: 2009 c.7 Sch.2 para.4, Sch.2 para.10
s.47, varied: 2009 c.7 Sch.2 para.9
s.48, applied: 2009 c.7 Sch.2 para.10
s.49, applied: 2009 c.7 Sch.2 para.6, Sch.2 para.10
s.51, varied: 2009 c.7 Sch.2 para.9
s.52, applied: 2009 c.7 Sch.2 para.10
s.52, varied: 2009 c.7 Sch.2 para.9
s.53, varied: 2009 c.7 Sch.2 para.9
s.54, applied: 2009 c.7 Sch.2 para.6, Sch.2 para.10
s.54, varied: 2009 c.7 Sch.2 para.9
s.55, applied: 2009 c.7 Sch.2 para.10
s.56, applied: 2009 c.7 Sch.2 para.10
s.93, amended: 2009 c.2 Sch.1 para.27
s.93, disapplied: SI 2009/55 Art.3
s.94, enabling: SI 2009/55
s.95, amended: 2009 c.2 Sch.1 para.28
s.95, applied: SI 2009/486 Reg.5
s.95, enabling: SI 2009/2393
s.96, enabling: SI 2009/2393
s.97, amended: 2009 c.2 Sch.1 para.29
s.99, applied: SI 2009/486 Reg.3, Reg.5
s.100, enabling: SI 2009/714
s.101, amended: 2009 c.2 Sch.1 para.30
s.123, enabling: SI 2009/321, SI 2009/560, SI 2009/2393
s.124, amended: 2009 c.2 Sch.1 para.31

28. Legal Deposit Libraries Act 2003
s.10, amended: 2009 c.25 Sch.23 Part 2

32. Crime (International Co-operation) Act 2003
Commencement Orders: SI 2009/2605 Art.2
Part 1 c.4, applied: SI 2009/613 Art.3, SI 2009/1764 Art.3
s.4, applied: SI 2009/613 Art.3, Art.4, SI 2009/1764 Art.4
s.4B, applied: SI 2009/613 Art.3, Art.4, SI 2009/1764 Art.4

2003– cont.

32. Crime (International Co-operation) Act 2003– *cont.*

s.6, referred to: SSI 2009/106 Art.2, Art.3, SSI 2009/206 Art.3, SSI 2009/441 Art.3

s.13, see *R. (on the application of Hafner) v Westminster Magistrates' Court* [2008] EWHC 524 (Admin), [2009] 1 W.L.R. 1005 (DC), Lord Phillips of Worth Matravers, L.C.J.

s.15, see *R. (on the application of Hafner) v Westminster Magistrates' Court* [2008] EWHC 524 (Admin), [2009] 1 W.L.R. 1005 (DC), Lord Phillips of Worth Matravers, L.C.J.

s.17, applied: SI 2009/3021 Art.4

s.18, applied: SI 2009/3021 Art.4

s.19, applied: SI 2009/3021 Art.4

s.21, enabling: SSI 2009/345

s.27, enabling: SI 2009/3021

s.31, applied: SI 2009/613 Art.3, Art.4, SI 2009/1764 Art.3

s.31, referred to: SSI 2009/106 Art.2, Art.3, SSI 2009/206 Art.2, SSI 2009/441 Art.2

s.32, applied: SI 2009/1764 Art.4

s.35, applied: SI 2009/613 Art.3, SI 2009/1764 Art.3, Art.4

s.37, referred to: SSI 2009/106 Art.2, SSI 2009/206 Art.2, Art.3

s.40, referred to: SSI 2009/106 Art.2, SSI 2009/206 Art.2, Art.3

s.43, applied: SI 2009/613 Art.3, SI 2009/1764 Art.3, Art.4

s.43, referred to: SSI 2009/106 Art.2, SSI 2009/206 Art.2, Art.3

s.44, applied: SI 2009/613 Art.3, SI 2009/1764 Art.3, Art.4

s.44, referred to: SSI 2009/106 Art.2, SSI 2009/206 Art.2, Art.3

s.45, applied: SI 2009/613 Art.3, SI 2009/1764 Art.3, Art.4

s.45, referred to: SSI 2009/106 Art.2, SSI 2009/206 Art.2, Art.3

s.47, applied: SI 2009/613 Art.3, Art.4, SI 2009/1764 Art.3

s.47, referred to: SSI 2009/106 Art.2, Art.3, SSI 2009/206 Art.2, SSI 2009/441 Art.2

s.48, applied: SI 2009/613 Art.3, Art.4, SI 2009/1764 Art.3

s.48, referred to: SSI 2009/106 Art.2, Art.3, SSI 2009/206 Art.2, SSI 2009/441 Art.2

s.50, applied: SI 2009/1764, SSI 2009/206, 2009/441

s.51, applied: SI 2009/613 Art.3, Art.4, SI 2009/1764 Art.3, Art.4

s.51, enabling: SI 2009/613, SI 2009/1764, SSI 2009/106, SSI 2009/206, SSI 2009/441

s.54, amended: 2009 c.25 Sch.21 para.93

s.94, enabling: SI 2009/2605

Sch.2 Part 2 para.15, applied: SI 2009/613 Art.3, Art.4, SI 2009/1764 Art.3

Sch.2 Part 2 para.15, referred to: SSI 2009/106 Art.2, Art.3, SSI 2009/206 Art.2, SSI 2009/441 Art.2

33. Waste and Emissions Trading Act 2003

applied: SI 2009/105 Sch.2 para.7

s.9, applied: SI 2009/105 Sch.2 para.8

37. Water Act 2003

Commencement Orders: SI 2009/359 Art.2

applied: 2009 c.2 Sch.2 Part 2, 2009 c.9 Sch.2 Part 35

s.58, referred to: SI 2009/359 Sch.1 para.1

s.104, enabling: SI 2009/359

s.105, enabling: SI 2009/359

2003– cont.

38. Anti-social Behaviour Act 2003

see *R. (on the application of Smith) v Snaresbrook Crown Court* [2008] EWHC 1282 (Admin), [2009] 1 W.L.R. 2024 (DC), Latham, L.J.

Part 1, see *R. (on the application of Smith) v Snaresbrook Crown Court* [2008] EWHC 1282 (Admin), [2009] 1 W.L.R. 2024 (DC), Latham, L.J.

s.2, see *Hampshire Police Authority v Smith* [2009] EWHC 174 (Admin), [2009] 4 All E.R. 316 (DC), Maurice Kay, L.J.; see *R. (on the application of Smith) v Snaresbrook Crown Court* [2008] EWHC 1282 (Admin), [2009] 1 W.L.R. 2024 (DC), Latham, L.J.; see *R. (on the application of Taylor) v Commissioner of Police of the Metropolis* [2009] EWHC 264 (Admin), (2009) 173 J.P. 121 (QBD (Admin)), Lloyd Jones, J.

s.5, see *R. (on the application of Smith) v Snaresbrook Crown Court* [2008] EWHC 1282 (Admin), [2009] 1 W.L.R. 2024 (DC), Latham, L.J.

s.30, see *Carter v Crown Prosecution Service* [2009] EWHC 2197 (Admin), (2009) 173 J.P. 590 (DC), Thomas, L.J.

s.31, see *Carter v Crown Prosecution Service* [2009] EWHC 2197 (Admin), (2009) 173 J.P. 590 (DC), Thomas, L.J.

39. Courts Act 2003

applied: 2009 c.2 Sch.2 Part 2, 2009 c.9 Sch.2 Part 13

Part 4, applied: 2009 c.25 s.148

s.4, applied: SI 2009/3184

s.4, enabling: SI 2009/3184

s.8, applied: SI 2009/2080

s.8, enabling: SI 2009/2080

s.41, amended: 2009 c.20 Sch.6 para.118

s.55, amended: 2009 c.25 s.146

s.55A, added: 2009 c.25 s.146

s.56, amended: 2009 c.25 s.146

s.58, applied: 2009 c.25 s.39

s.61, applied: 2009 c.25 s.39

s.69, enabling: SI 2009/2087

s.72, applied: SI 2009/2087

s.75, enabling: SI 2009/638

s.79, applied: SI 2009/638

s.92, see *R. (on the application of Hillingdon LBC) v Lord Chancellor* [2008] EWHC 2683 (Admin), [2009] C.P. Rep. 13 (DC), Dyson, L.J.

s.92, applied: SI 2009/1496, SI 2009/1497, SI 2009/1498, SI 2009/1499, SI 2009/2477 r.83

s.92, enabling: SI 2009/1496, SI 2009/1497, SI 2009/1498, SI 2009/1499

s.98, enabling: SI 2009/474

s.108, enabling: SI 2009/474, SI 2009/2080

Sch.3 Para.2, amended: 2009 c.25 Sch.21 para.46

Sch.4 para.8, referred to: 2009 c.25 Sch.22 para.46

Sch.5 Part 3 para.10, amended: 2009 c.24 Sch.2 para.13

Sch.6 para.2, amended: 2009 c.24 Sch.2 para.14

Sch.8 para.65, repealed: 2009 c.23 Sch.22 Part 5

Sch.8 para.302, repealed: 2009 c.25 Sch.23 Part 1

41. Extradition Act 2003

see *Chen v Romania* [2007] EWHC 520 (Admin), [2009] 1 W.L.R. 257 (DC), Scott Baker, L.J.; see *Mucelli v Albania* [2009] UKHL 2, [2009] 1 W.L.R. 276 (HL), Lord Phillips of Worth Matravers; see *Sonea v Mehedinti District Court* [2009] EWHC 89 (Admin), [2009] 2 All E.R. 821 (DC), Scott Baker, L.J.

2003– cont.

41. **Extradition Act 2003**–*cont.*

s.2, see *Kucera v Czech Republic* [2008] EWHC 414 (Admin), [2009] 1 W.L.R. 806 (DC), Richards, L.J.; see *Louca v Germany* [2008] EWHC 2907 (Admin), [2009] 2 All E.R. 719 (DC), Dyson, L.J.; see *Louca v Germany* [2009] UKSC 4, [2009] 1 W.L.R. 2550 (SC), Lord Hope (Deputy President); see *Pietrzak v Poland* [2008] EWHC 2138 (Admin), [2009] 1 W.L.R. 866 (DC), Latham, L.J.; see *Rana v Austria* [2008] EWHC 2975 (Admin), [2009] Lloyd's Rep. F.C. 71 (DC), Dyson, L.J.; see *Sonea v Mehedinti District Court* [2009] EWHC 89 (Admin), [2009] 2 All E.R. 821 (DC), Scott Baker, L.J.; see *Von Der Pahlen v Austria* [2009] EWHC 383 (Admin), [2009] Lloyd's Rep. F.C. 320 (QBD), Scott Baker, L.J.

s.6, amended: 2009 c.26 s.77

s.7, amended: 2009 c.26 s.77

s.8A, added: 2009 c.26 s.69

s.8B, added: 2009 c.26 s.69

s.10, see *Rana v Austria* [2008] EWHC 2975 (Admin), [2009] Lloyd's Rep. F.C. 71 (DC), Dyson, L.J.

s.11, see *Fasola (Dorothy May) v HM Advocate* [2009] HCJAC 3, 2009 J.C. 119 (HCJ), Lord Nimmo Smith; see *Louca v Germany* [2009] UKSC 4, [2009] 1 W.L.R. 2550 (SC), Lord Hope (Deputy President); see *Sonea v Mehedinti District Court* [2009] EWHC 89 (Admin), [2009] 2 All E.R. 821 (DC), Scott Baker, L.J.

s.14, see *Fasola (Dorothy May) v HM Advocate* [2009] HCJAC 3, 2009 J.C. 119 (HCJ), Lord Nimmo Smith; see *Gomes v Trinidad and Tobago* [2009] UKHL 21, [2009] 1 W.L.R. 1038 (HL), Lord Phillips of Worth Matravers; see *Lord Advocate v Trajer* 2009 J.C. 108 (HCJ), Lord Osborne; see *Von Der Pahlen v Austria* [2009] EWHC 383 (Admin), [2009] Lloyd's Rep. F.C. 320 (QBD), Scott Baker, L.J.

s.20, see *Louca v Germany* [2009] UKSC 4, [2009] 1 W.L.R. 2550 (SC), Lord Hope (Deputy President); see *Sonea v Mehedinti District Court* [2009] EWHC 89 (Admin), [2009] 2 All E.R. 821 (DC), Scott Baker, L.J.

s.21, see *Louca v Germany* [2009] UKSC 4, [2009] 1 W.L.R. 2550 (SC), Lord Hope (Deputy President); see *Sonea v Mehedinti District Court* [2009] EWHC 89 (Admin), [2009] 2 All E.R. 821 (DC), Scott Baker, L.J.

s.22, amended: 2009 c.26 s.71

s.23, amended: 2009 c.26 s.71

s.26, see *Mucelli v Albania* [2009] UKHL 2, [2009] 1 W.L.R. 276 (HL), Lord Phillips of Worth Matravers

s.29, see *Hungary v Fenyvesi* [2009] EWHC 231 (Admin), [2009] 4 All E.R. 324 (QBD (Admin)), Sir Anthony May (President, QB)

s.35, see *Mucelli v Albania* [2009] UKHL 2, [2009] 1 W.L.R. 276 (HL), Lord Phillips of Worth Matravers

s.59, substituted: 2009 c.26 s.72

s.64, see *Rana v Austria* [2008] EWHC 2975 (Admin), [2009] Lloyd's Rep. F.C. 71 (DC), Dyson, L.J.

s.65, see *Kucera v Czech Republic* [2008] EWHC 414 (Admin), [2009] 1 W.L.R. 806 (DC), Richards, L.J.

2003– cont.

41. **Extradition Act 2003**–*cont.*

s.67, see *R. (on the application of Hilali) v Westminster Magistrates' Court* [2008] EWHC 2892 (Admin), [2009] 1 All E.R. 834 (DC), Dyson, L.J.

s.68A, see *Sonea v Mehedinti District Court* [2009] EWHC 89 (Admin), [2009] 2 All E.R. 821 (DC), Scott Baker, L.J.

s.76A, added: 2009 c.26 s.70

s.76B, added: 2009 c.26 s.70

s.79, see *Chen v Romania* [2007] EWHC 520 (Admin), [2009] 1 W.L.R. 257 (DC), Scott Baker, L.J.

s.82, see *Chen v Romania* [2007] EWHC 520 (Admin), [2009] 1 W.L.R. 257 (DC), Scott Baker, L.J.; see *Gomes v Trinidad and Tobago* [2009] UKHL 21, [2009] 1 W.L.R. 1038 (HL), Lord Phillips of Worth Matravers

s.85, see *Chen v Romania* [2007] EWHC 520 (Admin), [2009] 1 W.L.R. 257 (DC), Scott Baker, L.J.

s.87, see *Chen v Romania* [2007] EWHC 520 (Admin), [2009] 1 W.L.R. 257 (DC), Scott Baker, L.J.

s.88, amended: 2009 c.26 s.71

s.89, amended: 2009 c.26 s.71

s.95, see *Norris v United States* [2009] EWHC 995 (QB), [2009] Lloyd's Rep. F.C. 475 (DC), Laws, L.J.

s.97, amended: 2009 c.26 s.71

s.98, amended: 2009 c.26 s.71

s.102, amended: 2009 c.26 s.71

s.103, see *Chen v Romania* [2007] EWHC 520 (Admin), [2009] 1 W.L.R. 257 (DC), Scott Baker, L.J.; see *Mucelli v Albania* [2009] UKHL 2, [2009] 1 W.L.R. 276 (HL), Lord Phillips of Worth Matravers; see *Norris v United States* [2009] EWHC 995 (QB), [2009] Lloyd's Rep. F.C. 475 (DC), Laws, L.J.

s.104, see *Chen v Romania* [2007] EWHC 520 (Admin), [2009] 1 W.L.R. 257 (DC), Scott Baker, L.J.; see *Hoholm v Norway* [2009] EWHC 1513 (Admin), Times, October 13, 2009 (QBD (Admin)), Stanley Burnton, L.J.

s.108, see *Norris v United States* [2009] EWHC 995 (QB), [2009] Lloyd's Rep. F.C. 475 (DC), Laws, L.J.

s.132, substituted: 2009 c.26 s.73

s.142, see *R. v Seddon (Neil)* [2009] EWCA Crim 483, [2009] 1 W.L.R. 2342 (CA (Crim Div)), Hughes, L.J. (V-P)

s.142, varied: SI 2009/2768 Art.3

s.143, repealed: 2009 c.26 Sch.8 Part 6

s.143, varied: SI 2009/2768 Art.3

s.144, repealed: 2009 c.26 Sch.8 Part 6

s.144, varied: SI 2009/2768 Art.3

s.145, amended: 2009 c.26 s.75

s.145, varied: SI 2009/2768 Art.3

s.146, see *R. v Seddon (Neil)* [2009] EWCA Crim 483, [2009] 1 W.L.R. 2342 (CA (Crim Div)), Hughes, L.J. (V-P)

s.146, varied: SI 2009/2768 Art.3

s.147, varied: SI 2009/2768 Art.3

s.148, varied: SI 2009/2768 Art.3

s.149, varied: SI 2009/2768 Art.3

s.150, varied: SI 2009/2768 Art.3

s.151, repealed: 2009 c.26 Sch.8 Part 6

s.151, varied: SI 2009/2768 Art.3

s.151A, added: 2009 c.26 s.76

s.151A, varied: SI 2009/2768 Art.3

2003– cont.

41. Extradition Act 2003–*cont.*
s.152, amended: 2009 c.26 s.75
s.152, varied: SI 2009/ 2768 Art.3
s.153, amended: 2009 c.26 s.74
s.153, varied: SI 2009/ 2768 Art.3
s.153A, added: 2009 c.26 s.74
s.153A, varied: SI 2009/ 2768 Art.3
s.153B, added: 2009 c.26 s.74
s.153B, varied: SI 2009/ 2768 Art.3
s.153C, added: 2009 c.26 s.74
s.153C, varied: SI 2009/ 2768 Art.3
s.153D, added: 2009 c.26 s.74
s.153D, varied: SI 2009/ 2768 Art.3
s.154, varied: SI 2009/ 2768 Art.3
s.155, varied: SI 2009/ 2768 Art.3
s.155A, applied: SI 2009/ 2768 Art.2, Art.3
s.155A, varied: SI 2009/ 2768 Art.3
s.155A, enabling: SI 2009/ 2768
s.185, amended: 2009 c.26 Sch.7 para.117
s.197, amended: 2009 c.26 s.74
s.197A, amended: 2009 c.26 s.71
s.204, substituted: 2009 c.26 s.67
s.206A, added: 2009 c.26 s.78
s.206B, added: 2009 c.26 s.78
s.206C, added: 2009 c.26 s.78
s.212, amended: 2009 c.26 s.68
s.216, amended: 2009 c.26 s.71

42. Sexual Offences Act 2003
see *HM Advocate v D* [2009] HCJAC 51, 2009 J.C.
215 (HCJ), Lord Nimmo Smith; see *R. v K
(Robert)* [2008] EWCA Crim 1923, [2009] 1 Cr.
App. R. 24 (CA (Crim Div)), Latham, L.J. (VP,
CA Crim); see *R. v Shi (Peiwen)* [2008] EWCA
Crim 1930, [2009] 1 Cr. App. R. (S.) 82 (CA
(Crim Div)), Hughes, L.J.; see *Wylie v M* 2009
S.L.T. (Sh Ct) 18 (Sh Ct (Grampian) (Fort
William)), Sheriff D C W Pyle
referred to: 2009 c.26 s.21
Part 2, see *R. (on the application of F) v Secretary of
State for the Home Department* [2008] EWHC
3170 (Admin), [2009] 2 Cr. App. R. (S.) 47
(DC), Latham, L.J.; see *R. v Davison
(Anthony)* [2008] EWCA Crim 2795, [2009] 2
Cr. App. R. (S.) 13 (CA (Crim Div)), Moses,
L.J.; see *R. v F* [2009] EWCA Crim 319, [2009]
2 Cr. App. R. (S.) 68 (CA (Crim Div)), Latham,
L.J. (VP, CA Crim)
s.1, see *R. v K (Robert)* [2008] EWCA Crim 1923,
[2009] 1 Cr. App. R. 24 (CA (Crim Div)),
Latham, L.J. (VP, CA Crim)
s.1, applied: 2009 asp 9 Sch.1 para.5, SI 2009/ 1059
Art.40
s.1, referred to: SI 2009/ 37 Sch.1 para.1, Sch.1
para.2, Sch.1 para.4
s.2, applied: 2009 asp 9 Sch.1 para.5
s.2, referred to: SI 2009/ 37 Sch.1 para.1, Sch.1
para.2, Sch.1 para.4
s.3, applied: 2009 asp 9 Sch.1 para.5, SI 2009/ 1168
Sch.1 para.1
s.3, referred to: SI 2009/ 37 Sch.1 para.2, Sch.1
para.4
s.4, applied: 2009 asp 9 Sch.1 para.5, SI 2009/ 1168
Sch.1 para.1
s.4, referred to: SI 2009/ 37 Sch.1 para.2, Sch.1
para.4
s.5, see *R. v G* [2008] UKHL 37, [2009] 1 A.C. 92
(HL), Lord Hoffmann
s.5, applied: 2009 asp 9 Sch.1 para.6
s.5, referred to: SI 2009/ 37 Sch.1 para.1, Sch.1 para.4

2003– cont.

42. Sexual Offences Act 2003– *cont.*
s.6, applied: 2009 asp 9 Sch.1 para.6
s.6, referred to: SI 2009/37 Sch.1 para.1, Sch.1
para.4
s.7, see *R. v B* [2008] EWCA Crim 830, [2009] 1 Cr.
App. R. (S.) 6 (CA (Crim Div)), Rix, L.J.
s.7, applied: 2009 asp 9 Sch.1 para.6, SI 2009/ 1168
Sch.1 para.1
s.7, referred to: SI 2009/ 37 Sch.1 para.1, Sch.1 para.4
s.8, applied: 2009 asp 9 Sch.1 para.6, SI 2009/ 1168
Sch.1 para.1
s.8, referred to: SI 2009/ 37 Sch.1 para.1, Sch.1
para.4
s.9, applied: 2009 asp 9 Sch.1 para.6, SI 2009/ 1168
Sch.1 para.1
s.9, referred to: SI 2009/ 37 Sch.1 para.2, Sch.1
para.4
s.10, applied: 2009 asp 9 Sch.1 para.6, SI 2009/ 1168
Sch.1 para.1
s.10, referred to: SI 2009/ 37 Sch.1 para.2, Sch.1
para.4
s.11, see *R. v B* [2008] EWCA Crim 830, [2009] 1 Cr.
App. R. (S.) 6 (CA (Crim Div)), Rix, L.J.; see *R.
v Bowling (Stephen David)* [2008] EWCA Crim
1148, [2009] 1 Cr. App. R. (S.) 23 (CA (Crim
Div)), Sir Igor Judge
s.11, applied: 2009 asp 9 Sch.1 para.6, SI 2009/ 1168
Sch.1 para.1
s.11, referred to: SI 2009/ 37 Sch.1 para.2, Sch.1
para.4
s.12, see *R. v B* [2008] EWCA Crim 830, [2009] 1 Cr.
App. R. (S.) 6 (CA (Crim Div)), Rix, L.J.
s.12, applied: 2009 asp 9 Sch.1 para.6, SI 2009/ 1168
Sch.1 para.1
s.12, referred to: SI 2009/ 37 Sch.1 para.2, Sch.1
para.4
s.13, see *R. v B* [2008] EWCA Crim 830, [2009] 1 Cr.
App. R. (S.) 6 (CA (Crim Div)), Rix, L.J.; see *R.
v G* [2008] UKHL 37, [2009] 1 A.C. 92 (HL),
Lord Hoffmann
s.13, applied: 2009 asp 9 Sch.1 para.6
s.13, referred to: SI 2009/ 37 Sch.1 para.4
s.14, see *R. v R* [2008] EWCA Crim 619, [2009] 1
W.L.R. 713 (CA (Crim Div)), Moses, L.J.
s.14, applied: 2009 asp 9 Sch.1 para.6, SI 2009/ 1168
Sch.1 para.1
s.14, referred to: SI 2009/ 37 Sch.1 para.4
s.15, applied: 2009 asp 9 Sch.1 para.6, Sch.1 para.17,
SI 2009/ 1168 Sch.1 para.1
s.15, referred to: SI 2009/ 37 Sch.1 para.2, Sch.1
para.4
s.16, applied: 2009 asp 9 Sch.1 para.5, Sch.1 para.17,
SI 2009/ 1547 Sch.3 para.3
s.16, referred to: SI 2009/ 37 Sch.1 para.2, Sch.1
para.4
s.17, applied: 2009 asp 9 Sch.1 para.5, Sch.1 para.17,
SI 2009/ 1547 Sch.3 para.3
s.17, referred to: SI 2009/ 37 Sch.1 para.2, Sch.1
para.4
s.18, applied: 2009 asp 9 Sch.1 para.5, Sch.1 para.17,
SI 2009/ 1547 Sch.3 para.3
s.18, referred to: SI 2009/ 37 Sch.1 para.2, Sch.1
para.4
s.19, applied: 2009 asp 9 Sch.1 para.5, Sch.1 para.17,
SI 2009/ 1547 Sch.3 para.3
s.19, referred to: SI 2009/ 37 Sch.1 para.2, Sch.1
para.4
s.20, referred to: SI 2009/ 37 Sch.1 para.2, Sch.1
para.4

2003– cont.

42. Sexual Offences Act 2003– *cont.*
s.25, applied: 2009 asp 9 Sch.1 para.5, SI 2009/1168 Sch.1 para.1
s.25, referred to: SI 2009/37 Sch.1 para.2, Sch.1 para.4
s.26, applied: 2009 asp 9 Sch.1 para.5
s.26, referred to: SI 2009/37 Sch.1 para.2, Sch.1 para.4
s.30, see *R. v C* [2008] EWCA Crim 1155, [2009] 1 Cr. App. R. 15 (CA (Crim Div)), Lord Philips, L.C.J.; see *R. v C* [2009] UKHL 42, [2009] 1 W.L.R. 1786 (HL), Lord Hope of Craighead
s.30, referred to: SI 2009/37 Sch.1 para.1, Sch.1 para.2, Sch.1 para.3
s.31, referred to: SI 2009/37 Sch.1 para.1, Sch.1 para.2, Sch.1 para.3
s.32, referred to: SI 2009/37 Sch.1 para.1, Sch.1 para.2, Sch.1 para.3
s.33, referred to: SI 2009/37 Sch.1 para.1, Sch.1 para.2, Sch.1 para.3
s.34, referred to: SI 2009/37 Sch.1 para.1, Sch.1 para.2, Sch.1 para.3
s.35, referred to: SI 2009/37 Sch.1 para.1, Sch.1 para.2, Sch.1 para.3
s.36, referred to: SI 2009/37 Sch.1 para.1, Sch.1 para.2, Sch.1 para.3
s.37, referred to: SI 2009/37 Sch.1 para.1, Sch.1 para.2, Sch.1 para.3
s.38, applied: 2009 asp 9 Sch.1 para.5
s.38, referred to: SI 2009/37 Sch.1 para.1, Sch.1 para.2, Sch.1 para.3
s.39, applied: 2009 asp 9 Sch.1 para.5
s.39, referred to: SI 2009/37 Sch.1 para.1, Sch.1 para.2, Sch.1 para.3
s.40, applied: 2009 asp 9 Sch.1 para.5
s.40, referred to: SI 2009/37 Sch.1 para.1, Sch.1 para.2, Sch.1 para.3
s.41, applied: 2009 asp 9 Sch.1 para.5
s.41, referred to: SI 2009/37 Sch.1 para.1, Sch.1 para.2, Sch.1 para.3
s.47, applied: 2009 asp 9 Sch.1 para.5, Sch.1 para.17, SI 2009/1168 Sch.1 para.1
s.47, referred to: SI 2009/37 Sch.1 para.2, Sch.1 para.4
s.48, applied: 2009 asp 9 Sch.1 para.5, Sch.1 para.17, SI 2009/1168 Sch.1 para.1
s.48, referred to: SI 2009/37 Sch.1 para.2, Sch.1 para.4
s.49, applied: 2009 asp 9 Sch.1 para.5, Sch.1 para.17, SI 2009/1168 Sch.1 para.1
s.49, referred to: SI 2009/37 Sch.1 para.2, Sch.1 para.4
s.50, applied: 2009 asp 9 Sch.1 para.5, Sch.1 para.17, SI 2009/1168 Sch.1 para.1
s.50, referred to: SI 2009/37 Sch.1 para.2, Sch.1 para.4
s.51A, added: 2009 c.26 s.19
s.52, applied: SI 2009/1168 Sch.1 para.1
s.52, referred to: SI 2009/37 Sch.1 para.2, Sch.1 para.4
s.53, referred to: SI 2009/37 Sch.1 para.2, Sch.1 para.4
s.53A, added: 2009 c.26 s.14
s.54, amended: 2009 c.26 Sch.7 para.24
s.57, applied: SI 2009/1168 Sch.1 para.1
s.57, referred to: SI 2009/37 Sch.1 para.2, Sch.1 para.4
s.58, applied: SI 2009/1168 Sch.1 para.1
s.58, referred to: SI 2009/37 Sch.1 para.2, Sch.1 para.4

2003– cont.

42. Sexual Offences Act 2003– *cont.*
s.59, applied: SI 2009/1168 Sch.1 para.1
s.59, referred to: SI 2009/37 Sch.1 para.2, Sch.1 para.4
s.61, applied: 2009 asp 9 Sch.1 para.5, SI 2009/1168 Sch.1 para.1
s.61, referred to: SI 2009/37 Sch.1 para.2, Sch.1 para.4
s.62, applied: SI 2009/1547 Sch.3 para.1
s.62, referred to: SI 2009/37 Sch.1 para.2, Sch.1 para.4
s.63, applied: SI 2009/1547 Sch.3 para.1
s.63, referred to: SI 2009/37 Sch.1 para.2, Sch.1 para.4
s.64, applied: SI 2009/1547 Sch.3 para.1
s.65, applied: SI 2009/1547 Sch.3 para.1
s.66, see *R. v Odam (Soloman Alexander)* [2008] EWCA Crim 1087, [2009] 1 Cr. App. R. (S.) 22 (CA (Crim Div)), Forbes, J.
s.66, applied: 2009 asp 9 Sch.1 para.5, Sch.1 para.17, SI 2009/1547 Sch.3 para.3
s.66, referred to: SI 2009/37 Sch.1 para.2, Sch.1 para.4
s.67, see *Police Service for Northern Ireland v MacRitchie* [2009] N.I. 84 (CA (NI)), Lord Kerr L.C.J.; see *R. v Hodgson (William John)* [2008] EWCA Crim 1180, [2009] 1 Cr. App. R. (S.) 27 (CA (Crim Div)), Aikens, J.
s.67, applied: 2009 asp 9 Sch.1 para.5, Sch.1 para.17
s.67, referred to: SI 2009/37 Sch.1 para.2, Sch.1 para.4
s.68, see *Police Service for Northern Ireland v MacRitchie* [2009] N.I. 84 (CA (NI)), Lord Kerr L.C.J.; see *R. v Bassett (Kevin)* [2008] EWCA Crim 1174, [2009] 1 W.L.R. 1032 (CA (Crim Div)), Hughes, L.J.
s.69, applied: SI 2009/1547 Sch.3 para.1, Sch.3 para.3
s.70, applied: SI 2009/1547 Sch.3 para.1, Sch.3 para.3
s.72, applied: SI 2009/1547 Sch.3 para.7
s.80, see *R. v Odam (Soloman Alexander)* [2008] EWCA Crim 1087, [2009] 1 Cr. App. R. (S.) 22 (CA (Crim Div)), Forbes, J.
s.82, see *R. (on the application of F) v Secretary of State for the Home Department* [2008] EWHC 3170 (Admin), [2009] 2 Cr. App. R. (S.) 47 (DC), Latham, L.J.
s.87, referred to: SI 2009/722 Reg.2
s.87, enabling: SI 2009/722
s.104, see *R. v Barley (Stuart John)* [2008] EWCA Crim 2466, [2009] 2 Cr. App. R. (S.) 2 (CA (Crim Div)), Toulson, L.J.; see *R. v Bowling (Stephen David)* [2008] EWCA Crim 1148, [2009] 1 Cr. App. R. (S.) 23 (CA (Crim Div)), Sir Igor Judge; see *R. v Ferguson (Mark Brandon)* [2008] EWCA Crim 2940, [2009] 2 Cr. App. R. (S.) 8 (CA (Crim Div)), Forbes, J.; see *R. v Hodgson (William John)* [2008] EWCA Crim 1180, [2009] 1 Cr. App. R. (S.) 27 (CA (Crim Div)), Aikens, J.
s.104, applied: SI 2009/1547 Reg.4
s.106, see *R. v Ferguson (Mark Brandon)* [2008] EWCA Crim 2940, [2009] 2 Cr. App. R. (S.) 8 (CA (Crim Div)), Forbes, J.
s.107, see *R. v Smith (Christopher Robert)* [2009] EWCA Crim 785, [2009] 2 Cr. App. R. (S.) 110 (CA (Crim Div)), Goldring, L.J.

2003–cont.

42. Sexual Offences Act 2003–*cont.*

s.114, see *R. (on the application of F) v Secretary of State for the Home Department* [2008] EWHC 3170 (Admin), [2009] 2 Cr. App. R. (S.) 47 (DC), Latham, L.J.

s.115, amended: 2009 c.26 s.23

s.115, repealed (in part): 2009 c.26 Sch.8 Part 2

s.116, amended: 2009 c.26 s.23

s.117, amended: 2009 c.26 s.24

s.117A, added: 2009 c.26 s.25

s.122, amended: 2009 c.26 s.25

s.123, applied: SI 2009/37 Reg.4, Reg.6

s.132A, added: 2009 c.26 s.22

s.133, varied: SI 2009/1059 Sch.1 para.52

s.136, amended: 2009 c.26 s.22

s.136A, added: 2009 c.26 Sch.2 para.1

s.136B, applied: 2009 c.26 s.21

s.136B, added: 2009 c.26 Sch.2 para.1

s.136C, added: 2009 c.26 Sch.2 para.1

s.136D, applied: 2009 c.26 s.21

s.136D, added: 2009 c.26 Sch.2 para.1

s.136E, added: 2009 c.26 Sch.2 para.1

s.136F, added: 2009 c.26 Sch.2 para.1

s.136G, added: 2009 c.26 Sch.2 para.1

s.136H, added: 2009 c.26 Sch.2 para.1

s.136I, added: 2009 c.26 Sch.2 para.1

s.136J, added: 2009 c.26 Sch.2 para.1

s.136K, added: 2009 c.26 Sch.2 para.1

s.136L, added: 2009 c.26 Sch.2 para.1

s.136M, added: 2009 c.26 Sch.2 para.1

s.136N, added: 2009 c.26 Sch.2 para.1

s.136O, added: 2009 c.26 Sch.2 para.1

s.136P, added: 2009 c.26 Sch.2 para.1

s.136Q, added: 2009 c.26 Sch.2 para.1

s.136R, added: 2009 c.26 Sch.2 para.1

s.137, varied: SI 2009/1059 Sch.1 para.52

s.138, amended: 2009 c.26 Sch.2 para.2

s.142, amended: 2009 c.26 Sch.2 para.3

s.142, repealed (in part): 2009 asp 9 Sch.6

Sch.1 para.3, repealed: 2009 c.26 Sch.8 Part 2

Sch.1 para.4, repealed: 2009 c.26 Sch.8 Part 2

Sch.3, see *R. v Davison (Anthony)* [2008] EWCA Crim 2795, [2009] 2 Cr. App. R. (S.) 13 (CA (Crim Div)), Moses, L.J.

Sch.3 para.18, see *R. v Davison (Anthony)* [2008] EWCA Crim 2795, [2009] 2 Cr. App. R. (S.) 13 (CA (Crim Div)), Moses, L.J.

Sch.3 para.33, see *R. v Odam (Soloman Alexander)* [2008] EWCA Crim 1087, [2009] 1 Cr. App. R. (S.) 22 (CA (Crim Div)), Forbes, J.

Sch.3 para.35B, added: 2009 c.25 Sch.21 para.62

Sch.3 para.36, amended: 2009 asp 9 Sch.5 para.5

Sch.3 para.41A, added: 2009 asp 9 Sch.5 para.5

Sch.3 para.42, repealed (in part): 2009 asp 9 Sch.6

Sch.3 para.59D, added: 2009 asp 9 Sch.5 para.5

Sch.3 para.59E, added: 2009 asp 9 Sch.5 para.5

Sch.3 para.59F, added: 2009 asp 9 Sch.5 para.5

Sch.3 para.59G, added: 2009 asp 9 Sch.5 para.5

Sch.3 para.59H, added: 2009 asp 9 Sch.5 para.5

Sch.3 para.59I, added: 2009 asp 9 Sch.5 para.5

Sch.3 para.59J, added: 2009 asp 9 Sch.5 para.5

Sch.3 para.59K, added: 2009 asp 9 Sch.5 para.5

Sch.3 para.59L, added: 2009 asp 9 Sch.5 para.5

Sch.3 para.59M, added: 2009 asp 9 Sch.5 para.5

Sch.3 para.59N, added: 2009 asp 9 Sch.5 para.5

Sch.3 para.59O, added: 2009 asp 9 Sch.5 para.5

Sch.3 para.59P, added: 2009 asp 9 Sch.5 para.5

Sch.3 para.59Q, added: 2009 asp 9 Sch.5 para.5

42. Sexual Offences Act 2003–*cont.*

Sch.3 para.59R, added: 2009 asp 9 Sch.5 para.5

Sch.3 para.59S, added: 2009 asp 9 Sch.5 para.5

Sch.3 para.59T, added: 2009 asp 9 Sch.5 para.5

Sch.3 para.59U, added: 2009 asp 9 Sch.5 para.5

Sch.3 para.59V, added: 2009 asp 9 Sch.5 para.5

Sch.3 para.59W, added: 2009 asp 9 Sch.5 para.5

Sch.3 para.59X, added: 2009 asp 9 Sch.5 para.5

Sch.3 para.59Y, added: 2009 asp 9 Sch.5 para.5

Sch.3 para.59Z, added: 2009 asp 9 Sch.5 para.5

Sch.3 para.59ZA, added: 2009 asp 9 Sch.5 para.5

Sch.3 para.59ZB, added: 2009 asp 9 Sch.5 para.5

Sch.3 para.59ZC, added: 2009 asp 9 Sch.5 para.5

Sch.3 para.59ZD, added: 2009 asp 9 Sch.5 para.5

Sch.3 para.59ZE, added: 2009 asp 9 Sch.5 para.5

Sch.3 para.59ZF, added: 2009 asp 9 Sch.5 para.5

Sch.3 para.59ZG, added: 2009 asp 9 Sch.5 para.5

Sch.3 para.59ZH, added: 2009 asp 9 Sch.5 para.5

Sch.3 para.59ZI, added: 2009 asp 9 Sch.5 para.5

Sch.3 para.59ZJ, added: 2009 asp 9 Sch.5 para.5

Sch.3 para.59ZK, added: 2009 asp 9 Sch.5 para.5

Sch.3 para.59ZL, added: 2009 asp 9 Sch.5 para.5

Sch.3 para.60, see *Wylie v M* 2009 S.L.T. (Sh Ct) 18 (Sh Ct (Grampian) (Fort William)), Sheriff D C W Pyle

Sch.3 para.60, amended: 2009 asp 9 Sch.5 para.5

Sch.3 para.92X, added: 2009 c.25 Sch.21 para.62

Sch.3 para.93, amended: 2009 c.25 Sch.21 para.62

Sch.3 para.93A, amended: 2009 c.25 Sch.21 para.62

Sch.3 para.93A, varied: SI 2009/1059 Sch.1 para.52

Sch.5 para.60ZA, added: 2009 c.26 Sch.7 para.25

Sch.5 para.106A, added: 2009 c.26 Sch.7 para.25

Sch.5 para.168ZA, added: 2009 c.26 Sch.7 para.25

Sch.6 para.33, repealed (in part): 2009 asp 9 Sch.6

43. Health and Social Care (Community Health and Standards) Act 2003

referred to: SI 2009/295

Part 2 c.3, applied: SI 2009/462 Sch.3 para.6

Part 2 c.5, applied: SI 2009/462 Sch.3 para.6

s.45, amended: 2009 c.21 Sch.1 para.5

s.45, referred to: SI 2009/1511 Sch.1

s.45, repealed (in part): 2009 c.21 Sch.1 para.5

s.47, referred to: SI 2009/1511 Sch.1

s.47A, applied: SI 2009/462 Sch.3 para.2, Sch.3 para.3

s.50, applied: SI 2009/462 Sch.3 para.2, Sch.3 para.8

s.50, varied: SI 2009/462 Sch.3 para.2

s.51, applied: SI 2009/462 Sch.3 para.3, Sch.3 para.8

s.51, varied: SI 2009/462 Sch.3 para.3

s.52, applied: SI 2009/462 Sch.3 para.3, Sch.3 para.6, Sch.3 para.8

s.52, varied: SI 2009/462 Sch.3 para.3

s.53, varied: SI 2009/462 Sch.3 para.4

s.54, applied: SI 2009/462 Sch.3 para.7

s.55, applied: SI 2009/462 Sch.3 para.8

s.55, varied: SI 2009/462 Sch.3 para.3

s.57, applied: SI 2009/462 Sch.3 para.8

s.57, varied: SI 2009/462 Sch.3 para.5

s.66, amended: SI 2009/462 Sch.3 para.15

s.66, applied: SI 2009/462 Sch.3 para.6

s.67, amended: SI 2009/462 Sch.3 para.16

s.67, applied: SI 2009/462 Sch.3 para.6

s.68, amended: SI 2009/462 Sch.3 para.17

s.68, applied: SI 2009/462 Sch.3 para.6

s.69, varied: SI 2009/462 Sch.3 para.18

s.69A, amended: SI 2009/462 Sch.3 para.19

2003– cont.

43. Health and Social Care (Community Health and Standards) Act 2003– cont.
s.77, applied: SI 2009/462 Sch.3 para.7
s.78, varied: SI 2009/462 Sch.3 para.3
s.79, applied: SI 2009/462 Sch.3 para.2
s.79, varied: SI 2009/462 Sch.3 para.2
s.80, varied: SI 2009/462 Sch.3 para.3
s.81, varied: SI 2009/462 Sch.3 para.4
s.82, varied: SI 2009/462 Sch.3 para.5
s.88, amended: SI 2009/462 Sch.3 para.20
s.88, applied: SI 2009/462 Sch.3 para.6
s.89, amended: SI 2009/462 Sch.3 para.21
s.89, applied: SI 2009/462 Sch.3 para.6
s.90, amended: SI 2009/462 Sch.3 para.22
s.90, applied: SI 2009/462 Sch.3 para.6
s.91, varied: SI 2009/462 Sch.3 para.23
s.113, enabling: SI 2009/309, SI 2009/1768
s.114, enabling: SI 2009/309, SI 2009/1768
s.115, enabling: SI 2009/309, SI 2009/1768
s.124, applied: SI 2009/462 Sch.3 para.9
s.153, enabling: SI 2009/316, SI 2009/834, SSI 2009/193
s.160, enabling: SI 2009/316, SSI 2009/193
s.168, enabling: SSI 2009/193
s.195, applied: SI 2009/316, SI 2009/834
s.195, enabling: SI 2009/309, SI 2009/316, SI 2009/834, SI 2009/1768, SSI 2009/193

44. Criminal Justice Act 2003
Commencement Orders: SI 2009/616 Art.2; SI 2009/2775 Art.2; SI 2009/2879 Art.2, Art.3
see *Attorney General's Reference (No.19 of 2008), Re* [2008] EWCA Crim 1760, [2009] 1 Cr. App. R. (S.) 69 (CA (Crim Div)), Latham, L.J.; see *Attorney General's Reference (No.24 of 2008), Re* [2008] EWCA Crim 2936, [2009] 3 All E.R. 839 (CA (Crim Div)), Thomas, L.J.; see *Brett v DPP* [2009] EWHC 440 (Admin), [2009] 1 W.L.R. 2530 (DC), Leveson, L.J.; see *R. (on the application of Taylor) v Southampton Magistrates Court* [2008] EWHC 3006 (Admin), (2009) 172 J.P. 17 (QBD (Admin)), Toulson, L.J.; see *R. (on the application of Thomas) v Greenwich Magistrates' Court* [2009] EWHC 1180 (Admin), (2009) 173 J.P. 345 (QBD (Admin)), Hickinbottom, J.; see *R. v Athwal (Bachan Kaur)* [2009] EWCA Crim 789, [2009] 1 W.L.R. 2430 (CA (Crim Div)), Maurice Kay, L.J.; see *R. v B* [2008] EWCA Crim 830, [2009] 1 Cr. App. R. (S.) 6 (CA (Crim Div)), Rix, L.J.; see *R. v Cross (Adam Stuart)* [2008] EWCA Crim 1194, [2009] 1 Cr. App. R. (S.) 34 (CA (Crim Div)), Dyson, L.J.; see *R. v Davison (Anthony)* [2008] EWCA Crim 2795, [2009] 2 Cr. App. R. (S.) 13 (CA (Crim Div)), Moses, L.J.; see *R. v Hills (Christopher Carl)* [2008] EWCA Crim 1871, [2009] 1 Cr. App. R. (S.) 75 (CA (Crim Div)), Latham, L.J.; see *R. v Horncastle (Michael Christopher)* [2009] EWCA Crim 964, [2009] 4 All E.R. 183 (CA (Crim Div)), Thomas, L.J.; see *R. v Lavery (Dominic Robert)* [2008] EWCA Crim 2499, [2009] 3 All E.R. 295 (CA (Crim Div)), Lord Judge, L.C.J.; see *R. v Mayers (Jordan)* [2008] EWCA Crim 2989, [2009] 1 W.L.R. 1915 (CA (Crim Div)), Lord Judge, L.C.J.; see *R. v Stannard (Raymond)* [2008] EWCA Crim 2789, [2009] 2 Cr. App. R. (S.) 21 (CA (Crim Div)), Lord Judge, L.C.J.; see *R. v Whittles (Jason)* [2009] EWCA Crim 580, [2009] 2 Cr. App. R. (S.) 102 (CA (Crim Div)), Rafferty, J.; see *R. v Z* [2009] EWCA Crim 20, [2009] 3 All E.R. 1015 (CA (Crim Div)), Stanley

2003– cont.

44. Criminal Justice Act 2003– cont.
see– cont.
Burnton, L.J.; see *Sharief v General Medical Council* [2009] EWHC 847 (Admin), [2009] LS Law Medical 389 (QBD (Admin)), Sir Thayne Forbes
Part 12, applied: SI 2009/2042 Reg.10
Part 12 c.1, applied: 2009 c.25 Sch.22 para.28
Part 12 c.6, applied: SI 2009/1059 Art.100, SI 2009/1887 Sch.1
Part 11, see *R. v A* [2008] EWCA Crim 2908, [2009] 1 W.L.R. 1947 (CA (Crim Div)), Lord Judge, L.C.J.
Part 12, see *Attorney General's Reference (No.55 of 2008), Re* [2008] EWCA Crim 2790, [2009] 1 W.L.R. 2158 (CA (Crim Div)), Lord Judge, L.C.J.
Part 3, see *R. (on the application of Guest) v DPP* [2009] EWHC 594 (Admin), [2009] 2 Cr. App. R. 26 (DC), Goldring, L.J.
s.23A, applied: SI 2009/2773 Art.2
s.23A, enabling: SI 2009/2773
s.29, applied: SI 2009/2879 Art.3
s.44, see *R. v T* [2009] EWCA Crim 1035, [2009] 3 All E.R. 1002 (CA (Crim Div)), Lord Judge, L.C.J.
s.46, see *R. v T* [2009] EWCA Crim 1035, [2009] 3 All E.R. 1002 (CA (Crim Div)), Lord Judge, L.C.J.
s.61, see *R. v A* [2008] EWCA Crim 2186, [2009] 1 W.L.R. 1661 (CA (Crim Div)), Scott Baker, L.J.
s.76, see *R. v A* [2008] EWCA Crim 2908, [2009] 1 W.L.R. 1947 (CA (Crim Div)), Lord Judge, L.C.J.; see *R. v G (G)* [2009] EWCA Crim 1207, Times, July 9, 2009 (CA (Crim Div)), Hughes, L.J.
s.78, see *R. v A* [2008] EWCA Crim 2908, [2009] 1 W.L.R. 1947 (CA (Crim Div)), Lord Judge, L.C.J.; see *R. v G (G)* [2009] EWCA Crim 1207, Times, July 9, 2009 (CA (Crim Div)), Hughes, L.J.
s.79, see *R. v A* [2008] EWCA Crim 2908, [2009] 1 W.L.R. 1947 (CA (Crim Div)), Lord Judge, L.C.J.; see *R. v G (G)* [2009] EWCA Crim 1207, Times, July 9, 2009 (CA (Crim Div)), Hughes, L.J.
s.98, see *DPP v Agyemang* [2009] EWHC 1542 (Admin), (2009) 173 J.P. 487 (QBD (Admin)), Richards, L.J.
s.100, see *W v H* [2008] EWHC 399 (QB), [2009] E.M.L.R. 11 (QBD), Tugendhat, J.
s.101, see *DPP v Agyemang* [2009] EWHC 1542 (Admin), (2009) 173 J.P. 487 (QBD (Admin)), Richards, L.J.; see *R. v Assani (Dale Steven)* [2008] EWCA Crim 2563, [2009] Crim. L.R. 514 (CA (Crim Div)), Maurice Kay, L.J.; see *R. v D* [2008] EWCA Crim 1156, [2009] 2 Cr. App. R. 17 (CA (Crim Div)), Rix, L.J.; see *R. v Freeman (Daniel Robert)* [2008] EWCA Crim 1863, [2009] 1 W.L.R. 2723 (CA (Crim Div)), Latham, L.J.; see *R. v Good (Gary)* [2008] EWCA Crim 2923, (2009) 173 J.P. 1 (CA (Crim Div)), Hooper, L.J.; see *R. v Hearne (David Henry)* [2009] EWCA Crim 103, (2009) 173 J.P. 97 (CA (Crim Div)), Moses, L.J.; see *R. v Johnson (Chad)* [2009] EWCA Crim 649, [2009] 2 Cr. App. R. 7 (CA (Crim Div)), Maurice Kay, L.J.; see *R. v Leonard (Mark Alan)* [2009] EWCA Crim 1251, (2009) 173 J.P. 366 (CA (Crim Div)), Aikens, L.J.; see *R. v McAllister (David)* [2008] EWCA Crim 1544,

2003– cont.

44. Criminal Justice Act 2003–*cont.*
  s.101–*cont.*
  [2009] 1 Cr. App. R. 10 (CA (Crim Div)), Moses, L.J.; see *R. v O'Dowd (Kevin)* [2009] EWCA Crim 905, [2009] 2 Cr. App. R. 16 (CA (Crim Div)), Scott Baker, L.J.; see *R. v Spittle (Brett George)* [2008] EWCA Crim 2537, [2009] R.T.R. 14 (CA (Crim Div)), Dyson, L.J.; see *R. v Woodhouse (Rupert Giles)* [2009] EWCA Crim 498, (2009) 173 J.P. 337 (CA (Crim Div)), Rix, L.J.; see *W v H* [2008] EWHC 399 (QB), [2009] E.M.L.R. 11 (QBD), Tugendhat, J.

  s.101, applied: SI 2009/ 1209 r.64, SI 2009/ 1211 r.64, r.65, SI 2009/ 2041 r.79
  s.101, referred to: SI 2009/ 1209 r.63, SI 2009/ 2041 r.78
  s.102, see *R. v D* [2008] EWCA Crim 1156, [2009] 2 Cr. App. R. 17 (CA (Crim Div)), Rix, L.J.
  s.103, see *R. v Johnson (Chad)* [2009] EWCA Crim 649, [2009] 2 Cr. App. R. 7 (CA (Crim Div)), Maurice Kay, L.J.; see *R. v O'Dowd (Kevin)* [2009] EWCA Crim 905, [2009] 2 Cr. App. R. 16 (CA (Crim Div)), Scott Baker, L.J.
  s.103, amended: 2009 c.25 Sch.17 para.1
  s.105, see *R. v Assani (Dale Steven)* [2008] EWCA Crim 2563, [2009] Crim. L.R. 514 (CA (Crim Div)), Maurice Kay, L.J.; see *R. v Good (Gary)* [2008] EWCA Crim 2923, (2009) 173 J.P. 1 (CA (Crim Div)), Hooper, L.J.
  s.106, see *R. v Assani (Dale Steven)* [2008] EWCA Crim 2563, [2009] Crim. L.R. 514 (CA (Crim Div)), Maurice Kay, L.J.
  s.108, amended: 2009 c.25 Sch.17 para.1
  s.111, enabling: SI 2009/ 1209, SI 2009/ 1211, SI 2009/ 2041
  s.112, varied: SI 2009/ 1059 Sch.1 para.53
  s.113, enabling: SI 2009/1209, SI 2009/ 1211, SI 2009/ 2041
  s.114, see *R. v Athwal (Bachan Kaur)* [2009] EWCA Crim 789, [2009] 1 W.L.R. 2430 (CA (Crim Div)), Maurice Kay, L.J.; see *R. v L* [2008] EWCA Crim 973, [2009] 1 W.L.R. 626 (CA (Crim Div)), Lord Phillips, L.C.J.; see *R. v Leonard (Mark Alan)* [2009] EWCA Crim 1251, (2009) 173 J.P. 366 (CA (Crim Div)), Aikens, L.J.; see *R. v Z* [2009] EWCA Crim 20, [2009] 3 All E.R. 1015 (CA (Crim Div)), Stanley Burnton, L.J.; see *Sharief v General Medical Council* [2009] EWHC 847 (Admin), [2009] LS Law Medical 389 (QBD (Admin)), Sir Thayne Forbes; see *West Midlands Probation Board v French* [2008] EWHC 2631 (Admin), [2009] 1 W.L.R. 1715 (DC), Scott Baker, L.J.
  s.114, applied: SI 2009/ 1209 r.66, SI 2009/ 1211 r.67, SI 2009/ 2041 r.81
  s.114, referred to: SI 2009/ 1209 r.66, SI 2009/ 1211 r.67, SI 2009/ 2041 r.81
  s.115, see *R. v Leonard (Mark Alan)* [2009] EWCA Crim 1251, (2009) 173 J.P. 366 (CA (Crim Div)), Aikens, L.J.
  s.116, see *R. v Horncastle (Michael Christopher)* [2009] UKSC 14 (SC), Lord Phillips (President); see *R. v Kamuhuza (Martin)* [2008] EWCA Crim 3060, (2009) 173 J.P. 55 (CA (Crim Div)), Thomas, L.J.; see *R. v T (D)* [2009] EWCA Crim 1213, (2009) 173 J.P. 425 (CA (Crim Div)), Thomas, L.J.; see *R. v Z* [2009] EWCA Crim 20, [2009] 3 All E.R. 1015 (CA (Crim Div)), Stanley Burnton, L.J.; see *West Midlands Probation Board v French* [2008]

2003– cont.

44. Criminal Justice Act 2003–*cont.*
  s.116–*cont.*
  EWHC 2631 (Admin), [2009] 1 W.L.R. 1715 (DC), Scott Baker, L.J.
  s.116, applied: SI 2009/ 1209 r.66, SI 2009/ 1211 r.67
  s.116, referred to: SI 2009/ 2041 r.81
  s.117, see *R. v Kamuhuza (Martin)* [2008] EWCA Crim 3060, (2009) 173 J.P. 55 (CA (Crim Div)), Thomas, L.J.; see *West Midlands Probation Board v French* [2008] EWHC 2631 (Admin), [2009] 1 W.L.R. 1715 (DC), Scott Baker, L.J.
  s.117, applied: SI 2009/ 1209 r.66, SI 2009/ 1211 r.67
  s.117, referred to: SI 2009/ 2041 r.81
  s.117, varied: SI 2009/ 1059 Sch.1 para.53
  s.118, see *R. v Athwal (Bachan Kaur)* [2009] EWCA Crim 789, [2009] 1 W.L.R. 2430 (CA (Crim Div)), Maurice Kay, L.J.; see *West Midlands Probation Board v French* [2008] EWHC 2631 (Admin), [2009] 1 W.L.R. 1715 (DC), Scott Baker, L.J.
  s.119, see *R. v Billingham (Mark Phillip)* [2009] EWCA Crim 19, [2009] 2 Cr. App. R. 20 (CA (Crim Div)), Stanley Burnton, L.J.; see *R. v Gibbons (Dean)* [2008] EWCA Crim 1574, (2009) 173 J.P. 260 (CA (Crim Div)), Hooper, L.J.
  s.120, see *R. v Athwal (Bachan Kaur)* [2009] EWCA Crim 789, [2009] 1 W.L.R. 2430 (CA (Crim Div)), Maurice Kay, L.J.
  s.120, repealed (in part): 2009 c.25 s.112, Sch.23 Part 3
  s.121, applied: SI 2009/ 1209 r.66, SI 2009/ 1211 r.67, SI 2009/ 2041 r.81
  s.124, see *R. v Horncastle (Michael Christopher)* [2009] EWCA Crim 964, [2009] 4 All E.R. 183 (CA (Crim Div)), Thomas, L.J.; see *R. v Horncastle (Michael Christopher)* [2009] UKSC 14 (SC), Lord Phillips (President)
  s.125, see *R. v Horncastle (Michael Christopher)* [2009] EWCA Crim 964, [2009] 4 All E.R. 183 (CA (Crim Div)), Thomas, L.J.; see *R. v Horncastle (Michael Christopher)* [2009] UKSC 14 (SC), Lord Phillips (President)
  s.126, see *R. v Horncastle (Michael Christopher)* [2009] UKSC 14 (SC), Lord Phillips (President)
  s.127, applied: SI 2009/ 1209 r.73, SI 2009/ 1211 r.74, SI 2009/ 2041 r.88
  s.132, enabling: SI 2009/ 1209, SI 2009/ 1211, SI 2009/ 2041
  s.134, varied: SI 2009/ 1059 Sch.1 para.53
  s.135, enabling: SI 2009/ 1209, SI 2009/ 1211, SI 2009/ 2041
  s.138, repealed (in part): 2009 c.25 s.111, Sch.23 Part 3
  s.142, varied: 2009 c.25 Sch.22 para.28
  s.142A, varied: 2009 c.25 Sch.22 para.28
  s.143, see *Attorney General's Reference (Nos.60, 62 and 63 of 2009), Re* [2009] EWCA Crim 2693, Times, December 24, 2009 (CA (Crim Div)), Lord Judge, L.C.J.; see *R. v Darwin (Anne Catherine)* [2009] EWCA Crim 860, [2009] 2 Cr. App. R. (S.) 115 (CA (Crim Div)), Lord Judge, L.C.J.; see *R. v Saw (Rebecca)* [2009] EWCA Crim 1, [2009] 2 All E.R. 1138 (CA (Crim Div)), Lord Judge, L.C.J.
  s.143, amended: 2009 c.25 Sch.17 para.6, Sch.23 Part 5
  s.143, varied: 2009 c.25 Sch.22 para.28, SI 2009/ 1059 Sch.1 para.53, SI 2009/ 2042 Reg.4
  s.144, applied: 2009 c.25 s.120, s.125
  s.144, disapplied: 2009 c.25 s.121
  s.144, varied: 2009 c.25 Sch.22 para.28
  s.145, varied: 2009 c.25 Sch.22 para.28

2003– cont.

44. Criminal Justice Act 2003– cont.

s.146, varied: 2009 c.25 Sch.22 para.28

s.147, varied: 2009 c.25 Sch.22 para.28

s.148, applied: 2009 c.25 s.125

s.148, varied: 2009 c.25 Sch.22 para.28

s.149, varied: 2009 c.25 Sch.22 para.28

s.150, varied: 2009 c.25 Sch.22 para.28

s.150A, varied: 2009 c.25 Sch.22 para.28

s.151, amended: 2009 c.25 Sch.17 para.8

s.151, varied: 2009 c.25 Sch.22 para.28, SI 2009/ 1059 Sch.1 para.53

s.152, applied: 2009 c.25 s.125

s.152, varied: 2009 c.25 Sch.22 para.28

s.153, see *R. v Whittles (Jason)* [2009] EWCA Crim 580, [2009] 2 Cr. App. R. (S.) 102 (CA (Crim Div)), Rafferty, J.

s.153, applied: 2009 c.25 s.125

s.153, varied: 2009 c.25 Sch.22 para.28

s.154, applied: 2009 c.13 s.10

s.154, referred to: 2009 c.12 s.40, 2009 c.25 Sch.22 para.12, Sch.22 para.13, Sch.22 para.14, SI 2009/ 1749 Art.14

s.154, varied: 2009 c.25 Sch.22 para.28

s.155, varied: 2009 c.25 Sch.22 para.28

s.156, varied: 2009 c.25 Sch.22 para.28

s.157, varied: 2009 c.25 Sch.22 para.28

s.158, varied: 2009 c.25 Sch.22 para.28

s.159, varied: 2009 c.25 Sch.22 para.28

s.160, varied: 2009 c.25 Sch.22 para.28

s.161, varied: 2009 c.25 Sch.22 para.28

s.161A, varied: 2009 c.25 Sch.22 para.28

s.161B, varied: 2009 c.25 Sch.22 para.28

s.162, varied: 2009 c.25 Sch.22 para.28

s.163, varied: 2009 c.25 Sch.22 para.28

s.164, applied: 2009 c.25 s.125

s.164, varied: 2009 c.25 Sch.22 para.28

s.165, applied: SI 2009/ 2041 r.114

s.165, varied: 2009 c.25 Sch.22 para.28

s.166, varied: 2009 c.25 Sch.22 para.28

s.167, repealed: 2009 c.25 Sch.23 Part 4

s.167, varied: 2009 c.25 Sch.22 para.28

s.168, repealed: 2009 c.25 Sch.23 Part 4

s.168, varied: 2009 c.25 Sch.22 para.28

s.169, repealed: 2009 c.25 Sch.23 Part 4

s.169, varied: 2009 c.25 Sch.22 para.28

s.170, see *R. v Saw (Rebecca)* [2009] EWCA Crim 1, [2009] 2 All E.R. 1138 (CA (Crim Div)), Lord Judge, L.C.J.

s.170, repealed: 2009 c.25 Sch.23 Part 4

s.170, varied: 2009 c.25 Sch.22 para.28

s.171, repealed: 2009 c.25 Sch.23 Part 4

s.171, varied: 2009 c.25 Sch.22 para.28

s.172, see *R. v Rigby (Paul)* [2008] EWCA Crim 1195, [2009] 1 Cr. App. R. (S.) 35 (CA (Crim Div)), Dyson, L.J.; see *R. v Saw (Rebecca)* [2009] EWCA Crim 1, [2009] 2 All E.R. 1138 (CA (Crim Div)), Lord Judge, L.C.J.

s.172, repealed: 2009 c.25 Sch.23 Part 4

s.172, varied: 2009 c.25 Sch.22 para.28

s.173, repealed: 2009 c.25 Sch.23 Part 4

s.173, varied: 2009 c.25 Sch.22 para.28

s.174, see *R. v Rigby (Paul)* [2008] EWCA Crim 1195, [2009] 1 Cr. App. R. (S.) 35 (CA (Crim Div)), Dyson, L.J.

s.174, amended: 2009 c.25 Sch.21 para.84

s.174, varied: 2009 c.25 Sch.22 para.28

s.175, varied: 2009 c.25 Sch.22 para.28

s.176, amended: 2009 c.25 Sch.23 Part 4

2003– cont.

44. Criminal Justice Act 2003– cont.

s.176, varied: 2009 c.25 Sch.22 para.28

s.177, see *R. v Davison (Anthony)* [2008] EWCA Crim 2795, [2009] 2 Cr. App. R. (S.) 13 (CA (Crim Div)), Moses, L.J.; see *R. v Kirby (Paul St John)* [2009] EWCA Crim 14, [2009] 2 Cr. App. R. (S.) 49 (CA (Crim Div)), Moses, L.J.

s.177, applied: 2009 c.25 s.131, SI 2009/ 1887 Sch.1

s.177, referred to: SI 2009/ 1887 Sch.2

s.181, see *R. (on the application of Noone) v Governor of Drake Hall Prison* [2008] EWCA Civ 1097, [2009] 1 W.L.R. 1321 (CA (Civ Div)), Sir Anthony Clarke, M.R.

s.182, see *R. (on the application of Noone) v Governor of Drake Hall Prison* [2008] EWCA Civ 1097, [2009] 1 W.L.R. 1321 (CA (Civ Div)), Sir Anthony Clarke, M.R.

s.186, applied: SI 2009/ 2041 r.114

s.189, see *R. v Zeca (Raul Joao)* [2009] EWCA Crim 133, [2009] 2 Cr. App. R. (S.) 65 (CA (Crim Div)), Lord Judge, L.C.J.

s.189, applied: 2009 c.25 s.131, SI 2009/ 1887 Sch.1

s.189, referred to: SI 2009/ 1887 Sch.2

s.199, see *R. v Kirby (Paul St John)* [2009] EWCA Crim 14, [2009] 2 Cr. App. R. (S.) 49 (CA (Crim Div)), Moses, L.J.

s.200, see *R. v Odam (Soloman Alexander)* [2008] EWCA Crim 1087, [2009] 1 Cr. App. R. (S.) 22 (CA (Crim Div)), Forbes, J.

s.200, referred to: SI 2009/ 1209 r.106, SI 2009/ 2041 r.144

s.207, amended: SI 2009/ 1182 Sch.5 para.7

s.207, referred to: SI 2009/ 1887 Sch.2

s.208, amended: SI 2009/ 1182 Sch.5 para.7

s.209, referred to: SI 2009/ 1887 Sch.1

s.212, referred to: SI 2009/ 1887 Sch.1

s.224, see *Attorney General's Reference (No.43 of 2009), Re* [2009] EWCA Crim 1925, Times, October 9, 2009 (CA (Crim Div)), Lord Judge, L.C.J.

s.225, see *Attorney General's Reference (No.43 of 2009), Re* [2009] EWCA Crim 1925, Times, October 9, 2009 (CA (Crim Div)), Lord Judge, L.C.J.; see *Attorney General's Reference (No.55 of 2008), Re* [2008] EWCA Crim 2790, [2009] 1 W.L.R. 2158 (CA (Crim Div)), Lord Judge, L.C.J.; see *R. v Bowling (Stephen David)* [2008] EWCA Crim 1148, [2009] 1 Cr. App. R. (S.) 23 (CA (Crim Div)), Sir Igor Judge; see *R. v Gorman (Daniel)* [2008] EWCA Crim 2907, [2009] 2 Cr. App. R. (S.) 36 (CA (Crim Div)), Hooper, L.J.; see *R. v Kehoe (Bridie Joanna)* [2008] EWCA Crim 819, [2009] 1 Cr. App. R. (S.) 9 (CA (Crim Div)), Lord Phillips of Worth Matravers, L.C.J.; see *R. v Kiely (Michael James)* [2009] EWCA Crim 756, [2009] 2 Cr. App. R. (S.) 111 (CA (Crim Div)), Scott Baker, L.J.; see *R. v L (D)* [2008] EWCA Crim 2669, [2009] 2 Cr. App. R. (S.) 44 (CA (Crim Div)), Moses, L.J.; see *R. v Lavery (Dominic Robert)* [2008] EWCA Crim 2499, [2009] 3 All E.R. 295 (CA (Crim Div)), Lord Judge, L.C.J.; see *R. v Stannard (Raymond)* [2008] EWCA Crim 2789, [2009] 2 Cr. App. R. (S.) 21 (CA (Crim Div)), Lord Judge, L.C.J.

s.225, applied: 2009 c.25 s.126, Sch.22 para.47, SI 2009/ 2657 r.48

s.226, see *R. v B* [2008] EWCA Crim 830, [2009] 1 Cr. App. R. (S.) 6 (CA (Crim Div)), Rix, L.J.; see *R. v C* [2008] EWCA Crim 2691, [2009] 2 Cr. App. R. (S.) 5 (CA (Crim Div)), Richards, J.

2003– cont.

44. Criminal Justice Act 2003–*cont.*

s.226, applied: 2009 c.25 s.126, Sch.22 para.47

s.227, see *Attorney General's Reference (No.55 of 2008), Re* [2008] EWCA Crim 2790, [2009] 1 W.L.R. 2158 (CA (Crim Div)), Lord Judge, L.C.J.

s.227, applied: 2009 c.25 s.126, Sch.22 para.47, SI 2009/ 2657 r.48

s.228, see *Attorney General's Reference (No.55 of 2008), Re* [2008] EWCA Crim 2790, [2009] 1 W.L.R. 2158 (CA (Crim Div)), Lord Judge, L.C.J.; see *R. v Lavery (Dominic Robert)* [2008] EWCA Crim 2499, [2009] 3 All E.R. 295 (CA (Crim Div)), Lord Judge, L.C.J.

s.228, applied: 2009 c.25 s.126, Sch.22 para.47

s.229, see *Attorney General's Reference (No.55 of 2008), Re* [2008] EWCA Crim 2790, [2009] 1 W.L.R. 2158 (CA (Crim Div)), Lord Judge, L.C.J.; see *R. v Bowling (Stephen David)* [2008] EWCA Crim 1148, [2009] 1 Cr. App. R. (S.) 23 (CA (Crim Div)), Sir Igor Judge; see *R. v Lavery (Dominic Robert)* [2008] EWCA Crim 2499, [2009] 3 All E.R. 295 (CA (Crim Div)), Lord Judge, L.C.J.; see *R. v Stannard (Raymond)* [2008] EWCA Crim 2789, [2009] 2 Cr. App. R. (S.) 21 (CA (Crim Div)), Lord Judge, L.C.J.

s.229, amended: 2009 c.25 Sch.21 para.95

s.229, varied: SI 2009/ 1059 Sch.1 para.53

s.237, varied: SI 2009/ 1059 Sch.1 para.53

s.239, enabling: SI 2009/408

s.240, see *R. v Metcalfe (Billy)* [2009] EWCA Crim 374, [2009] 2 Cr. App. R. (S.) 85 (CA (Crim Div)), Lord Judge, L.C.J.; see *R. v Nnaji (Ogechuku Ferdinand)* [2009] EWCA Crim 468, [2009] 2 Cr. App. R. (S.) 107 (CA (Crim Div)), Thomas, L.J.; see *R. v Vaughan (Carl Michael)* [2008] EWCA Crim 1613, [2009] 1 Cr. App. R. (S.) 63 (CA (Crim Div)), Hooper, L.J.

s.240, varied: SI 2009/ 2042 Reg.5, Reg.6, Reg.7, Reg.8, Reg.9

s.240A, see *Attorney General's Reference (No.6 of 2009), Re* [2009] EWCA Crim 1132, [2009] 2 Cr. App. R. (S.) 108 (CA (Crim Div)), Thomas, L.J.; see *R. v Sherif (Abdul)* [2008] EWCA Crim 2653, [2009] 2 Cr. App. R. (S.) 33 (CA (Crim Div)), Latham, L.J.

s.244, see *R. v Hussain (Mamoon)* [2008] EWCA Crim 1226, [2009] 1 Cr. App. R. (S.) 41 (CA (Crim Div)), Moses, L.J.

s.249, applied: SI 2009/ 1209 r.107

s.258, see *Wear Valley DC v Robson* [2008] EWCA Civ 1470, [2009] H.L.R. 27 (CA (Civ Div)), Laws, L.J.

s.265, see *R. v Whittles (Jason)* [2009] EWCA Crim 580, [2009] 2 Cr. App. R. (S.) 102 (CA (Crim Div)), Rafferty, J.

s.267, applied: SI 2009/ 1209 r.107

s.269, see *Attorney General's Reference (No.24 of 2008), Re* [2008] EWCA Crim 2936, [2009] 3 All E.R. 839 (CA (Crim Div)), Thomas, L.J.; see *R. (on the application of Wellington) v Secretary of State for the Home Department* [2008] UKHL 72, [2009] 1 A.C. 335 (HL), Lord Hoffmann; see *R. v Babamuboni (Diamond)* [2008] EWCA Crim 2505, [2009] 1 Cr. App. R. (S.) 51 (CA (Crim Div)), Forbes, J.; see *R. v Height (John)* [2008] EWCA Crim 2500, [2009] 1 Cr. App. R. (S.) 117 (CA (Crim Div)), Lord Judge, L.C.J.

s.269, amended: 2009 c.25 Sch.21 para.85

2003– cont.

44. Criminal Justice Act 2003–*cont.*

s.269, applied: 2009 c.25 s.125

s.270, see *Attorney General's Reference (No.24 of 2008), Re* [2008] EWCA Crim 2936, [2009] 3 All E.R. 839 (CA (Crim Div)), Thomas, L.J.

s.277, amended: 2009 c.25 Sch.21 para.86

s.280, referred to: 2009 c.25 s.30

s.281, referred to: 2009 c.25 Sch.6 para.10, 2009 c.26 s.106

s.282, applied: 2009 c.4 s.1207

s.282, referred to: 2009 c.11 s.18

s.311, applied: SI 2009/ 1209 r.108

s.329, see *Adorian v Commissioner of Police of the Metropolis* [2009] EWCA Civ 18, [2009] 1 W.L.R. 1859 (CA (Civ Div)), Sedley, L.J.

s.329, varied: SI 2009/ 1059 Sch.1 para.53

s.330, amended: 2009 c.25 Sch.21 para.87

s.330, enabling: SI 2009/ 616, SI 2009/ 3111

s.336, enabling: SI 2009/ 616, SI 2009/ 2775, SI 2009/ 2879, SI 2009/ 3111

s.337, varied: SI 2009/ 1059 Sch.1 para.53

s.338, referred to: 2009 c.25 s.181

Sch.3 Part 2 para.59, repealed: 2009 c.25 Sch.23 Part 1

Sch.6 para.5, enabling: SI 2009/ 1209, SI 2009/ 1211, SI 2009/ 2041

Sch.7 para.2, enabling: SI 2009/ 1209, SI 2009/ 1211, SI 2009/ 2041

Sch.8 Part 2 para.5, applied: SI 2009/ 1209 r.101, SI 2009/ 2041 r.140

Sch.8 Part 2 para.8, applied: SI 2009/ 1209 r.101, r.102, SI 2009/ 2041 r.140, r.141

Sch.8 Part 2 para.10, applied: SI 2009/ 1209 r.101, r.102, SI 2009/ 2041 r.141

Sch.8 Part 3 para.14, applied: SI 2009/ 1209 r.104, SI 2009/ 2041 r.142

Sch.8 Part 4 para.17, applied: SI 2009/ 1209 r.105, SI 2009/ 2041 r.143

Sch.8 Part 4 para.19, applied: SI 2009/ 2041 r.144

Sch.8 Part 4 para.20, applied: SI 2009/ 1209 r.106

Sch.8 Part 5 para.21, applied: SI 2009/ 1209 r.31, r.96

Sch.8 Part 5 para.23, applied: SI 2009/ 2041 r.44, r.114, Sch.2 para.17

Sch.10 para.1, disapplied: SI 2009/ 1209 r.109

Sch.12 para.2, see *R. v Zeca (Raul Joao)* [2009] EWCA Crim 133, [2009] 2 Cr. App. R. (S.) 65 (CA (Crim Div)), Lord Judge, L.C.J.

Sch.12 Part 2 para.12, referred to: SI 2009/ 2041 r.131

Sch.15 Part 1 para.59A, added: 2009 c.25 s.138

Sch.15 Part 1 para.59B, added: 2009 c.25 s.138

Sch.15 Part 1 para.59C, added: 2009 c.25 s.138

Sch.15 Part 1 para.59D, added: 2009 c.25 s.138

Sch.15 Part 1 para.60A, added: 2009 c.25 s.138

Sch.15 Part 1 para.60B, added: 2009 c.25 s.138

Sch.15 Part 1 para.60C, added: 2009 c.25 s.138

Sch.15 Part 1 para.63B, added: 2009 c.25 s.138

Sch.15 Part 1 para.63C, added: 2009 c.25 s.138

Sch.15 Part 1 para.63D, added: 2009 c.25 s.138

Sch.15 Part 1 para.63E, added: 2009 c.25 s.138

Sch.15 Part 1 para.63F, added: 2009 c.25 s.138

Sch.21, see *Attorney General's Reference (No.12 of 2008), Re* [2008] EWCA Crim 1060, [2009] 1 Cr. App. R. (S.) 18 (CA (Crim Div)), Lord Phillips of Worth Matravers, L.C.J.; see *Attorney General's Reference (No.24 of 2008), Re* [2008] EWCA Crim 2936, [2009] 3 All E.R. 839 (CA (Crim Div)), Thomas, L.J.; see *R. v Assani (Dale Steven)* [2008] EWCA Crim 2563, [2009]

2003–cont.

44. Criminal Justice Act 2003–*cont.*

Sch.21–*cont.*

Crim. L.R. 514 (CA (Crim Div)), Maurice Kay, L.J.; see *R. v Babamuboni (Diamond)* [2008] EWCA Crim 2505, [2009] 1 Cr. App. R. (S.) 51 (CA (Crim Div)), Forbes, J.; see *R. v Bonellie (Stephen)* [2008] EWCA Crim 1417, [2009] 1 Cr. App. R. (S.) 55 (CA (Crim Div)), Lord Phillips, L.C.J.; see *R. v Healy (John Michael)* [2008] EWCA Crim 2583, [2009] 2 Cr. App. R. (S.) 3 (CA (Crim Div)), Leveson, L.J.; see *R. v Height (John)* [2008] EWCA Crim 2500, [2009] 1 Cr. App. R. (S.) 117 (CA (Crim Div)), Lord Judge, L.C.J.; see *R. v Patterson (Rickell)* [2008] EWCA Crim 1018, [2009] 1 Cr. App. R. (S.) 19 (CA (Crim Div)), Hooper, L.J.

Sch.21, applied: 2009 c.25 s.125

Sch.21 para.4, see *R. v Height (John)* [2008] EWCA Crim 2500, [2009] 1 Cr. App. R. (S.) 117 (CA (Crim Div)), Lord Judge, L.C.J.

Sch.21 para.5, see *Attorney General's Reference (No.12 of 2008), Re* [2008] EWCA Crim 1060, [2009] 1 Cr. App. R. (S.) 18 (CA (Crim Div)), Lord Phillips of Worth Matravers, L.C.J.; see *Attorney General's Reference (Nos.25 & 26 of 2008), Re* [2008] EWCA Crim 2665, [2009] 1 Cr. App. R. (S.) 116 (CA (Crim Div)), Hallett, L.J. DBE; see *R. v Blue (Thomas)* [2008] EWCA Crim 769, [2009] 1 Cr. App. R. (S.) 2 (CA (Crim Div)), Gage, L.J.; see *R. v Bonellie (Stephen)* [2008] EWCA Crim 1417, [2009] 1 Cr. App. R. (S.) 55 (CA (Crim Div)), Lord Phillips, L.C.J.; see *R. v Davies (Gareth Talfryn)* [2008] EWCA Crim 1055, [2009] 1 Cr. App. R. (S.) 15 (CA (Crim Div)), Lord Phillips of Worth Matravers, L.C.J.; see *R. v Healy (John Michael)* [2008] EWCA Crim 2583, [2009] 2 Cr. App. R. (S.) 3 (CA (Crim Div)), Leveson, L.J.; see *R. v Height (John)* [2008] EWCA Crim 2500, [2009] 1 Cr. App. R. (S.) 117 (CA (Crim Div)), Lord Judge, L.C.J.; see *R. v Herbert (Ryan)* [2008] EWCA Crim 2501, [2009] 2 Cr. App. R. (S.) 9 (CA (Crim Div)), Lord Chief Justice; see *R. v Knight (Kate Marie)* [2008] EWCA Crim 1444, [2009] 1 Cr. App. R. (S.) 57 (CA (Crim Div)), Lord Philips, L.C.J.

Sch.21 para.11, see *R. v Patterson (Rickell)* [2008] EWCA Crim 1018, [2009] 1 Cr. App. R. (S.) 19 (CA (Crim Div)), Hooper, L.J.

Sch.21 para.11, amended: 2009 c.25 Sch.21 para.52, Sch.23 Part 2

Sch.22 para.10, varied: SI 2009/1059 Sch.1 para.53

Sch.25 para.12, repealed: 2009 c.23 Sch.22 Part 5

Sch.25 para.13, repealed: 2009 c.23 Sch.22 Part 5

Sch.25 para.70, repealed: 2009 c.23 Sch.22 Part 5

Sch.32 Part 1 para.130, repealed: 2009 c.24 Sch.7 Part 3

Sch.32 Part 1 para.131, repealed: 2009 c.24 Sch.7 Part 3

Sch.32 Part 1 para.132, repealed: 2009 c.24 Sch.7 Part 3

Sch.34A para.13A, added: 2009 c.25 Sch.21 para.63

Sch.35 para.2, repealed: 2009 c.26 Sch.8 Part 8

Sch.37 Part 9, amended: 2009 c.23 Sch.22 Part 5

Sch.38 para.2, repealed: 2009 c.25 Sch.21 para.88, Sch.23 Part 4

Sch.38 para.3, repealed: 2009 c.25 Sch.21 para.88, Sch.23 Part 4

2004

4. Justice (Northern Ireland) Act 2004

s.3, repealed: 2009 c.3 Sch.5 para.5

s.4, repealed: 2009 c.3 Sch.5 para.5

s.5, repealed: 2009 c.3 Sch.5 para.5

s.21, amended: 2009 c.25 s.147

Sch.1 para.3, repealed: 2009 c.3 Sch.5 para.5

Sch.3 para.5, amended: 2009 c.25 s.147

Sch.3 para.5A, added: 2009 c.25 s.147

Sch.3 para.6, amended: 2009 c.25 s.147

5. Planning and Compulsory Purchase Act 2004

Commencement Orders: SI 2009/384 Art.2

Part 2, applied: SI 2009/1254 Art.3, SI 2009/2467 Art.3

s.1, repealed: 2009 c.20 Sch.5 para.13, Sch.7 Part 4

s.2, repealed: 2009 c.20 Sch.5 para.13, Sch.7 Part 4

s.3, repealed: 2009 c.20 Sch.5 para.13, Sch.7 Part 4

s.4, repealed: 2009 c.20 Sch.5 para.13, Sch.7 Part 4

s.4A, repealed: 2009 c.20 Sch.5 para.13, Sch.7 Part 4

s.5, repealed: 2009 c.20 Sch.5 para.13, Sch.7 Part 4

s.6, repealed: 2009 c.20 Sch.5 para.13, Sch.7 Part 4

s.7, repealed: 2009 c.20 Sch.5 para.13, Sch.7 Part 4

s.8, repealed: 2009 c.20 Sch.5 para.13, Sch.7 Part 4

s.9, repealed: 2009 c.20 Sch.5 para.13, Sch.7 Part 4

s.10, repealed: 2009 c.20 Sch.5 para.13, Sch.7 Part 4

s.11, repealed: 2009 c.20 Sch.5 para.13, Sch.7 Part 4

s.12, repealed: 2009 c.20 Sch.5 para.13, Sch.7 Part 4

s.13, applied: 2009 c.20 s.69

s.15, varied: SI 2009/1254 Art.4, SI 2009/2467 Art.4

s.17, enabling: SI 2009/401

s.19, see *Capel Parish Council v Surrey CC* [2009] EWHC 350 (Admin), [2009] J.P.L. 1302 (QBD (Admin)), Collins, J.

s.19, amended: 2009 c.20 Sch.5 para.14

s.20, see *Capel Parish Council v Surrey CC* [2009] EWHC 350 (Admin), [2009] J.P.L. 1302 (QBD (Admin)), Collins, J.; see *Persimmon Homes (North East) Ltd v Blyth Valley BC* [2008] EWCA Civ 861, [2009] J.P.L. 335 (CA (Civ Div)), Keene, L.J.

s.24, amended: 2009 c.20 Sch.5 para.15

s.24, repealed (in part): 2009 c.20 Sch.5 para.15, Sch.7 Part 4

s.28, amended: 2009 c.20 Sch.5 para.16

s.29, enabling: SI 2009/1254, SI 2009/2467

s.36, enabling: SI 2009/401

s.37, amended: 2009 c.20 Sch.5 para.17

s.38, see *South Cambridgeshire DC v Secretary of State for Communities and Local Government* [2008] EWCA Civ 1010, [2009] J.P.L. 467 (CA (Civ Div)), Sir Mark Potter (President)

s.38, amended: 2009 c.20 s.82

s.39, amended: 2009 c.20 Sch.5 para.18

s.39, repealed (in part): 2009 c.20 Sch.5 para.18, Sch.7 Part 4

s.62, amended: 2009 c.2 Sch.2 para.5, Sch.2 para.6

s.62, varied: 2009 c.2 Sch.3 para.5, Sch.3 para.7

s.113, see *Persimmon Homes (North East) Ltd v Blyth Valley BC* [2008] EWCA Civ 861, [2009] J.P.L. 335 (CA (Civ Div)), Keene, L.J.

s.113, amended: 2009 c.20 Sch.5 para.19

s.121, enabling: SI 2009/384, SI 2009/2645

s.122, enabling: SI 2009/384, SI 2009/401, SI 2009/2645

Sch.8 para.1, see *R. (on the application of Roberts) v Secretary of State for Communities and Local Government* [2008] EWHC 677 (Admin), [2009] J.P.L. 81 (QBD (Admin)), Sullivan, J.

2004– cont.

6. Child Trust Funds Act 2004
s.2, amended: SI 2009/1117 Sch.2 para.1
s.5, enabling: SI 2009/694
s.9, amended: 2009 c.24 Sch.2 para.15
s.10, enabling: SI 2009/475
s.11, enabling: SI 2009/475
s.15, amended: SI 2009/3054 Sch.1 para.12
s.15, repealed (in part): SI 2009/3054 Sch.1 para.12
s.15, enabling: SI 2009/475
s.21, amended: SI 2009/56 Sch.1 para.415
s.23, amended: SI 2009/56 Sch.1 para.416
s.23, repealed (in part): SI 2009/56 Sch.1 para.416
s.24, repealed: SI 2009/56 Sch.1 para.417
s.28, applied: SI 2009/475
s.28, enabling: SI 2009/475, SI 2009/694
s.29, amended: SI 2009/56 Sch.1 para.418

7. Gender Recognition Act 2004
see *R. (on the application of B) v Secretary of State for Justice* [2009] EWHC 2220 (Admin), [2009] H.R.L.R. 35 (QBD (Admin)), David Elvin Q.C.
applied: 2009 asp 8 s.2
s.3, amended: SI 2009/1182 Sch.5 para.8
s.7, enabling: SI 2009/489
s.9, see *R. (on the application of B) v Secretary of State for Justice* [2009] EWHC 2220 (Admin), [2009] H.R.L.R. 35 (QBD (Admin)), David Elvin Q.C.
s.24, enabling: SI 2009/489
s.25, amended: SI 2009/1182 Sch.5 para.8
s.27, amended: SI 2009/1182 Sch.5 para.8
Sch.1 para.1, amended: SI 2009/1182 Sch.5 para.8

8. Higher Education Act 2004
s.24, enabling: SI 2009/3113
s.44, referred to: SI 2009/2737 Reg.3
s.47, enabling: SI 2009/3113

10. Age-Related Payments Act 2004
s.2, amended: 2009 c.24 Sch.2 para.16
s.2, repealed (in part): 2009 c.24 Sch.7 Part 1
s.8, amended: 2009 c.24 Sch.7 Part 1

11. Gangmasters (Licensing) Act 2004
disapplied: SI 2009/307 r.7
s.3, amended: SI 2009/463 Sch.2 para.10, SSI 2009/85 Sch.2 para.11
s.8, enabling: SI 2009/307
s.25, enabling: SI 2009/307

12. Finance Act 2004
referred to: SI 2009/1171 Reg.2
Part 3 c.3, applied: 2009 c.10 Sch.55 para.1, Sch.55 para.11, Sch.55 para.12, Sch.55 para.27, Sch.56 para.18
Part 4, applied: 2009 asp 1 Sch.1 para.81, 2009 c.10 Sch.35 para.18, SI 2009/227 Sch.1
Part 4 c.4, applied: SI 2009/470 Reg.29
s.34, repealed (in part): 2009 c.4 Sch.3 Part 1
s.38, repealed: 2009 c.4 Sch.3 Part 1
s.39, repealed: 2009 c.4 Sch.3 Part 1
s.45, repealed (in part): 2009 c.4 Sch.3 Part 1
s.48, repealed: 2009 c.4 Sch.3 Part 1
s.54, repealed: 2009 c.4 Sch.3 Part 1
s.59, amended: SI 2009/56 Sch.1 para.420
s.62, applied: 2009 c.10 Sch.56 para.1
s.67, amended: SI 2009/56 Sch.1 para.421
s.67, repealed (in part): SI 2009/56 Sch.1 para.421
s.70, applied: 2009 c.10 Sch.55 para.1
s.71, applied: 2009 c.4 s.1303
s.71, repealed (in part): 2009 c.4 Sch.3 Part 1
s.71, enabling: SI 2009/2030
s.83, amended: 2009 c.4 Sch.1 para.571

2004– cont.

12. Finance Act 2004–*cont.*
s.114, amended: SI 2009/56 Sch.1 para.422
s.131, amended: 2009 c.4 Sch.1 para.572
s.131, repealed: 2009 c.10 Sch.24 para.8
s.132, repealed: 2009 c.10 Sch.24 para.8
s.133, repealed: 2009 c.10 Sch.24 para.8
s.135, repealed: 2009 c.10 Sch.25 para.9
s.137, repealed (in part): 2009 c.4 Sch.3 Part 1
s.141, repealed: 2009 c.4 Sch.3 Part 1
s.156, amended: SI 2009/56 Sch.1 para.423
s.156, repealed (in part): SI 2009/56 Sch.1 para.423
s.159, amended: SI 2009/56 Sch.1 para.424
s.159, repealed (in part): SI 2009/56 Sch.1 para.424
s.164, applied: SI 2009/1171 Reg.3, Reg.4, Reg.5
s.164, repealed (in part): 2009 c.10 s.75
s.164, enabling: SI 2009/1171
s.165, applied: SI 2009/1171 Reg.2
s.166, applied: SI 2009/1171 Reg.2
s.166, referred to: 2009 c.10 Sch.35 para.15
s.168, applied: 2009 asp 1 Sch.3 para.14
s.169, applied: 2009 asp 1 Sch.1 para.75
s.169, referred to: 2009 asp 1 Sch.1 para.81
s.170, amended: SI 2009/56 Sch.1 para.425
s.170, repealed (in part): SI 2009/56 Sch.1 para.425
s.188, applied: SI 2009/1555 Sch.4 para.4, Sch.4 para.5, SI 2009/2158 Reg.9, Reg.10, SI 2009/2737 Sch.5 para.4, Sch.5 para.5, Sch.6 para.3, Sch.6 para.4, SI 2009/3359 Sch.2 para.3, Sch.2 para.4
s.188, referred to: SI 2009/1171 Reg.7
s.192, amended: 2009 c.10 Sch.2 para.11
s.193, applied: 2009 c.10 Sch.35 para.2
s.193, referred to: 2009 c.10 Sch.35 para.2
s.194, referred to: 2009 c.10 Sch.35 para.2
s.196, amended: 2009 c.4 Sch.1 para.573
s.196, applied: 2009 c.4 s.1221
s.196A, amended: 2009 c.4 Sch.1 para.574
s.196A, referred to: 2009 c.4 s.1247
s.197, amended: 2009 c.4 Sch.1 para.575
s.199, referred to: 2009 c.4 s.868
s.199A, amended: 2009 c.4 Sch.1 para.576
s.200, amended: 2009 c.4 Sch.1 para.577
s.200, applied: 2009 c.4 s.1247
s.205, applied: 2009 asp 1 Sch.1 para.99, 2009 c.10 Sch.35 para.18
s.205, referred to: 2009 c.10 Sch.35 para.18
s.208, amended: 2009 c.10 Sch.2 para.12
s.209, amended: 2009 c.10 Sch.2 para.13
s.212, applied: 2009 asp 1 Sch.1 para.45
s.214, applied: 2009 asp 1 Sch.1 para.89
s.215, amended: 2009 c.10 Sch.2 para.14
s.217, applied: 2009 asp 1 Sch.1 para.97, Sch.1 para.98
s.227, amended: 2009 c.10 Sch.2 para.15
s.227, applied: 2009 asp 1 Sch.1 para.89
s.228, referred to: 2009 c.10 Sch.35 para.1
s.229, applied: 2009 c.10 Sch.35 para.1, Sch.35 para.3, Sch.35 para.4
s.230, applied: 2009 c.10 Sch.35 para.3
s.230, varied: 2009 c.10 Sch.35 para.5, SI 2009/2031 Art.5
s.231, applied: 2009 c.10 Sch.35 para.3
s.231, varied: 2009 c.10 Sch.35 para.5
s.232, applied: 2009 c.10 Sch.35 para.3
s.232, varied: 2009 c.10 Sch.35 para.5
s.233, applied: 2009 c.10 Sch.35 para.3, Sch.35 para.16
s.233, referred to: SI 2009/2031 Art.5

2004– cont.

12. Finance Act 2004– *cont.*
s.233, varied: 2009 c.l0 Sch.35 para.5, SI 2009/2031 Art.5
s.234, applied: 2009 c.l0 Sch.35 para.3
s.234, varied: 2009 c.l0 Sch.35 para.5, SI 2009/2031 Art.5
s.235, applied: 2009 c.l0 Sch.35 para.3
s.235, varied: 2009 c.l0 Sch.35 para.5
s.236, applied: 2009 c.l0 Sch.35 para.3
s.236, varied: 2009 c.l0 Sch.35 para.5, Sch.35 para.6
s.237, applied: 2009 c.l0 Sch.35 para.3, SI 2009/2031 Art.5
s.237, varied: 2009 c.l0 Sch.35 para.5
s.239, referred to: 2009 asp 1 Sch.1 para.101
s.240, amended: 2009 c.l0 Sch.2 para.16
s.242, amended: 2009 c.l0 Sch.2 para.17
s.242, referred to: 2009 asp 1 Sch.1 para.101
s.246, amended: 2009 c.4 Sch.1 para.578
s.246, applied: 2009 c.4 s.868, s.1247
s.246, referred to: 2009 c.4 s.865
s.246A, amended: 2009 c.4 Sch.1 para.579
s.252, applied: SI 2009/3054 Art.8
s.252, repealed: SI 2009/3054 Sch.1 para.13
s.253, amended: SI 2009/56 Sch.1 para.426
s.253, applied: SI 2009/3054 Art.8
s.253, repealed (in part): SI 2009/56 Sch.1 para.426, SI 2009/3054 Sch.1 para.13
s.254, applied: 2009 c.l0 Sch.55 para.1, Sch.56 para.1
s.254, referred to: 2009 c.l0 Sch.56 para.1
s.259, applied: SI 2009/3054 Art.8
s.259, repealed: SI 2009/3054 Sch.1 para.13
s.269, amended: SI 2009/56 Sch.1 para.427
s.269, repealed (in part): SI 2009/56 Sch.1 para.427
s.271, amended: SI 2009/56 Sch.1 para.428
s.271, repealed (in part): SI 2009/56 Sch.1 para.428
s.280, amended: 2009 c.4 Sch.1 para.580, Sch.3 Part 1
s.281, repealed (in part): 2009 c.l0 s.75
s.282, amended: 2009 c.l0 s.75, Sch.2 para.18
s.282, enabling: SI 2009/3055
s.283, repealed (in part): 2009 c.l0 s.75
s.283, enabling: SI 2009/1172, SI 2009/1989
s.306, enabling: SI 2009/2033
s.306A, amended: SI 2009/56 Sch.1 para.429
s.306A, applied: SI 2009/275 Art.3
s.308, see *Revenue and Customs Commissioners v Mercury Tax Group Ltd* [2009] S.T.C. (S.C.D.) 307 (Sp Comm), John F Avery Jones
s.308, applied: SI 2009/2033 Reg.3
s.308A, amended: SI 2009/56 Sch.1 para.430
s.308A, applied: SI 2009/275 Art.3, SI 2009/2033 Reg.3
s.309, applied: SI 2009/2033 Reg.3
s.310, applied: SI 2009/2033 Reg.3
s.311, applied: SI 2009/611 Reg.1, SI 2009/612 Reg.1
s.312, applied: SI 2009/611 Reg.1, SI 2009/612 Reg.1
s.312, enabling: SI 2009/611
s.312A, applied: SI 2009/611 Reg.1, SI 2009/612 Reg.1
s.312A, enabling: SI 2009/611
s.313, amended: SI 2009/571 Sch.1 para.36
s.313, applied: SI 2009/611 Reg.1
s.313, enabling: SI 2009/611
s.313B, amended: SI 2009/56 Sch.1 para.431
s.313B, applied: SI 2009/275 Art.3
s.314A, amended: SI 2009/56 Sch.1 para.432
s.314A, applied: SI 2009/275 Art.3
s.317, enabling: SI 2009/2033
s.317A, repealed: SI 2009/56 Sch.1 para.433

2004– cont.

12. Finance Act 2004– *cont.*
s.318, amended: SI 2009/56 Sch.1 para.434
s.320, see *Heidelberg Graphic Equipment Ltd v Revenue and Customs Commissioners* [2009] EWHC 870 (Ch), [2009] S.T.C. 2334 (Ch D), Henderson, J.; see *Test Claimants in the FII Group Litigation v Revenue and Customs Commissioners* [2008] EWHC 2893 (Ch), [2009] S.T.C. 254 (Ch D), Henderson, J.
Sch.5 para.2, repealed: 2009 c.4 Sch.3 Part 1
Sch.5 para.5, repealed: 2009 c.4 Sch.3 Part 1
Sch.5 para.6, repealed: 2009 c.4 Sch.3 Part 1
Sch.5 para.7, repealed: 2009 c.4 Sch.3 Part 1
Sch.5 para.8, repealed: 2009 c.4 Sch.3 Part 1
Sch.5 para.14, repealed: 2009 c.4 Sch.3 Part 1
Sch.5 para.15, repealed: 2009 c.4 Sch.3 Part 1
Sch.5 para.16, repealed: 2009 c.4 Sch.3 Part 1
Sch.6 para.1, repealed: 2009 c.4 Sch.3 Part 1
Sch.6 para.9, repealed: 2009 c.4 Sch.3 Part 1
Sch.8 para.1, repealed: 2009 c.4 Sch.3 Part 1
Sch.8 para.2, repealed: 2009 c.4 Sch.3 Part 1
Sch.8 para.3, repealed: 2009 c.4 Sch.3 Part 1
Sch.8 para.4, repealed: 2009 c.4 Sch.3 Part 1
Sch.8 para.5, repealed: 2009 c.4 Sch.3 Part 1
Sch.8 para.6, repealed: 2009 c.4 Sch.3 Part 1
Sch.8 para.7, repealed: 2009 c.4 Sch.3 Part 1
Sch.9 para.1, repealed: 2009 c.4 Sch.3 Part 1
Sch.9 para.2, repealed: 2009 c.4 Sch.3 Part 1
Sch.9 para.3, repealed: 2009 c.4 Sch.3 Part 1
Sch.9 para.4, repealed: 2009 c.4 Sch.3 Part 1
Sch.9 para.5, repealed: 2009 c.4 Sch.3 Part 1
Sch.10 Part 1 para.1, repealed: 2009 c.4 Sch.3 Part 1
Sch.10 Part 1 para.2, repealed: 2009 c.4 Sch.3 Part 1
Sch.10 Part 1 para.3, repealed: 2009 c.4 Sch.3 Part 1
Sch.10 Part 1 para.4, repealed: 2009 c.4 Sch.3 Part 1
Sch.10 Part 1 para.6, repealed: 2009 c.4 Sch.3 Part 1
Sch.10 Part 1 para.8, repealed: 2009 c.4 Sch.3 Part 1
Sch.10 Part 1 para.9, repealed (in part): 2009 c.4 Sch.3 Part 1
Sch.10 Part 1 para.13, repealed: 2009 c.4 Sch.3 Part 1
Sch.10 Part 1 para.14, repealed: 2009 c.4 Sch.3 Part 1
Sch.10 Part 1 para.16, repealed: 2009 c.4 Sch.3 Part 1
Sch.10 Part 1 para.17, repealed: 2009 c.4 Sch.3 Part 1
Sch.10 Part 1 para.19, repealed: 2009 c.4 Sch.3 Part 1
Sch.10 Part 1 para.20, repealed: 2009 c.4 Sch.3 Part 1
Sch.10 Part 1 para.21, repealed: 2009 c.4 Sch.3 Part 1
Sch.10 Part 1 para.22, repealed: 2009 c.4 Sch.3 Part 1
Sch.10 Part 1 para.23, repealed: 2009 c.4 Sch.3 Part 1
Sch.10 Part 1 para.25, repealed: 2009 c.4 Sch.3 Part 1
Sch.10 Part 1 para.28, repealed: 2009 c.4 Sch.3 Part 1
Sch.10 Part 1 para.30, repealed: 2009 c.4 Sch.3 Part 1
Sch.10 Part 1 para.31, repealed: 2009 c.4 Sch.3 Part 1
Sch.10 Part 1 para.32, repealed: 2009 c.4 Sch.3 Part 1
Sch.10 Part 1 para.33, repealed: 2009 c.4 Sch.3 Part 1
Sch.10 Part 1 para.34, repealed: 2009 c.4 Sch.3 Part 1
Sch.10 Part 1 para.35, repealed: 2009 c.4 Sch.3 Part 1
Sch.10 Part 1 para.36, repealed: 2009 c.4 Sch.3 Part 1
Sch.10 Part 1 para.37, repealed: 2009 c.4 Sch.3 Part 1
Sch.10 Part 1 para.38, repealed: 2009 c.4 Sch.3 Part 1
Sch.10 Part 1 para.39, repealed: 2009 c.4 Sch.3 Part 1
Sch.10 Part 1 para.40, repealed: 2009 c.4 Sch.3 Part 1
Sch.10 Part 1 para.41, repealed: 2009 c.4 Sch.3 Part 1
Sch.10 Part 1 para.42, repealed: 2009 c.4 Sch.3 Part 1
Sch.10 Part 2 para.47, repealed: 2009 c.4 Sch.3 Part 1
Sch.10 Part 2 para.48, repealed: 2009 c.4 Sch.3 Part 1
Sch.10 Part 2 para.49, repealed: 2009 c.4 Sch.3 Part 1
Sch.10 Part 2 para.50, repealed: 2009 c.4 Sch.3 Part 1
Sch.10 Part 2 para.51, repealed: 2009 c.4 Sch.3 Part 1

2004–cont.

12. Finance Act 2004–*cont.*

Sch.10 Part 2 para.52, repealed: 2009 c.4 Sch.3 Part 1
Sch.10 Part 2 para.53, repealed: 2009 c.4 Sch.3 Part 1
Sch.10 Part 2 para.54, repealed: 2009 c.4 Sch.3 Part 1
Sch.10 Part 2 para.55, repealed: 2009 c.4 Sch.3 Part 1
Sch.10 Part 2 para.56, repealed: 2009 c.4 Sch.3 Part 1
Sch.10 Part 2 para.57, repealed: 2009 c.4 Sch.3 Part 1
Sch.10 Part 2 para.58, repealed: 2009 c.4 Sch.3 Part 1
Sch.10 Part 2 para.59, repealed: 2009 c.4 Sch.3 Part 1
Sch.10 Part 2 para.60, repealed: 2009 c.4 Sch.3 Part 1
Sch.10 Part 2 para.61, repealed: 2009 c.4 Sch.3 Part 1
Sch.10 Part 2 para.62, repealed: 2009 c.4 Sch.3 Part 1
Sch.10 Part 2 para.63, repealed: 2009 c.4 Sch.3 Part 1
Sch.10 Part 2 para.64, repealed: 2009 c.4 Sch.3 Part 1
Sch.10 Part 2 para.65, repealed: 2009 c.4 Sch.3 Part 1
Sch.10 Part 2 para.66, repealed: 2009 c.4 Sch.3 Part 1
Sch.10 Part 2 para.67, repealed: 2009 c.4 Sch.3 Part 1
Sch.10 Part 2 para.68, repealed: 2009 c.4 Sch.3 Part 1
Sch.10 Part 2 para.69, repealed: 2009 c.4 Sch.3 Part 1
Sch.10 Part 3 para.71, repealed: 2009 c.4 Sch.3 Part 1
Sch.10 Part 3 para.73, repealed: 2009 c.4 Sch.3 Part 1
Sch.11 Part 4 para.14A, added: SI 2009/1890 Art.6
Sch.16 para.5, repealed: 2009 c.4 Sch.3 Part 1
Sch.17 para.4, repealed: 2009 c.4 Sch.3 Part 1
Sch.17 para.7, repealed: 2009 c.4 Sch.3 Part 1
Sch.17 para.8, repealed: 2009 c.4 Sch.3 Part 1
Sch.18 Part 2 para.13, repealed (in part): 2009 c.10 Sch.8 para.10
Sch.21 para.1, repealed: SI 2009/2035 Sch.1 para.60
Sch.26 para.1, amended: 2009 c.4 Sch.1 para.581
Sch.26 para.1, repealed (in part): SI 2009/3001 Sch.2
Sch.26 para.2, amended: 2009 c.4 Sch.1 para.581
Sch.26 para.2, repealed (in part): SI 2009/3001 Sch.2
Sch.26 para.4, repealed: SI 2009/3001 Sch.2
Sch.26 para.5, repealed: SI 2009/3001 Sch.2
Sch.26 para.6, repealed: SI 2009/3001 Sch.2
Sch.26 para.7, repealed: SI 2009/3001 Sch.2
Sch.26 para.8, repealed: SI 2009/3001 Sch.2
Sch.26 para.9, repealed: SI 2009/3001 Sch.2
Sch.26 para.12, repealed: 2009 c.4 Sch.3 Part 1
Sch.26 para.13, repealed: SI 2009/3001 Sch.2
Sch.26 para.14, repealed: SI 2009/3001 Sch.2
Sch.26 para.15, repealed: SI 2009/3001 Sch.2
Sch.26 para.16, repealed: SI 2009/3001 Sch.2
Sch.28 Part 1 para.2, enabling: SI 2009/1311
Sch.28 Part 1 para.3, repealed (in part): 2009 c.10 s.75
Sch.28 Part 1 para.8, applied: SI 2009/1171 Reg.9
Sch.28 Part 2 para.17, repealed (in part): 2009 c.10 s.75
Sch.29 Part 1, applied: 2009 asp 1 Sch.1 para.42, Sch.1 para.45, Sch.1 para.55, Sch.1 para.72, Sch.1 para.91
Sch.29 Part 1 para.2, applied: 2009 asp 1 Sch.1 para.43
Sch.29 Part 1 para.7, applied: SI 2009/1171 Reg.10
Sch.29 Part 2, applied: 2009 asp 1 Sch.1 para.61, Sch.1 para.65, Sch.1 para.67, Sch.1 para.70
Sch.29A Part 2 para.9, repealed (in part): 2009 c.10 s.75
Sch.33, applied: 2009 c.10 Sch.35 para.16
Sch.33, referred to: SI 2009/2031 Art.5
Sch.33 para.6, amended: SI 2009/56 Sch.1 para.435
Sch.33 para.6, repealed (in part): SI 2009/56 Sch.1 para.435
Sch.34 para.7, enabling: SI 2009/2047
Sch.34 para.12, enabling: SI 2009/2047
Sch.34 para.15, applied: SI 2009/2047 Reg.1
Sch.34 para.19, enabling: SI 2009/2047

2004–cont.

12. Finance Act 2004–*cont.*

Sch.35 para.12, repealed: 2009 c.10 Sch.1 para.6
Sch.35 para.45, repealed: 2009 c.4 Sch.3 Part 1
Sch.35 para.49, repealed: 2009 c.10 s.126
Sch.35 para.50, repealed: 2009 c.4 Sch.3 Part 1
Sch.35 para.52, repealed: 2009 c.4 Sch.3 Part 1
Sch.35 para.53, repealed: 2009 c.4 Sch.3 Part 1
Sch.35 para.65, repealed (in part): 2009 c.10 s.126
Sch.36 Part 1 para.3, applied: 2009 asp 1 Sch.3 para.23
Sch.36 Part 1 para.3, enabling: SI 2009/3055
Sch.36 Part 2 para.12, referred to: SI 2009/1171 Reg.12
Sch.36 Part 3 para.22, applied: 2009 asp 1 Sch.3 para.12
Sch.36 Part 3 para.36, applied: 2009 asp 1 Sch.3 para.14
Sch.36 Part 4 para.49, amended: 2009 c.10 Sch.35 para.22
Sch.36 Part 4 para.51, applied: 2009 c.10 Sch.35 para.2, Sch.35 para.16
Sch.36 Part 4 para.51, referred to: SI 2009/2031 Art.5
Sch.36 Part 4 para.51, varied: SI 2009/2031 Art.5

17. Health Protection Agency Act 2004

referred to: 2009 c.21 s.40
s.3, applied: SI 2009/1348 Sch.2 para.4
s.10, applied: SI 2009/462 Sch.3 para.2
s.10, substituted: SI 2009/462 Art.13
s.10, varied: SI 2009/462 Sch.3 para.2
Sch.1 para.1, amended: 2009 c.21 Sch.3 para.5
Sch.1 para.29, amended: 2009 c.21 Sch.3 para.6

18. Traffic Management Act 2004

Commencement Orders: SI 2009/1095 Art.2
s.33, applied: SI 2009/1267 Reg.3, Reg.4, Reg.33
s.34, applied: SI 2009/1267 Reg.17, Reg.33, Reg.35
s.34, enabling: SI 2009/3141, SI 2009/3142, SI 2009/3148, SI 2009/3149, SI 2009/3158, SI 2009/3162, SI 2009/3163, SI 2009/3178, SI 2009/3179, SI 2009/3180, SI 2009/3186
s.36, applied: SI 2009/1267 Reg.17
s.37, applied: SI 2009/1267 Part 6, Reg.30
s.37, enabling: SI 2009/1267
s.39, enabling: SI 2009/1267, SI 2009/3141, SI 2009/3142, SI 2009/3148, SI 2009/3149, SI 2009/3158, SI 2009/3162, SI 2009/3163, SI 2009/3178, SI 2009/3179, SI 2009/3180, SI 2009/3186
s.72, enabling: SI 2009/478
s.73, enabling: SI 2009/478
s.78, enabling: SI 2009/478
s.79, enabling: SI 2009/478
s.89, enabling: SI 2009/478, SI 2009/715
s.99, enabling: SI 2009/1095
Sch.7, applied: SI 2009/1300 Art.50, SI 2009/2364 Art.34
Sch.8 Part 2 para.8, applied: SI 2009/19, SI 2009/24, SI 2009/305, SI 2009/306, SI 2009/326, SI 2009/439, SI 2009/464, SI 2009/596, SI 2009/715, SI 2009/3298
Sch.8 Part 2 para.8, enabling: SI 2009/19, SI 2009/24, SI 2009/305, SI 2009/306, SI 2009/326, SI 2009/439, SI 2009/464, SI 2009/596, SI 2009/715, SI 2009/3298
Sch.10 para.3, applied: SI 2009/19, SI 2009/24, SI 2009/305, SI 2009/306, SI 2009/326, SI 2009/439, SI 2009/464, SI 2009/596, SI 2009/715, SI 2009/3298

2004– cont.

18. Traffic Management Act 2004–*cont.*
Sch.10 para.3, enabling: SI 2009/19, SI 2009/24, SI 2009/305, SI 2009/306, SI 2009/326, SI 2009/439, SI 2009/464, SI 2009/596, SI 2009/715, SI 2009/3298

19. Asylum and Immigration (Treatment of Claimants, etc.) Act 2004
s.4, amended: 2009 c.11 s.54
s.4, referred to: SI 2009/37 Sch.1 para.2, Sch.1 para.4
s.8, see *JT (Cameroon) v Secretary of State for the Home Department* [2008] EWCA Civ 878, [2009] 1 W.L.R. 1411 (CA (Civ Div)), Pill, L.J.
s.19, applied: SI 2009/421 Reg.20
s.19, see *R. (on the application of Baiai) v Secretary of State for the Home Department* [2008] UKHL 53, [2009] 1 A.C. 287 (HL), Lord Bingham of Cornhill
s.21, applied: SI 2009/421 Reg.20
s.23, applied: SI 2009/421 Reg.20
s.42, applied: SI 2009/816
Sch.3 para.3, see *R. (on the application of Nasseri) v Secretary of State for the Home Department* [2009] UKHL 23, [2009] 2 W.L.R. 1190 (HL), Lord Hope of Craighead
Sch.3 para.4, see *R. (on the application of AM (Somalia)) v Secretary of State for the Home Department* [2009] EWCA Civ 114, [2009] Imm. A.R. 534 (CA (Civ Div)), Sedley, L.J.
Sch.3 para.5, see *R. (on the application of AM (Somalia)) v Secretary of State for the Home Department* [2009] EWCA Civ 114, [2009] Imm. A.R. 534 (CA (Civ Div)), Sedley, L.J.

20. Energy Act 2004
Commencement Orders: SI 2009/1269 Art.2, Art.3
s.27, amended: 2009 c.4 Sch.1 para.583
s.28, amended: 2009 c.4 Sch.1 para.584
s.37, amended: SI 2009/1941 Sch.1 para.220
s.44, amended: 2009 c.4 Sch.1 para.585
s.50, amended: SI 2009/1941 Sch.1 para.220
s.55, amended: 2009 c.26 Sch.7 para.11
s.82, referred to: 2009 c.19 s.2
s.84, amended: 2009 c.23 Sch.4 para.4
s.84, applied: SSI 2009/140 Art.5
s.84, referred to: SI 2009/153 Reg.31
s.85, applied: SI 2009/1743 Art.3
s.85, enabling: SI 2009/1739
s.87, enabling: SI 2009/1743
s.95, applied: 2009 c.23 s.12, s.13
s.95, varied: 2009 c.23 s.13
s.124, applied: SI 2009/843
s.124, enabling: SI 2009/843
s.126, enabling: SI 2009/843
s.132, enabling: SI 2009/843
s.171, amended: SI 2009/1941 Sch.1 para.220
s.173, applied: SI 2009/648 Art.3
s.173, referred to: SI 2009/648 Art.4
s.173, enabling: SI 2009/648
s.192, applied: SI 2009/843
s.192, enabling: SI 2009/843, SI 2009/1739, SI 2009/1743
s.196, amended: SI 2009/1941 Sch.1 para.220
s.198, enabling: SI 2009/1269
Sch.6 para.1, amended: SI 2009/1941 Sch.1 para.220
Sch.6 para.2, amended: SI 2009/1941 Sch.1 para.220
Sch.6 para.6, amended: SI 2009/1941 Sch.1 para.220
Sch.6 para.7, amended: SI 2009/1941 Sch.1 para.220
Sch.7 para.1, amended: SI 2009/1941 Sch.1 para.220
Sch.8 Part 1 para.1, amended: SI 2009/1941 Sch.1 para.220

2004– cont.

20. Energy Act 2004–*cont.*
Sch.9 Part 1 para.11, amended: 2009 c.4 Sch.1 para.586
Sch.9 Part 1 para.12, amended: 2009 c.4 Sch.1 para.586
Sch.9 Part 1 para.15, amended: 2009 c.4 Sch.1 para.586
Sch.9 Part 2 para.23, amended: 2009 c.4 Sch.1 para.586
Sch.9 Part 2 para.24, amended: 2009 c.4 Sch.1 para.586
Sch.9 Part 2 para.27, amended: 2009 c.4 Sch.1 para.586
Sch.9 Part 4 para.33, amended: 2009 c.4 Sch.1 para.586
Sch.16 para.1, varied: 2009 c.23 s.13
Sch.16 para.2, varied: 2009 c.23 s.13
Sch.16 para.3, disapplied: 2009 c.23 s.13
Sch.16 para.3, varied: 2009 c.23 s.13
Sch.16 para.4, disapplied: 2009 c.23 s.13
Sch.16 para.4, varied: 2009 c.23 s.13
Sch.16 para.5, varied: 2009 c.23 s.13
Sch.16 para.6, disapplied: 2009 c.23 s.13
Sch.16 para.6, varied: 2009 c.23 s.13
Sch.16 para.7, varied: 2009 c.23 s.13
Sch.16 para.8, varied: 2009 c.23 s.13
Sch.16 para.9, varied: 2009 c.23 s.13
Sch.20 Part 1 para.1, amended: SI 2009/1941 Sch.1 para.220
Sch.20 Part 3 para.33, amended: SI 2009/1941 Sch.1 para.220
Sch.20 Part 3 para.34, amended: SI 2009/1941 Sch.1 para.220
Sch.20 Part 3 para.35, amended: SI 2009/1941 Sch.1 para.220
Sch.20 Part 3 para.36, amended: SI 2009/1941 Sch.1 para.220
Sch.20 Part 3 para.37, amended: SI 2009/1941 Sch.1 para.220
Sch.20 Part 3 para.38, amended: SI 2009/1941 Sch.1 para.220
Sch.20 Part 3 para.39, amended: SI 2009/1941 Sch.1 para.220
Sch.20 Part 3 para.40, amended: SI 2009/1941 Sch.1 para.220

21. Fire and Rescue Services Act 2004
applied: SI 2009/2325 Art.22, SI 2009/3015 Art.105
s.2, amended: 2009 c.20 Sch.7 Part 4
s.2, applied: SI 2009/1360 Art.2, SI 2009/2393 Art.1
s.4, amended: 2009 c.20 Sch.7 Part 4
s.4, applied: SI 2009/1360 Art.2, SI 2009/2393 Art.1, SI 2009/2849
s.4, enabling: SI 2009/2849
s.24, amended: 2009 c.2 Sch.1 para.33
s.28, applied: SI 2009/1179 Art.2
s.28, enabling: SI 2009/1179
s.34, applied: SI 2009/1225
s.34, enabling: SI 2009/1225
s.60, enabling: SI 2009/1225, SI 2009/2849
s.62, enabling: SI 2009/1225, SI 2009/2849
Sch.1 para.69, repealed: SI 2009/818 Reg.4

22. Sustainable and Secure Buildings Act 2004
s.6, applied: SI 2009/3019 Art.2

23. Public Audit (Wales) Act 2004
s.13, applied: 2009 c.2 s.23, s.25
s.16, applied: 2009 c.2 s.46
s.20, applied: 2009 c.2 s.27

23. Public Audit (Wales) Act 2004–*cont.*
s.21, varied: 2009 c.2 s.27
s.41, amended: 2009 c.2 Sch.1 para.35
s.41, applied: 2009 c.2 s.23
s.54, amended: 2009 c.2 Sch.1 para.36
Sch.2 para.40, repealed: 2009 c.22 Sch.16 Part 9

25. Horserace Betting and Olympic Lottery Act 2004
s.2, amended: SI 2009/1941 Sch.1 para.221
s.5, amended: SI 2009/1941 Sch.1 para.221

27. Companies (Audit, Investigations and Community Enterprise) Act 2004
Part 2, disapplied: SI 2009/2437 Reg.18
s.16, amended: SI 2009/1941 Sch.1 para.222
s.30, enabling: SI 2009/1942
s.31, enabling: SI 2009/1942
s.32, amended: SI 2009/1941 Sch.1 para.223
s.32, repealed (in part): SI 2009/1941 Sch.1 para.223
s.32, enabling: SI 2009/1942
s.33, amended: SI 2009/1941 Sch.1 para.224
s.33, repealed (in part): SI 2009/1941 Sch.1 para.224, Sch.2
s.34, applied: SI 2009/1803 Reg.6
s.35, amended: SI 2009/1941 Sch.1 para.225
s.35, enabling: SI 2009/1942
s.36, substituted: SI 2009/1941 Sch.1 para.226
s.37, applied: SI 2009/1803 Reg.6
s.37, substituted: SI 2009/1941 Sch.1 para.227
s.37, enabling: SI 2009/1942
s.38, substituted: SI 2009/1941 Sch.1 para.227
s.39, amended: SI 2009/1941 Sch.1 para.228
s.40, amended: SI 2009/1941 Sch.1 para.229
s.40, repealed (in part): SI 2009/1942 Reg.2
s.40, enabling: SI 2009/1942
s.40A, amended: SI 2009/1941 Sch.1 para.230
s.45, amended: SI 2009/1941 Sch.1 para.231
s.46, amended: SI 2009/1941 Sch.1 para.232
s.49, amended: SI 2009/1941 Sch.1 para.233
s.51, amended: SI 2009/1941 Sch.1 para.234
s.52, amended: SI 2009/1941 Sch.1 para.235
s.53, amended: SI 2009/1941 Sch.1 para.236
s.54, substituted: SI 2009/1941 Sch.1 para.237
s.55, substituted: SI 2009/1941 Sch.1 para.237
s.56, enabling: SI 2009/1942
s.57, enabling: SI 2009/1942
s.58, repealed: SI 2009/1941 Sch.1 para.238
s.59, enabling: SI 2009/1942
s.60, amended: SI 2009/1941 Sch.1 para.239
s.62, amended: SI 2009/1941 Sch.1 para.240
s.62, applied: SI 2009/1942
s.62, enabling: SI 2009/1942
s.63, amended: SI 2009/1941 Sch.1 para.241
s.63, repealed (in part): SI 2009/1941 Sch.1 para.241
Sch.6 para.10, repealed: SI 2009/1941 Sch.2

28. Domestic Violence, Crime and Victims Act 2004
Commencement Orders: 2009 c.25 s.142, 2009 c.25 Sch.23 Part 5; SI 2009/2501 Art.2; SI 2009/2616 Art.2
s.5, see *R. v Ikram (Abid)* [2008] EWCA Crim 586, [2009] 1 W.L.R. 1419 (CA (Crim Div)), Sir Igor Judge (President, QB); see *R. v Khan (Uzma)* [2009] EWCA Crim 2, [2009] 1 W.L.R. 2036 (CA (Crim Div)), Lord Judge, L.C.J.
s.5, applied: SI 2009/1059 Art.13
s.5, referred to: SI 2009/37 Sch.1 para.2, Sch.1 para.4

28. Domestic Violence, Crime and Victims Act 2004– *cont.*
s.6, see *R. v Ikram (Abid)* [2008] EWCA Crim 586, [2009] 1 W.L.R. 1419 (CA (Crim Div)), Sir Igor Judge (President, QB)
s.6, applied: SI 2009/2041 r.104
s.8, varied: SI 2009/1059 Sch.1 para.54
s.32, applied: SI 2009/1603 r.44
s.48, amended: 2009 c.25 s.142
s.48, repealed (in part): 2009 c.25 Sch.23 Part 5
s.49, amended: 2009 c.25 s.142
s.49, repealed (in part): 2009 c.25 Sch.23 Part 5
s.50, repealed (in part): 2009 c.25 Sch.23 Part 5
s.55, amended: 2009 c.25 s.142
s.60, enabling: SI 2009/2501, SI 2009/2616
Sch.8 para.1, repealed: 2009 c.25 Sch.23 Part 5
Sch.8 para.2, repealed: 2009 c.25 Sch.23 Part 5
Sch.8 para.3, repealed: 2009 c.25 Sch.23 Part 5
Sch.8 para.4, repealed: 2009 c.25 Sch.23 Part 5
Sch.8 para.5, repealed: 2009 c.25 Sch.23 Part 5
Sch.8 para.6, repealed: 2009 c.25 Sch.23 Part 5
Sch.8 para.7, repealed: 2009 c.25 Sch.23 Part 5
Sch.8 para.8, repealed: 2009 c.25 Sch.23 Part 5
Sch.8 para.9, repealed: 2009 c.25 Sch.23 Part 5
Sch.8 para.10, repealed: 2009 c.25 Sch.23 Part 5
Sch.8 para.11, repealed: 2009 c.25 Sch.23 Part 5
Sch.9 para.1WA, added: SI 2009/2748 Sch.1 para.7
Sch.9 para.1XA, repealed: SI 2009/2748 Sch.1 para.7
Sch.9 para.3A, repealed: SI 2009/2748 Sch.1 para.7
Sch.9 para.9, repealed: 2009 c.25 Sch.23 Part 5
Sch.10 para.26, repealed: 2009 c.25 Sch.23 Part 1
Sch.10 para.27, repealed: 2009 c.25 Sch.23 Part 1

30. Human Tissue Act 2004
referred to: 2009 c.21 s.40
s.1, amended: 2009 c.25 Sch.21 para.48
s.5, amended: 2009 c.25 Sch.21 para.49
s.39, varied: SI 2009/1059 Sch.1 para.55
s.43, amended: 2009 c.25 Sch.21 para.50
Sch.2 para.9A, added: 2009 c.21 Sch.3 para.7
Sch.2 para.9B, added: 2009 c.21 Sch.3 para.7
Sch.2 para.9C, added: 2009 c.21 Sch.3 para.7
Sch.4 Part 2 para.5, varied: SI 2009/1059 Sch.1 para.55
Sch.6 para.3, repealed: 2009 c.25 Sch.23 Part 1

31. Children Act 2004
s.9A, added: 2009 c.22 s.195
s.10, amended: 2009 c.22 s.193
s.10, applied: 2009 c.22 s.252
s.10, repealed (in part): 2009 c.22 s.193, Sch.16 Part 5
s.11, applied: 2009 c.22 s.252
s.12, applied: 2009 c.22 s.252, SI 2009/1554 Reg.8, SI 2009/1563 Reg.3
s.12A, added: 2009 c.22 s.194
s.12A, applied: 2009 c.22 s.248
s.12B, added: 2009 c.22 s.194
s.12C, added: 2009 c.22 s.194
s.12C, applied: 2009 c.22 s.252
s.12D, added: 2009 c.22 s.194
s.12D, applied: 2009 c.22 s.252
s.13, amended: 2009 c.22 s.196
s.14, amended: 2009 c.22 s.196
s.14A, added: 2009 c.22 s.197
s.17, substituted: 2009 c.22 s.194
s.17A, applied: 2009 c.22 s.252
s.18, amended: 2009 c.22 s.194
s.20, applied: SI 2009/1360 Art.3
s.23, amended: 2009 c.22 s.194

2004– cont.

31. Children Act 2004– *cont.*
s.50, amended: 2009 c.22 s.194
s.66, amended: 2009 c.22 s.194, s.195

32. Armed Forces (Pensions and Compensation) Act 2004
s.1, applied: SI 2009/262 Art.2
s.1, enabling: SI 2009/262, SI 2009/544, SI 2009/3236
s.3, applied: SI 2009/262 Art.2
s.3, enabling: SI 2009/262
s.10, enabling: SI 2009/544, SI 2009/3236

33. Civil Partnership Act 2004
Commencement Orders: SI 2009/1941 Sch.1 para.242, Sch.2
see *Ladele v Islington LBC* [2009] I.C.R. 387 (EAT), Elias, J (President)
applied: SI 2009/845 Art.3, Art.4
referred to: 2009 c.24 s.58
s.86, amended: SI 2009/1892 Sch.1 para.4
s.88, enabling: SSI 2009/64, SSI 2009/314
s.94, enabling: SSI 2009/314
s.95, enabling: SSI 2009/64, SSI 2009/314
s.126, applied: SSI 2009/64, SSI 2009/314
Sch.5 Part 1, applied: SI 2009/1555 Sch.4 para.1, SI 2009/2737 Sch.5 para.1, Sch.6 para.1, SI 2009/3359 Sch.2 para.1
Sch.5 Part 2 para.6, applied: SI 2009/2737 Sch.5 para.1, Sch.6 para.1
Sch.5 Part 2 para.7, applied: SI 2009/2737 Sch.5 para.1, Sch.6 para.1
Sch.5 Part 6, applied: SI 2009/1555 Sch.4 para.1, SI 2009/3359 Sch.2 para.1
Sch.5 Part 7, applied: SI 2009/1555 Sch.4 para.1, SI 2009/3359 Sch.2 para.1
Sch.22 para.11, repealed: SI 2009/1941 Sch.1 para.242
Sch.22 para.12, repealed: SI 2009/1941 Sch.1 para.242
Sch.22 para.13, repealed: SI 2009/1941 Sch.1 para.242
Sch.22 para.14, repealed: SI 2009/1941 Sch.1 para.242
Sch.22 para.15, repealed: SI 2009/1941 Sch.1 para.242
Sch.22 para.16, repealed: SI 2009/1941 Sch.1 para.242
Sch.22 para.18, repealed: SI 2009/1941 Sch.1 para.242
Sch.23 Part 1 para.1, applied: SI 2009/421 Reg.20
Sch.24 Part 3 para.35, repealed: 2009 c.24 Sch.7 Part 2
Sch.24 Part 3 para.42, repealed: 2009 c.24 Sch.7 Part 1
Sch.24 Part 3 para.43, repealed: 2009 c.24 Sch.7 Part 1
Sch.24 Part 3 para.44, repealed: 2009 c.24 Sch.7 Part 1
Sch.24 Part 7 para.118, repealed: 2009 c.24 Sch.7 Part 3
Sch.24 Part 7 para.120, repealed: 2009 c.24 Sch.7 Part 3
Sch.24 Part 7 para.121, repealed: 2009 c.24 Sch.7 Part 3
Sch.24 Part 7 para.123, repealed: 2009 c.24 Sch.7 Part 1
Sch.27 para.165, repealed: SI 2009/534 Reg.9
Sch.29 para.68, repealed: SI 2009/1941 Sch.2
Sch.29 para.69, repealed: SI 2009/1941 Sch.2
Sch.29 para.70, repealed: SI 2009/1941 Sch.2

2004– cont.

33. Civil Partnership Act 2004– *cont.*
Sch.29 para.71, repealed: SI 2009/1941 Sch.2
Sch.29 para.72, repealed: SI 2009/1941 Sch.2
Sch.29 para.73, repealed: SI 2009/1941 Sch.2
Sch.29 para.74, repealed: SI 2009/1941 Sch.2
Sch.29 para.75, repealed: SI 2009/1941 Sch.2

34. Housing Act 2004
s.42, amended: SI 2009/1307 Sch.1 para.272
s.50, amended: SI 2009/1307 Sch.1 para.273
s.143, amended: SI 2009/1307 Sch.1 para.274
s.163, enabling: SI 2009/34
s.181, amended: SI 2009/1307 Sch.1 para.275
s.231, amended: SI 2009/1307 Sch.1 para.276
s.231, repealed (in part): SI 2009/1307 Sch.1 para.276
s.234, enabling: SI 2009/724, SI 2009/1915
s.250, applied: SI 2009/34
s.250, enabling: SI 2009/34
s.255, amended: SI 2009/1307 Sch.1 para.277
Sch.1 Part 3 para.19, amended: SI 2009/1307 Sch.1 para.278
Sch.1 Part 3 para.20, amended: SI 2009/1307 Sch.1 para.278
Sch.2 Part 3 para.14, amended: SI 2009/1307 Sch.1 para.279
Sch.2 Part 3 para.15, amended: SI 2009/1307 Sch.1 para.279
Sch.3 Part 3 para.11, amended: SI 2009/1307 Sch.1 para.280
Sch.5 Part 3 para.35, amended: SI 2009/1307 Sch.1 para.281
Sch.6 Part 3 para.27, amended: SI 2009/1307 Sch.1 para.282
Sch.6 Part 3 para.31, amended: SI 2009/1307 Sch.1 para.282
Sch.7 Part 4 para.29, amended: SI 2009/1307 Sch.1 para.283
Sch.7 Part 4 para.33, amended: SI 2009/1307 Sch.1 para.283
Sch.14 para.4, applied: SI 2009/2298 Reg.2
Sch.14 para.4, enabling: SI 2009/2298

35. Pensions Act 2004
Commencement Orders: SI 2009/325 Art.2; SI 2009/1542 Art.2
see *Independent Trustee Services Ltd v Hope* [2009] EWHC 2810 (Ch), [2009] Pens. L.R. 379 (Ch D), Henderson, J.
applied: SI 2009/1552
varied: SI 2009/317 Sch.1
Part 2, applied: 2009 c.10 s.73
s.13, applied: SI 2009/1888 Reg.2
s.14, applied: SI 2009/1888 Reg.2
s.17, applied: SI 2009/1888 Reg.2
s.38, applied: SI 2009/814 Art.5
s.38, enabling: SI 2009/1906
s.43, applied: SI 2009/814 Art.5
s.43, enabling: SI 2009/617
s.44, amended: SI 2009/1941 Sch.1 para.243
s.45, amended: SI 2009/1941 Sch.1 para.243
s.51, amended: SI 2009/1941 Sch.1 para.243
s.52, enabling: SI 2009/1906
s.57, amended: SI 2009/1941 Sch.1 para.243
s.69, enabling: SI 2009/617
s.72, applied: SI 2009/1888 Reg.2
s.87, amended: SI 2009/1941 Sch.1 para.243
s.91, enabling: SI 2009/1565, SI 2009/3068
s.101, applied: SI 2009/1888 Reg.2
s.121, amended: SI 2009/1941 Sch.1 para.243

2004– cont.

35. Pensions Act 2004– *cont.*
s.126, enabling: SI 2009/1906
s.129, enabling: SI 2009/451
s.130, enabling: SI 2009/451
s.134, enabling: SI 2009/1552
s.138, enabling: SI 2009/451
s.143, enabling: SI 2009/451
s.151, enabling: SI 2009/451
s.156, enabling: SI 2009/451
s.163, enabling: SI 2009/451
s.166, enabling: SI 2009/451
s.168, enabling: SI 2009/1851
s.177, applied: SI 2009/794 Art.2
s.178, applied: SI 2009/200, SI 2009/200 Art.2, SI 2009/794
s.178, enabling: SI 2009/200, SI 2009/794
s.179, enabling: SI 2009/451
s.182, referred to: 2009 c.10 s.73
s.182, enabling: SI 2009/1906
s.190, enabling: SI 2009/792, SI 2009/1851
s.201, amended: SI 2009/1941 Sch.1 para.243
s.221, enabling: SI 2009/1906
s.232, enabling: SI 2009/615
s.241, applied: 2009 asp 1 Sch.1 para.13
s.241, enabling: SI 2009/1906
s.242, enabling: SI 2009/615
s.243, amended: SI 2009/1941 Sch.1 para.243
s.243, enabling: SI 2009/615
s.248, amended: SI 2009/1941 Sch.1 para.243
s.249A, amended: SI 2009/1682 Sch.1 para.2
s.257, applied: SI 2009/814 Art.4
s.257, varied: SI 2009/3226 Art.12
s.258, applied: SI 2009/814 Art.4
s.258, varied: SI 2009/3226 Art.12
s.286, applied: 2009 c.10 s.73
s.286, enabling: SI 2009/792, SI 2009/1851
s.306, amended: SI 2009/1941 Sch.1 para.243
s.314, enabling: SI 2009/615
s.315, enabling: SI 2009/325, SI 2009/451, SI 2009/615, SI 2009/617, SI 2009/792, SI 2009/794, SI 2009/795, SI 2009/1542, SI 2009/1583, SI 2009/1851, SI 2009/1906
s.316, applied: SI 2009/792, SI 2009/794, SI 2009/795, SI 2009/1851
s.317, applied: SI 2009/451, SI 2009/617, SI 2009/792, SI 2009/1851, SI 2009/1888, SI 2009/1906
s.318, enabling: SI 2009/451, SI 2009/615, SI 2009/617, SI 2009/792, SI 2009/1552, SI 2009/1851, SI 2009/1888, SI 2009/1906
s.322, enabling: SI 2009/325, SI 2009/1542, SI 2009/1583
Sch.1 Part 4 para.21, enabling: SI 2009/1888
Sch.3, amended: SI 2009/1941 Sch.1 para.243
Sch.3, repealed: SI 2009/1941 Sch.1 para.243
Sch.7, see *Independent Trustee Services Ltd v Hope* [2009] EWHC 2810 (Ch), [2009] Pens. L.R. 379 (Ch D), Henderson, J.
Sch.7 para.26, applied: SI 2009/795 Art.2
Sch.7 para.26, enabling: SI 2009/795
Sch.7 para.27, enabling: SI 2009/795
Sch.7 para.33, enabling: SI 2009/451
Sch.8, amended: SI 2009/1941 Sch.1 para.243
Sch.8, repealed: SI 2009/1941 Sch.1 para.243

36. Civil Contingencies Act 2004
s.2, applied: 2009 asp 6 s.28
Sch.1 Part 1 para.11A, repealed: 2009 c.23 Sch.22 Part 8

2004– cont.

37. Hunting Act 2004
s.1, see *DPP v Wright* [2009] EWHC 105 (Admin), [2009] 3 All E.R. 726 (DC), Sir Anthony May (President, QB)
Sch.1, see *DPP v Wright* [2009] EWHC 105 (Admin), [2009] 3 All E.R. 726 (DC), Sir Anthony May (President, QB)
Sch.1 para.1, see *DPP v Wright* [2009] EWHC 105 (Admin), [2009] 3 All E.R. 726 (DC), Sir Anthony May (President, QB)

2005

2. Prevention of Terrorism Act 2005
see *A v United Kingdom (3455/05)* (2009) 49 E.H.R.R. 29 (ECHR (Grand Chamber)), Judge Costa (President); see *Secretary of State for the Home Department v F* [2008] EWCA Civ 1148, [2009] 2 W.L.R. 423 (CA (Civ Div)), Sir Anthony Clarke, M.R.; see *Secretary of State for the Home Department v F* [2009] UKHL 28, [2009] 3 W.L.R. 74 (HL), Lord Phillips of Worth Matravers
s.1, varied: SI 2009/554 Art.2
s.2, varied: SI 2009/554 Art.2
s.3, varied: SI 2009/554 Art.2
s.4, varied: SI 2009/554 Art.2
s.5, varied: SI 2009/554 Art.2
s.6, varied: SI 2009/554 Art.2
s.7, varied: SI 2009/554 Art.2
s.7A, varied: SI 2009/554 Art.2
s.7B, varied: SI 2009/554 Art.2
s.7C, varied: SI 2009/554 Art.2
s.8, varied: SI 2009/554 Art.2
s.9, varied: SI 2009/554 Art.2
s.10, see *AV v Secretary of State for the Home Department* [2008] EWHC 1895 (Admin), [2009] 1 W.L.R. 2318 (QBD (Admin)), Mitting, J.
s.13, applied: SI 2009/554
s.13, enabling: SI 2009/554
s.14, applied: SI 2009/554

4. Constitutional Reform Act 2005
Commencement Orders: SI 2009/1604 Art.2; SI 2009/1836 Sch.2
see *Bovale Ltd v Secretary of State for Communities and Local Government* [2009] EWCA Civ 171, [2009] 1 W.L.R. 2274 (CA (Civ Div)), Waller, L.J. (V-P)
applied: 2009 c.2 Sch.2 Part 2, 2009 c.9 Sch.2 Part 13, SI 2009/1603 r.9
Part 3, applied: 2009 c.13 Sch.1 para.1
Part 4 c.3, applied: 2009 c.25 Sch.3 para.14
s.40, applied: SI 2009/1603 r.11
s.41, amended: SI 2009/2958 Art.7
s.44, applied: SI 2009/1603 r.35
s.45, applied: SI 2009/1603
s.45, enabling: SI 2009/1603
s.52, applied: SI 2009/1603 r.45, SI 2009/2131
s.52, enabling: SI 2009/2131
s.109, referred to: 2009 c.25 s.35, s.43, s.44, Sch.3 para.13, Sch.4 para.5, Sch.7 para.11
s.118, applied: SI 2009/590, SI 2009/590 Art.3
s.118, enabling: SI 2009/590
s.120, applied: SI 2009/590
s.121, applied: SI 2009/590
s.134, applied: 2009 c.3 Sch.5 para.11
s.135, applied: 2009 c.3 Sch.5 para.11
s.135, disapplied: 2009 c.3 Sch.5 para.11
s.143, enabling: SI 2009/2468

2005–cont.

4. Constitutional Reform Act 2005–*cont.*
s.148, applied: SI 2009/1604
s.148, enabling: SI 2009/1604
Sch.1 Part 1, applied: 2009 c.25 s.45, SI 2009/582, SI 2009/1893
Sch.1 Part 2 para.19, repealed: 2009 c.25 Sch.23 Part 1
Sch.1 Part 2 para.20, repealed: 2009 c.25 Sch.23 Part 1
Sch.1 Part 2 para.21, repealed: 2009 c.25 Sch.23 Part 1
Sch.2, see *Practice Direction (Sup Ct: Upper Tribunal: Judicial Review Jurisdiction)* [2009] 1 W.L.R. 327 (Sup Ct), Lord Judge, L.C.J.
Sch.2 Part 1, applied: 2009 c.25 s.45
Sch.4 Part 1 para.34, repealed: SI 2009/1307 Sch.4
Sch.4 Part 1 para.193, repealed: 2009 c.25 Sch.23 Part 1
Sch.4 Part 1 para.194, repealed: 2009 c.25 Sch.23 Part 1
Sch.4 Part 1 para.195, repealed: 2009 c.25 Sch.23 Part 1
Sch.4 Part 1 para.357, repealed: 2009 c.25 Sch.23 Part 4
Sch.4 Part 1 para.358, repealed: 2009 c.25 Sch.23 Part 4
Sch.5 Part 1 para.115, amended: 2009 c.3 Sch.5 para.6
Sch.5 Part 1 para.116, repealed: 2009 c.3 Sch.5 para.6
Sch.5 Part 1 para.123, repealed: 2009 c.3 Sch.5 para.6
Sch.7 para.4, amended: 2009 c.3 Sch.5 para.7, 2009 c.25 s.134, Sch.23 Part 1, SI 2009/1307 Sch.1 para.285
Sch.9 Part 1 para.31, repealed: SI 2009/1836 Sch.2
Sch.10 para.3, applied: SSI 2009/312 Reg.9
Sch.11 Part 3 para.5, applied: SI 2009/2056 Art.36
Sch.11 Part 3 para.5, referred to: SI 2009/990 Art.5, SI 2009/1098 r.40, SI 2009/1209 r.111, SI 2009/1211 r.95
Sch.11 Part 3 para.5, varied: SI 2009/2044 Art.31
Sch.11 Part 3 para.6, amended: SI 2009/1941 Sch.2
Sch.11 Part 3 para.6, repealed (in part): SI 2009/1307 Sch.4
Sch.14, referred to: 2009 c.25 Sch.3 para.14
Sch.14 Part 3, amended: 2009 c.25 Sch.21 para.51, SI 2009/56 Sch.1 para.436, SI 2009/1307 Sch.1 para.286, SI 2009/1834 Sch.1 para.16
Sch.17 Part 3 para.36, repealed: 2009 c.3 Sch.5 para.8
Sch.17 Part 3 para.37, repealed: 2009 c.3 Sch.5 para.8
Sch.17 Part 3 para.38, repealed: 2009 c.3 Sch.5 para.8
Sch.17 Part 3 para.39, repealed: 2009 c.3 Sch.5 para.8

5. Income Tax (Trading and Other Income) Act 2005
applied: SI 2009/391 Reg.3
referred to: 2009 c.4 s.969
Part 2, applied: SI 2009/391 Reg.3, SI 2009/470 Reg.29
Part 2 c.10, applied: 2009 c.4 s.897
Part 2 c.16, applied: 2009 c.10 Sch.54 para.7
Part 3, applied: SI 2009/391 Reg.3
Part 3 c.4, applied: 2009 c.4 s.66, s.228, s.233, s.244
Part 4, applied: SI 2009/391 Reg.3
Part 4 c.3, applied: 2009 c.4 s.963

2005–cont.

5. Income Tax (Trading and Other Income) Act 2005–*cont.*
Part 4 c.5, applied: 2009 c.4 s.947
Part 4 c.6, applied: 2009 c.4 s.947
Part 4 c.8, applied: 2009 c.4 s.406
Part 5, applied: 2009 c.4 s.1301
Part 5 c.2, applied: 2009 c.4 s.1271
Part 5 c.5, applied: SI 2009/3001 Reg.20
Part 5 c.8, applied: SI 2009/3001 Reg.18, Reg.96, Reg.97
s.3, applied: SI 2009/2998 Reg.5
s.4, applied: SI 2009/2998 Reg.5
s.6, applied: SI 2009/2998 Reg.5
s.13, applied: 2009 c.4 s.1309
s.18, applied: 2009 c.4 s.190
s.22, amended: 2009 c.4 Sch.1 para.588
s.31, amended: 2009 c.10 Sch.11 para.35
s.35, applied: 2009 c.4 s.192
s.48, amended: 2009 c.4 Sch.1 para.589, Sch.3 Part 1, 2009 c.10 Sch.11 para.36
s.48, repealed (in part): 2009 c.10 Sch.11 para.36
s.49, amended: 2009 c.4 Sch.1 para.590, 2009 c.10 Sch.11 para.37
s.49, repealed (in part): 2009 c.10 Sch.11 para.37
s.50, repealed: 2009 c.10 Sch.11 para.38
s.50A, added: 2009 c.10 Sch.11 para.39
s.50B, added: 2009 c.10 Sch.11 para.39
s.50B, applied: 2009 c.4 s.1251
s.54, amended: SI 2009/56 Sch.1 para.438, SI 2009/571 Sch.1 para.38
s.57A, added: SI 2009/730 Art.3
s.60, amended: 2009 c.4 Sch.1 para.591
s.61, applied: 2009 c.4 s.230, s.235
s.63, applied: 2009 c.4 s.235
s.64, amended: 2009 c.4 Sch.1 para.592
s.65, amended: 2009 c.4 Sch.1 para.593
s.66, amended: 2009 c.4 Sch.1 para.594
s.67, amended: 2009 c.4 Sch.1 para.595
s.71, amended: 2009 c.4 Sch.1 para.596
s.75, repealed (in part): SI 2009/2035 Sch.1 para.42
s.79, repealed (in part): 2009 c.4 Sch.3 Part 1
s.79A, added: 2009 c.4 Sch.1 para.598
s.80, amended: 2009 c.4 Sch.1 para.599
s.88, amended: 2009 c.4 Sch.1 para.600
s.128, repealed: SI 2009/2035 Sch.1 para.43
s.146, referred to: 2009 c.4 s.897
s.148A, applied: 2009 c.10 Sch.33 para.6
s.148A, disapplied: 2009 c.10 Sch.33 para.5
s.148B, disapplied: 2009 c.10 Sch.33 para.7
s.148C, applied: 2009 c.10 Sch.33 para.8
s.148FD, added: 2009 c.10 Sch.33 para.2
s.149, amended: 2009 c.10 Sch.22 para.11
s.150, amended: 2009 c.10 Sch.22 para.11
s.155, amended: 2009 c.4 Sch.1 para.601, Sch.3 Part 1
s.158, amended: 2009 c.4 Sch.1 para.602
s.170, amended: 2009 c.4 Sch.1 para.603
s.170, applied: 2009 c.4 s.147
s.171, amended: 2009 c.4 Sch.1 para.604
s.175, amended: 2009 c.4 Sch.1 para.605
s.175, applied: 2009 c.4 s.169
s.176, amended: 2009 c.4 Sch.1 para.606
s.176, applied: 2009 c.4 s.169
s.177, amended: 2009 c.4 Sch.1 para.607
s.177, applied: 2009 c.4 s.169
s.178, amended: 2009 c.4 Sch.1 para.608
s.178, applied: 2009 c.4 s.169
s.180, amended: 2009 c.4 Sch.1 para.609
s.184, amended: 2009 c.4 Sch.1 para.610

5. Income Tax (Trading and Other Income) Act 2005 – *cont.*

s.186, amended: SI 2009/56 Sch.1 para.439
s.186, repealed (in part): SI 2009/56 Sch.1 para.439
s.194, amended: 2009 c.4 Sch.1 para.611
s.194, applied: 2009 c.4 s.178
s.218, amended: SI 2009/56 Sch.1 para.440
s.246, amended: 2009 c.4 Sch.1 para.612
s.246, applied: 2009 c.4 s.190
s.247, amended: 2009 c.10 Sch.11 para.40
s.249, amended: 2009 c.4 Sch.1 para.613
s.272, amended: 2009 c.10 Sch.11 para.41
s.274, amended: 2009 c.10 Sch.11 para.42
s.276, amended: 2009 c.4 Sch.1 para.614
s.277, applied: 2009 c.4 s.227, s.234
s.277, referred to: 2009 c.4 s.228, s.230
s.278, applied: 2009 c.4 s.227, s.234
s.278, referred to: 2009 c.4 s.230
s.279, amended: 2009 c.4 Sch.1 para.615
s.279, applied: 2009 c.4 s.227, s.234
s.279, referred to: 2009 c.4 s.228, s.230
s.280, applied: 2009 c.4 s.227, s.234
s.280, referred to: 2009 c.4 s.228, s.230
s.281, amended: 2009 c.4 Sch.1 para.616
s.281, applied: 2009 c.4 s.227, s.234
s.281, referred to: 2009 c.4 s.228, s.230
s.282, applied: 2009 c.4 s.227
s.282, referred to: 2009 c.4 s.228, s.230
s.287, amended: 2009 c.4 Sch.1 para.617, Sch.3 Part 1
s.288, amended: 2009 c.4 Sch.1 para.618, Sch.3 Part 1
s.288, applied: 2009 c.4 s.66, s.227, s.228, s.230, s.233, s.234, s.235
s.288, referred to: 2009 c.4 s.66
s.290, amended: 2009 c.4 Sch.1 para.619
s.292, applied: 2009 c.4 s.230, s.235
s.293, amended: 2009 c.4 Sch.1 para.620
s.294, amended: 2009 c.4 Sch.1 para.621
s.295, amended: 2009 c.4 Sch.1 para.622
s.296, amended: 2009 c.4 Sch.1 para.623
s.298, amended: 2009 c.4 Sch.1 para.624
s.299, amended: 2009 c.4 Sch.1 para.625
s.303, amended: 2009 c.4 Sch.1 para.626
s.304, amended: 2009 c.4 Sch.1 para.627
s.305, repealed: SI 2009/2035 Sch.1 para.44
s.316, applied: 2009 c.4 s.257
s.317, applied: 2009 c.4 s.257
s.318, amended: 2009 c.4 Sch.1 para.628
s.318, applied: 2009 c.4 s.257
s.353, applied: 2009 c.4 s.282
s.354, amended: 2009 c.10 Sch.11 para.43
s.356, amended: 2009 c.4 Sch.1 para.629
s.362, applied: 2009 c.4 s.282
s.367, amended: 2009 c.10 s.39
s.369, amended: 2009 c.10 s.33, s.39
s.369, applied: SI 2009/2998 Reg.6
s.378A, added: 2009 c.10 s.39
s.378A, amended: SI 2009/3001 Reg.128
s.378A, applied: SI 2009/3001 Reg.95, Reg.96
s.380, applied: 2009 c.4 s.414
s.380A, added: 2009 c.10 s.33
s.397, applied: 2009 c.10 Sch.54 para.14
s.397A, amended: 2009 c.10 Sch.19 para.2
s.397A, applied: 2009 c.10 Sch.54 para.14, SI 2009/3001 Reg.95
s.397AA, added: 2009 c.10 Sch.19 para.3
s.397AA, applied: SI 2009/3333 Reg.2
s.397B, amended: 2009 c.10 Sch.19 para.4
s.397BA, added: 2009 c.10 Sch.19 para.5

5. Income Tax (Trading and Other Income) Act 2005 – *cont.*

s.397BA, applied: SI 2009/3333, SI 2009/3333 Reg.2
s.397BA, enabling: SI 2009/3333
s.397C, amended: 2009 c.10 Sch.19 para.6
s.398, amended: 2009 c.10 Sch.19 para.7
s.407, applied: 2009 c.10 Sch.19 para.14
s.410, applied: 2009 c.4 s.947
s.413, amended: 2009 c.4 Sch.1 para.630
s.419, amended: 2009 c.4 Sch.1 para.631
s.419, applied: 2009 c.4 s.947
s.433, referred to: SI 2009/3001 Reg.25
s.466, amended: 2009 c.4 Sch.1 para.632
s.466, applied: 2009 c.4 s.947
s.496, amended: 2009 c.4 Sch.1 para.633
s.551, amended: 2009 c.10 Sch.25 para.9
s.552, repealed (in part): 2009 c.10 Sch.25 para.9
s.570, repealed: 2009 c.10 Sch.25 para.9
s.571, repealed: 2009 c.10 Sch.25 para.9
s.572, repealed: 2009 c.10 Sch.25 para.9
s.573, repealed: 2009 c.10 Sch.25 para.9
s.587, applied: 2009 c.4 s.1271
s.605, applied: 2009 c.4 s.952
s.629, applied: SI 2009/2998 Reg.3
s.632, amended: SI 2009/3001 Reg.128
s.640, amended: 2009 c.10 Sch.2 para.20
s.646, amended: SI 2009/56 Sch.1 para.441
s.648, amended: 2009 c.10 Sch.27 para.13
s.669, amended: 2009 c.10 Sch.2 para.21
s.671, amended: 2009 c.4 Sch.1 para.634
s.671, applied: 2009 c.4 s.954
s.685A, amended: 2009 c.10 Sch.2 para.22
s.688, disapplied: SI 2009/3001 Reg.18, Reg.96, Reg.97
s.689, disapplied: SI 2009/3001 Reg.18, Reg.96, Reg.97
s.694, enabling: SI 2009/1550, SI 2009/1994
s.695, enabling: SI 2009/1994
s.696, enabling: SI 2009/1994
s.697, enabling: SI 2009/1994
s.698, applied: SI 2009/2997 Reg.15
s.698, enabling: SI 2009/1994
s.699, enabling: SI 2009/1994
s.700, repealed: SI 2009/3054 Sch.1 para.14
s.700, enabling: SI 2009/1994
s.701, enabling: SI 2009/1550, SI 2009/1994
s.705, amended: 2009 c.10 Sch.26 para.2
s.706, amended: 2009 c.10 Sch.26 para.3, Sch.26 para.6, Sch.26 para.7, Sch.26 para.8
s.707, amended: 2009 c.10 Sch.26 para.4
s.708, amended: 2009 c.10 Sch.26 para.5, Sch.26 para.6
s.749A, added: 2009 c.4 Sch.1 para.635
s.752, amended: SI 2009/1890 Art.12
s.754, amended: 2009 c.4 Sch.1 para.636
s.755, amended: SI 2009/1890 Art.3
s.830, amended: SI 2009/3001 Reg.128
s.830, applied: SI 2009/3001 Reg.16, Reg.97
s.830, referred to: SI 2009/3001 Reg.11
s.839, amended: 2009 c.4 Sch.1 para.637, Sch.3 Part 1
s.847, amended: 2009 c.4 Sch.1 para.638
s.849, amended: 2009 c.4 Sch.1 para.639
s.850, substituted: 2009 c.4 Sch.1 para.640
s.860, amended: 2009 c.4 Sch.1 para.641
s.861, applied: 2009 c.4 s.1271
s.861, substituted: 2009 c.4 Sch.1 para.642
s.862, amended: 2009 c.4 Sch.1 para.643

2005–*cont.*

5. Income Tax (Trading and Other Income) Act 2005–*cont.*

s.862, repealed (in part): 2009 c.4 Sch.3 Part 1
s.869, amended: SI 2009/56 Sch.1 para.442, SI 2009/571 Sch.1 para.39
s.873, amended: 2009 c.10 Sch.19 para.8
s.881, repealed: 2009 c.4 Sch.3 Part 1
Sch.1 Part 1 para.6, repealed: 2009 c.4 Sch.3 Part 1
Sch.1 Part 1 para.7, repealed: 2009 c.4 Sch.3 Part 1
Sch.1 Part 1 para.9, repealed (in part): 2009 c.4 Sch.3 Part 1
Sch.1 Part 1 para.17, repealed: 2009 c.4 Sch.3 Part 1
Sch.1 Part 1 para.18, repealed: 2009 c.4 Sch.3 Part 1
Sch.1 Part 1 para.19, repealed: 2009 c.4 Sch.3 Part 1
Sch.1 Part 1 para.20, repealed: 2009 c.4 Sch.3 Part 1
Sch.1 Part 1 para.21, repealed: 2009 c.4 Sch.3 Part 1
Sch.1 Part 1 para.22, repealed: 2009 c.4 Sch.3 Part 1
Sch.1 Part 1 para.23, repealed: 2009 c.4 Sch.3 Part 1
Sch.1 Part 1 para.31, repealed: 2009 c.4 Sch.3 Part 1
Sch.1 Part 1 para.34, repealed (in part): 2009 c.4 Sch.3 Part 1
Sch.1 Part 1 para.44, repealed: 2009 c.4 Sch.3 Part 1
Sch.1 Part 1 para.46, repealed: 2009 c.4 Sch.3 Part 1
Sch.1 Part 1 para.48, repealed: 2009 c.4 Sch.3 Part 1
Sch.1 Part 1 para.49, repealed: 2009 c.4 Sch.3 Part 1
Sch.1 Part 1 para.50, repealed: 2009 c.4 Sch.3 Part 1
Sch.1 Part 1 para.56, repealed: 2009 c.4 Sch.3 Part 1
Sch.1 Part 1 para.57, repealed: 2009 c.4 Sch.3 Part 1
Sch.1 Part 1 para.58, repealed: 2009 c.4 Sch.3 Part 1
Sch.1 Part 1 para.60, repealed: 2009 c.4 Sch.3 Part 1
Sch.1 Part 1 para.62, repealed: 2009 c.4 Sch.3 Part 1
Sch.1 Part 1 para.63, repealed: 2009 c.4 Sch.3 Part 1
Sch.1 Part 1 para.64, repealed: 2009 c.4 Sch.3 Part 1
Sch.1 Part 1 para.65, repealed: 2009 c.4 Sch.3 Part 1
Sch.1 Part 1 para.66, repealed: 2009 c.4 Sch.3 Part 1
Sch.1 Part 1 para.67, repealed: 2009 c.4 Sch.3 Part 1
Sch.1 Part 1 para.68, repealed: 2009 c.4 Sch.3 Part 1
Sch.1 Part 1 para.69, repealed: 2009 c.4 Sch.3 Part 1
Sch.1 Part 1 para.70, repealed: 2009 c.4 Sch.3 Part 1
Sch.1 Part 1 para.71, repealed: 2009 c.4 Sch.3 Part 1
Sch.1 Part 1 para.72, repealed: 2009 c.4 Sch.3 Part 1
Sch.1 Part 1 para.73, repealed: 2009 c.4 Sch.3 Part 1
Sch.1 Part 1 para.74, repealed: 2009 c.4 Sch.3 Part 1
Sch.1 Part 1 para.77, repealed: 2009 c.4 Sch.3 Part 1
Sch.1 Part 1 para.78, repealed: 2009 c.4 Sch.3 Part 1
Sch.1 Part 1 para.79, repealed: 2009 c.4 Sch.3 Part 1
Sch.1 Part 1 para.80, repealed: 2009 c.4 Sch.3 Part 1
Sch.1 Part 1 para.81, repealed: 2009 c.4 Sch.3 Part 1
Sch.1 Part 1 para.82, repealed: 2009 c.4 Sch.3 Part 1
Sch.1 Part 1 para.83, repealed: 2009 c.4 Sch.3 Part 1
Sch.1 Part 1 para.84, repealed: 2009 c.4 Sch.3 Part 1
Sch.1 Part 1 para.85, repealed: 2009 c.4 Sch.3 Part 1
Sch.1 Part 1 para.90, repealed: 2009 c.4 Sch.3 Part 1
Sch.1 Part 1 para.92, repealed: 2009 c.4 Sch.3 Part 1
Sch.1 Part 1 para.95, repealed: 2009 c.4 Sch.3 Part 1
Sch.1 Part 1 para.97, repealed: 2009 c.4 Sch.3 Part 1
Sch.1 Part 1 para.107, repealed: 2009 c.4 Sch.3 Part 1
Sch.1 Part 1 para.124, repealed: 2009 c.10 Sch.1 para.6
Sch.1 Part 1 para.172, repealed: 2009 c.4 Sch.3 Part 1
Sch.1 Part 1 para.182, repealed: 2009 c.4 Sch.3 Part 1
Sch.1 Part 1 para.183, repealed: 2009 c.4 Sch.3 Part 1
Sch.1 Part 1 para.189, repealed: 2009 c.4 Sch.3 Part 1
Sch.1 Part 1 para.201, repealed: 2009 c.4 Sch.3 Part 1
Sch.1 Part 1 para.202, repealed: 2009 c.4 Sch.3 Part 1
Sch.1 Part 1 para.203, repealed: 2009 c.4 Sch.3 Part 1
Sch.1 Part 1 para.205, repealed: 2009 c.4 Sch.3 Part 1
Sch.1 Part 1 para.207, repealed: 2009 c.4 Sch.3 Part 1

2005–*cont.*

5. Income Tax (Trading and Other Income) Act 2005–*cont.*

Sch.1 Part 1 para.208, repealed: 2009 c.4 Sch.3 Part 1
Sch.1 Part 1 para.209, repealed: 2009 c.4 Sch.3 Part 1
Sch.1 Part 1 para.230, repealed: 2009 c.4 Sch.3 Part 1
Sch.1 Part 1 para.234, repealed: 2009 c.4 Sch.3 Part 1
Sch.1 Part 1 para.235, repealed: 2009 c.4 Sch.3 Part 1
Sch.1 Part 1 para.236, repealed: 2009 c.4 Sch.3 Part 1
Sch.1 Part 1 para.238, repealed: 2009 c.4 Sch.3 Part 1
Sch.1 Part 1 para.239, repealed: 2009 c.4 Sch.3 Part 1
Sch.1 Part 1 para.243, repealed: 2009 c.4 Sch.3 Part 1
Sch.1 Part 1 para.245, repealed: 2009 c.4 Sch.3 Part 1
Sch.1 Part 1 para.247, repealed: 2009 c.4 Sch.3 Part 1
Sch.1 Part 1 para.248, repealed: 2009 c.4 Sch.3 Part 1
Sch.1 Part 1 para.250, repealed: 2009 c.4 Sch.3 Part 1
Sch.1 Part 1 para.251, repealed: 2009 c.4 Sch.3 Part 1
Sch.1 Part 1 para.262, repealed: 2009 c.4 Sch.3 Part 1
Sch.1 Part 1 para.284, repealed: 2009 c.4 Sch.3 Part 1
Sch.1 Part 1 para.285, repealed: 2009 c.4 Sch.3 Part 1
Sch.1 Part 1 para.286, repealed: 2009 c.4 Sch.3 Part 1
Sch.1 Part 1 para.287, repealed: 2009 c.4 Sch.3 Part 1
Sch.1 Part 1 para.290, repealed: 2009 c.4 Sch.3 Part 1
Sch.1 Part 1 para.291, repealed (in part): 2009 c.4 Sch.3 Part 1, SI 2009/2035 Sch.1 para.60
Sch.1 Part 1 para.292, repealed: 2009 c.4 Sch.3 Part 1
Sch.1 Part 1 para.300, repealed: 2009 c.10 Sch.25 para.9
Sch.1 Part 1 para.308, repealed: SI 2009/3001 Sch.2
Sch.1 Part 1 para.309, repealed: SI 2009/3001 Sch.2
Sch.1 Part 1 para.312, repealed (in part): 2009 c.4 Sch.3 Part 1
Sch.1 Part 1 para.314, repealed (in part): 2009 c.4 Sch.3 Part 1
Sch.1 Part 1 para.321, repealed (in part): 2009 c.4 Sch.3 Part 1
Sch.1 Part 1 para.327, repealed: 2009 c.4 Sch.3 Part 1
Sch.1 Part 1 para.332, repealed: 2009 c.4 Sch.3 Part 1
Sch.1 Part 1 para.335, repealed: 2009 c.4 Sch.3 Part 1
Sch.1 Part 1 para.350, repealed: SI 2009/3001 Sch.2
Sch.1 Part 1 para.351, repealed (in part): 2009 c.4 Sch.3 Part 1
Sch.1 Part 1 para.352, repealed (in part): 2009 c.4 Sch.3 Part 1
Sch.1 Part 2 para.373, repealed: SI 2009/56 Sch.1 para.443
Sch.1 Part 2 para.374, repealed: SI 2009/56 Sch.1 para.443
Sch.1 Part 2 para.375, repealed: SI 2009/56 Sch.1 para.443
Sch.1 Part 2 para.378, repealed: 2009 c.4 Sch.3 Part 1
Sch.1 Part 2 para.383, repealed: SI 2009/56 Sch.1 para.443
Sch.1 Part 2 para.416, repealed (in part): 2009 c.4 Sch.3 Part 1
Sch.1 Part 2 para.418, repealed: 2009 c.4 Sch.3 Part 1
Sch.1 Part 2 para.451, repealed (in part): 2009 c.4 Sch.3 Part 1
Sch.1 Part 2 para.486, repealed: 2009 c.4 Sch.3 Part 1
Sch.1 Part 2 para.488, repealed: 2009 c.4 Sch.3 Part 1
Sch.1 Part 2 para.489, repealed: 2009 c.4 Sch.3 Part 1
Sch.1 Part 2 para.494, repealed (in part): 2009 c.4 Sch.3 Part 1
Sch.1 Part 2 para.500, repealed: 2009 c.4 Sch.3 Part 1
Sch.1 Part 2 para.502, repealed: 2009 c.4 Sch.3 Part 1
Sch.1 Part 2 para.506, repealed: 2009 c.4 Sch.3 Part 1
Sch.1 Part 2 para.509, repealed: 2009 c.4 Sch.3 Part 1
Sch.1 Part 2 para.520, repealed: 2009 c.4 Sch.3 Part 1
Sch.1 Part 2 para.576, repealed: 2009 c.4 Sch.3 Part 1
Sch.1 Part 2 para.578, repealed: 2009 c.4 Sch.3 Part 1

2005– cont.

5. **Income Tax (Trading and Other Income) Act 2005**– *cont.*
Sch.1 Part 2 para.583, repealed (in part): 2009 c.4 Sch.3 Part 1
Sch.1 Part 2 para.630, repealed: 2009 c.4 Sch.3 Part 1
Sch.2 Part 3 para.16, repealed: 2009 c.10 Sch.11 para.44
Sch.2 Part 3 para.17, repealed: 2009 c.10 Sch.11 para.44
Sch.2 Part 4 para.70, amended: 2009 c.4 Sch.1 para.646
Sch.2 Part 4 para.71, amended: 2009 c.4 Sch.1 para.646, SI 2009/ 2035 Sch.1 para.45
Sch.2 Part 6 para.109, amended: 2009 c.4 Sch.1 para.646
Sch.2 Part 11 para.153, repealed (in part): SI 2009/ 56 Sch.1 para.444
Sch.4 Part 1, amended: 2009 c.4 Sch.1 para.647, 2009 c.10 s.126
Sch.4 Part 2, amended: 2009 c.4 Sch.1 para.647, Sch.3 Part 1, 2009 c.10 Sch.2 para.23

6. **Child Benefit Act 2005**
referred to: 2009 c.24 s.58
Sch.1 Part 1 para.5, repealed: 2009 c.24 Sch.7 Part 2

7. **Finance Act 2005**
Part 2 c.5, applied: 2009 c.8 s.15, SI 2009/ 2998 Reg.3
s.40, amended: SI 2009/56 Sch.1 para.445
s.46, amended: SI 2009/ 2568 Art.2
s.47A, amended: 2009 c.4 Sch.1 para.649
s.48A, amended: 2009 c.4 Sch.1 para.650
s.48B, amended: 2009 c.4 Sch.1 para.651, 2009 c.10 Sch.61 para.27
s.48B, applied: 2009 c.10 Sch.61 para.2, Sch.61 para.4
s.48B, repealed (in part): 2009 c.4 Sch.3 Part 1
s.49, amended: 2009 c.4 Sch.1 para.652
s.49, applied: 2009 c.8 s.15, SI 2009/ 2998 Reg.3
s.49A, amended: 2009 c.4 Sch.1 para.653, SI 2009/ 2568 Art.2
s.49A, applied: 2009 c.8 s.15
s.50, repealed: 2009 c.4 Sch.3 Part 1
s.51, amended: 2009 c.4 Sch.3 Part 1
s.52, amended: 2009 c.4 Sch.3 Part 1
s.52, repealed (in part): 2009 c.4 Sch.3 Part 1
s.54, repealed: 2009 c.4 Sch.3 Part 1
s.54A, amended: 2009 c.4 Sch.1 para.658, Sch.3 Part 1
s.55, amended: 2009 c.4 Sch.3 Part 1
s.56, amended: 2009 c.4 Sch.1 para.660
s.56, repealed (in part): 2009 c.4 Sch.3 Part 1
s.57, amended: 2009 c.4 Sch.1 para.661, Sch.3 Part 1
s.60, see *Revenue and Customs Commissioners v Micro Fusion 2004-1 LLP* [2009] EWHC 1082 (Ch), [2009] S.T.C. 1741 (Ch D), Davis, J.
s.81, repealed: 2009 c.4 Sch.3 Part 1
s.83, amended: 2009 c.4 Sch.1 para.662
s.83, applied: 2009 c.4 s.519
s.84, applied: 2009 c.4 s.518
s.89, repealed: 2009 c.10 Sch.16 para.5
s.90, repealed: 2009 c.10 Sch.16 para.5
s.91, repealed (in part): 2009 c.4 Sch.3 Part 1
s.105, amended: 2009 c.4 Sch.1 para.663
Sch.2 para.2, repealed: 2009 c.4 Sch.3 Part 1
Sch.2 para.7, repealed: 2009 c.4 Sch.3 Part 1
Sch.2 para.8, amended: 2009 c.4 Sch.3 Part 1
Sch.2 para.10, amended: 2009 c.4 Sch.3 Part 1
Sch.2 para.11, amended: 2009 c.4 Sch.3 Part 1
Sch.2 para.12, amended: 2009 c.4 Sch.3 Part 1
Sch.2 para.13, amended: 2009 c.4 Sch.3 Part 1

2005– cont.

7. **Finance Act 2005**– *cont.*
Sch.4 Part 1 para.2, repealed: 2009 c.4 Sch.3 Part 1
Sch.4 Part 1 para.3, repealed: 2009 c.4 Sch.3 Part 1
Sch.4 Part 1 para.4, repealed: 2009 c.4 Sch.3 Part 1
Sch.4 Part 1 para.5, repealed: 2009 c.4 Sch.3 Part 1
Sch.4 Part 1 para.9, repealed: 2009 c.4 Sch.3 Part 1
Sch.4 Part 1 para.11, repealed: 2009 c.4 Sch.3 Part 1
Sch.4 Part 1 para.12, repealed: 2009 c.4 Sch.3 Part 1
Sch.4 Part 1 para.13, repealed: 2009 c.4 Sch.3 Part 1
Sch.4 Part 1 para.15, repealed: 2009 c.4 Sch.3 Part 1
Sch.4 Part 1 para.16, repealed: 2009 c.4 Sch.3 Part 1
Sch.4 Part 1 para.17, repealed: 2009 c.4 Sch.3 Part 1
Sch.4 Part 1 para.19, repealed: 2009 c.4 Sch.3 Part 1
Sch.4 Part 1 para.20, repealed: 2009 c.4 Sch.3 Part 1
Sch.4 Part 2 para.22, repealed: 2009 c.4 Sch.3 Part 1
Sch.4 Part 2 para.26, repealed: 2009 c.4 Sch.3 Part 1
Sch.4 Part 2 para.27, repealed: 2009 c.4 Sch.3 Part 1
Sch.4 Part 2 para.28, repealed: 2009 c.4 Sch.3 Part 1
Sch.4 Part 2 para.30, repealed: 2009 c.4 Sch.3 Part 1
Sch.4 Part 2 para.31, repealed: 2009 c.4 Sch.3 Part 1
Sch.4 Part 2 para.34, repealed: 2009 c.4 Sch.3 Part 1
Sch.4 Part 2 para.35, repealed: 2009 c.4 Sch.3 Part 1
Sch.4 Part 2 para.36, repealed: 2009 c.4 Sch.3 Part 1
Sch.4 Part 2 para.37, repealed: 2009 c.4 Sch.3 Part 1
Sch.4 Part 2 para.38, repealed: 2009 c.4 Sch.3 Part 1
Sch.4 Part 2 para.39, repealed: 2009 c.4 Sch.3 Part 1
Sch.4 Part 2 para.40, repealed: 2009 c.4 Sch.3 Part 1
Sch.4 Part 2 para.41, repealed: 2009 c.4 Sch.3 Part 1
Sch.4 Part 2 para.42, repealed: 2009 c.4 Sch.3 Part 1
Sch.4 Part 2 para.43, repealed: 2009 c.4 Sch.3 Part 1
Sch.4 Part 2 para.44, repealed: 2009 c.4 Sch.3 Part 1
Sch.4 Part 2 para.45, repealed: 2009 c.4 Sch.3 Part 1
Sch.4 Part 2 para.46, repealed: 2009 c.4 Sch.3 Part 1
Sch.4 Part 2 para.47, repealed: 2009 c.4 Sch.3 Part 1
Sch.4 Part 2 para.52, repealed: 2009 c.4 Sch.3 Part 1

9. **Mental Capacity Act 2005**
see *F, Re* (2009) 12 C.C.L. Rep. 530 (CP), Judge Marshall Q.C.; see *H (A Child), Re* (2009) 12 C.C.L. Rep. 695 (CP), Judge Hazel Marshall Q.C.; see *M, Re* [2009] EWHC 2525 (Fam), (2009) 12 C.C.L. Rep. 635 (CP), Munby, J.; see *S & S, Re* [2009] LS Law Medical 97 (CP), Judge Hazel Marshall Q.C.
applied: 2009 c.24 s.43, SI 2009/ 266 Reg.13, Reg.16, SI 2009/ 309 Reg.5, SI 2009/457 Reg.9, SI 2009/ 1887 Reg.8, Reg.12, SI 2009/ 2477 r.97
s.2, see *F, Re* (2009) 12 C.C.L. Rep. 530 (CP), Judge Marshall Q.C.; see *R. v C* [2009] UKHL 42, [2009] 1 W.L.R. 1786 (HL), Lord Hope of Craighead
s.3, see *Local Authority X v M* [2007] EWHC 2003 (Fam), [2009] 1 F.L.R. 443 (Fam Div), Munby, J.
s.4A, see *W Primary Care Trust v B* [2009] EWHC 1737 (Fam), (2009) 12 C.C.L. Rep. 488 (Fam Div), Roderic Wood, J.
s.9, applied: SI 2009/ 1887 Reg.5
s.15, see *F, Re* (2009) 12 C.C.L. Rep. 530 (CP), Judge Marshall Q.C.
s.16, see *W Primary Care Trust v B* [2009] EWHC 1737 (Fam), (2009) 12 C.C.L. Rep. 488 (Fam Div), Roderic Wood, J.
s.16, applied: SI 2009/ 1887 Reg.5
s.16A, see *W Primary Care Trust v B* [2009] EWHC 1737 (Fam), (2009) 12 C.C.L. Rep. 488 (Fam Div), Roderic Wood, J.
s.35, enabling: SI 2009/ 266, SI 2009/ 2376
s.44, referred to: SI 2009/37 Sch.1 para.2, Sch.1 para.4

2005–cont.

9. Mental Capacity Act 2005–*cont.*

s.48, see *F, Re* (2009) 12 C.C.L. Rep. 530 (CP), Judge Marshall Q.C.

s.49, see *F, Re* (2009) 12 C.C.L. Rep. 530 (CP), Judge Marshall Q.C.

s.51, see *Independent News and Media Ltd v A* [2009] EWHC 2858 (Fam), Times, November 17, 2009 (Fam Div), Hedley, J.

s.51, enabling: SI 2009/582

s.54, applied: SI 2009/513

s.54, enabling: SI 2009/513

s.58, enabling: SI 2009/514, SI 2009/1884

s.64, enabling: SI 2009/1884, SI 2009/2376

s.65, enabling: SI 2009/266, SI 2009/513, SI 2009/514, SI 2009/582, SI 2009/783, SI 2009/827, SI 2009/1884

Sch.A1, see *GJ v Foundation Trust* [2009] EWHC 2972 (Fam), (2009) 12 C.C.L. Rep. 600 (CP), Charles, J.

Sch.A1, applied: SI 2009/827 Reg.2, Reg.3, Reg.4, Reg.5

Sch.A1 Part 3 para.12, applied: SI 2009/783 Reg.13

Sch.A1 Part 4 para.24, applied: SI 2009/783 Reg.14

Sch.A1 Part 4 para.25, applied: SI 2009/783 Reg.14

Sch.A1 Part 4 para.29, applied: SI 2009/783 Reg.13

Sch.A1 Part 4 para.30, applied: SI 2009/783 Reg.14

Sch.A1 Part 4 para.31, enabling: SI 2009/783

Sch.A1 Part 4 para.33, enabling: SI 2009/783

Sch.A1 Part 4 para.47, enabling: SI 2009/783

Sch.A1 Part 4 para.68, applied: SI 2009/783 Reg.14

Sch.A1 Part 4 para.69, applied: SI 2009/783 Reg.10

Sch.A1 Part 4 para.70, enabling: SI 2009/783

Sch.A1 Part 5 para.76, applied: SI 2009/139 Sch.1 para.3, SI 2009/783 Reg.9, Reg.13

Sch.A1 Part 5 para.77, disapplied: SI 2009/139 Sch.1 para.4

Sch.A1 Part 5 para.78, varied: SI 2009/139 Sch.1 para.3

Sch.A1 Part 5 para.84, disapplied: SI 2009/139 Sch.1 para.4

Sch.A1 Part 5 para.85, disapplied: SI 2009/139 Sch.1 para.4

Sch.A1 Part 5 para.86, disapplied: SI 2009/139 Sch.1 para.4

Sch.A1 Part 9 para.129, enabling: SI 2009/783, SI 2009/827

Sch.A1 Part 9 para.130, enabling: SI 2009/783, SI 2009/827

Sch.A1 Part 10 para.138, enabling: SI 2009/266

Sch.A1 Part 10 para.142, enabling: SI 2009/266

Sch.A1 Part 10 para.143, enabling: SI 2009/266

Sch.A1 Part 10 para.144, enabling: SI 2009/266

Sch.A1 Part 10 para.145, enabling: SI 2009/266

Sch.A1 Part 10 para.147, enabling: SI 2009/266

Sch.A1 Part 10 para.148, enabling: SI 2009/266

Sch.A1 Part 12 para.162, applied: SI 2009/1360 Art.3

Sch.A1 Part 12 para.162, enabling: SI 2009/827

Sch.A1 Part 12 para.165, enabling: SI 2009/266

Sch.A1 Part 12 para.166, enabling: SI 2009/266

Sch.A1 Part 12 para.170, enabling: SI 2009/827

Sch.A1 Part 12 para.171, enabling: SI 2009/827

Sch.A1 Part 12 para.173, enabling: SI 2009/827

Sch.A1 Part 12 para.182, enabling: SI 2009/266

Sch.A1 Part 13 para.183, applied: SI 2009/783 Reg.14

Sch.A1 Part 13 para.183, enabling: SI 2009/783, SI 2009/827

Sch.1, enabling: SI 2009/1884

2005–cont.

9. Mental Capacity Act 2005–*cont.*

Sch.1A, see *W Primary Care Trust v B* [2009] EWHC 1737 (Fam), (2009) 12 C.C.L. Rep. 488 (Fam Div), Roderic Wood, J.

Sch.1A para.2, see *GJ v Foundation Trust* [2009] EWHC 2972 (Fam), (2009) 12 C.C.L. Rep. 600 (CP), Charles, J.

Sch.1A para.5, see *GJ v Foundation Trust* [2009] EWHC 2972 (Fam), (2009) 12 C.C.L. Rep. 600 (CP), Charles, J.; see *W Primary Care Trust v B* [2009] EWHC 1737 (Fam), (2009) 12 C.C.L. Rep. 488 (Fam Div), Roderic Wood, J.

Sch.1A para.12, see *GJ v Foundation Trust* [2009] EWHC 2972 (Fam), (2009) 12 C.C.L. Rep. 600 (CP), Charles, J.

Sch.1A para.16, see *W Primary Care Trust v B* [2009] EWHC 1737 (Fam), (2009) 12 C.C.L. Rep. 488 (Fam Div), Roderic Wood, J.

10. Public Services Ombudsman (Wales) Act 2005

Sch.3, amended: SI 2009/3019 Art.12

Sch.6 para.12, repealed (in part): 2009 c.21 Sch.6

11. Commissioners for Revenue and Customs Act 2005

see *Chilcott v Revenue and Customs Commissioners* [2009] S.T.C. (S.C.D.) 148 (Sp Comm), John Clark; see *Revenue and Customs Prosecutions Office v NE Plastics Ltd* [2008] EWHC 3560 (Admin), [2009] 2 Cr. App. R. 21 (DC), Maurice Kay, L.J.

applied: 2009 c.11 s.31, s.32

s.2, applied: 2009 c.11 s.3, s.11

s.5, applied: 2009 c.11 s.1, s.7

s.6, applied: 2009 c.11 s.3, s.11

s.9, applied: 2009 c.11 s.1, s.7

s.16A, added: 2009 c.10 s.92

s.18, referred to: 2009 c.4 s.1206

s.19, referred to: 2009 c.4 s.1207

s.23, amended: 2009 c.11 s.19

s.24, applied: 2009 c.11 s.7

s.25, applied: 2009 c.11 s.3, s.7, s.11

s.25A, applied: 2009 c.11 s.1, s.3, s.7, s.11

s.26, applied: 2009 c.11 s.7, s.11

s.30, applied: 2009 c.11 s.1, s.3, s.7, s.11

s.31, applied: 2009 c.11 s.1, s.3, s.7, s.11

s.32, applied: 2009 c.11 s.3, s.11

s.33, applied: 2009 c.11 s.1, s.3, s.7, s.11

s.44, referred to: 2009 c.11 s.32

Sch.1, referred to: 2009 c.11 s.2

Sch.2 Part 1 para.13A, substituted: 2009 c.26 Sch.7 para.116

Sch.4 para.132, repealed (in part): SI 2009/3054 Sch.1 para.16

Sch.4 para.133, repealed (in part): SI 2009/2035 Sch.1 para.60

12. Inquiries Act 2005

see *Hamill's Application for Judicial Review, Re* [2009] N.I. 103 (QBD (NI)), Weatherup, J.

applied: 2009 c.25 Sch.1 para.3, Sch.1 para.4, Sch.1 para.9, SSI 2009/268 Reg.6

s.5, applied: 2009 c.25 Sch.1 para.4

s.15, see *Hamill's Application for Judicial Review, Re* [2009] N.I. 103 (QBD (NI)), Weatherup, J.

14. Railways Act 2005

see *DPP v Inegbu* [2008] EWHC 3242 (Admin), [2009] 1 W.L.R. 2327 (DC), Latham, L.J.

applied: 2009 c.9 Sch.2 Part 7

s.6, applied: 2009 c.2 Sch.2 Part 2

s.16, amended: SI 2009/1941 Sch.1 para.246

s.22, disapplied: SI 2009/2726 Art.7

2005– *cont.*

14. Railways Act 2005– *cont.*
s.23, disapplied: SI 2009/2726 Art.7
s.24, disapplied: SI 2009/2726 Art.7
s.25, applied: SI 2009/2726 Art.10
s.25, enabling: SI 2009/2726, SI 2009/3336
s.26, disapplied: SI 2009/2726 Art.8
s.27, disapplied: SI 2009/2726 Art.8
s.28, disapplied: SI 2009/2726 Art.8
s.29, disapplied: SI 2009/2726 Art.9
s.30, disapplied: SI 2009/2726 Art.9
s.30, referred to: SSI 2009/371 Art.2
s.31, disapplied: SI 2009/2726 Art.9
s.33, amended: 2009 c.20 Sch.6 para.119
s.35, enabling: SI 2009/2973
s.38, enabling: SI 2009/2726, SI 2009/3336, SSI 2009/371
s.46, see *DPP v Inegbu* [2008] EWHC 3242 (Admin), [2009] 1 W.L.R. 2327 (DC), Latham, L.J.
s.56, enabling: SI 2009/3336
Sch.2 para.12, amended: SI 2009/1941 Sch.1 para.246
Sch.3 para.2, applied: SI 2009/1348
Sch.9 para.7, see *DPP v Inegbu* [2008] EWHC 3242 (Admin), [2009] 1 W.L.R. 2327 (DC), Latham, L.J.
Sch.10 Part 1 para.7, amended: 2009 c.4 Sch.1 para.667
Sch.10 Part 2 para.10, amended: 2009 c.4 Sch.1 para.667
Sch.10 Part 2 para.17, amended: 2009 c.4 Sch.1 para.667
Sch.10 Part 2 para.18, amended: 2009 c.4 Sch.1 para.667
Sch.10 Part 2 para.19, amended: 2009 c.4 Sch.1 para.667
Sch.10 Part 3 para.28, amended: 2009 c.4 Sch.1 para.667

15. Serious Organised Crime and Police Act 2005
Commencement Orders: 2009 c.26 Sch.8 Part 13
s.2A, referred to: 2009 c.25 s.170
s.3, amended: 2009 c.25 s.170, Sch.23 Part 7
s.30, applied: SI 2009/3269 Art.2
s.30, enabling: SI 2009/3269
s.33, amended: 2009 c.26 Sch.7 para.121
s.57, applied: SI 2009/3269 Art.2
s.57, enabling: SI 2009/3269
s.71, amended: 2009 c.25 s.113
s.72, amended: 2009 c.25 s.113
s.73, applied: 2009 c.25 s.125
s.73, disapplied: 2009 c.25 s.121
s.74, see *R. v G (G)* [2009] EWCA Crim 1207, Times, July 9, 2009 (CA (Crim Div)), Hughes, L.J.
s.74, applied: 2009 c.25 s.125
s.74, disapplied: 2009 c.25 s.121
s.75B, added: 2009 c.25 s.113
s.76, see *R. v Adams (Terrance)* [2008] EWCA Crim 914, [2009] 1 W.L.R. 301 (CA (Crim Div)), Latham, L.J.
s.76, applied: 2009 c.25 s.168
s.77, applied: 2009 c.25 s.168
s.78, applied: 2009 c.25 s.168
s.79, applied: 2009 c.25 s.168
s.80, applied: 2009 c.25 s.168
s.81, applied: 2009 c.25 s.168
s.120, repealed: 2009 c.26 Sch.8 Part 13
s.121, repealed (in part): 2009 c.26 Sch.8 Part 13
s.123, repealed (in part): 2009 c.26 Sch.8 Part 13
s.168, enabling: SI 2009/3215

2005– *cont.*

15. Serious Organised Crime and Police Act 2005– *cont.*
Sch.1 Part 4 para.20, amended: 2009 c.26 s.109
Sch.4 para.170, repealed: 2009 c.26 Sch.8 Part 13
Sch.4 para.171, repealed: 2009 c.26 Sch.8 Part 13
Sch.4 para.172, repealed: 2009 c.26 Sch.8 Part 13
Sch.9 para.10, repealed: 2009 c.26 Sch.8 Part 13
Sch.14 para.4, repealed (in part): 2009 c.26 Sch.8 Part 8
Sch.14 para.8, repealed (in part): 2009 c.26 Sch.8 Part 8

16. Clean Neighbourhoods and Environment Act 2005
see *R. v Kelleher (James Gerard)* [2008] EWCA Crim 3055, [2009] 2 Cr. App. R. (S.) 25 (CA (Crim Div)), Lord Judge, L.C.J.
Part 6 c.1, disapplied: SI 2009/2829 Art.3
s.55, applied: SI 2009/2829 Sch.1
s.55, referred to: SI 2009/2829 Sch.1
s.57, enabling: SI 2009/2829
s.66, referred to: SI 2009/2829
s.96, applied: SI 2009/486 Reg.5

17. Drugs Act 2005
Commencement Orders: 2009 c.26 Sch.8 Part 13
s.2, repealed: 2009 c.26 Sch.8 Part 13
s.5, repealed (in part): 2009 c.26 Sch.8 Part 13

18. Education Act 2005
Part 1, applied: 2009 c.22 s.137, SI 2009/817 Sch.1 para.3
Part 1 c.2, amended: 2009 c.22 s.225
s.5, applied: SI 2009/1360 Art.3
s.5, enabling: SI 2009/1564
s.8, applied: SI 2009/1360 Art.3
s.10A, added: 2009 c.22 s.225
s.14A, added: 2009 c.22 s.225
s.16A, added: 2009 c.22 s.225
s.18, amended: 2009 c.22 s.225
s.19, applied: SI 2009/3202
s.19, enabling: SI 2009/3202
s.20, amended: 2009 c.3 s.3
s.31, amended: 2009 c.3 s.3
s.48, enabling: SI 2009/1564
s.58, applied: 2009 c.22 s.137
s.102, enabling: SI 2009/1596
s.108, amended: 2009 c.22 Sch.6 para.57
s.114, enabling: SI 2009/2266
s.120, enabling: SI 2009/1596

19. Gambling Act 2005
Commencement Orders: 2009 c.26 Sch.8 Part 13
applied: SI 2009/665 Art.2
referred to: SI 2009/669 Sch.1 Part 3
s.2, amended: SSI 2009/248 Sch.1 para.12
s.25, amended: SSI 2009/248 Sch.1 para.12
s.69, varied: SI 2009/1059 Sch.1 para.56
s.69, enabling: SI 2009/1971
s.71, varied: SI 2009/1059 Sch.1 para.56
s.99, amended: SI 2009/207 Art.2
s.99, enabling: SI 2009/207
s.102, amended: SI 2009/1941 Sch.1 para.247
s.128, enabling: SI 2009/1971
s.132, enabling: SI 2009/1971
s.155, amended: SSI 2009/248 Sch.1 para.12
s.172, amended: SSI 2009/324 Art.2
s.172, applied: SI 2009/1970 Reg.3
s.172, enabling: SI 2009/324, SI 2009/1970
s.233, amended: SSI 2009/248 Sch.1 para.12
s.236, enabling: SI 2009/1502
s.274, amended: SSI 2009/248 Sch.2

2005–cont.

19. Gambling Act 2005–*cont.*
s.277, amended: SSI 2009/248 Sch.1 para.12
s.285, amended: SSI 2009/248 Sch.1 para.12
s.293, applied: SI 2009/1272 Reg.2, Reg.3
s.293, enabling: SI 2009/1272
s.355, applied: SI 2009/207, SI 2009/324, SI 2009/1502
s.355, enabling: SI 2009/1272, SI 2009/1502, SI 2009/1970, SI 2009/1971
Sch.11 Part 5 para.41, amended: SSI 2009/248 Sch.1 para.12
Sch.16 Part 2 para.17, repealed: 2009 c.26 Sch.8 Part 13

22. Finance (No.2) Act 2005
Commencement Orders: SI 2009/2094 Art.2
s.7, amended: 2009 c.10 Sch.2 para.24
s.10, repealed (in part): 2009 c.10 s.126
s.17, applied: 2009 c.4 s.490, s.587
s.17, repealed (in part): 2009 c.4 Sch.3 Part 1
s.17, enabling: SI 2009/2036, SI 2009/2199
s.18, amended: 2009 c.4 Sch.1 para.669
s.18, referred to: 2009 c.4 s.490, s.587
s.18, enabling: SI 2009/2036, SI 2009/2199
s.23, repealed (in part): 2009 c.4 Sch.3 Part 1, SI 2009/3001 Sch.2
s.26, amended: 2009 c.4 Sch.1 para.670, 2009 c.10 Sch.24 para.6
s.27, amended: 2009 c.4 Sch.1 para.671
s.36, repealed: 2009 c.10 Sch.12 para.4
s.41, repealed: 2009 c.4 Sch.3 Part 1
s.48, enabling: SI 2009/2094
s.54, repealed (in part): 2009 c.4 Sch.3 Part 1
s.55, repealed: 2009 c.4 Sch.3 Part 1
s.60, repealed: 2009 c.4 Sch.3 Part 1
s.63, repealed: 2009 c.4 Sch.3 Part 1
s.71, amended: 2009 c.4 Sch.1 para.672
Sch.2 para.20, repealed: 2009 c.4 Sch.3 Part 1
Sch.6 para.1, repealed: 2009 c.4 Sch.3 Part 1
Sch.6 para.4, repealed: 2009 c.4 Sch.3 Part 1
Sch.6 para.5, repealed: 2009 c.4 Sch.3 Part 1
Sch.6 para.6, repealed: 2009 c.4 Sch.3 Part 1
Sch.6 para.7, repealed: 2009 c.4 Sch.3 Part 1
Sch.6 para.9, repealed: 2009 c.4 Sch.3 Part 1
Sch.6 para.10, repealed: 2009 c.4 Sch.3 Part 1
Sch.6 para.11, repealed: 2009 c.4 Sch.3 Part 1
Sch.7 para.2, repealed: 2009 c.10 Sch.25 para.9
Sch.7 para.4, repealed: 2009 c.10 Sch.25 para.9
Sch.7 para.5, repealed: 2009 c.10 Sch.24 para.9
Sch.7 para.9, repealed: 2009 c.10 Sch.24 para.9
Sch.7 para.10, repealed: 2009 c.4 Sch.3 Part 1
Sch.7 para.11, repealed: 2009 c.4 Sch.3 Part 1
Sch.7 para.14, amended: 2009 c.4 Sch.1 para.674
Sch.7 para.15, repealed: 2009 c.4 Sch.3 Part 1
Sch.7 para.16, repealed: 2009 c.4 Sch.3 Part 1
Sch.7 para.17, repealed: 2009 c.4 Sch.3 Part 1
Sch.7 para.18, repealed: 2009 c.4 Sch.3 Part 1
Sch.7 para.20, repealed: 2009 c.4 Sch.3 Part 1
Sch.7 para.22, repealed: 2009 c.4 Sch.3 Part 1
Sch.7 para.23, repealed: 2009 c.4 Sch.3 Part 1
Sch.7 para.24, repealed: 2009 c.4 Sch.3 Part 1
Sch.8 para.4, repealed: 2009 c.4 Sch.3 Part 1
Sch.11 Part 2, amended: 2009 c.4 Sch.3 Part 1
Sch.11 Part 2 para.3, repealed: 2009 c.4 Sch.3 Part 1

2006

3. Equality Act 2006
s.77, see *Grainger Plc v Nicholson* Times, November 11, 2009 (EAT), Burton, J.

2006–cont.

5. Transport (Wales) Act 2006
s.8, enabling: SI 2009/2816, SI 2009/2915
s.9, applied: SI 2009/2816 Art.3
s.9, enabling: SI 2009/2816, SI 2009/2915
s.10, enabling: SI 2009/2816, SI 2009/2915

11. Terrorism Act 2006
s.6, see *R. v Da Costa (Kibley)* [2009] EWCA Crim 482, [2009] 2 Cr. App. R. (S.) 98 (CA (Crim Div)), Hughes, L.J. (V-P)
s.8, see *R. v Da Costa (Kibley)* [2009] EWCA Crim 482, [2009] 2 Cr. App. R. (S.) 98 (CA (Crim Div)), Hughes, L.J. (V-P)
s.25, applied: SI 2009/1883
s.25, disapplied: SI 2009/1883 Art.2
s.25, enabling: SI 2009/1883
s.36, amended: 2009 c.25 s.117

12. London Olympic Games and Paralympic Games Act 2006
Commencement Orders: SI 2009/2577 Art.2
s.4, amended: SI 2009/1307 Sch.1 para.287
s.11, applied: SI 2009/1573
s.11, enabling: SI 2009/1573
s.40, enabling: SI 2009/2577

13. Immigration, Asylum and Nationality Act 2006
s.12, see *R. (on the application of PE (Cameroon)) v Secretary of State for the Home Department* [2009] EWCA Civ 119, [2009] Q.B. 686 (CA (Civ Div)), Sedley, L.J.
s.15, enabling: SI 2009/2908
s.25, enabling: SI 2009/2908
s.36, amended: 2009 c.11 s.21
s.51, enabling: SI 2009/420, SI 2009/421, SI 2009/816
s.52, applied: SI 2009/420
s.52, enabling: SI 2009/421, SI 2009/816
s.54, see *MH (Syria) v Secretary of State for the Home Department* [2009] EWCA Civ 226, [2009] 3 All E.R. 564 (CA (Civ Div)), Ward, L.J.
s.58, repealed: 2009 c.11 Sch.1 Part 2

14. Consumer Credit Act 2006
s.55, repealed: SI 2009/1835 Sch.3
s.56, repealed (in part): SI 2009/1835 Sch.3
s.57, repealed: SI 2009/1835 Sch.3
s.58, repealed: SI 2009/1835 Sch.3
Sch.1, repealed: SI 2009/1835 Sch.3

15. Identity Cards Act 2006
Commencement Orders: SI 2009/2303 Art.2; SI 2009/2565 Art.2; SI 2009/3032 Art.2; SI 2009/3323 Art.2, Sch.1
applied: SI 2009/2575 Reg.7, Reg.8
s.2, applied: SI 2009/2572 Reg.2, SI 2009/2574 Reg.2
s.2, enabling: SI 2009/2572, SI 2009/2574
s.3, applied: SI 2009/2570
s.3, enabling: SI 2009/2570
s.5, applied: SI 2009/2795, SI 2009/2795 Reg.2, Reg.5, Reg.6
s.5, enabling: SI 2009/2795
s.6, applied: SI 2009/2794, SI 2009/2794 Reg.2, Reg.5, Reg.6, SI 2009/2795, SI 2009/2795 Reg.4, Reg.6, Reg.7, Reg.8, Reg.9, Reg.10, Reg.11, Reg.12, Reg.17, Reg.18
s.6, enabling: SI 2009/2794, SI 2009/2795
s.8, applied: SI 2009/2794, SI 2009/2794 Reg.7
s.8, enabling: SI 2009/2794, SI 2009/2795
s.9, applied: SI 2009/2570, SI 2009/2570 Art.3, Art.6
s.9, enabling: SI 2009/2570
s.10, applied: SI 2009/2795, SI 2009/2795 Reg.12, Reg.13, Reg.14, Reg.15, Reg.16

2006– cont.

15. Identity Cards Act 2006– *cont.*
s.10, enabling: SI 2009/2795
s.11, applied: SI 2009/2795 Reg.16, SI 2009/2805 Reg.4
s.11, enabling: SI 2009/2795
s.12, applied: SI 2009/2575 Reg.2, Reg.3, Reg.5, Reg.6, Reg.7, Reg.8
s.12, enabling: SI 2009/2575
s.17, applied: SI 2009/2570, SI 2009/2570 Art.8, SI 2009/2793, SI 2009/2793 Reg.2, Reg.3, Reg.4, Reg.5
s.17, enabling: SI 2009/2570, SI 2009/2793
s.18, applied: SI 2009/2793 Reg.3, Reg.4, Reg.5
s.19, applied: SI 2009/2793 Reg.3, Reg.4, Reg.5
s.20, applied: SI 2009/2570, SI 2009/2570 Art.9, SI 2009/2575 Reg.3, SI 2009/2793 Reg.3, Reg.4, Reg.5
s.20, enabling: SI 2009/2570
s.21, applied: SI 2009/2793
s.21, enabling: SI 2009/2793
s.25, see *R. v Okhotnikov (Ivan)* [2008] EWCA Crim 1190, [2009] 1 Cr. App. R. (S.) 33 (CA (Crim Div)), Hughes, L.J.
s.31, applied: SI 2009/2571 Reg.2, Reg.3, Reg.4
s.31, enabling: SI 2009/2571
s.32, applied: SI 2009/2571 Reg.3, Reg.4, Reg.5
s.32, enabling: SI 2009/2571
s.34, applied: SI 2009/2570
s.34, enabling: SI 2009/2570
s.35, applied: SI 2009/2805
s.35, enabling: SI 2009/2805
s.38, applied: SI 2009/2570, SI 2009/2570 Art.5, Art.6
s.38, enabling: SI 2009/2570
s.40, enabling: SI 2009/2571, SI 2009/2574, SI 2009/2575, SI 2009/2793, SI 2009/2794, SI 2009/2795, SI 2009/2805
s.42, enabling: SI 2009/2571, SI 2009/2572, SI 2009/2574, SI 2009/2575, SI 2009/2793, SI 2009/2794, SI 2009/2795
s.44, enabling: SI 2009/2303, SI 2009/2565, SI 2009/3032, SI 2009/3323
Sch.1, applied: SI 2009/2570 Art.9
Sch.1 para.6, amended: SI 2009/2570 Art.2
Sch.1 para.9, applied: SI 2009/2570 Art.9, SI 2009/2793 Reg.3, SI 2009/2795 Reg.17
Sch.1 para.9, referred to: SI 2009/2793 Reg.3

16. Natural Environment and Rural Communities Act 2006
Commencement Orders: 2009 c.23 Sch.22 Part 8
s.1, amended: 2009 c.23 s.311
s.7, applied: SI 2009/3264 Sch.2 para.1, SI 2009/3365 Sch.2 para.1
s.67, see *R. (on the application of Winchester College) v Hampshire CC* [2008] EWCA Civ 431, [2009] 1 W.L.R. 138 (CA (Civ Div)), Ward, L.J.
s.78, amended: SI 2009/229 Sch.2 para.4
s.79, amended: SI 2009/229 Sch.2 para.4
s.80, amended: SI 2009/229 Sch.2 para.4
s.82, amended: SI 2009/229 Sch.2 para.4
s.86, amended: SI 2009/229 Sch.2 para.4
s.98, amended: SI 2009/229 Sch.2 para.4
Sch.7 para.1A, added: 2009 c.23 Sch.14 para.20
Sch.10 para.1, amended: SI 2009/1941 Sch.1 para.255
Sch.11 Part 1 para.38, repealed: 2009 c.23 Sch.22 Part 4
Sch.11 Part 1 para.174, repealed: 2009 c.23 Sch.22 Part 8

2006– cont.

18. Work and Families Act 2006
s.14, applied: SI 2009/1903
s.14, enabling: SI 2009/1903
19. Climate Change and Sustainable Energy Act 2006
s.14, applied: SI 2009/3019 Art.2
21. Childcare Act 2006
Part 3, applied: SI 2009/1547 Reg.4, Reg.12
Part 3 c.2, applied: SI 2009/1547 Sch.1 para.19
Part 3 c.3, applied: SI 2009/1547 Reg.12, Sch.1 para.19
Part 3 c.4, applied: SI 2009/1547 Reg.10, Reg.12, Sch.1 para.19
s.3, amended: 2009 c.22 s.201
s.5A, added: 2009 c.22 s.198
s.5B, added: 2009 c.22 s.198
s.5C, added: 2009 c.22 s.198
s.5D, added: 2009 c.22 s.198
s.5E, added: 2009 c.22 s.198
s.5F, added: 2009 c.22 s.198
s.5G, added: 2009 c.22 s.198
s.8, applied: SI 2009/1554 Reg.6, Reg.9
s.35, enabling: SI 2009/1507
s.36, enabling: SI 2009/1507
s.39, referred to: SI 2009/1607 Reg.6
s.39, enabling: SI 2009/1549
s.41, amended: 2009 c.22 Sch.12 para.39
s.42, amended: 2009 c.22 s.160, Sch.12 para.40, Sch.16 Part 4
s.42, repealed (in part): 2009 c.22 Sch.12 para.40, Sch.16 Part 4
s.43, applied: SI 2009/1549
s.43, enabling: SI 2009/1549
s.44, amended: 2009 c.22 Sch.12 para.41
s.46, amended: 2009 c.22 Sch.12 para.42
s.49, applied: SI 2009/1360 Art.3
s.49, enabling: SI 2009/1508
s.59, applied: SI 2009/1545
s.59, enabling: SI 2009/1545, SI 2009/1547
s.60, applied: SI 2009/1360 Art.3
s.67, applied: SI 2009/1545
s.67, enabling: SI 2009/1545, SI 2009/1547
s.74, applied: SI 2009/1547 Reg.11
s.74, enabling: SI 2009/1547
s.75, enabling: SI 2009/1547
s.76, applied: SI 2009/1547 Reg.10
s.89, enabling: SI 2009/1507
s.98A, added: 2009 c.22 s.199
s.98B, added: 2009 c.22 s.199
s.98C, added: 2009 c.22 s.199
s.98D, added: 2009 c.22 s.199
s.98E, added: 2009 c.22 s.199
s.98F, added: 2009 c.22 s.199
s.98G, added: 2009 c.22 s.199
s.99, applied: SI 2009/1554 Reg.4, Reg.5, Reg.6, Reg.7, Reg.8, Reg.9
s.99, enabling: SI 2009/1554
s.104, enabling: SI 2009/1507, SI 2009/1508, SI 2009/1545, SI 2009/1547, SI 2009/1549, SI 2009/1554
Sch.1 para.2, repealed: 2009 c.22 Sch.16 Part 4
Sch.1 para.10, repealed (in part): 2009 c.22 Sch.16 Part 4
22. Electoral Administration Act 2006
Commencement Orders: SI 2009/1509 Art.2, Art.3
applied: 2009 c.9 Sch.2 Part 13, Sch.2 Part 57
referred to: 2009 c.2 Sch.2 Part 2

2006–cont.

22. Electoral Administration Act 2006–*cont.*
s.l, amended: 2009 c.12 s.28
s.2, amended: 2009 c.12 s.29
s.3A, added: 2009 c.12 s.28
s.6, amended: 2009 c.12 s.28
s.42, applied: SI 2009/813
s.42, enabling: SI 2009/813
s.62, amended: 2009 c.12 s.19
s.77, enabling: SI 2009/1509

25. Finance Act 2006
Part 4, applied: SI 2009/3315 Reg.5
s.28, repealed: 2009 c.4 Sch.3 Part 1
s.31, repealed: 2009 c.4 Sch.3 Part 1
s.32, repealed: 2009 c.4 Sch.3 Part 1
s.33, repealed: 2009 c.4 Sch.3 Part 1
s.34, repealed: 2009 c.4 Sch.3 Part 1
s.35, repealed: 2009 c.4 Sch.3 Part 1
s.36, repealed: 2009 c.4 Sch.3 Part 1
s.37, repealed: 2009 c.4 Sch.3 Part 1
s.38, repealed: 2009 c.4 Sch.3 Part 1
s.39, repealed: 2009 c.4 Sch.3 Part 1
s.40, repealed: 2009 c.4 Sch.3 Part 1
s.41, repealed: 2009 c.4 Sch.3 Part 1
s.42, amended: 2009 c.4 Sch.3 Part 1
s.43, repealed: 2009 c.4 Sch.3 Part 1
s.44, repealed: 2009 c.4 Sch.3 Part 1
s.45, repealed: 2009 c.4 Sch.3 Part 1
s.46, amended: 2009 c.4 Sch.1 para.679
s.47, amended: 2009 c.4 Sch.1 para.679
s.48, repealed: 2009 c.4 Sch.3 Part 1
s.49, repealed: 2009 c.4 Sch.3 Part 1
s.50, repealed: 2009 c.4 Sch.3 Part 1
s.51, repealed: 2009 c.4 Sch.3 Part 1
s.52, repealed: 2009 c.4 Sch.3 Part 1
s.53, repealed (in part): 2009 c.4 Sch.3 Part 1
s.77, repealed: 2009 c.4 Sch.3 Part 1
s.84, repealed (in part): 2009 c.10 s.126
s.93, repealed: 2009 c.4 Sch.3 Part 1
s.97, amended: 2009 c.4 Sch.1 para.683
s.98, enabling: SI 2009/2568
s.104, amended: 2009 c.4 Sch.1 para.684, 2009 c.10 Sch.34 para.2
s.106, amended: 2009 c.10 Sch.34 para.3
s.108, amended: 2009 c.10 Sch.34 para.4
s.109, amended: 2009 c.10 Sch.34 para.5
s.109, applied: SI 2009/3315 Reg.6
s.109, repealed (in part): 2009 c.10 Sch.34 para.5
s.112, amended: 2009 c.4 Sch.1 para.685
s.112, applied: SI 2009/3315 Reg.6
s.113, applied: 2009 c.10 Sch.15 para.76
s.115, amended: 2009 c.4 Sch.1 para.686, 2009 c.10 Sch.34 para.6
s.117, amended: 2009 c.4 Sch.3 Part 1, SI 2009/56 Sch.1 para.447
s.118, amended: 2009 c.10 Sch.34 para.7
s.120, amended: 2009 c.4 Sch.1 para.688
s.120, applied: 2009 c.10 Sch.15 para.58
s.121, amended: 2009 c.4 Sch.1 para.689
s.121, repealed (in part): 2009 c.4 Sch.3 Part 1
s.129, amended: SI 2009/56 Sch.1 para.448
s.129, applied: SI 2009/3315 Reg.6
s.133, amended: SI 2009/56 Sch.1 para.449
s.136, amended: 2009 c.4 Sch.1 para.690, 2009 c.10 Sch.12 para.3
s.136A, added: 2009 c.10 Sch.34 para.8
s.136A, applied: SI 2009/3315
s.136A, enabling: SI 2009/3315

2006–cont.

25. Finance Act 2006–*cont.*
s.139, amended: 2009 c.4 Sch.1 para.691, SI 2009/2859 Art.3
s.173, applied: SI 2009/226, SI 2009/227, SI 2009/228, SI 2009/3011, SI 2009/3012, SI 2009/3013
s.173, enabling: SI 2009/226, SI 2009/227, SI 2009/228, SI 2009/3011, SI 2009/3012, SI 2009/3013
s.174, referred to: SI 2009/404 Art.10
s.179, amended: 2009 c.4 Sch.1 para.692
Sch.2 para.1, repealed: 2009 c.4 Sch.3 Part 1
Sch.2 para.2, repealed: 2009 c.4 Sch.3 Part 1
Sch.2 para.3, repealed: 2009 c.4 Sch.3 Part 1
Sch.3 para.2, repealed (in part): 2009 c.4 Sch.3 Part 1
Sch.3 para.6, repealed: 2009 c.4 Sch.3 Part 1
Sch.3 para.7, repealed: 2009 c.4 Sch.3 Part 1
Sch.3 para.8, repealed: 2009 c.4 Sch.3 Part 1
Sch.3 para.9, repealed: 2009 c.4 Sch.3 Part 1
Sch.4 para.1, repealed: 2009 c.4 Sch.3 Part 1
Sch.4 para.2, repealed: 2009 c.4 Sch.3 Part 1
Sch.4 para.3, repealed: 2009 c.4 Sch.3 Part 1
Sch.4 para.4, repealed: 2009 c.4 Sch.3 Part 1
Sch.4 para.5, repealed: 2009 c.4 Sch.3 Part 1
Sch.4 para.6, repealed: 2009 c.4 Sch.3 Part 1
Sch.4 para.7, repealed: 2009 c.4 Sch.3 Part 1
Sch.4 para.8, repealed: 2009 c.4 Sch.3 Part 1
Sch.4 para.9, repealed: 2009 c.4 Sch.3 Part 1
Sch.4 para.10, repealed: 2009 c.4 Sch.3 Part 1
Sch.5 Part 1 para.1, repealed: 2009 c.4 Sch.3 Part 1
Sch.5 Part 1 para.2, repealed: 2009 c.4 Sch.3 Part 1
Sch.5 Part 1 para.3, repealed: 2009 c.4 Sch.3 Part 1
Sch.5 Part 1 para.4, repealed: 2009 c.4 Sch.3 Part 1
Sch.5 Part 1 para.5, repealed: 2009 c.4 Sch.3 Part 1
Sch.5 Part 1 para.6, repealed: 2009 c.4 Sch.3 Part 1
Sch.5 Part 1 para.7, repealed: 2009 c.4 Sch.3 Part 1
Sch.5 Part 1 para.8, repealed: 2009 c.4 Sch.3 Part 1
Sch.5 Part 1 para.9, repealed: 2009 c.4 Sch.3 Part 1
Sch.5 Part 1 para.10, repealed: 2009 c.4 Sch.3 Part 1
Sch.5 Part 1 para.11, repealed: 2009 c.4 Sch.3 Part 1
Sch.5 Part 1 para.12, repealed: 2009 c.4 Sch.3 Part 1
Sch.5 Part 1 para.13, repealed: 2009 c.4 Sch.3 Part 1
Sch.5 Part 1 para.14, repealed: 2009 c.4 Sch.3 Part 1
Sch.5 Part 2 para.24, repealed: 2009 c.4 Sch.3 Part 1
Sch.5 Part 2 para.25, repealed: 2009 c.4 Sch.3 Part 1
Sch.5 Part 4 para.30, repealed: 2009 c.4 Sch.3 Part 1
Sch.5 Part 4 para.31, repealed: 2009 c.4 Sch.3 Part 1
Sch.5 Part 4 para.32, repealed: 2009 c.4 Sch.3 Part 1
Sch.5 Part 4 para.33, repealed: 2009 c.4 Sch.3 Part 1
Sch.5 Part 4 para.34, repealed: 2009 c.4 Sch.3 Part 1
Sch.6 para.3, repealed: 2009 c.10 Sch.24 para.9
Sch.6 para.4, repealed: 2009 c.10 Sch.24 para.9
Sch.6 para.7, repealed: 2009 c.10 Sch.25 para.9
Sch.6 para.10, repealed (in part): 2009 c.4 Sch.3 Part 1
Sch.6 para.11, repealed: 2009 c.4 Sch.3 Part 1
Sch.6 para.12, repealed: 2009 c.4 Sch.3 Part 1
Sch.6 para.13, repealed: 2009 c.4 Sch.3 Part 1
Sch.6 para.14, repealed: 2009 c.4 Sch.3 Part 1
Sch.6 para.15, repealed: 2009 c.4 Sch.3 Part 1
Sch.6 para.16, repealed: 2009 c.4 Sch.3 Part 1
Sch.6 para.17, repealed: 2009 c.4 Sch.3 Part 1
Sch.6 para.18, repealed: 2009 c.4 Sch.3 Part 1
Sch.6 para.19, repealed: 2009 c.4 Sch.3 Part 1
Sch.6 para.21, repealed: 2009 c.4 Sch.3 Part 1
Sch.6 para.22, repealed: 2009 c.4 Sch.3 Part 1
Sch.6 para.23, repealed: 2009 c.4 Sch.3 Part 1
Sch.6 para.24, repealed: 2009 c.4 Sch.3 Part 1
Sch.10 Part 2 para.5, amended: 2009 c.4 Sch.1 para.695

25. Finance Act 2006–*cont.*
Sch.10 Part 2 para.6, amended: 2009 c.10 Sch.31 para.2
Sch.10 Part 2 para.7, amended: 2009 c.10 Sch.10 para.2, Sch.31 para.3
Sch.10 Part 2 para.7A, added: 2009 c.10 Sch.31 para.4
Sch.10 Part 2 para.13A, added: 2009 c.10 Sch.10 para.3
Sch.10 Part 2 para.17, amended: 2009 c.10 Sch.10 para.4, Sch.31 para.5
Sch.10 Part 2 para.17A, added: 2009 c.10 Sch.31 para.6
Sch.10 Part 2 para.22, amended: 2009 c.10 Sch.31 para.7
Sch.10 Part 3 para.23, amended: 2009 c.4 Sch.1 para.695, 2009 c.10 Sch.10 para.5
Sch.10 Part 3 para.23A, added: 2009 c.10 Sch.10 para.6
Sch.10 Part 3 para.28, amended: 2009 c.4 Sch.1 para.695
Sch.10 Part 3 para.32, amended: 2009 c.10 Sch.10 para.7
Sch.10 Part 4 para.38, amended: 2009 c.4 Sch.1 para.695
Sch.10 Part 4 para.39, amended: 2009 c.10 Sch.10 para.8
Sch.10 Part 4 para.40, repealed: 2009 c.10 Sch.31 para.8
Sch.10 Part 4 para.41, amended: 2009 c.10 Sch.31 para.9
Sch.10 Part 4 para.42, amended: 2009 c.10 Sch.31 para.10
Sch.10 Part 4 para.43, repealed (in part): 2009 c.4 Sch.3 Part 1
Sch.12 Part 3 para.46, repealed (in part): SI 2009/2035 Sch.1 para.60
Sch.12 Part 3 para.47, repealed: SI 2009/3001 Sch.2
Sch.15 Part 2 para.9, amended: 2009 c.4 Sch.1 para.696
Sch.15 Part 2 para.10, amended: 2009 c.4 Sch.1 para.696
Sch.15 Part 2 para.11, amended: 2009 c.4 Sch.1 para.696
Sch.15 Part 2 para.12, amended: 2009 c.4 Sch.1 para.696
Sch.15 Part 2 para.14, amended: 2009 c.4 Sch.1 para.696
Sch.16 Part 1 para.3, substituted: SI 2009/1482 Reg.2
Sch.16 Part 1 para.4, amended: 2009 c.4 Sch.1 para.697
Sch.16 Part 2 para.13, amended: 2009 c.4 Sch.1 para.697
Sch.16 Part 3 para.14, enabling: SI 2009/1482
Sch.17 para.11, amended: 2009 c.4 Sch.1 para.698
Sch.17 para.32, amended: 2009 c.4 Sch.1 para.698
Sch.17 para.32, repealed (in part): 2009 c.10 Sch.14 para.19
Sch.23 para.34, repealed (in part): 2009 c.10 s.75

26. Commons Act 2006
Part 1, applied: SI 2009/1300 Art.5, Art.35, Art.46
s.3, enabling: SI 2009/2018
s.15, see *R. (on the application of Lewis) v Redcar and Cleveland BC* [2009] EWCA Civ 3, [2009] 1 W.L.R. 1461 (CA (Civ Div)), Laws, L.J.
s.24, enabling: SI 2009/2018
s.59, enabling: SI 2009/2018
Sch.2, applied: SI 2009/1300 Art.5, Art.35, Art.46
Sch.3 para.2, enabling: SI 2009/2018

26. Commons Act 2006–*cont.*
Sch.3 para.4, enabling: SI 2009/2018

27. Housing Corporation (Delegation) etc Act 2006
s.1, repealed (in part): SI 2009/484 Sch.2

28. Health Act 2006
see *R. (on the application of G) v Nottinghamshire Healthcare NHS Trust* [2009] EWCA Civ 795, [2009] H.R.L.R. 31 (CA (Civ Div)), Lord Clarke of Stone-cum-Ebony MR
s.8, see *Blackpool BC v Howitt* [2008] EWHC 3300 (Admin), [2009] 4 All E.R. 154 (QBD (Admin)), Judge Denyer
s.60, applied: SI 2009/1182 Art.7, Art.8
Sch.4 para.6, substituted: 2009 c.21 Sch.3 para.8

29. Compensation Act 2006
s.3, see *Sienkiewicz v Greif (UK) Ltd* [2009] EWCA Civ 1159, Times, November 13, 2009 (CA (Civ Div)), Lord Clarke of Stone-cum-Ebony MR

32. Government of Wales Act 2006
applied: 2009 c.9 Sch.2 Part 57, 2009 c.23 s.324, SI 2009/3104 Reg.7
s.36, applied: 2009 c.4 s.6
s.37, amended: 2009 c.23 Sch.4 para.6
s.48, applied: SI 2009/2818 Sch.1 para.1
s.49, applied: 2009 c.4 s.1
s.50, applied: SI 2009/2818 Sch.1 para.1
s.52, applied: 2009 c.23 s.14
s.58, amended: 2009 c.23 Sch.4 para.6
s.58, applied: SI 2009/703, SI 2009/3019
s.58, varied: 2009 c.23 Sch.9 para.13
s.58, enabling: SI 2009/703, SI 2009/3019
s.59, amended: 2009 c.23 Sch.4 para.6
s.59, applied: SI 2009/2427, SI 2009/3140
s.59, varied: 2009 c.25 s.143
s.80, amended: 2009 c.23 Sch.4 para.6
s.80, applied: 2009 c.23 s.60
s.82, amended: 2009 c.23 Sch.4 para.6
s.82, applied: 2009 c.23 s.60
s.83, applied: 2009 c.23 s.27
s.94, amended: SI 2009/3006 Art.2
s.95, applied: SI 2009/1758, SI 2009/3006, SI 2009/3010
s.95, enabling: SI 2009/1758, SI 2009/3006, SI 2009/3010
s.96, applied: SI 2009/1603 r.41
s.99, applied: SI 2009/1603 r.41
s.101, amended: SI 2009/3006 Art.2
s.112, applied: SI 2009/1603 r.41
s.137, applied: 2009 c.4 Sch.1 para.7
s.138, applied: 2009 c.4 s.9, s.10, Sch.1 para.6
s.141, amended: SI 2009/1941 Sch.1 para.256
s.152, applied: 2009 c.23 s.60
s.155, amended: 2009 c.23 Sch.4 para.6
s.157, enabling: SI 2009/2958, SI 2009/3019
s.158, amended: 2009 c.23 s.43, Sch.22 Part 1
s.158, applied: 2009 c.23 s.322, SI 2009/1517 Art.1, SI 2009/3381 Reg.1
s.159, amended: 2009 c.23 Sch.4 para.6
s.160, enabling: SI 2009/2958
s.162, enabling: SI 2009/2958
Sch.2 para.3, varied: 2009 c.25 s.143
Sch.3 Part 1 para.4, amended: 2009 c.23 Sch.8 para.3
Sch.3 Part 1 para.4, repealed (in part): 2009 c.23 Sch.8 para.3, Sch.22 Part 2
Sch.3 Part 2 para.5, applied: 2009 c.23 s.60
Sch.4 para.1, disapplied: SI 2009/703 Art.3, SI 2009/3019 Art.7

2006–cont.

32. Government of Wales Act 2006–*cont.*
Sch.4 para.2, enabling: SI 2009/703, SI 2009/3019
Sch.5 Part 1, added: SI 2009/3010 Art.2
Sch.5 Part 1, amended: 2009 c.20 s.33, 2009 c.23 s.310, SI 2009/1758 Art.2, SI 2009/3006 Art.2, SI 2009/3010 Art.2, Art.3
Sch.5 Part 2 para.1, amended: SI 2009/3006 Art.2
Sch.5 Part 2 paraA.1, amended: SI 2009/3006 Art.2
Sch.5 Part 2 para.1, amended: SI 2009/3006 Art.2
Sch.5 Part 2 para.2, amended: SI 2009/3006 Art.2
Sch.5 Part 2 para.2A, amended: SI 2009/3006 Art.2
Sch.5 Part 2 para.3, amended: SI 2009/3006 Art.2
Sch.5 Part 2 para.4, amended: SI 2009/3006 Art.2
Sch.5 Part 2 para.5, amended: SI 2009/3006 Art.2
Sch.5 Part 2 para.6, amended: SI 2009/3006 Art.2
Sch.5 Part 3 para.6Z, added: SI 2009/3006 Art.2
Sch.5 Part 3 para.6Z, amended: SI 2009/3006 Art.2
Sch.5 Part 3 para.7, amended: SI 2009/3006 Art.2
Sch.5 Part 3 para.7A, amended: SI 2009/3006 Art.2
Sch.5 Part 3 para.8, amended: SI 2009/3006 Art.2
Sch.5 Part 3 para.9, amended: SI 2009/3006 Art.2
Sch.5 Part 3 para.10, amended: SI 2009/3006 Art.2
Sch.5 Part 3 para.11, amended: SI 2009/3006 Art.2
Sch.9 Part 5 para.29, applied: SI 2009/1603 r.41
Sch.9 Part 5 para.30, applied: SI 2009/1603 r.41
Sch.9 Part 5 para.32, enabling: SSI 2009/322, SSI 2009/323
Sch.11 para.35, amended: 2009 c.1 Sch.1 para.22

33. Northern Ireland (Miscellaneous Provisions) Act 2006
Commencement Orders: SI 2009/448 Art.2
s.28, repealed: 2009 c.3 Sch.5 para.9
s.31, enabling: SI 2009/448
Sch.4 Part 1 para.2, repealed: 2009 c.12 Sch.7
Sch.4 Part 1 para.3, repealed: 2009 c.12 Sch.7
Sch.4 Part 1 para.4, repealed (in part): 2009 c.12 Sch.7

35. Fraud Act 2006
s.1, applied: SI 2009/2773 Sch.1, SI 2009/2781 Sch.1
s.2, applied: SI 2009/214 Sch.2 para.6, SI 2009/1801 Sch.2 para.6
s.6, applied: SI 2009/2773 Sch.1, SI 2009/2781 Sch.1
s.7, applied: SI 2009/2773 Sch.1, SI 2009/2781 Sch.1
s.9, amended: SI 2009/1941 Sch.1 para.257
s.10, repealed: SI 2009/1941 Sch.2
s.11, applied: SI 2009/2773 Sch.1, SI 2009/2781 Sch.1
s.13, see *JSC BTA Bank v Ablyazov* [2009] EWCA Civ 1124, Times, November 12, 2009 (CA (Civ Div)), Pill, L.J.

36. Wireless Telegraphy Act 2006
see *T-Mobile (UK) Ltd v Office of Communications* [2008] EWCA Civ 1373, [2009] 1 W.L.R. 1565 (CA (Civ Div)), Tuckey, L.J.
applied: SI 2009/11 Reg.3
s.3, referred to: SI 2009/15 Art.2
s.5, applied: SI 2009/17 Reg.8
s.8, disapplied: SI 2009/65 Reg.3, SI 2009/1812 Reg.3, Reg.4, Reg.5, Reg.6, SI 2009/2517 Reg.4, Reg.8, Reg.12
s.8, enabling: SI 2009/65, SI 2009/1812, SI 2009/2517
s.9, amended: SI 2009/2979 Reg.13
s.9A, added: SI 2009/2979 Reg.13
s.12, enabling: SI 2009/66

2006–cont.

36. Wireless Telegraphy Act 2006–*cont.*
s.13, enabling: SI 2009/66
s.14, see *T-Mobile (UK) Ltd v Office of Communications* [2008] EWCA Civ 1373, [2009] 1 W.L.R. 1565 (CA (Civ Div)), Tuckey, L.J.
s.18, applied: SI 2009/16 Reg.2
s.18, enabling: SI 2009/16
s.29, enabling: SI 2009/15
s.30, enabling: SI 2009/17
s.31, enabling: SI 2009/14
s.39, amended: SI 2009/2979 Reg.13
s.47, see *R. v Judge (Paul Michael)* [2008] EWCA Crim 1820, [2009] 1 Cr. App. R. (S.) 74 (CA (Crim Div)), Hughes, L.J.
s.115, amended: SI 2009/2979 Reg.13
s.122, applied: SI 2009/14, SI 2009/15, SI 2009/16, SI 2009/17, SI 2009/65, SI 2009/66, SI 2009/1812, SI 2009/2517
s.122, enabling: SI 2009/14, SI 2009/17, SI 2009/66
Sch.2 para.1, enabling: SI 2009/16

38. Violent Crime Reduction Act 2006
Commencement Orders: SI 2009/1840 Art.2, Art.3
s.3, applied: SI 2009/2937 r.2, r.3, r.4, r.5, r.6
s.9, applied: SI 2009/2937 r.2, r.3, r.4
s.11, applied: SI 2009/2937 r.7
s.12, enabling: SI 2009/1839
s.13, applied: SI 2009/1839 Reg.10, Reg.11, SI 2009/2937 r.6
s.13, enabling: SI 2009/1839, SI 2009/2937
s.14, enabling: SI 2009/1839
s.27, amended: 2009 c.26 s.31
s.29, applied: 2009 c.25 s.125
s.47, varied: SI 2009/3074 Art.4
s.66, enabling: SI 2009/1840

39. Emergency Workers (Obstruction) Act 2006
s.2, see *R. v McMenemy (Claire)* [2009] EWCA Crim 42, [2009] 2 Cr. App. R. (S.) 57 (CA (Crim Div)), Keene, L.J.
s.4, see *R. v McMenemy (Claire)* [2009] EWCA Crim 42, [2009] 2 Cr. App. R. (S.) 57 (CA (Crim Div)), Keene, L.J.

40. Education and Inspections Act 2006
Commencement Orders: SI 2009/49 Art.2; SI 2009/1027 Art.3; SI 2009/2545 Art.3
s.7, see *R. (on the application of Chandler) v Secretary of State for Children, Schools and Families* [2009] EWHC 219 (Admin), [2009] Eu. L.R. 615 (QBD (Admin)), Forbes, J.
s.7, amended: 2009 c.22 s.126
s.7, applied: SI 2009/276 Reg.3
s.7, enabling: SI 2009/1556
s.8, applied: SI 2009/276 Reg.3
s.8, enabling: SI 2009/2984
s.9, applied: SI 2009/276 Reg.3
s.10, amended: 2009 c.22 s.126
s.10, applied: SI 2009/276 Reg.3
s.10, enabling: SI 2009/1556
s.11, applied: SI 2009/276 Reg.3
s.11, repealed (in part): 2009 c.22 Sch.16 Part 3
s.11, enabling: SI 2009/1556
s.12, applied: SI 2009/276 Reg.3
s.13, varied: SI 2009/276 Reg.3
s.15, applied: SI 2009/276 Reg.3
s.15, enabling: SI 2009/1556, SI 2009/3346
s.16, applied: SI 2009/276 Reg.3
s.17, varied: SI 2009/276 Reg.3
s.18, applied: SI 2009/276 Reg.3

40. Education and Inspections Act 2006–*cont.*
s.19, applied: SI 2009/276 Reg.3, SI 2009/1556 Reg.8
s.19, enabling: SI 2009/1556
s.20, applied: SI 2009/276 Reg.3
s.21, applied: SI 2009/276 Reg.3
s.21, enabling: SI 2009/1556
s.22, applied: SI 2009/276 Reg.3
s.23, applied: SI 2009/276 Reg.3
s.24, applied: SI 2009/276 Reg.3
s.28, applied: SI 2009/276 Reg.3
s.32, applied: SI 2009/276 Reg.3
s.59, amended: 2009 c.22 Sch.13 para.2
s.60, amended: 2009 c.22 Sch.13 para.3
s.60A, added: 2009 c.22 Sch.13 para.4
s.63, amended: 2009 c.22 Sch.13 para.5
s.64, amended: 2009 c.22 Sch.13 para.6
s.66, amended: 2009 c.22 Sch.13 para.7
s.67, amended: 2009 c.22 Sch.16 Part 6
s.69, amended: 2009 c.22 Sch.16 Part 6
s.69A, added: 2009 c.22 Sch.13 para.10
s.69B, added: 2009 c.22 Sch.13 para.10
s.73, amended: 2009 c.22 Sch.13 para.11
s.75, repealed: 2009 c.22 Sch.6 para.59, Sch.16 Part 2
s.81, repealed: 2009 c.22 s.57, Sch.16 Part 1
s.86, applied: 2009 c.3 s.9
s.88, referred to: SI 2009/2545 Art.4
s.89, referred to: SI 2009/2545 Art.4
s.89, varied: SI 2009/2545 Art.4
s.93A, added: 2009 c.22 s.246
s.94, amended: 2009 c.22 s.242
s.114, enabling: SI 2009/882, SI 2009/887, SI 2009/1740, SI 2009/2750, SI 2009/3007
s.118, applied: SI 2009/1360 Art.3
s.124, applied: SI 2009/1360 Art.3
s.125, see *R. (on the application of City College Birmingham) v Office for Standards in Education, Children Services and Skills* [2009] EWHC 2373 (Admin), [2009] E.L.R. 500 (QBD (Admin)), Burton, J.
s.125, applied: SI 2009/1360 Art.3
s.126, applied: SI 2009/1360 Art.3
s.128, applied: SI 2009/1360 Art.3
s.136, applied: SI 2009/1360 Art.3
s.155, enabling: SI 2009/2724
s.169, amended: 2009 c.26 s.81
s.171, amended: 2009 c.26 s.81
s.181, enabling: SI 2009/49, SI 2009/1027, SI 2009/1556, SI 2009/2545, SI 2009/2984
s.183, enabling: SI 2009/2724
s.188, enabling: SI 2009/49, SI 2009/1027, SI 2009/2545
Sch.2, applied: SI 2009/276 Reg.3
Sch.2 Part 2 para.8, enabling: SI 2009/1556
Sch.12 Part 2 para.9, amended: 2009 c.22 s.226, Sch.16 Part 8
Sch.12 Part 2 para.10, amended: 2009 c.22 s.226, Sch.16 Part 8
Sch.12 Part 2 para.11A, added: 2009 c.22 s.226
Sch.14 para.21, repealed: 2009 c.22 Sch.16 Part 4
Sch.14 para.25, repealed: 2009 c.22 Sch.16 Part 4

41. National Health Service Act 2006
see *R. (on the application of Harrison) v Secretary of State for Health* [2009] EWHC 574 (Admin), (2009) 12 C.C.L. Rep. 355 (QBD (Admin)), Silber, J.
applied: 2009 c.21 Sch.3 para.18

41. National Health Service Act 2006–*cont.*
s.1, see *R. (on the application of Harrison) v Secretary of State for Health* [2009] EWHC 574 (Admin), (2009) 12 C.C.L. Rep. 355 (QBD (Admin)), Silber, J.
s.2, see *R. (on the application of Harrison) v Secretary of State for Health* [2009] EWHC 574 (Admin), (2009) 12 C.C.L. Rep. 355 (QBD (Admin)), Silber, J.
s.7, enabling: SI 2009/112
s.8, enabling: SI 2009/112
s.12, applied: 2009 c.21 s.2
s.12A, added: 2009 c.21 s.11
s.12B, added: 2009 c.21 s.11
s.12C, added: 2009 c.21 s.11
s.12D, added: 2009 c.21 s.11
s.13, applied: SI 2009/2737 Reg.24
s.15, amended: 2009 c.21 s.29
s.16, amended: 2009 c.21 s.29
s.18, applied: SI 2009/2873, SI 2009/2874
s.18, enabling: SI 2009/2873, SI 2009/2874
s.25, applied: SI 2009/43, SI 2009/750, SI 2009/772 Art.3, SI 2009/1510, SI 2009/1577, SI 2009/3085
s.25, referred to: SI 2009/750 Art.3
s.25, enabling: SI 2009/43, SI 2009/750, SI 2009/772, SI 2009/1510, SI 2009/1577, SI 2009/3085, SI 2009/3086
s.28, applied: SI 2009/2737 Reg.24
s.44, amended: 2009 c.21 s.33
s.52A, added: 2009 c.21 s.15
s.52B, added: 2009 c.21 s.15
s.52C, added: 2009 c.21 s.15
s.52D, added: 2009 c.21 s.15
s.52E, added: 2009 c.21 s.15
s.53, amended: 2009 c.21 s.18
s.54, amended: 2009 c.21 s.18
s.65A, added: 2009 c.21 s.16
s.65B, added: 2009 c.21 s.16
s.65C, added: 2009 c.21 s.16
s.65D, added: 2009 c.21 s.16
s.65E, added: 2009 c.21 s.16
s.65F, added: 2009 c.21 s.16
s.65G, added: 2009 c.21 s.16
s.65H, added: 2009 c.21 s.16
s.65I, added: 2009 c.21 s.16
s.65J, added: 2009 c.21 s.16
s.65K, added: 2009 c.21 s.16
s.65L, added: 2009 c.21 s.16
s.65M, added: 2009 c.21 s.16
s.65N, added: 2009 c.21 s.16
s.65O, added: 2009 c.21 s.16
s.65P, added: 2009 c.21 s.17
s.65Q, added: 2009 c.21 s.17
s.65R, added: 2009 c.21 s.17
s.65S, added: 2009 c.21 s.17
s.65T, added: 2009 c.21 s.17
s.65U, added: 2009 c.21 s.17
s.65V, added: 2009 c.21 s.17
s.65W, added: 2009 c.21 s.17
s.65X, added: 2009 c.21 s.17
s.65Y, added: 2009 c.21 s.17
s.65Z, added: 2009 c.21 s.17
s.65Z1, added: 2009 c.21 s.17
s.65Z2, added: 2009 c.21 s.17
s.65Z3, added: 2009 c.21 s.17
s.75, applied: SI 2009/309 Reg.6
s.75, enabling: SI 2009/278
s.80, amended: 2009 c.21 Sch.1 para.7

2006–cont.

41. National Health Service Act 2006–*cont.*
s.83, applied: 2009 c.21 s.2
s.84, applied: 2009 c.21 s.2
s.88, enabling: SI 2009/2230
s.89, enabling: SI 2009/2205, SI 2009/2230
s.92, applied: 2009 c.21 s.2
s.94, enabling: SI 2009/2205, SI 2009/2230
s.100, applied: 2009 c.21 s.2
s.107, applied: 2009 c.21 s.2
s.115, enabling: SI 2009/409
s.117, applied: 2009 c.21 s.2
s.124, applied: 2009 c.21 s.8
s.126, applied: 2009 c.21 s.2
s.126, enabling: SI 2009/599, SI 2009/2205, SI 2009/3340
s.127, applied: 2009 c.21 s.2
s.128A, added: 2009 c.21 s.25
s.129, amended: 2009 c.21 s.26, s.27, Sch.6
s.129, repealed (in part): 2009 c.21 s.26, Sch.6
s.129, enabling: SI 2009/599, SI 2009/2205, SI 2009/3340
s.132, enabling: SI 2009/2205
s.134, amended: 2009 c.21 Sch.1 para.8
s.144, amended: 2009 c.21 s.29
s.150A, added: 2009 c.21 s.28
s.172, enabling: SI 2009/29, SI 2009/411, SI 2009/1166, SI 2009/2230
s.173, amended: 2009 c.21 Sch.1 para.7
s.174, enabling: SI 2009/411
s.175, see *R. (on the application of A) v Secretary of State for Health* [2009] EWCA Civ 225, (2009) 12 C.C.L. Rep. 213 (CA (Civ Div)), Ward, L.J.
s.175, enabling: SI 2009/1166
s.176, enabling: SI 2009/407
s.179, enabling: SI 2009/409
s.180, repealed (in part): 2009 c.21 s.34, Sch.6
s.182, enabling: SI 2009/411, SI 2009/1599, SI 2009/2230
s.183, enabling: SI 2009/411, SI 2009/1599
s.184, enabling: SI 2009/411, SI 2009/1599, SI 2009/2230
s.213, enabling: SI 2009/364, SI 2009/1928
s.217, enabling: SI 2009/364, SI 2009/1928
s.223, amended: SI 2009/1941 Sch.1 para.258
s.234, amended: 2009 c.21 Sch.1 para.7
s.242, amended: 2009 c.21 s.18
s.244, applied: SI 2009/1919 Reg.12
s.246, amended: 2009 c.21 Sch.1 para.9
s.262, enabling: SI 2009/3030
s.263, enabling: SI 2009/3030
s.266, enabling: SI 2009/3030
s.272, amended: 2009 c.21 s.18, Sch.1 para.10
s.272, enabling: SI 2009/29, SI 2009/43, SI 2009/112, SI 2009/278, SI 2009/364, SI 2009/407, SI 2009/409, SI 2009/411, SI 2009/599, SI 2009/750, SI 2009/772, SI 2009/1166, SI 2009/1510, SI 2009/1577, SI 2009/1599, SI 2009/1928, SI 2009/2205, SI 2009/2230, SI 2009/2873, SI 2009/2874, SI 2009/3030, SI 2009/3085, SI 2009/3086, SI 2009/3340
s.273, enabling: SI 2009/43, SI 2009/112, SI 2009/750, SI 2009/772, SI 2009/1510, SI 2009/1577, SI 2009/2873, SI 2009/2874, SI 2009/3085, SI 2009/3086
s.275, amended: 2009 c.21 s.18
s.275, enabling: SI 2009/2205, SI 2009/2230
s.276, amended: 2009 c.21 Sch.1 para.11, Sch.6
Sch.2 para.9, amended: 2009 c.21 Sch.3 para.10

2006–cont.

41. National Health Service Act 2006–*cont.*
Sch.3 Part 2 para.13, enabling: SI 2009/2873, SI 2009/2874
Sch.4 Part 1 para.5, enabling: SI 2009/43, SI 2009/750, SI 2009/772, SI 2009/1510, SI 2009/1577, SI 2009/3085, SI 2009/3086
Sch.4 Part 2 para.25, applied: SI 2009/772
Sch.4 Part 3 para.28, amended: 2009 c.21 s.18
Sch.4 Part 3 para.28, applied: SI 2009/750, SI 2009/772
Sch.4 Part 3 para.28, enabling: SI 2009/750, SI 2009/772
Sch.5 para.1, applied: SI 2009/618
Sch.5 para.1, enabling: SI 2009/618
Sch.6, referred to: 2009 c.21 s.40
Sch.6 para.5, amended: 2009 c.21 Sch.3 para.11
Sch.7 para.23, amended: SI 2009/1941 Sch.1 para.258
Sch.8 para.2, amended: 2009 c.21 Sch.3 para.12
Sch.8 para.2A, added: 2009 c.21 Sch.3 para.12
Sch.8A para.1, added: 2009 c.21 Sch.2
Sch.8A para.2, added: 2009 c.21 Sch.2
Sch.8A para.3, added: 2009 c.21 Sch.2
Sch.8A para.4, added: 2009 c.21 Sch.2
Sch.8A para.5, added: 2009 c.21 Sch.2
Sch.8A para.6, added: 2009 c.21 Sch.2
Sch.8A para.7, added: 2009 c.21 Sch.2
Sch.8A para.8, added: 2009 c.21 Sch.2
Sch.8A para.9, added: 2009 c.21 Sch.2
Sch.8A para.10, added: 2009 c.21 Sch.2
Sch.8A para.11, added: 2009 c.21 Sch.2
Sch.8A para.12, added: 2009 c.21 Sch.2
Sch.9 para.1, amended: 2009 c.21 s.18
Sch.12, applied: 2009 c.21 s.2
Sch.12 para.1, amended: 2009 c.21 s.29
Sch.12 para.1, repealed (in part): 2009 c.21 s.29, Sch.6
Sch.12 para.2, amended: 2009 c.21 s.29
Sch.12 para.2, enabling: SI 2009/599, SI 2009/2205
Sch.12 para.3, amended: 2009 c.21 s.29
Sch.12 para.3, enabling: SI 2009/599, SI 2009/2205
Sch.19, referred to: 2009 c.21 s.40
Sch.19 para.1, amended: 2009 c.21 Sch.3 para.13
Sch.19 para.5A, added: 2009 c.21 Sch.3 para.13

42. National Health Service (Wales) Act 2006
applied: 2009 c.21 Sch.3 para.18
referred to: 2009 c.21 s.37, s.40
Part 2, applied: SI 2009/3050 Art.2
Part 4, applied: SI 2009/3050 Art.3
s.1, referred to: SI 2009/1511 Sch.1
s.3, referred to: SI 2009/1511 Sch.1
s.4, referred to: SI 2009/1511 Sch.1
s.5, referred to: SI 2009/1511 Sch.1
s.6, referred to: SI 2009/1511 Sch.1
s.10, referred to: SI 2009/1511 Sch.1
s.11, applied: SI 2009/2737 Reg.24
s.11, enabling: SI 2009/778, SI 2009/1559, SI 2009/2617, SI 2009/3097
s.12, enabling: SI 2009/266, SI 2009/779, SI 2009/1511, SI 2009/3097
s.13, enabling: SI 2009/779, SI 2009/3097
s.14, referred to: SI 2009/1511 Sch.1
s.15, referred to: SI 2009/1511 Sch.1
s.17, referred to: SI 2009/1511 Sch.1
s.18, applied: SI 2009/2059
s.18, referred to: SI 2009/2058 Art.3

2006– cont.

42. National Health Service (Wales) Act 2006–
cont.
  s.18, enabling: SI 2009/ 201, SI 2009/ 1306, SI 2009/
    1558, SI 2009/ 2058, SI 2009/ 2059, SI 2009/ 2617,
    SI 2009/ 2618
  s.21, enabling: SI 2009/ 1035, SI 2009/ 1382
  s.22, applied: SI 2009/ 2737 Reg.24
  s.38, referred to: SI 2009/ 1511 Sch.1
  s.39, referred to: SI 2009/ 1511 Sch.1
  s.41, referred to: SI 2009/ 1511 Sch.1
  s.42, referred to: SI 2009/ 1511 Sch.1
  s.44, referred to: SI 2009/ 1511 Sch.1
  s.46, enabling: SI 2009/ 1838, SI 2009/ 1977
  s.50, referred to: SI 2009/ 1511 Sch.1
  s.51, referred to: SI 2009/ 1511 Sch.1
  s.53, referred to: SI 2009/ 1511 Sch.1
  s.54, referred to: SI 2009/ 1511 Sch.1
  s.55, referred to: SI 2009/ 1511 Sch.1
  s.56, referred to: SI 2009/ 1511 Sch.1
  s.57, referred to: SI 2009/ 1511 Sch.1
  s.59, referred to: SI 2009/ 1511 Sch.1
  s.61, enabling: SI 2009/ 456
  s.64, referred to: SI 2009/ 1511 Sch.1
  s.65, referred to: SI 2009/ 1511 Sch.1
  s.66, enabling: SI 2009/ 456
  s.67, referred to: SI 2009/ 1511 Sch.1
  s.68, referred to: SI 2009/ 1511 Sch.1
  s.69, referred to: SI 2009/ 1511 Sch.1
  s.70, referred to: SI 2009/ 1511 Sch.1
  s.71, referred to: SI 2009/ 1511 Sch.1
  s.71, enabling: SI 2009/ 311, SI 2009/ 589
  s.75, referred to: SI 2009/ 1511 Sch.1
  s.78, referred to: SI 2009/ 1511 Sch.1
  s.79, referred to: SI 2009/ 1511 Sch.1
  s.80, referred to: SI 2009/ 1511 Sch.1
  s.80, enabling: SI 2009/ 1491
  s.82, referred to: SI 2009/ 1511 Sch.1
  s.83, amended: 2009 c.21 s.30, Sch.6
  s.83, enabling: SI 2009/ 1491
  s.84, enabling: SI 2009/ 1491
  s.86, enabling: SI 2009/ 1491
  s.87, referred to: SI 2009/ 1511 Sch.1
  s.90, referred to: SI 2009/ 1511 Sch.1
  s.91, referred to: SI 2009/ 1511 Sch.1
  s.92, referred to: SI 2009/ 1511 Sch.1
  s.93, referred to: SI 2009/ 1511 Sch.1
  s.106A, added: 2009 c.21 s.31
  s.107, amended: 2009 c.21 s.31
  s.107, referred to: SI 2009/ 1511 Sch.1
  s.108, referred to: SI 2009/ 1511 Sch.1
  s.110, referred to: SI 2009/ 1511 Sch.1
  s.111, referred to: SI 2009/ 1511 Sch.1
  s.113, referred to: SI 2009/ 1511 Sch.1
  s.114, referred to: SI 2009/ 1511 Sch.1
  s.115, referred to: SI 2009/ 1511 Sch.1
  s.121, enabling: SI 2009/ 1175, SI 2009/ 2607
  s.124, enabling: SI 2009/ 1175, SI 2009/ 1512, SI
    2009/ 3005
  s.125, enabling: SI 2009/ 456
  s.128, enabling: SI 2009/ 311, SI 2009/ 589
  s.129, enabling: SI 2009/ 311, SI 2009/ 589
  s.130, enabling: SI 2009/ 54, SI 2009/ 589, SI 2009/
    709, SI 2009/ 2365, SI 2009/ 2607
  s.131, enabling: SI 2009/ 54, SI 2009/ 709, SI 2009/
    2365
  s.132, enabling: SI 2009/ 54, SI 2009/ 709, SI 2009/
    2365, SI 2009/ 2607
  s.137, referred to: SI 2009/ 1511 Sch.1

2006– cont.

42. National Health Service (Wales) Act 2006–
cont.
  s.138, referred to: SI 2009/ 1511 Sch.1
  s.159, referred to: SI 2009/ 1511 Sch.1
  s.163, referred to: SI 2009/ 1511 Sch.1
  s.166, referred to: SI 2009/ 1511 Sch.1
  s.170, amended: SI 2009/ 1941 Sch.1 para.259
  s.183, referred to: SI 2009/ 1511 Sch.1
  s.197, referred to: SI 2009/ 1511 Sch.1
  s.198, referred to: SI 2009/ 1511 Sch.1
  s.200, referred to: SI 2009/ 1511 Sch.1
  s.203, enabling: SI 2009/ 54, SI 2009/ 201, SI 2009/
    311, SI 2009/ 456, SI 2009/ 589, SI 2009/ 709, SI
    2009/ 778, SI 2009/ 1175, SI 2009/ 1382, SI 2009/
    1385, SI 2009/ 1491, SI 2009/ 1511, SI 2009/ 1512, SI
    2009/ 1558, SI 2009/ 1559, SI 2009/ 1824, SI 2009/
    1838, SI 2009/ 1977, SI 2009/ 2365, SI 2009/ 2607,
    SI 2009/ 2618, SI 2009/ 3097
  s.204, enabling: SI 2009/ 201, SI 2009/ 266, SI 2009/
    778, SI 2009/ 1306, SI 2009/ 1511, SI 2009/ 2059
  s.206, amended: 2009 c.21 s.18
  Sch.1 para.1, referred to: SI 2009/ 1511 Sch.1
  Sch.1 para.2, referred to: SI 2009/ 1511 Sch.1
  Sch.1 para.8, referred to: SI 2009/ 1511 Sch.1
  Sch.1 para.9, referred to: SI 2009/ 1511 Sch.1
  Sch.1 para.10, referred to: SI 2009/ 1511 Sch.1
  Sch.1 para.12, referred to: SI 2009/ 1511 Sch.1
  Sch.1 para.13, referred to: SI 2009/ 1511 Sch.1
  Sch.2 Part 1 para.4, enabling: SI 2009/ 779, SI
    2009/ 3097
  Sch.2 Part 1 para.7, applied: SI 2009/ 779
  Sch.2 Part 1 para.7, enabling: SI 2009/ 779
  Sch.2 Part 1 para.10, applied: SI 2009/ 779 Reg.17
  Sch.2 Part 2 para.11, enabling: SI 2009/ 778
  Sch.2 Part 2 para.12, enabling: SI 2009/ 778
  Sch.2 Part 3 para.21, enabling: SI 2009/ 1559
  Sch.2 Part 3 para.22, enabling: SI 2009/ 2617
  Sch.2 Part 3 para.23, enabling: SI 2009/ 2617
  Sch.2 Part 3 para.24, enabling: SI 2009/ 1559
  Sch.3 Part 1 para.4, enabling: SI 2009/ 201, SI 2009/
    1385
  Sch.3 Part 1 para.5, enabling: SI 2009/ 2058
  Sch.3 Part 1 para.7, enabling: SI 2009/ 2058
  Sch.3 Part 1 para.9, enabling: SI 2009/ 2617, SI
    2009/ 2618
  Sch.3 Part 1 para.11, applied: SI 2009/ 1385 Reg.24
  Sch.3 Part 3 para.28, applied: SI 2009/ 1306
  Sch.3 Part 3 para.28, enabling: SI 2009/ 1306
  Sch.3 Part 3 para.29, enabling: SI 2009/ 1558
  Sch.4 para.1, applied: SI 2009/ 1035, SI 2009/ 1382
  Sch.4 para.1, enabling: SI 2009/ 1035, SI 2009/ 1382
  Sch.5 para.5, amended: 2009 c.21 Sch.3 para.15
  Sch.6 para.1, referred to: SI 2009/ 1511 Sch.1
  Sch.6 para.2, referred to: SI 2009/ 1511 Sch.1
  Sch.6 para.3, referred to: SI 2009/ 1511 Sch.1
  Sch.6 para.4, referred to: SI 2009/ 1511 Sch.1
  Sch.6 para.5, referred to: SI 2009/ 1511 Sch.1
  Sch.6 para.7, referred to: SI 2009/ 1511 Sch.1
  Sch.7 para.1, amended: 2009 c.21 s.32
  Sch.7 para.1, repealed (in part): 2009 c.21 s.32, Sch.6
  Sch.7 para.3, amended: 2009 c.21 s.32
  Sch.10 para.2, amended: 2009 c.21 Sch.3 para.16,
    Sch.6
  Sch.10 para.2A, added: 2009 c.21 Sch.3 para.16
  Sch.13 para.1, amended: 2009 c.21 Sch.3 para.17
  Sch.13 para.5A, added: 2009 c.21 Sch.3 para.17

2006—cont.

43. National Health Service (Consequential Provisions) Act 2006
Sch.2 Part 2 para.16, amended: SI 2009/1511 Reg.7
Sch.2 Part 2 para.16, repealed (in part): SI 2009/1511 Reg.7

45. Animal Welfare Act 2006
see *Hanchett-Stamford v Attorney General* [2008] EWHC 330 (Ch), [2009] Ch. 173 (Ch D (Bristol)), Lewison, J.
s.8, repealed (in part): 2009 c.25 Sch.23 Part 5
s.10, applied: SI 2009/665 Art.2
s.34, applied: SSI 2009/141 Reg.4

46. Companies Act 2006
applied: 2009 c.1 s.82, s.83, s.93, 2009 c.4 s.46, s.764, SI 2009/209 Reg.20, Sch.3 para.19, SI 2009/1085 Reg.4, Reg.6, Reg.8, Reg.9, Reg.10, Reg.11, Reg.12, SI 2009/1209 r.9, SI 2009/1211 r.9, SI 2009/1804 Sch.1 para.1, SI 2009/1941 Art.3, SI 2009/2041 r.9, SI 2009/2436 Sch.2 para.10, Sch.2 para.37, SI 2009/2437 Reg.2, Reg.12, Reg.16, Reg.18, SI 2009/2477 r.58, SI 2009/2615 Reg.6, SI 2009/2767 Sch.1
disapplied: SI 2009/814 Art.3, SI 2009/2436 Sch.2 para.13, SI 2009/3226 Sch.1 para.28
referred to: 2009 c.1 s.166, 2009 c.20 s.44, SI 2009/357 r.4, SI 2009/1804 Reg.83, Sch.1 para.15, SI 2009/1941 Art.12, SI 2009/2436 Sch.2 para.1
varied: SI 2009/317 Sch.1
Part 3 c.3, applied: SI 2009/1803 Reg.6, Reg.8, SI 2009/1941 Sch.3 para.3
Part 7, applied: SI 2009/2101 Sch.1 para.7, Sch.1 para.8
Part 7, referred to: SI 2009/1941 Sch.3 para.2
Part 10 c.4, applied: SI 2009/814 Art.7
Part 10 c.8, applied: SI 2009/2400 Sch.2 para.9, Sch.2 para.10, SI 2009/2436 Sch.2 para.17
Part 10 c.8, referred to: SI 2009/2436 Sch.2 para.18
Part 15, applied: SI 2009/1803 Reg.6
Part 16, applied: 2009 c.20 s.40, SI 2009/2436 Reg.6
Part 16, disapplied: SI 2009/476 Art.5
Part 18 c.2, applied: SI 2009/2579 Sch.1 para.18, SI 2009/2604 Sch.1 para.18
Part 24, applied: SI 2009/1804 Sch.1 para.15, SI 2009/2436 Sch.2 para.37
Part 25, applied: SI 2009/214 Reg.11, SI 2009/1803 Reg.8, SI 2009/2101 Sch.1 para.7, Sch.1 para.9
Part 25, disapplied: 2009 c.1 s.252
Part 25, referred to: 2009 c.1 s.252
Part 30, applied: SI 2009/2425 Reg.6, SI 2009/2469 r.2
Part 34, applied: SI 2009/1085 Reg.9
Part 35, applied: SI 2009/1804 Sch.1 para.27
Part 35, referred to: SI 2009/1804 Reg.60
Part 26, see *Lehman Brothers International (Europe) (In Administration) (No.2), Re* [2009] EWCA Civ 1161, Times, November 12, 2009 (CA (Civ Div)), Lord Neuberger of Abbotsbury MR
s.1, applied: SI 2009/490 Art.3, SI 2009/2436 Reg.3, Reg.5
s.1, referred to: SI 2009/2437 Reg.24
s.3, referred to: SI 2009/1941 Art.13
s.10, applied: SI 2009/388 Art.2, SI 2009/2101 Sch.2 para.28
s.10, enabling: SI 2009/388
s.12, applied: SI 2009/214 Reg.9
s.14, applied: SI 2009/2101 Sch.1 para.7
s.17, referred to: SI 2009/2999 Reg.31
s.19, applied: SI 2009/2437 Reg.19

2006—cont.

46. Companies Act 2006—*cont.*
s.26, applied: SI 2009/1941 Art.5, SI 2009/2436 Sch.2 para.2, Sch.2 para.3
s.26, varied: SI 2009/2436 Sch.1 para.1
s.27, varied: SI 2009/2436 Sch.1 para.1
s.28, applied: SI 2009/1941 Art.5
s.31, applied: SI 2009/490 Art.3
s.32, applied: SI 2009/388 Art.2
s.32, enabling: SI 2009/388
s.33, applied: SI 2009/1941 Art.11
s.34, applied: SI 2009/1085 Reg.11, SI 2009/1803 Reg.6, SI 2009/2436 Sch.2 para.4
s.34, varied: SI 2009/2436 Sch.1 para.2
s.35, applied: SI 2009/1803 Reg.6, SI 2009/2436 Sch.2 para.5
s.35, varied: SI 2009/2436 Sch.1 para.2
s.39, applied: SI 2009/2436 Sch.1 para.3, Sch.2 para.6
s.40, see *Ford v Polymer Vision Ltd* [2009] EWHC 945 (Ch), [2009] 2 B.C.L.C. 160 (Ch D), Blackburne, J.
s.40, applied: SI 2009/2436 Sch.1 para.3
s.41, applied: SI 2009/2436 Sch.1 para.3
s.42, applied: SI 2009/1941 Art.6, SI 2009/2436 Sch.1 para.3
s.43, applied: SI 2009/1917 Reg.4, SI 2009/2436 Sch.1 para.3
s.43, varied: SI 2009/1804 Reg.4
s.44, see *Lovett v Carson Country Homes Ltd* [2009] EWHC 1143 (Ch), [2009] 2 B.C.L.C. 196 (Ch D), Davis, J.
s.44, applied: SI 2009/1917 Reg.4, SI 2009/2436 Sch.1 para.3, Sch.2 para.7
s.44, varied: SI 2009/1804 Reg.4
s.45, applied: SI 2009/2436 Sch.1 para.3
s.45, varied: SI 2009/1804 Reg.4
s.46, applied: SI 2009/1917 Reg.4, SI 2009/2436 Sch.1 para.3
s.46, varied: SI 2009/1804 Reg.4
s.47, applied: SI 2009/1804 Sch.1 para.2
s.47, varied: SI 2009/1804 Reg.4
s.48, applied: SI 2009/1917 Reg.5, SI 2009/2436 Sch.1 para.3
s.48, varied: SI 2009/1804 Reg.5
s.49, varied: SI 2009/1804 Reg.6
s.50, applied: SI 2009/2436 Sch.1 para.3
s.51, applied: SI 2009/1917 Reg.6, SI 2009/2436 Sch.1 para.3
s.51, varied: SI 2009/1804 Reg.7
s.52, varied: SI 2009/1804 Reg.7
s.53, substituted: SI 2009/1804 Reg.8
s.54, amended: SI 2009/1804 Reg.8, SI 2009/2958 Art.9
s.54, applied: SI 2009/214 Sch.1, SI 2009/1804 Sch.1 para.3, Sch.1 para.4, SI 2009/2982, SI 2009/2982 Reg.3, Reg.4
s.54, referred to: SI 2009/2982 Reg.2
s.54, substituted: SI 2009/1804 Reg.8
s.54, enabling: SI 2009/2982
s.55, applied: SI 2009/1804 Sch.1 para.3, Sch.1 para.4, SI 2009/2615 Reg.2, Reg.3, Reg.4, Reg.5, Reg.6
s.55, substituted: SI 2009/1804 Reg.8
s.55, enabling: SI 2009/2615
s.56, applied: SI 2009/1804 Sch.1 para.4
s.56, substituted: SI 2009/1804 Reg.8
s.56, enabling: SI 2009/2615, SI 2009/2982
s.57, applied: SI 2009/1804 Sch.1 para.3
s.57, varied: SI 2009/1804 Reg.9

46. Companies Act 2006– *cont.*
s.57, enabling: SI 2009/1085
s.59, applied: SI 2009/1085 Reg.5
s.60, applied: SI 2009/1085 Reg.5
s.60, enabling: SI 2009/1085
s.64, applied: SI 2009/2101 Sch.1 para.7
s.65, applied: SI 2009/1804 Sch.1 para.3, SI 2009/1941 Sch.3 para.2
s.65, varied: SI 2009/1804 Reg.10
s.65, enabling: SI 2009/1085, SI 2009/2404
s.66, applied: SI 2009/1085 Reg.7, SI 2009/1804 Sch.1 para.3
s.66, varied: SI 2009/1804 Reg.11
s.66, enabling: SI 2009/1085, SI 2009/2404
s.67, applied: SI 2009/2101 Sch.1 para.7, Sch.1 para.9
s.67, varied: SI 2009/1804 Reg.11
s.68, varied: SI 2009/1804 Reg.11
s.69, see *Barloworld Handling Ltd v Unilift South Wales Ltd* [2009] F.S.R. 21 (Arbitration), Judi Pike
s.69, varied: SI 2009/1804 Reg.12
s.70, varied: SI 2009/1804 Reg.12
s.71, varied: SI 2009/1804 Reg.12
s.72, varied: SI 2009/1804 Reg.12
s.73, applied: SI 2009/2101 Sch.1 para.7, Sch.1 para.9
s.73, varied: SI 2009/1804 Reg.12
s.74, applied: SI 2009/2101 Sch.1 para.7, Sch.1 para.9
s.74, varied: SI 2009/1804 Reg.12
s.75, varied: SI 2009/1804 Reg.13
s.76, varied: SI 2009/1804 Reg.13
s.78, applied: SI 2009/2101 Sch.1 para.8
s.80, applied: SI 2009/2101 Sch.1 para.7
s.82, applied: SI 2009/218
s.82, varied: SI 2009/1804 Reg.14, SI 2009/2436 Sch.1 para.4
s.82, enabling: SI 2009/218
s.83, varied: SI 2009/1804 Reg.14, SI 2009/2436 Sch.1 para.4
s.84, applied: SI 2009/814 Art.7, SI 2009/3226 Sch.5 para.1
s.84, varied: SI 2009/2436 Sch.1 para.4
s.85, varied: SI 2009/1804 Reg.15, SI 2009/2436 Sch.1 para.4
s.86, applied: SI 2009/2436 Sch.2 para.8
s.86, varied: SI 2009/1804 Reg.16, SI 2009/2436 Sch.1 para.5
s.87, applied: SI 2009/1803 Reg.4
s.87, varied: SI 2009/1804 Reg.16, SI 2009/2436 Sch.1 para.5
s.88, applied: SI 2009/1803 Reg.6, SI 2009/2615 Reg.2
s.88, referred to: SI 2009/2615 Reg.6
s.88, varied: SI 2009/1804 Reg.17
s.90, varied: SI 2009/1941 Sch.3 para.3
s.91, applied: SI 2009/2425 Reg.9, SI 2009/2437 Reg.9
s.91, varied: SI 2009/1941 Sch.3 para.3
s.92, applied: SI 2009/2437 Reg.9
s.92, varied: SI 2009/1941 Sch.3 para.3
s.93, applied: SI 2009/2437 Reg.9
s.93, varied: SI 2009/1941 Sch.3 para.3
s.94, applied: SI 2009/1803 Reg.7, Reg.8
s.94, varied: SI 2009/1941 Sch.3 para.3
s.95, varied: SI 2009/1941 Sch.3 para.3
s.96, varied: SI 2009/1941 Sch.3 para.3

46. Companies Act 2006– *cont.*
s.98, applied: SI 2009/1941 Sch.3 para.4, Sch.3 para.6
s.99, applied: SI 2009/1941 Sch.3 para.4
s.99, referred to: SI 2009/1941 Sch.3 para.4
s.108, applied: SI 2009/388 Art.2, SI 2009/2101 Sch.2 para.28
s.108, disapplied: SI 2009/2101 Sch.1 para.11
s.108, enabling: SI 2009/388
s.116, applied: SI 2009/214 Reg.10
s.117, applied: SI 2009/214 Reg.10
s.145, amended: SI 2009/1632 Reg.12, Reg.17
s.153, amended: SI 2009/1632 Reg.17
s.162, applied: SI 2009/814 Art.7, SI 2009/1804 Sch.1 para.5, SI 2009/2436 Sch.1 para.6, Sch.2 para.9, SI 2009/3226 Sch.5 para.1
s.162, referred to: SI 2009/1804 Sch.1 para.13, SI 2009/2437 Reg.7
s.162, varied: SI 2009/1804 Reg.18, SI 2009/2436 Sch.1 para.6
s.163, applied: SI 2009/1804 Sch.1 para.5, SI 2009/2436 Sch.1 para.6, Sch.2 para.11
s.163, referred to: SI 2009/2437 Reg.7
s.163, varied: SI 2009/1804 Reg.18
s.164, applied: SI 2009/2436 Sch.1 para.6
s.164, referred to: SI 2009/2437 Reg.7
s.164, varied: SI 2009/1804 Reg.18
s.165, applied: SI 2009/814 Art.7, SI 2009/1804 Sch.1 para.6, SI 2009/2436 Sch.1 para.6, SI 2009/3226 Sch.5 para.1
s.165, referred to: SI 2009/2437 Reg.7
s.165, varied: SI 2009/1804 Reg.18
s.166, applied: SI 2009/2436 Sch.1 para.6
s.167, applied: SI 2009/214 Reg.9, SI 2009/814 Art.7, SI 2009/2436 Sch.1 para.6, Sch.2 para.11, Sch.2 para.12, Sch.2 para.13, Sch.2 para.14, Sch.2 para.15, SI 2009/3226 Sch.5 para.1
s.170, applied: SI 2009/814 Art.7, SI 2009/3226 Sch.5 para.1
s.171, applied: SI 2009/814 Art.7, SI 2009/3226 Sch.5 para.1
s.172, applied: SI 2009/814 Art.7, SI 2009/3226 Sch.5 para.1
s.173, applied: SI 2009/814 Art.7, SI 2009/3226 Sch.5 para.1
s.174, applied: SI 2009/814 Art.7, SI 2009/3226 Sch.5 para.1
s.175, applied: SI 2009/814 Art.7, SI 2009/3226 Sch.5 para.1
s.176, applied: SI 2009/814 Art.7, SI 2009/3226 Sch.5 para.1
s.177, applied: SI 2009/814 Art.7, SI 2009/3226 Sch.5 para.1
s.182, applied: SI 2009/814 Art.7, SI 2009/3226 Sch.5 para.1
s.183, applied: SI 2009/814 Art.7, SI 2009/3226 Sch.5 para.1
s.184, applied: SI 2009/814 Art.7, SI 2009/3226 Sch.5 para.1
s.185, applied: SI 2009/814 Art.7, SI 2009/3226 Sch.5 para.1
s.186, applied: SI 2009/814 Art.7, SI 2009/3226 Sch.5 para.1
s.187, applied: SI 2009/814 Art.7, SI 2009/3226 Sch.5 para.1
s.188, applied: SI 2009/3226 Sch.5 para.1
s.189, applied: SI 2009/3226 Sch.5 para.1
s.190, applied: SI 2009/3226 Sch.5 para.1
s.191, applied: SI 2009/3226 Sch.5 para.1

2006–cont.

46. Companies Act 2006– *cont.*

s.192, applied: SI 2009/3226 Sch.5 para.1
s.193, applied: SI 2009/3226 Sch.5 para.1
s.194, applied: SI 2009/3226 Sch.5 para.1
s.195, applied: SI 2009/3226 Sch.5 para.1
s.196, applied: SI 2009/3226 Sch.5 para.1
s.197, applied: SI 2009/3226 Sch.5 para.1
s.198, applied: SI 2009/3226 Sch.5 para.1
s.199, applied: SI 2009/3226 Sch.5 para.1
s.200, applied: SI 2009/3226 Sch.5 para.1
s.201, applied: SI 2009/3226 Sch.5 para.1
s.202, applied: SI 2009/3226 Sch.5 para.1
s.203, applied: SI 2009/3226 Sch.5 para.1
s.204, applied: SI 2009/3226 Sch.5 para.1
s.205, applied: SI 2009/3226 Sch.5 para.1
s.206, applied: SI 2009/3226 Sch.5 para.1
s.207, applied: SI 2009/3226 Sch.5 para.1
s.208, applied: SI 2009/3226 Sch.5 para.1
s.209, applied: SI 2009/3226 Sch.5 para.1
s.210, applied: SI 2009/3226 Sch.5 para.1
s.211, applied: SI 2009/3226 Sch.5 para.1
s.212, applied: SI 2009/3226 Sch.5 para.1
s.213, applied: SI 2009/3226 Sch.5 para.1
s.214, applied: SI 2009/3226 Sch.5 para.1
s.215, applied: SI 2009/3226 Sch.5 para.1
s.216, applied: SI 2009/3226 Sch.5 para.1
s.217, applied: SI 2009/3226 Sch.5 para.1
s.218, applied: SI 2009/3226 Sch.5 para.1
s.219, applied: SI 2009/3226 Sch.5 para.1
s.220, applied: SI 2009/3226 Sch.5 para.1
s.221, applied: SI 2009/3226 Sch.5 para.1
s.222, applied: SI 2009/3226 Sch.5 para.1
s.223, applied: SI 2009/814 Art.7, SI 2009/3226 Sch.5 para.1
s.227, applied: SI 2009/814 Art.7, SI 2009/3226 Sch.5 para.1
s.228, applied: SI 2009/814 Art.7, SI 2009/3226 Sch.5 para.1
s.229, applied: SI 2009/814 Art.7, SI 2009/3226 Sch.5 para.1
s.230, applied: SI 2009/814 Art.7, SI 2009/3226 Sch.5 para.1
s.231, applied: SI 2009/814 Art.7, SI 2009/3226 Sch.5 para.1
s.235, referred to: SI 2009/2767 Sch.1
s.240, applied: SI 2009/1804 Sch.1 para.8, SI 2009/2436 Sch.1 para.7
s.240, varied: SI 2009/1804 Reg.19
s.241, applied: SI 2009/1804 Sch.1 para.8, SI 2009/2436 Sch.1 para.7
s.241, varied: SI 2009/1804 Reg.19
s.242, applied: SI 2009/1804 Sch.1 para.8, SI 2009/2101 Sch.3 para.1, SI 2009/2400 Sch.2 para.10, SI 2009/2436 Sch.1 para.7
s.242, disapplied: SI 2009/1804 Sch.1 para.9, SI 2009/2400 Sch.2 para.10, SI 2009/2436 Sch.2 para.18
s.242, referred to: SI 2009/2436 Sch.2 para.18
s.242, varied: SI 2009/1804 Reg.19
s.243, applied: SI 2009/214 Reg.2, SI 2009/1804 Sch.1 para.8, Sch.1 para.12, SI 2009/2400 Sch.2 para.13, SI 2009/2436 Sch.1 para.7
s.243, varied: SI 2009/1804 Reg.19, SI 2009/2436 Sch.1 para.7
s.243, enabling: SI 2009/214, SI 2009/2101
s.244, applied: SI 2009/1804 Sch.1 para.8, SI 2009/2436 Sch.1 para.7
s.244, varied: SI 2009/1804 Reg.19

2006–cont.

46. Companies Act 2006– *cont.*

s.245, applied: SI 2009/1804 Sch.1 para.8, Sch.1 para.10, SI 2009/2400 Sch.2 para.11, SI 2009/2436 Sch.1 para.7, Sch.2 para.19
s.245, varied: SI 2009/1804 Reg.19
s.246, applied: SI 2009/1804 Sch.1 para.8, SI 2009/2436 Sch.1 para.7
s.246, varied: SI 2009/1804 Reg.19
s.260, applied: SI 2009/814 Art.7, SI 2009/3226 Sch.5 para.1
s.261, applied: SI 2009/814 Art.7, SI 2009/3226 Sch.5 para.1
s.262, applied: SI 2009/814 Art.7, SI 2009/3226 Sch.5 para.1
s.263, applied: SI 2009/814 Art.7, SI 2009/3226 Sch.5 para.1
s.264, applied: SI 2009/814 Art.7, SI 2009/3226 Sch.5 para.1
s.265, applied: SI 2009/814 Art.7, SI 2009/3226 Sch.5 para.1
s.266, see *Wishart, Petitioner* [2009] CSIH 65, 2009 S.L.T. 812 (IH (Ex Div)), Lord Nimmo Smith; see *Wishart, Petitioner* [2009] CSOH 20, 2009 S.L.T. 376 (OH), Lord Glennie
s.266, applied: SI 2009/814 Art.7, SI 2009/3226 Sch.5 para.1
s.267, applied: SI 2009/814 Art.7, SI 2009/3226 Sch.5 para.1
s.268, see *Wishart, Petitioner* [2009] CSIH 65, 2009 S.L.T. 812 (IH (Ex Div)), Lord Nimmo Smith; see *Wishart, Petitioner* [2009] CSOH 20, 2009 S.L.T. 376 (OH), Lord Glennie
s.268, applied: SI 2009/814 Art.7, SI 2009/3226 Sch.5 para.1
s.269, applied: SI 2009/814 Art.7, SI 2009/3226 Sch.5 para.1
s.275, applied: SI 2009/2436 Sch.1 para.8, Sch.2 para.9, SI 2009/3226 Sch.5 para.1
s.275, varied: SI 2009/2436 Sch.1 para.8
s.276, applied: SI 2009/2436 Sch.1 para.8, Sch.2 para.11, Sch.2 para.13, Sch.2 para.15, SI 2009/3226 Sch.5 para.1
s.277, applied: SI 2009/2436 Sch.1 para.8, Sch.2 para.11
s.277, referred to: SI 2009/2437 Reg.7
s.278, applied: SI 2009/2436 Sch.1 para.8
s.278, referred to: SI 2009/2437 Reg.7
s.279, applied: SI 2009/2436 Sch.1 para.8
s.282, amended: SI 2009/1632 Reg.2, Reg.5
s.283, amended: SI 2009/1632 Reg.2, Reg.5
s.284, amended: SI 2009/1632 Reg.2
s.285, substituted: SI 2009/1632 Reg.3
s.302, applied: 2009 c.20 s.48
s.303, amended: SI 2009/1632 Reg.4
s.303, repealed (in part): SI 2009/1632 Reg.4
s.307, amended: SI 2009/1632 Reg.9
s.307A, added: SI 2009/1632 Reg.9
s.307A, referred to: SI 2009/1632 Reg.23
s.311, amended: SI 2009/1632 Reg.10
s.311A, added: SI 2009/1632 Reg.11
s.319A, added: SI 2009/1632 Reg.12
s.322A, added: SI 2009/1632 Reg.5
s.323, amended: SI 2009/1632 Reg.6
s.323, applied: SI 2009/1804 Reg.45, SI 2009/2477 r.54, r.67
s.324A, added: SI 2009/1632 Reg.7
s.327, amended: SI 2009/1632 Reg.13
s.330, amended: SI 2009/1632 Reg.13
s.333A, added: SI 2009/1632 Reg.13

2006– cont.

46. Companies Act 2006– *cont.*
s.334, amended: SI 2009/ 1632 Reg.14
s.336, amended: SI 2009/ 1632 Reg.15
s.337, amended: SI 2009/ 1632 Reg.15, Reg.16
s.338, amended: SI 2009/ 1632 Reg.15
s.338A, added: SI 2009/ 1632 Reg.17
s.338A, amended: SI 2009/ 1632 Reg.15
s.339, amended: SI 2009/ 1632 Reg.15
s.340, amended: SI 2009/ 1632 Reg.15
s.340A, added: SI 2009/ 1632 Reg.18
s.340A, amended: SI 2009/ 1632 Reg.15
s.340B, added: SI 2009/ 1632 Reg.18
s.340B, amended: SI 2009/ 1632 Reg.15
s.341, amended: SI 2009/ 1632 Reg.19
s.342, amended: SI 2009/ 1632 Reg.19
s.343, amended: SI 2009/ 1632 Reg.19
s.344, amended: SI 2009/ 1632 Reg.19
s.345, amended: SI 2009/ 1632 Reg.19
s.346, amended: SI 2009/ 1632 Reg.19
s.347, amended: SI 2009/ 1632 Reg.19
s.348, amended: SI 2009/ 1632 Reg.19
s.349, amended: SI 2009/ 1632 Reg.19
s.350, amended: SI 2009/ 1632 Reg.19
s.351, amended: SI 2009/ 1632 Reg.19
s.352, amended: SI 2009/ 1632 Reg.19
s.353, amended: SI 2009/ 1632 Reg.19
s.354, amended: SI 2009/ 1632 Reg.19
s.360, amended: SI 2009/ 1632 Reg.9, Reg.16, Reg.17, Reg.18
s.360A, added: SI 2009/ 1632 Reg.8
s.360B, added: SI 2009/ 1632 Reg.20
s.360C, added: SI 2009/ 1632 Reg.21
s.362, applied: SI 2009/ 2436 Sch.1 para.9, Sch.2 para.20
s.363, applied: SI 2009/ 2436 Sch.1 para.9, Sch.2 para.20
s.364, applied: SI 2009/ 2436 Sch.1 para.9, Sch.2 para.20
s.365, applied: SI 2009/ 2436 Sch.1 para.9, Sch.2 para.20
s.366, applied: SI 2009/ 2436 Sch.1 para.9, Sch.2 para.20
s.367, amended: SI 2009/ 1941 Sch.1 para.260
s.367, applied: SI 2009/ 2436 Sch.1 para.9, Sch.2 para.20
s.368, applied: SI 2009/ 2436 Sch.1 para.9, Sch.2 para.20
s.369, applied: SI 2009/ 2436 Sch.1 para.9, Sch.2 para.20
s.369, varied: SI 2009/ 2436 Sch.1 para.9
s.370, applied: SI 2009/ 2436 Sch.1 para.9, Sch.2 para.20
s.371, applied: SI 2009/ 2436 Sch.1 para.9, Sch.2 para.20
s.372, applied: SI 2009/ 2436 Sch.1 para.9, Sch.2 para.20
s.373, applied: SI 2009/ 2436 Sch.1 para.9, Sch.2 para.20
s.374, applied: SI 2009/ 2436 Sch.1 para.9, Sch.2 para.20
s.375, applied: SI 2009/ 2436 Sch.1 para.9, Sch.2 para.20
s.376, applied: SI 2009/ 2436 Sch.1 para.9, Sch.2 para.20
s.377, applied: SI 2009/ 2436 Sch.1 para.9, Sch.2 para.20
s.377, varied: SI 2009/ 2436 Sch.1 para.9
s.378, applied: SI 2009/ 2436 Sch.1 para.9, Sch.2 para.20

2006– cont.

46. Companies Act 2006– *cont.*
s.379, applied: SI 2009/ 2436 Sch.1 para.9, Sch.2 para.20
s.380, applied: SI 2009/ 2436 Sch.1 para.10, Sch.2 para.21
s.381, applied: SI 2009/ 2436 Sch.1 para.10, Sch.2 para.21
s.382, applied: SI 2009/ 2436 Sch.1 para.10, Sch.2 para.21, Sch.2 para.22
s.382, referred to: SI 2009/ 389 Reg.41
s.382A, applied: SI 2009/ 2436 Sch.1 para.10, Sch.2 para.21
s.382B, applied: SI 2009/ 2436 Sch.1 para.10, Sch.2 para.21
s.383, applied: SI 2009/ 2436 Sch.1 para.10, Sch.2 para.21, Sch.2 para.22
s.383, varied: SI 2009/ 2436 Sch.1 para.10
s.384, applied: SI 2009/ 2436 Sch.1 para.10, Sch.2 para.21, Sch.2 para.22
s.385, applied: SI 2009/ 2436 Sch.1 para.10, Sch.2 para.21
s.388, applied: SI 2009/ 1801 Sch.1
s.390, varied: SI 2009/ 1801 Reg.37, Reg.52
s.391, varied: SI 2009/ 1801 Reg.37, Reg.52
s.392, varied: SI 2009/ 1801 Reg.37, Reg.52
s.393, applied: SI 2009/ 2436 Sch.1 para.10, Sch.2 para.21
s.394, applied: SI 2009/ 2436 Sch.1 para.10, Sch.2 para.21
s.394, varied: SI 2009/ 1801 Reg.38, Reg.53
s.395, applied: SI 2009/ 2436 Sch.1 para.10, Sch.2 para.21
s.395, varied: SI 2009/ 1801 Reg.38, Reg.53
s.396, applied: SI 2009/ 2436 Sch.1 para.10, Sch.2 para.21
s.396, referred to: SI 2009/ 2999 Reg.31
s.396, varied: SI 2009/ 1801 Reg.38, Reg.53, SI 2009/ 2436 Sch.1 para.10
s.397, applied: SI 2009/ 2436 Sch.1 para.10, Sch.2 para.21
s.397, varied: SI 2009/ 1801 Reg.38, Reg.53
s.398, applied: SI 2009/ 2436 Sch.1 para.10, Sch.2 para.21
s.399, applied: SI 2009/ 2436 Sch.1 para.10, Sch.2 para.21
s.399, varied: SI 2009/ 1801 Reg.38, Reg.53
s.400, applied: SI 2009/ 1803 Reg.8, SI 2009/ 2436 Sch.1 para.10, Sch.2 para.21
s.401, applied: SI 2009/ 1803 Reg.8, SI 2009/ 2436 Sch.1 para.10, Sch.2 para.21
s.402, applied: SI 2009/ 2436 Sch.1 para.10, Sch.2 para.21
s.402, varied: SI 2009/ 1801 Reg.38, Reg.53
s.403, applied: SI 2009/ 2436 Sch.1 para.10, Sch.2 para.21
s.403, varied: SI 2009/ 1801 Reg.38, Reg.53
s.404, applied: SI 2009/ 2436 Sch.1 para.10, Sch.2 para.21
s.404, varied: SI 2009/ 1801 Reg.38, Reg.53, SI 2009/ 2436 Sch.1 para.10
s.405, applied: SI 2009/ 2436 Sch.1 para.10, Sch.2 para.21
s.405, varied: SI 2009/ 1801 Reg.38, Reg.53
s.406, applied: SI 2009/ 2436 Sch.1 para.10, Sch.2 para.21
s.406, varied: SI 2009/ 1801 Reg.38, Reg.53
s.407, applied: SI 2009/ 2436 Sch.1 para.10, Sch.2 para.21

2006–cont.

46. Companies Act 2006–*cont.*

s.408, applied: SI 2009/2436 Sch.1 para.10, Sch.2 para.21

s.409, applied: SI 2009/2436 Sch.1 para.10, Sch.2 para.21

s.409, varied: SI 2009/2436 Sch.1 para.10

s.410, applied: SI 2009/2436 Sch.1 para.10, Sch.2 para.21

s.410A, applied: SI 2009/2436 Sch.1 para.10, Sch.2 para.21

s.411, applied: SI 2009/2436 Sch.1 para.10, Sch.2 para.21

s.412, applied: SI 2009/2436 Sch.1 para.10, Sch.2 para.21

s.412, varied: SI 2009/2436 Sch.1 para.10

s.413, amended: SI 2009/3022 Reg.2

s.413, applied: SI 2009/2436 Sch.1 para.10, Sch.2 para.21

s.414, applied: SI 2009/1926 Reg.8, SI 2009/2436 Sch.1 para.10, Sch.2 para.21

s.414, varied: SI 2009/1801 Reg.39, Reg.54

s.415, applied: SI 2009/2436 Sch.1 para.10, Sch.2 para.21

s.415A, applied: SI 2009/2436 Sch.1 para.10, Sch.2 para.21

s.416, applied: SI 2009/2436 Sch.1 para.10, Sch.2 para.21

s.416, varied: SI 2009/2436 Sch.1 para.10

s.418, applied: SI 2009/2436 Sch.1 para.10, Sch.2 para.21

s.419, applied: SI 2009/2436 Sch.1 para.10, Sch.2 para.21

s.419A, added: SI 2009/1581 Reg.2

s.419A, applied: SI 2009/2436 Sch.1 para.10, Sch.2 para.21

s.421, varied: SI 2009/2436 Sch.1 para.10

s.423, applied: SI 2009/2436 Sch.1 para.10, Sch.2 para.21

s.424, applied: SI 2009/2436 Sch.1 para.10, Sch.2 para.21

s.425, applied: SI 2009/2436 Sch.1 para.10, Sch.2 para.21

s.426, applied: SI 2009/2436 Sch.1 para.10, Sch.2 para.21

s.426, varied: SI 2009/2436 Sch.1 para.10

s.427, applied: SI 2009/2436 Sch.1 para.10, Sch.2 para.21

s.427, varied: SI 2009/2436 Sch.1 para.10

s.428, applied: SI 2009/2436 Sch.1 para.10, Sch.2 para.21

s.428, varied: SI 2009/2436 Sch.1 para.10

s.429, applied: SI 2009/2436 Sch.1 para.10, Sch.2 para.21

s.430, applied: SI 2009/2436 Sch.1 para.10, Sch.2 para.21

s.431, applied: SI 2009/2436 Sch.1 para.10, Sch.2 para.21

s.432, applied: SI 2009/2436 Sch.1 para.10, Sch.2 para.21

s.433, applied: SI 2009/2436 Sch.1 para.10, Sch.2 para.21

s.434, applied: SI 2009/2436 Sch.1 para.10, Sch.2 para.21

s.435, applied: SI 2009/2436 Sch.1 para.10, Sch.2 para.21

s.436, applied: 2009 c.4 s.1046, s.1057, s.1094, s.1106, SI 2009/2436 Sch.1 para.10, Sch.2 para.21

s.441, applied: SI 2009/1803 Reg.8, SI 2009/2436 Sch.1 para.10, Sch.2 para.21

s.441, varied: SI 2009/1801 Reg.40, Reg.55, Reg.78

2006–cont.

46. Companies Act 2006–*cont.*

s.442, applied: SI 2009/2436 Sch.1 para.10, Sch.2 para.21

s.442, varied: SI 2009/1801 Reg.40, Reg.55

s.443, applied: SI 2009/2436 Sch.1 para.10, Sch.2 para.21

s.444, applied: SI 2009/2436 Sch.1 para.10, Sch.2 para.21

s.444, varied: SI 2009/2436 Sch.1 para.10

s.444A, amended: SI 2009/1581 Reg.10

s.444A, applied: SI 2009/2436 Sch.1 para.10, Sch.2 para.21

s.445, applied: SI 2009/2436 Sch.1 para.10, Sch.2 para.21

s.445, varied: SI 2009/2436 Sch.1 para.10

s.446, amended: SI 2009/1581 Reg.3

s.446, applied: SI 2009/2436 Sch.1 para.10, Sch.2 para.21

s.447, amended: SI 2009/1581 Reg.4

s.447, applied: SI 2009/2436 Sch.1 para.10, Sch.2 para.21

s.448, applied: SI 2009/2436 Sch.1 para.10, Sch.2 para.21

s.449, applied: SI 2009/2436 Sch.1 para.10, Sch.2 para.21

s.449, varied: SI 2009/2436 Sch.1 para.10

s.450, applied: SI 2009/2436 Sch.1 para.10, Sch.2 para.21

s.450, varied: SI 2009/2436 Sch.1 para.10

s.451, applied: SI 2009/2436 Sch.1 para.10, Sch.2 para.21

s.451, varied: SI 2009/1801 Reg.41, Reg.56

s.452, applied: SI 2009/2436 Sch.1 para.10, Sch.2 para.21

s.453, applied: SI 2009/2436 Sch.1 para.10, Sch.2 para.21

s.453, varied: SI 2009/2436 Sch.1 para.10

s.454, applied: SI 2009/2436 Sch.1 para.10, Sch.2 para.21

s.454, varied: SI 2009/2436 Sch.1 para.10

s.455, applied: SI 2009/2436 Sch.1 para.10, Sch.2 para.21

s.456, applied: SI 2009/2436 Sch.1 para.10, Sch.2 para.21

s.457, applied: SI 2009/2436 Sch.1 para.10, Sch.2 para.21

s.457, varied: SI 2009/2436 Sch.1 para.10

s.458, applied: SI 2009/2436 Sch.1 para.10, Sch.2 para.21

s.459, applied: SI 2009/2436 Sch.1 para.10, Sch.2 para.21

s.460, applied: SI 2009/2436 Sch.1 para.10, Sch.2 para.21

s.461, applied: SI 2009/2436 Sch.1 para.10, Sch.2 para.21

s.461, varied: SI 2009/317 Art.6

s.462, applied: SI 2009/2436 Sch.1 para.10, Sch.2 para.21

s.463, applied: SI 2009/2436 Sch.1 para.10, Sch.2 para.21

s.464, applied: SI 2009/2436 Sch.1 para.10, Sch.2 para.21

s.464, varied: SI 2009/2436 Sch.1 para.10

s.465, applied: SI 2009/2436 Sch.1 para.10, Sch.2 para.21, Sch.2 para.22

s.466, applied: SI 2009/2436 Sch.1 para.10, Sch.2 para.21, Sch.2 para.22

s.467, applied: SI 2009/2436 Sch.1 para.10, Sch.2 para.21, Sch.2 para.22

2006– cont.

46. Companies Act 2006–*cont.*

s.468, applied: SI 2009/2436 Sch.1 para.10, Sch.2 para.21

s.468, enabling: SI 2009/1581, SI 2009/3022

s.469, applied: SI 2009/2436 Sch.1 para.10, Sch.2 para.21

s.471, applied: SI 2009/2436 Sch.1 para.10, Sch.2 para.21

s.471, referred to: SI 2009/2331 Reg.9

s.471, varied: SI 2009/1801 Reg.42, Reg.57

s.472, applied: SI 2009/2436 Sch.1 para.10, Sch.2 para.21

s.472, varied: SI 2009/1801 Reg.42, Reg.57

s.472A, added: SI 2009/1581 Reg.5

s.472A, applied: SI 2009/2436 Sch.1 para.10, Sch.2 para.21

s.473, applied: SI 2009/1581, SI 2009/2436 Sch.1 para.10, Sch.2 para.21

s.474, amended: SI 2009/1342 Art.26

s.474, applied: SI 2009/2436 Sch.1 para.10, Sch.2 para.21

s.474, varied: SI 2009/1342 Art.31, SI 2009/1801 Reg.42, Reg.57

s.475, applied: SI 2009/476 Art.5, SI 2009/2436 Sch.1 para.11, Sch.2 para.23

s.476, applied: SI 2009/2436 Sch.1 para.11, Sch.2 para.23

s.477, applied: SI 2009/2436 Sch.1 para.11, Sch.2 para.23

s.478, applied: SI 2009/2436 Sch.1 para.11, Sch.2 para.23

s.479, applied: SI 2009/2436 Sch.1 para.11, Sch.2 para.23

s.480, applied: SI 2009/2436 Sch.1 para.11, Sch.2 para.23

s.481, applied: SI 2009/2436 Sch.1 para.11, Sch.2 para.23

s.482, amended: SI 2009/2958 Art.10

s.482, applied: SI 2009/476 Art.5

s.484, applied: SI 2009/2436 Sch.1 para.11, Sch.2 para.23

s.485, applied: SI 2009/2436 Sch.1 para.11, Sch.2 para.24

s.486, applied: SI 2009/2436 Sch.1 para.11, Sch.2 para.24

s.487, applied: SI 2009/2436 Sch.1 para.11, Sch.2 para.24

s.488, applied: SI 2009/2436 Sch.1 para.11, Sch.2 para.24

s.489, applied: SI 2009/2436 Sch.1 para.11, Sch.2 para.26

s.490, applied: SI 2009/2436 Sch.1 para.11, Sch.2 para.26

s.491, applied: SI 2009/2436 Sch.1 para.11, Sch.2 para.26

s.492, applied: SI 2009/2436 Sch.1 para.11, Sch.2 para.27

s.493, applied: SI 2009/2436 Sch.1 para.11, Sch.2 para.27

s.494, applied: SI 2009/2436 Sch.1 para.11, Sch.2 para.27

s.494, varied: SI 2009/2436 Sch.1 para.11

s.495, applied: SI 2009/2436 Sch.1 para.11, Sch.2 para.28

s.495, referred to: SI 2009/209 Reg.20

s.495, varied: 2009 c.20 s.44

s.496, applied: SI 2009/2436 Sch.1 para.11, Sch.2 para.28

s.496, varied: 2009 c.20 s.44

2006– cont.

46. Companies Act 2006–*cont.*

s.497, applied: SI 2009/2436 Sch.1 para.11, Sch.2 para.28

s.497, varied: 2009 c.20 s.44

s.497A, added: SI 2009/1581 Reg.6

s.497A, applied: SI 2009/2436 Sch.1 para.11, Sch.2 para.28

s.497A, varied: 2009 c.20 s.44

s.498, applied: SI 2009/2436 Sch.1 para.11, Sch.2 para.28

s.498, referred to: SI 2009/209 Reg.20

s.498, varied: 2009 c.20 s.44

s.498A, added: SI 2009/1581 Reg.7

s.498A, applied: SI 2009/2436 Sch.1 para.11

s.498A, varied: 2009 c.20 s.44

s.499, applied: SI 2009/2436 Sch.1 para.11, Sch.2 para.28

s.499, varied: 2009 c.20 s.44

s.500, applied: SI 2009/2436 Sch.1 para.11, Sch.2 para.28

s.500, varied: 2009 c.20 s.44

s.501, applied: SI 2009/2436 Sch.1 para.11, Sch.2 para.28

s.501, varied: 2009 c.20 s.44

s.502, applied: SI 2009/2436 Sch.1 para.11, Sch.2 para.29, Sch.2 para.30, Sch.2 para.32

s.503, applied: SI 2009/2436 Sch.1 para.11, Sch.2 para.28

s.504, applied: SI 2009/2436 Sch.1 para.11, Sch.2 para.28

s.504, varied: SI 2009/2436 Sch.1 para.11

s.505, applied: SI 2009/2436 Sch.1 para.11, Sch.2 para.28

s.506, applied: SI 2009/2436 Sch.1 para.11, Sch.2 para.28

s.507, applied: SI 2009/2436 Sch.1 para.11, Sch.2 para.28

s.508, applied: SI 2009/2436 Sch.1 para.11, Sch.2 para.28

s.509, applied: SI 2009/2436 Sch.1 para.11, Sch.2 para.28

s.510, applied: SI 2009/2436 Sch.1 para.11, Sch.2 para.30

s.511, applied: SI 2009/2436 Sch.1 para.11, Sch.2 para.30

s.512, applied: SI 2009/2436 Sch.1 para.11, Sch.2 para.30

s.513, applied: SI 2009/2436 Sch.1 para.11, Sch.2 para.30

s.514, applied: SI 2009/2436 Sch.1 para.11, Sch.2 para.31

s.515, applied: SI 2009/2436 Sch.1 para.11, Sch.2 para.31

s.516, applied: SI 2009/2436 Sch.1 para.11, Sch.2 para.32

s.517, applied: SI 2009/2436 Sch.1 para.11, Sch.2 para.32

s.518, applied: SI 2009/2436 Sch.1 para.11, Sch.2 para.32

s.519, applied: SI 2009/2436 Sch.1 para.11, Sch.2 para.33

s.520, applied: SI 2009/2436 Sch.1 para.11, Sch.2 para.33

s.521, applied: SI 2009/2436 Sch.1 para.11, Sch.2 para.33

s.522, applied: SI 2009/2436 Sch.1 para.11, Sch.2 para.33

s.523, applied: SI 2009/2436 Sch.1 para.11, Sch.2 para.33

2006–cont.

46. Companies Act 2006–*cont.*

s.524, applied: SI 2009/2436 Sch.1 para.11, Sch.2 para.33

s.525, applied: SI 2009/2436 Sch.1 para.11, Sch.2 para.33

s.526, applied: SI 2009/2436 Sch.1 para.11, Sch.2 para.34

s.527, applied: SI 2009/2436 Sch.2 para.35

s.532, applied: SI 2009/2436 Sch.1 para.11

s.533, applied: SI 2009/2436 Sch.1 para.11

s.534, applied: SI 2009/2436 Sch.1 para.11

s.535, applied: SI 2009/2436 Sch.1 para.11

s.536, applied: SI 2009/2436 Sch.1 para.11, Sch.2 para.36

s.537, applied: SI 2009/2436 Sch.1 para.11

s.538, applied: SI 2009/2436 Sch.1 para.11

s.538, varied: SI 2009/2436 Sch.1 para.11

s.538A, added: SI 2009/1581 Reg.8

s.549, amended: SI 2009/2561 Reg.2

s.555, applied: SI 2009/388 Art.2, Art.3, SI 2009/2101 Sch.2 para.28

s.555, enabling: SI 2009/388

s.556, applied: SI 2009/388 Art.2

s.556, enabling: SI 2009/388

s.560, amended: SI 2009/2561 Reg.2

s.561, repealed (in part): SI 2009/2561 Reg.2

s.562, amended: SI 2009/2022 Reg.2

s.562, enabling: SI 2009/2022

s.566, substituted: SI 2009/2561 Reg.2

s.573, amended: SI 2009/2561 Reg.2

s.583, applied: SI 2009/388 Art.4

s.583, enabling: SI 2009/388

s.584, applied: SI 2009/1941 Sch.3 para.9

s.585, applied: SI 2009/1941 Sch.3 para.9

s.586, applied: SI 2009/1941 Sch.3 para.9

s.587, applied: SI 2009/1941 Sch.3 para.9

s.601, amended: SI 2009/1941 Sch.1 para.260

s.601, repealed (in part): SI 2009/1941 Sch.1 para.260

s.619, applied: SI 2009/388 Art.2, SI 2009/2101 Sch.2 para.28

s.619, enabling: SI 2009/388

s.621, applied: SI 2009/388 Art.2, SI 2009/2101 Sch.2 para.28

s.621, enabling: SI 2009/388

s.625, applied: SI 2009/388 Art.2, SI 2009/2101 Sch.2 para.28

s.625, enabling: SI 2009/388

s.626, applied: SI 2009/1803 Reg.6

s.627, applied: SI 2009/388 Art.2, SI 2009/2101 Sch.2 para.28

s.627, enabling: SI 2009/388

s.641, applied: SI 2009/1803 Reg.6

s.644, applied: SI 2009/388 Art.2, SI 2009/2101 Sch.2 para.28

s.644, disapplied: SI 2009/2101 Sch.1 para.11

s.644, enabling: SI 2009/388

s.646, amended: SI 2009/2022 Reg.3

s.648, applied: SI 2009/2425 Reg.3

s.649, applied: SI 2009/388 Art.2, SI 2009/2101 Sch.2 para.28, SI 2009/2425 Reg.5

s.649, disapplied: SI 2009/2101 Sch.1 para.11

s.649, enabling: SI 2009/388

s.650, applied: SI 2009/2425 Reg.3, Reg.5, Reg.9

s.651, applied: SI 2009/2101 Sch.1 para.7

s.657, applied: SI 2009/1941

s.657, enabling: SI 2009/1941, SI 2009/2022

s.658, applied: 2009 c.4 s.674, s.682, s.819, s.821

2006–cont.

46. Companies Act 2006–*cont.*

s.658, referred to: 2009 c.4 s.421, s.431

s.662, applied: SI 2009/1803 Reg.6, SI 2009/2425 Reg.3, Reg.6, Reg.9

s.662, disapplied: SI 2009/1941 Sch.3 para.7

s.662, referred to: SI 2009/1941 Sch.3 para.2

s.663, applied: SI 2009/388 Art.2, SI 2009/2101 Sch.2 para.28

s.663, disapplied: SI 2009/1941 Sch.3 para.7

s.663, referred to: SI 2009/1941 Sch.3 para.2

s.663, enabling: SI 2009/388

s.664, applied: SI 2009/1803 Reg.6

s.664, disapplied: SI 2009/1941 Sch.3 para.7

s.664, referred to: SI 2009/1941 Sch.3 para.2

s.665, applied: SI 2009/2101 Sch.1 para.7

s.665, disapplied: SI 2009/1941 Sch.3 para.7

s.665, referred to: SI 2009/1941 Sch.3 para.2

s.666, disapplied: SI 2009/1941 Sch.3 para.7

s.666, referred to: SI 2009/1941 Sch.3 para.2

s.667, applied: SI 2009/2425 Reg.6

s.667, disapplied: SI 2009/1941 Sch.3 para.7

s.667, referred to: SI 2009/1941 Sch.3 para.2

s.668, applied: SI 2009/1941 Sch.3 para.7

s.668, disapplied: SI 2009/1941 Sch.3 para.7

s.668, referred to: SI 2009/1941 Sch.3 para.2

s.669, disapplied: SI 2009/1941 Sch.3 para.7

s.669, referred to: SI 2009/1941 Sch.3 para.2

s.670, applied: SI 2009/1941 Sch.3 para.7

s.677, referred to: SI 2009/2579 Sch.1 para.18, SI 2009/2604 Sch.1 para.18

s.689, applied: SI 2009/388 Art.2, SI 2009/2101 Sch.2 para.28

s.689, enabling: SI 2009/388

s.694, amended: SI 2009/2022 Reg.4

s.697, amended: SI 2009/2022 Reg.4

s.700, amended: SI 2009/2022 Reg.4

s.701, amended: SI 2009/2022 Reg.4

s.708, applied: SI 2009/388 Art.2, SI 2009/2101 Sch.2 para.28

s.708, enabling: SI 2009/388

s.714, applied: SI 2009/388 Art.5

s.714, enabling: SI 2009/388

s.725, applied: SI 2009/2022 Reg.5

s.725, repealed: SI 2009/2022 Reg.5

s.727, applied: SI 2009/388 Art.4

s.727, enabling: SI 2009/388

s.730, applied: SI 2009/388 Art.2, SI 2009/2101 Sch.2 para.28

s.730, enabling: SI 2009/388

s.732, applied: SI 2009/2022 Reg.5

s.737, enabling: SI 2009/2022

s.738, varied: SI 2009/1804 Reg.20

s.739, varied: SI 2009/1804 Reg.20

s.740, varied: SI 2009/1804 Reg.20

s.741, varied: SI 2009/1804 Reg.20

s.742, varied: SI 2009/1804 Reg.20

s.743, varied: SI 2009/1804 Reg.21

s.744, varied: SI 2009/1804 Reg.21

s.745, varied: SI 2009/1804 Reg.21

s.746, varied: SI 2009/1804 Reg.21

s.747, varied: SI 2009/1804 Reg.21

s.748, varied: SI 2009/1804 Reg.21

s.749, varied: SI 2009/1804 Reg.22

s.750, varied: SI 2009/1804 Reg.22

s.752, varied: SI 2009/1804 Reg.23

s.753, varied: SI 2009/1804 Reg.23

s.754, varied: SI 2009/1804 Reg.23

s.757, applied: SI 2009/2425 Reg.6

2006–cont.

46. Companies Act 2006–*cont.*
s.758, applied: SI 2009/2425 Reg.6
s.761, applied: SI 2009/2425 Reg.9
s.763, applied: SI 2009/2425 Reg.2
s.763, enabling: SI 2009/2425
s.766, enabling: SI 2009/2425
s.768, applied: SI 2009/2436 Sch.1 para.12
s.769, varied: SI 2009/1804 Reg.24
s.770, varied: SI 2009/1804 Reg.25
s.771, varied: SI 2009/1804 Reg.25
s.774, varied: SI 2009/1804 Reg.26
s.775, varied: SI 2009/1804 Reg.26
s.776, applied: SI 2009/814 Art.3
s.776, disapplied: SI 2009/814 Art.3, SI 2009/3226 Sch.1 para.28
s.776, varied: SI 2009/1804 Reg.27, SI 2009/3226 Sch.1 para.28
s.777, disapplied: SI 2009/814 Art.3, SI 2009/3226 Sch.1 para.28
s.778, applied: SI 2009/2436 Sch.1 para.12
s.778, disapplied: SI 2009/814 Art.3, SI 2009/3226 Sch.1 para.28
s.778, varied: SI 2009/1804 Reg.28, SI 2009/2436 Sch.1 para.12
s.782, varied: SI 2009/1804 Reg.29
s.784, applied: SI 2009/1889
s.784, enabling: SI 2009/1889
s.785, enabling: SI 2009/1889
s.788, enabling: SI 2009/1889
s.789, applied: SI 2009/1889
s.834, amended: 2009 c.10 Sch.22 para.11
s.839, amended: SI 2009/1941 Sch.1 para.260
s.854, applied: SI 2009/814 Art.7, SI 2009/1804 Sch.1 para.15, SI 2009/2101 Sch.1 para.7, Sch.1 para.9, SI 2009/2436 Sch.1 para.13, Sch.2 para.37, SI 2009/3226 Sch.5 para.1
s.854, varied: SI 2009/1804 Reg.30
s.855, applied: SI 2009/214 Reg.9, SI 2009/814 Art.7, SI 2009/1804 Sch.1 para.15, SI 2009/2436 Sch.1 para.13, Sch.2 para.37, SI 2009/3226 Sch.5 para.1
s.855, varied: SI 2009/1804 Reg.30, SI 2009/2436 Sch.1 para.13
s.855A, applied: SI 2009/814 Art.7, SI 2009/1804 Sch.1 para.15, SI 2009/2436 Sch.1 para.13, Sch.2 para.37, SI 2009/3226 Sch.5 para.1
s.855A, varied: SI 2009/1804 Reg.30
s.856, applied: SI 2009/814 Art.7, SI 2009/2436 Sch.1 para.13, Sch.2 para.37, SI 2009/3226 Sch.5 para.1
s.856A, applied: SI 2009/814 Art.7, SI 2009/2436 Sch.1 para.13, Sch.2 para.37, SI 2009/3226 Sch.5 para.1
s.856B, applied: SI 2009/814 Art.7, SI 2009/2436 Sch.1 para.13, Sch.2 para.37, SI 2009/3226 Sch.5 para.1
s.857, applied: SI 2009/814 Art.7, SI 2009/2436 Sch.1 para.13, Sch.2 para.37, SI 2009/3226 Sch.5 para.1
s.858, applied: SI 2009/814 Art.7, SI 2009/1804 Sch.1 para.15, SI 2009/2436 Sch.1 para.13, Sch.2 para.37, SI 2009/3226 Sch.5 para.1
s.858, varied: SI 2009/1804 Reg.31
s.859, applied: SI 2009/814 Art.7, SI 2009/2436 Sch.1 para.13, Sch.2 para.37
s.860, applied: SI 2009/1804 Sch.1 para.16
s.860, varied: SI 2009/1804 Reg.32
s.861, varied: SI 2009/1804 Reg.32
s.862, applied: SI 2009/1804 Sch.1 para.17

2006–cont.

46. Companies Act 2006–*cont.*
s.862, varied: SI 2009/1804 Reg.32
s.863, applied: SI 2009/1804 Sch.1 para.18
s.863, varied: SI 2009/1804 Reg.33
s.864, varied: SI 2009/1804 Reg.33
s.865, varied: SI 2009/1804 Reg.33
s.866, varied: SI 2009/1804 Reg.34
s.867, varied: SI 2009/1804 Reg.34
s.868, applied: SI 2009/1804 Sch.1 para.19
s.868, varied: SI 2009/1804 Reg.35
s.869, varied: SI 2009/1804 Reg.36
s.870, varied: SI 2009/1804 Reg.36
s.871, applied: SI 2009/1804 Sch.1 para.20
s.871, varied: SI 2009/1804 Reg.36
s.872, applied: SI 2009/1804 Sch.1 para.21
s.872, varied: SI 2009/1804 Reg.36
s.873, varied: SI 2009/1804 Reg.36
s.874, varied: SI 2009/1804 Reg.37
s.875, varied: SI 2009/1804 Reg.38
s.876, varied: SI 2009/1804 Reg.38
s.877, varied: SI 2009/1804 Reg.38
s.878, applied: SI 2009/1804 Sch.1 para.16
s.878, varied: SI 2009/1804 Reg.39
s.879, varied: SI 2009/1804 Reg.39
s.880, applied: SI 2009/1804 Sch.1 para.17
s.880, varied: SI 2009/1804 Reg.39
s.881, varied: SI 2009/1804 Reg.39
s.882, applied: SI 2009/1804 Sch.1 para.18
s.882, varied: SI 2009/1804 Reg.40
s.883, varied: SI 2009/1804 Reg.40
s.884, varied: SI 2009/1804 Reg.41
s.885, varied: SI 2009/1804 Reg.42
s.886, varied: SI 2009/1804 Reg.42
s.887, applied: SI 2009/1804 Sch.1 para.21
s.887, varied: SI 2009/1804 Reg.42
s.888, varied: SI 2009/1804 Reg.42
s.889, varied: SI 2009/1804 Reg.43
s.890, varied: SI 2009/1804 Reg.44
s.891, varied: SI 2009/1804 Reg.44
s.892, varied: SI 2009/1804 Reg.44
s.895, see *Lehman Brothers International (Europe) (In Administration) (No.2), Re* [2009] EWCA Civ 1161, Times, November 12, 2009 (CA (Civ Div)), Lord Neuberger of Abbotsbury MR
s.895, varied: SI 2009/1804 Reg.45
s.896, applied: SI 2009/1804 Reg.45
s.896, varied: SI 2009/1804 Reg.45
s.897, varied: SI 2009/1804 Reg.45
s.898, varied: SI 2009/1804 Reg.45
s.899, applied: SI 2009/1804 Reg.45
s.899, varied: SI 2009/1804 Reg.45, SI 2009/3056 Sch.1 para.3
s.900, varied: SI 2009/1804 Reg.45
s.938, amended: SI 2009/1941 Sch.1 para.260
s.948, applied: SI 2009/1208 Art.2
s.948, enabling: SI 2009/202, SI 2009/1208
s.965, enabling: SI 2009/1378
s.966, applied: SI 2009/2436 Sch.1 para.14
s.967, applied: SI 2009/2436 Sch.1 para.14
s.968, applied: SI 2009/2436 Sch.1 para.14
s.969, applied: SI 2009/2436 Sch.1 para.14
s.970, applied: SI 2009/2436 Sch.1 para.14
s.971, applied: SI 2009/2436 Sch.1 para.14
s.972, applied: SI 2009/2436 Sch.1 para.14
s.973, applied: SI 2009/2436 Sch.1 para.14
s.974, applied: SI 2009/2436 Sch.1 para.14
s.975, applied: SI 2009/2436 Sch.1 para.14
s.976, applied: SI 2009/2436 Sch.1 para.14

2006–cont.

46. Companies Act 2006–*cont.*

s.977, applied: SI 2009/2436 Sch.1 para.14
s.978, applied: SI 2009/2436 Sch.1 para.14
s.979, applied: SI 2009/2436 Sch.1 para.14
s.980, applied: SI 2009/2436 Sch.1 para.14
s.981, applied: SI 2009/2436 Sch.1 para.14
s.982, applied: SI 2009/2436 Sch.1 para.14
s.983, applied: SI 2009/2436 Sch.1 para.14
s.984, applied: SI 2009/2436 Sch.1 para.14
s.985, applied: SI 2009/2436 Sch.1 para.14
s.986, applied: SI 2009/2436 Sch.1 para.14
s.987, applied: SI 2009/2436 Sch.1 para.14
s.988, applied: SI 2009/2436 Sch.1 para.14
s.989, applied: SI 2009/2436 Sch.1 para.14
s.990, applied: SI 2009/2436 Sch.1 para.14
s.991, applied: SI 2009/2436 Sch.1 para.14
s.993, applied: SI 2009/2436 Sch.1 para.15, Sch.2 para.38
s.993, varied: SI 2009/1804 Reg.47, SI 2009/2436 Sch.2 para.38
s.994, see *Hawkes v Cuddy* [2009] EWCA Civ 291, [2009] 2 B.C.L.C. 427 (CA (Civ Div)), Moore-Bick, L.J.; see *Oak Investment Partners XII Ltd Partnership v Boughtwood* [2009] EWHC 176 (Ch), [2009] 1 B.C.L.C. 453 (Ch D (Companies Ct)), Sales, J; see *Wishart, Petitioner* [2009] CSIH 65, 2009 S.L.T. 812 (IH (Ex Div)), Lord Nimmo Smith
s.994, applied: SI 2009/2469 r.2, r.4
s.994, varied: SI 2009/1804 Reg.48
s.995, applied: SI 2009/2469 r.2
s.995, varied: SI 2009/1804 Reg.48
s.996, see *Oak Investment Partners XII Ltd Partnership v Boughtwood* [2009] EWHC 176 (Ch), [2009] 1 B.C.L.C. 453 (Ch D (Companies Ct)), Sales, J
s.996, applied: SI 2009/2437 Reg.22
s.996, varied: SI 2009/1804 Reg.48
s.997, varied: SI 2009/1804 Reg.49
s.999, applied: SI 2009/1803 Reg.6
s.1000, applied: SI 2009/1804 Sch.1 para.25
s.1000, varied: SI 2009/1804 Reg.50
s.1001, applied: SI 2009/1804 Sch.1 para.25
s.1001, varied: SI 2009/1804 Reg.50
s.1002, applied: SI 2009/1804 Sch.1 para.25
s.1002, varied: SI 2009/1804 Reg.50
s.1003, applied: SI 2009/1803 Reg.2, SI 2009/1804 Sch.1 para.25, SI 2009/2101 Sch.1 para.9
s.1003, varied: SI 2009/1804 Reg.51
s.1003, enabling: SI 2009/1803
s.1004, disapplied: SI 2009/1803 Reg.2
s.1004, varied: SI 2009/1804 Reg.51
s.1005, disapplied: SI 2009/1803 Reg.2
s.1005, varied: SI 2009/1804 Reg.51
s.1006, varied: SI 2009/1804 Reg.51
s.1007, varied: SI 2009/1804 Reg.51
s.1008, varied: SI 2009/1804 Reg.51
s.1009, varied: SI 2009/1804 Reg.51
s.1010, varied: SI 2009/1804 Reg.51
s.1011, varied: SI 2009/1804 Reg.51
s.1012, applied: SI 2009/1804 Sch.1 para.22, Sch.1 para.22A
s.1012, referred to: SI 2009/1804 Sch.1 para.26
s.1012, varied: SI 2009/805 Sch.1 para.18, Sch.1 para.31, SI 2009/1804 Reg.52
s.1013, applied: SI 2009/1804 Sch.1 para.22, Sch.1 para.22A
s.1013, varied: SI 2009/805 Sch.1 para.18, Sch.1 para.31, SI 2009/1804 Reg.52

2006–cont.

46. Companies Act 2006–*cont.*

s.1014, applied: SI 2009/1804 Sch.1 para.22, Sch.1 para.22A
s.1014, varied: SI 2009/805 Sch.1 para.18, Sch.1 para.31, SI 2009/1804 Reg.52
s.1015, applied: SI 2009/1804 Sch.1 para.22, Sch.1 para.22A
s.1015, varied: SI 2009/805 Sch.1 para.18, Sch.1 para.31, SI 2009/1804 Reg.53
s.1016, applied: SI 2009/1804 Sch.1 para.22, Sch.1 para.22A
s.1016, varied: SI 2009/805 Sch.1 para.18, Sch.1 para.31, SI 2009/1804 Reg.53
s.1017, applied: SI 2009/1804 Sch.1 para.22, Sch.1 para.22A
s.1017, varied: SI 2009/805 Sch.1 para.18, Sch.1 para.31, SI 2009/1804 Reg.53
s.1018, applied: SI 2009/1804 Sch.1 para.22, Sch.1 para.22A
s.1018, varied: SI 2009/805 Sch.1 para.18, Sch.1 para.31, SI 2009/1804 Reg.53
s.1019, applied: SI 2009/1804 Sch.1 para.22, Sch.1 para.22A
s.1019, varied: SI 2009/805 Sch.1 para.18, Sch.1 para.31, SI 2009/1804 Reg.53
s.1020, applied: SI 2009/1804 Sch.1 para.22, Sch.1 para.22A
s.1020, varied: SI 2009/805 Sch.1 para.18, Sch.1 para.31, SI 2009/1804 Reg.54
s.1021, applied: SI 2009/1804 Sch.1 para.22, Sch.1 para.22A
s.1021, varied: SI 2009/805 Sch.1 para.18, Sch.1 para.31, SI 2009/1804 Reg.54
s.1022, applied: SI 2009/1804 Sch.1 para.22, Sch.1 para.22A
s.1022, varied: SI 2009/805 Sch.1 para.18, Sch.1 para.31, SI 2009/1804 Reg.54
s.1023, applied: SI 2009/1804 Sch.1 para.22
s.1023, varied: SI 2009/805 Sch.1 para.18, Sch.1 para.31, SI 2009/1804 Reg.55
s.1024, disapplied: SI 2009/2101 Sch.1 para.11
s.1024, varied: SI 2009/1804 Reg.56
s.1025, varied: SI 2009/1804 Reg.56
s.1026, varied: SI 2009/1804 Reg.56
s.1027, varied: SI 2009/1804 Reg.56
s.1028, varied: SI 2009/1804 Reg.56
s.1029, applied: SI 2009/1804 Sch.1 para.24
s.1029, referred to: SI 2009/1804 Sch.1 para.25
s.1029, varied: SI 2009/1804 Reg.57
s.1030, applied: SI 2009/1804 Sch.1 para.24, Sch.1 para.25
s.1030, varied: SI 2009/1804 Reg.57
s.1031, applied: SI 2009/1804 Sch.1 para.24
s.1031, varied: SI 2009/1804 Reg.57
s.1032, applied: SI 2009/1804 Sch.1 para.24
s.1032, varied: SI 2009/1804 Reg.57
s.1033, applied: SI 2009/2101 Sch.1 para.7, Sch.1 para.9
s.1033, varied: SI 2009/1804 Reg.58
s.1034, applied: SI 2009/1804 Sch.1 para.26
s.1034, varied: SI 2009/805 Sch.1 para.18, Sch.1 para.31, SI 2009/1804 Reg.58, Sch.1 para.26
s.1040, applied: SI 2009/1085 Reg.13, SI 2009/2437 Reg.2
s.1042, enabling: SI 2009/2437
s.1043, enabling: SI 2009/2436
s.1044, referred to: SI 2009/2615 Reg.6
s.1045, enabling: SI 2009/1917
s.1046, applied: SI 2009/214 Reg.9, SI 2009/1801

2006–cont.

46. Companies Act 2006–*cont.*
s.1046, enabling: SI 2009/1801
s.1047, enabling: SI 2009/1801
s.1048, applied: SI 2009/1803 Reg.5, SI 2009/2101 Sch.1 para.10
s.1049, enabling: SI 2009/1801
s.1050, applied: SI 2009/2101 Sch.1 para.1
s.1050, enabling: SI 2009/1801
s.1051, applied: SI 2009/1801
s.1051, varied: SI 2009/1804 Reg.59
s.1051, enabling: SI 2009/1801
s.1052, applied: 2009 c.1 s.252, SI 2009/214 Reg.11
s.1052, enabling: SI 2009/1917
s.1053, applied: SI 2009/1801
s.1053, enabling: SI 2009/1801
s.1054, enabling: SI 2009/1801
s.1055, enabling: SI 2009/1801
s.1056, enabling: SI 2009/1801
s.1058, enabling: SI 2009/1801
s.1059A, added: SI 2009/1802 Art.3
s.1059A, varied: SI 2009/317 Art.6
s.1060, applied: SI 2009/1804 Reg.60, SI 2009/2436 Sch.1 para.17
s.1060, varied: SI 2009/317 Art.6
s.1061, amended: SI 2009/1802 Art.4
s.1061, applied: SI 2009/1804 Reg.60, SI 2009/2436 Sch.1 para.17
s.1061, repealed (in part): SI 2009/1802 Art.4
s.1061, varied: SI 2009/317 Art.6
s.1062, applied: SI 2009/1804 Reg.60, SI 2009/2436 Sch.1 para.17
s.1062, varied: SI 2009/317 Art.6
s.1063, applied: SI 2009/1804 Reg.60, Sch.1 para.36, SI 2009/2101 Reg.8, SI 2009/2392 Reg.6, SI 2009/2436 Sch.1 para.17, SI 2009/2492 Reg.4
s.1063, varied: SI 2009/317 Art.6
s.1063, enabling: SI 2009/2101, SI 2009/2392, SI 2009/2403, SI 2009/2439
s.1064, applied: SI 2009/1804 Sch.1 para.28, SI 2009/2437 Reg.12
s.1064, varied: SI 2009/317 Art.6, SI 2009/1804 Reg.61
s.1065, applied: SI 2009/1804 Sch.1 para.28, SI 2009/2101 Sch.2 para.7, Sch.2 para.11, Sch.2 para.12
s.1065, varied: SI 2009/317 Art.6, SI 2009/1804 Reg.61
s.1066, applied: SI 2009/1803 Reg.5
s.1066, varied: SI 2009/317 Art.6, SI 2009/1804 Reg.62, SI 2009/2436 Sch.1 para.18
s.1067, amended: SI 2009/1802 Art.5
s.1067, applied: SI 2009/1803 Reg.5
s.1067, varied: SI 2009/317 Art.6
s.1068, amended: SI 2009/1802 Art.6
s.1068, applied: SI 2009/1804 Reg.60, SI 2009/2436 Sch.1 para.17
s.1068, varied: SI 2009/317 Art.6
s.1069, applied: SI 2009/1804 Reg.60, SI 2009/2436 Sch.1 para.17
s.1069, varied: SI 2009/317 Art.6
s.1070, amended: SI 2009/1802 Art.7
s.1070, applied: SI 2009/1804 Reg.60, SI 2009/2436 Sch.1 para.17
s.1070, varied: SI 2009/317 Art.6
s.1071, applied: SI 2009/1804 Reg.60, SI 2009/2436 Sch.1 para.17
s.1071, varied: SI 2009/317 Art.6
s.1072, applied: SI 2009/1804 Reg.60, SI 2009/2436 Sch.1 para.17

2006–cont.

46. Companies Act 2006–*cont.*
s.1072, varied: SI 2009/317 Art.6
s.1073, applied: SI 2009/1804 Reg.60, SI 2009/2436 Sch.1 para.17
s.1073, varied: SI 2009/317 Art.6
s.1074, applied: SI 2009/1804 Reg.60, SI 2009/2436 Sch.1 para.17
s.1074, varied: SI 2009/317 Art.6
s.1075, amended: SI 2009/1802 Art.8
s.1075, applied: SI 2009/1804 Reg.60, SI 2009/2436 Sch.1 para.17
s.1075, varied: SI 2009/317 Art.6
s.1076, amended: SI 2009/1802 Art.9
s.1076, applied: SI 2009/1804 Reg.60, SI 2009/2436 Sch.1 para.17
s.1076, varied: SI 2009/317 Art.6
s.1077, varied: SI 2009/317 Art.6, SI 2009/1804 Reg.63, SI 2009/2436 Sch.1 para.19
s.1078, applied: SI 2009/1801 Reg.76
s.1078, varied: SI 2009/317 Art.6, SI 2009/1804 Reg.63, SI 2009/2436 Sch.1 para.19
s.1078, enabling: SI 2009/1801
s.1079, varied: SI 2009/317 Art.6, SI 2009/1804 Reg.63, SI 2009/2436 Sch.1 para.19
s.1080, amended: SI 2009/1802 Art.10
s.1080, applied: SI 2009/1804 Reg.60, SI 2009/2436 Sch.1 para.17, Sch.1 para.20
s.1080, varied: SI 2009/317 Art.6
s.1081, applied: SI 2009/1804 Sch.1 para.29
s.1081, varied: SI 2009/317 Art.6, SI 2009/1804 Reg.64
s.1081, enabling: SI 2009/1803
s.1082, varied: SI 2009/317 Art.6, SI 2009/1804 Reg.64
s.1083, amended: SI 2009/1802 Art.11
s.1083, applied: SI 2009/1804 Reg.60, SI 2009/2436 Sch.1 para.17
s.1083, varied: SI 2009/317 Art.6
s.1084, varied: SI 2009/317 Art.6, SI 2009/1804 Reg.65
s.1085, applied: SI 2009/2436 Sch.1 para.20
s.1085, varied: SI 2009/317 Art.6, SI 2009/1804 Reg.66
s.1086, applied: SI 2009/2436 Sch.1 para.20
s.1086, varied: SI 2009/317 Art.6, SI 2009/1804 Reg.66
s.1087, amended: SI 2009/1802 Art.12, SI 2009/1941 Sch.1 para.260
s.1087, applied: SI 2009/2436 Sch.1 para.20
s.1087, varied: SI 2009/317 Art.6, SI 2009/1804 Reg.66, SI 2009/2436 Sch.1 para.20
s.1088, applied: SI 2009/214, SI 2009/1941, SI 2009/2400 Sch.2 para.12, SI 2009/2436 Sch.1 para.20
s.1088, disapplied: SI 2009/2101 Sch.1 para.11
s.1088, varied: SI 2009/317 Art.6, SI 2009/1804 Reg.66, SI 2009/2436 Sch.1 para.20
s.1088, enabling: SI 2009/214, SI 2009/1941
s.1089, applied: SI 2009/2436 Sch.1 para.20
s.1089, varied: SI 2009/317 Art.6, SI 2009/1804 Reg.66
s.1090, applied: SI 2009/2436 Sch.1 para.20
s.1090, varied: SI 2009/317 Art.6, SI 2009/1804 Reg.66
s.1091, applied: SI 2009/2101 Sch.2 para.7, Sch.2 para.11, Sch.2 para.12, SI 2009/2403 Sch.2 para.3, Sch.2 para.7, Sch.2 para.8, SI 2009/2436 Sch.1 para.20
s.1091, varied: SI 2009/317 Art.6, SI 2009/1804 Reg.66, SI 2009/2436 Sch.1 para.20

2006–cont.

46. Companies Act 2006–*cont.*

s.1092, applied: SI 2009/1804 Reg.60, SI 2009/2436 Sch.1 para.17

s.1092, varied: SI 2009/317 Art.6

s.1093, applied: SI 2009/1804 Sch.1 para.30

s.1093, varied: SI 2009/317 Art.6, SI 2009/1804 Reg.67

s.1094, applied: SI 2009/1804 Sch.1 para.31

s.1094, disapplied: SI 2009/2101 Sch.1 para.11

s.1094, varied: SI 2009/317 Art.6, SI 2009/1804 Reg.67

s.1095, applied: SI 2009/1803, SI 2009/1803 Reg.5, SI 2009/1804 Sch.1 para.31

s.1095, disapplied: SI 2009/2101 Sch.1 para.11

s.1095, referred to: SI 2009/1803 Reg.5

s.1095, varied: SI 2009/317 Art.6, SI 2009/1804 Reg.67

s.1095, enabling: SI 2009/1803

s.1096, applied: SI 2009/1804 Sch.1 para.31

s.1096, varied: SI 2009/317 Art.6, SI 2009/1804 Reg.67

s.1097, applied: SI 2009/1804 Sch.1 para.31

s.1097, varied: SI 2009/317 Art.6, SI 2009/1804 Reg.67

s.1098, applied: SI 2009/1804 Sch.1 para.31

s.1098, varied: SI 2009/317 Art.6, SI 2009/1804 Reg.67

s.1099, applied: SI 2009/2101 Sch.2 para.12

s.1099, varied: SI 2009/317 Art.6

s.1100, varied: SI 2009/317 Art.6

s.1101, applied: SI 2009/1804

s.1101, varied: SI 2009/317 Art.6

s.1101, enabling: SI 2009/1804

s.1102, varied: SI 2009/317 Art.6

s.1102, enabling: SI 2009/2400

s.1103, varied: SI 2009/317 Art.6, SI 2009/1804 Reg.68

s.1104, referred to: SI 2009/1803 Reg.6

s.1104, varied: SI 2009/317 Art.6, SI 2009/1804 Reg.68

s.1104, enabling: SI 2009/1803

s.1105, applied: SI 2009/1801 Reg.78, SI 2009/1803 Reg.7, SI 2009/1917 Reg.27

s.1105, varied: SI 2009/317 Art.6, SI 2009/1804 Reg.68

s.1105, enabling: SI 2009/1801, SI 2009/1803, SI 2009/1917

s.1106, varied: SI 2009/317 Art.6, SI 2009/1804 Reg.68

s.1107, varied: SI 2009/317 Art.6, SI 2009/1804 Reg.68

s.1108, applied: SI 2009/1803 Reg.8, SI 2009/1804 Reg.60, SI 2009/2436 Sch.1 para.17

s.1108, disapplied: SI 2009/1803 Reg.8

s.1108, varied: SI 2009/317 Art.6

s.1108, enabling: SI 2009/1803, SI 2009/2399, SI 2009/2400

s.1109, amended: SI 2009/1802 Art.13

s.1109, applied: SI 2009/1804 Reg.60, SI 2009/2436 Sch.1 para.17

s.1109, varied: SI 2009/317 Art.6

s.1110, applied: SI 2009/1804 Reg.60, SI 2009/2436 Sch.1 para.17

s.1110, varied: SI 2009/317 Art.6

s.1111, applied: SI 2009/1804 Reg.60, SI 2009/2436 Sch.1 para.17

s.1111, varied: SI 2009/317 Art.6

2006–cont.

46. Companies Act 2006–*cont.*

s.1112, applied: SI 2009/214 Reg.16, Sch.2 para.6, SI 2009/1801 Sch.2 para.6, Sch.3 para.7, Sch.8 para.21, SI 2009/1804 Sch.1 para.11, Sch.1 para.12, Sch.1 para.32, SI 2009/2400 Sch.2 para.12, Sch.2 para.13

s.1112, varied: SI 2009/317 Art.6, SI 2009/1804 Reg.69

s.1113, varied: SI 2009/317 Art.6, SI 2009/1804 Reg.69

s.1114, applied: SI 2009/1804 Reg.60, SI 2009/2436 Sch.1 para.17

s.1114, varied: SI 2009/317 Art.6

s.1115, amended: SI 2009/1802 Art.14

s.1115, applied: SI 2009/1804 Reg.60, SI 2009/2436 Sch.1 para.17

s.1115, varied: SI 2009/317 Art.6

s.1116, amended: SI 2009/1802 Art.15

s.1116, applied: SI 2009/1804 Reg.60, SI 2009/2436 Sch.1 para.17

s.1116, varied: SI 2009/317 Art.6

s.1117, applied: SI 2009/1804 Reg.60, SI 2009/2436 Sch.1 para.17

s.1117, varied: SI 2009/317 Art.6

s.1118, applied: SI 2009/1804 Reg.60, SI 2009/2436 Sch.1 para.17

s.1118, varied: SI 2009/317 Art.6

s.1119, applied: SI 2009/1804 Reg.60, SI 2009/2436 Sch.1 para.17

s.1119, varied: SI 2009/317 Art.6

s.1120, repealed: SI 2009/1802 Art.16

s.1120, varied: SI 2009/317 Art.6

s.1121, varied: SI 2009/1804 Reg.70

s.1122, varied: SI 2009/1804 Reg.70

s.1125, varied: SI 2009/1804 Reg.71

s.1126, varied: SI 2009/1804 Reg.72

s.1127, varied: SI 2009/1804 Reg.73

s.1128, varied: SI 2009/1804 Reg.73

s.1129, varied: SI 2009/1804 Reg.73

s.1130, varied: SI 2009/1804 Reg.73

s.1131, varied: SI 2009/1804 Reg.73

s.1132, varied: SI 2009/1804 Reg.73

s.1133, varied: SI 2009/1804 Reg.73

s.1134, varied: SI 2009/1804 Reg.74

s.1135, varied: SI 2009/1804 Reg.74

s.1136, varied: SI 2009/1804 Reg.74

s.1137, varied: SI 2009/1804 Reg.74

s.1138, varied: SI 2009/1804 Reg.74

s.1139, varied: SI 2009/317 Art.6, SI 2009/1804 Reg.75

s.1140, amended: SI 2009/1941 Sch.1 para.260

s.1140, applied: SI 2009/1801 Reg.75

s.1140, varied: SI 2009/317 Art.6, SI 2009/1804 Reg.75

s.1140, enabling: SI 2009/1801

s.1141, varied: SI 2009/1804 Reg.75

s.1142, varied: SI 2009/1804 Reg.75

s.1154, amended: SI 2009/1941 Sch.1 para.260

s.1154, varied: SI 2009/1804 Reg.76

s.1155, varied: SI 2009/1804 Reg.76

s.1156, varied: SI 2009/1804 Reg.77

s.1156, enabling: SI 2009/2455

s.1157, varied: SI 2009/1804 Reg.77

s.1159, applied: SI 2009/509 Art.19

s.1159, referred to: 2009 c.10 Sch.53 para.7, SI 2009/307 Sch.1 para.1

s.1161, applied: 2009 c.1 s.65, s.68, s.71, s.234, SI 2009/389 Sch.1 para.14

s.1162, applied: SI 2009/389 Sch.1 para.14

2006– *cont.*

46. Companies Act 2006– *cont.*

s.1167, enabling: SI 2009/388, SI 2009/1803
s.1169, applied: 2009 c.10 Sch.15 para.3
s.1170A, added: SI 2009/1941 Sch.1 para.260
s.1170B, added: SI 2009/1941 Sch.1 para.260
s.1172, varied: SI 2009/1804 Reg.78
s.1173, applied: SI 2009/2657 r.8
s.1173, varied: SI 2009/1804 Reg.79
s.1193, amended: SI 2009/2958 Art.11
s.1193, applied: SI 2009/2982, SI 2009/2982 Reg.3, Reg.4
s.1193, referred to: SI 2009/2982 Reg.5
s.1193, enabling: SI 2009/2982
s.1194, applied: SI 2009/2615 Reg.3, Reg.5, Reg.6
s.1194, enabling: SI 2009/2615
s.1195, enabling: SI 2009/2615, SI 2009/2982
s.1197, enabling: SI 2009/1085, SI 2009/2404
s.1201, substituted: SI 2009/3182 Reg.2
s.1210, applied: SI 2009/2436 Reg.6
s.1210, enabling: SI 2009/2436
s.1212, applied: 2009 c.20 s.41
s.1214, applied: 2009 c.20 s.41
s.1231, amended: SI 2009/2958 Art.12
s.1255, applied: SI 2009/814 Art.7, SI 2009/3226 Sch.5 para.1
s.1284, applied: SI 2009/2436 Sch.2 para.39
s.1286, applied: SI 2009/1804 Sch.2 para.4
s.1288, varied: SI 2009/1804 Reg.80
s.1289, varied: SI 2009/1804 Reg.80
s.1290, applied: SI 2009/214, SI 2009/218, SI 2009/1581, SI 2009/1801, SI 2009/1802, SI 2009/1803, SI 2009/1804, SI 2009/1889, SI 2009/1890, SI 2009/1941, SI 2009/2022, SI 2009/2982
s.1290, varied: SI 2009/1804 Reg.80
s.1292, applied: SI 2009/1581, SI 2009/1802, SI 2009/1803
s.1292, varied: SI 2009/1804 Reg.81
s.1292, enabling: SI 2009/214, SI 2009/218, SI 2009/1085, SI 2009/1208, SI 2009/1581, SI 2009/1801, SI 2009/1802, SI 2009/1803, SI 2009/1804, SI 2009/1889, SI 2009/1917, SI 2009/1941, SI 2009/2022, SI 2009/2101, SI 2009/2392, SI 2009/2403, SI 2009/2404, SI 2009/2425, SI 2009/2436, SI 2009/2437, SI 2009/2476, SI 2009/2615, SI 2009/2982, SI 2009/3022
s.1294, applied: SI 2009/1802, SI 2009/1804, SI 2009/1889, SI 2009/1890, SI 2009/1941
s.1294, enabling: SI 2009/1801, SI 2009/1802, SI 2009/1804, SI 2009/1889, SI 2009/1890, SI 2009/1941
s.1296, enabling: SI 2009/1802, SI 2009/1804, SI 2009/1941, SI 2009/2392, SI 2009/2476
s.1297, applied: SI 2009/1941 Art.3
s.1297, referred to: SI 2009/1890 Art.1
s.1297, varied: SI 2009/1804 Reg.82
s.1300, enabling: SI 2009/1941, SI 2009/2476
Sch.2, referred to: SI 2009/1378 Art.2
Sch.2 Part 1 para.1, substituted: SI 2009/1208 Sch.1
Sch.2 Part 1 para.2, substituted: SI 2009/1208 Sch.1
Sch.2 Part 1 para.3, substituted: SI 2009/1208 Sch.1
Sch.2 Part 1 para.3A, added: SI 2009/202 Sch.1 para.1
Sch.2 Part 1 para.3A, substituted: SI 2009/1208 Sch.1
Sch.2 Part 1 para.4, substituted: SI 2009/1208 Sch.1
Sch.2 Part 1 para.5, substituted: SI 2009/1208 Sch.1
Sch.2 Part 1 para.5A, added: SI 2009/202 Sch.1 para.1

2006– *cont.*

46. Companies Act 2006– *cont.*

Sch.2 Part 1 para.5A, substituted: SI 2009/1208 Sch.1
Sch.2 Part 1 para.6, substituted: SI 2009/1208 Sch.1
Sch.2 Part 1 para.7, substituted: SI 2009/1208 Sch.1
Sch.2 Part 1 para.7, substituted: SI 2009/1208 Sch.1, SI 2009/1941 Sch.1 para.166
Sch.2 Part 1 para.7, substituted: SI 2009/1208 Sch.1
Sch.2 Part 1 para.7A, added: SI 2009/202 Sch.1 para.1
Sch.2 Part 1 para.7A, substituted: SI 2009/1208 Sch.1
Sch.2 Part 1 para.8, substituted: SI 2009/1208 Sch.1
Sch.2 Part 1 para.8, substituted: SI 2009/1208 Sch.1, SI 2009/1941 Sch.1 para.166
Sch.2 Part 1 para.8, substituted: SI 2009/1208 Sch.1
Sch.2 Part 1 para.9, substituted: SI 2009/1208 Sch.1
Sch.2 Part 1 para.10, substituted: SI 2009/1208 Sch.1
Sch.2 Part 1 para.11, substituted: SI 2009/1208 Sch.1
Sch.2 Part 1 para.12, substituted: SI 2009/1208 Sch.1
Sch.2 Part 1 para.12A, added: SI 2009/202 Sch.1 para.1
Sch.2 Part 1 para.12A, substituted: SI 2009/1208 Sch.1
Sch.2 Part 2 para.1, repealed: SI 2009/1941 Sch.1 para.166
Sch.2 Part 2 para.1, substituted: SI 2009/1208 Sch.1
Sch.2 Part 2 para.1, repealed: SI 2009/1941 Sch.1 para.166
Sch.2 Part 2 para.1, substituted: SI 2009/1208 Sch.1
Sch.2 Part 2 para.1, repealed: SI 2009/1941 Sch.1 para.166
Sch.2 Part 2 para.1, substituted: SI 2009/1208 Sch.1
Sch.2 Part 2 para.1, repealed: SI 2009/1941 Sch.1 para.166
Sch.2 Part 2 para.1, substituted: SI 2009/1208 Sch.1
Sch.2 Part 2 para.2, repealed: SI 2009/1941 Sch.1 para.166
Sch.2 Part 2 para.2, substituted: SI 2009/1208 Sch.1
Sch.2 Part 2 para.2, repealed: SI 2009/1941 Sch.1 para.166
Sch.2 Part 2 para.2, substituted: SI 2009/1208 Sch.1
Sch.2 Part 2 para.2, repealed: SI 2009/1941 Sch.1 para.166
Sch.2 Part 2 para.2, substituted: SI 2009/1208 Sch.1
Sch.2 Part 2 para.2, repealed: SI 2009/1941 Sch.1 para.166
Sch.2 Part 2 para.2, substituted: SI 2009/1208 Sch.1
Sch.2 Part 2 para.2, repealed: SI 2009/1941 Sch.1 para.166
Sch.2 Part 2 para.2, substituted: SI 2009/1208 Sch.1
Sch.2 Part 2 para.3, repealed: SI 2009/1941 Sch.1 para.166
Sch.2 Part 2 para.3, substituted: SI 2009/1208 Sch.1
Sch.2 Part 2 para.3, repealed: SI 2009/1941 Sch.1 para.166
Sch.2 Part 2 para.3, substituted: SI 2009/1208 Sch.1

2006–cont.

46. Companies Act 2006–*cont.*
Sch.2 Part 2 para.3, repealed: SI 2009/1941 Sch.1 para.166
Sch.2 Part 2 para.3, substituted: SI 2009/1208 Sch.1
Sch.2 Part 2 para.3, repealed: SI 2009/1941 Sch.1 para.166
Sch.2 Part 2 para.3, substituted: SI 2009/1208 Sch.1
Sch.2 Part 2 para.3, repealed: SI 2009/1941 Sch.1 para.166
Sch.2 Part 2 para.3, substituted: SI 2009/1208 Sch.1
Sch.2 Part 2 para.4, repealed: SI 2009/1941 Sch.1 para.166
Sch.2 Part 2 para.4, substituted: SI 2009/1208 Sch.1
Sch.2 Part 2 para.4, repealed: SI 2009/1941 Sch.1 para.166
Sch.2 Part 2 para.4, substituted: SI 2009/1208 Sch.1
Sch.2 Part 2 para.4, repealed: SI 2009/1941 Sch.1 para.166
Sch.2 Part 2 para.4, substituted: SI 2009/1208 Sch.1
Sch.2 Part 2 para.4, repealed: SI 2009/1941 Sch.1 para.166
Sch.2 Part 2 para.4, substituted: SI 2009/1208 Sch.1
Sch.2 Part 2 para.5, repealed: SI 2009/1941 Sch.1 para.166
Sch.2 Part 2 para.5, substituted: SI 2009/1208 Sch.1
Sch.2 Part 2 para.5, repealed: SI 2009/1941 Sch.1 para.166
Sch.2 Part 2 para.5, substituted: SI 2009/1208 Sch.1
Sch.2 Part 2 para.5, repealed: SI 2009/1941 Sch.1 para.166
Sch.2 Part 2 para.5, substituted: SI 2009/1208 Sch.1
Sch.2 Part 2 para.5, repealed: SI 2009/1941 Sch.1 para.166
Sch.2 Part 2 para.5, substituted: SI 2009/1208 Sch.1
Sch.2 Part 2 para.6, repealed: SI 2009/1941 Sch.1 para.166
Sch.2 Part 2 para.6, substituted: SI 2009/1208 Sch.1
Sch.2 Part 2 para.6, repealed: SI 2009/1941 Sch.1 para.166
Sch.2 Part 2 para.6, substituted: SI 2009/1208 Sch.1
Sch.2 Part 2 para.6, repealed: SI 2009/1941 Sch.1 para.166
Sch.2 Part 2 para.6, substituted: SI 2009/1208 Sch.1
Sch.2 Part 2 para.7, repealed: SI 2009/1941 Sch.1 para.166
Sch.2 Part 2 para.7, substituted: SI 2009/1208 Sch.1
Sch.2 Part 2 para.7, repealed: SI 2009/1941 Sch.1 para.166
Sch.2 Part 2 para.7, substituted: SI 2009/1208 Sch.1
Sch.2 Part 2 para.7, repealed: SI 2009/1941 Sch.1 para.166
Sch.2 Part 2 para.7, substituted: SI 2009/1208 Sch.1
Sch.2 Part 2 para.8, repealed: SI 2009/1941 Sch.1 para.166
Sch.2 Part 2 para.8, substituted: SI 2009/1208 Sch.1
Sch.2 Part 2 para.8, repealed: SI 2009/1941 Sch.1 para.166

2006–cont.

46. Companies Act 2006–*cont.*
Sch.2 Part 2 para.8, substituted: SI 2009/1208 Sch.1
Sch.2 Part 2 para.8, repealed: SI 2009/1941 Sch.1 para.166
Sch.2 Part 2 para.8, substituted: SI 2009/1208 Sch.1
Sch.2 Part 2 para.8, repealed: SI 2009/1941 Sch.1 para.166
Sch.2 Part 2 para.9, repealed: SI 2009/1941 Sch.1 para.166
Sch.2 Part 2 para.9, substituted: SI 2009/1208 Sch.1
Sch.2 Part 2 para.9, repealed: SI 2009/1941 Sch.1 para.166
Sch.2 Part 2 para.9, substituted: SI 2009/1208 Sch.1
Sch.2 Part 2 para.9, repealed: SI 2009/1941 Sch.1 para.166
Sch.2 Part 2 para.9, substituted: SI 2009/1208 Sch.1
Sch.2 Part 2 para.10, repealed: SI 2009/1941 Sch.1 para.166
Sch.2 Part 2 para.10, substituted: SI 2009/1208 Sch.1
Sch.2 Part 2 para.10, repealed: SI 2009/1941 Sch.1 para.166
Sch.2 Part 2 para.10, substituted: SI 2009/1208 Sch.1
Sch.2 Part 2 para.10, repealed: SI 2009/1941 Sch.1 para.166
Sch.2 Part 2 para.10, substituted: SI 2009/1208 Sch.1
Sch.2 Part 2 para.11, repealed: SI 2009/1941 Sch.1 para.166
Sch.2 Part 2 para.11, substituted: SI 2009/1208 Sch.1
Sch.2 Part 2 para.11, repealed: SI 2009/1941 Sch.1 para.166
Sch.2 Part 2 para.11, substituted: SI 2009/1208 Sch.1
Sch.2 Part 2 para.11, repealed: SI 2009/1941 Sch.1 para.166
Sch.2 Part 2 para.11, substituted: SI 2009/1208 Sch.1
Sch.2 Part 2 para.12, repealed: SI 2009/1941 Sch.1 para.166
Sch.2 Part 2 para.12, substituted: SI 2009/1208 Sch.1
Sch.2 Part 2 para.12, repealed: SI 2009/1941 Sch.1 para.166
Sch.2 Part 2 para.12, substituted: SI 2009/1208 Sch.1
Sch.2 Part 2 para.12, repealed: SI 2009/1941 Sch.1 para.166
Sch.2 Part 2 para.12, substituted: SI 2009/1208 Sch.1
Sch.2 Part 2 para.13, repealed: SI 2009/1941 Sch.1 para.166
Sch.2 Part 2 para.13, substituted: SI 2009/1208 Sch.1
Sch.2 Part 2 para.13, repealed: SI 2009/1941 Sch.1 para.166
Sch.2 Part 2 para.13, substituted: SI 2009/1208 Sch.1
Sch.2 Part 2 para.13, repealed: SI 2009/1941 Sch.1 para.166
Sch.2 Part 2 para.13, substituted: SI 2009/1208 Sch.1
Sch.2 Part 2 para.13, repealed: SI 2009/1941 Sch.1 para.166
Sch.2 Part 2 para.13, substituted: SI 2009/1208 Sch.1

2006–cont.

46. Companies Act 2006–*cont.*

Sch.2 Part 2 para.14, repealed: SI 2009/1941 Sch.1 para.166

Sch.2 Part 2 para.14, substituted: SI 2009/1208 Sch.1

Sch.2 Part 2 para.14, repealed: SI 2009/1941 Sch.1 para.166

Sch.2 Part 2 para.14, substituted: SI 2009/1208 Sch.1

Sch.2 Part 2 para.14, repealed: SI 2009/1941 Sch.1 para.166

Sch.2 Part 2 para.14, substituted: SI 2009/1208 Sch.1

Sch.2 Part 2 para.14A, added: SI 2009/202 Sch.1 para.2

Sch.2 Part 2 para.14A, repealed: SI 2009/1941 Sch.1 para.166

Sch.2 Part 2 para.14A, substituted: SI 2009/1208 Sch.1

Sch.2 Part 2 para.15, repealed: SI 2009/1941 Sch.1 para.166

Sch.2 Part 2 para.15, substituted: SI 2009/1208 Sch.1

Sch.2 Part 2 para.15, repealed: SI 2009/1941 Sch.1 para.166

Sch.2 Part 2 para.15, substituted: SI 2009/1208 Sch.1

Sch.2 Part 2 para.15, repealed: SI 2009/1941 Sch.1 para.166

Sch.2 Part 2 para.15, substituted: SI 2009/1208 Sch.1

Sch.2 Part 2 para.16, repealed: SI 2009/1941 Sch.1 para.166

Sch.2 Part 2 para.16, substituted: SI 2009/1208 Sch.1

Sch.2 Part 2 para.16, repealed: SI 2009/1941 Sch.1 para.166

Sch.2 Part 2 para.16, substituted: SI 2009/1208 Sch.1

Sch.2 Part 2 para.16, repealed: SI 2009/1941 Sch.1 para.166

Sch.2 Part 2 para.16, substituted: SI 2009/1208 Sch.1

Sch.2 Part 2 para.17, repealed: SI 2009/1941 Sch.1 para.166

Sch.2 Part 2 para.17, substituted: SI 2009/1208 Sch.1

Sch.2 Part 2 para.17, repealed: SI 2009/1941 Sch.1 para.166

Sch.2 Part 2 para.17, substituted: SI 2009/1208 Sch.1

Sch.2 Part 2 para.17, repealed: SI 2009/1941 Sch.1 para.166

Sch.2 Part 2 para.17, substituted: SI 2009/1208 Sch.1

Sch.2 Part 2 para.18, repealed: SI 2009/1941 Sch.1 para.166

Sch.2 Part 2 para.18, substituted: SI 2009/1208 Sch.1

Sch.2 Part 2 para.18, repealed: SI 2009/1941 Sch.1 para.166

Sch.2 Part 2 para.18, substituted: SI 2009/1208 Sch.1

Sch.2 Part 2 para.19, repealed: SI 2009/1941 Sch.1 para.166

Sch.2 Part 2 para.19, substituted: SI 2009/1208 Sch.1

Sch.2 Part 2 para.19, repealed: SI 2009/1941 Sch.1 para.166

2006–cont.

46. Companies Act 2006–*cont.*

Sch.2 Part 2 para.19, substituted: SI 2009/1208 Sch.1

Sch.2 Part 2 para.20, repealed: SI 2009/1941 Sch.1 para.166

Sch.2 Part 2 para.20, substituted: SI 2009/1208 Sch.1

Sch.2 Part 2 para.20, repealed: SI 2009/1941 Sch.1 para.166

Sch.2 Part 2 para.20, substituted: SI 2009/1208 Sch.1

Sch.2 Part 2 para.21, repealed: SI 2009/1941 Sch.1 para.166

Sch.2 Part 2 para.21, substituted: SI 2009/1208 Sch.1

Sch.2 Part 2 para.21, repealed: SI 2009/1941 Sch.1 para.166

Sch.2 Part 2 para.21, substituted: SI 2009/1208 Sch.1

Sch.2 Part 2 para.22, repealed: SI 2009/1941 Sch.1 para.166

Sch.2 Part 2 para.22, substituted: SI 2009/1208 Sch.1

Sch.2 Part 2 para.22, repealed: SI 2009/1941 Sch.1 para.166

Sch.2 Part 2 para.22, substituted: SI 2009/1208 Sch.1

Sch.2 Part 2 para.22A, added: SI 2009/202 Sch.1 para.2

Sch.2 Part 2 para.22A, repealed: SI 2009/1941 Sch.1 para.166

Sch.2 Part 2 para.22A, substituted: SI 2009/1208 Sch.1

Sch.2 Part 2 para.23, repealed: SI 2009/1941 Sch.1 para.166

Sch.2 Part 2 para.23, substituted: SI 2009/1208 Sch.1

Sch.2 Part 2 para.23, repealed: SI 2009/1941 Sch.1 para.166

Sch.2 Part 2 para.23, substituted: SI 2009/1208 Sch.1

Sch.2 Part 2 para.24, repealed: SI 2009/1941 Sch.1 para.166

Sch.2 Part 2 para.24, substituted: SI 2009/1208 Sch.1

Sch.2 Part 2 para.24, repealed: SI 2009/1941 Sch.1 para.166

Sch.2 Part 2 para.24, substituted: SI 2009/1208 Sch.1

Sch.2 Part 2 para.25, repealed: SI 2009/1941 Sch.1 para.166

Sch.2 Part 2 para.25, substituted: SI 2009/1208 Sch.1

Sch.2 Part 2 para.25, varied: SI 2009/317 Art.6

Sch.2 Part 2 para.25, repealed: SI 2009/1941 Sch.1 para.166

Sch.2 Part 2 para.25, substituted: SI 2009/1208 Sch.1

Sch.2 Part 2 para.25A, added: SI 2009/202 Sch.1 para.2

Sch.2 Part 2 para.25A, repealed: SI 2009/1941 Sch.1 para.166

Sch.2 Part 2 para.25A, substituted: SI 2009/1208 Sch.1

Sch.2 Part 2 para.25B, added: SI 2009/202 Sch.1 para.2

Sch.2 Part 2 para.25B, repealed: SI 2009/1941 Sch.1 para.166

Sch.2 Part 2 para.25B, substituted: SI 2009/1208 Sch.1

2006–cont.

46. Companies Act 2006–*cont.*

Sch.2 Part 2 para.26, repealed: SI 2009/1941 Sch.1 para.166

Sch.2 Part 2 para.26, substituted: SI 2009/1208 Sch.1

Sch.2 Part 2 para.26, repealed: SI 2009/1941 Sch.1 para.166

Sch.2 Part 2 para.26, substituted: SI 2009/1208 Sch.1

Sch.2 Part 2 para.27, repealed: SI 2009/1941 Sch.1 para.166

Sch.2 Part 2 para.27, substituted: SI 2009/1208 Sch.1

Sch.2 Part 2 para.27, repealed: SI 2009/1941 Sch.1 para.166

Sch.2 Part 2 para.27, substituted: SI 2009/1208 Sch.1

Sch.2 Part 2 para.27A, added: SI 2009/202 Sch.1 para.2

Sch.2 Part 2 para.27A, repealed: SI 2009/1941 Sch.1 para.166

Sch.2 Part 2 para.27A, substituted: SI 2009/1208 Sch.1

Sch.2 Part 2 para.27B, repealed: SI 2009/1941 Sch.1 para.166

Sch.2 Part 2 para.27B, substituted: SI 2009/1208 Sch.1

Sch.2 Part 2 para.28, repealed: SI 2009/1941 Sch.1 para.166

Sch.2 Part 2 para.28, substituted: SI 2009/1208 Sch.1

Sch.2 Part 2 para.28, repealed: SI 2009/1941 Sch.1 para.166

Sch.2 Part 2 para.28, substituted: SI 2009/1208 Sch.1

Sch.2 Part 2 para.29, repealed: SI 2009/1941 Sch.1 para.166

Sch.2 Part 2 para.29, substituted: SI 2009/1208 Sch.1

Sch.2 Part 2 para.29, repealed: SI 2009/1941 Sch.1 para.166

Sch.2 Part 2 para.29, substituted: SI 2009/1208 Sch.1

Sch.2 Part 2 para.29A, added: SI 2009/202 Sch.1 para.2

Sch.2 Part 2 para.29A, repealed: SI 2009/1941 Sch.1 para.166

Sch.2 Part 2 para.29A, substituted: SI 2009/1208 Sch.1

Sch.2 Part 2 para.30, repealed: SI 2009/1941 Sch.1 para.166

Sch.2 Part 2 para.30, substituted: SI 2009/1208 Sch.1

Sch.2 Part 2 para.30, varied: SI 2009/317 Art.6

Sch.2 Part 2 para.30, repealed: SI 2009/1941 Sch.1 para.166

Sch.2 Part 2 para.30, substituted: SI 2009/1208 Sch.1

Sch.2 Part 2 para.31, repealed: SI 2009/1941 Sch.1 para.166

Sch.2 Part 2 para.31, substituted: SI 2009/1208 Sch.1

Sch.2 Part 2 para.31, repealed: SI 2009/1941 Sch.1 para.166

Sch.2 Part 2 para.31, substituted: SI 2009/1208 Sch.1

Sch.2 Part 2 para.32, repealed: SI 2009/1941 Sch.1 para.166

Sch.2 Part 2 para.32, substituted: SI 2009/1208 Sch.1

2006–cont.

46. Companies Act 2006–*cont.*

Sch.2 Part 2 para.32, repealed: SI 2009/1941 Sch.1 para.166

Sch.2 Part 2 para.32, substituted: SI 2009/1208 Sch.1

Sch.2 Part 2 para.32A, added: SI 2009/202 Sch.1 para.2

Sch.2 Part 2 para.32A, repealed: SI 2009/1941 Sch.1 para.166

Sch.2 Part 2 para.32A, substituted: SI 2009/1208 Sch.1

Sch.2 Part 2 para.33, repealed: SI 2009/1941 Sch.1 para.166

Sch.2 Part 2 para.33, substituted: SI 2009/1208 Sch.1

Sch.2 Part 2 para.33, repealed: SI 2009/1941 Sch.1 para.166

Sch.2 Part 2 para.33, substituted: SI 2009/1208 Sch.1

Sch.2 Part 2 para.34, repealed: SI 2009/1941 Sch.1 para.166

Sch.2 Part 2 para.34, substituted: SI 2009/1208 Sch.1

Sch.2 Part 2 para.34, repealed: SI 2009/1941 Sch.1 para.166

Sch.2 Part 2 para.34, substituted: SI 2009/1208 Sch.1

Sch.2 Part 2 para.35, repealed: SI 2009/1941 Sch.1 para.166

Sch.2 Part 2 para.35, substituted: SI 2009/1208 Sch.1

Sch.2 Part 2 para.35, repealed: SI 2009/1941 Sch.1 para.166

Sch.2 Part 2 para.35, substituted: SI 2009/1208 Sch.1

Sch.2 Part 2 para.36, repealed: SI 2009/1941 Sch.1 para.166

Sch.2 Part 2 para.36, substituted: SI 2009/1208 Sch.1

Sch.2 Part 2 para.36, repealed: SI 2009/1941 Sch.1 para.166

Sch.2 Part 2 para.36, substituted: SI 2009/1208 Sch.1

Sch.2 Part 2 para.37, repealed: SI 2009/1941 Sch.1 para.166

Sch.2 Part 2 para.37, substituted: SI 2009/1208 Sch.1

Sch.2 Part 2 para.37, repealed: SI 2009/1941 Sch.1 para.166

Sch.2 Part 2 para.37, substituted: SI 2009/1208 Sch.1

Sch.2 Part 2 para.38, repealed: SI 2009/1941 Sch.1 para.166

Sch.2 Part 2 para.38, substituted: SI 2009/1208 Sch.1

Sch.2 Part 2 para.38, repealed: SI 2009/1941 Sch.1 para.166

Sch.2 Part 2 para.38, substituted: SI 2009/1208 Sch.1

Sch.2 Part 2 para.39, amended: SI 2009/202 Sch.1 para.2

Sch.2 Part 2 para.39, repealed: SI 2009/1941 Sch.1 para.166

Sch.2 Part 2 para.39, substituted: SI 2009/1208 Sch.1

Sch.2 Part 2 para.39, repealed: SI 2009/1941 Sch.1 para.166

Sch.2 Part 2 para.39, substituted: SI 2009/1208 Sch.1

2006–cont.

46. Companies Act 2006–*cont.*

Sch.2 Part 2 para.40, repealed: SI 2009/1941 Sch.1 para.166

Sch.2 Part 2 para.40, substituted: SI 2009/1208 Sch.1

Sch.2 Part 2 para.40, repealed: SI 2009/1941 Sch.1 para.166

Sch.2 Part 2 para.40, substituted: SI 2009/1208 Sch.1

Sch.2 Part 2 para.41, repealed: SI 2009/1941 Sch.1 para.166

Sch.2 Part 2 para.41, substituted: SI 2009/1208 Sch.1

Sch.2 Part 2 para.41, repealed: SI 2009/1941 Sch.1 para.166

Sch.2 Part 2 para.41, substituted: SI 2009/1208 Sch.1

Sch.2 Part 2 para.42, repealed: SI 2009/1941 Sch.1 para.166

Sch.2 Part 2 para.42, substituted: SI 2009/1208 Sch.1

Sch.2 Part 2 para.42, repealed: SI 2009/1941 Sch.1 para.166

Sch.2 Part 2 para.42, substituted: SI 2009/1208 Sch.1

Sch.2 Part 2 para.43, repealed: SI 2009/1941 Sch.1 para.166

Sch.2 Part 2 para.43, substituted: SI 2009/1208 Sch.1

Sch.2 Part 2 para.43, repealed: SI 2009/1941 Sch.1 para.166

Sch.2 Part 2 para.43, substituted: SI 2009/1208 Sch.1

Sch.2 Part 2 para.44, repealed: SI 2009/1941 Sch.1 para.166

Sch.2 Part 2 para.44, substituted: SI 2009/1208 Sch.1

Sch.2 Part 2 para.44, repealed: SI 2009/1941 Sch.1 para.166

Sch.2 Part 2 para.44, substituted: SI 2009/1208 Sch.1

Sch.2 Part 2 para.45, repealed: SI 2009/1941 Sch.1 para.166

Sch.2 Part 2 para.45, substituted: SI 2009/1208 Sch.1

Sch.2 Part 2 para.45, repealed: SI 2009/1941 Sch.1 para.166

Sch.2 Part 2 para.45, substituted: SI 2009/1208 Sch.1

Sch.2 Part 2 para.46, repealed: SI 2009/1941 Sch.1 para.166

Sch.2 Part 2 para.46, substituted: SI 2009/1208 Sch.1

Sch.2 Part 2 para.46, varied: SI 2009/317 Art.6

Sch.2 Part 2 para.46, repealed: SI 2009/1941 Sch.1 para.166

Sch.2 Part 2 para.46, substituted: SI 2009/1208 Sch.1

Sch.2 Part 2 para.47, repealed: SI 2009/1941 Sch.1 para.166

Sch.2 Part 2 para.47, substituted: SI 2009/1208 Sch.1

Sch.2 Part 2 para.47, repealed: SI 2009/1941 Sch.1 para.166

Sch.2 Part 2 para.47, substituted: SI 2009/1208 Sch.1

Sch.2 Part 2 para.48, repealed: SI 2009/1941 Sch.1 para.166

Sch.2 Part 2 para.48, substituted: SI 2009/1208 Sch.1

2006–cont.

46. Companies Act 2006–*cont.*

Sch.2 Part 2 para.48, repealed: SI 2009/1941 Sch.1 para.166

Sch.2 Part 2 para.48, substituted: SI 2009/1208 Sch.1

Sch.2 Part 2 para.48A, added: SI 2009/202 Sch.1 para.2

Sch.2 Part 2 para.48A, repealed: SI 2009/1941 Sch.1 para.166

Sch.2 Part 2 para.48A, substituted: SI 2009/1208 Sch.1

Sch.2 Part 2 para.49, repealed: SI 2009/1941 Sch.1 para.166

Sch.2 Part 2 para.49, substituted: SI 2009/1208 Sch.1

Sch.2 Part 2 para.49, repealed: SI 2009/1941 Sch.1 para.166

Sch.2 Part 2 para.49, substituted: SI 2009/1208 Sch.1

Sch.2 Part 2 para.50, repealed: SI 2009/1941 Sch.1 para.166

Sch.2 Part 2 para.50, substituted: SI 2009/1208 Sch.1

Sch.2 Part 2 para.50, repealed: SI 2009/1941 Sch.1 para.166

Sch.2 Part 2 para.50, substituted: SI 2009/1208 Sch.1

Sch.2 Part 2 para.51, repealed: SI 2009/1941 Sch.1 para.166

Sch.2 Part 2 para.51, substituted: SI 2009/1208 Sch.1

Sch.2 Part 2 para.51, repealed: SI 2009/1941 Sch.1 para.166

Sch.2 Part 2 para.51, substituted: SI 2009/1208 Sch.1

Sch.2 Part 2 para.52, repealed: SI 2009/1941 Sch.1 para.166

Sch.2 Part 2 para.52, substituted: SI 2009/1208 Sch.1

Sch.2 Part 2 para.52, varied: SI 2009/317 Art.6

Sch.2 Part 2 para.52, repealed: SI 2009/1941 Sch.1 para.166

Sch.2 Part 2 para.52, substituted: SI 2009/1208 Sch.1

Sch.2 Part 2 para.52A, added: SI 2009/202 Sch.1 para.2

Sch.2 Part 2 para.52A, repealed: SI 2009/1941 Sch.1 para.166

Sch.2 Part 2 para.52A, substituted: SI 2009/1208 Sch.1

Sch.2 Part 2 para.53, repealed: SI 2009/1941 Sch.1 para.166

Sch.2 Part 2 para.53, substituted: SI 2009/1208 Sch.1

Sch.2 Part 2 para.53, repealed: SI 2009/1941 Sch.1 para.166

Sch.2 Part 2 para.53, substituted: SI 2009/1208 Sch.1

Sch.2 Part 2 para.54, repealed: SI 2009/1941 Sch.1 para.166

Sch.2 Part 2 para.54, substituted: SI 2009/1208 Sch.1

Sch.2 Part 2 para.55, repealed: SI 2009/1941 Sch.1 para.166

Sch.2 Part 2 para.55, substituted: SI 2009/1208 Sch.1

Sch.2 Part 2 para.55A, added: SI 2009/202 Sch.1 para.2

Sch.2 Part 2 para.55A, repealed: SI 2009/1941 Sch.1 para.166

2006–cont.

46. Companies Act 2006–*cont.*

Sch.2 Part 2 para.55A, substituted: SI 2009/ 1208 Sch.1

Sch.2 Part 2 para.56, repealed: SI 2009/ 1941 Sch.1 para.166

Sch.2 Part 2 para.56, substituted: SI 2009/ 1208 Sch.1

Sch.2 Part 2 para.57, repealed: SI 2009/ 1941 Sch.1 para.166

Sch.2 Part 2 para.57, substituted: SI 2009/ 1208 Sch.1

Sch.2 Part 2 para.58, repealed: SI 2009/ 1941 Sch.1 para.166

Sch.2 Part 2 para.58, substituted: SI 2009/ 1208 Sch.1

Sch.2 Part 2 para.59, repealed: SI 2009/ 1941 Sch.1 para.166

Sch.2 Part 2 para.59, substituted: SI 2009/ 1208 Sch.1

Sch.2 Part 2 para.60, repealed: SI 2009/ 1941 Sch.1 para.166

Sch.2 Part 2 para.60, substituted: SI 2009/ 1208 Sch.1

Sch.2 Part 2 para.61, repealed: SI 2009/ 1941 Sch.1 para.166

Sch.2 Part 2 para.61, substituted: SI 2009/ 1208 Sch.1

Sch.2 Part 2 para.62, repealed: SI 2009/ 1941 Sch.1 para.166

Sch.2 Part 2 para.62, substituted: SI 2009/ 1208 Sch.1

Sch.2 Part 2 para.63, repealed: SI 2009/ 1941 Sch.1 para.166

Sch.2 Part 2 para.63, substituted: SI 2009/ 1208 Sch.1

Sch.2 Part 2 para.64, repealed: SI 2009/ 1941 Sch.1 para.166

Sch.2 Part 2 para.64, substituted: SI 2009/ 1208 Sch.1

Sch.2 Part 2 para.65, repealed: SI 2009/ 1941 Sch.1 para.166

Sch.2 Part 2 para.65, substituted: SI 2009/ 1208 Sch.1

Sch.2 Part 2 para.66, repealed: SI 2009/ 1941 Sch.1 para.166

Sch.2 Part 2 para.66, substituted: SI 2009/ 1208 Sch.1

Sch.2 Part 2 para.67, repealed: SI 2009/ 1941 Sch.1 para.166

Sch.2 Part 2 para.67, substituted: SI 2009/ 1208 Sch.1

Sch.2 Part 2 para.68, repealed: SI 2009/ 1941 Sch.1 para.166

Sch.2 Part 2 para.68, substituted: SI 2009/ 1208 Sch.1

Sch.2 Part 2 para.69, repealed: SI 2009/ 1941 Sch.1 para.166

Sch.2 Part 2 para.69, substituted: SI 2009/ 1208 Sch.1

Sch.2 Part 2 para.70, repealed: SI 2009/ 1941 Sch.1 para.166

Sch.2 Part 2 para.70, substituted: SI 2009/ 1208 Sch.1

Sch.2 Part 3 para.1, repealed: SI 2009/ 1941 Sch.1 para.166

Sch.2 Part 3 para.1, substituted: SI 2009/ 1208 Sch.1

Sch.2 Part 3 para.2, repealed: SI 2009/ 1941 Sch.1 para.166

Sch.2 Part 3 para.2, substituted: SI 2009/ 1208 Sch.1

2006–cont.

46. Companies Act 2006–*cont.*

Sch.2 Part 3 para.71, repealed: SI 2009/ 1941 Sch.1 para.166

Sch.2 Part 3 para.71, substituted: SI 2009/ 1208 Sch.1

Sch.2 Part 3 para.72, repealed: SI 2009/ 1941 Sch.1 para.166

Sch.2 Part 3 para.72, substituted: SI 2009/ 1208 Sch.1

Sch.2 Part 3 para.73, repealed: SI 2009/ 1941 Sch.1 para.166

Sch.2 Part 3 para.73, substituted: SI 2009/ 1208 Sch.1

Sch.7, applied: SI 2009/ 389 Sch.1 para.14

Sch.8, amended: SI 2009/ 1581 Reg.9, SI 2009/ 1632 Reg.21, SI 2009/ 1802 Art.17, SI 2009/ 1941 Sch.1 para.260, SI 2009/ 2561 Reg.2

47. Safeguarding Vulnerable Groups Act 2006

Commencement Orders: SI 2009/ 39 Art.2; SI 2009/ 1503 Art.2, Art.3; SI 2009/ 2610 Art.2; SI 2009/ 2611 Art.2, Art.3, Art.4, Sch.1

applied: SI 2009/ 26 Sch.1, SI 2009/ 263 Art.5, SI 2009/ 442 Art.5, SI 2009/ 468 Sch.1, SI 2009/ 1345 Art.5, SI 2009/ 1355 Sch.1, SI 2009/ 1633 Reg.2, Reg.3, SI 2009/ 1808 Art.5, SI 2009/ 1813 Sch.1, SI 2009/ 2558 Reg.2, Reg.3, SI 2009/ 2722 Reg.3

referred to: SI 2009/ 203 Art.10

s.1, amended: 2009 c.26 s.81

s.2, amended: 2009 c.26 s.81

s.2, applied: SI 2009/ 37 Reg.2, SSI 2009/ 4 Art.4, Art.5

s.3, applied: SI 2009/ 1547 Reg.8, SI 2009/ 1797 Art.5, SI 2009/ 2611 Art.3, SI 2009/ 2680 Sch.2 para.2, SSI 2009/ 4 Art.3

s.3, disapplied: SI 2009/ 2611 Art.5, Art.6, Art.7

s.3, enabling: SI 2009/ 1797

s.4, amended: 2009 c.26 s.81

s.5, enabling: SI 2009/ 2610

s.6, amended: 2009 c.21 Sch.1 para.13, 2009 c.26 s.81

s.8, amended: 2009 c.26 s.82

s.13, amended: 2009 c.26 s.82

s.15, amended: 2009 c.26 s.81, SI 2009/ 203 Art.13

s.21, amended: 2009 c.21 Sch.1 para.14, 2009 c.22 Sch.12 para.43, SI 2009/ 2610 Art.28, Art.30

s.21, enabling: SI 2009/ 2610

s.24, amended: 2009 c.26 s.83

s.24A, added: 2009 c.26 s.84

s.25, amended: 2009 c.26 s.81, s.84

s.28, varied: SI 2009/ 3215 Sch.2 para.1

s.30, amended: 2009 c.26 s.84, s.85

s.30, repealed (in part): 2009 c.26 s.85, Sch.8 Part 8

s.31, repealed (in part): 2009 c.26 s.87, Sch.8 Part 8

s.32, amended: 2009 c.26 s.86

s.32, repealed (in part): 2009 c.26 s.86, Sch.8 Part 8

s.34A, added: 2009 c.26 s.87

s.34B, added: 2009 c.26 s.87

s.34C, added: 2009 c.26 s.87

s.35, amended: 2009 c.26 s.81

s.35, applied: SI 2009/ 1350 Reg.1

s.36, amended: 2009 c.26 s.81

s.36, applied: SI 2009/ 1350 Reg.1

s.37, amended: 2009 c.26 s.81

s.38, amended: 2009 c.26 s.81

s.39, amended: 2009 c.26 s.81

s.39, applied: SI 2009/ 1350 Reg.1

s.40, amended: 2009 c.26 s.81

s.41, amended: 2009 c.26 s.81, SI 2009/ 1182 Sch.5 para.9

47. Safeguarding Vulnerable Groups Act 2006– *cont.*

s.42, amended: 2009 c.26 s.81

s.43, amended: 2009 c.26 s.81, SI 2009/ 1182 Sch.5 para.9

s.44, amended: 2009 c.26 s.81, SI 2009/ 1182 Sch.5 para.9

s.45, amended: 2009 c.26 s.81, SI 2009/ 1797 Art.6, SI 2009/ 2610 Art.30

s.45, enabling: SI 2009/ 1797

s.46, amended: 2009 c.26 s.81

s.47, amended: 2009 c.26 s.81

s.50, amended: 2009 c.26 s.81

s.50A, added: 2009 c.26 s.88

s.54, enabling: SI 2009/ 265

s.56, applied: SI 2009/ 12, SI 2009/ 37, SI 2009/ 39, SI 2009/ 1503, SI 2009/ 1548, SI 2009/ 1797, SI 2009/ 2610, SI 2009/ 2611

s.59, amended: 2009 c.21 Sch.1 para.15, Sch.6

s.59, applied: SI 2009/ 1548 Reg.2, SI 2009/ 1797 Art.2

s.59, enabling: SI 2009/ 1548, SI 2009/ 1797

s.60, enabling: SI 2009/ 1548

s.61, applied: SI 2009/ 12, SI 2009/ 37, SI 2009/ 2610

s.61, enabling: SI 2009/ 37, SI 2009/ 39, SI 2009/ 1503, SI 2009/ 2610, SI 2009/ 2611

s.64, enabling: SI 2009/ 12, SI 2009/ 37, SI 2009/ 2610, SI 2009/ 2611

s.65, enabling: SI 2009/ 39, SI 2009/ 1503, SI 2009/ 2610, SI 2009/ 2611

s.66, enabling: SI 2009/ 3215

Sch.1 para.1, amended: 2009 c.26 s.81

Sch.1 para.2, amended: 2009 c.26 s.81

Sch.1 para.3, amended: 2009 c.26 s.81

Sch.1 para.4, amended: 2009 c.26 s.81

Sch.1 para.5, amended: 2009 c.26 s.81

Sch.1 para.6, amended: 2009 c.26 s.81

Sch.1 para.7, amended: 2009 c.26 s.81

Sch.1 para.8, amended: 2009 c.26 s.81

Sch.1 para.9, amended: 2009 c.26 s.81

Sch.1 para.10, amended: 2009 c.26 s.81

Sch.1 para.11, amended: 2009 c.26 s.81

Sch.1 para.12, amended: 2009 c.26 s.81

Sch.1 para.13, amended: 2009 c.26 s.81

Sch.1 para.14, amended: 2009 c.26 s.81

Sch.1 para.15, amended: 2009 c.26 s.81

Sch.1 para.16, amended: 2009 c.26 s.81

Sch.2 para.1, amended: 2009 c.26 s.81

Sch.2 para.2, amended: 2009 c.26 s.81

Sch.3 Part 1 para.1, amended: 2009 c.26 s.89

Sch.3 Part 1 para.1, applied: SI 2009/ 37 Reg.3

Sch.3 Part 1 para.1, varied: SI 2009/ 12 Art.5, SI 2009/ 2610 Art.9

Sch.3 Part 1 para.1, enabling: SI 2009/ 37

Sch.3 Part 1 para.2, amended: 2009 c.26 s.81, s.89

Sch.3 Part 1 para.2, applied: SI 2009/ 37 Reg.4

Sch.3 Part 1 para.2, varied: SI 2009/ 12 Art.5, SI 2009/ 2610 Art.9

Sch.3 Part 1 para.2, enabling: SI 2009/ 37, SI 2009/ 2610

Sch.3 Part 1 para.3, amended: 2009 c.26 s.81

Sch.3 Part 1 para.3, varied: SI 2009/ 12 Art.5, SI 2009/ 2610 Art.23

Sch.3 Part 1 para.4, amended: 2009 c.26 s.81

Sch.3 Part 1 para.5, amended: 2009 c.26 s.81

Sch.3 Part 1 para.6, amended: 2009 c.26 s.81

Sch.3 Part 2 para.7, amended: 2009 c.26 s.89

Sch.3 Part 2 para.7, applied: SI 2009/ 37 Reg.5

47. Safeguarding Vulnerable Groups Act 2006– *cont.*

Sch.3 Part 2 para.7, varied: SI 2009/ 12 Art.5, SI 2009/ 2610 Art.9

Sch.3 Part 2 para.7, enabling: SI 2009/ 37

Sch.3 Part 2 para.8, amended: 2009 c.26 s.81, s.89

Sch.3 Part 2 para.8, applied: SI 2009/ 37 Reg.6

Sch.3 Part 2 para.8, varied: SI 2009/ 12 Art.5, SI 2009/ 2610 Art.9

Sch.3 Part 2 para.8, enabling: SI 2009/ 37, SI 2009/ 2610

Sch.3 Part 2 para.9, amended: 2009 c.26 s.81

Sch.3 Part 2 para.10, amended: 2009 c.26 s.81

Sch.3 Part 2 para.11, amended: 2009 c.26 s.81

Sch.3 Part 2 para.12, amended: 2009 c.26 s.81

Sch.3 Part 3 para.13, amended: 2009 c.26 s.81

Sch.3 Part 3 para.14, amended: 2009 c.26 s.81

Sch.3 Part 3 para.15, amended: 2009 c.26 s.81

Sch.3 Part 3 para.16, amended: 2009 c.26 s.81

Sch.3 Part 3 para.17, amended: 2009 c.26 s.81

Sch.3 Part 3 para.18, amended: 2009 c.26 s.81

Sch.3 Part 3 para.19, amended: 2009 c.26 s.81

Sch.3 Part 3 para.20, amended: 2009 c.26 s.81

Sch.3 Part 3 para.20, applied: SI 2009/ 12 Art.9, SI 2009/ 2610 Art.21

Sch.3 Part 3 para.21, amended: 2009 c.26 s.81

Sch.3 Part 3 para.23, amended: 2009 c.26 s.81

Sch.3 Part 3 para.24, amended: 2009 c.26 s.89

Sch.3 Part 3 para.24, enabling: SI 2009/ 37, SI 2009/ 2610

Sch.3 Part 3 para.25, amended: 2009 c.26 s.81

Sch.4 Part 1 para.1, amended: SI 2009/ 2610 Art.29, Art.30

Sch.4 Part 1 para.2, applied: SI 2009/ 1548 Reg.3

Sch.4 Part 1 para.2, enabling: SI 2009/ 1548

Sch.4 Part 1 para.3, amended: 2009 c.22 s.200, SI 2009/ 2610 Art.25

Sch.4 Part 1 para.4, amended: 2009 c.26 s.81, SI 2009/ 2610 Art.26

Sch.4 Part 1 para.6, enabling: SI 2009/ 1797

Sch.4 Part 2 para.7, amended: SI 2009/ 2610 Art.30

Sch.4 Part 2 para.7, applied: SI 2009/ 1548 Reg.4

Sch.4 Part 2 para.7, enabling: SI 2009/ 1548

Sch.4 Part 2 para.8, amended: 2009 c.26 s.81, SI 2009/ 2610 Art.27

Sch.4 Part 2 para.9, enabling: SI 2009/ 1797

Sch.5 Part 1 para.2, amended: 2009 c.26 s.81, SI 2009/ 203 Art.14

Sch.5 Part 4 para.12, amended: SI 2009/ 203 Art.14

Sch.5 Part 4 para.12A, added: SI 2009/ 203 Art.14

Sch.6 para.2, amended: SI 2009/ 203 Art.15

Sch.8 para.1, amended: 2009 c.26 s.81

Sch.8 para.2, amended: 2009 c.26 s.81

Sch.8 para.3, amended: 2009 c.26 s.81

Sch.9 Part 1 para.7, amended: 2009 c.26 s.81

Sch.9 Part 2 para.11, amended: 2009 c.26 s.81

Sch.9 Part 2 para.13, amended: 2009 c.26 s.81

Sch.9 Part 2 para.14, amended: 2009 c.26 s.81

Sch.9 Part 2 para.14, varied: SI 2009/ 3215 Sch.2 para.2, Sch.3 para.2, Sch.3 para.3, Sch.3 para.4

Sch.9 Part 2 para.15, amended: 2009 c.26 s.81

48. Police and Justice Act 2006

Commencement Orders: SI 2009/ 936 Art.2; SI 2009/ 1679 Art.2; SI 2009/ 2540 Art.2; SI 2009/ 2774 Art.2, Art.3

s.19, applied: SI 2009/ 942 Reg.7

s.20, applied: SI 2009/ 1919 Reg.12

s.20, referred to: SI 2009/ 942 Reg.5

2006– cont.

48. Police and Justice Act 2006–*cont.*
s.20, enabling: SI 2009/942
s.41, amended: 2009 c.11 s.30
s.41, enabling: SI 2009/2133
s.49, enabling: SI 2009/1679, SI 2009/2133, SI 2009/2774
s.53, enabling: SI 2009/936, SI 2009/1679, SI 2009/2540, SI 2009/2774
Sch.1 Part 1 para.3, amended: SI 2009/2054 Sch.1 para.30
Sch.1 Part 1 para.3, repealed (in part): SI 2009/2054 Sch.1 para.30
Sch.1 Part 7 para.78, repealed: 2009 c.26 Sch.8 Part 13
Sch.5 para.5, repealed (in part): 2009 c.26 Sch.8 Part 13

49. Road Safety Act 2006
s.11, enabling: SI 2009/493
s.20, repealed (in part): 2009 c.25 Sch.23 Part 1
s.21, repealed (in part): 2009 c.25 Sch.23 Part 1
s.35, referred to: 2009 c.25 Sch.22 para.30
Sch.2 para.33, repealed: 2009 c.24 Sch.7 Part 4
Sch.3 para.13, repealed (in part): 2009 c.26 Sch.8 Part 13
Sch.3 para.44, referred to: 2009 c.25 Sch.22 para.30
Sch.3 para.65, repealed (in part): 2009 c.24 Sch.7 Part 4
Sch.4, enabling: SI 2009/493
Sch.6, referred to: 2009 c.17 s.6

50. Charities Act 2006
Commencement Orders: SI 2009/1941 Sch.2; SI 2009/2648 Art.2
see *Hanchett-Stamford v Attorney General* [2008] EWHC 330 (Ch), [2009] Ch. 173 (Ch D (Bristol)), Lewison, J.
s.8, repealed (in part): SI 2009/1834 Sch.3
s.57, amended: SI 2009/1834 Sch.1 para.17
s.74, applied: SI 2009/1941
s.75, applied: SI 2009/1941
s.75, enabling: SI 2009/1941
s.78, enabling: SI 2009/841, SI 2009/2648
s.79, enabling: SI 2009/841, SI 2009/2648
Sch.3 para.1, repealed: SI 2009/1834 Sch.3
Sch.3 para.2, repealed: SI 2009/1834 Sch.3
Sch.3 para.3, repealed: SI 2009/1834 Sch.3
Sch.3 para.4, repealed: SI 2009/1834 Sch.3
Sch.3 para.5, repealed: SI 2009/1834 Sch.3
Sch.8 para.75, repealed: SI 2009/1941 Sch.2
Sch.8 para.208, repealed: SI 2009/1834 Sch.3

51. Legislative and Regulatory Reform Act 2006
Part 1, applied: SI 2009/1772
Part 1, referred to: SI 2009/1724
s.1, enabling: SI 2009/864, SI 2009/1375, SI 2009/1724, SI 2009/1772, SI 2009/1940
s.3, applied: SI 2009/864, SI 2009/1375, SI 2009/1940
s.3, referred to: SI 2009/1724, SI 2009/1772
s.13, applied: SI 2009/864, SI 2009/1375, SI 2009/1772, SI 2009/1940
s.13, referred to: SI 2009/1724
s.14, applied: SI 2009/864, SI 2009/1375, SI 2009/1772, SI 2009/1940
s.14, referred to: SI 2009/1724
s.15, applied: SI 2009/864, SI 2009/1375, SI 2009/1772, SI 2009/1940
s.15, referred to: SI 2009/1724
s.16, referred to: SI 2009/1375, SI 2009/1724
s.17, applied: SI 2009/864, SI 2009/1940
s.18, applied: SI 2009/1772
s.18, referred to: SI 2009/1772

2006– cont.

51. Legislative and Regulatory Reform Act 2006–*cont.*
s.21, applied: 2009 c.23 s.3
s.22, applied: 2009 c.23 s.3
s.24, applied: 2009 c.23 s.3, SI 2009/2981
s.24, disapplied: 2009 c.23 s.3
s.24, enabling: SI 2009/2981

52. Armed Forces Act 2006
Commencement Orders: SI 2009/812 Art.3; SI 2009/1167 Art.3, Art.4
applied: 2009 c.25 s.157, Sch.22 para.15, Sch.22 para.19, Sch.22 para.21, SI 2009/37 Sch.1 para.1, Sch.1 para.2, SI 2009/989 Art.1, Sch.1, SI 2009/1059 Art.4, Art.59, Art.60, Art.68, Art.152, Art.158, Art.174, Art.175, Art.181, Art.195, SI 2009/1091 Reg.13, SI 2009/1096 r.35, r.58, SI 2009/1209 Sch.2 para.4, SI 2009/1211 Sch.2 para.5, SI 2009/1749 Art.8, SI 2009/2041 Sch.2 para.5, Sch.2 para.21, SI 2009/2054 Sch.2 para.3, Sch.2 para.7, Sch.2 para.16, SI 2009/2056 Art.17
disapplied: SI 2009/832 Reg.9, Reg.10, Reg.11, Reg.12, SI 2009/1059 Art.115, SI 2009/1091 Reg.10, Reg.11, Reg.12
referred to: 2009 c.25 s.177, SI 2009/37 Sch.1 para.4, SI 2009/1059 Art.55, Art.80, Art.135, Sch.1 para.5, SI 2009/1091 Reg.9, SI 2009/2054 Sch.2 para.6
varied: SI 2009/826 Reg.3, SI 2009/1059 Sch.2 para.18
Part 1, applied: SI 2009/1109 Reg.3, Reg.12
Part 1, referred to: SI 2009/1059 Art.112, Art.117, Art.120, SI 2009/1109 Reg.12
Part 2, referred to: SI 2009/1059 Art.112, Art.117, Art.120
Part 2 c.3, applied: SI 2009/1059 Art.52
Part 2 c.3, referred to: SI 2009/1059 Art.44, Art.119
Part 3, applied: SI 2009/1059 Art.29, Art.33, SI 2009/2056 Art.14, Art.15, Art.16, Art.17, Art.23, Art.27, Art.28, Sch.4 para.10, Sch.4 para.11, Sch.4 para.19
Part 3, referred to: SI 2009/1059 Art.112, Art.117, Art.120
Part 3 c.1, applied: SI 2009/2056 Art.19, Art.31, Sch.4 para.12, Sch.4 para.23
Part 3 c.3, applied: SI 2009/2056 Art.19, Art.31, Sch.4 para.12, Sch.4 para.23
Part 4, applied: SI 2009/1059 Art.34, Art.168
Part 4, referred to: SI 2009/1059 Art.112, Art.117, Art.120
Part 5, applied: SI 2009/989 Sch.1, SI 2009/990 Art.1, SI 2009/1059 Art.44, Art.45, Art.46, Art.47, Art.48, Art.49, Art.51, Art.52, Art.53, Art.54, Art.119, SI 2009/1216 r.4, Sch.2 para.3, SI 2009/2041 r.156, Sch.2 para.27, SI 2009/2055 Reg.16
Part 5, referred to: 2009 c.25 Sch.22 para.15, SI 2009/1059 Art.42, Art.112, Art.117, Art.120
Part 6, referred to: SI 2009/1059 Art.112, Art.117, Art.120
Part 6 c.2, applied: SI 2009/1059 Art.64
Part 7, referred to: SI 2009/1059 Art.112, Art.117, Art.120
Part 8, referred to: SI 2009/1059 Art.112, Art.117, Art.120
Part 9, applied: SI 2009/2041 r.163
Part 9, referred to: SI 2009/1059 Art.7, Art.112, Art.117, Art.120
Part 10, referred to: SI 2009/1059 Art.112, Art.117, Art.120
Part 11, applied: SI 2009/2041 r.128

2006– cont.

52. Armed Forces Act 2006– *cont.*

Part 11, referred to: SI 2009/ 1059 Art.112, Art.117, Art.120

Part 12, applied: SI 2009/ 2041 r.128

Part 12, referred to: SI 2009/ 1059 Art.112, Art.117, Art.120

Part 13, applied: SI 2009/ 2041 r.128

Part 13, referred to: SI 2009/ 1059 Art.112, Art.117, Art.120

s.1, applied: 2009 c.25 s.159, SI 2009/ 1109 Reg.3, Reg.12

s.1, referred to: SI 2009/ 2056 Sch.3

s.1, varied: SI 2009/ 1059 Art.134

s.2, applied: 2009 c.25 s.159, SI 2009/ 826 Reg.4

s.2, referred to: SI 2009/ 2056 Sch.3

s.2, varied: SI 2009/ 826 Reg.4, SI 2009/ 1059 Art.134

s.3, applied: 2009 c.25 s.159

s.3, referred to: SI 2009/ 2056 Sch.3

s.3, varied: SI 2009/ 1059 Art.134

s.4, applied: 2009 c.25 s.159

s.4, referred to: SI 2009/ 2056 Sch.3

s.4, varied: SI 2009/ 1059 Art.134

s.5, applied: SI 2009/ 1109 Reg.3, Reg.12

s.5, varied: SI 2009/ 1059 Art.134

s.6, applied: 2009 c.25 s.159

s.6, referred to: SI 2009/ 2056 Sch.3

s.6, varied: SI 2009/ 1059 Art.134

s.7, applied: 2009 c.25 s.159

s.7, referred to: SI 2009/ 2056 Sch.3

s.7, varied: SI 2009/ 1059 Art.134

s.8, applied: SI 2009/ 833 Reg.3, Reg.4, Sch.1 para.2, SI 2009/ 1059 Art.42, Art.192, Art.199, Art.201, SI 2009/ 1090 Reg.3, Reg.4, Sch.1 para.2, SI 2009/ 1109 Reg.3, Reg.12

s.8, referred to: SI 2009/ 2056 Sch.3

s.8, varied: SI 2009/ 1059 Art.134

s.9, applied: SI 2009/ 1059 Art.199, Art.201, SI 2009/ 1109 Reg.3, Reg.12, SI 2009/ 1209 r.60

s.9, varied: SI 2009/ 1059 Art.134

s.10, applied: SI 2009/ 1209 r.61

s.10, varied: SI 2009/ 1059 Art.134

s.11, applied: SI 2009/ 826 Reg.4, SI 2009/ 1922 Sch.1

s.11, varied: SI 2009/ 826 Reg.4, SI 2009/ 1059 Art.134

s.12, applied: SI 2009/ 826 Reg.5

s.12, varied: SI 2009/ 826 Reg.5, SI 2009/ 1059 Art.134

s.13, varied: SI 2009/ 1059 Art.134

s.14, applied: SI 2009/ 1922 Sch.1

s.14, varied: SI 2009/ 1059 Art.134

s.15, applied: SI 2009/ 826 Reg.5

s.15, varied: SI 2009/ 1059 Art.134

s.16, varied: SI 2009/ 1059 Art.134

s.17, varied: SI 2009/ 1059 Art.134

s.18, varied: SI 2009/ 1059 Art.134

s.19, applied: SI 2009/ 826 Reg.5

s.19, varied: SI 2009/ 1059 Art.134

s.20, applied: SI 2009/ 826 Reg.4

s.20, varied: SI 2009/ 826 Reg.4, SI 2009/ 1059 Art.134

s.21, varied: SI 2009/ 1059 Art.134

s.22, applied: SI 2009/ 826 Reg.4

s.22, varied: SI 2009/ 826 Reg.4, SI 2009/ 1059 Art.134

s.23, varied: SI 2009/ 1059 Art.134

s.24, applied: SI 2009/ 1109 Reg.5, SI 2009/ 1922 Sch.1

2006– cont.

52. Armed Forces Act 2006– *cont.*

s.24, varied: SI 2009/ 1059 Art.134

s.25, varied: SI 2009/ 1059 Art.134

s.26, varied: SI 2009/ 1059 Art.134

s.27, applied: SI 2009/ 1922 Sch.1

s.27, varied: SI 2009/ 1059 Art.134

s.28, applied: SI 2009/ 1922 Sch.1

s.28, varied: SI 2009/ 1059 Art.134

s.29, applied: SI 2009/ 1922 Sch.1

s.29, varied: SI 2009/ 1059 Art.134

s.30, applied: SI 2009/ 1922 Sch.1

s.30, varied: SI 2009/ 1059 Art.134

s.31, referred to: SI 2009/ 2056 Sch.3

s.31, varied: SI 2009/ 1059 Art.134

s.32, varied: SI 2009/ 1059 Art.134

s.33, referred to: SI 2009/ 2056 Sch.3

s.33, varied: SI 2009/ 1059 Art.134

s.34, varied: SI 2009/ 1059 Art.134

s.35, varied: SI 2009/ 1059 Art.134

s.36, varied: SI 2009/ 1059 Art.134

s.37, varied: SI 2009/ 1059 Art.134

s.38, varied: SI 2009/ 1059 Art.134

s.39, applied: SI 2009/ 1922 Sch.1

s.39, referred to: SI 2009/ 2056 Sch.3

s.39, varied: SI 2009/ 1059 Art.134

s.40, applied: SI 2009/ 1922 Sch.1

s.40, referred to: SI 2009/ 2056 Sch.3

s.40, varied: SI 2009/ 1059 Art.134

s.41, varied: SI 2009/ 1059 Art.134

s.42, applied: SI 2009/ 37 Sch.1 para.1, Sch.1 para.2, SI 2009/ 991 Art.4, SI 2009/ 1059 Art.27, Art.28, Art.33, Art.40, Art.86, Art.87, Art.88, Art.133, Sch.1 para.32, Sch.1 para.34, SI 2009/ 2041 r.166, SI 2009/ 2054 Sch.2 para.18, SI 2009/ 2055 Reg.3, Reg.5, Reg.17, Sch.1 para.5

s.42, referred to: SI 2009/ 37 Sch.1 para.3, Sch.1 para.4, SI 2009/ 1059 Art.32

s.42, varied: SI 2009/ 1059 Art.134

s.43, varied: SI 2009/ 1059 Art.134

s.44, varied: SI 2009/ 1059 Art.134

s.45, varied: SI 2009/ 1059 Art.134

s.46, varied: SI 2009/ 1059 Art.134

s.47, varied: SI 2009/ 1059 Art.134

s.48, varied: SI 2009/ 1059 Art.134

s.49, applied: SI 2009/ 1094 Art.3

s.49, varied: SI 2009/ 1059 Art.134

s.49, enabling: SI 2009/ 1094

s.50, applied: 2009 c.25 Sch.22 para.21, SI 2009/ 1059 Art.168

s.50, referred to: 2009 c.25 Sch.22 para.15, Sch.22 para.21

s.50, varied: SI 2009/ 1059 Art.5, Art.134

s.51, applied: SI 2009/ 1059 Art.13, Art.168

s.51, varied: SI 2009/ 1059 Art.134

s.52, applied: SI 2009/ 1059 Art.15

s.52, referred to: SI 2009/ 1059 Art.47

s.52, varied: SI 2009/ 826 Reg.6, SI 2009/ 1059 Art.14, Art.134

s.53, applied: SI 2009/ 1059 Art.15, SI 2009/ 2041 r.157

s.53, varied: SI 2009/ 1059 Art.134

s.54, applied: SI 2009/ 1059 Art.16, Art.59, SI 2009/ 1216 r.3, r.5, Sch.2 para.4, SI 2009/ 2041 r.157

s.54, varied: SI 2009/ 1059 Art.134

s.55, varied: SI 2009/ 1059 Art.18, Art.134

s.56, varied: SI 2009/ 1059 Art.18, Art.134

s.57, referred to: SI 2009/ 1059 Art.19

2006– cont.

52. Armed Forces Act 2006– *cont.*

s.57, varied: SI 2009/ 1059 Art.18, Art.19, Art.20, Art.134

s.58, applied: SI 2009/ 1059 Art.20

s.58, varied: SI 2009/ 1059 Art.134

s.59, applied: SI 2009/ 1059 Art.21

s.59, varied: SI 2009/ 1059 Art.134

s.60, varied: SI 2009/ 1059 Art.134

s.61, applied: SI 2009/ 1059 Art.19

s.61, varied: SI 2009/ 1059 Art.134

s.62, applied: SI 2009/ 1059 Art.19

s.62, varied: SI 2009/ 1059 Art.22, Art.134

s.63, applied: SI 2009/ 1059 Art.168

s.63, referred to: SI 2009/ 1059 Art.27

s.63, varied: SI 2009/ 1059 Art.27, Art.134

s.64, applied: SI 2009/ 1059 Art.27

s.64, varied: SI 2009/ 1059 Art.27, Art.134

s.65, disapplied: SI 2009/ 1059 Art.27

s.65, varied: SI 2009/ 1059 Art.134

s.66, applied: SI 2009/ 1059 Art.28

s.66, varied: SI 2009/ 1059 Art.134

s.67, applied: SI 2009/ 826 Reg.4, SI 2009/ 1059 Art.30, Art.31, Art.168, SI 2009/ 1098 r.2, r.24, SI 2009/ 2056 Art.12, Art.13, Sch.4 para.8

s.67, varied: SI 2009/ 1059 Art.134

s.68, applied: SI 2009/ 1059 Art.168

s.68, varied: SI 2009/ 1059 Art.30, Art.134

s.69, applied: SI 2009/ 1059 Art.31, SI 2009/ 1097 Reg.10

s.69, varied: SI 2009/ 1059 Art.134

s.70, applied: SI 2009/ 1059 Art.31

s.70, referred to: SI 2009/ 1059 Art.31

s.70, varied: SI 2009/ 1059 Art.134

s.71, applied: SI 2009/ 1059 Art.31

s.71, disapplied: SI 2009/ 1059 Art.31

s.71, referred to: SI 2009/ 1059 Art.31

s.71, varied: SI 2009/ 1059 Art.134

s.72, varied: SI 2009/ 1059 Art.134

s.73, applied: SI 2009/ 2056 Art.17, Art.20, Art.29

s.73, referred to: SI 2009/ 1059 Art.31

s.73, varied: SI 2009/ 1059 Art.134

s.74, varied: SI 2009/ 1059 Art.134

s.74, enabling: SI 2009/ 2056

s.75, applied: SI 2009/ 2056 Art.3, Art.4, Sch.4 para.2, Sch.4 para.3

s.75, referred to: SI 2009/ 1059 Art.32

s.75, varied: SI 2009/ 1059 Art.134

s.76, applied: SI 2009/ 1059 Art.32, SI 2009/ 2056 Art.5, Art.23, Sch.4 para.4, Sch.4 para.15

s.76, referred to: SI 2009/ 1059 Art.32

s.76, varied: SI 2009/ 1059 Art.134

s.77, applied: SI 2009/ 1059 Art.32

s.77, referred to: SI 2009/ 1059 Art.32

s.77, varied: SI 2009/ 1059 Art.134

s.78, varied: SI 2009/ 1059 Art.134

s.79, varied: SI 2009/ 1059 Art.134

s.80, varied: SI 2009/ 1059 Art.134

s.81, varied: SI 2009/ 1059 Art.134

s.81, enabling: SI 2009/ 2056

s.82, varied: SI 2009/ 1059 Art.134

s.83, applied: SI 2009/ 1059 Art.33, SI 2009/ 2056 Art.7, Art.8, Art.15, Art.24, Art.29, Art.31, Sch.4 para.23

s.83, referred to: SI 2009/ 2056 Art.34

s.83, varied: SI 2009/ 1059 Art.134

s.84, applied: SI 2009/ 1059 Art.33, SI 2009/ 2056 Art.33, Sch.4 para.24

s.84, varied: SI 2009/ 1059 Art.134

2006– cont.

52. Armed Forces Act 2006– *cont.*

s.84, enabling: SI 2009/ 2056

s.85, varied: SI 2009/ 1059 Art.134

s.85, enabling: SI 2009/ 2056

s.86, varied: SI 2009/ 1059 Art.134

s.86, enabling: SI 2009/ 2056

s.87, applied: SI 2009/ 1059 Art.33, SI 2009/ 2056 Art.15, Art.19, Art.23, Art.34, Sch.4 para.12, Sch.4 para.15, Sch.4 para.25

s.87, disapplied: SI 2009/ 2056 Art.19, Art.28, Art.31, Sch.4 para.23

s.87, referred to: SI 2009/ 2056 Art.29, Art.34

s.87, varied: SI 2009/ 1059 Art.134

s.88, applied: SI 2009/ 1059 Art.33, SI 2009/ 2056 Art.15, Art.19, Art.23, Art.34, Sch.4 para.12, Sch.4 para.15

s.88, disapplied: SI 2009/ 2056 Art.19, Art.28, Art.31, Sch.4 para.23

s.88, referred to: SI 2009/ 2056 Art.29, Art.34

s.88, varied: SI 2009/ 1059 Art.134

s.89, applied: SI 2009/ 1059 Art.33, SI 2009/ 2056 Art.34, Sch.4 para.25

s.89, varied: SI 2009/ 1059 Art.134

s.89, enabling: SI 2009/ 2056

s.90, varied: SI 2009/ 1059 Art.134

s.91, applied: SI 2009/ 1059 Art.33

s.91, varied: SI 2009/ 1059 Art.134

s.92, applied: SI 2009/ 1059 Art.33, Art.168

s.92, varied: SI 2009/ 1059 Art.134

s.92, enabling: SI 2009/ 2056

s.93, applied: SI 2009/ 1059 Art.33

s.93, varied: SI 2009/ 1059 Art.134

s.93, enabling: SI 2009/ 2056

s.94, applied: SI 2009/ 1059 Art.33

s.94, varied: SI 2009/ 1059 Art.134

s.94, enabling: SI 2009/ 1923

s.95, varied: SI 2009/ 1059 Art.134

s.96, applied: SI 2009/ 2056 Art.12, Art.18, Art.34

s.96, varied: SI 2009/ 1059 Art.134

s.97, applied: SI 2009/ 1096 r.40

s.97, varied: SI 2009/ 1059 Art.134

s.98, applied: SI 2009/ 1059 Art.35, SI 2009/ 1097 Reg.3

s.98, referred to: SI 2009/ 1059 Art.36

s.98, varied: SI 2009/ 1059 Art.35, Art.39, Art.134

s.99, applied: SI 2009/ 1059 Art.36, Art.38, SI 2009/ 1096 r.58, SI 2009/ 1097 Reg.3, Reg.6

s.99, varied: SI 2009/ 1059 Art.39, Art.134

s.100, applied: SI 2009/ 1059 Art.36, Art.37, SI 2009/ 1097 Reg.3

s.100, varied: SI 2009/ 1059 Art.36, Art.39, Art.134

s.101, applied: SI 2009/ 1059 Art.38, SI 2009/ 1097 Reg.3, SI 2009/ 1098 r.24

s.101, varied: SI 2009/ 1059 Art.39, Art.134

s.102, applied: SI 2009/ 1059 Art.38, SI 2009/ 1097 Reg.3

s.102, varied: SI 2009/ 1059 Art.39, Art.134

s.103, varied: SI 2009/ 1059 Art.134

s.104, varied: SI 2009/ 1059 Art.134

s.104, enabling: SI 2009/ 1097

s.105, applied: SI 2009/ 1059 Art.40, SI 2009/ 1096 r.58, SI 2009/ 1098 r.27, r.29, r.30, r.31, r.32

s.105, varied: SI 2009/ 1059 Art.134

s.106, applied: SI 2009/ 1059 Art.40, SI 2009/ 1098 r.2

s.106, varied: SI 2009/ 1059 Art.134

2006–cont.

52. Armed Forces Act 2006–*cont.*

s.107, applied: SI 2009/1059 Art.21, Art.40, SI 2009/1098 r.2, r.25, r.27, r.29, r.31, SI 2009/1209 r.55, r.103, SI 2009/1211 r.56, SI 2009/2041 r.69, r.136, SI 2009/2044 Art.10

s.107, varied: SI 2009/1059 Art.134

s.108, applied: SI 2009/1059 Art.40, SI 2009/1098 r.2, r.27, r.30, r.31, r.35

s.108, varied: SI 2009/1059 Art.134

s.109, applied: SI 2009/1059 Art.40, SI 2009/1096 r.58, SI 2009/1098 r.2

s.109, varied: SI 2009/1059 Art.134

s.110, applied: SI 2009/1059 Art.31, Art.41, SI 2009/1098 r.2, r.26, r.31

s.110, varied: SI 2009/1059 Art.134

s.111, applied: SI 2009/1059 Art.31, Art.41, SI 2009/1098 r.2, r.26, r.31, SI 2009/1209 r.29, SI 2009/2041 r.42

s.111, varied: SI 2009/1059 Art.134, SI 2009/1209 r.28, r.29, SI 2009/2041 r.41, r.42

s.112, varied: SI 2009/1059 Art.134

s.112, enabling: SI 2009/1098

s.113, applied: SI 2009/1059 Art.43, Art.49

s.113, referred to: SI 2009/1059 Art.42

s.113, varied: SI 2009/1059 Art.134

s.114, applied: SI 2009/1059 Art.43, Art.49, SI 2009/2055 Reg.3

s.114, varied: SI 2009/1059 Art.134

s.114, enabling: SI 2009/2055

s.115, applied: SI 2009/1059 Art.43

s.115, varied: SI 2009/1059 Art.134

s.116, applied: SI 2009/1059 Art.49, Art.50, Art.168, SI 2009/2055 Reg.5, Reg.7, Reg.8, Reg.9

s.116, varied: SI 2009/1059 Art.134, Art.168

s.116, enabling: SI 2009/2055

s.117, varied: SI 2009/1059 Art.134

s.118, applied: SI 2009/1059 Art.168, SI 2009/2055 Reg.8

s.118, varied: SI 2009/1059 Art.134, Art.168

s.118, enabling: SI 2009/2055

s.119, applied: SI 2009/1059 Art.43, Art.50, Art.51, SI 2009/2055 Reg.10

s.119, varied: SI 2009/1059 Art.134

s.120, applied: SI 2009/988 Art.2, SI 2009/989 Sch.1, SI 2009/1098 r.25, SI 2009/2055 Reg.9, Reg.10, Reg.11, Reg.13, Sch.1 para.1

s.120, varied: SI 2009/1059 Art.134

s.121, applied: SI 2009/988 Art.2, SI 2009/989 Sch.1, SI 2009/1059 Art.51, SI 2009/2055 Reg.10, Reg.12, Reg.15

s.121, varied: SI 2009/1059 Art.134

s.122, applied: SI 2009/1098 r.25, SI 2009/2055 Reg.11, Reg.13, Sch.1 para.1

s.122, varied: SI 2009/1059 Art.134

s.123, applied: SI 2009/1216 r.3, r.26, SI 2009/2041 r.156, Sch.2 para.27, SI 2009/2055 Reg.13, Reg.15, Sch.1 para.1, Sch.1 para.3, Sch.1 para.4

s.123, varied: SI 2009/1059 Art.134

s.124, applied: SI 2009/1059 Art.48, Art.54

s.124, varied: SI 2009/1059 Art.134

s.125, applied: SI 2009/1059 Art.45, Art.48, Art.53, Art.61, SI 2009/1216 Sch.2 para.3, SI 2009/2041 r.60, r.156, r.157, Sch.2 para.28, SI 2009/2055 Reg.10, Reg.14, Reg.15, Sch.1 para.1, Sch.1 para.3, Sch.1 para.4

s.125, varied: SI 2009/1059 Art.134

s.125, enabling: SI 2009/2041

2006–cont.

52. Armed Forces Act 2006–*cont.*

s.126, applied: SI 2009/1059 Art.53, SI 2009/1209 r.47, SI 2009/2055 Reg.14, Reg.15, Sch.1 para.1, Sch.1 para.3, Sch.1 para.4

s.126, varied: SI 2009/1059 Art.134

s.127, applied: SI 2009/1059 Art.168, SI 2009/2041 r.61, SI 2009/2055 Reg.15

s.127, varied: SI 2009/1059 Art.134

s.128, applied: SI 2009/1209 r.37, r.40, r.47, SI 2009/2041 r.51, r.54, r.60

s.128, varied: SI 2009/1059 Art.134

s.128, enabling: SI 2009/2055

s.129, applied: SI 2009/1059 Art.54, SI 2009/1216 r.8, r.12, SI 2009/2041 r.156, r.157, r.160, r.164, Sch.2 para.26

s.129, disapplied: SI 2009/1216 r.12

s.129, varied: SI 2009/1059 Art.134

s.130, applied: SI 2009/1059 Art.61, SI 2009/2041 r.60

s.130, disapplied: SI 2009/1059 Art.61

s.130, varied: SI 2009/1059 Art.134

s.131, applied: SI 2009/1109 Reg.3, Reg.5, SI 2009/1216 r.22, r.23

s.131, varied: SI 2009/1059 Art.134

s.132, applied: SI 2009/1059 Art.68

s.132, varied: SI 2009/1059 Art.134

s.132, enabling: SI 2009/1215

s.133, applied: SI 2009/1059 Art.59, Art.60, Art.61, SI 2009/1211 r.15, r.86

s.133, varied: SI 2009/1059 Art.134

s.134, applied: SI 2009/1059 Art.59, Art.61, SI 2009/1211 r.15, r.86

s.134, varied: SI 2009/1059 Art.134

s.135, applied: SI 2009/1059 Art.59, Art.61, SI 2009/1211 r.15, r.86

s.135, varied: SI 2009/1059 Art.134

s.136, applied: SI 2009/1059 Art.59, Art.61, SI 2009/1211 r.15, r.86

s.136, varied: SI 2009/1059 Art.134

s.137, varied: SI 2009/1059 Art.134

s.138, applied: SI 2009/1059 Art.68

s.138, varied: SI 2009/1059 Art.134

s.138, enabling: SI 2009/1215

s.139, varied: SI 2009/1059 Art.134

s.140, varied: SI 2009/1059 Art.134

s.141, applied: SI 2009/988 Art.2, SI 2009/989 Sch.1, SI 2009/1059 Art.63, Art.64, SI 2009/1211 r.15, r.16, SI 2009/1216 r.8, r.22, r.23, r.31, r.34

s.141, varied: SI 2009/1059 Art.134

s.142, applied: SI 2009/1059 Art.64

s.142, varied: SI 2009/1059 Art.134

s.142, enabling: SI 2009/1211

s.143, varied: SI 2009/1059 Art.134

s.144, applied: SI 2009/1059 Art.65

s.144, varied: SI 2009/1059 Art.134

s.144, enabling: SI 2009/1211

s.145, disapplied: SI 2009/1211 r.90

s.145, varied: SI 2009/1059 Art.134

s.145, enabling: SI 2009/1211

s.146, applied: SI 2009/1059 Art.66, Art.67, Art.68

s.146, varied: SI 2009/1059 Art.134

s.147, applied: SI 2009/1059 Art.68, Art.98, SI 2009/1211 r.20, r.75, r.83

s.147, varied: SI 2009/1059 Art.66, Art.67, Art.68, Art.98, Art.134

s.147, enabling: SI 2009/1211

s.148, varied: SI 2009/1059 Art.134

s.149, applied: SI 2009/991 Art.3, SI 2009/1211 r.92, r.93

2006–cont.

52. Armed Forces Act 2006–*cont.*
s.149, varied: SI 2009/1059 Art.134
s.150, varied: SI 2009/1059 Art.134
s.151, applied: SI 2009/991 Art.3
s.151, varied: SI 2009/1059 Art.134
s.151, enabling: SI 2009/1211
s.152, applied: SI 2009/1059 Art.70, Art.71, Art.72, Art.73, SI 2009/1211 r.17, r.18
s.152, varied: SI 2009/1059 Art.72, Art.73, Art.134
s.153, applied: SI 2009/1059 Art.97
s.153, varied: SI 2009/1059 Art.134
s.153, enabling: SI 2009/1216
s.154, referred to: 2009 c.25 Sch.22 para.18
s.154, varied: SI 2009/1059 Art.134, SI 2009/2041 r.128
s.155, applied: SI 2009/1059 Art.74, SI 2009/2041 r.31
s.155, disapplied: SI 2009/2041 r.33
s.155, varied: SI 2009/1059 Art.134, SI 2009/2041 r.128
s.155, enabling: SI 2009/2041
s.156, applied: SI 2009/2041 r.31, r.33, r.160
s.156, varied: SI 2009/1059 Art.134, SI 2009/2041 r.128
s.157, applied: SI 2009/1059 Art.75, SI 2009/2041 r.31, r.33
s.157, varied: SI 2009/1059 Art.134, SI 2009/2041 r.128
s.157, enabling: SI 2009/2041
s.158, disapplied: SI 2009/2041 r.152
s.158, varied: SI 2009/1059 Art.134, SI 2009/2041 r.128
s.158, enabling: SI 2009/2041
s.159, varied: SI 2009/1059 Art.134, SI 2009/2041 r.128
s.160, varied: SI 2009/1059 Art.134, SI 2009/2041 r.128
s.161, referred to: SI 2009/1059 Art.27, Art.77
s.161, varied: SI 2009/1059 Art.134, SI 2009/2041 r.128
s.162, varied: SI 2009/1059 Art.134, SI 2009/2041 r.128
s.163, applied: SI 2009/991 Art.3, SI 2009/1059 Art.79, SI 2009/1169 Reg.3, SI 2009/2657
s.163, referred to: SI 2009/1059 Art.79
s.163, varied: SI 2009/1059 Art.134, SI 2009/2041 r.128
s.163, enabling: SI 2009/2041, SI 2009/2100
s.164, applied: SI 2009/992 Art.10, SI 2009/1059 Art.6, SI 2009/1215 Reg.8
s.164, referred to: SI 2009/991 Art.10, Art.14, SI 2009/992 Art.14, SI 2009/1059 Art.6, Art.8, SI 2009/2057 Reg.12
s.164, varied: SI 2009/1059 Art.134, SI 2009/2041 r.128
s.164, enabling: SI 2009/1215
s.165, applied: SI 2009/1059 Art.78, Art.94, SI 2009/2041 r.158, r.160, r.161, Sch.2 para.31, Sch.2 para.32
s.165, disapplied: SI 2009/2041 r.158, r.159, Sch.2 para.29, Sch.2 para.30
s.165, varied: SI 2009/1059 Art.78, Art.134, SI 2009/2041 r.128
s.165, enabling: SI 2009/2041
s.166, applied: SI 2009/2041 r.49
s.166, varied: SI 2009/1059 Art.134, SI 2009/2041 r.128
s.167, applied: SI 2009/1059 Art.82

2006–cont.

52. Armed Forces Act 2006–*cont.*
s.167, varied: SI 2009/1059 Art.134, SI 2009/2041 r.128
s.168, varied: SI 2009/1059 Art.134, SI 2009/2041 r.128
s.169, applied: SI 2009/1059 Art.80, Art.81, Art.83, SI 2009/1213 Reg.18, SI 2009/1922 Art.13, Sch.2 para.15, SI 2009/2054 Sch.2 para.17
s.169, varied: SI 2009/1059 Art.134, SI 2009/2041 r.128
s.170, referred to: SI 2009/1059 Art.122
s.170, varied: SI 2009/1059 Art.134, SI 2009/2041 r.128
s.170, enabling: SI 2009/1213
s.171, applied: SI 2009/1059 Art.81, SI 2009/1098 r.2, r.31
s.171, varied: SI 2009/1059 Art.134, SI 2009/2041 r.128
s.172, varied: SI 2009/1059 Art.134, SI 2009/2041 r.128
s.173, varied: SI 2009/1059 Art.134, SI 2009/2041 r.128
s.173, enabling: SI 2009/1214
s.174, varied: SI 2009/1059 Art.134, SI 2009/2041 r.128
s.174, enabling: SI 2009/1214
s.175, varied: SI 2009/1059 Art.134, SI 2009/2041 r.128
s.176, referred to: SI 2009/1059 Art.155
s.176, varied: SI 2009/1059 Art.134, SI 2009/2041 r.128
s.177, applied: SI 2009/2041 r.145, Sch.2 para.22
s.177, referred to: SI 2009/1059 Art.156
s.177, varied: SI 2009/1059 Art.134, SI 2009/2041 r.128
s.178, varied: SI 2009/1059 Art.134, SI 2009/2041 r.128
s.179, amended: SI 2009/1059 Sch.2 para.3
s.179, varied: SI 2009/1059 Art.134, Sch.2 para.14, SI 2009/2041 r.128
s.180, varied: SI 2009/1059 Art.134, SI 2009/2041 r.128
s.181, varied: SI 2009/1059 Art.134, SI 2009/2041 r.128
s.182, varied: SI 2009/1059 Art.134, SI 2009/2041 r.128
s.183, varied: SI 2009/1059 Art.134, SI 2009/2041 r.128
s.184, varied: SI 2009/1059 Art.134, SI 2009/2041 r.128
s.185, varied: SI 2009/1059 Art.134, SI 2009/2041 r.128
s.186, applied: SI 2009/1209 r.31, r.96, Sch.2 para.14, SI 2009/2041 r.44, Sch.2 para.16
s.186, varied: SI 2009/1059 Art.134, SI 2009/2041 r.128
s.187, disapplied: 2009 c.25 s.158
s.187, varied: SI 2009/1059 Art.134, SI 2009/2041 r.128
s.188, applied: SI 2009/1059 Art.85
s.188, varied: SI 2009/1059 Art.134, Sch.2 para.11, SI 2009/2041 r.128
s.189, applied: SI 2009/1059 Art.85
s.189, varied: SI 2009/1059 Art.134, SI 2009/2041 r.128
s.190, varied: SI 2009/1059 Art.134, SI 2009/2041 r.128
s.191, applied: SI 2009/1059 Art.93, Art.95, Art.96, Art.109, Art.117, Art.137, SI 2009/1216 r.7, r.8, r.23, r.30, r.31, r.34, SI 2009/2041 r.164, Sch.2 para.33
s.191, referred to: SI 2009/1059 Art.101, SI 2009/2041 r.132

52. Armed Forces Act 2006–*cont.*
s.191, varied: SI 2009/1059 Art.134, SI 2009/2041 r.128
s.192, applied: SI 2009/1059 Art.109
s.192, varied: SI 2009/1059 Art.134, SI 2009/2041 r.128
s.193, applied: SI 2009/1059 Art.93, Art.97, Art.98, Art.99, Art.137, Art.144, SI 2009/1211 r.86, SI 2009/1216 r.7, r.8, r.23, r.30, r.31, r.34, Sch.2 para.7
s.193, referred to: SI 2009/1059 Art.101
s.193, varied: SI 2009/1059 Art.134, SI 2009/2041 r.128
s.194, applied: SI 2009/1059 Art.97, SI 2009/1216 r.7, r.30, SI 2009/2041 r.164
s.194, varied: SI 2009/1059 Art.134, SI 2009/2041 r.128
s.195, applied: SI 2009/1216 r.8
s.195, referred to: SI 2009/1059 Art.70
s.195, varied: SI 2009/1059 Art.98, Art.134, SI 2009/2041 r.128
s.196, varied: SI 2009/1059 Art.134, SI 2009/2041 r.128
s.197, varied: SI 2009/1059 Art.134, SI 2009/2041 r.128
s.198, varied: SI 2009/1059 Art.134, SI 2009/2041 r.128
s.199, varied: SI 2009/1059 Art.134, SI 2009/2041 r.128
s.200, varied: SI 2009/1059 Art.134, SI 2009/2041 r.128
s.201, varied: SI 2009/1059 Art.134, SI 2009/2041 r.128
s.202, varied: SI 2009/1059 Art.134, SI 2009/2041 r.128
s.203, amended: SI 2009/1059 Sch.2 para.3
s.203, applied: SI 2009/1059 Art.90
s.203, varied: SI 2009/1059 Art.134, Sch.2 para.14, SI 2009/2041 r.128
s.204, varied: SI 2009/1059 Art.134, SI 2009/2041 r.128
s.205, amended: SI 2009/1059 Sch.2 para.3
s.205, varied: SI 2009/1059 Art.134, Sch.2 para.14, SI 2009/2041 r.128
s.206, varied: SI 2009/1059 Art.134, SI 2009/2041 r.128
s.207, varied: SI 2009/1059 Art.134, SI 2009/2041 r.128
s.208, amended: SI 2009/1059 Sch.2 para.5
s.208, varied: SI 2009/1059 Art.134, SI 2009/2041 r.128
s.209, amended: SI 2009/1059 Sch.2 para.5
s.209, applied: SI 2009/1059 Art.86, SI 2009/2041 r.29
s.209, varied: SI 2009/1059 Art.134, SI 2009/2041 r.128
s.210, varied: SI 2009/1059 Art.134, SI 2009/2041 r.128
s.211, amended: SI 2009/1059 Sch.2 para.5
s.211, applied: SI 2009/1216 r.3
s.211, varied: SI 2009/1059 Art.134, SI 2009/2041 r.128
s.212, amended: SI 2009/1059 Sch.2 para.5
s.212, varied: SI 2009/1059 Art.87, Art.134, SI 2009/2041 r.128
s.213, applied: SI 2009/1059 Art.87
s.213, varied: SI 2009/1059 Art.134, SI 2009/2041 r.128
s.214, referred to: SI 2009/2041 r.133
s.214, varied: SI 2009/1059 Art.134, SI 2009/2041 r.128
s.215, varied: SI 2009/1059 Art.134, SI 2009/2041 r.128
s.216, varied: SI 2009/1059 Art.134, SI 2009/2041 r.128
s.217, applied: SI 2009/1059 Art.88, Sch.2 para.6
s.217, varied: SI 2009/1059 Art.134, SI 2009/2041 r.128
s.218, applied: SI 2009/1059 Art.88
s.218, referred to: SI 2009/1059 Sch.2 para.6
s.218, varied: SI 2009/1059 Art.134, SI 2009/2041 r.128
s.219, applied: SI 2009/2657 r.48
s.219, varied: SI 2009/1059 Art.134, SI 2009/2041 r.128
s.220, referred to: SI 2009/2657 r.48
s.220, varied: SI 2009/1059 Art.134, SI 2009/2041 r.128
s.221, varied: SI 2009/1059 Art.134, SI 2009/2041 r.128
s.222, amended: SI 2009/1059 Sch.2 para.5
s.222, varied: SI 2009/1059 Art.134, SI 2009/2041 r.128
s.223, varied: SI 2009/1059 Art.134, SI 2009/2041 r.128
s.224, varied: SI 2009/1059 Art.134, SI 2009/2041 r.128
s.225, varied: SI 2009/1059 Art.134, SI 2009/2041 r.128
s.226, varied: SI 2009/1059 Art.134, SI 2009/2041 r.128
s.227, varied: SI 2009/1059 Art.134, SI 2009/2041 r.128

52. Armed Forces Act 2006–*cont.*
s.228, applied: SI 2009/1059 Art.110
s.228, varied: SI 2009/1059 Art.134, SI 2009/2041 r.128
s.229, applied: SI 2009/2041 r.148
s.229, varied: SI 2009/1059 Art.134, SI 2009/2041 r.128
s.230, applied: SI 2009/2041 r.148
s.230, varied: SI 2009/1059 Art.134, SI 2009/2041 r.128
s.231, varied: SI 2009/1059 Art.134, SI 2009/2041 r.128
s.232, applied: SI 2009/2041 r.149
s.232, varied: SI 2009/1059 Art.134, SI 2009/2041 r.128
s.233, applied: SI 2009/1059 Art.91, SI 2009/1209 r.96
s.233, varied: SI 2009/1059 Art.134, SI 2009/2041 r.128
s.234, varied: SI 2009/1059 Art.134, SI 2009/2041 r.128
s.235, applied: SI 2009/1059 Art.91, SI 2009/2041 r.150, Sch.2 para.24
s.235, varied: SI 2009/1059 Art.134, SI 2009/2041 r.128
s.236, applied: SI 2009/1059 Art.91, SI 2009/1212 Reg.2
s.236, varied: SI 2009/1059 Art.134, SI 2009/2041 r.128
s.237, disapplied: SI 2009/1059 Art.89
s.237, varied: SI 2009/1059 Art.134
s.238, amended: 2009 c.25 Sch.17 para.7, Sch.23 Part 5
s.238, varied: SI 2009/1059 Art.134
s.239, varied: SI 2009/1059 Art.134
s.240, varied: SI 2009/1059 Art.103, Art.134
s.241, varied: SI 2009/1059 Art.134
s.242, varied: SI 2009/1059 Art.134, SI 2009/2041 r.161
s.243, varied: SI 2009/1059 Art.134, SI 2009/2041 r.161
s.244, applied: SI 2009/1059 Art.95, Art.96, Art.97, Art.99, Art.105
s.244, varied: SI 2009/1059 Art.104, Art.134
s.245, applied: SI 2009/1059 Art.105
s.245, varied: SI 2009/1059 Art.105, Art.134
s.246, applied: SI 2009/1109 Reg.3
s.246, varied: SI 2009/1059 Art.106, Art.134, Sch.2 para.13
s.247, applied: SI 2009/1059 Art.106
s.247, varied: SI 2009/1059 Art.106, Art.134
s.248, varied: SI 2009/1059 Art.134, SI 2009/2041 r.161
s.249, applied: SI 2009/2041 r.147
s.249, varied: SI 2009/1059 Art.134
s.250, varied: SI 2009/1059 Art.134
.s.251, applied: SI 2009/2041 r.146, r.147, Sch.2 para.23
s.251, referred to: SI 2009/1059 Art.157
s.251, varied: SI 2009/1059 Art.134
s.252, applied: SI 2009/1211 r.88, SI 2009/1216 r.22, r.27, SI 2009/2041 r.117, r.123
s.252, disapplied: SI 2009/1059 Art.89
s.252, varied: SI 2009/1059 Art.134
s.253, applied: SI 2009/2041 r.123
s.253, varied: SI 2009/1059 Art.134
s.254, varied: SI 2009/1059 Art.134
s.255, applied: SI 2009/2041 r.161
s.255, varied: SI 2009/1059 Art.134
s.256, varied: SI 2009/1059 Art.134
s.257, varied: SI 2009/1059 Art.134
s.258, varied: SI 2009/1059 Art.134
s.259, amended: 2009 c.25 Sch.21 para.89
s.259, varied: SI 2009/1059 Art.134
s.260, applied: SI 2009/1059 Sch.2 para.7, Sch.2 para.9
s.260, disapplied: SI 2009/1059 Art.89
s.260, varied: SI 2009/1059 Art.134
s.261, applied: SI 2009/1059 Sch.2 para.7
s.261, disapplied: SI 2009/1059 Art.89
s.261, varied: SI 2009/1059 Art.134
s.262, varied: SI 2009/1059 Art.134

2006– cont.

52. Armed Forces Act 2006– *cont.*
s.263, amended: 2009 c.25 Sch.17 para.11
s.263, varied: SI 2009/1059 Art.134, Sch.2 para.12
s.264, varied: SI 2009/1059 Art.134
s.265, varied: SI 2009/1059 Art.134
s.266, varied: SI 2009/1059 Art.134
s.267, applied: SI 2009/2041 r.147
s.267, varied: SI 2009/1059 Art.134
s.268, applied: SI 2009/1059 Art.134
s.268, varied: SI 2009/1059 Art.134
s.269, varied: SI 2009/1059 Art.134
s.270, varied: SI 2009/1059 Art.134
s.270A, varied: SI 2009/1059 Art.134
s.270B, amended: 2009 c.25 Sch.17 para.9, Sch.23 Part 5
s.270B, varied: SI 2009/1059 Art.134
s.271, varied: SI 2009/1059 Art.134
s.271, enabling: SI 2009/2042
s.272, varied: SI 2009/1059 Art.134
s.273, applied: SI 2009/1059 Art.129, SI 2009/1168 Art.3, SI 2009/1169 Reg.5, Reg.6, Reg.7, Reg.8, SI 2009/2041 r.166, SI 2009/2657 r.54
s.273, disapplied: SI 2009/1059 Art.129
s.273, varied: SI 2009/1059 Art.129, Art.134
s.273, enabling: SI 2009/1168
s.274, applied: SI 2009/1169 Reg.6, Reg.8, SI 2009/2657 r.63, r.64
s.274, referred to: SI 2009/1059 Art.129
s.274, varied: SI 2009/1059 Art.129, Art.134
s.275, varied: SI 2009/1059 Art.134
s.275, enabling: SI 2009/1169
s.276, applied: SI 2009/1059 Art.130
s.276, disapplied: SI 2009/1059 Art.130
s.276, varied: SI 2009/1059 Art.130, Art.134
s.276A, disapplied: SI 2009/1059 Art.130
s.276A, varied: SI 2009/1059 Art.134
s.276B, disapplied: SI 2009/1059 Art.130
s.276B, varied: SI 2009/1059 Art.134
s.277, varied: SI 2009/1059 Art.134
s.278, applied: SI 2009/1059 Art.131
s.278, varied: SI 2009/1059 Art.134
s.279, applied: SI 2009/1059 Art.13, SI 2009/1209 r.22, r.34, r.42
s.279, disapplied: SI 2009/1059 Art.132
s.279, varied: SI 2009/1059 Art.134
s.280, referred to: SI 2009/1209 r.42
s.280, varied: SI 2009/1059 Art.134
s.280, enabling: SI 2009/1209
s.281, varied: SI 2009/1059 Art.134
s.282, varied: SI 2009/1059 Art.134
s.283, amended: SI 2009/1059 Sch.2 para.2
s.283, varied: SI 2009/1059 Art.134, Sch.2 para.9
s.284, referred to: SI 2009/1059 Art.133
s.284, varied: SI 2009/1059 Art.134
s.285, applied: SI 2009/1059 Art.134, Art.165, SI 2009/2041 r.125, r.126, r.127
s.285, disapplied: SI 2009/1059 Art.134
s.285, referred to: SI 2009/1059 Art.134
s.285, varied: SI 2009/1059 Art.134, Art.173
s.286, applied: SI 2009/1059 Art.134, SI 2009/2041 r.127
s.286, varied: SI 2009/1059 Art.134
s.286, enabling: SI 2009/2041
s.287, varied: SI 2009/1059 Art.134
s.288, varied: SI 2009/1059 Art.134
s.288, enabling: SI 2009/1209, SI 2009/2100
s.289, varied: SI 2009/1059 Art.134

2006– cont.

52. Armed Forces Act 2006– *cont.*
s.290, applied: SI 2009/1059 Art.137, Art.139, Art.142, SI 2009/1216 r.22, r.23, r.34
s.290, referred to: SI 2009/1059 Art.144
s.290, varied: SI 2009/1059 Art.134, Art.138, Art.139, Art.144
s.291, applied: SI 2009/1059 Art.137, Art.142, SI 2009/1216 r.22, r.23, r.34
s.291, referred to: SI 2009/1059 Art.144
s.291, varied: SI 2009/1059 Art.134, Art.140, Art.144
s.292, applied: SI 2009/1059 Art.137, Art.143
s.292, disapplied: SI 2009/1059 Art.143
s.292, referred to: SI 2009/1059 Art.144, SI 2009/1216 r.23, r.34
s.292, varied: SI 2009/1059 Art.134
s.293, applied: SI 2009/832 Reg.7, SI 2009/1091 Reg.7
s.293, varied: SI 2009/1059 Art.134
s.294, applied: SI 2009/1059 Art.145
s.294, varied: SI 2009/1059 Art.134
s.295, varied: SI 2009/826 Reg.3, SI 2009/1059 Art.134
s.296, referred to: SI 2009/1059 Art.146
s.296, varied: SI 2009/1059 Art.134
s.297, referred to: SI 2009/1059 Art.147
s.297, varied: SI 2009/1059 Art.134
s.298, disapplied: SI 2009/1059 Art.148
s.298, referred to: SI 2009/1059 Art.148
s.298, varied: SI 2009/1059 Art.134
s.299, referred to: SI 2009/1059 Art.149
s.299, varied: SI 2009/1059 Art.134
s.300, applied: SI 2009/1059 Art.149, Art.151
s.300, referred to: SI 2009/1059 Art.150
s.300, varied: SI 2009/1059 Art.134
s.300, enabling: SI 2009/1096
s.301, applied: SI 2009/1059 Art.151, SI 2009/1096 r.38
s.301, referred to: SI 2009/1059 Art.35
s.301, varied: SI 2009/1059 Art.134
s.302, referred to: SI 2009/1059 Art.152
s.302, varied: SI 2009/1059 Art.134
s.303, applied: SI 2009/1059 Art.31, Art.153
s.303, varied: SI 2009/1059 Art.134
s.304, referred to: SI 2009/1059 Art.154
s.304, varied: SI 2009/1059 Art.134, Sch.2 para.15
s.305, amended: SI 2009/1059 Sch.2 para.4
s.305, applied: SI 2009/1059 Art.177
s.305, varied: SI 2009/1059 Art.134
s.306, amended: SI 2009/1059 Sch.2 para.4
s.306, applied: SI 2009/1059 Art.177, SI 2009/1922 Art.12, Sch.2 para.14
s.306, varied: SI 2009/1059 Art.134
s.307, varied: SI 2009/1059 Art.134
s.308, referred to: SI 2009/1059 Art.177
s.308, varied: SI 2009/1059 Art.134
s.309, applied: SI 2009/988 Art.20, SI 2009/1059 Art.178, Art.179
s.309, varied: SI 2009/1059 Art.134
s.310, varied: SI 2009/1059 Art.134
s.311, applied: SI 2009/1059 Art.178, Art.179, SI 2009/1211 r.89, SI 2009/2041 r.151
s.311, varied: SI 2009/1059 Art.134
s.312, applied: SI 2009/1059 Art.178
s.312, varied: SI 2009/1059 Art.134
s.313, applied: SI 2009/1108 Reg.4, SI 2009/1110 r.8, r.11, r.23
s.313, varied: SI 2009/1059 Art.134, Art.180
s.313, enabling: SI 2009/1110

2006–cont.

52. Armed Forces Act 2006–*cont.*
s.314, applied: SI 2009/1059 Art.181
s.314, varied: SI 2009/1059 Art.134
s.315, applied: SI 2009/1059 Art.181, SI 2009/1108 Reg.4, Reg.5
s.315, varied: SI 2009/1059 Art.134
s.316, applied: SI 2009/1059 Art.181, Art.182, SI 2009/1108 Reg.3, Reg.4, Reg.5
s.316, varied: SI 2009/1059 Art.134
s.316, enabling: SI 2009/1108
s.317, applied: SI 2009/1059 Art.182, SI 2009/1110 r.8, r.11, r.23
s.317, varied: SI 2009/1059 Art.134
s.317, enabling: SI 2009/1110
s.318, applied: SI 2009/1059 Art.183
s.318, varied: SI 2009/1059 Art.134, Art.183
s.319, applied: SI 2009/1110 r.8
s.319, varied: SI 2009/1059 Art.134
s.319, enabling: SI 2009/1108
s.320, varied: SI 2009/1059 Art.134
s.321, varied: SI 2009/1059 Art.134
s.322, applied: SI 2009/2054 Sch.2 para.4
s.322, varied: SI 2009/1059 Art.134
s.322, enabling: SI 2009/1212
s.323, varied: SI 2009/1059 Art.134
s.323, enabling: SI 2009/2044, SI 2009/2056
s.324, varied: SI 2009/1059 Art.134
s.325, applied: SI 2009/1059 Art.186
s.325, varied: SI 2009/1059 Art.134
s.326, varied: SI 2009/1059 Art.134
s.327, varied: SI 2009/1059 Art.134
s.328, applied: SI 2009/831 Sch.1 para.7, Sch.1 para.8, Sch.1 para.10, SI 2009/1089 Sch.1 para.7, Sch.1 para.8, Sch.1 para.10, SI 2009/1112 Reg.4, SI 2009/1209 r.68, Sch.2 para.10, SI 2009/1211 r.69, Sch.2 para.11, SI 2009/2041 r.83, Sch.2 para.11
s.328, referred to: SI 2009/1059 Art.190
s.328, varied: SI 2009/1059 Art.190
s.328, enabling: SI 2009/831, SI 2009/832, SI 2009/833, SI 2009/1089, SI 2009/1090, SI 2009/1091, SI 2009/2057
s.329, applied: SI 2009/833 Reg.4, SI 2009/1090 Reg.4
s.329, referred to: SI 2009/1059 Art.191
s.329, enabling: SI 2009/831, SI 2009/1089
s.330, referred to: SI 2009/1059 Art.192
s.330, enabling: SI 2009/833, SI 2009/1090
s.331, applied: SI 2009/833 Reg.4, SI 2009/1090 Reg.4
s.331, referred to: SI 2009/1059 Art.193
s.331, enabling: SI 2009/832, SI 2009/1091
s.334, applied: SI 2009/1096 r.34
s.340, disapplied: SI 2009/835 Reg.2
s.340, enabling: SI 2009/835
s.341, applied: SI 2009/1212 Reg.5
s.342, applied: SI 2009/1059 Art.197, SI 2009/1212 Reg.5
s.342, referred to: SI 2009/1059 Art.198
s.342, enabling: SI 2009/1109
s.344, referred to: SI 2009/1059 Art.199
s.355, referred to: SI 2009/1059 Art.204
s.355, enabling: SI 2009/1093
s.362, referred to: SI 2009/1059 Art.188
s.367, applied: 2009 c.25 s.12
s.370, enabling: SI 2009/836
s.371, enabling: SI 2009/826
s.372, referred to: SI 2009/1059 Art.200

2006–cont.

52. Armed Forces Act 2006–*cont.*
s.372, enabling: SI 2009/1112
s.373, applied: SI 2009/2041, SI 2009/2042, SI 2009/2044, SI 2009/2054, SI 2009/2055, SI 2009/2056, SI 2009/2057
s.374, disapplied: SI 2009/826 Reg.4
s.374, varied: SI 2009/1059 Sch.2 para.16
s.379, enabling: SI 2009/2054
s.380, enabling: SI 2009/1059, SI 2009/2056
s.382, enabling: SI 2009/1752
s.383, enabling: SI 2009/812, SI 2009/1167
s.384, referred to: 2009 c.25 s.181
s.384, enabling: SI 2009/3215
Sch.2, applied: SI 2009/2041 r.29
Sch.2 para.12, amended: 2009 c.25 Sch.21 para.64
Sch.2 para.12, applied: SI 2009/1059 Art.42
Sch.3, applied: SI 2009/1209 r.31, SI 2009/2041 r.44
Sch.3 Part 1, applied: SI 2009/1059 Art.8, SI 2009/2041 r.27
Sch.3 Part 1 para.1, applied: SI 2009/1059 Art.8
Sch.3 Part 1 para.1, referred to: SI 2009/1059 Art.117
Sch.3 Part 1 para.1, varied: SI 2009/1059 Art.8, Art.134
Sch.3 Part 2, applied: SI 2009/2041 r.27
Sch.4, applied: SI 2009/1059 Art.80
Sch.5 Part 1 para.8, amended: SI 2009/1059 Sch.2 para.3, Sch.2 para.14
Sch.5 Part 1 para.8, repealed (in part): SI 2009/1059 Sch.2 para.14
Sch.5 Part 1 para.8, varied: SI 2009/1059 Sch.2 para.14
Sch.7 Part 2 para.8, applied: SI 2009/2041 r.131
Sch.8 para.53, referred to: 2009 c.25 Sch.22 para.22
Sch.10 para.1, enabling: SI 2009/1209
Sch.14 para.25, referred to: SI 2009/1059 Art.194
Sch.15, applied: SI 2009/1059 Art.19
Sch.15 Part 1 para.4, applied: SI 2009/836 Art.4, Sch.3 para.1
Sch.15 Part 1 para.5, applied: SI 2009/836 Art.2
Sch.15 Part 1 para.5, enabling: SI 2009/836
Sch.15 Part 1 para.6, applied: SI 2009/836 Art.3, Art.4, Sch.3 para.1
Sch.15 Part 1 para.6, enabling: SI 2009/836
Sch.15 Part 1 para.7, applied: 2009 c.25 s.12, SI 2009/1059 Art.19
Sch.15 Part 1 para.8, applied: SI 2009/836 Art.4, Sch.3 para.2
Sch.15 Part 1 para.9, applied: SI 2009/836 Art.4, Sch.3 para.1
Sch.15 Part 2 para.12, enabling: SI 2009/836
Sch.16 para.110, repealed: 2009 c.25 Sch.23 Part 1
Sch.16 para.111, repealed: 2009 c.25 Sch.23 Part 1

2007

1. Appropriation Act 2007
repealed: 2009 c.9 Sch.3
3. Income Tax Act 2007
referred to: 2009 c.4 s.969
Part 6 c.3, applied: SI 2009/3001 Reg.25
Part 7, applied: SI 2009/3001 Reg.25
Part 8, applied: SI 2009/3001 Reg.25
Part 8 c.2, applied: 2009 c.10 Sch.35 para.2
Part 13 c.2, applied: SI 2009/3001 Reg.24
Part 13 c.2, applied: SI 2009/3001 Reg.21
Part 14 c.A1, applied: SI 2009/3001 Reg.19
Part 15, applied: 2009 c.4 s.551
Part 15 c.15, applied: 2009 c.10 Sch.53 para.13
Part 15 c.8, referred to: 2009 c.4 s.976

2007– cont.

3. Income Tax Act 2007– *cont.*
s.2, amended: 2009 c.10 s.52, Sch.25 para.9
s.5, substituted: 2009 c.4 Sch.1 para.700
s.6, amended: 2009 c.10 s.6, Sch.2 para.2
s.8, amended: 2009 c.10 Sch.2 para.3
s.9, amended: 2009 c.10 s.6
s.10, amended: 2009 c.10 s.2, Sch.2 para.4
s.13, amended: 2009 c.10 Sch.2 para.5
s.21, disapplied: 2009 c.10 s.2
s.23, amended: 2009 c.10 Sch.1 para.6
s.23, applied: SI 2009/470 Reg.29
s.23, referred to: 2009 c.10 Sch.35 para.1
s.24, applied: 2009 c.10 Sch.35 para.2
s.26, amended: 2009 c.10 Sch.1 para.6
s.27, amended: 2009 c.10 Sch.1 para.6
s.29, amended: SI 2009/2859 Art.4
s.30, referred to: 2009 c.10 Sch.35 para.1
s.35, amended: 2009 c.10 s.3
s.35, referred to: 2009 c.10 s.3
s.35, substituted: 2009 c.10 s.4
s.36, amended: 2009 c.10 s.4
s.37, amended: 2009 c.10 s.4
s.57, amended: 2009 c.10 s.4
s.57, disapplied: 2009 c.10 s.3
s.61, varied: 2009 c.10 Sch.6 para.2
s.62, varied: 2009 c.10 Sch.6 para.2
s.63, varied: 2009 c.10 Sch.6 para.2
s.64, applied: 2009 c.10 Sch.6 para.1, SI 2009/470
Reg.29
s.64, referred to: 2009 c.10 Sch.6 para.2
s.66, applied: 2009 c.10 Sch.6 para.1
s.67, applied: 2009 c.10 Sch.6 para.1
s.68, applied: 2009 c.10 Sch.6 para.1
s.69, applied: 2009 c.10 Sch.6 para.1
s.70, applied: 2009 c.10 Sch.6 para.1
s.74B, applied: 2009 c.10 Sch.6 para.1
s.74C, applied: 2009 c.10 Sch.6 para.1
s.74D, applied: 2009 c.10 Sch.6 para.1
s.75, applied: 2009 c.10 Sch.6 para.1
s.76, applied: 2009 c.10 Sch.6 para.1
s.77, applied: 2009 c.10 Sch.6 para.1
s.78, applied: 2009 c.10 Sch.6 para.1
s.79, applied: 2009 c.10 Sch.6 para.1
s.80, applied: 2009 c.10 Sch.6 para.1
s.81, applied: 2009 c.10 Sch.6 para.1
s.96, applied: SI 2009/470 Reg.29
s.127, applied: SI 2009/470 Reg.29
s.127, varied: 2009 c.10 Sch.6 para.2
s.128, amended: 2009 c.10 s.68
s.128, applied: 2009 c.10 s.68, SI 2009/470 Reg.29
s.152, amended: 2009 c.10 s.69, SI 2009/3001
Reg.129
s.152, applied: 2009 c.10 s.69
s.153, referred to: 2009 c.10 s.69
s.158, amended: 2009 c.10 Sch.8 para.6
s.158, applied: 2009 c.10 Sch.8 para.13
s.158, repealed (in part): 2009 c.10 Sch.8 para.6
s.175, amended: 2009 c.10 Sch.8 para.7
s.239, amended: 2009 c.10 s.105
s.271, repealed (in part): SI 2009/2035 Sch.1
para.47
s.276, amended: 2009 c.4 Sch.1 para.701, SI 2009/
2860 Art.5
s.330, repealed (in part): SI 2009/2035 Sch.1 para.48
s.332, amended: 2009 c.10 Sch.22 para.11
s.341, amended: SI 2009/56 Sch.1 para.451
s.384A, added: 2009 c.10 Sch.30 para.1
s.414, amended: 2009 c.10 Sch.2 para.6

2007– cont.

3. Income Tax Act 2007– *cont.*
s.423, amended: 2009 c.10 Sch.1 para.6
s.424, amended: SI 2009/2859 Art.4
s.426, applied: 2009 c.10 Sch.35 para.2
s.482, amended: SI 2009/3001 Reg.129
s.489, amended: 2009 c.4 Sch.1 para.702
s.494, referred to: 2009 c.4 s.976
s.504, amended: 2009 c.10 Sch.19 para.13
s.504A, added: SI 2009/23 Art.5
s.515, amended: 2009 c.10 Sch.2 para.7
s.535, amended: SI 2009/3001 Reg.129
s.535, referred to: SI 2009/3001 Reg.31
s.538, repealed (in part): SI 2009/56 Sch.1 para.452
s.549, amended: SI 2009/1029 Reg.2
s.550, amended: 2009 c.4 Sch.1 para.703
s.557, amended: 2009 c.4 Sch.1 para.704, SI 2009/56
Sch.1 para.453
s.557, enabling: SI 2009/1029
s.582, enabling: SI 2009/2811
s.585, enabling: SI 2009/2810, SI 2009/2811
s.592, amended: 2009 c.10 Sch.19 para.13
s.593, amended: 2009 c.10 Sch.19 para.13
s.594, amended: 2009 c.10 Sch.19 para.13
s.674, amended: SI 2009/56 Sch.1 para.454
s.685, see *Grogan v Revenue and Customs
Commissioners* [2009] UKFTT 238 (TC)
(FTT (Tax)), Theodore Wallace
s.692, amended: SI 2009/56 Sch.1 para.455
s.697, amended: SI 2009/56 Sch.1 para.456
s.697, applied: SI 2009/275 Art.3
s.698, see *Grogan v Revenue and Customs
Commissioners* [2009] UKFTT 238 (TC)
(FTT (Tax)), Theodore Wallace
s.698, amended: SI 2009/56 Sch.1 para.457
s.703, repealed: SI 2009/2035 Sch.1 para.49
s.704, applied: SI 2009/56 Art.5, SI 2009/196 Art.9
s.704, repealed: SI 2009/56 Sch.1 para.458
s.705, amended: SI 2009/56 Sch.1 para.459
s.706, repealed: SI 2009/56 Sch.1 para.460
s.707, repealed: SI 2009/56 Sch.1 para.460
s.708, repealed: SI 2009/56 Sch.1 para.460
s.709, repealed: SI 2009/56 Sch.1 para.460
s.710, repealed: SI 2009/56 Sch.1 para.460
s.711, repealed: SI 2009/56 Sch.1 para.460
s.714, varied: SI 2009/3001 Reg.21
s.715, varied: SI 2009/3001 Reg.21
s.716, varied: SI 2009/3001 Reg.21
s.717, varied: SI 2009/3001 Reg.21
s.718, varied: SI 2009/3001 Reg.21
s.719, varied: SI 2009/3001 Reg.21
s.720, varied: SI 2009/3001 Reg.21
s.721, varied: SI 2009/3001 Reg.21
s.722, varied: SI 2009/3001 Reg.21
s.723, varied: SI 2009/3001 Reg.21
s.724, varied: SI 2009/3001 Reg.21
s.725, varied: SI 2009/3001 Reg.21
s.726, applied: SI 2009/3001 Reg.21
s.726, varied: SI 2009/3001 Reg.21
s.727, varied: SI 2009/3001 Reg.21
s.728, varied: SI 2009/3001 Reg.21
s.729, varied: SI 2009/3001 Reg.21
s.730, applied: SI 2009/3001 Reg.21
s.730, varied: SI 2009/3001 Reg.21
s.731, varied: SI 2009/3001 Reg.21
s.732, varied: SI 2009/3001 Reg.21
s.733, varied: SI 2009/3001 Reg.21
s.734, amended: SI 2009/3001 Reg.129
s.734, varied: SI 2009/3001 Reg.21

2007– cont.

3. Income Tax Act 2007– *cont.*

s.735, applied: SI 2009/3001 Reg.21
s.735, varied: SI 2009/3001 Reg.21
s.735A, varied: SI 2009/3001 Reg.21
s.736, varied: SI 2009/3001 Reg.21
s.737, varied: SI 2009/3001 Reg.21
s.738, varied: SI 2009/3001 Reg.21
s.739, varied: SI 2009/3001 Reg.21
s.740, varied: SI 2009/3001 Reg.21
s.741, varied: SI 2009/3001 Reg.21
s.742, varied: SI 2009/3001 Reg.21
s.743, varied: SI 2009/3001 Reg.21
s.744, varied: SI 2009/3001 Reg.21
s.745, varied: SI 2009/3001 Reg.21
s.746, varied: SI 2009/3001 Reg.21
s.747, varied: SI 2009/3001 Reg.21
s.748, varied: SI 2009/3001 Reg.21
s.749, varied: SI 2009/3001 Reg.21
s.750, varied: SI 2009/3001 Reg.21
s.751, amended: SI 2009/56 Sch.1 para.461
s.751, varied: SI 2009/3001 Reg.21
s.772, amended: SI 2009/2859 Art.4
s.777, amended: SI 2009/2859 Art.4
s.788, repealed: SI 2009/2035 Sch.1 para.50
s.809AZA, added: 2009 c.10 Sch.25 para.7
s.809AZB, added: 2009 c.10 Sch.25 para.7
s.809AZC, added: 2009 c.10 Sch.25 para.7
s.809AZD, added: 2009 c.10 Sch.25 para.7
s.809AZE, added: 2009 c.10 Sch.25 para.7
s.809AZF, added: 2009 c.10 Sch.25 para.7
s.809AZG, added: 2009 c.10 Sch.25 para.7
s.809B, applied: SI 2009/3001 Reg.19
s.809C, amended: 2009 c.10 Sch.27 para.2
s.809D, amended: 2009 c.10 Sch.27 para.3
s.809D, applied: SI 2009/3001 Reg.19
s.809E, amended: 2009 c.10 Sch.27 para.4
s.809E, applied: SI 2009/3001 Reg.19
s.809H, amended: 2009 c.10 Sch.27 para.5
s.809L, amended: 2009 c.10 Sch.27 para.6
s.809L, repealed (in part): 2009 c.10 Sch.27 para.6
s.809M, amended: 2009 c.10 Sch.27 para.7
s.809P, amended: 2009 c.10 Sch.27 para.8
s.809T, amended: 2009 c.10 Sch.27 para.9
s.809X, amended: 2009 c.10 Sch.27 para.10
s.809ZB, amended: 2009 c.10 Sch.32 para.10
s.809ZB, repealed (in part): 2009 c.10 Sch.32 para.10
s.809ZB, varied: 2009 c.10 Sch.32 para.11
s.809Z5, amended: 2009 c.10 Sch.27 para.11
s.809Z5, repealed (in part): 2009 c.10 Sch.27 para.11
s.811, amended: 2009 c.10 Sch.1 para.6
s.821, amended: SI 2009/23 Art.5
s.828A, added: 2009 c.10 s.52
s.828B, added: 2009 c.10 s.52
s.828C, added: 2009 c.10 s.52
s.828D, added: 2009 c.10 s.52
s.833, amended: 2009 c.10 Sch.1 para.6
s.835, amended: 2009 c.4 Sch.1 para.705
s.835, repealed (in part): 2009 c.4 Sch.3 Part 1
s.835A, added: 2009 c.4 Sch.1 para.706
s.848, applied: 2009 c.4 s.911, s.971
s.848, referred to: 2009 c.4 s.976
s.853, amended: SI 2009/1890 Art.3
s.862, repealed: SI 2009/2035 Sch.1 para.51
s.874, applied: 2009 c.10 s.45, SI 2009/2034 Reg.13
s.874, varied: SI 2009/2034 Reg.16
s.878, applied: SI 2009/3227 Reg.7
s.887, applied: 2009 c.4 s.397, s.500

2007– cont.

3. Income Tax Act 2007– *cont.*

s.899, amended: 2009 c.4 Sch.1 para.707
s.904, amended: 2009 c.4 Sch.1 para.708, SI 2009/23 Art.5
s.910, amended: 2009 c.4 Sch.1 para.709
s.910, applied: 2009 c.4 s.911, s.919, s.920
s.934, amended: 2009 c.4 Sch.1 para.710
s.937, amended: 2009 c.4 Sch.1 para.711
s.939, amended: 2009 c.4 Sch.1 para.712
s.941, amended: 2009 c.4 Sch.1 para.713, Sch.3 Part 1
s.941, applied: 2009 c.4 s.971
s.941, repealed (in part): 2009 c.4 Sch.3 Part 1
s.945, varied: SI 2009/2034 Reg.16
s.946, applied: 2009 c.10 Sch.53 para.13
s.946, varied: SI 2009/2034 Reg.16
s.947, varied: SI 2009/2034 Reg.16
s.948, amended: 2009 c.4 Sch.1 para.714
s.948, varied: SI 2009/2034 Reg.16
s.949, varied: SI 2009/2034 Reg.16
s.950, varied: SI 2009/2034 Reg.16
s.951, applied: 2009 c.10 Sch.53 para.13
s.951, varied: SI 2009/2034 Reg.16
s.952, varied: SI 2009/2034 Reg.16
s.953, applied: 2009 c.10 Sch.53 para.13
s.953, varied: SI 2009/2034 Reg.16
s.954, varied: SI 2009/2034 Reg.16
s.955, varied: SI 2009/2034 Reg.16
s.956, varied: SI 2009/2034 Reg.16
s.957, varied: SI 2009/2034 Reg.16
s.958, varied: SI 2009/2034 Reg.16
s.959, varied: SI 2009/2034 Reg.16
s.960, varied: SI 2009/2034 Reg.16
s.961, varied: SI 2009/2034 Reg.16
s.962, varied: SI 2009/2034 Reg.16
s.965, amended: 2009 c.4 Sch.1 para.715
s.966, applied: 2009 c.4 s.1203
s.971, amended: 2009 c.4 Sch.1 para.716
s.973, enabling: SI 2009/2036
s.974, enabling: SI 2009/2036
s.976, amended: 2009 c.4 Sch.1 para.717
s.979A, added: 2009 c.10 s.33
s.980, amended: 2009 c.4 Sch.1 para.718
s.980, referred to: 2009 c.4 s.570
s.989, amended: 2009 c.4 Sch.3 Part 1, 2009 c.10 Sch.2 para.8, Sch.19 para.13, SI 2009/56 Sch.1 para.462
s.993, applied: 2009 c.10 Sch.35 para.2, SI 2009/1171 Reg.2, SI 2009/3001 Reg.76, Reg.82
s.994, applied: SI 2009/3001 Reg.76, Reg.82
s.1007, amended: SI 2009/23 Art.5
s.1014, disapplied: 2009 c.10 Sch.22 para.14
s.1016, amended: 2009 c.10 Sch.25 para.9, SI 2009/3001 Reg.129, Sch.2
s.1017, amended: 2009 c.4 Sch.1 para.720
s.1028, enabling: SI 2009/23
s.1029, enabling: SI 2009/23, SI 2009/2859
Sch.1 Part 1 para.6, repealed: 2009 c.4 Sch.3 Part 1
Sch.1 Part 1 para.10, repealed: 2009 c.4 Sch.3 Part 1
Sch.1 Part 1 para.12, repealed: 2009 c.4 Sch.3 Part 1
Sch.1 Part 1 para.21, repealed: 2009 c.4 Sch.3 Part 1
Sch.1 Part 1 para.27, repealed: 2009 c.10 Sch.1 para.6
Sch.1 Part 1 para.28, repealed: 2009 c.10 Sch.1 para.6
Sch.1 Part 1 para.29, repealed: 2009 c.10 Sch.1 para.6
Sch.1 Part 1 para.30, repealed: 2009 c.10 Sch.1 para.6
Sch.1 Part 1 para.31, repealed: 2009 c.10 Sch.1 para.6
Sch.1 Part 1 para.32, repealed: 2009 c.10 Sch.1 para.6
Sch.1 Part 1 para.33, repealed: 2009 c.10 Sch.1 para.6
Sch.1 Part 1 para.34, repealed: 2009 c.10 Sch.1 para.6

2007–cont.

3. Income Tax Act 2007–*cont.*

Sch.1 Part 1 para.35, repealed: 2009 c.10 Sch.1 para.6

Sch.1 Part 1 para.36, repealed (in part): 2009 c.10 Sch.1 para.6

Sch.1 Part 1 para.37, repealed: 2009 c.10 Sch.1 para.6

Sch.1 Part 1 para.87, repealed (in part): 2009 c.4 Sch.3 Part 1

Sch.1 Part 1 para.91, repealed: 2009 c.4 Sch.3 Part 1

Sch.1 Part 1 para.107, repealed: 2009 c.4 Sch.3 Part 1

Sch.1 Part 1 para.109, repealed: 2009 c.4 Sch.3 Part 1

Sch.1 Part 1 para.114, repealed: 2009 c.4 Sch.3 Part 1

Sch.1 Part 1 para.134, repealed: 2009 c.4 Sch.3 Part 1

Sch.1 Part 1 para.160, repealed: SI 2009/2035 Sch.1 para.60

Sch.1 Part 1 para.163, repealed: SI 2009/2035 Sch.1 para.60

Sch.1 Part 1 para.172, repealed: 2009 c.10 Sch.24 para.9

Sch.1 Part 1 para.179, repealed: SI 2009/3001 Sch.2

Sch.1 Part 1 para.180, repealed: SI 2009/3001 Sch.2

Sch.1 Part 1 para.181, repealed: SI 2009/3001 Sch.2

Sch.1 Part 1 para.183, repealed: 2009 c.10 Sch.25 para.9

Sch.1 Part 1 para.193, amended: SI 2009/2859 Art.4

Sch.1 Part 1 para.232, repealed (in part): 2009 c.10 Sch.1 para.6

Sch.1 Part 2 para.243, repealed: SI 2009/56 Sch.1 para.463

Sch.1 Part 2 para.250, repealed: SI 2009/56 Sch.1 para.463

Sch.1 Part 2 para.255, repealed: SI 2009/56 Sch.1 para.463

Sch.1 Part 2 para.256, repealed: SI 2009/56 Sch.1 para.463

Sch.1 Part 2 para.267, repealed: SI 2009/56 Sch.1 para.463

Sch.1 Part 2 para.293, amended: 2009 c.10 Sch.8 para.9

Sch.1 Part 2 para.293, repealed (in part): 2009 c.10 Sch.8 para.9

Sch.1 Part 2 para.345, repealed (in part): 2009 c.10 Sch.8 para.10

Sch.1 Part 2 para.351, repealed: SI 2009/56 Sch.1 para.463

Sch.1 Part 2 para.371, repealed: 2009 c.4 Sch.3 Part 1

Sch.1 Part 2 para.372, repealed: 2009 c.4 Sch.3 Part 1

Sch.1 Part 2 para.373, repealed: 2009 c.4 Sch.3 Part 1, 2009 c.10 Sch.24 para.9

Sch.1 Part 2 para.374, repealed: 2009 c.4 Sch.3 Part 1

Sch.1 Part 2 para.375, repealed: 2009 c.4 Sch.3 Part 1

Sch.1 Part 2 para.376, repealed: 2009 c.4 Sch.3 Part 1

Sch.1 Part 2 para.422, repealed: 2009 c.4 Sch.3 Part 1

Sch.1 Part 2 para.439, repealed (in part): 2009 c.4 Sch.3 Part 1

Sch.1 Part 2 para.545, repealed: 2009 c.10 Sch.25 para.9

Sch.2 Part 4 para.14, repealed: 2009 c.10 Sch.1 para.6

Sch.2 Part 4 para.15, repealed: 2009 c.10 Sch.1 para.6

Sch.2 Part 4 para.16, repealed: 2009 c.10 Sch.1 para.6

Sch.2 Part 4 para.17, repealed: 2009 c.10 Sch.1 para.6

Sch.2 Part 15 para.155, repealed (in part): SI 2009/2035 Sch.1 para.52

Sch.3 Part 1, amended: SI 2009/2859 Art.4

Sch.4, amended: 2009 c.4 Sch.3 Part 1, 2009 c.10 Sch.2 para.9, Sch.25 para.9

5. Welfare Reform Act 2007

Commencement Orders: 2009 c.24 s.37; SI 2009/775 Art.2; SI 2009/1608 Art.2

2007–cont.

5. Welfare Reform Act 2007–*cont.*

applied: SI 2009/470 Reg.29

Part 1, applied: SI 2009/1555 Reg.121, Reg.138, SI 2009/2737 Reg.73, Reg.88, SSI 2009/48 Reg.6

s.1, amended: 2009 c.24 Sch.1 para.26

s.1, applied: SI 2009/212 Reg.2

s.1, repealed (in part): 2009 c.24 Sch.7 Part 1

s.3, enabling: SI 2009/2343

s.4, enabling: SI 2009/362, SI 2009/2655, SI 2009/3257

s.12, amended: 2009 c.24 s.3

s.12, enabling: SI 2009/2655

s.13, amended: 2009 c.24 s.3

s.14, amended: 2009 c.24 s.31

s.15, amended: 2009 c.24 s.10

s.15A, added: 2009 c.24 Sch.3 para.6

s.16, amended: 2009 c.24 Sch.3 para.8

s.17, enabling: SI 2009/583, SI 2009/1488, SI 2009/1575, SI 2009/2343, SI 2009/2655, SI 2009/3228

s.18, enabling: SI 2009/1488, SI 2009/2655

s.19, amended: 2009 c.24 s.28

s.19, applied: 2009 c.24 Sch.3 para.9

s.20, amended: 2009 c.24 s.6

s.24, amended: 2009 c.24 s.3, Sch.7 Part 1

s.24, enabling: SI 2009/362, SI 2009/583, SI 2009/1488, SI 2009/1575, SI 2009/2655, SI 2009/3228, SI 2009/3257

s.25, amended: 2009 c.24 Sch.3 para.8

s.25, enabling: SI 2009/362, SI 2009/583, SI 2009/1575, SI 2009/2655, SI 2009/3228, SI 2009/3257

s.26, amended: 2009 c.24 Sch.3 para.8

s.28, enabling: SI 2009/583

s.42, applied: SI 2009/2162 Art.2, SI 2009/2687 Art.2

s.42, enabling: SI 2009/2162, SI 2009/2687

s.68, enabling: SI 2009/775

s.70, enabling: SI 2009/775, SI 2009/1608

Sch.1 Part 1 para.1, amended: 2009 c.24 s.13

Sch.1 Part 2 para.6, amended: 2009 c.24 s.5, Sch.7 Part 1

Sch.1 Part 2 para.6, enabling: SI 2009/3228

Sch.1A para.1, added: 2009 c.24 Sch.3 para.7

Sch.1A para.1, applied: 2009 c.24 Sch.3 para.9

Sch.1A para.2, added: 2009 c.24 Sch.3 para.7

Sch.1A para.2, applied: 2009 c.24 Sch.3 para.9

Sch.1A para.3, added: 2009 c.24 Sch.3 para.7

Sch.1A para.3, applied: 2009 c.24 Sch.3 para.9

Sch.1A para.4, added: 2009 c.24 Sch.3 para.7

Sch.1A para.5, added: 2009 c.24 Sch.3 para.7

Sch.1A para.5, applied: 2009 c.24 Sch.3 para.9

Sch.1A para.6, added: 2009 c.24 Sch.3 para.7

Sch.1A para.6, applied: 2009 c.24 Sch.3 para.9

Sch.1A para.7, added: 2009 c.24 Sch.3 para.7

Sch.1A para.8, added: 2009 c.24 Sch.3 para.7

Sch.1A para.9, added: 2009 c.24 Sch.3 para.7

Sch.1A para.10, added: 2009 c.24 Sch.3 para.7

Sch.2 para.10, enabling: SI 2009/2343

Sch.2 para.10A, added: 2009 c.24 s.30

Sch.2 para.10A, amended: 2009 c.24 Sch.3 para.8

Sch.2 para.12, amended: 2009 c.24 Sch.3 para.8

Sch.2 para.13, amended: 2009 c.24 Sch.3 para.8

Sch.3 para.9, repealed (in part): 2009 c.24 Sch.7 Part 1, Sch.7 Part 2

Sch.3 para.12, repealed (in part): 2009 c.24 Sch.7 Part 3

Sch.3 para.20, repealed: 2009 c.24 Sch.7 Part 3

Sch.3 para.23, repealed (in part): 2009 c.24 Sch.7 Part 3

2007–cont.

5. Welfare Reform Act 2007–*cont.*
Sch.4 para.11, amended: 2009 c.24 Sch.2 para.17

6. Justice and Security (Northern Ireland) Act 2007
Commencement Orders: SI 2009/446 Art.2, Art.3
s.9, applied: SI 2009/2090, SI 2009/2090 Art.2
s.9, enabling: SI 2009/2090
s.48, enabling: SI 2009/446, SI 2009/3048
s.53, enabling: SI 2009/446
Sch.6, referred to: SI 2009/3048
Sch.6 para.1, repealed: SI 2009/3048 Art.4
Sch.6 para.2, repealed: SI 2009/3048 Art.4
Sch.6 para.3, repealed: SI 2009/3048 Art.4
Sch.6 para.4, repealed: SI 2009/3048 Art.4
Sch.6 para.5, repealed: SI 2009/3048 Art.4
Sch.6 para.6, repealed: SI 2009/3048 Art.4
Sch.6 para.7, repealed: SI 2009/3048 Art.4
Sch.6 para.8, repealed: SI 2009/3048 Art.4
Sch.6 para.9, repealed: SI 2009/3048 Art.4
Sch.6 para.10, repealed: SI 2009/3048 Art.4
Sch.6 para.11, repealed: SI 2009/3048 Art.4
Sch.6 para.12, repealed: SI 2009/3048 Art.4
Sch.6 para.13, repealed: SI 2009/3048 Art.4
Sch.6 para.14, repealed: SI 2009/3048 Art.4
Sch.6 para.15, repealed: SI 2009/3048 Art.4
Sch.6 para.16, repealed: SI 2009/3048 Art.4
Sch.6 para.17, repealed: SI 2009/3048 Art.4
Sch.6 para.18, repealed: SI 2009/3048 Art.4
Sch.6 para.19, repealed: SI 2009/3048 Art.4
Sch.6 para.20, repealed: SI 2009/3048 Art.4
Sch.6 para.21, repealed: SI 2009/3048 Art.4
Sch.6 para.22, repealed: SI 2009/3048 Art.4
Sch.6 para.23, repealed: SI 2009/3048 Art.4

10. Appropriation (No.2) Act 2007
repealed: 2009 c.9 Sch.3

11. Finance Act 2007
s.3, applied: 2009 c.10 s.8
s.9, repealed (in part): 2009 c.10 s.22
s.12, repealed: 2009 c.10 Sch.5 para.6
s.17, repealed: 2009 c.4 Sch.3 Part 1
s.28, repealed: 2009 c.4 Sch.3 Part 1
s.34, repealed (in part): 2009 c.4 Sch.3 Part 1
s.49, repealed: 2009 c.4 Sch.3 Part 1
s.50, repealed: 2009 c.4 Sch.3 Part 1
s.58, repealed (in part): 2009 c.4 Sch.3 Part 1
s.95, enabling: SI 2009/2978, SI 2009/3218
s.107, see *Test Claimants in the FII Group Litigation v Revenue and Customs Commissioners* [2008] EWHC 2893 (Ch), [2009] S.T.C. 254 (Ch D), Henderson, J.
s.108, repealed (in part): SI 2009/56 Sch.1 para.465
s.113, amended: 2009 c.4 Sch.1 para.723
Sch.3 Part 2 para.10, repealed: 2009 c.4 Sch.3 Part 1
Sch.5 para.11, repealed: 2009 c.4 Sch.3 Part 1
Sch.5 para.12, repealed: 2009 c.4 Sch.3 Part 1
Sch.5 para.13, repealed: 2009 c.4 Sch.3 Part 1
Sch.5 para.14, repealed: 2009 c.4 Sch.3 Part 1
Sch.5 para.15, repealed: 2009 c.4 Sch.3 Part 1
Sch.5 para.16, repealed: 2009 c.4 Sch.3 Part 1
Sch.5 para.18, repealed: 2009 c.4 Sch.3 Part 1
Sch.5 para.19, repealed: 2009 c.4 Sch.3 Part 1
Sch.6 para.2, repealed (in part): 2009 c.10 Sch.31 para.11
Sch.7 Part 1 para.19, repealed (in part): 2009 c.10 Sch.23 para.6
Sch.7 Part 1 para.56, added: 2009 c.10 Sch.16 para.5
Sch.7 Part 1 para.56, repealed: 2009 c.4 Sch.3 Part 1
Sch.7 Part 1 para.65, repealed: 2009 c.4 Sch.3 Part 1

2007–cont.

11. Finance Act 2007–*cont.*
Sch.7 Part 1 para.66, repealed: 2009 c.4 Sch.3 Part 1
Sch.7 Part 1 para.67, repealed: 2009 c.4 Sch.3 Part 1
Sch.7 Part 1 para.72, repealed: 2009 c.4 Sch.3 Part 1
Sch.7 Part 1 para.74, repealed: 2009 c.4 Sch.3 Part 1
Sch.7 Part 1 para.75, repealed: 2009 c.4 Sch.3 Part 1
Sch.7 Part 2, amended: 2009 c.4 Sch.1 para.725
Sch.7 Part 2 para.85, amended: 2009 c.4 Sch.1 para.725, Sch.3 Part 1
Sch.7 Part 2 para.86, amended: 2009 c.4 Sch.1 para.725
Sch.8 Part 1 para.20, repealed: 2009 c.4 Sch.3 Part 1
Sch.8 Part 1 para.25, repealed: 2009 c.4 Sch.3 Part 1
Sch.8 Part 1 para.26, repealed: 2009 c.4 Sch.3 Part 1
Sch.8 Part 1 para.27, repealed: 2009 c.4 Sch.3 Part 1
Sch.9 Part 1 para.1, repealed (in part): 2009 c.4 Sch.3 Part 1
Sch.10 para.4, repealed (in part): 2009 c.4 Sch.3 Part 1
Sch.10 para.6, repealed: 2009 c.4 Sch.3 Part 1
Sch.10 para.14, repealed (in part): 2009 c.4 Sch.3 Part 1
Sch.10 para.16, repealed (in part): 2009 c.4 Sch.3 Part 1
Sch.11 para.1, applied: SI 2009/1926 Reg.4, Reg.9, Reg.10
Sch.11 para.1, enabling: SI 2009/1926
Sch.11 para.2, amended: SI 2009/2035 Sch.1 para.53
Sch.11 para.3, applied: SI 2009/1926 Reg.6
Sch.11 para.3, referred to: SI 2009/1926 Reg.6
Sch.11 para.3, enabling: SI 2009/1926, SI 2009/2889
Sch.13 para.1, amended: 2009 c.4 Sch.1 para.726
Sch.13 para.2, repealed: 2009 c.4 Sch.3 Part 1
Sch.13 para.3, repealed: 2009 c.4 Sch.3 Part 1
Sch.13 para.4, repealed: 2009 c.4 Sch.3 Part 1
Sch.13 para.5, repealed: 2009 c.4 Sch.3 Part 1
Sch.13 para.7, repealed: 2009 c.4 Sch.3 Part 1
Sch.13 para.8, repealed: 2009 c.4 Sch.3 Part 1
Sch.13 para.9, repealed: 2009 c.4 Sch.3 Part 1
Sch.13 para.10, repealed: 2009 c.4 Sch.3 Part 1
Sch.13 para.12, repealed: 2009 c.4 Sch.3 Part 1
Sch.13 para.14, amended: 2009 c.4 Sch.1 para.726
Sch.13 para.15, amended: 2009 c.4 Sch.1 para.726
Sch.14 para.14, repealed: 2009 c.4 Sch.3 Part 1
Sch.14 para.15, repealed: 2009 c.4 Sch.3 Part 1
Sch.14 para.16, repealed: 2009 c.4 Sch.3 Part 1
Sch.14 para.17, repealed: 2009 c.4 Sch.3 Part 1
Sch.14 para.18, repealed: 2009 c.4 Sch.3 Part 1
Sch.24, applied: SI 2009/470 Reg.13, Reg.40
Sch.24, referred to: SI 2009/470 Reg.59
Sch.24 Part 1 para.1, varied: SI 2009/470 Reg.13, Reg.40
Sch.24 Part 1 para.1A, varied: SI 2009/470 Reg.13, Reg.40
Sch.24 Part 1 para.2, amended: 2009 c.10 Sch.57 para.2
Sch.24 Part 1 para.2, varied: SI 2009/470 Reg.13, Reg.40
Sch.24 Part 1 para.3, varied: SI 2009/470 Reg.13, Reg.40
Sch.24 Part 2 para.4, varied: SI 2009/470 Reg.13, Reg.40
Sch.24 Part 2 para.5, amended: 2009 c.10 Sch.57 para.3
Sch.24 Part 2 para.5, varied: SI 2009/470 Reg.13, Reg.40
Sch.24 Part 2 para.6, varied: SI 2009/470 Reg.13, Reg.40

2007– cont.

11. Finance Act 2007–*cont.*

Sch.24 Part 2 para.7, varied: SI 2009/470 Reg.13, Reg.40

Sch.24 Part 2 para.8, varied: SI 2009/470 Reg.13, Reg.40

Sch.24 Part 2 para.9, amended: 2009 c.10 Sch.57 para.4

Sch.24 Part 2 para.9, varied: SI 2009/470 Reg.13, Reg.40

Sch.24 Part 2 para.10, applied: 2009 c.10 s.94

Sch.24 Part 2 para.10, varied: SI 2009/470 Reg.13, Reg.40

Sch.24 Part 2 para.11, varied: SI 2009/470 Reg.13, Reg.40

Sch.24 Part 2 para.12, varied: SI 2009/470 Reg.13, Reg.40

Sch.24 Part 3 para.13, amended: 2009 c.10 Sch.57 para.5

Sch.24 Part 3 para.13, varied: SI 2009/470 Reg.13, Reg.40

Sch.24 Part 3 para.14, varied: SI 2009/470 Reg.13, Reg.40

Sch.24 Part 3 para.15, varied: SI 2009/470 Reg.13, Reg.40

Sch.24 Part 3 para.16, amended: 2009 c.10 Sch.57 para.6

Sch.24 Part 3 para.16, substituted: SI 2009/56 Sch.1 para.466

Sch.24 Part 3 para.16, varied: SI 2009/470 Reg.13, Reg.40

Sch.24 Part 3 para.17, amended: SI 2009/56 Sch.1 para.467

Sch.24 Part 3 para.17, varied: SI 2009/470 Reg.13, Reg.40

Sch.24 Part 4 para.18, varied: SI 2009/470 Reg.13, Reg.40

Sch.24 Part 4 para.19, amended: 2009 c.10 Sch.57 para.7

Sch.24 Part 4 para.19, varied: SI 2009/470 Reg.13, Reg.40

Sch.24 Part 4 para.20, varied: SI 2009/470 Reg.13, Reg.40

Sch.24 Part 4 para.21, varied: SI 2009/470 Reg.13, Reg.40

Sch.24 Part 5 para.22, varied: SI 2009/470 Reg.13, Reg.40

Sch.24 Part 5 para.23, varied: SI 2009/470 Reg.13, Reg.40

Sch.24 Part 5 para.23A, varied: SI 2009/470 Reg.13, Reg.40

Sch.24 Part 5 para.24, varied: SI 2009/470 Reg.13, Reg.40

Sch.24 Part 5 para.25, varied: SI 2009/470 Reg.13, Reg.40

Sch.24 Part 5 para.26, varied: SI 2009/470 Reg.13, Reg.40

Sch.24 Part 5 para.27, varied: SI 2009/470 Reg.13, Reg.40

Sch.24 Part 5 para.28, amended: 2009 c.4 Sch.1 para.727

Sch.24 Part 5 para.28, repealed (in part): 2009 c.4 Sch.1 para.727, 2009 c.10 Sch.57 para.8

Sch.24 Part 5 para.28, varied: SI 2009/470 Reg.13, Reg.40

Sch.24 Part 5 para.29, disapplied: SI 2009/571 Art.7

Sch.24 Part 5 para.29, varied: SI 2009/470 Reg.13, Reg.40

Sch.24 Part 5 para.30, amended: 2009 c.10 Sch.57 para.9

2007– cont.

11. Finance Act 2007–*cont.*

Sch.24 Part 5 para.30, varied: SI 2009/470 Reg.13, Reg.40

Sch.24 Part 5 para.31, amended: 2009 c.10 Sch.57 para.9

Sch.24 Part 5 para.31, varied: SI 2009/470 Reg.13, Reg.40

Sch.25 Part 4 para.17, repealed (in part): 2009 c.10 s.114

12. Mental Health Act 2007

Commencement Orders: SI 2009/139 Art.2

s.50, applied: SI 2009/783

s.56, enabling: SI 2009/139

13. Concessionary Bus Travel Act 2007

s.9, amended: 2009 c.20 Sch.6 para.120

15. Tribunals, Courts and Enforcement Act 2007

Commencement Orders: SI 2009/382 Art.2

see *DCC Realisations Ltd (In Liquidation) (formerly the Devon Cider Co Ltd), Re* [2009] EWHC 316 (Comm), [2009] S.T.C. 1390 (Ch D (Companies Ct)), David Donaldson Q.C.; see *Leicester City Council, Re* [2009] UKUT 155 (AAC), [2009] R.V.R. 306 (UT (AAC)), Edward Jacobs; see *Practice Direction (UT (Lands): Lands Tribunal: Interim Practice Directions and Guidance)* [2009] R.V.R. 208 (UT (Lands)), Carnwath, L.J. (SP)

applied: 2009 c.8 s.24, SI 2009/273 r.5, SI 2009/1976 r.5

s.7, applied: SI 2009/590 Art.3

s.7, enabling: SI 2009/196, SI 2009/1021, SI 2009/1590

s.9, see *Practice Direction (Sup Ct: Upper Tribunal: Judicial Review Jurisdiction)* [2009] 1 W.L.R. 327 (Sup Ct), Lord Judge, L.C.J.

s.9, enabling: SI 2009/273, SI 2009/1976

s.11, see *Practice Direction (Sup Ct: Upper Tribunal: Judicial Review Jurisdiction)* [2009] 1 W.L.R. 327 (Sup Ct), Lord Judge, L.C.J.

s.11, applied: 2009 c.8 s.25, SI 2009/275 Art.2, Art.3

s.11, varied: SI 2009/1834 Sch.4 para.3, SI 2009/1835 Sch.4 para.3, SI 2009/1836 Sch.3 para.3, SI 2009/1885 Sch.4 para.3

s.11, enabling: SI 2009/275

s.13, applied: SI 2009/275 Art.3

s.13, varied: SI 2009/1307 Sch.5 para.3, SI 2009/1885 Sch.4 para.4

s.13, enabling: SI 2009/275

s.15, see *Practice Direction (Sup Ct: Upper Tribunal: Judicial Review Jurisdiction)* [2009] 1 W.L.R. 327 (Sup Ct), Lord Judge, L.C.J.

s.16, enabling: SI 2009/274

s.18, see *Practice Direction (Sup Ct: Upper Tribunal: Judicial Review Jurisdiction)* [2009] 1 W.L.R. 327 (Sup Ct), Lord Judge, L.C.J.

s.19, see *R. (on the application of Hankinson) v Revenue and Customs Commissioners* [2009] EWHC 1774 (Admin), [2009] S.T.C. 2158 (QBD (Admin)), Kenneth Parker Q.C.

s.20, see *Currie, Petitioner* [2009] CSOH 145 (OH), Lord Hodge

s.20, amended: 2009 c.11 s.53

s.22, enabling: SI 2009/273, SI 2009/274, SI 2009/1975, SI 2009/1976

s.25, applied: SI 2009/273 r.7, SI 2009/1976 r.7

s.29, applied: SI 2009/273 r.10, SI 2009/1976 r.10

s.29, enabling: SI 2009/273, SI 2009/274, SI 2009/1975, SI 2009/1976

s.30, applied: 2009 c.11 s.58

s.30, enabling: SI 2009/56, SI 2009/1307, SI 2009/1834, SI 2009/1835, SI 2009/1836, SI 2009/1885

s.31, referred to: SI 2009/590 Art.3

2007– cont.

15. Tribunals, Courts and Enforcement Act 2007– *cont.*

s.31, enabling: SI 2009/56, SI 2009/1307, SI 2009/1834, SI 2009/1835, SI 2009/1836, SI 2009/1885

s.37, enabling: SI 2009/1836

s.38, enabling: SI 2009/56, SI 2009/1307, SI 2009/1834, SI 2009/1835, SI 2009/1836, SI 2009/1885

s.40, applied: SI 2009/56 Sch.3 para.12, SI 2009/121, SI 2009/273 r.4, SI 2009/1307 Sch.5 para.5, SI 2009/1834 Sch.4 para.5, SI 2009/1835 Sch.4 para.5, SI 2009/1836 Sch.3 para.5, SI 2009/1885 Sch.4 para.6

s.40, enabling: SI 2009/121

s.42, applied: SI 2009/1114

s.42, enabling: SI 2009/1114

s.44, applied: SSI 2009/211, SSI 2009/259, SSI 2009/260

s.49, applied: SI 2009/56, SI 2009/1307, SI 2009/1834, SI 2009/1835, SI 2009/1836, SI 2009/1885

s.50, applied: SI 2009/3070 Reg.5

s.51, applied: SI 2009/1307, SI 2009/3348

s.51, enabling: SI 2009/1307, SI 2009/3348

s.145, enabling: SI 2009/121, SI 2009/196, SI 2009/450, SI 2009/1307

s.148, enabling: SI 2009/382

Sch.2 para.2, enabling: SI 2009/1592

Sch.3 para.2, enabling: SI 2009/1592

Sch.4 Part 1 para.2, applied: SI 2009/590 Art.3

Sch.4 Part 1 para.5, applied: SI 2009/590 Art.3

Sch.5, enabling: SI 2009/273, SI 2009/274, SI 2009/1975, SI 2009/1976

Sch.5 Part 2 para.22, enabling: SI 2009/1975

Sch.5 Part 3 para.28, applied: SI 2009/273, SI 2009/274, SI 2009/1975, SI 2009/1976

Sch.5 Part 3 para.29, enabling: SI 2009/1975

Sch.5 Part 4 para.30, enabling: SI 2009/56, SI 2009/1834, SI 2009/1835, SI 2009/1885

Sch.6 Part 4, amended: SI 2009/1836 Art.4

Sch.7, applied: 2009 c.20 s.76, SI 2009/823, SI 2009/1500, SSI 2009/308

Sch.7 Part 3 para.24, applied: SI 2009/25, SI 2009/443, SI 2009/445, SI 2009/1099, SI 2009/1307, SI 2009/1964, SI 2009/1965, SI 2009/2089, SI 2009/2464, SI 2009/2578, SI 2009/3243, SI 2009/3245, SI 2009/3248, SI 2009/3293, SI 2009/3348, SSI 2009/183, SSI 2009/211, SSI 2009/259, SSI 2009/260

Sch.7 Part 4 para.25, enabling: SI 2009/3040

Sch.10 Part 1 para.5, repealed: SI 2009/1307 Sch.4

Sch.10 Part 1 para.11, repealed: SI 2009/1835 Sch.3

Sch.10 Part 1 para.23, repealed: SI 2009/1834 Sch.3

18. Statistics and Registration Service Act 2007

s.6, applied: SI 2009/753, SI 2009/753 Art.3

s.6, enabling: SI 2009/753

s.11, applied: SI 2009/2818

s.11, enabling: SI 2009/2818

s.12, applied: SI 2009/2818 Art.3

s.20, applied: SI 2009/277 Reg.5, SI 2009/3201 Reg.5, Reg.6

s.39, applied: SI 2009/3201 Reg.6

s.39, varied: SI 2009/277 Reg.6

s.47, applied: SI 2009/277, SI 2009/3201

s.47, enabling: SI 2009/277, SI 2009/3201

s.65, applied: SI 2009/277, SI 2009/753, SI 2009/2818, SI 2009/3201

Sch.3 para.14, repealed: 2009 c.20 Sch.7 Part 4

2007– cont.

19. Corporate Manslaughter and Corporate Homicide Act 2007

s.2, see *R. v Evans (Gemma)* [2009] EWCA Crim 650, [2009] 1 W.L.R. 1999 (CA (Crim Div)), Lord Judge, L.C.J.

Sch.1, amended: SI 2009/229 Sch.2 para.5, SI 2009/2748 Sch.1 para.8

Sch.2 para.1, repealed: 2009 c.25 Sch.23 Part 1

21. Offender Management Act 2007

Commencement Orders: SI 2009/32 Art.2, Art.3, Art.4, Art.5; SI 2009/547 Art.2

s.2, applied: 2009 c.20 s.2, s.23, s.123

s.2, referred to: SI 2009/504 Art.3

s.3, applied: 2009 c.20 s.2, s.123, SI 2009/504 Art.3

s.5, enabling: SI 2009/504

s.29, enabling: SI 2009/619

s.41, enabling: SI 2009/32, SI 2009/547

Sch.1 para.13, referred to: 2009 c.20 s.23

22. Pensions Act 2007

Commencement Orders: SI 2009/406 Art.2

s.27, enabling: SI 2009/2715, SI 2009/3094

s.30, enabling: SI 2009/406

Sch.1 Part 4 para.14, repealed: 2009 c.24 Sch.7 Part 2

Sch.1 Part 4 para.15, repealed: 2009 c.24 Sch.7 Part 2

Sch.1 Part 5 para.25, repealed: 2009 c.24 Sch.7 Part 1

23. Sustainable Communities Act 2007

applied: 2009 c.2 Sch.2 Part 2

25. Further Education and Training Act 2007

s.1, repealed: 2009 c.22 Sch.16 Part 2

s.2, repealed: 2009 c.22 Sch.16 Part 2

s.4, repealed: 2009 c.22 Sch.16 Part 2

s.5, repealed: 2009 c.22 Sch.16 Part 2

s.6, repealed: 2009 c.22 Sch.16 Part 2

s.7, repealed: 2009 c.22 Sch.16 Part 2

s.8, repealed: 2009 c.22 Sch.16 Part 2

s.9, repealed: 2009 c.22 Sch.16 Part 2

s.10, repealed: 2009 c.22 Sch.16 Part 2

s.11, repealed: 2009 c.22 Sch.6 para.61, Sch.16 Part 2

s.12, repealed: 2009 c.22 Sch.6 para.61, Sch.16 Part 2

s.13, repealed: 2009 c.22 Sch.6 para.61, Sch.16 Part 2

s.14, repealed: 2009 c.22 Sch.6 para.62, Sch.16 Part 2

s.15, repealed: 2009 c.22 Sch.6 para.62, Sch.16 Part 2

s.16, repealed: 2009 c.22 Sch.6 para.62, Sch.16 Part 2

26. Building Societies (Funding) and Mutual Societies (Transfers) Act 2007

Commencement Orders: SI 2009/36 Art.2

s.3, amended: SI 2009/1941 Sch.1 para.266

s.3, applied: SI 2009/509 Art.19

s.3, repealed (in part): SI 2009/1941 Sch.1 para.266

s.3, enabling: SI 2009/509

s.4, applied: SI 2009/509 Art.7

s.4, enabling: SI 2009/509

s.6, enabling: SI 2009/36

27. Serious Crime Act 2007

Commencement Orders: SSI 2009/224 Art.2

Part 2, applied: 2009 c.25 Sch.22 para.24, 2009 c.26 s.102, SI 2009/1059 Art.42

s.27, amended: SI 2009/1941 Sch.1 para.265

s.28, amended: SI 2009/1941 Sch.1 para.265

s.44, applied: 2009 c.25 s.159, SI 2009/1168 Sch.1 para.2

s.45, applied: 2009 c.25 s.159, SI 2009/1168 Sch.1 para.2

s.46, applied: 2009 c.25 s.159

s.51A, added: 2009 c.25 Sch.21 para.61

s.78, repealed: 2009 c.26 Sch.8 Part 4

s.80, repealed (in part): 2009 c.26 Sch.8 Part 5

s.94, enabling: SSI 2009/224

2007– cont.

27. Serious Crime Act 2007– *cont.*
Sch.1 Part 1 para.13, amended: 2009 c.23 Sch.22 Part 5
Sch.3 Part 2 para.27A, added: 2009 c.25 Sch.21 para.61
Sch.3 Part 4 para.42A, added: 2009 c.25 Sch.21 para.61
Sch.8 Part 4 para.107, repealed (in part): 2009 c.26 Sch.8 Part 5
Sch.8 Part 7 para.150, repealed: 2009 c.26 Sch.8 Part 4
Sch.8 Part 7 para.151, repealed: 2009 c.26 Sch.8 Part 4
Sch.8 Part 7 para.154, repealed: 2009 c.26 Sch.8 Part 4
Sch.10 para.3, repealed: 2009 c.26 Sch.8 Part 5
Sch.10 para.4, repealed: 2009 c.26 Sch.8 Part 5
Sch.10 para.5, repealed: 2009 c.26 Sch.8 Part 5
Sch.10 para.6, repealed: 2009 c.26 Sch.8 Part 5
Sch.10 para.9, repealed: 2009 c.26 Sch.8 Part 5
Sch.10 para.26, repealed: 2009 c.26 Sch.8 Part 5
Sch.10 para.27, repealed: 2009 c.26 Sch.8 Part 5
Sch.10 para.28, repealed: 2009 c.26 Sch.8 Part 5

28. Local Government and Public Involvement in Health Act 2007
Commencement Orders: SI 2009/959 Art.2; SI 2009/2539 Art.2
applied: SI 2009/467 Reg.1, SI 2009/2268 Reg.25, SI 2009/2271 Reg.3
Part 1 c.1, applied: 2009 c.20 s.60, s.63, SI 2009/5 Reg.1, SI 2009/276 Reg.1
Part 2 c.1, applied: 2009 c.20 s.60, Sch.2 para.2
Part 4 c.3, applied: 2009 c.20 s.60
s.4, amended: 2009 c.20 Sch.4 para.12
s.5, see *R. (on the application of Breckland DC) v Boundary Committee* [2009] EWCA Civ 239, [2009] B.L.G.R. 589 (CA (Civ Div)), Sir Anthony May (President, QB)
s.5, amended: 2009 c.20 Sch.4 para.13
s.6, see *R. (on the application of Breckland DC) v Boundary Committee* [2009] EWCA Civ 239, [2009] B.L.G.R. 589 (CA (Civ Div)), Sir Anthony May (President, QB)
s.6, amended: 2009 c.20 Sch.4 para.14
s.7, see *R. (on the application of Breckland DC) v Boundary Committee* [2009] EWCA Civ 239, [2009] B.L.G.R. 589 (CA (Civ Div)), Sir Anthony May (President, QB)
s.7, amended: 2009 c.20 Sch.4 para.15
s.7, applied: SI 2009/119
s.7, referred to: SI 2009/467 Reg.1
s.7, enabling: SI 2009/119, SI 2009/837, SI 2009/850
s.8, amended: 2009 c.20 s.65, Sch.4 para.16
s.9, amended: 2009 c.20 Sch.4 para.17
s.10, amended: 2009 c.20 s.65, Sch.4 para.18
s.11, amended: 2009 c.20 s.65
s.11, repealed (in part): 2009 c.20 s.65, Sch.4 para.16
s.11, enabling: SI 2009/119, SI 2009/837, SI 2009/850
s.12, amended: 2009 c.20 s.65, Sch.4 para.19
s.12, repealed (in part): 2009 c.20 Sch.7 Part 3
s.12, enabling: SI 2009/850
s.13, enabling: SI 2009/119, SI 2009/837, SI 2009/850
s.14, applied: SI 2009/486 Reg.3
s.14, enabling: SI 2009/5, SI 2009/276, SI 2009/467, SI 2009/486, SI 2009/532
s.16, applied: SI 2009/5 Reg.1, SI 2009/276 Reg.1
s.20, applied: SI 2009/276 Reg.1
s.23, amended: 2009 c.20 Sch.4 para.20, Sch.6 para.121, Sch.7 Part 3
s.36, amended: 2009 c.20 Sch.4 para.21

2007– cont.

28. Local Government and Public Involvement in Health Act 2007– *cont.*
s.41, amended: 2009 c.20 Sch.4 para.22
s.42, amended: 2009 c.20 Sch.4 para.23
s.43, amended: 2009 c.20 Sch.4 para.24
s.44, amended: 2009 c.20 Sch.4 para.25
s.45, amended: 2009 c.20 Sch.4 para.26
s.47, amended: 2009 c.20 Sch.4 para.26
s.50, amended: 2009 c.20 Sch.4 para.27
s.51, amended: 2009 c.20 Sch.4 para.28
s.52, amended: 2009 c.20 Sch.4 para.29
s.55, repealed: 2009 c.20 Sch.7 Part 3
s.56, repealed: 2009 c.20 Sch.7 Part 3
s.57, repealed: 2009 c.20 Sch.7 Part 3
s.59, amended: 2009 c.20 Sch.4 para.30
s.59, applied: 2009 c.20 s.60
s.86, amended: 2009 c.20 Sch.4 para.31
s.86, applied: SI 2009/276 Reg.1
s.92, amended: 2009 c.20 Sch.4 para.32
s.92, enabling: SI 2009/2786
s.96, amended: 2009 c.20 Sch.4 para.32
s.97, applied: SI 2009/276 Reg.1
s.98, amended: 2009 c.20 Sch.4 para.32
s.102, amended: 2009 c.20 Sch.4 para.33
s.104, amended: 2009 c.20 Sch.6 para.121
s.123, substituted: 2009 c.20 s.32
s.199, applied: SI 2009/2267 Reg.4, Reg.5
s.205, applied: SI 2009/105 Reg.2
s.205, enabling: SI 2009/105
s.206, applied: SI 2009/105 Sch.2 para.4
s.207, applied: 2009 c.20 s.2, s.35, s.123, SI 2009/1360 Art.2
s.212, applied: 2009 c.20 s.54
s.220, enabling: SI 2009/2267, SI 2009/2268, SI 2009/2271, SI 2009/2613
s.236, enabling: SI 2009/352 Reg.2
s.240, amended: 2009 c.20 Sch.4 para.34
s.240, applied: SI 2009/119, SI 2009/837, SI 2009/850
s.240, enabling: SI 2009/5, SI 2009/105, SI 2009/276, SI 2009/467, SI 2009/486, SI 2009/837
s.245, enabling: SI 2009/959, SI 2009/2539
Sch.1 Part 2 para.15, repealed: 2009 c.25 Sch.23 Part 1
Sch.1 Part 2 para.21, repealed: 2009 c.20 Sch.7 Part 4

29. Legal Services Act 2007
Commencement Orders: SI 2009/503 Art.2, Art.3, Art.4, Art.5; SI 2009/1365 Art.2; SI 2009/3250 Art.2, Art.3, Art.4, Art.5, Art.9
applied: SI 2009/1976 r.11
disapplied: SI 2009/3250 Art.6, Art.9
s.18, amended: SI 2009/3250 Art.3
s.18, repealed (in part): SI 2009/3233 Art.6, Art.7
s.25, amended: SI 2009/3250 Art.3
s.25, repealed (in part): SI 2009/3250 Art.3
s.30, applied: SI 2009/503 Art.6
s.30, enabling: SI 2009/503
s.37, applied: SI 2009/3249 r.2
s.37, enabling: SI 2009/3249
s.64, amended: SI 2009/3250 Art.3
s.69, applied: SI 2009/3339
s.69, enabling: SI 2009/3339
s.70, applied: SI 2009/3339
s.159, applied: SI 2009/3250 Art.7, Art.8
s.167, amended: SI 2009/3250 Art.3
s.168, amended: SI 2009/3250 Art.3
s.169, amended: SI 2009/3250 Art.3
s.171, amended: SI 2009/3250 Art.3

2007– cont.

29. Legal Services Act 2007– *cont.*
s.184, amended: SI 2009/3339 Art.2
s.204, enabling: SI 2009/503, SI 2009/1365, SI 2009/3249, SI 2009/3250
s.205, applied: SI 2009/3249
s.206, applied: SI 2009/1587, SI 2009/1589, SI 2009/3339, SI 2009/3348
s.208, enabling: SI 2009/500, SI 2009/503, SI 2009/1365, SI 2009/1587, SI 2009/1589, SI 2009/3233, SI 2009/3250, SI 2009/3348
s.211, enabling: SI 2009/503, SI 2009/1365, SI 2009/3250
Sch.4 Part 1 para.1, amended: SI 2009/3233 Art.3
Sch.5 Part 1 para.2A, added: SI 2009/3233 Art.4
Sch.5 Part 1 para.2A, applied: SI 2009/3233 Art.5, Art.6, Art.7
Sch.5 Part 2 para.4, amended: SI 2009/3250 Art.4
Sch.5 Part 2 para.4, repealed (in part): SI 2009/3250 Art.4
Sch.16 Part 2 para.81, varied: SI 2009/503 Art.4
Sch.17 Part 1 para.20, varied: SI 2009/503 Art.4
Sch.21 para.108, repealed: SI 2009/3054 Sch.1 para.16
Sch.22 para.5, applied: SI 2009/3233
Sch.22 para.5, enabling: SI 2009/3233
Sch.22 para.15, varied: SI 2009/503 Art.4
Sch.23, amended: 2009 c.25 Sch.23 Part 9
30. UK Borders Act 2007
s.2, amended: 2009 c.11 s.52
s.3, amended: 2009 c.11 s.52
s.5, applied: SI 2009/421 Reg.21
s.5, enabling: SI 2009/819, SI 2009/3321
s.6, applied: SI 2009/819, SI 2009/3321
s.6, enabling: SI 2009/819, SI 2009/3321
s.21, amended: 2009 c.11 s.34
s.21, repealed (in part): 2009 c.11 s.34, Sch.1 Part 4
s.24, amended: 2009 c.26 Sch.7 para.113
s.32, see *R. v Ovieriakhi (Valerie Ekiuwa)* [2009] EWCA Crim 452, [2009] 2 Cr. App. R. (S.) 91 (CA (Crim Div)), Lord Judge, L.C.J.
s.34, repealed: 2009 c.11 s.34
s.40, amended: 2009 c.11 s.47
s.41A, added: 2009 c.11 s.20
s.41B, added: 2009 c.11 s.20
s.42, amended: 2009 c.11 s.20
s.48, amended: 2009 c.11 s.28
s.48, applied: 2009 c.11 s.28
s.48, repealed (in part): 2009 c.11 s.28
s.53, amended: 2009 c.11 s.28
s.56, amended: 2009 c.11 s.28
s.60, amended: 2009 c.11 Sch.1 Part 3
31. Consolidated Fund Act 2007
repealed: 2009 c.9 Sch.3

2008

1. European Communities (Finance) Act 2008
s.1, added: SI 2009/1111 Art.2
s.2, applied: SI 2009/1111 Art.3
2. Banking (Special Provisions) Act 2008
referred to: 2009 c.1 s.259, s.262
s.3, enabling: SI 2009/320
s.5, enabling: SI 2009/790, SI 2009/791
s.6, enabling: SI 2009/308, SI 2009/310, SI 2009/320
s.8, enabling: SI 2009/308, SI 2009/320
s.9, applied: 2009 c.1 s.237
s.9, enabling: SI 2009/790, SI 2009/791
s.10, enabling: SI 2009/3227

2008– cont.

2. Banking (Special Provisions) Act 2008– *cont.*
s.12, referred to: 2009 c.1 s.237
s.12, enabling: SI 2009/308, SI 2009/310, SI 2009/320, SI 2009/790, SI 2009/791, SI 2009/3226
s.13, applied: SI 2009/790, SI 2009/791
s.13, enabling: SI 2009/308, SI 2009/310, SI 2009/320
s.14, enabling: SI 2009/310
s.16, disapplied: 2009 c.1 s.229
Sch.1, enabling: SI 2009/320
Sch.2, enabling: SI 2009/308, SI 2009/310, SI 2009/3226
3. Appropriation Act 2008
applied: 2009 c.2 Sch.1
referred to: 2009 c.2 s.5
4. Criminal Justice and Immigration Act 2008
Commencement Orders: SI 2009/140 Art.2; SI 2009/860 Art.2; SI 2009/1028 Art.2; SI 2009/1678 Art.2, Art.3; SI 2009/1679 Art.2; SI 2009/1842 Art.2; SI 2009/2606 Art.2, Art.3; SI 2009/2780 Art.2, Art.3; SI 2009/3074 Art.2, Art.3
see *Attorney General's Reference (No.55 of 2008), Re* [2008] EWCA Crim 2790, [2009] 1 W.L.R. 2158 (CA (Crim Div)), Lord Judge, L.C.J.; see *R. v Roberts (Stanley Frederick)* [2009] EWCA Crim 701, [2009] 2 Cr. App. R. (S.) 100 (CA (Crim Div)), Maurice Kay, L.J.; see *R. v Stannard (Raymond)* [2008] EWCA Crim 2789, [2009] 2 Cr. App. R. (S.) 21 (CA (Crim Div)), Lord Judge, L.C.J.
referred to: SI 2009/2019 Reg.2
Part 1, applied: 2009 c.25 s.131
s.11, amended: 2009 c.25 Sch.21 para.98
s.21, see *R. v Sherif (Abdul)* [2008] EWCA Crim 2653, [2009] 2 Cr. App. R. (S.) 33 (CA (Crim Div)), Latham, L.J.
s.22, see *R. v Nnaji (Ogechuku Ferdinand)* [2009] EWCA Crim 468, [2009] 2 Cr. App. R. (S.) 107 (CA (Crim Div)), Thomas, L.J.
s.27, repealed: 2009 c.25 Sch.23 Part 5
s.44, see *R. v A* [2008] EWCA Crim 2186, [2009] 1 W.L.R. 1661 (CA (Crim Div)), Scott Baker, L.J.
s.99, applied: SI 2009/2197 r.4
s.99, enabling: SI 2009/2197
s.100, applied: SI 2009/2197 r.2, r.4
s.101, applied: SI 2009/2197 r.2
s.103, applied: SI 2009/2197 r.3
s.104, applied: SI 2009/2197 r.2
s.110, applied: SI 2009/2019 Reg.11
s.110, enabling: SI 2009/2019
s.111, applied: SI 2009/2019 Reg.3, Reg.4, Reg.5, Reg.6, Reg.7, Reg.8, Reg.9, Reg.10
s.111, enabling: SI 2009/2019
s.112, applied: SI 2009/2019 Reg.10
s.135, amended: SI 2009/1307 Sch.1 para.288
s.135, repealed (in part): SI 2009/1307 Sch.1 para.288
s.147, applied: SI 2009/2019
s.147, enabling: SI 2009/2019
s.153, enabling: SI 2009/140, SI 2009/860, SI 2009/1028, SI 2009/1678, SI 2009/1842, SI 2009/2606, SI 2009/2780, SI 2009/3074
Sch.1 Part 2 para.20, amended: SI 2009/1182 Sch.5 para.10
Sch.1 Part 2 para.21, amended: SI 2009/1182 Sch.5 para.10
Sch.1 Part 2 para.26, applied: SI 2009/2950 Art.2
Sch.1 Part 2 para.26, enabling: SI 2009/2950

2008–cont.

4. Criminal Justice and Immigration Act 2008–
cont.
Sch.1 Part 3 para.30, amended: 2009 c.25 Sch.21 para.98, Sch.23 Part 9
Sch.4 Part 1 para.60, repealed (in part): 2009 c.25 Sch.23 Part 4
Sch.4 Part 1 para.65, repealed: 2009 c.24 Sch.7 Part 3
Sch.4 Part 1 para.66, repealed: 2009 c.24 Sch.7 Part 3
Sch.4 Part 1 para.67, repealed: 2009 c.24 Sch.7 Part 3
Sch.4 Part 1 para.76, amended: 2009 c.25 Sch.21 para.98
Sch.28 Part 1, amended: 2009 c.25 Sch.23 Part 4

6. Child Maintenance and Other Payments Act 2008
Commencement Orders: SI 2009/1314 Art.2; SI 2009/3072 Art.2
s.30, repealed: 2009 c.24 Sch.7 Part 4
s.57, enabling: SI 2009/396
s.59, amended: 2009 c.24 Sch.5 para.10, Sch.7 Part 4
s.62, enabling: SI 2009/1314, SI 2009/3072
Sch.3 Part 1 para.42, repealed: 2009 c.24 Sch.7 Part 4
Sch.3 Part 2 para.55, applied: SSI 2009/365 r.3
Sch.7 para.1, repealed (in part): 2009 c.24 Sch.7 Part 4
Sch.7 para.2, repealed (in part): 2009 c.24 Sch.7 Part 1

7. European Union (Amendment) Act 2008
Commencement Orders: SI 2009/3143 Art.2
s.8, enabling: SI 2009/3143
Sch.1 Part 2, applied: 2009 c.23 s.37

9. Finance Act 2008
Commencement Orders: SI 2009/404 Art.2; SI 2009/511 Art.2; SI 2009/571 Art.2; SI 2009/3024 Art.3, Art.4
varied: SI 2009/317 Sch.1
s.2, repealed (in part): 2009 c.10 Sch.1 para.6
s.3, amended: 2009 c.10 Sch.1 para.6
s.3, repealed (in part): 2009 c.10 Sch.1 para.6
s.7, referred to: 2009 c.10 s.8
s.26, repealed: 2009 c.4 Sch.3 Part 1
s.27, repealed: 2009 c.4 Sch.3 Part 1
s.28, repealed: 2009 c.4 Sch.3 Part 1
s.29, repealed: 2009 c.4 Sch.3 Part 1
s.30, repealed: 2009 c.4 Sch.3 Part 1
s.36, repealed (in part): 2009 c.4 Sch.3 Part 1
s.40A, added: 2009 c.10 Sch.22 para.2
s.40A, applied: 2009 c.10 Sch.22 para.6, SI 2009/3001 Reg.7, Reg.29, Reg.67, Reg.95, Reg.96
s.40B, added: 2009 c.10 Sch.22 para.2
s.40C, added: 2009 c.10 Sch.22 para.2
s.40C, applied: SI 2009/3001 Reg.5
s.40D, added: 2009 c.10 Sch.22 para.2
s.40D, applied: SI 2009/3001 Reg.6
s.40E, added: 2009 c.10 Sch.22 para.2
s.40F, added: 2009 c.10 Sch.22 para.2
s.40G, added: 2009 c.10 Sch.22 para.2
s.41, amended: 2009 c.10 Sch.22 para.3
s.41, applied: 2009 c.10 Sch.22 para.6
s.41, repealed (in part): 2009 c.10 Sch.22 para.3
s.41, enabling: SI 2009/3001, SI 2009/3139
s.42, amended: 2009 c.10 Sch.22 para.4
s.42, enabling: SI 2009/3001, SI 2009/3139
s.42A, added: 2009 c.10 Sch.22 para.5
s.42A, applied: SI 2009/3001
s.47, repealed (in part): 2009 c.10 Sch.28 para.9
s.49, repealed (in part): 2009 c.4 Sch.3 Part 1
s.58, repealed (in part): 2009 c.4 Sch.3 Part 1
s.64, repealed (in part): 2009 c.10 Sch.16 para.5
s.65, repealed: 2009 c.4 Sch.3 Part 1

2008–cont.

9. Finance Act 2008– *cont.*
s.73, repealed (in part): 2009 c.4 Sch.3 Part 1
s.77, amended: 2009 c.4 Sch.1 para.731
s.77, repealed (in part): 2009 c.4 Sch.3 Part 1, 2009 c.10 Sch.11 para.64
s.90, varied: SI 2009/470 Reg.62
s.91, varied: SI 2009/470 Reg.62
s.92, varied: SI 2009/470 Reg.62
s.93, varied: SI 2009/470 Reg.62
s.94, varied: SI 2009/470 Reg.62
s.95, varied: SI 2009/470 Reg.62
s.96, varied: SI 2009/470 Reg.62
s.97, varied: SI 2009/470 Reg.62
s.98, varied: SI 2009/470 Reg.62
s.99, varied: SI 2009/470 Reg.62
s.100, varied: SI 2009/470 Reg.62
s.101, varied: SI 2009/470 Reg.62
s.102, varied: SI 2009/470 Reg.62
s.103, varied: SI 2009/470 Reg.62
s.104, varied: SI 2009/470 Reg.62
s.105, varied: SI 2009/470 Reg.62
s.106, varied: SI 2009/470 Reg.62
s.107, varied: SI 2009/470 Reg.62
s.108, varied: SI 2009/470 Reg.62
s.109, varied: SI 2009/470 Reg.62
s.110, varied: SI 2009/470 Reg.62
s.111, varied: SI 2009/470 Reg.62
s.112, varied: SI 2009/470 Reg.62
s.113, enabling: SI 2009/404
s.115, enabling: SI 2009/402
s.118, enabling: SI 2009/403
s.119, repealed (in part): SI 2009/56 Sch.1 para.469
s.119, enabling: SI 2009/405
s.122, enabling: SI 2009/511, SI 2009/571
s.123, enabling: SI 2009/511
s.124, applied: SI 2009/56, SI 2009/777
s.124, enabling: SI 2009/56, SI 2009/777
s.128, enabling: SSI 2009/403
s.129, enabling: SI 2009/3024
s.136, applied: SI 2009/3073
s.136, enabling: SI 2009/3073
s.154, amended: 2009 c.4 Sch.1 para.732
s.160, enabling: SI 2009/730
s.165, amended: 2009 c.4 Sch.1 para.733
Sch.1 Part 2 para.44, repealed: 2009 c.4 Sch.3 Part 1
Sch.2 para.51, repealed: 2009 c.4 Sch.3 Part 1
Sch.7 Part 1 para.86, amended: 2009 c.10 Sch.27 para.14
Sch.7 Part 2 para.92, repealed: SI 2009/3001 Sch.2
Sch.7 Part 2 para.93, repealed: SI 2009/3001 Sch.2
Sch.7 Part 2 para.94, repealed: SI 2009/3001 Sch.2
Sch.7 Part 2 para.95, repealed: SI 2009/3001 Sch.2
Sch.7 Part 2 para.96, repealed: SI 2009/3001 Sch.2
Sch.7 Part 2 para.100, amended: SI 2009/3001 Reg.130
Sch.7 Part 2 para.101, amended: SI 2009/3001 Reg.130
Sch.7 Part 2 para.102, amended: SI 2009/3001 Reg.130
Sch.7 Part 2 para.161, repealed: SI 2009/56 Sch.1 para.470
Sch.8 para.1, repealed: 2009 c.4 Sch.3 Part 1
Sch.8 para.2, repealed: 2009 c.4 Sch.3 Part 1
Sch.8 para.3, repealed: 2009 c.4 Sch.3 Part 1
Sch.9 para.1, repealed: 2009 c.4 Sch.3 Part 1
Sch.9 para.2, repealed: 2009 c.4 Sch.3 Part 1
Sch.9 para.3, repealed: 2009 c.4 Sch.3 Part 1
Sch.10 Part 1 para.1, repealed: 2009 c.4 Sch.3 Part 1

2008– cont.

9. Finance Act 2008–*cont.*

Sch.10 Part 1 para.2, repealed: 2009 c.4 Sch.3 Part 1
Sch.10 Part 1 para.3, repealed: 2009 c.4 Sch.3 Part 1
Sch.10 Part 1 para.4, repealed: 2009 c.4 Sch.3 Part 1
Sch.10 Part 1 para.5, repealed: 2009 c.4 Sch.3 Part 1
Sch.10 Part 1 para.6, repealed: 2009 c.4 Sch.3 Part 1
Sch.10 Part 1 para.7, repealed: 2009 c.4 Sch.3 Part 1
Sch.10 Part 2 para.8, repealed: 2009 c.4 Sch.3 Part 1
Sch.10 Part 2 para.9, repealed: 2009 c.4 Sch.3 Part 1
Sch.10 Part 2 para.10, repealed: 2009 c.4 Sch.3 Part 1
Sch.13 para.1, repealed: 2009 c.4 Sch.3 Part 1
Sch.13 para.2, repealed: 2009 c.4 Sch.3 Part 1
Sch.13 para.3, repealed: 2009 c.4 Sch.3 Part 1
Sch.13 para.4, repealed: 2009 c.4 Sch.3 Part 1
Sch.13 para.5, repealed: 2009 c.4 Sch.3 Part 1
Sch.13 para.6, repealed: 2009 c.4 Sch.3 Part 1
Sch.13 para.7, repealed: 2009 c.4 Sch.3 Part 1
Sch.13 para.8, repealed: 2009 c.4 Sch.3 Part 1
Sch.15 Part 2 para.5, repealed: 2009 c.4 Sch.3 Part 1
Sch.15 Part 2 para.6, repealed: 2009 c.4 Sch.3 Part 1
Sch.15 Part 2 para.7, repealed: 2009 c.4 Sch.3 Part 1
Sch.15 Part 2 para.8, repealed: 2009 c.4 Sch.3 Part 1
Sch.15 Part 2 para.9, repealed: 2009 c.4 Sch.3 Part 1
Sch.15 Part 2 para.10, repealed: 2009 c.4 Sch.3 Part 1
Sch.17 para.4, amended: 2009 c.10 Sch.23 para.4
Sch.17 para.9, repealed (in part): 2009 c.4 Sch.3 Part 1
Sch.17 para.10, repealed (in part): 2009 c.10 Sch.23 para.6
Sch.17 para.12, repealed: 2009 c.4 Sch.3 Part 1
Sch.17 para.23, repealed: 2009 c.4 Sch.3 Part 1
Sch.17 para.28, repealed (in part): 2009 c.4 Sch.3 Part 1
Sch.17 para.29, repealed: 2009 c.4 Sch.3 Part 1, 2009 c.10 Sch.16 para.5
Sch.17 para.30, repealed: SI 2009/3001 Sch.2
Sch.17 para.36, repealed: 2009 c.4 Sch.3 Part 1
Sch.20 para.4, repealed: 2009 c.10 Sch.32 para.2
Sch.20 para.5, repealed: 2009 c.10 Sch.32 para.4
Sch.22 para.3, repealed: 2009 c.4 Sch.3 Part 1
Sch.22 para.4, repealed: 2009 c.4 Sch.3 Part 1
Sch.22 para.5, repealed: 2009 c.4 Sch.3 Part 1
Sch.22 para.6, repealed: 2009 c.4 Sch.3 Part 1
Sch.22 para.7, repealed: 2009 c.4 Sch.3 Part 1
Sch.22 para.8, repealed: 2009 c.4 Sch.3 Part 1
Sch.22 para.9, repealed: 2009 c.4 Sch.3 Part 1
Sch.22 para.10, repealed: 2009 c.4 Sch.3 Part 1
Sch.22 para.11, repealed: 2009 c.4 Sch.3 Part 1
Sch.22 para.12, repealed: 2009 c.4 Sch.3 Part 1
Sch.22 para.13, repealed: 2009 c.4 Sch.3 Part 1
Sch.22 para.14, repealed: 2009 c.4 Sch.3 Part 1
Sch.22 para.15, repealed: 2009 c.4 Sch.3 Part 1
Sch.22 para.16, repealed: 2009 c.4 Sch.3 Part 1
Sch.22 para.17, repealed (in part): 2009 c.4 Sch.3 Part 1
Sch.22 para.18, repealed: 2009 c.4 Sch.3 Part 1
Sch.22 para.19, repealed: 2009 c.4 Sch.3 Part 1
Sch.22 para.20, repealed: 2009 c.4 Sch.3 Part 1
Sch.25 Part 1 para.5, amended: 2009 c.4 Sch.1 para.737
Sch.25 Part 1 para.5, substituted: 2009 c.4 Sch.1 para.737
Sch.25 Part 1 para.6, repealed: 2009 c.10 s.126
Sch.29 para.2, repealed: 2009 c.10 s.75
Sch.35 para.10, repealed: 2009 c.4 Sch.3 Part 1
Sch.36, applied: SI 2009/1916 Reg.3, Reg.4
Sch.36, referred to: 2009 c.10 s.95, SI 2009/470 Reg.60
Sch.36 Part 1 para.1, varied: SI 2009/470 Reg.33, Reg.60, Reg.61

2008– cont.

9. Finance Act 2008–*cont.*

Sch.36 Part 1 para.2, amended: SI 2009/56 Sch.1 para.471
Sch.36 Part 1 para.2, varied: SI 2009/470 Reg.33, Reg.60, Reg.61
Sch.36 Part 1 para.3, amended: 2009 c.10 Sch.47 para.2, SI 2009/56 Sch.1 para.471
Sch.36 Part 1 para.3, varied: SI 2009/470 Reg.33, Reg.60, Reg.61
Sch.36 Part 1 para.4, amended: SI 2009/56 Sch.1 para.471
Sch.36 Part 1 para.4, varied: SI 2009/470 Reg.33, Reg.60, Reg.61
Sch.36 Part 1 para.5, amended: 2009 c.10 Sch.47 para.3, Sch.48 para.2, SI 2009/56 Sch.1 para.471
Sch.36 Part 1 para.5, varied: SI 2009/470 Reg.33, Reg.60, Reg.61
Sch.36 Part 1 para.6, amended: 2009 c.10 Sch.47 para.4, SI 2009/56 Sch.1 para.471
Sch.36 Part 1 para.6, varied: SI 2009/470 Reg.33, Reg.60, Reg.61
Sch.36 Part 1 para.7, varied: SI 2009/470 Reg.33, Reg.60, Reg.61
Sch.36 Part 1 para.8, varied: SI 2009/470 Reg.33, Reg.60, Reg.61
Sch.36 Part 1 para.9, varied: SI 2009/470 Reg.33, Reg.60, Reg.61
Sch.36 Part 2 para.10, amended: 2009 c.10 Sch.47 para.5, SI 2009/3054 Sch.1 para.15
Sch.36 Part 2 para.10, varied: SI 2009/470 Reg.33, Reg.60, Reg.61
Sch.36 Part 2 para.10A, added: 2009 c.10 Sch.48 para.3
Sch.36 Part 2 para.10A, amended: SI 2009/3054 Sch.1 para.15
Sch.36 Part 2 para.10A, varied: SI 2009/470 Reg.33, Reg.60, Reg.61
Sch.36 Part 2 para.11, amended: 2009 c.10 Sch.47 para.6, SI 2009/3054 Sch.1 para.15
Sch.36 Part 2 para.11, varied: SI 2009/470 Reg.33, Reg.60, Reg.61
Sch.36 Part 2 para.12, amended: 2009 c.10 Sch.47 para.7, Sch.48 para.4, SI 2009/56 Sch.1 para.471, SI 2009/3054 Sch.1 para.15
Sch.36 Part 2 para.12, varied: SI 2009/470 Reg.33, Reg.60, Reg.61
Sch.36 Part 2 para.12A, added: 2009 c.10 Sch.48 para.5
Sch.36 Part 2 para.12A, amended: SI 2009/3054 Sch.1 para.15
Sch.36 Part 2 para.12A, varied: SI 2009/470 Reg.33, Reg.60, Reg.61
Sch.36 Part 2 para.12B, added: 2009 c.10 Sch.48 para.5
Sch.36 Part 2 para.12B, amended: SI 2009/3054 Sch.1 para.15
Sch.36 Part 2 para.12B, varied: SI 2009/470 Reg.33, Reg.60, Reg.61
Sch.36 Part 2 para.13, amended: 2009 c.10 Sch.47 para.8, Sch.48 para.6, SI 2009/56 Sch.1 para.471, SI 2009/3054 Sch.1 para.15
Sch.36 Part 2 para.13, varied: SI 2009/470 Reg.33, Reg.60, Reg.61
Sch.36 Part 2 para.14, amended: SI 2009/3054 Sch.1 para.15
Sch.36 Part 2 para.14, varied: SI 2009/470 Reg.33, Reg.60, Reg.61
Sch.36 Part 3 para.15, varied: SI 2009/470 Reg.33, Reg.60, Reg.61

2008– cont.

9. Finance Act 2008– *cont.*

Sch.36 Part 3 para.16, varied: SI 2009/470 Reg.33, Reg.60, Reg.61

Sch.36 Part 3 para.17, amended: 2009 c.10 Sch.48 para.7

Sch.36 Part 3 para.17, varied: SI 2009/470 Reg.33, Reg.60, Reg.61

Sch.36 Part 4, amended: 2009 c.10 Sch.48 para.8

Sch.36 Part 4, amended: 2009 c.10 Sch.48 para.10

Sch.36 Part 4 para.18, varied: SI 2009/470 Reg.33, Reg.60, Reg.61

Sch.36 Part 4 para.19, varied: SI 2009/470 Reg.33, Reg.60, Reg.61

Sch.36 Part 4 para.20, varied: SI 2009/470 Reg.33, Reg.60, Reg.61

Sch.36 Part 4 para.21, amended: 2009 c.10 Sch.47 para.9, Sch.48 para.8

Sch.36 Part 4 para.21, varied: SI 2009/470 Reg.33, Reg.60, Reg.61

Sch.36 Part 4 para.21A, added: 2009 c.10 Sch.48 para.9

Sch.36 Part 4 para.21A, varied: SI 2009/470 Reg.33, Reg.60, Reg.61

Sch.36 Part 4 para.22, varied: SI 2009/470 Reg.33, Reg.60, Reg.61

Sch.36 Part 4 para.23, amended: SI 2009/56 Sch.1 para.471

Sch.36 Part 4 para.23, repealed (in part): SI 2009/56 Sch.1 para.471

Sch.36 Part 4 para.23, varied: SI 2009/470 Reg.33, Reg.60, Reg.61

Sch.36 Part 4 para.23, enabling: SI 2009/1916

Sch.36 Part 4 para.24, varied: SI 2009/470 Reg.33, Reg.60, Reg.61

Sch.36 Part 4 para.25, varied: SI 2009/470 Reg.33, Reg.60, Reg.61

Sch.36 Part 4 para.26, varied: SI 2009/470 Reg.33, Reg.60, Reg.61

Sch.36 Part 4 para.27, varied: SI 2009/470 Reg.33, Reg.60, Reg.61

Sch.36 Part 4 para.28, amended: 2009 c.10 Sch.48 para.10

Sch.36 Part 4 para.28, varied: SI 2009/470 Reg.33, Reg.60, Reg.61

Sch.36 para.5, see *Revenue and Customs Commissioners' Application (Approval to Serve 308 Notices on Financial Institiutions), Re (TC 174)* [2009] UKFTT 224 (TC), [2009] S.F.T.D. 780 (FTT (Tax)), John Avery Jones

Sch.36 Part 5 para.29, amended: SI 2009/56 Sch.1 para.471

Sch.36 Part 5 para.29, varied: SI 2009/470 Reg.33, Reg.60, Reg.61

Sch.36 Part 5 para.30, amended: SI 2009/56 Sch.1 para.471

Sch.36 Part 5 para.30, varied: SI 2009/470 Reg.33, Reg.60, Reg.61

Sch.36 Part 5 para.31, amended: SI 2009/56 Sch.1 para.471

Sch.36 Part 5 para.31, varied: SI 2009/470 Reg.33, Reg.60, Reg.61

Sch.36 Part 5 para.32, amended: SI 2009/56 Sch.1 para.471

Sch.36 Part 5 para.32, applied: 2009 c.10 Sch.49 para.4

Sch.36 Part 5 para.32, varied: SI 2009/470 Reg.33, Reg.60, Reg.61

Sch.36 Part 5 para.33, varied: SI 2009/470 Reg.33, Reg.60, Reg.61

2008– cont.

9. Finance Act 2008– *cont.*

Sch.36 Part 6 para.34, amended: SI 2009/56 Sch.1 para.471

Sch.36 Part 6 para.34, varied: SI 2009/470 Reg.33, Reg.60, Reg.61

Sch.36 Part 6 para.34A, added: 2009 c.10 Sch.48 para.11

Sch.36 Part 6 para.34A, varied: SI 2009/470 Reg.33, Reg.60, Reg.61

Sch.36 Part 6 para.34B, added: 2009 c.10 Sch.48 para.11

Sch.36 Part 6 para.34B, varied: SI 2009/470 Reg.33, Reg.60, Reg.61

Sch.36 Part 6 para.34C, added: 2009 c.10 Sch.48 para.11

Sch.36 Part 6 para.34C, varied: SI 2009/470 Reg.33, Reg.60, Reg.61

Sch.36 Part 6 para.35, amended: 2009 c.10 Sch.47 para.10, Sch.48 para.12, SI 2009/56 Sch.1 para.471

Sch.36 Part 6 para.35, repealed (in part): 2009 c.10 Sch.47 para.10

Sch.36 Part 6 para.35, varied: SI 2009/470 Reg.33, Reg.60, Reg.61

Sch.36 Part 6 para.36, varied: SI 2009/470 Reg.33, Reg.60, Reg.61

Sch.36 Part 6 para.37, amended: 2009 c.10 Sch.47 para.11, Sch.48 para.13, SI 2009/56 Sch.1 para.471

Sch.36 Part 6 para.37, repealed (in part): 2009 c.10 Sch.47 para.11

Sch.36 Part 6 para.37, varied: SI 2009/470 Reg.33, Reg.60, Reg.61

Sch.36 Part 6 para.37A, added: 2009 c.10 Sch.47 para.12

Sch.36 Part 6 para.37A, varied: SI 2009/470 Reg.33, Reg.60, Reg.61

Sch.36 Part 6 para.37B, added: 2009 c.10 Sch.47 para.12

Sch.36 Part 6 para.37B, varied: SI 2009/470 Reg.33, Reg.60, Reg.61

Sch.36 Part 6 para.38, varied: SI 2009/470 Reg.33, Reg.60, Reg.61

Sch.36 Part 7 para.39, amended: 2009 c.10 Sch.47 para.13, SI 2009/56 Sch.1 para.471

Sch.36 Part 7 para.39, applied: 2009 c.10 Sch.49 para.5

Sch.36 Part 7 para.39, varied: SI 2009/470 Reg.33, Reg.60, Reg.61

Sch.36 Part 7 para.40, amended: 2009 c.10 Sch.47 para.14

Sch.36 Part 7 para.40, varied: SI 2009/470 Reg.33, Reg.60, Reg.61

Sch.36 Part 7 para.40A, added: 2009 c.10 Sch.47 para.15

Sch.36 Part 7 para.40A, varied: SI 2009/470 Reg.33, Reg.60, Reg.61

Sch.36 Part 7 para.41, amended: 2009 c.10 Sch.47 para.16

Sch.36 Part 7 para.41, varied: SI 2009/470 Reg.33, Reg.60, Reg.61

Sch.36 Part 7 para.42, varied: SI 2009/470 Reg.33, Reg.60, Reg.61

Sch.36 Part 7 para.43, varied: SI 2009/470 Reg.33, Reg.60, Reg.61

Sch.36 Part 7 para.44, applied: 2009 c.10 Sch.49 para.5

Sch.36 Part 7 para.44, varied: SI 2009/470 Reg.33, Reg.60, Reg.61

2008–cont.

9. Finance Act 2008–*cont.*

Sch.36 Part 7 para.45, amended: SI 2009/56 Sch.1 para.471

Sch.36 Part 7 para.45, applied: 2009 c.10 Sch.49 para.5

Sch.36 Part 7 para.45, varied: SI 2009/470 Reg.33, Reg.60, Reg.61

Sch.36 Part 7 para.46, amended: 2009 c.10 Sch.47 para.17

Sch.36 Part 7 para.46, applied: 2009 c.10 Sch.49 para.5

Sch.36 Part 7 para.46, varied: SI 2009/470 Reg.33, Reg.60, Reg.61

Sch.36 Part 7 para.47, amended: 2009 c.10 Sch.47 para.18, SI 2009/56 Sch.1 para.471

Sch.36 Part 7 para.47, applied: 2009 c.10 Sch.49 para.5

Sch.36 Part 7 para.47, varied: SI 2009/470 Reg.33, Reg.60, Reg.61

Sch.36 Part 7 para.48, amended: 2009 c.10 Sch.47 para.19, SI 2009/56 Sch.1 para.471

Sch.36 Part 7 para.48, applied: 2009 c.10 Sch.49 para.5

Sch.36 Part 7 para.48, varied: SI 2009/470 Reg.33, Reg.60, Reg.61

Sch.36 Part 7 para.49, amended: 2009 c.10 Sch.47 para.20

Sch.36 Part 7 para.49, applied: 2009 c.10 Sch.49 para.5

Sch.36 Part 7 para.49, varied: SI 2009/470 Reg.33, Reg.60, Reg.61

Sch.36 Part 7 para.50, varied: SI 2009/470 Reg.33, Reg.60, Reg.61

Sch.36 Part 7 para.51, varied: SI 2009/470 Reg.33, Reg.60, Reg.61

Sch.36 Part 7 para.52, applied: 2009 c.10 Sch.49 para.5

Sch.36 Part 7 para.52, varied: SI 2009/470 Reg.33, Reg.60, Reg.61

Sch.36 Part 8 para.53, amended: SI 2009/56 Sch.1 para.471

Sch.36 Part 8 para.53, varied: SI 2009/470 Reg.33, Reg.60, Reg.61

Sch.36 Part 8 para.54, amended: SI 2009/56 Sch.1 para.471

Sch.36 Part 8 para.54, varied: SI 2009/470 Reg.33, Reg.60, Reg.61

Sch.36 Part 8 para.55, varied: SI 2009/470 Reg.33, Reg.60, Reg.61

Sch.36 Part 9 para.56, varied: SI 2009/470 Reg.33, Reg.60, Reg.61

Sch.36 Part 9 para.57, varied: SI 2009/470 Reg.33, Reg.60, Reg.61

Sch.36 Part 9 para.58, amended: SI 2009/56 Sch.1 para.471

Sch.36 Part 9 para.58, varied: SI 2009/470 Reg.33, Reg.60, Reg.61

Sch.36 Part 9 para.59, varied: SI 2009/470 Reg.33, Reg.60, Reg.61

Sch.36 Part 9 para.60, varied: SI 2009/470 Reg.33, Reg.60, Reg.61

Sch.36 Part 9 para.61, varied: SI 2009/470 Reg.33, Reg.60, Reg.61

Sch.36 Part 9 para.61A, added: 2009 c.10 Sch.48 para.14

Sch.36 Part 9 para.61A, varied: SI 2009/470 Reg.33, Reg.60, Reg.61

Sch.36 Part 9 para.62, amended: 2009 c.10 Sch.48 para.15

2008–cont.

9. Finance Act 2008–*cont.*

Sch.36 Part 9 para.62, varied: SI 2009/470 Reg.33, Reg.60, Reg.61

Sch.36 Part 9 para.63, amended: 2009 c.10 s.96, Sch.47 para.21

Sch.36 Part 9 para.63, varied: SI 2009/470 Reg.33, Reg.60, Reg.61

Sch.36 Part 9 para.64, amended: 2009 c.10 Sch.47 para.22

Sch.36 Part 9 para.64, varied: SI 2009/470 Reg.33, Reg.60, Reg.61

Sch.36 Part 10 para.65, varied: SI 2009/470 Reg.33, Reg.60, Reg.61

Sch.36 Part 10 para.66, varied: SI 2009/470 Reg.33, Reg.60, Reg.61

Sch.36 Part 10 para.67, varied: SI 2009/470 Reg.33, Reg.60, Reg.61

Sch.36 Part 10 para.68, disapplied: SI 2009/404 Art.4

Sch.36 Part 10 para.68, varied: SI 2009/470 Reg.33, Reg.60, Reg.61

Sch.36 Part 10 para.69, varied: SI 2009/470 Reg.33, Reg.60, Reg.61

Sch.36 Part 10 para.70, disapplied: SI 2009/404 Art.4

Sch.36 Part 10 para.70, varied: SI 2009/470 Reg.33, Reg.60, Reg.61

Sch.36 Part 10 para.71, disapplied: SI 2009/404 Art.3

Sch.36 Part 10 para.71, varied: SI 2009/470 Reg.33, Reg.60, Reg.61

Sch.36 Part 10 para.72, disapplied: SI 2009/404 Art.5

Sch.36 Part 10 para.72, varied: SI 2009/470 Reg.33, Reg.60, Reg.61

Sch.36 Part 10 para.73, disapplied: SI 2009/404 Art.6

Sch.36 Part 10 para.73, varied: SI 2009/470 Reg.33, Reg.60, Reg.61

Sch.36 Part 10 para.74, repealed: 2009 c.10 Sch.57 para.14

Sch.36 Part 10 para.74, varied: SI 2009/470 Reg.33, Reg.60, Reg.61

Sch.36 Part 10 para.75, disapplied: SI 2009/404 Art.3, Art.5

Sch.36 Part 10 para.75, varied: SI 2009/470 Reg.33, Reg.60, Reg.61

Sch.36 Part 10 para.76, disapplied: SI 2009/404 Art.4

Sch.36 Part 10 para.76, varied: SI 2009/470 Reg.33, Reg.60, Reg.61

Sch.36 Part 10 para.77, varied: SI 2009/470 Reg.33, Reg.60, Reg.61

Sch.36 Part 10 para.78, disapplied: SI 2009/404 Art.11

Sch.36 Part 10 para.78, varied: SI 2009/470 Reg.33, Reg.60, Reg.61

Sch.36 Part 10 para.79, varied: SI 2009/470 Reg.33, Reg.60, Reg.61

Sch.36 Part 10 para.80, disapplied: SI 2009/404 Art.6

Sch.36 Part 10 para.80, varied: SI 2009/470 Reg.33, Reg.60, Reg.61

Sch.36 Part 10 para.81, disapplied: SI 2009/404 Art.6

Sch.36 Part 10 para.81, varied: SI 2009/470 Reg.33, Reg.60, Reg.61

Sch.36 Part 10 para.82, disapplied: SI 2009/404 Art.6

2008–cont.

9. Finance Act 2008–*cont.*

Sch.36 Part 10 para.82, varied: SI 2009/470 Reg.33, Reg.60, Reg.61

Sch.36 Part 10 para.83, repealed (in part): SI 2009/2035 Sch.1 para.60

Sch.36 Part 10 para.83, varied: SI 2009/470 Reg.33, Reg.60, Reg.61

Sch.36 Part 10 para.84, disapplied: SI 2009/404 Art.9

Sch.36 Part 10 para.84, varied: SI 2009/470 Reg.33, Reg.60, Reg.61

Sch.36 Part 10 para.85, disapplied: SI 2009/404 Art.9

Sch.36 Part 10 para.85, varied: SI 2009/470 Reg.33, Reg.60, Reg.61

Sch.36 Part 10 para.86, varied: SI 2009/470 Reg.33, Reg.60, Reg.61

Sch.36 Part 10 para.87, varied: SI 2009/470 Reg.33, Reg.60, Reg.61

Sch.36 Part 10 para.88, varied: SI 2009/470 Reg.33, Reg.60, Reg.61

Sch.36 Part 10 para.89, varied: SI 2009/470 Reg.33, Reg.60, Reg.61

Sch.36 Part 10 para.90, disapplied: SI 2009/404 Art.9

Sch.36 Part 10 para.90, varied: SI 2009/470 Reg.33, Reg.60, Reg.61

Sch.36 Part 10 para.91, disapplied: SI 2009/404 Art.10

Sch.36 Part 10 para.91, varied: SI 2009/470 Reg.33, Reg.60, Reg.61

Sch.36 Part 10 para.92, disapplied: SI 2009/404 Art.12

Sch.36 Part 10 para.92, varied: SI 2009/470 Reg.33, Reg.60, Reg.61

Sch.39 para.17, repealed: 2009 c.4 Sch.3 Part 1

Sch.39 para.18, repealed: 2009 c.10 Sch.1 para.6

Sch.39 para.19, repealed: 2009 c.10 Sch.1 para.6

Sch.39 para.20, repealed: 2009 c.10 Sch.1 para.6

Sch.39 para.25, repealed: 2009 c.10 Sch.14 para.30

Sch.39 para.33, disapplied: SI 2009/403 Art.3

Sch.39 para.34, disapplied: SI 2009/403 Art.4

Sch.39 para.35, disapplied: SI 2009/403 Art.5

Sch.39 para.36, disapplied: SI 2009/403 Art.6

Sch.39 para.66, repealed: 2009 c.10 Sch.51 para.42

Sch.40 para.14, repealed: SI 2009/56 Sch.1 para.472

Sch.40 para.20, repealed (in part): 2009 c.10 Sch.57 para.14

Sch.41 para.13, applied: 2009 c.10 s.94

Sch.41 para.18, amended: 2009 c.10 Sch.57 para.11

Sch.41 para.18, substituted: SI 2009/56 Sch.1 para.473

Sch.41 para.19, amended: SI 2009/56 Sch.1 para.473

Sch.41 para.20, amended: SI 2009/56 Sch.1 para.473

Sch.41 para.21, amended: SI 2009/56 Sch.1 para.473

Sch.41 para.22, amended: 2009 c.10 Sch.57 para.12

Sch.43 Part 2 para.13, referred to: SI 2009/3024 Art.5

10. Sale of Student Loans Act 2008

s.5, enabling: SI 2009/470

s.6, enabling: SI 2009/470

13. Regulatory Enforcement and Sanctions Act 2008

Commencement Orders: SI 2009/550 Art.2

Part 2, applied: SI 2009/665 Art.2

s.4, applied: SI 2009/669 Sch.1 Part 2, Sch.1 Part 4

2008–cont.

13. Regulatory Enforcement and Sanctions Act 2008–*cont.*

s.4, referred to: SI 2009/669 Sch.1 Part 2, Sch.1 Part 4

s.24, enabling: SI 2009/669

s.27, applied: SI 2009/670 Art.3

s.28, applied: SI 2009/665 Art.2, SI 2009/670 Art.3, Art.4, Art.5, Art.6

s.28, disapplied: SI 2009/665 Art.3

s.28, enabling: SI 2009/665

s.29, enabling: SI 2009/665

s.39, applied: SI 2009/665 Art.2

s.42, applied: SI 2009/665 Art.2

s.46, applied: SI 2009/665 Art.2

s.76, enabling: SI 2009/550

Sch.3, amended: 2009 c.23 Sch.22 Part 4

Sch.4 para.1, applied: SI 2009/670 Art.13

Sch.4 para.2, applied: SI 2009/670 Art.13

Sch.4 para.3, applied: SI 2009/670 Art.13

Sch.4 para.6, enabling: SI 2009/670

Sch.5, amended: 2009 c.23 Sch.22 Part 4

Sch.6, amended: 2009 c.23 Sch.22 Part 4

Sch.7, amended: 2009 c.23 Sch.22 Part 4

14. Health and Social Care Act 2008

Commencement Orders: SI 2009/270 Art.2; SI 2009/462 Art.2, Art.3, Art.4, Art.5, Sch.1 para.1, para.2, para.3, para.4, para.5, para.6, para.7, para.8, para.9, para.10, para.11, para.12, para.13, para.14, para.15, para.16, para.17, para.18, para.19, para.20, para.21, para.22, para.23, para.24, para.25, para.26, para.27, para.28, para.29, para.30, para.31, para.32, para.33, para.34, para.35, para.36; SI 2009/631 Art.2; SI 2009/1310 Art.2; SI 2009/2567 Art.2, Art.3; SI 2009/2862 Art.2; SI 2009/3023 Art.2

Part 1, applied: SI 2009/660 Sch.2 para.2, Sch.2 para.6, Sch.2 para.9, Sch.2 para.10, SI 2009/3112 Sch.2 para.2, Sch.2 para.6, Sch.2 para.9, Sch.2 para.11

Part 1 c.2, applied: SI 2009/1360 Art.3, SI 2009/3112 Reg.4

s.8, applied: SI 2009/660 Reg.3

s.8, enabling: SI 2009/660

s.10, applied: SI 2009/660 Sch.1

s.10, disapplied: SI 2009/462 Art.7

s.10, enabling: SI 2009/3112

s.11, applied: SI 2009/462 Art.7

s.11, varied: SI 2009/3023 Art.3, Art.5

s.12, applied: SI 2009/660 Sch.2 para.3, SI 2009/3112 Reg.14, Sch.2 para.3, Sch.2 para.10

s.12, varied: SI 2009/3023 Art.6

s.13, applied: SI 2009/3112 Reg.5

s.13, enabling: SI 2009/3112

s.16, enabling: SI 2009/660, SI 2009/3112

s.17, applied: SI 2009/660 Sch.2 para.1, SI 2009/3112 Reg.6, Sch.2 para.1

s.17, enabling: SI 2009/3112

s.18, applied: SI 2009/660 Sch.2 para.1, SI 2009/3112 Sch.2 para.1

s.19, applied: SI 2009/660 Reg.9, SI 2009/3112 Reg.8

s.20, applied: SI 2009/660, SI 2009/3112

s.20, enabling: SI 2009/660, SI 2009/3112

s.26, applied: SI 2009/462 Art.7, SI 2009/660 Reg.9, SI 2009/3112 Reg.8

s.28, applied: SI 2009/462 Art.7, SI 2009/660 Reg.9, SI 2009/3112 Reg.8

s.29, applied: SI 2009/660 Reg.9, Sch.2 para.11, SI 2009/3112 Reg.8, Sch.2 para.13

2008– cont.

14. Health and Social Care Act 2008– *cont.*

s.30, applied: SI 2009/660 Reg.10, Sch.2 para.1, Sch.2 para.8, SI 2009/3112 Reg.9, Sch.2 para.1, Sch.2 para.8

s.30, enabling: SI 2009/660, SI 2009/3112

s.31, applied: SI 2009/660 Sch.2 para.1, Sch.2 para.3, SI 2009/3112 Sch.2 para.1, Sch.2 para.3

s.32, amended: SI 2009/56 Sch.1 para.474

s.32, applied: SI 2009/660 Sch.2 para.5, Sch.2 para.8, SI 2009/3112 Sch.2 para.5, Sch.2 para.8

s.32, referred to: SI 2009/660 Sch.2 para.8, SI 2009/3112 Sch.2 para.8

s.33, applied: SI 2009/660 Sch.1

s.34, applied: SI 2009/660 Sch.1

s.35, enabling: SI 2009/660

s.39, applied: SI 2009/660 Reg.10, SI 2009/3112 Reg.9

s.39, disapplied: SI 2009/660 Reg.9, SI 2009/3112 Reg.8

s.39, enabling: SI 2009/660, SI 2009/3112

s.41, enabling: SI 2009/3112

s.42, enabling: SI 2009/3112

s.48, applied: SI 2009/1360 Art.3

s.49, enabling: SI 2009/3049

s.50, applied: SI 2009/1360 Art.3

s.53, enabling: SI 2009/410

s.54, applied: SI 2009/1360 Art.3

s.59, enabling: SI 2009/410

s.60, applied: SI 2009/1360 Art.3

s.63, applied: SI 2009/660 Sch.1, SI 2009/3112 Sch.2 para.4, Sch.2 para.12

s.64, applied: SI 2009/660 Sch.1, SI 2009/3112 Sch.2 para.4, Sch.2 para.12

s.65, applied: SI 2009/660 Sch.1, SI 2009/3112 Sch.2 para.4, Sch.2 para.12

s.65, enabling: SI 2009/660, SI 2009/3112

s.76, applied: SI 2009/3112 Sch.2 para.2, Sch.2 para.9, Sch.2 para.11

s.76, disapplied: SI 2009/660 Sch.2 para.2, Sch.2 para.9, Sch.2 para.10

s.85, applied: SI 2009/3112 Reg.6

s.86, applied: SI 2009/660 Reg.7, Sch.2 para.4, SI 2009/3112 Sch.2 para.4, Sch.2 para.12

s.86, enabling: SI 2009/660

s.87, applied: SI 2009/3112 Sch.2 para.7

s.87, enabling: SI 2009/660

s.89, enabling: SI 2009/660, SI 2009/3112

s.94, applied: SI 2009/660 Reg.7

s.132, enabling: SI 2009/751

s.135, enabling: SI 2009/751

s.149, applied: SI 2009/649 Reg.8

s.150, applied: SI 2009/649 Reg.3, Reg.4, Reg.5, Reg.8

s.150, enabling: SI 2009/649

s.151, applied: SI 2009/649 Reg.8

s.152, applied: SI 2009/649 Reg.8

s.153, applied: SI 2009/649 Reg.8

s.154, applied: SI 2009/649 Reg.8

s.155, applied: SI 2009/649 Reg.8

s.156, amended: SI 2009/462 Art.14

s.156, applied: SI 2009/649 Reg.8

s.161, enabling: SI 2009/410, SI 2009/462, SI 2009/580, SI 2009/649, SI 2009/660, SI 2009/2722, SI 2009/3023, SI 2009/3049, SI 2009/3112

s.162, applied: SI 2009/660

s.167, enabling: SI 2009/462, SI 2009/580, SI 2009/3023

2008– cont.

14. Health and Social Care Act 2008– *cont.*

s.170, enabling: SI 2009/270, SI 2009/462, SI 2009/631, SI 2009/1310, SI 2009/2567, SI 2009/2862, SI 2009/3023

s.172, applied: SI 2009/270

Sch.5 Part 2 para.37, referred to: 2009 c.21 Sch.1 para.5

Sch.5 Part 2 para.38, referred to: 2009 c.21 Sch.1 para.5

Sch.6 para.4, applied: SI 2009/2722 Reg.2

Sch.6 para.5, enabling: SI 2009/2722

Sch.6 para.6, applied: SI 2009/2722 Reg.3

Sch.6 para.7, enabling: SI 2009/2722

15. Criminal Evidence (Witness Anonymity) Act 2008

see *R. v Mayers (Jordan)* [2008] EWCA Crim 2989, [2009] 1 W.L.R. 1915 (CA (Crim Div)), Lord Judge, L.C.J.

applied: 2009 c.25 Sch.22 para.16, Sch.22 para.18, Sch.22 para.19

s.1, repealed: 2009 c.25 Sch.23 Part 3

s.2, see *R. v Mayers (Jordan)* [2008] EWCA Crim 2989, [2009] 1 W.L.R. 1915 (CA (Crim Div)), Lord Judge, L.C.J.

s.2, repealed: 2009 c.25 Sch.23 Part 3

s.3, see *R. v Mayers (Jordan)* [2008] EWCA Crim 2989, [2009] 1 W.L.R. 1915 (CA (Crim Div)), Lord Judge, L.C.J.

s.3, applied: 2009 c.25 Sch.22 para.16

s.3, repealed: 2009 c.25 Sch.23 Part 3

s.4, see *R. v Mayers (Jordan)* [2008] EWCA Crim 2989, [2009] 1 W.L.R. 1915 (CA (Crim Div)), Lord Judge, L.C.J.; see *R. v Powar (Harbinder Singh)* [2009] EWCA Crim 594, [2009] 2 Cr. App. R. 8 (CA (Crim Div)), Hallett, L.J.

s.4, referred to: 2009 c.25 Sch.22 para.16

s.4, repealed: 2009 c.25 Sch.23 Part 3

s.5, see *R. v Mayers (Jordan)* [2008] EWCA Crim 2989, [2009] 1 W.L.R. 1915 (CA (Crim Div)), Lord Judge, L.C.J.

s.5, referred to: 2009 c.25 Sch.22 para.16

s.5, repealed: 2009 c.25 Sch.23 Part 3

s.6, applied: 2009 c.25 Sch.22 para.16

s.6, referred to: SI 2009/1059 Art.179

s.6, repealed: 2009 c.25 Sch.23 Part 3

s.7, see *R. v Mayers (Jordan)* [2008] EWCA Crim 2989, [2009] 1 W.L.R. 1915 (CA (Crim Div)), Lord Judge, L.C.J.

s.7, repealed: 2009 c.25 Sch.23 Part 3

s.8, repealed: 2009 c.25 Sch.23 Part 3

s.9, repealed: 2009 c.25 Sch.23 Part 3

s.10, repealed (in part): 2009 c.25 Sch.23 Part 3

s.11, see *R. v Powar (Harbinder Singh)* [2009] EWCA Crim 594, [2009] 2 Cr. App. R. 8 (CA (Crim Div)), Hallett, L.J.

s.11, applied: 2009 c.25 Sch.22 para.17

s.14, repealed: 2009 c.25 Sch.23 Part 3

17. Housing and Regeneration Act 2008

Commencement Orders: SI 2009/363 Art.2; SI 2009/415 Art.2, Art.3, Art.4; SI 2009/773 Art.2; SI 2009/803 Art.2, Art.3, Art.7, Art.8, Art.9, Art.10; SI 2009/1261 Art.2, Art.4; SI 2009/2096 Art.2, Art.3

see *Doherty v Birmingham City Council* [2008] UKHL 57, [2009] 1 A.C. 367 (HL), Lord Hope of Craighead

s.16, repealed: 2009 c.20 Sch.7 Part 4

s.32, applied: SI 2009/803 Art.2

s.33, applied: SI 2009/803 Art.2

2008– cont.

17. Housing and Regeneration Act 2008–*cont.*
s.34, referred to: SI 2009/803 Art.2
s.49, applied: SI 2009/801 Art.2
s.49, enabling: SI 2009/801
s.50, applied: SI 2009/801 Art.2
s.50, enabling: SI 2009/801
s.61, referred to: SI 2009/803 Art.2
s.64, enabling: SI 2009/484
s.67, enabling: SI 2009/484
s.112, amended: 2009 c.20 s.26
s.174, amended: 2009 c.20 s.26
s.196, amended: 2009 c.20 s.26
s.197, amended: 2009 c.20 s.26
s.216, amended: 2009 c.20 s.26
s.278A, added: 2009 c.20 s.26
s.320, applied: SI 2009/1260, SI 2009/1262
s.320, enabling: SI 2009/484, SI 2009/801
s.322, enabling: SI 2009/415, SI 2009/803, SI 2009/
2096
s.325, enabling: SI 2009/363, SI 2009/415, SI 2009/
773, SI 2009/803, SI 2009/1261, SI 2009/2096
Sch.2 Part 1 para.11, amended: SI 2009/1307 Sch.1
para.289
Sch.4 Part 1 para.8, amended: SI 2009/2748 Sch.1
para.9
Sch.4 Part 2 para.15, amended: SI 2009/2748 Sch.1
para.9
Sch.4 Part 5 para.40, amended: SI 2009/2748 Sch.1
para.9
Sch.11 Part 2, applied: SI 2009/1260 Art.2
Sch.11 Part 2 para.16, varied: SI 2009/1260 Art.3, SI
2009/1262 Art.3
Sch.11 Part 2 para.17, varied: SI 2009/1260 Art.4, SI
2009/1262 Art.4
Sch.11 Part 2 para.18, varied: SI 2009/1260 Art.5, SI
2009/1262 Art.5
Sch.11 Part 2 para.21, varied: SI 2009/1260 Art.6, SI
2009/1262 Art.6
Sch.11 Part 2 para.24, enabling: SI 2009/1260, SI
2009/1262
Sch.11 Part 2 para.26, varied: SI 2009/1260 Art.7, SI
2009/1262 Art.7
18. Crossrail Act 2008
s.4, amended: SI 2009/229 Sch.2 para.6
s.4, applied: SI 2009/229 Art.4
Sch.4 para.12, amended: SI 2009/229 Sch.2 para.6
Sch.4 para.12, applied: SI 2009/229 Art.4
Sch.6 Part 3 para.7, amended: SI 2009/1307 Sch.1
para.290
Sch.6 Part 3 para.14, amended: SI 2009/1307 Sch.1
para.290
Sch.6 Part 3 para.15, amended: SI 2009/1307 Sch.1
para.290
Sch.6 Part 3 para.16, amended: SI 2009/1307 Sch.1
para.290
Sch.7 Part 4 para.30, enabling: SI 2009/1312
Sch.7 Part 4 para.34, enabling: SI 2009/1312
Sch.7 Part 4 para.35, enabling: SI 2009/1312
Sch.13 Part 1 para.3, amended: 2009 c.4 Sch.1
para.739
Sch.13 Part 2 para.5, amended: 2009 c.4 Sch.1
para.739
Sch.13 Part 2 para.6, amended: 2009 c.4 Sch.1
para.739
Sch.13 Part 2 para.13, amended: 2009 c.4 Sch.1
para.739
Sch.13 Part 2 para.14, amended: 2009 c.4 Sch.1
para.739

2008– cont.

18. Crossrail Act 2008– *cont.*
Sch.13 Part 2 para.15, amended: 2009 c.4 Sch.1
para.739
Sch.13 Part 3 para.18, amended: 2009 c.4 Sch.1
para.739
Sch.13 Part 3 para.23, amended: 2009 c.4 Sch.1
para.739
Sch.13 Part 3 para.24, amended: 2009 c.4 Sch.1
para.739
Sch.13 Part 6 para.34, amended: 2009 c.4 Sch.1
para.739
Sch.13 Part 6 para.40, amended: 2009 c.4 Sch.1
para.739
Sch.17 Part 2 para.2, amended: SI 2009/229 Sch.2
para.6
Sch.17 Part 2 para.2, applied: SI 2009/229 Art.4
Sch.17 Part 2 para.13, amended: SI 2009/229 Sch.2
para.6
Sch.17 Part 2 para.13, applied: SI 2009/229 Art.4
Sch.17 Part 4 para.6, amended: SI 2009/2748 Sch.1
para.10
22. Human Fertilisation and Embryology Act 2008
Commencement Orders: SI 2009/479 Art.2, Art.3,
Art.4, Art.5, Art.6, Art.7, Sch.1 para.1; SI 2009/
2232 Art.2
applied: SI 2009/1892 Sch.1 para.15, Sch.4 para.2,
Sch.4 para.3, Sch.4 para.4, Sch.4 para.9, Sch.4
para.10, Sch.4 para.11
referred to: SI 2009/1892 Sch.4 para.1, Sch.4 para.8
s.20, applied: SI 2009/1892 Sch.4 para.10
s.24, applied: SI 2009/1892 Sch.4 para.13
s.24, referred to: SI 2009/1892 Sch.4 para.13
s.37, applied: SI 2009/479 Sch.1 para.1
s.37, referred to: SI 2009/479 Sch.1 para.1
s.44, applied: SI 2009/479 Sch.1 para.1
s.44, referred to: SI 2009/479 Sch.1 para.1
s.61, enabling: SI 2009/479, SI 2009/1892, SI 2009/
2232
s.64, enabling: SI 2009/1892, SI 2009/2478
s.68, enabling: SI 2009/479, SI 2009/2232
23. Children and Young Persons Act 2008
Commencement Orders: SI 2009/268 Art.2, Art.3;
SI 2009/323 Art.2, Art.3; SI 2009/728 Art.2; SI
2009/1921 Art.2; SI 2009/2273 Art.2; SI 2009/
3354 Art.2, Art.3
s.6, enabling: SI 2009/323
s.20, enabling: SI 2009/1538
s.34, referred to: SI 2009/268 Art.4
s.40, enabling: SI 2009/728, SI 2009/1921
s.44, applied: SI 2009/268
s.44, enabling: SI 2009/268, SI 2009/323, SI 2009/
728, SI 2009/1921, SI 2009/2273, SI 2009/3354
24. Employment Act 2008
Commencement Orders: SI 2009/603 Art.2
s.22, enabling: SI 2009/603
25. Education and Skills Act 2008
Commencement Orders: 2009 c.22 Sch.16 Part 10;
SI 2009/387 Art.2, Art.3; SI 2009/784 Art.2,
Art.3, Art.5; SI 2009/1513 Art.2, Art.3; SI
2009/1606 Art.2, Art.3, Art.4; SI 2009/3316
Art.2
Part 1, applied: 2009 c.22 s.83
Part 4 c.1, applied: SI 2009/1513 Art.2A
s.2, amended: 2009 c.22 s.37
s.2, applied: 2009 c.22 s.83, s.145
s.9, repealed: 2009 c.22 Sch.16 Part 4
s.15, repealed: 2009 c.22 Sch.16 Part 10
s.17, amended: 2009 c.22 s.254
s.66, amended: 2009 c.22 s.37

2008–cont.

25. Education and Skills Act 2008–*cont.*
s.68, applied: SI 2009/1563 Reg.3
s.69, amended: 2009 c.22 s.255
s.70, applied: SI 2009/1563 Reg.3
s.75, applied: SI 2009/1360 Art.3
s.76, amended: 2009 c.22 s.254
s.76, repealed (in part): 2009 c.22 Sch.16 Part 10
s.76A, added: 2009 c.22 s.255
s.94, applied: SI 2009/1607 Reg.6
s.95, applied: SI 2009/1513 Art.2A, SI 2009/1606
   Art.5, SI 2009/1607 Reg.2, Reg.4
s.108, applied: SI 2009/1513 Art.2A, SI 2009/1607
   Reg.1
s.109, applied: SI 2009/1607 Reg.1
s.111, varied: SI 2009/1513 Art.2A
s.111, enabling: SI 2009/1607
s.112, varied: SI 2009/1606 Art.5
s.117, varied: SI 2009/1606 Art.5
s.119, applied: SI 2009/1633 Reg.2, Reg.3
s.119, varied: SI 2009/1606 Art.5
s.119, enabling: SI 2009/1633
s.124, varied: SI 2009/1606 Art.5
s.127, varied: SI 2009/1606 Art.5
s.128, applied: SI 2009/1633 Reg.3, SI 2009/2558
   Reg.3
s.130, amended: 2009 c.26 s.81
s.137, varied: SI 2009/1606 Art.5
s.140, enabling: SI 2009/1607
s.141, amended: 2009 c.26 s.81
s.159, repealed (in part): 2009 c.22 Sch.16 Part 2
s.160, repealed (in part): 2009 c.22 Sch.16 Part 2
s.161, repealed: 2009 c.22 Sch.16 Part 4
s.162, repealed (in part): 2009 c.22 Sch.16 Part 4
s.163, repealed: 2009 c.22 Sch.16 Part 4
s.166, enabling: SI 2009/1607, SI 2009/1633
s.173, enabling: SI 2009/387, SI 2009/784, SI 2009/
   1513, SI 2009/1606, SI 2009/3316
Sch.1 Part 1 para.23, amended: 2009 c.26 s.81

26. Local Transport Act 2008
Commencement Orders: SI 2009/107 Art.2, Art.3,
   Art.4, Art.5, Sch.1 Part 1, Sch.2 para.4, Sch.2 Part
   1, Sch.3, Sch.4 Part 1, Sch.5; SI 2009/579 Art.2,
   Sch.1 para.2, para.3; SI 2009/3242 Art.2, Art.3;
   SI 2009/3294 Art.2
applied: SI 2009/1885 Art.2, Sch.4 para.1
s.8, referred to: SI 2009/107 Sch.2 para.1
s.9, referred to: SI 2009/107 Art.5
s.10, disapplied: SI 2009/579 Sch.1 para.1
s.10, referred to: SI 2009/107 Sch.2 para.2
s.44, referred to: SI 2009/3246 Reg.1, SI 2009/3247
   Reg.1
s.51, referred to: SI 2009/107 Sch.1 para.1
s.51, repealed (in part): SI 2009/1885 Sch.3
s.60, enabling: SI 2009/365, SI 2009/366
s.62, referred to: SI 2009/107 Sch.1 para.2
s.63, referred to: SI 2009/107 Sch.1 para.2
s.64, disapplied: SI 2009/579 Sch.1 para.2
s.64, referred to: SI 2009/107 Sch.2 para.4
s.71, disapplied: SI 2009/579 Sch.1 para.3
s.71, referred to: SI 2009/107 Sch.2 para.5
s.75, amended: SI 2009/1885 Sch.1 para.27
s.76, repealed: SI 2009/1885 Sch.3
s.78, applied: 2009 c.20 s.106, s.107
s.79, amended: 2009 c.20 Sch.6 para.123
s.84, applied: 2009 c.20 s.104
s.85, applied: 2009 c.20 s.104
s.86, amended: 2009 c.20 Sch.6 para.124
s.86, applied: 2009 c.20 s.104

2008–cont.

26. Local Transport Act 2008–*cont.*
s.87, amended: 2009 c.20 Sch.6 para.125
s.87, applied: 2009 c.20 s.104
s.88, amended: 2009 c.20 Sch.6 para.126
s.88, applied: 2009 c.20 s.104
s.88, referred to: 2009 c.20 s.104
s.89, applied: 2009 c.20 s.104
s.89A, added: 2009 c.20 Sch.6 para.127
s.90, amended: 2009 c.20 Sch.6 para.128
s.90, applied: 2009 c.20 s.106, s.107
s.91, amended: 2009 c.20 Sch.6 para.129
s.97, applied: 2009 c.20 s.104
s.102A, added: 2009 c.20 Sch.6 para.130
s.110, referred to: SI 2009/107 Sch.2 para.6
s.111, referred to: SI 2009/107 Sch.2 para.6
s.134, enabling: SI 2009/107, SI 2009/579, SI 2009/
   3242, SI 2009/3294

27. Climate Change Act 2008
Part 1, applied: SI 2009/1257 Reg.3
Part 3, applied: SI 2009/1258 Art.3
s.1, referred to: SI 2009/1259
s.4, applied: SI 2009/1259
s.5, amended: SI 2009/1258 Art.2
s.5, applied: SI 2009/1259
s.5, referred to: SI 2009/1258
s.5, repealed (in part): SI 2009/1258 Art.2
s.6, applied: SI 2009/1258
s.6, enabling: SI 2009/1258
s.7, applied: SI 2009/1258(a), SI 2009/1258(b)
s.8, applied: SI 2009/1259
s.8, enabling: SI 2009/1259
s.9, applied: SI 2009/1259
s.10, referred to: SI 2009/1259
s.11, applied: SI 2009/1258(c), SI 2009/1258(d), SI
   2009/1258
s.11, enabling: SI 2009/1258
s.26, enabling: SI 2009/1257
s.27, enabling: SI 2009/1257, SI 2009/3146
s.28, applied: SI 2009/1257(a), SI 2009/1257(b), SI
   2009/1257, SI 2009/3146
s.30, applied: SI 2009/1258 Art.4
s.30, enabling: SI 2009/1258
s.34, applied: SI 2009/1258(c), SI 2009/1259
s.56, applied: 2009 asp 12 s.53, s.55, s.56
s.90, enabling: SI 2009/1257, SI 2009/3146
s.91, applied: SI 2009/1257, SI 2009/1258, SI 2009/
   1259

28. Counter-Terrorism Act 2008
Commencement Orders: SI 2009/58 Art.2; SI
   2009/1256 Art.2; SI 2009/1493 Art.2
Part 4, applied: SI 2009/2493 Reg.3, Reg.5
s.52, applied: SI 2009/2493 Reg.2
s.52, enabling: SI 2009/2493
s.64, amended: SI 2009/1911 Art.2
s.64, repealed (in part): SI 2009/1911 Art.2
s.64, enabling: SI 2009/1893, SI 2009/1911
s.85, applied: SI 2009/2195 Art.2
s.86, applied: SI 2009/2195 Art.2
s.87, applied: SI 2009/2195 Art.2
s.87, enabling: SI 2009/2195
s.88, applied: SI 2009/2195 Art.2
s.89, applied: SI 2009/2195 Art.2
s.90, applied: SI 2009/2195 Art.2
s.96, enabling: SI 2009/2493
s.100, enabling: SI 2009/58, SI 2009/1256, SI 2009/
   1493
Sch.6 para.5, varied: SI 2009/1059 Sch.2 para.17
Sch.6 para.7, varied: SI 2009/1059 Sch.2 para.17

2008–cont.

28. Counter-Terrorism Act 2008–*cont.*
Sch.6 para.13, enabling: SI 2009/1059
Sch.7 Part 2 para.3, enabling: SI 2009/2725
Sch.7 Part 3 para.9, enabling: SI 2009/2725
Sch.7 Part 3 para.13, enabling: SI 2009/2725
Sch.7 Part 4 para.14, enabling: SI 2009/2725
Sch.7 Part 6 para.26, amended: SI 2009/777 Sch.1 para.2
Sch.7 Part 6 para.26A, added: SI 2009/777 Sch.1 para.3
Sch.7 Part 6 para.26B, added: SI 2009/777 Sch.1 para.3
Sch.7 Part 6 para.26C, added: SI 2009/777 Sch.1 para.3
Sch.7 Part 6 para.26D, added: SI 2009/777 Sch.1 para.3
Sch.7 Part 6 para.26E, added: SI 2009/777 Sch.1 para.3
Sch.7 Part 6 para.26F, added: SI 2009/777 Sch.1 para.3
Sch.7 Part 6 para.28, amended: SI 2009/777 Sch.1 para.4, SI 2009/1835 Sch.1 para.11
Sch.7 Part 6 para.28, repealed (in part): SI 2009/777 Sch.1 para.4, SI 2009/1835 Sch.1 para.11

29. Planning Act 2008
Commencement Orders: SI 2009/400 Art.2, Art.3, Art.4, Art.5, Art.6, Sch.1 Part 1, 2; SI 2009/1303 Art.2, Sch.1; SI 2009/2260 Art.2, Art.3, Art.4; SI 2009/2573 Art.2
Part 5, applied: SI 2009/2263 Reg.9, SI 2009/2264 Reg.5
Part 5 c.2, applied: 2009 c.23 s.23
Part 6, applied: 2009 c.23 s.23
s.7, applied: SI 2009/1302 Reg.3
s.7, enabling: SI 2009/1302
s.14, applied: 2009 c.23 s.12, s.13
s.15, applied: 2009 c.23 s.12, s.13
s.37, applied: SI 2009/2264 Reg.5
s.37, enabling: SI 2009/2264
s.38, applied: SI 2009/2265 Art.2
s.38, enabling: SI 2009/2265
s.42, applied: SI 2009/2263 Reg.6, SI 2009/2264 Reg.3
s.42, referred to: SI 2009/2264 Reg.12
s.42, substituted: 2009 c.23 s.23
s.42, enabling: SI 2009/2264
s.43, substituted: 2009 c.23 s.23
s.44, substituted: 2009 c.23 s.23
s.47, applied: SI 2009/2263 Reg.10
s.48, applied: SI 2009/2263 Reg.11, SI 2009/2264 Reg.4
s.48, enabling: SI 2009/2264
s.51, applied: SI 2009/2264 Reg.11
s.51, enabling: SI 2009/2264
s.53, amended: SI 2009/1307 Sch.1 para.292
s.55, amended: 2009 c.23 s.23
s.55, applied: SI 2009/2264 Reg.12
s.56, amended: 2009 c.23 s.23
s.56, applied: SI 2009/2263 Reg.13, SI 2009/2264 Reg.8, Reg.10, Sch.3
s.56, enabling: SI 2009/2264
s.58, applied: SI 2009/2264 Reg.10
s.58, enabling: SI 2009/2264
s.59, enabling: SI 2009/2264
s.102, amended: 2009 c.23 s.23
s.104, amended: 2009 c.23 s.58
s.148, repealed: 2009 c.23 Sch.8 para.4, Sch.22 Part 2
s.149, repealed: 2009 c.23 Sch.8 para.4, Sch.22 Part 2

2008–cont.

29. Planning Act 2008–*cont.*
s.149A, added: 2009 c.23 Sch.8 para.4
s.152, amended: SI 2009/1307 Sch.1 para.293
s.161, amended: 2009 c.23 Sch.8 para.4
s.165, amended: SI 2009/1307 Sch.1 para.294
s.179, repealed: 2009 c.20 Sch.7 Part 4
s.181, repealed: 2009 c.20 Sch.7 Part 4
s.192, amended: SI 2009/1307 Sch.1 para.295
s.219, amended: SI 2009/1307 Sch.1 para.296
s.229, referred to: SI 2009/2263 Reg.25
s.230, referred to: SI 2009/2263 Reg.25
s.231, referred to: SI 2009/2263 Reg.25
s.232, enabling: SI 2009/1302, SI 2009/2264
s.241, enabling: SI 2009/400, SI 2009/1303, SI 2009/2260, SI 2009/2573
Sch.4 para.1, amended: 2009 c.23 Sch.8 para.4
Sch.5 Part 1 para.27, referred to: 2009 c.23 Sch.9 para.2
Sch.5 Part 1 para.27, repealed: 2009 c.23 Sch.8 para.4, Sch.22 Part 2
Sch.5 Part 1 para.28, referred to: 2009 c.23 Sch.9 para.2
Sch.5 Part 1 para.28, repealed: 2009 c.23 Sch.8 para.4, Sch.22 Part 2
Sch.5 Part 1 para.29, referred to: 2009 c.23 Sch.9 para.4
Sch.5 Part 1 para.29, repealed: 2009 c.23 Sch.8 para.4, Sch.22 Part 2
Sch.5 Part 1 para.30, referred to: 2009 c.23 Sch.9 para.4
Sch.5 Part 1 para.30, repealed: 2009 c.23 Sch.8 para.4, Sch.22 Part 2
Sch.5 Part 1 para.30A, added: 2009 c.23 Sch.8 para.4
Sch.5 Part 1 para.30B, added: 2009 c.23 Sch.8 para.4
Sch.6 para.2, amended: 2009 c.23 Sch.8 para.4
Sch.6 para.5, amended: 2009 c.23 Sch.8 para.4
Sch.6 para.6, amended: SI 2009/1307 Sch.1 para.297
Sch.6 para.7, amended: SI 2009/1307 Sch.1 para.297
Sch.12 para.7, amended: SI 2009/1307 Sch.1 para.298
Sch.12 para.20, amended: SI 2009/1307 Sch.1 para.298
Sch.12 para.22, amended: SI 2009/1307 Sch.1 para.298

30. Pensions Act 2008
Commencement Orders: SI 2009/82 Art.2; SI 2009/809 Art.2; SI 2009/1566 Art.2
s.35, applied: SI 2009/1888 Reg.2
s.36, applied: SI 2009/1888 Reg.2
s.37, applied: SI 2009/1888 Reg.2
s.40, applied: SI 2009/1888 Reg.2
s.41, applied: SI 2009/1888 Reg.2
s.42, applied: SI 2009/1888 Reg.2
s.43, applied: SI 2009/1888 Reg.2
s.51, applied: SI 2009/1888 Reg.2
s.52, applied: SI 2009/1888 Reg.2
s.143, enabling: SI 2009/1566
s.144, enabling: SI 2009/809, SI 2009/1566
s.145, enabling: SI 2009/598
s.149, enabling: SI 2009/82, SI 2009/809, SI 2009/1566

31. Dormant Bank and Building Society Accounts Act 2008
Commencement Orders: SI 2009/490 Art.2, Art.3
applied: SI 2009/317 Art.7

2008– cont.

31. Dormant Bank and Building Society Accounts Act 2008– *cont.*
varied: SI 2009/317 Sch.1
s.l, applied: SI 2009/317 Art.7
s.2, applied: SI 2009/317 Art.7
s.5, varied: SI 2009/490 Art.3
s.31, enabling: SI 2009/490
Sch.1 para.1, varied: SI 2009/490 Art.3
Sch.1 para.2, varied: SI 2009/490 Art.3

32. Energy Act 2008
Commencement Orders: SI 2009/45 Art.2, Art.3, Art.4; SI 2009/559 Art.2; SI 2009/1270 Art.2; SI 2009/2809 Art.2, Art.3, Art.4
Part 1 c.2, applied: SI 2009/2813 Sch.1, SI 2009/2814 Sch.1 para.22
s.l, amended: 2009 c.23 Sch.4 para.5
s.l, applied: 2009 c.23 s.77, SI 2009/223 Art.2
s.l, enabling: SI 2009/223
s.2, applied: SI 2009/2809 Art.4, SI 2009/2813 Reg.3, SI 2009/2814 Reg.2, Sch.1 para.2
s.2, disapplied: SI 2009/2809 Art.3
s.4, applied: 2009 c.23 s.77, SI 2009/2809 Art.4, SI 2009/2814 Reg.2, Sch.1 para.2
s.5, enabling: SI 2009/2813
s.7, applied: SI 2009/2813 Reg.3
s.7, enabling: SI 2009/2813, SI 2009/2814
s.8, disapplied: SI 2009/2809 Art.3
s.15, applied: SI 2009/2813 Sch.1
s.18, applied: 2009 c.23 s.77
s.35, amended: 2009 c.23 Sch.4 para.5
s.38, enabling: SI 2009/556
s.79A, added: 2009 c.23 s.314
s.79B, added: 2009 c.23 s.314
s.79C, added: 2009 c.23 s.314
s.79D, added: 2009 c.23 s.314
s.79E, added: 2009 c.23 s.314
s.79F, added: 2009 c.23 s.314
s.79G, added: 2009 c.23 s.314
s.79H, added: 2009 c.23 s.314
s.79I, added: 2009 c.23 s.314
s.79J, added: 2009 c.23 s.314
s.79K, added: 2009 c.23 s.314
s.79L, added: 2009 c.23 s.314
s.79M, added: 2009 c.23 s.314
s.79N, added: 2009 c.23 s.314
s.79O, added: 2009 c.23 s.314
s.79P, added: 2009 c.23 s.314
s.79Q, added: 2009 c.23 s.314
s.104, enabling: SI 2009/2813, SI 2009/2814
s.105, amended: 2009 c.23 s.314
s.110, enabling: SI 2009/45, SI 2009/559, SI 2009/1270, SI 2009/2809

2. Learner Travel (Wales) Measure 2008 (c.02) 2008
Commencement Orders: SI 2009/371 Art.2, Sch.1 Part 1, 2; SI 2009/2819 Art.2
s.2, applied: SI 2009/569 Sch.1 para.1, Sch.1 para.3
s.3, applied: SI 2009/569 Sch.1 para.2, Sch.1 para.3
s.4, applied: SI 2009/569 Sch.1 para.2, Sch.1 para.4
s.6, applied: SI 2009/569 Sch.1 para.5
s.16, enabling: SI 2009/569
s.27, enabling: SI 2009/569
s.28, enabling: SI 2009/371, SI 2009/2819

2009

1. Banking Act 2009
Commencement Orders: SI 2009/296 Art.2, Art.3, Sch.1 para.1, para.2, para.3, para.4, para.5, para.6, para.7, para.8, para.9, para.10, para.11, para.12, para.13, para.14, para.15, para.16, para.17; SI 2009/1296 Art.2, Sch.1 para.1, para.2, para.3, para.4, para.5, para.6; SI 2009/2038 Art.2, Sch.1 para.1, para.2, para.3, para.4, para.5; SI 2009/3000 Art.2, Art.3, Art.4, Sch.1 para.1, para.2, para.3, para.4, para.5
Royal Assent, February 12, 2009
applied: SI 2009/350 r.4, SI 2009/356 r.3, r.16, r.188, r.209
referred to: SI 2009/351 r.4, SI 2009/356 r.6, SI 2009/357 r.4
Part 1, applied: SI 2009/319 Reg.7, SI 2009/350 r.27, SI 2009/351 r.96, SI 2009/356 r.187, SI 2009/357 r.35, SI 2009/805 Sch.2 para.2, SI 2009/807 Reg.5
Part 1, referred to: SI 2009/1805
Part 2, applied: SI 2009/317 Art.6, SI 2009/351 r.3, r.5, SI 2009/356 r.3, r.4, r.206, r.224, SI 2009/805 Sch.2 para.2, SI 2009/807 Reg.5, SI 2009/853 Reg.1
Part 2, referred to: SI 2009/351 r.3, SI 2009/356 r.3
Part 3, applied: SI 2009/314 Reg.8, SI 2009/317 Art.6, SI 2009/350 r.6, SI 2009/357 r.6, r.50, r.51, SI 2009/805 Sch.2 para.2, SI 2009/806 r.6, SI 2009/807 Reg.5, SI 2009/853 Reg.1
Part 3, referred to: SI 2009/806 r.40
Part 6, applied: SI 2009/3056 Reg.16
s.3, disapplied: SI 2009/312 Sch.1
s.11, applied: SI 2009/319 Reg.2, Reg.6, SI 2009/322 Art.2, SI 2009/350 r.13, SI 2009/357 r.15, SI 2009/806 r.13
s.12, applied: SI 2009/314 Reg.3, SI 2009/319 Reg.2, Reg.6, SI 2009/322 Art.2, SI 2009/350 r.21, SI 2009/357 r.29, r.61, SI 2009/806 r.20, r.41, SI 2009/807 Reg.11
s.13, applied: SI 2009/313 Reg.3, SI 2009/319 Reg.2, Reg.6, SI 2009/322 Art.2, SI 2009/807 Reg.3, Reg.11
s.34, applied: SI 2009/322 Art.7A
s.38, applied: SI 2009/1800 Art.9, Sch.2 para.3, Sch.2 para.4
s.38, referred to: SI 2009/322 Art.9
s.39, applied: SI 2009/319 Reg.2, SI 2009/322 Art.2, Art.3, Art.5, Art.6
s.42, applied: SI 2009/322 Art.2
s.43, applied: SI 2009/319 Reg.2, SI 2009/322 Art.2, Art.12
s.44, applied: SI 2009/322 Art.2, Art.8, Art.12
s.45, applied: SI 2009/313 Reg.3, SI 2009/319 Reg.2, SI 2009/322 Art.2, Art.12
s.46, applied: SI 2009/322 Art.2, Art.8, Art.12
s.47, applied: SI 2009/1826
s.47, enabling: SI 2009/322, SI 2009/1826
s.48, applied: SI 2009/1826
s.48, enabling: SI 2009/322, SI 2009/1826
s.49, enabling: SI 2009/1800
s.50, enabling: SI 2009/1800
s.52, enabling: SI 2009/1800
s.54, applied: SI 2009/319 Reg.4, SI 2009/807 Reg.7
s.54, enabling: SI 2009/1800
s.55, applied: SI 2009/319 Reg.4, SI 2009/1800 Sch.2 para.13, SI 2009/1810 Art.5, Art.11
s.55, enabling: SI 2009/1810
s.56, applied: SI 2009/319 Reg.4
s.56, enabling: SI 2009/1810

2009– cont.

1. **Banking Act 2009**–*cont.*

s.57, applied: SI 2009/319 Reg.7, SI 2009/1800 Sch.2 para.9

s.57, enabling: SI 2009/1800

s.58, enabling: SI 2009/1800

s.59, applied: SI 2009/319 Reg.4

s.59, enabling: SI 2009/1800

s.60, enabling: SI 2009/319

s.61, applied: SI 2009/807 Reg.5

s.61, enabling: SI 2009/1800

s.62, applied: SI 2009/1800

s.75, enabling: SI 2009/814, SI 2009/1805

s.82, applied: SI 2009/319 Reg.2, Reg.6, SI 2009/322 Art.2

s.83, applied: SI 2009/319 Reg.2, SI 2009/322 Art.2

s.84, referred to: SI 2009/814

s.90, varied: SI 2009/317 Art.3, SI 2009/805 Sch.1 para.2, Sch.1 para.3, Sch.1 para.4

s.91, applied: SI 2009/317 Art.7

s.91, varied: SI 2009/317 Art.3, SI 2009/805 Sch.1 para.2, Sch.1 para.3, Sch.1 para.4, Sch.1 para.7

s.92, varied: SI 2009/317 Art.3, SI 2009/805 Sch.1 para.2, Sch.1 para.3, Sch.1 para.4

s.93, varied: SI 2009/317 Art.3, SI 2009/805 Sch.1 para.2, Sch.1 para.3, Sch.1 para.4, Sch.1 para.8

s.94, varied: SI 2009/317 Art.3, SI 2009/805 Sch.1 para.2, Sch.1 para.3, Sch.1 para.4

s.95, applied: SI 2009/351 r.3, r.6, r.8, SI 2009/356 r.3

s.95, disapplied: SI 2009/356 r.188

s.95, varied: SI 2009/317 Art.3, SI 2009/805 Sch.1 para.2, Sch.1 para.3, Sch.1 para.4, Sch.1 para.9

s.96, varied: SI 2009/317 Art.3, SI 2009/805 Sch.1 para.2, Sch.1 para.3, Sch.1 para.4, Sch.1 para.10

s.97, varied: SI 2009/317 Art.3, SI 2009/805 Sch.1 para.2, Sch.1 para.3, Sch.1 para.4, Sch.1 para.11

s.98, varied: SI 2009/317 Art.3, SI 2009/805 Sch.1 para.2, Sch.1 para.3, Sch.1 para.4, Sch.1 para.12

s.99, varied: SI 2009/317 Art.3, SI 2009/805 Sch.1 para.2, Sch.1 para.3, Sch.1 para.4

s.100, applied: SI 2009/351 r.24, SI 2009/356 r.41

s.100, varied: SI 2009/317 Art.3, SI 2009/805 Sch.1 para.2, Sch.1 para.3, Sch.1 para.4

s.101, varied: SI 2009/317 Art.3, SI 2009/805 Sch.1 para.2, Sch.1 para.3, Sch.1 para.4

s.102, referred to: SI 2009/351 r.9, SI 2009/356 r.18

s.102, varied: SI 2009/317 Art.3, SI 2009/805 Sch.1 para.2, Sch.1 para.3, Sch.1 para.4

s.103, referred to: SI 2009/317 Art.6, SI 2009/351 r.8

s.103, varied: SI 2009/317 Art.3, SI 2009/805 Sch.1 para.2, Sch.1 para.3, Sch.1 para.4, Sch.1 para.13, SI 2009/3056 Sch.1 para.4

s.104, varied: SI 2009/317 Art.3, SI 2009/805 Sch.1 para.2, Sch.1 para.3, Sch.1 para.4, SI 2009/3056 Sch.1 para.4

s.105, varied: SI 2009/317 Art.3, SI 2009/805 Sch.1 para.2, Sch.1 para.3, Sch.1 para.4

s.106, varied: SI 2009/317 Art.3, SI 2009/805 Sch.1 para.2, Sch.1 para.3, Sch.1 para.4

s.107, varied: SI 2009/317 Art.3, SI 2009/805 Sch.1 para.2, Sch.1 para.3, Sch.1 para.4

s.108, varied: SI 2009/317 Art.3, SI 2009/805 Sch.1 para.2, Sch.1 para.3, Sch.1 para.4

s.109, applied: SI 2009/351 r.41, SI 2009/356 r.42

s.109, referred to: SI 2009/351 r.36

s.109, varied: SI 2009/317 Art.3, SI 2009/805 Sch.1 para.2, Sch.1 para.3, Sch.1 para.4

s.110, varied: SI 2009/317 Art.3, SI 2009/805 Sch.1 para.2, Sch.1 para.3, Sch.1 para.4

s.111, referred to: SI 2009/351 r.41

2009– cont.

1. **Banking Act 2009**–*cont.*

s.111, varied: SI 2009/317 Art.3, SI 2009/805 Sch.1 para.2, Sch.1 para.3, Sch.1 para.4

s.112, varied: SI 2009/317 Art.3, SI 2009/805 Sch.1 para.2, Sch.1 para.3, Sch.1 para.4

s.113, varied: SI 2009/317 Art.3, SI 2009/805 Sch.1 para.2, Sch.1 para.3, Sch.1 para.4, Sch.1 para.14

s.114, varied: SI 2009/317 Art.3, SI 2009/805 Sch.1 para.2, Sch.1 para.3, Sch.1 para.4, Sch.1 para.15

s.115, applied: SI 2009/351 r.44, SI 2009/356 r.96, SI 2009/805 Sch.1 para.18

s.115, varied: SI 2009/317 Art.3, SI 2009/805 Sch.1 para.2, Sch.1 para.3, Sch.1 para.4, Sch.1 para.16

s.116, applied: SI 2009/351 r.86, r.87, SI 2009/356 r.179, r.180

s.116, varied: SI 2009/317 Art.3, SI 2009/805 Sch.1 para.2, Sch.1 para.3, Sch.1 para.4, Sch.1 para.17

s.117, varied: SI 2009/317 Art.3, SI 2009/805 Sch.1 para.2, Sch.1 para.3, Sch.1 para.4, Sch.1 para.19

s.118, varied: SI 2009/317 Art.3, SI 2009/805 Sch.1 para.2, Sch.1 para.3, Sch.1 para.4, Sch.1 para.19

s.119, varied: SI 2009/317 Art.3, SI 2009/805 Sch.1 para.2, Sch.1 para.3, Sch.1 para.4, Sch.1 para.20

s.120, applied: SI 2009/350 r.13, SI 2009/356 r.10, SI 2009/357 r.12, r.15, r.22

s.120, varied: SI 2009/317 Art.3, SI 2009/805 Sch.1 para.2, Sch.1 para.3, Sch.1 para.4, Sch.1 para.21

s.121, varied: SI 2009/317 Art.3, SI 2009/805 Sch.1 para.2, Sch.1 para.3, Sch.1 para.4, Sch.1 para.21

s.122, varied: SI 2009/317 Art.3, SI 2009/805 Sch.1 para.2, Sch.1 para.3, Sch.1 para.4

s.123, varied: SI 2009/317 Art.3, SI 2009/805 Sch.1 para.2, Sch.1 para.3, Sch.1 para.4

s.124, varied: SI 2009/317 Art.3, SI 2009/805 Sch.1 para.2, Sch.1 para.3, Sch.1 para.4, Sch.1 para.22

s.125, applied: SI 2009/356

s.125, varied: SI 2009/317 Art.3, SI 2009/805 Sch.1 para.2, Sch.1 para.3, Sch.1 para.4

s.126, varied: SI 2009/317 Art.3, SI 2009/805 Sch.1 para.2, Sch.1 para.3, Sch.1 para.4

s.127, varied: SI 2009/317 Art.3, SI 2009/805 Sch.1 para.2, Sch.1 para.3, Sch.1 para.4

s.128, varied: SI 2009/317 Art.3, SI 2009/805 Sch.1 para.2, Sch.1 para.3, Sch.1 para.4

s.129, varied: SI 2009/317 Art.3, SI 2009/805 Sch.1 para.2, Sch.1 para.3, Sch.1 para.4

s.130, referred to: SI 2009/805

s.130, varied: SI 2009/317 Art.3, SI 2009/805 Sch.1 para.2, Sch.1 para.3, Sch.1 para.4, Sch.1 para.23

s.130, enabling: SI 2009/805

s.131, varied: SI 2009/317 Art.3, SI 2009/805 Sch.1 para.2, Sch.1 para.3, Sch.1 para.4, Sch.1 para.23

s.132, varied: SI 2009/317 Art.3, SI 2009/805 Sch.1 para.2, Sch.1 para.3, Sch.1 para.4, Sch.1 para.23

s.133, varied: SI 2009/317 Art.3, SI 2009/805 Sch.1 para.2, Sch.1 para.3, Sch.1 para.4, Sch.1 para.23

s.134, varied: SI 2009/317 Art.3, SI 2009/805 Sch.1 para.2, Sch.1 para.3, Sch.1 para.4, SI 2009/3056 Sch.1 para.4

s.135, varied: SI 2009/317 Art.3, SI 2009/805 Sch.1 para.2, Sch.1 para.3, Sch.1 para.4

s.135, enabling: SI 2009/317

s.136, varied: SI 2009/312, SI 2009/312 Sch.1, SI 2009/317 Art.3, SI 2009/805 Sch.1 para.2, Sch.1 para.3, Sch.1 para.4, Sch.1 para.32

s.137, varied: SI 2009/312 Sch.1, SI 2009/317 Art.3, SI 2009/805 Sch.1 para.2, Sch.1 para.3, Sch.1 para.4, Sch.1 para.32

2009– cont.

1. **Banking Act 2009**–*cont.*

s.138, varied: SI 2009/312, SI 2009/312 Sch.1, SI 2009/317 Art.3, SI 2009/805 Sch.1 para.2, Sch.1 para.3, Sch.1 para.4, Sch.1 para.32

s.138A, varied: SI 2009/313 Sch.1, SI 2009/317 Art.3, SI 2009/805 Sch.1 para.2, Sch.1 para.3, Sch.1 para.4, Sch.1 para.32

s.139, varied: SI 2009/312, SI 2009/312 Sch.1, SI 2009/313 Sch.1, SI 2009/317 Art.3, SI 2009/805 Sch.1 para.2, Sch.1 para.3, Sch.1 para.4, Sch.1 para.32

s.140, varied: SI 2009/312, SI 2009/312 Sch.1, SI 2009/317 Art.3, SI 2009/805 Sch.1 para.2, Sch.1 para.3, Sch.1 para.4, Sch.1 para.25, Sch.1 para.32

s.141, varied: SI 2009/317 Art.3, SI 2009/805 Sch.1 para.2, Sch.1 para.3, Sch.1 para.4, Sch.1 para.32

s.142, varied: SI 2009/312, SI 2009/317 Art.3, SI 2009/805 Sch.1 para.2, Sch.1 para.3, Sch.1 para.4, Sch.1 para.32

s.143, referred to: SI 2009/357 r.12

s.143, varied: SI 2009/312 Reg.3, Sch.1, SI 2009/313 Sch.1, SI 2009/317 Art.3, SI 2009/805 Sch.1 para.2, Sch.1 para.3, Sch.1 para.4, Sch.1 para.32

s.144, varied: SI 2009/317 Art.3, SI 2009/805 Sch.1 para.2, Sch.1 para.3, Sch.1 para.4, Sch.1 para.32

s.145, applied: SI 2009/350 r.21, r.22, r.23, r.24, r.31, r.38, SI 2009/357 r.29, SI 2009/805 Sch.1 para.29, SI 2009/806 r.20, r.37, r.40

s.145, referred to: SI 2009/317 Art.6, SI 2009/357 r.30, r.31, r.32, r.34, r.39, r.40, r.57, r.61, SI 2009/806 r.20, r.21, r.22, r.23, r.30, r.41

s.145, varied: SI 2009/312, SI 2009/312 Reg.4, Sch.1, SI 2009/317 Art.3, SI 2009/805 Sch.1 para.2, Sch.1 para.3, Sch.1 para.4, Sch.1 para.26, Sch.1 para.27, Sch.1 para.28, Sch.1 para.32, SI 2009/3056 Sch.1 para.4

s.146, varied: SI 2009/317 Art.3, SI 2009/805 Sch.1 para.2, Sch.1 para.3, Sch.1 para.4, Sch.1 para.32

s.147, applied: SI 2009/350 r.20, r.22, SI 2009/357 r.28, r.30, SI 2009/806 r.19, r.21

s.147, varied: SI 2009/312, SI 2009/317 Art.3, SI 2009/805 Sch.1 para.2, Sch.1 para.3, Sch.1 para.4, Sch.1 para.32

s.148, applied: SI 2009/314 Reg.3, Reg.5, Reg.6, Reg.7, Reg.8, Reg.9, Reg.10

s.148, referred to: SI 2009/314 Reg.4

s.148, varied: SI 2009/312, SI 2009/312 Sch.1, SI 2009/317 Art.3, SI 2009/805 Sch.1 para.2, Sch.1 para.3, Sch.1 para.4, Sch.1 para.32

s.148, enabling: SI 2009/314

s.149, applied: SI 2009/313 Reg.2, Reg.3

s.149, varied: SI 2009/317 Art.3, SI 2009/805 Sch.1 para.2, Sch.1 para.3, Sch.1 para.4, Sch.1 para.32

s.149, enabling: SI 2009/313

s.150, varied: SI 2009/312, SI 2009/312 Sch.1, SI 2009/313 Sch.1, SI 2009/317 Art.3, SI 2009/805 Sch.1 para.2, Sch.1 para.3, Sch.1 para.4, Sch.1 para.32

s.151, varied: SI 2009/312 Reg.3, Sch.1, SI 2009/317 Art.3, SI 2009/805 Sch.1 para.2, Sch.1 para.3, Sch.1 para.4, Sch.1 para.32

s.152, applied: SI 2009/312, SI 2009/313 Reg.3

s.152, varied: SI 2009/312, SI 2009/317 Art.3, SI 2009/805 Sch.1 para.2, Sch.1 para.3, Sch.1 para.4, Sch.1 para.32

s.152, enabling: SI 2009/312, SI 2009/805

s.153, applied: SI 2009/350 r.25, r.36, SI 2009/357 r.33, r.48, SI 2009/806 r.24

s.153, referred to: SI 2009/806 r.35, r.41

2009– cont.

1. **Banking Act 2009**–*cont.*

s.153, varied: SI 2009/312, SI 2009/317 Art.3, SI 2009/805 Sch.1 para.2, Sch.1 para.3, Sch.1 para.4, Sch.1 para.32

s.154, applied: SI 2009/350 r.20, r.21, r.37, SI 2009/357 r.28, r.29, r.49, SI 2009/806 r.19, r.20

s.154, referred to: SI 2009/806 r.36

s.154, varied: SI 2009/312, SI 2009/317 Art.3, SI 2009/805 Sch.1 para.2, Sch.1 para.3, Sch.1 para.4, Sch.1 para.32, Sch.1 para.33

s.155, varied: SI 2009/317 Art.3, SI 2009/805 Sch.1 para.2, Sch.1 para.3, Sch.1 para.4, Sch.1 para.32, Sch.1 para.34

s.156, varied: SI 2009/317 Art.3, SI 2009/805 Sch.1 para.2, Sch.1 para.3, Sch.1 para.4, Sch.1 para.32

s.157, varied: SI 2009/312, SI 2009/312 Sch.1, SI 2009/317 Art.3, SI 2009/805 Sch.1 para.2, Sch.1 para.3, Sch.1 para.4, Sch.1 para.32, Sch.1 para.35

s.158, applied: SI 2009/806 r.40

s.158, referred to: SI 2009/805

s.158, varied: SI 2009/317 Art.3, SI 2009/805 Sch.1 para.2, Sch.1 para.3, Sch.1 para.4, Sch.1 para.32, Sch.1 para.36

s.158, enabling: SI 2009/805

s.159, varied: SI 2009/317 Art.3, SI 2009/805 Sch.1 para.2, Sch.1 para.3, Sch.1 para.4, Sch.1 para.32, Sch.1 para.36

s.160, varied: SI 2009/317 Art.3, SI 2009/805 Sch.1 para.2, Sch.1 para.3, Sch.1 para.4, Sch.1 para.32

s.161, varied: SI 2009/317 Art.3, SI 2009/805 Sch.1 para.2, Sch.1 para.3, Sch.1 para.4, Sch.1 para.32

s.162, varied: SI 2009/317 Art.3, SI 2009/805 Sch.1 para.2, Sch.1 para.3, Sch.1 para.4, Sch.1 para.32

s.163, varied: SI 2009/317 Art.3, SI 2009/805 Sch.1 para.2, Sch.1 para.3, Sch.1 para.4, Sch.1 para.32, Sch.1 para.36

s.164, varied: SI 2009/317 Art.3, SI 2009/805 Sch.1 para.2, Sch.1 para.3, Sch.1 para.4, Sch.1 para.32, Sch.1 para.36

s.165, varied: SI 2009/317 Art.3, SI 2009/805 Sch.1 para.2, Sch.1 para.3, Sch.1 para.4, Sch.1 para.32

s.166, disapplied: SI 2009/805 Sch.1 para.37

s.166, varied: SI 2009/317 Art.3, SI 2009/805 Sch.1 para.2, Sch.1 para.3, Sch.1 para.4, Sch.1 para.32

s.167, varied: SI 2009/317 Art.3, SI 2009/805 Sch.1 para.2, Sch.1 para.3, Sch.1 para.4, Sch.1 para.32, SI 2009/3056 Sch.1 para.4

s.168, varied: SI 2009/317 Art.3, SI 2009/805 Sch.1 para.2, Sch.1 para.3, Sch.1 para.4, Sch.1 para.32

s.168, enabling: SI 2009/317

s.213, applied: SI 2009/3056 Reg.11, Reg.12, Reg.16, Reg.27, Reg.28

s.215, enabling: SI 2009/3056

s.216, enabling: SI 2009/3056

s.217, applied: SI 2009/3056 Reg.30

s.217, enabling: SI 2009/3056

s.218, applied: SI 2009/3056 Sch.3 para.4

s.218, enabling: SI 2009/3056

s.219, enabling: SI 2009/3056

s.220, applied: SI 2009/3056 Reg.27, Reg.28

s.220, enabling: SI 2009/3056

s.221, applied: SI 2009/3056 Reg.16

s.222, enabling: SI 2009/3056

s.223, applied: SI 2009/3056 Reg.11, Reg.12, Reg.16, Reg.28, Reg.31

s.223, enabling: SI 2009/3056

s.224, applied: SI 2009/3056 Reg.16

s.224, enabling: SI 2009/3056

s.226, enabling: SI 2009/3056

2009–cont.

1. Banking Act 2009–*cont.*
s.237, enabling: SI 2009/790, SI 2009/791
s.259, applied: SI 2009/312, SI 2009/313, SI 2009/
317, SI 2009/319, SI 2009/322, SI 2009/805
s.259, enabling: SI 2009/312, SI 2009/313, SI 2009/
314, SI 2009/319, SI 2009/322, SI 2009/805, SI
2009/814, SI 2009/1800, SI 2009/1805, SI
2009/1810, SI 2009/1826, SI 2009/3056
s.263, enabling: SI 2009/296, SI 2009/1296, SI
2009/2038, SI 2009/3000

01. Learning and Skills (Wales) Measure 2009
Commencement Orders: SI 2009/3174 Art.2
Royal Assent, May 13, 2009
s.48, enabling: SI 2009/3174
s.49, enabling: SI 2009/3174

2. Appropriation Act 2009
Royal Assent, March 12, 2009

3. Northern Ireland Act 2009
Commencement Orders: SI 2009/2466 Art.2
Royal Assent, March 12, 2009
s.5, enabling: SI 2009/2466
Sch.4 para.23, referred to: SI 2009/1307 Sch.1
para.226

4. Corporation Tax Act 2009
Royal Assent, March 26, 2009
applied: 2009 c.10 Sch.13 para.4
Part 3, applied: 2009 c.10 Sch.15 para.46, Sch.15
para.54, Sch.15 para.55, SI 2009/2971 Reg.8,
Reg.19, Reg.21, Reg.22, SI 2009/3227 Reg.4
Part 5, applied: 2009 c.10 Sch.15 para.46, Sch.15
para.54, Sch.15 para.55, Sch.24 para.15, SI
2009/2034 Reg.8, SI 2009/2971 Reg.8, Reg.19,
Reg.21, SI 2009/3173 Reg.15
Part 5, referred to: 2009 c.10 Sch.15 para.56, SI
2009/2034 Reg.8
Part 5 c.4, applied: SI 2009/3227 Reg.5
Part 5 c.8, applied: 2009 c.10 Sch.20 para.9
Part 6, applied: SI 2009/2971 Reg.8, Reg.19, Reg.21
Part 6 c.2A, applied: 2009 c.10 Sch.24 para.13
Part 6 c.7, referred to: 2009 c.10 Sch.24 para.14,
Sch.24 para.15
Part 7, applied: SI 2009/2034 Reg.8, SI 2009/2971
Reg.8, Reg.22
Part 7, referred to: SI 2009/2034 Reg.8
Part 7 c.3, substituted: 2009 c.10 Sch.21 para.5
Part 8, applied: SI 2009/2971 Reg.12, Reg.13,
Reg.28, Reg.29, SI 2009/3227 Reg.6
Part 8, referred to: SI 2009/3227 Reg.6
Part 9A, referred to: 2009 c.10 Sch.14 para.32
Part 10 c.8, applied: SI 2009/3001 Reg.16, Reg.18
Part 13, applied: SI 2009/1343 Art.2
Part 14 c.4, amended: 2009 c.10 Sch.7 para.12
Part 16, applied: 2009 c.10 Sch.15 para.65
s.1, amended: 2009 c.10 Sch.14 para.21
s.51, amended: 2009 c.10 Sch.11 para.46
s.56, amended: 2009 c.10 Sch.11 para.47
s.56, repealed (in part): 2009 c.10 Sch.11 para.47
s.57, amended: 2009 c.10 Sch.11 para.48
s.57, repealed (in part): 2009 c.10 Sch.11 para.48
s.58, repealed: 2009 c.10 Sch.11 para.49
s.58A, added: 2009 c.10 Sch.11 para.50
s.58B, added: 2009 c.10 Sch.11 para.50
s.61, disapplied: 2009 c.10 Sch.7 para.28
s.75, repealed (in part): SI 2009/2035 Sch.1 para.55
s.126, repealed: SI 2009/2035 Sch.1 para.56
s.130, amended: 2009 c.10 Sch.14 para.22
s.130, applied: SI 2009/3001 Reg.102, Reg.103
s.191, amended: 2009 c.10 Sch.11 para.51
s.210, amended: 2009 c.10 Sch.11 para.52

2009–cont.

4. Corporation Tax Act 2009–*cont.*
s.211, referred to: 2009 c.10 Sch.15 para.58
s.214, amended: 2009 c.10 Sch.11 para.53
s.245, repealed: SI 2009/2035 Sch.1 para.57
s.283, amended: 2009 c.10 Sch.11 para.54
s.297, applied: 2009 c.10 Sch.15 para.46, Sch.15
para.54, Sch.15 para.55
s.302, referred to: SI 2009/2034 Reg.11
s.311, amended: 2009 c.10 Sch.30 para.2
s.317, amended: 2009 c.10 Sch.30 para.2
s.328, amended: 2009 c.10 Sch.21 para.2
s.328A, added: 2009 c.10 Sch.21 para.3
s.328B, added: 2009 c.10 Sch.21 para.3
s.328C, added: 2009 c.10 Sch.21 para.3
s.328D, added: 2009 c.10 Sch.21 para.3
s.328E, added: 2009 c.10 Sch.21 para.3
s.328F, added: 2009 c.10 Sch.21 para.3
s.328G, added: 2009 c.10 Sch.21 para.3
s.328H, added: 2009 c.10 Sch.21 para.3
s.332, applied: SI 2009/2971 Reg.19, Reg.21
s.336, applied: SI 2009/2971 Reg.9, Reg.25, SI
2009/3227 Reg.5
s.336, referred to: SI 2009/2971 Reg.26
s.340, referred to: SI 2009/2971 Reg.26
s.344, applied: SI 2009/3227 Reg.5
s.344, referred to: SI 2009/2971 Reg.9, Reg.25
s.345, applied: SI 2009/2971 Reg.9, Reg.25
s.345, disapplied: SI 2009/2971 Reg.9, Reg.25
s.353, amended: 2009 c.10 s.42
s.353, repealed (in part): 2009 c.10 s.42
s.374, amended: 2009 c.10 Sch.20 para.2
s.375, amended: 2009 c.10 Sch.20 para.3
s.376, amended: 2009 c.10 Sch.20 para.4
s.377, substituted: 2009 c.10 Sch.20 para.5
s.383, applied: SI 2009/2860 Art.6
s.407, amended: 2009 c.10 Sch.20 para.6
s.407, applied: 2009 c.10 Sch.20 para.9
s.409, amended: 2009 c.10 Sch.20 para.7
s.409, applied: 2009 c.10 Sch.20 para.9
s.410, amended: 2009 c.10 Sch.20 para.8
s.418, amended: 2009 c.10 Sch.30 para.4
s.418A, added: 2009 c.10 Sch.30 para.4
s.457, applied: 2009 c.10 Sch.15 para.63
s.476, amended: 2009 c.10 s.42
s.477, amended: 2009 c.10 Sch.24 para.2, Sch.25
para.8
s.479, amended: 2009 c.10 s.42
s.480, applied: SI 2009/2971 Reg.19, Reg.22, Reg.24
s.481, amended: 2009 c.10 s.42
s.486A, added: 2009 c.10 Sch.24 para.3
s.486B, added: 2009 c.10 Sch.24 para.3
s.486B, applied: 2009 c.10 Sch.24 para.13
s.486C, added: 2009 c.10 Sch.24 para.3
s.486D, added: 2009 c.10 Sch.24 para.3
s.486D, applied: 2009 c.10 Sch.24 para.16
s.486E, added: 2009 c.10 Sch.24 para.3
s.486F, added: 2009 c.10 Sch.25 para.8
s.486G, added: 2009 c.10 Sch.25 para.8
s.489, amended: SI 2009/3001 Reg.131
s.490, amended: SI 2009/3001 Reg.131
s.490, applied: SI 2009/3001 Reg.104
s.502, amended: SI 2009/2568 Art.3
s.506, amended: SI 2009/2568 Art.3
s.514, amended: SI 2009/2860 Art.6
s.518, amended: SI 2009/2860 Art.6
s.521, enabling: SI 2009/2568
s.521A, added: 2009 c.10 Sch.24 para.4
s.521B, added: 2009 c.10 Sch.24 para.4

2009– cont.

4. Corporation Tax Act 2009– *cont.*
s.1156, amended: 2009 c.10 Sch.7 para.2
s.1157, amended: 2009 c.10 Sch.7 para.2
s.1158, amended: 2009 c.10 Sch.7 para.2
s.1159, amended: 2009 c.10 Sch.7 para.2
s.1160, amended: 2009 c.10 Sch.7 para.2
s.1161, amended: 2009 c.10 Sch.7 para.2, Sch.7 para.12
s.1161, repealed (in part): 2009 c.10 Sch.7 para.12
s.1162, amended: 2009 c.10 Sch.7 para.2
s.1162, substituted: 2009 c.10 Sch.7 para.13
s.1163, amended: 2009 c.10 Sch.7 para.2, Sch.7 para.14
s.1164, amended: 2009 c.10 Sch.7 para.2
s.1165, amended: 2009 c.10 Sch.7 para.2, Sch.7 para.15
s.1166, amended: 2009 c.10 Sch.7 para.2
s.1167, amended: 2009 c.10 Sch.7 para.2
s.1168, amended: 2009 c.10 Sch.7 para.2
s.1169, amended: 2009 c.10 Sch.7 para.2, Sch.7 para.16
s.1170, amended: 2009 c.10 Sch.7 para.2
s.1171, amended: 2009 c.10 Sch.7 para.2
s.1172, amended: 2009 c.10 Sch.7 para.2
s.1173, amended: 2009 c.10 Sch.7 para.2, Sch.7 para.17
s.1174, amended: 2009 c.10 Sch.7 para.2
s.1174, repealed: 2009 c.10 Sch.7 para.18
s.1175, amended: 2009 c.10 Sch.7 para.2, Sch.7 para.19
s.1175, substituted: 2009 c.10 Sch.7 para.19
s.1176, amended: 2009 c.10 Sch.7 para.2
s.1176, repealed: 2009 c.10 Sch.7 para.20
s.1177, amended: 2009 c.10 Sch.7 para.2
s.1178, amended: 2009 c.10 Sch.7 para.2, Sch.7 para.21
s.1178A, added: 2009 c.10 Sch.7 para.22
s.1178A, amended: 2009 c.10 Sch.7 para.2
s.1179, amended: 2009 c.10 Sch.7 para.2, Sch.7 para.23
s.1219, applied: 2009 c.10 Sch.15 para.65
s.1231, amended: 2009 c.10 Sch.11 para.56
s.1251, amended: 2009 c.10 Sch.11 para.57
s.1251, repealed (in part): 2009 c.10 Sch.11 para.57
s.1285, repealed: 2009 c.10 Sch.14 para.27
s.1310, amended: 2009 c.10 Sch.14 para.28
s.1310, applied: SI 2009/3314
s.1323, enabling: SI 2009/2860
s.1324, enabling: SI 2009/2860
Sch.1 Part 1 para.45, repealed: 2009 c.10 Sch.11 para.64
Sch.1 Part 1 para.174, repealed (in part): 2009 c.10 Sch.14 para.30
Sch.1 Part 1 para.214, repealed: 2009 c.10 Sch.25 para.9
Sch.1 Part 1 para.215, repealed: 2009 c.10 Sch.24 para.9
Sch.1 Part 1 para.230, repealed: 2009 c.10 Sch.25 para.9
Sch.1 Part 1 para.252, repealed: 2009 c.10 Sch.14 para.30
Sch.1 Part 1 para.253, repealed: 2009 c.10 Sch.14 para.30
Sch.1 Part 1 para.254, repealed: 2009 c.10 Sch.14 para.30
Sch.1 Part 2 para.307, repealed (in part): SI 2009/2035 Sch.1 para.60
Sch.1 Part 2 para.392, repealed (in part): 2009 c.10 Sch.14 para.30
Sch.1 Part 2 para.571, repealed: 2009 c.10 Sch.24 para.9
Sch.1 Part 2 para.651, repealed (in part): 2009 c.10 Sch.61 para.28
Sch.2 Part 6 para.16, repealed: 2009 c.10 Sch.11 para.58
Sch.2 Part 6 para.17, repealed: 2009 c.10 Sch.11 para.58

2009– cont.

4. Corporation Tax Act 2009– *cont.*
Sch.2 Part 8 para.71, amended: SI 2009/2860 Art.6
Sch.2 Part 9, amended: SI 2009/2860 Art.6
Sch.2 Part 9 para.73, amended: SI 2009/2860 Art.6
Sch.2 Part 9 para.74, amended: SI 2009/2860 Art.6
Sch.2 Part 9 para.75, amended: SI 2009/2860 Art.6
Sch.2 Part 21 para.137, amended: SI 2009/2035 Sch.1 para.59
Sch.2 Part 21 para.138, amended: SI 2009/2035 Sch.1 para.59
Sch.2 Part 21 para.138, repealed (in part): SI 2009/2035 Sch.1 para.59
Sch.3 Part 2, amended: SI 2009/2860 Art.6
Sch.4, amended: 2009 c.10 Sch.7 para.26, Sch.14 para.29, Sch.21 para.9, Sch.24 para.7, SI 2009/2860 Art.6
5. Industry and Exports (Financial Support) Act 2009
Royal Assent, May 21, 2009
6. Geneva Conventions and United Nations Personnel (Protocols) Act 2009
Commencement Orders: SI 2009/2892 Art.2
Royal Assent, July 02, 2009
s.3, enabling: SI 2009/2892
7. Business Rate Supplements Act 2009
Commencement Orders: SI 2009/2202 Art.2
Royal Assent, July 2, 2009
s.12, applied: SI 2009/2542 Reg.2
s.12, enabling: SI 2009/2542
s.18, applied: SI 2009/2543 Sch.2 para.2
s.19, applied: SI 2009/2543 Sch.2 para.2, Sch.2 para.5
s.20, applied: SI 2009/2543 Sch.2 para.5
s.29, enabling: SI 2009/2543
s.32, enabling: SI 2009/2202
Sch.3 para.2, enabling: SI 2009/2543
Sch.3 para.5, enabling: SI 2009/2543
8. Saving Gateway Accounts Act 2009
Commencement Orders: SI 2009/3332 Art.2
Royal Assent, July 02, 2009
s.2, applied: SI 2009/2997 Reg.5
s.2, enabling: SI 2009/2997
s.3, applied: SI 2009/2997 Reg.3, Reg.20
s.3, referred to: SI 2009/2997 Reg.4
s.3, repealed (in part): 2009 c.24 Sch.7 Part 1
s.3, enabling: SI 2009/2997
s.4, enabling: SI 2009/2997
s.5, enabling: SI 2009/2997
s.6, applied: SI 2009/2997 Reg.20
s.6, enabling: SI 2009/2997
s.7, enabling: SI 2009/2997
s.8, applied: SI 2009/2997 Reg.8
s.8, referred to: SI 2009/2997 Reg.9, Reg.10, Reg.22
s.8, enabling: SI 2009/2997
s.9, enabling: SI 2009/2997
s.10, enabling: SI 2009/2997
s.11, enabling: SI 2009/2997
s.12, enabling: SI 2009/2997
s.14, enabling: SI 2009/2998
s.16, enabling: SI 2009/2997
s.17, enabling: SI 2009/2997
s.19, applied: SI 2009/2997 Reg.21
s.20, applied: SI 2009/2997 Reg.21
s.21, applied: SI 2009/2997 Reg.21
s.23, applied: SI 2009/2997 Reg.15, Reg.20
s.24, enabling: SI 2009/2997, SI 2009/2998
s.28, applied: SI 2009/2998

2009– cont.

8. Saving Gateway Accounts Act 2009– *cont.*
s.28, enabling: SI 2009/2997, SI 2009/2998, SI 2009/3332
s.31, enabling: SI 2009/3332

9. Appropriation (No.2) Act 2009
Royal Assent, July 21, 2009

10. Finance Act 2009
Royal Assent, July 21, 2009
s.37, enabling: SI 2009/2192
s.45, enabling: SI 2009/2034
s.47, enabling: SI 2009/2039
s.95, enabling: SI 2009/2035
s.96, enabling: SI 2009/3054
s.124, enabling: SI 2009/2971
Sch.3 Part 1 para.2, applied: SI 2009/3127 Art.2
Sch.3 Part 2 para.15, enabling: SI 2009/3127
Sch.3 Part 5 para.22, enabling: SI 2009/3241
Sch.7 Part 3 para.27, enabling: SI 2009/2037
Sch.15 Part 3, applied: SI 2009/3173 Reg.4, Reg.5, Reg.8, Reg.9, Reg.13, Reg.19, Reg.28
Sch.15 Part 3 para.17, applied: SI 2009/3173 Reg.4, Reg.5, Reg.6, Reg.9, Reg.10, Reg.19
Sch.15 Part 3 para.17, disapplied: SI 2009/3173 Reg.7, Reg.8, Reg.9
Sch.15 Part 3 para.17, enabling: SI 2009/3173
Sch.15 Part 3 para.19, applied: SI 2009/3173 Reg.4, Reg.12
Sch.15 Part 3 para.20, applied: SI 2009/3173 Reg.4, Reg.9, Reg.13, Reg.24
Sch.15 Part 3 para.21, applied: SI 2009/3173 Reg.4, Reg.9, Reg.11, Reg.13
Sch.15 Part 3 para.24, enabling: SI 2009/3173
Sch.15 Part 3 para.25, applied: SI 2009/3173 Reg.15, Reg.18, Reg.32
Sch.15 Part 3 para.25, enabling: SI 2009/3173
Sch.15 Part 3 para.26, applied: SI 2009/3173 Reg.29
Sch.15 Part 3 para.26, enabling: SI 2009/3173
Sch.15 Part 4, applied: SI 2009/3173 Reg.19, Reg.20, Reg.23, Reg.24, Reg.28
Sch.15 Part 4 para.29, applied: SI 2009/3173 Reg.19, Reg.20, Reg.21, Reg.24, Reg.25
Sch.15 Part 4 para.29, disapplied: SI 2009/3173 Reg.20, Reg.22, Reg.23, Reg.24
Sch.15 Part 4 para.29, enabling: SI 2009/3173
Sch.15 Part 4 para.31, applied: SI 2009/3173 Reg.19, Reg.27
Sch.15 Part 4 para.32, applied: SI 2009/3173 Reg.19, Reg.28
Sch.15 Part 4 para.33, applied: SI 2009/3173 Reg.19, Reg.24, Reg.26, Reg.28, Reg.29
Sch.15 Part 4 para.36, enabling: SI 2009/3173
Sch.15 Part 4 para.38, enabling: SI 2009/3173
Sch.15 Part 5 para.40, applied: SI 2009/3173 Reg.13, Reg.28
Sch.15 Part 7 para.54, applied: SI 2009/3173 Reg.15
Sch.15 Part 7 para.60, applied: SI 2009/3313 Reg.2, Reg.4
Sch.15 Part 7 para.62, applied: SI 2009/3313, SI 2009/3313 Reg.5
Sch.15 Part 7 para.62, enabling: SI 2009/3313
Sch.15 Part 10 para.88, enabling: SI 2009/3217
Sch.16 Part 1 para.8, applied: 2009 c.4 s.931R, s.521B
Sch.17, applied: SI 2009/2192 Reg.5
Sch.17 Part 2 para.4, applied: SI 2009/2192 Reg.3
Sch.17 Part 2 para.4, enabling: SI 2009/2192
Sch.17 Part 2 para.6, applied: SI 2009/2192 Reg.2, Reg.6
Sch.17 Part 2 para.6, enabling: SI 2009/2192

2009– cont.

10. Finance Act 2009– *cont.*
Sch.17 Part 2 para.8, applied: SI 2009/2192 Reg.4, Reg.5
Sch.17 Part 2 para.8, enabling: SI 2009/2192
Sch.17 Part 2 para.9, enabling: SI 2009/2192
Sch.17 Part 3 para.14, enabling: SI 2009/2192
Sch.34 para.8, enabling: SI 2009/3315
Sch.35, referred to: SI 2009/2031 Art.2, Art.3
Sch.35 para.1, amended: SI 2009/2031 Art.4
Sch.35 para.1, varied: SI 2009/2031 Art.3
Sch.35 para.2, varied: SI 2009/2031 Art.3
Sch.35 para.3, referred to: SI 2009/2031 Art.5
Sch.35 para.3, varied: SI 2009/2031 Art.3
Sch.35 para.4, varied: SI 2009/2031 Art.3
Sch.35 para.5, varied: SI 2009/2031 Art.3
Sch.35 para.6, amended: SI 2009/2031 Art.6
Sch.35 para.6, varied: SI 2009/2031 Art.3
Sch.35 para.7, varied: SI 2009/2031 Art.3
Sch.35 para.8, amended: SI 2009/2031 Art.4
Sch.35 para.8, varied: SI 2009/2031 Art.3
Sch.35 para.9, amended: SI 2009/2031 Art.4
Sch.35 para.9, varied: SI 2009/2031 Art.3
Sch.35 para.10, amended: SI 2009/2031 Art.4
Sch.35 para.10, varied: SI 2009/2031 Art.3
Sch.35 para.11, amended: SI 2009/2031 Art.4
Sch.35 para.11, varied: SI 2009/2031 Art.3
Sch.35 para.12, varied: SI 2009/2031 Art.3
Sch.35 para.13, varied: SI 2009/2031 Art.3, Art.7
Sch.35 para.13A, varied: SI 2009/2031 Art.3
Sch.35 para.14, varied: SI 2009/2031 Art.3
Sch.35 para.15, amended: SI 2009/2031 Art.8
Sch.35 para.15, varied: SI 2009/2031 Art.3
Sch.35 para.16, amended: SI 2009/2031 Art.9
Sch.35 para.16, varied: SI 2009/2031 Art.3
Sch.35 para.17, amended: SI 2009/2031 Art.10
Sch.35 para.17, varied: SI 2009/2031 Art.3, Art.10
Sch.35 para.18, substituted: SI 2009/2031 Art.11
Sch.35 para.18, varied: SI 2009/2031 Art.3
Sch.35 para.19, varied: SI 2009/2031 Art.3
Sch.35 para.20, varied: SI 2009/2031 Art.3
Sch.35 para.20, enabling: SI 2009/2031
Sch.35 para.21, varied: SI 2009/2031 Art.3
Sch.35 para.22, varied: SI 2009/2031 Art.3
Sch.35 para.23, varied: SI 2009/2031 Art.3
Sch.61 Part 3, applied: SI 2009/2052 Reg.4, Reg.6
Sch.61 Part 3 para.5, applied: SI 2009/2052 Reg.3
Sch.61 Part 3 para.5, enabling: SI 2009/2052
Sch.61 Part 3 para.9, applied: SI 2009/2052 Reg.4
Sch.61 Part 3 para.9, enabling: SI 2009/2052
Sch.61 Part 3 para.18, applied: SI 2009/2052 Reg.5, Reg.6
Sch.61 Part 3 para.18, enabling: SI 2009/2052
Sch.61 Part 3 para.23, enabling: SI 2009/2052

11. Borders, Citizenship and Immigration Act 2009
Commencement Orders: SI 2009/2731 Art.2, Art.3, Art.4
Royal Assent, July 21, 2009
s.58, enabling: SI 2009/2731

12. Political Parties and Elections Act 2009
Commencement Orders: SI 2009/2395 Art.2, Art.3; SI 2009/3084 Art.3, Art.4, Art.5, Art.6
Royal Assent, July 21, 2009
s.43, enabling: SI 2009/2395, SI 2009/3084

13. Parliamentary Standards Act 2009
Commencement Orders: SI 2009/2500 Art.2; SI 2009/2612 Art.2
Royal Assent, July 21, 2009

2009– cont.

13. **Parliamentary Standards Act 2009**– *cont.*
    s.14, enabling: SI 2009/2500, SI 2009/2612
14. **Law Commission Act 2009**
    Royal Assent, November 12, 2009
15. **Autism Act 2009**
    Royal Assent, November 12, 2009
16. **Holocaust (Return of Cultural Objects) Act 2009**
    Royal Assent, November 12, 2009
17. **Driving Instruction (Suspension and Exemption Powers) Act 2009**
    Royal Assent, November 12, 2009
18. **Perpetuities and Accumulations Act 2009**
    Royal Assent, November 12, 2009
19. **Green Energy (Definition and Promotion) Act 2009**
    Royal Assent, November 12, 2009
20. **Local Democracy, Economic Development and Construction Act 2009**
    Commencement Orders: SI 2009/3087 Art.2; SI 2009/3318 Art.2, Art.3, Art.4
    Royal Assent, November 12, 2009
    s.148, enabling: SI 2009/3087, SI 2009/3318
21. **Health Act 2009**
    Royal Assent, November 12, 2009
22. **Apprenticeships, Skills, Children and Learning Act 2009**
    Commencement Orders: SI 2009/3317 Art.2, Sch.1; SI 2009/3341 Art.2
    Royal Assent, November 12, 2009
    s.262, enabling: SI 2009/3341
    s.269, enabling: SI 2009/3317
    Sch.9 para.2, enabling: SI 2009/3208
    Sch.15 para.1, applied: SI 2009/3337 Reg.2
    Sch.15 para.1, enabling: SI 2009/3337
23. **Marine and Coastal Access Act 2009**
    Commencement Orders: SI 2009/3345 Art.2, Art.3, Sch.1 para.2, para.3, para.4, para.5, para.6, para.7, para.8, para.9, para.10, para.11, para.12, para.13, para.14, para.15, para.16, para.17, para.18, para.19, para.20, para.21, para.22, para.23, para.24, para.25, para.26, para.27
    Royal Assent, November 12, 2009
    s.268, varied: SI 2009/3391 Art.7
    s.270, varied: SI 2009/3391 Art.7
    s.271, varied: SI 2009/3391 Art.7
    s.272, varied: SI 2009/3391 Art.7
    s.273, varied: SI 2009/3391 Art.7
    s.274, varied: SI 2009/3391 Art.7
    s.275, varied: SI 2009/3391 Art.7
    s.276, varied: SI 2009/3391 Art.7
    s.277, varied: SI 2009/3391 Art.7

2009– cont.

23. **Marine and Coastal Access Act 2009**– *cont.*
    s.278, varied: SI 2009/3391 Art.7
    s.316, enabling: SI 2009/3345
    s.324, enabling: SI 2009/3345
    Sch.18 para.1, varied: SI 2009/3391 Art.7
    Sch.18 para.2, varied: SI 2009/3391 Art.7
    Sch.18 para.3, varied: SI 2009/3391 Art.7
    Sch.18 para.4, varied: SI 2009/3391 Art.7
    Sch.18 para.5, varied: SI 2009/3391 Art.7
    Sch.18 para.6, varied: SI 2009/3391 Art.7
    Sch.18 para.7, varied: SI 2009/3391 Art.7
    Sch.18 para.8, varied: SI 2009/3391 Art.7
    Sch.18 para.9, varied: SI 2009/3391 Art.7
    Sch.18 para.10, varied: SI 2009/3391 Art.7
    Sch.18 para.11, varied: SI 2009/3391 Art.7
    Sch.18 para.12, varied: SI 2009/3391 Art.7
    Sch.18 para.13, varied: SI 2009/3391 Art.7
    Sch.18 para.14, varied: SI 2009/3391 Art.7
    Sch.18 para.15, varied: SI 2009/3391 Art.7
    Sch.18 para.16, varied: SI 2009/3391 Art.7
    Sch.18 para.17, varied: SI 2009/3391 Art.7
    Sch.18 para.18, varied: SI 2009/3391 Art.7
    Sch.18 para.19, varied: SI 2009/3391 Art.7
    Sch.18 para.20, varied: SI 2009/3391 Art.7
24. **Welfare Reform Act 2009**
    Royal Assent, November 12, 2009
25. **Coroners and Justice Act 2009**
    Commencement Orders: SI 2009/3253 Art.2, Art.3
    Royal Assent, November 12, 2009
    s.176, enabling: SI 2009/3253
    s.182, enabling: SI 2009/3253
26. **Policing and Crime Act 2009**
    Commencement Orders: SI 2009/3096 Art.2, Art.3, Art.4
    Royal Assent, November 12, 2009
    s.116, enabling: SI 2009/3096
27. **Consolidated Fund Act 2009**
    Royal Assent, December 16, 2009
02. **Local Government (Wales) Measure 2009**
    Commencement Orders: SI 2009/1796 Art.2; SI 2009/3272 Art.2, Art.3, Art.4, Sch.1, Sch.2, Sch.3
    s.53, enabling: SI 2009/1796, SI 2009/3272
03. **Healthy Eating in Schools (Wales) Measure 2009**
    Royal Assent, October 15, 2009
04. **National Assembly for Wales Commissioner for Standards Measure 2009**
    Royal Assent, December 09, 2009

STATUTORY INSTRUMENT CITATOR 2009

The Statutory Instrument Citator covers the period 2009 and is up to date to **March 1, 2010**. It comprises in a single table:

(i) Statutory Instruments amended, repealed, modified, etc. by Statute passed or Statutory Instrument issued during this period;
(ii) Statutory Instruments judicially considered during this period;
(iii) Statutory Intruments consolidated during this period; and
(iv) Statutory Instruments made under the powers of any Statutory Instrument issued during this period.

The material is arranged in numerical order under the relevant year.

Definitions of legislative effects:

"added"	: new provisions are inserted by subsequent legislation
"amended"	: text of legislation is modified by subsequent legislation
"applied"	: brought to bear, or exercised by subsequent legislation
"consolidated"	: used where previous legislation in the same subject area is brought together in subsequent legislation, with or without amendments
"disapplied"	: an exception made to the application of an earlier enactment
"enabling"	: giving power for the relevant SI to be made
"referred to"	: direction from other legislation without specific effect or application
"repealed"	: rescinded by subsequent legislation
"restored"	: reinstated by subsequent legislation (where previously repealed/revoked)
"substituted"	: text of provision is completely replaced by subsequent legislation
"varied"	: provisions modified in relation to their application to specified areas or circumstances, however the text itself remains unchanged

STATUTORY INSTRUMENTS ISSUED BY THE SCOTTISH PARLIAMENT

1999

1. **Environmental Impact Assessment (Scotland) Regulations 1999**
applied: SSI 2009/221 Reg.3
Reg.2, amended: SSI 2009/221 Reg.2
Reg.2A, revoked (in part): SSI 2009/343 Reg.3
Reg.3, amended: SSI 2009/221 Reg.2
Reg.3A, amended: SSI 2009/221 Reg.2
Reg.7, amended: SSI 2009/221 Reg.2
Reg.7, revoked (in part): SSI 2009/221 Reg.2
Reg.9, amended: SSI 2009/221 Reg.2
Reg.9A, added: SSI 2009/221 Reg.2
Reg.12, amended: SSI 2009/221 Reg.2
Reg.13, amended: SSI 2009/221 Reg.2
Reg.13, revoked (in part): SSI 2009/221 Reg.2
Reg.14, amended: SSI 2009/221 Reg.2
Reg.19, amended: SSI 2009/343 Reg.3
Reg.19, revoked (in part): SSI 2009/343 Reg.3
Reg.21B, amended: SSI 2009/221 Reg.2
Reg.21C, amended: SSI 2009/221 Reg.2
Reg.21D, amended: SSI 2009/221 Reg.2
Reg.21E, amended: SSI 2009/221 Reg.2

1999–cont.

1. **Environmental Impact Assessment (Scotland) Regulations 1999**–cont.
Reg.21G, amended: SSI 2009/221 Reg.2
Reg.21H, amended: SSI 2009/221 Reg.2
Reg.29, revoked: SSI 2009/343 Reg.3
Reg.30, revoked: SSI 2009/343 Reg.3
Reg.31, revoked: SSI 2009/343 Reg.3
Reg.32, revoked: SSI 2009/343 Reg.3
Reg.33, revoked: SSI 2009/343 Reg.3
Reg.34, revoked: SSI 2009/343 Reg.3
Reg.35, revoked: SSI 2009/343 Reg.3
Reg.36, revoked: SSI 2009/343 Reg.3
Reg.37, revoked: SSI 2009/343 Reg.3
Reg.38, revoked: SSI 2009/343 Reg.3
Reg.39, revoked: SSI 2009/343 Reg.3
Reg.43, amended: SSI 2009/343 Reg.3
Reg.45, amended: SSI 2009/221 Reg.2
Sch.1, referred to: SSI 2009/51 Sch.1
Sch.5, amended: SSI 2009/221 Reg.2
Sch.6, amended: SSI 2009/221 Reg.2
Sch.6A, amended: SSI 2009/221 Reg.2

1999– cont.

57. **National Health Service (Pharmaceutical Services) (Scotland) Amendment Regulations 1999**
revoked: SSI 2009/183 Sch.5
58. **Smoke Control Areas (Exempted Fireplaces) (Scotland) Order 1999**
revoked: SSI 2009/214 Sch.2
138. **The A96 Trunk Road (Great Northern Road/ Auchmill Road, Aberdeen) (Bus Lane and Traffic Management) Order 1999**
Art.2, amended: SSI 2009/204 Art.2
Art.4, amended: SSI 2009/204 Art.2

2000

7. **Sea Fishing (Enforcement of Community Control Measures) (Scotland) Order 2000**
Art.2, amended: SSI 2009/304 Art.2
Art.2A, added: SSI 2009/304 Art.2
Art.3, amended: SSI 2009/304 Art.2
Art.4, amended: SSI 2009/304 Art.2
Sch.1, amended: SSI 2009/304 Art.2
59. **Disabled Persons (Badges for Motor Vehicles) (Scotland) Regulations 2000**
Reg.12, applied: SSI 2009/146 Art.5
Reg.12, referred to: SSI 2009/95 Art.5, SSI 2009/149 Art.3
110. **Repayment of Student Loans (Scotland) Regulations 2000**
Reg.2, amended: SSI 2009/102 Reg.3
Reg.5, amended: SSI 2009/102 Reg.4
Reg.6, amended: SSI 2009/102 Reg.5
Reg.7, amended: SSI 2009/102 Reg.6
Reg.8, amended: SSI 2009/102 Reg.7
Reg.9, amended: SSI 2009/102 Reg.8
Reg.13A, amended: SSI 2009/102 Reg.9
121. **European Communities (Lawyer's Practice) (Scotland) Regulations 2000**
Reg.16, referred to: SI 2009/2999 Reg.31
201. **Seed Potatoes (Scotland) Regulations 2000**
applied: SSI 2009/306 Reg.3
Reg.2, amended: SSI 2009/226 Reg.3
Reg.3, applied: SSI 2009/306 Reg.2
Reg.8, amended: SSI 2009/226 Reg.4
Sch.6 para.1, amended: SSI 2009/226 Reg.5
Sch.6 para.2, amended: SSI 2009/226 Reg.5
227. **Sea Fish (Specified Sea Areas) (Regulation of Nets and Other Fishing Gear) (Scotland) Order 2000**
Art.2, amended: SSI 2009/165 Art.2
Art.3, amended: SSI 2009/165 Art.2
Art.4A, added: SSI 2009/165 Art.2
Art.5, amended: SSI 2009/165 Art.2
Art.6, amended: SSI 2009/165 Art.2
309. **Food Irradiation Provisions (Scotland) Regulations 2000**
Reg.2, revoked: SSI 2009/261 Reg.12
Reg.3, revoked: SSI 2009/261 Reg.12
Reg.4, revoked: SSI 2009/261 Reg.12
Reg.5, revoked: SSI 2009/261 Reg.12
Reg.6, revoked: SSI 2009/261 Reg.12
Reg.7, revoked: SSI 2009/261 Reg.12
Reg.8, revoked: SSI 2009/261 Reg.12
Reg.9, revoked: SSI 2009/261 Reg.12
Reg.10, revoked: SSI 2009/261 Reg.12
Reg.11, revoked: SSI 2009/261 Reg.12
Reg.12, revoked: SSI 2009/261 Reg.12
Reg.13, revoked: SSI 2009/261 Reg.12

2000– cont.

309. **Food Irradiation Provisions (Scotland) Regulations 2000–** *cont.*
Reg.14, revoked: SSI 2009/261 Reg.12
Reg.15, revoked: SSI 2009/261 Reg.12
Reg.16, revoked: SSI 2009/261 Reg.12
323. **Pollution Prevention and Control (Scotland) Regulations 2000**
Reg.1A, added: SSI 2009/336 Reg.2
Reg.2, amended: SSI 2009/247 Reg.6
Reg.9D, added: SSI 2009/247 Reg.6
330. **Diseases of Fish (Control) Amendment (Scotland) Regulations 2000**
revoked: SSI 2009/85 Sch.2 para.14
343. **Regulation of Investigatory Powers (Prescription of Offices, Ranks and Positions) (Scotland) Order 2000**
Sch.1, amended: SSI 2009/340 Art.2
364. **Brucellosis (Scotland) Regulations 2000**
revoked: SSI 2009/232 Sch.1

2001

16. **Smoke Control Areas (Exempt Fireplaces) (Scotland) Order 2001**
revoked: SSI 2009/214 Sch.2
50. **Less Favoured Area Support Scheme (Scotland) Regulations 2001**
Reg.13, applied: SSI 2009/376 Sch.1 para.11
Reg.20, amended: SSI 2009/376 Reg.11
70. **National Health Service (Pharmaceutical Services) (Scotland) Amendment Regulations 2001**
revoked: SSI 2009/183 Sch.5
87. **Regulation of Investigatory Powers (Prescription of Offices, Ranks and Positions) (Scotland) Amendment Order 2001**
revoked: SSI 2009/340 Art.3
128. **Limited Liability Partnerships (Scotland) Regulations 2001**
Sch.2, amended: SSI 2009/310 Sch.1 para.1
Sch.3, amended: SSI 2009/310 Sch.2 para.1
219. **Public Service Vehicles (Registration of Local Services) (Scotland) Regulations 2001**
Reg.13, amended: SSI 2009/151 Reg.2
223. **St Mary's Music School (Aided Places) (Scotland) Regulations 2001**
Appendix 1 para.4, amended: SSI 2009/429 Sch.1 para.7
Sch.1 Part III para.10, amended: SSI 2009/181 Reg.2
Sch.1 Part III para.13, amended: SSI 2009/181 Reg.2
Sch.1 Part III para.14, amended: SSI 2009/181 Reg.2
Sch.1 Part IV para.18, amended: SSI 2009/181 Reg.2
Sch.1 Part IV para.24, amended: SSI 2009/181 Reg.2
236. **Adoption of Children from Overseas (Scotland) Regulations 2001**
applied: SSI 2009/267 Art.8
Reg.3, applied: SSI 2009/267 Art.8, Art.9
Reg.3, referred to: SSI 2009/267 Art.8
300. **Rural Stewardship Scheme (Scotland) Regulations 2001**
applied: SSI 2009/376 Sch.1 para.23
Reg.18, amended: SSI 2009/376 Reg.11
302. **Health Boards (Membership and Procedure) (Scotland) Regulations 2001**
Reg.1, varied: SSI 2009/302 Sch.1 para.1
Reg.2, varied: SSI 2009/302 Sch.1 para.1
Reg.5, varied: SSI 2009/302 Sch.1 para.1
Reg.6, varied: SSI 2009/302 Sch.1 para.1
Reg.7, applied: SSI 2009/183 Sch.4 para.1

2001–cont.

409. Fish Health Amendment (Scotland) Regulations 2001
revoked: SSI 2009/85 Sch.2 para.15

2002

63. Children's Hearings (Legal Representation) (Scotland) Rules 2002
r.2, amended: SSI 2009/211 r.3
r.3, amended: SSI 2009/211 r.4
r.3A, added: SSI 2009/211 r.5
r.3B, added: SSI 2009/211 r.5
r.4, amended: SSI 2009/211 r.6
r.5, amended: SSI 2009/211 r.7

111. National Health Service (General Medical Services and Pharmaceutical Services) (Scotland) Amendment Regulations 2002
Reg.2, revoked: SSI 2009/183 Sch.5

113. Regulation of Care (Applications and Provision of Advice) (Scotland) Order 2002
Sch.1 para.20, amended: SSI 2009/429 Sch.1 para.3

114. Regulation of Care (Requirements as to Care Services) (Scotland) Regulations 2002
Reg.6, amended: SSI 2009/130 Reg.5

115. Regulation of Care (Registration and Registers) (Scotland) Regulations 2002
Reg.4, amended: SSI 2009/130 Reg.3

132. Act of Sederunt (Summary Cause Rules) 2002
Sch.1, referred to: SSI 2009/294 r.6
Sch.1 Appendix, amended: SSI 2009/107 Sch.4, SSI 2009/294 Sch.3, Sch.4
Sch.1 Part 1 para.1.1, amended: SSI 2009/164 r.4
Sch.1 Part 4 para.4.2A, added: SSI 2009/294 r.4
Sch.1 Part 4 para.4.4, amended: SSI 2009/294 r.11
Sch.1 Part 4 para.4.5, amended: SSI 2009/294 r.7
Sch.1 Part 5 para.5.5, amended: SSI 2009/294 r.11
Sch.1 Part 5 para.5.6, revoked (in part): SSI 2009/294 r.11
Sch.1 Part 6 para.6.A3, amended: SSI 2009/107 r.5
Sch.1 Part 6 para.6.A6, revoked: SSI 2009/107 r.5
Sch.1 Part 6 para.6.A8, added: SSI 2009/107 r.5
Sch.1 Part 7 para.7.2, amended: SSI 2009/294 r.4
Sch.1 Part 10 para.10.1, amended: SSI 2009/294 r.11
Sch.1 Part 10 para.10.1, revoked (in part): SSI 2009/294 r.11
Sch.1 Part 11 para.11.3, amended: SSI 2009/294 r.11
Sch.1 Part 22A para.22A.1, added: SSI 2009/294 r.15
Sch.1 Part 23 para.23.3, amended: SSI 2009/164 r.4

133. Act of Sederunt (Small Claim Rules) 2002
Sch.1, referred to: SSI 2009/294 r.6
Sch.1 Appendix 1, amended: SSI 2009/107 Sch.5, SSI 2009/294 Sch.5, Sch.6
Sch.1 Part 1 para.1.1, amended: SSI 2009/164 r.5
Sch.1 Part 4 para.4.2A, added: SSI 2009/294 r.5
Sch.1 Part 4 para.4.4, amended: SSI 2009/294 r.12
Sch.1 Part 7 para.7.A3, amended: SSI 2009/107 r.6
Sch.1 Part 7 para.7.A6, revoked: SSI 2009/107 r.6
Sch.1 Part 7 para.7.A8, added: SSI 2009/107 r.6
Sch.1 Part 8 para.8.2, amended: SSI 2009/294 r.5
Sch.1 Part 9 para.9.1, amended: SSI 2009/294 r.7
Sch.1 Part 11 para.11.1, revoked (in part): SSI 2009/294 r.12
Sch.1 Part 21 para.21.6, amended: SSI 2009/164 r.5

139. Less Favoured Area Support Scheme (Scotland) Regulations 2002
Reg.15, applied: SSI 2009/376 Sch.1 para.11
Reg.22, amended: SSI 2009/376 Reg.11

2002–cont.

153. National Health Service (General Medical Services and Pharmaceutical Services) (Scotland) Amendment (No.2) Regulations 2002
Reg.2, revoked (in part): SSI 2009/183 Sch.5

179. Food (Jelly Confectionery) (Emergency Control) (Scotland) Regulations 2002
revoked: SSI 2009/437 Reg.6

284. Food (Control of Irradiation) Amendment (Scotland) Regulations 2002
revoked: SSI 2009/261 Reg.12

303. Community Care (Personal Care and Nursing Care) (Scotland) Regulations 2002
Reg.2, amended: SSI 2009/138 Reg.2

389. Registration of Births, Deaths and Marriages (Fees) (Scotland) Order 2002
revoked: SSI 2009/65 Art.3

397. Food for Particular Nutritional Uses (Addition of Substances for Specific Nutritional Purposes) (Scotland) Regulations 2002
revoked: SSI 2009/427 Reg.6

494. Civil Legal Aid (Scotland) Regulations 2002
applied: SSI 2009/312 Reg.9
Reg.2, amended: SSI 2009/312 Reg.8
Reg.4, amended: SSI 2009/312 Reg.8
Reg.4, revoked (in part): SSI 2009/312 Reg.8
Reg.7, applied: SSI 2009/284 Sch.1
Reg.18, amended: SSI 2009/312 Reg.8, SSI 2009/429 Art.3, Sch.1 para.4
Reg.21, amended: SSI 2009/312 Reg.8
Reg.33, amended: SSI 2009/49 Reg.4
Reg.43, amended: SSI 2009/312 Reg.8
Reg.45, amended: SSI 2009/312 Reg.8

495. Advice and Assistance (Scotland) Amendment Regulations 2002
Reg.2, revoked (in part): SSI 2009/49 Sch.1 Part 1

560. Act of Sederunt (Debt Arrangement and Attachment (Scotland) Act 2002) 2002
Sch.1 para.8, amended: SSI 2009/107 r.7
Sch.1 para.22, substituted: SSI 2009/107 r.7
Sch.2, amended: SSI 2009/403 Art.2

566. Act of Sederunt (Fees of Messengers-at-Arms) (No.2) 2002
Sch.1 para.12A, added: SSI 2009/383 Art.2
Sch.1 para.13A, added: SSI 2009/383 Art.2
Sch.1 para.15, amended: SSI 2009/383 Art.2

567. Act of Sederunt (Fees of Sheriff Officers) (No.2) 2002
Sch.1 para.9, amended: SSI 2009/379 Art.3
Sch.1 para.12A, added: SSI 2009/379 Art.3
Sch.1 para.14A, added: SSI 2009/379 Art.3
Sch.1 para.17, amended: SSI 2009/379 Art.2, Art.3, Art.4

569. Proceeds of Crime Act 2002 (Cash Searches Constables in Scotland Code of Practice) Order 2002
revoked: SSI 2009/246 Art.1

2003

19. Intercountry Adoption (Hague Convention) (Scotland) Regulations 2003
applied: SSI 2009/267 Art.6, Art.7
revoked: SSI 2009/182 Reg.64

49. Civil Legal Aid (Scotland) Amendment Regulations 2003
Reg.5, revoked: SSI 2009/49 Sch.1 Part 2

67. Registration of Foreign Adoptions (Scotland) Regulations 2003
Reg.2A, added: SSI 2009/314 Reg.3

67. Registration of Foreign Adoptions (Scotland) Regulations 2003–*cont.*
Sch.1, amended: SSI 2009/314 Sch.1

94. Proceeds of Crime Act 2002 (Investigations Code of Practice) (Scotland) Order 2003
revoked: SSI 2009/245 Art.1

129. Less Favoured Area Support Scheme (Scotland) Regulations 2003
applied: SSI 2009/376 Sch.1 para.11
Reg.9, applied: SSI 2009/376 Sch.1 para.12
Reg.10, applied: SSI 2009/376 Sch.1 para.12
Reg.11, applied: SSI 2009/376 Sch.1 para.12
Reg.13, applied: SSI 2009/376 Sch.1 para.12
Reg.24, amended: SSI 2009/376 Reg.11

150. Regulation of Care (Requirements as to Limited Registration Services) (Scotland) Regulations 2003
Reg.4, amended: SSI 2009/130 Reg.7
Reg.5, amended: SSI 2009/90 Reg.3
Reg.7, amended: SSI 2009/90 Reg.4

163. Advice and Assistance (Scotland) Amendment Regulations 2003
Reg.5, revoked: SSI 2009/49 Sch.1 Part 1

176. Council Tax (Discounts) (Scotland) Consolidation and Amendment Order 2003
Art.3, amended: SI 2009/2054 Sch.1 para.23
Art.3, applied: SI 2009/2054 Sch.2 para.16

188. Non-Domestic Rating (Petrol Filling Stations, Public Houses and Hotels) (Scotland) Order 2003
revoked: SSI 2009/69 Art.4

209. SFGS Farmland Premium Scheme 2003
applied: SSI 2009/376 Sch.1 para.24
Art.14, applied: SSI 2009/376 Sch.1 para.24

231. Rehabilitation of Offenders Act 1974 (Exclusions and Exceptions) (Scotland) Order 2003
applied: SSI 2009/210 Sch.3 para.10
Art.2, amended: SSI 2009/271 Art.2
Sch.3 para.2, amended: SSI 2009/429 Sch.1 para.5
Sch.4 Part 1 para.8A, added: SI 2009/1182 Sch.4 para.28
Sch.4 Part 1 para.13, revoked: SI 2009/1182 Sch.4 para.9
Sch.4 Part 2 para.28, added: SSI 2009/271 Art.2
Sch.4 Part 2 para.29, added: SSI 2009/334 Art.4
Sch.4 Part 2 para.30, added: SSI 2009/334 Art.4
Sch.4 Part 2 para.31, added: SSI 2009/334 Art.4
Sch.4 Part 2 para.32, added: SSI 2009/334 Art.4
Sch.4 Part 4, amended: SI 2009/1182 Sch.4 para.9, Sch.4 para.28

235. Landfill (Scotland) Regulations 2003
Reg.2, amended: SSI 2009/247 Reg.7
Reg.11, amended: SSI 2009/247 Reg.7

240. A830 Trunk Road (Arisaig to Kinsadel) (40/30mph Speed Limit) Order 2003
revoked: SSI 2009/239 Art.4

278. Food Supplements (Scotland) Regulations 2003
Reg.2, amended: SSI 2009/438 Reg.2
Reg.3, amended: SSI 2009/438 Reg.2
Reg.5, amended: SSI 2009/438 Reg.2
Reg.5, revoked (in part): SSI 2009/438 Reg.2
Reg.6, amended: SSI 2009/438 Reg.2
Reg.12, added: SSI 2009/438 Reg.2
Sch.1, revoked: SSI 2009/438 Reg.2
Sch.2 para.A, revoked: SSI 2009/438 Reg.2
Sch.2 para.B, revoked: SSI 2009/438 Reg.2

293. Fruit Juices and Fruit Nectars (Scotland) Regulations 2003
Sch.3 para.2, substituted: SSI 2009/436 Reg.18

293. Fruit Juices and Fruit Nectars (Scotland) Regulations 2003–*cont.*
Sch.4 para.4, amended: SSI 2009/435 Reg.9
Sch.4 para.5, amended: SSI 2009/435 Reg.9
Sch.4 para.6, amended: SSI 2009/435 Reg.9

296. National Health Service (Pharmaceutical Services) (Scotland) Amendment Regulations 2003
revoked: SSI 2009/183 Sch.5

311. Condensed Milk and Dried Milk (Scotland) Regulations 2003
Sch.1, substituted: SSI 2009/436 Reg.18

350. Education (School Meals) (Scotland) Regulations 2003
revoked: SSI 2009/178 Reg.5

411. Animal By-Products (Scotland) Regulations 2003
Reg.2, amended: SSI 2009/7 Reg.2
Reg.5, amended: SSI 2009/7 Reg.2
Reg.9, amended: SSI 2009/7 Reg.2
Reg.21, applied: SSI 2009/230 Sch.1
Reg.51, revoked (in part): SSI 2009/7 Reg.2

415. Road Works (Inspection Fees) (Scotland) Regulations 2003
Reg.3, amended: SSI 2009/74 Reg.2

436. Smoke Control Area (Exempt Fireplaces) (Scotland) Order 2003
revoked: SSI 2009/214 Sch.2

452. Lands Tribunal for Scotland Rules 2003
Part I r.5A, added: SSI 2009/259 r.4
Part V r.13, amended: SSI 2009/259 r.5
Part V r.21, amended: SSI 2009/259 r.6
Part V r.28, amended: SSI 2009/259 r.7
r.2, amended: SSI 2009/259 r.3
Sch.1, amended: SSI 2009/259 r.8
Sch.2, amended: SSI 2009/259 r.8, Sch.1

460. National Health Service (Travelling Expenses and Remission of Charges) (Scotland) (No.2) Regulations 2003
applied: SSI 2009/183 Sch.1 para.4
Reg.4, amended: SSI 2009/124 Reg.2
Sch.1 Part I para.2, amended: SSI 2009/124 Reg.2

527. Specified Sugar Products (Scotland) Regulations 2003
Sch.1 Part I, substituted: SSI 2009/436 Reg.19

2004

6. Meat Products (Scotland) Regulations 2004
Sch.3 para.10, substituted: SSI 2009/436 Reg.18

38. National Health Service (Tribunal) (Scotland) Regulations 2004
referred to: SSI 2009/183 Sch.1 para.3
Reg.3, revoked (in part): SSI 2009/319 Sch.3 Part 2
Reg.26, applied: SSI 2009/183 Reg.5, Reg.8

39. National Health Service (Pharmaceutical Services) (Scotland) Amendment Regulations 2004
revoked: SSI 2009/183 Sch.5

49. Advice and Assistance (Scotland) Amendment Regulations 2004
revoked: SSI 2009/49 Sch.1 Part 1

50. Civil Legal Aid (Scotland) Amendment Regulations 2004
revoked: SSI 2009/49 Sch.1 Part 2

70. Less Favoured Area Support Scheme (Scotland) Regulations 2004
Reg.16, applied: SSI 2009/376 Sch.1 para.11

2004–cont.

83. Individual Learning Account (Scotland) Regulations 2004
Reg.3, amended: SSI 2009/176 Reg.2

88. Private Hire Car Drivers Licences (Carrying of Guide Dogs and Hearing Dogs) (Scotland) Regulations 2004
varied: SI 2009/2863 Reg.5

90. Food for Particular Nutritional Uses (Addition of Substances for Specific Nutritional Purposes) (Scotland) Amendment Regulations 2004
revoked: SSI 2009/427 Reg.6

115. National Health Service (General Medical Services Contracts) (Scotland) Regulations 2004
Reg.2, amended: SSI 2009/183 Sch.6 para.4

116. National Health Service (Primary Medical Services Section 17C Agreements) (Scotland) Regulations 2004
Reg.2, amended: SSI 2009/183 Sch.6 para.3

133. Jam and Similar Products (Scotland) Regulations 2004
Reg.2, amended: SSI 2009/436 Reg.18
Sch.2 para.1, amended: SSI 2009/436 Reg.18

143. Organic Aid (Scotland) Regulations 2004
applied: SSI 2009/376 Sch.1 para.20
Reg.20, applied: SSI 2009/376 Sch.1 para.20
Reg.25, amended: SSI 2009/376 Reg.11

187. Food (Jelly Mini-Cups) (Emergency Control) (Scotland) Regulations 2004
revoked: SSI 2009/437 Reg.6

212. Primary Medical Services (Consequential and Ancillary Amendments) (Scotland) Order 2004
Sch.1 para.4, revoked: SSI 2009/183 Sch.5

219. Town and Country Planning (Fees for Applications and Deemed Applications) (Scotland) Regulations 2004
Reg.1, amended: SSI 2009/222 Art.16
Reg.2, amended: SSI 2009/222 Art.16
Reg.3, amended: SSI 2009/222 Art.16
Reg.7, amended: SSI 2009/222 Art.16
Reg.8, amended: SSI 2009/222 Art.16
Sch.1 Part I para.1, amended: SSI 2009/222 Art.16
Sch.1 Part II para.2, amended: SSI 2009/222 Art.16
Sch.1 Part II para.3, amended: SSI 2009/222 Art.16
Sch.1 Part II para.4, amended: SSI 2009/222 Art.16
Sch.1 Part II para.5, amended: SSI 2009/222 Art.16
Sch.1 Part II para.6, amended: SSI 2009/222 Art.16
Sch.1 Part II para.7, amended: SSI 2009/222 Art.16
Sch.1 Part II para.8, amended: SSI 2009/222 Art.16
Sch.1 Part II para.9, amended: SSI 2009/222 Art.16
Sch.1 Part III para.10, amended: SSI 2009/222 Art.16
Sch.1 Part III para.10A, amended: SSI 2009/222 Art.16
Sch.1 Part III para.11, amended: SSI 2009/222 Art.16
Sch.1 Part III para.12, amended: SSI 2009/222 Art.16
Sch.1 Part III para.13, amended: SSI 2009/222 Art.16
Sch.1 Part III para.14, amended: SSI 2009/222 Art.16

224. Crofting Community Body Form of Application for Consent to Buy Croft Land etc and Notice of Minister's Decision (Scotland) Regulations 2004
revoked: SSI 2009/160 Reg.4

2004–cont.

233. Community Right to Buy (Forms) (Scotland) Regulations 2004
revoked: SSI 2009/156 Reg.7

257. Police (Scotland) Regulations 2004
Reg.11, amended: SSI 2009/372 Reg.4
Reg.31, amended: SSI 2009/372 Reg.4

292. National Health Service (Vocational Training for General Dental Practice) (Scotland) Regulations 2004
Reg.1, amended: SI 2009/2054 Sch.1 para.25

317. Oil and Fibre Plant Seed (Scotland) Regulations 2004
Reg.2, amended: SSI 2009/223 Reg.13
Reg.6, amended: SSI 2009/223 Reg.14
Reg.8B, added: SSI 2009/223 Reg.15
Reg.14, amended: SSI 2009/223 Reg.16
Reg.15, amended: SSI 2009/223 Reg.17
Reg.16, amended: SSI 2009/223 Reg.18
Reg.17, amended: SSI 2009/223 Reg.19
Sch.4A Part I para.1, added: SSI 2009/223 Sch.2
Sch.4A Part I para.2, added: SSI 2009/223 Sch.2
Sch.4A Part I para.3, added: SSI 2009/223 Sch.2
Sch.4A Part II, added: SSI 2009/223 Sch.2
Sch.4A Part III para.1, added: SSI 2009/223 Sch.2
Sch.4A Part III para.2, added: SSI 2009/223 Sch.2
Sch.4A Part IV para.1, added: SSI 2009/223 Sch.2
Sch.4A Part IV para.2, added: SSI 2009/223 Sch.2
Sch.4A Part IV para.3, added: SSI 2009/223 Sch.2
Sch.4A Part V, added: SSI 2009/223 Sch.2
Sch.6 Part II para.6B, added: SSI 2009/223 Reg.21

374. Mental Health Tribunal for Scotland (Appointment of Medical Members) Regulations 2004
Reg.2, amended: SSI 2009/359 Reg.2

375. Mental Health Tribunal for Scotland (Appointment of General Members) Regulations 2004
Reg.2, amended: SI 2009/1182 Sch.4 para.11

381. Agricultural Subsidies (Appeals) (Scotland) Regulations 2004
applied: SSI 2009/376 Reg.11
revoked: SSI 2009/376 Reg.11
Reg.4, applied: SSI 2009/376 Reg.11

406. Building (Scotland) Regulations 2004
Sch.1 para.21, amended: SSI 2009/119 Reg.2
Sch.3, amended: SSI 2009/119 Reg.2
Sch.3 para.2A, added: SSI 2009/119 Reg.2
Sch.3 para.2B, added: SSI 2009/119 Reg.2
Sch.3 para.2C, added: SSI 2009/119 Reg.2
Sch.3 para.21, amended: SSI 2009/119 Reg.2

411. Victim Notification (Prescribed Offences) (Scotland) Order 2004
Sch.1 para.30, substituted: SSI 2009/142 Art.2

413. Miscellaneous Food Additives Amendment (Scotland) Regulations 2004
Reg.3, referred to: SSI 2009/436 Reg.10

428. Building (Procedure) (Scotland) Regulations 2004
Reg.2, amended: SSI 2009/117 Reg.2
Reg.58, amended: SSI 2009/117 Reg.2

429. Mental Health (Advance Statements) (Prescribed Class of Persons) (Scotland) (No.2) Regulations 2004
Reg.2, amended: SI 2009/1182 Sch.4 para.12
Reg.2, revoked (in part): SI 2009/1182 Sch.4 para.12

430. Mental Health (Patient Representation) (Prescribed Persons) (Scotland) (No.2) Regulations 2004
Reg.2, amended: SI 2009/1182 Sch.4 para.13
Reg.2, revoked (in part): SI 2009/1182 Sch.4 para.13

2004– cont.

468. Debt Arrangement Scheme (Scotland) Regulations 2004
Reg.2, amended: SSI 2009/ 234 Reg.3
Reg.5, amended: SSI 2009/ 234 Reg.4
Reg.7, substituted: SSI 2009/ 234 Reg.5
Reg.8, revoked: SSI 2009/ 234 Reg.5
Reg.9, revoked: SSI 2009/ 234 Reg.5
Reg.10, revoked: SSI 2009/ 234 Reg.5
Reg.11, revoked: SSI 2009/ 234 Reg.5
Reg.12, revoked: SSI 2009/ 234 Reg.5
Reg.15, amended: SSI 2009/ 234 Reg.6
Reg.18, amended: SSI 2009/ 234 Reg.7
Reg.18, revoked (in part): SSI 2009/ 234 Reg.5
Reg.20, amended: SSI 2009/ 234 Reg.8
Reg.21, amended: SSI 2009/ 234 Reg.9
Reg.21, revoked (in part): SSI 2009/ 234 Reg.9
Reg.22, amended: SSI 2009/ 234 Reg.10
Reg.25, amended: SSI 2009/ 234 Reg.11
Reg.26, amended: SSI 2009/ 234 Reg.12
Reg.26, revoked (in part): SSI 2009/ 234 Reg.12
Reg.26A, added: SSI 2009/ 234 Reg.13
Reg.29, amended: SSI 2009/ 234 Reg.14
Reg.31, substituted: SSI 2009/ 234 Reg.15
Reg.31 A, amended: SSI 2009/ 234 Reg.16
Reg.33, amended: SSI 2009/ 234 Reg.17
Reg.35, amended: SSI 2009/ 234 Reg.18
Reg.37, substituted: SSI 2009/ 234 Reg.19
Reg.40, substituted: SSI 2009/ 234 Reg.20
Reg.41, amended: SSI 2009/ 234 Reg.21
Reg.42, amended: SSI 2009/ 234 Reg.22
Reg.43, amended: SSI 2009/ 234 Reg.23
Reg.43, revoked (in part): SSI 2009/ 234 Reg.5
Reg.45, substituted: SSI 2009/ 234 Reg.24
Reg.47, amended: SSI 2009/ 234 Reg.25
Reg.48, substituted: SSI 2009/ 234 Reg.26
Reg.49, amended: SSI 2009/ 234 Reg.27
Reg.49, revoked (in part): SSI 2009/ 234 Reg.27
Sch.1, amended: SSI 2009/ 234 Reg.28, Sch.1, Sch.2, Sch.3, Sch.4
Sch.4 para.1, revoked: SSI 2009/ 234 Reg.5
Sch.4 para.2, revoked: SSI 2009/ 234 Reg.5
Sch.4 para.3, revoked: SSI 2009/ 234 Reg.5
Sch.4 para.4, revoked: SSI 2009/ 234 Reg.5
Sch.4 para.5, revoked: SSI 2009/ 234 Reg.5
Sch.4 para.6, revoked: SSI 2009/ 234 Reg.5
Sch.5 para.8, amended: SSI 2009/ 234 Reg.5

518. Common Agricultural Policy Schemes (Cross-Compliance) (Scotland) Regulations 2004
applied: SSI 2009/ 376 Sch.1 para.9
Reg.2, amended: SSI 2009/ 391 Reg.16
Sch.1 Part IV para.18, amended: SSI 2009/ 391 Reg.17
Sch.1 Part V para.19, added: SSI 2009/ 391 Reg.18

520. Environmental Information (Scotland) Regulations 2004
Reg.10, applied: SI 2009/ 2263 Reg.9

2005

94. Colours in Food Amendment (Scotland) Regulations 2005
referred to: SSI 2009/ 436 Reg.7

111. Advice and Assistance (Scotland) Amendment Regulations 2005
revoked: SSI 2009/ 49 Sch.1 Part 1

112. Civil Legal Aid (Scotland) Amendment Regulations 2005
Reg.3, revoked: SSI 2009/ 49 Sch.1 Part 2

2005– cont.

112. Civil Legal Aid (Scotland) Amendment Regulations 2005– *cont.*
Reg.4, revoked (in part): SSI 2009/ 49 Sch.1 Part 2

117. Agricultural Subsidies (Appeals) (Scotland) Amendment Regulations 2005
revoked: SSI 2009/ 376 Reg.11

125. Gender Recognition (Disclosure of Information) (Scotland) Order 2005
varied: SI 2009/ 317 Sch.1
Art.5, amended: SI 2009/ 1182 Sch.4 para.29

127. Non-Domestic Rating (Valuation of Utilities) (Scotland) Order 2005
Art.4, amended: SSI 2009/ 196 Art.2
Art.7A, added: SSI 2009/ 112 Art.3
Sch.1, amended: SSI 2009/ 112 Art.4

143. Common Agricultural Policy Single Farm Payment and Support Schemes (Scotland) Regulations 2005
Reg.2, amended: SSI 2009/ 391 Reg.3, Reg.4
Reg.3, amended: SSI 2009/ 391 Reg.5
Reg.4, revoked (in part): SSI 2009/ 391 Reg.13
Reg.5, substituted: SSI 2009/ 391 Reg.6
Reg.6, revoked: SSI 2009/ 391 Reg.13
Reg.7, revoked: SSI 2009/ 391 Reg.13
Reg.8, revoked: SSI 2009/ 391 Reg.13
Reg.9, amended: SSI 2009/ 391 Reg.7
Reg.10, amended: SSI 2009/ 391 Reg.8
Reg.11, revoked: SSI 2009/ 391 Reg.13
Reg.12, revoked: SSI 2009/ 391 Reg.13
Reg.13, revoked: SSI 2009/ 391 Reg.13
Reg.14, revoked: SSI 2009/ 391 Reg.13
Reg.15, revoked: SSI 2009/ 391 Reg.13
Reg.16, revoked: SSI 2009/ 391 Reg.13
Reg.17, revoked: SSI 2009/ 391 Reg.13
Reg.18, revoked: SSI 2009/ 391 Reg.13
Reg.19, amended: SSI 2009/ 391 Reg.9
Reg.20, amended: SSI 2009/ 391 Reg.10
Reg.22, amended: SSI 2009/ 391 Reg.11
Sch.1 Part A para.1, revoked: SSI 2009/ 391 Reg.13
Sch.1 Part A para.2, revoked: SSI 2009/ 391 Reg.13
Sch.1 Part A para.3, revoked: SSI 2009/ 391 Reg.13
Sch.1 Part A para.4, revoked: SSI 2009/ 391 Reg.13
Sch.1 Part A para.5, revoked: SSI 2009/ 391 Reg.13
Sch.1 Part A para.6, revoked: SSI 2009/ 391 Reg.13
Sch.1 Part A para.7, revoked: SSI 2009/ 391 Reg.13
Sch.1 Part B para.8, revoked: SSI 2009/ 391 Reg.13
Sch.1 Part B para.9, revoked: SSI 2009/ 391 Reg.13
Sch.1 Part B para.10, revoked: SSI 2009/ 391 Reg.13
Sch.1 Part B para.11, revoked: SSI 2009/ 391 Reg.13
Sch.1 Part B para.12, revoked: SSI 2009/ 391 Reg.13
Sch.1 Part B para.13, revoked: SSI 2009/ 391 Reg.13
Sch.1 Part B para.14, revoked: SSI 2009/ 391 Reg.13
Sch.2 para.1, revoked: SSI 2009/ 391 Reg.13
Sch.2 para.2, revoked: SSI 2009/ 391 Reg.13
Sch.4 para.1, amended: SSI 2009/ 391 Reg.12
Sch.4 para.2, amended: SSI 2009/ 391 Reg.12
Sch.6, added: SSI 2009/ 391 Reg.14

152. Pensions Appeal Tribunals (Scotland) (Amendment) Rules 2005
r.5, revoked: SSI 2009/ 353 r.3
r.10, revoked: SSI 2009/ 353 r.3

214. Miscellaneous Food Additives Amendment (Scotland) Regulations 2005
Reg.3, referred to: SSI 2009/ 436 Reg.10
Reg.4, referred to: SSI 2009/ 436 Reg.10
Reg.5, referred to: SSI 2009/ 436 Reg.10
Reg.6, referred to: SSI 2009/ 436 Reg.10
Reg.7, referred to: SSI 2009/ 436 Reg.10

2005–cont.

214. Miscellaneous Food Additives Amendment (Scotland) Regulations 2005–cont.
Reg.8, referred to: SSI 2009/436 Reg.l0
Reg.9, referred to: SSI 2009/436 Reg.l0
Reg.l0, referred to: SSI 2009/436 Reg.l0
Reg.ll, referred to: SSI 2009/436 Reg.l0

216. Plant Health (Import Inspection Fees) (Scotland) Regulations 2005
Reg.2, amended: SSI 2009/8 Reg.3
Sch.2, amended: SSI 2009/305 Sch.l
Sch.2, substituted: SSI 2009/8 Reg.4, SSI 2009/305 Reg.4

223. Horse Passports (Scotland) Regulations 2005
revoked: SSI 2009/231 Reg.25

225. Land Management Contracts (Menu Scheme) (Scotland) Regulations 2005
applied: SSI 2009/376 Sch.l para.25

279. Seed Potatoes (Fees) (Scotland) Regulations 2005
revoked: SSI 2009/306 Reg.7

294. Food (Chilli, Chilli Products, Curcuma and Palm Oil) (Emergency Control) (Scotland) Regulations 2005
revoked: SSI 2009/446 Reg.52

318. Regulation of Care (Social Service Workers) (Scotland) Order 2005
Art.l, amended: SSI 2009/350 Art.2
Art.2, amended: SSI 2009/350 Art.2
Art.3, revoked (in part): SI 2009/1182 Sch.4 para.14

327. National Health Service (Pharmaceutical Services) (Scotland) Amendment Regulations 2005
revoked: SSI 2009/183 Sch.5

328. Cereal Seed (Scotland) Regulations 2005
Reg.2, amended: SSI 2009/223 Reg.3
Reg.6, amended: SSI 2009/223 Reg.4
Reg.9B, added: SSI 2009/223 Reg.5
Reg.l4, amended: SSI 2009/223 Reg.6
Reg.l5, amended: SSI 2009/223 Reg.7
Reg.l6, amended: SSI 2009/223 Reg.8
Reg.l7, amended: SSI 2009/223 Reg.9
Sch.4A Part I para.l, added: SSI 2009/223 Sch.l
Sch.4A Part I para.2, added: SSI 2009/223 Sch.l
Sch.4A Part I para.3, added: SSI 2009/223 Sch.l
Sch.4A Part II, added: SSI 2009/223 Sch.l
Sch.4A Part III para.l, added: SSI 2009/223 Sch.l
Sch.4A Part III para.2, added: SSI 2009/223 Sch.l
Sch.4A Part III para.3, added: SSI 2009/223 Sch.l
Sch.4A Part IV para.l, added: SSI 2009/223 Sch.l
Sch.4A Part IV para.2, added: SSI 2009/223 Sch.l
Sch.4A Part IV para.3, added: SSI 2009/223 Sch.l
Sch.4A Part IV para.4, added: SSI 2009/223 Sch.l
Sch.4A Part IV para.5, added: SSI 2009/223 Sch.l
Sch.4A Part V, added: SSI 2009/223 Sch.l
Sch.6 Part II para.6B, added: SSI 2009/223 Reg.ll

329. Fodder Plant Seed (Scotland) Regulations 2005
Reg.2, amended: SSI 2009/223 Reg.23
Reg.6, amended: SSI 2009/223 Reg.24
Reg.9B, added: SSI 2009/223 Reg.25
Reg.l4, amended: SSI 2009/223 Reg.26
Reg.l5, amended: SSI 2009/223 Reg.27
Reg.l6, amended: SSI 2009/223 Reg.28
Reg.l7, amended: SSI 2009/223 Reg.29
Sch.4A Part I para.l, added: SSI 2009/223 Sch.3
Sch.4A Part I para.2, added: SSI 2009/223 Sch.3
Sch.4A Part I para.3, added: SSI 2009/223 Sch.3
Sch.4A Part II, added: SSI 2009/223 Sch.3
Sch.4A Part III para.l, added: SSI 2009/223 Sch.3

2005–cont.

329. Fodder Plant Seed (Scotland) Regulations 2005–cont.
Sch.4A Part III para.2, added: SSI 2009/223 Sch.3
Sch.4A Part IV para.l, added: SSI 2009/223 Sch.3
Sch.4A Part IV para.2, added: SSI 2009/223 Sch.3
Sch.4A Part IV para.3, added: SSI 2009/223 Sch.3
Sch.4A Part V, added: SSI 2009/223 Sch.3
Sch.5 Part II para.26, amended: SSI 2009/330 Reg.2
Sch.6 Part II para.6B, added: SSI 2009/223 Reg.3l

348. Water Environment (Controlled Activities) (Scotland) Regulations 2005
Reg.2, amended: SSI 2009/420 Reg.4
Reg.4, amended: SSI 2009/420 Reg.4
Reg.l0, amended: SSI 2009/420 Reg.4
Reg.28, amended: SSI 2009/420 Reg.4
Sch.2 para.l, substituted: SSI 2009/420 Sch.l
Sch.2 para.2, substituted: SSI 2009/420 Sch.l
Sch.2 para.3, substituted: SSI 2009/420 Sch.l
Sch.3 Part 1, amended: SSI 2009/420 Reg.4
Sch.4 Part 1, substituted: SSI 2009/420 Sch.2
Sch.4 Part 2, substituted: SSI 2009/420 Sch.2
Sch.8 para.l, amended: SSI 2009/420 Reg.4

458. Registration of Civil Partnerships (Prescription of Forms, Publicisation and Errors) (Scotland) Regulations 2005
Sch.l, amended: SSI 2009/314 Sch.3
Sch.2, amended: SSI 2009/314 Sch.4
Sch.3, amended: SSI 2009/314 Sch.5

479. Tryptophan in Food (Scotland) Regulations 2005
Reg.2, amended: SSI 2009/427 Reg.5
Reg.5, amended: SSI 2009/427 Reg.5

565. Disability Discrimination (Public Authorities) (Statutory Duties) (Scotland) Regulations 2005
Sch.l Part I, amended: SSI 2009/248 Sch.l para.16

569. Less Favoured Area Support Scheme (Scotland) Regulations 2005
Reg.l6, applied: SSI 2009/376 Sch.l para.ll

605. Feeding Stuffs (Scotland) Regulations 2005
Sch.5, amended: SSI 2009/21 Reg.3, SSI 2009/373 Sch.l
Sch.7 Ch.A, amended: SSI 2009/21 Sch.l

608. Feed (Hygiene and Enforcement) (Scotland) Regulations 2005
Reg.2, amended: SSI 2009/263 Reg.2
Reg.4, amended: SSI 2009/263 Reg.2
Reg.l6, substituted: SSI 2009/263 Reg.2
Reg.32, amended: SSI 2009/263 Reg.2
Sch.l, amended: SSI 2009/446 Reg.5l

613. Plant Health (Scotland) Order 2005
Art.2, amended: SSI 2009/153 Art.3
Sch.l Part A, amended: SSI 2009/153 Art.4
Sch.l Part B, amended: SSI 2009/153 Art.5
Sch.2 Part A, amended: SSI 2009/153 Art.6
Sch.2 Part B, amended: SSI 2009/153 Art.6
Sch.4 Part A, amended: SSI 2009/153 Art.7
Sch.4 Part B, amended: SSI 2009/153 Art.7
Sch.6 Part A para.7, amended: SSI 2009/153 Art.8

618. National Health Service (Pharmaceutical Services) (Scotland) Amendment (No.2) Regulations 2005
revoked: SSI 2009/183 Sch.5

653. Transport of Animals (Cleansing and Disinfection) (Scotland) Regulations 2005
applied: SSI 2009/173 Sch.2 para.4

2006

1. **Public Contracts (Scotland) Regulations 2006**
applied: SSI 2009/428 Reg.3
Reg.2, amended: SSI 2009/428 Reg.2
Reg.16, amended: SSI 2009/428 Reg.2
Reg.17, amended: SSI 2009/428 Reg.2
Reg.18, amended: SSI 2009/428 Reg.2
Reg.19, amended: SSI 2009/428 Reg.2
Reg.20, amended: SSI 2009/428 Reg.2
Reg.23, amended: SSI 2009/428 Reg.2
Reg.23, referred to: SI 2009/2999 Reg.31
Reg.24, referred to: SI 2009/2999 Reg.31
Reg.25, referred to: SI 2009/2999 Reg.31
Reg.32, substituted: SSI 2009/428 Reg.2
Reg.33, amended: SSI 2009/428 Reg.2
Reg.47, substituted: SSI 2009/428 Reg.2
Reg.47A, added: SSI 2009/428 Reg.2
Reg.47B, added: SSI 2009/428 Reg.2
Reg.47C, added: SSI 2009/428 Reg.2

2. **Utilities Contracts (Scotland) Regulations 2006**
applied: SSI 2009/428 Reg.5
Reg.2, amended: SSI 2009/428 Reg.4
Reg.19, amended: SSI 2009/428 Reg.4
Reg.22, amended: SSI 2009/428 Reg.4
Reg.26, amended: SSI 2009/428 Reg.4
Reg.31, amended: SSI 2009/428 Reg.4
Reg.32, amended: SSI 2009/428 Reg.4
Reg.33, substituted: SSI 2009/428 Reg.4
Reg.34, amended: SSI 2009/428 Reg.4
Reg.44, revoked: SSI 2009/428 Reg.4
Reg.45, substituted: SSI 2009/428 Reg.4
Reg.45A, added: SSI 2009/428 Reg.4
Reg.45B, added: SSI 2009/428 Reg.4
Reg.45C, added: SSI 2009/428 Reg.4
Reg.46, revoked: SSI 2009/428 Reg.4

3. **Food Hygiene (Scotland) Regulations 2006**
Reg.5, applied: SSI 2009/446 Reg.3

24. **Crofting Counties Agricultural Grants (Scotland) Scheme 2006**
Art.6, applied: SSI 2009/376 Sch.1 para.27
Art.11A, applied: SSI 2009/376 Sch.1 para.27
Art.13, applied: SSI 2009/376 Sch.1 para.27

44. **Foot-and-Mouth Disease (Scotland) Order 2006**
Sch.2, applied: SSI 2009/173 Art.18

60. **Advice and Assistance (Scotland) Amendment Regulations 2006**
revoked: SSI 2009/49 Sch.1 Part 1

61. **Civil Legal Aid (Scotland) Amendment Regulations 2006**
revoked: SSI 2009/49 Sch.1 Part 2

73. **Sheep and Goats (Identification and Traceability) (Scotland) Regulations 2006**
revoked: SSI 2009/415 Sch.1

94. **Prisons and Young Offenders Institutions (Scotland) Rules 2006**
Part 1 r.2, amended: SI 2009/2054 Sch.1 para.31
Part 1 r.2, applied: SI 2009/2054 Sch.2 para.19
Part 1 r.5, amended: SSI 2009/248 Sch.1 para.17
Part 2 r.11, amended: SI 2009/2054 Sch.1 para.31
Part 2 r.11, applied: SI 2009/2054 Sch.2 para.19

96. **Police Act 1997 (Criminal Records) (Scotland) Regulations 2006**
Reg.4, amended: SSI 2009/216 Reg.2
Reg.7, amended: SSI 2009/40 Reg.3
Reg.8, amended: SI 2009/2054 Sch.1 para.32, SSI 2009/40 Reg.4
Reg.11, amended: SSI 2009/429 Sch.1 para.6
Reg.12, amended: SSI 2009/429 Sch.1 para.6

2006–cont.

96. **Police Act 1997 (Criminal Records) (Scotland) Regulations 2006–*cont.***
Reg.13, amended: SSI 2009/337 Art.5, SSI 2009/375 Art.4
Reg.13, revoked (in part): SSI 2009/337 Art.5
Reg.14, amended: SSI 2009/337 Art.5, SSI 2009/375 Art.4
Reg.14, revoked (in part): SSI 2009/337 Art.5
Reg.17, amended: SI 2009/2054 Sch.1 para.32
Reg.17, revoked (in part): SI 2009/2054 Sch.1 para.32

97. **Police Act 1997 (Criminal Records) (Registration) (Scotland) Regulations 2006**
Reg.7, amended: SI 2009/2054 Sch.1 para.33
Reg.7, revoked (in part): SI 2009/2054 Sch.1 para.33

143. **National Health Service (Pharmaceutical Services) (Scotland) Amendment Regulations 2006**
revoked: SSI 2009/183 Sch.5

245. **National Health Service (Pharmaceutical Services) (Scotland) Amendment (No.2) Regulations 2006**
revoked: SSI 2009/183 Sch.5

314. **Plastic Materials and Articles in Contact with Food (Scotland) Regulations 2006**
Sch.2 Part 1, applied: SSI 2009/30 Reg.18

320. **National Health Service (Pharmaceutical Services) (Scotland) Amendment (No.3) Regulations 2006**
revoked: SSI 2009/183 Sch.5

330. **National Health Service (Discipline Committees) (Scotland) Regulations 2006**
referred to: SSI 2009/183 Sch.1 para.3
Reg.2, amended: SSI 2009/183 Sch.6 para.5
Sch.2 para.1, amended: SSI 2009/308 Reg.2
Sch.1 para.1, amended: SSI 2009/308 Reg.2

333. **Education (Student Loans for Tuition Fees) (Scotland) Regulations 2006**
Reg.11, amended: SSI 2009/189 Reg.2
Sch.1 para.4, amended: SSI 2009/188 Reg.2
Sch.1 para.6A, added: SSI 2009/309 Reg.2

338. **Firefighters Compensation Scheme (Scotland) Order 2006**
Sch.1, amended: SSI 2009/184 Art.3

419. **Products of Animal Origin (Third Country Imports) (Scotland) Amendment (No.2) Regulations 2006**
revoked: SSI 2009/228 Reg.3

485. **Land Registration (Scotland) Rules 2006**
varied: SI 2009/317 Sch.1

486. **Community Right to Buy (Definition of Excluded Land) (Scotland) Order 2006**
revoked: SSI 2009/207 Art.3

556. **Food for Particular Nutritional Uses (Addition of Substances for Specific Nutritional Purposes) (Scotland) Amendment Regulations 2006**
revoked: SSI 2009/427 Reg.6

570. **Home Energy Efficiency Scheme (Scotland) Regulations 2006**
revoked: SSI 2009/48 Reg.9

575. **Registration Services (Fees, etc.) (Scotland) Regulations 2006**
Sch.2 Part II, amended: SSI 2009/64 Reg.2
Sch.3 Part I, amended: SSI 2009/64 Reg.2
Sch.3 Part II, amended: SSI 2009/64 Reg.2

2006–cont.

588. Personal Injuries (NHS Charges) (Amounts) (Scotland) Regulations 2006
Reg.2, amended: SSI 2009/193 Reg.2
Reg.2A, amended: SSI 2009/193 Reg.2
Reg.2B, added: SSI 2009/193 Reg.2
Reg.3, amended: SSI 2009/193 Reg.2
Reg.3A, added: SSI 2009/193 Reg.2
Reg.6, amended: SSI 2009/193 Reg.2

592. Personal Injuries (NHS Charges) (General) (Scotland) Regulations 2006
Reg.1, amended: SSI 2009/193 Reg.3
Reg.2, amended: SSI 2009/193 Reg.3
Reg.5, amended: SSI 2009/193 Reg.3

594. Sheep and Goats (Identification and Traceability) (Scotland) Amendment (No.2) Regulations 2006
revoked: SSI 2009/415 Sch.1

606. Welfare of Animals (Transport) (Scotland) Regulations 2006
Reg.2, amended: SSI 2009/339 Reg.2
Reg.2, referred to: SSI 2009/339
Reg.9, amended: SSI 2009/339 Reg.2
Reg.22, amended: SSI 2009/339 Reg.2
Reg.24A, added: SSI 2009/339 Reg.2
Reg.24B, added: SSI 2009/339 Reg.2

2007

1. Products of Animal Origin (Third Country Imports) (Scotland) Regulations 2007
Reg.4, amended: SSI 2009/228 Reg.2
Sch.1, referred to: SSI 2009/228
Sch.1 Part I para.1, substituted: SSI 2009/228 Sch.1
Sch.1 Part I para.2, substituted: SSI 2009/228 Sch.1
Sch.1 Part I para.3, substituted: SSI 2009/228 Sch.1
Sch.1 Part I para.4, substituted: SSI 2009/228 Sch.1
Sch.1 Part I para.5, substituted: SSI 2009/228 Sch.1
Sch.1 Part I para.6, substituted: SSI 2009/228 Sch.1
Sch.1 Part I para.7, substituted: SSI 2009/228 Sch.1
Sch.1 Part I para.8, substituted: SSI 2009/228 Sch.1
Sch.1 Part I para.9, substituted: SSI 2009/228 Sch.1
Sch.1 Part I para.10, substituted: SSI 2009/228 Sch.1
Sch.1 Part I para.11, substituted: SSI 2009/228 Sch.1
Sch.1 Part I para.12, substituted: SSI 2009/228 Sch.1
Sch.1 Part I para.13, substituted: SSI 2009/228 Sch.1
Sch.1 Part I para.14, substituted: SSI 2009/228 Sch.1
Sch.1 Part I para.15, substituted: SSI 2009/228 Sch.1
Sch.1 Part I para.16, substituted: SSI 2009/228 Sch.1
Sch.1 Part I para.17, substituted: SSI 2009/228 Sch.1
Sch.1 Part I para.18, substituted: SSI 2009/228 Sch.1
Sch.1 Part I para.19, substituted: SSI 2009/228 Sch.1
Sch.1 Part I para.20, substituted: SSI 2009/228 Sch.1
Sch.1 Part I para.21, substituted: SSI 2009/228 Sch.1
Sch.1 Part I para.22, substituted: SSI 2009/228 Sch.1
Sch.1 Part II para.1, substituted: SSI 2009/228 Sch.1
Sch.1 Part II para.2, substituted: SSI 2009/228 Sch.1
Sch.1 Part II para.3, substituted: SSI 2009/228 Sch.1
Sch.1 Part II para.4, substituted: SSI 2009/228 Sch.1
Sch.1 Part II para.5, substituted: SSI 2009/228 Sch.1
Sch.1 Part II para.6, substituted: SSI 2009/228 Sch.1
Sch.1 Part II para.7, substituted: SSI 2009/228 Sch.1
Sch.1 Part II para.8, substituted: SSI 2009/228 Sch.1
Sch.1 Part II para.9, substituted: SSI 2009/228 Sch.1
Sch.1 Part II para.10, substituted: SSI 2009/228 Sch.1
Sch.1 Part II para.11, substituted: SSI 2009/228 Sch.1
Sch.1 Part II para.12, substituted: SSI 2009/228 Sch.1
Sch.1 Part II para.13, substituted: SSI 2009/228 Sch.1
Sch.1 Part II para.14, substituted: SSI 2009/228 Sch.1

2007–cont.

1. Products of Animal Origin (Third Country Imports) (Scotland) Regulations 2007–*cont.*
Sch.1 Part II para.15, substituted: SSI 2009/228 Sch.1
Sch.1 Part II para.16, substituted: SSI 2009/228 Sch.1
Sch.1 Part II para.17, substituted: SSI 2009/228 Sch.1
Sch.1 Part II para.18, substituted: SSI 2009/228 Sch.1
Sch.1 Part II para.19, substituted: SSI 2009/228 Sch.1
Sch.1 Part II para.20, substituted: SSI 2009/228 Sch.1
Sch.1 Part II para.21, substituted: SSI 2009/228 Sch.1
Sch.1 Part II para.22, substituted: SSI 2009/228 Sch.1
Sch.1 Part II para.23, substituted: SSI 2009/228 Sch.1
Sch.1 Part II para.24, substituted: SSI 2009/228 Sch.1
Sch.1 Part II para.25, substituted: SSI 2009/228 Sch.1
Sch.1 Part II para.26, substituted: SSI 2009/228 Sch.1
Sch.1 Part II para.27, substituted: SSI 2009/228 Sch.1
Sch.1 Part II para.28, substituted: SSI 2009/228 Sch.1
Sch.1 Part II para.29, substituted: SSI 2009/228 Sch.1
Sch.1 Part II para.30, substituted: SSI 2009/228 Sch.1
Sch.1 Part II para.31, substituted: SSI 2009/228 Sch.1
Sch.1 Part III para.1, substituted: SSI 2009/228 Sch.1
Sch.1 Part III para.2, substituted: SSI 2009/228 Sch.1
Sch.1 Part III para.3, substituted: SSI 2009/228 Sch.1
Sch.1 Part III para.4, substituted: SSI 2009/228 Sch.1
Sch.1 Part III para.5, substituted: SSI 2009/228 Sch.1
Sch.1 Part III para.6, substituted: SSI 2009/228 Sch.1
Sch.1 Part III para.7, substituted: SSI 2009/228 Sch.1
Sch.1 Part III para.8, substituted: SSI 2009/228 Sch.1
Sch.1 Part III para.9, substituted: SSI 2009/228 Sch.1
Sch.1 Part III para.10, substituted: SSI 2009/228 Sch.1
Sch.1 Part IV para.1, substituted: SSI 2009/228 Sch.1
Sch.1 Part IV para.2, substituted: SSI 2009/228 Sch.1
Sch.1 Part IV para.3, substituted: SSI 2009/228 Sch.1
Sch.1 Part V para.1, substituted: SSI 2009/228 Sch.1
Sch.1 Part V para.2, substituted: SSI 2009/228 Sch.1
Sch.1 Part V para.3, substituted: SSI 2009/228 Sch.1
Sch.1 Part V para.4, substituted: SSI 2009/228 Sch.1
Sch.1 Part VI para.1, substituted: SSI 2009/228 Sch.1
Sch.1 Part VI para.2, substituted: SSI 2009/228 Sch.1
Sch.1 Part VII para.1, substituted: SSI 2009/228 Sch.1
Sch.1 Part VII para.2, substituted: SSI 2009/228 Sch.1
Sch.1 Part VII para.3, substituted: SSI 2009/228 Sch.1
Sch.1 Part VIII para.1, substituted: SSI 2009/228 Sch.1
Sch.1 Part VIII para.2, substituted: SSI 2009/228 Sch.1
Sch.1 Part VIII para.3, substituted: SSI 2009/228 Sch.1
Sch.1 Part VIII para.4, substituted: SSI 2009/228 Sch.1
Sch.1 Part VIII para.5, substituted: SSI 2009/228 Sch.1
Sch.1 Part VIII para.6, substituted: SSI 2009/228 Sch.1
Sch.1 Part VIII para.7, substituted: SSI 2009/228 Sch.1
Sch.1 Part VIII para.8, substituted: SSI 2009/228 Sch.1
Sch.1 Part VIII para.9, substituted: SSI 2009/228 Sch.1
Sch.1 Part VIII para.10, substituted: SSI 2009/228 Sch.1
Sch.1 Part VIII para.11, substituted: SSI 2009/228 Sch.1
Sch.1 Part VIII para.12, substituted: SSI 2009/228 Sch.1
Sch.1 Part VIII para.13, substituted: SSI 2009/228 Sch.1
Sch.1 Part VIII para.14, substituted: SSI 2009/228 Sch.1
Sch.1 Part VIII para.15, substituted: SSI 2009/228 Sch.1
Sch.1 Part VIII para.16, substituted: SSI 2009/228 Sch.1
Sch.1 Part VIII para.17, substituted: SSI 2009/228 Sch.1
Sch.1 Part VIII para.18, substituted: SSI 2009/228 Sch.1
Sch.1 Part VIII para.19, substituted: SSI 2009/228 Sch.1
Sch.1 Part VIII para.20, substituted: SSI 2009/228 Sch.1
Sch.1 Part IX para.1, substituted: SSI 2009/228 Sch.1
Sch.1 Part IX para.2, substituted: SSI 2009/228 Sch.1
Sch.1 Part IX para.3, substituted: SSI 2009/228 Sch.1
Sch.1 Part IX para.4, substituted: SSI 2009/228 Sch.1
Sch.1 Part IX para.5, substituted: SSI 2009/228 Sch.1
Sch.1 Part IX para.6, substituted: SSI 2009/228 Sch.1
Sch.1 Part IX para.7, substituted: SSI 2009/228 Sch.1

2007– cont.

2007– cont.

1. Products of Animal Origin (Third Country Imports) (Scotland) Regulations 2007– *cont.*
Sch.1 Part IX para.8, substituted: SSI 2009/228 Sch.1
Sch.1 Part IX para.9, substituted: SSI 2009/228 Sch.1
Sch.1 Part IX para.10, substituted: SSI 2009/228 Sch.1
Sch.1 Part IX para.11, substituted: SSI 2009/228 Sch.1
Sch.1 Part IX para.12, substituted: SSI 2009/228 Sch.1
Sch.1 Part IX para.13, substituted: SSI 2009/228 Sch.1
Sch.1 Part IX para.14, substituted: SSI 2009/228 Sch.1
Sch.1 Part IX para.15, substituted: SSI 2009/228 Sch.1
Sch.1 Part IX para.16, substituted: SSI 2009/228 Sch.1
Sch.1 Part IX para.17, substituted: SSI 2009/228 Sch.1
Sch.1 Part X para.1, substituted: SSI 2009/228 Sch.1
Sch.1 Part X para.2, substituted: SSI 2009/228 Sch.1
Sch.1 Part X para.3, substituted: SSI 2009/228 Sch.1
Sch.1 Part X para.4, substituted: SSI 2009/228 Sch.1
Sch.1 Part X para.5, substituted: SSI 2009/228 Sch.1
Sch.1 Part X para.6, substituted: SSI 2009/228 Sch.1
Sch.1 Part X para.7, substituted: SSI 2009/228 Sch.1
Sch.1 Part X para.8, substituted: SSI 2009/228 Sch.1
Sch.1 Part X para.9, substituted: SSI 2009/228 Sch.1
Sch.1 Part X para.10, substituted: SSI 2009/228 Sch.1
Sch.1 Part X para.11, substituted: SSI 2009/228 Sch.1
Sch.1 Part X para.12, substituted: SSI 2009/228 Sch.1
Sch.1 Part X para.13, substituted: SSI 2009/228 Sch.1
Sch.1 Part X para.14, substituted: SSI 2009/228 Sch.1
Sch.1 Part X para.15, substituted: SSI 2009/228 Sch.1
Sch.1 Part X para.16, substituted: SSI 2009/228 Sch.1
Sch.1 Part X para.17, substituted: SSI 2009/228 Sch.1
Sch.1 Part X para.18, substituted: SSI 2009/228 Sch.1
Sch.1 Part X para.19, substituted: SSI 2009/228 Sch.1
Sch.1 Part X para.20, substituted: SSI 2009/228 Sch.1
Sch.1 Part X para.21, substituted: SSI 2009/228 Sch.1
Sch.1 Part X para.22, substituted: SSI 2009/228 Sch.1
Sch.1 Part X para.23, substituted: SSI 2009/228 Sch.1
Sch.1 Part X para.24, substituted: SSI 2009/228 Sch.1
Sch.1 Part X para.25, substituted: SSI 2009/228 Sch.1
Sch.1 Part X para.26, substituted: SSI 2009/228 Sch.1
Sch.1 Part X para.27, substituted: SSI 2009/228 Sch.1
Sch.1 Part X para.28, substituted: SSI 2009/228 Sch.1
Sch.1 Part X para.29, substituted: SSI 2009/228 Sch.1
Sch.1 Part X para.30, substituted: SSI 2009/228 Sch.1
Sch.1 Part X para.31, substituted: SSI 2009/228 Sch.1
Sch.1 Part X para.32, substituted: SSI 2009/228 Sch.1
Sch.1 Part X para.33, substituted: SSI 2009/228 Sch.1
Sch.1 Part X para.34, substituted: SSI 2009/228 Sch.1
Sch.1 Part X para.35, substituted: SSI 2009/228 Sch.1
Sch.1 Part X para.36, substituted: SSI 2009/228 Sch.1
Sch.1 Part X para.37, substituted: SSI 2009/228 Sch.1
Sch.1 Part X para.38, substituted: SSI 2009/228 Sch.1
Sch.1 Part X para.39, substituted: SSI 2009/228 Sch.1
Sch.1 Part X para.40, substituted: SSI 2009/228 Sch.1
Sch.1 Part X para.41, substituted: SSI 2009/228 Sch.1
Sch.1 Part X para.42, substituted: SSI 2009/228 Sch.1
Sch.1 Part X para.43, substituted: SSI 2009/228 Sch.1
Sch.1 Part X para.44, substituted: SSI 2009/228 Sch.1
Sch.1 Part X para.45, substituted: SSI 2009/228 Sch.1
Sch.1 Part X para.46, substituted: SSI 2009/228 Sch.1
Sch.1 Part X para.47, substituted: SSI 2009/228 Sch.1
Sch.1 Part X para.48, substituted: SSI 2009/228 Sch.1
Sch.1 Part X para.49, substituted: SSI 2009/228 Sch.1
Sch.1 Part X para.50, substituted: SSI 2009/228 Sch.1
Sch.1 Part X para.51, substituted: SSI 2009/228 Sch.1
Sch.1 Part X para.52, substituted: SSI 2009/228 Sch.1
Sch.1 Part X para.53, substituted: SSI 2009/228 Sch.1
Sch.1 Part X para.54, substituted: SSI 2009/228 Sch.1
Sch.1 Part X para.55, substituted: SSI 2009/228 Sch.1
Sch.1 Part X para.56, substituted: SSI 2009/228 Sch.1

1. Products of Animal Origin (Third Country Imports) (Scotland) Regulations 2007– *cont.*
Sch.1 Part X para.57, substituted: SSI 2009/228 Sch.1
Sch.1 Part X para.58, substituted: SSI 2009/228 Sch.1
Sch.1 Part X para.59, substituted: SSI 2009/228 Sch.1
Sch.1 Part X para.60, substituted: SSI 2009/228 Sch.1
Sch.1 Part X para.61, substituted: SSI 2009/228 Sch.1
Sch.1 Part X para.62, substituted: SSI 2009/228 Sch.1
Sch.1 Part X para.63, substituted: SSI 2009/228 Sch.1
Sch.1 Part X para.64, substituted: SSI 2009/228 Sch.1
Sch.1 Part X para.65, substituted: SSI 2009/228 Sch.1
Sch.1 Part X para.66, substituted: SSI 2009/228 Sch.1
Sch.1 Part X para.67, substituted: SSI 2009/228 Sch.1
Sch.1 Part X para.68, substituted: SSI 2009/228 Sch.1
Sch.1 Part X para.69, substituted: SSI 2009/228 Sch.1
Sch.1 Part X para.70, substituted: SSI 2009/228 Sch.1
Sch.1 Part X para.71, substituted: SSI 2009/228 Sch.1
Sch.1 Part X para.72, substituted: SSI 2009/228 Sch.1
Sch.1 Part X para.73, substituted: SSI 2009/228 Sch.1
Sch.1 Part X para.74, substituted: SSI 2009/228 Sch.1
Sch.1 Part X para.75, substituted: SSI 2009/228 Sch.1
Sch.1 Part X para.76, substituted: SSI 2009/228 Sch.1
Sch.1 Part X para.77, substituted: SSI 2009/228 Sch.1
Sch.1 Part X para.78, substituted: SSI 2009/228 Sch.1
Sch.1 Part X para.79, substituted: SSI 2009/228 Sch.1
Sch.1 Part X para.80, substituted: SSI 2009/228 Sch.1
Sch.1 Part X para.81, substituted: SSI 2009/228 Sch.1
Sch.1 Part X para.82, substituted: SSI 2009/228 Sch.1
Sch.1 Part X para.83, substituted: SSI 2009/228 Sch.1
Sch.1 Part X para.84, substituted: SSI 2009/228 Sch.1
Sch.1 Part X para.85, substituted: SSI 2009/228 Sch.1
Sch.1 Part X para.86, substituted: SSI 2009/228 Sch.1
Sch.1 Part X para.87, substituted: SSI 2009/228 Sch.1
Sch.1 Part X para.88, substituted: SSI 2009/228 Sch.1
Sch.1 Part X para.89, substituted: SSI 2009/228 Sch.1
Sch.1 Part X para.90, substituted: SSI 2009/228 Sch.1
Sch.1 Part X para.91, substituted: SSI 2009/228 Sch.1
Sch.1 Part X para.92, substituted: SSI 2009/228 Sch.1
Sch.1 Part X para.93, substituted: SSI 2009/228 Sch.1
Sch.1 Part X para.94, substituted: SSI 2009/228 Sch.1
Sch.1 Part X para.95, substituted: SSI 2009/228 Sch.1
Sch.1 Part X para.96, substituted: SSI 2009/228 Sch.1
Sch.1 Part X para.97, substituted: SSI 2009/228 Sch.1
Sch.1 Part X para.98, substituted: SSI 2009/228 Sch.1
Sch.1 Part X para.99, substituted: SSI 2009/228 Sch.1
Sch.1 Part X para.100, substituted: SSI 2009/228 Sch.1
Sch.1 Part X para.101, substituted: SSI 2009/228 Sch.1
Sch.1 Part X para.102, substituted: SSI 2009/228 Sch.1
Sch.1 Part X para.103, substituted: SSI 2009/228 Sch.1
Sch.1 Part X para.104, substituted: SSI 2009/228 Sch.1
Sch.1 Part X para.105, substituted: SSI 2009/228 Sch.1
Sch.1 Part X para.106, substituted: SSI 2009/228 Sch.1
Sch.1 Part X para.107, substituted: SSI 2009/228 Sch.1
Sch.1 Part X para.108, substituted: SSI 2009/228 Sch.1
Sch.1 Part X para.109, substituted: SSI 2009/228 Sch.1
Sch.1 Part X para.110, substituted: SSI 2009/228 Sch.1
Sch.1 Part X para.111, substituted: SSI 2009/228 Sch.1
Sch.1 Part X para.112, substituted: SSI 2009/228 Sch.1
Sch.1 Part X para.113, substituted: SSI 2009/228 Sch.1
Sch.1 Part X para.114, substituted: SSI 2009/228 Sch.1
Sch.1 Part X para.115, substituted: SSI 2009/228 Sch.1
Sch.1 Part X para.116, substituted: SSI 2009/228 Sch.1
Sch.1 Part X para.117, substituted: SSI 2009/228 Sch.1
Sch.1 Part XI para.1, substituted: SSI 2009/228 Sch.1

29. Contaminants in Food (Scotland) Regulations 2007
revoked: SSI 2009/215 Reg.7

2007– cont.

30. Specified Animal Pathogens Amendment (Scotland) Order 2007
revoked: SSI 2009/45 Art.12

32. Sex Discrimination (Public Authorities) (Statutory Duties) (Scotland) Order 2007
Sch.1 Part I, amended: SSI 2009/248 Sch.1 para.18

39. Sea Fishing (Prohibition on the Removal of Shark Fins) (Scotland) Order 2007
Art.2, amended: SSI 2009/413 Art.2
Art.3, amended: SSI 2009/413 Art.2
Sch.1 Part 1, amended: SSI 2009/413 Art.2
Sch.1 Part 3, added: SSI 2009/413 Art.2

42. Scottish Local Government Elections Order 2007
Sch.1, amended: SSI 2009/36 Sch.1
Sch.1, applied: SSI 2009/35 Reg.15
Sch.4, amended: SSI 2009/36 Sch.2

59. Civil Legal Aid (Scotland) Amendment Regulations 2007
Reg.4, revoked (in part): SSI 2009/49 Sch.1 Part 2

60. Advice and Assistance (Scotland) Amendment Regulations 2007
Reg.2, revoked (in part): SSI 2009/49 Sch.1 Part 1
Reg.7, revoked: SSI 2009/49 Sch.1 Part 1

68. Police (Injury Benefit) (Scotland) Regulations 2007
Sch.3 para.6, amended: SSI 2009/185 Reg.7

113. Act of Sederunt (Registration Appeal Court) 2007
revoked: SSI 2009/12 Art.2

147. Tuberculosis (Scotland) Order 2007
Art.2, amended: SSI 2009/445 Art.2
Art.8, amended: SSI 2009/445 Art.2
Art.9A, added: SSI 2009/445 Art.2
Art.10, amended: SSI 2009/445 Art.2

149. Education Authority Bursaries (Scotland) Regulations 2007
applied: SI 2009/1562 Art.2
Reg.2, amended: SSI 2009/188 Reg.4
Sch.1 para.4, amended: SSI 2009/188 Reg.5
Sch.1 para.6A, added: SSI 2009/309 Reg.4
Sch.1 para.9, substituted: SSI 2009/188 Reg.5
Sch.2 para.2, amended: SSI 2009/309 Reg.5

151. Nursing and Midwifery Student Allowances (Scotland) Regulations 2007
applied: SI 2009/1555 Reg.5, Reg.116, Reg.133, Reg.150, SI 2009/2737 Reg.4, Reg.68, Reg.85, Reg.109
Reg.2, amended: SSI 2009/188 Reg.7
Sch.1 para.4, amended: SSI 2009/188 Reg.8
Sch.1 para.6A, added: SSI 2009/309 Reg.7
Sch.1 para.9, substituted: SSI 2009/188 Reg.8
Sch.2 para.2, amended: SSI 2009/309 Reg.8

152. Education (Fees and Awards) (Scotland) Regulations 2007
Reg.2, amended: SSI 2009/188 Reg.10, SSI 2009/309 Reg.10
Reg.5, amended: SSI 2009/309 Reg.11
Sch.1 para.4, amended: SSI 2009/188 Reg.11
Sch.1 para.6A, added: SSI 2009/309 Reg.12
Sch.1 para.9, amended: SSI 2009/188 Reg.11
Sch.2 para.4, amended: SSI 2009/188 Reg.12
Sch.2 para.6A, added: SSI 2009/309 Reg.13
Sch.2 para.11, amended: SSI 2009/309 Reg.13
Sch.3 para.3, amended: SSI 2009/188 Reg.13

153. Students Allowances (Scotland) Regulations 2007
Reg.2, amended: SSI 2009/188 Reg.15
Sch.1 para.4, amended: SSI 2009/188 Reg.16

2007– cont.

153. Students Allowances (Scotland) Regulations 2007– cont.
Sch.1 para.6A, added: SSI 2009/309 Reg.15
Sch.1 para.9, substituted: SSI 2009/188 Reg.16
Sch.2 para.2, amended: SSI 2009/309 Reg.16

154. Education (Student Loans) (Scotland) Regulations 2007
Reg.14, amended: SSI 2009/189 Reg.3
Sch.1 para.4, amended: SSI 2009/188 Reg.17
Sch.1 para.6A, added: SSI 2009/309 Reg.17

156. Education Maintenance Allowances (Scotland) Regulations 2007
Sch.1 para.4, amended: SSI 2009/188 Reg.18
Sch.1 para.6A, added: SSI 2009/309 Reg.18

170. Representation of the People (Absent Voting at Local Government Elections) (Scotland) Regulations 2007
Reg.2, amended: SSI 2009/35 Reg.6
Reg.2, revoked (in part): SSI 2009/35 Reg.5
Reg.2A, added: SSI 2009/35 Reg.5
Reg.3, amended: SSI 2009/35 Reg.7
Reg.3, revoked (in part): SSI 2009/35 Reg.7
Reg.4, substituted: SSI 2009/35 Reg.8
Reg.8, amended: SI 2009/1182 Sch.4 para.43
Reg.8, revoked (in part): SI 2009/1182 Sch.4 para.17
Reg.12, varied: SSI 2009/35 Reg.15
Reg.13, varied: SSI 2009/35 Reg.15
Reg.15A, added: SSI 2009/35 Reg.9
Reg.15B, added: SSI 2009/35 Reg.9
Reg.15C, added: SSI 2009/35 Reg.9
Reg.18A, added: SSI 2009/35 Reg.10
Reg.18A, amended: SSI 2009/94 Art.2
Reg.18A, revoked (in part): SSI 2009/94 Art.2

179. Radioactive Contaminated Land (Scotland) Regulations 2007
Reg.3, amended: SSI 2009/202 Reg.2
Reg.14, substituted: SSI 2009/202 Reg.2

194. Animals and Animal Products (Import and Export) (Scotland) Regulations 2007
applied: SSI 2009/173 Art.3
referred to: SSI 2009/227
Reg.1, amended: SSI 2009/227 Reg.2
Reg.4, amended: SSI 2009/227 Reg.2
Reg.23, amended: SSI 2009/227 Reg.2
Sch.1 para.1, revoked: SSI 2009/227 Reg.2
Sch.1 para.2, revoked: SSI 2009/227 Reg.2
Sch.3 Part I para.1, substituted: SSI 2009/227 Sch.1
Sch.3 Part I para.2, substituted: SSI 2009/227 Sch.1
Sch.3 Part I para.3, substituted: SSI 2009/227 Sch.1
Sch.3 Part I para.4, substituted: SSI 2009/227 Sch.1
Sch.3 Part I para.5, substituted: SSI 2009/227 Sch.1
Sch.3 Part I para.6, substituted: SSI 2009/227 Sch.1
Sch.3 Part I para.7, substituted: SSI 2009/227 Sch.1
Sch.3 Part I para.8, substituted: SSI 2009/227 Sch.1
Sch.3 Part I para.9, substituted: SSI 2009/227 Sch.1
Sch.3 Part I para.10, substituted: SSI 2009/227 Sch.1
Sch.3 Part I para.10A, substituted: SSI 2009/227 Sch.1
Sch.3 Part I para.11, substituted: SSI 2009/227 Sch.1
Sch.3 Part I para.12, substituted: SSI 2009/227 Sch.1
Sch.3 Part I para.13, substituted: SSI 2009/227 Sch.1
Sch.3 Part I para.14, substituted: SSI 2009/227 Sch.1
Sch.3 Part I para.15, substituted: SSI 2009/227 Sch.1
Sch.3 Part I para.16, substituted: SSI 2009/227 Sch.1
Sch.3 Part I para.17, substituted: SSI 2009/227 Sch.1
Sch.7 Part I para.1, substituted: SSI 2009/227 Sch.2
Sch.7 Part I para.2, substituted: SSI 2009/227 Sch.2
Sch.7 Part I para.3, substituted: SSI 2009/227 Sch.2
Sch.7 Part I para.4, substituted: SSI 2009/227 Sch.2

194. Animals and Animal Products (Import and Export) (Scotland) Regulations 2007– *cont.*
Sch.7 Part I para.5, substituted: SSI 2009/227 Sch.2
Sch.7 Part I para.6, substituted: SSI 2009/227 Sch.2
Sch.7 Part I para.7, substituted: SSI 2009/227 Sch.2
Sch.7 Part I para.8, substituted: SSI 2009/227 Sch.2
Sch.7 Part II para.1, substituted: SSI 2009/227 Sch.2
Sch.7 Part II para.2, substituted: SSI 2009/227 Sch.2
Sch.7 Part II para.3, substituted: SSI 2009/227 Sch.2
Sch.7 Part II para.4, substituted: SSI 2009/227 Sch.2
Sch.7 Part II para.5, substituted: SSI 2009/227 Sch.2
Sch.7 Part II para.6, substituted: SSI 2009/227 Sch.2
Sch.7 Part II para.7, substituted: SSI 2009/227 Sch.2
Sch.7 Part II para.8, substituted: SSI 2009/227 Sch.2
Sch.7 Part II para.9, substituted: SSI 2009/227 Sch.2
Sch.7 Part II para.10, substituted: SSI 2009/227 Sch.2
Sch.7 Part II para.11, substituted: SSI 2009/227 Sch.2
Sch.7 Part II para.12, substituted: SSI 2009/227 Sch.2
Sch.7 Part II para.13, substituted: SSI 2009/227 Sch.2
Sch.7 Part II para.14, substituted: SSI 2009/227 Sch.2
Sch.7 Part II para.15, substituted: SSI 2009/227 Sch.2
Sch.8 Part I para.3, amended: SSI 2009/227 Reg.2
Sch.8 Part I para.4, amended: SSI 2009/227 Reg.2
Sch.8 Part II para.4, amended: SSI 2009/227 Reg.2

208. National Health Service (Pharmaceutical Services) (Scotland) Amendment Regulations 2007
revoked: SSI 2009/183 Sch.5

217. Horse Passports (Scotland) Amendment Regulations 2007
revoked: SSI 2009/231 Reg.25

231. Regulation of Care (Scotland) Act 2001 (Minimum Frequency of Inspections) Order 2007
revoked: SSI 2009/131 Art.3

256. Prohibited Procedures on Protected Animals (Exemptions) (Scotland) Regulations 2007
Reg.2, amended: SSI 2009/47 Reg.2
Sch.1, substituted: SSI 2009/47 Reg.2
Sch.2, substituted: SSI 2009/47 Reg.2
Sch.3, substituted: SSI 2009/47 Reg.2
Sch.4, substituted: SSI 2009/47 Reg.2
Sch.5, substituted: SSI 2009/47 Reg.2
Sch.6, substituted: SSI 2009/47 Reg.2
Sch.7, substituted: SSI 2009/47 Reg.2
Sch.8, substituted: SSI 2009/47 Reg.2
Sch.9, substituted: SSI 2009/47 Reg.2
Sch.10, substituted: SSI 2009/47 Reg.2
Sch.11, substituted: SSI 2009/47 Reg.2
Sch.12, substituted: SSI 2009/47 Reg.2

263. Representation of the People (Postal Voting for Local Government Elections) (Scotland) Regulations 2007
Reg.3, amended: SSI 2009/128 Reg.3
Reg.19, amended: SSI 2009/128 Reg.4
Reg.22, amended: SSI 2009/128 Reg.5
Reg.24, amended: SSI 2009/128 Reg.6
Reg.24A, added: SSI 2009/128 Reg.7
Reg.24B, added: SSI 2009/128 Reg.7
Reg.29, amended: SSI 2009/128 Reg.8
Sch.1, amended: SSI 2009/128 Sch.1

267. Renewables Obligation (Scotland) Order 2007
applied: SI 2009/785 Art.61, SSI 2009/140 Art.61
revoked: SSI 2009/140 Art.61
Art.35, applied: SSI 2009/140 Art.61
Sch.1, applied: SSI 2009/140 Art.61

325. Addition of Vitamins, Minerals and Other Substances (Scotland) Regulations 2007
Reg.2, amended: SSI 2009/438 Reg.3

390. National Health Service (Pharmaceutical Services) (Scotland) Amendment (No.2) Regulations 2007
revoked: SSI 2009/183 Sch.5

412. Miscellaneous Food Additives and the Sweeteners in Food Amendment (Scotland) Regulations 2007
Reg.5, referred to: SSI 2009/436 Reg.10
Reg.6, referred to: SSI 2009/436 Reg.10
Reg.8, referred to: SSI 2009/436 Reg.10

436. Administrative Justice and Tribunals Council (Listed Tribunals) (Scotland) Order 2007
Sch.1, amended: SSI 2009/183 Sch.6 para.6

439. Less Favoured Area Support Scheme (Scotland) Regulations 2007
Reg.2, amended: SSI 2009/412 Reg.3
Reg.4, applied: SSI 2009/376 Sch.1 para.13
Reg.5, applied: SSI 2009/376 Sch.1 para.13
Reg.7, applied: SSI 2009/376 Sch.1 para.13
Reg.9, applied: SSI 2009/376 Sch.1 para.13
Reg.10, applied: SSI 2009/376 Sch.1 para.13
Reg.11, applied: SSI 2009/376 Sch.1 para.13
Reg.12, amended: SSI 2009/412 Reg.4
Reg.16, applied: SSI 2009/376 Sch.1 para.13
Reg.16A, applied: SSI 2009/376 Sch.1 para.13
Sch.1, amended: SSI 2009/412 Reg.5
Sch.3 Part I, substituted: SSI 2009/412 Reg.6
Sch.3 Part II, substituted: SSI 2009/412 Reg.6

441. A77 Trunk Road (Haggstone Climbing Lane and Glen App Carriageway Improvement) (Temporary Prohibition of Traffic, Temporary Prohibition of Overtaking and Temporary Speed Restriction) Order 2007
applied: SSI 2009/136
revoked: SSI 2009/136 Art.2

470. Contaminants in Food (Scotland) Amendment Regulations 2007
revoked: SSI 2009/215 Reg.7

471. Materials and Articles in Contact with Food (Scotland) Regulations 2007
Reg.2, amended: SSI 2009/30 Reg.23, SSI 2009/426 Reg.3
Reg.2, revoked (in part): SSI 2009/426 Reg.3
Reg.5A, added: SSI 2009/426 Reg.4
Reg.7A, added: SSI 2009/426 Reg.5
Reg.9, referred to: SSI 2009/30 Reg.13
Reg.10, amended: SSI 2009/30 Reg.23
Reg.11, amended: SSI 2009/30 Reg.23
Reg.13, amended: SSI 2009/426 Reg.6
Reg.15, substituted: SSI 2009/426 Reg.7
Reg.18, amended: SSI 2009/426 Reg.8

483. Natural Mineral Water, Spring Water and Bottled Drinking Water (Scotland) (No.2) Regulations 2007
Reg.2, amended: SSI 2009/273 Reg.3, Reg.4
Reg.4, amended: SSI 2009/273 Reg.4
Reg.8, amended: SSI 2009/273 Reg.5
Reg.9, amended: SSI 2009/273 Reg.6
Reg.16, amended: SSI 2009/273 Reg.7
Sch.4 para.4, amended: SSI 2009/273 Reg.8
Sch.4 para.5, amended: SSI 2009/273 Reg.8
Sch.4 para.8, amended: SSI 2009/273 Reg.8

485. Environmental Impact Assessment and Natural Habitats (Extraction of Minerals by Marine Dredging) (Scotland) Regulations 2007
Reg.2, amended: SSI 2009/333 Reg.2
Reg.2, revoked (in part): SSI 2009/333 Reg.2

2007– cont.

500. National Health Service (Pharmaceutical Services) (Scotland) Amendment (No.3) Regulations 2007
revoked: SSI 2009/ 183 Sch.5

520. Seed Potatoes (Fees) (Scotland) Amendment Regulations 2007
revoked: SSI 2009/ 306 Reg.7

522. Official Feed and Food Controls (Scotland) Regulations 2007
revoked: SSI 2009/ 446 Reg.52

539. Act of Sederunt (Lands Valuation Appeal Court) 2007
revoked: SSI 2009/ 295 Art.2

557. Education (Recognised Bodies) (Scotland) Order 2007
Sch.1, amended: SSI 2009/ 61 Art.3, Art.4, Art.5, Art.6, Art.7, Art.8, Art.9, Art.10, Art.11, Art.12, Art.13, Art.14, Art.15

558. Education (Listed Bodies) (Scotland) Order 2007
Sch.1 Part 1, amended: SSI 2009/ 60 Art.3, Art.4

559. Sheep and Goats (Identification and Traceability) (Scotland) Amendment Regulations 2007
revoked: SSI 2009/ 415 Sch.1

577. Zoonoses and Animal By-Products (Fees) (Scotland) Regulations 2007
revoked: SSI 2009/ 230 Reg.4

2008

13. National Assistance (Assessment of Resources) Amendment (Scotland) Regulations 2008
revoked: SSI 2009/ 72 Reg.5

14. National Assistance (Sums for Personal Requirements) (Scotland) Regulations 2008
revoked: SSI 2009/ 73 Reg.3

16. Scottish Road Works Register (Prescribed Fees and Amounts) Regulations 2008
Reg.2, amended: SSI 2009/ 26 Reg.4
Reg.3, applied: SSI 2009/ 26 Reg.3
Reg.4, revoked: SSI 2009/ 26 Reg.4
Sch.2, revoked: SSI 2009/ 26 Reg.4

27. National Health Service (Charges for Drugs and Appliances) (Scotland) Regulations 2008
Reg.2, amended: SSI 2009/ 183 Sch.6 para.7
Reg.3, amended: SSI 2009/ 37 Reg.2
Reg.4, amended: SSI 2009/ 37 Reg.2
Reg.5, amended: SSI 2009/ 37 Reg.2
Reg.7, amended: SSI 2009/ 37 Reg.2, SSI 2009/ 177 Reg.3
Reg.7, applied: SSI 2009/ 183 Sch.1 para.4
Reg.8, amended: SSI 2009/ 37 Reg.2
Reg.8, applied: SSI 2009/ 37 Reg.3
Reg.8, referred to: SSI 2009/ 37 Reg.3
Sch.1, amended: SSI 2009/ 37 Reg.2
Sch.1, applied: SSI 2009/ 37 Reg.3
Sch.2 para.1, added: SSI 2009/ 177 Reg.3
Sch.2 Part 1 para.1, added: SSI 2009/ 177 Reg.3
Sch.2 Part 1 para.2, added: SSI 2009/ 177 Reg.3
Sch.2 Part 1 para.3, added: SSI 2009/ 177 Reg.3
Sch.2 para.2, added: SSI 2009/ 177 Reg.3
Sch.2 Part 2 para.4, added: SSI 2009/ 177 Reg.3
Sch.2 para.3, added: SSI 2009/ 177 Reg.3
Sch.3 para.1, revoked: SSI 2009/ 183 Sch.5

29. Sea Fish (Prohibited Methods of Fishing) (Firth of Clyde) Order 2008
revoked: SSI 2009/ 38 Art.5

2008– cont.

31. Justice of the Peace Courts (Sheriffdom of Lothian and Borders) etc Order 2008
applied: SSI 2009/ 293 Art.4

33. Local Government Finance (Scotland) Order 2008
Art.2, revoked: SSI 2009/ 50 Art.5
Sch.1, amended: SSI 2009/ 50 Art.5

43. Road Works (Inspection Fees) (Scotland) Amendment Regulations 2008
revoked: SSI 2009/ 74 Reg.3

46. Police Grant (Scotland) Order 2008
Art.2, amended: SSI 2009/ 41 Art.2
Art.2, varied: SSI 2009/ 55 Art.3
Art.3, amended: SSI 2009/ 41 Art.2
Art.3, varied: SSI 2009/ 55 Art.3

47. Advice and Assistance (Scotland) Amendment Regulations 2008
revoked: SSI 2009/ 49 Sch.1 Part 1

48. Civil Legal Aid (Scotland) Amendment Regulations 2008
revoked: SSI 2009/ 49 Sch.1 Part 2

64. Agricultural Processing, Marketing and Co-operation Grants (Scotland) Regulations 2008
applied: SSI 2009/ 376 Sch.1 para.33

66. Leader Grants (Scotland) Regulations 2008
applied: SSI 2009/ 376 Sch.1 para.29

85. Non-Domestic Rates (Levying) (Scotland) Regulations 2008
revoked: SSI 2009/ 42 Reg.6

98. Meat (Official Controls Charges) (Scotland) Regulations 2008
revoked: SSI 2009/ 262 Reg.6

100. Rural Development Contracts (Rural Priorities) (Scotland) Regulations 2008
applied: SSI 2009/ 376 Sch.1 para.28
Reg.2, amended: SSI 2009/ 335 Reg.3, SSI 2009/ 411 Reg.3
Reg.7, amended: SSI 2009/ 335 Reg.4
Reg.9, amended: SSI 2009/ 335 Reg.5, SSI 2009/ 411 Reg.4
Reg.12, amended: SSI 2009/ 335 Reg.6
Sch.1, amended: SSI 2009/ 1 Reg.3, SSI 2009/ 335 Reg.7, SSI 2009/ 411 Reg.5
Sch.2 Part 1, amended: SSI 2009/ 1 Reg.4, SSI 2009/ 233 Reg.3, SSI 2009/ 335 Reg.8, SSI 2009/ 411 Reg.6, Sch.1
Sch.2 Part 1, revoked: SSI 2009/ 335 Reg.8
Sch.2 Part 1, substituted: SSI 2009/ 411 Reg.6
Sch.2 Part 2, added: SSI 2009/ 411 Sch.3
Sch.2 Part 2, amended: SSI 2009/ 1 Reg.5, SSI 2009/ 335 Reg.8, SSI 2009/ 411 Sch.2
Sch.2 Part 2, substituted: SSI 2009/ 233 Reg.4
Sch.3, amended: SSI 2009/ 335 Reg.9

115. Bankruptcy and Diligence etc (Scotland) Act 2007 (Commencement No.3, Savings and Transitionals) Order 2008
Art.12, amended: SSI 2009/ 67 Art.7

117. Police (Special Constables) (Scotland) Regulations 2008
Reg.2, amended: SSI 2009/ 372 Reg.3
Reg.8, amended: SSI 2009/ 372 Reg.3

127. Plastic Materials and Articles in Contact with Food (Scotland) Regulations 2008
applied: SSI 2009/ 30 Reg.5
revoked: SSI 2009/ 30 Reg.24

132. Renewables Obligation (Scotland) Amendment Order 2008
revoked: SSI 2009/ 140 Art.61

135. Forestry Challenge Funds (Scotland) Regulations 2008
applied: SSI 2009/376 Sch.1 para.32

137. Advice and Assistance (Financial Conditions) (Scotland) Regulations 2008
revoked: SSI 2009/143 Reg.8

138. Civil Legal Aid (Financial Conditions) (Scotland) Regulations 2008
revoked: SSI 2009/143 Reg.9

151. Sea Fishing (Enforcement of Community Quota and Third Country Fishing Measures and Restriction on Days at Sea) (Scotland) Order 2008
Part III, revoked: SSI 2009/317 Art.21
Part IV, revoked: SSI 2009/317 Art.21
Art.2, revoked: SSI 2009/317 Art.21
Art.3, revoked: SSI 2009/317 Art.21
Art.4, revoked: SSI 2009/317 Art.21
Art.5, revoked: SSI 2009/317 Art.21
Art.6, revoked: SSI 2009/317 Art.21
Art.21, revoked: SSI 2009/317 Art.21
Art.22, revoked: SSI 2009/317 Art.21
Art.23, revoked: SSI 2009/317 Art.21
Art.24, revoked: SSI 2009/317 Art.21
Art.25, revoked: SSI 2009/317 Art.21
Art.26, revoked: SSI 2009/317 Art.21
Art.27, revoked: SSI 2009/317 Art.21
Art.28, revoked: SSI 2009/317 Art.21
Art.29, revoked: SSI 2009/317 Art.21
Art.30, revoked: SSI 2009/317 Art.21
Art.31, revoked: SSI 2009/317 Art.21
Art.32, revoked: SSI 2009/317 Art.21
Art.33, revoked: SSI 2009/317 Art.21

158. Products of Animal Origin (Disease Control) (Scotland) Order 2008
Art.2, amended: SSI 2009/174 Art.3
Art.4, amended: SSI 2009/174 Art.4
Art.8, amended: SSI 2009/174 Art.5
Art.10, amended: SSI 2009/174 Art.6
Art.10, revoked (in part): SSI 2009/174 Art.6
Art.11, amended: SSI 2009/174 Art.7
Art.13, amended: SSI 2009/174 Art.8
Art.14, amended: SSI 2009/174 Art.9
Art.15, substituted: SSI 2009/174 Art.10
Art.16, amended: SSI 2009/174 Art.11
Sch.1 para.5, substituted: SSI 2009/173 Art.45
Sch.3 para.3A, added: SSI 2009/174 Art.12

159. Rural Development Contracts (Land Managers Options) (Scotland) Regulations 2008
applied: SSI 2009/376 Sch.1 para.30
Reg.2, amended: SSI 2009/155 Reg.2
Reg.5, amended: SSI 2009/155 Reg.2
Reg.8, amended: SSI 2009/155 Reg.2
Reg.10, amended: SSI 2009/155 Reg.2
Sch.1, amended: SSI 2009/155 Reg.2
Sch.2, amended: SSI 2009/155 Reg.2

162. Land Managers Skills Development Grants (Scotland) Regulations 2008
applied: SSI 2009/376 Sch.1 para.31

218. Official Feed and Food Controls (Scotland) Amendment Regulations 2008
revoked: SSI 2009/446 Reg.52

224. National Health Service Pension Scheme (Scotland) Regulations 2008
referred to: SSI 2009/19 Reg.23, Reg.87
Reg.2.A.1, amended: SSI 2009/19 Reg.24, SSI 2009/208 Reg.16
Reg.2.A.2, amended: SSI 2009/19 Reg.25

224. National Health Service Pension Scheme (Scotland) Regulations 2008–*cont.*
Reg.2.A.4, amended: SSI 2009/19 Reg.26
Reg.2.A.5, amended: SSI 2009/19 Reg.27
Reg.2.A.9, amended: SSI 2009/19 Reg.28, SSI 2009/208 Reg.17
Reg.2.A.10, amended: SSI 2009/208 Reg.18
Reg.2.B.1, amended: SSI 2009/19 Reg.29
Reg.2.B.2, amended: SSI 2009/19 Reg.30, SSI 2009/208 Reg.19
Reg.2.C.2, amended: SSI 2009/19 Reg.31, SSI 2009/208 Reg.20
Reg.2.C.5, amended: SSI 2009/19 Reg.32, SSI 2009/208 Reg.23
Reg.2.D.7, amended: SSI 2009/19 Reg.33, SSI 2009/208 Reg.27
Reg.2.D.9, amended: SSI 2009/19 Reg.34, SSI 2009/208 Reg.29
Reg.2.D.10, amended: SSI 2009/19 Reg.35
Reg.2.D.11, amended: SSI 2009/208 Reg.30
Reg.2.D.13, amended: SSI 2009/208 Reg.31
Reg.2.D.14, amended: SSI 2009/208 Reg.32
Reg.2.D.15, amended: SSI 2009/208 Reg.33
Reg.2.D.17, revoked (in part): SSI 2009/208 Reg.34
Reg.2.D.21, amended: SSI 2009/208 Reg.35
Reg.2.E.10, amended: SSI 2009/208 Reg.40
Reg.2.E.11, amended: SSI 2009/208 Reg.41
Reg.2.E.12, amended: SSI 2009/208 Reg.42
Reg.2.E.13, amended: SSI 2009/208 Reg.43
Reg.2.E.15, amended: SSI 2009/208 Reg.44
Reg.2.E.17, amended: SSI 2009/208 Reg.45
Reg.2.E.18, amended: SSI 2009/208 Reg.46
Reg.2.E.19, amended: SSI 2009/208 Reg.47
Reg.2.E.20A, added: SSI 2009/19 Reg.36
Reg.2.E.21, amended: SSI 2009/19 Reg.37
Reg.2.E.25, amended: SSI 2009/19 Reg.38, SSI 2009/208 Reg.48
Reg.2.F.6, amended: SSI 2009/19 Reg.39
Reg.2.F.8, amended: SSI 2009/19 Reg.40, SSI 2009/208 Reg.49
Reg.2.F.9, amended: SSI 2009/19 Reg.41
Reg.2.F.10, amended: SSI 2009/19 Reg.42
Reg.2.F.11, amended: SSI 2009/19 Reg.43
Reg.2.F.11, revoked (in part): SSI 2009/19 Reg.43
Reg.2.F.17, added: SSI 2009/19 Reg.44
Reg.2.H.2, substituted: SSI 2009/19 Reg.45
Reg.2.H.5, amended: SSI 2009/19 Reg.46
Reg.2.H.7, amended: SSI 2009/19 Reg.47
Reg.2.J.2, substituted: SSI 2009/19 Reg.48
Reg.2.J.5, revoked (in part): SSI 2009/208 Reg.51
Reg.2.J.7, amended: SSI 2009/19 Reg.49
Reg.2.J.9, amended: SSI 2009/19 Reg.50, SSI 2009/208 Reg.52
Reg.2.J.10, amended: SSI 2009/19 Reg.51
Reg.2.J.13, amended: SSI 2009/19 Reg.52
Reg.2.J.13, substituted: SSI 2009/208 Reg.53
Reg.3.A.1, amended: SSI 2009/19 Reg.53, SSI 2009/208 Reg.54
Reg.3.A.3, amended: SSI 2009/19 Reg.54
Reg.3.A.4, amended: SSI 2009/19 Reg.55
Reg.3.A.5, amended: SSI 2009/19 Reg.56
Reg.3.A.7, amended: SSI 2009/19 Reg.57
Reg.3.A.8, amended: SSI 2009/19 Reg.58
Reg.3.B.1, amended: SSI 2009/19 Reg.59
Reg.3.B.2, amended: SSI 2009/19 Reg.60, SSI 2009/208 Reg.55
Reg.3.B.5, amended: SSI 2009/19 Reg.61, SSI 2009/208 Reg.56

2008–cont.

224. National Health Service Pension Scheme (Scotland) Regulations 2008– *cont.*
Reg.3.C.2, amended: SSI 2009/19 Reg.62
Reg.3.C.3, amended: SSI 2009/19 Reg.63, SSI 2009/208 Reg.58
Reg.3.D.6, amended: SSI 2009/19 Reg.64
Reg.3.D.8, amended: SSI 2009/19 Reg.65, SSI 2009/208 Reg.63
Reg.3.D.9, amended: SSI 2009/19 Reg.66
Reg.3.D.10, amended: SSI 2009/208 Reg.64
Reg.3.D.11, amended: SSI 2009/208 Reg.65
Reg.3.D.13, revoked (in part): SSI 2009/208 Reg.66
Reg.3.D.17, amended: SSI 2009/208 Reg.67
Reg.3.E.8, amended: SSI 2009/208 Reg.72, SSI 2009/208 Reg.82
Reg.3.E.10, amended: SSI 2009/19 Reg.67, SSI 2009/208 Reg.73
Reg.3.E.11, amended: SSI 2009/208 Reg.74
Reg.3.E.12, amended: SSI 2009/208 Reg.75
Reg.3.E.13, amended: SSI 2009/208 Reg.76
Reg.3.E.15, amended: SSI 2009/208 Reg.77
Reg.3.E.17, amended: SSI 2009/208 Reg.78
Reg.3.E.18, amended: SSI 2009/208 Reg.79
Reg.3.E.19, amended: SSI 2009/208 Reg.80
Reg.3.E.20A, added: SSI 2009/19 Reg.68
Reg.3.E.21, amended: SSI 2009/19 Reg.69
Reg.3.E.25, amended: SSI 2009/19 Reg.70, SSI 2009/208 Reg.81
Reg.3.F.6, amended: SSI 2009/19 Reg.71
Reg.3.F.8, amended: SSI 2009/19 Reg.72
Reg.3.F.9, amended: SSI 2009/19 Reg.73
Reg.3.F.10, amended: SSI 2009/19 Reg.74
Reg.3.F.11, amended: SSI 2009/19 Reg.75
Reg.3.F.11, revoked (in part): SSI 2009/19 Reg.75
Reg.3.F.17, added: SSI 2009/19 Reg.76
Reg.3.H.2, substituted: SSI 2009/19 Reg.77,
Reg.3.J.2, substituted: SSI 2009/19 Reg.78
Reg.3.J.7, amended: SSI 2009/19 Reg.79
Reg.3.J.9, amended: SSI 2009/19 Reg.80, SSI 2009/208 Reg.85
Reg.3.J.10, amended: SSI 2009/19 Reg.81
Reg.3.J.13, amended: SSI 2009/19 Reg.82
Reg.3.J.13, substituted: SSI 2009/208 Reg.86
Reg.4.A.2, amended: SSI 2009/19 Reg.83
Reg.4.D.1, amended: SSI 2009/19 Reg.84
Reg.4.D.2, amended: SSI 2009/19 Reg.85

228. Local Government Pension Scheme (Administration) (Scotland) Regulations 2008
Reg.3, amended: SSI 2009/93 Reg.10
Reg.8, amended: SSI 2009/93 Reg.11
Reg.12, amended: SSI 2009/93 Reg.12
Reg.35, amended: SSI 2009/187 Reg.31
Reg.38A, added: SSI 2009/187 Reg.32
Reg.60A, added: SSI 2009/187 Reg.33

229. Local Government Pension Scheme (Transitional Provisions) (Scotland) Regulations 2008
Reg.4, amended: SSI 2009/187 Reg.34
Reg.15, amended: SSI 2009/93 Reg.14
Sch.2 para.1, amended: SSI 2009/93 Reg.15
Sch.2 para.4, amended: SSI 2009/93 Reg.15, SSI 2009/187 Reg.34
Sch.2 para.6, revoked (in part): SSI 2009/93 Reg.15

230. Local Government Pension Scheme (Benefits, Membership and Contributions) (Scotland) Regulations 2008
Reg.2, amended: SSI 2009/93 Reg.3
Reg.3, amended: SSI 2009/93 Reg.4
Reg.11, amended: SSI 2009/93 Reg.5

2008–cont.

230. Local Government Pension Scheme (Benefits, Membership and Contributions) (Scotland) Regulations 2008– *cont.*
Reg.20, revoked (in part): SSI 2009/187 Reg.29
Reg.29, amended: SSI 2009/93 Reg.6
Reg.31, amended: SSI 2009/93 Reg.7, SSI 2009/187 Reg.29

236. Court of Session etc Fees Amendment Order 2008
Sch.2, amended: SSI 2009/88 Art.3
Sch.3, amended: SSI 2009/88 Art.4
Sch.3, revoked: SSI 2009/88 Art.4

239. Sheriff Court Fees Amendment Order 2008
Sch.2, amended: SSI 2009/89 Art.3
Sch.3, amended: SSI 2009/89 Art.4

261. Plastic Materials and Articles in Contact with Food (Scotland) Amendment Regulations 2008
Reg.2, revoked: SSI 2009/30 Reg.24

266. Control of Salmonella in Poultry (Scotland) Order 2008
revoked: SSI 2009/229 Art.19

296. Smoke Control Areas (Exempt Fireplaces) (Scotland) (No.2) Order 2008
revoked: SSI 2009/214 Sch.2

298. Action Programme for Nitrate Vulnerable Zones (Scotland) Regulations 2008
Reg.3, amended: SSI 2009/447 Reg.3
Reg.5, amended: SSI 2009/447 Reg.4
Reg.14, amended: SSI 2009/447 Reg.5
Reg.14A, added: SSI 2009/447 Reg.6
Reg.14B, added: SSI 2009/447 Reg.6
Reg.25, amended: SSI 2009/447 Reg.7
Sch.1, amended: SSI 2009/447 Reg.8
Sch.1, substituted: SSI 2009/447 Reg.8
Sch.3, amended: SSI 2009/447 Reg.9
Sch.3 Part C, amended: SSI 2009/447 Reg.9

363. Justice of the Peace Courts (Sheriffdom of Tayside, Central and Fife) Order 2008
applied: SSI 2009/20 Art.2
Art.8, added: SSI 2009/20 Art.2
Sch.4, added: SSI 2009/20 Art.2

368. Sheep and Goats (Identification and Traceability) (Scotland) Amendment Regulations 2008
revoked: SSI 2009/415 Sch.1

378. Zoonoses and Animal By-Products (Fees) (Scotland) Amendment Regulations 2008
revoked: SSI 2009/230 Reg.4

386. Book of Scottish Connections Regulations 2008
Sch.5, amended: SSI 2009/314 Sch.6
Sch.6, amended: SSI 2009/314 Sch.7
Sch.7, amended: SSI 2009/314 Sch.8
Sch.8, amended: SSI 2009/314 Sch.9

394. Action Programme for Nitrate Vulnerable Zones (Scotland) Amendment Regulations 2008
Reg.3, revoked: SSI 2009/447 Reg.10

423. Zoonoses and Animal By-Products (Fees) (Scotland) Amendment (No.2) Regulations 2008
revoked: SSI 2009/230 Reg.4

426. Town and Country Planning (Development Planning) (Scotland) Regulations 2008
Reg.1, amended: SSI 2009/378 Reg.2
Reg.3, amended: SSI 2009/378 Reg.2
Reg.10, amended: SSI 2009/378 Reg.2
Reg.24, amended: SSI 2009/220 Reg.6
Reg.30, amended: SSI 2009/343 Reg.4

427. Planning etc (Scotland) Act 2006 (Development Planning) (Saving, Transitional and Consequential Provisions) Order 2008
Art.1, amended: SSI 2009/18 Art.2

2008–cont.

427. Planning etc (Scotland) Act 2006 (Development Planning) (Saving, Transitional and Consequential Provisions) Order 2008–*cont.*
Art.3, amended: SSI 2009/344 Art.2
Art.5, amended: SSI 2009/344 Art.2

432. Town and Country Planning (Development Management Procedure) (Scotland) Regulations 2008
Reg.2, amended: SSI 2009/220 Reg.7
Reg.3, amended: SSI 2009/220 Reg.7
Reg.13, amended: SSI 2009/220 Reg.7
Reg.20, amended: SSI 2009/220 Reg.7
Reg.20, applied: SSI 2009/257 Reg.2
Reg.24, substituted: 2009 asp 6 s.42
Reg.27, amended: SSI 2009/220 Reg.7
Reg.43, applied: SSI 2009/257 Reg.3
Reg.45, amended: SSI 2009/220 Reg.7
Reg.47, amended: SSI 2009/220 Reg.7
Sch.2 para.3, amended: SSI 2009/220 Reg.7

433. Town and Country Planning (Schemes of Delegation and Local Review Procedure) (Scotland) Regulations 2008
Reg.10, amended: SSI 2009/220 Reg.5

434. Town and Country Planning (Appeals) (Scotland) Regulations 2008
Reg.5, amended: SSI 2009/220 Reg.4
Reg.19, amended: SSI 2009/220 Reg.4

2009

4. Protection of Vulnerable Groups (Scotland) Act 2007 (Transitory Provisions in Consequence of the Safeguarding Vulnerable Groups Act 2006) Order 2009
revoked: SSI 2009/337 Art.6

31. Victim Statements (Prescribed Offences) (Scotland) Order 2009
revoked: SSI 2009/71 Art.2

41. Police Grant (Variation) (Scotland) Order 2009
revoked: SSI 2009/55 Art.2

45. Specified Animal Pathogens (Scotland) Order 2009
applied: SSI 2009/173 Art.3
Sch.1 Part 1 para.34A, added: SSI 2009/394 Art.2

48. Home Energy Assistance Scheme (Scotland) Regulations 2009
Reg.2, amended: SSI 2009/392 Reg.3
Reg.8, substituted: SSI 2009/392 Reg.4

50. Local Government Finance Act 1992 (Scotland) Order 2009
Sch.1, substituted: SSI 2009/132 Sch.1

68. Diligence (Scotland) Regulations 2009
Reg.2, amended: SSI 2009/396 Reg.2
Reg.3, amended: SSI 2009/396 Reg.2
Reg.3A, added: SSI 2009/396 Reg.2
Sch.2, amended: SSI 2009/396 Reg.2
Sch.3, amended: SSI 2009/396 Reg.2
Sch.4, amended: SSI 2009/396 Reg.2
Sch.5, amended: SSI 2009/396 Reg.2
Sch.6, amended: SSI 2009/396 Reg.2

91. Regulation of Care (Fitness of Employees in Relation to Care Services) (Scotland) Regulations 2009
revoked: SSI 2009/118 Reg.17

98. Diligence against Earnings (Variation) (Scotland) Regulations 2009
revoked: SSI 2009/133 Reg.2

2009–cont.

115. Justice of the Peace Courts (Sheriffdom of South Strathclyde, Dumfries and Galloway) Order 2009
revoked: SSI 2009/180 Art.2

116. Criminal Proceedings etc (Reform) (Scotland) Act 2007 (Commencement No.7) Order 2009
revoked: SSI 2009/238 Art.1

118. Regulation of Care (Fitness of Employees in Relation to Care Services) (Scotland) (No.2) Regulations 2009
Reg.1, amended: SSI 2009/349 Reg.2
Reg.3, amended: SSI 2009/349 Reg.2
Reg.6A, added: SSI 2009/349 Reg.2
Reg.15A, added: SSI 2009/349 Reg.2
Reg.15B, added: SSI 2009/349 Reg.2
Reg.15C, added: SSI 2009/349 Reg.2

140. Renewables Obligation (Scotland) Order 2009
Art.33, referred to: SSI 2009/276
Sch.2 Part 1 para.1, amended: SSI 2009/276 Art.2
Sch.2 Part 2, amended: SSI 2009/276 Art.2

154. Adoption Agencies (Scotland) Regulations 2009
applied: SSI 2009/267 Art.5, SSI 2009/268 Reg.9
Part IV, applied: SSI 2009/182 Reg.7, Reg.50
Part V, applied: SSI 2009/182 Reg.7, Reg.50
Part VIII, applied: SSI 2009/182 Reg.5, Reg.14
Reg.6, applied: SSI 2009/182 Reg.8
Reg.6, varied: SSI 2009/182 Reg.62
Reg.7, varied: SSI 2009/182 Reg.62
Reg.8, varied: SSI 2009/182 Reg.62
Reg.9, varied: SSI 2009/182 Reg.62
Reg.10, applied: SSI 2009/284 Sch.1
Reg.10, varied: SSI 2009/182 Reg.62
Reg.11, varied: SSI 2009/182 Reg.62
Reg.13, varied: SSI 2009/182 Reg.62
Reg.14, referred to: SSI 2009/268 Reg.6
Reg.14, varied: SSI 2009/182 Reg.62

154. Adoption Agencies (Scotland) Regulations 2009–*cont.*
Reg.15, varied: SSI 2009/182 Reg.62
Reg.16, varied: SSI 2009/182 Reg.62
Reg.17, varied: SSI 2009/182 Reg.62
Reg.18, applied: SSI 2009/182 Reg.8, Reg.41, Reg.50
Reg.18, referred to: SSI 2009/182 Reg.8, Reg.41, Reg.50
Reg.21, varied: SSI 2009/182 Reg.62
Reg.24, referred to: SSI 2009/268 Reg.6
Reg.24, varied: SSI 2009/182 Reg.62
Reg.25, applied: SSI 2009/182 Reg.50, SSI 2009/284 Sch.1
Reg.25, referred to: SSI 2009/182 Reg.8
Reg.25, varied: SSI 2009/182 Reg.62
Reg.26, applied: SSI 2009/182 Reg.50
Sch.1 Part I, referred to: SSI 2009/182 Reg.16
Sch.1 Part II, referred to: SSI 2009/182 Reg.48
Sch.1 Part III para.13, referred to: SSI 2009/268 Reg.11

163. Act of Sederunt (Sections 25 to 29 of the Law Reform (Miscellaneous Provisions) (Scotland) Act 1990) (Association of Commercial Attorneys) 2009
applied: SSI 2009/162 Art.2

177. National Health Service (Pharmaceutical Services, Charges for Drugs and Appliances and Charges to Overseas Visitors) (Scotland) Amendment Regulations 2009
Reg.2, revoked: SSI 2009/183 Sch.5

182. Adoptions with a Foreign Element (Scotland) Regulations 2009
Part 3, applied: SSI 2009/284 Sch.1

2009– cont.

182. Adoptions with a Foreign Element (Scotland) Regulations 2009– *cont.*
Reg.4, disapplied: SSI 2009/267 Art.8
Reg.5, applied: SSI 2009/267 Art.9
Reg.7, applied: SSI 2009/284 Sch.1
Reg.8, applied: SSI 2009/284 Sch.1
Reg.50, applied: SSI 2009/284 Sch.1

183. National Health Service (Pharmaceutical Services) (Scotland) Regulations 2009
Reg.8, amended: SSI 2009/209 Reg.2
Reg.9, amended: SSI 2009/209 Reg.2
Reg.11, amended: SSI 2009/209 Reg.2
Reg.15, amended: SSI 2009/209 Reg.2
Sch.1 para.4, amended: SSI 2009/209 Reg.2
Sch.2, amended: SSI 2009/209 Reg.2
Sch.6 para.1, amended: SSI 2009/209 Reg.2
Sch.6 para.2, amended: SSI 2009/209 Reg.2

210. Looked After Children (Scotland) Regulations 2009
Reg.33, amended: SSI 2009/290 Reg.2
Reg.45, amended: SSI 2009/290 Reg.2
Reg.46, amended: SSI 2009/290 Reg.2
Reg.48, amended: SSI 2009/290 Reg.2
Sch.3 para.1, amended: SSI 2009/290 Reg.2
Sch.3 para.2, amended: SSI 2009/290 Reg.2
Sch.3 para.9, amended: SSI 2009/290 Reg.2
Sch.3 para.11, amended: SSI 2009/290 Reg.2
Sch.3 para.13, amended: SSI 2009/290 Reg.2
Sch.3 para.14, amended: SSI 2009/290 Reg.2
Sch.4 para.7, amended: SSI 2009/290 Reg.2

230. Zoonoses and Animal By-Products (Fees) (Scotland) Regulations 2009
Reg.2, amended: SSI 2009/416 Reg.2
Sch.1, amended: SSI 2009/416 Reg.2

233. Rural Development Contracts (Rural Priorities) (Scotland) Amendment (No.2) Regulations 2009
Reg.3, revoked (in part): SSI 2009/335 Reg.10

2009– cont.

234. Debt Arrangement Scheme (Scotland) Amendment Regulations 2009
revoked: SSI 2009/258 Reg.2

242. Health Boards (Membership and Elections) (Scotland) Act 2009 (Commencement No.1) Order 2009
applied: SSI 2009/352 Reg.3

268. Adoption (Disclosure of Information and Medical Information about Natural Parents) (Scotland) Regulations 2009
applied: SSI 2009/154 Reg.28

294. Act of Sederunt (Sheriff Court Rules) (Miscellaneous Amendments) 2009
r.2, amended: SSI 2009/402 r.2
r.3, amended: SSI 2009/402 r.2
r.4, amended: SSI 2009/402 r.2
r.5, amended: SSI 2009/402 r.2

317. Sea Fishing (Enforcement of Community Quota and Third Country Fishing Measures and Restriction on Days at Sea) (Scotland) Order 2009
Art.12, amended: SSI 2009/338 Art.2

319. Public Health etc (Scotland) Act 2008 (Commencement No 2, Savings and Consequential Provisions) Order 2009
Art.3, revoked (in part): SSI 2009/404 Art.3

331. Justice of the Peace Courts (Sheriffdom of North Strathclyde) etc Order 2009
Art.9, added: SSI 2009/409 Art.2
Sch.4, added: SSI 2009/409 Art.2

409. Justice of the Peace Courts (Sheriffdom of North Strathclyde) etc Amendment Order 2009
referred to: SSI 2009/331 Sch.4

428. Public Contracts and Utilities Contracts (Scotland) Amendment Regulations 2009
Reg.2, amended: SSI 2009/439 Reg.2

STATUTORY RULES ISSUED BY THE UK PARLIAMENT

1883

Rules of the Supreme Court 1883
see *A v Payne* [2009] EWHC 736 (Fam), [2009] 2 F.L.R. 463 (Fam Div), Sir Mark Potter (President)

1898

496. Light Railways (Costs) Rules 1898
referred to: SI 2009/500 Sch.1 Part 2

1899

141. Benefices Rules 1899
referred to: SI 2009/500 Sch.1 Part 2

1904

256. Rules with Respect to Applications under The Railways (Electrical Power) Act 1904
referred to: SI 2009/500 Sch.1 Part 2

1907

1020. Limited Partnerships Rules 1907
revoked (in part): SI 2009/2160 r.2

1923

1624. Babbacombe Cliff Light Railway Order 1923
Art.3, amended: SI 2009/872 Art.7
Art.14, revoked: SI 2009/872 Sch.1
Art.15, revoked: SI 2009/872 Sch.1
Art.16, revoked (in part): SI 2009/872 Sch.1
Art.17, revoked (in part): SI 2009/872 Sch.1
Art.19, revoked: SI 2009/872 Sch.1
Art.20, revoked: SI 2009/872 Sch.1
Art.23, revoked: SI 2009/872 Sch.1
Art.25, revoked: SI 2009/872 Sch.1

1925

1093. Land Registration Rules 1925
referred to: SI 2009/500 Sch.1 Part 2

1926

1078. Regulations relating to mechanical power on the Babbacombe Cliff Light Railway 1926
revoked: SI 2009/872 Sch.1

1927

196. Ministry of Transport (Light Railways Procedure) Rules 1927
referred to: SI 2009/500 Sch.1 Part 2

1939

90. Liverpool-Leeds-Hull Trunk Road (Hambleton By-Pass) Order 1939
revoked: SI 2009/283 Art.4
91. Liverpool-Leeds-Hull Trunk Road (Monk Fryston Diversion) Order 1939
revoked: SI 2009/283 Art.4

1942

270. Visiting Forces (Military Courts-Martial) Order 1942
Art.1, amended: SI 2009/2054 Sch.1 para.2

1948

1411. Civil Aviation (Births, Deaths and Missing Persons) Regulations 1948
Appendix 1, amended: SI 2009/1892 Sch.1 para.5
Appendix 2, amended: SI 2009/1892 Sch.1 para.5
Appendix 3, amended: SI 2009/1892 Sch.1 para.5
Reg.2, amended: SI 2009/1892 Sch.1 para.5
Reg.8, substituted: SI 2009/1892 Sch.1 para.5

1952

161. Lands Tribunal (Statutory Undertakers Compensation Jurisdiction) Order 1952
Art.3, amended: SI 2009/1307 Sch.2 para.2
Art.8, amended: SI 2009/1307 Sch.2 para.3
1215. Double Taxation Relief (Taxes on Income) (Guernsey) Order 1952
Sch.1, referred to: SI 2009/3011 Art.3
1216. Double Taxation Relief (Taxes on Income) (Jersey) Order 1952
Sch.1, applied: SI 2009/3012 Art.3

1954

796. Non-Contentious Probate Rules, 1954
referred to: SI 2009/500 Sch.1 Part 2
1255. Landlord and Tenant (Determination of Rateable Value Procedure) Rules 1954
r.8, amended: SI 2009/1307 Sch.2 para.5
Sch.1, amended: SI 2009/1307 Sch.2 para.6

1955

725. Babbacombe Cliff Lift Railway (Amendment) Regulations 1955
revoked: SI 2009/872 Sch.1
1205. Double Taxation Relief (Taxes on Income) (Isle of Man) Order 1955
referred to: SI 2009/228 Sch.1
Sch.1, added: SI 2009/228 Sch.1
Sch.1, referred to: SI 2009/228 Art.3
Sch.1, revoked: SI 2009/228 Sch.1
Sch.1, substituted: SI 2009/228 Sch.1

1956

552. Rules of the Supreme Court (Non-Contentious Probate Costs) 1956
referred to: SI 2009/500 Sch.1 Part 2

1957

331. Rotherham Main Mine (Employment Below Ground) Special Regulations 1957
revoked: SI 2009/693 Sch.2
448. Watford and South of St Albans-Redbourn-Kidney Wood, Luton, Special Road Scheme 1957
Art.1A, added: SI 2009/776 Art.2
Sch.1, substituted: SI 2009/776 Sch.1

1958

1168. Newman Spinney Mine (Electricity) Special Regulations 1958
revoked: SI 2009/693 Sch.2
1678. Loch Aline Mine (Diesel Vehicles) Special Regulations 1958
revoked: SI 2009/693 Sch.2

1959

141. Sandwith Anhydrite Mine (Electricity) Special Regulations 1959
revoked: SI 2009/693 Sch.2
406. Service Departments Registers Order 1959
Art.3A, amended: SI 2009/1736 Art.2
Art.3A(3A), amended: SI 2009/1736 Art.2
Art.3A(3B), amended: SI 2009/1736 Art.2
Art.3B, amended: SI 2009/1736 Art.3
640. Foreign Compensation Commission (Egyptian Claims) Rules 1959
referred to: SI 2009/500 Sch.1 Part 2, Sch.2 Part 2
715. Government Oil Pipe-Lines Regulations 1959
Reg.7, amended: SI 2009/1307 Sch.2 para.7
1011. Subwealden Mine (Diesel Vehicles) Special Regulations 1959
revoked: SI 2009/693 Sch.2
1335. Diseases of Animals (Ascertainment of Compensation) Order 1959
Art.4, disapplied: SSI 2009/232 Art.19
1520. Middleton-by-Wirksworth Limestone Mine (Diesel Vehicles) Special Regulations 1959
revoked: SI 2009/693 Sch.2

1960

132. Linby Mine (Refuge Holes) Special Regulations 1960
revoked: SI 2009/693 Sch.2
133. Parsonage Mine (Refuge Holes) Special Regulations 1960
revoked: SI 2009/693 Sch.2
194. Opencast Coal (Fees) Regulations 1960
Sch.1, amended: SI 2009/1307 Sch.2 para.8
718. Sandwith Anhydrite Mine (Explosives) Special Regulations 1960
revoked: SI 2009/693 Sch.2
724. Billingham Mine (Explosives) Special Regulations 1960
revoked: SI 2009/693 Sch.2
1118. Riber Mine (Explosives) Special Regulations 1960
revoked: SI 2009/693 Sch.2

1960– cont.

1291. Woodside Nos 2 and 3 Mine (Diesel Vehicles) Special Regulations 1960
revoked: SI 2009/ 693 Sch.2

1956. Visiting Forces (Canadian Military and Air Forces) Order 1960
Art.2, amended: SI 2009/ 2054 Sch.1 para.3
Art.3, amended: SI 2009/ 2054 Sch.1 para.3
Art.3, applied: SI 2009/ 2054 Sch.2 para.1
Art.4, amended: SI 2009/ 2054 Sch.1 para.3
Art.4, applied: SI 2009/ 2054 Sch.2 para.1

2347. Moorgreen (Waterloo) Mine (Diesel Vehicles) Special Regulations 1960
revoked: SI 2009/ 693 Sch.2

1961

59. Sovereign Base Areas of Akrotiri and Dhekelia (Appeals to Privy Council) Order in Council 1961
revoked (in part): SI 2009/ 224 Art.5

241. Bestwood Mine (Diesel Vehicles) Special Regulations 1961
revoked: SI 2009/ 693 Sch.2

1273. Bates Mine (Diesel Vehicles) Special Regulations 1961
revoked: SI 2009/ 693 Sch.2

1973. Hartley Bank Mine (Diesel Vehicles) Special Regulations 1961
revoked: SI 2009/ 693 Sch.2

2305. Sandwith Anhydrite Mine (Diesel Vehicles) Special Regulations 1961
revoked: SI 2009/ 693 Sch.2

2444. Grimethorpe Mine (Diesel Vehicles) Special Regulations 1961
revoked: SI 2009/ 693 Sch.2

2445. Lynemouth Mine (Diesel Vehicles and Storage Battery Vehicles) Special Regulations 1961
revoked: SI 2009/ 693 Sch.2

1962

13. Dollar Nos 4 and 5 Mine (Diesel Vehicles) Special Regulations 1962
revoked: SI 2009/ 693 Sch.2

49. Lingdale Mine (Diesel Vehicles) Special Regulations 1962
revoked: SI 2009/ 693 Sch.2

617. Golborne Mine (Diesel Vehicles) Special Regulations 1962
revoked: SI 2009/ 693 Sch.2

719. Usworth Mine (Diesel Vehicles) Special Regulations 1962
revoked: SI 2009/ 693 Sch.2

735. Lea Hall Mine (Diesel Vehicles) Special Regulations 1962
revoked: SI 2009/ 693 Sch.2

763. North Skelton Mine (Diesel Vehicles) Special Regulations 1962
revoked: SI 2009/ 693 Sch.2

931. Calverton Mine (Diesel Vehicles) Special Regulations 1962
revoked: SI 2009/ 693 Sch.2

1002. New Stamphill Mine (Diesel Vehicles) Special Regulations 1962
revoked: SI 2009/ 693 Sch.2

1020. Coppice Mine (Diesel Vehicles) Special Regulations 1962
revoked: SI 2009/ 693 Sch.2

1962– cont.

1094. Brightling Mine (Diesel Vehicles) Special Regulations 1962
revoked: SI 2009/ 693 Sch.2

1096. Horden Mine (Diesel Vehicles) Special Regulations 1962
revoked: SI 2009/ 693 Sch.2

1286. Sutton Manor Mine (Steam Boilers) Special Regulations 1962
revoked: SI 2009/ 693 Sch.2

1650. Jamaica (Procedure in Appeals to Privy Council) Order in Council 1962
revoked (in part): SI 2009/ 224 Art.5

1676. Easington Mine (Diesel Vehicles) Special Regulations 1962
revoked: SI 2009/ 693 Sch.2

1729. Boldon Mine (Diesel Vehicles) Special Regulations 1962
revoked: SI 2009/ 693 Sch.2

1730. Harton Mine (Diesel Vehicles) Special Regulations 1962
revoked: SI 2009/ 693 Sch.2

1731. Heworth Mine (Diesel Vehicles) Special Regulations 1962
revoked: SI 2009/ 693 Sch.2

1732. Wardley Mine (Diesel Vehicles) Special Regulations 1962
revoked: SI 2009/ 693 Sch.2

1733. Washington "F&rdquo Mine (Diesel Vehicles) Special Regulations 1962
revoked: SI 2009/ 693 Sch.2

2059. Rufford Mine (Diesel Vehicles) Special Regulations 1962
revoked: SI 2009/ 693 Sch.2

2114. Trelewis Drift Mine (Diesel Vehicles) Special Regulations 1962
revoked: SI 2009/ 693 Sch.2

2193. Wharncliffe Woodmoor 4 and 5 Mine (Diesel Vehicles) Special Regulations 1962
revoked: SI 2009/ 693 Sch.2

2512. Seaham Mine (Diesel Vehicles) Special Regulations 1962
revoked: SI 2009/ 693 Sch.2

2578. Denby Grange Mine (Refuge Holes) Special Regulations 1962
revoked: SI 2009/ 693 Sch.2

1963

28. Bold Mine (Diesel Vehicles) Special Regulations 1963
revoked: SI 2009/ 693 Sch.2

45. Newstead Mine (Diesel Vehicles) Special Regulations 1963
revoked: SI 2009/ 693 Sch.2

118. Dawdon Mine (Diesel Vehicles) Special Regulations 1963
revoked: SI 2009/ 693 Sch.2

132. Lambton "D&rdquo Mine (Diesel Vehicles) Special Regulations 1963
revoked: SI 2009/ 693 Sch.2

353. Herrington Mine (Diesel Vehicles) Special Regulations 1963
revoked: SI 2009/ 693 Sch.2

825. Thoresby Mine (Diesel Vehicles) Special Regulations 1963
revoked: SI 2009/ 693 Sch.2

889. Mainsforth Mine (Diesel Vehicles) Special Regulations 1963
revoked: SI 2009/ 693 Sch.2

1963– cont.

1035. **Cousland No.2 Mine (Diesel Vehicles) Special Regulations 1963**
revoked: SI 2009/693 Sch.2

1096. **Westoe Mine (Diesel Vehicles) Special Regulations 1963**
revoked: SI 2009/693 Sch.2

1117. **Ledston Luck Mine (Diesel Vehicles) Special Regulations 1963**
revoked: SI 2009/693 Sch.2

1137. **Nostell Mine (Refuge Holes) Special Regulations 1963**
revoked: SI 2009/693 Sch.2

1197. **Hem Heath Mine (Diesel Vehicles) Special Regulations 1963**
revoked: SI 2009/693 Sch.2

1335. **Abernant Mine (Diesel Vehicles) Special Regulations 1963**
revoked: SI 2009/693 Sch.2

1469. **Skelpie Mine (Diesel Vehicles) Special Regulations 1963**
revoked: SI 2009/693 Sch.2

1470. **Blaengwrach New Mine (Diesel Vehicles) Special Regulations 1963**
revoked: SI 2009/693 Sch.2

1536. **Albion Mine (Diesel Vehicles) Special Regulations 1963**
revoked: SI 2009/693 Sch.2

1545. **Markham Main Mine (Steam Boilers) Special Regulations 1963**
revoked: SI 2009/693 Sch.2

1618. **Silverwood Mine (Diesel Vehicles) Special Regulations 1963**
revoked: SI 2009/693 Sch.2

1778. **Fforchaman Mine (Diesel Vehicles) Special Regulations 1963**
revoked: SI 2009/693 Sch.2

1964

239. **Merry Lees Mine (Diesel Vehicles) Special Regulations 1964**
revoked: SI 2009/693 Sch.2

378. **Harelawhill Mine (Diesel Vehicles) Special Regulations 1964**
revoked: SI 2009/693 Sch.2

379. **Marley Hill Mine (Diesel Vehicles) Special Regulations 1964**
revoked: SI 2009/693 Sch.2

388. **Prison Rules 1964**
referred to: SI 2009/500 Sch.1 Part 2, Sch.2 Part 2

533. **Notification of Employment of Persons Order 1964**
revoked: SI 2009/605 Reg.2

539. **Prince of Wales Mine (Diesel Vehicles) Special Regulations 1964**
revoked: SI 2009/693 Sch.2

567. **Kellingley Mine (Diesel Vehicles) Special Regulations 1964**
revoked: SI 2009/693 Sch.2

616. **Ormonde Mine (Diesel Vehicles) Special Regulations 1964**
revoked: SI 2009/693 Sch.2

660. **Eden/South Medomsley Mine (Diesel Vehicles) Special Regulations 1964**
revoked: SI 2009/693 Sch.2

669. **Denby Hall Mine (Diesel Vehicles) Special Regulations 1964**
revoked: SI 2009/693 Sch.2

1964– cont.

899. **Newbiggin Mine (Diesel Vehicles) Special Regulations 1964**
revoked: SI 2009/693 Sch.2

1000. **Foreign Marriage (Armed Forces) Order 1964**
Art.1, amended: SI 2009/2054 Sch.1 para.4
Art.2, amended: SI 2009/2054 Sch.1 para.4

1086. **Industrial Training (Engineering Board) Order 1964**
Sch.1 para.1, applied: SI 2009/548 Art.8

1225. **Cwmgwili Mine (Diesel Vehicles) Special Regulations 1964**
revoked: SI 2009/693 Sch.2

1418. **Ryhope Mine (Diesel Vehicles) Special Regulations 1964**
revoked: SI 2009/693 Sch.2

1476. **Wearmouth Mine (Diesel Vehicles) Special Regulations 1964**
revoked: SI 2009/693 Sch.2

1614. **Pleasley Mine (Diesel Vehicles) Special Regulations 1964**
revoked: SI 2009/693 Sch.2

1755. **Ecclesiastical Jurisdiction (Discipline) Rules 1964**
r.49, applied: SI 2009/2107 Sch.2 para.4

1773. **Nailstone Mine (Precautions against Inrushes) Special Regulations 1964**
revoked: SI 2009/693 Sch.2

1846. **St Helena Court of Appeal (Appeal to Privy Council) Order 1964**
applied: SI 2009/3204 Art.4
revoked (in part): SI 2009/224 Art.5
Art.2, amended: SI 2009/3204 Art.3
Art.3, amended: SI 2009/3204 Art.3

1952. **Huncoat Mine (Diesel Vehicles) Special Regulations 1964**
revoked: SI 2009/693 Sch.2

2007. **Pensions (Polish Forces) Scheme 1964**
Art.11, amended: SI 2009/436 Art.3
Art.11, substituted: SI 2009/436 Art.3
Art.11A, added: SI 2009/436 Art.4

2042. **Bahama Islands (Procedure in Appeals to Privy Council) Order 1964**
revoked (in part): SI 2009/224 Art.5

1965

41. **Blackhall Mine (Diesel Vehicles) Special Regulations 1965**
revoked: SI 2009/693 Sch.2

251. **Ecclesiastical Jurisdiction (Faculty Appeals) Rules 1965**
referred to: SI 2009/500 Sch.1 Part 2

272. **Langley Park Mine (Diesel Vehicles) Special Regulations 1965**
revoked: SI 2009/693 Sch.2

539. **Brandon Pit House Mine (Diesel Vehicles) Special Regulations 1965**
revoked: SI 2009/693 Sch.2

592. **British Antarctic Territory Court of Appeal (Appeal to Privy Council) Order 1965**
revoked (in part): SI 2009/224 Art.5

759. **South Crofty Mine (Locomotives) Special Regulations 1965**
revoked: SI 2009/693 Sch.2

1101. **Industrial Tribunals (England and Wales) Regulations 1965**
referred to: SI 2009/500 Sch.1 Part 2

1965–cont.

1194. Bevercotes Mine (Diesel Vehicles) Special Regulations 1965
revoked: SI 2009/693 Sch.2

1203. United Kingdom Forces (Jurisdiction of Colonial Courts) Order 1965
Art.2, amended: SI 2009/2054 Sch.1 para.5

1430. Fishburn Mine (Diesel Vehicles) Special Regulations 1965
revoked: SI 2009/693 Sch.2

1500. County Court Funds Rules 1965
referred to: SI 2009/500 Sch.1 Part 2

1506. Performing Right Tribunal Rules 1965
referred to: SI 2009/500 Sch.1 Part 2

1535. International Headquarters and Defence Organisations (Designation and Privileges) Order 1965
Sch.1 Part I, substituted: SI 2009/704 Art.3
Sch.1 Part II, substituted: SI 2009/704 Art.3

1687. Transport Tribunals Rules 1965
referred to: SI 2009/500 Sch.1 Part 2

1699. Stafford Mine (Diesel Vehicles) Special Regulations 1965
revoked: SI 2009/693 Sch.2

1776. Rules of the Supreme Court (Revision) 1965
referred to: SI 2009/500 Sch.2 Part 2
see *P-B (Children) (Contact Order: Committal: Penal Notice), Re* [2009] EWCA Civ 143, [2009] 2 F.L.R. 66 (CA (Civ Div)), Thorpe, L.J.
Ord.15 r.6, see *O v O* [2008] EWHC 3031 (Fam), [2009] 1 F.L.R. 1036 (Fam Div), Munby, J.
Ord.52 r.5, see *R. v M* [2008] EWCA Crim 1901, [2009] 1 W.L.R. 1179 (CA (Crim Div)), Toulson, L.J.

1863. Turks and Caicos Islands (Appeal to Privy Council) Order 1965
revoked (in part): SI 2009/224 Art.5

1915. Astley Green Mine (Steam Boilers) Special Regulations 1965
revoked: SI 2009/693 Sch.2

1997. Trimdon Grange Mine (Diesel Vehicles) Special Regulations 1965
revoked: SI 2009/693 Sch.2

1966

141. East Hetton Mine (Diesel Vehicles) Special Regulations 1966
revoked: SI 2009/693 Sch.2

350. Dean and Chapter Nos 1, 2 and 3 Mine (Diesel Vehicles) Special Regulations 1966
revoked: SI 2009/693 Sch.2

475. Thorny Bank Mine (Diesel Vehicles) Special Regulations 1966
revoked: SI 2009/693 Sch.2

507. Export of Horses (Veterinary Examination) Order 1966
Art.2, amended: SI 2009/2713 Art.2
Art.3, amended: SI 2009/2713 Art.2

777. Cairn Hill Mine (Refuge Holes) Special Regulations 1966
revoked: SI 2009/693 Sch.2

979. Arley Mine (Diesel Vehicles) Special Regulations 1966
revoked: SI 2009/693 Sch.2

1073. Mineral Hydrocarbons in Food Regulations 1966
Reg.3, amended: SI 2009/3238 Reg.18, SI 2009/3378 Reg.18, SSI 2009/436 Reg.18

1966–cont.

1325. Sallet Hole Mine (Storage Battery Locomotives) Special Regulations 1966
revoked: SI 2009/693 Sch.2

1456. Barbados (Procedure in Appeals to Privy Council) Order 1966
revoked: SI 2009/224 Art.4

1471. Commons Registration (General) Regulations 1966
referred to: SI 2009/500 Sch.1 Part 2

1967

149. Capital Gains Tax Regulations 1967
Reg.2, amended: SI 2009/56 Sch.2 para.2
Reg.8, amended: SI 2009/56 Sch.2 para.3
Reg.9, amended: SI 2009/56 Sch.2 para.4
Reg.9, revoked (in part): SI 2009/56 Sch.2 para.4
Reg.12, amended: SI 2009/56 Sch.2 para.5
Reg.17, revoked: SI 2009/56 Sch.2 para.6

224. West Indies Associated States (Appeals to Privy Council) Order 1967
revoked (in part): SI 2009/224 Art.5

233. Montserrat (Appeals to Privy Council) Order 1967
revoked (in part): SI 2009/224 Art.5

234. Virgin Islands (Appeals to Privy Council) Order 1967
revoked (in part): SI 2009/224 Art.5

480. Carriage by Air Acts (Application of Provisions) Order 1967
Sch.1, see *Laroche v Spirit of Adventure (UK) Ltd* [2009] EWCA Civ 12, [2009] Q.B. 778 (CA (Civ Div)), Mummery, L.J.

956. Ellington Mine (Diesel Vehicles and Storage Battery Vehicles) Special Regulations 1967
revoked: SI 2009/693 Sch.2

1002. Faculty Jurisdiction Rules 1967
referred to: SI 2009/500 Sch.1 Part 2

1150. Judicial Committee (Veterinary Surgeons Rules) Order 1967
revoked: SI 2009/224 Art.4

1291. Haig Mine (Diesel Vehicles) Special Regulations 1967
revoked: SI 2009/693 Sch.2

1310. Industrial and Provident Societies Regulations 1967
referred to: SI 2009/500 Sch.1 Part 2

1335. Glebe Mine (Locomotives and Diesel Vehicles) Special Regulations 1967
revoked: SI 2009/693 Sch.2

1545. Groverake Mine (Storage Battery Locomotives) Special Regulations 1967
revoked: SI 2009/693 Sch.2

1756. British Railways Board (Totnes and Ashburton) Light Railway Order 1967
Art.5, revoked: SI 2009/3281 Sch.2
Sch.1, revoked: SI 2009/3281 Sch.2

1968

1071. Courts-Martial Appeal Rules 1968
applied: SI 2009/2657 Sch.4 para.3
revoked: SI 2009/2657 Sch.5
r.3, applied: SI 2009/2657 Sch.4 para.3

1295. Fauld Mine (Diesel Vehicles) Special Regulations 1968
revoked: SI 2009/693 Sch.2

1968–cont.

1672. Registers of Drainage Boards Regulations 1968
Reg.13, amended: SI 2009/1307 Sch.2 para.9

1862. Inter-Governmental Maritime Consultative Organisation (Immunities and Privileges) Order 1968
revoked (in part): SSI 2009/44 Art.3

1969

17. Town and Country Planning (Tree Preservation Order) Regulations 1969
Sch.1, applied: SI 2009/1300 Art.24

508. British Railways Board (Totnes and Ashburton) Light Railway (Transfer) Order 1969
revoked: SI 2009/3281 Sch.2

559. Brenkley Mine (Endless Rope Haulage) Special Regulations 1969
revoked: SI 2009/693 Sch.2

727. Bagworth Mine (Pass-Byes) (Revocation) Special Regulations 1969
revoked: SI 2009/693 Sch.2

799. Lynemouth Mine (Cable Reel Shuttle Cars) Special Regulations 1969
revoked: SI 2009/693 Sch.2

800. Ellington Mine (Cable Reel Shuttle Cars) Special Regulations 1969
revoked: SI 2009/693 Sch.2

842. Foreign Compensation Commission (Union of Soviet Socialist Republics) Rules Approval Instrument 1969
referred to: SI 2009/500 Sch.1 Part 2, Sch.2 Part 2

1377. Prince of Wales Mine (Captive Rail Diesel Locomotives) Special Regulations 1969
revoked: SI 2009/693 Sch.2

1437. Air Navigation (Investigation of Combined Military and Civil Air Accidents) Regulations 1969
referred to: SI 2009/500 Sch.1 Part 2

1592. Whiteheaps Mine (Storage Battery Locomotives) Special Regulations 1969
revoked: SI 2009/693 Sch.2

1876. Blackdene Mine (Storage Battery Locomotives) Special Regulations 1969
revoked: SI 2009/693 Sch.2

1970

36. Bullcliffe Wood Mine (Suspended Chair Haulage Apparatus) Special Regulations 1970
revoked: SI 2009/693 Sch.2

376. National Insurance (Industrial Injuries) (Colliery Workers Supplementary Scheme) Amendment &amp Consolidation Order 1970
referred to: SI 2009/500 Sch.1 Part 2

596. General Medical Council Disciplinary Committee (Procedure) Rules Order of Council 1970
referred to: SI 2009/500 Sch.2 Part 2

613. Aberpergwm Mine (Diesel Vehicles) Special Regulations 1970
revoked: SI 2009/693 Sch.2

1114. Gambia Appeals to Judicial Committee Order 1970
revoked: SI 2009/224 Art.4

1122. Blidworth Mine (Man-riding) (Revocation) Special Regulations 1970
revoked: SI 2009/693 Sch.2

1174. New Stubbin Mine (Diesel Vehicles) (Revocation) Special Regulations 1970
revoked: SI 2009/693 Sch.2

1970–cont.

1230. Creswell Mine (Winding and Haulage) Special Regulations 1970
revoked: SI 2009/693 Sch.2

1428. Maltby Main Mine (Methane Gas-Fired Steam Boilers) Special Regulations 1970
revoked: SI 2009/693 Sch.2

1539. Foreign Marriage Order 1970
applied: SI 2009/700 Sch.1 Part VI

1696. Restriction on Agreements (Estate Agents) Order 1970
referred to: SI 2009/500 Sch.1 Part 2

1971

28. West Cannock No.5 Mine (Diesel Vehicles) Special Regulations 1971
revoked: SI 2009/693 Sch.2

50. Winsford Rock Salt Mine (Diesel Vehicles and Storage Battery Vehicles) Special Regulations 1971
revoked: SI 2009/693 Sch.2

111. Lynemouth Mine (Cable Reel Shuttle Cars) (Amendment) Special Regulations 1971
revoked: SI 2009/693 Sch.2

131. Public Health (Aircraft) (Scotland) Regulations 1971
Reg.2, amended: SSI 2009/319 Sch.2 para.7

132. Public Health (Ships) (Scotland) Regulations 1971
Reg.2, amended: SSI 2009/319 Sch.2 para.6

139. Ellington Mine (Cable Reel Shuttle Cars) (Amendment) Special Regulations 1971
revoked: SI 2009/693 Sch.2

218. Lands Tribunal for Scotland Rules 1971
Sch.2, amended: SSI 2009/260 r.2

729. Farm and Garden Chemicals Regulations 1971
Reg.3, applied: SI 2009/716 Reg.7
Reg.4, applied: SI 2009/716 Reg.7

1253. Indictment Rules 1971
r.4, see *R. v Marchese (Maria Del Carmen)* [2008] EWCA Crim 389, [2009] 1 W.L.R. 992 (CA (Crim Div)), Lord Phillips of Worth Matravers, L.C.J.
r.7, see *R. v K (Robert)* [2008] EWCA Crim 1923, [2009] 1 Cr. App. R. 24 (CA (Crim Div)), Latham, L.J. (VP, CA Crim)
r.9, see *R. v Roberts (Patrice)* [2008] EWCA Crim 1304, [2009] 1 Cr. App. R. 20 (CA (Crim Div)), Latham, L.J. (VP, CA Crim)

1267. Medicines (Surgical Materials) Order 1971
applied: SI 2009/389 Sch.3 para.6

1325. Silverwood Mine (Methane Gas-Fired Steam Boilers) Special Regulations 1971
revoked: SI 2009/693 Sch.2

1450. Medicines (Exemption from Licences) (Special and Transitional Cases) Order 1971
Art.2, applied: SI 2009/389 Reg.24, Sch.1 para.30

1578. Ashington Mine (Endless Rope Haulage) Special Regulations 1971
revoked: SI 2009/693 Sch.2

1703. Littleton Mine (Refuge Holes) Special Regulations 1971
revoked: SI 2009/693 Sch.2

1704. Riddings Drift Mine (Rope Hauled Sledge) Special Regulations 1971
revoked: SI 2009/693 Sch.2

1972

71. Pensions Increase (Judicial Pensions) Regulations 1972
Sch.1 para.15, revoked: SI 2009/1307 Sch.2 para.10

118. Inter-Governmental Maritime Consultative Organization (Immunities and Privileges) (Amendment) Order 1972
revoked (in part): SSI 2009/44 Art.3

189. Southampton Airport (Designation) (Detention and Sale of Aircraft) Order 1972
revoked: SI 2009/2350 Sch.2

371. Cotgrave Mine (Electric Lighting for Cinematography) Special Regulations 1972
revoked: SI 2009/693 Sch.2

764. National Savings Bank Regulations 1972
Reg.2B, referred to: 2009 c.10 s.125
Reg.2BA, referred to: 2009 c.10 s.125
Reg.2BB, referred to: 2009 c.10 s.125

765. Premium Savings Bonds Regulations 1972
Reg.15, applied: SI 2009/1263 Reg.4
Reg.15, revoked: SI 2009/1263 Reg.5
Reg.15A, added: SI 2009/1263 Reg.5

798. Courts-Martial Appeal (Amendment) Rules 1972
revoked: SI 2009/2657 Sch.5

984. Marblaegis Mine (Diesel Vehicles) Special Regulations 1972
revoked: SI 2009/693 Sch.2

1101. Cayman Islands (Constitution) Order 1972
revoked: SI 2009/1379 Sch.1
Sch.2, applied: SI 2009/1379 Art.9

1139. Solicitors Remuneration Order 1972
referred to: SI 2009/500 Sch.1 Part 2

1163. Hatfield/Thorne Mine (Chain Haulage) Special Regulations 1972
revoked: SI 2009/693 Sch.2

1179. Easington Mine (Man-riding) (Revocation) Special Regulations 1972
revoked: SI 2009/693 Sch.2

1180. Savile Mine (Rope Hauled Sledge) Special Regulations 1972
revoked: SI 2009/693 Sch.2

1265. Health and Personal Social Services (Northern Ireland) Order 1972
Art.16, applied: SI 2009/2737 Reg.24

1351. Creswell Mine (Light Water Container Barrier) Special Regulations 1972
revoked: SI 2009/693 Sch.2

1357. Vane Tempest Mine (Endless Rope Haulage) Special Regulations 1972
revoked: SI 2009/693 Sch.2

1364. Vane Tempest Mine (Diesel Vehicles) (Revocation) Special Regulations 1972
revoked: SI 2009/693 Sch.2

1389. Ledston Luck Mine (Rope Hauled Sledge) Special Regulations 1972
revoked: SI 2009/693 Sch.2

1513. Hovercraft (Births, Deaths and Missing Persons) Regulations 1972
Appendix 1, amended: SI 2009/1892 Sch.1 para.6
Appendix 2, amended: SI 2009/1892 Sch.1 para.6
Appendix 3, amended: SI 2009/1892 Sch.1 para.6
Reg.2, amended: SI 2009/1892 Sch.1 para.6
Reg.6, amended: SI 2009/1892 Sch.1 para.6
Reg.7, substituted: SI 2009/1892 Sch.1 para.6

1630. Hucknall Mine (Endless Rope Haulage) Special Regulations 1972
revoked: SI 2009/693 Sch.2

1972– cont.

1635. Merchant Shipping (Maintenance of Seamen's Dependants) Regulations 1972
Reg.4, amended: SI 2009/462 Sch.5 para.1

1736. Lydd Airport (Designation) (Detention and Sale of Aircraft) Order 1972
revoked: SI 2009/2350 Sch.2

1831. Glass Houghton Mine (Rope Hauled Sledge) Special Regulations 1972
revoked: SI 2009/693 Sch.2

1952. Bentinck Mine (Endless Rope Haulage) Special Regulations 1972
revoked: SI 2009/693 Sch.2

1980. Swine Vesicular Disease Order 1972
revoked (in part): SI 2009/1299 Reg.47, SI 2009/1372 Reg.47, SSI 2009/173 Art.45

2014. Swine Vesicular Disease (Compensation) Order 1972
revoked (in part): SI 2009/1299 Reg.47, SI 2009/1372 Reg.47, SSI 2009/173 Art.45

2036. Newstead Mine (Endless Rope Haulage) Special Regulations 1972
revoked: SI 2009/693 Sch.2

1973

8. Factories Act General Register Order 1973
revoked: SI 2009/605 Reg.4

19. Adoption (Designation of Overseas Adoptions) Order 1973
applied: SSI 2009/267 Art.12

22. Grading of Horticultural Produce (Amendment) Regulations 1973
revoked (in part): SI 2009/1361 Reg.21, SI 2009/1551 Reg.21, SSI 2009/225 Reg.23

69. Drainage (Northern Ireland) Order 1973
Sch.1, amended: SI 2009/225 Art.4
Sch.1, applied: SI 2009/225 Art.4

101. Swine Vesicular Disease (Amendment) Order 1973
revoked (in part): SI 2009/1299 Reg.47, SI 2009/1372 Reg.47, SSI 2009/173 Art.45

270. Naval Detention Quarters Rules 1973
revoked: SI 2009/1096 r.2

371. Longriggs Mine (Diesel Vehicles) Special Regulations 1973
revoked: SI 2009/693 Sch.2

495. Pensions Increase (Judicial Pensions) (Amendment) Regulations 1973
Sch.1 para.10, revoked: SI 2009/1307 Sch.4

686. Walkways Regulations 1973
Reg.3, applied: SI 2009/721 Sch.1 para.8
Reg.4, applied: SI 2009/721 Sch.1 para.8
Reg.5, applied: SI 2009/721 Sch.1 para.8
Reg.6, applied: SI 2009/721 Sch.1 para.8

737. Nostell Mine (Endless Rope Haulage) Special Regulations 1973
revoked: SI 2009/693 Sch.2

900. Clerks to General Commissioners (Compensation) Regulations 1973
revoked: SI 2009/56 Sch.2 para.187

917. Pye Hill Mine (Endless Rope Haulage) Special Regulations 1973
revoked: SI 2009/693 Sch.2

940. Savile Mine (Diesel Vehicles) Special Regulations 1973
revoked: SI 2009/693 Sch.2

1003. Calverton Mine (Endless Rope Haulage) Special Regulations 1973
revoked: SI 2009/693 Sch.2

1973– cont.

1005. Cadley Hill Mine (Endless Rope Haulage) Special Regulations 1973
revoked: SI 2009/693 Sch.2

1041. Annesley Mine (Endless Rope Haulage) Special Regulations 1973
revoked: SI 2009/693 Sch.2

1042. Whitwick Mine (Endless Rope Haulage) Special Regulations 1973
revoked: SI 2009/693 Sch.2

1043. Cotgrave Mine (Endless Rope Haulage) Special Regulations 1973
revoked: SI 2009/693 Sch.2

1044. Linby Mine (Endless Rope Haulage) Special Regulations 1973
revoked: SI 2009/693 Sch.2

1073. Gedling Mine (Endless Rope Haulage) Special Regulations 1973
revoked: SI 2009/693 Sch.2

1074. Babbington Mine (Endless Rope Haulage) Special Regulations 1973
revoked: SI 2009/693 Sch.2

1081. Bahamas (Procedure in Appeals to Privy Council) (Amendment) Order 1973
revoked (in part): SI 2009/224 Art.5

1084. Turks and Caicos Islands (Appeal to Privy Council) (Amendment) Order 1973
revoked (in part): SI 2009/224 Art.5

1206. Ash Grove No 1 Mine (Diesel Vehicles) Special Regulations 1973
revoked: SI 2009/693 Sch.2

1339. Creswell Mine (Light Water Container Barrier) Special Regulations 1973
revoked: SI 2009/693 Sch.2

1499. Bagworth Mine (Endless Rope Haulage) Special Regulations 1973
revoked: SI 2009/693 Sch.2

1513. Statutory Rules (Northern Ireland) Order 1973
applied: 2009 c.23 s.316

1524. Rawdon Mine (Endless Rope Haulage) Special Regulations 1973
revoked: SI 2009/693 Sch.2

1633. Moorgreen Mine (Endless Rope Haulage) Special Regulations 1973
revoked: SI 2009/693 Sch.2

1689. Bates Mine (Endless Rope Haulage) Special Regulations 1973
revoked: SI 2009/693 Sch.2

1822. Medicines (Pharmacies) (Applications for Registration and Fees) Regulations 1973
Reg.3, amended: SI 2009/3071 Reg.2
Reg.3A, added: SI 2009/2502 Reg.2

1952. Crystal Glass (Descriptions) Regulations 1973
referred to: SI 2009/669 Sch.1 Part 2

1954. Pensions Increase (Compensation to Clerks to General Commissioners) Regulations 1973
revoked: SI 2009/56 Sch.2 para.187

1958. Isles of Scilly (Sale of Intoxicating Liquor) Order 1973
referred to: SI 2009/500 Sch.1 Part 2

1974

29. National Health Service (Venereal Diseases) Regulations 1974
Reg.2, amended: SI 2009/1824 Sch.1 para.1

455. National Health Service (Service Committees and Tribunal) Regulations 1974
referred to: SI 2009/500 Sch.1 Part 2

1974– cont.

502. Motorways Traffic (Speed Limit) Regulations 1974
see *Robbie the Pict v Service* [2009] HCJAC 49, 2009 S.C.L. 944 (HCJ), Lord Carloway

710. Elsecar Main Mine (Diesel Vehicles) Special Regulations 1974
revoked: SI 2009/693 Sch.2

984. Pensions Increase (Judicial Pensions) (Amendment) Regulations 1974
Sch.1 para.10, revoked: SI 2009/1307 Sch.4

985. Pensions Increase (Judicial Pensions) Regulations 1974
Sch.1 para.5, revoked: SI 2009/1307 Sch.2 para.11

1101. Cynheidre/Pentremawr (Escape Breathing Apparatus) Special Regulations 1974
revoked: SI 2009/693 Sch.2

1176. Bilsthorpe Mine (Endless Rope Haulage) Special Regulations 1974
revoked: SI 2009/693 Sch.2

1242. Town and Country Planning (Compensation and Certificates) Regulations 1974
Reg.7, amended: SI 2009/1307 Sch.2 para.13
Reg.12, amended: SI 2009/1307 Sch.2 para.14
Reg.15, amended: SI 2009/1307 Sch.2 para.15
Sch.2 para.4, amended: SI 2009/1307 Sch.2 para.16

1286. Land Charges Rules 1974
r.10, amended: SI 2009/1307 Sch.2 para.17

1837. Legal Officers Fees Order 1974
referred to: SI 2009/500 Sch.1 Part 2

1866. Rixey Park Mine (Storage Battery Locomotives) Special Regulations 1974
revoked: SI 2009/693 Sch.2

1917. Collins Green Mine (Employment Below Ground) Special Regulations 1974
revoked: SI 2009/693 Sch.2

1963. Desford Mine (Endless Rope Haulage) Special Regulations 1974
revoked: SI 2009/693 Sch.2

2034. Agriculture (Tractor Cabs) Regulations 1974
applied: SI 2009/515 Reg.3

2049. Silverdale Mine (Endless Rope Haulage) Special Regulations 1974
revoked: SI 2009/693 Sch.2

2112. Whitwick Mine (Diesel Vehicles) Special Regulations 1974
revoked: SI 2009/693 Sch.2

2198. Markham Main Mine (Endless Rope Haulage) Special Regulations 1974
revoked: SI 2009/693 Sch.2

2199. Frickley/South Elmsall Mine (Endless Rope Haulage) Special Regulations 1974
revoked: SI 2009/693 Sch.2

2200. Ellistown Mine (Endless Rope Haulage) Special Regulations 1974
revoked: SI 2009/693 Sch.2

2201. Hatfield/Thorne Mine (Endless Rope Haulage) Special Regulations 1974
revoked: SI 2009/693 Sch.2

2212. Rabies (Control) Order 1974
Art.2, amended: SI 2009/2713 Art.2
Art.4, amended: SI 2009/2713 Art.2
Art.5, amended: SI 2009/2713 Art.3
Sch.2, amended: SI 2009/2713 Art.3

2217. Santon Main Mine (Diesel Vehicles) Special Regulations 1974
revoked: SI 2009/693 Sch.2

2218. Askern Mine (Endless Rope Haulage) Special Regulations 1974
revoked: SI 2009/693 Sch.2

1974– cont.

2219. Kellingley Mine (Endless Rope Haulage) Special Regulations 1974
revoked: SI 2009/693 Sch.2

2220. Measham Mine (Endless Rope Haulage) Special Regulations 1974
revoked: SI 2009/693 Sch.2

2224. Kiveton Park Mine (Diesel Vehicles) Special Regulations 1974
revoked: SI 2009/693 Sch.2

1975

148. Town and Country Planning (Tree Preservation Order) (Amendment) and (Trees in Conservation Areas) (Exempted Cases) Regulations 1975
Reg.3, applied: SI 2009/1300 Art.24

299. Lands Tribunal Rules 1975
referred to: SI 2009/500 Sch.1 Part 2

434. Industrial Training (Transfer of the Activities of Establishments) Order 1975
applied: SI 2009/549 Sch.1

493. Social Security (Benefit) (Members of the Forces) Regulations 1975
Reg.3, amended: SI 2009/2054 Sch.1 para.7
Reg.3, applied: SI 2009/2054 Sch.2 para.3

539. Act of Sederunt (Commissary Business) 1975
Sch.1, amended: SSI 2009/292 Art.2

556. Social Security (Credits) Regulations 1975
applied: SI 2009/1562 Art.2
Reg.3, amended: SI 2009/2206 Reg.29
Reg.9A, amended: SI 2009/2206 Reg.30

563. Social Security Benefit (Persons Abroad) Regulations 1975
see *Secretary of State for Work and Pensions v Yates* [2009] EWCA Civ 479, [2009] Pens. L.R. 217 (CA (Civ Div)), Lord Clarke of Stone-cum-Ebony MR
Reg.5, applied: SI 2009/607 Reg.3, SI 2009/810 Reg.3
Reg.5, see *Secretary of State for Work and Pensions v Yates* [2009] EWCA Civ 479, [2009] Pens. L.R. 217 (CA (Civ Div)), Lord Clarke of Stone-cum-Ebony MR

1023. Rehabilitation of Offenders Act 1974 (Exceptions) Order 1975
Art.2, amended: SI 2009/1818 Art.3
Art.3, amended: SI 2009/1818 Art.4
Art.4, amended: SI 2009/1818 Art.5
Art.6, added: SI 2009/1818 Art.6
Sch.1 Part I para.4, substituted: SI 2009/1182 Sch.4 para.37
Sch.1 Part I para.13, revoked: SI 2009/1182 Sch.4 para.1
Sch.1 Part II para.12A, added: SI 2009/1818 Art.7
Sch.1 Part II para.14A, added: SI 2009/1818 Art.7
Sch.1 Part II para.38, amended: 2009 c.26 s.81
Sch.1 Part II para.44, added: SI 2009/1818 Art.7
Sch.1 Part III para.11, added: SI 2009/1818 Art.7
Sch.1 Part IV, amended: SI 2009/1182 Sch.4 para.1, Sch.4 para.37, SI 2009/1818 Art.7

1078. Shilbottle Mine (Endless Rope Haulage) Special Regulations 1975
revoked: SI 2009/693 Sch.2

1135. Schools General (Scotland) Regulations 1975
Reg.3, amended: SSI 2009/319 Sch.2 para.8
Reg.6, amended: SSI 2009/319 Sch.2 para.8

1975– cont.

1157. Industrial Training (Transfer of the Activities of Establishments) (No.2) Order 1975
applied: SI 2009/549 Sch.1

1507. Tuvalu (Appeals to Privy Council) Order 1975
revoked (in part): SI 2009/224 Art.5

1803. Supreme Court Funds Rules 1975
referred to: SI 2009/500 Sch.1 Part 2

2125. Calibration of Tanks of Vessels (EEC Requirements) Regulations 1975
referred to: SI 2009/669 Sch.1 Part 4

1976

27. Baddesley Mine (Endless Rope Haulage) Special Regulations 1976
revoked: SI 2009/693 Sch.2

28. Birch Coppice Mine (Endless Rope Haulage) Special Regulations 1976
revoked: SI 2009/693 Sch.2

43. High Moor Mine (Endless Rope Haulage) Special Regulations 1976
revoked: SI 2009/693 Sch.2

44. Warsop Main Mine (Endless Rope Haulage) Special Regulations 1976
revoked: SI 2009/693 Sch.2

82. Snibston Mine (Endless Rope Haulage) Special Regulations 1976
revoked: SI 2009/693 Sch.2

396. Industrial Training (Transfer of the Activities of Establishments) Order 1976
applied: SI 2009/549 Sch.1

409. Social Security (Invalid Care Allowance) Regulations 1976
Reg.2A, amended: SI 2009/471 Reg.2

479. Monktonhall Mine (Endless Rope Haulage) Special Regulations 1976
revoked: SI 2009/693 Sch.2

480. Snibston Mine (Diesel Vehicles) Special Regulations 1976
revoked: SI 2009/693 Sch.2

482. Bogside Mine (Endless Rope Haulage) Special Regulations 1976
revoked: SI 2009/693 Sch.2

483. Polkemmet Mine (Endless Rope Haulage) Special Regulations 1976
revoked: SI 2009/693 Sch.2

484. Arkwright Mine (Endless Rope Haulage) Special Regulations 1976
substituted: SI 2009/693 Sch.2

485. Bolsover Mine (Endless Rope Haulage) Special Regulations 1976
revoked: SI 2009/693 Sch.2

486. Shirebrook Mine (Endless Rope Haulage) Special Regulations 1976
revoked: SI 2009/693 Sch.2

487. Westthorpe Mine (Endless Rope Haulage) Special Regulations 1976
revoked: SI 2009/693 Sch.2

556. Daw Mill Mine (Endless Rope Haulage) Regulations 1976
revoked: SI 2009/693 Sch.2

967. Whitwell Mine (Endless Rope Haulage) Special Regulations 1976
revoked: SI 2009/693 Sch.2

1019. Offshore Installations (Operational Safety, Health and Welfare) Regulations 1976
Reg.5, see *Spencer-Franks v Kellogg Brown & Root Ltd* [2008] UKHL 46, [2009] 1 All E.R. 269 (HL), Lord Hoffmann

1976– cont.

1042. Sex Discrimination (Northern Ireland) Order 1976
applied: SI 2009/ 1059 Art.196
Part I, applied: SI 2009/ 1059 Art.196
Part II, applied: SI 2009/ 1059 Art.196
Part III, applied: SI 2009/ 1059 Art.196
Part IV, applied: SI 2009/ 1059 Art.196
Part V, applied: SI 2009/ 1059 Art.196
Part VI, applied: SI 2009/ 1059 Art.196
Part VII, applied: SI 2009/ 1059 Art.196
Part VIII, applied: SI 2009/ 1059 Art.196
Part IX, applied: SI 2009/ 1059 Art.196
Art.2, applied: SI 2009/ 1059 Art.196
Art.8, applied: SI 2009/ 1059 Art.196
Art.24, applied: SI 2009/ 1059 Art.196
Art.25, applied: SI 2009/ 1059 Art.196
Art.63, applied: SI 2009/ 1059 Art.196
Art.63A, see *Nelson v Newry and Mourne DC* [2009] NICA 24, [2009] I.R.L.R. 548 (CA (NI)), Higgins, L.J.
Art.77, applied: SI 2009/ 1059 Art.196
Art.77A, applied: SI 2009/ 1059 Art.196
Art.84A, applied: SI 2009/ 1059 Art.196
Art.107, applied: SI 2009/ 1059 Art.196
Art.141, applied: SI 2009/ 1059 Art.196
Art.146, applied: SI 2009/ 1059 Art.196
Sch.1, applied: SI 2009/ 1059 Art.196
Sch.2, applied: SI 2009/ 1059 Art.196
Sch.3, applied: SI 2009/ 1059 Art.196
Sch.4, applied: SI 2009/ 1059 Art.196
Sch.5, applied: SI 2009/ 1059 Art.196
Sch.6, applied: SI 2009/ 1059 Art.196
Sch.7, applied: SI 2009/ 1059 Art.196

1073. Police (Scotland) Regulations 1976
Reg.42, see *Robb v Tayside Joint Police Board* 2009 S.L.T. (Lands Tr) 23 (Lands Tr (Scot)), J N Wright QC
Reg.66, see *Robb v Tayside Joint Police Board* 2009 S.L.T. (Lands Tr) 23 (Lands Tr (Scot)), J N Wright QC

1213. Pharmacy (Northern Ireland) Order 1976
applied: SI 2009/ 2722 Reg.3

1445. Seafield Mine (Endless Rope Haulage) Special Regulations 1976
revoked: SI 2009/ 693 Sch.2

1607. Solsgirth Nos 1 &amp 2 Mine (Endless Rope Haulage) Special Regulations 1976
revoked: SI 2009/ 693 Sch.2

1608. Killoch Mine (Endless Rope Haulage) Special Regulations 1976
revoked: SI 2009/ 693 Sch.2

1609. Bilston Glen Mine (Endless Rope Haulage) Special Regulations 1976
revoked: SI 2009/ 693 Sch.2

1610. New Hucknall Mine (Endless Rope Haulage) Special Regulations 1976
revoked: SI 2009/ 693 Sch.2

1612. Cardowan Mine (Endless Rope Haulage) Regulations 1976
revoked: SI 2009/ 693 Sch.2

1635. Industrial Training (Transfer of the Activities of Establishments) (No.2) Order 1976
applied: SI 2009/ 549 Sch.1

1654. Yorkshire Main Mine (Endless Rope Haulage) Regulations 1976
revoked: SI 2009/ 693 Sch.2

1655. Frances Mine (Endless Rope Haulage) Regulations 1976
revoked: SI 2009/ 693 Sch.2

1976– cont.

1733. High Moor Mine (Diesel Vehicles) Regulations 1976
revoked: SI 2009/ 693 Sch.2

1734. Markham Mine (Diesel Vehicles) Regulations 1976
revoked: SI 2009/ 693 Sch.2

1777. Hong Kong Supreme Court (Admiralty Procedure) Rules Order 1976
referred to: SI 2009/ 500 Sch.2 Part 2

1827. Blackdene Mine (Storage Battery Locomotives) Special Regulations 1976
revoked: SI 2009/ 693 Sch.2

1915. Trinidad and Tobago Appeals to Judicial Committee Order 1976
revoked (in part): SI 2009/ 224 Art.5

2012. National Savings Stock Register Regulations 1976
Reg.43, applied: SI 2009/ 1263 Reg.3, Reg.6
Reg.43, disapplied: SI 2009/ 1263 Reg.3
Reg.43, revoked: SI 2009/ 1263 Reg.7
Reg.43A, added: SI 2009/ 1263 Reg.7
Reg.43A, disapplied: SI 2009/ 1263 Reg.3
Reg.44, disapplied: SI 2009/ 1263 Reg.3
Reg.44, revoked: SI 2009/ 1263 Reg.7

2046. Bentinck Mine (Diesel Engined Stone Dusting Machine) Regulations 1976
revoked: SI 2009/ 693 Sch.2

2052. High Moor Mine (Cable Reel Shuttle Cars) Regulations 1976
revoked: SI 2009/ 693 Sch.2

2110. Industrial Training (Transfer of the Activities of Establishments) (No.3) Order 1976
applied: SI 2009/ 549 Sch.1

1977

8. Local Government Area Changes (Scotland) Regulations 1977
applied: SSI 2009/ 368 Art.3, SSI 2009/ 442 Art.3

84. Internal Drainage Boards (Acquisition of New Interests and Rights) Regulations 1977
Reg.11, amended: SI 2009/ 1307 Sch.2 para.18
Reg.11, substituted: SI 2009/ 1307 Sch.2 para.18

203. Bentley Mine (Endless Rope Haulage) Regulations 1977
revoked: SI 2009/ 693 Sch.2

225. Murton Mine (Endless Rope Haulage) Regulations 1977
revoked: SI 2009/ 693 Sch.2

243. Donisthorpe Mine (Endless Rope Haulage) Regulations 1977
revoked: SI 2009/ 693 Sch.2

343. Social Security Benefit (Dependency) Regulations 1977
Sch.2 Part I para.2B, amended: SI 2009/ 607 Reg.4

344. Matrimonial Causes Rules 1977
referred to: SI 2009/ 500 Sch.1 Part 2

483. Rossington Mine (Endless Rope Haulage) Regulations 1977
revoked: SI 2009/ 693 Sch.2

577. Police (Withdrawn, Anonymous Etc Complaints) Regulations 1977
referred to: SI 2009/ 500 Sch.1 Part 2

658. Goldthorpe/Highgate Mine (Endless Rope Haulage) Regulations 1977
revoked: SI 2009/ 693 Sch.2

735. Ireland Mine (Diesel Vehicles) Regulations 1977
revoked: SI 2009/ 693 Sch.2

1977– cont.

737. Dinnington Main Mine (Revocation of Special Regulations) Regulations 1977
revoked: SI 2009/ 693 Sch.2

917. Blaenserchan Mine (Diesel Vehicles) Regulations 1977
revoked: SI 2009/ 693 Sch.2

932. Measuring Container Bottles (EEC Requirements) Regulations 1977
referred to: SI 2009/ 669 Sch.1 Part 4

944. Importation of Animals Order 1977
Art.2, amended: SI 2009/ 2713 Art.2
Art.4, amended: SI 2009/ 2713 Art.2
Art.5, amended: SI 2009/ 2713 Art.2

985. Local Land Charges Rules 1977
r.10, amended: SI 2009/ 1307 Sch.2 para.20
Sch.3, amended: SI 2009/ 1307 Sch.2 para.22, SI 2009/ 2494 r.3

1140. Aerosol Dispensers (EEC Requirements) Regulations 1977
applied: SI 2009/ 2824 Reg.8
referred to: SI 2009/ 669 Sch.1 Part 4
revoked: SI 2009/ 2824 Sch.1 para.1
Reg.3, amended: SI 2009/ 663 Reg.6

1210. National Savings Bank (Investment Deposits) (Limits) Order 1977
Art.3B, amended: SI 2009/ 2460 Art.4
Art.3B, varied: SI 2009/ 2460 Art.5

1247. Criminal Damage (Compensation) (Northern Ireland) Order 1977
Art.4A, added: SI 2009/ 884 Art.3

1457. Plymouth Port Health Authority Order 1977
Art.1, amended: SI 2009/ 837 Art.15

1459. River Blyth Port Health Authority Order 1977
Art.1, amended: SI 2009/ 837 Art.16
Art.1, revoked (in part): SI 2009/ 837 Art.16
Art.2, amended: SI 2009/ 837 Art.16
Art.3, revoked: SI 2009/ 837 Art.16
Art.5, revoked: SI 2009/ 837 Art.16
Art.6, amended: SI 2009/ 837 Art.16
Art.7, revoked: SI 2009/ 837 Art.16
Art.8, revoked: SI 2009/ 837 Art.16
Art.9, revoked: SI 2009/ 837 Art.16

1460. Manchester Port Health Authority Order 1977
Art.1, amended: SI 2009/ 837 Art.14
Art.2, amended: SI 2009/ 837 Art.14
Art.8, substituted: SI 2009/ 837 Art.14

1593. Parsonage Mine (Endless Rope Haulage) Regulations 1977
revoked: SI 2009/ 693 Sch.2

1696. Hapton Valley Mine (Diesel Vehicles) Regulations 1977
revoked: SI 2009/ 693 Sch.2

1753. Alcoholometers and Alcohol Hydrometers (EEC Requirements) Regulations 1977
referred to: SI 2009/ 669 Sch.1 Part 4

1758. Treeton Mine (Refuge Holes) Special Regulations 1977
revoked: SI 2009/ 693 Sch.2

1855. Golborne Mine (Endless Rope Haulage) Regulations 1977
revoked: SI 2009/ 693 Sch.2

1951. Industrial Training (Transfer of the Activities of Establishments) Order 1977
applied: SI 2009/ 549 Sch.1

1977– cont.

2036. Cynheidre/Pentremawr Mine (Escape Breathing Apparatus) (Amendment) Regulations 1977
revoked: SI 2009/ 693 Sch.2

2106. Cwmgwili Mine (Escape Breathing Apparatus) Regulations 1977
revoked: SI 2009/ 693 Sch.2

2157. Rates (Northern Ireland) Order 1977
Sch.9B, amended: 2009 c.3 Sch.4 para.9
Sch.9B, revoked (in part): 2009 c.3 Sch.4 para.9
Sch.9B, substituted: 2009 c.3 Sch.4 para.9
Sch.12, amended: SI 2009/ 1941 Sch.1 para.38

1978

20. Pharmaceutical Society (Statutory Committee) Order of Council 1978
referred to: SI 2009/ 500 Sch.1 Part 2

33. Gascoigne Wood Mine (Refuge Holes) Regulations 1978
revoked: SI 2009/ 693 Sch.2

119. Thoresby Mine (Cable Reel Load-Haul-Dump Vehicles) Regulations 1978
revoked: SI 2009/ 693 Sch.2

393. Social Security (Graduated Retirement Benefit) (No.2) Regulations 1978
Sch.2 para.1, varied: SI 2009/ 497 Art.12
Sch.2 para.2, varied: SI 2009/ 497 Art.12
Sch.2 para.3, varied: SI 2009/ 497 Art.12
Sch.2 para.4, varied: SI 2009/ 497 Art.12

448. Industrial Training (Transfer of the Activities of Establishments) Order 1978
applied: SI 2009/ 549 Sch.1

761. Sallet Hole Nos 1 and 2 Mines (Diesel Vehicles) Regulations 1978
revoked: SI 2009/ 693 Sch.2

1047. Protection of Children (Northern Ireland) Order 1978
Art.3, applied: 2009 asp 9 Sch.1 para.12, SI 2009/ 1547 Sch.3 para.3, SSI 2009/ 182 Sch.1 para.17
Art.3, referred to: SI 2009/ 37 Sch.1 para.2, Sch.1 para.4
Art.3B, amended: 2009 c.25 s.69
Art.4, applied: 2009 c.25 s.67
Sch.1, applied: 2009 c.25 s.67

1049. Pollution Control and Local Government (Northern Ireland) Order 1978
Art.65, referred to: SI 2009/ 2037 Art.5
Art.66, referred to: SI 2009/ 2037 Art.5

1159. Income Tax (Life Assurance Premium Relief) Regulations 1978
Reg.10, amended: SI 2009/ 56 Sch.2 para.7

1225. Industrial Training (Transfer of the Activities of Establishments) (No.2) Order 1978
applied: SI 2009/ 549 Sch.1

1376. Trelewis Drift Mine (Diesel Vehicles) Regulations 1978
revoked: SI 2009/ 693 Sch.2

1485. Brucellosis and Tuberculosis Compensation (Scotland) Order 1978
referred to: SSI 2009/ 232 Art.27
revoked: SSI 2009/ 232 Sch.1
Art.3, applied: SSI 2009/ 232 Art.27

1535. Control of Off-Street Parking (England and Wales) Order 1978
Sch.1 Part IV para.22, amended: SI 2009/ 1307 Sch.2 para.23

1978– cont.

1643. Industrial Training (Transfer of the Activities of Establishments) (No.3) Order 1978
applied: SI 2009/549 Sch.1

1689. Social Security (Categorisation of Earners) Regulations 1978
Reg.1, see *Oleochem (Scotland) Ltd v Revenue and Customs Commissioners* [2009] S.T.C. (S.C.D.) 205 (Sp Comm), J Gordon Reid Q.C.
Sch.3, see *Oleochem (Scotland) Ltd v Revenue and Customs Commissioners* [2009] S.T.C. (S.C.D.) 205 (Sp Comm), J Gordon Reid Q.C.

1723. Compressed Acetylene (Importation) Regulations 1978
applied: SI 2009/515 Sch.8 Part 3

1908. Rehabilitation of Offenders (Northern Ireland) Order 1978
varied: SI 2009/1059 Sch.1 para.17
Art.8, amended: 2009 c.25 s.158

1979

132. Alcohol Tables Regulations 1979
referred to: SI 2009/669 Sch.1 Part 2

294. Aircraft and Shipbuilding Industries (Northern Ireland) Order 1979
Art.2, amended: SI 2009/1941 Sch.1 para.41

399. Matrimonial Causes (Costs) Rules 1979
referred to: SI 2009/500 Sch.1 Part 2

521. European Assembly Election Petition Rules 1979
referred to: SI 2009/1118 r.2
r.2, revoked (in part): SI 2009/1118 r.4
r.5, amended: SI 2009/1118 r.5

591. Social Security (Contributions) Regulations 1979
Reg.19, see *Mason v Revenue and Customs Commissioners* [2009] UKFTT 139 (TC), [2009] S.F.T.D. 369 (FTT (Tax)), Howard M Nowlan

597. Social Security (Overlapping Benefits) Regulations 1979
applied: SI 2009/1562 Art.2

642. Social Security (Widow's Benefit and Retirement Pensions) Regulations 1979
Reg.1, amended: SI 2009/2206 Reg.6
Reg.1A, amended: SI 2009/471 Reg.3
Reg.2, amended: SI 2009/2206 Reg.7
Reg.2, revoked (in part): SI 2009/2206 Reg.7
Reg.3, amended: SI 2009/2206 Reg.8
Reg.3, revoked (in part): SI 2009/2206 Reg.8
Reg.4, amended: SI 2009/2206 Reg.9
Reg.6, amended: SI 2009/2206 Reg.11
Reg.6, revoked (in part): SI 2009/2206 Reg.11
Reg.6, substituted: SI 2009/2206 Reg.10
Reg.6A, added: SI 2009/2206 Reg.12
Reg.6B, added: SI 2009/2206 Reg.12
Reg.8, amended: SI 2009/2206 Reg.13
Reg.8, revoked (in part): SI 2009/2206 Reg.13
Reg.8A, added: SI 2009/2206 Reg.14
Sch.1 para.1, amended: SI 2009/2206 Reg.15

643. Social Security (Widow's Benefit, Retirement Pensions and Other Benefits) (Transitional) Regulations 1979
Reg.2, amended: SI 2009/2206 Reg.17
Reg.3, amended: SI 2009/2206 Reg.18, Reg.19
Reg.7, amended: SI 2009/2206 Reg.20, Reg.21
Reg.13, amended: SI 2009/2206 Reg.22

1979– cont.

720. Kiribati Appeals to Judicial Committee Order 1979
revoked (in part): SI 2009/224 Art.5

793. Industrial Training (Transfer of the Activities of Establishments) Order 1979
applied: SI 2009/549 Sch.1

924. Inheritance (Provision for Family and Dependants) (Northern Ireland) Order 1979
Art.21, applied: 2009 c.10 Sch.53 para.8, Sch.54 para.10

937. Industrial and Provident Societies (Credit Unions) Regulations 1979
referred to: SI 2009/500 Sch.1 Part 2

1085. Fowey Port Health Authority Order 1979
Art.1, amended: SI 2009/837 Art.18
Art.1, revoked (in part): SI 2009/837 Art.18
Art.2, amended: SI 2009/837 Art.18
Art.2, revoked (in part): SI 2009/837 Art.18
Art.3, revoked: SI 2009/837 Art.18
Art.5, revoked: SI 2009/837 Art.18
Art.6, amended: SI 2009/837 Art.18
Art.6, revoked (in part): SI 2009/837 Art.18
Art.7, amended: SI 2009/837 Art.18
Art.9, revoked: SI 2009/837 Art.18
Art.10, revoked: SI 2009/837 Art.18

1293. High Moor Mine (Cable Reel Load-Haul-Dump Vehicles) Regulations 1979
revoked: SI 2009/693 Sch.2

1379. Taximeters (EEC Requirements) Regulations 1979
referred to: SI 2009/669 Sch.1 Part 4

1456. Imprisonment and Detention (Army) Rules 1979
applied: SI 2009/1096 r.63
revoked: SI 2009/1096 r.2
Part VII r.83, applied: SI 2009/1096 r.77
Part VII r.85, applied: SI 2009/1096 r.77

1532. Boulby Mine (Diesel Vehicles) Regulations 1979
revoked: SI 2009/693 Sch.2

1573. Statutory Rules (Northern Ireland) Order 1979
applied: 2009 c.4 s.106, 2009 c.21 s.37, s.40, 2009 c.22 s.262

1577. Merchant Shipping (Returns of Births and Deaths) Regulations 1979
Reg.11, added: SI 2009/1892 Sch.1 para.8
Reg.11, amended: SI 2009/1892 Sch.1 para.8
Sch.1 para.3, amended: SI 2009/1892 Sch.1 para.8

1644. National Health Service (Vocational Training) Regulations 1979
referred to: SI 2009/500 Sch.1 Part 2

1714. Perjury (Northern Ireland) Order 1979
Art.10, applied: 2009 c.23 s.263

1769. Whitwell Mine (Teleplatform Haulage and Refuge Holes) Regulations 1979
revoked: SI 2009/693 Sch.2

1980

51. Consumer Credit (Total Charge for Credit) Regulations 1980
applied: SI 2009/470 Reg.21

187. INMARSAT (Immunities and Privileges) Order 1980
revoked (in part): SSI 2009/44 Art.3

397. County Courts (Northern Ireland) Order 1980
applied: SI 2009/3015 Art.243

1980 – cont.

538. Merchant Shipping (Life-Saving Appliances) Regulations 1980
Sch.15 Part III, applied: SI 2009/3015 Sch.4 para.5

568. Double Taxation Relief (Taxes on Income) (The United States of America) Order 1980
see *Bayfine UK Products v Revenue and Customs Commissioners* [2009] S.T.C. (S.C.D.) 43 (Sp Comm), John F Avery Jones
Sch.1, see *Bayfine UK Products v Revenue and Customs Commissioners* [2009] S.T.C. (S.C.D.) 43 (Sp Comm), John F Avery Jones

704. Criminal Justice (Northern Ireland) Order 1980
Art.8A, added: 2009 c.25 Sch.16 para.1
Art.8B, added: 2009 c.25 Sch.16 para.1
Art.9, applied: 2009 asp 9 Sch.1 para.22, SI 2009/1547 Sch.3 para.3
Art.9, referred to: SI 2009/37 Sch.1 para.2, Sch.1 para.4

821. Supreme Court Fees Order 1980
referred to: SI 2009/500 Sch.1 Part 2

860. General Medical Council (Fraud or Error in relation to Registration) Rules Order of Council 1980
referred to: SI 2009/500 Sch.2 Part 2

1203. Sallet Hole No.2 Mine (Storage Battery Locomotives) Special Regulations 1980
revoked: SI 2009/693 Sch.2

1330. Penwith Port Health Authority order 1980
Art.1, amended: SI 2009/837 Art.19

1474. Harworth Mine (Cable Reel Load-Haul-Dump Vehicles) Regulations 1980
revoked: SI 2009/693 Sch.2

1705. Point of Ayr Mine (Diesel Vehicles) Regulations 1980
revoked: SI 2009/693 Sch.2

1753. Industrial Training (Transfer of the Activities of Establishments) (No.2) Order 1980
applied: SI 2009/549 Sch.1

1923. Medicines (Sale or Supply) (Miscellaneous Provisions) Regulations 1980
Reg.1, amended: SI 2009/3063 Reg.3
Reg.5, amended: SI 2009/3063 Reg.3

1924. Medicines (Pharmacy and General Sale Exemption) Order 1980
Art.1, amended: SI 2009/3062 Art.4
Art.7A, added: SI 2009/1165 Art.5
Sch.1 Part I, amended: SI 2009/3062 Art.4
Sch.1 Part II, amended: SI 2009/3062 Art.4

1961. Double Taxation Relief (Taxes on Income) (Netherlands) Order 1980
see *Laerstate BV v Revenue and Customs Commissioners* [2009] UKFTT 209 (TC), [2009] S.F.T.D. 551 (FTT (Tax)), John F Avery Jones

2005. Imprisonment and Detention (Air Force) Rules 1980
revoked: SI 2009/1096 r.2

1981

15. Public Bodies Land (Appropriate Ministers) Order 1981
Art.2, applied: SI 2009/229 Art.4

154. Road Traffic (Northern Ireland) Order 1981
Part II, applied: SI 2009/2793 Reg.2
Art.31A, applied: SI 2009/717 Sch.3 para.2

1981 – cont.

226. Judgments Enforcement (Northern Ireland) Order 1981
applied: 2009 c.1 s.134
Art.2, amended: SI 2009/1941 Sch.1 para.49
Art.46, applied: SI 2009/1917 Reg.18
Art.58, amended: SI 2009/1941 Sch.1 para.49

228. Legal Aid, Advice and Assistance (Northern Ireland) Order 1981
Part II, applied: SI 2009/2131 Sch.2 para.1
Sch.1, amended: 2009 c.26 Sch.7 para.45, Sch.7 para.97

234. Judgments Enforcement (Northern Ireland) Order 1981
applied: SI 2009/470 Reg.51

257. Public Service Vehicles (Conditions of Fitness, Equipment, Use and Certification) Regulations 1981
Reg.3, amended: SI 2009/141 Reg.2
Reg.4A, substituted: SI 2009/141 Reg.2
Reg.6, applied: SI 2009/365 Reg.6
Reg.6, referred to: SI 2009/366 Reg.5
Reg.7, applied: SI 2009/365 Reg.6
Reg.8, applied: SI 2009/365 Reg.6
Reg.9, applied: SI 2009/365 Reg.6
Reg.10, applied: SI 2009/365 Reg.6
Reg.11, applied: SI 2009/365 Reg.6
Reg.12, applied: SI 2009/365 Reg.6
Reg.13, applied: SI 2009/365 Reg.6
Reg.14, applied: SI 2009/365 Reg.6
Reg.15, applied: SI 2009/365 Reg.6
Reg.16, applied: SI 2009/365 Reg.6
Reg.17, applied: SI 2009/365 Reg.6
Reg.18, applied: SI 2009/365 Reg.6
Reg.19, applied: SI 2009/365 Reg.6
Reg.20, applied: SI 2009/365 Reg.6
Reg.21, applied: SI 2009/365 Reg.6
Reg.22, applied: SI 2009/365 Reg.6
Reg.23, applied: SI 2009/365 Reg.6
Reg.24, applied: SI 2009/365 Reg.6
Reg.25, applied: SI 2009/365 Reg.6
Reg.26, applied: SI 2009/365 Reg.6
Reg.27, applied: SI 2009/365 Reg.6
Reg.28, applied: SI 2009/365 Reg.6
Reg.28A, applied: SI 2009/365 Reg.6
Reg.29, applied: SI 2009/365 Reg.6
Reg.30, applied: SI 2009/365 Reg.6
Reg.31, applied: SI 2009/365 Reg.6
Reg.32, applied: SI 2009/365 Reg.6
Reg.33, applied: SI 2009/365 Reg.6
Reg.33, referred to: SI 2009/366 Reg.5
Reg.35, applied: SI 2009/365 Reg.6
Reg.35, referred to: SI 2009/366 Reg.5
Reg.36, applied: SI 2009/365 Reg.6
Reg.37, applied: SI 2009/365 Reg.6
Reg.38, applied: SI 2009/365 Reg.6
Reg.39, applied: SI 2009/365 Reg.6
Reg.40, applied: SI 2009/365 Reg.6
Reg.41, applied: SI 2009/365 Reg.6
Reg.42, applied: SI 2009/365 Reg.6
Reg.43, applied: SI 2009/365 Reg.6
Reg.44, applied: SI 2009/365 Reg.6
Reg.44, referred to: SI 2009/366 Reg.5
Reg.45A, applied: SI 2009/365 Reg.6
Reg.45A, referred to: SI 2009/366 Reg.5
Reg.46, amended: SI 2009/877 Reg.3
Reg.50, amended: SI 2009/877 Reg.3
Reg.53, amended: SI 2009/877 Reg.3
Reg.57, amended: SI 2009/877 Reg.3

1981– cont.

500. Pensions Appeal Tribunals (Scotland) Rules 1981
referred to: SSI 2009/ 353 r.1
r.2, revoked (in part): SSI 2009/ 353 r.2
r.9, amended: SSI 2009/ 353 r.2
r.9, substituted: SSI 2009/ 353 r.2
r.16, amended: SSI 2009/ 353 r.2
r.18, amended: SSI 2009/ 353 r.2
r.24, amended: SSI 2009/ 353 r.2
r.24, substituted: SSI 2009/ 353 r.2
r.30, amended: SSI 2009/ 353 r.2

552. Magistrates Courts Rules 1981
applied: SI 2009/ 470 Reg.51
r.3A, added: SI 2009/ 3362 r.3
r.47, amended: SI 2009/ 2054 Sch.1 para.8
r.47, applied: SI 2009/ 2054 Sch.2 para.4

917. Health and Safety (First-Aid) Regulations 1981
Reg.3, applied: SI 2009/ 515 Reg.18, Reg.20

1041. Industrial Training (Transfer of the Activities of Establishments) Order 1981
applied: SI 2009/ 549 Sch.1

1121. Double Taxation Relief (Taxes on Income) (Mauritius) Order 1981
see *Smallwood v Revenue and Customs Commissioners* [2009] EWHC 777 (Ch), [2009] S.T.C. 1222 (Ch D), Mann, J.

1448. Brucellosis and Tuberculosis Compensation (Scotland) Amendment Order 1981
revoked: SSI 2009/ 232 Sch.1

1502. Glebe Mine (Locomotives and Diesel Vehicles) Special Regulations 1981
revoked: SI 2009/ 693 Sch.2

1518. Estate Agents (Appeals) Regulations 1981
revoked: SI 2009/ 1836 Sch.2
Reg.19, applied: SI 2009/ 1836 Art.3

1549. Aerosol Dispensers (EEC Requirements) (Amendment) Regulations 1981
revoked: SI 2009/ 2824 Sch.1 para.2

1675. Magistrates Courts (Northern Ireland) Order 1981
applied: SI 2009/ 2297 Reg.44, SI 2009/ 2890 Reg.21, Reg.23
see *Tierney's Application for Judicial Review, Re* [2009] N.I. 77 (QBD (NI)), Lord Kerr L.C.J.
Art.19, disapplied: SI 2009/ 886 Art.12, SI 2009/ 1749 Art.14
Art.20, see *DPP v Long* [2009] N.I. 10 (CA (NI)), Campbell, L.J.
Art.95, applied: SI 2009/ 1850 Art.10, SSI 2009/ 317 Art.13
Art.115, see *Tierney's Application for Judicial Review, Re* [2009] N.I. 77 (QBD (NI)), Lord Kerr L.C.J.
Art.146, applied: SI 2009/ 1896 Sch.1 para.6, SI 2009/ 1899 Sch.1 para.6, SI 2009/ 2194 Reg.9
Sch.4, applied: SI 2009/ 209 Reg.118, SI 2009/ 216 Reg.10, SI 2009/ 261 Reg.52, SI 2009/ 3263 Reg.12
Sch.4, referred to: SI 2009/ 842 Reg.28

1685. Company and Business Names Regulations 1981
revoked: SI 2009/ 2615 Reg.7

1687. County Court Rules 1981
see *P-B (Children) (Contact Order: Committal: Penal Notice), Re* [2009] EWCA Civ 143, [2009] 2 F.L.R. 66 (CA (Civ Div)), Thorpe, L.J.

1981– cont.

1687. County Court Rules 1981– *cont.*
Ord.29 r.1, see *P-B (Children) (Contact Order: Committal: Penal Notice), Re* [2009] EWCA Civ 143, [2009] 2 F.L.R. 66 (CA (Civ Div)), Thorpe, L.J.
Ord.37 r.1, see *Roult v North West SHA* [2009] EWCA Civ 444, [2009] P.I.Q.R. P18 (CA (Civ Div)), Carnwath, L.J.

1694. Motor Vehicles (Tests) Regulations 1981
Reg.20, amended: SI 2009/ 643 Reg.3, SI 2009/ 802 Reg.2
Reg.25, amended: SI 2009/ 643 Reg.4
Sch.2 para.1, amended: SI 2009/ 643 Reg.5
Sch.2 para.2, amended: SI 2009/ 643 Reg.5

1794. Transfer of Undertakings (Protection of Employment) Regulations 1981
see *Alemo-Herron v Parkwood Leisure Ltd* [2009] 2 C.M.L.R. 40 (EAT), Judge McMullen Q.C.; see *Dynamex Friction Ltd v Amicus* [2008] EWCA Civ 381, [2009] I.C.R. 511 (CA (Civ Div)), Ward, L.J.; see *Metropolitan Resources Ltd v Churchill Dulwich Ltd (In Liquidation)* [2009] I.C.R. 1380 (EAT), Judge Burke Q.C.; see *Small v Boots Co Plc* [2009] I.R.L.R. 328 (EAT), Slade, J.; see *Sodexo Ltd v Gutridge* [2009] EWCA Civ 729, [2009] I.C.R. 1486 (CA (Civ Div)), Pill, L.J.; see *Sodexo Ltd v Gutridge* [2009] I.C.R. 70 (EAT), Elias, J.; see *Swissport (UK) Ltd (In Liquidation) v Aer Lingus Ltd* [2007] EWHC 1089 (Ch), [2009] B.C.C. 113 (Ch D), Peter Prescott Q.C.
Reg.5, see *Alemo-Herron v Parkwood Leisure Ltd* [2009] 2 C.M.L.R. 40 (EAT), Judge McMullen Q.C.; see *Coutinho v Rank Nemo (DMS) Ltd* [2009] EWCA Civ 454, [2009] I.C.R. 1296 (CA (Civ Div)), Mummery, L.J.; see *Dynamex Friction Ltd v Amicus* [2008] EWCA Civ 381, [2009] I.C.R. 511 (CA (Civ Div)), Ward, L.J.
Reg.6, see *Alemo-Herron v Parkwood Leisure Ltd* [2009] 2 C.M.L.R. 40 (EAT), Judge McMullen Q.C.
Reg.8, see *Dynamex Friction Ltd v Amicus* [2008] EWCA Civ 381, [2009] I.C.R. 511 (CA (Civ Div)), Ward, L.J.
Reg.10, see *Small v Boots Co Plc* [2009] I.R.L.R. 328 (EAT), Slade, J.

1982

92. Oil Taxation (Gas Banking Schemes) Regulations 1982
Reg.5, applied: SI 2009/ 229 Art.4
Reg.7, amended: SI 2009/ 56 Sch.2 para.8

218. Poisons Rules 1982
applied: SSI 2009/ 183 Sch.1 para.4
Sch.4, disapplied: SSI 2009/ 183 Sch.1 para.4
Sch.5, disapplied: SSI 2009/ 183 Sch.1 para.4
Sch.12 Part I para.6, amended: SSI 2009/ 319 Sch.3 Part 2

387. Grading of Horticultural Produce (Forms of Labels) Regulations 1982
revoked (in part): SI 2009/ 1361 Reg.21, SI 2009/ 1551 Reg.21, SSI 2009/ 225 Reg.23

448. Smoke Control Areas (Exempted Fireplaces) (Scotland) Order 1982
revoked: SSI 2009/ 214 Sch.2

709. Inter-Governmental Maritime Consultative Organisation (Immunities and Privileges) (Amendment) Order 1982
revoked (in part): SSI 2009/ 44 Art.3

1982– cont.

719. Public Lending Right Scheme 1982 (Commencement) Order 1982
Part V para.46, amended: SI 2009/ 3259 Art.2

1070. British Protectorates, Protected States and Protected Persons Order 1982
Art.3, substituted: SI 2009/ 1892 Sch.1 para.10
Art.4, amended: SI 2009/ 1892 Sch.1 para.10
Art.7, amended: SI 2009/ 1892 Sch.1 para.10

1083. Industrial Development (Northern Ireland) Order 1982
Art.7, applied: 2009 c.4 s.102, s.1252
Art.9, applied: 2009 c.4 s.102, s.1252
Art.15, amended: SI 2009/ 1941 Sch.1 para.53
Art.30, applied: 2009 c.4 s.102, s.1252

1109. Crown Court Rules 1982
Part llA r.5A, added: SI 2009/ 3361 r.3
Sch.3 Part III, amended: SI 2009/ 3361 r.4

1110. Foreign Compensation Commission (Czechoslovakia) Rules Approval Instrument 1982
referred to: SI 2009/ 500 Sch.1 Part 2

1123. Registration of Overseas Births and Deaths Regulations 1982
Reg.5, amended: SI 2009/ 1892 Sch.1 para.9
Reg.7, amended: SI 2009/ 1892 Sch.1 para.9

1163. Motorways Traffic (England and Wales) Regulations 1982
Reg.3, varied: SI 2009/ 1571 Reg.3
Reg.4, varied: SI 2009/ 1571 Reg.3
Reg.5A, varied: SI 2009/ 1571 Reg.3
Reg.7, referred to: SI 2009/ 2247 Reg.4
Reg.7, varied: SI 2009/ 1571 Reg.3
Reg.9, varied: SI 2009/ 1571 Reg.3
Reg.12, varied: SI 2009/ 1571 Reg.3
Reg.14, varied: SI 2009/ 1571 Reg.3

1221. Wildlife and Countryside (Registration and Ringing of Certain Captive Birds) Regulations 1982
revoked (in part): SSI 2009/ 419 Reg.7

1236. Income Tax (Interest Relief) Regulations 1982
Reg.14, amended: SI 2009/ 56 Sch.2 para.10
Reg.19, amended: SI 2009/ 56 Sch.2 para.11
Reg.19, revoked (in part): SI 2009/ 56 Sch.2 para.11

1271. Motor Vehicles (Type Approval for Goods Vehicles) (Great Britain) Regulations 1982
Reg.2, amended: SI 2009/ 2084 Reg.3
Reg.2A, amended: SI 2009/ 2084 Reg.4
Reg.4, amended: SI 2009/ 2084 Reg.5
Reg.4, revoked (in part): SI 2009/ 2084 Reg.5
Sch.1 Part I, amended: SI 2009/ 2084 Reg.6
Sch.1 Part II para.2, revoked: SI 2009/ 2084 Reg.7
Sch.1 Part II para.3, revoked: SI 2009/ 2084 Reg.7
Sch.2 Part I, amended: SI 2009/ 2084 Reg.8
Sch.2 Part II, amended: SI 2009/ 2084 Reg.9

1408. Social Security (General Benefit) Regulations 1982
Reg.2, amended: SI 2009/ 2054 Sch.1 para.9
Reg.2, applied: SI 2009/ 2054 Sch.2 para.5
Reg.16, amended: SI 2009/ 2343 Reg.2

1489. Workmen's Compensation (Supplementation) Scheme 1982
Art.5, amended: SI 2009/ 664 Art.2
Sch.1 Part I, substituted: SI 2009/ 664 Art.3
Sch.1 Part II, substituted: SI 2009/ 664 Art.3

1536. Homosexual Offences (Northern Ireland) Order 1982
Art.7, referred to: SI 2009/ 37 Sch.1 para.2, Sch.1 para.4

1982– cont.

1536. Homosexual Offences (Northern Ireland) Order 1982– *cont.*
Art.8, referred to: SI 2009/ 37 Sch.1 para.2, Sch.1 para.4

1653. Company and Business Names (Amendment) Regulations 1982
revoked: SI 2009/ 2615 Reg.7

1676. Judicial Committee (General Appellate Jurisdiction) Rules Order 1982
revoked: SI 2009/ 224 Art.4

1706. County Court Fees Order 1982
referred to: SI 2009/ 500 Sch.1 Part 2

1875. Trunk Roads (Route A83) (Restricted Road) (Inveraray) Order 1982
revoked: SSI 2009/ 111 Art.3

1983

179. Manchester Ship Canal Revision Order 1983
revoked: SI 2009/ 2579 Sch.2

344. Aujeszky's Disease Order 1983
Art.19, amended: SI 2009/ 2713 Art.4
Sch.1, amended: SI 2009/ 2713 Art.4

569. Detention Centre Rules 1983
referred to: SI 2009/ 500 Sch.1 Part 2

570. Youth Custody Centre Rules 1983
referred to: SI 2009/ 500 Sch.1 Part 2

585. Licensed Dealers (Conduct of Business) Rules 1983
referred to: SI 2009/ 500 Sch.1 Part 2

587. Dealers in Securities (Licensing) Regulations 1983
referred to: SI 2009/ 500 Sch.1 Part 2

686. Personal Injuries (Civilians) Scheme 1983
applied: SI 2009/ 212 Reg.2
Art.14, applied: SSI 2009/ 48 Reg.6
Art.15, applied: SSI 2009/ 48 Reg.6
Art.16, applied: SSI 2009/ 48 Reg.6
Art.20, amended: SI 2009/ 438 Sch.1 para.1
Art.25A, applied: SSI 2009/ 48 Reg.6
Art.26A, applied: SI 2009/ 438 Art.3
Art.26A, substituted: SI 2009/ 438 Sch.1 para.2
Art.43, applied: SSI 2009/ 48 Reg.6
Art.44, applied: SSI 2009/ 48 Reg.6
Art.48A, applied: SI 2009/ 438 Reg.6
Art.49A, applied: SI 2009/ 438 Art.3
Sch.2, amended: SI 2009/ 438 Sch.1 para.3
Sch.3, substituted: SI 2009/ 438 Sch.2
Sch.4, substituted: SI 2009/ 438 Sch.3

711. Mines (Endless Rope Haulage) Regulations 1983
revoked: SI 2009/ 693 Sch.2

712. Point of Ayr and Cadley Hill Mines (Drift) Regulations 1983
revoked: SI 2009/ 693 Sch.2

713. Civil Courts Order 1983
referred to: SI 2009/ 2455 Art.1
Art.10A, added: SI 2009/ 2455 Art.3
Sch.3, amended: SI 2009/ 2455 Art.4, SI 2009/ 3320 Art.3

914. Weighing Equipment (Beltweighers) Regulations 1983
Reg.12A, varied: SI 2009/ 3045 Reg.5

942. Mental Health Review Tribunal Rules 1983
r.6, see *R. (on the application of N) v Mental Health Review Tribunal* [2008] EWHC 3383 (Admin), (2009) 106 B.M.L.R. 64 (QBD (Admin)), Justice Plender

1983– cont.

942. Mental Health Review Tribunal Rules 1983–
cont.
r.12, see *Roberts v Nottinghamshire Healthcare NHS Trust* [2008] EWHC 1934 (QB), [2009] F.S.R. 4 (QBD), Cranston, J.
r.29, see *R. (on the application of Rayner) v Secretary of State for the Home Department* [2008] EWCA Civ 176, [2009] 1 W.L.R. 310 (CA (Civ Div)), Ward, L.J.

1053. Grading of Horticultural Produce (Amendment) Regulations 1983
revoked (in part): SI 2009/1361 Reg.21, SI 2009/1551 Reg.21, SSI 2009/225 Reg.23

1106. Merchant Shipping (Prevention of Oil Pollution) Order 1983
Art.3, enabled: SI 2009/1210

1109. Anguilla (Appeals to Privy Council) Order 1983
revoked (in part): SI 2009/224 Art.5

1114. Health Service Commissioner for England (Mental Health Act Commission) Order 1983
revoked: SI 2009/462 Sch.6

1120. Criminal Attempts and Conspiracy (Northern Ireland) Order 1983
Art.3, amended: 2009 c.25 Sch.21 para.59
Art.9A, amended: 2009 c.25 s.72

1140. Classification and Labelling of Explosives Regulations 1983
applied: SI 2009/515 Sch.8 Part 7, Sch.8 Part 8

1222. Trunk Roads (Route A76) (Mauchline) (Prohibition of Waiting) Order 1983
revoked: SSI 2009/146 Art.7

1360. Houghton Main Mine (Steam Boilers) Regulations 1983
revoked: SI 2009/693 Sch.2

1390. Measuring Equipment (Liquid Fuel delivered from Road Tankers) Regulations 1983
Reg.11A, amended: SI 2009/3045 Reg.3
Reg.16A, amended: SI 2009/3045 Reg.3

1573. Smoke Control Areas (Exempted Fireplaces) (Scotland) Order 1983
revoked: SSI 2009/214 Sch.2

1656. Measuring Equipment (Intoxicating Liquor) Regulations 1983
Reg.1, amended: SI 2009/2463 Reg.3
Reg.7A, amended: SI 2009/3045 Reg.3
Reg.9, amended: SI 2009/2463 Reg.4
Reg.11A, added: SI 2009/2463 Reg.5
Reg.11B, added: SI 2009/2463 Reg.5
Reg.12, amended: SI 2009/2463 Reg.6

1888. British Indian Ocean Territory (Appeals to Privy Council) Order 1983
revoked (in part): SI 2009/224 Art.5

1984

126. Cayman Islands (Constitution) (Amendment) Order 1984
applied: SI 2009/3206 Art.4
revoked: SI 2009/1379 Sch.1

176. Goods Vehicles (Operators Licences, Qualifications and Fees) Regulations 1984
referred to: SI 2009/500 Sch.1 Part 2

252. High Court of Justiciary Fees Order 1984
Art.2A, amended: SSI 2009/87 Art.2

360. District Electoral Areas Commissioner (Northern Ireland) Order 1984
Sch.2, amended: SI 2009/3016 Art.2

1984– cont.

552. Coroners Rules 1984
Part I r.2, amended: SI 2009/3348 Art.6
Part VI r.20, amended: SI 2009/3348 Art.6
r.36, see *R. (on the application of Farah) v HM Coroner for Southampton and New Forest District of Hampshire* [2009] EWHC 1605 (Admin), (2009) 173 J.P. 457 (QBD (Admin)), Silber, J.
r.43, see *R. (on the application of Lewis) v HM Coroner for the Mid and North Division of Shropshire* [2009] EWHC 661 (Admin), (2009) 108 B.M.L.R. 87 (QBD (Admin)), Sir Thayne Forbes

748. Road Transport (International Passenger Services) Regulations 1984
Reg.14, amended: SI 2009/879 Reg.2
Reg.19, applied: SI 2009/483 Art.2
Reg.19, referred to: SI 2009/491 Sch.1 Part 2, SI 2009/492 Sch.1 Part 2

887. Deeds of Arrangement Fees Order 1984
Art.3, amended: SI 2009/2748 Sch.1 para.11

1151. Cayman Islands (Appeals to Privy Council) Order 1984
revoked (in part): SI 2009/224 Art.5
Art.2, amended: SI 2009/3206 Art.3

1805. Smoke Control Areas (Exempted Fireplaces) (Scotland) Order 1984
revoked: SSI 2009/214 Sch.2

1890. Freight Containers (Safety Convention) Regulations 1984
applied: SI 2009/515 Reg.4

2035. Court of Protection Rules 1984
referred to: SI 2009/500 Sch.1 Part 2

1985

315. Smoke Control Areas (Exempted Fireplaces) (Scotland) Order 1985
revoked: SSI 2009/214 Sch.2

444. Falkland Islands Constitution Order 1985
applied: SI 2009/3205 Art.4

445. Falkland Islands (Appeals to Privy Council) Order 1985
applied: SI 2009/3205 Art.1
revoked (in part): SI 2009/224 Art.5
Art.2, amended: SI 2009/3205 Art.3

450. South Georgia and South Sandwich Islands (Appeals to Privy Council) Order 1985
revoked (in part): SI 2009/224 Art.5

520. Police (Complaints) (General) Regulations 1985
referred to: SI 2009/500 Sch.1 Part 2

680. Companies (Unregistered Companies) Regulations 1985
revoked: SI 2009/2436 Reg.8
Reg.6, referred to: SI 2009/2436 Sch.2 para.2

754. Foreign Limitation Periods (Northern Ireland) Order 1985
Art.9, amended: SI 2009/3064 Reg.4

777. Units of Measurement Regulations 1985
referred to: SI 2009/669 Sch.1 Part 4

960. Films Co-Production Agreements Order 1985
Sch.1, substituted: SI 2009/3009 Art.2

967. Social Security (Industrial Injuries) (Prescribed Diseases) Regulations 1985
Sch.1 Part I, amended: SI 2009/1396 Reg.2

1162. Kellingley Mine (Steam Boilers) Regulations 1985
revoked: SI 2009/693 Sch.2

1985– cont.

1199. Gibraltar (Appeals to Privy Council) Order 1985
revoked (in part): SI 2009/224 Art.5
Art.2, amended: SI 2009/3207 Art.3

1204. Betting, Gaming, Lotteries and Amusements (Northern Ireland) Order 1985
Art.7, amended: SI 2009/1941 Sch.1 para.65
Art.61, amended: SI 2009/1941 Sch.1 para.65
Art.84, amended: SI 2009/1941 Sch.1 para.65
Art.109, amended: SI 2009/1941 Sch.1 para.65
Art.141, amended: SI 2009/1941 Sch.1 para.65
Art.155, amended: SI 2009/1941 Sch.1 para.65

1205. Credit Unions (Northern Ireland) Order 1985
referred to: 2009 c.1 s.89
Art.2, referred to: 2009 c.1 s.134, s.167
Art.68, substituted: SI 2009/1941 Sch.1 para.66

1262. Gascoigne Wood Mine (Refuge Platforms) Regulations 1985
revoked: SI 2009/693 Sch.2

1279. Aerosol Dispensers (EEC Requirements) and the Cosmetic Products (Amendment) Regulations 1985
revoked: SI 2009/2824 Sch.1 para.3

1638. Child Abduction (Northern Ireland) Order 1985
Art.3, referred to: SI 2009/37 Sch.1 para.2, Sch.1 para.4
Art.4, referred to: SI 2009/37 Sch.1 para.2, Sch.1 para.4

1662. Industrial Training (Transfer of the Activities of Establishments) Order 1985
applied: SI 2009/549 Sch.1

1807. Register of County Court Judgments Regulations 1985
referred to: SI 2009/500 Sch.1 Part 2

1929. Occupational Pension Schemes (Discharge of Liability) Regulations 1985
Reg.4, see *Easterly Ltd v Headway Plc* [2009] EWCA Civ 793, [2009] Pens. L.R. 279 (CA (Civ Div)), Lord Neuberger of Abbotsbury

1983. Commonwealth Countries and Republic of Ireland (Immunities and Privileges) Order 1985
Art.9, substituted: SI 2009/1741 Art.2
Sch.1, substituted: SI 2009/1741 Art.3

2026. Caseins and Caseinates Regulations 1985
Sch.1 Part II, amended: SI 2009/3235 Reg.8, SSI 2009/435 Reg.8

1986

26. Textile Products (Indications of Fibre Content) Regulations 1986
Reg.4, amended: SI 2009/551 Reg.2, SI 2009/1034 Reg.3
Reg.8, amended: SI 2009/551 Reg.2, SI 2009/1034 Reg.3
Sch.1 para.7, amended: SI 2009/551 Reg.2, SI 2009/1034 Reg.3

127. Court of Protection (Enduring Powers of Attorney) Rules 1986
referred to: SI 2009/500 Sch.1 Part 2

225. Control of Off-Street Parking (England and Wales) (Metropolitan Districts) Order 1986
Sch.1 Part IV para.22, amended: SI 2009/1307 Sch.2 para.24

590. Value Added Tax Tribunals Rules 1986
revoked: SI 2009/56 Sch.2 para.187

1986– cont.

590. Value Added Tax Tribunals Rules 1986– *cont.*
r.4, applied: SI 2009/56 Sch.3 para.2, Sch.3 para.3, Sch.3 para.4
r.6, see *Revenue and Customs Commissioners v Grattan Plc* [2009] EWHC 364 (Ch), [2009] S.T.C. 882 (Ch D), Lewison, J.
r.23, see *Revenue and Customs Commissioners v Grattan Plc* [2009] EWHC 364 (Ch), [2009] S.T.C. 882 (Ch D), Lewison, J.
r.28, see *Mobile Export 365 Ltd v Revenue and Customs Commissioners* [2009] EWHC 797 (Ch), [2009] 2 C.M.L.R. 46 (Ch D), Sir Andrew Park

594. Education and Libraries (Northern Ireland) Order 1986
applied: 2009 c.4 s.71
Art.2, applied: SI 2009/1369 Reg.2
Art.70, applied: SI 2009/1547 Reg.7
Art.88A, applied: SI 2009/1547 Reg.7

595. Mental Health (Northern Ireland) Order 1986
Art.119, referred to: SI 2009/37 Sch.1 para.2, Sch.1 para.4
Art.121, referred to: SI 2009/37 Sch.1 para.2, Sch.1 para.4
Art.122, applied: SI 2009/37 Sch.1 para.2
Art.122, referred to: SI 2009/37 Sch.1 para.1, Sch.1 para.2, Sch.1 para.3, Sch.1 para.4
Art.123, applied: 2009 asp 9 Sch.1 para.21
Art.123, referred to: SI 2009/37 Sch.1 para.1, Sch.1 para.2, Sch.1 para.3
Art.124, referred to: SI 2009/37 Sch.1 para.2, Sch.1 para.4
Art.125, referred to: SI 2009/37 Sch.1 para.2, Sch.1 para.4
Sch.3 para.1, amended: 2009 c.3 Sch.4 para.20
Sch.3 para.2, amended: 2009 c.3 Sch.4 para.20
Sch.3 para.2, substituted: 2009 c.3 Sch.4 para.20
Sch.3 para.3, amended: 2009 c.3 Sch.4 para.20

887. Dental Auxiliaries Regulations 1986
referred to: SI 2009/1182 Art.9

975. National Health Service (General Ophthalmic Services) Regulations 1986
Reg.13, amended: SI 2009/589 Reg.7

1032. Companies (Northern Ireland) Order 1986
applied: SI 2009/1801 Sch.8 para.3, Sch.8 para.9, Sch.8 para.15, Sch.8 para.16, Sch.8 para.17, SI 2009/1804 Sch.1 para.15, Sch.1 para.16, Sch.1 para.18, Sch.1 para.22, Sch.1 para.35, SI 2009/2436 Sch.2 para.10, Sch.2 para.13, Sch.2 para.21, Sch.2 para.22, Sch.2 para.37
referred to: SI 2009/1801 Sch.8 para.31, SI 2009/1804 Sch.1 para.34, SI 2009/2101 Sch.4 para.2, SI 2009/2436 Sch.2 para.1, Sch.2 para.40
varied: SI 2009/317 Sch.1
Part XIII, applied: SI 2009/214 Reg.11, SI 2009/1917 Sch.1 para.2, Sch.1 para.3, Sch.1 para.4, SI 2009/2101 Sch.4 para.1
Part XIII, referred to: 2009 c.1 s.252
Part XV, applied: SI 2009/214 Sch.1, SI 2009/1801 Sch.1, SI 2009/1804 Sch.2 para.4
Part XXIII, applied: SI 2009/1801 Sch.8 para.2, SI 2009/2101 Sch.4 para.1
Art.3, applied: SI 2009/490 Art.3
Art.21, applied: SI 2009/214 Reg.9
Art.29, applied: SI 2009/2436 Sch.2 para.2, Sch.2 para.3, Sch.2 para.4
Art.45, applied: SI 2009/2436 Sch.2 para.6
Art.46A, applied: SI 2009/2436 Sch.2 para.7
Art.48, applied: SI 2009/1804 Sch.1 para.2

1986–cont.

1032. Companies (Northern Ireland) Order 1986–
cont.
Art.149, applied: SI 2009/2425 Reg.9
Art.296, applied: SI 2009/214 Reg.9
Art.314, referred to: SI 2009/1941 Art.9
Art.315, referred to: SI 2009/1941 Art.9
Art.371, applied: SI 2009/214 Reg.9, SI 2009/1804 Sch.1 para.15, SI 2009/2101 Sch.4 para.1
Art.372, applied: SI 2009/1804 Sch.1 para.15
Art.394, applied: SI 2009/2436 Sch.2 para.24
Art.398, applied: SI 2009/2436 Sch.2 para.30, Sch.2 para.32
Art.401A, applied: SI 2009/2436 Sch.2 para.33
Art.401B, applied: SI 2009/2436 Sch.2 para.33
Art.407, applied: SI 2009/1804 Sch.1 para.17
Art.408, applied: SI 2009/1804 Sch.1 para.19, SI 2009/1917 Sch.1 para.5
Art.411, applied: SI 2009/1804 Sch.1 para.21, SI 2009/1917 Sch.1 para.7
Art.413, applied: SI 2009/1804 Sch.1 para.20, SI 2009/1917 Sch.1 para.6
Art.438, applied: SI 2009/2436 Sch.2 para.39
Art.440, applied: SI 2009/214 Sch.1, SI 2009/1801 Sch.1
Art.449, applied: SI 2009/2436 Sch.2 para.39
Art.451, applied: SI 2009/2436 Sch.2 para.38
Art.451, disapplied: SI 2009/2436 Sch.2 para.38
Art.602, applied: SI 2009/1804 Sch.1 para.23
Art.603, applied: SI 2009/1804 Sch.1 para.25
Art.603A, applied: SI 2009/1804 Sch.1 para.25
Art.604, applied: SI 2009/1804 Sch.1 para.23, Sch.1 para.25
Art.605, applied: SI 2009/1804 Sch.1 para.22A, Sch.1 para.26
Art.607, applied: SI 2009/1804 Sch.1 para.22A
Art.640A, applied: SI 2009/1801 Sch.8 para.15, Sch.8 para.16
Art.641, applied: SI 2009/214 Reg.9, SI 2009/1801 Sch.8 para.9, Sch.8 para.12, Sch.8 para.15, Sch.8 para.16
Art.641, disapplied: SI 2009/1801 Sch.8 para.14
Art.642, applied: SI 2009/214 Reg.9, SI 2009/1801 Sch.8 para.15, Sch.8 para.16
Art.647, applied: SI 2009/1801 Sch.8 para.14
Art.648A, applied: SI 2009/1801 Sch.8 para.4
Art.648AA, applied: SI 2009/1801 Sch.8 para.23
Art.649, applied: SI 2009/1801 Sch.8 para.23, Sch.8 para.24
Art.652, applied: SI 2009/1801 Sch.8 para.23, Sch.8 para.24
Art.652P, applied: SI 2009/1801 Sch.8 para.27, Sch.8 para.28
Art.652Q, applied: SI 2009/1801 Sch.8 para.29
Art.656B, applied: SI 2009/2436 Sch.2 para.40
Art.656B, referred to: SI 2009/1801 Sch.8 para.31, SI 2009/1804 Sch.1 para.34
Art.657, applied: SI 2009/1804 Sch.1 para.36
Art.657, referred to: SI 2009/1804 Sch.1 para.36
Art.659A, referred to: SI 2009/1804 Sch.1 para.33
Art.663, applied: SI 2009/1801 Sch.8 para.10
Art.674, applied: SI 2009/1941 Art.13
Art.674, varied: SI 2009/1941 Art.13
Sch.2, varied: SI 2009/317 Sch.1
Sch.20A, applied: SI 2009/1801 Sch.8 para.3, Sch.8 para.6, Sch.8 para.7, Sch.8 para.14, Sch.8 para.15, Sch.8 para.16, Sch.8 para.17
Sch.20C, applied: SI 2009/1801 Sch.8 para.25, Sch.8 para.26

1032. Companies (Northern Ireland) Order 1986–
cont.
Sch.20D, applied: SI 2009/1801 Sch.8 para.8, Sch.8 para.23, Sch.8 para.24, Sch.8 para.25
Sch.23, applied: SI 2009/1804 Sch.1 para.35
1035. Companies Consolidation (Consequential Provisions) (Northern Ireland) Order 1986
applied: SI 2009/1941 Art.12
1046. Occupational Pension Schemes (Disclosure of Information) Regulations 1986
referred to: SI 2009/500 Sch.1 Part 2
1078. Road Vehicles (Construction and Use) Regulations 1986
Reg.3, amended: SI 2009/2196 Reg.3
Reg.3, applied: SI 2009/365 Reg.6, SI 2009/366 Reg.5, SI 2009/1899 Reg.2
Reg.27, referred to: SI 2009/492 Sch.2
Reg.33, amended: SI 2009/142 Reg.3
Reg.36A, amended: SI 2009/142 Reg.4
Reg.36A, applied: SI 2009/492 Sch.2
Reg.36A, revoked (in part): SI 2009/142 Reg.4
Reg.36B, amended: SI 2009/142 Reg.5
Reg.36B, applied: SI 2009/492 Sch.2
Reg.36B, revoked (in part): SI 2009/142 Reg.5
Reg.37, amended: SI 2009/3221 Reg.2
Reg.41, applied: SI 2009/365 Reg.6
Reg.41, referred to: SI 2009/366 Reg.5
Reg.41A, applied: SI 2009/365 Reg.6
Reg.41A, referred to: SI 2009/366 Reg.5
Reg.41A, substituted: SI 2009/142 Reg.6
Reg.42, applied: SI 2009/365 Reg.6
Reg.42, referred to: SI 2009/366 Reg.5
Reg.43, applied: SI 2009/365 Reg.6
Reg.43, referred to: SI 2009/366 Reg.5
Reg.53C, substituted: SI 2009/142 Reg.7
Reg.61B, added: SI 2009/2196 Reg.4
Reg.66, applied: SI 2009/492 Sch.2
Reg.75, referred to: SI 2009/492 Sch.2
Reg.76, referred to: SI 2009/492 Sch.2
Reg.80, referred to: SI 2009/492 Sch.2
Reg.100, applied: SI 2009/492 Sch.2
Sch.2, amended: SI 2009/142 Reg.8, SI 2009/2196 Reg.5
Sch.2A Part I para.1, amended: SI 2009/2196 Reg.6
Sch.2A Part II para.9C, added: SI 2009/2196 Reg.6
Sch.7B Part I para.7, amended: SI 2009/1806 Reg.2
Sch.7XA Part I para.1, amended: SI 2009/2196 Reg.7
Sch.7XA Part II para.2, amended: SI 2009/2196 Reg.7
Sch.7XA Part II para.2, revoked (in part): SI 2009/2196 Reg.7
Sch.7XA Part III para.7, amended: SI 2009/2196 Reg.7
1082. Units of Measurement Regulations 1986
Reg.7, amended: SI 2009/3046 Reg.3
Sch.1 para.1, amended: SI 2009/3046 Reg.4
Sch.1 para.2, amended: SI 2009/3046 Reg.4, Sch.1
Sch.1 para.2, revoked (in part): SI 2009/3046 Reg.4
1159. Child Abduction and Custody (Parties to Conventions) Order 1986
Sch.1, substituted: SI 2009/702 Sch.1
Sch.2, substituted: SI 2009/702 Sch.1
1245. Community Bus Regulations 1986
revoked: SI 2009/366 Sch.1

1986–cont.

1320. Weighing Equipment (Filling and Discontinuous Totalisting Automatic Weighing Machines) Regulations 1986
Reg.12A, amended: SI 2009/3045 Reg.3
1330. Fixed Penalty (Procedure) Regulations 1986
Reg.1, amended: SI 2009/494 Reg.3
Reg.2, amended: SI 2009/494 Reg.3
Reg.3, amended: SI 2009/494 Reg.3
Reg.4, amended: SI 2009/494 Reg.3
Reg.6, amended: SI 2009/494 Reg.3
Reg.8, amended: SI 2009/494 Reg.3
Sch.1, amended: SI 2009/494 Reg.4
1335. Costs in Criminal Cases (General) Regulations 1986
Reg.3, see *R. (on the application of Crowch) v DPP* [2008] EWHC 948 (Admin), [2009] P.N.L.R. 1 (QBD (Admin)), Davis, J.
Reg.3B, revoked (in part): SI 2009/2720 Reg.3
Reg.3C, amended: SI 2009/2720 Reg.4
Reg.3C, revoked (in part): SI 2009/2720 Reg.4
Reg.3F, revoked (in part): SI 2009/2720 Reg.5
Reg.3G, revoked: SI 2009/2720 Reg.6
Reg.3H, amended: SI 2009/2720 Reg.7
Reg.3H, revoked (in part): SI 2009/2720 Reg.7
Reg.7, applied: SI 2009/2720 Reg.1
Reg.7, substituted: SI 2009/2720 Reg.8
Reg.7, see *R. v Dodd (Costs)* [2009] 2 Costs L.R. 368 (Sup Ct Costs Office), Costs Judge Gordon-Saker
Reg.11, see *Brewer v Secretary of State for Justice* [2009] EWHC 987 (QB), [2009] 3 All E.R. 861 (QBD), Holroyde, J
Reg.13, amended: SI 2009/2720 Reg.9
Reg.13, substituted: SI 2009/2720 Reg.9
Reg.16, amended: SI 2009/2720 Reg.9
Reg.25, amended: SI 2009/2720 Reg.10
1347. Aerodromes (Designation) (Detention and Sale of Aircraft) (No.2) Order 1986
revoked (in part): SI 2009/2350 Sch.2
1399. Land Registration Fee Order 1986
referred to: SI 2009/500 Sch.1 Part 2
1442. Registration of Marriages Regulations 1986
Sch.1, amended: SI 2009/2806 Sch.1
1510. Control of Pesticides Regulations 1986
applied: SI 2009/153 Sch.3 para.1, SI 2009/716 Reg.9, SI 2009/995 Sch.3 para.1
1629. Public Service Vehicles (Traffic Commissioners Publication and Inquiries) Regulations 1986
Reg.3, amended: SI 2009/443 Sch.1 para.1
Reg.3, applied: SI 2009/1964 Reg.12
1671. Public Service Vehicles (Registration of Local Services) Regulations 1986
Reg.4A, added: SI 2009/3245 Sch.1 para.1
Reg.5, amended: SI 2009/443 Sch.1 para.2, SI 2009/3245 Sch.1 para.1
Reg.5, disapplied: SI 2009/3245 Reg.3
Reg.6, disapplied: SI 2009/3245 Reg.3
Reg.7, amended: SI 2009/3245 Sch.1 para.1
Reg.7, disapplied: SI 2009/3245 Reg.3
Reg.8, amended: SI 2009/3245 Sch.1 para.1
Reg.8, disapplied: SI 2009/3245 Reg.3
Reg.9A, amended: SI 2009/3245 Sch.1 para.1
Reg.12, amended: SI 2009/878 Reg.2
1682. Measuring Equipment (Measures of Length) Regulations 1986
Reg.17A, amended: SI 2009/3045 Reg.3
1711. Stamp Duty Reserve Tax Regulations 1986
Reg.2, amended: SI 2009/56 Sch.2 para.13

1986–cont.

1711. Stamp Duty Reserve Tax Regulations 1986–cont.
Reg.8, amended: SI 2009/56 Sch.2 para.14, SI 2009/1307 Sch.2 para.25
Reg.8, revoked (in part): SI 2009/56 Sch.2 para.14
Reg.9, substituted: SI 2009/56 Sch.2 para.15
Reg.10, revoked: SI 2009/56 Sch.2 para.16
Sch.1 Part I, amended: SI 2009/56 Sch.2 para.17
Sch.1 Part II, amended: SI 2009/56 Sch.2 para.20, Sch.2 para.21, SI 2009/1890 Art.3
Sch.1 Part II, revoked: SI 2009/56 Sch.2 para.20
Sch.1 Part II, substituted: SI 2009/56 Sch.2 para.19, Sch.2 para.20
1915. Insolvency (Scotland) Rules 1986
applied: SI 2009/350 r.7, SI 2009/351 r.3, SI 2009/806 r.7
referred to: SI 2009/350 r.7, SI 2009/351 r.3, SI 2009/806 r.8, r.38
varied: SI 2009/350 r.41, SI 2009/351 r.3, SI 2009/3056 Sch.1 para.5
Part I r.1.4, amended: SI 2009/662 Sch.1 para.1
Part I r.1.16, amended: SI 2009/662 Sch.1 para.1
Part I r.1.17, amended: SI 2009/662 Sch.1 para.1
Part I r.1.18A, amended: SI 2009/662 Sch.1 para.1
Part I r.1.19, amended: SI 2009/662 Sch.1 para.1
Part I r.1.20, amended: SI 2009/662 Sch.1 para.1
Part I r.1.26, amended: SI 2009/662 Sch.1 para.1
Part I r.1.30, amended: SI 2009/662 Sch.1 para.1, Sch.1 para.2
Part I r.1.31, amended: SI 2009/662 Sch.1 para.1
Part I r.1.32, amended: SI 2009/662 Sch.1 para.1, Sch.1 para.3
Part I r.1.34, amended: SI 2009/662 Sch.1 para.1
Part I r.1.35, amended: SI 2009/662 Sch.1 para.1
Part I r.1.37, amended: SI 2009/662 Sch.1 para.1
Part I r.1.44, amended: SI 2009/662 Sch.1 para.1
Part I r.1.45, amended: SI 2009/662 Sch.1 para.1
Part 2 r.2.19, amended: SI 2009/662 Sch.1 para.4
Part 2 r.2.19, referred to: SI 2009/806 r.34
Part 2 r.2.19, varied: SI 2009/350 r.42, SI 2009/806 r.41
Part 2 r.2.20, applied: SI 2009/350 r.42, SI 2009/806 r.41
Part 2 r.2.21, applied: SI 2009/350 r.42, SI 2009/806 r.41
Part 2 r.2.22, applied: SI 2009/350 r.20, r.21, SI 2009/806 r.19, r.20
Part 2 r.2.22, varied: SI 2009/350 r.42, SI 2009/806 r.41
Part 2 r.2.23, varied: SI 2009/350 r.42, SI 2009/806 r.41
Part 2 r.2.24, applied: SI 2009/350 r.42, SI 2009/806 r.41
Part 2 r.2.25, amended: SI 2009/662 Sch.1 para.5, Sch.1 para.6
Part 2 r.2.25, disapplied: SI 2009/350 r.42, SI 2009/806 r.41
Part 2 r.2.25, varied: SI 2009/350 r.42
Part 2 r.2.26, varied: SI 2009/350 r.42, SI 2009/806 r.41
Part 2 r.2.26A, added: SI 2009/662 Sch.1 para.7
Part 2 r.2.26A, varied: SI 2009/350 r.42
Part 2 r.2.27, varied: SI 2009/350 r.42, SI 2009/806 r.41
Part 2 r.2.28, applied: SI 2009/350 r.42
Part 2 r.2.29, applied: SI 2009/350 r.42
Part 2 r.2.31, varied: SI 2009/350 r.42, SI 2009/806 r.41
Part 2 r.2.33, applied: SI 2009/350 r.42
Part 2 r.2.34, amended: SI 2009/662 Sch.1 para.8, Sch.1 para.9
Part 2 r.2.34, varied: SI 2009/350 r.42, SI 2009/806 r.41
Part 2 r.2.35, applied: SI 2009/350 r.42
Part 2 r.2.36, varied: SI 2009/350 r.42
Part 2 r.2.37, varied: SI 2009/350 r.42, SI 2009/806 r.41
Part 2 r.2.38, applied: SI 2009/350 r.30, SI 2009/806 r.29

1986– cont.

1915. Insolvency (Scotland) Rules 1986– *cont.*

Part 2 r.2.38, disapplied: SI 2009/ 350 r.42, SI 2009/ 806 r.41

Part 2 r.2.39, applied: SI 2009/ 350 r.20, r.21, SI 2009/ 806 r.19, r.20

Part 2 r.2.39, varied: SI 2009/ 350 r.42, SI 2009/ 806 r.41

Part 2 r.2.39A, varied: SI 2009/ 350 r.42, SI 2009/ 806 r.41

Part 2 r.2.39B, varied: SI 2009/ 350 r.42

Part 2 r.2.40, applied: SI 2009/ 806 r.41

Part 2 r.2.40, varied: SI 2009/ 350 r.42

Part 2 r.2.41, varied: SI 2009/ 350 r.42, SI 2009/ 806 r.41

Part 2 r.2.41A, applied: SI 2009/ 806 r.41

Part 2 r.2.41A, varied: SI 2009/ 350 r.42

Part 2 r.2.42, applied: SI 2009/ 806 r.41

Part 2 r.2.42, varied: SI 2009/ 350 r.42

Part 2 r.2.45, amended: SI 2009/ 662 Sch.1 para.10, Sch.1 para.11

Part 2 r.2.45, disapplied: SI 2009/ 350 r.42, SI 2009/ 806 r.41

Part 2 r.2.46, varied: SI 2009/ 350 r.42, SI 2009/ 806 r.41

Part 2 r.2.48, disapplied: SI 2009/ 350 r.42, SI 2009/ 806 r.41

Part 2 r.2.49, varied: SI 2009/ 350 r.42, SI 2009/ 806 r.41

Part 2 r.2.50, applied: SI 2009/ 806 r.41

Part 2 r.2.50, varied: SI 2009/ 350 r.42

Part 2 r.2.51, applied: SI 2009/ 350 r.42, SI 2009/ 806 r.41

Part 2 r.2.52, applied: SI 2009/ 350 r.42, SI 2009/ 806 r.41

Part 2 r.2.53, varied: SI 2009/ 350 r.42, SI 2009/ 806 r.41

Part 2 r.2.54, applied: SI 2009/ 350 r.42, SI 2009/ 806 r.41

Part 2 r.2.55, applied: SI 2009/ 350 r.42, SI 2009/ 806 r.41

Part 2 r.2.55, referred to: SI 2009/ 806 r.34

Part 2 r.2.56, varied: SI 2009/ 350 r.42, SI 2009/ 806 r.41

Part 3 r.3.8, applied: SI 2009/ 806 r.41

Part 4 r.4.1, applied: SI 2009/ 351 r.11

Part 4 r.4.1, disapplied: SI 2009/ 350 r.42, SI 2009/ 806 r.41

Part 4 r.4.1, varied: SI 2009/ 351 r.11

Part 4 r.4.2, disapplied: SI 2009/ 350 r.42, SI 2009/ 806 r.41

Part 4 r.4.3, applied: SI 2009/ 350 r.42, SI 2009/ 351 r.13, SI 2009/ 806 r.41

Part 4 r.4.4, applied: SI 2009/ 350 r.42, SI 2009/ 351 r.14, SI 2009/ 806 r.41

Part 4 r.4.5, applied: SI 2009/ 350 r.42, SI 2009/ 351 r.15, SI 2009/ 806 r.41

Part 4 r.4.6, applied: SI 2009/ 351 r.16

Part 4 r.4.6, varied: SI 2009/ 350 r.42, SI 2009/ 351 r.16, SI 2009/ 806 r.41

Part 4 r.4.7, applied: SI 2009/ 351 r.17

Part 4 r.4.7, varied: SI 2009/ 351 r.17

Part 4 r.4.8, applied: SI 2009/ 351 r.18

Part 4 r.4.9, applied: SI 2009/ 351 r.19

Part 4 r.4.11, applied: SI 2009/ 351 r.22

Part 4 r.4.11, varied: SI 2009/ 351 r.22

Part 4 r.4.13, applied: SI 2009/ 351 r.25

Part 4 r.4.14, applied: SI 2009/ 351 r.26

Part 4 r.4.15, applied: SI 2009/ 351 r.27

Part 4 r.4.16, applied: SI 2009/ 351 r.28

Part 4 r.4.16, varied: SI 2009/ 351 r.28

Part 4 r.4.17, applied: SI 2009/ 351 r.29

Part 4 r.4.17, varied: SI 2009/ 351 r.29

Part 4 r.4.19, applied: SI 2009/ 351 r.42

Part 4 r.4.20, applied: SI 2009/ 351 r.10, r.42

Part 4 r.4.21, applied: SI 2009/ 351 r.33, r.42

Part 4 r.4.22, applied: SI 2009/ 351 r.34

Part 4 r.4.22, varied: SI 2009/ 351 r.34

Part 4 r.4.24, applied: SI 2009/ 351 r.37

1986– cont.

1915. Insolvency (Scotland) Rules 1986– *cont.*

Part 4 r.4.24, varied: SI 2009/ 351 r.37

Part 4 r.4.27, applied: SI 2009/ 351 r.40

Part 4 r.4.32, applied: SI 2009/ 351 r.45

Part 4 r.4.33, applied: SI 2009/ 351 r.46

Part 4 r.4.34, applied: SI 2009/ 351 r.47

Part 4 r.4.35, applied: SI 2009/ 351 r.48

Part 4 r.4.36, amended: SI 2009/ 351 r.51

Part 4 r.4.36, applied: SI 2009/ 351 r.51

Part 4 r.4.37, applied: SI 2009/ 351 r.52

Part 4 r.4.37, varied: SI 2009/ 351 r.52

Part 4 r.4.38, applied: SI 2009/ 351 r.55

Part 4 r.4.38, varied: SI 2009/ 351 r.55

Part 4 r.4.39, applied: SI 2009/ 351 r.56

Part 4 r.4.41, applied: SI 2009/ 351 r.58

Part 4 r.4.41, varied: SI 2009/ 351 r.58

Part 4 r.4.42, applied: SI 2009/ 351 r.59

Part 4 r.4.43, applied: SI 2009/ 351 r.60

Part 4 r.4.43, varied: SI 2009/ 351 r.60

Part 4 r.4.44, applied: SI 2009/ 351 r.61

Part 4 r.4.45, applied: SI 2009/ 351 r.62

Part 4 r.4.46, applied: SI 2009/ 351 r.63

Part 4 r.4.47, applied: SI 2009/ 351 r.64

Part 4 r.4.48, applied: SI 2009/ 351 r.65

Part 4 r.4.49, applied: SI 2009/ 351 r.66

Part 4 r.4.50, applied: SI 2009/ 351 r.67

Part 4 r.4.51, applied: SI 2009/ 351 r.68

Part 4 r.4.52, applied: SI 2009/ 351 r.69

Part 4 r.4.53, applied: SI 2009/ 351 r.70

Part 4 r.4.54, applied: SI 2009/ 351 r.71

Part 4 r.4.55, applied: SI 2009/ 351 r.72

Part 4 r.4.55, varied: SI 2009/ 351 r.72

Part 4 r.4.56, applied: SI 2009/ 351 r.73

Part 4 r.4.56, varied: SI 2009/ 351 r.73

Part 4 r.4.57, applied: SI 2009/ 351 r.74

Part 4 r.4.58, applied: SI 2009/ 351 r.75

Part 4 r.4.59, applied: SI 2009/ 351 r.76

Part 4 r.4.59, varied: SI 2009/ 351 r.76

Part 4 r.4.59A, applied: SI 2009/ 351 r.77

Part 4 r.4.66, applied: SI 2009/ 351 r.78

Part 4 r.4.67, applied: SI 2009/ 351 r.79

Part 4 r.4.68, applied: SI 2009/ 351 r.80

Part 4 r.4.69, applied: SI 2009/ 351 r.81

Part 4 r.4.70, applied: SI 2009/ 351 r.82

Part 4 r.4.71, applied: SI 2009/ 351 r.83

Part 4 r.4.72, applied: SI 2009/ 351 r.84

Part 4 r.4.73, applied: SI 2009/ 351 r.85

Part 4 r.4.76, applied: SI 2009/ 351 r.88

Part 4 r.4.77, applied: SI 2009/ 351 r.89

Part 4 r.4.78, applied: SI 2009/ 351 r.90

Part 4 r.4.78, varied: SI 2009/ 351 r.90

Part 4 r.4.79, applied: SI 2009/ 351 r.92

Part 4 r.4.80, applied: SI 2009/ 351 r.93

Part 4 r.4.80, varied: SI 2009/ 351 r.93

Part 4 r.4.81, applied: SI 2009/ 351 r.94

Part 4 r.4.82, applied: SI 2009/ 351 r.95

Part 4 r.4.82, varied: SI 2009/ 351 r.95

Part 7 r.7.1, disapplied: SI 2009/ 806 r.41

Part 7 r.7.2, applied: SI 2009/ 351 r.97, SI 2009/ 806 r.41

Part 7 r.7.3, amended: SI 2009/ 662 Sch.1 para.12, Sch.1 para.13

Part 7 r.7.3, applied: SI 2009/ 351 r.98

Part 7 r.7.3, varied: SI 2009/ 351 r.98

Part 7 r.7.4, disapplied: SI 2009/ 806 r.41

Part 7 r.7.6, applied: SI 2009/ 351 r.100, SI 2009/ 806 r.23

Part 7 r.7.6, referred to: SI 2009/ 350 r.24, SI 2009/ 351 r.101

Part 7 r.7.6, varied: SI 2009/ 351 r.100

1986–cont.

1915. Insolvency (Scotland) Rules 1986–*cont.*
Part 7 r.7.7, applied: SI 2009/351 r.102
Part 7 r.7.8, applied: SI 2009/351 r.103
Part 7 r.7.9, applied: SI 2009/351 r.104
Part 7 r.7.10, applied: SI 2009/351 r.105
Part 7 r.7.11, applied: SI 2009/351 r.106
Part 7 r.7.12, applied: SI 2009/351 r.107
Part 7 r.7.13, applied: SI 2009/351 r.108
Part 7 r.7.13A, applied: SI 2009/350 r.42, SI 2009/351 r.109, SI 2009/806 r.41
Part 7 r.7.13B, applied: SI 2009/350 r.42, SI 2009/351 r.110, SI 2009/806 r.41
Part 7 r.7.13B, varied: SI 2009/351 r.110
Part 7 r.7.14, applied: SI 2009/350 r.42, SI 2009/351 r.111
Part 7 r.7.15, applied: SI 2009/350 r.42, SI 2009/351 r.112
Part 7 r.7.16, applied: SI 2009/350 r.42, SI 2009/351 r.113
Part 7 r.7.17, applied: SI 2009/350 r.42, SI 2009/351 r.114
Part 7 r.7.18, applied: SI 2009/350 r.42, SI 2009/351 r.115
Part 7 r.7.18, varied: SI 2009/351 r.115
Part 7 r.7.19, applied: SI 2009/350 r.42, SI 2009/351 r.116
Part 7 r.7.20, applied: SI 2009/351 r.117
Part 7 r.7.20, varied: SI 2009/350 r.42, SI 2009/351 r.117, SI 2009/806 r.41
Part 7 r.7.21, applied: SI 2009/350 r.42, SI 2009/351 r.118
Part 7 r.7.21, varied: SI 2009/351 r.118
Part 7 r.7.22, applied: SI 2009/351 r.120
Part 7 r.7.22, varied: SI 2009/350 r.42, SI 2009/806 r.41
Part 7 r.7.23, applied: SI 2009/350 r.42, SI 2009/351 r.121
Part 7 r.7.24, applied: SI 2009/350 r.42, SI 2009/351 r.122
Part 7 r.7.24, varied: SI 2009/351 r.122
Part 7 r.7.25, applied: SI 2009/350 r.42, SI 2009/351 r.123
Part 7 r.7.26, applied: SI 2009/351 r.124
Part 7 r.7.26, varied: SI 2009/350 r.42, SI 2009/351 r.124, SI 2009/806 r.41
Part 7 r.7.27, applied: SI 2009/350 r.42, SI 2009/351 r.125
Part 7 r.7.27, varied: SI 2009/806 r.41
Part 7 r.7.28, applied: SI 2009/350 r.42, SI 2009/351 r.126, SI 2009/806 r.41
Part 7 r.7.28, varied: SI 2009/351 r.126
Part 7 r.7.29, applied: SI 2009/350 r.42, SI 2009/806 r.41
Part 7 r.7.31, applied: SI 2009/350 r.42, SI 2009/351 r.128, SI 2009/806 r.41
Part 7 r.7.32, applied: SI 2009/350 r.42, SI 2009/351 r.129, SI 2009/806 r.41
Part 7 r.7.33, applied: SI 2009/350 r.42, SI 2009/351 r.130, SI 2009/806 r.41
Part 7 r.7.33, varied: SI 2009/351 r.130
Part 7 r.7.34, applied: SI 2009/350 r.42, SI 2009/351 r.131, SI 2009/806 r.41
Part 7 r.7.35, applied: SI 2009/350 r.42, SI 2009/806 r.41
Part 7 r.7.36, applied: SI 2009/351 r.132
Sch.3, applied: SI 2009/351 r.23
Sch.5, amended: SI 2009/662 Sch.1 Part 2, SI 2009/2375 Sch.2
Sch.5, applied: SI 2009/351 r.127
Sch.5, substituted: SI 2009/662 Sch.1 Part 2

1925. Insolvency Rules 1986
applied: SI 2009/356 r.3, r.5, r.283, SI 2009/357 r.7, r.8, r.27, r.50, r.58, SI 2009/2477 r.92, r.102
disapplied: SI 2009/2477 r.5
referred to: SI 2009/2477 r.3
varied: SI 2009/2477 r.5
see *Courts Plc (In Liquidation), Re* [2008] EWHC 2339 (Ch), [2009] 1 W.L.R. 1499 (Ch D (Companies Ct)), Blackburne, J.; see *Kaupthing Singer & Friedlander Ltd (In Administration), Re* [2009] EWHC 2308 (Ch), (2009) 153(38) S.J.L.B. 30 (Ch D (Companies

1986–cont.

1925. Insolvency Rules 1986–*cont.*
see–*cont.*
Ct)), Norris, J.; see *Official Receiver v McKay* [2009] EWCA Civ 467, [2009] B.P.I.R. 1061 (CA (Civ Div)), Mummery, L.J.
Part 0 r.0.2, amended: SI 2009/2472 r.4
Part 1 r.1.4, amended: SI 2009/642 r.5
Part 1 r.1.21, amended: SI 2009/642 r.5
Part 1 r.1.22A, amended: SI 2009/642 r.5, SI 2009/2472 r.5
Part 1 r.1.23, amended: SI 2009/642 r.5
Part 1 r.1.24, amended: SI 2009/642 r.5
Part 1 r.1.25, amended: SI 2009/642 r.5
Part 1 r.1.36, amended: SI 2009/642 r.5
Part 1 r.1.40, amended: SI 2009/642 r.6
Part 1 r.1.40, substituted: SI 2009/642 r.5
Part 1 r.1.41, amended: SI 2009/642 r.5, SI 2009/2472 r.6
Part 1 r.1.42, amended: SI 2009/642 r.5, r.7
Part 1 r.1.43, amended: SI 2009/642 r.5
Part 1 r.1.44, amended: SI 2009/642 r.5
Part 1 r.1.46, amended: SI 2009/642 r.5
Part 1 r.1.53, amended: SI 2009/642 r.5
Part 1 r.1.54, amended: SI 2009/642 r.5
Part 2, applied: SI 2009/2477 r.11
Part 2 r.2.12, referred to: SI 2009/357 r.23
Part 2 r.2.27, amended: SI 2009/642 r.8
Part 2 r.2.27, varied: SI 2009/357 r.61
Part 2 r.2.28, applied: SI 2009/357 r.61
Part 2 r.2.29, applied: SI 2009/357 r.61
Part 2 r.2.30, applied: SI 2009/357 r.28, r.29
Part 2 r.2.30, varied: SI 2009/357 r.61
Part 2 r.2.31, varied: SI 2009/357 r.61
Part 2 r.2.32, applied: SI 2009/357 r.61
Part 2 r.2.33, amended: SI 2009/642 r.9
Part 2 r.2.33, disapplied: SI 2009/357 r.61
Part 2 r.2.34, amended: SI 2009/642 r.10
Part 2 r.2.34, varied: SI 2009/357 r.61
Part 2 r.2.35, varied: SI 2009/357 r.61
Part 2 r.2.36, applied: SI 2009/357 r.61
Part 2 r.2.37, applied: SI 2009/357 r.32
Part 2 r.2.37, varied: SI 2009/357 r.61
Part 2 r.2.38, applied: SI 2009/357 r.61
Part 2 r.2.39, applied: SI 2009/357 r.61
Part 2 r.2.40, applied: SI 2009/357 r.61
Part 2 r.2.41, applied: SI 2009/357 r.61
Part 2 r.2.42, applied: SI 2009/357 r.61
Part 2 r.2.43, applied: SI 2009/357 r.61
Part 2 r.2.44, applied: SI 2009/357 r.61
Part 2 r.2.45, amended: SI 2009/642 r.11
Part 2 r.2.45, varied: SI 2009/357 r.61
Part 2 r.2.46, applied: SI 2009/357 r.61
Part 2 r.2.47, applied: SI 2009/357 r.38
Part 2 r.2.47, disapplied: SI 2009/357 r.61
Part 2 r.2.48, disapplied: SI 2009/357 r.61
Part 2 r.2.49, amended: SI 2009/2472 r.7
Part 2 r.2.49, disapplied: SI 2009/357 r.61
Part 2 r.2.50, applied: SI 2009/357 r.61
Part 2 r.2.51, amended: SI 2009/2472 r.8
Part 2 r.2.51, applied: SI 2009/357 r.61
Part 2 r.2.52, applied: SI 2009/357 r.61
Part 2 r.2.53, applied: SI 2009/357 r.61
Part 2 r.2.54, applied: SI 2009/357 r.61
Part 2 r.2.55, amended: SI 2009/2472 r.8
Part 2 r.2.55, applied: SI 2009/357 r.61
Part 2 r.2.56, applied: SI 2009/357 r.61
Part 2 r.2.57, applied: SI 2009/357 r.61
Part 2 r.2.58, applied: SI 2009/357 r.61

1986– cont.

1925.   Insolvency Rules 1986–*cont.*
Part 2 r.2.59, applied: SI 2009/ 357 r.61
Part 2 r.2.60, applied: SI 2009/ 357 r.61
Part 2 r.2.61, applied: SI 2009/ 357 r.61
Part 2 r.2.62, applied: SI 2009/ 357 r.61
Part 2 r.2.63, applied: SI 2009/ 357 r.61
Part 2 r.2.64, varied: SI 2009/ 357 r.61
Part 2 r.2.65, applied: SI 2009/ 357 r.61
Part 2 r.2.66, varied: SI 2009/ 357 r.61
Part 2 r.2.67, varied: SI 2009/ 357 r.61
Part 2 r.2.68, applied: SI 2009/ 357 r.61
Part 2 r.2.69, applied: SI 2009/ 357 r.61
Part 2 r.2.70, applied: SI 2009/ 357 r.61
Part 2 r.2.71, applied: SI 2009/ 357 r.61
Part 2 r.2.72, applied: SI 2009/ 357 r.61
Part 2 r.2.73, applied: SI 2009/ 357 r.61
Part 2 r.2.74, applied: SI 2009/ 357 r.61
Part 2 r.2.75, applied: SI 2009/ 357 r.61
Part 2 r.2.76, applied: SI 2009/ 357 r.61
Part 2 r.2.77, applied: SI 2009/ 357 r.61
Part 2 r.2.78, varied: SI 2009/ 357 r.61
Part 2 r.2.79, applied: SI 2009/ 357 r.61
Part 2 r.2.80, varied: SI 2009/ 357 r.61
Part 2 r.2.81, applied: SI 2009/ 357 r.61
Part 2 r.2.82, applied: SI 2009/ 357 r.61
Part 2 r.2.83, applied: SI 2009/ 357 r.61
Part 2 r.2.84, applied: SI 2009/ 357 r.61
Part 2 r.2.85, applied: SI 2009/ 357 r.61
Part 2 r.2.86, applied: SI 2009/ 357 r.61
Part 2 r.2.87, applied: SI 2009/ 357 r.61
Part 2 r.2.88, applied: SI 2009/ 357 r.61
Part 2 r.2.89, applied: SI 2009/ 357 r.61
Part 2 r.2.90, applied: SI 2009/ 357 r.61
Part 2 r.2.91, applied: SI 2009/ 357 r.61
Part 2 r.2.92, applied: SI 2009/ 357 r.61
Part 2 r.2.93, applied: SI 2009/ 357 r.61
Part 2 r.2.94, applied: SI 2009/ 357 r.61
Part 2 r.2.95, amended: SI 2009/ 642 r.12
Part 2 r.2.95, varied: SI 2009/ 357 r.61
Part 2 r.2.96, applied: SI 2009/ 357 r.61
Part 2 r.2.97, applied: SI 2009/ 357 r.61
Part 2 r.2.98, varied: SI 2009/ 357 r.61
Part 2 r.2.99, applied: SI 2009/ 357 r.61
Part 2 r.2.100, varied: SI 2009/ 357 r.61
Part 2 r.2.101, applied: SI 2009/ 357 r.61
Part 2 r.2.102, amended: SI 2009/ 642 r.5
Part 2 r.2.102, applied: SI 2009/ 357 r.61
Part 2 r.2.103, varied: SI 2009/ 357 r.61
Part 2 r.2.104, applied: SI 2009/ 357 r.61
Part 2 r.2.105, varied: SI 2009/ 357 r.61
Part 2 r.2.106, applied: SI 2009/ 357 r.28, r.29
Part 2 r.2.106, varied: SI 2009/ 357 r.61
Part 2 r.2.107, applied: SI 2009/ 357 r.61
Part 2 r.2.108, varied: SI 2009/ 357 r.61
Part 2 r.2.109, varied: SI 2009/ 357 r.61
Part 2 r.2.110, varied: SI 2009/ 357 r.61
Part 2 r.2.113, amended: SI 2009/ 642 r.13
Part 2 r.2.113, disapplied: SI 2009/ 357 r.61
Part 2 r.2.113, referred to: SI 2009/ 357 r.48
Part 2 r.2.114, varied: SI 2009/ 357 r.61
Part 2 r.2.118, disapplied: SI 2009/ 357 r.61
Part 2 r.2.118, referred to: SI 2009/ 357 r.49
Part 2 r.2.119, varied: SI 2009/ 357 r.61
Part 2 r.2.120, varied: SI 2009/ 357 r.61
Part 2 r.2.121, applied: SI 2009/ 357 r.61
Part 2 r.2.122, varied: SI 2009/ 357 r.61
Part 2 r.2.123, applied: SI 2009/ 357 r.61
Part 2 r.2.124, applied: SI 2009/ 357 r.61

1986– cont.

1925.   Insolvency Rules 1986–*cont.*
Part 2 r.2.125, varied: SI 2009/ 357 r.61
Part 2 r.2.126, applied: SI 2009/ 357 r.61
Part 2 r.2.127, applied: SI 2009/ 357 r.47, r.61
Part 2 r.2.128, applied: SI 2009/ 357 r.47, r.61
Part 2 r.2.129, applied: SI 2009/ 357 r.61
Part 3 r.3.2, amended: SI 2009/ 642 r.14
Part 3 r.3.8, amended: SI 2009/ 642 r.15
Part 3 r.3.9, amended: SI 2009/ 642 r.16
Part 3 r.3.17, amended: SI 2009/ 2472 r.8
Part 3 r.3.21, amended: SI 2009/ 2472 r.8
Part 3 r.3.31, amended: SI 2009/ 642 r.5
Part 3 r.3.34, amended: SI 2009/ 642 r.5
Part 3 r.3.35, amended: SI 2009/ 642 r.5, SI 2009/ 2472 r.9
Part 3 r.3.36, amended: SI 2009/ 642 r.5
Part 3 r.3.38, amended: SI 2009/ 2472 r.10
Part 3 r.3.39, amended: SI 2009/ 642 r.17
Part 4, referred to: SI 2009/ 356 r.3
Part 4 r.4.1, varied: SI 2009/ 356 r.3
Part 4 r.4.2, amended: SI 2009/ 2472 r.11
Part 4 r.4.2, varied: SI 2009/ 356 r.3
Part 4 r.4.3, varied: SI 2009/ 356 r.3
Part 4 r.4.4, varied: SI 2009/ 356 r.3
Part 4 r.4.5, varied: SI 2009/ 356 r.3
Part 4 r.4.6, varied: SI 2009/ 356 r.3
Part 4 r.4.7, varied: SI 2009/ 356 r.3
Part 4 r.4.8, amended: SI 2009/ 2472 r.12
Part 4 r.4.8, varied: SI 2009/ 356 r.3
Part 4 r.4.9, applied: SI 2009/ 356 r.9
Part 4 r.4.9, varied: SI 2009/ 356 r.3
Part 4 r.4.10, varied: SI 2009/ 356 r.3
Part 4 r.4.11, amended: SI 2009/ 2472 r.13
Part 4 r.4.11, substituted: SI 2009/ 642 r.18
Part 4 r.4.11, varied: SI 2009/ 356 r.3
Part 4 r.4.12, varied: SI 2009/ 356 r.3
Part 4 r.4.13, varied: SI 2009/ 356 r.3
Part 4 r.4.14, amended: SI 2009/ 642 r.19
Part 4 r.4.14, applied: SI 2009/ 356 r.13
Part 4 r.4.14, varied: SI 2009/ 356 r.3, r.13
Part 4 r.4.15, applied: SI 2009/ 356 r.14
Part 4 r.4.15, varied: SI 2009/ 356 r.3, r.14
Part 4 r.4.16, varied: SI 2009/ 356 r.3
Part 4 r.4.17, varied: SI 2009/ 356 r.3
Part 4 r.4.18, amended: SI 2009/ 642 r.5
Part 4 r.4.18, varied: SI 2009/ 356 r.3
Part 4 r.4.19, varied: SI 2009/ 356 r.3
Part 4 r.4.20, amended: SI 2009/ 642 r.5
Part 4 r.4.20, varied: SI 2009/ 356 r.3
Part 4 r.4.21, amended: SI 2009/ 642 r.5, r.20
Part 4 r.4.21, varied: SI 2009/ 356 r.3
Part 4 r.4.21A, applied: SI 2009/ 356 r.19
Part 4 r.4.21A, substituted: SI 2009/ 642 r.21
Part 4 r.4.21A, varied: SI 2009/ 356 r.3
Part 4 r.4.21B, added: SI 2009/ 642 r.21
Part 4 r.4.21B, varied: SI 2009/ 356 r.3
Part 4 r.4.22, varied: SI 2009/ 356 r.3
Part 4 r.4.23, varied: SI 2009/ 356 r.3
Part 4 r.4.24, varied: SI 2009/ 356 r.3
Part 4 r.4.25, disapplied: SI 2009/ 357 r.61
Part 4 r.4.25, varied: SI 2009/ 356 r.3
Part 4 r.4.25A, amended: SI 2009/ 642 r.5, r.22
Part 4 r.4.25A, disapplied: SI 2009/ 357 r.61
Part 4 r.4.25A, varied: SI 2009/ 356 r.3
Part 4 r.4.26, amended: SI 2009/ 642 r.5
Part 4 r.4.26, applied: SI 2009/ 357 r.45
Part 4 r.4.26, disapplied: SI 2009/ 357 r.61
Part 4 r.4.26, varied: SI 2009/ 356 r.3

1986–cont.

1925. Insolvency Rules 1986–*cont.*

Part 4 r.4.27, varied: SI 2009/ 356 r.3
Part 4 r.4.28, applied: SI 2009/ 356 r.23, SI 2009/ 357 r.61
Part 4 r.4.28, varied: SI 2009/ 356 r.3
Part 4 r.4.29, applied: SI 2009/ 356 r.24, SI 2009/ 357 r.61
Part 4 r.4.29, varied: SI 2009/ 356 r.3
Part 4 r.4.30, applied: SI 2009/ 356 r.25
Part 4 r.4.30, varied: SI 2009/ 356 r.3, r.25, SI 2009/ 357 r.61
Part 4 r.4.31, amended: SI 2009/ 642 r.23
Part 4 r.4.31, applied: SI 2009/ 356 r.26
Part 4 r.4.31, varied: SI 2009/ 356 r.3, r.26, SI 2009/ 357 r.61
Part 4 r.4.32, applied: SI 2009/ 356 r.27
Part 4 r.4.32, varied: SI 2009/ 356 r.3, r.27
Part 4 r.4.33, applied: SI 2009/ 356 r.28
Part 4 r.4.33, varied: SI 2009/ 356 r.3, r.28
Part 4 r.4.34, amended: SI 2009/ 642 r.5
Part 4 r.4.34, varied: SI 2009/ 356 r.3
Part 4 r.4.34A, amended: SI 2009/ 642 r.5
Part 4 r.4.34A, varied: SI 2009/ 356 r.3
Part 4 r.4.35, applied: SI 2009/ 356 r.29
Part 4 r.4.35, varied: SI 2009/ 356 r.3, r.29
Part 4 r.4.36, applied: SI 2009/ 356 r.30
Part 4 r.4.36, varied: SI 2009/ 356 r.3, r.30
Part 4 r.4.37, applied: SI 2009/ 356 r.31
Part 4 r.4.37, varied: SI 2009/ 356 r.3, r.31
Part 4 r.4.38, varied: SI 2009/ 356 r.3
Part 4 r.4.39, applied: SI 2009/ 356 r.32
Part 4 r.4.39, varied: SI 2009/ 356 r.3, r.32
Part 4 r.4.40, varied: SI 2009/ 356 r.3
Part 4 r.4.41, varied: SI 2009/ 356 r.3
Part 4 r.4.42, applied: SI 2009/ 356 r.33
Part 4 r.4.42, varied: SI 2009/ 356 r.3, r.33
Part 4 r.4.43, varied: SI 2009/ 356 r.3
Part 4 r.4.44, applied: SI 2009/ 356 r.35
Part 4 r.4.44, varied: SI 2009/ 356 r.3
Part 4 r.4.45, applied: SI 2009/ 356 r.36
Part 4 r.4.45, varied: SI 2009/ 356 r.3, r.36
Part 4 r.4.46, applied: SI 2009/ 356 r.37
Part 4 r.4.46, varied: SI 2009/ 356 r.3
Part 4 r.4.47, applied: SI 2009/ 356 r.38
Part 4 r.4.47, varied: SI 2009/ 356 r.3, r.38
Part 4 r.4.48, applied: SI 2009/ 356 r.39
Part 4 r.4.48, varied: SI 2009/ 356 r.3, r.39
Part 4 r.4.49, varied: SI 2009/ 356 r.3
Part 4 r.4.49A, varied: SI 2009/ 356 r.3
Part 4 r.4.50, amended: SI 2009/ 642 r.5, r.24
Part 4 r.4.50, varied: SI 2009/ 356 r.3
Part 4 r.4.51, varied: SI 2009/ 356 r.3
Part 4 r.4.52, varied: SI 2009/ 356 r.3
Part 4 r.4.53, varied: SI 2009/ 356 r.3
Part 4 r.4.53A, varied: SI 2009/ 356 r.3
Part 4 r.4.53B, varied: SI 2009/ 356 r.3
Part 4 r.4.54, amended: SI 2009/ 642 r.25
Part 4 r.4.54, applied: SI 2009/ 356 r.42
Part 4 r.4.54, varied: SI 2009/ 356 r.3
Part 4 r.4.55, varied: SI 2009/ 356 r.3
Part 4 r.4.56, varied: SI 2009/ 356 r.3
Part 4 r.4.57, applied: SI 2009/ 356 r.44, r.45
Part 4 r.4.57, referred to: SI 2009/ 356 r.45
Part 4 r.4.57, varied: SI 2009/ 356 r.3
Part 4 r.4.58, applied: SI 2009/ 356 r.46
Part 4 r.4.58, varied: SI 2009/ 356 r.3
Part 4 r.4.59, applied: SI 2009/ 356 r.47
Part 4 r.4.59, varied: SI 2009/ 356 r.3
Part 4 r.4.60, applied: SI 2009/ 356 r.48
Part 4 r.4.60, varied: SI 2009/ 356 r.3

1986–cont.

1925. Insolvency Rules 1986–*cont.*

Part 4 r.4.61, applied: SI 2009/ 356 r.49
Part 4 r.4.61, varied: SI 2009/ 356 r.3
Part 4 r.4.62, varied: SI 2009/ 356 r.3
Part 4 r.4.63, applied: SI 2009/ 356 r.50
Part 4 r.4.63, varied: SI 2009/ 356 r.3
Part 4 r.4.64, amended: SI 2009/ 642 r.5
Part 4 r.4.64, applied: SI 2009/ 356 r.51
Part 4 r.4.64, varied: SI 2009/ 356 r.3
Part 4 r.4.65, applied: SI 2009/ 356 r.52
Part 4 r.4.65, varied: SI 2009/ 356 r.3, r.52
Part 4 r.4.66, varied: SI 2009/ 356 r.3
Part 4 r.4.67, applied: SI 2009/ 356 r.53
Part 4 r.4.67, varied: SI 2009/ 356 r.3, r.53
Part 4 r.4.68, varied: SI 2009/ 356 r.3
Part 4 r.4.69, applied: SI 2009/ 356 r.54
Part 4 r.4.69, varied: SI 2009/ 356 r.3
Part 4 r.4.70, applied: SI 2009/ 356 r.55
Part 4 r.4.70, varied: SI 2009/ 356 r.3, r.55
Part 4 r.4.71, applied: SI 2009/ 356 r.56
Part 4 r.4.71, varied: SI 2009/ 356 r.3
Part 4 r.4.72, varied: SI 2009/ 356 r.3
Part 4 r.4.73, applied: SI 2009/ 356 r.57
Part 4 r.4.73, varied: SI 2009/ 356 r.3, r.57
Part 4 r.4.74, applied: SI 2009/ 356 r.58
Part 4 r.4.74, varied: SI 2009/ 356 r.3
Part 4 r.4.75, applied: SI 2009/ 356 r.59
Part 4 r.4.75, varied: SI 2009/ 356 r.3
Part 4 r.4.76, varied: SI 2009/ 356 r.3
Part 4 r.4.77, applied: SI 2009/ 356 r.60
Part 4 r.4.77, varied: SI 2009/ 356 r.3, r.60
Part 4 r.4.78, applied: SI 2009/ 356 r.61
Part 4 r.4.78, varied: SI 2009/ 356 r.3, r.61
Part 4 r.4.79, applied: SI 2009/ 356 r.62
Part 4 r.4.79, varied: SI 2009/ 356 r.3
Part 4 r.4.80, amended: SI 2009/ 642 r.5
Part 4 r.4.80, varied: SI 2009/ 356 r.3
Part 4 r.4.81, applied: SI 2009/ 356 r.63
Part 4 r.4.81, varied: SI 2009/ 356 r.3
Part 4 r.4.82, amended: SI 2009/ 642 r.5
Part 4 r.4.82, applied: SI 2009/ 356 r.64
Part 4 r.4.82, varied: SI 2009/ 356 r.3
Part 4 r.4.83, applied: SI 2009/ 356 r.65
Part 4 r.4.83, varied: SI 2009/ 356 r.3, r.65
Part 4 r.4.84, applied: SI 2009/ 356 r.66
Part 4 r.4.84, varied: SI 2009/ 356 r.3
Part 4 r.4.85, applied: SI 2009/ 356 r.67
Part 4 r.4.85, varied: SI 2009/ 356 r.3
Part 4 r.4.86, applied: SI 2009/ 356 r.68, r.72
Part 4 r.4.86, varied: SI 2009/ 356 r.3
Part 4 r.4.87, applied: SI 2009/ 356 r.69
Part 4 r.4.87, varied: SI 2009/ 356 r.3
Part 4 r.4.88, applied: SI 2009/ 356 r.70
Part 4 r.4.88, varied: SI 2009/ 356 r.3
Part 4 r.4.89, applied: SI 2009/ 356 r.71
Part 4 r.4.89, varied: SI 2009/ 356 r.3
Part 4 r.4.90, varied: SI 2009/ 356 r.3
Part 4 r.4.91, applied: SI 2009/ 356 r.74
Part 4 r.4.91, varied: SI 2009/ 356 r.3, r.74
Part 4 r.4.92, applied: SI 2009/ 356 r.75
Part 4 r.4.92, varied: SI 2009/ 356 r.3, r.75
Part 4 r.4.93, applied: SI 2009/ 356 r.76
Part 4 r.4.93, varied: SI 2009/ 356 r.3, r.76
Part 4 r.4.94, applied: SI 2009/ 356 r.77
Part 4 r.4.94, varied: SI 2009/ 356 r.3, r.77
Part 4 r.4.95, applied: SI 2009/ 356 r.78
Part 4 r.4.95, varied: SI 2009/ 356 r.3
Part 4 r.4.96, applied: SI 2009/ 356 r.79

1986–cont.

1925. Insolvency Rules 1986–*cont.*
Part 4 r.4.96, varied: SI 2009/356 r.3, r.79
Part 4 r.4.97, applied: SI 2009/356 r.80
Part 4 r.4.97, varied: SI 2009/356 r.3
Part 4 r.4.98, applied: SI 2009/356 r.81
Part 4 r.4.98, varied: SI 2009/356 r.3
Part 4 r.4.99, applied: SI 2009/356 r.82
Part 4 r.4.99, varied: SI 2009/356 r.3
Part 4 r.4.100, applied: SI 2009/356 r.84
Part 4 r.4.100, varied: SI 2009/356 r.3, r.84
Part 4 r.4.101, amended: SI 2009/642 r.5
Part 4 r.4.101, varied: SI 2009/356 r.3
Part 4 r.4.101A, varied: SI 2009/356 r.3
Part 4 r.4.102, amended: SI 2009/642 r.26
Part 4 r.4.102, varied: SI 2009/356 r.3
Part 4 r.4.103, amended: SI 2009/642 r.27
Part 4 r.4.103, varied: SI 2009/356 r.3
Part 4 r.4.104, varied: SI 2009/356 r.3
Part 4 r.4.105, applied: SI 2009/356 r.85
Part 4 r.4.105, varied: SI 2009/356 r.3, r.85
Part 4 r.4.106, amended: SI 2009/642 r.5, r.28
Part 4 r.4.106, varied: SI 2009/356 r.3
Part 4 r.4.107, amended: SI 2009/642 r.5
Part 4 r.4.107, varied: SI 2009/356 r.3
Part 4 r.4.108, applied: SI 2009/356 r.87
Part 4 r.4.108, varied: SI 2009/356 r.3, r.87
Part 4 r.4.109, amended: SI 2009/642 r.5
Part 4 r.4.109, varied: SI 2009/356 r.3
Part 4 r.4.110, amended: SI 2009/642 r.5
Part 4 r.4.110, varied: SI 2009/356 r.3
Part 4 r.4.111, amended: SI 2009/642 r.5
Part 4 r.4.111, varied: SI 2009/356 r.3
Part 4 r.4.112, applied: SI 2009/356 r.89
Part 4 r.4.112, varied: SI 2009/356 r.3
Part 4 r.4.113, applied: SI 2009/356 r.90
Part 4 r.4.113, varied: SI 2009/356 r.3, r.90
Part 4 r.4.114, varied: SI 2009/356 r.3
Part 4 r.4.115, applied: SI 2009/356 r.91
Part 4 r.4.115, varied: SI 2009/356 r.3, r.91
Part 4 r.4.116, applied: SI 2009/356 r.92
Part 4 r.4.116, varied: SI 2009/356 r.3, r.92
Part 4 r.4.117, amended: SI 2009/642 r.5
Part 4 r.4.117, varied: SI 2009/356 r.3
Part 4 r.4.118, applied: SI 2009/356 r.93
Part 4 r.4.118, varied: SI 2009/356 r.3
Part 4 r.4.119, applied: SI 2009/356 r.94
Part 4 r.4.119, varied: SI 2009/356 r.3, r.94
Part 4 r.4.120, amended: SI 2009/642 r.5
Part 4 r.4.120, varied: SI 2009/356 r.3
Part 4 r.4.121, applied: SI 2009/356 r.95
Part 4 r.4.121, varied: SI 2009/356 r.3, r.95
Part 4 r.4.122, varied: SI 2009/356 r.3
Part 4 r.4.123, amended: SI 2009/642 r.5
Part 4 r.4.123, varied: SI 2009/356 r.3
Part 4 r.4.124, varied: SI 2009/356 r.3
Part 4 r.4.125, varied: SI 2009/356 r.3
Part 4 r.4.125A, applied: SI 2009/356 r.97
Part 4 r.4.125A, varied: SI 2009/356 r.3, r.97
Part 4 r.4.126, varied: SI 2009/356 r.3
Part 4 r.4.127, applied: SI 2009/356 r.98
Part 4 r.4.127, varied: SI 2009/356 r.3, r.98
Part 4 r.4.127A, applied: SI 2009/356 r.99
Part 4 r.4.127A, varied: SI 2009/356 r.3, r.99
Part 4 r.4.127B, applied: SI 2009/356 r.100, SI 2009/357 r.61
Part 4 r.4.127B, varied: SI 2009/356 r.3, r.100
Part 4 r.4.128, applied: SI 2009/356 r.101
Part 4 r.4.128, varied: SI 2009/356 r.3

1986–cont.

1925. Insolvency Rules 1986–*cont.*
Part 4 r.4.129, applied: SI 2009/356 r.102
Part 4 r.4.129, varied: SI 2009/356 r.3
Part 4 r.4.130, applied: SI 2009/356 r.103
Part 4 r.4.130, varied: SI 2009/356 r.3
Part 4 r.4.131, applied: SI 2009/356 r.104
Part 4 r.4.131, varied: SI 2009/356 r.3
Part 4 r.4.132, varied: SI 2009/356 r.3
Part 4 r.4.133, varied: SI 2009/356 r.3
Part 4 r.4.134, amended: SI 2009/642 r.5
Part 4 r.4.134, applied: SI 2009/356 r.108
Part 4 r.4.134, varied: SI 2009/356 r.3, r.108
Part 4 r.4.135, amended: SI 2009/642 r.5
Part 4 r.4.135, varied: SI 2009/356 r.3
Part 4 r.4.136, varied: SI 2009/356 r.3
Part 4 r.4.137, applied: SI 2009/356 r.110
Part 4 r.4.137, varied: SI 2009/356 r.3, r.110
Part 4 r.4.138, amended: SI 2009/642 r.5
Part 4 r.4.138, applied: SI 2009/356 r.111
Part 4 r.4.138, varied: SI 2009/356 r.3, r.111
Part 4 r.4.139, amended: SI 2009/642 r.5
Part 4 r.4.139, varied: SI 2009/356 r.3
Part 4 r.4.140, varied: SI 2009/356 r.3
Part 4 r.4.141, varied: SI 2009/356 r.3
Part 4 r.4.142, amended: SI 2009/642 r.5
Part 4 r.4.142, varied: SI 2009/356 r.3
Part 4 r.4.143, amended: SI 2009/642 r.5
Part 4 r.4.143, varied: SI 2009/356 r.3
Part 4 r.4.144, amended: SI 2009/642 r.5
Part 4 r.4.144, varied: SI 2009/356 r.3
Part 4 r.4.145, varied: SI 2009/356 r.3
Part 4 r.4.146, amended: SI 2009/642 r.5
Part 4 r.4.146, varied: SI 2009/356 r.3
Part 4 r.4.147, varied: SI 2009/356 r.3
Part 4 r.4.148, amended: SI 2009/642 r.5
Part 4 r.4.148, varied: SI 2009/356 r.3
Part 4 r.4.148A, varied: SI 2009/356 r.3
Part 4 r.4.148B, varied: SI 2009/356 r.3
Part 4 r.4.149, applied: SI 2009/356 r.112
Part 4 r.4.149, varied: SI 2009/356 r.3, r.112
Part 4 r.4.150, applied: SI 2009/356 r.113
Part 4 r.4.150, varied: SI 2009/356 r.3
Part 4 r.4.151, varied: SI 2009/356 r.3
Part 4 r.4.152, applied: SI 2009/356 r.115
Part 4 r.4.152, varied: SI 2009/356 r.3, r.115
Part 4 r.4.153, amended: SI 2009/642 r.5, SI 2009/2472 r.8
Part 4 r.4.153, applied: SI 2009/356 r.116
Part 4 r.4.153, varied: SI 2009/356 r.3, r.116
Part 4 r.4.154, applied: SI 2009/356 r.117
Part 4 r.4.154, varied: SI 2009/356 r.3, r.117
Part 4 r.4.155, applied: SI 2009/356 r.118
Part 4 r.4.155, varied: SI 2009/356 r.3
Part 4 r.4.156, applied: SI 2009/356 r.119
Part 4 r.4.156, varied: SI 2009/356 r.3
Part 4 r.4.157, applied: SI 2009/356 r.120
Part 4 r.4.157, varied: SI 2009/356 r.3
Part 4 r.4.158, varied: SI 2009/356 r.3
Part 4 r.4.159, amended: SI 2009/2472 r.8
Part 4 r.4.159, applied: SI 2009/356 r.122
Part 4 r.4.159, varied: SI 2009/356 r.3, r.122
Part 4 r.4.160, applied: SI 2009/356 r.123
Part 4 r.4.160, varied: SI 2009/356 r.3
Part 4 r.4.161, applied: SI 2009/356 r.124
Part 4 r.4.161, varied: SI 2009/356 r.3
Part 4 r.4.162, applied: SI 2009/356 r.125
Part 4 r.4.162, varied: SI 2009/356 r.3
Part 4 r.4.163, applied: SI 2009/356 r.126

1986–cont.

1925. Insolvency Rules 1986–*cont.*

Part 4 r.4.163, varied: SI 2009/356 r.3
Part 4 r.4.164, applied: SI 2009/356 r.127
Part 4 r.4.164, varied: SI 2009/356 r.3
Part 4 r.4.165, applied: SI 2009/356 r.128
Part 4 r.4.165, varied: SI 2009/356 r.3
Part 4 r.4.166, varied: SI 2009/356 r.3
Part 4 r.4.167, applied: SI 2009/356 r.129
Part 4 r.4.167, varied: SI 2009/356 r.3
Part 4 r.4.168, applied: SI 2009/356 r.130
Part 4 r.4.168, varied: SI 2009/356 r.3
Part 4 r.4.169, applied: SI 2009/356 r.131
Part 4 r.4.169, varied: SI 2009/356 r.3
Part 4 r.4.170, applied: SI 2009/356 r.132
Part 4 r.4.170, varied: SI 2009/356 r.3
Part 4 r.4.171, amended: SI 2009/642 r.5
Part 4 r.4.171, applied: SI 2009/356 r.133
Part 4 r.4.171, varied: SI 2009/356 r.3, r.133
Part 4 r.4.172, applied: SI 2009/356 r.134
Part 4 r.4.172, varied: SI 2009/356 r.3, r.134
Part 4 r.4.172A, applied: SI 2009/356 r.135
Part 4 r.4.172A, varied: SI 2009/356 r.3, r.135
Part 4 r.4.173, varied: SI 2009/356 r.3
Part 4 r.4.174, varied: SI 2009/356 r.3
Part 4 r.4.175, varied: SI 2009/356 r.3
Part 4 r.4.176, varied: SI 2009/356 r.3
Part 4 r.4.177, varied: SI 2009/356 r.3
Part 4 r.4.178, varied: SI 2009/356 r.3
Part 4 r.4.179, applied: SI 2009/356 r.136
Part 4 r.4.179, varied: SI 2009/356 r.3
Part 4 r.4.180, applied: SI 2009/356 r.138
Part 4 r.4.180, varied: SI 2009/356 r.3
Part 4 r.4.181, applied: SI 2009/356 r.139
Part 4 r.4.181, varied: SI 2009/356 r.3
Part 4 r.4.182, applied: SI 2009/356 r.140
Part 4 r.4.182, varied: SI 2009/356 r.3
Part 4 r.4.182A, amended: SI 2009/642 r.29
Part 4 r.4.182A, varied: SI 2009/356 r.3
Part 4 r.4.183, applied: SI 2009/356 r.141
Part 4 r.4.183, varied: SI 2009/356 r.3
Part 4 r.4.184, applied: SI 2009/356 r.142
Part 4 r.4.184, varied: SI 2009/356 r.3, r.142
Part 4 r.4.185, applied: SI 2009/356 r.143
Part 4 r.4.185, varied: SI 2009/356 r.3
Part 4 r.4.186, applied: SI 2009/356 r.144
Part 4 r.4.186, varied: SI 2009/356 r.3, r.144
Part 4 r.4.187, applied: SI 2009/356 r.145, SI 2009/357 r.61
Part 4 r.4.187, varied: SI 2009/356 r.3
Part 4 r.4.188, amended: SI 2009/642 r.5
Part 4 r.4.188, applied: SI 2009/356 r.146, SI 2009/357 r.61
Part 4 r.4.188, varied: SI 2009/356 r.3
Part 4 r.4.189, applied: SI 2009/356 r.147, SI 2009/357 r.61
Part 4 r.4.189, varied: SI 2009/356 r.3
Part 4 r.4.190, applied: SI 2009/356 r.148, SI 2009/357 r.61
Part 4 r.4.190, varied: SI 2009/356 r.3
Part 4 r.4.191, applied: SI 2009/356 r.149, SI 2009/357 r.61
Part 4 r.4.191, varied: SI 2009/356 r.3
Part 4 r.4.192, applied: SI 2009/356 r.150, SI 2009/357 r.61
Part 4 r.4.192, varied: SI 2009/356 r.3
Part 4 r.4.193, applied: SI 2009/356 r.151, SI 2009/357 r.61
Part 4 r.4.193, varied: SI 2009/356 r.3, r.151

1986–cont.

1925. Insolvency Rules 1986–*cont.*

Part 4 r.4.194, applied: SI 2009/356 r.152, SI 2009/357 r.61
Part 4 r.4.194, varied: SI 2009/356 r.3
Part 4 r.4.195, applied: SI 2009/356 r.153
Part 4 r.4.195, varied: SI 2009/356 r.3
Part 4 r.4.196, applied: SI 2009/356 r.155
Part 4 r.4.196, varied: SI 2009/356 r.3
Part 4 r.4.197, applied: SI 2009/356 r.156
Part 4 r.4.197, varied: SI 2009/356 r.3
Part 4 r.4.198, amended: SI 2009/642 r.5
Part 4 r.4.198, applied: SI 2009/356 r.157
Part 4 r.4.198, varied: SI 2009/356 r.3
Part 4 r.4.199, applied: SI 2009/356 r.158
Part 4 r.4.199, varied: SI 2009/356 r.3
Part 4 r.4.200, applied: SI 2009/356 r.159
Part 4 r.4.200, varied: SI 2009/356 r.3, r.159
Part 4 r.4.201, varied: SI 2009/356 r.3
Part 4 r.4.202, applied: SI 2009/356 r.161
Part 4 r.4.202, varied: SI 2009/356 r.3
Part 4 r.4.203, applied: SI 2009/356 r.162
Part 4 r.4.203, varied: SI 2009/356 r.3
Part 4 r.4.204, applied: SI 2009/356 r.163
Part 4 r.4.204, varied: SI 2009/356 r.3
Part 4 r.4.205, applied: SI 2009/356 r.164
Part 4 r.4.205, varied: SI 2009/356 r.3
Part 4 r.4.206, applied: SI 2009/356 r.165
Part 4 r.4.206, varied: SI 2009/356 r.3
Part 4 r.4.207, applied: SI 2009/356 r.166
Part 4 r.4.207, varied: SI 2009/356 r.3
Part 4 r.4.208, applied: SI 2009/356 r.167
Part 4 r.4.208, varied: SI 2009/356 r.3
Part 4 r.4.209, applied: SI 2009/356 r.168
Part 4 r.4.209, varied: SI 2009/356 r.3
Part 4 r.4.210, applied: SI 2009/356 r.169
Part 4 r.4.210, varied: SI 2009/356 r.3
Part 4 r.4.211, amended: SI 2009/642 r.5
Part 4 r.4.211, varied: SI 2009/356 r.3
Part 4 r.4.212, amended: SI 2009/642 r.30
Part 4 r.4.212, varied: SI 2009/356 r.3
Part 4 r.4.213, amended: SI 2009/642 r.5
Part 4 r.4.213, varied: SI 2009/356 r.3
Part 4 r.4.214, varied: SI 2009/356 r.3
Part 4 r.4.215, varied: SI 2009/356 r.3
Part 4 r.4.216, varied: SI 2009/356 r.3
Part 4 r.4.217, varied: SI 2009/356 r.3
Part 4 r.4.218, applied: SI 2009/356 r.170
Part 4 r.4.218, varied: SI 2009/356 r.3, r.170
Part 4 r.4.218A, applied: SI 2009/356 r.171
Part 4 r.4.218A, varied: SI 2009/356 r.3
Part 4 r.4.218B, applied: SI 2009/356 r.172
Part 4 r.4.218B, varied: SI 2009/356 r.3
Part 4 r.4.218C, applied: SI 2009/356 r.173
Part 4 r.4.218C, varied: SI 2009/356 r.3
Part 4 r.4.218D, applied: SI 2009/356 r.174
Part 4 r.4.218D, varied: SI 2009/356 r.3
Part 4 r.4.218E, applied: SI 2009/356 r.175
Part 4 r.4.218E, varied: SI 2009/356 r.3
Part 4 r.4.219, varied: SI 2009/356 r.3
Part 4 r.4.220, applied: SI 2009/356 r.176
Part 4 r.4.220, varied: SI 2009/356 r.3
Part 4 r.4.221, applied: SI 2009/356 r.177
Part 4 r.4.221, varied: SI 2009/356 r.3
Part 4 r.4.222, applied: SI 2009/356 r.178
Part 4 r.4.222, varied: SI 2009/356 r.3
Part 4 r.4.223, amended: SI 2009/642 r.5
Part 4 r.4.223, varied: SI 2009/356 r.3
Part 4 r.4.224, varied: SI 2009/356 r.3

1986– cont.

1925. Insolvency Rules 1986–*cont.*

Part 4 r.4.225, varied: SI 2009/356 r.3
Part 4 r.4.226, applied: SI 2009/356 r.181
Part 4 r.4.226, varied: SI 2009/356 r.3, r.181
Part 4 r.4.227, applied: SI 2009/356 r.183
Part 4 r.4.227, varied: SI 2009/356 r.3
Part 4 r.4.228, applied: SI 2009/356 r.184
Part 4 r.4.228, varied: SI 2009/356 r.3, r.184
Part 4 r.4.229, applied: SI 2009/356 r.185
Part 4 r.4.229, varied: SI 2009/356 r.3, r.185
Part 4 r.4.230, amended: SI 2009/2472 r.14
Part 4 r.4.230, applied: SI 2009/356 r.186
Part 4 r.4.230, varied: SI 2009/356 r.3, r.186
Part 4 r.4.231, varied: SI 2009/356 r.3
Part 5, applied: SI 2009/645 Art.7
Part 5 r.5.4, amended: SI 2009/642 r.5
Part 5 r.5.10, amended: SI 2009/642 r.5
Part 5 r.5.24, amended: SI 2009/642 r.5
Part 5 r.5.26, amended: SI 2009/642 r.5
Part 5 r.5.29, amended: SI 2009/642 r.5
Part 5 r.5.30, amended: SI 2009/642 r.5
Part 5 r.5.60, amended: SI 2009/642 r.31
Part 5A r.5A.1, added: SI 2009/642 Sch.1
Part 5A r.5A.2, added: SI 2009/642 Sch.1
Part 5A r.5A.3, added: SI 2009/642 Sch.1
Part 5A r.5A.4, added: SI 2009/642 Sch.1
Part 5A r.5A.5, added: SI 2009/642 Sch.1
Part 5A r.5A.6, added: SI 2009/642 Sch.1
Part 5A r.5A.7, added: SI 2009/642 Sch.1
Part 5A r.5A.8, added: SI 2009/642 Sch.1
Part 5A r.5A.9, added: SI 2009/642 Sch.1
Part 5A r.5A.10, added: SI 2009/642 Sch.1
Part 5A r.5A.11, added: SI 2009/642 Sch.1
Part 5A r.5A.12, added: SI 2009/642 Sch.1
Part 5A r.5A.13, added: SI 2009/642 Sch.1
Part 5A r.5A.14, added: SI 2009/642 Sch.1
Part 5A r.5A.15, added: SI 2009/642 Sch.1
Part 5A r.5A.16, added: SI 2009/642 Sch.1
Part 5A r.5A.17, added: SI 2009/642 Sch.1
Part 5A r.5A.18, added: SI 2009/642 Sch.1
Part 5A r.5A.19, added: SI 2009/642 Sch.1
Part 5A r.5A.20, added: SI 2009/642 Sch.1
Part 5A r.5A.21, added: SI 2009/642 Sch.1
Part 5A r.5A.22, added: SI 2009/642 Sch.1
Part 5A r.5A.23, added: SI 2009/642 Sch.1
Part 5A r.5A.24, added: SI 2009/642 Sch.1
Part 5A r.5A.24, amended: SI 2009/2472 r.15
Part 5A r.5A.25, added: SI 2009/642 Sch.1
Part 5A r.5A.26, added: SI 2009/642 Sch.1
Part 5A r.5A.27, added: SI 2009/642 Sch.1
Part 6, added: SI 2009/642 r.47
Part 6 r.6.3, amended: SI 2009/642 r.33
Part 6 r.6.3, disapplied: SI 2009/642 r.3
Part 6 r.6.4, amended: SI 2009/642 r.34
Part 6 r.6.4, disapplied: SI 2009/642 r.3
Part 6 r.6.5, amended: SI 2009/642 r.5
Part 6 r.6.11, amended: SI 2009/642 r.35
Part 6 r.6.11, disapplied: SI 2009/642 r.3
Part 6 r.6.13, amended: SI 2009/642 r.5
Part 6 r.6.28, amended: SI 2009/642 r.5
Part 6 r.6.29, amended: SI 2009/642 r.5
Part 6 r.6.33, amended: SI 2009/642 r.5
Part 6 r.6.34, amended: SI 2009/642 r.5, r.36
Part 6 r.6.35, amended: SI 2009/642 r.37
Part 6 r.6.42, amended: SI 2009/642 r.5
Part 6 r.6.43, amended: SI 2009/642 r.5
Part 6 r.6.44, amended: SI 2009/642 r.5
Part 6 r.6.45, amended: SI 2009/642 r.5

1986– cont.

1925. Insolvency Rules 1986–*cont.*

Part 6 r.6.46, amended: SI 2009/642 r.5, r.38
Part 6 r.6.47, amended: SI 2009/642 r.39
Part 6 r.6.52, amended: SI 2009/642 r.5
Part 6 r.6.79, amended: SI 2009/642 r.5, r.40
Part 6 r.6.81, amended: SI 2009/642 r.41
Part 6 r.6.89, amended: SI 2009/642 r.5
Part 6 r.6.103, amended: SI 2009/642 r.5
Part 6 r.6.104, amended: SI 2009/642 r.5
Part 6 r.6.124, amended: SI 2009/642 r.42
Part 6 r.6.125, amended: SI 2009/642 r.5
Part 6 r.6.127, amended: SI 2009/642 r.5
Part 6 r.6.128, amended: SI 2009/642 r.5
Part 6 r.6.133, amended: SI 2009/642 r.5
Part 6 r.6.134, amended: SI 2009/642 r.43
Part 6 r.6.144, amended: SI 2009/642 r.5
Part 6 r.6.146, amended: SI 2009/642 r.5
Part 6 r.6.151, amended: SI 2009/642 r.5
Part 6 r.6.172, amended: SI 2009/642 r.5, r.44
Part 6 r.6.173, amended: SI 2009/642 r.5
Part 6 r.6.179, amended: SI 2009/642 r.5
Part 6 r.6.190, amended: SI 2009/642 r.5
Part 6 r.6.191, amended: SI 2009/642 r.5
Part 6 r.6.192, amended: SI 2009/642 r.5
Part 6 r.6.193, amended: SI 2009/642 r.5
Part 6 r.6.194, amended: SI 2009/642 r.5
Part 6 r.6.195, amended: SI 2009/642 r.5
Part 6 r.6.200, amended: SI 2009/642 r.5
Part 6 r.6.203, amended: SI 2009/2472 r.16
Part 6 r.6.204, amended: SI 2009/642 r.5
Part 6 r.6.212, amended: SI 2009/642 r.5
Part 6 r.6.213, amended: SI 2009/642 r.5, r.45
Part 6 r.6.220, amended: SI 2009/642 r.5, r.46
Part 6 r.6.235, amended: SI 2009/642 r.5
Part 6A r.6A.1, amended: SI 2009/642 r.48
Part 6A r.6A.4, amended: SI 2009/642 r.49
Part 6A r.6A.5A, added: SI 2009/642 r.50
Part 6A r.6A.5B, added: SI 2009/642 r.50
Part 6A r.6A.7A, added: SI 2009/642 r.51
Part 6A r.6A.7B, added: SI 2009/642 r.51
Part 6A r.6A.8, amended: SI 2009/642 r.52
Part 7, referred to: SI 2009/356 r.3
Part 7 r.7.1, varied: SI 2009/356 r.3, SI 2009/357 r.61
Part 7 r.7.2, amended: SI 2009/642 r.53
Part 7 r.7.2, applied: SI 2009/356 r.189, SI 2009/357 r.61
Part 7 r.7.2, varied: SI 2009/356 r.3
Part 7 r.7.3, applied: SI 2009/356 r.190, SI 2009/357 r.61
Part 7 r.7.3, varied: SI 2009/356 r.3
Part 7 r.7.3A, applied: SI 2009/356 r.191, SI 2009/357 r.61
Part 7 r.7.3A, varied: SI 2009/356 r.3, r.191
Part 7 r.7.4, applied: SI 2009/356 r.192, SI 2009/357 r.61
Part 7 r.7.4, varied: SI 2009/356 r.3
Part 7 r.7.4A, applied: SI 2009/356 r.193, SI 2009/357 r.61
Part 7 r.7.4A, varied: SI 2009/356 r.3, r.193
Part 7 r.7.5, amended: SI 2009/642 r.5
Part 7 r.7.5, applied: SI 2009/356 r.194, SI 2009/357 r.61
Part 7 r.7.5, varied: SI 2009/356 r.3
Part 7 r.7.6, applied: SI 2009/356 r.195, SI 2009/357 r.61
Part 7 r.7.6, varied: SI 2009/356 r.3
Part 7 r.7.7, applied: SI 2009/356 r.196, SI 2009/357 r.61
Part 7 r.7.7, varied: SI 2009/356 r.3
Part 7 r.7.8, applied: SI 2009/356 r.197, SI 2009/357 r.61
Part 7 r.7.8, varied: SI 2009/356 r.3, r.197
Part 7 r.7.9, applied: SI 2009/357 r.61
Part 7 r.7.9, varied: SI 2009/356 r.3
Part 7 r.7.10, applied: SI 2009/356 r.199, SI 2009/357 r.61

1986–cont.

1925. Insolvency Rules 1986–*cont.*

Part 7 r.7.10, varied: SI 2009/356 r.3

Part 7 r.7.11, amended: SI 2009/642 r.54

Part 7 r.7.11, varied: SI 2009/356 r.3

Part 7 r.7.12, amended: SI 2009/642 r.55

Part 7 r.7.12, varied: SI 2009/356 r.3

Part 7 r.7.13, amended: SI 2009/642 r.56

Part 7 r.7.13, varied: SI 2009/356 r.3

Part 7 r.7.14, amended: SI 2009/642 r.5

Part 7 r.7.14, varied: SI 2009/356 r.3

Part 7 r.7.15, varied: SI 2009/356 r.3

Part 7 r.7.16, amended: SI 2009/642 r.57

Part 7 r.7.16, applied: SI 2009/356 r.200, SI 2009/357 r.61

Part 7 r.7.16, varied: SI 2009/356 r.3, r.200

Part 7 r.7.17, applied: SI 2009/356 r.201, SI 2009/357 r.61

Part 7 r.7.17, varied: SI 2009/356 r.3

Part 7 r.7.18, varied: SI 2009/356 r.3

Part 7 r.7.19, applied: SI 2009/356 r.202, SI 2009/357 r.61

Part 7 r.7.19, varied: SI 2009/356 r.3, r.202

Part 7 r.7.20, applied: SI 2009/357 r.61

Part 7 r.7.20, varied: SI 2009/356 r.3

Part 7 r.7.21, amended: SI 2009/642 r.58

Part 7 r.7.21, applied: SI 2009/357 r.61

Part 7 r.7.21, varied: SI 2009/356 r.3

Part 7 r.7.22, varied: SI 2009/356 r.3

Part 7 r.7.23, amended: SI 2009/642 r.5, r.59

Part 7 r.7.23, applied: SI 2009/356 r.205, SI 2009/357 r.61

Part 7 r.7.23, varied: SI 2009/356 r.3, r.205

Part 7 r.7.24, varied: SI 2009/356 r.3

Part 7 r.7.25, varied: SI 2009/356 r.3

Part 7 r.7.26, amended: SI 2009/642 r.60

Part 7 r.7.26, varied: SI 2009/356 r.3

Part 7 r.7.27, applied: SI 2009/356 r.207, SI 2009/357 r.61

Part 7 r.7.27, varied: SI 2009/356 r.3

Part 7 r.7.28, amended: SI 2009/642 r.5

Part 7 r.7.28, applied: SI 2009/356 r.208, SI 2009/357 r.56, r.61

Part 7 r.7.28, varied: SI 2009/356 r.3

Part 7 r.7.29, varied: SI 2009/356 r.3

Part 7 r.7.30, applied: SI 2009/357 r.61

Part 7 r.7.30, varied: SI 2009/356 r.3

Part 7 r.7.31, amended: SI 2009/642 r.61

Part 7 r.7.31, disapplied: SI 2009/357 r.61

Part 7 r.7.31, varied: SI 2009/356 r.3

Part 7 r.7.32, applied: SI 2009/356 r.210, SI 2009/357 r.61

Part 7 r.7.32, revoked: SI 2009/642 r.62

Part 7 r.7.32, varied: SI 2009/356 r.3, r.210

Part 7 r.7.33, applied: SI 2009/356 r.211, SI 2009/357 r.61

Part 7 r.7.33, varied: SI 2009/356 r.3

Part 7 r.7.34, applied: SI 2009/356 r.212, SI 2009/357 r.61

Part 7 r.7.34, varied: SI 2009/356 r.3, r.212

Part 7 r.7.35, applied: SI 2009/356 r.213, SI 2009/357 r.61

Part 7 r.7.35, varied: SI 2009/356 r.3, r.213

Part 7 r.7.36, amended: SI 2009/642 r.5

Part 7 r.7.36, applied: SI 2009/356 r.214, SI 2009/357 r.61

Part 7 r.7.36, varied: SI 2009/356 r.3, r.214

Part 7 r.7.37, varied: SI 2009/356 r.3

Part 7 r.7.38, applied: SI 2009/356 r.215, SI 2009/357 r.61

Part 7 r.7.38, varied: SI 2009/356 r.3

Part 7 r.7.39, applied: SI 2009/356 r.216, SI 2009/357 r.61

Part 7 r.7.39, varied: SI 2009/356 r.3, r.216

Part 7 r.7.40, amended: SI 2009/642 r.63

Part 7 r.7.40, applied: SI 2009/356 r.217, SI 2009/357 r.61

Part 7 r.7.40, varied: SI 2009/356 r.3, r.217

1986–cont.

1925. Insolvency Rules 1986–*cont.*

Part 7 r.7.41, amended: SI 2009/642 r.64

Part 7 r.7.41, applied: SI 2009/356 r.218, SI 2009/357 r.61

Part 7 r.7.41, varied: SI 2009/356 r.3, r.218

Part 7 r.7.42, applied: SI 2009/356 r.219, SI 2009/357 r.61

Part 7 r.7.42, varied: SI 2009/356 r.3

Part 7 r.7.43, applied: SI 2009/356 r.220, SI 2009/357 r.61

Part 7 r.7.43, varied: SI 2009/356 r.3, r.220

Part 7 r.7.44, applied: SI 2009/356 r.221, SI 2009/357 r.61

Part 7 r.7.44, varied: SI 2009/356 r.3, r.221

Part 7 r.7.45, applied: SI 2009/356 r.222, SI 2009/357 r.61

Part 7 r.7.45, varied: SI 2009/356 r.3, r.222

Part 7 r.7.46, applied: SI 2009/356 r.223, SI 2009/357 r.61

Part 7 r.7.46, varied: SI 2009/356 r.3

Part 7 r.7.47, varied: SI 2009/356 r.3, SI 2009/357 r.61

Part 7 r.7.48, varied: SI 2009/356 r.3

Part 7 r.7.49, applied: SI 2009/357 r.61

Part 7 r.7.49, varied: SI 2009/356 r.3

Part 7 r.7.50, applied: SI 2009/356 r.226

Part 7 r.7.50, varied: SI 2009/356 r.3, r.226

Part 7 r.7.51, varied: SI 2009/356 r.3, SI 2009/357 r.61

Part 7 r.7.52, varied: SI 2009/356 r.3

Part 7 r.7.53, applied: SI 2009/356 r.228, SI 2009/357 r.61

Part 7 r.7.53, varied: SI 2009/356 r.3, r.228

Part 7 r.7.54, applied: SI 2009/357 r.61

Part 7 r.7.54, varied: SI 2009/356 r.3

Part 7 r.7.55, applied: SI 2009/357 r.61

Part 7 r.7.55, varied: SI 2009/356 r.3

Part 7 r.7.56, applied: SI 2009/357 r.61

Part 7 r.7.56, varied: SI 2009/356 r.3

Part 7 r.7.57, varied: SI 2009/356 r.3

Part 7 r.7.58, amended: SI 2009/642 r.5

Part 7 r.7.58, applied: SI 2009/356 r.230, SI 2009/357 r.61

Part 7 r.7.58, varied: SI 2009/356 r.3

Part 7 r.7.59, applied: SI 2009/356 r.231, SI 2009/357 r.61

Part 7 r.7.59, varied: SI 2009/356 r.3

Part 7 r.7.60, applied: SI 2009/356 r.232, SI 2009/357 r.61

Part 7 r.7.60, varied: SI 2009/356 r.3, r.232

Part 7 r.7.61, applied: SI 2009/356 r.233, SI 2009/357 r.61

Part 7 r.7.61, varied: SI 2009/356 r.3

Part 7 r.7.62, varied: SI 2009/356 r.3

Part 7 r.7.63, amended: SI 2009/642 r.5

Part 7 r.7.63, varied: SI 2009/356 r.3

Part 7 r.7.64, amended: SI 2009/642 r.65

Part 7 r.7.64, varied: SI 2009/356 r.3

Part 8, referred to: SI 2009/356 r.3

Part 8 r.8.1, applied: SI 2009/356 r.234, SI 2009/357 r.61

Part 8 r.8.1, varied: SI 2009/356 r.3, r.234

Part 8 r.8.2, applied: SI 2009/356 r.235, SI 2009/357 r.61

Part 8 r.8.2, varied: SI 2009/356 r.3

Part 8 r.8.3, applied: SI 2009/356 r.236, SI 2009/357 r.61

Part 8 r.8.3, varied: SI 2009/356 r.3, r.236

Part 8 r.8.4, amended: SI 2009/642 r.5

Part 8 r.8.4, applied: SI 2009/356 r.237, SI 2009/357 r.61

Part 8 r.8.4, varied: SI 2009/356 r.3

Part 8 r.8.5, applied: SI 2009/356 r.238, SI 2009/357 r.61

Part 8 r.8.5, varied: SI 2009/356 r.3, r.238

Part 8 r.8.6, applied: SI 2009/356 r.239, SI 2009/357 r.61

Part 8 r.8.6, varied: SI 2009/356 r.3

Part 8 r.8.7, amended: SI 2009/2472 r.8

Part 8 r.8.7, applied: SI 2009/356 r.240

1986–cont.

1925. Insolvency Rules 1986–*cont.*

Part 8 r.8.7, varied: SI 2009/ 356 r.3, r.240, SI 2009/ 357 r.61
Part 8 r.8.8, varied: SI 2009/ 356 r.3
Part 9, referred to: SI 2009/ 356 r.3
Part 9 r.9.1, amended: SI 2009/ 642 r.66
Part 9 r.9.1, varied: SI 2009/ 356 r.3, SI 2009/ 357 r.61
Part 9 r.9.2, applied: SI 2009/356 r.242, SI 2009/357 r.61
Part 9 r.9.2, varied: SI 2009/ 356 r.3
Part 9 r.9.3, amended: SI 2009/ 642 r.5
Part 9 r.9.3, applied: SI 2009/356 r.243, SI 2009/357 r.61
Part 9 r.9.3, varied: SI 2009/ 356 r.3
Part 9 r.9.4, amended: SI 2009/ 642 r.67
Part 9 r.9.4, applied: SI 2009/356 r.244, SI 2009/357 r.61
Part 9 r.9.4, varied: SI 2009/ 356 r.3
Part 9 r.9.5, applied: SI 2009/356 r.245, SI 2009/357 r.61
Part 9 r.9.5, varied: SI 2009/ 356 r.3
Part 9 r.9.6, amended: SI 2009/ 642 r.68
Part 9 r.9.6, applied: SI 2009/356 r.246, SI 2009/357 r.61
Part 9 r.9.6, varied: SI 2009/ 356 r.3, r.246
Part 10 r.10.2, amended: SI 2009/ 642 r.69
Part 10 r.10.4, amended: SI 2009/ 642 r.70
Part 11, referred to: SI 2009/ 356 r.3
Part 11 r.11.1, applied: SI 2009/ 357 r.61
Part 11 r.11.1, varied: SI 2009/ 356 r.3
Part 11 r.11.2, amended: SI 2009/ 642 r.71
Part 11 r.11.2, applied: SI 2009/ 356 r.248, SI 2009/ 357 r.61
Part 11 r.11.2, varied: SI 2009/ 356 r.3, r.248
Part 11 r.11.3, applied: SI 2009/ 356 r.249, SI 2009/ 357 r.61
Part 11 r.11.3, varied: SI 2009/ 356 r.3, r.249
Part 11 r.11.4, applied: SI 2009/ 356 r.250, SI 2009/ 357 r.61
Part 11 r.11.4, varied: SI 2009/ 356 r.3
Part 11 r.11.5, applied: SI 2009/ 356 r.251, SI 2009/ 357 r.61
Part 11 r.11.5, varied: SI 2009/ 356 r.3
Part 11 r.11.6, applied: SI 2009/ 356 r.252, SI 2009/ 357 r.61
Part 11 r.11.6, varied: SI 2009/ 356 r.3, r.252
Part 11 r.11.7, applied: SI 2009/ 356 r.253, SI 2009/ 357 r.61
Part 11 r.11.7, varied: SI 2009/ 356 r.3
Part 11 r.11.8, applied: SI 2009/ 356 r.254, SI 2009/ 357 r.61
Part 11 r.11.8, varied: SI 2009/ 356 r.3
Part 11 r.11.9, amended: SI 2009/ 642 r.5
Part 11 r.11.9, applied: SI 2009/ 356 r.255, SI 2009/ 357 r.61
Part 11 r.11.9, varied: SI 2009/ 356 r.3
Part 11 r.11.10, applied: SI 2009/ 356 r.256, SI 2009/ 357 r.61
Part 11 r.11.10, varied: SI 2009/ 356 r.3
Part 11 r.11.11, applied: SI 2009/ 356 r.257, SI 2009/ 357 r.61
Part 11 r.11.11, varied: SI 2009/ 356 r.3
Part 11 r.11.12, applied: SI 2009/ 356 r.258, SI 2009/ 357 r.61
Part 11 r.11.12, varied: SI 2009/ 356 r.3
Part 11 r.11.13, applied: SI 2009/ 356 r.259
Part 11 r.11.13, varied: SI 2009/356 r.3, r.259, SI 2009/ 357 r.61
Part 12, referred to: SI 2009/ 356 r.3
Part 12 r.12.1, amended: SI 2009/ 642 r.72
Part 12 r.12.1, enabled: SI 2009/ 482
Part 12 r.12.1, varied: SI 2009/ 356 r.3, SI 2009/ 357 r.61

1986–cont.

1925. Insolvency Rules 1986–*cont.*

Part 12 r.12.2, applied: SI 2009/ 357 r.61
Part 12 r.12.2, varied: SI 2009/ 356 r.3
Part 12 r.12.3, applied: SI 2009/ 357 r.61
Part 12 r.12.3, varied: SI 2009/ 356 r.3
Part 12 r.12.4, applied: SI 2009/ 356 r.263, SI 2009/ 357 r.61
Part 12 r.12.4, varied: SI 2009/ 356 r.3, r.263
Part 12 r.12.4A, amended: SI 2009/ 2472 r.8
Part 12 r.12.4A, applied: SI 2009/ 356 r.264
Part 12 r.12.4A, varied: SI 2009/ 356 r.3, r.264, SI 2009/ 357 r.61
Part 12 r.12.5, applied: SI 2009/ 356 r.265, SI 2009/ 357 r.61
Part 12 r.12.5, varied: SI 2009/ 356 r.3
Part 12 r.12.6, applied: SI 2009/ 356 r.266, SI 2009/ 357 r.61
Part 12 r.12.6, varied: SI 2009/ 356 r.3, r.266
Part 12 r.12.7, varied: SI 2009/ 356 r.3
Part 12 r.12.8, applied: SI 2009/ 356 r.267, SI 2009/ 357 r.61
Part 12 r.12.8, varied: SI 2009/ 356 r.3, r.267
Part 12 r.12.9, applied: SI 2009/ 356 r.268, SI 2009/ 357 r.61
Part 12 r.12.9, varied: SI 2009/ 356 r.3
Part 12 r.12.10, applied: SI 2009/ 356 r.269
Part 12 r.12.10, varied: SI 2009/356 r.3, SI 2009/357 r.61
Part 12 r.12.11, varied: SI 2009/356 r.3, SI 2009/357 r.61
Part 12 r.12.12, varied: SI 2009/356 r.3, SI 2009/357 r.61
Part 12 r.12.13, applied: SI 2009/ 356 r.272, SI 2009/ 357 r.61
Part 12 r.12.13, varied: SI 2009/ 356 r.3, r.272
Part 12 r.12.14, applied: SI 2009/ 356 r.273, SI 2009/ 357 r.61
Part 12 r.12.14, varied: SI 2009/ 356 r.3
Part 12 r.12.15, applied: SI 2009/ 356 r.274, SI 2009/ 357 r.61
Part 12 r.12.15, varied: SI 2009/ 356 r.3
Part 12 r.12.15A, applied: SI 2009/ 356 r.275, SI 2009/ 357 r.61
Part 12 r.12.15A, varied: SI 2009/ 356 r.3
Part 12 r.12.16, applied: SI 2009/ 356 r.276, SI 2009/ 357 r.61
Part 12 r.12.16, varied: SI 2009/ 356 r.3
Part 12 r.12.17, applied: SI 2009/ 357 r.61
Part 12 r.12.17, varied: SI 2009/ 356 r.3
Part 12 r.12.18, applied: SI 2009/ 356 r.278, SI 2009/ 357 r.61
Part 12 r.12.18, varied: SI 2009/ 356 r.3
Part 12 r.12.19, varied: SI 2009/ 356 r.3
Part 12 r.12.20, amended: SI 2009/ 642 r.5
Part 12 r.12.20, applied: SI 2009/356 r.280, SI 2009/ 357 r.61
Part 12 r.12.20, varied: SI 2009/ 356 r.3
Part 12 r.12.21, applied: SI 2009/ 356 r.281, SI 2009/ 357 r.61
Part 12 r.12.21, varied: SI 2009/ 356 r.3, r.281
Part 12 r.12.22, amended: SI 2009/ 642 r.73
Part 12 r.12.22, applied: SI 2009/356 r.282, SI 2009/ 357 r.61
Part 12 r.12.22, varied: SI 2009/ 356 r.3, r.282
Part 13, referred to: SI 2009/ 356 r.3
Part 13 r.13.1, applied: SI 2009/ 357 r.61
Part 13 r.13.1, varied: SI 2009/ 356 r.3
Part 13 r.13.2, applied: SI 2009/ 356 r.284, SI 2009/ 357 r.61
Part 13 r.13.2, varied: SI 2009/ 356 r.3, r.284
Part 13 r.13.3, amended: SI 2009/ 642 r.74

1986–cont.

1925. Insolvency Rules 1986–*cont.*

Part 13 r.13.3, applied: SI 2009/356 r.285, SI 2009/357 r.61

Part 13 r.13.3, varied: SI 2009/356 r.3

Part 13 r.13.4, applied: SI 2009/356 r.286, SI 2009/357 r.61

Part 13 r.13.4, varied: SI 2009/356 r.3

Part 13 r.13.5, applied: SI 2009/357 r.61

Part 13 r.13.5, varied: SI 2009/356 r.3

Part 13 r.13.6, applied: SI 2009/357 r.61

Part 13 r.13.6, varied: SI 2009/356 r.3

Part 13 r.13.7, applied: SI 2009/357 r.61

Part 13 r.13.7, varied: SI 2009/356 r.3

Part 13 r.13.8, amended: SI 2009/642 r.75

Part 13 r.13.8, applied: SI 2009/357 r.61

Part 13 r.13.8, varied: SI 2009/356 r.3

Part 13 r.13.9, applied: SI 2009/357 r.61

Part 13 r.13.9, varied: SI 2009/356 r.3

Part 13 r.13.10, applied: SI 2009/357 r.61

Part 13 r.13.10, varied: SI 2009/356 r.3

Part 13 r.13.11, applied: SI 2009/357 r.61

Part 13 r.13.11, varied: SI 2009/356 r.3

Part 13 r.13.12, applied: SI 2009/356 r.291, SI 2009/357 r.61

Part 13 r.13.12, varied: SI 2009/356 r.3, r.291

Part 13 r.13.12A, applied: SI 2009/357 r.61

Part 13 r.13.12A, varied: SI 2009/356 r.3

Part 13 r.13.13, amended: SI 2009/642 r.76, SI 2009/2748 Sch.1 para.12

Part 13 r.13.13, applied: SI 2009/356 r.292, SI 2009/357 r.61

Part 13 r.13.13, varied: SI 2009/356 r.3, r.292

Part 13 r.13.14, varied: SI 2009/356 r.3

r.2.4, see *Kayley Vending Ltd, Re* [2009] EWHC 904 (Ch), [2009] B.C.C. 578 (Ch D (Birmingham)), Judge Cooke

r.2.67, see *Kayley Vending Ltd, Re* [2009] EWHC 904 (Ch), [2009] B.C.C. 578 (Ch D (Birmingham)), Judge Cooke

r.2.85, see *Kaupthing Singer & Friedlander Ltd (In Administration), Re* [2009] EWHC 2308 (Ch), (2009) 153(38) S.J.L.B. 30 (Ch D (Companies Ct)), Norris, J.

r.2.86, see *Kaupthing Singer & Friedlander Ltd (In Administration), Re* [2009] EWHC 2308 (Ch), (2009) 153(38) S.J.L.B. 30 (Ch D (Companies Ct)), Norris, J.

r.2.87, see *Kaupthing Singer & Friedlander Ltd (In Administration), Re* [2009] EWHC 2308 (Ch), (2009) 153(38) S.J.L.B. 30 (Ch D (Companies Ct)), Norris, J.

r.2.88, see *Kaupthing Singer & Friedlander Ltd (In Administration), Re* [2009] EWHC 2308 (Ch), (2009) 153(38) S.J.L.B. 30 (Ch D (Companies Ct)), Norris, J.

r.2.97, see *Kaupthing Singer & Friedlander Ltd (In Administration), Re* [2009] EWHC 2308 (Ch), (2009) 153(38) S.J.L.B. 30 (Ch D (Companies Ct)), Norris, J.

r.2.105, see *Kaupthing Singer & Friedlander Ltd (In Administration), Re* [2009] EWHC 2308 (Ch), (2009) 153(38) S.J.L.B. 30 (Ch D (Companies Ct)), Norris, J.

r.4.70, see *Power v Petrus Estates Ltd* [2008] EWHC 2607 (Ch), [2009] 1 B.C.L.C. 250 (Ch D (Companies Ct)), Lewison, J.

r.4.86, see *Kaupthing Singer & Friedlander Ltd (In Administration), Re* [2009] EWHC 2308 (Ch), (2009) 153(38) S.J.L.B. 30 (Ch D (Companies Ct)), Norris, J.

1986–cont.

1925. Insolvency Rules 1986–*cont.*

r.4.90, see *Rayden v Edwardo Ltd (In Members' Voluntary Liquidation)* [2008] EWHC 2689 (Comm), [2009] B.P.I.R. 892 (QBD (Comm)), Gloster, J.

r.4.99, see *Kaupthing Singer & Friedlander Ltd (In Administration), Re* [2009] EWHC 2308 (Ch), (2009) 153(38) S.J.L.B. 30 (Ch D (Companies Ct)), Norris, J.

r.4.184, see *Gresham International Ltd (In Liquidation) v Moonie* [2009] EWHC 1093 (Ch), [2009] 2 B.C.L.C. 256 (Ch D), Peter Smith, J.

r.5.22, see *Tradition (UK) Ltd v Ahmed* [2008] EWHC 2946 (Ch), [2009] B.P.I.R. 626 (Ch D), Andrew Simmonds Q.C.

r.5.23, see *Tradition (UK) Ltd v Ahmed* [2008] EWHC 2946 (Ch), [2009] B.P.I.R. 626 (Ch D), Andrew Simmonds Q.C.

r.6.5, see *Ahmed v Landstone Leisure Ltd* [2009] EWHC 125 (Ch), [2009] B.P.I.R. 227 (Ch D (Birmingham)), Judge Purle Q.C.

r.6.13, see *Trustee in Bankruptcy of St John Poulton v Ministry of Justice* [2009] EWHC 2123 (Ch), [2009] B.P.I.R. 1512 (Ch D), Judge Hazel Marshall Q.C.

r.6.25, see *Watts v Newham LBC* [2009] EWHC 377 (Ch), [2009] B.P.I.R. 718 (Ch D), Stephen Smith Q.C.

r.6.106, see *Official Receiver v McKay* [2009] EWCA Civ 467, [2009] B.P.I.R. 1061 (CA (Civ Div)), Mummery, L.J.

r.6.107, see *Official Receiver v McKay* [2009] EWCA Civ 467, [2009] B.P.I.R. 1061 (CA (Civ Div)), Mummery, L.J.

r.6.175, see *Rottmann v Brittain* [2009] EWCA Civ 473, [2009] B.P.I.R. 1148 (CA (Civ Div)), Ward, L.J.

r.6.224, see *Bank of Baroda v Patel* [2008] EWHC 3390 (Ch), [2009] 2 F.L.R. 753 (Ch D), Sales, J

r.7.31, see *Kayley Vending Ltd, Re* [2009] EWHC 904 (Ch), [2009] B.C.C. 578 (Ch D (Birmingham)), Judge Cooke

r.7.48, see *Bailey v Dargue* [2008] EWHC 2903 (Ch), [2009] B.P.I.R. 1 (Ch D (Manchester)), Judge Hodge Q.C.

r.9.3, see *Rottmann, Re* [2008] EWHC 1794 (Ch), [2009] Bus. L.R. 284 (Ch D), Judge Kaye Q.C.

r.9.4, see *Rottmann, Re* [2008] EWHC 1794 (Ch), [2009] Bus. L.R. 284 (Ch D), Judge Kaye Q.C.

r.12.2, see *International Sections Ltd (In Liquidation), Re* [2009] EWHC 137 (Ch), [2009] B.C.C. 574 (Ch D (Birmingham)), Judge Purle Q.C.

Sch.1, applied: SI 2009/356 r.40, Sch.1 para.1

Sch.1 para.1, varied: SI 2009/356 Sch.1 para.1

Sch.1 para.2, varied: SI 2009/356 Sch.1 para.1

Sch.1 para.3, varied: SI 2009/356 Sch.1 para.1

Sch.1 para.4, varied: SI 2009/356 Sch.1 para.1

Sch.1 para.5, varied: SI 2009/356 Sch.1 para.1

Sch.1 para.6, varied: SI 2009/356 Sch.1 para.1

Sch.2, amended: SI 2009/642 r.77

Sch.4, amended: SI 2009/642 Sch.2 para.1, Sch.2 para.2, Sch.2 para.3, SI 2009/2472 r.17

Sch.5, applied: SI 2009/356 Sch.1 para.1, SI 2009/357 r.61

Sch.6, applied: SI 2009/356 Sch.1 para.1, SI 2009/357 r.61

1986–cont.

1953. Air Navigation (Investigation of Air Accidents involving Civil and Military Aircraft or Installations) Regulations 1986
referred to: SI 2009/500 Sch.1 Part 2

1960. Statutory Maternity Pay (General) Regulations 1986
Reg.6, amended: SI 2009/497 Art.10

1996. Insolvency Proceedings (Monetary Limits) Order 1986
Art.3, amended: SI 2009/465 Art.2
Sch.1 Part II, amended: SI 2009/465 Art.3

2000. Companies (Unfair Prejudice Applications) Proceedings Rules 1986
revoked: SI 2009/2469 r.1

2128. Passenger and Goods Vehicles (Recording Equipment) (Approval of fitters and workshops) (Fees) Regulations 1986
Reg.3, amended: SI 2009/866 Reg.2

2211. Charitable Deductions (Approved Schemes) Regulations 1986
Reg.8, amended: SI 2009/56 Sch.2 para.22

2288. Value Added Tax Tribunals Appeals Order 1986
revoked: SI 2009/56 Sch.2 para.187

1987

37. Dangerous Substances in Harbour Areas Regulations 1987
Part IX, applied: SI 2009/515 Reg.11

257. Police Pensions Regulations 1987
referred to: SSI 2009/185 Reg.2
see *Rooney v Strathclyde Joint Police Board* 2009 S.C. 73 (IH (Ex Div)), Lord Reed
Reg.1, amended: SI 2009/2060 Sch.1 para.8
Reg.1, revoked (in part): SI 2009/2060 Sch.1 para.8
Reg.1, amended: SI 2009/2060 Sch.1 para.11
Reg.1, amended: SI 2009/2060 Sch.1 para.12
Reg.1, added: SSI 2009/185 Reg.4
Reg.2, added: SSI 2009/185 Reg.4
Reg.2A, amended: SI 2009/2060 Sch.1 para.9
Reg.3, added: SSI 2009/185 Reg.4
Reg.4, amended: SI 2009/2060 Sch.1 para.13
Reg.4, added: SSI 2009/185 Reg.5
Reg.4, revoked (in part): SSI 2009/185 Reg.5
Reg.5, added: SSI 2009/185 Reg.6
Reg.5, see *Carruthers v Dumfries and Galloway Council* 2009 S.L.T. (Sh Ct) 127 (Sh Ct (South Strathclyde) (Dumfries)), Sheriff K A Ross
Reg.6, amended: SI 2009/2060 Sch.1 para.2
Reg.6, added: SSI 2009/185 Reg.6
Reg.8, amended: SI 2009/2060 Sch.1 para.10, SSI 2009/185 Reg.3
Reg.12, amended: SI 2009/2060 Sch.1 para.3
Reg.12, see *Corkindale v Police Medical Appeal Board* [2006] EWHC 3362 (Admin), [2009] I.C.R. 63 (QBD (Admin)), Underhill, J.; see *R. (on the application of Ashton) v Police Medical Appeal Board* [2008] EWHC 1833 (Admin), [2009] I.C.R. 51 (QBD (Admin)), Charles, J.
Reg.16, amended: SI 2009/2060 Sch.1 para.4
Reg.17, amended: SI 2009/2060 Sch.1 para.5
Reg.18, amended: SI 2009/2060 Sch.1 para.6
Reg.19, amended: SI 2009/2060 Sch.1 para.7
Sch.A, amended: SI 2009/2060 Sch.1 para.14
Sch.A, see *R. (on the application of Ashton) v Police Medical Appeal Board* [2008] EWHC 1833 (Admin), [2009] I.C.R. 51 (QBD (Admin)), Charles, J.

1987–cont.

383. Smoke Control Areas (Exempted Fireplaces) (Scotland) Order 1987
revoked: SSI 2009/214 Sch.2

416. Social Security (Maternity Allowance) Regulations 1987
Reg.1A, substituted: SI 2009/471 Reg.4

470. Merchant Shipping (Prevention and Control of Pollution) Order 1987
Art.3, enabled: SI 2009/1210
Art.5, enabled: SI 2009/1210

764. Town and Country Planning (Use Classes) Order 1987
Sch.1, see *R. (on the application of Tendring DC) v Secretary of State for Communities and Local Government* [2008] EWHC 2122 (Admin), [2009] J.P.L. 350 (QBD (Admin)), Sullivan, J.
Sch.1 para.1, see *Cocktails Ltd v Secretary of State for Communities and Local Government* [2008] EWCA Civ 1523, [2009] J.P.L. 953 (CA (Civ Div)), Pill, L.J.

773. Patronage (Benefices) Rules 1987
applied: SI 2009/2105 Sch.1 Part II

790. Infectious Diseases of Horses Order 1987
Art.3, amended: SI 2009/2713 Art.2
Art.4, amended: SI 2009/2713 Art.2
Art.7, amended: SI 2009/2713 Art.2
Art.9, amended: SI 2009/2713 Art.2
Sch.1, amended: SI 2009/2713 Art.2, Art.5

821. Court Funds Rules 1987
see *Petroleo Brasilieiro SA v ENE Kos 1 Ltd* [2009] EWCA Civ 1127, Times, November 5, 2009 (CA (Civ Div)), Waller, L.J.
Part A r.2, amended: SI 2009/1307 Sch.2 para.27
Part I r.7, amended: SI 2009/1307 Sch.2 para.28
Part I r.8, amended: SI 2009/1307 Sch.2 para.29
Part VIII r.55, amended: SI 2009/2748 Sch.1 para.13
r.16, see *Petroleo Brasilieiro SA v ENE Kos 1 Ltd* [2009] EWCA Civ 1127, Times, November 5, 2009 (CA (Civ Div)), Waller, L.J.

851. Police Regulations 1987
referred to: SI 2009/500 Sch.1 Part 2

1110. Personal Pension Schemes (Disclosure of Information) Regulations 1987
Reg.1, amended: SI 2009/598 Art.2
Reg.5, amended: SI 2009/598 Art.2
Sch.1 para.12, amended: SI 2009/598 Art.2
Sch.1 para.13, amended: SI 2009/598 Art.2
Sch.2 para.4, amended: SI 2009/598 Art.2
Sch.2 para.11, amended: SI 2009/598 Art.2

1230. Minibus and Other Section 19 Permit Buses Regulations 1987
revoked: SI 2009/365 Sch.1

1377. Aerodromes (Designation) (Detention and Sale of Aircraft) Order 1987
revoked (in part): SI 2009/2350 Sch.2

1496. Insurance Brokers Registration Council (Indemnity Insurance and Grants Scheme) Rules Approval Order 1987
referred to: SI 2009/500 Sch.1 Part 2

1806. Value Added Tax (Tour Operators) Order 1987
Art.3, amended: SI 2009/3166 Art.3
Art.3, revoked (in part): SI 2009/3166 Art.3
Art.5, amended: 2009 c.10 Sch.36 para.13
Art.5, revoked (in part): 2009 c.10 Sch.36 para.13
Art.5, varied: 2009 c.10 Sch.36 para.13
Art.7, amended: SI 2009/3166 Art.4
Art.9A, added: SI 2009/3166 Art.5

1987– cont.

1806. Value Added Tax (Tour Operators) Order 1987– *cont.*
Art.12, amended: SI 2009/3166 Art.6
1850. Local Government Superannuation (Scotland) Regulations 1987
Part E Reg.E6, amended: SSI 2009/186 Reg.8
Part U Reg.U1, added: SSI 2009/186 Reg.9
Part U Reg.U2, added: SSI 2009/186 Reg.9
Part U Reg.U3, added: SSI 2009/186 Reg.9
Part U Reg.U4, added: SSI 2009/186 Reg.9, Reg.10
Part U Reg.U4, revoked: SSI 2009/186 Reg.10
Part U Reg.U5, added: SSI 2009/186 Reg.9, Reg.11
Part U Reg.U6, added: SSI 2009/186 Reg.9, Reg.11
1967. Income Support (General) Regulations 1987
referred to: SI 2009/497 Art.16
Part V, amended: SI 2009/2655 Reg.2
Reg.2, amended: SI 2009/583 Reg.2, SI 2009/2655 Reg.2
Reg.2A, amended: SI 2009/471 Reg.5
Reg.4, amended: SI 2009/3152 Reg.3
Reg.4ZA, amended: SI 2009/583 Reg.2, SI 2009/3152 Reg.3
Reg.4ZA, revoked (in part): SI 2009/2655 Reg.2
Reg.6, revoked (in part): SI 2009/3228 Reg.4
Reg.13, revoked (in part): SI 2009/2655 Reg.2
Reg.15, varied: SI 2009/497 Art.17
Reg.17, amended: SI 2009/3228 Reg.3
Reg.17, referred to: SI 2009/497 Art.16
Reg.18, amended: SI 2009/3228 Reg.3
Reg.18, referred to: SI 2009/497 Art.16
Reg.21, referred to: SI 2009/497 Art.16
Reg.21, revoked (in part): SI 2009/583 Reg.2
Reg.21AA, amended: SI 2009/362 Reg.2
Reg.22A, referred to: SI 2009/497 Sch.4
Reg.22B, added: SI 2009/3228 Reg.3
Reg.25, amended: SI 2009/2655 Reg.2
Reg.30, amended: SI 2009/583 Reg.2
Reg.35, amended: SI 2009/2655 Reg.2
Reg.39, amended: SI 2009/583 Reg.2
Reg.39D, amended: SI 2009/583 Reg.2
Reg.40, amended: SI 2009/2655 Reg.2
Reg.42, amended: SI 2009/583 Reg.2, SI 2009/2655 Reg.2
Reg.54, amended: SI 2009/2655 Reg.2
Reg.55, amended: SI 2009/2655 Reg.2
Reg.57, amended: SI 2009/2655 Reg.2
Reg.57, revoked (in part): SI 2009/2655 Reg.2
Reg.58, amended: SI 2009/2655 Reg.2
Reg.59, amended: SI 2009/2655 Reg.2
Reg.61, amended: SI 2009/583 Reg.2, SI 2009/2655 Reg.2, SI 2009/3152 Reg.3
Reg.62, amended: SI 2009/583 Reg.2, SI 2009/1575 Reg.2
Reg.66A, amended: SI 2009/583 Reg.2, SI 2009/1575 Reg.2, SI 2009/3152 Reg.3
Reg.70, revoked: SI 2009/3228 Reg.2
Reg.71, referred to: SI 2009/497 Art.16, Sch.4
Reg.71, revoked: SI 2009/3228 Reg.2
Reg.72, revoked: SI 2009/3228 Reg.2
Sch.1 B, amended: SI 2009/3152 Reg.3
Sch.1 B, substituted: SI 2009/2655 Reg.2
Sch.1 B para.2, amended: SI 2009/2655 Reg.2
Sch.1 B para.2A, added: SI 2009/2655 Reg.2
Sch.1 B para.3, amended: SI 2009/583 Reg.2
Sch.1 B para.7, revoked (in part): SI 2009/3152 Reg.2
Sch.1 B para.8, revoked: SI 2009/3228 Reg.4
Sch.1 B para.9, revoked: SI 2009/3228 Reg.4

1987– cont.

1967. Income Support (General) Regulations 1987– *cont.*
Sch.1 B para.10, revoked: SI 2009/3152 Reg.2
Sch.1 B para.12, revoked: SI 2009/3152 Reg.2
Sch.1 B para.13, revoked: SI 2009/3152 Reg.2
Sch.1 B para.15A, added: SI 2009/583 Reg.2
Sch.1 B para.15A, amended: SI 2009/2655 Reg.2
Sch.1 B para.21, substituted: SI 2009/3228 Reg.3
Sch.1 B para.28, amended: SI 2009/583 Reg.2
Sch.2 Part I, referred to: SI 2009/497 Art.16
Sch.2 Part I para.1, substituted: SI 2009/497 Sch.2
Sch.2 Part I para.1A, substituted: SI 2009/497 Sch.2
Sch.2 Part I para.1ZA, substituted: SI 2009/497 Sch.2
Sch.2 Part I para.2, substituted: SI 2009/497 Sch.2
Sch.2 Part II para.3, amended: SI 2009/497 Art.16
Sch.2 Part III para.7, amended: SI 2009/583 Reg.2
Sch.2 Part III para.9, amended: SI 2009/1488 Reg.3
Sch.2 Part III para.10, amended: SI 2009/1488 Reg.3
Sch.2 Part III para.11, amended: SI 2009/1488 Reg.3
Sch.2 Part III para.13A, amended: SI 2009/1488 Reg.3
Sch.2 Part III para.13A, referred to: SI 2009/497 Art.16
Sch.2 Part III para.14, referred to: SI 2009/497 Art.16
Sch.2 Part IV, referred to: SI 2009/497 Art.16
Sch.2 Part IV para.15, substituted: SI 2009/497 Sch.3
Sch.3 para.3, amended: SI 2009/583 Reg.2, SI 2009/2655 Reg.2
Sch.3 para.5, referred to: SI 2009/497 Sch.4
Sch.3 para.6, referred to: SI 2009/497 Sch.4
Sch.3 para.7, referred to: SI 2009/497 Sch.4
Sch.3 para.8, referred to: SI 2009/497 Sch.4
Sch.3 para.10, referred to: SI 2009/497 Sch.4
Sch.3 para.11, referred to: SI 2009/497 Sch.4
Sch.3 para.12, referred to: SI 2009/497 Sch.4
Sch.3 para.14, amended: SI 2009/2655 Reg.2
Sch.3 para.18, amended: SI 2009/497 Art.16
Sch.3 para.18, referred to: SI 2009/497 Art.16
Sch.4 para.10, see *Peters v East Midlands SHA* [2009] EWCA Civ 145, [2009] 3 W.L.R. 737 (CA (Civ Div)), Sir Anthony Clarke, M.R.
Sch.7, referred to: SI 2009/497 Sch.4
Sch.7, see *R. (on the application of M) v Secretary of State for Work and Pensions* [2008] UKHL 63, [2009] 1 A.C. 311 (HL), Lord Hope of Craighead
Sch.7, referred to: SI 2009/497 Sch.4
Sch.8 para.1, amended: SI 2009/2655 Reg.2
Sch.8 para.2, amended: SI 2009/2655 Reg.2
Sch.9 para.2A, added: SI 2009/2655 Reg.2
Sch.9 para.16, amended: SI 2009/2655 Reg.2
Sch.9 para.25, amended: SI 2009/2655 Reg.2
Sch.9 para.58, amended: SI 2009/583 Reg.2
Sch.9 para.73, substituted: SI 2009/2655 Reg.2
Sch.10 para.4, amended: SI 2009/1488 Reg.4
Sch.10 para.39A, added: SI 2009/583 Reg.2
Sch.10 para.44, see *Peters v East Midlands SHA* [2009] EWCA Civ 145, [2009] 3 W.L.R. 737 (CA (Civ Div)), Sir Anthony Clarke, M.R.
Sch.10 para.67, amended: SI 2009/583 Reg.2
1968. Social Security (Claims and Payments) Regulations 1987
applied: SI 2009/1562 Art.2

1987– cont.

1968. Social Security (Claims and Payments) Regulations 1987– *cont.*
Reg.2, amended: SI 2009/1490 Reg.2, SI 2009/3229 Reg.2
Reg.3, amended: SI 2009/1490 Reg.2
Reg.4, amended: SI 2009/1490 Reg.2, SI 2009/2655 Reg.3
Reg.4, revoked (in part): SI 2009/1490 Reg.2
Reg.4D, amended: SI 2009/2655 Reg.3
Reg.4G, amended: SI 2009/2655 Reg.3
Reg.4H, amended: SI 2009/2655 Reg.3
Reg.5, amended: SI 2009/1490 Reg.2
Reg.6, amended: SI 2009/1490 Reg.2
Reg.16, amended: SI 2009/604 Reg.2, SI 2009/3229 Reg.2
Reg.19, see *Leicester City Council, Re* [2009] UKUT 155 (AAC), [2009] R.V.R. 306 (UT (AAC)), Edward Jacobs
Reg.22, amended: SI 2009/604 Reg.2, SI 2009/3229 Reg.2
Reg.22A, added: SI 2009/604 Reg.2
Reg.22A, applied: SI 2009/609 Reg.2, Reg.3
Reg.22B, added: SI 2009/604 Reg.2
Reg.22C, added: SI 2009/3229 Reg.2
Reg.22D, added: SI 2009/3229 Reg.2
Reg.24, amended: SI 2009/604 Reg.2
Reg.24, applied: SI 2009/609 Reg.3
Reg.24, revoked (in part): SI 2009/604 Reg.2
Reg.26B, amended: SI 2009/3229 Reg.2
Reg.26BA, added: SI 2009/3229 Reg.2
Reg.32B, amended: SI 2009/1490 Reg.2
Reg.33, applied: SI 2009/2997 Reg.13
Reg.34A, applied: SI 2009/609 Reg.2, Reg.3
Reg.34B, applied: SI 2009/609 Reg.2, Reg.3
Reg.35, applied: SI 2009/609 Reg.2, Reg.3
Reg.36, amended: SI 2009/1488 Reg.6
Sch.2, see *Leicester City Council, Re* [2009] UKUT 155 (AAC), [2009] R.V.R. 306 (UT (AAC)), Edward Jacobs
Sch.6 para.5, amended: SI 2009/3229 Reg.2
Sch.6 para.6, revoked: SI 2009/604 Reg.2
Sch.7 para.1, applied: SI 2009/609 Reg.3
Sch.7 para.2, amended: SI 2009/604 Reg.2
Sch.7 para.2ZA, added: SI 2009/604 Reg.2
Sch.7 para.2ZA, applied: SI 2009/609 Reg.2
Sch.7 para.3, applied: SI 2009/609 Reg.3
Sch.9 para.4, amended: SI 2009/607 Reg.5
Sch.9 para.4A, amended: SI 2009/1490 Reg.2
Sch.9 para.4A, revoked (in part): SI 2009/1490 Reg.2
Sch.9A para.7, amended: SI 2009/583 Reg.3
2023. Insolvent Companies (Disqualification of Unfit Directors) Proceedings Rules 1987
varied: SI 2009/317 Sch.1
2024. Non-Contentious Probate Rules 1987
r.2, amended: SI 2009/3348 Art.7
r.32, amended: SI 2009/1893 r.3
2048. Charities (Northern Ireland) Order 1987
amended: SI 2009/1941 Sch.1 para.92
applied: SI 2009/1941 Art.6
revoked (in part): SI 2009/1941 Sch.1 para.92
2088. Registration of Births and Deaths Regulations 1987
Reg.2, amended: SI 2009/2165 Reg.2
Reg.3, amended: SI 2009/2165 Reg.3
Reg.6, amended: SI 2009/2165 Reg.4
Reg.7, amended: SI 2009/2165 Reg.5
Reg.8, substituted: SI 2009/2165 Reg.6

1987– cont.

2088. Registration of Births and Deaths Regulations 1987– *cont.*
Reg.9, amended: SI 2009/2165 Reg.7
Reg.10, amended: SI 2009/2165 Reg.8
Reg.13, amended: SI 2009/2165 Reg.9
Reg.16, substituted: SI 2009/2165 Reg.10
Reg.17, substituted: SI 2009/2165 Reg.11
Reg.18, substituted: SI 2009/2165 Reg.12
Reg.19, amended: SI 2009/2165 Reg.13
Reg.20, substituted: SI 2009/2165 Reg.14
Reg.21, amended: SI 2009/2165 Reg.15
Reg.22, amended: SI 2009/2165 Reg.16
Reg.23, amended: SI 2009/2165 Reg.17
Reg.26, amended: SI 2009/2165 Reg.18
Reg.34A, amended: SI 2009/2165 Reg.19
Reg.42, amended: SI 2009/2165 Reg.20
Reg.55, amended: SI 2009/2165 Reg.21
Reg.56, amended: SI 2009/2165 Reg.22
Reg.63, amended: SI 2009/2165 Reg.23
Sch.2, amended: SI 2009/2165 Sch.1
2089. Registration of Births and Deaths (Welsh Language) Regulations 1987
Sch.2, amended: SI 2009/2165 Sch.2
Sch.3, amended: SI 2009/2165 Sch.3
2174. General Medical Council Health Committee (Procedure) Rules Order of Council 1987
referred to: SI 2009/500 Sch.2 Part 2
2197. Civil Jurisdiction (Offshore Activities) Order 1987
Art.1, applied: SI 2009/515 Reg.17
Art.1, referred to: SI 2009/2813 Sch.1, SI 2009/2814 Sch.1 para.22
2199. Cayman Islands (Constitution) (Amendment) Order 1987
revoked: SI 2009/1379 Sch.1
2203. Adoption (Northern Ireland) Order 1987
amended: 2009 c.3 Sch.4 para.21
Art.9, see *P (A Child) (Adoption: Unmarried Couples), Re* [2008] UKHL 38, [2009] 1 A.C. 173 (HL (NI)), Lord Hoffmann
Art.14, see *P (A Child) (Adoption: Unmarried Couples), Re* [2008] UKHL 38, [2009] 1 A.C. 173 (HL (NI)), Lord Hoffmann
Sch.1, amended: 2009 c.3 Sch.4 para.21
2229. Aerodromes (Designation) (Detention and Sale of Aircraft) (No.2) Order 1987
revoked (in part): SI 2009/2350 Sch.2
2244. Secretary of State's Traffic Orders (Procedure) (Scotland) Regulations 1987
Part II, applied: SSI 2009/13, SSI 2009/14, SSI 2009/15, SSI 2009/46, SSI 2009/79, SSI 2009/84, SSI 2009/95, SSI 2009/111, SSI 2009/146, SSI 2009/148, SSI 2009/149, SSI 2009/204, SSI 2009/239, SSI 2009/241

1988

93. Department of Trade and Industry (Fees) Order 1988
Art.5, applied: SI 2009/2089
Art.7, applied: SI 2009/2089
Sch.1 Part II, applied: SI 2009/2089
Sch.1 Part IV, applied: SI 2009/2089
Sch.2 Part I, applied: SI 2009/2089
Sch.2 Part II, applied: SI 2009/2089
120. Capacity Serving Measures (Intoxicating Liquor) Regulations 1988
Reg.10, amended: SI 2009/3045 Reg.3

1988– cont.

186. Measuring Instruments (EEC Requirements) Regulations 1988
referred to: SI 2009/669 Sch.1 Part 4

296. Measuring Instruments (EEC Requirements) (Gas Volume Meters) Regulations 1988
referred to: SI 2009/669 Sch.1 Part 4

370. International Carriage of Dangerous Goods by Road (Fees) Regulations 1988
Reg.3, amended: SI 2009/856 Reg.2
Reg.3A, amended: SI 2009/856 Reg.2
Reg.4, amended: SI 2009/856 Reg.2
Reg.5, amended: SI 2009/856 Reg.2
Reg.6, amended: SI 2009/856 Reg.2

371. International Transport of Goods under Cover of TIR Carnets (Fees) Regulations 1988
Reg.3, amended: SI 2009/861 Reg.2
Reg.4, amended: SI 2009/861 Reg.2
Reg.5, amended: SI 2009/861 Reg.2

559. Crofting Counties Agricultural Grants (Scotland) Scheme 1988
Art.8, applied: SSI 2009/376 Sch.1 para.26
Art.12B, applied: SSI 2009/376 Sch.1 para.26

629. Land Registration (Official Searches) Rules 1988
referred to: SI 2009/500 Sch.1 Part 2

643. Department of Transport (Fees) Order 1988
applied: SI 2009/718, SI 2009/855, SI 2009/856, SI 2009/866, SI 2009/879
referred to: SI 2009/643, SI 2009/844
Sch.1, amended: SI 2009/711 Art.10
Sch.2 para.1, amended: SI 2009/1885 Sch.2 para.1

646. Banking Act 1987 (Exempt Transactions) Regulations 1988
referred to: SI 2009/500 Sch.2 Part 2

664. Social Security (Payments on account, Overpayments and Recovery) Regulations 1988
Reg.20, applied: SI 2009/470 Reg.51

665. Land Registration Fee Order 1988
referred to: SI 2009/500 Sch.1 Part 2

668. Pneumoconiosis etc (Workers Compensation) (Payment of Claims) Regulations 1988
Reg.5, amended: SI 2009/747 Reg.2
Reg.6, amended: SI 2009/747 Reg.2
Reg.8, amended: SI 2009/747 Reg.2
Sch.1 Part 1, substituted: SI 2009/747 Sch.1
Sch.1 Part 2, substituted: SI 2009/747 Sch.1

895. Weights and Measures (Knitting Yarns) Order 1988
Art.2, amended: SI 2009/663 Reg.3
Art.3, amended: SI 2009/663 Reg.3

913. Magistrates Courts (Children and Young Persons) Rules 1988
referred to: SI 2009/500 Sch.1 Part 2

1213. Petroleum (Production) (Seaward Areas) Regulations 1988
Reg.5, amended: SI 2009/229 Sch.2 para.7
Reg.7, amended: SI 2009/229 Sch.2 para.7
Reg.9, amended: SI 2009/3283 Reg.2
Sch.3, amended: SI 2009/229 Sch.2 para.7

1291. Farm Woodland Scheme 1988
applied: SSI 2009/376 Sch.1 para.14

1418. Judicial Pensions (Preservation of Benefits) Order 1988
Sch.1, amended: SI 2009/1307 Sch.2 para.30

1420. Judicial Pensions (Requisite Benefits) Order 1988
Sch.1, amended: SI 2009/1307 Sch.2 para.31

1988– cont.

1478. Goods Vehicles (Plating and Testing) Regulations 1988
Reg.12, amended: SI 2009/799 Reg.3, Reg.6
Reg.12, revoked (in part): SI 2009/799 Reg.3
Reg.16, amended: SI 2009/799 Reg.4, Reg.6, SI 2009/3220 Reg.17
Reg.16, revoked (in part): SI 2009/799 Reg.4
Reg.25, amended: SI 2009/799 Reg.6
Reg.34, amended: SI 2009/799 Reg.5, Reg.6
Reg.37B, amended: SI 2009/799 Reg.6
Reg.41, amended: SI 2009/799 Reg.6
Sch.3 Part I para.2, amended: SI 2009/3220 Reg.17

1695. Criminal Justice Act 1987 (Dismissal of Transferred Charges) Rules 1988
referred to: SI 2009/500 Sch.1 Part 2

1699. Criminal Justice Act 1987 (Preparatory Hearings) Rules 1988
referred to: SI 2009/500 Sch.1 Part 2

1700. Criminal Justice Act 1987 (Preparatory Hearings) (Interlocutory Appeals) Rules 1988
referred to: SI 2009/500 Sch.1 Part 2

1724. Social Fund Cold Weather Payments (General) Regulations 1988
Reg.3, varied: SI 2009/2649 Reg.3
Sch.1, substituted: SI 2009/2649 Sch.1
Sch.2, substituted: SI 2009/2649 Sch.2

1842. St Helena Constitution Order 1988
applied: SI 2009/3204 Art.4
revoked: SI 2009/1751 Art.3

1847. Criminal Justice (Evidence, Etc.) (Northern Ireland) Order 1988
amended: 2009 c.25 s.69
applied: 2009 asp 9 Sch.1 para.9, SI 2009/1547 Sch.3 para.3, SSI 2009/182 Sch.1 para.18
referred to: SI 2009/37 Sch.1 para.2, Sch.1 para.4

1852. Scotch Whisky (Northern Ireland) Order 1988
revoked: SI 2009/2890 Reg.2

2013. Act of Sederunt (Proceedings in the Sheriff Court under the Debtors (Scotland) Act 1987) 1988
Part VA r.69A, added: SSI 2009/107 r.2
Part VA r.69B, added: SSI 2009/107 r.2
Part VA r.69C, added: SSI 2009/107 r.2
Part VA r.69D, added: SSI 2009/107 r.2
Part VA r.69E, added: SSI 2009/107 r.2
Part VA r.69E, amended: SSI 2009/294 r.13
Part VA r.69F, added: SSI 2009/107 r.2
Part VA r.69G, added: SSI 2009/107 r.2
Sch.1, amended: SSI 2009/107 Sch.1, SSI 2009/294 r.8, r.9

2039. Weights and Measures (Intoxicating Liquor) Order 1988
Art.1, amended: SI 2009/663 Reg.4
Art.3A, added: SI 2009/663 Reg.4
Art.4, revoked: SI 2009/663 Reg.4
Art.7, amended: SI 2009/663 Reg.4
Sch.A1, added: SI 2009/663 Sch.1
Sch.1 Part I, amended: SI 2009/663 Reg.4
Sch.1 Part II, amended: SI 2009/663 Reg.4
Sch.1 Part III, amended: SI 2009/663 Reg.4

2040. Weights and Measures (Miscellaneous Foods) Order 1988
Art.3, amended: SI 2009/663 Reg.5
Art.6, amended: SI 2009/663 Reg.5
Art.11, revoked (in part): SI 2009/663 Reg.5

2050. Distress for Rent Rules 1988
Appendix 2, added: SI 2009/873 r.5
Appendix 2, amended: SI 2009/873 r.5

1988– cont.

2050. Distress for Rent Rules 1988– *cont.*
Appendix 2, revoked: SI 2009/ 873 r.5
Appendix 3, amended: SI 2009/ 873 r.6
r.4, amended: SI 2009/ 873 r.3
r.13, amended: SI 2009/ 873 r.4

2075. Falmouth and Truro Port Health Authority Order 1988
Art.1, amended: SI 2009/ 837 Art.17
Art.2, revoked: SI 2009/ 837 Art.17
Art.3, amended: SI 2009/ 837 Art.17
Art.3, revoked (in part): SI 2009/ 837 Art.17
Art.4, revoked: SI 2009/ 837 Art.17
Art.6, revoked: SI 2009/ 837 Art.17
Art.7, amended: SI 2009/ 837 Art.17
Art.8, amended: SI 2009/ 837 Art.17
Art.9, revoked: SI 2009/ 837 Art.17
Art.10, revoked: SI 2009/ 837 Art.17

2256. Church of England Pensions Regulations 1988
Reg.17, amended: SI 2009/ 2109 Reg.2

1989

19. Criminal Appeal (Reviews of Sentencing) Rules 1989
referred to: SI 2009/ 500 Sch.1 Part 2

28. Financial Services Act 1986 (Single Property Schemes) (Exemption) Regulations 1989
referred to: SI 2009/ 500 Sch.1 Part 2

155. St Helena Constitution Order 1989
revoked: SI 2009/ 1751 Art.3

193. Town and Country Planning (Fees for Applications and Deemed Applications) Regulations 1989
Reg.10A, amended: SI 2009/ 851 Reg.2
Reg.11A, amended: SI 2009/ 851 Reg.2
Sch.1 Part I para.4, amended: SI 2009/ 851 Reg.2
Sch.1 Part I para.6, amended: SI 2009/ 851 Reg.2
Sch.1 Part I para.7, amended: SI 2009/ 851 Reg.2
Sch.1 Part I para.7A, amended: SI 2009/ 851 Reg.2
Sch.1 Part I para.7B, amended: SI 2009/ 851 Reg.2
Sch.1 Part I para.15, amended: SI 2009/ 851 Reg.2
Sch.1 Part II, referred to: SI 2009/ 851 Reg.2
Sch.1 Part II, substituted: SI 2009/ 851 Sch.1
Sch.2, referred to: SI 2009/ 851 Reg.2
Sch.2, substituted: SI 2009/ 851 Sch.2

306. National Health Service (Charges to Overseas Visitors) Regulations 1989
see *R. (on the application of A) v Secretary of State for Health* [2009] EWCA Civ 225, (2009) 12 C.C.L. Rep. 213 (CA (Civ Div)), Ward, L.J.
Reg.1, amended: SI 2009/ 1824 Sch.1 para.2
Reg.2, amended: SI 2009/ 1824 Sch.1 para.2
Reg.4, amended: SI 2009/ 1512 Reg.2, SI 2009/ 1824 Sch.1 para.2
Reg.8, amended: SI 2009/ 1824 Sch.1 para.2
Sch.1 Part IV, amended: SI 2009/ 1166 Reg.3, SI 2009/ 1175 Reg.3
Sch.2, amended: SI 2009/ 1512 Reg.3, SI 2009/ 3005 Reg.2

339. Civil Legal Aid (General) Regulations 1989
Reg.100, see *Legal Services Commission v Thipthorpe* [2009] B.P.I.R. 1399 (CC (Chelmsford)), Judge Murfitt
Reg.105, see *Legal Services Commission v Thipthorpe* [2009] B.P.I.R. 1399 (CC (Chelmsford)), Judge Murfitt

340. Legal Advice and Assistance Regulations 1989
Reg.3, amended: SI 2009/ 2054 Sch.1 para.10
Reg.3, applied: SI 2009/ 2054 Sch.2 para.6

1989– cont.

341. Legal Advice and Assistance (Duty Solicitor) (Remuneration) Regulations 1989
referred to: SI 2009/ 500 Sch.1 Part 2

342. Legal Advice and Assistance at Police Stations (Remuneration) Regulations 1989
referred to: SI 2009/ 500 Sch.1 Part 2

343. Legal Aid in Criminal and Care Proceedings (Costs) Regulations 1989
referred to: SI 2009/ 500 Sch.1 Part 2

344. Legal Aid in Criminal and Care Proceedings (General) Regulations 1989
referred to: SI 2009/ 500 Sch.1 Part 2

364. National Health Service (Charges to Overseas Visitors) (Scotland) Regulations 1989
Sch.1, amended: SSI 2009/ 177 Reg.4

438. Community Charges (Administration and Enforcement) Regulations 1989
applied: SI 2009/ 470 Reg.51

439. Valuation and Community Charge Tribunals Regulations 1989
varied: SI 2009/ 2271 Reg.3
Part IV, applied: SI 2009/ 2271 Reg.4
Reg.1, varied: SI 2009/ 2271 Sch.1 Part 1, Sch.1 Part 2
Reg.1A, revoked (in part): SI 2009/ 2271 Reg.3
Reg.2, revoked (in part): SI 2009/ 2271 Reg.3
Reg.2, varied: SI 2009/ 2271 Sch.1 Part 2
Reg.3, revoked (in part): SI 2009/ 2271 Reg.3
Reg.4, revoked (in part): SI 2009/ 2271 Reg.3
Reg.5, revoked (in part): SI 2009/ 2271 Reg.3
Reg.6, revoked (in part): SI 2009/ 2271 Reg.3
Reg.7, revoked (in part): SI 2009/ 2271 Reg.3
Reg.8, revoked (in part): SI 2009/ 2271 Reg.3
Reg.9, revoked (in part): SI 2009/ 2271 Reg.3
Reg.10, revoked (in part): SI 2009/ 2271 Reg.3
Reg.11, revoked (in part): SI 2009/ 2271 Reg.3
Reg.12, revoked (in part): SI 2009/ 2271 Reg.3
Reg.13, revoked (in part): SI 2009/ 2271 Reg.3
Reg.14, revoked (in part): SI 2009/ 2271 Reg.3
Reg.15, varied: SI 2009/ 2271 Sch.1 Part 1, Sch.1 Part 2
Reg.16, varied: SI 2009/ 2271 Sch.1 Part 1, Sch.1 Part 2
Reg.17, varied: SI 2009/ 2271 Sch.1 Part 1, Sch.1 Part 2
Reg.18, applied: SI 2009/ 2271 Reg.4
Reg.18, varied: SI 2009/ 2271 Sch.1 Part 1, Sch.1 Part 2
Reg.19, varied: SI 2009/ 2271 Sch.1 Part 1, Sch.1 Part 2
Reg.20, varied: SI 2009/ 2271 Sch.1 Part 1, Sch.1 Part 2
Reg.21, varied: SI 2009/ 2271 Sch.1 Part 1, Sch.1 Part 2
Reg.22, varied: SI 2009/ 2271 Sch.1 Part 1, Sch.1 Part 2
Reg.23, varied: SI 2009/ 2271 Sch.1 Part 1, Sch.1 Part 2
Reg.24, varied: SI 2009/ 2271 Sch.1 Part 1, Sch.1 Part 2
Reg.25, varied: SI 2009/ 2271 Sch.1 Part 1, Sch.1 Part 2
Reg.26, varied: SI 2009/ 2271 Sch.1 Part 1, Sch.1 Part 2
Reg.27, varied: SI 2009/ 2271 Sch.1 Part 2
Reg.28, varied: SI 2009/ 2271 Sch.1 Part 1, Sch.1 Part 2
Reg.29, varied: SI 2009/ 2271 Sch.1 Part 1, Sch.1 Part 2
Reg.30, varied: SI 2009/ 2271 Sch.1 Part 1, Sch.1 Part 2
Reg.31, amended: SI 2009/ 1307 Sch.2 para.33
Reg.31, applied: SI 2009/ 2271 Reg.4
Reg.31, varied: SI 2009/ 2271 Sch.1 Part 1, Sch.1 Part 2
Reg.32, varied: SI 2009/ 2271 Sch.1 Part 1, Sch.1 Part 2
Reg.33, varied: SI 2009/ 2271 Sch.1 Part 1, Sch.1 Part 2
Reg.34, revoked (in part): SI 2009/ 2271 Reg.3
Reg.35, revoked (in part): SI 2009/ 2271 Reg.3
Reg.36, revoked (in part): SI 2009/ 2271 Reg.3
Reg.37, revoked (in part): SI 2009/ 2271 Reg.3
Reg.38, revoked (in part): SI 2009/ 2271 Reg.3
Reg.39, revoked (in part): SI 2009/ 2271 Reg.3
Reg.40, revoked (in part): SI 2009/ 2271 Reg.3

1989–cont.

439. Valuation and Community Charge Tribunals Regulations 1989–*cont.*
Reg.41, revoked (in part): SI 2009/2271 Reg.3
Reg.42, revoked (in part): SI 2009/2271 Reg.3
Reg.43, revoked (in part): SI 2009/2271 Reg.3
Reg.44, revoked (in part): SI 2009/2271 Reg.3
Reg.45, revoked (in part): SI 2009/2271 Reg.3
Reg.46, revoked (in part): SI 2009/2271 Reg.3
Reg.47, revoked (in part): SI 2009/2271 Reg.3
Reg.48, revoked (in part): SI 2009/2271 Reg.3
Reg.49, amended: SI 2009/1307 Sch.2 para.34
Reg.49, revoked (in part): SI 2009/2271 Reg.3
Reg.50, revoked (in part): SI 2009/2271 Reg.3
Reg.51, revoked (in part): SI 2009/2271 Reg.3
Reg.51, see *R. (on the application of Fayad) v London South East Valuation Tribunal* [2008] EWHC 2531 (Admin), [2009] R.A. 157 (QBD (Admin)), Neil Garnham Q.C.; see *R. (on the application of Kinsley) v Barnet Magistrates Court* [2009] EWHC 464 (Admin), [2009] R.V.R. 133 (QBD (Admin)), Judge Raynor Q.C.
Reg.52, revoked (in part): SI 2009/2271 Reg.3
Sch.1, amended: SI 2009/119 Art.4, Art.7
Sch.1, revoked (in part): SI 2009/2271 Reg.3
Sch.2 para.1, revoked (in part): SI 2009/2271 Reg.3
Sch.2 para.2, revoked (in part): SI 2009/2271 Reg.3
Sch.2 para.3, revoked (in part): SI 2009/2271 Reg.3
Sch.2 para.4, revoked (in part): SI 2009/2271 Reg.3
Sch.2 para.5, revoked (in part): SI 2009/2271 Reg.3
Sch.2 para.6, revoked (in part): SI 2009/2271 Reg.3
Sch.3, revoked (in part): SI 2009/2271 Reg.3
Sch.4, revoked (in part): SI 2009/2271 Reg.3

550. Legal Advice and Assistance (Scope) Regulations 1989
referred to: SI 2009/500 Sch.1 Part 2

638. European Economic Interest Grouping Regulations 1989
Reg.1, amended: SI 2009/2399 Reg.4
Reg.2, amended: SI 2009/2399 Reg.5
Reg.3, amended: SI 2009/2399 Reg.6
Reg.4, amended: SI 2009/2399 Reg.7
Reg.5, amended: SI 2009/2399 Reg.8
Reg.5, revoked (in part): SI 2009/2399 Reg.8
Reg.6, amended: SI 2009/2399 Reg.9
Reg.7, amended: SI 2009/2399 Reg.10
Reg.8, amended: SI 2009/2399 Reg.11
Reg.9, amended: SI 2009/2399 Reg.12
Reg.9, applied: SI 2009/2403 Sch.1 para.5
Reg.10, amended: SI 2009/2399 Reg.13
Reg.11, amended: SI 2009/2399 Reg.14
Reg.11, applied: SI 2009/2403 Sch.1 para.5
Reg.11, revoked (in part): SI 2009/2399 Reg.14
Reg.12, amended: SI 2009/2399 Reg.15
Reg.12, applied: SI 2009/2403 Sch.1 para.5
Reg.12A, added: SI 2009/2399 Reg.16
Reg.13, amended: SI 2009/2399 Reg.17
Reg.17, revoked: SI 2009/2399 Reg.18
Reg.18, amended: SI 2009/2399 Reg.19
Reg.19, amended: SI 2009/2399 Reg.20
Reg.20, amended: SI 2009/2399 Reg.21
Sch.2, substituted: SI 2009/2399 Sch.1
Sch.4 Part 1 para.1, revoked: SI 2009/2399 Reg.23
Sch.4 Part 1 para.2, revoked: SI 2009/2399 Reg.23
Sch.4 Part 1 para.3, revoked: SI 2009/2399 Reg.23
Sch.4 Part 1 para.4, revoked: SI 2009/2399 Reg.23
Sch.4 Part 1 para.5, amended: SI 2009/2399 Reg.23
Sch.4 Part 1 para.8, amended: SI 2009/2399 Reg.23

1989–cont.

638. European Economic Interest Grouping Regulations 1989–*cont.*
Sch.4 Part 1 para.10, amended: SI 2009/2399 Reg.23
Sch.4 Part 1 para.14, revoked: SI 2009/2399 Reg.23
Sch.4 Part 1 para.15, revoked: SI 2009/2399 Reg.23
Sch.4 Part 1 para.16, revoked: SI 2009/2399 Reg.23
Sch.4 Part 1 para.17, revoked: SI 2009/2399 Reg.23
Sch.4 Part 1 para.18, revoked: SI 2009/2399 Reg.23
Sch.4 Part 1 para.19, revoked: SI 2009/2399 Reg.23
Sch.4 Part 1 para.20, revoked: SI 2009/2399 Reg.23
Sch.4 Part 1 para.21, revoked: SI 2009/2399 Reg.23
Sch.4 Part 1 para.22, revoked: SI 2009/2399 Reg.23
Sch.4 Part 1 para.23, revoked: SI 2009/2399 Reg.23
Sch.4 Part 1 para.26, applied: SI 2009/2403 Sch.1 para.5
Sch.4 Part 2 para.1, substituted: SI 2009/2399 Reg.23
Sch.4 Part 2 para.2, substituted: SI 2009/2399 Reg.23

682. Health and Safety Information for Employees Regulations 1989
Reg.3, amended: SI 2009/606 Reg.2
Reg.5, amended: SI 2009/606 Reg.2

878. Tuberculosis (Deer) Order 1989
Art.2, amended: SI 2009/2713 Art.2
Art.4, amended: SI 2009/2713 Art.2
Art.5, amended: SI 2009/2713 Art.2
Art.7, amended: SI 2009/2713 Art.2

888. Smoke Control Areas (Exempted Fireplaces) (Scotland) Order 1989
revoked: SSI 2009/214 Sch.2

1058. Non-Domestic Rating (Collection and Enforcement) (Local Lists) Regulations 1989
Reg.1, amended: SI 2009/2706 Art.3
Reg.2, amended: SI 2009/2706 Art.4
Reg.4, see *JJB Sports Plc v Telford and Wrekin BC* [2008] EWHC 2870 (Admin), [2009] R.A. 33 (QBD (Admin)), Timothy Brennan Q.C.; see *R. (on the application of Waltham Forest LBC) v Waltham Forest Magistrates Court* [2008] EWHC 3579 (Admin), [2009] R.A. 181 (QBD (Admin)), David Holgate QC
Reg.5, see *JJB Sports Plc v Telford and Wrekin BC* [2008] EWHC 2870 (Admin), [2009] R.A. 33 (QBD (Admin)), Timothy Brennan Q.C.; see *R. (on the application of Waltham Forest LBC) v Waltham Forest Magistrates Court* [2008] EWHC 3579 (Admin), [2009] R.A. 181 (QBD (Admin)), David Holgate QC
Reg.7A, added: SI 2009/204 Reg.2, SI 2009/461 Reg.2
Reg.7B, added: SI 2009/1597 Reg.2
Reg.7C, added: SI 2009/2154 Reg.2
Sch.1C, added: SI 2009/1597 Sch.2
Sch.1A para.1, added: SI 2009/204 Sch.1, SI 2009/461 Sch.1
Sch.1A para.2, added: SI 2009/204 Sch.1, SI 2009/461 Sch.1
Sch.1A para.3, added: SI 2009/204 Sch.1, SI 2009/461 Sch.1
Sch.1A para.4, added: SI 2009/204 Sch.1, SI 2009/461 Sch.1
Sch.1A para.5, added: SI 2009/204 Sch.1, SI 2009/461 Sch.1
Sch.1A para.6, added: SI 2009/204 Sch.1, SI 2009/461 Sch.1
Sch.1A para.7, added: SI 2009/204 Sch.1, SI 2009/461 Sch.1

1058. Non-Domestic Rating (Collection and Enforcement) (Local Lists) Regulations 1989–*cont.*
Sch.1A para.8, added: SI 2009/204 Sch.1, SI 2009/461 Sch.1
Sch.1A para.9, added: SI 2009/204 Sch.1, SI 2009/461 Sch.1
Sch.1A para.10, added: SI 2009/204 Sch.1, SI 2009/461 Sch.1
Sch.1A para.11, added: SI 2009/204 Sch.1, SI 2009/461 Sch.1
Sch.1A para.12, added: SI 2009/204 Sch.1, SI 2009/461 Sch.1
Sch.1A para.13, added: SI 2009/204 Sch.1, SI 2009/461 Sch.1
Sch.1A para.14, added: SI 2009/204 Sch.1, SI 2009/461 Sch.1
Sch.1A para.15, added: SI 2009/204 Sch.1, SI 2009/461 Sch.1
Sch.1A para.16, added: SI 2009/204 Sch.1, SI 2009/461 Sch.1
Sch.1A para.17, added: SI 2009/204 Sch.1, SI 2009/461 Sch.1
Sch.1A para.18, added: SI 2009/204 Sch.1, SI 2009/461 Sch.1
Sch.1A para.19, added: SI 2009/204 Sch.1, SI 2009/461 Sch.1
Sch.1A para.20, added: SI 2009/204 Sch.1, SI 2009/461 Sch.1
Sch.1A para.21, added: SI 2009/204 Sch.1, SI 2009/461 Sch.1
Sch.1A para.22, added: SI 2009/204 Sch.1, SI 2009/461 Sch.1
Sch.1B para.1, added: SI 2009/1597 Sch.1
Sch.1B para.2, added: SI 2009/1597 Sch.1
Sch.1B para.3, added: SI 2009/1597 Sch.1
Sch.1B para.4, added: SI 2009/1597 Sch.1
Sch.1B para.5, added: SI 2009/1597 Sch.1
Sch.1B para.6, added: SI 2009/1597 Sch.1
Sch.1B para.7, added: SI 2009/1597 Sch.1
Sch.1B para.8, added: SI 2009/1597 Sch.1
Sch.1B para.9, added: SI 2009/1597 Sch.1
Sch.1B para.10, added: SI 2009/1597 Sch.1
Sch.1B para.11, added: SI 2009/1597 Sch.1
Sch.1B para.12, added: SI 2009/1597 Sch.1
Sch.1B para.13, added: SI 2009/1597 Sch.1
Sch.1B para.14, added: SI 2009/1597 Sch.1
Sch.1B para.15, added: SI 2009/1597 Sch.1
Sch.1B para.16, added: SI 2009/1597 Sch.1
Sch.1B para.17, added: SI 2009/1597 Sch.1
Sch.1B para.18, added: SI 2009/1597 Sch.1
Sch.1B para.19, added: SI 2009/1597 Sch.1
Sch.1B para.20, added: SI 2009/1597 Sch.1
Sch.1B para.21, added: SI 2009/1597 Sch.1
Sch.1B para.22, added: SI 2009/1597 Sch.1
Sch.1B para.23, added: SI 2009/1597 Sch.1
Sch.1D para.1, added: SI 2009/2154 Sch.1
Sch.1D para.2, added: SI 2009/2154 Sch.1
Sch.1D para.3, added: SI 2009/2154 Sch.1
Sch.1D para.4, added: SI 2009/2154 Sch.1
Sch.1D para.5, added: SI 2009/2154 Sch.1
Sch.1D para.6, added: SI 2009/2154 Sch.1
Sch.1D para.7, added: SI 2009/2154 Sch.1
Sch.1D para.8, added: SI 2009/2154 Sch.1
Sch.1D para.9, added: SI 2009/2154 Sch.1
Sch.1D para.10, added: SI 2009/2154 Sch.1
Sch.1D para.11, added: SI 2009/2154 Sch.1
Sch.1D para.12, added: SI 2009/2154 Sch.1
Sch.1D para.13, added: SI 2009/2154 Sch.1
Sch.1D para.14, added: SI 2009/2154 Sch.1

1060. Non-Domestic Rating (Miscellaneous Provisions) Regulations 1989
Reg.3, amended: SI 2009/1307 Sch.2 para.35
1130. Design Right (Proceedings before Comptroller) Rules 1989
r.6, amended: SI 2009/3348 Art.8
r.23, amended: SI 2009/546 r.3
Sch.1, amended: SI 2009/546 r.4
1263. Sludge (Use in Agriculture) Regulations 1989
Reg.2, applied: SSI 2009/266 Sch.1 para.2
1297. Taxes (Interest Rate) Regulations 1989
Reg.2, amended: SI 2009/2032 Reg.3
Reg.2A, revoked: SI 2009/2032 Reg.4
Reg.3A, amended: SI 2009/2032 Reg.8
Reg.3AA, amended: SI 2009/2032 Reg.5
Reg.3AA, revoked (in part): SI 2009/2032 Reg.5
Reg.3AAA, added: SI 2009/2032 Reg.6
Reg.3AB, amended: SI 2009/2032 Reg.7
Reg.3B, amended: SI 2009/2032 Reg.9
Reg.3BA, amended: SI 2009/2032 Reg.10
Reg.3BB, amended: SI 2009/2032 Reg.11
Reg.4, amended: SI 2009/2032 Reg.12
Reg.4A, added: SI 2009/2032 Reg.13
Reg.5, amended: SI 2009/199 Reg.2
Reg.6, amended: SI 2009/2032 Reg.14
1339. Limitation (Northern Ireland) Order 1989
applied: SI 2009/1941 Art.11
Art.4, referred to: SI 2009/1941 Art.11
Art.4, revoked (in part): SI 2009/1941 Sch.1 para.105
Art.15, referred to: SI 2009/1941 Art.11
Art.15, revoked (in part): SI 2009/1941 Sch.1 para.105
Art.72A, amended: 2009 c.26 s.62
Art.72B, amended: 2009 c.26 s.62
Art.72C, added: 2009 c.25 s.171
Art.72C, applied: 2009 c.25 s.163
1341. Police and Criminal Evidence (Northern Ireland) Order 1989
applied: 2009 c.11 s.22, s.23, 2009 c.1 s.194
see *C's Application for Judicial Review, Re* [2009] UKHL 15, [2009] 1 A.C. 908 (HL (NI)), Lord Phillips of Worth Matravers
Art.37, amended: 2009 c.26 Sch.7 para.124, Sch.8 Part 13
Art.37, revoked (in part): 2009 c.26 Sch.7 para.124, Sch.8 Part 13
Art.40, amended: 2009 c.26 Sch.7 para.124
Art.40, revoked (in part): 2009 c.26 Sch.7 para.124, Sch.8 Part 13
Art.61, revoked (in part): 2009 c.26 Sch.7 para.128, Sch.8 Part 13
Art.63, revoked (in part): 2009 c.26 Sch.7 para.128, Sch.8 Part 13
Art.70, varied: SI 2009/1059 Sch.1 para.31
Art.71, amended: 2009 c.25 Sch.17 para.16
Art.72, amended: 2009 c.25 Sch.17 para.17
Art.73, amended: 2009 c.25 Sch.17 para.18
Art.85, applied: 2009 c.11 s.23
1355. Cider and Perry Regulations 1989
disapplied: SI 2009/1022 Art.3
Reg.11, see *DCC Realisations Ltd (In Liquidation) (formerly the Devon Cider Co Ltd), Re* [2009] EWHC 316 (Comm), [2009] S.T.C. 1390 (Ch D (Companies Ct)), David Donaldson Q.C.
Reg.13, see *DCC Realisations Ltd (In Liquidation) (formerly the Devon Cider Co Ltd), Re* [2009] EWHC 316 (Comm), [2009] S.T.C. 1390 (Ch D (Companies Ct)), David Donaldson Q.C.

1989– cont.

1356. Wine and Made-wine Regulations 1989
disapplied: SI 2009/ 1022 Art.3
1401. Fire Precautions (Sub-surface Railway Stations) Regulations 1989
revoked (in part): SI 2009/ 782 Reg.13
1490. Civil Legal Aid (Scotland) (Fees) Regulations 1989
applied: SSI 2009/ 312 Reg.9
Reg.2, amended: SSI 2009/ 312 Reg.3
Reg.5, amended: SSI 2009/ 203 Reg.4, Reg.5, SSI 2009/ 312 Reg.3
Reg.10, amended: SSI 2009/ 312 Reg.3
Reg.12A, amended: SSI 2009/ 312 Reg.3
Sch.2, referred to: SSI 2009/ 203 Reg.2
Sch.2 para.2, substituted: SSI 2009/ 203 Reg.6
Sch.2 Part 2, substituted: SSI 2009/ 203 Sch.1
Sch.5, amended: SSI 2009/ 203 Reg.7
Sch.6, referred to: SSI 2009/ 203 Reg.2
Sch.6 Part I, amended: SSI 2009/ 203 Reg.8
Sch.6 Part II, amended: SSI 2009/ 203 Reg.8
Sch.6 Part II para.1, amended: SSI 2009/ 203 Reg.8
Sch.6 Part II para.1, substituted: SSI 2009/ 203 Reg.8
Sch.6 Part II para.2, amended: SSI 2009/ 203 Reg.8
Sch.6 Part II para.2, substituted: SSI 2009/ 203 Reg.8
Sch.6 Part II para.3, amended: SSI 2009/ 203 Reg.8
Sch.6 Part II para.4, amended: SSI 2009/ 203 Reg.8
Sch.6 Part II para.5, amended: SSI 2009/ 203 Reg.8
Sch.6 Part II para.6, amended: SSI 2009/ 203 Reg.8
Sch.6 Part II para.7, amended: SSI 2009/ 203 Reg.8
Sch.6 Part II para.7A, amended: SSI 2009/ 203 Reg.8
Sch.6 Part II para.8, amended: SSI 2009/ 203 Reg.8
Sch.6 Part II para.9, amended: SSI 2009/ 203 Reg.8
Sch.6 Part II para.10, amended: SSI 2009/ 203 Reg.8
Sch.6 Part II para.11, amended: SSI 2009/ 203 Reg.8
Sch.6 Part II para.12, amended: SSI 2009/ 203 Reg.8
Sch.6 Part II para.13, amended: SSI 2009/ 203 Reg.8
Sch.6 Part II para.14, amended: SSI 2009/ 203 Reg.8
Sch.6 Part II para.14A, amended: SSI 2009/ 203 Reg.8
Sch.6 Part II para.14B, amended: SSI 2009/ 203 Reg.8
Sch.6 Part II para.15, amended: SSI 2009/ 203 Reg.8
Sch.6 Part II para.16, amended: SSI 2009/ 203 Reg.8
Sch.6 Part II para.17, amended: SSI 2009/ 203 Reg.8
Sch.6 Part II para.18, amended: SSI 2009/ 203 Reg.8
Sch.6 Part II para.19, amended: SSI 2009/ 203 Reg.8
Sch.6 Part II para.20, amended: SSI 2009/ 203 Reg.8
Sch.6 Part II para.21, amended: SSI 2009/ 203 Reg.8
Sch.6 Part II para.22, amended: SSI 2009/ 203 Reg.8
Sch.6 Part II para.23, amended: SSI 2009/ 203 Reg.8
Sch.6 Part II para.24, amended: SSI 2009/ 203 Reg.8
Sch.6 Part III, amended: SSI 2009/ 203 Reg.8
Sch.6 Part III para.1, amended: SSI 2009/ 203 Reg.8
Sch.6 Part III para.2, amended: SSI 2009/ 203 Reg.8
Sch.6 Part III para.3, amended: SSI 2009/ 203 Reg.8
Sch.6 Part III para.4, amended: SSI 2009/ 203 Reg.8
Sch.6 Part III para.5, amended: SSI 2009/ 203 Reg.8
Sch.6 Part III para.5A, amended: SSI 2009/ 203 Reg.8
Sch.6 Part III para.6, amended: SSI 2009/ 203 Reg.8
Sch.6 Part III para.7, amended: SSI 2009/ 203 Reg.8
Sch.7, amended: SSI 2009/ 203 Reg.9
Sch.7 para.1, added: SSI 2009/ 203 Reg.9
1491. Criminal Legal Aid (Scotland) (Fees) Regulations 1989
applied: SSI 2009/ 312 Reg.9
Reg.2, amended: SSI 2009/ 312 Reg.4
Reg.11, amended: SSI 2009/ 312 Reg.4
Reg.11A, amended: SSI 2009/ 312 Reg.4

1989– cont.

1491. Criminal Legal Aid (Scotland) (Fees) Regulations 1989– cont.
Sch.1, amended: SSI 2009/ 312 Reg.4
Sch.1 para.1, amended: SSI 2009/ 312 Reg.4
Sch.1 para.2, amended: SSI 2009/ 312 Reg.4
Sch.1 para.3, amended: SSI 2009/ 312 Reg.4
Sch.1 para.4, amended: SSI 2009/ 312 Reg.4
Sch.1 para.5, amended: SSI 2009/ 312 Reg.4
Sch.1 para.6, amended: SSI 2009/ 312 Reg.4
Sch.3 para.1, amended: SSI 2009/ 312 Reg.4
Sch.3 para.2, amended: SSI 2009/ 312 Reg.4
1597. Magistrates Courts (Extradition) Rules 1989
referred to: SI 2009/ 500 Sch.1 Part 2
1671. Offshore Installations and Pipeline Works (First-Aid) Regulations 1989
Reg.5, applied: SI 2009/ 515 Reg.19
1796. Road Vehicles Lighting Regulations 1989
Reg.3, amended: SI 2009/ 3220 Reg.3
Reg.9B, amended: SI 2009/ 3220 Reg.4
Reg.11, amended: SI 2009/ 3220 Reg.5
Reg.18, amended: SI 2009/ 3220 Reg.6
Reg.20, amended: SI 2009/ 3220 Reg.7
Reg.20A, added: SI 2009/ 3220 Reg.8
Reg.24, amended: SI 2009/ 3220 Reg.9
Sch.1, amended: SI 2009/ 3220 Reg.10
Sch.1, substituted: SI 2009/ 3220 Reg.10
Sch.7 Part I para.1, amended: SI 2009/ 3220 Reg.11
Sch.7 Part I para.3, amended: SI 2009/ 3220 Reg.11
Sch.7 Part I para.4, amended: SI 2009/ 3220 Reg.11
Sch.7 Part I para.5, amended: SI 2009/ 3220 Reg.11
Sch.7 Part III, amended: SI 2009/ 3220 Reg.11
Sch.14 para.1, amended: SI 2009/ 3220 Reg.12
Sch.14 para.4, amended: SI 2009/ 3220 Reg.12
Sch.14 para.10, amended: SI 2009/ 3220 Reg.12
Sch.14 para.11, amended: SI 2009/ 3220 Reg.12
Sch.17 Part II, substituted: SI 2009/ 3220 Reg.13
Sch.18 Part I para.2, amended: SI 2009/ 3220 Reg.14
Sch.18 Part I para.3, amended: SI 2009/ 3220 Reg.14
Sch.18 Part II, substituted: SI 2009/ 3220 Reg.14
Sch.19 Part I para.5, amended: SI 2009/ 3220 Reg.15
Sch.19 Part I para.8, amended: SI 2009/ 3220 Reg.15
Sch.21 Part I para.2, amended: SI 2009/ 3220 Reg.16
Sch.21 Part I para.3, amended: SI 2009/ 3220 Reg.16
2250. Public Health (Notification of Infectious Diseases) (Scotland) Amendment Regulations 1989
revoked: SSI 2009/ 404 Sch.4 Part 2
2260. Non-Domestic Rating (Collection and Enforcement) (Central Lists) Regulations 1989
Reg.2, amended: SI 2009/ 2706 Art.6
Reg.3, substituted: SI 2009/ 2706 Art.7
Reg.7A, added: SI 2009/ 1597 Reg.3
Reg.7B, added: SI 2009/ 2154 Reg.3
Sch.1 Part I para.1, substituted: SI 2009/ 1597 Reg.3
Sch.1 Part I para.2, substituted: SI 2009/ 1597 Reg.3
Sch.1 Part I para.3, substituted: SI 2009/ 1597 Reg.3
Sch.1 Part I para.4, substituted: SI 2009/ 1597 Reg.3
Sch.1 Part I para.5, substituted: SI 2009/ 1597 Reg.3
Sch.1 Part II para.6, substituted: SI 2009/ 1597 Reg.3
Sch.1 Part II para.7, substituted: SI 2009/ 1597 Reg.3
Sch.1 Part II para.7A, substituted: SI 2009/ 1597 Reg.3
Sch.1 Part II para.7B, substituted: SI 2009/ 1597 Reg.3
Sch.1 Part II para.7C, substituted: SI 2009/ 1597 Reg.3
Sch.1 Part II para.8, substituted: SI 2009/ 1597 Reg.3
Sch.1A para.1, added: SI 2009/ 1597 Sch.3
Sch.1A para.2, added: SI 2009/ 1597 Sch.3
Sch.1A para.3, added: SI 2009/ 1597 Sch.3
Sch.1A para.4, added: SI 2009/ 1597 Sch.3

1989– cont.

2260. Non-Domestic Rating (Collection and Enforcement) (Central Lists) Regulations 1989– *cont.*

Sch.1A para.5, added: SI 2009/1597 Sch.3
Sch.1A para.6, added: SI 2009/1597 Sch.3
Sch.1A para.7, added: SI 2009/1597 Sch.3
Sch.1A para.8, added: SI 2009/1597 Sch.3
Sch.1A para.9, added: SI 2009/1597 Sch.3
Sch.1A para.10, added: SI 2009/1597 Sch.3
Sch.1A para.11, added: SI 2009/1597 Sch.3
Sch.1A para.12, added: SI 2009/1597 Sch.3
Sch.1A para.13, added: SI 2009/1597 Sch.3
Sch.1A para.14, added: SI 2009/1597 Sch.3
Sch.1A para.15, added: SI 2009/1597 Sch.3
Sch.1A para.16, added: SI 2009/1597 Sch.3
Sch.1A para.17, added: SI 2009/1597 Sch.3
Sch.1A para.18, added: SI 2009/1597 Sch.3
Sch.1A para.19, added: SI 2009/1597 Sch.3
Sch.1A para.20, added: SI 2009/1597 Sch.3
Sch.1A para.21, added: SI 2009/1597 Sch.3
Sch.1A para.22, added: SI 2009/1597 Sch.3
Sch.1B para.1, added: SI 2009/2154 Sch.2
Sch.1B para.2, added: SI 2009/2154 Sch.2
Sch.1B para.3, added: SI 2009/2154 Sch.2
Sch.1B para.4, added: SI 2009/2154 Sch.2
Sch.1B para.5, added: SI 2009/2154 Sch.2
Sch.1B para.6, added: SI 2009/2154 Sch.2
Sch.1B para.7, added: SI 2009/2154 Sch.2
Sch.1B para.8, added: SI 2009/2154 Sch.2
Sch.1B para.9, added: SI 2009/2154 Sch.2
Sch.1B para.10, added: SI 2009/2154 Sch.2
Sch.1B para.11, added: SI 2009/2154 Sch.2
Sch.1B para.12, added: SI 2009/2154 Sch.2
Sch.1B para.13, added: SI 2009/2154 Sch.2
Sch.1B para.14, added: SI 2009/2154 Sch.2

2396. Brunei (Appeals) Order 1989

Art.4, revoked: SI 2009/224 Art.4
Sch.2 para.1, revoked: SI 2009/224 Art.4
Sch.2 para.2, revoked: SI 2009/224 Art.4
Sch.2 para.3, revoked: SI 2009/224 Art.4
Sch.2 para.4, revoked: SI 2009/224 Art.4
Sch.2 para.5, revoked: SI 2009/224 Art.4
Sch.2 para.6, revoked: SI 2009/224 Art.4
Sch.2 para.7, revoked: SI 2009/224 Art.4
Sch.2 para.8, revoked: SI 2009/224 Art.4
Sch.2 para.9, revoked: SI 2009/224 Art.4
Sch.2 para.10, revoked: SI 2009/224 Art.4
Sch.2 para.11, revoked: SI 2009/224 Art.4
Sch.2 para.12, revoked: SI 2009/224 Art.4
Sch.2 para.13, revoked: SI 2009/224 Art.4
Sch.2 para.14, revoked: SI 2009/224 Art.4

2399. Falkland Islands Courts (Overseas Jurisdiction) Order 1989

amended: SI 2009/1737 Art.2

2404. Companies (Northern Ireland) Order 1989

Part II, applied: SI 2009/26 Sch.1, SI 2009/263 Art.5, SI 2009/442 Art.5, SI 2009/468 Sch.1, SI 2009/1345 Art.5, SI 2009/1355 Sch.1, SI 2009/1808 Art.5, SI 2009/1813 Sch.1, SI 2009/1941 Art.4, SI 2009/2471 Reg.5, Reg.9, SI 2009/2722 Reg.3
Part XI, applied: SI 2009/457 Reg.9

2405. Insolvency (Northern Ireland) Order 1989

applied: SI 2009/457 Reg.9, SI 2009/1801 Reg.69, Reg.70
referred to: SI 2009/1804 Sch.2 para.3, SI 2009/1941 Art.8
Part II, applied: SI 2009/1801 Reg.71

1989– cont.

2405. Insolvency (Northern Ireland) Order 1989– *cont.*

Part III, applied: SI 2009/1801 Reg.71
Part V, amended: SI 2009/1941 Sch.1 para.111
Art.2, amended: SI 2009/1941 Sch.1 para.106
Art.2, varied: SI 2009/3056 Sch.1 para.2
Art.3, applied: SI 2009/214 Sch.1, SI 2009/1801 Sch.1
Art.3, amended: SI 2009/1941 Sch.1 para.106
Art.4, amended: SI 2009/1941 Sch.1 para.106
Art.5, amended: SI 2009/1941 Sch.1 para.106
Art.5, revoked (in part): SI 2009/1941 Sch.1 para.106
Art.12, amended: SI 2009/1941 Sch.1 para.106
Art.13, amended: SI 2009/1941 Sch.1 para.106
Art.13, revoked (in part): SI 2009/1941 Sch.1 para.106
Art.14, amended: SI 2009/1941 Sch.1 para.107
Art.17, varied: SI 2009/3056 Sch.1 para.2
Art.20A, amended: SI 2009/1941 Sch.1 para.107
Art.27, amended: 2009 c.26 Sch.7 para.64, SI 2009/1941 Sch.1 para.109
Art.28, amended: SI 2009/1941 Sch.1 para.109
Art.30, amended: SI 2009/1941 Sch.1 para.109
Art.33, amended: SI 2009/1941 Sch.1 para.109
Art.36, amended: SI 2009/1941 Sch.1 para.109
Art.39, amended: SI 2009/1941 Sch.1 para.109
Art.39A, added: SI 2009/1941 Sch.1 para.110
Art.49, applied: SI 2009/1801 Reg.63
Art.52, varied: SI 2009/3056 Sch.1 para.2
Art.53, amended: SI 2009/1941 Sch.1 para.110
Art.60, substituted: SI 2009/1941 Sch.1 para.111
Art.61, amended: SI 2009/1941 Sch.1 para.111
Art.62, referred to: SI 2009/1941 Art.9
Art.62, revoked: SI 2009/1941 Sch.1 para.111
Art.63, amended: SI 2009/1941 Sch.1 para.111
Art.63, revoked (in part): SI 2009/1941 Sch.1 para.111
Art.64, amended: SI 2009/1941 Sch.1 para.111
Art.65, amended: SI 2009/1941 Sch.1 para.111
Art.69, amended: SI 2009/1941 Sch.1 para.111
Art.70, amended: SI 2009/1941 Sch.1 para.111
Art.96, amended: SI 2009/1941 Sch.1 para.111
Art.98, amended: SI 2009/1941 Sch.1 para.111
Art.102, amended: SI 2009/1941 Sch.1 para.111
Art.104, amended: SI 2009/2400 Reg.41
Art.104, revoked (in part): SI 2009/1941 Sch.1 para.111
Art.104A, amended: SI 2009/1941 Sch.1 para.111
Art.104B, added: SI 2009/2400 Reg.41
Art.106, amended: SI 2009/1941 Sch.1 para.111
Art.106, varied: SI 2009/3056 Sch.1 para.2
Art.108, varied: SI 2009/3056 Sch.1 para.2
Art.110, amended: SI 2009/1941 Sch.1 para.111
Art.110, varied: SI 2009/3056 Sch.1 para.2
Art.115, applied: 2009 c.4 s.322, s.357, SI 2009/317 Art.6
Art.121, varied: SI 2009/3056 Sch.1 para.2
Art.125, amended: SI 2009/1941 Sch.1 para.111
Art.126, amended: SI 2009/1941 Sch.1 para.111
Art.127, amended: SI 2009/1941 Sch.1 para.111
Art.136, amended: SI 2009/1941 Sch.1 para.111
Art.137, amended: SI 2009/1941 Sch.1 para.111
Art.140, varied: SI 2009/3056 Sch.1 para.2
Art.142, varied: SI 2009/3056 Sch.1 para.2
Art.158, amended: SI 2009/1941 Sch.1 para.111
Art.159, applied: SI 2009/1801 Reg.63
Art.164, amended: SI 2009/1941 Sch.1 para.111
Art.166, amended: SI 2009/1941 Sch.1 para.111
Art.176, revoked (in part): SI 2009/1941 Sch.1 para.111
Art.178, amended: SI 2009/1941 Sch.1 para.111
Art.179, revoked (in part): SI 2009/1941 Sch.1 para.111
Art.180, amended: SI 2009/1941 Sch.1 para.111
Art.181, amended: SI 2009/1941 Sch.1 para.111

1989–cont.

2405. Insolvency (Northern Ireland) Order 1989– *cont.*
Art.182, amended: SI 2009/1941 Sch.1 para.111
Art.183, amended: SI 2009/1941 Sch.1 para.111
Art.184, substituted: SI 2009/1941 Sch.1 para.112
Art.185, amended: SI 2009/1941 Sch.1 para.112
Art.190, revoked (in part): SI 2009/1941 Sch.1 para.112
Art.193, amended: SI 2009/1941 Sch.1 para.112
Art.193, revoked (in part): SI 2009/1941 Sch.1 para.112
Art.279A, amended: 2009 c.26 Sch.7 para.60
Art.279AA, added: 2009 c.26 Sch.7 para.61
Art.279B, amended: 2009 c.26 Sch.7 para.62
Art.279BA, added: 2009 c.26 Sch.7 para.63
Art.280, applied: SI 2009/470 Reg.80
Art.283, applied: SI 2009/470 Reg.80
Art.309, see *Official Receiver for Northern Ireland v Rooney* [2009] 2 F.L.R. 1437 (Ch D (NI)), Weir, J.
Art.359, amended: SI 2009/1941 Sch.1 para.113
Art.381, revoked (in part): SI 2009/1941 Sch.2
Art.386, added: SI 2009/1941 Sch.1 para.115
Art.387, added: SI 2009/1941 Sch.1 para.115
Sch.A1, amended: SI 2009/1941 Sch.1 para.107, SI 2009/2400 Reg.41
Sch.A1, applied: SI 2009/1801 Reg.63
Sch.A1, varied: SI 2009/3056 Sch.1 para.2
Sch.B1, amended: SI 2009/1941 Sch.1 para.108
Sch.B1, applied: 2009 c.4 s.323, SI 2009/1801 Reg.63, SI 2009/1941 Art.8
Sch.B1, varied: SI 2009/3056 Sch.1 para.2
Sch.2A, applied: SI 2009/263 Art.5, SI 2009/442 Art.5, SI 2009/468 Sch.1, SI 2009/1345 Art.5, SI 2009/1355 Sch.1, SI 2009/1808 Art.5, SI 2009/1813 Sch.1, SI 2009/2722 Reg.3
Sch.7, amended: SI 2009/1941 Sch.1 para.114
Sch.8, amended: SI 2009/1941 Sch.1 para.114

2487. Tore-Ullapool Trunk Road (A835) (Garve) (40mph Speed Limit) Order 1989
revoked: SSI 2009/46 Art.4

3405. Insolvency (Northern Ireland) Order 1989
Art.279A(1)(b), amended: 2009 c.26 Sch.8 Part 4

1990

126. Surface Waters (Dangerous Substances) (Classification) (Scotland) Regulations 1990
revoked: SSI 2009/420 Sch.3

172. Land Registration Fee Order 1990
referred to: SI 2009/500 Sch.1 Part 2

314. Land Registration Rules 1990
referred to: SI 2009/500 Sch.1 Part 2

507. Town and Country Planning (Appeals) (Written Submissions Procedure) (Scotland) Regulations 1990
Reg.2, amended: SSI 2009/220 Reg.2
Reg.5, revoked: SSI 2009/220 Reg.2
Reg.6, amended: SSI 2009/220 Reg.2
Reg.6, revoked (in part): SSI 2009/220 Reg.2
Sch.1 para.1, revoked: SSI 2009/220 Reg.2
Sch.1 para.2, revoked: SSI 2009/220 Reg.2
Sch.1 para.3, revoked: SSI 2009/220 Reg.2
Sch.1 para.4, revoked: SSI 2009/220 Reg.2
Sch.1 para.5, revoked: SSI 2009/220 Reg.2
Sch.1 para.7, revoked: SSI 2009/220 Reg.2

779. Housing Corporation Advances (Increase of Limit) Order 1990
revoked: SI 2009/484 Sch.2

1990–cont.

928. Industrial Training (Transfer of the Activities of Establishment) Order 1990
applied: SI 2009/549 Sch.1

1271. Dingwall-Ullapool Trunk Road (A893) (Shore Street, Ullapool) (Prohibition of Waiting) Order 1990
revoked: SSI 2009/79 Art.10

1454. Patent Agents (Non-recognition of Certain Agents by Comptroller) Rules 1990
r.2, amended: SI 2009/3348 Art.9
r.2, substituted: SI 2009/3348 Art.9
r.3, amended: SI 2009/3348 Art.9

1457. Register of Patent Agents Rules 1990
revoked (in part): SI 2009/3348 Art.24

1458. Register of Trade Mark Agents Rules 1990
revoked (in part): SI 2009/3348 Art.24

1504. Companies (No.2) (Northern Ireland) Order 1990
varied: SI 2009/317 Sch.1

1506. Education (Student Loans) (Northern Ireland) Order 1990
applied: SI 2009/470 Reg.16, Reg.19, SI 2009/1555 Reg.5, SI 2009/2737 Reg.4

1519. Planning (Listed Buildings and Conservation Areas) Regulations 1990
Reg.3, amended: SI 2009/2262 Reg.2
Reg.3A, amended: SI 2009/2262 Reg.2
Reg.3B, substituted: SI 2009/1026 Reg.2
Sch.4 Part 1, substituted: SI 2009/2711 Reg.2
Sch.4 Part 2, substituted: SI 2009/2711 Reg.2

1527. Aerodromes (Designation) (Detention and Sale of Aircraft) Order 1990
revoked (in part): SI 2009/2350 Sch.2

1730. Housing (Prescribed Forms) (No.2) Regulations 1990
Sch.1, amended: SI 2009/1307 Sch.2 para.36

1904. Non-Domestic Rating (Payment of Interest) Regulations 1990
Reg.3, amended: SI 2009/1307 Sch.2 para.37

2024. National Health Service Trusts (Membership and Procedure) Regulations 1990
Reg.1, amended: SI 2009/1385 Reg.26
Reg.1A, added: SI 2009/1385 Reg.26

2035. Overhead Lines (Exemption) Regulations 1990
applied: SI 2009/640 Reg.6
revoked (in part): SI 2009/640 Reg.1
Reg.5, applied: SI 2009/640 Reg.6

2145. Civil Aviation Act 1982 (Jersey) Order 1990
Sch.1 Part II para.29, amended: SI 2009/1307 Sch.2 para.38

2360. Public Lending Right Scheme 1982 (Commencement of Variations) Order 1990
Part V para.46, varied: SI 2009/3259 Art.2

2457. Smoke Control Areas (Exempted Fireplaces) (No.2) Order 1990
revoked (in part): SSI 2009/214 Sch.2

2463. Food Safety (Sampling and Qualifications) Regulations 1990
varied: SI 2009/3255 Reg.38, SI 2009/3376 Reg.38, SSI 2009/446 Reg.38
Reg.6, applied: SI 2009/3379 Reg.4
Reg.6, referred to: SI 2009/3230 Reg.4
Reg.6, varied: SSI 2009/437 Reg.4
Reg.7, applied: SI 2009/3379 Reg.4
Reg.7, referred to: SI 2009/3230 Reg.4
Reg.7, varied: SSI 2009/437 Reg.4
Reg.8, applied: SI 2009/3379 Reg.4
Reg.8, referred to: SI 2009/3230 Reg.4
Reg.8, varied: SSI 2009/437 Reg.4

1990–cont.

2463. Food Safety (Sampling and Qualifications) Regulations 1990–*cont.*
Reg.9, varied: SI 2009/3379 Reg.5, SSI 2009/437 Reg.5
Sch.1, amended: SI 2009/205 Reg.25, SI 2009/481 Reg.25, SI 2009/1223 Reg.6, SI 2009/1386 Reg.6, SSI 2009/30 Reg.22, SSI 2009/215 Reg.6
Sch.3, referred to: SI 2009/3255 Reg.38, SI 2009/3376 Reg.38, SSI 2009/446 Reg.38

2485. Legal Services Ombudsman (Jurisdiction) Order 1990
revoked: SI 2009/3250 Sch.1

2490. Food (Control of Irradiation) Regulations 1990
revoked (in part): SI 2009/1584 Reg.12, SI 2009/1795 Reg.12, SSI 2009/261 Reg.12

2639. Health Education Board for Scotland Order 1990
Sch.1 Part III, amended: SSI 2009/166 Sch.1 para.1

1991

167. Occupational Pension Schemes (Preservation of Benefit) Regulations 1991
Reg.5, substituted: SI 2009/2930 Reg.2
Reg.9, see *Easterly Ltd v Headway Plc* [2009] EWCA Civ 793, [2009] Pens. L.R. 279 (CA (Civ Div)), Lord Neuberger of Abbotsbury
Reg.27B, amended: SI 2009/615 Reg.2

168. Occupational Pension Schemes (Revaluation) Regulations 1991
Reg.13A, added: SI 2009/615 Reg.3

478. Wildlife and Countryside (Registration and Ringing of Certain Captive Birds) (Amendment) Regulations 1991
revoked (in part): SSI 2009/419 Reg.7

509. National Health Service Trusts (Pharmaceutical Services Remuneration Special Arrangement) Order 1991
revoked (in part): SI 2009/1824 Art.2

724. High Court and County Courts Jurisdiction Order 1991
amended: SI 2009/577 Art.6
Art.4A, substituted: SI 2009/577 Art.2
Art.5, amended: SI 2009/577 Art.3
Art.8, amended: SI 2009/577 Art.4
Art.8A, amended: SI 2009/577 Art.5
Art.9, amended: SI 2009/577 Art.7
Art.9, amended: SI 2009/577 Art.6

875. Buying Agency Trading Fund Order 1991
referred to: SI 2009/81
Art.3, amended: SI 2009/647 Art.2
Sch.1, substituted: SI 2009/81 Sch.1
Sch.1 para.1, substituted: SI 2009/81 Sch.1
Sch.1 para.2, substituted: SI 2009/81 Sch.1

880. Financial Markets and Insolvency Regulations 1991
varied: SI 2009/317 Sch.1
Reg.2, amended: SI 2009/853 Reg.3
Reg.7, amended: SI 2009/853 Reg.3
Reg.10, amended: SI 2009/853 Reg.3
Reg.11, amended: SI 2009/853 Reg.3
Reg.16, amended: SI 2009/853 Reg.3
Reg.16, revoked (in part): SI 2009/853 Reg.3

1063. Manchester Ship Canal Harbour Revision Order 1991
revoked: SI 2009/2579 Sch.2

1991–cont.

1220. Planning (Northern Ireland) Order 1991
applied: SI 2009/890 Sch.7 para.8, SI 2009/2301 Sch.4 para.3, SI 2009/3130 Sch.2 para.3
referred to: SI 2009/2037 Art.5

1247. Family Proceedings Rules 1991
referred to: SI 2009/857 r.2
see *H (Children) (Care Proceedings: Disclosure), Re* [2009] EWCA Civ 704, [2009] 2 F.L.R. 1531 (CA (Civ Div)), Thorpe, L.J.
Part I r.1.2, amended: SI 2009/636 r.4
Part III r.3.13, amended: SI 2009/636 r.5
Part III r.3.14, substituted: SI 2009/2027 r.4
Part IV r.4.1, amended: SI 2009/636 r.6, r.7, SI 2009/2027 r.5
Part IV r.4.2, amended: SI 2009/636 r.6
Part IV r.4.3, amended: SI 2009/636 r.6
Part IV r.4.4, amended: SI 2009/636 r.6, r.8, SI 2009/2027 r.6
Part IV r.4.4A, amended: SI 2009/636 r.6
Part IV r.4.5, amended: SI 2009/636 r.6
Part IV r.4.6, amended: SI 2009/636 r.6
Part IV r.4.7, amended: SI 2009/636 r.6
Part IV r.4.8, amended: SI 2009/636 r.6
Part IV r.4.9, amended: SI 2009/636 r.6, SI 2009/2027 r.7
Part IV r.4.10, amended: SI 2009/636 r.6
Part IV r.4.11, amended: SI 2009/636 r.6
Part IV r.4.11A, amended: SI 2009/636 r.6
Part IV r.4.11AA, amended: SI 2009/636 r.6
Part IV r.4.11B, amended: SI 2009/636 r.6
Part IV r.4.12, amended: SI 2009/636 r.6
Part IV r.4.13, amended: SI 2009/636 r.6
Part IV r.4.13A, amended: SI 2009/636 r.6
Part IV r.4.13B, amended: SI 2009/636 r.6
Part IV r.4.14, amended: SI 2009/636 r.6
Part IV r.4.15, amended: SI 2009/636 r.6
Part IV r.4.16, amended: SI 2009/636 r.6
Part IV r.4.17, amended: SI 2009/636 r.6
Part IV r.4.17A, amended: SI 2009/636 r.6
Part IV r.4.17AA, amended: SI 2009/636 r.6
Part IV r.4.18, amended: SI 2009/636 r.6
Part IV r.4.19, amended: SI 2009/636 r.6
Part IV r.4.20, amended: SI 2009/636 r.6
Part IV r.4.21, amended: SI 2009/636 r.6
Part IV r.4.21AA, amended: SI 2009/636 r.6
Part IV r.4.21A, amended: SI 2009/636 r.6
Part IV r.4.21B, amended: SI 2009/636 r.6
Part IV r.4.22, amended: SI 2009/636 r.6
Part IV r.4.22, revoked: SI 2009/636 r.9
Part IV r.4.23, amended: SI 2009/636 r.6
Part IV r.4.24, amended: SI 2009/636 r.6
Part IV r.4.24A, amended: SI 2009/636 r.6
Part IV r.4.25, amended: SI 2009/636 r.6
Part IV r.4.26, amended: SI 2009/636 r.6
Part IV r.4.27, amended: SI 2009/636 r.6
Part IV r.4.27A, amended: SI 2009/636 r.6
Part IV r.4.28, amended: SI 2009/636 r.6
Part IVA r.4A.1, amended: SI 2009/2027 r.8
Part VII r.7.28, revoked: SI 2009/636 r.9
Part VIII r.8.A1, added: SI 2009/636 r.10
Part VIII r.8.A1, substituted: SI 2009/2027 r.9
Part VIII r.8.1, amended: SI 2009/636 r.11
Part VIII r.8.1A, revoked: SI 2009/636 r.9
Part VIII r.8.1B, revoked: SI 2009/636 r.9
Part VIII r.8.2, amended: SI 2009/2027 r.10
Part VIII r.8.2, substituted: SI 2009/636 r.12
Part VIII r.8.2A, amended: SI 2009/2027 r.11
Part VIII r.8.2A, substituted: SI 2009/636 r.12

1991– cont.

1247. Family Proceedings Rules 1991– cont.

Part VIII r.8.2B, amended: SI 2009/2027 r.12

Part VIII r.8.2B, substituted: SI 2009/636 r.12

Part VIII r.8.2C, substituted: SI 2009/636 r.12, SI 2009/2027 r.13

Part VIII r.8.2D, substituted: SI 2009/636 r.12

Part VIII r.8.2E, amended: SI 2009/2027 r.14

Part VIII r.8.2E, substituted: SI 2009/636 r.12

Part VIII r.8.2F, amended: SI 2009/2027 r.15

Part VIII r.8.2F, substituted: SI 2009/636 r.12

Part VIII r.8.2FF, added: SI 2009/2027 r.16

Part VIII r.8.2FF, substituted: SI 2009/636 r.12

Part VIII r.8.2G, amended: SI 2009/2027 r.17

Part VIII r.8.2G, substituted: SI 2009/636 r.12

Part VIII r.8.2H, substituted: SI 2009/636 r.12

Part VIII r.8.3, amended: SI 2009/636 r.13

Part IX r.9.3, amended: SI 2009/636 r.14

Part X r.10.20, amended: SI 2009/857 r.4

Part X r.10.20A, revoked: SI 2009/857 r.4

Part X r.10.21A, amended: SI 2009/857 r.4

Part X r.10.28, added: SI 2009/857 r.4

Part XI r.11.1, added: SI 2009/857 r.5

Part XI r.11.2, added: SI 2009/857 r.5

Part XI r.11.3, added: SI 2009/857 r.5

Part XI r.11.4, added: SI 2009/857 r.5

Part XI r.11.5, added: SI 2009/857 r.5

Part XI r.11.6, added: SI 2009/857 r.5

Part XI r.11.7, added: SI 2009/857 r.5

Part XI r.11.8, added: SI 2009/857 r.5

Part XI r.11.9, added: SI 2009/857 r.5

Part XI r.11.9, amended: SI 2009/3348 Art.10

Appendix 1, amended: SI 2009/636 Sch.1

Appendix 1, substituted: SI 2009/2027 Sch.1, Sch.2

Appendix 3, amended: SI 2009/636 r.16, SI 2009/2027 r.20

Part XI, see *H (Children) (Care Proceedings: Disclosure), Re* [2009] EWCA Civ 704, [2009] 2 F.L.R. 1531 (CA (Civ Div)), Thorpe, L.J.; see *N (A Child) (Family Proceedings: Disclosure), Re* [2009] EWHC 1663 (Fam), [2009] 2 F.L.R. 1152 (Fam Div), Munby, J.

r.1.2, see *Judge v Judge* [2008] EWCA Civ 1458, [2009] 1 F.L.R. 1287 (CA (Civ Div)), Longmore, L.J.

r.2.61A, see *R. v K* [2009] EWCA Crim 1640, [2009] S.T.C. 2553 (CA (Crim Div)), Moore-Bick, L.J.

r.2.61E, see *Myerson v Myerson* [2008] EWCA Civ 1376, [2009] 1 F.L.R. 826 (CA (Civ Div)), Thorpe, L.J.

r.2.61F, see *R. v K* [2009] EWCA Crim 1640, [2009] S.T.C. 2553 (CA (Crim Div)), Moore-Bick, L.J.

r.2.71, see *Judge v Judge* [2008] EWCA Civ 1458, [2009] 1 F.L.R. 1287 (CA (Civ Div)), Longmore, L.J.

r.4.16, see *X (A Child) (Residence and Contact: Rights of Media Attendance), Re* [2009] EWHC 1728 (Fam), [2009] E.M.L.R. 26 (Fam Div), Sir Mark Potter (President, Fam)

r.4.23, see *H (Children) (Care Proceedings: Disclosure), Re* [2009] EWCA Civ 704, [2009] 2 F.L.R. 1531 (CA (Civ Div)), Thorpe, L.J.

r.8.1A, see *Practice Direction (Fam Div: Family Proceedings: Appeals)* [2009] 1 W.L.R. 1103 (Fam Div), Sir Mark Potter (President, Fam)

r.8.2, see *Practice Direction (Fam Div: Family Proceedings: Appeals)* [2009] 1 W.L.R. 1103 (Fam Div), Sir Mark Potter (President, Fam)

1991– cont.

1247. Family Proceedings Rules 1991– cont.

r.8.2H, see *Practice Direction (Fam Div: Family Proceedings: Appeals)* [2009] 1 W.L.R. 1103 (Fam Div), Sir Mark Potter (President, Fam)

r.10.20, see *P (Care Proceedings: Disclosure), Re* [2008] EWHC 2197 (Fam), [2009] 2 F.L.R. 1039 (Fam Div), Judge Hunt

r.10.20A, see *A v Payne* [2009] EWHC 736 (Fam), [2009] 2 F.L.R. 463 (Fam Div), Sir Mark Potter (President); see *H (Children) (Care Proceedings: Disclosure), Re* [2009] EWCA Civ 704, [2009] 2 F.L.R. 1531 (CA (Civ Div)), Thorpe, L.J.

r.10.27, see *Judge v Judge* [2008] EWCA Civ 1458, [2009] 1 F.L.R. 1287 (CA (Civ Div)), Longmore, L.J.

r.10.28, see *D v D (Divorce: Media Presence)* [2009] EWHC 946 (Fam), [2009] 2 F.L.R. 324 (Fam Div), Charles, J.; see *Practice Direction (Fam Div: Family Proceedings: Media Representatives)* [2009] 1 W.L.R. 1111 (Fam Div), Sir Mark Potter (President, Fam); see *Practice Statement (Fam Div: Family Proceedings: Media Representatives: Applications)* [2009] 1 W.L.R. 1119 (Fam Div), Sir Mark Potter (President, Fam); see *Spencer v Spencer* [2009] EWHC 1529 (Fam), [2009] E.M.L.R. 25 (Fam Div), Munby, J.; see *X (A Child) (Residence and Contact: Rights of Media Attendance), Re* [2009] EWHC 1728 (Fam), [2009] E.M.L.R. 26 (Fam Div), Sir Mark Potter (President, Fam)

r.11.2, see *N (A Child) (Family Proceedings: Disclosure), Re* [2009] EWHC 1663 (Fam), [2009] 2 F.L.R. 1152 (Fam Div), Munby, J.

r.11.4, see *N (A Child) (Family Proceedings: Disclosure), Re* [2009] EWHC 1663 (Fam), [2009] 2 F.L.R. 1152 (Fam Div), Munby, J.

1395. Family Proceedings Courts (Children Act 1989) Rules 1991

see *Practice Statement (Fam Div: Family Proceedings: Media Representatives: Applications)* [2009] 1 W.L.R. 1119 (Fam Div), Sir Mark Potter (President, Fam)

Part I r.2, amended: SI 2009/637 r.4, r.5, SI 2009/2025 r.3

Part I r.2A, added: SI 2009/637 r.6

Part II r.4, amended: SI 2009/637 r.7, r.8, SI 2009/2025 r.4

Part II r.9, amended: SI 2009/2025 r.5

Part II r.16, amended: SI 2009/858 r.4

Part II r.16, revoked (in part): SI 2009/858 r.4

Part II r.16A, added: SI 2009/858 r.5

Part II r.21, amended: SI 2009/637 r.9

Part IIA r.21A, amended: SI 2009/2025 r.6

Part III r.23, amended: SI 2009/858 r.7

Part III r.23A, revoked: SI 2009/858 r.8

Part IIC r.21Q, added: SI 2009/858 r.6

Part IIC r.21R, added: SI 2009/858 r.6

Part IIC r.21T, added: SI 2009/858 r.6

Part IIC r.21U, added: SI 2009/858 r.6

Part IIC r.21V, added: SI 2009/858 r.6

Part IIC r.21W, added: SI 2009/858 r.6

Part IIC r.21X, added: SI 2009/858 r.6

Part IIC r.21Y, added: SI 2009/858 r.6

Part IIC r.21Y, amended: SI 2009/3348 Art.11

r.16A, see *Practice Direction (Fam Div: Family Proceedings: Media Representatives: Magistrates' Courts)* [2009] 1 W.L.R. 1115 (Fam Div), Sir Mark Potter (President, Fam); see

1991– cont.

1395. Family Proceedings Courts (Children Act 1989) Rules 1991– *cont.*

r.16A – *cont.*

Practice Statement (Fam Div: Family Proceedings: Media Representatives: Applications) [2009] 1 W.L.R. 1119 (Fam Div), Sir Mark Potter (President, Fam)

s.art IIC r.21S, added: SI 2009/858 r.6

Sch.1, amended: SI 2009/637 Sch.1, SI 2009/2025 Sch.1

Sch.2, amended: SI 2009/637 r.11, SI 2009/2025 r.8

1478. Parental Responsibility Agreement Regulations 1991

Reg.2, amended: SI 2009/2026 Reg.3

Sch.1, substituted: SI 2009/2026 Sch.1

1531. Control of Explosives Regulations 1991

referred to: SI 2009/693 Reg.2

Reg.2, amended: SI 2009/693 Sch.1 para.1

Reg.3, amended: SI 2009/693 Sch.1 para.1

Reg.4, applied: SI 2009/515 Reg.9, Sch.8 Part 9

Reg.4, revoked (in part): SI 2009/693 Sch.1 para.1

Reg.5, amended: SI 2009/693 Sch.1 para.1

Reg.5, revoked (in part): SI 2009/693 Sch.1 para.1

Reg.14, amended: SI 2009/693 Sch.1 para.1

Reg.14, applied: SI 2009/693 Reg.2

Reg.15, amended: SI 2009/693 Sch.1 para.1

Sch.1, substituted: SI 2009/693 Sch.1 para.1

Sch.1 Part 1, substituted: SI 2009/693 Sch.1 para.1

Sch.1 Part 2, substituted: SI 2009/693 Sch.1 para.1

1540. Human Fertilisation and Embryology (Statutory Storage Period) Regulations 1991

applied: SI 2009/1582 Reg.8

revoked: SI 2009/1582 Reg.9

1559. Income Support (General) Amendment No 4 Regulations 1991

Reg.22, revoked: SI 2009/3228 Reg.4

Reg.23, revoked: SI 2009/3228 Reg.4

Reg.24, revoked: SI 2009/3228 Reg.4

1588. Human Fertilisation and Embryology (Special Exemptions) Regulations 1991

revoked: SI 2009/1918 Reg.4

1620. Construction Products Regulations 1991

referred to: SI 2009/669 Sch.2 Part 2

1672. Civil Aviation Authority Regulations 1991

applied: SI 2009/41 Reg.26

Reg.3, amended: SI 2009/41 Reg.36

1719. Nuclear Material (Offences) Act 1983 (Isle of Man) Order 1991

revoked: SI 2009/3203 Art.4

1795. Companies House Trading Fund Order 1991

referred to: SI 2009/2622

Art.2, amended: SI 2009/2622 Art.2

Art.3, amended: SI 2009/2622 Art.2, SI 2009/2748 Sch.1 para.14

Art.4, amended: SI 2009/2748 Sch.1 para.14

Art.5, amended: SI 2009/2622 Art.2

Sch.1, referred to: SI 2009/2622

1796. Patent Office Trading Fund Order 1991

Art.2, amended: SI 2009/2748 Sch.1 para.15

Art.3, amended: SI 2009/2748 Sch.1 para.15

1889. Human Fertilisation and Embryology Authority (Licence Committees and Appeals) Regulations 1991

applied: SI 2009/1892 Sch.4 para.10

revoked: SI 2009/1891 Reg.32

1991. Family Proceedings Courts (Matrimonial Proceedings etc.) Rules 1991

Sch.1, amended: SI 2009/2025 Sch.2

1991– cont.

1997. Companies Act 1989 (Eligibility for Appointment as Company Auditor) (Consequential Amendments) Regulations 1991

Sch.1 para.59, revoked (in part): SI 2009/484 Sch.2

2512. Ancient Monuments (Claims for Compensation) (England) Regulations 1991

Sch.1 Part 1, amended: SI 2009/1307 Sch.2 para.39

Sch.1 Part 2, amended: SI 2009/1307 Sch.2 para.39

2628. Child Support (Northern Ireland) Order 1991 (N.I.23) 1991

applied: SI 2009/1109 Reg.10

Art.27, amended: 2009 c.24 Sch.6 para.24

Art.41, amended: SI 2009/1941 Sch.1 para.128

2684. Solicitors Recognised Bodies Order 1991

amended: SI 2009/500 Art.2

Art.1, amended: SI 2009/500 Art.2

Art.3, amended: SI 2009/500 Art.2

Sch.1, amended: SI 2009/500 Art.2, Sch.1 Part 1, Sch.1 Part 2, SI 2009/2054 Sch.1 para.12

Sch.2, amended: SI 2009/500 Art.2, Sch.2 Part 1, Sch.2 Part 2

2749. Simple Pressure Vessels (Safety) Regulations 1991

referred to: SI 2009/669 Sch.1 Part 4, Sch.2 Part 2

2790. Private Water Supplies Regulations 1991

revoked (in part): SI 2009/3101 Reg.22

2814. Anthrax Order 1991

Art.2, amended: SI 2009/2713 Art.2

Art.4, amended: SI 2009/2713 Art.2

Art.7, amended: SI 2009/2713 Art.2

Art.9, amended: SI 2009/2713 Art.2

2831. Registered Foreign Lawyers Order 1991

revoked: SI 2009/1589 Art.2

2872. Children and Young Persons (Protection from Tobacco) (Northern Ireland) Order 1991

Art.4A, added: 2009 c.21 s.23

2880. Double Taxation Relief (Taxes on Income) (Isle of Man) Order 1991

Sch.1, referred to: SI 2009/228 Art.3

2890. Social Security (Disability Living Allowance) Regulations 1991

Reg.4, amended: SI 2009/497 Art.13

2892. Smoke Control Areas (Exempted Fireplaces) Order 1991

revoked (in part): SSI 2009/214 Sch.2

1992

129. Firemen's Pension Scheme Order 1992

see *R. (on the application of London Fire & Emergency Planning Authority) v Board of Medical Referees* [2008] EWCA Civ 1515, [2009] I.C.R. 697 (CA (Civ Div)), Tuckey, L.J.

Sch.1 Part I, added: SI 2009/1226 Sch.1 para.2

Sch.1 Part I, amended: SI 2009/1226 Sch.1 para.2

Sch.1 Part II, added: SI 2009/1226 Sch.1 para.2

Sch.1 Part II, amended: SI 2009/1226 Sch.1 para.2

Sch.2, added: SI 2009/1226 Sch.1 para.1, SSI 2009/184 Sch.1 para.2, Sch.1 para.3, Sch.1 para.4

Sch.2, revoked (in part): SSI 2009/184 Sch.1 para.3

Sch.2, substituted: SI 2009/1226 Sch.1 para.2, SSI 2009/184 Sch.1 para.1

Sch.2, see *R. (on the application of London Fire & Emergency Planning Authority) v Board of Medical Referees* [2008] EWCA Civ 1515, [2009] I.C.R. 697 (CA (Civ Div)), Tuckey, L.J.

223. Town and Country Planning (General Permitted Development) (Scotland) Order 1992

Sch.1 Part 1A para.6A, added: SSI 2009/34 Sch.1

Sch.1 Part 1A para.6B, added: SSI 2009/34 Sch.1

Sch.1 Part 1A para.6C, added: SSI 2009/34 Sch.1

Sch.1 Part 1A para.6D, added: SSI 2009/34 Sch.1

Sch.1 Part 1A para.6E, added: SSI 2009/34 Sch.1

Sch.1 Part 1A para.6F, added: SSI 2009/34 Sch.1

224. Town and Country Planning (General Development Procedure) (Scotland) Order 1992

Art.14, see *Vattenfall Wind Power Ltd v Scottish Ministers* [2009] CSIH 27, 2009 S.C. 444 (IH (2 Div)), The Lord Justice Clerk (Gill)

Art.23, see *Vattenfall Wind Power Ltd v Scottish Ministers* [2009] CSIH 27, 2009 S.C. 444 (IH (2 Div)), The Lord Justice Clerk (Gill)

226. Cayman Islands (Constitution) (Amendment) Order 1992

revoked: SI 2009/1379 Sch.1

230. Civil Aviation Act 1982 (Guernsey) Order 1992

Sch.1 Part I, amended: SI 2009/1307 Sch.2 para.40

Sch.1 Part II para.29, substituted: SI 2009/1307 Sch.2 para.40

231. Electricity (Northern Ireland) Order 1992

Art.3, applied: SSI 2009/140 Art.2

Art.35, applied: SSI 2009/140 Art.19

Art.35, referred to: SI 2009/785 Art.19

Art.39, applied: SI 2009/785 Art.58, SSI 2009/140 Art.58

Art.73, amended: SI 2009/1941 Sch.1 para.135

Art.79, amended: SI 2009/1941 Sch.1 para.135

Sch.11 para.1, amended: SI 2009/1941 Sch.1 para.135

347. Protection of Wrecks (Designation No.1) Order 1992

revoked: SI 2009/2394 Art.3

548. Council Tax (Discount Disregards) Order 1992

Art.2, amended: SI 2009/2054 Sch.1 para.13

Art.2, applied: SI 2009/2054 Sch.2 para.7

Sch.1 para.4, see *R. (on the application of Fayad) v London South East Valuation Tribunal* [2008] EWHC 2531 (Admin), [2009] R.A. 157 (QBD (Admin)), Neil Garnham Q.C.

549. Council Tax (Chargeable Dwellings) Order 1992

Art.3, applied: SI 2009/2270 Reg.4, Reg.11

Art.4, applied: SI 2009/2270 Reg.4

550. Council Tax (Situation and Valuation of Dwellings) Regulations 1992

see *Chilton-Merryweather (Listing Officer) v Hunt* [2008] EWCA Civ 1025, [2009] Env. L.R. 16 (CA (Civ Div)), Waller, L.J.

Reg.6, see *Domblides v Listing Officer* [2008] EWHC 3271 (Admin), [2009] R.V.R. 5 (QBD (Admin)), Judge Bidder QC

551. Council Tax (Liability for Owners) Regulations 1992

Reg.2, see *Jackson v Cambridge City Council* [2008] EWHC 2529 (Admin), [2009] R.A. 21 (QBD (Admin)), Burnett, J.; see *R. (on the application of Salmon) v Feltham Magistrates' Court* [2008] EWHC 3507 (Admin), [2009] R.V.R. 160 (QBD (Admin)), Stadlen, J.; see *Watts v Preston City Council* [2009] EWHC 2179 (Admin), [2009] R.A. 334 (QBD (Admin)), Langstaff, J.

554. Council Tax (Reductions for Disabilities) Regulations 1992

applied: SI 2009/3193 Sch.1 para.26

referred to: SI 2009/3193 Sch.1 para.16

574. Surface Waters (Dangerous Substances) (Classification) (Scotland) Regulations 1992

revoked: SSI 2009/420 Sch.3

588. Controlled Waste Regulations 1992

Reg.7A, see *R. (on the application of Thames Water Utilities Ltd) v Bromley Magistrates' Court* [2008] EWHC 1763 (Admin), [2009] 1 W.L.R. 1247 (DC), Carnwath, L.J.

Sch.4 para.2, revoked (in part): SSI 2009/248 Sch.1 para.13

Sch.4 para.2A, added: SSI 2009/248 Sch.1 para.13

612. Local Authorities (Calculation of Council Tax Base) Regulations 1992

applied: SI 2009/3193 Reg.2

613. Council Tax (Administration and Enforcement) Regulations 1992

applied: SI 2009/470 Reg.51

see *R. (on the application of Salmon) v Feltham Magistrates' Court* [2008] EWHC 3507 (Admin), [2009] R.V.R. 160 (QBD (Admin)), Stadlen, J.

Reg.1, amended: SI 2009/2706 Art.9

Reg.2, amended: SI 2009/2706 Art.10

Reg.23, see *R. (on the application of Kinsley) v Barnet LBC* [2008] EWHC 2013 (Admin), [2009] R.V.R. 34 (QBD (Admin)), Mitting, J.

Reg.34, see *R. (on the application of Salmon) v Feltham Magistrates' Court* [2008] EWHC 3507 (Admin), [2009] R.V.R. 160 (QBD (Admin)), Stadlen, J.

Reg.36A, see *R. (on the application of Mohammed) v Southwark LBC* [2009] EWHC 311 (Admin), [2009] B.P.I.R. 882 (QBD (Admin)), Geraldine Andrews QC

656. Planning (Hazardous Substances) Regulations 1992

Reg.2, amended: SI 2009/1901 Reg.2

Reg.3, applied: SI 2009/1901 Reg.3

Reg.4, amended: SI 2009/1901 Reg.2

Sch.1 Part A, referred to: SI 2009/1901 Reg.3

Sch.1 Part A, substituted: SI 2009/1901 Sch.1

Sch.1 Part B, referred to: SI 2009/1901 Reg.3

Sch.1 Part B, substituted: SI 2009/1901 Sch.1

Sch.1 Part C, substituted: SI 2009/1901 Sch.1

Sch.1 Part D, substituted: SI 2009/1901 Sch.1

662. National Health Service (Pharmaceutical Services) Regulations 1992

Reg.2, amended: SI 2009/1491 Reg.2

Reg.4, amended: SI 2009/1491 Reg.3

Reg.5, amended: SI 2009/1491 Reg.4

Reg.6, amended: SI 2009/1491 Reg.5

Reg.7, amended: SI 2009/1491 Reg.6

Reg.9, amended: SI 2009/1491 Reg.7

Reg.10, amended: SI 2009/1491 Reg.8

Reg.11, substituted: SI 2009/1491 Reg.10

Reg.11ZA, added: SI 2009/1491 Reg.9

Reg.12, substituted: SI 2009/1491 Reg.11

Reg.13, substituted: SI 2009/1491 Reg.12

Reg.20, substituted: SI 2009/1491 Reg.13

Reg.21, substituted: SI 2009/1491 Reg.14

Reg.21A, substituted: SI 2009/1491 Reg.15

Reg.21B, amended: SI 2009/1491 Reg.16

Reg.21C, amended: SI 2009/1491 Reg.17

Reg.21D, added: SI 2009/1491 Reg.18

Reg.21E, added: SI 2009/1491 Reg.18

1992– cont.

662. National Health Service (Pharmaceutical Services) Regulations 1992– *cont.*
Reg.21F, added: SI 2009/1491 Reg.18
Reg.21G, added: SI 2009/1491 Reg.18
Reg.21H, added: SI 2009/1491 Reg.18
Sch.2 Part VI para.34, substituted: SI 2009/1491 Reg.1
Sch.2 Part VI para.35, substituted: SI 2009/1491 Reg.1
Sch.2 Part VI para.36, substituted: SI 2009/1491 Reg.1
Sch.2 Part VI para.37, substituted: SI 2009/1491 Reg.1
Sch.2 Part VI para.38, substituted: SI 2009/1491 Reg.1
Sch.2 Part VI para.39, substituted: SI 2009/1491 Reg.1
Sch.2 Part VI para.40, substituted: SI 2009/1491 Reg.1
Sch.2 Part VI para.41, substituted: SI 2009/1491 Reg.1
Sch.2 Part VI para.42, substituted: SI 2009/1491 Reg.1

666. Town and Country Planning (Control of Advertisements) Regulations 1992
Reg.6, see *R. (on the application of Clear Channel UK Ltd) v Hammersmith and Fulham LBC* [2009] EWHC 465 (Admin), [2009] 22 E.G. 120 (QBD (Admin)), Irwin, J.

807. Industrial Relations (Northern Ireland) Order 1992
Art.2, amended: SI 2009/1941 Sch.1 para.136
Art.3, amended: SI 2009/1941 Sch.1 para.136
Art.7, amended: SI 2009/1941 Sch.1 para.136
Art.11, amended: SI 2009/1941 Sch.1 para.136

810. Local Government (Miscellaneous Provisions) (Northern Ireland) Order 1992
Art.18, amended: SI 2009/1941 Sch.1 para.137

905. Farm Woodland Premium Scheme 1992
applied: SSI 2009/376 Sch.1 para.15

926. Dart Valley Light Railway Plc (Totnes and Ashburton) Light Railway (Transfer) Order 1992
revoked: SI 2009/3281 Sch.2

1190. Gas Transit (EEC Requirements) Regulations 1992
Reg.4, amended: SI 2009/229 Sch.2 para.8

1196. Company and Business Names (Amendment) Regulations 1992
revoked: SI 2009/2615 Reg.7

1227. Legal Aid in Contempt of Court Proceedings (Scotland) Regulations 1992
applied: SSI 2009/312 Reg.9
Reg.2, amended: SSI 2009/312 Reg.5

1228. Legal Aid in Contempt of Court Proceedings (Scotland) (Fees) Regulations 1992
applied: SSI 2009/312 Reg.9
Reg.2, amended: SSI 2009/312 Reg.5

1492. Town and Country Planning General Regulations 1992
Sch.2, amended: SI 2009/1307 Sch.2 para.41

1675. Road Works (Qualifications of Supervisors and Operatives) (Scotland) Regulations 1992
applied: SI 2009/2257 Reg.7

1687. Street Works (Qualifications of Supervisors and Operatives) Regulations 1992
applied: SI 2009/2257 Reg.7
Reg.1A, added: SI 2009/2257 Reg.3
Reg.3, applied: SI 2009/2257 Reg.11
Reg.4, applied: SI 2009/2257 Reg.11

1689. Street Works (Reinstatement) Regulations 1992
Reg.3, applied: SI 2009/721 Sch.2 para.7

1691. Street Works (Maintenance) Regulations 1992
Reg.3, applied: SI 2009/721 Sch.2 para.9
Reg.4, applied: SI 2009/721 Sch.2 para.9

1992– cont.

1708. Housing (Service Charge Loans) Regulations 1992
Reg.6, amended: SI 2009/602 Reg.2
Sch.2 para.1, amended: SI 2009/602 Reg.3

1725. Housing (Northern Ireland) Order 1992
Art.3, amended: SI 2009/1941 Sch.1 para.138
Art.23, amended: SI 2009/1941 Sch.1 para.138
Art.27, amended: SI 2009/1941 Sch.1 para.138
Art.28, amended: SI 2009/1941 Sch.1 para.138
Art.29, amended: SI 2009/1941 Sch.1 para.138

1813. Child Support (Maintenance Assessment Procedure) Regulations 1992
applied: SI 2009/1562 Art.2
Reg.20, amended: SI 2009/2909 Reg.3
Reg.23, amended: SI 2009/2909 Reg.3
Sch.1, applied: SI 2009/2909 Reg.5
Sch.1 para.1, amended: SI 2009/396 Reg.2
Sch.1 para.1, substituted: SI 2009/2909 Reg.3
Sch.1 para.2, substituted: SI 2009/2909 Reg.3
Sch.1 para.4, amended: SI 2009/2909 Reg.3
Sch.1 para.5, revoked: SI 2009/2909 Reg.3
Sch.1 para.6, substituted: SI 2009/2909 Reg.3

1815. Child Support (Maintenance Assessments and Special Cases) Regulations 1992
applied: SI 2009/1562 Art.2
Reg.1, amended: SI 2009/736 Reg.3
Reg.9, amended: SI 2009/736 Reg.3
Reg.18, amended: SI 2009/736 Reg.3
Sch.2 para.15A, added: SI 2009/736 Reg.3

1816. Child Support (Arrears, Interest and Adjustment of Maintenance Assessments) Regulations 1992
Reg.2, revoked: SI 2009/3151 Sch.1
Reg.3, revoked: SI 2009/3151 Sch.1
Reg.4, revoked: SI 2009/3151 Sch.1
Reg.5, revoked: SI 2009/3151 Sch.1
Reg.6, revoked: SI 2009/3151 Sch.1
Reg.7, revoked: SI 2009/3151 Sch.1
Reg.8, referred to: SI 2009/3151 Reg.3
Reg.9, revoked: SI 2009/3151 Sch.1
Reg.10, amended: SI 2009/396 Reg.3
Reg.10, applied: SI 2009/3151 Reg.15
Reg.10, revoked: SI 2009/3151 Sch.1
Reg.10A, applied: SI 2009/3151 Reg.15
Reg.10B, applied: SI 2009/3151 Reg.15
Reg.11, applied: SI 2009/3151 Reg.15
Reg.11, revoked: SI 2009/3151 Sch.1
Reg.12, applied: SI 2009/3151 Reg.15
Reg.12, revoked: SI 2009/3151 Sch.1
Reg.13, applied: SI 2009/3151 Reg.15
Reg.13, revoked: SI 2009/3151 Sch.1
Reg.14, applied: SI 2009/3151 Reg.15
Reg.14, revoked: SI 2009/3151 Sch.1
Reg.15, applied: SI 2009/3151 Reg.15
Reg.15, revoked: SI 2009/3151 Sch.1
Reg.16, applied: SI 2009/3151 Reg.15
Reg.16, revoked: SI 2009/3151 Sch.1
Reg.17, applied: SI 2009/3151 Reg.15
Reg.17, revoked: SI 2009/3151 Sch.1

1878. Act of Sederunt (Fees of Witnesses and Shorthand Writers in the Sheriff Court) 1992
Sch.2 para.1, amended: SSI 2009/103 Art.2
Sch.2 para.4, amended: SSI 2009/103 Art.2
Sch.2 para.5, amended: SSI 2009/103 Art.2

1919. Environmentally Sensitive Areas (Loch Lomond) Designation Order 1992
Art.5A, applied: SSI 2009/376 Sch.1 para.18
Art.5D, applied: SSI 2009/376 Sch.1 para.17

1992– cont.

1920. Environmentally Sensitive Areas (Breadalbane) Designation Order 1992
Art.5A, applied: SSI 2009/376 Sch.1 para.18
Art.5D, applied: SSI 2009/376 Sch.1 para.17
1978. Food Additives Labelling Regulations 1992
revoked (in part): SI 2009/3238 Reg.20, SI 2009/3378 Reg.20, SSI 2009/436 Reg.20
1989. Child Support (Collection and Enforcement) Regulations 1992
applied: SI 2009/470 Reg.51
see *Bird v Secretary of State for Work and Pensions* [2008] EWHC 3159 (Admin), [2009] 2 F.L.R. 660 (QBD (Admin)), Slade, J.
Reg.25A, added: SI 2009/1815 Reg.2
Reg.25AA, added: SI 2009/1815 Reg.2
Reg.25AB, added: SI 2009/1815 Reg.2
Reg.25AC, added: SI 2009/1815 Reg.2
Reg.25AD, added: SI 2009/1815 Reg.2
Reg.25B, added: SI 2009/1815 Reg.2
Reg.25C, added: SI 2009/1815 Reg.2
Reg.25D, added: SI 2009/1815 Reg.2
Reg.25E, added: SI 2009/1815 Reg.2
Reg.25F, added: SI 2009/1815 Reg.2
Reg.25G, added: SI 2009/1815 Reg.2
Reg.25H, added: SI 2009/1815 Reg.2
Reg.25I, added: SI 2009/1815 Reg.2
Reg.25J, added: SI 2009/1815 Reg.2
Reg.25K, added: SI 2009/1815 Reg.2
Reg.25L, added: SI 2009/1815 Reg.2
Reg.25M, added: SI 2009/1815 Reg.2
Reg.25N, added: SI 2009/1815 Reg.2
Reg.25O, added: SI 2009/1815 Reg.2
Reg.25P, added: SI 2009/1815 Reg.2
Reg.25Q, added: SI 2009/1815 Reg.2
Reg.25R, added: SI 2009/1815 Reg.2
Reg.25T, added: SI 2009/1815 Reg.2
Reg.25U, added: SI 2009/1815 Reg.2
Reg.25V, added: SI 2009/1815 Reg.2
Reg.25W, added: SI 2009/1815 Reg.2
Reg.25X, added: SI 2009/1815 Reg.2
Reg.25Y, added: SI 2009/1815 Reg.2
Reg.25Z, added: SI 2009/1815 Reg.2
s.art IIIA Reg.25S, added: SI 2009/1815 Reg.2
2051. Management of Health and Safety at Work Regulations 1992
see *Spencer v Secretary of State for Work and Pensions* [2008] EWCA Civ 750, [2009] Q.B. 358 (CA (Civ Div)), Waller, L.J.
2071. Magistrates Courts (Children and Young Persons) Rules 1992
Part III r.14, amended: SI 2009/1892 Sch.1 para.11
2086. Town and Country Planning (Enforcement of Control) (No.2) (Scotland) Regulations 1992
Reg.5, amended: SSI 2009/220 Reg.3
Reg.5, applied: SSI 2009/220 Reg.3
Reg.6, amended: SSI 2009/220 Reg.3
Reg.6, applied: SSI 2009/220 Reg.3
Reg.6, revoked (in part): SSI 2009/220 Reg.3
Reg.7, amended: SSI 2009/220 Reg.3
Reg.8, amended: SSI 2009/220 Reg.3
Reg.8, applied: SSI 2009/220 Reg.3
2184. Non-Domestic Rating (Payment of Interest) (Scotland) Regulations 1992
Reg.3, amended: SSI 2009/76 Reg.3
Reg.4, amended: SSI 2009/76 Reg.4
Reg.5, revoked: SSI 2009/76 Reg.5
Reg.6, revoked: SSI 2009/76 Reg.5

1992– cont.

2356. Merchant Shipping (Categorisation of Waters) Regulations 1992
see *Oleochem (Scotland) Ltd v Revenue and Customs Commissioners* [2009] S.T.C. (S.C.D.) 205 (Sp Comm), J Gordon Reid Q.C.
2414. Town and Country Planning (Simplified Planning Zones) Regulations 1992
Reg.2, amended: SI 2009/801 Art.3
Reg.3, amended: SI 2009/801 Art.3
2428. Local Authorities (Funds) (England) Regulations 1992
Reg.2, varied: SI 2009/5 Sch.1 para.1
Reg.5, varied: SI 2009/5 Sch.1 para.2
Reg.7, referred to: SI 2009/2543 Sch.2 para.10
Reg.8, applied: SI 2009/2543 Sch.2 para.10
Reg.8, varied: SI 2009/2543 Sch.2 para.10
Reg.11, varied: SI 2009/5 Sch.1 para.3
Sch.2 Part I para.2, amended: SI 2009/2543 Reg.5
2559. North Staffordshire Hospital Centre National Health Service Trust (Establishment) Order 1992
Art.1, amended: SI 2009/3085 Art.2
Art.3, amended: SI 2009/3085 Art.3
Art.4, amended: SI 2009/3085 Art.4
Art.7, amended: SI 2009/3085 Art.5
2645. Child Support (Maintenance Arrangements and Jurisdiction) Regulations 1992
Reg.7, revoked: SI 2009/2909 Reg.2
2790. Statistics of Trade (Customs and Excise) Regulations 1992
see *Revenue and Customs Prosecutions Office v NE Plastics Ltd* [2008] EWHC 3560 (Admin), [2009] 2 Cr. App. R. 21 (DC), Maurice Kay, L.J.
Reg.3, amended: SI 2009/2974 Reg.2
2793. Manual Handling Operations Regulations 1992
see *Egan v Central Manchester and Manchester Children's University Hospitals NHS Trust* [2008] EWCA Civ 1424, [2009] I.C.R. 585 (CA (Civ Div)), Sedley, L.J.
Reg.4, see *Egan v Central Manchester and Manchester Children's University Hospitals NHS Trust* [2008] EWCA Civ 1424, [2009] I.C.R. 585 (CA (Civ Div)), Sedley, L.J.; see *Kerr v Stiell Facilities Ltd* [2009] CSOH 67, 2009 S.L.T. 851 (OH), Lord Hodge
2811. Smoke Control Areas (Exempted Fireplaces) Order 1992
revoked (in part): SSI 2009/214 Sch.2
2843. Road Traffic Offenders (Prescribed Devices) (No.2) Order 1992
see *Robbie the Pict v Crown Prosecution Service* [2009] EWHC 1176 (Admin), Times, May 14, 2009 (QBD (Admin)), Davis, J.
2977. National Assistance (Assessment of Resources) Regulations 1992
Reg.2, amended: SSI 2009/381 Reg.2
Reg.20, amended: SI 2009/597 Reg.3, SSI 2009/72 Reg.2
Reg.28, amended: SI 2009/597 Reg.4, SSI 2009/72 Reg.3
Reg.28A, amended: SI 2009/632 Reg.4
Sch.3 Part I para.28G, amended: SSI 2009/72 Reg.4
Sch.3 Part I para.28H, amended: SI 2009/597 Reg.5, SI 2009/632 Reg.5
Sch.4 para.2, amended: SI 2009/462 Sch.5 para.2, SI 2009/632 Reg.6
Sch.4 para.2, substituted: SI 2009/632 Reg.6, SSI 2009/381 Reg.3

1992– cont.

2985. Street Works (Registers, Notices, Directions and Designations) Regulations 1992
applied: SI 2009/303 Reg.9, SI 2009/1268 Reg.8
Reg.2, applied: SI 2009/303 Reg.9, SI 2009/1268 Reg.8

2992. Licensing of Air Carriers Regulations 1992
revoked: SI 2009/41 Sch.1

2993. Access for Community Air Carriers to Intra-Community Air Routes Regulations 1992
revoked: SI 2009/41 Sch.1

2994. Air Fares Regulations 1992
revoked: SI 2009/41 Sch.1

3004. Workplace (Health, Safety and Welfare) Regulations 1992
see *Munro v Aberdeen City Council* [2009] CSOH 129, 2009 S.L.T. 964 (OH), Lord Malcolm
Reg.5, see *Munro v Aberdeen City Council* [2009] CSOH 129, 2009 S.L.T. 964 (OH), Lord Malcolm
Reg.12, see *Burgess v Napier University* [2009] CSOH 6, 2009 Rep. L.R. 55 (OH), Lady Dorrian; see *Craner v Dorset CC* [2008] EWCA Civ 1323, [2009] I.C.R. 563 (CA (Civ Div)), Sedley, L.J.; see *Munro v Aberdeen City Council*[2009] CSOH 129, 2009 S.L.T. 964 (OH), Lord Malcolm

3073. Supply of Machinery (Safety) Regulations 1992
referred to: SI 2009/669 Sch.1 Part 4, Sch.2 Part 2

3077. Goods Vehicles (Community Authorisations) Regulations 1992
applied: SI 2009/1885 Art.2, Sch.4 para.1
Reg.3, applied: SI 2009/483 Art.2
Reg.3, referred to: SI 2009/491 Sch.1 Part 2, SI 2009/492 Sch.1 Part 2
Reg.6, amended: SI 2009/1885 Sch.2 para.2
Reg.7, applied: SI 2009/483 Art.2
Reg.7, referred to: SI 2009/491 Sch.1 Part 2, SI 2009/492 Sch.1 Part 2

3082. Non-Domestic Rating Contributions (England) Regulations 1992
referred to: SI 2009/3095 Reg.2
Reg.6, varied: SI 2009/1597 Reg.5
Sch.1 Part 1 para.1, amended: SI 2009/3095 Reg.3
Sch.1 Part 1 para.4, amended: SI 2009/1307 Sch.2 para.42, SI 2009/3095 Reg.3
Sch.2, applied: SI 2009/2543 Sch.2 para.3
Sch.2 Part 1 para.2, amended: SI 2009/3095 Reg.4
Sch.2 Part 1 para.8, amended: SI 2009/3095 Reg.4

3106. Gloucestershire Airport (Designation) (Detention and Sale of Aircraft) Order 1992
revoked: SI 2009/2350 Sch.2

3121. Value Added Tax (Place of Supply of Services) Order 1992
Art.17, see *Arachchige v Revenue and Customs Commissioners* [2009] B.V.C. 2003 (V&DTr (London)), Charles Hellier (Chairman)
Art.18, see *Arachchige v Revenue and Customs Commissioners* [2009] B.V.C. 2003 (V&DTr (London)), Charles Hellier (Chairman)
Art.21, see *Arachchige v Revenue and Customs Commissioners* [2009] B.V.C. 2003 (V&DTr (London)), Charles Hellier (Chairman); see *Arachchige v Revenue and Customs Commissioners* [2009] EWHC 1077 (Ch), [2009] S.T.C. 1729 (Ch D), Lewison, J.

3122. Value Added Tax (Cars) Order 1992
Art.8, see *Pendragon Plc v Revenue and Customs Commissioners* [2009] UKFTT 192 (TC) (FTT (Tax)), Adrian Shipwright

1992– cont.

3135. Excise Goods (Holding, Movement, Warehousing and REDS) Regulations 1992
see *R. v Khan (Robert)* [2009] EWCA Crim 588, Times, April 23, 2009 (CA (Crim Div)), Hughes, L.J. (V-P)
Reg.5, see *R. v Khan (Robert)* [2009] EWCA Crim 588, Times, April 23, 2009 (CA (Crim Div)), Hughes, L.J. (V-P)

3179. Oversea Companies and Credit and Financial Institutions (Branch Disclosure) Regulations 1992
revoked: SI 2009/1801 Reg.79

3222. Value Added Tax (Input Tax) Order 1992
Art.2, amended: SI 2009/217 Art.2

3238. Non-Domestic Rating Contributions (Wales) Regulations 1992
Reg.6, varied: SI 2009/2154 Reg.5
Sch.4, substituted: SI 2009/3147 Sch.1

3288. Package Travel, Package Holidays and Package Tours Regulations 1992
referred to: SI 2009/669 Sch.1 Part 2

1993

100. Air Fares (Amendment) Regulations 1993
revoked: SI 2009/41 Sch.1

101. Licensing of Air Carriers (Amendment) Regulations 1993
revoked: SI 2009/41 Sch.1

231. Air Navigation (Third Amendment) Order 1993
applied: SI 2009/2268 Reg.25

252. Non-Domestic Rating (Demand Notices) (Wales) Regulations 1993
Reg.2, varied: SI 2009/2154 Reg.4

290. Council Tax (Alteration of Lists and Appeals) Regulations 1993
revoked (in part): SI 2009/2270 Reg.14
see *Chilton-Merryweather (Listing Officer) v Hunt* [2008] EWCA Civ 1025, [2009] Env. L.R. 16 (CA (Civ Div)), Waller, L.J.
Reg.30, amended: SI 2009/1307 Sch.2 para.43
Reg.32, see *R. (on the application of Kinsley) v Barnet LBC* [2008] EWHC 2013 (Admin), [2009] R.V.R. 34 (QBD (Admin)), Mitting, J.

291. Non-Domestic Rating (Alteration of Lists and Appeals) Regulations 1993
revoked (in part): SI 2009/2268 Reg.25
Reg.2, varied: SI 2009/2268 Sch.1
Reg.4, varied: SI 2009/2268 Sch.1
Reg.4A, see *Kendrick (Valuation Officer), Re* [2009] R.A. 145 (Lands Tr), George Bartlett Q.C. (President, LTr); see *Tuplin v Focus (DIY) Ltd*[2009] UKUT 118 (LC), [2009] R.A. 226 (UT (Lands)), George Bartlett Q.C. (President, LTr)
Reg.4A, varied: SI 2009/2268 Sch.1
Reg.5, varied: SI 2009/2268 Sch.1
Reg.5A, see *Tuplin v Focus (DIY) Ltd* [2009] UKUT 118 (LC), [2009] R.A. 226 (UT (Lands)), George Bartlett Q.C. (President, LTr)
Reg.7, varied: SI 2009/2268 Sch.1
Reg.11, see *Metropolitan Police Service v Fernley (Valuation Officer)* [2009] R.A. 254 (VT)
Reg.12, varied: SI 2009/2268 Sch.1
Reg.13A, varied: SI 2009/2268 Sch.1
Reg.18, varied: SI 2009/2268 Sch.1
Reg.20, varied: SI 2009/2268 Sch.1
Reg.28, varied: SI 2009/2268 Sch.1
Reg.32, varied: SI 2009/2268 Sch.1

1993– cont.

291. Non-Domestic Rating (Alteration of Lists and Appeals) Regulations 1993– *cont.*
Reg.33, varied: SI 2009/2268 Sch.1
Reg.34, see *Metropolitan Police Service v Fernley (Valuation Officer)* [2009] R.A. 254 (VT)
Reg.35, varied: SI 2009/2268 Sch.1
Reg.36, varied: SI 2009/2268 Sch.1
Reg.37, varied: SI 2009/2268 Sch.1
Reg.38, varied: SI 2009/2268 Sch.1
Reg.39, varied: SI 2009/2268 Sch.1
Reg.40, varied: SI 2009/2268 Sch.1
Reg.41, varied: SI 2009/2268 Sch.1
Reg.43, varied: SI 2009/2268 Sch.1
Reg.44, varied: SI 2009/2268 Sch.1
Reg.45, varied: SI 2009/2268 Sch.1
Reg.46, varied: SI 2009/2268 Sch.1
Reg.47, varied: SI 2009/2268 Sch.1
Reg.48, varied: SI 2009/2268 Sch.1
Reg.49, varied: SI 2009/2268 Sch.1

323. Town and Country Planning (Hazardous Substances) (Scotland) Regulations 1993
referred to: SSI 2009/378 Reg.4
Reg.2, amended: SSI 2009/378 Reg.3
Reg.4, amended: SSI 2009/378 Reg.3
Sch.1 Part A, substituted: SSI 2009/378 Sch.1
Sch.1 Part A para.1, substituted: SSI 2009/378 Sch.1
Sch.1 Part A para.2, substituted: SSI 2009/378 Sch.1
Sch.1 Part A para.3, substituted: SSI 2009/378 Sch.1
Sch.1 Part A para.4, substituted: SSI 2009/378 Sch.1
Sch.1 Part A para.5, substituted: SSI 2009/378 Sch.1
Sch.1 Part A para.6, substituted: SSI 2009/378 Sch.1
Sch.1 Part A para.7, substituted: SSI 2009/378 Sch.1
Sch.1 Part A para.8, substituted: SSI 2009/378 Sch.1
Sch.1 Part B, substituted: SSI 2009/378 Sch.1
Sch.1 Part B para.1, substituted: SSI 2009/378 Sch.1
Sch.1 Part B para.2, substituted: SSI 2009/378 Sch.1
Sch.1 Part B para.3, substituted: SSI 2009/378 Sch.1
Sch.1 Part B para.4, substituted: SSI 2009/378 Sch.1
Sch.1 Part B para.5, substituted: SSI 2009/378 Sch.1
Sch.1 Part C, substituted: SSI 2009/378 Sch.1
Sch.1 Part C para.1, substituted: SSI 2009/378 Sch.1
Sch.1 Part C para.2, substituted: SSI 2009/378 Sch.1
Sch.1 Part D, substituted: SSI 2009/378 Sch.1
Sch.2, amended: SSI 2009/378 Reg.3

486. Bankruptcy Fees (Scotland) Regulations 1993
Reg.3, amended: SSI 2009/97 Reg.2
Reg.4, amended: SSI 2009/97 Reg.2
Reg.4, substituted: SSI 2009/97 Reg.2
Sch.1 Part I, substituted: SSI 2009/97 Sch.1
Sch.1 Part II, amended: SSI 2009/97 Sch.1
Sch.1 Part II, substituted: SSI 2009/97 Sch.1

558. University of Paisley (Scotland) Order of Council 1993
Art.2, amended: SSI 2009/194 Art.3
Art.5, amended: SSI 2009/194 Art.4
Art.6, amended: SSI 2009/194 Art.5
Art.7, revoked (in part): SSI 2009/194 Art.6
Art.9, revoked: SSI 2009/194 Art.6
Art.9A, added: SSI 2009/194 Art.7
Art.12, amended: SSI 2009/194 Art.8
Sch.1 paraB, amended: SSI 2009/194 Art.9
Sch.1 paraC, amended: SSI 2009/194 Art.9
Sch.1 paraD, amended: SSI 2009/194 Art.9
Sch.1 paraE, amended: SSI 2009/194 Art.9
Sch.2 Part I para.1, substituted: SSI 2009/194 Art.10
Sch.2 Part I para.2, substituted: SSI 2009/194 Art.10
Sch.2 Part I para.3, substituted: SSI 2009/194 Art.10
Sch.2 Part I para.4, substituted: SSI 2009/194 Art.10

1993– cont.

558. University of Paisley (Scotland) Order of Council 1993– *cont.*
Sch.2 Part I para.5, substituted: SSI 2009/194 Art.10
Sch.2 Part I para.5A, substituted: SSI 2009/194 Art.10
Sch.2 Part II para.7, amended: SSI 2009/194 Art.11

604. Civil Jurisdiction and Judgments (Authentic Instruments and Court Settlements) Order 1993
disapplied: SI 2009/3131 Reg.46

627. Family Proceedings Courts (Child Support Act 1991) Rules 1993
r.5, amended: SI 2009/858 r.9

913. Child Support (Miscellaneous Amendments) Regulations 1993
Reg.35, revoked: SI 2009/3151 Sch.1
Reg.36, revoked: SI 2009/3151 Sch.1
Reg.37, revoked: SI 2009/3151 Sch.1
Reg.38, revoked: SI 2009/3151 Sch.1
Reg.39, revoked: SI 2009/3151 Sch.1
Reg.40, revoked: SI 2009/3151 Sch.1

920. Act of Sederunt (Child Support Rules) 1993
Art.1, amended: SSI 2009/365 r.2
Art.2, amended: SSI 2009/365 r.2
Art.5, amended: SSI 2009/365 r.2
Art.5AA, added: SSI 2009/365 r.2
Art.5AB, added: SSI 2009/365 r.2
Art.5AC, added: SSI 2009/365 r.2
Sch.1, amended: SSI 2009/365 r.2, Sch.1

970. Civil Legal Aid (Financial Conditions and Contributions) (Scotland) Regulations 1993
revoked: SSI 2009/143 Reg.9

994. National Health Service (Appointment of Consultants) (Scotland) Regulations 1993
revoked: SSI 2009/166 Reg.8

996. Environmentally Sensitive Areas (Central Southern Uplands) Designation Order 1993
Art.5A, applied: SSI 2009/376 Sch.1 para.18
Art.5D, applied: SSI 2009/376 Sch.1 para.17

997. Environmentally Sensitive Areas (Western Southern Uplands) Designation Order 1993
Art.5A, applied: SSI 2009/376 Sch.1 para.18
Art.5D, applied: SSI 2009/376 Sch.1 para.17

1026. Cranfield Airport (Designation) (Detention and Sale of Aircraft) Order 1993
revoked: SI 2009/2350 Sch.2

1228. Beer Regulations 1993
disapplied: SI 2009/1022 Art.3

1366. Crop Residues (Burning) Regulations 1993
applied: SI 2009/3365 Sch.1 para.1
Reg.4, applied: SI 2009/3264 Sch.1 para.1, SI 2009/3365 Sch.1 para.1
Reg.5, applied: SI 2009/3264 Sch.1 para.1, SI 2009/3365 Sch.1 para.1

1698. Road Traffic Offenders (Prescribed Devices) Order 1993
see *Robbie the Pict v Service* [2009] HCJAC 49, 2009 S.C.L. 944 (HCJ), Lord Carloway
Art.2, see *Robbie the Pict v Service* [2009] HCJAC 49, 2009 S.C.L. 944 (HCJ), Lord Carloway

1956. Act of Sederunt (Sheriff Court Ordinary Cause Rules) 1993
see *Kevan M Smith Ltd v Tevendale* 2009 S.L.T. (Sh Ct) 21 (Sh Ct (Grampian) (Aberdeen)), Sheriff Principal Sir S S T Young, Bt, QC
Sch.1, see *B v B* 2009 S.L.T. (Sh Ct) 43 (Sh Ct (Lothian) (Edinburgh)), Sheriff Principal E F Bowen, QC; see *Campbell v Chief Constable of the Northern Constabulary* 2009 S.L.T. (Sh

1993– cont.

1956. Act of Sederunt (Sheriff Court Ordinary Cause Rules) 1993– *cont.*
Sch.1– *cont.*
Ct) 2 (Sh Ct (Grampian) (Dingwall)), Sheriff Principal Sir S S T Young, Bt, QC

2004. Income Tax (Manufactured Overseas Dividends) Regulations 1993
Reg.7, revoked (in part): SI 2009/ 2811 Reg.2

2277. Smoke Control Areas (Exempted Fireplaces) Order 1993
revoked (in part): SSI 2009/ 214 Sch.2

2345. Environmentally Sensitive Areas (Cairngorms Straths) Designation Order 1993
Art.5A, applied: SSI 2009/ 376 Sch.1 para.18
Art.5D, applied: SSI 2009/ 376 Sch.1 para.17

2551. George Eliot Hospital National Health Service Trust (Establishment) Order 1993
Art.1, amended: SI 2009/ 1510 Art.2
Art.3, amended: SI 2009/ 1510 Art.3

2574. Royal Wolverhampton Hospitals National Health Service Trust (Establishment) Order 1993
Art.1, amended: SI 2009/ 3086 Art.2
Art.3, amended: SI 2009/ 3086 Art.3
Art.4, amended: SI 2009/ 3086 Art.4
Art.7, amended: SI 2009/ 3086 Art.5

2643. Worthing and Southlands Hospitals National Health Service Trust (Establishment) Order 1993
revoked: SI 2009/ 750 Art.6

2767. Environmentally Sensitive Areas (Central Borders) Designation Order 1993
Art.5A, applied: SSI 2009/ 376 Sch.1 para.18
Art.5D, applied: SSI 2009/ 376 Sch.1 para.17

2768. Environmentally Sensitive Areas (Stewartry) Designation Order 1993
Art.5A, applied: SSI 2009/ 376 Sch.1 para.18
Art.5D, applied: SSI 2009/ 376 Sch.1 para.17

2810. Education and Libraries (Northern Ireland) Order 1993
Art.19, amended: SI 2009/ 1941 Sch.1 para.146

2838. Velindre National Health Service Trust (Establishment) Order 1993
Art.3, revoked (in part): SI 2009/ 2059 Art.2

3039. Licensing of Air Carriers (Second Amendment and Other Provisions) Regulations 1993
revoked: SI 2009/ 41 Sch.1

3040. Access for Community Air Carriers to Intra-Community Air Routes (Amendment and Other Provisions) Regulations 1993
Reg.2, revoked: SI 2009/ 41 Sch.1
Reg.3, revoked: SI 2009/ 41 Sch.1

3041. Air Fares (Second Amendment) Regulations 1993
revoked: SI 2009/ 41 Sch.1

3053. Commercial Agents (Council Directive) Regulations 1993
see *Berry v Laytons* [2009] EWHC 1591 (QB), [2009] E.C.C. 34 (QBD), Sharp, J.; see *Sagal (t/a Bunz UK) v Atelier Bunz GmbH* [2009] EWCA Civ 700, [2009] Bus. L.R. 1527 (CA (Civ Div)), Laws, L.J.
Reg.2, see *Accentuate Ltd v Asigra Inc* [2009] EWHC 2655 (QB), [2009] 2 Lloyd's Rep. 599 (QBD), Tugendhat, J.
Reg.7, see *Berry v Laytons* [2009] EWHC 1591 (QB), [2009] E.C.C. 34 (QBD), Sharp, J.
Reg.8, see *Berry v Laytons* [2009] EWHC 1591 (QB), [2009] E.C.C. 34 (QBD), Sharp, J.

1993– cont.

3053. Commercial Agents (Council Directive) Regulations 1993– *cont.*
Reg.17, see *Accentuate Ltd v Asigra Inc* [2009] EWHC 2655 (QB), [2009] 2 Lloyd's Rep. 599 (QBD), Tugendhat, J.; see *Berry v Laytons* [2009] EWHC 1591 (QB), [2009] E.C.C. 34 (QBD), Sharp, J.; see *Scottish Power Energy Retail Ltd v Taskforce Contracts Ltd* 2009 S.C.L.R. 137 (OH), Lord Menzies

3080. Act of Sederunt (Fees of Solicitors in the Sheriff Court) (Amendment and Further Provisions) 1993
Sch.1 Part 1, amended: SSI 2009/ 81 Sch.1
Sch.1 Part 1, added: SSI 2009/ 321 Sch.1
Sch.1 Part 1, amended: SSI 2009/ 81 Sch.1, SSI 2009/ 321 Art.2
Sch.1 Part 1 para.1, amended: SSI 2009/ 81 Sch.1
Sch.1 Part 1 para.2, amended: SSI 2009/ 81 Sch.1
Sch.1 Part 1 para.3, amended: SSI 2009/ 81 Sch.1

3136. Environmentally Sensitive Areas (Argyll Islands) Designation Order 1993
Art.5A, applied: SSI 2009/ 376 Sch.1 para.18
Art.5D, applied: SSI 2009/ 376 Sch.1 para.17

3143. Cayman Islands (Constitution) (Amendment) Order 1993
revoked: SI 2009/ 1379 Sch.1

3149. Environmentally Sensitive Areas (Machair of the Uists and Benbecula, Barra and Vatersay) Designation Order 1993
Art.5A, applied: SSI 2009/ 376 Sch.1 para.18
Art.5D, applied: SSI 2009/ 376 Sch.1 para.17

3150. Environmentally Sensitive Areas (Shetland Islands) Designation Order 1993
Art.5A, applied: SSI 2009/ 376 Sch.1 para.18
Art.5D, applied: SSI 2009/ 376 Sch.1 para.17

3212. Lottery Duty Regulations 1993
Sch.1 para.2, amended: SI 2009/ 1890 Art.3

3253. Parliamentary Pensions (Consolidation and Amendment) Regulations 1993
applied: SI 2009/ 1920 Reg.16
Part J, applied: SI 2009/ 1920 Reg.16
Reg.1, amended: SI 2009/ 3154 Reg.3
Reg.1, amended: SI 2009/ 3154 Reg.5
Reg.1, applied: SI 2009/ 1920 Reg.16
Reg.1, amended: SI 2009/ 1920 Reg.3
Reg.1, applied: SI 2009/ 1920 Reg.1, Reg.16
Reg.2, amended: SI 2009/ 3154 Reg.2
Reg.2, amended: SI 2009/ 3154 Reg.4
Reg.2, amended: SI 2009/ 3154 Reg.6
Reg.2, applied: SI 2009/ 1920 Reg.16
Reg.2, revoked (in part): SI 2009/ 3154 Reg.6
Reg.2, applied: SI 2009/ 1920 Reg.16
Reg.2, amended: SI 2009/ 1920 Reg.4
Reg.3, applied: SI 2009/ 1920 Reg.16
Reg.3, amended: SI 2009/ 1920 Reg.5
Reg.3, revoked (in part): SI 2009/ 1920 Reg.5
Reg.3, amended: SI 2009/ 1920 Reg.13
Reg.4, amended: SI 2009/ 3154 Reg.7
Reg.4, applied: SI 2009/ 1920 Reg.16
Reg.4, revoked (in part): SI 2009/ 3154 Reg.7
Reg.4, amended: SI 2009/ 1920 Reg.6
Reg.4, amended: SI 2009/ 1920 Reg.10
Reg.4A, revoked: SI 2009/ 1920 Reg.7
Reg.5, amended: SI 2009/ 3154 Reg.8
Reg.5, substituted: SI 2009/ 1920 Reg.8
Reg.5, amended: SI 2009/ 1920 Reg.11
Reg.5A, added: SI 2009/ 1920 Reg.9
Reg.6, added: SI 2009/ 1920 Reg.9
Reg.7, applied: SI 2009/ 1920 Reg.16

1993– cont.

3253. Parliamentary Pensions (Consolidation and Amendment) Regulations 1993– *cont.*
Reg.8, amended: SI 2009/1920 Reg.2
Reg.8, amended: SI 2009/1920 Reg.12
Sch.2 para.1, amended: SI 2009/1920 Reg.14
Sch.2 para.4, amended: SI 2009/3154 Reg.9
Sch.6 para.5, amended: SI 2009/1920 Reg.15
Sch.6 para.6, amended: SI 2009/1920 Reg.15

1994

105. Medicines (Homoeopathic Medicinal Products for Human Use) Regulations 1994
Reg.14, amended: SI 2009/389 Reg.50
Reg.15, amended: SI 2009/389 Reg.50
Reg.15A, added: SI 2009/389 Reg.50
Sch.2 para.3, amended: SI 2009/389 Reg.50
Sch.2A para.2, amended: SI 2009/389 Reg.50

117. Companies (Welsh Language Forms and Documents) Regulations 1994
Reg.4, revoked: SI 2009/1803 Reg.6

166. Royal West Sussex National Health Service Trust (Establishment) Order 1994
revoked: SI 2009/750 Art.6

426. Airports (Northern Ireland) Order 1994
Art.2, amended: SI 2009/1941 Sch.1 para.149
Art.32, amended: SI 2009/1941 Sch.1 para.149
Art.51, amended: SI 2009/1941 Sch.1 para.149
Art.57, amended: SI 2009/1941 Sch.1 para.149

570. Channel Tunnel (Security) Order 1994
Sch.2 para.7, amended: SI 2009/1307 Sch.2 para.44
Sch.2 para.7A, added: SI 2009/1307 Sch.2 para.44
Sch.2 para.8, revoked (in part): SI 2009/1307 Sch.2 para.44
Sch.2 para.9, revoked (in part): SI 2009/1307 Sch.2 para.44

573. Railways (London Regional Transport) (Exemptions) Order 1994
Art.2, amended: SI 2009/3336 Art.2
Art.2A, added: SI 2009/3336 Art.2
Art.2B, added: SI 2009/3336 Art.2
Art.3, substituted: SI 2009/3336 Art.2
Art.4, substituted: SI 2009/3336 Art.2
Art.5, amended: SI 2009/3336 Art.2
Art.6, amended: SI 2009/3336 Art.2
Art.7, added: SI 2009/3336 Art.2

606. Railways (Class and Miscellaneous Exemptions) Order 1994
Art.1, applied: SI 2009/2726 Art.12, Art.13, Art.14
Art.3, applied: SI 2009/2726 Art.11
Art.5, applied: SI 2009/2726 Art.11
Art.6, applied: SI 2009/2726 Art.11
Art.7, applied: SI 2009/2726 Art.12, Art.13, Art.14

607. Railways (Alternative Closure Procedure) Order 1994
Art.1, applied: SI 2009/2726 Art.15
Art.2, applied: SI 2009/2726 Art.15

652. Education (Special Schools) Regulations 1994
Reg.7, amended: SI 2009/2544 Reg.2

867. Local Government Changes for England Regulations 1994
applied: SI 2009/1611 Reg.19

950. Foreign Companies (Execution of Documents) Regulations 1994
revoked: SI 2009/1917 Reg.7

955. Travellers Allowances Order 1994
Art.2, referred to: SI 2009/3172 Art.1
Sch.1, amended: SI 2009/3172 Art.3

1994– cont.

1056. Waste Management Licensing Regulations 1994
applied: SI 2009/716 Reg.3
Reg.1, amended: SSI 2009/247 Reg.4
Reg.12C, added: SSI 2009/247 Reg.4
Reg.12D, added: SSI 2009/247 Reg.4
Reg.17, amended: SSI 2009/247 Reg.4
Sch.3 para.17, amended: SSI 2009/247 Reg.4
Sch.3 para.18, amended: SSI 2009/247 Reg.4
Sch.3 para.36, amended: SSI 2009/247 Reg.4
Sch.3 para.39, amended: SSI 2009/247 Reg.4
Sch.3 para.45, amended: SSI 2009/247 Reg.4

1151. Wildlife and Countryside Act 1981 (Variation of Schedule 4) Order 1994
Art.3, revoked (in part): SI 2009/780 Art.3, SSI 2009/418 Art.3

1152. Wildlife and Countryside (Registration and Ringing of Certain Captive Birds) (Amendment) Regulations 1994
revoked (in part): SSI 2009/419 Reg.7

1438. Bail (Amendment) Act 1993 (Prescription of Prosecuting Authorities) Order 1994
Sch.1, amended: SI 2009/2748 Sch.1 para.16

1443. Act of Sederunt (Rules of the Court of Session 1994) 1994
Appendix 1, amended: SSI 2009/63 Sch.1, SSI 2009/104 r.2, Sch.1
Sch.2 Part 2 para.5.1A, substituted: SSI 2009/63 r.3
Sch.2 Part 3 para.14A.3, amended: SSI 2009/104 r.2
Sch.2 Part 3 para.16.15, amended: SSI 2009/104 r.2
Sch.2 Part 3 para.16.15, revoked (in part): SSI 2009/104 r.2
Sch.2 Part 3 para.16.16, added: SSI 2009/104 r.2
Sch.2 Part 3 para.23.2, revoked (in part): SSI 2009/387 r.2
Sch.2 Part 3 para.23.2, substituted: SSI 2009/387 r.2
Sch.2 Part 3 para.23.3, amended: SSI 2009/387 r.2
Sch.2 Part 3 para.23.3, substituted: SSI 2009/387 r.2
Sch.2 Part 3 para.23.4, amended: SSI 2009/387 r.2
Sch.2 Part 3 para.23.4, substituted: SSI 2009/387 r.2
Sch.2 Part 3 para.23.5, amended: SSI 2009/387 r.2
Sch.2 Part 3 para.23.5, substituted: SSI 2009/387 r.2
Sch.2 Part 3 para.23.6, amended: SSI 2009/387 r.2
Sch.2 Part 3 para.23.6, substituted: SSI 2009/387 r.2
Sch.2 Part 3 para.23.7, substituted: SSI 2009/387 r.2
Sch.2 Part 3 para.23.8, substituted: SSI 2009/387 r.2
Sch.2 Part 3 para.23.9, substituted: SSI 2009/387 r.2
Sch.2 Part 3 para.23.10, substituted: SSI 2009/387 r.2
Sch.2 Part 3 para.23.11, substituted: SSI 2009/387 r.2
Sch.2 Part 3 para.23.12, substituted: SSI 2009/387 r.2
Sch.2 Part 3 para.23.13, substituted: SSI 2009/387 r.2
Sch.2 Part 3 para.23.14, substituted: SSI 2009/387 r.2
Sch.2 Part 3 para.23.15, substituted: SSI 2009/387 r.2
Sch.2 Part 3 para.25A.1, amended: SSI 2009/323 Art.2
Sch.2 Part 3 para.25A.8, amended: SSI 2009/323 Art.2
Sch.2 Part 3 para.25A.9, amended: SSI 2009/323 Art.2
Sch.2 Part 3 para.25A.10, amended: SSI 2009/323 Art.2
Sch.2 Part 3 para.25A.11, amended: SSI 2009/323 Art.2
Sch.2 Part 3 para.25.2, amended: SSI 2009/104 r.2
Sch.2 Part 3 para.26.3, amended: SSI 2009/104 r.2
Sch.2 Part 3 para.33.9, amended: SSI 2009/63 r.3
Sch.2 Part 3 para.41.20, amended: SSI 2009/63 r.4
Sch.2 Part 3 para.41.23, revoked (in part): SSI 2009/114 r.2
Sch.2 Part 3 para.41.24, revoked: SSI 2009/114 r.2
Sch.2 Part 3 para.41.25, revoked: SSI 2009/114 r.2
Sch.2 Part 3 para.41.26, amended: SSI 2009/114 r.2

1994– cont.

1443. Act of Sederunt (Rules of the Court of Session 1994) 1994– *cont.*

Sch.2 Part 3 para.42.16, amended: SSI 2009/82 Sch.1, SSI 2009/105 r.2

Sch.2 Part 4 para.43.1, amended: SSI 2009/63 r.5

Sch.2 Part 4 para.49.7, amended: SSI 2009/104 r.2

Sch.2 Part 4 para.52.3, substituted: SSI 2009/63 r.6

Sch.2 Part 4 para.59.1, amended: SSI 2009/104 r.2

Sch.2 Part 4 para.59.1, revoked (in part): SSI 2009/104 r.2

Sch.2 Part 5, applied: SI 2009/351 r.6, r.11

Sch.2 Part 5, applied: SI 2009/806 r.41

Sch.2 Part 5 para.74.1, amended: SSI 2009/63 r.3

Sch.2 Part 5 para.74.2, amended: SSI 2009/63 r.3

Sch.2 Part 5 para.74.3, amended: SSI 2009/63 r.3

Sch.2 Part 5 para.74.9, amended: SSI 2009/63 r.3

Sch.2 Part 5 para.74.15A, added: SSI 2009/63 r.3

Sch.2 Part 5 para.74.32B, added: SSI 2009/63 r.3

Sch.2 Part 5 para.74.32B, amended: SSI 2009/135 r.2

Sch.2 Part 5 para.74.35, added: SSI 2009/63 r.3

Sch.2 Part 5 para.74.36, added: SSI 2009/63 r.3

Sch.2 Part 5 para.74.37, added: SSI 2009/63 r.3

Sch.2 Part 5 para.74.38, added: SSI 2009/63 r.3

Sch.2 Part 5 para.74.39, added: SSI 2009/63 r.3

Sch.2 Part 5 para.74.40, added: SSI 2009/63 r.3

Sch.2 Part 5 para.74.41, added: SSI 2009/63 r.3

Sch.2 Part 5 para.74.42, added: SSI 2009/63 r.3

Sch.2 Part 5 para.74.43, added: SSI 2009/63 r.3

Sch.2 Part 5 para.74.44, added: SSI 2009/63 r.3

Sch.2 Part 5 para.74.45, added: SSI 2009/63 r.3

Sch.2 Part 5 para.74.46, added: SSI 2009/63 r.3

Sch.2 Part 5 para.74.47, added: SSI 2009/63 r.3

Sch.2 Part 5 para.74.48, added: SSI 2009/63 r.3

Sch.2 Part 5 para.74.49, added: SSI 2009/63 r.3

Sch.2 Part 5 para.74.49, amended: SSI 2009/135 r.2

Sch.2 Part 5 para.74.50, added: SSI 2009/63 r.3

Sch.2 Part 5 para.74.51, added: SSI 2009/135 r.2

Sch.2 Part 5 para.96.9, amended: SSI 2009/63 r.7

Sch.2 para.36.2, see *Scottish Ministers v Stirton* [2009] CSOH 61, 2009 S.C.L.R. 541 (OH), Lord Mackay of Drumadoon

Sch.2 para.38.3, see *Robertson, Petitioner (No 2)* [2009] CSIH 59, 2009 S.C.L.R. 773 (IH (1 Div)), The Lord President (Hamilton); see *Robertson, Petitioner (No.1)* [2009] CSIH 58 (IH (1 Div)), The Lord President (Hamilton)

Sch.2 para.38.7, see *Robertson, Petitioner (No 2)* [2009] CSIH 59, 2009 S.C.L.R. 773 (IH (1 Div)), The Lord President (Hamilton)

Sch.2 para.41.20, see *Y v Law Society of Scotland* [2009] CSIH 32, 2009 S.C. 430 (IH (Ex Div)), Lord Carloway

Sch.2 para.42.4, see *McLean v Zonal Retail Data Systems Ltd* [2009] CSOH 12, 2009 S.C.L.R. 763 (OH), Lord Hodge

Sch.2 para.42.13, see *JA McClelland & Sons (Auctioneers) Ltd v IR Robertson & Partners Ltd* [2009] CSOH 11, 2009 S.L.T. 531 (OH), Lord Hodge; see *McLean v Zonal Retail Data Systems Ltd* [2009] CSOH 12, 2009 S.C.L.R. 763 (OH), Lord Hodge

Sch.2 para.42.14, see *JA McClelland & Sons (Auctioneers) Ltd v IR Robertson & Partners Ltd* [2009] CSOH 11, 2009 S.L.T. 531 (OH), Lord Hodge

Sch.2 para.42.16, see *JA McClelland & Sons (Auctioneers) Ltd v IR Robertson & Partners Ltd* [2009] CSOH 11, 2009 S.L.T. 531 (OH), Lord Hodge

1994– cont.

1443. Act of Sederunt (Rules of the Court of Session 1994) 1994– *cont.*

Sch.2 para.43.11, see *Cameron v Gellatly* [2009] CSOH 82, 2009 S.C. 639 (OH), Lord Malcolm

1447. Diseases of Fish (Control) Regulations 1994

revoked (in part): SI 2009/463 Sch.2 para.11, SSI 2009/85 Sch.2 para.12

1642. International Headquarters and Defence Organisations (Designation and Privileges) (Amendment) Order 1994

revoked: SI 2009/704 Art.4

1701. Organic Aid (Scotland) Regulations 1994

applied: SSI 2009/376 Sch.1 para.19

Reg.12, applied: SSI 2009/376 Sch.1 para.19

1731. Access for Community Air Carriers to Intra-Community Air Routes (Second Amendment and other Provisions) Regulations 1994

Reg.2, revoked: SI 2009/41 Sch.1

Reg.3, revoked: SI 2009/41 Sch.1

1732. Licensing of Air Carriers (Third Amendment and other Provisions) Regulations 1994

revoked: SI 2009/41 Sch.1

1735. Air Fares (Third Amendment) Regulations 1994

revoked: SI 2009/41 Sch.1

1737. Aircraft Operators (Accounts and Records) Regulations 1994

Sch.1, amended: SI 2009/2051 Reg.3

1738. Air Passenger Duty Regulations 1994

Reg.9, amended: SI 2009/2045 Reg.2

Sch.3, revoked: SI 2009/2045 Reg.2

1811. Special Commissioners (Jurisdiction and Procedure) Regulations 1994

revoked: SI 2009/56 Sch.2 para.187

1812. General Commissioners (Jurisdiction and Procedure) Regulations 1994

revoked: SI 2009/56 Sch.2 para.187

Reg.17, varied: SI 2009/56 Sch.3 para.11

Reg.20, varied: SI 2009/56 Sch.3 para.11

Reg.21, varied: SI 2009/56 Sch.3 para.11

Reg.22, varied: SI 2009/56 Sch.3 para.11

Reg.23, varied: SI 2009/56 Sch.3 para.11

Reg.24, varied: SI 2009/56 Sch.3 para.11

1885. Local Authorities (Charges for Land Searches) Regulations 1994

applied: SI 2009/369 Reg.3

revoked (in part): SI 2009/369 Reg.3

1895. Immigration (European Economic Area) Order 1994

see *OP (Colombia) v Secretary of State for the Home Department* [2009] Imm. A.R. 233 (AIT), CMG Ockelton (Deputy President)

1932. Medicines (Advertising) Regulations 1994

referred to: SI 2009/669 Sch.1 Part 2

1978. Value Added Tax Tribunals Appeals (Northern Ireland) Order 1994

revoked: SI 2009/56 Sch.2 para.187

2095. Police (Scotland) Amendment Regulations 1994

see *Robb v Tayside Joint Police Board* 2009 S.L.T. (Lands Tr) 23 (Lands Tr (Scot)), J N Wright QC

2184. Fire Precautions (Sub-surface Railway Stations) (Amendment) Regulations 1994

revoked (in part): SI 2009/782 Reg.13

2507. Insolvency Regulations 1994

varied: SI 2009/317 Sch.1

Reg.3, amended: SI 2009/2748 Sch.1 para.17

Sch.2, substituted: SI 2009/482 Reg.2

1994– cont.

2576. British Coal Staff Superannuation Scheme (Modification) Regulations 1994
applied: SI 2009/229 Art.4

2577. Mineworkers Pension Scheme (Modification) Regulations 1994
applied: SI 2009/229 Art.4

2616. Solicitors (Non-Contentious Business) Remuneration Order 1994
applied: SI 2009/2105 Sch.1 Part II, SI 2009/2107 Sch.1 Part B, Sch.2 para.1, Sch.2 para.4
revoked: SI 2009/1931 Art.1
Art.2, amended: SI 2009/500 Art.3

2710. Habitats (Scotland) Regulations 1994
applied: SSI 2009/376 Sch.1 para.21
Reg.12, applied: SSI 2009/376 Sch.1 para.21

2716. Conservation (Natural Habitats, &c.) Regulations 1994
applied: 2009 c.23 s.158, SI 2009/153 Sch.1 para.5, SI 2009/995 Sch.1 para.5
referred to: SI 2009/2325 Art.38
Part IVA, applied: SSI 2009/53 Reg.2
Reg.2, amended: SI 2009/6 Reg.3
Reg.3, amended: SI 2009/2438 Reg.4
Reg.4, amended: SI 2009/6 Reg.4
Reg.8, applied: 2009 asp 6 s.23
Reg.16, amended: SI 2009/1307 Sch.2 para.46
Reg.22, amended: SI 2009/2438 Reg.10
Reg.23, amended: SI 2009/2438 Reg.10
Reg.24, amended: SI 2009/2438 Reg.10
Reg.25, substituted: SI 2009/2438 Reg.10
Reg.27A, added: SI 2009/2438 Reg.10
Reg.36, substituted: 2009 c.23 Sch.11 para.4
Reg.37, amended: SI 2009/2438 Reg.5
Reg.37A, amended: SI 2009/6 Reg.5
Reg.37B, amended: SI 2009/6 Reg.6
Reg.39, amended: SI 2009/6 Reg.7
Reg.39, revoked (in part): SI 2009/6 Reg.7
Reg.40, amended: SI 2009/6 Reg.8
Reg.41A, amended: SI 2009/6 Reg.9
Reg.41B, amended: SI 2009/6 Reg.10
Reg.44, amended: SI 2009/6 Reg.11
Reg.48, applied: SI 2009/2264 Reg.5, SI 2009/2325 Art.38
Reg.54, amended: SSI 2009/222 Art.14
Reg.59, amended: SI 2009/1307 Sch.2 para.47
Reg.60, disapplied: SI 2009/2325 Art.38
Reg.67A, added: SI 2009/2438 Reg.6
Reg.67B, added: SI 2009/2438 Reg.6
Reg.68, substituted: SI 2009/2438 Reg.6
Reg.71, varied: 2009 c.23 s.12
Reg.72, varied: 2009 c.23 s.12
Reg.73, varied: 2009 c.23 s.12
Reg.74, amended: SI 2009/1307 Sch.2 para.48
Reg.74, varied: 2009 c.23 s.12
Reg.78, amended: SI 2009/1307 Sch.2 para.49
Reg.82, amended: SI 2009/1307 Sch.2 para.50
Reg.84C, added: SI 2009/2438 Reg.9
Reg.84D, added: SI 2009/3160 Reg.11
Reg.85A, amended: SSI 2009/343 Reg.2
Reg.85F, added: SI 2009/2438 Reg.7, Reg.8
Reg.89, amended: SI 2009/2438 Reg.11
Reg.90, amended: SI 2009/2438 Reg.11
Reg.91, amended: SI 2009/2438 Reg.11
Reg.92, amended: SI 2009/1307 Sch.2 para.51, SI 2009/2438 Reg.11
Reg.96, amended: SI 2009/1307 Sch.2 para.52
Sch.1 para.2, amended: SI 2009/2438 Reg.11

1994– cont.

2795. Criminal Justice (Northern Ireland) Order 1994
Art.11, applied: 2009 c.25 s.164

2809. Ports (Northern Ireland) Order 1994
Art.2, amended: SI 2009/1941 Sch.1 para.150
Art.3, amended: SI 2009/1941 Sch.1 para.150
Art.5, amended: SI 2009/1941 Sch.1 para.150

2841. Urban Waste Water Treatment (England and Wales) Regulations 1994
see *R. (on the application of Thames Water Utilities Ltd) v Bromley Magistrates' Court* [2008] EWHC 1763 (Admin), [2009] 1 W.L.R. 1247 (DC), Carnwath, L.J.

2946. Social Security (Incapacity Benefit) Regulations 1994
Reg.2A, amended: SI 2009/471 Reg.6
Reg.8, amended: SI 2009/2343 Reg.3
Reg.10, amended: SI 2009/497 Art.14
Reg.20A, added: SI 2009/792 Reg.2

3024. Charitable Institutions (Fund-Raising) Regulations 1994
Reg.7, amended: SI 2009/1060 Reg.3
Reg.7, applied: SI 2009/1060 Reg.4
Reg.7, referred to: SI 2009/1060 Reg.4

3144. Medicines for Human Use (Marketing Authorisations Etc.) Regulations 1994
applied: SI 2009/389 Reg.42, SSI 2009/45 Art.5
Reg.1, amended: SI 2009/3222 Reg.9
Reg.4, applied: SI 2009/389 Reg.18
Sch.1 para.1, amended: SI 2009/3063 Reg.2
Sch.1 para.2, amended: SI 2009/3063 Reg.2
Sch.2 Part 1 para.1, amended: SI 2009/3222 Reg.9
Sch.2 Part 1 para.5, applied: SI 2009/389 Sch.5 para.2
Sch.2 Part 2 para.11, referred to: SI 2009/389 Reg.37
Sch.2 Part 3 para.16, referred to: SI 2009/389 Reg.37
Sch.2 para.7, substituted: SI 2009/2820 Reg.2
Sch.3 para.1, see *R. v Patel (Hitendra)* [2009] EWCA Crim 2311, Times, November 19, 2009 (CA (Crim Div)), Hooper, L.J.
Sch.3 para.3A, amended: SI 2009/3222 Reg.9
Sch.5 para.9, added: SI 2009/1164 Reg.2

3200. Non-Domestic Rating (Unoccupied Property) (Scotland) Regulations 1994
varied: SI 2009/317 Sch.1

3208. Double Taxation Relief (Taxes on Income) (Isle of Man) Order 1994
Sch.1, referred to: SI 2009/228 Art.3

3209. Double Taxation Relief (Taxes on Income) (Guernsey) Order 1994
Sch.1, referred to: SI 2009/3011 Art.3

3210. Double Taxation Relief (Taxes on Income) (Jersey) Order 1994
Sch.1, applied: SI 2009/3012 Art.3

3260. Electrical Equipment (Safety) Regulations 1994
referred to: SI 2009/669 Sch.1 Part 4, Sch.2 Part 2

3279. Non-Domestic Rating (Chargeable Amounts) Regulations 1994
Reg.36, see *Monster Worldwide Ltd (also t/a TMP Worldwide) v Westminster City Council* [2009] R.V.R. 186 (Ch D), Master Bragge
Sch.2, see *Monster Worldwide Ltd (also t/a TMP Worldwide) v Westminster City Council* [2009] R.V.R. 186 (Ch D), Master Bragge

1995

204. Toys (Safety) Regulations 1995
referred to: SI 2009/669 Sch.1 Part 4, Sch.2 Part 2

300. National Health Service Pension Scheme Regulations 1995
referred to: SI 2009/381 Reg.2

Reg.1, amended: SI 2009/1298 Reg.2, SI 2009/2446 Sch.1 para.1

Reg.1, amended: SI 2009/2446 Sch.1 para.1

Reg.1, amended: SI 2009/381 Reg.4, SI 2009/2446 Sch.1 para.1

Reg.1, amended: SI 2009/2446 Sch.1 para.1

Reg.1, amended: SI 2009/2446 Sch.1 para.3

Reg.1, amended: SI 2009/381 Reg.9, SI 2009/2446 Sch.1 para.1, Sch.1 para.2

Reg.1, amended: SI 2009/2446 Sch.1 para.1

Reg.1A, amended: SI 2009/381 Reg.12

Reg.2, amended: SI 2009/2446 Reg.3, Sch.1 para.1, Sch.1 para.2

Reg.2, amended: SI 2009/2446 Sch.1 para.1, Sch.1 para.2

Reg.2, amended: SI 2009/2446 Sch.1 para.1

Reg.2A, amended: SI 2009/2446 Sch.1 para.1

Reg.2B, amended: SI 2009/381 Reg.5, SI 2009/2446 Reg.4

Reg.3, see *R. (on the application of Parish) v Pensions Ombudsman* [2009] EWHC 32 (Admin), [2009] Pens. L.R. 91 (QBD (Admin)), Keith, J.

Reg.3, amended: SI 2009/2446 Sch.1 para.1

Reg.3, see *R. (on the application of Parish) v Pensions Ombudsman* [2009] EWHC 32 (Admin), [2009] Pens. L.R. 91 (QBD (Admin)), Keith, J.

Reg.3, amended: SI 2009/381 Reg.3, SI 2009/1298 Reg.2, SI 2009/2446 Sch.1 para.1

Reg.3, see *R. (on the application of Parish) v Pensions Ombudsman* [2009] EWHC 32 (Admin), [2009] Pens. L.R. 91 (QBD (Admin)), Keith, J.

Reg.3, amended: SI 2009/2446 Sch.1 para.1

Reg.3, see *R. (on the application of Parish) v Pensions Ombudsman* [2009] EWHC 32 (Admin), [2009] Pens. L.R. 91 (QBD (Admin)), Keith, J.

Reg.3, see *R. (on the application of Parish) v Pensions Ombudsman* [2009] EWHC 32 (Admin), [2009] Pens. L.R. 91 (QBD (Admin)), Keith, J.

Reg.3, amended: SI 2009/2446 Reg.5, Sch.1 para.1

Reg.3, see *R. (on the application of Parish) v Pensions Ombudsman* [2009] EWHC 32 (Admin), [2009] Pens. L.R. 91 (QBD (Admin)), Keith, J.

Reg.3, amended: SI 2009/2446 Reg.7, Sch.1 para.1

Reg.3, see *R. (on the application of Parish) v Pensions Ombudsman* [2009] EWHC 32 (Admin), [2009] Pens. L.R. 91 (QBD (Admin)), Keith, J.

Reg.3, amended: SI 2009/2446 Sch.1 para.1

Reg.3, see *R. (on the application of Parish) v Pensions Ombudsman* [2009] EWHC 32 (Admin), [2009] Pens. L.R. 91 (QBD (Admin)), Keith, J.

Reg.3, see *R. (on the application of Parish) v Pensions Ombudsman* [2009] EWHC 32 (Admin), [2009] Pens. L.R. 91 (QBD (Admin)), Keith, J.

1995– cont.

300. National Health Service Pension Scheme Regulations 1995– *cont.*

Reg.3, see *R. (on the application of Parish) v Pensions Ombudsman* [2009] EWHC 32 (Admin), [2009] Pens. L.R. 91 (QBD (Admin)), Keith, J.

Reg.3, see *R. (on the application of Parish) v Pensions Ombudsman* [2009] EWHC 32 (Admin), [2009] Pens. L.R. 91 (QBD (Admin)), Keith, J.

Reg.3A, amended: SI 2009/2446 Sch.1 para.1

Reg.4, amended: SI 2009/2446 Sch.1 para.1

Reg.4, amended: SI 2009/381 Reg.8, SI 2009/2446 Reg.8, Sch.1 para.1

Reg.4, amended: SI 2009/2446 Sch.1 para.1

Reg.4, amended: SI 2009/2446 Sch.1 para.4

Reg.4, amended: SI 2009/2446 Sch.1 para.1

Reg.5, amended: SI 2009/2446 Sch.1 para.1

Reg.6, amended: SI 2009/381 Reg.6

Reg.6, amended: SI 2009/2446 Sch.1 para.1

Reg.7, amended: SI 2009/381 Reg.7

Reg.7, amended: SI 2009/2446 Sch.1 para.1

Reg.7, amended: SI 2009/2446 Sch.1 para.1, Sch.1 para.2

Reg.7, amended: SI 2009/2446 Sch.1 para.1

Reg.8, amended: SI 2009/2446 Sch.1 para.1, Sch.1 para.4

Reg.8, amended: SI 2009/381 Reg.11

Reg.8A, amended: SI 2009/2446 Sch.1 para.1

Reg.9, amended: SI 2009/2446 Sch.1 para.1

Reg.12, amended: SI 2009/2446 Sch.1 para.1

Reg.14, amended: SI 2009/2446 Reg.6

Reg.16, amended: SI 2009/2446 Sch.1 para.1

s.art S Reg.1, amended: SI 2009/2446 Sch.1 para.1

s.art S Reg.2, amended: SI 2009/2446 Sch.1 para.1

s.art S Reg.3A, amended: SI 2009/381 Reg.10

Sch.2 para.2, amended: SI 2009/2446 Sch.1 para.1

Sch.2 para.2A, amended: SI 2009/2446 Sch.1 para.1

Sch.2 para.4, amended: SI 2009/2446 Sch.1 para.1

Sch.2 para.9, amended: SI 2009/2446 Reg.9, Sch.1 para.1

Sch.2 para.9A, amended: SI 2009/2446 Sch.1 para.1

Sch.2 para.10, amended: SI 2009/381 Reg.13, SI 2009/2446 Sch.1 para.1

Sch.2 para.11A, amended: SI 2009/2446 Reg.9, Sch.1 para.1

Sch.2 para.14, amended: SI 2009/2446 Sch.1 para.1

Sch.2 para.14, substituted: SI 2009/381 Reg.13

Sch.2 para.18, amended: SI 2009/2446 Sch.1 para.1

Sch.2 para.21, amended: SI 2009/2446 Sch.1 para.1

Sch.2 para.22, amended: SI 2009/2446 Sch.1 para.1

Sch.2 para.23, amended: SI 2009/2446 Sch.1 para.1

Sch.2 para.23, substituted: SI 2009/381 Reg.13

Sch.2A para.2, revoked: SI 2009/381 Reg.14

Sch.2A para.3, amended: SI 2009/381 Reg.14, SI 2009/2446 Sch.1 para.1

Sch.2A para.3A, added: SI 2009/381 Reg.14

Sch.2A para.3B, added: SI 2009/381 Reg.14

Sch.2A para.4, amended: SI 2009/381 Reg.14

Sch.2A para.5, amended: SI 2009/381 Reg.14

Sch.2A para.6, amended: SI 2009/2446 Sch.1 para.1

Sch.2A para.7, amended: SI 2009/381 Reg.14, SI 2009/2446 Sch.1 para.1

Sch.2A para.8, amended: SI 2009/2446 Sch.1 para.1

Sch.2A para.9, amended: SI 2009/2446 Sch.1 para.1

Sch.2A para.12, revoked (in part): SI 2009/381 Reg.14

Sch.2A para.13, revoked (in part): SI 2009/381 Reg.14

Sch.2A para.16, added: SI 2009/381 Reg.14

1995– cont.

310. Social Security (Incapacity Benefit) (Transitional) Regulations 1995
Reg.l, amended: SI 2009/ 1488 Reg.8
Reg.18, amended: SI 2009/ 497 Art.15
Reg.18, varied: SI 2009/ 497 Art.15

311. Social Security (Incapacity for Work) (General) Regulations 1995
see *Sheffield Forgemasters International Ltd v Fox* [2009] I.C.R. 333 (EAT), Silber, J.
Reg.6, applied: SI 2009/ 3152 Reg.2
Reg.10A, see *Sheffield Forgemasters International Ltd v Fox* [2009] I.C.R. 333 (EAT), Silber, J.
Reg.16, see *Sheffield Forgemasters International Ltd v Fox* [2009] I.C.R. 333 (EAT), Silber, J.
Reg.17, amended: SI 2009/ 2343 Reg.4
Reg.17, see *Sheffield Forgemasters International Ltd v Fox* [2009] I.C.R. 333 (EAT), Silber, J.
Reg.25, see *Sheffield Forgemasters International Ltd v Fox* [2009] I.C.R. 333 (EAT), Silber, J.
Reg.28, applied: SI 2009/ 3152 Reg.2

365. National Health Service Superannuation Scheme (Scotland) Regulations 1995
referred to: SSI 2009/ 19 Reg.2, Reg.87
Reg.l, amended: SSI 2009/ 19 Reg.5, SSI 2009/ 208 Reg.4
Reg.l, substituted: SSI 2009/ 19 Reg.16
Reg.2, amended: SSI 2009/ 19 Reg.3
Reg.2, amended: SSI 2009/ 19 Reg.4
Reg.2, amended: SSI 2009/ 19 Reg.9
Reg.2, amended: SSI 2009/ 19 Reg.19, SSI 2009/ 208 Reg.12
Reg.2B, amended: SSI 2009/ 19 Reg.6, SSI 2009/ 208 Reg.5
Reg.3, amended: SSI 2009/ 208 Reg.3
Reg.3, amended: SSI 2009/ 19 Reg.10
Reg.3, amended: SSI 2009/ 19 Reg.12
Reg.4, amended: SSI 2009/ 208 Reg.9
Reg.6, amended: SSI 2009/ 19 Reg.7, SSI 2009/ 208 Reg.6
Reg.6, amended: SSI 2009/ 19 Reg.17
Reg.6A, added: SSI 2009/ 19 Reg.11
Reg.7, amended: SSI 2009/ 208 Reg.7
Reg.9, amended: SSI 2009/ 19 Reg.8
Reg.9, amended: SSI 2009/ 19 Reg.18, SSI 2009/ 208 Reg.11
Reg.11, amended: SSI 2009/ 208 Reg.8
Reg.12, amended: SSI 2009/ 19 Reg.20
Reg.20A, added: SSI 2009/ 19 Reg.21
Reg.S2, amended: SSI 2009/ 19 Reg.13
Reg.S3A, amended: SSI 2009/ 208 Reg.10
Reg.S4, amended: SSI 2009/ 19 Reg.14
Reg.S4A, amended: SSI 2009/ 19 Reg.15
Sch.l Part II para.3, amended: SSI 2009/ 19 Reg.22
Sch.l Part III para.9, amended: SSI 2009/ 19 Reg.22
Sch.l Part III para.9, revoked (in part): SSI 2009/ 19 Reg.22
Sch.l Part IV para.10, amended: SSI 2009/ 19 Reg.22, SSI 2009/ 208 Reg.13
Sch.l Part V para.14, substituted: SSI 2009/ 208 Reg.13
Sch.l Part XII para.23, substituted: SSI 2009/ 208 Reg.13
Sch.l A para.5, revoked (in part): SSI 2009/ 208 Reg.14
Sch.l A para.9, revoked (in part): SSI 2009/ 208 Reg.14
Sch.l A para.10, revoked (in part): SSI 2009/ 208 Reg.14

414. National Health Service (Pharmaceutical Services) (Scotland) Regulations 1995
revoked: SSI 2009/ 183 Sch.5
Reg.l, applied: SSI 2009/ 183 Reg.10
Reg.2, amended: SSI 2009/ 177 Reg.2

1995– cont.

414. National Health Service (Pharmaceutical Services) (Scotland) Regulations 1995– *cont.*
Reg.5ZA, added: SSI 2009/ 177 Reg.2
Reg.8, amended: SSI 2009/ 177 Reg.2
Reg.11, amended: SSI 2009/ 177 Reg.2
Sch.l para.3, amended: SSI 2009/ 177 Reg.2
Sch.l para.4, amended: SSI 2009/ 177 Reg.2

418. Town and Country Planning (General Permitted Development) Order 1995
referred to: 2009 c.19 s.3, s.4
Art.l, amended: SI 2009/ 2193 Art.2
Art.3, applied: SI 2009/ 2325 Art.38
Sch.2, see *Cocktails Ltd v Secretary of State for Communities and Local Government* [2008] EWCA Civ 1523, [2009] J.P.L. 953 (CA (Civ Div)), Pill, L.J.; see *R. (on the application of Gore) v Secretary of State for Communities and Local Government* [2008] EWHC 3278 (Admin), [2009] J.P.L. 931 (QBD (Admin)), Sullivan, J.
Sch.2 Part 1 para.A.1, amended: SI 2009/ 2193 Art.2
Sch.2 Part 1 para.C.1, substituted: SI 2009/ 2193 Art.2
Sch.2 Part 11, applied: SI 2009/ 2325 Art.38
Sch.2 Part 40 para.A, added: SI 2009/ 2193 Art.2
Sch.2 Part 40 para.B, added: SI 2009/ 2193 Art.2
Sch.2 Part 40 para.C, added: SI 2009/ 2193 Art.2
Sch.2 Part 40 para.D, added: SI 2009/ 2193 Art.2
Sch.2 Part 40 para.E, added: SI 2009/ 2193 Art.2
Sch.2 Part 40 para.F, added: SI 2009/ 2193 Art.2
Sch.2 Part 40, added: SI 2009/ 2193 Art.2
Sch.2 Part 40 para.A.1, added: SI 2009/ 2193 Art.2
Sch.2 Part 40 para.B.1, added: SI 2009/ 2193 Art.2
Sch.2 Part 40 para.E.1, added: SI 2009/ 2193 Art.2
Sch.2 Part 40 para.F.1, added: SI 2009/ 2193 Art.2
Sch.2 Part 40 para.A.2, added: SI 2009/ 2193 Art.2
Sch.2 Part 40 para.B.2, added: SI 2009/ 2193 Art.2

419. Town and Country Planning (General Development Procedure) Order 1995
Art.1, amended: SI 2009/ 453 Art.3
Art.2B, revoked (in part): SI 2009/ 1304 Art.2
Art.4C, amended: SI 2009/ 2261 Art.2
Art.4D, substituted: SI 2009/ 1024 Art.2
Art.4E, amended: SI 2009/ 2261 Art.2
Art.4E, revoked (in part): SI 2009/ 2261 Art.2
Art.4F, added: SI 2009/ 2261 Art.2
Art.8, see *R. (on the application of Guiney) v Greenwich LBC* [2008] EWHC 2012 (Admin), [2009] J.P.L. 211 (QBD (Admin)), Judge Mackie Q.C.
Art.10, amended: SI 2009/ 453 Art.4, SI 2009/ 2261 Art.2
Art.10B, added: SI 2009/ 2261 Art.2
Art.11A, amended: SI 2009/ 2261 Art.2
Art.16, applied: SI 2009/ 229 Art.4
Art.22, see *R. (on the application of Aldergate Projects Ltd) v Nottinghamshire CC* [2008] EWHC 2881 (Admin), [2009] J.P.L. 939 (QBD (Admin)), Collins, J.
Art.23, amended: SI 2009/ 453 Art.5
Art.25, amended: SI 2009/ 1024 Art.2
Sch.l Part 2, amended: SI 2009/ 453 Art.6
Sch.2 Part 1, amended: SI 2009/ 453 Sch.1 Part 1, Sch.1 Part 2
Sch.3, amended: SI 2009/ 453 Art.6

449. Medical Devices (Consultation Requirements) (Fees) Regulations 1995
Reg.3, amended: SI 2009/ 383 Reg.2
Reg.3A, amended: SI 2009/ 383 Reg.2

1995–cont.

490. Antarctic Regulations 1995
Sch.l, amended: SI 2009/2354 Reg.2, Sch.l

731. Welfare of Animals (Slaughter or Killing) Regulations 1995
Sch.9, see *R. (on the application of Royal Society for the Prevention of Cruelty to Animals) v Secretary of State for the Environment, Food and Rural Affairs* [2008] EWHC 2321 (Admin), [2009] 1 C.M.L.R. 12 (QBD (Admin)), Sir Robin Auld

735. Measuring Equipment (Capacity Measures and Testing Equipment) Regulations 1995
Reg.16, amended: SI 2009/3045 Reg.3

738. Offshore Installations and Pipeline Works (Management and Administration) Regulations 1995
Reg.3, see *Spowage v Revenue and Customs Commissioners* [2009] UKFTT 142 (TC), [2009] S.F.T.D. 393 (FTT (Tax)), J Gordon Reid Q.C.

755. Children (Northern Ireland) Order 1995
applied: SI 2009/2057 Reg.5
Part XI, applied: SI 2009/1547 Sch.1 para.19
Art.2, applied: SI 2009/421 Reg.6, SI 2009/816 Reg.16
Art.7, amended: 2009 c.24 Sch.6 para.26
Art.50, applied: SI 2009/1547 Sch.1 para.2
Art.53, applied: SI 2009/1107 Reg.5
Art.68, applied: SI 2009/1547 Sch.3 para.3
Art.69, applied: SI 2009/1547 Sch.3 para.3
Art.79, applied: SI 2009/1547 Sch.3 para.3
Art.80, applied: SI 2009/1547 Sch.1 para.16
Art.81, applied: SI 2009/1547 Sch.3 para.3
Art.82, applied: SI 2009/1547 Sch.1 para.16
Art.95, applied: SI 2009/1547 Sch.3 para.3
Art.96, applied: SI 2009/1547 Sch.1 para.16
Art.97, applied: SI 2009/1547 Sch.3 para.3
Art.98, applied: SI 2009/1547 Sch.1 para.16
Art.110, applied: SI 2009/1547 Sch.1 para.17
Art.117, applied: SI 2009/1547 Sch.3 para.3
Art.132, applied: SI 2009/1547 Sch.3 para.3

866. National Health Service (Injury Benefits) Regulations 1995
Reg.2, amended: SI 2009/381 Reg.85, SI 2009/2446 Reg.104
Reg.2A, amended: SI 2009/381 Reg.86
Reg.4, amended: SI 2009/381 Reg.87
Reg.13, amended: SI 2009/381 Reg.88

939. Ministry of Defence Police (Police Committee) Regulations 1995
revoked: SI 2009/1609 Reg.1

1014. Measuring Equipment (Liquid Fuel and Lubricants) Regulations 1995
Reg.8, amended: SI 2009/3045 Reg.3

1032. United Nations Arms Embargoes (Dependent Territories) Order 1995
Art.11, varied: SI 2009/888 Art.2, Sch.2

1045. Child Support and Income Support (Amendment) Regulations 1995
Reg.7, revoked: SI 2009/3151 Sch.l
Reg.8, revoked: SI 2009/3151 Sch.l
Reg.9, revoked: SI 2009/3151 Sch.l
Reg.10, revoked: SI 2009/3151 Sch.l
Reg.11, revoked: SI 2009/3151 Sch.l

1046. Excise Goods (Drawback) Regulations 1995
Reg.5, amended: SI 2009/1023 Reg.3
Reg.13, amended: SI 2009/1023 Reg.4

1995–cont.

1054. Civil Aviation (Air Travel Organisers Licensing) Regulations 1995
applied: SI 2009/41 Reg.10

1268. Value Added Tax (Special Provisions) Order 1995
Art.5, see *Pendragon Plc v Revenue and Customs Commissioners* [2009] UKFTT 192 (TC) (FTT (Tax)), Adrian Shipwright; see *Royal Bank of Scotland Group Plc v Revenue and Customs Commissioners* [2009] B.V.C. 2212 (V&DTr (London)), John F Avery Jones (Chairman)

1436. Petroleum (Production) (Landward Areas) Regulations 1995
Reg.5, amended: SI 2009/229 Sch.2 para.9
Reg.7, amended: SI 2009/229 Sch.2 para.9
Reg.10, amended: SI 2009/3283 Reg.2
Sch.4 para.1, amended: SI 2009/229 Sch.2 para.9
Sch.5 para.1, amended: SI 2009/229 Sch.2 para.9

1455. Vehicle Excise (Design Weight Certificate) Regulations 1995
Sch.1 para.1, amended: SI 2009/881 Reg.2
Sch.1 para.4, amended: SI 2009/881 Reg.2

1544. Eggs (Marketing Standards) Regulations 1995
applied: SI 2009/2163 Reg.40
revoked (in part): SI 2009/793 Sch.1
varied: SI 2009/793 Reg.22

1614. Adoption (Designation of Overseas Adoptions) (Variation) (Scotland) Order 1995
applied: SSI 2009/267 Art.12

1629. Gas Appliances (Safety) Regulations 1995
referred to: SI 2009/669 Sch.1 Part 4, Sch.2 Part 2

1755. Equine Viral Arteritis Order 1995
Art.3, amended: SI 2009/2713 Art.2
Art.4, amended: SI 2009/2713 Art.2
Art.6, amended: SI 2009/2713 Art.2
Sch.1 Part 1 para.3, amended: SI 2009/2713 Art.2
Sch.1 Part 1 para.5, amended: SI 2009/2713 Art.2
Sch.1 Part II para.7, amended: SI 2009/2713 Art.2

1804. Units of Measurement Regulations 1995
referred to: SI 2009/669 Sch.1 Part 4

1945. Fees in the Registers of Scotland Order 1995
Sch.1 Part I, substituted: SSI 2009/171 Art.3
Sch.1 Part I para.A, substituted: SSI 2009/171 Art.3
Sch.1 Part XII, added: SSI 2009/171 Art.5
Sch.1 Part XII, substituted: SSI 2009/171 Art.4

1979. Venture Capital Trust Regulations 1995
Reg.4, amended: SI 2009/56 Sch.2 para.24
Reg.5, amended: SI 2009/56 Sch.2 para.25
Reg.6, amended: SI 2009/56 Sch.2 para.26
Reg.7, amended: SI 2009/56 Sch.2 para.27

1986. Contracting Out (Highway Functions) Order 1995
Art.1, revoked (in part): SI 2009/721 Art.4
Art.2, revoked: SI 2009/721 Art.4
Sch.1 para.1, revoked: SI 2009/721 Art.4
Sch.1 para.2, revoked: SI 2009/721 Art.4
Sch.1 para.3, revoked: SI 2009/721 Art.4
Sch.1 para.4, revoked: SI 2009/721 Art.4
Sch.1 para.5, revoked: SI 2009/721 Art.4
Sch.2 para.1, revoked: SI 2009/721 Art.4
Sch.2 para.2, revoked: SI 2009/721 Art.4
Sch.2 para.3, revoked: SI 2009/721 Art.4
Sch.2 para.4, revoked: SI 2009/721 Art.4
Sch.2 para.5, revoked: SI 2009/721 Art.4
Sch.2 para.6, revoked: SI 2009/721 Art.4
Sch.2 para.7, revoked: SI 2009/721 Art.4
Sch.2 para.8, revoked: SI 2009/721 Art.4
Sch.2 para.9, revoked: SI 2009/721 Art.4

1995– cont.

1986. Contracting Out (Highway Functions) Order 1995– *cont.*
Sch.2 para.l0, revoked: SI 2009/ 721 Art.4
Sch.2 para.ll, revoked: SI 2009/ 721 Art.4
Sch.2 para.l2, revoked: SI 2009/ 721 Art.4
Sch.3 para.l, revoked: SI 2009/ 721 Art.4
Sch.3 para.2, revoked: SI 2009/ 721 Art.4
Sch.3 para.3, revoked: SI 2009/ 721 Art.4
Sch.3 para.4, revoked: SI 2009/ 721 Art.4
Sch.3 para.5, revoked: SI 2009/ 721 Art.4
Sch.3 para.6, revoked: SI 2009/ 721 Art.4
Sch.3 para.7, revoked: SI 2009/ 721 Art.4
Sch.3 para.8, revoked: SI 2009/ 721 Art.4

2089. Education (Pupil Registration) Regulations 1995
applied: SI 2009/ 3355 Sch.2 para.4

2427. Spring Traps Approval Order 1995
Sch.1 Part II, amended: SI 2009/ 2166 Art.2

2456. Local Government (Assistants for Political Groups) (Remuneration) Order 1995
revoked (in part): SI 2009/ 40 Art.4

2475. Aerodromes (Designation) (Detention and Sale of Aircraft) Order 1995
revoked (in part): SI 2009/ 2350 Sch.2

2489. Footwear (Indication of Composition) Labelling Regulations 1995
referred to: SI 2009/ 669 Sch.1 Part 4

2518. Value Added Tax Regulations 1995
see *R. (on the application of BMWAG) v Revenue and Customs Commissioners* [2009] EWCA Civ 77, [2009] S.T.C. 963 (CA (Civ Div)), Pill, L.J.
Part XX, applied: SI 2009/ 3241 Reg.18
Part XX, amended: SI 2009/ 3241 Reg.15
Part XXI, amended: SI 2009/ 3241 Reg.17
Reg.15A, added: SI 2009/ 3241 Reg.3
Reg.21, substituted: SI 2009/ 3241 Reg.4
Reg.22, substituted: SI 2009/ 3241 Reg.5
Reg.22A, added: SI 2009/ 3241 Reg.6
Reg.22B, added: SI 2009/ 3241 Reg.6
Reg.22C, added: SI 2009/ 3241 Reg.6
Reg.23, revoked: SI 2009/ 3241 Reg.7
Reg.24, see *Brunel Motor Co Ltd v Revenue and Customs Commissioners* [2009] EWCA Civ 118, [2009] S.T.C. 1146 (CA (Civ Div)), Sir Andrew Morritt (Chancellor)
Reg.25, amended: SI 2009/ 2978 Reg.3
Reg.25, revoked (in part): SI 2009/ 2978 Reg.3
Reg.25, see *Revenue and Customs Commissioners v Raj Restaurant* [2009] S.T.C.729 (IH (Ex Div)), Lord Nimmo Smith
Reg.25A, added: SI 2009/ 2978 Reg.4
Reg.29, amended: SI 2009/ 586 Reg.3
Reg.34, amended: SI 2009/ 586 Reg.4
Reg.38, amended: SI 2009/ 586 Reg.5
Reg.38, revoked (in part): SI 2009/ 586 Reg.5
Reg.38, see *Brunel Motor Co Ltd v Revenue and Customs Commissioners* [2009] EWCA Civ 118, [2009] S.T.C. 1146 (CA (Civ Div)), Sir Andrew Morritt (Chancellor)
Reg.40, amended: SI 2009/ 2978 Reg.5
Reg.55K, amended: SI 2009/ 3241 Reg.9
Reg.55L, amended: SI 2009/ 586 Reg.6
Reg.55L, revoked (in part): SI 2009/ 586 Reg.6
Reg.55M, amended: SI 2009/ 586 Reg.7
Reg.67, see *Boots Co Plc v Revenue and Customs Commissioners* [2009] EWHC 487 (Ch), [2009] S.T.C. 1577 (Ch D), Patten, J.
Reg.82, substituted: SI 2009/ 3241 Reg.l0
Reg.84, amended: SI 2009/ 1967 Reg.3

1995– cont.

2518. Value Added Tax Regulations 1995– *cont.*
Reg.93, amended: SI 2009/ 1967 Reg.4, Reg.5
Reg.94B, amended: SI 2009/ 1967 Reg.6
Reg.99, amended: SI 2009/ 820 Reg.3
Reg.l01, amended: SI 2009/ 820 Reg.4
Reg.101, see *Royal Bank of Scotland Group Plc v Revenue and Customs Commissioners (C-488/07)* [2009] S.T.C. 461 (ECJ (8th Chamber)), Judge von Danwitz (President)
Reg.102, amended: SI 2009/ 820 Reg.5
Reg.l02, see *Loughborough University v Revenue and Customs Commissioners* [2009] UKFTT 91 (TC), [2009] S.F.T.D. 200 (FTT (Tax)), Richard Barlow
Reg.l02A, see *Loughborough University v Revenue and Customs Commissioners* [2009] UKFTT 91 (TC), [2009] S.F.T.D. 200 (FTT (Tax)), Richard Barlow
Reg.l02B, see *Loughborough University v Revenue and Customs Commissioners* [2009] UKFTT 91 (TC), [2009] S.F.T.D. 200 (FTT (Tax)), Richard Barlow
Reg.l02C, see *Loughborough University v Revenue and Customs Commissioners* [2009] UKFTT 91 (TC), [2009] S.F.T.D. 200 (FTT (Tax)), Richard Barlow
Reg.103, amended: SI 2009/ 820 Reg.6
Reg.l03B, amended: SI 2009/ 820 Reg.7
Reg.107, amended: SI 2009/ 820 Reg.8
Reg.107B, amended: SI 2009/ 820 Reg.9
Reg.107F, added: SI 2009/ 820 Reg.10
Reg.109, see *Community Housing Association Ltd v Revenue and Customs Commissioners* [2009] EWHC 455 (Ch), [2009] S.T.C. 1324 (Ch D), Sales, J
Reg.111, amended: SI 2009/ 586 Reg.8
Reg.112, see *Shurgard Storage Centres UK Ltd v Revenue and Customs Commissioners* [2009] B.V.C. 2139 (V&DTr (London)), Rodney P Huggins (Chairman)
Reg.113, see *Shurgard Storage Centres UK Ltd v Revenue and Customs Commissioners* [2009] B.V.C. 2139 (V&DTr (London)), Rodney P Huggins (Chairman)
Reg.115, amended: SI 2009/ 586 Reg.9
Reg.129, see *Martin-Jenkins v Revenue and Customs Commissioners* [2009] UKFTT 99 (TC), [2009] S.F.T.D. 192 (FTT (Tax)), John Walters Q.C.
Reg.165A, amended: SI 2009/ 586 Reg.l0
Reg.173, amended: SI 2009/ 3241 Reg.11
Reg.173A, added: SI 2009/ 3241 Reg.12
Reg.173B, added: SI 2009/ 3241 Reg.12
Reg.173C, added: SI 2009/ 3241 Reg.12
Reg.173D, added: SI 2009/ 3241 Reg.12
Reg.173E, added: SI 2009/ 3241 Reg.12
Reg.173F, added: SI 2009/ 3241 Reg.12
Reg.173G, added: SI 2009/ 3241 Reg.12
Reg.173H, added: SI 2009/ 3241 Reg.12
Reg.173I, added: SI 2009/ 3241 Reg.12
Reg.173J, added: SI 2009/ 3241 Reg.12
Reg.173K, added: SI 2009/ 3241 Reg.12
Reg.173L, added: SI 2009/ 3241 Reg.12
Reg.173M, added: SI 2009/ 3241 Reg.12
Reg.173N, added: SI 2009/ 3241 Reg.12
Reg.173O, added: SI 2009/ 3241 Reg.12
Reg.173P, added: SI 2009/ 3241 Reg.12
Reg.173Q, added: SI 2009/ 3241 Reg.12
Reg.173R, added: SI 2009/ 3241 Reg.12

1995– cont.

2518. Value Added Tax Regulations 1995– *cont.*
Reg.173T, added: SI 2009/3241 Reg.12
Reg.173U, added: SI 2009/3241 Reg.12
Reg.173V, added: SI 2009/3241 Reg.12
Reg.173W, added: SI 2009/3241 Reg.12
Reg.173X, added: SI 2009/3241 Reg.12
Reg.174, revoked: SI 2009/3241 Reg.13
Reg.175, revoked: SI 2009/3241 Reg.13
Reg.176, revoked: SI 2009/3241 Reg.13
Reg.177, revoked: SI 2009/3241 Reg.13
Reg.178, revoked: SI 2009/3241 Reg.13
Reg.179, revoked: SI 2009/3241 Reg.13
Reg.181, amended: SI 2009/3241 Reg.14
Reg.182, revoked: SI 2009/3241 Reg.15
Reg.183, revoked: SI 2009/3241 Reg.15
Reg.194, amended: SI 2009/3241 Reg.16
Reg.195, revoked: SI 2009/3241 Reg.17
Reg.201, amended: SI 2009/1967 Reg.7
Reg.201A, added: SI 2009/1967 Reg.8
Sch.1, amended: SI 2009/1967 Sch.1
Sch.1, substituted: SI 2009/2978 Sch.1, SI 2009/3241 Sch.1

2696. Charities Act 1993 (Substitution of Sums) Order 1995
Art.2, revoked (in part): SI 2009/508 Art.17

2863. Town and Country Planning (Minerals) Regulations 1995
Sch.1, amended: SI 2009/1307 Sch.2 para.53

2869. Goods Vehicles (Licensing of Operators) Regulations 1995
Sch.4 para.2, amended: SI 2009/1307 Sch.2 para.54

2902. Taxation of Income from Land (Non-residents) Regulations 1995
Reg.6, amended: SI 2009/56 Sch.2 para.29
Reg.6, revoked (in part): SI 2009/56 Sch.2 para.29
Reg.9, amended: SI 2009/56 Sch.2 para.30
Reg.17, amended: SI 2009/56 Sch.2 para.31
Reg.17, revoked (in part): SI 2009/56 Sch.2 para.31
Reg.19, amended: SI 2009/56 Sch.2 para.32
Reg.19, revoked (in part): SI 2009/56 Sch.2 para.32

2908. Public Service Vehicles (Operators Licences) Regulations 1995
Reg.3, amended: SI 2009/786 Reg.2
Reg.11, amended: SI 2009/786 Reg.2
Reg.11, revoked (in part): SI 2009/786 Reg.2
Sch.1 para.2, amended: SSI 2009/248 Sch.3

2909. Public Service Vehicles (Operators Licences) (Fees) Regulations 1995
Reg.2, amended: SI 2009/787 Reg.2
Reg.3, amended: SI 2009/787 Reg.2
Reg.3, applied: SI 2009/787 Reg.3
Reg.4, revoked (in part): SI 2009/787 Reg.2
Sch.1, amended: SI 2009/787 Reg.2, Sch.1

2922. Animal Health Orders (Divisional Veterinary Manager Amendment) Order 1995
revoked (in part): SI 2009/2713 Art.9

3000. Goods Vehicles (Licensing of Operators) (Fees) Regulations 1995
Reg.2, amended: SI 2009/804 Reg.2, Reg.4
Reg.3, amended: SI 2009/804 Reg.2, Reg.4
Reg.3, applied: SI 2009/804 Reg.3
Reg.3, revoked (in part): SI 2009/804 Reg.2, Reg.4
Reg.4, amended: SI 2009/804 Reg.2
Sch.1 Part I, amended: SI 2009/804 Reg.2
Sch.1 Part I, revoked: SI 2009/804 Reg.4
Sch.1 Part II, amended: SI 2009/804 Reg.2, Sch.1
Sch.1 Part II, revoked: SI 2009/804 Reg.4

1995– cont.

3022. Company and Business Names (Amendment) Regulations 1995
revoked: SI 2009/2615 Reg.7

3123. Sweeteners in Food Regulations 1995
applied: SI 2009/3238 Reg.13, SI 2009/3378 Reg.13
revoked (in part): SI 2009/3238 Reg.20, SI 2009/3378 Reg.20, SSI 2009/436 Reg.20
Reg.2, amended: SI 2009/891 Reg.3, SI 2009/1092 Reg.3, SSI 2009/167 Reg.3
Reg.3, referred to: SSI 2009/436 Reg.13
Reg.4, referred to: SSI 2009/436 Reg.13
Reg.5, referred to: SSI 2009/436 Reg.13
Reg.6, referred to: SSI 2009/436 Reg.13
Reg.7, referred to: SSI 2009/436 Reg.13

3124. Colours in Food Regulations 1995
applied: SI 2009/3238 Reg.7, SI 2009/3378 Reg.7, SSI 2009/436 Reg.7
revoked (in part): SI 2009/3238 Reg.20, SI 2009/3378 Reg.20, SSI 2009/436 Reg.20
Reg.2, amended: SI 2009/891 Reg.2, SI 2009/1092 Reg.2, SSI 2009/167 Reg.2

3128. Merchant Shipping (Port State Control) Regulations 1995
Reg.11, varied: SI 2009/2796 Reg.13
Reg.12, varied: SI 2009/2796 Reg.13

3158. Adopted Children Register and Parental Order Register (Form of Entry) (Scotland) Regulations 1995
Sch.1, amended: SSI 2009/314 Sch.1
Sch.2, amended: SSI 2009/314 Sch.2

3187. Miscellaneous Food Additives Regulations 1995
applied: SI 2009/3238 Reg.10, SI 2009/3378 Reg.10, SSI 2009/436 Reg.10
revoked (in part): SI 2009/3238 Reg.20, SI 2009/3378 Reg.20, SSI 2009/436 Reg.20
Reg.2, amended: SI 2009/891 Reg.4, SI 2009/1092 Reg.4, SSI 2009/167 Reg.4

3192. Retirement Age of General Commissioners Order 1995
revoked: SI 2009/56 Sch.2 para.187

3213. Pensions (Northern Ireland) Order 1995
varied: SI 2009/317 Sch.1
Art.22, amended: SI 2009/1941 Sch.1 para.158

3218. North Wales Fire Services (Combination Scheme) Order 1995
Sch.1, varied: SI 2009/2849 Art.2

3229. Mid and West Wales Fire Services (Combination Scheme) Order 1995
Sch.1, varied: SI 2009/2849 Art.2

3230. South Wales Fire Services (Combination Scheme) Order 1995
Sch.1, varied: SI 2009/2849 Art.2

1996

177. National Health Service (General Dental Services) (Scotland) Regulations 1996
Reg.2, amended: SSI 2009/183 Sch.6 para.1
Sch.1 Part II para.8, amended: SSI 2009/96 Reg.2
Sch.1 Part II para.9, amended: SSI 2009/96 Reg.2

206. Income Support (General) (Jobseeker's Allowance Consequential Amendments) Regulations 1996
Reg.1, amended: SI 2009/604 Reg.3

207. Jobseeker's Allowance Regulations 1996
applied: SI 2009/1562 Art.2
referred to: SI 2009/497 Art.24
Part VIII, amended: SI 2009/2655 Reg.4

1996–cont.

207. Jobseeker's Allowance Regulations 1996–cont.
Reg.1, amended: SI 2009/480 Reg.2, SI 2009/583 Reg.4, SI 2009/1488 Reg.10, SI 2009/2655 Reg.4
Reg.2A, amended: SI 2009/471 Reg.7
Reg.11, amended: SI 2009/583 Reg.4
Reg.19, amended: SI 2009/583 Reg.4
Reg.49, amended: SI 2009/1488 Reg.11
Reg.51, revoked (in part): SI 2009/583 Reg.4
Reg.53, revoked (in part): SI 2009/3228 Reg.4
Reg.57, amended: SI 2009/583 Reg.4
Reg.60, amended: SI 2009/2655 Reg.4
Reg.69, amended: SI 2009/480 Reg.2, SI 2009/2710 Reg.2
Reg.73, amended: SI 2009/480 Reg.2
Reg.75, amended: SI 2009/480 Reg.2, SI 2009/583 Reg.4
Reg.79, amended: SI 2009/497 Art.23
Reg.83, amended: SI 2009/3228 Reg.3
Reg.83, referred to: SI 2009/497 Art.24
Reg.84, amended: SI 2009/3228 Reg.3
Reg.84, referred to: SI 2009/497 Art.24
Reg.85, referred to: SI 2009/497 Art.24
Reg.85, revoked (in part): SI 2009/583 Reg.4
Reg.85A, amended: SI 2009/362 Reg.3
Reg.86A, amended: SI 2009/3228 Reg.3
Reg.86B, amended: SI 2009/3228 Reg.3
Reg.89, amended: SI 2009/2655 Reg.4
Reg.95, amended: SI 2009/583 Reg.4
Reg.98, amended: SI 2009/2655 Reg.4
Reg.102, amended: SI 2009/583 Reg.4
Reg.102D, amended: SI 2009/583 Reg.4
Reg.103, amended: SI 2009/2655 Reg.4
Reg.105, amended: SI 2009/480 Reg.2, SI 2009/583 Reg.4, SI 2009/2655 Reg.4
Reg.113, amended: SI 2009/480 Reg.2
Reg.117, amended: SI 2009/2655 Reg.4
Reg.118, amended: SI 2009/2655 Reg.4
Reg.121, amended: SI 2009/2655 Reg.4
Reg.121, revoked (in part): SI 2009/2655 Reg.4
Reg.122, amended: SI 2009/2655 Reg.4
Reg.123, amended: SI 2009/2655 Reg.4
Reg.130, amended: SI 2009/583 Reg.4, SI 2009/2655 Reg.4
Reg.131, amended: SI 2009/583 Reg.4, SI 2009/1575 Reg.2
Reg.136, amended: SI 2009/1575 Reg.2
Reg.140, amended: SI 2009/480 Reg.2
Reg.140A, amended: SI 2009/480 Reg.2
Reg.145, referred to: SI 2009/497 Sch.16
Reg.146A, amended: SI 2009/480 Reg.2
Reg.146B, amended: SI 2009/480 Reg.2
Reg.146G, referred to: SI 2009/497 Sch.16
Reg.147, revoked: SI 2009/3228 Reg.2
Reg.148, referred to: SI 2009/497 Art.24, Sch.16
Reg.148, revoked: SI 2009/3228 Reg.2
Reg.148A, referred to: SI 2009/497 Sch.16
Reg.148A, revoked: SI 2009/3228 Reg.2
Reg.149, revoked: SI 2009/3228 Reg.2
Reg.163, amended: SI 2009/583 Reg.4
Reg.170, amended: SI 2009/583 Reg.4
Reg.172, amended: SI 2009/497 Art.25
Sch.A1 para.7, revoked: SI 2009/3228 Reg.4
Sch.A1 para.8, revoked: SI 2009/3228 Reg.4
Sch.A1 para.13, substituted: SI 2009/1488 Reg.12
Sch.A1 para.16, amended: SI 2009/583 Reg.4
Sch.1 Part I, referred to: SI 2009/497 Art.24
Sch.1 Part I para.1, amended: SI 2009/497 Sch.13, SI 2009/1575 Reg.3

207. Jobseeker's Allowance Regulations 1996–cont.
Sch.1 Part I para.2, amended: SI 2009/497 Sch.13
Sch.1 Part I para.3, amended: SI 2009/497 Sch.13
Sch.1 Part II para.4, amended: SI 2009/497 Art.24
Sch.1 Part III para.8, amended: SI 2009/583 Reg.4
Sch.1 Part III para.10, amended: SI 2009/1488 Reg.13
Sch.1 Part III para.12, amended: SI 2009/1488 Reg.13
Sch.1 Part III para.13, amended: SI 2009/1488 Reg.13
Sch.1 Part III para.15A, amended: SI 2009/1488 Reg.13
Sch.1 Part III para.15A, referred to: SI 2009/497 Art.24
Sch.1 Part III para.16, referred to: SI 2009/497 Art.24
Sch.1 Part IV, amended: SI 2009/497 Sch.14, SI 2009/1488 Reg.13
Sch.1 Part IV, referred to: SI 2009/497 Art.24
Sch.1 Part IVA para.20D, amended: SI 2009/583 Reg.4
Sch.1 Part IVA para.20E, amended: SI 2009/1488 Reg.13
Sch.1 Part IVA para.20F, amended: SI 2009/1488 Reg.13
Sch.1 Part IVA para.20G, amended: SI 2009/1488 Reg.13
Sch.1 Part IVA para.20IA, amended: SI 2009/1488 Reg.13
Sch.1 Part IVB, referred to: SI 2009/497 Art.24
Sch.1 Part IVB para.20M, amended: SI 2009/497 Sch.15, SI 2009/1488 Reg.13
Sch.2 para.3, amended: SI 2009/583 Reg.4
Sch.2 para.5, referred to: SI 2009/497 Sch.16
Sch.2 para.6, referred to: SI 2009/497 Sch.16
Sch.2 para.7, referred to: SI 2009/497 Sch.16
Sch.2 para.8, amended: SI 2009/1488 Reg.14
Sch.2 para.9, referred to: SI 2009/497 Sch.16
Sch.2 para.10, referred to: SI 2009/497 Sch.16
Sch.2 para.13, amended: SI 2009/480 Reg.2, SI 2009/2655 Reg.4
Sch.2 para.17, amended: SI 2009/497 Art.24
Sch.2 para.17, referred to: SI 2009/497 Art.24
Sch.6 para.1, amended: SI 2009/2655 Reg.4
Sch.6 para.5, amended: SI 2009/1488 Reg.15
Sch.6A para.1, amended: SI 2009/1488 Reg.16
Sch.7 para.2A, added: SI 2009/2655 Reg.4
Sch.7 para.17, amended: SI 2009/2655 Reg.4
Sch.7 para.26, amended: SI 2009/2655 Reg.4
Sch.7 para.56, amended: SI 2009/583 Reg.4
Sch.7 para.64, amended: SI 2009/2655 Reg.4
Sch.7 para.70, substituted: SI 2009/2655 Reg.4
Sch.8 para.4, amended: SI 2009/1488 Reg.17
Sch.8 para.37A, added: SI 2009/583 Reg.4
Sch.8 para.60, amended: SI 2009/583 Reg.4

221. Police (Promotion) (Scotland) Regulations 1996
Reg.1, amended: SSI 2009/372 Reg.2
Reg.2, revoked (in part): SSI 2009/372 Reg.2
Reg.8, amended: SSI 2009/372 Reg.2
Reg.9, amended: SSI 2009/372 Reg.2

270. International Sea-Bed Authority (Immunities and Privileges) Order 1996
revoked (in part): SSI 2009/44 Art.3

272. International Tribunal for the Law of the Sea (Immunities and Privileges) Order 1996
revoked (in part): SSI 2009/44 Art.3

375

274. Education (Northern Ireland) Order 1996
Art.22, amended: 2009 c.3 Sch.4 para.26
282. Merchant Shipping (Prevention of Pollution) (Law of the Sea Convention) Order 1996
Art.2, amended: 2009 c.23 Sch.4 para.3
Art.2, enabled: SI 2009/1210
375. Human Fertilisation and Embryology (Statutory Storage Period for Embryos) Regulations 1996
applied: SI 2009/1582 Reg.6
revoked: SI 2009/1582 Reg.9
513. Act of Adjournal (Criminal Procedure Rules) 1996
Sch.2 Appendix, added: SSI 2009/345 r.3
Sch.2 Appendix, amended: SSI 2009/144 r.4, r.6, Sch.1 Part 1, Sch.1 Part 2, SSI 2009/244 Sch.1, SSI 2009/345 r.3, Sch.1 Part 1, Sch.1 Part 2
Sch.2 Appendix, referred to: SSI 2009/144 r.2, r.3
Sch.2 Part III, added: SSI 2009/144 r.2
Sch.2 Part IV, added: SSI 2009/144 r.3
Sch.2 Part VII, amended: SSI 2009/144 r.4
Sch.2 Part VII, added: SSI 2009/144 r.5
Sch.2 Part VII, added: SSI 2009/345 r.4
Sch.2 Part VII para.28.2, amended: SSI 2009/144 r.4
Sch.2 Part VII para.29B.1, added: SSI 2009/243 r.2
Sch.2 Part VII para.29B.2, added: SSI 2009/243 r.2
Sch.2 Part VII para.29B.3, added: SSI 2009/243 r.2
Sch.2 Part VII para.29B.4, added: SSI 2009/243 r.2
Sch.2 Part VII para.29B.5, added: SSI 2009/243 r.2
Sch.2 Part VII para.29B.6, added: SSI 2009/243 r.2
Sch.2 Part VII para.29B.7, added: SSI 2009/243 r.2
Sch.2 Part VII para.29B.8, added: SSI 2009/243 r.2
Sch.2 Part VII para.29B.9, added: SSI 2009/243 r.2
Sch.2 Part VII para.36.9A, added: SSI 2009/345 r.2
Sch.2 Part VII para.36.9B, added: SSI 2009/345 r.2
Sch.2 Part VII para.36.9C, added: SSI 2009/345 r.2
Sch.2 Part VII para.37AA.1, amended: SSI 2009/244 r.2
Sch.2 Part VII para.37AA.5, amended: SSI 2009/244 r.2
Sch.2 Part VII para.37AA.5A, added: SSI 2009/244 r.2
Sch.2 Part VII para.37AA.5B, added: SSI 2009/244 r.2
Sch.2 Part VII para.37AA.5C, added: SSI 2009/244 r.2
Sch.2 Part VII para.37AA.5D, added: SSI 2009/244 r.2
Sch.2 Part VII para.37AA.5E, added: SSI 2009/244 r.2
Sch.2 Part VII para.37AA.5F, added: SSI 2009/244 r.2
Sch.2 Part VII para.37AA.5G, added: SSI 2009/244 r.2
Sch.2 Part VII para.40.1, amended: SSI 2009/322 r.2
Sch.2 Part VII para.40.8, amended: SSI 2009/322 r.2
Sch.2 Part VII para.40.9, amended: SSI 2009/322 r.2
Sch.2 Part VII para.40.10, amended: SSI 2009/322 r.2
Sch.2 Part VII para.40.11, amended: SSI 2009/322 r.2
Sch.2 Part VII para.51.1, amended: SSI 2009/144 r.6
Sch.2 para.40.2, see *Allison (Steven Edward) v HM Advocate* [2009] HCJAC 23, 2009 S.L.T. 550 (HCJ), Lord Osborne
551. Gas Safety (Management) Regulations 1996
applied: SI 2009/515 Reg.15, Sch.12
Reg.11, applied: SI 2009/515 Sch.12
600. Energy Information (Washing Machines) Regulations 1996
referred to: SI 2009/669 Sch.1 Part 4
Reg.2, amended: SI 2009/2559 Reg.2
Reg.2A, added: SI 2009/2559 Reg.2
Sch.5 Part I para.2A, added: SI 2009/2559 Reg.2
601. Energy Information (Tumble Driers) Regulations 1996
referred to: SI 2009/669 Sch.1 Part 4
Reg.2, amended: SI 2009/2559 Reg.3
Reg.2A, added: SI 2009/2559 Reg.3

601. Energy Information (Tumble Driers) Regulations 1996–*cont.*
Sch.5 Part I para.2A, added: SI 2009/2559 Reg.3
615. Education (Areas to which Pupils and Students Belong) Regulations 1996
Reg.2, amended: SI 2009/1301 Reg.2, SI 2009/1338 Reg.2
Reg.3, amended: SI 2009/1301 Reg.2, SI 2009/1338 Reg.2
Reg.3, revoked (in part): SI 2009/1301 Reg.2, SI 2009/1338 Reg.2
Reg.4, amended: SI 2009/1301 Reg.2, SI 2009/1338 Reg.2
Reg.5, amended: SI 2009/1301 Reg.2, SI 2009/1338 Reg.2
Reg.6, amended: SI 2009/1301 Reg.2, SI 2009/1338 Reg.2
Reg.7, amended: SI 2009/1301 Reg.2, SI 2009/1338 Reg.2
Reg.7, revoked (in part): SI 2009/1301 Reg.2, SI 2009/1338 Reg.2
Reg.8, revoked (in part): SI 2009/1301 Reg.2, SI 2009/1338 Reg.2
Reg.9, revoked (in part): SI 2009/1301 Reg.2, SI 2009/1338 Reg.2
Reg.10, revoked (in part): SI 2009/1301 Reg.2, SI 2009/1338 Reg.2
Reg.11, revoked (in part): SI 2009/1301 Reg.2, SI 2009/1338 Reg.2
707. Health Authorities (Membership and Procedure) Regulations 1996
Sch.2, amended: SI 2009/462 Sch.5 para.3
708. National Health Service (Functions of Health Authorities and Administration Arrangements) Regulations 1996
revoked: SI 2009/1511 Reg.6
Reg.5, revoked (in part): SI 2009/462 Sch.5 para.4
717. Health Service Commissioner for England (Authorities for the Ashworth, Broadmoor and Rampton Hospitals) Order 1996
revoked: SI 2009/883 Art.2
725. Business Tenancies (Northern Ireland) Order 1996
Art.31, amended: SI 2009/1941 Sch.1 para.164
775. Occupational Pension Schemes (Discharge of Protected Rights on Winding Up) Regulations 1996
Reg.5, amended: SI 2009/2930 Reg.3
825. Pipelines Safety Regulations 1996
applied: SI 2009/515 Reg.15
Sch.2 para.10, amended: SI 2009/716 Sch.6
840. National Health Service (Pharmaceutical Services) (Scotland) Amendment Regulations 1996
revoked: SSI 2009/183 Sch.5
913. Offshore Installations and Wells (Design and Construction, etc.) Regulations 1996
see *Spencer-Franks v Kellogg Brown & Root Ltd* [2008] UKHL 46, [2009] 1 All E.R. 269 (HL), Lord Hoffmann
943. Insurance Companies (Accounts and Statements) Regulations 1996
Sch.4, see *Legal & General Assurance Society Ltd v Revenue and Customs Commissioners* [2009] UKFTT 225 (TC), [2009] S.F.T.D. 701 (FTT (Tax)), John F Avery Jones
972. Special Waste Regulations 1996
applied: SI 2009/716 Reg.3

1996–cont.

1005. Sheriff Court Districts (Alteration of Boundaries) Order 1996
Sch.l, amended: SSI 2009/293 Art.2

1021. Lands Tribunal (Fees) Rules 1996
revoked: SI 2009/1307 Sch.4

1022. Lands Tribunal Rules 1996
applied: SI 2009/1307 Art.4
see *Practice Direction (UT (Lands): Lands Tribunal: Interim Practice Directions and Guidance)* [2009] R.V.R. 208 (UT (Lands)), Carnwath, L.J. (SP)
Part I r.l, substituted: SI 2009/1307 Sch.2 para.56
Part I r.2, amended: SI 2009/1307 Sch.2 para.57
Part I r.2, revoked (in part): SI 2009/1307 Sch.2 para.57
Part I r.2A, added: SI 2009/1307 Sch.2 para.58
Part II r.3, revoked: SI 2009/1307 Sch.2 para.59
Part II r.5, amended: SI 2009/1307 Sch.2 para.60
Part IIA r.5A, amended: SI 2009/1307 Sch.2 para.61
Part IIA r.5B, amended: SI 2009/1307 Sch.2 para.62
Part IIA r.5C, amended: SI 2009/1307 Sch.2 para.63
Part III r.6, amended: SI 2009/1307 Sch.2 para.64
Part III r.6, applied: SI 2009/1114 Sch.1
Part IV r.9, amended: SI 2009/1307 Sch.2 para.65
Part IV r.10, amended: SI 2009/1307 Sch.2 para.66
Part IV r.10, applied: SI 2009/1114 Sch.1
Part V r.13, applied: SI 2009/1114 Sch.1
Part V r.16, amended: SI 2009/1307 Sch.2 para.67
Part V r.17, amended: SI 2009/1307 Sch.2 para.68
Part V r.17, referred to: SI 2009/1114 Sch.1
Part V r.19, amended: SI 2009/1307 Sch.2 para.69
Part VI r.21, amended: SI 2009/1307 Sch.2 para.70
Part VI r.21, applied: SI 2009/1114 Sch.1
Part VII r.26, amended: SI 2009/1307 Sch.2 para.71
Part VII r.26A, amended: SI 2009/1307 Sch.2 para.72
Part VIII r.27, applied: SI 2009/1114 Sch.1
Part VIII r.28, amended: SI 2009/1307 Sch.2 para.73
Part VIII r.29A, revoked: SI 2009/1307 Sch.2 para.74
Part VIII r.30, amended: SI 2009/1307 Sch.2 para.75
Part VIII r.31, amended: SI 2009/1307 Sch.2 para.76
Part VIII r.31, revoked (in part): SI 2009/1307 Sch.2 para.76
Part VIII r.32, amended: SI 2009/1307 Sch.2 para.77
Part VIII r.33, amended: SI 2009/1307 Sch.2 para.78
Part VIII r.37, amended: SI 2009/1307 Sch.2 para.79
Part VIII r.38, amended: SI 2009/1307 Sch.2 para.80
Part VIII r.38, referred to: SI 2009/1114 Sch.1
Part VIII r.38, revoked (in part): SI 2009/1307 Sch.2 para.80
Part VIII r.39, amended: SI 2009/1307 Sch.2 para.81
Part VIII r.43, amended: SI 2009/1307 Sch.2 para.82
Part VIII r.45, amended: SI 2009/1307 Sch.2 para.83
Part VIII r.47, amended: SI 2009/1307 Sch.2 para.84
Part VIII r.48, amended: SI 2009/1307 Sch.2 para.85
Part VIII r.50, amended: SI 2009/1307 Sch.2 para.86
Part VIII r.51, referred to: SI 2009/1114 Sch.1
Part VIII r.52, amended: SI 2009/1307 Sch.2 para.87
Part VIII r.52, referred to: SI 2009/1114 Sch.1
Part VIII r.52, revoked (in part): SI 2009/1307 Sch.2 para.87
Part VIII r.54, amended: SI 2009/1307 Sch.2 para.88
Part VIII r.54, revoked (in part): SI 2009/1307 Sch.2 para.88

1996–cont.

1022. Lands Tribunal Rules 1996–*cont.*
Part VIII r.56, amended: SI 2009/1307 Sch.2 para.89
Part IX r.57, substituted: SI 2009/1307 Sch.2 para.90
Sch.l, amended: SI 2009/1307 Sch.2 para.91
Sch.2, revoked: SI 2009/1307 Sch.2 para.92

1108. Smoke Control Areas (Exempted Fireplaces) Order 1996
revoked (in part): SSI 2009/214 Sch.2

1141. Juries (Northern Ireland) Order 1996
Art.26C, amended: 2009 c.3 s.3

1172. Occupational Pension Schemes (Contracting-out) Regulations 1996
Reg.1, amended: SI 2009/2930 Reg.4
Reg.1, revoked (in part): SI 2009/598 Art.3
Reg.9, amended: SI 2009/615 Reg.4
Reg.12, amended: SI 2009/615 Reg.4
Reg.20, amended: SI 2009/2930 Reg.4
Reg.23, revoked (in part): SI 2009/598 Art.3
Reg.39, amended: SI 2009/598 Art.3
Reg.60, amended: SI 2009/2930 Reg.4
Reg.63, amended: SI 2009/598 Art.3
Reg.69A, added: SI 2009/846 Reg.2
Reg.69B, added: SI 2009/846 Reg.2
Reg.73, amended: SI 2009/598 Art.3
Reg.76A, amended: SI 2009/598 Art.3

1174. Armed Forces (Protection of Children of Service Families) Regulations 1996
applied: SI 2009/1107 Reg.15
revoked: SI 2009/1107 Reg.2
Reg.5, applied: SI 2009/1107 Reg.13
Reg.6, applied: SI 2009/1107 Reg.14
Reg.7, applied: SI 2009/1107 Reg.15
Reg.8, applied: SI 2009/1107 Reg.16
Reg.9, applied: SI 2009/1107 Reg.17

1243. National Park Authorities (England) Order 1996
Sch.1 Part 1, amended: SI 2009/557 Art.2
Sch.1 Part 2, amended: SI 2009/557 Art.2, SI 2009/837 Art.23

1296. United Nations (International Tribunal) (Rwanda) Order 1996
Art.2, amended: SI 2009/2054 Sch.1 para.14
Art.2, applied: SI 2009/2054 Sch.2 para.8

1299. Proceeds of Crime (Northern Ireland) Order 1996
Sch.2, amended: SI 2009/1941 Sch.1 para.165

1320. Road Traffic Offenders (Northern Ireland) Order 1996
Art.35, amended: 2009 c.25 Sch.21 para.92
Art.36, amended: 2009 c.25 Sch.21 para.92
Art.37, amended: 2009 c.25 Sch.21 para.92
Art.38A, amended: 2009 c.25 Sch.21 para.92
Art.40, amended: 2009 c.25 Sch.21 para.92
Art.40A, added: 2009 c.25 Sch.16 para.4
Art.40B, added: 2009 c.25 Sch.16 para.4
Art.42, amended: 2009 c.25 Sch.21 para.92
Art.47, amended: 2009 c.25 Sch.21 para.92
Art.52, amended: 2009 c.25 Sch.21 para.92

1358. Brucellosis and Tuberculosis Compensation (Scotland) Amendment Order 1996
revoked: SSI 2009/232 Sch.l

1455. Disability Discrimination (Meaning of Disability) Regulations 1996
Reg.3, see *Governors of X Endowed Primary School v Special Educational Needs and Disability Tribunal* [2009] EWHC 1842 (Admin), [2009] I.R.L.R. 1007 (QBD (Admin)), Lloyd-Jones J.

1996– cont.

1455. Disability Discrimination (Meaning of Disability) Regulations 1996– *cont.*

Reg.4, see *Governors of X Endowed Primary School v Special Educational Needs and Disability Tribunal* [2009] EWHC 1842 (Admin), [2009] I.R.L.R. 1007 (QBD (Admin)), Lloyd-Jones J.

1462. Contracting-out (Transfer and Transfer Payment) Regulations 1996

Reg.1, amended: SI 2009/615 Reg.5

1469. Financial Markets and Insolvency Regulations 1996

varied: SI 2009/317 Sch.1

1499. Food Labelling Regulations 1996

Reg.2, amended: SI 2009/2538 Reg.2, SI 2009/2705 Reg.2, SI 2009/3235 Reg.7, SSI 2009/328 Reg.2, SSI 2009/435 Reg.7

Reg.14, amended: SI 2009/3235 Reg.7, SSI 2009/435 Reg.7

Reg.17, amended: SI 2009/3235 Reg.7, SSI 2009/435 Reg.7

Reg.17, substituted: SSI 2009/435 Reg.7

Reg.50, amended: SI 2009/2538 Reg.3, SI 2009/2705 Reg.3, SI 2009/2801 Reg.2, SI 2009/2880 Reg.2, SSI 2009/328 Reg.2, SSI 2009/374 Reg.2

Sch.4, amended: SI 2009/3235 Reg.7, SSI 2009/435 Reg.7

Sch.6 Part II, amended: SI 2009/2538 Sch.1, Sch.2, SI 2009/2705 Sch.1, Sch.2, SSI 2009/328 Sch.1, Sch.2

Sch.7 Part I para.5, amended: SI 2009/2538 Reg.2, SI 2009/2705 Reg.2, SSI 2009/328 Reg.2

1504. National Health Service (General Medical Services, Pharmaceutical Services and Charges for Drugs and Appliances) (Scotland) Amendment Regulations 1996

Reg.3, revoked: SSI 2009/183 Sch.5

1527. Landfill Tax Regulations 1996

Reg.10, amended: SI 2009/1930 Reg.2

Reg.11, amended: SI 2009/1930 Reg.2

Reg.12, amended: SI 2009/1930 Reg.2

Reg.13, amended: SI 2009/1930 Reg.2

Reg.14, amended: SI 2009/1930 Reg.2

Reg.14A, amended: SI 2009/1930 Reg.2

Reg.14B, amended: SI 2009/1930 Reg.2

Reg.14C, amended: SI 2009/1930 Reg.2

Reg.14D, amended: SI 2009/1930 Reg.2

Reg.14E, amended: SI 2009/1930 Reg.2

Reg.14F, amended: SI 2009/1930 Reg.2

Reg.14G, amended: SI 2009/1930 Reg.2

Reg.14H, amended: SI 2009/1930 Reg.2

Reg.15, amended: SI 2009/1930 Reg.2

Reg.16, amended: SI 2009/1930 Reg.2

Reg.16A, added: SI 2009/1930 Reg.2

Reg.16A, amended: SI 2009/1930 Reg.2

Reg.16A, applied: SI 2009/1929 Art.3

Reg.21, amended: SI 2009/1930 Reg.2

Reg.33, amended: SI 2009/1890 Art.4

Reg.38, revoked: SI 2009/1930 Reg.2

Reg.39, revoked: SI 2009/1930 Reg.2

Reg.40, revoked: SI 2009/1930 Reg.2

Reg.42, amended: SI 2009/1930 Reg.2

Sch.1, amended: SI 2009/1930 Reg.2

1537. Personal and Occupational Pension Schemes (Protected Rights) Regulations 1996

Reg.8, amended: SI 2009/2930 Reg.5

1632. Deregulation and Contracting Out (Northern Ireland) Order 1996

Art.2, amended: SI 2009/1941 Sch.1 para.166

1996– cont.

1632. Deregulation and Contracting Out (Northern Ireland) Order 1996– *cont.*

Art.2, varied: SI 2009/1941 Art.7

Art.11, revoked (in part): SI 2009/1941 Sch.1 para.166

Art.11, varied: SI 2009/1941 Art.7

Art.12, amended: SI 2009/1941 Sch.1 para.166

Sch.2 Part I para.1, varied: SI 2009/1941 Art.7

Sch.2 Part I para.2, substituted: SI 2009/1941 Sch.1 para.166

Sch.2 Part I para.2, varied: SI 2009/1941 Art.7

Sch.2 Part I para.3, substituted: SI 2009/1941 Sch.1 para.166

Sch.2 Part I para.3, varied: SI 2009/1941 Art.7

Sch.2 Part I para.3A, varied: SI 2009/1941 Art.7

Sch.2 Part I para.4, varied: SI 2009/1941 Art.7

Sch.2 Part I para.5, varied: SI 2009/1941 Art.7

Sch.2 Part I para.6, varied: SI 2009/1941 Art.7

Sch.2 Part I para.7, varied: SI 2009/1941 Art.7

Sch.2 Part I para.8, varied: SI 2009/1941 Art.7

1655. Occupational Pension Schemes (Disclosure of Information) Regulations 1996

Reg.11, amended: SI 2009/615 Reg.6

Sch.1 para.18, amended: SI 2009/1906 Sch.1 para.1

Sch.2 para.6AA, amended: SI 2009/598 Art.4

Sch.2 para.9, amended: SI 2009/598 Art.4

Sch.2 para.10, amended: SI 2009/598 Art.4

1656. Work in Compressed Air Regulations 1996

applied: SI 2009/515 Sch.5

1679. Occupational Pension Schemes (Indexation) Regulations 1996

Reg.5, added: SI 2009/615 Reg.7

1725. Eggs (Marketing Standards) (Amendment) Regulations 1996

revoked (in part): SI 2009/793 Sch.1

1847. Occupational Pension Schemes (Transfer Values) Regulations 1996

Reg.11, amended: SI 2009/615 Reg.8

1909. Insolvent Companies (Reports on Conduct of Directors) Rules 1996

varied: SI 2009/317 Sch.1

1919. Employment Rights (Northern Ireland) Order 1996

varied: SI 2009/317 Sch.1

Part I, applied: SI 2009/2402 Reg.27

Part XI, applied: SI 2009/2402 Reg.29

Art.67A, applied: SI 2009/2402 Reg.24, Reg.29, Reg.31

Art.71, applied: SI 2009/2402 Reg.32

Art.72, applied: SI 2009/2402 Reg.32

Art.90, applied: SI 2009/2402 Reg.27

Art.137, see *McConnell v Bombardier Aerospace/ Short Brothers Plc* [2009] I.R.L.R. 201 (CA (NI)), Higgins, L.J.

Art.137, amended: SI 2009/2402 Reg.30

Art.140, amended: SI 2009/2402 Reg.30

Art.163, see *McConnell v Bombardier Aerospace/ Short Brothers Plc* [2009] I.R.L.R. 201 (CA (NI)), Higgins, L.J.

Art.164, see *McConnell v Bombardier Aerospace/ Short Brothers Plc* [2009] I.R.L.R. 201 (CA (NI)), Higgins, L.J.

Art.174, see *McConnell v Bombardier Aerospace/ Short Brothers Plc* [2009] I.R.L.R. 201 (CA (NI)), Higgins, L.J.

Art.202, applied: 2009 c.4 s.81, s.1243

Art.237, amended: SI 2009/2054 Sch.1 para.15

Art.237, applied: SI 2009/2054 Sch.2 para.9

1996–cont.

1921. Industrial Tribunals (Northern Ireland) Order 1996
see *SCA Packaging Ltd v Boyle* [2009] UKHL 37, [2009] 4 All E.R. 1181 (HL (NI)), Lord Hope of Craighead
Art.20, amended: SI 2009/2402 Reg.33
Art.20, applied: SI 2009/2402 Reg.37

1977. Occupational Pension Schemes (Mixed Benefit Contracted-out Schemes) Regulations 1996
Reg.4, amended: SI 2009/598 Art.5
Reg.4, revoked (in part): SI 2009/598 Art.5

2128. Merchant Shipping (Prevention of Pollution) (Limits) Regulations 1996
Sch.1, referred to: SI 2009/223 Art.2

2154. Merchant Shipping (Prevention of Oil Pollution) Regulations 1996
Reg.1, amended: SI 2009/1210 Reg.4
Reg.10, amended: SI 2009/1210 Reg.4
Reg.11, amended: SI 2009/1210 Reg.4
Reg.11A, added: SI 2009/1210 Reg.4
Reg.11B, added: SI 2009/1210 Reg.4
Reg.11C, added: SI 2009/1210 Reg.4
Reg.12, amended: SI 2009/1210 Reg.4
Reg.12, revoked (in part): SI 2009/1210 Reg.4
Reg.13, amended: SI 2009/1210 Reg.4
Reg.13, revoked (in part): SI 2009/1210 Reg.4
Reg.16, amended: SI 2009/1210 Reg.4
Reg.22, amended: SI 2009/1210 Reg.4
Reg.32, revoked (in part): SI 2009/1210 Reg.4
Reg.35A, added: SI 2009/1210 Reg.4
Reg.36, revoked (in part): SI 2009/1210 Reg.4
Reg.36A, added: SI 2009/1210 Reg.4
Reg.37, amended: SI 2009/1210 Reg.4

2421. Aerosol Dispensers (EEC Requirements) (Amendment) Regulations 1996
revoked: SI 2009/2824 Sch.1 para.4

2447. Advice and Assistance (Scotland) Regulations 1996
Reg.16, amended: SSI 2009/49 Reg.3

2489. Local Authorities Traffic Orders (Procedure) (England and Wales) Regulations 1996
Reg.18, amended: SI 2009/1116 Reg.2

2503. Chemical Weapons (Notification) Regulations 1996
Reg.3, amended: SI 2009/229 Sch.2 para.10

2549. Parental Responsibilities and Parental Rights Agreement (Scotland) Regulations 1996
Reg.2, amended: SSI 2009/191 Reg.2
Reg.3, added: SSI 2009/191 Reg.2
Sch.1, amended: SSI 2009/191 Reg.2
Sch.2, added: SSI 2009/191 Reg.2

2555. Criminal Legal Aid (Scotland) Regulations 1996
applied: SSI 2009/312 Reg.9
Reg.2, amended: SSI 2009/312 Reg.6
Reg.4, amended: SSI 2009/312 Reg.6
Reg.14, amended: SSI 2009/312 Reg.6

2628. Specified Diseases (Notification) Order 1996
Art.2, amended: SI 2009/2713 Art.2
Art.5, amended: SI 2009/2713 Art.2

2714. Greater Manchester (Light Rapid Transit System) (Eccles Extension) Order 1996
Art.2, applied: SI 2009/1100 Art.7
Art.4, applied: SI 2009/1100 Art.7
Art.7, applied: SI 2009/1100 Art.7
Art.8, applied: SI 2009/1100 Art.7
Art.9, applied: SI 2009/1100 Art.7

1996–cont.

2714. Greater Manchester (Light Rapid Transit System) (Eccles Extension) Order 1996– cont.
Art.11, applied: SI 2009/1100 Art.7
Art.11, varied: SI 2009/1100 Art.7
Art.12, applied: SI 2009/1100 Art.7
Art.13, applied: SI 2009/1100 Art.7
Art.16, applied: SI 2009/1100 Art.7
Art.20, applied: SI 2009/1100 Art.7
Art.22, applied: SI 2009/1100 Art.7
Art.23, applied: SI 2009/1100 Art.7
Art.35, applied: SI 2009/1100 Art.7
Art.37, applied: SI 2009/1100 Art.7
Art.38, applied: SI 2009/1100 Art.7
Art.40, applied: SI 2009/1100 Art.7
Art.41, applied: SI 2009/1100 Art.7
Art.42, applied: SI 2009/1100 Art.7
Art.44, applied: SI 2009/1100 Art.7
Art.45, applied: SI 2009/1100 Art.7
Art.46, applied: SI 2009/1100 Art.7
Art.47, applied: SI 2009/1100 Art.7
Art.60, applied: SI 2009/1100 Art.7

2745. Social Security Benefit (Computation of Earnings) Regulations 1996
Reg.2, applied: SI 2009/497 Art.6
Reg.9, amended: SI 2009/2678 Reg.2
Reg.11, amended: SI 2009/2678 Reg.2

2890. Housing Renewal Grants Regulations 1996
applied: SI 2009/1562 Art.2
Reg.2, amended: SI 2009/1807 Reg.3
Reg.10, amended: SI 2009/1807 Reg.3
Reg.19, amended: SI 2009/1807 Reg.3
Sch.1 Part I para.1, amended: SI 2009/1807 Reg.3
Sch.1 Part III para.12, amended: SI 2009/1807 Reg.3
Sch.1 Part III para.13A, substituted: SI 2009/1807 Reg.3
Sch.2 para.12, amended: SI 2009/1807 Reg.3
Sch.3 para.4, amended: SI 2009/1807 Reg.3
Sch.3 para.4B, added: SI 2009/1087 Reg.3
Sch.3 para.6, substituted: SI 2009/1807 Reg.3
Sch.3 para.11, amended: SI 2009/480 Reg.4
Sch.3 para.50A, added: SI 2009/1087 Reg.3
Sch.3 para.50B, added: SI 2009/1087 Reg.3
Sch.4 para.6, amended: SI 2009/1807 Reg.3
Sch.4 para.9, amended: SI 2009/1087 Reg.3, SI 2009/1807 Reg.3
Sch.4 para.67, added: SI 2009/1087 Reg.3

2907. Child Support Departure Direction and Consequential Amendments Regulations 1996
Reg.1, amended: SI 2009/736 Reg.2
Reg.24, substituted: SI 2009/736 Reg.2

2918. Bedfordshire Fire Services (Combination Scheme) Order 1996
Sch.1 Part II para.3, amended: SI 2009/119 Art.2
Sch.1 Part III para.11, applied: SI 2009/119 Sch.1 para.1
Sch.1 Part III para.12, applied: SI 2009/119 Sch.1 para.1
Sch.1 Part III para.13, applied: SI 2009/119 Sch.1 para.1
Sch.1 Part III para.14, applied: SI 2009/119 Sch.1 para.1
Sch.1 Part III para.15, applied: SI 2009/119 Sch.1 para.1
Sch.1 Part III para.16, applied: SI 2009/119 Sch.1 para.1

1996–cont.

3010. Merchant Shipping (Dangerous or Noxious Liquid Substances in Bulk) Regulations 1996
Reg.14, amended: SI 2009/1210 Reg.5
3087. Community Bus (Amendment) Regulations 1996
revoked: SI 2009/366 Sch.1
3088. Minibus and Other Section 19 Permit Buses (Amendment) Regulations 1996
revoked: SI 2009/365 Sch.1
3124. Products of Animal Origin (Import and Export) Regulations 1996
Reg.1, amended: SI 2009/2712 Reg.2
Reg.13, amended: SI 2009/2712 Reg.2
Reg.16, amended: SI 2009/2712 Reg.2
3126. Occupational Pension Schemes (Winding Up) Regulations 1996
Reg.8, amended: SI 2009/615 Reg.9, SI 2009/2930 Reg.6
Reg.8, revoked (in part): SI 2009/615 Reg.9
3158. Licensing (Northern Ireland) Order 1996
referred to: 2009 c.26 s.30
3160. Criminal Justice (Northern Ireland) Order 1996
Art.6, disapplied: 2009 c.25 s.158
3205. Local Authorities (Contracting Out of Allocation of Housing and Homelessness Functions) Order 1996
see *De-Winter Heald v Brent LBC* [2009] EWCA Civ 930, [2009] H.R.L.R. 34 (CA (Civ Div)), Sedley, L.J.
3257. Adoption Allowance (Scotland) Regulations 1996
applied: SSI 2009/152 Reg.17
3261. Children's Hearings (Scotland) Rules 1996
Part IV r.20, amended: SSI 2009/307 r.2
Part V r.22, amended: SSI 2009/429 Sch.1 para.2
Part VI r.31, applied: SSI 2009/169 Reg.3
Sch.1, amended: SSI 2009/429 Sch.1 para.2
3262. Arrangements to Look After Children (Scotland) Regulations 1996
applied: SSI 2009/210 Reg.50
revoked: SSI 2009/210 Reg.52
3263. Fostering of Children (Scotland) Regulations 1996
applied: SSI 2009/210 Reg.50
revoked: SSI 2009/210 Reg.52
Reg.9, applied: SSI 2009/210 Reg.51
Reg.12, applied: SSI 2009/210 Reg.50
Reg.13, applied: SSI 2009/210 Reg.50
Reg.13, referred to: SSI 2009/210 Reg.50
Reg.14, applied: SSI 2009/210 Reg.50
Reg.14, referred to: SSI 2009/210 Reg.50
3266. Adoption Agencies (Scotland) Regulations 1996
applied: SSI 2009/154 Reg.27, SSI 2009/267 Art.5
3267. Children (Reciprocal Enforcement of Prescribed Orders etc (England and Wales and Northern Ireland)) (Scotland) Regulations 1996
Reg.1, amended: SSI 2009/429 Sch.1 para.1
Reg.4, amended: SSI 2009/429 Sch.1 para.1
Reg.5, amended: SSI 2009/429 Sch.1 para.1

1997

16. Criminal Justice and Public Order Act 1994 (Application to the Armed Forces) Order 1997
revoked: SI 2009/990 Art.3

1997–cont.

172. Standing Civilian Courts Order 1997
applied: SI 2009/1059 Art.44, SI 2009/1209 Sch.2 para.4
varied: SI 2009/1209 Sch.2 para.8
Art.6, applied: SI 2009/1059 Art.52
Art.13, applied: SI 2009/1059 Art.52
Art.17, applied: SI 2009/1059 Art.52
Art.21, applied: SI 2009/1209 Sch.2 para.6
Art.35, applied: SI 2009/1209 Sch.2 para.7
Art.39, varied: SI 2009/1209 Sch.2 para.8
Art.44, applied: SI 2009/1059 Art.52
291. Act of Sederunt (Child Care and Maintenance Rules) 1997
Part 2, revoked: SSI 2009/284 r.4
Part 2 r.2.1, amended: SSI 2009/284 r.4, SSI 2009/294 r.17
Part 2 r.2.3, revoked: SSI 2009/284 r.4
Part 2 r.2.4, revoked: SSI 2009/284 r.4
Part 5 r.5.1, amended: SSI 2009/29 r.2
Part 5 r.5.16A, amended: SSI 2009/29 r.2
Part 5 r.5.17A, added: SSI 2009/29 r.2
Part 5 r.5.22, amended: SSI 2009/29 r.2
Part 5 r.5.22A, added: SSI 2009/29 r.2
Part 5 r.5.22B, added: SSI 2009/29 r.2
Part 5 r.5.23, amended: SSI 2009/29 r.2
Part 5 r.5.23A, added: SSI 2009/29 r.2
Part 5 r.5.23B, added: SSI 2009/29 r.2
Part 5 r.5.23C, added: SSI 2009/29 r.2
Part 5 r.5.23D, added: SSI 2009/29 r.2
Part 5 r.5.37A, added: SSI 2009/29 r.2
Part 5 r.5.37B, added: SSI 2009/29 r.2
Part 5 r.5.37C, added: SSI 2009/29 r.2
Part 5 r.5.38, amended: SSI 2009/449 r.2
Part 5 r.5.38, substituted: SSI 2009/449 r.2
302. Civil Jurisdiction and Judgments Act 1982 (Interim Relief) Order 1997
see *ETI Euro Telecom International NV v Bolivia* [2008] EWCA Civ 880, [2009] 1 W.L.R. 665 (CA (Civ Div)), Tuckey, L.J.
Art.2, amended: SI 2009/3131 Reg.26
330. Countryside Premium Scheme (Scotland) Regulations 1997
applied: SSI 2009/376 Sch.1 para.22
Reg.12, applied: SSI 2009/376 Sch.1 para.22
420. Town and Country Planning (Determination of Appeals by Appointed Persons) (Prescribed Classes) Regulations 1997
Reg.3, amended: SI 2009/380 Reg.2
Reg.4, amended: SI 2009/380 Reg.2
470. Personal Pension Schemes (Appropriate Schemes) Regulations 1997
Reg.8, revoked (in part): SI 2009/598 Art.6
Reg.15, amended: SI 2009/615 Reg.10
494. Bedfordshire (Coroners) Order 1997
Art.2, revoked (in part): SI 2009/837 Art.29
534. Customs Reviews and Appeals (Tariff and Origin) Regulations 1997
Reg.3, amended: SI 2009/56 Sch.2 para.34
Reg.4, amended: SI 2009/56 Sch.2 para.35
Reg.5, amended: SI 2009/56 Sch.2 para.36
Reg.6, amended: SI 2009/56 Sch.2 para.37
562. Merchant Shipping (Light Dues) Regulations 1997
Sch.2 Part II para.3, amended: SI 2009/1371 Reg.2
579. Courts-Martial and Standing Civilian Courts (Army and Royal Air Force) (Additional Powers on Trial of Civilians) Regulations 1997
applied: SI 2009/1059 Art.174

1997– cont.

579. Courts-Martial and Standing Civilian Courts (Army and Royal Air Force) (Additional Powers on Trial of Civilians) Regulations 1997–*cont.*
Reg.3, applied: SI 2009/1059 Art.175
Reg.11, applied: SI 2009/1059 Art.175
Sch.2 Part II, applied: SI 2009/1059 Art.175

580. Courts-Martial Appeal (Amendment) Rules 1997
revoked: SI 2009/2657 Sch.5

687. Sheriff Court Fees Order 1997
Art.2, amended: SSI 2009/89 Art.2
Art.4, amended: SSI 2009/89 Art.2
Art.5, amended: SSI 2009/89 Art.2
Art.7, amended: SSI 2009/89 Art.2
Art.8, amended: SSI 2009/89 Art.2
Art.9, amended: SSI 2009/89 Art.2
Art.10, amended: SSI 2009/89 Art.2

688. Court of Session etc Fees Order 1997
Art.5, amended: SSI 2009/88 Art.2
Art.5A, amended: SSI 2009/88 Art.2
Art.5B, amended: SSI 2009/88 Art.2

690. Legal Aid (Scotland) (Children) Regulations 1997
applied: SSI 2009/312 Reg.9
Reg.2, amended: SSI 2009/312 Reg.7

696. National Health Service (Pharmaceutical Services) (Scotland) Amendment Regulations 1997
revoked: SSI 2009/183 Sch.5

750. Town and Country Planning Appeals (Determination by Appointed Person) (Inquiries Procedure) (Scotland) Rules 1997
r.2, amended: SSI 2009/212 r.3
r.2, revoked (in part): SSI 2009/212 r.3

784. Occupational Pension Schemes (Discharge of Liability) Regulations 1997
see *Easterly Ltd v Headway Plc* [2009] EWCA Civ 793, [2009] Pens. L.R. 279 (CA (Civ Div)), Lord Neuberger of Abbotsbury
Reg.5, see *Easterly Ltd v Headway Plc* [2009] EWCA Civ 793, [2009] Pens. L.R. 279 (CA (Civ Div)), Lord Neuberger of Abbotsbury

785. Occupational Pension Schemes (Assignment, Forfeiture, Bankruptcy etc.) Regulations 1997
Reg.2, amended: SI 2009/2930 Reg.7

796. Town and Country Planning (Inquiries Procedure) (Scotland) Rules 1997
r.2, amended: SSI 2009/212 r.2
r.2, revoked (in part): SSI 2009/212 r.2
r.3, amended: SSI 2009/212 r.2

818. National Health Service (Optical Charges and Payments) Regulations 1997
Reg.1, amended: SI 2009/311 Reg.2, SI 2009/409 Reg.2, SI 2009/589 Reg.2, SI 2009/1824 Sch.1 para.3
Reg.2, amended: SI 2009/1824 Sch.1 para.3
Reg.8, amended: SI 2009/409 Reg.2, SI 2009/589 Reg.3, SI 2009/1824 Sch.1 para.3
Reg.10, amended: SI 2009/1824 Sch.1 para.3
Reg.12, applied: SI 2009/409 Reg.3, SI 2009/589 Reg.6
Reg.17, applied: SI 2009/409 Reg.3, SI 2009/589 Reg.6
Reg.19, amended: SI 2009/409 Reg.2, SI 2009/589 Reg.4
Sch.1, amended: SI 2009/409 Reg.2, SI 2009/589 Reg.5, SI 2009/1824 Sch.1 para.3

1997– cont.

818. National Health Service (Optical Charges and Payments) Regulations 1997– *cont.*
Sch.2 para.1, amended: SI 2009/409 Reg.2, SI 2009/589 Reg.5, SI 2009/1824 Sch.1 para.3
Sch.2 para.2, amended: SI 2009/409 Reg.2, SI 2009/589 Reg.5
Sch.3, substituted: SI 2009/409 Reg.2, SI 2009/589 Sch.1

828. Farm Woodland (Amendment) Scheme 1997
applied: SSI 2009/376 Sch.1 para.16

869. Race Relations (Northern Ireland) Order 1997
Art.71, applied: SI 2009/1059 Art.196

873. Driving Standards Agency Trading Fund Order 1997
Art.6, amended: SI 2009/469 Art.2

932. Jobseeker's Allowance (Members of the Forces) (Northern Ireland) Regulations 1997
Reg.4, amended: SI 2009/2054 Sch.1 para.16
Reg.4, applied: SI 2009/2054 Sch.2 para.10

946. Occupational Pension Schemes (Age-related Payments) Regulations 1997
Reg.10, amended: SI 2009/615 Reg.11

1160. Hedgerows Regulations 1997
applied: SI 2009/3264 Sch.1 para.7, SI 2009/3365 Sch.1 para.1
Reg.5, applied: SI 2009/3264 Sch.1 para.1, SI 2009/3365 Sch.1 para.1
Reg.14, amended: SI 2009/1307 Sch.2 para.93

1183. Social Security (Recovery of Benefits) (Northern Ireland) Order 1997
Sch.1 Part I para.2, varied: SI 2009/1059 Sch.1 para.42

1331. Surface Waters (Fishlife) (Classification) Regulations 1997
Reg.1, amended: SI 2009/1264 Reg.2
Reg.6, amended: SI 2009/1264 Reg.2
Sch.1 Part I, amended: SI 2009/1264 Reg.2

1332. Surface Waters (Shellfish) (Classification) Regulations 1997
Reg.1, amended: SI 2009/1266 Reg.2
Reg.2, amended: SI 2009/1266 Reg.2
Reg.6, amended: SI 2009/1266 Reg.2

1335. Novel Foods and Novel Food Ingredients Regulations 1997
Reg.2, amended: SI 2009/3235 Reg.10, SSI 2009/435 Reg.10

1372. Control of Trade in Endangered Species (Enforcement) Regulations 1997
Reg.2, amended: SI 2009/1773 Reg.2
Reg.8A, added: SI 2009/1773 Reg.3

1414. Eggs (Marketing Standards) (Amendment) Regulations 1997
revoked (in part): SI 2009/793 Sch.1

1421. Control of Trade in Endangered Species (Fees) Regulations 1997
revoked: SI 2009/496 Reg.7

1524. Value Added Tax (Place of Supply of Services) (Amendment) Order 1997
see *Arachchige v Revenue and Customs Commissioners* [2009] EWHC 1077 (Ch), [2009] S.T.C. 1729 (Ch D), Lewison, J.

1611. International Monetary Fund (Limit on Lending) Order 1997
revoked: SI 2009/1830 Art.3

1612. Local Government Pension Scheme Regulations 1997
see *Booth v Oldham MBC* [2009] EWCA Civ 880, [2009] Pens. L.R. 325 (CA (Civ Div)), Laws, L.J.;
see *R. (on the application of South Tyneside*

1997– cont.

1612. Local Government Pension Scheme Regulations 1997– cont.

see– cont.

MBC) v Lord Chancellor [2009] EWCA Civ 299, [2009] I.C.R. 1352 (CA (Civ Div)), Sedley, L.J.

Reg.27, see *Booth v Oldham MBC* [2009] EWCA Civ 880, [2009] Pens. L.R. 325 (CA (Civ Div)), Laws, L.J.

Reg.31, see *Hamilton v Monmouthshire CC* [2008] EWHC 3101 (Ch), [2009] Pens. L.R. 31 (Ch D (Bristol)), Lewison, J.

Reg.77, see *R. (on the application of South Tyneside MBC) v Lord Chancellor* [2009] EWCA Civ 299, [2009] I.C.R. 1352 (CA (Civ Div)), Sedley, L.J.

Reg.79, see *R. (on the application of South Tyneside MBC) v Lord Chancellor* [2009] EWCA Civ 299, [2009] I.C.R. 1352 (CA (Civ Div)), Sedley, L.J.

Reg.97, see *Booth v Oldham MBC* [2009] EWCA Civ 880, [2009] Pens. L.R. 325 (CA (Civ Div)), Laws, L.J.

Sch.1, see *R. (on the application of South Tyneside MBC) v Lord Chancellor* [2009] EWCA Civ 299, [2009] I.C.R. 1352 (CA (Civ Div)), Sedley, L.J.

1624. Energy Information (Combined Washer-driers) Regulations 1997

referred to: SI 2009/669 Sch.1 Part 4

Reg.2, amended: SI 2009/2559 Reg.4

Reg.2A, added: SI 2009/2559 Reg.4

Sch.5 Part I para.2A, added: SI 2009/2559 Reg.4

1729. Animals and Animal Products (Examination for Residues and Maximum Residue Limits) Regulations 1997

Reg.2, amended: SI 2009/1925 Reg.2

Reg.3, amended: SI 2009/1925 Reg.2

Reg.3, revoked (in part): SI 2009/1925 Reg.2

Reg.4, substituted: SI 2009/1925 Reg.2

Reg.5, amended: SI 2009/1925 Reg.2

Reg.5, revoked (in part): SI 2009/1925 Reg.2

Reg.9, amended: SI 2009/1925 Reg.2

Reg.26, amended: SI 2009/1925 Reg.2

Reg.27, amended: SI 2009/1925 Reg.2

Reg.27, revoked (in part): SI 2009/1925 Reg.2

Reg.28A, revoked: SI 2009/1925 Reg.2

1772. Further Education (Northern Ireland) Order 1997

amended: SI 2009/1941 Sch.1 para.170

applied: 2009 c.4 s.71

Art.14, amended: SI 2009/1941 Sch.1 para.170

1830. Prescription Only Medicines (Human Use) Order 1997

Art.1, revoked (in part): SI 2009/1165 Art.2

Art.8, amended: SI 2009/1165 Art.3

Art.8, referred to: SSI 2009/183 Sch.1 para.4

Art.12C, applied: SSI 2009/183 Sch.1 para.4, Sch.1 para.10

Art.12F, added: SI 2009/1165 Art.4

Sch.5 Part II, amended: SI 2009/3062 Art.3

Sch.5 Part III, amended: SI 2009/3062 Art.3

1881. Fish Health Regulations 1997

revoked (in part): SI 2009/463 Sch.2 para.12, SSI 2009/85 Sch.2 para.13

1968. Education (Assisted Places) Regulations 1997

Reg.10, amended: SI 2009/1561 Reg.2

Sch.2 para.1, amended: SI 2009/1561 Reg.2

Sch.2 para.2, amended: SI 2009/1561 Reg.2

1969. Education (Assisted Places) (Incidental Expenses) Regulations 1997

Reg.2, amended: SI 2009/1560 Reg.2

Reg.4, amended: SI 2009/1560 Reg.2

1997– cont.

1984. Rent Officers (Housing Benefit Functions) Order 1997

Sch.3B para.2, amended: SI 2009/2459 Art.2

1995. Rent Officers (Housing Benefit Functions) (Scotland) Order 1997

Sch.3B para.2, amended: SI 2009/2459 Art.3

2161. Race Relations (Complaints to Employment Tribunals) (Armed Forces) Regulations 1997

Reg.2, amended: SI 2009/2054 Sch.1 para.17

Reg.2, applied: SI 2009/2054 Sch.2 para.11

2162. Equal Pay (Complaints to Employment Tribunals) (Armed Forces) Regulations 1997

Reg.2, amended: SI 2009/2054 Sch.1 para.18

Reg.2, applied: SI 2009/2054 Sch.2 para.12

2163. Sex Discrimination (Complaints to Employment Tribunals) (Armed Forces) Regulations 1997

Reg.2, amended: SI 2009/2054 Sch.1 para.19

Reg.2, applied: SI 2009/2054 Sch.2 para.13

2196. Gaming Duty Regulations 1997

Reg.5, amended: SI 2009/2046 Reg.4

2348. Registration of Births, Still-births, Deaths and Marriages (Prescription of Forms) (Scotland) Regulations 1997

Sch.1, amended: SSI 2009/315 Sch.1

Sch.2, amended: SSI 2009/315 Sch.2

Sch.8, amended: SSI 2009/315 Sch.3

Sch.9, amended: SSI 2009/315 Sch.4

Sch.10, amended: SSI 2009/315 Sch.5

Sch.15A, amended: SSI 2009/315 Sch.6

Sch.17, amended: SSI 2009/315 Sch.7

Sch.18, amended: SSI 2009/315 Sch.8

Sch.19, amended: SSI 2009/315 Sch.9

Sch.20, amended: SSI 2009/315 Sch.10

Sch.21, amended: SSI 2009/315 Sch.11

Sch.22, amended: SSI 2009/315 Sch.12

2349. Marriage (Prescription of Forms) (Scotland) Regulations 1997

Sch.1, amended: SSI 2009/315 Sch.13

Sch.3, amended: SSI 2009/315 Sch.14

2367. Merchant Shipping (Dangerous Goods and Marine Pollutants) Regulations 1997

applied: SI 2009/716 Reg.6, Reg.8

2537. Imported Food Regulations 1997

Reg.2, amended: SSI 2009/319 Sch.3 Part 2

2697. Cheshire Fire Services (Combination Scheme) Order 1997

Sch.1 Part II para.3, amended: SI 2009/119 Art.5

Sch.1 Part III para.11, applied: SI 2009/119 Sch.1 para.2

Sch.1 Part III para.12, applied: SI 2009/119 Sch.1 para.2

Sch.1 Part III para.13, applied: SI 2009/119 Sch.1 para.2

Sch.1 Part III para.14, applied: SI 2009/119 Sch.1 para.2

Sch.1 Part III para.15, applied: SI 2009/119 Sch.1 para.2

Sch.1 Part III para.16, applied: SI 2009/119 Sch.1 para.2

2778. Waste and Contaminated Land (Northern Ireland) Order 1997

Art.2, amended: SI 2009/1941 Sch.1 para.171

2780. Civil Jurisdiction and Judgments Act 1982 (Provisional and Protective Measures) (Scotland) Order 1997

Art.2, amended: SI 2009/3131 Reg.27

Art.3, amended: SI 2009/3131 Reg.27

STATUTORY INSTRUMENT CITATOR 2009 **1998**

1997– cont.

2792. Non-Domestic Rating (Rural Settlements) (England) Order 1997
Art.3, amended: SI 2009/3176 Art.2

2916. Minibus and Other Section 19 Permit Buses (Amendment) Regulations 1997
revoked: SI 2009/365 Sch.1

2917. Community Bus (Amendment) Regulations 1997
revoked: SI 2009/366 Sch.1

2962. Merchant Shipping and Fishing Vessels (Health and Safety at Work) Regulations 1997
Reg.28, see *Club Cruise Entertainment & Travelling Services Europe BV v Department for Transport (The Van Gogh)* [2008] EWHC 2794 (Comm), [2009] 1 All E.R. (Comm) 955 (QBD (Comm)), Flaux, J.

2984. Deregulation (Northern Ireland) Order 1997
Art.5, revoked: SI 2009/1941 Sch.2

3001. Teachers Pensions Regulations 1997
applied: SI 2009/12 Art.9, Art.12, SI 2009/2610 Art.21
varied: SI 2009/2610 Art.16
Reg.4, applied: SI 2009/12 Art.12
Reg.4, varied: SI 2009/2610 Art.16
Reg.9, applied: SI 2009/12 Art.12, SI 2009/2610 Art.16

3009. Smoke Control Areas (Exempted Fireplaces) Order 1997
revoked (in part): SSI 2009/214 Sch.2

3032. Copyright and Rights in Databases Regulations 1997
see *Magical Marking Ltd v Holly* [2008] EWHC 2428 (Ch), [2009] E.C.C. 10 (Ch D), Norris, J.
Reg.16, see *Exchange Communications Ltd v Masheder* [2009] CSOH 135, 2009 S.L.T. 1141 (OH), Temporary Judge M Wise, QC; see *Magical Marking Ltd v Holly* [2008] EWHC 2428 (Ch), [2009] E.C.C. 10 (Ch D), Norris, J.

3061. Town and Country Planning (Use Classes) (Scotland) Order 1997
Sch.1 para.7, amended: SSI 2009/248 Sch.1 para.14

1998

192. Local Government (Discretionary Payments and Injury Benefits) (Scotland) Regulations 1998
Reg.2, amended: SSI 2009/187 Reg.3
Reg.5, amended: SSI 2009/187 Reg.4
Reg.6, amended: SSI 2009/187 Reg.5
Reg.8, amended: SSI 2009/187 Reg.6
Reg.9, amended: SSI 2009/187 Reg.7
Reg.10, amended: SSI 2009/187 Reg.8
Reg.11, amended: SSI 2009/187 Reg.9
Reg.16, amended: SSI 2009/187 Reg.10
Reg.17, amended: SSI 2009/187 Reg.11
Reg.18, amended: SSI 2009/187 Reg.12
Reg.20, amended: SSI 2009/187 Reg.13
Reg.21, amended: SSI 2009/187 Reg.14
Reg.24, amended: SSI 2009/187 Reg.15
Reg.25, amended: SSI 2009/187 Reg.16
Reg.29, amended: SSI 2009/187 Reg.17
Reg.31, amended: SSI 2009/187 Reg.18
Reg.34, amended: SSI 2009/187 Reg.19
Reg.35, amended: SSI 2009/187 Reg.20
Reg.38, amended: SSI 2009/187 Reg.21
Reg.41, amended: SSI 2009/187 Reg.22
Reg.44, amended: SSI 2009/187 Reg.23

1998– cont.

192. Local Government (Discretionary Payments and Injury Benefits) (Scotland) Regulations 1998– *cont.*
Reg.45, amended: SSI 2009/187 Reg.24
Reg.46, amended: SSI 2009/187 Reg.25
Reg.49A, added: SSI 2009/187 Reg.26
Reg.49B, added: SSI 2009/187 Reg.26
Reg.51, amended: SSI 2009/187 Reg.28
Reg.51A, amended: SSI 2009/187 Reg.27

212. Building Societies (Transfer of Business) Regulations 1998
Reg.2, varied: SI 2009/509 Art.14
Reg.3, varied: SI 2009/509 Art.15
Sch.1 Part I para.4, varied: SI 2009/509 Art.16
Sch.1 Part I para.9, varied: SI 2009/509 Art.16
Sch.1 Part I para.21, varied: SI 2009/509 Art.16
Sch.1 Part II para.2, varied: SI 2009/509 Art.16
Sch.1 Part II para.3, varied: SI 2009/509 Art.16
Sch.1 Part II para.4, varied: SI 2009/509 Art.16
Sch.1 Part II para.5, varied: SI 2009/509 Art.16
Sch.1 Part II para.6, varied: SI 2009/509 Art.16
Sch.1 Part II para.11, varied: SI 2009/509 Art.16
Sch.1 Part II para.12, varied: SI 2009/509 Art.16
Sch.1 Part II para.13, varied: SI 2009/509 Art.16
Sch.1 Part III para.1A, varied: SI 2009/509 Art.16
Sch.1 Part III para.5, varied: SI 2009/509 Art.16
Sch.1 Part V para.1, varied: SI 2009/509 Art.16
Sch.1 Part V para.2, varied: SI 2009/509 Art.16
Sch.1 Part V para.3, varied: SI 2009/509 Art.16
Sch.1 Part V para.4, varied: SI 2009/509 Art.16
Sch.1 Part V para.5, varied: SI 2009/509 Art.16
Sch.1 Part V para.6, varied: SI 2009/509 Art.16
Sch.1 Part V para.7, varied: SI 2009/509 Art.16
Sch.2 para.2, varied: SI 2009/509 Art.17
Sch.2 para.3, varied: SI 2009/509 Art.17
Sch.2 para.5, varied: SI 2009/509 Art.17

250. Surface Waters (Dangerous Substances) (Classification) (Scotland) Regulations 1998
revoked: SSI 2009/420 Sch.3

366. Local Government Pension Scheme (Scotland) Regulations 1998
Reg.39, amended: SSI 2009/186 Reg.3
Reg.161, added: SSI 2009/186 Reg.4
Reg.162, added: SSI 2009/186 Reg.4
Reg.163, added: SSI 2009/186 Reg.4
Reg.164, added: SSI 2009/186 Reg.4, Reg.5
Reg.164, revoked: SSI 2009/186 Reg.5
Reg.165, added: SSI 2009/186 Reg.4, Reg.6
Reg.165A, added: SSI 2009/186 Reg.4, Reg.6

463. Specified Animal Pathogens Order 1998
revoked (in part): SSI 2009/45 Art.12

472. Secure Training Centre Rules 1998
see *R. (on the application of Pounder) v HM Coroner for North and South Districts of Durham and Darlington* [2009] EWHC 76 (Admin), [2009] 3 All E.R. 150 (QBD (Admin)), Blake, J

494. Health and Safety (Enforcing Authority) Regulations 1998
Reg.2, amended: SI 2009/716 Sch.6
Reg.3, disapplied: SI 2009/716 Reg.14
Reg.4, amended: SI 2009/693 Sch.1 para.2
Sch.1 para.1, amended: SI 2009/716 Sch.6

504. Building Societies (Accounts and Related Provisions) Regulations 1998
Sch.8 para.4, amended: SI 2009/1391 Reg.2

562. Income-related Benefits (Subsidy to Authorities) Order 1998
Art.6, amended: SI 2009/ 30 Art.2
Art.14, amended: SI 2009/ 2580 Art.2
Art.17, substituted: SI 2009/ 2580 Art.2
Sch.1, substituted: SI 2009/ 30 Sch.1
Sch.4A Part I para.1, amended: SI 2009/ 2564 Sch.1 para.2
Sch.4A Part II para.2, amended: SI 2009/ 2564 Sch.1 para.3
Sch.4A Part II para.3, amended: SI 2009/ 2564 Sch.1 para.4
Sch.4A Part III, substituted: SI 2009/ 2564 Sch.1 para.5
Sch.4A Part V, substituted: SI 2009/ 2564 Sch.1 para.6
Sch.7, added: SI 2009/ 2580 Art.2

642. National Health Service (Optical Charges and Payments) (Scotland) Regulations 1998
Reg.8, amended: SSI 2009/ 288 Reg.2
Reg.12, amended: SSI 2009/ 288 Reg.2
Reg.12A, amended: SSI 2009/ 288 Reg.2
Reg.15, amended: SSI 2009/ 288 Reg.2
Reg.16, amended: SSI 2009/ 288 Reg.2
Reg.19, amended: SSI 2009/ 86 Reg.2
Reg.20, amended: SSI 2009/ 288 Reg.2
Sch.1, amended: SSI 2009/ 86 Reg.2
Sch.2, substituted: SSI 2009/ 86 Sch.1
Sch.3 para.1, amended: SSI 2009/ 86 Reg.2
Sch.3 para.2, amended: SSI 2009/ 86 Reg.2

649. Scheme for Construction Contracts (England and Wales) Regulations 1998
see *Vision Homes Ltd v Lancsville Construction Ltd* [2009] EWHC 2042 (TCC), [2009] B.L.R. 525 (QBD (TCC)), Christopher Clarke, J.
Sch.1 para.2, see *Vision Homes Ltd v Lancsville Construction Ltd* [2009] EWHC 2042 (TCC), [2009] B.L.R. 525 (QBD (TCC)), Christopher Clarke, J.
Sch.1 para.23, see *HS Works Ltd v Enterprise Managed Services Ltd* [2009] EWHC 729 (TCC), [2009] B.L.R. 378 (QBD (TCC)), Akenhead, J.

678. Welsh Ambulance Services National Health Service Trust (Establishment) Order 1998
Art.4, amended: SI 2009/ 201 Art.2

935. Legal Services Ombudsman (Jurisdiction) (Amendment) Order 1998
revoked: SI 2009/ 3250 Sch.1

1056. Merchant Shipping (Oil Pollution Preparedness, Response and Co-operation Convention) Regulations 1998
Reg.4, amended: SI 2009/ 229 Sch.2 para.11
Reg.4, applied: SI 2009/ 229 Art.4

1344. Surface Waters (Dangerous Substances) (Classification) (Scotland) (No.2) Regulations 1998
revoked: SSI 2009/ 420 Sch.3

1376. Plastic Materials and Articles in Contact with Food Regulations 1998
Sch.2 Part I, referred to: SI 2009/ 481 Reg.21

1461. Air Passenger Duty and Other Indirect Taxes (Interest Rate) Regulations 1998
Reg.2, amended: SI 2009/ 2032 Reg.16
Reg.2A, revoked: SI 2009/ 2032 Reg.17
Reg.4, amended: SI 2009/ 56 Sch.2 para.39
Reg.5, amended: SI 2009/ 56 Sch.2 para.40, SI 2009/ 2032 Reg.18

1506. Social Security (Northern Ireland) Order 1998
applied: 2009 c.8 s.24
Part II, applied: 2009 c.8 s.25
Part II, varied: 2009 c.8 s.25
Art.2, enabled: SI 2009/ 3268
Art.6, amended: 2009 c.3 Sch.4 para.29
Art.7, amended: 2009 c.3 Sch.4 para.30
Art.9, applied: SI 2009/ 810 Reg.2
Art.10, enabled: SI 2009/ 713, SI 2009/ 751, SI 2009/ 3268
Art.10A, enabled: SI 2009/ 713
Art.11, enabled: SI 2009/ 3268
Art.11A, amended: SI 2009/ 56 Sch.2 para.42
Art.13, enabled: SI 2009/ 713, SI 2009/ 751, SI 2009/ 3268
Art.15, applied: 2009 c.8 s.25
Art.24A, amended: SI 2009/ 56 Sch.2 para.43
Art.39, amended: SI 2009/ 56 Sch.2 para.44
Art.74, enabled: SI 2009/ 713, SI 2009/ 751, SI 2009/ 3268
Sch.1, amended: 2009 c.3 Sch.4 para.31

1594. National Health Service (Scotland) (Injury Benefits) Regulations 1998
referred to: SSI 2009/ 19 Reg.87
Reg.2, amended: SSI 2009/ 208 Reg.88
Reg.4, amended: SSI 2009/ 19 Reg.86, SSI 2009/ 208 Reg.89
Reg.13, amended: SSI 2009/ 208 Reg.90

1665. Eggs (Marketing Standards) (Amendment) Regulations 1998
revoked (in part): SI 2009/ 793 Sch.1

1759. Education (Northern Ireland) Order 1998
Art.3, applied: SI 2009/ 2737 Reg.85, Reg.101
Art.8, applied: SI 2009/ 2737 Reg.85, Reg.101
Art.87, applied: SI 2009/ 1369 Reg.2

1760. Education (Student Support) (Northern Ireland) Order 1998
applied: SI 2009/ 470 Reg.19
Art.3, applied: SI 2009/ 1555 Reg.120, Reg.137, Reg.140, SI 2009/ 2737 Reg.72
Art.8, applied: SI 2009/ 1555 Reg.120, Reg.137, Reg.140, SI 2009/ 2737 Reg.72

1764. Trial of the Pyx Order 1998
Art.4, amended: SI 2009/ 2748 Sch.1 para.18
Art.15, amended: SI 2009/ 2748 Sch.1 para.18

1827. Coventry Airport (Designation) (Detention and Sale of Aircraft) Order 1998
revoked: SI 2009/ 2350 Sch.2

1831. Local Government Pension Scheme (Management and Investment of Funds) Regulations 1998
revoked: SI 2009/ 3093 Sch.2

1833. Working Time Regulations 1998
see *Craig v Transocean International Resources Ltd* [2009] I.R.L.R. 519 (EAT (SC)), Lady Smith; see *Inland Revenue Commissioners v Ainsworth* [2009] UKHL 31, [2009] 4 All E.R. 1205 (HL), Lord Hope of Craighead
Reg.2, see *Redrow Homes (Yorkshire) Ltd v Buckborough* [2009] I.R.L.R. 34 (EAT), Judge Burke Q.C.
Reg.12, see *Corps of Commissionaries Management Ltd v Hughes* [2009] I.C.R. 345 (EAT), Silber, J.
Reg.13, see *Inland Revenue Commissioners v Ainsworth* [2009] UKHL 31, [2009] 4 All E.R. 1205 (HL), Lord Hope of Craighead

1998– cont.

1833. Working Time Regulations 1998– *cont.*

Reg.14, see *Inland Revenue Commissioners v Ainsworth* [2009] UKHL 31, [2009] 4 All E.R. 1205 (HL), Lord Hope of Craighead

Reg.16, see *British Airways Plc v Williams* [2009] EWCA Civ 281, [2009] I.C.R. 906 (CA (Civ Div)), Ward, L.J.

Reg.24, see *Corps of Commissionaries Management Ltd v Hughes* [2009] I.C.R. 345 (EAT), Silber, J.

Reg.25A, amended: SI 2009/1567 Reg.2, SI 2009/2766 Reg.2

Reg.30, see *Corps of Commissionaries Management Ltd v Hughes* [2009] I.C.R. 345 (EAT), Silber, J.

Reg.35, amended: SI 2009/3348 Art.22, Art.23

Sch.2A, added: SI 2009/1567 Reg.3

Sch.2A, amended: SI 2009/2766 Reg.3

1870. Individual Savings Account Regulations 1998

applied: SI 2009/3328 Reg.12

varied: SI 2009/317 Sch.1

Reg.2, amended: SI 2009/1994 Reg.3

Reg.4, amended: SI 2009/1550 Reg.3, Reg.4, Reg.5, Reg.7, Reg.8, Reg.9, SI 2009/1994 Reg.4

Reg.5A, substituted: SI 2009/1994 Reg.5

Reg.7, amended: SI 2009/1994 Reg.6

Reg.10, amended: SI 2009/1550 Reg.6

Reg.12, amended: SI 2009/1994 Reg.7

Reg.18, amended: SI 2009/56 Sch.2 para.46

Reg.18, revoked (in part): SI 2009/56 Sch.2 para.46

Reg.21, amended: SI 2009/1994 Reg.8

Reg.21, revoked (in part): SI 2009/1994 Reg.8

Reg.27, amended: SI 2009/56 Sch.2 para.47

Reg.31, amended: SI 2009/1994 Reg.9

1901. Family Proceedings (Amendment) Rules 1998

see *Practice Direction (Fam Div: Requests to Inspect Files Following Pronouncements of Decrees Nisi)* [2009] 2 F.L.R. 1079 (Fam Div)

r.2, see *Practice Direction (Fam Div: Requests to Inspect Files Following Pronouncements of Decrees Nisi)* [2009] 2 F.L.R. 1079 (Fam Div)

1943. Education (Infant Class Sizes) (Wales) Regulations 1998

Sch.1 para.2A, added: SI 2009/828 Reg.3

Sch.1 para.5, amended: SI 2009/828 Reg.4

Sch.1 para.5A, added: SI 2009/828 Reg.5

Sch.1 para.5B, added: SI 2009/828 Reg.5

Sch.1 para.6, substituted: SI 2009/828 Reg.6

Sch.1 para.9, amended: SI 2009/828 Reg.7

1967. Assured and Protected Tenancies (Lettings to Students) Regulations 1998

Sch.2, amended: SI 2009/1825 Reg.2

2003. Education (Student Support) Regulations 1998

applied: SI 2009/1555 Reg.4, SI 2009/2737 Reg.3

2051. Motor Vehicles (EC Type Approval) Regulations 1998

applied: SI 2009/717 Reg.42

revoked: SI 2009/717 Sch.1

2181. Brucellosis and Tuberculosis (Scotland) Compensation Amendment Order 1998

revoked: SSI 2009/232 Sch.1

2224. National Health Service (Pilot Schemes for Personal Dental Services Miscellaneous Provisions and Consequential Amendments) Regulations 1998

Reg.8, revoked (in part): SSI 2009/183 Sch.5

1998– cont.

2306. Provision and Use of Work Equipment Regulations 1998

see *Spencer-Franks v Kellogg Brown & Root Ltd* [2008] UKHL 46, [2009] 1 All E.R. 269 (HL), Lord Hoffmann

Reg.2, see *Smith v Northamptonshire CC* [2009] UKHL 27, [2009] 4 All E.R. 557 (HL), Lord Hope of Craighead; see *Spencer-Franks v Kellogg Brown & Root Ltd* [2008] UKHL 46, [2009] 1 All E.R. 269 (HL), Lord Hoffmann

Reg.3, see *Smith v Northamptonshire CC* [2009] UKHL 27, [2009] 4 All E.R. 557 (HL), Lord Hope of Craighead

Reg.4, see *McLellan v Dundee City Council* [2009] CSOH 9, 2009 Rep. L.R. 61 (OH), Lord Hodge

Reg.5, see *Smith v Northamptonshire CC* [2009] UKHL 27, [2009] 4 All E.R. 557 (HL), Lord Hope of Craighead

Reg.7, see *McLellan v Dundee City Council* [2009] CSOH 9, 2009 Rep. L.R. 61 (OH), Lord Hodge

Reg.8, see *McLellan v Dundee City Council* [2009] CSOH 9, 2009 Rep. L.R. 61 (OH), Lord Hodge

Reg.9, see *McLellan v Dundee City Council* [2009] CSOH 9, 2009 Rep. L.R. 61 (OH), Lord Hodge

Reg.11, see *McLellan v Dundee City Council* [2009] CSOH 9, 2009 Rep. L.R. 61 (OH), Lord Hodge

Reg.22, see *McLellan v Dundee City Council* [2009] CSOH 9, 2009 Rep. L.R. 61 (OH), Lord Hodge

2452. Crime and Disorder Strategies (Prescribed Descriptions) Order 1998

revoked (in part): SI 2009/3050 Art.4

Art.3, amended: SI 2009/2054 Sch.1 para.20

2513. Crime and Disorder Strategies (Prescribed Descriptions) (Amendment) Order 1998

revoked (in part): SI 2009/3050 Art.4

2535. Religious Character of Schools (Designation Procedure) Regulations 1998

referred to: SI 2009/3273

2573. Employers Liability (Compulsory Insurance) Regulations 1998

Sch.2 para.7, revoked (in part): SI 2009/801 Art.3

2746. Groundwater Regulations 1998

applied: SI 2009/153 Sch.3 para.1, SI 2009/995 Sch.3 para.1

revoked (in part): SI 2009/2902 Reg.25

3031. National Health Service (Pharmaceutical Services) (Scotland) Amendment Regulations 1998

revoked: SSI 2009/183 Sch.5

3084. Water (Prevention of Pollution) (Code of Practice) Order 1998

revoked (in part): SI 2009/46 Art.3

3111. Road Vehicles (Authorised Weight) Regulations 1998

Reg.4, referred to: SI 2009/492 Sch.2

Sch.1, referred to: SI 2009/492 Sch.2

3132. Civil Procedure Rules 1998

applied: SI 2009/273 r.10, SI 2009/356 r.227, SI 2009/1976 r.10, SI 2009/2469 r.2, SI 2009/2477 r.95

disapplied: SI 2009/356 r.227, SI 2009/2477 r.100

varied: SI 2009/2477 r.100

see *Al Rawi v Security Service* [2009] EWHC 2959 (QB), Times, November 24, 2009 (QBD), Silber, J.; see *Mastercigars Direct Ltd v Withers LLP* [2009] EWHC 993 (Ch), [2009] C.P. Rep. 35 (Ch D), Morgan, J.; see *McFaddens (A Firm) v Platford* [2009] EWHC 126 (TCC), [2009] P.N.L.R. 26 (QBD (TCC)), Judge Toulmin

1998– cont.

3132. Civil Procedure Rules 1998– *cont.*

see– *cont.*

Q.C.; see *Mucelli v Albania* [2009] UKHL 2, [2009] 1 W.L.R. 276 (HL), Lord Phillips of Worth Matravers; see *Petroleo Brasilieiro SA v ENE Kos 1 Ltd* [2009] EWCA Civ 1127, Times, November 5, 2009 (CA (Civ Div)), Waller, L.J.; see *R. (on the application of Compton) v Wiltshire Primary Care Trust* [2008] EWCA Civ 749, [2009] 1 W.L.R. 1436 (CA (Civ Div)), Waller, L.J.; see *R. (on the application of Kinsley) v Barnet Magistrates Court* [2009] EWHC 464 (Admin), [2009] R.V.R. 133 (QBD (Admin)), Judge Raynor Q.C.; see *Raja v Van Hoogstraten* [2008] EWCA Civ 1444, [2009] 1 W.L.R. 1143 (CA (Civ Div)), Mummery, L.J.; see *Red River UK Ltd v Sheikh* [2009] EWCA Civ 643, [2009] C.P. Rep. 41 (CA (Civ Div)), Sir Anthony Clarke, M.R.; see *Roberts v Gill & Co* [2008] EWCA Civ 803, [2009] 1 W.L.R. 531 (CA (Civ Div)), Pill, L.J.

Part 2 r.2.3, amended: SI 2009/3390 r.3
Part 2 r.2.8, amended: SI 2009/3390 r.3
Part 2 r.2.8, applied: SI 2009/2477 r.121
Part 3 r.3.1, applied: SI 2009/2477 r.121
Part 5, disapplied: SI 2009/2477 r.81
Part 5 r.5.4, amended: SI 2009/3390 r.4
Part 5 r.5.4B, amended: SI 2009/3390 r.4
Part 5 r.5.4C, amended: SI 2009/3390 r.4
Part 6, applied: SI 2009/356 r.270, r.271, SI 2009/2477 r.122
Part 6 r.6.2, amended: SI 2009/3390 r.5
Part 6 r.6.3, amended: SI 2009/2092 r.3, SI 2009/3390 r.5
Part 6 r.6.4, applied: SI 2009/356 r.271
Part 6 r.6.5, amended: SI 2009/3390 r.5
Part 6 r.6.6, amended: SI 2009/3390 r.5
Part 6 r.6.7, substituted: SI 2009/3390 r.5
Part 6 r.6.10, amended: SI 2009/3390 r.5
Part 6 r.6.20, amended: SI 2009/2092 r.3, SI 2009/3390 r.5
Part 6 r.6.23, amended: SI 2009/3390 r.5
Part 6 r.6.26, amended: SI 2009/3390 r.5
Part 6 r.6.31, amended: SI 2009/3131 Reg.29
Part 6 r.6.33, amended: SI 2009/3131 Reg.30, Reg.31
Part 6 r.6.35, amended: SI 2009/3390 r.5
Part 6 r.6.36, amended: SI 2009/3390 r.5
Part 6 r.6.37, amended: SI 2009/3390 r.5
Part 6 r.6.41, amended: SI 2009/3390 r.5
Part 6 r.6.41, applied: SI 2009/356 r.271
Part 6 r.6.42, amended: SI 2009/3390 r.5
Part 6 r.6.43, amended: SI 2009/3390 r.5
Part 6 r.6.52, amended: SI 2009/2092 r.3
Part 7 r.7.1, amended: SI 2009/3390 r.6
Part 7 r.7.2, amended: SI 2009/3390 r.6
Part 7 r.7.2A, amended: SI 2009/3390 r.6
Part 7 r.7.4, amended: SI 2009/3390 r.6
Part 7 r.7.10, amended: SI 2009/3390 r.6
Part 7 r.7.12, amended: SI 2009/3390 r.6
Part 8 r.8.2, amended: SI 2009/3390 r.7
Part 8 r.8.3, amended: SI 2009/3390 r.7
Part 9 r.9.2, revoked (in part): SI 2009/3390 r.8
Part 10 r.10.3, amended: SI 2009/3390 r.9
Part 12 r.12.11, amended: SI 2009/3131 Reg.32, Reg.33
Part 14 r.14.1A, amended: SI 2009/3390 r.10
Part 15 r.15.6, amended: SI 2009/3390 r.11
Part 16 r.16.2, amended: SI 2009/3390 r.12
Part 18, applied: SI 2009/2477 r.108
Part 19 r.19.4A, amended: SI 2009/3390 r.13

1998– cont.

3132. Civil Procedure Rules 1998– *cont.*

Part 19 r.19.9A, amended: SI 2009/3390 r.13
Part 19 r.19.11, amended: SI 2009/3390 r.13
Part 21, applied: SI 2009/2477 r.70, r.97
Part 22, applied: SI 2009/356 r.3
Part 22 r.22.1, varied: SI 2009/357 r.60
Part 22 r.22.2, varied: SI 2009/357 r.60
Part 22 r.22.3, varied: SI 2009/357 r.60
Part 22 r.22.4, varied: SI 2009/357 r.60
Part 25 r.25.13, amended: SI 2009/3131 Reg.34
Part 27 r.27.4, amended: SI 2009/3390 r.14
Part 27 r.27.14, amended: SI 2009/3390 r.14
Part 29, applied: SI 2009/356 r.227
Part 29, referred to: SI 2009/2477 r.100
Part 30 r.30.1, amended: SI 2009/3390 r.15
Part 30 r.30.6, amended: SI 2009/3390 r.15
Part 31, applied: SI 2009/2477 r.108
Part 32, applied: SI 2009/2477 r.75
Part 32 r.32.8, amended: SI 2009/3390 r.16
Part 32 r.32.16, amended: SI 2009/3390 r.16
Part 34 r.34.7, amended: SI 2009/3390 r.17
Part 34 r.34.8, amended: SI 2009/3390 r.17
Part 34 r.34.19, amended: SI 2009/2092 r.4
Part 34 r.34.22, amended: SI 2009/3390 r.17
Part 35 r.35.2, substituted: SI 2009/2092 r.5
Part 35 r.35.3, amended: SI 2009/2092 r.5
Part 35 r.35.4, amended: SI 2009/2092 r.5, SI 2009/3390 r.18
Part 35 r.35.5, amended: SI 2009/2092 r.5
Part 35 r.35.6, amended: SI 2009/2092 r.5
Part 35 r.35.7, substituted: SI 2009/2092 r.5
Part 35 r.35.8, amended: SI 2009/2092 r.5
Part 35 r.35.9, amended: SI 2009/2092 r.5
Part 35 r.35.10, amended: SI 2009/2092 r.5, SI 2009/3390 r.18
Part 35 r.35.12, amended: SI 2009/2092 r.5
Part 35 r.35.14, amended: SI 2009/2092 r.5
Part 35 r.35.15, substituted: SI 2009/2092 r.5
Part 36 r.36.5, amended: SI 2009/3390 r.19
Part 37, applied: SI 2009/2477 r.107
Part 40 r.40.2, amended: SI 2009/3390 r.20
Part 40 r.40.18, amended: SI 2009/3390 r.20
Part 41 r.41.7, amended: SI 2009/3390 r.21
Part 41 r.41.9, amended: SI 2009/3390 r.21
Part 41 r.41.10, amended: SI 2009/3390 r.21
Part 43, applied: SI 2009/2477 r.87
Part 43 r.43.2, amended: SI 2009/2092 r.6
Part 44, applied: SI 2009/2092 r.23, SI 2009/2477 r.87
Part 44 r.44.3B, amended: SI 2009/2092 r.7, SI 2009/3390 r.22
Part 44 r.44.7, amended: SI 2009/3390 r.22
Part 44 r.44.12A, amended: SI 2009/2092 r.7
Part 44 r.44.12B, added: SI 2009/2092 r.7
Part 44 r.44.15, amended: SI 2009/3390 r.22
Part 44 r.44.17, amended: SI 2009/3390 r.22
Part 44 r.44.19, amended: SI 2009/3390 r.22
Part 45, applied: SI 2009/2477 r.87
Part 45 r.45.1, amended: SI 2009/3390 r.23
Part 45 r.45.9, amended: SI 2009/3390 r.23
Part 45 r.45.23, amended: SI 2009/3390 r.23
Part 46 r.46.3, amended: SI 2009/3390 r.24
Part 47, applied: SI 2009/2477 r.87, r.88, r.90
Part 47 r.47.1, amended: SI 2009/3390 r.25
Part 47 r.47.3, amended: SI 2009/3390 r.25
Part 47 r.47.4, amended: SI 2009/2092 r.8, SI 2009/3390 r.25
Part 47 r.47.6, amended: SI 2009/3390 r.25

1998– cont.

3132. Civil Procedure Rules 1998–*cont.*
Part 47 r.47.9, amended: SI 2009/3390 r.25
Part 47 r.47.11, amended: SI 2009/3390 r.25
Part 47 r.47.12, amended: SI 2009/3390 r.25
Part 47 r.47.13, amended: SI 2009/3390 r.25
Part 47 r.47.14, amended: SI 2009/3390 r.25
Part 47 r.47.16, amended: SI 2009/3390 r.25
Part 47 r.47.19, amended: SI 2009/3390 r.25
Part 48, applied: SI 2009/2477 r.87
Part 48 r.48.3, amended: SI 2009/3390 r.26
Part 48 r.48.5, amended: SI 2009/3390 r.26
Part 48 r.48.6, amended: SI 2009/3390 r.26
Part 49 r.49, substituted: SI 2009/2092 r.9
Part 51 r.51.1, amended: SI 2009/3390 r.27
Part 52, applied: SI 2009/356 r.225, SI 2009/2477
    r.99
Part 52 r.52.2, amended: SI 2009/3390 r.28
Part 52 r.52.3, amended: SI 2009/3390 r.28
Part 52 r.52.6, amended: SI 2009/3390 r.28
Part 52 r.52.7, amended: SI 2009/3390 r.28
Part 52 r.52.16, amended: SI 2009/2092 r.10
Part 52 r.52.17, amended: SI 2009/3390 r.28
Part 54, revoked: SI 2009/3390 r.29
Part 54 r.54.6, amended: SI 2009/3390 r.29
Part 55 r.55.3, amended: SI 2009/3390 r.30
Part 55 r.55.4, amended: SI 2009/3390 r.30
Part 55 r.55.10, amended: SI 2009/2092 r.11
Part 55 r.55.13, amended: SI 2009/3390 r.30
Part 55 r.55.14, amended: SI 2009/3390 r.30
Part 55 r.55.22, amended: SI 2009/3390 r.30
Part 55 r.55.23, amended: SI 2009/3390 r.30
Part 55 r.55.24, amended: SI 2009/3390 r.30
Part 55 r.55.25, amended: SI 2009/3390 r.30
Part 56 r.56.2, amended: SI 2009/3390 r.31
Part 56 r.56.3, amended: SI 2009/3390 r.31
Part 57 r.57.4, amended: SI 2009/3390 r.32
Part 57 r.57.5, amended: SI 2009/3390 r.32
Part 57 r.57.12, amended: SI 2009/3390 r.32
Part 57 r.57.13, amended: SI 2009/3390 r.32
Part 57 r.57.15, amended: SI 2009/3390 r.32
Part 57 r.57.16, amended: SI 2009/3390 r.32
Part 58 r.58.1, amended: SI 2009/3390 r.33
Part 58 r.58.13, amended: SI 2009/3390 r.33
Part 59 r.59.1, amended: SI 2009/3390 r.34
Part 59 r.59.11, amended: SI 2009/3390 r.34
Part 60 r.60.1, amended: SI 2009/3390 r.35
Part 60 r.60.4, amended: SI 2009/3390 r.35
Part 60 r.60.6, amended: SI 2009/3390 r.35
Part 61 r.61.1, amended: SI 2009/3390 r.36
Part 61 r.61.3, amended: SI 2009/3390 r.36
Part 61 r.61.4, amended: SI 2009/3390 r.36
Part 61 r.61.5, amended: SI 2009/3390 r.36
Part 61 r.61.7, amended: SI 2009/3390 r.36
Part 61 r.61.8, amended: SI 2009/3390 r.36
Part 61 r.61.9, amended: SI 2009/3390 r.36
Part 61 r.61.11, amended: SI 2009/3390 r.36
Part 62 r.62.1, amended: SI 2009/3390 r.37
Part 62 r.62.3, amended: SI 2009/3390 r.37
Part 62 r.62.7, amended: SI 2009/3390 r.37
Part 63 r.63.1, amended: SI 2009/3390 r.38
Part 63 r.63.1, revoked (in part): SI 2009/3390 r.38
Part 63 r.63.1, substituted: SI 2009/2092 Sch.1
Part 63 r.63.2, substituted: SI 2009/2092 Sch.1
Part 63 r.63.3, substituted: SI 2009/2092 Sch.1
Part 63 r.63.4, substituted: SI 2009/2092 Sch.1
Part 63 r.63.4A, substituted: SI 2009/2092 Sch.1
Part 63 r.63.5, substituted: SI 2009/2092 Sch.1
Part 63 r.63.6, amended: SI 2009/3390 r.38

1998– cont.

3132. Civil Procedure Rules 1998–*cont.*
Part 63 r.63.6, substituted: SI 2009/2092 Sch.1
Part 63 r.63.7, substituted: SI 2009/2092 Sch.1
Part 63 r.63.8, amended: SI 2009/3390 r.38
Part 63 r.63.8, substituted: SI 2009/2092 Sch.1
Part 63 r.63.9, amended: SI 2009/3390 r.38
Part 63 r.63.9, substituted: SI 2009/2092 Sch.1
Part 63 r.63.10, substituted: SI 2009/2092 Sch.1
Part 63 r.63.11, substituted: SI 2009/2092 Sch.1
Part 63 r.63.12, substituted: SI 2009/2092 Sch.1
Part 63 r.63.13, amended: SI 2009/3390 r.38
Part 63 r.63.13, substituted: SI 2009/2092 Sch.1
Part 63 r.63.14, substituted: SI 2009/2092 Sch.1
Part 63 r.63.15, substituted: SI 2009/2092 Sch.1
Part 63 r.63.16, substituted: SI 2009/2092 Sch.1
Part 63 r.63.17, substituted: SI 2009/2092 Sch.1
Part 64 r.64.1, amended: SI 2009/3390 r.39
Part 64 r.64.6, amended: SI 2009/3390 r.39
Part 65, added: SI 2009/2092 Sch.2
Part 65 r.65.1, amended: SI 2009/2092 r.13
Part 65 r.65.3, amended: SI 2009/3390 r.40
Part 65 r.65.14, amended: SI 2009/3390 r.40
Part 67 r.67.1, amended: SI 2009/3390 r.41
Part 67 r.67.3, amended: SI 2009/3390 r.41
Part 68 r.68.1, amended: SI 2009/2092 r.14
Part 68 r.68.2, amended: SI 2009/2092 r.14, SI
    2009/3390 r.42
Part 68 r.68.2A, added: SI 2009/2092 r.14
Part 68 r.68.3, amended: SI 2009/2092 r.14
Part 69 r.69.2, amended: SI 2009/3390 r.43
Part 69 r.69.6, amended: SI 2009/3390 r.43
Part 69 r.69.8, amended: SI 2009/3390 r.43
Part 70 r.70.2, amended: SI 2009/3390 r.44
Part 70 r.70.5, amended: SI 2009/3390 r.44
Part 71 r.71.2, amended: SI 2009/3390 r.45
Part 72 r.72.3, amended: SI 2009/3390 r.46
Part 72 r.72.4, amended: SI 2009/3390 r.46
Part 73 r.73.3, amended: SI 2009/3390 r.47
Part 73 r.73.13, amended: SI 2009/3390 r.47
Part 73 r.73.17, amended: SI 2009/3390 r.47
Part 73 r.73.22, amended: SI 2009/3390 r.47
Part 74 r.74.1, amended: SI 2009/3131 Reg.35, SI
    2009/3390 r.48
Part 74 r.74.2, amended: SI 2009/3131 Reg.36
Part 74 r.74.3, amended: SI 2009/3131 Reg.37
Part 74 r.74.4, amended: SI 2009/3131 Reg.38
Part 74 r.74.5, amended: SI 2009/3131 Reg.39
Part 74 r.74.6, amended: SI 2009/2092 r.15, SI 2009/
    3131 Reg.40
Part 74 r.74.8, amended: SI 2009/3131 Reg.41
Part 74 r.74.10, amended: SI 2009/3131 Reg.42
Part 74 r.74.11, substituted: SI 2009/3131 Reg.43
Part 74 r.74.12, amended: SI 2009/3131 Reg.44
Part 74 r.74.15, amended: SI 2009/2092 r.15
Part 74 r.74.25, amended: SI 2009/2092 r.15
Part 75 r.75.1, amended: SI 2009/3390 r.49
Part 75 r.75.3, amended: SI 2009/3390 r.49
Part 75 r.75.5, amended: SI 2009/3390 r.49
Part 76 r.76.10, amended: SI 2009/2092 r.16
Part 76 r.76.12, amended: SI 2009/3390 r.50
Part 76 r.76.16, amended: SI 2009/3390 r.50
Part 76 r.76.19, amended: SI 2009/2092 r.16
Part 76 r.76.24, amended: SI 2009/2092 r.16
Part 76 r.76.26, amended: SI 2009/2092 r.16
Part 77 r.77.2, amended: SI 2009/3390 r.51
Part 77 r.77.3, amended: SI 2009/3390 r.51
Part 77 r.77.5, amended: SI 2009/3390 r.51
Part 78 r.78.1, amended: SI 2009/3390 r.52

1998– cont.

3132. Civil Procedure Rules 1998– *cont.*

Part 79, added: SI 2009/ 2092 r.18

Part 79 r.79.1, amended: SI 2009/ 2092 r.17, r.18

Part 79 r.79.2, amended: SI 2009/ 2092 r.17

Part 79 r.79.3, amended: SI 2009/ 2092 r.17

Part 79 r.79.4, amended: SI 2009/ 2092 r.17

Part 79 r.79.5, amended: SI 2009/ 2092 r.17

Part 79 r.79.6, amended: SI 2009/ 2092 r.17

Part 79 r.79.7, amended: SI 2009/ 2092 r.17

Part 79 r.79.8, amended: SI 2009/ 2092 r.17

Part 79 r.79.9, amended: SI 2009/ 2092 r.17

Part 79 r.79.10, amended: SI 2009/ 2092 r.17

Part 79 r.79.11, amended: SI 2009/ 2092 r.17

Part 79 r.79.12, amended: SI 2009/ 2092 r.17

Part 79 r.79.13, amended: SI 2009/ 2092 r.17

Part 79 r.79.14, amended: SI 2009/ 2092 r.17

Part 79 r.79.15, amended: SI 2009/ 2092 r.17, r.18

Part 79 r.79.16, amended: SI 2009/ 2092 r.17

Part 79 r.79.17, amended: SI 2009/ 2092 r.17, r.18

Part 79 r.79.18, amended: SI 2009/ 2092 r.17, r.18

Part 79 r.79.19, amended: SI 2009/ 2092 r.17

Part 79 r.79.20, amended: SI 2009/ 2092 r.17

Part 79 r.79.21, amended: SI 2009/ 2092 r.17

Part 79 r.79.22, amended: SI 2009/ 2092 r.17, r.18

Part 79 r.79.23, amended: SI 2009/ 2092 r.17, r.18

Part 79 r.79.24, amended: SI 2009/ 2092 r.17

Part 79 r.79.25, amended: SI 2009/ 2092 r.17

Part 79 r.79.26, amended: SI 2009/ 2092 r.17

Part 79 r.79.27, amended: SI 2009/ 2092 r.17

Part 79 r.79.28, amended: SI 2009/ 2092 r.17, r.18

Part 79 r.79.29, amended: SI 2009/ 2092 r.17, r.18

Part 79 r.79.30, amended: SI 2009/ 2092 r.17, r.18

Part 79 r.79.31, amended: SI 2009/ 2092 r.17

Part 11, see *Dunn v Parole Board* [2008] EWCA Civ 374, [2009] 1 W.L.R. 728 (CA (Civ Div)), Smith, L.J.; see *Maple Leaf Macro Volatility Master Fund v Rouvroy* [2009] EWHC 257 (Comm), [2009] 2 All E.R. (Comm) 287 (QBD (Comm)), Andrew Smith, J.

Part 19, see *Smithson v Hamilton* [2008] EWCA Civ 996, [2009] I.C.R. 1 (CA (Civ Div)), Mummery, L.J.

Part 24, see *W v H* [2008] EWHC 399 (QB), [2009] E.M.L.R. 11 (QBD), Tugendhat, J.

Part 36, see *Bray (t/a Building Co) v Bishop* [2009] EWCA Civ 768, [2009] T.C.L.R. 9 (CA (Civ Div)), Longmore, L.J.; see *C v W* [2008] EWCA Civ 1459, [2009] 4 All E.R. 1129 (CA (Civ Div)), Arden, L.J.; see *Carver v BAA Plc* [2008] EWCA Civ 412, [2009] 1 W.L.R. 113 (CA (Civ Div)), Ward, L.J.; see *Fitzpatrick Contractors Ltd v Tyco Fire and Integrated Solutions (UK) Ltd (formerly Wormald Ansul (UK) Ltd)* [2009] EWHC 274 (TCC), [2009] B.L.R. 144 (QBD (TCC)), Coulson, J.; see *Ritchie (Deceased), Re (Costs)* [2009] W.T.L.R. 885 (Ch D (Leeds)), Judge Behrens

Part 38, see *Sheltam Rail Co (Proprietary) Ltd v Mirambo Holdings Ltd* [2008] EWHC 829 (Comm), [2009] Bus. L.R. 302 (QBD (Comm)), Aikens, J.

Part 44, see *Smith v Springford* [2008] EWHC 3446 (Ch), [2009] W.T.L.R. 705 (Ch D), Norris, J.

Part 52, see *Bracknell Forest BC v Green* [2009] EWCA Civ 238, [2009] C.P. Rep. 31 (CA (Civ Div)), Mummery, L.J.

Part 53, see *W v H* [2008] EWHC 399 (QB), [2009] E.M.L.R. 11 (QBD), Tugendhat, J.

1998– cont.

3132. Civil Procedure Rules 1998– *cont.*

Part 54, see *Jones v Powys Local Health Board* [2008] EWHC 2562 (Admin), (2009) 12 C.C.L. Rep. 68 (QBD (Admin)), Plender, J

Part 55, see *Secretary of State for the Environment, Food and Rural Affairs v Meier* [2009] UKSC 11, [2009] 1 W.L.R. 2780 (SC), Lord Rodger

Part 62, see *National Navigation Co v Endesa Generacion SA (The Wadi Sudr)* [2009] EWHC 196 (Comm), [2009] 1 Lloyd's Rep. 666 (QBD (Comm)), Gloster, J.; see *Sheltam Rail Co (Proprietary) Ltd v Mirambo Holdings Ltd* [2008] EWHC 829 (Comm), [2009] Bus. L.R. 302 (QBD (Comm)), Aikens, J.

Part 67, see *Mastercigars Direct Ltd v Withers LLP* [2007] EWHC 2733 (Ch), [2009] 1 W.L.R. 881 (Ch D), Morgan, J.

Part 72, see *Kier Regional Ltd (t/a Wallis) v City & General (Holborn) Ltd* [2008] EWHC 2454 (TCC), [2009] B.L.R. 90 (QBD (TCC)), Coulson, J.; see *Westacre Investments Inc v Yugoimport SDPR* [2008] EWHC 801 (Comm), [2009] 1 All E.R. (Comm) 780 (QBD (Comm)), Tomlinson, J.

Part 76, see *Secretary of State for the Home Department v F* [2008] EWCA Civ 1148, [2009] 2 W.L.R. 423 (CA (Civ Div)), Sir Anthony Clarke, M.R.

Part 8, see *Bovale Ltd v Secretary of State for Communities and Local Government* [2009] EWCA Civ 171, [2009] 1 W.L.R. 2274 (CA (Civ Div)), Waller, L.J. (V-P); see *Brewer v Supreme Court Costs Office* [2009] EWHC 986 (QB), [2009] 3 Costs L.R. 462 (QBD (Admin)), Holroyde, J; see *British Telecommunications Plc v SAE Group Inc* [2009] EWHC 252 (TCC), [2009] B.L.R. 231 (QBD (TCC)), Ramsey, J.; see *Howell v Lees-Millais* [2009] EWHC 1754 (Ch), [2009] W.T.L.R. 1163 (Ch D), Sir John Lindsay; see *Office of Fair Trading v Foxtons Ltd* [2008] EWHC 1662 (Ch), [2009] Eu. L.R. 32 (Ch D), Morgan, J.; see *PD Teesport Ltd, Re* [2009] EWHC 1693 (Ch), [2009] Pens. L.R. 263 (Ch D), Proudman, J; see *Perpetual Trustee Co Ltd v BNY Corporate Trustee Services Ltd* [2009] EWHC 1912 (Ch), [2009] 2 B.C.L.C. 400 (Ch D), Sir Andrew Morritt (Chancellor); see *Walter Lilly & Co Ltd v DMW Developments Ltd* [2008] EWHC 3139 (TCC), [2009] T.C.L.R. 3 (QBD (TCC)), Coulson, J.

r.1.1, see *National Grid Electricity Transmission Plc v ABB Ltd* [2009] EWHC 1326 (Ch), [2009] U.K.C.L.R. 838 (Ch D), Sir Andrew Morritt (Chancellor)

r.1.4, see *Leaflet Co Ltd v Royal Mail Group Ltd* [2008] EWHC 3514 (Ch), [2009] U.K.C.L.R. 323 (Ch D), Sir Andrew Morritt (Chancellor)

r.2.1, see *Bailey v Dargue* [2008] EWHC 2903 (Ch), [2009] B.P.I.R. 1 (Ch D (Manchester)), Judge Hodge Q.C.

r.3.1, see *Business Environment Bow Lane Ltd v Deanwater Estates Ltd* [2009] EWHC 2014 (Ch), [2009] 45 E.G. 106 (Ch D), Mann, J.; see *Littlewoods Retail Ltd v Revenue and Customs Commissioners* [2008] EWHC 2622 (QB), [2009] S.T.C. 22 (QBD), Sir Charles Gray

r.3.2, see *Beloit Walmsley Ltd, Re* [2008] EWHC 1888 (Ch), [2009] 1 B.C.L.C. 584 (Ch D (Manchester)), Judge Pelling Q.C.

r.3.4, see *Marstons Plc (formerly t/a Wolverhampton and Dudley Breweries Plc) v Charman* [2009] EWCA Civ 719, [2009] C.P.

1998– cont.

3132. Civil Procedure Rules 1998– *cont.*

r.3.4– *cont.*

Rep. 42 (CA (Civ Div)),Ward, L.J.; see *Williams v Lishman Sidwell Campbell & Price Ltd* [2009] EWHC 1322 (QB), [2009] P.N.L.R. 34 (QBD), Judge Reddihough

r.3.5, see *Serious Fraud Office v Lexi Holdings Plc (In Administration)* [2008] EWCA Crim 1443, [2009] Q.B. 376 (CA (Crim Div)), Keene, L.J.

r.3.9, see *North Tyneside Primary Care Trust v Aynsley* [2009] I.C.R. 1333 (EAT), Underhill, J.; see *Tarn Insurance Services Ltd v Kirby* [2009] EWCA Civ 19, [2009] C.P. Rep. 22 (CA (Civ Div)), Waller, L.J. (V-P)

r.3.11, see *Supperstone v Hurst* [2009] EWHC 1271 (Ch), [2009] 1 W.L.R. 2306 (Ch D), Bernard Livesey Q.C.

r.5.4C, see *S v Rochdale MBC* [2008] EWHC 3283 (Fam), [2009] 1 F.L.R. 1090 (Fam Div), Munby, J.

r.6.7, see *Mucelli v Albania* [2009] UKHL 2, [2009] 1 W.L.R. 276 (HL), Lord Phillips of Worth Matravers

r.6.20, see *Accentuate Ltd v Asigra Inc* [2009] EWHC 2655 (QB), [2009] 2 Lloyd's Rep. 599 (QBD), Tugendhat, J.; see *Cherney v Deripaska* [2008] EWHC 1530 (Comm), [2009] 1 All E.R. (Comm) 333 (QBD (Comm)), Christopher Clarke, J.; see *Elektrim SA v Vivendi Holdings 1 Corp* [2008] EWCA Civ 1178, [2009] 2 All E.R. (Comm) 213 (CA (Civ Div)), Sir Anthony May (President, QB); see *Greene Wood & McClean LLP v Templeton Insurance Ltd* [2008] EWHC 1593 (Comm), [2009] Lloyd's Rep. I.R. 61 (QBD (Comm)), Teare, J.; see *Greene Wood & McClean LLP v Templeton Insurance Ltd* [2009] EWCA Civ 65, [2009] 1 W.L.R. 2013 (CA (Civ Div)), Sir Anthony Clarke, M.R.; see *NML Capital Ltd v Argentina* [2009] EWHC 110 (Comm), [2009] Q.B. 579 (QBD (Comm)), Blair, J.; see *Novus Aviation Ltd v Onur Air Tasimacilik AS* [2009] EWCA Civ 122, [2009] 1 Lloyd's Rep. 576 (CA (Civ Div)), Sir Mark Potter (President, Fam); see *Sharab v Prince Al-Waleed Bin Tala Bin Abdal-Aziz-Al-Saud* [2009] EWCA Civ 353, [2009] 2 Lloyd's Rep. 160 (CA (Civ Div)), Arden, L.J.; see *Vitol SA v Capri Marine Ltd* [2008] EWHC 378 (Comm), [2009] Bus. L.R. 271 (QBD (Comm)), Tomlinson, J.

r.6.21, see *Greene Wood & McClean LLP v Templeton Insurance Ltd* [2009] EWCA Civ 65, [2009] 1 W.L.R. 2013 (CA (Civ Div)), Sir Anthony Clarke, M.R.

r.6.30, see *Masri v Consolidated Contractors International Co SAL* [2008] EWCA Civ 876, [2009] 2 W.L.R. 699 (CA (Civ Div)), Sir Anthony Clarke, M.R.; see *Vitol SA v Capri Marine Ltd* [2008] EWHC 378 (Comm), [2009] Bus. L.R. 271 (QBD (Comm)), Tomlinson, J.

r.6.37, see *Metropolitan International Schools Ltd (t/a SkillsTrain and t/a Train2Game) v Designtechnica Corp (t/a Digital Trends)* [2009] EWHC 1765 (QB), [2009] E.M.L.R. 27 (QBD), Eady, J.

r.6.44, see *Wilhelm Finance Inc v Ente Administrador Del Astillero Rio Santiago* [2009] EWHC 1074 (Comm), [2009] 1 C.L.C. 867 (QBD (Comm)), Teare, J.

r.7.11, see *A v B (Investigatory Powers Tribunal: Jurisdiction)* [2009] EWCA Civ 24, [2009] 3 W.L.R. 717 (CA (Civ Div)), Laws, L.J.

1998– cont.

3132. Civil Procedure Rules 1998– *cont.*

r.8.7, see *Angel Solicitors v Jenkins O'Dowd & Barth* [2009] EWHC 46 (Ch), [2009] 1 W.L.R. 1220 (Ch D), Judge Hodge Q.C.

r.16.4, see *Pickthall v Hill Dickinson LLP* [2008] EWHC 3409 (Ch), [2009] B.P.I.R. 114 (Ch D), Judge Waksman QC

r.16.6, see *Kaupthing Singer and Friedlander Ltd (In Administration), Re* [2009] EWHC 740 (Ch), [2009] 2 Lloyd's Rep. 154 (Ch D), Sir Andrew Morritt (Chancellor)

r.17.2, see *Law Society v Shah* [2008] EWHC 2515 (Ch), [2009] 1 W.L.R. 2254 (Ch D), Norris, J.

r.17.4, see *Law Society v Shah* [2008] EWHC 2515 (Ch), [2009] 1 W.L.R. 2254 (Ch D), Norris, J.; see *Parker v SJ Berwin & Co* [2008] EWHC 3017 (QB), [2009] P.N.L.R. 17 (QBD), Hamblen, J; see *Roberts v Gill & Co* [2008] EWCA Civ 803, [2009] 1 W.L.R. 531 (CA (Civ Div)), Pill, L.J.

r.19.2, see *Angel Solicitors v Jenkins O'Dowd & Barth* [2009] EWHC 46 (Ch), [2009] 1 W.L.R. 1220 (Ch D), Judge Hodge Q.C.; see *Dornoch Ltd v Westminster International BV* [2009] EWHC 201 (Admlty), [2009] I.L.Pr. 37 (QBD (Admlty)), Tomlinson, J.; see *Dunlop Haywards (DHL) Ltd (formerly Dunlop Heywood Lorenz Ltd) v Erinaceous Insurance Services Ltd (formerly Hanover Park Commercial Ltd)* [2009] EWCA Civ 354, [2009] Lloyd's Rep. I.R. 464 (CA (Civ Div)), Rix, L.J.; see *Football Association Premier League Ltd v QC Leisure* [2008] EWHC 2897 (Ch), [2009] 1 W.L.R. 1603 (Ch D), Kitchin, J.; see *PD Teesport Ltd, Re* [2009] EWHC 1693 (Ch), [2009] Pens. L.R. 263 (Ch D), Proudman, J; see *Ruttle Plant Hire Ltd v Secretary of State for the Environment, Food and Rural Affairs* [2008] EWHC 238 (TCC), [2009] 1 All E.R. 448 (QBD (TCC)), Ramsey, J.

r.19.3, see *HLB Kidsons (A Firm) v Lloyd's Underwriters* [2008] EWHC 2415 (Comm), [2009] 1 All E.R. (Comm) 760 (QBD (Comm)), Judge Mackie Q.C.

r.19.4, see *PD Teesport Ltd, Re* [2009] EWHC 1693 (Ch), [2009] Pens. L.R. 263 (Ch D), Proudman, J

r.19.5, see *Roberts v Gill & Co* [2008] EWCA Civ 803, [2009] 1 W.L.R. 531 (CA (Civ Div)), Pill, L.J.

r.19.6, see *Emerald Supplies Ltd v British Airways Plc* [2009] EWHC 741 (Ch), [2009] 3 W.L.R. 1200 (Ch D), Sir Andrew Morritt (Chancellor)

r.19.7, see *PD Teesport Ltd, Re* [2009] EWHC 1693 (Ch), [2009] Pens. L.R. 263 (Ch D), Proudman, J; see *Smithson v Hamilton* [2008] EWCA Civ 996, [2009] I.C.R. 1 (CA (Civ Div)), Mummery, L.J.

r.19.8, see *Austin v Southwark LBC* [2009] EWCA Civ 66, [2009] 25 E.G. 138 (CA (Civ Div)), Pill, L.J.

r.20.7, see *Angel Solicitors v Jenkins O'Dowd & Barth* [2009] EWHC 46 (Ch), [2009] 1 W.L.R. 1220 (Ch D), Judge Hodge Q.C.

r.23.8, see *R. (on the application of Compton) v Wiltshire Primary Care Trust* [2008] EWCA Civ 749, [2009] 1 W.L.R. 1436 (CA (Civ Div)), Waller, L.J.

r.23.9, see *Raja v Van Hoogstraten* [2008] EWCA Civ 1444, [2009] 1 W.L.R. 1143 (CA (Civ Div)), Mummery, L.J.

r.23.10, see *Raja v Van Hoogstraten* [2008] EWCA Civ 1444, [2009] 1 W.L.R. 1143 (CA (Civ Div)), Mummery, L.J.

1998– cont.

3132. Civil Procedure Rules 1998–*cont.*

r.25.7, see *Heidelberg Graphic Equipment Ltd v Revenue and Customs Commissioners* [2009] EWHC 870 (Ch), [2009] S.T.C. 2334 (Ch D), Henderson, J.; see *P v Taunton and Somerset NHS Trust* [2009] EWHC 1965 (QB), [2009] LS Law Medical 598 (QBD), Blair, J.

r.25.13, see *Jirehouse Capital v Beller* [2008] EWCA Civ 908, [2009] 1 W.L.R. 751 (CA (Civ Div)), Mummery, L.J.

r.31.3, see *Expandable Ltd v Rubin* [2007] EWHC 2463 (Ch), [2009] B.C.C. 443 (Ch D), Patten, J.; see *Webster v Ridgeway Foundation School Governors* [2009] EWHC 1140 (QB), [2009] E.L.R. 439 (QBD), Nicol, J.

r.31.6, see *OCS Group Ltd v Wells* [2008] EWHC 919 (QB), [2009] 1 W.L.R. 1895 (QBD), Nelson, J.

r.31.7, see *Digicel (St Lucia) Ltd v Cable & Wireless Plc* [2008] EWHC 2522 (Ch), [2009] 2 All E.R. 1094 (Ch D), Morgan, J.

r.31.12, see *Digicel (St Lucia) Ltd v Cable & Wireless Plc* [2008] EWHC 2522 (Ch), [2009] 2 All E.R. 1094 (Ch D), Morgan, J.

r.31.14, see *Barr v Biffa Waste Services Ltd* [2009] EWHC 1033 (TCC), (2009) 25 Const. L.J. 547 (QBD (TCC)), Coulson, J.; see *Expandable Ltd v Rubin* [2007] EWHC 2463 (Ch), [2009] B.C.C. 443 (Ch D), Patten, J.

r.31.16, see *EDO Corp v Ultra Electronics Ltd* [2009] EWHC 682 (Ch), [2009] Bus. L.R. 1306 (Ch D), Bernard Livesey Q.C.; see *OCS Group Ltd v Wells* [2008] EWHC 919 (QB), [2009] 1 W.L.R. 1895 (QBD), Nelson, J.

r.31.17, see *Flood v Times Newspapers Ltd* [2009] EWHC 411 (QB), [2009] E.M.L.R. 18 (QBD), Eady, J.

r.31.19, see *Expandable Ltd v Rubin* [2007] EWHC 2463 (Ch), [2009] B.C.C. 443 (Ch D), Patten, J.

r.31.22, see *SITA UK Group Holdings Ltd v Serruys* [2009] EWHC 869 (QB), [2009] S.T.C. 1595 (QBD), Jack, J.

r.32.1, see *Serious Organised Crime Agency v Olden* [2009] EWHC 610 (QB), [2009] Lloyd's Rep. F.C. 375 (QBD), Holroyde, J

r.36.10, see *Fitzpatrick Contractors Ltd v Tyco Fire and Integrated Solutions (UK) Ltd (formerly Wormald Ansul (UK) Ltd)* [2009] EWHC 274 (TCC), [2009] B.L.R. 144 (QBD (TCC)), Coulson, J.

r.36.14, see *Carver v BAA Plc* [2008] EWCA Civ 412, [2009] 1 W.L.R. 113 (CA (Civ Div)), Ward, L.J.; see *Fitzpatrick Contractors Ltd v Tyco Fire and Integrated Solutions (UK) Ltd (formerly Wormald Ansul (UK) Ltd)* [2009] EWHC 274 (TCC), [2009] B.L.R. 144 (QBD (TCC)), Coulson, J.

r.38.2, see *Sheltam Rail Co (Proprietary) Ltd v Mirambo Holdings Ltd* [2008] EWHC 829 (Comm), [2009] Bus. L.R. 302 (QBD (Comm)), Aikens, J.

r.38.4, see *Sheltam Rail Co (Proprietary) Ltd v Mirambo Holdings Ltd* [2008] EWHC 829 (Comm), [2009] Bus. L.R. 302 (QBD (Comm)), Aikens, J.

r.39.2, see *Revenue and Customs Commissioners v Banerjee* [2009] EWHC 1229 (Ch), [2009] 3 All E.R. 930 (Ch D), Henderson, J.

r.40.8, see *Gater Assets Ltd v Nak Naftogaz Ukrainiy* [2008] EWHC 1108 (Comm), [2009] Bus. L.R. 396 (QBD (Comm)), Beatson, J.

1998– cont.

3132. Civil Procedure Rules 1998–*cont.*

r.44.3, see *Ben Hashem v Ali Shayif* [2009] EWHC 864 (Fam), [2009] 2 F.L.R. 896 (Fam Div), Munby, J.; see *Edwards Lifesciences AG v Cook Biotech Inc (Costs)* [2009] EWHC 1443 (Pat), [2009] F.S.R. 28 (Ch D (Patents Ct)), Kitchin, J.; see *Fitzpatrick Contractors Ltd v Tyco Fire and Integrated Solutions (UK) Ltd (formerly Wormald Ansul (UK) Ltd)* [2009] EWHC 274 (TCC), [2009] B.L.R. 144 (QBD (TCC)), Coulson, J.; see *Judge v Judge* [2008] EWCA Civ 1458, [2009] 1 F.L.R. 1287 (CA (Civ Div)), Longmore, L.J.; see *Krysia Maritime Inc v Intership Ltd (The Krysia)* [2008] EWHC 1880 (Admlty), [2009] 1 All E.R. (Comm) 292 (QBD (Admlty)), Aikens, J.; see *Peakman v Linbrooke Services Ltd* [2008] EWCA Civ 1239, [2009] C.P. Rep. 14 (CA (Civ Div)), Mummery, L.J.; see *Raymond Saul & Co v Holden* [2008] EWHC 8565 (Ch), [2009] B.P.I.R. 50 (Ch D), Richard Snowden QC; see *Vedalease Ltd v Cascabel Investments Ltd* [2009] 29 E.G. 100 (CC (Central London)), Judge Hazel Marshall Q.C.

r.45.11, see *Kilby v Gawith* [2008] EWCA Civ 812, [2009] 1 W.L.R. 853 (CA (Civ Div)), Sir Anthony Clarke, M.R.

r.48.2, see *Bank of Baroda v Patel* [2008] EWHC 3390 (Ch), [2009] 2 F.L.R. 753 (Ch D), Sales, J; see *Dean & Dean (A Firm) v Angel Airlines SA* [2009] EWHC 447 (Ch), [2009] B.P.I.R. 409 (Ch D), Patten, J.

r.52.1, see *Bailey v Dargue* [2008] EWHC 2903 (Ch), [2009] B.P.I.R. 1 (Ch D (Manchester)), Judge Hodge Q.C.

r.52.9, see *Calltel Telecom Ltd v Revenue and Customs Commissioners* [2008] EWHC 2107 (Ch), [2009] Bus. L.R. 513 (Ch D), Briggs, J.; see *Dadourian Group International Inc v Simms (Damages)* [2009] EWCA Civ 169, [2009] 1 Lloyd's Rep. 601 (CA (Civ Div)), Arden, L.J.; see *R. (on the application of Compton) v Wiltshire Primary Care Trust* [2008] EWCA Civ 749, [2009] 1 W.L.R. 1436 (CA (Civ Div)), Waller, L.J.

r.52.10, see *Hicks v Russell Jones & Walker* [2007] EWCA Civ 844, [2009] 1 W.L.R. 487 (CA (Civ Div)), Lloyds, L.J.

r.52.11, see *Mastercigars Direct Ltd v Withers LLP* [2009] EWHC 993 (Ch), [2009] C.P. Rep. 35 (Ch D), Morgan, J.

r.52.13, see *B (A Child) (Residence: Second Appeal), Re* [2009] EWCA Civ 545, [2009] 2 F.L.R. 632 (CA (Civ Div)), Wall, L.J.

r.54.5, see *Finn-Kelcey v Milton Keynes BC* [2008] EWCA Civ 1067, [2009] Env. L.R. 17 (CA (Civ Div)), Keene, L.J.

r.62.9, see *ASM Shipping Ltd of India v TTMI Ltd of England (The Amer Energy)* [2009] 1 Lloyd's Rep. 293 (QBD (Comm)), Flaux, J.

r.62.18, see *Norsk Hydro ASA v State Property Fund of Ukraine* [2002] EWHC 2120 (Admin), [2009] Bus. L.R. 558 (QBD (Admin)), Gross, J.

r.63.7, see *Research in Motion UK Ltd v Visto Corp* [2008] EWHC 3026 (Pat), [2009] F.S.R. 10 (Ch D (Patents Ct)), Arnold, J.

r.71.2, see *Masri v Consolidated Contractors International Co SAL* [2008] EWCA Civ 876, [2009] 2 W.L.R. 699 (CA (Civ Div)), Sir Anthony Clarke, M.R.; see *Vitol SA v Capri Marine Ltd* [2008] EWHC 378 (Comm), [2009] Bus. L.R. 271 (QBD (Comm)), Tomlinson, J.

1998– cont.

3132. Civil Procedure Rules 1998– *cont.*

r.72.3, see *Westacre Investments Inc v Yugoimport SDPR* [2008] EWHC 801 (Comm), [2009] 1 All E.R. (Comm) 780 (QBD (Comm)), Tomlinson, J.

r.72.9, see *Beechwood Construction Ltd v Afza* [2008] EWHC 2671 (Ch), [2009] B.P.I.R. 7 (Ch D), Judge Behrens

r.73.10, see *Close Invoice Finance Ltd v Pile* [2008] EWHC 1580 (Ch), [2009] 1 F.L.R. 873 (Ch D), Judge Purle Q.C.

Sch.1 Part 45 para.2, amended: SI 2009/3390 r.53

Sch.1 Part 45 para.12, amended: SI 2009/3390 r.53

Sch.1 Part 46 para.6, amended: SI 2009/2092 r.19

Sch.1 Part 46 para.8, amended: SI 2009/3390 r.54

Sch.1 Ord.46 r.8, see *H v N* [2009] EWHC 640 (Fam), [2009] 1 W.L.R. 2335 (Fam Div), Pamela Scriven Q.C.

Sch.1 Ord.47, see *Kier Regional Ltd (t/a Wallis) v City & General (Holborn) Ltd* [2008] EWHC 2454 (TCC), [2009] B.L.R. 90 (QBD (TCC)), Coulson, J.

Sch.1 Part 54 para.6, amended: SI 2009/3390 r.55

Sch.1 Part 54 para.10, amended: SI 2009/3390 r.55

Sch.1 Part 79 para.9, amended: SI 2009/2092 r.20, SI 2009/3390 r.56

Sch.1 Part 109 para.1, amended: SI 2009/2092 r.21

Sch.1 Part 109 para.3, amended: SI 2009/2092 r.21

Sch.1 Part 109 para.4, amended: SI 2009/2092 r.21, SI 2009/3390 r.57

Sch.2 Part 1 para.6, amended: SI 2009/2092 r.22

3162. Fair Employment and Treatment (Northern Ireland) Order 1998

see *McConkey v Simon Community* [2009] UKHL 24, [2009] N.I. 297 (HL (NI)), Lord Phillips of Worth Matravers

Art.2, see *McConkey v Simon Community* [2009] UKHL 24, [2009] N.I. 297 (HL (NI)), Lord Phillips of Worth Matravers

Art.69, amended: SI 2009/1941 Sch.1 para.175

Art.82, amended: 2009 c.3 Sch.4 para.32

3175. Corporation Tax (Instalment Payments) Regulations 1998

Reg.6, amended: SI 2009/56 Sch.2 para.49

3186. Building Societies (Business Names) Regulations 1998

Sch.1, amended: SI 2009/2748 Sch.1 para.19

3218. Parole Board (Transfer of Functions) Order 1998

referred to: 2009 c.25 s.145, Sch.22 para.43

3314. North West Wales National Health Service Trust (Establishment) Order 1998

revoked: SI 2009/1306 Sch.1

3321. Gwent Healthcare National Health Service Trust (Establishment) Order 1998

revoked: SI 2009/1306 Sch.1

1999

71. Allocation of Housing and Homelessness (Review Procedures) Regulations 1999

Reg.2, see *De-Winter Heald v Brent LBC* [2009] EWCA Civ 930, [2009] H.R.L.R. 34 (CA (Civ Div)), Sedley, L.J.

Reg.8, see *Banks v Kingston-upon-Thames RLBC* [2008] EWCA Civ 1443, [2009] H.L.R. 29 (CA (Civ Div)), Longmore, L.J.; see *Lambeth LBC v Johnston* [2008] EWCA Civ 690, [2009] H.L.R. 10 (CA (Civ Div)), Smith, L.J.

1999– cont.

293. Town and Country Planning (Environmental Impact Assessment) (England and Wales) Regulations 1999

applied: SI 2009/3342 Reg.52

see *Finn-Kelcey v Milton Keynes BC* [2008] EWCA Civ 1067, [2009] Env. L.R. 17 (CA (Civ Div)), Keene, L.J.; see *R. (on the application of Baker) v Bath and North East Somerset DC* [2009] EWHC 595 (Admin), [2009] Env. L.R. 27 (QBD (Admin)), Collins, J.

Part VIII, applied: SI 2009/3342 Reg.52

Reg.4, see *R. (on the application of Baker) v Bath and North East Somerset DC* [2009] EWHC 595 (Admin), [2009] Env. L.R. 27 (QBD (Admin)), Collins, J.

Reg.5, see *R. (on the application of Aldergate Projects Ltd) v Nottinghamshire CC* [2008] EWHC 2881 (Admin), [2009] J.P.L. 939 (QBD (Admin)), Collins, J.

Reg.19, see *Finn-Kelcey v Milton Keynes BC* [2008] EWCA Civ 1067, [2009] Env. L.R. 17 (CA (Civ Div)), Keene, L.J.; see *Finn-Kelcey v Milton Keynes BC* [2008] EWHC 1650 (Admin), [2009] Env. L.R. 4 (QBD (Admin)), Collins, J.

Sch.2, see *R. (on the application of Aldergate Projects Ltd) v Nottinghamshire CC* [2008] EWHC 2881 (Admin), [2009] J.P.L. 939 (QBD (Admin)), Collins, J.

483. Crime and Disorder Strategies (Prescribed Descriptions) (Amendment) Order 1999

revoked (in part): SI 2009/3050 Art.4

584. National Minimum Wage Regulations 1999

see *Smith v Oxfordshire Learning Disability NHS Trust* [2009] I.C.R. 1395 (EAT), Underhill, J. (President)

Reg.2, see *Smith v Oxfordshire Learning Disability NHS Trust* [2009] I.C.R. 1395 (EAT), Underhill, J. (President)

Reg.11, amended: SI 2009/1902 Reg.2

Reg.12, amended: SI 2009/1902 Reg.3

Reg.13, amended: SI 2009/1902 Reg.4

Reg.14, see *Smith v Oxfordshire Learning Disability NHS Trust* [2009] I.C.R. 1395 (EAT), Underhill, J. (President)

Reg.30, see *Revenue and Customs Commissioners v Annabel's (Berkeley Square) Ltd* [2009] EWCA Civ 361, [2009] 4 All E.R. 55 (CA (Civ Div)), Mummery, L.J.

Reg.31, amended: SI 2009/1902 Reg.5

Reg.31, see *Smith v Oxfordshire Learning Disability NHS Trust* [2009] I.C.R. 1395 (EAT), Underhill, J. (President)

Reg.36, amended: SI 2009/1902 Reg.6

648. Planning and Compensation Act 1991 (Amendment of Schedule 18) Order 1999

Art.2, revoked (in part): SI 2009/1307 Sch.4

662. Water (Northern Ireland) Order 1999

Art.46, amended: SI 2009/1941 Sch.1 para.180

665. Judicial Committee (Devolution Issues) Rules Order 1999

revoked: SI 2009/224 Art.4

671. Social Security Contributions (Transfer of Functions, etc.) (Northern Ireland) Order 1999

Art.9, amended: SI 2009/56 Sch.2 para.51

Art.10, amended: SI 2009/56 Sch.2 para.52

Art.11, amended: SI 2009/56 Sch.2 para.53

Art.11, revoked (in part): SI 2009/56 Sch.2 para.53

Art.12, amended: SI 2009/56 Sch.2 para.54, SI 2009/777 Art.5

1999– cont.

671. Social Security Contributions (Transfer of Functions, etc.) (Northern Ireland) Order 1999– *cont.*
Art.12, revoked (in part): SI 2009/56 Sch.2 para.54
Art.13, amended: SI 2009/56 Sch.2 para.55
Art.18, substituted: SI 2009/56 Sch.2 para.56

672. National Assembly for Wales (Transfer of Functions) Order 1999
Sch.1, amended: SI 2009/463 Sch.2 para.13

704. Education (Transition to New Framework) (School Organisation Proposals) Regulations 1999
Reg.1, amended: SI 2009/1556 Reg.2

728. Prison Rules 1999
Part I r.2, amended: SI 2009/3082 Sch.1 para.1
Part II r.20, substituted: SI 2009/3082 Sch.1 para.2
Part II r.21, amended: SI 2009/3082 Sch.1 para.4
Part II r.24, amended: SI 2009/3082 Sch.1 para.4
Part II r.31, amended: SI 2009/3082 Sch.1 para.3
Part II r.35A, amended: SI 2009/3082 Sch.1 para.5
Part II r.38, amended: SI 2009/3082 Sch.1 para.6
Part II r.39, amended: SI 2009/3082 Sch.1 para.7
Part II r.43, amended: SI 2009/3082 Sch.1 para.8
Part II r.45, amended: SI 2009/3082 Sch.1 para.4
Part II r.49, amended: SI 2009/3082 Sch.1 para.4, Sch.1 para.9
Part II r.58, amended: SI 2009/3082 Sch.1 para.4
r.43, see *R. (on the application of Coleman) v Governor of Wayland Prison* [2009] EWHC 1005 (Admin), Times, April 23, 2009 (QBD), Dobbs, J.

743. Control of Major Accident Hazards Regulations 1999
Reg.22, applied: SI 2009/1595 Reg.2

778. Motor Vehicles (EC Type Approval) (Amendment) Regulations 1999
revoked: SI 2009/717 Sch.1

881. Overseas Insurers (Tax Representatives) Regulations 1999
Reg.13, amended: SI 2009/56 Sch.2 para.58
Reg.13, revoked (in part): SI 2009/56 Sch.2 para.58

903. Education (Individual Pupil Information) (Prescribed Persons) Regulations 1999
revoked: SI 2009/1563 Sch.1
Reg.3, amended: SI 2009/213 Reg.2

929. Act of Sederunt (Summary Applications, Statutory Applications and Appeals etc Rules) 1999
referred to: SSI 2009/294 r.6
Part I r.1.2, amended: SSI 2009/164 r.3
Part 2 r.2.4, amended: SSI 2009/294 r.3
Part 2 r.2.18A, added: SSI 2009/107 r.4
Part 2 r.2.22, amended: SSI 2009/294 r.3
Part 3, added: SSI 2009/109 r.2
Part 3, added: SSI 2009/294 r.18
Part 3, added: SSI 2009/320 r.2
r.3.1.2, see *Manning v Manning* [2009] CSIH 67, 2009 S.L.T. 743 (IH (Ex Div)), Lord Clarke
r.3.1.3, see *Manning v Manning* [2009] CSIH 67, 2009 S.L.T. 743 (IH (Ex Div)), Lord Clarke
Sch.1, amended: SSI 2009/107 Sch.3, SSI 2009/294 r.3, Sch.2, SSI 2009/320 Sch.1

991. Social Security and Child Support (Decisions and Appeals) Regulations 1999
Reg.3, amended: SI 2009/659 Reg.2, SI 2009/1490 Reg.3
Reg.3, revoked (in part): SI 2009/1490 Reg.3
Reg.3A, amended: SI 2009/396 Reg.4
Reg.3A, revoked (in part): SI 2009/396 Reg.4

1999– cont.

991. Social Security and Child Support (Decisions and Appeals) Regulations 1999– *cont.*
Reg.4, amended: SI 2009/396 Reg.4
Reg.6A, substituted: SI 2009/396 Reg.4
Reg.6B, amended: SI 2009/396 Reg.4
Reg.6B, revoked (in part): SI 2009/396 Reg.4
Reg.7, amended: SI 2009/1490 Reg.3
Reg.7B, substituted: SI 2009/396 Reg.4
Reg.7C, amended: SI 2009/396 Reg.4
Reg.15A, amended: SI 2009/396 Reg.4
Reg.15B, amended: SI 2009/396 Reg.4
Reg.15C, amended: SI 2009/396 Reg.4
Reg.15C, revoked (in part): SI 2009/396 Reg.4
Reg.15D, revoked: SI 2009/396 Reg.4
Reg.23, amended: SI 2009/396 Reg.4
Reg.24, amended: SI 2009/396 Reg.4
Reg.26, amended: SI 2009/2715 Art.2
Reg.30, amended: SI 2009/396 Reg.4
Reg.30A, amended: SI 2009/396 Reg.4
Reg.30A, applied: SI 2009/3151 Reg.15
Reg.30A, revoked: SI 2009/3151 Sch.1
Reg.34, varied: SI 2009/3151 Reg.12
Sch.3D para.1, added: SI 2009/396 Reg.4
Sch.3D para.2, added: SI 2009/396 Reg.4
Sch.3D para.3, added: SI 2009/396 Reg.4
Sch.3D para.4, added: SI 2009/396 Reg.4
Sch.3D para.5, added: SI 2009/396 Reg.4
Sch.3D para.6, added: SI 2009/396 Reg.4
Sch.3D para.7, added: SI 2009/396 Reg.4
Sch.3D para.8, added: SI 2009/396 Reg.4
Sch.3D para.9, added: SI 2009/396 Reg.4
Sch.3D para.10, added: SI 2009/396 Reg.4
Sch.3D para.11, added: SI 2009/396 Reg.4
Sch.3D para.12, added: SI 2009/396 Reg.4

1006. Anti-Pollution Works Regulations 1999
Reg.2, amended: SI 2009/3104 Reg.6
Sch.1 para.6, amended: SI 2009/1307 Sch.2 para.94
Sch.1 para.6, revoked (in part): SI 2009/1307 Sch.2 para.94

1026. Highways (Traffic Calming) Regulations 1999
referred to: SI 2009/1300 Art.8

1027. Social Security Contributions (Decisions and Appeals) Regulations 1999
Reg.3, amended: SI 2009/56 Sch.2 para.60
Reg.5, amended: SI 2009/56 Sch.2 para.61
Reg.7, substituted: SI 2009/56 Sch.2 para.62
Reg.8, revoked: SI 2009/56 Sch.2 para.63
Reg.8A, revoked: SI 2009/56 Sch.2 para.63
Reg.9, amended: SI 2009/56 Sch.2 para.64
Reg.10, amended: SI 2009/56 Sch.2 para.65
Reg.11, amended: SI 2009/56 Sch.2 para.66
Reg.12, substituted: SI 2009/56 Sch.2 para.67, SI 2009/777 Art.6

1048. Street Works Register (Registration Fees) Regulations 1999
applied: SI 2009/721 Sch.2 para.10

1082. Scotland Act 1998 (Transitory and Transitional Provisions) (Scottish Parliamentary Pension Scheme) Order 1999
applied: 2009 asp 1 Sch.3 para.2, Sch.3 para.6, Sch.3 para.7, Sch.3 para.8, Sch.3 para.9, Sch.3 para.10, Sch.3 para.12, Sch.3 para.13, Sch.3 para.15, Sch.3 para.22
referred to: 2009 asp 1 s.3
varied: 2009 asp 1 s.3
applied: 2009 asp 1 Sch.3 para.9
Part D, applied: 2009 asp 1 Sch.3 para.15, Sch.3 para.16

1082. Scotland Act 1998 (Transitory and Transitional Provisions) (Scottish Parliamentary Pension Scheme) Order 1999–*cont.*
Part Q, applied: 2009 asp 1 Sch.3 para.18
Part R, applied: 2009 asp 1 Sch.3 para.19
Part S, applied: 2009 asp 1 Sch.3 para.21
Part S Art.1, varied: 2009 asp 1 s.3
Part S Art.2, applied: 2009 asp 1 Sch.3 para.21
Part S Art.2, varied: 2009 asp 1 s.3
Part S Art.3, varied: 2009 asp 1 s.3
Art.1, applied: 2009 asp 1 Sch.3 para.2
Art.1, applied: 2009 asp 1 Sch.3 para.17
Art.1, applied: 2009 asp 1 Sch.3 para.9
Art.2, applied: 2009 asp 1 Sch.3 para.9
Art.2, referred to: 2009 asp 1 Sch.3 para.9
Art.3, applied: 2009 asp 1 Sch.3 para.18
Art.3, referred to: 2009 asp 1 Sch.3 para.2, Sch.3 para.10, Sch.3 para.19, Sch.3 para.21, Sch.3 para.22
Art.3, varied: 2009 asp 1 Sch.3 para.5
Art.4, applied: 2009 asp 1 Sch.3 para.14
Art.6, applied: 2009 asp 1 Sch.3 para.17, Sch.3 para.20
s.art S, applied: 2009 asp 1 Sch.3 para.21
s.art S Art.1, varied: 2009 asp 1 s.3
s.art S Art.2, applied: 2009 asp 1 Sch.3 para.21
s.art S Art.2, varied: 2009 asp 1 s.3
s.art S Art.3, varied: 2009 asp 1 s.3
Sch.4, applied: 2009 asp 1 Sch.3 para.12
Sch.5, applied: 2009 asp 1 Sch.3 para.6, Sch.3 para.17, Sch.3 para.18
Sch.6, applied: 2009 asp 1 Sch.3 para.19
Sch.6 para.3, amended: 2009 asp 1 Sch.3 para.19
Sch.6 para.3, revoked (in part): 2009 asp 1 Sch.3 para.19
Sch.6 para.4, applied: 2009 asp 1 Sch.3 para.18
Sch.6 para.4, revoked (in part): 2009 asp 1 Sch.3 para.19
Sch.6 para.9, amended: 2009 asp 1 Sch.3 para.19
Sch.6 para.10, revoked: 2009 asp 1 Sch.3 para.19
Sch.6 para.11, revoked: 2009 asp 1 Sch.3 para.19

1096. Scotland Act 1998 (Transitory and Transitional Provisions) (Statutory Instruments) Order 1999
Art.5, varied: 2009 asp 1 s.3
Art.7, varied: 2009 asp 1 s.3
Art.8, varied: 2009 asp 1 s.3

1322. Public Service Vehicles (Community Licences) Regulations 1999
applied: SI 2009/1885 Art.2, Sch.4 para.1
Reg.2, amended: SI 2009/1885 Sch.2 para.4
Reg.3, applied: SI 2009/483 Art.2
Reg.3, referred to: SI 2009/491 Sch.1 Part 2, SI 2009/492 Sch.1 Part 2
Reg.6, amended: SI 2009/1885 Sch.2 para.5
Reg.7, applied: SI 2009/483 Art.2
Reg.7, referred to: SI 2009/491 Sch.1 Part 2, SI 2009/492 Sch.1 Part 2

1347. Act of Sederunt (Proceedings for Determination of Devolution Issues Rules) 1999
Art.2, amended: SSI 2009/323 Art.3
Art.10, amended: SSI 2009/323 Art.3
Art.11, substituted: SSI 2009/323 Art.3
Art.12, amended: SSI 2009/323 Art.3
Art.13, amended: SSI 2009/323 Art.3
Art.14, amended: SSI 2009/323 Art.3
Sch.2 para.1, amended: SSI 2009/323 Art.3
Sch.2 para.2, amended: SSI 2009/323 Art.3

1347. Act of Sederunt (Proceedings for Determination of Devolution Issues Rules) 1999–*cont.*
Sch.2 para.3, amended: SSI 2009/323 Art.3
Sch.2 para.4, amended: SSI 2009/323 Art.3
Sch.2 para.5, amended: SSI 2009/323 Art.3

1517. Energy Information (Lamps) Regulations 1999
referred to: SI 2009/669 Sch.1 Part 4
Reg.2, amended: SI 2009/2559 Reg.5
Reg.2A, added: SI 2009/2559 Reg.5
Sch.4 Part I para.2A, added: SI 2009/2559 Reg.5

1549. Public Interest Disclosure (Prescribed Persons) Order 1999
Sch.1, amended: SI 2009/462 Sch.5 para.5, SI 2009/2457 Sch.1, SI 2009/2748 Sch.1 para.20

1619. General Teaching Council for Wales (Constitution) Regulations 1999
Reg.2, amended: SI 2009/1352 Reg.2
Reg.5, amended: SI 2009/1352 Reg.2
Reg.10, amended: SI 2009/1352 Reg.2
Sch.1 Part 1, amended: SI 2009/1352 Reg.2
Sch.1 Part 2, amended: SI 2009/1352 Reg.2

1621. Registration of Marriages (Welsh Language) Regulations 1999
Reg.2, amended: SI 2009/2806 Reg.3
Sch.1, amended: SI 2009/2806 Reg.3, Sch.2

1676. Energy Information (Dishwashers) Regulations 1999
referred to: SI 2009/669 Sch.1 Part 4
Reg.2, amended: SI 2009/2559 Reg.6
Reg.2A, added: SI 2009/2559 Reg.6
Sch.5 Part I para.2A, added: SI 2009/2559 Reg.6

1726. General Teaching Council for England (Constitution) Regulations 1999
Reg.5, amended: SI 2009/1924 Reg.3
Reg.10, amended: SI 2009/1924 Reg.3

1735. International Headquarters and Defence Organisations (Designation and Privileges) (Amendment) Order 1999
revoked: SI 2009/704 Art.4

1736. Visiting Forces and International Headquarters (Application of Law) Order 1999
applied: SI 2009/2054 Sch.2 para.14
Art.2, amended: SI 2009/2054 Sch.1 para.21
Art.18, substituted: SI 2009/2054 Sch.1 para.21
Sch.1 Part II, amended: SI 2009/705 Art.4
Sch.2, substituted: SI 2009/705 Art.5
Sch.6, amended: SI 2009/2054 Sch.1 para.21, SSI 2009/248 Sch.1 para.15, Sch.3
Sch.7 para.1, amended: SI 2009/2054 Sch.1 para.21
Sch.7 para.2, substituted: SI 2009/2054 Sch.1 para.21
Sch.7 para.4, amended: SI 2009/2054 Sch.1 para.21
Sch.7 para.4, revoked (in part): SI 2009/2054 Sch.1 para.21
Sch.7 para.5, amended: SI 2009/2054 Sch.1 para.21
Sch.7 para.6, revoked: SI 2009/2054 Sch.1 para.21
Sch.8 para.2, amended: SI 2009/2054 Sch.1 para.21
Sch.8 para.3, amended: SI 2009/2054 Sch.1 para.21
Sch.8 para.5, amended: SI 2009/2054 Sch.1 para.21
Sch.8 para.6, amended: SI 2009/2054 Sch.1 para.21

1748. Scotland Act 1998 (Functions Exercisable in or as Regards Scotland) Order 1999
Sch.1 para.4, revoked: SI 2009/56 Sch.2 para.72

1780. Education (Maintained Special Schools) (Wales) Regulations 1999
Reg.12, substituted: SI 2009/48 Reg.2

1812. Education (School Information) (Wales) Regulations 1999
applied: SI 2009/569 Reg.4

1999– cont.

1812. Education (School Information) (Wales) Regulations 1999– cont.
Sch.1 Part I para.8, revoked: SI 2009/569 Reg.2
Sch.1 Part II para.19, revoked: SI 2009/569 Reg.2
Sch.1 Part II para.20, revoked: SI 2009/569 Reg.2

1856. General Chiropractic Council (Registration) Rules Order of Council 1999
applied: SI 2009/27 Sch.1
Sch.1, amended: SI 2009/2305 Sch.1
Sch.1, applied: SI 2009/27 Sch.1
Sch.1, referred to: SI 2009/27 Sch.1
Sch.1, revoked: SI 2009/2305 Sch.1
Sch.1, substituted: SI 2009/2305 Sch.1

1876. Cross-Border Credit Transfers Regulations 1999
revoked: SI 2009/209 Sch.6 para.2

1892. Town and Country Planning (Trees) Regulations 1999
see *Palm Developments Ltd v Secretary of State for Communities and Local Government* [2009] EWHC 220 (Admin), [2009] 2 P. & C.R. 16 (QBD (Admin)), Cranston, J.
Reg.10, applied: SI 2009/1300 Art.24
Sch.1, applied: SI 2009/1300 Art.24

1957. Merchant Shipping (Marine Equipment) Regulations 1999
Reg.2, amended: SI 2009/2021 Reg.3
Reg.6, amended: SI 2009/2021 Reg.4

2001. Pressure Equipment Regulations 1999
referred to: SI 2009/669 Sch.1 Part 4, Sch.2 Part 2
Sch.2, applied: SI 2009/261 Reg.20

2083. Unfair Terms in Consumer Contracts Regulations 1999
referred to: SI 2009/669 Sch.1 Part 2
see *Direct Line Insurance Plc v Fox* [2009] EWHC 386 (QB), [2009] 1 All E.R. (Comm) 1017 (QBD), Judge Richard Seymour Q.C.; see *Maple Leaf Macro Volatility Master Fund v Rouvroy* [2009] EWHC 257 (Comm), [2009] 2 All E.R. (Comm) 287 (QBD (Comm)), Andrew Smith, J.; see *Office of Fair Trading v Abbey National Plc* [2009] UKSC 6, [2009] 3 W.L.R. 1215 (SC), Lord Phillips; see *Office of Fair Trading v Foxtons Ltd* [2009] EWHC 1681 (Ch), Times, July 29, 2009 (Ch D), Mann, J.
Reg.5, see *Office of Fair Trading v Foxtons Ltd* [2008] EWHC 1662 (Ch), [2009] Eu. L.R. 32 (Ch D), Morgan, J.
Reg.6, see *Office of Fair Trading v Abbey National Plc* [2009] EWCA Civ 116, [2009] 2 W.L.R. 1286 (CA (Civ Div)), Sir Anthony Clarke, M.R.; see *Office of Fair Trading v Abbey National Plc* [2009] UKSC 6, [2009] 3 W.L.R. 1215 (SC), Lord Phillips; see *Office of Fair Trading v Foxtons Ltd* [2009] EWHC 1681 (Ch), Times, July 29, 2009 (Ch D), Mann, J.
Reg.7, see *Office of Fair Trading v Foxtons Ltd* [2009] EWHC 1681 (Ch), Times, July 29, 2009 (Ch D), Mann, J.; see *Peabody Trust Governors v Reeve* [2008] EWHC 1432 (Ch), [2009] L. & T.R. 6 (Ch D), Gabriel Moss Q.C.
Reg.8, see *Barclays Bank Plc v Kufner* [2008] EWHC 2319 (Comm), [2009] 1 All E.R. (Comm) 1 (QBD (Comm)), Field, J.; see *Peabody Trust Governors v Reeve* [2008] EWHC 1432 (Ch), [2009] L. & T.R. 6 (Ch D), Gabriel Moss Q.C.
Reg.12, see *Office of Fair Trading v Foxtons Ltd* [2008] EWHC 1662 (Ch), [2009] Eu. L.R. 32 (Ch D), Morgan, J.

1999– cont.

2083. Unfair Terms in Consumer Contracts Regulations 1999– cont.
Sch.2 para.1, see *Mylcrist Builders Ltd v Buck* [2008] EWHC 2172 (TCC), [2009] 2 All E.R. (Comm) 259 (QBD (TCC)), Ramsey, J.

2106. Local Authorities (Contracting Out of Highway Functions) Order 1999
revoked: SI 2009/721 Art.4
Sch.2 para.1, applied: SI 2009/721 Art.4
Sch.2 para.10, applied: SI 2009/721 Art.4

2149. Motor Vehicles (Type Approval and Approval Marks) (Fees) Regulations 1999
Reg.3, amended: SI 2009/719 Reg.3
Reg.5A, added: SI 2009/719 Reg.4
Reg.6, amended: SI 2009/719 Reg.5
Reg.9, amended: SI 2009/719 Reg.6
Sch.1 Part I, amended: SI 2009/719 Reg.7
Sch.1 Part II, amended: SI 2009/719 Reg.7
Sch.1 Part III, amended: SI 2009/719 Reg.7
Sch.1 Part III, referred to: SI 2009/719 Reg.7
Sch.1 Part III, substituted: SI 2009/719 Sch.1
Sch.1 Part IV, amended: SI 2009/719 Reg.7
Sch.4 Part III, referred to: SI 2009/719 Reg.8
Sch.4 Part III, substituted: SI 2009/719 Sch.2
Sch.5 Part I, revoked: SI 2009/719 Reg.9
Sch.5 Part II, revoked: SI 2009/719 Reg.9
Sch.5 Part III, revoked: SI 2009/719 Reg.9

2228. Environmental Impact Assessment (Forestry) (England and Wales) Regulations 1999
applied: SI 2009/3365 Sch.1 para.1
Reg.4, applied: SI 2009/3264 Sch.1 para.1, SI 2009/3365 Sch.1 para.1
Reg.22, applied: SI 2009/3264 Sch.1 para.1, SI 2009/3365 Sch.1 para.1

2257. Education (Non-Maintained Special Schools) (England) Regulations 1999
Reg.2, amended: SI 2009/1924 Reg.2
Sch.1 Part I para.3C, amended: SI 2009/1924 Reg.2

2263. Education (Student Support) (Dance and Drama) Regulations 1999
Reg.4, applied: SI 2009/1555 Reg.14
Reg.4, referred to: SI 2009/2737 Reg.13

2277. Redundancy Payments (Continuity of Employment in Local Government, etc.) (Modification) Order 1999
Sch.1 para.17B, revoked: SI 2009/462 Sch.5 para.6
Sch.1 para.17C, revoked: SI 2009/462 Sch.5 para.6
Sch.1 para.44, revoked (in part): SI 2009/801 Art.3

2324. Motor Vehicles (EC Type Approval) (Amendment No.2) Regulations 1999
revoked: SI 2009/717 Sch.1

2537. Stamp Duty (Collection and Recovery of Penalties) Regulations 1999
Sch.1 Part I, amended: SI 2009/56 Sch.2 para.70
Sch.1 Part II, amended: SI 2009/56 Sch.2 para.71, SI 2009/1890 Art.3
Sch.1 Part II, revoked: SI 2009/56 Sch.2 para.71

2864. Motor Vehicles (Driving Licences) Regulations 1999
Reg.3, amended: SI 2009/788 Reg.3
Reg.3A, amended: SI 2009/788 Reg.4
Reg.4, applied: SI 2009/365 Reg.2
Reg.22, amended: SI 2009/788 Reg.5
Reg.23, amended: SI 2009/788 Reg.6
Reg.24, amended: SI 2009/788 Reg.7
Reg.25, amended: SI 2009/788 Reg.8
Reg.30, amended: SI 2009/788 Reg.9
Reg.31, amended: SI 2009/788 Reg.10
Reg.32, amended: SI 2009/788 Reg.11

1999–cont.

2864. Motor Vehicles (Driving Licences) Regulations 1999–cont.
Reg.34, amended: SI 2009/788 Reg.12
Reg.34, applied: SI 2009/788 Reg.33
Reg.35, amended: SI 2009/788 Reg.13
Reg.36, amended: SI 2009/788 Reg.14
Reg.37, amended: SI 2009/788 Reg.15
Reg.38, amended: SI 2009/788 Reg.16
Reg.39, amended: SI 2009/788 Reg.17
Reg.40, amended: SI 2009/788 Reg.18
Reg.40A, amended: SI 2009/788 Reg.19
Reg.40B, amended: SI 2009/788 Reg.20, SI 2009/2362 Reg.2
Reg.40B, disapplied: SI 2009/788 Reg.33
Reg.40B, revoked (in part): SI 2009/788 Reg.20
Reg.40C, amended: SI 2009/788 Reg.21
Reg.40C, varied: SI 2009/788 Reg.33
Reg.43, amended: SI 2009/788 Reg.22
Reg.44, amended: SI 2009/788 Reg.23
Reg.46, amended: SI 2009/788 Reg.24
Reg.47, amended: SI 2009/788 Reg.25
Reg.47B, amended: SI 2009/788 Reg.26
Reg.48, amended: SI 2009/788 Reg.27
Sch.3 Part 1, amended: SI 2009/788 Reg.28
Sch.5, substituted: SI 2009/788 Sch.1
Sch.5 Part 1, substituted: SI 2009/788 Sch.1
Sch.5 Part 2, substituted: SI 2009/788 Sch.1
Sch.8A, added: SI 2009/788 Sch.2
Sch.8 Part 1 paraD, revoked (in part): SI 2009/788 Reg.30
Sch.10D Part 1, added: SI 2009/788 Sch.3
Sch.10D Part 2, added: SI 2009/788 Sch.3

2905. Legal Services Ombudsman (Jurisdiction) (Amendment) Order 1999
revoked: SI 2009/3250 Sch.1

2920. Motor Cycles Etc (EC Type Approval) Regulations 1999
Sch.1, amended: SI 2009/3266 Reg.2

2975. Corporation Tax (Simplified Arrangements for Group Relief) Regulations 1999
varied: SI 2009/317 Sch.1

2979. Financial Markets and Insolvency (Settlement Finality) Regulations 1999
varied: SI 2009/317 Sch.1
Reg.2, applied: SI 2009/322 Art.1
Reg.6, amended: SI 2009/1972 Reg.3
Reg.14, amended: SI 2009/1972 Reg.4
Reg.15, amended: SI 2009/1972 Reg.5
Reg.16, amended: SI 2009/1972 Reg.6
Reg.19, amended: SI 2009/1972 Reg.7

3137. Chartered Institute of Patent Agents Order 1999
revoked: SI 2009/3250 Sch.1

3219. Tax Credits (Payment by Employers) Regulations 1999
Reg.7, applied: SI 2009/470 Reg.54

3232. Ionising Radiations Regulations 1999
applied: SI 2009/515 Reg.8, Sch.5
Reg.6, disapplied: SI 2009/515 Sch.7
Reg.20, applied: SI 2009/1348 Sch.2 para.3
Reg.21, applied: SI 2009/515 Reg.8, Sch.7, SI 2009/1348 Sch.2 para.3
Reg.22, applied: SI 2009/1348 Sch.2 para.3
Reg.23, applied: SI 2009/1348 Sch.2 para.3
Reg.24, applied: SI 2009/1348 Sch.2 para.3
Reg.25, applied: SI 2009/1348 Sch.2 para.3
Reg.26, applied: SI 2009/1348 Sch.2 para.3
Reg.35, applied: SI 2009/515 Sch.7

1999–cont.

3232. Ionising Radiations Regulations 1999–cont.
Sch.1 para.1, applied: SI 2009/515 Reg.8, Sch.7
Sch.4, applied: SI 2009/1348 Sch.2 para.4
Sch.4 Part I para.1, applied: SI 2009/1348 Sch.2 para.3
Sch.4 Part I para.1, referred to: SI 2009/1348 Sch.2 para.3
Sch.4 Part I para.2, applied: SI 2009/1348 Sch.2 para.3
Sch.4 Part I para.2, referred to: SI 2009/1348 Sch.2 para.3
Sch.4 Part I para.6, applied: SI 2009/1348 Sch.2 para.3
Sch.4 Part I para.7, applied: SI 2009/1348 Sch.2 para.3
Sch.4 Part I para.8, applied: SI 2009/1348 Sch.2 para.3

3242. Management of Health and Safety at Work Regulations 1999
Reg.3, see *McLellan v Dundee City Council* [2009] CSOH 9, 2009 Rep. L.R. 61 (OH), Lord Hodge; see *R. v TDG (UK) Ltd* [2008] EWCA Crim 1963, [2009] 1 Cr. App. R. (S.) 81 (CA (Crim Div)), Gage, L.J.

3259. Local Government Pension Scheme (Management and Investment of Funds) (Amendment) Regulations 1999
revoked: SI 2009/3093 Sch.2

3292. Special Commissioners (Jurisdiction and Procedure) (Amendment) Regulations 1999
revoked: SI 2009/56 Sch.2 para.187

3293. General Commissioners (Jurisdiction and Procedure) (Amendment) Regulations 1999
revoked: SI 2009/56 Sch.2 para.187

3294. Special Commissioners (Amendment of the Taxes Management Act 1970) Regulations 1999
revoked: SI 2009/56 Sch.2 para.187

3323. Transnational Information and Consultation of Employees Regulations 1999
Reg.41, amended: SI 2009/3348 Art.22, Art.23
Reg.46A, substituted: SI 2009/2401 Reg.40, SI 2009/2402 Reg.38

3379. Non-Domestic Rating (Chargeable Amounts) (England) Regulations 1999
Reg.36, revoked: SI 2009/3343 Reg.19
Reg.37, revoked: SI 2009/3343 Reg.19

3413. Road Transport (Passenger Vehicles Cabotage) Regulations 1999
applied: SI 2009/1885 Art.2, Sch.4 para.1
Reg.3, applied: SI 2009/483 Art.2
Reg.3, referred to: SI 2009/491 Sch.1 Part 2, SI 2009/492 Sch.1 Part 2
Reg.4, applied: SI 2009/483 Art.2
Reg.4, referred to: SI 2009/491 Sch.1 Part 2, SI 2009/492 Sch.1 Part 2
Reg.6, amended: SI 2009/1885 Sch.2 para.6
Reg.7, applied: SI 2009/483 Art.2
Reg.7, referred to: SI 2009/491 Sch.1 Part 2, SI 2009/492 Sch.1 Part 2

3451. Cardiff and Vale National Health Service Trust Establishment Order 1999
revoked: SI 2009/1306 Sch.1

2000

51. Sea Fishing (Enforcement of Community Control Measures) Order 2000
Art.2, amended: SI 2009/1847 Art.2

2000– cont.

51. Sea Fishing (Enforcement of Community Control Measures) Order 2000– *cont.*
Art.2A, added: SI 2009/ 1847 Art.2
Art.3, amended: SI 2009/ 1847 Art.2
Art.4, amended: SI 2009/ 1847 Art.2
Sch.1, amended: SI 2009/ 1847 Art.2

188. Data Protection (Notification and Notification Fees) Regulations 2000
Reg.3, amended: SI 2009/ 1677 Reg.2
Reg.7, substituted: SI 2009/ 1677 Reg.3
Reg.14, substituted: SI 2009/ 1677 Reg.4
Sch.1 para.1, amended: SI 2009/ 1677 Reg.2
Sch.1 para.6, added: SI 2009/ 1677 Reg.2

241. General Osteopathic Council (Professional Conduct Committee) (Procedure) Rules Order of Council 2000
Sch., added: SI 2009/ 1182 Sch.4 para.19
Sch., amended: SI 2009/ 1182 Sch.4 para.19

288. Special Commissioners (Jurisdiction and Procedure) (Amendment) Regulations 2000
revoked: SI 2009/ 56 Sch.2 para.187

300. Crime and Disorder Strategies (Prescribed Descriptions) (Amendment) Order 2000
revoked (in part): SI 2009/ 3050 Art.4

388. Weighing Equipment (Automatic Gravimetric Filling Instruments) Regulations 2000
Reg.6A, amended: SI 2009/ 3045 Reg.3

419. Data Protection (Miscellaneous Subject Access Exemptions) Order 2000
Sch.1 Part I, substituted: SI 2009/ 1892 Sch.3 para.1

441. Community Legal Service (Costs) Regulations 2000
Reg.2, amended: SI 2009/ 3348 Art.12
Reg.10, amended: SI 2009/ 2468 Art.4
Reg.18, see *Beechwood Construction Ltd v Afza* [2008] EWHC 2671 (Ch), [2009] B.P.I.R. 7 (Ch D), Judge Behrens
Reg.19, see *Beechwood Construction Ltd v Afza* [2008] EWHC 2671 (Ch), [2009] B.P.I.R. 7 (Ch D), Judge Behrens
Reg.20, see *Beechwood Construction Ltd v Afza* [2008] EWHC 2671 (Ch), [2009] B.P.I.R. 7 (Ch D), Judge Behrens

516. Community Legal Service (Financial) Regulations 2000
referred to: SI 2009/ 502 Reg.2
Reg.2, amended: SI 2009/ 3348 Art.13
Reg.3, amended: SI 2009/ 502 Reg.5
Reg.4, amended: SI 2009/ 1894 Reg.3
Reg.5, amended: SI 2009/ 502 Reg.6
Reg.5A, amended: SI 2009/ 502 Reg.7
Reg.12, applied: SSI 2009/ 86 Reg.3
Reg.15, amended: SI 2009/ 1894 Reg.4
Reg.15, applied: SI 2009/ 502 Reg.3, SI 2009/ 3312 Reg.1
Reg.17, applied: SSI 2009/ 86 Reg.3
Reg.19, amended: SI 2009/ 1887 Reg.19
Reg.20, amended: SI 2009/ 502 Reg.8
Reg.24A, added: SI 2009/ 3312 Reg.2
Reg.35, amended: SI 2009/ 502 Reg.9
Reg.38, amended: SI 2009/ 502 Reg.10
Reg.40, amended: SI 2009/ 2468 Art.5

540. Valuation for Rating (Plant and Machinery) (England) Regulations 2000
see *Leda Properties Ltd v Howells (Valuation Officer)* [2009] R.A. 165 (Lands Tr), George Bartlett Q.C. (President, LTr)
Sch.1, referred to: SI 2009/ 2268 Reg.4

2000– cont.

617. NHS Bodies and Local Authorities Partnership Arrangements Regulations 2000
Reg.5, amended: SI 2009/ 278 Reg.2

619. National Health Service Pension Scheme (Additional Voluntary Contributions) Regulations 2000
Reg.20, amended: SI 2009/ 2446 Reg.105
Sch.2 para.6, amended: SI 2009/ 2446 Reg.105
Sch.2 para.14, amended: SI 2009/ 2446 Reg.105

620. National Health Service (Charges for Drugs and Appliances) Regulations 2000
Reg.3, amended: SI 2009/ 411 Reg.2
Reg.4, amended: SI 2009/ 411 Reg.2
Reg.4A, amended: SI 2009/ 411 Reg.2
Reg.5, amended: SI 2009/ 411 Reg.2, SI 2009/ 1166 Reg.2
Reg.6, amended: SI 2009/ 411 Reg.2
Reg.6A, amended: SI 2009/ 411 Reg.2
Reg.7, amended: SI 2009/ 29 Reg.2
Reg.7C, added: SI 2009/ 2230 Reg.2
Reg.8, amended: SI 2009/ 29 Reg.3
Reg.9, amended: SI 2009/ 411 Reg.2
Reg.9, applied: SI 2009/ 411 Reg.3
Sch.1, amended: SI 2009/ 411 Reg.2
Sch.1, referred to: SI 2009/ 411 Reg.3

627. Community Legal Service (Funding) Order 2000
Art.2, amended: SI 2009/ 2468 Art.6

636. Social Security (Immigration and Asylum) Consequential Amendments Regulations 2000
Reg.2, amended: SI 2009/ 3228 Reg.3
Reg.12, revoked (in part): SI 2009/ 3228 Reg.2

643. Licensed Conveyancers (Compensation for Inadequate Professional Services) Order 2000
revoked: SI 2009/ 501 Art.3

656. Food Standards Act 1999 (Transitional and Consequential Provisions and Savings) (England and Wales) Regulations 2000
Reg.14, applied: SI 2009/ 2825
Reg.14, referred to: SI 2009/ 28

692. Conditional Fee Agreements Regulations 2000
Reg.4, see *Birmingham City Council v Forde* [2009] EWHC 12 (QB), [2009] 1 W.L.R. 2732 (QBD (Birmingham)), Christopher Clarke, J.; see *Tankard v John Fredricks Plastics Ltd* [2008] EWCA Civ 1375, [2009] 1 W.L.R. 1731 (CA (Civ Div)), Sir Anthony Clarke, M.R.

704. Asylum Support Regulations 2000
Reg.10, amended: SI 2009/ 1388 Reg.2

727. Social Security Contributions (Intermediaries) Regulations 2000
Reg.6, see *Revenue and Customs Commissioners v Larkstar Data Ltd* [2008] EWHC 3284 (Ch), [2009] S.T.C. 1161 (Ch D), Sir Donald Rattee

729. Social Fund Winter Fuel Payment Regulations 2000
Reg.1, amended: SI 2009/ 1488 Reg.19
Reg.2, amended: SI 2009/ 1488 Reg.20
Reg.2, varied: SI 2009/ 1489 Reg.2
Reg.3, amended: SI 2009/ 1488 Reg.21

738. European Communities (Designation) Order 2000
referred to: SI 2009/ 1349

824. Community Legal Service (Cost Protection) Regulations 2000
see *Liverpool Freeport Electronics Ltd v Habib Bank Ltd* [2009] EWHC 861 (QB), [2009] 3 Costs L.R. 434 (QBD), Jack, J.

2000—cont.

824. Community Legal Service (Cost Protection) Regulations 2000—cont.
Reg.2, amended: SI 2009/3348 Art.14
Reg.5, amended: SI 2009/2468 Art.3
Reg.5, see *Aehmed v Legal Services Commission* [2009] EWCA Civ 572, [2009] 3 Costs L.R. 425 (CA (Civ Div)), Sedley, L.J.

869. Motor Vehicles (EC Type Approval) (Amendment) Regulations 2000
revoked: SI 2009/717 Sch.1

897. Social Security (Work-focused Interviews) Regulations 2000
referred to: SI 2009/1541 Reg.3
Reg.12, disapplied: SI 2009/1541 Reg.3
Reg.12, referred to: SI 2009/1541 Reg.3

932. Weighing Equipment (Non-automatic Weighing Machines) Regulations 2000
Reg.18, amended: SI 2009/3045 Reg.3

941. Civil Procedure (Modification of Enactments) Order 2000
revoked: SI 2009/1307 Sch.4

944. Education (Student Loans) (Repayment) Regulations 2000
applied: SI 2009/470 Reg.54
revoked: SI 2009/470 Sch.1
Reg.7, amended: SI 2009/56 Sch.2 para.73
Reg.45, revoked (in part): SI 2009/56 Sch.2 para.73

1038. General Osteopathic Council (Application for Registration and Fees) Rules Order of Council 2000
Sch.1, applied: SI 2009/1993 Sch.1
Sch.1, disapplied: SI 2009/1993 Sch.1
Sch.1, substituted: SI 2009/1993 Sch.1

1048. Pensions on Divorce etc (Provision of Information) Regulations 2000
Reg.1, amended: SI 2009/615 Reg.12
Reg.9, amended: SI 2009/615 Reg.12

1049. Pensions on Divorce etc (Charging) Regulations 2000
Reg.1, amended: SI 2009/615 Reg.13
Reg.9, amended: SI 2009/615 Reg.13

1053. Pension Sharing (Implementation and Discharge of Liability) Regulations 2000
Reg.1, amended: SI 2009/598 Art.7, SI 2009/615 Reg.14
Reg.13, revoked: SI 2009/598 Art.7
Reg.15, amended: SI 2009/2930 Reg.8

1054. Pension Sharing (Pension Credit Benefit) Regulations 2000
Reg.1, amended: SI 2009/598 Art.8, SI 2009/615 Reg.15
Reg.3, substituted: SI 2009/615 Reg.15, SI 2009/2930 Reg.9
Reg.4, substituted: SI 2009/615 Reg.15
Reg.7, amended: SI 2009/615 Reg.15
Reg.7, revoked (in part): SI 2009/615 Reg.15
Reg.10, revoked (in part): SI 2009/598 Art.8
Reg.13, amended: SI 2009/615 Reg.15
Reg.16, revoked: SI 2009/598 Art.8
Reg.17, revoked: SI 2009/598 Art.8
Reg.18, revoked: SI 2009/598 Art.8
Reg.19, revoked: SI 2009/598 Art.8
Reg.20, amended: SI 2009/598 Art.8
Reg.21, amended: SI 2009/598 Art.8
Reg.21, revoked (in part): SI 2009/598 Art.8
Reg.22, amended: SI 2009/615 Reg.15
Reg.22, revoked (in part): SI 2009/598 Art.8
Reg.35, revoked (in part): SI 2009/598 Art.8

2000—cont.

1055. Pension Sharing (Safeguarded Rights) Regulations 2000
revoked: SI 2009/598 Art.9

1059. Ionising Radiation (Medical Exposure) Regulations 2000
Reg.2, amended: SI 2009/462 Sch.5 para.7

1119. European Communities (Lawyer's Practice) Regulations 2000
Reg.2, amended: SI 2009/1587 Art.2
Reg.11, amended: SI 2009/1587 Art.2
Reg.16, referred to: SI 2009/2999 Reg.31
Reg.29, amended: SI 2009/1587 Art.2
Sch.1, amended: SI 2009/1587 Art.2
Sch.3 Part 2, amended: SI 2009/1587 Art.2
Sch.3 Part 3, amended: SI 2009/1587 Art.2
Sch.4, added: SI 2009/1587 Art.3
Sch.4 para.1, amended: SI 2009/1587 Art.3
Sch.4 para.1, revoked (in part): SI 2009/1587 Art.3
Sch.4 para.3, revoked: SI 2009/1587 Art.3
Sch.4 para.4, revoked: SI 2009/1587 Art.3
Sch.4 para.5, revoked: SI 2009/1587 Art.3
Sch.4 para.6, revoked: SI 2009/1587 Art.3
Sch.4 para.7, amended: SI 2009/1587 Art.3
Sch.4 para.8, amended: SI 2009/1587 Art.3
Sch.4 para.8, revoked (in part): SI 2009/1587 Art.3
Sch.4 para.9, amended: SI 2009/1587 Art.3
Sch.4 para.9, revoked (in part): SI 2009/1587 Art.3
Sch.4 para.10, amended: SI 2009/1587 Art.3
Sch.4 para.11, substituted: SI 2009/1587 Art.3
Sch.4 para.15, revoked: SI 2009/1587 Art.3
Sch.4 para.16, revoked (in part): SI 2009/3348 Art.15
Sch.4 para.17, amended: SI 2009/1587 Art.3
Sch.4 para.18, revoked: SI 2009/1587 Art.3
Sch.4 para.20, amended: SI 2009/1587 Art.3
Sch.4 para.23, revoked: SI 2009/1587 Art.3
Sch.4 para.24, substituted: SI 2009/1587 Art.3

1403. Stakeholder Pension Schemes Regulations 2000
Reg.3, amended: SI 2009/615 Reg.16
Reg.21, amended: SI 2009/615 Reg.16

1413. Barking, Havering and Redbridge Hospitals National Health Service Trust (Establishment) Order 2000
Art.1, amended: SI 2009/43 Art.2, Art.3
Art.2, amended: SI 2009/43 Art.3
Art.3, amended: SI 2009/43 Art.4
Art.4, substituted: SI 2009/43 Art.5

1472. Burma (Freezing of Funds) Regulations 2000
revoked: SI 2009/1495 Reg.24

1551. Part-time Workers (Prevention of Less Favourable Treatment) Regulations 2000
see *Carl v University of Sheffield* [2009] 3 C.M.L.R. 21 (EAT), Judge Peter Clark; see *Department of Constitutional Affairs v O'Brien* [2008] EWCA Civ 1448, [2009] 2 C.M.L.R. 15 (CA (Civ Div)), Sir Andrew Morritt (Chancellor)
Reg.5, see *Carl v University of Sheffield* [2009] 3 C.M.L.R. 21 (EAT), Judge Peter Clark
Reg.17, see *Department of Constitutional Affairs v O'Brien* [2008] EWCA Civ 1448, [2009] 2 C.M.L.R. 15 (CA (Civ Div)), Sir Andrew Morritt (Chancellor)

1562. Air Navigation Order 2000
see *Laroche v Spirit of Adventure (UK) Ltd* [2009] EWCA Civ 12, [2009] Q.B. 778 (CA (Civ Div)), Mummery, L.J.

2000 – cont.

1563. Scotland Act 1998 (Transfer of Functions to the Scottish Ministers etc.) Order 2000
Art.4, revoked: 2009 c.24 Sch.7 Part 3

1624. Town and Country Planning (Inquiries Procedure) (England) Rules 2000
r.2, amended: SI 2009/455 r.4
r.3A, added: SI 2009/455 r.4
r.4, amended: SI 2009/455 r.4
r.6, amended: SI 2009/455 r.4
r.6, revoked (in part): SI 2009/455 r.4
r.9, amended: SI 2009/455 r.4
r.14, amended: SI 2009/455 r.4
r.15, amended: SI 2009/455 r.4
r.17, amended: SI 2009/455 r.4
r.21, amended: SI 2009/455 r.4
r.23, amended: SI 2009/455 r.4
r.23, revoked (in part): SI 2009/455 r.4

1625. Town and Country Planning Appeals (Determination by Inspectors) (Inquiries Procedure) (England) Rules 2000
r.2, amended: SI 2009/455 r.3
r.3A, added: SI 2009/455 r.3
r.4, amended: SI 2009/455 r.3
r.5, amended: SI 2009/455 r.3
r.6, amended: SI 2009/455 r.3
r.6, revoked (in part): SI 2009/455 r.3
r.9, amended: SI 2009/455 r.3
r.13, amended: SI 2009/455 r.3
r.15, amended: SI 2009/455 r.3
r.16, amended: SI 2009/455 r.3
r.18, amended: SI 2009/455 r.3
r.24, amended: SI 2009/455 r.3
r.24, revoked (in part): SI 2009/455 r.3

1626. Town and Country Planning (Hearings Procedure) (England) Rules 2000
r.2, amended: SI 2009/455 r.2
r.3A, added: SI 2009/455 r.2
r.4, amended: SI 2009/455 r.2
r.5, amended: SI 2009/455 r.2
r.6, amended: SI 2009/455 r.2
r.6, revoked (in part): SI 2009/455 r.2
r.8, amended: SI 2009/455 r.2
r.13, amended: SI 2009/455 r.2
r.14, amended: SI 2009/455 r.2
r.20, amended: SI 2009/455 r.2
r.20, revoked (in part): SI 2009/455 r.2

1628. Town and Country Planning (Appeals) (Written Representations Procedure) (England) Regulations 2000
revoked: SI 2009/452 Reg.20

1816. Pitcairn (Appeals to Privy Council) Order 2000
revoked (in part): SI 2009/224 Art.5

1927. Electricity Works (Environmental Impact Assessment) (England and Wales) Regulations 2000
varied: 2009 c.23 s.12

1941. General Teaching Council for Wales (Additional Functions) Order 2000
Sch.1 Part I para.2, amended: SI 2009/1351 Art.2
Sch.1 Part I para.3A, added: SI 2009/1351 Art.2
Sch.1 Part II para.19A, added: SI 2009/1351 Art.2
Sch.1 Part II para.22A, added: SI 2009/1351 Art.2
Sch.1 Part II para.23C, added: SI 2009/1351 Art.2
Sch.1 Part II para.23D, added: SI 2009/1351 Art.2

1970. Public Service Vehicles Accessibility Regulations 2000
Reg.5, amended: SI 2009/143 Reg.2

2000 – cont.

1970. Public Service Vehicles Accessibility Regulations 2000 *– cont.*
Reg.7, amended: SI 2009/876 Reg.2
Reg.12, amended: SI 2009/876 Reg.2
Reg.17, amended: SI 2009/876 Reg.2
Reg.18, amended: SI 2009/876 Reg.2
Sch.1, applied: SI 2009/717 Sch.4 Part 2, Sch.5 Part 4
Sch.2, applied: SI 2009/717 Sch.4 Part 2, Sch.5 Part 4

1979. General Teaching Council for Wales (Functions) Regulations 2000
Reg.2, amended: SI 2009/1353 Reg.2
Reg.4A, revoked: SI 2009/1353 Reg.2
Reg.18A, added: SI 2009/1353 Reg.2
Sch.1 para.22C, added: SI 2009/1353 Reg.2
Sch.1 para.22D, added: SI 2009/1353 Reg.2
Sch.1 para.25, added: SI 2009/1353 Reg.2
Sch.2 para.11A, amended: SI 2009/1353 Reg.2
Sch.2 para.12A, added: SI 2009/1353 Reg.2
Sch.2 para.13C, added: SI 2009/1353 Reg.2
Sch.2 para.13D, added: SI 2009/1353 Reg.2
Sch.2 para.15, added: SI 2009/1353 Reg.2

2030. Changing of School Session Times (Wales) Regulations 2000
revoked: SI 2009/572 Reg.2

2047. Faculty Jurisdiction Rules 2000
referred to: SI 2009/2105 Sch.1 Part I

2048. Faculty Jurisdiction (Care of Places of Worship) Rules 2000
referred to: SI 2009/2105 Sch.1 Part I

2055. Brucellosis (England) Order 2000
Art.2, amended: SI 2009/2713 Art.2

2056. Enzootic Bovine Leukosis (England) Order 2000
Art.2, amended: SI 2009/2713 Art.2
Art.3, amended: SI 2009/2713 Art.2
Art.4, amended: SI 2009/2713 Art.6
Art.5, amended: SI 2009/2713 Art.6

2129. Tonnage Tax (Training Requirement) Regulations 2000
applied: SI 2009/2304 Reg.2
Reg.15, amended: SI 2009/2304 Reg.3
Reg.21, amended: SI 2009/2304 Reg.3

2228. Courts-Martial Appeal (Amendment) Rules 2000
revoked: SI 2009/2657 Sch.5

2254. Food Irradiation Provisions (England) Regulations 2000
Reg.2, revoked: SI 2009/1584 Reg.12
Reg.3, revoked: SI 2009/1584 Reg.12
Reg.4, revoked: SI 2009/1584 Reg.12
Reg.5, revoked: SI 2009/1584 Reg.12
Reg.6, revoked: SI 2009/1584 Reg.12
Reg.7, revoked: SI 2009/1584 Reg.12
Reg.8, revoked: SI 2009/1584 Reg.12
Reg.9, revoked: SI 2009/1584 Reg.12
Reg.10, revoked: SI 2009/1584 Reg.12
Reg.11, revoked: SI 2009/1584 Reg.12
Reg.12, revoked: SI 2009/1584 Reg.12
Reg.13, revoked: SI 2009/1584 Reg.12
Reg.14, revoked: SI 2009/1584 Reg.12
Reg.15, revoked: SI 2009/1584 Reg.12
Reg.16, revoked: SI 2009/1584 Reg.12

2000–cont.

2326. Immigration (European Economic Area) Regulations 2000

see *Jeleniewicz v Secretary of State for Work and Pensions* [2008] EWCA Civ 1163, [2009] 1 C.M.L.R. 21 (CA (Civ Div)), Mummery, L.J.

2334. Consumer Protection (Distance Selling) Regulations 2000

referred to: SI 2009/669 Sch.1 Part 2

Reg.21, revoked: SI 2009/209 Sch.6 para.3

2370. Summary Appeal Court (Navy) Rules 2000

applied: SI 2009/1211 Sch.2 para.7, Sch.2 para.9

Part II r.8, applied: SI 2009/1211 Sch.2 para.8

Part II r.9, applied: SI 2009/1211 Sch.2 para.8

Part II r.12, applied: SI 2009/1211 Sch.2 para.8

2371. Summary Appeal Court (Army) Rules 2000

applied: SI 2009/1211 Sch.2 para.7, Sch.2 para.9

Part II r.8, applied: SI 2009/1211 Sch.2 para.8

Part II r.9, applied: SI 2009/1211 Sch.2 para.8

Part II r.12, applied: SI 2009/1211 Sch.2 para.8

2372. Summary Appeal Court (Air Force) Rules 2000

applied: SI 2009/1211 Sch.2 para.7, Sch.2 para.9

Part II r.8, applied: SI 2009/1211 Sch.2 para.8

Part II r.9, applied: SI 2009/1211 Sch.2 para.8

Part II r.12, applied: SI 2009/1211 Sch.2 para.8

2531. Building Regulations 2000

Part VA, applied: SI 2009/3019 Art.4

Reg.2, amended: SI 2009/1219 Reg.2

Reg.6, amended: SI 2009/1219 Reg.2

Reg.8, amended: SI 2009/1219 Reg.2

Reg.9, amended: SI 2009/1219 Reg.2

Reg.12, applied: SI 2009/1219 Reg.5, Reg.6, Reg.7

Reg.13, revoked (in part): SI 2009/1219 Reg.2

Reg.14, amended: SI 2009/1219 Reg.2

Reg.15, applied: SI 2009/1219 Reg.5

Reg.17, amended: SI 2009/1219 Reg.2

Reg.17A, applied: SI 2009/3019 Art.4

Reg.17B, applied: SI 2009/3019 Art.4

Reg.17E, applied: SI 2009/3019 Art.4

Reg.17F, applied: SI 2009/3019 Art.4

Reg.17K, added: SI 2009/1219 Reg.2

Reg.17K, amended: SI 2009/2397 Reg.2

Reg.20, amended: SI 2009/1219 Reg.2

Reg.20E, added: SI 2009/1219 Reg.2

Reg.22, amended: SI 2009/1219 Reg.2

Reg.22A, revoked: SI 2009/2397 Reg.2

Reg.22A, varied: SI 2009/2397 Reg.2

Reg.22B, amended: SI 2009/1219 Reg.2

Sch.1, amended: SI 2009/1219 Sch.1

Sch.2A, amended: SI 2009/466 Reg.2, SI 2009/1219 Reg.2, SI 2009/2397 Reg.2

Sch.2B para.1, amended: SI 2009/1219 Reg.2

2532. Building (Approved Inspectors etc.) Regulations 2000

Reg.11, amended: SI 2009/1219 Reg.3

Reg.12, applied: SI 2009/3019 Art.4

Reg.12E, added: SI 2009/1219 Reg.3

Reg.31A, amended: SI 2009/1219 Reg.3

2552. Local Government Pension Scheme (Management and Investment of Funds) (Amendment) Regulations 2000

revoked: SI 2009/3093 Sch.2

2665. Investigatory Powers Tribunal Rules 2000

see *A v B (Investigatory Powers Tribunal: Jurisdiction)* [2009] EWCA Civ 24, [2009] 3 W.L.R. 717 (CA (Civ Div)), Laws, L.J.

2000–cont.

2724. Immigration (Designation of Travel Bans) Order 2000

Sch.1 Part 1, substituted: SI 2009/3044 Sch.1

Sch.1 Part 2, substituted: SI 2009/3044 Sch.1

2730. Motor Vehicles (EC Type Approval) (Amendment) (No.2) Regulations 2000

revoked: SI 2009/717 Sch.1

2792. Fixed Penalty Order 2000

Art.1A, added: SI 2009/488 Art.2

Art.2, amended: SI 2009/488 Art.3

Art.2A, added: SI 2009/488 Art.4

Sch.1, amended: SI 2009/488 Art.5, SI 2009/1487 Art.2

Sch.2 para.1, added: SI 2009/488 Art.6

Sch.2 para.2, added: SI 2009/488 Art.6

Sch.2 para.3, added: SI 2009/488 Art.6

Sch.2 para.4, added: SI 2009/488 Art.6

Sch.2 para.5, added: SI 2009/488 Art.6

Sch.2 para.6, added: SI 2009/488 Art.6

2831. Genetically Modified Organisms (Contained Use) Regulations 2000

applied: SI 2009/515 Reg.13

Reg.2, amended: SI 2009/1892 Sch.3 para.2

Reg.14, applied: SI 2009/515 Reg.13

Reg.15, applied: SI 2009/515 Reg.13

Reg.24, amended: SI 2009/693 Sch.1 para.3

2853. Local Authorities (Functions and Responsibilities) (England) Regulations 2000

Reg.4, see *R. (on the application of Domb) v Hammersmith and Fulham LBC* [2008] EWHC 3277 (Admin), [2009] B.L.G.R. 340 (QBD (Admin)), Sir Michael Harrison

Reg.5, see *R. (on the application of Domb) v Hammersmith and Fulham LBC* [2008] EWHC 3277 (Admin), [2009] B.L.G.R. 340 (QBD (Admin)), Sir Michael Harrison

Sch.4, see *R. (on the application of Domb) v Hammersmith and Fulham LBC* [2008] EWHC 3277 (Admin), [2009] B.L.G.R. 340 (QBD (Admin)), Sir Michael Harrison

2871. Road Traffic (Permitted Parking Area and Special Parking Area) (County of Bedfordshire) (Borough of Bedford) Order 2000

revoked: SI 2009/715 Art.2

3025. Local Government Pension Scheme (Pension Sharing on Divorce) Regulations 2000

Reg.4, revoked: SI 2009/3093 Sch.2

3027. School Government (Terms of Reference)(Wales) Regulations 2000

Reg.2, amended: SI 2009/2159 Reg.11

Reg.10, revoked (in part): SI 2009/2159 Reg.11

3042. Energy Crops Regulations 2000

applied: SI 2009/3264 Sch.2 para.1, SI 2009/3365 Sch.2 para.1

3184. Water Supply (Water Quality) Regulations 2000

Reg.31, applied: SI 2009/3101 Reg.5

3185. Child Support (Decisions and Appeals) (Amendment) Regulations 2000

Reg.10, amended: SI 2009/3151 Sch.1

Reg.12, revoked: SI 2009/3151 Sch.1

3186. Child Support (Transitional Provisions) Regulations 2000

Reg.28, varied: SI 2009/2909 Reg.5

3236. Non-automatic Weighing Instruments Regulations 2000

referred to: SI 2009/669 Sch.1 Part 4

2000– cont.

3242. Iraq (United Nations Sanctions) (Overseas Territories) Order 2000
Art.11, varied: SI 2009/ 888 Art.2
Sch.2, varied: SI 2009/ 888 Art.2, Art.5

3255. Social Security (Australia) Order 2000
see *Secretary of State for Work and Pensions v Burley* [2008] EWCA Civ 376, [2009] 1 W.L.R. 241 (CA (Civ Div)), Mummery, L.J.

3290. General Chiropractic Council (Professional Conduct Committee) Rules Order of Council 2000
Sch.1, added: SI 2009/ 1182 Sch.4 para.20
Sch.1, amended: SI 2009/ 1182 Sch.4 para.20

3314. Street Works (Sharing of Costs of Works) (England) Regulations 2000
applied: SI 2009/ 721 Sch.2 para.8

3371. Young Offender Institution Rules 2000
Part I r.2, amended: SI 2009/ 3082 Sch.2 para.1
Part II r.11, amended: SI 2009/ 3082 Sch.2 para.5
Part II r.16, amended: SI 2009/ 3082 Sch.2 para.6
Part II r.17, amended: SI 2009/ 3082 Sch.2 para.7
Part II r.20, amended: SI 2009/ 3082 Sch.2 para.4
Part II r.27, substituted: SI 2009/ 3082 Sch.2 para.2
Part II r.28, amended: SI 2009/ 3082 Sch.2 para.4
Part II r.37, amended: SI 2009/ 3082 Sch.2 para.3
Part II r.48, amended: SI 2009/ 3082 Sch.2 para.8
Part II r.49, amended: SI 2009/ 3082 Sch.2 para.4
Part II r.52, amended: SI 2009/ 3082 Sch.2 para.4, Sch.2 para.9
Part II r.61, amended: SI 2009/ 3082 Sch.2 para.4

2001

7. Climate Change Levy (Registration and Miscellaneous Provisions) Regulations 2001
Reg.6, amended: SI 2009/ 1890 Art.4

25. Motor Vehicles (Approval) Regulations 2001
Reg.3, amended: SI 2009/ 815 Reg.2
Reg.4, amended: SI 2009/ 815 Reg.2
Reg.5, amended: SI 2009/ 815 Reg.2
Reg.6, revoked (in part): SI 2009/ 815 Reg.2
Sch.2 para.1, amended: SI 2009/ 815 Reg.2
Sch.3, amended: SI 2009/ 815 Reg.2

55. Units of Measurement Regulations 2001
Reg.2, amended: SI 2009/ 3046 Reg.5
Reg.3, revoked: SI 2009/ 3046 Reg.5
Reg.4, revoked (in part): SI 2009/ 3046 Reg.5

85. Weights and Measures (Metrication Amendments) Regulations 2001
Reg.2, revoked: SI 2009/ 3045 Reg.4
Reg.3, revoked (in part): SI 2009/ 3045 Reg.4

155. Child Support (Maintenance Calculations and Special Cases) Regulations 2001
Reg.5, revoked (in part): SI 2009/ 396 Reg.5
Reg.11, see *W v Secretary of State for Work and Pensions* [2009] CSIH 21, 2009 S.C. 340 (IH (1 Div)), Lord President Hamilton

156. Child Support (Variations) Regulations (2000) 2001
Reg.1, amended: SI 2009/ 736 Reg.4
Reg.19, see *Secretary of State for Work and Pensions v Wincott* [2009] EWCA Civ 113, [2009] 1 F.L.R. 1222 (CA (Civ Div)), Sedley, L.J.
Reg.19, amended: SI 2009/ 736 Reg.4

157. Child Support (Maintenance Calculation Procedure) Regulations 2001
applied: SI 2009/ 1562 Art.2
Sch.1, applied: SI 2009/ 2909 Reg.5
Sch.1 para.1, substituted: SI 2009/ 2909 Reg.4

2001– cont.

157. Child Support (Maintenance Calculation Procedure) Regulations 2001– *cont.*
Sch.1 para.2, substituted: SI 2009/ 2909 Reg.4
Sch.1 para.4, amended: SI 2009/ 2909 Reg.4
Sch.1 para.5, revoked: SI 2009/ 2909 Reg.4
Sch.1 para.6, substituted: SI 2009/ 2909 Reg.4

162. Child Support (Collection and Enforcement and Miscellaneous Amendments) Regulations 2001
Reg.5, revoked (in part): SI 2009/ 3151 Sch.1

238. Detention Centre Rules 2001
see *Yarl's Wood Immigration Ltd v Bedfordshire Police Authority* [2008] EWHC 2207 (Comm), [2009] 1 All E.R. 886 (QBD (Comm)), Beatson, J.
r.9, see *R. (on the application of SK (Zimbabwe)) v Secretary of State for the Home Department* [2008] EWCA Civ 1204, [2009] 1 W.L.R. 1527 (CA (Civ Div)), Laws, L.J.

259. Company and Business Names (Amendment) Regulations 2001
revoked: SI 2009/ 2615 Reg.7

341. Representation of the People (England and Wales) Regulations 2001
Reg.13, amended: SI 2009/ 725 Reg.3
Reg.31 I, amended: SI 2009/ 725 Reg.6
Reg.31 J, amended: SI 2009/ 725 Reg.7
Reg.53, amended: SI 2009/ 1182 Sch.4 para.39
Reg.53, revoked (in part): SI 2009/ 1182 Sch.4 para.2
Reg.99, amended: SI 2009/ 725 Reg.8
Sch.4, amended: SI 2009/ 725 Reg.4
Sch.4A, added: SI 2009/ 725 Reg.5

354. Aerodromes (Designation) (Chargeable Air Services) Order 2001
revoked: SI 2009/ 189 Art.2

497. Representation of the People (Scotland) Regulations 2001
applied: SSI 2009/ 35 Reg.12
Reg.13, amended: SI 2009/ 725 Reg.10
Reg.31 I, amended: SI 2009/ 725 Reg.13
Reg.31 J, amended: SI 2009/ 725 Reg.14
Reg.50A, added: SSI 2009/ 35 Reg.3
Reg.53, amended: SI 2009/ 1182 Sch.4 para.40
Reg.53, revoked (in part): SI 2009/ 1182 Sch.4 para.3
Reg.98, amended: SI 2009/ 725 Reg.15
Sch.4, amended: SI 2009/ 725 Reg.11
Sch.4A, added: SI 2009/ 725 Reg.12

544. Financial Services and Markets Act 2000 (Regulated Activities) Order 2001
Art.3, amended: SI 2009/ 1342 Art.3
Art.4, amended: SI 2009/ 1389 Art.3
Art.7, amended: SI 2009/ 500 Art.3
Art.9AB, added: SI 2009/ 209 Sch.6 para.4
Art.9L, added: SI 2009/ 209 Sch.6 para.4
Art.16, referred to: SI 2009/ 3226 Sch.3
Art.25E, added: SI 2009/ 1342 Art.4
Art.25E, referred to: SI 2009/ 1342 Art.32
Art.26, amended: SI 2009/ 1342 Art.5
Art.27, amended: SI 2009/ 1342 Art.6
Art.28A, amended: SI 2009/ 1342 Art.7
Art.29, amended: SI 2009/ 1342 Art.8
Art.29, applied: SI 2009/ 1342 Sch.1 para.8
Art.29A, amended: SI 2009/ 1342 Art.9
Art.29A, applied: SI 2009/ 1342 Sch.1 para.9
Art.33, amended: SI 2009/ 1342 Art.10
Art.33A, amended: SI 2009/ 1342 Art.11
Art.36, amended: SI 2009/ 1342 Art.12

2001–cont.

544. Financial Services and Markets Act 2000 (Regulated Activities) Order 2001–*cont.*

Art.53, see *Financial Services Authority v Bayshore Nominees Ltd* [2009] EWHC 285 (Ch), [2009] Lloyd's Rep. F.C. 398 (Ch D), Floyd, J

Art.53D, added: SI 2009/1342 Art.13

Art.53D, referred to: SI 2009/1342 Art.32

Art.54, amended: SI 2009/1342 Art.14

Art.54A, amended: SI 2009/1342 Art.15

Art.55, amended: SI 2009/1342 Art.16

Art.63J, added: SI 2009/1342 Art.17

Art.63J, referred to: SI 2009/1342 Art.32

Art.63K, added: SI 2009/1342 Art.17

Art.63L, added: SI 2009/1342 Art.17

Art.63M, added: SI 2009/1342 Art.17

Art.63N, added: SI 2009/1389 Art.4

Art.64, amended: SI 2009/1389 Art.5

Art.64, referred to: SI 2009/1342 Art.32

Art.66, amended: SI 2009/1342 Art.18

Art.67, amended: SI 2009/1342 Art.19

Art.72, amended: SI 2009/1342 Art.20

Art.88C, added: SI 2009/1342 Art.21

Art.89, amended: SI 2009/1342 Art.22

561. Road Vehicles (Display of Registration Marks) Regulations 2001

applied: SI 2009/717 Sch.4 Part 2, Sch.5 Part 2, Sch.5 Part 4

Reg.2, amended: SI 2009/811 Reg.3

Reg.16, substituted: SI 2009/811 Reg.4

600. Special Educational Needs Tribunal Regulations 2001

Reg.32, see *Hammersmith and Fulham LBC v First-Tier Tribunal (Health, Education and Social Care Chamber)* [2009] EWHC 1694 (Admin), [2009] E.L.R. 486 (QBD (Admin)), Cranston, J.

Reg.34, see *Hammersmith and Fulham LBC v First-Tier Tribunal (Health, Education and Social Care Chamber)* [2009] EWHC 1694 (Admin), [2009] E.L.R. 486 (QBD (Admin)), Cranston, J.

Reg.36, see *H v East Sussex CC* [2009] EWCA Civ 249, [2009] E.L.R. 161 (CA (Civ Div)), Waller, L.J. (V-P)

686. Common Agricultural Policy (Wine) (England and Northern Ireland) Regulations 2001

revoked (in part): SI 2009/386 Reg.17

Reg.3, see *R. (on the application of Sovio Wines Ltd) v Food Standards Agency (Wine Standards Branch)* [2009] EWHC 382 (Admin), Times, April 9, 2009 (QBD (Admin)), Dobbs, J.

769. Social Security (Crediting and Treatment of Contributions, and National Insurance Numbers) Regulations 2001

Reg.4, amended: SI 2009/659 Reg.3

Reg.6C, added: SI 2009/659 Reg.3

855. Criminal Defence Service (Funding) Order 2001

Sch.1 para.14, see *R. v Al-Goni (Costs)* [2009] 2 Costs L.R. 356 (Sup Ct Costs Office), Costs Judge Rogers

Sch.4 para.9, see *R. v Al-Goni (Costs)* [2009] 2 Costs L.R. 356 (Sup Ct Costs Office), Costs Judge Rogers

856. Criminal Defence Service (Recovery of Defence Costs Orders) Regulations 2001

Reg.2, amended: SI 2009/2468 Art.7

Reg.4, amended: SI 2009/3352 Reg.2

2001–cont.

880. Biocidal Products Regulations 2001

applied: SI 2009/153 Sch.3 para.1, SI 2009/995 Sch.3 para.1

Reg.2, amended: SI 2009/716 Sch.6

Sch.4 para.13, amended: SI 2009/716 Sch.6

Sch.6 para.6, amended: SI 2009/716 Sch.6

Sch.7 para.4, amended: SI 2009/716 Sch.6

922. Buying Agency Trading Fund (Amendment) (Change of Name) Order 2001

revoked: SI 2009/647 Art.3

967. Companies (Disqualification Orders) Regulations 2001

revoked: SI 2009/2471 Reg.3

971. Education (Student Loans) (Repayment) (Amendment) Regulations 2001

revoked: SI 2009/470 Sch.1

995. Financial Services and Markets Act 2000 (Recognition Requirements for Investment Exchanges and Clearing Houses) Regulations 2001

Reg.3, amended: SI 2009/853 Reg.4

Sch.Part II para.10, amended: SI 2009/853 Reg.4

Sch.Part II para.12, amended: SI 2009/853 Reg.4

Sch.Part II para.12A, added: SI 2009/853 Reg.4

Sch.Part II para.14, amended: SI 2009/853 Reg.4

Sch.Part II para.15, amended: SI 2009/853 Reg.4

Sch.Part IV para.24, amended: SI 2009/853 Reg.4

Sch.Part IV para.25, amended: SI 2009/853 Reg.4

Sch.Part IV para.25A, added: SI 2009/853 Reg.4

Sch.Part IV para.27, amended: SI 2009/853 Reg.4

Sch.Part IV para.28, amended: SI 2009/853 Reg.4

1004. Social Security (Contributions) Regulations 2001

applied: SI 2009/470 Reg.45, Reg.46

Reg.1, amended: SI 2009/600 Reg.3, SI 2009/1890 Art.3

Reg.10, amended: SI 2009/591 Reg.3

Reg.11, amended: SI 2009/111 Reg.3

Reg.15, applied: SI 2009/470 Reg.47

Reg.75, amended: SI 2009/600 Reg.4

Reg.87, amended: SI 2009/600 Reg.5

Reg.87A, added: SI 2009/600 Reg.6

Reg.87B, added: SI 2009/600 Reg.6

Reg.87C, added: SI 2009/600 Reg.6

Reg.87D, added: SI 2009/600 Reg.6

Reg.87E, added: SI 2009/600 Reg.6

Reg.87F, added: SI 2009/600 Reg.6

Reg.87G, added: SI 2009/600 Reg.6

Reg.90K, amended: SI 2009/2028 Reg.3

Reg.90M, amended: SI 2009/2028 Reg.5

Reg.90M, substituted: SI 2009/2028 Reg.4

Reg.90N, amended: SI 2009/2028 Reg.6

Reg.90N, revoked (in part): SI 2009/2028 Reg.6

Reg.90O, amended: SI 2009/2028 Reg.7

Reg.90P, amended: SI 2009/2028 Reg.8

Reg.90Q, amended: SI 2009/56 Sch.2 para.75

Reg.90Q, revoked (in part): SI 2009/56 Sch.2 para.75

Reg.115, see *Oleochem (Scotland) Ltd v Revenue and Customs Commissioners* [2009] S.T.C. (S.C.D.) 205 (Sp Comm), J Gordon Reid Q.C.

Reg.117, see *Oleochem (Scotland) Ltd v Revenue and Customs Commissioners* [2009] S.T.C. (S.C.D.) 205 (Sp Comm), J Gordon Reid Q.C.

Reg.125, amended: SI 2009/696 Reg.2

Sch.3 Part V para.9, amended: SI 2009/600 Reg.7

Sch.4 Part I para.1, amended: SI 2009/600 Reg.8

Sch.4 Part II para.7, amended: SI 2009/111 Reg.4

2001—cont.

1004. Social Security (Contributions) Regulations 2001—*cont.*

Sch.4 Part II para.9, amended: SI 2009/111 Reg.4

Sch.4 Part II para.9, applied: SI 2009/470 Reg.53

Sch.4 Part IIIA para.29B, amended: SI 2009/600 Reg.8

Sch.4 Part IIIA para.29D, amended: SI 2009/600 Reg.8

Sch.4 Part IIIA para.29F, amended: SI 2009/600 Reg.8

Sch.4 Part IIIA para.29G, revoked (in part): SI 2009/56 Sch.2 para.76

Sch.4 Part IIIA para.29H, amended: SI 2009/56 Sch.2 para.76

Sch.4 Part IIIA para.29J, amended: SI 2009/56 Sch.2 para.76

Sch.4 Part III para.11, applied: SI 2009/470 Reg.54

Sch.4 Part III para.15, amended: SI 2009/600 Reg.8

Sch.4 Part III para.22, amended: SI 2009/111 Reg.4

Sch.4 Part III para.26, substituted: SI 2009/600 Reg.8

1077. Community Legal Service (Funding) (Counsel in Family Proceedings) Order 2001

Art.2, amended: SI 2009/1854 Art.3

Art.4, amended: SI 2009/2468 Art.9

Art.9, amended: SI 2009/1854 Art.4

Art.9, revoked (in part): SI 2009/1854 Art.4

Art.16, amended: SI 2009/1854 Art.5

Sch.1 para.1, amended: SI 2009/1854 Art.6

Sch.1 para.2, amended: SI 2009/1854 Art.7

Sch.1 para.3, amended: SI 2009/1854 Art.8

Sch.1 para.4, amended: SI 2009/1854 Art.9

1090. Limited Liability Partnerships Regulations 2001

applied: SI 2009/1804 Sch.2 para.4, SI 2009/2101 Sch.4 para.1

Reg.2A, added: SI 2009/1804 Sch.3 para.13

Reg.4, amended: SI 2009/1804 Sch.3 para.13

Reg.4, revoked (in part): SI 2009/1804 Sch.3 para.13, SI 2009/1941 Sch.1 para.192

Reg.5, amended: SI 2009/1941 Sch.1 para.192

Reg.6, applied: SI 2009/1804 Sch.2 para.3

Reg.10, amended: SI 2009/1804 Sch.3 para.13

Sch.2 Part I, amended: SI 2009/1804 Sch.3 para.13

Sch.5 para.9, revoked: SI 2009/1804 Sch.3 para.13, SI 2009/1941 Sch.2

Sch.5 para.10, revoked: SI 2009/1804 Sch.3 para.13, SI 2009/1941 Sch.2

Sch.5 para.11, revoked: SI 2009/1804 Sch.3 para.13, SI 2009/1941 Sch.2

Sch.6 Part I para.4, revoked: SI 2009/1804 Sch.3 para.13

Sch.6 Part I para.5, revoked: SI 2009/1804 Sch.3 para.13

Sch.6 Part III para.1, revoked: SI 2009/1804 Sch.3 para.13

1137. Climate Change Levy (Solid Fuel) Regulations 2001

revoked: SI 2009/3338 Reg.2

1167. Discretionary Financial Assistance Regulations 2001

see *R. (on the application of Gargett) v Lambeth LBC* [2008] EWCA Civ 1450, [2009] B.L.G.R. 527 (CA (Civ Div)), Mummery, L.J.

Reg.2, see *R. (on the application of Gargett) v Lambeth LBC* [2008] EWCA Civ 1450, [2009] B.L.G.R. 527 (CA (Civ Div)), Mummery, L.J.

2001—cont.

1167. Discretionary Financial Assistance Regulations 2001—*cont.*

Reg.4, see *R. (on the application of Gargett) v Lambeth LBC* [2008] EWCA Civ 1450, [2009] B.L.G.R. 527 (CA (Civ Div)), Mummery, L.J.

1177. Financial Services and Markets Act 2000 (Carrying on Regulated Activities by Way of Business) Order 2001

Art.3D, added: SI 2009/1342 Art.27

1184. European Parliamentary Elections (Franchise of Relevant Citizens of the Union) Regulations 2001

Reg.8, amended: SI 2009/726 Reg.2

Reg.9, amended: SI 2009/726 Reg.2

Sch., substituted: SI 2009/726 Sch.1

1201. Financial Services and Markets Act 2000 (Exemption) Order 2001

Sch.Part I para.15B, added: SI 2009/118 Art.2

Sch.Part IV para.47, amended: SI 2009/1342 Art.28

Sch.Part IV para.48, amended: SI 2009/1342 Art.28

Sch.Part IV para.50, amended: SI 2009/264 Art.2

1208. Weighing Equipment (Beltweighers) Regulations 2001

Reg.8, amended: SI 2009/3045 Reg.3

Reg.15, applied: SI 2009/1850 Art.7

1227. Financial Services and Markets Act 2000 (Professions) (Non-Exempt Activities) Order 2001

Art.2, amended: SI 2009/1342 Art.29

Art.6G, added: SI 2009/1342 Art.29

Art.6H, added: SI 2009/1342 Art.29

1228. Open-Ended Investment Companies Regulations 2001

Reg.1, amended: SI 2009/553 Reg.2

Reg.2, amended: SI 2009/553 Reg.2

Reg.30, applied: SI 2009/214 Sch.1, SI 2009/1801 Sch.1

Sch.4 para.4A, added: SI 2009/553 Reg.2

Sch.4 para.4B, added: SI 2009/553 Reg.2

Sch.4 para.4C, added: SI 2009/553 Reg.2

Sch.4 para.5, amended: SI 2009/553 Reg.2

Sch.4 para.6, amended: SI 2009/553 Reg.2

Sch.7 Part I para.3, revoked: SI 2009/1941 Sch.2

Sch.7 Part I para.4, revoked: SI 2009/1941 Sch.2

Sch.7 Part I para.5, revoked: SI 2009/1941 Sch.2

Sch.7 Part I para.6, revoked: SI 2009/1941 Sch.2

Sch.7 Part I para.7, revoked: SI 2009/1941 Sch.2

Sch.7 Part I para.8, revoked: SI 2009/1941 Sch.2

Sch.7 Part I para.9, revoked: SI 2009/1941 Sch.2

1232. Food Irradiation Provisions (Wales) Regulations 2001

Reg.2, revoked: SI 2009/1795 Reg.12

Reg.3, revoked: SI 2009/1795 Reg.12

Reg.4, revoked: SI 2009/1795 Reg.12

Reg.5, revoked: SI 2009/1795 Reg.12

Reg.6, revoked: SI 2009/1795 Reg.12

Reg.7, revoked: SI 2009/1795 Reg.12

Reg.8, revoked: SI 2009/1795 Reg.12

Reg.9, revoked: SI 2009/1795 Reg.12

Reg.10, revoked: SI 2009/1795 Reg.12

Reg.11, revoked: SI 2009/1795 Reg.12

Reg.12, revoked: SI 2009/1795 Reg.12

Reg.13, revoked: SI 2009/1795 Reg.12

Reg.14, revoked: SI 2009/1795 Reg.12

Reg.15, revoked: SI 2009/1795 Reg.12

Reg.16, revoked: SI 2009/1795 Reg.12

2001– cont.

1268. General Teaching Council for England (Disciplinary Functions) Regulations 2001
varied: SI 2009/3200 Reg.5
Reg.9, varied: SI 2009/12 Art.13, SI 2009/2610 Art.17

1281. Street Works (Charges for Unreasonably Prolonged Occupation of the Highway) (England) Regulations 2001
applied: SI 2009/303 Reg.4
revoked: SI 2009/303 Reg.2
Reg.4, applied: SI 2009/721 Sch.2 para.15
Reg.5, applied: SI 2009/721 Sch.2 para.15
Reg.6, applied: SI 2009/721 Sch.2 para.15
Reg.7, applied: SI 2009/721 Sch.2 para.15

1304. General Commissioners of Income Tax (Costs) Regulations 2001
revoked: SI 2009/56 Sch.2 para.187
varied: SI 2009/56 Sch.3 para.11

1323. Additional Pension and Social Security Pensions (Home Responsibilities) (Amendment) Regulations 2001
Reg.1, amended: SI 2009/2206 Reg.24
Reg.2, amended: SI 2009/2206 Reg.25
Reg.3, amended: SI 2009/2206 Reg.26
Reg.5A, added: SI 2009/2206 Reg.27

1420. Financial Services and Markets Act 2000 (Service of Notices) Regulations 2001
applied: SI 2009/209 Sch.5 para.9

1424. General Teaching Council for Wales (Disciplinary Functions) Regulations 2001
varied: SI 2009/3200 Reg.5
Reg.9, amended: 2009 c.26 s.81, SI 2009/1354 Reg.2, SI 2009/2161 Reg.3
Reg.9, varied: SI 2009/12 Art.14
Reg.18A, added: SI 2009/1354 Reg.2

1437. Criminal Defence Service (General) (No.2) Regulations 2001
applied: SI 2009/2054 Sch.2 para.15
Part IV, amended: SI 2009/2468 Art.8
Reg.2, amended: SI 2009/1853 Reg.3, SI 2009/2468 Art.8, SI 2009/2876 Reg.3
Reg.2, revoked (in part): SI 2009/1853 Reg.3
Reg.3, amended: SI 2009/2167 Reg.2, SI 2009/2777 Reg.2, SI 2009/2876 Reg.4
Reg.5, amended: SI 2009/2054 Sch.1 para.22
Reg.7, substituted: SI 2009/2876 Reg.5
Reg.8, added: SI 2009/2876 Reg.6
Reg.9, substituted: SI 2009/2876 Reg.7
Reg.10, amended: SI 2009/2468 Art.8
Reg.10A, added: SI 2009/1853 Reg.4
Reg.10A, revoked: SI 2009/1853 Reg.4
Reg.12, see *R. (on the application of Taylor) v Westminster Magistrates Court* [2009] EWHC 1498 (Admin), (2009) 173 J.P. 405 (DC), Pill, L.J.
Reg.13, amended: SI 2009/2468 Art.8
Reg.14, amended: SI 2009/1853 Reg.5, SI 2009/2468 Art.8, SI 2009/2876 Reg.8
Reg.14, revoked (in part): SI 2009/1853 Reg.5, SI 2009/2876 Reg.8
Reg.15, amended: SI 2009/2876 Reg.9
Reg.16, amended: SI 2009/1853 Reg.6
Reg.16, revoked (in part): SI 2009/1853 Reg.6
Reg.16A, substituted: SI 2009/1853 Reg.7

1449. City of Stoke-on-Trent (Electoral Changes) Order 2001
Art.3, revoked: SI 2009/2734 Art.3

1701. Noise Emission in the Environment by Equipment for use Outdoors Regulations 2001
Reg.12, amended: SI 2009/2748 Sch.1 para.21

2001– cont.

1712. Tobacco Products Regulations 2001
see *R. v Khan (Robert)* [2009] EWCA Crim 588, Times, April 23, 2009 (CA (Crim Div)), Hughes, L.J. (V-P)
Reg.13, see *R. v Khan (Robert)* [2009] EWCA Crim 588, Times, April 23, 2009 (CA (Crim Div)), Hughes, L.J. (V-P); see *R. v M* [2009] EWCA Crim 214, [2009] 2 Cr. App. R. (S.) 66 (CA (Crim Div)), Toulson, L.J.

1754. Offshore Petroleum Activities (Conservation of Habitats) Regulations 2001
applied: SI 2009/153 Sch.1 para.5

2127. Health and Safety at Work etc Act 1974 (Application outside Great Britain) Order 2001
applied: SI 2009/716 Reg.16
Art.4, revoked (in part): SI 2009/1750 Art.2
Art.8A, added: SI 2009/1750 Art.2
Art.8B, added: SI 2009/1750 Art.2
Sch.1, revoked: SI 2009/1750 Art.2

2188. Financial Services and Markets Act 2000 (Disclosure of Confidential Information) Regulations 2001
Reg.2, varied: SI 2009/209 Sch.5 para.10
Reg.5, varied: SI 2009/209 Sch.5 para.10
Reg.8, varied: SI 2009/209 Sch.5 para.10
Reg.9, varied: SI 2009/209 Sch.5 para.10
Reg.11, varied: SI 2009/209 Sch.5 para.10
Sch.1 Part 1, varied: SI 2009/209 Sch.5 para.10
Sch.2, amended: SI 2009/2877 Reg.2

2281. Local Government Investigations (Functions of Monitoring Officers and Standards Committees)(Wales) Regulations 2001
applied: SI 2009/2578 Reg.1
Reg.4, amended: SI 2009/2578 Reg.4
Reg.8, amended: SI 2009/2578 Reg.4
Reg.10, amended: SI 2009/2578 Reg.4
Reg.11, amended: SI 2009/2578 Reg.4

2288. Adjudications by Case Tribunals and Interim Case Tribunals (Wales) Regulations 2001
applied: SI 2009/2578 Reg.1
Sch.1 para.1, amended: SI 2009/2578 Reg.6
Sch.1 para.9, substituted: SI 2009/2578 Reg.6
Sch.1 para.16, amended: SI 2009/2578 Reg.6
Sch.1 para.16, revoked (in part): SI 2009/2578 Reg.6

2476. Financial Services and Markets Tribunal Rules 2001
varied: SI 2009/1810 Art.14
Part I r.2, varied: SI 2009/1810 Art.21
Part II r.4, varied: SI 2009/1810 Art.20, Art.22
Part II r.5, varied: SI 2009/1810 Art.20, Art.23
Part II r.6, varied: SI 2009/1810 Art.20, Art.24
Part II r.7, varied: SI 2009/1810 Art.20, Art.24
Part II r.8, varied: SI 2009/1810 Art.20, Art.24
Part II r.10, varied: SI 2009/1810 Art.20, Art.25
Part II r.10A, varied: SI 2009/1810 Art.26
Part II r.10B, varied: SI 2009/1810 Art.26
Part II r.11, varied: SI 2009/1810 Art.20, Art.24
Part II r.12, varied: SI 2009/1810 Art.24
Part II r.14, varied: SI 2009/1810 Art.20, Art.24
Part II r.15, varied: SI 2009/1810 Art.20, Art.24
Part III r.19, varied: SI 2009/1810 Art.20, Art.27
Part IV r.23, varied: SI 2009/1810 Art.20, Art.24
Part V r.27, varied: SI 2009/1810 Art.20
Part V r.31, varied: SI 2009/1810 Art.20

2486. Motor Vehicles (Approval) (Fees) Regulations 2001
Reg.4, amended: SI 2009/863 Reg.3, Reg.4
Reg.5, amended: SI 2009/863 Reg.3

2541. Capital Allowances (Energy-saving Plant and Machinery) Order 2001
Art.2, amended: SI 2009/1863 Art.3
Art.3, amended: SI 2009/1863 Art.4
Art.5, amended: SI 2009/1863 Art.5

2550. Welsh Language Schemes (Public Bodies) Order 2001
Sch.1, amended: SI 2009/462 Sch.5 para.8

2599. Northern Ireland Assembly (Elections) Order 2001
Appendix 1, substituted: SI 2009/256 Sch.1
Appendix 1 para.1, substituted: SI 2009/256 Sch.1
Appendix 1 para.2, substituted: SI 2009/256 Sch.1
Appendix 1 para.3, substituted: SI 2009/256 Sch.1
Appendix 1 para.4, substituted: SI 2009/256 Sch.1
Art.2, amended: SI 2009/256 Art.2
Art.3, substituted: SI 2009/256 Art.3
Art.4, amended: SI 2009/256 Art.4
Art.6, amended: SI 2009/256 Art.5
Art.6, applied: SI 2009/256 Art.1
Art.6A, added: SI 2009/256 Art.6
Art.6A, applied: SI 2009/256 Art.1
Art.6B, added: SI 2009/256 Art.6
Art.6B, applied: SI 2009/256 Art.1
Art.7, amended: SI 2009/256 Art.7
Art.7, applied: SI 2009/256 Art.1
Sch.1, substituted: SI 2009/256 Sch.1
Sch.2, substituted: SI 2009/256 Sch.2

2635. Financial Services and Markets Act 2000 (Law Applicable to Contracts of Insurance) Regulations 2001
Reg.3, amended: SI 2009/3075 Reg.2

2638. Financial Services and Markets Act 2000 (Controllers) (Exemption) Order 2001
revoked: SI 2009/774 Art.7

2709. Education (Foundation Body) (Wales) Regulations 2001
Sch.2 para.5, amended: SI 2009/2544 Reg.3

2809. Motor Vehicles (EC Type Approval) (Amendment) Regulations 2001
revoked: SI 2009/717 Sch.1

2975. Radiation (Emergency Preparedness and Public Information) Regulations 2001
Reg.14, applied: SI 2009/515 Reg.8, Sch.7

3074. Children (Leaving Care) Social Security Benefits Regulations 2001
Reg.2, amended: SI 2009/3152 Reg.3
Reg.2, revoked (in part): SI 2009/3152 Reg.3

3210. Social Security (Jobcentre Plus Interviews) Regulations 2001
referred to: SI 2009/1541 Reg.3
Reg.11, disapplied: SI 2009/1541 Reg.3
Reg.11, referred to: SI 2009/1541 Reg.3

3338. Financial Services and Markets Act 2000 (Controllers) (Exemption) (No.2) Order 2001
revoked: SI 2009/774 Art.7

3352. Railway Administration Order Rules 2001
Part 1 r.1.2, amended: SI 2009/2748 Sch.1 para.22

3365. Terrorism (United Nations Measures) Order 2001
applied: SI 2009/1747 Art.26

3366. Terrorism (United Nations Measures) (Overseas Territories) Order 2001
Art.11, varied: SI 2009/888 Art.2
Sch.2 para.1, varied: SI 2009/888 Art.2
Sch.2 para.2, varied: SI 2009/888 Art.2
Sch.2 para.3, varied: SI 2009/888 Art.2
Sch.2 para.4, varied: SI 2009/888 Art.2

3366. Terrorism (United Nations Measures) (Overseas Territories) Order 2001–*cont.*
Sch.2 para.5, varied: SI 2009/888 Art.2
Sch.2 para.6, varied: SI 2009/888 Art.2
Sch.2 para.7, varied: SI 2009/888 Art.2

3455. Education (Special Educational Needs) (England) (Consolidation) Regulations 2001
Reg.19, see *R. (on the application of M) v East Sussex CC* [2009] EWHC 1651 (Admin), Times, May 12, 2009 (QBD), Timothy Brennan Q.C.

3458. Race Relations Act 1976 (Statutory Duties) Order 2001
Sch.3, amended: SI 2009/3019 Art.13

3510. Seeds (National Lists of Varieties) Regulations 2001
Reg.2, amended: SI 2009/1273 Reg.3
Reg.5, amended: SI 2009/1273 Reg.4
Reg.6, amended: SI 2009/1273 Reg.5
Reg.7, amended: SI 2009/1273 Reg.6
Reg.12, amended: SI 2009/1273 Reg.7
Sch.2 Part I para.1A, added: SI 2009/1273 Reg.8
Sch.2 Part III, amended: SI 2009/1273 Reg.8

3539. Contracting Out of Functions (Tribunal Staff) Order 2001
revoked: SI 2009/1307 Sch.4
Art.2, amended: SI 2009/121 Art.3

3606. Goods Vehicles (Authorisation of International Journeys) (Fees) Regulations 2001
Reg.2, amended: SI 2009/855 Reg.2
Reg.3, amended: SI 2009/855 Reg.3
Reg.3, revoked (in part): SI 2009/855 Reg.3
Sch.1, amended: SI 2009/855 Reg.4

3625. Financial Services and Markets Act 2000 (Control of Business Transfers) (Requirements on Applicants) Regulations 2001
substituted: SI 2009/1390 Reg.2
Reg.1, amended: SI 2009/1390 Reg.2
Reg.3, see *Names at Lloyds, Re* [2008] EWHC 2960 (Ch), [2009] Bus. L.R. 509 (Ch D), Floyd, J
Reg.5, amended: SI 2009/1390 Reg.2
Reg.6, amended: SI 2009/1390 Reg.2

3629. Financial Services and Markets Act 2000 (Consequential Amendments) (Taxes) Order 2001
Art.16, revoked (in part): 2009 c.4 Sch.3 Part 1

3635. Insurers (Winding Up) Rules 2001
see *Whiteley Insurance Consultants (A Firm), Re* [2008] EWHC 1782 (Ch), [2009] Bus. L.R. 418 (Ch D (Companies Ct)), David Richards, J.
r.6, see *Whiteley Insurance Consultants (A Firm), Re* [2008] EWHC 1782 (Ch), [2009] Bus. L.R. 418 (Ch D (Companies Ct)), David Richards, J.

3649. Financial Services and Markets Act 2000 (Consequential Amendments and Repeals) Order 2001
Art.574, revoked: SI 2009/3093 Sch.2
Art.575, revoked: SI 2009/3093 Sch.2
Art.576, revoked: SI 2009/3093 Sch.2
Art.577, revoked: SI 2009/3093 Sch.2
Art.578, revoked: SI 2009/3093 Sch.2

3662. Bolton Primary Care Trust (Establishment) Order 2001
Art.1, amended: SI 2009/2874 Art.2
Art.2, amended: SI 2009/2874 Art.2

3698. Contracting Out (Administrative and Other Court Staff) Order 2001
Art.3, revoked: SI 2009/56 Sch.2 para.77

2001–cont.

3755. Uncertificated Securities Regulations 2001
see *Kaupthing Singer and Friedlander Ltd (In Administration), Re* [2009] EWHC 740 (Ch), [2009] 2 Lloyd's Rep. 154 (Ch D), Sir Andrew Morritt (Chancellor)
Reg.3, amended: SI 2009/1889 Art.2
Reg.16, amended: SI 2009/1889 Art.2
Reg.18, amended: SI 2009/1889 Art.2
Reg.20, amended: SI 2009/1889 Art.2
Reg.21, amended: SI 2009/1889 Art.2
Reg.22, amended: SI 2009/1889 Art.2
Reg.23, amended: SI 2009/1889 Art.2
Reg.24, amended: SI 2009/1889 Art.2
Reg.26, amended: SI 2009/1889 Art.2
Reg.27, amended: SI 2009/1889 Art.2
Reg.28, amended: SI 2009/1889 Art.2
Reg.32, amended: SI 2009/1889 Art.2
Reg.33, amended: SI 2009/1889 Art.2
Reg.38, amended: SI 2009/1889 Art.2
Reg.40, amended: SI 2009/1889 Art.2
Reg.41, amended: SI 2009/1889 Art.2
Reg.42, amended: SI 2009/1889 Art.2
Reg.49, revoked (in part): SI 2009/1889 Art.2
Sch.4 para.2, amended: SI 2009/1889 Art.2
Sch.4 para.3, amended: SI 2009/1889 Art.2
Sch.4 para.4, amended: SI 2009/1889 Art.2
Sch.4 para.5, amended: SI 2009/1889 Art.2
Sch.4 para.6, amended: SI 2009/1889 Art.2
Sch.4 para.6, revoked (in part): SI 2009/1889 Art.2
Sch.4 para.7, amended: SI 2009/1889 Art.2
Sch.4 para.8, amended: SI 2009/1889 Art.2
Sch.4 para.9, amended: SI 2009/1889 Art.2
Sch.4 para.10, amended: SI 2009/1889 Art.2
Sch.4 para.11, amended: SI 2009/1889 Art.2
Sch.4 para.14, amended: SI 2009/1889 Art.2
Sch.4 para.15, amended: SI 2009/1889 Art.2
Sch.4 para.16, amended: SI 2009/1889 Art.2
Sch.4 para.16, revoked (in part): SI 2009/1889 Art.2
Sch.4 para.18, amended: SI 2009/1889 Art.2
Sch.4 para.19, amended: SI 2009/1889 Art.2
Sch.4 para.20, amended: SI 2009/1889 Art.2
Sch.4 para.21, amended: SI 2009/1889 Art.2
Sch.5, revoked: SI 2009/1889 Art.2

3911. Water Supply (Water Quality) Regulations 2001
amended: SI 2009/1824 Sch.1 para.4
Reg.2, amended: SI 2009/1824 Sch.1 para.4

3929. Civil Jurisdiction and Judgments Order 2001
Sch.1 para.4, amended: SI 2009/871 Art.10
Sch.1 para.12, see *Gomez v Gomez-Monche Vives* [2008] EWCA Civ 1065, [2009] Ch. 245 (CA (Civ Div)), Jacob, L.J.
Sch.3 para.24, revoked: 2009 c.24 Sch.7 Part 1

3965. Care Homes Regulations 2001
Reg.2, amended: SI 2009/462 Sch.2 para.5, SI 2009/1182 Sch.4 para.4
Reg.19, amended: SI 2009/1895 Reg.9
Reg.19, revoked (in part): SI 2009/1895 Reg.9
Sch.2 para.7, substituted: SI 2009/1895 Reg.9

3967. Children's Homes Regulations 2001
Sch.2, substituted: SI 2009/1895 Reg.4

3968. Private and Voluntary Health Care (England) Regulations 2001
Reg.2, amended: SI 2009/462 Sch.2 para.5, SI 2009/1182 Sch.4 para.5
Reg.3, amended: SI 2009/1892 Sch.3 para.3
Sch.2, substituted: SI 2009/1895 Reg.12
Sch.3 Part II, amended: SI 2009/1892 Sch.3 para.3

2001–cont.

3969. National Care Standards Commission (Registration) Regulations 2001
Sch.2 para.4, substituted: SI 2009/1895 Reg.13
Sch.2 para.10, amended: SI 2009/1895 Reg.13
Sch.3 Part II para.12, revoked: SI 2009/1895 Reg.13
Sch.3 Part II para.13, substituted: SI 2009/1895 Reg.13

3981. Goods Vehicles (Enforcement Powers) Regulations 2001
applied: SI 2009/1885 Art.2, Sch.4 para.1
Reg.4, substituted: SI 2009/1965 Reg.3
Reg.5, amended: SI 2009/1965 Reg.4
Reg.6, amended: SI 2009/1965 Reg.5
Reg.7, revoked: SI 2009/1965 Reg.6
Reg.9, amended: SI 2009/1965 Reg.7
Reg.10, amended: SI 2009/1965 Reg.8
Reg.10, revoked (in part): SI 2009/1965 Reg.8
Reg.11, amended: SI 2009/1965 Reg.9
Reg.12, amended: SI 2009/1965 Reg.10
Reg.13, amended: SI 2009/1885 Sch.2 para.8
Reg.13, revoked (in part): SI 2009/1885 Sch.2 para.8
Reg.14, amended: SI 2009/1885 Sch.2 para.9, SI 2009/1965 Reg.11
Reg.15, amended: SI 2009/1885 Sch.2 para.10, SI 2009/1965 Reg.12
Reg.18, amended: SI 2009/1965 Reg.13
Reg.18, revoked (in part): SI 2009/1965 Reg.13
Reg.23, added: SI 2009/1965 Reg.14

3997. Misuse of Drugs (Designation) Order 2001
Sch.1 Part I para.1, amended: SI 2009/3135 Art.2
Sch.1 Part II para.3, added: SI 2009/3135 Art.3

3998. Misuse of Drugs Regulations 2001
applied: SSI 2009/183 Sch.1 para.4
referred to: SI 2009/2297 Sch.3 para.6
Reg.4B, added: SI 2009/3136 Reg.3
Sch.1 para.1, amended: SI 2009/3136 Reg.4
Sch.2 para.1, amended: SI 2009/3136 Reg.4
Sch.4, disapplied: SSI 2009/183 Sch.1 para.4
Sch.4, referred to: SSI 2009/183 Sch.1 para.4
Sch.4 Part I para.1, amended: SI 2009/3136 Reg.4
Sch.4 Part II para.1, amended: SI 2009/3136 Reg.4
Sch.4 Part II para.4, amended: SI 2009/3136 Reg.4
Sch.5, disapplied: SSI 2009/183 Sch.1 para.4
Sch.5, referred to: SSI 2009/183 Sch.1 para.4

3999. Tonnage Tax (Training Requirement) (Amendment) Regulations 2001
revoked: SI 2009/2304 Sch.1

4023. Social Security Contributions (Decisions and Appeals) (Amendment) Regulations 2001
revoked: SI 2009/56 Sch.2 para.187

4024. Referrals to the Special Commissioners Regulations 2001
revoked: SI 2009/56 Sch.2 para.187

4061. Local Authorities (Contracting Out of Highway Functions) (England) Order 2001
revoked: SI 2009/721 Art.4

2002

57. Fostering Services Regulations 2002
Reg.24, amended: SI 2009/394 Reg.2
Reg.26, amended: SI 2009/394 Reg.3
Reg.27, applied: SI 2009/395 Reg.4
Reg.28, applied: SI 2009/395 Reg.4
Reg.28, substituted: SI 2009/394 Reg.4
Reg.29, applied: SI 2009/395 Reg.4
Reg.29, substituted: SI 2009/394 Reg.4
Reg.29A, added: SI 2009/394 Reg.5

2002– cont.

57. Fostering Services Regulations 2002–*cont.*
Reg.29A, applied: SI 2009/ 395 Reg.13
Sch.1 para.2, substituted: SI 2009/ 1895 Reg.5
Sch.3 para.13, substituted: SI 2009/ 1895 Reg.5

112. Al-Qa'ida and Taliban (United Nations Measures) (Overseas Territories) Order 2002
Art.19, varied: SI 2009/ 888 Art.2
Sch.2 para.1, varied: SI 2009/ 888 Art.2
Sch.2 para.2, varied: SI 2009/ 888 Art.2
Sch.2 para.3, varied: SI 2009/ 888 Art.2
Sch.2 para.4, varied: SI 2009/ 888 Art.2
Sch.2 para.5, varied: SI 2009/ 888 Art.2
Sch.2 para.6, varied: SI 2009/ 888 Art.2
Sch.2 para.7, varied: SI 2009/ 888 Art.2
Sch.2 para.8, varied: SI 2009/ 888 Art.2
Sch.2 para.9, varied: SI 2009/ 888 Art.2

233. Police Act 1997 (Criminal Records) Regulations 2002
Reg.2, amended: SI 2009/ 1882 Reg.2
Reg.4, amended: SI 2009/ 2428 Reg.2
Reg.5A, amended: SI 2009/ 1882 Reg.3
Reg.5A, applied: SI 2009/ 1882 Reg.5, Reg.6, SI 2009/ 3297 Reg.6
Reg.5A, revoked (in part): SI 2009/ 1882 Reg.3
Reg.5B, revoked: SI 2009/ 1882 Reg.4
Reg.5C, revoked: SI 2009/ 1882 Reg.4
Reg.6, revoked: SI 2009/ 1882 Reg.4
Reg.7, revoked: SI 2009/ 1882 Reg.4
Reg.8, revoked: SI 2009/ 1882 Reg.4
Reg.8A, revoked: SI 2009/ 1882 Reg.4
Reg.10, amended: SI 2009/ 460 Reg.3
Reg.11, amended: SI 2009/ 460 Reg.3

253. Nursing and Midwifery Order (2001) 2002
applied: SI 2009/ 2722 Reg.3
Art.3, applied: SI 2009/ 2894 Sch.1
Art.3, enabled: SI 2009/ 2894
Art.5, amended: SI 2009/ 1182 Sch.4 para.38
Art.5, applied: SI 2009/ 783 Reg.5
Art.6A, amended: SI 2009/ 1182 Sch.4 para.38
Art.21, amended: SI 2009/ 1182 Sch.4 para.38
Art.25, amended: SI 2009/ 1182 Sch.4 para.38
Art.27, revoked (in part): SI 2009/ 1182 Sch.4 para.38
Art.37, amended: SI 2009/ 1182 Sch.4 para.38
Art.47, applied: SI 2009/ 2894, SI 2009/ 2894 Sch.1
Art.48, applied: SI 2009/ 2894
Sch.1 Part I para.1B, amended: SI 2009/ 1182 Sch.4 para.38
Sch.1 Part II para.17, amended: SI 2009/ 1182 Sch.4 para.38
Sch.1 Part II para.17, applied: SI 2009/ 2894 Sch.1
Sch.1 Part II para.17, enabled: SI 2009/ 2894
Sch.1 Part II para.18, revoked (in part): SI 2009/ 1182 Sch.4 para.38

254. Health Professions Order 2001. 2002
applied: SI 2009/ 2722 Reg.3
referred to: SI 2009/ 1182 Art.8
Art.3, amended: SI 2009/ 1182 Sch.2 para.1
Art.3, applied: SI 2009/ 1182 Art.8
Art.3, enabled: SI 2009/ 1345
Art.3, revoked (in part): SI 2009/ 1182 Sch.2 para.1
Art.5, amended: SI 2009/ 1182 Sch.2 para.2
Art.7, applied: SI 2009/ 272, SI 2009/ 1355
Art.7, enabled: SI 2009/ 272, SI 2009/ 1355
Art.9, enabled: SI 2009/ 272, SI 2009/ 1355
Art.9, referred to: SI 2009/ 1182 Art.4
Art.13, amended: SI 2009/ 1182 Sch.2 para.3
Art.13, referred to: SI 2009/ 1182 Art.4

2002– cont.

254. Health Professions Order 2001. 2002–*cont.*
Art.21, amended: SI 2009/ 1182 Sch.2 para.4
Art.22, amended: 2009 c.26 s.81, SI 2009/ 1182 Sch.2 para.5
Art.25, amended: SI 2009/ 1182 Sch.2 para.6
Art.25, revoked (in part): SI 2009/ 1182 Sch.2 para.6
Art.26, enabled: SI 2009/ 1355
Art.27, revoked (in part): SI 2009/ 1182 Sch.2 para.7
Art.31, applied: SI 2009/ 1355 Sch.1
Art.32, amended: SI 2009/ 1182 Sch.2 para.8
Art.32, enabled: SI 2009/ 1355
Art.33, enabled: SI 2009/ 272
Art.37, amended: SI 2009/ 1182 Sch.2 para.9
Art.37, enabled: SI 2009/ 1355
Art.39, amended: SI 2009/ 1182 Sch.2 para.10
Art.39, referred to: SI 2009/ 1182 Art.4
Art.41, amended: SI 2009/ 1182 Sch.2 para.11
Art.41, applied: SI 2009/ 272, SI 2009/ 1355
Art.41, enabled: SI 2009/ 272
Art.42, amended: SI 2009/ 1182 Sch.2 para.12
Art.42, applied: SI 2009/ 272, SI 2009/ 1355
Art.44, substituted: SI 2009/ 1182 Sch.2 para.13
Art.46, amended: SI 2009/ 1182 Sch.2 para.14
Sch.1 Part I para.1, amended: SI 2009/ 1182 Sch.2 para.17, Sch.2 para.18
Sch.1 Part I para.1, substituted: SI 2009/ 1182 Sch.2 para.15
Sch.1 Part I para.1A, applied: SI 2009/ 1345 Art.6
Sch.1 Part I para.1B, enabled: SI 2009/ 1345
Sch.1 Part I para.2, amended: SI 2009/ 1182 Sch.2 para.17, Sch.2 para.18
Sch.1 Part I para.2, substituted: SI 2009/ 1182 Sch.2 para.15
Sch.1 Part I para.3, amended: SI 2009/ 1182 Sch.2 para.18
Sch.1 Part I para.3, substituted: SI 2009/ 1182 Sch.2 para.15
Sch.1 Part I para.4, substituted: SI 2009/ 1182 Sch.2 para.15
Sch.1 Part I para.5, substituted: SI 2009/ 1182 Sch.2 para.15
Sch.1 Part I para.6, substituted: SI 2009/ 1182 Sch.2 para.15
Sch.1 Part I para.7, substituted: SI 2009/ 1182 Sch.2 para.15
Sch.1 Part I para.8, substituted: SI 2009/ 1182 Sch.2 para.15
Sch.1 Part I para.9, amended: SI 2009/ 1182 Sch.2 para.17, Sch.2 para.18
Sch.1 Part I para.9, substituted: SI 2009/ 1182 Sch.2 para.15
Sch.1 Part I para.10, substituted: SI 2009/ 1182 Sch.2 para.15
Sch.1 Part I para.11, substituted: SI 2009/ 1182 Sch.2 para.15
Sch.1 Part I para.12, substituted: SI 2009/ 1182 Sch.2 para.15
Sch.1 Part I para.13, substituted: SI 2009/ 1182 Sch.2 para.15
Sch.1 Part I para.14, revoked (in part): SI 2009/ 1182 Sch.2 para.15
Sch.1 Part I para.15, amended: SI 2009/ 1182 Sch.2 para.15
Sch.1 Part I para.16, revoked (in part): SI 2009/ 1182 Sch.2 para.15
Sch.1 Part II para.17, amended: SI 2009/ 1182 Sch.2 para.15
Sch.1 Part II para.18, enabled: SI 2009/ 1355

2002–cont.

254. Health Professions Order 2001. 2002–*cont.*
Sch.1 Part II para.18, substituted: SI 2009/1182 Sch.2 para.15
Sch.1 Part II para.19, amended: SI 2009/1182 Sch.2 para.15
Sch.1 Part II para.19, revoked (in part): SI 2009/1182 Sch.2 para.15
Sch.2 para.6, revoked: SI 2009/1182 Sch.2 para.17
Sch.3 para.1, amended: SI 2009/1182 Sch.2 para.16

263. Carriage by Air Acts (Implementation of the Montreal Convention 1999) Order 2002
see *Cowden v British Airways Plc* [2009] 2 Lloyd's Rep. 653 (CC (Stoke on Trent)), Judge Orrell Q.C.

282. Health and Safety at Work etc Act 1974 (Application to Environmentally Hazardous Substances) Regulations 2002
Reg.2, amended: SI 2009/318 Reg.2

284. Diseases of Fish (Control) (Amendment) (England and Wales) Regulations 2002
revoked: SI 2009/463 Sch.2 para.14

324. Care Homes (Wales) Regulations 2002
Reg.2, amended: SI 2009/1182 Sch.4 para.6
Reg.3, amended: SI 2009/1824 Sch.1 para.5
Reg.7, amended: SI 2009/2541 Reg.11
Reg.9, amended: SI 2009/2541 Reg.11
Reg.19, amended: SI 2009/2541 Reg.11
Reg.19, revoked (in part): SI 2009/2541 Reg.11
Reg.43, amended: SI 2009/2541 Reg.11
Sch.2 para.2, substituted: SI 2009/2541 Reg.11
Sch.2 para.7, revoked: SI 2009/2541 Reg.11
Sch.2 para.8, revoked: SI 2009/2541 Reg.11

325. Private and Voluntary Health Care (Wales) Regulations 2002
Reg.2, amended: SI 2009/1182 Sch.4 para.7
Reg.3, amended: SI 2009/1892 Sch.3 para.4
Reg.9, amended: SI 2009/2541 Reg.14
Reg.11, amended: SI 2009/2541 Reg.14
Reg.18, amended: SI 2009/2541 Reg.14
Reg.24, amended: SI 2009/3258 Reg.2
Sch.2 para.2, substituted: SI 2009/2541 Reg.14
Sch.2 para.8, revoked: SI 2009/2541 Reg.14
Sch.2 para.9, revoked: SI 2009/2541 Reg.14
Sch.3 Part II para.2, amended: SI 2009/1892 Sch.3 para.4

327. Children's Homes (Wales) Regulations 2002
Reg.6, amended: SI 2009/2541 Reg.6
Reg.6, revoked (in part): SI 2009/2541 Reg.6
Reg.8, amended: SI 2009/2541 Reg.6
Reg.8, revoked (in part): SI 2009/2541 Reg.6
Reg.26, amended: SI 2009/2541 Reg.6
Sch.2 para.2, substituted: SI 2009/2541 Reg.6
Sch.2 para.7, revoked: SI 2009/2541 Reg.6
Sch.2 para.8, revoked: SI 2009/2541 Reg.6

339. Relevant Authorities (Standards Committee) (Dispensations) Regulations 2002
revoked: SI 2009/1255 Reg.19

446. Police Act 1997 (Enhanced Criminal Record Certificates) (Protection of Vulnerable Adults) Regulations 2002
revoked: SI 2009/1882 Reg.7

502. Companies (Competent Authority) (Fees) Regulations 2002
revoked: SI 2009/2101 Sch.5

503. Limited Liability Partnerships (Competent Authority) (Fees) Regulations 2002
revoked: SI 2009/2101 Sch.5

2002–cont.

528. Environmental Protection (Controls on Ozone-Depleting Substances) Regulations 2002
Reg.15, applied: SI 2009/665 Art.2

614. London Service Permits (Appeals) Regulations 2002
revoked: SI 2009/1885 Sch.3

618. Medical Devices Regulations 2002
applied: SI 2009/716 Reg.3
referred to: SI 2009/669 Sch.2 Part 2
see *Hyaltech Ltd, Petitioners* 2009 S.L.T. 92 (IH (Ex Div)), Lady Paton
Reg.2, see *Hyaltech Ltd, Petitioners* 2009 S.L.T. 92 (IH (Ex Div)), Lady Paton
Reg.54, amended: SI 2009/383 Reg.3
Reg.55, amended: SI 2009/383 Reg.3
Reg.56, amended: SI 2009/383 Reg.3

770. Lands Tribunal (Fees) (Amendment) Rules 2002
revoked: SI 2009/1307 Sch.4

794. Ministry of Agriculture, Fisheries and Food (Dissolution) Order 2002
Art.2, applied: SI 2009/2825
Art.2, referred to: SI 2009/28
Art.6, applied: SI 2009/2825
Art.6, referred to: SI 2009/28
Sch.1 para.21, revoked (in part): SI 2009/463 Sch.2 para.15, SSI 2009/85 Sch.2 para.16

796. Criminal Injuries Compensation (Northern Ireland) Order 2002
Art.7, amended: 2009 c.3 Sch.4 para.39
Art.7, revoked (in part): 2009 c.3 Sch.4 para.39
Art.13, amended: 2009 c.3 Sch.4 para.40

812. Child Minding and Day Care (Wales) Regulations 2002
Reg.2, amended: SI 2009/3265 Reg.2
Reg.4, amended: SI 2009/2541 Reg.2, SI 2009/3265 Reg.2
Reg.4, revoked (in part): SI 2009/2541 Reg.2
Reg.4B, amended: SI 2009/2541 Reg.2
Reg.4B, revoked (in part): SI 2009/2541 Reg.2
Reg.16, amended: SI 2009/2541 Reg.2
Sch.2 para.2, substituted: SI 2009/2541 Reg.2
Sch.2 para.7, revoked: SI 2009/2541 Reg.2
Sch.2 para.8, revoked: SI 2009/2541 Reg.2
Sch.3 para.14, added: SI 2009/3265 Reg.2

826. Zimbabwe (Freezing of Funds, other Financial Assets or Economic Resources) Regulations 2002
revoked: SI 2009/847 Reg.17

913. Limited Liability Partnerships (No.2) Regulations 2002
revoked: SI 2009/1804 Sch.3 para.17

915. Limited Liability Partnerships (Particulars of Usual Residential Address) (Confidentiality Orders) Regulations 2002
applied: SI 2009/1804 Sch.1 para.11, Sch.1 para.14
referred to: SI 2009/1804 Sch.1 para.12
revoked: SI 2009/1804 Sch.3 para.17

919. Registration of Social Care and Independent Health Care (Wales) Regulations 2002
Reg.2, amended: SI 2009/3265 Reg.3
Reg.17, amended: SI 2009/3265 Reg.3
Reg.17, revoked (in part): SI 2009/3265 Reg.3
Sch.1 Part I para.3, amended: SI 2009/1824 Sch.1 para.6
Sch.2 para.4, substituted: SI 2009/2541 Reg.16
Sch.2 para.8, amended: SI 2009/1824 Sch.1 para.6
Sch.2 para.9A, substituted: SI 2009/2541 Reg.16
Sch.2 para.10, amended: SI 2009/2541 Reg.16

2002– cont.

919. Registration of Social Care and Independent Health Care (Wales) Regulations 2002– *cont.*
Sch.3 Part II para.12, revoked: SI 2009/2541 Reg.16
Sch.3 Part II para.13, substituted: SI 2009/2541 Reg.16
Sch.3 Part II para.13A, substituted: SI 2009/2541 Reg.16
Sch.7 Part I para.2, amended: SI 2009/3265 Reg.3
Sch.8 para.4, substituted: SI 2009/2541 Reg.16
Sch.8 para.5, amended: SI 2009/3265 Reg.3
Sch.8 para.9, revoked: SI 2009/2541 Reg.16
Sch.8 para.10, amended: SI 2009/2541 Reg.16

931. Food (Jelly Confectionery) (Emergency Control) (England) Regulations 2002
revoked: SI 2009/3230 Reg.6

1016. Travel Concessions (Eligible Services) Order 2002
Art.3, amended: SI 2009/575 Art.2
Art.4, added: SI 2009/575 Art.2

1077. Overseas Territories (Zimbabwe) (Restrictive Measures) Order 2002
Art.19, varied: SI 2009/888 Art.2
Sch.2 para.1, amended: SI 2009/888 Art.5
Sch.2 para.1, varied: SI 2009/888 Art.2
Sch.2 para.2, varied: SI 2009/888 Art.2
Sch.2 para.3, varied: SI 2009/888 Art.2
Sch.2 para.4, varied: SI 2009/888 Art.2
Sch.2 para.5, varied: SI 2009/888 Art.2
Sch.2 para.6, varied: SI 2009/888 Art.2
Sch.2 para.7, varied: SI 2009/888 Art.2
Sch.2 para.8, varied: SI 2009/888 Art.2
Sch.2 para.9, varied: SI 2009/888 Art.2

1090. Food (Jelly Confectionery) (Emergency Control) (Wales) Regulations 2002
revoked: SI 2009/3379 Reg.6

1144. Personal Protective Equipment Regulations 2002
referred to: SI 2009/669 Sch.1 Part 4, Sch.2 Part 2

1341. Mid Yorkshire Hospitals National Health Service Trust (Establishment) and the Pinderfields and Pontefract Hospitals National Health Service Trust and the Dewsbury Health Care National Health Service Trust (Dissolution) Order 2002
Art.1, amended: SI 2009/1577 Art.2
Art.3, amended: SI 2009/1577 Art.3

1394. School Teacher Appraisal (Wales) Regulations 2002
referred to: SI 2009/2159 Reg.2
Reg.3, amended: SI 2009/2159 Reg.4, SI 2009/2864 Reg.2
Reg.4, amended: SI 2009/2159 Reg.5, SI 2009/2864 Reg.2
Reg.15, amended: SI 2009/2159 Reg.6
Reg.22, amended: SI 2009/2159 Reg.7, SI 2009/2864 Reg.2
Reg.29, amended: SI 2009/2159 Reg.8
Reg.34, added: SI 2009/2159 Reg.9
Reg.35, added: SI 2009/2159 Reg.9
Reg.36, added: SI 2009/2159 Reg.9
Reg.37, added: SI 2009/2159 Reg.9
Reg.38, added: SI 2009/2159 Reg.9
Reg.38, added: SI 2009/2864 Reg.2
Reg.39, added: SI 2009/2159 Reg.9
Reg.40, added: SI 2009/2159 Reg.9
Reg.41, added: SI 2009/2159 Reg.9
Reg.42, added: SI 2009/2159 Reg.9
Reg.43, added: SI 2009/2159 Reg.9
Reg.43, amended: SI 2009/2864 Reg.2

2002– cont.

1394. School Teacher Appraisal (Wales) Regulations 2002– *cont.*
Reg.44, added: SI 2009/2159 Reg.9
Reg.45, added: SI 2009/2159 Reg.9

1397. Secretaries of State for Education and Skills and for Work and Pensions Order 2002
Sch.1 Part I para.7, revoked: 2009 c.24 Sch.7 Part 1

1457. Regulatory Reform (Carer's Allowance) Order 2002
referred to: 2009 c.24 s.58
Sch.1 para.2, revoked (in part): 2009 c.24 Sch.7 Part 2

1689. Chemicals (Hazard Information and Packaging for Supply) Regulations 2002
referred to: SI 2009/669 Sch.1 Part 4
revoked: SI 2009/716 Sch.7

1703. Social Security (Jobcentre Plus Interviews) Regulations 2002
Reg.2, amended: SI 2009/3152 Reg.3
Reg.16, amended: SI 2009/1541 Reg.3
Reg.16, applied: SI 2009/1541 Reg.3

1792. State Pension Credit Regulations 2002
referred to: SI 2009/497 Art.26
see *Patmalniece v Secretary of State for Work and Pensions* [2009] EWCA Civ 621, [2009] 4 All E.R. 738 (CA (Civ Div)), Lord Clarke
Reg.1, amended: SI 2009/2655 Reg.5, SI 2009/3229 Reg.3
Reg.1A, added: SI 2009/471 Reg.8
Reg.2, amended: SI 2009/362 Reg.4
Reg.2, see *Patmalniece v Secretary of State for Work and Pensions* [2009] EWCA Civ 621, [2009] 4 All E.R. 738 (CA (Civ Div)), Lord Clarke
Reg.6, amended: SI 2009/497 Art.26
Reg.6, referred to: SI 2009/497 Sch.17
Reg.7, amended: SI 2009/497 Art.26
Reg.7, referred to: SI 2009/497 Art.26, Sch.17
Reg.13A, amended: SI 2009/3229 Reg.3
Reg.13A, revoked (in part): SI 2009/3229 Reg.3
Reg.13B, amended: SI 2009/3229 Reg.3
Reg.15, amended: SI 2009/583 Reg.5, SI 2009/1676 Reg.3
Reg.15, revoked (in part): SI 2009/1676 Reg.3
Reg.17, amended: SI 2009/583 Reg.5
Reg.17A, amended: SI 2009/2655 Reg.5
Reg.18, amended: SI 2009/2655 Reg.5
Sch.2 para.4, amended: SI 2009/583 Reg.5
Sch.2 para.6, referred to: SI 2009/497 Sch.17
Sch.2 para.7, referred to: SI 2009/497 Sch.17
Sch.2 para.8, referred to: SI 2009/497 Sch.17
Sch.2 para.9, referred to: SI 2009/497 Sch.17
Sch.2 para.14, amended: SI 2009/497 Art.26
Sch.2 para.14, referred to: SI 2009/497 Art.26
Sch.3 para.1, amended: SI 2009/497 Art.26
Sch.3 para.2, referred to: SI 2009/497 Sch.17
Sch.4 para.1, amended: SI 2009/2655 Reg.5
Sch.5 Part I para.4, amended: SI 2009/1488 Reg.23
Sch.5 Part I para.15, amended: SI 2009/583 Reg.5
Sch.5 Part I para.23B, added: SI 2009/583 Reg.5

1817. Food for Particular Nutritional Uses (Addition of Substances for Specific Nutritional Purposes) (England) Regulations 2002
revoked: SI 2009/3051 Reg.6

1834. Companies (Disqualification Orders) (Amendment No 2) Regulations 2002
revoked: SI 2009/2471 Reg.3

1835. Motor Vehicles (EC Type Approval) (Amendment) Regulations 2002
revoked: SI 2009/717 Sch.1

2002–cont.

1837. Penalties for Disorderly Behaviour (Amount of Penalty) Order 2002
Sch.1 Part I, substituted: SI 2009/83 Sch.1
Sch.1 Part II, substituted: SI 2009/83 Sch.1

1852. Local Government Pensions Scheme (Management and Investment of Funds) (Amendment) Regulations 2002
revoked: SI 2009/3093 Sch.2

1922. Food (Control of Irradiation) (Amendment) (England) Regulations 2002
revoked: SI 2009/1584 Reg.12

1983. Education (Middle School) (England) Regulations 2002
Reg.2, amended: SI 2009/1556 Reg.3
Reg.5, amended: SI 2009/1556 Reg.3
Reg.6, amended: SI 2009/1556 Reg.3
Reg.7, amended: SI 2009/1556 Reg.3
Reg.7, revoked (in part): SI 2009/1556 Reg.3

2005. Working Tax Credit (Entitlement and Maximum Rate) Regulations 2002
Reg.4, amended: SI 2009/697 Reg.3
Reg.5, amended: SI 2009/1829 Reg.3
Reg.5A, amended: SI 2009/1829 Reg.4
Reg.6, amended: SI 2009/1829 Reg.5
Reg.7, amended: SI 2009/1829 Reg.6
Reg.7A, amended: SI 2009/1829 Reg.7
Reg.7B, amended: SI 2009/1829 Reg.7
Reg.7C, amended: SI 2009/1829 Reg.7
Reg.7D, applied: SI 2009/830 Art.2, SI 2009/1673 Art.2, SSI 2009/178 Reg.3, Reg.4
Reg.7D, substituted: SI 2009/1829 Reg.8
Reg.8, amended: SI 2009/1829 Reg.9
Reg.11, amended: SI 2009/697 Reg.4, SI 2009/2887 Reg.3
Reg.14, amended: SI 2009/697 Reg.5, SI 2009/2887 Reg.4
Reg.14, revoked (in part): SI 2009/697 Reg.5
Sch.2, amended: SI 2009/800 Sch.1

2006. Tax Credits (Definition and Calculation of Income) Regulations 2002
Reg.4, amended: SI 2009/2887 Reg.6
Reg.7, amended: SI 2009/697 Reg.7
Reg.19, amended: SI 2009/697 Reg.8, SI 2009/2887 Reg.7

2007. Child Tax Credit Regulations 2002
Reg.3, amended: SI 2009/697 Reg.10
Reg.7, amended: SI 2009/800 Reg.2

2008. Tax Credits (Income Thresholds and Determination of Rates) Regulations 2002
Reg.3, amended: SI 2009/800 Reg.4
Reg.8, amended: SI 2009/800 Reg.4

2014. Tax Credits (Claims and Notifications) Regulations 2002
Reg.2, amended: SI 2009/697 Reg.12
Reg.4, amended: SI 2009/697 Reg.13
Reg.5, amended: SI 2009/697 Reg.14
Reg.7, amended: SI 2009/2887 Reg.8
Reg.8, amended: SI 2009/2887 Reg.8
Reg.8, substituted: SI 2009/697 Reg.15
Reg.11, amended: SI 2009/697 Reg.16
Reg.18, applied: SI 2009/2997 Reg.13
Reg.25, amended: SI 2009/697 Reg.17
Reg.26, substituted: SI 2009/697 Reg.18
Reg.26A, substituted: SI 2009/697 Reg.19

2051. Homelessness (Priority Need for Accommodation) (England) Order 2002
Art.3, see *R. (on the application of G) v Southwark LBC* [2009] UKHL 26, [2009] 1 W.L.R. 1299 (HL), Lord Hope of Craighead

2002–cont.

2086. Education (Teacher Student Loans) (Repayment etc.) Regulations 2002
applied: SI 2009/470 Reg.15

2087. Education (Student Loans) (Repayment) (Amendment) Regulations 2002
revoked: SI 2009/470 Sch.1

2092. Street Works (Inspection Fees) (England) Regulations 2002
Reg.3, amended: SI 2009/104 Reg.3
Reg.3, applied: SI 2009/721 Sch.2 para.6

2172. Working Tax Credit (Payment by Employers) Regulations 2002
applied: SI 2009/470 Reg.54

2173. Tax Credits (Payments by the Commissioners) Regulations 2002
Reg.11, amended: SI 2009/56 Sch.2 para.78

2265. Tonnage Tax (Training Requirement) (Amendment) Regulations 2002
revoked: SI 2009/2304 Sch.1

2326. Police and Criminal Evidence Act 1984 (Department of Trade and Industry Investigations) Order 2002
Art.2, amended: SI 2009/2748 Sch.1 para.23
Art.3, amended: SI 2009/2748 Sch.1 para.23
Art.4, amended: SI 2009/2748 Sch.1 para.23

2375. National Health Service (Functions of Strategic Health Authorities and Primary Care Trusts and Administration Arrangements) (England) Regulations 2002
Reg.10, revoked (in part): SI 2009/462 Sch.5 para.9
Sch.5, substituted: SI 2009/112 Reg.2

2403. M60 Motorway (Junction 25) (Speed Limit) Regulations 2002
revoked: SI 2009/3061 Reg.2

2443. Genetically Modified Organisms (Deliberate Release) Regulations 2002
Reg.2, amended: SI 2009/1892 Sch.3 para.5

2530. Zimbabwe (Freezing of Funds, other Financial Assets or Economic Resources) (Amendment) Regulations 2002
revoked: SI 2009/847 Reg.17

2631. Somalia (United Nations Sanctions) (Overseas Territories) Order 2002
Art.15, varied: SI 2009/888 Art.2
Sch.2 para.1, varied: SI 2009/888 Art.2
Sch.2 para.2, varied: SI 2009/888 Art.2
Sch.2 para.3, varied: SI 2009/888 Art.2
Sch.2 para.4, varied: SI 2009/888 Art.2
Sch.2 para.5, varied: SI 2009/888 Art.2
Sch.2 para.6, varied: SI 2009/888 Art.2
Sch.2 para.7, varied: SI 2009/888 Art.2
Sch.2 para.8, varied: SI 2009/888 Art.2

2665. Electricity Safety, Quality and Continuity Regulations 2002
Reg.1, amended: SI 2009/639 Reg.2

2675. Control of Asbestos at Work Regulations 2002
Reg.7, see *R. v LCH Contracts Ltd* [2009] EWCA Crim 902, [2009] 2 Cr. App. R. (S.) 101 (CA (Crim Div)), Maurice Kay, L.J.
Reg.15, see *R. v LCH Contracts Ltd* [2009] EWCA Crim 902, [2009] 2 Cr. App. R. (S.) 101 (CA (Crim Div)), Maurice Kay, L.J.

2676. Control of Lead at Work Regulations 2002
applied: SI 2009/515 Reg.7
Reg.2, amended: SI 2009/716 Sch.6

2677. Control of Substances Hazardous to Health Regulations 2002
applied: SI 2009/515 Sch.5

2002– cont.

2677. Control of Substances Hazardous to Health Regulations 2002– *cont.*
Reg.2, amended: SI 2009/716 Sch.6

2704. General Chiropractic Council (Registration of Chiropractors with Foreign Qualifications) Rules Order of Council 2002
Sch.1 Part II para.6, applied: SI 2009/27 Sch.1

2742. Road Vehicles (Registration and Licensing) Regulations 2002
applied: SI 2009/2325 Art.21
Sch.2 para.1, amended: SI 2009/3103 Reg.3
Sch.2 para.1A, added: SI 2009/3103 Reg.4
Sch.2 para.2, amended: SI 2009/3103 Reg.5
Sch.2 para.5, amended: SI 2009/3103 Reg.6
Sch.2 para.5, substituted: SI 2009/3103 Reg.6
Sch.2 para.6, amended: SI 2009/3103 Reg.7
Sch.2 para.8, amended: SI 2009/3103 Reg.8
Sch.2 para.12, amended: SI 2009/3103 Reg.9
Sch.2 para.13, amended: SI 2009/880 Reg.3, SI 2009/3103 Reg.10
Sch.3 para.7, amended: SI 2009/880 Reg.4

2743. Motor Vehicles (EC Type Approval) (Amendment) (No.2) Regulations 2002
revoked: SI 2009/717 Sch.1

2776. Dangerous Substances and Explosive Atmospheres Regulations 2002
Reg.2, amended: SI 2009/716 Sch.6
Reg.10, applied: SI 2009/716 Reg.7

2786. Air Navigation (Dangerous Goods) Regulations 2002
applied: SI 2009/716 Reg.6, Reg.8
Reg.3, amended: SI 2009/1492 Reg.2

2818. Statutory Paternity Pay and Statutory Adoption Pay (Weekly Rates) Regulations 2002
Reg.2, amended: SI 2009/497 Art.11
Reg.3, amended: SI 2009/497 Art.11

2832. Freedom of Information (Excluded Welsh Authorities) Order 2002
Sch.1 Part II, amended: SI 2009/56 Sch.2 para.79

2859. Education (Student Loans) (Repayment) (Amendment) (No.2) Regulations 2002
revoked: SI 2009/470 Sch.1

2926. Tax Credits (Appeals) Regulations 2002
Reg.3, amended: SI 2009/56 Sch.2 para.81
Reg.12, amended: SI 2009/56 Sch.2 para.82

2939. Food for Particular Nutritional Uses (Addition of Substances for Specific Nutritional Purposes) (Wales) Regulations 2002
revoked: SI 2009/3254 Reg.6

2972. Employment Tribunals (Enforcement of Orders in Other Jurisdictions) (Scotland) Regulations 2002
Reg.3, amended: SI 2009/3131 Reg.45
Sch.1, revoked: SI 2009/3131 Reg.45

2976. General Commissioners and Special Commissioners (Jurisdiction and Procedure) (Amendment) Regulations 2002
revoked: SI 2009/56 Sch.2 para.187

2978. School Companies Regulations 2002
Sch.1 para.8A, added: SI 2009/1924 Reg.4

3017. Quality Partnership Schemes (Existing Facilities) (Wales) Regulations 2002
revoked: SI 2009/3293 Reg.1

3045. Sale and Supply of Goods to Consumers Regulations 2002
referred to: SI 2009/669 Sch.1 Part 2

2002– cont.

3113. Traffic Signs Regulations and General Directions 2002
applied: SI 2009/1300 Art.70, SSI 2009/92 Art.2, SSI 2009/241 Art.2
referred to: SSI 2009/46 Art.3
Part II, applied: SSI 2009/56 Art.3, Art.4, Art.5, SSI 2009/57 Art.3, Art.4, Art.5, SSI 2009/58 Art.3, Art.4, Art.5, SSI 2009/59 Art.3, Art.4, Art.5, SSI 2009/62 Art.2, SSI 2009/77 Art.2, SSI 2009/78 Art.3, SSI 2009/113 Art.2, SSI 2009/127 Art.3, Art.4, Art.5, SSI 2009/161 Art.3, Art.4, Art.5, SSI 2009/175 Art.2, SSI 2009/195 Art.2, Art.3, Art.4, SSI 2009/201 Art.3, Art.4, Art.5, SSI 2009/237 Art.2, SSI 2009/252 Art.3, Art.4, Art.5, SSI 2009/253 Art.3, Art.4, Art.5, SSI 2009/254 Art.3, Art.4, Art.5, SSI 2009/255 Art.3, Art.4, Art.5, SSI 2009/265 Art.2, SSI 2009/272 Art.2, Art.3, Art.4, SSI 2009/274 Art.2, SSI 2009/278 Art.2, SSI 2009/279 Art.3, Art.4, Art.5
Part II, referred to: SSI 2009/22 Art.3, Art.4, Art.5, SSI 2009/23 Art.3, Art.4, Art.5, SSI 2009/24 Art.3, Art.4, Art.5, SSI 2009/25 Art.3, Art.4, Art.5, SSI 2009/123 Art.3, Art.4, Art.5, SSI 2009/125 Art.3, Art.4, Art.5, SSI 2009/126 Art.3, Art.4, Art.5, SSI 2009/157 Art.3, Art.4, Art.5, SSI 2009/158 Art.3, Art.4, Art.5, SSI 2009/159 Art.3, Art.4, Art.5, SSI 2009/198 Art.3, Art.4, Art.5, SSI 2009/199 Art.3, Art.4, Art.5, SSI 2009/200 Art.3, Art.4, Art.5, SSI 2009/289 Art.2
Reg.10, referred to: SI 2009/492 Sch.1 Part 1

3150. Company Directors Disqualification (Northern Ireland) Order 2002
applied: SI 2009/26 Sch.1, SI 2009/263 Art.5, SI 2009/442 Art.5, SI 2009/457 Reg.9, SI 2009/468 Sch.1, SI 2009/1345 Art.5, SI 2009/1355 Sch.1, SI 2009/1808 Art.5, SI 2009/1813 Sch.1, SI 2009/1941 Art.4, SI 2009/2471 Reg.5, Reg.9, SI 2009/2722 Reg.3
Art.2, amended: SI 2009/1941 Sch.1 para.204
Art.6, amended: SI 2009/1941 Sch.1 para.205
Art.8, amended: SI 2009/1941 Sch.1 para.206
Art.11, amended: SI 2009/1941 Sch.1 para.207
Art.13, revoked (in part): SI 2009/1941 Sch.1 para.208
Art.14, amended: SI 2009/1941 Sch.1 para.209
Art.15, amended: SI 2009/1941 Sch.1 para.210
Art.22, amended: SI 2009/1941 Sch.1 para.211
Art.23, amended: SI 2009/1941 Sch.1 para.209
Art.24, amended: SI 2009/1941 Sch.1 para.209
Art.24D, added: SI 2009/1941 Sch.1 para.212
Art.24E, added: SI 2009/1941 Sch.1 para.212
Art.25, amended: SI 2009/1941 Sch.1 para.213
Art.25A, amended: SI 2009/1941 Sch.1 para.214
Sch.1 Part I para.1, amended: SI 2009/1941 Sch.1 para.215
Sch.1 Part I para.3, amended: SI 2009/1941 Sch.1 para.215
Sch.1 Part I para.4, substituted: SI 2009/1941 Sch.1 para.215
Sch.1 Part I para.6, revoked: SI 2009/1941 Sch.1 para.215
Sch.1 Part I para.7, revoked: SI 2009/1941 Sch.1 para.215
Sch.1 Part II para.10, amended: SI 2009/1941 Sch.1 para.215
Sch.1 Part II para.11, amended: SI 2009/1941 Sch.1 para.215
Sch.1 Part II para.12, amended: SI 2009/1941 Sch.1 para.215

2002– cont.

3171. Beet Seed (England) Regulations 2002
Reg.2, amended: SI 2009/1274 Reg.4
Reg.18A, added: SI 2009/1274 Reg.5
Reg.20, amended: SI 2009/1274 Reg.6
Reg.21, amended: SI 2009/1274 Reg.7
Reg.23, amended: SI 2009/1274 Reg.8
Sch.8 Part VI para.19, added: SI 2009/1274 Reg.9

3172. Fodder Plant Seed (England) Regulations 2002
Reg.2, amended: SI 2009/1274 Reg.11
Reg.20A, added: SI 2009/1274 Reg.12
Reg.23, amended: SI 2009/1274 Reg.13
Reg.24, amended: SI 2009/1274 Reg.14
Reg.26, amended: SI 2009/1274 Reg.15
Sch.8 Part IX para.45, added: SI 2009/1274 Reg.16

3173. Cereal Seed (England) Regulations 2002
Reg.2, amended: SI 2009/1274 Reg.18
Reg.20A, added: SI 2009/1274 Reg.19
Reg.23, amended: SI 2009/1274 Reg.20
Reg.24, amended: SI 2009/1274 Reg.21
Reg.26, amended: SI 2009/1274 Reg.22
Sch.8 Part VIII para.35, added: SI 2009/1274 Reg.23

3174. Oil and Fibre Plant Seed (England) Regulations 2002
Reg.2, amended: SI 2009/1274 Reg.25
Reg.19A, added: SI 2009/1274 Reg.26
Reg.23, amended: SI 2009/1274 Reg.27
Reg.24, amended: SI 2009/1274 Reg.28
Reg.26, amended: SI 2009/1274 Reg.29
Sch.8 Part IX para.39, added: SI 2009/1274 Reg.30

3177. School Companies (Private Finance Initiative Companies) Regulations 2002
Sch.1 para.8A, added: SI 2009/1924 Reg.5

3178. Education (Pupil Exclusions and Appeals) (Maintained Schools) (England) Regulations 2002
Reg.7A, see *R. (on the application of V) v Independent Appeal Panel for Tom Hood School* [2009] EWHC 369 (Admin), [2009] B.L.G.R. 691 (QBD (Admin)), Silber, J.
Sch.1 para.1, see *R. (on the application of P) v Haringey LBC* [2008] EWHC 2357 (Admin), [2009] E.L.R. 49 (QBD (Admin)), Mr David Elvin QC

3200. Education (Student Support) (No.2) Regulations 2002
applied: SI 2009/2737 Reg.3

3212. Nurses Agencies Regulations 2002
Reg.2, amended: SI 2009/462 Sch.2 para.5
Reg.12, amended: SI 2009/1895 Reg.11
Reg.12, revoked (in part): SI 2009/1895 Reg.11
Sch.2 para.2, substituted: SI 2009/1895 Reg.11
Sch.3 para.13, substituted: SI 2009/1895 Reg.11

3213. Residential Family Centres Regulations 2002
Sch.2 para.2, substituted: SI 2009/1895 Reg.7

3214. Domiciliary Care Agencies Regulations 2002
Reg.2, amended: SI 2009/462 Sch.2 para.5
Reg.12, amended: SI 2009/1895 Reg.10
Reg.12, revoked (in part): SI 2009/1895 Reg.10
Sch.2 para.2, substituted: SI 2009/1895 Reg.10
Sch.3 para.13, substituted: SI 2009/1895 Reg.10

3236. Flexible Working (Eligibility, Complaints and Remedies) Regulations 2002
Reg.3A, substituted: SI 2009/595 Reg.2

2003

74. Wireless Telegraphy (Exemption) Regulations 2003
see *Floe Telecom Ltd (In Administration) v Office of Communications* [2009] EWCA Civ 47, [2009] Bus. L.R. 1116 (CA (Civ Div)), Mummery, L.J.

96. Community Investment Tax Relief (Accreditation of Community Development Finance Institutions) Regulations 2003
Reg.2, amended: SI 2009/2748 Sch.1 para.24
Reg.7, amended: SI 2009/2748 Sch.1 para.24
Reg.13, amended: SI 2009/2748 Sch.1 para.24
Reg.15, amended: SI 2009/2748 Sch.1 para.24
Reg.16, amended: SI 2009/56 Sch.2 para.83, SI 2009/2748 Sch.1 para.24

114. Common Agricultural Policy (Wine) (England and Northern Ireland) (Amendment) Regulations 2003
revoked (in part): SI 2009/386 Reg.17

120. Proceeds of Crime Act 2002 (Commencement No.4, Transitional Provisions and Savings) Order 2003
see *R. v Anwoir (Ilham)* [2008] EWCA Crim 1354, [2009] 1 W.L.R. 980 (CA (Crim Div)), Latham, L.J.

148. Local Health Boards (Establishment) (Wales) Order 2003
applied: SI 2009/778 Art.7
Sch.1, substituted: SI 2009/778 Sch.3

149. Local Health Boards (Constitution, Membership and Procedures) (Wales) Regulations 2003
applied: SI 2009/779 Reg.19
revoked: SI 2009/779 Reg.22

150. Local Health Boards (Functions) (Wales) Regulations 2003
referred to: SI 2009/1511 Reg.4
revoked: SI 2009/1511 Reg.6

172. Proceeds of Crime Act 2002 (References to Financial Investigators) Order 2003
revoked: SI 2009/975 Sch.2

192. Child Support, Pensions and Social Security Act 2000 (Commencement No.12) Order 2003
Art.3, applied: SI 2009/396 Reg.7

237. Fostering Services (Wales) Regulations 2003
Reg.38, see *A (A Child) (Residential Assessment), Re* [2009] EWHC 865 (Fam), [2009] 2 F.L.R. 443 (Fam Div), Munby, J.
Sch.1 para.2, substituted: SI 2009/2541 Reg.7
Sch.3 para.13, substituted: SI 2009/2541 Reg.7

239. Allocation of Housing (Wales) Regulations 2003
Reg.5, amended: SI 2009/393 Reg.2

282. Income and Corporation Taxes (Electronic Communications) Regulations 2003
Reg.1, amended: SI 2009/3218 Sch.1 para.1, Sch.1 para.2
Reg.2, amended: SI 2009/3218 Sch.1 para.3, Sch.1 para.4
Reg.3, amended: SI 2009/3218 Sch.1 para.5, Sch.1 para.6, Sch.1 para.7, Sch.1 para.8, Sch.1 para.9
Reg.3A, added: SI 2009/3218 Sch.1 para.10
Reg.5, amended: SI 2009/3218 Sch.1 para.11
Reg.10, amended: SI 2009/3218 Sch.1 para.12, Sch.1 para.13

2003– cont.

333. Proceeds of Crime Act 2002 (Commencement No 5, Transitional Provisions, Savings and Amendment) Order 2003
Art.3, see *Crown Prosecution Service v Moulden* [2008] EWCA Crim 2648, [2009] 1 W.L.R. 1173 (CA (Crim Div)), Pill, L.J.

336. Proceeds of Crime Act 2002 (Exemptions from Civil Recovery) Order 2003
Sch.1 Part 2, amended: SI 2009/2054 Sch.1 para.24

367. Voluntary Adoption Agencies and the Adoption Agencies (Miscellaneous Amendments) Regulations 2003
Sch.2 para.2, substituted: SI 2009/1898 Reg.2

370. Local Authority Adoption Service (England) Regulations 2003
Sch.3 para.2, substituted: SI 2009/1895 Reg.6

399. Movement of Animals (Restrictions) (Wales) Order 2003
Art.5, substituted: SI 2009/2940 Art.2
Art.6, revoked: SI 2009/2940 Art.2
Art.10, amended: SI 2009/2940 Art.2

403. Nuclear Industries Security Regulations 2003
Reg.23, amended: SI 2009/229 Sch.2 para.12
Reg.23, applied: SI 2009/229 Art.4
Reg.24, amended: SI 2009/229 Sch.2 para.12
Reg.24, applied: SI 2009/229 Art.4

410. Strategic Investment and Regeneration of Sites (Northern Ireland) Order 2003
Art.5, amended: SI 2009/1941 Sch.1 para.219

417. Protection of Children and Vulnerable Adults (Northern Ireland) Order 2003
Part II, applied: SI 2009/1547 Sch.1 para.23
Art.3, applied: SI 2009/1547 Sch.1 para.23, SI 2009/1633 Reg.3, SI 2009/2558 Reg.3
Art.23, applied: SI 2009/1633 Reg.3, SI 2009/2558 Reg.3
Art.24, applied: SI 2009/1633 Reg.3, SI 2009/2558 Reg.3
Art.30, applied: SSI 2009/39 Art.2

419. Energy (Northern Ireland) Order 2003
Art.42, applied: SSI 2009/140 Art.42
Art.43, applied: SSI 2009/140 Art.42
Art.44, applied: SSI 2009/140 Art.42
Art.45, applied: SSI 2009/140 Art.42
Art.46, applied: SSI 2009/140 Art.42
Art.47, applied: SSI 2009/140 Art.42
Art.48, applied: SSI 2009/140 Art.42
Art.49, applied: SSI 2009/140 Art.42
Art.50, applied: SSI 2009/140 Art.42
Art.51, applied: SSI 2009/140 Art.42
Art.52, applied: SI 2009/785 Art.7, Art.9, SSI 2009/140 Art.36
Art.53, applied: SI 2009/785 Art.7, Art.9
Art.54, applied: SI 2009/785 Art.7, Art.9
Art.54, referred to: SI 2009/785 Art.17, SSI 2009/140 Art.15, Art.17
Art.54D, applied: SI 2009/785 Art.7, Art.9
Art.55, applied: SI 2009/785 Art.7, Art.9
Art.55A, applied: SI 2009/785 Art.7, Art.9
Art.55F, applied: SI 2009/785 Art.7, Art.9

431. Health and Personal Social Services (Quality, Improvement and Regulation) (Northern Ireland) Order 2003
applied: SI 2009/1547 Sch.1 para.15
Sch.2 para.1, amended: 2009 c.3 Sch.4 para.41
Sch.2 para.2, amended: 2009 c.3 Sch.4 para.41
Sch.2 para.3, amended: 2009 c.3 Sch.4 para.41
Sch.2 para.7, revoked: 2009 c.3 Sch.4 para.41

2003– cont.

435. Access to Justice (Northern Ireland) Order 2003
Sch.2 para.2, amended: 2009 c.26 Sch.7 para.96, Sch.7 para.112, Sch.8 Part 4
Sch.2 para.3, amended: 2009 c.26 Sch.7 para.96

491. Mid Devon (Parishes) Order 2003
applied: SI 2009/542 Art.3

492. Child Benefit and Guardian's Allowance (Administration) Regulations 2003
Reg.2, amended: SI 2009/3268 Reg.3
Reg.5, amended: SI 2009/3268 Reg.3
Reg.19, amended: SI 2009/3268 Reg.3
Reg.26, amended: SI 2009/3268 Reg.3
Reg.26, revoked (in part): SI 2009/3268 Reg.3

495. Guardian's Allowance (General) Regulations 2003
Reg.10, amended: SI 2009/3268 Reg.6

531. Proceeds of Crime Act 2002 (Commencement No 5) (Amendment of Transitional Provisions) Order 2003
Art.3, see *R. v Stapleton (Rosie)* [2008] EWCA Crim 1308, [2009] 1 Cr. App. R. (S.) 38 (CA (Crim Div)), Latham, L.J.

533. Accounts and Audit Regulations 2003
see *Veolia ES Nottinghamshire Ltd v Nottinghamshire CC* [2009] EWHC 2382 (Admin), Times, October 15, 2009 (QBD (Admin)), Cranston, J.
Reg.2, amended: SI 2009/473 Reg.3
Reg.4, applied: SI 2009/276 Reg.11
Reg.4, varied: SI 2009/276 Reg.11
Reg.7, amended: SI 2009/3322 Reg.4
Reg.7, varied: SI 2009/276 Reg.9, Reg.10
Reg.7B, added: SI 2009/473 Reg.4
Reg.10, amended: SI 2009/473 Reg.5
Reg.10, varied: SI 2009/276 Reg.9, Reg.10
Reg.11, varied: SI 2009/276 Reg.9
Reg.12, amended: SI 2009/473 Reg.6
Reg.17, amended: SI 2009/473 Reg.7
Reg.21, amended: SI 2009/473 Reg.8

542. Education (Supply of Information) (Wales) Regulations 2003
revoked: SI 2009/1350 Reg.2
Reg.4, applied: SI 2009/12 Art.2, Art.3, SI 2009/2610 Art.18
Reg.6, applied: SI 2009/12 Art.2, Art.3, SI 2009/2610 Art.18

548. British Nationality (General) Regulations 2003
Reg.14, substituted: SI 2009/3363 Reg.3
Sch.2 para.1A, added: SI 2009/3363 Reg.4
Sch.2 para.5, revoked: SI 2009/3363 Reg.4
Sch.2 para.10, substituted: SI 2009/3363 Reg.4
Sch.2 para.11, substituted: SI 2009/3363 Reg.4
Sch.2 para.11A, added: SI 2009/3363 Reg.4

628. National Assistance (Sums for Personal Requirements) (England) Regulations 2003
Reg.2, amended: SI 2009/597 Reg.2

658. Immigration (Notices) Regulations 2003
see *JN (Cameroon) v Secretary of State for the Home Department* [2009] EWCA Civ 307, [2009] Imm. A.R. 615 (CA (Civ Div)), Rix, L.J.; see *MA (Somalia) v Secretary of State for Home Department* [2009] EWCA Civ 4, [2009] Imm. A.R. 413 (CA (Civ Div)), Laws, L.J.; see *MS (Palestinian Territories) v Secretary of State for the Home Department* [2009] EWCA Civ 17, [2009] Imm. A.R. 464 (CA (Civ Div)), Rix, L.J.
Reg.2, amended: SI 2009/1117 Sch.2 para.2

2003– cont.

658. Immigration (Notices) Regulations 2003– *cont.*
Reg.5, see *JN (Cameroon) v Secretary of State for the Home Department* [2009] EWCA Civ 307, [2009] Imm. A.R. 615 (CA (Civ Div)), Rix, L.J.

751. Energy Information (Household Electric Ovens) Regulations 2003
referred to: SI 2009/669 Sch.1 Part 4
Reg.2, amended: SI 2009/2559 Reg.7
Reg.2A, added: SI 2009/2559 Reg.7
Sch.6 Part I para.2A, added: SI 2009/2559 Reg.7

762. Community Care, Services for Carers and Children's Services (Direct Payments) (England) Regulations 2003
revoked: SI 2009/1887 Sch.3

781. Residential Family Centres (Wales) Regulations 2003
see *A (A Child) (Residential Assessment), Re* [2009] EWHC 865 (Fam), [2009] 2 F.L.R. 443 (Fam Div), Munby, J.
Reg.5, amended: SI 2009/2541 Reg.9
Reg.5, revoked (in part): SI 2009/2541 Reg.9
Reg.7, amended: SI 2009/2541 Reg.9
Reg.7, revoked (in part): SI 2009/2541 Reg.9
Sch.2 para.2, substituted: SI 2009/2541 Reg.9
Sch.2 para.7, revoked: SI 2009/2541 Reg.9

813. Health Authorities (Transfer of Functions, Staff, Property, Rights and Liabilities and Abolition) (Wales) Order 2003
referred to: SI 2009/1511 Reg.4

815. Powys Local Health Board (Additional Functions) (Regulations 2003
revoked: SI 2009/1511 Reg.6

816. Local Health Boards (Functions) (Amendment) Regulations 2003
revoked: SI 2009/1511 Reg.6

916. Child Benefit and Guardian's Allowance (Decisions and Appeals) Regulations 2003
Reg.2, amended: SI 2009/3268 Reg.4

938. Tax Credits Act 2002 (Commencement No 3 and Transitional Provisions and Savings) Order 2003
Art.3, referred to: SI 2009/775 Art.3
Art.4, referred to: SI 2009/775 Art.3

968. Special Commissioners (Jurisdiction and Procedure) (Amendment) Regulations 2003
revoked: SI 2009/56 Sch.2 para.187

1019. Motor Vehicles (EC Type Approval) (Amendment) Regulations 2003
revoked: SI 2009/717 Sch.1

1038. Education (National Curriculum) (Key Stage 2 Assessment Arrangements) (England) Order 2003
Art.5, amended: SI 2009/1585 Art.2
Art.11, amended: SI 2009/1585 Art.2

1039. Education (National Curriculum) (Key Stage 3 Assessment Arrangements) (England) Order 2003
Art.12, substituted: SI 2009/1585 Art.3

1078. Diseases of Poultry (England) Order 2003
Art.3, amended: SI 2009/2713 Art.2
Art.4, amended: SI 2009/2713 Art.2

1184. Education (Prohibition from Teaching or Working with Children) Regulations 2003
applied: SI 2009/37 Reg.3, Reg.4
Reg.4, see *R. (on the application of G) v X School Governors* [2009] EWHC 504 (Admin), [2009] I.R.L.R. 434 (QBD (Admin)), Stephen Morris QC

2003– cont.

1184. Education (Prohibition from Teaching or Working with Children) Regulations 2003– *cont.*
Reg.4, applied: SI 2009/12 Art.2, Art.3, SI 2009/2610 Art.18
Reg.4, varied: SI 2009/12 Art.4
Reg.8, applied: SI 2009/37 Reg.3, Reg.4
Reg.13, see *Secretary of State for Children, Schools and Families v Philliskirk* [2008] EWHC 2838 (Admin), [2009] E.L.R. 68 (QBD (Admin)), Collins, J.
Sch.1 Part 1 para.7, varied: SI 2009/12 Art.3
Sch.1 Part 2 para.7, varied: SI 2009/12 Art.3
Sch.2 Part 1 para.12, varied: SI 2009/12 Art.4
Sch.2 Part 2, referred to: SI 2009/37 Reg.3, Reg.4
Sch.2 Part 3, referred to: SI 2009/37 Reg.4
Sch.2 Part 4, referred to: SI 2009/37 Reg.4
Sch.2 Part 5, referred to: SI 2009/37 Reg.4

1185. Immigration (Passenger Transit Visa) Order 2003
Art.2, amended: SI 2009/198 Art.2, SI 2009/1032 Art.3, SI 2009/1229 Art.4, SI 2009/1233 Art.3
Art.2, revoked (in part): SI 2009/1229 Art.4
Sch.1, amended: SI 2009/198 Art.2, SI 2009/1032 Art.3, SI 2009/1229 Art.4

1209. Health Professions Council (Practice Committees) (Constitution) Rules Order of Council 2003
revoked: SI 2009/1182 Sch.4 para.36

1247. Criminal Justice (Northern Ireland) Order 2003
Art.18, applied: 2009 asp 9 Sch.1 para.18
Art.19, applied: 2009 asp 9 Sch.1 para.18
Art.19, referred to: SI 2009/37 Sch.1 para.2, Sch.1 para.4
Art.20, applied: 2009 asp 9 Sch.1 para.18
Art.20, referred to: SI 2009/37 Sch.1 para.2, Sch.1 para.4
Art.21, applied: 2009 asp 9 Sch.1 para.18
Art.21, referred to: SI 2009/37 Sch.1 para.2, Sch.1 para.4

1250. General and Specialist Medical Practice (Education, Training and Qualifications) Order 2003
Art.8, referred to: SI 2009/385 Sch.1
Art.11, referred to: SI 2009/385 Sch.1
Art.11A, referred to: SI 2009/385 Sch.1
Art.12, referred to: SI 2009/385 Sch.1
Art.13, referred to: SI 2009/385 Sch.1
Art.14, referred to: SI 2009/385 Sch.1
Art.14A, referred to: SI 2009/385 Sch.1
Art.15, referred to: SI 2009/385 Sch.1
Art.15A, referred to: SI 2009/385 Sch.1
Art.15B, referred to: SI 2009/385 Sch.1
Art.16, referred to: SI 2009/385 Sch.1
Art.17, referred to: SI 2009/385 Sch.1
Art.18, referred to: SI 2009/385 Sch.1
Art.19, referred to: SI 2009/385 Sch.1
Art.20, referred to: SI 2009/385 Sch.1
Art.21, referred to: SI 2009/385 Sch.1
Art.24, enabled: SI 2009/385
Art.24, referred to: SI 2009/385 Sch.1
Art.25, applied: SI 2009/385
Art.25, enabled: SI 2009/385
Sch.1, referred to: SI 2009/385 Sch.1
Sch.3, referred to: SI 2009/385 Sch.1
Sch.3 Part 1, amended: SI 2009/1846 Art.2
Sch.3 Part 2, amended: SI 2009/1846 Art.2
Sch.7A Part 2, referred to: SI 2009/385 Sch.1

2003–cont.

1326. Government Resources and Accounts Act 2000 (Audit of Public Bodies) Order 2003
Art.16, revoked (in part): SI 2009/484 Sch.2

1370. Enterprise Act 2002 (Merger Fees and Determination of Turnover) Order 2003
Art.5, amended: SI 2009/2396 Art.2

1372. Competition Appeal Tribunal Rules 2003
r.16, see *Barclays Bank Plc v Competition Commission* [2009] CAT 15, [2009] Comp. A.R. 242 (CAT), Briggs, J.
r.31, see *BCL Old Co Ltd v BASF SE* [2009] C.P. Rep. 9 (CAT), Barling, J; see *BCL Old Co Ltd v BASF SE* [2009] EWCA Civ 434, [2009] Bus. L.R. 1516 (CA (Civ Div)), Waller, L.J.; see *Emerson Electric Co v Morgan Crucible Co Plc* [2009] Comp. A.R. 7 (CAT), Barling, J. (President)
r.55, see *Consumers' Association v JJB Sports Plc* [2009] CAT 2, [2009] Comp. A.R. 117 (CAT), Lord Carlile of Berriew Q.C.; see *Emerson Electric Co v Morgan Crucible Co Plc* [2009] Comp. A.R. 7 (CAT), Barling, J. (President); see *Tesco Plc v Competition Commission (Costs)* [2009] CAT 26, [2009] Comp. A.R. 429 (CAT), Barling, J. (President)

1377. School Governance (Procedures) (England) Regulations 2003
Reg.16, amended: SI 2009/2680 Reg.10
Reg.17, amended: SI 2009/2680 Reg.10

1382. Tax Credits (Employer Penalty Appeals) Regulations 2003
Reg.3, amended: SI 2009/56 Sch.2 para.85
Reg.4, revoked: SI 2009/56 Sch.2 para.86
Reg.5, revoked: SI 2009/56 Sch.2 para.86
Reg.6, revoked: SI 2009/56 Sch.2 para.86
Reg.7, amended: SI 2009/56 Sch.2 para.87
Reg.8, revoked: SI 2009/56 Sch.2 para.88
Reg.10, substituted: SI 2009/56 Sch.2 para.89

1387. Food Supplements (England) Regulations 2003
Reg.2, amended: SI 2009/3251 Reg.2
Reg.3, amended: SI 2009/3251 Reg.2
Reg.5, amended: SI 2009/3251 Reg.2
Reg.5, revoked (in part): SI 2009/3251 Reg.2
Reg.6, amended: SI 2009/3251 Reg.2
Reg.12, added: SI 2009/3251 Reg.2
Sch.1, revoked: SI 2009/3251 Reg.2
Sch.2 para.A, revoked: SI 2009/3251 Reg.2
Sch.2 para.B, revoked: SI 2009/3251 Reg.2

1417. Land Registration Rules 2003
varied: SI 2009/317 Sch.1
see *Parkinson v Hawthorne* [2008] EWHC 3499 (Ch), [2009] 1 W.L.R. 1665 (Ch D), Patten, J.
Part 9 r.111A, added: SI 2009/1996 r.3
Sch.1, amended: SI 2009/1996 r.4, SI 2009/2748 Sch.1 para.25
Sch.1A, amended: SI 2009/1996 r.5
Sch.1A, applied: SI 2009/1996 r.9
Sch.2, applied: SI 2009/1393 Art.2, SI 2009/2727 Art.2
Sch.5, amended: SI 2009/56 Sch.2 para.90, SI 2009/2748 Sch.1 para.25
Sch.9, amended: SI 2009/1996 r.6, r.7, r.8

1476. Financial Services and Markets Act 2000 (Regulated Activities) (Amendment) (No.2) Order 2003
see *Whiteley Insurance Consultants (A Firm), Re* [2008] EWHC 1782 (Ch), [2009] Bus. L.R. 418 (Ch D (Companies Ct)), David Richards, J.
Art.21, revoked: SI 2009/774 Art.7

2003–cont.

1483. Local Authorities (Code of Conduct) (Local Determination) Regulations 2003
applied: SI 2009/486 Reg.6

1511. Creosote (Prohibition on Use and Marketing)(No.2) Regulations 2003
referred to: SI 2009/669 Sch.1 Part 4

1515. Cayman Islands (Constitution) (Amendment) Order 2003
revoked: SI 2009/1379 Sch.1

1516. Iraq (United Nations Sanctions) (Overseas Territories) Order 2003
Art.19, varied: SI 2009/888 Art.2
Sch.2 para.1, varied: SI 2009/888 Art.2
Sch.2 para.2, varied: SI 2009/888 Art.2
Sch.2 para.3, varied: SI 2009/888 Art.2
Sch.2 para.4, varied: SI 2009/888 Art.2
Sch.2 para.5, varied: SI 2009/888 Art.2
Sch.2 para.6, varied: SI 2009/888 Art.2
Sch.2 para.7, varied: SI 2009/888 Art.2
Sch.2 para.8, varied: SI 2009/888 Art.2

1517. Copyright (Bermuda) Order 2003
revoked: SI 2009/2749 Art.2

1563. Specified Sugar Products (England) Regulations 2003
Sch.1, amended: SI 2009/3238 Reg.19

1564. Fruit Juices and Fruit Nectars (England) Regulations 2003
Sch.3 para.6, substituted: SI 2009/3238 Reg.18
Sch.4 para.4, amended: SI 2009/3235 Reg.9
Sch.4 para.5, amended: SI 2009/3235 Reg.9
Sch.4 para.6, amended: SI 2009/3235 Reg.9

1571. Health Professions (Parts of and Entries in the Register) Order of Council 2003
Art.6A, added: SI 2009/1182 Sch.4 para.8
Sch.1, amended: SI 2009/1182 Sch.4 para.8

1572. Health Professions Council (Registration and Fees) Rules Order of Council 2003
Sch.1, added: SI 2009/1355 Sch.1
Sch.1, amended: SI 2009/272 Sch.1, SI 2009/1355 Sch.1
Sch.1, substituted: SI 2009/1355 Sch.1

1574. Health Professions Council (Investigating Committee) Procedure Rules Order of Council 2003
Sch.1, amended: SI 2009/1355 Sch.1

1575. Health Professions Council (Conduct and Competence Committee) (Procedure) Rules Order of Council 2003
Sch.1, added: SI 2009/1182 Sch.4 para.21
Sch.1, amended: SI 2009/1182 Sch.4 para.21, SI 2009/1355 Sch.1

1576. Health Professions Council (Health Committee) (Procedure) Rules Order of Council 2003
Sch.1, amended: SI 2009/1355 Sch.1

1579. Health Professions Council (Registration Appeals) Rules Order of Council 2003
Sch.1, added: SI 2009/1355 Sch.1
Sch.1, amended: SI 2009/1355 Sch.1
Sch.1, substituted: SI 2009/1182 Sch.4 para.10, SI 2009/1355 Sch.1

1596. Condensed Milk and Dried Milk (England) Regulations 2003
Sch.1, amended: SI 2009/3238 Reg.18

1660. Employment Equality (Religion or Belief) Regulations 2003
see *Ladele v Islington LBC* [2009] I.C.R. 387 (EAT), Elias, J (President)

2003– cont.

1660. Employment Equality (Religion or Belief) Regulations 2003– *cont.*
Reg.3, see *Ladele v Islington LBC* [2009] I.C.R. 387 (EAT), Elias, J (President)
Reg.5, see *Ladele v Islington LBC* [2009] I.C.R. 387 (EAT), Elias, J (President); see *Saini v All Saints Haque Centre* [2009] 1 C.M.L.R. 38 (EAT), Lady Smith
Sch.4 Part 1 para.2, amended: SI 2009/3348 Art.22, Art.23

1661. Employment Equality (Sexual Orientation) Regulations 2003
Reg.5, see *English v Thomas Sanderson Blinds Ltd* [2008] EWCA Civ 1421, [2009] 2 All E.R. 468 (CA (Civ Div)), Laws, L.J.
Sch.4 Part 1 para.2, amended: SI 2009/3348 Art.22, Art.23

1662. Education (School Teachers Qualifications) (England) Regulations 2003
Sch.2 Part 1 para.5, amended: SI 2009/3156 Reg.4
Sch.2 Part 1 para.6, substituted: SI 2009/3156 Reg.5
Sch.2 Part 1 para.7, amended: SI 2009/3156 Reg.6
Sch.2 Part 1 para.7A, added: SI 2009/3156 Reg.7
Sch.2 Part 1 para.11, amended: SI 2009/3156 Reg.8
Sch.2 Part 1 para.11, revoked (in part): SI 2009/3156 Reg.8

1663. Education (Specified Work and Registration) (England) Regulations 2003
Reg.6, referred to: SI 2009/3200 Reg.6

1719. Food Supplements (Wales) Regulations 2003
Reg.2, amended: SI 2009/3252 Reg.2
Reg.3, amended: SI 2009/3252 Reg.2
Reg.5, amended: SI 2009/3252 Reg.2
Reg.5, revoked (in part): SI 2009/3252 Reg.2
Reg.6, amended: SI 2009/3252 Reg.2
Reg.12, added: SI 2009/3252 Reg.2
Sch.1, revoked: SI 2009/3252 Reg.2
Sch.2, revoked: SI 2009/3252 Reg.2
Sch.2 para.1, revoked: SI 2009/3252 Reg.2
Sch.2 para.2, revoked: SI 2009/3252 Reg.2
Sch.2 para.3, revoked: SI 2009/3252 Reg.2
Sch.2 para.4, revoked: SI 2009/3252 Reg.2
Sch.2 para.5, revoked: SI 2009/3252 Reg.2
Sch.2 para.6, revoked: SI 2009/3252 Reg.2
Sch.2 para.7, revoked: SI 2009/3252 Reg.2
Sch.2 para.8, revoked: SI 2009/3252 Reg.2
Sch.2 para.9, revoked: SI 2009/3252 Reg.2
Sch.2 para.10, revoked: SI 2009/3252 Reg.2
Sch.2 para.11, revoked: SI 2009/3252 Reg.2
Sch.2 para.12, revoked: SI 2009/3252 Reg.2
Sch.2 para.13, revoked: SI 2009/3252 Reg.2

1724. Transport of Animals (Cleansing and Disinfection) (England) (No.3) Order 2003
Sch.2, applied: SI 2009/1299 Sch.2 para.4, Sch.2 para.6

1809. Merchant Shipping and Fishing Vessels (Port Waste Reception Facilities) Regulations 2003
Reg.2, amended: SI 2009/1176 Reg.2
Reg.11, amended: SI 2009/1176 Reg.2
Reg.12, amended: SI 2009/1176 Reg.2
Reg.17, amended: SI 2009/1176 Reg.2
Sch.2, amended: SI 2009/1176 Reg.2

1810. Burma (Freezing of Funds) (Amendment) Regulations 2003
revoked: SI 2009/1495 Reg.24

1879. Judicial Committee (General Appellate Jurisdiction) Rules (Amendment) Order 2003
revoked: SI 2009/224 Art.4

2003– cont.

1880. Judicial Committee (Devolution Issues) Rules (Amendment) Order 2003
revoked: SI 2009/224 Art.4

1910. Education (Independent School Standards) (England) Regulations 2003
Reg.4, amended: SI 2009/1924 Reg.6
Sch.1 para.4, amended: SI 2009/1924 Reg.6
Sch.1 para.4B, amended: SI 2009/1924 Reg.6
Sch.1 para.4C, amended: SI 2009/1924 Reg.6

1917. Education (Teacher Student Loans) (Repayment etc.) Regulations 2003
applied: SI 2009/470 Reg.29
Reg.3, applied: SI 2009/470 Reg.16

1926. Education (Independent School Inspection Fees and Publication) (England) Regulations 2003
Reg.5, applied: SI 2009/1607 Reg.5

1934. Education (Provision of Information by Independent Schools) (England) Regulations 2003
Reg.4, amended: SI 2009/1924 Reg.6
Reg.8, amended: 2009 c.26 s.81, SI 2009/37 Reg.7
Reg.8, revoked (in part): SI 2009/37 Reg.7
Reg.10A, added: SI 2009/37 Reg.7
Reg.10A, amended: 2009 c.26 s.81
Sch.1 Part 5 para.20, amended: 2009 c.26 s.81, SI 2009/37 Reg.7

1941. Packaging (Essential Requirements) Regulations 2003
Reg.6, amended: SI 2009/1504 Reg.2
Reg.6, disapplied: SI 2009/1504 Reg.3
Reg.6, referred to: SI 2009/1504 Reg.3
Sch.2, referred to: SI 2009/1504 Reg.3

1960. Motor Cycles Etc (Single Vehicle Approval) (Fees) Regulations 2003
Reg.3, amended: SI 2009/865 Reg.2
Reg.4, amended: SI 2009/865 Reg.2
Reg.6, amended: SI 2009/865 Reg.2
Reg.8, amended: SI 2009/865 Reg.2

1963. School Staffing (England) Regulations 2003
revoked: SI 2009/2680 Sch.1
Reg.3, amended: SI 2009/1924 Reg.8
Reg.11, amended: SI 2009/1924 Reg.8
Reg.15A, amended: SI 2009/1924 Reg.8
Reg.18A, amended: SI 2009/1924 Reg.8
Reg.20, amended: SI 2009/1924 Reg.8
Reg.24A, amended: SI 2009/1924 Reg.8
Reg.26A, amended: SI 2009/1924 Reg.8

1968. Transport of Animals (Cleansing and Disinfection) (Wales) (No.3) Order 2003
Sch.2, applied: SI 2009/1372 Sch.2 para.4, Sch.2 para.6

1998. Road Vehicles (Authorisation of Special Types) (General) Order 2003
applied: SI 2009/717 Sch.4 Part 2, Sch.5 Part 4

2066. Collective Investment Schemes (Miscellaneous Amendments) Regulations 2003
Reg.13, revoked (in part): SI 2009/3093 Sch.2

2075. Meat Products (England) Regulations 2003
Sch.3 para.10, amended: SI 2009/3238 Reg.18

2076. Capital Allowances (Environmentally Beneficial Plant and Machinery) Order 2003
Art.2, amended: SI 2009/1864 Art.2

2099. Leasehold Valuation Tribunals (Procedure) (England) Regulations 2003
Reg.14, see *Earl Cadogan v Erkman* [2009] 1 E.G.L.R. 87 (Lands Tr), George Bartlett Q.C. (President)
Reg.20, amended: SI 2009/1307 Sch.2 para.95

2003–cont.

2120. RTM Companies (Memorandum and Articles of Association) (England) Regulations 2003
revoked: SI 2009/2767 Reg.3

2273. Armed Forces (Entry, Search and Seizure) Order 2003
applied: SI 2009/2056 Sch.4 para.15, Sch.4 para.19, Sch.4 para.20, Sch.4 para.21, Sch.4 para.23
Art.3, applied: SI 2009/2056 Sch.4 para.2, Sch.4 para.4
Art.4, applied: SI 2009/2056 Sch.4 para.3, Sch.4 para.4
Art.5, applied: SI 2009/2056 Sch.4 para.4
Art.8, applied: SI 2009/2056 Sch.4 para.5, Sch.4 para.7
Art.9, applied: SI 2009/2056 Sch.4 para.5, Sch.4 para.6, Sch.4 para.11
Art.10, applied: SI 2009/2056 Sch.4 para.5, Sch.4 para.7
Art.13, applied: SI 2009/2056 Sch.4 para.8
Art.14, applied: SI 2009/2056 Sch.4 para.11
Art.15, applied: SI 2009/2056 Sch.4 para.11
Art.15, disapplied: SI 2009/2056 Sch.4 para.20, Sch.4 para.21, Sch.4 para.23
Art.16, applied: SI 2009/2056 Sch.4 para.10
Sch.1, applied: SI 2009/2056 Sch.4 para.5, Sch.4 para.7

2314. Religious Character of Schools (Designation Procedure) (Independent Schools) (England) Regulations 2003
applied: SI 2009/510
referred to: SI 2009/2198, SI 2009/3276

2320. Tonnage Tax (Training Requirement) (Amendment) Regulations 2003
Reg.2, revoked: SI 2009/2304 Sch.1
Reg.4, revoked: SI 2009/2304 Sch.1
Reg.5, revoked: SI 2009/2304 Sch.1

2321. Medicines for Human Use (Fees and Miscellaneous Amendments) Regulations 2003
Reg.9, revoked: SI 2009/389 Reg.51
Reg.10, revoked: SI 2009/389 Reg.51
Reg.11, revoked: SI 2009/389 Reg.51
Reg.12, revoked: SI 2009/389 Reg.51
Reg.13, revoked: SI 2009/389 Reg.51

2329. Classical Swine Fever (England) Order 2003
Art.2, amended: SI 2009/2713 Art.2
Art.4, amended: SI 2009/2713 Art.2
Art.13, amended: SI 2009/2713 Art.2
Sch.1 Part I para.8, amended: SI 2009/2713 Art.2
Sch.1 Part II para.20, amended: SI 2009/2713 Art.2
Sch.2 Part I para.5, amended: SI 2009/2713 Art.2
Sch.2 Part II para.9, amended: SI 2009/2713 Art.2

2382. National Health Service (Travel Expenses and Remission of Charges) Regulations 2003
Reg.5, amended: SI 2009/411 Reg.4
Sch.1, amended: SI 2009/411 Reg.5, SI 2009/1599 Reg.2

2426. Privacy and Electronic Communications (EC Directive) Regulations 2003
applied: SI 2009/1976 r.19

2428. Motor Vehicles (EC Type Approval) (Amendment) (No.2) Regulations 2003
revoked: SI 2009/717 Sch.1

2495. Income Tax (Incentive Payments for Voluntary Electronic Communication of PAYE Returns) Regulations 2003
Reg.4, amended: SI 2009/1890 Art.3
Reg.6, amended: SI 2009/56 Sch.2 para.91

2527. Nurses Agencies (Wales) Regulations 2003
Reg.2, amended: SI 2009/1824 Sch.1 para.7

2003–cont.

2527. Nurses Agencies (Wales) Regulations 2003–cont.
Reg.3, amended: SI 2009/1824 Sch.1 para.7
Reg.7, amended: SI 2009/2541 Reg.13
Reg.9, amended: SI 2009/2541 Reg.13
Reg.12, amended: SI 2009/2541 Reg.13
Reg.19, amended: SI 2009/1824 Sch.1 para.7
Sch.2 para.2, substituted: SI 2009/2541 Reg.13
Sch.2 para.9, revoked: SI 2009/2541 Reg.13
Sch.2 para.10, revoked: SI 2009/2541 Reg.13
Sch.3 para.4, substituted: SI 2009/2541 Reg.13
Sch.3 para.5, revoked: SI 2009/2541 Reg.13
Sch.3 para.14, revoked: SI 2009/2541 Reg.13

2553. Electronic Communications Code (Conditions and Restrictions) Regulations 2003
Reg.2, amended: SI 2009/584 Sch.1 para.1
Reg.5, amended: SI 2009/584 Sch.1 para.2
Reg.8, amended: SI 2009/584 Sch.1 para.3

2613. Council Tax and Non-Domestic Rating (Demand Notices) (England) Regulations 2003
disapplied: SI 2009/3193 Reg.1
Reg.1, varied: SI 2009/1597 Reg.4
Sch.2 Part 1 para.7, amended: SI 2009/355 Reg.3
Sch.2 Part 3 para.3, amended: SI 2009/355 Reg.4

2627. Democratic Republic of the Congo (Restrictive Measures) (Overseas Territories) Order 2003
Art.15, varied: SI 2009/888 Art.2
Sch.2 para.1, varied: SI 2009/888 Art.2
Sch.2 para.2, varied: SI 2009/888 Art.2
Sch.2 para.3, varied: SI 2009/888 Art.2
Sch.2 para.4, varied: SI 2009/888 Art.2
Sch.2 para.5, varied: SI 2009/888 Art.2
Sch.2 para.6, varied: SI 2009/888 Art.2
Sch.2 para.7, varied: SI 2009/888 Art.2
Sch.2 para.8, varied: SI 2009/888 Art.2

2682. Income Tax (Pay As You Earn) Regulations 2003
varied: SI 2009/470 Reg.70
Reg.2, amended: SI 2009/56 Sch.2 para.93
Reg.2, see *R. (on the application of Oriel Support Ltd) v Revenue and Customs Commissioners* [2009] EWCA Civ 401, [2009] S.T.C. 1397 (CA (Civ Div)), Sir Anthony Clarke, M.R.
Reg.4, see *R. (on the application of Oriel Support Ltd) v Revenue and Customs Commissioners* [2009] EWCA Civ 401, [2009] S.T.C. 1397 (CA (Civ Div)), Sir Anthony Clarke, M.R.
Reg.10, see *R. (on the application of Oriel Support Ltd) v Revenue and Customs Commissioners* [2009] EWCA Civ 401, [2009] S.T.C. 1397 (CA (Civ Div)), Sir Anthony Clarke, M.R.
Reg.12, see *R. (on the application of Oriel Support Ltd) v Revenue and Customs Commissioners* [2009] EWCA Civ 401, [2009] S.T.C. 1397 (CA (Civ Div)), Sir Anthony Clarke, M.R.
Reg.18, amended: SI 2009/56 Sch.2 para.94
Reg.18, revoked (in part): SI 2009/56 Sch.2 para.94
Reg.19, amended: SI 2009/56 Sch.2 para.95
Reg.21, see *R. (on the application of Oriel Support Ltd) v Revenue and Customs Commissioners* [2009] EWCA Civ 401, [2009] S.T.C. 1397 (CA (Civ Div)), Sir Anthony Clarke, M.R.
Reg.46, amended: SI 2009/588 Reg.3
Reg.47, amended: SI 2009/588 Reg.3
Reg.48, amended: SI 2009/588 Reg.3
Reg.49, amended: SI 2009/588 Reg.3
Reg.67, applied: SI 2009/470 Reg.53
Reg.72A, amended: SI 2009/56 Sch.2 para.96

2003– cont.

2682. Income Tax (Pay As You Earn) Regulations 2003– *cont.*
Reg.72B, amended: SI 2009/56 Sch.2 para.97
Reg.72C, amended: SI 2009/56 Sch.2 para.98
Reg.72D, amended: SI 2009/56 Sch.2 para.99
Reg.72D, revoked (in part): SI 2009/56 Sch.2 para.99
Reg.72G, amended: SI 2009/56 Sch.2 para.100
Reg.78, amended: SI 2009/588 Reg.4
Reg.79, amended: SI 2009/588 Reg.5
Reg.80, see *ECL Solutions Ltd v Revenue and Customs Commissioners* [2009] S.T.C. (S.C.D.) 90 (Sp Comm), Theodore Wallace; see *Littlewood (t/a JL Window & Door Services) v Revenue and Customs Commissioners* [2009] S.T.C. (S.C.D.) 243 (Sp Comm), John Clark; see *Patel v Marquette Partners (UK) Ltd* [2009] I.C.R. 569 (EAT), Judge McMullen Q.C.
Reg.80, amended: SI 2009/56 Sch.2 para.101
Reg.80, revoked (in part): SI 2009/56 Sch.2 para.101
Reg.80, see *Littlewood (t/a JL Window & Door Services) v Revenue and Customs Commissioners* [2009] S.T.C. (S.C.D.) 243 (Sp Comm), John Clark
Reg.81A, amended: SI 2009/56 Sch.2 para.102
Reg.84, applied: SI 2009/470 Reg.57
Reg.90, amended: SI 2009/588 Reg.9
Reg.97, substituted: SI 2009/588 Reg.6
Reg.97G, revoked (in part): SI 2009/56 Sch.2 para.103
Reg.97H, amended: SI 2009/56 Sch.2 para.104
Reg.97J, amended: SI 2009/56 Sch.2 para.105
Reg.98, applied: SI 2009/470 Reg.47
Reg.99, applied: SI 2009/470 Reg.47
Reg.110, revoked (in part): SI 2009/56 Sch.2 para.106
Reg.122, amended: SI 2009/588 Reg.10
Reg.126, revoked (in part): SI 2009/56 Sch.2 para.107
Reg.127, amended: SI 2009/56 Sch.2 para.108
Reg.127, revoked (in part): SI 2009/56 Sch.2 para.108
Reg.128, amended: SI 2009/56 Sch.2 para.109
Reg.150, amended: SI 2009/588 Reg.7
Reg.174, amended: SI 2009/588 Reg.7
Reg.184B, amended: SI 2009/588 Reg.7, SI 2009/2029 Reg.3
Reg.202, varied: SI 2009/470 Reg.70
Reg.203, amended: SI 2009/2029 Reg.4
Reg.203, applied: SI 2009/470 Reg.68
Reg.203, varied: SI 2009/470 Reg.70
Reg.204, amended: SI 2009/56 Sch.2 para.110
Reg.205, substituted: SI 2009/2029 Reg.5
Reg.206, amended: SI 2009/2029 Reg.7
Reg.206, substituted: SI 2009/2029 Reg.6
Reg.206A, added: SI 2009/2029 Reg.8
Reg.207, revoked (in part): SI 2009/2029 Reg.9
Reg.208, amended: SI 2009/2029 Reg.10
Reg.209, substituted: SI 2009/2029 Reg.11
Reg.210, amended: SI 2009/2029 Reg.13
Reg.210, substituted: SI 2009/2029 Reg.12
Reg.210, varied: SI 2009/470 Reg.70
Reg.210A, substituted: SI 2009/2029 Reg.14
Reg.210C, amended: SI 2009/2029 Reg.15
Reg.217, amended: SI 2009/56 Sch.2 para.111
Reg.217, revoked (in part): SI 2009/56 Sch.2 para.111
Reg.218, amended: SI 2009/588 Reg.8

2003– cont.

2719. Local Government Pension Scheme (Management and Investment of Funds) (Amendment) Regulations 2003
revoked: SI 2009/3093 Sch.2

2725. School Staffing (England) (Amendment) Regulations 2003
revoked: SI 2009/2680 Sch.1

2759. Export of Objects of Cultural Interest (Control) Order 2003
Art.1, amended: SI 2009/2164 Art.2

2761. Weighing Equipment (Automatic Catchweighing Instruments) Regulations 2003
Reg.7, amended: SI 2009/3045 Reg.3

2764. Export of Goods, Transfer of Technology and Provision of Technical Assistance (Control) Order 2003
see *R. (on the application of Hasan) v Secretary of State for Trade and Industry* [2008] EWCA Civ 1312, [2009] 3 All E.R. 539 (CA (Civ Div)), Sir Anthony May (President, QB)

2821. Organic Products (Imports from Third Countries) Regulations 2003
revoked: SI 2009/842 Reg.32

2837. Stamp Duty Land Tax (Administration) Regulations 2003
referred to: SI 2009/56 Sch.2 para.112
Reg.2, amended: SI 2009/56 Sch.2 para.113
Reg.15, amended: SI 2009/56 Sch.2 para.114
Reg.19, revoked (in part): SI 2009/56 Sch.2 para.115
Reg.20, amended: SI 2009/56 Sch.2 para.116
Reg.21, amended: SI 2009/56 Sch.2 para.117
Reg.22, amended: SI 2009/56 Sch.2 para.118
Reg.22, revoked (in part): SI 2009/56 Sch.2 para.118
Reg.23, amended: SI 2009/56 Sch.2 para.119

2913. African Swine Fever (England) Order 2003
Art.2, amended: SI 2009/2713 Art.2
Art.4, amended: SI 2009/2713 Art.2
Art.13, amended: SI 2009/2713 Art.2
Sch.1 Part 1 para.9, amended: SI 2009/2713 Art.2
Sch.1 Part 2 para.11, amended: SI 2009/2713 Art.2
Sch.2 Part 1 para.5, amended: SI 2009/2713 Art.2
Sch.2 Part 2 para.3, amended: SI 2009/2713 Art.2

2994. Department for Transport (Driver Licensing and Vehicle Registration Fees) Order 2003
referred to: SI 2009/788

3011. Council Tax (Prescribed Classes of Dwellings) (England) Regulations 2003
Sch.1 para.1, see *Lever v Southwark LBC* [2009] EWHC 536 (Admin), [2009] R.V.R. 137 (QBD (Admin)), Judge Raynor Q.C.

3041. Fruit Juices and Fruit Nectars (Wales) Regulations 2003
Sch.3 para.6, substituted: SI 2009/3378 Reg.18

3047. Specified Sugar Products (Wales) Regulations 2003
Sch.1, amended: SI 2009/3378 Reg.19

3049. Merchant Shipping (Working Time Inland Waterways) Regulations 2003
Reg.19, amended: SI 2009/3348 Art.23

3053. Condensed Milk and Dried Milk (Wales) Regulations 2003
Sch.1, substituted: SI 2009/3378 Reg.18

3102. Export (Penalty) Regulations 2003
referred to: SI 2009/56 Sch.2 para.120
Reg.2, amended: SI 2009/56 Sch.2 para.121
Reg.6, amended: SI 2009/56 Sch.2 para.122
Reg.9, amended: SI 2009/56 Sch.2 para.123
Reg.9A, added: SI 2009/56 Sch.2 para.124

2003–cont.

3102. Export (Penalty) Regulations 2003–*cont.*
Reg.9B, added: SI 2009/56 Sch.2 para.124
Reg.9C, added: SI 2009/56 Sch.2 para.124
Reg.9D, added: SI 2009/56 Sch.2 para.124
Reg.9E, added: SI 2009/56 Sch.2 para.124
Reg.9F, added: SI 2009/56 Sch.2 para.124
Reg.10, revoked: SI 2009/56 Sch.2 para.125
Reg.11, revoked: SI 2009/56 Sch.2 para.125
Reg.12, revoked: SI 2009/56 Sch.2 para.125
Reg.13, substituted: SI 2009/56 Sch.2 para.126

3113. Customs (Contravention of a Relevant Rule) Regulations 2003
Reg.2, amended: SI 2009/3164 Reg.3
Sch.1, amended: SI 2009/3164 Reg.4, Reg.5, Reg.6, Reg.7

3120. Jam and Similar Products (England) Regulations 2003
Reg.2, amended: SI 2009/3238 Reg.18
Sch.2 para.1, amended: SI 2009/3238 Reg.18

3143. Income and Corporation Taxes (Electronic Certificates of Deduction of Tax and Tax Credit) Regulations 2003
Reg.2, amended: SI 2009/2050 Reg.2

3146. Local Authorities (Capital Finance and Accounting) (England) Regulations 2003
Reg.14, amended: SI 2009/2272 Reg.3
Reg.30G, added: SI 2009/321 Reg.3
Reg.31, amended: SI 2009/321 Reg.4

3171. Regulation of Investigatory Powers (Directed Surveillance and Covert Human Intelligence Sources) Order 2003
Sch.1 Part I, amended: SI 2009/229 Sch.2 para.13, SI 2009/462 Sch.5 para.10

3190. Commission for Social Care Inspection (Membership) Regulations 2003
revoked: SI 2009/462 Sch.6

3195. Communications (Bailiwick of Guernsey) Order 2003
applied: SI 2009/505

3197. Communications (Jersey) Order 2003
applied: SI 2009/505

3198. Communications (Isle of Man) Order 2003
applied: SI 2009/505

3226. Financial Collateral Arrangements (No.2) Regulations 2003
applied: 2009 c.1 s.255
varied: SI 2009/317 Sch.1
see *R. (on the application of Cukurova Finance International Ltd) v HM Treasury* [2008] EWHC 2567 (Admin), [2009] Eu. L.R. 317 (QBD (Admin)), Moses, L.J.
Reg.3, applied: SI 2009/322 Art.1
Reg.4, amended: SI 2009/2462 Reg.2
Reg.5, amended: SI 2009/2462 Reg.2
Reg.6A, added: SI 2009/2462 Reg.2
Reg.7, revoked: SI 2009/2462 Reg.2
Reg.10, amended: SI 2009/2462 Reg.2
Reg.11, revoked (in part): SI 2009/2462 Reg.2
Reg.17, see *R. (on the application of Cukurova Finance International Ltd) v HM Treasury* [2008] EWHC 2567 (Admin), [2009] Eu. L.R. 317 (QBD (Admin)), Moses, L.J.

3230. Independent Schools (Provision of Information) (Wales) Regulations 2003
Reg.2, amended: SI 2009/2544 Reg.5

3233. Independent Schools (Religious Character of Schools) (Designation Procedure) (Wales) Regulations 2003
referred to: SI 2009/1218

2003–cont.

3234. Independent School Standards (Wales) Regulations 2003
Reg.2, amended: SI 2009/2544 Reg.4
Sch.1 para.4, amended: SI 2009/2544 Reg.4

3235. Wildlife and Countryside (Registration, Ringing and Marking of Certain Captive Birds) (Wales) Regulations 2003
Reg.2, amended: SI 2009/1733 Reg.3
Reg.3, amended: SI 2009/1733 Reg.4
Reg.5, amended: SI 2009/1733 Reg.5
Sch.1, added: SI 2009/1733 Reg.6

3239. Local Authorities (Capital Finance and Accounting) (Wales) Regulations 2003
Reg.24G, added: SI 2009/560 Reg.2

3242. Water Environment (Water Framework Directive) (England and Wales) Regulations 2003
Reg.5, applied: SI 2009/3042 Reg.23

3279. Commission for Healthcare Audit and Inspection (Membership) Regulations 2003
revoked: SI 2009/462 Sch.6

3310. Controls on Certain Azo Dyes and "Blue Colourant Regulations 2003
referred to: SI 2009/669 Sch.1 Part 4

3319. Conduct of Employment Agencies and Employment Businesses Regulations 2003
Reg.14, see *Joseph v Spiller* [2009] EWCA Civ 1075, Times, October 30, 2009 (CA (Civ Div)), Pill, L.J.

3363. Insolvency Practitioners and Insolvency Services Account (Fees) Order 2003
varied: SI 2009/317 Sch.1
Art.2, amended: SI 2009/487 Art.3
Art.2, applied: SI 2009/487 Art.4
Art.2, disapplied: SI 2009/487 Art.4
Art.3, amended: SI 2009/487 Art.5, SI 2009/3081 Reg.3
Sch.1 para.2, amended: SI 2009/487 Art.6

2004

8. Proceeds of Crime Act 2002 (References to Financial Investigators) (Amendment) Order 2004
revoked: SI 2009/975 Sch.2

73. Motor Vehicle (EC Type Approval) (Amendment) Regulations 2004
revoked: SI 2009/717 Sch.1

102. Price Marking Order 2004
Art.11, amended: SI 2009/3231 Art.2

219. Domiciliary Care Agencies (Wales) Regulations 2004
Sch.2 para.3, substituted: SI 2009/2541 Reg.12
Sch.2 para.11, revoked: SI 2009/2541 Reg.12
Sch.3 para.4, substituted: SI 2009/2541 Reg.12
Sch.3 para.13, revoked: SI 2009/2541 Reg.12

291. National Health Service (General Medical Services Contracts) Regulations 2004
Reg.2, amended: SI 2009/2205 Reg.35, SI 2009/2230 Reg.3
Sch.6 Part 3 para.38, amended: SI 2009/2230 Reg.3
Sch.6 Part 3 para.39, amended: SI 2009/2230 Reg.3
Sch.6 Part 3 para.42, amended: SI 2009/2230 Reg.3
Sch.6 Part 3 para.43, amended: SI 2009/2230 Reg.3
Sch.6 Part 6 para.92, substituted: SI 2009/309 Sch.1 para.3
Sch.6 Part 6 para.93, revoked: SI 2009/309 Sch.1 para.3
Sch.6 Part 6 para.94, revoked: SI 2009/309 Sch.1 para.3

2004–cont.

291. National Health Service (General Medical Services Contracts) Regulations 2004–*cont.*
Sch.6 Part 6 para.95, revoked: SI 2009/309 Sch.1 para.3
Sch.6 Part 6 para.96, revoked: SI 2009/309 Sch.1 para.3
Sch.6 Part 6 para.97, amended: SI 2009/309 Sch.1 para.3
Sch.6 Part 6 para.98, revoked: SI 2009/309 Sch.1 para.3

293. European Parliamentary Elections Regulations 2004
applied: SI 2009/1069 Art.8, SI 2009/1077 Art.7, SI 2009/1120 Sch.1 para.4
Appendix 1, substituted: SI 2009/186 Sch.2
Appendix 2, substituted: SI 2009/186 Sch.3
Reg.2, amended: SI 2009/186 Reg.3
Reg.4, revoked (in part): SI 2009/186 Reg.4
Reg.5, amended: SI 2009/186 Reg.5
Reg.6, amended: SI 2009/186 Reg.6
Reg.8, amended: SI 2009/186 Reg.8
Reg.9, amended: SI 2009/186 Reg.9
Reg.13, revoked: SI 2009/186 Reg.10
Reg.15, amended: SI 2009/186 Reg.11
Reg.15, applied: SI 2009/1120 Art.5
Reg.15, enabled: SI 2009/1069, SI 2009/1077, SI 2009/1120
Reg.17, amended: SI 2009/186 Reg.12
Reg.19, amended: SI 2009/186 Reg.13
Reg.21, amended: SI 2009/186 Reg.14
Reg.24, amended: SI 2009/186 Reg.15
Reg.25, amended: SI 2009/186 Reg.16
Reg.26, amended: SI 2009/186 Reg.17
Reg.28, amended: SI 2009/186 Reg.18
Reg.29, amended: SI 2009/186 Reg.19
Reg.31, amended: SI 2009/186 Reg.20
Reg.32, amended: SI 2009/186 Reg.21
Reg.36, amended: SI 2009/186 Reg.22
Reg.43, amended: SI 2009/186 Reg.23
Reg.45, amended: SI 2009/186 Reg.24
Reg.46, amended: SI 2009/186 Reg.25
Reg.51, amended: SI 2009/186 Reg.26
Reg.52, referred to: SI 2009/781 Art.6
Reg.60, amended: SI 2009/186 Reg.27
Reg.61, amended: SI 2009/186 Reg.27
Reg.62, amended: SI 2009/186 Reg.28
Reg.63, amended: SI 2009/186 Reg.29
Reg.65, amended: SI 2009/186 Reg.30
Reg.74, substituted: SI 2009/186 Reg.31
Reg.79, amended: SI 2009/186 Reg.32
Reg.86, amended: SI 2009/186 Reg.33
Reg.89, amended: SI 2009/186 Reg.34
Reg.103, revoked: SI 2009/186 Reg.35
Reg.109, amended: SI 2009/186 Reg.36
Reg.114, substituted: SI 2009/186 Reg.37
Reg.120, enabled: SI 2009/1118
Reg.122A, added: SI 2009/186 Reg.38
Sch.A1, added: SI 2009/186 Sch.1
Sch.A1, referred to: SI 2009/186 Reg.7
Sch.1, referred to: SI 2009/186 Reg.39
Sch.1 Part 1 para.1, substituted: SI 2009/186 Sch.2
Sch.1 Part 1 para.2, substituted: SI 2009/186 Sch.2
Sch.1 Part 2 para.3, substituted: SI 2009/186 Sch.2
Sch.1 Part 2 para.4, referred to: SI 2009/781 Art.4
Sch.1 Part 2 para.4, substituted: SI 2009/186 Sch.2
Sch.1 Part 2 para.5, substituted: SI 2009/186 Sch.2
Sch.1 Part 2 para.6, substituted: SI 2009/186 Sch.2
Sch.1 Part 2 para.7, substituted: SI 2009/186 Sch.2

2004–cont.

293. European Parliamentary Elections Regulations 2004–*cont.*
Sch.1 Part 2 para.8, substituted: SI 2009/186 Sch.2
Sch.1 Part 2 para.9, substituted: SI 2009/186 Sch.2
Sch.1 Part 2 para.10, substituted: SI 2009/186 Sch.2
Sch.1 Part 2 para.11, substituted: SI 2009/186 Sch.2
Sch.1 Part 2 para.12, substituted: SI 2009/186 Sch.2
Sch.1 Part 2 para.13, substituted: SI 2009/186 Sch.2
Sch.1 Part 2 para.14, substituted: SI 2009/186 Sch.2
Sch.1 Part 2 para.15, substituted: SI 2009/186 Sch.2
Sch.1 Part 2 para.16, substituted: SI 2009/186 Sch.2
Sch.1 Part 2 para.17, substituted: SI 2009/186 Sch.2
Sch.1 Part 2 para.18, substituted: SI 2009/186 Sch.2
Sch.1 Part 2 para.19, substituted: SI 2009/186 Sch.2
Sch.1 Part 2 para.20, substituted: SI 2009/186 Sch.2
Sch.1 Part 3 para.20, substituted: SI 2009/186 Sch.2
Sch.1 Part 3 para.21, substituted: SI 2009/186 Sch.2
Sch.1 Part 3 para.22, substituted: SI 2009/186 Sch.2
Sch.1 Part 3 para.22, referred to: SI 2009/781 Art.4, Art.6
Sch.1 Part 3 para.22, substituted: SI 2009/186 Sch.2
Sch.1 Part 3 para.23, substituted: SI 2009/186 Sch.2
Sch.1 Part 3 para.23, referred to: SI 2009/781 Art.6
Sch.1 Part 3 para.23, substituted: SI 2009/186 Sch.2
Sch.1 Part 3 para.24, substituted: SI 2009/186 Sch.2
Sch.1 Part 3 para.25, substituted: SI 2009/186 Sch.2
Sch.1 Part 3 para.26, substituted: SI 2009/186 Sch.2
Sch.1 Part 3 para.27, substituted: SI 2009/186 Sch.2
Sch.1 Part 3 para.28, substituted: SI 2009/186 Sch.2
Sch.1 Part 3 para.29, substituted: SI 2009/186 Sch.2
Sch.1 Part 3 para.30, substituted: SI 2009/186 Sch.2
Sch.1 Part 3 para.31, substituted: SI 2009/186 Sch.2
Sch.1 Part 3 para.31, referred to: SI 2009/781 Art.6
Sch.1 Part 3 para.31, substituted: SI 2009/186 Sch.2
Sch.1 Part 3 para.32, substituted: SI 2009/186 Sch.2
Sch.1 Part 3 para.32, referred to: SI 2009/781 Art.6
Sch.1 Part 3 para.32, substituted: SI 2009/186 Sch.2
Sch.1 Part 3 para.33, substituted: SI 2009/186 Sch.2
Sch.1 Part 3 para.34, substituted: SI 2009/186 Sch.2
Sch.1 Part 3 para.35, substituted: SI 2009/186 Sch.2
Sch.1 Part 3 para.36, substituted: SI 2009/186 Sch.2
Sch.1 Part 3 para.36, referred to: SI 2009/781 Art.5
Sch.1 Part 3 para.36, substituted: SI 2009/186 Sch.2
Sch.1 Part 3 para.37, substituted: SI 2009/186 Sch.2
Sch.1 Part 3 para.38, substituted: SI 2009/186 Sch.2
Sch.1 Part 3 para.39, substituted: SI 2009/186 Sch.2
Sch.1 Part 3 para.39, referred to: SI 2009/781 Art.5
Sch.1 Part 3 para.39, substituted: SI 2009/186 Sch.2
Sch.1 Part 3 para.40, substituted: SI 2009/186 Sch.2
Sch.1 Part 3 para.41, substituted: SI 2009/186 Sch.2
Sch.1 Part 3 para.42, substituted: SI 2009/186 Sch.2
Sch.1 Part 3 para.43, substituted: SI 2009/186 Sch.2
Sch.1 Part 3 para.43, referred to: SI 2009/781 Art.5
Sch.1 Part 3 para.43, substituted: SI 2009/186 Sch.2
Sch.1 Part 3 para.44, substituted: SI 2009/186 Sch.2
Sch.1 Part 3 para.45, substituted: SI 2009/186 Sch.2
Sch.1 Part 3 para.46, substituted: SI 2009/186 Sch.2
Sch.1 Part 3 para.47, substituted: SI 2009/186 Sch.2
Sch.1 Part 3 para.48, substituted: SI 2009/186 Sch.2
Sch.1 Part 3 para.49, substituted: SI 2009/186 Sch.2
Sch.1 Part 3 para.50, substituted: SI 2009/186 Sch.2
Sch.1 Part 3 para.51, substituted: SI 2009/186 Sch.2
Sch.1 Part 3 para.52, substituted: SI 2009/186 Sch.2
Sch.1 Part 3 para.53, substituted: SI 2009/186 Sch.2
Sch.1 Part 3 para.53, amended: SI 2009/848 Reg.2
Sch.1 Part 3 para.53, substituted: SI 2009/186 Sch.2
Sch.1 Part 3 para.54, substituted: SI 2009/186 Sch.2
Sch.1 Part 3 para.55, substituted: SI 2009/186 Sch.2

2004–cont.

293. European Parliamentary Elections Regulations 2004–*cont.*

Sch.1 Part 3 para.56, substituted: SI 2009/ 186 Sch.2
Sch.1 Part 3 para.57, substituted: SI 2009/ 186 Sch.2
Sch.1 Part 3 para.58, substituted: SI 2009/ 186 Sch.2
Sch.1 Part 3 para.59, substituted: SI 2009/ 186 Sch.2
Sch.1 Part 3 para.60, substituted: SI 2009/ 186 Sch.2
Sch.1 Part 4 para.56, substituted: SI 2009/ 186 Sch.2
Sch.1 Part 4 para.57, substituted: SI 2009/ 186 Sch.2
Sch.1 Part 4 para.61, substituted: SI 2009/ 186 Sch.2
Sch.1 Part 4 para.62, substituted: SI 2009/ 186 Sch.2
Sch.1 Part 5 para.58, substituted: SI 2009/ 186 Sch.2
Sch.1 Part 5 para.59, substituted: SI 2009/ 186 Sch.2
Sch.1 Part 5 para.60, substituted: SI 2009/ 186 Sch.2
Sch.1 Part 5 para.61, substituted: SI 2009/ 186 Sch.2
Sch.1 Part 5 para.63, substituted: SI 2009/ 186 Sch.2
Sch.1 Part 5 para.64, substituted: SI 2009/ 186 Sch.2
Sch.1 Part 5 para.65, substituted: SI 2009/ 186 Sch.2
Sch.1 Part 5 para.66, substituted: SI 2009/ 186 Sch.2
Sch.1 Part 6 para.67, substituted: SI 2009/ 186 Sch.2
Sch.1 Part 6 para.68, substituted: SI 2009/ 186 Sch.2
Sch.1 Part 6 para.69, substituted: SI 2009/ 186 Sch.2
Sch.1 Part 6 para.70, substituted: SI 2009/ 186 Sch.2
Sch.1 Part 6 para.71, substituted: SI 2009/ 186 Sch.2
Sch.1 Part 6 para.72, substituted: SI 2009/ 186 Sch.2
Sch.1 Part 7, substituted: SI 2009/ 186 Sch.2
Sch.2, referred to: SI 2009/ 186 Reg.40
Sch.2 Part 1 para.1, substituted: SI 2009/ 186 Sch.3
Sch.2 Part 1 para.2, substituted: SI 2009/ 186 Sch.3
Sch.2 Part 1 para.3, substituted: SI 2009/ 186 Sch.3
Sch.2 Part 1 para.4, substituted: SI 2009/ 186 Sch.3
Sch.2 Part 1 para.5, substituted: SI 2009/ 186 Sch.3
Sch.2 Part 1 para.6, referred to: SI 2009/ 781 Art.6
Sch.2 Part 1 para.6, substituted: SI 2009/ 186 Sch.3
Sch.2 Part 1 para.7, substituted: SI 2009/ 186 Sch.3
Sch.2 Part 1 para.8, substituted: SI 2009/ 186 Sch.3
Sch.2 Part 1 para.9, substituted: SI 2009/ 186 Sch.3
Sch.2 Part 1 para.10, substituted: SI 2009/ 186 Sch.3
Sch.2 Part 1 para.11, substituted: SI 2009/ 186 Sch.3
Sch.2 Part 2 para.9, substituted: SI 2009/ 186 Sch.3
Sch.2 Part 2 para.10, substituted: SI 2009/ 186 Sch.3
Sch.2 Part 2 para.11, substituted: SI 2009/ 186 Sch.3
Sch.2 Part 2 para.12, substituted: SI 2009/ 186 Sch.3
Sch.2 Part 2 para.13, substituted: SI 2009/ 186 Sch.3
Sch.2 Part 2 para.14, substituted: SI 2009/ 186 Sch.3
Sch.2 Part 2 para.15, substituted: SI 2009/ 186 Sch.3
Sch.2 Part 2 para.16, substituted: SI 2009/ 186 Sch.3
Sch.2 Part 2 para.17, substituted: SI 2009/ 186 Sch.3
Sch.2 Part 2 para.18, substituted: SI 2009/ 186 Sch.3
Sch.2 Part 2 para.19, substituted: SI 2009/ 186 Sch.3
Sch.2 Part 2 para.20, substituted: SI 2009/ 186 Sch.3
Sch.2 Part 2 para.21, substituted: SI 2009/ 186 Sch.3
Sch.2 Part 2 para.22, substituted: SI 2009/ 186 Sch.3
Sch.2 Part 2 para.23, substituted: SI 2009/ 186 Sch.3
Sch.2 Part 2 para.24, substituted: SI 2009/186 Sch.3
Sch.2 Part 2 para.25, substituted: SI 2009/ 186 Sch.3
Sch.2 Part 2 para.26, substituted: SI 2009/ 186 Sch.3
Sch.2 Part 2 para.27, substituted: SI 2009/ 186 Sch.3
Sch.2 Part 2 para.28, substituted: SI 2009/ 186 Sch.3
Sch.2 Part 2 para.29, substituted: SI 2009/ 186 Sch.3
Sch.2 Part 2 para.30, substituted: SI 2009/ 186 Sch.3
Sch.2 Part 2 para.31, substituted: SI 2009/ 186 Sch.3
Sch.2 Part 2 para.32, substituted: SI 2009/ 186 Sch.3
Sch.2 Part 2 para.33, substituted: SI 2009/ 186 Sch.3
Sch.2 Part 2 para.34, substituted: SI 2009/ 186 Sch.3
Sch.2 Part 3 para.26, substituted: SI 2009/ 186 Sch.3
Sch.2 Part 3 para.27, substituted: SI 2009/ 186 Sch.3
Sch.2 Part 3 para.28, substituted: SI 2009/ 186 Sch.3

2004–cont.

293. European Parliamentary Elections Regulations 2004–*cont.*

Sch.2 Part 3 para.29, substituted: SI 2009/ 186 Sch.3
Sch.2 Part 3 para.30, substituted: SI 2009/ 186 Sch.3
Sch.2 Part 3 para.31, substituted: SI 2009/ 186 Sch.3
Sch.2 Part 3 para.32, substituted: SI 2009/ 186 Sch.3
Sch.2 Part 3 para.33, substituted: SI 2009/ 186 Sch.3
Sch.2 Part 3 para.34, substituted: SI 2009/ 186 Sch.3
Sch.2 Part 3 para.35, substituted: SI 2009/ 186 Sch.3
Sch.2 Part 3 para.36, substituted: SI 2009/ 186 Sch.3
Sch.2 Part 3 para.36, amended: SI 2009/ 848 Reg.2
Sch.2 Part 3 para.36, substituted: SI 2009/ 186 Sch.3
Sch.2 Part 3 para.37, substituted: SI 2009/ 186 Sch.3
Sch.2 Part 3 para.38, substituted: SI 2009/ 186 Sch.3
Sch.2 Part 3 para.39, substituted: SI 2009/ 186 Sch.3
Sch.2 Part 3 para.39, amended: SI 2009/ 848 Reg.2
Sch.2 Part 3 para.39, substituted: SI 2009/ 186 Sch.3
Sch.2 Part 3 para.40, substituted: SI 2009/ 186 Sch.3
Sch.2 Part 3 para.41, substituted: SI 2009/ 186 Sch.3
Sch.2 Part 3 para.42, substituted: SI 2009/ 186 Sch.3
Sch.2 Part 3 para.43, substituted: SI 2009/ 186 Sch.3
Sch.2 Part 3 para.44, substituted: SI 2009/ 186 Sch.3
Sch.2 Part 3 para.45, substituted: SI 2009/ 186 Sch.3
Sch.2 Part 3 para.46, substituted: SI 2009/ 186 Sch.3
Sch.2 Part 3 para.47, substituted: SI 2009/ 186 Sch.3
Sch.2 Part 3 para.48, substituted: SI 2009/ 186 Sch.3
Sch.2 Part 3 para.49, substituted: SI 2009/ 186 Sch.3
Sch.2 Part 3 para.50, substituted: SI 2009/ 186 Sch.3
Sch.2 Part 3 para.51, substituted: SI 2009/ 186 Sch.3
Sch.2 Part 3 para.52, substituted: SI 2009/ 186 Sch.3
Sch.2 Part 4 para.40, substituted: SI 2009/ 186 Sch.3
Sch.2 Part 4 para.41, substituted: SI 2009/ 186 Sch.3
Sch.2 Part 4 para.42, referred to: SI 2009/ 781 Art.6
Sch.2 Part 4 para.42, substituted: SI 2009/ 186 Sch.3
Sch.2 Part 4 para.43, substituted: SI 2009/ 186 Sch.3
Sch.2 Part 4 para.44, substituted: SI 2009/ 186 Sch.3
Sch.2 Part 4 para.45, substituted: SI 2009/ 186 Sch.3
Sch.2 Part 4 para.46, substituted: SI 2009/ 186 Sch.3
Sch.2 Part 4 para.47, substituted: SI 2009/ 186 Sch.3
Sch.2 Part 4 para.48, substituted: SI 2009/ 186 Sch.3
Sch.2 Part 4 para.49, substituted: SI 2009/ 186 Sch.3
Sch.2 Part 4 para.50, substituted: SI 2009/ 186 Sch.3
Sch.2 Part 4 para.51, substituted: SI 2009/ 186 Sch.3
Sch.2 Part 4 para.52, substituted: SI 2009/ 186 Sch.3
Sch.2 Part 4 para.53, substituted: SI 2009/ 186 Sch.3
Sch.2 Part 4 para.54, amended: SI 2009/ 848 Reg.2
Sch.2 Part 4 para.54, substituted: SI 2009/ 186 Sch.3
Sch.2 Part 4 para.55, substituted: SI 2009/ 186 Sch.3
Sch.2 Part 4 para.56, substituted: SI 2009/ 186 Sch.3
Sch.2 Part 4 para.57, substituted: SI 2009/ 186 Sch.3
Sch.2 Part 4 para.58, substituted: SI 2009/ 186 Sch.3
Sch.2 Part 4 para.59, substituted: SI 2009/ 186 Sch.3
Sch.2 Part 4 para.60, substituted: SI 2009/ 186 Sch.3
Sch.2 Part 4 para.61, substituted: SI 2009/ 186 Sch.3
Sch.2 Part 4 para.62, substituted: SI 2009/ 186 Sch.3
Sch.2 Part 4 para.63, substituted: SI 2009/ 186 Sch.3
Sch.2 Part 4 para.64, substituted: SI 2009/ 186 Sch.3
Sch.2 Part 4 para.65, substituted: SI 2009/ 186 Sch.3
Sch.2 Part 4 para.66, substituted: SI 2009/ 186 Sch.3
Sch.2 Part 4 para.67, substituted: SI 2009/ 186 Sch.3
Sch.2 Part 4 para.68, substituted: SI 2009/ 186 Sch.3
Sch.2 Part 4 para.69, substituted: SI 2009/ 186 Sch.3
Sch.2 Part 4 para.70, amended: SI 2009/ 848 Reg.2
Sch.2 Part 4 para.70, referred to: SI 2009/ 781 Art.6
Sch.2 Part 4 para.70, substituted: SI 2009/ 186 Sch.3
Sch.2 Part 5, substituted: SI 2009/ 186 Sch.3
Sch.3, referred to: SI 2009/ 186 Reg.41
Sch.3 Part 1 para.1, substituted: SI 2009/ 186 Sch.4

2004– cont.

293. European Parliamentary Elections Regulations 2004– cont.

Sch.3 Part 1 para.2, substituted: SI 2009/186 Sch.4
Sch.3 Part 1 para.3, substituted: SI 2009/186 Sch.4
Sch.3 Part 1 para.4, substituted: SI 2009/186 Sch.4
Sch.3 Part 1 para.5, substituted: SI 2009/186 Sch.4
Sch.3 Part 1 para.6, substituted: SI 2009/186 Sch.4
Sch.3 Part 1 para.7, substituted: SI 2009/186 Sch.4
Sch.3 Part 1 para.8, referred to: SI 2009/781 Art.6
Sch.3 Part 1 para.8, substituted: SI 2009/186 Sch.4
Sch.3 Part 1 para.9, substituted: SI 2009/186 Sch.4
Sch.3 Part 1 para.10, substituted: SI 2009/186 Sch.4
Sch.3 Part 1 para.11, substituted: SI 2009/186 Sch.4
Sch.3 Part 1 para.12, substituted: SI 2009/186 Sch.4
Sch.3 Part 1 para.13, substituted: SI 2009/186 Sch.4
Sch.3 Part 1 para.14, substituted: SI 2009/186 Sch.4
Sch.3 Part 1 para.15, substituted: SI 2009/186 Sch.4
Sch.3 Part 1 para.16, substituted: SI 2009/186 Sch.4
Sch.3 Part 1 para.17, substituted: SI 2009/186 Sch.4
Sch.3 Part 1 para.18, substituted: SI 2009/186 Sch.4
Sch.3 Part 1 para.19, substituted: SI 2009/186 Sch.4
Sch.3 Part 1 para.20, substituted: SI 2009/186 Sch.4
Sch.3 Part 1 para.21, substituted: SI 2009/186 Sch.4
Sch.3 Part 1 para.22, substituted: SI 2009/186 Sch.4
Sch.3 Part 1 para.23, substituted: SI 2009/186 Sch.4
Sch.3 Part 1 para.24, substituted: SI 2009/186 Sch.4
Sch.3 Part 1 para.25, substituted: SI 2009/186 Sch.4
Sch.3 Part 1 para.26, substituted: SI 2009/186 Sch.4
Sch.3 Part 1 para.27, substituted: SI 2009/186 Sch.4
Sch.3 Part 1 para.28, referred to: SI 2009/781 Art.6
Sch.3 Part 1 para.28, substituted: SI 2009/186 Sch.4
Sch.3 Part 1 para.29, referred to: SI 2009/781 Art.5
Sch.3 Part 1 para.29, substituted: SI 2009/186 Sch.4
Sch.3 Part 2 para.1, substituted: SI 2009/186 Sch.4
Sch.3 Part 2 para.2, substituted: SI 2009/186 Sch.4
Sch.3 Part 2 para.3, substituted: SI 2009/186 Sch.4
Sch.3 Part 2 para.4, substituted: SI 2009/186 Sch.4
Sch.3 Part 2 para.5, substituted: SI 2009/186 Sch.4
Sch.3 Part 2 para.6, substituted: SI 2009/186 Sch.4
Sch.3 Part 2 para.7, substituted: SI 2009/186 Sch.4
Sch.3 Part 2 para.8, substituted: SI 2009/186 Sch.4
Sch.3 Part 2 para.9, substituted: SI 2009/186 Sch.4
Sch.3 Part 2 para.10, substituted: SI 2009/186 Sch.4
Sch.3 Part 2 para.11, substituted: SI 2009/186 Sch.4
Sch.3 Part 2 para.12, substituted: SI 2009/186 Sch.4
Sch.3 Part 2 para.13, substituted: SI 2009/186 Sch.4
Sch.3 Part 2 para.14, substituted: SI 2009/186 Sch.4
Sch.3 Part 2 para.15, substituted: SI 2009/186 Sch.4
Sch.3 Part 2 para.16, substituted: SI 2009/186 Sch.4
Sch.3 Part 2 para.17, substituted: SI 2009/186 Sch.4
Sch.3 Part 2 para.18, substituted: SI 2009/186 Sch.4
Sch.3 Part 2 para.19, substituted: SI 2009/186 Sch.4
Sch.3 Part 2 para.20, substituted: SI 2009/186 Sch.4
Sch.3 Part 2 para.21, substituted: SI 2009/186 Sch.4
Sch.3 Part 2 para.22, substituted: SI 2009/186 Sch.4
Sch.3 Part 2 para.23, substituted: SI 2009/186 Sch.4
Sch.3 Part 2 para.24, substituted: SI 2009/186 Sch.4
Sch.3 Part 2 para.25, substituted: SI 2009/186 Sch.4
Sch.3 Part 2 para.26, substituted: SI 2009/186 Sch.4
Sch.3 Part 2 para.27, substituted: SI 2009/186 Sch.4
Sch.3 Part 2 para.28, substituted: SI 2009/186 Sch.4
Sch.4 Part 1 para.2, amended: SI 2009/186 Reg.42
Sch.4 Part 2 para.4, amended: SI 2009/186 Reg.42, SI 2009/2054 Sch.1 para.26
Sch.4 Part 2 para.4, applied: SI 2009/2054 Sch.2 para.17
Sch.4 Part 2 para.6, amended: SI 2009/186 Reg.42
Sch.4 Part 2 para.7, amended: SI 2009/186 Reg.42

2004– cont.

293. European Parliamentary Elections Regulations 2004– cont.

Sch.4 Part 2 para.7, revoked: SI 2009/186 Reg.42
Sch.4 Part 2 para.10, amended: SI 2009/186 Reg.42
Sch.4 Part 2 para.11, amended: SI 2009/186 Reg.42
Sch.4 Part 2 para.15, amended: SI 2009/186 Reg.42
Sch.4 Part 2 para.17, amended: SI 2009/186 Reg.42
Sch.4 Part 2 para.18, amended: SI 2009/186 Reg.42
Sch.4 Part 2 para.20, amended: SI 2009/186 Reg.42
Sch.5 para.1, revoked: SI 2009/186 Reg.43
Sch.5 para.2, revoked: SI 2009/186 Reg.43
Sch.5 para.3, revoked: SI 2009/186 Reg.43
Sch.5 para.4, revoked: SI 2009/186 Reg.43
Sch.5 para.5, revoked: SI 2009/186 Reg.43
Sch.5 para.6, revoked: SI 2009/186 Reg.43
Sch.5 para.7, revoked: SI 2009/186 Reg.43
Sch.5 para.8, revoked: SI 2009/186 Reg.43
Sch.5 para.9, revoked: SI 2009/186 Reg.43
Sch.5 para.10, revoked: SI 2009/186 Reg.43
Sch.5 para.11, revoked: SI 2009/186 Reg.43
Sch.6 Part 1 para.1, amended: SI 2009/186 Reg.44
Sch.6 Part 3 para.10, substituted: SI 2009/186 Reg.44
Sch.7A, referred to: SI 2009/186 Reg.45
Sch.7A Part 1 para.1, added: SI 2009/186 Sch.5
Sch.7A Part 1 para.2, added: SI 2009/186 Sch.5
Sch.7A Part 1 para.3, added: SI 2009/186 Sch.5
Sch.7A Part 1 para.4, added: SI 2009/186 Sch.5
Sch.7A Part 1 para.5, added: SI 2009/186 Sch.5
Sch.7A Part 1 para.6, added: SI 2009/186 Sch.5
Sch.7A Part 2 para.7, added: SI 2009/186 Sch.5
Sch.7A Part 2 para.8, added: SI 2009/186 Sch.5
Sch.7A Part 2 para.9, added: SI 2009/186 Sch.5
Sch.7A Part 2 para.10, added: SI 2009/186 Sch.5
Sch.7A Part 2 para.11, added: SI 2009/186 Sch.5
Sch.7A Part 2 para.12, added: SI 2009/186 Sch.5
Sch.7A Part 2 para.13, added: SI 2009/186 Sch.5

307. Communications (Bailiwick of Guernsey) Order 2004

applied: SI 2009/505

308. Broadcasting and Communications (Jersey) Order 2004

applied: SI 2009/505

349. Sudan (Restrictive Measures) (Overseas Territories) Order 2004

Art.15, varied: SI 2009/888 Art.2
Sch.2 para.1, varied: SI 2009/888 Art.2
Sch.2 para.2, varied: SI 2009/888 Art.2
Sch.2 para.3, varied: SI 2009/888 Art.2
Sch.2 para.4, varied: SI 2009/888 Art.2
Sch.2 para.5, varied: SI 2009/888 Art.2
Sch.2 para.6, varied: SI 2009/888 Art.2
Sch.2 para.7, varied: SI 2009/888 Art.2
Sch.2 para.8, varied: SI 2009/888 Art.2

352. Petroleum Licensing (Exploration and Production) (Seaward and Landward Areas) Regulations 2004

Reg.2, amended: SI 2009/3283 Reg.3
Reg.3, disapplied: SI 2009/2814 Reg.3
Sch.1, disapplied: SI 2009/2814 Reg.3
Sch.1 para.1, amended: SI 2009/229 Sch.2 para.14
Sch.6 para.1, amended: SI 2009/229 Sch.2 para.14, SI 2009/3283 Reg.3

478. National Health Service (General Medical Services Contracts) (Wales) Regulations 2004

Sch.6 Part 5 para.89, substituted: SI 2009/462 Sch.5 para.11

2004–cont.

478. National Health Service (General Medical Services Contracts) (Wales) Regulations 2004–*cont.*
Sch.6 Part 6 para.95, revoked (in part): SI 2009/462 Sch.5 para.11

553. Jam and Similar Products (Wales) Regulations 2004
Reg.2, amended: SI 2009/3378 Reg.18
Sch.2 para.1, amended: SI 2009/3378 Reg.18

555. Commission for Social Care Inspection (Explanation and Co-operation) Regulations 2004
revoked: SI 2009/462 Sch.6
Reg.2, applied: SI 2009/462 Sch.3 para.6
Reg.2, varied: SI 2009/462 Sch.3 para.6

557. Commission for Healthcare Audit and Inspection (Explanation, Statements of Action and Co-operation) Regulations 2004
revoked: SI 2009/462 Sch.6
Reg.2, applied: SI 2009/462 Sch.3 para.6
Reg.2, varied: SI 2009/462 Sch.3 para.6
Reg.3, applied: SI 2009/462 Sch.3 para.6
Reg.3, varied: SI 2009/462 Sch.3 para.6

568. Carriage of Dangerous Goods and Use of Transportable Pressure Equipment Regulations 2004
Sch.2 para.4, applied: SI 2009/1348 Reg.14

593. Insolvency Proceedings (Fees) Order 2004
Art.4, amended: SI 2009/645 Art.4
Art.5, amended: SI 2009/645 Art.4
Art.6, amended: SI 2009/645 Art.4
Art.7, amended: SI 2009/645 Art.4
Sch.2 para.1, amended: SI 2009/645 Art.5
Sch.2 para.2, amended: SI 2009/645 Art.6

615. Commission for Social Care Inspection (Children's Rights Director) Regulations 2004
revoked: SI 2009/462 Sch.6

627. National Health Service (Personal Medical Services Agreements) Regulations 2004
Reg.2, amended: SI 2009/2205 Reg.36, SI 2009/2230 Reg.4
Sch.5 Part 3 para.37, amended: SI 2009/2230 Reg.4
Sch.5 Part 3 para.38, amended: SI 2009/2230 Reg.4
Sch.5 Part 3 para.41, amended: SI 2009/2230 Reg.4
Sch.5 Part 3 para.42, amended: SI 2009/2230 Reg.4
Sch.5 Part 6 para.86, substituted: SI 2009/309 Sch.1 para.4
Sch.5 Part 6 para.87, revoked: SI 2009/309 Sch.1 para.4
Sch.5 Part 6 para.88, revoked: SI 2009/309 Sch.1 para.4
Sch.5 Part 6 para.89, revoked: SI 2009/309 Sch.1 para.4
Sch.5 Part 6 para.90, revoked: SI 2009/309 Sch.1 para.4
Sch.5 Part 6 para.91, amended: SI 2009/309 Sch.1 para.4
Sch.5 Part 6 para.92, revoked: SI 2009/309 Sch.1 para.4

629. National Health Service (General Medical Services Contracts) (Prescription of Drugs etc.) Regulations 2004
Sch.2, amended: SI 2009/2230 Reg.5

643. Police (Complaints and Misconduct) Regulations 2004
referred to: SI 2009/3070 Reg.4
Reg.12, applied: SI 2009/3069 Reg.19, Reg.35, Reg.55
Reg.14A, applied: SI 2009/3069 Reg.19, Reg.35, Reg.55

2004–cont.

652. Ministry of Defence Police Appeal Tribunals Regulations 2004
revoked: SI 2009/3070 Reg.2

653. Ministry of Defence Police (Conduct) Regulations 2004
revoked: SI 2009/3069 Reg.2

654. Ministry of Defence Police (Conduct) (Senior Officers) Regulations 2004
revoked: SI 2009/3069 Reg.2

664. Health and Social Care (Community Health and Standards) Act 2003 (Commission for Healthcare Audit and Inspection and Commission for Social Care Inspection) (Transitional and Consequential Provisions) Order 2004
revoked: SI 2009/462 Sch.6

692. Communications (Television Licensing) Regulations 2004
Sch.1, amended: SI 2009/505 Reg.3
Sch.2 Part 1 para.1, revoked (in part): SI 2009/505 Reg.4
Sch.2 Part 1 para.2, amended: SI 2009/505 Reg.4
Sch.2 Part 2 para.5, amended: SI 2009/505 Reg.4, Sch.1
Sch.2 Part 2 para.6, amended: SI 2009/505 Reg.4, Sch.1
Sch.2 Part 2 para.7, amended: SI 2009/505 Reg.4, Sch.1
Sch.2 Part 3 para.8, revoked (in part): SI 2009/505 Reg.4
Sch.2 Part 3 para.9, amended: SI 2009/505 Reg.4
Sch.2 Part 3 para.11, amended: SI 2009/505 Reg.4
Sch.2 Part 3 para.12, amended: SI 2009/505 Reg.4
Sch.2 Part 3 para.13, amended: SI 2009/505 Reg.4
Sch.2 Part 3 para.14, amended: SI 2009/505 Reg.4
Sch.2 Part 3 para.15, amended: SI 2009/505 Reg.4
Sch.2 Part 3 para.16, amended: SI 2009/505 Reg.4
Sch.2 Part 3 para.17, amended: SI 2009/505 Reg.4
Sch.3 Part 1, amended: SI 2009/505 Reg.5
Sch.3 Part 2 para.1, amended: SI 2009/505 Reg.5
Sch.5 para.1, amended: SI 2009/505 Reg.6
Sch.5 para.3, amended: SI 2009/505 Reg.6

747. Children (Leaving Care) Social Security Benefits (Scotland) Regulations 2004
Reg.2, amended: SI 2009/3152 Reg.3
Reg.2, revoked (in part): SI 2009/3152 Reg.3

752. Employment Act 2002 (Dispute Resolution) Regulations 2004
see *N v Lewisham LBC* [2009] I.C.R. 1538 (EAT), Burton, J.; see *Remploy Ltd v Shaw* [2009] I.C.R. 1159 (EAT), Judge McMullen Q.C.
Reg.2, see *N v Lewisham LBC* [2009] I.C.R. 1538 (EAT), Burton, J.; see *Suffolk Mental Health Partnership NHS Trust v Hurst* [2009] I.C.R. 281 (EAT), Elias, J (President)
Reg.15, see *Corps of Commissionaries Management Ltd v Hughes* [2009] I.C.R. 345 (EAT), Silber, J.; see *Remploy Ltd v Shaw* [2009] I.C.R. 1159 (EAT), Judge McMullen Q.C.

754. Compromise Agreements (Description of Person) Order 2004
Art.2, amended: SI 2009/3348 Art.22

756. Civil Aviation (Working Time) Regulations 2004
Reg.4, see *British Airways Plc v Williams* [2009] EWCA Civ 281, [2009] I.C.R. 906 (CA (Civ Div)), Ward, L.J.

816. Zimbabwe (Freezing of Funds and Economic Resources) Regulations 2004
revoked: SI 2009/847 Reg.17

2004 – cont.

953. Scotland Act 1998 (Designation of Receipts) Order 2004
revoked: SI 2009/537 Art.3

1022. National Health Service (General Medical Services Contracts) (Prescription of Drugs Etc.) (Wales) Regulations 2004
Sch.2, amended: SI 2009/1838 Reg.2, SI 2009/1977 Reg.2

1031. Medicines for Human Use (Clinical Trials) Regulations 2004
applied: SI 2009/389 Sch.1 para.32, SI 2009/716 Reg.3
Reg.18, applied: SI 2009/389 Reg.34
Reg.19, applied: SI 2009/389 Reg.34
Reg.20, applied: SI 2009/389 Reg.34
Reg.24, applied: SI 2009/389 Reg.19
Reg.28, applied: SI 2009/389 Reg.30
Reg.30, amended: SI 2009/1164 Reg.3
Reg.44, applied: SI 2009/389 Reg.18
Sch.3 Part 2 para.11, applied: SI 2009/389 Sch.1 para.32
Sch.5 para.3, referred to: SI 2009/389 Reg.37
Sch.8 para.4, referred to: SI 2009/389 Reg.37

1034. Crime (International Co-operation) Act 2003 (Designation of Prosecuting Authorities) Order 2004
Art.2, amended: SI 2009/2748 Sch.1 para.26

1045. Credit Institutions (Reorganisation and Winding up) Regulations 2004
varied: SI 2009/317 Sch.1
Reg.2, varied: SI 2009/3226 Sch.2
Reg.9, varied: SI 2009/3226 Sch.2
Reg.10, varied: SI 2009/3226 Sch.2
Reg.12A, varied: SI 2009/3226 Sch.2
Reg.19, varied: SI 2009/3226 Sch.2
Reg.21, varied: SI 2009/3226 Sch.2

1046. Common Agricultural Policy (Wine) (England and Northern Ireland) (Amendment) Regulations 2004
revoked (in part): SI 2009/386 Reg.17

1072. Greater Manchester (Light Rapid Transit System) (Exemptions) Order 2004
revoked: SI 2009/2726 Art.18

1077. Competition Act 1998 (Concurrency) Regulations 2004
Reg.7, see *R. (on the application of Cityhook Ltd) v Office of Fair Trading* [2009] EWHC 204 (Admin), [2009] U.K.C.L.R. 657 (QBD (Admin)), Foskett, J.; see *R. (on the application of Cityhook Ltd) v Office of Fair Trading* [2009] EWHC 57 (Admin), [2009] U.K.C.L.R. 255 (QBD (Admin)), Foskett, J.

1175. Education (Student Loans) (Repayment) (Amendment) Regulations 2004
revoked: SI 2009/470 Sch.1

1192. Courts Boards Areas Order 2004
Sch.1, amended: SI 2009/3184 Art.4, Art.5

1219. Accession (Immigration and Worker Registration) Regulations 2004
Reg.1, amended: SI 2009/892 Reg.2
Reg.2, amended: SI 2009/2426 Reg.3

1246. European Parliament (Disqualification) (United Kingdom and Gibraltar) Order 2004
revoked: SI 2009/190 Art.2

1256. EC/Swiss Air Transport Agreement (Consequential Amendments) Regulations 2004
Reg.2, revoked (in part): SI 2009/41 Sch.1
Reg.3, revoked: SI 2009/41 Sch.1
Reg.4, revoked: SI 2009/41 Sch.1

2004 – cont.

1256. EC/Swiss Air Transport Agreement (Consequential Amendments) Regulations 2004– *cont.*
Reg.5, revoked: SI 2009/41 Sch.1
Reg.6, revoked: SI 2009/41 Sch.1
Reg.10, revoked: SI 2009/41 Sch.1

1267. European Parliamentary Elections (Northern Ireland) Regulations 2004
Appendix 1, substituted: SI 2009/813 Sch.1
Appendix 2, substituted: SI 2009/813 Sch.2
Reg.2A, added: SI 2009/813 Reg.4
Reg.6, amended: SI 2009/813 Reg.5
Reg.7, amended: SI 2009/813 Reg.6
Reg.8, amended: SI 2009/813 Reg.7
Reg.11, amended: SI 2009/813 Reg.8
Reg.12A, added: SI 2009/813 Reg.9
Reg.14, revoked: SI 2009/813 Reg.10
Reg.16, amended: SI 2009/813 Reg.11
Reg.16, applied: SI 2009/1143 Art.3
Reg.16, enabled: SI 2009/1143
Reg.17, applied: SI 2009/1143 Art.3
Reg.18, amended: SI 2009/813 Reg.12
Reg.22, amended: SI 2009/813 Reg.13
Reg.24, amended: SI 2009/813 Reg.14
Reg.25, amended: SI 2009/813 Reg.15
Reg.26, amended: SI 2009/813 Reg.16
Reg.29, amended: SI 2009/813 Reg.17
Reg.29, substituted: SI 2009/813 Reg.17
Reg.30, amended: SI 2009/813 Reg.18
Reg.31, amended: SI 2009/813 Reg.19
Reg.32, amended: SI 2009/813 Reg.20
Reg.33, amended: SI 2009/813 Reg.21
Reg.39, amended: SI 2009/813 Reg.22
Reg.41, amended: SI 2009/813 Reg.23
Reg.42, amended: SI 2009/813 Reg.24
Reg.47, amended: SI 2009/813 Reg.25
Reg.51, revoked (in part): SI 2009/813 Reg.26
Reg.54, amended: SI 2009/813 Reg.27
Reg.55, substituted: SI 2009/813 Reg.28
Reg.56, substituted: SI 2009/813 Reg.28
Reg.57, amended: SI 2009/813 Reg.29
Reg.68, amended: SI 2009/813 Reg.30
Reg.73, amended: SI 2009/813 Reg.31
Reg.79, amended: SI 2009/813 Reg.32
Reg.81, amended: SI 2009/813 Reg.33
Reg.84, substituted: SI 2009/813 Reg.34
Reg.89, amended: SI 2009/813 Reg.35
Reg.99, amended: SI 2009/813 Reg.36
Reg.111A, added: SI 2009/813 Reg.37
Sch.1 Part I para.1, substituted: SI 2009/813 Sch.1
Sch.1 Part I para.2, substituted: SI 2009/813 Sch.1
Sch.1 Part II para.3, substituted: SI 2009/813 Sch.1
Sch.1 Part II para.4, substituted: SI 2009/813 Sch.1
Sch.1 Part II para.5, substituted: SI 2009/813 Sch.1
Sch.1 Part II para.6, substituted: SI 2009/813 Sch.1
Sch.1 Part II para.7, substituted: SI 2009/813 Sch.1
Sch.1 Part II para.8, substituted: SI 2009/813 Sch.1
Sch.1 Part II para.9, substituted: SI 2009/813 Sch.1
Sch.1 Part II para.10, substituted: SI 2009/813 Sch.1
Sch.1 Part II para.11, substituted: SI 2009/813 Sch.1
Sch.1 Part II para.12, substituted: SI 2009/813 Sch.1
Sch.1 Part II para.13, substituted: SI 2009/813 Sch.1
Sch.1 Part II para.14, substituted: SI 2009/813 Sch.1
Sch.1 Part II para.15, substituted: SI 2009/813 Sch.1
Sch.1 Part II para.16, substituted: SI 2009/813 Sch.1
Sch.1 Part II para.17, applied: SI 2009/1143 Art.3
Sch.1 Part II para.17, substituted: SI 2009/813 Sch.1
Sch.1 Part III para.18, substituted: SI 2009/813 Sch.1

2004–cont.

1267. European Parliamentary Elections (Northern Ireland) Regulations 2004–*cont.*

Sch.1 Part III para.19, substituted: SI 2009/813 Sch.1
Sch.1 Part III para.20, substituted: SI 2009/813 Sch.1
Sch.1 Part III para.21, substituted: SI 2009/813 Sch.1
Sch.1 Part III para.22, substituted: SI 2009/813 Sch.1
Sch.1 Part III para.23, substituted: SI 2009/813 Sch.1
Sch.1 Part III para.24, substituted: SI 2009/813 Sch.1
Sch.1 Part III para.25, substituted: SI 2009/813 Sch.1
Sch.1 Part III para.26, substituted: SI 2009/813 Sch.1
Sch.1 Part III para.27, substituted: SI 2009/813 Sch.1
Sch.1 Part III para.28, substituted: SI 2009/813 Sch.1
Sch.1 Part III para.29, substituted: SI 2009/813 Sch.1
Sch.1 Part III para.30, substituted: SI 2009/813 Sch.1
Sch.1 Part III para.31, substituted: SI 2009/813 Sch.1
Sch.1 Part III para.32, substituted: SI 2009/813 Sch.1
Sch.1 Part III para.33, substituted: SI 2009/813 Sch.1
Sch.1 Part III para.34, substituted: SI 2009/813 Sch.1
Sch.1 Part III para.35, substituted: SI 2009/813 Sch.1
Sch.1 Part III para.36, substituted: SI 2009/813 Sch.1
Sch.1 Part III para.37, substituted: SI 2009/813 Sch.1
Sch.1 Part III para.38, substituted: SI 2009/813 Sch.1
Sch.1 Part III para.39, substituted: SI 2009/813 Sch.1
Sch.1 Part III para.40, substituted: SI 2009/813 Sch.1
Sch.1 Part III para.41, substituted: SI 2009/813 Sch.1
Sch.1 Part III para.42, substituted: SI 2009/813 Sch.1
Sch.1 Part III para.43, substituted: SI 2009/813 Sch.1
Sch.1 Part III para.44, substituted: SI 2009/813 Sch.1
Sch.1 Part III para.45, substituted: SI 2009/813 Sch.1
Sch.1 Part III para.46, substituted: SI 2009/813 Sch.1
Sch.1 Part III para.47, substituted: SI 2009/813 Sch.1
Sch.1 Part III para.48, substituted: SI 2009/813 Sch.1
Sch.1 Part III para.49, substituted: SI 2009/813 Sch.1
Sch.1 Part III para.50, substituted: SI 2009/813 Sch.1
Sch.1 Part III para.51, substituted: SI 2009/813 Sch.1
Sch.1 Part III para.52, substituted: SI 2009/813 Sch.1
Sch.1 Part III para.53, substituted: SI 2009/813 Sch.1
Sch.1 Part III para.54, substituted: SI 2009/813 Sch.1
Sch.1 Part III para.55, substituted: SI 2009/813 Sch.1
Sch.1 Part III para.56, substituted: SI 2009/813 Sch.1
Sch.1 Part III para.57, substituted: SI 2009/813 Sch.1
Sch.1 Part III para.58, substituted: SI 2009/813 Sch.1
Sch.1 Part III para.59, substituted: SI 2009/813 Sch.1
Sch.1 Part IV para.60, substituted: SI 2009/813 Sch.1
Sch.1 Part IV para.61, substituted: SI 2009/813 Sch.1
Sch.1 Part V para.62, substituted: SI 2009/813 Sch.1
Sch.1 Part V para.63, substituted: SI 2009/813 Sch.1
Sch.1 Part V para.64, substituted: SI 2009/813 Sch.1
Sch.1 Part V para.65, substituted: SI 2009/813 Sch.1
Sch.1 Part VI para.66, substituted: SI 2009/813 Sch.1
Sch.2 Part I para.1, substituted: SI 2009/813 Sch.2
Sch.2 Part I para.2, substituted: SI 2009/813 Sch.2
Sch.2 Part I para.3, substituted: SI 2009/813 Sch.2
Sch.2 Part I para.4, substituted: SI 2009/813 Sch.2
Sch.2 Part I para.5, substituted: SI 2009/813 Sch.2
Sch.2 Part I para.6, substituted: SI 2009/813 Sch.2
Sch.2 Part I para.7, substituted: SI 2009/813 Sch.2
Sch.2 Part I para.8, substituted: SI 2009/813 Sch.2
Sch.2 Part I para.9, substituted: SI 2009/813 Sch.2
Sch.2 Part I para.10, substituted: SI 2009/813 Sch.2
Sch.2 Part I para.11, substituted: SI 2009/813 Sch.2
Sch.2 Part I para.12, substituted: SI 2009/813 Sch.2
Sch.2 Part I para.13, substituted: SI 2009/813 Sch.2
Sch.2 Part I para.14, substituted: SI 2009/813 Sch.2
Sch.2 Part II para.15, substituted: SI 2009/813 Sch.2
Sch.2 Part II para.16, substituted: SI 2009/813 Sch.2
Sch.2 Part II para.17, substituted: SI 2009/813 Sch.2
Sch.2 Part II para.18, substituted: SI 2009/813 Sch.2

2004–cont.

1267. European Parliamentary Elections (Northern Ireland) Regulations 2004–*cont.*

Sch.2 Part II para.19, substituted: SI 2009/813 Sch.2
Sch.2 Part II para.20, substituted: SI 2009/813 Sch.2
Sch.2 Part II para.21, substituted: SI 2009/813 Sch.2
Sch.2 Part II para.22, substituted: SI 2009/813 Sch.2
Sch.2 Part II para.23, substituted: SI 2009/813 Sch.2
Sch.2 Part II para.24, substituted: SI 2009/813 Sch.2
Sch.2 Part II para.25, substituted: SI 2009/813 Sch.2
Sch.2 Part II para.26, substituted: SI 2009/813 Sch.2
Sch.2 Part II para.27, substituted: SI 2009/813 Sch.2
Sch.2 Part II para.28, substituted: SI 2009/813 Sch.2
Sch.2 Part II para.29, substituted: SI 2009/813 Sch.2
Sch.2 Part II para.30, substituted: SI 2009/813 Sch.2
Sch.2 Part II para.31, substituted: SI 2009/813 Sch.2
Sch.2 Part II para.32, substituted: SI 2009/813 Sch.2
Sch.2 Part II para.33, substituted: SI 2009/813 Sch.2
Sch.2 Part II para.34, substituted: SI 2009/813 Sch.2
Sch.2 Part II para.35, substituted: SI 2009/813 Sch.2
Sch.2 Part II para.36, substituted: SI 2009/813 Sch.2
Sch.6 para.1, substituted: SI 2009/813 Sch.4
Sch.6 para.2, substituted: SI 2009/813 Sch.4
Sch.6 para.3, substituted: SI 2009/813 Sch.4
Sch.6 para.4, substituted: SI 2009/813 Sch.4
Sch.6 para.5, substituted: SI 2009/813 Sch.4
Sch.6 para.6, substituted: SI 2009/813 Sch.4
Sch.6 para.7, substituted: SI 2009/813 Sch.4
Sch.6 para.8, substituted: SI 2009/813 Sch.4
Sch.6 para.9, substituted: SI 2009/813 Sch.4
Sch.6 para.10, substituted: SI 2009/813 Sch.4
Sch.6 para.11, substituted: SI 2009/813 Sch.4
Sch.6 para.12, substituted: SI 2009/813 Sch.4
Sch.6 para.13, substituted: SI 2009/813 Sch.4
Sch.6 para.14, substituted: SI 2009/813 Sch.4
Sch.6 para.15, substituted: SI 2009/813 Sch.4
Sch.6 para.16, substituted: SI 2009/813 Sch.4
Sch.6 para.17, substituted: SI 2009/813 Sch.4
Sch.6 para.18, substituted: SI 2009/813 Sch.4
Sch.6 para.19, substituted: SI 2009/813 Sch.4
Sch.6 para.20, substituted: SI 2009/813 Sch.4

1298. European Parliamentary Elections (Returning Officers Charges) (Great Britain and Gibraltar) Order 2004

revoked: SI 2009/1069 Art.3

1299. European Parliamentary Elections (Local Returning Officers Charges) (Great Britain and Gibraltar) Order 2004

revoked (in part): SI 2009/1077 Art.2, SI 2009/1120 Art.3

1300. Measuring Instruments (EEC Requirements) (Fees) Regulations 2004

Sch.1, amended: SI 2009/2748 Sch.1 para.27

1363. Stamp Duty Land Tax (Appeals) Regulations 2004

revoked: SI 2009/56 Sch.2 para.187

1373. European Parliamentary Elections (Welsh Forms) Order 2004

revoked: SI 2009/781 Art.3

1377. Education (Individual Pupil Information) (Prescribed Persons) (England) (Amendment) Regulations 2004

revoked: SI 2009/1563 Sch.1

1396. Meat Products (Wales) Regulations 2004

Sch.3 para.1, substituted: SI 2009/3378 Reg.18

1397. Horse Passports (England) Regulations 2004

revoked: SI 2009/1611 Reg.25

2004—cont.

1405. European Parliamentary Elections (Returning Officer's Charges) (Northern Ireland) Order 2004
revoked: SI 2009/ 1143 Art.2

1450. Child Trust Funds Regulations 2004
Reg.2, amended: SI 2009/475 Reg.3
Reg.5, amended: SI 2009/694 Reg.3
Reg.7, amended: SI 2009/475 Reg.4
Reg.7A, added: SI 2009/475 Reg.5
Reg.22, amended: SI 2009/475 Reg.6
Reg.28, amended: SI 2009/56 Sch.2 para.127
Reg.30, amended: SI 2009/475 Reg.7

1464. Recreational Craft Regulations 2004
referred to: SI 2009/669 Sch.1 Part 4, Sch.2 Part 2
see *Nicolle v Saunders Morgan Harris Ltd* [2008] EWHC 1518 (TCC), [2009] P.N.L.R. 8 (QBD (TCC)), Judge David Wilcox

1468. Energy Information (Household Refrigerators and Freezers) Regulations 2004
referred to: SI 2009/669 Sch.1 Part 4
Reg.2, amended: SI 2009/2559 Reg.8
Reg.2A, added: SI 2009/2559 Reg.8
Sch.6 Part 1 para.2A, added: SI 2009/2559 Reg.8

1501. Criminal Justice (Evidence) (Northern Ireland) Order 2004
Art.8, amended: 2009 c.25 Sch.17 para.2
Art.13, amended: 2009 c.25 Sch.17 para.2
Art.33, see *Public Prosecution Service v McGowan* [2009] N.I. 1 (CA (NI)), Lord Kerr L.C.J.
Art.36, see *Public Prosecution Service v Duddy* [2009] N.I. 19 (CA (NI)), Lord Kerr L.C.J.

1511. Human Fertilisation and Embryology Authority (Disclosure of Donor Information) Regulations 2004
applied: SI 2009/1892 Sch.4 para.13
referred to: SI 2009/1892 Sch.4 para.13
Reg.1, amended: SI 2009/1892 Sch.3 para.6
Reg.2, amended: SI 2009/1892 Sch.3 para.6

1517. Enterprise Act 2002 (Bodies Designated to make Super-complaints) Order 2004
Sch.1, substituted: SI 2009/2079 Art.2

1604. Organic Products Regulations 2004
revoked: SI 2009/842 Reg.32

1679. Demoted Tenancies (Review of Decisions)(England) Regulations 2004
see *R. (on the application of Gilboy) v Liverpool City Council* [2008] EWCA Civ 751, [2009] Q.B. 699 (CA (Civ Div)), Waller, L.J. (V-P)

1705. Local Government (Best Value Authorities) (Power to Trade) (England) Order 2004
revoked: SI 2009/2393 Art.3

1713. Fishing Vessels (Working Time Sea-fishermen) Regulations 2004
Reg.20, amended: SI 2009/3348 Art.23

1742. Wales Centre for Health (Constitution, Membership and Procedures) Regulations 2004
revoked: SI 2009/2623 Art.7

1744. Education (Specified Work and Registration) (Wales) Regulations 2004
Reg.6, referred to: SI 2009/3200 Reg.6

1748. Community Care, Services for Carers and Children's Services (Direct Payments) (Wales) Regulations 2004
applied: SI 2009/212 Reg.2

1756. Adult Placement Schemes (Wales)Regulations 2004
Sch.3 para.2, substituted: SI 2009/2541 Reg.10

2004—cont.

1761. Nursing and Midwifery Council (Fitness to Practise) Rules Order of Council 2004
Sch.1, added: SI 2009/1182 Sch.4 para.22
Sch.1, amended: SI 2009/1182 Sch.4 para.22

1765. Nurses and Midwives (Parts of and Entries in the Register) Order of Council 2004
Art.1, amended: SSI 2009/183 Sch.6 para.2

1767. Nursing and Midwifery Council (Education, Registration and Registration Appeals) Rules Order of Council 2004
Sch.1, substituted: SI 2009/1182 Sch.4 para.41

1768. National Health Service (Complaints) Regulations 2004
applied: SI 2009/309 Reg.8, Reg.20, Sch.1 para.8
revoked: SI 2009/309 Reg.22
Part II, applied: SI 2009/309 Reg.20
Reg.1, applied: SI 2009/309 Sch.1 para.8
Reg.2, applied: SI 2009/309 Sch.1 para.8
Reg.3, applied: SI 2009/309 Sch.1 para.8
Reg.3A, applied: SI 2009/309 Sch.1 para.8
Reg.3B, applied: SI 2009/309 Sch.1 para.8
Reg.4, applied: SI 2009/309 Sch.1 para.8
Reg.5, applied: SI 2009/309 Sch.1 para.8
Reg.6, applied: SI 2009/309 Sch.1 para.8
Reg.7, applied: SI 2009/309 Reg.20, Sch.1 para.8
Reg.8, applied: SI 2009/309 Sch.1 para.8
Reg.9, applied: SI 2009/309 Sch.1 para.8
Reg.10, applied: SI 2009/309 Sch.1 para.8
Reg.11, applied: SI 2009/309 Sch.1 para.8
Reg.12, applied: SI 2009/309 Sch.1 para.8
Reg.13, applied: SI 2009/309 Sch.1 para.8
Reg.13, varied: SI 2009/309 Reg.20, Sch.1 para.8
Reg.14, applied: SI 2009/309 Reg.20, Sch.1 para.8
Reg.14, disapplied: SI 2009/309 Reg.20
Reg.15, applied: SI 2009/309 Reg.21
Reg.15, disapplied: SI 2009/309 Reg.20
Reg.16, disapplied: SI 2009/309 Reg.20
Reg.17, disapplied: SI 2009/309 Reg.20
Reg.18, disapplied: SI 2009/309 Reg.20
Reg.19, disapplied: SI 2009/309 Reg.20
Reg.20, disapplied: SI 2009/309 Reg.20
Reg.21, disapplied: SI 2009/309 Reg.20
Reg.22, disapplied: SI 2009/309 Reg.20
Reg.23, applied: SI 2009/309 Sch.1 para.8
Reg.24, applied: SI 2009/309 Sch.1 para.8

1771. Health Act 1999 (Consequential Amendments) (Nursing and Midwifery) Order 2004
Sch.1 Part 2 para.43, revoked: SSI 2009/183 Sch.5

1777. Cotswolds Area of Outstanding Natural Beauty (Establishment of Conservation Board) Order 2004
Art.4, amended: SI 2009/837 Art.21
Art.23A, added: SI 2009/1579 Art.2
Sch.1, amended: SI 2009/837 Art.21

1778. Chilterns Area of Outstanding Natural Beauty (Establishment of Conservation Board) Order 2004
Art.4, amended: SI 2009/837 Art.20
Art.23A, added: SSI 2009/1578 Art.2
Sch.1, amended: SI 2009/837 Art.20

1829. Commonhold Regulations 2004
Reg.2, amended: SI 2009/2363 Reg.3
Reg.12, amended: SI 2009/2363 Reg.4
Reg.13, revoked: SI 2009/2363 Reg.5
Reg.14, amended: SI 2009/2363 Reg.6
Reg.14, revoked (in part): SI 2009/2363 Reg.6
Reg.19, amended: SI 2009/2363 Reg.7
Sch.1, revoked: SI 2009/2363 Reg.8

2004–cont.

1829. Commonhold Regulations 2004–cont.
Sch.2, substituted: SI 2009/2363 Sch.1
Sch.3, amended: SI 2009/2363 Reg.10

1830. Commonhold (Land Registration) Rules 2004
r.4, amended: SI 2009/2024 r.3
r.19, amended: SI 2009/2024 r.4
r.23, amended: SI 2009/2024 r.5
r.28, amended: SI 2009/2024 r.6
Sch.1, amended: SI 2009/2024 r.7

1861. Employment Tribunals (Constitution and Rules of Procedure) Regulations 2004
Reg.8, applied: SI 2009/590 Art.3
Reg.16, applied: SI 2009/515 Reg.17
Sch.1, applied: SI 2009/515 Reg.17
Sch.1 para.8, see *North Tyneside Primary Care Trust v Aynsley* [2009] I.C.R. 1333 (EAT), Underhill, J.
Sch.1 para.10, see *Davidson v M* [2009] CSIH 70, 2009 S.L.T. 1009 (IH (Ex Div)), Lord Nimmo Smith; see *North Tyneside Primary Care Trust v Aynsley* [2009] I.C.R. 1333 (EAT), Underhill, J.
Sch.1 para.18, see *Force One Utilities Ltd v Hatfield* [2009] I.R.L.R. 45 (EAT), Elias, J (President)
Sch.1 para.25, see *Davidson v M* [2009] CSIH 70, 2009 S.L.T. 1009 (IH (Ex Div)), Lord Nimmo Smith
Sch.1 para.28, see *North Tyneside Primary Care Trust v Aynsley* [2009] I.C.R. 1333 (EAT), Underhill, J.
Sch.1 para.33, see *North Tyneside Primary Care Trust v Aynsley* [2009] I.C.R. 1333 (EAT), Underhill, J.
Sch.1 para.34, see *Hutchison 3G UK Ltd v Francois* [2009] EWCA Civ 405, [2009] I.C.R. 1323 (CA (Civ Div)), Mummery, L.J.; see *North Tyneside Primary Care Trust v Aynsley* [2009] I.C.R. 1333 (EAT), Underhill, J.
Sch.1 para.50, see *Davidson v M* [2009] CSIH 70, 2009 S.L.T. 1009 (IH (Ex Div)), Lord Nimmo Smith; see *Tradition Securities & Futures SA v Times Newspapers Ltd* [2009] I.R.L.R. 354 (EAT), Underhill, J.
Sch.1 para.60, see *Davidson v M* [2009] CSIH 70, 2009 S.L.T. 1009 (IH (Ex Div)), Lord Nimmo Smith
Sch.1 para.61, amended: SI 2009/2748 Sch.1 para.28
Sch.4, applied: SI 2009/515 Reg.17
Sch.6 para.5, see *Suffolk Mental Health Partnership NHS Trust v Hurst* [2009] I.C.R. 281 (EAT), Elias, J (President)

1863. Tax Avoidance Schemes (Prescribed Descriptions of Arrangements) Regulations 2004
Sch.1 para.6, see *Revenue and Customs Commissioners v Mercury Tax Group Ltd* [2009] S.T.C. (S.C.D.) 307 (Sp Comm), John F Avery Jones
Sch.1 para.7, see *Revenue and Customs Commissioners v Mercury Tax Group Ltd* [2009] S.T.C. (S.C.D.) 307 (Sp Comm), John F Avery Jones

1864. Tax Avoidance Schemes (Information) Regulations 2004
Reg.4, applied: SI 2009/2033 Reg.3
Reg.7, substituted: SI 2009/611 Reg.3
Reg.8, referred to: SI 2009/611 Reg.1
Reg.8, substituted: SI 2009/611 Reg.4

2004–cont.

1910. Nationality, Immigration and Asylum Act 2002 (Specification of Particularly Serious Crimes) Order 2004
see *EN (Serbia) v Secretary of State for the Home Department* [2009] EWCA Civ 630, [2009] I.N.L.R. 459 (CA (Civ Div)), Laws, L.J.

1931. Value Added Tax (Groups eligibility) Order 2004
Art.3, amended: SI 2009/1890 Art.4

1940. Companies (Disqualification Orders) (Amendment) Regulations 2004
revoked: SI 2009/2471 Reg.3

1964. Fur Farming (Compensation Scheme) (England) Order 2004
Art.5, amended: SI 2009/1307 Sch.2 para.97
Art.6, amended: SI 2009/1307 Sch.2 para.98

1972. Care Standards Act 2000 (Extension of the Application of Part 2 to Adult Placement Schemes) (England) Regulations 2004
Reg.2, amended: SI 2009/462 Sch.2 para.6

1979. Burma (Restrictive Measures) (Overseas Territories) Order 2004
revoked: SI 2009/3008 Art.31
Art.8, applied: SI 2009/3008 Art.11
Art.19, varied: SI 2009/888 Art.2
Sch.2 para.1, varied: SI 2009/888 Art.2
Sch.2 para.2, varied: SI 2009/888 Art.2
Sch.2 para.3, varied: SI 2009/888 Art.2
Sch.2 para.4, varied: SI 2009/888 Art.2
Sch.2 para.5, varied: SI 2009/888 Art.2
Sch.2 para.6, varied: SI 2009/888 Art.2
Sch.2 para.7, varied: SI 2009/888 Art.2
Sch.2 para.8, varied: SI 2009/888 Art.2
Sch.2 para.9, varied: SI 2009/888 Art.2

2029. Cayman Islands (Constitution) (Amendment) Order 2004
revoked: SI 2009/1379 Sch.1

2071. Adult Placement Schemes (England) Regulations 2004
Reg.3, amended: SI 2009/462 Sch.2 para.7
Reg.4, amended: SI 2009/462 Sch.2 para.7
Reg.5, amended: SI 2009/462 Sch.2 para.7
Reg.6, amended: SI 2009/462 Sch.2 para.7
Reg.8, amended: SI 2009/462 Sch.2 para.7
Reg.9, amended: SI 2009/462 Sch.2 para.7
Reg.12, amended: SI 2009/462 Sch.2 para.7
Reg.22, amended: SI 2009/462 Sch.2 para.7
Reg.23, amended: SI 2009/462 Sch.2 para.7
Reg.24, amended: SI 2009/462 Sch.2 para.7
Reg.24A, amended: SI 2009/462 Sch.2 para.7
Reg.25, amended: SI 2009/462 Sch.2 para.7
Reg.26, amended: SI 2009/462 Sch.2 para.7
Reg.28, amended: SI 2009/462 Sch.2 para.7
Reg.29, amended: SI 2009/462 Sch.2 para.7
Reg.30, amended: SI 2009/462 Sch.2 para.7
Reg.31, amended: SI 2009/462 Sch.2 para.7
Reg.32, amended: SI 2009/462 Sch.2 para.7
Reg.33, amended: SI 2009/462 Sch.2 para.7
Reg.34, amended: SI 2009/462 Sch.2 para.7
Reg.35, amended: SI 2009/462 Sch.2 para.7
Reg.36, amended: SI 2009/462 Sch.2 para.7
Reg.37, amended: SI 2009/462 Sch.2 para.7
Reg.39, amended: SI 2009/462 Sch.2 para.7
Sch.2 para.2, substituted: SI 2009/1895 Reg.8
Sch.3 para.2, substituted: SI 2009/1895 Reg.8

2095. Financial Services (Distance Marketing) Regulations 2004
Reg.7, amended: SI 2009/209 Sch.6 para.5

2004-cont.

2095. Financial Services (Distance Marketing) Regulations 2004—*cont.*
Reg.8, amended: SI 2009/209 Sch.6 para.5
Reg.14, revoked: SI 2009/209 Sch.6 para.5

2143. Veterinary Surgeons (Registration Appeals) Rules Order of Council 2004
applied: SI 2009/2474 Sch.1
revoked: SI 2009/2474 Art.3

2186. Motor Vehicles (EC Type Approval) (Amendment) (No.2) Regulations 2004
Reg.1, revoked: SI 2009/717 Sch.1
Reg.2, revoked: SI 2009/717 Sch.1
Reg.3, revoked: SI 2009/717 Sch.1
Reg.4, revoked: SI 2009/717 Sch.1
Reg.5, revoked: SI 2009/717 Sch.1

2199. Venture Capital Trust (Winding up and Mergers) (Tax) Regulations 2004
referred to: SI 2009/56 Sch.2 para.128
Reg.10, amended: SI 2009/56 Sch.2 para.129
Reg.10, applied: SI 2009/275 Art.3

2201. Finance Act 2002, Schedule 26, Parts 2 and 9 (Amendment) Order 2004
revoked: 2009 c.4 Sch.3 Part 1

2202. Planning and Compulsory Purchase Act 2004 (Commencement No.2, Transitional Provisions and Savings) Order 2004
see *R. (on the application of Stamford Chamber of Trade and Commerce) v Secretary of State for Communities and Local Government* [2009] EWHC 719 (Admin), [2009] 2 P. & C.R. 19 (QBD (Admin)), Rabinder Singh Q.C.

2204. Town and Country Planning (Local Development) (England) Regulations 2004
Reg.2, amended: SI 2009/401 Reg.2
Reg.6, amended: SI 2009/401 Reg.2
Reg.8, amended: SI 2009/401 Reg.2
Reg.8, revoked (in part): SI 2009/401 Reg.2
Reg.16, revoked (in part): SI 2009/401 Reg.2
Reg.17, revoked (in part): SI 2009/401 Reg.2
Reg.24, amended: SI 2009/401 Reg.2
Reg.24, revoked (in part): SI 2009/401 Reg.2
Reg.26, revoked (in part): SI 2009/401 Reg.2
Reg.27, amended: SI 2009/401 Reg.2
Reg.30, amended: SI 2009/401 Reg.2
Reg.30, revoked (in part): SI 2009/401 Reg.2

2255. Tonnage Tax (Training Requirement) (Amendment) Regulations 2004
revoked: SI 2009/2304 Sch.1

2307. Local Government (Best Value Authorities) (Power to Trade) (England) (Amendment) Order 2004
revoked: SI 2009/2393 Art.3

2310. Finance Act 2004, Sections 38 to 40 and 45 and Schedule 6 (Consequential Amendment of Enactments) Order 2004
Sch.1 Part 2 para.4, revoked (in part): 2009 c.4 Sch.3 Part 1
Sch.1 Part 2 para.5, revoked: 2009 c.4 Sch.3 Part 1
Sch.1 Part 2 para.6, revoked: 2009 c.4 Sch.3 Part 1
Sch.1 Part 2 para.22, revoked: 2009 c.4 Sch.3 Part 1
Sch.1 Part 10 para.58, revoked: 2009 c.4 Sch.3 Part 1
Sch.1 Part 10 para.59, revoked: 2009 c.4 Sch.3 Part 1
Sch.1 Part 10 para.60, revoked: 2009 c.4 Sch.3 Part 1
Sch.1 Part 10 para.61, revoked: 2009 c.4 Sch.3 Part 1
Sch.1 Part 10 para.62, revoked: 2009 c.4 Sch.3 Part 1
Sch.1 Part 10 para.63, revoked: 2009 c.4 Sch.3 Part 1
Sch.1 Part 11 para.64, revoked: 2009 c.4 Sch.3 Part 1

2004-cont.

2326. European Public Limited-Liability Company Regulations 2004
added: SI 2009/2400 Reg.15
Reg.1, amended: SI 2009/2400 Reg.4
Reg.3, amended: SI 2009/2400 Reg.5
Reg.5, amended: SI 2009/2400 Reg.6
Reg.5, referred to: SI 2009/1803 Reg.8
Reg.6, amended: SI 2009/2400 Reg.7
Reg.6, referred to: SI 2009/1803 Reg.8
Reg.7, amended: SI 2009/2400 Reg.8
Reg.7, referred to: SI 2009/1803 Reg.8
Reg.8, amended: SI 2009/2400 Reg.9
Reg.8, referred to: SI 2009/1803 Reg.8
Reg.9, amended: SI 2009/2400 Reg.10
Reg.9, referred to: SI 2009/1803 Reg.8
Reg.10, amended: SI 2009/2400 Reg.11
Reg.10, referred to: SI 2009/1803 Reg.8
Reg.11, amended: SI 2009/2400 Reg.12
Reg.11, referred to: SI 2009/1803 Reg.8
Reg.12, amended: SI 2009/2400 Reg.13
Reg.13, amended: SI 2009/2400 Reg.14
Reg.13A, added: SI 2009/2400 Reg.15
Reg.13A, disapplied: SI 2009/2400 Reg.15
Reg.14, amended: SI 2009/2400 Reg.16
Reg.14, substituted: SI 2009/2400 Reg.16
Reg.16, revoked: SI 2009/2400 Reg.17
Reg.17, revoked: SI 2009/2400 Reg.17
Reg.18, revoked: SI 2009/2400 Reg.17
Reg.19, revoked: SI 2009/2400 Reg.17
Reg.20, revoked: SI 2009/2400 Reg.17
Reg.21, revoked: SI 2009/2400 Reg.17
Reg.22, revoked: SI 2009/2400 Reg.17
Reg.23, revoked: SI 2009/2400 Reg.17
Reg.24, revoked: SI 2009/2400 Reg.17
Reg.25, revoked: SI 2009/2400 Reg.17
Reg.26, revoked: SI 2009/2400 Reg.17
Reg.27, revoked: SI 2009/2400 Reg.17
Reg.28, revoked: SI 2009/2400 Reg.17
Reg.29, revoked: SI 2009/2400 Reg.17
Reg.30, revoked: SI 2009/2400 Reg.17
Reg.31, revoked: SI 2009/2400 Reg.17
Reg.32, revoked: SI 2009/2400 Reg.17
Reg.33, revoked: SI 2009/2400 Reg.17
Reg.34, revoked: SI 2009/2400 Reg.17
Reg.35, revoked: SI 2009/2400 Reg.17
Reg.36, revoked: SI 2009/2400 Reg.17
Reg.37, revoked: SI 2009/2400 Reg.17
Reg.38, revoked: SI 2009/2400 Reg.17
Reg.39, revoked: SI 2009/2400 Reg.17
Reg.40, revoked: SI 2009/2400 Reg.17
Reg.41, revoked: SI 2009/2400 Reg.17
Reg.42, revoked: SI 2009/2400 Reg.17
Reg.43, revoked: SI 2009/2400 Reg.17
Reg.44, revoked: SI 2009/2400 Reg.17
Reg.45, revoked: SI 2009/2400 Reg.17
Reg.46, revoked: SI 2009/2400 Reg.17
Reg.47, revoked: SI 2009/2400 Reg.17
Reg.48, revoked: SI 2009/2400 Reg.17
Reg.49, revoked: SI 2009/2400 Reg.17
Reg.50, revoked: SI 2009/2400 Reg.17
Reg.51, revoked: SI 2009/2400 Reg.17
Reg.52, amended: SI 2009/3348 Art.23
Reg.52, revoked: SI 2009/2400 Reg.17
Reg.53, revoked: SI 2009/2400 Reg.17
Reg.54, revoked: SI 2009/2400 Reg.17
Reg.56, amended: SI 2009/2400 Reg.18
Reg.60, revoked: SI 2009/2400 Reg.19
Reg.68, amended: SI 2009/2400 Reg.20

2004– cont.

2326. European Public Limited-Liability Company Regulations 2004– *cont.*
Reg.68, applied: SI 2009/1803 Reg.8
Reg.69, amended: SI 2009/2400 Reg.21
Reg.70, amended: SI 2009/2400 Reg.22
Reg.72, amended: SI 2009/2400 Reg.23
Reg.73, amended: SI 2009/2400 Reg.24
Reg.74, amended: SI 2009/2400 Reg.25
Reg.75, amended: SI 2009/2400 Reg.26
Reg.76, amended: SI 2009/2400 Reg.27
Reg.79, applied: SI 2009/214 Reg.9, SI 2009/2400 Sch.2 para.7, Sch.2 para.14
Reg.79, substituted: SI 2009/2400 Reg.28
Reg.80, applied: SI 2009/2400 Sch.2 para.3, Sch.2 para.7
Reg.80, substituted: SI 2009/2400 Reg.28
Reg.80B, applied: SI 2009/2400 Sch.2 para.6
Reg.80C, applied: SI 2009/214 Reg.9, SI 2009/2400 Sch.2 para.3, Sch.2 para.4, Sch.2 para.5, Sch.2 para.6, Sch.2 para.7
Reg.81, amended: SI 2009/2400 Reg.29
Reg.82, amended: SI 2009/2400 Reg.30
Reg.82, applied: SI 2009/1803 Reg.8
Reg.83, amended: SI 2009/2400 Reg.31
Reg.85, amended: SI 2009/2400 Reg.32
Reg.85, applied: SI 2009/1803 Reg.8
Reg.86, amended: SI 2009/2400 Reg.33
Reg.86, applied: SI 2009/1803 Reg.8
Reg.87, amended: SI 2009/2400 Reg.34
Reg.87, revoked (in part): SI 2009/2400 Reg.34
Reg.88, amended: SI 2009/2400 Reg.35
Sch.1, substituted: SI 2009/2400 Sch.1
Sch.1A para.1, added: SI 2009/2400 Reg.37
Sch.1A para.2, added: SI 2009/2400 Reg.37
Sch.1A para.3, added: SI 2009/2400 Reg.37
Sch.1A para.4, added: SI 2009/2400 Reg.37
Sch.1A para.5, added: SI 2009/2400 Reg.37
Sch.1A para.6, added: SI 2009/2400 Reg.37
Sch.2 para.1, substituted: SI 2009/2400 Reg.38
Sch.2 para.2, substituted: SI 2009/2400 Reg.38
Sch.2 para.3, substituted: SI 2009/2400 Reg.38
Sch.2 para.4, substituted: SI 2009/2400 Reg.38
Sch.2 para.5, substituted: SI 2009/2400 Reg.38
Sch.3 Part 1, revoked: SI 2009/2400 Reg.39
Sch.3 Part 1 para.2, revoked: SI 2009/2400 Reg.39
Sch.3 Part 1 para.3, revoked: SI 2009/2400 Reg.39
Sch.3 Part 1 para.4, revoked: SI 2009/2400 Reg.39
Sch.3 Part 1 para.5, revoked: SI 2009/2400 Reg.39
Sch.3 Part 2 para.6, revoked: SI 2009/2400 Reg.39
Sch.3 Part 3 para.7, revoked: SI 2009/2400 Reg.39
Sch.4 para.1, amended: SI 2009/2400 Reg.40
Sch.4 para.1, revoked: SI 2009/2400 Reg.40
Sch.4 para.2, amended: SI 2009/2400 Reg.40
Sch.4 para.3, amended: SI 2009/2400 Reg.40
Sch.4 para.4, amended: SI 2009/2400 Reg.40
Sch.4 para.5, amended: SI 2009/2400 Reg.40
Sch.4 para.5, substituted: SI 2009/2400 Reg.40
Sch.4 para.6, amended: SI 2009/2400 Reg.40
Sch.4 para.7, amended: SI 2009/2400 Reg.40
Sch.4 para.8, amended: SI 2009/2400 Reg.40
Sch.4 para.8, revoked: SI 2009/2400 Reg.40
Sch.4 para.9, amended: SI 2009/2400 Reg.40
Sch.4 para.10, amended: SI 2009/2400 Reg.40
Sch.4 para.10, revoked: SI 2009/2400 Reg.40
Sch.4 para.11, amended: SI 2009/2400 Reg.40

2407. European Public Limited-Liability Company (Fees) Regulations 2004
applied: SI 2009/2492 Reg.2, Reg.3, Reg.4

2004– cont.

2407. European Public Limited-Liability Company (Fees) Regulations 2004– *cont.*
revoked: SI 2009/2492 Sch.2

2573. Local Government (Best Value Authorities) (Power to Trade) (England) (Amendment No.2) Order 2004
revoked: SI 2009/2393 Art.3

2595. Compulsory Purchase of Land (Prescribed Forms) (Ministers) Regulations 2004
Sch.1, amended: SI 2009/1307 Sch.2 para.99

2601. Miscellaneous Food Additives (Amendment) (England) Regulations 2004
Reg.3, applied: SI 2009/3238 Reg.10

2607. General Medical Council (Fitness to Practise) (Disqualifying Decisions and Determinations by Regulatory Bodies) Procedure Rules Order of Council 2004
Sch.1, amended: SI 2009/2765 Sch.1

2608. General Medical Council (Fitness to Practise) Rules Order of Council 2004
see *Cheatle v General Medical Council* [2009] EWHC 645 (Admin), [2009] LS Law Medical 299 (QBD (Admin)), Cranston, J.
Sch.1, added: SI 2009/1182 Sch.4 para.23, SI 2009/1913 Sch.1
Sch.1, amended: SI 2009/1182 Sch.4 para.23, SI 2009/1913 Sch.1
Sch.1, substituted: SI 2009/1913 Sch.1

2609. General Medical Council (Voluntary Erasure and Restoration following Voluntary Erasure) Regulations Order of Council 2004
Sch.1, amended: SI 2009/2763 Sch.1
Sch.1, revoked: SI 2009/2763 Sch.1

2611. General Medical Council (Constitution of Panels and Investigation Committee) Rules Order of Council 2004
Sch.1, amended: SI 2009/2751 Sch.1

2612. General Medical Council (Restoration following Administrative Erasure) Regulations Order of Council 2004
Sch.1, amended: SI 2009/2764 Sch.1

2620. Limited Liability Partnerships (Fees) Regulations 2004
Reg.1, revoked (in part): SI 2009/2101 Sch.5
Reg.2, revoked (in part): SI 2009/2101 Sch.5
Reg.3, revoked (in part): SI 2009/2101 Sch.5
Reg.4, revoked (in part): SI 2009/2101 Sch.5
Reg.5, revoked (in part): SI 2009/2101 Sch.5
Sch.1 para.1, revoked (in part): SI 2009/2101 Sch.5
Sch.1 para.2, revoked (in part): SI 2009/2101 Sch.5
Sch.1 para.3, revoked (in part): SI 2009/2101 Sch.5
Sch.1 para.4, revoked (in part): SI 2009/2101 Sch.5
Sch.1 para.5, revoked (in part): SI 2009/2101 Sch.5
Sch.2, revoked (in part): SI 2009/2101 Sch.5
Sch.2 para.1, revoked (in part): SI 2009/2101 Sch.5
Sch.2 para.2, revoked (in part): SI 2009/2101 Sch.5
Sch.2 para.3, revoked (in part): SI 2009/2101 Sch.5
Sch.2 para.4, revoked (in part): SI 2009/2101 Sch.5
Sch.2 para.5, revoked (in part): SI 2009/2101 Sch.5
Sch.2 para.6, revoked (in part): SI 2009/2101 Sch.5
Sch.3, revoked (in part): SI 2009/2101 Sch.5

2621. Companies (Fees) Regulations 2004
Reg.1, revoked (in part): SI 2009/2101 Sch.5
Reg.2, revoked (in part): SI 2009/2101 Sch.5
Reg.3, revoked (in part): SI 2009/2101 Sch.5
Reg.4, revoked (in part): SI 2009/2101 Sch.5
Reg.5, revoked (in part): SI 2009/2101 Sch.5
Sch.1 para.1, revoked (in part): SI 2009/2101 Sch.5
Sch.1 para.2, revoked (in part): SI 2009/2101 Sch.5

2004– cont.

2621. Companies (Fees) Regulations 2004– *cont.*
Sch.l para.3, revoked (in part): SI 2009/2101 Sch.5
Sch.l para.4, revoked (in part): SI 2009/2101 Sch.5
Sch.l para.5, revoked (in part): SI 2009/2101 Sch.5
Sch.2, revoked (in part): SI 2009/2101 Sch.5
Sch.2 para.l, revoked (in part): SI 2009/2101 Sch.5
Sch.2 para.2, revoked (in part): SI 2009/2101 Sch.5
Sch.2 para.3, revoked (in part): SI 2009/2101 Sch.5
Sch.2 para.4, revoked (in part): SI 2009/2101 Sch.5
Sch.2 para.5, revoked (in part): SI 2009/2101 Sch.5
Sch.2 para.6, revoked (in part): SI 2009/2101 Sch.5
Sch.3, revoked (in part): SI 2009/2101 Sch.5
Sch.4, revoked (in part): SI 2009/2101 Sch.5

2622. Exemption From Tax For Certain Interest Payments Regulations 2004
Reg.9, amended: SI 2009/56 Sch.2 para.130

2643. European Economic Interest Grouping (Fees) Regulations 2004
applied: SI 2009/2492 Reg.2, Reg.3, Reg.4
Reg.l, revoked: SI 2009/2492 Sch.2
Reg.2, revoked: SI 2009/2492 Sch.2
Reg.3, revoked: SI 2009/2492 Sch.2
Reg.4, revoked: SI 2009/2492 Sch.2
Reg.5, revoked: SI 2009/2492 Sch.2
Sch.l, revoked: SI 2009/2492 Sch.2
Sch.2, revoked: SI 2009/2492 Sch.2

2673. Cayman Islands (Constitution) (Amendment No.2) Order 2004
revoked: SI 2009/1379 Sch.l

2695. Disqualification from Caring for Children (Wales) Regulations 2004
Sch.l Part I para.3, amended: SI 2009/2541 Reg.3
Sch.l Part III para.33, substituted: SI 2009/2541 Reg.3
Sch.l Part III para.34, substituted: SI 2009/2541 Reg.3

2752. Education (Student Loans) (Repayment) (Amendment) (No.2) Regulations 2004
revoked: SI 2009/470 Sch.l

2757. Legal Services Ombudsman (Extension of Remit) Regulations 2004
revoked: SI 2009/3250 Sch.l

2817. County of Shropshire (Electoral Changes) Order 2004
revoked: SI 2009/529 Art.3

2821. County of Wiltshire (Electoral Changes) Order 2004
revoked: SI 2009/531 Art.3

2858. Education (School Performance Targets) (England) Regulations 2004
Reg.5, amended: SI 2009/1596 Reg.2
Sch.lA, substituted: SI 2009/1596 Reg.2

2881. Oil and Fibre Plant Seed (Wales) Regulations 2004
applied: SI 2009/1356 Reg.2
Reg.2, amended: SI 2009/1356 Reg.25
Reg.19A, added: SI 2009/1356 Reg.26
Reg.23, amended: SI 2009/1356 Reg.27
Reg.24, amended: SI 2009/1356 Reg.28
Reg.26, amended: SI 2009/1356 Reg.29
Sch.8 Part IX para.39, added: SI 2009/1356 Reg.30

2987. Health and Social Care (Community Health and Standards) Act 2003 (Commission for Healthcare Audit and Inspection and Commission for Social Care Inspection) (Consequential Provisions) Order 2004
revoked: SI 2009/462 Sch.6

2004– cont.

3039. International Criminal Tribunal for the former Yugoslavia (Restrictive Measures) (Overseas Territories) Order 2004
Art.9, varied: SI 2009/888 Art.2
Sch.2 para.l, varied: SI 2009/888 Art.2
Sch.2 para.2, varied: SI 2009/888 Art.2
Sch.2 para.3, varied: SI 2009/888 Art.2
Sch.2 para.4, varied: SI 2009/888 Art.2
Sch.2 para.5, varied: SI 2009/888 Art.2
Sch.2 para.6, varied: SI 2009/888 Art.2
Sch.2 para.7, varied: SI 2009/888 Art.2
Sch.2 para.8, varied: SI 2009/888 Art.2

3101. Export of Goods, Transfer of Technology and Provision of Technical Assistance (Control) (Overseas Territories) Order 2004
Sch.2 Part VI para.16, amended: SI 2009/3212 Art.2
Sch.2 Part VI para.16, varied: SI 2009/888 Art.2
Sch.4 para.l, varied: SI 2009/888 Art.2
Sch.4 para.2, varied: SI 2009/888 Art.2
Sch.4 para.3, varied: SI 2009/888 Art.2
Sch.4 para.4, varied: SI 2009/888 Art.2
Sch.4 para.5, varied: SI 2009/888 Art.2
Sch.4 para.6, varied: SI 2009/888 Art.2
Sch.4 para.7, varied: SI 2009/888 Art.2
Sch.4 para.8, varied: SI 2009/888 Art.2

3102. Trade in Goods (Control) (Overseas Territories) Order 2004
Sch.2 Part 2 para.9, varied: SI 2009/888 Art.2
Sch.5 para.l, varied: SI 2009/888 Art.2
Sch.5 para.2, amended: SI 2009/888 Art.5
Sch.5 para.2, varied: SI 2009/888 Art.2
Sch.5 para.3, varied: SI 2009/888 Art.2
Sch.5 para.4, varied: SI 2009/888 Art.2
Sch.5 para.5, varied: SI 2009/888 Art.2
Sch.5 para.6, varied: SI 2009/888 Art.2
Sch.5 para.7, varied: SI 2009/888 Art.2

3103. Trade in Controlled Goods (Embargoed Destinations) (Overseas Territories) Order 2004
Sch.2 Part 3 para.8, varied: SI 2009/888 Art.2
Sch.5 para.l, amended: SI 2009/888 Art.5
Sch.5 para.l, varied: SI 2009/888 Art.2
Sch.5 para.2, amended: SI 2009/888 Art.5
Sch.5 para.2, varied: SI 2009/888 Art.2
Sch.5 para.3, amended: SI 2009/888 Art.5
Sch.5 para.3, varied: SI 2009/888 Art.2
Sch.5 para.4, varied: SI 2009/888 Art.2
Sch.5 para.5, varied: SI 2009/888 Art.2
Sch.5 para.6, varied: SI 2009/888 Art.2
Sch.5 para.7, varied: SI 2009/888 Art.2

3120. Non-Contentious Probate Fees Order 2004
Sch.lA para.l, substituted: SI 2009/1497 Sch.l
Sch.lA para.2, substituted: SI 2009/1497 Sch.l
Sch.lA para.3, substituted: SI 2009/1497 Sch.l
Sch.lA para.4, substituted: SI 2009/1497 Sch.l
Sch.lA para.5, substituted: SI 2009/1497 Sch.l
Sch.lA para.6, substituted: SI 2009/1497 Sch.l
Sch.lA para.7, substituted: SI 2009/1497 Sch.l
Sch.lA para.8, substituted: SI 2009/1497 Sch.l
Sch.lA para.9, substituted: SI 2009/1497 Sch.l

3125. Race Relations Act 1976 (Statutory Duties) Order 2004
Art.2, varied: SI 2009/462 Sch.5 para.12
Art.3, varied: SI 2009/462 Sch.5 para.12
Sch.l, amended: SI 2009/462 Sch.5 para.13
Sch.l, varied: SI 2009/462 Sch.5 para.12

2004– cont.

3148. Value Added Tax (Place of Supply of Goods) Order 2004
Art.6, amended: SI 2009/215 Art.3

3151. Non-Domestic Rating (Stud Farms) (England) Order 2004
revoked: SI 2009/3177 Art.3

3155. Wireless Telegraphy (Register) Regulations 2004
Sch.1 Part 8, amended: SI 2009/14 Reg.2

3214. Air Navigation (Dangerous Goods)(Amendment) Regulations 2004
revoked: SI 2009/1492 Reg.3

3256. Loan Relationships and Derivative Contracts (Disregard and Bringing into Account of Profits and Losses) Regulations 2004
Reg.6, amended: SI 2009/1886 Reg.4
Reg.7A, added: SI 2009/1886 Reg.5
Reg.9, disapplied: 2009 c.4 s.616
Reg.10A, added: SI 2009/1886 Reg.6
Reg.13, added: SI 2009/1886 Reg.7

3267. Finance Act 2000, Schedule 20 (Definition of Small or Medium-Sized Enterprise) Order 2004
revoked: 2009 c.4 Sch.3 Part 1

3270. Finance Act 2002, Schedule 26, Parts 2 and 9 (Amendment No.2) Order 2004
revoked: 2009 c.4 Sch.3 Part 1

3271. Loan Relationships and Derivative Contracts (Change Of Accounting Practice) Regulations 2004
Reg.3A, applied: SI 2009/2971 Reg.8

3315. Non-Domestic Rating (Small Business Rate Relief) (England) Order 2004
referred to: SI 2009/354 Art.2
Art.2, revoked: SI 2009/354 Art.3
Art.3, amended: SI 2009/354 Art.4, SI 2009/3175 Art.3
Art.6, amended: SI 2009/354 Art.5, SI 2009/3175 Art.4
Sch.1, substituted: SI 2009/3175 Art.5

3333. Burma (Restrictive Measures) (Overseas Territories) (Amendment) Order 2004
applied: SI 2009/3008 Art.19
revoked: SI 2009/3008 Art.31

3339. Proceeds of Crime Act 2002 (References to Financial Investigators) (Amendment No 2) Order 2004
revoked: SI 2009/975 Sch.2

3348. Sweeteners in Food (Amendment) (England) Regulations 2004
Reg.3, applied: SI 2009/3238 Reg.13
Reg.4, applied: SI 2009/3238 Reg.13
Reg.5, applied: SI 2009/3238 Reg.13
Reg.6, applied: SI 2009/3238 Reg.13
Reg.7, applied: SI 2009/3238 Reg.13

3349. Biofuel (Labelling) Regulations 2004
referred to: SI 2009/669 Sch.1 Part 4
Reg.3, amended: SI 2009/3277 Reg.3
Sch.1 Part 1 para.2, amended: SI 2009/3277 Reg.4

3385. Common Agricultural Policy Single Payment Scheme (Set-aside) (England) Regulations 2004
revoked: SI 2009/3102 Reg.9

3386. Control of Substances Hazardous to Health (Amendment) Regulations 2004
Reg.3, revoked: SI 2009/716 Sch.7

3387. Non-Domestic Rating (Chargeable Amounts) (England) Regulations 2004
Reg.19, applied: SI 2009/2268 Reg.25

2004– cont.

3391. Environmental Information Regulations 2004
applied: 2009 c.23 s.24, SI 2009/1976 r.19, SI 2009/2263 Reg.9, SI 2009/3342 Reg.16, Reg.36
see *Finn-Kelcey v Milton Keynes BC* [2008] EWCA Civ 1067, [2009] Env. L.R. 17 (CA (Civ Div)), Keene, L.J.
Reg.5, see *R. (on the application of Office of Communications) v Information Commissioner* [2008] EWHC 1445 (Admin), [2009] Env. L.R. 1 (QBD (Admin)), Laws, L.J.
Reg.12, see *R. (on the application of Office of Communications) v Information Commissioner* [2008] EWHC 1445 (Admin), [2009] Env. L.R. 1 (QBD (Admin)), Laws, L.J.; see *R. (on the application of Office of Communications) v Information Commissioner* [2009] EWCA Civ 90, Times, February 27, 2009 (CA (Civ Div)), Waller, L.J. (V-P)
Reg.18, applied: SI 2009/1976 r.19, r.22

3426. Information and Consultation of Employees Regulations 2004
Reg.14, see *Darnton v Bournemouth University* [2009] I.R.L.R. 4 (CAC), John Purcell (Chairman)
Reg.40, amended: SI 2009/3348 Art.22, Art.23

3435. A63 Trunk Road (Barlby Junction to Bridge Farm) (Detrunking) Order 2004
revoked: SI 2009/283 Art.4

3436. A63 Trunk Road (Osgodby Bypass) Order 2004
revoked: SI 2009/283 Art.4

2005

14. Information Tribunal (Enforcement Appeals) Rules 2005
see *Galloway v Information Commissioner* (2009) 108 B.M.L.R. 50 (Information Tr), Claire Taylor

15. Immigration (Procedure for Marriage) Regulations 2005
see *R. (on the application of Baiai) v Secretary of State for the Home Department* [2008] UKHL 53, [2009] 1 A.C. 287 (HL), Lord Bingham of Cornhill

42. Licensing Act 2003 (Premises licences and club premises certificates) Regulations 2005
Reg.2, amended: SI 2009/1809 Reg.2, SI 2009/3159 Reg.3
Reg.10, substituted: SI 2009/1809 Reg.2
Reg.12, substituted: SI 2009/1809 Reg.2
Reg.13, amended: SI 2009/1809 Reg.2
Reg.13A, added: SI 2009/1809 Reg.2
Reg.13B, added: SI 2009/1809 Reg.2
Reg.19, amended: SI 2009/1809 Reg.2
Reg.19A, added: SI 2009/1809 Reg.2
Reg.21, amended: SI 2009/1809 Reg.2
Reg.21, substituted: SI 2009/3159 Reg.4
Reg.21A, added: SI 2009/3159 Reg.5
Reg.21B, added: SI 2009/3159 Reg.5
Reg.22, amended: SI 2009/1809 Reg.2
Reg.23, amended: SI 2009/3159 Reg.6
Reg.25, amended: SI 2009/1809 Reg.2
Reg.26A, added: SI 2009/1809 Reg.2
Reg.26A, amended: SI 2009/3159 Reg.7
Reg.27, amended: SI 2009/1809 Reg.2
Reg.27, substituted: SI 2009/3159 Reg.8
Reg.27A, added: SI 2009/3159 Reg.8
Reg.28, amended: SI 2009/3159 Reg.9

2005–cont.

42. Licensing Act 2003 (Premises licences and club premises certificates) Regulations 2005–*cont.*
Reg.28, substituted: SI 2009/1809 Reg.2
Reg.39B, added: SI 2009/3159 Reg.10
Sch.4A, added: SI 2009/1809 Sch.1
Sch.4B, added: SI 2009/1809 Sch.1

43. Licensing Act 2003 (Licensing authority's register) (other information) Regulations 2005
Reg.2, amended: SI 2009/1809 Reg.3

50. Blood Safety and Quality Regulations 2005
Reg.7, amended: SI 2009/3307 Reg.2
Reg.7, revoked (in part): SI 2009/3307 Reg.2
Reg.22, amended: SI 2009/372 Reg.2

52. Education (Student Support) Regulations 2005
applied: SI 2009/2737 Reg.3

79. Licensing Act 2003 (Fees) Regulations 2005
Reg.4A, added: SI 2009/1809 Reg.4
Reg.6A, added: SI 2009/1809 Reg.4
Sch.6, amended: SI 2009/1809 Reg.4

157. Local Authorities Plans and Strategies (Disapplication) (England) Order 2005
applied: SI 2009/486 Reg.4
Art.2, amended: SI 2009/714 Art.3
Art.3, amended: SI 2009/714 Art.4
Art.4, amended: SI 2009/714 Art.5
Art.6, amended: SI 2009/714 Art.6
Art.7, amended: SI 2009/714 Art.7
Art.8, amended: SI 2009/714 Art.8
Sch.2 Part 1 para.1, amended: SI 2009/714 Art.7

168. County of Cornwall (Electoral Changes) Order 2005
Art.1, revoked (in part): SI 2009/850 Art.6
Art.3, revoked: SI 2009/850 Art.6
Art.6, revoked: SI 2009/850 Art.6
Art.7, revoked: SI 2009/850 Art.6
Art.8, revoked: SI 2009/850 Art.6
Sch.1, revoked: SI 2009/850 Art.6

191. Child Trust Funds (Non-tax Appeals) Regulations 2005
referred to: SI 2009/56 Sch.2 para.131
Reg.1, revoked (in part): SI 2009/56 Sch.2 para.132
Reg.4, amended: SI 2009/56 Sch.2 para.133
Reg.14, amended: SI 2009/56 Sch.2 para.134

210. Sexual Offences Act 2003 (Prescribed Police Stations) Regulations 2005
revoked: SI 2009/722 Reg.3

218. Common Agricultural Policy Single Payment and Support Schemes (Integrated Administration and Control System) Regulations 2005
applied: SI 2009/3263 Reg.3, Reg.15, SSI 2009/376 Reg.3
revoked: SI 2009/3263 Reg.15

219. Common Agricultural Policy Single Payment and Support Schemes Regulations 2005
revoked: SI 2009/3102 Reg.9
Reg.3, referred to: SI 2009/1771 Reg.4
Reg.5, referred to: SI 2009/1771 Reg.5

230. Asylum and Immigration Tribunal (Procedure) Rules 2005
see *NB (Guinea) v Secretary of State for the Home Department* [2008] EWCA Civ 1229, [2009] Imm. A.R. 337 (CA (Civ Div)), Ward, L.J.
r.9, see *JH (Zimbabwe) v Secretary of State for the Home Department* [2009] EWCA Civ 78, [2009] Imm. A.R. 499 (CA (Civ Div)), Laws, L.J.
r.23, see *NB (Guinea) v Secretary of State for the Home Department* [2008] EWCA Civ 1229, [2009] Imm. A.R. 337 (CA (Civ Div)), Ward, L.J.

2005–cont.

230. Asylum and Immigration Tribunal (Procedure) Rules 2005–*cont.*
r.59, see *NB (Guinea) v Secretary of State for the Home Department* [2008] EWCA Civ 1229, [2009] Imm. A.R. 337 (CA (Civ Div)), Ward, L.J.

231. Horse Passports (Wales) Regulations 2005
revoked: SI 2009/2470 Reg.25

240. Institute of Trade Mark Attorneys Order 2005
revoked: SI 2009/3250 Sch.1

242. Ivory Coast (Restrictive Measures) (Overseas Territories) Order 2005
Art.19, varied: SI 2009/888 Art.2
Sch.2 para.1, varied: SI 2009/888 Art.2
Sch.2 para.2, varied: SI 2009/888 Art.2
Sch.2 para.3, varied: SI 2009/888 Art.2
Sch.2 para.4, varied: SI 2009/888 Art.2
Sch.2 para.5, varied: SI 2009/888 Art.2
Sch.2 para.6, varied: SI 2009/888 Art.2
Sch.2 para.7, varied: SI 2009/888 Art.2
Sch.2 para.8, varied: SI 2009/888 Art.2
Sch.2 para.9, varied: SI 2009/888 Art.2

255. Pensions (Northern Ireland) Order 2005
varied: SI 2009/317 Sch.1
Art.2, amended: SI 2009/1941 Sch.1 para.252
Art.40, amended: SI 2009/1941 Sch.1 para.252
Art.41, amended: SI 2009/1941 Sch.1 para.252
Art.47, amended: SI 2009/1941 Sch.1 para.252
Art.53, amended: SI 2009/1941 Sch.1 para.252
Art.100, revoked: SI 2009/1941 Sch.2
Art.105, amended: SI 2009/1941 Sch.1 para.252
Art.220, amended: SI 2009/1941 Sch.1 para.252
Art.225, amended: SI 2009/1941 Sch.1 para.252
Sch.3, amended: SI 2009/1941 Sch.1 para.252
Sch.7, amended: SI 2009/1941 Sch.1 para.252
Sch.10 para.2, revoked: SI 2009/1941 Sch.2

259. Miscellaneous Food Additives (Amendment) (Wales) Regulations 2005
Reg.3, applied: SI 2009/3378 Reg.10

340. General Commissioners (Jurisdiction and Procedure) (Amendment) Regulations 2005
revoked: SI 2009/56 Sch.2 para.187

341. Special Commissioners (Jurisdiction and Procedure) (Amendment) Regulations 2005
revoked: SI 2009/56 Sch.2 para.187

360. Common Agricultural Policy Single Payment and Support Schemes (Wales) Regulations 2005
Reg.2, amended: SI 2009/3129 Reg.3
Reg.5A, added: SI 2009/3129 Reg.4
Reg.6, substituted: SI 2009/3129 Reg.5
Reg.10, substituted: SI 2009/3129 Reg.6

384. Criminal Procedure Rules 2005
referred to: SI 2009/2087 r.2
see *R. v O'Dowd (Kevin)* [2009] EWCA Crim 905, [2009] 2 Cr. App. R. 16 (CA (Crim Div)), Scott Baker, L.J.; see *R. v S Ltd* [2009] EWCA Crim 85, [2009] 2 Cr. App. R. 11 (CA (Crim Div)), Moses, L.J.
Part 2 r.2.1, amended: SI 2009/2087 r.3
Part 3 r.3.8, amended: SI 2009/2087 r.4
Part 4 r.4.7, amended: SI 2009/2087 r.5
Part 5 r.5.1, substituted: SI 2009/2087 Sch.1
Part 5 r.5.2, substituted: SI 2009/2087 Sch.1
Part 5 r.5.3, substituted: SI 2009/2087 Sch.1
Part 5 r.5.4, substituted: SI 2009/2087 Sch.1
Part 5 r.5.5, substituted: SI 2009/2087 Sch.1
Part 5 r.5.6, substituted: SI 2009/2087 Sch.1
Part 5 r.5.7, substituted: SI 2009/2087 Sch.1

2005 – cont.

384. Criminal Procedure Rules 2005–*cont.*

Part 6 r.6.1, substituted: SI 2009/ 2087 Sch.2
Part 6 r.6.2, substituted: SI 2009/ 2087 Sch.2
Part 6 r.6.3, substituted: SI 2009/ 2087 Sch.2
Part 6 r.6.4, substituted: SI 2009/ 2087 Sch.2
Part 6 r.6.5, substituted: SI 2009/ 2087 Sch.2
Part 6 r.6.6, substituted: SI 2009/ 2087 Sch.2
Part 6 r.6.7, substituted: SI 2009/ 2087 Sch.2
Part 6 r.6.8, substituted: SI 2009/ 2087 Sch.2
Part 6 r.6.9, substituted: SI 2009/ 2087 Sch.2
Part 6 r.6.10, substituted: SI 2009/ 2087 Sch.2
Part 6 r.6.11, substituted: SI 2009/ 2087 Sch.2
Part 6 r.6.12, substituted: SI 2009/ 2087 Sch.2
Part 6 r.6.13, substituted: SI 2009/ 2087 Sch.2
Part 6 r.6.14, substituted: SI 2009/ 2087 Sch.2
Part 6 r.6.15, substituted: SI 2009/ 2087 Sch.2
Part 6 r.6.16, substituted: SI 2009/ 2087 Sch.2
Part 6 r.6.17, substituted: SI 2009/ 2087 Sch.2
Part 6 r.6.18, substituted: SI 2009/ 2087 Sch.2
Part 6 r.6.19, substituted: SI 2009/ 2087 Sch.2
Part 6 r.6.20, substituted: SI 2009/ 2087 Sch.2
Part 6 r.6.21, substituted: SI 2009/ 2087 Sch.2
Part 6 r.6.22, substituted: SI 2009/ 2087 Sch.2
Part 14 r.14.1, amended: SI 2009/ 2087 r.9
Part 16 r.16.11, amended: SI 2009/ 2087 r.10
Part 17 r.17.2, amended: SI 2009/ 2087 r.11
Part 19 r.19.2, amended: SI 2009/ 2087 r.13
Part 19 r.19.26, added: SI 2009/ 2087 r.13
Part 19 r.19.26, amended: SI 2009/ 2087 r.12
Part 19 r.19.27, added: SI 2009/ 2087 r.13
Part 19 r.19.27, amended: SI 2009/ 2087 r.12
Part 22 r.1, substituted: SI 2009/ 2087 Sch.3
Part 22 r.22.1, substituted: SI 2009/ 2087 Sch.3
Part 22 r.22.2, substituted: SI 2009/ 2087 Sch.3
Part 22 r.22.3, substituted: SI 2009/ 2087 Sch.3
Part 22 r.22.4, substituted: SI 2009/ 2087 Sch.3
Part 22 r.22.5, substituted: SI 2009/ 2087 Sch.3
Part 22 r.22.6, substituted: SI 2009/ 2087 Sch.3
Part 22 r.22.7, substituted: SI 2009/ 2087 Sch.3
Part 22 r.22.8, substituted: SI 2009/ 2087 Sch.3
Part 22 r.22.9, substituted: SI 2009/ 2087 Sch.3
Part 23 r.1, revoked: SI 2009/ 2087 r.15
Part 24 r.24.1, revoked: SI 2009/ 2087 r.15
Part 24 r.24.2, revoked: SI 2009/ 2087 r.15
Part 24 r.24.3, revoked: SI 2009/ 2087 r.15
Part 25 r.25.1, revoked: SI 2009/ 2087 r.15
Part 25 r.25.2, revoked: SI 2009/ 2087 r.15
Part 25 r.25.3, revoked: SI 2009/ 2087 r.15
Part 25 r.25.4, revoked: SI 2009/ 2087 r.15
Part 25 r.25.5, revoked: SI 2009/ 2087 r.15
Part 25 r.25.6, revoked: SI 2009/ 2087 r.15
Part 25 r.25.7, revoked: SI 2009/ 2087 r.15
Part 25 r.25.8, revoked: SI 2009/ 2087 r.15
Part 26 r.26.1, revoked: SI 2009/ 2087 r.15
Part 26 r.26.2, revoked: SI 2009/ 2087 r.15
Part 26 r.26.3, revoked: SI 2009/ 2087 r.15
Part 26 r.26.4, revoked: SI 2009/ 2087 r.15
Part 26 r.26.5, revoked: SI 2009/ 2087 r.15
Part 27 r.27.1, substituted: SI 2009/ 2087 Sch.4
Part 27 r.27.2, substituted: SI 2009/ 2087 Sch.4
Part 27 r.27.3, substituted: SI 2009/ 2087 Sch.4
Part 27 r.27.4, substituted: SI 2009/ 2087 Sch.4
Part 32 r.32.1, amended: SI 2009/ 2087 r.17
Part 32 r.32.2, amended: SI 2009/ 2087 r.17
Part 32 r.32.3, amended: SI 2009/ 2087 r.17
Part 32 r.32.4, amended: SI 2009/ 2087 r.17
Part 32 r.32.5, amended: SI 2009/ 2087 r.17
Part 32 r.32.6, amended: SI 2009/ 2087 r.17

2005 – cont.

384. Criminal Procedure Rules 2005–*cont.*

Part 32 r.32.7, amended: SI 2009/ 2087 r.17
Part 32 r.32.8, amended: SI 2009/ 2087 r.17
Part 32 r.32.9, amended: SI 2009/ 2087 r.17
Part 32 r.32.10, added: SI 2009/ 2087 r.17
Part 32 r.32.10, amended: SI 2009/ 2087 r.17
Part 33 r.1, substituted: SI 2009/ 2087 Sch.5
Part 33 r.33.1, substituted: SI 2009/ 2087 Sch.5
Part 33 r.33.2, substituted: SI 2009/ 2087 Sch.5
Part 33 r.33.3, substituted: SI 2009/ 2087 Sch.5
Part 33 r.33.4, substituted: SI 2009/ 2087 Sch.5
Part 33 r.33.5, substituted: SI 2009/ 2087 Sch.5
Part 33 r.33.6, substituted: SI 2009/ 2087 Sch.5
Part 33 r.33.7, substituted: SI 2009/ 2087 Sch.5
Part 33 r.33.8, substituted: SI 2009/ 2087 Sch.5
Part 33 r.33.9, substituted: SI 2009/ 2087 Sch.5
Part 34, see *R. v Kamuhuza (Martin)* [2008] EWCA Crim 3060, (2009) 173 J.P. 55 (CA (Crim Div)), Thomas, L.J.
Part 39 r.39.1, amended: SI 2009/ 2087 r.19
Part 59 r.59.1, amended: SI 2009/ 2087 r.20
Part 59 r.59.2, amended: SI 2009/ 2087 r.20
Part 59 r.59.3, amended: SI 2009/ 2087 r.20
Part 59 r.59.4, amended: SI 2009/ 2087 r.20
Part 59 r.59.5, amended: SI 2009/ 2087 r.20
Part 59 r.59.6, added: SI 2009/ 2087 r.21
Part 59 r.59.6, amended: SI 2009/ 2087 r.20
Part 61 r.61.19, amended: SI 2009/ 2087 r.22
Part 61 r.61.20, amended: SI 2009/ 2087 r.22
Part 61 r.61.21, amended: SI 2009/ 2087 r.22
Part 62 r.62.1, substituted: SI 2009/ 2087 Sch.6
Part 62 r.62.2, substituted: SI 2009/ 2087 Sch.6
Part 62 r.62.3, substituted: SI 2009/ 2087 Sch.6
Part 62 r.62.4, substituted: SI 2009/ 2087 Sch.6
Part 62 r.62.5, substituted: SI 2009/ 2087 Sch.6
Part 62 r.62.6, substituted: SI 2009/ 2087 Sch.6
Part 62 r.62.7, substituted: SI 2009/ 2087 Sch.6
Part 62 r.62.8, substituted: SI 2009/ 2087 Sch.6
Part 62 r.62.9, substituted: SI 2009/ 2087 Sch.6
Part 62 r.62.10, substituted: SI 2009/ 2087 Sch.6
Part 62 r.62.11, substituted: SI 2009/ 2087 Sch.6
Part 62 r.62.12, substituted: SI 2009/ 2087 Sch.6
Part 63 r.63.1, amended: SI 2009/ 2087 r.24
Part 63 r.63.8, amended: SI 2009/ 2087 r.24
Part 63 r.63.10, amended: SI 2009/ 2087 r.24
Part 64 r.64.7, amended: SI 2009/ 2087 r.25
Part 65 r.65.1, amended: SI 2009/ 2087 r.26
Part 65 r.65.3, amended: SI 2009/ 2087 r.26
Part 65 r.65.6, amended: SI 2009/ 2087 r.26
Part 68 r.68.3, amended: SI 2009/ 2087 r.27
Part 68 r.68.4, amended: SI 2009/ 2087 r.28
Part 68 r.68.8, amended: SI 2009/ 2087 r.29
Part 71 r.71.1, amended: SI 2009/ 2087 r.30
Part 71 r.71.2, amended: SI 2009/ 2087 r.30
Part 71 r.71.3, amended: SI 2009/ 2087 r.30
Part 71 r.71.4, amended: SI 2009/ 2087 r.30
Part 71 r.71.5, amended: SI 2009/ 2087 r.30
Part 71 r.71.6, amended: SI 2009/ 2087 r.30
Part 71 r.71.7, amended: SI 2009/ 2087 r.30
Part 71 r.71.8, amended: SI 2009/ 2087 r.30
Part 71 r.71.9, amended: SI 2009/ 2087 r.30
Part 71 r.71.10, amended: SI 2009/ 2087 r.30
Part 71 r.71.11, amended: SI 2009/ 2087 r.30
Part 71 r.71.12, amended: SI 2009/ 2087 r.30
Part 74 r.74.1, amended: SI 2009/ 2087 r.31
Part 74 r.74.2, amended: SI 2009/ 2087 r.31
Part 74 r.74.3, amended: SI 2009/ 2087 r.31
Part 74 r.74.4, amended: SI 2009/ 2087 r.31

2005–cont.

384. Criminal Procedure Rules 2005–*cont.*
Part 76 r.1, substituted: SI 2009/2087 Sch.7
Part 76 r.76.1, substituted: SI 2009/2087 Sch.7
Part 76 r.76.2, substituted: SI 2009/2087 Sch.7
Part 76 r.76.3, substituted: SI 2009/2087 Sch.7
Part 76 r.76.4, substituted: SI 2009/2087 Sch.7
Part 76 r.76.5, substituted: SI 2009/2087 Sch.7
Part 76 r.76.6, substituted: SI 2009/2087 Sch.7
Part 76 r.76.7, substituted: SI 2009/2087 Sch.7
Part 76 r.76.8, substituted: SI 2009/2087 Sch.7
Part 76 r.76.9, substituted: SI 2009/2087 Sch.7
Part 76 r.76.10, substituted: SI 2009/2087 Sch.7
Part 76 r.76.11, substituted: SI 2009/2087 Sch.7
Part 76 r.76.12, substituted: SI 2009/2087 Sch.7
Part 76 r.76.13, substituted: SI 2009/2087 Sch.7
Part 76 r.76.14, substituted: SI 2009/2087 Sch.7
Part 77 r.1, revoked: SI 2009/2087 r.33
Part 78 r.78.1, revoked: SI 2009/2087 r.33
Part 78 r.78.2, revoked: SI 2009/2087 r.33
Part 78 r.78.3, revoked: SI 2009/2087 r.33
Part 78 r.78.4, revoked: SI 2009/2087 r.33
Part 78 r.78.5, revoked: SI 2009/2087 r.33
Part 78 r.78.6, revoked: SI 2009/2087 r.33
Part 78 r.78.7, revoked: SI 2009/2087 r.33
Part 22, see *Practice Direction (Sen Cts: Criminal Proceedings: Additional Forms)* [2009] 1 W.L.R. 2239 (Sen Cts), Lord Judge, L.C.J.
Part 27, see *Practice Direction (Sen Cts: Criminal Proceedings: Additional Forms)* [2009] 1 W.L.R. 2239 (Sen Cts), Lord Judge, L.C.J.
Part 34, see *R. v Kamuhuza (Martin)* [2008] EWCA Crim 3060, (2009) 173 J.P. 55 (CA (Crim Div)), Thomas, L.J.
Part 62, see *Practice Direction (Sen Cts: Criminal Proceedings: Additional Forms)* [2009] 1 W.L.R. 2239 (Sen Cts), Lord Judge, L.C.J.
r.4.7, see *R. v Popat (Harish)* [2008] EWCA Crim 1921, (2009) 172 J.P. 24 (CA (Crim Div)), Hughes, L.J.
r.4.10, see *Gidden v Chief Constable of Humberside* [2009] EWHC 2924 (Admin), (2009) 173 J.P. 609 (DC), Elias, L.J.
r.14.2, see *R. v Roberts (Patrice)* [2008] EWCA Crim 1304, [2009] 1 Cr. App. R. 20 (CA (Crim Div)), Latham, L.J. (VP, CA Crim)
r.57.8, see *T v B* [2008] EWHC 3000 (Fam), [2009] 1 F.L.R. 1231 (Fam Div), Sir Mark Potter (President, Fam)

386. Proceeds of Crime Act 2002 (References to Financial Investigators) (Amendment) Order 2005
revoked: SI 2009/975 Sch.2

389. Adoption Agencies Regulations 2005
Part 4, see *R. (on the application of T) v Newham LBC* [2008] EWHC 2640 (Admin), [2009] 1 F.L.R. 311 (QBD (Admin)), Bennett, J.
Part 5, see *R. (on the application of T) v Newham LBC* [2008] EWHC 2640 (Admin), [2009] 1 F.L.R. 311 (QBD (Admin)), Bennett, J.
Reg.14, amended: SI 2009/1892 Sch.1 para.13
Reg.23, amended: SI 2009/1895 Reg.2
Reg.23, applied: SSI 2009/182 Reg.15
Reg.25, applied: SI 2009/395 Reg.11
Reg.27, applied: SI 2009/395 Reg.3
Reg.28, applied: SI 2009/395 Reg.11
Reg.35, see *C (A Child) (Adoption: Parental Consent), Re* [2008] EWHC 2555 (Fam), [2009] Fam. 83 (Fam Div), Eleanor King, J
Sch.3 Part 1 para.2, referred to: SSI 2009/182 Reg.15

2005–cont.

389. Adoption Agencies Regulations 2005–*cont.*
Sch.3 Part 1 para.3, referred to: SSI 2009/182 Reg.15
Sch.3 Part 1 para.4, referred to: SSI 2009/182 Reg.15
Sch.3 Part 1 para.5, referred to: SSI 2009/182 Reg.15
Sch.3 Part 1 para.6, referred to: SSI 2009/182 Reg.15
Sch.3 Part 1 para.7, referred to: SSI 2009/182 Reg.15
Sch.3 Part 1 para.8, referred to: SSI 2009/182 Reg.15
Sch.3 Part 1 para.9, referred to: SSI 2009/182 Reg.15
Sch.3 Part 1 para.10, referred to: SSI 2009/182 Reg.15
Sch.3 Part 1 para.11, referred to: SSI 2009/182 Reg.15
Sch.3 Part 2, applied: SSI 2009/182 Reg.15

390. Tractor etc (EC Type-Approval) Regulations 2005
Reg.2, amended: SI 2009/3266 Reg.3

391. Electricity (Fuel Mix Disclosure) Regulations 2005
Sch.1, amended: SI 2009/229 Sch.2 para.15

392. Adoptions with a Foreign Element Regulations 2005
Reg.19, amended: SI 2009/2563 Reg.2
Reg.20, amended: SI 2009/2563 Reg.2

400. General Medical Council (Registration Appeals Panels Procedure) Rules Order of Council 2005
Sch.1, amended: SI 2009/2752 Sch.1
Sch.1, substituted: SI 2009/2752 Sch.1

421. New Forest National Park Authority (Establishment) Order 2005
Art.5, amended: SI 2009/837 Art.22
Art.5, revoked (in part): SI 2009/837 Art.22

437. Armed Forces Early Departure Payments Scheme Order 2005
referred to: SI 2009/544 Art.2
Art.7, substituted: SI 2009/544 Art.3
Art.11, amended: SI 2009/544 Art.4
Art.12, amended: SI 2009/544 Art.5

438. Armed Forces Pension Scheme Order 2005
referred to: SI 2009/544 Art.6
Sch.1, added: SI 2009/544 Art.8, Art.9, Art.12
Sch.1, amended: SI 2009/544 Art.8, Art.9, Art.12
Sch.1, revoked: SI 2009/544 Art.12
Sch.1, substituted: SI 2009/544 Art.7, Art.10, Art.11, Art.12

439. Armed Forces and Reserve Forces (Compensation Scheme) Order 2005
Art.20, applied: SI 2009/3236 Art.2
Sch.4, amended: SI 2009/3236 Art.2

446. Courts-Martial Appeal (Amendment) Rules 2005
revoked: SI 2009/2657 Sch.5

448. Gangmasters (Licensing Authority) Regulations 2005
Sch.2, amended: SI 2009/2748 Sch.1 para.29

454. Social Security (Graduated Retirement Benefit) Regulations 2005
Sch.1 Part 1 para.1, varied: SI 2009/497 Art.12
Sch.1 Part 1 para.2, varied: SI 2009/497 Art.12
Sch.1 Part 1 para.3, varied: SI 2009/497 Art.12
Sch.1 Part 1 para.4, varied: SI 2009/497 Art.12
Sch.1 Part 1 para.5, varied: SI 2009/497 Art.12
Sch.1 Part 1 para.6, varied: SI 2009/497 Art.12
Sch.1 Part 1 para.7, varied: SI 2009/497 Art.12
Sch.1 Part 1 para.8, varied: SI 2009/497 Art.12
Sch.1 Part 1 para.9, varied: SI 2009/497 Art.12
Sch.1 Part 1 para.10, varied: SI 2009/497 Art.12
Sch.1 Part 2A para.20A, varied: SI 2009/497 Art.12
Sch.1 Part 2A para.20B, varied: SI 2009/497 Art.12
Sch.1 Part 2A para.20C, varied: SI 2009/497 Art.12

2005–cont.

454. Social Security (Graduated Retirement Benefit) Regulations 2005–*cont.*

Sch.1 Part 2A para.20D, varied: SI 2009/497 Art.12
Sch.1 Part 2 para.11, varied: SI 2009/497 Art.12
Sch.1 Part 2 para.12, varied: SI 2009/497 Art.12
Sch.1 Part 2 para.13, varied: SI 2009/497 Art.12
Sch.1 Part 2 para.14, varied: SI 2009/497 Art.12
Sch.1 Part 2 para.15, varied: SI 2009/497 Art.12
Sch.1 Part 2 para.16, varied: SI 2009/497 Art.12
Sch.1 Part 2 para.17, varied: SI 2009/497 Art.12
Sch.1 Part 2 para.18, varied: SI 2009/497 Art.12
Sch.1 Part 2 para.19, varied: SI 2009/497 Art.12
Sch.1 Part 2 para.20, varied: SI 2009/497 Art.12
Sch.1 Part 2 para.20ZA, varied: SI 2009/497 Art.12
Sch.1 Part 2 para.20ZB, varied: SI 2009/497 Art.12
Sch.1 Part 3 para.21, varied: SI 2009/497 Art.12

474. Damages (Government and Health Service Bodies) Order 2005

Sch.1 Part 1, amended: SI 2009/229 Sch.2 para.16, SI 2009/2748 Sch.1 para.30

489. Legal Services Ombudsman (Jurisdiction) (Amendment) Order 2005

revoked: SI 2009/3250 Sch.1

500. Health and Social Care Information Centre Regulations 2005

Reg.1, amended: SI 2009/462 Sch.5 para.14
Reg.1, revoked (in part): SI 2009/462 Sch.5 para.14

519. Colours in Food (Amendment) (England) Regulations 2005

applied: SI 2009/3238 Reg.7

524. Insolvency Practitioners Regulations 2005

varied: SI 2009/317 Sch.1
Reg.5, amended: SI 2009/2748 Sch.1 para.31
Reg.7, amended: SI 2009/3081 Sch.1 para.3
Reg.8, amended: SI 2009/3081 Sch.1 para.4
Reg.8A, added: SI 2009/3081 Sch.1 para.4
Reg.10, revoked: SI 2009/3081 Sch.1 para.5
Reg.11, amended: SI 2009/3081 Sch.1 para.6
Reg.12, amended: SI 2009/3081 Sch.1 para.7
Sch.2 Part 1 para.1, amended: SI 2009/3081 Sch.1 para.8
Sch.2 Part 2, amended: SI 2009/3081 Sch.1 para.8
Sch.2 Part 2 para.2A, added: SI 2009/3081 Sch.1 para.8
Sch.2 Part 2 para.3, amended: SI 2009/3081 Sch.1 para.8
Sch.2 Part 2 para.8A, added: SI 2009/3081 Sch.1 para.8
Sch.2 Part 2 para.8B, added: SI 2009/3081 Sch.1 para.8
Sch.2 Part 2 para.8C, added: SI 2009/3081 Sch.1 para.8
Sch.2 Part 2 para.8D, added: SI 2009/3081 Sch.1 para.8
Sch.2 Part 2 para.8E, added: SI 2009/3081 Sch.1 para.8
Sch.2 Part 3 para.9, amended: SI 2009/3081 Sch.1 para.8
Sch.2 Part 3 para.10, amended: SI 2009/3081 Sch.1 para.8
Sch.2 Part 3 para.10, substituted: SI 2009/3081 Sch.1 para.8
Sch.2 Part 3 para.11, amended: SI 2009/3081 Sch.1 para.8
Sch.3 para.2, amended: SI 2009/3081 Sch.1 para.9
Sch.3 para.4, substituted: SI 2009/3081 Sch.1 para.9

554. Local Justice Areas Order 2005

Sch.1, amended: SI 2009/2080 Art.3

2005–cont.

581. Penalties for Disorderly Behaviour (Amount of Penalty) (Amendment) Order 2005

revoked: SI 2009/83 Art.3

590. Pension Protection Fund (Entry Rules) Regulations 2005

varied: SI 2009/317 Sch.1
Reg.1, amended: SI 2009/451 Reg.2
Reg.2, amended: SI 2009/1906 Sch.1 para.2
Reg.6, amended: SI 2009/317 Art.8
Reg.7, amended: SI 2009/451 Reg.2
Reg.10, amended: SI 2009/451 Reg.2
Reg.15, substituted: SI 2009/1552 Reg.2
Reg.17, amended: SI 2009/451 Reg.2
Reg.25, amended: SI 2009/451 Reg.2

631. Health and Social Care (Community Health and Standards) Act 2003 (Commission for Healthcare Audit and Inspection) (Transitional Provisions) Order 2005

revoked: SI 2009/462 Sch.6

641. National Health Service (Pharmaceutical Services) Regulations 2005

Reg.2, amended: SI 2009/2205 Reg.3, SI 2009/3340 Reg.2
Reg.7A, added: SI 2009/2205 Reg.4
Reg.12, amended: SI 2009/2205 Reg.5
Reg.13, amended: SI 2009/2205 Reg.6
Reg.17A, added: SI 2009/2205 Reg.7
Reg.23, revoked (in part): SI 2009/2205 Reg.8
Reg.25, amended: SI 2009/599 Reg.2
Reg.27, amended: SI 2009/2205 Reg.9
Reg.28, amended: SI 2009/2205 Reg.10
Reg.33, revoked (in part): SI 2009/2205 Reg.11
Reg.37, amended: SI 2009/2205 Reg.12
Reg.53, amended: SI 2009/2205 Reg.13
Reg.60, amended: SI 2009/2205 Reg.14
Reg.65A, added: SI 2009/2205 Reg.15
Reg.67, amended: SI 2009/599 Reg.2
Reg.69B, added: SI 2009/2205 Reg.16
Sch.1 Part 2 para.6, substituted: SI 2009/3340 Reg.4
Sch.1 Part 2 para.9, amended: SI 2009/3340 Reg.5
Sch.1 Part 2 para.10, amended: SI 2009/3340 Reg.6
Sch.1 Part 2 para.10, substituted: SI 2009/3340 Reg.6
Sch.1 Part 2 para.11A, added: SI 2009/3340 Reg.7
Sch.1 Part 2 para.19, amended: SI 2009/3340 Reg.8
Sch.1 Part 3 para.22, amended: SI 2009/2205 Reg.17
Sch.1 Part 3 para.25, amended: SI 2009/2205 Reg.18
Sch.1 Part 3 para.25A, added: SI 2009/2205 Reg.19
Sch.1 Part 4 para.26, amended: SI 2009/3340 Reg.9
Sch.1 Part 4 para.28, amended: SI 2009/2205 Reg.20, SI 2009/3340 Reg.10
Sch.1 Part 4 para.31, amended: SI 2009/2205 Reg.21
Sch.1 Part 4 para.32, substituted: SI 2009/309 Sch.1 para.1
Sch.1 Part 5 para.34, amended: SI 2009/2205 Reg.22
Sch.1 Part 5 para.37, amended: SI 2009/3340 Reg.11
Sch.2 para.8, amended: SI 2009/2205 Reg.23
Sch.2 para.9, amended: SI 2009/309 Sch.1 para.1
Sch.3 para.4, amended: SI 2009/3340 Reg.13
Sch.3 para.4A, added: SI 2009/3340 Reg.14
Sch.3 para.5, amended: SI 2009/3340 Reg.15
Sch.3 para.6, amended: SI 2009/3340 Reg.16
Sch.3 para.7, amended: SI 2009/3340 Reg.17
Sch.3 para.7, substituted: SI 2009/3340 Reg.17
Sch.3 para.8, amended: SI 2009/3340 Reg.18
Sch.3 para.8, substituted: SI 2009/3340 Reg.18
Sch.3 para.9A, added: SI 2009/3340 Reg.19
Sch.3 para.9B, added: SI 2009/3340 Reg.19
Sch.3 para.10, amended: SI 2009/2205 Reg.24

2005–cont.

641. National Health Service (Pharmaceutical Services) Regulations 2005–*cont.*
Sch.3 para.10, revoked (in part): SI 2009/2205 Reg.24
Sch.3 para.13A, added: SI 2009/2205 Reg.25, SI 2009/3340 Reg.20
Sch.3 para.15, amended: SI 2009/3340 Reg.21
Sch.3 para.18, amended: SI 2009/2205 Reg.26
Sch.3 para.19, substituted: SI 2009/309 Sch.1 para.1
Sch.3 para.21, amended: SI 2009/2205 Reg.27
Sch.3 para.24, amended: SI 2009/3340 Reg.22
Sch.4 Part 1 para.5, amended: SI 2009/2205 Reg.28

646. Finance Act 2002, Schedule 26, Parts 2 and 9 (Amendment) Order 2005
revoked: 2009 c.4 Sch.3 Part 1

659. Non-Domestic Rating (Alteration of Lists and Appeals) (England) Regulations 2005
applied: SI 2009/2268 Reg.25
revoked: SI 2009/2268 Reg.25
Reg.4, amended: SI 2009/1307 Sch.2 para.101
Reg.8, amended: SI 2009/1307 Sch.2 para.102
Reg.17, amended: SI 2009/1307 Sch.2 para.103
Reg.17A, applied: SI 2009/2268 Reg.20
Reg.35, amended: SI 2009/1307 Sch.2 para.104
Reg.37, amended: SI 2009/1307 Sch.2 para.105
Reg.37, revoked (in part): SI 2009/1307 Sch.2 para.105
Reg.39, amended: SI 2009/1307 Sch.2 para.106

670. Pension Protection Fund (Compensation) Regulations 2005
Reg.15, amended: SI 2009/809 Art.3
Reg.15A, added: SI 2009/451 Reg.3

672. Pension Protection Fund (Valuation) Regulations 2005
Reg.1, amended: SI 2009/451 Reg.4

678. Occupational Pension Schemes (Employer Debt) Regulations 2005
Reg.4, amended: SI 2009/1906 Sch.1 para.3

703. Occupational Pension Schemes (Independent Trustee) Regulations 2005
Reg.13, amended: SI 2009/615 Reg.17

706. Occupational Pension Schemes (Winding up etc.) Regulations 2005
Reg.3, amended: SI 2009/1906 Sch.1 para.4

888. Disclosure of Adoption Information (Post-Commencement Adoptions) Regulations 2005
Reg.2, amended: SI 2009/1892 Sch.1 para.14
Reg.15, applied: SI 2009/395 Reg.12

894. Hazardous Waste (England and Wales) Regulations 2005
applied: SI 2009/716 Reg.3
referred to: SI 2009/507 Reg.2
Reg.5, amended: SI 2009/507 Reg.3
Reg.6, referred to: SI 2009/2263 Sch.1 para.9
Reg.12, amended: SI 2009/507 Reg.4
Reg.13, substituted: SI 2009/507 Reg.5
Reg.14, substituted: SI 2009/507 Reg.6
Reg.14A, added: SI 2009/507 Reg.7
Reg.21, amended: SI 2009/507 Reg.8
Reg.23, substituted: SI 2009/507 Reg.9
Reg.26, amended: SI 2009/507 Reg.10
Reg.30, substituted: SI 2009/507 Reg.11
Reg.32, amended: SI 2009/507 Reg.12
Reg.42, amended: SI 2009/507 Reg.13
Reg.48, amended: SI 2009/507 Reg.14
Reg.49, amended: SI 2009/507 Reg.15
Reg.70, amended: SI 2009/507 Reg.16

2005–cont.

900. Pensions Regulator (Notifiable Events) Regulations 2005
Reg.1, amended: SI 2009/617 Reg.3
Reg.2, revoked (in part): SI 2009/617 Reg.3

907. Child Trust Funds (Appeals) (Northern Ireland) Regulations 2005
Reg.1, revoked (in part): SI 2009/56 Sch.2 para.135

912. Gender Recognition Register Regulations 2005
Reg.1, amended: SI 2009/1892 Sch.1 para.15
Sch.1 Part 2, amended: SI 2009/1892 Sch.1 para.15
Sch.2 Part 3, amended: SI 2009/1892 Sch.1 para.15
Sch.3, amended: SI 2009/1892 Sch.1 para.15
Sch.6, amended: SI 2009/1892 Sch.1 para.15
Sch.8 Part 3, amended: SI 2009/1892 Sch.1 para.15
Sch.9, amended: SI 2009/1892 Sch.1 para.15

916. Gender Recognition (Disclosure of Information) (England, Wales and Northern Ireland) (No.2) Order 2005
varied: SI 2009/317 Sch.1

931. Pensions Regulator (Contribution Notices and Restoration Orders) Regulations 2005
Reg.3, amended: SI 2009/1906 Sch.1 para.5

950. Criminal Justice Act 2003 (Commencement No.8 and Transitional and Saving Provisions) Order 2005
see *Gibson v Secretary of State for Justice* [2008] EWCA Civ 177, [2009] Q.B. 204 (CA (Civ Div)), Sir Anthony Clarke, M.R.
Art.2, amended: SI 2009/616 Art.2, SI 2009/3111 Art.2
Art.2, revoked (in part): SI 2009/3111 Art.2
Art.4, amended: SI 2009/616 Art.2
Art.4, revoked: SI 2009/3111 Art.2
Sch.2 Part 2 para.7, substituted: SI 2009/3111 Art.2
Sch.2 Part 2 para.11, amended: SI 2009/3111 Art.2
Sch.2 Part 2 para.12, amended: SI 2009/3111 Art.2
Sch.2 para.23, see *Gibson v Secretary of State for Justice* [2008] EWCA Civ 177, [2009] Q.B. 204 (CA (Civ Div)), Sir Anthony Clarke, M.R.

965. Pensions Appeal Commissioners (Procedure) (Northern Ireland) Regulations 2005
Reg.2, amended: SI 2009/459 Reg.2
Reg.3, amended: SI 2009/459 Reg.2
Reg.6, amended: SI 2009/459 Reg.2
Reg.9, amended: SI 2009/459 Reg.2
Reg.11, amended: SI 2009/459 Reg.2
Reg.15, amended: SI 2009/459 Reg.2
Reg.25, amended: SI 2009/459 Reg.2
Reg.26, amended: SI 2009/459 Reg.2

966. Community Legal Service (Asylum and Immigration Appeals) Regulations 2005
Reg.3, amended: SI 2009/3348 Art.16

990. Child Trust Funds (Appeals) Regulations 2005
Reg.1, revoked (in part): SI 2009/56 Sch.2 para.136

992. Occupational and Personal Pension Schemes (Pension Liberation) Regulations 2005
Reg.2, amended: SI 2009/598 Art.10

1032. Education (Review of Staffing Structure) (England) Regulations 2005
revoked: SI 2009/2680 Sch.1

1082. Manufacture and Storage of Explosives Regulations 2005
referred to: SI 2009/693 Reg.2
Reg.2, amended: SI 2009/693 Sch.1 para.4
Reg.2, applied: SI 2009/515 Sch.8 Part 1
Reg.3, amended: SI 2009/693 Sch.1 para.4
Reg.3, applied: SI 2009/693 Reg.2
Reg.5, amended: SI 2009/693 Sch.1 para.4
Reg.7, amended: SI 2009/693 Sch.1 para.4

2005–cont.

1082. Manufacture and Storage of Explosives Regulations 2005–*cont.*
Reg.9, amended: SI 2009/693 Sch.1 para.4
Reg.9, applied: SI 2009/515 Sch.8 Part 1
Reg.10, amended: SI 2009/693 Sch.1 para.4
Reg.10, applied: SI 2009/515 Sch.8 Part 1, Sch.8 Part 2
Reg.11, amended: SI 2009/693 Sch.1 para.4
Reg.11, applied: SI 2009/515 Sch.8 Part 2
Reg.13, amended: SI 2009/693 Sch.1 para.4
Reg.13, referred to: SI 2009/693
Reg.16, amended: SI 2009/693 Sch.1 para.4
Reg.16, applied: SI 2009/515 Sch.8 Part 1, Sch.8 Part 2
Reg.17, amended: SI 2009/693 Sch.1 para.4
Reg.18, amended: SI 2009/693 Sch.1 para.4
Reg.19, substituted: SI 2009/693 Sch.1 para.4
Reg.20, applied: SI 2009/515 Sch.8 Part 1, Sch.8 Part 2
Reg.20, substituted: SI 2009/693 Sch.1 para.4
Reg.21, amended: SI 2009/693 Sch.1 para.4
Reg.25A, added: SI 2009/693 Sch.1 para.4
Reg.27, revoked (in part): SI 2009/693 Sch.1 para.4
Sch.1 para.1, amended: SI 2009/693 Sch.1 para.4
Sch.1 para.1, applied: SI 2009/515 Reg.9
Sch.1 para.3, amended: SI 2009/693 Sch.1 para.4
Sch.4 para.2, amended: SI 2009/693 Sch.1 para.4
Sch.4 para.3, amended: SI 2009/693 Sch.1 para.4
Sch.4 para.4, amended: SI 2009/693 Sch.1 para.4
Sch.4 para.7A, added: SI 2009/693 Sch.1 para.4

1085. Planning (Listed Buildings and Conservation Areas) (Amendment) (England) Regulations 2005
revoked: SI 2009/2711 Reg.3

1087. Common Agricultural Policy Single Payment and Support Schemes (Amendment) Regulations 2005
revoked: SI 2009/3102 Reg.9

1099. Miscellaneous Food Additives (Amendment) (England) Regulations 2005
Reg.3, applied: SI 2009/3238 Reg.10
Reg.4, applied: SI 2009/3238 Reg.10
Reg.5, applied: SI 2009/3238 Reg.10
Reg.6, applied: SI 2009/3238 Reg.10
Reg.7, applied: SI 2009/3238 Reg.10
Reg.8, applied: SI 2009/3238 Reg.10
Reg.9, applied: SI 2009/3238 Reg.10
Reg.10, applied: SI 2009/3238 Reg.10
Reg.11, applied: SI 2009/3238 Reg.10

1138. Judicial Committee (Devolution Issues) Rules (Amendment) Order 2005
revoked: SI 2009/224 Art.4

1139. Judicial Committee (General Appellate Jurisdiction) Rules (Amendment) Order 2005
revoked: SI 2009/224 Art.4

1156. Sweeteners in Food (Amendment) (Wales) Regulations 2005
Reg.3, referred to: SI 2009/3378 Reg.13
Reg.4, referred to: SI 2009/3378 Reg.13
Reg.5, referred to: SI 2009/3378 Reg.13
Reg.6, referred to: SI 2009/3378 Reg.13
Reg.7, referred to: SI 2009/3378 Reg.13

1207. Fodder Plant Seed (Wales) Regulations 2005
referred to: SI 2009/1356 Reg.2
Reg.2, amended: SI 2009/1356 Reg.11
Reg.20A, added: SI 2009/1356 Reg.12
Reg.23, amended: SI 2009/1356 Reg.13
Reg.24, amended: SI 2009/1356 Reg.14
Reg.26, amended: SI 2009/1356 Reg.15

2005–cont.

1207. Fodder Plant Seed (Wales) Regulations 2005–*cont.*
Sch.8 Part VIII para.42, amended: SI 2009/1356 Reg.16
Sch.8 Part VIII para.43, amended: SI 2009/1356 Reg.16
Sch.8 Part VIII para.44, amended: SI 2009/1356 Reg.16
Sch.8 Part IX para.45, added: SI 2009/1356 Reg.16

1258. Sudan (United Nations Measures) (Overseas Territories) Order 2005
Art.9, varied: SI 2009/888 Art.2
Sch.2 para.1, varied: SI 2009/888 Art.2
Sch.2 para.2, varied: SI 2009/888 Art.2
Sch.2 para.3, varied: SI 2009/888 Art.2
Sch.2 para.4, varied: SI 2009/888 Art.2
Sch.2 para.5, varied: SI 2009/888 Art.2
Sch.2 para.6, varied: SI 2009/888 Art.2
Sch.2 para.7, varied: SI 2009/888 Art.2
Sch.2 para.8, varied: SI 2009/888 Art.2

1260. Child Abduction and Custody (Parties to Conventions) (Amendment) Order 2005
revoked: SI 2009/702 Art.2

1311. Miscellaneous Food Additives (Amendment) (No.2) (Wales) Regulations 2005
Reg.3, referred to: SI 2009/3378 Reg.10
Reg.4, referred to: SI 2009/3378 Reg.10
Reg.5, referred to: SI 2009/3378 Reg.10
Reg.6, referred to: SI 2009/3378 Reg.10
Reg.7, referred to: SI 2009/3378 Reg.10
Reg.8, referred to: SI 2009/3378 Reg.10
Reg.9, referred to: SI 2009/3378 Reg.10
Reg.10, referred to: SI 2009/3378 Reg.10
Reg.11, referred to: SI 2009/3378 Reg.10

1313. Adoption Agencies (Wales) Regulations 2005
Reg.2, amended: SI 2009/1892 Sch.1 para.16
Reg.3, amended: SI 2009/1892 Sch.1 para.16
Reg.14, amended: SI 2009/1892 Sch.1 para.16
Reg.17, amended: SI 2009/1892 Sch.1 para.16
Reg.19, amended: SI 2009/1892 Sch.1 para.16
Reg.23, amended: SI 2009/2541 Reg.4
Reg.34, amended: SI 2009/1892 Sch.1 para.16
Reg.39, amended: SI 2009/1892 Sch.1 para.16
Sch.1 Part 1 para.13, amended: SI 2009/1892 Sch.1 para.16
Sch.1 Part 1 para.14, amended: SI 2009/1892 Sch.1 para.16
Sch.1 Part 3, amended: SI 2009/1892 Sch.1 para.16
Sch.1 Part 3 para.16, substituted: SI 2009/1892 Sch.1 para.16
Sch.1 Part 3 para.17, substituted: SI 2009/1892 Sch.1 para.16
Sch.1 Part 3 para.27, amended: SI 2009/1892 Sch.1 para.16

1378. Wireless Telegraphy (Licence Charges) Regulations 2005
Reg.3, amended: SI 2009/66 Reg.3
Sch.2, amended: SI 2009/66 Reg.4
Sch.8 Part 2, amended: SI 2009/66 Reg.5

1398. Education (Admission Appeals Arrangements) (Wales) Regulations 2005
Reg.6, amended: SI 2009/823 Reg.2
Sch.2 para.1, amended: SI 2009/1500 Reg.2
Sch.2 para.1, substituted: SI 2009/823 Reg.2
Sch.2 para.2, amended: SI 2009/1500 Reg.2
Sch.2 para.2, substituted: SI 2009/823 Reg.2

1435. Plant Protection Products Regulations 2005
applied: SI 2009/153 Sch.3 para.1, SI 2009/995 Sch.3 para.1

2005 – cont.

1442. Food (Chilli, Chilli Products, Curcuma and Palm Oil) (Emergency Control) (England) Regulations 2005
revoked: SI 2009/3255 Reg.52

1452. Law Reform (Miscellaneous Provisions) (Northern Ireland) Order 2005
Art.4, revoked (in part): SI 2009/1941 Sch.2

1455. Insolvency (Northern Ireland) Order 2005
Art.10, amended: SI 2009/1941 Sch.1 para.253
Sch.2 para.12, revoked: SI 2009/1941 Sch.2
Sch.2 para.13, revoked: SI 2009/1941 Sch.2
Sch.2 para.14, revoked: SI 2009/1941 Sch.2
Sch.2 para.15, revoked: SI 2009/1941 Sch.2
Sch.2 para.16, revoked: SI 2009/1941 Sch.2
Sch.2 para.17, revoked: SI 2009/1941 Sch.2

1461. Democratic Republic of the Congo (United Nations Sanctions) (Overseas Territories) Order 2005
Art.9, varied: SI 2009/888 Art.2
Sch.2 para.1, varied: SI 2009/888 Art.2
Sch.2 para.2, varied: SI 2009/888 Art.2
Sch.2 para.3, varied: SI 2009/888 Art.2
Sch.2 para.4, varied: SI 2009/888 Art.2
Sch.2 para.5, varied: SI 2009/888 Art.2
Sch.2 para.6, varied: SI 2009/888 Art.2
Sch.2 para.7, varied: SI 2009/888 Art.2
Sch.2 para.8, varied: SI 2009/888 Art.2

1474. General Optical Council (Committee Constitution Rules) Order of Council 2005
Sch.1, amended: 2009 c.26 s.81

1475. General Optical Council (Fitness to Practise Rules) Order of Council 2005
Sch.1, added: SI 2009/1182 Sch.4 para.24
Sch.1, amended: SI 2009/1182 Sch.4 para.24

1514. Adoption Support Agencies (Wales) Regulations 2005
Sch.2 para.2, substituted: SI 2009/2541 Reg.5

1526. Burma (Financial Sanctions) Regulations 2005
revoked: SI 2009/1495 Reg.24

1529. Financial Services and Markets Act 2000 (Financial Promotion) Order 2005
Art.28B, amended: SI 2009/1342 Art.30
Art.73, amended: SI 2009/1342 Art.30
Sch.1 Part I para.10I, added: SI 2009/1342 Art.30
Sch.1 Part I para.10J, added: SI 2009/1342 Art.30
Sch.1 Part I para.10K, added: SI 2009/1342 Art.30
Sch.1 Part II para.26C, added: SI 2009/1342 Art.30
Sch.1 Part II para.27, amended: SI 2009/1342 Art.30
Sch.1 Part II para.28, amended: SI 2009/1342 Art.30

1530. Home Energy Efficiency Scheme (England) Regulations 2005
Reg.4, amended: SI 2009/1816 Reg.3
Reg.6, amended: SI 2009/1816 Reg.3

1531. Energy Information (Household Air Conditioners) Regulations 2005
applied: SI 2009/515 Reg.9

1536. Summary Appeal Courts (Amendment) Rules 2005
revoked: SI 2009/1211 r.97

1540. Food (Chilli, Chilli Products, Curcuma and Palm Oil) (Emergency Control) (Wales) Regulations 2005
revoked: SI 2009/3376 Reg.52

1541. Regulatory Reform (Fire Safety) Order 2005
applied: SI 2009/665 Art.2
Art.24, enabled: SI 2009/782

2005 – cont.

1605. Registration of Fish Buyers and Sellers and Designation of Fish Auction Sites Regulations 2005
Reg.1, amended: SI 2009/1309 Reg.2
Reg.13, amended: SI 2009/1309 Reg.2
Reg.15, substituted: SI 2009/1309 Reg.2

1625. Health Professions Council (Practice Committees and Registration) (Amendment) Rules Order of Council 2005
Sch.1, revoked: SI 2009/1182 Sch.4 para.36

1628. Colours in Food (Amendment) (Wales) Regulations 2005
applied: SI 2009/3378 Reg.7

1643. Control of Noise at Work Regulations 2005
referred to: SI 2009/693 Reg.2
Reg.7, amended: SI 2009/693 Sch.1 para.5
Reg.14, applied: SI 2009/693 Reg.2

1671. M42 (Junctions 3A to 7) (Actively Managed Hard Shoulder and Variable Speed Limits) Regulations 2005
Sch.1 para.1, amended: SI 2009/1568 Reg.3

1717. Scallop Fishing (Wales) Order 2005
revoked: SI 2009/2721 Art.5

1720. Pensions Act 2004 (Commencement No.6, Transitional Provisions and Savings) Order 2005
Art.4, revoked (in part): SI 2009/1583 Art.2

1721. Street Works (Sharing of Costs of Works) (Wales) Regulations 2005
applied: SI 2009/721 Sch.2 para.8
Reg.6, applied: SI 2009/1267 Reg.33

1726. Energy Information (Household Air Conditioners) (No.2) Regulations 2005
referred to: SI 2009/669 Sch.1 Part 4
Reg.2, amended: SI 2009/2559 Reg.9
Reg.2A, added: SI 2009/2559 Reg.9
Sch.4 Part I para.2A, added: SI 2009/2559 Reg.9

1788. Community Interest Company Regulations 2005
Reg.2, amended: SI 2009/1942 Reg.3
Reg.5, substituted: SI 2009/1942 Reg.4
Reg.6A, added: SI 2009/1942 Reg.5
Reg.7, amended: SI 2009/1942 Reg.6
Reg.7, substituted: SI 2009/1942 Reg.7
Reg.8, amended: SI 2009/1942 Reg.6
Reg.8, substituted: SI 2009/1942 Reg.8
Reg.9, amended: SI 2009/1942 Reg.6
Reg.10, amended: SI 2009/1942 Reg.6
Reg.11, referred to: SI 2009/1803 Reg.6
Reg.12, amended: SI 2009/1942 Reg.9
Reg.12, referred to: SI 2009/1803 Reg.6
Reg.13, amended: SI 2009/1942 Reg.10
Reg.14, amended: SI 2009/1942 Reg.11
Reg.15, amended: SI 2009/1942 Reg.12
Reg.16, amended: SI 2009/1942 Reg.13
Reg.17, amended: SI 2009/1942 Reg.14
Reg.23, amended: SI 2009/1942 Reg.15
Reg.26, amended: SI 2009/1942 Reg.16
Reg.34, amended: SI 2009/1942 Reg.17
Reg.34, revoked (in part): SI 2009/1942 Reg.17
Sch.1 para.1, amended: SI 2009/1942 Reg.18, Reg.19, Reg.20
Sch.1 para.2, amended: SI 2009/1942 Reg.18
Sch.1 para.3, amended: SI 2009/1942 Reg.18
Sch.1 para.3, revoked (in part): SI 2009/1942 Reg.21
Sch.1 para.4, amended: SI 2009/1942 Reg.18, Reg.22

2005– cont.

1788. Community Interest Company Regulations 2005–*cont.*
Sch.1 para.4, revoked (in part): SI 2009/1942 Reg.22
Sch.2 para.1, amended: SI 2009/1942 Reg.18, Reg.19, Reg.20
Sch.2 para.2, amended: SI 2009/1942 Reg.18
Sch.2 para.3, amended: SI 2009/1942 Reg.18
Sch.2 para.3, revoked (in part): SI 2009/1942 Reg.21
Sch.2 para.4, amended: SI 2009/1942 Reg.18, Reg.22
Sch.2 para.4, revoked (in part): SI 2009/1942 Reg.22
Sch.3 para.1, amended: SI 2009/1942 Reg.18, Reg.19, Reg.20
Sch.3 para.2, amended: SI 2009/1942 Reg.18
Sch.3 para.3, amended: SI 2009/1942 Reg.18
Sch.3 para.3, revoked (in part): SI 2009/1942 Reg.21
Sch.3 para.4, amended: SI 2009/1942 Reg.18, Reg.22
Sch.3 para.4, revoked (in part): SI 2009/1942 Reg.22
Sch.5, substituted: SI 2009/1942 Reg.23
1803. General Product Safety Regulations 2005
referred to: SI 2009/669 Sch.1 Part 4, Sch.2 Part 2
Reg.11, applied: SI 2009/665 Art.2
Reg.12, applied: SI 2009/665 Art.2
Reg.13, applied: SI 2009/665 Art.2
Reg.14, applied: SI 2009/665 Art.2
Reg.15, applied: SI 2009/665 Art.2
1806. Hazardous Waste (Wales) Regulations 2005
applied: SI 2009/716 Reg.3
Reg.5, amended: SI 2009/2861 Reg.3
Reg.12, amended: SI 2009/2861 Reg.4
Reg.13, substituted: SI 2009/2861 Reg.5
Reg.14, substituted: SI 2009/2861 Reg.6
Reg.14A, added: SI 2009/2861 Reg.7
Reg.21, amended: SI 2009/2861 Reg.8
Reg.23, substituted: SI 2009/2861 Reg.9
Reg.26, amended: SI 2009/2861 Reg.10
Reg.30, substituted: SI 2009/2861 Reg.11
Reg.32, amended: SI 2009/2861 Reg.12
Reg.42, amended: SI 2009/2861 Reg.13
Reg.48, amended: SI 2009/2861 Reg.14
Reg.49, amended: SI 2009/2861 Reg.15
1902. Motor Cars (Driving Instruction) Regulations 2005
Reg.17, amended: SI 2009/844 Reg.2
1910. Education (Review of Staffing Structure) (Wales) Regulations 2005
Reg.5, revoked: SI 2009/2708 Reg.2
1963. Colleges of Education (Northern Ireland) Order 2005
Art.7, amended: SI 2009/1941 Sch.1 para.254
1964. Traffic Management (Northern Ireland) Order 2005
Art.29, amended: 2009 c.3 Sch.4 para.42
Art.29, revoked (in part): 2009 c.3 Sch.4 para.42
1970. Air Navigation Order 2005
revoked: SI 2009/3015 Sch.1
Part 10, applied: SI 2009/1742 Art.1
Art.70, enabled: SI 2009/1492
Art.73, applied: SI 2009/1094 Art.3
Art.74, applied: SI 2009/1094 Art.3
Art.75, applied: SI 2009/1094 Art.3
Art.77, applied: SI 2009/1094 Art.3

2005– cont.

1970. Air Navigation Order 2005–*cont.*
Art.78, applied: SI 2009/1094 Art.3
Art.95, enabled: SI 2009/2169
Art.96, enabled: SI 2009/2020
Art.107, substituted: SI 2009/1742 Art.3
Art.107A, substituted: SI 2009/1742 Art.3
Art.107B, substituted: SI 2009/1742 Art.3
Art.107C, substituted: SI 2009/1742 Art.3
Art.108, substituted: SI 2009/1742 Art.3
Art.108A, substituted: SI 2009/1742 Art.3
Art.108B, substituted: SI 2009/1742 Art.3
Art.108C, substituted: SI 2009/1742 Art.3
Art.108D, substituted: SI 2009/1742 Art.3
Art.109, substituted: SI 2009/1742 Art.3
Art.109A, substituted: SI 2009/1742 Art.3
Art.110, substituted: SI 2009/1742 Art.3
Art.111, substituted: SI 2009/1742 Art.3
Art.112, substituted: SI 2009/1742 Art.3
Art.113, substituted: SI 2009/1742 Art.3
Art.114, substituted: SI 2009/1742 Art.3
Art.115, substituted: SI 2009/1742 Art.3
Art.116, substituted: SI 2009/1742 Art.3
Art.117, substituted: SI 2009/1742 Art.3
Art.117A, substituted: SI 2009/1742 Art.3
Art.117B, substituted: SI 2009/1742 Art.3
Art.118, substituted: SI 2009/1742 Art.3
Art.119, substituted: SI 2009/1742 Art.3
Art.119A, substituted: SI 2009/1742 Art.3
Art.119B, substituted: SI 2009/1742 Art.3
Art.119C, substituted: SI 2009/1742 Art.3
Art.120, substituted: SI 2009/1742 Art.3
Art.120A, substituted: SI 2009/1742 Art.3
Art.136, enabled: SI 2009/1605
Art.138, amended: SI 2009/41 Reg.37
Art.145, amended: SI 2009/1742 Art.5
Art.148, amended: SI 2009/1742 Art.6
Art.155, amended: SI 2009/1742 Art.7
Art.167, amended: SI 2009/1742 Art.8
Sch.11 Part A para.1, substituted: SI 2009/1742 Art.4
Sch.11 Part A para.2, substituted: SI 2009/1742 Art.4
Sch.11 Part B para.1, substituted: SI 2009/1742 Art.4
Sch.11 Part B para.2, substituted: SI 2009/1742 Art.4
Sch.11 Part B para.3, substituted: SI 2009/1742 Art.4
Sch.11 Part B para.4, substituted: SI 2009/1742 Art.4
Sch.14 Part A, amended: SI 2009/1742 Art.9
Sch.14 Part B, amended: SI 2009/1742 Art.9
1973. Children Act 2004 (Joint Area Reviews) Regulations 2005
Sch.1 para.1, amended: SI 2009/462 Sch.5 para.15
Sch.1 para.7, substituted: SI 2009/462 Sch.5 para.15
1986. Financial Assistance Scheme Regulations 2005
applied: SI 2009/1851 Reg.36, Reg.37
varied: SI 2009/317 Sch.1, SI 2009/1851 Reg.38
Reg.2, amended: SI 2009/1851 Reg.4, Reg.7
Reg.4, amended: SI 2009/1851 Reg.5, Reg.7
Reg.5, amended: SI 2009/1851 Reg.6
Reg.5A, revoked: SI 2009/1851 Reg.6
Reg.6, substituted: SI 2009/1851 Reg.8
Reg.7, revoked: SI 2009/1851 Reg.6
Reg.8, revoked: SI 2009/1851 Reg.6
Reg.12A, amended: SI 2009/1851 Reg.7
Reg.12B, amended: SI 2009/1851 Reg.7
Reg.13, amended: SI 2009/1851 Reg.7
Reg.14, amended: SI 2009/1851 Reg.7, Reg.9
Reg.14A, added: SI 2009/1851 Reg.10
Reg.14B, added: SI 2009/1851 Reg.10
Reg.16A, added: SI 2009/1851 Reg.11
Reg.16B, added: SI 2009/1851 Reg.11

2005–cont.

1986. Financial Assistance Scheme Regulations 2005–*cont.*

Reg.17, amended: SI 2009/792 Reg.4, SI 2009/1851 Reg.7, Reg.12, Reg.17

Reg.17A, amended: SI 2009/792 Reg.5, SI 2009/1851 Reg.13, Reg.17

Reg.17B, amended: SI 2009/792 Reg.6, SI 2009/1851 Reg.7, Reg.14, Reg.17

Reg.17C, added: SI 2009/792 Reg.7

Reg.17C, amended: SI 2009/1851 Reg.15

Reg.18, amended: SI 2009/792 Reg.8, SI 2009/1851 Reg.7, Reg.16, Reg.17

Reg.18, revoked (in part): SI 2009/1851 Reg.16

Reg.19, amended: SI 2009/1851 Reg.17

Reg.20, amended: SI 2009/1851 Reg.7, Reg.17

Sch.1 para.1, amended: SI 2009/1851 Reg.7

Sch.1 para.2, amended: SI 2009/1851 Reg.7

Sch.1 para.3ZA, added: SI 2009/1851 Reg.18

Sch.1 para.3ZB, added: SI 2009/1851 Reg.18

Sch.1 para.3ZC, added: SI 2009/1851 Reg.18

Sch.1 para.3ZD, added: SI 2009/1851 Reg.18

Sch.1 para.3ZE, added: SI 2009/1851 Reg.18

Sch.1 para.5, amended: SI 2009/1851 Reg.18

Sch.1 para.9, amended: SI 2009/1851 Reg.7

Sch.1 para.10, revoked (in part): SI 2009/1851 Reg.18

Sch.1 para.11, amended: SI 2009/1851 Reg.7, Reg.18

Sch.1 para.12, amended: SI 2009/1851 Reg.7

Sch.1 para.14, amended: SI 2009/1851 Reg.7

Sch.1 para.14, revoked (in part): SI 2009/1851 Reg.18

Sch.1 para.17, added: SI 2009/1851 Reg.18

Sch.1 para.18, added: SI 2009/1851 Reg.18

Sch.2 para.1, amended: SI 2009/1851 Reg.19

Sch.2 para.2, amended: SI 2009/1851 Reg.7, Reg.20

Sch.2 para.2, revoked (in part): SI 2009/1851 Reg.20

Sch.2 para.2A, added: SI 2009/1851 Reg.21

Sch.2 para.3, amended: SI 2009/1851 Reg.7, Reg.22

Sch.2 para.4, amended: SI 2009/792 Reg.9, SI 2009/1851 Reg.7, Reg.23

Sch.2 para.4, revoked (in part): SI 2009/1851 Reg.23

Sch.2 para.4A, added: SI 2009/1851 Reg.24

Sch.2 para.4B, added: SI 2009/1851 Reg.24

Sch.2 para.5, amended: SI 2009/792 Reg.9, SI 2009/1851 Reg.7, Reg.25

Sch.2 para.5, revoked (in part): SI 2009/1851 Reg.25

Sch.2 para.5A, added: SI 2009/792 Reg.9

Sch.2 para.5B, added: SI 2009/1851 Reg.26

Sch.2 para.7, amended: SI 2009/1851 Reg.27

Sch.2 para.9, amended: SI 2009/792 Reg.9

Sch.2 para.9, substituted: SI 2009/1851 Reg.28

Sch.2 para.10, amended: SI 2009/792 Reg.9, SI 2009/1851 Reg.7, Reg.29

Sch.2 para.10A, added: SI 2009/1851 Reg.30

Sch.2A para.2, amended: SI 2009/1851 Reg.31

Sch.2A para.2A, added: SI 2009/1851 Reg.31

Sch.2A para.3, added: SI 2009/1851 Reg.31

Sch.2A para.3A, added: SI 2009/1851 Reg.31

Sch.2A para.4, revoked: SI 2009/1851 Reg.31

Sch.2A para.5, amended: SI 2009/1851 Reg.31

Sch.2A para.6, added: SI 2009/1851 Reg.31

Sch.2A para.7, amended: SI 2009/1851 Reg.31

Sch.2A para.9, added: SI 2009/1851 Reg.31

Sch.2A para.10, added: SI 2009/1851 Reg.31

Sch.2A para.11, added: SI 2009/1851 Reg.31

2005–cont.

1994. Financial Assistance Scheme (Internal Review) Regulations 2005

Reg.1, amended: SI 2009/1851 Reg.33

Reg.2, amended: SI 2009/792 Reg.10, SI 2009/1851 Reg.33

Reg.3, amended: SI 2009/792 Reg.10, SI 2009/1851 Reg.33

Reg.4, amended: SI 2009/1851 Reg.33

Reg.5, amended: SI 2009/792 Reg.10, SI 2009/1851 Reg.33

Reg.6, amended: SI 2009/792 Reg.10, SI 2009/1851 Reg.33

Reg.8, amended: SI 2009/1851 Reg.33

Reg.10, amended: SI 2009/1851 Reg.33

Reg.11, amended: SI 2009/792 Reg.10, SI 2009/1851 Reg.33

Reg.16, amended: SI 2009/792 Reg.10, SI 2009/1851 Reg.33

Reg.18, added: SI 2009/1851 Reg.33

2004. Local Government Pension Scheme and Management and Investment of Funds (Amendment) Regulations 2005

revoked: SI 2009/3093 Sch.2

2038. Education (School Inspection) (England) Regulations 2005

Reg.3, substituted: SI 2009/1564 Reg.3

Reg.10, substituted: SI 2009/1564 Reg.4

2045. Income Tax (Construction Industry Scheme) Regulations 2005

referred to: SI 2009/56 Sch.2 para.137

Reg.2, amended: SI 2009/56 Sch.2 para.138

Reg.9, amended: SI 2009/56 Sch.2 para.139

Reg.13, amended: SI 2009/56 Sch.2 para.140

Reg.13, revoked (in part): SI 2009/56 Sch.2 para.140

Reg.25, revoked (in part): SI 2009/56 Sch.2 para.141

Reg.48, amended: SI 2009/2030 Reg.2

Reg.59, amended: SI 2009/56 Sch.2 para.142

Reg.59, revoked (in part): SI 2009/56 Sch.2 para.142

2078. Mental Health (Care and Treatment) (Scotland) Act 2003 (Consequential Provisions) Order 2005

Sch.2 para.25, revoked: SI 2009/1887 Sch.3

2082. Finance Act 2002, Schedule 26, Parts 2 and 9 (Amendment No.2) Order 2005

revoked: 2009 c.4 Sch.3 Part 1

2114. Civil Partnership Act 2004 (Amendments to Subordinate Legislation) Order 2005

Art.2, amended: SI 2009/1887 Sch.3

Sch.4 Part 2 para.5, revoked (in part): SI 2009/1887 Sch.3

2115. Town and Country Planning (Major Infrastructure Project Inquiries Procedure) (England) Rules 2005

r.13, amended: SI 2009/455 r.5

r.21, amended: SI 2009/455 r.5

2122. Criminal Justice Act 2003 (Commencement No.8 and Transitional and Saving Provisions) Order 2005 (Supplementary Provisions) Order 2005

see *R. (on the application of Noone) v Governor of Drake Hall Prison* [2008] EWCA Civ 1097, [2009] 1 W.L.R. 1321 (CA (Civ Div)), Sir Anthony Clarke, M.R.

2184. Occupational Pension Schemes (Fraud Compensation Payments and Miscellaneous Amendments) Regulations 2005

Reg.2, amended: SI 2009/1906 Sch.1 para.6

2005– cont.

2188. Pensions Regulator (Financial Support Directions etc.) Regulations 2005
Reg.5, substituted: SI 2009/617 Reg.2
2189. Financial Assistance Scheme (Provision of Information and Administration of Payments) Regulations 2005
Reg.2, amended: SI 2009/1851 Reg.32
Reg.3, amended: SI 2009/1851 Reg.32
Reg.5, amended: SI 2009/1851 Reg.32
Reg.6, amended: SI 2009/1851 Reg.32
Reg.7, amended: SI 2009/1851 Reg.32
Reg.8, amended: SI 2009/1851 Reg.32
Sch.1 para.1, amended: SI 2009/792 Reg.11, SI 2009/1851 Reg.32
Sch.1 para.1, revoked (in part): SI 2009/1851 Reg.32
Sch.1 para.2, added: SI 2009/1851 Reg.32
Sch.2 para.1, amended: SI 2009/792 Reg.11
Sch.2 para.2, added: SI 2009/1851 Reg.32
2295. Tonnage Tax (Training Requirement) (Amendment) Regulations 2005
revoked: SI 2009/2304 Sch.1
2305. Conditional Fee Agreements (Revocation) Regulations 2005
see *Birmingham City Council v Forde* [2009] EWHC 12 (QB), [2009] 1 W.L.R. 2732 (QBD (Birmingham)), Christopher Clarke, J.
2347. Animal By-Products Regulations 2005
Reg.21, applied: SI 2009/2043 Sch.1
Reg.29, amended: SI 2009/1119 Reg.2
2364. Compromise Agreements (Description of Person) Order 2005
Art.2, amended: SI 2009/3348 Art.22
2365. Specified Body (Consumer Claims) Order 2005
see *Consumers' Association v JJB Sports Plc* [2009] CAT 2, [2009] Comp. A.R. 117 (CAT), Lord Carlile of Berriew Q.C.
2450. Education (Local Education Authority Performance Targets) (England) Regulations 2005
Sch.1 para.3, amended: SI 2009/1596 Reg.3
2454. Motor Vehicles (EC Type Approval) (Amendment) Regulations 2005
revoked: SI 2009/717 Sch.1
2483. Energy Administration Rules 2005
Part 15 r.186, amended: SI 2009/2748 Sch.1 para.32
2517. Plant Health (Forestry) Order 2005
Art.2, amended: SI 2009/594 Art.2, SI 2009/3020 Art.2
Sch.1 para.1a, added: SI 2009/594 Art.2
Sch.1 para.4za, added: SI 2009/594 Art.2
Sch.2 Part A, added: SI 2009/594 Art.2
Sch.2 Part A, amended: SI 2009/594 Art.2
Sch.3, amended: SI 2009/3020 Art.2
Sch.4 Part A, amended: SI 2009/594 Art.2, SI 2009/3020 Art.2
Sch.4 Part B, amended: SI 2009/594 Art.2
Sch.5 Part A para.3, substituted: SI 2009/594 Art.2
Sch.5 Part A para.4, amended: SI 2009/594 Art.2
Sch.6 Part A para.4a, added: SI 2009/594 Art.2
Sch.7 Part A para.4a, added: SI 2009/594 Art.2
2530. Plant Health (England) Order 2005
Art.2, amended: SI 2009/587 Art.2
Sch.1 Part A para.11a, added: SI 2009/587 Art.2
Sch.1 Part A para.15, substituted: SI 2009/587 Art.2
Sch.1 Part A para.26a, added: SI 2009/587 Art.2
Sch.1 Part B para.1a, added: SI 2009/587 Art.2
Sch.2 Part A, added: SI 2009/587 Art.2
Sch.2 Part A, amended: SI 2009/587 Art.2

2005– cont.

2530. Plant Health (England) Order 2005– *cont.*
Sch.2 Part B, amended: SI 2009/587 Art.2
Sch.4 Part A, amended: SI 2009/587 Art.2
Sch.4 Part B, amended: SI 2009/587 Art.2
Sch.6 Part A para.7, amended: SI 2009/587 Art.2
2571. Chemicals (Hazard Information and Packaging for Supply) (Amendment) Regulations 2005
revoked: SI 2009/716 Sch.7
2628. Railways (Provision etc of Railway Facilities) (Exemptions) Order 2005
applied: SI 2009/2726 Art.16
Sch.2 para.1, amended: SI 2009/3336 Art.3
Sch.2 para.3A, added: SI 2009/3336 Art.3
Sch.2 para.3B, added: SI 2009/3336 Art.3
2630. Tryptophan in Food (England) Regulations 2005
Reg.2, amended: SI 2009/3051 Reg.5
Reg.5, amended: SI 2009/3051 Reg.5
2689. Access to Information (Post-Commencement Adoptions) (Wales) Regulations 2005
Reg.2, amended: SI 2009/1892 Sch.1 para.17
2690. Education (Student Loans) (Repayment) (Amendment) Regulations 2005
revoked: SI 2009/470 Sch.1
2720. Adoption Support Agencies (England) and Adoption Agencies (Miscellaneous Amendments) Regulations 2005
Sch.2 para.2, substituted: SI 2009/1895 Reg.3
2722. Planning and Compulsory Purchase Act 2004 (Commencement No.4 and Consequential, Transitional and Savings Provisions) (Wales) Order 2005
Sch.1, amended: SI 2009/2645 Art.2
2750. Medicines (Traditional Herbal Medicinal Products for Human Use) Regulations 2005
referred to: SI 2009/669 Sch.1 Part 4, Sch.2 Part 2
Reg.5, applied: SI 2009/389 Reg.42
Reg.6, applied: SI 2009/389 Reg.18
Reg.8, applied: SI 2009/389 Sch.5 para.3
Sch.2 Part 2 para.12, referred to: SI 2009/389 Reg.37
Sch.2 Part 3 para.17, referred to: SI 2009/389 Reg.37
Sch.2 Part 4 para.20, referred to: SI 2009/389 Reg.37
2761. Civil Partnership (Registration Abroad and Certificates) Order 2005
applied: SI 2009/700 Sch.1 Part VI
2773. Volatile Organic Compounds in Paints, Varnishes and Vehicle Refinishing Products Regulations 2005
Reg.7, amended: SI 2009/3145 Reg.2
2789. Medicines for Human Use (Manufacturing, Wholesale Dealing and Miscellaneous Amendments) Regulations 2005
Reg.8, amended: SI 2009/1164 Reg.4
2795. Family Procedure (Adoption) Rules 2005
Part 2 r.6, amended: SI 2009/3348 Art.17
Part 8 r.78, amended: SI 2009/3348 Art.17
Part 9 r.95, amended: SI 2009/638 r.2
2892. Terrorism Act 2000 (Proscribed Organisations) (Amendment) Order 2005
see *AV v Secretary of State for the Home Department* [2008] EWHC 1895 (Admin), [2009] 1 W.L.R. 2318 (QBD (Admin)), Mitting, J.
2914. Government of Maintained Schools (Wales) Regulations 2005
Sch.5 para.9, amended: SI 2009/2544 Reg.6

2005–cont.

2914. Government of Maintained Schools (Wales) Regulations 2005–*cont.*
Sch.5 para.12, amended: SI 2009/2544 Reg.6

2925. Health and Social Care (Community Health and Standards) Act 2003 Commencement (No.8) Order 2005
Art.3, revoked: SI 2009/462 Sch.6

2966. Disability Discrimination (Public Authorities) (Statutory Duties) Regulations 2005
Sch.1 Part I, amended: SI 2009/462 Sch.5 para.16
Sch.2, amended: SI 2009/229 Sch.2 para.17, SI 2009/2748 Sch.1 para.33

2992. Common Agricultural Policy (Wine) (England and Northern Ireland) (Amendment) Regulations 2005
revoked (in part): SI 2009/386 Reg.17

3036. Cereal Seed (Wales) Regulations 2005
referred to: SI 2009/1356 Reg.2
Reg.2, amended: SI 2009/1356 Reg.18
Reg.20A, added: SI 2009/1356 Reg.19
Reg.23, amended: SI 2009/1356 Reg.20
Reg.24, amended: SI 2009/1356 Reg.21
Reg.26, amended: SI 2009/1356 Reg.22
Sch.8 Part VIII para.35, added: SI 2009/1356 Reg.23

3037. Beet Seed (Wales) Regulations 2005
referred to: SI 2009/1356 Reg.2
Reg.2, amended: SI 2009/1356 Reg.4
Reg.18A, added: SI 2009/1356 Reg.5
Reg.20, amended: SI 2009/1356 Reg.6
Reg.21, amended: SI 2009/1356 Reg.7
Reg.23, amended: SI 2009/1356 Reg.8
Sch.8 Part VI para.19, added: SI 2009/1356 Reg.9

3049. Railways Infrastructure (Access and Management) Regulations 2005
Reg.3, amended: SI 2009/1122 Reg.2
Reg.3, revoked (in part): SI 2009/1122 Reg.2
Reg.5, substituted: SI 2009/1122 Reg.2
Reg.6, amended: SI 2009/1122 Reg.2
Reg.13, amended: SI 2009/1122 Reg.2
Reg.16, amended: SI 2009/1122 Reg.2
Reg.18, amended: SI 2009/1122 Reg.2
Reg.28, amended: SI 2009/1122 Reg.2
Reg.28, revoked (in part): SI 2009/1122 Reg.2
Reg.29A, added: SI 2009/1122 Reg.2
Reg.31, amended: SI 2009/1122 Reg.2
Reg.33, amended: SI 2009/1122 Reg.2
Reg.34, amended: SI 2009/1122 Reg.2
Reg.35, revoked: SI 2009/1122 Reg.2
Reg.36, amended: SI 2009/1122 Reg.2
Sch.3 para.3, amended: SI 2009/1122 Reg.2
Sch.3 para.6, amended: SI 2009/1122 Reg.2

3050. Railway (Licensing of Railway Undertakings) Regulations 2005
Sch.2 para.4, amended: SI 2009/2054 Sch.1 para.27
Sch.2 para.4, applied: SI 2009/2054 Sch.2 para.18

3100. Sheep and Goats (Records, Identification and Movement) (England) Order 2005
Art.14, applied: SI 2009/138 Sch.5 para.4
Art.17, applied: SI 2009/138 Sch.5 para.4
Art.20, applied: SI 2009/138 Sch.5 para.4

3111. Tryptophan in Food (Wales) Regulations 2005
Reg.2, amended: SI 2009/3254 Reg.5
Reg.5, amended: SI 2009/3254 Reg.5

3117. Offshore Installations (Safety Case) Regulations 2005
applied: SI 2009/515 Reg.14, Sch.11

2005–cont.

3117. Offshore Installations (Safety Case) Regulations 2005–*cont.*
Reg.2, amended: SI 2009/229 Sch.2 para.18
Reg.2, applied: SI 2009/515 Reg.17
Reg.6, amended: SI 2009/229 Sch.2 para.18
Reg.6, applied: SI 2009/515 Sch.11
Reg.9, applied: SI 2009/515 Sch.11
Reg.23, applied: SI 2009/515 Sch.11

3153. Renewable Energy Zone (Designation of Area) (Scottish Ministers) Order 2005
applied: SSI 2009/140 Art.17

3181. Proceeds of Crime Act 2002 (External Requests and Orders) Order 2005
see *King v Serious Fraud Office* [2009] UKHL 17, [2009] 1 W.L.R.718 (HL), Lord Phillips of Worth Matravers
Art.6, see *King v Serious Fraud Office* [2009] UKHL 17, [2009] 1 W.L.R. 718 (HL), Lord Phillips of Worth Matravers
Art.7, see *King v Serious Fraud Office* [2009] UKHL 17, [2009] 1 W.L.R. 718 (HL), Lord Phillips of Worth Matravers
Art.8, see *King v Serious Fraud Office* [2009] UKHL 17, [2009] 1 W.L.R. 718 (HL), Lord Phillips of Worth Matravers
Art.18, see *King v Serious Fraud Office* [2009] UKHL 17, [2009] 1 W.L.R. 718 (HL), Lord Phillips of Worth Matravers
Art.28, see *King v Serious Fraud Office* [2009] UKHL 17, [2009] 1 W.L.R. 718 (HL), Lord Phillips of Worth Matravers
Sch.5, amended: SI 2009/2054 Sch.1 para.28

3188. Civil Partnership (Armed Forces) Order 2005
Art.4, substituted: SI 2009/2054 Sch.1 para.29

3207. Channel Tunnel (International Arrangements) Order 2005
Art.2, amended: SI 2009/2081 Art.2
Art.3, amended: SI 2009/2081 Art.2
Art.5, amended: SI 2009/2081 Art.2
Art.6, added: SI 2009/2081 Art.2
Art.7, added: SI 2009/2081 Art.2
Sch.1, disapplied: SI 2009/2081 Art.3
Sch.1, substituted: SI 2009/2081 Sch.1

3239. Qualifications, Curriculum and Assessment Authority for Wales (Transfer of Functions to the National Assembly for Wales and Abolition) Order 2005
applied: SI 2009/1220
Sch.1 para.7, revoked: 2009 c.22 Sch.16 Part 4
Sch.1 para.22, revoked: 2009 c.22 Sch.16 Part 4
Sch.1 para.23, revoked: 2009 c.22 Sch.16 Part 4
Sch.1 para.24, revoked: 2009 c.22 Sch.16 Part 4

3257. Export Control (Uzbekistan) Order 2005
Art.1, amended: SI 2009/1174 Art.2

3262. Healthy Start Scheme and Welfare Food (Amendment) Regulations 2005
Reg.3, amended: SI 2009/295 Reg.2
Reg.8, amended: SI 2009/295 Reg.3
Sch.2 para.4, amended: SI 2009/295 Reg.4

3273. Financial Assistance Scheme (Appeals) Regulations 2005
Reg.2, amended: SI 2009/792 Reg.12, SI 2009/1851 Reg.34
Reg.6, amended: SI 2009/792 Reg.12, SI 2009/1851 Reg.34
Reg.17, amended: SI 2009/792 Reg.12, SI 2009/1851 Reg.34
Reg.23, amended: SI 2009/1851 Reg.34

2005–cont.

3280. Feed (Hygiene and Enforcement) (England) Regulations 2005
Reg.17, applied: SI 2009/665 Art.2
Reg.22, applied: SI 2009/665 Art.2
Sch.1, substituted: SI 2009/3255 Sch.7

3281. Feeding Stuffs (England) Regulations 2005
Sch.5, amended: SI 2009/28 Reg.3, SI 2009/2825 Sch.1
Sch.7 Ch.A, amended: SI 2009/28 Sch.1

3332. Independent Review of Determinations (Adoption) Regulations 2005
applied: SI 2009/268 Art.4
revoked: SI 2009/395 Reg.22

3338. Lloyd's Underwriters (Tax) Regulations 2005
Reg.5, applied: SI 2009/404 Art.8
Reg.5A, added: SI 2009/2889 Reg.2

3356. Air Navigation (Dangerous Goods) (Amendment) Regulations 2005
revoked: SI 2009/1492 Reg.3

3361. National Health Service (General Dental Services Contracts) Regulations 2005
Sch.3 Part 5A para.46A, added: SI 2009/309 Sch.1 para.5
Sch.3 Part 5 para.44, amended: SI 2009/462 Sch.5 para.17
Sch.3 Part 5 para.46, substituted: SI 2009/462 Sch.5 para.17
Sch.3 Part 6 para.47, amended: SI 2009/309 Sch.1 para.5
Sch.3 Part 6 para.51, amended: SI 2009/309 Sch.1 para.5

3368. Feed (Hygiene and Enforcement) (Wales) Regulations 2005
Reg.17, applied: SI 2009/665 Art.2
Reg.22, applied: SI 2009/665 Art.2
Sch.1, substituted: SI 2009/3376 Sch.7

3373. National Health Service (Personal Dental Services Agreements) Regulations 2005
see *R. (on the application of Crouch) v South Birmingham Primary Care Trust* [2008] EWCA Civ 1365, [2009] I.C.R. 461 (CA (Civ Div)), Sir Anthony Clarke, M.R.
Sch.3, see *R. (on the application of Crouch) v South Birmingham Primary Care Trust* [2008] EWCA Civ 1365, [2009] I.C.R. 461 (CA (Civ Div)), Sir Anthony Clarke, M.R.
Sch.3 Part 5A para.46A, added: SI 2009/309 Sch.1 para.6
Sch.3 Part 5 para.44, amended: SI 2009/462 Sch.5 para.18
Sch.3 Part 5 para.46, substituted: SI 2009/462 Sch.5 para.18
Sch.3 Part 6 para.47, amended: SI 2009/309 Sch.1 para.6
Sch.3 Part 6 para.51, amended: SI 2009/309 Sch.1 para.6
Sch.3 para.67, see *R. (on the application of Crouch) v South Birmingham Primary Care Trust* [2008] EWCA Civ 1365, [2009] I.C.R. 461 (CA (Civ Div)), Sir Anthony Clarke, M.R.
Sch.3 para.68, see *R. (on the application of Crouch) v South Birmingham Primary Care Trust* [2008] EWCA Civ 1365, [2009] I.C.R. 461 (CA (Civ Div)), Sir Anthony Clarke, M.R.
Sch.3 para.72, see *R. (on the application of Crouch) v South Birmingham Primary Care Trust* [2008] EWCA Civ 1365, [2009] I.C.R. 461 (CA (Civ Div)), Sir Anthony Clarke, M.R.

2005–cont.

3376. Research and Development Tax Relief (Definition of "Small or Medium-Sized Enterprise") Order 2005
revoked: 2009 c.4 Sch.3 Part 1

3377. Occupational Pension Schemes (Scheme Funding) Regulations 2005
Reg.17, amended: SI 2009/615 Reg.18, SI 2009/1906 Sch.1 para.7
Sch.2 para.9, amended: SI 2009/615 Reg.18

3378. Occupational Pension Schemes (Investment) Regulations 2005
Reg.12, amended: SI 2009/615 Reg.19
Reg.13, amended: SI 2009/615 Reg.19
Reg.13, revoked (in part): SI 2009/615 Reg.19
Reg.15A, added: SI 2009/615 Reg.19
Reg.16, amended: SI 2009/615 Reg.19
Reg.17, amended: SI 2009/615 Reg.19
Reg.17, revoked (in part): SI 2009/615 Reg.19

3380. Occupational Pension Schemes (Regulatory Own Funds) Regulations 2005
Reg.15, amended: SI 2009/1906 Sch.1 para.8

3381. Occupational Pension Schemes (Cross-border Activities) Regulations 2005
Sch.2 para.5, amended: SI 2009/598 Art.11

3382. Proceeds of Crime Act 2002 (Legal Expenses in Civil Recovery Proceedings) Regulations 2005
Reg.2, amended: SI 2009/3348 Art.18

3440. Finance Act 2002, Schedule 26 (Parts 2 and 9) (Amendment No 3) Order 2005
revoked: 2009 c.4 Sch.3 Part 1

3448. Registered Pension Schemes (Relief at Source) Regulations 2005
referred to: SI 2009/56 Sch.2 para.143
Reg.2, amended: SI 2009/56 Sch.2 para.144
Reg.12, amended: SI 2009/56 Sch.2 para.145
Reg.14, revoked (in part): SI 2009/571 Sch.2 para.41

3457. Taxes Management Act 1970 (Modifications to Schedule 3 for Pension Scheme Appeals) Order 2005
revoked: SI 2009/56 Sch.2 para.187

3459. Common Agricultural Policy Single Payment and Support Schemes (Cross-compliance) (England) Regulations 2005
revoked: SI 2009/3264 Sch.3

3460. Common Agricultural Policy Single Payment Scheme (Set-aside) (England) (Amendment) Regulations 2005
revoked: SI 2009/3102 Reg.9

3472. Hydrocarbon Oil (Registered Remote Markers) Regulations 2005
Reg.13, amended: SI 2009/56 Sch.2 para.146

3477. National Health Service (Dental Charges) Regulations 2005
Reg.4, amended: SI 2009/407 Reg.2

3478. Armed Forces Proceedings (Costs) Regulations 2005
revoked: SI 2009/993 Reg.8

3524. Insolvency Practitioners and Insolvency Services Account (Fees) (Amendment) (No.2) Order 2005
revoked: SI 2009/487 Art.1

3595. Register of Judgments, Orders and Fines Regulations 2005
amended: SI 2009/474 Reg.5
amended: SI 2009/474 Reg.9
amended: SI 2009/474 Reg.14
Reg.3, amended: SI 2009/474 Reg.3
Reg.5, amended: SI 2009/474 Reg.4

2005– cont.

3595. Register of Judgments, Orders and Fines Regulations 2005– *cont.*
Reg.8, amended: SI 2009/474 Reg.6
Reg.9A, added: SI 2009/474 Reg.7
Reg.10, amended: SI 2009/474 Reg.8
Reg.11, amended: SI 2009/474 Reg.10
Reg.14, amended: SI 2009/474 Reg.11
Reg.18, amended: SI 2009/474 Reg.12
Reg.20, amended: SI 2009/474 Reg.13
Reg.21, amended: SI 2009/474 Reg.15
Reg.26, amended: SI 2009/474 Reg.16

2006

5. Public Contracts Regulations 2006
applied: SI 2009/3244 Reg.9
see *Federal Security Services Ltd v Chief Constable of Northern Ireland* [2009] NICh 3, [2009] Eu. L.R. 774 (Ch D (NI)), Deeny, J.; see *Federal Security Services Ltd v Northern Ireland Court Service* [2009] NIQB 15, [2009] Eu. L.R. 739 (QBD (NI)), McCloskey, J.; see *McLaughlin & Harvey Ltd v Department of Finance and Personnel* [2009] B.L.R. 104 (QBD (NI)), Deeny, J.; see *R. (on the application of Chandler) v Secretary of State for Children, Schools and Families* [2009] EWHC 219 (Admin), [2009] Eu. L.R. 615 (QBD (Admin)), Forbes, J.
Reg.2, amended: SI 2009/2992 Reg.4
Reg.4, see *Amaryllis Ltd v HM Treasury* [2009] EWHC 1666 (TCC), [2009] B.L.R. 425 (QBD (TCC)), Coulson, J.
Reg.20, amended: SI 2009/2992 Reg.5
Reg.23, referred to: SI 2009/2999 Reg.31
Reg.24, referred to: SI 2009/2999 Reg.31
Reg.25, referred to: SI 2009/2999 Reg.31
Reg.29A, added: SI 2009/2992 Reg.6
Reg.31, amended: SI 2009/2992 Reg.7
Reg.32, amended: SI 2009/2992 Reg.8
Reg.32, revoked (in part): SI 2009/2992 Reg.8
Reg.32A, added: SI 2009/2992 Reg.9
Reg.47, substituted: SI 2009/2992 Reg.10
Reg.47, see *Federal Security Services Ltd v Chief Constable of Northern Ireland* [2009] NICh 3, [2009] Eu. L.R. 774 (Ch D (NI)), Deeny, J.; see *Henry Bros (Magherafelt) Ltd (t/a Woodvale Construction Co Ltd) v Department of Education for Northern Ireland* [2009] B.L.R. 174 (QBD (NI)), Coghlin, L.J.; see *McLaughlin & Harvey Ltd v Department of Finance and Personnel* [2009] B.L.R. 104 (QBD (NI)), Deeny, J.
Reg.47A, substituted: SI 2009/2992 Reg.10
Reg.47B, substituted: SI 2009/2992 Reg.10
Reg.47C, substituted: SI 2009/2992 Reg.10
Reg.47D, substituted: SI 2009/2992 Reg.10
Reg.47E, substituted: SI 2009/2992 Reg.10
Reg.47F, substituted: SI 2009/2992 Reg.10
Reg.47G, substituted: SI 2009/2992 Reg.10
Reg.47H, substituted: SI 2009/2992 Reg.10
Reg.47I, substituted: SI 2009/2992 Reg.10
Reg.47J, substituted: SI 2009/2992 Reg.10
Reg.47K, substituted: SI 2009/2992 Reg.10
Reg.47L, substituted: SI 2009/2992 Reg.10
Reg.47M, substituted: SI 2009/2992 Reg.10
Reg.47N, substituted: SI 2009/2992 Reg.10
Reg.47O, substituted: SI 2009/2992 Reg.10
Reg.47P, substituted: SI 2009/2992 Reg.10

2006– cont.

5. Public Contracts Regulations 2006– *cont.*
Sch.1, amended: SI 2009/1307 Sch.2 para.107
6. Utilities Contracts Regulations 2006
applied: SI 2009/3244 Reg.9
Reg.2, amended: SI 2009/3100 Reg.4
Reg.16, amended: SI 2009/3100 Reg.5
Reg.16, applied: SI 2009/3100 Reg.13
Reg.19, amended: SI 2009/3100 Reg.6
Reg.29A, added: SI 2009/3100 Reg.7
Reg.32, amended: SI 2009/3100 Reg.8
Reg.33, amended: SI 2009/3100 Reg.9
Reg.33, revoked (in part): SI 2009/3100 Reg.9
Reg.33A, added: SI 2009/3100 Reg.10
Reg.44, revoked: SI 2009/3100 Reg.11
Reg.45, substituted: SI 2009/3100 Reg.12
Reg.45A, substituted: SI 2009/3100 Reg.12
Reg.45B, substituted: SI 2009/3100 Reg.12
Reg.45C, substituted: SI 2009/3100 Reg.12
Reg.45D, substituted: SI 2009/3100 Reg.12
Reg.45E, substituted: SI 2009/3100 Reg.12
Reg.45F, substituted: SI 2009/3100 Reg.12
Reg.45G, substituted: SI 2009/3100 Reg.12
Reg.45H, substituted: SI 2009/3100 Reg.12
Reg.45I, substituted: SI 2009/3100 Reg.12
Reg.45J, substituted: SI 2009/3100 Reg.12
Reg.45K, substituted: SI 2009/3100 Reg.12
Reg.45L, substituted: SI 2009/3100 Reg.12
Reg.45M, substituted: SI 2009/3100 Reg.12
Reg.45N, substituted: SI 2009/3100 Reg.12
Reg.45O, substituted: SI 2009/3100 Reg.12
Reg.45P, substituted: SI 2009/3100 Reg.12
Reg.45Q, substituted: SI 2009/3100 Reg.12
Reg.45R, substituted: SI 2009/3100 Reg.12
Reg.46, substituted: SI 2009/3100 Reg.12
s.Art.9 Reg.45S, substituted: SI 2009/3100 Reg.12
14. Food Hygiene (England) Regulations 2006
applied: SI 2009/3255 Reg.3
Reg.6, applied: SI 2009/665 Art.2
Reg.8, applied: SI 2009/665 Art.2
Reg.9, applied: SI 2009/665 Art.2
Reg.27, applied: SI 2009/665 Art.2
31. Food Hygiene (Wales) Regulations 2006
referred to: SI 2009/3376 Reg.3
Reg.5, applied: SI 2009/3376 Reg.3
Reg.6, applied: SI 2009/665 Art.2
Reg.8, applied: SI 2009/665 Art.2
Reg.9, applied: SI 2009/665 Art.2
Reg.27, applied: SI 2009/665 Art.2
57. Proceeds of Crime Act 2002 (References to Financial Investigators) (Amendment) Order 2006
revoked: SI 2009/975 Sch.2
60. Climate Change Agreements (Eligible Facilities) Regulations 2006
Sch.1 para.13, added: SI 2009/2458 Reg.2
Sch.1 para.14, added: SI 2009/2458 Reg.2
Sch.1 para.15, added: SI 2009/2458 Reg.2
91. Transport for London (Best Value) (Contracting Out of Investment and Highway Functions) Order 2006
Art.3, referred to: SI 2009/721 Art.4
Art.3, revoked: SI 2009/721 Art.4
116. Feeding Stuffs (Wales) Regulations 2006
Sch.5, amended: SI 2009/106 Reg.2, SI 2009/2881 Sch.1
Sch.7, amended: SI 2009/106 Sch.1

2006–cont.

131. Registered Pension Schemes (Enhanced Lifetime Allowance) Regulations 2006
referred to: SI 2009/56 Sch.2 para.147
Reg.2, amended: SI 2009/56 Sch.2 para.148
Reg.12, amended: SI 2009/56 Sch.2 para.149
Reg.12, revoked (in part): SI 2009/56 Sch.2 para.149
Reg.14, amended: SI 2009/56 Sch.2 para.150
Reg.14, revoked (in part): SI 2009/56 Sch.2 para.150
Reg.14A, amended: SI 2009/56 Sch.2 para.151
Reg.14A, revoked (in part): SI 2009/56 Sch.2 para.151
Reg.24, amended: SI 2009/56 Sch.2 para.152
Reg.24, revoked (in part): SI 2009/56 Sch.2 para.152

138. Pension Schemes (Reduction in Pension Rates) Regulations 2006
Reg.3, substituted: SI 2009/1311 Reg.2
Reg.4, substituted: SI 2009/1311 Reg.2
Reg.5, substituted: SI 2009/1311 Reg.2

142. Motor Vehicles (EC Type Approval) (Amendment) Regulations 2006
revoked: SI 2009/717 Sch.1

168. Cattle Compensation (England) Order 2006
see *R. (on the application of Partridge Farms Ltd) v Secretary of State for the Environment, Food and Rural Affairs* [2009] EWCA Civ 284, [2009] Eu. L.R. 816 (CA (Civ Div)), Ward, L.J.
Art.3, see *R. (on the application of Partridge Farms Ltd) v Secretary of State for the Environment, Food and Rural Affairs* [2009] EWCA Civ 284, [2009] Eu. L.R. 816 (CA (Civ Div)), Ward, L.J.

179. Foot-and-Mouth Disease (Wales) Order 2006
applied: SI 2009/1372 Reg.4

182. Foot-and-Mouth Disease (England) Order 2006
applied: SI 2009/1299 Reg.4
Art.2, amended: SI 2009/2713 Art.2
Art.9, amended: SI 2009/2713 Art.2, Art.7
Sch.8 para.1, amended: SI 2009/2713 Art.2

183. Foot-and-Mouth Disease (Control of Vaccination) (England) Regulations 2006
Reg.2, amended: SI 2009/2712 Reg.3
Reg.21, amended: SI 2009/2712 Reg.3
Reg.23, amended: SI 2009/2712 Reg.3

202. Duty Stamps Regulations 2006
Reg.10, amended: SI 2009/571 Sch.2 para.43

207. Pensions Schemes (Application of UK Provisions to Relevant Non-UK Schemes) Regulations 2006
Reg.15, amended: SI 2009/2047 Reg.3, Reg.4, Reg.5, Reg.6, Reg.7, Reg.8, Reg.9, Reg.10

213. Housing Benefit Regulations 2006
applied: SI 2009/1562 Art.2
referred to: SI 2009/497 Art.19
Reg.2, amended: SI 2009/583 Reg.6, SI 2009/2655 Reg.6
Reg.4, amended: SI 2009/471 Reg.9
Reg.7, amended: SI 2009/583 Reg.6
Reg.10, amended: SI 2009/362 Reg.5
Reg.12L, added: SI 2009/614 Reg.2
Reg.13D, amended: SI 2009/614 Reg.2
Reg.13D, revoked (in part): SI 2009/614 Reg.2
Reg.27, referred to: SI 2009/497 Art.19
Reg.28, amended: SI 2009/1848 Reg.2
Reg.35, amended: SI 2009/2655 Reg.6
Reg.36, amended: SI 2009/583 Reg.6
Reg.37, amended: SI 2009/583 Reg.6
Reg.39, amended: SI 2009/583 Reg.6

2006–cont.

213. Housing Benefit Regulations 2006–*cont.*
Reg.42, amended: SI 2009/480 Reg.3, SI 2009/2655 Reg.6
Reg.49, amended: SI 2009/480 Reg.3
Reg.53, amended: SI 2009/583 Reg.6
Reg.56, amended: SI 2009/583 Reg.6
Reg.59, amended: SI 2009/583 Reg.6, SI 2009/1575 Reg.2
Reg.63, revoked (in part): SI 2009/583 Reg.6
Reg.64, amended: SI 2009/1575 Reg.2
Reg.74, amended: SI 2009/497 Art.19
Reg.74, referred to: SI 2009/497 Art.19
Reg.83, amended: SI 2009/1488 Reg.25
Reg.102, amended: SI 2009/2608 Reg.2
Reg.102, revoked (in part): SI 2009/2608 Reg.2
Reg.104A, added: SI 2009/2608 Reg.2
Sch.1 Part 1 para.2, amended: SI 2009/497 Art.19
Sch.1 Part 2 para.6, amended: SI 2009/497 Art.19
Sch.3 Part 1, referred to: SI 2009/497 Art.19
Sch.3 Part 1 para.1, amended: SI 2009/583 Reg.6
Sch.3 Part 1 para.1A, added: SI 2009/497 Sch.5
Sch.3 Part 1 para.1A, amended: SI 2009/497 Sch.5
Sch.3 Part 1 para.2, amended: SI 2009/497 Sch.5
Sch.3 Part 2 para.3, amended: SI 2009/497 Art.19, SI 2009/583 Reg.6
Sch.3 Part 2 para.3, referred to: SI 2009/497 Art.19
Sch.3 Part 3 para.7, amended: SI 2009/583 Reg.6
Sch.3 Part 3 para.12, amended: SI 2009/1488 Reg.26
Sch.3 Part 3 para.14, amended: SI 2009/583 Reg.6
Sch.3 Part 3 para.15, amended: SI 2009/1488 Reg.26
Sch.3 Part 4, amended: SI 2009/497 Sch.6
Sch.3 Part 4, referred to: SI 2009/497 Art.19
Sch.3 Part 6 para.25, amended: SI 2009/497 Art.19
Sch.3 Part 6 para.26, amended: SI 2009/497 Art.19
Sch.4 para.1, amended: SI 2009/2655 Reg.6
Sch.4 para.2, amended: SI 2009/2655 Reg.6
Sch.4 para.2A, added: SI 2009/583 Reg.6
Sch.4 para.3, amended: SI 2009/1488 Reg.27
Sch.4 para.10A, added: SI 2009/2608 Reg.2
Sch.4 para.17, amended: SI 2009/497 Art.19, SI 2009/2608 Reg.2
Sch.5 para.2A, added: SI 2009/2655 Reg.6
Sch.5 para.15, amended: SI 2009/2655 Reg.6
Sch.5 para.25, amended: SI 2009/2655 Reg.6
Sch.5 para.47A, substituted: SI 2009/2655 Reg.6
Sch.5 para.56, amended: SI 2009/497 Art.19
Sch.5 para.57, amended: SI 2009/583 Reg.6
Sch.5 para.65, added: SI 2009/1848 Reg.3
Sch.6 para.4, amended: SI 2009/1488 Reg.28
Sch.6 para.41A, added: SI 2009/583 Reg.6
Sch.6 para.58, amended: SI 2009/583 Reg.6

214. Housing Benefit (Persons who have attained the qualifying age for state pension credit) Regulations 2006
applied: SI 2009/1562 Art.2
referred to: SI 2009/497 Art.20
Reg.2, amended: SI 2009/583 Reg.7, SI 2009/2655 Reg.7
Reg.4, amended: SI 2009/471 Reg.10
Reg.7, amended: SI 2009/583 Reg.7
Reg.10, amended: SI 2009/362 Reg.6
Reg.12L, added: SI 2009/614 Reg.3
Reg.13D, amended: SI 2009/614 Reg.3
Reg.13D, revoked (in part): SI 2009/614 Reg.3
Reg.27, amended: SI 2009/2608 Reg.3

214. Housing Benefit (Persons who have attained the qualifying age for state pension credit) Regulations 2006–*cont.*
Reg.29, amended: SI 2009/583 Reg.7, SI 2009/1676 Reg.5
Reg.29, revoked (in part): SI 2009/1676 Reg.5
Reg.30, referred to: SI 2009/497 Art.20
Reg.31, amended: SI 2009/1848 Reg.2
Reg.33, amended: SI 2009/583 Reg.7
Reg.35, amended: SI 2009/2655 Reg.7
Reg.36, amended: SI 2009/583 Reg.7
Reg.40, amended: SI 2009/583 Reg.7
Reg.41, amended: SI 2009/2655 Reg.7
Reg.55, amended: SI 2009/497 Art.20
Reg.55, referred to: SI 2009/497 Art.20
Reg.64, amended: SI 2009/1488 Reg.30
Reg.83, amended: SI 2009/2608 Reg.3
Reg.83, revoked (in part): SI 2009/2608 Reg.3
Reg.85A, added: SI 2009/2608 Reg.3
Sch.1 Part 1 para.2, amended: SI 2009/497 Art.20
Sch.1 Part 2 para.6, amended: SI 2009/497 Art.20
Sch.3 Part 1, referred to: SI 2009/497 Art.20
Sch.3 Part 1 para.1, substituted: SI 2009/497 Sch.7
Sch.3 Part 1 para.2, substituted: SI 2009/497 Sch.7
Sch.3 Part 2 para.3, amended: SI 2009/497 Art.20
Sch.3 Part 2 para.3, referred to: SI 2009/497 Art.20
Sch.3 Part 3 para.5, amended: SI 2009/583 Reg.7
Sch.3 Part 4, amended: SI 2009/497 Sch.8
Sch.3 Part 4, referred to: SI 2009/497 Art.20
Sch.3 Part 4, substituted: SI 2009/497 Sch.8
Sch.4 para.5, amended: SI 2009/583 Reg.7
Sch.4 para.5A, added: SI 2009/2608 Reg.3
Sch.4 para.8, amended: SI 2009/583 Reg.7
Sch.4 para.9, amended: SI 2009/497 Art.20
Sch.5 para.1, amended: SI 2009/2655 Reg.7
Sch.5 para.21, amended: SI 2009/497 Art.20
Sch.5 para.24, substituted: SI 2009/1676 Reg.6
Sch.6 Part 1 para.4, amended: SI 2009/1488 Reg.31
Sch.6 Part 1 para.26C, added: SI 2009/583 Reg.7

215. Council Tax Benefit Regulations 2006
applied: SI 2009/1562 Art.2
referred to: SI 2009/497 Art.21, SI 2009/3193 Sch.1 para.16
Reg.2, amended: SI 2009/583 Reg.8, SI 2009/2655 Reg.8
Reg.4, substituted: SI 2009/471 Reg.11
Reg.7, amended: SI 2009/362 Reg.7
Reg.8, amended: SI 2009/583 Reg.8
Reg.17, referred to: SI 2009/497 Art.21
Reg.18, amended: SI 2009/1848 Reg.2
Reg.25, amended: SI 2009/2655 Reg.8
Reg.26, amended: SI 2009/583 Reg.8
Reg.27, amended: SI 2009/583 Reg.8
Reg.29, amended: SI 2009/583 Reg.8
Reg.32, amended: SI 2009/480 Reg.3, SI 2009/2655 Reg.8
Reg.39, amended: SI 2009/480 Reg.3
Reg.43, amended: SI 2009/583 Reg.8
Reg.45, amended: SI 2009/583 Reg.8
Reg.46, amended: SI 2009/583 Reg.8, SI 2009/1575 Reg.2
Reg.50, revoked (in part): SI 2009/583 Reg.8
Reg.51, amended: SI 2009/1575 Reg.2
Reg.58, amended: SI 2009/497 Art.21
Reg.58, referred to: SI 2009/497 Art.21
Reg.69, amended: SI 2009/1488 Reg.33
Sch.1 Part 1, referred to: SI 2009/497 Art.21
Sch.1 Part 1 para.1, substituted: SI 2009/497 Sch.9

215. Council Tax Benefit Regulations 2006–*cont.*
Sch.1 Part 1 para.1A, added: SI 2009/583 Reg.8
Sch.1 Part 1 para.1A, substituted: SI 2009/497 Sch.9
Sch.1 Part 1 para.2, substituted: SI 2009/497 Sch.9
Sch.1 Part 2 para.3, amended: SI 2009/497 Art.21, SI 2009/583 Reg.8
Sch.1 Part 2 para.3, referred to: SI 2009/497 Art.21
Sch.1 Part 3 para.7, amended: SI 2009/583 Reg.8
Sch.1 Part 3 para.12, amended: SI 2009/1488 Reg.34
Sch.1 Part 3 para.14, amended: SI 2009/583 Reg.8
Sch.1 Part 3 para.15, amended: SI 2009/1488 Reg.34
Sch.1 Part 4, referred to: SI 2009/497 Art.21
Sch.1 Part 4, substituted: SI 2009/497 Sch.10
Sch.1 Part 6 para.25, amended: SI 2009/497 Art.21
Sch.1 Part 6 para.26, amended: SI 2009/497 Art.21
Sch.2 para.1, amended: SI 2009/497 Art.21
Sch.3 para.1, amended: SI 2009/2655 Reg.8
Sch.3 para.2, amended: SI 2009/2655 Reg.8
Sch.3 para.2A, added: SI 2009/583 Reg.8
Sch.3 para.3, amended: SI 2009/1488 Reg.35
Sch.3 para.10A, added: SI 2009/2608 Reg.4
Sch.3 para.16, amended: SI 2009/497 Art.21, SI 2009/2608 Reg.4
Sch.4 para.2A, added: SI 2009/2655 Reg.8
Sch.4 para.16, amended: SI 2009/2655 Reg.8
Sch.4 para.26, amended: SI 2009/2655 Reg.8
Sch.4 para.43, amended: SI 2009/583 Reg.8
Sch.4 para.48A, substituted: SI 2009/2655 Reg.8
Sch.4 para.56, amended: SI 2009/497 Art.21
Sch.4 para.57, amended: SI 2009/583 Reg.8
Sch.4 para.66, added: SI 2009/1848 Reg.3
Sch.5 para.4, amended: SI 2009/1488 Reg.36
Sch.5 para.41A, added: SI 2009/583 Reg.8
Sch.5 para.60, amended: SI 2009/583 Reg.8

216. Council Tax Benefit (Persons who have attained the qualifying age for state pension credit) Regulations 2006
applied: SI 2009/1562 Art.2
referred to: SI 2009/497 Art.22, SI 2009/3193 Sch.1 para.16
see *Leicester City Council, Re* [2009] UKUT 155 (AAC), [2009] R.V.R. 306 (UT (AAC)), Edward Jacobs
Reg.2, amended: SI 2009/583 Reg.9, SI 2009/2655 Reg.9
Reg.4, substituted: SI 2009/471 Reg.12
Reg.7, amended: SI 2009/362 Reg.8
Reg.8, amended: SI 2009/583 Reg.9
Reg.17, amended: SI 2009/2608 Reg.5
Reg.19, amended: SI 2009/583 Reg.9, SI 2009/1676 Reg.8
Reg.19, revoked (in part): SI 2009/1676 Reg.8
Reg.20, referred to: SI 2009/497 Art.22
Reg.21, amended: SI 2009/1848 Reg.2
Reg.23, amended: SI 2009/583 Reg.9
Reg.25, amended: SI 2009/2655 Reg.9
Reg.26, amended: SI 2009/583 Reg.9
Reg.30, amended: SI 2009/583 Reg.9
Reg.31, amended: SI 2009/2655 Reg.9
Reg.42, amended: SI 2009/497 Art.22
Reg.42, referred to: SI 2009/497 Art.22
Reg.53, amended: SI 2009/1488 Reg.38
Reg.53, see *Leicester City Council, Re* [2009] UKUT 155 (AAC), [2009] R.V.R. 306 (UT (AAC)), Edward Jacobs

2006–cont.

216. Council Tax Benefit (Persons who have attained the qualifying age for state pension credit) Regulations 2006–*cont.*
Sch.1 Part 1, referred to: SI 2009/497 Art.22
Sch.1 Part 1 para.1, substituted: SI 2009/497 Sch.11
Sch.1 Part 1 para.2, substituted: SI 2009/497 Sch.11
Sch.1 Part 2 para.3, amended: SI 2009/497 Art.22
Sch.1 Part 2 para.3, referred to: SI 2009/497 Art.22
Sch.1 Part 3 para.5, amended: SI 2009/583 Reg.9
Sch.1 Part 3 para.6, amended: SI 2009/583 Reg.9
Sch.1 Part 4, amended: SI 2009/497 Sch.12
Sch.1 Part 4, referred to: SI 2009/497 Art.22
Sch.1 Part 4, substituted: SI 2009/497 Sch.12
Sch.2 para.5, amended: SI 2009/583 Reg.9
Sch.2 para.5A, added: SI 2009/2608 Reg.5
Sch.2 para.9, amended: SI 2009/497 Art.22
Sch.3 para.1, amended: SI 2009/2655 Reg.9
Sch.3 para.21, amended: SI 2009/497 Art.22
Sch.3 para.23, substituted: SI 2009/1676 Reg.9
Sch.4 Part 1 para.4, amended: SI 2009/1488 Reg.39
Sch.4 Part 1 para.26B, added: SI 2009/583 Reg.9
Sch.4 Part 1 para.26B, substituted: SI 2009/2608 Reg.5
Sch.6 para.1, amended: SI 2009/497 Art.22

217. Housing Benefit and Council Tax Benefit (Consequential Provisions) Regulations 2006
Sch.3 para.5, amended: SI 2009/1488 Reg.41

223. Child Benefit (General) Regulations 2006
Reg.1, amended: SI 2009/3268 Reg.5
Reg.4, amended: SI 2009/3268 Reg.5
Reg.5, amended: SI 2009/3268 Reg.5

239. Common Agricultural Policy Single Payment and Support Schemes (Amendment) Regulations 2006
revoked: SI 2009/3102 Reg.9

246. Transfer of Undertakings (Protection of Employment) Regulations 2006
applied: 2009 c.20 s.62, s.115, SI 2009/486 Reg.7, SI 2009/814 Art.4
see *Amicus v UCATT* [2009] I.C.R. 852 (EAT (SC)), Lady Smith; see *Marra v Express Gifts Ltd* [2009] B.P.I.R. 508 (ET), Judge Russell; see *Royal Mail Group Ltd v Communication Workers Union* [2009] I.C.R. 357 (EAT), Elias, J.; see *Tapere v South London and Maudsley NHS Trust* [2009] I.C.R. 1563 (EAT), Judge Hand; see *UCATT v Glasgow City Council* [2009] I.R.L.R. 253 (EAT (SC)), Lady Smith
Reg.3, disapplied: SI 2009/486 Reg.7
Reg.3, see *Metropolitan Resources Ltd v Churchill Dulwich Ltd (In Liquidation)* [2009] I.C.R. 1380 (EAT), Judge Burke Q.C.
Reg.4, see *Marra v Express Gifts Ltd* [2009] B.P.I.R. 508 (ET), Judge Russell; see *Oakland v Wellswood (Yorkshire) Ltd* [2009] I.R.L.R. 250 (EAT), Judge Peter Clark; see *Royal Mail Group Ltd v Communication Workers Union* [2009] I.C.R. 357 (EAT), Elias, J.; see *Tapere v South London and Maudsley NHS Trust* [2009] I.C.R. 1563 (EAT), Judge Hand
Reg.7, see *Marra v Express Gifts Ltd* [2009] B.P.I.R. 508 (ET), Judge Russell
Reg.8, see *Marra v Express Gifts Ltd* [2009] B.P.I.R. 508 (ET), Judge Russell; see *Oakland v Wellswood (Yorkshire) Ltd* [2009] I.R.L.R. 250 (EAT), Judge Peter Clark
Reg.11, amended: SI 2009/592 Reg.2
Reg.13, see *Amicus v UCATT* [2009] I.C.R. 852 (EAT (SC)), Lady Smith; see *Royal Mail Group Ltd v Communication Workers Union*

2006–cont.

246. Transfer of Undertakings (Protection of Employment) Regulations 2006–*cont.*
Reg.13–*cont.*
[2009] I.C.R. 357 (EAT), Elias, J.; see *UCATT v Glasgow City Council* [2009] I.R.L.R. 253 (EAT (SC)), Lady Smith
Reg.15, see *UCATT v Glasgow City Council* [2009] I.R.L.R. 253 (EAT (SC)), Lady Smith
Sch.1 para.10, amended: SI 2009/592 Reg.2

301. Common Agricultural Policy Single Payment and Support Schemes (Amendment No 2) Regulations 2006
revoked: SI 2009/3102 Reg.9

310. Uzbekistan (Restrictive Measures) (Overseas Territories) Order 2006
Art.15, varied: SI 2009/888 Art.2
Sch.2 para.1, varied: SI 2009/888 Art.2
Sch.2 para.2, varied: SI 2009/888 Art.2
Sch.2 para.3, varied: SI 2009/888 Art.2
Sch.2 para.4, varied: SI 2009/888 Art.2
Sch.2 para.5, varied: SI 2009/888 Art.2
Sch.2 para.6, varied: SI 2009/888 Art.2
Sch.2 para.7, varied: SI 2009/888 Art.2
Sch.2 para.8, varied: SI 2009/888 Art.2

311. Lebanon and Syria (United Nations Measures) (Overseas Territories) Order 2006
Art.11, varied: SI 2009/888 Art.2
Sch.2 para.1, varied: SI 2009/888 Art.2
Sch.2 para.2, varied: SI 2009/888 Art.2
Sch.2 para.3, varied: SI 2009/888 Art.2
Sch.2 para.4, varied: SI 2009/888 Art.2
Sch.2 para.5, varied: SI 2009/888 Art.2
Sch.2 para.6, varied: SI 2009/888 Art.2, Art.5
Sch.2 para.7, varied: SI 2009/888 Art.2
Sch.2 para.8, varied: SI 2009/888 Art.2
Sch.2 para.9, varied: SI 2009/888 Art.2

343. Pensions Act 2004 (PPF Payments and FAS Payments) (Consequential Provisions) Order 2006
Sch.1 Part 1 para.1, revoked (in part): 2009 c.24 Sch.7 Part 2

346. Artist's Resale Right Regulations 2006
Reg.17, amended: SI 2009/2792 Reg.2

349. Occupational and Personal Pension Schemes (Consultation by Employers and Miscellaneous Amendment) Regulations 2006
Reg.18, amended: SI 2009/615 Reg.20
Reg.18A, added: SI 2009/615 Reg.20
Sch.1 para.13, amended: SI 2009/3348 Art.22, Art.23

372. Management of Houses in Multiple Occupation (England) Regulations 2006
Reg.6, amended: SI 2009/724 Reg.2

373. Licensing and Management of Houses in Multiple Occupation and Other Houses (Miscellaneous Provisions) (England) Regulations 2006
Reg.11, amended: SI 2009/1307 Sch.2 para.109
Reg.12, amended: SI 2009/1307 Sch.2 para.110
Reg.13, amended: SI 2009/1307 Sch.2 para.111

405. Greater Manchester (Light Rapid Transit System) Order 2006
Art.4, amended: SI 2009/1100 Art.7

428. Private Security Industry Act 2001 (Exemption) (Aviation Security) Regulations 2006
amended: SI 2009/2964 Reg.2
Reg.1, revoked (in part): SI 2009/2964 Reg.2

2006–cont.

489. National Health Service (Personal Dental Services Agreements) (Wales) Regulations 2006
Sch.2 Part 1 para.2, amended: SI 2009/456 Reg.5
Sch.3 Part 5 para.44, amended: SI 2009/462 Sch.5 para.19
Sch.3 Part 5 para.46, substituted: SI 2009/462 Sch.5 para.19
Sch.3 Part 6 para.51, revoked (in part): SI 2009/462 Sch.5 para.19

490. National Health Service (General Dental Services Contracts) (Wales) Regulations 2006
Sch.2 Part 1 para.2, amended: SI 2009/456 Reg.4
Sch.3 Part 5 para.44, amended: SI 2009/462 Sch.5 para.20
Sch.3 Part 5 para.46, substituted: SI 2009/462 Sch.5 para.20
Sch.3 Part 6 para.51, revoked (in part): SI 2009/462 Sch.5 para.20

491. National Health Service (Dental Charges) (Wales) Regulations 2006
Sch.3, amended: SI 2009/456 Reg.3

552. National Health Service (Local Pharmaceutical Services etc.) Regulations 2006
Reg.2, amended: SI 2009/599 Reg.3, SI 2009/2205 Reg.30
Reg.4, amended: SI 2009/599 Reg.4
Reg.14A, added: SI 2009/599 Reg.5
Reg.15, amended: SI 2009/599 Reg.6, SI 2009/2205 Reg.31
Reg.16, amended: SI 2009/2205 Reg.32
Reg.16A, added: SI 2009/2205 Reg.33
Sch.2 para.15, amended: SI 2009/2205 Reg.34
Sch.2 para.25, substituted: SI 2009/309 Sch.1 para.2
Sch.2 para.26A, added: SI 2009/2205 Reg.34

557. Health and Safety (Enforcing Authority for Railways and Other Guided Transport Systems) Regulations 2006
Reg.3, amended: SI 2009/1348 Reg.32

558. Occupational Pension Schemes (Fraud Compensation Levy) Regulations 2006
Reg.11, amended: SI 2009/615 Reg.21

562. General Dental Services, Personal Dental Services and Abolition of the Dental Practice Board Transitional and Consequential Provisions Order 2006
Art.5, applied: SI 2009/309 Sch.1 para.8
Art.6, applied: SI 2009/309 Sch.1 para.8
Art.21, applied: SI 2009/309 Sch.1 para.8
Art.22, applied: SI 2009/309 Sch.1 para.8

570. Registered Pension Schemes and Overseas Pension Schemes (Electronic Communication of Returns and Information) Regulations 2006
Reg.2, amended: SI 2009/56 Sch.2 para.153
Sch.2, amended: SI 2009/56 Sch.2 para.153

572. Taxation of Pension Schemes (Transitional Provisions) Order 2006
Art.23A, added: SI 2009/1172 Art.3
Art.23B, added: SI 2009/1172 Art.3
Art.23C, added: SI 2009/1172 Art.3
Art.23D, added: SI 2009/1172 Art.3
Art.34, substituted: SI 2009/1989 Art.2

580. Pension Protection Fund (General and Miscellaneous Amendments) Regulations 2006
Reg.3, substituted: SI 2009/451 Reg.5
Reg.4, amended: SI 2009/451 Reg.5

2006–cont.

580. Pension Protection Fund (General and Miscellaneous Amendments) Regulations 2006–cont.
Reg.4A, added: SI 2009/451 Reg.5

606. Naval, Military and Air Forces Etc (Disablement and Death) Service Pensions Order 2006
applied: SI 2009/212 Reg.2
Part II, applied: SSI 2009/48 Reg.6
Art.7, amended: SI 2009/706 Art.2
Art.7, revoked (in part): SI 2009/706 Art.2
Art.8, amended: SI 2009/706 Art.3
Art.8, referred to: SI 2009/706 Art.18
Art.10, amended: SI 2009/706 Art.4
Art.10, referred to: SI 2009/706 Art.18
Art.14, amended: SI 2009/706 Art.5
Art.14, referred to: SI 2009/706 Art.18
Art.15, amended: SI 2009/706 Art.6
Art.20, applied: SSI 2009/48 Reg.6
Art.22, amended: SI 2009/706 Art.7
Art.23, amended: SI 2009/706 Art.8
Art.32, applied: SI 2009/706 Art.18
Art.32, substituted: SI 2009/706 Art.9
Art.34, amended: SI 2009/706 Art.10
Art.41, see *R. (on the application of Bunce) v Pensions Appeal Tribunal* [2009] EWCA Civ 451, Times, April 15, 2009 (CA (Civ Div)), Laws, L.J.
Art.42, see *R. (on the application of Bunce) v Pensions Appeal Tribunal* [2009] EWCA Civ 451, Times, April 15, 2009 (CA (Civ Div)), Laws, L.J.
Art.50, amended: SI 2009/706 Art.11
Art.50, applied: SI 2009/706 Art.18
Art.55, applied: SI 2009/706 Art.18
Art.55, revoked: SI 2009/706 Art.12
Art.56, amended: SI 2009/706 Art.13
Art.56, applied: SI 2009/706 Art.18
Art.61, amended: SI 2009/706 Art.14
Art.61, applied: SI 2009/706 Art.18
Sch.1 Part II, amended: SI 2009/706 Sch.1
Sch.1 Part III, amended: SI 2009/706 Sch.2
Sch.1 Part IV, amended: SI 2009/706 Sch.3
Sch.1 Part V, amended: SI 2009/706 Art.15
Sch.2 Part II, amended: SI 2009/706 Sch.4
Sch.2 Part III, amended: SI 2009/706 Sch.5
Sch.4 Part II para.8, applied: SSI 2009/48 Reg.6
Sch.6 Part II, amended: SI 2009/706 Art.17

659. Weights and Measures (Packaged Goods) Regulations 2006
referred to: SI 2009/669 Sch.1 Part 4

680. Lord Chancellor (Transfer of Functions and Supplementary Provisions) Order 2006
Sch.1 para.54, revoked: SI 2009/1307 Sch.4

714. Occupational Pension Schemes (Member-nominated Trustees and Directors) Regulations 2006
Reg.2, amended: SI 2009/1906 Sch.1 para.9
Reg.3, amended: SI 2009/615 Reg.22
Reg.5, amended: SI 2009/615 Reg.22

750. Police Act 1997 (Criminal Records) (Registration) Regulations 2006
Reg.3, amended: SI 2009/203 Art.17
Reg.4, amended: SI 2009/203 Art.18
Reg.7, amended: SI 2009/203 Art.19
Reg.10, amended: SI 2009/203 Art.20

758. Gender Recognition (Application Fees) Order 2006
Art.2, amended: SI 2009/489 Art.3

2006–cont.

758. Gender Recognition (Application Fees) Order 2006–*cont.*
Art.3, amended: SI 2009/489 Art.4
Art.5, amended: SI 2009/489 Art.5

759. Occupational Pension Schemes (Modification of Schemes) Regulations 2006
Reg.8, substituted: SI 2009/1906 Sch.1 para.10

779. Controls on Dogs (Non-application to Designated Land) Order 2006
revoked: SI 2009/2829 Art.4

831. Residential Property Tribunal Procedure (England) Regulations 2006
Reg.35, amended: SI 2009/1307 Sch.2 para.112

843. Loan Relationships and Derivative Contracts (Disregard and Bringing into Account of Profits and Losses) Regulations 2006
revoked: 2009 c.10 Sch.21 para.10

873. Staffing of Maintained Schools (Wales) Regulations 2006
Reg.3, amended: SI 2009/2544 Reg.7
Reg.5A, added: SI 2009/2708 Reg.4
Reg.9A, amended: SI 2009/2544 Reg.7
Reg.15A, amended: SI 2009/2544 Reg.7
Reg.18A, amended: SI 2009/2544 Reg.7
Reg.20A, amended: SI 2009/2544 Reg.7
Reg.24A, amended: SI 2009/2544 Reg.7
Reg.26A, amended: SI 2009/2544 Reg.7

932. Police (Injury Benefit) Regulations 2006
see *Merseyside Police Authority v Police Medical Appeal Board* [2009] EWHC 88 (Admin), (2009) 107 B.M.L.R. 22 (QBD (Admin)), Cranston, J.
Reg.3, amended: SI 2009/2060 Sch.1 para.16
Reg.6, amended: SI 2009/2060 Sch.1 para.17
Reg.6, see *Merseyside Police Authority v Police Medical Appeal Board* [2009] EWHC 88 (Admin), (2009) 107 B.M.L.R. 22 (QBD (Admin)), Cranston, J.
Reg.39, amended: SI 2009/2060 Sch.1 para.18
Sch.1, amended: SI 2009/2060 Sch.1 para.19

937. Waste Management (England and Wales) Regulations 2006
Reg.3, revoked: SI 2009/3381 Reg.14

948. Town and Country Planning (Fees for Applications and Deemed Applications) (Amendment) (Wales) Regulations 2006
revoked: SI 2009/851 Reg.3

959. Income Tax (Trading and Other Income) Act 2005 (Consequential Amendments) Order 2006
Art.5, revoked: 2009 c.4 Sch.3 Part 1

964. Authorised Investment Funds (Tax) Regulations 2006
Part 5, amended: SI 2009/2036 Reg.26
Reg.2, amended: SI 2009/2036 Reg.3
Reg.6, amended: SI 2009/2036 Reg.4
Reg.8, amended: SI 2009/56 Sch.2 para.155, SI 2009/2036 Reg.5
Reg.9A, added: SI 2009/2036 Reg.6
Reg.9B, added: SI 2009/2036 Reg.6
Reg.13, amended: SI 2009/2036 Reg.7
Reg.14B, amended: SI 2009/2036 Reg.8
Reg.14B, revoked (in part): SI 2009/2036 Reg.8
Reg.14C, revoked: SI 2009/2036 Reg.9
Reg.14D, revoked: SI 2009/2036 Reg.9
Reg.14E, added: SI 2009/2036 Reg.10
Reg.14F, added: SI 2009/2036 Reg.10
Reg.14G, added: SI 2009/2036 Reg.10
Reg.14H, added: SI 2009/2036 Reg.10

2006–cont.

964. Authorised Investment Funds (Tax) Regulations 2006–*cont.*
Reg.14I, added: SI 2009/2036 Reg.10
Reg.14J, added: SI 2009/2036 Reg.10
Reg.14K, added: SI 2009/2036 Reg.10
Reg.14L, added: SI 2009/2036 Reg.10
Reg.14M, added: SI 2009/2036 Reg.10
Reg.14N, added: SI 2009/2036 Reg.10
Reg.17, amended: SI 2009/2036 Reg.11
Reg.48, amended: SI 2009/2036 Reg.12
Reg.51, amended: SI 2009/2036 Reg.13
Reg.52B, added: SI 2009/2036 Reg.14
Reg.52C, added: SI 2009/2036 Reg.14
Reg.52D, added: SI 2009/2036 Reg.14
Reg.52E, added: SI 2009/2036 Reg.14
Reg.69D, amended: SI 2009/2036 Reg.15
Reg.69DA, revoked: SI 2009/2036 Reg.16
Reg.69J, revoked: SI 2009/2036 Reg.17
Reg.69O, amended: SI 2009/2036 Reg.18
Reg.69P, amended: SI 2009/2036 Reg.19
Reg.69Q, amended: SI 2009/2036 Reg.20
Reg.69T, amended: SI 2009/56 Sch.2 para.156
Reg.69U, revoked: SI 2009/2036 Reg.21
Reg.69Z8, amended: SI 2009/2036 Reg.22
Reg.69Z11, amended: SI 2009/56 Sch.2 para.157
Reg.69Z34, substituted: SI 2009/2036 Reg.23
Reg.69Z38, amended: SI 2009/56 Sch.2 para.158
Reg.69Z42, added: SI 2009/2036 Reg.24
Reg.69Z43, added: SI 2009/2036 Reg.24
Reg.69Z44, added: SI 2009/2036 Reg.24
Reg.69Z45, added: SI 2009/2036 Reg.24
Reg.69Z46, added: SI 2009/2036 Reg.24
Reg.69Z47, added: SI 2009/2036 Reg.24
Reg.69Z48, added: SI 2009/2036 Reg.24
Reg.69Z49, added: SI 2009/2036 Reg.24
Reg.69Z50, added: SI 2009/2036 Reg.24
Reg.69Z51, added: SI 2009/2036 Reg.24
Reg.69Z52, added: SI 2009/2036 Reg.24
Reg.69Z53, added: SI 2009/2036 Reg.24
Reg.69Z54, added: SI 2009/2036 Reg.24
Reg.69Z55, added: SI 2009/2036 Reg.24
Reg.69Z56, added: SI 2009/2036 Reg.24
Reg.69Z57, added: SI 2009/2036 Reg.24
Reg.69Z58, added: SI 2009/2036 Reg.24
Reg.69Z59, added: SI 2009/2036 Reg.24
Reg.69Z60, added: SI 2009/2036 Reg.24
Reg.69Z61, added: SI 2009/2036 Reg.24
Reg.69Z62, added: SI 2009/2036 Reg.24
Reg.69Z63, added: SI 2009/2036 Reg.24
Reg.69Z64, added: SI 2009/2036 Reg.24
Reg.69Z65, added: SI 2009/2036 Reg.24
Reg.69Z66, added: SI 2009/2036 Reg.24
Reg.69Z67, added: SI 2009/2036 Reg.24
Reg.69Z68, added: SI 2009/2036 Reg.24
Reg.69Z69, added: SI 2009/2036 Reg.24
Reg.69Z70, added: SI 2009/2036 Reg.24
Reg.69Z71, added: SI 2009/2036 Reg.24
Reg.69Z72, added: SI 2009/2036 Reg.24
Reg.69Z73, added: SI 2009/2036 Reg.24
Reg.70, amended: SI 2009/2036 Reg.25
Reg.71, amended: SI 2009/2036 Reg.26, Reg.27
Reg.72, amended: SI 2009/2036 Reg.26, Reg.28
Reg.74, amended: SI 2009/2036 Reg.29
Reg.95, amended: SI 2009/2036 Reg.30
Reg.95, revoked: 2009 c.4 Sch.3 Part 1
Reg.96, amended: SI 2009/2036 Reg.31
Sch.1 Part 1, amended: SI 2009/2036 Reg.32
Sch.1 Part 2, amended: SI 2009/2036 Reg.32

2006–cont.

989. Common Agricultural Policy Single Payment and Support Schemes (Amendment) (No.3) Regulations 2006
revoked: SI 2009/3102 Reg.9

1003. Immigration (European Economic Area) Regulations 2006
applied: SI 2009/2794 Reg.3, SI 2009/2795 Sch.1 para.8, Sch.1 para.23, Sch.2 para.4, Sch.2 para.9, Sch.2 para.18, Sch.3 para.24

see *B (Netherlands) v Secretary of State for the Home Department* [2008] EWCA Civ 806, [2009] Q.B. 536 (CA (Civ Div)), Waller, L.J.; see *CS (Brazil) v Secretary of State for the Home Department* [2009] EWCA Civ 480, [2009] 2 F.L.R. 928 (CA (Civ Div)), Laws, L.J.; see *EN (Kenya) v Secretary of State for the Home Department* [2009] Imm. A.R. 1 (AIT), CMG Ockelton (Deputy President); see *KG (Sri Lanka) v Secretary of State for the Home Department* [2008] EWCA Civ 13, [2009] Eu. L.R. 289 (CA (Civ Div)), Buxton, L.J.

Reg.2, amended: SI 2009/1117 Sch.1 para.1
Reg.3, amended: SI 2009/1117 Sch.1 para.2
Reg.4, see *HB (Algeria) v Secretary of State for the Home Department* [2009] Imm. A.R. 38 (AIT), Senior Immigration Judge Storey
Reg.6, see *Barry v Southwark LBC* [2008] EWCA Civ 1440, [2009] 2 C.M.L.R. 11 (CA (Civ Div)), Arden, L.J.
Reg.7, see *CS (Brazil) v Secretary of State for the Home Department* [2009] EWCA Civ 480, [2009] 2 F.L.R. 928 (CA (Civ Div)), Laws, L.J.; see *EN (Kenya) v Secretary of State for the Home Department* [2009] Imm. A.R. 1 (AIT), CMG Ockelton (Deputy President)
Reg.8, see *Bigia v Entry Clearance Officer* [2009] EWCA Civ 79, [2009] 2 C.M.L.R. 42 (CA (Civ Div)), Sir Anthony Clarke, M.R.; see *CS (Brazil) v Secretary of State for the Home Department* [2009] EWCA Civ 480, [2009] 2 F.L.R. 928 (CA (Civ Div)), Laws, L.J.; see *KG (Sri Lanka) v Secretary of State for the Home Department* [2008] EWCA Civ 13, [2009] Eu. L.R. 289 (CA (Civ Div)), Buxton, L.J.; see *YB (Ivory Coast) v Secretary of State for the Home Department* [2009] Imm. A.R. 18 (AIT), Senior Immigration Judge Storey
Reg.9, see *HB (Algeria) v Secretary of State for the Home Department* [2009] Imm. A.R. 38 (AIT), Senior Immigration Judge Storey
Reg.10, see *CS (Brazil) v Secretary of State for the Home Department* [2009] EWCA Civ 480, [2009] 2 F.L.R. 928 (CA (Civ Div)), Laws, L.J.
Reg.12, amended: SI 2009/1117 Sch.1 para.3
Reg.12, see *Bigia v Entry Clearance Officer* [2009] EWCA Civ 79, [2009] 2 C.M.L.R. 42 (CA (Civ Div)), Sir Anthony Clarke, M.R.
Reg.14, see *HB (Algeria) v Secretary of State for the Home Department* [2009] Imm. A.R. 38 (AIT), Senior Immigration Judge Storey
Reg.15, see *OP (Colombia) v Secretary of State for the Home Department* [2009] Imm. A.R. 233 (AIT), CMG Ockelton (Deputy President)
Reg.16, see *CS (Brazil) v Secretary of State for the Home Department* [2009] EWCA Civ 480, [2009] 2 F.L.R. 928 (CA (Civ Div)), Laws, L.J.
Reg.17, amended: SI 2009/1117 Sch.1 para.4
Reg.17, see *CS (Brazil) v Secretary of State for the Home Department* [2009] EWCA Civ 480, [2009] 2 F.L.R. 928 (CA (Civ Div)), Laws, L.J.; see *HB (Algeria) v Secretary of State for the*

2006–cont.

1003. Immigration (European Economic Area) Regulations 2006–*cont.*
Reg.17–*cont.*
Home Department [2009] Imm. A.R. 38 (AIT), Senior Immigration Judge Storey
Reg.18, amended: SI 2009/1117 Sch.1 para.5
Reg.19, amended: SI 2009/1117 Sch.1 para.6
Reg.20, amended: SI 2009/1117 Sch.1 para.7
Reg.21, see *B (Netherlands) v Secretary of State for the Home Department* [2008] EWCA Civ 806, [2009] Q.B. 536 (CA (Civ Div)), Waller, L.J.; see *BF (Portugal) v Secretary of State for the Home Department* [2009] EWCA Civ 923, Times, August 18, 2009 (CA (Civ Div)), Jacob, L.J.; see *LG (Italy) v Secretary of State for the Home Department* [2009] UKAIT 24, [2009] Imm. A.R. 691 (AIT), Carnwath, L.J.
Reg.22, amended: SI 2009/1117 Sch.1 para.8
Reg.23, amended: SI 2009/1117 Sch.1 para.9
Reg.24, amended: SI 2009/1117 Sch.1 para.10
Reg.24A, added: SI 2009/1117 Sch.1 para.11
Reg.27, amended: SI 2009/1117 Sch.1 para.12

1004. Renewables Obligation Order 2006
applied: SI 2009/785 Art.61, SSI 2009/140 Art.61
revoked: SI 2009/785 Art.61
Art.28, applied: SI 2009/785 Art.61
Sch.1, applied: SI 2009/785 Art.61

1009. Social Security (Reduced Rates of Class 1 Contributions, Rebates and Minimum Contributions) Order 2006
Art.4, amended: SI 2009/3094 Art.2
Art.4, revoked (in part): SI 2009/3094 Art.2
Sch.5, amended: SI 2009/3094 Art.3
Sch.5, revoked: SI 2009/3094 Art.3
Sch.6, amended: SI 2009/3094 Art.3
Sch.6, revoked: SI 2009/3094 Art.3

1030. Cross-Border Insolvency Regulations 2006
see *D/S Norden A/S v Samsun Logix Corp* [2009] EWHC 2304 (Ch), [2009] B.P.I.R. 1367 (Ch D (Companies Ct)), Guy Newey Q.C.; see *Samsun Logix Corp v DEF* [2009] EWHC 576 (Ch), [2009] B.P.I.R. 1502 (Ch D), Morgan, J.; see *Stanford International Bank Ltd (In Receivership), Re* [2009] EWHC 1441 (Ch), [2009] B.P.I.R. 1157 (Ch D (Companies Ct)), Lewison, J.; see *SwissAir Schweizerische Luftverkehr-Aktiengesellschaft, Re* [2009] EWHC 2099 (Ch), [2009] B.P.I.R. 1505 (Ch D (Companies Ct)), David Richards, J.
Reg.1, amended: SI 2009/1941 Sch.1 para.264
Reg.2, see *Gerrard, Petitioner* [2009] CSOH 76, 2009 S.C. 593 (OH), Lord Glennie
Reg.3, see *Gerrard, Petitioner* [2009] CSOH 76, 2009 S.C. 593 (OH), Lord Glennie
Reg.5, see *Gerrard, Petitioner* [2009] CSOH 76, 2009 S.C. 593 (OH), Lord Glennie
Reg.6, see *Gerrard, Petitioner* [2009] CSOH 76, 2009 S.C. 593 (OH), Lord Glennie
Sch.1, see *Bernard L Madoff Investment Securities LLC, Re* [2009] EWHC 442 (Ch), [2009] 2 B.C.L.C. 78 (Ch D), Lewison, J.; see *SwissAir Schweizerische Luftverkehr-Aktiengesellschaft, Re* [2009] EWHC 2099 (Ch), [2009] B.P.I.R. 1505 (Ch D (Companies Ct)), David Richards, J.
Sch.2 Part 1 para.1, amended: SI 2009/1941 Sch.1 para.264
Sch.2 Part 2 para.3, amended: SI 2009/1941 Sch.1 para.264
Sch.2 Part 6 para.25, amended: SI 2009/1941 Sch.1 para.264

2006–cont.

1030. Cross-Border Insolvency Regulations 2006–
cont.
Sch.2 Part 9 para.46, amended: SI 2009/1941 Sch.1
para.264
Sch.2 para.17, see *D/S Norden A/S v Samsun Logix
Corp* [2009] EWHC 2304 (Ch), [2009] B.P.I.R.
1367 (Ch D (Companies Ct)), Guy Newey Q.C.
Sch.3 Part 1 para.1, amended: SI 2009/1941 Sch.1
para.264
Sch.3 Part 3 para.6, amended: SI 2009/1941 Sch.1
para.264
Sch.3 Part 3 para.9, amended: SI 2009/1941 Sch.1
para.264
Sch.4 para.1, amended: SI 2009/1941 Sch.1
para.264
Sch.4 para.3, revoked: SI 2009/1941 Sch.1 para.264
Sch.5, amended: SI 2009/1941 Sch.1 para.264

1031. Employment Equality (Age) Regulations 2006
see *R. (on the application of British Medical
Association) v General Medical Council* [2008]
EWHC 2602 (Admin), Times, January 19, 2009
(QBD (Admin)), Burnett, J.; see *R. (on the
application of Incorporated Trustees of the
National Council on Ageing (Age Concern
England)) v Secretary of State for Business,
Enterprise and Regulatory Reform (C-388/07)*
[2009] All E.R. (EC) 619 (ECJ (3rd Chamber)),
Judge Rosas (President); see *Rolls-Royce Plc v
Unite the Union* [2008] EWHC 2420 (QB), [2009]
1 C.M.L.R. 17 (QBD), Sir Thomas Morison
Reg.3, see *Rolls-Royce Plc v Unite the Union* [2008]
EWHC 2420 (QB), [2009] 1 C.M.L.R. 17 (QBD),
Sir Thomas Morison; see *Tower Hamlets LBC v
Wooster* [2009] I.R.L.R. 980 (EAT), Underhill, J.
(President)
Reg.32, see *Rolls-Royce Plc v Unite the Union*
[2008] EWHC 2420 (QB), [2009] 1 C.M.L.R. 17
(QBD), Sir Thomas Morison
Sch.2 Part 1 para.1, amended: SI 2009/598 Art.12
Sch.5 Part 1 para.2, amended: SI 2009/3348
Art.22, Art.23

**1067. School Staffing (England) (Amendment) Regu-
lations 2006**
revoked: SI 2009/2680 Sch.1

**1078. Monkseaton Community High School
(Governing Body Procedures) Order 2006**
applied: SI 2009/558
Art.3, substituted: SI 2009/558 Art.2

**1092. Air Navigation (Dangerous Goods) (Amend-
ment) Regulations 2006**
revoked: SI 2009/1492 Reg.3

1161. Seed Potatoes (England) Regulations 2006
referred to: SI 2009/2342 Reg.2
Reg.2, amended: SI 2009/2342 Reg.3
Reg.4A, added: SI 2009/2342 Reg.4
Sch.2 Part I para.8A, added: SI 2009/2342 Reg.5

**1182. Investment Trusts and Venture Capital Trusts
(Definition of Capital Profits, Gains or
Losses) Order 2006**
revoked: 2009 c.4 Sch.3 Part 1

**1255. Measuring Instruments (Automatic Discontin-
uous Totalisers) Regulations 2006**
referred to: SI 2009/669 Sch.1 Part 4

**1256. Measuring Instruments (Automatic Rail-
weighbridges) Regulations 2006**
referred to: SI 2009/669 Sch.1 Part 4

**1257. Measuring Instruments (Automatic Catch-
weighers) Regulations 2006**
referred to: SI 2009/669 Sch.1 Part 4

2006–cont.

**1258. Measuring Instruments (Automatic Gravi-
metric Filling Instruments) Regulations 2006**
referred to: SI 2009/669 Sch.1 Part 4

**1259. Measuring Instruments (Beltweighers) Regula-
tions 2006**
referred to: SI 2009/669 Sch.1 Part 4

**1264. Measuring Instruments (Capacity Serving
Measures) Regulations 2006**
referred to: SI 2009/669 Sch.1 Part 4

**1266. Measuring Instruments (Liquid Fuel and
Lubricants) Regulations 2006**
referred to: SI 2009/669 Sch.1 Part 4

**1267. Measuring Instruments (Material Measures of
Length) Regulations 2006**
referred to: SI 2009/669 Sch.1 Part 4

**1268. Measuring Instruments (Cold-water Meters)
Regulations 2006**
referred to: SI 2009/669 Sch.1 Part 4

**1269. Measuring Instruments (Liquid Fuel delivered
from Road Tankers) Regulations 2006**
referred to: SI 2009/669 Sch.1 Part 4

**1294. Allocation of Housing and Homelessness
(Eligibility) (England) Regulations 2006**
Reg.4, amended: SI 2009/358 Reg.2
Reg.6, see *Barry v Southwark LBC* [2008] EWCA
Civ 1440, [2009] 2 C.M.L.R. 11 (CA (Civ Div)),
Arden, L.J.
Reg.6, amended: SI 2009/358 Reg.2

1332. Land Registration Fee Order 2006
disapplied: SI 2009/845 Sch.4
revoked: SI 2009/845 Art.15

**1349. Products of Animal Origin (Third Country
Imports) (Wales) (Amendment) (No.2) Regulations 2006**
revoked: SI 2009/1088 Reg.3

**1380. Contaminated Land (England) Regulations
2006**
Sch.2 para.5, amended: SI 2009/1307 Sch.2
para.113
Sch.2 para.6, amended: SI 2009/1307 Sch.2
para.113

**1384. Civil Aviation (Safety of Third-Country
Aircraft) Regulations 2006**
Reg.14, revoked: SI 2009/3015 Sch.1
Reg.15, revoked: SI 2009/3015 Sch.1
Reg.16, revoked: SI 2009/3015 Sch.1
Reg.17, revoked: SI 2009/3015 Sch.1

**1390. British Citizenship (Designated Service) Order
2006**
Sch.2 para.3, substituted: SI 2009/2054 Sch.1
para.34
Sch.2 para.15, applied: SI 2009/2958 Art.6
Sch.2 para.15, revoked: SI 2009/2958 Art.4

**1401. Plastic Materials and Articles in Contact with
Food (England) Regulations 2006**
Sch.2 Part 1, referred to: SI 2009/205 Reg.21

**1466. Transport and Works (Applications and
Objections Procedure) (England and Wales)
Rules 2006**
applied: SI 2009/872, SI 2009/1100, SI 2009/1300,
SI 2009/2364, SI 2009/2728

**1471. Animals and Animal Products (Import and
Export) (England) Regulations 2006**
applied: SI 2009/1299 Reg.4

**1499. Common Agricultural Policy (Wine) (England
and Northern Ireland) (Amendment) Regulations 2006**
revoked (in part): SI 2009/386 Reg.17

2006–cont.

1505. Education (Individual Pupil Information) (Prescribed Persons) (Amendment) Regulations 2006
revoked: SI 2009/ 1563 Sch.1

1510. Ozone Depleting Substances (Qualifications) Regulations 2006
revoked: SI 2009/ 216 Reg.12

1532. Street Works (Inspection Fees) (Wales) Regulations 2006
Reg.3, amended: SI 2009/ 258 Reg.3
Reg.3, applied: SI 2009/ 721 Sch.2 para.6

1536. Animals and Animal Products (Import and Export) (Wales) Regulations 2006
applied: SI 2009/ 1372 Reg.4
Reg.1, amended: SI 2009/ 390 Reg.2
Reg.35, amended: SI 2009/ 390 Reg.2
Sch.1 para.1, revoked: SI 2009/ 390 Reg.2
Sch.1 para.2, revoked: SI 2009/ 390 Reg.2
Sch.2, substituted: SI 2009/ 390 Sch.1
Sch.3 Part I para.1, substituted: SI 2009/ 390 Sch.1
Sch.3 Part I para.2, substituted: SI 2009/ 390 Sch.1
Sch.3 Part I para.3, substituted: SI 2009/ 390 Sch.1
Sch.3 Part I para.4, substituted: SI 2009/ 390 Sch.1
Sch.3 Part I para.5, substituted: SI 2009/ 390 Sch.1
Sch.3 Part I para.6, substituted: SI 2009/ 390 Sch.1
Sch.3 Part I para.7, substituted: SI 2009/ 390 Sch.1
Sch.3 Part I para.8, substituted: SI 2009/ 390 Sch.1
Sch.3 Part I para.9, substituted: SI 2009/ 390 Sch.1
Sch.3 Part I para.10, substituted: SI 2009/ 390 Sch.1
Sch.3 Part I para.10A, substituted: SI 2009/ 390 Sch.1
Sch.3 Part I para.11, substituted: SI 2009/ 390 Sch.1
Sch.3 Part I para.12, substituted: SI 2009/ 390 Sch.1
Sch.3 Part I para.13, substituted: SI 2009/ 390 Sch.1
Sch.3 Part I para.14, substituted: SI 2009/ 390 Sch.1
Sch.3 Part I para.15, substituted: SI 2009/ 390 Sch.1
Sch.3 Part I para.16, substituted: SI 2009/ 390 Sch.1
Sch.3 Part I para.17, substituted: SI 2009/ 390 Sch.1
Sch.3 Part I para.18, substituted: SI 2009/ 390 Sch.1
Sch.3 Part II para.1, substituted: SI 2009/ 390 Sch.1
Sch.3 Part II para.2, substituted: SI 2009/ 390 Sch.1
Sch.3 Part II para.3, substituted: SI 2009/ 390 Sch.1
Sch.3 Part III para.1, substituted: SI 2009/ 390 Sch.1
Sch.3 Part III para.2, substituted: SI 2009/ 390 Sch.1
Sch.3 Part III para.3, substituted: SI 2009/ 390 Sch.1
Sch.3 Part III para.4, substituted: SI 2009/ 390 Sch.1
Sch.3 Part III para.5, substituted: SI 2009/ 390 Sch.1
Sch.3 Part III para.6, substituted: SI 2009/ 390 Sch.1
Sch.7 Part I para.1, substituted: SI 2009/ 390 Sch.1
Sch.7 Part I para.2, substituted: SI 2009/ 390 Sch.1
Sch.7 Part I para.3, substituted: SI 2009/ 390 Sch.1
Sch.7 Part I para.4, substituted: SI 2009/ 390 Sch.1
Sch.7 Part I para.5, substituted: SI 2009/ 390 Sch.1
Sch.7 Part I para.6, substituted: SI 2009/ 390 Sch.1
Sch.7 Part I para.7, substituted: SI 2009/ 390 Sch.1
Sch.7 Part I para.8, substituted: SI 2009/ 390 Sch.1
Sch.7 Part II para.1, substituted: SI 2009/ 390 Sch.1
Sch.7 Part II para.2, substituted: SI 2009/ 390 Sch.1
Sch.7 Part II para.3, substituted: SI 2009/ 390 Sch.1
Sch.7 Part II para.4, substituted: SI 2009/ 390 Sch.1
Sch.7 Part II para.5, substituted: SI 2009/ 390 Sch.1
Sch.7 Part II para.6, substituted: SI 2009/ 390 Sch.1
Sch.7 Part II para.7, substituted: SI 2009/ 390 Sch.1

2006–cont.

1536. Animals and Animal Products (Import and Export) (Wales) Regulations 2006–*cont.*
Sch.7 Part II para.8, substituted: SI 2009/ 390 Sch.1
Sch.7 Part II para.9, substituted: SI 2009/ 390 Sch.1
Sch.7 Part II para.10, substituted: SI 2009/ 390 Sch.1
Sch.7 Part II para.11, substituted: SI 2009/ 390 Sch.1
Sch.7 Part II para.12, substituted: SI 2009/ 390 Sch.1
Sch.7 Part II para.13, substituted: SI 2009/ 390 Sch.1
Sch.7 Part II para.14, substituted: SI 2009/ 390 Sch.1
Sch.7 Part II para.15, substituted: SI 2009/ 390 Sch.1
Sch.7 Part II para.16, substituted: SI 2009/ 390 Sch.1
Sch.7 Part II para.17, substituted: SI 2009/ 390 Sch.1
Sch.7 Part II para.18, substituted: SI 2009/ 390 Sch.1
Sch.7 Part II para.19, substituted: SI 2009/ 390 Sch.1
Sch.7 Part II para.20, substituted: SI 2009/ 390 Sch.1
Sch.7 Part II para.21, substituted: SI 2009/ 390 Sch.1
Sch.7 Part II para.22, substituted: SI 2009/ 390 Sch.1
Sch.7 Part II para.23, substituted: SI 2009/ 390 Sch.1
Sch.7 Part II para.24, substituted: SI 2009/ 390 Sch.1
Sch.7 Part II para.25, substituted: SI 2009/ 390 Sch.1

1540. Eggs (Marketing Standards) (Amendment) (England and Wales) Regulations 2006
revoked (in part): SI 2009/ 793 Sch.1

1543. Tax Avoidance Schemes (Prescribed Descriptions of Arrangements) Regulations 2006
Reg.5, amended: SI 2009/ 2033 Reg.2
Reg.9, amended: SI 2009/ 1890 Art.3
Reg.17A, added: SI 2009/ 2033 Reg.2
Reg.18, applied: SI 2009/ 2033 Reg.3

1643. Plant Health (Wales) Order 2006
Art.2, amended: SI 2009/ 1376 Art.2
Sch.1 Part A para.11a, added: SI 2009/ 1376 Art.2
Sch.1 Part A para.15, substituted: SI 2009/ 1376 Art.2
Sch.1 Part A para.26a, added: SI 2009/ 1376 Art.2
Sch.1 Part B para.1a, amended: SI 2009/ 1376 Art.2
Sch.2 Part A, amended: SI 2009/ 1376 Art.2
Sch.2 Part B, amended: SI 2009/ 1376 Art.2
Sch.4 Part A, amended: SI 2009/ 1376 Art.2
Sch.4 Part B, amended: SI 2009/ 1376 Art.2
Sch.6 Part A para.7, amended: SI 2009/ 1376 Art.2

1663. General Dental Council (Fitness to Practise) Rules Order of Council 2006
Sch.1, added: SI 2009/ 1182 Sch.4 para.25
Sch.1, amended: SI 2009/ 1182 Sch.4 para.25

1664. General Dental Council (Appointments Committee and Appointment of Members of Committees) Rules Order of Council 2006
Sch.1, revoked: SI 2009/ 1813 Sch.1

1665. General Dental Council (Constitution of Committees) Order of Council 2006
revoked: SI 2009/ 1182 Sch.4 para.35

1666. General Dental Council (Constitution) Order of Council 2006
revoked: SI 2009/ 1182 Sch.4 para.34

2006–cont.

1681. Local Authority Social Services Complaints (England) Regulations 2006
applied: SI 2009/309 Reg.8, Reg.19
revoked: SI 2009/309 Reg.22
see *R. (on the application of F) v Wirral BC* [2009] EWHC 1626 (Admin), [2009] B.L.G.R. 905 (QBD (Admin)), McCombe, J.
Reg.5, applied: SI 2009/309 Reg.19
Reg.7, see *R. (on the application of F) v Wirral BC* [2009] EWHC 1626 (Admin), [2009] B.L.G.R. 905 (QBD (Admin)), McCombe, J.
Reg.8, applied: SI 2009/309 Reg.19
Reg.9, see *R. (on the application of F) v Wirral BC* [2009] EWHC 1626 (Admin), [2009] B.L.G.R. 905 (QBD (Admin)), McCombe, J.

1695. Motor Vehicles (EC Type Approval) (Amendment No 2) Regulations 2006
revoked: SI 2009/717 Sch.1

1713. Management of Houses in Multiple Occupation (Wales) Regulations 2006
Reg.6, amended: SI 2009/1915 Reg.2

1786. Courts-Martial (Prosecution Appeals) Order 2006
applied: SI 2009/2044 Art.32
referred to: SI 2009/2044 Art.32
Art.7, varied: SI 2009/2044 Art.32
Art.11, varied: SI 2009/2044 Art.32

1788. Courts-Martial (Prosecution Appeals) (Supplementary Provisions) Order 2006
revoked: SI 2009/2044 Art.1

1832. Mental Capacity Act 2005 (Independent Mental Capacity Advocates) (General) Regulations 2006
Reg.5, amended: SI 2009/2376 Reg.2

1846. Export of Radioactive Sources (Control) Order 2006
Art.2, amended: SI 2009/585 Sch.1 para.1
Art.5, amended: SI 2009/585 Sch.1 para.2
Art.8, substituted: SI 2009/585 Sch.1 para.3

1863. Assembly Learning Grants and Loans (Higher Education) (Wales) (Amendment) Regulations 2006
applied: SI 2009/2737 Reg.3

1879. Plant Health (Import Inspection Fees) (England) Regulations 2006
Sch.2, amended: SI 2009/2053 Sch.1
Sch.2, substituted: SI 2009/2053 Reg.4

1909. Belarus (Restrictive Measures) (Overseas Territories) Order 2006
Art.9, varied: SI 2009/888 Art.2
Sch.2 para.1, varied: SI 2009/888 Art.2
Sch.2 para.2, varied: SI 2009/888 Art.2
Sch.2 para.3, varied: SI 2009/888 Art.2
Sch.2 para.4, varied: SI 2009/888 Art.2
Sch.2 para.5, varied: SI 2009/888 Art.2
Sch.2 para.6, varied: SI 2009/888 Art.2
Sch.2 para.7, varied: SI 2009/888 Art.2
Sch.2 para.8, varied: SI 2009/888 Art.2

1913. Turks and Caicos Islands Constitution Order 2006
Sch.2, added: SI 2009/701 Sch.1 para.1, Sch.1 para.3, Sch.1 para.4, Sch.1 para.5, Sch.1 para.6, Sch.1 para.8
Sch.2, amended: SI 2009/701 Sch.1 para.2, Sch.1 para.3, Sch.1 para.5, Sch.1 para.7, Sch.1 para.9, Sch.1 para.10, Sch.1 para.11
Sch.2, revoked: SI 2009/701 Sch.1 para.1, Sch.1 para.3, Sch.1 para.4, Sch.1 para.5, Sch.1 para.6, Sch.1 para.8

2006–cont.

1954. Transport and Works (Model Clauses for Railways and Tramways) Order 2006
Sch.1, amended: SI 2009/1307 Sch.2 para.115
Sch.1, substituted: SI 2009/1307 Sch.2 para.115
Sch.2, amended: SI 2009/1307 Sch.2 para.116
Sch.2, substituted: SI 2009/1307 Sch.2 para.116

1970. Sea Fishing (Enforcement of Annual Community and Third Country Fishing Measures) (England) Order 2006
revoked: SI 2009/1850 Art.19

1975. Registered Designs Rules 2006
Part 6 r.42, amended: SI 2009/546 r.6
Part 6 r.43, amended: SI 2009/546 r.7

2009. Education (Student Loans)(Repayment)(Amendment) Regulations 2006
revoked: SI 2009/470 Sch.1

2015. Police and Criminal Evidence Act 1984 (Application to the Armed Forces) Order 2006
revoked: SI 2009/1922 Art.18

2059. European Cooperative Society (Involvement of Employees) Regulations 2006
Reg.41, amended: SI 2009/3348 Art.22, Art.23

2072. Primary Care Trusts (Establishment and Dissolution) (England) Order 2006
Sch.1, amended: SI 2009/2873 Art.2
Sch.2, amended: SI 2009/2873 Art.2

2075. Environmental Stewardship (England) and Organic Products (Amendment) Regulations 2006
Reg.2, revoked: SI 2009/842 Reg.32

2229. Tonnage Tax (Training Requirement) (Amendment) Regulations 2006
revoked: SI 2009/2304 Sch.1

2238. Environmental Noise (England) Regulations 2006
referred to: SI 2009/1610
Reg.2, amended: SI 2009/1610 Reg.3
Reg.3, amended: SI 2009/1610 Reg.4
Reg.13, substituted: SI 2009/1610 Reg.5
Reg.14, substituted: SI 2009/1610 Reg.6
Reg.14A, added: SI 2009/1610 Reg.6
Reg.15, amended: SI 2009/1610 Reg.7
Reg.29, amended: SI 2009/1610 Reg.8
Reg.30, substituted: SI 2009/1610 Reg.9

2285. Charges for Residues Surveillance Regulations 2006
Reg.3, amended: SI 2009/2779 Reg.2
Sch.1, amended: SI 2009/2779 Sch.1

2312. Non-Domestic Rating (Alteration of Lists and Appeals) (England) (Amendment) Regulations 2006
revoked: SI 2009/2268 Reg.25

2316. Air Navigation (Amendment) Order 2006
revoked: SI 2009/3015 Sch.1

2326. Criminal Justice and Public Order Act 1994 (Application to the Armed Forces) Order 2006
revoked: SI 2009/990 Art.3

2369. Tobacco Advertising and Promotion Act 2002 etc (Amendment) Regulations 2006
Reg.7, revoked: 2009 c.21 Sch.6

2373. Gangmasters (Licensing Conditions) (No.2) Rules 2006
revoked: SI 2009/307 r.10

2409. Motor Vehicles (EC Type Approval) (Amendment No.3) Regulations 2006
revoked: SI 2009/717 Sch.1

2006–cont.

2492. Criminal Defence Service (Financial Eligibility) Regulations 2006
Reg.2, amended: SI 2009/1887 Reg.19, SI 2009/2878 Reg.3
Reg.3, substituted: SI 2009/2878 Reg.4
Reg.5, amended: SI 2009/2878 Reg.5
Reg.7, amended: SI 2009/2878 Reg.6
Reg.10, amended: SI 2009/2878 Reg.7
Reg.11, revoked (in part): SI 2009/2878 Reg.8

2493. Criminal Defence Service (Representation Orders and Consequential Amendments) Regulations 2006
Reg.2, amended: SI 2009/3331 Reg.3
Reg.4, substituted: SI 2009/3331 Reg.4
Reg.4A, added: SI 2009/3331 Reg.5
Reg.5, amended: SI 2009/3331 Reg.6

2494. Criminal Defence Service (Representation Orders Appeals etc.) Regulations 2006
Reg.3, amended: SI 2009/3329 Reg.3
Reg.3, revoked (in part): SI 2009/3329 Reg.3
Reg.6, substituted: SI 2009/3329 Reg.4
Reg.8, revoked: SI 2009/3329 Reg.5

2522. Environmental Impact Assessment (Agriculture) (England) (No.2) Regulations 2006
applied: SI 2009/3365 Sch.1 para.1
Reg.4, applied: SI 2009/3264 Sch.1 para.1, SI 2009/3365 Sch.1 para.1
Reg.9, applied: SI 2009/3264 Sch.1 para.1, SI 2009/3365 Sch.1 para.1
Reg.26, applied: SI 2009/3264 Sch.1 para.1, SI 2009/3365 Sch.1 para.1
Reg.28, applied: SI 2009/3264 Sch.1 para.1, SI 2009/3365 Sch.1 para.1
Reg.37, revoked: SI 2009/3264 Sch.3
Sch.4 para.9, amended: SI 2009/1307 Sch.2 para.117

2525. Refugee or Person in Need of International Protection (Qualification) Regulations 2006
see *SH (Palestinian Territories) v Secretary of State for the Home Department* [2008] EWCA Civ 1150, [2009] Imm. A.R. 306 (CA (Civ Div)), Scott Baker, L.J.
Reg.5, see *SH (Palestinian Territories) v Secretary of State for the Home Department* [2008] EWCA Civ 1150, [2009] Imm. A.R. 306 (CA (Civ Div)), Scott Baker, L.J.

2601. Education (Information About Individual Pupils) (England) Regulations 2006
Sch.1, referred to: SI 2009/1563 Reg.3

2629. Environmental Noise (Wales) Regulations 2006
Reg.2, amended: SI 2009/47 Reg.3
Reg.3, amended: SI 2009/47 Reg.4
Reg.13, substituted: SI 2009/47 Reg.5
Reg.14, revoked: SI 2009/47 Reg.8
Reg.15, amended: SI 2009/47 Reg.6
Reg.30, substituted: SI 2009/47 Reg.7

2646. Homelessness (Wales) Regulations 2006
Reg.4, amended: SI 2009/393 Reg.3

2657. Terrorism (United Nations Measures) Order 2006
applied: SI 2009/1747 Art.26
revoked: SI 2009/1747 Art.26
see *Av HM Treasury* [2008] EWCA Civ 1187, [2009] 3 W.L.R. 25 (CA (Civ Div)), Sir Anthony Clarke, M.R.
Art.4, applied: SI 2009/1747 Art.26
Art.7, applied: SI 2009/209 Reg.13

2006–cont.

2657. Terrorism (United Nations Measures) Order 2006– *cont.*
Art.7, see *Av HM Treasury* [2008] EWCA Civ 1187, [2009] 3 W.L.R. 25 (CA (Civ Div)), Sir Anthony Clarke, M.R.
Art.8, applied: SI 2009/209 Reg.13
Art.8, see *Av HM Treasury* [2008] EWCA Civ 1187, [2009] 3 W.L.R. 25 (CA (Civ Div)), Sir Anthony Clarke, M.R.
Art.10, applied: SI 2009/209 Reg.13
Art.20, applied: SI 2009/1747 Art.26

2697. Plant Health (Fees) (Forestry) Regulations 2006
Sch.3A, substituted: SI 2009/2956 Reg.2

2701. Avian Influenza (Preventive Measures) (England) Regulations 2006
Reg.13, amended: SI 2009/2712 Reg.4

2702. Avian Influenza and Influenza of Avian Origin in Mammals (England) (No.2) Order 2006
Art.9, amended: SI 2009/2713 Art.2
Art.9, revoked (in part): SI 2009/2713 Art.8

2703. Avian Influenza (Vaccination) (England) Regulations 2006
Reg.11, amended: SI 2009/2712 Reg.5

2739. Control of Asbestos Regulations 2006
applied: SI 2009/515 Reg.5, Reg.6, Sch.5
Sch.2 para.1, amended: SI 2009/716 Sch.6

2816. Motor Vehicles (EC Type Approval) (Amendment No.4) Regulations 2006
revoked: SI 2009/717 Sch.1

2832. Plant Health (Import Inspection Fees) (Wales) (No.2) Regulations 2006
Reg.4, amended: SI 2009/398 Reg.2
Sch.2, substituted: SI 2009/398 Reg.2, SI 2009/3140 Reg.2

2841. Products of Animal Origin (Third Country Imports) (England) Regulations 2006
Reg.4, amended: SI 2009/875 Reg.2

2867. Real Estate Investment Trusts (Assessment and Recovery of Tax) Regulations 2006
Reg.7, amended: SI 2009/2036 Reg.33

2886. Youth Justice and Criminal Evidence Act 1999 (Application to Courts-Martial) Order 2006
revoked: SI 2009/2083 Art.14

2887. Youth Justice and Criminal Evidence Act 1999 (Application to the Courts-Martial Appeal Court) Order 2006
revoked: SI 2009/2083 Art.14

2888. Youth Justice and Criminal Evidence Act 1999 (Application to Standing Civilian Courts) Order 2006
revoked: SI 2009/2083 Art.14

2889. Courts-Martial (Royal Navy, Army and Royal Air Force) (Evidence) Rules 2006
revoked: SI 2009/2100 r.16

2890. Criminal Justice Act 1988 (Application to Service Courts) (Evidence) Order 2006
revoked: SI 2009/994 Art.2

2891. Standing Civilian Courts (Evidence) Rules 2006
revoked: SI 2009/2100 r.16

2913. Scotland Act 1998 (River Tweed) Order 2006
Sch.1, amended: SI 2009/837 Art.27

2914. Local Government (Early Termination of Employment) (Discretionary Compensation) (England and Wales) Regulations 2006
Reg.2, amended: SI 2009/3150 Reg.3
Reg.4, amended: SI 2009/3150 Reg.4

2006–cont.

2914. Local Government (Early Termination of Employment) (Discretionary Compensation) (England and Wales) Regulations 2006– *cont.*
Reg.6, amended: SI 2009/3150 Reg.5
Reg.9, amended: SI 2009/3150 Reg.6

2917. Royal Marines Terms of Service Regulations 2006
varied: SI 2009/1059 Art.191
Reg.2, amended: SI 2009/831 Reg.10, SI 2009/1089 Reg.10
Reg.3, amended: SI 2009/831 Reg.11, SI 2009/1089 Reg.11
Reg.3, revoked (in part): SI 2009/831 Reg.11, SI 2009/1089 Reg.11
Reg.4, applied: SI 2009/1089 Sch.1 para.6
Reg.6, substituted: SI 2009/831 Reg.12, SI 2009/1089 Reg.12
Reg.7, amended: SI 2009/831 Reg.13, SI 2009/1089 Reg.13
Reg.7, applied: SI 2009/831 Sch.1 para.7
Reg.7, referred to: SI 2009/831 Sch.1 para.7
Reg.7, revoked (in part): SI 2009/831 Reg.13, SI 2009/1089 Reg.13
Reg.7, varied: SI 2009/831 Sch.1 para.7
Reg.8A, added: SI 2009/831 Reg.14, SI 2009/1089 Reg.14
Sch.1, revoked: SI 2009/831 Reg.15, SI 2009/1089 Reg.15

2918. Royal Navy Terms of Service (Ratings) Regulations 2006
applied: SI 2009/1089 Sch.1 para.2
varied: SI 2009/1059 Art.191
Reg.2, amended: SI 2009/831 Reg.3, SI 2009/1089 Reg.3
Reg.3, amended: SI 2009/831 Reg.4, SI 2009/1089 Reg.4
Reg.3, applied: SI 2009/831 Sch.1 para.5, SI 2009/1089 Sch.1 para.5
Reg.3, disapplied: SI 2009/1089 Sch.1 para.2
Reg.3, revoked (in part): SI 2009/831 Reg.4, SI 2009/1089 Reg.4
Reg.4, applied: SI 2009/1089 Sch.1 para.3
Reg.6, substituted: SI 2009/831 Reg.5, SI 2009/1089 Reg.5
Reg.7, amended: SI 2009/831 Reg.6, SI 2009/1089 Reg.6
Reg.7, applied: SI 2009/1089 Sch.1 para.4
Reg.7, revoked (in part): SI 2009/831 Reg.6, SI 2009/1089 Reg.6
Reg.7, varied: SI 2009/831 Sch.1 para.4
Reg.8, amended: SI 2009/831 Reg.7, SI 2009/1089 Reg.7
Reg.8, applied: SI 2009/831 Sch.1 para.5
Reg.8A, added: SI 2009/831 Reg.8, SI 2009/1089 Reg.8
Reg.10, applied: SI 2009/831 Sch.1 para.2, SI 2009/1089 Sch.1 para.2
Sch.1, revoked: SI 2009/831 Reg.9, SI 2009/1089 Reg.9

2929. Seed Potatoes (Wales) Regulations 2006
Reg.2, amended: SI 2009/2980 Reg.2
Reg.4A, added: SI 2009/2980 Reg.2
Sch.2 Part I para.8A, added: SI 2009/2980 Reg.2

2930. Sex Discrimination Act 1975 (Public Authorities) (Statutory Duties) Order 2006
Art.2, varied: SI 2009/462 Sch.5 para.21
Sch.1, amended: SI 2009/462 Sch.5 para.22

2006–cont.

2952. Al-Qaida and Taliban (United Nations Measures) Order 2006
see *A v HM Treasury* [2008] EWCA Civ 1187, [2009] 3 W.L.R. 25 (CA (Civ Div)), Sir Anthony Clarke, M.R.; see *AV v Secretary of State for the Home Department* [2008] EWHC 1895 (Admin), [2009] 1 W.L.R. 2318 (QBD (Admin)), Mitting, J.; see *Hay v HM Treasury* [2009] EWHC 1677 (Admin), [2009] Lloyd's Rep. F.C. 547 (QBD (Admin)), Owen, J.; see *R. (on the application of K) v HM Treasury* [2009] EWHC 1643 (Admin), [2009] Lloyd's Rep. F.C. 533 (QBD (Admin)), Burton, J.
Art.3, see *Hay v HM Treasury* [2009] EWHC 1677 (Admin), [2009] Lloyd's Rep. F.C. 547 (QBD (Admin)), Owen, J.
Art.5, see *A v HM Treasury* [2008] EWCA Civ 1187, [2009] 3 W.L.R. 25 (CA (Civ Div)), Sir Anthony Clarke, M.R.
Art.7, applied: SI 2009/209 Reg.13
Art.8, applied: SI 2009/209 Reg.13
Art.10, applied: SI 2009/209 Reg.13

2993. Regional Transport Planning (Wales) Order 2006
Art.5, amended: SI 2009/109 Art.2

3102. Local Government (Best Value Authorities) (Power to Trade) (Amendment) (England) Order 2006
revoked: SI 2009/2393 Art.3

3145. Immigration (Certificate of Entitlement to Right of Abode in the United Kingdom) Regulations 2006
Reg.2, amended: SI 2009/1892 Sch.1 para.18
Sch.1, amended: SI 2009/1892 Sch.1 para.18

3148. Controlled Drugs (Supervision of Management and Use) Regulations 2006
Reg.2, amended: SI 2009/462 Sch.5 para.23
Reg.4, amended: SI 2009/462 Sch.5 para.23
Reg.12, amended: SI 2009/462 Sch.5 para.23
Reg.12, revoked (in part): SI 2009/462 Sch.5 para.23
Reg.16, amended: SI 2009/462 Sch.5 para.23
Reg.16, revoked (in part): SI 2009/462 Sch.5 para.23
Reg.18, amended: SI 2009/462 Sch.5 para.23
Reg.18, revoked (in part): SI 2009/462 Sch.5 para.23
Reg.19, amended: SI 2009/462 Sch.5 para.23
Reg.19, revoked (in part): SI 2009/462 Sch.5 para.23
Reg.21, amended: SI 2009/462 Sch.5 para.23
Reg.22, amended: SI 2009/462 Sch.5 para.23
Reg.22, revoked (in part): SI 2009/462 Sch.5 para.23

3156. Education (Student Support) (European Institutions) (No.2) Regulations 2006
Reg.17, amended: SI 2009/1576 Reg.2
Reg.19, amended: SI 2009/1576 Reg.2

3197. School Staffing (England) (Amendment) (No.2) Regulations 2006
revoked: SI 2009/2680 Sch.1

3199. Further Education (Providers of Education) (England) Regulations 2006
Reg.3, amended: SI 2009/1924 Reg.9
Reg.5, amended: SI 2009/1924 Reg.9
Reg.13, amended: SI 2009/1924 Reg.9
Reg.17, amended: SI 2009/1924 Reg.9
Reg.18, amended: SI 2009/1924 Reg.9
Sch.1 Part 1 para.3, amended: SI 2009/1924 Reg.9
Sch.1 Part 2 para.2, amended: SI 2009/1924 Reg.9

2006–cont.

3243. Armed Forces (Entry, Search and Seizure) Order 2006

Art.3, applied: SI 2009/2056 Sch.4 para.13, Sch.4 para.14, Sch.4 para.15, Sch.4 para.19, Sch.4 para.20, Sch.4 para.21, Sch.4 para.23

Art.4, applied: SI 2009/2056 Sch.4 para.13, Sch.4 para.14, Sch.4 para.15, Sch.4 para.19, Sch.4 para.20, Sch.4 para.21, Sch.4 para.23

Art.5, applied: SI 2009/2056 Sch.4 para.13

Art.6, applied: SI 2009/2056 Sch.4 para.14

Art.6, referred to: SI 2009/2056 Sch.4 para.14

Art.12, applied: SI 2009/2056 Sch.4 para.20

Art.14, applied: SI 2009/2056 Sch.4 para.21

3254. Common Agricultural Policy Single Payment and Support Schemes (Cross-compliance) (England) (Amendment) Regulations 2006

revoked: SI 2009/3264 Sch.3

3269. Finance Act 2002, Schedule 26, (Parts 2 and 9) (Amendment) Order 2006

revoked: 2009 c.4 Sch.3 Part 1

3285. Gambling (Personal Licence Fees) Regulations 2006

Reg.3, amended: SI 2009/1971 Reg.3

Reg.4, amended: SI 2009/1971 Reg.4

3289. Waste Electrical and Electronic Equipment Regulations 2006

referred to: SI 2009/2957 Reg.2

Reg.2, amended: SI 2009/2957 Sch.1 para.1

Reg.8, amended: SI 2009/2957 Sch.1 para.2

Reg.10, amended: SI 2009/2957 Sch.1 para.3

Reg.20, amended: SI 2009/2957 Sch.1 para.4

Reg.22, amended: SI 2009/2957 Sch.1 para.5

Reg.26, amended: SI 2009/2957 Sch.1 para.6

Reg.26, revoked (in part): SI 2009/2957 Sch.1 para.6

Reg.27, amended: SI 2009/2957 Sch.1 para.7

Reg.28, amended: SI 2009/2957 Sch.1 para.8

Reg.29, amended: SI 2009/2957 Sch.1 para.9

Reg.33, amended: SI 2009/2957 Sch.1 para.10

Reg.34, revoked (in part): SI 2009/2957 Sch.1 para.11

Reg.41, amended: SI 2009/2957 Sch.1 para.12

Reg.41, revoked (in part): SI 2009/2957 Sch.1 para.12

Reg.43, amended: SI 2009/2957 Sch.1 para.13

Reg.46, amended: SI 2009/2957 Sch.1 para.14

Reg.47, amended: SI 2009/2957 Sch.1 para.15

Reg.52, amended: SI 2009/2957 Sch.1 para.16

Reg.52, revoked (in part): SI 2009/2957 Sch.1 para.16

Reg.58, revoked (in part): SI 2009/2957 Sch.1 para.17

Reg.59A, revoked: SI 2009/2957 Sch.1 para.18

Reg.73, applied: SI 2009/890 Reg.52, Sch.3 para.7

Sch.6 para.14, amended: SI 2009/2957 Sch.1 para.19

Sch.7 Part 3, amended: SI 2009/2957 Sch.1 para.20

Sch.7 Part 4 para.5, amended: SI 2009/2957 Sch.1 para.20

Sch.8 Part 1 para.6, amended: SI 2009/2957 Sch.1 para.21

Sch.8 Part 2 para.2, revoked: SI 2009/2957 Sch.1 para.21

Sch.8 Part 2 para.3, revoked: SI 2009/2957 Sch.1 para.21

Sch.8 Part 2 para.7, substituted: SI 2009/2957 Sch.1 para.21

Sch.8 Part 2 para.8, amended: SI 2009/2957 Sch.1 para.21

2006–cont.

3289. Waste Electrical and Electronic Equipment Regulations 2006– *cont.*

Sch.8 Part 2 para.8B, amended: SI 2009/2957 Sch.1 para.21

Sch.8 Part 2 para.9, revoked (in part): SI 2009/2957 Sch.1 para.21

Sch.8 Part 2 para.10, amended: SI 2009/2957 Sch.1 para.21

Sch.8 Part 2 para.12, added: SI 2009/2957 Sch.1 para.21

Sch.8 Part 2 para.13, added: SI 2009/2957 Sch.1 para.21

Sch.8 Part 2 para.14, added: SI 2009/2957 Sch.1 para.21

Sch.8 Part 3 para.1, substituted: SI 2009/2957 Sch.1 para.21

Sch.8 Part 3 para.5, substituted: SI 2009/2957 Sch.1 para.21

Sch.8 Part 3 para.5A, amended: SI 2009/2957 Sch.1 para.21

Sch.8 Part 3 para.6, revoked (in part): SI 2009/2957 Sch.1 para.21

Sch.8 Part 3 para.7, substituted: SI 2009/2957 Sch.1 para.21

Sch.8 Part 3 para.8, added: SI 2009/2957 Sch.1 para.21

Sch.8 Part 3 para.9, added: SI 2009/2957 Sch.1 para.21

3295. Town and Country Planning (Environmental Impact Assessment) (Amendment) Regulations 2006

see *Finn-Kelcey v Milton Keynes BC* [2008] EWCA Civ 1067, [2009] Env. L.R. 17 (CA (Civ Div)), Keene, L.J.

3304. Local Elections (Principal Areas) (England and Wales) Rules 2006

see *Pilling v Reynolds* [2008] EWHC 316 (QB), [2009] 1 All E.R. 163 (DC), Tugendhat, J.

Sch.2, see *Aehmed v Legal Services Commission* [2009] EWCA Civ 572, [2009] 3 Costs L.R. 425 (CA (Civ Div)), Sedley, L.J.; see *Pilling v Reynolds* [2008] EWHC 316 (QB), [2009] 1 All E.R. 163 (DC), Tugendhat, J.

3316. Planning (Listed Buildings and Conservation Areas) (Amendment) (Wales) Regulations 2006

revoked: SI 2009/1026 Reg.3

3317. Accession (Immigration and Worker Authorisation) Regulations 2006

Reg.2, amended: SI 2009/2426 Reg.2

Reg.3, substituted: SI 2009/2426 Reg.2

Sch.1, amended: SI 2009/2748 Sch.1 para.34

3327. North Korea (United Nations Measures) (Overseas Territories) Order 2006

Art.2, amended: SI 2009/1746 Art.2

Art.7, substituted: SI 2009/1746 Art.3

Art.8A, added: SI 2009/1746 Art.4

Art.23, amended: SI 2009/1746 Art.5

Art.23, varied: SI 2009/888 Art.2

Sch.2 para.1, amended: SI 2009/1746 Art.6

Sch.2 para.1, varied: SI 2009/888 Art.2

Sch.2 para.2, varied: SI 2009/888 Art.2

Sch.2 para.3, amended: SI 2009/888 Art.5

Sch.2 para.3, varied: SI 2009/888 Art.2

Sch.2 para.4, amended: SI 2009/888 Art.5

Sch.2 para.4, varied: SI 2009/888 Art.2

Sch.2 para.5, amended: SI 2009/888 Art.5

Sch.2 para.5, varied: SI 2009/888 Art.2

Sch.2 para.6, varied: SI 2009/888 Art.2

2006–cont.

3327. North Korea (United Nations Measures) (Overseas Territories) Order 2006–cont.
Sch.2 para.7, varied: SI 2009/888 Art.2, Art.5
Sch.2 para.8, varied: SI 2009/888 Art.2
Sch.2 para.9, varied: SI 2009/888 Art.2
Sch.2 para.10, varied: SI 2009/888 Art.2

3333. Association of Law Costs Draftsmen Order 2006
revoked: SI 2009/3250 Sch.1

3334. National Assembly for Wales (Transfer of Functions) (No.2) Order 2006
Art.4, applied: SI 2009/3210

3335. National Assembly for Wales (Disqualification) Order 2006
Sch.1 Part 1, amended: SI 2009/462 Sch.5 para.24, SI 2009/1307 Sch.2 para.118

3336. Water and Sewerage Services (Northern Ireland) Order 2006
Art.2, amended: SI 2009/1941 Sch.1 para.263
Art.268, amended: SI 2009/1941 Sch.1 para.263
Art.269, amended: SI 2009/1941 Sch.1 para.263
Art.271, amended: SI 2009/1941 Sch.1 para.263
Art.276, amended: SI 2009/1941 Sch.1 para.263

3343. Rural Development Programmes (Wales) Regulations 2006
Reg.2, amended: SI 2009/3270 Reg.2
Reg.3, amended: SI 2009/3270 Reg.2
Reg.4, amended: SI 2009/3270 Reg.2
Reg.6, amended: SI 2009/3270 Reg.2
Reg.7, amended: SI 2009/3270 Reg.2
Reg.8, amended: SI 2009/3270 Reg.2
Reg.9, amended: SI 2009/3270 Reg.2
Sch.1 para.4, substituted: SI 2009/3270 Reg.2
Sch.1 para.5, substituted: SI 2009/3270 Reg.2
Sch.1 para.6, substituted: SI 2009/3270 Reg.2

3362. Legal Services Ombudsman (Jurisdiction) (Amendment) Order 2006
revoked: SI 2009/3250 Sch.1

3388. Personal Injuries (NHS Charges) (General) and Road Traffic (NHS Charges) (Amendment) Regulations 2006
Reg.1, amended: SI 2009/316 Sch.2 para.1
Reg.2, amended: SI 2009/316 Sch.2 para.2
Reg.5, amended: SI 2009/316 Sch.2 para.3

3411. Private Security Industry Act 2001 (Duration of Licence) (No.2) Order 2006
Art.1, revoked (in part): SI 2009/635 Art.2

3415. Police Pensions Regulations 2006
Reg.3, amended: SI 2009/2060 Sch.1 para.21
Reg.4, amended: SI 2009/2060 Sch.1 para.22
Reg.5, amended: SI 2009/2060 Sch.1 para.23
Reg.6, amended: SI 2009/2060 Sch.2 para.2
Reg.17, amended: SI 2009/2060 Sch.1 para.24
Reg.18, amended: SI 2009/2060 Sch.1 para.25
Reg.19, amended: SI 2009/2060 Sch.1 para.26
Reg.20, amended: SI 2009/2060 Sch.1 para.27
Reg.23, amended: SI 2009/2060 Sch.1 para.28
Reg.51, amended: SI 2009/2060 Sch.1 para.29
Reg.52, amended: SI 2009/2060 Sch.1 para.30
Sch.1, amended: SI 2009/2060 Sch.1 para.31
Sch.2 para.9, amended: SI 2009/2060 Sch.2 para.3
Sch.3 para.19, added: SI 2009/2060 Sch.2 para.4

3418. Electromagnetic Compatibility Regulations 2006
referred to: SI 2009/669 Sch.1 Part 4

2006–cont.

3428. Companies Act 2006 (Commencement No.1, Transitional Provisions and Savings) Order 2006
Sch.5 Part 3 para.6, applied: SI 2009/2392 Reg.6
Sch.5 Part 3 para.6, revoked (in part): SI 2009/2392 Reg.7

3435. Civil Procedure (Amendment No.3) Rules 2006
see *Carver v BAA Plc* [2008] EWCA Civ 412, [2009] 1 W.L.R. 113 (CA (Civ Div)), Ward, L.J.
r.7, see *Carver v BAA Plc* [2008] EWCA Civ 412, [2009] 1 W.L.R. 113 (CA (Civ Div)), Ward, L.J.

2007

22. Air Passenger Duty (Rate) (Qualifying Territories) Order 2007
revoked: 2009 c.10 Sch.5 para.2

28. Air Navigation (Dangerous Goods) (Amendment) Regulations 2007
revoked: SI 2009/1492 Reg.3

115. Personal Injuries (NHS Charges) (Amounts) Regulations 2007
applied: SI 2009/316 Reg.4
Reg.2, amended: SI 2009/316 Sch.1 para.1
Reg.3A, added: SI 2009/316 Sch.1 para.2

121. National Health Service (Free Prescriptions and Charges for Drugs and Appliances) (Wales) Regulations 2007
Reg.2, amended: SI 2009/2607 Reg.2
Reg.3, amended: SI 2009/2607 Reg.3
Reg.4, amended: SI 2009/2607 Reg.4
Reg.7A, added: SI 2009/1175 Reg.2
Reg.8, amended: SI 2009/2607 Reg.5
Reg.9, amended: SI 2009/2607 Reg.6
Reg.11A, added: SI 2009/2607 Reg.7

126. Financial Services and Markets Act 2000 (Markets in Financial Instruments) Regulations 2007
Sch.2 para.10, revoked: SI 2009/534 Reg.9
Sch.5 para.20, revoked: SI 2009/534 Reg.9

210. Contaminants in Food (England) Regulations 2007
revoked: SI 2009/1223 Reg.7

236. National Assembly for Wales (Representation of the People) Order 2007
Sch.1 para.4, amended: SI 2009/1182 Sch.4 para.42
Sch.1 para.4, revoked (in part): SI 2009/1182 Sch.4 para.16

266. Copyright (Certification of Licensing Scheme for Educational Recording of Broadcasts) (Educational Recording Agency Limited) Order 2007
referred to: SI 2009/20
Sch.1, amended: SI 2009/20 Art.2
Sch.1, referred to: SI 2009/20 Art.2
Sch.1, substituted: SI 2009/20 Sch.1

274. Air Navigation (Amendment) Order 2007
revoked: SI 2009/3015 Sch.1

276. Patents (Convention Countries) Order 2007
Sch.1, amended: SI 2009/2746 Art.2

277. Designs (Convention Countries) Order 2007
Sch.1, amended: SI 2009/2747 Art.2

285. Scottish Parliament (Disqualification) Order 2007
Sch.1 Part I, amended: SI 2009/56 Sch.2 para.159

288. Police and Criminal Evidence (Amendment) (Northern Ireland) Order 2007
Art.30, revoked (in part): 2009 c.26 Sch.8 Part 13

2007–cont.

288. Police and Criminal Evidence (Amendment) (Northern Ireland) Order 2007–*cont.*
Art.33, revoked (in part): 2009 c.26 Sch.8 Part 13
289. Pharmacists and Pharmacy Technicians Order 2007
applied: SI 2009/2722 Reg.3
Art.2, amended: SI 2009/1182 Sch.3 para.1
Art.2, revoked (in part): SI 2009/1182 Sch.3 para.1
Art.3, amended: SI 2009/1182 Sch.3 para.2
Art.4, amended: SI 2009/1182 Sch.3 para.3
Art.4, revoked (in part): SI 2009/1182 Sch.3 para.3
Art.6, amended: SI 2009/1182 Sch.3 para.4
Art.7, amended: SI 2009/1182 Sch.3 para.5
Art.19A, added: SI 2009/1182 Sch.3 para.6
Art.19B, added: SI 2009/1182 Sch.3 para.6
Art.22, amended: SI 2009/1182 Sch.3 para.7
Art.23, amended: SI 2009/1182 Sch.3 para.8
Art.24, amended: SI 2009/1182 Sch.3 para.9
Art.25, amended: SI 2009/1182 Sch.3 para.10
Art.30, amended: SI 2009/1182 Sch.3 para.11
Art.32, amended: SI 2009/1182 Sch.3 para.12
Art.34, amended: SI 2009/1182 Sch.3 para.13
Art.40, amended: SI 2009/1182 Sch.3 para.14
Art.42, amended: SI 2009/1182 Sch.3 para.15
Art.44, amended: SI 2009/1182 Sch.3 para.16
Art.44, revoked (in part): SI 2009/1182 Sch.3 para.16
Art.46, amended: SI 2009/1182 Sch.3 para.17
Art.46, revoked (in part): SI 2009/1182 Sch.3 para.17
Art.48, amended: 2009 c.26 s.81, SI 2009/1182 Sch.3 para.18
Art.49, amended: SI 2009/1182 Sch.3 para.19
Art.49, revoked (in part): SI 2009/1182 Sch.3 para.19
Art.53, amended: SI 2009/1182 Sch.3 para.20
Art.54, amended: SI 2009/1182 Sch.3 para.21
Art.56, amended: SI 2009/1182 Sch.3 para.22
Art.58, amended: SI 2009/1182 Sch.3 para.23
Art.66, amended: SI 2009/1182 Sch.3 para.24
Art.69, amended: SI 2009/1182 Sch.3 para.25
Sch.1 Part 2 para.18, revoked: SSI 2009/183 Sch.5
Sch.2 Part 1 para.1, amended: SI 2009/1182 Sch.3 para.26
Sch.2 Part 2 para.6, amended: SI 2009/1182 Sch.3 para.26
292. Guarantees of Origin of Electricity Produced from High-efficiency Cogeneration Regulations 2007
Reg.2, amended: SI 2009/229 Sch.2 para.19
Reg.2, applied: SI 2009/229 Art.5
Reg.3, amended: SI 2009/229 Sch.2 para.19
Reg.3, applied: SI 2009/229 Art.5
315. Local Health Boards (Functions) (Wales) (Amendment) Regulations 2007
revoked: SI 2009/1511 Reg.6
318. Companies Acts (Unregistered Companies) Regulations 2007
revoked: SI 2009/2436 Reg.8
376. Products of Animal Origin (Third Country Imports) (Wales) Regulations 2007
Reg.4, amended: SI 2009/1088 Reg.2
Sch.1 Part I para.1, substituted: SI 2009/392 Sch.1
Sch.1 Part I para.2, substituted: SI 2009/392 Sch.1
Sch.1 Part I para.3, substituted: SI 2009/392 Sch.1
Sch.1 Part I para.4, substituted: SI 2009/392 Sch.1
Sch.1 Part I para.5, substituted: SI 2009/392 Sch.1
Sch.1 Part I para.6, substituted: SI 2009/392 Sch.1

2007–cont.

376. Products of Animal Origin (Third Country Imports) (Wales) Regulations 2007–*cont.*
Sch.1 Part I para.7, substituted: SI 2009/392 Sch.1
Sch.1 Part I para.8, substituted: SI 2009/392 Sch.1
Sch.1 Part I para.9, substituted: SI 2009/392 Sch.1
Sch.1 Part I para.10, substituted: SI 2009/392 Sch.1
Sch.1 Part I para.11, substituted: SI 2009/392 Sch.1
Sch.1 Part I para.12, substituted: SI 2009/392 Sch.1
Sch.1 Part I para.13, substituted: SI 2009/392 Sch.1
Sch.1 Part I para.14, substituted: SI 2009/392 Sch.1
Sch.1 Part I para.15, substituted: SI 2009/392 Sch.1
Sch.1 Part I para.16, substituted: SI 2009/392 Sch.1
Sch.1 Part I para.17, substituted: SI 2009/392 Sch.1
Sch.1 Part I para.18, substituted: SI 2009/392 Sch.1
Sch.1 Part I para.19, substituted: SI 2009/392 Sch.1
Sch.1 Part I para.20, substituted: SI 2009/392 Sch.1
Sch.1 Part I para.21, substituted: SI 2009/392 Sch.1
Sch.1 Part I para.22, substituted: SI 2009/392 Sch.1
Sch.1 Part II para.1, substituted: SI 2009/392 Sch.1
Sch.1 Part II para.2, substituted: SI 2009/392 Sch.1
Sch.1 Part II para.3, substituted: SI 2009/392 Sch.1
Sch.1 Part II para.4, substituted: SI 2009/392 Sch.1
Sch.1 Part II para.5, substituted: SI 2009/392 Sch.1
Sch.1 Part II para.6, substituted: SI 2009/392 Sch.1
Sch.1 Part II para.7, substituted: SI 2009/392 Sch.1
Sch.1 Part II para.8, substituted: SI 2009/392 Sch.1
Sch.1 Part II para.9, substituted: SI 2009/392 Sch.1
Sch.1 Part II para.10, substituted: SI 2009/392 Sch.1
Sch.1 Part II para.11, substituted: SI 2009/392 Sch.1
Sch.1 Part II para.12, substituted: SI 2009/392 Sch.1
Sch.1 Part II para.13, substituted: SI 2009/392 Sch.1
Sch.1 Part II para.14, substituted: SI 2009/392 Sch.1
Sch.1 Part II para.15, substituted: SI 2009/392 Sch.1
Sch.1 Part II para.16, substituted: SI 2009/392 Sch.1
Sch.1 Part II para.17, substituted: SI 2009/392 Sch.1
Sch.1 Part II para.18, substituted: SI 2009/392 Sch.1
Sch.1 Part II para.19, substituted: SI 2009/392 Sch.1
Sch.1 Part II para.20, substituted: SI 2009/392 Sch.1
Sch.1 Part II para.21, substituted: SI 2009/392 Sch.1
Sch.1 Part II para.22, substituted: SI 2009/392 Sch.1
Sch.1 Part II para.23, substituted: SI 2009/392 Sch.1
Sch.1 Part II para.24, substituted: SI 2009/392 Sch.1
Sch.1 Part II para.25, substituted: SI 2009/392 Sch.1
Sch.1 Part II para.26, substituted: SI 2009/392 Sch.1
Sch.1 Part II para.27, substituted: SI 2009/392 Sch.1
Sch.1 Part II para.28, substituted: SI 2009/392 Sch.1
Sch.1 Part II para.29, substituted: SI 2009/392 Sch.1
Sch.1 Part II para.30, substituted: SI 2009/392 Sch.1
Sch.1 Part II para.31, substituted: SI 2009/392 Sch.1
Sch.1 Part III para.1, substituted: SI 2009/392 Sch.1
Sch.1 Part III para.2, substituted: SI 2009/392 Sch.1
Sch.1 Part III para.3, substituted: SI 2009/392 Sch.1
Sch.1 Part III para.4, substituted: SI 2009/392 Sch.1
Sch.1 Part III para.5, substituted: SI 2009/392 Sch.1
Sch.1 Part III para.6, substituted: SI 2009/392 Sch.1

2007– cont.

376. Products of Animal Origin (Third Country Imports) (Wales) Regulations 2007– *cont.*

Sch.1 Part III para.7, substituted: SI 2009/ 392 Sch.1
Sch.1 Part III para.8, substituted: SI 2009/392 Sch.1
Sch.1 Part III para.9, substituted: SI 2009/ 392 Sch.1
Sch.1 Part III para.10, substituted: SI 2009/ 392 Sch.1
Sch.1 Part IV para.1, substituted: SI 2009/ 392 Sch.1
Sch.1 Part IV para.2, substituted: SI 2009/ 392 Sch.1
Sch.1 Part IV para.3, substituted: SI 2009/ 392 Sch.1
Sch.1 Part V para.1, substituted: SI 2009/ 392 Sch.1
Sch.1 Part V para.2, substituted: SI 2009/ 392 Sch.1
Sch.1 Part V para.3, substituted: SI 2009/ 392 Sch.1
Sch.1 Part V para.4, substituted: SI 2009/ 392 Sch.1
Sch.1 Part VI para.1, substituted: SI 2009/ 392 Sch.1
Sch.1 Part VI para.2, substituted: SI 2009/ 392 Sch.1
Sch.1 Part VII para.1, substituted: SI 2009/ 392 Sch.1
Sch.1 Part VII para.2, substituted: SI 2009/ 392 Sch.1
Sch.1 Part VII para.3, substituted: SI 2009/ 392 Sch.1
Sch.1 Part VIII para.1, substituted: SI 2009/ 392 Sch.1
Sch.1 Part VIII para.2, substituted: SI 2009/ 392 Sch.1
Sch.1 Part VIII para.3, substituted: SI 2009/ 392 Sch.1
Sch.1 Part VIII para.4, substituted: SI 2009/ 392 Sch.1
Sch.1 Part VIII para.5, substituted: SI 2009/ 392 Sch.1
Sch.1 Part VIII para.6, substituted: SI 2009/ 392 Sch.1
Sch.1 Part VIII para.7, substituted: SI 2009/ 392 Sch.1
Sch.1 Part VIII para.8, substituted: SI 2009/ 392 Sch.1
Sch.1 Part VIII para.9, substituted: SI 2009/ 392 Sch.1
Sch.1 Part VIII para.10, substituted: SI 2009/ 392 Sch.1
Sch.1 Part VIII para.11, substituted: SI 2009/ 392 Sch.1
Sch.1 Part VIII para.12, substituted: SI 2009/ 392 Sch.1
Sch.1 Part VIII para.13, substituted: SI 2009/ 392 Sch.1
Sch.1 Part VIII para.14, substituted: SI 2009/ 392 Sch.1
Sch.1 Part VIII para.15, substituted: SI 2009/ 392 Sch.1
Sch.1 Part VIII para.16, substituted: SI 2009/ 392 Sch.1
Sch.1 Part VIII para.17, substituted: SI 2009/ 392 Sch.1
Sch.1 Part VIII para.18, substituted: SI 2009/ 392 Sch.1
Sch.1 Part VIII para.19, substituted: SI 2009/ 392 Sch.1
Sch.1 Part VIII para.20, substituted: SI 2009/ 392 Sch.1
Sch.1 Part IX para.1, substituted: SI 2009/ 392 Sch.1
Sch.1 Part IX para.2, substituted: SI 2009/ 392 Sch.1
Sch.1 Part IX para.3, substituted: SI 2009/ 392 Sch.1
Sch.1 Part IX para.4, substituted: SI 2009/ 392 Sch.1
Sch.1 Part IX para.5, substituted: SI 2009/ 392 Sch.1
Sch.1 Part IX para.6, substituted: SI 2009/ 392 Sch.1
Sch.1 Part IX para.7, substituted: SI 2009/ 392 Sch.1
Sch.1 Part IX para.8, substituted: SI 2009/ 392 Sch.1
Sch.1 Part IX para.9, substituted: SI 2009/ 392 Sch.1
Sch.1 Part IX para.10, substituted: SI 2009/ 392 Sch.1
Sch.1 Part IX para.11, substituted: SI 2009/ 392 Sch.1
Sch.1 Part IX para.12, substituted: SI 2009/ 392 Sch.1
Sch.1 Part IX para.13, substituted: SI 2009/ 392 Sch.1
Sch.1 Part IX para.14, substituted: SI 2009/ 392 Sch.1
Sch.1 Part IX para.15, substituted: SI 2009/ 392 Sch.1
Sch.1 Part IX para.16, substituted: SI 2009/ 392 Sch.1
Sch.1 Part IX para.17, substituted: SI 2009/ 392 Sch.1
Sch.1 Part X para.1, substituted: SI 2009/ 392 Sch.1
Sch.1 Part X para.2, substituted: SI 2009/ 392 Sch.1
Sch.1 Part X para.3, substituted: SI 2009/ 392 Sch.1
Sch.1 Part X para.4, substituted: SI 2009/ 392 Sch.1
Sch.1 Part X para.5, substituted: SI 2009/ 392 Sch.1
Sch.1 Part X para.6, substituted: SI 2009/ 392 Sch.1
Sch.1 Part X para.7, substituted: SI 2009/ 392 Sch.1
Sch.1 Part X para.8, substituted: SI 2009/ 392 Sch.1
Sch.1 Part X para.9, substituted: SI 2009/ 392 Sch.1
Sch.1 Part X para.10, substituted: SI 2009/ 392 Sch.1
Sch.1 Part X para.11, substituted: SI 2009/ 392 Sch.1
Sch.1 Part X para.12, substituted: SI 2009/ 392 Sch.1
Sch.1 Part X para.13, substituted: SI 2009/ 392 Sch.1

2007– cont.

376. Products of Animal Origin (Third Country Imports) (Wales) Regulations 2007– *cont.*

Sch.1 Part X para.14, substituted: SI 2009/ 392 Sch.1
Sch.1 Part X para.15, substituted: SI 2009/ 392 Sch.1
Sch.1 Part X para.16, substituted: SI 2009/ 392 Sch.1
Sch.1 Part X para.17, substituted: SI 2009/ 392 Sch.1
Sch.1 Part X para.18, substituted: SI 2009/ 392 Sch.1
Sch.1 Part X para.19, substituted: SI 2009/ 392 Sch.1
Sch.1 Part X para.20, substituted: SI 2009/ 392 Sch.1
Sch.1 Part X para.21, substituted: SI 2009/ 392 Sch.1
Sch.1 Part X para.22, substituted: SI 2009/ 392 Sch.1
Sch.1 Part X para.23, substituted: SI 2009/ 392 Sch.1
Sch.1 Part X para.24, substituted: SI 2009/ 392 Sch.1
Sch.1 Part X para.25, substituted: SI 2009/ 392 Sch.1
Sch.1 Part X para.26, substituted: SI 2009/ 392 Sch.1
Sch.1 Part X para.27, substituted: SI 2009/ 392 Sch.1
Sch.1 Part X para.28, substituted: SI 2009/ 392 Sch.1
Sch.1 Part X para.29, substituted: SI 2009/ 392 Sch.1
Sch.1 Part X para.30, substituted: SI 2009/ 392 Sch.1
Sch.1 Part X para.31, substituted: SI 2009/ 392 Sch.1
Sch.1 Part X para.32, substituted: SI 2009/ 392 Sch.1
Sch.1 Part X para.33, substituted: SI 2009/ 392 Sch.1
Sch.1 Part X para.34, substituted: SI 2009/ 392 Sch.1
Sch.1 Part X para.35, substituted: SI 2009/ 392 Sch.1
Sch.1 Part X para.36, substituted: SI 2009/ 392 Sch.1
Sch.1 Part X para.37, substituted: SI 2009/ 392 Sch.1
Sch.1 Part X para.38, substituted: SI 2009/ 392 Sch.1
Sch.1 Part X para.39, substituted: SI 2009/ 392 Sch.1
Sch.1 Part X para.40, substituted: SI 2009/ 392 Sch.1
Sch.1 Part X para.41, substituted: SI 2009/ 392 Sch.1
Sch.1 Part X para.42, substituted: SI 2009/ 392 Sch.1
Sch.1 Part X para.43, substituted: SI 2009/ 392 Sch.1
Sch.1 Part X para.44, substituted: SI 2009/ 392 Sch.1
Sch.1 Part X para.45, substituted: SI 2009/ 392 Sch.1
Sch.1 Part X para.46, substituted: SI 2009/ 392 Sch.1
Sch.1 Part X para.47, substituted: SI 2009/ 392 Sch.1
Sch.1 Part X para.48, substituted: SI 2009/ 392 Sch.1
Sch.1 Part X para.49, substituted: SI 2009/ 392 Sch.1
Sch.1 Part X para.50, substituted: SI 2009/ 392 Sch.1
Sch.1 Part X para.51, substituted: SI 2009/ 392 Sch.1
Sch.1 Part X para.52, substituted: SI 2009/ 392 Sch.1
Sch.1 Part X para.53, substituted: SI 2009/ 392 Sch.1
Sch.1 Part X para.54, substituted: SI 2009/ 392 Sch.1
Sch.1 Part X para.55, substituted: SI 2009/ 392 Sch.1
Sch.1 Part X para.56, substituted: SI 2009/ 392 Sch.1
Sch.1 Part X para.57, substituted: SI 2009/ 392 Sch.1
Sch.1 Part X para.58, substituted: SI 2009/ 392 Sch.1
Sch.1 Part X para.59, substituted: SI 2009/ 392 Sch.1
Sch.1 Part X para.60, substituted: SI 2009/ 392 Sch.1
Sch.1 Part X para.61, substituted: SI 2009/ 392 Sch.1
Sch.1 Part X para.62, substituted: SI 2009/ 392 Sch.1
Sch.1 Part X para.63, substituted: SI 2009/ 392 Sch.1
Sch.1 Part X para.64, substituted: SI 2009/ 392 Sch.1
Sch.1 Part X para.65, substituted: SI 2009/ 392 Sch.1
Sch.1 Part X para.66, substituted: SI 2009/ 392 Sch.1
Sch.1 Part X para.67, substituted: SI 2009/ 392 Sch.1
Sch.1 Part X para.68, substituted: SI 2009/ 392 Sch.1
Sch.1 Part X para.69, substituted: SI 2009/ 392 Sch.1
Sch.1 Part X para.70, substituted: SI 2009/ 392 Sch.1
Sch.1 Part X para.71, substituted: SI 2009/ 392 Sch.1
Sch.1 Part X para.72, substituted: SI 2009/ 392 Sch.1
Sch.1 Part X para.73, substituted: SI 2009/ 392 Sch.1
Sch.1 Part X para.74, substituted: SI 2009/ 392 Sch.1
Sch.1 Part X para.75, substituted: SI 2009/ 392 Sch.1
Sch.1 Part X para.76, substituted: SI 2009/ 392 Sch.1
Sch.1 Part X para.77, substituted: SI 2009/ 392 Sch.1
Sch.1 Part X para.78, substituted: SI 2009/ 392 Sch.1
Sch.1 Part X para.79, substituted: SI 2009/ 392 Sch.1

376. Products of Animal Origin (Third Country Imports) (Wales) Regulations 2007– *cont.*
Sch.1 Part X para.80, substituted: SI 2009/392 Sch.1
Sch.1 Part X para.81, substituted: SI 2009/392 Sch.1
Sch.1 Part X para.82, substituted: SI 2009/392 Sch.1
Sch.1 Part X para.83, substituted: SI 2009/392 Sch.1
Sch.1 Part X para.84, substituted: SI 2009/392 Sch.1
Sch.1 Part X para.85, substituted: SI 2009/392 Sch.1
Sch.1 Part X para.86, substituted: SI 2009/392 Sch.1
Sch.1 Part X para.87, substituted: SI 2009/392 Sch.1
Sch.1 Part X para.88, substituted: SI 2009/392 Sch.1
Sch.1 Part X para.89, substituted: SI 2009/392 Sch.1
Sch.1 Part X para.90, substituted: SI 2009/392 Sch.1
Sch.1 Part X para.91, substituted: SI 2009/392 Sch.1
Sch.1 Part X para.92, substituted: SI 2009/392 Sch.1
Sch.1 Part X para.93, substituted: SI 2009/392 Sch.1
Sch.1 Part X para.94, substituted: SI 2009/392 Sch.1
Sch.1 Part X para.95, substituted: SI 2009/392 Sch.1
Sch.1 Part X para.96, substituted: SI 2009/392 Sch.1
Sch.1 Part X para.97, substituted: SI 2009/392 Sch.1
Sch.1 Part X para.98, substituted: SI 2009/392 Sch.1
Sch.1 Part X para.99, substituted: SI 2009/392 Sch.1
Sch.1 Part X para.100, substituted: SI 2009/392 Sch.1
Sch.1 Part X para.101, substituted: SI 2009/392 Sch.1
Sch.1 Part X para.102, substituted: SI 2009/392 Sch.1
Sch.1 Part X para.103, substituted: SI 2009/392 Sch.1
Sch.1 Part X para.104, substituted: SI 2009/392 Sch.1
Sch.1 Part X para.105, substituted: SI 2009/392 Sch.1
Sch.1 Part X para.106, substituted: SI 2009/392 Sch.1
Sch.1 Part X para.107, substituted: SI 2009/392 Sch.1
Sch.1 Part X para.108, substituted: SI 2009/392 Sch.1
Sch.1 Part X para.109, substituted: SI 2009/392 Sch.1
Sch.1 Part X para.110, substituted: SI 2009/392 Sch.1
Sch.1 Part X para.111, substituted: SI 2009/392 Sch.1
Sch.1 Part X para.112, substituted: SI 2009/392 Sch.1
Sch.1 Part X para.113, substituted: SI 2009/392 Sch.1
Sch.1 Part X para.114, substituted: SI 2009/392 Sch.1
Sch.1 Part X para.115, substituted: SI 2009/392 Sch.1
Sch.1 Part X para.116, substituted: SI 2009/392 Sch.1
Sch.1 Part X para.117, substituted: SI 2009/392 Sch.1
Sch.1 Part X para.118, substituted: SI 2009/392 Sch.1
Sch.1 Part XI para.1, substituted: SI 2009/392 Sch.1

385. Local Government (Best Value Authorities) (Power to Trade) (England) (Amendment) Order 2007
revoked: SI 2009/2393 Art.3

391. Criminal Justice Act 2003 (Commencement No.8 and Transitional and Saving Provisions) (Amendment) Order 2007
revoked: SI 2009/616 Art.3

397. Local Authorities (Alternative Arrangements) (Wales) Regulations 2007
Sch.1, revoked: SI 2009/2993 Reg.3
Sch.2 para.18, substituted: SI 2009/2993 Reg.4
Sch.2 para.24, substituted: SI 2009/2993 Reg.4
Sch.3, amended: SI 2009/2993 Reg.5

399. Local Authorities (Executive Arrangements) (Functions and Responsibilities) (Wales) Regulations 2007
Sch.1, revoked: SI 2009/2983 Reg.3
Sch.2 para.18, substituted: SI 2009/2983 Reg.4
Sch.2 para.24, substituted: SI 2009/2983 Reg.4
Sch.3, amended: SI 2009/2983 Reg.5

441. Royal Pharmaceutical Society of Great Britain (Registration Rules) Order of Council 2007
Sch.1, added: SI 2009/1182 Sch.4 para.30
Sch.1, amended: SI 2009/1182 Sch.4 para.26, Sch.4 para.30, Sch.4 para.45

441. Royal Pharmaceutical Society of Great Britain (Registration Rules) Order of Council 2007– *cont.*
Sch.1, revoked: SI 2009/1182 Sch.4 para.30

442. Royal Pharmaceutical Society of Great Britain (Fitness to Practise and Disqualification etc Rules) Order of Council 2007
Sch.1, added: SI 2009/1182 Sch.4 para.27
Sch.1, amended: SI 2009/1182 Sch.4 para.27
Sch.1, revoked: SI 2009/1182 Sch.4 para.31

448. Diseases of Animals (Approved Disinfectants) (England) Order 2007
Art.3, applied: SI 2009/839 Art.2

480. Aylesbury Vale (Parish Electoral Arrangements and Electoral Changes) Order 2007
Sch.4, amended: SI 2009/536 Art.2

529. Cattle Identification Regulations 2007
Sch.2, applied: SI 2009/138 Sch.5 para.1

556. Commission for Social Care Inspection (Fees and Frequency of Inspections) Regulations 2007
Reg.4, amended: SI 2009/462 Sch.2 para.8
Reg.6, amended: SI 2009/462 Sch.2 para.8

561. Royal Pharmaceutical Society of Great Britain (Fitness to Practise and Registration Appeals Committees and their Advisers Rules) Order of Council 2007
Sch.1, amended: SI 2009/1182 Sch.4 para.32
Sch.1, revoked: SI 2009/1182 Sch.4 para.32

605. Vehicle Drivers (Certificates of Professional Competence) Regulations 2007
applied: SI 2009/1885 Art.2, Sch.4 para.1
Reg.6A, amended: SI 2009/1885 Sch.2 para.11
Reg.10, referred to: SI 2009/491 Sch.1 Part 2
Reg.11, applied: SI 2009/483 Art.2
Reg.11, referred to: SI 2009/491 Sch.1 Part 2, SI 2009/492 Sch.1 Part 2
Reg.13, referred to: SI 2009/491 Sch.1 Part 2

633. Common Agricultural Policy Single Payment Scheme (Set-aside) (England) (Amendment) Regulations 2007
revoked: SI 2009/3102 Reg.9

650. Royal Air Force Terms of Service Regulations 2007
varied: SI 2009/1059 Art.191
Reg.2, amended: SI 2009/831 Reg.23, SI 2009/1089 Reg.23
Reg.2, applied: SI 2009/831 Sch.1 para.10
Reg.2, revoked (in part): SI 2009/831 Reg.23, SI 2009/1089 Reg.23
Reg.3, amended: SI 2009/831 Reg.24, SI 2009/1089 Reg.24
Reg.3, revoked (in part): SI 2009/831 Reg.24, SI 2009/1089 Reg.24
Reg.8, amended: SI 2009/831 Reg.25, SI 2009/1089 Reg.25
Reg.8, revoked (in part): SI 2009/831 Reg.25, SI 2009/1089 Reg.25
Reg.12, amended: SI 2009/831 Reg.26, SI 2009/1089 Reg.26
Reg.17, revoked: SI 2009/831 Reg.27, SI 2009/1089 Reg.27
Sch.1, revoked: SI 2009/831 Reg.27, SI 2009/1089 Reg.27
Sch.2 para.1, amended: SI 2009/831 Reg.28, SI 2009/1089 Reg.28

675. Judicial Pensions and Retirement Act 1993 (Addition of Qualifying Judicial Offices) Order 2007
Art.2, revoked: SI 2009/1834 Sch.3

691. Minibus and Other Section 19 Permit Buses (Amendment) Regulations 2007
revoked: SI 2009/365 Sch.1

694. Her Majesty's Chief Inspector of Education, Children's Services and Skills (Fees and Frequency of Inspections) (Children's Homes etc.) Regulations 2007
applied: SI 2009/2724 Reg.5
Reg.16, amended: SI 2009/2724 Reg.2
Reg.17, amended: SI 2009/2724 Reg.3
Reg.18, amended: SI 2009/2724 Reg.4

710. Courts-Martial Appeal (Amendment) Rules 2007
revoked: SI 2009/2657 Sch.5

723. Childcare (Disqualification) Regulations 2007
revoked: SI 2009/1547 Reg.3

734. Rules of the Air Regulations 2007
applied: SI 2009/3015 Art.107, Art.109, Art.211, Sch.4 para.5, Sch.7 Part A
Sch.1, added: SI 2009/2169 Reg.2
Sch.1, substituted: SI 2009/2169 Reg.3

740. Tuberculosis (England) Order 2007
Art.3, amended: SI 2009/2713 Art.2
Art.5, amended: SI 2009/2713 Art.2
Art.6, amended: SI 2009/2713 Art.2
Art.9, amended: SI 2009/2713 Art.2
Art.13, amended: SI 2009/2713 Art.2

765. Smoke-free (Exemptions and Vehicles) Regulations 2007
Reg.5, see *R. (on the application of G) v Nottinghamshire Healthcare NHS Trust* [2009] EWCA Civ 795, [2009] H.R.L.R. 31 (CA (Civ Div)), Lord Clarke of Stone-cum-Ebony MR
Reg.10, see *R. (on the application of G) v Nottinghamshire Healthcare NHS Trust* [2009] EWCA Civ 795, [2009] H.R.L.R. 31 (CA (Civ Div)), Lord Clarke of Stone-cum-Ebony MR

785. National Insurance Contributions (Application of Part 7 of the Finance Act 2004) Regulations 2007
Reg.2, amended: SI 2009/208 Reg.3
Reg.4, amended: SI 2009/208 Reg.3
Reg.5A, amended: SI 2009/208 Reg.3
Reg.5A, applied: SI 2009/275 Art.3
Reg.7A, amended: SI 2009/208 Reg.3
Reg.7A, applied: SI 2009/275 Art.3
Reg.10, applied: SI 2009/612 Reg.1
Reg.11, applied: SI 2009/612 Reg.1
Reg.11A, applied: SI 2009/612 Reg.1
Reg.12B, amended: SI 2009/208 Reg.3
Reg.12B, applied: SI 2009/275 Art.3
Reg.12C, amended: SI 2009/208 Reg.3
Reg.12C, applied: SI 2009/275 Art.3
Reg.13A, revoked: SI 2009/208 Reg.3
Reg.15, revoked (in part): SI 2009/208 Reg.3
Reg.17, amended: SI 2009/612 Reg.2

807. Immigration and Nationality (Fees) Order 2007
Art.2, amended: SI 2009/420 Art.2
Art.3, amended: SI 2009/420 Art.2
Art.3, applied: SI 2009/421 Reg.3, Reg.4, Reg.12, Reg.15, Reg.16, Reg.17, Reg.18, Reg.19, Reg.20, Reg.21, Reg.22, Reg.23, Reg.24, Reg.29, Reg.30, SI 2009/816 Reg.3, Reg.4, Reg.5, Reg.6, Reg.7,

807. Immigration and Nationality (Fees) Order 2007– *cont.*
Art.3, applied:–*cont.*
Reg.8, Reg.9, Reg.10, Reg.20, Reg.21, Reg.23, Reg.24, Reg.25, Reg.28, Reg.30
Art.4, applied: SI 2009/421 Reg.26, Reg.27, Reg.28, SI 2009/816 Reg.22
Art.5, applied: SI 2009/421 Reg.25, SI 2009/816 Reg.29
Art.6, added: SI 2009/420 Art.2
Art.6, applied: SI 2009/421 Reg.31

808. Private Security Industry Act 2001 (Approved Contractor Scheme) Regulations 2007
Reg.1, amended: SI 2009/633 Reg.2
Reg.1, revoked (in part): SI 2009/633 Reg.2

810. Private Security Industry Act 2001 (Licences) Regulations 2007
Reg.1, revoked (in part): SI 2009/634 Reg.2
Reg.6, amended: SI 2009/634 Reg.2
Sch.1, amended: SI 2009/2398 Sch.1
Sch.1, referred to: SI 2009/2398 Reg.2

840. Contaminants in Food (Wales) Regulations 2007
revoked: SI 2009/1386 Reg.7

852. Mental Capacity Act 2005 (Independent Mental Capacity Advocates) (Wales) Regulations 2007
Reg.2, amended: SI 2009/266 Reg.18
Reg.5, amended: SI 2009/266 Reg.19

855. Motor Vehicles (EC Type Approval) (Amendment) Regulations 2007
revoked: SI 2009/717 Sch.1

865. Pension Protection Fund (Closed Schemes) Regulations 2007
Sch.1 Part 1 para.1, amended: SI 2009/451 Reg.6

871. Producer Responsibility Obligations (Packaging Waste) Regulations 2007
applied: SI 2009/890 Reg.52, Sch.3 para.7
Reg.38, amended: SSI 2009/248 Sch.1 para.19

912. Policing (Miscellaneous Provisions) (Northern Ireland) Order 2007
Art.6, revoked (in part): 2009 c.26 Sch.8 Part 13
Sch.4 para.1, revoked (in part): 2009 c.26 Sch.8 Part 13
Sch.4 para.2, revoked: 2009 c.26 Sch.8 Part 13
Sch.4 para.3, revoked: 2009 c.26 Sch.8 Part 13
Sch.4 para.4, revoked: 2009 c.26 Sch.8 Part 13
Sch.4 para.5, revoked: 2009 c.26 Sch.8 Part 13

913. Electricity (Single Wholesale Market) (Northern Ireland) Order 2007
Art.3, amended: SI 2009/1941 Sch.1 para.268

916. Road Traffic (Northern Ireland) Order 2007
Art.81, revoked: 2009 c.26 Sch.7 para.132, Sch.8 Part 13

934. Regulation of Investigatory Powers (Authorisations Extending to Scotland) Order 2007
Sch.1, amended: SI 2009/2748 Sch.1 para.35, SI 2009/3403 Art.2

936. Immigration and Nationality (Cost Recovery Fees) Regulations 2007
revoked: SI 2009/421 Reg.33

937. Scottish Parliament (Elections etc.) Order 2007
applied: SSI 2009/35 Reg.12
Appendix 1, amended: SI 2009/1978 Art.14
Art.46, amended: SI 2009/1978 Art.3
Art.50, amended: SI 2009/1978 Art.4
Art.52, amended: SI 2009/1978 Art.5
Art.52, revoked (in part): SI 2009/1978 Art.5
Art.53, amended: SI 2009/1978 Art.6

2007– cont.

937. Scottish Parliament (Elections etc.) Order 2007– cont.

Art.55, amended: SI 2009/ 1978 Art.7

Art.55, revoked (in part): SI 2009/ 1978 Art.7

Sch.2, added: SI 2009/ 1978 Art.9

Sch.2, amended: SI 2009/ 1978 Art.8, Art.9, Art.10, Art.11

Sch.2, revoked: SI 2009/ 1978 Art.9, Art.10, Art.11

Sch.2, substituted: SI 2009/ 1978 Art.10

Sch.3 para.3, amended: SI 2009/ 1182 Sch.4 para.44

Sch.3 para.3, revoked (in part): SI 2009/ 1182 Sch.4 para.15

Sch.5 Part II para.18, amended: SI 2009/ 1978 Art.12

Sch.5 Part II para.18, substituted: SI 2009/ 1978 Art.12

Sch.5 Part III para.36, amended: SI 2009/ 1978 Art.13

Sch.5 Part III para.36, substituted: SI 2009/ 1978 Art.13

948. Loan Relationships and Derivative Contracts (Disregard and Bringing into Account of Profits and Losses) (Amendment) Regulations 2007

revoked: 2009 c.4 Sch.3 Part 1

950. Loan Relationships and Derivative Contracts (Change of Accounting Practice) (Amendment) Regulations 2007

revoked: 2009 c.4 Sch.3 Part 1

953. Local Health Boards (Constitution, Membership and Procedures) (Wales) (Amendment) Regulations 2007

revoked: SI 2009/ 779 Reg.22

957. School Governance (Constitution) (England) Regulations 2007

Sch.6 para.9, amended: SI 2009/ 1924 Reg.10

Sch.6 para.11, amended: SI 2009/ 1924 Reg.10

958. School Governance (New Schools) (England) Regulations 2007

Sch.2 para.8, amended: SI 2009/ 1924 Reg.11

Sch.2 para.10, amended: SI 2009/ 1924 Reg.11

960. School Governance (Federations) (England) Regulations 2007

Reg.8, amended: SI 2009/ 1556 Reg.4

Reg.9, amended: SI 2009/ 1556 Reg.4

Reg.37, amended: SI 2009/ 1556 Reg.4

Reg.42, amended: SI 2009/ 1556 Reg.4

991. Energy Performance of Buildings (Certificates and Inspections) (England and Wales) Regulations 2007

varied: SI 2009/ 3019 Art.6

Reg.9, applied: SI 2009/ 3019 Art.4

Reg.14, amended: SI 2009/ 1900 Reg.2

Reg.35B, substituted: SI 2009/ 1900 Reg.2

Reg.37, substituted: SI 2009/ 1900 Reg.2

1050. Corporation Tax (Taxation of Films) (Transitional Provisions) Regulations 2007

revoked: 2009 c.4 Sch.3 Part 1

1066. Atomic Weapons Establishment (AWE) Aldermaston Byelaws 2007

see *Tabernacle v Secretary of State for Defence* [2009] EWCA Civ 23, Times, February 25, 2009 (CA (Civ Div)), Laws, L.J.

Reg.7, see *Tabernacle v Secretary of State for Defence* [2009] EWCA Civ 23, Times, February 25, 2009 (CA (Civ Div)), Laws, L.J.

1072. Firefighters Pension Scheme (Wales) Order 2007

Sch.1, added: SI 2009/ 1225 Sch.1 para.3, Sch.1 para.4, Sch.1 para.6, Sch.1 para.9

1072. Firefighters Pension Scheme (Wales) Order 2007– cont.

Sch.1, amended: SI 2009/ 1225 Sch.1 para.1, Sch.1 para.2, Sch.1 para.4, Sch.1 para.5, Sch.1 para.7, Sch.1 para.8, Sch.1 para.9, Sch.1 para.10, Sch.1 para.12, Sch.1 para.13

Sch.1, revoked: SI 2009/ 1225 Sch.1 para.10

Sch.1, substituted: SI 2009/ 1225 Sch.1 para.2, Sch.1 para.3, Sch.1 para.5, Sch.1 para.6, Sch.1 para.7, Sch.1 para.9, Sch.1 para.11

1078. Renewables Obligation Order 2006 (Amendment) Order 2007

revoked: SI 2009/ 785 Art.61

1093. Companies Act 2006 (Commencement No.2, Consequential Amendments, Transitional Provisions and Savings) Order 2007

Sch.4 Part 1 para.7, revoked: SI 2009/ 1941 Sch.2

Sch.4 Part 1 para.8, revoked: SI 2009/ 1941 Sch.2

Sch.4 Part 1 para.17, revoked: SI 2009/ 1941 Sch.2

Sch.4 Part 1 para.18, revoked: SI 2009/ 1941 Sch.2

Sch.4 Part 1 para.19, revoked: SI 2009/ 1941 Sch.2

Sch.4 Part 1 para.20, revoked: SI 2009/ 1941 Sch.2

Sch.4 Part 2 para.31, revoked: SI 2009/ 1941 Sch.2

Sch.4 Part 2 para.32, revoked: SI 2009/ 1941 Sch.2

1098. Police, Public Order and Criminal Justice (Scotland) Act 2006 (Consequential Provisions and Modifications) Order 2007

Art.1, revoked (in part): 2009 c.26 s.106, Sch.8 Part 11

Art.5, revoked: 2009 c.26 s.106, Sch.8 Part 11

1104. National Health Service (Travelling Expenses and Remission of Charges) (Wales) Regulations 2007

Reg.2, amended: SI 2009/ 1824 Sch.1 para.8

Reg.5, amended: SI 2009/ 709 Reg.2

Reg.11, amended: SI 2009/ 1824 Sch.1 para.8

Reg.14, amended: SI 2009/ 54 Reg.2

Sch.1, amended: SI 2009/ 54 Reg.3, Reg.4, SI 2009/ 709 Reg.3, SI 2009/ 2365 Reg.2

1158. Immigration and Nationality (Fees) Regulations 2007

revoked: SI 2009/ 816 Reg.32

1166. Local Government Pension Scheme (Benefits, Membership and Contributions) Regulations 2007

Reg.1, amended: SI 2009/ 3150 Reg.8

Reg.4, amended: SI 2009/ 3150 Reg.9

Reg.10, substituted: SI 2009/ 3150 Reg.10

Reg.12A, added: SI 2009/ 3150 Reg.11

Reg.12B, added: SI 2009/ 3150 Reg.11

Reg.13, amended: SI 2009/ 3150 Reg.12

Reg.13A, added: SI 2009/ 3150 Reg.13

Reg.14A, added: SI 2009/ 3150 Reg.14

Reg.27, amended: SI 2009/ 3150 Reg.15

Reg.38, substituted: SI 2009/ 3150 Reg.16

Reg.40, revoked: SI 2009/ 1025 Reg.2

1174. Criminal Defence Service (Funding) Order 2007

Art.2, amended: SI 2009/ 1843 Art.3, SI 2009/ 2468 Art.10

Art.3, amended: SI 2009/ 2468 Art.10

Art.4, amended: SI 2009/ 2468 Art.10

Art.6, amended: SI 2009/ 1843 Art.4

Art.9, amended: SI 2009/ 2468 Art.10

Art.10, amended: SI 2009/ 1843 Art.5

Art.10A, added: SI 2009/ 1843 Art.6

Art.10A, revoked: SI 2009/ 1843 Art.6

Art.14, amended: SI 2009/ 1843 Art.7

Art.29, amended: SI 2009/ 1843 Art.8

Sch.1 Part 4 para.8, amended: SI 2009/ 1843 Art.9

461

2007– cont.

1174. Criminal Defence Service (Funding) Order 2007– *cont.*

Sch.1 Part 4 para.9, amended: SI 2009/1843 Art.10

Sch.1 Part 4 para.11, amended: SI 2009/2086 Art.3, Art.4

Sch.1 Part 4 para.19, amended: SI 2009/2086 Art.5

Sch.1 para.5, see *R. v Agbobu (Costs)* [2009] 2 Costs L.R. 374 (Sup Ct Costs Office), Costs Judge Gordon-Saker

Sch.1 Part 5 para.20, amended: SI 2009/1843 Art.11

Sch.1 Part 5 para.24A, added: SI 2009/1843 Art.12

Sch.1 Part 6, referred to: SI 2009/3328 Reg.9

Sch.2 Part 1 para.2, amended: SI 2009/1843 Art.14

Sch.2 Part 1 para.2, revoked (in part): SI 2009/1843 Art.13

Sch.2 Part 2 para.7, amended: SI 2009/1843 Art.15, Art.16

Sch.2 Part 2 para.8, amended: SI 2009/1843 Art.17

Sch.2 Part 2 para.10, amended: SI 2009/1843 Art.18, Art.19, Art.20, Art.21, Art.22

Sch.2 Part 3 para.12A, added: SI 2009/1843 Art.23

Sch.2 Part 3 para.14, amended: SI 2009/1843 Art.25, Art.26, Art.27

Sch.2 Part 3 para.14, revoked (in part): SI 2009/1843 Art.24

Sch.2 Part 3 para.15, amended: SI 2009/1843 Art.28

Sch.2 Part 4 para.25, amended: SI 2009/1843 Art.29

Sch.2 Part 4 para.25, revoked (in part): SI 2009/1843 Art.29

Sch.2 para.12, see *R. v Sturmer (Costs)* [2009] 2 Costs L.R. 364 (Sup Ct Costs Office), Costs Judge Gordon-Saker

Sch.2 para.16, see *R. v Agbobu (Costs)* [2009] 2 Costs L.R. 374 (Sup Ct Costs Office), Costs Judge Gordon-Saker

1253. Lasting Powers of Attorney, Enduring Powers of Attorney and Public Guardian Regulations 2007

Reg.18, amended: SI 2009/1884 Reg.3

Reg.32, amended: SI 2009/1884 Reg.4

Sch.1, referred to: SI 2009/1884 Reg.2

Sch.1 Part 1, substituted: SI 2009/1884 Sch.1

Sch.1 Part 2, substituted: SI 2009/1884 Sch.1

1257. Service Charges (Summary of Rights and Obligations, and Transitional Provision) (England) Regulations 2007

Reg.3, amended: SI 2009/1307 Sch.2 para.119

1258. Administration Charges (Summary of Rights and Obligations) (England) Regulations 2007

Reg.2, amended: SI 2009/1307 Sch.2 para.120

1287. School Organisation (Requirements as to Foundations) (England) Regulations 2007

Sch.1 para.1, amended: SI 2009/1924 Reg.12

1288. School Organisation (Establishment and Discontinuance of Schools) (England) Regulations 2007

varied: SI 2009/276 Reg.3

Reg.2, amended: SI 2009/2984 Reg.3

Reg.4, amended: SI 2009/1556 Reg.5

Reg.9, amended: SI 2009/2984 Reg.4

Reg.12, amended: SI 2009/1556 Reg.5

Reg.12A, added: SI 2009/1556 Reg.5

Reg.13, amended: SI 2009/1556 Reg.5

Reg.20, see *R. (on the application of Elphinstone) v Westminster City Council* [2008] EWCA Civ 1069, [2009] B.L.G.R. 158 (CA (Civ Div)), Thorpe, L.J.

Reg.20, amended: SI 2009/1556 Reg.5

Sch.2 Part 2 para.41, amended: SI 2009/1556 Reg.5

2007– cont.

1288. School Organisation (Establishment and Discontinuance of Schools) (England) Regulations 2007– *cont.*

Sch.3 Part 2 para.50, amended: SI 2009/1556 Reg.5

Sch.4, see *R. (on the application of Elphinstone) v Westminster City Council* [2008] EWCA Civ 1069, [2009] B.L.G.R. 158 (CA (Civ Div)), Thorpe, L.J.

Sch.4 para.11, see *R. (on the application of Elphinstone) v Westminster City Council* [2008] EWCA Civ 1069, [2009] B.L.G.R. 158 (CA (Civ Div)), Thorpe, L.J.

Sch.4 para.20, amended: SI 2009/1556 Reg.5

Sch.5 Part 4 para.27, amended: SI 2009/1556 Reg.5

Sch.5 Part 6 para.51, amended: SI 2009/1556 Reg.5

Sch.5 Part 7 para.58, revoked: SI 2009/1556 Reg.5

1289. School Organisation (Prescribed Alterations to Maintained Schools) (England) Regulations 2007

varied: SI 2009/276 Reg.3

Sch.1 Part 2 para.15, amended: SI 2009/1556 Reg.6

Sch.2 Part 1 para.2, revoked: SI 2009/1556 Reg.6

Sch.2 Part 2 para.13, revoked: SI 2009/1556 Reg.6

Sch.3 Part 1 para.16, substituted: SI 2009/1556 Reg.6

Sch.3 Part 1 para.25A, amended: SI 2009/1556 Reg.6

Sch.3 Part 2 para.28, amended: SI 2009/1556 Reg.6

Sch.3 Part 2 para.29, amended: SI 2009/1556 Reg.6

Sch.3 Part 2 para.29, revoked (in part): SI 2009/1556 Reg.6

Sch.3 Part 2 para.38, amended: SI 2009/1556 Reg.6

Sch.4 Part 1 para.2, revoked: SI 2009/1556 Reg.6

Sch.4 Part 4 para.19, revoked: SI 2009/1556 Reg.6

Sch.5 Part 1 para.16, substituted: SI 2009/1556 Reg.6

Sch.5 Part 1 para.25A, amended: SI 2009/1556 Reg.6

Sch.5 Part 2 para.28, amended: SI 2009/1556 Reg.6

Sch.5 Part 2 para.29, amended: SI 2009/1556 Reg.6

Sch.5 Part 2 para.29, revoked (in part): SI 2009/1556 Reg.6

Sch.5 Part 2 para.38, amended: SI 2009/1556 Reg.6

1298. Courts-Martial Appeal (Amendment No.2) Rules 2007

revoked: SI 2009/2657 Sch.5

1315. Veterinary Surgery (Artificial Insemination) Order 2007

Art.1, amended: SI 2009/2769 Art.2

Art.3, amended: SI 2009/2769 Art.2

1351. Safeguarding Vulnerable Groups (Northern Ireland) Order 2007

applied: SI 2009/26 Sch.1, SI 2009/263 Art.5, SI 2009/442 Art.5, SI 2009/468 Sch.1, SI 2009/1345 Art.5, SI 2009/1355 Sch.1, SI 2009/1808 Art.5, SI 2009/1813 Sch.1, SI 2009/2722 Reg.3

Art.2, amended: 2009 c.26 s.81

Art.2, applied: SI 2009/1633 Reg.3, SI 2009/2558 Reg.3

Art.5, amended: 2009 c.26 s.81

Art.6, amended: 2009 c.26 s.81

Art.6, applied: SI 2009/12 Art.6A, Art.7A, SI 2009/1797 Art.5

Art.7, applied: SSI 2009/316 Art.2

Art.8, amended: 2009 c.26 s.81

Art.10, amended: 2009 c.26 s.81

Art.19, amended: 2009 c.26 s.81

Art.29, amended: 2009 c.26 s.81

Art.33, revoked (in part): 2009 c.26 s.90, Sch.8 Part 8

2007– cont.

1351. Safeguarding Vulnerable Groups (Northern Ireland) Order 2007– cont.
Art.36A, added: 2009 c.26 s.90
Art.36B, added: 2009 c.26 s.90
Art.36C, added: 2009 c.26 s.90
Art.37, amended: 2009 c.26 s.81
Art.38, amended: 2009 c.26 s.81
Art.39, amended: 2009 c.26 s.81
Art.40, amended: 2009 c.26 s.81
Art.41, amended: 2009 c.26 s.81
Art.42, amended: 2009 c.26 s.81
Art.43, amended: 2009 c.26 s.81
Art.44, amended: 2009 c.26 s.81
Art.45, amended: 2009 c.26 s.81
Art.46, amended: 2009 c.26 s.81, SI 2009/1182 Sch.5 para.13
Art.46, referred to: SI 2009/1182 Art.1
Art.47, amended: 2009 c.26 s.81
Art.48, amended: 2009 c.26 s.81
Art.49, amended: 2009 c.26 s.81
Art.52, amended: 2009 c.26 s.81
Art.52A, added: 2009 c.26 s.91
Sch.1 Part I para.1, amended: 2009 c.26 s.92
Sch.1 Part I para.2, amended: 2009 c.26 s.81, s.92
Sch.1 Part I para.3, amended: 2009 c.26 s.81
Sch.1 Part I para.4, amended: 2009 c.26 s.81
Sch.1 Part I para.5, amended: 2009 c.26 s.81
Sch.1 Part I para.6, amended: 2009 c.26 s.81
Sch.1 Part II para.7, amended: 2009 c.26 s.92
Sch.1 Part II para.8, amended: 2009 c.26 s.81, s.92
Sch.1 Part II para.9, amended: 2009 c.26 s.81
Sch.1 Part II para.10, amended: 2009 c.26 s.81
Sch.1 Part II para.11, amended: 2009 c.26 s.81
Sch.1 Part II para.12, amended: 2009 c.26 s.81
Sch.1 Part III para.13, amended: 2009 c.26 s.81
Sch.1 Part III para.14, amended: 2009 c.26 s.81
Sch.1 Part III para.15, amended: 2009 c.26 s.81
Sch.1 Part III para.16, amended: 2009 c.26 s.81
Sch.1 Part III para.17, amended: 2009 c.26 s.81
Sch.1 Part III para.18, amended: 2009 c.26 s.81
Sch.1 Part III para.19, amended: 2009 c.26 s.81
Sch.1 Part III para.20, amended: 2009 c.26 s.81
Sch.1 Part III para.21, amended: 2009 c.26 s.81
Sch.1 Part III para.23, amended: 2009 c.26 s.81
Sch.1 Part III para.24, amended: 2009 c.26 s.92
Sch.1 Part III para.25, amended: 2009 c.26 s.81
Sch.2 Part I para.4, amended: 2009 c.26 s.81
Sch.2 Part II para.8, amended: 2009 c.26 s.81
Sch.3 Part I para.2, amended: 2009 c.26 s.81
Sch.6 para.1, amended: 2009 c.26 s.81
Sch.6 para.2, amended: 2009 c.26 s.81
Sch.6 para.3, amended: 2009 c.26 s.81

1357. Local Authority Adoption Service (Wales) Regulations 2007
Reg.7, amended: SI 2009/1892 Sch.1 para.19
Reg.9, amended: SI 2009/1892 Sch.1 para.19
Sch.3 para.2, substituted: SI 2009/2541 Reg.8

1509. Control of Cash (Penalties) Regulations 2007
amended: SI 2009/56 Sch.2 para.163
Reg.2, amended: SI 2009/56 Sch.2 para.161
Reg.3, amended: SI 2009/56 Sch.2 para.162
Reg.4, amended: SI 2009/56 Sch.2 para.163
Reg.4, revoked (in part): SI 2009/56 Sch.2 para.163
Reg.4A, added: SI 2009/56 Sch.2 para.164
Reg.4B, added: SI 2009/56 Sch.2 para.164
Reg.4C, added: SI 2009/56 Sch.2 para.164
Reg.4D, added: SI 2009/56 Sch.2 para.164
Reg.4E, added: SI 2009/56 Sch.2 para.164

2007– cont.

1509. Control of Cash (Penalties) Regulations 2007– cont.
Reg.4F, added: SI 2009/56 Sch.2 para.164
Reg.5, substituted: SI 2009/56 Sch.2 para.165
Reg.6, amended: SI 2009/56 Sch.2 para.166
Reg.7, substituted: SI 2009/56 Sch.2 para.167

1518. Marine Works (Environmental Impact Assessment) Regulations 2007
applied: SSI 2009/27 Art.10
Reg.2, amended: SI 2009/2258 Reg.2

1520. Road Tunnel Safety Regulations 2007
Reg.2, amended: SI 2009/64 Reg.3
Reg.5, revoked (in part): SI 2009/64 Reg.4
Reg.9, amended: SI 2009/64 Reg.5
Reg.12, revoked (in part): SI 2009/64 Reg.6
Reg.13, amended: SI 2009/64 Reg.7
Reg.15, amended: SI 2009/64 Reg.8
Reg.20, amended: SI 2009/64 Reg.9
Sch.1, amended: SI 2009/64 Reg.10

1522. Human Fertilisation and Embryology (Quality and Safety) Regulations 2007
Reg.1, amended: SI 2009/1892 Sch.3 para.8

1523. Human Tissue (Quality and Safety for Human Application) Regulations 2007
Reg.5, amended: SI 2009/1892 Sch.3 para.7

1573. Carriage of Dangerous Goods and Use of Transportable Pressure Equipment Regulations 2007
applied: SI 2009/716 Reg.6, Reg.8, SI 2009/1348 Reg.25
revoked: SI 2009/1348 Reg.33
Reg.9, applied: SI 2009/1348 Reg.12
Reg.10, applied: SI 2009/1348 Reg.12
Reg.66, applied: SI 2009/1348 Reg.30
Reg.67, applied: SI 2009/1348 Reg.25
Reg.69, applied: SI 2009/1348 Reg.30
Reg.70, applied: SI 2009/1348 Reg.30
Sch.3 para.5, applied: SI 2009/1348 Reg.14

1619. Housing Benefit and Council Tax Benefit (War Pension Disregards) Regulations 2007
Sch.1 Part 1 para.1, amended: SI 2009/2655 Reg.10
Sch.1 Part 1 para.1, substituted: SI 2009/3389 Reg.2
Sch.1 Part 2 para.2, amended: SI 2009/2655 Reg.10
Sch.1 Part 2 para.2, substituted: SI 2009/3389 Reg.2
Sch.1 Part 2 para.3, amended: SI 2009/2655 Reg.10
Sch.1 Part 2 para.3, revoked: SI 2009/2655 Reg.10
Sch.1 Part 2 para.3, substituted: SI 2009/3389 Reg.2

1631. Addition of Vitamins, Minerals and Other Substances (England) Regulations 2007
Reg.2, amended: SI 2009/3251 Reg.3

1655. Civil Jurisdiction and Judgments Regulations 2007
Sch.1 Part 1 para.16, revoked: 2009 c.24 Sch.7 Part 1

1667. Home Information Pack (No.2) Regulations 2007
Reg.14, amended: SI 2009/34 Reg.3

1681. Parliamentary Constituencies (England) Order 2007
Sch.1, amended: SI 2009/698 Sch.1

1683. Education (Student Loans) (Repayment) (Amendment) Regulations 2007
revoked: SI 2009/470 Sch.1

1709. Secure Training Centre (Amendment) Rules 2007
see *R. (on the application of C) v Secretary of State for Justice* [2008] EWCA Civ 882, [2009] Q.B. 657 (CA (Civ Div)), Buxton, L.J.

1744. Court of Protection Rules 2007

Part 3 r.6, amended: SI 2009/582 r.3, SI 2009/3348 Art.19

Part 8 r.51, amended: SI 2009/582 r.4

Part 10A r.82A, added: SI 2009/582 r.5

r.90, see *Independent News and Media Ltd v A* [2009] EWHC 2858 (Fam), Times, November 17, 2009 (Fam Div), Hedley, J.

r.91, see *Independent News and Media Ltd v A* [2009] EWHC 2858 (Fam), Times, November 17, 2009 (Fam Div), Hedley, J.

r.93, see *Independent News and Media Ltd v A* [2009] EWHC 2858 (Fam), Times, November 17, 2009 (Fam Div), Hedley, J.

1745. Court of Protection Fees Order 2007

Art.7, amended: SI 2009/513 Art.3

Art.7, revoked (in part): SI 2009/513 Art.3

Art.8, amended: SI 2009/513 Art.4

Sch.1, amended: SI 2009/513 Art.5

1771. Early Years Foundation Stage (Welfare Requirements) Regulations 2007

Reg.3, amended: SI 2009/1549 Reg.3

Reg.8A, added: SI 2009/1549 Reg.4

1777. Gambling Act 2005 (Limits on Prize Gaming) Regulations 2007

revoked: SI 2009/1272 Reg.4

1778. Miscellaneous Food Additives and the Sweeteners in Food (Amendment) (England) Regulations 2007

Reg.5, applied: SI 2009/3238 Reg.10

Reg.6, applied: SI 2009/3238 Reg.10

Reg.8, applied: SI 2009/3238 Reg.10

1842. Offshore Marine Conservation (Natural Habitats, &c.) Regulations 2007

applied: SI 2009/153 Sch.1 para.5

Reg.32, amended: SI 2009/7 Reg.3

Reg.39, amended: SI 2009/7 Reg.4

Reg.40, amended: SI 2009/7 Reg.5

Reg.44, amended: SI 2009/7 Reg.6

Reg.45, amended: SI 2009/7 Reg.7

Reg.46, amended: SI 2009/7 Reg.8

Reg.47, amended: SI 2009/7 Reg.9

1864. Further Education (Principals Qualifications) (England) Regulations 2007

Reg.2, amended: SI 2009/472 Reg.3

Reg.3, amended: SI 2009/472 Reg.4

Reg.5, amended: SI 2009/472 Reg.5, SI 2009/2049 Reg.3

Reg.5, substituted: SI 2009/472 Reg.5

1892. Police Act 1997 (Criminal Records) (Amendment No 2) Regulations 2007

Reg.2, amended: 2009 c.26 s.81

1903. Licensing and Management of Houses in Multiple Occupation (Additional Provisions) (England) Regulations 2007

Reg.7, amended: SI 2009/724 Reg.3

1932. Police Pension Fund Regulations 2007

Reg.2, amended: SI 2009/2060 Sch.1 para.33

Reg.12A, amended: SI 2009/2060 Sch.1 para.34

Reg.12B, added: SI 2009/2060 Sch.1 para.35

1933. Mobile Roaming (European Communities) Regulations 2007

Reg.1, amended: SI 2009/1591 Sch.1 para.1

Reg.5, amended: SI 2009/1591 Sch.1 para.2

Reg.5, disapplied: SI 2009/1591 Reg.3

Reg.13, applied: SI 2009/1591 Reg.3

1943. Common Agricultural Policy (Wine) (England and Northern Ireland) (Amendment) Regulations 2007

revoked (in part): SI 2009/386 Reg.17

1951. Street Works (Registers, Notices, Directions and Designations) (England) Regulations 2007

Reg.4, applied: SI 2009/721 Sch.2 para.11

Reg.6, applied: SI 2009/721 Sch.2 para.11

Reg.7, applied: SI 2009/721 Sch.2 para.11

Reg.9, applied: SI 2009/721 Sch.2 para.11

Reg.10, applied: SI 2009/721 Sch.2 para.11

Reg.11, applied: SI 2009/721 Sch.2 para.11

Reg.12, applied: SI 2009/721 Sch.2 para.11

Reg.13, applied: SI 2009/721 Sch.2 para.11

Reg.14, applied: SI 2009/721 Sch.2 para.11

Reg.15, applied: SI 2009/721 Sch.2 para.11

Reg.16, applied: SI 2009/721 Sch.2 para.11

1952. Street Works (Fixed Penalty) (England) Regulations 2007

Reg.5, applied: SI 2009/721 Sch.2 para.13

1984. Addition of Vitamins, Minerals and Other Substances (Wales) Regulations 2007

Reg.2, amended: SI 2009/3252 Reg.3

2003. Heather and Grass etc Burning (England) Regulations 2007

applied: SI 2009/3365 Sch.1 para.1

Reg.5, applied: SI 2009/3264 Sch.1 para.1, SI 2009/3365 Sch.1 para.1

Reg.6, applied: SI 2009/3264 Sch.1 para.1, SI 2009/3365 Sch.1 para.1

Reg.10, revoked: SI 2009/3264 Sch.3

2037. Ecodesign for Energy-Using Products Regulations 2007

Reg.2, amended: SI 2009/2560 Reg.3

Reg.6A, added: SI 2009/2560 Reg.4

Reg.8, amended: SI 2009/2560 Reg.5

Reg.10, amended: SI 2009/2560 Reg.14

Reg.16, amended: SI 2009/2560 Reg.6

Reg.18, amended: SI 2009/2560 Reg.7, Reg.14

Reg.18, revoked (in part): SI 2009/2560 Reg.7

Reg.19, amended: SI 2009/2560 Reg.14

Reg.20, amended: SI 2009/2560 Reg.7, Reg.14

Reg.21, substituted: SI 2009/2560 Reg.7

Reg.22, amended: SI 2009/2560 Reg.7

Reg.23, substituted: SI 2009/2560 Reg.8

Reg.25, substituted: SI 2009/2560 Reg.8

Reg.27A, added: SI 2009/2560 Reg.8

Sch.1 Part 1 para.1, substituted: SI 2009/2560 Reg.9

Sch.1 Part 1 para.2, amended: SI 2009/2560 Reg.9

Sch.1 Part 5 para.1, added: SI 2009/2560 Reg.10

Sch.3 Part 5 para.1, added: SI 2009/2560 Reg.11

Sch.5 para.4, amended: SI 2009/2560 Reg.12

Sch.9 Part 4 para.2, amended: SI 2009/2560 Reg.14

Sch.9 Part 4 para.3, amended: SI 2009/2560 Reg.14

Sch.9 Part 5 para.2, revoked: SI 2009/2560 Reg.13

Sch.9 Part 5 para.3, revoked: SI 2009/2560 Reg.13

Sch.9 Part 5 para.4, revoked: SI 2009/2560 Reg.13

Sch.9 Part 5 para.5, revoked: SI 2009/2560 Reg.13

Sch.9 Part 5 para.6, revoked: SI 2009/2560 Reg.13

2050. Education (Individual Pupil Information) (Prescribed Persons) (Amendment) Regulations 2007

revoked: SI 2009/1563 Sch.1

2051. Public Guardian (Fees, etc) Regulations 2007

Reg.2, amended: SI 2009/514 Reg.3

Reg.4A, added: SI 2009/514 Reg.4

2051. Public Guardian (Fees, etc) Regulations 2007– *cont.*
Reg.5A, added: SI 2009/514 Reg.5
Reg.7, amended: SI 2009/514 Reg.6
Reg.8, amended: SI 2009/514 Reg.7
Reg.9, amended: SI 2009/514 Reg.8
Sch.1, amended: SI 2009/514 Reg.9

2084. Wireless Telegraphy (Ultra-Wideband Equipment) (Exemption) Regulations 2007
revoked: SI 2009/2517 Reg.2

2090. Income Tax (Exemption of Minor Benefits) (Amendment) Regulations 2007
revoked: SI 2009/695 Reg.2

2128. Secretary of State for Justice Order 2007
Sch.1 Part 2 para.12, revoked: SI 2009/2657 Sch.5

2149. Rehabilitation of Offenders Act 1974 (Exceptions) (Amendment) (England and Wales) Order 2007
Art.7, amended: 2009 c.26 s.81

2157. Money Laundering Regulations 2007
applied: SI 2009/209 Reg.6, Reg.13, Reg.25, Reg.29, Sch.2 para.6, SI 2009/214 Sch.2 para.7, SI 2009/1801 Sch.2 para.7, SI 2009/2997 Reg.13
Reg.2, amended: SI 2009/209 Sch.6 para.6, SI 2009/1912 Reg.2
Reg.17, amended: SI 2009/209 Sch.6 para.6
Reg.22, amended: SI 2009/209 Sch.6 para.6
Reg.23, amended: SI 2009/209 Sch.6 para.6
Reg.25, amended: SI 2009/209 Sch.6 para.6
Reg.26, amended: SI 2009/209 Sch.6 para.6
Reg.29, amended: SI 2009/56 Sch.2 para.169
Reg.30, amended: SI 2009/56 Sch.2 para.170
Reg.42, amended: SI 2009/56 Sch.2 para.171
Reg.43, amended: SI 2009/56 Sch.2 para.172
Reg.43A, added: SI 2009/56 Sch.2 para.173
Reg.43B, added: SI 2009/56 Sch.2 para.173
Reg.43C, added: SI 2009/56 Sch.2 para.173
Reg.43D, added: SI 2009/56 Sch.2 para.173
Reg.43E, added: SI 2009/56 Sch.2 para.173
Reg.43F, added: SI 2009/56 Sch.2 para.173
Reg.44, amended: SI 2009/1835 Sch.2 para.1
Reg.44, revoked (in part): SI 2009/56 Sch.2 para.174, SI 2009/1835 Sch.2 para.1
Reg.49A, added: SI 2009/209 Sch.6 para.6
Reg.49A, applied: SI 2009/209 Reg.119
Reg.50, amended: SI 2009/209 Sch.6 para.6
Sch.1, amended: SI 2009/209 Sch.6 para.6
Sch.5 Part 1 para.1, substituted: SI 2009/56 Sch.2 para.175

2158. Categories of Gaming Machine Regulations 2007
Reg.3, substituted: SI 2009/1502 Reg.2
Reg.4, amended: SI 2009/1502 Reg.2

2163. Value Added Tax (Betting, Gaming and Lotteries) Order 2007
revoked: 2009 c.10 s.113

2167. Gaming Duty (Amendment) Regulations 2007
revoked: SI 2009/2046 Reg.3

2186. Verification of Information in Passport Applications Etc.(Specified Persons) Order 2007
revoked: SI 2009/2570 Art.4

2194. Companies Act 2006 (Commencement No.3, Consequential Amendments, Transitional Provisions and Savings) Order 2007
Sch.3 para.23A, amended: SI 2009/1632 Reg.22
Sch.4 Part 3 para.40, revoked: SI 2009/1941 Sch.2

2199. Data Retention (EC Directive) Regulations 2007
revoked: SI 2009/859 Reg.12

2220. Persons Providing Education at Further Education Institutions in Wales (Conditions) Regulations 2007
Reg.3, amended: SI 2009/2544 Reg.8
Reg.5, amended: SI 2009/2544 Reg.8
Reg.8, amended: SI 2009/2730 Reg.2
Reg.13, amended: SI 2009/2544 Reg.8
Reg.17, amended: SI 2009/2544 Reg.8
Reg.18, amended: SI 2009/2544 Reg.8
Sch.1 Part 1 para.3, amended: SI 2009/2544 Reg.8
Sch.1 Part 2 para.2, amended: SI 2009/2544 Reg.8

2245. Eggs and Chicks (England) Regulations 2007
applied: SI 2009/2163 Reg.40

2260. Education (Supply of Information about the School Workforce) (No.2) (England) Regulations 2007
Reg.3, amended: SI 2009/2266 Reg.3
Reg.8, amended: SI 2009/2266 Reg.4
Sch.1 para.1, substituted: SI 2009/2266 Reg.5
Sch.1 Part 1 para.1, revoked: SI 2009/2266 Reg.5
Sch.1 Part 1 para.1, substituted: SI 2009/2266 Reg.5
Sch.1 Part 1 para.2, revoked: SI 2009/2266 Reg.5
Sch.1 Part 1 para.2, substituted: SI 2009/2266 Reg.5
Sch.1 Part 1 para.3, revoked: SI 2009/2266 Reg.5
Sch.1 Part 1 para.3, substituted: SI 2009/2266 Reg.5
Sch.1 Part 1 para.4, revoked: SI 2009/2266 Reg.5
Sch.1 Part 1 para.4, substituted: SI 2009/2266 Reg.5
Sch.1 Part 1 para.5, revoked: SI 2009/2266 Reg.5
Sch.1 Part 1 para.5, substituted: SI 2009/2266 Reg.5
Sch.1 Part 1 para.6, revoked: SI 2009/2266 Reg.5
Sch.1 Part 1 para.6, substituted: SI 2009/2266 Reg.5
Sch.1 Part 1 para.7, revoked: SI 2009/2266 Reg.5
Sch.1 Part 1 para.7, substituted: SI 2009/2266 Reg.5
Sch.1 para.2, substituted: SI 2009/2266 Reg.5
Sch.1 Part 2 para.8, revoked: SI 2009/2266 Reg.5
Sch.1 Part 2 para.8, substituted: SI 2009/2266 Reg.5
Sch.1 Part 2 para.9, revoked: SI 2009/2266 Reg.5
Sch.1 Part 2 para.9, substituted: SI 2009/2266 Reg.5
Sch.1 Part 2 para.10, revoked: SI 2009/2266 Reg.5
Sch.1 Part 2 para.10, substituted: SI 2009/2266 Reg.5
Sch.1 Part 2 para.11, revoked: SI 2009/2266 Reg.5
Sch.1 Part 2 para.11, substituted: SI 2009/2266 Reg.5
Sch.1 Part 2 para.12, revoked: SI 2009/2266 Reg.5
Sch.1 Part 2 para.12, substituted: SI 2009/2266 Reg.5
Sch.1 Part 2 para.13, revoked: SI 2009/2266 Reg.5
Sch.1 Part 2 para.13, substituted: SI 2009/2266 Reg.5
Sch.1 Part 2 para.14, revoked: SI 2009/2266 Reg.5
Sch.1 Part 2 para.14, substituted: SI 2009/2266 Reg.5
Sch.1 Part 2 para.15, revoked: SI 2009/2266 Reg.5
Sch.1 Part 2 para.15, substituted: SI 2009/2266 Reg.5
Sch.1 Part 2 para.16, revoked: SI 2009/2266 Reg.5
Sch.1 Part 2 para.16, substituted: SI 2009/2266 Reg.5
Sch.1 Part 2 para.17, revoked: SI 2009/2266 Reg.5
Sch.1 Part 2 para.17, substituted: SI 2009/2266 Reg.5
Sch.1 Part 2 para.18, revoked: SI 2009/2266 Reg.5
Sch.1 Part 2 para.18, substituted: SI 2009/2266 Reg.5
Sch.1 para.3, substituted: SI 2009/2266 Reg.5
Sch.1 para.4, substituted: SI 2009/2266 Reg.5
Sch.1 para.5, substituted: SI 2009/2266 Reg.5
Sch.1 para.6, substituted: SI 2009/2266 Reg.5
Sch.1 para.7, substituted: SI 2009/2266 Reg.5
Sch.1 para.9, substituted: SI 2009/2266 Reg.5
Sch.1 para.10, substituted: SI 2009/2266 Reg.5
Sch.1 para.11, substituted: SI 2009/2266 Reg.5
Sch.1 para.12, substituted: SI 2009/2266 Reg.5
Sch.1 para.13, substituted: SI 2009/2266 Reg.5
Sch.1 para.14, substituted: SI 2009/2266 Reg.5
Sch.1 para.15, substituted: SI 2009/2266 Reg.5

2007– cont.

2260. Education (Supply of Information about the School Workforce) (No.2) (England) Regulations 2007– cont.
Sch.1 para.16, substituted: SI 2009/ 2266 Reg.5
Sch.1 para.17, substituted: SI 2009/ 2266 Reg.5
Sch.1 para.18, substituted: SI 2009/ 2266 Reg.5

2311. Education Maintenance Allowances (Wales) Regulations 2007
revoked: SI 2009/ 825 Reg.2

2312. Assembly Learning Grants and Loans (Higher Education) (Wales) (Amendment) Regulations 2007
applied: SI 2009/ 2737 Reg.3

2324. Education (School Performance Information) (England) Regulations 2007
Reg.7, revoked: SI 2009/ 646 Reg.2
Reg.14, revoked (in part): SI 2009/ 646 Reg.2
Sch.3 para.1, revoked: SI 2009/ 646 Reg.2
Sch.3 para.2, revoked: SI 2009/ 646 Reg.2
Sch.3 para.3, revoked: SI 2009/ 646 Reg.2
Sch.3 para.4, revoked: SI 2009/ 646 Reg.2
Sch.3 para.5, revoked: SI 2009/ 646 Reg.2
Sch.4 Part 1 para.2, revoked (in part): SI 2009/ 646 Reg.2
Sch.6 para.3, revoked: SI 2009/ 646 Reg.2
Sch.6 para.9, revoked: SI 2009/ 646 Reg.2
Sch.6 para.10, revoked: SI 2009/ 646 Reg.2
Sch.8 Part 2 para.1, amended: SI 2009/ 646 Reg.2
Sch.8 Part 4 para.1, revoked: SI 2009/ 646 Reg.2
Sch.8 Part 4 para.2, revoked: SI 2009/ 646 Reg.2

2351. Value Added Tax Tribunals (Amendment) Rules 2007
revoked: SI 2009/ 56 Sch.1 para.228

2440. Wireless Telegraphy (Ultra-Wideband Equipment) (Exemption) (Amendment) Regulations 2007
revoked: SI 2009/ 2517 Reg.2

2441. Community Legal Service (Funding) Order 2007
Art.2, applied: SI 2009/ 2468 Art.6
Art.3, amended: SI 2009/ 2468 Art.11
Art.5, amended: SI 2009/ 2468 Art.11

2482. Tonnage Tax (Training Requirement) (Amendment) Regulations 2007
revoked: SI 2009/ 2304 Sch.1

2488. Manufactured Interest (Tax) Regulations 2007
revoked: SI 2009/ 2810 Reg.2

2500. Common Agricultural Policy Single Payment and Support Schemes (Cross-compliance) (England) (Amendment) Regulations 2007
revoked: SI 2009/ 3264 Sch.3

2501. Political Parties, Elections and Referendums Act 2000 (Northern Ireland Political Parties) Order 2007
Art.11, amended: SI 2009/ 2748 Sch.1 para.36

2543. Local Government (Best Value Authorities) (Power to Trade) (England) (Amendment No.2) Order 2007
revoked: SI 2009/ 2393 Art.3

2781. European Communities (Recognition of Professional Qualifications) Regulations 2007
applied: SI 2009/ 1885 Art.2, Sch.4 para.1
Part 2, applied: SI 2009/ 2257 Reg.6
Reg.9, applied: SI 2009/ 3200 Reg.3
Reg.11, referred to: SI 2009/ 2999 Reg.31, SI 2009/ 3200 Reg.4, Reg.6
Reg.12, referred to: SI 2009/ 2999 Reg.31, SI 2009/ 3200 Reg.4, Reg.6

2007– cont.

2781. European Communities (Recognition of Professional Qualifications) Regulations 2007– cont.
Reg.22, applied: SI 2009/ 2257 Reg.4, Reg.5
Reg.25, applied: SI 2009/ 2257 Reg.5
Reg.25, referred to: SI 2009/ 2257 Reg.4, Reg.5
Reg.31, referred to: SI 2009/ 2999 Reg.31
Reg.32, referred to: SI 2009/ 2999 Reg.31
Reg.33, referred to: SI 2009/ 2999 Reg.31
Sch.1 Part 1, amended: SI 2009/ 1182 Sch.4 para.18, Sch.4 para.33
Sch.1 Part 2, amended: SI 2009/ 1182 Sch.4 para.18
Sch.2, amended: SI 2009/ 1182 Sch.4 para.18, Sch.4 para.33
Sch.5, amended: SI 2009/ 1587 Art.4, SI 2009/ 1885 Sch.2 para.12

2785. Natural Mineral Water, Spring Water and Bottled Drinking Water (England) Regulations 2007
disapplied: SI 2009/ 3101 Reg.3
Reg.2, amended: SI 2009/ 1598 Reg.3, Reg.4
Reg.4, amended: SI 2009/ 1598 Reg.4
Reg.8, amended: SI 2009/ 1598 Reg.5
Reg.9, amended: SI 2009/ 1598 Reg.6
Reg.16, amended: SI 2009/ 1598 Reg.7
Sch.4 para.4, substituted: SI 2009/ 1598 Reg.8
Sch.4 para.5, amended: SI 2009/ 1598 Reg.8
Sch.4 para.8, substituted: SI 2009/ 1598 Reg.8

2790. Materials and Articles in Contact with Food (England) Regulations 2007
Reg.2, amended: SI 2009/ 205 Reg.26, SI 2009/ 2938 Reg.3
Reg.2, revoked (in part): SI 2009/ 2938 Reg.3
Reg.4A, added: SI 2009/ 2938 Reg.4
Reg.6A, added: SI 2009/ 2938 Reg.5
Reg.9, referred to: SI 2009/ 205 Reg.13
Reg.10, amended: SI 2009/ 205 Reg.26
Reg.11, amended: SI 2009/ 205 Reg.26
Reg.13, amended: SI 2009/ 2938 Reg.6
Reg.14, substituted: SI 2009/ 2938 Reg.7
Reg.18, amended: SI 2009/ 2938 Reg.8
Reg.21, amended: SI 2009/ 2938 Reg.9

2794. Education (Listed Bodies) (Wales) Order 2007
Sch.1 Part I, amended: SI 2009/ 710 Art.2

2795. Education (Recognised Bodies) (Wales) Order 2007
Sch.1, amended: SI 2009/ 667 Art.3, Art.4

2868. Housing Benefit (Local Housing Allowance and Information Sharing) Amendment Regulations 2007
Reg.14, referred to: SI 2009/ 497 Art.19

2869. Housing Benefit (State Pension Credit) (Local Housing Allowance and Information Sharing) Amendment Regulations 2007
Reg.14, applied: SI 2009/ 497 Art.20

2951. Administrative Justice and Tribunals Council (Listed Tribunals) Order 2007
Art.2, amended: SI 2009/ 1307 Sch.2 para.121, SI 2009/ 1834 Sch.2 para.1, SI 2009/ 1835 Sch.2 para.2, SI 2009/ 3040 Art.3

2974. Companies (Cross-Border Mergers) Regulations 2007
referred to: SI 2009/ 2437 Reg.18
varied: SI 2009/ 317 Sch.1
Reg.1, varied: SI 2009/ 1804 Reg.46
Reg.2, varied: SI 2009/ 1804 Reg.46
Reg.3, varied: SI 2009/ 1804 Reg.46
Reg.4, varied: SI 2009/ 1804 Reg.46
Reg.5, varied: SI 2009/ 1804 Reg.46

2007– cont.

2974. Companies (Cross-Border Mergers) Regulations 2007– *cont.*
Reg.6, varied: SI 2009/1804 Reg.46
Reg.7, varied: SI 2009/1804 Reg.46
Reg.8, varied: SI 2009/1804 Reg.46
Reg.9, varied: SI 2009/1804 Reg.46
Reg.10, varied: SI 2009/1804 Reg.46
Reg.11, varied: SI 2009/1804 Reg.46
Reg.12, varied: SI 2009/1804 Reg.46
Reg.13, varied: SI 2009/1804 Reg.46
Reg.14, varied: SI 2009/1804 Reg.46
Reg.15, varied: SI 2009/1804 Reg.46
Reg.16, varied: SI 2009/1804 Reg.46
Reg.17, varied: SI 2009/1804 Reg.46
Reg.18, varied: SI 2009/1804 Reg.46
Reg.19, varied: SI 2009/1804 Reg.46
Reg.20, varied: SI 2009/1804 Reg.46
Reg.21, varied: SI 2009/1804 Reg.46
Reg.62, amended: SI 2009/3348 Art.22, Art.23
Reg.65, varied: SI 2009/1804 Reg.46
Reg.66, varied: SI 2009/1804 Reg.46

2978. Education (Pupil Referral Units) (Management Committees etc.) (England) Regulations 2007
Sch.2 para.8, amended: SI 2009/1924 Reg.13
Sch.2 para.10, amended: SI 2009/1924 Reg.13

2983. Contaminants in Food (England) (Amendment) (No.2) Regulations 2007
revoked: SI 2009/1223 Reg.7

3005. General Dental Council (Appointments Committee and Appointment of Members of Committees) (Amendment) Rules Order of Council 2007
Sch.1, revoked: SI 2009/1813 Sch.1

3072. Renewable Transport Fuel Obligations Order 2007
Art.3, amended: SI 2009/843 Art.3
Art.3, revoked (in part): SI 2009/843 Art.3
Art.4, amended: SI 2009/843 Art.4
Art.5, amended: SI 2009/843 Art.5
Art.5, revoked (in part): SI 2009/843 Art.5

3135. Motor Vehicles (EC Type Approval) (Amendment No.2) Regulations 2007
revoked: SI 2009/717 Sch.1

3152. Company and Business Names (Amendment) (No.2) Regulations 2007
revoked: SI 2009/2615 Reg.7

3159. Air Navigation (Dangerous Goods) (Amendment) (No.2) Regulations 2007
revoked: SI 2009/1492 Reg.3

3165. Natural Mineral Water, Spring Water and Bottled Drinking Water (Wales) Regulations 2007
Reg.2, amended: SI 2009/1897 Reg.3, Reg.4
Reg.4, amended: SI 2009/1897 Reg.4
Reg.8, amended: SI 2009/1897 Reg.5
Reg.9, amended: SI 2009/1897 Reg.6
Sch.4 para.4, substituted: SI 2009/1897 Reg.7
Sch.4 para.5, amended: SI 2009/1897 Reg.7
Sch.4 para.8, substituted: SI 2009/1897 Reg.7

3172. General Dental Council (Constitution) (Amendment) Order of Council 2007
revoked: SI 2009/1182 Sch.4 para.34

3175. Police and Criminal Evidence Act 1984 (Application to Revenue and Customs) Order 2007
applied: 2009 c.11 s.22
Art.2, disapplied: 2009 c.11 s.22
Art.7, disapplied: 2009 c.11 s.22

2007– cont.

3175. Police and Criminal Evidence Act 1984 (Application to Revenue and Customs) Order 2007– *cont.*
Art.19, disapplied: 2009 c.11 s.22

3182. Common Agricultural Policy Single Payment and Support Schemes (Amendment) Regulations 2007
revoked: SI 2009/3102 Reg.9

3185. Official Feed and Food Controls (England) Regulations 2007
revoked: SI 2009/3255 Reg.52

3219. Felixstowe Dock and Railway Harbour Revision Order 2007
disapplied: SI 2009/2259 Art.3
Art.3, revoked: SI 2009/2259 Art.4
Sch.1, revoked: SI 2009/2259 Art.4
Sch.2 Part 2 para.2, amended: SI 2009/2259 Art.4

3229. Licensing and Management of Houses in Multiple Occupation (Additional Provisions) (Wales) Regulations 2007
Reg.7, amended: SI 2009/1915 Reg.3

3252. Materials and Articles in Contact with Food (Wales) Regulations 2007
Reg.2, amended: SI 2009/481 Reg.26, SI 2009/3105 Reg.3
Reg.2, revoked (in part): SI 2009/3105 Reg.3
Reg.4A, added: SI 2009/3105 Reg.4
Reg.6A, added: SI 2009/3105 Reg.5
Reg.9, referred to: SI 2009/481 Reg.13
Reg.10, amended: SI 2009/481 Reg.26
Reg.11, amended: SI 2009/481 Reg.26
Reg.13, amended: SI 2009/3105 Reg.6
Reg.14, substituted: SI 2009/3105 Reg.7
Reg.18, amended: SI 2009/3105 Reg.8
Reg.21, amended: SI 2009/3105 Reg.9

3279. Animals and Animal Products (Import and Export) (Wales) (Amendment) Regulations 2007
Reg.2, revoked (in part): SI 2009/390 Reg.3

3282. Medicines (Pharmacies) (Applications for Registration and Fees) Amendment Regulations 2007
revoked: SI 2009/3071 Reg.3

3284. Grants for Fishing and Aquaculture Industries Regulations 2007
Reg.3, amended: SI 2009/1309 Reg.3

3290. Immigration (Restrictions on Employment) Order 2007
Art.6, amended: SI 2009/2908 Art.3
Sch.1 Part LIST.A para.1, amended: SI 2009/2908 Art.4
Sch.1 Part LIST.A para.2, substituted: SI 2009/2908 Art.4

3291. Patents Rules 2007
Part 9 r.103, amended: SI 2009/546 r.9
Part 9 r.104, amended: SI 2009/546 r.10

3292. Patents (Fees) Rules 2007
r.3, amended: SI 2009/2089 r.21
r.3A, added: SI 2009/2089 r.22

3294. Official Feed and Food Controls (Wales) Regulations 2007
revoked: SI 2009/3376 Reg.52

3298. Transfer of Funds (Information on the Payer) Regulations 2007
Reg.2, amended: SI 2009/1912 Reg.3
Reg.11, amended: SI 2009/56 Sch.2 para.177
Reg.12, amended: SI 2009/56 Sch.2 para.178
Reg.12A, added: SI 2009/56 Sch.2 para.179
Reg.12B, added: SI 2009/56 Sch.2 para.179

2007–cont.

3298. Transfer of Funds (Information on the Payer) Regulations 2007–*cont.*
Reg.12C, added: SI 2009/56 Sch.2 para.179
Reg.12D, added: SI 2009/56 Sch.2 para.179
Reg.12E, added: SI 2009/56 Sch.2 para.179
Reg.12F, added: SI 2009/56 Sch.2 para.179
Reg.13, amended: SI 2009/56 Sch.2 para.180
Reg.13, revoked (in part): SI 2009/56 Sch.2 para.180
Sch.2 para.2, substituted: SI 2009/56 Sch.2 para.181

3368. Contaminants in Food (Wales) (Amendment) Regulations 2007
revoked: SI 2009/1386 Reg.7

3382. Army Terms of Service Regulations 2007
varied: SI 2009/1059 Art.191
Reg.2, amended: SI 2009/831 Reg.16, SI 2009/1089 Reg.16
Reg.2, applied: SI 2009/831 Sch.1 para.8
Reg.7, amended: SI 2009/831 Reg.17, SI 2009/1089 Reg.17
Reg.9, amended: SI 2009/831 Reg.18, SI 2009/1089 Reg.18
Reg.9, revoked (in part): SI 2009/831 Reg.18, SI 2009/1089 Reg.18
Reg.14, amended: SI 2009/831 Reg.19, SI 2009/1089 Reg.19
Reg.16A, added: SI 2009/831 Reg.20, SI 2009/1089 Reg.20
Reg.17, revoked: SI 2009/831 Reg.21, SI 2009/1089 Reg.21
Reg.19, amended: SI 2009/831 Reg.22, SI 2009/1089 Reg.22

3431. Loan Relationships and Derivative Contracts (Disregard and Bringing into Account of Profits and Losses) (Amendment No 2) Regulations 2007
revoked: 2009 c.4 Sch.3 Part 1

3432. Loan Relationships and Derivative Contracts (Change of Accounting Practice) (Amendment) (No.2) Regulations 2007
revoked: 2009 c.4 Sch.3 Part 1

3442. Courts-Martial (Army) Rules 2007
Part 6 r.37, applied: SI 2009/2041 Sch.2 para.2
Part 6 r.38, applied: SI 2009/2041 Sch.2 para.2

3443. Courts-Martial (Royal Navy) Rules 2007
Part 6 r.34, applied: SI 2009/2041 Sch.2 para.2
Part 6 r.35, applied: SI 2009/2041 Sch.2 para.2
Part 10 r.62, applied: SI 2009/2041 Sch.2 para.2
Part 10 r.65, applied: SI 2009/2041 Sch.2 para.2

3444. Courts-Martial (Royal Air Force) Rules 2007
Part 6 r.37, applied: SI 2009/2041 Sch.2 para.2
Part 6 r.38, applied: SI 2009/2041 Sch.2 para.2

3467. Air Navigation (Amendment) (No.2) Order 2007
revoked: SI 2009/3015 Sch.1

3483. Civil Enforcement of Parking Contraventions (England) General Regulations 2007
Reg.2, revoked (in part): SI 2009/478 Reg.4
Reg.6, substituted: SI 2009/478 Reg.5

3493. Sheep and Goats (Records, Identification and Movement) (England) Order 2007
revoked: SI 2009/3219 Art.42

3494. Statutory Auditors and Third Country Auditors Regulations 2007
Reg.15, revoked (in part): SI 2009/2798 Reg.2

3506. Income Tax Act 2007 (Amendment) (No.3) Order 2007
Art.3, revoked (in part): SI 2009/2859 Art.5

2007–cont.

3509. Education (Student Loans) (Re Payment) (Amendment) (Wales) Regulations 2007
revoked: SI 2009/470 Sch.1

3521. Infant Formula and Follow-on Formula (England) Regulations 2007
see *R. (on the application of Infant and Dietetic Foods Association Ltd) v Secretary of State for Health* [2008] EWHC 575 (Admin), [2009] Eu. L.R. 1 (QBD (Admin)), Mitting, J.

3537. Employer-Financed Retirement Benefits (Excluded Benefits for Tax Purposes) Regulations 2007
Reg.3, amended: SI 2009/2886 Reg.3
Sch.1 Part 3 para.17, added: SI 2009/2886 Reg.4

3538. Environmental Permitting (England and Wales) Regulations 2007
applied: SI 2009/153 Reg.10, Reg.11, Sch.3 para.1, SI 2009/995 Reg.10, Reg.11, Sch.3 para.1, SI 2009/1927 Reg.9, SI 2009/2902 Reg.13
referred to: SI 2009/2902 Reg.14
Reg.2, amended: SI 2009/890 Sch.8 para.2, SI 2009/1799 Reg.3, SI 2009/3381 Reg.3
Reg.5, substituted: SI 2009/3381 Reg.4
Reg.8, amended: SI 2009/1799 Reg.4
Reg.12, substituted: SI 2009/1799 Reg.5
Reg.17, substituted: SI 2009/1799 Reg.6
Reg.22, amended: SI 2009/3381 Reg.5
Reg.24, amended: SI 2009/1799 Reg.7
Reg.31, amended: SI 2009/1799 Reg.8
Reg.32, amended: SI 2009/1799 Reg.9
Reg.33, amended: SI 2009/1799 Reg.10
Reg.35, amended: SI 2009/890 Sch.8 para.2, SI 2009/1799 Reg.11
Reg.36, applied: SI 2009/665 Art.2
Reg.37, applied: SI 2009/665 Art.2
Reg.38, amended: SI 2009/1799 Reg.12, SI 2009/3381 Reg.6
Reg.42, amended: SI 2009/1799 Reg.13
Reg.46, amended: SI 2009/1799 Reg.14
Reg.63, amended: SI 2009/1799 Reg.15
Reg.68, substituted: SI 2009/3381 Reg.7
Reg.68A, added: SI 2009/890 Sch.8 para.2
Reg.71, amended: SI 2009/1799 Reg.16
Reg.71, substituted: SI 2009/1799 Reg.16
Reg.71A, added: SI 2009/1799 Reg.16
Reg.71B, added: SI 2009/3381 Reg.8
Reg.72, amended: SI 2009/1307 Sch.2 para.123, SI 2009/1799 Reg.17
Sch.1 Part 2, amended: SI 2009/1799 Reg.18
Sch.1 Part 2 para.1, amended: SI 2009/3381 Reg.9
Sch.2 para.1, substituted: SI 2009/3381 Sch.1
Sch.2 para.2, substituted: SI 2009/3381 Sch.1
Sch.2 para.3, substituted: SI 2009/3381 Sch.1
Sch.2 para.4, substituted: SI 2009/3381 Sch.1
Sch.2 para.5, substituted: SI 2009/3381 Sch.1
Sch.2 para.6, substituted: SI 2009/3381 Sch.1
Sch.2 para.7, substituted: SI 2009/3381 Sch.1
Sch.2 para.8, substituted: SI 2009/3381 Sch.1
Sch.2 para.9, substituted: SI 2009/3381 Sch.1
Sch.2 para.10, substituted: SI 2009/3381 Sch.1
Sch.2 para.11, substituted: SI 2009/3381 Sch.1
Sch.2 para.12, substituted: SI 2009/3381 Sch.1
Sch.2 para.13, substituted: SI 2009/3381 Sch.1
Sch.3 Part 1 para.1, substituted: SI 2009/3381 Sch.2
Sch.3 Part 1 para.2, substituted: SI 2009/3381 Sch.2
Sch.3 Part 1 para.3, substituted: SI 2009/3381 Sch.2
Sch.3 Part 1 para.4, substituted: SI 2009/3381 Sch.2
Sch.3 Part 1 para.5, amended: SI 2009/1799 Reg.19

2007– cont.

3538. Environmental Permitting (England and Wales) Regulations 2007– *cont.*
Sch.3 Part 1 para.5, substituted: SI 2009/3381 Sch.2
Sch.3 Part 1 para.6, substituted: SI 2009/3381 Sch.2
Sch.3 Part 1 para.7, substituted: SI 2009/3381 Sch.2
Sch.3 Part 1 para.8, substituted: SI 2009/3381 Sch.2
Sch.3 Part 1 para.9, substituted: SI 2009/3381 Sch.2
Sch.3 Part 1 para.10, substituted: SI 2009/3381 Sch.2
Sch.3 Part 1 para.11, substituted: SI 2009/3381 Sch.2
Sch.3 Part 1 para.12, substituted: SI 2009/3381 Sch.2
Sch.3 Part 1 para.13, substituted: SI 2009/3381 Sch.2
Sch.3 Part 1 para.14, substituted: SI 2009/3381 Sch.2
Sch.3 Part 1 para.15, substituted: SI 2009/3381 Sch.2
Sch.3 Part 1 para.16, substituted: SI 2009/3381 Sch.2
Sch.3 Part 1 para.17, substituted: SI 2009/3381 Sch.2
Sch.3 Part 1 para.18, substituted: SI 2009/3381 Sch.2
Sch.3 Part 1 para.19, substituted: SI 2009/3381 Sch.2
Sch.3 Part 1 para.20, substituted: SI 2009/3381 Sch.2
Sch.3 Part 1 para.21, substituted: SI 2009/3381 Sch.2
Sch.3 Part 1 para.22, substituted: SI 2009/3381 Sch.2
Sch.3 Part 1 para.23, substituted: SI 2009/3381 Sch.2
Sch.3 Part 1 para.24, substituted: SI 2009/3381 Sch.2
Sch.3 Part 1 para.25, substituted: SI 2009/3381 Sch.2
Sch.3 Part 1 para.26, substituted: SI 2009/3381 Sch.2
Sch.3 Part 1 para.27, substituted: SI 2009/3381 Sch.2
Sch.3 Part 1 para.28, substituted: SI 2009/3381 Sch.2
Sch.3 Part 1 para.29, amended: SI 2009/1799 Reg.19
Sch.3 Part 1 para.29, substituted: SI 2009/3381 Sch.2
Sch.3 Part 1 para.30, substituted: SI 2009/3381 Sch.2
Sch.3 Part 1 para.31, substituted: SI 2009/3381 Sch.2
Sch.3 Part 1 para.32, substituted: SI 2009/3381 Sch.2
Sch.3 Part 1 para.33, substituted: SI 2009/3381 Sch.2
Sch.3 Part 1 para.34, substituted: SI 2009/3381 Sch.2
Sch.3 Part 1 para.35, substituted: SI 2009/3381 Sch.2
Sch.3 Part 1 para.36, substituted: SI 2009/3381 Sch.2
Sch.3 Part 1 para.37, substituted: SI 2009/3381 Sch.2
Sch.3 Part 1 para.38, substituted: SI 2009/3381 Sch.2
Sch.3 Part 1 para.39, substituted: SI 2009/3381 Sch.2
Sch.3 Part 1 para.40, substituted: SI 2009/3381 Sch.2
Sch.3 Part 1 para.41, substituted: SI 2009/3381 Sch.2
Sch.3 Part 1 para.42, substituted: SI 2009/3381 Sch.2
Sch.3 Part 1 para.43, substituted: SI 2009/3381 Sch.2
Sch.3 Part 1 para.44, substituted: SI 2009/3381 Sch.2
Sch.3 Part 1 para.45, substituted: SI 2009/3381 Sch.2
Sch.3 Part 1 para.46, substituted: SI 2009/3381 Sch.2
Sch.3 Part 1 para.47, substituted: SI 2009/3381 Sch.2
Sch.3 Part 1 para.48, substituted: SI 2009/3381 Sch.2
Sch.3 Part 2 para.49, substituted: SI 2009/3381 Sch.2
Sch.3 Part 2 para.50, substituted: SI 2009/3381 Sch.2
Sch.3 Part 2 para.51, substituted: SI 2009/3381 Sch.2
Sch.3 Part 2 para.52, substituted: SI 2009/3381 Sch.2
Sch.3 Part 2 para.53, added: SI 2009/890 Sch.8 para.2
Sch.3 Part 2 para.53, substituted: SI 2009/3381 Sch.2
Sch.5 Part 1 para.1, amended: SI 2009/1799 Reg.20
Sch.5 Part 1 para.5, amended: SI 2009/1799 Reg.20
Sch.5 Part 1 para.10, amended: SI 2009/1799 Reg.20
Sch.5 Part 1 para.16, amended: SI 2009/1799 Reg.20
Sch.5 Part 2 para.26, amended: SI 2009/1307 Sch.2 para.124
Sch.6 para.3, amended: SI 2009/1799 Reg.21
Sch.6 para.3, revoked (in part): SI 2009/1799 Reg.21
Sch.7 para.2, amended: SI 2009/1799 Reg.22
Sch.7 para.5, amended: SI 2009/1799 Reg.22
Sch.7 para.8, amended: SI 2009/1799 Reg.22
Sch.8 para.2, amended: SI 2009/1799 Reg.23
Sch.8 para.4, amended: SI 2009/1799 Reg.23
Sch.8 para.5, amended: SI 2009/1799 Reg.23
Sch.8 para.7, amended: SI 2009/1799 Reg.23

2007– cont.

3538. Environmental Permitting (England and Wales) Regulations 2007– *cont.*
Sch.10 para.1, revoked (in part): SI 2009/1799 Reg.24
Sch.18A para.1, added: SI 2009/890 Sch.8 para.2
Sch.18A para.2, added: SI 2009/890 Sch.8 para.2
Sch.18B para.1, added: SI 2009/1799 Sch.1
Sch.18B para.2, added: SI 2009/1799 Sch.1
Sch.18B para.3, added: SI 2009/1799 Sch.1
Sch.18B para.4, added: SI 2009/1799 Sch.1
Sch.18B para.5, added: SI 2009/1799 Sch.1
Sch.18B para.6, added: SI 2009/1799 Sch.1
Sch.18B para.7, added: SI 2009/1799 Sch.1
Sch.18B para.8, added: SI 2009/1799 Sch.1
Sch.18B para.9, added: SI 2009/1799 Sch.1
Sch.18B para.10, added: SI 2009/1799 Sch.1
Sch.18B para.11, added: SI 2009/1799 Sch.1
Sch.18B para.12, added: SI 2009/1799 Sch.1
Sch.18B para.13, added: SI 2009/1799 Sch.1
Sch.18B para.14, added: SI 2009/1799 Sch.1
Sch.19 para.1, amended: SI 2009/1799 Reg.26, SI 2009/3381 Reg.12
Sch.20 para.1, amended: SI 2009/1799 Reg.27
Sch.20 para.6, amended: SI 2009/1799 Reg.27

3544. Legislative and Regulatory Reform (Regulatory Functions) Order 2007
Art.1, amended: SI 2009/2981 Art.3
Sch.1 Part 1, amended: SI 2009/2981 Art.4
Sch.1 Part 1A, added: SI 2009/2981 Art.4
Sch.1 Part 2, amended: SI 2009/2981 Art.4
Sch.1 Part 3, amended: SI 2009/2824 Sch.1 para.5, SI 2009/2981 Art.4
Sch.1 Part 5, added: SI 2009/2981 Sch.1
Sch.1 Part 6, added: SI 2009/2981 Sch.1
Sch.1 Part 7, added: SI 2009/2981 Sch.1
Sch.1 Part 8, added: SI 2009/2981 Sch.1
Sch.1 Part 9, added: SI 2009/2981 Sch.1
Sch.1 Part 10, added: SI 2009/2981 Sch.1
Sch.1 Part 11, added: SI 2009/2981 Sch.1
Sch.1 Part 12, added: SI 2009/2981 Sch.1
Sch.1 Part 13, added: SI 2009/2981 Sch.1

3545. Safeguarding Vulnerable Groups Act 2006 (Commencement No.1) Order 2007
Art.3, amended: 2009 c.26 s.81

3612. General Commissioners and Special Commissioners (Jurisdiction and Procedure) (Amendment) Regulations 2007
revoked: SI 2009/56 Sch.1 para.36, Sch.2 para.187

2008

3. Insolvency Practitioners and Insolvency Services Account (Fees) (Amendment) Order 2008
revoked: SI 2009/487 Art.1

4. Information as to Provision of Education (England) Regulations 2008
Sch.1 para.4, amended: SI 2009/1556 Reg.7

15. Textile Products (Determination of Composition) Regulations 2008
referred to: SI 2009/669 Sch.1 Part 4

16. Safeguarding Vulnerable Groups Act 2006 (Barred List Prescribed Information) Regulations 2008
Reg.1, amended: 2009 c.26 s.81

18. Assembly Learning Grants (European Institutions) (Wales) Regulations 2008
revoked: SI 2009/3359 Reg.4
Reg.18, amended: SI 2009/2157 Reg.4
Reg.19, amended: SI 2009/2157 Reg.5

2008–cont.

18. **Assembly Learning Grants (European Institutions) (Wales) Regulations 2008**–*cont.*
Reg.20, amended: SI 2009/2157 Reg.6, Reg.7
37. **Restriction of the Use of Certain Hazardous Substances in Electrical and Electronic Equipment Regulations 2008**
Reg.3, amended: SI 2009/581 Reg.2
Reg.10, amended: SI 2009/581 Reg.2
Reg.13, amended: SI 2009/581 Reg.2
Reg.13, revoked (in part): SI 2009/581 Reg.2
Reg.14, substituted: SI 2009/581 Reg.2
Reg.15, substituted: SI 2009/581 Reg.2
41. **Fluorinated Greenhouse Gases Regulations 2008**
revoked: SI 2009/261 Reg.2
Reg.19, applied: SI 2009/261 Reg.43
Reg.24, applied: SI 2009/665 Art.2
48. **Absent Voting (Transitional Provisions) (Scotland) Regulations 2008**
applied: SSI 2009/35 Reg.12
80. **Common Agricultural Policy Single Payment and Support Schemes (Cross-compliance) (England) (Amendment) Regulations 2008**
revoked: SI 2009/3264 Sch.3
97. **Ozone Depleting Substances (Qualifications) (Amendment) Regulations 2008**
revoked: SI 2009/216 Reg.12
101. **Street Works (Registers, Notices, Directions and Designations) (Wales) Regulations 2008**
Reg.4, applied: SI 2009/721 Sch.2 para.12
Reg.6, applied: SI 2009/721 Sch.2 para.12
Reg.7, applied: SI 2009/721 Sch.2 para.12
Reg.9, applied: SI 2009/721 Sch.2 para.12
Reg.10, applied: SI 2009/721 Sch.2 para.12
Reg.11, applied: SI 2009/721 Sch.2 para.12
Reg.12, applied: SI 2009/721 Sch.2 para.12
Reg.13, applied: SI 2009/721 Sch.2 para.12
Reg.14, applied: SI 2009/721 Sch.2 para.12
Reg.15, applied: SI 2009/721 Sch.2 para.12
Reg.16, applied: SI 2009/721 Sch.2 para.12
102. **Street Works (Fixed Penalty) (Wales) Regulations 2008**
Reg.5, applied: SI 2009/721 Sch.2 para.14
130. **Sheep and Goats (Records, Identification and Movement) (Wales) Order 2008**
revoked: SI 2009/3364 Art.45
135. **British Citizenship (Designated Service) (Amendment) Order 2008**
revoked: SI 2009/2958 Art.5
138. **Miscellaneous Food Additives and the Sweeteners in Food (Amendment) (Wales) Regulations 2008**
Reg.5, referred to: SI 2009/3378 Reg.10
Reg.6, referred to: SI 2009/3378 Reg.10
Reg.8, referred to: SI 2009/3378 Reg.10
188. **Electricity and Gas (Carbon Emissions Reduction) Order 2008**
applied: SI 2009/1905 Art.14
Art.2, amended: SI 2009/1904 Art.3
Art.3, amended: SI 2009/1904 Art.4
Art.9, amended: SI 2009/1905 Art.28
Art.9, substituted: SI 2009/1904 Art.5
Art.12, amended: SI 2009/1904 Art.6
Art.15, amended: SI 2009/1904 Art.7
Art.19, amended: SI 2009/1904 Art.8
Sch.A1 para.1, added: SI 2009/1904 Art.9
Sch.A1 para.2, added: SI 2009/1904 Art.9
Sch.A1 para.3, added: SI 2009/1904 Art.9
Sch.A1 para.4, added: SI 2009/1904 Art.9

2008–cont.

188. **Electricity and Gas (Carbon Emissions Reduction) Order 2008**–*cont.*
Sch.A1 para.5, added: SI 2009/1904 Art.9
Sch.2 para.2, amended: SI 2009/1904 Art.10
212. **Independent Police Complaints Commission (Immigration and Asylum Enforcement Functions) Regulations 2008**
revoked (in part): SI 2009/2133 Reg.72
218. **Immigration and Nationality (Cost Recovery Fees)(Amendment) Regulations 2008**
revoked: SI 2009/421 Reg.33
221. **Charity Tribunal Rules 2008**
revoked: SI 2009/1834 Sch.3
225. **Petroleum Licensing (Production) (Seaward Areas) Regulations 2008**
Reg.1, amended: SI 2009/3283 Reg.4
Sch.1 para.1, amended: SI 2009/229 Sch.2 para.20
Sch.1 para.2, amended: SI 2009/3283 Reg.4
Sch.1 para.3, amended: SI 2009/3283 Reg.4
Sch.1 para.5, amended: SI 2009/3283 Reg.4
Sch.1 para.30, amended: SI 2009/3283 Reg.4
238. **Local Government Pension Scheme (Transitional Provisions) Regulations 2008**
Reg.3, amended: SI 2009/3150 Reg.18
Reg.7, substituted: SI 2009/3150 Reg.19
Sch.2 para.3, amended: SI 2009/3150 Reg.20
239. **Local Government Pension Scheme (Administration) Regulations 2008**
Reg.4, amended: SI 2009/3150 Reg.22
Reg.8A, added: SI 2009/447 Reg.3
Reg.9, amended: SI 2009/3150 Reg.23
Reg.12, amended: SI 2009/447 Reg.4
Reg.13, amended: SI 2009/3150 Reg.24
Reg.24A, added: SI 2009/3150 Reg.25
Reg.24B, added: SI 2009/3150 Reg.25
Reg.25, applied: SI 2009/3093 Reg.4
Reg.29, applied: SI 2009/3150 Reg.32
Reg.36A, added: SI 2009/1025 Reg.3
Reg.38, amended: SI 2009/3150 Reg.26
Reg.38A, added: SI 2009/1025 Reg.3
Reg.39, applied: SI 2009/3093 Reg.4
Reg.40, applied: SI 2009/3093 Reg.4
Reg.40, substituted: SI 2009/3150 Reg.27
Reg.40A, added: SI 2009/3150 Reg.28
Reg.40A, applied: SI 2009/3093 Reg.4
Reg.41, applied: SI 2009/3093 Reg.4
Reg.44, applied: SI 2009/3093 Reg.4
Reg.50A, added: SI 2009/3150 Reg.29
Reg.74, amended: SI 2009/3150 Reg.30
Sch.1, amended: SI 2009/3150 Reg.31
Sch.4, applied: SI 2009/3093 Reg.4
300. **Judicial Committee (General Appellate Jurisdiction) Rules (Amendment) Order 2008**
revoked: SI 2009/224 Art.4
307. **Scottish Parliament (Elections etc.) (Amendment) Order 2008**
applied: SSI 2009/35 Reg.12
346. **Regulated Covered Bonds Regulations 2008**
varied: SI 2009/317 Sch.1
373. **Companies (Revision of Defective Accounts and Reports) Regulations 2008**
referred to: SI 2009/1803 Reg.6
377. **Education (Budget Statements) (England) Regulations 2008**
Reg.2, amended: SI 2009/444 Reg.2
Reg.4, applied: SI 2009/444 Reg.1
Reg.4, revoked (in part): SI 2009/444 Reg.2
Sch.2 Part 2, amended: SI 2009/444 Reg.2

377. **Education (Budget Statements) (England) Regulations 2008**–*cont.*
Sch.2 Part 3, amended: SI 2009/444 Reg.2
Sch.2 Part 4, amended: SI 2009/444 Reg.2
Sch.3 Part 2, amended: SI 2009/444 Reg.2
Sch.3 Part 3, amended: SI 2009/444 Reg.2
Sch.3 Part 4, amended: SI 2009/444 Reg.2
378. **Northern Ireland Arms Decommissioning Act 1997 (Amnesty Period) Order 2008**
revoked: SI 2009/281 Art.3
386. **Non-Domestic Rating (Unoccupied Property) (England) Regulations 2008**
Reg.4, varied: SI 2009/353 Reg.2
409. **Small Companies and Groups (Accounts and Directors Report) Regulations 2008**
Reg.12, amended: SI 2009/1581 Reg.11
Sch.7 Part 2 para.6, added: SI 2009/1581 Reg.11
410. **Large and Medium-sized Companies and Groups (Accounts and Reports) Regulations 2008**
Reg.12, amended: SI 2009/1581 Reg.12
Sch.3 Part 2 para.50, applied: SI 2009/1926 Reg.4, Reg.9, Reg.10
Sch.3 Part 2 para.51, applied: SI 2009/1926 Reg.4, Reg.9, Reg.10
Sch.3 Part 2 para.53, applied: SI 2009/1926 Reg.8
Sch.6 Part 2 para.30, referred to: SI 2009/1803 Reg.6
Sch.8 Part 3 para.13, amended: SI 2009/1581 Reg.12
Sch.9 Part 2 para.8, added: SI 2009/1581 Reg.12
432. **Northern Rock plc Transfer Order 2008**
referred to: SI 2009/3226
447. **Meat (Official Controls Charges) (England) Regulations 2008**
revoked: SI 2009/1574 Reg.6
465. **Products of Animal Origin (Disease Control) (England) Regulations 2008**
Reg.2, amended: SI 2009/1297 Reg.3
Reg.3, amended: SI 2009/1297 Reg.4
Reg.7, amended: SI 2009/1297 Reg.5
Reg.9, amended: SI 2009/1297 Reg.6
Reg.9, revoked (in part): SI 2009/1297 Reg.6
Reg.10, amended: SI 2009/1297 Reg.7
Reg.12, amended: SI 2009/1297 Reg.8
Reg.13, amended: SI 2009/1297 Reg.9
Reg.14, substituted: SI 2009/1297 Reg.10
Reg.15, amended: SI 2009/1297 Reg.11
Sch.3 para.3A, added: SI 2009/1297 Reg.12
473. **Safeguarding Vulnerable Groups Act 2006 (Transitional Provisions) Order 2008**
applied: SI 2009/12 Art.9
Art.2, amended: 2009 c.26 s.81, SI 2009/37 Sch.8
Art.2, applied: SI 2009/12 Art.6, Art.6A, SI 2009/2611 Art.3, Art.5, Art.7
Art.3, applied: SI 2009/12 Art.6, Art.6A, SI 2009/2611 Art.5, Art.7
Art.4, applied: SI 2009/12 Art.7, SI 2009/2611 Art.6
Art.4, disapplied: SI 2009/12 Art.7A
490. **Wiltshire (Structural Change) Order 2008**
Art.3, amended: SI 2009/837 Art.6
491. **Cornwall (Structural Change) Order 2008**
applied: SI 2009/850, SI 2009/2325
Art.3, amended: SI 2009/837 Art.3
492. **Shropshire (Structural Change) Order 2008**
Art.3, amended: SI 2009/837 Art.5
493. **County Durham (Structural Change) Order 2008**
Art.3, amended: SI 2009/837 Art.7

494. **Northumberland (Structural Change) Order 2008**
Art.3, amended: SI 2009/837 Art.4
495. **Companies (Trading Disclosures) Regulations 2008**
Reg.3, amended: SI 2009/218 Reg.2
Reg.4, amended: SI 2009/218 Reg.3
Reg.7, amended: SI 2009/218 Reg.4
514. **Smoke Control Areas (Authorised Fuels) (England) Regulations 2008**
Sch.1 para.18, amended: SI 2009/2191 Reg.2
Sch.1 para.43A, added: SI 2009/2191 Reg.2
518. **Aerodromes (Designation) (Chargeable Air Services) (Amendment) Order 2008**
revoked: SI 2009/189 Art.2
529. **Education (Student Support) Regulations 2008**
Reg.65, amended: SI 2009/862 Reg.3, Reg.4
Reg.71, amended: SI 2009/862 Reg.5
538. **Assembly Learning Grant (Further Education) Regulations 2008**
revoked: SI 2009/2158 Reg.19
540. **Street Works (Registers, Notices, Directions and Designations) (Wales) (No.2) Regulations 2008**
Sch.1 Part 2 para.7, varied: SI 2009/1267 Reg.38
542. **Police Act 1997 (Criminal Records)(Disclosure) Regulations (Northern Ireland) 2008**
Reg.2, amended: SI 2009/2495 Reg.2
Reg.2, revoked (in part): SI 2009/2495 Reg.2
Reg.4, substituted: SI 2009/3334 Reg.2
Reg.8, amended: SI 2009/1798 Reg.3
Reg.9, amended: SI 2009/3334 Reg.2
Reg.9, substituted: SI 2009/2495 Reg.2
Reg.9A, added: SI 2009/2495 Reg.2
Reg.11, added: SI 2009/1798 Reg.3
Reg.11, substituted: SI 2009/3334 Reg.2
544. **Immigration and Nationality (Fees)(Amendment) Regulations 2008**
revoked: SI 2009/816 Reg.32
546. **Education (Student Loans) (Repayment) (Amendment) Regulations 2008**
revoked: SI 2009/470 Sch.1
552. **Medicines (Products for Human Use-Fees) Regulations 2008**
revoked: SI 2009/389 Reg.51
554. **Postgraduate Medical Education and Training Board (Fees) Rules Order 2008**
revoked: SI 2009/385 Sch.1
559. **Prevention of Terrorism Act 2005 (Continuance in force of sections 1 to 9) Order 2008**
Art.2, applied: SI 2009/554 Art.2
562. **Income Tax (Purchased Life Annuities) Regulations 2008**
Reg.20, amended: SI 2009/56 Sch.2 para.183
Reg.20, revoked (in part): SI 2009/56 Sch.2 para.183
574. **Serious Organised Crime and Police Act 2005 and Serious Crime Act 2007 (Consequential and Supplementary Amendments to Secondary Legislation) Order 2008**
Sch.1 para.4, revoked: SI 2009/56 Sch.2 para.184
590. **FCO Services Trading Fund Order 2008**
Art.4, amended: SI 2009/1362 Art.2
601. **Meat (Official Controls Charges) (Wales) Regulations 2008**
revoked: SI 2009/1557 Reg.6
630. **Police Authority Regulations 2008**
applied: SI 2009/119 Sch.2 para.1, Sch.2 para.2
Reg.7, applied: SI 2009/119 Sch.2 para.1

2008—cont.

632. Social Security Benefits Up-rating Order 2008
revoked: SI 2009/497 Art.28

634. Cheshire (Structural Changes) Order 2008
referred to: SI 2009/119

635. Criminal Procedure and Investigations Act 1996 (Application to the Armed Forces) Order 2008
applied: SI 2009/988 Art.21
referred to: SI 2009/988 Art.21
revoked: SI 2009/988 Art.3

638. Gangmasters (Licensing Conditions) (No.2) (Amendment) Rules 2008
revoked: SI 2009/307 r.10

648. Criminal Procedure and Investigations Act 1996 (Code of Practice) (Armed Forces) Order 2008
revoked: SI 2009/989 Art.2

652. Diseases of Animals (Approved Disinfectants) (Fees) (England) Order 2008
revoked: SI 2009/839 Art.3

653. National Health Service Pension Scheme Regulations 2008
referred to: SI 2009/381 Reg.15
Part 2, added: SI 2009/2446 Reg.52
Part 3, added: SI 2009/2446 Reg.94
Reg.1, amended: SI 2009/381 Reg.16, SI 2009/2446 Reg.13, Sch.2 para.1
Reg.1, amended: SI 2009/2446 Reg.17, Sch.2 para.1, Sch.2 para.2, Sch.2 para.3, Sch.2 para.4
Reg.1, amended: SI 2009/2446 Sch.2 para.1
Reg.1, amended: SI 2009/2446 Reg.25
Reg.1, amended: SI 2009/381 Reg.36
Reg.1, amended: SI 2009/2446 Sch.2 para.1
Reg.1, amended: SI 2009/381 Reg.53, SI 2009/2446 Reg.53, Sch.2 para.1
Reg.1, amended: SI 2009/2446 Reg.59, Sch.2 para.1, Sch.2 para.2, Sch.2 para.3, Sch.2 para.4
Reg.1, amended: SI 2009/2446 Sch.2 para.1
Reg.1, amended: SI 2009/2446 Reg.67
Reg.1, amended: SI 2009/381 Reg.66
Reg.1, amended: SI 2009/2446 Sch.2 para.1
Reg.1, amended: SI 2009/2446 Reg.96
Reg.1, amended: SI 2009/2446 Reg.102
Reg.1, amended: SI 2009/2446 Sch.2 para.2, Sch.2 para.3
Reg.1A, added: SI 2009/2446 Reg.18
Reg.1A, added: SI 2009/2446 Reg.60
Reg.2, amended: SI 2009/2446 Reg.14, Sch.2 para.1, Sch.2 para.2, Sch.2 para.3
Reg.2, amended: SI 2009/381 Reg.19, SI 2009/1298 Reg.3, SI 2009/2446 Sch.2 para.1, Sch.2 para.2, Sch.2 para.3
Reg.2, amended: SI 2009/381 Reg.20
Reg.2, amended: SI 2009/381 Reg.23
Reg.2, amended: SI 2009/2446 Reg.35
Reg.2, amended: SI 2009/2446 Sch.2 para.1
Reg.2, amended: SI 2009/381 Reg.54, SI 2009/2446 Sch.2 para.1, Sch.2 para.2, Sch.2 para.3
Reg.2, substituted: SI 2009/381 Reg.55
Reg.2, amended: SI 2009/381 Reg.56
Reg.2, amended: SI 2009/2446 Reg.76
Reg.2, amended: SI 2009/2446 Sch.2 para.1
Reg.2, amended: SI 2009/2446 Reg.95
Reg.2, amended: SI 2009/2446 Reg.97
Reg.3, amended: SI 2009/2446 Reg.12
Reg.3, amended: SI 2009/2446 Sch.2 para.1
Reg.3, substituted: SI 2009/381 Reg.21
Reg.3, amended: SI 2009/2446 Reg.26

2008—cont.

653. National Health Service Pension Scheme Regulations 2008—*cont.*
Reg.3, amended: SI 2009/381 Reg.37, SI 2009/2446 Reg.36, Sch.2 para.1
Reg.3, amended: SI 2009/2446 Sch.2 para.1
Reg.3, amended: SI 2009/2446 Reg.54, Sch.2 para.1, Sch.2 para.2
Reg.3, amended: SI 2009/2446 Sch.2 para.1
Reg.3, amended: SI 2009/2446 Reg.68
Reg.3, amended: SI 2009/381 Reg.67, SI 2009/2446 Reg.77, Sch.2 para.1
Reg.3, amended: SI 2009/2446 Sch.2 para.1
Reg.3, amended: SI 2009/2446 Reg.98
Reg.4, amended: SI 2009/2446 Sch.2 para.1
Reg.4, substituted: SI 2009/381 Reg.22
Reg.4, amended: SI 2009/381 Reg.24, SI 2009/2446 Reg.27
Reg.4, amended: SI 2009/381 Reg.38, SI 2009/2446 Reg.37
Reg.4, revoked (in part): SI 2009/2446 Reg.37
Reg.4, amended: SI 2009/2446 Sch.2 para.1
Reg.4, amended: SI 2009/381 Reg.57, SI 2009/2446 Reg.69
Reg.4, amended: SI 2009/381 Reg.68, SI 2009/2446 Reg.78
Reg.4, revoked (in part): SI 2009/2446 Reg.78
Reg.4, amended: SI 2009/2446 Sch.2 para.1
Reg.5, amended: SI 2009/2446 Reg.15, Sch.2 para.1, Sch.2 para.2
Reg.5, amended: SI 2009/2446 Sch.2 para.1
Reg.5, amended: SI 2009/2446 Reg.19, Sch.2 para.1
Reg.5, amended: SI 2009/381 Reg.25, SI 2009/2446 Reg.28
Reg.5, amended: SI 2009/381 Reg.48
Reg.5, amended: SI 2009/2446 Sch.2 para.1
Reg.5, revoked (in part): SI 2009/381 Reg.49
Reg.5, amended: SI 2009/2446 Reg.55, Sch.2 para.1, Sch.2 para.2
Reg.5, amended: SI 2009/2446 Sch.2 para.1
Reg.5, amended: SI 2009/381 Reg.58, SI 2009/2446 Reg.70
Reg.5, amended: SI 2009/381 Reg.79
Reg.5, amended: SI 2009/2446 Sch.2 para.1
Reg.5, revoked (in part): SI 2009/381 Reg.80
Reg.6, amended: SI 2009/2446 Sch.2 para.1
Reg.6, amended: SI 2009/381 Reg.26, SI 2009/2446 Sch.2 para.1
Reg.6, amended: SI 2009/2446 Sch.2 para.1
Reg.6, amended: SI 2009/2446 Reg.46
Reg.6, amended: SI 2009/2446 Sch.2 para.1
Reg.6, amended: SI 2009/2446 Reg.61
Reg.6, amended: SI 2009/381 Reg.59, SI 2009/2446 Sch.2 para.1
Reg.6, amended: SI 2009/2446 Sch.2 para.1
Reg.6, amended: SI 2009/2446 Reg.87
Reg.7, amended: SI 2009/2446 Sch.2 para.1
Reg.7, amended: SI 2009/381 Reg.27
Reg.7, amended: SI 2009/381 Reg.39, SI 2009/2446 Reg.38
Reg.7, amended: SI 2009/2446 Sch.2 para.1
Reg.7, amended: SI 2009/2446 Reg.56
Reg.7, amended: SI 2009/2446 Sch.2 para.1
Reg.7, amended: SI 2009/381 Reg.60, SI 2009/2446 Reg.71
Reg.7, amended: SI 2009/381 Reg.69, SI 2009/2446 Reg.79
Reg.7, amended: SI 2009/2446 Sch.2 para.1
Reg.7A, added: SI 2009/2446 Reg.99
Reg.8, amended: SI 2009/2446 Sch.2 para.1

2008–cont.

653. National Health Service Pension Scheme Regulations 2008–*cont.*

Reg.8, amended: SI 2009/2446 Reg.20

Reg.8, amended: SI 2009/381 Reg.28, SI 2009/2446 Reg.29

Reg.8, amended: SI 2009/2446 Reg.47, Sch.2 para.1

Reg.8, amended: SI 2009/2446 Sch.2 para.1

Reg.8, amended: SI 2009/2446 Reg.62

Reg.8, amended: SI 2009/381 Reg.61, SI 2009/2446 Reg.72

Reg.8, amended: SI 2009/381 Reg.70

Reg.8, amended: SI 2009/2446 Reg.88, Sch.2 para.1

Reg.8, amended: SI 2009/2446 Sch.2 para.1

Reg.8, substituted: SI 2009/2446 Reg.100

Reg.9, amended: SI 2009/381 Reg.17, SI 2009/2446 Sch.2 para.1

Reg.9, amended: SI 2009/2446 Sch.2 para.1

Reg.9, amended: SI 2009/381 Reg.29, SI 2009/2446 Reg.30

Reg.9, amended: SI 2009/2446 Sch.2 para.1

Reg.9, amended: SI 2009/381 Reg.50, SI 2009/2446 Reg.51, Sch.2 para.1

Reg.9, amended: SI 2009/2446 Reg.63

Reg.9, amended: SI 2009/2446 Reg.73

Reg.9, amended: SI 2009/2446 Reg.89, Sch.2 para.1

Reg.9, amended: SI 2009/381 Reg.81, SI 2009/2446 Reg.93, Sch.2 para.1

Reg.10, amended: SI 2009/381 Reg.18, SI 2009/2446 Reg.16

Reg.10, amended: SI 2009/2446 Reg.21

Reg.10, amended: SI 2009/2446 Reg.31

Reg.10, amended: SI 2009/381 Reg.40, SI 2009/2446 Reg.39, Sch.2 para.1

Reg.10, amended: SI 2009/2446 Reg.48, Sch.2 para.1

Reg.10, amended: SI 2009/2446 Sch.2 para.1

Reg.10, amended: SI 2009/381 Reg.62, SI 2009/2446 Reg.74, Sch.2 para.1

Reg.10, amended: SI 2009/381 Reg.71, SI 2009/2446 Reg.80, Sch.2 para.1

Reg.10, substituted: SI 2009/2446 Reg.90

Reg.10, amended: SI 2009/2446 Sch.2 para.1

Reg.11, amended: SI 2009/2446 Reg.22

Reg.11, amended: SI 2009/381 Reg.30, SI 2009/2446 Reg.32

Reg.11, amended: SI 2009/381 Reg.41, SI 2009/2446 Reg.40, Sch.2 para.1

Reg.11, amended: SI 2009/2446 Reg.49, Sch.2 para.1

Reg.11, amended: SI 2009/381 Reg.51

Reg.11, revoked: SI 2009/2446 Reg.57

Reg.11, amended: SI 2009/381 Reg.63

Reg.11, amended: SI 2009/381 Reg.72, SI 2009/2446 Reg.81, Sch.2 para.1

Reg.11, amended: SI 2009/2446 Reg.91, Sch.2 para.1

Reg.11, substituted: SI 2009/2446 Reg.91

Reg.11, amended: SI 2009/381 Reg.82

Reg.11, added: SI 2009/2446 Reg.101

Reg.12, amended: SI 2009/2446 Sch.2 para.1

Reg.12, amended: SI 2009/381 Reg.42, SI 2009/2446 Reg.41, Sch.2 para.1

Reg.12, amended: SI 2009/2446 Reg.50

Reg.12, amended: SI 2009/2446 Reg.64

Reg.12, substituted: SI 2009/2446 Reg.75

Reg.12, amended: SI 2009/381 Reg.73, SI 2009/2446 Reg.82, Sch.2 para.1

Reg.12, amended: SI 2009/2446 Reg.92

Reg.12, substituted: SI 2009/2446 Reg.92

2008–cont.

653. National Health Service Pension Scheme Regulations 2008–*cont.*

Reg.13, amended: SI 2009/381 Reg.31, SI 2009/2446 Sch.2 para.1

Reg.13, amended: SI 2009/381 Reg.43

Reg.13, amended: SI 2009/2446 Sch.2 para.1

Reg.13, amended: SI 2009/2446 Reg.58

Reg.13, revoked: SI 2009/381 Reg.64

Reg.13, amended: SI 2009/381 Reg.74

Reg.13, amended: SI 2009/2446 Sch.2 para.1

Reg.14, amended: SI 2009/2446 Reg.23

Reg.14, amended: SI 2009/381 Reg.32, SI 2009/2446 Reg.33, Sch.2 para.1

Reg.14, amended: SI 2009/2446 Sch.2 para.1

Reg.14, substituted: SI 2009/381 Reg.52

Reg.14, amended: SI 2009/2446 Reg.65

Reg.14, amended: SI 2009/2446 Sch.2 para.1

Reg.14, substituted: SI 2009/381 Reg.83

Reg.15, amended: SI 2009/2446 Sch.2 para.1

Reg.15, amended: SI 2009/381 Reg.33

Reg.15, amended: SI 2009/381 Reg.44, SI 2009/2446 Sch.2 para.1

Reg.15, amended: SI 2009/2446 Sch.2 para.1

Reg.15, amended: SI 2009/2446 Reg.66

Reg.15, amended: SI 2009/381 Reg.75, SI 2009/2446 Sch.2 para.1

Reg.15, amended: SI 2009/2446 Sch.2 para.1

Reg.16, amended: SI 2009/2446 Reg.24

Reg.16, substituted: SI 2009/2446 Reg.34

Reg.16, amended: SI 2009/2446 Sch.2 para.1

Reg.17, revoked: SI 2009/381 Reg.34

Reg.17, amended: SI 2009/381 Reg.45, SI 2009/2446 Reg.42

Reg.17, amended: SI 2009/2446 Sch.2 para.1, Sch.2 para.2, Sch.2 para.5

Reg.17, amended: SI 2009/381 Reg.65, SI 2009/2446 Sch.2 para.1

Reg.17, amended: SI 2009/381 Reg.76, SI 2009/2446 Reg.83

Reg.17, amended: SI 2009/2446 Sch.2 para.1, Sch.2 para.2

Reg.18, amended: SI 2009/2446 Sch.2 para.1

Reg.18, amended: SI 2009/381 Reg.46, SI 2009/2446 Reg.43

Reg.18, amended: SI 2009/2446 Sch.2 para.1

Reg.18, amended: SI 2009/381 Reg.77, SI 2009/2446 Reg.84

Reg.19, amended: SI 2009/381 Reg.47, SI 2009/2446 Reg.44

Reg.19, amended: SI 2009/381 Reg.78, SI 2009/2446 Reg.85

Reg.21, amended: SI 2009/381 Reg.35, SI 2009/2446 Sch.2 para.1

Reg.21, amended: SI 2009/2446 Reg.45

Reg.21, amended: SI 2009/2446 Reg.86

Reg.22, amended: SI 2009/2446 Sch.2 para.1

Reg.25, amended: SI 2009/2446 Sch.2 para.1

Reg.26, amended: SI 2009/2446 Sch.2 para.1

667. Social Security Benefits Up-rating Regulations 2008

revoked: SI 2009/607 Reg.6

668. Consumer Credit Appeals Tribunal Rules 2008

revoked: SI 2009/1835 Sch.3

676. Consular Fees Order 2008

revoked: SI 2009/700 Sch.2

677. Copyright and Performances (Application to Other Countries) Order 2008

Sch.1, amended: SI 2009/2745 Art.2

2008–cont.

712. Hywel Dda National Health Service Trust (Establishment) Order 2008
revoked: SI 2009/1306 Sch.1

716. Abertawe Bro Morgannwg University National Health Service Trust (Establishment) Order 2008
revoked: SI 2009/1306 Sch.1

717. Cwm Taf National Health Service Trust (Establishment) Order 2008
revoked: SI 2009/1306 Sch.1

718. Northern Rock plc Compensation Scheme Order 2008
Sch.1, amended: SI 2009/791 Art.3, Art.4

729. Companies (Authorised Minimum) Regulations 2008
Reg.2, revoked: SI 2009/2425 Reg.8

736. Health and Safety (Fees) Regulations 2008
applied: SI 2009/1595 Reg.2
revoked: SI 2009/515 Reg.21

743. National Assistance (Assessment of Resources and Sums for Personal Requirements) (Amendment) (Wales) Regulations 2008
Reg.2, revoked: SI 2009/632 Reg.3
Reg.3, revoked: SI 2009/632 Reg.3
Reg.4, revoked: SI 2009/632 Reg.3
Reg.5, revoked: SI 2009/632 Reg.3

760. Asylum Support (Amendment) Regulations 2008
revoked: SI 2009/1388 Reg.3

794. Employment and Support Allowance Regulations 2008
referred to: SI 2009/497 Art.27
Part 10, amended: SI 2009/2655 Reg.11
Reg.2, amended: SI 2009/583 Reg.10, SI 2009/2655 Reg.11
Reg.2A, added: SI 2009/471 Reg.13
Reg.43, revoked (in part): SI 2009/3228 Reg.4
Reg.45, amended: SI 2009/2343 Reg.5
Reg.61, amended: SI 2009/2655 Reg.11
Reg.67, amended: SI 2009/3228 Reg.3
Reg.68, amended: SI 2009/3228 Reg.3
Reg.70, amended: SI 2009/362 Reg.9
Reg.76, amended: SI 2009/2343 Reg.5
Reg.85, amended: SI 2009/2655 Reg.11
Reg.91, amended: SI 2009/583 Reg.10
Reg.92, amended: SI 2009/583 Reg.10
Reg.93, amended: SI 2009/583 Reg.10
Reg.93, revoked (in part): SI 2009/583 Reg.10
Reg.94, amended: SI 2009/583 Reg.10
Reg.95, amended: SI 2009/2655 Reg.11
Reg.104, amended: SI 2009/2655 Reg.11
Reg.106, amended: SI 2009/2655 Reg.11
Reg.107, amended: SI 2009/2655 Reg.11
Reg.108, amended: SI 2009/2655 Reg.11
Reg.119, amended: SI 2009/2655 Reg.11
Reg.120, amended: SI 2009/2655 Reg.11
Reg.123, amended: SI 2009/2655 Reg.11
Reg.123, revoked (in part): SI 2009/2655 Reg.11
Reg.124, amended: SI 2009/2655 Reg.11
Reg.125, amended: SI 2009/2655 Reg.11
Reg.131, amended: SI 2009/583 Reg.10, SI 2009/2655 Reg.11
Reg.132, amended: SI 2009/583 Reg.10, SI 2009/1575 Reg.2
Reg.137, amended: SI 2009/1575 Reg.2
Reg.153, revoked (in part): SI 2009/2655 Reg.11
Reg.158, amended: SI 2009/1488 Reg.43
Reg.162, revoked: SI 2009/3228 Reg.2

2008–cont.

794. Employment and Support Allowance Regulations 2008–*cont.*
Reg.163, referred to: SI 2009/497 Sch.20
Reg.163, revoked: SI 2009/3228 Reg.2
Reg.164, revoked: SI 2009/3228 Reg.2
Sch.4 Part 1, referred to: SI 2009/497 Art.27
Sch.4 Part 1 para.1, amended: SI 2009/2655 Reg.11
Sch.4 Part 1 para.1, substituted: SI 2009/497 Sch.18
Sch.4 Part 2 para.4, amended: SI 2009/583 Reg.10
Sch.4 Part 3, referred to: SI 2009/497 Art.27
Sch.4 Part 3 para.11, substituted: SI 2009/497 Sch.19
Sch.4 Part 4 para.12, amended: SI 2009/497 Art.27
Sch.4 Part 4 para.13, amended: SI 2009/497 Art.27
Sch.6 para.5, amended: SI 2009/583 Reg.10, SI 2009/2655 Reg.11
Sch.6 para.7, referred to: SI 2009/497 Sch.20
Sch.6 para.8, referred to: SI 2009/497 Sch.20
Sch.6 para.11, referred to: SI 2009/497 Sch.20
Sch.6 para.12, referred to: SI 2009/497 Sch.20
Sch.6 para.13, referred to: SI 2009/497 Sch.20
Sch.6 para.15, amended: SI 2009/2655 Reg.11
Sch.6 para.19, amended: SI 2009/497 Art.27
Sch.6 para.19, referred to: SI 2009/497 Art.27
Sch.7 para.1, amended: SI 2009/2655 Reg.11
Sch.7 para.2, amended: SI 2009/2655 Reg.11
Sch.7 para.5, amended: SI 2009/2343 Reg.5
Sch.7 para.6, amended: SI 2009/2343 Reg.5
Sch.7 para.7, amended: SI 2009/2343 Reg.5
Sch.8 para.2A, added: SI 2009/2655 Reg.11
Sch.8 para.17, amended: SI 2009/2655 Reg.11
Sch.8 para.26, amended: SI 2009/2655 Reg.11
Sch.8 para.53, amended: SI 2009/583 Reg.10
Sch.8 para.60, substituted: SI 2009/2655 Reg.11
Sch.9 para.4, amended: SI 2009/1488 Reg.44
Sch.9 para.38A, added: SI 2009/583 Reg.10
Sch.9 para.56, amended: SI 2009/583 Reg.10

795. Employment and Support Allowance (Transitional Provisions) Regulations 2008
Reg.2, applied: SI 2009/3152 Reg.2

907. Bedfordshire (Structural Changes) Order 2008
referred to: SI 2009/119
Art.16, amended: SI 2009/837 Art.2
Art.26, amended: SI 2009/837 Art.2

909. Pension Protection Fund (Pension Compensation Cap) Order 2008
revoked: SI 2009/795 Art.3

911. Occupational Pension Schemes (Levy Ceiling) Order 2008
revoked: SI 2009/794 Art.3

916. Plastic Materials and Articles in Contact with Food (England) Regulations 2008
applied: SI 2009/205 Reg.5
revoked: SI 2009/205 Reg.27

928. Official Statistics Order 2008
revoked: SI 2009/753 Art.2

930. Safeguarding Vulnerable Groups Act 2006 (Commencement No 1) (Northern Ireland) Order 2008
Art.2, amended: 2009 c.26 s.81

944. Specified Animal Pathogens Order 2008
applied: SI 2009/1299 Reg.4
Sch.1 Part 1 para.34A, added: SI 2009/3083 Art.3
Sch.2 para.2, amended: SI 2009/3083 Art.4

945. Charities Act 2006 (Commencement No 4, Transitional Provisions and Savings) Order 2008
amended: SI 2009/841 Art.2

2008–cont.

945. Charities Act 2006 (Commencement No 4, Transitional Provisions and Savings) Order 2008–*cont.*
Art.2A, added: SI 2009/841 Art.2
Art.3, amended: SI 2009/841 Art.2
Art.10, amended: SI 2009/841 Art.2
Sch.1A, added: SI 2009/841 Art.2
Sch.2, amended: SI 2009/841 Art.2

948. Companies Act 2006 (Consequential Amendments etc) Order 2008
Sch.1 Part 1 para.1, revoked (in part): SI 2009/484 Sch.2

950. Protection of Military Remains Act 1986 (Designation of Vessels and Controlled Sites) Order 2008
revoked: SI 2009/3380 Art.4

954. Companies Act 2006 (Consequential Amendments) (Taxes and National Insurance) Order 2008
Art.21, revoked: 2009 c.4 Sch.3 Part 1

960. Legislative Reform (Health and Safety Executive) Order 2008
Sch.3, amended: SI 2009/716 Sch.7

962. Bluetongue Regulations 2008
Reg.8, amended: SI 2009/2712 Reg.6
Reg.8, revoked (in part): SI 2009/2712 Reg.6
Reg.11, amended: SI 2009/2712 Reg.6

975. Childcare (General Childcare Register) Regulations 2008
Sch.3 para.2, amended: SI 2009/1545 Reg.3
Sch.3 para.18, amended: SI 2009/1545 Reg.4
Sch.6 para.3, amended: SI 2009/1545 Reg.6
Sch.6 para.3A, added: SI 2009/1545 Reg.7
Sch.6 para.11, amended: SI 2009/1545 Reg.8
Sch.6 para.19, amended: SI 2009/1545 Reg.9

1052. Magistrates Courts Fees Order 2008
see *R. (on the application of Hillingdon LBC) v Lord Chancellor* [2008] EWHC 2683 (Admin), [2009] C.P. Rep. 13 (DC), Dyson, L.J.
Sch.1, substituted: SI 2009/1496 Sch.1
Sch.2 para.1, amended: SI 2009/1496 Art.4
Sch.2 para.3, amended: SI 2009/1496 Art.5, Art.6, Art.7
Sch.2 para.5, amended: SI 2009/1496 Art.8

1053. Civil Proceedings Fees Order 2008
Sch.1, amended: SI 2009/1498 Art.3, Art.4, Art.5, Art.6, Art.7, Art.8, Art.9, Art.10, Art.11, Art.12, Art.13, Art.14, Art.15, Art.16, Art.17
Sch.2 para.1, amended: SI 2009/1498 Art.18
Sch.2 para.3, amended: SI 2009/1498 Art.19, Art.20, Art.21
Sch.2 para.5, amended: SI 2009/1498 Art.22

1054. Family Proceedings Fees Order 2008
see *R. (on the application of Hillingdon LBC) v Lord Chancellor* [2008] EWHC 2683 (Admin), [2009] C.P. Rep. 13 (DC), Dyson, L.J.
Sch.1, amended: SI 2009/1499 Art.3, Art.4, Art.5, Art.6, Art.7, Art.8, Art.9, Art.10, Art.11, Art.12, Art.13, Art.14, Art.15, Art.16, Art.17, Art.18, Art.19, Art.20, Art.21
Sch.2 para.1, amended: SI 2009/1499 Art.22
Sch.2 para.3, amended: SI 2009/1499 Art.23, Art.24, Art.25
Sch.2 para.5, amended: SI 2009/1499 Art.26

1085. Standards Committee (England) Regulations 2008
applied: SI 2009/276 Reg.6
varied: SI 2009/276 Reg.7
Part 3, applied: SI 2009/276 Reg.5

2008–cont.

1085. Standards Committee (England) Regulations 2008–*cont.*
Reg.5, varied: SI 2009/1255 Reg.14
Reg.7, varied: SI 2009/1255 Reg.14
Reg.10, applied: SI 2009/276 Reg.7
Reg.11, applied: SI 2009/1255 Reg.9, Reg.10
Reg.11, varied: SI 2009/1255 Reg.9, Reg.10
Reg.13, applied: SI 2009/276 Reg.6, SI 2009/1255 Reg.9, Reg.10
Reg.13, varied: SI 2009/1255 Reg.9, Reg.10
Reg.14, applied: SI 2009/276 Reg.6, SI 2009/1255 Reg.9, Reg.10
Reg.14, varied: SI 2009/1255 Reg.9, Reg.10
Reg.16, applied: SI 2009/1255 Reg.9, Reg.10
Reg.16, varied: SI 2009/1255 Reg.9, Reg.10
Reg.17, applied: SI 2009/276 Reg.6
Reg.17, varied: SI 2009/276 Reg.5
Reg.18, applied: SI 2009/276 Reg.6
Reg.19, applied: SI 2009/276 Reg.5, Reg.6

1087. Control of Major Accident Hazard (Amendment) Regulations 2008
applied: SI 2009/1595 Reg.2

1139. Common Agricultural Policy Single Payment and Support Schemes (Amendment) Regulations 2008
revoked: SI 2009/3102 Reg.9

1181. Commission for Healthcare Audit and Inspection (Defence Medical Services) Regulations 2008
applied: SI 2009/462 Sch.3 para.9
revoked: SI 2009/462 Sch.6

1183. Immigration (Biometric Registration) (Pilot) Regulations 2008
applied: SI 2009/421 Reg.21

1184. Mental Health (Hospital, Guardianship and Treatment) (England) Regulations 2008
Reg.2, amended: SI 2009/462 Sch.5 para.25
Reg.30, amended: SI 2009/462 Sch.5 para.25
Reg.30, varied: SI 2009/462 Sch.4 para.15

1185. General Ophthalmic Services Contracts Regulations 2008
Sch.1 Part 4A para.21A, added: SI 2009/309 Sch.1 para.7
Sch.1 Part 5 para.22, amended: SI 2009/309 Sch.1 para.7
Sch.1 Part 5 para.26, amended: SI 2009/309 Sch.1 para.7

1186. Primary Ophthalmic Services Regulations 2008
Reg.3, amended: SI 2009/409 Reg.4

1188. Food Labelling (Declaration of Allergens) (England) Regulations 2008
Reg.2, revoked (in part): SI 2009/2801 Reg.3

1206. Mental Health (Approved Mental Health Professionals) (Approval) (England) Regulations 2008
Sch.1, varied: SI 2009/1357 Art.3

1216. Criminal Justice (Northern Ireland) Order 2008
Art.91A, added: 2009 c.25 Sch.16 para.6
Art.91B, added: 2009 c.25 Sch.16 para.6
Sch.1 para.25A, added: 2009 c.25 s.139
Sch.1 para.26A, added: 2009 c.25 s.139
Sch.1 para.31ZA, added: 2009 c.25 s.139
Sch.2 Part 1 para.27A, added: 2009 c.25 s.139
Sch.2 Part 1 para.28A, added: 2009 c.25 s.139
Sch.2 Part 1 para.31A, added: 2009 c.25 s.139
Sch.4 para.1, varied: SI 2009/1357 Art.3

2008–cont.

1261. London Gateway Port Harbour Empowerment Order 2008
Art.2, amended: SI 2009/1307 Sch.2 para.125

1268. Food Labelling (Declaration of Allergens) (Wales) Regulations 2008
Reg.2, revoked (in part): SI 2009/2880 Reg.3

1270. Specified Animal Pathogens (Wales) Order 2008
applied: SI 2009/1372 Reg.4
Sch.1 Part 1 para.34A, added: SI 2009/3234 Art.3
Sch.2 para.2, amended: SI 2009/3234 Art.4

1273. Assembly Learning Grants and Loans (Higher Education) (Wales) Regulations 2008
applied: SI 2009/2737 Reg.3

1275. Products of Animal Origin (Disease Control) (Wales) Regulations 2008
Reg.2, amended: SI 2009/1373 Reg.3
Reg.3, amended: SI 2009/1373 Reg.4, SI 2009/1910 Reg.2
Reg.7, amended: SI 2009/1373 Reg.5
Reg.9, amended: SI 2009/1373 Reg.6
Reg.9, revoked (in part): SI 2009/1373 Reg.6
Reg.10, amended: SI 2009/1373 Reg.7
Reg.12, amended: SI 2009/1373 Reg.8
Reg.13, amended: SI 2009/1373 Reg.9
Reg.14, substituted: SI 2009/1373 Reg.10
Reg.15, amended: SI 2009/1373 Reg.11
Sch.3 para.3A, added: SI 2009/1373 Reg.12

1277. Consumer Protection from Unfair Trading Regulations 2008
referred to: SI 2009/669 Sch.1 Part 2

1284. Cosmetic Products (Safety) Regulations 2008
applied: SI 2009/716 Reg.3
referred to: SI 2009/669 Sch.1 Part 4, Sch.2 Part 2
Sch.2 para.56, added: SI 2009/1346 Reg.2
Sch.2 para.56, substituted: SI 2009/2562 Sch.1
Sch.2 para.56i, added: SI 2009/796 Reg.2, SI 2009/1346 Reg.2
Sch.2 para.56i, substituted: SI 2009/2562 Sch.1
Sch.2 para.57, added: SI 2009/1346 Reg.2
Sch.2 para.57, substituted: SI 2009/2562 Sch.1
Sch.2 para.60, added: SI 2009/3367 Reg.2
Sch.3, amended: SI 2009/796 Sch.1, SI 2009/1346 Reg.2, Sch.1
Sch.4 Part 1, amended: SI 2009/796 Reg.2, SI 2009/1346 Sch.2, SI 2009/2562 Sch.2
Sch.4 Part 2, amended: SI 2009/796 Reg.2, SI 2009/2562 Reg.2, SI 2009/3367 Reg.2
Sch.4 Part 2, revoked: SI 2009/2562 Reg.2
Sch.7 Part 1, amended: SI 2009/1346 Reg.2

1324. Assembly Learning Grants (European Institutions) (Wales) (Amendment) Regulations 2008
revoked: SI 2009/3359 Reg.4

1337. Immigration and Nationality (Cost Recovery Fees) (Amendment No.2) Regulations 2008
revoked: SI 2009/421 Reg.33

1419. Local Government (Structural and Boundary Changes) (Staffing) Regulations 2008
Reg.4, amended: SI 2009/276 Reg.13

1432. Financial Assistance Scheme (Miscellaneous Provisions) Regulations 2008
Reg.8, applied: SI 2009/1851 Reg.38
Reg.8, revoked: SI 2009/1851 Reg.35
Reg.8, varied: SI 2009/1851 Reg.38

1463. Authorised Investment Funds (Tax) (Amendment No.2) Regulations 2008
revoked: 2009 c.4 Sch.3 Part 1

2008–cont.

1465. Community Bus (Amendment) Regulations 2008
revoked: SI 2009/366 Sch.1

1485. Nursing and Midwifery (Amendment) Order 2008
Sch.1 para.4, amended: 2009 c.26 s.81
Sch.2 para.1, amended: 2009 c.26 s.81

1513. Civil Enforcement of Parking Contraventions (England) General (Amendment) Regulations 2008
revoked: SI 2009/478 Reg.2

1521. Finance Act 2007, Section 17(2) (Corporation Tax Deduction for Expenditure on Energy-Saving Items) (Appointed Day) Order 2008
revoked: 2009 c.4 Sch.3 Part 1

1575. Education (Outturn Statements) (England) Regulations 2008
revoked: SI 2009/1586 Reg.3

1582. Education (Student Support) (No.2) Regulations 2008
applied: SI 2009/1555 Reg.4, SI 2009/1562 Art.2
Part 4, revoked: SI 2009/1555 Reg.4
Part 5, revoked: SI 2009/1555 Reg.4
Part 6, revoked: SI 2009/1555 Reg.4
Part 7, revoked: SI 2009/1555 Reg.4
Part 10, revoked: SI 2009/1555 Reg.4
Reg.1, revoked: SI 2009/1555 Reg.4
Reg.2, amended: SI 2009/1555 Sch.5 para.1
Reg.2, revoked: SI 2009/1555 Reg.4
Reg.3, revoked: SI 2009/1555 Reg.4
Reg.4, applied: SI 2009/1555 Reg.4
Reg.4, revoked (in part): SI 2009/470 Reg.2, SI 2009/1555 Reg.4
Reg.5, revoked: SI 2009/1555 Reg.4
Reg.6, revoked: SI 2009/1555 Reg.4
Reg.7, revoked: SI 2009/1555 Reg.4
Reg.8, revoked: SI 2009/1555 Reg.4
Reg.9, revoked: SI 2009/1555 Reg.4
Reg.10, revoked: SI 2009/1555 Reg.4
Reg.11, revoked: SI 2009/1555 Reg.4
Reg.12, revoked: SI 2009/1555 Reg.4
Reg.14, amended: SI 2009/1555 Sch.5 para.2
Reg.20, amended: SI 2009/1555 Sch.5 para.3
Reg.27, amended: SI 2009/1555 Sch.5 para.4
Reg.28, amended: SI 2009/1555 Sch.5 para.5
Reg.29, amended: SI 2009/1555 Sch.5 para.6
Reg.93, revoked (in part): SI 2009/470 Reg.2, SI 2009/1555 Reg.4, Reg.4
Reg.94, revoked (in part): SI 2009/470 Reg.2, SI 2009/1555 Reg.4, Reg.4
Reg.95, revoked: SI 2009/1555 Reg.4
Reg.96, revoked: SI 2009/1555 Reg.4
Reg.97, revoked: SI 2009/1555 Reg.4
Reg.98, revoked: SI 2009/1555 Reg.4
Reg.99, revoked: SI 2009/1555 Reg.4
Reg.100, revoked: SI 2009/1555 Reg.4
Reg.101, revoked: SI 2009/1555 Reg.4
Reg.102, revoked: SI 2009/1555 Reg.4
Reg.115, revoked: SI 2009/1555 Reg.4
Reg.116, revoked: SI 2009/1555 Reg.4
Reg.117, revoked: SI 2009/1555 Reg.4
Reg.118, revoked: SI 2009/1555 Reg.4
Reg.119, amended: SI 2009/1555 Sch.5 para.7
Reg.119, revoked: SI 2009/1555 Reg.4
Reg.120, revoked: SI 2009/1555 Reg.4
Reg.121, revoked: SI 2009/1555 Reg.4
Reg.122, revoked: SI 2009/1555 Reg.4
Reg.123, revoked: SI 2009/1555 Reg.4

2008–cont.

1582. Education (Student Support) (No.2) Regulations 2008–*cont.*

Reg.124, revoked: SI 2009/1555 Reg.4
Reg.125, revoked: SI 2009/1555 Reg.4
Reg.126, revoked: SI 2009/1555 Reg.4
Reg.127, revoked: SI 2009/1555 Reg.4
Reg.128, revoked: SI 2009/1555 Reg.4
Reg.129, revoked: SI 2009/1555 Reg.4
Reg.130, revoked: SI 2009/1555 Reg.4
Reg.131, revoked: SI 2009/1555 Reg.4
Reg.132, revoked: SI 2009/1555 Reg.4
Reg.133, revoked: SI 2009/1555 Reg.4
Reg.134, revoked: SI 2009/1555 Reg.4
Reg.135, revoked: SI 2009/1555 Reg.4
Reg.136, amended: SI 2009/1555 Sch.5 para.8
Reg.136, revoked: SI 2009/1555 Reg.4
Reg.137, revoked: SI 2009/1555 Reg.4
Reg.138, revoked: SI 2009/1555 Reg.4
Reg.139, revoked: SI 2009/1555 Reg.4
Reg.140, revoked: SI 2009/1555 Reg.4
Reg.141, revoked: SI 2009/1555 Reg.4
Reg.142, revoked: SI 2009/1555 Reg.4
Reg.143, revoked: SI 2009/1555 Reg.4
Reg.144, revoked: SI 2009/1555 Reg.4
Reg.145, revoked: SI 2009/1555 Reg.4
Reg.146, revoked: SI 2009/1555 Reg.4
Reg.147, revoked: SI 2009/1555 Reg.4
Reg.148, revoked: SI 2009/1555 Reg.4
Reg.149, revoked: SI 2009/1555 Reg.4
Reg.150, revoked: SI 2009/1555 Reg.4
Reg.151, revoked: SI 2009/1555 Reg.4
Reg.152, revoked: SI 2009/1555 Reg.4
Reg.153, revoked: SI 2009/1555 Reg.4
Reg.154, revoked: SI 2009/1555 Reg.4
Reg.155, revoked: SI 2009/1555 Reg.4
Reg.156, revoked: SI 2009/1555 Reg.4
Reg.157, revoked: SI 2009/1555 Reg.4
Reg.158, revoked: SI 2009/1555 Reg.4
Sch.1 Part 1 para.1, revoked: SI 2009/1555 Reg.4
Sch.1 Part 2, revoked: SI 2009/1555 Reg.4
Sch.5 para.1, revoked: SI 2009/1555 Reg.4
Sch.5 para.2, revoked: SI 2009/1555 Reg.4
Sch.5 para.3, revoked: SI 2009/1555 Reg.4
Sch.5 para.4, revoked: SI 2009/1555 Reg.4
Sch.5 para.5, revoked: SI 2009/1555 Reg.4
Sch.5 para.6, revoked: SI 2009/1555 Reg.4
Sch.5 para.7, revoked: SI 2009/1555 Reg.4
Sch.5 para.8, revoked: SI 2009/1555 Reg.4
Sch.5 para.9, revoked: SI 2009/1555 Reg.4

1584. Lyme Bay Designated Area (Fishing Restrictions) Order 2008

Art.3, amended: SI 2009/1675 Art.2

1592. Data Protection Act 1998 (Commencement No.2) Order 2008

Art.2, amended: 2009 c.26 s.81

1596. Social Security (Recovery of Benefits) (Lump Sum Payments) Regulations 2008

Reg.7, amended: SI 2009/1494 Reg.2

1642. Plastic Materials and Articles in Contact with Food (England) (Amendment) Regulations 2008

Reg.2, revoked: SI 2009/205 Reg.27
Reg.3, revoked: SI 2009/205 Reg.27
Reg.4, revoked: SI 2009/205 Reg.27

1648. North Wales National Health Service Trust (Establishment) Order 2008

revoked: SI 2009/1306 Sch.1

2008–cont.

1654. Magnetic Toys (Safety) Regulations 2008

revoked: SI 2009/1347 Reg.2

1682. Plastic Materials and Articles in Contact with Food (Wales) (No.2) Regulations 2008

applied: SI 2009/481 Reg.5
revoked: SI 2009/481 Reg.27

1695. Immigration and Nationality (Fees) (Amendment No.2) Regulations 2008

revoked: SI 2009/816 Reg.32

1700. Primary Ophthalmic Services Amendment, Transitional and Consequential Provisions Regulations 2008

Reg.4, applied: SI 2009/309 Sch.1 para.8
Reg.5, applied: SI 2009/309 Sch.1 para.8

1718. Eggs and Chicks (England) Regulations 2008

applied: SI 2009/2163 Reg.40
revoked: SI 2009/2163 Reg.2

1722. Childcare (Provision of Information About Young Children) (England) Regulations 2008

Reg.1, revoked (in part): SI 2009/1554 Reg.3
Reg.2, revoked (in part): SI 2009/1554 Reg.3
Reg.3, revoked (in part): SI 2009/1554 Reg.3
Reg.4, revoked (in part): SI 2009/1554 Reg.3
Reg.5, revoked (in part): SI 2009/1554 Reg.3
Reg.6, revoked (in part): SI 2009/1554 Reg.3
Reg.7, revoked (in part): SI 2009/1554 Reg.3
Reg.8, revoked (in part): SI 2009/1554 Reg.3
Reg.9, revoked: SI 2009/1563 Sch.1
Reg.10, revoked (in part): SI 2009/1554 Reg.3
Sch.1 Part 1 para.1, revoked (in part): SI 2009/1554 Reg.3
Sch.1 Part 1 para.2, revoked (in part): SI 2009/1554 Reg.3
Sch.1 Part 2 para.3, revoked (in part): SI 2009/1554 Reg.3
Sch.1 Part 2 para.4, revoked (in part): SI 2009/1554 Reg.3
Sch.1 Part 2 para.5, revoked (in part): SI 2009/1554 Reg.3
Sch.1 Part 2 para.6, revoked (in part): SI 2009/1554 Reg.3
Sch.1 Part 2 para.7, revoked (in part): SI 2009/1554 Reg.3
Sch.1 Part 2 para.8, revoked (in part): SI 2009/1554 Reg.3
Sch.1 Part 2 para.9, revoked (in part): SI 2009/1554 Reg.3
Sch.1 Part 2 para.10, revoked (in part): SI 2009/1554 Reg.3
Sch.1 Part 2 para.11, revoked (in part): SI 2009/1554 Reg.3
Sch.1 Part 2 para.12, revoked (in part): SI 2009/1554 Reg.3
Sch.1 Part 2 para.13, revoked (in part): SI 2009/1554 Reg.3

1729. Childcare (Inspections) Regulations 2008

Reg.3, amended: SI 2009/1508 Reg.2

1737. Political Parties, Elections and Referendums Act 2000 (Northern Ireland Political Parties) Order 2008

Art.11, amended: SI 2009/2748 Sch.1 para.37

1738. Company Names Adjudicator Rules 2008

r.5, see *Barloworld Handling Ltd v Unilift South Wales Ltd* [2009] F.S.R. 21 (Arbitration), Judi Pike

1740. Childcare (Disqualification) (Amendment) Regulations 2008

revoked: SI 2009/1547 Reg.3

1769. Sexual Offences (Northern Ireland) Order 2008

Part 3, applied: SI 2009/1547 Sch.3 para.3

Art.5, applied: 2009 asp 9 Sch.1 para.2, SSI 2009/182 Sch.1 para.6

Art.5, referred to: SI 2009/37 Sch.1 para.1, Sch.1 para.2, Sch.1 para.4

Art.6, applied: 2009 asp 9 Sch.1 para.2, SSI 2009/182 Sch.1 para.7

Art.6, referred to: SI 2009/37 Sch.1 para.1, Sch.1 para.2, Sch.1 para.4

Art.7, applied: 2009 asp 9 Sch.1 para.2

Art.7, referred to: SI 2009/37 Sch.1 para.2, Sch.1 para.4

Art.8, applied: 2009 asp 9 Sch.1 para.2, SSI 2009/182 Sch.1 para.8

Art.8, referred to: SI 2009/37 Sch.1 para.2, Sch.1 para.4

Art.12, applied: 2009 asp 9 Sch.1 para.3, SSI 2009/182 Sch.1 para.9

Art.12, referred to: SI 2009/37 Sch.1 para.1, Sch.1 para.4

Art.13, applied: 2009 asp 9 Sch.1 para.3

Art.13, referred to: SI 2009/37 Sch.1 para.1, Sch.1 para.4

Art.14, applied: 2009 asp 9 Sch.1 para.3

Art.14, referred to: SI 2009/37 Sch.1 para.1, Sch.1 para.4

Art.15, applied: 2009 asp 9 Sch.1 para.3

Art.15, referred to: SI 2009/37 Sch.1 para.1, Sch.1 para.4

Art.16, applied: 2009 asp 9 Sch.1 para.3

Art.16, referred to: SI 2009/37 Sch.1 para.2, Sch.1 para.4

Art.17, applied: 2009 asp 9 Sch.1 para.3

Art.17, referred to: SI 2009/37 Sch.1 para.2, Sch.1 para.4

Art.18, applied: 2009 asp 9 Sch.1 para.3

Art.18, referred to: SI 2009/37 Sch.1 para.2, Sch.1 para.4

Art.19, applied: 2009 asp 9 Sch.1 para.3

Art.19, referred to: SI 2009/37 Sch.1 para.2, Sch.1 para.4

Art.20, applied: 2009 asp 9 Sch.1 para.3

Art.21, applied: 2009 asp 9 Sch.1 para.3

Art.21, referred to: SI 2009/37 Sch.1 para.2, Sch.1 para.4

Art.22, applied: 2009 asp 9 Sch.1 para.3

Art.22, referred to: SI 2009/37 Sch.1 para.2, Sch.1 para.4

Art.23, applied: 2009 asp 9 Sch.1 para.2

Art.23, referred to: SI 2009/37 Sch.1 para.2, Sch.1 para.4

Art.24, applied: 2009 asp 9 Sch.1 para.2

Art.24, referred to: SI 2009/37 Sch.1 para.2, Sch.1 para.4

Art.25, applied: 2009 asp 9 Sch.1 para.2

Art.25, referred to: SI 2009/37 Sch.1 para.2, Sch.1 para.4

Art.26, applied: 2009 asp 9 Sch.1 para.2

Art.26, referred to: SI 2009/37 Sch.1 para.2, Sch.1 para.4

Art.27, referred to: SI 2009/37 Sch.1 para.2, Sch.1 para.4

Art.32, applied: 2009 asp 9 Sch.1 para.2, SSI 2009/182 Sch.1 para.10

Art.32, referred to: SI 2009/37 Sch.1 para.2, Sch.1 para.4

Art.33, applied: 2009 asp 9 Sch.1 para.2, SSI 2009/182 Sch.1 para.11

1769. Sexual Offences (Northern Ireland) Order 2008–*cont.*

Art.33, referred to: SI 2009/37 Sch.1 para.2, Sch.1 para.4

Art.37, applied: 2009 asp 9 Sch.1 para.2

Art.37, referred to: SI 2009/37 Sch.1 para.2, Sch.1 para.4

Art.38, applied: 2009 asp 9 Sch.1 para.2

Art.38, referred to: SI 2009/37 Sch.1 para.2, Sch.1 para.4

Art.39, applied: 2009 asp 9 Sch.1 para.2

Art.39, referred to: SI 2009/37 Sch.1 para.2, Sch.1 para.4

Art.40, applied: 2009 asp 9 Sch.1 para.2

Art.40, referred to: SI 2009/37 Sch.1 para.2, Sch.1 para.4

Art.43, applied: SSI 2009/182 Sch.1 para.12

Art.43, referred to: SI 2009/37 Sch.1 para.1, Sch.1 para.2, Sch.1 para.3

Art.44, applied: SSI 2009/182 Sch.1 para.13

Art.44, referred to: SI 2009/37 Sch.1 para.1, Sch.1 para.2, Sch.1 para.3

Art.45, referred to: SI 2009/37 Sch.1 para.1, Sch.1 para.2, Sch.1 para.3

Art.46, referred to: SI 2009/37 Sch.1 para.1, Sch.1 para.2, Sch.1 para.3

Art.47, applied: SSI 2009/182 Sch.1 para.14

Art.47, referred to: SI 2009/37 Sch.1 para.1, Sch.1 para.2, Sch.1 para.3

Art.48, applied: SSI 2009/182 Sch.1 para.15

Art.48, referred to: SI 2009/37 Sch.1 para.1, Sch.1 para.2, Sch.1 para.3

Art.49, referred to: SI 2009/37 Sch.1 para.1, Sch.1 para.2, Sch.1 para.3

Art.50, referred to: SI 2009/37 Sch.1 para.1, Sch.1 para.2, Sch.1 para.3

Art.51, applied: 2009 asp 9 Sch.1 para.2

Art.51, referred to: SI 2009/37 Sch.1 para.1, Sch.1 para.2, Sch.1 para.3

Art.52, applied: 2009 asp 9 Sch.1 para.2

Art.52, referred to: SI 2009/37 Sch.1 para.1, Sch.1 para.2, Sch.1 para.3

Art.53, applied: 2009 asp 9 Sch.1 para.2

Art.53, referred to: SI 2009/37 Sch.1 para.1, Sch.1 para.2, Sch.1 para.3

Art.54, applied: 2009 asp 9 Sch.1 para.2

Art.54, referred to: SI 2009/37 Sch.1 para.1, Sch.1 para.2, Sch.1 para.3

Art.58, amended: 2009 c.26 Sch.7 para.26, Sch.8 Part 2

Art.58, revoked (in part): 2009 c.26 Sch.7 para.26, Sch.8 Part 2

Art.60, substituted: 2009 c.26 s.20

Art.61, substituted: 2009 c.26 s.20

Art.62, referred to: SI 2009/37 Sch.1 para.2, Sch.1 para.4

Art.63, referred to: SI 2009/37 Sch.1 para.2, Sch.1 para.4

Art.64A, added: 2009 c.26 s.15

Art.65, applied: 2009 asp 9 Sch.1 para.2

Art.65, referred to: SI 2009/37 Sch.1 para.2, Sch.1 para.4

Art.66, referred to: SI 2009/37 Sch.1 para.2, Sch.1 para.4

Art.67, referred to: SI 2009/37 Sch.1 para.2, Sch.1 para.4

Art.70, applied: 2009 asp 9 Sch.1 para.2, SI 2009/1547 Sch.3 para.3

2008–cont.

1769. Sexual Offences (Northern Ireland) Order 2008–*cont.*
Art.70, referred to: SI 2009/37 Sch.1 para.2, Sch.1 para.4
Art.71, applied: 2009 asp 9 Sch.1 para.2
Art.71, referred to: SI 2009/37 Sch.1 para.2, Sch.1 para.4
Art.73, applied: SI 2009/1547 Sch.3 para.3
Art.74, applied: SI 2009/1547 Sch.3 para.3

1774. Health Care and Associated Professions (Miscellaneous Amendments) Order 2008
Art.1, enabled: SI 2009/666
Art.5, revoked: SI 2009/1182 Art.7
Sch.1 para.15, amended: 2009 c.26 s.81
Sch.2 para.2, amended: 2009 c.26 s.81
Sch.3 para.4, amended: 2009 c.26 s.81
Sch.4 para.4, amended: 2009 c.26 s.81

1778. Social Fund Winter Fuel Payment (Temporary Increase) Regulations 2008
revoked: SI 2009/1489 Reg.3

1782. Air Navigation (Amendment) Order 2008
revoked: SI 2009/3015 Sch.1

1783. Films Co-Production Agreements (Amendment) Order 2008
revoked: SI 2009/3009 Art.3

1797. Trade Marks Rules 2008
r.2, amended: SI 2009/2089 r.4
r.5, amended: SI 2009/2089 r.5, r.6, r.7, r.8
r.11, amended: SI 2009/546 r.12
r.12, amended: SI 2009/546 r.13
r.13, amended: SI 2009/2089 r.9
r.26, amended: SI 2009/2089 r.10
r.28, amended: SI 2009/2089 r.11
r.28, revoked (in part): SI 2009/2089 r.12
r.54, see *AVON GRIPSTER Trade Mark* [2009] R.P.C. 17 (TMR), Allan James
r.74, see *AVON GRIPSTER Trade Mark* [2009] R.P.C. 17 (TMR), Allan James
r.77, amended: SI 2009/2089 r.13

1801. Education (Independent School Inspection Fees and Publication) (England) Regulations 2008
Reg.4, applied: SI 2009/1607 Reg.5
Reg.4, revoked: SI 2009/1607 Reg.9
Reg.5, applied: SI 2009/1607 Reg.5
Reg.5, revoked: SI 2009/1607 Reg.9
Reg.6, revoked: SI 2009/1607 Reg.9
Reg.7, revoked: SI 2009/1607 Reg.9

1804. Childcare (Fees) Regulations 2008
Reg.3, amended: SI 2009/1507 Reg.2
Reg.4, amended: SI 2009/1507 Reg.2
Reg.9, amended: SI 2009/1507 Reg.2
Reg.10, amended: SI 2009/1507 Reg.2

1814. Stamp Duty and Stamp Duty Reserve Tax (Investment Exchanges and Clearing Houses) (European Central Counterparty Limited and the Turquoise Multilateral Trading Facility) Regulations 2008
revoked: SI 2009/1827 Reg.6

1858. Mental Capacity (Deprivation of Liberty Standard Authorisations, Assessments and Ordinary Residence) Regulations 2008
Reg.3, amended: SI 2009/827 Reg.6
Reg.5, varied: SI 2009/1357 Art.3
Reg.13, varied: SI 2009/139 Sch.1 para.2
Reg.19, amended: SI 2009/827 Reg.6

1880. Finance Act 2007, Section 50 (Appointed Day) Order 2008
revoked: 2009 c.4 Sch.3 Part 1

2008–cont.

1894. National Minimum Wage Regulations 1999 (Amendment) Regulations 2008
Reg.3, revoked: SI 2009/1902 Reg.8
Reg.5, revoked: SI 2009/1902 Reg.8
Reg.6, revoked: SI 2009/1902 Reg.8

1911. Limited Liability Partnerships (Accounts and Audit) (Application of Companies Act 2006) Regulations 2008
applied: SI 2009/1804 Sch.1 para.35
Part 17, amended: SI 2009/1804 Sch.3 para.15
Reg.3, amended: SI 2009/1804 Sch.3 para.15
Reg.6, amended: SI 2009/1804 Sch.3 para.16
Reg.6, substituted: SI 2009/1804 Sch.3 para.16
Reg.24, amended: SI 2009/1804 Sch.3 para.16
Reg.24, substituted: SI 2009/1804 Sch.3 para.16
Reg.32, amended: SI 2009/1804 Sch.3 para.15
Reg.39, applied: SI 2009/209 Reg.20
Reg.40, amended: SI 2009/1804 Sch.3 para.16
Reg.40, applied: SI 2009/209 Reg.20
Reg.40, substituted: SI 2009/1804 Sch.3 para.16
Reg.49, amended: SI 2009/1804 Sch.3 para.15
Reg.50, amended: SI 2009/1804 Sch.3 para.15
Reg.54, amended: SI 2009/1804 Sch.3 para.15
Reg.55, amended: SI 2009/1804 Sch.3 para.15
Reg.56, amended: SI 2009/1804 Sch.3 para.15
Reg.57, amended: SI 2009/1804 Sch.3 para.15

1925. Finance Act 2008, Section 30 (Appointed Day) Order 2008
revoked: 2009 c.4 Sch.3 Part 1

1928. Finance Act 2008, Section 29 (Appointed Day) Order 2008
revoked: 2009 c.4 Sch.3 Part 1

1929. Finance Act 2008, Section 28 (Appointed Day) Order 2008
revoked: 2009 c.4 Sch.3 Part 1

1930. Finance Act 2008, Section 27 (Appointed Day) Order 2008
revoked: 2009 c.4 Sch.3 Part 1

1943. Air Navigation (Dangerous Goods) (Amendment) Regulations 2008
revoked: SI 2009/1492 Reg.3

1948. Taxes (Fees for Payment by Telephone) Regulations 2008
revoked: SI 2009/3073 Reg.3

1958. Trade Marks (Fees) Rules 2008
Sch.1, amended: SI 2009/2089 r.15, r.16, r.17, r.18, r.19

1961. Commons Registration (England) Regulations 2008
Reg.7, amended: SI 2009/2018 Reg.2
Reg.9, amended: SI 2009/2018 Reg.2
Reg.18, amended: SI 2009/2018 Reg.2
Reg.21, amended: SI 2009/2018 Reg.2
Reg.26, amended: SI 2009/2018 Reg.2
Reg.27, amended: SI 2009/2018 Reg.2
Reg.39, amended: SI 2009/2018 Reg.2
Reg.41, amended: SI 2009/2018 Reg.2
Reg.42, amended: SI 2009/2018 Reg.2
Sch.4 para.18, amended: SI 2009/2018 Reg.2
Sch.6 para.2, amended: SI 2009/2018 Reg.2

1969. Legal Officers (Annual Fees) Order 2008
revoked: SI 2009/2107 Art.4

1970. Ecclesiastical Judges, Legal Officers and Others (Fees) Order 2008
revoked: SI 2009/2105 Art.3

1976. Private Dentistry (Wales) Regulations 2008
Reg.5, amended: SI 2009/2541 Reg.15
Reg.13, amended: SI 2009/2541 Reg.15
Sch.2 para.2, substituted: SI 2009/2541 Reg.15

2008–cont.

2035. Designation of Rural Primary Schools (England) Order 2008
revoked: SI 2009/3346 Art.3

2094. Education (Student Support) (Amendment) (No.2) Regulations 2008
revoked: SI 2009/1555 Reg.4

2108. Export and Import of Dangerous Chemicals Regulations 2008
Reg.5, revoked (in part): SI 2009/716 Sch.7

2114. Welfare Reform Act (Relevant Enactment) Order 2008
revoked: SI 2009/2162 Art.3

2140. Assembly Learning Grants and Loans (Higher Education) (Wales) (Amendment) Regulations 2008
applied: SI 2009/2737 Reg.3

2141. School Milk (Wales) Regulations 2008
Reg.2, amended: SI 2009/108 Reg.2
Reg.3, amended: SI 2009/108 Reg.2

2155. Education (School Teachers Pay and Conditions) Order 2008
revoked: SI 2009/2132 Art.3

2176. Local Government (Structural Changes) (Transfer of Functions, Property, Rights and Liabilities) Regulations 2008
Reg.6, amended: SI 2009/5 Reg.7
Reg.7, disapplied: SI 2009/467 Reg.3
Reg.10, applied: SI 2009/276 Reg.9
Reg.11, disapplied: SI 2009/467 Reg.3
Reg.12, disapplied: SI 2009/467 Reg.3
Reg.13, disapplied: SI 2009/467 Reg.3

2206. Trade Marks (International Registration) Order 2008
Sch.2 para.7, amended: SI 2009/2464 Art.3
Sch.6, amended: SI 2009/2464 Art.4

2264. Tonnage Tax (Training Requirement) (Amendment) Regulations 2008
revoked: SI 2009/2304 Sch.1

2265. Social Fund (Applications and Miscellaneous Provisions) Regulations 2008
Reg.2, substituted: SI 2009/3033 Reg.2
Reg.5, amended: SI 2009/3033 Reg.2
Reg.6, amended: SI 2009/3033 Reg.2
Reg.6, substituted: SI 2009/2655 Reg.12
Reg.7, amended: SI 2009/3033 Reg.2

2297. Veterinary Medicines Regulations 2008
Reg.1, revoked: SI 2009/2297 Reg.45
Reg.2, applied: SI 2009/716 Reg.3
Reg.2, revoked: SI 2009/2297 Reg.45
Reg.3, revoked: SI 2009/2297 Reg.45
Reg.4, revoked: SI 2009/2297 Reg.45
Reg.5, revoked: SI 2009/2297 Reg.45
Reg.6, revoked: SI 2009/2297 Reg.45
Reg.7, revoked: SI 2009/2297 Reg.45
Reg.8, revoked: SI 2009/2297 Reg.45
Reg.9, revoked: SI 2009/2297 Reg.45
Reg.10, revoked: SI 2009/2297 Reg.45
Reg.11, revoked: SI 2009/2297 Reg.45
Reg.12, revoked: SI 2009/2297 Reg.45
Reg.13, revoked: SI 2009/2297 Reg.45
Reg.14, revoked: SI 2009/2297 Reg.45
Reg.15, revoked: SI 2009/2297 Reg.45
Reg.16, revoked: SI 2009/2297 Reg.45
Reg.17, revoked: SI 2009/2297 Reg.45
Reg.18, revoked: SI 2009/2297 Reg.45
Reg.19, revoked: SI 2009/2297 Reg.45
Reg.20, revoked: SI 2009/2297 Reg.45
Reg.21, revoked: SI 2009/2297 Reg.45

2008–cont.

2297. Veterinary Medicines Regulations 2008–*cont.*
Reg.22, revoked: SI 2009/2297 Reg.45
Reg.23, revoked: SI 2009/2297 Reg.45
Reg.24, revoked: SI 2009/2297 Reg.45
Reg.25, revoked: SI 2009/2297 Reg.45
Reg.26, revoked: SI 2009/2297 Reg.45
Reg.27, revoked: SI 2009/2297 Reg.45
Reg.28, revoked: SI 2009/2297 Reg.45
Reg.29, revoked: SI 2009/2297 Reg.45
Reg.30, revoked: SI 2009/2297 Reg.45
Reg.31, revoked: SI 2009/2297 Reg.45
Reg.32, revoked: SI 2009/2297 Reg.45
Reg.33, revoked: SI 2009/2297 Reg.45
Reg.34, revoked: SI 2009/2297 Reg.45
Reg.35, revoked: SI 2009/2297 Reg.45
Reg.36, revoked: SI 2009/2297 Reg.45
Reg.37, revoked: SI 2009/2297 Reg.45
Reg.38, revoked: SI 2009/2297 Reg.45
Reg.39, revoked: SI 2009/2297 Reg.45
Reg.40, revoked: SI 2009/2297 Reg.45
Reg.41, revoked: SI 2009/2297 Reg.45
Reg.42, revoked: SI 2009/2297 Reg.45
Reg.43, revoked: SI 2009/2297 Reg.45
Reg.44, revoked: SI 2009/2297 Reg.45
Reg.45, revoked (in part): SI 2009/2297 Reg.45
Sch.1 Part 1 para.1, revoked: SI 2009/2297 Reg.45
Sch.1 Part 1 para.2, revoked: SI 2009/2297 Reg.45
Sch.1 Part 1 para.3, revoked: SI 2009/2297 Reg.45
Sch.1 Part 1 para.4, revoked: SI 2009/2297 Reg.45
Sch.1 Part 1 para.5, revoked: SI 2009/2297 Reg.45
Sch.1 Part 2 para.6, revoked: SI 2009/2297 Reg.45
Sch.1 Part 2 para.7, revoked: SI 2009/2297 Reg.45
Sch.1 Part 2 para.8, revoked: SI 2009/2297 Reg.45
Sch.1 Part 2 para.9, revoked: SI 2009/2297 Reg.45
Sch.1 Part 2 para.10, revoked: SI 2009/2297 Reg.45
Sch.1 Part 2 para.11, revoked: SI 2009/2297 Reg.45
Sch.1 Part 2 para.12, revoked: SI 2009/2297 Reg.45
Sch.1 Part 2 para.13, revoked: SI 2009/2297 Reg.45
Sch.1 Part 2 para.14, revoked: SI 2009/2297 Reg.45
Sch.1 Part 2 para.15, revoked: SI 2009/2297 Reg.45
Sch.1 Part 2 para.16, revoked: SI 2009/2297 Reg.45
Sch.1 Part 3 para.17, revoked: SI 2009/2297 Reg.45
Sch.1 Part 3 para.18, revoked: SI 2009/2297 Reg.45
Sch.1 Part 3 para.19, revoked: SI 2009/2297 Reg.45
Sch.1 Part 3 para.20, revoked: SI 2009/2297 Reg.45
Sch.1 Part 3 para.21, revoked: SI 2009/2297 Reg.45
Sch.1 Part 3 para.22, revoked: SI 2009/2297 Reg.45
Sch.1 Part 3 para.23, revoked: SI 2009/2297 Reg.45
Sch.1 Part 3 para.24, revoked: SI 2009/2297 Reg.45
Sch.1 Part 3 para.25, revoked: SI 2009/2297 Reg.45
Sch.1 Part 3 para.26, revoked: SI 2009/2297 Reg.45
Sch.1 Part 3 para.27, revoked: SI 2009/2297 Reg.45
Sch.1 Part 3 para.28, revoked: SI 2009/2297 Reg.45
Sch.1 Part 3 para.29, revoked: SI 2009/2297 Reg.45
Sch.1 Part 3 para.30, revoked: SI 2009/2297 Reg.45
Sch.1 Part 3 para.31, revoked: SI 2009/2297 Reg.45
Sch.1 Part 3 para.32, revoked: SI 2009/2297 Reg.45
Sch.1 Part 4 para.33, revoked: SI 2009/2297 Reg.45
Sch.1 Part 4 para.34, revoked: SI 2009/2297 Reg.45
Sch.1 Part 4 para.35, revoked: SI 2009/2297 Reg.45
Sch.1 Part 4 para.36, revoked: SI 2009/2297 Reg.45
Sch.1 Part 4 para.37, revoked: SI 2009/2297 Reg.45
Sch.1 Part 5 para.38, revoked: SI 2009/2297 Reg.45
Sch.1 Part 5 para.39, revoked: SI 2009/2297 Reg.45
Sch.1 Part 5 para.40, revoked: SI 2009/2297 Reg.45
Sch.1 Part 5 para.41, revoked: SI 2009/2297 Reg.45
Sch.1 Part 6 para.42, revoked: SI 2009/2297 Reg.45
Sch.1 Part 6 para.43, revoked: SI 2009/2297 Reg.45

2008–cont.

2297. Veterinary Medicines Regulations 2008–*cont.*

Sch.1 Part 6 para.44, revoked: SI 2009/ 2297 Reg.45
Sch.1 Part 7 para.45, revoked: SI 2009/ 2297 Reg.45
Sch.1 Part 7 para.46, revoked: SI 2009/ 2297 Reg.45
Sch.1 Part 7 para.47, revoked: SI 2009/ 2297 Reg.45
Sch.1 Part 7 para.48, revoked: SI 2009/ 2297 Reg.45
Sch.1 Part 7 para.49, revoked: SI 2009/ 2297 Reg.45
Sch.1 Part 7 para.50, revoked: SI 2009/ 2297 Reg.45
Sch.1 Part 7 para.51, revoked: SI 2009/ 2297 Reg.45
Sch.1 Part 7 para.52, revoked: SI 2009/ 2297 Reg.45
Sch.1 Part 7 para.53, revoked: SI 2009/ 2297 Reg.45
Sch.1 Part 7 para.54, revoked: SI 2009/ 2297 Reg.45
Sch.1 Part 8 para.55, revoked: SI 2009/ 2297 Reg.45
Sch.1 Part 8 para.56, revoked: SI 2009/ 2297 Reg.45
Sch.1 Part 8 para.57, revoked: SI 2009/ 2297 Reg.45
Sch.1 Part 8 para.58, revoked: SI 2009/ 2297 Reg.45
Sch.1 Part 8 para.59, revoked: SI 2009/ 2297 Reg.45
Sch.1 Part 8 para.60, revoked: SI 2009/ 2297 Reg.45
Sch.1 Part 8 para.61, revoked: SI 2009/ 2297 Reg.45
Sch.1 Part 9 para.62, revoked: SI 2009/ 2297 Reg.45
Sch.1 Part 9 para.63, revoked: SI 2009/ 2297 Reg.45
Sch.1 Part 9 para.64, revoked: SI 2009/ 2297 Reg.45
Sch.1 Part 9 para.65, revoked: SI 2009/ 2297 Reg.45
Sch.1 Part 9 para.66, revoked: SI 2009/ 2297 Reg.45
Sch.1 Part 9 para.67, revoked: SI 2009/ 2297 Reg.45
Sch.2 Part 1 para.1, revoked: SI 2009/ 2297 Reg.45
Sch.2 Part 1 para.2, revoked: SI 2009/ 2297 Reg.45
Sch.2 Part 1 para.3, revoked: SI 2009/ 2297 Reg.45
Sch.2 Part 1 para.4, revoked: SI 2009/ 2297 Reg.45
Sch.2 Part 1 para.5, revoked: SI 2009/ 2297 Reg.45
Sch.2 Part 1 para.6, revoked: SI 2009/ 2297 Reg.45
Sch.2 Part 1 para.7, revoked: SI 2009/ 2297 Reg.45
Sch.2 Part 1 para.8, revoked: SI 2009/ 2297 Reg.45
Sch.2 Part 1 para.9, revoked: SI 2009/ 2297 Reg.45
Sch.2 Part 1 para.10, revoked: SI 2009/ 2297 Reg.45
Sch.2 Part 1 para.11, revoked: SI 2009/ 2297 Reg.45
Sch.2 Part 1 para.12, revoked: SI 2009/ 2297 Reg.45
Sch.2 Part 1 para.13, revoked: SI 2009/ 2297 Reg.45
Sch.2 Part 2 para.14, revoked: SI 2009/ 2297 Reg.45
Sch.2 Part 2 para.15, revoked: SI 2009/ 2297 Reg.45
Sch.2 Part 2 para.16, revoked: SI 2009/ 2297 Reg.45
Sch.2 Part 2 para.17, revoked: SI 2009/ 2297 Reg.45
Sch.2 Part 2 para.18, revoked: SI 2009/ 2297 Reg.45
Sch.2 Part 2 para.19, revoked: SI 2009/ 2297 Reg.45
Sch.2 Part 3 para.20, revoked: SI 2009/ 2297 Reg.45
Sch.2 Part 3 para.21, revoked: SI 2009/ 2297 Reg.45
Sch.2 Part 3 para.22, revoked: SI 2009/ 2297 Reg.45
Sch.2 Part 3 para.23, revoked: SI 2009/ 2297 Reg.45
Sch.2 Part 3 para.24, revoked: SI 2009/ 2297 Reg.45
Sch.2 Part 4 para.25, revoked: SI 2009/ 2297 Reg.45
Sch.2 Part 4 para.26, revoked: SI 2009/ 2297 Reg.45
Sch.2 Part 4 para.27, revoked: SI 2009/ 2297 Reg.45
Sch.2 Part 4 para.28, revoked: SI 2009/ 2297 Reg.45
Sch.2 Part 4 para.29, revoked: SI 2009/ 2297 Reg.45
Sch.2 Part 5 para.30, revoked: SI 2009/ 2297 Reg.45
Sch.2 Part 5 para.31, revoked: SI 2009/ 2297 Reg.45
Sch.2 Part 5 para.32, revoked: SI 2009/ 2297 Reg.45
Sch.2 Part 5 para.33, revoked: SI 2009/ 2297 Reg.45
Sch.2 Part 5 para.34, revoked: SI 2009/ 2297 Reg.45
Sch.3 Part 1 para.1, revoked: SI 2009/ 2297 Reg.45
Sch.3 Part 1 para.2, revoked: SI 2009/ 2297 Reg.45
Sch.3 Part 1 para.3, revoked: SI 2009/ 2297 Reg.45
Sch.3 Part 1 para.4, revoked: SI 2009/ 2297 Reg.45
Sch.3 Part 1 para.5, revoked: SI 2009/ 2297 Reg.45
Sch.3 Part 1 para.6, revoked: SI 2009/ 2297 Reg.45
Sch.3 Part 1 para.7, revoked: SI 2009/ 2297 Reg.45
Sch.3 Part 1 para.8, revoked: SI 2009/ 2297 Reg.45
Sch.3 Part 1 para.9, revoked: SI 2009/ 2297 Reg.45

2008–cont.

2297. Veterinary Medicines Regulations 2008–*cont.*

Sch.3 Part 1 para.10, revoked: SI 2009/ 2297 Reg.45
Sch.3 Part 1 para.11, revoked: SI 2009/ 2297 Reg.45
Sch.3 Part 1 para.12, revoked: SI 2009/ 2297 Reg.45
Sch.3 Part 1 para.13, revoked: SI 2009/ 2297 Reg.45
Sch.3 Part 1 para.14, revoked: SI 2009/ 2297 Reg.45
Sch.3 Part 1 para.15, revoked: SI 2009/ 2297 Reg.45
Sch.3 Part 2 para.16, revoked: SI 2009/ 2297 Reg.45
Sch.3 Part 2 para.17, revoked: SI 2009/ 2297 Reg.45
Sch.3 Part 2 para.18, revoked: SI 2009/ 2297 Reg.45
Sch.3 Part 2 para.19, revoked: SI 2009/ 2297 Reg.45
Sch.3 Part 2 para.20, revoked: SI 2009/ 2297 Reg.45
Sch.3 Part 2 para.21, revoked: SI 2009/ 2297 Reg.45
Sch.3 Part 3 para.22, revoked: SI 2009/ 2297 Reg.45
Sch.3 Part 3 para.23, revoked: SI 2009/ 2297 Reg.45
Sch.4 para.1, revoked: SI 2009/ 2297 Reg.45
Sch.4 para.2, revoked: SI 2009/ 2297 Reg.45
Sch.4 para.3, revoked: SI 2009/ 2297 Reg.45
Sch.4 para.4, revoked: SI 2009/ 2297 Reg.45
Sch.4 para.5, revoked: SI 2009/ 2297 Reg.45
Sch.4 para.6, revoked: SI 2009/ 2297 Reg.45
Sch.4 para.7, revoked: SI 2009/ 2297 Reg.45
Sch.4 para.8, revoked: SI 2009/ 2297 Reg.45
Sch.4 para.9, revoked: SI 2009/ 2297 Reg.45
Sch.5 para.1, revoked: SI 2009/ 2297 Reg.45
Sch.5 para.2, revoked: SI 2009/ 2297 Reg.45
Sch.5 para.3, revoked: SI 2009/ 2297 Reg.45
Sch.5 para.4, revoked: SI 2009/ 2297 Reg.45
Sch.5 para.5, revoked: SI 2009/ 2297 Reg.45
Sch.5 para.6, revoked: SI 2009/ 2297 Reg.45
Sch.5 para.7, revoked: SI 2009/ 2297 Reg.45
Sch.5 para.8, revoked: SI 2009/ 2297 Reg.45
Sch.5 para.9, revoked: SI 2009/ 2297 Reg.45
Sch.5 para.10, revoked: SI 2009/ 2297 Reg.45
Sch.5 para.11, revoked: SI 2009/ 2297 Reg.45
Sch.5 para.12, revoked: SI 2009/ 2297 Reg.45
Sch.5 para.13, revoked: SI 2009/ 2297 Reg.45
Sch.5 para.14, revoked: SI 2009/ 2297 Reg.45
Sch.5 para.15, revoked: SI 2009/ 2297 Reg.45
Sch.5 para.16, revoked: SI 2009/ 2297 Reg.45
Sch.5 para.17, revoked: SI 2009/ 2297 Reg.45
Sch.5 para.18, revoked: SI 2009/ 2297 Reg.45
Sch.5 para.19, revoked: SI 2009/ 2297 Reg.45
Sch.5 para.20, revoked: SI 2009/ 2297 Reg.45
Sch.5 para.21, revoked: SI 2009/ 2297 Reg.45
Sch.5 para.22, revoked: SI 2009/ 2297 Reg.45
Sch.5 para.23, revoked: SI 2009/ 2297 Reg.45
Sch.5 para.24, revoked: SI 2009/ 2297 Reg.45
Sch.5 para.25, revoked: SI 2009/ 2297 Reg.45
Sch.5 para.26, revoked: SI 2009/ 2297 Reg.45
Sch.5 para.27, revoked: SI 2009/ 2297 Reg.45
Sch.6 para.1, revoked: SI 2009/ 2297 Reg.45
Sch.6 para.2, revoked: SI 2009/ 2297 Reg.45
Sch.6 para.3, revoked: SI 2009/ 2297 Reg.45
Sch.6 para.4, revoked: SI 2009/ 2297 Reg.45
Sch.6 para.5, revoked: SI 2009/ 2297 Reg.45
Sch.6 para.6, revoked: SI 2009/ 2297 Reg.45
Sch.6 para.7, revoked: SI 2009/ 2297 Reg.45
Sch.6 para.8, revoked: SI 2009/ 2297 Reg.45
Sch.6 para.9, revoked: SI 2009/ 2297 Reg.45
Sch.7 Part 1 para.1, revoked: SI 2009/ 2297 Reg.45
Sch.7 Part 1 para.2, revoked: SI 2009/ 2297 Reg.45
Sch.7 Part 1 para.3, revoked: SI 2009/ 2297 Reg.45
Sch.7 Part 1 para.4, revoked: SI 2009/ 2297 Reg.45
Sch.7 Part 1 para.5, revoked: SI 2009/ 2297 Reg.45
Sch.7 Part 1 para.6, revoked: SI 2009/ 2297 Reg.45
Sch.7 Part 2 para.7, revoked: SI 2009/ 2297 Reg.45
Sch.7 Part 2 para.8, revoked: SI 2009/ 2297 Reg.45

2008–cont.

2297. Veterinary Medicines Regulations 2008–*cont.*
Sch.7 Part 2 para.9, revoked: SI 2009/2297 Reg.45
Sch.7 Part 2 para.10, revoked: SI 2009/2297 Reg.45
Sch.7 Part 2 para.11, revoked: SI 2009/2297 Reg.45
Sch.7 Part 2 para.12, revoked: SI 2009/2297 Reg.45
Sch.7 Part 2 para.13, revoked: SI 2009/2297 Reg.45
Sch.7 Part 2 para.14, revoked: SI 2009/2297 Reg.45
Sch.7 Part 2 para.15, revoked: SI 2009/2297 Reg.45
Sch.7 Part 2 para.16, revoked: SI 2009/2297 Reg.45
Sch.7 Part 2 para.17, revoked: SI 2009/2297 Reg.45
Sch.7 Part 2 para.18, revoked: SI 2009/2297 Reg.45
Sch.7 Part 2 para.19, revoked: SI 2009/2297 Reg.45
Sch.7 Part 2 para.20, revoked: SI 2009/2297 Reg.45
Sch.7 Part 2 para.21, revoked: SI 2009/2297 Reg.45
Sch.7 Part 2 para.22, revoked: SI 2009/2297 Reg.45
Sch.7 Part 2 para.23, revoked: SI 2009/2297 Reg.45
Sch.7 Part 2 para.24, revoked: SI 2009/2297 Reg.45
Sch.7 Part 2 para.25, revoked: SI 2009/2297 Reg.45
Sch.7 Part 2 para.26, revoked: SI 2009/2297 Reg.45
Sch.7 Part 3 para.27, revoked: SI 2009/2297 Reg.45
Sch.7 Part 3 para.28, revoked: SI 2009/2297 Reg.45
Sch.7 Part 3 para.29, revoked: SI 2009/2297 Reg.45
Sch.7 Part 3 para.30, revoked: SI 2009/2297 Reg.45
Sch.7 Part 3 para.31, revoked: SI 2009/2297 Reg.45
Sch.7 Part 3 para.32, revoked: SI 2009/2297 Reg.45
Sch.7 Part 3 para.33, revoked: SI 2009/2297 Reg.45
Sch.7 Part 3 para.34, revoked: SI 2009/2297 Reg.45
Sch.7 Part 3 para.35, revoked: SI 2009/2297 Reg.45
Sch.7 Part 3 para.36, revoked: SI 2009/2297 Reg.45
Sch.7 Part 3 para.37, revoked: SI 2009/2297 Reg.45
Sch.7 Part 4 para.38, revoked: SI 2009/2297 Reg.45
Sch.7 Part 4 para.39, revoked: SI 2009/2297 Reg.45
Sch.7 Part 4 para.40, revoked: SI 2009/2297 Reg.45
Sch.7 Part 4 para.41, revoked: SI 2009/2297 Reg.45
Sch.7 Part 5 para.42, revoked: SI 2009/2297 Reg.45
Sch.7 Part 5 para.43, revoked: SI 2009/2297 Reg.45
Sch.7 Part 5 para.44, revoked: SI 2009/2297 Reg.45
Sch.7 Part 6 para.45, revoked: SI 2009/2297 Reg.45
Sch.7 Part 6 para.46, revoked: SI 2009/2297 Reg.45
Sch.7 Part 6 para.47, revoked: SI 2009/2297 Reg.45
Sch.7 Part 6 para.48, revoked: SI 2009/2297 Reg.45
Sch.7 Part 6 para.49, revoked: SI 2009/2297 Reg.45
Sch.7 Part 6 para.50, revoked: SI 2009/2297 Reg.45
Sch.7 Part 6 para.51, revoked: SI 2009/2297 Reg.45
Sch.7 Part 6 para.52, revoked: SI 2009/2297 Reg.45
Sch.7 Part 6 para.53, revoked: SI 2009/2297 Reg.45
Sch.7 Part 6 para.54, revoked: SI 2009/2297 Reg.45
Sch.7 Part 6 para.55, revoked: SI 2009/2297 Reg.45
Sch.7 Part 6 para.56, revoked: SI 2009/2297 Reg.45
Sch.7 Part 6 para.57, revoked: SI 2009/2297 Reg.45
Sch.7 Part 6 para.58, revoked: SI 2009/2297 Reg.45
Sch.7 Part 6 para.58A, revoked: SI 2009/2297 Reg.45
Sch.7 Part 6 para.59, revoked: SI 2009/2297 Reg.45
Sch.7 Part 6 para.60, revoked: SI 2009/2297 Reg.45
Sch.7 Part 6 para.61, revoked: SI 2009/2297 Reg.45
Sch.7 Part 6 para.62, revoked: SI 2009/2297 Reg.45
Sch.7 Part 6 para.63, revoked: SI 2009/2297 Reg.45

2337. Chemicals (Hazard Information and Packaging for Supply) (Amendment) Regulations 2008
revoked: SI 2009/716 Sch.7

2338. Stamp Duty Land Tax (Variation of Part 4 of the Finance Act 2003) Regulations 2008
revoked: 2009 c.10 s.10

2008–cont.

2339. Stamp Duty Land Tax (Exemption of Certain Acquisitions of Residential Property) Regulations 2008
revoked: 2009 c.10 s.10

2343. Smoke Control Areas (Exempted Fireplaces) (England) (No.2) Order 2008
revoked: SI 2009/449 Art.3

2346. Houses in Multiple Occupation (Specified Educational Establishments) (England) Regulations 2008
revoked: SI 2009/2298 Reg.3

2349. Nitrate Pollution Prevention Regulations 2008
applied: SI 2009/3264 Sch.1 para.8, SI 2009/3365 Sch.1 para.1
Reg.3, amended: SI 2009/3160 Reg.3
Reg.6, substituted: SI 2009/3160 Reg.3
Reg.12, amended: SI 2009/3160 Reg.4
Reg.13A, added: SI 2009/3160 Reg.5
Reg.13B, added: SI 2009/3160 Reg.5
Reg.13C, added: SI 2009/3160 Reg.5
Reg.13D, added: SI 2009/3160 Reg.5
Reg.13E, added: SI 2009/3160 Reg.5
Reg.13F, added: SI 2009/3160 Reg.5
Reg.15, amended: SI 2009/3160 Reg.6
Reg.16, amended: SI 2009/3160 Reg.6
Reg.18, applied: SI 2009/3365 Sch.1 para.8
Reg.20, applied: SI 2009/3264 Sch.1 para.1, SI 2009/3365 Sch.1 para.1
Reg.20, substituted: SI 2009/3160 Reg.7
Reg.21, applied: SI 2009/3264 Sch.1 para.1, SI 2009/3365 Sch.1 para.1
Reg.22, substituted: SI 2009/3160 Reg.7
Reg.27, amended: SI 2009/3160 Reg.8
Reg.42, amended: SI 2009/3160 Reg.9
Sch.1, substituted: SI 2009/3160 Sch.1
Sch.2 Part 1, substituted: SI 2009/3160 Sch.1
Sch.2 Part 2 para.1, substituted: SI 2009/3160 Sch.1
Sch.2 Part 2 para.2, substituted: SI 2009/3160 Sch.1
Sch.3, substituted: SI 2009/3160 Sch.1

2375. Gas (Applications for Licences and Extensions and Restrictions of Licences) Regulations 2008
revoked: SI 2009/3190 Reg.1

2376. Electricity (Applications for Licences, Modifications of an Area and Extensions and Restrictions of Licences) Regulations 2008
revoked: SI 2009/3191 Reg.1

2425. Local Government Pension Scheme (Miscellaneous) Regulations 2008
Reg.11, revoked: SI 2009/3093 Sch.2
Reg.12, revoked: SI 2009/3093 Sch.2
Reg.13, revoked: SI 2009/3093 Sch.2
Reg.14, revoked: SI 2009/3093 Sch.2

2429. Air Navigation (Dangerous Goods) (Amendment) (No.2) Regulations 2008
revoked: SI 2009/1492 Reg.3

2436. Mental Health (Approval of Persons to be Approved Mental Health Professionals) (Wales) Regulations 2008
Sch.1 para.1, varied: SI 2009/1357 Art.3

2470. Parochial Fees Order 2008
revoked: SI 2009/2106 Art.5

2499. Non-Domestic Rating (Unoccupied Property) (Wales) Regulations 2008
Reg.4, amended: SI 2009/255 Reg.2

2546. Bradford &amp Bingley plc Transfer of Securities and Property etc Order 2008
Art.6, amended: SI 2009/320 Art.2
Art.33, amended: SI 2009/320 Art.2

2008–cont.

2551. Child Support Information Regulations 2008
Reg.14, substituted: SI 2009/396 Reg.6

2553. Nursing and Midwifery Council (Constitution) Order 2008
Art.5, amended: 2009 c.26 s.81

2554. General Medical Council (Constitution) Order 2008
Art.5, amended: 2009 c.26 s.81

2644. Heritable Bank plc Transfer of Certain Rights and Liabilities Order 2008
Art.13, referred to: SI 2009/310 Art.2
Art.15, amended: SI 2009/310 Art.4
Art.23, amended: SI 2009/310 Art.4
Art.23, varied: SI 2009/310 Art.3

2668. Landsbanki Freezing Order 2008
revoked: SI 2009/1392 Art.2

2674. Kaupthing Singer &amp Friedlander Limited Transfer of Certain Rights and Liabilities Order 2008
Art.14, amended: SI 2009/308 Art.2
Art.16, amended: SI 2009/308 Art.2
Art.21, amended: SI 2009/308 Art.2

2684. First-tier Tribunal and Upper Tribunal (Chambers) Order 2008
applied: SI 2009/273 r.1
Art.2, amended: SI 2009/196 Art.3, SI 2009/1590 Art.3
Art.3, amended: SI 2009/196 Art.4, SI 2009/1021 Art.3, SI 2009/1590 Art.4
Art.5A, added: SI 2009/196 Art.5
Art.5B, added: SI 2009/1590 Art.5
Art.6, amended: SI 2009/1021 Art.4, SI 2009/1590 Art.6
Art.6, substituted: SI 2009/196 Art.6
Art.7, amended: SI 2009/196 Art.7, SI 2009/1590 Art.7
Art.8, added: SI 2009/196 Art.8
Art.8, substituted: SI 2009/1590 Art.8
Art.9, added: SI 2009/1021 Art.5
Art.9A, added: SI 2009/1021 Art.5
Art.10, added: SI 2009/1021 Art.5

2685. Tribunal Procedure (First-tier Tribunal) (Social Entitlement Chamber) Rules 2008
Part 1 r.1, amended: SI 2009/274 r.2
Part 3 r.23, amended: SI 2009/1975 r.3
Sch.1, substituted: SI 2009/1975 r.4

2686. Tribunal Procedure (First-tier Tribunal) (War Pensions and Armed Forces Compensation Chamber) Rules 2008
Part 3 r.21, amended: SI 2009/1975 r.5

2692. Qualifications for Appointment of Members to the First-tier Tribunal and Upper Tribunal Order 2008
Art.1, substituted: SI 2009/1592 Art.3
Art.2, amended: SI 2009/1592 Art.4

2696. Tribunals, Courts and Enforcement Act 2007 (Commencement No.6 and Transitional Provisions) Order 2008
Art.4, amended: SI 2009/56 Sch.3 para.11

2698. Tribunal Procedure (Upper Tribunal) Rules 2008
applied: SI 2009/1964 Reg.16
Part 1 r.1, amended: SI 2009/274 r.5, SI 2009/1975 r.8
Part 1 r.1, revoked (in part): SI 2009/274 r.5
Part 2 r.5, amended: SI 2009/1975 r.9
Part 2 r.8, amended: SI 2009/274 r.6
Part 2 r.9, substituted: SI 2009/1975 r.10
Part 2 r.10, amended: SI 2009/1975 r.11

2008–cont.

2698. Tribunal Procedure (Upper Tribunal) Rules 2008–cont.
Part 2 r.10, revoked (in part): SI 2009/1975 r.11
Part 2 r.10, substituted: SI 2009/274 r.7
Part 2 r.11, amended: SI 2009/274 r.8, SI 2009/1975 r.12
Part 2 r.12, amended: SI 2009/274 r.9
Part 2 r.13, amended: SI 2009/274 r.10
Part 2 r.14, amended: SI 2009/1975 r.13
Part 2 r.14, revoked (in part): SI 2009/1975 r.13
Part 2 r.16, amended: SI 2009/274 r.11
Part 2 r.20, amended: SI 2009/274 r.12
Part 2 r.20A, added: SI 2009/1975 r.14
Part 3 r.21, amended: SI 2009/274 r.13
Part 3 r.21, revoked (in part): SI 2009/1975 r.15
Part 3 r.21, varied: SI 2009/196 Art.9
Part 3 r.22, amended: SI 2009/274 r.13, r.14, SI 2009/1975 r.16
Part 3 r.23, amended: SI 2009/274 r.13, SI 2009/1975 r.17
Part 3 r.24, amended: SI 2009/274 r.13, r.15, SI 2009/1975 r.18
Part 3 r.25, amended: SI 2009/274 r.13
Part 3 r.26, amended: SI 2009/274 r.13
Part 3 r.26A, added: SI 2009/274 r.16
Part 3 r.26A, amended: SI 2009/274 r.13, SI 2009/1975 r.19
Part 4 r.28, amended: SI 2009/274 r.17
Part 4 r.29, amended: SI 2009/274 r.18
Part 5 r.37, amended: SI 2009/274 r.19, SI 2009/1975 r.20
Part 6 r.39, amended: SI 2009/274 r.20
Part 6 r.40, amended: SI 2009/274 r.21, SI 2009/1975 r.21
Part 7 r.41, amended: SI 2009/274 r.22
Part 7 r.44, amended: SI 2009/274 r.23
Sch.1 para.1, added: SI 2009/1975 r.22
Sch.1 para.2, added: SI 2009/1975 r.22
Sch.1 para.3, added: SI 2009/1975 r.22
Sch.1 para.4, added: SI 2009/1975 r.22
Sch.1 para.5, added: SI 2009/1975 r.22
Sch.1 para.6, added: SI 2009/1975 r.22
Sch.1 para.7, added: SI 2009/1975 r.22
Sch.1 para.8, added: SI 2009/1975 r.22
Sch.1 para.9, added: SI 2009/1975 r.22
Sch.1 para.10, added: SI 2009/1975 r.22
Sch.1 para.11, added: SI 2009/1975 r.22

2699. Tribunal Procedure (First-tier Tribunal) (Health, Education and Social Care Chamber) Rules 2008
Sch.1, amended: SI 2009/1975 r.6

2700. Discipline of Judges (Designation) Order 2008
revoked: SI 2009/590 Art.2

2705. Mental Health Review Tribunal for Wales Rules 2008
Part 1 r.2, amended: SI 2009/3348 Art.20

2707. Appeals (Excluded Decisions) Order 2008
revoked: SI 2009/275 Art.4
Art.2, revoked (in part): SI 2009/56 Sch.2 para.185

2708. Agricultural Holdings (Units of Production) (England) Order 2008
revoked: SI 2009/2762 Art.3

2715. Education (Student Loans) (Repayment) (Amendment) (No.2) Regulations 2008
revoked: SI 2009/470 Sch.1

2716. Zoonoses and Animal By-Products (Fees) (Wales) Regulations 2008
Reg.2, amended: SI 2009/2427 Reg.2

2008–cont.

2766. Landsbanki Freezing (Amendment) Order 2008
revoked: SI 2009/1392 Art.2

2767. Social Security (Miscellaneous Amendments) (No.6) Regulations 2008
Reg.2, amended: SI 2009/2655 Reg.13

2780. Appeals (Excluded Decisions) (Amendment) Order 2008
revoked: SI 2009/275 Art.4

2790. Immigration and Nationality (Cost Recovery Fees) (Amendment No.3) Regulations 2008
revoked: SI 2009/421 Reg.33

2795. Cat and Dog Fur (Control of Import, Export and Placing on the Market) Regulations 2008
Reg.3, amended: SI 2009/1056 Reg.2
Reg.4, amended: SI 2009/1056 Reg.2
Reg.4, revoked (in part): SI 2009/1056 Reg.2
Reg.5, amended: SI 2009/1056 Reg.2

2828. Mental Health Act 2007 (Consequential Amendments) Order 2008
Art.18, revoked (in part): SI 2009/1887 Sch.3

2833. Transfer of Tribunal Functions Order 2008
applied: SI 2009/1307 Art.5
Sch.3 para.102, revoked: 2009 c.24 Sch.7 Part 3
Sch.3 para.191, revoked (in part): SI 2009/56 Sch.2 para.186

2836. Allocation and Transfer of Proceedings Order 2008
Art.3, substituted: SI 2009/871 Art.11
Sch.1, amended: SI 2009/3319 Art.3

2839. Transfer of Housing Corporation Functions (Modifications and Transitional Provisions) Order 2008
Sch.1 para.3, revoked (in part): SI 2009/484 Sch.2
Sch.1 para.5, revoked (in part): SI 2009/484 Sch.2

2841. Cremation (England and Wales) Regulations 2008
Reg.2, see *R. (on the application of Ghai) v Newcastle City Council* [2009] EWHC 978 (Admin), Times, May 18, 2009 (QBD (Admin)), Cranston, J.
Reg.13, see *R. (on the application of Ghai) v Newcastle City Council* [2009] EWHC 978 (Admin), Times, May 18, 2009 (QBD (Admin)), Cranston, J.

2844. Motor Vehicles (EC Type Approval) (Amendment) Regulations 2008
revoked: SI 2009/717 Sch.1

2852. REACH Enforcement Regulations 2008
Sch.3 Part 1 para.1, amended: SI 2009/716 Sch.6
Sch.10 Part 3 para.1, revoked: SI 2009/716 Sch.7
Sch.10 Part 3 para.2, revoked: SI 2009/716 Sch.7
Sch.10 Part 3 para.3, revoked: SI 2009/716 Sch.7
Sch.10 Part 3 para.4, revoked: SI 2009/716 Sch.7

2860. Companies Act 2006 (Commencement No.8, Transitional Provisions and Savings) Order 2008
Art.3, amended: SI 2009/2476 Reg.2
Sch.1 Part 1, amended: SI 2009/1941 Art.13
Sch.1 Part 2, amended: SI 2009/1941 Art.13
Sch.2, applied: SI 2009/1804 Sch.1 para.27
Sch.2, added: SI 2009/2476 Reg.2
Sch.2 para.1, applied: SI 2009/1941 Art.3
Sch.2 para.9, applied: SI 2009/1941 Art.5
Sch.2 para.36, applied: SI 2009/214 Reg.13
Sch.2 para.36, referred to: SI 2009/214 Reg.13
Sch.2 para.88, substituted: SI 2009/2476 Reg.2
Sch.2 para.93, applied: SI 2009/2437 Reg.24
Sch.2 para.97, substituted: SI 2009/1802 Sch.1

2008–cont.

2860. Companies Act 2006 (Commencement No.8, Transitional Provisions and Savings) Order 2008– *cont.*
Sch.2 para.98, substituted: SI 2009/1802 Sch.1
Sch.2 para.99, substituted: SI 2009/1802 Sch.1
Sch.2 para.100, substituted: SI 2009/1802 Sch.1
Sch.2 para.101, substituted: SI 2009/1802 Sch.1
Sch.2 para.102, substituted: SI 2009/1802 Sch.1
Sch.2 para.103, substituted: SI 2009/1802 Sch.1
Sch.2 para.104, substituted: SI 2009/1802 Sch.1
Sch.2 para.105, substituted: SI 2009/1802 Sch.1
Sch.2 para.106, substituted: SI 2009/1802 Sch.1
Sch.2 para.107, substituted: SI 2009/1802 Sch.1
Sch.2 para.108, substituted: SI 2009/1802 Sch.1
Sch.2 para.109, substituted: SI 2009/1802 Sch.1
Sch.2 para.114A, added: SI 2009/2476 Reg.2

2867. Local Government (Structural Changes) (Transitional Arrangements) (No.2) Regulations 2008
Reg.4, disapplied: SI 2009/486 Reg.3
Reg.14, applied: SI 2009/486 Reg.3
Reg.19, amended: SI 2009/276 Reg.14

2908. Crossrail (Planning Appeals) (Written Representations Procedure) (England) Regulations 2008
Sch.2, amended: SI 2009/1312 Reg.2

2927. Council for Healthcare Regulatory Excellence (Appointment, Procedure etc.) Regulations 2008
Reg.2, amended: 2009 c.26 s.81

2928. Social Security (Incapacity Benefit Work-focused Interviews) Regulations 2008
referred to: SI 2009/1541 Reg.3
Reg.2, amended: SI 2009/1541 Reg.2, SI 2009/3152 Reg.3
Reg.3, amended: SI 2009/1541 Reg.2
Reg.8, amended: SI 2009/1541 Reg.2
Reg.9, amended: SI 2009/1541 Reg.2
Reg.9, applied: SI 2009/1541 Reg.3
Reg.12, amended: SI 2009/1541 Reg.2
Sch.1, added: SI 2009/1541 Reg.2

2938. Case Tribunals (England) Regulations 2008
Reg.5, applied: SI 2009/1976 r.17

2939. Education (Student Support) (Amendment) (No.3) Regulations 2008
revoked: SI 2009/1555 Reg.4

2945. Education (Special Educational Needs Co-ordinators) (England) Regulations 2008
Reg.3, amended: SI 2009/1387 Reg.2

2946. Medicines (Pharmacies) (Applications for Registration and Fees) Amendment Regulations 2008
revoked: SI 2009/3071 Reg.3

2995. Judicial Appointments Order 2008
Art.2, amended: SI 2009/3348 Art.21
Art.5, amended: SI 2009/3348 Art.21
Art.6, amended: SI 2009/3348 Art.21
Art.8, amended: SI 2009/3348 Art.21
Sch.1 Part 1, amended: SI 2009/1307 Sch.2 para.126

3017. Immigration and Nationality (Fees) (Amendment No.3) Regulations 2008
revoked: SI 2009/816 Reg.32

3020. Value Added Tax (Change of Rate) Order 2008
revoked: 2009 c.10 s.9

3022. Local Government (Structural Changes) (Finance) Regulations 2008
Reg.8, applied: SI 2009/5 Reg.6

2008–cont.

3026. Alcoholic Liquor Duties (Surcharges) and Tobacco Products Duty Order 2008
revoked (in part): 2009 c.10 s.11, s.12

3047. General Chiropractic Council (Constitution) Order 2008
Art.5, amended: 2009 c.26 s.81

3048. Immigration (Biometric Registration) Regulations 2008
Reg.2, amended: SI 2009/3321 Reg.3
Reg.3, amended: SI 2009/3321 Reg.4
Reg.3, substituted: SI 2009/819 Reg.3
Reg.4, amended: SI 2009/3321 Reg.5
Reg.4, substituted: SI 2009/819 Reg.4
Reg.13, amended: SI 2009/819 Reg.5
Reg.16, amended: SI 2009/819 Reg.6
Reg.17, amended: SI 2009/819 Reg.7
Reg.19, amended: SI 2009/819 Reg.8

3052. Immigration (Designation of Travel Bans) (Amendment) Order 2008
revoked: SI 2009/3044 Art.3

3054. Education (Student Support) (European Institutions) (Amendment) (No.2) Regulations 2008
Sch.1, amended: SI 2009/1576 Reg.3

3062. Alcoholic Liquor (Surcharge on Spirits Duty) Order 2008
revoked: 2009 c.10 s.11

3071. Childcare (Provision of Information About Young Children) (England) (Amendment) Regulations 2008
revoked: SI 2009/1554 Reg.3

3089. School Admissions (Admission Arrangements) (England) Regulations 2008
Reg.31, revoked (in part): SI 2009/1099 Reg.2
Reg.31A, added: SI 2009/1099 Reg.2

3092. Education (Admissions Appeals Arrangements) (England) (Amendment) Regulations 2008
Reg.1, amended: SI 2009/25 Reg.2

3100. Smoke Control Areas (Authorised Fuels) (Wales) Regulations 2008
Sch.1 para.8A, added: SI 2009/3225 Reg.3
Sch.1 para.41A, added: SI 2009/3225 Reg.3
Sch.1 para.42A, added: SI 2009/3225 Reg.3

3101. Smoke Control Areas (Exempted Fireplaces) (Wales) Order 2008
revoked: SI 2009/3224 Art.3

3109. Health in Pregnancy Grant (Administration) Regulations 2008
Reg.12, applied: SI 2009/713 Reg.9

3113. General Optical Council (Committee Constitution) (Amendment) Rules Order of Council 2008
Sch.1, amended: 2009 c.26 s.81

3114. Assembly Learning Grants (European Institutions) (Wales) (Amendment) (No.2) Regulations 2008
revoked: SI 2009/3359 Reg.4

3115. Parliamentary Commissioner Order 2008
Sch.1, amended: 2009 c.26 s.81

3122. Companies Act 2006 (Extension of Takeover Panel Provisions) (Isle of Man) Order 2008
Sch.1 para.9, revoked: SI 2009/1378 Art.3
Sch.1 para.10, revoked: SI 2009/1378 Art.3

3127. Cayman Islands (Constitution) (Amendment) Order 2008
revoked: SI 2009/1379 Sch.1

3131. Medical Profession (Miscellaneous Amendments) Order 2008
Art.1, enabled: SI 2009/280, SI 2009/2200

2008–cont.

3148. Nursing and Midwifery Council (Midwifery and Practice Committees) (Constitution) Rules Order of Council 2008
Sch.1, amended: 2009 c.26 s.81, SI 2009/2894 Sch.1

3150. Health Care and Associated Professions (Miscellaneous Amendments) Order 2008 (Commencement No 2) Order of Council 2008
Art.2, amended: SI 2009/666 Art.2

3158. UK Borders Act 2007 (Code of Practice on Children) Order 2008
revoked: 2009 c.11 Sch.1 Part 4

3166. Mental Health Act 1983 (Independent Mental Health Advocates) (England) Regulations 2008
Reg.6, amended: SI 2009/2376 Reg.3

3168. Health and Social Care Act 2008 (Commencement No.6, Transitory and Transitional Provisions) Order 2008
Art.6, applied: SI 2009/462 Art.7

3170. Assembly Learning Grants and Loans (Higher Education) (Wales) (No.2) Regulations 2008
revoked: SI 2009/2737 Reg.3
Reg.2, amended: SI 2009/2156 Reg.3
Reg.5, amended: SI 2009/2156 Reg.5
Reg.6, amended: SI 2009/2156 Reg.6, SI 2009/2737 Reg.118
Reg.42, amended: SI 2009/2737 Reg.118
Reg.49, amended: SI 2009/2737 Reg.118
Reg.51, revoked: SI 2009/470 Reg.2
Reg.60, amended: SI 2009/2156 Reg.8, Reg.9
Reg.80, amended: SI 2009/2156 Reg.10
Reg.82, amended: SI 2009/2737 Reg.118
Sch.1 Part 2, referred to: SI 2009/2158 Reg.3
Sch.1 Part 2 para.9, amended: SI 2009/2156 Reg.11
Sch.1 Part 2 para.9, referred to: SI 2009/2158 Reg.3

3195. Social Security (Housing Costs Special Arrangements) (Amendment and Modification) Regulations 2008
Reg.3, amended: SI 2009/3257 Reg.2
Reg.6, amended: SI 2009/3257 Reg.3
Reg.8, substituted: SI 2009/3257 Reg.4
Reg.11, amended: SI 2009/3257 Reg.5
Reg.12, amended: SI 2009/3257 Reg.6

3196. Zoonoses and Animal By-Products (Fees) (England) (No.2) Regulations 2008
revoked: SI 2009/2043 Reg.4

3200. Agricultural Holdings (Units of Production) (Wales) (No.2) Order 2008
revoked: SI 2009/3232 Art.3

3201. Land Registration (Proper Office) Order 2008
revoked: SI 2009/1393 Art.4

3206. Spirit Drinks Regulations 2008
Reg.5, applied: SI 2009/2890 Reg.15
Sch.2 Part 2, amended: SI 2009/3235 Reg.11

3231. Export Control Order 2008
applied: SI 2009/1749 Art.3, Art.6
Art.2, amended: SI 2009/2151 Sch.1 para.1
Art.8, substituted: SI 2009/2151 Sch.1 para.2
Art.9A, added: SI 2009/1852 Art.2
Art.26, amended: SI 2009/2151 Sch.1 para.3
Art.28, amended: SI 2009/2151 Sch.1 para.4
Art.29, amended: SI 2009/2151 Sch.1 para.5
Art.31, amended: SI 2009/2151 Sch.1 para.6
Art.32, amended: SI 2009/2151 Sch.1 para.7
Art.33, amended: SI 2009/2748 Sch.1 para.38
Art.35, amended: SI 2009/1305 Art.2, SI 2009/2151 Sch.1 para.8
Art.40, amended: SI 2009/2151 Sch.1 para.9

2008–cont.

3231. Export Control Order 2008–*cont.*
Art.44, amended: SI 2009/2748 Sch.1 para.38
Sch.1 Part 2 para.11, substituted: SI 2009/1305 Art.3
Sch.1 Part 2 para.12, amended: SI 2009/1305 Art.3
Sch.2 Part 1, amended: SI 2009/1305 Sch.1, SI 2009/2151 Sch.1 para.10
Sch.2 Part 2, substituted: SI 2009/2151 Sch.1 para.11
Sch.3, amended: SI 2009/2151 Sch.1 para.12
Sch.4 Part 2, amended: SI 2009/2969 Art.2
Sch.4 Part 4, amended: SI 2009/1305 Art.5, SI 2009/2969 Art.2

3238. General Dental Council (Constitution) (Amendment) Order of Council 2008
revoked: SI 2009/1182 Sch.4 para.34

3239. Controlled Drugs (Supervision of Management and Use) (Wales) Regulations 2008
Reg.12, amended: SI 2009/1824 Sch.1 para.9

3249. Bradford &amp Bingley plc Compensation Scheme Order 2008
Sch.1, added: SI 2009/790 Art.3, Art.4

3258. Health Service Branded Medicines (Control of Prices and Supply of Information) (No.2) Regulations 2008
Reg.2, amended: SI 2009/3030 Reg.2

3263. Severn Bridges Tolls Order 2008
revoked: SI 2009/3358 Art.3

3267. Charities Act 2006 (Commencement No 5, Transitional and Transitory Provisions and Savings) Order 2008
amended: SI 2009/2648 Art.3
Art.1, amended: SI 2009/2648 Art.3
Art.6, amended: SI 2009/2648 Art.3
Art.11, amended: SI 2009/2648 Art.3
Art.11A, added: SI 2009/2648 Art.3
Art.12, amended: SI 2009/2648 Art.3
Art.13, amended: SI 2009/2648 Art.3
Art.14, substituted: SI 2009/2648 Art.3
Art.15, amended: SI 2009/2648 Art.3
Art.16, substituted: SI 2009/2648 Art.3
Art.17, substituted: SI 2009/2648 Art.3
Art.18, added: SI 2009/2648 Art.3
Art.19, added: SI 2009/2648 Art.3
Art.20, added: SI 2009/2648 Art.3
Art.21, added: SI 2009/2648 Art.3
Art.22, added: SI 2009/2648 Art.3
Art.23, added: SI 2009/2648 Art.3
Art.24, added: SI 2009/2648 Art.3
Art.25, added: SI 2009/2648 Art.3
Art.26, added: SI 2009/2648 Art.3
Art.27, added: SI 2009/2648 Art.3

3297. Penalties for Disorderly Behaviour (Amount of Penalty) (Amendment) Order 2008
revoked: SI 2009/83 Art.3

2009

5. Local Government (Structural Changes) (Further Financial Provisions and Amendment) Regulations 2009
Reg.6, applied: SI 2009/467 Reg.12

12. Safeguarding Vulnerable Groups Act 2006 (Transitory Provisions) Order 2009
applied: SSI 2009/4 Art.4, Art.5
revoked: SI 2009/2610 Art.3
Art.6A, added: SI 2009/265 Art.2
Art.7A, added: SI 2009/265 Art.2

2009–cont.

26. General Chiropractic Council (Constitution of the Statutory Committees) Rules Order of Council 2009
Sch.1, added: SI 2009/2738 Sch.1
Sch.1, amended: 2009 c.26 s.81
Sch.1, substituted: SI 2009/2738 Sch.1

37. Safeguarding Vulnerable Groups Act 2006 (Prescribed Criteria and Miscellaneous Provisions) Regulations 2009
Reg.7, amended: 2009 c.26 s.81
Sch.1 para.2, amended: SI 2009/2610 Art.24
Sch.1 para.4, amended: SI 2009/2610 Art.24

41. Operation of Air Services in the Community Regulations 2009
Reg.37, revoked: SI 2009/3015 Sch.1

56. Transfer of Tribunal Functions and Revenue and Customs Appeals Order 2009
applied: SI 2009/1307 Art.5
Sch.1 para.74, revoked (in part): SI 2009/777 Art.7
Sch.2 para.67, revoked: SI 2009/777 Art.7
Sch.3 para.11, applied: SI 2009/196 Art.9

63. Bank Administration Rules (Northern Ireland) 2009
varied: SI 2009/3056 Sch.1 para.7

122. Bank Insolvency (No.2) Rules (Northern Ireland) 2009
varied: SI 2009/3056 Sch.1 para.8

153. Environmental Damage (Prevention and Remediation) Regulations 2009
Reg.6, amended: SI 2009/3275 Reg.3
Sch.1 para.5, amended: SI 2009/3275 Reg.4

157. Waste Batteries and Accumulators (Charges) Regulations (Northern Ireland) 2009
applied: SI 2009/890 Reg.13

194. Stamp Duty and Stamp Duty Reserve Tax (Investment Exchanges and Clearing Houses) Regulations (No.2) 2009
revoked: SI 2009/2977 Reg.6

202. Companies Act 2006 (Amendment of Schedule 2) Order 2009
revoked: SI 2009/1208 Art.3

209. Payment Services Regulations 2009
Reg.1, applied: SI 2009/2475 Reg.1
Reg.5, applied: SI 2009/2475 Reg.1
Reg.10, applied: SI 2009/2475 Reg.1
Reg.10A, added: SI 2009/2475 Reg.3
Reg.10A, applied: SI 2009/2475 Reg.1
Reg.12, applied: SI 2009/2475 Reg.1
Reg.13, amended: SI 2009/1912 Reg.4
Reg.29, applied: SI 2009/2475 Reg.1
Reg.42, amended: SI 2009/2475 Reg.4
Reg.43, amended: SI 2009/2475 Reg.5
Reg.47, amended: SI 2009/2475 Reg.6
Reg.51, amended: SI 2009/2475 Reg.7
Reg.66, amended: SI 2009/2475 Reg.8
Reg.69, amended: SI 2009/2475 Reg.9
Reg.72, amended: SI 2009/2475 Reg.10
Reg.110, amended: SI 2009/2475 Reg.11
Reg.127, added: SI 2009/2475 Reg.12
Sch.7 para.1, added: SI 2009/2475 Reg.13
Sch.7 para.2, added: SI 2009/2475 Reg.13
Sch.7 para.3, added: SI 2009/2475 Reg.13

213. Education (Individual Pupil Information) (Prescribed Persons) (Amendment) (England) Regulations 2009
revoked: SI 2009/1563 Sch.1

214. Companies (Disclosure of Address) Regulations 2009
varied: SI 2009/1804 Sch.1 para.12

2009– cont.

214. Companies (Disclosure of Address) Regulations 2009– cont.
Part 1, applied: SI 2009/1804 Sch.1 para.11, Sch.1 para.12
Part 2, applied: SI 2009/1804 Sch.1 para.12
Part 3, applied: SI 2009/1804 Sch.1 para.11
Part 4, applied: SI 2009/1804 Sch.1 para.11, Sch.1 para.12
Reg.1, amended: SI 2009/2400 Reg.42
Reg.2, applied: SI 2009/2101 Sch.3 para.1
Reg.3, applied: SI 2009/2101 Sch.3 para.1
Reg.7, varied: SI 2009/2437 Reg.7
Reg.9, amended: SI 2009/1941 Sch.1 para.270, SI 2009/2400 Reg.42
Reg.11, amended: SI 2009/1941 Sch.1 para.270

262. Armed Forces (Pensions) (Prescribed Modification) Order 2009
Art.2, applied: SI 2009/544

263. General Osteopathic Council (Constitution) Order 2009
Art.5, amended: 2009 c.26 s.81

273. Tribunal Procedure (First-tier Tribunal) (Tax Chamber) Rules 2009
r.5, see *R. (on the application of Hankinson) v Revenue and Customs Commissioners* [2009] EWHC 1774 (Admin), [2009] S.T.C. 2158 (QBD (Admin)), Kenneth Parker Q.C.
r.28, see *R. (on the application of Hankinson) v Revenue and Customs Commissioners* [2009] EWHC 1774 (Admin), [2009] S.T.C. 2158 (QBD (Admin)), Kenneth Parker Q.C.

303. Street Works (Charges for Unreasonably Prolonged Occupation of the Highway) (England) Regulations 2009
Reg.15, amended: SI 2009/1178 Reg.2

309. Local Authority Social Services and National Health Service Complaints (England) Regulations 2009
Reg.1, amended: SI 2009/1768 Reg.2
Reg.6, amended: SI 2009/1768 Reg.3
Reg.8, amended: SI 2009/1768 Reg.4

312. Banking Act 2009 (Bank Administration) (Modification for Application to Banks in Temporary Public Ownership) Regulations 2009
varied: SI 2009/805 Sch.2 para.1, Sch.2 para.2
Reg.1, varied: SI 2009/805 Sch.2 para.2
Reg.2, varied: SI 2009/805 Sch.2 para.2, Sch.2 para.5
Reg.4, varied: SI 2009/805 Sch.2 para.2
Sch.1, varied: SI 2009/805 Sch.2 para.2, Sch.2 para.5

313. Banking Act 2009 (Bank Administration) (Modification for Application to Multiple Transfers) Regulations 2009
varied: SI 2009/805 Sch.2 para.1, Sch.2 para.2
Reg.1, varied: SI 2009/805 Sch.2 para.2, Sch.2 para.4
Reg.2, varied: SI 2009/805 Sch.2 para.2
Reg.3, varied: SI 2009/805 Sch.2 para.2, Sch.2 para.4
Sch.1, varied: SI 2009/805 Sch.2 para.2

314. Bank Administration (Sharing Information) Regulations 2009
varied: SI 2009/805 Sch.2 para.1, Sch.2 para.2
Reg.1, varied: SI 2009/805 Sch.2 para.2
Reg.2, varied: SI 2009/805 Sch.2 para.2
Reg.3, varied: SI 2009/805 Sch.2 para.2
Reg.4, varied: SI 2009/805 Sch.2 para.2

2009– cont.

314. Bank Administration (Sharing Information) Regulations 2009– cont.
Reg.5, varied: SI 2009/805 Sch.2 para.2
Reg.6, varied: SI 2009/805 Sch.2 para.2
Reg.7, varied: SI 2009/805 Sch.2 para.2
Reg.8, varied: SI 2009/805 Sch.2 para.2
Reg.9, varied: SI 2009/805 Sch.2 para.2
Reg.10, varied: SI 2009/805 Sch.2 para.2
Sch.1, varied: SI 2009/805 Sch.2 para.2

316. Personal Injuries (NHS Charges) Amendment Regulations 2009
Reg.4, amended: SI 2009/834 Reg.2

317. Banking Act 2009 (Parts 2 and 3 Consequential Amendments) Order 2009
varied: SI 2009/805 Sch.2 para.1, Sch.2 para.2
Art.3, varied: SI 2009/805 Sch.2 para.2, Sch.2 para.3
Art.4, varied: SI 2009/805 Sch.2 para.3
Art.5, varied: SI 2009/805 Sch.2 para.2, Sch.2 para.3
Art.6, varied: SI 2009/805 Sch.2 para.2, Sch.2 para.3
Art.7, varied: SI 2009/805 Sch.2 para.2, Sch.2 para.3
Art.8, varied: SI 2009/805 Sch.2 para.3
Art.9, varied: SI 2009/805 Sch.2 para.3
Sch.1, varied: SI 2009/805 Sch.2 para.3

319. Banking Act 2009 (Third Party Compensation Arrangements for Partial Property Transfers) Regulations 2009
Reg.3, applied: SI 2009/1800

322. Banking Act 2009 (Restriction of Partial Property Transfers) Order 2009
Art.1, amended: SI 2009/1826 Art.3
Art.3, amended: SI 2009/1826 Art.4
Art.5, amended: SI 2009/1826 Art.5
Art.7A, added: SI 2009/1826 Art.6
Art.8, amended: SI 2009/1826 Art.7

350. Bank Administration (Scotland) Rules 2009
varied: SI 2009/3056 Sch.1 para.9

351. Bank Insolvency (Scotland) Rules 2009
varied: SI 2009/3056 Sch.1 para.10

389. Medicines (Products for Human Use) (Fees) Regulations 2009
Reg.18, revoked (in part): SI 2009/3222 Reg.3
Reg.18A, added: SI 2009/3222 Reg.4
Reg.20, amended: SI 2009/3222 Reg.5
Reg.20A, added: SI 2009/3222 Reg.6
Sch.1 Part 1 para.2, amended: SI 2009/3222 Reg.7
Sch.1 Part 1 para.4, revoked: SI 2009/3222 Reg.7
Sch.1 Part 1 para.5, amended: SI 2009/3222 Reg.7
Sch.1 Part 1 para.22, amended: SI 2009/3222 Reg.7
Sch.1 Part 1 para.23, amended: SI 2009/3222 Reg.7
Sch.1 Part 4 para.35, revoked: SI 2009/3222 Reg.7
Sch.1 Part 4 para.35A, added: SI 2009/3222 Reg.7
Sch.1 Part 4 para.37, amended: SI 2009/3222 Reg.7
Sch.1 Part 4 para.46, amended: SI 2009/3222 Reg.7
Sch.1 Part 4 para.46A, added: SI 2009/3222 Reg.7
Sch.1 Part 4 para.47, revoked: SI 2009/3222 Reg.7
Sch.1 Part 4 para.47A, added: SI 2009/3222 Reg.7
Sch.1 Part 4 para.48, amended: SI 2009/3222 Reg.7
Sch.1 Part 5 para.49, amended: SI 2009/3222 Reg.7
Sch.7 para.1, amended: SI 2009/3222 Reg.8

396. Child Support (Miscellaneous Amendments) Regulations 2009
Reg.3, revoked: SI 2009/3151 Sch.1
Reg.4, revoked (in part): SI 2009/3151 Sch.1

2009–cont.

397. **Stamp Duty and Stamp Duty Reserve Tax (Investment Exchanges and Clearing Houses) Regulations (No.3) 2009**
revoked: SI 2009/2976 Reg.6

442. **General Optical Council (Constitution) Order 2009**
Art.5, amended: 2009 c.26 s.81

445. **Quality Partnership Schemes (England) Regulations 2009**
Reg.13, amended: SI 2009/3248 Reg.2

449. **Smoke Control Areas (Exempted Fireplaces) (England) Order 2009**
revoked: SI 2009/2190 Art.3

457. **Debt Relief Orders (Designation of Competent Authorities) Regulations 2009**
Reg.10, amended: SI 2009/1553 Reg.2

462. **Health and Social Care Act 2008 (Commencement No.9, Consequential Amendments and Transitory, Transitional and Saving Provisions) Order 2009**
Art.1, amended: SI 2009/580 Art.2
Sch.5 para.2, substituted: SI 2009/580 Art.2

468. **General Osteopathic Council (Constitution of the Statutory Committees) Rules Order of Council 2009**
Sch.1, amended: 2009 c.26 s.81

479. **Human Fertilisation and Embryology Act 2008 (Commencement No.1 and Transitional Provisions) Order 2009**
Art.6, amended: SI 2009/2232 Art.3

485. **Asylum Support (Amendment) Regulations 2009**
revoked: SI 2009/641 Reg.2

497. **Social Security Benefits Up-rating Order 2009**
applied: SI 2009/607 Reg.3

515. **Health and Safety (Fees) Regulations 2009**
applied: SI 2009/1595 Reg.2

551. **Textile Products (Indications of Fibre Content) (Amendment) Regulations 2009**
revoked: SI 2009/1034 Reg.2

616. **Criminal Justice Act 2003 (Commencement No.8 and Transitional and Saving Provisions) (Amendment) Order 2009**
revoked: SI 2009/3111 Art.3

660. **Health and Social Care Act 2008 (Registration of Regulated Activities) Regulations 2009**
Reg.3, applied: SI 2009/3049 Reg.2

700. **Consular Fees Order 2009**
Sch.1 Part III, substituted: SI 2009/1745 Art.2
Sch.1 Part IV, substituted: SI 2009/1745 Art.2

701. **Turks and Caicos Islands Constitution (Interim Amendment) Order 2009**
Art.1, amended: SI 2009/1755 Art.2
Art.4, amended: SI 2009/1755 Art.3
Art.5, amended: SI 2009/1755 Art.3
Art.6, amended: SI 2009/1755 Art.3
Art.7, amended: SI 2009/1755 Art.4
Art.8, amended: SI 2009/1755 Art.4
Art.9, amended: SI 2009/1755 Art.5

711. **Department for Transport (Fees) Order 2009**
applied: SI 2009/787, SI 2009/799, SI 2009/802, SI 2009/804, SI 2009/863, SI 2009/876, SI 2009/877, SI 2009/878, SI 2009/880
Sch.1 Part 2 para.10, substituted: SI 2009/1885 Sch.2 para.13

713. **Health in Pregnancy Grant (Notices, Revisions and Appeals) Regulations 2009**
revoked: SI 2009/751 Reg.11

2009–cont.

717. **Road Vehicles (Approval) Regulations 2009**
Reg.27, applied: SI 2009/718 Reg.3, Reg.4, Reg.5
Reg.27, referred to: SI 2009/718 Reg.4, Reg.5, Reg.6
Reg.37, applied: SI 2009/718 Reg.8
Reg.38, applied: SI 2009/718 Reg.11
Sch.5 Part 2, applied: SI 2009/718 Reg.6
Sch.5 Part 3, applied: SI 2009/718 Reg.6
Sch.5 Part 4, applied: SI 2009/718 Reg.6

778. **Local Health Boards (Establishment and Dissolution) (Wales) Order 2009**
Sch.2, referred to: SI 2009/779 Sch.2 para.2
Sch.3, referred to: SI 2009/779 Sch.2 para.2

779. **Local Health Boards (Constitution, Membership and Procedures) (Wales) Regulations 2009**
Reg.17, applied: SI 2009/3097 Reg.10

783. **Mental Capacity (Deprivation of Liberty Assessments, Standard Authorisations and Disputes about Residence) (Wales) Regulations 2009**
Reg.5, varied: SI 2009/1357 Art.3

785. **Renewables Obligation Order 2009**
Art.6, applied: SSI 2009/140 Art.7
Art.7, applied: SSI 2009/140 Art.8
Art.9, applied: SSI 2009/140 Art.9

797. **Guardian's Allowance Up-rating Order 2009**
applied: SI 2009/810 Reg.2, Reg.3

798. **Guardian's Allowance Up-rating (Northern Ireland) Order 2009**
applied: SI 2009/810 Reg.2, Reg.3

805. **Building Societies (Insolvency and Special Administration) Order 2009**
Sch.1 Part 3 para.30, applied: SI 2009/806 r.36

807. **Financial Services and Markets Act 2000 (Contribution to Costs of Special Resolution Regime) Regulations 2009**
Reg.8, applied: SI 2009/1800 Art.11

831. **Armed Forces (Terms of Service) (Amendment) Regulations 2009**
revoked: SI 2009/1089 Reg.30

832. **Armed Forces (Discharge and Transfer to the Reserve Forces) Regulations 2009**
revoked: SI 2009/1091 Reg.16

833. **Armed Forces (Forfeiture of Service) Regulations 2009**
revoked: SI 2009/1090 Reg.7

857. **Family Proceedings (Amendment) (No.2) Rules 2009**
see *Spencer v Spencer* [2009] EWHC 1529 (Fam), [2009] E.M.L.R. 25 (Fam Div), Munby, J.

862. **Education (Student Support) Regulations 2008 (Amendment) Regulations 2009**
revoked: SI 2009/1555 Reg.4

871. **Access to Justice Act 1999 (Destination of Appeals) (Family Proceedings) Order 2009**
see *Practice Direction (Fam Div: Family Proceedings: Written Reasons)* [2009] 1 W.L.R. 1109 (Sup Ct), Lord Judge, L.C.J.

890. **Waste Batteries and Accumulators Regulations 2009**
Sch.8 para.2, revoked (in part): SI 2009/3381 Reg.15

975. **Proceeds of Crime Act 2002 (References to Financial Investigators) Order 2009**
Art.1, amended: SI 2009/2707 Art.3
Sch.1, amended: SI 2009/2748 Sch.1 para.39
Sch.1, substituted: SI 2009/2707 Sch.1

2009–cont.

988. Criminal Procedure and Investigations Act 1996 (Application to the Armed Forces) Order 2009
Art.4, applied: SI 2009/1211 r.64, r.66, r.67, SI 2009/2041 r.81, r.97
Art.4, referred to: SI 2009/2041 r.78, r.80
Art.13, referred to: SI 2009/989 Sch.1

1032. Immigration (Passenger Transit Visa) (Amendment) (No.2) Order 2009
revoked: SI 2009/1229 Art.3

1035. National Health Service Trusts (Originating Capital) (Wales) Order 2009
Sch.1, substituted: SI 2009/1382 Sch.1

1059. Armed Forces Act 2006 (Transitional Provisions etc) Order 2009
Art.16, applied: SI 2009/1216 Sch.2 para.4
Art.44, applied: SI 2009/1216 Sch.2 para.3
Art.46, applied: SI 2009/1216 Sch.2 para.3
Art.47, applied: SI 2009/1216 Sch.2 para.3
Art.54, applied: SI 2009/1216 Sch.2 para.3
Art.55, applied: SI 2009/1216 Sch.2 para.5
Art.93, applied: SI 2009/1216 Sch.2 para.5
Art.96, applied: SI 2009/1216 Sch.2 para.12

1085. Company and Business Names (Miscellaneous Provisions) Regulations 2009
Reg.13, amended: SI 2009/2404 Reg.2
Sch.2 para.3, amended: SI 2009/2404 Reg.2

1169. Armed Forces (Review of Court Martial Sentence) (Supplementary Provision) Regulations 2009
Reg.7, referred to: SI 2009/2657 r.57, r.58
Reg.9, referred to: SI 2009/2657 r.57

1182. Health Care and Associated Professions (Miscellaneous Amendments and Practitioner Psychologists) Order 2009
Art.1, applied: SI 2009/1357
Art.1, enabled: SI 2009/1357
Art.7, applied: SI 2009/1358 Art.2
Art.7, enabled: SI 2009/1358, SI 2009/1808
Art.9, enabled: SI 2009/1357
Sch.1 para.7, amended: 2009 c.26 s.81
Sch.1 para.8, amended: 2009 c.26 s.81
Sch.2 para.5, amended: 2009 c.26 s.81
Sch.3 para.18, amended: 2009 c.26 s.81
Sch.4 Part 2 para.19, amended: 2009 c.26 s.81
Sch.4 Part 2 para.20, amended: 2009 c.26 s.81
Sch.4 Part 2 para.21, amended: 2009 c.26 s.81
Sch.4 Part 2 para.22, amended: 2009 c.26 s.81
Sch.4 Part 2 para.23, amended: 2009 c.26 s.81
Sch.4 Part 2 para.24, amended: 2009 c.26 s.81
Sch.4 Part 2 para.25, amended: 2009 c.26 s.81
Sch.4 Part 2 para.27, amended: 2009 c.26 s.81

1208. Companies Act 2006 (Amendment of Schedule 2) (No.2) Order 2009
referred to: SI 2009/1378 Art.2

1219. Building and Approved Inspectors (Amendment) Regulations 2009
Reg.1, amended: SI 2009/2465 Reg.2
Reg.5, amended: SI 2009/2465 Reg.2
Reg.6, amended: SI 2009/2465 Reg.2
Reg.7, amended: SI 2009/2465 Reg.2
Reg.8, amended: SI 2009/2465 Reg.2

1231. Berwick Upon Tweed Harbour Revision (Constitution) Order 2009
Art.5, amended: SI 2009/3382 Art.7
Art.5, revoked (in part): SI 2009/3382 Art.7

1257. Carbon Accounting Regulations 2009
Reg.5, applied: SI 2009/1258 Art.3

2009–cont.

1257. Carbon Accounting Regulations 2009– *cont.*
Reg.6, amended: SI 2009/3146 Reg.2
Reg.6, applied: SI 2009/1258 Art.3

1268. Street Works (Charges for Unreasonably Prolonged Occupation of the Highway) (Wales) Regulations 2009
Reg.5, applied: SI 2009/1267 Reg.33

1306. National Health Service Trusts (Dissolution) (Wales) Order 2009
Sch.1, referred to: SI 2009/779 Sch.2 para.2

1345. Health Professions Council (Constitution) Order 2009
Art.5, amended: 2009 c.26 s.81

1350. Education (Supply of Information) (Wales) Regulations 2009
Reg.1, amended: 2009 c.26 s.81

1354. General Teaching Council for Wales (Disciplinary Functions) (Amendment) Regulations 2009
Reg.2, revoked: SI 2009/2161 Reg.2

1355. Health Professions Council (Practice Committees and Miscellaneous Amendments Rules) Order of Council 2009
Sch.1, amended: 2009 c.26 s.81

1363. Fixed Penalty (Amendment) (No.2) Order 2009
revoked: SI 2009/1487 Art.3

1372. Swine Vesicular Disease (Wales) Regulations 2009
Reg.41, amended: SI 2009/1580 Reg.3

1374. Offshore Installations (Safety Zones) Order 2009
revoked: SI 2009/2099 Art.3

1393. Land Registration (Proper Office) Order 2009
revoked: SI 2009/2727 Art.4

1397. Human Fertilisation and Embryology (Procedure for Revocation, Variation or Refusal of Licences) Regulations 2009
Reg.4, amended: SI 2009/2088 Reg.2
Reg.10, revoked: SI 2009/2088 Reg.2
Reg.15, revoked (in part): SI 2009/2088 Reg.2

1513. Education and Skills Act 2008 (Commencement No.3) Order 2009
Art.2A, added: SI 2009/1606 Art.7

1582. Human Fertilisation and Embryology (Statutory Storage Period for Embryos and Gametes) Regulations 2009
Reg.2, amended: SI 2009/2581 Reg.2
Reg.3, amended: SI 2009/2581 Reg.2, Reg.3
Reg.4, amended: SI 2009/2581 Reg.2
Reg.5, amended: SI 2009/2581 Reg.2
Reg.6, amended: SI 2009/2581 Reg.2
Reg.7, amended: SI 2009/2581 Reg.2
Reg.8, amended: SI 2009/2581 Reg.2

1603. Supreme Court Rules 2009
Part 3 r.18, applied: SI 2009/2131 Sch.1
Part 3 r.21, applied: SI 2009/2131 Sch.1
Part 7 r.52, applied: SI 2009/2131 Sch.1

1742. Air Navigation (Amendment) Order 2009
revoked: SI 2009/3015 Sch.1

1747. Terrorism (United Nations Measures) Order 2009
Art.10, applied: SI 2009/209 Reg.13
Art.11, applied: SI 2009/209 Reg.13
Art.12, applied: SI 2009/209 Reg.13
Art.13, applied: SI 2009/209 Reg.13
Art.14, applied: SI 2009/209 Reg.13
Art.16, applied: SI 2009/209 Reg.13

2009—cont.

1749. North Korea (United Nations Sanctions) Order 2009
Art.1, amended: SI 2009/3213 Art.3
Art.2, amended: SI 2009/3213 Art.4
Art.3, amended: SI 2009/3213 Art.5
Art.4, amended: SI 2009/3213 Art.5
Art.4, revoked (in part): SI 2009/3213 Art.6
Art.5, amended: SI 2009/3213 Art.5
Art.6, amended: SI 2009/3213 Art.7
Art.8, substituted: SI 2009/3213 Art.8
Art.8A, added: SI 2009/3213 Art.9
Art.8B, added: SI 2009/3213 Art.9
Art.11, substituted: SI 2009/3213 Art.10
Art.13, substituted: SI 2009/3213 Art.11
Art.14, amended: SI 2009/3213 Art.12
Sch.3 Part 1 para.1, added: SI 2009/3213 Art.13
Sch.3 Part 1 para.2, added: SI 2009/3213 Art.13
Sch.3 Part 1 para.3, added: SI 2009/3213 Art.13
Sch.3 Part 1 para.4, added: SI 2009/3213 Art.13
Sch.3 Part 1 para.5, added: SI 2009/3213 Art.13
Sch.3 Part 1 para.6, added: SI 2009/3213 Art.13
Sch.3 Part 1 para.7, added: SI 2009/3213 Art.13
Sch.3 Part 1 para.8, added: SI 2009/3213 Art.13
Sch.3 Part 2 para.9, added: SI 2009/3213 Art.13
Sch.3 Part 2 para.10, added: SI 2009/3213 Art.13
Sch.3 Part 2 para.11, added: SI 2009/3213 Art.13
Sch.3 Part 2 para.12, added: SI 2009/3213 Art.13
Sch.3 Part 2 para.13, added: SI 2009/3213 Art.13
Sch.3 Part 2 para.14, added: SI 2009/3213 Art.13
Sch.3 Part 3 para.15, added: SI 2009/3213 Art.13
Sch.3 para.4, added: SI 2009/3213 Art.13
Sch.3 para.15, added: SI 2009/3213 Art.13
Sch.4, added: SI 2009/3213 Art.14

1800. Dunfermline Building Society Compensation Scheme, Resolution Fund and Third Party Compensation Order 2009
Art.4, referred to: SI 2009/1810 Art.6, Art.8, Art.9, Art.10, Art.11
Art.5, applied: SI 2009/1810 Art.4
Sch.2, applied: SI 2009/1810 Art.12
Sch.2 Part 2 para.4, applied: SI 2009/1810 Art.12
Sch.2 Part 3 para.10, applied: SI 2009/1810 Art.12

1801. Overseas Companies Regulations 2009
referred to: SI 2009/2999 Reg.31
Part 2, applied: SI 2009/2101 Sch.1 para.10
Part 3, applied: SI 2009/2101 Sch.1 para.10
Part 5, applied: SI 2009/2101 Sch.1 para.10
Part 6, applied: SI 2009/2101 Sch.1 para.10
Part 6, applied: SI 2009/1803 Reg.8
Reg.4, applied: SI 2009/1803 Reg.5
Reg.7, applied: SI 2009/1803 Reg.4
Reg.8, applied: SI 2009/1803 Reg.8
Reg.9, applied: SI 2009/1803 Reg.8
Reg.13, applied: SI 2009/1803 Reg.4, Reg.5
Reg.14, applied: SI 2009/1803 Reg.8
Reg.15, applied: SI 2009/1803 Reg.8
Reg.21, applied: SI 2009/2101 Sch.3 para.1
Reg.23, applied: SI 2009/2101 Sch.3 para.1
Reg.23, referred to: SI 2009/2101 Sch.4 para.1
Reg.24, applied: SI 2009/2101 Sch.3 para.1
Reg.24, referred to: SI 2009/2101 Sch.4 para.1
Reg.25, referred to: SI 2009/2101 Sch.4 para.1
Reg.26, referred to: SI 2009/2101 Sch.4 para.1
Reg.32, applied: SI 2009/1803 Reg.8
Reg.45, applied: SI 2009/1803 Reg.8
Reg.46, applied: SI 2009/1803 Reg.8
Sch.8 Part 5 para.23, referred to: SI 2009/2101 Sch.4 para.1

2009—cont.

1801. Overseas Companies Regulations 2009—*cont.*
Sch.8 Part 5 para.24, referred to: SI 2009/2101 Sch.4 para.1
Sch.8 Part 6 para.25, referred to: SI 2009/2101 Sch.4 para.1
Sch.8 Part 6 para.26, referred to: SI 2009/2101 Sch.4 para.1

1802. Companies Act 2006 (Part 35) (Consequential Amendments, Transitional Provisions and Savings) Order 2009
Sch.1, applied: SI 2009/1804 Sch.1 para.27

1803. Registrar of Companies and Applications for Striking Off Regulations 2009
Reg.8, amended: SI 2009/2399 Reg.24, SI 2009/2400 Reg.43

1804. Limited Liability Partnerships (Application of Companies Act 2006) Regulations 2009
Part 9, applied: SI 2009/2101 Sch.1 para.9
Reg.8, amended: SI 2009/2995 Reg.2
Reg.8, applied: SI 2009/2615, SI 2009/2982, SI 2009/2982 Reg.2
Reg.8, referred to: SI 2009/2615 Reg.2
Reg.11, applied: SI 2009/2101 Sch.1 para.9
Reg.12, applied: SI 2009/2101 Sch.1 para.9
Reg.17, referred to: SI 2009/2615 Reg.2
Reg.19, applied: SI 2009/2101 Sch.3 para.1
Reg.30, applied: SI 2009/2101 Sch.1 para.9
Reg.51, applied: SI 2009/2101 Sch.1 para.9
Reg.56, applied: SI 2009/2101 Sch.1 para.11
Reg.58, applied: SI 2009/2101 Sch.1 para.9
Reg.61, applied: SI 2009/2101 Sch.2 para.7, Sch.2 para.11, Sch.2 para.12
Reg.66, applied: SI 2009/2101 Sch.1 para.11, Sch.2 para.7, Sch.2 para.11, Sch.2 para.12
Reg.67, applied: SI 2009/2101 Sch.1 para.11
Reg.81, applied: SI 2009/2615, SI 2009/2982
Sch.1 Part 7 para.22, substituted: SI 2009/2476 Reg.3
Sch.3 Part 2 para.13, amended: SI 2009/1833 Reg.2

1808. General Dental Council (Constitution) Order 2009
Art.5, amended: 2009 c.26 s.81

1813. General Dental Council (Constitution of Committees) Rules Order of Council 2009
Sch.1, amended: 2009 c.26 s.81

1831. Stamp Duty and Stamp Duty Reserve Tax (Investment Exchanges and Clearing Houses) Regulations (No.10) 2009
revoked: SI 2009/2975 Reg.6

1882. Police Act 1997 (Criminal Records) (No.2) Regulations 2009
Reg.5, applied: SI 2009/3297 Reg.7
Reg.6, applied: SI 2009/3297 Reg.8

1891. Human Fertilisation and Embryology (Appeals) Regulations 2009
applied: SI 2009/1892 Sch.4 para.10
Reg.16, applied: SI 2009/1892 Sch.4 para.10

1892. Human Fertilisation and Embryology (Consequential Amendments and Transitional and Saving Provisions) Order 2009
Sch.4 para.9, applied: SI 2009/1891 Reg.32
Sch.4 para.10, applied: SI 2009/1891 Reg.32

1924. Education (Miscellaneous Amendments relating to Safeguarding Children) (England) Regulations 2009
Reg.8, revoked: SI 2009/2680 Sch.1

2031. Special Annual Allowance Charge (Application to Members of Currently-Relieved Non-UK Pension Schemes) Order 2009
Art.4, applied: 2009 c.10 Sch.35 para.6
Art.5, applied: 2009 c.10 Sch.35 para.6

2009– cont.

2036. Authorised Investment Funds (Tax) (Amendment) Regulations 2009
Reg.30, revoked: SI 2009/2199 Reg.2
2087. Criminal Procedure (Amendment) Rules 2009
see *Practice Direction (Sen Cts: Criminal Proceedings: Additional Forms)* [2009] 1 W.L.R. 2239 (Sen Cts), Lord Judge, L.C.J.
2098. Housing (Right to Enfranchise) (Designated Protected Areas) (England) Order 2009
referred to: SI 2009/2096 Art.3
2101. Registrar of Companies (Fees) (Companies, Overseas Companies and Limited Liability Partnerships) Regulations 2009
Reg.2A, added: SI 2009/2439 Reg.3
Reg.4A, added: SI 2009/2439 Reg.4
Sch.1 Part 2 para.7, amended: SI 2009/2439 Reg.5
2157. Assembly Learning Grants (European Institutions) (Wales) (Amendment) Regulations 2009
revoked: SI 2009/3359 Reg.4
2161. General Teaching Council for Wales (Disciplinary Functions) (Amendment No 2) Regulations 2009
Reg.3, amended: 2009 c.26 s.81
2190. Smoke Control Areas (Exempted Fireplaces) (England) (No.2) Order 2009
revoked: SI 2009/2302 Art.3
2263. Infrastructure Planning (Environmental Impact Assessment) Regulations 2009
applied: SI 2009/2264 Reg.5
2264. Infrastructure Planning (Applications Prescribed Forms and Procedure) Regulations 2009
Reg.10, applied: SI 2009/2263 Reg.14
2267. Valuation Tribunal for England (Membership and Transitional Provisions) Regulations 2009
Reg.5, amended: SI 2009/2613 Reg.2
2268. Non-Domestic Rating (Alteration of Lists and Appeals) (England) Regulations 2009
applied: SI 2009/2269 Reg.42, Reg.44
referred to: SI 2009/2269 Reg.28
Reg.8, applied: SI 2009/2269 Reg.2, Reg.5, Reg.19
Reg.12, applied: SI 2009/2269 Reg.2
Reg.13, applied: SI 2009/2269 Reg.2, Reg.5, Reg.7, Reg.19, Reg.33, Reg.38
Reg.19, applied: SI 2009/2269 Reg.2
Reg.24, applied: SI 2009/2269 Reg.17
2269. Valuation Tribunal for England (Council Tax and Rating Appeals) (Procedure) Regulations 2009
applied: SI 2009/2267 Reg.6, Reg.7, SI 2009/2268 Reg.25
varied: SI 2009/2268 Reg.20
Reg.2, applied: SI 2009/2270 Reg.2
Reg.4, applied: SI 2009/2268 Reg.8
Reg.7, applied: SI 2009/2268 Reg.19
Reg.19, applied: SI 2009/2270 Reg.10
Reg.31, applied: SI 2009/2268 Reg.8
Reg.32, referred to: SI 2009/2270 Reg.4
Reg.35, applied: SI 2009/2270 Reg.11
Reg.38, applied: SI 2009/2270 Reg.11
Reg.44, applied: SI 2009/2270 Reg.7
2270. Council Tax (Alteration of Lists and Appeals) (England) Regulations 2009
referred to: SI 2009/2269 Reg.28
Reg.7, applied: SI 2009/2269 Reg.5, Reg.19, Reg.24
Reg.10, applied: SI 2009/2269 Reg.2, Reg.5, Reg.7, Reg.19, Reg.22, Reg.25, Reg.27, Reg.33, Reg.38
Reg.11, applied: SI 2009/2269 Reg.38
Reg.13, applied: SI 2009/2269 Reg.19

2009– cont.

2397. Building (Amendment No.2) Regulations 2009
Reg.1, amended: SI 2009/2465 Reg.3
2403. Registrar of Companies (Fees) (European Economic Interest Grouping and European Public Limited-Liability Company) Regulations 2009
Sch.1, applied: SI 2009/2492 Reg.4
Sch.1, disapplied: SI 2009/2492 Reg.2, Reg.3
2478. Human Fertilisation and Embryology (Supplementary Provision) Order 2009
Art.2, applied: SI 2009/1582 Reg.3
2610. Safeguarding Vulnerable Groups Act 2006 (Regulated Activity, Miscellaneous and Transitional Provisions and Commencement No 5) Order 2009
Art.11, amended: 2009 c.26 s.81
Art.12, amended: 2009 c.26 s.81
Art.17, amended: 2009 c.26 s.81
2611. Safeguarding Vulnerable Groups Act 2006 (Commencement No 6, Transitional Provisions and Savings) Order 2009
Art.3, amended: 2009 c.26 s.81
2623. Wales Centre for Health (Transfer of Functions, Property, Rights and Liabilities and Abolition) (Wales) Order 2009
Art.4, applied: SI 2009/2618 Art.3
Art.5, applied: SI 2009/2618 Art.4
Sch.1, applied: SI 2009/2618 Art.3
2957. Waste Electrical and Electronic Equipment (Amendment) Regulations 2009
Sch.1 para.8, amended: SI 2009/3216 Reg.2
2997. Saving Gateway Accounts Regulations 2009
Reg.10, applied: SI 2009/2998 Reg.5
Reg.11, applied: SI 2009/2998 Reg.3, Reg.5
Reg.12, applied: SI 2009/2998 Reg.5
Reg.13, applied: SI 2009/2998 Reg.5
Reg.14, applied: SI 2009/2998 Reg.5
Reg.15, applied: SI 2009/2998 Reg.5
Reg.16, applied: SI 2009/2998 Reg.5
Reg.17, applied: SI 2009/2998 Reg.5
Reg.18, applied: SI 2009/2998 Reg.5
Reg.19, applied: SI 2009/2998 Reg.5
Reg.20, applied: SI 2009/2998 Reg.5
Reg.21, applied: SI 2009/2998 Reg.5
2998. Saving Gateway Accounts (No.2) Regulations 2009
Reg.3, applied: SI 2009/2997 Reg.10
3001. Offshore Funds (Tax) Regulations 2009
Reg.54, amended: SI 2009/3139 Reg.3
Reg.94, amended: SI 2009/3139 Reg.4
Sch.1 para.1, amended: SI 2009/3139 Reg.5
Sch.1 para.3, amended: SI 2009/3139 Reg.5
Sch.1 para.3A, added: SI 2009/3139 Reg.5
Sch.1 para.3B, added: SI 2009/3139 Reg.5
Sch.1 para.3C, added: SI 2009/3139 Reg.5
3041. Children Act 1989 (Amendment of Miscellaneous Regulations) (Wales) Regulations 2009
revoked: SI 2009/3265 Reg.4
3069. Ministry of Defence Police (Conduct) Regulations 2009
referred to: SI 2009/3070 Reg.4
Reg.36, applied: SI 2009/3070 Reg.9
Reg.56, applied: SI 2009/3070 Reg.9
3264. Agriculture (Cross compliance) Regulations 2009
revoked: SI 2009/3365 Reg.8
3382. Berwick upon Tweed (Closure of Spittal Quay) Harbour Revision Order 2009
applied: SI 2009/1231 Art.5